October 26-30, 2015
Brisbane, Australia

Association for
Computing Machinery

Advancing Computing as a Science & Profession

MM'15

Proceedings of the 2015 ACM
Multimedia Conference

Sponsored by:

ACM SIGMM

Supported by:

The University of Queensland, NSF, FX PAL, Baidu, UESTC, Google, QUT, Alibaba Group, University of Sydney, Brisbane, HUAWEI, IBM Research, Microsoft Research, HTC, Facebook, Yahoo! Labs, & cisra

Association for
Computing Machinery

Advancing Computing as a Science & Profession

The Association for Computing Machinery
2 Penn Plaza, Suite 701
New York, New York 10121-0701

ISBN: 978-1-4503-3459-4 (Digital)

ISBN: 978-1-4503-4112-7 (Print)

Additional copies may be ordered prepaid from:

ACM Order Department
PO Box 30777
New York, NY 10087-0777, USA

Phone: 1-800-342-6626 (USA and Canada)
+1-212-626-0500 (Global)
Fax: +1-212-944-1318
E-mail: acmhelp@acm.org
Hours of Operation: 8:30 am – 4:30 pm ET

Printed in the USA

General Chairs' Welcome

It is our great pleasure to welcome you to the *2015 ACM MULTIMEDIA* Conference, the premier conference for multimedia experts and practitioners from across academia and industry. This year we are in beautiful Brisbane, Australia, our first time in this wonderful country and we're delighted to be here and looking forward to experiencing some of the delights and treasures this great country has to offer.

This year's conference is the 23rd in the annual series continues our tradition to bring together a wide and diverse set of activities including panel sessions, tutorials, a series of workshops, technical demos, an open source software competition, a doctoral symposium, an interactive art exhibition, a video program and of course scientific papers and posters including special sessions on brave new ideas and grand challenges, as well as "regular" topics. What a busy week we are going to have!

One of the great parts of the program that we have lined up for you is the two keynote talks. On Tuesday October 27th, Judy Kay from the University of Sydney will talk about "*Harnessing Big Personal Data, with scrutable user modeling for privacy and control*", bringing her extensive background in Human-Computer Interaction to the really topical issue of personal data, and how to manage and use it for good and practical purposes. On Thursday October 29th, Zhengyou Zhang from Microsoft Research will talk about *"Vision-enhanced Immersive Interaction and Remote Collaboration with Large Touch Displays"* where he will address issues like telepresence and computer supported cooperative work and how those technologies have, and continue to develop.

We are immensely grateful to the University of Queensland, our hosts and local organizers, for inviting us here to Brisbane and for organizing such a great event. We also thank our gold sponsors ACM SIGMM, the University of Queensland, the National Science Foundation, FXPAL, Baidu, and the University of Electronic Science and Technology China, our silver sponsors Google, Queensland University of Technology, the Alibaba Group, the University of Sydney and Brisbane Marketing, and our bronze sponsors Huawei, IBM Research, Microsoft Research, HTC, Facebook and Yahoo! Labs. Without their support this conference would simply not be what it is today.

Of course putting together *MULTIMEDIA 2015* was a team effort and there are large number of people we should thank including authors, the program committee, area chairs, chairs of a myriad of other conference-related functions, local organizers and volunteers. We would like to make a special call out to Roger Zimmerman and Yongdong Zhang, our proceedings chairs, for the enormous amount of work they have done in the background to bring all this material together into one volume.

Finally, we hope that you will find the program for *Multimedia 2015* interesting and thought-provoking and that you use the opportunity to share and exchange ideas with other researchers and practitioners from around the world.

Welcome to Brisbane.

Xiaofang Zhou
The University of Queensland, Australia

Alan F. Smeaton
Dublin City University, Ireland

Qi Tian
The University of Texas at San Antonio, USA

ACM MULTIMEDIA'15 General Chairs

Message from Technical Program Chairs

We are pleased to introduce to you the Technical Program for the ACM International Conference on Multimedia (ACM Multimedia) 2015, for its first appearance in the Southern hemisphere. While adopting the best practices from previous ACM Multimedia conferences, this year we also introduced some changes on the research areas, the review process, and the conference program to reflect and ensure the greatest interests of researchers in our multimedia community.

Fifteen research areas of interest were grouped into four research themes, including a System Theme (covering Multimedia Telepresence and Virtual/Augmented Reality, Multimedia Systems and Middleware, Multimedia Transport and Delivery, Mobile Multimedia), an Experience Theme (covering Multimedia for Collaboration in Education & Distributed Environments, Multimedia HCI and Quality of Experience, Music, Speech and Audio Processing in Multimedia, Multimedia Authoring and Enrichment), an Understanding Theme (covering Deep Learning for Multimedia, Multimodal Analysis and Description, Multimedia and Vision), and an Engagement Theme (covering Multimedia Art, Entertainment and Culture, Multimedia Search and Recommendation, Social Multimedia, Emotional and Social Signals In Multimedia). In particular, the area of Multimedia and Vision was introduced to reach out to the relevant community that mainly deals with processing vision-related multimedia data.

This year, CMT was used to manage paper submissions and each research theme was set up as a track in the system. While CMT worked well for most steps in the review process, moving submissions across tracks was not allowed. In CMT, the Conflict of Interest (CoI) was easily handled by authors who had to specify the conflicting domains, Area Chairs and reviewers before they could make submissions.

Each research theme was overseen by one Technical Program Chair. For each area, a team of Area Chairs (ACs) of one to five members was recruited to handle the paper review process. In total, 37 ACs were appointed. Technical Program Chairs firstly assigned three or four reviewers and one or two ACs to each full and short submission. ACs then monitored the review process, coordinated discussions based on feedback, assessed the submissions based on reviews, and provided meta-recommendations as the inputs for the Technical Programme Committee (TPC) meeting.

While the general practices for ACs as stated in previous ACM Multimedia conferences were followed, this year we introduced the pairing relationship between two ACs to look at all borderline papers. If a submission received an initial borderline recommendation, another AC with relevant expertise was brought in to provide another examination of the submission before a final decision was made.

Regarding the paper submission and review process,

- As in 2014, there was no pre-submission of abstracts. Submissions of full and short papers were separated from each other, with the short paper submission deadline being one month later than the deadline for full paper submissions.
- As in 2014, for full papers, a two-stage review process was applied. Authors were invited to submit a rebuttal based on the first stage reviews. The reviewers were then asked to consider the rebuttal, to revise their reviews accordingly, and to enter discussion with other reviewers aiming to improve review consensus on each paper. The results of the second round reviews and discussion were then summarized by the ACs into meta-reviews, which included

tentative recommendations, to be discussed and finalized during the TPC meeting. In the second stage review, authors had the opportunity to talk to the Authors' Advocate if they felt they had issues with the reviews.

- For any submission with a borderline recommendation, an additional AC was paired with the initially assigned AC to provide a second recommendation, to be further discussed and finalized during the TPC meeting.
- Submissions from Technical Program Chairs and ACs were handled personally by non-conflicting Technical Program Chairs.
- In total, 252 full and 386 short paper submissions were received by their respective deadlines and entered the regular review process.
- The table below gives the exact submission numbers across research areas.

Area	**Full**	**Short**
Multimedia Telepresence and Virtual/Augmented Reality	12	11
Multimedia Systems and Middleware	16	23
Multimedia Transport and Delivery	11	8
Mobile Multimedia	16	15
Multimedia for Collaboration in Education & Distributed Environments	8	5
Multimedia HCI and Quality of Experience	16	17
Music, Speech and Audio Processing in Multimedia	7	18
Multimedia Authoring and Enrichment	3	8
Deep Learning for Multimedia	8	34
Multimodal Analysis and Description	26	43
Multimedia and Vision	43	94
Multimedia Art, Entertainment and Culture	16	11
Multimedia Search and Recommendation	40	59
Social Multimedia	18	17
Emotional and Social Signals In Multimedia	12	23
Total	**252**	**386**

Decisions on full and short paper acceptances were made at the one-day TPC meeting held at Fudan University on 22 June 2015. All four Technical Program Chairs attended the meeting and handled their own themes in four different rooms separately. The emphasis of the TPC meeting was on high-score, borderline, and controversial paper submissions. The discussion was intensive, taking into account all the available data, including reviews, the authors' rebuttals, the discussions, the initial recommendations by the ACs (in the form of a meta review) and the reviews performed by other ACs during the meeting. Technical Program Chairs and ACs were requested to leave the room when a conflicting submission was discussed.

After the meeting, the four TPC Chairs met to make final decisions, taking quality and balance of different tracks into consideration. By end of the day, we accepted 56 full and 117 short papers, leading to acceptance rates of 22.2% and 30.3% for full and short papers, respectively. Eight high quality full paper submissions had also been suggested to be accepted as short papers.

In a change from previous years, we also arranged a poster session for orally presented papers, including full and BNI papers, to be presented as posters to increase interactions among conference attendees. A number of TOMM papers published in 2014 were also invited to be presented in this poster session, to promote their research results as reported in TOMM.

The Technical Program Committee has worked really hard to ensure that the technical program of the conference is of the highest possible quality. Unfortunately, we couldn't include every single quality paper into the program. We really appreciate all the efforts and inputs from ACs and reviewers towards the exciting technical program.

We look forward to seeing you in the season of Spring, in Brisbane, Australia.

Dick C.A. Bulterman
FXPal, USA

Heng Tao Shen
The University of Queensland, Australia

Ketan Mayer-Patel
The University of North Carolina, USA

Shuicheng Yan
National University of Singapore

Message from SIGMM Chair

T-Shaped Vision, New Initiative, and Great Tradition

Different from other professional societies, the technical activities in ACM are organized around SIG, which stands for Special Interest Group. Each SIG is focused on a specific disciplinary area. In our case, it's *Multimedia*, a relatively broad but vaguely defined field covering a wide spectrum of aspects surrounding multimedia – computing, communications, and applications. However, there is a unique force that makes our community continue to excel and thrive: it's the dynamic *cross-disciplinary* nature of the intellectual pursuit of novel solutions in response to grand challenges facing the community at various times, starting with streaming and storage of multimedia data in the 90's, to rich media interaction (including overcoming the semantic gap in accessing web-scale multimedia), large-scale media sensing and processing over distributed platforms (including Internet of Things), collaborative environments incorporating rich sensory data and peta-scale networks, finally to the emerging cognitive multimedia systems involving affective computing and sociopsychological study.

The outcomes of such dynamic interdisciplinary efforts are both deep and broad, underscoring an important theme identified in the recent SIGMM retreat held in November 2014. A concrete recommendation made by 28 volunteer leaders in that retreat was ***the T-shaped vision for SIGMM*** - SIGMM should continue to embrace both depth (the vertical line of T) and breadth (the horizontal bar of T). We should welcome and encourage research of "X and Multimedia" (X being works from other individual "narrow" disciplines), while aiming to develop the core foundation of our field, including but not limited to multimedia integration, experience, representation, devices, contexts, and distributed computing.

I am delighted to see this upcoming ACM Multimedia Conference demonstrates excellent execution of the above T-shaped vision. The technical program, including an impressive array of regular and special activities, fully embodies the balanced spirit. You can find in-depth studies of foundational topics as well as applications of multimedia solutions in many practical domains.

This year also marks the launching of an important initiative – the inaugural ***SIGMM Multimedia Frontiers Workshop***, featuring 12 rising star researchers in multimedia. These speakers will share their achievements and visions through invited talks, followed by open dialogs with senior members in the community. These rising members are at the height of their career and, together with the senior colleagues, in perfect positions to shape the future direction of the community. The workshop has been organized with broad input from the Executive Committee and many other volunteers, but the list of speakers is by no means complete. We look forward to continuing this new initiative in the future to benefit from views from other rising members.

A great tradition at ACMMM is celebration of the extraordinary achievements of SIGMM members. This year we are privileged to recognize the exceptional achievements of the following members: Dr. Tat-Seng Chua for SIGMM Technical Achievement Award, Dr. Yu-Gang Jiang for SIGMM Rising Star Award, and Dr. Ting Yao for SIGMM Best Ph.D. Thesis Award. These are the prestigious honors bestowed upon members for their outstanding contributions. Each recipient will address the conference audience in plenary presentations to share their exciting accomplishments. We thank the award committees (chaired by Rainer Lienhart and Shin'ichi Satoh) for their hard work in making the selections from the nominations.

Finally, we are all profoundly indebted to the organizing team of ACM Multimedia 2015 for their devoted efforts that make ACMMM15 possible and more importantly sustains the success of SIGMM. We salute them for their invaluable leadership and contributions!

Shih-Fu Chang
Columbia University, USA
ACM SIGMM Chair

Table of Contents

Session: Multimedia Grand Challenge

Session: Brave New Ideas

Session 4: Multimedia and Vision

Session Chair: Mohan S. Kankanhalli *(National University of Singapore)*

Session 5: Multimedia Art, Entertainment and Culture

Session Chair: Phoebe Chen *(La Trobe University)*

Session 6: Telepresence, Virtual, and Augmented Reality

Session Chair: Klara Nahrstedt *(UIUC)*

Session: Session 7: Actions and Events

Session Chair: Nicu Sebe *(University of Trento)*

Session 8: Video Systems

Session Chair: Wu-Chi Feng *(Portland State University)*

Session 9: Deep Learning and Multimedia

Session Chair: Cees G. M. Snoek *(University of Amsterdam)*

Session 10: Multimedia Quality Perception

Session Chair: Bart Thomee *(Yahoo Research)*

Session 11: Multimedia Networking

Session Chair: Ketan Mayer-Patel *(University of North Carolina)*

Session 12: Data Imperfectness for Multimedia

Session Chair: Meng Wang *(Hefei Institute of Technology)*

Session 13: Multimedia Experiences and Expectations

Session Chair: Dick C. A. Bulterman *(FXPAL)*

Doctoral Symposium

Open Source Software Competition

Art Exhibit

Session Chairs: Ann Morrison *(Aalborg University)* and Stephen Viller *(The University of Queensland)*

Videos/Demos 1

Session Chair: Alejandro Jaimes *(Yahoo! Spain)*

Demos 2

Session Chair: Zheng-Jun Zha *(Hefei Institute of Intelligent Machines, Chinese Academy of Sciences)*

Poster Session 1

Session Chair: Jun Zhou *(Griffith University)*

Poster Session 2

Session Chair: Dian Tjondronegoro *(Queensland University of Technology)*

Tutorials

Workshop Summaries

MM 2015 Conference Organization

General Chairs:	Xiaofang Zhou *(The University of Queensland, Australia)* Alan F. Smeaton *(Dublin City University, Ireland)* Qi Tian *(The University of Texas at San Antonio, USA)*
Technical Program Committee Chairs:	Dick C.A. Bulterman *(FXPAL, USA)* Heng Tao Shen *(The University of Queensland, Australia)* Ketan Mayer-Patel *(The University of North Carolina, USA)* Shuicheng Yan *(National University of Singapore, Singapore)*
Author's Advocate:	Wei Tsang Ooi *(National University of Singapore, Singapore)*
Brave New Idea Chairs:	Yong Rui *(Microsoft Research Asia, China)* Nicu Sebe *(University of Trento, Italy)* Xuelong Li *(OPTical IMagery Analysis and Learning (OPTIMAL), China)*
Multimedia Grand Challenge Chairs:	Michael Lew *(Leiden University, The Netherlands)* Jie Yang *(National Science Foundation, USA)*
Technical Demo Chairs:	Alejandro Jaimes *(Yahoo!, Spain)* Zheng-Jun Zha *(Hefei Institute of Intelligent Machines, Chinese Academy of Sciences, China)*
Interactive Arts Chairs:	Stephen Viller *(The University of Queensland, Australia)* Ann Morrison *(Aalborg University, Denmark)*
Panel Chairs:	Chang Wen Chen *(University at Buffalo, USA)* Zhi-Hua Zhou *(Nanjing University, China)*
Open Source Software Competition Chairs:	Marco Bertini *(University of Florence, Italy)* Xian-Sheng Hua *(Alibaba, China)* Tao Mei *(Microsoft Research Asia, China)*
Video Program Chairs:	Shin'ichi Satoh *(National Institute of Informatics, Japan)* Meng Wang *(Hefei University of Technology, China)* Jinman Kim *(The University of Sydney, Australia)*
Doctoral Symposium Chairs:	Cees G. M. Snoek *(University of Amsterdam & Qualcomm Research Netherlands, The Netherlands)* Hervé Jégou *(Facebook AI Research, France)*

Tutorials Chairs: Rainer Lienhart *(University of Augsburg, Germany)*
Thomas Plagemann *(University of Oslo, Norway)*
Zhiyong Wang *(The University of Sydney, Australia)*

Workshop Chairs: Alan Hanjalic *(Delft University of Technology, The Netherlands)*
Lexing Xie *(Australian National University, Australia)*
Svetha Venkatesh *(Deakin University, Australia)*

Sponsorship Chairs: Abdulmotaleb El Saddik *(University of Ottawa, Canada)*
Rong Yan *(Snapchat Inc, USA)*
Kiyoharu Aizawa *(University of Tokyo, Japan)*
Zhengyou Zhang *(Microsoft Research, USA)*

Travel Grant Chairs: Xiangjian (Sean) He *(University of Technology Sydney, Australia)*
Yang Yang *(University of Electronic Science and Technology, China)*

Publicity Chairs: Jiebo Luo *(University of Rochester, USA)*
Lei Zhang *(Microsoft Research, USA)*
Weidong Cai *(The University of Sydney, Australia)*

History Preservation Chairs: K. Selçuk Candan *(Arizona State University, USA)*
Chong-Wah Ngo *(City University of Hong Kong, Hong Kong)*

Local Organization Chairs: Xue Li *(University of Queensland, Australia)*
Dian Tjondronegoro *(Queensland University of Technology, Australia)*

Finance Chair: Zi Huang *(The University of Queensland, Australia)*

Proceedings Chairs: Roger Zimmermann *(National University of Singapore, Singapore)*
Yongdong Zhang *(Chinese Academy of Science, China)*

Web and Social Media Chairs: Lorna Macdonald *(The University of Queensland, Australia)*
Jun Zhou *(Griffith University, Australia)*

MM 2015 Area Chairs

Multimedia Telepresence and Virtual/Augmented Reality:	Klara Nahrstedt *(UIUC, USA)* Wanmin Wu *(Ricoh Innovations, USA)*
Multimedia Systems and Middleware:	Wu-Chi Feng *(Portland State University, USA)* Kuan-Ta Chen *(Academia Sinica, Taiwan)*
Multimedia Transport and Delivery:	Ali C. Begen *(Cisco Systems, USA)* Christian Timmerer *(Alpen-Adria-University Klagenfurt, Austria)*
Mobile Multimedia:	Jochen Huber *(MIT Media Lab, USA)* Winston Hsu *(National Taiwan University, Taiwan)*
Multimedia for Collaboration in Education & Distributed Environments:	Matt Cooper *(FXPAL, USA)*
Multimedia HCI and Quality of Experience:	Bart Thomee *(Yahoo, USA)*
Music, Speech and Audio Processing in Multimedia:	Ye Wang *(National University of Singapore, Singapore)*
Multimedia Authoring and Enrichment:	Pablo Cesar *(CWI, The Netherlands)*
Deep Learning for Multimedia:	Greg Corrado *(Google, USA)* Ming Yang *(Facebook, USA)*
Multimodal Analysis and Description:	Mohan S. Kankanhalli *(National University of Singapore, Singapore)* Xian-Sheng Hua *(Microsoft Research, USA)* Qiong Liu *(FXPAL, USA)* Guo-Jun Qi *(University of Central Florida, USA)* Benoit Huet *(Eurecom, France)*
Multimedia and Vision:	Nicu Sebe *(University of Trento, Italy)* Gang Hua *(Stevens Institute of Technology, USA)* Yaser Sheikh *(CMU, USA)* Meng Wang *(Hefei Institute of Technology, China)* Cees G. M. Snoek *(University of Amsterdam & Qualcomm Research Netherlands, The Netherlands)*

Multimedia Art, Entertainment and Culture: James Z. Wang *(Pennsylvania State University, USA)*
Vincent Oria *(New Jersey Institute of Technology, USA)*

Multimedia Search and Recommendation: John R. Smith *(IBM, USA)*
Jingdong Wang *(Microsoft Research Asia, China)*
Phoebe Chen *(University of Latrobe, Australia)*
Chunhua Shen *(Adelaide University, Australia)*
Zi Huang *(University of Queensland, Australia)*

Social Multimedia: Mei Tao *(Microsoft Research Asia, China)*
Peng Cui *(Tsinghua University, China)*

Emotional and Social Signals In Multimedia: Hayley Hung *(Technical University of Delft, The Netherlands)*
Hatice Gunes *(Queen Mary University of London, UK)*
Mohammad Soleymani *(University of Geneva, Switzerland)*
Emily Mower Provost *(University of Michigan, USA)*

MM 2015 Program Committee

Abhinav Dhall
Aisling Kelliher
Aixin Sun
Ajita John
Albert Ali Salah
Alexander Raake
Ali C. Begen
Amirhossein Habibian
Amy Pavel
Andreas Girgensohn
Andrew Hines
Andrew Jones
Andrew Maas
Andrew Perkis
Anna Hilsmann
Arefin Ahsan
Arnold Smeulders
Arslan Basharat
Balakrishnan Prabhakaran
Baochun Li
Bart Thomee
Benoit Huet
Benoit Favre
Bin Cui
Bin Li
Bingbing Ni
Björn W. Schuller
Brais Martinez
Bruce Thomas
Bruno Lepri
Caifeng Shan
Carl James Debono
Carl S. Marshall
Carsten Griwodz
Cathal Gurrin
Cees G. M. Snoek
Cha Zhang
Changsheng Xu
Cheng Deng
Cheng-Hsin Hsu
Chenqiang Gao
Chong-Wah Ngo
Christian Timmerer
Christoph Trattner
Christopher Peters
Chunhua Shen
Chun-Ying Huang
Cynthia Liem
Cyril Concolato
Dacheng Tao
Damian Borth
Daniel Overholt
Daragh Byrne
David Grunberg
David Imseng
Deyu Meng
Dhiraj Joshi
Dinesh Jayagopi
Dong Liu
Eakta Jain
Eckehard Steinbach
Eduardo Veas
Emily Mower Provost
Eng-Jon Ong
Erik Mannens
Fei Wu
Feiping Nie
Felix Yu
Feng Zheng
Fernando Pereira
Florian Metze
Fons Kuijk
Francesc Alias
Frank Nack
Frank Shipman
Fred Charles
Fumin Shen
Gang Hua
Gene Cheung
George Tzanetakis
Gerald Friedland
Go Irie
Graham Percival
Greg Corrado
Gregorij Kurillo
Grenville Armitage
Gualtiero Volpe
Guillaume Chanel
Guillaume Gravier
Guo-Jun Qi
Guosheng Lin
Gustavo Carneiro
Gwendal Simon
Haichao Zhang
Hamid Izadinia
Hanwang Zhang
Hao Tang
Haoxiang Li
Harald Wuest
Hari Sundaram
Hatice Gunes
Hayley Hung
Hayrettin Gurkok
Herman Engelbrecht
Hong Lu
Houqiang Li
Huan Li
Huchuan Lu
Huiyu Zhou
Ian Kegel
Ichiro Ide
Ilaria Bartolini
Ishan Vaishnavi
Jacopo Staiano
James Wang
Jan van Gemert
Jan Willem Kleinrouweler
Jasper Uijlings
Jean-Charles Bazin
Jenny Benois-Pineau
Jeremy R. Cooperstock
Jiajun Liu
Jialie Shen
Jianbing Shen
Jianfei Cai
Jiang Wang
Jiangtao Cui
Jianmin Li
Jie Shao
Jiebo Luo
Jim Vaughan
Jingdong Wang
Jinhui Tang
Jinqiao Wang
Jitao Sang
Jochen Huber
John Kender
John R. Smith
John Tang
Joke Kort
Jonathan Ventura
Jonghwa Kim
Jordi Luque
Jörg Ott
Jose Alvarez
Ju Fan
Judith Redi
Juergen Geiger
Jun Zhou
Junfeng He
Jungong Han
Junping Zhang
Junsong Yuan
Kaiming He
Kathy Clawson
Kazuhiro Otsuka
Kazuya Takeda
Ke Hu
Ketan Mayer-Patel
Kevin Almeroth
Kevin Gao
Khiet Truong
Khurram Soomro
Klara Nahrstedt
Kuan-Ta Chen
Lamberto Ballan
Laurent Amsaleg
Lea Skorin-Kapov
Lei Chen
Lei Zhang
Lianli Gao
Lie Lu
Lijun Zhang
Ling Shao
Lingfen Sun
Lingqiao Liu
Litao Yu
Longfei Zhang
Lu Jiang
Luca Aiello
Lucjan Janowski
Luming Zhang
Luoqi Liu
Lynda Hardman

MM 2015 Grand Challenge Program Committee

Chairs: Michael Lew *(Leiden University, The Netherlands)*
Jie Yang *(National Science Foundation, USA)*

Program Committee: **IBM – New York City 360°**
John Smith *(IBM, USA)*
Liangliang Cao *(IBM,USA)*
Michele Merler *(IBM, USA)*
Yuan-Chi Chang *(IBM,USA)*

Microsoft – MSR-Bing Image Retrieval Challenge
Hongzhi Li *(Columbia University, USA)*
Yuxiao Hu *(Microsoft, USA)*
Zhangyang Wang *(UIUC, USA)*

Yahoo – Yahoo-Flickr Event Summarization Challenge
Adrian Popescu *(CEA-LIST, France)*
Bart Thomee *(Yahoo Labs, USA)*
Bogdan Ionescu *(LAPI, University Politehnica of Bucharest, Romania)*
Debanjan Mahata *(University of Arkansas at Little Rock, USA)*
Raphael Troncy *(Eurecom, France)*
Vasileios Mezaris *(CERTH-ITI, Greece)*

MM 2015 Doctoral Symposium Program Committee

Chairs: Cees G. M. Snoek *(University of Amsterdam & Qualcomm Research Netherlands, The Netherlands)*
Hervé Jégou *(Facebook AI Research, France)*

Program Committee: Relja Arandjelovic *(Inria, France)*
Susanne Boll *(University of Oldenburg, Germany)*
Dick C.A. Bulterman *(FXPAL, USA)*
Shih-Fu Chang *(Columbia University, USA)*
Tat-Seng Chua *(National University of Singapore, Singapore)*
Alan Hanjalic *(Delft University of Technology, The Netherlands)*
Xian-Sheng Hua *(Alibaba Group, China)*
Alexis Joly *(Inria, France)*
Thomas Mensink *(University of Amsterdam, The Netherlands)*
Bernard Merialdo *(Eurecom, France)*
Dinh Phung *(Deakin University, Australia)*
Georges Quénot *(Laboratory of Informatics of Grenoble, France)*
Miriam Redi *(Yahoo! Research, UK)*
Shin'ichi Satoh *(NII, Japan)*
Ronan Sicre *(Inria, France)*
Giorgos Tolias *(Inria, France)*
Lexing Xie *(Australian National University, Australia)*

MM 2015 Technical Demos Program Committee

Chairs: Alejandro Jaimes *(Yahoo!, Spain)*
Zheng-Jun Zha *(Hefei Institute of Intelligent Machines, Chinese Academy of Sciences)*

Program Committee: Marco Beritini *(ESADE, Spain)*
Junjie Cai *(University of Texas at San Antonio, USA)*
Yang Cao *(University of Science and Technology of China, China)*
Shu-Ching Chen *(Florida International University, USA)*
Jian Chen *(Institute of Automation, CAS, China)*
Wen-Huang Cheng *(Academia SINICA, Taiwan)*
Cheng Deng *(Xidian University, China)*
Lu Fang *(University of Science and Technology of China, China)*
Alex Hauptman *(Carnegie-Mellon University, USA)*
Steven Hoi *(Singapore Management University, Singapore)*
Wolfgang Hurst *(Utrecht University, Netherlands)*
Ichiro Ide *(Nagoya University, Japan)*
Alejandro Jaimes *(Yahoo!, USA)*
Yannis Kalantidis *(Yahoo!, USA)*
Yiannis Kompatsiaris *(Informatics and Telematics Institute, Greece)*
Hyowon Lee *(Singapore University of Technology and Design, Singapore)*
Liang Li *(University of Chinese Academy of Sciences, China)*
Dong Liu *(University of Science and Technology of China, China)*
Vasileios Mezaris *(CERTH-ITI, Greece)*
Bingbing Ni *(Advanced Digital Sciences Center, Singapore)*
Naoko Nitta *(Osaka University, Japan)*
Vincent Oria *(New Jersey Institute of Technology, USA)*
Stefan Rueger *(The Open University, UK)*
Jitao Sang *(Institute of Automation, CAS, China)*
Shin'ichi Satoh *(National Institute of Informatics, Japan)*
Klaus Schoeffmann *(Klagenfurt University, Austria)*
Xinmei Tian *(University of Science and Technology of China, China)*
Changhu Wang *(Microsoft Research Asia, China)*
Qi Wang *(Northwestern Polytechnical University, China)*
Jinqiao Wang *(Institute of Automation, CAS, China)*
Xiangyu Wang *(Institute for Infocomm Research, Singapore)*
Zilei Wang *(University of Science and Technology of China, China)*
Marcel Worring *(University of Amsterdam, Netherlands)*
Yang Yang *(University of Electronic Science and Technology of China)*
Kuiyuan Yang *(Microsoft Research Asia, China)*
Xin Yang *(Huazhong University of Science and Technology, China)*

Program Committee (continued):

Ting Yao *(Microsoft Research Asia, China)*
Zheng-Jun Zha *(Hefei Institute of Intelligent Machines, CAS, China)*
Hanwang Zhang *(National University of Singapore, Singapore)*
Shiliang Zhang *(Beijing University, China)*
Yan-Tao Zheng *(Snapchat Inc., USA)*
Wengang Zhou *(University of Science and Technology of China, China)*
Roger Zimmermann *(National University of Singapore, Singapore)*

MM 2015 Open Source Software Competition Organization Committee

Chairs: Marco Bertini *(University of Florence, Italy)*
Xian-Sheng Hua *(Alibaba, China)*
Tao Mei *(Microsoft Research Asia, China)*

Program Committee: Andreas Girgensohn *(FXPAL, USA)*
Anthony Vetro *(Mitsubishi Electric Research Laboratories, USA)*
Samson Cheung *(University of Kentucky, USA)*
Steven Hoi *(Singapore Management University, Singapore)*
Peng Cui *(Tsinghua University, China)*
Chia-Wen Lin *(National Tsing Hua University, Taiwan)*
Dan Ellis *(Columbia University, USA)*
Meng Wang *(Hefei University of Technology, China)*
Junfeng He *(Facebook, USA)*
Ichiro Ide *(Nagoya University, Japan)*
Yangqing Jia *(Google, USA)*
Jingdong Wang *(Microsoft Research Asia, China)*
Rongrong Ji *(Xiamen University, China)*
Kuiyuan Yang *(Microsoft Research Asia, China)*
Lei Zhang *(Microsoft Research, USA)*
Liangliang Cao *(Yahoo! Labs, USA)*
Qiong Liu *(FXPAL,USA)*
Marco Bertini *(University of Florence, Italy)*
Ioannis Pitas *(University of Thessaloniki, Greece)*
Kuan-Ta Chen *(Academia Sinica, Taiwan)*
Kwang-Ting (Tim) Cheng *(University of California, Santa Barbara, USA)*
Vicky Zhao *(University of Alberta, Canada)*
Winston Hsu *(National Taiwan University, Taiwan)*
Lynn Wilcox *(FXPAL, USA)*
Xiaoyan Sun *(Microsoft Research Asia, China)*
Yan-Yin Chen *(FXPAL, USA)*
Yi Yang *(University of Technology, Sydney, Australia)*
Yimin Zhang *(Intel, China)*
Yu-Gang Jiang *(Fudan University, China)*
Zhou Wang *(University of Waterloo, Canada)*

MM 2015 Brave New Idea Organization Committee

Chairs:
Yong Rui *(Microsoft Research Asia, China)*
Nicu Sebe *(University of Trento, Italy)*
Xuelong Li *(OPTical IMagery Analysis and Learning (OPTIMAL), China)*

Program Committee:
Abdulmotaleb El Saddik *(University of Ottawa, Canada)*
Benoit Huet *(Eurecom, France)*
Bo Du *(Wuhan University, China)*
Bo Luo *(University of Kansas, USA)*
Bruno Lepri *(FBK, Italy)*
Cha Zhang *(Microsoft Research, USA)*
Cheng Deng *(Xidian University, China)*
Chong-Wah Ngo *(Hong Kong University of Science & Technology, Hong Kong)*
Dong Liu *(Columbia University, USA)*
Gene Cheung *(National Institute of Informatics, Japan)*
Gerald Friedland *(International Computer Science Institute, USA)*
Jacopo Staiano *(UPMC-Sorbonne Universitees, France)*
Jian Zhang *(University of Technology Sydney, Australia)*
Jianfei Cai *(Nanyang Technological University, Singapore)*
Jiebo Luo *(University of Rochester, USA)*
Kaiqi Huang *(Chinese Academy of Sciences, China)*
Kuan-Ta Chen *(Academia Sinica, Taiwan)*
Lei Zhang *(Microsoft Research Asia, China)*
Lexing Xie *(Australian National University, Australia)*
Ling Shao *(Northumbria University, UK)*
Lyndon Kennedy *(Yahoo Labs, USA)*
Marco Cristani *(University of Verona, Italy)*
Martha Larson *(TU Delft, Netherlands)*
Mohammad Soleymani *(University of Geneva, Switzerland)*
Munmun De Choudhury *(Georgia Tech, USA)*
Nannan Wang *(Xidian University, China)*
Peng Cui *(Tsinghua University, China)*
Ramanathan Subramanian *(Advanced Digital Sciences Center, Singapore)*
Raymond Fu *(Northeastern University, USA)*
Shin'ichi Satoh *(National Institute of Informatics, Japan)*
Stefan Winkler *(Advanced Digital Sciences Center, Singapore)*
Tao Mei *(Microsoft Research Asia, China)*
Ting Yao *(Microsoft Research Asia, China)*
Vasileios Mezaris *(CERTH-ITI, Greece)*
Winston Hsu *(National Taiwan University, Taiwan)*
Xian-Sheng Hua *(Microsoft Research, USA)*
Xiaogang Wang *(The Chinese University of Hong Kong, Hong Kong)*
Xing Xie *(Microsoft Research Asia, China)*
Yi Yang *(University of Technology Sydney, Australia)*
Yongsheng Dong *(Chinese Academy of Sciences, China)*

MM 2015 Sponsor & Supporters

Sponsor:

Gold Supporters:

Silver Supporters:

Bronze Supporters:

Supporter:

ACM SIGMM/TOMM 2015
Award Announcements

The ACM Special Interest Group in Multimedia (SIGMM) and ACM Transactions on Multimedia Computing, Communications and Applications (TOMM) are pleased to announce the following awards for 2015 recognizing outstanding achievements and services made in the multimedia community.

SIGMM Technical Achievement Award
Dr. Tat-Seng Chua, National University of Singapore

SIGMM Rising Star Award
Dr. Yu-Gang Jiang, Fudan University

SIGMM Best Ph.D. Thesis Award
Dr. Ting Yao, City University of Hong Kong (currently Microsoft Research)

TOMM Nicolas D. Georganas Best Paper Award
"A Quality of Experience Model for Haptic Virtual Environments" by Abdelwahab Hamam, Abdulmotaleb El Saddik, and Jihad Alja'am, published in TOMM, Vol. 10, Issue 3, 2014

TOMM Best Associate Editor Award
Dr. Pradeep K. Atrey, State University of New York, Albany

Additional information of each award and recipient is available: http://www.sigmm.org/

Awards will be presented in the annual SIGMM event, ACM Multimedia Conference, held in Brisbane, Australia during October 26-30, 2015.

ACM is the professional society of computer scientists, and SIGMM is the special interest group on multimedia. TOMCCAP is the flagship journal publication of SIGMM.

ACM Multimedia 2016

The 24th ACM International Conference on Multimedia
October 15-19, 2016 Amsterdam, The Netherlands

About ACM Multimedia 2016

Since the founding of ACM SIGMM in 1993, ACM Multimedia has been the worldwide premier conference and a key world event to display scientific achievements and innovative industrial products in the multimedia field. At ACM Multimedia 2016, we will celebrate its twenty-forth iteration with an extensive program consisting of technical sessions covering all aspects of the multimedia field in forms of oral and poster presentations, tutorials, panels, exhibits, demonstrations and workshops, bringing into focus the principal subjects of investigation, competitions of research teams on challenging problems, and also an interactive art program stimulating artists and computer scientists to meet and discover together the frontiers of artistic communication. Details and updates will be published on the conference's website: www.acmmm.org/2016.

Call for Contributions

ACM Multimedia 2016 solicits submissions of contributions for the following programs (partial list, please visit the website for details):

- Regular scientific papers
- Brave new idea papers
- Interactive art exhibition
- Open source software competition
- Multimedia grand challenge competition
- Tutorials
- Panels
- Doctoral symposium
- Technical demonstrations
- Workshops

Important Dates

The dates for submissions to the abovementioned contribution categories and other key dates will be provided on the conference website. Please check the website frequently for the latest news and updates.

Conference Location – Amsterdam, The Netherlands

The conference will be held at the *Tuschinski Theater* in Amsterdam, a beautiful 1921 historic building in Jugendstil style. Amsterdam is a renowned tourist destination with its famous canals, museums and relaxed atmosphere. It has optimal accessibility by plane from almost everywhere in the world. It also has a very extensive public transport system, although the city center is small enough to make walking a rewarding experience.

Accommodation caters for any budget from 5 star hotels to youth hostels all in close vicinity of the conference venue. Amsterdam is in the top-5 of creative hotspots in the world and is hosting the head offices for leading international companies such as Philips, Booking.com and TomTom.

Association for Computing Machinery

SIGMM

ACMmultimedia

XXX

2016

The *fertilized forests* Decision Forest Library

Christoph Lassner
University of Augsburg
Universitätsstr. 6a
86159 Augsburg, Germany
Christoph.Lassner@informatik.uni-augsburg.de

Rainer Lienhart
University of Augsburg
Universitätsstr. 6a
86159 Augsburg, Germany
Rainer.Lienhart@informatik.uni-augsburg.de

ABSTRACT

Since the introduction of Random Forests in the 80's they have been a frequently used statistical tool for a variety of machine learning tasks. Many different training algorithms and model adaptions demonstrate the versatility of the forests. This variety resulted in a fragmentation of research and code, since each adaption requires its own algorithms and representations.

In 2011, Criminisi and Shotton developed a unifying Decision Forest model for many tasks. By identifying the reusable parts and specifying clear interfaces, we extend this approach to an object oriented representation and implementation. This has the great advantage that research on specific parts of the Decision Forest model can be done 'locally' by reusing well-tested and high-performance components.

Our *fertilized forests* library is open source and easy to extend. It provides components allowing for parallelization up to node optimization level to exploit modern many core architectures. Additionally, the library provides consistent and easy-to-maintain interfaces to C++, Python and Matlab and offers cross-platform and cross-interface persistence.

Categories and Subject Descriptors

G.4 [**Mathematics of Computing**]: Mathematical Software;
D.2.2 [**Software**]: Software engineering—*Design tools and techniques, Software libraries*;
I.2.6 [**Computing methodologies**]: Artificial intelligence—*Learning*

General Terms

Algorithms, Design, Experimentation

Keywords

Decision Forests; Object Oriented Implementation; Open Source; Parallel Implementation; Machine Learning

MM'15, October 26–30, 2015, Brisbane, Australia.

ACM 978-1-4503-3459-4/15/10...$15.00
DOI: http://dx.doi.org/10.1145/2733373.2807407.

1. INTRODUCTION

The basic idea of Decision Trees, hierarchical splitting of data with the aim of an increasingly informative grouping, is appealingly simple. This leads on the one hand to many possible refinements and specializations. On the other hand, many researchers have created their own, hand-tailored implementation for their specific needs. This is especially true for the "classic" algorithms of the early days of Decision Forests[1], because each of the algorithms was created for a specific data type and purpose. But if not implemented with thorough testing and proper thoughts about efficiency, even a simple algorithm may be erroneous or inefficient.

However, in their work [6], Criminisi and Shotton developed a unifying Decision Forest Model suitable for many tasks and data types, making many of these dedicated algorithms obsolete. Furthermore, this new model provides a solid foundation for an object oriented framework with high reusability of components.

With the recent developments in Decision Forest theory and in computing technology, the benefits of such an object oriented framework compared to hand-tailored problem oriented implementations are becoming increasingly important. Computing platforms with significantly more than 40 CPUs render tree-level parallelism insufficient to exploit their power, when memory intensive models such as Hough Forests [10] with fewer trees than CPUs are trained. On the theoretical side, recent algorithmic extensions such as Alternating Decision Forests [17] or, as mentioned before, Hough Forests, merely use and recombine existing algorithmic parts. We tackle this problem by providing an open source library for Decision Forest training.

With clear interfaces and strong locality, the library classes remain easy to understand and easy to alter and extend. While not going as far as to use SSE optimizations, the library is written in highly templated C++ and optimized thoroughly without destroying code readability. At the same time, OpenMP is used to create nested parallelization on tree and node optimization level, which allows to make use of many cores even when training fewer trees than cores.

The open source library is available under a permissive license with extensive documentation and examples. It provides clean and consistent interfaces to C++, Python and Matlab. With the idea to be easily extendable, it features an interface generator that automatically keeps the interfaces up-to-date with changes.

[1]Similar to [6], we use the phrase "Decision Forest" as a synonym for "Random Forest". The new term emphasizes the reference to the new, but equivalent, theoretical framework.

Name	License	Core lang.	Available bindings	OS ind.	Parallelization	Type aware	Extend.	Setups
fertilized forests	BSD	C++	Python, Matlab	✓	Trees & Nodes	✓	✓	2295
scikit-learn [15]	BSD	Cython	Python	✓	Trees			32
OpenCV [3]	BSD	C++	Python	✓		✓		9
Sherwood [5]	MSR-LA	C++	C#		Nodes		✓	5
ALGLIB [2]	GPL 2+	C	C#, VB.NET, Python	✓				1
WEKA [11]	GPL 2	Java	Python	✓				4

Table 1: Overview over Decision Forest libraries. The column "Type aware" refers to whether a library can treat input data in its native data type. The column "Extend." (extendable) refers to whether it is possible without much overhead to extend the implemented algorithms of the library. "Setups" summarizes how many different training setups can be realized with the library.

While the library is significantly more flexible than others with these features, it stays competitive in terms of speed and learning performance (an evaluation is given in Section 4). With a strong focus on computer vision applications, it features last years winner of the ACM Multimedia Open-Source Software Competition, CAFFE [13], as part of the library that can be used for feature extraction. For making this possible, we contributed a platform independent build system to the project, making CAFFE available on Windows, and integrated parts of it into our own library.

2. FEATURES

The library tackles many of the software engineering challenges in its domain by using an **object oriented model** of Decision Forests. This has several advantages:

Local parameterization Instead of having few, overparameterized factory functions, parameters are local to the objects they are related to. This means, that new parameterized objects can easily be created, without having to bloat parameter lists with default values.

Recombination It is natural to recombine objects to create new, meaningful forest types. E.g., Hough Forests can be created by reusing regression and classification threshold optimizers and just adding two new objects.

Code encapsulation Semantically close code is automatically grouped together. This makes understanding and extending the code of a class easier, since only the class's interface must be understood to enhance it.

Inheritance Minor modifications to existing algorithms can be created by inheriting from their defining classes. Not the entire functionality must be rewritten, only the most relevant parts.

The library currently contains classes for all classification and regression concepts described in [6], but has been extended with a state-of-the art implementation of Hough Forests, two variants of boosting, several strategies for split optimization and many entropy functions, including the recently described induced entropies [14].

Deterministic, nested parallelism To be able to fully exploit modern many core architectures, the library supports deterministic, nested parallelism down to node optimization level. While coarse-grained tree-level parallelism is insufficient on modern machines, an additional parallelization step during node optimization offers a second level of fine-grained parallelism. When carefully implemented, race conditions can be avoided while maintaining good parallelization behavior. This guarantees the same, deterministic results independent of the number of used threads.

Templated classes The library has been created with multimedia and computer vision applications in mind. In the age of big data, the sampled signals are getting so large that inflating the data only to adjust its data type becomes permissively wasteful, e.g., increasing the amount of image data by four only to convert its data type from `unsigned byte` to `float`. To avoid this, all library classes are templated with the relevant types of the data they process. To take the hassle away of re-typing the template parameters frequently and to reflect this concept in the non-templated languages MATLAB and Python, a factory object is used that receives the template parameters once and then creates all library objects correctly templated for the user's convenience.

OS independence Being compatible to the gcc, Intel and Microsoft Visual C++ compilers, the library can be used on all major platforms. The build system is realized with SCons[2] and can hence be used on all platforms where a Python distribution is available.

Interfaces The library offers completely consistent interfaces to C++, MATLAB and Python. Convenient updating and complete consistency is ensured by using an easy to use interface generator written in Python that comes with the library.

OS and interface independent persistence By using Boost serialization text archives for persistence across all interfaces, the library objects can be serialized and deserialized across all possible platforms and interfaces. This allows training trees on a large HPC Linux cluster and then performing analyses, e.g., in Python on Windows.

2.1 Comparison with existing libraries

There are countless libraries for Decision Forest training available (an overview over the most relevant ones is given in Table 1). However, most of them are outdated concerning the supported algorithms and none of them offers a comparably versatile combination of open source code, OS availability, cross platform serialization and number and completeness of interfaces.

Interestingly, there is no other Decision Forest library with support for MATLAB, but its built-in Decision Forest implementation is outdated and slow (more than two orders of magnitude slower than our implementation). Thus, our library could be a good alternative for computer vision researchers in this environment. It is, however, necessary to note, that while a lot of care has been taken to copy as few data as possible in the general library design, a copy of parameters from and to MATLAB is necessary due to its column major storage order concept.

[2] `http://www.scons.org`

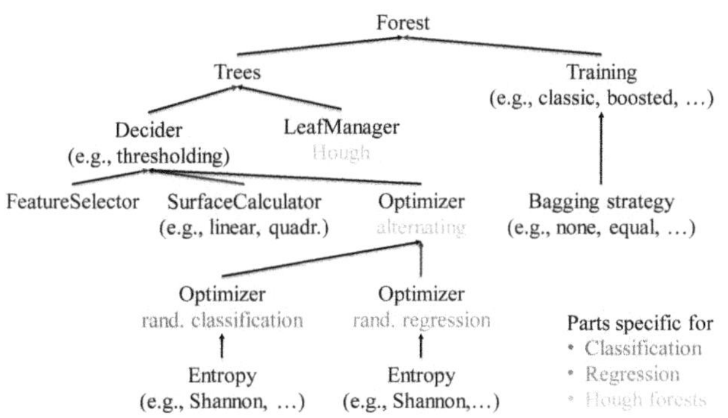

Figure 1: Hough Forest object structure. Arrows represent 'is-using' relations.

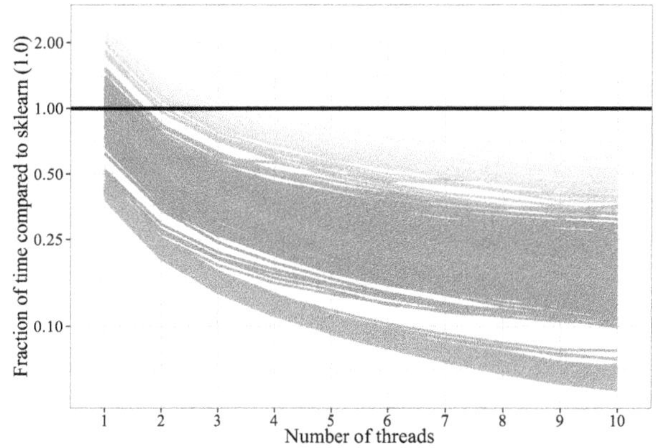

Figure 2: Runtime comparison with scikit-learn.

While most of the other software listed as representative selection in Table 1 is competitive in the historically relevant areas such as single-threaded runtime and platform availability, few are data type aware, and no other supports nested parallelism and is nearly as versatile and easy to extend. Our aim is to excel in this area by creating a library that is well suited for the dynamic process of research.

3. LIBRARY DESIGN

The library's design is general enough to enable efficient recombination of components and to enable benefits by inheritance, but still groups related code together closely. Figure 1 shows an overview of the objects necessary to represent a Hough Forest. This specific scenario has been selected, because it illustrates many of the benefits well.

By exchanging the *LeafManager*, which controls the information stored at leafs, as well as the *Optimizer*, which optimizes the thresholds according to the data annotations, it is possible already to change the objective function and the resulting model. This can, e.g., be used to create a classification or regression forest. By adding two new classes, a *HoughLeafManager* and an *AlternatingOptimizer*, and by reusing existing classes, the completely different concept of a Hough Forest can be defined.

Parallelization is implemented in the *Training* and *Decider* objects. All objects being located lower in the hierarchy automatically benefit of this parallelization without explicitly implementing it.

4. EVALUATION

To give the reader an impression of the performance of the library, we did some experiments with the competing library 'scikit-learn'. We selected that library as competitor, since (a) we appreciate its impact on the machine learning community and its high popularity, (b) used it in some ways as inspiration for our project, and (c) the parameterization of this library is similar enough to ours to allow a fair comparison.

Runtime It is not straightforward to set up an experiment resulting in a reliable statement about library speeds: specifics of the data can bias results in favor of each candidate, or a specific parameter setting can as well strongly influence the results removing its generality.

Therefore, we came up with the idea to use 100 runs with randomly (but equivalently) sampled parameter settings on each of three large scale, computer vision datasets (chars74k [9], MNIST [1] and USPS [12]). This results in a large set of overall runs under diverse conditions, and we hope that it provides a better impression of performance.

While parallelization over trees trivially has a good parallelization behavior, this is not necessarily true for deterministic parallelization over the node optimization. To visualize the behavior of our library in this specific case, we varied the number of threads for node optimization.

The results are visualized in Figure 2. For each run, the corresponding runtime of scikit-learn was used as normalization (hence the straight line at height 1.0). All other lines show the traces of our library. The brightness of the color is higher for traces closer to the mean trace.

The first important results are the performance values for one thread. There are a few runs for certain parameter settings where the runtime of our library goes up to more than twice of the runtime of scikit-learn. The mean, however, is at about 1.0, with the start of a solid trace at little more than a third of the runtime of scikit-learn (the y-axis is logarithmic). For an increasing number of threads, the library shows good parallelization behavior peaking out in the best cases at substantially smaller values than 0.1, even though only 10 threads have been used.

We identified the ability to parallelize beyond tree level to be of critical importance. Dantone et al. report a training time of 3 hours on a 700 CPU cluster for their Hough Forest human pose estimation implementation [8]. Since our university does not have a comparably sized cluster, we exploited our local infrastructure using our library. It comprises of only 64 CPUs, of which two times twenty are part of server systems. Even though Dantone's original model only uses 10 trees, we could fully exploit our computing power and reduced the training time by more than an order of magnitude to 2.5 hours on our infrastructure.

Classification performance In Figure 3, we provide a comparison of F1-scores with scikit-learn on five large scale computer vision classification datasets (parameters were again randomly sampled 100 times). The x-axis shows the various datasets, where the left of each pair of columns shows the fertilized forests performance, and the right the scikit-learn performance. The datasets, from left to right, are chars74k [9], g50c [4], letter [1], MNIST [1] and USPS [12].

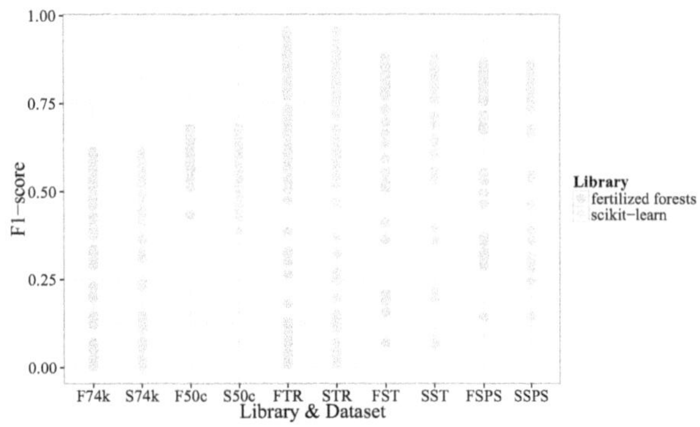

Figure 3: F1-score comparison with scikit-learn.

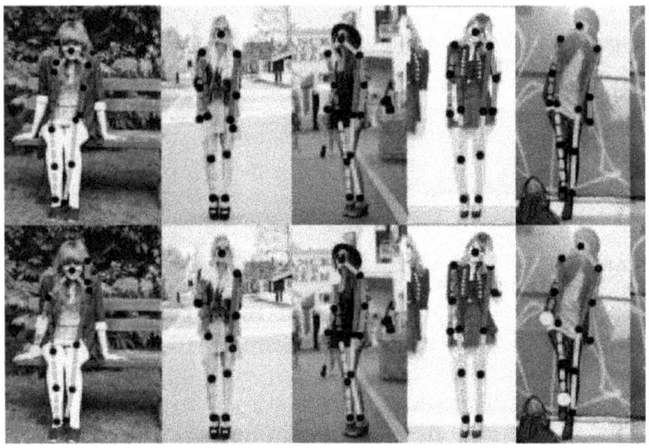

Figure 4: Human pose estimation with Decision Forests using the fertilized forests library (c.t. [14]). The samples are part of the FashionPose dataset [7].

The y-axis shows the F1-score[3], since some of the datasets have a high number of classes and are not perfectly balanced. The authors of scikit-learn have implemented various heuristics in addition to the traditional Decision Forest algorithm. We went through the source code and added them to our library, as well as one new heuristic. This gives the fertilized forests sometimes a slight edge over the scikit-learn implementation (visible, e.g., for the g50c dataset).

5. APPLICATIONS

The library is well-tested and has been applied in many scenarios. It is in use for research at the Multimedia Computing and Computer Vision Lab and the Institute for Software Engineering at the University of Augsburg, the Information Processing Lab at the University of Washington and the Max Planck Institute for Intelligent Systems in Tübingen.

The first two research projects were a work on uncertainty sampling for model abstraction [16] and on induced entropies for Decision Forests [14]. Whereas the first one mainly used the probabilistic regression features of the library, the second used nearly all features of the library and shows how the simplicity of replacing algorithmic building blocks of Decision Forests can support research in this field. Figure 4 shows some samples of the implemented human pose estimation algorithm and improvements (marked with a yellow dot in the bottom row) while using a different entropy measure.

[3] $F_1 = \frac{2 \cdot \text{precision} \cdot \text{recall}}{\text{precision} + \text{recall}}$.

6. SOURCE & ACKNOWLEDGEMENTS

The main source of information around the library, including API documentation, examples, FAQ page and news section, is the website `http://www.fertilized-forests.org`. The source code is available at `https://github.com/ChrislS/fertilized-forests`.

We thank the students Moritz Einfalt, Philipp Harzig and Christian Diller for their contributions. Furthermore, we thank Matthias Dantone and Jürgen Gall for the permission to use their Hough Forest feature extraction code.

7. REFERENCES

[1] K. Bache and M. Lichman. UCI machine learning repository. `http://archive.ics.uci.edu/ml`.

[2] S. Bochkanov. Alglib. `http://www.alglib.net`.

[3] G. Bradski. Opencv. `http://www.opencv.org`.

[4] O. Chapelle, B. Schölkopf, and A. Zien, editors. *Semi-Supervised Learning.* MIT Press, 2006.

[5] A. Criminisi and J. Shotton, editors. *Decision Forests for Computer Vision and Medical Image Analysis.* Springer-Verlag London, 2013.

[6] A. Criminisi, J. Shotton, and E. Konukoglu. Decision forests for classification, regression, density estimation, manifold learning and semi-supervised learning. Technical Report MSR-TR-2011-114, MS Res., 2011.

[7] M. Dantone, J. Gall, C. Leistner, and L. V. Gool. Human Pose Estimation using Body Parts Dependent Joint Regressors. In *Proc. of the IEEE CVPR*, 2013.

[8] M. Dantone, J. Gall, C. Leistner, and L. V. Gool. Body Parts Dependent Joint Regressors for Human Pose Estimation in Still Images. *IEEE TPAMI*, 36(11):2131–2143, November 2014.

[9] T. E. de Campos, B. R. Babu, and M. Varma. Character recognition in natural images. In *Proc. of the VISAPP*, February 2009.

[10] J. Gall, A. Yao, N. Razavi, L. V. Gool, and V. Lempitsky. Hough Forests for Object Detection, Tracking and Action Recognition. *IEEE TPAMI*, 33(11):2188 – 2202, 2011.

[11] M. Hall, E. Frank, G. Holmes, B. Pfahringer, P. Reutemann, and I. H. Witten. The weka data mining software: An update. *SIGKDD Expl.*, 11, 2009.

[12] J. Hull. A database for handwritten text recognition research. *IEEE TPAMI*, 16(5):550–554, May 1994.

[13] Y. Jia, E. Shelhamer, J. Donahue, S. Karayev, J. Long, R. Girshick, S. Guadarrama, and T. Darrell. Caffe: Convolutional architecture for fast feature embedding. *ACM MM Open Source Comp.*, 2014.

[14] C. Lassner and R. Lienhart. Norm-induced entropies for decision forests. In *Proc.of the IEEE WACV*, 2015.

[15] F. Pedregosa, G. Varoquaux, A. Gramfort, V. Michel, B. Thirion, O. Grisel, M. Blondel, P. Prettenhofer, R. Weiss, V. Dubourg, J. Vanderplas, A. Passos, D. Cournapeau, M. Brucher, M. Perrot, and E. Duchesnay. Scikit-learn: Machine learning in Python. *JMLR*, 12:2825–2830, 2011.

[16] A. Schiendorfer, C. Lassner, G. Anders, W. Reif, and R. Lienhart. Active learning for abstract models of collectives. In *Proc. of the SAOS workshop*, 2015.

[17] S. Schulter, P. Wohlhart, C. Leistner, A. Saffari, P. M. Roth, and H. Bischof. Alternating Decision Forests. In *Proc. of the IEEE CVPR*, 2013.

SINGA: A Distributed Deep Learning Platform

Beng Chin Ooi†, Kian-Lee Tan†, Sheng Wang†, Wei Wang†, Qingchao Cai†,
Gang Chen§, Jinyang Gao†, Zhaojing Luo†, Anthony K. H. Tung†, Yuan Wang‡, Zhongle Xie†,
Meihui Zhang¶, Kaiping Zheng†
†National University of Singapore, §Zhejiang University, China, ‡NetEase, Inc., China,
¶ Singapore University of Technology and Design
†{ooibc, tankl, wangsh, wangwei, caiqc, jinyang.gao, zhaojing, atung, zhongle,
kaiping}@comp.nus.edu.sg, §cg@zju.edu.cn,
‡wangyuan@corp.netease.com, ¶meihui_zhang@sutd.edu.sg

ABSTRACT

Deep learning has shown outstanding performance in various machine learning tasks. However, the deep complex model structure and massive training data make it expensive to train. In this paper, we present a distributed deep learning system, called SINGA, for training big models over large datasets. An intuitive programming model based on the layer abstraction is provided, which supports a variety of popular deep learning models. SINGA architecture supports both synchronous and asynchronous training frameworks. Hybrid training frameworks can also be customized to achieve good scalability. SINGA provides different neural net partitioning schemes for training large models. SINGA is an Apache Incubator project released under Apache License 2.

Categories and Subject Descriptors

I.5.1 [**Pattern Recognition**]: Models—*Neural Nets*; H.3.4 [**Information Storage and Retrieval**]: Systems and Software—*Distributed System*

General Terms

Design, Experimentation, Performance

Keywords

Deep learning; Distributed training

1. INTRODUCTION

There has been a surge of interests, from both industry and academia, in deep learning. On one hand, deep learning has been shown to achieve (and even surpass) the accuracy of state-of-the-art algorithms in a variety of tasks, e.g., image classification [4] and multi-modal data analysis [9, 10]. On the other hand, to improve runtime performance, distributed training systems have also been proposed in recent years, e.g., Google's DistBelief [1], Torch used by Facebook [7], Baidu's DeepImage [11], Caffe [3] and Purine [6]. These studies showed that deep learning models can benefit from deeper structures and larger training datasets.

However, there are two major challenges to develop a distributed deep learning system. First, deep learning models have a large number of parameters, which would incur huge amount of communication overhead to synchronize nodes when these are updated. Consequently, the scalability in terms of training time to reach certain accuracy is a challenge. Second, it is non-trivial for programmers to develop and train models with deep and complex model structures. Distributed training further increases the burden of programmers, e.g., data and model partitioning, and network communication. This problem is exacerbated if data scientists with little deep learning background are expected to work with deep learning models.

In this paper, we present SINGA[1], a general distributed deep learning platform. SINGA is designed with an intuitive programming model that supports a variety of popular deep learning models, namely feed-forward models including convolution neural networks (CNN), energy models like restricted Boltzmann machine (RBM), and recurrent neural networks (RNN). Many built-in layers are provided for training popular deep learning models. SINGA architecture is sufficiently flexible to run synchronous, asynchronous and hybrid training frameworks. Synchronous training improves the efficiency of one iteration, and asynchronous training improves the convergence rate. Given a fixed budget (e.g., cluster size), users can run a hybrid framework that maximizes the scalability by trading off between the efficiency and convergence rate. SINGA also supports different neural net partitioning schemes to parallelize the training of large models, namely partitioning on batch dimension, feature dimension or hybrid partitioning. GPU support and integration with cluster management software like Mesos will be added in near future.

2. OVERVIEW

The stochastic gradient descent (SGD) algorithm is used in SINGA to train parameters of deep learning models. The training workload is distributed over worker and server units as shown in Figure 1. In each iteration, every worker calls *TrainOneBatch* function to compute parameter gradients.

MM'15, October 26–30, 2015, Brisbane, Australia.

ACM 978-1-4503-3459-4/15/10 ...$15.00.
DOI: http://dx.doi.org/10.1145/2733373.2807410 .

[1]http://www.comp.nus.edu.sg/~dbsystem/singa

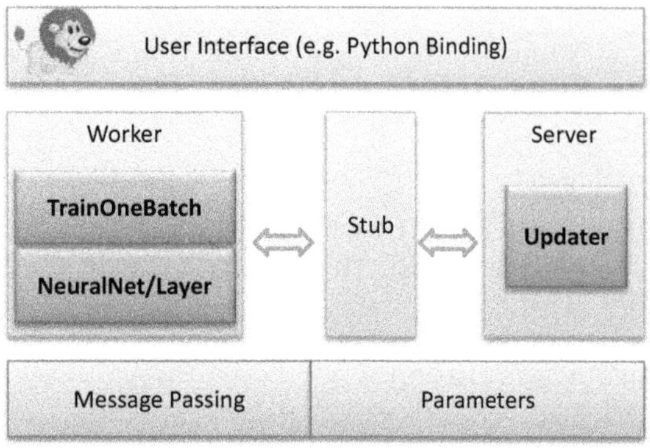

Figure 1: SINGA software stack.

TrainOneBatch takes a *NeuralNet* object representing the neural net, and visits layers of the *NeuralNet* in certain order. The resultant gradients are sent to the local stub that aggregates the requests and forwards them to corresponding servers for updating. Servers reply to workers with the updated parameters for the next iteration. To start a training job, users submit a job configuration consisting of four components: 1) a *NeuralNet* describing the neural net structure with the detailed layer setting and their connections (Section 3.1); 2) a *TrainOneBatch* algorithm which is tailored for different model categories (Section 3.2); 3) an *Updater* defining the protocol for updating parameters at the server side (Section 3.3); 4) a *Cluster Topology* specifying the distributed architecture (Section 4) of workers and servers.

3. PROGRAMMING MODEL

In this section, we describe the first three components of the job configuration. SINGA has provided many built-in implementations for these components. They are also modular and extensible for customization. Users can submit their training job on a single node after configuring these three parts. To conduct distributed training, users need to set the cluster topology as discussed in Section 4.

3.1 NeuralNet

Neural net representation. SINGA represents a neural net using a data structure called *NeuralNet*, which consists of a set of unidirectionally connected layers. Users configure the *NeuralNet* by listing all layers of the neural net and specifying each layer's source layer names. This representation is natural for feed-forward models, e.g., CNN and MLP. For energy models including RBM, DBM, etc., their connections are undirected. To represent these models using *NeuralNet*, users can simply replace each connection with two directed connections. In other words, for each pair of connected layers, their source layer field should include each other's name. For recurrent neural networks, users can remove the recurrent connections by unrolling the recurrent layer. For example, in Figure 2, the original layer is unrolled into a new layer with 4 layers managed inside the new layer. In this way, the model is like a normal feed-forward model, thus can be configured similarly. When SINGA creates the *NeuralNet* instance, it also partitions the original neural net according to user's configuration to support parallel training of large models. Partitioning strategies include:

1. Partitioning all layers into different subsets.

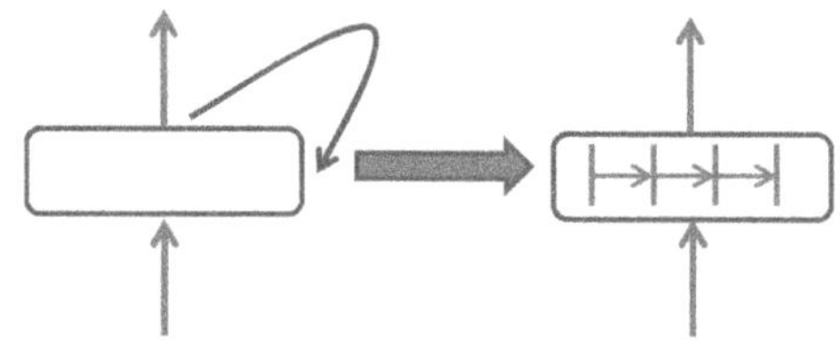

Figure 2: Unroll a recurrent layer into 4 (internal) layers.

```
Layer:
Vector<Layer> srclayer
Blob feature
Func ComputeFeature(phase)
Func ComputeGradient()

Param:
Blob data, gradient
```

Figure 3: Base layer class.

2. Partitioning each singe layer into sub-layers on batch dimension.
3. Partitioning each singe layer into sub-layers on feature dimension.
4. Hybrid partitioning of strategy 1, 2 and 3.

More details on partitioning are discussed in [8].

Layer. Layers of a neural net are represented by instances of Layer classes. Figure 3 shows the base layer class which includes two fields and two functions. The *srclayer* vector records all source layers. The *feature* blob consists of a set of feature vectors, e.g., one vector per image, computed from the source layers. For a recurrent layer in RNN, the feature blob contains one vector per internal layer. If a layer has parameters, these parameters are declared using type *Param* which consists of a *data* and a *gradient* blob for parameter values and gradients respectively. The *ComputeFeature* function evaluates the feature blob by transforming (e.g. convolution and pooling) features from the source layers. *ComputeGradient* computes the gradients of parameters associated with this layer. These two functions are invoked by the *TrainOneBatch* function during training (Section 3.2). SINGA has provided many built-in layers, which can be used directly to create neural nets. Users can also extend the layer class to implement their own feature transformation logics as long as the two base functions are overridden to be consistent with the *TrainOneBatch* function. Besides the common fields like name and type, layer configuration contains some specific fields as well, e.g. file path for data layers. The layers in SINGA are categorized as follows according to their functionalities,

- *Data layers* for loading records (e.g., images) from disk, HDFS or network into memory.
- *Parser layers* for parsing features, labels, etc. from records.
- *Neuron layers* for feature transformation, e.g., convolution, pooling, dropout, etc.
- *Loss layers* for measuring the training objective loss, e.g., cross entropy-loss or Euclidean loss.

- *Output layers* for outputting the prediction results (e.g., probabilities of each category) onto disk or network.
- *Connection layers* for connecting layers when the neural net is partitioned.

3.2 TrainOneBatch

For each SGD iteration, every worker calls the *TrainOneBatch* function to compute gradients of parameters associated with local layers (i.e., layers dispatched to it). SINGA has implemented two algorithms for the *TrainOneBatch* function. Users select the corresponding algorithm for their model in the configuration. Algorithm 1 shows the back-propagation (BP) algorithm [5] for feed-forward models and recurrent neural networks. It forwards (Line 1-3) features through all local layers and backwards gradients in the reverse order (Line 4-6). Since RNN models are unrolled into feed-forward models (*ComputeFeature* and *ComputeGradient* functions compute for all internal layers), Algorithm 1 runs as the back-propagation through time (BPTT) algorithm for them. Algorithm 2 illustrates the contrastive divergence (CD) algorithm [2] for energy models. Parameter gradients are computed (Line 7-9) after the positive phase (Line 1-3) and negative phase (Line 4-6). *kCD* controls the number of Gibbs sampling iterations in the negative phase. In both algorithms, the *Collect* function is blocked until the parameters are fetched from servers. The *Update* function returns immediately after sending the gradients.

Algorithm 1: BPTrainOneBatch

```
  Input: net
1 foreach layer in net.local_layers do
2     Collect(layer.params()) // receive parameters
3     layer.ComputeFeature(kFprop) // forward prop
4 foreach layer in reverse(net.local_layers) do
5     layer.ComputeGradient()// backward prop
6     Update(layer.params())// send gradients
```

3.3 Updater

SINGA comes with many popular protocols for updating parameter values based on gradients. If users want to implement their own updating protocols, they can extend the base Updater to override the *Update* function.

4. DISTRIBUTED TRAINING

4.1 System Architecture

The logical system architecture is shown in Fig. 4. There are two types of execution units, namely workers and servers. Workers compute the parameter updates (e.g., the gradients), while servers maintain up-to-date parameters and handle get/update requests from workers. In each iteration, workers collect fresh parameters from servers and issue update requests to servers after the computation. A number of workers/servers are logically grouped as a worker/server group. A *worker group* loads a subset of the training data and computes the parameter gradients for a complete model replica, denoted as ParamShard. SINGA provides different strategies (i.e., data parallelism, model parallelism and hybrid parallelism) to distribute the workload within a worker group. Workers in the same group run synchronously, while different worker groups run asynchronously. A *server group* maintains one replica of the full model parameters (i.e., a ParamShard), handling requests from multiple worker groups. Neighboring server groups synchronize their parameters periodically.

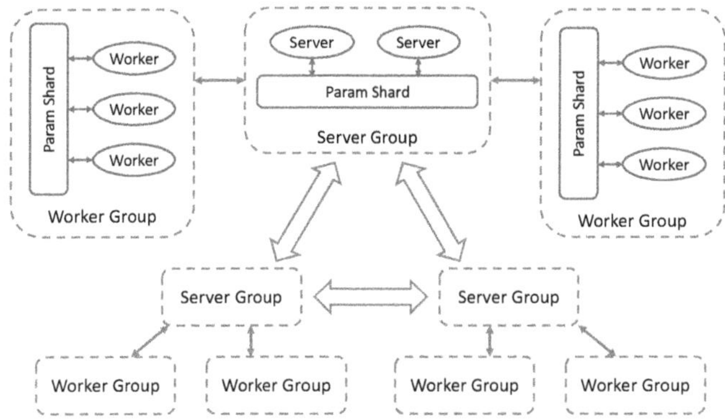

Figure 4: Logical architecture of SINGA.

Algorithm 2: CDTrainOneBatch

```
  Input: net, kCD
1 foreach layer in net.local_layers do
2     Collect(layer.params()) // receive parameters
3     layer.ComputeFeature(kPostive)// pos phase
4 foreach k in 1...kCD do
5     foreach layer in net.local_layers do
6         layer.ComputeFeature(kNegative) // neg phase
7 foreach layer in net.local_layers do
8     layer.ComputeGradient();
9     Update(layer.params())// send gradients
```

4.2 System Implementation

In SINGA implementation, each execution unit (worker or server) is a thread. As a process may contain multiple threads, there could be multiple (worker/server) groups in one process. It is also possible that one group spans across multiple processes. When starting up a SINGA process, after all execution units are launched, the main thread runs as a stub thread as shown in Figure 1, which aggregates local requests and sends them to remote stubs. Hence, each unit only sends and receives messages from its local stub. SINGA defines general communication APIs on top of ZeroMQ[2] and MPI. Users can choose the underlying implementation (ZeroMQ or MPI) at compile time. If two execution units manage the same parameter partition and they are in the same process, SINGA can leverage the shared memory to reduce communication cost.

4.3 Training Frameworks

SINGA supports various synchronous and asynchronous training frameworks. Users can change the cluster topology configuration to run different frameworks. Here we illustrate how users can train with SINGA using popular distributed training frameworks.

[2]http://zeromq.org/

Sandblaster. This is a synchronous framework used by Google Brain [1]. The training dataset is partitioned into multiple nodes. In one iteration, all nodes fetch up-to-date parameters from parameter servers and sends requests back to update parameters. To run this framework with n nodes, we configure SINGA as follows:

- A single worker group with x workers.
- A single server group with $n - x$ servers.

AllReduce. This is a synchronous framework used by Baidu's DeepImage [11]. There is no concept of server. Each worker computes gradients of one model replica and maintains a subset of parameters. In one iteration, every node fetches up-to-date parameters from all other nodes and sends parameter gradients back to corresponding nodes. To run this framework with n nodes, we configure SINGA as follows:

- A single worker group with n workers.
- A single server group with n servers.
- One worker and one server in each node/process.

Downpour. This is an asynchronous framework used by Google Brain [1]. The training process is similar to Sandblaster. One major difference is that there are multiple groups running asynchronously. Each group of nodes run without awareness of other groups. To run this framework with n nodes, we configure SINGA as follows:

- x worker groups, each with y workers.
- A single server group with $n - x \cdot y$ servers.

Distributed Hogwild. This is an asynchronous framework used by Caffe [3]. Each node maintains a local replica of parameters. In an iteration, each node computes gradients for one model replica and updates them locally. To ensure accuracy and convergence, nodes must exchange updates with others periodically. To run this framework with n nodes, we configure SINGA as follows:

- n worker groups, each with one worker.
- n server groups, each with one server.
- One worker and one server in each node/process.

All training frameworks have their own advantages and limitations. Synchronous training can accelerate the speed for one iteration as the workload is distributed to multiple workers. However, it is limited to small or medium size clusters, because the synchronization delay is large as the cluster size increases. Asynchronous training can improve the convergence rate to some degree, but the improvement becomes small when there are too many model replicas.

SINGA provides users a unified platform for verifying the performance of different frameworks (e.g., convergence rate, computation time) under the same environmental setting. Moreover, users can run hybrid training by launching multiple server groups and worker groups: using multiple server (groups) can alleviate the communication bottleneck at server sides; using multiple worker groups can improve the convergence rate; using multiple workers in a group can accelerate each training iteration. Given a fixed budget (e.g., number of nodes in a cluster), there lies the opportunity to find the optimal hybrid training framework that trades off between the convergence rate and efficiency to achieve the minimal training time.

5. AVAILABILITY

The code and documentation of SINGA is available on the incubator website[3] under Apache License 2. Installation guide and quick start examples are also provided. Sample applications and extensive performance evaluations are presented in [8].

6. ACKNOWLEDGMENTS

This work was in part supported by the National Research Foundation, Prime Minister's Office, Singapore under its Competitive Research Programme (CRP Award No. NRF-CRP8-2011-08) and A*STAR project 1321202073. Gang Chen's work was supported by National Natural Science Foundation of China (NSFC) Grant No. 61472348. We would like to thank the SINGA team members and NetEase for their contributions to the implementation of the Apache SINGA system, and the anonymous reviewers for their insightful and constructive comments.

7. REFERENCES

[1] J. Dean, G. Corrado, R. Monga, K. Chen, M. Devin, Q. V. Le, M. Z. Mao, M. Ranzato, A. W. Senior, P. A. Tucker, K. Yang, and A. Y. Ng. Large scale distributed deep networks. In *NIPS*, pages 1232–1240, 2012.

[2] G. E. Hinton. Training products of experts by minimizing contrastive divergence. *Neural Computation*, 14(8):1771–1800, 2002.

[3] Y. Jia, E. Shelhamer, J. Donahue, S. Karayev, J. Long, R. Girshick, S. Guadarrama, and T. Darrell. Caffe: Convolutional architecture for fast feature embedding. *arXiv preprint arXiv:1408.5093*, 2014.

[4] A. Krizhevsky, I. Sutskever, and G. E. Hinton. Imagenet classification with deep convolutional neural networks. In *NIPS*, pages 1106–1114, 2012.

[5] Y. LeCun, L. Bottou, G. B. Orr, and K. Müller. Effiicient backprop. In *Neural Networks: Tricks of the Trade*, pages 9–50, 1996.

[6] M. Lin, S. Li, X. Luo, and S. Yan. Purine: A bi-graph based deep learning framework. *CoRR*, abs/1412.6249, 2014.

[7] N. Vasilache, J. Johnson, M. Mathieu, S. Chintala, S. Piantino, and Y. LeCun. Fast convolutional nets with fbfft: A GPU performance evaluation. *CoRR*, abs/1412.7580, 2014.

[8] W. Wang, G. Chen, T. T. A. Dinh, J. Gao, B. C. Ooi, K.-L. Tan, and S. Wang. SINGA: Putting deep learning in the hands of multimedia users. *MM*, 2015.

[9] W. Wang, B. C. Ooi, X. Yang, D. Zhang, and Y. Zhuang. Effective multi-modal retrieval based on stacked auto-encoders. *PVLDB*, 7(8):649–660, 2014.

[10] W. Wang, X. Yang, B. C. Ooi, D. Zhang, and Y. Zhuang. Effective deep learning-based multi-modal retrieval. *The VLDB Journal*, pages 1–23, 2015.

[11] R. Wu, S. Yan, Y. Shan, Q. Dang, and G. Sun. Deep image: Scaling up image recognition. *CoRR*, abs/1501.02876, 2015.

[3]`http://singa.incubator.apache.org/`

MatConvNet

Convolutional Neural Networks for MATLAB

Andrea Vedaldi
University of Oxford
vedaldi@robots.ox.ac.uk

Karel Lenc
University of Oxford
lenc@robots.ox.ac.uk

ABSTRACT

MatConvNet is an open source implementation of Convolutional Neural Networks (CNNs) with a deep integration in the MATLAB environment. The toolbox is designed with an emphasis on simplicity and flexibility. It exposes the building blocks of CNNs as easy-to-use MATLAB functions, providing routines for computing convolutions with filter banks, feature pooling, normalisation, and much more. MatConvNet can be easily extended, often using only MATLAB code, allowing fast prototyping of new CNN architectures. At the same time, it supports efficient computation on CPU and GPU, allowing to train complex models on large datasets such as ImageNet ILSVRC containing millions of training examples.

Categories and Subject Descriptors

D.0 [**Software**]: General; I.2.10 [**Artificial Intelligence**]: Vision and Scene Understanding

General Terms

Algorithm, design, prototyping

Keywords

Computer vision; image understanding; machine learning; deep learning; convolutional neural networks

1. INTRODUCTION

MatConvNet is a MATLAB toolbox implementing *Convolutional Neural Networks* (CNN) for computer vision applications. Since the breakthrough work of [4], CNNs have had a major impact in computer vision, and image understanding in particular, essentially replacing traditional image representations such as the ones implemented in our own VLFeat [8] open source library.

While most CNNs are obtained by composing simple linear and non-linear filtering operations such as convolution and rectification, their implementation is far from trivial.

MM'15, October 26–30, 2015, Brisbane, Australia.

ACM 978-1-4503-3459-4/15/10 ...$15.00.
DOI: http://dx.doi.org/10.1145/2733373.2807412.

```
% install and compile MatConvNet (run once)
untar(['http://www.vlfeat.org/matconvnet/download/' ...
  'matconvnet-1.0-beta12.tar.gz']) ;
cd matconvnet-1.0-beta12
run matlab/vl_compilenn

% download a pre-trained CNN from the web (run once)
urlwrite(...
 'http://www.vlfeat.org/matconvnet/models/imagenet-vgg-f.mat', ...
 'imagenet-vgg-f.mat') ;

% setup MatConvNet
run matlab/vl_setupnn

% load the pre-trained CNN
net = load('imagenet-vgg-f.mat') ;

% load and preprocess an image
im = imread('peppers.png') ;
im_ = imresize(single(im), net.normalization.imageSize(1:2)) ;
im_ = im_ - net.normalization.averageImage ;

% run the CNN
res = vl_simplenn(net, im_) ;

% show the classification result
scores = squeeze(gather(res(end).x
[bestScore, best] = max(scores) ;
figure(1) ; clf ; imagesc(im) ;
title(sprintf('%s (%d), score %.3f',...
net.classes.description{best}, best, bestScore)) ;
```

Figure 1: A complete example including download, installing, compiling and running MatConvNet to classify one of MATLAB stock images using a large CNN pre-trained on ImageNet.

The reason is that CNNs need to be learned from vast amounts of data, often millions of images, requiring very efficient implementations. As most CNN libraries, MatConvNet achieves this by using a variety of optimisations and, chiefly, by supporting computations on GPUs.

Numerous other machine learning, deep learning, and CNN open source libraries exist. To cite some of the most popular ones: CudaConvNet,[1] Torch,[2] Theano,[3] and Caffe[4]. Many of these libraries are well supported, with dozens of active contributors and large user bases. Therefore, why creating yet another library?

[1] https://code.google.com/p/cuda-convnet/
[2] http://cilvr.nyu.edu/doku.php?id=code:start
[3] http://deeplearning.net/software/theano/
[4] http://caffe.berkeleyvision.org

The key motivation for developing MatConvNet was to provide an environment particularly friendly and efficient for researchers to use in their investigations.[5] MatConvNet achieves this by its deep integration in the MATLAB environment, which is one of the most popular development environments in computer vision research as well as in many other areas. In particular, MatConvNet exposes as simple MATLAB commands CNN building blocks such as convolution, normalisation and pooling (section 2); these can then be combined and extended with ease to create CNN architectures. While many of such blocks use optimised CPU and GPU implementations written in C++ and CUDA (section 4), MATLAB native support for GPU computation means that it is often possible to write new blocks in MATLAB directly while maintaining computational efficiency. Compared to writing new CNN components using lower level languages, this is an important simplification that can significantly accelerate testing new ideas. Using MATLAB also provides a bridge towards other areas; for instance, MatConvNet was recently used by the University of Arizona in planetary science, as summarised in this NVIDIA blogpost.[6]

MatConvNet can learn large CNN models such AlexNet [4] and the very deep networks of [6] from millions of images. Pre-trained versions of several of these powerful models can be downloaded from the MatConvNet home page. (section 3). While powerful, MatConvNet remains simple to use and install. The implementation is fully self-contained, requiring only MATLAB and a compatible C++ compiler (using the GPU code requires the freely-available CUDA DevKit and a suitable NVIDIA GPU). As demonstrated in figure 1 and section 1.1, it is possible to download, compile, and install MatConvNet using three MATLAB commands. Several fully-functional examples demonstrating how small and large networks can be learned are included. Importantly, several *standard pre-trained network* can be immediately downloaded and used in applications. A manual with a complete technical description of the toolbox is maintained along with the toolbox.[7] These features make MatConvNet useful in an educational context too.[8]

MatConvNet is open-source released under a BSD-like license. It can be downloaded from http://www.vlfeat.org/matconvnet as well as from GitHub.[9]

1.1 Getting started

MatConvNet is simple to install and use. Figure 1 provides a complete example that classifies an image using a latest-generation deep convolutional neural network. The example includes downloading MatConvNet, compiling the package, downloading a pre-trained CNN model, and evaluating the latter on one of MATLAB's stock images.

[5]While from a user perspective MatConvNet currently relies on MATLAB, the library is being developed with a clean separation between MATLAB code and the C++ and CUDA core; therefore, in the future the library may be extended to allow processing convolutional networks independently of MATLAB.

[6]http://devblogs.nvidia.com/parallelforall/deep-learning-image-understanding-planetary-science/

[7]http://www.vlfeat.org/matconvnet/matconvnet-manual.pdf

[8]An example laboratory experience based on MatConvNet can be downloaded from http://www.robots.ox.ac.uk/~vgg/practicals/cnn/index.html.

[9]http://ww.github.com/matconvnet

The key command in this example is **vl_simplenn**, a wrapper that takes as input the CNN **net** and the pre-processed image **im_** and produces as output a structure **res** of results. This particular wrapper can be used to model networks that have a simple structure, namely a *chain* of operations. Examining the code of **vl_simplenn** (**edit** ↩ **vl_simplenn** in MATLAB) we note that the wrapper transforms the data sequentially, applying a number of MATLAB functions as specified by the network configuration. These function, discussed in detail in section 2, are called "building blocks" and constitute the backbone of MatConvNet.

While most blocks implement simple operations, what makes them non trivial is their efficiency (section 4) as well as support for backpropagation (section 2.2) to allow learning CNNs. Next, we demonstrate how to use one of such building blocks directly. For the sake of the example, consider convolving an image with a bank of linear filters. Start by reading an image in MATLAB, say using **im** ↩ = **single**(**imread**('peppers.png')), obtaining a $H \times W \times D$ array **im**, where $D = 3$ is the number of colour channels in the image. Then create a bank of $K = 16$ random filters of size 3×3 using **f** = randn(3,3,3,16,'single'). Finally, convolve the image with the filters by using the command **y** = **vl_nnconv**(**x**,**f**,[]). This results in an array **y** with K channels, one for each of the K filters in the bank.

While users are encouraged to make use of the blocks directly to create new architectures, MatConvNet provides wrappers such as **vl_simplenn** for standard CNN architectures such as AlexNet [4] or Network-in-Network [5]. Furthermore, the library provides numerous examples (in the **examples/** subdirectory), including code to learn a variety models on the MNIST, CIFAR, and ImageNet datasets. All these examples use the **examples/cnn_train** training code, which is an implementation of stochastic gradient descent (section 2.1). While this training code is perfectly serviceable and quite flexible, it remains in the **examples/** subdirectory as it is somewhat problem-specific. Users are welcome to implement their optimisers.

2. BUILDING BLOCKS

At the core of MatConvNet there is a library of CNN building blocks, such as the convolution operator **vl_nnconv** seen above. This section discusses in detail these building blocks and their design.

2.1 Overview of the available blocks

In order to understand the design of the building blocks, it is necessary to first review the fundamentals of CNNs. On the outset, a *Convolutional Neural Network* (CNN) is a function f mapping data $\mathbf{x}$, for example an image, to an output vector $\mathbf{y}$. The function $f = f_L \circ \cdots \circ f_1$ is the composition of a sequence of simpler functions f_l, which we call *computational blocks* or *layers*. Let $\mathbf{x}_1, \mathbf{x}_2, \ldots, \mathbf{x}_L$ be the outputs of each layer in the network, and let $\mathbf{x}_0 = \mathbf{x}$ denote the network input. Each output $\mathbf{x}_l = f_l(\mathbf{x}_{l-1}; \mathbf{w}_l)$ is computed from the previous output $\mathbf{x}_{l-1}$ by applying the function f_l with parameters $\mathbf{w}_l$. The data flowing through the network has a spatial structure; namely, $\mathbf{x}_l \in \mathbb{R}^{H_l \times W_l \times D_l}$ is a 3D array whose first two dimensions are interpreted as spatial coordinates (it therefore represents a feature field). A fourth non-singleton dimension in the array allows processing *batches* of images in parallel, which is important for efficiency. The network is called *convolutional* because the functions f_l act as local and translation invariant operators (i.e. non-linear filters).

MatConvNet includes a variety of building blocks, contained in the `matlab/` directory, such as `vl_nnconv` (convolution), `vl_nnconvt` (convolution transpose or deconvolution), `vl_nnpool` (max and average pooling), `vl_nnrelu` (ReLU activation), `vl_nnsigmoid` (sigmoid activation), `vl_nnsoftmax` (softmax operator), `vl_nnloss` (classification log-loss), `vl_nnbnorm` (batch normalization), `vl_nnspnorm` (spatial normalization), `vl_nnnormalize` (cross-channel normalization), or `vl_nnpdist` (p-distance). The library of blocks is sufficiently extensive that many interesting state-of-the-art network can be implemented and learned using the toolbox, or even ported from other toolboxes such as Caffe.

CNNs are used as classifiers or regressors. In the example of figure 1, the output $\hat{\mathbf{y}} = f(\mathbf{x})$ is a vector of probabilities, one for each of a 1,000 possible image labels (dog, cat, trilobite, ...). If $\mathbf{y}$ is the true label of image $\mathbf{x}$, we can measure the CNN performance by a loss function $\ell_{\mathbf{y}}(\hat{\mathbf{y}}) \in \mathbb{R}$ which assigns a penalty to classification errors. The CNN parameters can then be tuned or *learned* to minimise this loss averaged over a large dataset of labelled example images.

Learning generally uses a variant of *stochastic gradient descent* (SGD). While this is an efficient method (for this type of problems), networks may contain several million parameters and need to be trained on millions of images; thus, efficiency is a paramount in MatConvNet design, as further discussed in section 4. SGD requires also to compute the CNN derivatives, as explained in the next section.

2.2 Backpropagation

The fundamental operation to learn a network is computing the derivative of the loss with respect to the network parameters (as this is required for gradient descent). This is obtained using an algorithm called *backpropagation*, which is an application of the chain rule for derivatives:

$$\frac{d}{d\mathbf{w}_l^\top}\ell_{\mathbf{y}}(f(\mathbf{x};\mathbf{w}_1,\ldots,\mathbf{w}_L)) \\ = \frac{d[\ell_{\mathbf{y}} \circ f_L \circ \ldots f_{l+1}](\mathbf{x}_l)}{d\mathbf{x}_l^\top}\frac{df_l(\mathbf{x}_{l-1};\mathbf{w}_l)}{d\mathbf{w}_l^\top}$$

where for notational simplicity that data and parameters are identified with vectors (which is always possible up to stacking). Note that the formula involves computing the derivative of parts of the network with respect to the data; these are obtained in a similar manner, and require computing the derivative "one level up". Overall derivatives are computed by backtracking from the last layer (output) to the first (input).

Since the loss function output is scalar, the dimension of all the intermediate derivatives is the same as the corresponding parameter. For example, $d[\ell_{\mathbf{y}} \circ f_L \circ \ldots f_{l+1}]/d\mathbf{x}_l^\top$ has $H_lW_lD_l$ components, equal to the number of elements of $\mathbf{x}_l$. Compare this to a Jacobian such as $df_l/d\mathbf{x}_{l-1}^\top$ that has $H_lW_lD_lH_{l-1}W_{l-1}D_{l-1}$ components instead.

The key in implementing backpropagation efficiently is to store only the smaller derivatives, leaving the intermediate calculations of the larger Jacobians implicit. This is best illustrated with an example. Consider a layer f such as the convolution operator implemented by `vl_nnconv`. In the so called "forward" mode, one calls the function as `y` ↩ `= vl_nnconv(x,w,[])` to convolve input `x` and obtain output `y`. In the "backward mode", one calls `[dzdx, dzdw]` = ↩ `vl_nnconv(x,w,[],dzdy)`. To understand this syntax, imagine that f is connected to the "rest of the network", denoted $z(\cdot)$, terminating in a scalar loss:

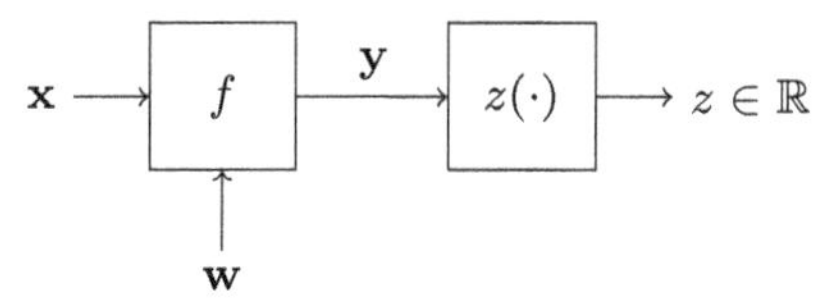

Here `dzdy` is the derivative $dz/d\mathbf{y}$ of the downstream subnetwork $z(\cdot)$, `dzdx` the derivative $d[z \circ f]/d\mathbf{x}$ of the upstream subnetwork (i.e. prefixed by f), and `dzdx` and `dzdw` the corresponding derivatives w.r.t. `x` and `w`.

As explained above, `dzdx`, `dzdw`, and `dzdy` have the same dimension of `x`, `w`, and `y`. In this manner, the computation of larger Jacobians is encapsulated in the function call and never carried explicitly. Another way of looking at this is that, instead of computing a derivative such as $d\mathbf{y}/d\mathbf{w}$, one always computes a projection of the type $\langle dz/d\mathbf{y}, d\mathbf{y}/d\mathbf{w}\rangle$.

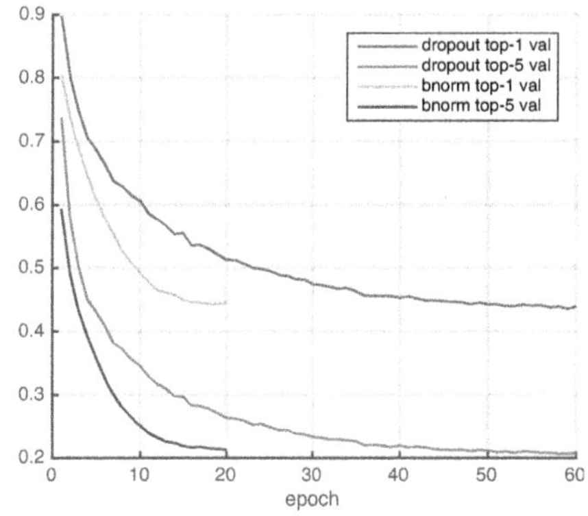

Figure 2: Training AlexNet on ImageNet ILSVRC: dropout vs batch normalisation.

3. DOCUMENTATION AND EXAMPLES

There are three main sources of information about MatConvNet. First, the website contains descriptions of all the functions and several examples and tutorials.[10] Second, there is a PDF manual containing a great deal of technical details about the toolbox, including detailed mathematical descriptions of the building blocks. Third, MatConvNet ships with several examples (section 1.1).

Most examples are fully self-contained. For example, in order to run the MNIST example, it suffices to point MATLAB to the MatConvNet root directory and type `addpath examples` followed by `cnn_mnist`. Due to the problem size, the ImageNet ILSVRC example requires some more preparation, including downloading and preprocessing the images (using the bundled script `utils/preprocess-imagenet.sh`). Several advanced examples are included as well. For example, figure 2 illustrates the top-1 and top-5 validation errors as a model similar to AlexNet [4] is trained using either standard dropout regularisation or the recent *batch normalisation* technique of [3]. The latter is shown to converge in about one third of the

[10]See also `http://www.robots.ox.ac.uk/~vgg/practicals/cnn/index.html`.

epochs (passes through the training data) required by the former.

The MatConvNet website contains also numerous *pre-trained* models, i.e. large CNNs trained on ImageNet ILSVRC that can be downloaded and used as a starting point for many other problems [1]. These include: AlexNet [4], VGG-S, VGG-M, VGG-S [1], and VGG-VD-16, and VGG-VD-19 [7]. The example code of figure 1 shows how one such models can be used in a few lines of MATLAB code.

4. SPEED

Efficiency is very important for working with CNNs. MatConvNet supports using NVIDIA GPUs as it includes CUDA implementations of all algorithms (or relies on MATLAB CUDA support).

To use the GPU (provided that suitable hardware is available and the toolbox has been compiled with GPU support), one simply converts the arguments to `gpuArrays` in MATLAB, as in `y = vl_nnconv(gpuArray(x), gpuArray(w), [])`. In this manner, switching between CPU and GPU is fully transparent. Note that MatConvNet can also make use of the NVIDIA CuDNN library which significant speed and space benefits.

Next we evaluate the performance of MatConvNet when training large architectures on the ImageNet ILSVRC 2012 challenge data [2]. The test machine is a Dell server with two Intel Xeon CPU E5-2667 v2 clocked at 3.30 GHz (each CPU has eight cores), 256 GB of RAM, and four NVIDIA Titan Black GPUs (only one of which is used unless otherwise noted). Experiments use MatConvNet beta12, CuDNN v2, and MATLAB R2015a. The data is preprocessed to avoid rescaling images on the fly in MATLAB and stored in a RAM disk for faster access. The code uses the `vl_imreadjpeg` command to read large batches of JPEG images from disk in a number of separate threads. The driver `examples/cnn_imagenet.m` is used in all experiments.

We train the models discussed in section 3 on ImageNet ILSVRC. Table 1 reports the training speed as number of images per second processed by stochastic gradient descent. AlexNet trains at about 264 images/s with CuDNN, which is about 40% faster than the vanilla GPU implementation (using CuBLAS) and more than 10 times faster than using the CPUs. Furthermore, we note that, despite MATLAB overhead, the implementation speed is comparable to Caffe (they report 253 images/s with cuDNN and a Titan – a slightly slower GPU than the Titan Black used here). Note also that, as the model grows in size, the size of a SGD batch must be decreased (to fit in the GPU memory), increasing the overhead impact somewhat.

Table 2 reports the speed on VGG-VD-16, a very large model, using multiple GPUs. In this case, the batch size is set to 264 images. These are further divided in sub-batches of 22 images each to fit in the GPU memory; the latter are then distributed among one to four GPUs on the same machine. While there is a substantial communication overhead, training speed increases from 20 images/s to 45. Addressing this overhead is one of the medium term goals of the library.

model	batch sz.	CPU	GPU	CuDNN
AlexNet	256	22.1	192.4	264.1
VGG-F	256	21.4	211.4	289.7
VGG-M	128	7.8	116.5	136.6
VGG-S	128	7.4	96.2	110.1
VGG-VD-16	24	1.7	18.4	20.0
VGG-VD-19	24	1.5	15.7	16.5

Table 1: ImageNet training speed (images/s).

num GPUs	1	2	3	4
VGG-VD-16 speed	20.0	22.20	38.18	44.8

Table 2: Multiple GPU speed (images/s).

5. CONCLUSIONS

MatConvNet is a novel framework for experimenting with deep convolutional networks that is deeply integrated in MATLAB and allows easy experimentation with novel ideas. MatConvNet is already sufficient for advanced research in deep learning; despite being introduced less than a year ago, it is already citied 24 times in arXiv papers, and has been used in several papers published at the recent CVPR 2015 conference.

As CNNs are a rapidly moving target, MatConvNet is developing fast. So far there have been 12 ad-interim releases incrementally adding new features to the toolbox. Several new features, including support for DAGs, will be included in the upcoming releases starting in August 2015. The goal is to ensure that MatConvNet will stay current for the next several years of research in deep learning.

Acknowledgments. We kindly thank NVIDIA supporting this project by providing us with top-of-the-line GPUs and Mathworks for ongoing discussion on how to improve the library. Andrea Vedaldi is partially supported by the ERC StG 196773 and Karel Lenc by a DTA of the University of Oxford.

6. REFERENCES

[1] K. Chatfield, K. Simonyan, A. Vedaldi, and A. Zisserman. Return of the devil in the details: Delving deep into convolutional nets. In *Proc. BMVC*, 2014.

[2] J. Deng, W. Dong, R. Socher, L.-J. Li, K. Li, and L. Fei-Fei. ImageNet: A Large-Scale Hierarchical Image Database. In *Proc. CVPR*, 2009.

[3] S. Ioffe and C. Szegedy. Batch normalization: Accelerating deep network training by reducing internal covariate shift. *CoRR*, 2015.

[4] A. Krizhevsky, I. Sutskever, and G. E. Hinton. Imagenet classification with deep convolutional neural networks. In *Proc. NIPS*, 2012.

[5] M. Lin, Q. Chen, and S. Yan. Network in network. *CoRR*, abs/1312.4400, 2013.

[6] K. Simonyan, A. Vedaldi, and A. Zisserman. Deep inside convolutional networks: Visualising image classification models and saliency maps. In *Proc. ICLR*, 2014.

[7] K. Simonyan and A. Zisserman. Very deep convolutional networks for large-scale image recognition. *CoRR*, abs/1409.1556, 2014.

[8] A. Vedaldi and B. Fulkerson. VLFeat – An open and portable library of computer vision algorithms. In *Proc. ACM Int. Conf. on Multimedia*, 2010.

Theia: A Fast and Scalable Structure-from-Motion Library

Chris Sweeney Tobias Höllerer Matthew Turk
University of California Santa Barbara
2104 Harold Frank Hall
Santa Barbara, USA
{cmsweeney, holl, mturk}@cs.ucsb.edu

ABSTRACT

The Theia library provides students, researchers, and industry experts with a clean C++ library including a state-of-the-art Structure-from-Motion pipeline and a vast collection of multi-view geometry tools and algorithms that utilize image and video inputs to create high quality 3D reconstructions. The library is BSD licensed with strict Google C++ style guide adherence and comprehensive unit test coverage. All algorithms are intentionally designed to be scalable, and multithreaded computation is utilized automatically whenever possible. Theia is very modular so that all algorithms can be easily extended, modified, or used independently of the rest of the library. Feature extraction, image matching, RANSAC, pose estimation and SfM methods may all be chosen at runtime, enabling simple experimentation and fine-tuning for obtaining high quality SfM reconstructions. Since being released in February 2015 Theia has gathered an active community of users spanning graduate students, industry members, and computer vision experts.

Categories and Subject Descriptors

I.4.5 [**Computer Vision**]: Reconstruction; I.4.9 [**Computer Vision**]: Applications—*structure-from-motion*

Keywords

Computer vision, Structure-from-Motion, multi-view geometry

1. INTRODUCTION

The proliferation of online photo collections, such as Google Street View and Flickr, has allowed for large-scale mapping of urban environments via structure from motion (SfM)[15]. In particular, famous landmarks around the world have been captured by thousands or even millions of images and can be densely reconstructed using SfM. The 3D reconstructions obtained from SfM can be useful for an array of applications such as autonomous navigation, virtual tourism, and even disaster relief. While the benefits of SfM are clear, few publicly available tools exist for creating 3D reconstructions from SfM, and none of the currently available software is specifically geared towards large-scale SfM.

MM'15, October 26–30, 2015, Brisbane, Australia.
© 2015 ACM. ISBN 978-1-4503-3459-4/15/10 ...$15.00.
DOI: http://dx.doi.org/10.1145/2733373.2807405.

Figure 1: We are able to reconstruct Notre Dame from over 500 images in less than 120 seconds using Theia, compared to over 11 minutes using alternative software such as VisualSfM.

In this paper we introduce Theia, a fast and scalable SfM library designed to be simple to understand and easy to extend. Theia is intended to provide computer vision researchers and academics with a set of multi-view geometry tools that are useful as individual components while also providing full out-of-the-box SfM pipelines that are efficient and robust. The library utilizes the SSE optimized Eigen[1] library for matrix operations and Ceres Solver[2] for large-scale, multi-threaded nonlinear optimization. The code is extensively covered by unit tests and features significant, useful logging tools for performance evaluation and debugging. CMake[3] is used to ensure cross-platform portability and a simple build and installation process. Theia is well documented within the code and on the library's website[4]. To make this library as useful as possible for other researchers, we have also provided compatible I/O interfaces with match-

[1]`http://eigen.tuxfamily.org`
[2]`http://ceres-solver.org`
[3]`http://www.cmake.org`
[4]`http://www.theia-sfm.org`

Table 1: **Our RANSAC class is comprised of a `Sampler` class and a `QualityMeasurement` class that allow for alternative RANSAC approaches to be easily implemented. The table below outlines the RANSAC variants implemented in Theia by combining different sampling and quality measurement strategies.**

	Random Sampler	Progressive Sampler	EVT Sampler	SPRT Sampler
Inlier	RANSAC [5]	PROSAC [4]	EVSAC [6]	-
MLE	MLESAC [20]	MLE + PROSAC	MLE + EVSAC	ARRSAC [14]

ing and reconstruction files computed by Bundler[5] and VisualSFM[6] as well as interfaces to several benchmark datasets.

1.1 Comparison to other software

There are several open-source SfM libraries available, but they differ from Theia in some key features. The Bundler library robustly computes 3D reconstructions with incremental SfM, limiting the ability to scale (see Section 3 for a comparison of incremental and global SfM). VisualSfM is a closed-source software that contains an incremental SfM pipeline that utilizes multi-threading and GPU programming for high efficiency; however, the scalability is still limited because of the incremental nature of the pipeline. OpenMVG[7] is a SfM library with an active community that implements both an incremental SfM and global SfM pipeline; however, the focus of OpenMVG is on high accuracy for small to medium-sized problems and many of the methods were not designed with scalability in mind. Further, OpenMVG does not adhere to a consistent style guide and is not particularly modular, making it more difficult to extend and develop for casual users. The primary goals of the Theia library are usability, extendibility, and scalability.

2. OVERVIEW OF FEATURES

In this section we provide an overview of the core algorithms of Theia. The core features are modular so although they contribute to Theia's SfM pipeline, they may still be used independently. As such, the interface to the core features is typically generic and not dependent on Theia-specific data types. The library contains a large number of useful algorithms for multi-view geometry, linear algebra, and optimization.

2.1 Feature Extraction

Detecting salient image points is a fundamental aspect of computer vision. Feature detection and extraction methods that produce distinctive, repeatable image points and descriptors are desired for a wide range of applications such as object detection, image recognition, and multi-view stereo. In Theia, we implement a generic keypoint detector and feature descriptor extraction interface so that various types of image feature methods may be implemented and seamlessly integrated into the library. Further, this abstract interface allows the user to select the desired feature extraction method at run-time. The library currently contains implementations for SIFT, BRIEF, BRISK, FREAK, and AGAST features with support for AKAZE in development.

2.2 Feature Matching

To determine which images observe similar views of a scene, features are matched across images. There are currently two methods for feature matching in Theia: brute forces and a cascade hashing [3] that is over two orders of magnitude faster than brute force matching. Feature matching is also built with a generic interface so that new matching techniques may be seamlessly added and integrated into the library. The abstract matching interface utilizes dynamic thread-pooling to optimize for multi-threaded performance, allowing Theia users to implement new matching techniques while getting the multi-threaded performance for free.

2.3 RANSAC

Random sample and consensus, or RANSAC, is one of the most commonly used algorithms in Computer Vision. As a result, much research has gone into making RANSAC extensions and variants that increase the efficiency or accuracy of the estimation. We have implemented a templated class that makes using RANSAC for estimation extremely easy as well as simple to extend. The user defines an **`Estimator`** class that estimates a model from a set of data. This allows the user to easily deploy any RANSAC class for a variety of tasks without having to rewrite the RANSAC-specific code.

Further, the RANSAC class itself is composed of an abstract **`Sampler`** class that samples the data and a **`QualityMeasurement`** class that determines how a model fits the data. For standard RANSAC, the **`Sampler`** class performs random sampling and the **`QualityMeasurement`** class counts the number of inliers in the data. These classes can be used to implement different RANSAC methods. For instance, using a maximum likelihood error as the **`QualityMeasurement`** would result in MLESAC[20] as shown in Table 1. RANSAC [5], PROSAC [4], MLESAC [20], ARRSAC [14], and EVSAC [6] have been implemented with this generic RANSAC interface.

2.4 Pose Estimation

A fundamental problem in multi-view geometry is the ability to determine a camera's pose in a scene. This library implements numerous state-of-the-art pose estimation methods with generic interfaces so that they may be used independently of Theia's SfM pipeline. In addition to tcomprisedhe standard absolute and relative pose problems, we also implement methods for multi-camera systems, partially calibrated cameras, and scenarios where IMU information is available (*e.g.*, the vertical direction is known from IMU sensors). The following state-of-the-art solvers are currently implemented:

- Absolute pose: P3P [10], PnP [9]
- 4-point algorithm for absolute pose and focal length [1]
- 5-point algorithm for absolute pose, focal length, and radial distortion parameter(s) [11]
- Relative pose: 5-point essential matrix [16], 7-point fundamental matrix [7], 8-point fundamental matrix [8]

[5] `http://www.cs.cornell.edu/~snavely/bundler`
[6] `http://ccwu.me/vsfm`
[7] `http://openmvg.readthedocs.org`

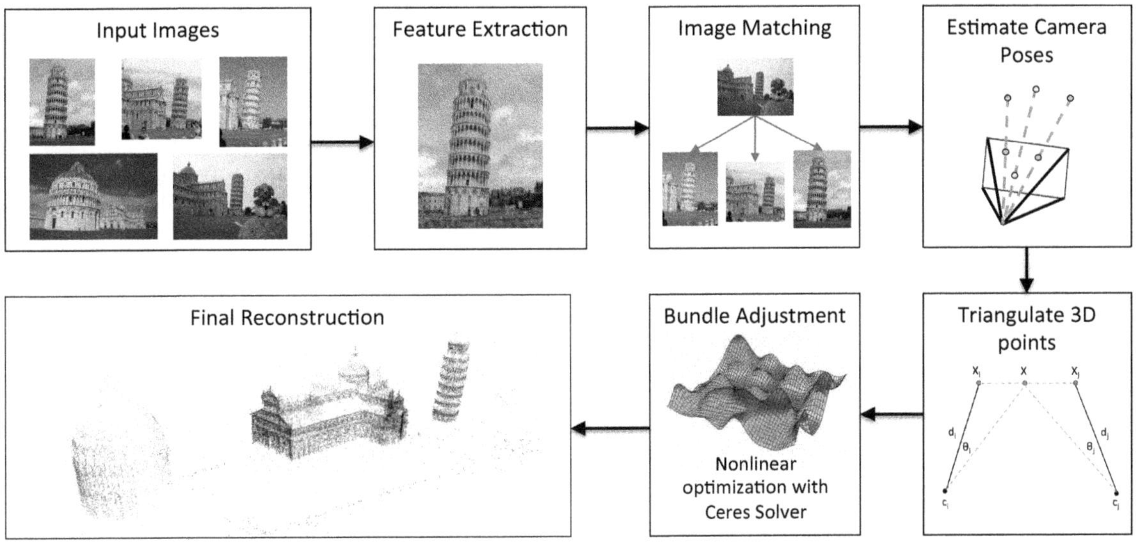

Figure 2: Overview of the global SfM pipeline implemented in Theia. In contrast to incremental SfM, each step in a global SfM pipeline is fully parallelizable and thus extremely scalable. Each step in Theia's SfM pipeline is modular and can be modified at runtime *e.g.*, to use different feature descriptors or pose estimation algorithms.

- Relative pose with known vertical direction: 3-point relative pose [17], 4-point for multi-camera systems [17]
- Homography from 4 points [7]
- Similarity transformations: from 3D-3D correspondences [21], from 2D-3D correspondences [18], from 2D-2D correspondences [19]

2.5 Mathematics and Optimization

We make a number of useful mathematics tools available as part of the library:

- A scalable L_1 minimizer
- Polynomial solvers (closed form and iterative)
- Sparse matrix eigen-decomposition
- RQ matrix decomposition
- Bundle Adjustment

3. SFM PIPELINE

At the core of Theia is the SfM module. Theia contains Incremental and Globabl SfM pipelines, but we only describe the Global SfM pipeline here (*c.f.* Figure 2). By combining the modular features presented in Section 2, we create SfM pipelines that are simple to follow, easily extendable, and highly scalable. The Incremental pipeline follows a standard sequential SfM procedure [15]. The Global SfM pipeline takes a set of pairwise relative poses between cameras as input, and outputs the orientation and position of all cameras in a global reference frame. The camera poses are computed through motion averaging algorithms. These global methods are inherently parallelizable and only require a single bundle adjustment, which is generally the most expensive part of SfM. This is in contrast to incremental SfM methods that add one new image at a time repeatedly perform bundle adjustment, making them slower and less scalable than global SfM methods. Our global SfM pipeline is summarized with the following steps: in Ojai

1. **Feature Extraction:** We extract feature descriptors (in parallel) at salient points within images. The feature type may be chosen at run-time for convenience.
2. **Image Matching:** After features are extracted, images must be matched to determine two-view geometry between images that observe the same scene. By default, Theia uses the extremely fast cascade hashing method [3] to compute image matches with multiple threads, though the matching technique may also be chosen at run-time.
3. **Estimate Camera Poses:** We use the geometrically verified two-view matches from the previous step to estimate camera poses with global motion averaging schemes. Camera orientations are estimated with either a robust orientation estimation algorithm [2] or with an L_2 averaging scheme [12]. After camera orientations are estimated, the camera positions are robustly estimated with a nonlinear position optimization [22]. The robust position estimation method of [13] is currently in development and will soon be integrated into the library.
4. **Triangulate 3D Points:** After camera poses are estimated, 3D points are triangulated in parallel and refined with a nonlinear optimization.
5. **Bundle Adjustment:** As a final step, camera poses and 3D points are refined with a nonlinear optimization to minimize reprojection error. We use the Ceres Solver for scalable multi-threaded optimization to ensure high quality results are obtained efficiently.

Table 2: Efficiency evaluation (in seconds) of Theia vs VisualSfM for large reconstructions using 8 threads. The number of images is given in parentheses for each dataset.

	VisualSfM	Theia
Notre Dame (553)	687	118
Pisa (481)	621	142
Trevi (1259)	2467	387

3.1 ReconstructionBuilder

The simplest way to create a 3D reconstruction with Theia is to utilize the `ReconstructionBuilder` class. This class takes images as input and outputs 3D reconstructions created from the input images. The caller may choose to use Incremental or Global SfM at runtime. The options set in the `ReconstructionBuilder` control parameters for feature extraction, matching, pose estimation, triangulation, and bundle adjustment. Creating a reconstruction can be done in just a few lines of code:

```
ReconstructionBuilder builder(options);
for (const std::string& image : image_files)
    builder.AddImage(image);

std::vector<Reconstruction*> reconstructions;
builder.BuildReconstruction(&reconstructions);
```

3.2 Performance

Theia achieves state-of-the-art performance on large scale datasets both in terms of efficiency and accuracy. Timing results for several large scale datasets are shown in Table 2, and more results are available on the Theia website.

4. CONCLUSIONS

In this paper, we have presented a comprehensive multi-view geometry library, Theia, that focuses on large-scale SfM. In addition to state-of-the-art scalable SfM pipelines, the library provides numerous tools that are useful for students, researchers, and industry experts in the field of multi-view geometry. Theia contains clean code that is well documented (with code comments and the website) and easy to extend. The modular design allows for users to easily implement and experiment with new algorithms within our current pipeline without having to implement a full end-to-end SfM pipeline themselves. Theia has already gathered a large number of diverse users from universities, startups, and industry and we hope to continue to gather users and active contributors from the open-source community.

5. ACKNOWLEDGMENTS

This work was supported in part by NSF Grant IIS-1219261, ONR Grant N00014-14-1-0133, and NSF Graduate Research Fellowship Grant DGE-1144085

6. REFERENCES

[1] M. Bujnak, Z. Kukelova, and T. Pajdla. A general solution to the p4p problem for camera with unknown focal length. In *CVPR*. IEEE, 2008.

[2] A. Chatterjee and V. M. Govindu. Efficient and robust large-scale rotation averaging. In *ICCV*. IEEE, 2013.

[3] J. Cheng, C. Leng, J. Wu, H. Cui, and H. Lu. Fast and accurate image matching with cascade hashing for 3d reconstruction. In *CVPR*. IEEE, 2014.

[4] O. Chum and J. Matas. Matching with PROSAC-progressive sample consensus. In *CVPR*, 2005.

[5] M. A. Fischler and R. C. Bolles. Random sample consensus: a paradigm for model fitting with applications to image analysis and automated cartography. *Communications of the ACM*, 1981.

[6] V. Fragoso, P. Sen, S. Rodriguez, and M. Turk. EVSAC: Accelerating Hypotheses Generation by Modeling Matching Scores with Extreme Value Theory. In *ICCV*. IEEE, 2013.

[7] R. Hartley and A. Zisserman. *Multiple view geometry in computer vision*. Cambridge university press, 2003.

[8] R. I. Hartley. In defense of the eight-point algorithm. *T-PAMI*, 1997.

[9] J. Hesch and S. Roumeliotis. A direct least-squares (dls) solution for pnp. In *ICCV*. IEEE, 2011.

[10] L. Kneip, D. Scaramuzza, and R. Siegwart. A novel parametrization of the perspective-three-point problem for a direct computation of absolute camera position and orientation. In *CVPR*. IEEE, 2011.

[11] Z. Kukelova, M. Bujnak, and T. Pajdla. Real-time solution to the absolute pose problem with unknown radial distortion and focal length. In *ICCV*. IEEE, 2013.

[12] D. Martinec and T. Pajdla. Robust rotation and translation estimation in multiview reconstruction. In *CVPR*. IEEE, 2007.

[13] O. Ozyesil and A. Singer. Robust camera location estimation by convex programming. In *CVPR*, 2015.

[14] R. Raguram, J.-M. Frahm, and M. Pollefeys. A comparative analysis of ransac techniques leading to adaptive real-time random sample consensus. In *ECCV*. Springer, 2008.

[15] N. Snavely, S. M. Seitz, and R. Szeliski. Photo tourism: exploring photo collections in 3d. In *ACM TOG*. ACM, 2006.

[16] H. Stewenius, C. Engels, and D. Nistér. Recent developments on direct relative orientation. *ISPRS Journal of Photogrammetry and Remote Sensing*, 2006.

[17] C. Sweeney, J. Flynn, and M. Turk. Solving for relative pose with a partially known rotation is a quadratic eigenvalue problem. In *3DV*. IEEE, 2014.

[18] C. Sweeney, V. Fragoso, T. Hollerer, and M. Turk. gdls: A scalable solution to the generalized pose and scale problem. In *ECCV*. Springer, 2014.

[19] C. Sweeney, L. Kneip, T. Hollerer, and M. Turk. Computing similarity transformations from only image correspondences. In *Proceedings of CVPR*, 2015.

[20] P. H. Torr and A. Zisserman. MLESAC: A new robust estimator with application to estimating image geometry. *Computer Vision and Image Understanding*, 2000.

[21] S. Umeyama. Least-squares estimation of transformation parameters between two point patterns. *IEEE T-PAMI*, 1991.

[22] K. Wilson and N. Snavely. Robust global translations with 1dsfm. In *ECCV*. Springer, 2014.

eRS - A System to Facilitate Emotion Recognition in Movies

Joël Dumoulin, Diana Affi, Elena Mugellini, Omar Abou Khaled
HumanTech Institute, University of Applied Sciences
Fribourg, Switzerland
[name.surname]@hes-so.ch

SUBMITTED to ACM MULTIMEDIA 2015 OPEN SOURCE SOFTWARE COMPETITION

ABSTRACT

We present e*RS*, an open-source system whose purpose is to facilitate the workflow of emotion recognition in movies, released under the MIT license. The system consists of a Django project and an AngularJS web application. It allows to easily create emotional video datasets, process the videos, extract the features and model the emotion. All data is exposed by a REST API, making it available not only to the e*RS* web application, but also to other applications. All visualizations are interactive and linked to the playing video, allowing researchers to easily analyze the results of their algorithms. The system currently runs on Linux and OS X. e*RS* can be extended, to integrate new features and algorithms needed in the different steps of emotion recognition in movies.

Categories and Subject Descriptors

H.3.1 [**Information Storage and Retrieval**]: Content Analysis and Indexing; H.3.3 [**Information Storage and Retrieval**]: Information Search and Retrieval

General Terms

Algorithms; Design; Experimentation

Keywords

Open Source; Sentiment Analysis; Video Analysis

1. INTRODUCTION

In recent years, there has been a growing interest in research on multimedia retrieval based on concepts such as emotion. Proposed by Hanjalic *et al.* [6], *affective content analysis* is a well used approach that suggests to extract and model the affective content of a video (using both audio and video features) corresponding to the emotions (type and intensity) that are expected to arise in the user while watching the video. For researchers, the workflow to apply this kind of approach in order to model the emotion present in movies usually consists of the following steps. First, datasets of videos are created, corresponding to a specific video database or a specific experiment objective. Then, videos are processed in order to extract features. Finally, the features are used to model the emotion. If many great libraries and toolboxes are available for processing audio and video files (i.e., OpenCV [1], OpenSMILE [3]), using these libraries, managing the files and the extracted data, analyzing and comparing results can be a tedious task. Particularly when it comes to analyzing results, trying to map a static two dimensional plot with a dynamic playing video.

The goal of the e*RS* system is to facilitate this workflow (illustrated in Figure 1) for researchers, providing them with a backend handling of the processing tasks, and a web application allowing to easily manage all the data and the tasks, while helping them as well to analyze results thanks to interactive visualizations.

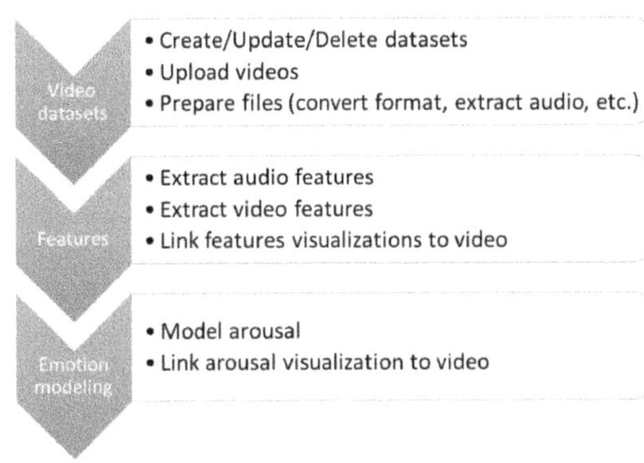

Figure 1: System workflow overview - 1) Video datasets management 2) Features extraction and visualization 3) Emotion modeling

2. OVERALL ARCHITECTURE

The e*RS* system consists of two main parts as shown in Figure 2: the backend and the frontend.

2.1 Backend

The backend is expected to be run on a server, allowing to take advantage of high computational capabilities, required by tasks such as video conversions, features extraction and

MM'15, October 26–30, 2015, Brisbane, Australia.

ACM 978-1-4503-3459-4/15/10 ...$15.00.
DOI: http://dx.doi.org/10.1145/2733373.2807409 .

emotion modeling. It consists of a Django[1] project and is therefore written in Python. For each dataset, all videos files are stored in folders according to their emotional class. All datasets and videos metadata are stored in a relational database. The default relational database management system used is MySQL, but it can be replaced by any other Django supported database type (i.e., PostgreSQL, Oracle).

The time consuming tasks are launched as Celery[2] asynchronous tasks (Celery is a distributed task queue library), using a Redis[3] message broker.

2.2 Frontend

The frontend is an HTML5 web application, developed with the AngularJS[4] JavaScript framework. The role of this web application is to offer a pleasant and easy to use interface to the system users, allowing to launch tasks on the backend and retrieve data for analysis, with the use of interactive visualizations.

It can have access to the data by two different ways: through a Representational State Transfer (REST) API and through a WebSocket endpoint. The choice of the REST API is motivated by the idea that other applications than the e*RS* web application could have access to the data and take advantage of it. The use of the WebSocket[5] endpoint allows to provide monitoring capabilities, by establishing a full duplex communication between the frontend and the backend. It is therefore possible to launch time consuming tasks in an asynchronous manner, close the browser, and when the web application will be launched the next time it will be updated with the current state of the tasks, thanks to the push communication model.

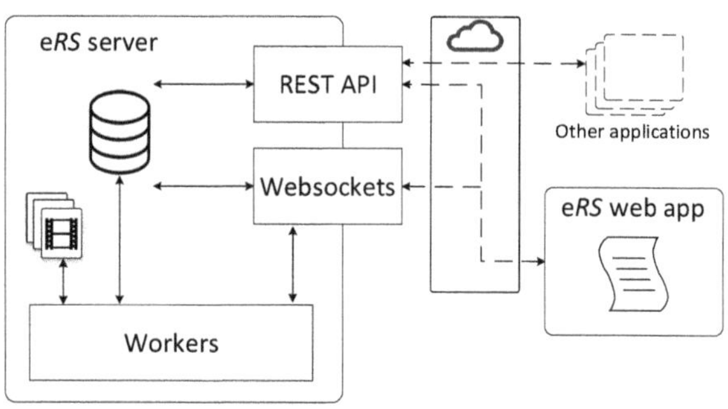

Figure 2: Overall architecture - the server stores the videos and all the associated data ; as the extracted data (datasets and video metadata, features, emotion values, etc.) are available through a REST API, the e*RS* web application but also other applications can access them ; the e*RS* web application launches processing tasks asynchronously and monitors them through the WebSockets endpoint.

3. ERS FUNCTIONALITIES

In this section, an overview of the functionalities provided by the e*RS* system are described.

[1]https://www.djangoproject.com/
[2]http://www.celeryproject.org/
[3]http://redis.io/
[4]https://angularjs.org/
[5]https://www.websocket.org/

3.1 Video datasets management

Video datasets can be created, updated and removed. Videos can be uploaded to the server directly through the web application. It is also possible to add the files in the correct folders on the server and ask the application to scan for available videos. Once added to the system, videos have to be converted in a format so they can be processed by standard libraries (i.e., OpenCV [1]) and their audio channel is extracted into Waveform Audio Format files (WAV) in order to be processed by OpenSMILE [3].

As shown in Figure 3, monitoring indications are helping the researcher to always know the state of each task applied to a dataset and to the videos. This aspect is important, as the different tasks (i.e., shot boundaries detection, features extraction, emotion modeling) may take a long time (depending on the size of the processed video) and can lead to issues.

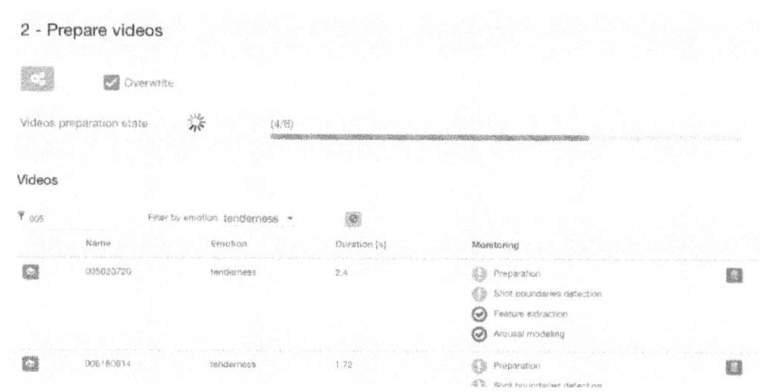

Figure 3: Time consuming tasks are launched asynchronously and their status is updated in real time by push thanks to the WebSockets protocol.

3.2 Features extraction and visualization

Emotions in movies are conveyed through both audio and visual channels. The e*RS* system allows to easily select the desired features to be extracted, depending on the intended objectives. Once extracted, the features can be visualized for each video. As features extraction can be a time consuming task, it is important that the researcher can easily select which features are needed, in order to not extract all the features. The features are then stored in the database, so they can be easily retrieved for a specific video.

Any newly added audio or visual features in the backend will automatically be available for use (selection for features extraction, visualization) in the frontend without any additional line of code.

3.2.1 Audio features

Multiple audio features are available for extraction from the video clips. Those features are inspired from challenges [8, 9] organized in order to create a baseline for affect recognition in audio, as well as from research focusing on emotion recognition in movies [5] and music [2].

The audio features are extracted using the OpenSMILE [3] tool which enables specifying the framing and windowing over an audio file, as well as it gives the possibility to apply functions on the retrieved features. The following list presents the implemented audio features and their descriptions [4]:

Energy: intensity measuring the distribution of power.

Mel-Frequency Cepstral Coefficients (MFCC): a representation of the short-term power spectrum of a sound, based on a linear cosine transform of a log power spectrum on a nonlinear mel scale of frequency. The first 12 coefficients are available.

Pitch (Voice Prob): the voicing probability computed from the ACF(Auto correlation function).

Pitch (F0): the fundamental frequency computed from the Cepstrum.

LSP: the 8 line spectral pair frequencies computed from 8 LPC coefficients.

Loudness and Intensity: the loudness as the normalized intensity raised to a power of 0.3.

Zero-Crossings: the rate of sign-changes along a signal, i.e., the rate at which the signal changes from positive to negative or back.

Spectral (User defined band energies): rectangular summation of FFT magnitudes over the following frequency bands: 0-250, 0-650, 250-650, 1000-4000, 3010-9123.

Spectral Rolloff: the frequency below which X% of the magnitude distribution is concentrated. It is available for the following values of X: 25-50-75-90.

Spectral Flux: the squared difference between the normalized magnitudes of successive spectral distributions.

Spectral Centroid: a measure used in digital signal processing to characterize a spectrum. It indicates where the "center of mass" of the spectrum is. Perceptually, it has a robust connection with the impression of "brightness" of a sound.

As shown in the literature, functionals describing features and their distribution have a big role in classifying the emotions. The following functions are automatically computed on the features over a window of 1 second: *range*, *skeweness*, *kurtosis*, *minimum*, *maximum* and *mean*.

3.2.2 Video features

Two video features are currently supported by the system: shot cut density and brightness. To compute the shot cut density, shot boundaries detection has to be applied first. In order to ease this task, a dedicated view is provided in the web interface. It is possible to configure a list of algorithms (currently supported algorithms are Color Histograms and Edge Change Ratio) and specify a value for the threshold and the weight of the algorithm (if several algorithms are used). Once executed the resulting shot boundaries can be viewed thanks to an interactive visualization linked to the video. It is also possible to provide a ground truth for the shot boundaries values and compute the precision/recall of the resulting shot boundaries detection. As shown in Figure 4, the interactive visualization uses a color box around the playing video, associated to the type of the shot boundary (green for true positives, red for false positives and orange for misses), in order to better understand the result of the algorithm configuration. The shot cut density is then calculated with the following formula as proposed by Wang et al. [10]:

$$c(k) = e^{(1-n(k))/r} \quad (1)$$

where $n(k)$ is the number of frames including the k-th video frame and r is a constant determining the distribution of the values.

Figure 4: Shot boundaries detection result interactive visualization, with a color box mapped to the type of the shot boundary (true positive, false positive, miss). The video shown here is an excerpt of the movie The Visitors, part of the FilmStim emotional dataset [7].

The brightness is considered as a feature varying with emotions. For instance, dark scenes are used to express negative emotions such as fear and sadness. For each frame, the brightness is calculated over each pixel using the following formula and the mean of these values is computed.

$$brightness(p) = \sqrt{0.299R^2 + 0.587G^2 + 0.144B^2} \quad (2)$$

3.2.3 Features visualizations

Plenty of different features can be extracted and for each audio feature several functions are applied, leading to the availability of a huge amount of data. The researcher can choose which features and which functions to visualize (as shown in Figure 5) in order to reduce the amount of data to load. It is therefore possible to focus on the important features and analyze them according to the displayed video.

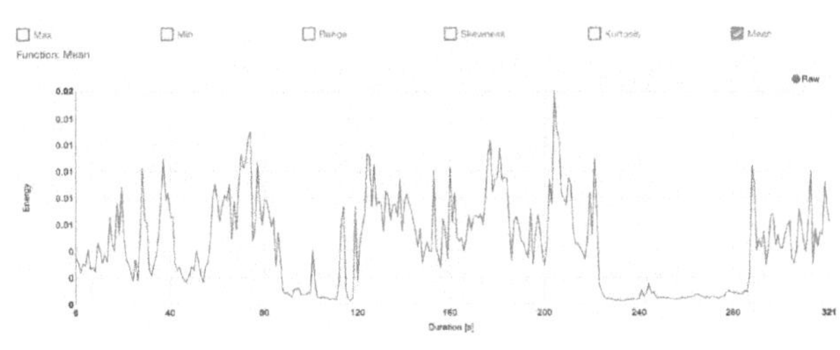

Figure 5: Features functions selection

3.3 Emotion modeling

The emotion modeling is based on an arousal curve generation. Arousal is one one the two main axis of the affective content, with the valence. It corresponds to the intensity of the emotion that is expected to arise in the user while watching the movie.

3.3.1 *Arousal curve generation*

The arousal is modeled with an approach inspired by the one presented by Wang *et al.* [10]. It consists of a combination of features by applying normalization, smoothing and linear weighted summarization for the fusion. The features can be easily selected among the already extracted features list on the web interface. For instance, the sound energy and the shot cut density are two features to be used for modeling the excitement of movies. Figure 6 shows the arousal curve obtained with these two features for a sequence of Saving Private Ryan (part of the FilmStim dataset [7]).

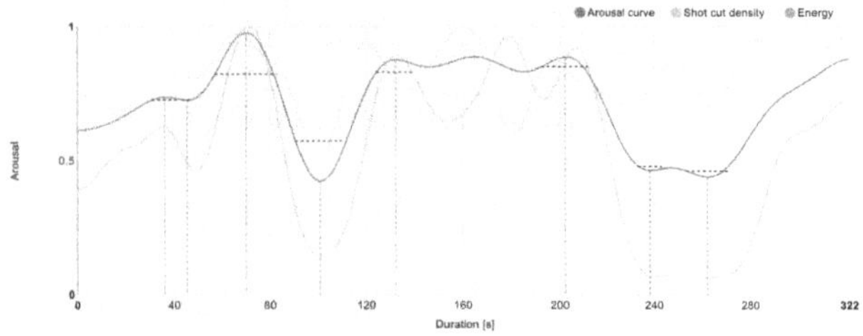

Figure 6: Arousal modeling - arousal curve obtained with sound energy and shot cut density features

3.3.2 *High and low arousal partitioning*

The arousal curve can be exploited to define more interesting and less interesting parts. To define these scenes we first detect the crests and troughs of the arousal curve. The first derivative of the curve is then calculated in order to determine the transition points around these minima and maxima. Finally the partition between the transition points is restrained so the values contained in it will be near (68%) the minimal or maximal value whether it is a trough or a crest.

3.4 Dynamic visualizations

One important functionality of the e*RS* web application is that all visualizations are linked to the playing video. When the video is played, a timeline is updated on each visible visualization ; it is also possible to click on each of them on a specific position (for instance a peek in the arousal curve) to seek the video at this time. It allows the researcher to analyze the resulting data in the best way.

4. APPLICATIONS

e*RS* has been recently used by students in several Bachelor and Master projects in the University of Applied Sciences of Fribourg, where the goal was to extract emotion information of movies+ and take advantage of this information. For instance, one project used e*RS* to define the less interesting parts of a movie and propose advertisements to the viewer on a second screen application during these moments, without interrupting the display of the movie on the television. Another project maps the arousal level of the movie with the intensity of a dynamic ambient lighting system connected with a smart television, in order to create an immersive movie viewing experience.

We expect our system to be useful to students and researchers who have to manage video datasets for emotion recognition purpose and want to easily test their algorithms and analyze the results.

5. CONCLUSION

We presented e*RS*, an open-source system to facilitate the emotion recognition in movies workflow. The system consists of a backend storing the data and processing the videos, a web application accompanying the researcher through the whole emotion recognition workflow and a REST API making the data available for other applications. In our future work, we will focus on expanding the system by adding valence modeling and classification functionalities and we will also add support for more video features. The detailed information about e*RS* is available on the official project web page[6] and on the GitHub project page[7].

6. ACKNOWLEDGMENTS

We would like to thank Célin Chassot, former bachelor student at HES-SO, for his contribution in the development of some functionalities prototypes.

7. REFERENCES

[1] G. Bradski. *Dr. Dobb's Journal of Software Tools.*

[2] W. C. Chiang, J. S. Wang, and Y. L. Hsu. A Music Emotion Recognition Algorithm with Hierarchical SVM Based Classifiers. *2014 International Symposium on Computer, Consumer and Control*, pages 1249–1252, June 2014.

[3] F. Eyben, F. Weninger, F. Gross, and B. Schuller. Recent developments in opensmile, the munich open-source multimedia feature extractor. In *Proceedings of the 21st ACM International Conference on Multimedia*, MM '13, pages 835–838, New York, NY, USA, 2013. ACM.

[4] F. Eyben, M. Woellmer, and B. Schuller. the Munich open Speech and Music Interpretation by Large Space Extraction toolkit. 2010.

[5] T. Giannakopoulos, A. Pikrakis, and S. Theodoridis. A dimensional approach to emotion recognition of speech from movies. pages 65–68, 2009.

[6] A. Hanjalic. Affective video content representation and modeling. *IEEE Transactions on Multimedia*, 7(1):669–676, 2005.

[7] A. Schaefer, F. Nils, X. Sanchez, and P. Philippot. Assessing the effectiveness of a large database of emotion-eliciting films: A new tool for emotion researchers. *Cognition and Emotion*, 24(7):1153–1172, 2010.

[8] B. Schuller, S. Steidl, A. Batliner, F. Burkhardt, L. Devillers, M. Christian, and S. Narayanan. The INTERSPEECH 2010 Paralinguistic Challenge. In *Proc. Interspeech*, 2010.

[9] M. Valstar, K. Smith, F. Eyben, T. U. München, and R. Cowie. AVEC 2014 - 3D Dimensional Affect and Depression Recognition Challenge. 2014.

[10] Z. Wang, J. Yu, Y. He, and T. Guan. Affection arousal based highlight extraction for soccer video. *Multimedia Tools and Applications*, pages 1–28, July 2013.

[6] http://ers.ilab-research.ch/#/

[7] https://github.com/dumoulinj/ers/

WATSS: a Web Annotation Tool for Surveillance Scenarios

Federico Bartoli
University of Florence
federico.bartoli@unifi.it

Lorenzo Seidenari
University of Florence
lorenzo.seidenari@unifi.it

Giuseppe Lisanti
University of Florence
giuseppe.lisanti@unifi.it

Svebor Karaman
Columbia University
svebor.karaman@columbia.edu

Alberto Del Bimbo
University of Florence
alberto.delbimbo@unifi.it

ABSTRACT

In this paper, we present a web based annotation tool we developed allowing creating collaboratively a detailed ground truth for datasets related to visual surveillance and behavior understanding. The system persistence is based on a relational database and the user interface is designed using HTML5, Javascript and CSS. Our tool can easily manage datasets with multiple cameras. It allows annotating a person location in the image, its identity, its body and head gaze, as well as a potential occlusion or group membership. We justify each annotation type with regards to current trends of research in the computer vision community. We further detail how our interface can be used to annotate each of these annotations type. We conclude the paper with an usability evaluation of our system.

Categories and Subject Descriptors

H.3.7 [**Digital Libraries**]: Collection; H.5.2 [**User Interfaces**]: Graphical user interfaces (GUI)

General Terms

Experimentation

Keywords

Annotation; Surveillance

1. INTRODUCTION

The computer vision and pattern recognition community is always seeking more challenging and realistic datasets to work on. Such datasets have been the main driver of recent major advancements in machine learning and pattern recognition. Challenges, associated with public datasets have also pushed researchers to develop methods to go beyond the state-of-the-art. PASCAL VOC [10] had been and is still advancing the accuracy of object recognition, detection and segmentation. A major break-through in image recognition has been recently made possible thanks to the large ImageNet taxonomy [7] allowing to train a deep convolutional neural network with a sufficient amount of data [12].

MM'15, October 26–30, 2015, Brisbane, Australia.

ACM 978-1-4503-3459-4/15/10 ...$15.00.
DOI: http://dx.doi.org/10.1145/2733373.2807411.

Recently, researchers started to address the problem of group behavior understanding. Collective behavior understanding, like standing in groups or queuing up has been addressed in [1, 6]. The problem of person to person interaction has been tackled in [3, 17] showing that modelling social behavior can improve tracking performance. Dataset to study group behavior will often be recorded in mildly crowded environments therefore knowing whether a body is fully visible or partially occluded allows to evaluate how the methods are able to cope with occlusion. Moreover, one of the most important social cue is gaze, usually defined as a coarse gaze by the head pose since it is often not possible to detect the real gaze of a person from far field camera.

Dataset annotation is a time consuming and expensive task to perform. Recently large datasets have been annotated with crowd sourcing. Crowd sourcing usually relies on platforms like Amazon Mechanical Turk (AMT), where "turkers" are paid to perform annotations. To properly exploit AMT web based annotation interfaces [18,20] are needed.

In this paper we present an open-source tool we have developed to annotate the MuseumVisitors dataset [2]. This dataset of person and group behavior understanding, can be used for tracking, detection and coarse gaze estimation. We recorded this dataset at the National Museum of Bargello in Florence, Italy as part of the MNEMOSYNE project [11]. We designed the tool as a web application in order to easily gather annotations from multiple users and to allow concurrent annotations. The tool had to deal with multiple kinds of information thus needing a user interface designed specifically for the task. Annotators can insert groups and people identities, gaze and body occlusion.

2. RELATED TOOLS AND DATASETS

In this section we first review some publicly released annotation tools and then discuss the related datasets limitations that triggered the development of the WATSS tool.

2.1 Annotation tools

The LabelMe annotation tool [18] is focused on annotating scenes providing web based tools and mobile applications to annotate, using polygons, the outline of objects. Tools to annotate surveillance videos have been recently proposed such as VIPER [13] and VATIC [20]. These tools usually support annotations like bounding boxes, polygons and ellipses, as they are mostly developed for object detection. VATIC allows to specify a finite set of attribute per every object such as "walking" for "person" objects. The main drawback of a tool like VIPER is that is meant to be used locally instead of online, therefore the gathering of annotations from multiple sources can become difficult and there is no way of connecting the tool with crowdsourcing platforms. VATIC is a more modern online tool that can be used for crowdsourcing at scale, although their data model is extremely focused on detection and structured detection of objects [22]. The possibility to add attributes gives some flexibility to the data model but is not enough to manage the diversity of data needed for behavior understanding.

2.2 Group and occlusion detection datasets

Person detection is widely studied in literature and many datasets have been publicly released, each one with different characteristics. However, there is a lack of datasets with group annotation, that can be used for example in group detection, tracking and behavior analysis. Moreover, very few datasets have gaze annotation. In this section we briefly review some currently available datasets that contain groups or occlusion annotations.

Group detection.

The CAVIAR dataset [5] was released in 2003 for behavior analysis purposes. It consists of two sets of experiments, each one composed by a set of video clips taken from different cameras. These sequences were recorded acting out different scenarios of interest for different behaviors. It comes with groups annotations and it can be exploited for group detection, tracking or behavior analysis.

The Friends Meet (FM) dataset was recently proposed in [3] specifically for group detection and tracking. It contains groups of people that evolve, appear and disappear spontaneously, and experience split and merge events. It is composed of 53 sequences, for a total of 16286 frames. The sequences are partitioned in a synthetic set without any complex object representation and dynamics, and a real dataset.

Occlusion detection.

Recently a lot of techniques have been focusing on person detection with occlusions handling [14,16,21]. However, due to the lack of datasets with occlusion annotations it is difficult to produce a quantitative measure of this phenomenon and compare with other methods. The Daimler Pedestrian Detection Benchmark dataset [9] is a set of images captured from a vehicle-mounted calibrated stereo camera rig that is moving in an urban environment. It contains bounding boxes annotations for pedestrians and non-pedestrians in the scene. No additional annotation are provided about visible (or occluded) part of each pedestrian. However, the test set is split between non-occluded and partially-occluded. The Caltech dataset [8] is composed of 250000 frames extracted from 10 hours of videos acquired from a vehicle driving through regular traffic in an urban environment.

3. WATSS ANNOTATION TOOL

Most of current datasets are targeted for a single task, such as: person detection with occlusion, group detection and/or behavior analysis. Moreover, to the best of our knowledge no open source annotation tools are available to easily produce all the annotations needed to build a dataset covering jointly all these tasks.

We hence developed a web-based annotation tool to annotate our MuseumVisitors Dataset [2] and we made the source code publicly available. This dataset is a great example of what is needed in a modern visual surveillance dataset. In our case we want as much information as possible so we developed functionalities to annotate position, person identity, gaze, occlusion persons and group membership.

3.1 Annotation protocol

We propose the following annotation protocol. First of all people bounding boxes must be defined, a bounding box can be positioned and rescaled to better fit a person. If a person is partially occluded, a secondary bounding box annotation corresponding only to the visible part of the person can be defined as shown in Fig. 3(a).

Annotators can provide identities for pedestrians associating a single identifier on all frames of all cameras. Identities are easily assigned thanks to our *Add person* interface showing avatars of already enrolled identities as show in Fig. 2.

In presence of groups, annotators can also associate a group identifier that is common to all frames of all cameras. Finally, it is possible to specify body orientation and gaze with a quantization of 5 degrees as shown in Fig. 3(b).

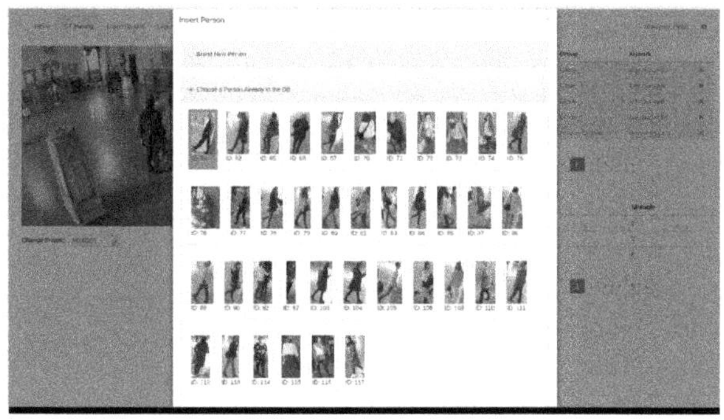

Figure 2: Add person view. Annotators can add a new identity or select from a one previously inserted.

(a) (b)

Figure 3: *(a)* The solid green rectangle represents the bounding box selected for the annotation while the green dashed rectangle corresponds to the visible (not occluded) area; *(b)* The cone visualizes the annotation of the gaze.

3.2 The web based annotation tool

We designed a user friendly web interface to ease the tedious task of a detailed surveillance videos annotation. Implementing the tool as a web platform allows concurrent annotation. In fact, multiple annotators can be easily tasked

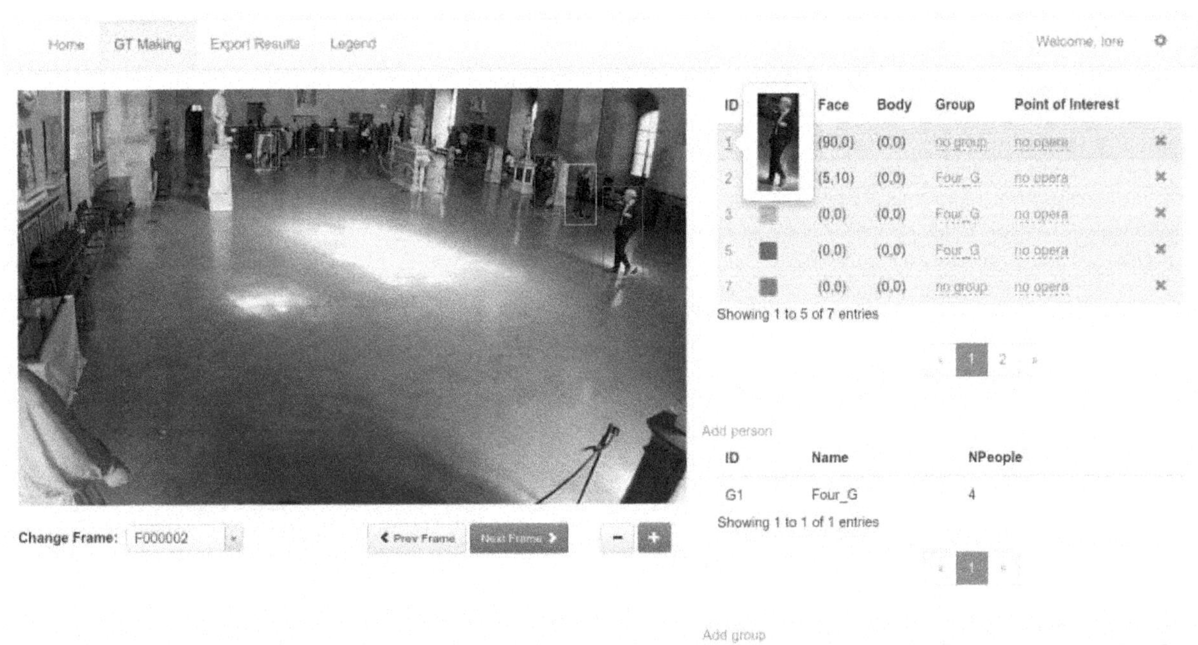

Figure 1: Web interface. Showing several persons bounding boxes and the pop-up avatar for the first one.

with a different range of frames to annotate. Moreover the interface implement a function to point an annotator to the next un-annotated frame. In Fig. 1 we show the interface.

On the top of the interface we have a menu bar with different options: *GTmaking*, *Export results* and *Legend*. If a user selects *GT making* the annotation tool asks for username and allows to chose the camera and frame to annotate, if none is specified the annotation process will start from the latest frame annotated by the user.

On the *left-top* part of the interface, we show the chosen frame along with some already annotated bounding boxes. By selecting one of the bounding boxes the dashed rectangle become solid and the user is able to move and resize the bounding box. Once a bounding box is selected the user can also specify different information about that annotation, such as: the visible area (occlusion), the direction of the body and the gaze. A new bounding boxes can be added by clicking "Add person".

On the *left-bottom* part of the interface, we put some video related buttons that allows to navigate through the frames and zoom-in or out on the image (annotators can zoom also by scrolling with the mouse or touchpad).

In the *right-top* part of the interface we put one table summarizing the information about each individual, like the person identifier (ID), the color of the bounding box, the gaze direction (Face), the body direction (Body), the group of which the selected user is part of (Group) and if it is standing by a particular object in the scene or not (Object).

In the *right-bottom* part of the interface we put, instead, a table summarizing the groups information, like the identifier of the group (ID), the name of the group (Name) and the number of persons that are part of the group (NPeople). A new group can be added by clicking "Add group" below the table.

The tool now supports CSV exporting, clicking on export data triggers the generation of an archive containing the CSV files with the annotated data.

In order to make this tool intuitive and ease the annotation process we defined a series of keyboard shortcuts to speed-up the process. These shortcuts are summarized in the *Legend* section of the annotation tool. Moreover, once a frame is annotated, the successive frame will have the same bounding boxes as a starting point for the new annotations, in order to overcome the necessity of re-defining from scratch every person annotation at every frame.

3.3 Usability evaluation

To evaluate the usability of the proposed annotation tool we used the System Usability Scale (SUS) [4], which is a Likert scale. The form to create a Likert [19] scale is built by presenting a set of questions and asking the respondent to choose a degree of agreement in a fixed point scale, from strongly disagree to strongly agree (in our case 1 to 5). It is not just a forced choice questionnaire. Questions are selected in order to present extreme cases and alternating positive and negative statements. The alternation of positive and negative statements is a way of making sure that the respondent reads carefully. The selection of extreme scenarios is instead a way of removing bias. The SUS questionnaire was build selecting among a pool of 50 questions, those leading to the most extreme responses.

We report our usability study result in Table 1. As suggested by Nielsen [15] five system users are enough to find the 85% of usability issues of interfaces. Regarding the SUS score our system obtained an average score of 70. We noted that all users found to be confident using the system (item 10), and the system easy to learn and use (items 2,3). We also found that many user gave a neutral response to item 6; this is probably caused by the diversity of annotations requested, but it is also room for improvement.

4. CONCLUSION

We presented a web annotation system designed for annotating multi-camera video sequences typical of surveillance scenarios.

We tested WATSS annotating our publicly released MuseumVisitors dataset comprised of 96972 detections, and

	Str. Dis.	Dis.	Neutr.	Agr.	Str. Agr.
1. I think that I would like to use this system to perform an annotation task	0	0	2	2	1
2. I imagine that most people would learn to use this system very quickly	1	**3**	0	1	0
3. I found the system very cumbersome to use	2	2	0	1	0
4. I thought the system was easy to use	0	1	0	**4**	0
5. I think that I would need the help of a technical person to use this system	2	2	1	0	0
6. I found the various functions in this system were well integrated	0	0	**4**	1	0
7. I thought there was too much inconsistency in this system	2	2	0	1	0
8. I found the system unnecessarily complex	2	2	0	1	0
9. I needed to learn a lot of things before I could get going with this system	2	2	0	0	1
10. I felt very confident using the system	1	0	1	2	1

Table 1: Result of our SUS usability study. We report frequencies of each answers. Most frequent items are reported in bold.

gazes, 101 persons' identities over 9477 frames from four cameras. This is the work of 5 people performed through our interface for 20 days: roughly 3 man/months. We evaluated the system usability using the well known SUS scale finding that the system is considered easy to learn and use and annotators felt productive and confident in using it.

The tool is available on bitbucket at `https://bitbucket.org/fbert/watss`[1] under GPLv3 License. We provide installation scripts to feed frames into the system that can be tested at `http://150.217.35.152/watss`. We release our MuseumVisitors dataset together with the tool so that annotations can be visualized on a real world scenario.

With respect to a tool like VATIC we have a specific interface to annotate occlusions and user gaze. Moreover we are able to easily annotate user identity by showing the annotator previous persons frames. Our system provides suggestions for bounding boxes and gazes for subsequent frames so that annotators have to perform a simpler tuning task instead of redefining all scene entities from scratch. Considering the complexity of the scenarios usually involved we are not able, at the moment, to allow the interpolation of coarsely annotated sequences via tracking as in [20]. We plan in the future to add more sensible proposals for unannotated frames both for gaze and detections in order to reduce the complexity of the annotation process.

Acknowledgments. Lorenzo Seidenari is supported by "THE SOCIAL MUSEUM AND SMART TOURISM", MIUR project no. CTN01_00034_23154_SMST.

5. REFERENCES

[1] M. Amer, P. Lei, and S. Todorovic. Hirf: Hierarchical random field for collective activity recognition in videos. In *Proc of ECCV*, 2014.

[2] F. Bartoli, G. Lisanti, S. Seidenari, Lorenzo Karaman, and A. Del Bimbo. Museumvisitors: a dataset for pedestrian and group detection, gaze estimation and behavior understanding. In *Proc. of CVPR Int.'l Workshop on Group And Crowd Behavior Analysis And Understanding*, Boston, USA, 2015.

[3] L. Bazzani, V. Murino, and M. Cristani. Decentralized particle filter for joint individual-group tracking. In *Proc. of CVPR*, 2012.

[4] J. Brooke. Sus-a quick and dirty usability scale. *Usability evaluation in industry*, 189(194):4–7, 1996.

[5] CAVIAR. Test case scenarios. `http://homepages.inf.ed.ac.uk/rbf/CAVIAR/`.

[6] W. Choi and S. Savarese. A unified framework for multi-target tracking and collective activity recognition. In *Proc. of ECCV*, 2012.

[7] J. Deng, W. Dong, R. Socher, L.-J. Li, K. Li, and L. Fei-Fei. ImageNet: A Large-Scale Hierarchical Image Database. In *Proc. of CVPR*, 2009.

[8] P. Dollár, C. Wojek, B. Schiele, and P. Perona. Pedestrian detection: An evaluation of the state of the art. *PAMI*, 34(4):743–761, April 2012.

[9] M. Enzweiler, A. Eigenstetter, B. Schiele, and D. M. Gavrila. Multi-cue pedestrian classification with partial occlusion handling. In *Proc. of CVPR*, 2010.

[10] M. Everingham, L. Van Gool, C. K. Williams, J. Winn, and A. Zisserman. The pascal visual object classes (voc) challenge. *Int. J. Comput. Vision*, 88(2):303–338, June 2010.

[11] S. Karaman, A. D. Bagdanov, L. Landucci, G. D'Amico, A. Ferracani, D. Pezzatini, and A. Del Bimbo. Personalized multimedia content delivery on an interactive table by passive observation of museum visitors. *Multimedia Tools and Applications*, pages 1–25, 2014.

[12] A. Krizhevsky, I. Sutskever, and G. E. Hinton. Imagenet classification with deep convolutional neural networks. In *Proc. of NIPS*. 2012.

[13] V. Mariano, J. Min, J.-H. Park, R. Kasturi, D. Mihalcik, D. Doermann, and T. Drayer. Performance evaluation of object detection algorithms. international conference on pattern recognition. In *In Proc. of ICPR*, 2002.

[14] M. Mathias, R. Benenson, R. Timofte, and L. Van Gool. Handling occlusions with franken-classifiers. In *Proc. of ICCV*, 2013.

[15] J. Nielsen and R. Molich. Heuristic evaluation of user interfaces. In *Proceedings of the SIGCHI Conference on Human Factors in Computing Systems*, CHI '90, pages 249–256, New York, NY, USA, 1990. ACM.

[16] W. Ouyang and X. Wang. Single-pedestrian detection aided by multi-pedestrian detection. In *Proc. of CVPR*, 2013.

[17] S. Pellegrini, A. Ess, K. Schindler, and L. Van Gool. You'll never walk alone: Modeling social behavior for multi-target tracking. In *Proc. of ICCV*, 2009.

[18] B. C. Russell, A. A. Torralba, and F. W. T. Murphy, K. P. Labelme: a database and web-based tool for image annotation. *International Journal of Computer Vision*, 77:157–173, May 2008.

[19] W. M. Trochim et al. Likert scaling. *Research methods knowledge base*, 2, 2006.

[20] C. Vondrick, D. Patterson, and D. Ramanan. Efficiently scaling up crowdsourced video annotation. *International Journal of Computer Vision*, pages 1–21.

[21] P. Wohlhart, M. Donoser, P. M. Roth, and H. Bischof. Detecting partially occluded objects with an implicit shape model random field. In *Proc. of ACCV*, 2012.

[22] Y. Yang and D. Ramanan. Articulated pose estimation with flexible mixtures-of-parts. In *Computer Vision and Pattern Recognition (CVPR), 2011 IEEE Conference on*, pages 1385–1392. IEEE, 2011.

[1]Direct download: `https://goo.gl/cgihhr`

Aurio: Audio Processing, Analysis and Retrieval

Mario Guggenberger
Institute of Information Technology
Alpen-Adria-Universität Klagenfurt
9020 Klagenfurt am Wörthersee, Austria
mg@itec.aau.at

ABSTRACT

Aurio is an open source software library written for audio-based processing, analysis, and retrieval of audio and video recordings. The novelty of this library is the implementation of a number of fingerprinting and time warping algorithms to retrieve, match and synchronize media streams, which no other library currently offers. It is designed with simplicity, performance and versatility in mind, can be easily integrated into .NET applications, and offers a collection of many basic signal processing methods. It can read many file formats, offers multiple export abilities for further processing, and contains various UI widgets for graphical applications. Built upon the Aurio library, *AudioAlign* is an additionally released open source application for the (semi-)automatic synchronization of media recordings.

Categories and Subject Descriptors

D.2.13 [**Software Engineering**]: Reusable Software—*reusable libraries*; H.3.1 [**Information Storage and Retrieval**]: Content Analysis and Indexing

Keywords

Audio, features, fingerprinting, dynamic time warping, synchronization, retrieval, processing, open source software

1. INTRODUCTION

The widespread usage of portable and ubiquitous multimedia capable devices that allow easy recording and thus creation of new content has led to an abundance of media recordings that are either kept in the local archives of users or shared across various online platforms. The big question is how all these files can be managed, and while this can be manually done if an archive is small, it gets tedious or even overwhelming when it grows. This is an area where the multimedia retrieval community is actively researching for new helpful tools and methods, and many tools and methods with high impact have been proposed in recent years.

MM'15, October 26–30, 2015, Brisbane, Australia.

DOI: http://dx.doi.org/10.1145/2733373.2807408.

For audio content management, the probably most helpful tool is fingerprinting [3], enabling music discovery tools that tell which song is playing on the radio [23], improving music library management through metadata retrieval [22] and duplicate detection, and helping content creators with broadcast monitoring. Researchers have also shown its use for the synchronization of multiple media recordings captured at an event [17,19]. Another older but nonetheless interesting invention is dynamic time warping [20] for the nonlinear alignment of data series, that can be used to synchronize different song interpretations [4] or to follow scores [1].

We think that these two methods fit well together, and that there is a lack of easy to use libraries that implement these methods. We therefore present *Aurio*, an audio library that implements these methods and makes them easily accessible, on top of a collection of basic reusable building blocks that allow for rapid experimentation, prototyping and implementation of additional high-level features and methods.

2. ARCHITECTURE

Aurio[1] is a library written in C# for the .NET Framework, and designed with simplicity, performance, and versatility in mind. Due to the nature of managed .NET code, this library cannot be as effective as purely native code, but critical sections are implemented in unsafe code to minimize the impact and overhead of the managed runtime.

The core module *Aurio* contains classes for file I/O, 32-bit floating point block-based stream processing, audio playback, various data structures, utility functions, FFT, resampling, audio features, and various audio matching algorithms, described in more detail in Section 3. Aurio comes with a few additional modules that are essentially interfaces to 3rd party native libraries that it makes use of. *Aurio.FFmpeg* handles file input and support of various audio and video (container) formats through the well-known FFmpeg[2] library. *Aurio.PFFFT* interfaces with the PFFFT[3] library for FFT calculation, and there is optional support for the FFTW library [10] through *Aurio.FFTW* and the purely managed Exocortex.DSP library[4]. For resampling, Aurio uses the Sox Resampler[5] through *Aurio.Soxr* by default, while libsamplerate[6] is optionally available through

[1]`https://github.com/protyposis/Aurio`
[2]`http://ffmpeg.org/`
[3]`https://bitbucket.org/jpommier/pffft`
[4]`http://exocortex.org/dsp/`
[5]`http://sourceforge.net/p/soxr/`
[6]`http://www.mega-nerd.com/SRC/`

Aurio.LibSampleRate. Reading and writing of wave files, and audio playback is handled through NAudio[7]. The optional module *Aurio.WaveControls* depends on Aurio and provides multiple audio-related UI widgets.

Although written for Windows, it should be portable to the Mono framework[8] for use on other OS' like Linux, OS X and possibly Android for which almost all external dependencies are available. The two exceptions are the optional UI widget module based on the Windows Presentation Foundation API and the audio playback functionality using the NAudio library, which are both Windows-only. The library supports x86 and x64 architectures and automatically loads the appropriate native dependencies.

3. FEATURES

The stream-based audio processing engine in Aurio works similar to conventional I/O stream implementations in Java and .NET. All available streams implement a common interface and can be chained together to achieve certain goals, through which complex processing can be achieved very easily and logically. A chain of streams must start with a source where audio data is initially read from, continue with intermediate processing or analysis streams, and optionally end in a sink stream where the final data is written to. Currently supported sources are wave files through NAudio, various file formats through FFmpeg, raw memory, and a sine generator. Intermediate streams are available for concatenation of multiple streams, cropping of start and end positions, (double) buffering, data monitoring (e.g. for online calculation of spectrograms and correlations), mixing multiple input streams into one output stream, mono down- and up-conversion, time offsetting, phase inversion, resampling, time warping for nonlinear time stretching, visualization with seamless zooming, and volume clipping, metering, balancing and leveling. All higher level features and algorithms in Aurio build upon this interface and require a stream as input, and all streams and features check the format of its input stream and reject it with an exception and a meaningful message in case it is not supported.

Conversion from the time into the frequency domain can be achieved through one of the FFT implementations, for which multiple utility functions for magnitude calculation, normalization and scale conversion are available. The library also provides all commonly used window functions, and a class for automatic sequential windowing of sample streams. Based on the windowing are implementations for calculating spectrograms with the short-time Fourier transform (STFT), calculating chromagrams [2], and the Continuous Frequency Activation feature [21] for music detection.

The included data structures are commonly used buffers, moving average calculation methods, a undirected graph implementation with minimal spanning tree and connected component calculation, and various memory efficient matrix representations including the diagonal matrix and two kinds of sparse matrices.

3.1 Fingerprinting and Matching

The key features of Aurio that distinguish the library from other audio processing and retrieval libraries are the fingerprinting and matching methods.

[7]`http://naudio.codeplex.com/`

[8]`http://www.mono-project.com/`

Fingerprinting systems all share the same basic idea of transforming a stream of audio samples from known tracks into a series of hashes that are stored in a hash table and later used for lookup operations with hashes from unknown tracks [3]. The differences lie in the way the hashes are calculated and matched, but even there, many ideas are shared. Four fingerprinting methods are currently implemented. The first one is a well-known and widely used method usually referred to as "Philips fingerprinting", developed by Haitsma and Kalker at Philips Research [15]. Hashes are calculated by simply detecting onsets in the spectrogram and mapping them to a 32-bit integer bitmap, which proved to be working very well with noisy data. The second is probably the most famous algorithm by Wang because of its use in the popular smartphone app Shazam, therefore usually referred to as the "Shazam algorithm" [23]. Compared to the first method, Wang uses an intelligent approach to achieve a reduced number of more sparsely distributed hashes with greater entropy by selecting only the most prominent peaks that most likely survive high noise ("constellation map"), and forming pairs between each peak and the peaks in a defined target zone. The hashes are a concatenation of the two frequency bin indices and the temporal distance of a pair's peaks, resulting in 24-bit data stored in a 32-bit integer. Tests have shown even better resilience to noise than the Philips approach. A more recent method is Echoprint by Ellis et al. [8], built for The Echo Nest corporation that has been acquired by Spotify. It differentiates itself from Wang's method by first whitening the stream, then splitting the spectrum into 8 sub-bands, and detecting peaks and forming peak pairs separately in each band. Hashes are formed from the distances between two consecutive pairs' peaks and their band index, truncated to 20 bits but stored in 32-bit integers. Their distribution is even sparser with an average distance of one second between peaks. Its original application is music identification with over-the-air support, but compared to the previous two methods it does not work very well with high noise. The fourth method is named Chromaprint [18] and is based on ideas from [2, 16]. Chromaprint computes a chromagram, smooths and normalizes it over time, and then applies 16 classifiers frame by frame consisting of a filtering and quantization step, whose results are concatenated to a 32-bit hash. This method has been developed for audio file identification and is used by the MusicBrainz project [22] for metadata tagging. It is not designed for noise and over-the-air applications.

All methods are exactly documented, except for Wang's which is only described conceptually but has an unofficial open source library available [6]. For the Philips method, all crucial parameters are specified in the original paper [15], Echoprint and Chromaprint even offer official open source libraries [18,25]. Although there are implementations available, Aurio reimplements all methods from scratch to allow for stream-based processing of arbitrarily long input streams with constant memory usage. It also provides the ability to parameterize most variable settings through profiles, and each method comes with at least a default profile. The Echoprint and Chromaprint default profiles are compatible with the official libraries and produce the same hash output.

For retrieval, Aurio provides an accompanying hash storage for each fingerprinting method, backed by a hash table or SQLite[9]. Generated hashes can be written to the storage, which can then be queried for matches. Because Aurio is optimized for media synchronization, the hash stores do not just return a result telling if one track matches another, but they return exact matching positions of hashes within tracks. This essentially means that Aurio can be used to determine which temporal position within one track matches a temporal position within another track.

The accuracy of a match strongly depends on the granularity of the hashes, e.g. the Philips method returns much more accurate matches than Echoprint using the default settings. Aurio implements various methods for calculating the cross-correlation between stream segments, which can be used to improve the accuracy up to the sample level [13]. It also implements the common dynamic time warping method [20], and the improved on-line time warping [5] method. Given a single matching point, both can be used to calculate a series of matching points over the whole runtime of stream pairs, which effectively provides means for nonlinear synchronization, and the detection of time drift [12], cuts and drop-outs.

3.2 UI Widgets

To support building applications with graphical user interfaces, Aurio.WaveControls offers a range of widgets commonly found in audio and video analysis and editing tools. The *spectrogram* widget renders spectrograms and other 2D-grams, e.g. chromagrams, with configurable color gradients. The *graph* widget renders audio waves, windows, spectra and other kinds of value series. The *wave view* widget is the most elaborate control that can render arbitrarily long audio tracks with scrolling and continuous zooming between the whole track and single samples, and offers bitmap- and vector-based rendering modes. Additional widgets include a time scale, correlation meter, VU meter, and volume control slider.

3.3 Demo Applications

Included with the library are multiple tools, test applications and unit tests that serve as examples on how the library can be used. Among the interesting demos is a benchmark of the fingerprinting methods, which runs a file through all algorithms and prints the required computation time. It is useful for optimizing and monitoring the impact of changes in the algorithms and their many parameters. Another is a multi-track media player where multiple files can be mixed together and played back through a simple GUI. A demo application for the Philips fingerprinting algorithms allows the graphical inspection of the hash table and calculated fingerprints. For the Shazam fingerprinting, there is a demo that displays the constellation map on a spectrogram.

4. AUDIOALIGN

AudioAlign[10] is a Windows application shown in Figure 1, jointly developed with and built upon the Aurio library. Its main purpose is the (semi-)automatic synchronization of audio and video recordings. Other use-cases include the evaluation of fingerprinting algorithms and their configuration parameters, comparison of file sources, analysis of differences

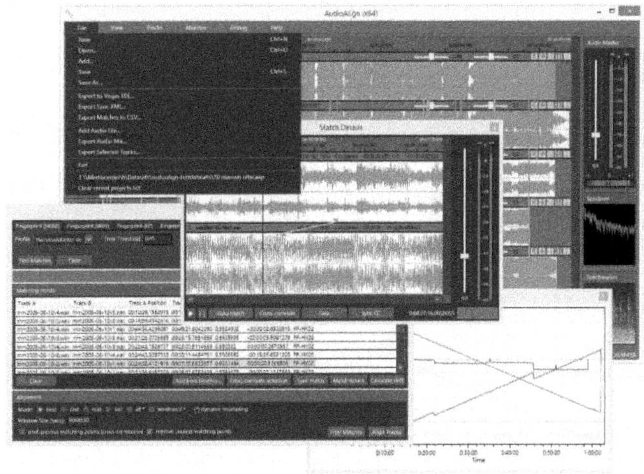

Figure 1: AudioAlign main window, file menu options, matching window, alignment graph, and match detail window.

in distinct live performances of artists, automatic synchronization of multiple audio tracks of different languages or formats, the synchronization of different cover interpretations of a musical piece, and dubbing of vocal recordings. It provides a simple multitrack timeline editor similar to common digital audio editors and video cutting tools, but does not offer direct audio editing abilities. Instead, it serves as a front end to Aurio's fingerprinting and matching algorithms, uses almost all of the core library's functionality and all the UI widgets, and is additionally designed to speed up processing by parallelizing tasks over multiple CPU cores.

To synchronize multiple recordings of an event, they can be dragged into the timeline or added through the menu. Because Aurio supports many file formats, it can also load videos downloaded from online video platforms like YouTube. Once the timeline is populated, tracks can be shifted across the scrollable and zoomable timeline which displays the audio waveforms. This way, tracks can be synchronized manually by specifying synchronization points through the *Match & Align* window. Playback can be started from any position within the timeline, and controls attached to each track allow basic balancing and mixing of parallel tracks to inspect their synchronization by listening. An instance of the application with its timeline and all its settings makes up a project that can be saved and loaded through the file menu. When a desirable synchronization has been achieved, a mixdown of the whole timeline or of separate selected tracks can be rendered into audio files. The timeline can also be exported to the Sony Vegas Pro video editor[11], where presynchronized video clips can easily be further processed, e.g. to create a multicamera cut. Of course, the real value is not the manual timeline adjustment but the available algorithms. A populated timeline can be automatically synchronized from the Match & Align window by first executing a fingerprinting algorithm, after which the discovered matching points are displayed on the timeline, and then carrying out an alignment step where the matching points are filtered by adjustable criteria and the tracks are temporally adjusted on the timeline. Relations between tracks and their

[9] `http://sqlite.org/`

[10] `https://github.com/protyposis/AudioAlign`

[11] `http://www.sonycreativesoftware.com/vegaspro`

matching points can be inspected in the *Alignment Graph* window that is also shown in Figure 1. Additional and more fine-grained matching points can be obtained through the dynamic time warping and cross-correlation options.

AudioAlign has already been presented as a demo [11] and has been used to create a synchronization ground truth for the Jiku Mobile Video Dataset [13]. Its sources are made available together with Aurio to serve as a reference application for the Aurio library.

5. LICENSE & PATENTS

Both Aurio and AudioAlign are available as open source software under the GNU Affero General Public License Version 3 [9]. Aurio contains methods protected by patents that can legally only be used under certain conditions. In Europe, these conditions are private use and research. For other uses, all users are encouraged to clarify the legal situation before using these methods. This particularly applies to the Philips and Shazam fingerprinting methods which are protected in many regions of the world [14, 24], and Echoprint which is protected in the US [7].

6. REFERENCES

[1] A. Arzt. Score following with dynamic time warping. Master's thesis, Vienna University of Technology, Vienna, Austria, 2008.

[2] M. Bartsch and G. Wakefield. Audio thumbnailing of popular music using chroma-based representations. *Multimedia, IEEE Transactions on*, 7(1):96–104, Feb 2005.

[3] P. Cano, E. Batlle, T. Kalker, and J. Haitsma. A review of audio fingerprinting. *Journal of VLSI signal processing systems for signal, image and video technology*, 41(3):271–284, 2005.

[4] S. Dixon. An on-line time warping algorithm for tracking musical performances. In *Proceedings of the 19th international joint conference on Artificial intelligence*, IJCAI'05, pages 1727–1728, San Francisco, CA, USA, 2005. Morgan Kaufmann Publishers Inc.

[5] S. Dixon. An on-line time warping algorithm for tracking musical performances. In *Proceedings of the International Joint Conference on Artificial Intelligence (IJCAI-05)*, pages 1727–1728, 2005.

[6] D. Ellis. Robust landmark-based audio fingerprinting. Web resource: `http://labrosa.ee.columbia.edu/matlab/fingerprint/` , 2009. Accessed 2015-05-20.

[7] D. Ellis and B. Whitman. Musical fingerprinting based on onset intervals. US Patent US20130139673, June 6 2013. Priority date Dec. 2 2011.

[8] D. Ellis, B. Whitman, and A. Porter. Echoprint - an open music identification service. In *Proceedings of the 12th International Society for Music Information Retrieval Conference (ISMIR 2011)*, Miami, Florida, 2011.

[9] Free Software Foundation, Inc. GNU Affero General Public License Version 3 (AGPLv3). Web resource: `http://www.gnu.org/licenses/agpl-3.0.txt`, Nov. 19 2007. Accessed 2015-05-20.

[10] M. Frigo and S. G. Johnson. The design and implementation of FFTW3. *Proceedings of the IEEE*, 93(2):216–231, 2005. Special issue on "Program Generation, Optimization, and Platform Adaptation".

[11] M. Guggenberger, M. Lux, and L. Böszörmenyi. Audioalign - synchronization of A/V-streams based on audio data. In *Multimedia (ISM), 2012 IEEE International Symposium on*, pages 382–383, 2012.

[12] M. Guggenberger, M. Lux, and L. Böszörmenyi. An analysis of time drift in hand-held recording devices. In *MultiMedia Modeling*, volume 8935 of *Lecture Notes in Computer Science*, pages 203–213. Springer International Publishing, 2015.

[13] M. Guggenberger, M. Lux, and L. Böszörmenyi. A synchronization ground truth for the jiku mobile video dataset. In *MultiMedia Modeling*, volume 8936 of *Lecture Notes in Computer Science*, pages 87–98. Springer International Publishing, 2015.

[14] J. Haitsma, A. Kalker, C. Baggen, and J. Oostveen. Generating and matching hashes of multimedia content. WIPO publication WO/2002/065782, Aug. 22 2002. Priority date Feb. 2 2001.

[15] J. Haitsma and T. Kalker. A highly robust audio fingerprinting system. In *Proceedings of the 3rd International Conference on Music Information Retrieval (ISMIR)*, Paris, France, 2002.

[16] D. Jang, C. Yoo, S. Lee, S. Kim, and T. Kalker. Pairwise boosted audio fingerprint. *Information Forensics and Security, IEEE Transactions on*, 4(4):995–1004, Dec 2009.

[17] L. Kennedy and M. Naaman. Less talk, more rock: Automated organization of community-contributed collections of concert videos. In *Proceedings of the 18th International Conference on World Wide Web*, WWW '09, pages 311–320, New York, NY, USA, 2009. ACM.

[18] L. Lalinský. AcoustID Chromaprint. Web resource: `https://acoustid.org/chromaprint`, 2011. Accessed: 2015-05-20.

[19] A. Llagostera Casanovas and A. Cavallaro. Audio-visual events for multi-camera synchronization. *Multimedia Tools and Applications*, pages 1–24, 2014.

[20] M. Müller. Dynamic time warping. In *Information Retrieval for Music and Motion*, pages 69–84. Springer Berlin Heidelberg, 2007.

[21] K. Seyerlehner, G. Widmer, T. Pohle, and M. Schedl. Automatic music detection in television productions. In *Proceedings of the Int. Conf. on Digital Audio Effects (DAFx-2007)*, 2007.

[22] A. Swartz. Musicbrainz: A semantic web service. *Intelligent Systems, IEEE*, 17(1):76–77, Jan 2002.

[23] A. L.-C. Wang. An industrial strength audio search algorithm. In *Proceedings of the Fourth International Conference on Music Information Retrieval (ISMIR 2003)*, pages 7–13, 2003.

[24] A. L.-C. Wang and J. O. Smith III. Method for search in an audio database. WIPO publication WO/2002/011123, Feb. 7 2002. Priority date Aug. 31 2000.

[25] B. Whitman, A. Porter, D. Ellis, et al. Echoprint Codegen. Web resource: `http://echoprint.me/codegen`, 2011. Accessed 2015-05-20.

Amalia.js : an Open-Source Metadata Driven HTML5 Multimedia Player

Nicolas Hervé, Pierre Letessier, Mathieu Derval, Hakim Nabi
Institut National de l'Audiovisuel - INA
Bry-sur-Marne, France
nherve@ina.fr

ABSTRACT

Amalia.js is a new extensible and versatile HTML5 multimedia player that allows you to view any type of metadata synchronized with your video or audio streams. It manages metadata that are localized both temporally and spatially. They can also be hierarchical. Several visualization plugins have already been developped, enabling amalia.js to be deployed in a huge variety of web applications. We believe it can be used in various research areas to quickly visualize analysis results and to share them with the community. Amalia.js is an open-source software under a GPL license. It is available for download at `http://ina-foss.github.io/amalia.js`.

Categories and Subject Descriptors

H.5.4 [**Information Interfaces and Presentation**]: Hypertext/Hypermedia; I.3.8 [**Computer Graphics**]: Applications

General Terms

Algorithms, Design, Documentation

Keywords

multimedia, player, metadata, plugin, html5

1. INTRODUCTION

The INA Research Department is working on several multimedia document analysis topics : audio segmentation, speaker diarization and recognition, visual segmentation, visual object detection, text/audio synchronization, ... As part of our Research Area [1], several of our prototypes have to be developped as web applications so as to be easily accessible. Among these prototypes, most of them are used to analyze video streams and enhance their metadata. However, the analysis being at different levels (keyframes, video segments, audio channels, associated synopses, one video alone or relative to a corpus, ...) results are obtained in very different natures, often needing quite specific approaches to be presented to the end user. It is also common that a user interaction is required as part of research on the navigation aid or data mining in large multimedia data sets. Finally, it is sometimes useful to engage the user by asking him to confirm the results of automatic algorithms or to annotate the media and thus create groundtruth. Despite the disparity in research fields and resulting interfaces, working on a common object, a video, allows us to set a generic framework in which we hope to insert all of our work. The objective is to develop a universal media player, extensible and accessible through a web browser allowing on one hand to present all the results of video and audio analysis algorithms and also to be a solid foundation for applications of manual or semi-automatic annotation. The main characteristics expected of such a player are: ergonomics, ease of technical integration, genericity of the manipulated metadata and the use cases addressed, scalability, related tools and technical robustness.

After studying the various existing solutions, we concluded that it was better to develop our own software to meet all of our needs. Furthermore, we believe that this kind of tool can be useful to others. This is the case in all the areas of image analysis: biology, medicine, satellite, cultural heritage, sport ... Whatever the field of analysis, we always need to be able to quickly and easily view the results of the methods we are developing. This problem is particularly true as we often manipulate large amount of videos. Developing visualization and annotation tools is often a tedious task that deserves to be pooled. Thus, we choose to share it as an open-source project under a GPL license.

Amalia.js is composed of three main parts that will be described in the following sections : the unified metadata format, the core player and the visualization plugins.

[1] `http://research.ina.fr`

MM'15, October 26–30, 2015, Brisbane, Australia.

ACM 978-1-4503-3459-4/15/10 ...$15.00.
DOI: http://dx.doi.org/10.1145/2733373.2807406 .

2. PREVIOUS WORK

2.1 Metadata Format

We need a unified metadata model that will be used to convey all the necessary informations for the visualization plugins of our player. We already mentioned the huge diversity of analysis result types that can be produced for a media stream. Thus, the main difficulty in choosing or defining a metadata model is to ensure it will be generic enough and stable. Many formats already exist to represent technical or indexing metadata on video and audio streams. Amoung the most common one can find Dublin Core [2], MPEG-7 [3], Cinelab data model (Advene project) [1] or the Open Annotation Data Model [3]. Work on creating such a model is conducted for several years in our Research Department. One can cite the work done around Feria [2] that allowed such thinking and formalized the representation of metadata temporally positioned on a stream. This paper also showed why MPEG-7 is unable to fulfil all our requirements.

2.2 Web Players

The list of available HTML5 video players is growing every day. Among the well known softwares in this category, we can cite JWPlayer, video.js or Popcorn.js [4]. A good overview is available with a comparison matrix [5]. However, there are only a few players able to synchronize metadata with the playback of the stream. Generally they are limited to the display of subtitles or clickable overlays for ads insertion in the video. Some tools meet quite the needs we have presented. Most of them are developed in research labs. This is the case of the IRI player [6]. There are also some tools for video annotation, like Vatic [7] and the Open Video Annotation Project [7]. In [5] an HTML5 player is presented with a special attention on non-linear navigation and user annotations. VideoJot [6] allows the user to annotate both spatially and temporally. These two software seems promising but, unfortunately, they are not publicly available.

3. AMALIA SOFTWARE ARCHITECTURE

3.1 Metadata Model

The existing formats either do not allow for an accurate representation of temporal metadata or they are too complex to implement. Indeed, we need a representation format of the information for displaying them in the player. This means it must be easy to parse and to be in a standard language for HTML5 developments, typically JSON. Thus, algorithms for analyzing multimedia streams retain, if they need it, their own data model, which can be richer and more complex than the one used for the player.

The main principle of amalia.js is to have a unified metadata model. Ensuring that all the metadata types are consistent and use the same standards will facilitate their use and enable us to design generic visualization plugins. A typical usage of amalia.js is to have a video file with a few metadata blocks. When instantiating the player, a binding has to be done between the metadata blocks and the visualization plugins so as to decide which metadata is displayed and in which way. It is possible to have a single metadata block bound with several visualization plugins, each one responsible for displaying a specific facet of the data.

A generic metadata model has thus been designed, it is intended to represent all the metadata of a media stream. It is able to describe both the audio and video of a content, technical informations, any documentary notes and all the results of automatic metadata extraction algorithms. Currently, this model is only able to manage metadata of a single stream. For analysis results of a corpus, involving links between streams (clustering, mining, similarity detection ...), a specific data model extension has to be created and is currently investigated. A full XML schema (XSD) has been written to represent this metadata model. This schema has much more elements than what is strictly needed to display simple metadata with amalia.js. The current version is 0.2.5. We use this schema to automatically generate Java classes using Jaxb and Jackson to serialize the metadata stream in JSON. The amalia-model project [8] is the reference implementation. It comes with several helper methods through a general factory and is also available on the Central Maven Repository. This JSON format is currently the only supported metadata format.

The model is generic and extensible, it is able to represent any metadata that is :

- localized temporally in the stream : at a given timecode (*tc*) or during a specific time segment (*tcin*, *tcout*)
- localized spatially in a video frame : currently ellipses and rectangles bounding boxes are available
- hierarchical : each metadata is associated to a specific level (*tclevel*)
- labeled : each metadata may have a label
- scored : each metadata may have a confidence scored
- extended : each metadata can have its own additionnal data that is not represented in this model

Each metadata block has a unique *id* that is used for the binding with the visualization plugins. A metadata block should only represent a coherent and homogeneous bunch of data. If you need to display distinct types of data, or even several blocks of data of the same type (e.g. the output of different versions of the same algorithm), you should provide them in separate blocks of metadata. One can find example of JSON files on the web site.

3.2 The core player

There are two main difficulties identified for such a project. First, we have to cope with the HTML5 restrictions. Although major progress has been made with the latest versions of HTML, there are still some difficulties compared to the development of desktop applications. This is particularly true for the multimedia streams management (codecs and synchronization). Unfortunately, we also still have to deal with the web browsers diversity. This is especially true with the emergence of mobile devices. Thus, we have to ensure our player is working fine on a huge variety of web browsers, including tablets and smartphones. It has to follow the responsive design guidelines. Secondly, we must ensure that the software architecture enables the player to support the various plugins that will be developed and that it does not put too many constraints on future developments. Furthermore, we must guarantee the good overall performances of the whole system.

For our player development, we could have started with an existing software and adapt it. However, the main development effort is on the visualization plugins management infrastructure and the metadata synchronization. It quickly

[2] `http://dublincore.org`

[3] `http://www.openannotation.org/spec/core`

[4] `http://popcornjs.org`

[5] `http://html5video.org/wiki/HTML5_Video_Player_Comparison`

[6] `http://www.iri.centrepompidou.fr/outils/metadata-player-2`

[7] `http://www.openvideoannotation.org`

[8] amalia-model project : `https://github.com/ina-foss/amalia-model`

Figure 1: Amalia.js player interface

appears more complex and time-consuming to adapt existing software rather than developing a new one from start. Indeed the basic functionalities of a media player are now managed by web browsers, the additional cost to manage these features (mainly the player control bar) is minimal compared to adapting an existing software. Amalia.js core is mainly an event-driven framework based on a plugin architecture. Both the internal technical components and the visualization widgets are plugins. This way, we can easily extend and modify the behaviour of the player or adapt it to an evolving technical environment. The core player is responsible for the overall configuration, the media asset being played, the plugins management (instantiation, configuration), the metadata management (loading, parsing, keeping up-to-date), the binding between metadata blocks and visualization plugins and the event loop (user interaction, synchronization between the plugins and the stream playback, metadata update notification). It provides an API for the plugins to access the metadata and to control the stream playback. The loading and parsing of the metadata blocks are two technical plugins. They are responsible for, respectively, the transmission protocol and the data format. We have implemented two protocols. The first, and simplest, is loading a full list of metadata blocks from an URL. On the server side, this URL can be a simple JSON file (such as the demonstrations on the amalia.js web site) or a dynamic web application using, for example, the amalia-model implementation (such as DigInPix [4]). The second protocol uses web sockets. We can thus manage metadata streaming to the player. This feature is particularly interesting when one need real-time synchronization of the metadata. It is the case, for example, with collaborative annotation of a media stream or if we need to display the results of an automatic analysis algorithm as they are produced. As already mentioned, we currently only support the JSON format of our metadata model. But, as the parsing of these data is also a plugin, it can easily be replaced so as to manage another data representation. The binding between a metadata block and a visualization plugin can be achieved in two ways. One can either bind them statically when configuring the player (using the metadata block *id*) or use the dynamic binding that will associate metadata blocks and plugins based on the data types.

The figure 1 shows the amalia.js player default layout. Indeed, the control bar is a plugin which contains many widgets. The global layout and the visual aspect of these widgets can easily be modified so as to adapt the player to your application visual design.

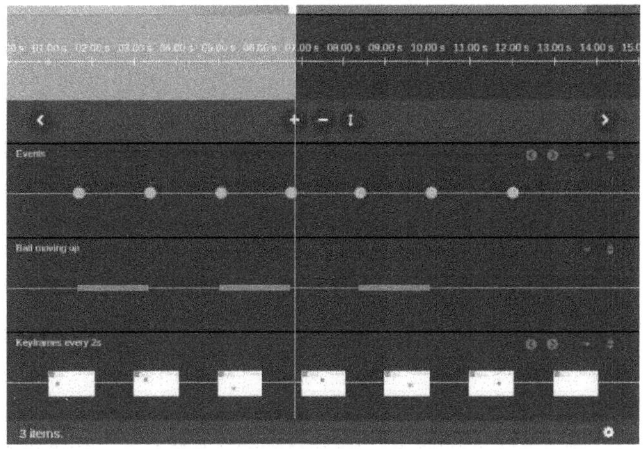

Figure 2: The timeline plugin

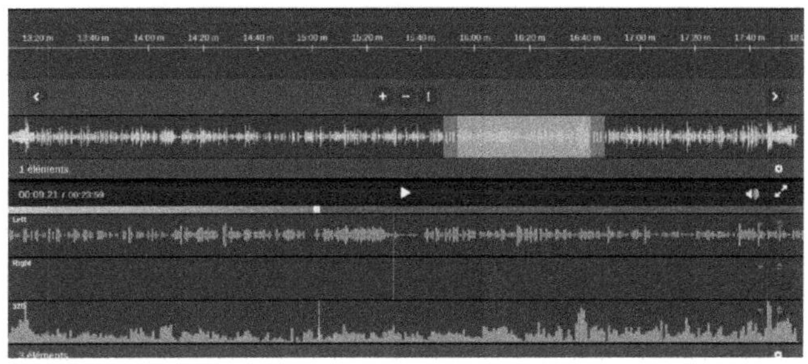

Figure 3: The histogram visualization for the timeline plugin

3.3 Visualization Plugins

3.3.1 *Timeline*

The purpose of this plugin is to represent all the timecoded metadata on a timeline. This plugin is composed of two parts. At the top, the time axis where you can navigate and zoom in the timeline. Below the time axis, all the timelines are displayed. For a given media stream, one can display as many timelines as desired, each of which may be bound to a different metadata block and displayed with a specific type of line. For the moment, we have four types of lines :

- cuepoint: simple temporal points (tc field)
- segment: temporal segments (tcin and tcout fields)
- image: temporal points with images, typically keyframes (tc and thumb fields)
- histogram: any information that is temporally distributed

The three first types of lines are used in the figure 2. The histogram visualization is presented in figure 3 where a wave form is displayed. One can notice that an audio stream is played as no video playback window is displayed. Furthermore, the timeline plugin is instanciated twice and bound each time on the same metadata block. Once with the zoom enabled (at the top), and once with the zoom disabled.

The timeline is synchronized with the player, a progress bar indicates the current position in the media and a click on any object represented in the timeline will seek in the media at the correct timecode. Optionnaly, the hierarchical structure of the metadata can be exploited. One can associated a level in the data hierarchy with a zoom level of the player. This option is particularly usefull when too many data are available and when we choose to display only the most important ones at a first glance. The other data will only be displayed if the user chooses to zoom in and explore a specific part of the metadata

3.3.2 Caption and synchonized text

Textual metadata can be displayed by two specific plugins: caption and synchonized text. Depending on the textual metadata you have, it may be usefull to exploit its hierarchical structure. Typically, one may choose to have the words, sentences and paragraphs of a text temporally localized. In such a case, one would choose a specific *tclevel* for each level of text. When binding a text metadata block with one of the text visualization plugin, one has to choose which level will be displayed. The caption plugin is relatively conventional and simply used to represent the text over the video. It is used to display subtitles. The synchronized text plugin allows you to browse all the text in a specific window and synchronize the playback with the video.

3.3.3 Overlay

This plugin is used to visualize objects detected in the video with bounding boxes. Moreover, it is able to track them. A track is represented by a series of spatial locations. The exact position of the bounding box is then extrapolated by the plugin during the playback of the video.

3.3.4 Edition

Apart from the new technical or visualization plugins, we are currently working on the editing version of amalia.js. This will allow us to enter or correct metadata directly through the player. We plan to use this version in groundtruth management applications so as to enable the creation of huge research datasets used to train supervised algorithms or to assess analysis methods performances. Entering information in the player is also a feature that could be useful for any business applications dealing with temporal annotations of multimedia streams. The current version is shown in figure 4.

4. CONCLUSION AND FUTURE WORK

We have developped a HTML5 media player with its synchronized metadata visualization plugins. This software is used in some of our research prototypes : DigInPix [4] and SyncNotes [9]. It is also used at INA for professional applications. We provide it as an open-source software in the hope it will be usefull, especially in the multimedia analysis community. The work is not yet finished. We are currently developing the edition version of the plugins and improving the server side libraries so as to ease applications development. Furthermore, new visualization plugins will be available shortly. We encourage anyone to participate by providing their own plugins or help us with existing ones.

[9] `http://syncnotes.ina.fr/en`

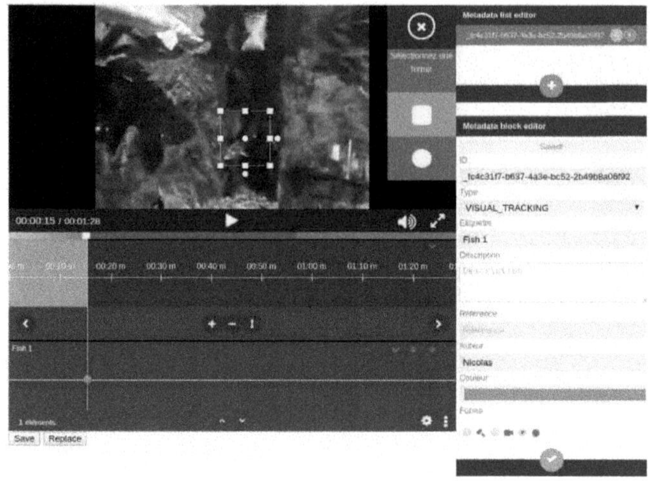

Figure 4: The edition application

Acknowledgments

We wish to thank the main developer of this software that, unfortunately, can not be in the authors list for legal reasons.

5. REFERENCES

[1] O. Aubert and Y. Prié. Advene: An open-source framework for integrating and visualising audiovisual metadata. In *Proceedings of the 15th International Conference on Multimedia*, MULTIMEDIA '07, pages 1005–1008, New York, NY, USA, 2007. ACM.

[2] V. Brunie, J. Carrive, and L. Vinet. Ingénierie des documents audiovisuels : le projet feria. une approche centrée sur la description des contenus. *Technique et Science de l'Information*, 2006.

[3] S.-F. Chang, A. Puri, T. Sikora, and H. Zhang. Introduction to the special issue on mpeg-7. *IEEE Transactions on Circuits and Systems for Video Technology*, 11(6):685–687, 2001.

[4] P. Letessier, N. Hervé, A. Joly, H. Nabi, M. Derval, and O. Buisson. Diginpix: visual named-entities identification in images and videos. In *ACM International Conference on Multimedia Retrieval*, 2015.

[5] B. Meixner, B. Siegel, P. Schultes, F. Lehner, and H. Kosch. An html5 player for interactive non-linear video with time-based collaborative annotations. In *Proceedings of International Conference on Advances in Mobile Computing & Multimedia*, MoMM '13, pages 490:490–490:499, New York, NY, USA, 2013. ACM.

[6] M. Riegler, M. Lux, V. Charvillat, A. Carlier, R. Vliegendhart, and M. Larson. Videojot: A multifunctional video annotation tool. In *Proceedings of International Conference on Multimedia Retrieval*, ICMR '14, pages 534:534–534:537, New York, NY, USA, 2014. ACM.

[7] C. Vondrick, D. Patterson, and D. Ramanan. Efficiently scaling up crowdsourced video annotation. *International Journal of Computer Vision*, pages 1–21. 10.1007/s11263-012-0564-1.

SIVA Suite: Framework for Hypervideo Creation, Playback and Management

Britta Meixner
University of Passau
Passau, Germany
meixner@fim.uni-passau.de

Stefan John
University of Passau
Passau, Germany
stefan.john@uni-passau.de

Christian Handschigl
University of Passau
Passau, Germany
christian.handschigl@uni-passau.de

SUBMITTED to ACM MULTIMEDIA 2015 OPEN SOURCE SOFTWARE COMPETITION

ABSTRACT

Due to their structure, hypervideos are well suited for different scenarios. Compared to traditional linear videos, they have advantages especially in e-learning and training, where the study matter can be fitted to the needs of the viewer. In this paper we present the SIVA Suite, an open source framework for the creation, playback, and administration of hypervideos. The SIVA Suite consists of an authoring tool, an HTML5 hypervideo player, and a Web server for user and video management. This framework has been successfully used for the creation of hypervideos in different use cases, e.g. a medical hypervideo training. It was evaluated in several usability tests and improved step-by-step since 2008.

Categories and Subject Descriptors

H.5.4 [**INFORMATION INTERFACES AND PRESENTATION**]: Hypertext/Hypermedia

Keywords

Authoring tool, Player, Management server, Hypervideo, Multimedia, Scene graph, Annotations

1. INTRODUCTION

For the term hypervideo no universal definition can be found. Usually it refers to a compound of video scenes linked to each other or to additional multimedia elements. In our work, scenes and navigational elements are arranged in a graph, called scene graph, to define the navigational structure of a hypervideo. Annotations offering additional information can be added to single scenes or the whole video. For this purpose, images, text, pdf files, audio files, and even other videos may be used. As a supplement to the video structure defined by the scene graph, further navigational elements like a table of contents and a keyword search enable the viewer to jump to certain entry points.

Hypervideos can be used for different use cases like e-learning, virtual tours, sports training, interactive video stories, mobile help systems, or memory training. Depending on the use case one or another function may be more important. Requirements for a medical training realized with hypervideos can for example be found in [5], a demo video can be found on the project homepage[1].

First hypervideos were created in 1996 by Sawhney [6] with the use case of a cafe. Instead of programs specialized for the creation of hypervideos, common multimedia editing software was used. In the following years, different tools were presented. One of the most advanced was Hyper-Hitchcock [7] which could be used for the creation of detail-on-demand hypervideos with one main storyline and entry points for more detailed video explanations. However, an open source version of the software could not be found. With new technologies like HTML5, CSS 3, and JavaScript, web-based tools like Klynt [2] emerged. It allows the creation of hypervideos with focus on different media types. Klynt provides many useful features but can not be extended or customized due to the proprietary licensing.

In this paper we present the SIVA Suite, an open source framework for the creation, playback, and administration of hypervideos.

2. SOFTWARE COMPONENTS

The SIVA Suite consists of an authoring tool, the SIVA Producer, a hypervideo player with extended controls and display areas, the SIVA Player, and a Web server for user, group, and video management, the SIVA Server. These components will be described in detail hereafter including implementation details as well as installation instructions and licensing. The suite is available at the project's GitHub repository (`https://github.com/SIVAteam/SIVA-Suite`).

2.1 SIVA Producer

The SIVA Producer is used for the production of hypervideos consisting of main video scenes and multimedia annotations like images, videos, audio files, or text. The main video scenes are linked with each other in a scene graph, each of them may have one or more multimedia annotations. Further navigational structures are a table of contents as well

[1] `http://siva.uni-passau.de/mirkul/projekte/BB_Trainer` only in German (accessed May 20, 2015)

MM'15, October 26–30, 2015, Brisbane, Australia.
© 2015 ACM. ISBN 978-1-4503-3459-4/15/10 ...$15.00.
DOI: http://dx.doi.org/10.1145/2733373.2807413.

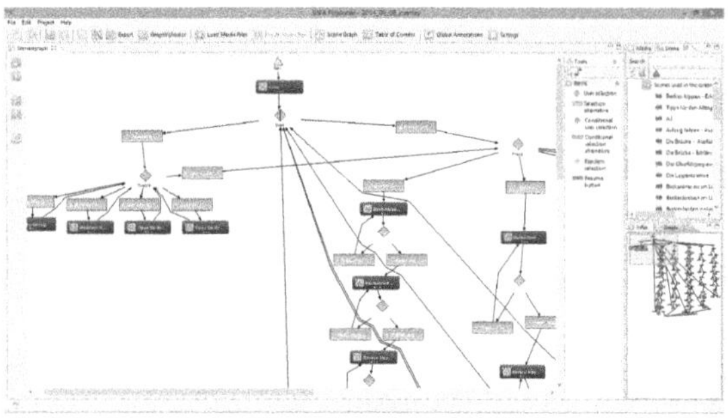

Figure 1: Screenshot of the SIVA Producer with the scene graph (left side) and the media repository (right side)

as the definition of keywords which can then be searched for in the player.

2.1.1 *Main Features*

Hypervideos are created step by step in the SIVA Producer. When a new project is created the appearance of the associated player can be customized. Afterwards, media files are imported into the media repository (see Figure 1, right side, top). The Producer uses each media file in its original format during the creation process. From videos, scenes can be extracted and tagged with keywords. Those will be added to the scene repository from where they can be dragged to the scene graph to create the hypervideo structure. A scene graph consists of a defined start and an end, as well as several scenes and connection/branching elements (see Figure 1, left side) allowing advanced navigation options during playback of the video. These are:

- Forward button: A single button with only one label. It can be used to interrupt a linear sequence of scenes.
- Standard selection: Users may select one of the attached paths to continue playback.
- Random selection: One of the attached paths will be selected at random without user interaction.
- Conditional selection: For attached paths, conditions can be defined which have to be fulfilled before the path is unlocked for playback.

In order to produce a valid and exportable scene graph two conditions have to be met. First, only one start scene is allowed. Second, every scene has to be connected by some path to the start and to the end of the video.

Each scene in the scene graph may have one or more multimedia annotations. To add an annotation, a media file can either be dragged from the media repository and dropped on a scene, or an annotation editor can be used to customize its timing and appearance. The editor also allows to add keywords by which annotations can easily be accessed in the player. Additionally, a hotspot can be added to the scene which invokes the display of the annotation only after a viewer clicks the marked area. Besides annotations which are displayed with scenes, global annotations which are displayed during the whole hypervideo can be added with a separate editor.

The table of contents editor is used to create a tree structure of entries with meaningful headlines. A scene from the scene graph can be linked with one of the entries in the table of contents.

In a last step, finished hypervideo projects with valid scene graphs are exported for the player. The structure of the hypervideo with all possible actions is imported into a JSON file. The media files are transformed and transcoded for the desired target platform.

The SIVA Producer furthermore provides a function for handing over a project to another computer. The validity of the scene graph can be checked with a validation function. Further descriptions of the SIVA Producer as well as usability tests for an easier and more efficient creation of hypervideos can be found in [4]. A help for the SIVA Producer can be found in the menu under "Help ▷ Help Contents".

2.1.2 *Implementation*

For now, the SIVA Producer is only available as a 32-bit Windows application. Implemented in Java 1.6, it is based on version 3.8.2 of the Eclipse Rich Client Platform (RCP)[2]. Supporting the OSGi standard, RCP allows for the separation of distinct concerns. In our case, major players like the model, the UI, and the transcoding functionality are split into separate bundles. Additionally, the RCP framework simplifies the integration of standard features. Among others, project creation wizards, undo/redo functionality, and a help system were added to the SIVA Producer.

For the handling of media files, we rely on third party projects. The transcoding and manipulation of videos as well as the extraction of video frames is done with ffmpeg[3]. In various editors, the SIVA Producer offers embedded media players. Therefore, facilitated by the vlcj Java bindings[4], the libraries of the VLC player[5] are used. Both, ffmpeg as well as the VLC player, support a large variety of video and audio codecs allowing the SIVA Producer to work with all media formats required by HTML5 video elements.

2.1.3 *Installation and Licenses*

The SIVA Producer is released in the form of a single setup file. The installation follows the standard procedure for Windows applications offering an installation wizard.

Being based on the Eclipse RCP, the SIVA Producer is licensed under the terms of the Eclipse Public License (EPL).

2.2 SIVA Player

The SIVA Player is used to play the hypervideo created in the SIVA Producer. The structure and media elements of the hypervideo are described in a JSON file which conforms to the XML structure described in [3]. The player was tested and improved in several user tests (among others with elderly people). See [8] for further descriptions of the tests and their results.

2.2.1 *Main Features*

The player provides a main video view on the left side and an annotation panel on the right side of the player area (see Figure 2). A click on one of the annotations opens its contents in full screen mode for additional interactions (like browsing an image gallery or watching a video), while the

[2] `http://www.eclipse.org/eclipse/` (accessed May 20, 2015)

[3] `http://www.ffmpeg.org/` (accessed May 20, 2015)

[4] `http://capricasoftware.co.uk/\#/projects/vlcj` (accessed May 20, 2015)

[5] `http://www.videolan.org/vlc/index.html` (accessed May 20, 2015)

Figure 2: Screenshot of the SIVA Player with the video area (left side) and the annotation area (right side)

player pauses the main video in the background. The player furthermore provides extended navigation elements beyond the well known timeline and control buttons. If a fork in the video occurs, a button panel is provided at the left side of the main video area where the viewer has to select the next scene. Furthermore, a table of contents and a keyword search are available if the author of the hypervideo provided the required information. The latter performs a live search and refines the search results with every keystroke. The player also provides multiple language support if the author provides translations for all text and media elements. Besides clicking or tapping the buttons, the basic functions of the player can also be controlled using the keyboard, namely with space bar, ESC button, left and right arrow button.

All actions of the user can be recorded if logging is enabled by the author. The player transmits the actions to the server every 60 seconds as well as when the player starts or the video ends, if it is used in online mode. If the player is used in offline mode, logging data is collected and transmitted to the server when a connection can be established.

To make the player usable for a wide range of use cases, it provides a simple design which can be customized by the author. It is for example possible to select a primary and a secondary color, to determine the width of the annotation panel, etc. Furthermore, configurations in HTML are possible. Using a responsive design, the player cannot only be used on desktop PCs having varying screen sizes but also on mobile devices in landscape and portrait mode. The player can be used online over the internet or in offline mode when all files are stored at the end user device.

2.2.2 *Implementation*

The player's implementation consists of HTML5, CSS 3, JavaScript, and SVG. The usage of these web technologies with their wide range of functions offered by APIs enabled us to create a lightweight and portable hypervideo player. HTML5 comes with built-in video support without the need of further plug-ins. JavaScript is used to control the videos and to listen to the video events. While JavaScript is also responsible for creating the view according to the hypervideo configuration, CSS 3 and SVG are used for browser optimized design and animation.

Modern browsers like Mozilla Firefox, Google Chrome, Apple Safari, Internet Explorer and Opera are capable of executing the SIVA Player independent of the available operating system. Therefor it can be even executed on mobile browsers. A current version of the browser and the availability of an MPEG4 or WebM codec are the only prerequisites.

To ease selecting and manipulating the DOM we use jQuery 1.9.1[6] and jQuery Mobile 1.4.2[7] rather than basic JavaScript. Besides cross-browser support, both frameworks come with lots of plug-ins[8] satisfying almost any need. Furthermore, the Modernizr library2[9] in version 2.7.1 is used to ensure the support of HTML5 videos and the availability of features which are not available on all modern browsers (e.g. full screen mode).

2.2.3 *Installation and Licenses*

The SIVA Producer provides an HTML export profile. If this export profile is used, the result contains the hypervideo files as well as an HTML file and the SIVA Player files. The HTML file links it all together. The exported player is as large as the browser window by default. Since the player works on the local file system as long as all files are unpacked and correctly linked, it can be put into an installer or on portable media like CDs to make the distribution easier for end users. To integrate the SIVA Player into a website the body part of the exported HTML file has to be copied and the paths have to be adapted.

The SIVA Player is licensed under the terms of the GPLv3.

2.3 SIVA Server

The SIVA Server provides a platform for hypervideos and evaluations based on logging data. Furthermore, it provides a user and rights management for videos protected by copyright.

2.3.1 *Main Features*

The server application is used to manage users, user groups, and videos. Videos exported by the producer are uploaded in the Web interface, extracted by the server, and can then be viewed on the server. It is furthermore possible to provide a link to a video, for example when the video is also available as a Chrome App [1], or a download for a zip file. The latter can be extracted locally on the end user device and watched without internet connection.

Users may have different roles (like user, admin, etc.) and rights according to their roles. Furthermore, each user may be member of one or more groups. The accessibility of videos can be assigned at group level. This ensures that the visibility of videos is satisfied according to the demands of the author or copyright limitations. A help for the SIVA Server can be found on its start page.

The server furthermore provides the SIVA Player Stats, the back end for the logging functionality of the player. This part of the application facilitates analyzing and evaluating the logged usage data. Watching, searching, exporting, or visualizing these data can be done video based. One of the currently available diagram views is the Sunburst diagram (see Figure 3), which shows how often certain paths were taken in a video by the viewers. Another diagram is a Treemap which shows the different scenes of the video and the events in these scenes. Thereby, the sizes of the boxes are representing the frequency of occurrence of one single event. This part of the application is only accessible for administrators registered in the front-end.

[6] `https://jquery.com/` (accessed May 20, 2015)
[7] `https://jquerymobile.com/` (accessed May 20, 2015)
[8] `https://plugins.jquery.com/` (accessed May 20, 2015)
[9] `http://modernizr.com/` (accessed May 20, 2015)

Figure 3: Screenshot of the SIVA Player Stats with the Sunburst diagram

2.3.2 *Implementation*

The SIVA Server is split into two parts. The first and main part of the application provides the user, group, and video management, as well as APIs for authentication and logging. It is written in Java 7 and uses JavaServer Faces Mojarra in Version 2.2.4[10] for a stable and efficient front-end system that deals with large hypervideo files and plenty of logging traffic. For storing data, a PostgreSQL[11] database is currently used. It ensures reliability and data integrity by applying to the ACID properties. Since the support of other database systems might be desired we used a modular design that allows exchanging by providing a package implementing the interfaces. The SIVA Player Stats back-end application is written in PHP 5 to allow easy and fast adaption and extension for evaluation purposes. For visualization, D3.js charts[12] are used.

2.3.3 *Installation and Licenses*

For the installation of the front-end we recommend Apache Tomcat 7[13] and PostgreSQL 9.1[14] or newer. Additionally credentials to an SMTP account are needed. The WAR archive can then be uploaded via the Tomcat manager or put directly into Tomcat's webapp folder. After successfully deploying the archive an installation page will appear when opening the font-end's URL in a browser. The installation is completed after filling all fields. For customizing the appearance of the front-end images, CSS files and other files can be stored persistently in the configuration folder. There is also a branding configuration file that allows to change the texts of some pages (e.g. home or privacy). An Apache 2 webserver[15] is required for the installation of the SIVA Player Stats back-end. PHP in version 5.4 or newer has to be installed and the Apache module mod_rewrite has to be enabled. The files of the back-end can then be put into the virtual host's folder. The back-end can then be opened in the browser to complete the installation. The SIVA Server is licensed under the terms of the GPLv3.

[10] `http://www.oracle.com/technetwork/java/javaee/javaserverfaces-139869.html` (accessed May 20, 2015)
[11] `http://www.postgresql.org/` (accessed May 20, 2015)
[12] `http://d3js.org/` (accessed May 20, 2015)
[13] `https://tomcat.apache.org/index.html` (accessed May 20, 2015)
[14] `http://www.postgresql.org/` (accessed May 20, 2015)
[15] `http://httpd.apache.org/` (accessed May 20, 2015)

3. CONCLUSIONS

In this paper we present the SIVA Suite, an open source framework for the creation, playback, and administration of hypervideos. The authoring tool, the SIVA Producer, provides several editors like a scene graph or annotation editors, as well as an export function. The hypervideo player, the SIVA Player, has extended controls and display areas as well as an intuitive design. The Web server, the SIVA Server, provides functions for user, group, and video management. This framework, especially the authoring tool and the player were successfully used for the creation and playback of several hypervideos, like a medical hypervideo training. Both were evaluated in several usability tests and improved step-by-step since 2008.

4. ACKNOWLEDGMENTS

The SIVA Suite was designed and implemented at the Passau University in four different projects which partially built upon each other. They were partially funded by the European Social Fonds and the Bayrisches Staatsministerium für Wissenschaft, Forschung und Kunst (Bavarian State Ministry for Sciences, Research and the Arts). Furthermore, it was funded by the Bundesministerium für Bildung und Forschung (German Federal Ministry of Education and Research) (BMBF) under project number 03V0633. We furthermore want to thank all (former) colleagues and students who contributed to the software.

5. REFERENCES

[1] Google. What are chrome apps? Website (accessed May 18, 2015), 2015. https://developer.chrome.com/apps/about_apps.

[2] Honkytonk Films. Klynt. Website (accessed May 18, 2015), 2015. http://www.klynt.net/.

[3] B. Meixner and H. Kosch. Interactive non-linear video: Definition and xml structure. In *Proc. of the 2012 ACM Symp. on Document Engineering*, DocEng '12, pages 49–58, New York, NY, USA, 2012. ACM.

[4] B. Meixner, K. Matusik, C. Grill, and H. Kosch. Towards an easy to use authoring tool for interactive non-linear video. *Multimedia Tools Appl.*, 70(2):1251–1276, May 2014.

[5] B. Meixner, K. Tonndorf, S. John, C. Handschigl, K. Hofmann, and M. Granitzer. A multimedia help system for a medical scenario in a rehabilitation clinic. In *Proc. of the 14th Intl. Conf. on Knowledge Technologies and Data-driven Business*, i-KNOW '14, pages 25:1–25:8, New York, NY, USA, 2014. ACM.

[6] N. Sawhney, D. Balcom, and I. Smith. Hypercafe: narrative and aesthetic properties of hypervideo. In *Proc. of the 7th ACM Conf. on Hypertext. HYPERTEXT '96*, pages 1–10, New York, NY, USA, 1996. ACM.

[7] F. Shipman, A. Girgensohn, and L. Wilcox. Authoring, viewing, and generating hypervideo: An overview of hyper-hitchcock. *ACM Trans. Multimedia Comput. Commun. Appl.*, 5(2):15:1–15:19, Nov. 2008.

[8] K. Tonndorf, C. Handschigl, J. Winscheid, and M. Granitzer. The effect of non-linear structures on the usage of hypervideo for physical training. In *2014 IEEE International Conference on Multimedia and Expo (ICME)*, page to appear. IEEE, 2015.

Using Handmade Controllers for Interactive Projection Mapping

Alinta Krauth
Artist/Griffith University
154 Upper Coomera Rd
Witheren, Queensland
+61 439 540 895
a.krauth@griffith.edu.au

ABSTRACT
In this short paper I will look at the use of hand-made gaming controllers for my own interactive artworks, in particular the technology behind the interactive projection mapping artwork *Shadows blister those who try to touch*, exhibited at ACM MM 2015 in Brisbane. In this installation, interactions between viewer and artwork give new life to older forms of interactive hardware and traditional art media. Its set up also creates previously unexplored connections between new and old software, and has caused me to postulate that the aesthetic of interactive controllers can, and perhaps should, be considered in the artistic process. In new media art, hardware can be a part of the artwork – not just a peripheral.

Categories and Subject Descriptors
J.5 [Computer Applications]: Arts and Humanities: Fine arts.

General Terms
Documentation, Performance, Design, Experimentation, Theory.

Keywords
Projection Mapping; Interactive Art; Interactive Controllers; Joystick; Button; Arcade; Interaction; Mixed Media; New Media Art.

1. INTRODUCTION
In this paper I look at previously unmade connections between software and hardware in my own projection mapping artworks. In particular, I discuss the creation and purpose of bespoke controllers in my interactive works such as *Shadows blister those who try to touch*, exhibited at ACM MM 2015 in Brisbane. I examine how the interactions between viewer and artwork created by this work give new life to older forms of interactive hardware, create previously unexplored connections between software, and remind the viewer that interactive controllers can and should be just as much a part of the aesthetic, rather than apart from the aesthetic. When looked at in this frame of mind, instructions become art, and both 'old' and 'new' technologies and art media can work together to new effect.

In recent decades artists have attempted to bring interactive elements into projection mapping works, though this is still not the norm. Since 2010 this has become much easier with technologies made commonplace, such as the Xbox Kinect (https://www.microsoft.com/en-us/kinectforwindows/develop) and the Leap Motion (https://www.leapmotion.com). In my artwork *Shadows blister those who try to touch* and in my projection mapping works more generally, I use pre-existing software packages and technology from the 1980s to control the work. I attempt to find new software and hardware combinations in order to create interactive site-specific pieces that combine new and traditional media, and allow audiences to engage in the social, political and education issues the works bring to the fore.

MM'15, October 26 - 30, 2015, Brisbane, Australia

ACM 978-1-4503-3459-4/15/10…$15.00
DOI: http://dx.doi.org/10.1145/2733373.2808104

2. 'SHADOWS BLISTER THOSE WHO TRY TO TOUCH'
Shadows blister those who try to touch shown at ACM MM 2015 is an interactive projection mapped piece created using several different software packages. The first is Adobe Photoshop (http://www.adobe.com/au/products/photoshop.html), where I created images to become frame-by-frame animations. These images were often hand-drawn or painted onto paper, then digitised, in order to cement connections between traditional and new media. The images were then imported into a game designing program, in this case GameSalad (http://www.gamesalad.com), in order to turn the still images into animations and to create the interactive elements. The artwork was thus packaged as an .app file. This output is projection mapped to a wall-mounted sculpture, fabricated out of recycled plastic and cardboard materials.

Installing this work required the sculpture to be stuck to a wall, and the projection mapping software MadMapper (http://www.madmapper.com) was used to create an output to fit this sculpture, requiring around 200 digital surfaces. However, at the time of creating this artwork MadMapper did not natively allow interactive inputs (beyond having a live webcam mode). In order to be able to import the interactive piece, a program called Syphoner (http://syphoner.sigma6.ch) was used.

A bespoke control box using simple arcade buttons connects to the hidden computer. I made this box out of wood, adding traditional art media such as paint and clay. The outcome is a rectangular white controller with two options to press – two large red buttons signifying left and right. Protruding from this box are copper and gold coloured pipes, further customised with black ink and paint. This box sits on a tall plinth.

By using traditional art media, hand-made and hand-drawn elements, and technology made famous in the 1980s, the controller for this piece was unique and unbranded. It attempted to do something new with something old, while also aesthetically contributing to the work as a whole. While these software and hardware components are readily available and used extensively in their own right, the combination is under-explored. By using pre-existing programs, hardware, and media in new ways, and with new combinations, we can create digital artworks that are distinct in look, and distinct in the ways in which the audience can interact.

3. NEW VS. OLD IS SO YESTERDAY

My experiments with interactive screen based artworks and site-specific projection mapping works have led me to believe that what one might consider older forms of technology and creative craft are still incredibly relevant to new media art. They have also led me to believe that technology used to create viewer interaction (whether it is touch based or gesture based) must also be a part of the art. I have often attempted to revamp older hardware and combine the digital with the real. For example, I have used canvases painted with reactive paint to create touch controllers that double as paintings in *An Argument in Parallel Incompleteness: Canvas Edition*, 2015 (http://alintakrauth.com/an_argument). This is a screen-based interactive art/poetry world. Another example is turning arcade game buttons and joysticks into steampunk[1] sculpture as the controller for *Un[tram]melled*, 2015 (http://alintakrauth.com/untrammelled). *Un[tram]melled* is an interactive projection work, mapped to 1930s powerhouse machinery originally used to power the tram network of Brisbane, Australia.

Is it possible to create works like this that live beyond the media that they are made with, or will the medium always be the message? (McLuhan 1964). It is easy to become obsessed with the newness of new technologies, and forget that art is predominantly about the content. However, by using older components to new effect, such as a bespoke arcade button set up to control a projection-mapped artwork (such as *Un[tram]melled)*, the user may more easily understand how the interaction will occur, and can perhaps even reminisce. By contrast, using touchable paintings to control a digital work plays on the concept of the real/digital dichotomy, and creates an unexpected situation for the viewer where they must do what they have previously been told not to do – touch paintings in an art gallery. This also reminds the viewer that projection mapping can first and foremost be a work of art, not simply a spectacle or an experimentation with technology.

While many recent interactive artworks attempt to hide their interactive controllers or incorporate them as screens in the artwork[2], there are still a lot of interactive projection mapping works out there that are happy for the audience to clearly see branded peripherals[3]. While this technology can excite an audience, it may potentially take away from the work's aesthetic. I believe that moving away from the obsession with the 'new new', and looking back to previous hardware, is one way (among others) to reconsider this.

---

[1] A trend of using 19th century machinery parts to create modern design and fashion.

[2] For example Ethno Tekh's 'Flow' exhibited in 2015 for *Pause Festival*, Melbourne Australia (http://www.ethnotekh.com/project/flow).

[3] Some works at the *Gertrude Street Projection Festival* 2015, which I also had work in, would be testament to this (http://gspf.com.au).

4. INSTRUCTIONS AS ART

I believe that interaction can be intrinsically tied to instruction. In many of my interactive artworks, there is no right or wrong in how one interacts, however, audience members can sometimes feel the need to follow normalised social rules for interaction. While there may be very few rules as to how one behaves inside these artworks, audience members must initially understand how to interact – whether it is by gesture, movement, touch, or other peripherals. This is true even in many artworks where interaction is purposefully surprising.

I initially became interesting in the idea of instructions as art when making screen-based works. I found that in my screen-based works, my audience saw themselves as being inside a game world where they were expecting to only travel in one 'correct' direction. I wanted them to explore these on-screen worlds at their leisure, however I also wanted them to feel as though they were progressing onto new areas. To overcome this, instructional symbols such as arrows became a part of the art itself (Krauth 2014). Similar notions of instructions becoming art are seen in other artists' screen-based works, such as *Evidence of Everything Exploding* by Jason Nelson (Krauth 2014; http://www.secrettechnology.com/explode/evidence.html).

These artful on-screen instructions began translating themselves into the real-world game controllers seen in my projection mapping artworks. Arcade controls used in new ways are one such reply to the issue of instruction, as these controls live in a liminal space between being well known to the general public, yet generally being unbranded and malleable in design. Thus, while my controllers can look very different for each artwork, for most of my viewers they are approachable and need no introduction; they are instructional art.

5. CONCLUSION

The technical set up for *Shadows blister those who try to touch* is just one example of how projection mapping artists, and interactive artists more widely, could approach interaction from another way – not by continuously looking for new interactive hardware and software, but by returning to older hardware and creating little-used software combinations. The use of hand-made controllers based on arcade buttons and joysticks in my artworks is one way to intrinsically include the controls as a part of the work's aesthetic, and one way to promote one's own artistic craft in controller fabrication. By celebrating technology based on its usefulness, rather than its newness, and by celebrating traditional art media such as painting and sculpture in new projection mapping works, we can create bridges of contact between art media, and remind ourselves as artists, and our audiences, that concept and content is what is most important.

6. REFERENCES

[1] Adobe Photoshop Homepage. http://www.adobe.com/au/products/photoshop.html accessed 30th July 2015.

[2] Developing with Kinect – Microsoft. https://www.microsoft.com/en-us/kinectforwindows/develop accessed 29th July 2015.

[3] GameSalad homepage. http://www.gamesalad.com accessed 29th July 2015.

[4] Krauth, A. 2014. Instructions as Art: Digital Writers as Modern-day Renaissance People. In *Cordite Poetry Review*

Online (5th Dec). http://cordite.org.au/guncotton/instructions-as-art-digital-writers/ accessed 24th July 2015.

[5] Krauth, A. 2015. *Untrammelled* documentation. http://alintakrauth.com/untrammelled accessed 29th Jul 2015.

[6] Krauth, A. 2015. *An Argument in Parallel Incompleteness* documentation. http://alintakrauth.com/an_argument accessed 29th Jul 2015.

[7] Leap Motion Homepage. https://www.leapmotion.com accessed 29th July 2015.

[8] MadMapper homepage. http://www.madmapper.com accessed 29th July 2015.

[9] McLuhan, M. 1964. *Understanding Media: The extensions of man.* Mentor, New York.

[10] Nelson, J. 2012. *Evidence of Everything Exploding.* http://www.secrettechnology.com/explode/evidence.html accessed 29th July 2015.

[11] Syphoner homepage. http://syphoner.sigma6.ch accessed 29th July 2015.

3D Printing and Camera Mapping: Dialectic of Virtual and Reality

He-Lin Luo
National Taiwan University

I-Chun Chen
Taipei National University of the Arts

Yi-Ping Hung
National Taiwan University

Video link: https://www.youtube.com/watch?v=p724rx_qGY8

Abstract
"What is virtuality? What is reality?" This is the concept that lies at the heart of this work, *Digital Buddha*, which incorporates mathematical formulas and elements of industrial design to create an abstract and geometric kinetic physical sculpture. After using a camera to capture a video of this sculpture, the recording is then calculated and decoded into a realistic sculpture of Buddha residing within a virtual image. In reality, you would not be able to see the original shape of the sculpture. In the virtual world, however, you are able to see the sculpture in its entirety.

The concepts of "Buddha" and "media" behind *Digital Buddha* serve as a salute to Nam June Paik's *TV Buddha*. Starting from the analogous Buddha, the media has become more informationized, as well as reflects the transitions between Buddha and the media in the digital era of 2000.

After being influenced by the digital and Internet age, media now relies on transmissions through concepts of "coding" and "decoding," where it becomes the products of computing and displaying. In the 21st century, the Internet revolution has brought high speeds to the distribution of media. Technology has allowed digital reproduction to better represent manifestations of reality.

MM'15, October 26 - 30, 2015, Brisbane, Australia
Copyright 2015 ACM ISBN. 978-1-4503-3459-4/15/10…$15.00
DOI: http://dx.doi.org/10.1145/2733373.2808105

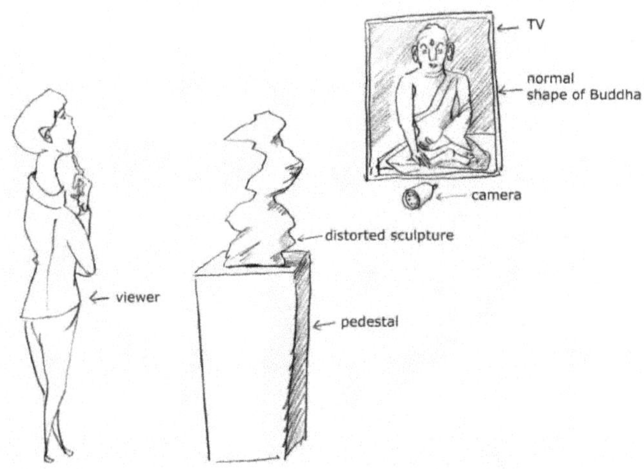

Figure: Schematic diagram of *Digital Buddh*a

Massive amounts of media information are like seawater inundating every aspect daily life, making images omnipresent. As life is assaulted with such massive amounts of images, the lines between virtuality and reality can become blurred, enabling the possibility for virtual images to replace or even transcend reality.

Drag A Star – the Social Media in Outer Space

James She
HKUST-NIE Social Media Lab.
Hong Kong University of Sci. & Tech.
Hong Kong
eejames@ust.hk

Carmen Ng
JM Network
Hong Kong
carmenng@joinmerit.com

Desmond Leung
Desmond Leung Media Arts
Hong Kong
desmond@desmondleung.net

ABSTRACT

"Drag A Star" is an interactive installation artwork that gives audiences an immersive and stunning interactive experience to remember the myth of making wishes upon a shooting star. Through the interactions with the display, audiences can learn about meteorites from outer space based on scientific and artistic perspectives by catching a shooting star with their smartphones. Audiences can send their wishes to a shooting star through their smartphones, while being able to read and reply the wishes from others at the same time. The piece was created based on the latest technologies of digital display, screen smart-device interactions, mobile applications, and web-based messaging systems. Extensive scientific, artistic and design efforts were integrated to create these cyber-physical interactive experiences between shooting stars and audiences. The artistic statement of this installation, akin to many ancient myths about wishing upon shooting stars, is about the possibility of catching a shooting star physically through technologies, and realizing someone's wish after reading them. Hence the existence of shooting stars could likely be the social media in outer space - a world where a connection is made between other beings in the Universe. A high-definition video about this artwork is available at http://smedia.ust.hk/dragastar/.

Categories and Subject Descriptors

J.5 [Computer Applications]: Arts and Humanities - arts, fine and performing; I.4.8 [Computing Methodologies]: gesture processing and recognition.

General Terms

Performance, Design, Experimentation, Human Factors.

Keywords

Interactive Artworks; Shooting Stars; Screen-Smart Device Interaction; Smartphones and Mobile Applications.

1. Introduction

1.1 Artistic Statement

Once upon a time in ancient Greece, there lived the Gods of Olympus [1]. From time to time, curiosity drove the gods to peek over the edge of the Universe; during that process, stars would be knocked over as they looked down from high above [2]. Make a wish, they say, when you see a falling star. It is the moment in time when the realm of immortals is opened briefly, and people on Earth make wishes directly to the gods and the stars above. These wishes may eventually come true when the gods are moved by the hopes and dreams of everyday people. Nowadays, people may not believe in such a myth so beautiful; the possibility to realize and actualize a wish when they share their wishes to others in the Universe. Recent scientific discoveries revealed that the meteorites themselves, like hard drives, retain memories of their origins and their travels [3]. So fascinated by these memories of meteorites, artists have tried to utilize the unique compositions in a meteoroid to create artistic representations that are easily understood by everyone [4]. With the advances in interactive and smartphone technologies today, our belief is in the future where stars can be caught on the fly with just a "dragging" gesture through our smartphones; the opportunity lies in sending out our own wishes with the stars, or even reading out and realizing the wishing messages of others. This is an interactive artwork with scientific, artistic and professional design efforts to engage the rebirth in the meanings and experiences of the myth. Now, the night sky is where humans on Earth are connected by Draggable Stars - to read and send messages of wishes from others or even from higher beings in the Universe. If an audience manages to "drag" a star into his/her smartphone before it vanishes and read the messages inside a meteoroid, one may send a wish back to the farthest corners of the Universe. Like the ancient myth, someone out there may happen to have the chance or the power to realize the wishes of others when they catch the same Draggable Stars. A smartphone by then is no longer just for connecting everyone on Earth through today's social media platform, but also allows us to interact with others in the Universe through our wishes and others over these Draggable Stars; in this way shooting stars are a representation of the social media in outer space!

1.2 Related Technologies and Artworks

New advancements in digital media, smart devices and interactive technologies [5] are always pushing new and innovative dimensions for art pieces in the artistic and media-related fields. [6] proposed a cyber-physical interactive broadcast/multicast media system, it allows users to interact and collect content from digital displays through user smartphones with an intuitive hand gesture. The technology was, however, only applicable to image content on a display for user interaction. [7] As the first attempt to use emerging screen-smart devices in conjunction with interactive technologies on an art installation, it allows audiences to interact and keep a snapshot of an animated painting in the smartphones. On the other hand, [4] we have collaborated on artistic visualizations inspired by unique memories of meteoroids, where the art installation does not involve any interaction with audiences. [8] Some space-themed films were produced with 3D technologies to give the audience an impression of touchable content that could be sought out. However, it does not involve any

MM'15, October 26–30, 2015, Brisbane, Australia.

ACM 978-1-4503-3459-4/15/10…$15.00.
DOI: http://dx.doi.org/10.1145/2733373.2808106

interaction with the audience. This interactive artwork will be one of the first attempts to fill and bridge missing gaps across these related works in the technical, art and industrial communities.

2. THE ART AND USER EXPERIENCES

2.1 Drag A Star

Fig. 1. Drag A Star - the interactive artwork and user interactions.

Fig. 1 shows how our interactive artwork, "Drag A Star", looks like and how audiences would experience and interact with the installation. A large visual wall formed by a high-resolution LED display (any high resolution projector or TV in suitable sizes would suffice) was the first interaction point for the audience; a video was ran continuously to give audiences an impression of being under a night sky along with a short introduction about the piece. A draggable device from CyPhy Media [9] was connected to the display with programmed content for various interactive scenarios, enabling robust screen-smart device interactions that would allow audiences to catch a random shooting star on the display - simply with smartphones installed with our mobile application.

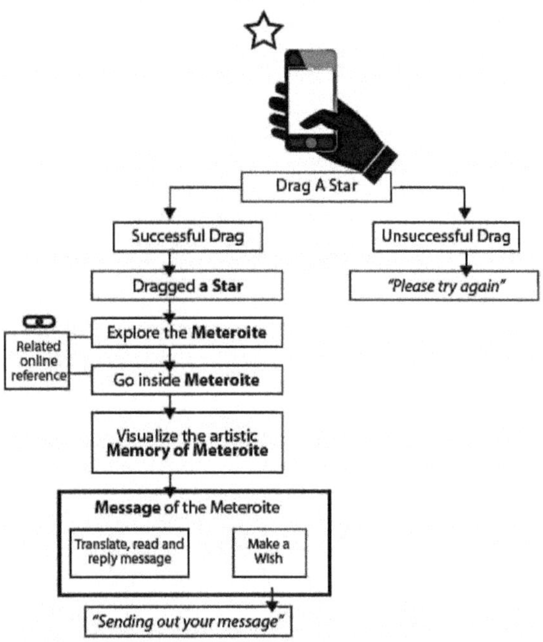

Fig. 2. Flow chat of user interactive experiences on smartphones.

An audience may miss the chance to catch a star in time just like real life experience. For those who have successfully "dragged" the star, they could experience an interesting journey of learning and discovery about the shooting star from scientific and artistic perspectives, enhanced by imaginative interactions with their smartphones. Audiences can read and reply wishes of others after exploring the memories of the meteorites, or make a wish on the same draggable star on hand. Fig. 2 describes the flow chat of the designed user interactive experience on user smartphones. More technical details to achieve these setups will be described in the next section. To convey our expected artistic statements over interactions, aesthetic and convincing content about these shooting stars were produced acutely for the display and the user's smartphones. These contents were produced aesthetically and reliably from comprehensive scientific data about each Draggable Star (i.e., meteoroids). The aesthetic merits of the content will be described in the following.

2.2 The Time-lapse Night Sky

The content on the display was designed to give the audience a stunning and aesthetic night sky, which was the first user interface that attracts and engages audiences to start the interactions with the installation through their smartphones. The night sky provides not only a beautiful and immersive feeling full of stars in the darkest and most crowded nights known to man, but the random appearance of the shooting stars on the screen were realistically produced with particle system techniques that challenge audiences to catch a star with a simple "dragging" gestures directly through their smartphones with a dash of sheer luck.

Fig. 3. A snapshot of the time-lapse night sky video.

2.3 Draggable Stars

When an audience successfully catches a Draggable Star in his/her smartphone, one could zoom in the associated meteoroid to explore the multi-layered information and understand the star from scientific evidence and artistic visualization of the memories inside the meteoroid. Furthermore, the audience could read or reply the wishes from others, in addition to simply making a new wish. With our comprehensive scientific survey, a collection of discovered meteoroids with their multi-layered content were produced aesthetically and sampled in Table 1. Fig. 4 shows an example of a meteoroid and the associated multi-layered information that could be experienced by the audience on the smartphones once he/she has successfully "caught" the particular Draggable Star on the smartphone:

Scientific layers - one can see the compositions and structural patterns of the elements inside a meteoroid (Fig. 4b and c) that were surveyed from comprehensive scientific reports - but aesthetically produced to give audiences an appealing characteristic;

Artistic layers - one can see an artistic visualization unique to the particular meteoroid based on the corresponding composition extracted from artistic productions of Meteoroid Memories Series [reference]. Each of these artistic visualizations will dissolve into an artistic decoding user interface to firm a connection to me imaginative layers (Fig. 4d and e);

Imaginative layers - After decoding memories of meteoroids, it was imagined that scientific breakthroughs in the near future would allow us to read and reply wishes to others, or to create your own new wishes much like how messaging works in our social media systems today. While sending back the stars with our own wishes or replies, one may be able to connect with new friends or to even realize the wishes of others (Fig. 4f and g).

3. TECHNICAL DESIGNS

To support our artistic statements, Fig. 5 was the technical design of our installation that gives audiences an intuitive interaction that starts from dragging a star, to exploring the multi-layered content about the meteorite, and to even interact with others on their wishes through a web-based messaging platform. These interaction processes must be very robust and responsive, but also scalable to any size of the audience at the site of the installation. The technical designs involve the following 3 aspects of interactions: 1) draggable star-audience interaction (or screen-smart device interaction); 2) exploring draggable stars on smartphones; 3) audience interaction through wish-messaging.

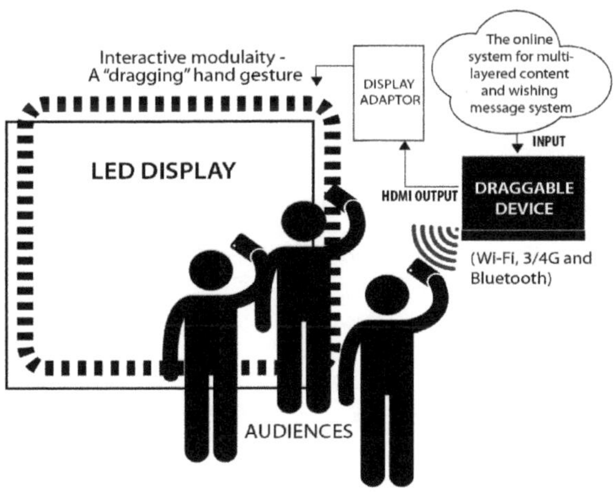

Fig. 5. Technical designs of the involved interactions.

3.1 Draggable Star-Audience Interactions

This installation was designed to mimic real-life situations where multiple shooting stars occasionally fly over the night sky; multiple audiences may try to catch the same or different stars with their smartphones before the star vanishes. There were chances that an audience may not be able to catch any star. The interaction must be able to synchronize with the audience's dragging gesture when the shooting stars appear on the display randomly, and the installation must react to the dragging gestures of multiple audiences at the same time. Such real-time and scalable screen-smart device interactions for multiple users was implemented through CyPhy draggable device [9], in which the device will synchronize the visual situations of a running video on a digital display and the real-time gesture movements learnt by the mobile application in user smartphones.

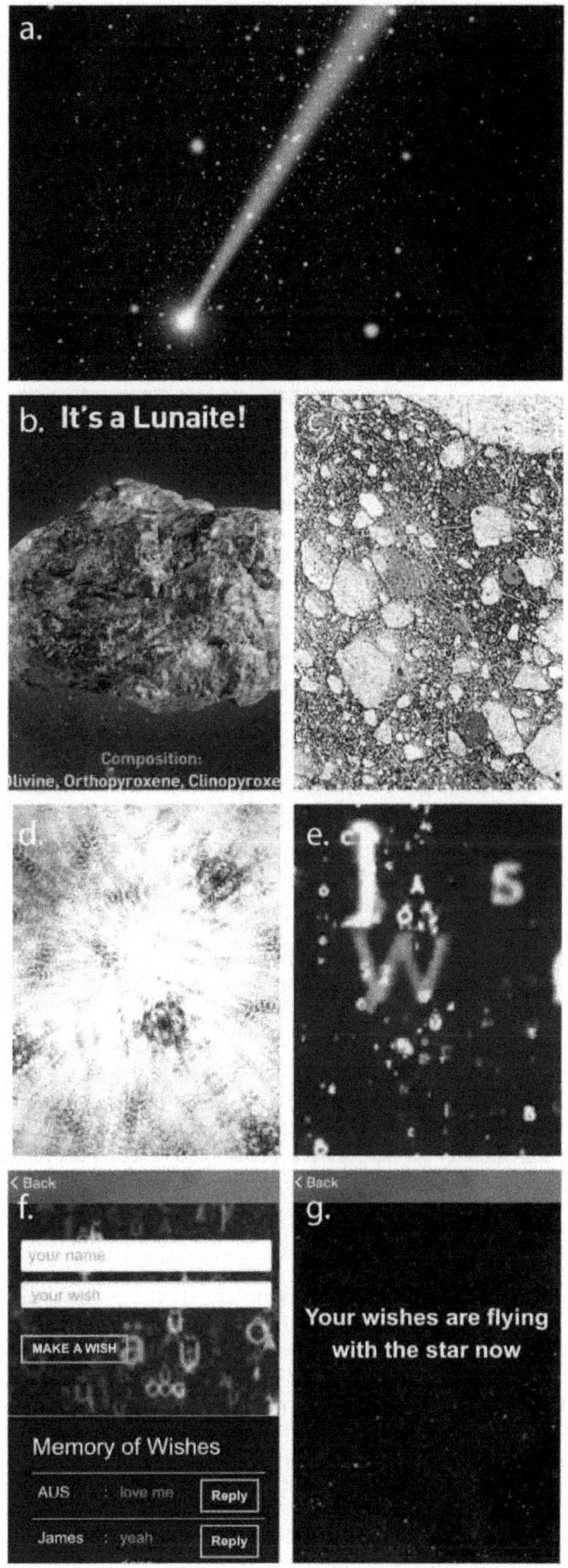

Fig. 4. Interface and content designs of a draggable star.

3.2 Exploring Draggable Star

When an audience successfully drags a star into his/her smartphone, an image of a random but unique meteorite corresponding to a Draggable Star would show up on the smartphone. There were clickable links on this image in the mobile application that directs audiences to external scientific information about the compositions, cross-sectional views and astronomical details of the meteoroid. Audiences who only want to explore the artistic visualization of the meteorite memories may click and further explore inside the meteorite and reach the imaginative wish-messaging interface at the end.

3.3 Audience Interactions Through Wish-Messaging

When an audience finishes the artistic visualization of the meteorite memory, these visualizations will be decoded and transformed into an interface that allows audience to make wishes through an online wish-messaging system. Audience may read and reply wishes from others, or to send out a new wish. Eventually, someone may have the chance or power to realize someone else's wishes much like the tales from classical mythology - the interactions between audiences were stored in the memory of each Draggable Star over the wish-messaging system.

3.4 Robustness, Transportability and Scalability

Robustness: The piece was designed to scale the interactions for a large number of audiences up to the limit of the Wi-Fi infrastructure in a gallery or museum, or the range over a collection of Bluetooth transmitters. In summary, the installation should able to handle up interactions up to at least 200 audiences based on the proven records from previous works by us [1, 2].

Transportability: The installation is very transportable and could be easily re-setup by simply bringing the draggable devices to any site with suitable digital display and the availability of Wi-Fi or mobile Internet access as all the content, messaging systems and interactions were already pre-loaded and accessible online through the compact draggable device. Smartphone wise, audiences would simply be able to use their own.

Scalability: The installation can be deployed with most high definition displays or projectors as along as an HDMI input of the display unit and Internet access (i.e., Wi-Fi and 3G/4G) for user smartphones are in place. Unlike some installations, which require dedicated interaction devices for the audience, our installation simply uses any number of participating audience's smartphones as long as the mobile application has been downloaded.

4. CONCLUSION

This interactive art installation tries to engage the audience with an immersive and interactive experience, in allowing audiences to recall and re-live the myth of the shooting star. Our draggable night sky was in fact a social media platform that allows audiences to send out their own wishes, and to even play the role of ancient Greek gods who could read wishes of others and realize wishes for those in need. To achieve these artistic ideas, high-quality and comprehensive artistic, scientific and design efforts were extensively produced and integrated as described in earlier sections. This installation has induced an on-going research for more advanced screen-smart device interactions and also aesthetic developments for decoding the memories of meteoroids. Meanwhile, this installation will be developed as an educational and artistic 3D space-themed film with user smartphone interactions in venues such as cinemas or space museums.

5. ACKNOWLEDGMENTS

Thanks to CyPhy Media Limited for sponsoring the uses of LED, draggable devices, and voice over efforts by Mr. Gavin Ng.

6. REFERENCES

[1] Fresco by Giulio Romano. 1532-1535. The Gods of Olympus", Chamber of Giants, Palazzo Te, Mantua, Italy

[2] Day Translations. 2012. Wishing Upon A Star: Is it true or just a myth? (Dec. 7, 2012). http://www.daytranslations.com/blog/2012/12/wishing-upon-a-star-is-it-true-or-just-a-myth-62

[3] Simon Redfern. 2015. Meteorite is 'hard drive' from space. Science and Environment. (Jan. 21, 2015). http://www.bbc.com/news/science-environment-30916692

[4] D. Leung. 2015. Meteorite Memory Series. Methods of Arts. (Mar. 16-20, 2015). Connecting Space Hong Kong.

[5] J. She, J. Crowcroft, H. Fu, F. Li. 2014. Convergence of interactive displays with smart mobile devices for effective advertising: A survey. ACM Transactions on Multimedia Computing, Communications, and Applications. 10, 2 (Feb. 2014), 17.1-17.6

[6] J. She, J. Crowcroft, H. Fu, P.H. Ho. 2013. Smart Signage: A draggable cyber-physical broadcast/multicast media system. IEEE Transaction on Emerging Technologies on Computing. 2, 2 (Sep. 2013), 232-243.

[7] J. She. 2014. i-LiberTango. Stonehenge New Media Arts Exhibition. Hong Kong. https://www.youtube.com/watch?v=prsLA8JVxUk

[8] Journey to Space. (2015) Kennedy Space Center. US.

[9] Draggable Device, CyPhy Media http://www.cyphymedia.com/products/draggable-devices

Table 1. Selected Draggable Stars on User Smartphones

Draggable Stars	Meteorites/ Composition	Parent body
	Imilac / Iron, Nickel, Gallium	Unknown
	Martian Meteorite/ Olivine, Orthopyroxene, Phyric	Mars
	Lunaite/ Plagioclase, Pigeonite, Olivine	Moon

Disturbed System: Recreating Sculptor's Experience of Their Medium With Haptics and Generated Sound

Oksana Krzyhanivska
University of Calgary
2500 University Drive NW
Calgary, Canada
okryzhan@ucalgary.ca

Simon Fay
University of Calgary
2500 University Drive NW
Calgary, Canada
simonjohnfay@gmail.com

Jeffrey E. Boyd
University of Calgary
2500 University Drive NW
Calgary, Canada
jboyd@ucalgary.ca

ABSTRACT

This paper discusses a collaborative project that inquires about the possibilities of the tactile sensation in art and its ability to reestablish human sensory relationships with consumer technology. It introduces the visitor to the interaction style practiced by the artists with their medium. The described interactive sculpture predisposes the visitor to explore tactile interaction as an aesthetic experience within multimodal multisensory system. *Disturbed System* takes the visitor's experience with the artwork into unfamiliar sensory territory. Touching the soft silicone surface of the sculpture provides electronic feedback of embedded vibration and directional spatialized sound in an installation format. The artwork presents this sensory information in a form of unexpected assemblage of pulsing organic sculptural surfaces and emitting sound. It also places visitors in a shared interactive space, an aura of traveling sound warped by their touch of the sculpture. This shared interaction investigates relationships between nature, artifice, technology, human body and human social group behavior.

Categories and Subject Descriptors

H.5.2 [**User Interfaces**]: Auditory (non-speech) feedback; Haptic I/O; H.5.5 [**Sound and Music Computing**]: Methodologies and techniques; Signal analysis, synthesis, and processing; I.2.9 [**Robotics**]: Sensors; J.5 [**Arts and Humanities**]: Arts, fine and performing;Fine arts; Music;Performing arts

General Terms

Exerimentation, Human Factors, Performance

Keywords

Group interaction; touch; physical computing; haptic feedback; generative sound; consumer electronics; spatialized sound; multi-sensory; immersion; information interfaces and presentation

MM'15, October 26–30, 2015, Brisbane, Australia.

DOI: http://dx.doi.org/10.1145/2733373.2808107.

1. INTRODUCTION

Figure 1: Disturbed System (2015). The soft silicone material disguises 8 built-in speakers that emit directional sound along with 4 external spatialized speakers.

This research project emerges from the idea of metaphorically sharing of the artist's experience of touching sculptural material with the visitors. Recreating artist's poetic relationship with the artwork aims to transform the notion of presentation into a creative active experience for the visitors [6, 7]. Unlike visitors' experiences in exhibitions, artists experience their work at a physical level during the fabrication. Artists sense the scent of oil paint, the texture of modeling clay, and the varying resistance of carved stone.

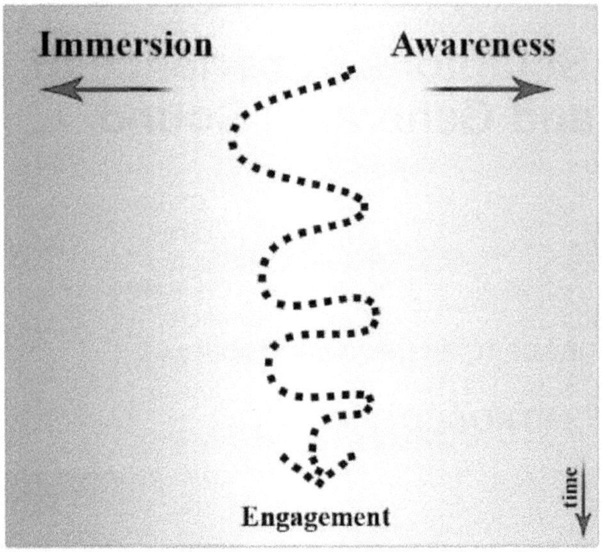

Figure 2: Structure of Experience. The artist's experience with the sculptures during production. The artist experiences oscillating periods of immersion and awareness from the first encounter with the work. This oscillating pattern between the two extremes translates into the presentation of the interaction to the audience. Elements of the sculptures such as pulsing vibrations and generated sound invite closer investigation, while artifice of colours, flesh-like appearance and reference to internal organs repel the audience.

Disturbed System (Figure 1) recreates the sensory experience of the sculptor who in their creative practice employs resins, conductive materials, electronics, coding, 3d printing and digital modeling.

Disturbed System demonstrates to the visitors the embodied connection between the artist and their medium, which authors Brodsky [2] and Vallega-Neu [9] describe as conscious experience in their analysis of perceiving art work. The authors provide examples how the making and viewing of art happens through a full body experience. Furthermore, artist's perception of the art work initiates at the moment of the first contact with the medium before completion and undergoes a non-linear evolution (refer to Figure 2).

While engaging in the full body experience of art requires training for some viewers, current interactive technology enables artists to create an accessible guidance to the embodied experience for untrained audience. Writings of Brodsky [2] Vallega-Neu [9] assist in establishing guidelines for this art research in simulating artist's own full body experience with the interactive sculpture. These guidlines derive from Merleau-Ponty's [5] and Dewey's [3] theories about perception and embodiment discussed in the context of experiencing the making and perceiving art [2, 9].

The lived-through physical connection of the artist and their material is evident in Richard Serra's film *Hand Catching Lead* (1968) and Matthew Barney's relationship with prosthetic grade plastics and petroleum jelly in *Cremaster Cycle* (1994-2002). Both in Serra's and Barney's films the artists document their process of manipulating their sculptural material of choice, demonstrating their ways of interaction with the medium. Taking the idea of sharing the artistic experience further, interactive sound sculpture *Disturbed System* metaphorically utilizes tactile interaction, electronics, generated sound and spatailization to engage the visitor in embodied experience of the sculptural material (refer to Figure 1).

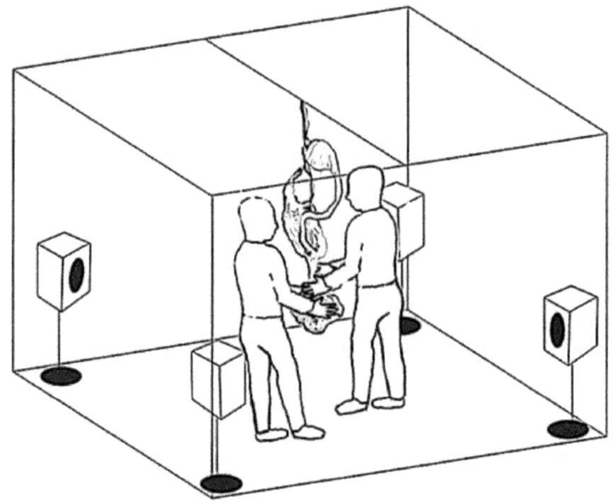

Figure 3: Layout of the interactive space around installation *Disturbed System*. The sculpture is located in the middle of the exhibition area suspended from the ceiling or a support structure. The sculpture is wired to the computer and the speakers over the ceiling. Some wires are exposed with the organic tissue appearing to grow around the wires. The image illustrates two visitors interacting with the organically shaped sculpture. Visitors stroke, squeeze and fold its surfaces to produce spatialized distortions in computer generated speech, activate musical notes and vibration in the touched areas.

Our approach to recreation of artist's experience of the sculpture involves consumer-grade electronics found in cell phones, touch devices and personal computers. Habitual integration of this technology in everyday life provides visitors with an accessible interaction style. However, the artists placed this technology in a context of an organic object referencing a generic internal body organ in order to transform the habitual interaction with technology into engaging conscious experience. Communicating to the audience the involvement of the artist's experience with the sculpture in the making, addresses problems of disengaged interaction in art noted by a cultural critic Alan Kirby. In his *Digimodernism* [4], Kirby regards popular modes of interactivity as a mindless passive activity. He attributes shift in nature of interaction to new technologies, cultural, economical and social forces. The user directly creates the content of the meaning with "the fingers and thumbs that key and press and click" [4]. This meaning is changeable, expanding and impermanent, as illustrated with multiple authors that contribute to Wikipedia, YouTube, Twitter, blogs, and user reviews. Development of information technologies and mobile telecommunications change social interaction through texting, vote-in reality television, social networks, and blogs [4]. This change affects the making of meaning within art, literary texts and cinema. *Disturbed System* attempts to bring awareness of these social issues to the visitors.

2. OVERVIEW

The current work, *Disturbed System* explores human tactile interaction with silicone and technology as part of the art series *Raw*. The two other sculptures of the series engaged the visitor through combinations of haptics with conceptual art, and haptics combined with performance. Attempting to create a multi-sensory experience of the sculpture, *Disturbed System* engages the visitors with addition of haptics and sound. This installation places visitors within a virtual immersive sonic environment in the physical exhibition space.

Visitors are invited to touch an object that references disassembled body tissue (Figure 1). This object emits a synthetic, distorted voice speaking gibberish, which structurally resembles English. *Disturbed System* slowly starts to growl quietly from the embedded speakers when visitors stop touching it. The growling changes into voice once the visitors overcome their discomfort of the presented object and engage in touching the sculpture (refer to Figure 4). At this time the voice-like sound moves from the inside of the sculpture to the surrounding speakers and changes over to playing music. The volume of the generated notes and distortions rises the longer one holds the sculpture. With more visitors activating the sensors a program puts together the notes into a sequence. The sensors within the surface play separate synthesized notes, regulate volume and activate different distortions of the generated voice. The sound is louder, but gentler. The sculpture becomes an interface for performing music activated by the participating audience.

Emitted sound travels around the locations of the visitors' touches in relationship to the sculptural surface (Figure 3). This spatialization effect allows the simulation of a space aura, which distorts based on the number of visitors interacting with the piece. *Disturbed System* evokes a feeling of discomfort while presenting the visitors with familiar technology disguised within an unfamiliar object. Combination of the tactile and sonic feedback draws visitors' attention to the familiar daily experiences of touching technology, authenticity of feedback, physical sensations, nature and artifice.

3. ENGAGING PARTICIPATION

The proposed structure of interaction with the sculptures produced within the scope of this research, follows the narrative development of the artist and artwork relationship. This narrative attempts to engage the viewer through alternating states of engagement and awareness, which occur to the artist at various stages of fabrication. This pattern engages the artist in acquiring tacit knowledge and thinking through the processes related to manipulation of materials. The periods of immersive involvment with sculptural materials interchange with periods of alertness when the artist stretches the capabilities of their medium. These periods of alertness are identified by problem solving, resistance of materials to desired application methods and unexpected challenges.

The narrative structure of fabrication provides a sense of evolution in the artistic concept, in creation of the meaning of the work and in communicating ideas to the audience. In the case of *Disturbed System*, design of 3D printed prototypes, application of silicone, incorporation of electronics and software integration follow the same narrative pattern of experiencing the fabrication process. Figure 2 illustrates this pattern, which defines the structure of the visitors' encounter with the discussed sculptures. The iterative practice of manual sculptural production allows to refine and fill in the details in the methodology of integrating haptics into sculpture. The chosen haptic technology metaphorically references tactile interaction with sculptural materials.

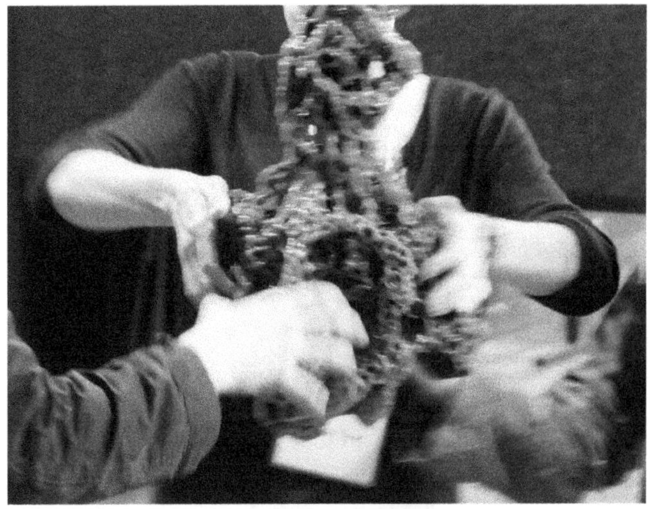

Figure 4: The visitors manipulate the generated sound by holding and squeezing four sides of the*Disturbed System*. The amount of physical involvement with the sculpture references the physicality of producing the sculpture.

Following this structure of experiencing the sculpture, audience is invited to approach the sculpture, which lures the visitors with the artificial voice coming from internal speakers. At first, the visitor must overcome the discomfort of approaching a brightly coloured object resembling an unidentified organ suspended by a hook from the ceiling. At this stage the visitor experiences a stage of awareness while encountering an unfamiliar object for the first time.

After the initial disquiet, the visitor sees the textural detail of the sculpture, which appears clearly modeled and artificial. Once the visitor touches the sculptural surface with enough effort to trigger the sensors, the sculpture starts to play notes, buzzes and pulses with vibration. After a short delay the sound of notes moves towards the outside speakers (Figure 3).

Notes forming a musical sequence provide balancing immersive periods of engagement with the sculpture. Upon loosening the grip on the material, the disengaged sensors transform the emitted sound into distorted voice and then into growling from the inside of the sculpture (Figure 5). The reaction of the sculpture and the artificiality of the voice produce a shift in the visitor's experience bringing the visitor out of the state of immersion into engaged awareness. Both of the induced states involve a strong physical perception of the sculpture through touch and sonic feedback.

3.1 Phenomenological approach to Artwork-Interface

Design approach of *Disturbed System*, which serves an object-interface for generating sound, commends inquiry for

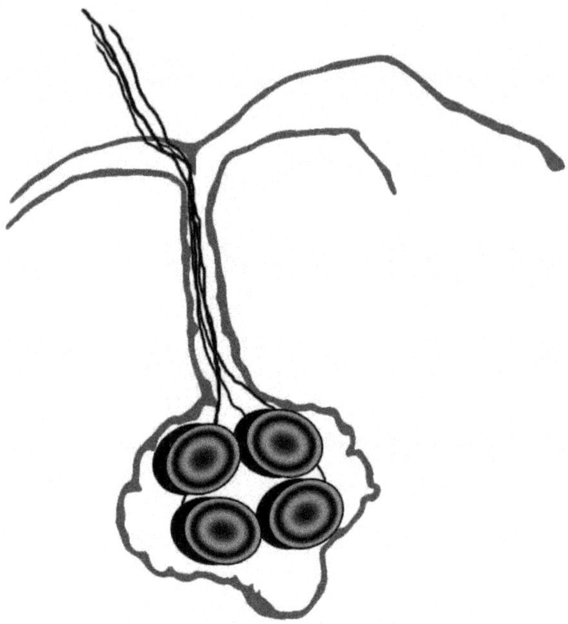

Figure 5: The illustration of the cross-section of the lower area of *Disturbed System* containing internal speakers, which direct sound from the specific areas of the sculpture, corresponding to the touched sensors. Visitors can clearly hear this sound in close proximity to the sculpture. The low volume of emitting computer-generated voice invites visitors to listen closer and pick up the sculpture

an alternative to the established approach of interface design in human-machine interaction field. In contrast to the pragmatic goal of effective, habitual and effortless interaction with technology, the entertainment industry, art and advertising focus on engaging the audience's attention for prolonged time periods, creating awareness of the physical interface, strive to reformulate the experience of their medium, embodiment and continuing discovery.

Designers David Bolter and Diane Gromala discuss these two approaches and identify the increasing interest in making the users aware of the interfaces [1]. Authors describe a number of interactive art installations as examples of successful implementation of exposed interfaces and embodied experiences. However, authors do not provide detailed analysis of why this design approach significantly contributes in presentation of artistic and media content.

Producing of the sculptures in the *Raw* series, including *Disturbed System*, contributes tacit knowledge to the discussion. This knowledge identifies how the physicality of experience and awareness of the interface assists in creating meaning and communicating the content with the audience. More so, referencing research in phenomenology in addition to psychology and neuroscience, allows the artist to analyze and design an approach that is suitable to communicating complex social concepts and pose difficult questions.In the case of the *Raw* interactive sculpture series these are the questions about relationship of humanity with machines, integration of technology in everyday life, body augmentation and artificial life among others. With these sculptures, visitors are confronted with alternative experiences of tactile interaction with technology, and with presentation of interactive technology as a soft organic form.

3.2 Perception of Experience

The proposed structure of interaction with touchable sculptures evolves from studies of human perceptual experience. Methodology of analyzing experience through phenomenology allows the artist to create a system of subjective non-biased evaluation of the artwork and interaction while fabricating the sculpture. It allows to systematically and consciously alter the design of the final outcome prior to presenting it for public judgment. Sculptural fabrication allows the artist to analyze haptic interaction through a practice-based approach to understanding perceptual experience, a popular subject matter in philosophy, art and cognitive science, which is still not fully understood. This is due to the fact that human experience contains components that are difficult to empirically quantify and measure. While complimenting empirical science, the tacit insight from the production and display of the sculptures elaborates on the knowledge about human experience. This is possible through encountering experience through simultaneous high-level holistic and low-level physical degrees of perception.

4. FUTURE WORK

Pursuing the study of interactive experiences in art continues evolving the sculpture. Our current project suggests a sensory and musical contrast between the body contact and proximity of the visitors. Through technique similar to those described in our ISMAR[8] paper, the sculpture can utilize the ultrasound transducers to estimate the location of visitors around the sculpture. Addition of the proximity sensing promises a mapped spatialization of sound emitted from and around the sculpture. It also provides for opportunities to include other modes of feedback and variations of generated sound based on the type of interaction.

5. REFERENCES

[1] J. D. Bolter and D. Gromala. *Windows and Mirrors âĂŞ Interaction Design, Digital Art, and the Myth of Transparency.* MIT Press, USA, 2003.

[2] J. Brodsky. How to "see" with the whole body. *Visual Studies*, 17(2).

[3] J. Dewey. *Art as Experience.* Perigee Books, New York, 1980.

[4] A. Kirby. *Digimodernism: How New Technologies Dismantle the Postmodern and Reconfigure Our Culture.* Bloomsbury Publishing, London, 2009.

[5] M. Merleau-Ponty. *The Visible and the Invisible.* 1968.

[6] A. Noë. Experience and experiment in art. *Journal of Consciousness Studies*, 7(8-9), 2000.

[7] A. Noë. *Varieties of Presense.* Harvard University Press, USA, 2010.

[8] J. E. B. Oksana Kryzhanivska. Body topography: Simulating human form. In *Proceedings of the IEEE and ACM International Symposium on Augmented Reality, 2012*, 2012.

[9] D. Vallega-Neu. *The bodily dimension in thinking.* State University of New York Press, New York, USA, 2006.

The Real Time Rolling Shutter

David Monaghan and Noel E. O'Connor
Insight centre for data analytics
Dublin City University, Ireland
david.monaghan@dcu.ie

Anne Cleary and Denis Connolly
Paris, France
connollycleary@noos.fr

ABSTRACT

From an early age children are often told either, you are creative you should do art but stay away from science and maths. Or that you are mathematical you should do science but you're not that creative. Compounding this there also exist some traditional barriers of artistic rhetoric that say, "don't touch, don't think and don't be creative, we've already done that for you, you can just look...". The Real Time Rolling Shutter is part of a collaborative Art/Science partnership whose core tenets are in complete contrast to this. The Art/Science exhibitions we have created have invited the public to become part of the exhibition by utilising augmented digital mirrors, Kinects, feed-back camera and projector systems and augmented reality perception helmets. The fundamental underlying principles we are trying to adhere to are to foster curiosity, intrigue, wonderment and amazement and we endeavour to draw the audience into the interactive nature of our exhibits and exclaim to everyone that you can be what ever you chose to be, and that everyone can be creative, everyone can be an artist, everyone can be a scientist... all it takes is an inquisitive mind, so come and explore the real-time rolling shutter and be creative.

Keywords

Virtual Mirror, Visual Perception, Rolling Shutter, Interactive Artworks

1. INTRODUCTION

In early 2011 some scientists and some artists began to talk. From humble beginnings and email debates, regarding the definitions of science and art, the interactions and crossovers within the fields of art, design and science stemmed an unique collaboration of Art and Science. This collaboration has lead to a series of engaging interactive science/art collaborative pieces that reflect different aspects of how we perceive the world around us. Under the lead of Professor Noel O'Connor at CLARITY (now called Insight) in Dublin City University Dr. David Monaghan has headed the scientific aspects of this collaboration and together with Dr. Philip Kelly has mentored a team of undergraduate Summer interns that have worked on various technical and engaging scientific challenges embedded in these art works. Anne Cleary and Denis Connolly are fast becoming known as Ireland's foremost new-media artists, easily incorporating innovative new technologies into their work to produce art that is both engaging and significant. They are the only two living Irish artists to have had an exhibition in the Pompidou Centre [2]. As relatively new artists on the scene they are causing a stir within the art community with their playful yet socially aware approach to interactive digital exhibitions. Much of Cleary and Connolly's work is collaborative, with a strong socio-political aspect, both through its subject matter and in its engagement with people. They coined the term "observer participation" to describe their work, which is committed to affirming the active role of the public in art.

The result of this collaboration has been a series of exhibits that leverage emerging sensing technology and image processing that have been exhibited in Farmleigh House, Limerick City Gallery of Art, Solstice Arts Centre, Navan and Kerry County Museum, Tralee before moving to the Centre Culturel Irlandais in Paris. Recently, the Rolling Shutter exhibit was selected to represent Ireland on "Europe Day" in Paris. It was unveiled to the public on May 9th by the Mayor of Paris Bertrand Delanoë in the presence of Mr Dinny McGinley, Delegate Minister of State for Arts Heritage and the Gaeltacht, and the Irish Ambassador to France Mr Paul Kavanagh.

MM'15, October 26–30, 2015, Brisbane, Australia

ACM. 978-1-4503-3459-4/15/10 ...$15.00.
DOI: http://dx.doi.org/10.1145/2733373.2808110.

2. PREVIOUS WORKS

What follows in this section is a brief overview of the some of our previous art/science exhibitions. By explaining some of these pieces my hope is to convey some of the axiomatic fundamental principles that we are trying to encapsulate within the Real Time Rolling Shutter.

Daniel Finnegan, a talented young computer scientist studying in UCD at the time worked with us for 3 months (mentored by Dr. Kelly and Dr. Monaghan) to develop "virtual reality" helmets for the Cleary/Connolly that allow the wearer to experience the world upside down or as a negative image. It uses android phones as the lens in a specially constructed helmet designed by Irish SME ape.ie. This work is a reboot of George Stratton's classic perceptual adaption experiment in the late 19th century. Stratton was a world-famous US psychologist who pioneered the study of perception in vision. He used prims to create "upside glasses" which he wore for 8 days running so that his vision system

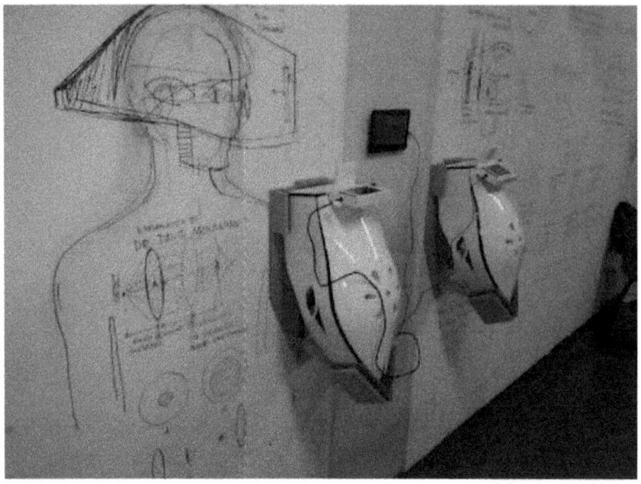

Figure 1: The VR helmets we made for Dublin Contemporary in September 2011

Figure 2: The Dot-Man Exhibition

ultimately adapted to this view of the world. The helmets we designed were exhibited at Dublin Contemporary 2011, see fig 1, were they were cited as the "Stand Out Exhibit" according to one reviewer (Guide2Dublin).

Dr Philip Kelly and Dr David Monaghan developed software for the "Dot Man" exhibit that uses a Microsoft Kinect to show a representation of the viewer as 13 points of light on a black background. This is a re-imagining of the seminal experiments by Swedish psychophysicist Gunnar Johansson on the perception of human bodies in motion. It shows how humans have evolved to recognize human motion, even with very little information and in the presence of large distractions. The "Joining the Dots" exhibit allows the viewer to become a "DotMan" by standing in front of a digital mirror that translates their body into a set of connected dots superimposed into a whirling representation of the stars in the universe.

A large collection of different visually interactive pieces, including the VR perception helmets and the dot-man piece,

Figure 3: Dr. David Monaghan, Dr. Noel O'Connor, Dr. Phil Kelly of Insight (formerly Clarity) with Denis Connolly at the opening of Hall of Mirrors at Farmleigh, 15 March 2012

were brought together to form the Hall of Mirrors exhibition. Designed to align with Dublin City of Science, the various exhibits were collected into a public exhibition in Farmleigh House, from 15 March - 22 July 2012. The exhibition, entitled Digital Hall of Mirrors was designed to be interactive, hands on and fun! Opened by Brian Hayes TD, the exhibition attracted over 15,000 visitors during its run, including a large number of school visits.

Cleary and Connolly secured a commission, entitled Look Both Ways, from the Rail Procurement Agency, one aim of which was to bring these experiences to your mobile phone. Once again, funded a talented undergraduate student to work on this. Conor Gallagher, now a graduate of DCU's Digital Media Engineering degree programme and a Research Assistant in CLARITY, (mentored by Dr. Monaghan) developed an App for both iPhone and Android that is freely available on Google Play Store and Apple's App Store. This App allows visitors to effectively bring home some of the digital exhibitions with them [3].

3. THE REAL TIME ROLLING SHUTTER

Inspired and conceptualized by Cleary-Connolly who worked closely with Dr. David Monaghan who created, firstly an off-line rolling shutter programme followed by the real time software. The objective is to create a mirror-like rolling shutter where the image develops from bottom to top over 4 seconds. This is inspired by a 100-year-old photograph by Jacques Henri Lartigue, which led to the well known (in photographic circles) "Mystery of the Slanting Car", see fig 5.

The car in this photo appeared to lean forward while the spectators appear to be tilting backwards. This expression of movement and is all down to the design of Lartigue's rolling shutter camera and the fact that the photographer was taking the photo from a car moving more slowly than the race car.

The Real Time Rolling Shutter extends this concept by using a virtual digital mirror and shows the exaggerated effects of a rolling shutter camera. Time is expressed a geometric distortion and, as in a fairground hall of mirrors,

Figure 4: Irish Minister of State for the Office of Public Works Brian Hayes, Dr. David Monaghan, Prof. Noel O'Connor and Anne Cleary at the opening of Hall of Mirrors at Farmleigh, 15 March 2012

Figure 5: Lartigue's photo of the slanting car in 1913

Figure 6: Lartigue's Rolling Shutter camera

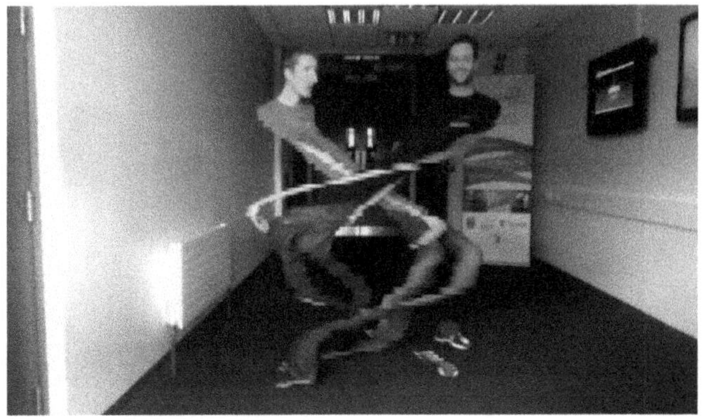

Figure 7: The Real Time Rolling Shutter being demonstrated by Dr. David Monaghan Conor Gallagher at Dublin City University

Figure 8: The Real Time Rolling Shutter at Limerick City Art Gallery during the launch of the a show on interact digital art. Here Dr. David Monaghan can be seen being inter-tangled by Anne Cleary and Denis Connolly as the demonstrate the exhibition

the experience is as much fun as it is challenging. To fully experience what the real time rolling shutter does please see this youtube video clip [4] and also [5].

The Real Time Shutter was displayed at the Centre Culturel Irlandais in Paris before being selected to represent Ireland on "Europe Day" in Paris [6, 1]. It was unveiled to the public on May 9th by the Mayor of Paris Bertrand DelanoÃń in the presence of Mr Dinny McGinley, Delegate Minister of State for Arts Heritage and the Gaeltacht, and the Irish Ambassador to France Mr Paul Kavanagh. It was also exhibited by the artists at the Irish booth at the European Parliament Open Day, 4th May 2013, at the invitation of An Taoiseach.

4. THE 2015 ACM MULTIMEDIA EXHIBITION

At the 12th edition of the Interactive Arts Programme at ACM MM 2015 we plan to exhibit the Real Time Rolling Shutter piece. Practically, this will consist of a large TV screen or projector and screen, depending on the venue, a laptop and a web camera as the only equipment needed. The main aim to this piece to draw in the audience, engage them, allow them to play and have fun but at the same time challenging them to think, to analyse, to be creative and

Figure 9: The Real Time Rolling Shutter being demonstrated by Denis Connolly and Vincent O'Shea

Figure 10: The Real Time Rolling Shutter at "Europe Day" in Paris in May 2013

most of all to simply be curious! We are certain that the real time rolling shutter exhibition will be as popular in ACM Multimedia as it has been at the various Art exhibitions where we have displayed it. We have found that each time we display it, that different people find different ways to interact and play with it. We believe that this piece would make an excellent addition to the ACM MM Art exhibition and that the artist merit aligns extremely well with the philosophy of the ACM MM Art Exhibition.

This exhibition can either be display on a small screen on the side of a wall or on a large 20 foot screen, as seen in fig. 10, either way it has never failed to intrigue and engage audiences of all walks of life.

5. ACKNOWLEDGMENTS

The research that lead to this paper was supported in part by Science Foundation Ireland. The Authors would like to acknowledge the Scientific and Artistic contribution of Patrick Cavanagh, Vincent O'Shea, Greg Keely, Daniel Finegan, Conor Gallagher and Philip Kelly.

6. REFERENCES

[1] Cleary connolly at the irish cultural heritage centre. www.cultureireland.ie/eu2013/event/look-both-ways-a-multimedia-installation.

[2] Cleary connolly website. http://www.connolly-cleary.com.

[3] Look both ways. http://www.connolly-cleary.com/LookBothWays/LookBothWays.html.

[4] Real time rolling shutter demo video1. http://www.youtube.com/watch?v=-HlHxq16pp8.

[5] Real time rolling shutter demo video2. https://www.youtube.com/watch?v=Fg9Ph53ka2I.

[6] Rolling shutter in brussels and paris. http://www.dcu.ie/news/2013/may/s0513r.shtml.

Query-by-Emoji Video Search

Spencer Cappallo[†] Thomas Mensink[†] Cees G. M. Snoek[†‡]
[†]University of Amsterdam [‡]Qualcomm Research Netherlands
{cappallo, tmensink, cgmsnoek}@uva.nl

ABSTRACT

This technical demo presents Emoji2Video, a query-by-emoji interface for exploring video collections. Ideogram-based video search and representation presents an opportunity for an intuitive, visual interface and concise non-textual summary of video contents, in a form factor that is ideal for small screens. The demo allows users to build search strings comprised of ideograms which are used to query a large dataset of YouTube videos. The system returns a list of the top-ranking videos for the user query along with an emoji summary of the video contents so that users may make an informed decision whether to view a video or refine their search terms. The ranking of the videos is done in a zero-shot, multi-modal manner that employs an embedding space to exploit semantic relationships between user-selected ideograms and the video's visual and textual content.

1. INTRODUCTION

The internet is perpetually inundated with new videos, but the methods for interfacing with this exponentially growing data remain static. There is a need to investigate new, alternative approaches for exploration of large video datasets, with a focus on interaction that translates seamlessly to new mobile platforms such as smartwatches. We present Emoji2Video as a new means of interaction and representation for large databases of multi-modal video and text.

Emoji2Video allows users to query any dataset of visual media using emoji. Emoji present a unique opportunity for visual representation and exploration. As a set of intuitive iconography, emoji are able to transcend language, age, and culture boundaries. Furthermore, the use of ideograms maintains a strictly visual language of interaction between search construction and video results. In this way, using emoji helps to decrease the semantic gap between the query grammar and the visual media. Furthermore, the native support of emoji from companies like Google and Apple makes them uniquely well-positioned as a means for video search via smart watches and phones, with a square form factor that integrates seamlessly into touch interfaces.

MM'15, October 26–30, 2015, Brisbane, Australia.
ACM 978-1-4503-3459-4/15/10.
DOI: http://dx.doi.org/10.1145/2733373.2807961.

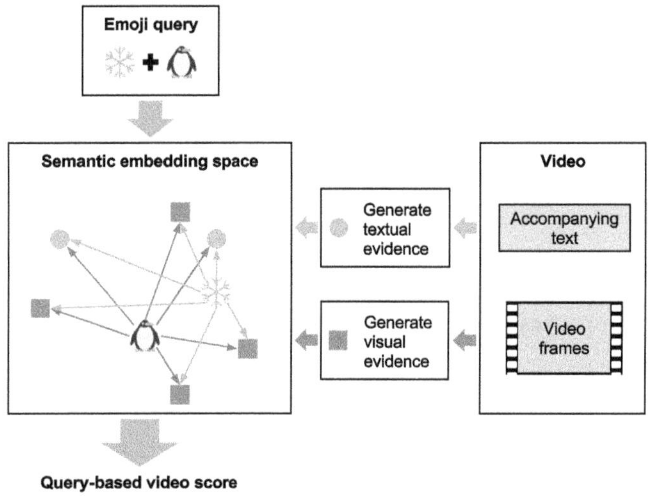

Figure 1: Illustration of video scoring for emoji. Query emoji are inserted into a space trained to capture semantic similarity. The concepts detected in the visual data of the video along with the textual concepts present in the video title are also placed in the same space. Videos are thus ranked based on the calculation of their similarity to the query emoji within this semantic space.

Emoji are becoming increasingly popular as a form of communication, and have steadily gained the attention of major companies. Microsoft's Bing has begun supporting search-by-emoji,[1] while Instagram has recently investigated users' use of emoji within their network.[2]

Our demo uses emoji as a set of ideograms, but the underlying architecture is zero-shot and therefore trivially adaptable to any arbitrary set of ideograms. Emoji are simply an ideal test case due to their pervasive presence, which renders users instantly familiar with the range of ideograms available. Furthermore, the popularity of emoji suggests that they have sufficiently descriptive semantics for a wide range of scenarios. These properties make them an ideal test bed

[1] http://blogs.bing.com/search/2014/10/27/do-you-speak-emoji-bing-does/

[2] http://instagram-engineering.tumblr.com/post/117889701472/emojineering-part-1-machine-learning-for-emoji

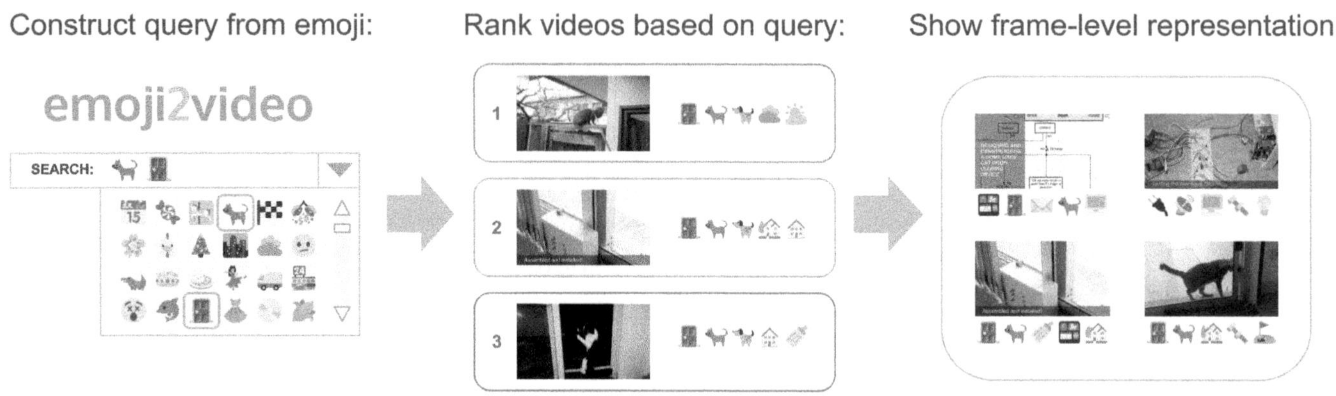

Figure 2: Users construct emoji queries through a web app interface which are used to return a ranked list of videos. Thumbnails of the videos are shown along with at-a-glance emoji representations of video content. Users can then either select a video for viewing or refine their query. An exploded view of several frames from the video can also be viewed, along with their respective frame-level emoji representations.

for exploration into ideogram-based search and representation of video, especially for small screens.

2. EMOJI2VIDEO SEARCH ENGINE

Our technical demo system utilizes emoji-based search queries to return videos from the VideoStory46k dataset [2]. This dataset consists of 46,000 videos harvested from YouTube, and as such is a reasonable proxy for the breadth and nature of content on video-sharing websites. The system is multi-modal, relying on both the frames of the videos and the video titles to generate searchable emoji-based representations. This is an extension of our previous work [1] on zero-shot emoji representation to a video search application.

Our approach relies on a word2vec [3] semantic embedding space, within which we can relate visual, textual, and emoji concepts. Visual evidence is collected through the application of deep-learning based concept detectors [4] on the video frames, and textual evidence is harvested from the title text of the YouTube videos.[1]

2.1 User Experience

In our demo, users are presented with a search interface similar to those commonly found on the mobile web. However, instead of users typing text strings to compose the search query, they are presented with a panel of emoji to choose from. As users compose and refine their query, videos are ranked according to this query. The results are displayed in an ordered list with a thumbnail of each video, along with an emoji-based summary of the video contents. The emoji representation is generated using the entirety of the video along with its title, and so may capture information about the content of the video that is not present in a single thumbnail image. This at-a-glance visual summary allows users to make an informed decision about which of the returned videos they want to view.

As the user refines their query, suggestions for other emoji to include are made by grouping the emoji within the semantic space. When a user has found a video they are interested in, they can choose to view that video, or see an expansion of some frames of the video along with their emoji representations. An overview of the core experience along with the system's results for an example query is given in Figure 2.

2.2 Video Summarization

Emoji-based representations are calculated on a frame-level across the video. At the frame-level, a smaller weight is applied to evidence from the video's title than to the local, frame-specific visual information. The mean of the frame-level representations is used to calculate the video-level emoji representation. In this way, the video-level representation provides an ideogrammatical summary of the visual content across the video. The demo is run as a web app, and could therefore be accessed by any internet-capable devices networked to the server, providing compact emoji summarization of videos for devices where screen real estate may be at a premium.

Our demo presents a new way of interacting with large numbers of videos. Emoji2Video allows us to leverage the increasingly familiar emoji ideograms to provide an interface for quickly exploring video datasets in a form that can be used on smart watches, smart phones, and by users of any language, age, or culture.

Acknowledgments This research is supported by the STW STORY project and the Dutch national program COMMIT.

3. REFERENCES

[1] S. Cappallo, T. Mensink, and C. G. M. Snoek. Image2emoji: Zero-shot emoji prediction for visual media. In *ACM MM*. ACM, 2015.

[2] A. Habibian, T. Mensink, and C. G. M. Snoek. Videostory: A new multimedia embedding for few-example recognition and translation of events. In *ACM MM*. ACM, 2014.

[3] T. Mikolov, I. Sutskever, K. Chen, G. S. Corrado, and J. Dean. Distributed representations of words and phrases and their compositionality. In *NIPS*, 2013.

[4] C. Szegedy, W. Liu, Y. Jia, P. Sermanet, S. Reed, D. Anguelov, D. Erhan, V. Vanhoucke, and A. Rabinovich. Going deeper with convolutions. In *CVPR*, 2015.

Dive into Remote Events: Omnidirectional Video Streaming with Acoustic Immersion

Daisuke Ochi, Kenta Niwa, Akio Kameda, Yutaka Kunita, and Akira Kojima
NTT Media Intelligence Laboratories
1-1 Hikarino-oka, Yokosuka-Shi, Japan
{ochi.daisuke, niwa.kenta, kameda.akio, kunita.yutaka, kojima.akira}@lab.ntt.co.jp

ABSTRACT

We propose a system that can provide the physical presence of remote events through a head mount display (HMD) and a headphone. It can stream omnidirectional video within a limited network bandwidth at a high bitrate without sending regions that users are not viewing. It can also reproduce binaural sounds by convoluting head related transfer functions and angular region-wise separated signals. Technical demos of the system using an Oculus Rift HMD with a headphone will be performed to enable users to experience the visual and acoustic immersion it provides.

Categories and Subject Descriptors

H.5.1 [Information Interfaces and Presentation]: Multimedia Information Systems—Video, Audio input/output; H.5.2 [Information Interfaces and Presentation]: User Interfaces—Prototyping

General Terms

Design

Keywords

Omnidirectional Video; Sound source separation; Head mount display; Video streaming

1. INTRODUCTION

Simulating one's physical presence as if one were in a remote place has been a challenging issue in the virtual reality (VR) field. A huge number of VR researchers, programmers, and engineers have been trying to tackle this issue from many aspects. In particular, reproducing the human visual sense in a remote place has been gathering attention recently, backed by many releases of sophisticated devices, omnidirectional cameras, and head mount displays (HMDs). Watching omnidirectional video taken by a camera through HMD makes it possible for people to feel a sense of remote presence easily.

MM'15, October 26–30, 2015, Brisbane, Australia.
ACM 978-1-4503-3459-4/15/10.
http://dx.doi.org/10.1145/2733373.2807963.

Achieving remote presence by transferring omnidirectional video has one major issue: the size of the video becomes very large when we send it clearly so as to appeal to the visual sense. Although people are currently forced to experience the remote presence by downloading the huge video in advance or preparing wider network bandwidth, a more efficient way to transfer has been required.

On the other hand, in the real world it is obvious that people use not only the visual sense but also their other senses to understand what is going on around them. To take the hearing sense as an example, in any discussion of omnidirectional immersion acoustic immersion plays an important role, e.g., when hazards spring up from dead angles (blind spots) or when people are playing a ball game while getting help from their teammates calling them from behind. Thus, for achieving omnidirectional immersion, practical capturing and simple reproduction of sounds has been required.

To address these issues, we propose an omnidirectional video streaming system with acoustic immersion that can allow people to immerse themselves in remote events with an ordinary network environment, including a mobile network and simple equipment such as an HMD and a headphone. It was achieved by making use of our previous work involving video streaming [1,2] and sound isolation [3] techniques. We developed a prototype for it and it showed that recorded omnidirectional video and sound could be reproduced well enough to enable viewers to feel that they were actually at the remote place.

2. SYSTEM OVERVIEW

To simulate the physical presence of remote events, two different techniques are used in our prototype. One is for capturing omnidirectional video and one for capturing omnidirectional sounds (Fig.1).

2.1 Video Streaming System

The system [1,2] enables us to efficiently stream omnidirectional video that normally has extremely high resolution, i.e. 4K or more. In the system, we first capture an omnidirectional video as a rectangular-shaped one using an omnidirectional camera. The video is then divided into many overlapped tile-shaped videos after copying it in low resolution that covers the whole area in one tile-shaped video. We then encode both every divided tile-shaped video in advance at higher bitrate and the low-resolution video at lower bitrate by H.264 (MPEG-4 AVC) codec. The user watching the video wears an HMD that is equipped with an acceleration and orientation sensor to sense the user's gazing direction. It

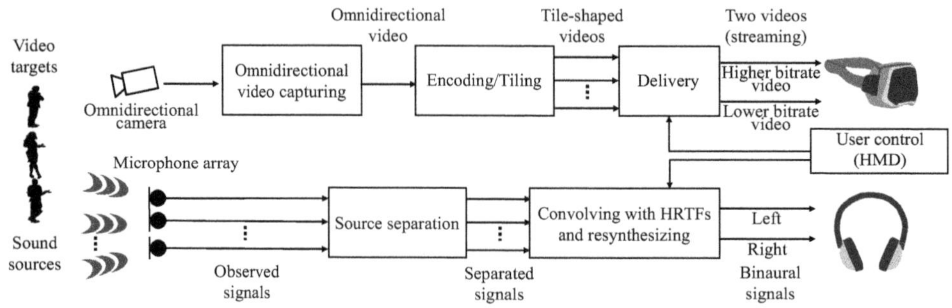

Figure 1: Overview of our prototype system.

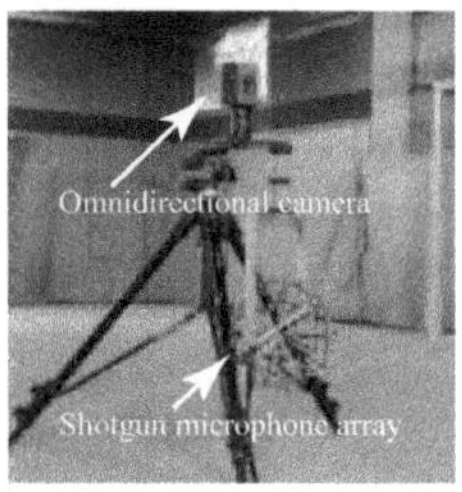

Figure 2: Capturing part of the system.

Figure 3: Examples of user's view.

is used to request and fetch one of the higher-bitrate videos according to the direction. After the video is fetched, it is remapped with the simultaneously requested lower-bitrate video in the spherical coordinates and rendered.

This technique can reduce the network bandwidth requirement because viewers no longer need to receive higher-bitrate videos for regions they are not viewing.

2.2 Sound System

We assemble an array of multiple shotgun microphones spherically to pre-enhance the signals for each direction. The array, however, should ideally be on the same place as the omnidirectional camera. Consequently, we place it below the camera and some distance from it so as not to block the camera's vision, assuming that the human hearing sense is not so sensitive. In the post-process, we first applied our sound source separation technique, which is based on the power spectrum density (PSD) estimation in the beamspace method [3] for angular region-wise source enhancement. To extract well-separated angular region-wise omnidirectional sounds without any sound leaking from neighboring microphones, the Wiener gains are adjusted. The binaural sounds corresponding to the user's gazing direction can be resynthesized after convolution of the separated sounds and head-related transfer functions (HRTFs) [4,5]. This technique enables users to get clear and immersive sounds through their headphones.

3. DEMONSTRATIONS

In demonstrations, the system showed immersive soccer content recorded by the capturing part of the prototype (Fig.2), Point Grey's Ladybug3 omnidirectional camera, and our microphone array. The original size of the captured video was 3840×1920 pixels and its frame rate was 30 fps. We assigned 5 Mbps for the higher-bitrate videos and 2 Mbps for the lower-bitrate one. The higher-bitrate video came in about five seconds after the request due to network latency and the client's video buffering. The array had 20 shotgun microphones on the vertex of a regular dodecahedron with a diameter of 0.4 m. Each captured sound was 48 kHz without any compression. The distance between the camera and the array was about 0.5 m. Users were able to watch the content with an HMD (Oculus VR's Oculus Rift Development Kit2) and a headphone (Audio-Technica's ATH-A500X) through an audio interface (Roland's OCTA-CAPTURE). When they moved their heads, they were able to experience the corresponding video and sounds (Fig.3).

4. CONCLUSION

We have developed and here propose a system that can provide physical presence of remote events. Applying streaming and sound source separation techniques we had previously developed, the system streams omnidirectional video efficiently while reproducing acoustic immersion through a head mount display and a headphone.

In future, it will be necessary for us to show our system's validity by conducting user studies regarding such factors as video and sound quality and usability.

5. REFERENCES

[1] D. Ochi, S. Iwaki, Y. Kunita, J. Hirose, K. Fujii, and A. Kojima, HMD Viewing Spherical Streaming System, *Proc. ACM MM 2014*, November 2014.

[2] D. Ochi, S. Iwaki, K. Akio, Y. Kunita, and A. Kojima, Live Streaming System for Omnidirectional Video, *Proc. IEEE VR 2015*, March 2015.

[3] Y. Hioka, K. Furuya, K. Kobayashi, K. Niwa, and Y. Haneda, Underdetermined sound source separation using power spectrum density estimated by combination of directivity gain, *IEEE trans. on Audio, Speech, and Language*, Vol.21, No.6, pp.1240-1250, 2013.

[4] K. Niwa, T. Nishino, and K. Takeda, Encoding large array signals into a 3D sound field representation for selective listening point audio based on blind source separation, *Proc. ICASSP 2008*, 181-184, 2008.

[5] Nagoya University, Head Related Transfer Functions, *http://www.sp.m.is.nagoya-u.ac.jp/HRTF/*.

Movie's Affect Communication Using Multisensory Modalities

Joël Dumoulin, Diana Affi,
Elena Mugellini, Omar Abou Khaled
HumanTech Institute
University of Applied Sciences
Fribourg, Switzerland
[name.surname]@hes-so.ch

Marco Bertini, Alberto Del Bimbo
MICC
University of Florence
Florence, Italy
[name.surname]@unifi.it

ABSTRACT

The goal of the system presented in this demo is to make possible for the visually and hearing impaired audience to live empathetic viewing experiences using their home theatre. In this work we suggest the incorporation of new emotion communication modalities into the standard television, to provide the targeted audience with sensations that they do not have the opportunity to enjoy because of their disability.

Categories and Subject Descriptors

H.5.1 [**INFORMATION INTERFACES AND PRESENTATION**]: Multimedia Information Systems—*Video*

Keywords

Sentiment analysis; video analysis; affect communication

1. INTRODUCTION

There are lots of competitors in the television market, that need to differentiate themselves providing new functionalities to their products and to respond to the needs of consumers. Increasing the immersion of viewers in movies is one of the axes of the evolution of television experience. Hearing and visually impaired people are a special and challenging audience. In fact, some solutions exist to provide these people with the semantic content of the video using for instance subtitles for the hearing impaired and audio-description for the visually impaired, but solutions that bring them the emotions contained in the movies are not so common yet. In this paper, emotion communication modalities compatible with televisions are presented in order to assure more immersion and empathic sensations to the viewers.

2. RELATED WORK

Many new technologies have appeared adding synchronised devices to the home theatre aiming to enhance the TV viewing experience. Second screen apps such as Syfy Sync [1] are developed to work together with Philips Hue lights in order to change the room lightning (color and intensity) at key moments (particular scenes, such as extreme weather, or intense violence) of the TV shows. More advanced features, such as Microsoft's IllumiRoom [3] project, augment the area surrounding a television screen with projected visualizations to enhance the traditional living room entertainment experience. The audio cue is also being enhanced by working on 3D sound audio system embedded in the new generation TVs. Researches also focused on emotional subtitles [4] in order to express emotions in originally static text. These techniques do enhance the TV viewing experience but do not offer any substitutes for the malfunctioning senses of the impaired viewers.

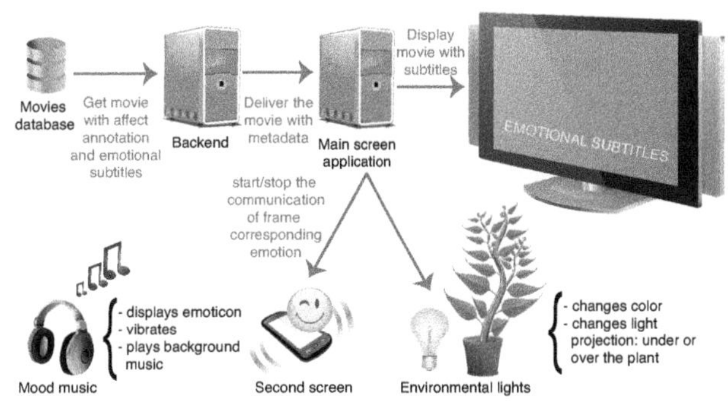

Figure 1: System setup

3. SYSTEM OVERVIEW

The system is composed of a backend application, a main screen application and a set of different emotion communication devices: the TV monitor displaying the movie and the special subtitles, environmental lights, and a second screen application.

In the database, each second of each movie is annotated, showing seven probability values corresponding to the seven basic emotions: *anger*, *disgust*, *fear*, *happiness*, *sadness*, *surprise* and *neutral*. The highest value denotes the emotion mostly perceived in the given scene. This annotation is obtained after a previous processing step applied on the movie in the backend. First, multiple visual and audio features are extracted from each frame per second and over one second long audio clips respectively. Then a previously trained classifier on emotion annotated video datasets, is applied on these features in order to recognise the emotions for each sec-

MM'15, October 26–30, 2015, Brisbane, Australia.
ACM 978-1-4503-3459-4/15/10.
DOI: http://dx.doi.org/10.1145/2733373.2807965 .

(a) (b) (c) (d)

Figure 2: Emotion communication via Philips Hue lights: a) TV rear mounted LightStrip b) Blooms setup c) Lighting from beneath for negative emotions d) Lighting from above for positive emotions.

ond of the movie. For classification, a Random Forrest Tree is used after training it on the Acted Facial Expressions in the Wild dataset (AFEW) and the FilmStim dataset. The best result of 32% of accuracy is obtained when using audio features inspired from the INTERSPEECH 2010 challenge and deep learning based visual features addressing both visual content and sentiment [2].

When watching a movie, first the movie is loaded with its emotional annotation and subtitles from the database to the backend application. Then, the video file and the subtitles are sent to the main screen application where the movie is played. While playing, the main screen application sends a command to all the emotion communication modalities to display the emotion corresponding to the current frame.

3.1 Emotion communication devices

Multiple devices and techniques are used to convey emotions to the users while watching a movie. The backend application synchronises these devices with the video player in order to present the right emotion at the right time:

Environmental lights Two Philips Hue Blooms and one Philips Hue LightStrip are used for expressing emotions via lights (see Figure 2). The strip LED light, attached to the borders of the TV screen, changes colours according to the current emotion, while the Hue light, in addition of changing colours, modifies the projection type. In fact, two Hue LED's are used in order to enlighten a plant in two different ways: either from above or from beneath it. This difference of light projection is used to differentiate between positive and negative emotions respectively. As for the colours red is used for anger, green for disgust, blue for fear, yellow for happiness, grey for sadness and pink for surprise.

Second screen A mobile application is developed on the Android platform to accompany the viewers during their movie. The application is controlled by the backend that sends at each second, the corresponding emotion that needs to be presented on the second screen. A *translator layer* is implemented that takes the emotion value and fires accordingly three different events:

1. Displays on the screen the corresponding smiley face (see Figure 3).
2. Plays a background music that is lyrics free and with low volume so it will not disturb the viewer from not hearing the movie's audio but just enough to set a certain mood.
3. Starts a vibrations that will stimulate the viewer - who is supposed to hold the mobile phone in his hand, about some event occurence. The different emotions have different stimuli or vibration patterns as shown in Figure 4.

Figure 3: Emoticons shown on a second screen.

Emotion	Vibration pattern
Anger	●_●_●
Disgust	●_⬬_
Fear	●_●_
Happiness	⬬_⬬_⬬
Sadness	⬬___
Surprise	⬬_●_

Figure 4: Vibration patterns for each emotion

Monitor display On the monitor displaying the movie, subtitles are added as well. These subtitles change font, colour and size according to the emotion they convey. CSS classes are created for each emotion and are attributed for each sentence in the movie. The subtitles are generated automatically using the Google Speech Recognition API and saved in a WebVTT file (Web Video Text Tracks format).

The association of colors and emoticons to emotions has been evaluated with a survey conducted on 126 men and 87 women aged between 17 and 60 (avg. 24).

4. CONCLUSION

The designed system presents multiple techniques and devices that can encode an emotional information and deliver it to the television audience. Each of these proposed techniques do target a different sense in order to ensure their effectiveness on hearing and visually impaired viewers. With this solution, the TV viewing experience is enhanced by delivering more immersion for the global users and better content delivery for the targeted audience.

5. REFERENCES

[1] The internet of things: Wifi lights + interactive tv. `https://www.gloto.com/2015/05/the-internet-of-things-wifi-lights-interactive-tv/`. Accessed on May 2015.

[2] T. Chen, D. Borth, T. Darrell, and S.-F. Chang. DeepSentiBank: Visual sentiment concept classification with deep convolutional neural networks. *arXiv:1410.8586*, 2014.

[3] Microsoft. Illumiroom. `http://research.microsoft.com/en-us/projects/illumiroom/`. Accessed on May 2015.

[4] J. Ohene-djan and R. Shipsey. E-Subtitles : Emotional Subtitles as a Technology to assist the Deaf and Hearing-Impaired when Learning from Television and Film. In *Proc. of ICALT*, pages 2–4, 2006.

QOEYE:A Data Driven Platform for QoE Visualization and System Performance Monitoring

Chao Zhou, Lifeng Sun, Wenming Shi, and Shiqiang Yang
Tsinghua National Laboratory for Information Science and Technology
Department of Computer Science and Technology, Tsinghua University
{zhouc13@mails., sunlf@,swm12@mails., yangshq@}tsinghua.edu.cn

ABSTRACT

The stunning increase of video streaming has been a major part of the network flow in the past few years. It is essential for content providers to manage more flow servers to satisfy the demands of users. Therefore, to effectively manage large-scale servers and to identify problems, service node become crucial to guarantee video user experience. The rule-based approach that the traditional service providers use is effective but could hardly be applied to large-scale server clusters, let alone in a joint service resources and the maximization of user experience. Unlike traditional rule-based QoS monitoring platform, we design a framework on a basis of user experience metrics to detect the quality of service. In line with the characteristics of IP addresses, we also design a method to quickly pinpoint the fault location.

Categories and Subject Descriptors

H.5.1 [**Multimedia Information systems**]

Keywords

QoE; monitoring platform; visualization

1. INTRODUCTION

In the past few years, video streaming has occupied a major part of the network flow. In order to meet the increasing user demands, content providers deploy more servers and create more methods including cloud computing, multi-CDN and DASH[3], to raise efficiency of server resources.

With the expanse of server scale, traditional ways to monitor servers are no longer useful. Content providers could monitor every QoS parameter(e.g., RTT, CPU, memory, bandwidth) by running rule-based scripts[4] in the background in the old days, which does not work now when facing the enormous scale of server clusters. Operators can quickly figure out the position of network congestion or bad performance of servers , including high CPU load and bandwidth filled, and migrate those excessive load to other well-

MM'15, October 26–30, 2015, Brisbane, Australia.
ACM 978-1-4503-3459-4/15/10.
DOI:http://dx.doi.org/10.1145/2733373.2807968 .

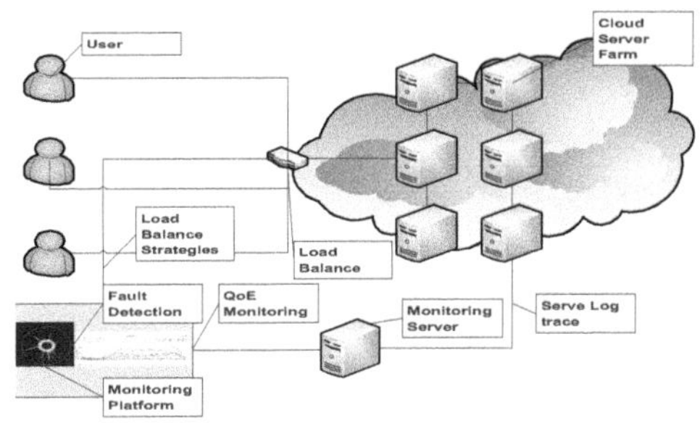

Figure 1: Platform Architecture of QOEYE.

performed server but in trouble with being confused by the complicated architecture of lots of servers.

There is an agreement that improving quality of experience (QoE) is crucial to sustain these revenue models, especially when users' expectation of video quality is steadily rising[1].It is also proved that multi-quality metrics can be represented by the engagement-centric model.

Jeffrey Pang[4] designed a visualization tool that can be used by operators to find faults that were not noticed before. However, it visualizes all the IP prefixes into the same level and can only show one dimension of parameter, which is inapplicable in our platform.

Our work mainly focuses on three aspects. First of all, we employ user engagement as QoE metric in reflection of the server's performance. Secondly, we design a novel visualization process to represent server faults and to guide the maximization of server resources utilization. Thirdly, we deploy a user-friendly application with a interactive design.

2. SYSTEM OVERVIEW

The architecture of our monitoring platform is shown as Fig.1. We use the real trace from China content provider BesTV as our data source. We collected video streaming logs from BesTV servers to our monitoring server. We then analyze the log data, provide some statistics and find fault location. Content providers can gain considerable benefits from our platform by modifying load balance strategies based on QoE monitoring metrics and server statement visualization.

2.1 QoE Monitoring Metric

We utilize the percent of playtime in the whole video as the only QoE metric to represent the server statement because users tend to have a long viewing duration with a good server, in other words, when with a terrible network

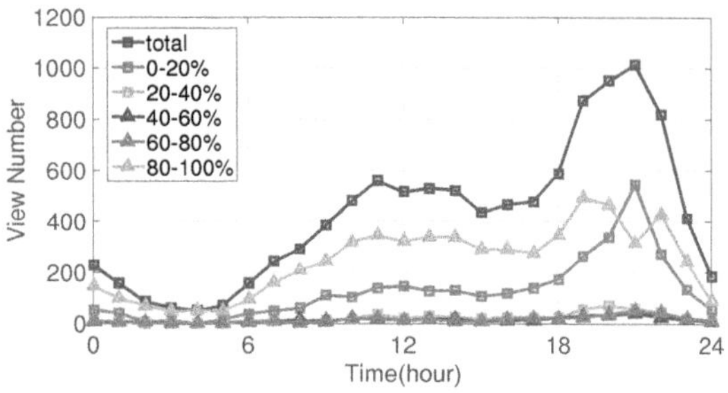

Figure 2: a server tendency chart based on QoE metric during one day

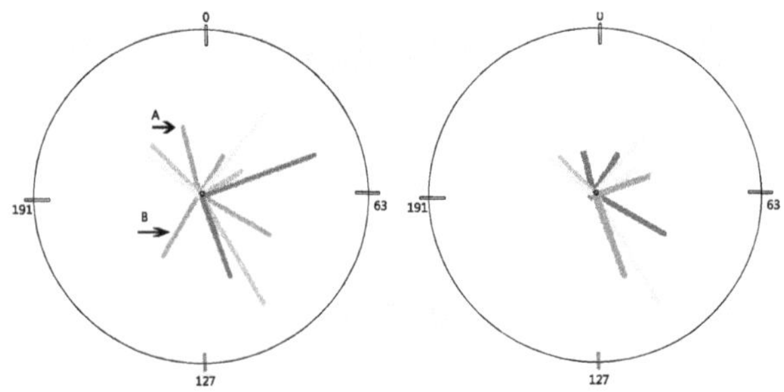

Figure 3: the performance of same areas servers which represent IP prefix aggregation

condition, users will shut down the video rather than patiently wait to watch. Meanwhile, from the perspective of providers, they can profit more with more playtime and more advertisements put into the video. Therefore, we design a tendency chart with QoE metrics and server load to find out the meaning of the sharped decrease of QoE metric's line.

We divide the percent of playtime into 5 sections(e.g. 0-20%...).Our problem then turns into maximizing the numbers of highest part of percent(80-100%) while minimizing those of the lowest part(0-20%).We can detect bad performance as soon as possible despite the complicated QoS metrics influence.Fig.2 shows a sharped decrease of the number of people who watch 80-100% of playtime in comparison with a huge increase of 0-20%. It suggests that this server has a bad performance in peak hour while we can't even notice it when we just monitor with the traditional QoS metrics.

2.2 Server Statement Visualization

An effective visualization method can help people to understand Internet characteristic[2]. By using the characteristics that the same IP prefixes are more likely to be geographically close, we hash the prefixes in a circle, each of which represents a server.An IP address can be divided into 4 parts so the total level of this circle is 4. We count the same IP prefixes as a line. In addition, we use line colors and lengths to encode QoS and QoE metrics to understand the relationship between them.

Fig.3 represents level 0 of two same areas servers. We choose colors to demonstrate user engagement and lengths for start delay. The arrows of A means that all the user performance of this server operates under IP prefix of 240.x.x.x. The performance on the left in this prefix has a bad QoE(red color) and a terrible start delay(long length), while the right one has a good QoE(blue) and a fine start delay(short).Based on this chart, content providers can migrate some users under 240.x.x.x from left server to the right. An anomaly spike (B arrows) appears in the left one but not in the right, which is probably caused by improper load balance strategies that lead the user request to the remote server. Therefore, content providers can modify their load balance strategies to maximize a joint of user experience and server resources.

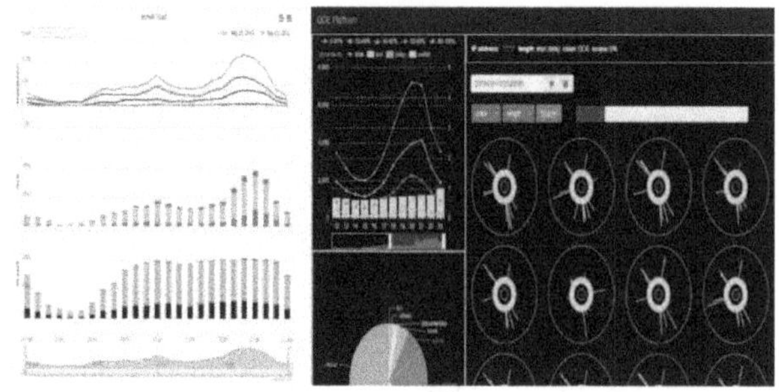

Figure 4: User Interface of QOEYE

3. DEMONSTRATION SETUP

With QOEYE platform on the web page shown in Fig.4, users can easily select a server and ISP with no geographic restrictions, as well as all-around statistics, including user distribution, DASH switch time with time varying, and the percentage of video type which can reflect people preferences. Users can select a date to see the user engagement's temporal variation as well.

4. CONCLUSION

We propose a data driven platform with novel visualization method, enabling content providers to monitor large-scale server clusters. It simplifies the dimensions of monitoring, rapidly orients fault location and help content provider to modify the load balance strategies to maximize the utilization of resources.

5. ACKNOWLEDGMENT

This work is supported by the National Natural Science Foundation of China under Grant No.61272231 and 61472204, Beijing Key Laboratory of Networked Multimedia.

6. REFERENCES

[1] A. Balachandran, V. Sekar, A. Akella, S. Seshan, I. Stoica, and H. Zhang. Developing a predictive model of quality of experience for internet video. In *ACM SIGCOMM Computer Communication Review*, volume 43, pages 339–350. ACM, 2013.

[2] H. Burch and B. Cheswick. Mapping the internet. *Computer*, 32(4):97–98, 1999.

[3] J. Jiang, V. Sekar, and H. Zhang. Improving fairness, efficiency, and stability in http-based adaptive video streaming with festive. In *Proceedings of the 8th international conference on Emerging networking experiments and technologies*, pages 97–108. ACM, 2012.

[4] J. Pang, S. Sen, O. Spatscheck, and S. Venkataraman. Internet-scale visualization and detection of performance events. Citeseer.

AR in Hand: Egocentric Palm Pose Tracking and Gesture Recognition for Augmented Reality Applications

Hui Liang[1], Junsong Yuan[2], Daniel Thalmann[1], Nadia Magnenat-Thalmann[1]
[1]Institute for Media Innovation, [2]School of Electrical and Electronics Engineering
50 Nanyang Avenue, Nanyang Technological University, Singapore
{lianghui,jsyuan,danielthalmann,nadiathalmann}@ntu.edu.sg

ABSTRACT

Wearable devices such as Microsoft Hololens and Google glass are highly popular in recent years. As traditional input hardware is difficult to use on such platforms, vision-based hand pose tracking and gesture control techniques are more suitable alternatives. This demo shows the possibility to interact with 3D contents with bare hands on wearable devices by two Augmented Reality applications, including virtual teapot manipulation and fountain animation in hand. Technically, we use a head-mounted depth camera to capture the RGB-D images from egocentric view, and adopt the random forest to regress for the palm pose and classify the hand gesture simultaneously via a spatial-voting framework. The predicted pose and gesture are used to render the 3D virtual objects, which are overlaid onto the hand region in input RGB images with camera calibration parameters for seamless virtual and real scene synthesis.

Categories and Subject Descriptors

H.1.2 [**Models and Principles**]: User/Machine Systems—*Human information processing*; I.4.8 [**Image Processing and Computer Vision**]: Scene Analysis—*Depth cues, Tracking*

Keywords

Augmented Reality, Gesture Recognition, Palm Pose Estimation.

1. INTRODUCTION

Augmented Reality (AR) applications are now getting increasingly popular with the wearable devices such as Microsoft HoloLens and Google glass, which provide users enhanced reality by synthesizing real visual cues with virtual graphics. As portability matters much for wearable devices, the traditional input tools like mouse and keyboard are very inconvenient to carry and use on such platforms. By comparison, vision-based hand gesture control is more suitable, since no separate hardware is needed and it is more straightforward for users to directly use their bare hands and fingers to fulfill the various control and manipulative tasks. Despite that there exist several AR systems that are built upon vision-based hand tracking and gesture recognition [6, 2, 3], they still have limitations, *e.g.* sensitivity to hand posture variations or working in quite limited viewpoints.

MM'15, October 26–30, 2015, Brisbane, Australia.
ACM 978-1-4503-3459-4/15/10.
DOI: http://dx.doi.org/10.1145/2733373.2807972.

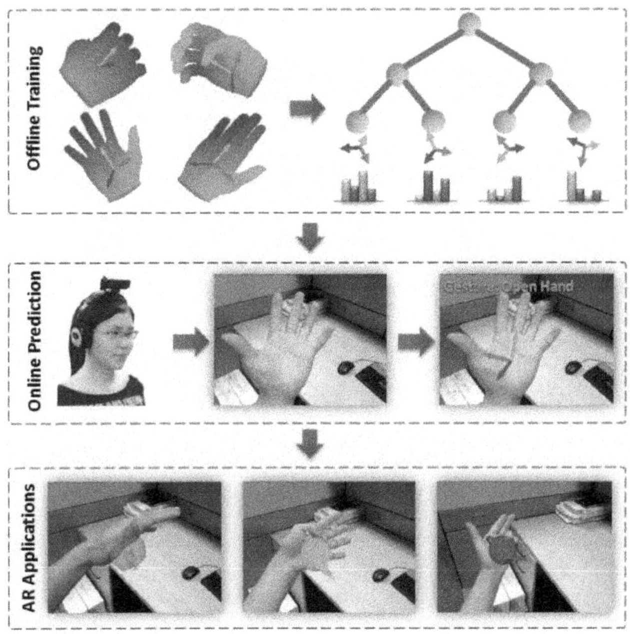

Figure 1: Framework of our AR system via egocentric palm pose tracking and gesture recognition.

In this demo we present an AR system to allow users to manipulate virtual objects freely with their bare hands based on our joint palm pose tracking and gesture recognition algorithm, so that the virtual objects are visually put upon the palm for arbitrary poses in the RGB images and the hand gestures are used to change the object appearance, *e.g.*, color. The framework of our system is shown in Fig. 1, in which we use a head-mounted SoftKinetic DS325 sensor to capture both the RGB and depth images of user's hand from egocentric view and predict the 6-DOF palm pose and recognize hand gesture simultaneously from the input depth images. The depth and color cameras of the SoftKinetic sensor are calibrated in advance to transform the 3D palm position and rotation recovered from the depth images to the coordinate

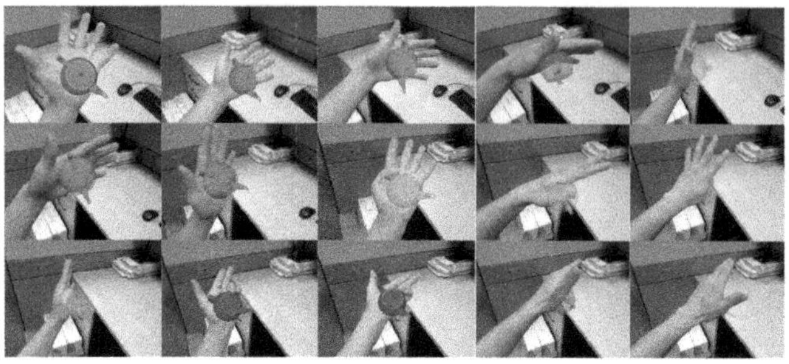

Figure 2: Teapot inspection and color selection.

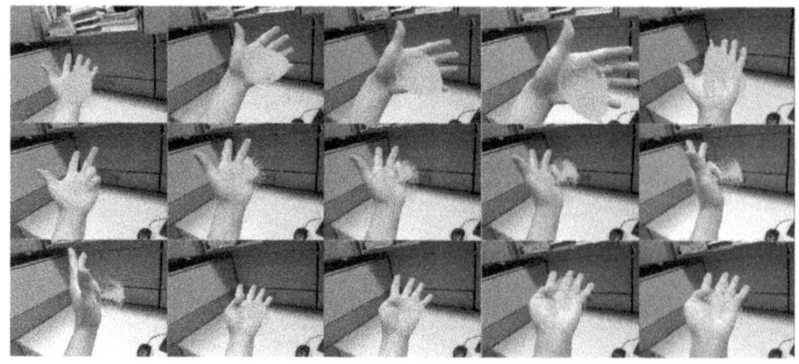

Figure 3: Fountain animation in hand.

system centered at the color camera. The virtual objects are then rendered according to the transformed palm pose and hand gesture, and projected onto the image plane with OpenGL, which is then overlaid on the RGB image.

Technically, a random forest [4] is trained offline for joint regression of palm pose and classification of hand gestures so that they can be predicted together. Following previous work on spatial-voting based pose estimation and gesture recognition [7, 5], the random forest is learned to map the local features of spatially-distributed voting pixels to the probabilistic votes for either palm pose or gesture class. During online testing, a set of voting pixels are randomly sampled within the hand region in the depth image, which then retrieve their votes for palm pose and hand gesture with the random forest. The final pose and gesture predictions are obtained by MAP inference via a linearly weighting model of the per-pixel pose and gesture votes. Moreover, as such a linear weighting model with uniform weights tends to produce ambiguous predictions, we learn an optimal weighting model to fuse the per-pixel votes, which proves quite robust against noisy inputs. A Kalman filter is used to further smooth palm pose prediction in successive frames.

2. APPLICATION SCENARIOS

The goal of this demo is to showcase two AR applications built upon our joint palm pose tracking and hand gesture recognition algorithms, which allow users to interact with virtual objects with their bare hands. The system recognizes three hand gestures to change the object appearance and predicts unconstrained 6D palm pose to change the viewpoint for object inspection. The resolution of the depth images is 320×240. The program is coded in C++/OpenCV, and tested on a PC with Intel i5 750 CPU and 4G RAM. The average time cost to process one frame is less than 40ms, which is sufficient for real-time interaction.

In the first application users can manipulate and inspect a static teapot from different perspectives and use different gestures to change its color. Particularly, to get realistic visual feedback, we define a visibility term for the teapot based on hand rotation angles to reflect hand-object occlusion, which is implemented via controlling the transparency effect in OpenGL with the roll angle of the palm. That is, the teapot is fully opaque when the palm is facing the camera, and becomes gradually transparent when it rotates backwards. The user interface is shown in Fig. 2.

In the second application users can view a fountain animation in their hands and use different gestures to change the fountain style, as illustrated in Fig. 3. For fountain simulation we adopt the algorithm in [1], which models the fountain as a discrete set of water drops and changes their velocity by simulated gravity force. The different fountain styles are simulated by setting different numbers and initial velocities of water drops. The palm position and orientation are used as the origin to simulate the gravity force, and the water drops thus visually fall towards the palm plane.

3. CONCLUSION

This demo presents two AR applications built upon our unified 6-DOF palm pose tracking and gesture recognition algorithm, including static teapot manipulation and fountain animation in hand. Based on the recovered palm pose and camera calibration parameters, the virtual objects are rendered and overlaid onto the hand in the input RGB images, which provides seamless virtual and real scene synthesis. The program runs in real-time, and is particularly suitable for interaction on wearable devices.

4. ACKNOWLEDGMENT

This research, which is carried out at BeingThere Centre, is supported by the Singapore National Research Foundation under its International Research Centre @ Singapore Funding Initiative and administered by the IDM Programme Office.

5. REFERENCES

[1] Fountain simulation. http://www.codecolony.de.

[2] O. Akman, R. Poelman, W. Caarls, and P. Jonker. Multi-cue hand detection and tracking for a head-mounted augmented reality system. *Machine Vision and Applications*, 24(5):931–946, July 2013.

[3] M. Asad and G. Slabaugh. Hand orientation regression using random forest for augmented reality. In *Augmented and Virtual Reality*, pages 159–174, 2014.

[4] L. Breiman. Random forests. *Mach. Learning*, 45(1):5–32, 2001.

[5] C. Keskin, F. Kirac, Y. E. Kara, and L. Akarun. Hand pose estimation and hand shape classification using multi-layered randomized decision forests. In *European Conf. Computer Vision*, 2012.

[6] T. Lee and T. Hollerer. Handy ar: Markerless inspection of augmented reality objects using fingertip tracking. In *IEEE Int'l Symposium on Wearable Computers*, pages 83–90, 2007.

[7] C. Xu and L. Cheng. Efficient hand pose estimation from a single depth image. In *IEEE Int'l Conf. Computer Vision*, 2013.

PPTLens: Create Digital Objects with Sketch Images

Changcheng Xiao*
Shanghai Jiao Tong University
Shanghai, China
xchangcheng@gmail.com

Changhu Wang†
Microsoft Research
Beijing, China
chw@microsoft.com

Liqing Zhang
Shanghai Jiao Tong University
Shanghai, China
zhang-lq@cs.sjtu.edu.cn

ABSTRACT

In this work, we introduce the PPTLens system to convert sketch images captured by smart phones to digital flowcharts in PowerPoint. Different from existing sketch recognition system, which is based on hand-drawn strokes, PPTLens enables users to use sketch images as inputs directly. It's more challenging since strokes extracted from sketch images might not only be very messy, but also without temporal information of the drawings. To implement the 'Image to Object' (I2O) scenario, we propose a novel sketch image recognition framework, including an effective stroke extraction strategy and a novel offline sketch parsing algorithm. By enabling sketch images as inputs, our system makes flowchart/diagram production much more convenient and easier.

Categories and Subject Descriptors

H.3.1 [**Information Storage and Retrieval**]: Content Analysis and Indexing; H.5.2 [**User Interfaces**]: User-centered Design

Keywords

Offline Sketch Recognition; Sketched Flowchart Recognition

1. INTRODUCTION

Drawing flowcharts and diagrams on a whiteboard or tablet is an effective way for users to convey and express information. Although with the development of touch-screen devices, increasing research is conducted on hand-drawn flowchart or diagram recognition, most work targets at interpreting online drawings with temporal information (online sketch recognition), with little effort on understanding sketch images captured by smart phones (offline sketch parsing). However, it will make flowchart/diagram production much more convenient and easier if we can use sketch images as inputs, especially with the popularity of smart phones.

*Changcheng Xiao performed this work while being an intern at Microsoft Research Asia.
†Corresponding author.

MM'15, October 26–30, 2015, Brisbane, Australia.
ACM 978-1-4503-3459-4/15/10.
DOI: http://dx.doi.org/10.1145/2733373.2807974 .

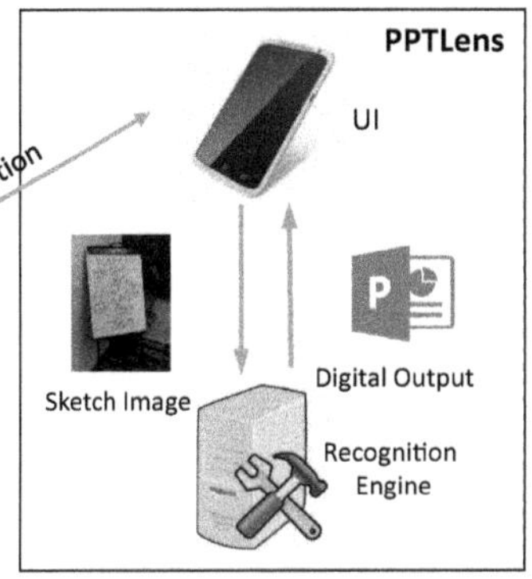

Figure 1: Illustration of the PPTLens system. Users can take a photo of the sketched flowchart, which can be automatically converted to a digital flowchart in PowerPoint with shape symbols and arrows replaced by form digital objects.

In spite of the increasing interest in building system that can automatically recognize sketch images, there is still a huge gap between sketch images and digital objects. This gap mainly comes from the following two aspects: **1) the challenges of extracting strokes from sketch images.** Different from online sketch recognition [5], in which strokes can be obtained directly from the user interface, it's very challenging to extract strokes from sketch images. On the one hand, sketch images may have uneven drawing quality and large variations of luminous intensity, resulting in low stroke extraction recall. On the other hand, the missing of drawing orders results in high error rate for the stroke construction. **2) the challenges of offline sketch parsing.** To recognize the symbols of a sketch, a typical approach in the literature is to first generate a number of candidate stroke groups, followed by the recognition of each group [3, 4]. Theoretically, for N strokes, there will be 2^N different stroke groups to recognize. To avoid the exponentially growing recognition cost, several constraints are leveraged, such as temporal constraint [1] and spatial constraint [4]. However, the strokes extracted from sketch images might be very messy, resulting in much more groups. Moreover, the unavailable of the temporal constraint makes it harder to reduce the search space.

To bridge the gap between sketch images and digital objects, in this work, we first propose an effective stroke ex-

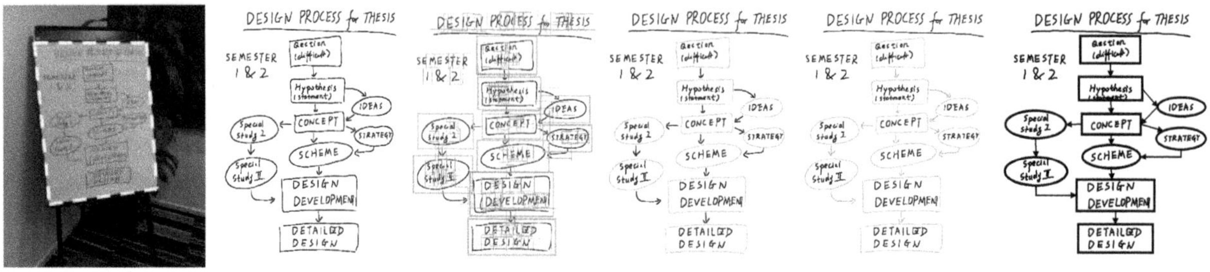

(a) Source Image (b) Extracted Strokes (c) Shapeness Estimation (d) Shape Recognition (e) Shape-Guided Sketch Parsing (f) Object Generation

Figure 2: Illustration of the sketch image recognition framework. Given a hand-drawn flowchart image, we first detect the region with sketched contents (a), and extract strokes from the detected region (b). Then a large number of stroke groups are generated as candidates (red&green bounding boxes), followed by the shapeness estimation algorithm to select a few 'good' candidates (green bounding boxes) in (c). The selected 'good' candidates are then fed into a robust recognizer to predict their specific shape types in (d), followed by the shape-guided parsing to recognize all other parts (e). The final sketch parsing results are converted to a digital flowchart in PowerPoint that can be further edited (f).

traction strategy, which is based on the observation that sketches hold almost fixed stroke width. The main process of our stroke extraction strategy is: 1) detect the borders of the whiteboard/paper, then crop and rectify the image [6], 2) binarize the image by leveraging the Stroke Width Transform [2] and MRF optimization, 3) extract the skeleton of the binary image and construct strokes. To reduce the search space of sketch recognition efficiently, we propose the idea of shapeness estimation, measuring how likely a stroke group could be a *good* shape. Owing to the shapeness estimation process, our system can efficiently remove most of the *bad* shape groups while still preserve high recall for the *good* shape groups.

Based on the above technologies, we present a novel sketch image recognition framework (Fig. 2) and build the PPTLens system to recognize camera-captured sketch images and convert them to digital flowcharts in PowerPoint.

2. SYSTEM OVERVIEW

In this section, we introduce the main functions of the PPTLens system from the following two aspects:

System Input

The input of the PPTLens system should be an image, containing a flowchart drawn on a whiteboard or a paper. A typical flowchart, as in Fig. 2, mainly contains three categories of objects, i.e., shape symbols, non-shape symbols and noises. The five basic shape symbols are process (rectangle), decision (diamond), terminator (ellipse), data (parallelogram) and connection (circle). The two non-shape symbols are arrow and text. In this work, we mainly recognize the five shape symbols and arrows while leaving the text recognition for future work.

System Output

The output of the PPTLens system is a PowerPoint file with three slides. The first slide contains all the strokes extracted from the sketch image. The second slide contains the unrecognized strokes and the formal digital objects replacing recognized strokes. The third slide contains the original input image.

Fig. 3 shows two example sketch images and their corresponding results of the PPTLens system.

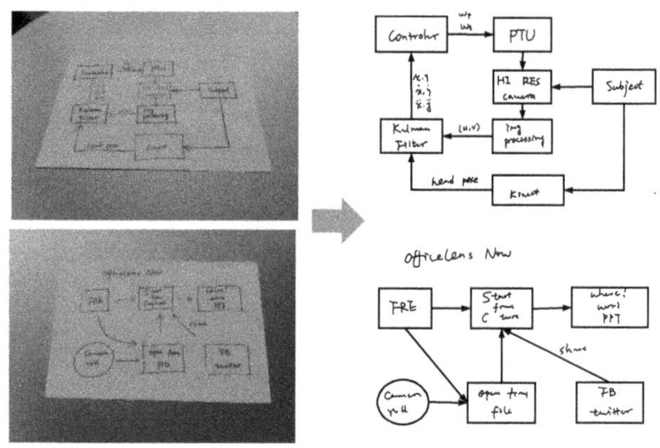

Figure 3: Example sketch images and corresponding results.

3. ACKNOWLEDGMENTS

The work of first and third authors was supported by the National Natural Science Foundation of China (Grant No. 61272251) and National Key Basic Research Program of China (Grant No. 2015CB856004).

4. REFERENCES

[1] C. Carton, A. Lemaitre, and B. Couasnon. Fusion of statistical and structural information for flowchart recognition. In *ICDAR*, 2013.

[2] B. Epshtein, E. Ofek, and Y. Wexler. Detecting text in natural scenes with stroke width transform. *CVPR*, 2010.

[3] L. B. Kara and T. F. Stahovich. Hierarchical parsing and recognition of hand-sketched diagrams. *UIST*, 2004.

[4] E. J. Peterson, T. F. Stahovich, E. Doi, and C. Alvarado. Grouping Strokes into Shapes in Hand-Drawn Diagrams. *Artificial Intelligence*, 2010.

[5] J. Wu, C. Wang, L. Zhang, and Y. Rui. Sketch Recognition with Natural Correction and Editing. AAAI, 2014.

[6] Z. Zhang and L. W. He. Whiteboard scanning and image enhancement. *Digital Signal Processing*, 2007.

A Multi-Modal 3D Capturing Platform for Learning and Preservation of Traditional Sports and Games

François Destelle, Amin Ahmadi, Kieran Moran and Noel E. O'Connor
INSIGHT, Dublin City University, Ireland
francois.destelle@dcu.ie

Nikolaos Zioulis, Anargyros Chatzitofis, Dimitrios Zarpalas and Petros Daras
ITI-CERTH
Thessaloniki, Greece

Luis Unzueta, Jon Goenetxea, Mikel Rodriguez and Maria T. Linaza
Vicomtech-IK4
San Sebastián, Spain

Yvain Tisserand, Nadia Magnenat Thalmann
MIRALab, University of Geneva, Switzerland

ABSTRACT

We present a demonstration of a multi-modal 3D capturing platform coupled to a motion comparison system. This work is focused on the preservation of Traditional Sports and Games, namely the Gaelic sports from Ireland and Basque sports from France and Spain. Users can learn, compare and compete in the performance of sporting gestures and compare themselves to real athletes. Our online gesture database provides a way to preserve and display a wide range of sporting gestures. The capturing devices utilised are Kinect 2 sensors and wearable inertial sensors, where the number required varies based on the requested scenario. The fusion of these two capture modalities, coupled to our inverse kinematic algorithm, allow us to synthesize a fluid and reliable 3D model of the user gestures over time. Our novel comparison algorithms provide the user with a performance score and a set of comparison curves (i.e. joint angles and angular velocities), providing a precise and valuable feedback for coaches and players.

Categories and Subject Descriptors

I.4.5/7 [**Computing Methodologies**]: Image Processing and Computer Vision—*Reconstruction, Feature Measurement*

General Terms

Capture, Tracking, Measurement, Comparison.

Keywords

Motion capture, Sensor Fusion, Vision, Motion Retargeting.

MM'15, October26–30,2015, Brisbane, Australia.
ACM 978-1-4503-3459-4/15/10.
DOI: http://dx.doi.org/10.1145/2733373.2807977.

1. INTRODUCTION

Traditional Sports and Games (TSG) are a strong part of a society's identity and a strong mechanism for the promotion of cultural diversity. European examples include Gaelic games (Hurling, Football, etc.) in Ireland, Basque Pelota (and variants) in Spain, among many others.

Our project [1] aims to preserve and promote these TSG, that may be under the threat of disappearing and losing their social and community value. This demonstration software platform implements three different scenarios: *Play& Learn*, *Coach&Train* and *Interact&Preserve*. The first one is dedicated to children at home and allows the user to learn TSG gestures and compare himself to local existing heroes. The second one is more technical and aims to provide coaches with a precise measurement tool in order to improve an athlete's performance. This scenario is close to the first one but it uses up to 4 Kinect sensors and up to 9 Wearable Inertial Measurement Units (WIMUs). The last one is intended for a museum or other exhibition place. It preserves the TSG sporting gestures into an accessible online database of captured gestures.

A key feature of our framework is the cost to achieve our goals. Given the budget-constrained conditions under which most TSG clubs operate, it was imperative that our aims be achievable in a cost-effective manner. To this end, we used open source software wherever possible, putting the creation of such digital exhibitions within reach of even modest budgets.

2. SYSTEM DESCRIPTION

The platform that includes all our scenarios is embedded in a single application, and the game engine Unity [2] was employed to allow us to create the 3D interactive environment.

Motion Capture Framework.

Our main platform handles four Kinect sensors and up

[1] RePlay project: www.fp7-replay.eu
[2] www.unity3d.com

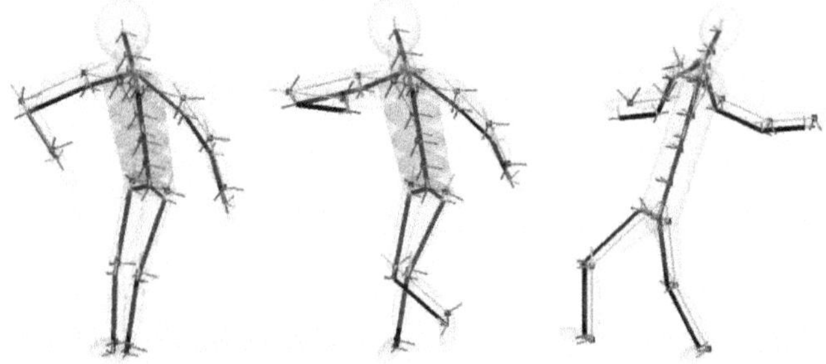

Figure 1: Transformation of a captured fused skeleton (black stickman) to the normalized avatar (yellow avatar) for motion retargeting.

to nine WIMUs. The multi-Kinect setup enables the creation of the athlete's full body 3D reconstruction, providing a photo-realistic visualization of the performed skill [3]. Each Kinect version 2 sensor requires a different machine, thus involving a network design. This client-server design uses a fast and reliable TCP/IP implementation, where each receiver machine is a client and where the main machine running the Unity 3D main software fulfills the server role. Moreover, as one machine alone can't easily handle more than 7 paired Bluetooth devices, especially at high framerate (100Hz or 256Hz), we use this multi-machine framework to also handle the Bluetooth reception of inertial data. Each client receives the WIMU data packet via Bluetooth at a fixed framerate, this packet is then used to compute the resulting local orientation changes of each sensor, using the efficient Madgwick rotational estimator [4].

Multi-modal Sensor Fusion.

The first step of our capturing pipeline is the fusion of the captured Kinect skeleton and the rotational information computed from the WIMUs. The whole process is described in [1], it uses one frame from the Kinect tracking algorithm to create a skeleton reference. This reference is then animated using solely the rotational information provided by the WIMUs. The fused Kinect-WIMUs skeleton provides a much more fluid, reliable and high-framerate model of the human gesture than the Kinect tracking algorithm.

Real-time Motion Retargeting.

The system could be used by a wide range of people, so a high variability of body part sizes is expected. Thus, we need to set a common integration framework for both the captured skeleton and the reference one from the elite ('gold standard') athlete to which they are compared. This representation constructs a normalized skeleton from any captured user, through real-time motion retargeting. The motion retargeting could be summarized as inverse kinematics (IK) solvers integrated with an objective function optimization for space-time constraints [2]. This kinematic representation of the virtual human has more segments and joints than those tracked by the sensors, see Fig. 1. It also insures a constant size for each bone and provides biomechanical constraints on the joint orientations to finally achieve a natural preservation of the performed skill properties.

[3]3D Photorealistic reconstruction: www.youtube.com/watch?v=gu72_g2GOQk
[4]Sebastian O.H. Madgwick, 30/09/2010: www.x-io.co.uk/open-source-imu-and-ahrs-algorithms

Figure 2: Pictures taken from our live demo, a Gaelic (left) and a Basque player (right).

Motion Comparison Algorithms.

The last part of our pipeline is the evaluation of the user's gesture against the one performed by the elite athlete. It compares two skeletons obtained by our IK algorithms applied to both the reference skeleton captured using a full motion capture system (Vicon, UK) and the skeleton obtained by our sensor fusion. We extract a number of geometric features including hierarchical rotations, linear/angular velocities, joint angles and kinetic energy. A dynamic time warping technique is used for both global and local temporal alignment of the multi-spectral signal. We then use a novel weighted scheme to obtain a global scoring from the overall performance of the user. These important weights are defined for each gesture by real coaches and biomechanical experts. While the scoring is a global performance indicator, our graphical interface also provides a rendering of all the local information for each joint of the skeleton over time.

3. DEMONSTRATION

The demonstration will consist of the *Coach&Train* scenario, involving one Kinect sensor and nine WIMUs. Two laptops will be used in order to receive the information coming from the WIMUs via Bluetooth. The RePlay exhibition will be showcased on a main large screen in front of the user, while the Kinect camera will be placed below it. A short video detailing the main RePlay platform and showing graphically the steps involved will also be displayed.

4. ACKNOWLEDGMENTS

The work presented in this paper was supported by the European Commission under contract FP7-601170 RePlay.

5. REFERENCES

[1] F. Destelle, A. Ahmadi, N. E. O'Connor et al. Low-cost accurate skeleton tracking based on fusion of kinect and wearable inertial sensors. In *EUSIPCO '14*, pages 371–375, Sept 2014.

[2] L. Unzueta, J. Goenetxea, M. Rodriguez, and M. Linaza. Viewpoint-dependent 3d human body posing for sports legacy recovery from images and video. In *EUSIPCO '14*, pages 361–365, Sept 2014.

Analysing Audience Response to Performing Events

A Web Platform for Interactive Exploration of Physiological Sensor Data

Thomas Röggla
CWI
Science Park 123
Amsterdam, Netherlands
t.roggla@cwi.nl

Chen Wang
CWI
Science Park 123
Amsterdam, Netherlands
c.wang@cwi.nl

Pablo Cesar
CWI
Science Park 123
Amsterdam, Netherlands
p.s.cesar@cwi.nl

ABSTRACT

This paper presents a web interface for the exploration of audience response to a performing arts event. The platform temporally synchronises data obtained from physiological sensors with video recordings. More concretely, it is geared towards people from the creative industry, e.g. theatre directors, who want to gain deeper insights into how audiences perceive their performances. The platform takes the raw data from sensors and corresponding video recordings and visualises both synchronised in a more digestible manner. This document presents the major features of the application and explains the reasoning behind its various visualisations and interactive capabilities and how it can benefit performing artists.

Categories and Subject Descriptors

H.5.m. [**Information Interfaces and Presentation (e.g. HCI)**]: multimedia information systems, user interfaces

General Terms

Experimentation, Human Factors

Keywords

Physiological Sensors, Visualisation, Web Technologies

1. INTRODUCTION

The field of physiological sensors has become an active area of research because it allows researchers to measure parameters of the human physiology and to link them to psychological concepts such as emotion, attention or engagement [3]. The data obtained from these sensors is comprised of streams of numbers, which in themselves are rather meaningless. It takes domain knowledge as well as mathematical tools to interpret this data and assign it some meaning.

Our previous research in the context of theatre performances, where audience members were equipped with GSR (*Galvanic Skin Response*) sensors, has shown that people who might profit from such measurements, namely performers or directors, often have trouble interpreting the results. What is presented in this paper is a web-based tool which allows the user to play back video recordings of performances where audience members were wearing physiological sensors. The platform takes in the raw sensor data, which needs to be in temporal synchronisation with the video recordings and presents it in the form of various visualisations, making it easier to interpret and understand. The data and video recordings used for testing the web application were taken from our previous experiments [4].

The main design goals behind the platform, besides enabling easier interpretation of sensor data, was to foster collaboration by allowing multiple users, e.g. theatre directors, to annotate sections of the video recording. To make the experience more interactive, the user can jump around in the recording and see the performance from different camera angles to gain a more complete picture of the audience's reaction to a piece, thereby providing artists with a better user experience in the most unobtrusive way.

The contribution of this tool is to provide creative people with a means of post-performance analysis of audience reaction. More concretely, users of the application can seek to random parts of the performance and observe the stage and the audience in the video and cross-reference it with the sensor data. Different from existing tools like [1, 3], we focus on user reaction and engagement and provide a way for performing artists to assess it in a more intuitive way, whereas previous work did not include sensor data at all or only did so in a laboratory setting.

2. APPROACH

To achieve this, we have implemented a web interface taking advantage of web technologies including *HTML5 video playback* and interactive charts using SVG and JavaScript. The application is backed by a web server serving the content and a database holding the sensor data. This makes sure that the application works anywhere the user has access to the Internet via a reasonably modern web browser. Furthermore, in this way, the data is kept in a centralised location, which enables several users to interact with the application at once. To protect access to the data, each user has to log in with a personal password.

While we did set a handful of basic requirements for the application ourselves, such as video playback and the possibility to switch between camera angles, the main bulk of the features was developed using direct input from artists. We

MM'15 October 26-30, 2015, Brisbane, Australia
ACM 978-1-4503-3459-4/15/10.
DOI: http://dx.doi.org/10.1145/2733373.2807976 .

followed a human-centered approach, involving users from the very beginning in one-on-one interviews and focus group discussions. Performing artists were also asked in the final evaluation process, which involved them testing and rating it using the CSI (*Creativity Support Index*) defined in [2], which gives us a comparable value for different factors of creativity, such as *Collaboration*, *Enjoyment*, *Exploration*, *Expressiveness*, *Immersion*, and *Results Worth Effort*.

2.1 Video Page

Figure 1 illustrates the top part of the video page of the application, which shows the video playback window, simple playback controls, controls for changing the camera angles and the seek bar, with which the user can jump to arbitrary positions in the timeline.

Figure 1: Video page of the application, playing back a video in a browser window

The red sections overlaid on certain parts of the timeline represent textual annotations which have been left by users. An annotation is displayed for as long as the timeline scrubber intersects with the red section. In the figure, the timeline scrubber is currently positioned over such an annotation and its content is displayed in the area below the timeline. This control field can also be used to add new annotations or delete the current one. Artists saw this annotation mechanism as a very important feature, as it allows them to tie comments and notes to specific points in time.

The elements below the annotation controls are devoted to an individual audience member's sensor measurements at the current point in the timeline. The table contains one entry for each audience member, while the arrows represent whether the sensor response is currently on the rise, decline or if it stays within a certain threshold. This is meant to give an indication whether the person wearing the sensor is currently getting more engaged with the performance, indicated by a green arrow pointing up, or if, on the other extreme, starts losing interest, which is indicated by a red arrow pointing down.

Figure 2 shows the remaining part of the video page. It contains detailed line charts showing the evolution of the sensor response for the duration of the entire performance. The user can view an individual's response curve by selecting a participant's name in the table in Figure 1. The averaged sensor response of the entire audience is always displayed below that. These line charts double as seek bars, allowing the user to exactly pinpoint a location and see what happening at that specific point in time by clicking on it.

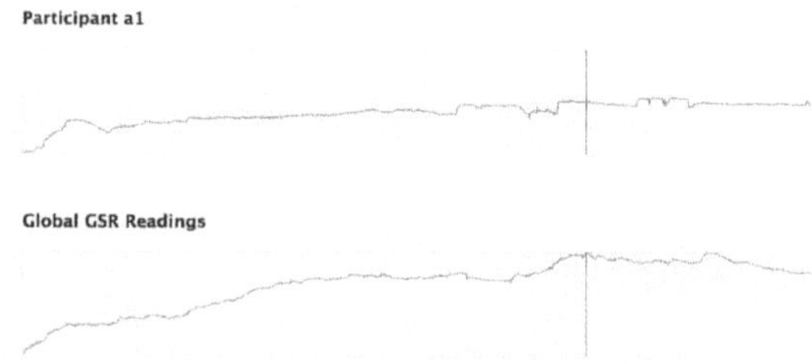

Figure 2: Lower part of the video page, with individual response curve and an average for the whole audience.

3. CONCLUSION

In the evaluation process, we had testers use the application and rate it using CSI, giving an indication about how well it supports the creative process. In the results, the testers rated the factors of *Exploration* and *Collaboration* the highest, which largely coincides with our design goals.

After these tests and more discussions with potential end users, which supplied us with another round of feedback, we were able to conclude that the tool could be a valuable tool for artists to gauge an audience's reaction to a performance in an easy way. More specifically, it gives them a means to see which parts of a performance are perceived well and which parts still might have room for improvement. The annotation system was added with this use case in mind.

Finally, one should also note that even though the example of the application given in this paper displays GSR data, it can be used to visualise any type of sensor data from any number of users, as long as it is quantifiable, i.e. it is comprised of a stream of numbers and can be reasonably displayed on a temporal axis. The application is designed in such a way that it could display data from multiple sources at once, provided that they are in temporal synchrony with video recordings. The example also uses two video recordings, but in practice, the application can support any number of recordings.

While the results from the testers were positive and largely coincided with our expectations, we believe that the tool still requires more real-world testing to really prove its usefulness and collect more valuable feedback to improve user experience, usability and add potential new features.

4. REFERENCES

[1] D. Cabral et al. Evaluation of a multimodal video annotator for contemporary dance. In *Proceedings of the International Working Conference on Advanced Visual Interfaces*, AVI '12, pages 572–579, 2012.

[2] E. Cherry et al. Quantifying the creativity support of digital tools through the creativity support index. *ACM Trans. Comput.-Hum. Interact.*, 21(4):21:1–21:25, 2014.

[3] C. Latulipe et al. Love, hate, arousal and engagement: exploring audience responses to performing arts. In *Proceedings of CHI*, pages 1845–1854, 2011.

[4] C. Wang et al. Sensing a live audience. In *Proceedings of CHI*, CHI '14, pages 1909–1912, 2014.

MPEG-DASH for Low Latency and Hybrid Streaming Services

Jean Le Feuvre, Cyril Concolato, Nassima Bouzakaria, Viet-Thanh-Trung Nguyen
Telecom ParisTech; Institut Mines-Telecom; CNRS LTCI
46, rue Barrault
75013 PARIS, France

{lefeuvre, concolato, bouzakaria, vnguyen}@telecom-parsitech.fr

ABSTRACT
While over-the-top video distribution is now widely deployed, it still suffers from much higher latencies than traditional broadcast, typically from a few seconds up to half a minute. In this paper, we demonstrate a novel DASH system with latency close to broadcast channels, and show how such a system can be used to enable combined broadcast and broadband services while keeping the client buffering requirements on the broadcast link low.

Categories and Subject Descriptors
C.2.4 [**Computer-Communication Networks**]: Distributed Systems – *client/server.*

General Terms
Algorithms, Performance, Experimentation, Standardization.

Keywords
Adaptive Streaming; Hybrid Broadcast Broadband; Low Latency.

1. INTRODUCTION
Video streaming today represents a large fraction of the Internet traffic. Among the streaming methods, HTTP adaptive streaming solutions are the most popular. In particular, the MPEG-DASH (Dynamic Adaptive Streaming over HTTP) standard [1] is foreseen as the future interoperable solution for various types of services, from on demand to live. One of the drawbacks of HTTP adaptive streaming solutions, including of MPEG-DASH, is the associated latency, which can be in the order of tens of seconds when deployed with typical parameters in some systems. Such latency may be acceptable for on demand services but is not acceptable for live events, especially when compared to existing broadcast solutions. This paper describes first the demonstration of open-source software used in the realization of an end-to-end audio/video delivery system using MPEG-DASH. This system is capable of low-latency, in the order of a frame duration (excluding the encoding time), similar to conventional RTP-based streaming. This is unique to the best of the authors' knowledge. Additionally, with such a system, it becomes possible to efficiently combine broadcast services, which can deliver the same content to a large audience with a reasonable latency, together with HTTP adaptive streaming services, which can deliver personalized content to individual users. This demonstration also shows the use of the MPEG-TEMI (Timeline and External Media Information) standard [2] to achieve the combination of MPEG-2 TS-based broadcast services and DASH-based services to offer hybrid broadcast/broadband services, using scalable HEVC videos. Finally, MPEG-DASH live services rely on accurate UTC timing configuration of both server and clients to locate the live edge, using e.g. common NTP servers. The demonstration shows how MPEG-DASH services can be accurately synchronized to broadcast events even if NTP servers are absent.

MM'15, October 26-30, 2015, Brisbane, Australia
ACM 978-1-4503-3459-4/15/10.
http://dx.doi.org/10.1145/2733373.2807977

2. SYSTEM ARCHITECTURE

2.1 Low-latency live DASH streaming

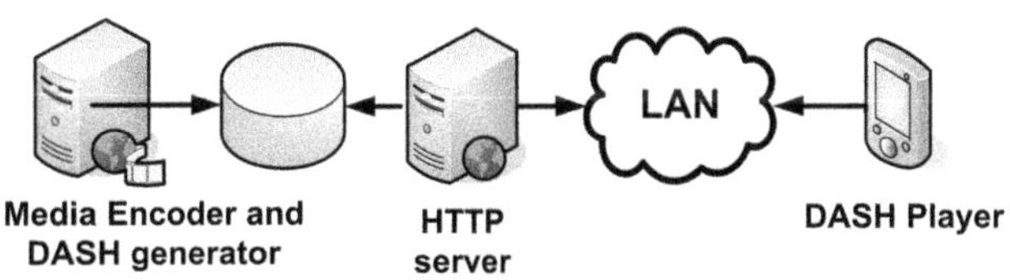

Figure 1 Architecture of the low-latency streaming system

In previous work [3], an analysis of the latency of live streaming services using MPEG-DASH was presented, indicating that the major component inducing latency was the segmentation process. This paper presented a method capable of achieving low latency, as low as frame duration, based on HTTP/1.1 chunked-transfer encoding and on a specific packaging using the ISO Base Media File Format (ISOBMFF) movie fragments. The system, demonstrating such results, is depicted in Figure 1 and composed of the following open-source tools, developed within the GPAC[1] project [4]:

- A live MPEG-DASH encoder, called DashCast. This tool encodes, using FFmpeg[2], raw audio and video frames, captured from a web cam or from screen captures, into multiple MPEG-4 AVC|H.264 and AAC streams of different qualities, and packages them in ISOBMFF compliant media segments. It also produces MPEG-DASH Media Presentation Descriptions (MPD) describing the service. To achieve low latency, the

[1] http://www.gpac.io

[2] http://www.ffmpeg.org

video encoder uses a low-latency coding profile without bidirectional prediction; and segments are flushed to disk and published as small fragments as soon as ready.

- An HTTP/1.1 compliant server[3], written as a NodeJS[4] module, is used to deliver both the MPD and media segments. To achieve low latency, the server detects when new movie fragments are flushed on disk and pushes them immediately using HTTP/1.1 chunked-transfer encoding.
- An MPEG-DASH player, called MP4Client. This tool reads the DASH MPD, selects an appropriate stream quality and fetches the media segments. To achieve low latency, the de-jittering network buffer is configured to a small value. Movie fragments are read progressively and frames from these fragments are dispatched to the decoder immediately.

Different settings are demonstrated for the encoder (group of pictures size), for the client buffer (de-jittering buffer size), and for the packager (movie fragment duration).

2.2 Hybrid Broadcast/Broadband Delivery

Hybrid broadcast/broadband services allow providing additional, personalized content on the broadband channel, synchronized to the mass content delivered over the broadcast channel. One challenge in such hybrid scenario is that typical broadcast channels feature a constant latency, usually lower than HTTP streaming services. Extending broadcast services with HTTP streaming services requires accurately synchronizing data from both channels, possibly at the frame level (e.g. for scalable enhancement) without introducing additional buffers and latency. In our test bed, we observed a delay of 1 to 2 s on a DVB-T2 link fed by IP multicast. Given such delay, with the use of low latency DASH as described previously, i.e. with fragments pushed in typical CDN early, the broadband data can arrive at the receiver before the corresponding broadcast data. This can guarantee a proper synchronization.

When the broadband content to be synchronized with the broadcast is live content, i.e. not entirely available at the beginning of the session, MPEG-DASH requires the use of 'dynamic' MPD, which implies accurate UTC clock sampling at both server and client sides in order to locate the live edge. This requirement may not be always satisfied: different, not accurately synchronized NTP servers may be used by client and servers; or no NTP may be available at the client side. The latest DASH standard specifies that a specific time server may be indicated in the MPD. This approach requires the client to fetch the time information before processing segments, therefore introducing an additional delay. In order to avoid this, in this demonstration, we inject NTP used by the DASH origin server in the broadcast, thereby helping the client find the live edge unambiguously.

In this demonstration, the system depicted in Figure 2 is as follows:

- A low latency MPEG-DASH broadband channel is produced with the system described in Section 2.1, with the exception that the live encoder is replaced by a live simulator. This simulator uses as input an HEVC enhancement layer stored in an MP4 file.
- A broadcast channel is simulated by the use of an IP multicast delivery of an MPEG-2 Transport Stream (TS), generated from the base HEVC layer. The MPEG-2 TS PCR information is randomly initialized at startup to demonstrate synchronization aspects, and enriched with location, i.e. the HTTP URL of the DASH session, and timing information, i.e. UTC and PCR-to-DASH-time mapping, compatible with the TEMI standard.
- A hybrid broadcast/broadband client runs on a separate machine, with inaccurate UTC settings. It uses NTP information from the broadcast stream to locate the live edge despite its clock configuration and plays the video reconstructed from the base and enhancement layers.

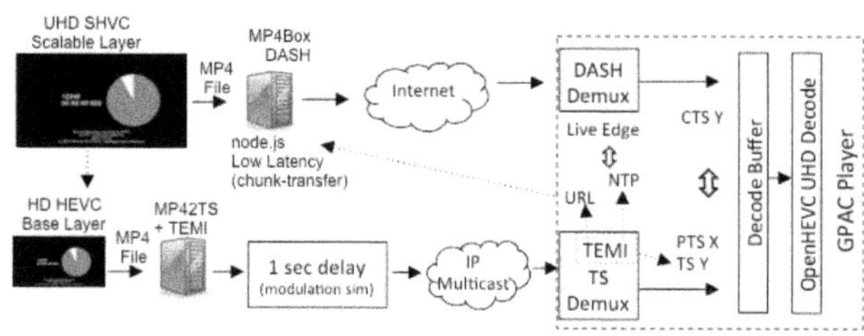

Figure 2 Demonstration of low-latency hybrid broadcast broadband service using MPEG-DASH and MPEG-

Different settings are demonstrated for the low-latency packager (movie fragment duration), for the multicast (propagation delay) and for the client (de-jittering buffer size).

3. CONCLUSION

We demonstrate a unique low latency DASH system for both broadband and hybrid broadcast/broadband delivery chains, based on open source tools and standards. In future works, we plan to extend these tools by enabling live encoding in the hybrid chain.

4. ACKNOWLEDGMENTS

This work is supported by the European Celtic-Plus H2B2VS[5] and 4Ever 2[6] projects funded by the French government.

5. REFERENCES

[1] Stockhammer, T. 2011. Dynamic adaptive streaming over HTTP --: standards and design principles. In Proc. of ACM MMSys '11. pp. 133-144. DOI=10.1145/1943552.1943572

[2] ISO/IEC 13818-1:2015:Amd.2 Timeline and External Media Information

[3] Bouzakaria, N., Concolato, C., & Le Feuvre, J. 2014. Overhead and performance of low latency live streaming using MPEG-DASH. In Proc. of IEEE IISA 2014. pp. 92-97.

[4] Le Feuvre, J, Concolato, C, Dufourd, J-C, Bouqueau, R, and Moissinac, J-C. 2011. Experimenting with multimedia advances using GPAC. In Proc. of ACM MM '11. pp. 715-718. DOI=10.1145/2072298.2072427

[3] https://github.com/gpac/node-gpac-dash

[4] https://nodejs.org/

[5] http://h2b2vs.epfl.ch/

[6] http://www.4ever2-project.com/

eMosic: Mobile Media Pushing through Social Emotion Sensing

Jheng-Wei Peng[a,b,c], Shih-Wei Sun[a,b], Wen-Huang Cheng[c], and Yi-Hsuan Yang[c]
[a]Department of New Media Art, Taipei National University of the Arts, Taiwan
[b]Center for Art and Technology, Taipei National University of the Arts, Taiwan
[c]Research Center for Information Technology Innovation, Academia Sinica, Taiwan
away0421@gmail.com,swsun@newmedia.tnua.edu.tw,{whcheng,yang}@citi.sinica.edu.tw

Keywords

Media pushing, mobile device, face recognition, emotional music, social media

1. INTRODUCTION

Checking the information on a mobile device is a very common behavior in our daily life. Statistically, as reported by [1], users check their smartphones on average 110 times per day. By checking a mobile device, it is lack of displaying the emotion of a user according to an automatic process. In this paper, a media pushing scheme is proposed according to a vision-based emotion sensing to trigger the proposed media pushing services, i.e. the emotional music delivery and the social media visualization.

2. VISION-BASED EMOTION SENSING

As shown from the left of Fig. 1, when a user is using and holding a mobile device, the user's face can be captured from the built-in frontal camera on the mobile device. We applied a principled optimization method [2] to reliably detect a user's face. The positions of the user's eyes, eyebrows, nose, mouth, and the boundary of the users face are applied to determine the expression of a user. Furthermore, the recognized facial expressions are linked to the representative emotion features to trig the proposed media pushing services.

3. EMOTION-BASED MUSIC RETRIEVAL

Following [3], we formulate a regression problem by viewing valence and arousal as real values in [−1, 1]. As Fig. 2 shows, the valence-arousal space provides a ready canvas for visualizing affective terms and for music retrieval. Then two regression models can be trained to predict the VA values, respectively. Given the acoustic features of a song, regression models are employed to learn the mapping between acoustic features to VA values. In our prototype system, we employ the PsySound toolbox (available from http://psysound.wikidot.com/) to compute psychoacoustic features including loudness, sound pressure level, sharpness, dissonance, and tonalness of music, most of which have been found related to emotion perception by psychologists [3]. We train SVR models using a dataset of 60 English Pop songs with VA annotations [3]. After training, the regression models can be applied to any test song. As shown in the middle of Fig. 1, the recognized emotion feature from the detected face is used for emotion-based music retrieval.

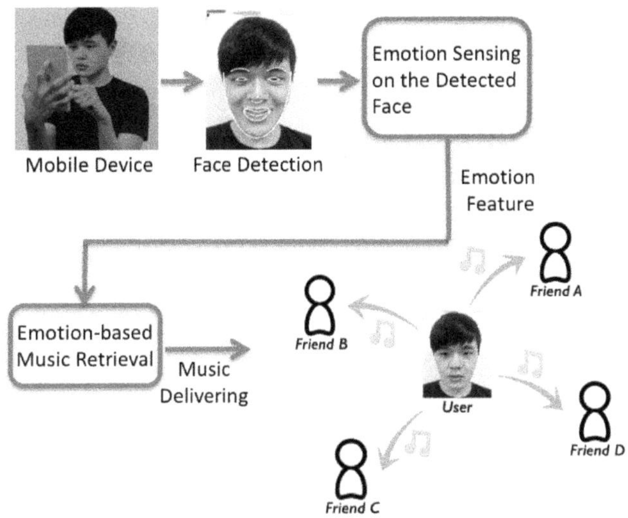

Figure 1: Overview of the proposed media pushing services to push the emotional media to a user.

4. MEDIA PUSHING SERVICES

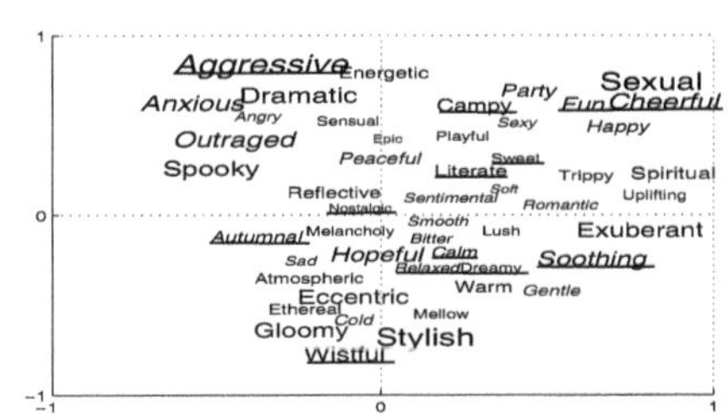

Figure 2: Tag cloud of affective terms deployed over the valence-arousal emotion space.

MM'15, October 26–30, 2015, Brisbane, Australia.
ACM 978-1-4503-3459-4/15/10.
DOI: http://dx.doi.org/10.1145/2733373.2807979.

As shown by the right-most part of Fig. 1, the recognized emotion belonging to the user is utilized to trigger the music retrieval process from a local/cloud-based music database. The retrieved music with the corresponding emotion of the user is pushed to the social members (friends) of the user. First, an audio pushing service is enabled by applying [3]'s method on music emotion recognition, which employs a hybrid set of energy, rhythm, timbre and tonal descriptors of music to characterize the affective content of a musical piece on the valence-arousal two-dimensional emotion space. As there is a one-to-one mapping between the four facial expressions and the four quadrants of the emotion space, in our implementation we randomly select a song with the sensed emotion of a user. On the other hand, the face recognition result from the built-in camera can authenticate the user's identity, connect and push the media to the user from a social service, e.g. music file on iTunes in the local/cloud space.

5. IMPLEMENTATION

In our current implementation, the face detection process is executed on a mobile device. When a user is using a mobile device, as shown in Fig. 3 (a), to browse the online information, the proposed eMosic is background executed, as conceptually shown in Fig. 3 (b). The relative positions of the eyes, eyebrows, nose, mouth, and the facial boundary is detected by the white lines depicted in Fig. 3 (c). On the other hand, the retrieved music is depicted by the white point in the emotional space in Fig. 3 (d). We should notice that, the face detection, expression recognition, and music clustering processes are background executed.

When another user is using a mobile device (the tablet on the right of Fig. 4 (a)) to listen to music, the music information of the tablet is shown on the screen of the mobile device. When the emotion of the social member (friend of the user) is recognized, the retrieved music with the corresponding emotion belonging to the social member is pushed to the user, as shown by the yellow banner in Fig. 4 (b). At the same time, if the user is interested in the social member, by checking the detail of the yellow banner on the top, the detail information about the emotion of the social member is displayed on the screen, as shown in Fig. 4 (c).

In our user study, by setting the installation in a tech-art gallery, the expression recognition rate is about 80% from 20 user's testing for four different emotions: happy, angry, sad, and relaxing, as shown in Fig. 3 (e). Most of the users are attracted by proposed media pushing experience from the facial expression recognition.

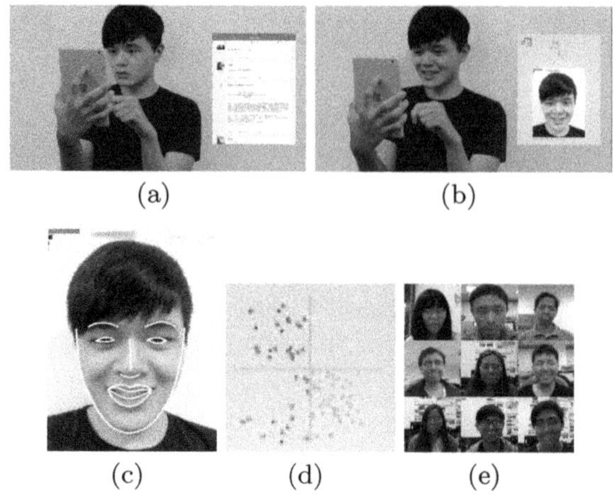

Figure 3: The emotion sensing scenario: (a) when a user is web surfing on a mobile device, (b) the proposed eMosic is background sensing the user's emotion from a mobile device, (c) the detected face expression from the built-in camera on a mobile device, (d) the pushed and retrieved music in the emotional space, and (e) the detected relative positions of the eyes, eyebrows, nose, mouth, and face boudaries of the users.

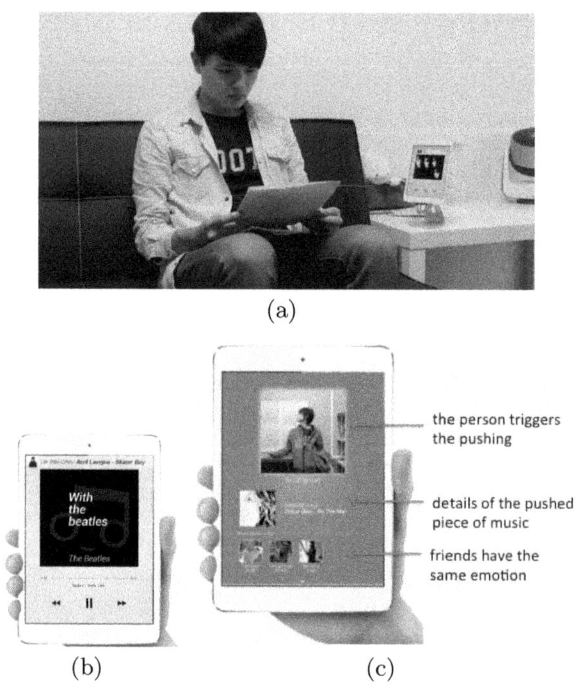

Figure 4: The media pushing scenario: (a) a user using a mobile device listening to music, (b) the pushed emotional music (yellow banner) from the friend belonging to the user in the same social network, and (c) the detail information of the pushed music.

6. REFERENCES

[1] S. Chu. *http://www.idigitaltimes.com/articles/20259/20131008/checkphone-locket-app-data-users-smartphone.htm*.

[2] J. M. Saragih, S. Lucey, and J. F. Cohn. Face alignment through subspace constrained mean-shifts. In *ICCV*, 2009.

[3] Y.-H. Yang and H. H. Chen. *Music Emotion Recognition*. CRC Press, 2011.

PITAGORA: Recommending Users and Local Experts in an Airport Social Network

Andrea Ferracani, Daniele Pezzatini, Andrea Benericetti, Marco Guiducci, Alberto Del Bimbo
Università degli Studi di Firenze - MICC
Firenze, Italy
[name.surname]@unifi.it

ABSTRACT

In this demo we present PITAGORA[1]: a mobile web contextual social network designed for the check-in area of an airport. The app provides recommendation of potential friends, local experts and targeted services. Recommendation is hybrid and combines social media analysis and collaborative filtering techniques. Users' recommendation has been evaluated through a user study with good results.

Categories and Subject Descriptors

H.3.1 [**Information Storage and Retrieval**]: Content Analysis And Indexing; H.5.m [**Information Storage and Retrieval**]: Information Interfaces And Presentation—*Miscellaneous*

General Terms

Experimentation, Contextual Social Networking, Mobile Web Application

Keywords

Social Media Analysis, User Profiling, Local Experts Recommendation, Users Recommendation

1. MOTIVATIONS AND PREVIOUS WORK

Knowledge extracted from online social networks (e.g. Facebook and LinkedIn), combined with information about users' location, can be exploited to build more targeted contextual services, such as recommendation of people and facilities.
In this demo we present PITAGORA, a mobile social network which exploits analysis of social media to provide friend and local experts recommendation in the check-in area of an airport. The proposed analysis techniques and recommendation approaches can be applied also in other domains where social applications may be used to offer contextual services.

[1]Demo video available at http://bit.ly/1GgtUrN

ACM Multimedia '15 Brisbane, Australia
ACM 978-1-4503-3459-4/15/10.
DOI: http://dx.doi.org/10.1145/2733373.2807980.

In the check-in area of an airport people basically have little time but also the opportunity to get in touch with other people. Usually, passengers are in airports for business or leisure and, in both cases, it has been demonstrated that they are more open to social interactions than usual [1]. In this context, recommendation systems and interfaces can be really valuable provided you take into account the motivations and needs of users temporary co-located in the same place. In the case of an airport check-in area, for example, the passenger's destination and the reason of the travel (professional or not) can be essential infos to improve general-purpose recommenders.

Section 2 describes the social network and gives insights on the user interface (Section. 2.1) and the two main recommendation modules: friends prediction in Section 2.2 and local experts suggestion in Section 2.3. Recommender evaluation is conducted in Section 3.

2. THE SOCIAL NETWORK

PITAGORA has been developed as a mobile web application available in the check-in area of an airport. The goal of the application is to improve passengers experience providing an enhanced people recommender by exploiting situational information. The application allows the user to search and display flight infos, to check the presence of passengers on his same flight and to communicate with them through a realtime chat. Recommendations are mainly constituted by suggestions of other users who share the same interests. Users are also provided with a recommendation of local experts, present at the airport, on the basis of their flight destination. The system uses an hybrid approach to the recommendation problem combining content-based and collaborative filtering. As well-known in literature hybrid approaches give better results solving issues related to the large amount and the sparsity of the data.

2.1 User Interface

The user interface is composed by two main views: 1) a search view and a 2) browsing view. At the first access the user is provided with an autosuggest search input which allows to identify his/her own flight. Once the user has selected the flight, the interface proposes a sliding menu based panel (i.e. browsing view) organised in several sections: 1) profile: it displays flight infos, allows to login with both Facebook and LinkedIn and provides recommendation of destination-based local experts; 2) leisure: it provides recommendation of users weighting more Facebook data; 3) professional: it provides recommendation of users weighting more LinkedIn data; 4) chat: it allows to chat in realtime; 5) search flight: it can be used to go back to the search view. Recommendations are shown as lists of records which behave as an accordion: each item can be expanded to show things in common between users: demographic info, Facebook 'likes' (leisure), connections, groups and companies followed (professional). Users can be ordered by similarity or organised visually with a taxonomy of categories. Leisure recommendations contemplate also retails in the airport semantically matching user interests (e.g. liquor store if the user likes dry gin and tequila). Contextual retail suggestions can be exploited by the user in the chat to invite other users for dating.

2.2 Data Analysis and Users' Recommendation

Users are profiled analysing data extracted from Facebook and LinkedIn accounts. The different nature of this data is exploited in order to obtain recommendations concerning leisure (Facebook) and professional aspects (LinkedIn). When the user logs into the system the following data are extracted: *a*) demographic infos, connections, level of education, job history (Facebook and LinkedIn); *b*) page 'likes', photo albums (Facebook) *c*) groups and companies followed (LinkedIn). Profiles are described as vectors of pages on which users have expressed a 'like' and groups or companies followed. In order to solve the sparsity problem, a co-occurrence matrix is used to infer additional possible resources of interests. Users' recommendation is then achieved with a standard user-based algorithm considering the distribution of user's interests and computing a nearest-N users' neighbourhood with the Euclidean distance. Sparsity reduction is performed offline, using an item-based algorithm. Demographic data and professional history infos are used to adjust features' intra-weights for recommendation. Performance of the users' recommender is evaluated in Section 3.

2.3 Local Experts Recommendation

The goal of the local experts recommender is to suggest users that have an high level of travel experience about the flight city or region destination. The identification of local experts is obtained through the analysis of social media extracted from Facebook. In particular, user travels and location history are computed analysing geo-tagged pictures: travels are identified considering photos and photo albums metadata, birthplaces and places of residence and exploited to produce destination-based recommendations.
The proposed method for local experts estimation builds upon some approaches [2] where human location history is exploited to recommend points of interests in geographical areas: count of city visits, social media analysis, user activity in the social network and cities' correlation are used in PITAGORA to estimate the user travel experience per city. Given a set of users U and a set of visited cities C, a matrix V is defined where the item v_{ij} of V represents how many times the user u_i has visited the city c_j. Visited cities are computed by analysing data from Facebook, as stated above, but to reduce the sparsity problem also data from user's activity in the social network is exploited: selections of flight destinations are considered as visits. The travel experience E of users is calculated iteratively on the basis of the number of travels in cities as follows: $E_n = E_{n-1} \cdot V \cdot V^T$. E_n indicates the vector E at the n iteration that is initialised with $E_0 = (1, 1, \cdots, 1)$. The vector E is then normalised, dividing by its highest value. The correlation $CORR(c_i, c_j)$ between two cities c_i and c_j is expressed as $CORR(c_i, c_j) = \sum_{u_k \in U'} \alpha * e_k$. U' represents the group of users who has visited both c_i and c_j, e_k is the component of E relative to the user u_k. The weight factor α, with $0 < \alpha \leq 1$ is defined taking into account the Euclidean distance between latitude and longitude of the two cities. Finally, we compute the level of experience of a user u for a given city c. To this end, we define n_k as the number of visits of the user u in the city c_k, based on previous activity on the network (i.e. previous flight destinations). In addition the number of geo-tagged photos p_k that the user has published in c_k is extracted from Facebook. On this basis a rating $exp_{u,c}$ can be assigned to a user for a city as $exp_{u,c} = \sum_{k=0}^{|C|} (1 + p_k) * n_k * CORR(c, c_k)$. Furthermore, if a user lives (or has lived) in c or if she had educational/professional experiences in the city a *bonus* to the rating $exp_{u,c}$ is given. Local experts whose score is greater than a threshold are shown as a list of recommendation, in descending order, in a dedicated view.

3. EVALUATION

The proposed users' recommendation system is based on the ranking of user similarities and can be seen as an information retrieval system, considering a user as a query term. To evaluate the relevance of the recommendations the normalised Cumulative Discounted Gain (nDCG) measure has been used. Relevance scores are computed comparing the list of recommended users with the ideal list given by the user. The ground truth has been collected asking 150 users to express a relevance score (on a 0 to 3 scale) for the first J people suggested by the system. In this experiment, a logarithm with base 2 is used to ensure all positions are discounted. The nDCG for the top-J item results in values of 0.767 with j=5 and 0.872 for j=10.

4. CONCLUSIONS

In this demo we present PITAGORA, a mobile airport social network featuring users' recommendation and suggestion of local experts. Novel approaches are proposed which take into account profiling techniques from social media analysis (e.g. Facebook and LinkedIn) and inferred ratings for users' neighbourhood detection and identification. An evaluation of the effectiveness of the solutions is provided through a user study based on the nDCG measure which shows good results.

5. ACKNOWLEDGMENTS

PITAGORA - Innovative technologies and processes for Airport Management R&D project was supported by the Regional Government of Tuscany (POR CReO - Bando Unico R&S 2012) and the European Regional Development Fund.

6. REFERENCES

[1] Z. Rubin. Disclosing oneself to a stranger: Reciprocity and its limits. *Journal of Experimental Social Psychology*, 11(3):233 – 260, 1975.
[2] Y. Zheng, L. Zhang, X. Xie, and W.-Y. Ma. Mining correlation between locations using human location history. In *Proceedings of the 17th ACM SIGSPATIAL International Conference on Advances in Geographic Information Systems*, GIS '09, pages 472–475, New York, NY, USA, 2009. ACM.

A System for Video Recommendation using Visual Saliency, Crowdsourced and Automatic Annotations

Andrea Ferracani, Daniele Pezzatini, Marco Bertini
Saverio Meucci, Alberto Del Bimbo
Università degli Studi di Firenze - MICC
[name.surname]@unifi.it

ABSTRACT

In this paper we present a system for content-based video recommendation that exploits visual saliency to better represent video features and content[1]. Visual saliency is used to select relevant frames to be presented in a web-based interface to tag and annotate video frames in a social network; it is also employed to summarize video content to create a more effective video representation used in the recommender system. The system exploits automatic annotations from CNN-based classifiers on salient frames and user generated annotations. We evaluate several baseline approaches and show how the proposed method improves over them.

Categories and Subject Descriptors

H.3.5 [**Information Storage and Retrieval**]: Online Information Services; H.4 [**Information Systems Applications**]: Miscellaneous

General Terms

Algorithms, Design, Experimentation

Keywords

Social video tagging, automatic video tagging, item-based video recommendation, visual saliency

1. INTRODUCTION

A typical item-based video recommender builds its prediction model considering user preferences for videos, expressed as ratings, and suggests potentially interesting videos comparing distributions of such ratings. The proposed system adopts an hybrid approach in which a brief but comprehensive representation of video content, derived from video analysis and concepts extraction from user activity can improve the performance of a standard recommender based on collaborative filtering (i.e. using ratings).

Video recommendation can drive users to watch other videos, much more than direct searching for new videos, as shown in [5]. The approaches presented in the scientific literature are typically based on textual analysis of the metadata that accompany a video, that is sometimes complemented by some multimedia content analysis. The YouTube recommendation system, described in [1], uses two broad classes of data: *i)* content data, such as the raw video streams and video metadata such as title, description etc., and *ii)* user activity data, either explicit (e.g. video rating/liking) and implicit (watching a video for a long time).

2. THE SYSTEM

The architecture of our system has been implemented in a beta version of a social network that exploits user profiling techniques to propose to the user targeted recommendations of videos, topic of interests and similar users in the network. This is achieved initially by analysing data from other online profiles (i.e. Facebook) and then tracking user's activities on the social network, like number of video views, click-through data, video annotation and rating. Users can share and annotate videos at frame level using concepts derived from Wikipedia. All these concepts are clustered in 54 categories using Fuzzy K-Means in a two-levels taxonomy of interests (12 macro and 42 micro-categories such as Music and Jazz music, inspired by the taxonomy of Vimeo) and classified using a semantic distance [2] with a nearest neighbour approach. All the resources categorised in videos are then used to build a vector describing video content exploited in the recommender.

Video analysis is performed to improve the interaction of users with the system, and to obtain content-based representation of videos, in order to compute the recommendation. Automatic video annotations are extracted using a classifier which exploits convolutional neural networks (CNN) on most salient frames. Automatic annotations are categorised using the semantic relatedness measure weighted according to the confidence returned by the classifier. Fig. 1 shows an overview of the workflow used to collect and annotate videos.

Visual saliency. Visual saliency is used *i)* at the interface level to propose to the users possible frames of interest through a carousel above the video player, to ease the addition of comments and annotations; *ii)* at the automatic annotation level to reduce the computational cost of processing all the frames. Videos are preprocessed to eliminate letterboxing, then visual saliency maps, computed with the iLab Neuromorphic Toolkit [3], are extracted for all the frames of a video. The salient frames to be used in the system interface are selected by identifying the peaks of salience of

[1]Demo video available at http://bit.ly/1FYloeQ

MM'15, October 26–30, 2015, Brisbane, Australia.
ACM 978-1-4503-3459-4/15/10.
DOI: http://dx.doi.org/10.1145/2733373.2807982.

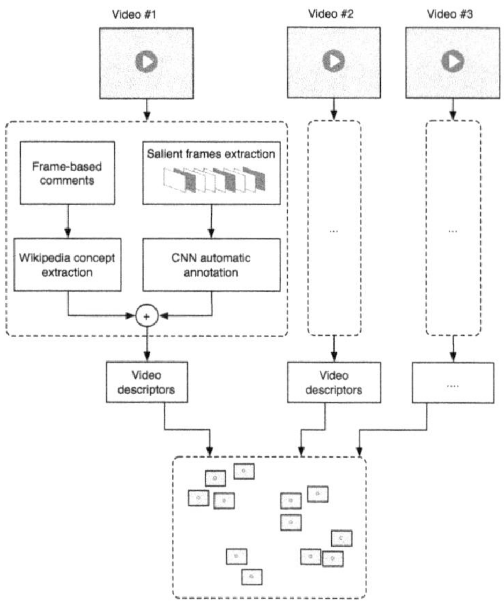

Figure 1: System overview: manual annotation, automatic video content analysis and representation.

the video using the crest detection algorithm proposed in [4]. The frames used in automatic annotation are selected computing the average saliency of the video and choosing those above the average, to have a denser sampling of video content.

Crowdsourced annotations. Users can comment videos at frame level and can add semantic references to Wikipedia entities in comments using an autosuggest widget. A carousel of the most salient frames is also shown above the video player as a video summary (see Fig. 2). Users can click on an image in the carousel and jump directly to the correspondent frame in the video at the exact timecode, to facilitate fast and accurate annotations.

A vector of categories C, with dimension equal to the number of categories of the taxonomy, is used to represent video content according to the comments of the users. Each category is assigned with a weight which indicates the affinity between category and video contents. C is defined by calculating for each category the average of the semantic distance of each annotation to the categories of the taxonomy. This semantic relatedness between the terms is obtained using the Web Link Based Measure [2].

Figure 2: Frame selection from the salient frames carousel.

Visual features. In the proposed system video frames are subsampled according to their visual saliency, considering that visual saliency allows to make a targeted selection of these frames, allowing the system to scale while maintaining a reasonably dense sampling of video content. The convolutional network implemented uses the LibCCV[2] library, and it is trained on the ImageNet ILSVRC 2014 dataset to detect 1000 synsets. Video content is represented using a Bag-of-words approach, applied to the 1,000 synsets, selecting for each video the probabilities that obtained a score above a predefined threshold.

Recommender. The recommender implements an item-based collaborative filtering that builds an item-item matrix determining similarity relationships between pairs of items. Then the recommendation step uses the most similar items to a user's already-rated items to generate a list of recommendations. Videos are represented using a feature vector that concatenates the histogram of the categories of the manual comments and the BoW description obtained using the CNN classifier on most salient frames. User's general rating on a video is built combining explicit and implicit activity on the content itself. Users can explicitly vote a video on a 5 point scale through a visual widget. At the same time, implicit rating is computed taking into account number of visualizations, frame browsing and comments added to every video.

A dataset has been collected by hiring 812 workers from the Microworkers web site, and asking them to use the system to upload their favorite videos, annotate and comment some shots that were more interesting to them and to provide ratings for some videos. The dataset is composed by 632 videos, of which 468 were annotated with 1956 comments and 1802 annotations. 613 videos were rated by 950 of 1059 total network users. Comparing the performance of the system, in terms of Root Mean Square Error (RMSE), with a standard item-based recommender implemented in Apache Mahout shows an improvement of $\sim 26\%$.

3. CONCLUSIONS

In this paper we have presented a system that performs item-based video recommendation using a content based description of videos obtained from crowdsourced and automatic annotations. Visual saliency is exploited to present the most relevant frames to the users and to reduce the number of frames to be processed. Experiments show that the proposed method improves over the standard implementation of an item-based algorithm.

References

[1] J. Davidson, B. Liebald, J. Liu, P. Nandy, T. Van Vleet, U. Gargi, S. Gupta, Y. He, M. Lambert, B. Livingston, and D. Sampath. The YouTube video recommendation system. In *Proc. of ACM RecSys*, 2010.

[2] D. Milne and I. H. Witten. Learning to link with Wikipedia. In *Proc. of ACM CIKM*, 2008.

[3] V. Navalpakkam and L. Itti. Modeling the influence of task on attention. *Vision Research*, 45(2), 2005.

[4] Z. Wang, J. Yu, Y. He, and T. Guan. Affection arousal based highlight extraction for soccer video. *Multimedia Tools and Applications*, 73(1), 2014.

[5] R. Zhou, S. Khemmarat, and L. Gao. The impact of YouTube recommendation system on video views. In *Proc. of ACM SIGCOMM IMC*, 2010.

[2]http://libccv.org/

A Semantic Geo-Tagged Multimedia-Based Routing in a Crowdsourced Big Data Environment

Faizan Ur Rehman[1, 2], Ahmed Lbath[1], Abdullah Murad[2, 3], Md. Abdur Rahman[2, 4], Bilal Sadiq[2], Akhlaq Ahmad[2, 5], Ahmad Qamar[2, 6], Saleh Basalamah[2, 4]

[1]Department of Computer Science, LIG, University of Grenoble Alpes, France, {[2]KACST GIS Technology Innovation Center, [3]Innovation and Entrepreneurship Institute, [4]College of Computer and Information Systems}, Umm Al-Qura University, Saudi Arabia, [5]KICT, International Islamic University Malaysia, [6] University Sains Malaysia

{faizan.ur-rehman, ahmed.lbath}@imag.fr, {aamurad, marahman, rmsadiq, aajee, amqamar, smbasalamah}@uqu.edu.sa

ABSTRACT

Traditional routing algorithms for calculating the fastest or shortest path become ineffective or difficult to use when both source and destination are dynamic or unknown. To solve the problem, we propose a novel semantic routing system that leverages geo-tagged rich crowdsourced multimedia information such as images, audio, video and text to add semantics to the conventional routing. Our proposed system includes a Semantic Multimedia Routing Algorithm (SMRA) that uses an indexed spatial big data environment to answer multimedia spatio-temporal queries in real-time. The results are customized to the users' smartphone bandwidth and resolution requirements. The system has been designed to be able to handle a very large number of multimedia spatio-temporal requests at any given moment. A proof of concept of the system will be demonstrated through two scenarios. These are 1) multimedia enhanced routing and 2) finding lost individuals in a large crowd using multimedia. We plan to test the system's performance and usability during Hajj 2015, where over four million pilgrims from all over the world gather to perform their rituals.

Categories and Subject Descriptors

H.2.8 [**Database Applications**]: Spatial databases and GIS
H.2.4 [**Information Systems**]: Query Processing

General Terms

Design, Algorithms.

Keywords

Crowdsourcing, Geo-Tagged Multimedia, Semantic Multimedia Routing, Spatio-temporal Multimedia Queries.

1. INTRODUCTION

Hajj poses a unique challenge to existing routing applications due to the fact that more than 4 million pilgrims with diversity in language, level of education, and culture come to Makkah city mostly for the first time with limited or no prior knowledge of using routing through smartphone [1]. Hence, finding lost individuals or POIs in such a large crowd poses a great difficulty for pilgrims, event organizers, ministries, governments, health industries, emergency departments, and family members. The recent advancements in technologies have contributed in making the high-speed network more available and the location and multimedia enabled smartphones more accessible. As a result, the number of pilgrims sharing geo-tagged multimedia data, which carries semantics, have increased manifold, making crowdsourcing a reality. We argue that adding semantics in routing with the help of multimedia could make it easier for pilgrims with limited or no prior experience of map-based routing techniques to find each other and locate POIs.

In this context, we present a novel semantic multimedia enabled routing mechanism to display routes that is easy to understand and can be used by most users. The system also provides constraint and context-aware multimedia information for POI exploring service. This will further help users to know the semantics of route with respect to their current location in real-time. For example, in case a user submits a query for a hotel, the system will show live results from all the nearby hotels with dynamic information such as vacancies, charges, images of nearby landmarks, available public and private parking with images, customer reviews and traffic constraints.

Although geo-tagged multimedia has been used in many scenarios in the past but none has used in the field of adding semantics to routing. For example, in [2], the authors have used geo-tagged tweets to identify traffic constraints such as accidents and roadblocks whereas in [3] the authors have used a semantic algorithm to recommend interested POIs based on data collected from Foursquare and Instagram. Our system stands out from [2, 3] in that it 1) collects the source and destination of the route from the geo-tagged multimedia information submitted in real-time for route discovery 2) shows the publicly available POIs with multimedia associated with it within a certain radius of the calculated route to semantically help the user(s) and 3) indexes the different types of multimedia data separately in a spatial big data repository for an efficient real-time retrieval. Moreover, we have enhanced the indexing method [4] to support different types of real-time multimedia data with high arrival rates.

2. HIGH-LEVEL ARCHITECTURE

Figure 1 shows the high-level architecture of the system. The system augments multimedia element to conventional routing using SMRA. Apart from the aggregated geo-tagged multimedia data, the system uses road network represented as graph G = (N, E) where N and E are the nodes and edges respectively for calculating the route. We divide the spatial area into cells; each

MM'15, October 26-30, 2015, Brisbane, Australia
ACM 978-1-4503-3459-4/15/10.
http://dx.doi.org/10.1145/2733373.2807985

cell is of size (one latitude degree * one longitude degree), using a grid approach for efficient retrieval of multimedia data and traffic constraints. Constraints include user choice, accidents and roadblocks. The system aggregates both the publicly available geo-tagged data from social media (crowdsourced data) such as Twitter, Flickr, Instagram and destination, metadata of the multimedia, date and time, and multimedia payload including audio, video, image, text, location, time and user profile.

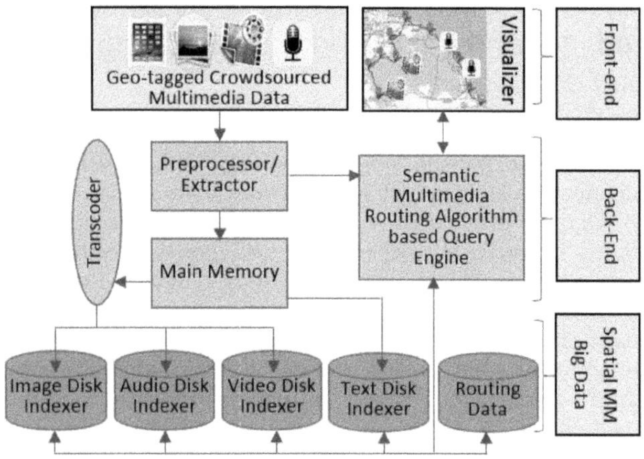

Figure 1. High-level architecture

The preprocessor receives the crowdsourced multimedia data for extracting the location of user and media and input data for spatio-temporal queries (see Figure 2(B)), which is forwarded to the query engine and main memory respectively. Then, the system preprocesses the data and index in the main memory temporarily to answer the fast retrieval of recent data. Based on a predefined threshold value, a flushing process moves data from the main memory to the Spatial Multimedia Big Data repository, where we employ multiple indexers for each type of geo-tagged multimedia data that are stored in big data repository and indexed based on location and meta-data. Each multimedia data is labeled with nearby edge ID and cell ID. The Transcoder transforms the multimedia data in different resolutions to support diversified user bandwidth and resolution and finally stores the original and transcoded media in the Spatial Multimedia Big Data. SMRA based Query engine processes the spatio-temporal queries by fetching the routing information, user constraint such as bandwidth and resolution, media preference and data type etc. from the preprocessor, generates dynamic route, augments geo-tagged media with appropriate resolution and shares the resultant route to the visualization interface (see **Figure 3**). Visualizer displays the results of multimedia enhanced spatio-temporal queries on a map, both online and offline.

3. DEMONSTRATION SCENARIOS

To validate our approach, we developed a prototype based on twitter data as social media and user generated data through our developed smartphone application for Saudi Arabia. The following two scenarios were selected to demonstrate the system's capability.

Scenario-1 Multimedia enhanced routing: It add semantics to the traditional routing to make it more effective in helping users, for example, in a simple navigation scenario such as "take a right turn after the Radisson Hotel" would be more effective if an image of the hotel were also displayed. In this scenario, the system displays the geo-tagged multimedia data along with the conventional route using the query pseudo code shown in **Figure 2** and the corresponding visualization is shown in **Figure 3(A)**. As shown in **Figure 2**, we extend the traditional routing by adding several semantical elements into it (see **Figure 2(B)**) such as type and source of media, types of POIs, and temporal range.

```
SELECT * FROM mmData JOIN
  ((SELECT * FROM shortest_path(          <-[A]        [B]->
      ……………))
AS route ON mmData.gid = route.gid
Where (mmData.msgType = 'Image' or mmData.msgType =
'Text') and (mmData.source = 'Twitter' or mmData.source =
'OwnApp') and (mmData.poiType = 'SuperMarket' or
mmData.poiType = 'Restaurant') and mmData.date >=
'2015/05/25';
```

Figure 2. A) Conventional shortest path query and B) spatio-temporal query operator to support multimedia enhanced routing

Scenario-2 Finding lost individuals in a large crowd using multimedia: In this scenario, users can share just geo-tagged multimedia data with each other and the system extracts the locations from that geo-tagged data and provides multimedia aided navigation as shown in **Figure 3(B)**.

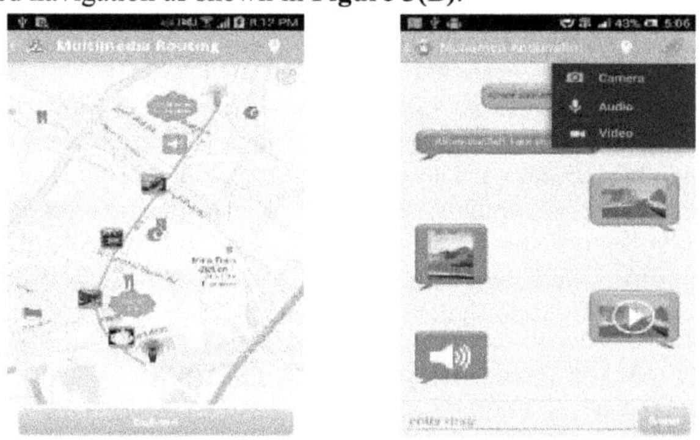

(A) (B)

Figure 3. Scenarios where multimedia is used to add semantics A) multimedia enhanced routing and B) finding lost individuals

4. ACKNOWLEDGMENT

This project was fully supported by the NSTIP strategic technologies program (11-INF1683-10, 11-INF1700-10 and 13-INF2455-10) in the Kingdom of Saudi Arabia.

5. REFERENCES

[1] A. Ahmad et al. A Framework for Crowd-Sourced Data Collection and Context-Aware Services in Hajj and Umrah. IEEE/ACS 11th International Confserence on Computer Systems and Applications (AICCSA), pp.405-412, November 2014.

[2] F. U. Rehman et al. Toward dynamic path recommender system based on social network data. Proc. 7th ACM SIGSPATIAL, IWCTS '14, pp. 64–69, November 2014.

[3] X. Wang et al. Semantic-Based Location Recommendation With Multimodal Venue Semantics. Multimedia, IEEE Transactions, vol.17, no.3, pp. 409,419, March 2015.

[4] A. Magdy et al. Taghreed: a system for querying, analyzing, and visualizing geotagged microblogs. Proc. 22nd ACM SIGSPATIAL, 163-172, November 2014.

Crowdsourced Multimedia Enhanced Spatio-temporal Constraint Based on-Demand Social Network for Group Mobility

Bilal Sadiq[1], Md. Abdur Rahman[1, 2], Abdullah Murad[1, 3], Muhammad Shahid[4], Faizan Ur Rehman[1, 5], Ahmed Lbath[5], Akhlaq Ahmad[6, 7], Ahmad Qamar[2, 8],
{[1]KACST GIS Technology Innovation Center, [2]College of Computer and Information Systems, [3]Innovation and Entrepreneurship Institute, [6]College of Engineering and Islamic Architecture} Umm Al-Qura University, Saudi Arabia, [4]Ministry of Science and Technology, Pakistan,[5]Department of Computer Science, LIG, University of Grenoble Alpes, France, [7]KICT, International Islamic University, Malaysia, [8]University Sains Malaysia
bsadiq@gistic.org, {faizan.ur-rehman, ahmed.lbath}@imag.fr, toujoursaami@yahoo.com, {marahman, aajee, aamurad, amqamar}@uqu.edu.sa

ABSTRACT
This paper presents a system that enables efficient and scalable real-time user and vehicle discovery using textual, audio and video mechanisms. The system allows users to group together for shared intra-city transportation with the aid of multimedia that helps individuals to 1) find community of common interest (CoCI), 2) locate individual users in a large crowd and 3) locate vehicles for mobility in an efficient and cost effective manner. The system is a pilot project and will be deployed during Hajj 2015 when over three million pilgrims from all over the world visit Makkah, Saudi Arabia.

Categories and Subject Descriptors
H.5.1 [Multimedia Information Systems];

H.3 [Information Storage and Retrieval]: Content Analysis and indexing

General Terms
Design; Human Factors

Keywords
Taxi Services; Smart City, Crowdsourcing, Group Mobility

1. INTRODUCTION
Millions of Muslims from all over the world gather to perform Hajj in Makkah, Saudi Arabia every year. To perform the Hajj rituals, which comprise of several spatio-temporal activities, such as stay in Arafat area on the 9th day of the 12th month of the Hijri calendar from noon to sunset, the whole crowd has to move from one location to another within a certain time under multiple resource constraints such as number of available vehicles and free seats, etc. To provide cost effective rides to users is challenging to efficiently utilize transportation resources with respect to increase in demand. Besides mobility, the other challenge is to efficiently and effectively form a community of common interest (CoCI) on an ad-hoc basis, which requires the satisfaction of several constraints for group mobility due to unfamiliar environment, old age people, language barrier, fear of travelling alone, lack of knowledge about roads and surrounding areas and ambiguous travel plans. Similar scenarios may arise in other situations such as tourism, Olympic Games, tournaments, Kumbh Mela, etc.

To address the ensuing challenges in such foreign environments, we have devised a multimedia based system that allows users to search places of interest and announce them within a huge crowd to find and create social network of CoCI. In order to form the CoCI, users can share and locate each other using text, images, audio and video. Users can also share their constraints such as maximum fare that they can afford, time of traveling, pick up point, language or company preference, etc. Once a CoCI is formed, the system allows broadcasting the constraints along with multimedia information such as location, images of persons and surroundings, etc., with the taxi drivers in a certain geo-zone [5]. Moreover, taxi owners within the geo-zone can respond to the group with multimedia information [3] such as image of the taxi and driver, number plate, make and model, etc. In case the CoCI wants to meet at a certain place, the system allows them to share their geo-tagged multimedia information for efficient rendezvous point discovery and share with the vehicle owner. The system also allows the vehicle owner to share real-time location with CoCI.

A large crowd moving in a tight spatio-temporal zone can generate a huge amount of data. To efficiently store, retrieve and visualize this real-time multimedia data for assisting in group mobility scenarios, we have devised a system architecture that digests the high arrival rate of huge crowdsourced geo-tagged multimedia data and manages it using a big data repository[4]. This system is envisioned to help city planners in evacuating a very large crowd under multiple spatio-temporal constraints [1].

MM'15, October 26-30, 2015, Brisbane, Australia
ACM 978-1-4503-3459-4/15/10.
http://dx.doi.org/10.1145/2733373.2807986

2. HIGH-LEVEL ARCHITECTURE
Figure 1 shows the high-level architecture of our proposed system. The **Client Layer** generates the real-time multimedia and sensory data from smartphones and vehicles respectively that is passed to the **API Server Layer**. The **API Server Layer** consists of several components to manage and process data between **Client** and **Big Data Layer** as illustrated. The **Big Data Layer**

addresses efficient data storage, retrieval, recovery, and indexing requirements by extending the architecture presented in [2]. The **Indexer** digests high arrival rates of data and efficiently creates the search space within the **main memory**. The **query optimizer** receives user requests and generates an optimized query plan in order to hit the system indexes efficiently and delivers the complete plan to the query processor to execute. The **recovery manager** serves as a triple-redundancy model for supporting main-memory contents. Whenever there is memory crash, the system is restore using the backup copies from the permanent memory. To support complex and real-time user query and diversified high volume data arrival rates of multimedia data, **relational, in memory** and **HDFS** as NoSQL databases are used.

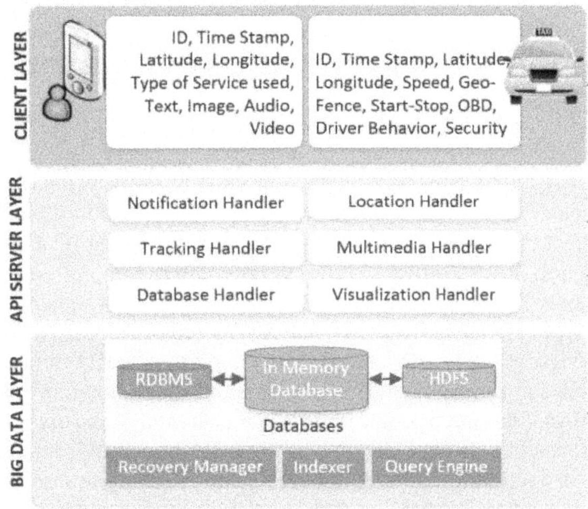

Figure 1. System architecture to support multimedia for group mobility

The client application is being implemented in terms of Android app, which communicates with the **API Server** through the REST API's. The **API server** consists of several services, such as **Notification Handler,** which is responsible to broadcast notification to the community within a geo-zone using the **Google Cloud Messaging**. **Location** and **Tracking handler** uses the mobile and vehicle sensors to get the GPS fixes. **Visualization Handler** is responsible for generating reports and on map multimedia presentation using the **Open Street Map**. We uses the **Spatial Hadoop** as *NoSQL*, **Postgres** as *relational* and **Apache Geode** as *in-memory* open source database management system.

The API server is deployed on Amazon using LINUX environment. The hardware used is "c4.4xlarge (62 ECUs, 16 vCPUs, 2.9 GHz, Intel Xeon E5-2666v3, 30 GiB memory, EBS only)", which has a higher ratio of CPU to memory and the lowest cost per CPU among all Amazon EC2 instance types. It is recommended for running CPU-bound scale out applications e.g. high traffic front end fleets etc. The Auto scale service is used to scale up and down according to the requirements with the help of Cloud Watch.

3. DEMONSTRATION SCENARIO

The following two scenarios will be demonstrated to show the group mobility with the aid of multimedia.

(A) Scenario 1- Group Mobility for CoOI: Suppose a ***person A*** wants to visit holy places in Makkah. The person wants the system to accommodate several factors such as resource constraints, language barrier or uncomfortable in travelling alone. ***A*** intends to locate real time co-passenger and the taxi for shared transportation. Our developed app will enable the person ***A*** to announce his interest, constraints, source and target locations. The system will generate and broadcast a multimedia notification with his current and target locations to visit with profile attributes (age, sex, picture etc.). Suppose a ***Person B*** receives this message and responds positively. Both the users can be grouped and establish a communication channel to allow sharing text, images, audio and video information. If a ***Person C*** is also interested, he can join the group and the chat session by replying to the message, the system will add him in the group and now he can also share the multimedia information and can see the multimedia information shared among group members.

Once the group agrees on the meeting point, the system will allow each person on the map to see each one's live trail and also share geo-tagged multimedia data. The group admin can broadcast a multimedia message, which contains details about itinerary, constraints, and user profiles to potential taxi drivers. The interested drivers within a geo-zone can replay with fair amount, available seats, and multimedia information regarding driver and vehicle, which will be received by all group members. Once a vehicle is selected, the group admin can send back the confirmation to the specific taxi driver. After acknowledging the confirmation, the taxi driver will be part of the ad-hoc social network and send/receive multimedia information to the group. For example, the group can see the live location of the taxi, the taxi driver can receive multimedia messages from the group and so on and so forth.

(B) Scenario 2-Finding Passenger for Predefined Route: A driver ***D*** announces his complete route, acceptable temporary destinations around the route, number of seats available, and fair rate, in addition to multimedia information regarding driver and the vehicle. The status and the number of seats' availability are broadcasted and visible to the passengers within an appropriate and dynamically sized geo-zone. The passengers who want to go to the same destination and are within the geo-zone along the route will be able to communicate with the driver using multimedia. The driver can share potential passenger(s) its current location, estimated travelling time, the appropriate pick up time and location after a certain time interval in real time.

4. ACKNOWLEDGEMENT

We extend our gratitude to King Abdul Aziz City for Science and Technology for funding this research project through NSTIP grant number 11-INF1683-10, 11-INF1700-10 and 13-INF2455-10.

5. REFERENCES

[1] Batty, M. 2013. Big data, smart cities and city planning. *Dialogues in Human Geography*. 3, 3, 274–279.

[2] Magdy, A. et al. 2014. Taghreed. *Proceedings of the 22nd ACM SIGSPATIAL International Conference on Advances in Geographic Information Systems - SIGSPATIAL '14*, 163–172.

[3] Mehta, T. and Narmawala, Z. 2011. Survey on multimedia transmission using Network Coding over Wireless Networks. *2011 Nirma University International Conference on Engineering*, 1–6.

[4] Sharma, S. and Mangat, V. 2015. Technology and Trends to Handle Big Data: Survey. *2015 Fifth International Conference on Advanced Computing & Communication Technologies*, 266–271.

[5] Zhang, J. et al. 2011. Data-Driven Intelligent Transportation Systems: A Survey. *IEEE Transactions on Intelligent Transportation Systems*. 12, 4, 1624–1639.

A Multi-sensory Gesture-Based Login Environment

Ahmad Qamar[1,6], Abdullah Murad[3,4], Md. Abdur Rahman[1]; Faizan Ur Rehman[3,5], Akhlaq Ahmad[2,6] Bilal Sadiq[4]; Saleh Basalamah[1,4]
{[1]College of Computer and Information Systems, [2]College of Engineering and Islamic Architecture, [3]KACST GIS Technology Innovation Center, [4]Innovation and Entrepreneurship Institute} Umm Al-Qura University, Makkah, KSA
[5]Department of Computer Science, LIG, University of Grenoble Alpes, France
[6]School of Computer Sciences, Universiti Sains Malaysia, [7]Kulliyyah of Information and Communication Technology, International Islamic University, Malaysia
{amqamar, aamurad, marahman, fsrehman, aajee, smbasalamah}@uqu.edu.sa, bsadiq@gistic.org

ABSTRACT
Logging on to a system using a conventional keyboard may not be feasible in certain environments, such as, in a surgical operation theatre or in an industrial manufacturing facility. We have developed a multi-sensory gesture based login system that allows a user to access secure information using body gestures. The system can be configured to use different types of gestures according to the type of sensors available to the user. We have proposed a simple scheme to represent all alphanumeric characters required for password entry as gestures within the multi-sensory environment. Our scheme is scalable enough to support sensors that detect a large number of gestures to those that can only accept a few. This allows the system to be used in a variety of situations such as usage by disabled persons with limited ability to perform gestures. We are in the midst of deploying our developed system in a clinical environment.

Categories and Subject Descriptors
H.1.2 [**User/Machine Systems**]: Human Factors.

K.4.2 [**Social Issues**]: Assistive technologies for persons with disabilities

General Terms
Human Factors; Accessibility

Keywords
Leap; Myo; Accessibility; Login.

1. INTRODUCTION
The traditional method of accessing a computer system by entering login credentials through a keyboard is difficult to practice in certain work environments. Examples of such environments are a surgical operation room or an industrial manufacturing facility where a subject is not able to access the keyboard due to fear of contamination or environmental hazards. Similar issues arise with physically challenged individuals who face difficulty in using a keyboard due to hand disability. A number of alternative accessibility methods have been developed, such as finger print-based solutions used by mobile phones[1], face recognition for gaming via Kinect[2] and tap pattern based login for touch screens[3]. All of these solutions, however, cannot function efficiently in the above mentioned environments where both the face and the fingers are fully or partially covered by clothes, gloves or masks.

In this paper, we propose a solution to the problem of contactless login by providing an environment whereby a user can log on to a system using body gestures. The gestures can be performed by fingers, hands or any part of the body, depending upon the type of sensors available to the user for detecting those gestures. Most of the work done with gesture based interfacing to date has been concerned with performing software actions or controlling hardware devices[4][5]. In [6], the authors have shown that gesture based login with a single gesture using Kinect can result in a very low equal error rate (ERR). We have devised a scheme to flexibly map a set of gestures to any set of alphanumeric characters. This allows us to add a gesture based authentication layer to any conventional alphanumeric password based environment. As a proof of concept, we have implemented the system using the Leap Motion controller[7] and the Myo electromyography (EMG) sensor from Thalmic Labs[8].

The remainder of the paper is organized as follows: Section 2 describes the details of the system architecture. Section 3 illustrates the implementation details. Section 4 highlights the demo scenario.

2. SYSTEM ARCHITECTURE

Table 1 : A sample mapping of gestures to characters

Left Hand Fingers	Right Hand Fingers	Base 5 Code	Decimal Code	Character
2	1	21	11	A
2	2	22	12	B
2	3	23	13	C
2	4	24	14	D

The multi-sensory environment we have used to test our concept consists of a Leap Motion controller which has the ability to detect a wide range of hand gestures with sub-millimeter accuracy[9]. It can also detect rotational gestures such as forearm pronation and supination. The infrared cameras allow it to differentiate between the right and the left hand. We have adopted gestures with fingers flexed outwards to represent a base5 code. The first 25 codes can thus be generated with 5 fingers from each hand, both hands being in the pronated state. Since each hand can either be in the pronated or supinated state, the total number of states that can be represented with two hands is 4. This gives us a total of 25x4=100 different detectable gestures. The total number of characters in the ASCII set used for password entry is 95[10]. A sample mapping of gestures to characters is shown in table 1.

MM'15, October 26-30, 2015, Brisbane, Australia
ACM 978-1-4503-3459-4/15/10.
http://dx.doi.org/10.1145/2733373.2807987

Another sensor that we have used in our multi-sensory environment is the Myo EMG sensor. The Myo has the ability to interpret five hand gestures from electromyographic signals produced by hand muscle activity. These include touching the thumb with the pinky, spreading the fingers, making a fist and flexing (wave in) and extending the wrist (wave out). In addition to that, it can measure the amount of pronation and supination angle. We have reserved these gestures for activities required to move around the form elements. In our currently implemented environment, flexing and extending the wrist using MYO makes the cursor move forward or backward. Touching the middle finger with the pinky performs the backspace action by deleting the character to the left of the cursor. Spreading the fingers apart moves the cursor to the next tab while making a fist performs the reverse tab action by moving the focus to the previous field. Touching the pinky when a button has the focus performs the button press activity.

To provide support for an environment where a user has a single sensor with a restricted set of detectable gestures, we have adopted a different scheme. To use the Myo only for login, we have reserved the wave in gesture for entering the tens digit and the wave out gesture for representing the units digit for the decimal representation of the code. To enter 31, for example, a user needs to perform the wave in gesture 3 times and the wave out gesture one time. After that the user makes a fist to indicate end of character entry. Touching the pinky allows the user to cancel input and start all over. When all characters have been entered, the user makes the "fingers spread" gesture to jump to the next field. To press the submit button, the user makes a fist gesture when the button receives focus. In this way, we have used four gestures for character entry and a fifth one for switching between the different data entry objects on the screen.

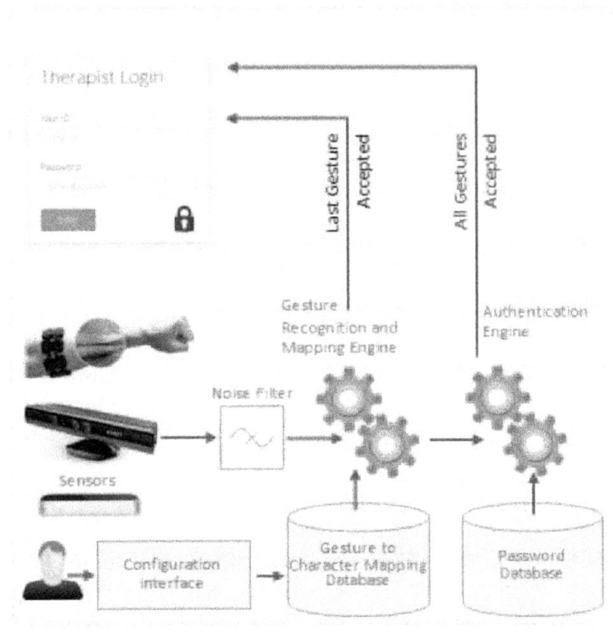

Figure 1: System Architecture

Figure 1 shows the major components of the system. Motion capture **Sensors** record the movement of related body parts and send the output to the **Noise Filter** which removes invalid input from the data stream. Data is then fed to the **Gesture Recognition and Mapping Engine,** which interprets gestures from the motion frames and converts it to a character using the **Gesture to Character Mapping Database**. This database is updated using the **Configuration Interface**, which allows a user to personalize the login characters from the available options and sensors. Text characters obtained from the mapping table are then sent to the screen. On end of input, the user performs a special gesture to switch to the next field. Another gesture is used to press the submit button. The password is verified by the **Authentication Engine** using the **Password Database**.

3. IMPLEMENTATION AND DEMONSTRATION SCENARIO

We have tested the system on a 2GHz machine with 4GB RAM running Windows 8 using Leap SDK v2 and Myo SDK v0.8.1.

For the purpose of demonstration, we will show a software environment that allows users to login using hand and arm based gestures.

4. ACKNOWLEDGMENTS

This project was supported by the NSTIP strategic technologies program (11-INF1700-10) and (11-INF1703-10) of the Kingdom of Saudi Arabia.

5. REFERENCES

[1] Jain, A., Ross, A. and Prabharkar, S. 2004. An introduction to biometrics. *IEEE Transactions On Circuits and System for Video Technology*, *14*, 1, 4 - 20.

[2] Min, R.; Kose, N. and Dugelay, J.-L. 2014. KinectFaceDB: A Kinect Database for Face Recognition. *IEEE Transactions on Systems, Man, and Cybernetics: Systems*, *44*, 11, 1534 - 1548.

[3] Meng, Y., Wong, D. S., Schlegel, R., and Kwok, L.-f. 2013. Touch gestures based biometric authentication scheme for touchscreen mobile phones. *Information Security and Cryptology*, *7763*, 331-350.

[4] Rahman, ASM Mahfujur, Hossain, M. Anwar, Parra, Jorge and Saddik, Abdulmotaleb El. 2009. Motion-path based gesture interaction with smart home services. In *Proceedings of the 17th ACM international conference on Multimedia (MM '09)*. ACM, New York, NY, USA, 761-764.

[5] Qamar, A., Khan, A. R., Husain, S. O., Rahman, A. and Basalamah, S. 2015. A Multi-Sensory Gesture-Based Occupational Therapy Environment for Controlling Home Appliances. In *Proceedings of ACM International Conference on Multimedia Retrieval, (ACM ICMR)*, June 23-26.

[6] Wu, J., Ishwar, P., Konrad, J., 2014. The value of posture, build and dynamics in gesture-based user authentication. In *Proceedings of IEEE International Joint Conference on Biometrics (IJCB)*, 1-8.

[7] http://www.leapmotion.com.

[8] https://www.thalmic.com/en/myo/.

[9] Weichert, F., Bachmann, D., Rudak, B., & Fisseler, D. 2013. "Analysis of the accuracy and robustness of the Leap Motion Controller". *Sensors*, *13*(5), 6380-6393.

[10] Arstechnica.com, 2015. Anatomy of a hack: How crackers ransack passwords like "qeadzcwrsfxv1331". http://arstechnica.com/security/2013/05/how-crackers-make-minced-meat-out-of-your-passwords/2.

Hand-Object Sense: A Hand-held Object Recognition System Based on RGB-D Information

Xiong Lv, Shuqiang Jiang, Luis Herranz, Shuang Wang
Key Laboratory of Intelligent Information Processing, Institute of Computing Technology Chinese Academy of Sciences, Beijing 100190, China
{xiong.lv,luis.herranz,shuang.wang}@vipl.ict.ac.cn; sqjiang@ict.ac.cn

ABSTRACT

Hand-held objects play an important role in human-human and human-machine interaction. It can be used as a reference for understanding user intentions or user requirements. In this technical demonstration, we introduce an object recognition system called Hand-Object Sense that can automatically recognize the object held by user. This system first detects and segments the hand-held object by exploiting skeleton information combined with depth information. Second, in the object recognition stage, this system exploits features computed in different ways and fuses them to improve the recognition accuracy. Our system can recognize objects in real-time and have a good tolerance to angle and scale transformation. Furthermore, it has a good generalization capability for unknown objects.

Categories and Subject Descriptors

I.4.6 [Image Processing and Computer Vision]: Segmentation—***Region growing, partitioning; Edge and feature detection***; **I.5.4 [Pattern Recognition]: Application**—***Computer vision***

Keywords

RGB-D, hand-held object recognition, feature fusion

1. INTRODUCTION

Object recognition has many applications in human-machine interaction, information retrieval, mobile visual assistance, video surveillance etc. Specifically, hand-held object recognition is a special and important case of object recognition as it can not only help machine obtain more information about the user but also know some implicit intentions or interests of the user. Therefore, we propose a hand-held object recognition system called Hand-Object Sense.

Traditional object recognition based on RGB image meets the following problems: 1) clutter background makes it difficult to segment the object; 2) the same objects may have various visual appearances; 3) objects from different classes may look similar. With the availability of inexpensive RGB-D devices (e.g. Kinect), depth information can be exploited to alleviate these problems. Nevertheless, how to precisely locate and segment the object from background and extract representative and discriminative features to describe the object is still a challenging problem.

This system is developed based on our previous work[1], which takes advantage of RGB-D devices and uses specific segmentation technique based on skeleton and depth information to find hand-held objects. Thus it can effectively eliminate the background. Then a rich object representation is obtained by fusing different kind of features.

Hand-Object Sense can segment and recognize objects held by the user in real-time and simultaneously recognize the objects held in both hands. The system can allow the user rotate and move the objects freely.

2. HAND-HELD OBJECT RECOGNITION SYSTEM

2.1 Framework

We now briefly describe the Hand-Object Sense framework. The details of the algorithm were elaborated in our previous work [1]. The block diagram of our framework is shown in Figure 1. The main steps are object segmentation, feature extraction, feature fusion and object recognition.

2.1.1 Hand-held Object Segmentation

First, we use the hand position located by Kinect API as the seed. Then the object mask is obtained using a region-growing algorithm. This algorithm examines the neighbors of the points in the seed set and includes them in the seed set when they are at a similar depth as the hand. Finally, we use the seed set to get the object region and its corresponding depth region.

2.1.2 Feature Extraction

When the RGB and depth regions of the object are acquired, we extract features from them. Point cloud is built by using RGB and depth information. In order to have a comprehensive and representative description of the object. We use three features together to represent object. They are Ensemble Shape Functions (ESF), Circular Color Cubic Higher-order Local Auto-Correlation descriptor (C^3-HALC) and Global Radius-based Surface Descriptor (GRSD).

MM'15, October 26–30, 2015, Brisbane, Australia.
ACM 978-1-4503-3459-4/15/10.
DOI: http://dx.doi.org/10.1145/2733373.2807990.

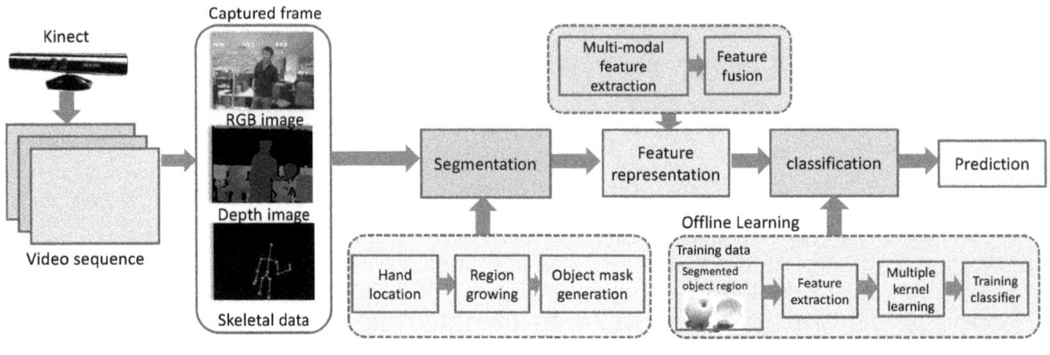

Figure 1: Hand-Object Sense Framework

2.1.3 Feature Fusion and Recognition

Different fusion methods lead to a very different classification performance. We consider two operations to fuse features: concatenation and multiple kernel learning (MKL). For MKL, we implement Gaussian kernels and polynomial kernels. After fusion, we train an SVM to predict the object category.

For each hand, we use the same procedure to predict the object category. The SVM and MKL are trained on our Hand-held object dataset(HOD) dataset[1], which contains 16 daily categories.

2.2 System Architecture

In order to effectively executes segmenting and recognizing simultaneously and ensure that our system can be implemented in real-time. We take advantage of parallel processing, Hand-Object Sense is implemented with a multi-thread architecture. Each thread runs as a separate module. In this way, we divide Hand-Object Sense into four modules: UI, segmentation, feature extraction and object recognition. Each of them is ran with a thread.

We use a voting scheme combining the predictions obtained from several video frames to improve the prediction accuracy. The voting window is 10, which means that we use the majority of the predicted label in 10 frames as the current label.

In human-machine interaction, we simultaneously use two hands, which requires our system to recognize the objects in both hands. We utilize the skeletal data to locate both hands and repeat the above operations for each of them.

2.3 Evaluation

Object recognition can be categorized into instance level and category level object recognition[2]. For instance-level object recognition, it indicates recognizing a concrete object, category-level object recognition indicates recognizing a basic concept. Thus, category-level object recognition has a better generalization capability for new objects. This demonstration focuses on category-level object recognition.

HOD dataset[1] was used to evaluate the performance of our Hand-Object Sense. We trained our classifier and MKL on the HOD dataset. The experiment was performed on a laptop with Intel Core i5 3.10GHz processor and 16GB DDR3, running Windows7. HOD contains 16 categories and each category includes 4 instances. We used all the 16 categories to train our system.

We invited 5 subjects to test our system with 16 categories. In the test, the 16 kinds of testing objects are the same category with the training data but different instances, user can hold object in single hand or both hands. It validates the generalization capability and robustness of our system. The average test accuracy is 65.96% and the recognition time is in real-time.

3. CONCLUSION AND FUTURE WORK

In this demo, we have presented Hand-Object Sense, a hand-held object recognition system. We employ a region-growing algorithm to segment objects and feature fusion for recognition. Hand-Object Sense works stably with high accuracy and scalability.

In the future, we will add more daily categories to make recognition more extensive. More features (e.g. deep features) and fusing method will be explored to make the recognition more robust. Furthermore, we will investigate incremental learning and more applications of our system and deploy the system into intelligent interaction platform.

Acknowledgement

This work was supported in part by the National Basic Research 973 Program of China under Grant No. 2012CB316400, the National Natural Science Foundation of China under Grant Nos. 61322212 and 61450110446, the National High Technology Research and Development 863 Program of China under Grant No. 2014AA015202, and the Chinese Academy of Sciences Fellowships for Young International Scientists under Grant No. 2011Y1GB05. This work is also funded by Lenovo Outstanding Young Scientists Program (LOYS).

4. REFERENCES

[1] Xiong Lv, Shuqiang Jiang, Luis Herranz, and Shuang Wang. Rgb-d hand-held object recognition based on heterogeneous feature fusion. *Journal of Computer Science and Technology*, 30(2):340–352, 2015.

[2] Shuang Wang and Shuqiang Jiang. Instre: A new benchmark for instance-level object retrieval and recognition. *ACM Trans. Multimedia Comput. Commun. Appl.*, 11(3):37:1–37:21, February 2015.

A Cross-media Sentiment Analytics Platform For Microblog

Chao Chen, Fuhai Chen, Donglin Cao, and Rongrong Ji
{catlnMud,cfh3c}@stu.xmu.edu.cn, {another,rrji}@xmu.edu.cn
Department of Cognitive Science, School of Information Science and Engineering, Xiamen University,
Xiamen, Fujian, P. R. China, 361005

ABSTRACT

In this demo, a cross-media public sentiment analysis system is presented. The system presents and visualizes the sentiments of microblog data by organizing the results by region, topic, and content, respectively. Such sentiment is obtained by fusing of sentiment classification scores from both visual and textual channel. In such a way, social multimedia sentiment is shown in a multi-level and user-friendly form.

1. INTRODUCTION

These years have witnessed a rapid development of social network, which provides a novel way for social media users to express their emotion. Sina Weibo, as one of the most popular social network platforms in China, has owned 143 million monthly active user by 2014 March, which grows by 10.9% compared with 2013 December. Due to the increasing popularity and influence of microblog, sentiment analysis on Weibo becomes essential for enterprise to monitor product marketing as well as for government to monitor public sentiment.

However, traditional research on sentiment analysis typically focuses on the textual domain. In many cases, the textual information can be missing while the visual content might become the only channel for expression user emotion. And with the widespread popularity of mobile devices nowadays, it becomes more convenient and more natural to post or transpond images and videos in the social network platform. Therefore, cross-media public sentiment analysis system is necessary under such a circumstance.

In this demo, we show a cross-media sentiment analysis platform that integrates several existing and state-of-the-art visual and cross-media sentiment analysis algorithm proposed in the recent literature [6][1][8][3][5][4]. To collect the Weibo data, we adopt a novel verification code recognizing algorithm proposed in [7] to crack the Sina. For analyzing sentiments in the Chinese language, adopt a textual sentiment analysis algorithm scheme proposed in [6].For analyzing sentiments for visual domain, we adopt a well-used visual sentiment detection scheme, *i.e.*, the SentiBank detector proposed in [1]. To achieve cross-media sentiment analysis for fusing sentiment classification results from both textual and visual modalities, we adopt a novel hypergraph learning scheme proposed in [3], and also propose multi-modal correlation model in [5]. And meanwhile, deep learning based scheme is also investigated [9]. A more detailed description of the algorithm we adopted in this paper, please refer to the work in [2].

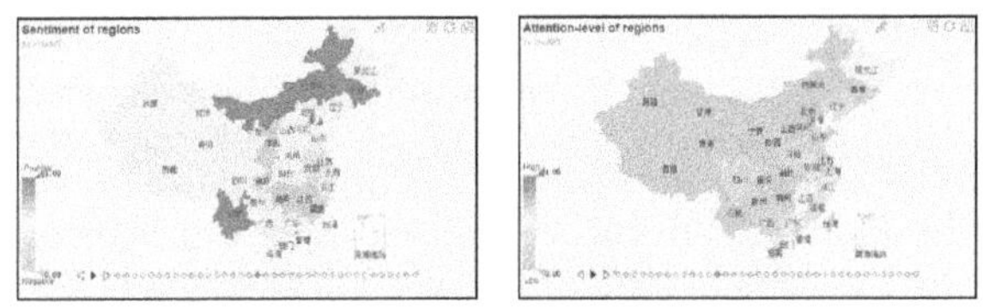

(a) Map of sentiment (b) Map of attention level

Figure 1: Geographical region based view for microblog sentiment visualization in terms of either relative or absolute distribution percentages

Given the above cutting-edge algorithm as the core of our system, in this demo we mainly demonstrate the following aspects for visualizing cross-media sentiment: First, we present sentiment in three modalities, *i.e.*, region-based modality, topic-based modality and microblog-based modality. Second, we introduce a very user-friendly interaction scheme, which allows the users to navigate and browse our analytics results fluently.

2. SYSTEM DEMO AND CASE

We have crawled over 6,500,000 Sina Weibo data with the dates ranging from 2013-1-1 to 2014-10-1. For each day, we adopt a hot topic list from the hottest topics of Sina Weibo website to initialize the seed for crawling. Then, we simulate the user browsing by searching the Weibo interface with the seed words. Image, text, gif, as well as the user information are captured. For the demo purpose, we used 3,373,080 posts of users ranging from 2013-10 to 2014-2. And as mentioned in previous section, our system shows sentiment results in three module, region-based module, topic-based module and Microblog-based module. The demo system adopt a style like Sina Weibo by using its css file, developed using html+css/javascript programming language for web user interface and java/php/cpp for backstage. And we adopt a plug-in from Baidu called Echarts for Data visualization. Here is the link of our demo: http://v.youku.com/v_show/id_XOTQ5NTU1MDIO.html?from=y1.7-1.2.

MM'15, October 26-30, 2015, Brisbane, Australia.
© 2015 ACM. ISBN 978-1-4503-3459-4/15/10 ...$15.00.
DOI: http://dx.doi.org/10.1145/2733373.2807398.

Figure 2: Geographical maps in the city level together with the most-concerned topic for this region

2.1 Region-based Sentiment Analysis

As showed in Fig.1(a) and Fig.1(b), the sentiment analysis results are presented in a national map with province-level resolution. Users can select and click into one certain province in this map, and details of this province and related illustrates will be given beneath the map as shown in Fig.2. If users want to focus on one certain topic which they are interested in, they can input the name in the topic selection cell on the top of the map and specific data he or she wants will be returned to the interface.

Here, we given two modes with respect to the popularity, that is, the "attention-level" that shows the percentage of topic popularity as an absolute measurement while the "sentiment-level" that shows percentage of people with different sentiment. There is an example in Fig.1, sentiment-level mode(Fig.1(a)) and attention-level(Fig.1(b)) mode, where the colors of related areas change accordingly over time. In the sentiment-level mode, warm tone and cool tone represent the positive and negative sentiment level, respectively. In attention-level mode different colors of warm toned and cool tone colors stand for high or low attention level. Both levels are available for both global and local region maps. For example, Fig.1(b) shows people in coastal region tend to be more concerned about the topic "coming of typhoon the 'tian tu'"and their sentiments are more negative as showed in Fig.1(a) and Fig.2.

2.2 Topic-based Sentiment Analysis

In topic-based sentiment analysis module, based on the period of time selected in the pervious module, we list the topics according to their follower number as showed in Fig.3(a). And for one specific topic we have two statistical graphs demonstrated to show the detailed information, including: (1). a line graph for the changes of the users number on three different sentiments levels (positive, negative and neutral) which are marked in different colors , and (2). a pie graph which presents the proportion of this three kinds of users with different sentiments as shown in Fig.3(b).

This module indicates the detail information of a certain topic. For example, Fig.3(a) shows that "coming of typhoon 'TianTu'" is the hottest topic and Fig.3(b) shows when typhoon is coming it draws a lot of attention with high positive sentiment (probably excited we assume) and high negative sentiment. After the typhoon "TianTu", the number of people with negative sentiment goes down quickly but the one with positive sentiment marks the peak again. It is an interesting phenomena we get in this case which might refers to that users may showed both excited and fear at the very beginning but when typhoon attenuated, those two kinds of people joined together and share one single positive sentiment which is probably joyful we assume.

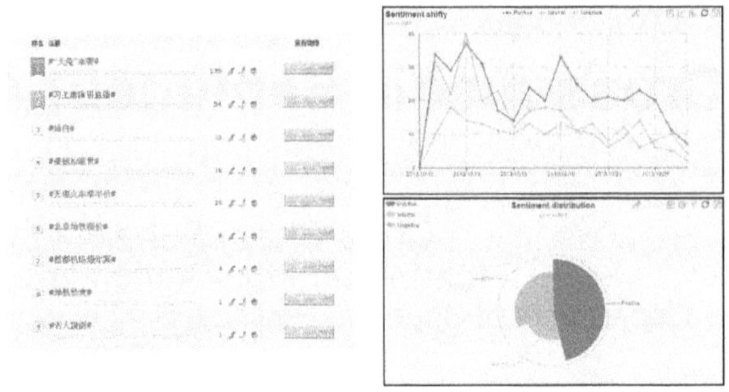

(a) List of topics (b) Statistical graph

Figure 3: Topic popularity and its statistical graph on positive, negative, and neutral

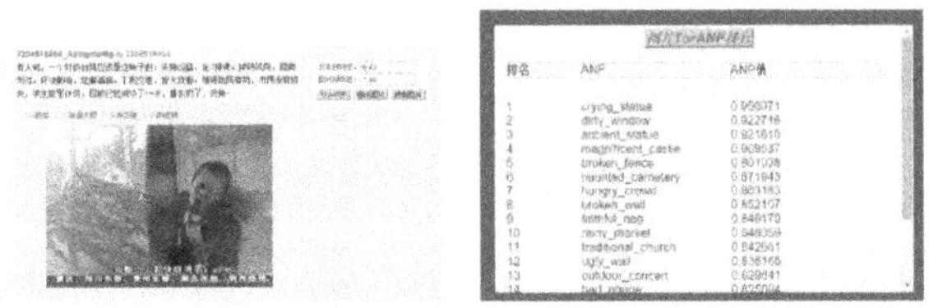

(a) Microblog analysis (b) ANP list

Figure 4: Microblog analysis example and ANPs

2.3 Microblog-based Sentiment Analysis

Related to the topic chosen in pervious module, each microblog post is presented by topic name, id of users, textual content, visual content, location of users and cross-media sentiment analysis result, respectively. Sentiment analysis results include textual sentiment polarity, visual sentiment polarity, entire sentiment polarity of multimedia, and top ANPs [1] given by our algorithm,respectively. For example, in Fig.4(a) there is a reporter in rainstorm, our system gives negative numbers on both text and image which means negative sentiment for this microblog post and the top ANPs of this image is showed in Fig.4(b).

3. CONCLUSION

While the existing sentiment analysis systems typically reside on the textual domain, for microblog the textual words are typically missing. In this paper, we present a demo for cross-media sentiment analysis. Our key innovation lies in a novel and multi-level way to present the analysis results, *a.k.a.*, we propose to organize the sentiments of the Weibo microblog data by region, by topic, and by content, allowing an interactive digest and manipulation of the prediction results towards a very user-friendly visualization. Therefore, our system has achieved a good improvement in terms of the user experience.

4. ACKNOWLEDGEMENTS

This work is supported by the Special Fund for Earthquake Research in the Public Interest No.201508025, the Nature Science Foundation of China (No. 61422210 and No. 61373076), the Fundamental Research Funds for the Central Universities (No.2013121026), and the 985 Project of Xiamen University.

5. REFERENCES

[1] D. Borth, R. Ji, T. Chen, T. Breuel, and S.-F. Chang. Large-scale visual sentiment ontology and detectors using adjective noun pairs. In *Proceedings of the 21st ACM international conference on Multimedia*, pages 223–232. ACM, 2013.

[2] D. Cao, R. Ji, D. Lin, and S. Li. A cross-media public sentiment analysis system for microblog. *Multimedia Systems*, pages 1–8, 2014.

[3] F. Chen, Y. Gao, D. Cao, and R. Ji. Multimodal hypergraph learning for microblog sentiment prediction. In *Proceedings of the IEEE International Conference on Multimedia and Expo*, pages 1–6. IEEE, 2015.

[4] R. Ji, D. Cao, and D. Lin. Cross-modality sentiment analysis for social multimedia. In *Proceedings of the IEEE International Conference on Multimedia Big Data*, pages 28–31. IEEE, 2015.

[5] L. Li, D. Cao, S. Li, and R. Ji. Sentiment analysis of chinese micro-blog based on multi-modal correlation model. In *IEEE Xplore Digital Library*. IEEE, 2015.

[6] B. Pang, L. Lee, and S. Vaithyanathan. Thumbs up? sentiment classification using machine learning techniques. In *Proceedings of the Conference on Empirical Methods in Natural Language Processing*, pages 79–86, 2002.

[7] Y. Shen, R. Ji, D. Cao, and M. Wang. Hacking chinese touclick captcha by multi-scale corner structure model with fast pattern matching. In *Proceedings of the ACM International Conference on Multimedia*, pages 853–856. ACM, 2014.

[8] M. Wang, D. Cao, L. Li, S. Li, and R. Ji. Microblog sentiment analysis based on cross-media bag-of-words model. In *Proceedings of International Conference on Internet Multimedia Computing and Service*, page 76. ACM, 2014.

[9] Q. You, J. Luo, H. Jin, and J. Yang. Robust image sentiment analysis using progressively trained and domain transferred deep networks. In *The Twenty-Ninth AAAI Conference on Artificial Intelligence*, 2015.

A Unsupervised Person Re-identification Method Using Model Based Representation and Ranking

Chao Liang[1,2], Bingyue Huang[1], Ruimin Hu[1,2,*], Chunjie Zhang[3], Xiaoyuan Jing[1], Jing Xiao[1,2]

[1] Computer School, Wuhan University, Wuhan, China, 430079
[2] Collaborative Innovation Center of Geospatial Technology, Wuhan, China, 430079
[3] University of Chinese Academy of Sciences, Beijing, China, 100049
{cliang@whu.edu.cn}

ABSTRACT

As a core technique supporting the multi-camera tracking task, person re-identification attracts increasing research interests in both academic and industrial communities. Its aim is to match individuals across a group of spatially non-overlapping surveillance cameras, which are usually interfered by various imaging conditions and object motions. Current methods mainly focus on robust feature representation and accurate distance measure, where intensive computations and expensive training samples prohibit their practical applications. To address the above problems, this paper proposes a new unsupervised person re-identification method featured by its competitive accuracy and high efficiency. Both merits stem from model based person image representation and ranking, with which, merely 4-dimension pixel-level features can achieve over 20% matching rate at Rank 1 on the challenging VIPeR dataset.

Categories and Subject Descriptors

H.3.3 [**Information Search and Retrieval**]: Retrieval models, Search process; H.4.m [**Information Systems Applications**]: Miscellaneous

General Terms

Theory, Experimentation, Performance

Keywords

person re-identification, model representation and ranking

1. INTRODUCTION

With the rapid expansion of networking surveillance, more and more pedestrian activities in public zones can be faithfully recorded by various cameras installed in city buses, businesses, public schools and subway stations. In this condition, matching individuals across a group of spatially non-overlapping cameras, a.k.a., person re-identification, has become an emergent problem of great importance. However, person re-identification currently remains an unsolved problem due to difficulties caused by view variation, scale zooming and illumination change (see Fig. 1), making different persons appear more alike than the same person in various cameras.

Figure 1: Examples of appearance changes caused by variant views, lighting and scales. Each column shows two images of the same person taken from two different cameras.

To address the above challenges, previous research mainly focus on two directions: feature representation and distance measure. The former aims to construct discriminative visual descriptions that are robust and stable among different cameras [4, 9, 10], while the latter focuses on utilizing abundant training samples to learn a proper distance metric, where feature distance of the same person is smaller than that of different persons [16, 8]. However, in many practical applications, e.g., criminal investigation or suspect tracking, timeliness and respond speed are equally important, if not more, than re-identification accuracy. This no doubt severely limits the employment of complex feature description in the real-world scenario. Furthermore, considering massive cameras in the large-scale networking surveillance environment, learning a proper metric for each pair of involved cameras is usually difficult or even unrealistic due to the lack of sufficient training samples.

Motivated by the wide success of mixture models in both image classification [1] and speaker verification [13], this paper proposes a model based person re-identification method.

*indicates corresponding author

ACM Multimedia '15 Sydney, Australia
© 2015 ACM. ISBN 978-1-4503-3459-4/15/10 ...$15.00.
DOI: http://dx.doi.org/10.1145/2733373.2807399.

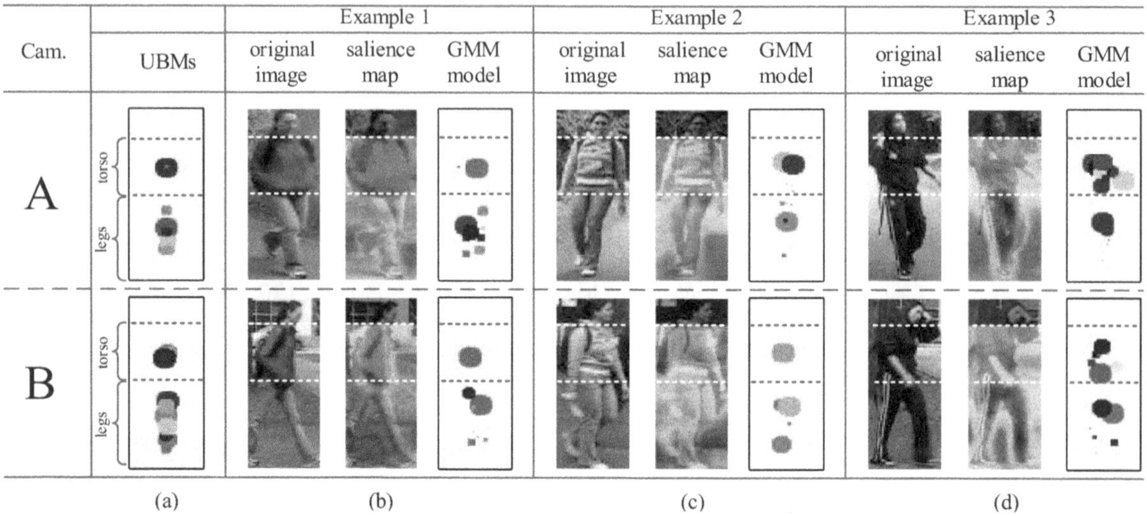

Figure 2: Illustrations of trained UBMs and adapted personal GMMs. (a) torso and leg UBMs trained under two separate cameras; (b)-(d) Three examples of person image modeling processes. In UBMs and personal GMMs, each circle corresponds to a Gaussian component, where its mean vector is represented as the position and color of the circle, and its weights is illustrated as the circle diameter.

Its core idea is adopting probabilistic model to organize and describe the spatial feature distribution of person images, which is assumed to be more robust than individual image features to environment changes and external interference. In particular, a salience weighted universal background model-Gaussian mixture model (UBM-GMM) procedure [13] is introduced to generate accurate person image model with limited observations, e.g., in VIPeR dataset there is only one image for each person in a camera. Thereafter, manifold ranking based on approximate model-to-model distance is conducted to generate globally consistent person re-identification results.

Compared with existing methods, our contribution lies in proposing a new unsupervised person re-identification method with merits of competitive accuracy as well as high efficiency. Its key foundation is model based person image representation, which endows simple pixel-level features with robust discrimination power. Moreover, instead of direct ranking based on pairwise probe-to-gallery comparison, manifold ranking on the union of probe and whole gallery set not only provides more accurate ranking results, but also validates our novelties from previous work [18].

2. PERSON IMAGE MODELING

To generate both robust and discriminative person image model with limited observations, a salience weighted UBM-GMM procedure is discussed in this section.

2.1 Body Part Oriented UBM training

UBM aims to model the common feature distribution that partially shared by individuals in a category. In person re-identification, the common feature distribution first varies camera by camera. On this basis, considering the common dressing habit of the public, i.e., the upper body is usually covered by clothes and the lower body by trousers or skirts, UBMs are further categorized to denote different body parts. In this paper, we train torso and leg UBMs for each camera as shown in Fig.2(a). Intrinsically, UBM is a GMM that can be written as

$$p(x|\lambda) = \sum_k w_k \cdot \mathcal{N}_k(x) \tag{1}$$

where $\lambda = \{\{w_k\}, \{\mu_k\}, \{\Sigma_k\}\}$ is the model parameter set and w_k is the mixture weight of the kth Gaussian component

$$\mathcal{N}_k(x) = \frac{1}{(2\pi)^{\frac{d}{2}}|\Sigma_k|^{\frac{1}{2}}} \exp\left\{-\frac{1}{2}(x-\mu_k)^\top \Sigma_k^{-1}(x-\mu_k)\right\} \tag{2}$$

with feature dimension d, mean vector μ_k and covariance matrix Σ_k. For the sake of strong scalability, a unsupervised EM algorithm [5] is adopted to train UBM with adaptive component number as shown in Fig.2 (a).

2.2 Salience Weighted Model Adaptation

Compared to person-independent UBMs, model adaptation step aims to generate person-specific GMMs for both probe and gallery images. For the sake of effective matching, model adaptation is not just to accurately restore feature distributions of a person image, but more importantly, to preserve those salient features helpful to identification [15].

Given a UBM λ and a set of person image features $X = \{x_i\}$, both coming from the same body part and camera. The salience value s_i of feature x_i is defined as

$$s_i = 1 - \frac{p(x_i|\lambda) - \min_{x_i \in X}[p(x_i|\lambda)]}{\max_{x_i \in X}[p(x_i|\lambda)] - \min_{x_i \in X}[p(x_i|\lambda)]} \tag{3}$$

From which, salience weighted sufficient statistics are

$$n_k = \sum_i s_i \cdot p(k|x_i) \tag{4}$$

$$E_k(x) = \frac{1}{n_k}\sum_i s_i \cdot p(k|x_i) \cdot x_i \tag{5}$$

$$E_k(x^2) = \frac{1}{n_k}\sum_i s_i \cdot p(k|x_i) \cdot x_i^2 \tag{6}$$

and the person image model can be finally adapted from the corresponding UBM [13] as shown in Fig.2 (b)-(d).

Table 1: Comparative results on VIPeR dataset.

Methods	Retrieval Accuracy (%)				Feature Dimesion
	@ 1	@ 5	@ 10	@ 20	
Ours	**20.25**	37.03	52.53	**68.05**	**81**
ℓ_1 [11]	9.43	20.03	27.06	34.68	-
ℓ_2 [11]	10.95	23.92	31.39	44.11	-
MRank [11]	11.42	24.27	33.73	44.11	2,784
SDALF [4]	19.87	38.89	49.37	65.73	1,633
USL [15]	19.95	**43.04**	**53.80**	67.72	201,600
ELF [7]	12	31	41	58	200
RankSVM [12]	14.83	37.12	50.19	65.66	2,784
PRDC [16]	16.01	37.09	51.27	65.95	2,784

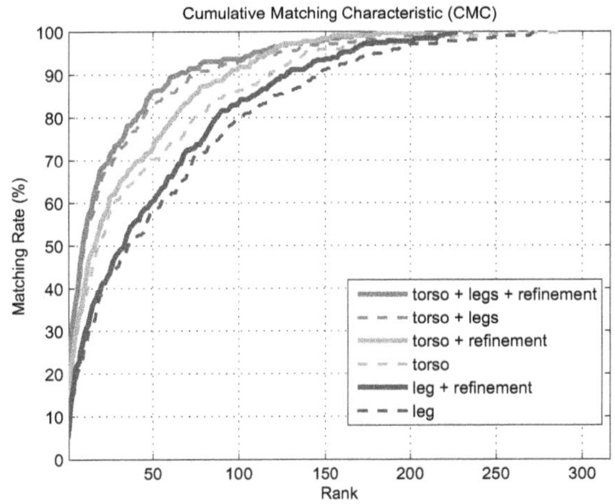

Figure 3: Effects of individual body parts and manifold based ranking refinement.

3. PERSON MODEL RANKING

This section discusses key steps in the image ranking phrase, including pairwise distance based image ranking and manifold based ranking refinement.

3.1 Pairwise Distance Based Ranking

Given the model based representation for both probe and galleries, their image distances depend on the comparison between two probabilistic distributions. For GMMs, classic KL divergence does not have a closed-form expression, which leads to various approximation methods. With a comprehensive consideration on both accuracy and complexity, this paper adopts unscented transform (UT) based approximation [6] to measure the distance between GMMs.

It is worthy noting that we are currently able to generate a ranking result through pairwise comparison between the probe and each gallery. However, as a approximation estimation, UT based distance measure inevitably deviates from the true KL divergence. Together with the separate pairwise matching manner, above deviation error will be exactly propagated to the final ranking process, leading to inaccurate retrieval results.

3.2 Manifold Based Ranking Refinement

Motivated by [11], rich information and structure inherent in the gallery set is exploited to improve the above pairwise ranking result.

More precisely, given a probe q and gallery set $\{g_j\}_{j=1}^N$ we first construct a weighted graph $\mathcal{G} = \langle \mathcal{V}, \mathcal{E}, \mathcal{W} \rangle$, where $\mathcal{V} = \{v_i\} = \{q \cup \{g_j\}\}$ represents the node set, $\mathcal{W} = \{w_{i,j}\} \in \mathbb{R}^{(N+1)\times(N+1)}$ are weight matrix defined by the node similarity

$$w_{i,j} = \exp\{-D_{\text{UT}}(\lambda^{v_i}||\lambda^{v_j})/\sigma^2\} \quad (7)$$

for $i \neq j$ and $w_{i,i} = 0$, $D_{\text{UT}} = \alpha \times D_{\text{UT}}^{\text{torso}} + (1-\alpha) \times D_{\text{UT}}^{\text{leg}}$ is a linear combination of torso and leg part model distances, σ is a scaling parameter. Here, we need to emphasize that the weight matrix $\mathcal{W}$ is no longer symmetric due to the asymmetric UT based distance measure.

Given the above model based weighted graph $\mathcal{G}$, initial pairwise ranking scores can be further updated through information propagation along its global manifold structure. Due to limited space, we omit following regular derivations and suggest interest readers to reference classic manifold ranking algorithm [17] for more technical details.

4. EXPERIMENTAL RESULTS

In this section, the proposed approach is validated by comparing with several state-of-the-art person re-identification methods on the public VIPeR [2] and ETHZ [3] datasets.

4.1 Implementation Details

In the image representation phrase, fixed vertical ratios, i.e., 0.2 and 0.5, are used to extract body parts. Then, 4-dimension pixel-level features, i.e., y-axis position, hue, saturation and value, are extracted for person image modeling, and diagonal covariance matrixes are adopted to restrict the model complexity in the UBM training. In the image ranking phrase, we adopt the equal weight scheme with $\alpha = 0.5$ to combine torso and leg part distances with $\sigma = 1$. For ease and fair comparison, cumulative matching characteristic (CMC) curve [14] is adopted as the evaluation criterion.

4.2 VIPeR Dataset

Data description. The VIPeR dataset contains two views of 632 persons. Each pair is made up of images of the same person taken from two individual cameras, under different viewpoint, pose and light conditions. Viewpoint variation is the most significant cause of the appearance change with most of matched image pairs containing one front/back view and one side-view.

Comparative results with baselines. As can be seen from Table 1, the proposed method achieves obvious superiority over most of unsupervised learning methods, including ℓ_1, ℓ_2 and MRank, with an average improvement of more than 15% − 20%. Furthermore, even compared with part supervised learning methods, e.g., RankSVM and PRDC, there are obviously higher CMC scores in the top-20 ranks. In particular, compared with two state-of-the-art unsupervised methods, SDALF and USL, the proposed method achieves comparable performance, i.e., CMC@1 and @20 are 20.25% and 68.05% for ours, versus 19.87% and 65.73% for SDALF, and 19.95% and 67.72% for USL (without additional fusion with other methods [15] for fair comparison hereafter in this paper), given our 81-dimension model parameters for each image versus 1,633-dimension features for SDALF and 201,600-dimension features for USL.

Table 2: Comparative CMC results (%) at rank $1-7$ on ETHZ dataset.

Methods	SEQ.#1							SEQ.#2							SEQ.#3						
	1	2	3	4	5	6	7	1	2	3	4	5	6	7	1	2	3	4	5	6	7
Ours	72	**79**	**82**	**85**	**86**	**88**	**89**	72	80	**85**	**87**	**89**	**90**	**92**	83	88	90	92	93	94	95
SDALF [4]	65	73	77	79	81	82	84	64	74	79	83	85	87	89	76	83	86	88	90	92	93
USL [15]	**72**	78	82	84	86	87	88	**74**	**81**	84	86	88	89	90	**89**	**94**	**96**	**97**	**98**	**98**	**99**

Effects of different implementations. Fig.3 shows various retrieval performances under different model ranking implementations. Here, we mainly focus on two factors, different body parts and manifold based ranking refinement. First, through comparing the red group (full body), green group (torso part) and blue group (leg part), we find that the torso is more useful than leg part, which can be ascribe to more abundant and discriminative information contained in clothes than trousers. Moreover, the full body, i.e., the combination of torso and legs, provides the most complete information for person re-identification. Second, through comparing the solid line and broken line in each color group, we find that the ranking refinement step can consistently improve the corresponding pairwise matching result, with an average improvement of $2-3\%$, which validates the effectiveness of manifold structure in the rank optimization.

4.3 ETHZ Dataset

Data description. This ETHZ dataset contains three video sequences captured from moving cameras. It contains a large number of different people in uncontrolled conditions. Following the settings in [4, 15], we use a single-shot evaluation strategy. For each person, one image is randomly selected to build gallery set while the rest images form the probe set. Each image in probe is matched to every gallery image and the correct matched rank is obtained.

Comparative results with baselines. As can be seen from Table 2, the proposed method consistently outperforms SDALF method, with an average advantage of 5%, on all three video sequences. In particular, in comparison with USL, ours is generally better in first two sequences, i.e., with higher CMC values after rank 1 and 2, respectively. For the last video sequence, the proposed method encounters severe degradation, with a relative lag of 6% to that of USL, which is mainly ascribed to inaccurate body part division and insufficient UBM training due to limited observations from only 28 person tracks.

5. CONCLUSIONS AND FUTURE WORK

In this work, we have proposed a novel unsupervised person re-identification method with model based representation and ranking. Specifically, through regional UBM training and salience weighted modeling adaptation, person images are represented as a group of robust and discriminative GMMs. Thereafter, UT based model distance is introduced to give an initial similarity score, from which a more accurate ranking result is obtained based on the manifold ranking.

In the future, our research work has two directions: 1) study multi-graph based manifold learning algorithm to make better use of the part-specific model representation; 2) investigate practical disposition and operation strategies to apply the proposed model based person re-identification method.

Acknowledgement. The research was supported by National Nature Science Foundation of China (61231015, 61172173, 61303114, 61170023, 61303154), National High Technology Research and Development Program of China (2015AA016306), Technology Research Project of Ministry of Public Security (2014JSYJA016), Nature Science Foundation of Hubei Province (2014CFB712), Specialized Research Fund for Doctoral Program of Higher Education (20130141120024), Fundamental Research Funds for the Central Universities (2042014kf0250, 2042014kf0025), China Postdoctoral Science Foundation (2014M562058) and Scientific Research Foundation for the Returned Overseas Chinese Scholars ([2014]1685).

6. REFERENCES

[1] C. Beecks, A. M. Ivanescu, S. Kirchhoff, and T. Seidl. Modeling image similarity by gaussian mixture models and the signature quadratic form distance. In *ICCV*, pages 1754–1761, 2011.

[2] S. B. D. Gray and H. Tao. Evaluating appearance models for recognition, reacquisition, and tracking. In *PETS*, 2007.

[3] A. Ess, B. Leibe, and L. J. V. Gool. Depth and appearance for mobile scene analysis. In *ICCV*, pages 1–8, 2007.

[4] M. Farenzena, L. Bazzani, A. Perina, V. Murino, and M. Cristani. Person re-identification by symmetry-driven accumulation of local features. In *CVPR*, 2010.

[5] M. A. T. Figueiredo and A. K. Jain. Unsupervised learning of finite mixture models. *TPAMI*, 24(3):381–396, 2002.

[6] J. Goldberger, S. Gordon, and H. Greenspan. An efficient image similarity measure based on approximations of kl-divergence between two gaussian mixtures. In *ICCV*, pages 487–493, 2003.

[7] D. Gray and H. Tao. Viewpoint invariant pedestrian recognition with an ensemble of localized features. In *ECCV*, 2008.

[8] M. Kostinger, M. Hirzer, P. Wohlhart, P. Roth, and H. Bischof. Large scale metric learning from equivalence constraints. In *CVPR*, 2012.

[9] I. Kviatkovsky, A. Adam, and E. Rivlin. Color invariants for person reidentification. *TPAMI*, 35(7):1622–1634, 2013.

[10] W. Li, R. Zhao, T. Xiao, and X. Wang. Deepreid: Deep filter pairing neural network for person re-identification. In *CVPR*, pages 152–159, 2014.

[11] C. C. Loy, C. Liu, and S. Gong. Person re-identification by manifold ranking. In *ICIP*, pages 3567–3571, 2013.

[12] B. Prosser, W. Zheng, S. Gong, and T. Xiang. Person re-identification by support vector ranking. In *BMVC*, pages 1–11, 2010.

[13] D. A. Reynolds, T. F. Quatieri, and R. B. Dunn. Speaker verification using adapted gaussian mixture models. *DSP*, 10(1-3):19–41, 2000.

[14] X. Wang, G. Doretto, T. Sebastian, J. Rittscher, and P. H. Tu. Shape and appearance context modeling. In *ICCV*, pages 1–8, 2007.

[15] R. Zhao, W. Ouyang, and X. Wang. Unsupervised salience learning for person re-identification. In *CVPR*, pages 3586–3593, 2013.

[16] W.-S. Zheng, S. Gong, and T. Xiang. Person re-identification by probabilistic relative distance comparison. In *CVPR*, 2011.

[17] D. Zhou, J. Weston, A. Gretton, O. Bousquet, and B. Schölkopf. Ranking on data manifolds. In *NIPS*, pages 169–176, 2003.

[18] X. Zhou, X. Zhuang, S. Yan, S. Chang, M. Hasegawa-Johnson, and T. S. Huang. Sift-bag kernel for video event analysis. In *MM*, pages 229–238, 2008.

Evolution of a Tabletop Telepresence System through Art and Technology

Tony Dunnigan, John Doherty, Daniel Avrahami, Jacob Biehl,
Patrick Chiu, Chelhwon Kim, Qiong Liu, Henry Tang, Lynn Wilcox
FX Palo Alto Laboratory
3174 Porter Drive
Palo Alto, CA, USA
tonyd@fxpal.com

ABSTRACT
New technologies arise in a number of ways. They may come from advances in scientific research, through new combinations of existing technologies, or by simply imagining what might be possible in the future. This video describes the evolution of Tabletop Telepresence, a system for remote collaboration through desktop videoconferencing combined with a digital desk. Tabletop Telepresence began as a collection of camera, projector, videoconferencing and user interaction technologies. Working together; artists and research scientists combined these technologies into a means of sharing paper documents between remote desktops, interacting with those documents, requesting services (such as translation), and communicating through a videoconference.

Categories and Subject Descriptors
H.4.m [**INFORMATION SYSTEMS APPLICATIONS**]: Miscellaneous.

General Terms
Design, Human Factors.

Keywords
Digital desk, tabletop systems, telepresence.

1. INTRODUCTION
Teleconferencing systems have been steadily improving, both in audio/video transmission quality and in the user interfaces to control them. These systems support screen sharing during video conferencing, but sharing paper documents, or other tangible objects, requires users to present them to videoconferencing cameras in an unnatural way. Dedicated overhead cameras are better at capturing paper documents while users interact with them on a tabletop surface. As researchers develop these technologies, concept artists depict how they can be combined and extended to create novel work environments. This video illustrates the evolution of Tabletop Telepresence, a system for desktop conferencing that combines the usual "talking heads" with a shared desktop environment.

2. INSPIRATION
The digital desk was described over 20 years ago as a means to seamlessly work with paper documents and electronic content on a desk [8]. The system involved a camera that recognized documents and user activity on the desktop and a projector that displayed digital content. A related system [6] used a low-resolution video camera to capture selected parts of paper documents.

Improvements in camera/projector systems allowed the creation of vision-based gesture interfaces ([3], [7]), and rich document interactions [5]. In these, the user interacts with an interface projected on the desktop along with paper documents to control applications such as document services on a digital desk. High resolution cameras also enabled the capture of document pages on a tabletop surface with sufficient quality for OCR [4].

Concept artists working among researchers saw examples of teleconferencing technologies and digital desks, and imagined a system that combined the two in a novel manner. The first concept was a conferencing system in which a paper document on one side of a videoconference could be printed at the other end. This involved using a camera to capture the document, transferring the document image to the remote site for printing, and providing a projected interface controlled by gestures. This was later enhanced with the addition of document translation, which leveraged a web-based document service for OCR of the document image and then translation before printing at the remote location.

3. DEVELOPMENT
We were able to build a working prototype of the system that emerged from the concept art. We added a projector-camera module to our existing tabletop document capture system [4] to provide a vision-based user interface [7], and to support projection of a document on the tabletop. We integrated the Google Translation service to process the captured document OCR results into Japanese or other languages.

Figure 1. Concept of teleconferencing with a digital desk.

DOI: http://dx.doi.org/10.1145/2733373.2807400

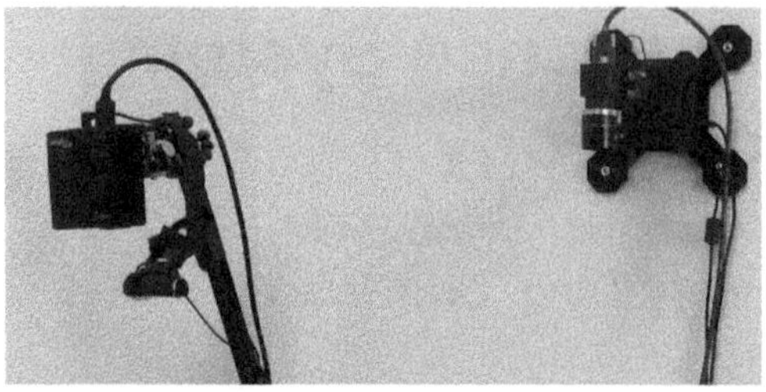

(a)

(b)

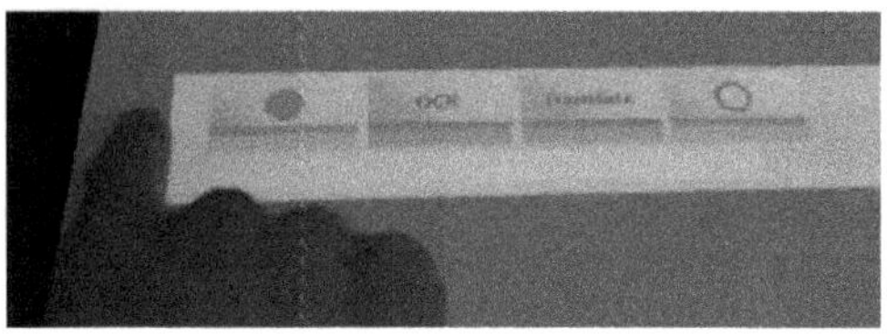

(c)

Figure 2. (a) Projector-camera module and 4K camera mounted on a pan-tilt unit. (b) A user interface toolbar and a captured document are projected on the left side of the table. (c) Close-up of toolbar.

The the tabletop system hardware consists of a Point Grey Flea3 4K video camera for document capture, which is mounted on a pan-tilt robot turret that scans the entire tabletop surface. The document capture occurs in two stages: first by detecting document pages on a cluttered tabletop based on a text probability map, and then by capturing a sequence of overlapping frames of the detected page which are fused into a high quality image that can be processed by OCR [4].

The projector-camera unit is made up of a generic webcam and a lightweight Optoma pico projector. The projected user interface widgets use vision-based techniques that monitor patterns of occlusion on the widgets' hotspots to recognize swipe gestures and button press gestures [7].

Although teleconferencing functions are not integrated into the current system, researchers assumed that teleconferencing could be added with standard systems like Skype or Hangouts. Our concept artists then produced additional illustrations and videos that depict systems with teleconferencing and remote printing capabilities.

4. CONCEPT EXTENSIONS

As video conferencing has become more common, its limitations have become more obvious. Remote participants in meetings consistently report that they feel less "present" than their co-located counterparts. To mitigate this problem, a new generation of telepresence devices is being developed. These devices provide remote collaborators with an enhanced sense of embodiment in environments to which they connect. In particular, we built a prototype telepresence robot called Jarvis [1]. Jarvis consists of an articulated display with a camera, speaker and microphone that can be actively or passively controlled by a remote participant.

Figure 3. Concept of Tabletop Telepresence with Jarvis.

Inspired by Jarvis, concept artists added embodied telepresence to the developing Tabletop Telepresence system. This again resulted in a new round of illustrations and videos.

5. CONCLUSIONS

Concept art has long contributed to product and industrial design, helping manufacturers iteratively improve their product offerings. This video shows how introducing concept art into the early stages of research broadens its scope and helps us iterate into the future.

6. REFERENCES

[1] Biehl, J., Avrahami, D., & Dunnigan, A. Not really there: Understanding embodied communication affordances in team perception and participation. *Proc. CSCW '15.*

[2] Golovchinsky, G., Qvarfordt, P., van Melle, B., Carter, S. Dunnigan, T., DICE: designing conference rooms for usability. *Proc. CHI '09*, pp. 1015-1024.

[3] Kjeldsen, R., Pingali, G., Hartman, J., Levas, T., Podlaseck, M. Interacting with steerable projected displays. *Intl. Conf. on Automatic Face and Gesture Recognition (FGR '02)*, pp. 402-407.

[4] Kim, C., Chiu, P., Tang, H. High-quality capture of documents on a cluttered tabletop with a 4K video camera. *Proceedings of ACM DocEng 2015.*

[5] Liao, C., Tang, H., Liu, Q., Chiu, P., Chen, F. FACT: fine-grained cross-media interaction with documents via a portable hybrid paper-laptop interface. *Proc. ACM Multimedia '10*, pp. 361-370.

[6] Newman, W., Dance, C., Taylor, A., Taylor, S., Taylor, M., Aldhous, T. CamWorks: a video-based tool for efficient capture from paper source documents. *Proc. ICMCS '99*, pp 647–653.

[7] Tang, H., Chiu, P., Liu, Q. Gesture Viewport: Interacting with media content using finger gestures on any surface. *ICME '15 demo.*

[8] Wellner, P. The DigitalDesk Calculator: Tangible manipulation on a desk top display. *Proc. UIST '91*, pp. 27-33.

LiveTraj: Real-Time Trajectory Tracking over Live Video Streams

Tom Z. J. Fu[1] Jianbing Ding[1, 2] Richard T. B. Ma[3, 1] Marianne Winslett[1, 4]
Yin Yang[5, 1] Zhenjie Zhang[1] Yong Pei[1] Bingbing Ni[1]

[1]Advanced Digital Sciences Center, Illinois at Singapore Pte. Ltd.
[2]School of Information Science and Technology, Sun Yat-sen University
[3]School of Computing, National University of Singapore
[4]Department of Computer Science, University of Illinois at Urbana-Champaign
[5]College of Science and Engineering, Hamad Bin Khalifa University

{tom.fu, jianbing.d, tbma, winslett, yin.yang, zhenjie, pei.yong, bingbing.ni}@adsc.com.sg

ABSTRACT

We present LiveTraj, a novel system for tracking trajectories in a live video stream in real time, backed by a cloud platform. Although trajectory tracking is a well-studied topic in computer vision, so far most attention has been devoted to improving the *accuracy* of trajectory tracking, rather than the *efficiency*. To our knowledge, LiveTraj is the first that achieves real-time efficiency in trajectory tracking, which can be a key enabler in many important applications such as video surveillance, action recognition and robotics. LiveTraj is based on a state-of-the-art approach to (offline) trajectory tracking; its main innovation is to adapt this base solution to run on an elastic cloud platform to achieve real-time tracking speed at an affordable cost.

The video demo shows the offline base solution and LiveTraj side by side, both running on a video stream containing human actions. Besides demonstrating the real-time efficiency of LiveTraj, our video demo also exhibits important system parameters to the audience such as latency and cloud resource usage for different components of the system. Further, if the conference venue provides sufficiently fast Internet connection to our cloud platform, *we also plan to demonstrate LiveTraj on-site*, during which we will show LiveTraj identifying and tracking trajectories from a live video stream captured by a camera.

Categories and Subject Descriptors

I.2.10 [**Artificial Intelligence**]: Vision and Scene Understanding – *video analysis*; I.3 [**Computer Graphics**]: Hardware Architecture – *parallel processing.*

General Terms

Performance, Design

Keywords

Real-time video analysis, trajectory tracking, elastic cloud.

MM'15, October 26–30, 2015, Brisbane, Queensland, Australia.
© 2015 ACM. ISBN 978-1-4503-3459-4/15/10 …$15.00.
DOI: http://dx.doi.org/10.1145/2733373.2807401

1. INTRODUCTION

We present LiveTraj, a real-time trajectory tracking system over live videos, running on an elastic cloud platform. Unlike the majority of existing trajectory tracking systems, LiveTraj features real-time processing, which means that its throughput must keep up with the frame rate of the video stream at all times. This capability is critical in many applications, including video surveillance, robotics, autonomous vehicles, etc. For instance, LiveTraj can be deployed to extract human body movements from a surveillance video feed; such movements can be further analyzed to recognize public security threats as well as socially undesirable actions such as fighting. Additionally, LiveTraj can be used to monitor people flows in a crowded area such as a city square during a major festival, which helps prevent accidents such as stampedes, such as the one happened in Shanghai on the New Year's Eve in 2014[1].

One main technical challenge in building LiveTraj is that the workload for video trajectory tracking can be highly dynamic, depending on the content of the video. Figure 1 shows two snapshots from our demo video. In Figure 1a, a man is clapping his hands; clearly, there are only a small number of the extracted trajectories (shown in green lines), which concentrate on the part of the video frame centering on his hands. In contrast, in Figure 1b, where two people are walking, LiveTraj identifies and tracks a much larger number of trajectories. As we explain in Section 3, the workload of LiveTraj depends on the number of trajectories being tracked; hence, the frame shown in Figure 1b incurs significantly higher workload compared to that in Figure 1a. Since LiveTraj runs in real-time, the former frame (Figure 1b) also requires more computational power than the latter (Figure 1a) in order to keep up with the video frame rate. In general, the amount of work can vary from frame to frame in an unpredictable manner, depending on the number of detected trajectories. Provisioning computational resources based on the peak workload would lead to considerable idle time and, thus, waste of resources.

Our solution in LiveTraj is to employ an elastic cloud system to support such fluctuating workload. In particular, the backend of LiveTraj is based on Resa [12], a cloud-based real-time stream processing system built by the authors. Resa includes DRS [5], a dynamic resource scheduler that optimally allocates cloud resources such as CPU cores to different system components, such that overall resource usage is minimized, while ensuring real-time response. Since most cloud providers have a pay-as-you-go

[1] http://en.wikipedia.org/wiki/2014_Shanghai_stampede

pricing scheme, such optimized resource allocation effectively reduces the financial cost for running a real-time trajectory monitoring system. Additionally, Resa also contains a component for efficiently migrating workload between different nodes in a cluster, which facilitates dynamic node additions / removals, and ensures load balancing [3].

(a) Low workload frame (b) High workload frame
Figure 1. Examples of real-time trajectory tracking

LiveTraj is based on an existing state-of-the-art offline trajectory tracking algorithm [15], which achieves high accuracy. In fact, two of our team members have won the ICPR-HARL 2012 competition[2] using an improved version of this algorithm [9]. The main idea is to start new trajectories at dense points [14], and tracks trajectories using optic flows [11]. Note that adapting this algorithm to the cloud platform is non-trivial, as it involves complex data flows containing a loop, as elaborated in Section 3. Further, LiveTraj reduces communication costs between different nodes in the cloud through novel partitioning schemes, avoids redundant computations, and facilitates balanced workloads in different nodes. These designs help LiveTraj achieve real-time response using only a small amount of cloud resources. Our video demo shows that LiveTraj processes a video stream with 640×480 resolution in real time, using merely 7 commodity nodes.

We have prepared both a video demo and an on-site demo. The video demo compares LiveTraj side-by-side with its base algorithm [15], which is so slow that its output video barely moves. Additionally, our video demo also monitors key system performance measurements, e.g., the response time and resource consumption of different system components. The on-site demo will also show the effectiveness and efficiency of LiveTraj at analyzing a live video stream captured by a camera. A pre-requisite of the on-site demo is that the conference venue provides sufficiently fast Internet connection to our cloud platform, so that the live video can be streamed in real time to the cloud servers that run LiveTraj, and at the same time the results of LiveTraj can be streamed back for on-site presentation.In the following, Section 2 overviews related systems. Sections 3 presents LiveTraj. Section 4 describes our video demo as well as the proposed on-site demo. Section 5 concludes with directions for future work.

2. BACKGROUND

Offline video trajectory tracking. Tracking trajectories in an input video is a well-studied problem in computer vision. In the following we overview the offline tracking algorithm [15] used in LiveTraj, which is a state-of-the-art method for video trajectory tracking. Figure 2 illustrates the major components of this method. Specifically, each input video frame is analyzed by two independent components: dense point extraction and optic flow generation. A dense point [14] marks the beginning of a new trajectory, where as an optic flow [11] tracks the movements of pixels in the video frame. After that, the main trajectory tracking module generates trajectories by combining the dense points, the current set of tracked trajectories, and the optic flows.

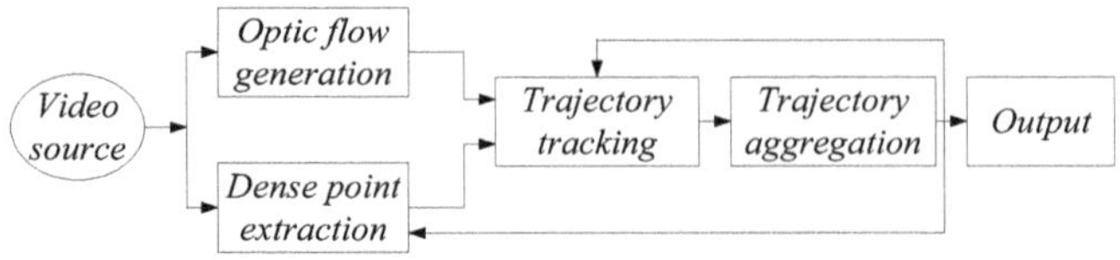

Figure 2. Offline video trajectory tracking algorithm [15]

In particular, for each dense point, the algorithm starts a new trajectory, and later on uses the optic flow to compute its next point. Similarly, for each existing trajectory, the tracking module uses the optic flow to check whether the trajectory has ended, and, if not, the position of the next point on the trajectory. Finally, the generated trajectories are aggregated (e.g., to remove duplicates) and reported to the user. Meanwhile, the results are fed back to the dense point extraction module (e.g., to eliminate dense points on existing trajectories) as well as the trajectory tracking module.

Cloud-based stream processing. Recently, several real-time, cloud-based stream processing systems have been built for applications involving "fast data", which include Apache Storm [13] and its successor Twitter Heron [7], Apache S4 [10], Apache Samza [1], StreamCloud [6] and Apache Spark Streaming [16]. Our Resa system [12] builds on top of Apache Storm, and adds various elasticity features. In particular, a key component of Resa is DRS [5], which, along with a dynamic workload migration module [3] and a resource negotiator called Abacus [17], provides support for *elastic resource allocation*, meaning that resources can be dynamically added to or removed from an application to match its current workload. Further, the resource allocation in DRS is optimized to minimize total resource usage, while satisfying the real-time response constraint. LiveTraj is based on Resa and uses DRS to manage resource allocations.

3. LIVETRAJ

LiveTraj adapts its base trajectory tracking algorithm described in Section 2 to run on an elastic cloud platform. Our main design goals are to (i) minimize redundant computations, (ii) reduce communication costs between nodes in the cloud, (iii) allow a high degree of parallelism and (iv) enable dynamic node additions and removals to match the current workload. Specifically, LiveTraj is based on Resa (described in Section 2), an enhanced version of Apache Storm. Each video manipulation operation in the algorithm, shown in Figure 2, is implemented as a *bolt* (i.e., logical operator) executed by multiple nodes, while the input frame arrive at the system via a *spout* (i.e., streaming source). The output of the system is presented on screen using FFmpeg[3].

We first focus on the dense point extraction bolt, which has two input streams: the input video frame and the current trajectories (from the trajectory aggregation operator shown in Figure 2). The output of this operator consists of dense points sampled in the video frame that are not already on any of the current trajectories. According to Ref. [15], to identify dense points, the algorithm uniformly samples coordinates in the input video frame, and then tests each of these coordinates based on the brightness of the corresponding pixel in the input frame. Figure 3 illustrates the parallel execution of the dense point extractor. In particular, LiveTraj partitions the frame into different regions, and assigns one region to a *dense point evaluator*, each running in a separate thread. Then, the sampled coordinates are grouped according to the partitioning, and routed to the corresponding dense point evaluator. Meanwhile, coordinates on current

[2] http://liris.cnrs.fr/harl2012

[3] https://www.ffmpeg.org

trajectories are similarly grouped by a *point dispatcher*, and routed accordingly. Such partitioning and routing minimizes network transmissions as each node is only fed the pixels and trajectory points it needs. To balance the workload of different nodes, we set the number of regions (a tunable parameter) to be larger than the number of nodes for the operator, and assign each node multiple regions. This design avoids stragglers (i.e., slow nodes forming the bottleneck of the entire system) caused by very dense regions, as the workload is partitioned in finer units. Finally, as the dense point evaluators are stateless, nodes can be added to or removed from the operator at run time, enabling dynamic elasticity provided by the underlying Resa platform.

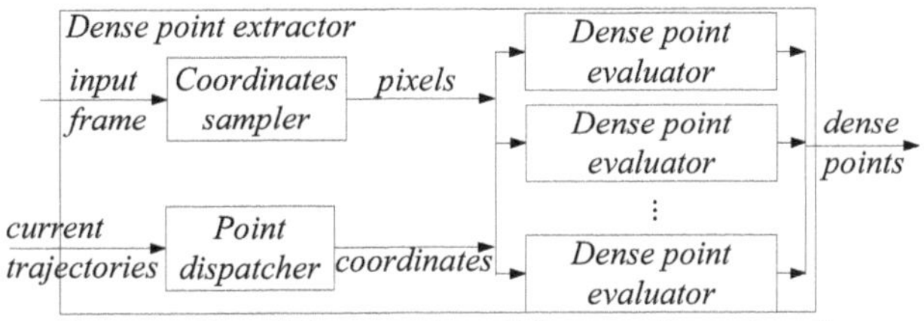

Figure 3. Parallel execution of dense point extraction

The optic flow generation operator is executed by multiple nodes in parallel similarly to the dense point extractor. An additional challenge here is that the generation of optic flows involves (i) comparing two frames at consecutive time instances and (ii) multiple pixels in determining the value of the flow in each coordinate. (i) means that the operator is *stateful*, i.e., each node must store the previous frame and compare with the current one. Hence, node additions and removals (necessary for elasticity) become non-trivial as a new node does not immediately possess the necessary states to work (i.e., pixels on the previous frame) on its inputs. Fortunately, these are handled by the DRS module of the underlying Resa platform, which performs operator state migrations transparently [3][5]. Regarding (ii), each node cannot simply handle a region in the frame, as is the case in the dense point extractor, as the computation at one coordinates relies on the surrounding pixels. A naive solution is to broadcast the entire input frame to each node, which, however, incurs a high communication overhead. Our solution in LiveTraj is to split the frame into overlapping *patches* [8]; each patch contains a partition of the frame, as well as the pixels surrounding the partition, as illustrated in Figure 4. This design effectively reduces the amount of network transmissions, thus improving system scalability.

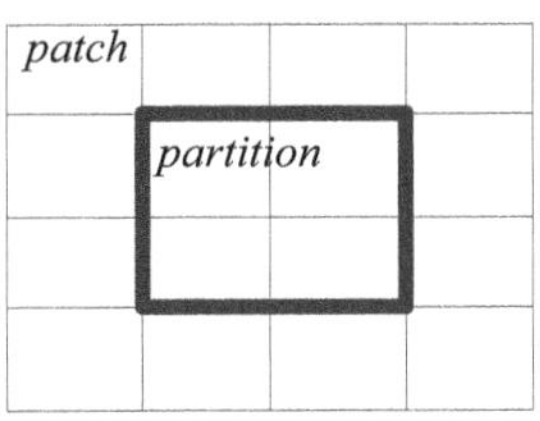

Figure 4. Example of frame partition and patch

Finally, we examine the trajectory tracking operator, which involves three inputs: the current trajectories, the dense points detected from the input frame, and the optic flows of the input frame. The main idea of this operator is to "grow" a trajectory, either an existing one or a new one starting at a dense point, by adding one more coordinate computed from the optic flow. Note that it is possible that the optic flow indicates that there is no more coordinate on this trajectory in the input frame, ending the trajectory. The parallelization of this operator is similar to that of the dense point extractor, except that each node is assigned trajectories rather than pixels and coordinates. Grouping of the trajectories is performed according to their last coordinates (or the newly identified dense points for new trajectories). We omit further details for brevity. Observe that the workload of this operator depends on the number of extracted dense points and current trajectories: when there are numerous trajectories being tracked (e.g., in Figure 1b), the system has heavier workload, which may necessitate node additions. Conversely, when there are few trajectories (Figure 1a), the amount of workload drops and the system can release some nodes. Our elastic Resa platform handles such resource changes efficiently and effectively, which reduces resource costs while ensuring real-time response.

4. DEMONSTRATION SCENARIO

Video demo. Figure 5 shows a screenshot of our video demo. The panel on the left monitors important performance measurements of different components of the system, e.g., dense point extraction and optic flow computation. The performance indicators include response time, resource consumption, etc. In the center we present the output video streams of both the offline algorithm and LiveTraj side by side. The output video of LiveTraj plays smoothly, whereas the output for the offline algorithm barely moves at all. Finally, the bottom of the demo video displays the command lines and textual outputs of the two systems, which inform the audience of their status updates.

Figure 5. Screen shot of the video demo

The video demo was recorded while LiveTraj was running on 8 nodes, each equipped with an Intel quad-core 3.4GHz CPU and 24GB RAM. Following common practice, we dedicate one node as the master node, running Nimbus (the master node of Apache Storm as well as Resa) and Apache Zookeeper server [2], used in Storm and Resa. Hence, there are 7 worker nodes in total. The input video is from the ChaLearn Looking at People 2014 Challenge [4], which has a resolution of 640×480, at 30 frames per second. The input video is specifically designed for human pose, gesture and action recognition [4]. Note that given sufficient resources, LiveTraj could handle video streams with much higher resolutions. We chose this one due to limitations of the file size in the submission system.

On-site demo. The planned on-site live demo uses LiveTraj to track trajectories of an arbitrary input stream captured by a camera. For instance, the audience can stand in front of the camera and perform arbitrary body movements, and LiveTraj will mark these movements in real time. The audience can then observe the effectiveness (i.e., accuracy) and efficiency (i.e., in terms of output smoothness and result delay) of LiveTraj. Note that the onsite demo is only possible when the conference venue provides sufficiently fast Internet connection, since all computations will be performed remotely on our cloud servers. For the same reason, the resolution of the input video will be tuned according to the Internet speed at the conference site.

5. CONCLUSIONS AND FUTURE WORK

We propose to demonstrate LiveTraj, a real-time video trajectory tracking system running on an elastic cloud platform. LiveTraj is based on a state-of-the-art offline trajectory tracking algorithm using dense points and optic flows, and it adapts this algorithm to the elastic cloud environment through a number of innovative designs as well as the underlying Resa platform. Our video demo compares the efficiency of LiveTraj with the offline base solution, and presents to the audience the smooth and low-lag output stream of the former. Given sufficiently fast Internet connection at the conference venue, we will also show an onsite demo that further enriches the audience's experience by letting them try LiveTraj using a live video stream captured on site.

6. ACKNOWLEDGEMENTS

This study is supported by the research grant for the Human-Centered Cyber-physical Systems Programme at the Advanced Digital Sciences Center from Singapore's Agency for Science, Technology and Research (A*STAR). Ding is partially supported by NSF of China under Grant 61173081, and also supported by GZSI's grant 2013Y2-00046.

7. REFERENCES

[1] Apache Samsa. *http://samza.apache.org* .

[2] Apache Zookeeper. *https://zookeeper.apache.org/* .

[3] Ding, J., Fu, T., Ma, R., Winslett, M., Yang, Y., Zhang, Z., Chao, H. Optimal Operator State Migration for Elastic Data Stream Processing. *CoRR*, 1501.03619, 2015.

[4] Escalera, S., Baró, X., Gonzàlez, J., Bautista, M., Madadi, M., Reyes, M., Ponce-López, V., Escalante, H., Shotton, J., Guyon, I. ChaLearn Looking at People Challenge 2014: Dataset and Results. In *Proc. ECCV Workshops*, 2014.

[5] Fu, T., Ding, J., Ma, R., Winslett, M., Yang, Y., Zhang, Z. DRS: Dynamic Resource Scheduling for Real-Time Analytics over Fast Streams. In *Proc. IEEE ICDCS*, 2015.

[6] Gulisano, V., Jiménez-Peris, R., Patiño-Martínez, M., Soriente, C., Valduriez, P. StreamCloud: an Elastic and Scalable Data Stream System. *IEEE TPDS*, 23(12): 2351-2365, 2012.

[7] Kulkarni, S., Bhagat, N., Fu, M., Kedigehalli, V., Kellogg, C., Mittal, S., Patel, J., Ramasamy, K., Taneja, S. Twitter Heron: Stream Processing at Scale. In *Proc. ACM SIGMOD*, 2015.

[8] Lindeberg, T. Scale Invariant Feature Transform. *Scholarpedia*, 7(5): 10491, 2012.

[9] Ni, B., Pei, Y., Moulin, P., Yan, S. Multi-Level Depth and Image Fusion for Human Activity Detection. *IEEE TSMC (B)*, 43(5): 1383-1394, 2013.

[10] Neumeyer, L., Robbins, B., Nair, A., Kesari, A. S4: Distributed Stream Computing Platform. In *Proc. IEEE ICDM KDCloud Workshop*, 2010.

[11] O'Donovan, P. Optical Flow: Techniques and Applications. Technical Report 502425, University of Saskatchewan, 2005.

[12] Tan, T, Ma, R., Winslett, M., Yang, Y., Yong, Y., Zhang, Z. Resa: Realtime Elastic Streaming Analytics in the Cloud. In *Proc. ACM SIGMOD*, 2013, poster.

[13] Toshniwal, A., Taneja, S., Shukla, A., Ramasamy, K., Patel, J. M., Kulkarni, S., Jackson, J., Gade, K., Fu, M., Donham, et al. Storm@Twitter. In *Proc. ACM SIGMOD*, 2014.

[14] Wang, H., Kläser, A., Schmid, C., Liu, C.-L. Action Recognition by Dense Trajectories. In *Proc. CVPR*, 2011.

[15] Wang, H., Kläser, A., Schmid, C., Liu, C.-L. Dense Trajectories and Motion Boundary Descriptors for Action Recognition. *IJCV*, 103(1): 60-79, 2013.

[16] Zaharia, M., Das, T., Li, H., Shenker, S., Stoica, I. Discretize Streams: an Efficient and Fault-Tolerant Model for Stream Processing on Large Clusters. In *Proc. ACM SOSP*, 2013.

[17] Zhang, Z., Ma, R., Ding, J., Yang, Y. ABACUS: An Auction-Based Approach to Cloud Service Differentiation. In *Proc. IEEE IC2E*, 2013.

[18] Zhang, Z., Shu, H., Chong, Z., Lu, H., Yang, Y. C-Cube: Elastic Continuous Clustering in the Cloud. In *Proc. IEEE ICDE*, 2013.

Automatic Accident Detection and Alarm System

Zhuo Wei
Shield Lab, Huawei
International Pte. Ltd.
wei.zhuo@huawei.com

Swee-Won Lo
Singapore Management
University, Singapore
sweewon.lo.2009@smu.edu.sg

Yu Liang
Wuhan University,
China
liangyu@whu.edu.cn

Tieyan Li
Shield Lab, Huawei
International Pte. Ltd.
li.tieyan@huawei.com

Jialie Shen
Singapore Management
University, Singapore
jlshen@smu.edu.sg

Robert H. Deng
Singapore Management
University, Singapore
robertdeng@smu.edu.sg

ABSTRACT

Accident detection and alarm system is very important to detect possible accidents or dangers for people using their mobile devices while walking, i.e., distracted walking. In this paper, we introduce an automatic accident detection and alarm system, called AutoADAS, which is fully implemented and tested on real mobile devices. The proposed system can be activated either manually or automatically. Under the manual mode, user activates the system before distracted walking while under the automatic mode, a "user behaviour profiling" module is used to recognize (distracted) walking behaviours and an "object detection" module is activated. Using image processing and camera field of view, the distance and angle between the user and detected objects are estimated and then used to identify whether any potential accidents can happen. The "accident analysis and prediction" module includes: temporal alarm that inputs the user's walking speed and distance with respect to the detected objects and outputs temporal accident prediction; spatial alarm that inputs the user's walking direction and angle with respect to the detected objects and outputs spatial accident prediction. Once the proposed system positively predicts a potential accident, the "alarm and suggestion" module alerts the user with text, sound or vibration.

Categories and Subject Descriptors

I.4 [**Image Processing and Computer Vision**]: Applications

Keywords

Smartphone; Sensor; Machine learning

1. INTRODUCTION

Intelligent mobile devices such as smartphones and tablets have become one of our essential day-to-day tools. They can simultaneously function as communication, entertainment and work-related tools via multitude of applications such as text messages, emails, electronic payment, online gaming and entertainment. Hence, pedestrians are increasingly being seen walking down the street engaging in their mobile devices; this has also rendered them to be accident-prone due to distracted walking. A research study conducted by Ohio State University found that injuries involving pedestrians on their mobile devices have more than doubled between 2005 and 2010[2]. Aside from the texting-while-walking statistics, there have been numerous incidents concerning distracted walking in the recent years that have made headlines, e.g., a woman fell into a fountain at the Pennsylvania mall while texting in January 2011; a tourist in Australia walked off a pier in December while checking Facebook on her phone. A few research study also found that 53% of adult smartphones users have been involved in a distracted walking encounter[3]. It is thus necessary for accident detection and alarm systems to be in place to prevent such accidents due to distracted walking. For example, in a bid to avoid "text walking" collisions, a Belgian city has been provided with dedicated temporary "text walking lanes" for pedestrians who are glued to their mobile phones. Such prevention measures have been given considerable attention in the industry. In 2014, Apple Inc. developed a "transparent texting" technology where the mobile device's rear-facing camera continuously capture images of the environment in front of the pedestrian. These images are shown as background within a text messaging session currently in use so the pedestrian can continuously be aware of any obstacles in front. However, this application cannot be used when multimedia applications are in use since it requires ample amount of space to render visual information. Furthermore, pedestrian is not always able to pay attention to the background while texting and there is no automatic push alerts. A pedestrian collision detection system is also developed by Denso Corporation, a global automotive components manufacturer. Here, a vehicle-side collision detection module is mounted inside a vehicle to detect collision with pedestrian through wireless communication between the vehicle and user's mobile device. This method relies on devices which can detect collision and requires communication between the pedestrian and vehicle, but some obstacles do not have such detection and communication capability. In [1], the CrashAlert scheme is applied to design a collision de-

MM'15, October 26–30, 2015, Brisbane, Australia.
© 2015 ACM. ISBN 978-1-4503-3459-4/15/10 ...$15.00.
DOI: http://dx.doi.org/10.1145/2733373.2807402.

tection system via extending a user's peripheral alertness during distracted walking. This is achieved by mounting a depth camera on the mobile device and displaying the depth camera's image as a minimal footprint on the mobile device; a red alert is then forwarded to the user on a potential accident. This scheme requires a mobile device augmented with a depth camera to calculate object distance and location.

In this paper, we propose an automatic accident detection and alarm system, called AutoADAS, which is fully implemented for the mobile devices. The system consists of four modules: firstly, it makes use of sensors on the mobile device to run the user behavior profiling module and decide when to automatically activate the device. Based on the sensors' feedback, the object detection module is turned on to identify objects of interest such as obstacles and pedestrians, and estimate their positions (distance and angle) with respect to the user. The accident analysis and prediction module assesses the probability of possible accidents and the alarm and suggestion module then sends an alert to the user.

2. AUTOMATIC ACCIDENT DETECTION AND ALARM SYSTEM

This section gives a detail introduction of AutoADAS and its four key modules.

2.1 User Behavior Profiling Module

Today mobile devices such as smartphones and tabelets are equipped with various sensors such as barometer, accelerometer and gyroscope.

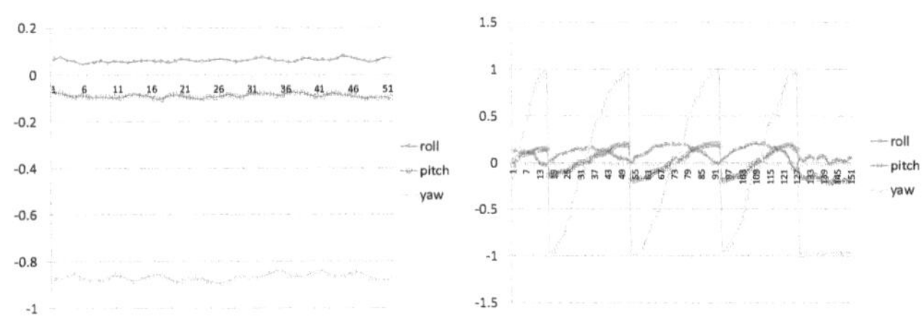

(a) Straight. (b) Turning.

Figure 1: The yaw, pitch and roll axes of a gyroscope when user walks.

In this system, we make use of gyroscope and accelerometer to detect user's walking direction and speed, respectively. When a user walks, gyroscope detects three orthogonal axes, namely, yaw, pitch and roll as shown in Figure 1. The parameter of interest in this study is the *yaw* axis which measures the device direction (left or right) given the direction of its motion. As for Google Nexus 5, the yaw value decreases as user turns right and increases as user turns left. Hence, it can be used to infer user's walking direction and evaluate whether an accident is prone to happen when combined with other modules. For example, if a detected object is on the left and in front of a user while the user's walking direction is towards the right, then there will be no accident detection. Let yaw_t be the yaw value at time t and yaw_{t-1} be the yaw value at time $t-1$. When yaw_t and yaw_{t-1} have the same sign, let $\Delta = \mathsf{yaw}_t - \mathsf{yaw}_{(y-1)}$, the system infers that the user walking direction is "left" if Δ is positive; otherwise, the direction is "right". When yaw_t and yaw_{t-1} have different signs, let $\omega = \mathsf{yaw}_t + \mathsf{yaw}_{t-1}$, we say that the user's walking direction is straight or has changed suddenly when $\omega > 0.1$. If $\mathsf{yaw}_t > 0.5$ or -0.1 and $\omega < 0.1$, then the walking direction is "left"; otherwise, it is "right".

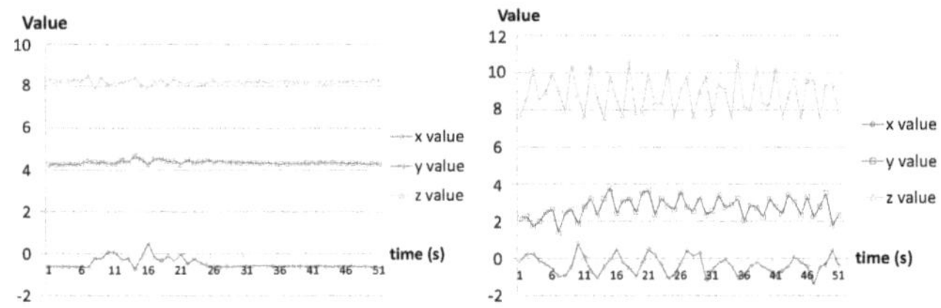

(a) Standing. (b) Walking.

Figure 2: The distribution of x, y and z values of accelerometer.

Accelerometer can be used to infer the user's walking speed. Figure 2(a) illustrates the x, y and z values of the accelerometer when a user is static. Figure 2(b) illustrates changes in the x, y and z values as the user walks. Based on the peak and trough frequencies, the system can infer the user's number of walking steps, s_w, and the step length, l_w using machine learning. Then, the walking speed is calculated as *speed* $= (s_w \times l_w)/\Delta t$, where Δt is the time span over where s_w and l_w were measured.

2.2 Object Detection Module

The object detection module consists of five core components: image processing, feature extraction, classification, object recognition, and position estimation. Assuming that the user holds the mobile device in vertical position and the views in front of the user is captured by the rear camera, the module proceeds as follow.

Let $\mathbf{I}$ be the front view image captured by the camera. The image $\mathbf{I}$ is first converted into gray image $\mathbf{I}_g$ in order to reduce subsequent computation complexity; note that $\mathbf{I}_g$ could be scaled based on device processor and memory capacity. Feature is then extracted from $\mathbf{I}_g$ and by using classifiers (from open sources, e.g., Opencv classifiers or training data, e.g., using Support Vector Machine), object of interest (e.g., other pedestrians or obstacles) can be recognized. Considering that the object of interest may be in full or partial view, the classifiers can be trained based on different datasets, e.g., full body, upper or lower body only. Once objects of interest are recognized, the position in relative to the user is estimated in terms of *angle* (i.e., straight/left/right) and *distance* (i.e., far/close). Both parameters are obtained using the camera position.

On the one hand, the distance between the user and object of interest can be estimated by following way. Assuming that camera focus is constant and camera height is h, which can be configured by the users based on their height, the distance d_O can be calculated as in Figure 3(a).

$$d_O = h/\mathtt{tan}(\phi/2) \tag{1}$$

Figure 3(b) illustrates d_i and the corresponding positions in the image and shows a linear relationship between real and pixel distance. Since the camera focus is constant, each image is of the same resolution. Hence, the object distance

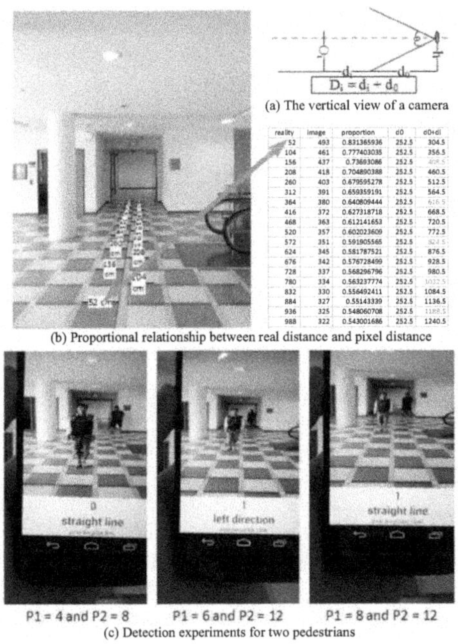

Figure 3: The proportional relationship between real distance and pixel distance.

can be estimated based on its position and size and the real distance D is calculated as follow.

$$D = d_0 + d_i \tag{2}$$

Figure 3(c) illustrates the distance experiments for two pedestrians. The distance between the user and the pedestrians can be estimated, where Pi is distance from the ith pedestrian;

On the other hand, similarly, the angle ψ between the user and object of interest can be estimated as shown in Figure 4(a). The angle on image I, ϕ^I, is calculated, where (w, h) is the image resolution. The reality angle ϕ is estimated by using the proportional relationship between real angle and pixel angle as shown in Figure 4(b). The example at the figure shows that when the reality angle are 45, 30, and 15 degrees to the left, the arccot values are about 0.647, 1.084, and 2.198 on the image, respectively. Figure 5 illustrates the angle estimation results for a human object.

2.3 Accident Analysis and Prediction Module

The output parameters from the user behavior profiling and object detection modules are then analyzed in the accident analysis and prediction module as shown in Figure 6. The danger prediction P is given by spatial $\phi(t)$ and temporal $d(t)$ predictions:

$$P = \int_0^t \frac{d(t)}{\cos(\phi(t))} - \frac{d(t+\Delta t}{\cos(\phi(t+\Delta t))}, \text{ where} \tag{3}$$

$$\phi(t) = F_s(angle, direction) \tag{4}$$

$$d(t) = F_t(spccd, distance) \tag{5}$$

, where P, F_s and F_t are logical discriminants. The spatial prediction $\phi(t)$ depends on the user's walking direction and the angle between the user and the object of interest, where an angle threshold should be set, e.g., no less than 30 degrees. The temporal prediction $d(t)$ depends on the user's walking speed and distance between the user and the object of interest, where a distance threshold should be set, e.g., no less than 10m. When both spatial and temporal alarms are true, the user will be alerted. For example, if a user is walking straight with an object right in front (i.e., angle = 0 degree), and the distance between the user and object is less than 5m while the walking speed will result in collision within 4-5s, both spatial and temporal alarms are true, and the user will be alerted. However, if in similar spatial prediction parameters but the distance is more than 10m with a walking speed of less than 0.5m/s, then the user will not be alerted since the temporal alarm is false.

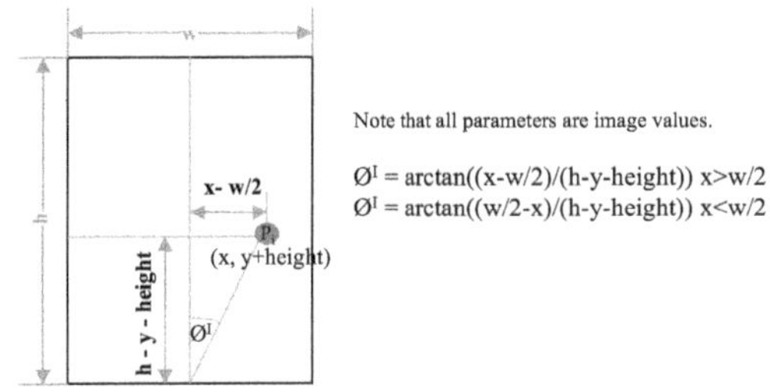

(a) Angle ϕ^I calculation at I.

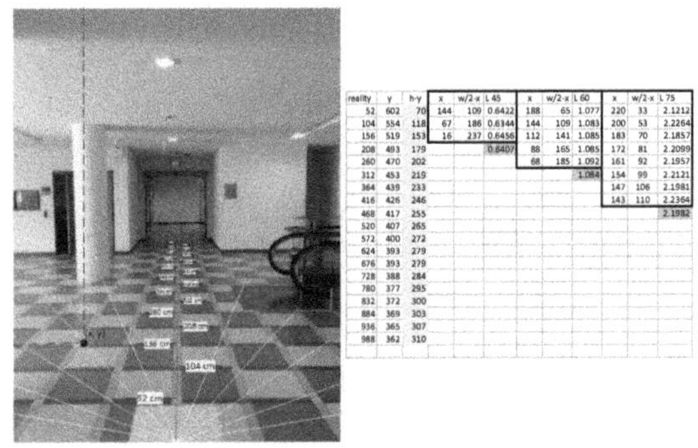

(b) The linear relationship between real angle and pixel angle.

Figure 4: Angle calculation.

2.4 Alarm and Suggestion Module

Once the accident analysis and prediction module detects that the user is prone to an accident, this module will alert the user through either text messaging, alert tone or device vibration. In addition, this module can further display popup advices such as "stop walking", or advice the user to "turn 30 degrees to your left".

3. EXPERIMENTS AND DISCUSSIONS

AutoADAS is demonstrated to recognize pedestrians in front of mobile users. Our experiments are performed on Android platforms (Samsung Galaxy 4, Huawei P6, and Google Nexus 5) in indoor and outdoor environments, in order to evaluate the performance. Experimental results show that AutoADAS can accurately predict accidents in

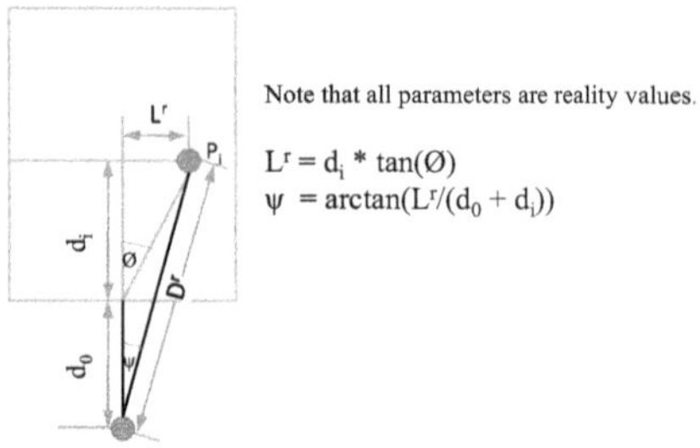

(a) The real angle ψ between pedestrians and objects.

(b) Experiments of angle.

Figure 5: Angle calculation.

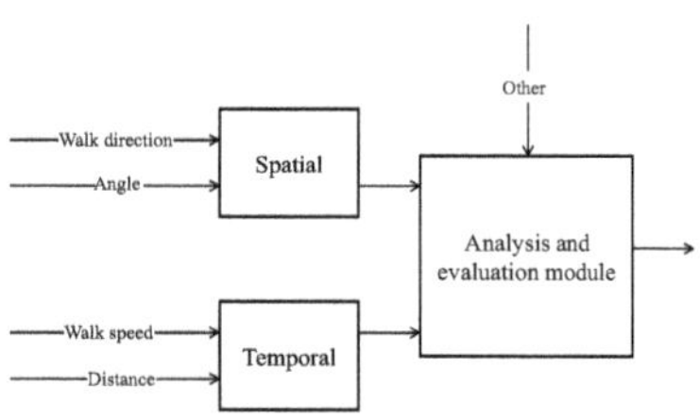

Figure 6: Spatial and temporal evaluations.

real time for mobile users. Specifically, sensors detect user behavior, where error margins for walk direction is about 5 degrees and walking speed is 0.1m/s; and image processing estimates objects position, where orientation is about 10 degrees drift and distance is about 0.5m drift error.

3.1 Discussions

Although our demonstrations show that mobile devices were hold vertically, commercially available devices such as the Vivo's OPPO N1 smartphones have camera that can be rotated up to 206 degrees to emulate vertical position during device usage. The proposed system also depends on accuracy of object detection, which is affected by photo quality (lighting or appearance), but this does not affect the system's accident detection performance.

3.1.1 Usability

Since user behavior estimation and object detection are less complex, the proposed system is real-time; it guarantees that predicted potential accident can be conveyed to the user immediately. The proposed system can be activated either manually or automatically, depending on the need of a user. For the manual model, a user activates the system prior to distracted walking while for the automatic model, the system is automatically started once the user behavior profiling module detects distracted walking behavior. Furthermore, accident prediction is based upon both spatial and temporal alarms that takes into account of not only detected objects in front of the user, but also the user's walking speed and the distance between the user and the object. The alarm can be customized depending on the urgency of required actions. In addition, the proposed system is fully integrated with the mobile device and does not require any additional mounting on the mobile device.

3.1.2 Extension

Apart from preventing accidents during distracted walking, AutoADAS can also be used to assist visually-impaired users in case of accidents, or to alert them of other pedestrians, obstacles, hazardous places, or important signs such as traffic lights. For example, when walking on tactile paving, the object detection module scans for obstacles, signs of hazardous places in front of the user. The accident analysis and prediction module then computes the spatial and temporal predictions and will decide if the users are accident-prone. If yes, the alarm and suggestion module will alert the user by sound or vibration, which could be customize to convey whether the users should stop, turn left or turn right.

The system can also be used for users who walk and call, where after detecting that a user is walking while calling, the system will be activated and alerts the user by sound or vibration to avoid accidents.

4. CONCLUSION

To decrease the number of potential accidents due to distracted walking while using mobile devices, we introduce an automatic accident detection and alarm system that has been fully integrated into the mobile devices. It exploits the sensors available on mobile devices to infer the user's walking behavior (e.g., walking direction and speed), and utilizes image processing and camera FOV to estimate the distance and angle between the user and detected objects. Then, the system uses the above information to predict and evaluate if potential accidents could happen with temporal and spatial alarms. Finally, the proposed system raises an alert and provides advices to the user (via text, sound or vibration) once a potential accident happens.

5. REFERENCES

[1] J. D. Hincapie-Ramos and P. Irani. CrashAlert: Enhancing peripheral alertness for eyes-busy mobile interaction while walking. In *Proceedings of the SIGCHI Conference on Human Factors in Computing Systems*, pages 3385–3388, 2013.

[2] J. L. Nasar and D. Troyer. Pedestrian injuries due to mobile phone use in public places. *Accident Analysis & Prevention*, 57(0):91 – 95, 2013.

[3] A. Smith. More than half of cell owners affected by 'distracted walking', January 2014.

Visible Light Communication via Temporal Psycho-Visual Modulation

Chunjia Hu
Institute of Image Communication and Information Processing
Shanghai Jiao Tong University
Shanghai, China
hcj-sjtu@sjtu.edu.cn

Guangtao Zhai
Institute of Image Communication and Information Processing
Shanghai Jiao Tong University
Shanghai, China
zhaiguangtao@sjtu.edu.cn

Zhongpai Gao
Institute of Image Communication and Information Processing
Shanghai Jiao Tong University
Shanghai, China
gaozhongpai@sjtu.edu.cn

ABSTRACT

ARAR In this paper we propose a new paradigm for visible light communication (VLC) using the emerging display technology of Temporal Psycho-Visual Modulation (TPVM) that exploits the interaction between human visual system and modern electro-optical display devices. Unlike traditional VLC, no specifically designed light emitter and receiver are required. In the proposed system, light projector is used as the information source and digital cameras act as information decoder. The emitted light is designed in a specific way such that it can carry meaningful information (or simply works as an illumination source) for human eyes while other message can be decoded by the digital camera due to the fundamental difference in the imaging mechanism of the human eye and digital devices. We further describe two applications of this new type of VLC in ubiquitous augmented reality and illegal camcorder-recording prevention with extensive experimental results.

Keywords

Augmented reality; Temporal Psychovisual Modulation; TPVM

1. INTRODUCTION

Electric light, after its invention, has played an important role in our daily life. Recent years, some technology has emerged using electric light more than a light source. For example, visible light communication (VLC) [1] has been introduced to modulate light principally used for illumination to carry information. However, VLC system relies on specific modules. Only with those modules, can we receive and decode the information transferred via light. The modulated light itself is not meaningful to human eyes or cameras.

Another popular technology these days is augmented reality[2], which supplements the real world with virtual (computer-generated) objects that appear to coexist in the same space as the real world. It combines real and virtual objects in a real environment and registers them with each other. The dominant implementation of augmented reality system involves a symbol, a camera sensor and a screen. The symbol is used as an identification, indicating the information and the location of the virtual objects that should appear on the screen. It can be either a barcode (e.g., QR code) or a specific image. When the camera detects the symbol, the system presents the preset virtual objects in the real environment on the screen. One obvious drawback of this kind of augmented reality system is that both the identification symbol and the virtual object should be preset in the database and require a specific program used for recognizing and rendering. Meanwhile, for the system using barcode as the symbol, the barcode is not meaningful to human, but it occupies a large space in the real world. For those using the specific image for identification, the accuracy of the recognizing process depends heavily on the environment. The computational complexity of both recognizing and rendering process is not low.

In this paper, we present a new paradigm for VLC, which

Figure 1: Illustration of the proposed visible light communication system.

MM'15, October 26–30, 2015, Brisbane, Australia.

DOI: http://dx.doi.org/10.1145/2733373.2807404.

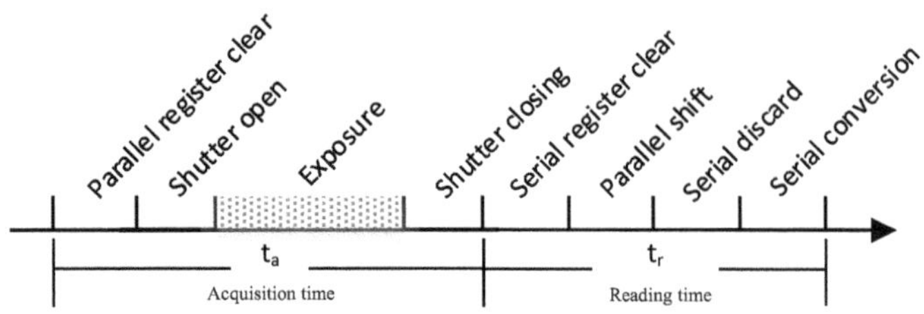

Figure 2: Time slices of one frame recorded by full frame CCD in digital cameras. The frame rate f of the digital cameras is determined by the frame acquisition time t_a and frame read time t_r as $f = 1/(t_a + t_r)$.

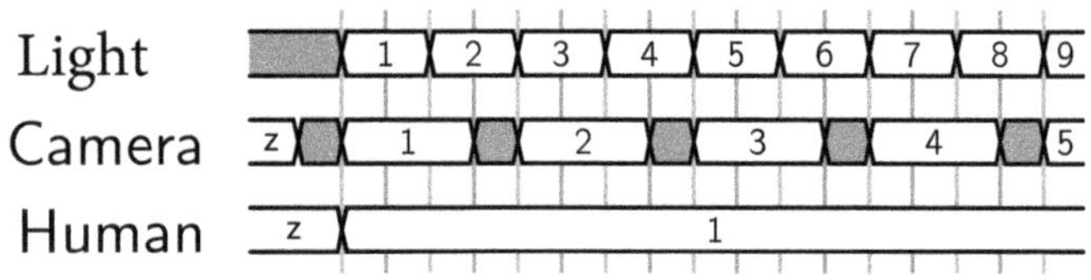

Figure 3: Timing diagram for TPVM display. The black blocks represent no signal is emitted or received. The number blocks represent the frames are emitted or received.2012acm

seems to be a normal light source for human eye, while users can get the imperceptible information through their camera, as shown in Fig.1.

2. PHILOSOPHY

The design of our special light exploits the difference in image formation mechanism between human visual perception and video capture of digital cameras. For human eyes, we form steady image in our human visual system by continuous integration of light field. While for digital sensors, their sample process is discrete.

Charge-coupled device (CCD) and complimentary metal oxide semiconductor (CMOS) are two types of commonly used sensors in the market. Fig. 2 shows the time schedule of imaging process for a single frame by full frame CCD in digital cameras. There are two periods in the imaging process, which are frame acquisition time t_a and frame read time t_r. Only during the acquisition time t_a the shutter is open to the light source. Then, the shutter closes during the frame read time t_r to process the data captured and clear the register. The digital cameras cannot capture all the information from the light source due to the 'blackout' period due to CCD's working mechanism. CMOS works much like CCD except that each column of sensors have independent image acquisition process.

As analysis above, digital camera cannot fully record all the optical signals emitted from the light with high refresh rate. Therefore, human eyes and digital imaging sensors apply different temporal convolution kernels to light sources when forming images. Based on this difference, we can design optical signals in the way that human and imaging sensors perceive drastically different images. To achieve this goal, as shown in Fig. 3, the refresh rate of the light should be in the same order as a camera shutting period $(t_a + t_r)$. More specifically, there should be more than two refresh of the light during a camera shutting period. Fortunately, the LED based lights support high refresh rate. For LED displays, refresh rate of 300 Hz is a standard and it is possible to reach more than 1200 Hz at a moment. BenQ DLP® Projector TH681[1] can support full HD resolution (1920 × 1080) with triple flash (144 Hz). The TI DLP7000 chipset[2], a flexible light steering solution for industrial, medical and scientific applications, even provides 32,552 Hz refresh rate. However, the shutter period of normal imaging sensors (e.g., those embedded in the mobile phones or smart glasses), only support the highest frame rate of 60Hz. Thus, with the off-the-shelf products, we can achieve the mismatch between the image captured by human eye and electronic eyes. Now it comes to the problem that how to modulate the high refreshing light to achieve the different images simultaneously.

3. DISPLAY MODEL

3.1 Temporal Psychovisual Modulation

As new paradigms of information display, Temporal and Spatial Psychovisual Modulation (TPVM and SPVM) [7], [4] are recently proposed as ingenious interplay of signal processing, optoelectronics, and psychophysics. TPVM uses the psychovisual redundancy in refresh rate of the modern optoelectronic displays. The main stream liquid crystal displays such as LCD and LED support 120Hz or higher refresh rate output nowadays. While the human visual system (HVS) cannot differentiate quick changes above about 60Hz under most conditions. TPVM exploits the redundant frames to provide different contents to different observers simultaneously. The so-called atom frames are broadcasted at a speed several times higher than that the HVS can recognize. And the viewers can use their own display-synchronized shutter glasses to temporally weight the atom frames. Through different glasses, people can see different images on the same screen at the same time. There are many applications based on TPVM paradigm. e.g., backward compatible stereoscopic display [6], camcorder defeating [9] and multi-subtitle exhibition [5].

3.2 Human Eyes View

The VLC system should provide basic illumination function as the normal light for human eyes view. As in the TPVM framework, the human eyes cannot discriminate light refreshing higher than the critical flicker frequency, which is 60Hz. We let the light emit a subframe sequence x_i at a refresh rate of 120Hz or higher, instead of the frame of conventional display. HVS perceive the high speed frames with continuously integral kernel. This process be expressed by:

$$I_1 = \sum_i x_i \tag{1}$$

, where I_1 is the human eyes view and x_i is the subframes presented by the light, i is the number of the subframe.

3.3 Digital Imaging Sensor View

Besides, the VLC system provide a digital imaging sensor view which is different from the human eyes view. As analyzed in Section II, the imaging process of the digital sensor involves the acquisition and reading time. The sampling

[1]BenQ TH681: http://benq.eu/product/projector/th681
[2]TI DLP7000 chipset: http://www.ti.com/product/dlp7000

process is discrete thus it cannot record all the subframes emitted from the light. Here we can assume that the longer the digital sensor is exposed to signal light, the higher the intensity of the image will be. We add a weight function to indicate the degree of exposure:

$$w_i = t_e/t_f \tag{2}$$

, where w_i is corresponding weight of each subframe, t_e is the exposure time of each subframe to the rolling sensor and t_f is the total time each subframe is displayed by the light. Thus, we can express the imaging process of digital sensor by a weighted kernel:

$$I_2 = \sum_i w_i x_i \tag{3}$$

, where I_2 is the digital imaging sensor view and x_i is the subframes presented by the light, w_i is corresponding weight of each subframe.

3.4 Multi-view Solution

To achieve simultaneous display of two different views (i.e., both I_1 and I_2 are meaningful), the system should satisfy the following equation:

$$\min\left\{\left\|Y_1 - \sum_i x_i\right\| + \lambda\left\|Y_2 - \sum_i w_i x_i\right\|\right\} \tag{4}$$

,where Y_1 and Y_2 are the preset images to be displayed for the view I_1 and I_2. In this paper, we need Y_1 equal to a constant, which is used for normal illumination. The augmented reality view is achieved in I_2, so that the user can use their camera to acquire more information of the real object. Thus,

$$\begin{cases} Y_1 = C \\ Y_2 = V \end{cases} \tag{5}$$

,where C is a constant and V is the virtual image of the augmented reality.

For a 120Hz refresh rate light ($i = 2$), here we can give a simple solution to the system:

$$\begin{cases} x_1 = C - V \\ x_2 = V \end{cases} \tag{6}$$

which means the two subframes to shift between the virtual image and its complementary. In that way, the human eye view is

$$I_1 = \sum_i x_i = C - V + V = C \tag{7}$$

When using digital sensors, due to the fact that the camera shutter is not sync to the refresh of the display, only one of the two weight w_i is dominant for each exposure. That is, the sensor record either x_1 or x_2 with a larger weight. The digital imaging sensor view comes to

$$I_2 = \sum_i w_i x_i = w_1(C-V)+w_2V = w_1C+(w_2-w_1)V \tag{8}$$

Thus, the captured view can be either V or its complementary $C - V$. Both of the views are meaningful to the HVS, as shown in the experimental results.

The multi-view visible light communication system is realized. In the next section, we will discuss the interesting applications of this novel function.

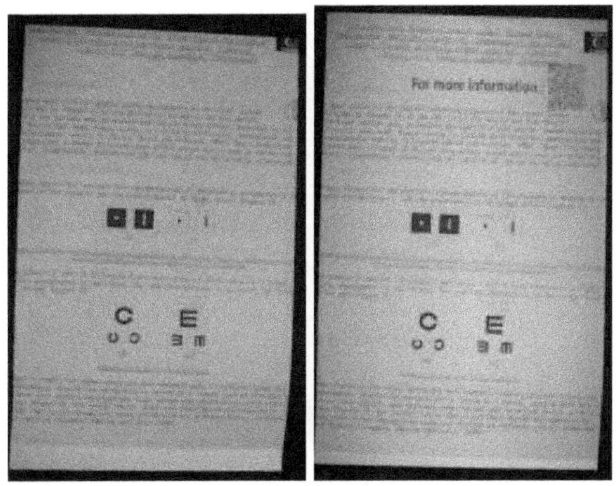

Figure 4: Augmented Reality Solution. The left is the normal view for the human eyes view. And the right is the digital camera view with a QR code embedded for more information. Both the two views are clear and not conflicting with each other.

4. APPLICATIONS AND EXPERIMENT RESULTS

In our implementation, we use the TI DLP® LightCrafter^{TM} 4500[3] as our light source. The light refreshes at the pattern of 120Hz. To acquire the view for human eyes, we set Cannon EOS 5d camera's exposure time as 1 second to simulate the HVS. The figures of camera view are taken by different popular mobile phones on the market. All of the cameras of the mobile phones apply default setting.

4.1 Augmented Reality

The visible light communication system via TPVM provides a brand new approach of augmented reality. For example, in a museum, the exhibits can be lightened by the augmented light. For those who are interested in the exhibits, they just need to take out their cameras or smart phones to get a augmented view. No extra application is required to be installed and no limitation on the performance of the smart phones and cameras. Meanwhile, the two different views are not conflicting with each other. In some international exhibition, the light can also work as a simple translator. The native speakers can read the original documents directly while those need translation can see through their camera view. As shown in Fig.4, we add a QR code pattern into the document. For those want to get more information about the document, he can use his camera to get the link via QR code. More experiment results of augmented reality are given in the supplementary video.

4.2 Illegal Camcorder-recording Prevention

Another interesting application of this novel light is illegal recording defeating. Privacy protection achieves great attention these days. Some existing solutions[3] use the infrared light that can be captured by the sensor but imperceptible to human eyes. Yamada et al.[8] proposed to embed infrared lights on glasses for preventing privacy invasion through un-

[3]Datasheet available: http://www.ti.com/tool/dlplcr4500evm

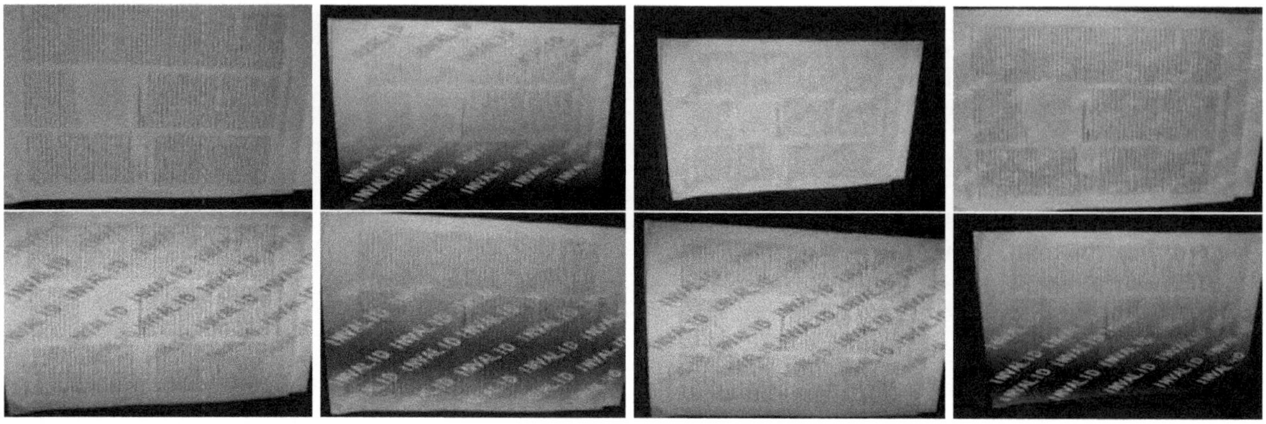

Figure 5: Illegal Camcorder-recording Prevention. Subfigure (a) is the normal view for human eyes. The rest are taken by different cameras. From left to right are: (b) iPhone 6 Plus, (c)iPhone 5, (d)Samsung S5, (e)Samsung S4 (f)Google Nexus 5 (g)Huawei P6 (h)XiaoMi 4
We can come to the conclusion that the defeating camcorder system can jam the recording of most of the mobile phones on the market.

intentional capture of facial images. However, the infrared lights are harmful to human eyes. Furthermore, most cameras these days has coating film that filter the infrared light. A better solution to defeating camcorder is necessary. We can use the proposed multi-view light to realize this function. For Eq.6, we can set the camera view V to a disturbing watermark. Then, the lightened objects become read only, which means we can only see the object but it is not available for cameras. The captured images are shown in Fig.5. We tested many kinds of popular cameras and mobile phones from the market, and all of images taken are stamped with a watermark of 'Invalid'. We can even use some barcode as the watermark pattern to track the illegal recording.

5. CONCLUSIONS

Visible light communication use light as a source to convey information. However, the information transmitted is only meaningful to specific modules, not to human eyes. In this paper, we propose a novel visible light communication solution. The system exploit the different imaging mechanism to provide two different views simultaneously. It provide normal illumination for HVS. Meanwhile, if the user use the digital cameras to capture images, the hidden virtual display will be visible. Based on this brand new function, we further list two applications of this kind of light. It can be used for both augmented reality and illegal recording defeating. We test our system on different kinds of cameras and the experiment results are provided.

6. ACKNOWLEDGEMENTS

This work was supported in part by NSFC (61422112, 61331014, 61371146).

7. REFERENCES

[1] S. Arnon. *Visible light communication.* Cambridge University Press, 2015.
[2] R. Azuma, Y. Baillot, R. Behringer, S. Feiner, S. Julier, and B. MacIntyre. Recent advances in augmented reality. *Computer Graphics and Applications, IEEE*, 21(6):34–47, Nov 2001.
[3] I. Echizen, T. Yamada, and S. Gohshi. Ir hiding: method for preventing illegal recording of videos based on differences in sensory perception between humans and devices. In *Transactions on Data Hiding and Multimedia Security VII*, pages 34–51. Springer, 2012.
[4] C. Hu, G. Zhai, Z. Gao, and X. Min. Information security display system based on spatial psychovisual modulation. In *Multimedia and Expo (ICME), 2014 IEEE International Conference on*, pages 1–4. IEEE, 2014.
[5] C. Hu, G. Zhai, Z. Gao, and X. Min. Simultaneous triple subtitles exhibition via temporal psychovisual modulation. In *Industrial Electronics and Applications (ICIEA), 2014 IEEE 9th Conference on*, pages 944–947. IEEE, 2014.
[6] X. Wu and G. Zhai. Backward compatible stereoscopic displays via temporal psychovisual modulation. In *SIGGRAPH Asia 2012 Emerging Technologies*, page 4. ACM, 2012.
[7] X. Wu and G. Zhai. Temporal psychovisual modulation: A new paradigm of information display [exploratory dsp]. *Signal Processing Magazine, IEEE*, 30(1):136–141, 2013.
[8] T. Yamada, S. Gohshi, and I. Echizen. Use of invisible noise signals to prevent privacy invasion through face recognition from camera images. In *Proceedings of the 20th ACM international conference on Multimedia*, pages 1315–1316. ACM, 2012.
[9] G. Zhai and X. Wu. Defeating camcorder piracy by temporal psychovisual modulation. *Journal of Display Technology*, 10(9):754–757, 2014.

What shall I look like after N years ?

Xiangbo Shu[1,2]
shuxb104@gmail.com

Jinhui Tang[1,*]
jinhuitang@njust.edu.cn

Luoqi Liu[2]
llq667@gmail.com

Zhiheng Niu[2]
niuzhiheng@nus.edu.sg

Shuicheng Yan[2]
eleyans@nus.edu.sg

[1]School of Computer Science and Engineering, Nanjing University of Science and Technology, China
[2]Department of Electrical and Computer Engineering, National University of Singapore, Singapore

ABSTRACT

—*"What shall I look like after N years?"*
In this paper, we present an Auto Age Progression system, which automatically renders a series of aging faces in the future age ranges and generates an aging sequence (aging video) covering the entire life for an individual input. In the offline stage, a set of age-range specific dictionaries are learned from the constructed database, where the dictionary bases corresponding to the same index yet from different dictionaries form a particular aging process pattern across different age groups, and a linear combination of these patterns expresses a particular personalized aging process. In the online stage, for an input face of an individual, our system renders the aging faces corresponding to different age ranges through the aging dictionaries, and then generates an age progression by the presented face morphing technology.

Categories and Subject Descriptors

J.5 [**Arts and humanities**]: Arts, fine and performing

Keywords

Age progression system, face aging, face morhping

1. INTRODUCTION

Age progression has found application in some domains such as authentication systems, finding lost children, and entertainment. Recently, some demos/Apps related to face aging have been developed. For example, Face Transformer[1] and AgingBooth[2] are receiving great interest. However, these demos/Apps require some manually operations, which are not very convenient. Besides, the generated aging faces for different inputs are very similar, and not many personalized characteristics are preserved. Furthermore, the aging faces correspond to the coarse age periods, i.e., Teenager, Adulthood, Older.

*Corresponding author
[1]http://cherry.dcs.aber.ac.uk/Transformer/
[2]http://www.piviandco.com/apps/agingbooth/

MM'15, October 26–30, 2015, Brisbane, Australia.
© 2015 ACM. ISBN 978-1-4503-3459-4/15/10 ...$15.00.
DOI: http://dx.doi.org/10.1145/2733373.2807962.

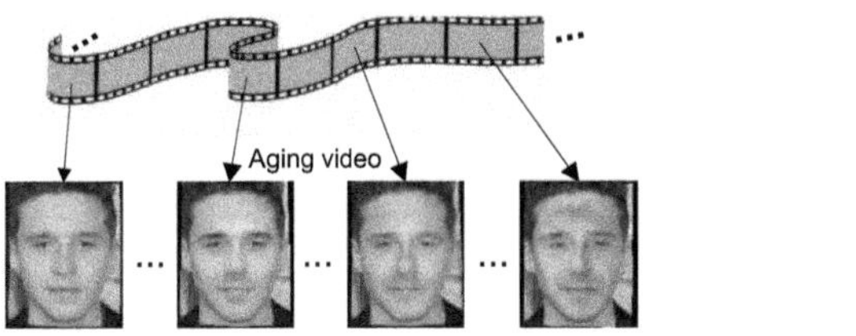

Figure 1. The unfold frames of aging video generated by our demo. An face photo of individual (on the left top) is shot or loaded, then our presented demo automatically generates an aging sequence (aging video) covering one's whole life.

Therefore, we develop an Auto Age Progression system, which can render a series of aging faces in the future age ranges (one age range spans no more than 10 years) and generate a whole aging sequence covering the entire life for an individual input. Figure 1 shows the unfold frames of an aging video for an input face. Compared to the previous Apps, our system has two advantages: (1) **Automatic & Personalized**: our system can automatically render the aging face in a personalized way by the proposed aging bases; (2) **More Visualized**: our system can generate a whole aging video densely covering the entire life.

Technically, we firstly collect the intra-person aging pairs from the Web and the available databases, and then we design a corresponding aging dictionary to represent the aging characteristics in one age group. Finally, all aging dictionaries are simultaneously trained by a personality-aware dictionary learning model on the collected data. Above steps are offline operation.

In our system, we load or photograph an input face. The face is first aligned by the face alignment technology. Then its gender and age will be estimated by the gender and age estimators. The aging face in one age range will be rendered by calling the aging dictionary, which is saved in the backstage. After rendering all aging faces, we generate more dense aging faces between the aging faces of the two nearest age ranges by the face morph technology. A loop-play video is made by stringing all the aging faces. Figure 2 shows the interface of our auto age progression system.

2. TECHNOLOGY

2.1 Data Collection

We download a large number of intra-person face photos covering different ages from Bing, and two other databases, CACD database [1] and MORPH aging database [3]. We select the photos with approximately frontal faces and relatively natural illumi-

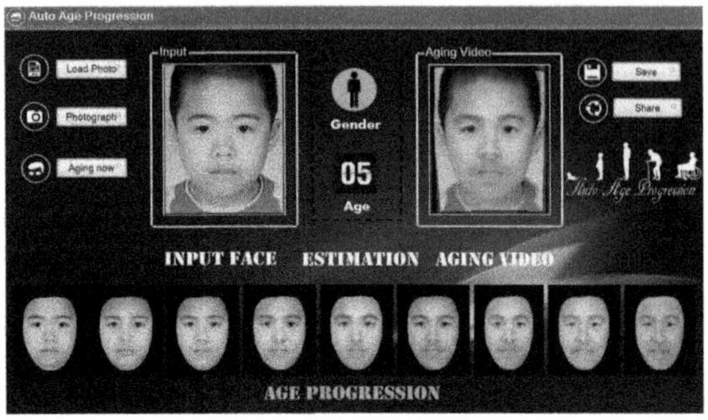

Figure 2. Interface of the presented system. When an input face photo is loaded/photographed, the system first estimates his/her age and gender, and shows aging faces in different age ranges, as well as an aging video from now to future playing in the loop.

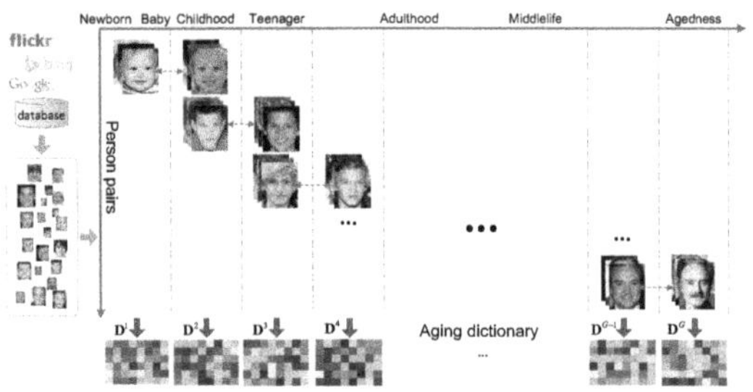

Figure 3. Data collection and aging dictionary learning. $\mathbf{D}^g$ denotes an aging dictionary of the age group g. We collect short-term aging face pairs and then train the aging dictionary.

nation, and then use collection flow [2] to correct all the faces to common neutral expressions. We divide all images into 18 age groups (i.e., $G = 9$): 0-5, 6-10, 11-15, 16-20, 21-30, 31-40, 41-50, 51-60, 61-80 of two genders. Actually, the aging faces of most subjects fall into only one or two age groups (i.e. most persons have face photos covering no more than 20 years). Therefore, we further select those intra-person face photos which densely fall into two neighboring age groups. Finally, As shown in Figure 3, the training database contains 3,200 face aging pairs.

2.2 Aging Dictionary Learning

Let $\{\mathbf{x}_i^g, \mathbf{y}_i^g\}$ denote a face aging pair of the person i in the age group g. Assuming m face aging pairs covering two neighboring age groups, we train two aging dictionaries for male and female, respectively. For the age group g and $g+1$ ($g = 1, 2, \cdots, G-1$), we define their aging dictionaries $\mathbf{D}^g$ and $\mathbf{D}^{g+1}$ to capture the corresponding aging characteristics, which will be learned in the following.

$$\begin{aligned}
&\min_{\mathbf{D}^g,\mathbf{D}^{g+1}} \sum_{i=1}^{m} \{\|\mathbf{x}_i^g - \mathbf{H}^g\mathbf{D}^g\mathbf{a}_i^g - \mathbf{p}_i^g\|_2^2 \\
&\qquad + \|\mathbf{y}_i^g - \mathbf{H}^{g+1}\mathbf{D}^{g+1}\mathbf{a}_i^g - \mathbf{p}_i^g\|_2^2\} \\
&s.t.\ \mathbf{a}_i^g = \arg\min_{\mathbf{z}_i^g} \|\mathbf{x}_i^g - \mathbf{H}^g\mathbf{D}^g\mathbf{z}_i^g - \mathbf{p}_i^g\|_2^2 + \lambda_1\|\mathbf{z}_i^g\|_1 + \lambda_2\|\mathbf{z}_i^g\|_2^2 \\
&\quad \mathbf{p}_i^g = \arg\min_{\mathbf{q}_i^g} \|\mathbf{x}_i^g - \mathbf{H}^g\mathbf{D}^g\mathbf{a}_i^g - \mathbf{q}_i^g\|_2^2 + \gamma\|\mathbf{q}_i^g\|_1 \\
&\quad \|\mathbf{D}^c(:,l)\|_2 \le 1,\ i = 1,...,m,\ l = 1,...,k,\ and\, c = \{g, g+1\},
\end{aligned} \tag{1}$$

where $\mathbf{a}_i^g$ and $\mathbf{p}_i^g$ are the representation coefficient and personalized layer respectively, and the latter is invariant in the aging process, i.e., mole. λ_1, λ_2 and γ are the parameters to control the corresponding terms. The optimizing of Eq. (1) can be solved by referring to bi-level optimization in the paper [4].

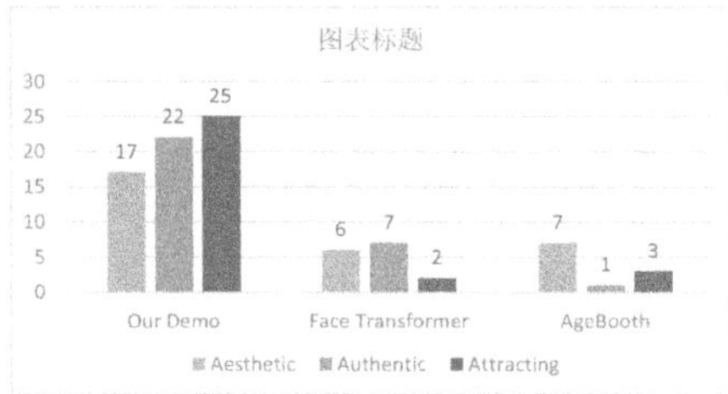

Figure 4. Evaluation of the aging show from the 30 volunteers. The vertical axis is the number of persons.

2.3 Age Progression and Aging video

For a given face $\mathbf{x}$ belonging to the age group g[3], we can render its aging faces $\{\mathbf{x}^{g+1}, ..., \mathbf{x}^G\}$. The coefficient and personalized layer are optimized by solving the following optimization:

$$\begin{cases}
\mathbf{a}^g = \arg\min_{\mathbf{z}^g} \|\mathbf{x}^g - \mathbf{H}^g\mathbf{D}^g\mathbf{z}^g - \mathbf{p}^g\|_2^2 + \lambda_1\|\mathbf{z}^g\|_1 + \lambda_2\|\mathbf{z}^g\|_2^2 \\
\mathbf{p}^g = \arg\min_{\mathbf{q}^g} \|\mathbf{x}^g - \mathbf{H}^g\mathbf{D}^g\mathbf{a}^g - \mathbf{q}^g\|_2^2 + \gamma\|\mathbf{q}^g\|_1
\end{cases}. \tag{2}$$

Then the aging face is $\mathbf{x}^{g+1} = \mathbf{x}^g - \mathbf{H}^{g+1}\mathbf{D}^{g+1}\mathbf{z}^g - \mathbf{p}^g$. For one aging face, we blend into the original face to obtain the blending face; for two arbitrary aging faces $\mathbf{x}^{g+j}$ and $\mathbf{x}^{g+j+1}$ in the neighboring age ranges, we morph their blending faces with different weights by the face morphing technology. Finally, we make a video by stringing all aging faces and view the played faces according to the age axis. An age progression example is shown in Figure 1.

3. EVALUATIONS

We compare our aging system with two other Apps: Face Transformer and AgeBooth. The properties of the aging system are evaluated in three aspects: aesthetic, authentic, attracting. 30 volunteers (12 females and 28 males who are students, staffs and businessmen ranged from 18 to 50 years old) participate in the user study. We conduct user study by making participants vote for some aging results of two apps and our system on 20 input faces: 10 females and 10 males. The average voting results of three aspects are shown in Figure 4. We can see that our system has gained the highest voting support in all the three aspects. The Face Transfer and AgeBooth are comparable with each other.

4. CONCLUSION

In this paper, we proposed an auto age progression system. This system can automatically render a series of aging faces in the future age ranges and generates a whole aging sequence covering the entire life for an individual input. The supplementary slides can be found at http://t.cn/R2Ja5kO.

5. ACKNOWLEDGEMENTS

This work was partially supported by the National Basic Research Program of China (973 Program) under Grant 2014CB347600, the Program for New Century Excellent Talents in University under Grant NCET-12-0632, the Natural Science Foundation of Jiangsu Province under Grant BK2012033.

6. REFERENCES

[1] B.-C. Chen, C.-S. Chen, and W. H. Hsu. Cross-age reference coding for age-invariant face recognition and retrieval. In *ECCV*. 2014.
[2] I. Kemelmacher-Shlizerman and S. M. Seitz. Collection flow. In *CVPR*, 2012.
[3] K. Ricanek and T. Tesafaye. Morph: A longitudinal image database of normal adult age-progression. In *FG*, 2006.
[4] J. Yang, Z. Wang, Z. Lin, S. Cohen, and T. Huang. Coupled dictionary training for image super-resolution. *TIP*, 21(8):3467–3478, 2012.

[3]The age and gender are estimated by age and gender estimators.

Searching and Browsing Live, Web-based Meetings

Scott Carter, Laurent Denoue, Matthew Cooper
FX Palo Alto Laboratory, Inc.
3174 Porter Drive
Palo Alto, CA 94304
carter,denoue,cooper@fxpal.com

ABSTRACT

Establishing common ground is one of the key problems for any form of communication. The problem is particularly pronounced in remote meetings, in which participants can easily lose track of the details of dialogue for any number of reasons. In this demo we present a web-based tool, MixMeet, that allows teleconferencing participants to search the contents of *live* meetings so they can rapidly retrieve previously shared content to get on the same page, correct a misunderstanding, or discuss a new idea.

Categories and Subject Descriptors

H.5.2 [**Information Interfaces and Presentation (e.g., HCI)**]: User Interfaces

Keywords

Teleconferencing; web; search

1. INTRODUCTION

Past work in teleconferencing recording and retrieval has focused on systems and methods to capture content in instrumented spaces and to access and search media post hoc [1], as well as methods to help users late to a meeting "catch up" to real-time via the rapid presentation of key information [2]. On the other hand, less work has focused on searching and recovering material presented during lightweight, web-based meetings. This functionality can be particularly useful in a long meeting during which participants are sharing digital content via screensharing.

For example, consider the following scenario: John, an interaction designer, is sharing his designs during a teleconference with Maria, a product manager. He uses screensharing to page through several designs constructed in a variety of different applications. Half an hour into the meeting, Maria realizes that a design John is currently showing would work best alongside another he showed ten minutes earlier. Using current web-based meeting tools, which provide support for searching through meeting content post hoc, Maria would have to verbally describe the content and hope that John could find it and re-share it.

MixMeet is a web-based teleconferencing tool we built that can simplify this process (Figure 1). With MixMeet Maria can quickly retrieve the design she is looking for either by searching (Figures 2, 3) or browsing (Figure 4). MixMeet creates a browsable and searchable keyframe archive per participant during live meetings. Frames from participants' streams are saved at regular intervals in real time during the meeting. Users can adjust a range slider on each participant's stream to view archived frames (Figure 4 left). Users can also hover over the main timeline to view archived frames from the stream that is currently in full-screen mode. At the same time, MixMeet utilizes live content analysis and interface techniques to make it possible to index and search content. Users can type a query into the search box at any time, and search matches are visualized either as marks on the appropriate range slider (Figure 3) or, when the user searches in a separate search panel, inline.

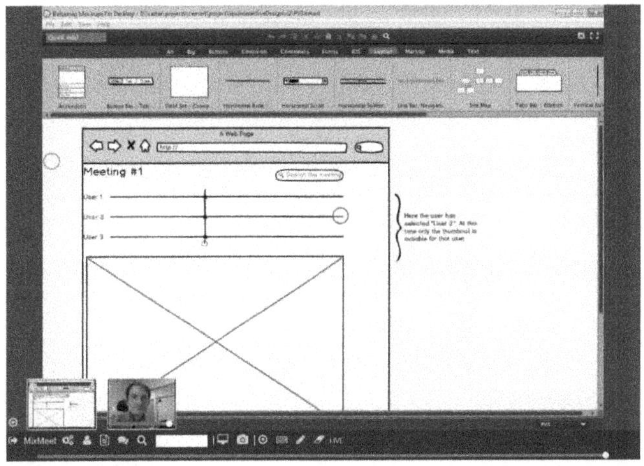

Figure 1: The MixMeet interface. Here, one user shares his webcam while the other shares a region of her screen. Participants can browse captured keyframes for each stream using range sliders. The slider of the currently selected, fullscreen stream is positioned at the bottom of the interface, while the other slider is positioned at the bottom of the remote participant's live, thumbnailed video.

MM '15, October 26-30, 2015, Brisbane, Australia
ACM 978-1-4503-3459-4/15/10.
DOI: http://dx.doi.org/10.1145/2733373.2807964.

Figure 2: Searching a live meeting. The search term 'meeting' has a single hit, indicated in white on the main timeline.

2. INDEXES

MixMeet analyses video, audio, and metadata streams continuously to generate searchable content:

- *Speech* MixMeet generates a speech-to-text transcript on the fly using Google's Web Speech API running in continuous mode.
- *OCR* MixMeet can stream either webcams or screen regions. A Javascript-based OCR engine analyses screen content. Users connecting via a mobile device can take advantage of a server-side OCR engine.
- *Annotations* MixMeet also supports live, content-based annotations [3]. Annotated screen content is weighted preferentially for matching frames with search terms.
- *Mouse events* MixMeet records and forwards mouse events to remote clients. These events are also weighted preferentially during search.

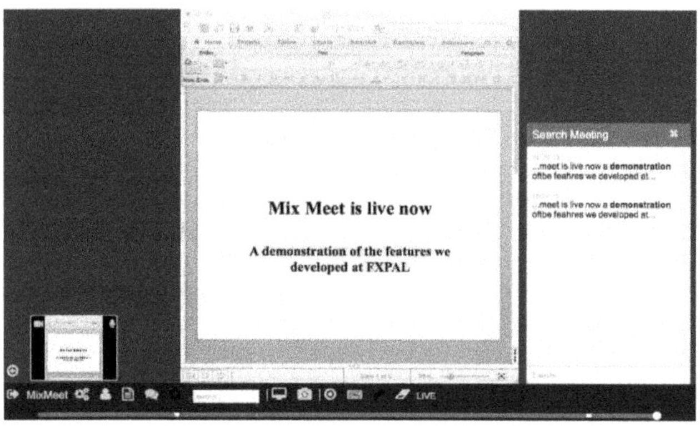

Figure 3: The search box shows OCR or Speech to Text that match the query 'demonstration'; for each result, the system shows the time and a small snippet of text around the match.

3. ORIENTATION-BASED BROWSING

Many remote participants use teleconferencing to meet with a group of collocated people. This scenario often involves a tablet device with a single camera that is rotated during the meeting so that the remote participant can see different co-located members or resources (e.g., whiteboards) in the room. These rotations can be controlled by the remote participant via a table-top device (such as a Kubi[1]) or by a local participant manually moving the tablet to frame other participants when appropriate. MixMeet listens to DeviceOrientationEvents that modern browsers generate to detect these changes and index archived keyframes appropriately. The client further bins these orientation events into

Figure 4: (Left) Users can browse to frames archived earlier in the meeting with the range slider. (Right) Orientation events are automatically detected and used to help users navigate meetings. In this case, the user moved his tablet device away from his face and toward a whiteboard. The remote interface automatically generated an interactor showing previous directions the camera had pointed during the meeting (black rectangle), the current direction (red), and directions not yet used in this meeting (light gray). Clicking on any black rectangle shows the most recent frame from that direction. Clicking on the red rectangle sets the stream to the live view.

four categories: front, left, right, and back. When a device has keyframes saved from at least two positions, a small interactor appears above the appropriate participant's stream allowing remote users to directly navigate back to the last keyframe stored from each direction (Figure 4 right).

4. CONCLUSIONS AND FUTURE WORK

Using content analysis, indexing, and search and browsing interfaces, MixMeet can make content shared in live meetings more useful. As work practices become more distributed, the context of meetings will continue to evolve, and the types of devices people use to follow meetings remotely will change. As such, we are investigating ways for people to search, browse, and otherwise actively participate in live meetings from other interfaces, including wearables.

5. REFERENCES

[1] Cutler, R., Rui, Y., Gupta, A., Cadiz, J.J., Tashev, I., He, L., Colburn, A., Zhang, Z., Liu, Z., and Silverberg, S. Distributed Meetings: A Meeting Capture and Broadcasting System. *Proceedings of ACM Multimedia*, 503–512. 2002.

[2] Junuzovic, S., Inkpen, K., Hegde, R., Zhang, Z., Tang, J., and Brooks, C. What Did I Miss?: In-meeting Review Using Multimodal Accelerated Instant Replay (Air) Conferencing. *Proceedings of the SIGCHI Conference on Human Factors in Computing Systems*, 513–522. 2011.

[3] Denoue, L., Cooper, M., Girgensohn, A., and Carter, S. Building digital project rooms for web meetings. *Proceedings of the ACM Symposium on Document Engineering*, 135–138. 2014.

[1] https://www.revolverobotics.com/

Deep Face Beautification

Jianshu Li [1,5]
jianshu@u.nus.edu

Chao Xiong [2]
superx21@gmail.com

Luoqi Liu [4]
llq667@gmail.com

Xiangbo Shu [3,4]
shuxb104@gmail.com

Shuicheng Yan [4]
eleyans@nus.edu.sg

[1] School of Computing, National University of Singapore, Singapore
[2] Department of Electrical and Electronic Engineering, Imperial College London, U.K.
[3] School of Computer Science and Engineering, Nanjing University of Science and Technology, P. R. China
[4] Department of Electrical and Computer Engineering, National University of Singapore, Singapore
[5] SAP Research and Innovation Singapore, SAP Asia Pte Ltd

ABSTRACT

The beautification of human photos usually requires professional editing softwares, which are difficult for most users. In this technical demonstration, we propose a deep face beautification framework, which is able to automatically modify the geometrical structure of a face so as to boost the attractiveness. A learning based approach is adopted to capture the underlying relations between the facial shape and the attractiveness via training the Deep Beauty Predictor (DBP). Relying on the pre-trained DBP, we construct the BeAuty SHaper (BASH) to infer the "flows" of landmarks towards the maximal aesthetic level. BASH modifies the facial landmarks with the direct guidance of the beauty score estimated by DBP.

Categories and Subject Descriptors

J.5 [**Arts and Humanities**]: Arts, fine and performing

Keywords

Facial beautification; Face morphing

1. INTRODUCTION

The pursuit of beauty roots deeply in the intrinsic spirit of human beings and people incline to show their most attractive side to others by retouching the portraits. However, the aesthetic enhancement of photos usually has high requirements on the skills of using some professional editing softwares, such as Photoshop. Such barrier makes it difficult for most users to beautify photos by themselves. Therefore, automatic beautification of human face photos becomes a topic of great importance, which is demonstrated in this work. Despite the importance and great commercial potential, prior efforts on the statistical study of beauty are limited. Most previous works [4, 3] focus on the analysis of facial attractiveness. The work in [2] enhances facial attractiveness, but the score predictor is built on a simple linear regressor, whose discriminative capability is limited in capturing the complex underlying rules of aesthetic evaluation.

The recent success of deep learning has stimulated many applications in various research fields [1]. Deep neural network is able to learn a highly abstract and nonlinear feature representation with regard to the given objective, which makes it a suitable tool to capture the implicit link between facial geometry structure and attractiveness. In this demo, we use deep neural networks to automatically beautify facial images. We first learn the relation between facial geometrical structure and beauty level. Then with a photo of a human face, we can predict the beauty score, based on which the structure of facial landmarks is reshaped towards the maximal level of beauty. The face image is then warped according to the transformed landmarks to produce the beautified face.

In our demo, we process the user's input face image and display the result in real time. The interface is shown in Figure 1.

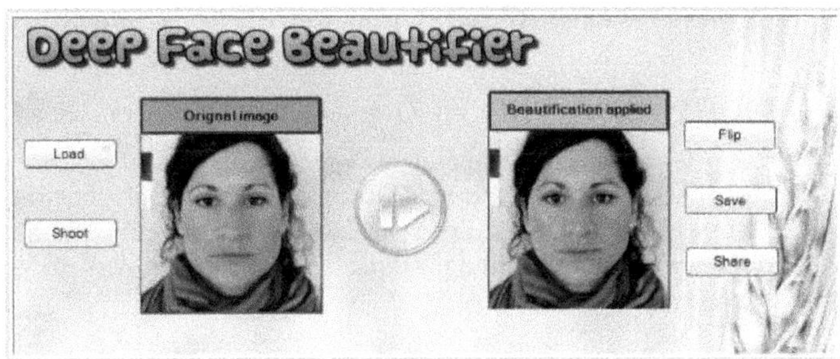

Figure 1: User interface of our demo

2. TECHNOLOGY

2.1 Training Dataset

Several datasets have been released for the studies on human attractiveness in literature. The Multi-Modality Beauty (M^2B) dataset in [4] is used to train our model. M^2B database includes facial, dressing images and audio files of 1,240 females, and provides corresponding attractiveness score for each modality. The scores are in the range of 1 to 10, where 1 is the lowest beauty level and 10 is the highest. During the training process of our model, only information in terms of the face images is employed.

MM'15, October 26–30, 2015, Brisbane, Australia.
ACM978-1-4503-3459-4/15/10.
DOI: http://dx.doi.org/10.1145/2733373.2807966.

2.2 Deep Beauty Predictor

A fully-connected deep neural network is adopted to learn the beauty score prediction, which is called Deep Beauty Predictor (DBP). The input feature vector of DBP is the concatenation of the facial landmarks' coordinates. Assume we are given n training samples $\{\boldsymbol{X}_i, i = 1, 2, ..., n\}$ with corresponding beauty scores $\{s_i, i = 1, 2, ..., n\}$. The DBP network aims at solving a regression problem with regard to the following objective

$$\mathcal{L} = \sum_{i=1}^{n} (\mathcal{F}(\boldsymbol{X}_i) - s_i)^2 + \alpha ||\boldsymbol{W}||^2, \tag{1}$$

where $\mathcal{F}$ denotes the feature mapping of the network, and $|| \cdot ||^2$ is the ℓ-2 regularizer on the network weights to reduce over-fitting. The objective can be optimized with standard Stochastic Gradient Descent (SGD).

In this demo, DBP follows a four-layered structure, and the numbers of hidden units are 800, 800, 300 and 1 respectively. Each of the first three layers is followed by ReLU as the activation function. The output of the last layer is used to compute the regression cost as in Eqn. (1), and thus the dimension should be 1. To reduce the impact of over-fitting, drop-out is adopted after each of the first three layers, and the drop-out rate is set as 0.3. The weight decay parameter α in Eqn. (1) is set as 0.1. As for the training of DBP, the initial learning rate is set to 0.001, and decreased by 50% every 2,000 iterations. The maximal iteration number is set as 20,000.

2.3 BeAuty SHaper with Deep Input Gradient

BeAuty SHaper (BASH) focuses on inferring the "flows" of landmark points such that the resulting beauty score of the transformed landmark locations is maximized. The flow is defined as a displacement vector, denoted as $\Delta \boldsymbol{T}$, from the original locations. The flows of landmarks define the characteristics of the reshaping motion. We inherit the pre-trained DBP in the BASH module, and utilize DBP to infer the landmark flows which can maximize the corresponding beauty score.

Let us denote the input landmark feature of the testing image i as $\boldsymbol{X}_i$, and the estimated beauty score of DBP can be formulated as

$$\tilde{s}_i = \mathcal{F}(\boldsymbol{X}_i + \Delta \boldsymbol{T}_i), \tag{2}$$

where $\mathcal{F}(\cdot)$ is the same mapping as described above and $\tilde{s}_i$ is the beauty score of the transformed landmark features. The objective is defined with regard to $\Delta \boldsymbol{T}_i$, and penalizes on the gap between the current beauty score and the maximal beauty score. In particular, we define a cost as follows,

$$\mathcal{L}_{beauty} = |\tilde{s}_i - M| \tag{3}$$

where M is the maximal beauty score, which is 10 on the currently used training dataset.

Based on Eqn. (2) and Eqn. (3), it can be observed that the gradient with regard to $\Delta \boldsymbol{T}_i$ actually equals the gradient in terms of the input vectors for DBP. In this work, the displacement vector is inferred via computing its gradient, referred to as the deep input gradient. By minimizing the cost in Eqn. (3), the network automatically moves the key landmarks towards the locations with the highest rating of beauty.

To retain the semantic relations between facial landmarks, we include a constraint defined with the aid of Probabilistic Principal Component Analysis (PPCA). We train a PPCA model on the high-score face images to capture the underlying distribution of the desired facial landmark structure. Accordingly, we penalize the negative log-likelihood of transformed landmark positions by introducing the following constraint:

$$\mathcal{L}_{ppca} = -ln(Pr(\boldsymbol{X}_i + \Delta \boldsymbol{T}_i | \boldsymbol{\mu}, \boldsymbol{P}\boldsymbol{P}^T + \sigma^2 \boldsymbol{I})). \tag{4}$$

By minimizing $\mathcal{L}_{ppca}$, the transformed shape model is enforced to follow the same distribution of the targeted beauty group of high attractiveness. The resulting model, therefore, avoids the violation of relative semantic positions among facial landmarks.

In summary, the objective of the BASH module integrates the aforementioned two costs as

$$\mathcal{L} = \mathcal{L}_{beauty} + \beta_1 \cdot \mathcal{L}_{ppca}. \tag{5}$$

The corresponding gradient with regard to $\Delta \boldsymbol{T}_i$ is computed as follows,

$$\begin{aligned} \frac{\partial \mathcal{L}}{\partial \Delta \boldsymbol{T}_i} = & \frac{\partial \mathcal{L}_{beauty}}{\partial \Delta \boldsymbol{T}_i} + \\ & 2\beta_1 \left[(\boldsymbol{P}\boldsymbol{P}^T + \sigma^2 \boldsymbol{I})^{-1} \cdot (\boldsymbol{X}_i + \Delta \boldsymbol{T}_i - \boldsymbol{\mu}) \right], \end{aligned} \tag{6}$$

where the first term refers to the deep input gradient. It is noted that optimization with regard to the displacement vector is non-convex due to the high non-linearity of DBP, and thus is conducted in an iterative manner. In particular, we follow the gradient descent method to iteratively update the displacement vector, which is initialized as an all-zero vector. In each inference iteration, the gradient w.r.t. $\Delta \boldsymbol{T}_i$ is computed to transform the present facial landmark structure. Finally, the inferred displacement is acquired as the combination of the input gradients derived in all the iterations.

After we obtain the displacement vectors, standard image warping techniques are applied to produce the beautified image.

3. EXPERIMENT

We compare our face beautification method with the work in [2]. The proposed method is more natural and personalized compared with SVR-beauty. SVR-beauty tends to morph the landmarks towards the mean shape, while our method learns an adaptive transformation for a different shape vector. As the standard to rate the level of attractiveness is vague, 26 volunteers are invited to quantitatively rate the beautified results of our method and SVR-beauty. According to the statistics of the user study, most beautified images show aesthetic improvements over the original copies for our method. In comparison, the number for SVR-beauty is lower. The volunteers also give a higher rating of our method in terms of naturalness: the inferred shape transformations are generally considered as smooth and natural. In summary, the proposed framework gives satisfying performance for facial beautification based on the evaluation from the users.

4. CONCLUSION

In this demo, we showcase an automatic face beautification framework. It performs the beautification task in a learning-based manner and generates personalized and natural beautification results. The beautification of human faces within videos also has very promising application potential. In future, we shall further extend the proposed framework to handle beautification tasks in videos.

5. REFERENCES

[1] A. Krizhevsky, I. Sutskever, and G. E. Hinton. Imagenet classification with deep convolutional neural networks. In *NIPS*, 2012.

[2] T. Leyvand, D. Cohen-Or, G. Dror, and D. Lischinski. Data-driven enhancement of facial attractiveness. *TOG*, 2008.

[3] L. Liu, J. Xing, S. Liu, H. Xu, X. Zhou, and S. Yan. Wow! you are so beautiful today! *ACM TOMM*, 2014.

[4] T. V. Nguyen, S. Liu, B. Ni, J. Tan, Y. Rui, and S. Yan. Sense beauty via face, dressing, and/or voice. In *ACM MM*, 2012.

Pan360: INS Assisted 360-Degree Panorama (Demo Description)

Yu-Hsin Lin
HTC Research, Taipei
peach09142000@gmail.com

Yu-Mei Chen
HTC Research, Taipei
yumei_chen@htc.com

Lun-Cheng Chu
HTC Research, Taipei
seamyself@gmail.com

Andre Chen
HTC Research, Taipei
andre.hl.chen@gmail.com

Scott Chien-Hung Liao
HTC Research, Taipei
scottcliao@gmail.com

Edward Y. Chang
HTC Research, Taipei
edward_chang@htc.com

ABSTRACT

This article describes Pan360, a $360° \times 180°$ panorama capturing and viewing product developed and launched by our team, and our demo plan.

Categories and Subject Descriptors

I.4 [**IMAGE PROCESSING AND COMPUTER VISION**]: Applications

Keywords

Panorama, INS-assisted System

1. INTRODUCTION

Recently, two types of devices to generate full-view panorama images are made available in the consumer market. First, a one-shot device such as THETA by Ricoh[4], which customizes two 180° fisheye lenses. Second, a multiple-shot device such as a smart-phone equipped with proprietary stitching software. The one-shot type could generate a panorama in real-time due to the prior knowledge of its hardware configuration, and the stitching result is usually without artifact. The multiple-shot devices are much more popular than one-shot due to the proliferation of the smartphones. Several multiple-shot panorama applications exist, such as PhotoSynth [3] and PhotoSphere [2]. PhotoSynth allows a user to browse stitched results using gestures. The quality is high but the drawbacks are time-consuming stitching algorithm and the unconstrained user interface in capturing mode, unable to guide users to take pictures in a correct order. On the other hand, PhotoSphere solves the UI problem by showing sensor-guided indicators. However, without camera preview features, serious artifacts often occur, e.g., ghost effect and motion blur, with PhotoSphere.

We developed and launched Pan360 on HTC flagship phones, and also launched PanOMG on Google Play. Pan360 is an INS (Inertial Navigation System) assisted panorama application. Pan360 calibrates a gyroscope and fuses its signals with the signals of an accelerometer to provide shooting targets for a panorama shooter. Whereas the detailed technical specifications and related work are documented in our technical report [1], our Pan360 demonstration shows four key features: 1) gyro calibration, 2) shooting target generation, 3) sensor-guided panorama viewing, and 4) photo taking when viewing a panorama. We also compare panorama stitching speed and quality with PhotoSynth and PhotoSphere.

MM'15, October 26–30, 2015, Brisbane, Australia.
ACM 978-1-4503-3459-4/15/10.
DOI: http://dx.doi.org/10.1145/2733373.2807967 .

Gyro Calibrtion

The UI presented in Figs. 1(b) and (c) shows that Pan360 requires a user to hold the camera steadily to perform calibration. The rectangle in the middle of the screen is filled with an orange color from left to right in time, during which gyro measurements are collected and the biased factor computed. This simple and timely calibration performed before each panorama capturing sequence remedies the fact that the bias can change in time and is temperature-dependent.

Shooting Target Generation

After calibration, several virtual rectangles are dynamically generated and equally spread out on the surface of a virtual sphere for user to aim. These rectangle targets guide users to translate and rotate the device to capture them one after another (Figs. 1(d) and (e)). Once the camera center and indicator completely overlap, the camera captures a photo frame and its orientations generated by the sensors. Meanwhile, the captured position becomes transparent to notify the user to aim for the next target. In addition, a mini-map at the upper-left corner of the screen shows the capturing progress, i.e., which rectangles have been filled and which have not. The users can stop or capture more rectangles. Once the shooting has completed, Pan360 stitches all captured frames (Fig. 1(f)). To achieve cross-platform compatibility, we adopt Google PhotoSphere XMP metadata format.

Sensor-Guided Panorama Viewing

There are two modes in Pan360: capturing and viewing. In the viewing mode, the panoramic image is projected onto a spherical environment, and the user can navigate the viewpoint by motion sensor, touch gesture, or default motion.

Users can browse panoramas in HTC photo gallery (Fig. 2(a)). If a panoramic photo is selected and the Pan360

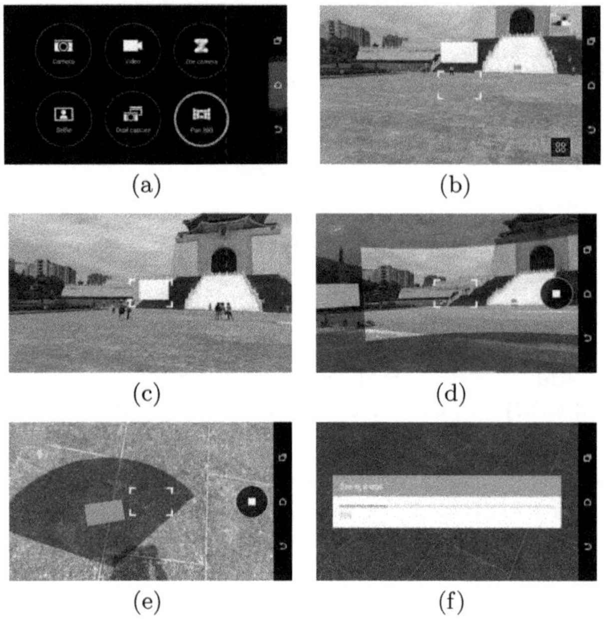

Figure 1: Steps of capturing panorama. (a) A user switches to Pan360 mode in the HTC camera app. (b) The user aims at a white rectangle. (c) The white rectangle is filled with orange for showing the progress of calibration. (d) Once the calibration is done, other rectangular indicators appear. The user captures one by one. (e) The last rectangle to aim at. (f) Pan360 stitches all captured frames.

icon is tapped, the device enters the panorama viewing mode (Fig. 2(b)). In this mode, Pan360 renders a sphere mesh with the selected panorama mapped onto the sphere according to the XMP metadata. A mini-map on the upper-left corner shows the scene coverage. Pan360 supports three browsing ways. First, the view direction is controlled by INS. The downward direction of the sphere is always aligned with gravity. Thus, the sphere always locks on the absolute orientation in the real world no matter how the device rotates and translates. Fig. 3 illustrates this scenario. In the second way, a user can change his/her view direction by single-finger scrolling, rotate view orientation by two-finger rotation, and zoom by pinch. The default field of view is 60°. The angle of the circular sector on the mini-map changes with zooming (Figs. 2(e) and (f)). In the third way of viewing, Pan360 generates an animated panorama by automatically rotating the viewing direction. A user can take a photo in the viewing mode as if the photo was captured in the original scene.

2. CONCLUDING REMARKS

We developed Pan360 on HTC smart phone M8 equipped with Quad-core 2.5 GHz Krait 400, Adreno 330 GPU and 2 GB RAM. The size of input images is 1280×720. Pan360 can capture up to 44 images with a 69.6° horizontal field of view, which forms a whole sphere ($360° \times 180°$) and renders into a 4096×2048 photo. We collected 2,728 test cases for reproducing panoramic photos during algorithm developement. To test overall system performance, we ran all test cases on M8. Each case contains 17 images on average. Our system stitches them in 7.63 seconds per case on average.

Figure 2: Steps of viewing panorama. (a) A user selects a panorama. (b) The user can tap the icon to explore it in 3D immersive view. (c) As the user enters the virtual view, he can identify his current orientation by the orientation indicator on the upper-left corner. (d) The user turns to another direction. (e) The user pinches the screen to zoom out. (f) The user unpinches the screen to zoom in.

Figure 3: Illustration of the view direction controlled by INS.

We also ran all 430 44-image cases and the stitching time is 21.77 seconds on average, significantly shorter than the stitching time of a $360° \times 180°$ panorama by PhotoSynth (average 44.6 seconds on iPhone 4S) or PhotoSphere (average 48.8 seconds on M8). Selected test cases, stitched results and quality comparisons with other competitors are documented in the extended version [1]. Our work is a embedded feature of the built-in camera application in HTC Sense 6.0 and its later versions.

Producing good panoramic photos with traditional cameras is a challenging task, since it requires massive photography and post-production techniques. The high-performance Pan360 not only provides augmented reality UI for guiding users to create high-quality results, but also gives users more impressive viewing experiences via immersive virtual reality.

3. REFERENCES

[1] Pan360 extended version. http://infolab.stanford.edu/~echang/pan360.html.

[2] Google. PhotoSphere. https://www.google.com/maps/about/contribute/photosphere/.

[3] Microsoft. PhotoSynth. https://photosynth.net/.

[4] Ricoh. Theta. https://theta360.com/.

HeartHealth: New Adventures in Serious Gaming *

David Monaghan, Freddie Honohan, Edmond Mitchell and Noel O'Connor
Insight Centre for Data Analytics
Dublin City University, Ireland
david.monaghan@dcu.ie

Anargyros Chatzitofis, Dimitrios Zarpalas and Petros Daras
The Centre for Research and Technology, Hellas
Thessaloniki, Greece
tofis@iti.gr

ABSTRACT

We present a novel, low-cost, interactive, exercise-based rehabilitation system. Our research involves the investigation and development of patient-centric, sensor-based rehabilitation games and surrounding technologies. HeartHealth is designed to provide a safe, personalised and fun exercise environment that could be deployed in any exercise based rehabilitation program. HeartHealth utilises a cloud-based patient information management system built on FIWARE Generic Enablers[1],and motion tracking coupled with our sophisticated motion comparison algorithms. Users can record customised exercises through a *doctors* interface and then play the rehabilitation game where they must perform a sequence of their exercises in order to complete the game scenario. Their exercises are monitored, recorded and compared by our Motion Evaluation software and real-time feedback is than given based on the users performance.

Categories and Subject Descriptors

I.4.5 [**Computing Methodologies**]: Image Processing and Computer Vision—*Reconstruction*

General Terms

Cardiovascular Disease, Rehabilitation, Serious Games

Keywords

Motion capture, 3D Vision, Exercise Rehabilitation.

1. INTRODUCTION

The significant benefits of integrating exercise into rehabilitation are well recognized for a broad range of medical conditions[2]. However, despite the known benefits of exercise, uptake and adherence are very low, especially amongst those with medical conditions such as Cardiovascular disease (under 10% - W.H.O.). Patient adherence to prescribed exercise **is crucial** in both disease prevention and rehabilitation. The development of intuitive, low-cost, personalized home-based exercise monitoring systems can help address these issues by encouraging exercise adherence through a captivating Serious Game that provides real-time feedback.

A Serious Game can be thought of as any game that has been designed for any purpose other than entertainment. Inspired by the success of video games and through their inherent ability to capture and keep a persons attention, serious games have grown into a significant research area [1]. Serious games in rehabilitation have been used for successful balance re-training, rheumatoid arthritis rehabilitation [2], rehabilitation following stroke that often necessitates upper limb rehabilitation [3]. Recently it was reported that the application of home-based exercise programs for cardiac rehabilitation carried the possibility of providing much higher adherence rates [4]. However, to date none of these systems have fully utilised a culmination of captivating story-based scenarios, intuitive human computer interaction and sophisticated motion analysis software present in our system.

2. THE HEARTHEALTH SYSTEM

2.1 Target Population

The target population group for our research are phase 4 cardiovascular disease patients who have been prescribed exercise-based rehabilitation, for which the adherence rates are low. We define Phase 4 of Cardiac Rehabilitation (CR), although the definition varies from country to country, as home or community based CR, in which patients try to sustain long-term behaviour change typically with encouragement by CR staff. Although the HeartHealth project specifically targets individuals at phase 4 CR, current work is being pursued to introduce this technology earlier in the CR process.

2.2 Use Case Scenario

Typically when a clinician sees a patient he/she prescribes a set of CR exercises, however adherence rates remain low for a variety of reasons. Four well recognised reasons are (1) there is no real motivation; exercises may be boring; exercises are not personalised, (2) patients do not train sufficiently or they perform the exercises incorrectly, (3) patients

*The HeartHealth project is supported by the European Commission under contract FP7-604691 FI-STAR.
[1]http://catalogue.fiware.org/enablers

[2]World Health Organization 2011

MM'15, MM'15, October 26-30, 2015, Brisbane, Australia
ACM 978-1-4503-3459-4/15/10
http://dx.doi.org/10.1145/2733373.2807969

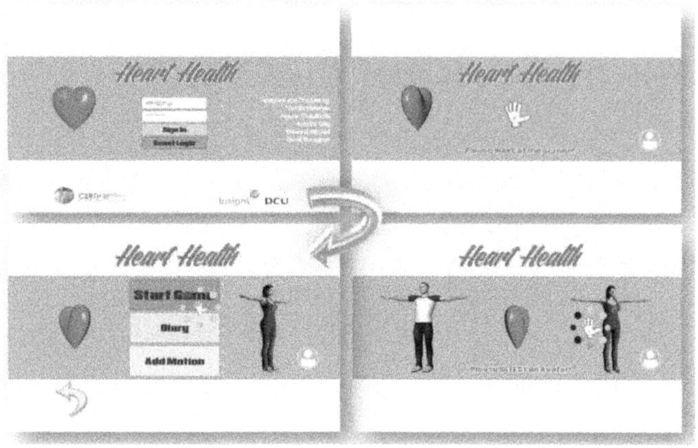

Figure 1: Clockwise from the top-left: the login page; the Kinect Scanning screen where the system waits to track a user, allowing for Hands-Free navigation; the patient can select an avatar to use during the game using the timer-hand; the main menu

do not know when they should increase (progress) the degree of exercise difficulty (i.e. frequency, intensity, tempo), and (4) the clinician must rely on the patients honesty and subjective evaluation when evaluating the effectiveness of their CR program design. The HeartHealth system allows clinicians to tailor a personalised CR programme for a patient, based on their individual mobility limitations. The system than empowers the patient to take ownership of their rehabilitation journey by enabling them to keep a rehabilitation diary, recorded automatically in the game, and by providing a fun and personalised game through which they can perform their exercise rehabilitation.

2.3 System Description

HeartHealth utilises open-source computer gaming technology, called the Unity3D game engine, in order to maintain a low-cost prerogative. There are many components within the HeartHealth system but one of the core ones is the Motion Evaluation Specific Enabler (S.E.)[3]. This module was created in-house and hosted on the Fi-Star cloud. It provides highly accurate human motion evaluation by utilising a Dynamic Time Wrapping approach for comparing motion capture skeletal sequences. Our Motion Evaluation S.E. can evaluate and compare skeletal sequences from any motion capture arrangement as long as the sequences are stored in the h-anim[4] motion capture format. The HeartHealth system allows a clinician to record any required exercise motions, which are performed by a patient. These exercises then form the basis of the patients CR and are stored securely online in the patients account and are utilised during the course of game. During the game the patients motions are recorded, via a fusion of data from the Microsoft Kinect V2 and body worn accelerometers, and sent to the evaluation S.E. for comparison. The results are then used to assess the patients progress through his/her rehabilitation journey and are securely stored in their exercise diary for them to review later or for a doctor to remotely analyse. Screen shots of the HeartHealth system can be seen in fig.1 and fig. 2, and user testing with CVD patients can be seen in fig. 3.

[3]http://catalogue.fi-star.eu/enablers/motion-evaluation
[4]www.h-anim.org/

Figure 2: Clockwise from the top-left: the intro information for the warm-up scene; the warm up scene where the patient has to collect the green apples and try to avoid the red apples; the rehabilitation scene where the patient follows the trainer avatar and is given real-time feedback; the practice scene where the patient can practice their personalised exercises

.

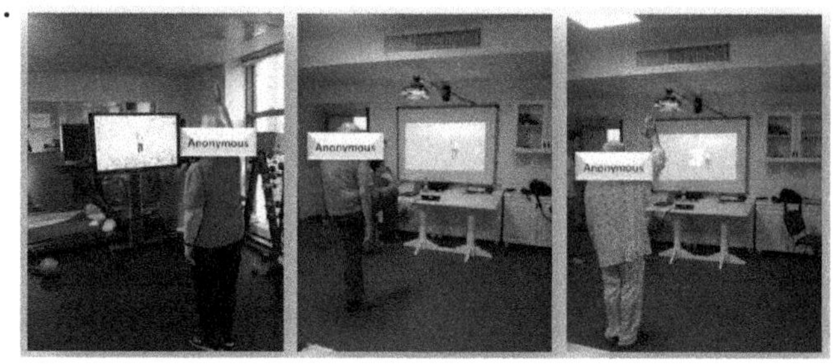

Figure 3: User trials of the HeartHealth system at Dublin City University in Ireland and Bagdasar-Arseni Emergency Clinical Hospital in Bucharest

3. DEMONSTRATION

The demonstration will consist of a laptop with a special 3D-screen, or 3D-projector depending on space, coupled with 3D glasses. The heartHealth game will be showcased and users will be shown how to record individualised rehabilitation exercises. Then they can proceed to play through the rehabilitation game from a patients perspective. Users will need to wear the 3D glasses in order to experience the 3D effect. A non-3D version will also be available as will a *local* system in case of internet connectivity issues. A poster detailing the motivations behind and current state of our research on behaviour change coupled with low-cost home-based rehabilitation gaming technologies will also be shown.

4. REFERENCES

[1] P. Rego, et al. Serious games for rehab: A survey and a classification towards a taxonomy, Information Systems and Technologies *IEEE CISTI*, pp. 1-6, 2010.

[2] V. Metsis et al. Computer aided rehab. for patients with rheumatoid arthritis *IEE ICNC*, pp. 97-102, 2013.

[3] G. Alankus et al. Towards customizable games for stroke rehabilitation *SIGCHI*, pp. 2113-2122, 2010.

[4] D. Soares et al. Home-Based Programs and Application of New Technologies in Cardiac Rehabilitation *Int J Phys Med Rehabil*, pp.2, 2013.

Challenged Content Delivery Network: Eliminating the Digital Divide

Hua-Jun Hong[1], Shu-Ting Wang[1], Chih-Pin Tan[1], Tarek El-Ganainy[2], Khaled A. Harras[3], Cheng-Hsin Hsu[1], and Mohamed Hefeeda[2]

[1]Department of Computer Science, National Tsing Hua University, Taiwan
[2]Qatar Computing Research Institute, HBKU, Qatar
[3]School of Computer Science, Carnegie Mellon University, Qatar

ABSTRACT

We present a complete system, called Challenged Content Delivery Network (CCDN), to efficiently deliver multimedia content to mobile users who live in developing countries, rural areas, or over-populated cities with no or weak network infrastructure. These mobile users do not have always-on Internet access. We demo our CCDN, implemented on a Linux server, Raspberry Pi proxies, and Android phones from three aspects: multimedia, networking, and machine learning tools. We propose multiple optimization algorithm modules that compute personalized distribution plans, and maximize the overall user experience. CCDN allows people living in area with challenged networks access to multimedia content, like news reports, using mobile devices, such as smartphones. This in turn will help in eliminating the digital divide, which refers to information inequality to persons with different Internet accessing abilities.

Categories and Subject Descriptors: H.3 [Information Storage and Retrieval]: Systems and Software

Keywords: Multimedia; Challenged Networks; Content Distribution; Mobile Devices; Offline Access

1. INTRODUCTION

Using mobile devices to watch online multimedia content is getting increasingly popular. However, in developing countries, rural areas, or over-populated cities, many mobile users do not have Internet access. For instance, only 15% of mobile users have mobile Internet access in Africa [1], because of weak or non-existing network infrastructure. Therefore, people in these areas have little chance to access online multimedia content, such as news, advertisements, and movies. That is, they suffer from *digital divide* from other parts of the world. Digital divide refers to information inequality to persons with different Internet accessing abilities. Fig. 1 shows one day of Amy who does not have Internet access at home. Online multimedia content providers cannot efficiently deliver content to Amy even after hiring Content Delivery Network (CDN) providers, because traditional CDNs take end-to-end connectivity as granted. On the other hand, Amy's mobile device is not always isolated from the Internet. Amy may run into other people and WiFi access points in crowded places, such as schools, city halls, and markets.

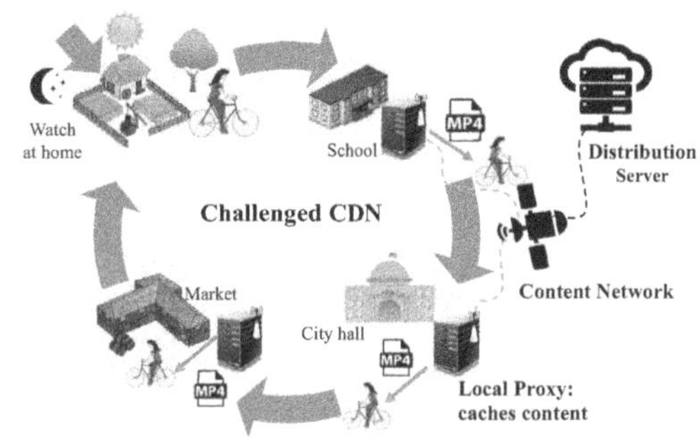

Figure 1: How CCDN helps people who suffer from digital divide.

In this demo, we present the CCDN system for: (i) mobile users without stable Internet access to prefetch multimedia content, and (ii) service providers to deliver their multimedia content to more people. Our CCDN system consists of several entities: a *distribution server*, several *local proxies*, and many *mobile clients*. Local proxies are intelligent WiFi access points with storage spaces, which are deployed at crowded places. Local proxies retrieve online multimedia content from a distribution server over the Internet, and send it to near-by users running our mobile app over WiFi. The crux of our proposed CCDN is to make decisions on *when and which online content to transfer to which mobile client in order to achieve the highest overall user experience*. We refer to such decisions as *distribution plans*, which are periodically computed on the distribution server using a carefully designed algorithm. Several multimedia, networking, and machine learning tools are leveraged to derive the distribution plans. The plans are sent to local proxies, which relay the plans to mobile clients. The mobile clients follow their plans to download multimedia content.

2. CHALLENGED CDN: OUR SOLUTION

Fig 2 depicts the system architecture of our CCDN. The distribution planning algorithm guides mobile devices to intelligently and automatically download multimedia content:

This work was partially supported by the Ministry of Science and Technology of Taiwan, #102-2221-E-007-062-MY3.

MM'15, October 26–30, 2015, Brisbane, Australia.
ACM 978-1-4503-3459-4/15/10.
DOI: http://dx.doi.org/10.1145/2733373.2807970. .

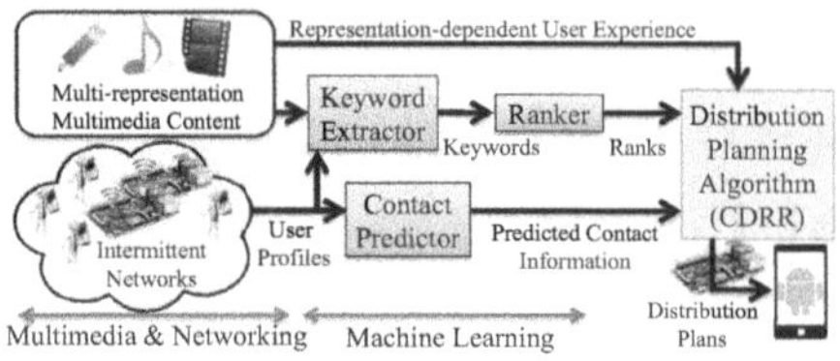

Figure 2: The system architecture of our CCDN.

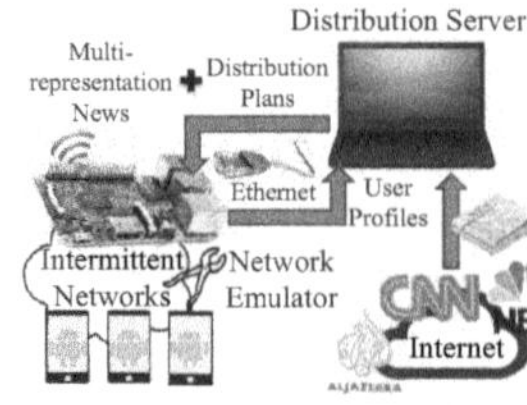

Figure 3: The setup of the demonstrations.

(i) at the best time, (ii) with the highest viewing probability, and (iii) from the best sender. Specifically, we propose an efficient algorithm, Contact-Driven Round Robin (CDRR), which: (i) uses less resources (energy, disk, and network) to send content leading to higher user experience, (ii) sends more content to users with more chances to spread it out, and (iii) receives content from users with less chances to relay it to others. Several supporting components are described in the following.

Multi-representation multimedia content. A multimedia content may have three representations: article, audio, and video. The video can be further transcoded to different resolutions. Different representations of the same multimedia content give different user experience improvement which typically follows a decreasing function. For example, when a mobile user first downloads an article, the user will have significant user experience improvement. In contrast, moving from medium- to high-resolution video only leads to little improvement. Moreover, different users have diverse interests, and won't view uninterested content. We extract keywords of multimedia content and user interests to create personalized ranks. Multi-representation helps CCDN to gracefully adapt to diverse and dynamic environments.

User profiles in challenged networks. We deploy local proxies and leverage contacts to disseminate multimedia content over intermittent networks. In the mobile client, we keep track of user profiles, including clicked multimedia content and contact information. Contact information consists of trajectory, contact duration, and throughput of each contact. These historical user profiles are processed for the inputs of CDRR algorithm.

Machine learning modules. CCDN employs three machine learning modules: keyword extractor, ranker, and contact predictor. The keyword extractor, implementing LDA [2], is responsible for extracting the keywords of online content and user-clicked (interested) content. The ranker uses the keywords to compute per-user ranks using some ranking tools, such as LambdaMART [3]. The contact predictor estimates the contact information of mobile users in the future using popular algorithms, such as trajectory pattern [4]. CCDN provides a modularized platform for testing machine learning algorithms.

3. DEMONSTRATIONS

We design experiments to demonstrate our CCDN from three aspects: multi-representation multimedia content, intermittent networks, and matching user interests. As illustrated in Fig 3, we setup a testbed composed of Android phones running our mobile client, a Raspberry Pi running the local proxy, and a laptop running the distribution server. In this demo, the distribution server crawls daily news reports. However, CCDN also works for other types of content. Details on the experiments are given below.

Multi-representation multimedia content. Sending different representations allow us to distribute more news reports under limited resources, such as network bandwidth. We install network emulator on the local proxy to throttle the available bandwidth so as to mimic challenged networks. We will show that only very few news reports can be distributed without multi-representation content.

Intermittent networks. To show the robustness of our CCDN under challenged networks, we deploy our system in a rural area, and collect contact traces. We use the traces to drive the network emulator and local proxy so as to recreate a challenged network. In particular, once we reach the first contact in the trace, we enable the WiFi interface of a local proxy, and configure the network emulator to the measured throughput in the trace. Our mobile client will associate with the local proxy and download news reports. We follow the trace, and turn off the WiFi interface on the local proxy to emulate the disconnection. We turn on the WiFi interface once contact starts, and configure the network emulator following the trace. These steps are repeated until we finish the whole trace. The mobile client will download news reports whenever the WiFi interface is on.

Matching interests. Different users have different user interests on different types of news reports. We leverage user profiles to estimate user interests and compute per-user ranks of each news report. We will demonstrate that CCDN distributes different news reports to mobile users with diverse user interests. Moreover, a mobile user tends to receive better representations for more interested news reports.

4. CONCLUSION

We presented a complete CCDN system for multimedia content delivery in challenged networks. The current multimedia content providers, such as CNN, YouTube, and Al Jazeera, provide mobile apps that offer fresh online multimedia content. However, most apps require always-on Internet access, and thus they do not work for people with challenged networks. Some of them provide offline access, which requires users to manually download favorite multimedia content, which is tedious. Hence, we believe that the proposed CCDN will help service providers to deliver more content to more users in a cost-effective way.

References

[1] How do we accelerate Internet access in Africa? `http://tinyurl.com/q9ksjwg`, 2013.

[2] D. Blei, A. Ng, and M. Jordan. Latent dirichlet allocation. *Journal of Machine Learning Research*, 3:993–1022, 2003.

[3] C. Burges. From ranknet to LambdaRank to LambdaMART: An overview. Technical report, Microsoft Research, 2010.

[4] A. Monreale, F. Pinelli, R. Trasarti, and F. Giannotti. Wherenext: A location predictor on trajectory pattern mining. In *Proc. of ACM Conference on Knowledge Discovery and Data Mining (KDD'09)*, 2009.

OmniViewer: Enabling Multi-modal 3D DASH

Zhenhuan Gao Shannon Chen Klara Nahrstedt

Department of Computer Science
University of Illinois at Urbana-Champaign
{zgao11, cchen116, klara}@illinois.edu

ABSTRACT

This paper presents OmniViewer, a multi-modal 3D video streaming system based on Dynamic Adaptive Streaming over HTTP (DASH) standard. OmniViewer allows users to view arbitrary side of a performer by choosing the view angle from 0°to 360°. Besides, according to the current available bandwidth, it can also adaptively change the bitrate of rendered 3D video for both smooth and high-quality view rendering. Finally, OmniViewer extends traditional DASH implementation to support multi-modal data streaming besides video and audio.

Categories and Subject Descriptors

H.5.1 [**Multimedia Information Systems**]: Artificial, augmented, and virtual realities

Keywords

3D; Real-time; DASH; View

1. INTRODUCTION

3D Tele-immersion (3DTI) system enables remote users to view the local scene and even to interact with local users in a virtual 3D space, which has promoted lots of potential applications such as remote physiotherapy [1]. Furthermore, in a traditional 2D on-demand video streaming system, the interactivity of the end users choosing any viewpoint is not available except if the number of streams is equal to the number of possible views. In contrast, 3DTI enables interactivity of users from any viewpoint. Thus, free view is the trump of 3D over 2D. Gao et al. presented FreeViewer [2], a 3DTI system offering free-view feature. However, transmission of such huge 3D data without encoding necessitates high bandwidth and is not feasible for commercial use. Therefore, 3D video recording, compresssion and streaming are further challenges in 3D systems.

To the best of our knowledge, there is no 3D video streaming standard which can fit the rendering and streaming part of 3D systems like 3DTI system. We also notice that in 2D video streaming, the popularity of DASH (defined by ISO/IEC 23009-1) skyrockets and an increasing number of commercial streaming services are adopting this new standard. While the benefits of DASH is clear for 2D streaming, the research of DASH in 3DTI is not well understood. Therefore, we present OmniViewer, a complete multi-modal on-demand 3D video streaming solution based on DASH.

Same as with FreeViewer, OmniViewer uses four 3D camera streams to cover the whole 360°view. Each 3D stream is encoded with multiple bitrates as a normal 2D stream, containing a pair of color frame and depth frame. The user is able to set any view angle to watch the performer from. Also, to be consistent with DASH standard, Omniviewer can adaptively change the bitrates of streams to achieve the best possible media quality of the chosen view. Moreover, since fundamentally DASH is ignorant of content and encoder/decoder, we introduce multi-modal data (eg. Kinect skeleton, heartbeat sensor data) into OmniViewer to support multi-modal media streaming, expanding the scope of DASH to more general use cases.

In summary, the contributions of Omniviewer lie in four major aspects:

- 3D video recording. OmniViewer leverages 2D video en-/decoding technique to store and retrieve monoscopic 3D video segments in a natural way.
- Omni-view rendering. OmniViewer offers the user to view the 3D video from any view angle at any time through a natural user interface.
- Adaptive 3D streaming. On top of DASH, OmniViewer always provisions the best media quality while keeps the total bitrate under current available bandwidth.
- Multi-modal media support. OmniViewer supports any type of media including but not limiting to video and audio giving more flexibility in applications.

2. SYSTEM OVERVIEW

This section gives an overview of the system architecture including both server and client sides.

2.1 OmniViewer Server

2.1.1 Recording

As illustrated in Figure 1(a), we still adopt four 3D cameras (Kinect). In order to fit DASH, we represent each 3D camera video as a 2D video where each 2D frame consists of

MM'15, October 26–30, 2015, Brisbane, Australia.
ACM 978-1-4503-3459-4/15/10.
DOI: http://dx.doi.org/10.1145/2733373.2807971 .

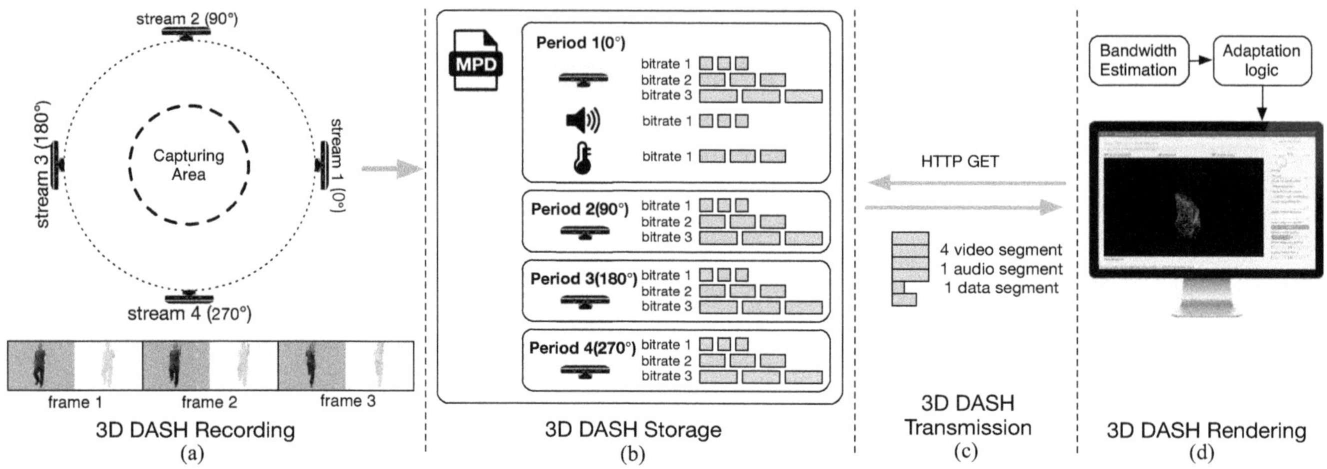

Figure 1: OmniViewer System Overview

a pair of color (RGB) and depth (Gray) frames, stitched together horizontally. Then we compress these four 2D videos using H.264 codec with different bitrates and slice them into 1s DASH segments using MP4Box [3]. For audio, we only need one stream and apply similar operation. For other media data, in our case we incorporate skeleton and heartbeat data, encoding them in JSON file, one file per segment including the data for each frame.

2.1.2 *Storage*

In DASH, a media presentation description (MPD) file is required to describe segment information. To be specific, the media presentation defines the video sequence with one or more consecutive periods that break up the video from start to finish. Each period contains one or more adaptation sets that contain the content of one modality data, video, audio, etc. Each adaptation set contains multiple representations, which represents the streams with different qualities.

In 3D DASH, since we have four video streams, OmniViewer leverages period customization to support streaming four video streams concurrently. We configure the MPD file in OmniViewer system with four periods and each of them contains a video adaptation set consisting of the same number of representations with the same qualities. For example, in Figure 1(b), we show a MPD for a 3D video that includes 4 camera-related periods, and each segment in each period includes data of 1s under different bitrates (the small blocks). As for audio and other data, we only need one stream for each modality. Thus, we choose to put their adaptation sets into the first period (period 1(0°) in Figure 1(b)) and let the client read them from the first period. Considering DASH is audio/video codec agnostic, we set other data segment in the form of JSON and implement our own en-/decoder in the recording step and in the client. All the generated segments and customized MPD file are stored in a standard static webserver.

2.2 OmniViewer Client

We implement all the components of OmniViewer client based on the open-source sample player that comes with libdash [4], an open-source C++ library which implements the full MPEG-DASH standard defined by ISO/IEC 23009-1. After the OmniViewer client downloads the MPD file, it analyzes the information of periods, adaptation sets and representations. Then, it opens two decoders, audio/video decoder and our own JSON decoder, and six buffers, four for videos, another for audio, and the last one for other data except for A/V data. When all the data, required for the current frame, are available, the frame will be rendered in an OpenGL 3D context. At any time, the human viewer is able to choose the preferred view angle from the OmniViewer client GUI. Then the OmniViewer client will select the required two neighbouring video streams, decode the 3D point clouds, merge them into a partial 3D model by geometrical relationship and finally render the frame according to the computed viewpoint. Also, when the bandwidth fluctuates greatly, the client will correspondingly adapt the bitrates of media streams to keep smooth and high-quality rendering.

3. ACKNOWLEDGEMENTS

This presented work does not represent opinions of NSF. The presented material is based on our work supported by NSF Grant CNS 10-12194, CNS 09-64081 and Deutsche Telecom Gift funding.

4. CONCLUSIONS

In this demo paper, we present OmniViewer, the multimodal 3D DASH framwork, that supports free-view, adaptive, multi-modal 3D video streaming. OmniViewer combines DASH, 3D and multi-modal data together, which expands the current scope of both DASH and 3D systems. The versatility and flexibility of OmniViewer can be leveraged to fit many use cases, such as remote physiotherapy, entertainmnet and other 3D activities.

5. REFERENCES

[1] Klara Nahrstedt. 3D Teleimmersion for Remote Injury Assessment. In *Proceedings of the 2012 International Workshop on Socially-aware Multimedia*, SAM '12, pages 21–24, New York, NY, USA, 2012. ACM.

[2] Zhenhuan Gao, Shannon Chen, and Klara Nahrstedt. FreeViewer: An Intelligent Director for 3D Tele-Immersion System. In *Proceedings of the ACM International Conference on Multimedia*, MM '14, pages 755–756, New York, NY, USA, 2014. ACM.

[3] MP4Box. `http://gpac.wp.mines-telecom.fr/mp4box/`.

[4] Libdash. `http://github.com/bitmovin/libdash`.

Large Video Event Ontology Browsing, Search and Tagging (EventNet Demo)

Hongliang Xu, Guangnan Ye, Yitong Li, Dong Liu, Shih-Fu Chang
Department of Electrical Engineering, Columbia University, New York, NY 10027, USA
{hx2168, gy2179, yl3029, dl2713, sc250}@columbia.edu

ABSTRACT

EventNet is the largest video event ontology existent today, consisting of 500 events and 4,490 event-specific concepts systematically discovered from the crowdsource forum like WikiHow. Such sources offer rich information about events happening in everyday lives. Additionally, it includes automatic detection models for the constituent events and concepts using deep learning with around $95K$ training videos from YouTube. In this demo, we present several novel functions of *EventNet*: 1) interactive ontology browsing, 2) semantic event search, and 3) tagging of user-loaded videos via open web interfaces. The system is the first in allowing users to explore rich hierarchical structures among video events, relations between concepts and events, and automatic detection of events and concepts embedded in user-uploaded videos in a live fashion.

Categories and Subject Descriptors

I.2.10 [**ARTIFICIAL INTELLIGENCE**]: Vision and Scene Understanding—*Video Analysis*

Keywords

EventNet Ontology Browsing; Event Search; Automatic Video Tagging; Structured Video Event Ontology

1. INTRODUCTION

Recent advances in computer vision and multimedia have shown impressive progresses in automatic recognition of objects, actions, and events [3, 4, 5]. Significant performance gains have been periodically reported thanks to the availability of large data sources and sophisticated learning models. However, a few major questions remain open: what classes should be included in the recognition task and what structural relations might exist among classes?

Motivated by these challenges, we have developed a systematic process to discover common events that are relevant to human activities (e.g., "wedding", "dance party") or procedural tasks (e.g., "cooking", "car repair"). We focus on events that can be manifested visually in the video data and are with a reasonable level of details. Using data mining and machine learning processes, our efforts have resulted in an EventNet event ontology [6], which consists of 500 high level events and 4,490 semantic concepts relevant to the discovered events.

MM'15, October 26–30, 2015, Brisbane, Australia.
ACM 978-1-4503-3459-4/15/10.
DOI: http://dx.doi.org/10.1145/2733373.2807973.

Figure 1: Interface for event ontology browsing. Example videos and related concepts of the selected event are shown.

In this demo, we present new functions of the EventNet system: interactive browser, semantic search, and live tagging of user-uploaded videos. In each of the modules, we emphasize the unique ontological structure embedded in EventNet and utilize it to achieve novel experience. For example, the event browser leverages the hierarchical event structure discovered from the crowdsource forum WikiHow [2] to facilitate intuitive exploration of events, the search engine focuses on retrieval of hierarchical paths containing interested events rather than events as independent entities, and finally the live detection module applies the event models and the associated concept models to explain why a specific event is detected in an uploaded video. To the best of our knowledge, the EventNet system is the largest video event ontology and the first interactive system allowing users to explore high level events and associated concepts in videos in a systematic structured manner.

2. BRIEF SUMMARY OF EVENTNET

EventNet ontology is discovered from WikiHow, an online forum teaching how to perform various how-to tasks in human daily life. Topics covered in such sources are also frequently captured in videos. WikiHow organizes topics into categories (currently 2,803) using a hierarchical structure. The top layer contains 19 broad categories, and each category is further divided into subcategories that correspond to specialized subclasses or different facets of the parent category. The events in EventNet are found by first systematically inspecting articles in each category and then choosing an event that can be manifested by visual content (such as "bike riding", "apply makeup") . This process results in a total of 500

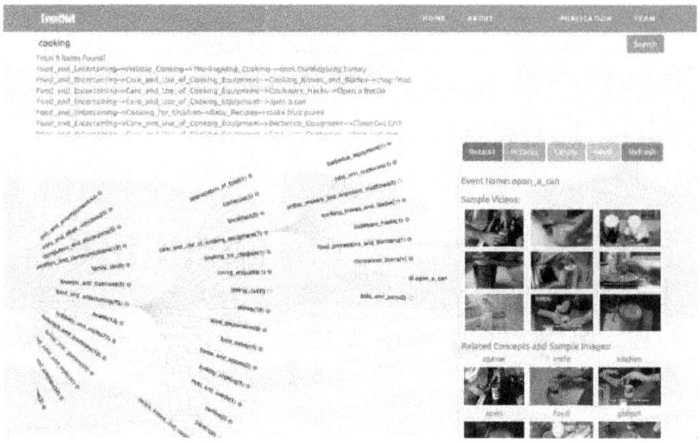

Figure 2: Interface for searching events embedded in the EventNet ontology.

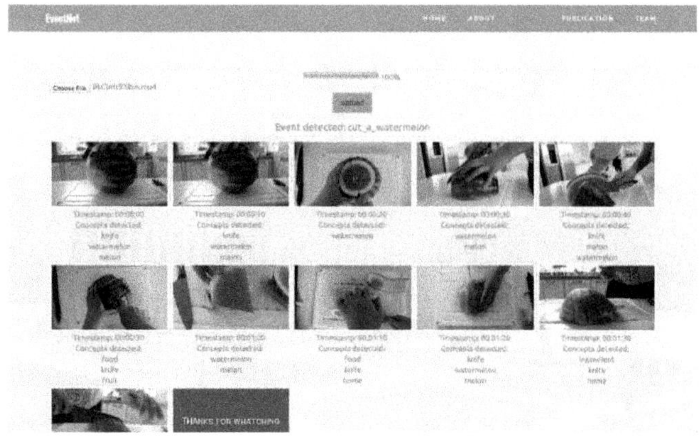

Figure 3: Interface of automatic tagging of user uploaded videos.

events, which are attached to the hierarchical ontology of WikiHow. For each event, we further use it as a textual query to search YouTube videos and discover event-specific concepts from the textual tags contained in the returned videos. This results in $4,490$ concepts in total. The pipeline mentioned above is systematic and productive, combining the rich information captured by the large crowdsource repository (WikiHow) about frequent events in human lives, and the almost unlimited video content available in online sources like YouTube.

With the large number of events and concepts, we crawl around $95K$ YouTube as training data for model learning. For event model, we use the video frames to train an AlexNet structure CNN model [4] over the 500 events. For concept model, we first extract the $4,096$-dimensional feature in the second last layer of the event model computed over each frame, and then train a binary SVM as the concept model. Details about EventNet construction can be seen in [6].

3. DEMO SYSTEM

Function I: Event Ontology Browser. Our system supports users to browse EventNet tree ontology in an interactive and intuitive manner. When a user clicks on a non-leaf category node, it expands the child category nodes together with any event attached to this category (the event node is filled in red while the category node is in green). When the user clicks on an event, it shows the exemplary videos of this event with a dynamic GIF showing animation of keyframes extracted from a sample video. Concepts specific to the event are also shown with representative keyframes of the concept. We specifically adopt the expandable, rotatable tree as the visualization tool (as shown in Figure 1) since it maintains a nice balance between the depth and breadth of the scope when the user navigates through layers and siblings in the tree.

Function II: Semantic Search of Events in the Ontology. We adopt a unique search interface that is different from conventional ones by allowing users to find hierarchical paths matching user interest, instead of treating events as independent units. This design is important for fully leveraging the ontology structure information in EventNet. For each event in EventNet, we generate its text representation by combining all words of the category names from root node to the current category containing the event plus the name of the event. Such texts are used to set up search indexes in Java Lucene [1]. When the user searches for keywords, the system will return all the paths in the index that contain the query keywords. If the query contains more than one words, the path that has more matched keywords will be ranked higher in the search result. After the search, users can click on each returned event, and our system will dynamically expand the corresponding path of this event and visualize it using the tree browser described in the previous section. This not only helps users quickly find target events, but also help suggest additional events to the user by showing events that may exist in the sibling categories in the EventNet hierarchy. Figure 2 shows the interface of the search function.

Function III: Automatic Video Tagging. EventNet includes an upload function that allows users to upload any video and use pre-trained detection models to predict events and concepts present in the video. For each uploaded video, EventNet extracts one frame every 10 seconds. Each frame is then resized to 256 by 256 pixels and fed to the deep learning model described earlier. We average the 500-dimensional detection scores across all extracted frames and use the average score vector as the event detection scores of the video. To present the final detection result, we only show the top event with highest score as the event prediction of the video. For concept detection, we use the feature in the second last layer of the deep learning model computed over each frame, and then apply the binary SVM classifiers to compute the concept scores on each frame. We show the top-ranked predicted concepts under each sampled frame of the uploaded video. Figure 3 shows the tagging results of event and concept for a uploaded video, indicating the high accuracy of the tagging result. It is worth mentioning that our tagging system is very fast and satisfies real-time requirement. For example, when we upload 10 MB video, the tagging system can generate the tagging results in 5 seconds on a single regular workstation, demonstrating the high efficiency of the system.

4. CONCLUSION

This paper demonstrates novel functions on EventNet, the largest event ontology existent today with a hierarchical structure extracted from the popular crowdsource forum WikiHow. The system provides efficient event browsing and search interfaces, and supports live video tagging with high accuracy. It also provides a flexible framework for future scaling up by allowing users to add new event nodes to the ontology structure.

5. REFERENCES

[1] `https://lucene.apache.org/core/`.

[2] `http://www.wikihow.com/Main-Page`.

[3] Y.-G. Jiang, S. Bhattacharya, S.-F. Chang, M. Shah. High-level event recognition in unconstrained videos. In *IJMIR*, 2013.

[4] A. Krizhevsky, I. Sutskever, and G. Hinton. ImageNet Classification with Deep Convolutional Neural Networks. In *NIPS*, 2012.

[5] S. Khurram, A. R. Zamir, and M. Shah. Ucf101: A dataset of 101 human actions classes from videos in the wild. In *arXiv:1212.0402*, 2012.

[6] G. Ye, Y. Li, H. Xu, D. Liu, and S.-F. Chang. EventNet: A Large Scale Structured Concept Library for Complex Event Detection in Video. In *ACMMM*, 2015.

MASTER: Multi-platform Application Streaming Toolkits for Elastic Resources

Yusen Li Yunhua Deng Ronald Seet Xueyan Tang Wentong Cai
Nanyang Technological University, Singapore
{liys, yhdeng, ronaldseet, asxytang, aswtcai}@ntu.edu.sg

ABSTRACT

In this demonstration, we propose MASTER, a set of toolkits for cross-platform application streaming that is able to utilize elastic resources on public clouds. MASTER has many useful features. It provides full control of resource acquisition and request dispatching, requires only a browser on the client side for user interactions, and incorporates an input transformer to assist touchscreen device users to naturally interact with desktop applications that need keystroke and mouse control. MASTER also supports session concurrency (serving multiple streaming sessions on a single cloud server instance), thereby improving resource utilization and cutting the cloud bill.

Categories and Subject Descriptors

H.5 [**Information Systems Applications**]: Multimedia Information Systems

Keywords

Application streaming, multi-platform, elastic resources

1. INTRODUCTION

Resource-intensive applications, such as high-end video gaming, 3D modeling, CAD, physical simulation, scientific visualization, and medical imaging, typically consume vast computation (CPU and GPU), memory, and storage resources, making them difficult to run on today's mass-market mobile devices such as laptops, tablets and smart phones. Recently, video-based streaming from the cloud has been considered as a viable means to let more users on more devices enjoy this class of applications that are supposed to run on costly workstations (Figure 1). In addition to *removal of device constraints*, there are several other important benefits provided by interactively streaming the application from the cloud to users: *instant-on* – the application can be used immediately, without time-consuming software downloads and installations; *cross-platform* – the application can reach to multiple device platforms without any code modification; *improved-security* – the application binary is securely stored in the cloud, avoiding theft or reverse engineering.

MM'15, October 26-30, 2015, Brisbane, Australia
ACM 978-1-4503-3459-4/15/10.
http://dx.doi.org/10.1145/2733373.2807978

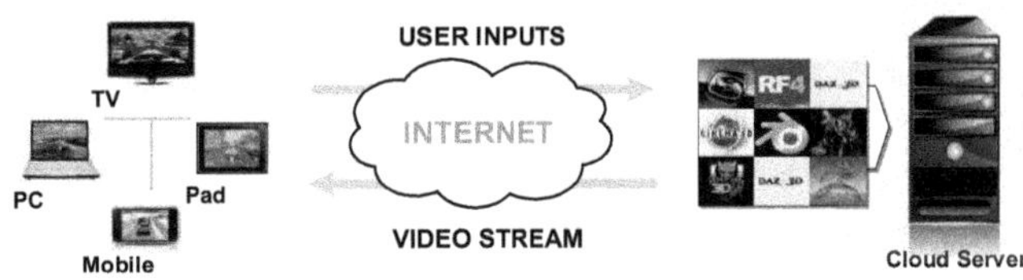

Figure 1: Streaming applications from cloud servers to clients.

In recent years, video games have been successfully streamed from the cloud to players (known as *cloud gaming*). Currently, there are two major cloud gaming services: Sony's PlayStation Now[1] and nVidia's SHIELD[2]. These cloud gaming services run on their respective private clouds, offer their own or third-party games to the players, and require the players to buy designated consoles.

Meanwhile, Amazon has launched an application streaming service called AppStream[3] that helps customers deploy their resource-intensive applications onto Amazon EC2[4] without code modifications, and stream them to targeted users on nearly any device. Currently, AppStream customers can only deploy their applications onto limited regions of Amazon EC2, so users far away from those supported regions may suffer from poor interactivity performance due to high network latencies. Furthermore, customers cannot control *resource acquisition* and *request dispatching*, thus it is hard for them to strive for cost-performance optimization.

Motivated by observing the above constraints found in existing systems, we have developed MASTER, a set of toolkits that serves those customers who intend to not only stream their resource-intensive applications from public clouds to users anywhere on any device, but also fully control the associated resource acquisition and request dispatching. We started this project in early 2013 and have been gradually adding new functions and features to the toolkits.

Besides controllability, there are several additional features that technically make MASTER unique compared to those systems developed by other researchers for cloud gaming, such as GamingAnywhere [1] (the first open-source cloud gaming system), Rhizome [5] (similar to the former except for explicit supports for hardware-based encoding/decoding), and LiveRender [4] (based on graphics-based streaming rather than video-based streaming used by the previous two and ours). First, MASTER is designed to stream any resource-intensive application (not limited to video games)

[1] `https://www.playstation.com/en-us/explore/psnow/`. Sony has acquired two pioneering cloud gaming companies GaiKai and OnLive, and integrated their technologies into its cloud gaming service.

[2] `http://shield.nvidia.com/`

[3] `http://aws.amazon.com/appstream/`

[4] `http://aws.amazon.com/ec2/`

to users anywhere on any device, as it utilizes public clouds as the underlying server infrastructure and requires only a browser on the client side for user interactions. Second, we have designed a Javascript input transformer to assist touchscreen device users to naturally interact with desktop applications that need keyboard and mouse inputs without any code modification or plugin installation. Finally, MASTER can support session concurrency (serving multiple streaming sessions on one single cloud server) without relying on virtualization. Existing systems, however, all require machine virtualization for implementing session concurrency, making it difficult and inefficient to realize on public clouds as multiple virtual machines have to be created on top of a cloud server instance which is already a virtual machine by itself. We present the key features and the demonstration of MASTER in the following sections.

2. KEY FEATURES

2.1 High Controllability

High controllability is a key feature that differentiates MASTER from existing commercial products. According to our empirical studies on Amazon AppStream, customers have very limited controllability on the deployment and operation of their application streaming. For example, they can choose only two regions of Amazon EC2[5] to place servers, which restricts their applications from reaching users in wider geographic areas due to latency constraints. In addition, only one streaming session is hosted by each server that is actually very powerful (G2 instance), which results in low resource utilization and excessive operational cost.

In contrast, with MASTER, application providers can deploy their applications in the servers located in any region on Amazon EC2 or any other public clouds, to reach as many users as possible without violating latency constraints. Furthermore, they can operate multiple streaming sessions on one cloud server, which can greatly improve resource utilization and cut down the cloud bill. In addition, they can even dynamically choose to use on-demand or reserved instances to optimize resource acquisition and request dispatching by leveraging request arrival patterns and session lengths. This indeed reveals the scientific value of MASTER as a testbed for studying related cloud resource optimization problems [2] [3]. Figure 2 illustrates the controllability concepts of MASTER.

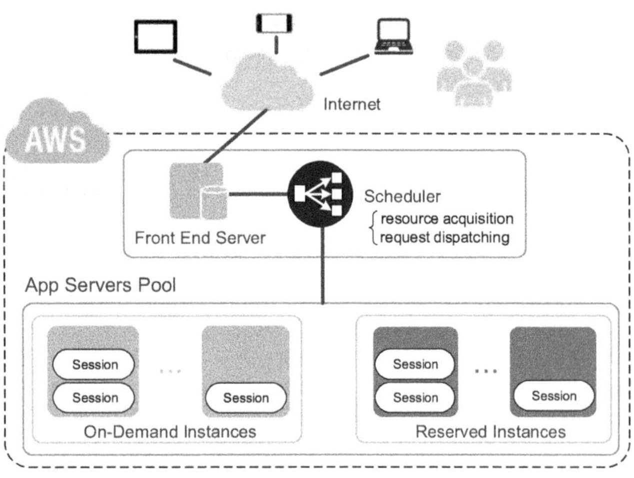

Figure 2: Application streaming under your control.

[5]US East (N.Virginia) and Asia Pacific (Tokyo) only.

2.2 High Adaptability

Our system enables the cloud server to adapt the streaming session to the client device's screen size, estimated bandwidth availability, and quality preference indicated by the client for guaranteeing smooth interaction while minimizing the resource consumption. Specifically, the knowledge of screen size helps prevent unnecessarily high video resolution that will not be useful to the client, the estimated bandwidth capacity helps adjust the video bitrate for smooth video transmission, and the quality preference gives the client the freedom to control the video size manually.

Besides considering the above factors, MASTER also takes into account the nature of client devices. Specifically, MASTER provides an input transformer interface that can facilitate clients on touchscreen devices (e.g. mobile phones or tablets) to interact with desktop applications that require keystroke and mouse control. The input transformer is written in Javascript and can be automatically loaded into the browser of the mobile device, without any code modification on the application being streamed.

3. DEMONSTRATION

In this demo, we will show, from the application provider's perspective, how to setup MASTER onto a server that is a GPU instance on Amazon EC2. We will choose the datacenter of Amazon EC2 that is closest to the conference venue to deploy MASTER, in order to achieve low-latency application streaming to the audience. We will prepare a set of representative thin client devices, including a laptop, a tablet PC, and a mobile phone, for the audience to interact with the applications streamed from the cloud using browsers. The audience will be invited to interact with some typical resource-intensive applications, including a complex 3D virtual environment and a professional 3D graphics modeling software. They will access the streaming sessions simultaneously to demonstrate the session concurrency ability of MASTER.

4. ACKNOWLEDGMENTS

This research is supported by Multi-plAtform Game Innovation Centre (MAGIC), funded by the Singapore National Research Foundation under its IDM Futures Funding Initiative and administered by the Interactive & Digital Media Programme Office, Media Development Authority. This research is also supported by Singapore Ministry of Education Academic Research Fund Tier 2 under Grant MOE2013-T2-2-067, and by an AWS in Education Research Grant award. We would like to thank Hanying Zheng and many undergraduate students involved in the project for their contributions.

5. REFERENCES

[1] C.-Y. Huang, K.-T. Chen, D.-Y. Chen, H.-J. Hsu, and C.-H. Hsu. Gaminganywhere: The first open source cloud gaming system. *ACM TOMCCAP*, 10(1s):10:1–10:25, Jan. 2014.

[2] Y. Li, X. Tang, and W. Cai. Let's depart together: Efficient play request dispatching in cloud gaming. In *Proc. NetGames*, pages 1–6, 2014.

[3] Y. Li, X. Tang, and W. Cai. On dynamic bin packing for resource allocation in the cloud. In *Proc. ACM SPAA*, pages 2–11, 2014.

[4] L. Lin, X. Liao, G. Tan, H. Jin, X. Yang, W. Zhang, and B. Li. Liverender: A cloud gaming system based on compressed graphics streaming. In *Proc. ACM MM*, pages 347–356, 2014.

[5] R. Shea, D. Fu, and J. Liu. Rhizome: Utilizing the public cloud to provide 3D gaming infrastructure. In *Proc. ACM MMSys*, pages 97–100, 2015.

smArt: Open and Interactive Indoor Cultural Data

Andrea Ferracani, Daniele Pezzatini, Alberto Del Bimbo, Riccardo Del Chiaro, Franco Yang, Maurizio Sanesi
Università degli Studi di Firenze - MICC
Firenze, Italy
[name.surname]@unifi.it

ABSTRACT

In this demo we present smArt[1], a low-cost framework to quickly set up indoor exhibits featuring a smart navigation system for museums. The framework is web-based and allows the design on a digital map of a sensorized museum environment and the dynamic and assisted definition of the multimedia materials and sensors associated to the artworks. The knowledge-base uses semantic technologies and it is exploited by museum visitors to get directions and to have multimedia insights in a natural way. Indoor localisation and routing is provided taking advantage of active and passive sensors advertisements and user interactions. In this way we overcome the Global Positioning System (GPS) unavailability issue in indoor environments.

Categories and Subject Descriptors

H.4 [**Information Systems Applications**]: Miscellaneous; J.5 [**Computer Applications**]: Arts and Humanities—*Architecture*

General Terms

Theory, Design, Cultural Data Curation, Installations

Keywords

Cultural heritage, web applications, beacon, sensors, Open Linked Data, Museum guide

1. CONTEXT AND MOTIVATION

The problem of linking physical spaces with structured data is urgent considering from the one hand the opportunities offered by the evolution of the semantic web and from the other the increasing adoption of the so-called Internet-Of-Things (IOT). Furthermore, managers in the cultural heritage need easy to use tools to promote, curate and publish cultural data that may be exploited at several levels by students, tourists, professionals, researchers and so on. To this end tools have to provide museum curators with facilities for artworks' search, browsing and collection, and not at least the opportunity to make cultural resources available as public structured data on the web. At the same time, nowadays, real spaces can easily be made reactive and low-cost solutions are desirable. smArt fulfills these requirements and provides a tool where cultural resources can be browsed and published, from and on the web, using a big and extendable repository (i.e. DBPedia dataset[2]). Data can be enriched with sensors information for *ad hoc* deployable installations. In details, the web application allows to associate artworks in a semi-automatic way with different types of sensors and features proximity sensing and routing in an indoor environment. This is not trivial: in fact while tourism electronic guides for outdoor are widespread and provide access to contextual multimedia data relying on GPS technology, things are more difficult in indoor where GPS is not available. Sub-room indoor localisation is an active area of research which includes applications in reactive indoor spaces. smArt exploits Bluetooth Low Energy (BLE) beaconing, in synergy with other tools, as an indoor positioning and routing technology. Bluetooth Estimote Beacons[3] and automatic generated QR codes can be automatically and manually associated to artworks or locations in the knowledge-base and then physically positioned. Cited technologies are low or without cost and don't involve an infrastructural overhead: two common requirements for cultural public institutions.

[1]Demo video: https://vimeo.com/miccunifi/smart

MM'15, October 26–30, 2015, Brisbane, Australia.
ACM 978-1-4503-3459-4/15/10.
DOI: http://dx.doi.org/10.1145/2733373.2807981.

2. THE SYSTEM

The system is mainly composed by two modules: 1) a web-based application for the semi-automatic ingestion and management of Open Linked Data regarding the cities of Venice, Rome and Florence in Italy; 2) a mobile Android application which exploits the data generated by the web app and reacts to the expected signals in the real environment.

2.1 Configuring the environment: the Web Application

The web application is used for the ingestion, creation and management of data concerning museums. It provides a graphical user interface for building data and components mashups in order to configure a sensorized environment. Users are enabled to 'pipe' several interface components and

[2]See http://bit.ly/1HxOUVI
[3]See http://bit.ly/1d7dZdB

then set up rules for how content should be modified. There are three main components: 1) City Component: it allows to choose cities from which to select public multimedia data; 2) Museum Component: it is used to collect, aggregate and enrich data about museums and artworks from DBPedia through Open Linked Data; 3) Sensor Component: it can be applied to artwork collections in order to automatically associate physical sensors. Components are managed and organised on the interface using a drag-and-drop paradigm. A component is shown as a circle icon with a label and an image. When dragged on other components icons can make appear contextual menus in order to apply modifiers. The Museum Component provides contextual panels to search museums, select and associate sensors to artworks (i.e. Beacons or QR codes). Furthermore, for each museum the user can: 1) interactively draw the museum map of the environment to be sensorized; 2) decide the location of the artworks; 3) define the access point to the museum halls and finally 4) mark out all the trajectories that visitors can use to reach the artworks. All this infos are then used by the mobile application to provide localisation and routing systems to museum visitors. The web app has been developed in HTML5 for the client and uses PHP and MySQL on the server for metadata storing. Storing and communication with the semantic knowledge-base is performed through RDF and Sparql Queries to a self-hosted DBPedia endpoint. The knowledge-base is reachable on a self-hosted Virtuoso Server[4] and it uses triple-store dumps of Wikipedia frequently and automatically updated.

2.2 Mobile App, Localisation and Routing

smArt mobile application allows the visitor to localise herself in the indoor museum and provides a routing system to guide the user to artworks of interest on the basis of the data generated by the web application. The app has been designed with the aim to enhance the user experience of a visitor approaching or searching for an artwork and provides multimedia insights exploiting natural interaction paradigms. It is well known that GPS is not working in indoor locations due to the poor signal coverage. Furthermore, indoor localisation is particularly challenging for several reasons: presence of obstacles and moving people, interference caused by other electronic devices etc. Standard solutions contemplate active (QR code scanning, NFC) and passive sensors (beacon bluetooth for proximity detection or triangulation for exact location). smArt exploits bluetooth beacons which are cheap and well supported and require a low level of interaction. As an alternative each artwork can be automatically or manually associated to QR codes which have no cost but need more user participation.
The app has been developed as an Android application and uses an SQL Lite database generated by the web application and stored on a server. The interface has been designed following the Google guidelines for material design. The main interface is map based and provides outdoor navigation. Through a sliding-up panel the user can check his localisation and browse all the nearby museums where an interactive exhibit has been set up. Google directions are also provided. When a user approaches a museum she is notified on the app interface of the possibility to switch to an indoor map visualisation. The map is rendered in real-time on the device using canvas and vector shapes. Zoom and drag gestures are enabled. Artworks equipped with a sensor are visualised on the map as icons. Once the user has localised herself or the app has identified her location, the user can select any artwork on the map or using the sliding panel in order to be suggested with the shortest path to it. User location is acquired when the app receives the unique identifying information broadcasted by a beacon via bluetooth or when the user scans a QR code associated with an artwork or provided as a localisation hotspot in the museum. A background service is always active and listens to BLE advertisements. When the device receives the signal, the user is notified and contextual artwork multimedia data are shown.
The indoor engine is in charge to draw and manage the map and the navigation system: paths are computed modelling the information about museum rooms and artworks as a graph of traversable spots. Spots have been defined and arranged by the web app user on the map and can be sensorized artworks, path spot, door spot or museum visitor localisation spots. The shortest path to an artwork is estimated on the fly by the indoor engine using the Dijkstra's algorithm and then visualised on the map. The engine provides also a completely automatic system to calculate the shortest path in the case that the web app user has not marked the path spots required to navigate from an artwork or a localisation in a room to another. This is achieved using automatic 2D polygon convex partitioning of the museum map: the Hertel-Mehlhorn algorithm is exploited which is never worse than $2r + 1$ pieces, where r is the number of reflex vertices. Once the polygon is partitioned the center of mass of each partition is identified and treated as a path spot to be used in the graph by the Dijkstra's algorithm to build the itinerary from the user position to the artwork of interest. The algorithm allows to face situations where the map is a regular polygon but paths from an artwork or a localisation in a room to a target artwork in another room could cross the museum hall walls resulting in a wrong feedback to the user.

[4]See http://bit.ly/1BqKEVP

3. CONCLUSIONS AND FUTURE WORK

In this demo we present a web-based framework designed for museum curators to manage and set up easily interactive exhibits in a sensorized environment. Museums, artworks and associated multimedia materials are retrieved from and saved to the web using Open Linked Data. Artworks can be placed on the map and associated with cheap and easy to install actuators to be placed in the real museum environment. Exploiting these data museum visitors equipped with an *ad hoc* mobile app can enjoy interactive exhibits in an effective and natural way. Future work will focus on the refinement of methods for the reduction of localisation errors using BLE technology. A good starting point are the results in [1].

4. REFERENCES

[1] P. Martin, B.-J. Ho, N. Grupen, S. Muñoz, and M. Srivastava. An ibeacon primer for indoor localization: Demo abstract. In *Proceedings of the 1st ACM Conference on Embedded Systems for Energy-Efficient Buildings*, BuildSys '14, pages 190–191, New York, NY, USA, 2014. ACM.

i-Diary: A Crowdsource-based Spatio-Temporal Multimedia Enhanced Points of Interest Authoring Tool

Akhlaq Ahmad[1, 2], Faizan Ur Rehman[3, 4], Md. Abdur Rahman[3, 5], Abdullah Murad[3, 6], Ahmad Qamar[5, 7], Bilal Sadiq[3], Salah Basalamah[3], Mohamed Ridza Wahiddin[1]

[1]KICT, International Islamic University, Malaysia, ([2]College of Engineering and Islamic Architecture, [3]KACST GIS Technology Innovation Center, [5]College of Computer and Information Systems, [6]Innovation and Entrepreneurship Institute) Umm Al Qura University, Makkah, Saudi Arabia, [4]Dept. of Computer Science, LIG, University of Grenoble Alpes, France, [7]University Sains Malaysia,

Email: {aajee, fsrehman, marahman, aamurad, amqamar, sabasalamah}@uqu.edu.sa, bsadiq@gistic.org, mridza@iium.edu.my

ABSTRACT

Aggregating interesting spatio-temporal events of daily life in a diary used to be favorite pastime for many individuals. However, crescive use of social media through portable digital devices is replacing traditional diary writing. Thanks to ubiquity of smartphones, people can now add multiple media types in order to record joyful moments and events with a time line. In this paper, we propose a spatio-temporal multimedia authoring tool by leveraging the ubiquity of geo-tagged multimedia that represents activities of interest to the user and allowing users to aggregate the multimedia for generating a digital diary. The authoring tool allows users to aggregate one's own spatial media with that of publicly available geo-tagged multimedia artifacts. The complex digital diary can then be saved into a big data repository for personal use as well as for sharing with a community of interest (COI). During the authoring process, the system allows a novel visualization technique of browsing clustered multiple points of interests (CMPOI) at a single GPS location, thereby exploring POIs in a multi-story building, shopping mall, etc. To facilitate efficient and user friendly discovery of CMPOIs, the authoring environment also supports spatio-temporal multimedia queries such as range and KNN (K nearest neighbor) queries from the big data environment. We plan to incorporate this multimedia authoring tool with our existing large scale multimedia supported crowdsourcing environment that is envisioned to support millions of pilgrims during the Hajj 2015 event.

Categories and Subject Descriptors

H.2.4 [**Systems**] Multimedia Database

H.2.8 [**Database Applications**] Spatial Database and GIS.

General Terms

Design, Human factors

Keywords

Geo-tagged Multimedia, Community of Interest, Authoring tool, Spatio-Temporal Activities.

MM'15, October 26-30, 2015, Brisbane, Australia

ACM 978-1-4503-3459-4/15/10.

http://dx.doi.org/10.1145/2733373.2807983

1. INTRODUCTION

People add descriptions about points of interest (POI) in their diary. Due to the advancements of several technologies such as high speed internet, smartphones with location and multimedia capability, people can now capture rich digital information about any POI such as its location, type, images, audio, video, reviews, and things around the POI, to name a few. Once captured, this rich location-aware multimedia data and its metadata can be instantly shared with one's community of interest (COI). Combining such crowdsourced geo-tagged multimedia information provides a semantically rich multimedia diary, such as a favorite shopping diary, an emergency evacuation diary, a health diary, etc. People can thus create personalized multimedia diaries or can share certain aspects of the compiled digital diary with their COIs. Personal diaries remain private with limited circulation among people of interest, however, if one can establish a shareable multimedia diary with selective attributes, the beneficiaries can speed up their learning processes and perform well in some specific tasks such as emergency situation, leisure trip, journalism, tourism, etc. domains [1].

Adjoining a temporal dimension to the co-located multimedia data helps in segregating it from the rest of the data collected during multiple visits to the same location. This could happen in routine life when users visit a multi-story shopping mall, park, library, etc., physically or virtually [2][3]. Semantics added to POI collected from abundant heterogeneous user generated crowdsourced content helps to explore multimedia data with location similarity [4]. In a large crowd with culturally diverse profiles, different spatio-temporal activities such as lost and found or navigation to POIs are of common interest [5]. Users can get benefit from other users' past experience through their shared multimedia information.

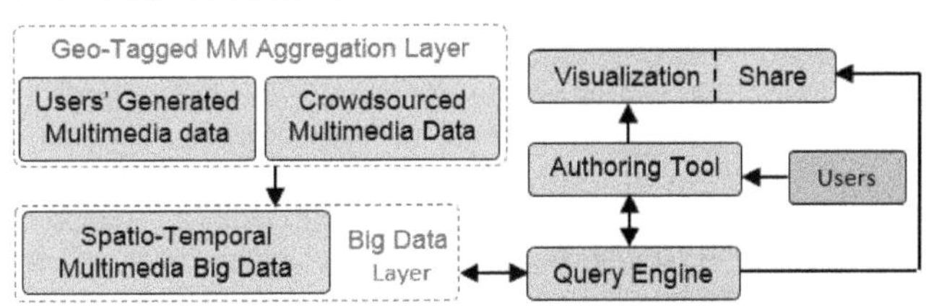

Figure 1: High Level System Architecture

In this paper, we present an authoring tool that allows users to extract geo-tagged multimedia artifacts from aggregated multimedia data and crowd sourced social media sources. This tool facilitates users to compile digital diaries for personal use as well as for sharing with COI to guide them in performing similar activities. In addition, we introduce a technique of multimedia based browsing of co-located CMPOI to help users choose POIs in a multistory building, shopping mall, etc. Moreover this tool supports multimedia tagging, which is important to create metadata, supporting search for a particular event and or POI.

In this paper, we intend to demonstrate two different scenarios. First, we will show how to collect geo-tagged multimedia POIs using crowdsourcing architecture and save these in a big data environment. Our proposed authoring tool can then be used to search these private or publicly shared POIs using KNN and range spatial queries to aggregate and add multiple attributes to compile the geo-tagged multimedia diary, save it in a big data environment and share it with one's COI. The second scenario takes into consideration multiple points of interests located at a single GPS location. The tool allows visualizing, aggregating, and saving these multiple POIs in a big data environment as a multimedia diary, and then sharing it with one's COI.

2. SYSTEM ARCHITECTURE

Figure 1 shows the high-level architecture with multiple layers. **Multimedia aggregation layer** allows collecting geo-tagged multimedia POIs from a very large crowd using our developed smartphone application. In the **big data layer**, the multimedia data is indexed spatially and temporally. A user interacts with the authoring tool through a user interface which supports selecting multiple attributes regarding a POI. The **authoring tool** offers multiple options to select multimedia objects from a timeline, including objects related to a point in time or a period of time such as an event or a journey. These selections will generate a multimedia diary on the **visualization** screen based on the data fetched from the big data layer through the **query engine**. The user has an option to share a multimedia diary with other people of interest. Depending on the available bandwidth and memory, users can visualize multiple views on the screen. For multiple points of interest at a single location we propose a tree-based visualization as shown in **Figure 2**.

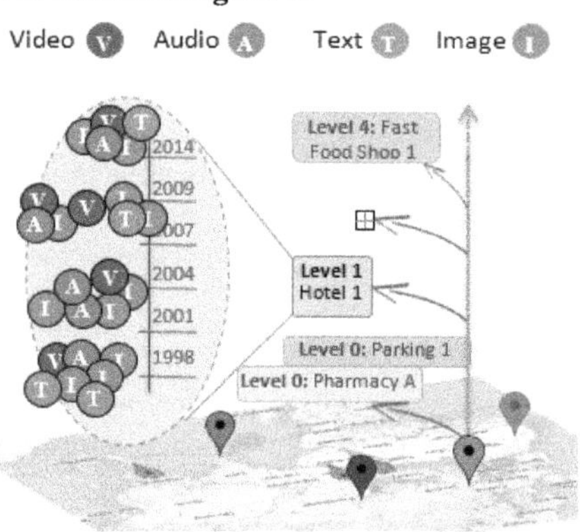

Figure 2: A Multilevel Co-located POI Browsing Interface

This visualization is proposed to elaborate co-located multimedia data objects collected by users at the same location such as a multistory building or a shopping mall, etc. A branch (Level 1 in **Figure 2**) that comes out of the stem represents the temporal dimension of a single POI with chronological order of the multimedia objects.

3. IMPLEMENTATION

We have developed an Android smart phone app [6] to collect the multimedia POIs and designed a web interface (see **Figure 3**) for authoring and sharing a collection of customized POIs. To collect the POIs from pilgrims, we deployed the system during Hajj 2014 where pilgrims from more than 95 countries downloaded our app. The front end of the system is a web application that communicates with the backend through HTTP REST API, which passes and receives the parameters in JSON. The backend comprises of a big data repository that is deployed in Amazon EC2 c3.4xlarge machines for processing crowdsourced and user generated multimedia data.

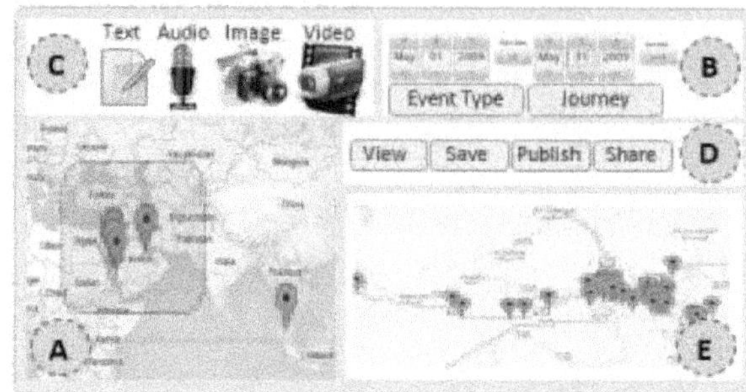

Figure 3: The Authoring Interface

4. DEMONSTRATION SCENARIOS

Scenario 1: A user interacts with system through a web-based authoring tool that provides the user with an interface to select the POIs by dragging the mouse over the map in a spatial browser (Figure 3(A)), to select the date range and event type or journey (Figure 3(B)), and to drag multimedia objects (Figure 3(C)). By different authoring options shown in Figure 3(D), one can author the diary and produce an output as shown in Figure 3(E) for a specific event such as shopping, rituals, vacations, etc. At the end of authoring process, one can save the diary privately or share it with a community of interest. The authoring tool is customized for desktop and smartphone web browsers.

Scenario 2: A user generates a diary with multiple selections where some POIs appear on a single GPS location. The visualization layer will show all POIs in an expanded view as shown in Figure 2. Once the user selects a single Multimedia object, the system displays all related information and the authoring tool will allow the user to save it privately or publically.

5. ACKNOWLEDGEMENT

We extend our gratitude to King Abdul Aziz City for Science and Technology (KACST), Kingdom of Saudi Arabia for funding this research project through NSTIP grant number 11-INF1683-10, 11-INF1700-10 and 13-INF2455-10.

6. REFERENCES

[1] Vazirgiannis, M. et al. 1998. Spatio-temporal composition and indexing for large multimedia applications. *Multimedia Systems*. 6, 4 (1998), 284–298.

[2] Rahman, M.A. and Anwar Hossain, M. 2004. Lornav: A demo of a virtual reality tool for navigation and authoring of learning object repositories. *Proceedings - Eighth IEEE International Symposium on Distributed Simulation and Real-Time Applications, DS-RT 2004*. (2004), 240–243.

[3] El Saddik, A. et al. 2005. Authoring multimedia objects in collaborative ambient intelligent virtual environment. *HAVE 2005: IEEE International Workshop on Haptic Audio Visual Environments and their Applications*. October (2005), 159–164.

[4] Wang, X. et al. 2015. Semantic-Based Location Recommendation With Multimodal Venue Semantics. 17, 3 (2015), 409–419.

[5] Ahmad, A. et al. 2014. A Framework for Crowd-Sourced Data Collection and Context-Aware Services in Hajj and Umrah. *Computer Systems and Applications (AICCSA), 2014 IEEE/ACS 11th International Conference* (2014), 405–412.

[6] https://play.google.com/store/apps/details?id=com.hajjandumrah&hl=en

[7] https://haj.gov.sa

B-box Mixer: An Interactive UI for Generating B-box Music

Yi-Zhu Dai, Ting-Chia Lee, Xin-Yu Kuo, Tse-Yu Pan and Min-Chun Hu
Department of Computer Science and Information Engineering,
National Cheng Kung University, Taiwan
{p268846, carry8241, bassy, panju328, trimy}@mislab.csie.ncku.edu.tw

ABSTRACT

B-box is a form of vocal percussion that imitates rhythms in various types of sound, especially musical instruments. As b-box becoming popular, more and more people want to learn b-box and make their own b-box music. However, not everyone has the talent for generating harmonic b-box music. In this work, we develop an interactive system which helps the user easily compose b-box music given two inputs: an unaccompanied vocal song and a piece of b-box rhythm. The audio signals of the two inputs are analyzed and adaptively matched on the basis of their beats. The state of the art beat detection technique does not perform well on vocal songs. Hence, we propose to partition the song into short segments and estimate the average tempo for each segment so that the adjustment of tempo will not be affected too much by the wrongly detected beats. With the proposed system, people who love b-box or are not familiar with b-box can enjoy producing their own b-box music.

Categories and Subject Descriptors

H.5.1 & H5.5 [**Information Interfaces and Presentation**]: Multimedia Information Systems & Sound and Music Computing – *Audio input/output & Methodologies and techniques; signal analysis, synthesis, and processing.*

General Terms

Algorithms, Design, Human Factors

Keywords

Audio processing, B-box music, Beat detection, Beat alignment.

1. INTRODUCTION

Originated in America, b-box is one of the elements in hip-hop culture. It is a form of vocal percussion that imitates rhythms in various types of sound such as drum beats or any musical instruments using one's mouth, lips, tongue, and voice. Nowadays, b-box has become a popular music or street culture that arouses people's interests. For a b-box beginner, it is difficult to sing and b-box at the same time, and specific devices/software are needed. The audio mixers in the market are too complicated to operate for generating harmonic b-box music. Hence, we develop a user friendly system that allows the user to generate music with b-box accompaniment by simply choosing an unaccompanied vocal song and a piece of b-box rhythm. Figure 1 shows the framework of the proposed B-Box Mixer system. The note onset detection method is applied to detect the beats of the unaccompanied vocal song and the b-box. After that, we can adjust the tempo of b-box to fit the song and finally match the beats of the two tracks. Please see the demo video in https://goo.gl/15ZW37 for more details.

MM'15, October 26-30, 2015, Brisbane, Australia
ACM 978-1-4503-3459-4/15/10.
http://dx.doi.org/10.1145/2733373.2807984

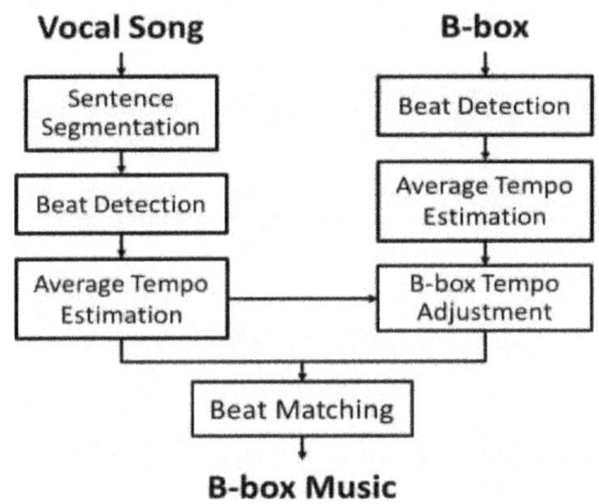

Figure 1. The framework of the proposed B-box Mixer.

2. TEMPO ANALYSIS

Given an unaccompanied vocal song and a piece of b-box rhythm, we focus on matching the beats of the two tracks. Since the vocal song are usually longer and might contain sentences with different tempos, we segment the song into sentences before analyzing the beat locations and calculating the average tempo for each sentence. In contrast, a piece of b-box rhythm is usually shorter and with consistent tempo. Hence, we directly apply beat detection to estimate its overall tempo.

2.1 Sentence Segmentation

The unaccompanied vocal song is segmented into sentences by locating time instances which are with low energy for a long enough duration. Note that the beginning of the recorded vocal song usually contains a short period of silence because the user usually starts singing with a time delay after pushing the recording button. Hence, the maximum energy of the first 0.25 seconds of the song is set as the threshold to discriminate whether the energy is low enough to be considered as the silence part between sentences. For every 0.25 seconds of the song, we evaluate the percentage of samples whose energy is lower than the threshold. If the percentage is larger than 88%, we consider this 0.25 seconds as silent and can be a partition point. At last, we use erosion and dilation to eliminate the fractional parts.

2.2 Beat Detection

In the implementation of beat detection, we apply the note onset detection method proposed in [1]. First, we find out all the time indexes with local maximum (peaks) of the input signal. A non-maximum suppression step is further applied to filter the result since there might be some peaks which are too close and some of them should be ignored. The indexes of the remaining peaks will be the detected beat locations.

2.3 Average Tempo Estimation

With the detected beat locations (for each sentence or for each piece of b-box rhythm), we compute the distance (in terms of samples) between successive beats and find out the mode of the distance values to be the average tempo.

3. MUSIC REMIX

After analyzing the average tempo of unaccompanied vocal song and b-box, we adjust the tempo of b-box so that it can be remixed with the unaccompanied song appropriately.

3.1 Tempo Adjustment

In order to adjust the b-box input $\boldsymbol{B}$ to a proper average tempo, the scaling magnitude S is computed by: $S = \frac{AT_s}{AT_b}$, where AT_s is the average tempo of unaccompanied vocal song, and AT_b is the average tempo of the b-box. Then, we compute the distance (in terms of samples) of every successive beats detected in $\boldsymbol{B}$ and scale the distance by S to obtain a new tempo-adjusted b-box $\boldsymbol{B'}$ whose average tempo equals to the vocal song's tempo.

3.2 Beat Matching

If we align the starting beat of $\boldsymbol{B'}$ with the starting beat of the unaccompanied vocal song and directly repeat $\boldsymbol{B'}$ until the song ends, the misalignment of beats will drift and result in seriously unsynchronized sound effect between the two tracks. This problem is caused by two reasons: 1) The tempo of the vocal song is not always the same. 2) The break duration between two successive sentences of the vocal song might be slightly different due to the impreciseness of the singer. Therefore, we propose three beat aligning methods to frequently realign these two tracks so that the drifting misalignment can be reduced.

- **Realignment by adjusting B-box per 5 Seconds:** The vocal song is unchanged. Repeat $\boldsymbol{B'}$ but realign the first beat of a $\boldsymbol{B'}$ when it is going to be aligned with the next 5 seconds of the vocal song.
- **Realignment by adjusting B-box per Sentence:** The vocal song is unchanged. Repeat $\boldsymbol{B'}$ but realign the first beat of a $\boldsymbol{B'}$ when it is going to be aligned with a new sentence of the vocal song.
- **Realignment by adjusting each sentence of the vocal song:**

  Different from the previous two methods, the b-box $\boldsymbol{B'}$ is repeated directly. In contrast, the first beat of each sentence of the vocal song is realigned with the first beat of the upcoming $\boldsymbol{B'}$. This method can prevent the two tracks from being silent at the same time.

In the first two methods, we adjust the b-box to fit the unaccompanied vocal song. However, we have to split some b-box $\boldsymbol{B'}$ to realign the next matching cycle, and the b-box or/and the song track will sound like being skipped. In the third method, we adjust the unaccompanied vocal song so that we can prevent the resulting music from being choppy.

4. EXPERIMENTAL RESULTS

To evaluate the proposed system, we recorded 10 unaccompanied songs and 10 pieces of b-box rhythms by ourselves. Before remixing, we detect the beats of the vocal song and the b-box correspondingly. Figure 2 shows the beat detection results of the two inputs colored as blue. The horizontal axis and the vertical axis represent time and amplitude respectively, the vertical red lines are the beat locations we detected, and the vertical green lines show the ground truth. Figure 3 shows the sentence segmentation result of a vocal song. The vertical yellow lines represent the beginnings of sentences, and the vertical green lines show the ground truth. The remixing result without beat alignment and with the proposed three aligning methods are presented in the demo video: https://goo.gl/15ZW37.

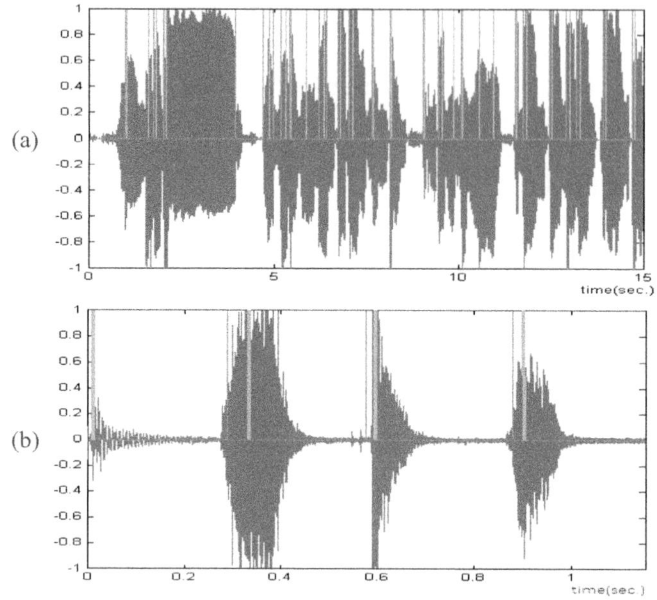

Figure 2. (a) Beat detection result of the b-box input. (b) Beat detection result of unaccompanied vocal song.

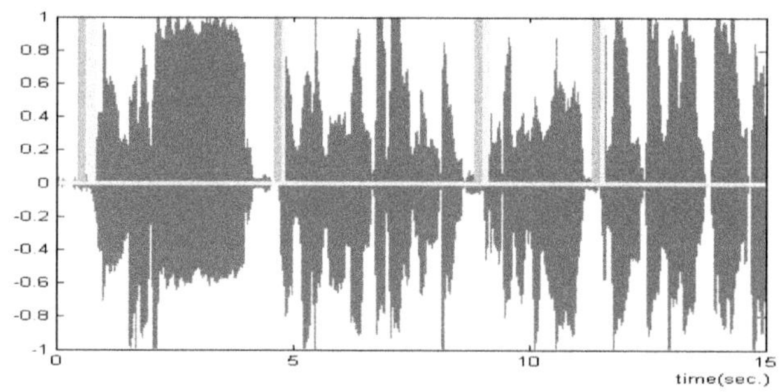

Figure 3. Example result of sentence segmentation for an unaccompanied vocal song.

5. CONCLUSIONS

We presented an interactive user interface to easily generate b-box music. After selecting or recording a song and a b-box piece, our system will estimate and adjust the tempo of the inputs and match the beats of the vocal song and the b-box tracks. In addition, the volume of the two tracks and the speed of the b-box can also be adjusted by users. Experimental results show that our work has a good performance in tempo analysis. However, though we proposed three methods to align the two tracks, we could not determine which one can get the best quality (it depends on the inputs). Currently, we provide all the three methods for the user to generate the final b-box music and the user can choose the one they like through the user interface. In the future, we would like to use machine learning techniques to automatically recommend the best matching result to our users. After that, people can make their music with more ease.

6. REFERENCES

[1] Piano Note Detection: http://www.oercommons.org/courses/matlab-code-that-implements-piano-note-detection/view

DeepFont: A System for Font Recognition and Similarity

Zhangyang Wang[1] Jianchao Yang[3] Hailin Jin[2] Jonathan Brandt [2] Eli Shechtman[2]
Aseem Agarwala [4] Zhaowen Wang [2] Yuyan Song [2] Joseph Hsieh [2] Sarah Kong [2]
Thomas S. Huang [1]
[1]University of Illinois at Urbana-Champaign, Urbana, IL, 61801, USA
[2]Adobe Research, San Jose, CA, 95110
[3]Snapchat Inc, Venice, CA, 90291
[4]Google Inc, Mountain View, CA, 94043
{zwang119, t-huang1}@illinois.edu, jianchao.yang@snapchat.com,
{hljin, jbrandt, elishe, zhawang, yusong, hsieh, sakong}@adobe.com, aseem@agarwala.org

ABSTRACT

We develop the *DeepFont* system, a large-scale learning-based solution for automatic font identification, organization and selection. In this proposed technical demonstration, we will give our audience a tour to the DeepFont system, with the focus on its impacts on real consumer products, including but not limited to: 1) a cloud-based iOS App for font recognition; 2) a web-based tool for font similarity evaluation and discovery.

Categories and Subject Descriptors

I.4.7 [**Image Processing and Computer Vision**]: Feature measurement; I.4.10 [**Image Processing and Computer Vision**]: Image Representation; I.5 [**Pattern Recognition**]: Classifier design and evaluation

Keywords

Visual Font Recognition; Deep Learning; Domain Adaptation; Model Compression

1. INTRODUCTION

Automatic visual font identification (VFR) and similar font suggestion from an image has been on the wish list of many designers. The human identification process calls for high expertise, and proves to be extremely tedious and error-prone. Despite the existence of several tools and websites assisting the VFR task, they rely on tedious human interactions and high-quality manual pre-processing of images, with the outcome accuracies still being unsatisfactory. In addition, existing softwares usually adopt simple interfaces of linear lists to exhaustively explore the entire font space, which is unrealistic for most users.

We develop the powerful *DeepFont* system, a large-scale learning-based automatic font identification solution. Without any dependence on character segmentation or content text, the DeepFont system obtains an impressive performance on vast real-word data, covering an extensive variety of font categories, and accompanied with complicated background clutters, size and ratio variations, as well as perspective distortions. Furthermore, DeepFont also facilitates font organization and selection during the design process.

2. TECHNICAL NOVELTY

The underlying technical novelty of DeepFont has been throughly discussed in our full paper [1]. It exploits a Convolutional Neural Network (CNN) decomposition approach, using a domain adaptation technique derived from a Stacked Convolutional Auto-Encoder (SCAE) that exploits massive unlabeled real-world text images, combined with synthetic data preprocessed in a specific way. The contributions of DeepFont can be briefly summarized in three-folds:

- **Domain Adapted CNN** It is very easy to generate lots of rendered font examples but very hard to obtain labeled real-world images for supervised training. The real-to-synthetic domain gap caused poor generalization to new real data in previous VFR methods. We address this *domain mismatch* problem by leveraging synthetic data to obtain effective classification features, while introducing a new domain adaptation technique with the help of unlabeled real-world data.
- **Learning-based Model Compression** We introduce a novel learning-based approach to obtain a *losslessly compressible model*. By adopting an aggressive compression strategy, the obtained "mini" model could become less than 40 megabytes in storage, with negligible performance degradation.
- **AdobeVFR Dataset** A large set of *labeled real-world* images as well as a large corpus of unlabeled real-world data are collected for both training and testing, which is the first of its kind and has been publicly released[1]. We also leverage a large training corpus of labeled synthetic data augmented in a specific way.

MM'15, October 26–30, 2015, Brisbane, Australia.
 ACM 978-1-4503-3459-4/15/10.
http://dx.doi.org/10.1145/2733373.2807988.

[1]atlaswang.com/deepfont.html

3. DEMONSTRATION

3.1 Font Recognition

Fig. 1 shows successful VFR examples using DeepFont, captured from our preliminary demonstration interface. In Fig. 1 (a), given a real-world query image, top-5 font recognition results are presented, sorted by their confidence weights from high to low[2]. DeepFont shows its proven ability to correctly recognize many more challenging real-world examples, such as those in Fig. 1 (b).

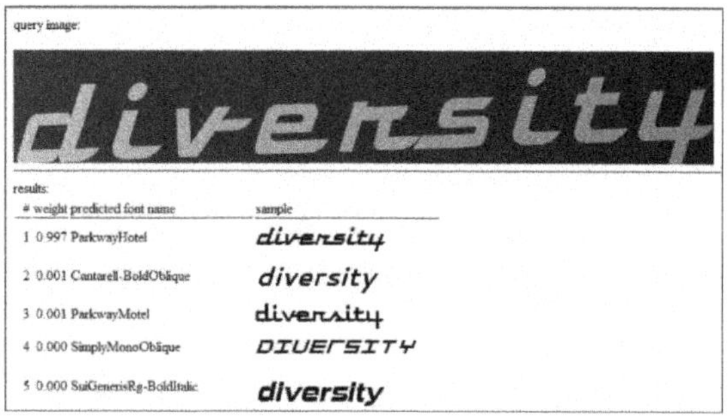

(a)

(b)

Figure 1: (a) A successful VFR example with the DeepFont system. The top row is a query image, and the results are sorted by their confidence weights. (b) More correctly recognized real-world images with DeepFont.

Moreover, we have further developed a **cloud-based iOS App**, whose screenshot is shown in Fig. 2. It launches a light iOS application which uploads a image of the cropped text region to the cloud server and sends back query results. Similar features have been implemented in the Photoshop software, which enables users to recognize typefaces of texts in images/graphics within the Photoshop software, and supports advanced features such as text font editing.

3.2 Discover Similarity Between Fonts

There are a variety of font selection tasks with different goals and requirements. One designer may wish to match a font to the style of a particular image. Another may wish to find a free font which looks similar to a commercial font such as Helvetica. A third may simply be exploring a large set of fonts such as Adobe TypeKit or Google Web Fonts. Exhaustively exploring the entire space of fonts using an alphabetical listing is unrealistic for most users. The font similarity measure is thus very helpful for font selection, organization, browsing, and suggestion.

[2]The texts are input manually for rendering purposes only. The font recognition process itself does not read any text.

Figure 2: The font recognition feature in the cloud-based iOS App.

(a)

Figure 3: An examples of the DeepFont font similarity. The top is the query image, and the renderings with the most similar fonts are returned.

The DeepFont system provides us with a smart solution to measure font similarity. We use the hidden layer activations as the high-level features describing font visual appearances. We then extract such features from all samples in a large synthetic Dataset, obtaining 100 feature vectors per class. and averaging them class-wise in order for one representative vector per class. Finally, we calculate the Euclidean distance between the representative vectors of two font classes as their similarity measure. We develop a **web-based tool** for font similarity evaluation and discovery, as illustrated in Fig. 3. Note that although the result fonts may belong to different font families from the query, they share perceivably identifiable visual similarities.

4. REFERENCES

[1] Z. Wang, J. Yang, H. Jin, E. Shechtman, A. Agarwala, J. Brandt and T. Huang, "DeepFont: Identify Your Font from An Image", In *Proceedings of ACM International Conference on Multimedia*, 2015.

ObjectMinutiae: Fingerprinting for Object Authentication

Tzu-Yun Lin
Research Center for IT Innovation, Academia Sinica, Taipei, Taiwan
power6188@gmail.com

Yu-Chiang Frank Wang
Research Center for IT Innovation, Academia Sinica, Taipei, Taiwan
ycwang@citi.sinica.edu.tw

Sean Moss-Pultz
Bitmark, Inc.
Taipei, Taiwan
sean@bitmark.com

ABSTRACT

In this work, we present *ObjectMinutiae*, which is a framework for authenticating different objects or materials via extracting and matching their fingerprints. Unlike biometrics fingerprinting processes, which use patterns such as ridge ending and bifurcation points as the interest points, our work applies stereo photometric techniques for reconstructing objects' local image regions that contain the surface texture information. The interest points of the recovered image regions can be detected and described by state-of-the-art computer vision algorithms. Together with dimension reduction and hashing techniques, our proposed system is able to perform object verification using compact image features. With neutral and different torturing conditions, preliminary results on multiple types of papers support the use of our framework for practical object authentication tasks.

Categories and Subject Descriptors

H.4 [**Information Systems Applications**]: Miscellaneous

Keywords

object fingerprinting, photometric stereo, keypoints detection, binary descriptor

1. INTRODUCTION

Forgery has been a serious issue in business marketing. Valuable items such as works of art, official documents, and luxury goods often require certain procedures (e.g., watermark, bar code, RFID, etc.) or even expert verification of an item's authenticity. Unfortunately, it is still possible to replicate or even tamper with such authentication processes. Thus, performing material authentication for practical applications can be a very challenging problem.

A desirable solution would be something akin to biometric methods for human identification and verification. Such a process would identify distinctive patterns or key features that could be used to uniquely authenticate an item. Once such patterns are extracted, together with proper hashing or encryption techniques, the resulting features can be compact yet non-replicable, thereby securing the authentication process without requiring additional human verification.

Recently, a number of solutions for object fingerprinting were proposed [2, 3, 5], which generally aim at extracting and encoding the surface texture of objects. In addition, physical properties like textural randomness are further taken into consideration when encoding their extracted features. Nevertheless, the above solutions generally rely on sophisticated machinery settings or require precise alignment. In our work, we present *ObjectMinutiae*, which advances stereo photometric techniques for capturing the local image regions of objects containing surface textural information. By utilizing state-of-the-art computer vision algorithms, ObjectMinutiae produces a set of keypoints with compact features, which enables one to perform image matching for object authentication.

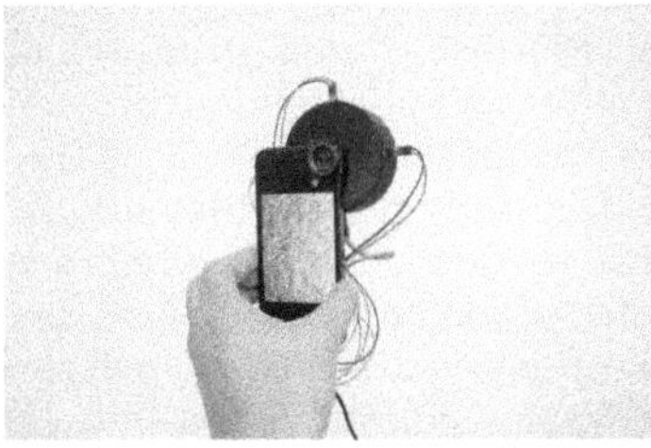

Figure 1: The prototype of our device.

2. OUR METHOD

2.1 Image Sensing

Given an object or a material, we apply the photometric stereo method of [7] to extract the surface textural information of a region of interest (ROI). As illustrated in Figure 1, we currently consider an Apple iPhone5 with Olloclip 21X macro lens and a 3D-printed photometric stereo mask for implementation. For our device, we set up 4 white light LEDs mounted inside the mask (at 0, 90, 180, and 270 degrees) in such a way that each LED can be controlled independently. Compared to recent approaches like [5, 6] which simply capture one image from the ROI, our derived output via stereo photometric techniques would contain detailed information about the surface texture. This allows us to extract unique fingerprints for verification as discussed later.

MM'15, October 26–30, 2015, Brisbane, Australia.
ACM 978-1-4503-3459-4/15/10.
DOI: http://dx.doi.org/10.1145/2733373.2807989.

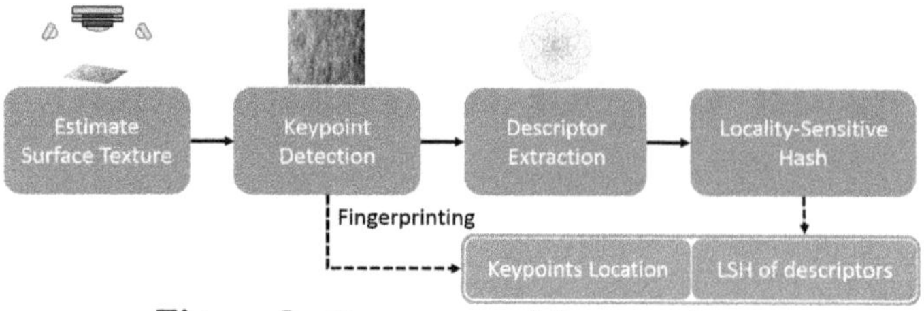

Figure 2: Our proposed framework.

2.2 Fingerprinting

Figure 2 illustrates our framework for object fingerprinting. Once the gradient image of the ROI is derived, the local interest points (i.e., keypoints) are identified and described by FAST [4] and FREAK [1] descriptors, respectively.

In addition, we further apply random projection and locality-sensitive hashing, which allow us to encode the extracted descriptors and reduce their feature dimensions. As a result, only compact information will be required to be stored, processed, and matched for our proposed framework. In our work, we only keep fewer than 300 keypoints for each ROI, while each descriptor requires only 64 bits. Adding the locations of the keypoints results in a fingerprint size for the ROI that is only about 25K bits.

2.3 Authentication Procedure

1. For a ROI, we take 4 images with lighting from 4 different horizontal and vertical directions (i.e., 0, 90, 180, and 270 degrees). Using photometric stereo techniques, we can derive the resulting gradient image describing the surface textural information.

2. We apply FAST keypoint detector to identify the local interest points of the ROI (fewer than 300), while each is described by a FREAK descriptor.

3. For encoding and dimension reduction purposes, we apply random projection on each descriptor with locality-sensitive hashing to reduce each descriptor to a 64-bit binary string. The collection of the binary strings for all descriptors forms as a set of unique minutiae that represents as an object's fingerprint.

4. Once the fingerprints of both gallery and query images are obtained, verification can be performed by matching the corresponding fingerprints.

3. EVALUATION

To evaluate the performance of our verification process, we consider 10 different art paper samples of the same material. For each paper type, we apply two types of tampering processes, rubbing and soaking before acquiring a gradient image, which make the verification task more practical yet difficult. The rubbing process involves vigorously rubbing the paper with an eraser, whereas the soaking process involves soaking the paper in water for an hour.

For each condition(untampered, rubbed, and soaked) of each paper sample, we capture two gradient images separated by a time interval. Thus, a total of $10 \times 3 \times 2 = 60$ samples would be available for our verification tests. As a result, we have 360 genuine pairs corresponding to different tampering conditions of the same piece of art paper, while 3240 imposter pairs can be obtained. To compare our work with existing methods, we consider the baseline method of [5, 6] which take only 1 photographic (not gradient) image for the ROI, with the use of our descriptors for matching.

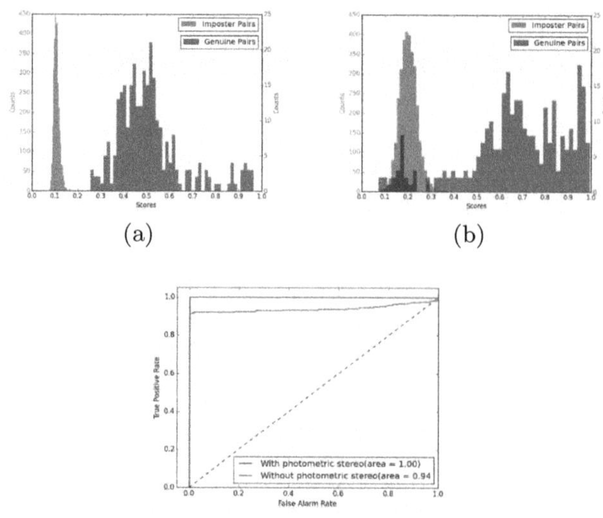

Figure 3: Matching score distributions of (a) ours and (b) baseline approach. The ROC curve is shown in (c).

Figures 3(a) and 3(b) show the matching score distributions for the genuine and imposter pairs using our and baseline approaches, respectively. It can be seen that, our proposed method was able to distinguish between genuine and imposter pairs, while the standard approach failed to do so. In addition, we plot and compare the ROC curves (i.e., true positive rate (TPR) vs. false alarm rate (FAR)) in Figure 3(c), which also confirms the effectiveness of our approach.

It is worth noting that, our work does not require precise alignment when extracting the object fingerprints. This is due to our use of robust keypoint descriptors. Another advantage is that, with LSH techniques noted in Section 2, the size of the encoded fingerprints is only about 25K bits. As a result, our proposed framework is not only applicable for offline verification tests, but also prevents possible forgery of the object of interest using our encoded fingerprints.

4. REFERENCES

[1] A. Alahi et al. Freak: Fast retina keypoint. In *CVPR'12*.

[2] J. D. Buchanan et al. Forgery: "fingerprinting" documents and packaging. *Nature*, 2005.

[3] W. Clarkson et al. Fingerprinting blank paper using commodity scanners. In *SP'09*.

[4] E. Rosten et al. Faster and better: A machine learning approach to corner detection. *PAMI'10*.

[5] A. Sharma et al. Paperspeckle: microscopic fingerprinting of paper. In *ACM CCS'11*, 2011.

[6] T. Takahashi et al. Fibar: Fingerprint imaging by binary angular reflection for individual identification of metal parts. In *EST'14*.

[7] R. J. Woodham. Photometric method for determining surface orientation from multiple images. *Optical Engineering*, 1980.

Hyper Video Browser: Search and Hyperlinking in Broadcast Media

Maria Eskevich, Huynh Nguyen, Mathilde Sahuguet, Benoit Huet
EURECOM, Sophia Antipolis, France
huet@eurecom.fr

ABSTRACT

Massive amounts of digital media is being produced and consumed daily on the Internet. Efficient access to relevant information is of key importance in contemporary society. The Hyper Video Browser provides multiple navigation means within the content of a media repository. Our system utilizes the state of the art multimodal content analysis and indexing techniques, at multiple temporal granularity, in order to satisfy the user need by suggesting relevant material. We integrate two intuitive interfaces: for search and browsing through the video archive, and for further hyperlinking to the related content while enjoying some video content. The novelty of this work includes a multi-faceted search and browsing interface for navigating in video collections and the dynamic suggestion of hyperlinks related to a media fragment content, rather than the entire video, being viewed. The approach was evaluated on the MediaEval Search and Hyperlinking task, demonstrating its effectiveness at locating accurately relevant content in a big media archive.

Categories and Subject Descriptors

H.5.1 [**Information Interfaces and Presentation**]: Multimedia Information Systems; H.5.4 [**Information Interfaces and Presentation**]: HyperText/Hypermedia

Keywords

Multimedia Search, Media Fragment, Hyperlinking

1. INTRODUCTION

Video traffic steadily increases to the level of representing two thirds of Internet communications within the next two years[1]. The number of online media platforms featuring professional (e.g. broadcast) and user contributed content is rising, together with the amount of media content available for consumption. With the sheer volume of data available, finding relevant information becomes a challenge, as in the case of videos, the search is less straightforward due to the lack of interpretability of their content. New online tools providing flexible, on-demand and relevant media documents are urgently needed to help users navigate in the media maze that a large-scale collection represents. To this end, we propose a Hyper Video Browser allowing for fine-grained media browsing, searching and hyperlinking within video collections. Fine-grained access to media content is achieved by computing and indexing descriptors and metadata at both the whole document and the media fragment level[2]. The proposed system may also be seen as an integrated second screen demonstrator, allowing viewers to actively search for additional content, cf. Figure 2, and proposing/recommending content related to the media fragment the user is watching dynamically, cf. Figure 3. It differs from common video search engines (i.e. YouTube, Dailymotion) by operating at finer-temporal scale and by taking video content into account throughout the process. The dataset from the MediaEval 2014 Search and Hyperlinking task [2], containing 2323 broadcast programs from various genre and totaling 1697 hours of content has been processed by our system as presented in Section 2. These media files are indexed and processed as a collection of 76240 topically coherent media fragments in order to become entirely available for users to browse, search and navigate though hyperlinks based on their content as detailed in Section 2.3.

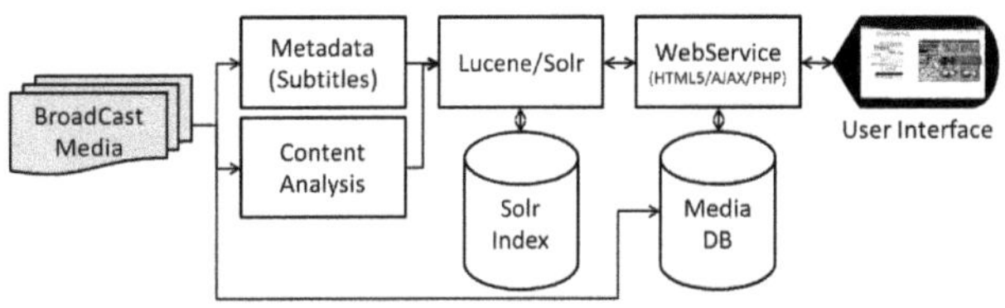

Figure 1: System Architecture Overview

2. SYSTEM ARCHITECTURE

The "Hyper Video Browser" architecture, as depicted in Figure 1, is composed of both offline and online processing components. Multimodal content analysis and indexing (using Lucene/Solr[3]) is performed offline, whenever a new video is added to the archive. A Web-service issues queries to the Solr index at run-time corresponding to the user activity.

2.1 Content Analysis

When a new multimedia document is ingested into the Hyper Video Browser, it is stored into the media database and processed at two levels: the entire document, where various metadata are available, i.e. title, cast, description, broadcast

[1] Cisco Visual Networking Index

[2] W3C Recommendation

[3] http://lucene.apache.org

MM'15, October 26–30, 2015, Brisbane, Australia.
ACM 978-1-4503-3459-4/15/10.
http://dx.doi.org/10.1145/2733373.2812618.

Figure 2: The Search/Browse Interface

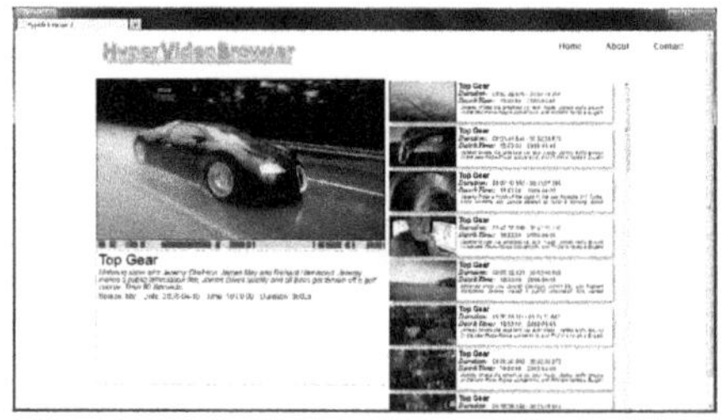

Figure 3: The Hyperlinking Interface

time, and the media fragment. The media fragments are defined using a complex segmentation procedure. Firstly, each video is segmented into shots. Then subtitles corresponding to each shot are extracted. Visual concept detection and optical character recognition are carried out on the key-frame associated to each shot [3]. Finally, the shots are grouped into larger segments (scenes or media fragments), based on visual similarity and temporal consistency [4].

2.2 Content Indexing & Searching

Both the metadata available with the broadcast and the extracted content are entered in a Lucene/Solr index at different granularities: video/scene/shot levels, allowing for precise jump-in point to be detected. Multimedia documents are represented by textual fields (for the textual metadata) and floating point fields (for the visual concept detector responses). When searching using text query, Solr's default TF-IDF-based text search is performed. When searching for visual concepts, the query is composed of range queries on the corresponding visual concepts. When searching for visual information using free text queries, the relevant visual concepts are identified based on their semantic WordNet distance with the query keywords. Multimodal queries are achieved by extending the textual query with range queries on the values of the selected visual concepts.

Hyperlinking is accomplished by automatically crafting a multimodal query from the currently played media fragment. The text query is compiled by extracting keywords from the subtitles aligned between the start and end time of the media fragment. Visual concepts scores are taken from the corresponding indexed data of the media fragment keyframes. If the media fragment contains more than one shot, the highest score over all shots for each concept is used.

2.3 Novel Media Browsing Interface

The interface has been designed with simplicity in mind and is composed of only two views: "Search and Browse" versus "Hyperlinking".

Figure 2 depicts the Hyper Video Browser home screen which is devised for browsing and searching for relevant media within the collection. It is composed of two main parts. The left hand side, provides rapid textual access to the media archive. It features a clickable animated tag-cloud, which can be selected to visualise the dataset content through various facets: Cast, Title, Description and Visual Concepts in our case. Other dimensions, such as Genre could easily be added along with one showing the user's favorite tags. Clicking on a tag, issues a textual search for the corresponding keyword/concept, which results in the presentation of a ranked list of media fragments. It is also possible to issue a free text query using the search field. Following the MediaEval Search and Hyperlinking scenario, the query may contain an additional field describing the visual content of the target video (e.g. 'visual:="visual description"'). The right hand side of the interface is contextualized so that a selection of 9 media fragments corresponding to a keyword randomly selected from the tag-cloud is displayed, providing a visual entry point to the collection, until the user issues a request. When a request is made, a ranked list of media fragment is shown (keyframe and metadata).

Upon selecting a video from the main screen, the user enters the second view panel: the hyperlinking player. Figure 3 shows a list of hyperlinks whose content relates to the content of the video fragment currently playing (on the left). When a new scene (media fragment) is reached, the system automatically constructs and issues a query to the Solr index for related content, and the hyperlinks are updated. Selecting a hyperlink results in its playing and an update in relevant hyperlinks suggestions on the right. A textual description of the program and the current fragment is dynamically displayed below the player. A bi-colored temporal stripe underneath the displayed video gives direct access to individual media fragments and provides insight upon the program structure. These functionalities empower the viewer to explore and reach media content more effectively.

3. CONCLUSION

The Hyper Video Browser endeavors to facilitate user access to multimedia content. The novel media browsing interface provides effective skimming using categorized tag-clouds, allows to perform textual and visual searches (using natural language queries) and offers hyperlinks to media containing related content dynamically while playing the selected video. The system performed among the best of MediaEval Search and Hyperlinking task, indicating the relevance and accuracy of the system [1].

4. ACKNOWLEDGEMENTS

This work has been partially supported by Bpifrance within the NexGen-TV Project, under grant number F1504054U.

5. REFERENCES

[1] E. Apostolidis, V. Mezaris, M. Sahuguet, B. Huet, B. Cervenková, D. Stein, S. Eickeler, J. L. Redondo Garcia, R. Troncy, and L. Pikora. Automatic fine-grained hyperlinking of videos within a closed collection using scene segmentation. In *ACMMM 2014, 22nd ACM International Conference on Multimedia*, Orlando, Florida, USA, 11 2014.

[2] M. Eskevich, R. Aly, D. N. Racca, R. Ordelman, S. Chen, and G. J. Jones. The Search and Hyperlinking Task at MediaEval 2014. In *Proceedings of MediaEval 2014 Workshop*, Barcelona, Catalunya, Spain, 2014.

[3] H. Le, Q. Bui, B. Huet, B. Cervenková, J. Bouchner, E. E. Apostolidis, F. Markatopoulou, A. Pournaras, V. Mezaris, D. Stein, S. Eickeler, and M. Stadtschnitzer. LinkedTV at MediaEval 2014 Search and Hyperlinking Task. In *Proceedings of MediaEval 2014 Workshop*, Barcelona, Catalunya, Spain, 2014.

[4] P. Sidiropoulos, V. Mezaris, I. Kompatsiaris, H. Meinedo, M. Bugalho, and I. Trancoso. Temporal video segmentation to scenes using high-level audiovisual features. *IEEE Trans. Circuits Syst. Video Techn.*, 21(8):1163–1177, 2011.

Joint Modeling of Users' Interests and Mobility Patterns for Point-of-Interest Recommendation

Hongzhi Yin[†] Bin Cui[§] Zi Huang[†] Weiqing Wang[†] Xian Wu[‡] Xiaofang Zhou[†,‡]
[†]The University of Queensland, School of Information Technology and Electrical Engineering, Qld 4072, Australia
[§]Key Lab of High Confidence Software Technologies (MOE), School of EECS, Peking University
[‡]School of Computer Science and Technology, Soochow University, China
[†]{h.yin1, weiqingwang}@uq.edu.au [†]{huang, zxf}@itee.uq.edu.au
[§]bin.cui@pku.edu.cn [‡]wuxian@suda.edu.cn

ABSTRACT

Point-of-Interest (POI) recommendation has become an important means to help people discover interesting places, especially when users travel out of town. However, extreme sparsity of user-POI matrix creates a severe challenge. To cope with this challenge, we propose a unified probabilistic generative model, *Topic-Region Model (TRM)*, to simultaneously discover the semantic, temporal and spatial patterns of users' check-in activities, and to model their joint effect on users' decision-making for POIs. We conduct extensive experiments to evaluate the performance of our TRM on two real large-scale datasets, and the experimental results clearly demonstrate that TRM outperforms the state-of-art methods.

Categories and Subject Descriptors

H.3.3 [**Information Search and Retrieval**]: Information Filtering

Keywords

Recommender system; Location-based service; Probabilistic generative model; Joint Modeling

1. INTRODUCTION

The rapid development of Web 2.0, location acquisition and wireless communication technologies have fostered a number of location-based social networks (LBSNs), such as Foursquare and Facebook Places. In these LBSNs, users can post their physical locations or geo-tagged information in the form of "check-in", and share their visiting experiences for points of interest (POI). In LBSNs, it is crucial to utilize user check-in data to make personalized POI recommendation, which helps users know new POIs and explore new places and facilitates advertisers to launch mobile advertisements.

One of the most important problems for POI recommendation is how to deal with a severe challenge stemming from extreme sparsity of user-POI interaction matrix. There are millions of POIs in LBSNs, but a user can only visit a limited number of them. Moreover, the observation of travel locality exacerbates this problem. The observation of travel locality [5] made on LBSNs shows that the check-in records generated by users in their non-home cities only take up 0.47% of the ones generated in their home cities [11].

MM'15, October 26–30, 2015, Brisbane, Australia.
 ISBN 978-1-4503-3459-4/15/10 ...$15.00.
DOI: http://dx.doi.org/10.1145/2733373.2806339.

This observation aggravates the data sparsity problem with POI recommendation for out-of-town users [3, 17].

The most popular approach in recommender systems is *collaborative filtering* [1]. There exists a considerable body of research [5, 13, 6, 3, 4] which deposits people's check-in history into user-POI matrix. Based on the matrix, a collaborative filtering-based method is then employed to infer the user's preference regarding each unvisited POI. The core idea of collaborative filtering is that similar users provide clues for making recommendation. Due to travel locality, most of these similar users are more likely to live in the same region with the target user. As a recommendation is made by considering POIs visited by the similar users, most of the recommended POIs would be located in the target user's home town. So, these CF-based methods cannot be directly applied to the POI recommendation for out-of-town users [3, 17].

To deal with the issue of data sparsity, especially for the out-of-town recommendation scenario, we propose a unified probabilistic generative model, namely Topic-Region Model (TRM), to simultaneously discover the semantic, temporal and spatial patterns of users' check-in activities, and model their joint effect on users' check-in behaviors. (1) Semantic Patterns. A recent analysis of the Whrrl dataset shows that the check-in activities of users exhibit a strong semantic regularity [12], e.g., the entropy of semantic categories in individual user's visited POIs is very small. (2) Temporal Patterns. As observed in [18, 4], users' activity contents exhibit strong temporal cyclic patterns in terms of hour of the day. For example, a user is more likely to go to a restaurant rather than a bar at lunch time. (3) Spatial Patterns. Many recent studies show that people tend to explore POIs near the ones that they have visited before [14]. So, POIs visited by users often form spatial clusters [6].

Note that while there are some recent studies [17, 18, 4, 6] that exploit one of the above patterns to improve POI recommendation, they lack an integrated analysis of their joint effect to deal with the issue of data sparsity, especially in the out-of-town scenario.

The remainder of the paper is organized as follows. Section 2 details TRM model. We deploy TRM to POI recommendation in Section 3. We report the experimental results in Section 4. Section 5 concludes the paper.

2. JOINT MODELING OF USER CHECK-IN ACTIVITIES

In this section, we first formulate the problem definition, and then present our proposed TRM.

2.1 Problem Formulation

Definition 1. **(POI)** A POI is defined as a uniquely identified specific site. In our model, a POI has three attributes: identifier,

Variable	Interpretation
$\boldsymbol{\vartheta_u}$	the spatial patterns of user u, expressed by a multinomial distribution over a set of regions
$\boldsymbol{\theta_u}$	the interests of user u, expressed by a multinomial distribution over a set of topics
$\boldsymbol{\phi_z}$	a multinomial distribution over words specific to topic z
$\boldsymbol{\psi_z}$	a multinomial distribution over time slots specific to topic z
$\boldsymbol{\varphi_{z,r}}$	a multinomial distribution over POI IDs specific to topic-region (z, r)
$\boldsymbol{\mu_r}$	the mean location of region r
$\boldsymbol{\Sigma_r}$	the location covariance of region r
$\gamma, \alpha, \beta, \eta, \tau$	Dirichlet priors to multinomial distributions $\boldsymbol{\vartheta_u}$, $\boldsymbol{\theta_u}$, $\boldsymbol{\phi_z}$, $\boldsymbol{\psi_z}$ and $\boldsymbol{\varphi_{z,r}}$, respectively

Table 1: Notations of parameters

location and contents. We use v to represent a POI identifier and l_v to denote its corresponding location attribute in terms of longitude and latitude coordinates. Besides, we use the notation W_v to denote the set of words describing POI v, such as tags and categories.

Definition 2. **(User Home Location)** We define a user's home location as the place where she lives, denoted as l_u. For a user whose home location is not explicitly given, we adopt the method developed by [11] which discretizes the world into 25 by $25km$ cells and defines the home location as the average position of check-ins in the cell with most of his/her check-ins.

Definition 3. **(Check-in Activity)** A check-in activity is represented by a five tuple $(u,\ v,\ l_v,\ W_v,\ t)$ that means user u visits POI v at time t.

Definition 4. **(User Profile)** For each user u, we create a user profile D_u, which is a set of check-in activities associated with user u. The dataset D used in our model consists of user profiles, i.e., $D = \{D_u : u \in U\}$ where U is the set of users.

Definition 5. **(Topic)** Given a collection of words W, a topic z is defined as a multinomial distribution over W, i.e., $\boldsymbol{\phi_z} = \{\phi_{z,w} : w \in W\}$ where each component $\phi_{z,w}$ denotes the probability of topic z generating word w.

PROBLEM 1. ***(POI Recommendation)*** *Given a target user u with her current location l and time t (that is, the query is $q = (u,\ t,\ l)$), our goal is to recommend a list of POIs that u would be interested in. Given a distance threshold d, the problem becomes an* ***out-of-town recommendation*** *if the distance between her current location and her home location (that is, $|l - l_u|$) is greater than d. Otherwise, the problem is a* ***home-town recommendation****.*

Following related studies [3, 10], we set $d = 100km$.

2.2 Model Description

For ease of presentation, we first list the notations used in TRM in Table 1. Figure 1 shows the graphical representation of TRM where users' check-in records are modeled as observed random variables. As a POI has both semantic and geographical attributes, we introduce two latent random variables, topic z and region r, which are responsible for generating them, respectively. Based on the two latent factors, TRM aims to model users' interests and spatial patterns as well as their joint effect on users' visiting behaviors.

User Interest Modeling. Inspired by the early work about user interest modeling [9, 17], TRM adopts latent topics to characterize users' interests to overcome the data sparsity. Specifically, we infer individual user's interest distribution over a set of topics according to the contents (e.g., tags and categories) of his/her checked-in POIs, denoted as $\boldsymbol{\theta_u}$. Thus, a user is associated with a topic distribution, from which topics of check-in activities are sampled.

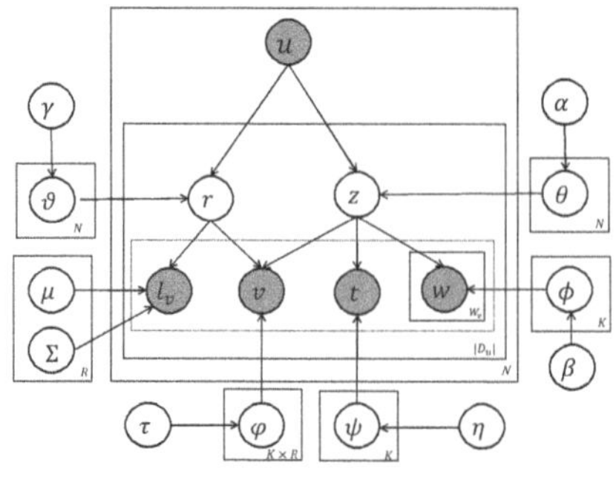

Figure 1: The Graphical Representation of TRM

Unfortunately, based on recent analysis of LBSNs data [12], about 30% of all POIs lack any meaningful content information. To address this problem, we exploit the association between the contents of checked-in POIs and the check-in time through latent topic z, since the check-in time provides important clues about the semantic content of POIs. Technically, each topic z in our TRM is not only associated with a word distribution $\boldsymbol{\phi_z}$, but also with a distribution over time $\boldsymbol{\psi_z}$. Thus, the introduction of check-in time is helpful to infer the topics of POIs whose contents are not available. To integrate the check-in time information to the topic discovery process, we employ the widely adopted discretization method in [4, 18] to split a day into hourly-based slots.

User Spatial Pattern Modeling. The spatial clustering phenomenon indicates that users are most likely to visit a number of POIs and these POIs are usually limited to some geographical regions [14]. In this component, the geographical space is divided into R regions. We apply a multinomial distribution $\boldsymbol{\vartheta_u}$ over regions to model u's spatial patterns. Following the literatures [8, 7], we assume a Gaussian distribution for each region r, and the location for POI v is characterized by $l_v \sim \mathcal{N}(\boldsymbol{\mu_r}, \boldsymbol{\Sigma_r})$, as follows:

$$P(l_v|\boldsymbol{\mu_r}, \boldsymbol{\Sigma_r}) = \frac{1}{2\pi\sqrt{|\boldsymbol{\Sigma_r}|}} \exp\left(\frac{-(l_v - \boldsymbol{\mu_r})^T \boldsymbol{\Sigma}_r^{-1}(l_v - \boldsymbol{\mu_r})}{2}\right) \quad (1)$$

where $\boldsymbol{\mu_r}$ and $\boldsymbol{\Sigma_r}$ denote the mean vector and covariance matrix.

Modeling The Joint Effect. As a POI has both semantic and geographical attributes, the propensity of a user u for a POI v is determined by the joint effect of u's personal interests and spatial mobility patterns. To model this joint effect, we introduce a joint latent factor topic-region which is responsible for generating the IDs of visited POIs, i.e., a topic-region (z, r) is associated with a distribution over POI IDs (that is $\boldsymbol{\varphi_{z,r}}$). As a matter of fact, a topic-region represents a geographical area in which POIs have same or similar semantics (e.g., categories or functions).

2.3 Model Inference

Exact inference for TRM model is difficult due to the intractable normalizing constant of the posterior distribution, we therefore exploit collapsed Gibbs sampling for approximate inference, following the studies [17, 16, 15]. As for the hyperparameters α, β, γ, η and τ, for simplicity, we take fixed values, i.e., $\alpha = 50/K$, $\gamma = 50/R$ and $\beta = \eta = \tau = 0.01$. At each iteration of our Gibbs sampler, for each user check-in record, we sample both the corresponding topic indicator z and the region indicator r. Below, we present the sampling formulas.

Sample topic indicator z according to:

$$P(z|\boldsymbol{z_{\neg u,v}}, \boldsymbol{r}, \boldsymbol{v}, \boldsymbol{l_v}, \boldsymbol{W_v}, \boldsymbol{t}, u, \cdot) \propto \frac{n_{u,z}^{\neg u,v} + \alpha}{\sum_{z'}(n_{u,z'}^{\neg u,v} + \alpha)} \times$$
$$\frac{n_{z,t}^{\neg u,v} + \eta}{\sum_{t'}(n_{z,t'}^{\neg u,v} + \eta)} \frac{n_{z,r,v}^{\neg u,v} + \tau}{\sum_{v'}(n_{z,r,v'}^{\neg u,v} + \tau)} \prod_{w \in W_v} \frac{n_{z,w}^{\neg u,v} + \beta}{\sum_{w'}(n_{z,w'}^{\neg u,v} + \beta)} \quad (2)$$

where $\boldsymbol{z}_{\neg u,v}$ represents topic assignments for all check-in records except the current one, $n_{u,z}$ is the number of times that latent topic z has been sampled from the interest distribution of user u, $n_{z,w}$ is the number of times that word w is generated from topic z, and $n_{z,t}$ is the number of times that time slot t is generated from topic z; $n_{z,r,v}$ is the number of times that POI v is generated by topic-region (z, r); the number $n^{\neg u,v}$ with superscript $\neg u, v$ denotes a quantity excluding the current instance.

Sample region indicator r according to:

$$P(r|\boldsymbol{r}_{\neg u,v}, \boldsymbol{z}, \boldsymbol{v}, \boldsymbol{l_v}, \boldsymbol{W_v}, \boldsymbol{t}, u, \cdot) \propto \frac{n_{u,r}^{\neg u,v}+\gamma}{\sum_{r'}(n_{u,r'}^{\neg u,v}+\gamma)} \frac{n_{z,r,v}^{\neg u,v}+\tau}{\sum_{v'}(n_{z,r,v'}^{\neg u,v}+\tau)} P(l_v|\boldsymbol{\mu_r}, \boldsymbol{\Sigma_r}) \quad (3)$$

where $n_{u,r}$ is the number of times that region r has been sampled from the spatial distribution of user u.

After each iteration, we employ the method of moments to update the Gaussian distribution parameters (i.e., $\boldsymbol{\mu}$ and $\boldsymbol{\Sigma}$):

$$\boldsymbol{\mu_r} = E(r) = \frac{1}{|S_r|}\sum_{v\in S_r} l_v \quad (4)$$

$$\boldsymbol{\Sigma_r} = D(r) = \frac{1}{|S_r|-1}\sum_{v\in S_r}(l_v-\boldsymbol{\mu_r})(l_v-\boldsymbol{\mu_r})^T \quad (5)$$

where S_r denotes the set of POIs associated with latent region r.

3. POI RECOMMENDATION USING TRM

Once we have learnt the model parameter set $\hat{\boldsymbol{\Psi}} = \{\hat{\boldsymbol{\theta}}, \hat{\boldsymbol{\vartheta}}, \hat{\boldsymbol{\phi}}, \hat{\boldsymbol{\varphi}}, \hat{\boldsymbol{\psi}}, \hat{\boldsymbol{\mu}}, \hat{\boldsymbol{\Sigma}}\}$, given a target user u with the current time t and location l, i.e., $q = (u, t, l)$, we compute a probability of user u checking-in each unvisited POI v as in Equation 6, and then select top-k POIs with highest probabilities for the target user.

$$P(v|u,t,l,\hat{\boldsymbol{\Psi}}) = \frac{P(v,t|u,l,\hat{\boldsymbol{\Psi}})}{\sum_{v'}P(v',t|u,l,\hat{\boldsymbol{\Psi}})} \propto P(v,t|u,l,\hat{\boldsymbol{\Psi}}) \quad (6)$$

where $P(v,t|u,l,\hat{\boldsymbol{\Psi}})$ is calculated as follows:

$$P(v,t|u,l,\hat{\boldsymbol{\Psi}}) = \sum_r P(r|l,\hat{\boldsymbol{\Psi}})P(v,t|u,r,\hat{\boldsymbol{\Psi}}) \quad (7)$$

where $P(r|l,\hat{\boldsymbol{\Psi}})$ denotes the probability of user u choosing region r given his current location l, and it is computed as in Equation 8 according to Bayes rule, in which the prior probability of latent region r can be estimated using Equation 9.

$$P(r|l,\hat{\boldsymbol{\Psi}}) = \frac{P(r)P(l|r,\hat{\boldsymbol{\Psi}})}{\sum_{r'}P(r')P(l|r',\hat{\boldsymbol{\Psi}})} \propto P(r)P(l|r,\hat{\boldsymbol{\Psi}}) \quad (8)$$

$$P(r) = \sum_u P(r|u)P(u) = \sum_u \frac{N_u+\kappa}{\sum_{u'}(N_{u'}+\kappa)}\hat{\vartheta}_{u',r} \quad (9)$$

where N_u denotes the number of check-ins generated by user u. In order to avoid overfitting, we introduce the Dirichlet prior parameter κ to play the role of pseudocount. The second part of Equation 7, $P(v,t|u,r,\hat{\boldsymbol{\Psi}})$, is computed as follows.

$$P(v,t|u,r,\hat{\boldsymbol{\Psi}}) = \sum_z P(z|u,\hat{\boldsymbol{\Psi}})P(t|z,\hat{\boldsymbol{\Psi}})P(v|z,r,\hat{\boldsymbol{\Psi}}) \quad (10)$$

Based on Equations (7-10), the original Equation 6 can be reformulated as follows.

$$\begin{aligned} &P(v|u,t,l,\hat{\boldsymbol{\Psi}}) \\ &\propto \sum_r \Big[P(r)P(l|r,\hat{\boldsymbol{\Psi}})\sum_z P(z|u,\hat{\boldsymbol{\Psi}})P(t|z,\hat{\boldsymbol{\Psi}})P(v|z,r,\hat{\boldsymbol{\Psi}})\Big] \\ &= \sum_r \Big[P(r)P(l|\hat{\boldsymbol{\mu}}_{\boldsymbol{r}},\hat{\boldsymbol{\Sigma}}_{\boldsymbol{r}})\sum_z \hat{\theta}_{u,z}\hat{\psi}_{z,t}\hat{\varphi}_{z,r,v}\Big] \end{aligned} \quad (11)$$

4. EXPERIMENTS

In this section, we first describe the settings of experiments and then demonstrate the experimental results.

4.1 Experimental Settings

4.1.1 Datasets

Foursquare. This dataset contains the check-in history of 4,163 users who live in the California, USA. For each user, it contains her social networks, check-in POI IDs, location of each check-in POI in terms of latitude and longitude, check-in time and the contents of each check-in POI. The total number of check-in records is 483,813, and the total number of social relationship is 32,512.

Twitter. This dataset is based on the publicly available twitter dataset [2]. But the original dataset does not contain the category and tag information about each POI. So, we crawled the content information associated with each POI from Foursquare with the help of its publicly available API [1]. The enhanced dataset contains 114,058 users and 1434,668 check-ins.

4.1.2 Comparative Approaches

TACF. TACF is the state-of-the-art time-aware POI recommendation method [18], which is a collaborative filtering model considering *temporal effect*.

GeoMF. GeoMF is a weighted matrix factorization model that exploits the *spatial patterns* of users' check-in activities [6].

LCA-LDA. LCA-LDA is a location-content-aware recommender model which is developed to support POI recommendation for users traveling in new cities [17].

UPS-CF. UPS-CF, proposed in [3], is a collaborative recommendation framework which incorporates social influence to support out-of-town recommendation.

4.1.3 Evaluation methods

For each user, we divide the user's activity records into a training set and a test set. For the scenario of home-town recommendation, we randomly select 30% of the activity records occurring at the user's home town as test set, and use the remaining activity records as the training set. Similarly, for the scenario of out-of-town recommendation, we randomly select 30% of the activity records generated by the user when he/she travels out of town as the test set.

To evaluate the recommendation methods, we adopt the evaluation methodology and measurement Accuracy@k proposed in [17, 16]. Specifically, for each activity record $(u,\ v,\ l_v,\ W_v,\ t)$ in the test set, we define hit@k as either the value 1, if the ground truth POI v appears in the top-k results, or the value 0, if otherwise. The overall Accuracy@k is defined by averaging over all test cases:

$$Accuracy@k = \frac{\#hit@k}{\#tests}$$

where $\#hit@k$ denotes the number of hits in the test set, and $\#tests$ is the number of all test cases.

4.2 Experimental Results

Figure 2(a) presents the recommendation accuracy in the scenario of out-of-town recommendation where the accuracy of TRM is about 0.122 when $k = 10$, and 0.151 when $k = 20$ (i.e., the model has a probability of 12.2% of placing an appealing POI in the top-10 and 15.1% of placing it in the top-20). Clearly, TRM outperforms other competitor models significantly, and the advantages of TRM are very obvious in this scenario. Several observations are

[1] https://developer.foursquare.com/

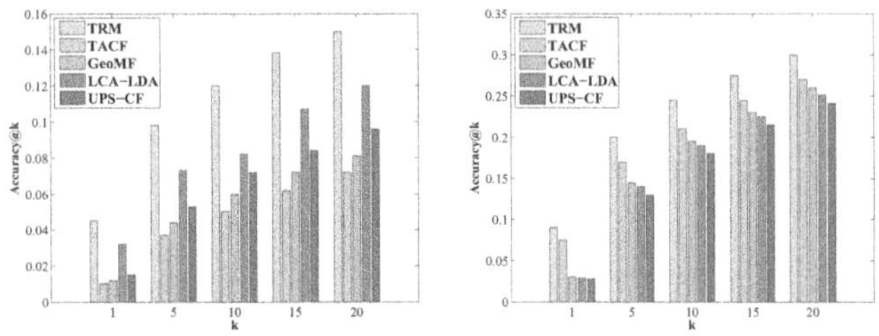

(a) Out-of-town Recommendation (b) Home-town Recommendation

Figure 2: Top-k Performance on Foursquare Dataset

made from the results: 1) TACF, UPS-CF and GeoMF drop behind TRM and LCA-LDA, showing the advantages of exploiting the semantic patterns of users' check-in activities. This is because users have very few check-in activity records in out-of-town regions, and these CF-based or matrix factorization-based methods suffer from the severe data sparsity, while the contents of user activities can serve as the medium to transfer users' interests inferred at home town to out-of-town regions. 2) TRM achieves much higher recommendation accuracy than LCA-LDA, showing the benefits of considering both temporal and geographical patterns.

In Figure 2(b), we report the performance of all recommendation models for the home-town scenario. From the figure, we can see that the recommendation accuracies of all methods are higher in Figure 2(b) than that in Figure 2(a). Besides, both LCA-LDA and GeoMF outperform TACF in Figure 2(a) while TACF slightly exceeds both of them in Figure 2(b) due to its incorporation of temporal patterns, showing that time-aware collaborative filtering method better suits the setting where the user-POI matrix is not sparse, and the model-based methods, especially the ones which integrate semantic patterns of users' activities are more capable of overcoming the difficulty of data sparsity in the out-of-town scenario. By the comparison between LCA-LDA and GeoMF in Figure 2(a) and 2(b), we observe that exploiting semantic patterns is more beneficial in out-town recommendation scenario while exploiting spatial patterns is more important in the home-town recommendation. Another observation is that the performance gap between our TRM and other competitor methods is not as big as in Figure 2(a), showing that the performance difference among recommendation methods become less obvious when the issue of data sparsity is not serious. The comparisons between Figure 2(a) and 2(b) also reveal that the two scenarios are intrinsically different, and should be separately evaluated.

Figure 3 reports the performance of the recommendation models on the Twitter dataset. We do not compare our model with UPS-CF since this dataset does not contain user social network information. From the figure, we can see that the trend of comparison result is similar to that presented in Figure 2, and the main difference is that all recommendation methods achieve lower accuracy. This may be because each user in the Foursquare dataset has more check-in records on average than users in the Twitter dataset.

5. CONCLUSION AND FUTURE WORK

In this paper, we proposed a unified probabilistic generative model TRM to model users' check-in activities in LBSNs, which simultaneously exploits the semantic, temporal and geographical patterns and also models their joint effect on users' visiting behaviors. We conducted extensive experiments to evaluate the performance of TRM on two real datasets, and the results showed TRM effectively overcomes the data sparsity and significantly improves recommendation accuracy, especially when users travel out of town.

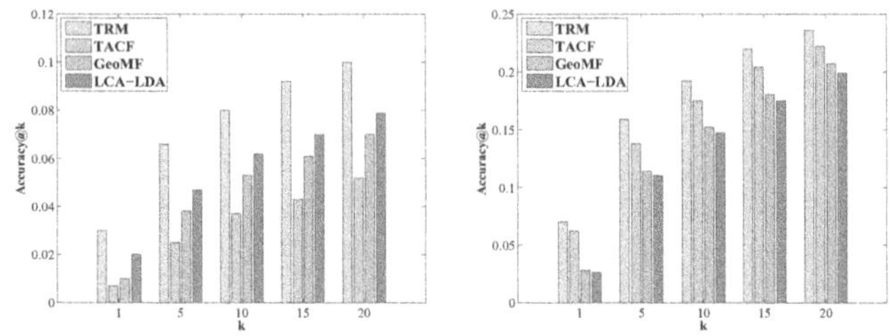

(a) Out-of-town Recommendation (b) Home-town Recommendation

Figure 3: Top-k Performance on Twitter Dataset

6. ACKNOWLEDGEMENT

The work described in this paper is partially supported by ARC Discovery Project (DP140103171), the National Natural Science Foundation of China (Grant No. 61272155 and No. 61232006) and 973 program (No. 2014CB340405).

7. REFERENCES

[1] G. Adomavicius and A. Tuzhilin. Toward the next generation of recommender systems: a survey of the state-of-the-art and possible extensions. *Knowledge and Data Engineering, IEEE Transactions on*, 17(6):734 – 749, june 2005.

[2] Z. Cheng, J. Caverlee, K. Lee, and D. Z. Sui. Exploring millions of footprints in location sharing services. In *ICWSM*, 2011.

[3] G. Ference, M. Ye, and W.-C. Lee. Location recommendation for out-of-town users in location-based social networks. In *CIKM*, pages 721–726, 2013.

[4] H. Gao, J. Tang, X. Hu, and H. Liu. Exploring temporal effects for location recommendation on location-based social networks. In *RecSys*, pages 93–100, 2013.

[5] J. J. Levandoski, M. Sarwat, A. Eldawy, and M. F. Mokbel. Lars: A location-aware recommender system. In *ICDE*, pages 450–461, 2012.

[6] D. Lian, C. Zhao, X. Xie, G. Sun, E. Chen, and Y. Rui. Geomf: Joint geographical modeling and matrix factorization for point-of-interest recommendation. In *KDD*, pages 831–840, 2014.

[7] M. Lichman and P. Smyth. Modeling human location data with mixtures of kernel densities. In *KDD*, pages 35–44, 2014.

[8] B. Liu, Y. Fu, Z. Yao, and H. Xiong. Learning geographical preferences for point-of-interest recommendation. In *KDD*, pages 1043–1051, 2013.

[9] B. Liu and H. Xiong. Point-of-interest recommendation in location based social networks with topic and location awareness. In *SDM*, pages 396–404, 2013.

[10] D. Mok, B. Wellman, and J. Carrasco. Does distance matter in the age of the internet? *Urban Studies*, 47(13):2747–2783, 2010.

[11] S. Scellato, A. Noulas, R. Lambiotte, and C. Mascolo. Socio-spatial properties of online location-based social networks. In *ICWSM*, 2011.

[12] M. Ye, D. Shou, W.-C. Lee, P. Yin, and K. Janowicz. On the semantic annotation of places in location-based social networks. In *KDD*, pages 520–528, 2011.

[13] M. Ye, P. Yin, and W.-C. Lee. Location recommendation for location-based social networks. In *GIS*, pages 458–461, 2010.

[14] M. Ye, P. Yin, W.-C. Lee, and D.-L. Lee. Exploiting geographical influence for collaborative point-of-interest recommendation. In *SIGIR*, pages 325–334, 2011.

[15] H. Yin, B. Cui, L. Chen, Z. Hu, and C. Zhang. Modeling location-based user rating profiles for personalized recommendation. *ACM Trans. Knowl. Discov. Data*, 9(3):19:1–19:41, Apr. 2015.

[16] H. Yin, B. Cui, Y. Sun, Z. Hu, and L. Chen. Lcars: A spatial item recommender system. *ACM Trans. Inf. Syst.*, 32(3):11:1–11:37, July 2014.

[17] H. Yin, Y. Sun, B. Cui, Z. Hu, and L. Chen. Lcars: A location-content-aware recommender system. In *KDD*, pages 221–229, 2013.

[18] Q. Yuan, G. Cong, Z. Ma, A. Sun, and N. M. Thalmann. Time-aware point-of-interest recommendation. In *SIGIR*, pages 363–372, 2013.

SHOE: Sibling Hashing with Output Embeddings

Sravanthi Bondugula, Varun Manjunatha, Larry S. Davis, David Doermann
University of Maryland, College Park, MD, 20742, USA
sravb@cs.umd.edu, varunm@cs.umd.edu, lsd@umiacs.umd.edu, doermann@umd.edu

ABSTRACT

We present a supervised binary encoding scheme for image retrieval that learns projections by taking into account similarity between classes obtained from output embeddings. Our motivation is that binary hash codes learned in this way improve the visual quality of retrieval results by ranking related (or "sibling") class images before unrelated class images. We employ a sequential greedy optimization that learns relationship aware projections by minimizing the difference between inner products of binary codes and output embedding vectors. We develop a joint optimization framework to learn projections which improve the accuracy of supervised hashing over the current state of the art with respect to standard and sibling evaluation metrics. We further obtain discriminative features learned from correlations of kernelized input CNN features and output embeddings, which significantly boosts performance. Experiments are performed on three datasets: CUB-2011, SUN-Attribute and ImageNet ILSVRC 2010, where we show significant improvement in sibling performance metrics over state-of-the-art supervised hashing techniques, while maintaining performance with respect to standard metrics.

Categories and Subject Descriptors

H.3 [**Information Storage and Retrieval**]: Content Analysis and Indexing, Information Search and Retrieval

General Terms

Hashing, Retrieval, Sibling classes

Keywords

Supervised Hashing, Sibling Hashing, Output Embeddings

1. INTRODUCTION

Supervised Image Hashing [1, 8, 7] is a method which maps images belonging to the same class to similar binary codes. Recent approaches include Supervised Hashing with Kernels [8], which construct binary projections sequentially by greedily minimizing the difference between Hamming distances and similarity of pairs of data points; and FastHash [7] which employs Boosted Decision Trees as hash functions and utilizes a GraphCut based method for binary code inference. In this work, we develop a new approach to Supervised Hashing, which we motivate with the example shown in Figure 1. Consider an image retrieval problem that involves a database of animals and a query image of a leopard. Now consider the following three scenarios :

1. If the retrieval algorithm returns images of leopards, we can deem the result to be absolutely satisfactory.
2. If the retrieval algorithm returns images of dolphins, whales or sharks, we consider the results to be absolutely unsatisfactory because not only are dolphins not leopards, they do not look anything at all like leopards.
3. If the retrieval algorithm returns the image of a jaguar or a tiger, we would be reasonably satisfied with the results. Although a jaguar is not the same as a leopard, it is semantically similar to one.

In this example, leopards, dolphins, whales, sharks, jaguars and tigers all belong to different categories. However, some of these categories are more closely related to each other than to other categories. Animals which fall under the "big cat" (*Panthera*) genus are related to each other, as are the large aquatic vertebrates like dolphins, sharks and whales. We designate the related categories as "siblings". The question now becomes : how can we construct hash functions

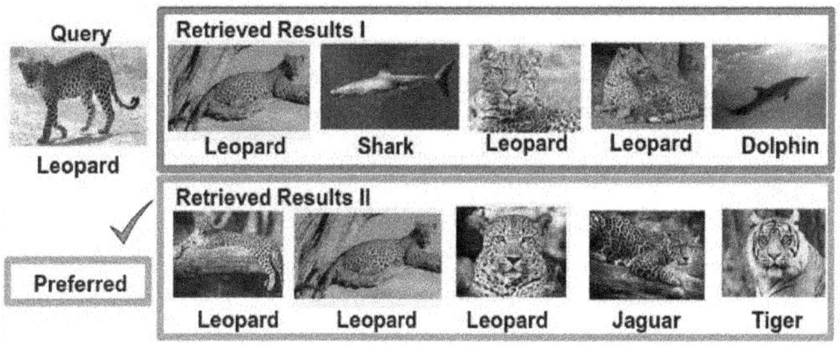

Figure 1: We prefer results II over I because they tend to retrieve images of classes(jaguar and tiger) related to the class label of the query(leopard), rather than unrelated classes(sharks and dolphins).

MM'15, October 26–30, 2015, Brisbane, Australia.
© 2015 ACM. ISBN 978-1-4503-3459-4/15/10 ...$15.00.
DOI: http://dx.doi.org/10.1145/2733373.2806340.

that rank sibling class images ahead of unrelated class images? Traditional supervised hashing algorithms like [8, 7] use discrete binary labels to compute similarity between classes. We, on the other hand, consider information outside of the image domain to define inter-class relationships.

To study the relationships between categories, Weinberger *et al.* [11] suggested the concept of "output embeddings" - vector representations of category information in Euclidean space. There has been extensive work on "input embeddings", which are vector-space representations of images [5], but less work has been done on output embeddings, which map similar category labels to similar vectors in Euclidean space. For example, in an output embedding space of animals, we would expect to have embeddings for labels so that chimpanzees, orangutans and gorillas are near each other as are leopards, cheetas, tigers and jaguars. Output embeddings can be data-dependent, such as [6, 10] which uses attributes or Linnean taxonomies to obtain vector representations for classes, or data-independent, like [4] where the embeddings for each class are random vectors containing ± 1.

Our method, which uses output embeddings to construct hash codes in a supervised framework is called SHOE: Sibling Hashing with Output Embeddings. Our motivation for doing this is the following : it is our belief that in the case of Supervised Hashing, a more desirable algorithm will retrieve images of sibling classes ahead of images of unrelated classes, while maintaining the retrieval performance for images of the same class. This improves the overall visual quality of retrieved results.

The contributions of our paper are as follows : 1) To the best of our knowledge, our approach is the first to introduce the problem of learning supervised hash functions using the modality of output embeddings. 2) We propose a joint learning method to solve the above problem, and experimentally validate our method. 3) We propose two new evaluation criteria - "sibling metrics" and "weighted sibling metrics", for gauging the efficacy of our method. 4) We significantly boost retrieval performance by applying Canonical Correlation Analysis on input features, and learn hash functions using output embeddings on these features.

The remainder of this paper is arranged as follows. In Section 2 we describe our hashing framework, and carry out experiments in Section 3 and conclude in Section 4.

2. METHOD

2.1 SHOE

Given a training set $M = \{(x_1, y_1), ..., (x_N, y_N)\}$ of N (image,label) pairs with $x_i \in \mathcal{X}$ and $y_i \in \mathcal{Y}$, let $\phi : \mathcal{X} \rightarrow \bar{\mathcal{X}} \in \mathcal{R}^d$ be the input embedding function and $\psi : \mathcal{Y} \rightarrow \bar{\mathcal{Y}} \in \mathcal{R}^e$ be the output embedding function. We wish to learn binary codes b_i, b_j of length c (i.e., $b_i \in \{-1, 1\}^c$) such that for pairs of training images, the Hamming distance $(d_H(b_i, b_j))$ between the codes preserve the distance between their class labels (given by their corresponding output embedding vectors). In other words, for a given query image, retrieved results of sibling(unrelated) classes ought to be ranked higher(lower). Utilizing the equivalence between inner product of binary codes and Hamming distances [8], $2d_H(b_i, b_j) = c - b_i^T b_j$, where $b_i^T b_j$ is the inner product of the binary codes b_i and b_j and the traditional hyperplane hash function definition($h(x) = sgn(wx)$), w is the projection vector), we obtain the following objective function:

$$\min_{\mathcal{H}} \sum_{i=1}^{N} \sum_{j=1}^{N} (\frac{1}{c} \sum_{l=1}^{c} h_l(\phi(x_i)) h_l(\phi(x_j)) - \bar{\psi}(y_i)^T \bar{\psi}(y_j))^2 \quad (1)$$

where $\mathcal{H} = \{h_l | l = 1, \ldots, c\}$ denote the c hash functions to be learned. Equivalently, we want to learn c projection vectors ($W = [w_1, \ldots, w_c] \in \mathcal{R}^{c \times d}$). Note that the normalized inner product of binary codes lies between -1 and 1 and the dot product of the unit normalized output embedding vectors(denoted by $o_{ij} = \bar{\psi}(y_i)^T \bar{\psi}(y_j)$) also lies between -1 and 1 and therefore, the equivalence. The objective ensures that the learned binary codes preserve the similarity between output embeddings, which is required for our goal of ranking related neighbors before farthest neighbors. This is similar to the KSH[8] objective function, except that KSH assumes that o_{ij} takes only values $1(-1)$ for similar(dissimilar) pairs defined with semantic information. Their work also accommodates the definition of the $o_{ij} = 0$ for related pairs but only for metric neighbors. Our work is different from theirs, as we emphasize the learning of binary codes that preserve the similarity between the classes, given by o_{ij}. Regardless of the definition of o_{ij}, our optimization is similar, and so we employ a similar sequential greedy optimization. We refer the reader to [8] for further details.

2.2 SHOE Revisited

We observe that using similarity directly from output embeddings reduces the performance of retrieving same class images, while improving the retrieval of sibling class images. Let θ measure the similarity between a class and a related class and we wish to learn such a similarity value that maximizes both the performance of same class and related class pairs. To do this, we split the objective function of Equation (1) into three parts - for identical classes, sibling classes and unrelated classes, respectively. We also empirically observe that precision and recall metrics improve for negative values of θ. Therefore, we add regularizer term $\lambda \|\theta + 1\|^2$ to the objective function, which becomes small when θ lies close to -1. For easier notation, we denote $h_{l_i} = h_l(\phi(x_i))$. Our modified objective function now becomes :

$$\min_{W,\theta} \sum_{\substack{i,j \in \text{ same} \\ \text{class}}}^{N} \sum^{N} (\frac{1}{c} \sum_{l=1}^{c} h_{l_i} h_{l_j} - 1)^2 + \sum_{\substack{i,j \in \text{ sibling} \\ \text{class}}}^{N} \sum^{N} (\frac{1}{c} \sum_{l=1}^{c} h_{l_i} h_{l_j} - \theta)^2$$
$$+ \sum_{\substack{i,j \in \text{ unrelated} \\ \text{class}}}^{N} \sum^{N} (\frac{1}{c} \sum_{l=1}^{c} h_{l_i} h_{l_j} + 1)^2 + \lambda \|\theta + 1\|^2 \quad (2)$$

We solve the above objective function in a two-step process, where we first learn the hash functions and then the similarity value θ. Let $\mathcal{H}_{ij_c} = \frac{1}{c} \sum_{l=1}^{c} h_{l_i} h_{l_j}$ and given $\mathcal{H}_{ij_c}$, we compute the derivative of Equation (2) w.r.t θ, set it to 0 and solve for each θ. We obtain :

$$\theta = \theta_c = \frac{\sum_{\substack{i,j \in \text{ sibling} \\ \text{class}}}^{N} \sum^{N} (\mathcal{H}_{ij_c} - \lambda)}{c(n_{sib} + \lambda)} \quad (3)$$

where n_{sib} is the number of sibling pairs in the training data. We have thus obtained a closed form solution for the

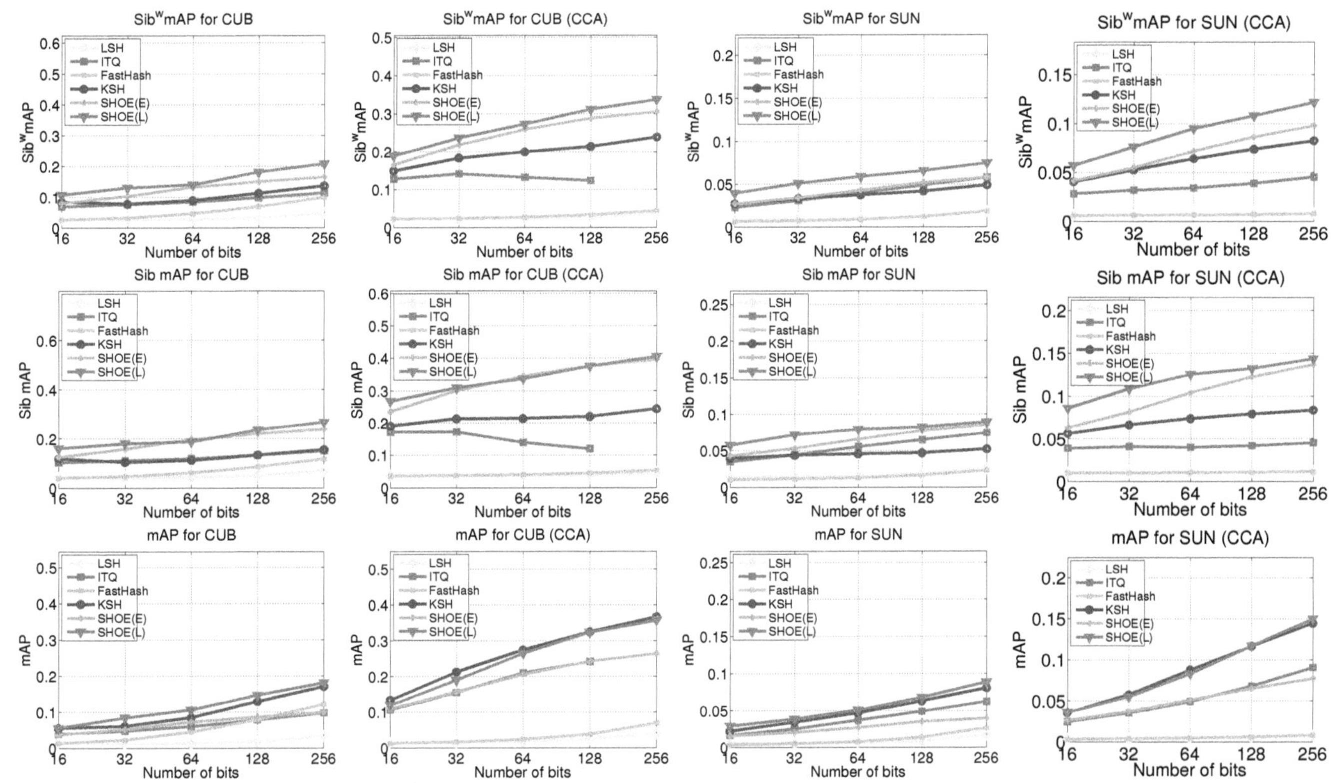

Figure 2: Retrieval on CUB-2011(first and second column) and SUN(third and fourth column) dataset comparing our methods SHOE(E) and SHOE(L) with the state-of-the art hashing techniques.

optimal θ. However, we cannot calculate θ directly as we do not learn all the bits at once. Therefore, we employ a two step alternate optimization procedure that first learns the bits and then an approximate θ_l value calculated from the previously learned bits. For the first iteration, we use an initial θ_0 value, computed from the similarity of the output embeddings. The two step optimization procedure for learning the lth hash function is:

1. Step 1 : We optimize for Equation (1), keeping θ_{l-1} constant and updating the projection vector W, thus learning hash-code bits $h_l(\phi(x_i))$.

2. Step 2 : We keep the hash-code bits $h_l(\phi(x_i))$ constant and learn θ_l for each image pair using Equation (3).

2.3 Evaluation Criteria

Standard metrics like precision, recall and mAP defined for semantic neighbors are not sufficient to evaluate the retrieval of the sibling class images. To measure this, we define sibling metrics. Let $R_y : (y_i, y_j) \rightarrow rank$ return the rank of class y_j for a query class y_i, $0 \leq rank \leq L$, where L is the number of classes and $Sib^w_m(y_i, y_j, R_y) \rightarrow \frac{m - R_y(y_i,y_j)}{m} * \mathbb{I}(R_y(y_i, y_j) \leq m)$ gives the sibling weight between the classes, when only m sibling classes are considered. We use $m = 5$. The ranking R_y is computed by sorting the distance between the output embedding vectors $\psi(y)$ and $\psi(y^*)$, $y^* \in \mathcal{Y} \setminus y$. The sibling metrics for a query q are defined as(y_{q_l} refers to the class of the lth retrieved image):

$$s^w_{precision_q}@k = \frac{\sum_{l=1}^{k} Sib^w_m(y_q, y_{q_l}, R_y)}{k} \quad (4)$$

$$s^w_{recall_q}@k = \frac{\sum_{l=1}^{k} Sib^w_m(y_q, y_{q_l}, R_y)}{\sum_{p=1}^{L} \mathcal{N}_l * \mathbb{I}(Sib^w_m(y_q, y_p, R))} \quad (5)$$

$$s^w_{AP_q} = \sum_{k=1}^{N} s_{precision_q}@k \times \triangle s_{recall_q}@k \quad (6)$$

$$s^w_{mAP} = \frac{\sum_{q=1}^{Q} s_{AP_q}}{Q} \quad (7)$$

3. EXPERIMENTS

We evaluate our method on Caltech-UCSD-2011 Birds (CUB) [12], the SUN Attribute [9] and ILSVRC 2010 [2] datasets. We extract CNN features of the fc7 layer[5] and further kernelize them to take the form :$[\kappa(x, x_1), .., \kappa(x, x_p)]$ where κ is a radial basis kernel, and p is the cardinality of a subset of training sample, designated as "anchor points".

Output Embeddings/Train-Test Partitions: For CUB dataset, we use the 312 mean-centered real-valued attribute vectors as output embeddings and only select 2000 samples for training and $p = 300$ anchor points. We use the whole train set for retrieval and all the test images as queries. For ImageNet experiments, we obtain output embeddings using the method of Tsochantaridis[10]. We uniformly select 2 images per class as a test set and use the rest of the 1.2 million images as retrieval set. We select 5000 images and

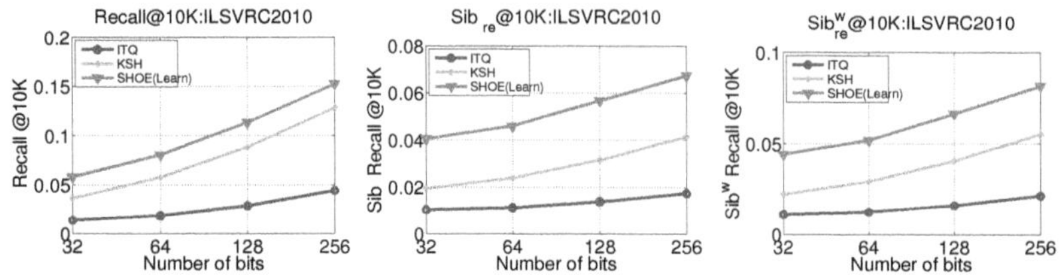

Method	pre	s_{pre}	s^w_{pre}
SHOE(L)+CCA	24.5	**32.6**	**29.1**
KSH+CCA	**24.8**	30.4	28.0
ITQ+CCA	6.5	10.8	9.9
Method	mAP	s_{mAP}	s^w_{mAP}
SHOE(L)+CCA	**0.039**	**0.021**	**0.022**
KSH+CCA	0.036	0.010	0.014
ITQ+CCA	0.005	0.001	0.002

Figure 3: Retrieval on ILSVRC2010 dataset comparing SHOE with the state-of-the art hashing techniques. Table reports the performance for 256 bits. We use Kernelized CNN features with CCA.

3000 anchor points for training. For SUN dataset, we use the 102 real valued attributes as output embeddings. We partition the dataset into equal retrieval and test sets and only use a subset of 3585 and 1434 images as training and anchor point images respectively. For all the datasets, we define the ground truth using class labels.

Results: Two variants of SHOE are used - SHOE(E), which uses raw output embeddings as in Section 2.1, and SHOE(L), which is learned using the method in Section 2.2. We compare with the state-of-the-art methods[1] : KSH[8], FastHash[7], ITQ[3] and LSH[1] in Supervised Hashing literature and present the results in Figure 2.

In Figure 2, the rows represent weighted sibling, sibling and mAP metrics. The first two columns represent experiments without and with CCA projections on the CUB dataset, while the latter two columns represent the same on the SUN Attribute dataset. We notice that without CCA projections, we outperform the baselines on standard metrics, and comfortably outperform on sibling metrics. With output embedded CCA projections, our method performs as well as the best baseline on standard metrics, and comfortably outperforms on sibling metrics. CCA projections significantly improve the performance for SHOE, KSH and ITQ, while it lowers the performance for FastHash and LSH. Results on the ILSVRC2010 dataset in Figure 3 show that with CCA features, SHOE surpasses KSH on recall@10K and sibling precision metrics, while performing as well as KSH on precision@50 and mAP. Qualitative results which compares SHOE and KSH can be found in Figure 4.

Figure 4: The first query is of an ovenbird. SHOE retrieves more ovenbirds than KSH. The second query is of a Brewer black-bird. Neither SHOE nor KSH retrieve Brewer black-birds. However, SHOE returns ravens(sibling classes of Brewer black-birds), whereas KSH retrieves pileated woodpeckers(unrelated to black-birds). Here, blue borders represent sibling classes.

4. CONCLUSION

The key idea in our paper is to learn binary codes that respect the relationship between classes. We utilize output embeddings to define the similarity between classes and obtain binary codes that preserve class order. To the best of our knowledge, ours is the first work to do so. We devised a method to learn class similarity jointly with the hash function, along with new metrics for their evaluation. It is our belief that this scheme improves overall visual quality of the retrieval system, and we have validated this experimentally with sibling metrics. Our method, called SHOE, achieves state-of-the art image retrieval results with and without CCA projections over multiple datasets.

5. REFERENCES

[1] M. S. Charikar. Similarity estimation techniques from rounding algorithms. STOC, 2002.

[2] J. Deng, W. Dong, R. Socher, L.-J. Li, K. Li, and L. Fei-Fei. ImageNet: A Large-Scale Hierarchical Image Database. In *CVPR*, 2009.

[3] Y. Gong and S. Lazebnik. Iterative quantization: A procrustean approach to learning binary codes. In *CVPR*, 2011.

[4] D. Hsu, S. Kakade, J. Langford, and T. Zhang. Multi-label prediction via compressed sensing. In *NIPS*, 2009.

[5] A. Krizhevsky, I. Sutskever, and G. E. Hinton. Imagenet classification with deep convolutional neural networks. In *NIPS*, 2012.

[6] C. H. Lampert, H. Nickisch, and S. Harmeling. Learning to detect unseen object classes by between-class attribute transfer. In *CVPR*, 2009.

[7] G. Lin, C. Shen, Q. Shi, A. van den Hengel, and D. Suter. Fast supervised hashing with decision trees for high-dimensional data. In *CVPR*, 2014.

[8] W. Liu, J. Wang, R. Ji, Y.-G. Jiang, and S.-F. Chang. Supervised hashing with kernels. In *CVPR*, 2012.

[9] G. Patterson, C. Xu, H. Su, and J. Hays. The sun attribute database: Beyond categories for deeper scene understanding. *ICCV*, 2014.

[10] I. Tsochantaridis, T. Joachims, T. Hofmann, and Y. Altun. Large margin methods for structured and interdependent output variables. *JMLR*, Dec. 2005.

[11] K. Q. Weinberger and O. Chapelle. Large margin taxonomy embedding for document categorization. In *NIPS*. 2009.

[12] P. Welinder, S. Branson, T. Mita, C. Wah, F. Schroff, S. Belongie, and P. Perona. Caltech-UCSD Birds 200. Technical Report CNS-TR-2010-001, 2010.

[1]We use their publicly available implementations

Supervised Hashing with Pseudo Labels for Scalable Multimedia Retrieval

Jingkuan Song
University of Trento
jingkuan.song@unitn.it

LianLi Gao
University of Electronic Science and Technology of China
lianli.gao@uestc.edu.cn

Yan Yan
University of Trento
yan@disi.unitn.it

Dongxiang Zhang
National University of Singapore
zhangdo@comp.nus.edu.sg

Nicu Sebe
University of Trento
sebe@disi.unitn.it

ABSTRACT

There is an increasing interest in using hash codes for efficient multimedia retrieval and data storage. The hash functions are learned in such a way that the hash codes can preserve essential properties of the original space or the label information. Then the Hamming distance of the hash codes can approximate the data similarity. Existing works have demonstrated the success of many supervised hashing models. However, labeling data is time and labor consuming, especially for scalable datasets. In order to utilize the supervised hashing models to improve the discriminative power of hash codes, we propose a Supervised Hashing with Pseudo Labels (SHPL) which uses the cluster centers of the training data to generate pseudo labels, based on which the hash codes can be generated using the criteria of supervised hashing. More specifically, we utilize linear discriminant analysis (LDA) with trace ratio criterion as a showcase for hash functions learning and during the optimization, we prove that the pseudo labels and the hash codes can be jointly learned and iteratively updated in an unified framework. The learned hash functions can harness the discriminant power of trace ratio criterion, and thus can achieve better performance. Experimental results on three large-scale unlabeled datasets (i.e., SIFT1M, GIST1M, and SIFT1B) demonstrate the superior performance of our SHPL over existing hashing methods.

Categories and Subject Descriptors

H.3.3 [**Information Systems**]: INFORMATION STORAGE AND RETRIEVAL—*Search process*

Keywords

Hashing; multimedia retrieval; pseudo labels

MM'15, October 26–30, 2015, Brisbane, Australia.
 ISBN 978-1-4503-3459-4/15/10 ...$15.00.
DOI: http://dx.doi.org/10.1145/2733373.2806341 .

1. INTRODUCTION

Recently, learning-based hashing methods [10, 15, 5, 7, 11, 12] have become the mainstream for scalable ANN due to their compact binary representation and efficient Hamming distance calculation. Such approaches map data points to compact binary codes through a hash function. Hashing methods can be categorized as unsupervised and supervised. The unsupervised learning of the hash functions is usually based on the criterion of preserving important properties of the training data points. Typical approaches preserve the consistency property (i.e., the similarity of binary codes should be consistent with that of the original data points) [16, 5], the similarity alignment property (i.e., the Hamming distance of the binary code should approximate the Euclidean distance of the original data points) [6], the order preserving property (i.e., the order of a reference data item computed from the original space and the Hamming space should be aligned) [9], etc. A fundamental limitation of property-preserving hashing methods is that different methods try to preserve varied properties according to the applications, and thus the performance may degrade when a specifically designed hashing method is applied to another application. On the other hand, supervised hashing is designed to preserve some label-based similarity [7, 2, 13]. For example, Strecha *et al.* [13] developed a supervised hashing which maximizes the between-class Hamming distance and minimizes the within-class Hamming distance. [7, 2] proposed learning the hash codes which can approximate the pairwise label similarity. The performance for supervised hashing methods is usually significantly superior to unsupervised methods. However, the supervised information is scarce, especially for scalable datasets.

Inspired by this, in this paper, we propose a Supervised Hashing with Pseudo Labels (SHPL) which makes use the self-generated cluster centers of the training data as supervision information to improve the effectiveness of the hash codes. It is worth highlighting the following contributions:

- We propose a general framework to learn hashing code in a supervised way to improve the effectiveness of hashing methods by using some pseudo labels. We then prove that the pseudo supervision information and the hash codes can be jointly learned and iteratively updated in an unified framework.
- We further integrate the pseudo labels strategy to unsupervised hashing model, which can potentially improve the search accuracy of hash codes.

- We successfully show it to work on a huge dataset SIFT1B (1 billion data points). Experimental results on three popular datasets show superior performance compared to other unsupervised hashing methods.

2. SUPERVISED HASHING WITH PSEUDO LABELS

In this section, we introduce our algorithm. We first introduce the notations which will be used in the rest of the paper.

Suppose there is a dataset $X = [x_1, ..., x_N] \in \mathbb{R}^{M\times N}$, where N is the number of data points and M is the dimensionality of each x_i. Their hash codes are $Y = [y_1, ..., y_N] \in \mathbb{R}^{L\times N}$ where L is the code length for each y_i. For supervised hashing methods, different criteria are utilized to preserve the label information [13, 14, 8]. Based on these criteria to be preserved, different objective functions are given. Without loss of generality, we utilize LDA with trace ratio criterion (similar to LDAH [13]) as a showcase for hash functions learning and demonstrate how it is incorporated into our framework. Note that some other criterion like label-similarity preserving [14, 8] can also be applied to our framework.

The loss function for LDA trace ratio based hashing method is:

$$\ell_{SHPL}(Y) = \frac{tr(S_b)}{tr(S_w)},\ s.t.\ Y \in \{0,1\}^{N\times L} \tag{1}$$

where S_w represents within-class scatter matrix, and S_b is the between-class scatter matrix. They are defined as:

$$\begin{aligned} S_w &= \sum_{k=1}^{C}\sum_{x_i\in\Omega_k}(y_i - c_k)(y_i - c_k)^T \\ S_b &= \sum_{k=1}^{C} n_k(c_k - \overline{y})(c_k - \overline{y})^T \end{aligned} \tag{2}$$

where y_i is the corresponding hash code for a date point x_i, Ω_k indicates the data points in the k-th class and c_k is the mean of hash codes in the k-th class. $\overline{y}$ is the mean of all hash codes Y. We also define the total scatter matrix S_t as:

$$S_t = S_b + S_w = \sum_{i=1}^{N}(y_i - \overline{y})(y_i - \overline{y})^T \tag{3}$$

Suppose the data has been centralized, i.e., $\overline{x} = 0$. We denote the pseudo labels as F, and we define a cluster centroid matrix C to include the centroid vector of the hash codes in each class as $C = [c_1, ..., c_K]$. We use a linear hash function, i.e., $y_i = sgn\left(W^T x_i\right)$. This objective function is intractable and we follow [8, 16] to apply the spectral relaxation trick to drop the sign functions. Then $\overline{y} = 0$. Thus S_b, S_w and S_t can be rewritten as:

$$\begin{aligned} S_w &= (W^T X - CF^T)(W^T X - CF^T)^T \\ S_b &= CF^T FC^T \\ S_t &= W^T XX^T W \end{aligned} \tag{4}$$

Then the objective function becomes:

$$\ell_{SHPL}(W, W^T W = I) = \frac{tr(CF^T FC^T)}{tr\left((W^T X - CF^T)(W^T X - CF^T)^T\right)} \tag{5}$$

Because $S_t = S_w + S_b$, optimizing (1) is equivalent to optimize $\frac{tr(S_b)}{tr(S_t)}$. The problem is that we do not know the class labels F. Then, the final objective function for our SHPL becomes:

$$\begin{aligned} &\ell_{SHPL}(W, F, C) = \frac{tr(CF^T FC^T)}{tr(W^T XX^T W)} \\ &s.t. \begin{cases} F \in \{0,1\}^{N\times K} \\ \|f_i\|_1 = 1 \\ W^T W = I \end{cases} \end{aligned} \tag{6}$$

where $\|\cdot\|_1$ is the l_1 norm. The second constraint $\|f_i\|_1 = 1$ requires that each x_i belongs to a single class.

2.1 Solution

There are three unknown variables in (6), namely W, C and F. Using the class indicator matrix F, we can represent each cluster centroid c_k as:

$$c_k = \frac{1}{size\left(\prod(k)\right)} \sum_{y_i\in\prod(k)} y_i \tag{7}$$

where $\prod(k)$ indicates the set of data points in class k. Then, C can be reformulated in a matrix form:

$$C = W^T XF\left(F^T F\right)^{-1} \tag{8}$$

Then, (6) becomes:

$$\begin{aligned} &\ell_{SHPL}(W, F) = \frac{tr\left(W^T XF(F^T F)^{-1} F^T X^T W\right)}{tr(W^T XX^T W)} \\ &s.t. \begin{cases} F \in \{0,1\}^{N\times K} \\ \|f_i\|_1 = 1 \\ W^T W = I \end{cases} \end{aligned} \tag{9}$$

We utilize coordinate descent to optimize (9). We firstly fix F and update W, and then fix update W by fixing F. They are updated iteratively until convergence. The solution is illustrated in Algorithm (1).

Update W: Given F, obviously solving problem (9) is to minimize the trace ratio LDA w.r.t. W:

$$\ell\left(W, W^T W = I\right) = \frac{tr\left(W^T XF(F^T F)^{-1} F^T X^T W\right)}{tr\left(W^T XX^T W\right)} \tag{10}$$

which can be directly solved with the generalized eigenvalue decomposition (GEVD) method:

$$XF\left(F^T F\right)^{-1} F^T X^T w_l = \lambda_l XX^T w_l \tag{11}$$

where λ_l is the l-th largest eigenvalue of the GEVD with the corresponding eigenvector w_l, and w_l constitutes the l-th column vector of the matrix W.

When W is fixed, $tr(W^T XX^T W)$ is irrelevant to F. Thus, we need to maximize the following problem *w.r.t* F:

$$\begin{aligned} &\ell(F) = tr\left(W^T XF(F^T F)^{-1} F^T X^T W\right) \\ &s.t. \begin{cases} F \in \{0,1\}^{N\times K} \\ \|f_i\|_1 = 1 \end{cases} \end{aligned} \tag{12}$$

It is still difficult to solve due to the intractable constraints in (12). Because $tr(W^T XX^T W)$ is a constant now (W is fixed), maximizing between-class distance in problem (12) is equivalent to minimizing within-class distance. Problem (12) is equivalent to the following problem:

$$\ell(F) = \left\|W^T X - CF^T\right\|_F^2, s.t. \begin{cases} F \in \{0,1\}^{N\times K} \\ \|f_i\|_1 = 1 \end{cases} \tag{13}$$

Problem (13) can be easily solved by alternating optimization, i.e., iteratively optimizing C when F is fixed and optimizing F when C is fixed.

Update C: Each cluster center c_k is the mean of all data points in the class k. C can be updated using (7).

Update F: Since each data point belongs to one class, x_i is assigned to its closest cluster center c_k. Therefore, f_i is a column vector with its k-th element being 1 and others being 0.

After we get W, the hash codes for x_i can be generated by $sgn(W^T x_i)$.

Algorithm 1 Solution for the SHPL

Input: Initialized F;
Output: F, W;
1: **repeat**
2: Fix F, update W according to Eqn.(11);
3: **repeat**
4: Fix W and F, update C according to classical K-means, each c_k is the mean of the y_i within the same class;
5: Fix W and C, update F;
6: **until** convergence or max iteration is reached.
7: **until** convergence or max iteration is reached.
8: **return** F, W;

3. PSEUDO LABELS FOR UNSUPERVISED HASHING

The pseudo label strategy can also be integrated to unsupervised hashing models to improve the performance of hash codes. A typical unsupervised hashing preserving global similarity can be formulated as the following loss function:

$$\ell(Y) = \sum_{ij} w_{ij} \|y_i - y_j\|_H, \; s.t. \; Y^T Y = I, \; y_i \in \{0,1\}^L \quad (14)$$

where y_i is the hash code for the data point x_i, L is the hash code length, and W is the affinity matrix [1].

Suppose we also have pseudo labels f_i for each data point x_i. Suppose there are K classes and each data point belongs to a single class. Then we can have K cluster centers. It is reasonable to assume that data points from the same class should have similar hash codes. Based on these clustering centers, the class label f_i for each x_i can be updated as:

$$k_i^* = \arg \min_{k \in \{1,\ldots,K\}} \|\mathbf{x}_i - \mathbf{c}_k\|_2^2 \quad (15)$$

where c_k is the cluster center for x_i. The problem is that we do not have the cluster centers. Actually, by taking each bucket with the same hash codes as a class, we can build a connection between y_i and k_i as:

$$y_i = b(k_i), \; k_i = r(y_i) \quad (16)$$

where $r(.)$ converts a binary code y_i into an integer k_i and $b(.)$ converts an integer k_i to a binary code y_i.

The solution is omitted due to the space limit.

4. EXPERIMENTS

We evaluate our algorithm on the task of high-dimensional approximate nearest neighbor (ANN) search. Firstly, we study the influence of the parameters in our algorithm. Then, we compare our results with state-of-the-art algorithms on three standard datasets.

4.1 Settings

Experiments are conducted on three widely-used high-dimensional datasets: SIFT1M [14], GIST1M [14], and SIFT1B [14]. Each dataset comprises of disjoint one training set, one query set, and one base database (on which the search is performed). SIFT1M provides 10^5 training points, 10^4 query points and 10^6 database points with each point being a 128-dimensional SIFT descriptor. GIST1M provides 5×10^5 training points, 10^3 query points and 10^6 database points with each point being a 960-dimensional GIST feature. SIFT1B is composed of 10^8 training points, 10^4 query points and as large as 10^9 database points. Following [10], we use the first 10^6 training points on the SIFT1B datasets. The whole training set is used on SIFT1M and GIST1M.

ANN search is conducted to evaluate our proposed approaches, and two indicators are reported, namely Recall *vs.* K (top-K results) and Mean Average Precision (MAP).

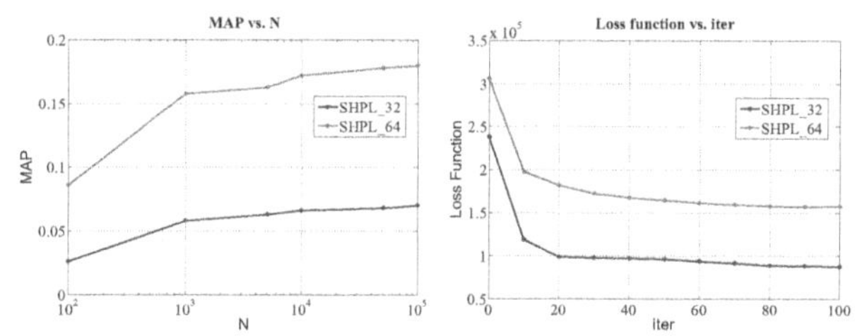

(a) Performance variance with N (b) Number of iterations

Figure 1: Parameters study with code length 32 and 64 on SIFT1M

We compare our SHPL with other state-of-the-art hashing algorithms, such as spectral hashing (SH) [16], iterative quantization (ITQ) hashing [3] and K-means Hashing (KMH) [4]. Some other hashing methods (e.g, minimal loss hashing (MLH) [9], PCA hashing (PCAH) [14]) are not compared here because they are outperformed by these compared methods.

4.2 Parameters

There are several parameters, e.g., the size of the training datasets N and the number of iteration $iter$, affecting the performance of our algorithm. In this subsection, we study the performance variance with different parameters. Due to the space limit, we only report the results on the SIFT1M dataset. The default settings for SIFT1M are: $iter = 50$ and $N = 10^5$. The size of training dataset N affects the training speed and model accuracy. We tune $N = 10^3, 5\times10^3, 10^4, 5\times10^4, 10^5$, and illustrate the performance changes in Fig. 1(a). There is an increasing trend with the rising of N. When N reaches 10^4, further increasing the training number will not improve the MAP significantly. The loss function in each iteration is shown in Fig. 1(b). The loss function drops dramatically in the first 20 iterations, and then keeps stable after 40 iterations. This indicates the efficiency of our solution.

4.3 Results

Fig. 2 shows the comparisons of different unsupervised hashing methods on the three unlabeled datasets. We have tested L=32 and L=64. We used the codes provided by the authors to compare different algorithms. For KMH, the bit number of each subspace is 8 for L=32 and $L = 64$. Larger bit number will increase the performance of KMH, but will cause out-of-memory for our computer. For the other algorithms, the default settings are used. From these figures, we have the following observations:

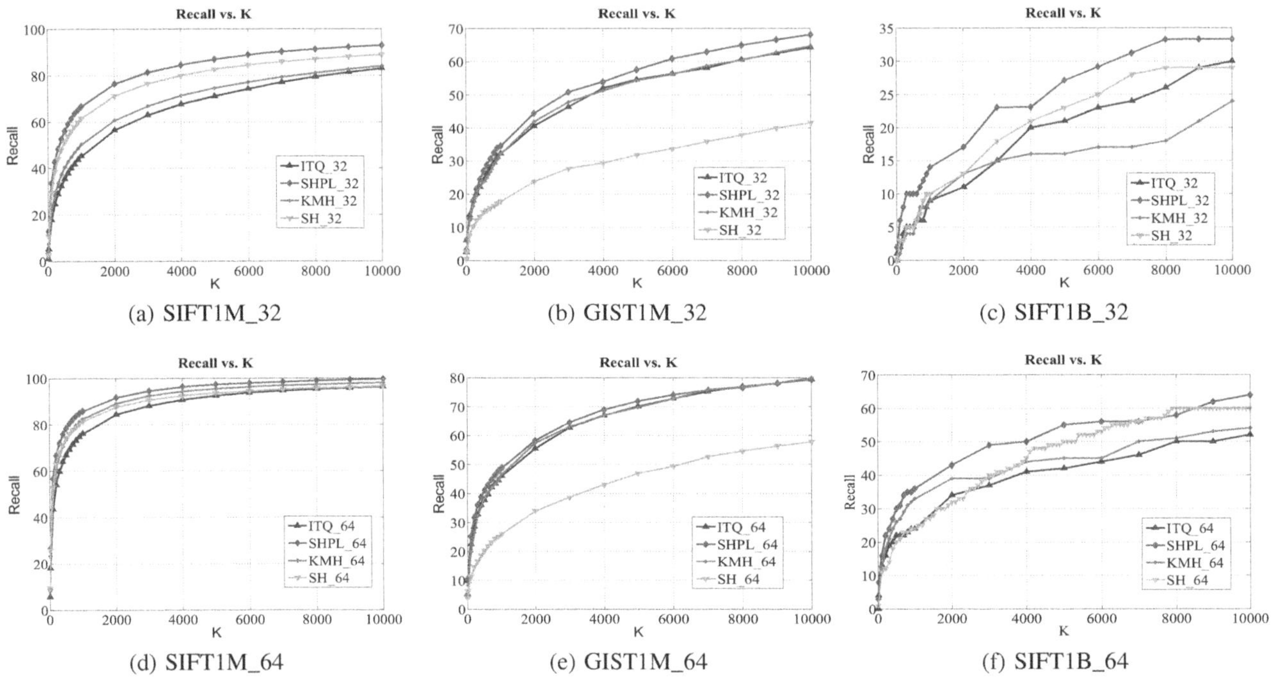

(a) SIFT1M_32 (b) GIST1M_32 (c) SIFT1B_32

(d) SIFT1M_64 (e) GIST1M_64 (f) SIFT1B_64

Figure 2: The comparison of different unsupervised hashing methods with code length 32 and 64

- Our method consistently outperforms the other hashing methods in all datasets. In SIFT1M and SIFT1B datasets, the improvement of SHPL over the other methods is more significant, compared with that in GIST1M dataset. Also, the improvements gap between SHPL and other hashing methods is larger in the case of $L = 32$, than that of $L = 64$.
- With the increase of code length, the performance of different hashing methods is improved accordingly. More specifically, the recall improvements of KMH (20%-28%) and ITQ (20%-25%) are generally more significant than SH (10%-15%) on SIFT1M and SIFT1B dataset, while the improvements on GIST1M dataset are more consistent.
- SH performs surprisingly well in SIFT1M and SIFT1B datasets, but it is inferior in GIST1M dataset. KMH is competitive in most settings, especially when the code length is 64 bits.

5. CONCLUSION

In this work, we propose a Supervised Hashing with Pseudo Labels (SHPL), a general framework which uses the supervised hashing models to improve the effectiveness of hashing methods by the pseudo label strategy. It is shown that SHPL has stronger discriminative power and thus achieves better performance. The pseudo label strategy can also be integrated to unsupervised hashing models. Experiments on three large-scale datasets demonstrate that SHPL obtains superior accuracy over existing hashing methods.

6. ACKNOWLEDGMENTS

The work of Jingkuan Song, Yan Yan and Nicu Sebe has been partially supported by the EC project xLiMe. The work of Lianli Gao is partially supported by the Fundamental Research Funds for the Central Universities of China under grant No.ZYGX2014J063 and No.ZYGX2014Z007.

7. REFERENCES

[1] L. Gao, J. Song, F. Nie, Y. Yan, N. Sebe, and H. T. Shen. Optimal graph leaning with partial tags and multiple features for image and video annotation. In *CVPR*, 2015.

[2] T. Ge, K. He, and J. Sun. Graph cuts for supervised binary coding. In *ECCV*, 2014.

[3] Y. Gong, S. Lazebnik, A. Gordo, and F. Perronnin. Iterative quantization: A procrustean approach to learning binary codes for large-scale image retrieval. *TPAMI*, 35(12):2916–2929, 2013.

[4] K. He, F. Wen, and J. Sun. K-means hashing: An affinity-preserving quantization method for learning binary compact codes. In *CVPR*, 2013.

[5] G. Irie, Z. Li, X. Wu, and S. Chang. Locally linear hashing for extracting non-linear manifolds. In *CVPR*, 2014.

[6] B. Kulis and T. Darrell. Learning to hash with binary reconstructive embeddings. In *NIPS*, 2009.

[7] G. Lin, C. Shen, Q. Shi, A. van den Hengel, and D. Suter. Fast supervised hashing with decision trees for high-dimensional data. In *CVPR*, 2014.

[8] W. Liu, J. Wang, R. Ji, Y. Jiang, and S. Chang. Supervised hashing with kernels. In *CVPR*, 2012.

[9] M. Norouzi and D. J. Fleet. Minimal loss hashing for compact binary codes. In *ICML*, 2011.

[10] M. Norouzi and D. J. Fleet. Cartesian k-means. In *CVPR*, 2013.

[11] J. Song, Y. Yang, Z. Huang, H. T. Shen, and R. Hong. Multiple feature hashing for real-time large scale near-duplicate video retrieval. In *ACM MM*, 2011.

[12] J. Song, Y. Yang, Y. Yang, Z. Huang, and H. T. Shen. Inter-media hashing for large-scale retrieval from heterogeneous data sources. In *SIGMOD*, 2013.

[13] C. Strecha, A. M. Bronstein, M. M. Bronstein, and P. Fua. Ldahash: Improved matching with smaller descriptors. *TPAMI*, 34(1):66–78, 2012.

[14] J. Wang, S. Kumar, and S. Chang. Semi-supervised hashing for large-scale search. *TPAMI*, 34(12):2393–2406, 2012.

[15] J. Wang, H. T. Shen, J. Song, and J. Ji. Hashing for similarity search: A survey. *CoRR*, abs/1408.2927, 2014.

[16] Y. Weiss, A. Torralba, and R. Fergus. Spectral hashing. In *NIPS*, 2008.

Multi-view Latent Hashing for Efficient Multimedia Search

Xiaobo Shen[†,♮,*], Fumin Shen[‡], Quan-Sen Sun[†], Yun-Hao Yuan[§]
[†]School of Computer Science and Engineering, Nanjing University of Science and Technology
[‡]School of Computer Science and Engineering, University of Electronic Science and Technology of China
[§]Department of Computer Science and Technology, Jiangnan University
[♮]School of Information Technology and Electrical Engineering, The University of Queensland
{njust.shenxiaobo, fumin.shen}@gmail.com, sunquansen@njust.edu.cn, yyhzbh@163.com

ABSTRACT

Hashing techniques have attracted broad research interests in recent multimedia studies. However, most of existing hashing methods focus on learning binary codes from data with only one single view, and thus cannot fully utilize the rich information from multiple views of data. In this paper, we propose a novel unsupervised hashing approach, dubbed multi-view latent hashing (MVLH), to effectively incorporate multi-view data into hash code learning. Specifically, the binary codes are learned by the latent factors shared by multiple views from an unified kernel feature space, where the weights of different views are adaptively learned according to the reconstruction error with each view. We then propose to solve the associate optimization problem with an efficient alternating algorithm. To obtain high-quality binary codes, we provide a novel scheme to directly learn the codes without resorting to continuous relaxations, where each bit is efficiently computed in a closed form. We evaluate the proposed method on several large-scale datasets and the results demonstrate the superiority of our method over several other state-of-the-art methods.

Categories and Subject Descriptors

H.3.3 [**Information Storage and Retrieval**]: Information Search and Retrieval; I.2.6 [**Artificial Intelligence**]: Learning

General Terms

Algorithms, Experimentation, Theory

Keywords

Hashing, multi-view, matrix factorization, multimedia search

1. INTRODUCTION

Recent years have witnessed the rapid success of hashing techniques for approximate nearest neighbor (ANN) search in many multimedia applications. The basic idea of hashing is to encoding documents, images, videos, or other types of data in the original high-dimensional space into a set of binary codes, by which effective similarity search can be performed in the Hamming space with very low cost for both storage and computation. Locality Sensitive Hashing (LSH) [2] is one of the most well-known *data-independent* hashing methods, which generates the hash functions by random projections. To generate more effective compact binary codes, many *data-dependent* or *learning based* methods have recently been proposed to learn the hash functions from the training data available. Some representative works in this category include Spectral Hashing (SH) [12], Anchor Graph Hashing (AGH) [6], Iterative Quantization (ITQ) [3], Inductive Manifold Hashing (IMH) [9, 10], Supervised Discrete Hashing [8], etc. However, forgoing methods focus on learning binary codes from data with only one single view (i.e., using single feature), and cannot be directly applied to data described as different features.

Recently, some efforts [15, 4, 1, 11, 14, 7, 5] have been made towards effective hash code learning from data with multiple views. They can be mainly divided into two categories: *cross-view hashing* (CVH) and *multi-view hashing* (MVH). CVH [15, 4, 1] aims to support cross-modal retrival where a query of one view can search for the relevant results of another view, while the prupose of MVH is to learn better codes by leveraging multiple views than single-view hashing. Clearly, this work mainly focuses on the hashing problem of the second category, where some representative works include Multiple Feature Hashing (MFH) [11], Composite Hashing with Multiple Information Sources (CHMIS) [14], Multiple Feature Kernel Hashing (MFKH) [7], Multi-View Spectral Hashing (SU-MVSH) [5]. However, these methods share some common drawbacks. First, they mainly apply spectral, graph techniques (e.g., kNN graph) to model the similarities between data points. In general, the time cost of constructing the similarity matrix for n data points is $O(n^2)$, which is not practical for large scale applications. Besides, the similarity matrix by this method is usually sensitive to data noises. Second, the discrete constraints imposed on binary hash codes often make the associate optimization problem difficult to solve. These methods simply discard the discrete constraint to obtain a relaxed problem, by which the continuous outputs are then thresholded for binarization. However, this simple optimization scheme may suffer from large quantization loss, which makes obtained binary codes sub-optimal.

*X. Shen's contribution was made when he was visiting The University of Queensland.

MM'15, October 26–30, 2015, Brisbane, Australia.

DOI: http://dx.doi.org/10.1145/2733373.2806342.

Based on the above considerations, in this paper, we propose a novel multi-view hashing approach by leveraging data with multiple views. We investigate this approach from the following aspects. First, an unified kernel feature space is formed with multiple views, the weights of which are adaptively learned according to the reconstruction errors. Second, the proposed problem is formulated as a matrix factorization (MF) problem, where hash codes are learned by the binary latent factors, which can thus uncover the semantics shared by multiple views. Third, an efficient algorithm is further presented to solve the proposed problem in an alternative manner. More importantly, in contrast with existing approaches, we provide a novel scheme to directly learn the binary codes bit by bit without continuous relaxations.

2. PROPOSED METHOD

2.1 Problem Setup

Suppose that $O = \{o_i\}_{i=1}^N$ is a set of objects, and we are given its corresponding features $\{X^{(m)} = [x_1^{(m)}, \ldots, x_N^{(m)}] \in \mathbb{R}^{d_m \times N}\}_{m=1}^M$, where d_m is the dimension of the m-th view, M is the number of views, N is the number of objects. We also denote an integrated binary code matrix $V = \{v_i\}_{i=1}^N \in \{-1,1\}^{c \times N}$, where v_i is the binary code associated with o_i, and c is the code length. The aim of MVLH is to learn V which can well preserve the similarities between objects with high probability.

2.2 Integrated Kernel Feature Mapping

It has been shown that kernel function is a quite popular and effective technique to exploit the structure information of multimedia objects. Thus, in this paper, by Empirical Kernel Mapping (EKM) [13], we *explicitly* formulate a series of mapping functions $\varphi_m \colon \chi^{(m)} \to \mathcal{F}^{(m)} (m = 1, \ldots, M)$ to mapping the input spaces of each view into the M corresponding feature spaces $\{\mathcal{F}^{(m)}\}_{m=1}^M$ with M different kernels.

More specifically, we first construct the corresponding set of L landmarks, i.e., $\{z_l^{(m)}\}_{l=1}^L (m = 1, \ldots, M)$ in each view, which can be obtained by clustering [6] or randomly chosen from the original N samples. Then in each view, kernel matrix $K^{(m)} = [\text{ker}_{ij}^{(m)}] \in \mathbb{R}^{L \times L}$ can be further constructed corresponding to its embedding function $\varphi_m(\cdot)$, that means we have $\text{ker}_{ij}^{(m)} = \varphi_m(z_i^{(m)})^T \varphi_m(z_j^{(m)})$. If the rank of $K^{(m)}$ is r_m, then $K^{(m)}$ can be decomposed as

$$K^{(m)} = Q^{(m)} \Lambda^{(m)} Q^{(m)T} \tag{1}$$

where $\Lambda^{(m)} \in \mathbb{R}^{r_m \times r_m}$ is a diagonal matrix consisting of the r_m positive eigenvalues of $K^{(m)}$, and $Q^{(m)} \in \mathbb{R}^{L \times r_m}$ consists of the corresponding orthonormal eigenvectors. Thus, the explicit mapping (i.e., EKM) is given as $\varphi_m \colon \chi^{(m)} \to \mathcal{F}^{(m)}$

$$x^{(m)} \to \left(\Lambda^{(m)}\right)^{(-1/2)} Q^{(m)T} \left[\text{ker}\left(x^{(m)}, z_1^{(m)}\right), \ldots, \text{ker}\left(x^{(m)}, z_L^{(m)}\right)\right] \tag{2}$$

To this end, we define our integrated nonlinear kernel feature as follows

$$\varphi(X) = \left[\mu_1^{1/2} \varphi_1^T \left(X^{(1)}\right), \ldots, \mu_M^{1/2} \varphi_M^T \left(X^{(M)}\right)\right]^T \tag{3}$$

where $\mu = [\mu_1, \ldots, \mu_M]^T$ is a weighting vector, μ_m measures the weight of the m-th view in the learning process. We will show how to adaptively learn these weights in the later subsection.

2.3 Formulation

We now elaborate the formulation of our proposed multi-view hashing method, which jointly exploits the consistent latent information from multi-view data. Its main idea is to apply matrix factorization in the constructed unified kernel feature space so as to learn compact integrated binary codes, which are composed of latent factors shared by multiple views. To this end, we formulate our hashing problem as follows

$$\begin{aligned} \min_{U,V,\mu} \quad & F = \|\varphi(X) - UV\|_F^2 + \lambda \|U\|_F^2 \\ \text{s.t.} \quad & V \in \{-1,1\}^{c \times N} \\ & \sum_{m=1}^M \mu_m = 1, \mu_m \geq 0 \end{aligned} \tag{4}$$

where U can be viewed as the basis matrix, and it can be also defined as $U = [\mu_1^{1/2} U^{(1)T}, \ldots, \mu_M^{1/2} U^{(M)T}]^T \in \mathbb{R}^{r \times c}$, $U^{(m)} \in \mathbb{R}^{r_m \times c}$ is the basis matrix in the m-th view, $r = \sum_{m=1}^M r_m$. The first term in (4) models the matrix reconstruction error under binary codes, the second one is a regularization term on basis matrix, λ is a nonnegative parameter to tradeoff these two terms. We will detail its optimization in the next subsection.

2.4 Optimization Solution

As we can see, there is no closed form solution in (4), and this joint optimization function is not convex over all variables simultaneously. Therefore, we present an iterative optimization algorithm as follows.

Fixing V and μ, optimize U. Generally speaking, it is a regularized least square problem to U, thus by setting $\partial F / \partial U = 0$, we have

$$U = \varphi(X) V^T (VV^T + \lambda I)^{-1} \tag{5}$$

where I is the identity matrix.

Fixing U and μ, optimize V. To optimize V is a challenging task (NP-hard problem) due to the discrete constraints. In contrast with most existing approaches which simply drop the discrete constraints for relaxation, we provide a different scheme to directly optimize this problem.

By dropping some irrelevant terms of V, we can transform (4) into the following form

$$\begin{aligned} \min_{V} \quad & -2\text{tr}\left(\varphi(X)^T UV\right) + \|UV\|_F^2 \\ \text{s.t.} \quad & V \in \{-1,1\}^{c \times N} \end{aligned} \tag{6}$$

It is still difficult to find a closed-form solution for the above formulation. However, if we optimize one row of V at a time while fixing all other rows, there will be luckily a closed-form solution. Thus we can optimize V bit by bit, the solution process for the i-th bit (i-th row of V) is as follow.

Let $v^T \in \{-1,1\}^{1 \times N}$ denotes the i-th row of V, and $\bar{V} \in \{-1,1\}^{(c-1) \times N}$ denotes all other rows in V excluding v^T. Similarly, let $u \in \mathbb{R}^{r \times 1}$ denotes the i-th column of U, and $\bar{U} \in \mathbb{R}^{r \times (c-1)}$ denotes all other columns in U excluding u^T. Then we can obtain

$$\begin{aligned} \text{tr}\left(\varphi(X)^T UV\right) &= \text{tr}\left(\varphi(X)^T (uv^T + \bar{U}\bar{V})\right) \\ &= \text{tr}\left(\varphi(X)^T uv^T\right) + const \end{aligned} \tag{7}$$

Similarly,

$$\begin{aligned}\|UV\|_F^2 &= \|uv^T + \bar{U}\bar{V}\|_F^2 \\ &= \|vu^T\|_F^2 + 2\mathrm{tr}(vu^T\bar{U}\bar{V}) + \|\bar{U}\bar{V}\|_F^2 \\ &= 2\mathrm{tr}(vu^T\bar{U}\bar{V}) + const\end{aligned} \tag{8}$$

here $\|vu^T\|_F^2 = \mathrm{tr}(vu^Tuv^T) = cu^Tu = const$.
Substitute (7), (8) into (6), and we obtain the following optimization problem

$$\begin{aligned}\min_{v} \quad & \left(\bar{V}^T\bar{U}^Tu - \varphi(X)^Tu\right)^T v \\ \text{s.t.} \quad & v \in \{-1,1\}^{N\times 1}\end{aligned} \tag{9}$$

This problem has a closed-form solution

$$v = \mathrm{sign}\left((\varphi(X)^T - \bar{V}^T\bar{U}^T)u\right) \tag{10}$$

where sign(·) is the sign function.
Fixing U and V, optimize μ. Put definition of $\varphi(X)$ and U into (4), we can obtain the following problem:

$$\begin{aligned}\min_{\mu} \quad & \sum_{m=1}^{M} \mu_m \left(\|\varphi_m(X^{(m)}) - U^{(m)}V\|_F^2 + \lambda\|U^{(m)}\|_F^2\right) \\ \text{s.t.} \quad & \sum_{m=1}^{M} \mu_m = 1, \mu_m \geq 0\end{aligned} \tag{11}$$

The solution of μ is $\mu_m = 1$ corresponding to the minimum $\left(\|\varphi_m(X^{(m)}) - U^{(m)}V\|_F^2 + \lambda\|U^{(m)}\|_F^2\right)$ over all views, and $\mu_m = 0$ otherwise. In this situation, this solution finally selects only one view, but ignores exploiting the complementary information of other views. To overcome this limitation, we adopt the following technique: set $\mu_m \leftarrow \mu_m^t$, $t > 1$. Through this trick, the new optimization problem can be reformulated as

$$\begin{aligned}\min_{\mu} \quad & \sum_{m=1}^{M} \mu_m^t h_m \\ \text{s.t.} \quad & \sum_{m=1}^{M} \mu_m = 1, \mu_m \geq 0\end{aligned} \tag{12}$$

where $h_m = \|\varphi_m(X^{(m)}) - U^{(m)}V\|_F^2 + \lambda\|U^{(m)}\|_F^2$. The Lagrange function can be constructed as:

$$L(\mu, \zeta) = \sum_{m=1}^{M} \mu_m^t h_m - \zeta\left(\sum_{m=1}^{M} \mu_m - 1\right) \tag{13}$$

we can obtain μ_m as follows:

$$\mu_m = \frac{(1/h_m)^{1/(t-1)}}{\sum_{m=1}^{M}(1/h_m)^{1/(t-1)}} \tag{14}$$

The detailed procedure of proposed algorithm is listed in Algorithm 1.

2.5 Out-of-Sample Extension

Since a hashing scheme should be able to generate the hash code for any data point beyond the training dataset, here we address the out-of-example extension of MVLH model. The basic idea is to reconstruct the binary code using those of its nearest neighbors in the unified feature space. Specifically, for a new data point $\{x_q^{(m)}\}_{m=1}^M$, we first compute its integrated feature $\varphi(x_q)$ using (3), then obtain its binary code as

$$v_q = \mathrm{sign}\left(\frac{\sum_{i=1}^{N} w_{iq}v_i}{\sum_{i=1}^{N} w_{iq}}\right) \tag{15}$$

where v_i is the hash code of the i-th sample in the training set, w_{iq} is a similarity measurement between x_i and x_q, and defined as $w_{iq} = \exp\left(-\|\varphi(x_i) - \varphi(x_q)\|^2/\sigma^2\right)$ if $x_i \in N_k(x_q)$, and $w_{iq} = 0$ otherwise, σ is the bandwidth parameter.

Algorithm 1: Multi-view Latent Hashing (MVLH)

INPUT: Training set $\{X^{(m)} \in \mathbb{R}^{d_m \times N}\}_{m=1}^M$; code length c; number of anchor points L; parameters λ, t.
OUTPUT: Binary codes $V = \{v_i\}_{i=1}^N \in \{-1,1\}^{c\times N}$.
Initialization:
1. Initialize V as a $\{-1,1\}$ matrix randomly, and $\mu_m = 1/M$;
2. Construct the landmark set $\{z_l^{(m)}\}_{l=1}^L$ for each view;
3. Define the integrated kernel feature $\varphi(X)$ using (3).
Repeat
4. Update U using (5);
5. Iteratively update V bit by bit using (10);
6. Update μ_m using (14).
Until *Convergence*

---

3. EXPERIMENTAL RESULTS

In this section, we evaluate our proposed hashing method in image retrieval by comparing with some state-of-the-art methods in the unsupervised settings. These methods can be divided into two categories: (1) multi-view hashing methods, including MFH [11], CHMIS [14], MFKH [7], SU-MVSH [5]; (2) single-view hashing methods, including SH [12], AGH [6]. Since single-view methods cannot deal with multi-view data directly, we first concatenate multiple features as one feature. Note that our proposed method is unsupervised, thus for a fair comparison, we do not incorporate label information into constructing similarity matrices for all comparing methods.

3.1 Datasets and Protocols

Two well-known benchmark datasets: CIFAR-10 and Caltech256 are adopted for experiment. CIFAR-10 contains 60,000 32×32 color images of 10 classes and 6,000 images in each class. The Caltech256 dataset contains a total of 30,607 images of 256 object categories with more than 80 images per category. Similar to existing works [11, 14, 7, 5], to construct the multi-view data, we extract two following visual features for each dataset: (1) gist feature; (2) bag of visual words quantized from dense sift features as the global and local feature, respectively. In all our experiments, we apply Gaussian RBF kernels for each feature.

For evaluation, for each dataset, we randomly sample 3,000 images as the training data, 1,000 images as queries, and the remaining images as the database, respectively. Ground truths are defined by the class labels. Two protocols are adopted: (1) Hamming ranking, (2) hash lookup within Hamming radius 2. We report the widely used measures including precision curve, recall curve, F_1 measure, and mean average precision (MAP) from 8 to 64 bits.

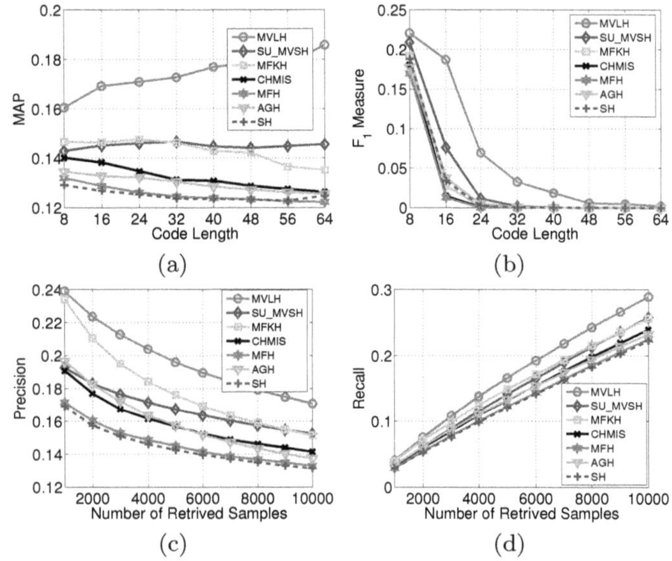

Figure 1: Performance comparisions on CIFAR-10 dataset. (a) MAP, (b) F_1 measure within Hamming radius 2 using hashing lookup, (c) Precision curve using 24-bit codes, (d) Recall curve using 24-bit codes.

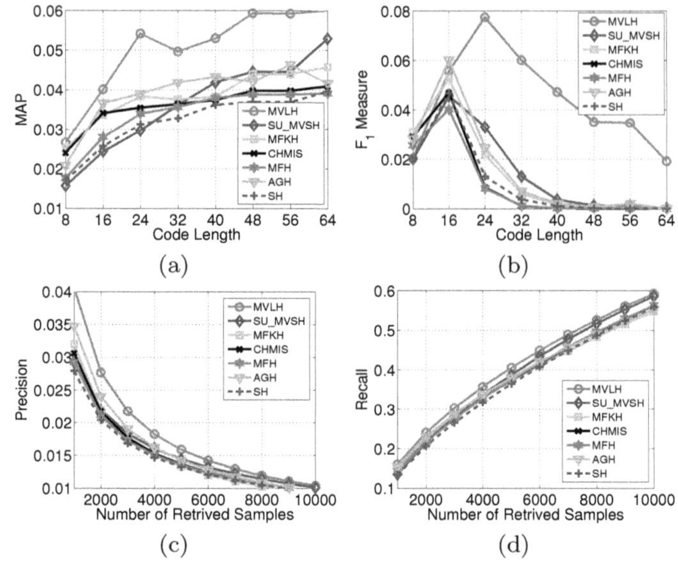

Figure 2: Performance comparisions on Caltech256 dataset. (a) MAP, (b) F_1 measure within Hamming radius 2 using hashing lookup, (c) Precision curve using 24-bit codes, (d) Recall curve using 24-bit codes.

3.2 Results and Discussions

The experimental results on CIFAR-10 and Caltech256 are shown in Fig. 1, Fig. 2, respectively. Fig. 1(a) and Fig. 2(a) show MAPs with varying code lengths, where we can clearly see that MVLH consistently outperforms comparing methods for all code lengths. As code length increases, MAP performances of MVLH improve more significantly than those of most comparing methods, some of which even drop to varying degress on CIFAR-10 dataset. This indicates that MVLH can perform better with longer codes. F_1 measures of hashing lookup within Hamming radius 2 are reported in Fig. 1(b), Fig. 2(b). Although F_1 measures of all methods drop due to the increased sparsity of the Hamming space with longer code length, MVLH still obviously achieves best performances. Especially after a point (32 bits on CIFAR-10, 40 bits on Caltech256), F_1 measures of all compared methods approach to 0, while those of MVLH are still relatively high.

For further evaluation, we also report precision and recall curves with 24-bit codes in Fig. 1(c-d), Fig. 2(c-d). From these results, we can confirm again that, compared with other methods, MVLH consistently achieves better performances with varying degrees on different number of retrieved samples.

4. CONCLUSIONS

This work focused on learning compact binary codes from multi-view data. We proposed a novel method, dubbed multi-view latent hashing (MVLH), which learned hash codes by the latent binary factors from an unified kernel space formed with multi-view features of data. Specifically, to reveal the nonlinear data structures of different views, we first explicitly constructed an unified kernel feature space, then further applied matrix factorization to learn the latent factors as the target binary codes. As such, the generated binary codes were able to convey consistent semantic information shared by multiple views. Furthermore, we designed a novel alternative algorithm to solve the proposed problem, where high-quality hash codes were learned by directly optimizing the problem with binary constraints. Experimental results have validated the effectiveness of the proposed method on several large-scale datasets.

5. ACKNOWLEDGMENTS

This work is supported by the National Science Foundation of China (Grant No. 61273251, 61402203).

References

[1] G. Ding, Y. Guo, and J. Zhou. Collective matrix factorization hashing for multimodal data. In *CVPR*, pages 2083–2090, 2014.
[2] A. Gionis, P. Indyk, R. Motwani, et al. Similarity search in high dimensions via hashing. In *VLDB*, pages 518–529, 1999.
[3] Y. Gong, S. Lazebnik, A. Gordo, and F. Perronnin. Iterative quantization: A procrustean approach to learning binary codes for large-scale image retrieval. *TPAMI*, 35(12):2916–2929, 2013.
[4] Y. Hu, Z. Jin, H. Ren, D. Cai, and X. He. Iterative multi-view hashing for cross media indexing. In *MM*, pages 527–536, 2014.
[5] S. Kim, Y. Kang, and S. Choi. Sequential spectral learning to hash with multiple representations. In *ECCV*, pages 538–551. 2012.
[6] W. Liu, J. Wang, S. Kumar, and S.-F. Chang. Hashing with graphs. In *ICML*, pages 1–8, 2011.
[7] X. Liu, J. He, D. Liu, and B. Lang. Compact kernel hashing with multiple features. In *MM*, pages 881–884, 2012.
[8] F. Shen, C. Shen, W. Liu, and H. Tao Shen. Supervised discrete hashing. In *CVPR*, pages 37–45, 2015.
[9] F. Shen, C. Shen, Q. Shi, A. Van Den Hengel, and Z. Tang. Inductive hashing on manifolds. In *CVPR*, pages 1562–1569, 2013.
[10] F. Shen, C. Shen, Q. Shi, A. van den Hengel, Z. Tang, and H. T. Shen. Hashing on nonlinear manifolds. *TIP*, 24(6):1839–1851, 2015.
[11] J. Song, Y. Yang, Z. Huang, H. T. Shen, and R. Hong. Multiple feature hashing for real-time large scale near-duplicate video retrieval. In *MM*, pages 423–432, 2011.
[12] Y. Weiss, A. Torralba, and R. Fergus. Spectral hashing. In *NIPS*, pages 1753–1760, 2009.
[13] H. Xiong, M. Swamy, and M. O. Ahmad. Optimizing the kernel in the empirical feature space. *TNN*, 16(2):460–474, 2005.
[14] D. Zhang, F. Wang, and L. Si. Composite hashing with multiple information sources. In *SIGIR*, pages 225–234, 2011.
[15] X. Zhu, Z. Huang, H. T. Shen, and X. Zhao. Linear cross-modal hashing for efficient multimedia search. In *MM*, pages 143–152, 2013.

Jointly Estimating Interactions and Head, Body Pose of Interactors from Distant Social Scenes

Ramanathan Subramanian[1], Jagannadan Varadarajan[1], Elisa Ricci[2,3], Oswald Lanz[2], Stefan Winkler[1]
[1]Advanced Digital Sciences Center (ADSC), University of Illinois at Urbana-Champaign, Singapore, [2]Fondazione Bruno Kessler, Trento, Italy. [3]University of Perugia, Italy
Subramanian.R,vjagan,Stefan.Winkler@adsc.com.sg, eliricci,lanz@fbk.eu

ABSTRACT

We present **joint** estimation of *F-formations* and *head, body pose* of interactors in a social scene captured by surveillance cameras. Unlike prior works that have focused on (a) discovering F-formations based on head pose and position cues, or (b) jointly learned head and body pose of individuals based on anatomic constraints, we exploit positional and pose cues characterizing interactors and interactions to jointly infer both (a) and (b). We show how the joint inference framework benefits both F-formation and head, body pose estimation accuracy via experiments on two social datasets.

Categories and Subject Descriptors

H.1.2 [**User/Machine Systems**]: Human information processing; I.5.4 [**Pattern Recognition Applications**]: Computer vision

General Terms

Algorithms, Measurement, Human Factors

Keywords

F-formations; Head and Body Pose; Joint Estimation; Social Scenes

1. INTRODUCTION

Following considerable research progress in the areas of computer vision and multimodal analysis, examination of complex phenomena such as *social interactions* is now possible. Social interactions are commonplace in our daily lives and have been extensively studied by psychologists in a variety of contexts. Social interactions provide a wealth of information concerning individual and group behavior, and while most automated social interaction analysis methods have focused on round-table meetings [8], recent works have examined unstructured meeting scenes [11] (*e.g.*, cocktail party) involving free-standing conversational groups (FCGs). FCGs naturally emerge in social settings, and individuals constituting an FCG are characterized by mutual scene locations and head/body orientations resulting in distinct spatial patterns known as F-formations.

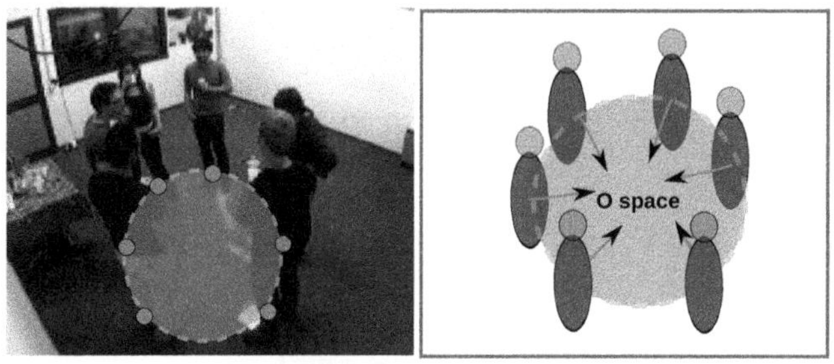

Figure 1: (Left) Social scene from the *Cocktail-Party* dataset [11]. We *jointly* estimate F-formations and the head, body pose of targets exploiting the interation-interactor relationship in terms of positional and pose constraints. Red circles denote targets' feet positions and O-space corresponding to the F-formation is shown via the circular region connecting target positions. (Right) Body pose of interactors serves as our primary cue for determining the O-space center and the corresponding F-formation.

F-formations (FFs) are primarily detected using visual cues [4,9] and FF detection from a distant social scene captured by surveillance cameras is challenging as seen in Fig.1. Fig.1 (left) shows an FCG comprising six targets– despite being a small group, most targets are partially or severely occluded and are captured at low-resolution, making head and body pose estimation difficult. An F-formation is defined via the O-space (Fig.1 (right)), which is the smallest empty convex space encompassed by the interactors. The body orientation of targets better defines the O-space geometrically[1] as compared to head pose which can frequently change during conversations. Still, head pose is typically used for FF detection [4,7,9] due to severe body occlusions.

We present the first work to exploit the *social context* to *jointly* estimate targets' head and body pose and F-formations in a social scene. Prior pose estimation (PE) works have jointly learned head and body pose of individuals based on anatomic constraints [2,3], while FF detection works have mainly used position and head pose cues [4,9]. Differently, we exploit positional and pose constraints governing the *synergetic* interaction-interactor relationship in

[1]FF members typically orient their bodies towards the O-space center.

MM'15, October 26–30, 2015, Brisbane, Australia.
Copyright 2015 ACM. ISBN 978-1-4503-3459-4/15/10 ...$15.00.
DOI: http://dx.doi.org/10.1145/2733373.2806343.

social scenes to jointly infer both FFs and pose of targets. Specifically, FFs are characterized by mutual locations and head, body orientations of interactors, and conversely, interactors are constrained in terms of the head and body pose they can exhibit, motivating the need for joint learning. Our multimodal framework[2] (i) exploits both annotated and unlabeled examples to learn the range of possible joint head-body orientations, (ii) employs positional and pose-based constraints relating interactors to discover FFs, and (iii) progressively refines pose estimates of interactors based on the gained FF knowledge and vice-versa.

Contributions: (i) We present a multimodal framework for jointly estimating targets' head, body orientations and F-formations in social scenes. We show the benefit of joint learning via experiments on two social datasets. (ii) Different from prior works, we primarily use body orientation for estimating F-formations. Precise body pose estimates are computed via coupled head-body pose learning, and knowledge of F-formations.

2. SOCIAL SCENE ANALYSIS

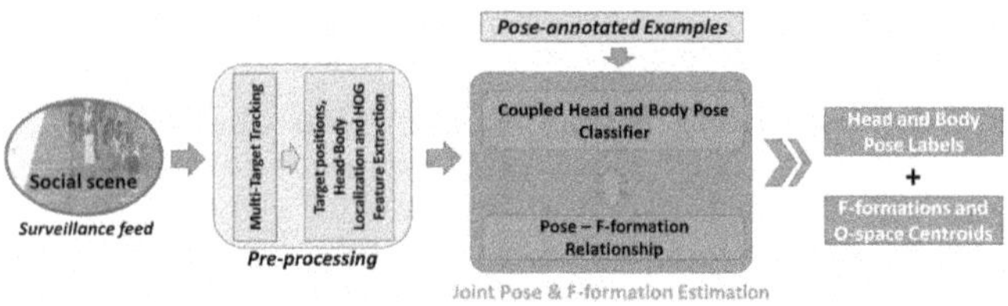

Figure 2: Our social scene analysis framework.

Overview: An overview of our social scene analysis (SSA) method is presented in Fig.2. Given the surveillance video of a social gathering, we apply multi-target tracking to estimate the feet positions of targets in the scene. As in [10], a 3-D head-plus-shoulder model is registered to each target via shape matching with color information provided by the tracker to output head coordinates. The body region is then determined as the portion lying between the head and feet coordinates. Head and body images are respectively normalized to 20×20 and 80×60 pixels, and HoG features are extracted over 4×4 cells, resulting in 775 and 2480-dimensional head and body descriptors. These features and target positions are input to our SSA algorithm to output (a) head, body pose along with FF membership for each target, and (b) O-space centroids for the detected FFs.

2.1 Joint pose and FF learning

Given a T-frame surveillance video of a social scene with K persons (targets), we assume to have the head and body crops for each target k at each frame t. In other words, for each target k, we have a set of samples $\mathcal{S}_k = \{\mathbf{x}^B_{k,t}, \mathbf{x}^H_{k,t}\}_{t=1}^T$, where $\mathbf{x}^B_{k,t} \in I\!R^{D_B}, \mathbf{x}^H_{k,t} \in I\!R^{D_H}$ are the head and body HOG descriptors of dimensionality D_B and D_H respectively. For each frame t, we also have the tracker-output ground position for each target k, $k = 1, \dots, K$, *i.e.*, over the video length, for each target k we have a set $\mathcal{P}_k = \{\mathbf{p}_{k,t}\}_{t=1}^T$ with $\mathbf{p}_{k,t} = (p^x_{k,t}, p^y_{k,t})$ respectively denoting (x, y) feet positions.

[2]Even though our approach is vision-based, we employ multiple cues such as target positions, their head, body pose and FF membership in our model.

In addition to social scene features, we also assume to have training data from an (independent) annotated dataset, $\mathcal{T}_B = \{(\hat{\mathbf{x}}^B_i, y^B_i\}_{i=1}^{N_B}$, $\mathcal{T}_H = \{(\hat{\mathbf{x}}^H_i, y^H_i\}_{i=1}^{N_H}$, where $\hat{\mathbf{x}}^B_i \in I\!R^{D_B}$, $\hat{\mathbf{x}}^H_i \in I\!R^{D_H}$ denote HOG body and head descriptors, while $y^B_i \in \{0,1\}^{C_B}$, $y^H_i \in \{0,1\}^{C_H}$ are the corresponding labels (*i.e.*, $y^B_i = [0, 0, \dots, 1, \dots, 0]$, $y^H_i = [0, 0, \dots, 1, \dots, 0]$ where the position of the non-zero element indicates the class label of the training sample). In this work, we quantize the set of possible head and body pose directions into $C_H = C_B = 8$ possible classes, each denoting a 45° head/body *pan* range.

We define matrices $\mathbf{X}^B_k \in I\!R^{D_B \times K} = [\mathbf{x}^B_{k,1}, \dots, \mathbf{x}^B_{k,T}]$ and $\mathbf{X}^H_k \in I\!R^{D_H \times K} = [\mathbf{x}^H_{k,1}, \dots, \mathbf{x}^H_{k,T}]$ obtained by concatenating head and body features for target k, and define global matrices $\mathbf{X}^B \in I\!R^{D_B \times KT} = [\mathbf{X}^B_1, \dots, \mathbf{X}^B_K]$ and $\mathbf{X}^H \in I\!R^{D_H \times KT} = [\mathbf{X}^H_1, \dots, \mathbf{X}^H_K]$ collating features for all targets. Similarly, the matrix $\mathbf{P}$ is defined as $\mathbf{P} = [\mathbf{P}_1, \dots \mathbf{P}_T]$, where $\mathbf{P}_t = [\mathbf{p}_{1,t}, \dots, \mathbf{p}_{K,t}]$, *i.e.*, $\mathbf{P} \in I\!R^{2 \times KT}$ contains feet positions of all targets over the video length. We also consider matrices $\hat{\mathbf{X}}^B \in I\!R^{D_B \times N_B} = [\hat{\mathbf{x}}^B_1, \dots, \hat{\mathbf{x}}^B_{N_B}]$ and $\mathbf{Y}^B = [y^B_1, \dots, y^B_{N_B}]$, obtained by concatenating head, body features and corresponding labels from the annotated data. Similarly, $\hat{\mathbf{X}}^H \in I\!R^{D_H \times N_H} = [\hat{\mathbf{x}}^H_1, \dots, \hat{\mathbf{x}}^H_{N_H}]$ and $\mathbf{Y}^H = [y^H_1, \dots, y^H_{N_H}]$.

We propose a joint framework to infer the head and body pose of all the targets in the social scene along with FFs. More formally, we propose to jointly learn head and body pose classifiers $f^H : D_H \to I\!R^{C_H}$ and $f^B : D_B \to I\!R^{C_B}$, and respectively parametrized by matrices $\mathbf{\Theta}_B \in I\!R^{C_B \times D_B}$ and $\mathbf{\Theta}_H \in I\!R^{C_H \times D_H}$, and indirectly infer F-formations based on shared cluster memberships. We propose to solve the following optimization problem:

$$\min_{\mathbf{\Theta}_B, \mathbf{\Theta}_H, \mathbf{\Theta}_F} \quad \mathcal{L}_{\mathbf{\Theta}_B, \mathbf{\Theta}_H}(\hat{\mathbf{X}}^B, \hat{\mathbf{X}}^H, \mathbf{Y}^B, \mathbf{Y}^H) \qquad (1)$$
$$+\lambda_U \mathcal{U}_{\mathbf{\Theta}_B, \mathbf{\Theta}_H}(\mathbf{X}^B, \mathbf{X}^H) + \lambda_F \mathcal{F}_{\mathbf{\Theta}_B, \mathbf{\Theta}_F}(\mathbf{X}^B, \mathbf{P})$$

where $\mathbf{\Theta}_F$ denotes FF parameters. The objective function is the sum of three terms. The first term $\mathcal{L}(\cdot)$ leverages annotated data to learn both the head and body pose classifiers. Formally, we minimize the training error on labeled head and body samples, while regularizing the classifiers to reflect the distribution of the training examples. The second term $\mathcal{U}(\cdot)$ exploits unlabeled examples gathered from the social scene to improve PE performance. The last term models the relationship between targets' body pose and FFs. Intuitively, if the precise body orientation of interactors is known, F-formations can be detected. Conversely, if FFs are known, body pose of interactors can be enforced/refined. The parameters λ_U and λ_F regulates the importance of the three terms. We now describe loss functions $\mathcal{L}(\cdot)$, $\mathcal{U}(\cdot)$ and $\mathcal{F}(\cdot)$.

Training loss: The first term $\mathcal{L}(\cdot)$ in Eq(1) implements the traditional trade-off between minimization of the empirical error on labeled data and regularization. More formally, considering the head and body training data, we define $\mathcal{L}(\cdot) = \mathcal{L}^H(\cdot) + \mathcal{L}^B(\cdot)$ and:

$$\mathcal{L}^{\triangle} = \|\mathbf{Y}_{\triangle} - \mathbf{\Theta}_{\triangle}\hat{\mathbf{X}}_{\triangle}\|^2 + \lambda_r \|\mathbf{\Theta}_{\triangle}\|^2$$
$$+\lambda_g \sum_{(i,j) \in \mathcal{G}_{\triangle}} \gamma^{\triangle}_{ij} \|\boldsymbol{\theta}^{c_i}_{\triangle} - \boldsymbol{\theta}^{c_j}_{\triangle}\|_2$$

where $\triangle = \{B, H\}$. The last term enforces that similar classifiers, corresponding to columns $\boldsymbol{\theta}^{c_i}_{\triangle}$ of the matrix $\mathbf{\Theta}_{\triangle}$, are obtained for neighboring poses. This is achieved by defining an appropriate pose graph $\mathcal{G}_{\triangle}$ such that $\gamma^{\triangle}_{ij} = 1$

if the classes c_i and c_j correspond to similar head/body orientations. The parameters λ_g and λ_r regulate the trade-off between loss and regularization.

Unsupervised loss: Since one would expect unlabeled data from the social scene to be consistent with the distribution of the labeled data (this is the assumption in semi-supervised manifold learning), we propose to integrate unlabeled data information by adopting a graph-based regularization term as typically done in semi-supervised methods [12]. The assumption is that the manifold in which data are embedded can be approximated by a weighted discrete graph whose vertices are identified with (labeled and unlabeled) training examples. The proposed unsupervised data term $\mathcal{U}(\cdot)$ in Eq(1) is defined as $\mathcal{U}(\cdot) = \mathcal{U}^B(\cdot) + \mathcal{U}^H(\cdot) + \mathcal{U}^P(\cdot)$, where:

$$\mathcal{U}^{\triangle} = \mathbf{\Theta}'_{\triangle}\mathbf{L}_{\triangle}\mathbf{\Theta}_{\triangle}$$

where $\triangle = \{B, H\}$ and $\mathbf{L}_{\triangle}$ is the Laplacian matrix defined as $\mathbf{L}_{\triangle} \in I\!R^{M_\triangle \times M_\triangle}$, $\mathbf{L}_{\triangle} = \mathbf{D}_{\triangle} - \mathbf{A}_{\triangle}$, where $\mathbf{D}_{\triangle} = \mathrm{diag}(d_i)$, $i = 1, \ldots, M_\triangle$, $d_i = \sum_{j=1}^{M_\triangle}[A_\triangle]_{ij}$ and $M_\triangle = N_\triangle + KT$ is the total number of labeled and unlabeled data. The $M_\triangle \times M_\triangle$ adjacency matrix $\mathbf{A}_\triangle$ is defined such that $[A_\triangle]_{ij} = 1$ if the i-th sample is one of the k-nearest neighbors of j and zero otherwise. The term $\mathcal{U}^P$ couples head and body pose estimates on unlabeled data based on human anatomic constraints (*e.g.*, the body and head cannot be oppositely oriented) and it is defined as follows:

$$\begin{aligned}\mathcal{U}^P &= \sum_{k=1}^{K}\sum_{t=1}^{T}\|f^B(\mathbf{x}^B_{k,t}) - f^H(\mathbf{x}^H_{k,t})\|^2 \qquad (2)\\ &= \|\mathbf{\Theta}_H\mathbf{X}_H - \mathbf{\Theta}_B\mathbf{X}_B\|^2\end{aligned}$$

F-formation loss: The third term in the objective function Eq(1) models the relationship between interactors' body pose and the F-formations. Our aim is to iteratively exploit the targets' FF membership for refining body pose estimates as interactors tend to orient towards the O-space center, and conversely, to detect FFs from the body pose of interactors. We consider the interactions between **pairs of targets** and compute at each frame t, the angle β^t_{kq} of the line connecting targets q, k. We formulate FF detection as the problem of learning a set of parameters $\mathbf{\Theta}_F = \{\boldsymbol{C}_t, \boldsymbol{Z}_t\}$, where $z_{kt} \in \boldsymbol{Z}_t \in I\!R^{K\times K}$. At each frame t, we aim to learn both $\boldsymbol{C}_t$, the matrix of O-space centers and the FF membership matrix $\mathbf{Z}_t$. To learn $\boldsymbol{C}_t, \boldsymbol{Z}_t$, we define loss $\mathcal{F}_P$ as follows:

$$\begin{aligned}\mathcal{F}_P = &\sum_{t=1}^{T}\|\hat{\mathbf{P}}_t - \mathbf{C}_t\mathbf{Z}_t\|^2 \qquad (3)\\ &+\gamma_p\sum_{t=1}^{T}\sum_{k,q=1}^{K}\delta^t_{kq}\|\eta^B_{k,t} - \beta^t_{kq}\|^2(\mathbf{z}_{k,t})^T\mathbf{z}_{q,t}\end{aligned}$$

and we minimize it imposing $\mathbf{C}_t, \mathbf{Z}_t \geq 0$. In (3), γ_p is a user-defined parameter, $\mathbf{z}_{k,t}$ denotes the k-th column of the matrix $\mathbf{Z}_t$, δ^t_{kq} is an indicator function, *i.e.* $\delta^t_{kq} = I(\|\mathbf{p}_{k,t} - \mathbf{p}_{q,t}\|^2 < \tau)$ and τ is a user-defined threshold. $\eta_{k,t}$ denotes transformation from $f_B(x^B_{k,t})$ to a real-valued angle obtained by computing the weighted average vector $\sum_{i=1}^{C_B/C_H}\hat{y}_i\vec{n_{\alpha_i}}$, where $\vec{n_{\alpha_i}}$ is the unit vector corresponding to α_i. The proposed function $\mathcal{F}_P(\cdot)$ aims to jointly learn the F-formation detection parameters and the body classifier $\mathbf{\Theta}_B$. Intuitively, minimizing $\mathcal{F}_P(\cdot)$, we enforce that targets belonging to the same FF (*i.e.*, with same membership $\mathbf{z}_{k,t}$) should have the body pose almost aligned with the direction individuated by the angle β_{kq}. On the other hand, detection of FFs is influenced by the body pose of targets, *i.e.*, targets belong to the same FF if they are close-by, and their body orientation is consistent with β_{kq}.

Optimization: To solve the optimization problem (1), we adopt an alternating optimization approach solving for pose classifiers $\mathbf{\Theta}_\triangle$ having $\mathbf{\Theta}_F$ fixed, and solving with respect to $\mathbf{\Theta}_F$ when the pose classifiers are known.

3. EXPERIMENTAL RESULTS

3.1 Datasets

We evaluate our framework on the *CocktailParty* (CP) and *CoffeeBreak* (CB) social datasets. **CocktailParty** [11] is a 30-minute video recording of a social event involving six targets in a 30m^2 room, and recorded using four synchronized wall-mounted cameras. We only use images from Camera 1 for analysis. Target positions are logged via a tracker, while head and body orientations are manually assigned to one of $N_C = 8$ class labels denoting a quantized 45° head/body pan, while F-formation annotations are available for every 75th frame. **CoffeeBreak** comprises a maximum of 14 targets, organized in groups of 2-3 persons. Target positions are annotated using a tracker, while head and body pose are assigned to one of eight classes. F-formations are annotated for two sequences of lengths 45 and 75 frames respectively. as auxiliary data, we used 1000 frames from the DPOSE dataset [5] which contains head pose measurements, while body pose is computed via walking direction as in [2].

3.2 Quantitative evaluation

Algorithm parameters for our method and other baselines were tuned using a small validation set. To evaluate head, body pose estimation (HBPE) accuracy, we use the mean angular error (in degrees) as defined in [3]. F-formation estimation (FFE) accuracy is evaluated using F1-score as described in [4, 9]. Table 1 shows the average HBPE errors on the CP, CB datasets. Maximum error of about 72° is obtained for both when the objective function involves only the training error (L), which is within two pose classes. Additionally incorporating unlabeled scene examples (L+U) and coupling head and body pose learning (L+U+H/B) considerably reduces HBPE error, while exploiting knowledge of FFs (L+U+H/B+FF) further minimizes the error to produce the best performance. We compare our approach with the state-of-the-art for joint HBPE [3]. Our algorithm performs significantly better than [3] on both datasets as the *social context* is taken into account, and other cues (*e.g.*, velocity direction) are ineffective when targets are mostly static and heavily occluded. FFE results are compared with the state-of-the-art in Table 2. Specifically, we compare with the linear Hough transform method (HVFF lin) [4], its non-linear (HVFF ent) [6] and multi-scale extensions [7] (HVFF ms). Evidently, we achieve the best performance on both datasets as we primarily use body orientation for detecting FFs, and refine body pose estimates via coupled HBPE.

3.3 Qualitative Results

Fig.3 presents some qualitative results with our algorithm. Specifically, we show the inferred head and body pose for each target along with the detected F-formations. First two columns in Fig.3 present results on CP. Despite being a small group, severe occlusions are observed for conversing targets making HBPE challenging. Note that most of the

Figure 3: Qualitative results on the CP (Columns 1,2) and CB (Columns 3,4) datasets: Pies on the ground located at targets' feet positions denote body pose, while arrows denote head pose. FF members are shown connected (Figure best viewed under zoom).

Table 1: Mean HBPE error with various cues.

	CP		CB	
Method	Head	Body	Head	Body
L	67.3	71.4	68.3	72.6
L + U	61.3	64.7	59.8	62.3
L + U + H/B	58.9	61.6	55.3	59.6
L + U + H/B + FF	**51.7**	**55.3**	**49.6**	**51.4**
Chen *et al.* [3]	58.3	62.7	56.1	60.2

Table 2: FFE evaluation via precison (pre), recall (rec) and F1-scores (F1).

	CP			CB		
Method	pre	rec	F1	pre	rec	F1
HVFF lin [4]	0.64	0.72	0.68	0.74	0.85	0.78
HVFF ent [6]	0.78	0.82	0.79	0.81	0.78	0.79
HVFF ms [7]	0.79	0.80	0.79	0.78	0.85	0.81
Our	0.79	0.82	**0.82**	0.82	0.84	**0.83**

head, body pose and FF estimates are still accurate, demonstrating the effectiveness of our joint learning framework. In column 1, the target coded in yellow is incorrectly left out of the FF. Also, while HPE outputs for the green and yellow targets are erroneous, their body pose is estimated correctly. This is because we link FFs with the body pose of interactors, and progressively refine both body pose and FF estimates upon gaining knowledge of the other. All estimates are correct for the frame in column 2, including for the singleton yellow target who moves away from the group. Columns 3 and 4 show exemplar results on the CB dataset, which also captures a densely crowded social gathering over a large area. Here again, we notice that FF and body pose estimates are generally more correct than targets' head pose estimates. Overall, these results demonstrate the effectiveness of our approach for HBPE and FFE on challenging social datasets.

4. CONCLUSION

Our multimodal social scene analysis framework exploits positional and pose constraints relating interactors to improve both HBPE and FFE accuracy for social scenes involving persistent and considerable occlusions. Different from prior works, we employ body pose of interactors as the primary cue for determining F-formations, and progressively refine both body pose and F-formation estimates via an alternating optimization strategy. Nevertheless, difficulties in studying small groups point to the extreme challenges posed to vision-based tracking and pose estimation while dealing with large groups– incorporating multi-sensory information can help alleviate limitations of purely vision-based analysis [1], and will be the focus of future work.

5. ACKNOWLEDGEMENT

This study is supported by the research grant for ADSC's Human-Centered Cyber-physical Systems (HCCS) Program from Singapore's Agency for Science, Technology and Research (A*STAR).

6. REFERENCES

[1] X. Alameda-Pineda, J. Staiano, R. Subramanian, L. M. Batrinca, E. Ricci, B. Lepri, O. Lanz, and N. Sebe. SALSA: A novel dataset for multimodal group behavior analysis. *CoRR*, abs, 2015.

[2] B. Benfold and I. Reid. Unsupervised learning of a scene-specific coarse gaze estimator. In *ICCV*, 2011.

[3] C. Chen and J. M. Odobez. We are not contortionists: coupled adaptive learning for head and body orientation estimation in surveillance video. In *CVPR*, 2012.

[4] M. Cristani, L. Bazzani, G. Paggetti, A. Fossati, D. Tosato, A. Del Bue, G. Menegaz, and V. Murino. Social interaction discovery by statistical analysis of f-formations. In *BMVC*, 2011.

[5] A. K. Rajagopal, R. Subramanian, E. Ricci, R. L. Vieriu, O. Lanz, N. Sebe, et al. Exploring transfer learning approaches for head pose classification from multi-view surveillance images. *IJCV*, 109(1-2):146–167, 2014.

[6] F. Setti, H. Hung, and M. Cristani. Group detection in still images by f-formation modeling: A comparative study. In *WIAMIS*, 2013.

[7] F. Setti, O. Lanz, R. Ferrario, V. Murino, and M. Cristani. Multi-scale f-formation discovery for group detection. In *ICIP*, 2013.

[8] J. Staiano, B. Lepri, R. Subramanian, N. Sebe, and F. Pianesi. Automatic modeling of personality states in small group interactions. In *ACMMM*, 2011.

[9] S. Vascon, E. Z. Mequanint, M. Cristani, H. Hung, M. Pelillo, and V. Murino. A game theoretic probabilistic approach for detecting conversational groups. In *ACCV*, 2014.

[10] Y. Yan, E. Ricci, R. Subramanian, O. Lanz, and N. Sebe. No matter where you are: Flexible graph-guided multi-task learning for multi-view head pose classification under target motion. In *ICCV*, 2013.

[11] G. Zen, B. Lepri, E. Ricci, and O. Lanz. Space speaks: towards socially and personality aware visual surveillance. In *MPVA*. ACM, 2010.

[12] X. Zhu and A. B. Goldberg. Introduction to semi-supervised learning. *Synthesis lectures on artificial intelligence and machine learning*, 3(1):1–130, 2009.

Exploring Viewable Angle Information in Georeferenced Video Search

Gang Hu Jie Shao Lianli Gao Yang Yang
School of Computer Science & Engineering, University of Electronic Science and Technology of China
hugang@std.uestc.edu.cn {shaojie,lianli.gao,yang.yang}@uestc.edu.cn

ABSTRACT

As positioning data and other sensor information such as orientation measurement became powerful contextual features generated by mobile devices during video recording, a model capturing geographic field-of-view (FOV) has been developed for georeferenced video search. The accurate representation of an FOV is through the geometric shape of a circular sector. However, previous work simply employed a rectilinear vector model to represent the coverage area of a video scene. In this study, we propose to use a novel circular sector model with beginning-ending vectors for FOV representation which additionally explores viewable angle information. Its major advantage is that it leads to a more accurate georeferenced video search without false positives or false negatives (which occur in previous model using single vector). We demonstrate how our model can be applied to perform different types of overlap queries for spatial data selection in a unified framework, while providing competitive performance in terms of efficiency.

Categories and Subject Descriptors

H.2.4 [**Database Management**]: System—*multimedia databases*

General Terms

Algorithms, Experimentation

Keywords

Georeferenced video search; meta-data; viewable angle

1. INTRODUCTION

With the development of mobile and sensor technologies, many videos now can be tagged with geographic properties while being collected, such as camera locations from GPS and camera directions from digital compasses. Previous work [1, 3] demonstrated that field-of-view (FOV) information can be used to model the coverage area of a video scene. In this model, the following are important factors that should be captured (see Figure 1(a)): (1) **camera location**: geographic coordinates (longitude, latitude and optional height) obtained from GPS related services, which can be represented by $P(x, y)$ (or $P(x, y, z)$ in 3D space); (2) **camera direction**: horizontal angle from a particular direction (such as north) obtained from sensors such as digital compass, which can be represented by a vector V_c; (3) **visible distance**: distance from P is R at which objects in the scene can be recognized by observers, calculated from camera lens parameter [2]; (4) **viewable angle**: θ describes the angular extent of the scene imaged by the camera, which can be calculated from camera lens parameter [2] as well.

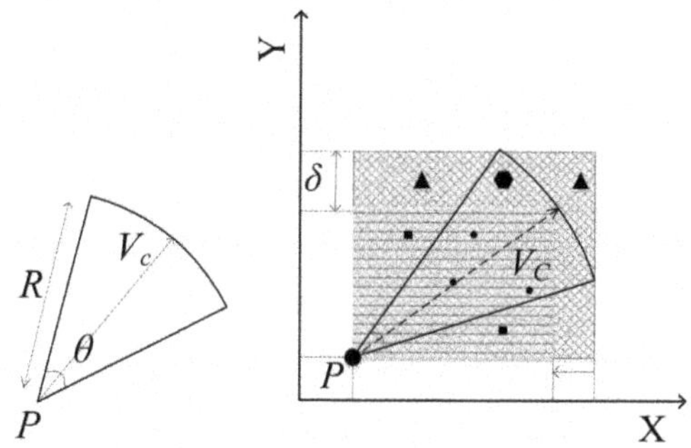

(a) FOV model. (b) Problem with single vector.

Figure 1: Field-of-view model.

The FOV model can collect and fuse multiple sensor streams and provide comprehensive information about the viewable scene. Thus, video search problem can be transformed into a *spatial data selection* problem. Each FOV can be regarded as a spatial object such that videos can be organized, indexed and searched in support of georeferenced video search. Compared with traditional feature-based video search dealing with visual signals, the captured geographic meta-data from camera-attached sensors have a great potential to aid in the indexing and searching of georeferenced video data at the high semantic level, which is preferred by humans.

Previous work [3] derived from the FOV model simply used a single rectilinear vector approach to combine camera location, direction and visible distance information. The direction of the vector V_c represents central camera direction and the norm of V_c represents visible distance. The idea is to use the simplified model with filter-refinement steps to find possibly matching candidates quickly. The shortcoming of this approach is that it inevitably brings false negative (exemplified by an octagon dot in Figure 1(b)) and false positive (exemplified by two square dots in Figure 1(b)), as the single vector model treats X and Y dimensions individually. To amend this problem, [3] further considered an overestimation constant δ to enlarge the search area. However, it may bring additional false positive (exemplified by two triangle dots in Figure 1(b)).

MM'15, October 26–30, 2015, Brisbane, Australia.
© 2015 ACM. ISBN 978-1-4503-3459-4/15/10 ...$15.00.
DOI: http://dx.doi.org/10.1145/2733373.2806344.

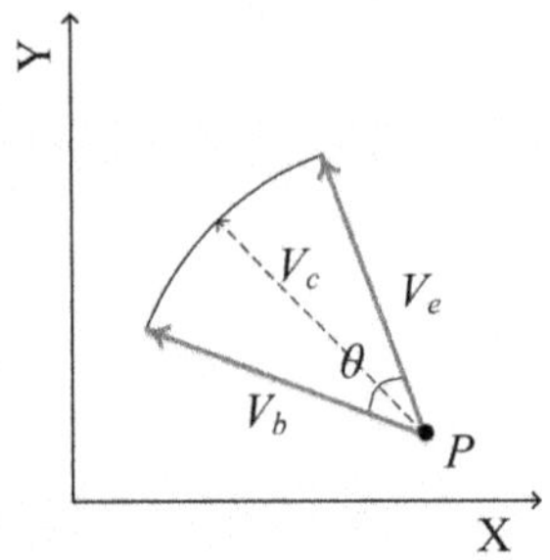

Figure 2: Beginning-ending vectors for FOV model.

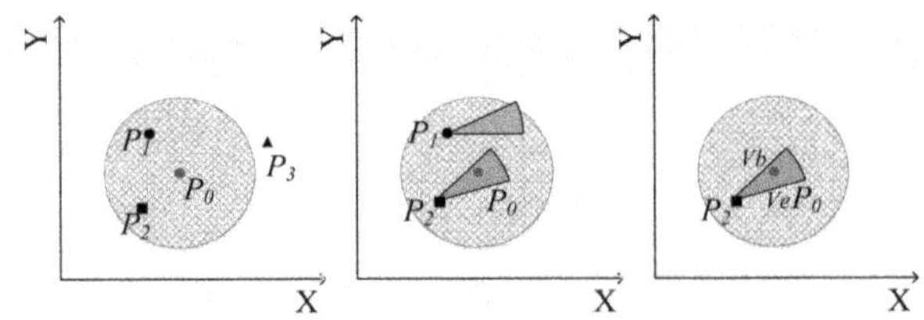

(a) Filtering. (b) Refinement. (c) Final result.

Figure 3: Processing point query.

The above false negatives and false positives are resulted from the simplified rectilinear vector model in which an FOV is reduced to a single vector to facilitate query processing. In this work, we propose a new model for versatile georeferenced video search and related algorithms for query processing. This circular sector model for FOV representation additionally explores viewable angle information with beginning-ending vectors (in Section 2). Its major advantage is that it leads to an accurate georeferenced video search without false positives or false negatives. We apply our model to process different types of overlap queries in georeferenced video search (in Section 3), and demonstrate the important effect of viewable angle (in Section 4). Finally, we give conclusions with remark on future work (in Section 5).

2. OUR MODEL

Based on available meta-data collected from video cameras, our model utilizes all the information fused from different georeferenced data sources. In the beginning-ending vector representation for FOV model (shown in Figure 2), location information is still represented by $P(x, y)$. The information of camera direction, viewable angle and visible distance are combined together into two vectors V_b and V_e (beginning and ending vectors, according to clockwise direction). It is easy to see $||V_b|| = ||V_e||$ (i.e., their norms are equal). Thus, the field-of-view can be represented by a circular sector. The angle between V_b and V_e reflects viewable angle, and the central direction of the camera can be represented by the central direction of the angle between V_b and V_e.

In this way, we can represent an FOV by a tuple $< T, P, V_b, V_e >$ (T is the time stamp at which the video scene is recorded). Next, we will demonstrate how to process different overlap queries with this new model in georeferenced video search, including *point query*, *direction query*, and *circle query*. All of them have real applications in different cases. As we can see, the major advantage of our mode is its query accuracy. Unlike previous single vector model, it can avoid false positive and false negative. In addition, it does not involve complex parameter like overestimation constant needed by the single vector model [3].

3. QUERY PROCESSING ALGORITHMS

In this section, we demonstrate how to apply our model using both beginning and ending vectors to facilitate processing different types of overlap queries in georeferenced video search.

3.1 Point Query

DEFINITION 1 (POINT QUERY). *In a two-dimensional coordinate system X-Y, given a query point p_0 with its FOV $p_0 :< T_0, P_0, V_{b0}, V_{e0} >$, find all points which overlap p_0 in its field-of-view $p_k :< T_k, P_k, V_{bk}, V_{ek} >$.*

Point query is to retrieval those video scenes that cover the query location. All cameras have their maximum visible distances. From the above definition it can be seen that all the video frames in the search space beyond the maximum visible distance should be disqualified. This can be achieved by checking the distance between P_x and P_0 (lines 1-2 of Algorithm 1). If $|P_0 P_x| > ||V_{bx}||$, it can be disregard safely. As shown in Figure 3(a) , P_3 is an example of the points which should be disqualified, while P_1 and P_2 are candidates after the filtering in the first step. From Figure 3(b) we can see that for P_1, although it is in the shadow, actually it does not overlap with P_0 and thus should not be an answer. The key issue of the second refinement step is how to further disregard points like P_1 but retain points like P_2. We propose to use directional information of beginning and ending vectors (lines 3-7 of Algorithm 1). The essence is to check the absolute value of the angular difference between $< \overrightarrow{P_x P_0}, V_{xb} >$ and $< \overrightarrow{P_x P_0}, V_{xe} >$. If it equals to the angle between the beginning and ending vectors of P_x, it means the FOV of P_x covers P_0, and thus should be added to the answer set Q_k.

Algorithm 1 Point Query

Input:
query point $p_0 :< T_0, P_0, V_{b0}, V_{e0} >$.
Output:
point set Q_k.
Description:

1: $R_x \leftarrow getDistance(P_0, P_x)$; //compute distance of P_0 and P_x
2: **if** $R_x \leq ||V_{bx}||$ **then**
3: $< \overrightarrow{P_x P_0}, V_{xb} > \leftarrow getAngle(\overrightarrow{P_x P_0}, V_{xb})$;
4: $< \overrightarrow{P_x P_0}, V_{xe} > \leftarrow getAngle(\overrightarrow{P_x P_0}, V_{xe})$;
5: $< V_{xb}, V_{xe} > \leftarrow getAngle(V_{xb}, V_{xe})$;
6: **if** $| < \overrightarrow{P_x P_0}, V_{xb} > - < \overrightarrow{P_x P_0}, V_{xe} > | = < V_{xb}, V_{xe} >$ **then**
7: Add P_x to Q_k;
8: **end if**
9: **end if**
10: **return** Q_k;

3.2 Direction Query

DEFINITION 2 (DIRECTION QUERY). *In a two-dimensional coordinate system X-Y, given a query point p_0 with its FOV $p_0 :< T_0, P_0, V_{b0}, V_{e0} >$ and a direction constraint V, find all points which overlap p_0 in its field-of-view $p_k :< T_k, P_k, V_{bk}, V_{ek} >$ and locate on the direction V of P_0.*

Camera direction (defined as a line of sight from the camera to the query point) often plays an important role in georeferenced video search. For instance, people may be only interested in those scenes for a given landmark captured from a particular direction.

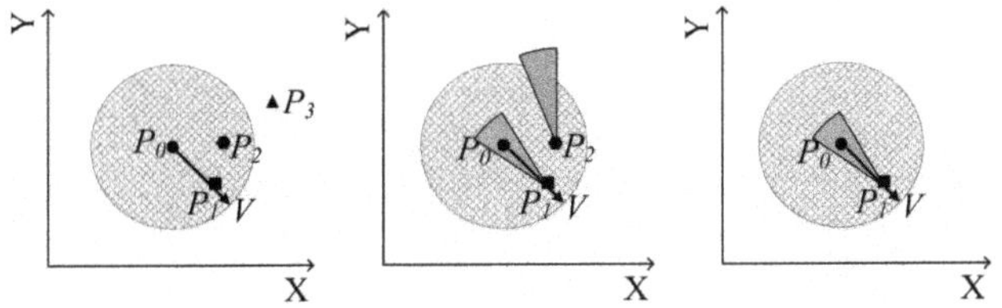

(a) Filtering. (b) Refinement. (c) Final result.

Figure 4: Processing direction query.

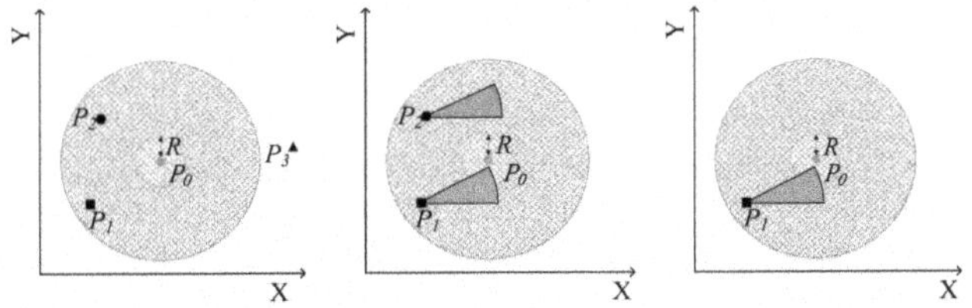

(a) Filtering. (b) Refinement. (c) Final result.

Figure 5: Processing circle query.

With the direction constraint V, the only difference of Algorithm 2 to process direction query from Algorithm 1 is in line 3. This additional condition makes sure that the vector from P_x to P_0 is on the line segment of the specified direction of V (m can be any negative real number). Algorithm 2 also uses filter-refinement steps which are similar to Algorithm 1 (lines 4-9 of using directional information of beginning and ending vectors for overlap checking are same with Algorithm 1). As shown in Figure 4(a), P_3 is firstly disregarded by distance check. Then, P_2 is disregarded by direction check as shown in Figure 4(b). Finally, P_1 is added to the answer set in Figure 4(c).

Algorithm 2 Direction Query

Input:
query point $p_0 :< T_0, P_0, V_{b0}, V_{e0} >$, direction constraint V.
Output:
point set Q_k.
Description:
1: $R_x \leftarrow getDistance(P_0, P_x)$; //compute distance of P_0 and P_x
2: **if** $R_x \leq ||V_{bx}||$ **then**
3: **if** $\overrightarrow{P_xP_0} = m * V$ **then**
4: $< \overrightarrow{P_xP_0}, V_{xb} > \leftarrow getAngle(\overrightarrow{P_xP_0}, V_{xb})$;
5: $< \overrightarrow{P_xP_0}, V_{xe} > \leftarrow getAngle(\overrightarrow{P_xP_0}, V_{xe})$;
6: $< V_{xb}, V_{xe} > \leftarrow getAngle(V_{xb}, V_{xe})$;
7: **if** $| < \overrightarrow{P_xP_0}, V_{xb} > - < \overrightarrow{P_xP_0}, V_{xe} > | = < V_{xb}, V_{xe} >$ **then**
8: Add P_x to Q_k;
9: **end if**
10: **end if**
11: **end if**
12: **return** Q_k;

3.3 Circle Query

DEFINITION 3 (CIRCLE QUERY). *In a two-dimanional coordinate system X-Y, given a query point p_0 with its FOV $p_0 :< T_0, P_0, V_{b0}, V_{e0} >$ and a circle centered at p_0 with radius R, find all points whose field-of-view $p_k :< T_k, P_k, V_{bk}, V_{ek} >$ overlaps the circle.*

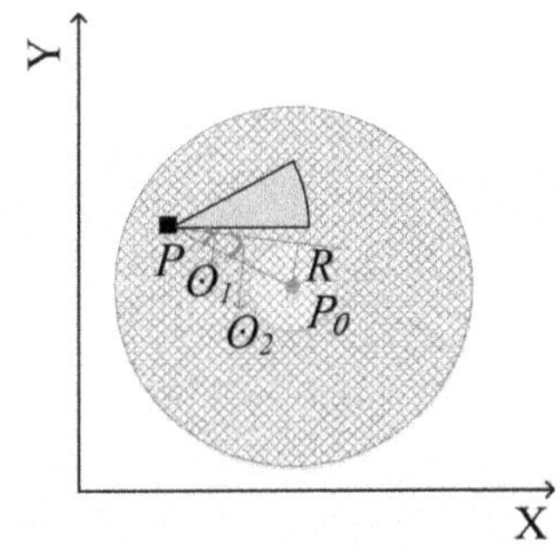

Figure 6: Chamfer angle for circle overlap check.

The rationale of using circle query is due to the fact that most real-life objects (e.g., buildings) have certain spatial extent that may not be appropriately modeled as a point at the center. For instance, when retrieving relevant georeferenced videos of a stadium, some scenes with their FOVs only overlapping with part of the stadium but not covering its geographic center are still needed. Thus, a radius R is introduced to reflect the geographic extent of the query. From Figure 5 we can clearly see that although the FOV of P_1 does not cover the query point, it overlaps the query circle of radius R, and thus should be in the answer set. Algorithm 3 to process circle query is derived from Algorithm 1, but with a different filtering strategy (line 3). After the distance check, we get some candidates. The key point here is to find the points that overlap the query circle. As we can see in Figure 6, the angle between the FOV of P and the circle can be denoted as θ_1, and the chamfer angle between the FOV and the circle can be denoted as θ_2. If $\theta_1 > \theta_2$, the FOV of P does not overlap the circle. Otherwise, it will be returned as an answer. Note that, in line 6 of Algorithm 3, we should also confider another case that the center of the query circle is covered by the FOV (which is equivalent to the case of a point query).

Algorithm 3 Circle Query

Input:
query point $p_0 :< T_0, P_0, V_{b0}, V_{e0} >$, circle radius R.
Output:
point set Q_k.
Description:
1: $R_x \leftarrow getDistance(P_0, P_x)$; //compute distance of P_0 and P_x
2: **if** $R_x + R \leq ||V_{bx}||$ **then**
3: $< \overrightarrow{P_xP_0}, V_{xb} > \leftarrow getAngle(\overrightarrow{P_xP_0}, V_{xb})$;
4: $< \overrightarrow{P_xP_0}, V_{xe} > \leftarrow getAngle(\overrightarrow{P_xP_0}, V_{xe})$;
5: $< V_{xb}, V_{xe} > \leftarrow getAngle(V_{xb}, V_{xe})$;
6: **if** $| < \overrightarrow{P_xP_0}, V_{xb} > - < \overrightarrow{P_xP_0}, V_{xe} > | \neq < V_{xb}, V_{xe} >$ or $\theta_1 \leq \theta_2$ **then**
7: Add P_x to Q_k;
8: **end if**
9: **end if**
10: **return** Q_k;

4. EVALUATION

4.1 Data Collection

The purpose of exploring viewable angle information with the proposed model is to improve the accuracy of georeferenced video search. In our evaluation, we employed the same method described in [1] for experimental data collection: a camera to record videos, a compass to get directions and a GPS to get locations. Note that, as the data collected by sensors may be inaccurate, recently a system

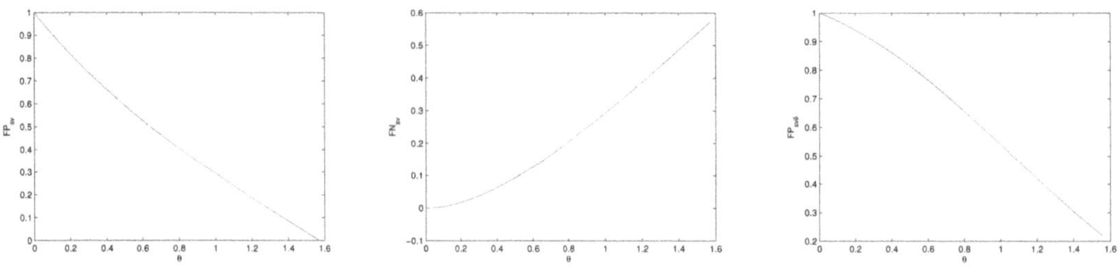

(a) False positive rate. (b) False negative rate. (c) False positive rate with δ.

Figure 7: Query accuracy of single vector model.

Id	$PositionX$	$PositionY$	V_{xb}	V_{yb}	V_{xe}	V_{ye}
115	-24.00	-3.00	9.90	5.40	0.81	11.25
...	...	...	...	...	...	...

Table 1: Database schema for experimental meta-data.

has been introduced for data correction [5]. However, in this work we do not take the incorrectness of data into count but focus on the effect of viewable angle in terms of query accuracy.

We used a mobile phone (Samsung Galaxy Note 3) to collect the test data. The device has a rear lens with 13 million pixels, supporting the UHD 30 fps and FHD 30 fps models to capture image or video streams, and GPS/GLONASS/Beidou for position and direction acquisition. Based on calculation methods in [2] we can get its viewable angle θ is $\pi/3$ (i.e., 60°) and its maximum visible distance is 250m. We created a local database using MySQL to store the experimental meta-data collected. The table includes seven fields as shown in Table 1 (a sample data record is given).

4.2 Results

To compare our proposal with previous model using single vector [3], we measure the following performance indicators: (1) **false positive rate of single vector model** (FP_{SV}); (2) **false negative rate of single vector model** (FN_{SV}); and (3) **false positive rate of single vector model with overestimation constant** ($FP_{SV\delta}$). From Figure 1(b), we can derive through theoretical analysis that:

$$FP_{SV} = \tan\left((\frac{\pi}{2} - \theta)/2\right),$$

$$FN_{SV} = \theta + \tan\left((\frac{\pi}{2} - \theta)/2\right) - 1,$$

$$FP_{SV\delta} = 1 - \frac{\theta}{2\cos\left((\frac{\pi}{2} - \theta)/2\right)}.$$

where θ is the viewable angle. Figure 7 shows analytical results of the above performance indicators with respect to θ, ranging from 0 to $\pi/2$. Most angles of FOVs are between $\pi/4$ to $5\pi/12$ in real-life, so we pay more attention to this range. As we can see, FP_{SV} decreases with the increase of θ. When θ varies from 45° to 75°, FP_{SV} varies from 0.412 to 0.137. FN_{SV} increases with the increasing of θ. When θ varies from 45° to 75°, FN_{SV} varies from 0.1996 to 0.4406. When the overestimation constant δ is taken into account, $FP_{SV\delta}$ varies from 0.6648 to 0.3567 with θ varying from 45° to 75°. All these have verified that viewable angle is a very important factor that should not be neglected. In particular, when δ is used to enlarge the search area, although false negatives no longer appear, false positive rate becomes increasing (we can see that by comparing Figure 7(a) and Figure 7(c)). In contrast, our model theoretically guarantees to achieve accurate georeferenced video search without false positives or false negatives.

We also conducted experiments with the real data collected, in order to test the correct ratio of the answers returned by our approach (by manually inspecting those actual spatial objects). In our experiment evaluation, the correct ratio is at least 89.332% (due to inaccurate sensor information and passible other reasons, accuaccy of our approach is not 100%, but it is already much higher than using single vector model). Meanwhile, our approach has a competitive response time for each kind of queries (point query, direction query and circle query) compared with previous model of [3].

5. CONCLUSIONS AND FUTURE WORK

In this paper, we propose a novel model to transform the video search problem to spatial query. It can effectively fuse all meta information obtained during video recording and can be used to handel different types of overlap queries in georeferenced video search. Through the theoretical analysis, we prove the viewable angle is a very important factor which should not be neglected. Our experiments conducted in a real environment also confirms the proposed model is highly accurate . For future work, we will further investigate query efficiency issue for large scale databases [4], and more meta-data to describe image/video, such as height information in 3D space.

Acknowledgments

This work is supported by the Fundamental Research Funds for the Central Universities of China under grants No.ZYGX2014Z007 and No.ZYGX2014J063.

6. REFERENCES

[1] S. A. Ay, R. Zimmermann, and S. H. Kim. Viewable scene modeling for geospatial video search. In *Proceedings of the 16th International Conference on Multimedia 2008, Vancouver, British Columbia, Canada, October 26-31, 2008*, pages 309–318, 2008.

[2] E. Hecht. *Optics*. Addison-Wesley Publishing Company, 4th edition, 2001.

[3] S. H. Kim, S. A. Ay, B. Yu, and R. Zimmermann. Vector model in support of versatile georeferenced video search. In *Proceedings of the First Annual ACM SIGMM Conference on Multimedia Systems, MMSys 2010, Phoenix, Arizona, USA, February 22-23, 2010*, pages 235–246, 2010.

[4] H. Ma, S. A. Ay, R. Zimmermann, and S. H. Kim. Large-scale geo-tagged video indexing and queries. *GeoInformatica*, 18(4):671–697, 2014.

[5] G. Wang, B. Seo, Y. Yin, R. Zimmermann, and Z. Shen. OSCOR: an orientation sensor data correction system for mobile generated contents. In *ACM Multimedia Conference, MM '13, Barcelona, Spain, October 21-25, 2013*, pages 439–440, 2013.

Topic Hypergraph Hashing for Mobile Image Retrieval

Lei Zhu‡, Jialie Shen‡, Liang Xie§
‡School of Information Systems, Singapore Management University, Singapore
§School of Science, Wuhan University of Technology, Wuhan, 430070, China
leizhu0608@gmail.com, jlshen@smu.edu.sg, whutxl@hotmail.com

ABSTRACT

Hashing is one of the promising techniques to support efficient Mobile Image Retrieval (MIR). However, most of existing hashing strategies simply rely on low-level features, which inevitably makes the generated hashing codes less discriminative. Moreover, many of them fail to exploit complex and high-order semantic correlations between images. Motivated by these observations, we propose a novel unsupervised hashing scheme, called *Topic Hypergraph Hashing* (THH), to address these limitations. A unified topic hypergraph, where images and topics are represented with independent vertices and hyperedges respectively, is first constructed to model latent semantics of images and their correlations. With topic hypergraph model, hashing codes and functions are then learned by simultaneously preserving similarity consistence and semantic correlation. Experiments on standard datasets demonstrate that THH can achieve superior performance compared with several state-of-the-art techniques, and it is more suitable for MIR.

Categories and Subject Descriptors

H.3.1 [**Content Analysis and Indexing**]: Indexing Methods; H.3.3 [**Information Search and Retrieval**]: Search Process

Keywords

Mobile Image Retrieval, High-order Semantic Correlations, Topic Hypergraph Hashing

1. INTRODUCTION

The recent decades have witnessed rapid growth of social image websites (e.g, Flickr[1] and Instagram[2]). As a result, huge amount of images have been uploaded and shared on the Web. On the other hand, with fast popularity of smart mobile devices, Mobile Image Retrieval (MIR) is gaining in importance due to potential applications. The most popular and naive approach to support MIR is text based search, where user needs to input textual information as query. However, it is very time-consuming and less robust. Thus, Content-based Mobile Image Retrieval (CBMIR) [6], where only visual images are uploaded as query example, becomes more popular and convenient retrieval paradigm.

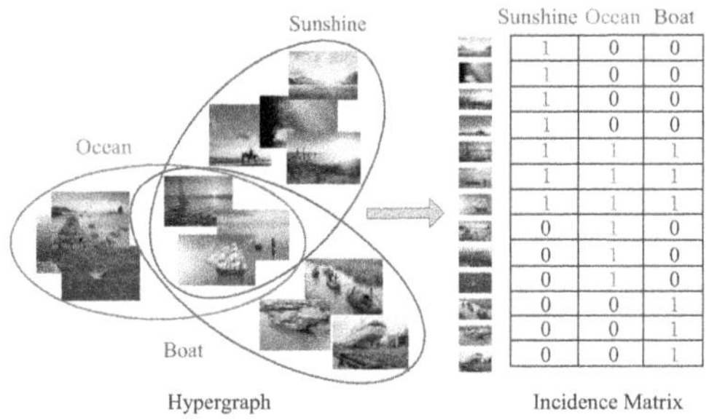

Figure 1: Semantic correlations of images are actually high-order. This study describes them with a unified topic hypergraph and preserves them in hashing codes. The above figure presents a typical topic hypergraph and its corresponding incidence matrix.

Retrieval efficiency is important to real world CBMIR system. To support fast query response, various hashing techniques can be applied as indexing structure [13, 10, 15, 12, 8, 4]. The core idea is to transform raw high-dimensional visual features into compact binary codes, where retrieval process can be conducted with efficient bit operations. Unfortunately, they generally suffer from two major limitations when being directly applied to CBMIR:

- CBMIR is only based on visual queries. Therefore, most hashing schemes rely on only low-level visual features. Due to the semantic gap, they cannot represent the latent semantics of images effectively. On the other hand, it is common that real world Web images (e.g., those from Flickr or Wiki[3]) for CBMIR are accompanied with informative tags or textual descriptions, which can be leveraged to enrich the semantics of hashing codes. Cross-Modal/Media Hashing (CMH) [5, 14, 11] can leverage the associated textual information to assist hashing in visual space and be applied to CBMIR. However, the main aim of CMH is to support accurate retrieval ***across*** image and text. Therefore, CMH generally treats the involved visual and textual information equally, and consequently the semantics of images shared in the common Hamming space are very limited.
- Most existing hashing strategies perform learning on pairwise similarities of images which cannot capture high-order

[1] https://www.flickr.com/
[2] https://instagram.com/
[3] https://www.wikipedia.org/

MM'15, October 26–30, 2015, Brisbane, Australia.
© 2015 ACM. ISBN 978-1-4503-3459-4/15/10 ...$15.00.
DOI: http://dx.doi.org/10.1145/2733373.2806345.

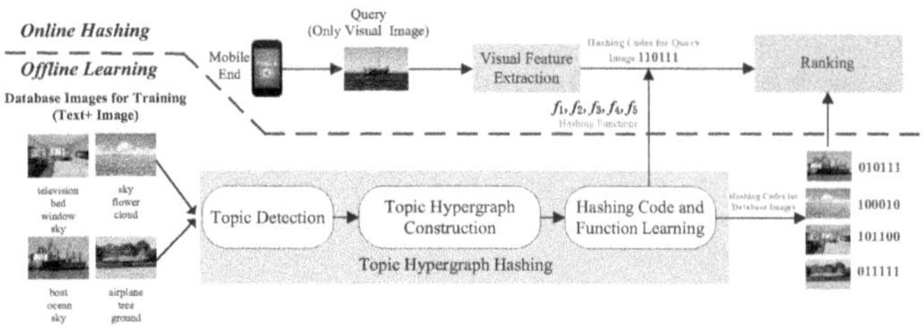

Figure 2: Framework of the THH-based CBMIR system. This figure is best viewed with pdf magnification.

semantic correlations of real world images (as shown in Figure 1). It is common that a single image can represent more than one semantic concept, and images may jointly describe several semantic concepts. On the other hand, even in Hamming space, we can find that correlations of images are high-order, assuming that each hashing bit represents a latent concept. Hence, it is particularly important to learn hashing codes and functions with high-order semantic correlation preserving.

Motivated by the above observations, we propose a novel hashing scheme, *Topic Hypergraph Hashing* (THH), for efficient CBMIR. The core idea of THH is to learn hashing codes with high-order semantic correlation preserving, and simultaneously leverage the associated textual modality to enrich semantics of hashing codes. More specifically, semantic topics describing latent semantics of images are detected by jointly considering visual contents of images and their associated textual descriptions. Then, high-order semantic correlations of images are effectively modelled with a unified topic hypergraph, where images and topics are considered as independent vertices and hyperedges respectively. Finally, hashing learning is conducted to map high-dimensional visual features into compact binary codes, and learn hashing functions for online retrieval. Figure 2 illustrates the main framework of THH-based CBMIR system.

2. TOPIC HYPERGRAPH HASHING

Let $X^m = [x_1^m, x_2^m, ..., x_N^m] \in \mathbb{R}^{d_m \times N}, m = 1, 2$ denote features of database images extracted from visual and textual contents respectively, d_1, d_2 denote the dimension of visual and textual feature, N is the number of database images. Denote hashing codes of database images to be learned as $Z = [z_1, z_2, ..., z_N] \in \mathbb{R}^{L \times N}$, and a group of hashing functions as $\mathbf{F} = \{f_1, f_2, .., f_L\}$, where $z_n = [z_{1n}, z_{2n}, ..., z_{Ln}]^{\mathrm{T}} \in \mathbb{R}^{L \times 1}$ are the hashing codes of the n_{th} image, each hashing function f_l is a mapping: $\mathbb{R}^{d_m} \mapsto \{0, 1\}$, $l = 1, 2, ..., L$, L is the length of the hashing codes.

2.1 Topic Detection

Most database images for CBMIR are augmented with texts, and they jointly describe the same semantic topic. These heterogeneous modalities carry out rich and complementary information [2]. Therefore, it is promising way to leverage auxiliary textual modality to detect topics. Furthermore, since the multimedia data that describe the same semantic topic usually have similar visual and textual distributions, they are naturally from the same semantic clusters. Motivated by these important observations, this study resorts to two-step graph partition to facilitate topic detection.

Step 1. Visual and textual graph are constructed to characterize correlations of images from different viewpoints. Denote $G^m, m = 1, 2$ as two graphs, and $S^m \in \mathbb{R}^{N \times N}, m = 1, 2$ are their corresponding similarity matrices. Formally, the element at i_{th} row and j_{th} column in S^m can be calculated as (α is smoothing factor)

$$S_{ij}^m = \begin{cases} exp\left(-\frac{||x_i^m - x_j^m||^2}{\alpha}\right) & \text{if} x_i^m \in \mathcal{N}_k(x_j^m) \text{ or } x_j^m \in \mathcal{N}_k(x_i^m) \\ 0 & \text{otherwise} \end{cases} \tag{1}$$

where $\mathcal{N}_k(x)$ denotes the set of k nearest neighbor of x.

Step 2. Perform spectral clustering [1] on the fused semantic graph to detect L topics[4]. In this case, database images are transformed as $Y = [y_1, y_2, ..., y_N] \in \mathbb{R}^{L \times N}$. The detected topics are represented as $T = [t_1, t_2, ..., t_L] \in \mathbb{R}^{L \times L}$.

2.2 Topic Hypergraph Construction

Semantic correlations of real world images are complex and high-order. This study models them with a unified topic hypergraph, where images and the detected topics are considered as vertices and hyperedges, respectively. In this way, hyperedges can represent latent semantics, and hypergraph can represent high-order semantic correlations. With topic hypergraph model, an image can represent several semantic topics, and several images jointly describe the same semantic topic. In addition, several images may be included in more than one topic. High-order semantic correlations are naturally represented.

In this study, $THG = (V, E, W)$ denotes topic hypergraph, $V = \{v_n\}_{n=1}^N$ denotes the vertex set, $E = \{e_l\}_{l=1}^L$ denotes the hyperedge set, $W = \{w(e_l)\}_{l=1}^L$ denotes the weight set for hyperedges, $w(e_l)$ is weight of hyperedge e_l. A topic and its q nearest vertices jointly comprise a hyperedge[5]. Topic hypergraph can also be represented with an $L \times N$ incidence matrix H. For example, the incidence value between hyperedge e_l and vertex v_n in H is given as

$$h(e_l, v_n) = \begin{cases} 1 & y_n \in \mathcal{N}_q(t_l) \\ 0 & \text{otherwise} \end{cases} \tag{2}$$

The degree of hyperedge is calculated as the number of images that belong to it. Hence, for hyperedge e_l, its degree $\delta(e_l)$ is

$$\delta(e_l) = \sum_{n=1}^{N} h(e_l, v_n) \tag{3}$$

For simplicity, the weights of hyperedge are all set to 1, $w(e_l) = 1$. The degree of each vertex is defined as the number of hyperedges that the vertex belongs to,

$$d(v_n) = \sum_{n=1}^{N} w(e_l)h(e_l, v_n) = \sum_{n=1}^{N} h(e_l, v_n) \tag{4}$$

Denote $\Delta \in \mathbb{R}^{N \times N}$ as Laplacian matrix of topic hypergraph, which can be calculated as

$$\Delta = I - D_v^{-1/2} H D_w D_e^{-1} H^T D_v^{-1/2} \tag{5}$$

where D_v, D_e, and D_w are the diagonal matrices of the vertex degrees, edge degrees, and hyperedge weights, respectively.

2.3 Hashing Code Learning

By leveraging topic hypergraph, hashing codes and functions are learnt by simultaneously preserving similarity consistence and semantic correlation. Thus, the objective of hashing code learning

[4] In this study, the best performance of THH is achieved when k is set to 8, α is set to 100, weights for visual and textual graph are set to 0.2 and 0.8, respectively, $S_{ij} = 0.2S_{ij}^1 + 0.8S_{ij}^2$

[5] In this study, the best performance of THH is achieved when q is set to 7

should first minimize the average Hamming distances between images, which are included in the same hyperedges. In principle, images belonging to more same hyperedges should be mapped with shorter Hamming distances. Moreover, we should enforce the high-order semantic correlations of images to be preserved in the binary hashing codes. In this study, we explicitly minimize the distances between the rotated incidence matrix and hashing codes. Motivated by the these considerations, the objective function can be formulated as[6]

$$\min_{Z,R} \Omega(Z,R) = \frac{1}{2}\sum_{l=1}^{L}\sum_{i,j=1}^{N} \frac{w(e_l)h(e_l,v_i)h(e_l,v_j)}{\delta(e_l)} \cdot \left(\frac{z_i}{\sqrt{d(v_i)}} - \frac{z_j}{\sqrt{d(v_j)}}\right)^2 + \mu\sum_{l=1}^{L}\sum_{i=1}^{N}\left(\sum_{l'=1}^{L} R_{ll'}h(e_{l'},v_i) - z_{li}\right)^2$$

$$s.t. \quad \sum_{n=1}^{N} z_n = 0, \frac{1}{N}\sum_{n=1}^{N} z_n z_n^{\mathrm{T}} = I, z_n \in \{-1,1\}^L \tag{6}$$

where $\mu > 0$ is the factor that adjusts the balance between two terms, $R \in \mathbb{R}^{L \times L}$ is rotation matrix which aligns incidence values in H to hashing codes in Z, $R_{ll'}$ is the element in the l_{th} row and l'_{th} column in R. The objective function can be represented with following compact form,

$$\min_{Z,R} \Omega(Z,R) = trace(Z\Delta Z^{\mathrm{T}}) + \mu||RH - Z||_F^2 \tag{7}$$

where $||\cdot||_F$ is Frobenius norm, $trace(\cdot)$ is the trace function.

By setting the derivative of Eq.(7) w.r.t R to zero, we can obtain that

$$R = ZH^{\mathrm{T}}(HH^{\mathrm{T}})^{-1} \tag{8}$$

Then, R in Eq.(7) is substituted with $R = ZH^{\mathrm{T}}(HH^{\mathrm{T}})^{-1}$, and the objective function is transformed as

$$\min_{Z} \Omega(Z) = trace(Z\Delta' Z^{\mathrm{T}})$$

$$s.t. \quad \sum_{n=1}^{N} z_n = 0, \frac{1}{N}\sum_{n=1}^{N} z_n z_n^{\mathrm{T}} = I, z_n \in \{-1,1\}^L, \mu > 0 \tag{9}$$

where $\Delta' = \Delta - 2\mu H^{\mathrm{T}}(HH^{\mathrm{T}})^{-1}H$. The above formula can be solved effectively with recently proposed Sequential Projection Learning (SPL) [12].

2.4 Hashing Function Learning

After obtaining hashing codes, we apply linear projection to learn hashing functions. Formally,

$$Z = P^{\mathrm{T}}X^1 \tag{10}$$

where $P \in \mathbb{R}^{d_1 \times L}$ denotes the projection matrix, X^1 denotes the visual features of images. The main objective for learning P is to reduce the loss between the newly generated hashing codes and the projected ones. With this aim, the objective function can be represented as

$$\min_{P} O(P) = \min_{P} ||Z - P^{\mathrm{T}}X^1||_F^2 + \eta||P||_F^2 \tag{11}$$

where $||Z - P^{\mathrm{T}}X^1||^2$ is the loss term, the regulation term $||P||_F$ is used to avoid overfitting, $\eta > 0$ is the factor that balances these two terms (similar to η). Hashing functions can be constructed as

$$\mathbf{F}(x) = \frac{sgn(P^{\mathrm{T}}x - b) + 1}{2}, b = \frac{P^{\mathrm{T}}X^1\mathbf{1}}{N} \tag{12}$$

[6]we substitute 0 in incidence H with -1 in objective function

3. EXPERIMENTS

3.1 Experimental Datasets

In this study, experiments are conducted on two publicly available multi-modal datasets: **Wiki** [9], and **NUS-WIDE** [3], to empirically validate the effectiveness of THH. Each dataset is partitioned into query set, learning set, and database set. Queries are only visual images, and database images are comprised of visual images and textual descriptions. This experimental setting matches the practical retrieval scenario of CBMIR, where queries are visual image and out of database, and are continuously uploaded for querying when time passes by.

- **Wiki** consists of 2,866 multimedia documents in 10 semantic categories. Visual contents and textual contents are represented by 1000-D Bag-of-Visual-Words (BoVW) and 2000-D Bag-of-Words (BoW) respectively. Images are considered to be relevant only if they belong to the same category. 5% images are used as query set and the remaining images are used as training set and database set.

- **NUS-WIDE** is comprised of 269,648 images labelled into 81 concepts. We preserve 10 most common concepts and the corresponding 186,643 pairs. Images are represented by 500-D BoVW. Textual features are 1000-D binary BoW. Images are considered to be relevant if they share at least one concept. 1% images are used as query set, 10000 images are used as training set, and the remaining images are used as database set.

3.2 Evaluation Metrics

In this experimental study, mean Average Precision (mAP) [11] is adopted as the evaluation metric. For a given query, Average Precision (AP) is calculated as

$$AP = \frac{1}{Q}\sum_{r=1}^{NR} Pre(r)\theta(r) \tag{13}$$

where NR is the total number of retrieved images, Q is the number of relevant images in retrieved set, $Pre(r)$ denotes the precision of top r retrieval images, and $\theta(r)$ is indicator function which equals to 1 if the r_{th} image is relevant to query, and vice versa. mAP is defined as the average of the AP of all queries. In experiments, NR is set to 100 to collect experimental results. Furthermore, *Precision-Scope* curve [7] is also reported to reflect the retrieval performance variations with respect to the number of retrieved images.

3.3 Compared Approaches

Since THH is unsupervised, for comparison fairness, we compare THH with several state-of-the-art unsupervised single feature-based hashing and CMH approaches. Single-feature based hashing approaches used for comparison include: SKLSH [8], SPH [13], PCAH [12], LSI [10], STH [15], ITQ [4]. CMH approaches used for evaluation include CVH [5], CHMIS [14], IMH [11]. Note that, parameters of all compared approaches are adjusted to maximize the performance according to the relevant literature.

3.4 Experimental Results

Main results are shown in Figure 3. We can clearly observe from the figure that THH consistently outperforms all the compared approaches on both two datasets. For example, on **NUS-WIDE**, the highest mAP of THH is 51.86%, which is more than 2% better than the second best mAP 49.19% achieved by ITQ on 128 bits. Furthermore, using 16bits, THH can achieve mAP 49.18% which is

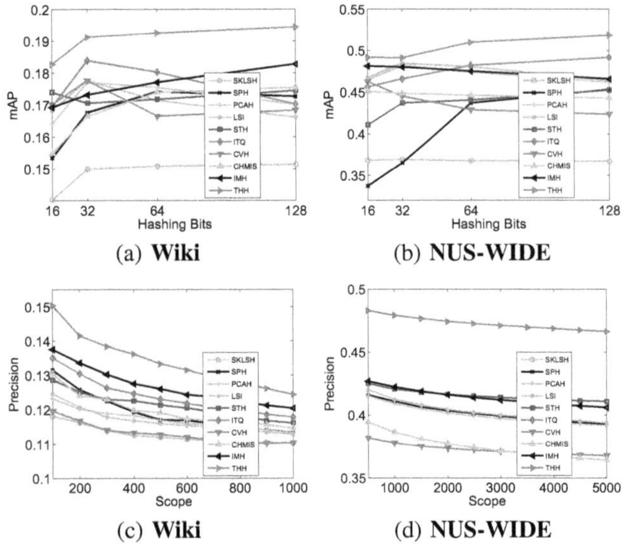

(a) **Wiki** (b) **NUS-WIDE**

(c) **Wiki** (d) **NUS-WIDE**

Figure 3: Performance comparison results. (a) and (b) present mAP variations of all approaches with hashing bits. (d) and (c) present *Precision-Scope* curves of all approaches when code length is fixed on 128 bits.

comparable with 49.19%. Obviously, in this case, THH has faster retrieval speed due to shorter hashing codes. These desirable properties enable THH to become promising retrieval paradigm of CBMIR, where the memory space of mobile and data transmission speed of wireless network is limited.

Besides, we can obtain two insightful observations:

- It is interesting to find that CMH approaches even perform worse than single-feature based hashing in some cases. The reason is that: The aim of CMH is to achieve fast retrieval ***across*** heterogeneous modalities. Therefore, seeking the shared space of heterogeneous modalities is the main formulation objective of CMH. In this way, the discovered common semantic space of heterogeneous modalities in CMH can principally preserve semantic correlations of different modalities. But it may even lose the valuable semantics besides the common part in original visual features. CMH may not be the best suited for CBMIR.
- On **Wiki**, CVH can even achieve even better performance than IMH on several code lengths. It demonstrates that, CVH performs better than IMH on preserving semantic information of original visual feature in process of shared space discovery. More importantly, it shows that performance on cross-modal retrieval obtained by CMH approaches may be not consistent with the performance on CBMIR. The advantages of some CMH approaches on cross-modal retrieval may not be held on CBMIR.

Furthermore, Figure 4 presents performance variations of THH with the parameters μ and η on **Wiki** dataset. μ and η are used in Eq.(6) and Eq.(11) respectively to play trade-off between regularization term and empirical loss. We study performance when μ and η vary from $\{10^{-4}, 10^{-2}, 10^{-1}, 1, 10, 10^2, 10^4\}$. In particular, we fix one parameter and observe the retrieval performance when the other parameter is varied. For μ, performance of THH first increases with μ, and then becomes steady after certain point. For η, performance of THH first increases with η before a certain point,

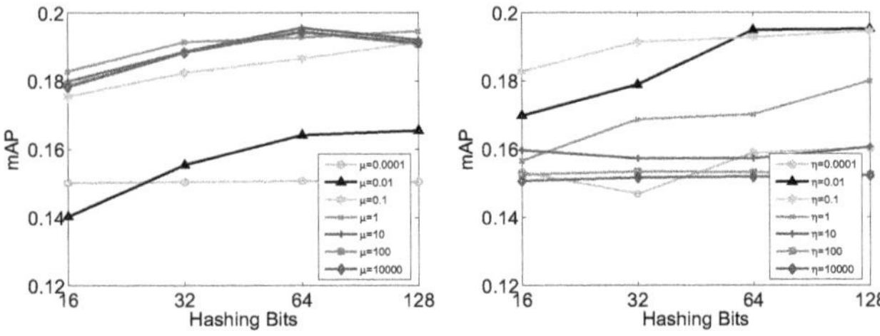

Figure 4: Performance variations of THH with parameters μ and η on Wiki.

and then decreases after that. In this case, the best performance of THH can be achieved when $\mu = 1, \eta = 0.1$.

4. CONCLUSIONS

CBMIR is a practical retrieval paradigm to support convenient MIR. Most database images for CBMIR are associated with informative texts and they are not fully exploited for hashing scheme development yet. In this study, we propose a novel scheme to leverage them to enhance the effectiveness of hashing in visual space. More importantly, we perform hashing learning on a unified topic hypergraph, which makes the learned hashing codes preserve more latent high-order semantic correlations between images. The results gained from experiments on standard datasets demonstrate the promising effectiveness of the proposed approach.

5. ACKNOWLEDGMENTS

Lei Zhu and Jialie Shen are supported by the Singapore Ministry of Education Academic Research Fund Tier 2 (MOE Ref: MOE2013-T2-2-156), and Microsoft Research Faculty Grant (FY14-RES-OPP-048).

6. REFERENCES

[1] F. R. Bach and M. I. Jordan. Learning spectral clustering. In *NIPS*, pages 305–312, 2003.

[2] Z. Cheng, J. Shen, and H. Miao. The effects of multiple query evidences on social image retrieval. *MMSJ*, pages 1–15, 2014.

[3] T.-S. Chua, J. Tang, R. Hong, H. Li, Z. Luo, and Y. Zheng. Nus-wide: A real-world web image database from national university of singapore. In *CIVR*, pages 48:1–48:9, 2009.

[4] Y. Gong, S. Lazebnik, A. Gordo, and F. Perronnin. Iterative quantization: A procrustean approach to learning binary codes for large-scale image retrieval. *TPAMI*, 35(12):2916–2929, 2013.

[5] S. Kumar and R. Udupa. Learning hash functions for cross-view similarity search. In *IJCAI*, pages 1360–1365, 2011.

[6] G. Lan, H. Qi, K. Li, K. Lin, W. Qu, and Z. Li. A framework of mobile visual search based on the weighted matching of dominant descriptor. In *MM*, pages 1181–1184, 2014.

[7] V. A. Nguyen, J. Lu, and M. N. Do. Supervised discriminative hashing for compact binary codes. In *MM*, pages 989–992, 2014.

[8] M. Raginsky and S. Lazebnik. Locality-sensitive binary codes from shift-invariant kernels. In *NIPS*, pages 1509–1517, 2009.

[9] N. Rasiwasia, J. Costa Pereira, E. Coviello, G. Doyle, G. R. Lanckriet, R. Levy, and N. Vasconcelos. A new approach to cross-modal multimedia retrieval. In *MM*, pages 251–260, 2010.

[10] R. Salakhutdinov and G. Hinton. Semantic hashing. *Int. J. Approx. Reasoning*, 50(7):969–978, 2009.

[11] J. Song, Y. Yang, Y. Yang, Z. Huang, and H. T. Shen. Inter-media hashing for large-scale retrieval from heterogeneous data sources. In *SIGMOD*, pages 785–796, 2013.

[12] J. Wang, S. Kumar, and S.-F. Chang. Sequential projection learning for hashing with compact codes. In *ICML*, pages 1127–1134, 2010.

[13] Y. Weiss, A. Torralba, and R. Fergus. Spectral hashing. In *NIPS*, pages 1753–1760, 2008.

[14] D. Zhang, F. Wang, and L. Si. Composite hashing with multiple information sources. In *SIGIR*, pages 225–234, 2011.

[15] D. Zhang, J. Wang, D. Cai, and J. Lu. Self-taught hashing for fast similarity search. In *SIGIR*, pages 18–25, 2010.

Semi-supervised Coupled Dictionary Learning for Cross-modal Retrieval in Internet Images and Texts

Xing Xu
Kyushu University
Fukuoka, Japan
xing@limu.ait.kyushu-u.ac.jp

Yang Yang
University of Electronic Science and Technology of China
Chengdu, China
dlyyang@gmail.com

Atsushi Shimada
Kyushu University
Fukuoka, Japan
atsushi@limu.ait.kyushu-u.ac.jp

Rin-ichiro Taniguchi
Kyushu University
Fukuoka, Japan
rin@kyudai.jp

Li He
Qualcomm R&D Center
San Diego, USA
lih@qti.qualcomm.com

ABSTRACT

Nowadays massive amount of images and texts has been emerging on the Internet, arousing the demand of effective cross-modal retrieval. To eliminate the heterogeneity between the modalities of images and texts, the existing subspace learning methods try to learn a common latent subspace under which cross-modal matching can be performed. However, these methods usually require fully paired samples (images with corresponding texts) and also ignore the class label information along with the paired samples. Indeed, the class label information can reduce the semantic gap between different modalities and explicitly guide the subspace learning procedure. In addition, the large quantities of unpaired samples (images or texts) may provide useful side information to enrich the representations from learned subspace. Thus, in this paper we propose a novel model for cross-modal retrieval problem. It consists of 1) a semi-supervised coupled dictionary learning step to generate homogeneously sparse representations for different modalities based on both paired and unpaired samples; 2) a coupled feature mapping step to project the sparse representations of different modalities into a common subspace defined by class label information to perform cross-modal matching. Experiments on a large scale web image dataset MIRFlickr-1M with both fully paired and unpaired settings show the effectiveness of the proposed model on the cross-modal retrieval task.

Categories and Subject Descriptors

H.3.3 [**Information Storage and Retrieval**]: Information Search and Retrieval

MM'15, October 26–30, 2015, Brisbane, Australia.
 ISBN 978-1-4503-3459-4/15/10 ...$15.00.
DOI: http://dx.doi.org/10.1145/2733373.2806346.

General Terms

Algorithms, Experimentation, Performance

Keywords

Cross-modal Retrieval, Semi-supervised learning, Coupled Dictionary Learning

1. INTRODUCTION

During the last decade, there has been a tremendous volume of multimedia data emerging on the Internet. Usually, the data come from different input channels and are usually paired with one-to-one correspondences. For examples, images are associated with texts, videos contain visual and audio signals. Recently, jointly modeling the Internet images and associated texts has gained much attentions in the multimedia research field [7, 9, 10], resulting in a variety of cross-modal retrieval scenarios: 1) "*Text2Img*": given a text query (document or several words), finding the most related image; 2) "*Img2Text*": given an image query, finding the words or phrases that best describe the image. Indeed, there are several challenges existing in the cross-modal retrieval problem: 1) the images and texts have different representations. For example, images are usually represented using real-valued and dense feature descriptors, whereas texts are represented as discrete sparse word count vectors; 2) the different modalities of visual and textual features cannot be matched directly with each other since they have distinct statistical properties; 3) the high level semantic description of texts and the extracted low level visual descriptors lead to semantic gap between the modalities of images and texts.

To eliminate the diversities between the different modalities, a number of recent approaches that are are concentrated on latent subspace learning have been proposed, such as Canonical Correlation Analysis (CCA) [3] and its extensions [1, 2, 6]. These methods are designed to learn a common subspace, in which the correlations in paired samples can also be well preserved and the projected features of different modalities can be measured directly. However, these methods have two limitations: 1) they do not utilize the class label information (e.g., categories or attributes of im-

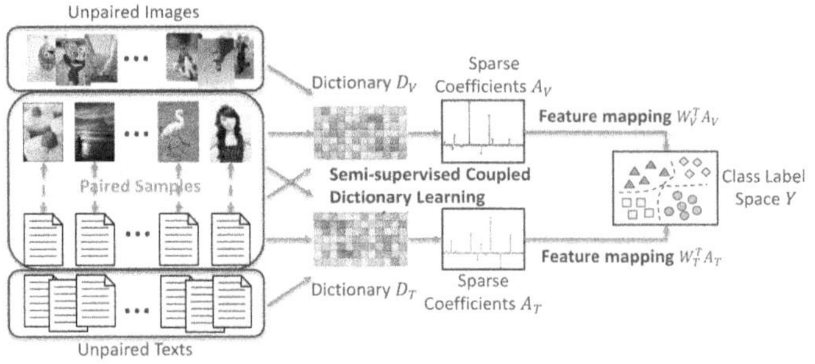

Figure 1: Flowchart of the proposed model.

ages) along with the paired samples; 2) they require fully paired training samples, where a paired sample should consist of an image and its corresponding text. They cannot handle the more common data on the web that are weakly paired or unpaired, such as images with noisy texts or without texts. Indeed, the class label information would be very helpful to explicitly guide the subspace learning and reduce the semantic gap between the modalities of images and texts. And the unpaired samples can provide useful side information and enrich the representations of learned subspace.

In this work, to tackle the limitations of these methods, we propose a novel model for cross-modal retrieval problem. The proposed model, as shown in Fig. 1, consists of two steps: *semi-supervised coupled dictionary learning* and *coupled feature mapping*. In the first step, to deal with paired and unpaired samples simultaneously, we develop a semi-supervised coupled dictionary learning algorithm that transforms the original features of different modalities into homogeneously sparse representations. In the second step, with the class label information, we derive an efficient feature mapping scheme that projects the learned sparse representations of the paired samples into a discriminant subspace defined by class information.

The novelty and advantages of our work include: 1) a practical solution that can efficiently handle paired and unpaired data, as well as the valuable class information; 2) a novel model with different methodology based on semi-supervised coupled dictionary learning and feature mapping schemes, comparing with the most recent works [5] (facilitating blob based image features) and [7] (using deep learning architecture). Experiments on a large scale web image dataset with both fully paired and unpaired settings show the effectiveness of the proposed model.

The rest of the paper is organized as follows. In Section 2, we describe the details of the proposed model. Section 3 reports the experimental results and the conclusion is summarized in Section 4.

2. THE PROPOSED MODEL

Let $\mathbf{Z} = \{\mathbf{Z}^p \cup \mathbf{Z}^u\}$ denote a collection of training samples with features from two different modalities. $\mathbf{Z}^p = \{(\mathbf{v}_i, \mathbf{t}_i)\}|_{i=1}^{N^p}$ contains the paired samples, such as the images and their associated texts, where a paired sample $(\mathbf{v}_i, \mathbf{t}_i)$ consists of d_1 dimensional visual feature $\mathbf{v}_i$ and d_2 dimensional text feature $\mathbf{t}_i$. $\mathbf{V}^p = [\mathbf{v}_1, ..., \mathbf{v}_{N^p}] \in \mathbb{R}^{d_1 \times N^p}$ and $\mathbf{T}^p = [\mathbf{t}_1, ..., \mathbf{t}_{N^p}] \in \mathbb{R}^{d_2 \times N^p}$ are feature matrices of paired images and texts, respectively. $\mathbf{Z}^u = \{(\mathbf{v}_j,)|_{j=1}^{N_v^u} \cup (, \mathbf{t}_k)|_{k=1}^{N_t^u}\}$ is the subset of N^u unpaired samples including N_v^u images without associated texts and N_t^u texts without corresponding images. Similarly, $\mathbf{V}^u \in \mathbb{R}^{d_1 \times N_v^u}$ and $\mathbf{T}^u \in \mathbb{R}^{d_2 \times N_t^u}$ are feature matrix of unpaired images and texts, respectively. Specifically, for the top m paired samples in $\mathbf{Z}^p$ ($m \leq N^p$), besides the one-to-one correspondences of visual and text features, they also have class label information $\{\mathbf{y}_i\}_{i=1}^t$. Here $\mathbf{y}_i \in \{0, 1\}^{c \times 1}$ is a c dimensional binary class indicator vector.

For the cross-modal retrieval problems, our primary goal is to learn a representative latent subspace that can get rid of the heterogeneity between different modalities and incorporate the relationships across modalities, by utilizing both paired and unpaired training samples. In addition, an explicit mapping function is also required to ensure the learned space to be discriminant based on the class information of the paired training samples.

2.1 Semi-supervised Coupled Dictionary Learning

To handle both paired and unpaired samples of two different modalities, we employ sparse representation from dictionary learning for each modality since it has been shown to be very effective in data representation and reconstruction problems. Specifically, we introduce a semi-supervised coupled dictionary learning method that learns two two dictionaries $\mathbf{D}_V \in \mathbb{R}^{d_1 \times k_1}$ and $\mathbf{D}_T \in \mathbb{R}^{d_2 \times k_2}$ of two modalities, and the paired samples are used to carry the relationship between different modalities while the unpaired samples are introduced to exploit the marginal distribution for obtaining robust sparse representations. The proposed method can be formulated to minimize the following objective function

$$E(\mathbf{D}_V, \mathbf{D}_T, \mathbf{A}_V, \mathbf{A}_T) = E^u(\mathbf{D}_V, \mathbf{A}_V^u) + E^u(\mathbf{D}_T, \mathbf{A}_T^u) + E^p(\mathbf{D}_V, \mathbf{D}_T, \mathbf{A}_V^p, \mathbf{A}_T^p), \quad (1)$$

where $\{\mathbf{A}_V^p, \mathbf{A}_T^p\}$ and $\{\mathbf{A}_V^u, \mathbf{A}_T^u\}$ are the sparse coefficients for paired and unpaired samples of two modalities, respectively. Specifically, to guarantee that the sparse representations of the two modalities well reconstruct the unpaired samples, in Eq. 1 we have

$$E^u(\mathbf{D}_V, \mathbf{A}_V^u) = \|\mathbf{V}^u - \mathbf{D}_V \mathbf{A}_V^u\|_F^2 + \sigma_V^u \|\mathbf{A}_V^u\|_1, \quad (2)$$

$$E^u(\mathbf{D}_T, \mathbf{A}_T^u) = \|\mathbf{T}^u - \mathbf{D}_T \mathbf{A}_T^u\|_F^2 + \sigma_T^u \|\mathbf{A}_T^u\|_1, \quad (3)$$

which are standard form of sparse coding. And the useful information in unpaired samples can be reflected in the dictionaries of the two modalities. Furthermore, to ensure the dictionaries of two modalities to be coupled, we impose a function $f(\mathbf{A}_V^p, \mathbf{A}_T^p)$ to relate the sparse representations of two modalities of the paired samples. Then for the paired samples, in Eq. 1, we have

$$E^p(\mathbf{D}_V, \mathbf{D}_T, \mathbf{A}_V^p, \mathbf{A}_T^p) = \|\mathbf{V}^p - \mathbf{D}_V \mathbf{A}_V^p\|_F^2 + \|\mathbf{T}^p - \mathbf{D}_T \mathbf{A}_T^p\|_F^2 + \sigma^p(\|\mathbf{A}_V^p\|_1 + \|\mathbf{A}_T^p\|_1) + f(\mathbf{A}_V^p, \mathbf{A}_T^p), \quad (4)$$
$$s.t. \quad \|\mathbf{d}_{v,i}\|_2 \leq 1, \|\mathbf{d}_{t,i}\|_2 \leq 1, \forall i.$$

Inspired by [4], we introduce a k_c dimensional common feature space $\mathcal{P}$ for $f(\mathbf{A}_V^p, \mathbf{A}_T^p)$ so that each pair of samples from $\mathbf{A}_V^p$ and $\mathbf{A}_T^p$ can be transformed to the points of $\mathbf{P}_T$ and $\mathbf{P}_V$ in space $\mathcal{P}$ mutually. Here we restrict $k_c = k_1 = k_2$ so that different modalities of data are comparable in $\mathcal{P}$.

The formulation of $f(\mathbf{A}_V^p, \mathbf{A}_T^p)$ is derived as

$$f(\mathbf{A}_V^p, \mathbf{A}_T^p) = \gamma(\|\mathbf{A}_V^p - \mathbf{U}_V^{-1}\mathbf{P}_T\|_F^2 + \|\mathbf{A}_T^p - \mathbf{U}_T^{-1}\mathbf{P}_V\|_F^2) + \mu(\|\mathbf{U}_V^{-1}\|_F^2 + \|\mathbf{U}_T^{-1}\|_F^2), \quad (5)$$

where $\mathbf{U}_V \in \mathbb{R}^{k_c \times k_1}$ and $\mathbf{U}_T \in \mathbb{R}^{k_c \times k_2}$ are the transform matrices for two modalities. The regularized constraints on $\mathbf{U}_V$ and $\mathbf{U}_T$ ensure numerical stability and avoid overfitting. It can be learned that the constraints in Eq. 5 shows the ability of recovering the sparse representations in one modality using data from the other, hence the relationship across different modalities can be efficiently incorporated in the sparse representations.

2.2 Coupled Feature Mapping

Let $\mathbf{Y} = [\mathbf{y}_1, \mathbf{y}_2, ..., \mathbf{y}_n] \in \mathbb{R}^{c \times m}$ be the class label matrix of the paired samples $\{(\mathbf{v}_i, \mathbf{t}_i)\}|_{i=1}^m$. The coupled feature mapping aims to learn two projection matrices $\mathbf{W}_V \in \mathbb{R}^{k_1 \times c}$ and $\mathbf{W}_T \in \mathbb{R}^{k_2 \times c}$, which map the sparse representations $\mathbf{A}_{v_i}^p|_{i=1}^m$ and $\mathbf{A}_{t_i}^p|_{i=1}^m$ of the two modalities for the paired samples into the common subspace defined by class labels.

In order to minimize the errors of projecting the sparse representations of each modality to the label space, besides the basic ridge regression form, we also employ the coupled feature selection scheme proposed in [8], to select relevant and discriminative features from the sparse representations and to enhance the relevance across different modalities. The objective function of the coupled feature mapping procedure can be derived as

$$\min_{\mathbf{W}_V, \mathbf{W}_T} \frac{1}{2}(\|\mathbf{W}_V^\top \mathbf{A}_V^p - \mathbf{Y}\|_F^2 + \|\mathbf{W}_T^\top \mathbf{A}_T^p - \mathbf{Y}\|_F^2) \quad (6)$$
$$+ \lambda_1(\|\mathbf{W}_V\|_{21} + \|\mathbf{W}_T\|_{21}) + \lambda_2\|[\mathbf{W}_V^\top \mathbf{A}_V^p \mathbf{W}_T^\top \mathbf{A}_T^p]\|_*,$$

where the L_{21} norm $\|\cdot\|_{21}$ is used to select features from coupled feature space jointly, the trace norm $\|\cdot\|_*$ encodes the correlations of different modalities with a low-rank constraint. Note that Eq. 6 differs from [8] in that coupled feature selection is performed on sparse representations $\mathbf{A}_V^p$ and $\mathbf{A}_T^p$ to leverage the merit from coupled dictionary learning, rather than on the original features in [8].

2.3 Solution

The objective function in Eq. 1 is convex with each of the variables of dictionaries $\{\mathbf{D}_V, \mathbf{D}_T\}$, sparse representations $\{\mathbf{A}_V, \mathbf{A}_T\}$ and transform matrices $\{\mathbf{U}_V, \mathbf{U}_T\}$ when fixing the other variables. They can be iteratively updated in an alternating manner. Similar as in [4], We utilize the sparse modeling software SPAMS[1] to efficiently implement the optimization algorithm. In addition, we use the iterative algorithm developed in [8] to optimize Eq. 6.

In the testing phase, given a paired sample $(\hat{\mathbf{v}}, \hat{\mathbf{t}})$, we first generate the sparse representations $\hat{\mathbf{A}}_{\hat{v}}$ and $\hat{\mathbf{A}}_{\hat{t}}$ based on learned dictionaries $\mathbf{D}_V$ and $\mathbf{D}_T$, respectively. Then we can project $\hat{\mathbf{A}}_{\hat{v}}$ and $\hat{\mathbf{A}}_{\hat{t}}$ into the class label space through the learned projection matrices $\mathbf{W}_V$ and $\mathbf{W}_T$, respectively. To perform cross-modal retrieval, we take a sample of one modal data (i.e., an image) as the query to retrieval the other modality of it (i.e., the texts). Even if an unpaired sample with one missing modality is given, we can still reconstruct its missing modality using the similar pipeline.

[1]http://spams-devel.gforge.inria.fr/

3. EXPERIMENTS

We evaluate the effectiveness of the proposed model on a large scale web image dataset MIRFlickr-1M. This dataset consists of one million web images retrieved from Flickr website along with their user assigned tags. Among the 1 million images, a subset of 25K images have been manually annotated with 38 class labels such as object and scene categories, where each image may belong to several classes. The remaining subset of 975K images have no class labels. For the feature representation of image and text, we use the features extracted in [7]. Specifically, each image is represented by 3,857 dimensional features by concatenating SIFT, Gist and MPEG-7 descriptors. Each text input is represented using a vocabulary of the 2,000 most frequent tags in the 1 million collection, and the average number of tags associated with an image is 5. Since there are 128,501 images which do not have any tags, thus in our experiment the number of paired and unpaired samples are $N^p = 871,499$ and $N_v^u = 128,501$, respectively. For the evaluation, the standard metric of mean average precision (MAP) is used for the cross-modal retrieval: Img2Text and Text2Img tasks. Besides, we also evaluate our model on classification task for the paired samples with class labels and the results are reported using MAP of samples and top-50 predictions (Prec@50) for multi-label classification. Note that for all the metrics, larger numerical value indicates better performance. In the training stage, we empirically set the parameters σ, γ, μ and dictionary size to 0.01, 0.0001, 0.001, 350 for the semi-supervised coupled dictionary learning procedure; and the parameters λ_1 and λ_2 to 0.1 and 0.001 for the coupled feature mapping procedure, respectively. In testing phase, the cosine distance is adopt as similarity measure to select the best matches.

3.1 Results on Fully Paired Setting

We first evaluate the proposed model on fully paired setting. Specifically, we use the subset of the 25K paired samples with class labels and randomly allocate 10K, 5K, 10K images for training, validation and testing, respectively. And we report the averaged results over five random splits of the 25K paired samples. Three typical subspace learning methods of Kernel CCA (KCCA) [1], MultiView CCA (MCCA) [2] and LCFS [8] are compared with the proposed semi-supervised dictionary learning scheme. Then a baseline using ridge regression (RR), two recent works of LGCFL [5] and DBM [7] are compared with the proposed model. We implement the KCCA and LGCFL algorithm according to the instructions in the corresponding papers and refer to the code of the other methods from the authors' websites.

Task	Cross-modal retrieval		Classification	
Method	Img2Text	Text2Img	MAP	Prec@50
KCCA [1]	0.579	0.589	-	-
MCCA [2]	0.557	0.551	-	-
RR	-	-	0.432	0.712
LCFS [8]	0.533	0.546	0.449	0.762
LGCFL [5]	0.596	0.599	0.504	0.811
DBM [7]	0.600	0.607	0.526	0.791
Proposed	0.612	0.624	0.532	0.824

Table 1: Overall results on the subset of 25K paired samples under fully paired setting.

Table 1 shows the overall performance of these methods on cross-modal retrieval task and classification task. On the cross-modal task, the proposed model achieves higher MAP scores than the subspace learning methods of KCCA, MCCA and LCFS, showing the effectiveness of the coupled dictionary learning scheme in the proposed model on learning representative subspace. In addition, the proposed model also outperforms the two recent works of LGCFL and DBM, indicating that the learned sparse representations in the proposed model is effective and reliable to get rid of the diversity between different modalities on the paired setting. On the classification task, the propose model performs much better than the baseline of RR that only uses image modality to learn model, showing that combining both image and text modalities improves the accuracy of classification task than using single image modality. Moreover, the proposed model achieves the best performance comparing with the other methods, indicating that with small number of paired training samples, the proposed model is able to enhance the relationship across different modalities by leveraging the useful class label information.

3.2 Results on Partially Paired Setting

We then evaluate the proposed model on partially paired setting, with the training samples containing both paired samples and unpaired samples. We consider the subset of 25K paired samples with class labels as the start point, and gradually add the remaining paired and unpaired samples for training until covering the entire 1 million samples. We still report the evaluation results on the 25K subset. The proposed model is compared with the LGCFL and DBM methods that can also handle partially paired setting. Specifically, for the LGCFL method we first use the model trained on the 25K subset to predict class labels for the remaining samples, and then conduct experiment on the entire dataset of 1 million samples with partially paired setting.

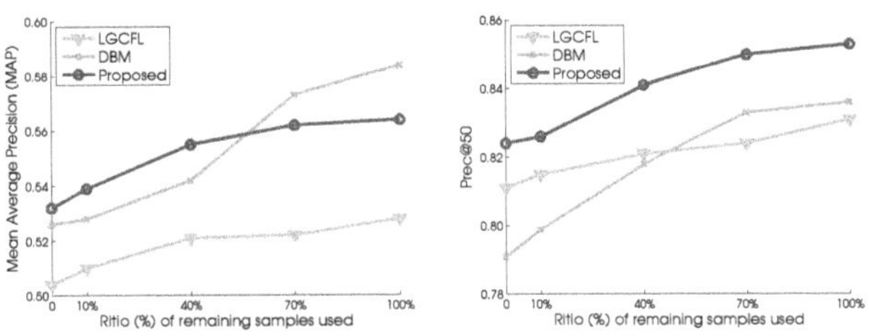

(a) MAP (b) Prec@50

Figure 2: Effects of using different ratio of remaining samples on classification task.

Fig. 2 shows the MAP and Prec@50 scores on classification task with different ratio of remaining samples added gradually, from 10% to 100%. We can observe that for all three methods further improvements can be made by using more additional data. In particular, for the proposed model, the performance consistently increases when more samples are added. The reason is that the semi-supervised learning manner can incorporate the unimodal data of unpaired samples in the coupled dictionary learning step, which enhances to obtain robust sparse representations for both modalities. The proposed model performs better than the LGCFL method and it is more robust to tackle heterogeneous feature representations of different modalities, whereas the LGCFL method is elaborately designed for blob based image features and requires class label information even for unpaired samples. Moreover, the proposed model obtains comparable result with the DBM method, which uses deep Boltzmann machine to learn joint space of image and text modalities. Compared with the sophisticated deep architecture in DBM, the proposed model is simpler and promising to cope with large scale data and to obtain competitive performance under the partially paired setting. Table 2 depicts the overall

Task	Cross-modal retrieval		Classification	
Method	Img2Text	Text2Img	MAP	Prec@50
LGCFL [5]	0.598	0.601	0.528	0.831
DBM [7]	0.602	0.611	0.584	0.836
Proposed	0.619	0.631	0.564	0.853
Proposed (CNN)	0.640	0.652	0.678	0.884

Table 2: Overall results on entire collection of 1 million samples under partially paired setting.

results of the three method on the entire collection of 1 million samples under partially paired setting. And we can obtain similar observation from Table 2 that the proposed model performs comparable with the two recent works and further benefits from using features extracted from the popular VGG Net of deep convolutional neural network.

4. CONCLUSION

In this paper, we propose a novel model solving the practical cross-modal retrieval problem. To handle both paired and unpaired samples simultaneously, we propose a semi-supervised coupled dictionary learning scheme to generate homogeneously sparse representations for different modalities. We then use coupled feature mapping scheme to project the sparse representations of different modalities into the class label space for cross-modal matching. Experiments on a large scale web image dataset with both fully paired and unpaired settings show the effectiveness of our proposal.

Acknowledgements

This research has been partly supported by Grant-in-Aid for Scientific Research (B), Grant Number 24300074.

5. REFERENCES

[1] L. Ballan, T. Uricchio, L. Seidenari, and A. Bimbo. A cross media model for automatic image annotation. In *ICMR*, 2014.

[2] Y. Gong, Q. Ke, M. Isard, and S. Lazebnik. A multi-view embedding space for modeling internet images, tags, and their semantics. *IJCV*, 106:210–233, 2014.

[3] D. R. Hardoon, S. R. Szedmak, and J. R. Shawe-taylor. Canonical correlation analysis: An overview with application to learning methods. *Neural Comput.*, 16(12):2639–2664, 2004.

[4] D. Huang and Y. Wang. Coupled dictionary and feature space learning with applications to cross-domain image synthesis and recognition. In *ICCV*, pages 2496–2503, 2013.

[5] C. Kang, S. Xiang, S. Liao, C. Xu, and C. Pan. Learning consistent feature representation for cross-modal multimedia retrieval. *TMM*, 17(3):370–381, 2015.

[6] N. Rasiwasia, J. Costa Pereira, E. Coviello, G. Doyle, G. Lanckriet, R. Levy, and N. Vasconcelos. A new approach to cross-modal multimedia retrieval. In *ACM MM*, 2010.

[7] N. Srivastava and R. Salakhutdinov. Multimodal learning with deep boltzmann machines. *JMLR*, 15:2949–2980, 2014.

[8] K. Wang, R. He, W. Wang, L. Wang, and T. Tan. Learning coupled feature spaces for cross-modal matching. In *ICCV*, pages 2088–2095, 2013.

[9] Y. Yang, Y. Yang, and H. T. Shen. Effective transfer tagging from image to video. *ACM Trans. Multimedia Comput. Commun. Appl.*, 9(2):1–20, 2013.

[10] Y. Yang, Z.-J. Zha, Y. Gao, X. Zhu, and T.-S. Chua. Exploiting web images for semantic video indexing via robust sample-specific loss. *TMM*, 17(2):246–256, 2015.

Vocabulary Expansion Using Word Vectors for Video Semantic Indexing *

Nakamasa Inoue
Tokyo Institute of Technology, Tokyo, Japan
inoue@ks.cs.titech.ac.jp

Koichi Shinoda
Tokyo Institute of Technology, Tokyo, Japan
shinoda@cs.titech.ac.jp

ABSTRACT

We propose vocabulary expansion for video semantic indexing. From many semantic concept detectors obtained by using training data, we make detectors for concepts not included in training data. First, we introduce Mikolov's word vectors to represent a word by a low-dimensional vector. Second, we represent a new concept by a weighted sum of concepts in training data in the word vector space. Finally, we use the same weighting coefficients for combining detectors to make a new detector. In our experiments, we evaluate our methods on the TRECVID Video Semantic Indexing (SIN) Task. We train our models with Google News text documents and ImageNET images to generate new semantic detectors for SIN task. We show that our method performs as well as SVMs trained with 100 TRECVID example videos.

Categories and Subject Descriptors

I.4 [**Computing Methodologies**]: Image Processing and Computer Vision; I.4.9 [**Applications**]: Multimedia Search and Recommendation

Keywords

Semantic Indexing; Video Search; Word Vectors; Deep Learning

1. INTRODUCTION

A large amount of video data has made been available on the Internet with advances in information and communication technologies. Semantic indexing is one of the most important techniques in multimedia applications including video search, surveillance and robot vision. Here, semantic indexing is the process to detect semantic concepts of objects, events, and scenes, e.g., *Bus*, *Airplane*, *Dancing*, and *Landscape*. Since the diversity of semantic concepts is very large, it has been a challenging task to bridge the semantic gap between low-level features and high-level semantics.

Most previous studies have focused on supervised learning methods such as support vector machines (SVMs) with Fisher vectors [1], and deep convolutional neural networks (CNNs) [2]. The Fisher vectors extend bag-of-visual-words [10] to a probabilistic framework by introducing Gaussian mixture models. SVMs are often trained for each semantic concept with them. Deep CNNs [2] typically have more than five layers for convolution and pooling, in which the input is a raw image and the output is a set of detection scores for each semantic concept. With most of these approaches, training images are required to be manually annotated. For example, to train a CNN for detecting object categories, several thousands of training images or videos are needed for each category.

Several methods use text data appeared with each image/video to decrease such annotation costs. For example, Joint embedding [3, 4] estimates a concept category from the text data appearing with their images at the same time, for example, on the same web page. But such a co-occurrence based approach cannot be used to detect an unseen concept in training data, i.e., a concept whose corresponding text data are not available in the training phase.

In natural language processing, word embedding methods have shown to be effective to capture semantic relationships between words. Their typical applications include machine translation [5], and web-document classification [6]. For example, word-vector representation proposed by Mikolov et. al [7] represents a word by a low-dimensional vector. They reported that the distance between semantically similar words tends to be smaller in the word vector space. Its interesting property is that semantic regularities are captured with vector operations for addition and subtraction. For example, a result of $\phi(\text{King}) - \phi(\text{Man}) + \phi(\text{Woman})$ is close to $\phi(\text{Queen})$ where $\phi(w)$ is a word vector of a word w. This may be also helpful to explore the relationship between semantic concepts in video.

In this paper, we propose a vocabulary expansion method based on word vectors for semantic indexing. From pre-trained semantic-concept detectors, we make detectors for out-of-vocabulary concepts, i.e., concepts not included in training data, by using word vectors. To the best of our knowledge, applying word vectors to vocabulary expansion for video semantic indexing is novel. By introducing word vectors, we expect that our framework provides general semantic concept detectors, which are effective for detecting

*(Produces the permission block, and copyright information). For use with SIG-ALTERNATE.CLS. Supported by ACM.

MM'15, October 26–30, 2015, Brisbane, Australia.

ACM 978-1-4503-3459-4/15/10 ...$15.00.
DOI: http://dx.doi.org/10.1145/2733373.2806347 .

various semantic concepts in Internet videos. In our experiments, our method is evaluated on the TRECVID Video Semantic Indexing Task [9]. We train our model without TRECVID data by using the Google News documents [7] and the ImageNET [8] dataset and show that our method performs as well as SVMs trained with 100 example videos for each TRECVID semantic concept with Fisher-vector representation.

The rest of this paper is organized as follows. Section 2 presents the proposed framework. Section 3 shows experimental evaluations, and Section 4 describes conclusion and future work.

2. PROPOSED METHOD

Let x be a video and $\mathcal{W}$ be a set of words. We assume the word vectors $\phi(w) \in \mathbb{R}^d$ for all the words in $\mathcal{W}$ are obtained by introducing a word embedding method (e.g.,[7]). Our goal is to build visual concept detectors for each word.

The easiest way is to train detectors $f_w(x)$ (e.g., SVMs) for each $w \in \mathcal{W}$. However, this is not always a reasonable solution for real applications such as video search allowing users to enter any query words since the size of $\mathcal{W}$ is often large. To solve this problem, we build a detector for $w \notin \mathcal{C}$ from pre-trained detectors by using word vectors, where we assume pre-trained detectors for a subset $\mathcal{C} \subset \mathcal{W}$ are given.

We first approximate a word vector for $w \notin \mathcal{C}$ with the word vectors for words in $\mathcal{C}$ by

$$\bar{\phi}(w) = \sum_{i=1}^{N} \alpha_i \phi(w_i), \tag{1}$$

where $\bar{\phi}(w)$ is an approximation of a word vector $\phi(w)$, N is the number of words in $\mathcal{C}$, w_i is the i-th word in $\mathcal{C}$, and α_i is a weighting coefficient. We then use the same weighting coefficients for making a detector by

$$f_w(x) = \sum_{i=1}^{N} \alpha_i f_{w_i}(x). \tag{2}$$

Here we assume that those concepts (words) semantically similar to each other have similar visual features.

The following subsections present three methods using 1) vector quantization (VQ), 2) k-nearest neighbor search (KNN), and 3) Gaussian mixture models (GMMs), to determine the weighting coefficients in Eq. (1).

2.1 Vector Quantization

Approximating a word by the most similar word by applying vector quantization to word vectors is the simplest way to obtain the weighting coefficients. α_i is given by

$$\alpha_i = \begin{cases} 1 & \text{if } i = \operatorname*{argmin}_i d(\phi(w), \phi(w_i)) \\ 0 & \text{otherwise} \end{cases}, \tag{3}$$

where $d(\cdot,\cdot)$ is the distance between two word vectors. For example, cosine distance between word vectors [7] can be introduced to here.

2.2 k-Nearest Neighbor Search

The k-nearest neighbor (KNN) search, which provides k similar words, is an extension of VQ to assign more than one similar words to a given word. With KNN, we set the weighting coefficients as

$$\alpha_i = \begin{cases} \frac{1}{k} & \text{if } i \in \mathrm{KNN}(w) \\ 0 & \text{otherwise} \end{cases}, \tag{4}$$

where $\mathrm{KNN}(w)$ is a set of k nearest words of w based on the distance measure $d(\cdot,\cdot)$ in Sec. 2.1.

2.3 Gaussian Mixture Models

Gaussian mixture models (GMMs) capture variance information for each pre-defined words and provide soft weighting for α_i as

$$\alpha_i = \frac{\pi_i \mathcal{N}(\phi(w)|\phi(w_i), \Sigma_i)}{\sum_{i=1}^{N} \pi_i \mathcal{N}(\phi(w)|\phi(w_i), \Sigma_i)}, \tag{5}$$

where $\phi(w)$ is a word vector, π_i is a mixture coefficient, and $\mathcal{N}(\cdot|\phi(w_i), \Sigma_i)$ is a pdf of Gaussian distribution with a mean vector $\phi(w_i)$ and a covariance matrix Σ_i for the i-th mixture component. Note that the word vectors for pre-determined words are used as mean vectors.

To estimate the covariance matrixes and the mixture coefficients from the set of word vectors for $\mathcal{W}$, we use the Expectation Maximization (EM) algorithm. Note that $\mathcal{W}$ includes words $w \notin \mathcal{C}$. In the M-step, the parameters are updated by

$$\pi_i = \frac{1}{|\mathcal{W}|} \sum_{w \in \mathcal{W}} c_{iw}, \tag{6}$$

$$\Sigma_i = \frac{1}{\sum_{w \in \mathcal{W}} c_{iw}} \sum_{w \in \mathcal{W}} c_{iw} (\phi(w) - \phi(w_i))(\phi(w) - \phi(w_i))^T \tag{7}$$

where c_{iw} is a *responsibility* of w to the i-th mixture component. The responsibilities are computed in the E-step as

$$c_{iw} = \frac{\pi_i \mathcal{N}(\phi(w)|\phi(w_i), \Sigma_i)}{\sum_{i=1}^{N} \pi_i \mathcal{N}(\phi(w)|\phi(w_i), \Sigma_i)}. \tag{8}$$

For the initialization values, we use $\pi_i = \frac{1}{N}$ and $\Sigma_i = I$ where I is the identity matrix.

2.4 Extension to a Set of Words

To further extend the discriminative function f to accept a set of words e.g., Airplane+Flying, we simply make the average vector as follows. Let $s = \{w^t\}_{t=1}^{T}$ be a set of word vectors. The average vector $\phi(s)$ is given by

$$\phi(s) = \sum_{t=1}^{T} \phi(w^t). \tag{9}$$

By approximating this vector in the same way as Eq. (1), the three methods presented in Sec. 2.1 to 2.3 are applied in the same way to build a detector for s.

3. EXPERIMENTS

3.1 Experimental Setup

We evaluate our method on the TRECVID 2010 Semantic Indexing dataset, which consists of 11,556 Internet video clips with creative commons licenses. Each video clip is divided into video shots based on the switching of a camera. Shot boundaries and a key-frame for each shot are provided with the dataset. The total number of video shots is 264,673, which is divided into 119,685 for training and 144,988 for testing. Only the key-frame images of the testing set are used to evaluate our methods.

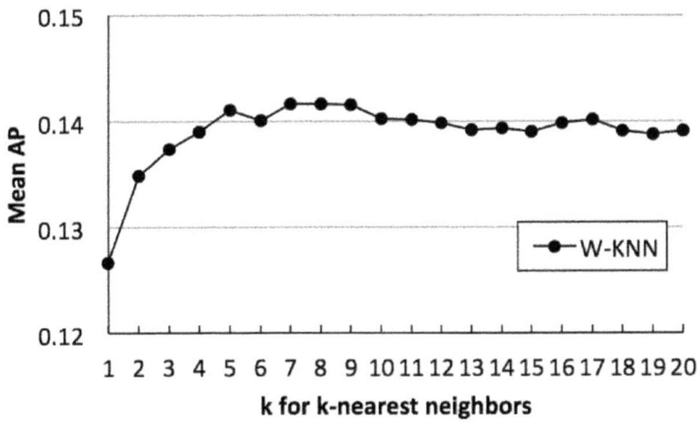

Figure 1: Evaluation using different k for k-nearest neighbor search.

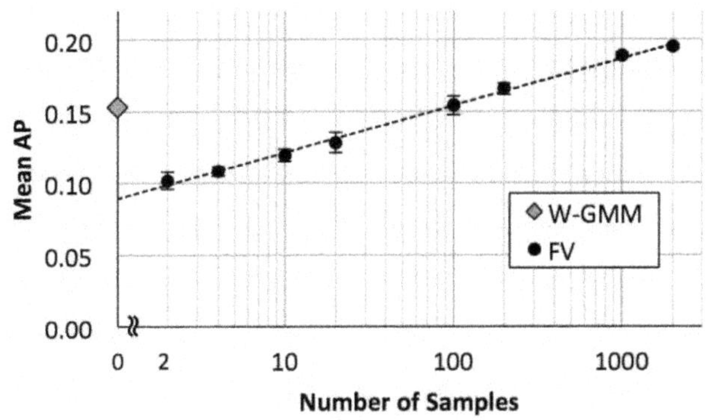

Figure 2: Comparison with Fisher vectors using different numbers of training samples.

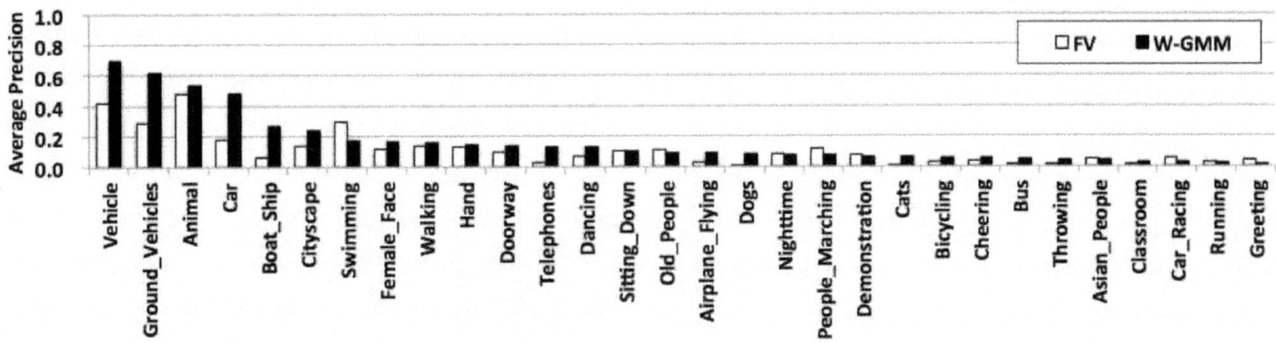

Figure 3: Average Precision (AP) by semantic concepts. AP for randomly sampled 30 of 346 semantic concepts are reported. FV: Fisher vectors of dense SIFT features. SVMs are trained on randomly sampled two examples, one for positive and one for negative. W-GMM: our word-based model using a GMM (Sec 2.3).

Table 1: Mean AP on TRECVID by methods. W-VQ, W-KNN, W-GMM: our word-vector based methods presented in Sec. 2, Fisher Vector: SVMs trained on one positive and one negative samples with Fisher vectors.

Method	Mean AP
W-VQ	0.127
W-KNN ($k = 10$)	0.140
W-GMM	**0.153**
Fisher Vector (one example) [1]	0.101

The task is to detect 346 semantic concepts including objects, events, and scenes, e.g., Boat, AirplaneFlying, Dancing, Walking, Basketball and Cityscape, from video shots. For semantic concepts presented by more than one word, we apply the method in Sec. 2.4. The evaluation measure is Mean Average Precision (Mean AP) over the 346 semantic concepts [1].

For the pre-trained concept detectors in Sec. 2, a CNN trained with 1,000 objects in the ImageNET Challenge 2012 [8] is used with the Caffe implementation [15]. Note that semantic concepts on TRECVID and the objects on ImageNET are exclusive. For the distance measure between words, cosine distance between 300-dimension word representations in [7] is used. This measure is trained on the Google News dataset, which has 100 billion words with 3 million synsets. We use the word2vec implementation [7]. We compare our methods with a baseline using SVMs with Fisher vectors (FV) trained for each 346 semantic concepts trained by using annotations provided in the TRECVID dataset. We follow the FV extraction process with dense SIFT features in [1].

[1]We use annotations provided in TRECVID 2014 to compute average precision, since the official annotations in 2010 only has 30 semantic concepts.

3.2 Experimental Results

Main Results

Table 1 compares Mean AP for word-based vector quantization (W-VQ), k-nearest neighbor search (W-KNN), and the Gaussian mixture model (W-GMM). We see that W-GMM outperforms the others. This shows that soft weighting in a GMM is effective for representing a semantic concepts by pre-determined objects.

For the parameter k in W-KNN, $k \geq 5$ is reasonable as shown in Figure 1. However, W-GMM is better than the best result of W-KNN using different k. This shows the effectiveness of probabilistic estimation of word distribution presented in Sec. 2.3.

Comparison with Fisher Vector

Comparison with Fisher Vector (FV) representation [1] is shown in Table 1. With FV, SVMs are trained for each semantic concept in TRECVID with randomly sampled two examples, one for positive and one for negative. The Mean AP shown in the table is the average value of ten repeated experiments. We see that the FV performs worse than our methods. This is because the number of training samples is not enough to train SVMs.

In Figure 2, the number of training samples for FV is increased from 2 to 2,000. The result of W-GMM is also plotted on the figure. We conclude that W-GMM, which uses no examples from TRECVID, performs as well as SVMs trained with 100 example videos for each TRECVID semantic concept.

Analysis

Figure 3 shows AP for randomly sampled 30 of 346 semantic concepts. We see that our W-GMM performs well for objects such as vehicles and animals. As shown in Figure 4, which analyzes the relation between word vectors and visual features, vehicles and animals are separated into two clusters. This confirms our assumption that semantically similar concepts tend to have similar visual features. We conclude that this tendency helped to detect concepts in TRECVID that are not included in training data.

On the other hand, it is difficult to detect actions from video. For example, for a concept of "Swimming", concepts about actions with motion detectors and/or motion features should be added to the pre-trained detector to improve the action detection performance.

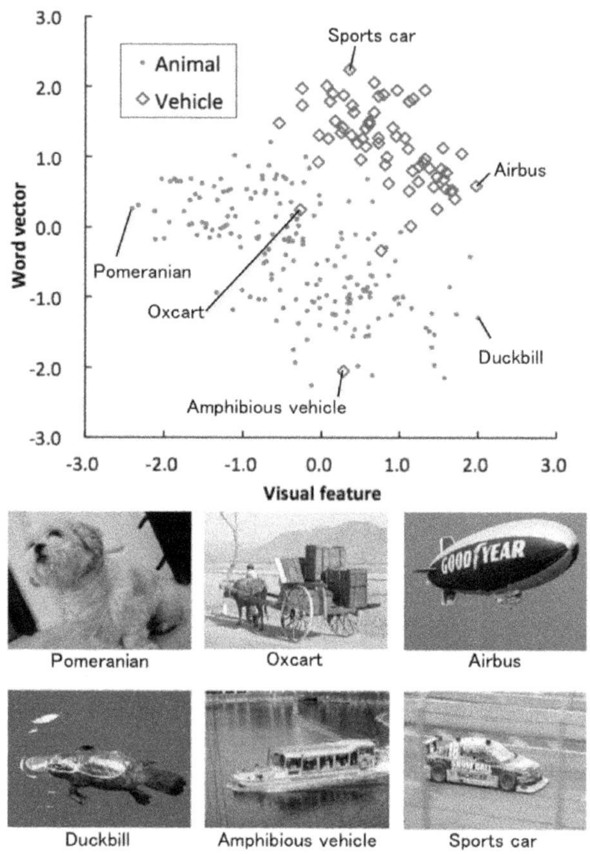

Figure 4: Analysis for Vehicles and Animals. The first principal components for word vectors and visual features are used for visualization. Visual features are obtained from the penultimate layer of the CNN, and are averaged on randomly sampled 100 images for each concept.

4. CONCLUSION

We proposed vocabulary expansion for video semantic indexing without any additional training with annoations. From pre-trained semantic-concept detectors, we made detectors for out-of-vocabulary concepts. Our experiments showed that the word-vector based Gaussian mixture models (W-GMM) performed the best and as well as SVMs trained with 100 example videos for each TRECVID semantic concept. Our future work will focus on motion analysis for semantic indexing to detect actions and events in videos.

5. REFERENCES

[1] F. Perronnin, S. Jorge, and T. Mensink. Improving the fisher kernel for large-scale image classification. *Proc. ECCV*, pp.143–156, 2010.

[2] A. Krizhevsky, I.Sutskever, and G.E. Hinton. ImageNet Classification with Deep Convolutional Neural Networks. *Proc. NIPS*, pp.1–9, 2012.

[3] J. Weston, et al. Large Scale Image Annotation: Learning to Rank with Joint Word-Image Embeddings. *Porc. ECML*, 2010

[4] A. Frome, et al. Devise: A deep visual-semantic embedding model. *Proc. NIPS*, 2013.

[5] T. Mikolov, et al. Distributed Representations of Words and Phrases and their Compositionality. *Proc. NIPS*, 2013.

[6] D. Jacob, et al. Fast and Robust Neural Network Joint Models for Statistical Machine Translation. *Proc. ACL*, 2014.

[7] T. Mikolov, et al. Efficient Estimation of Word Representations in Vector Space. *Proc. ICLR*, 2013.

[8] J. Den, et al. ImageNet: A Large-Scale Hierarchical Image Database. *Proc. CVPR*, 2009.

[9] P. Over, et. al. TRECVID 2013 – An Overview of the Goals, Tasks, Data, Evaluation Mechanisms and Metrics. *Proc. TRECVID workshop*, 2013.

[10] G. Csurka, et al. Visual categorization with bags of keypoints. *Proc. ECCV SLCV*, pp.59–74, 2004.

[11] K. Chatfield, et al. The devil is in the details: an evaluation of recent feature encoding methods. *Proc. BMVC*, pp.1–12, 2011.

[12] J. Wang, et al. Locality-constrained linear coding for image classification. *Proc. CVPR*, pp.3360–3367, 2010.

[13] X. Zhou, et al. Image classification using super-vector coding of local image descriptors. *Proc. ECCV*, pp.141–154, 2010.

[14] C.G.M. Snoek, et. al. The MediaMill TRECVID 2012 Semantic Video Search Engine. *Proc. TRECVID workshop*, 2012.

[15] Y. Jia, et al. Caffe: Convolutional Architecture for Fast Feature Embedding. *Proc. ACM Multimedia Open Source Competition*, 2014.

Filter-Invariant Image Classification on Social Media Photos

Yu-Hsiu Chen, Ting-Hsuan Chao, Sheng-Yi Bai, Yen-Liang Lin, Wen-Chin Chen, Winston H. Hsu

National Taiwan University, Taipei, Taiwan

ABSTRACT

With the popularity of social media nowadays, tons of photos are uploaded everyday. To understand the image content, image classification becomes a very essential technique for plenty of applications (e.g., object detection, image caption generation). Convolutional Neural Network (CNN) has been shown as the state-of-the-art approach for image classification. However, one of the characteristics in social media photos is that they are often applied with photo filters, especially on Instagram. We find that prior works do not aware of this trend in social media photos and fail on filtered images. Thus, we propose a novel CNN architecture that utilizes the power of pairwise constraint by combining Siamese network and the proposed adaptive margin contrastive loss with our discriminative pair sampling method to solve the problem of filter bias. To the best of our knowledge, this is the first work to tackle filter bias on CNN and achieve state-of-the-art performance on a filtered subset of ILSVRC2012.

Categories and Subject Descriptors

I.5.4 [**Computing Methodologies**]: PATTERN RECOGNITION—*Applications*

Keywords

Convolutional Neural Network (CNN); Siamese Network; Image Classification; Photo Filter; Filter Bias

1. INTRODUCTION

With the emergence of social media in recent years, lots of photos are uploaded everyday (e.g., 70M photos per day on instagram[1]). Understanding the stories behind the photos is becoming a strong need for analyzing the user behavior on social media. With widespread photo editing and sharing services like Instagram and Facebook, people can easily change the lighting and the color tone by applying filters

[1]https://instagram.com/press/

MM'15, October 26–30, 2015, Brisbane, Australia.

ACM 978-1-4503-3459-4/15/10 ...$15.00.
DOI: http://dx.doi.org/10.1145/2733373.2806348 .

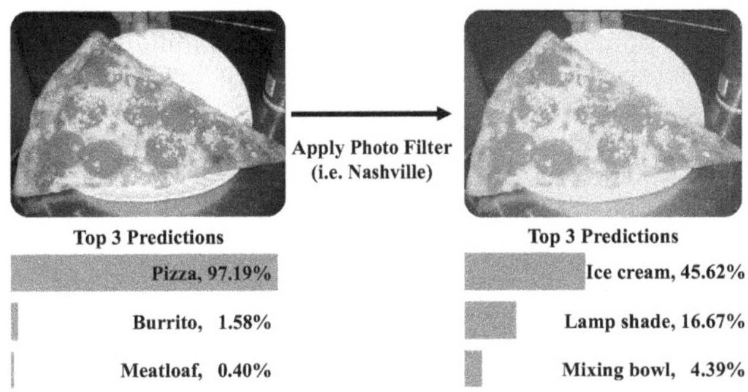

Figure 1: An example shows that a correctly predicted image with high confidence will be mispredicted after applying photo filters. In this case, the photo is applied with "Nashville" filter on Instagram. We call this phenomenon filter bias.

(e.g., Hudson available in Instagram) with just a few clicks. Based on the statistics of Instagram images, around 54% of photos have been enhanced by filters.[2] Thus, considering the side effects brought by the filtered images has become an issue that we cannot neglect.

Recently, deep learning is playing an important role in image classification. Convolutional Neural Networks (CNN), like AlexNet [6], VGG-Net [10] and GoogLeNet [11], achieve state-of-the-art performance. However, most of the traditional models ignore the effects brought by photo filters in image classification. For instance, as Figure 1 shows, a normal image which is predicted correctly with high confidence would be messed up after applying filters while humans can still recognize it correctly. Besides, Table 1 shows that the performance of most of the well-known models would degrade drastically after simply applying filters to validation images (e.g., top-5 accuracy from 80% to 54% on AlexNet [6]). These results suggest the previous work in machine learning, even with the state-of-the-art performance, are vulnerable to the filtered images. We call this phenomenon **filter bias**.

A lot of work has been published on image classification with CNN, but few of them take care of the filter bias. Domain adaptation tackles the problem of domain shift by adapting one model from a source domain to another target domain. In this scenario, we can treat one filter as one domain and use domain adaptation works, such as [9, 14] to deal with the filter bias. However, it might be hard to get filter information of a photo on social media. In addition, if we treat one filter as one domain, there would be infinitely

[2]http://filterfakers.com/filterguide

Table 1: **The top-1/top-5 accuracy on the original and filtered images. The performance among most of the state-of-the-art CNN models degrades severely after applying filters to the same validation set (ILSVRC2012 Val). Here, we use filter "Valencia" available on Instagram.**

ILSVRC2012 Val	Without filter	With filter
AlexNet [6]	56.87%/80.30%	30.14%/53.70%
VGG-Net [10]	68.27%/92.50%	50.95%/74.58%
GoogLeNet [11]	68.70%/88.90%	47.85%/73.02%

many domains that we need to adapt to since we can easily change the parameters of a filter (e.g., the lighting and the color tone) to generate a brand new filter. Moreover, the focus of domain adaptation works is limited to one-to-one, or many-to-one domain adaptation, and it might be problematic to adapt to the domains of all filters.

Guo and Wang [3] discover the problem that a filtered image would harm the descriptor of SIFT and try to learn a more robust domain-invariant descriptor. However, it is limited in a shallow model and test on a small scale of data and filter types. Recent works [12, 2] explore the adversarial examples that can easily "hack" the deep CNN models. We can take any arbitrary image and fool a state-of-the-art CNN model to classify it as whatever class we want while the noises we added are almost imperceptible to the human eye. These works give us hints about the root of filter bias and imply that it is not dependent on the CNN architecture, i.e., it might be suffered from the linear nature of CNN.

Thus, we propose a pairwise regularization method and a discriminative pair sampling technique to relieve the filter bias and learn representations that are more robust and filter-invariant. Meanwhile, we also create a challenging filtered image dataset—Filter100—that contains around 1 million filtered photos. To the best of our knowledge, this is the first work to address the problem of filter bias on CNN-based image classification on social media photos.

2. PROPOSED METHOD

As we stated in the previous section, we attempt to learn filter-invariant representations that are less vulnerable to filtered images. The intuitive way to solve this problem is data augmentation. It is easy to generate filtered images from original images; however, it is hard to generate and include all types of filtered images for training since the size of training data would grow excessively and training models on this scale of images is unrealistic. Hence, we introduce a novel CNN architecture which learns robust representations by integrating a Siamese network with our proposed adaptive margin contrastive loss. Moreover, the discriminative pair sampling prevents the size of training data from overgrowth and improves the performance. We start by generating affordable types of filtered images and use a pairwise constraint to regularize the classification loss which helps filter-invariant representation learning.

2.1 CNN Structure

We propose a novel CNN architecture, which is illustrated in Figure 2. It is a Siamese network with both columns composed by AlexNet [6] and two additional adaptive margin contrastive losses between them to force these layers to learn filter-invariant representations. A Siamese network is a weakly-supervised learning structure first proposed by [1]. It learns the similarity relationship from labeled pairs of data as similar or dissimilar. Though Siamese is a two-column architecture, the parameters of the layers on both columns are identical. It has been shown that Siamese networks are very effective for learning invariant representations [4, 13].

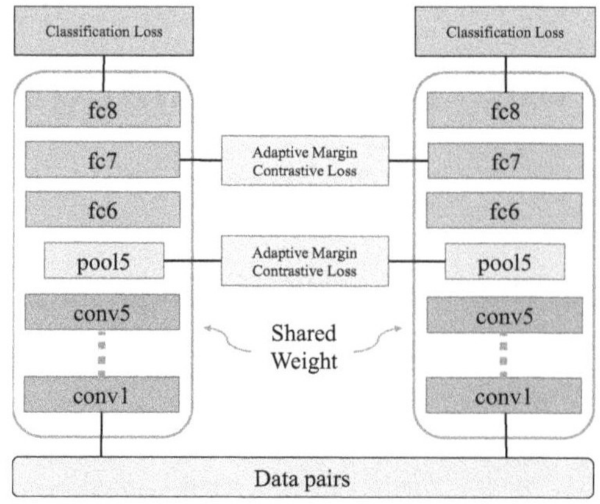

Figure 2: **Our proposed CNN architecture for filter-invariant representations learning. It is a Siamese network composed of two AlexNet [6] and the additional adaptive margin contrastive loss. Combining the classification loss with two adaptive margin contrastive losses helps us to learn both semantic meaningful and filter-invariant representations.**

2.2 Pairwise Definition For Siamese Network

For Siamese network, it requires pairwise data for the training process. First, we define the similar and dissimilar pairs in our work. We treat the image pairs that are generated from the same image but with different types of filters (we treat original images as one kind of filtered images) as similar pair. Since the two filtered images are exactly generated from the same original image, we expect their representations to be more similar and try to make these two embeddings closer (e.g., dog images in Figure 3). For the dissimilar pairs, we sample those image pairs that have the same filter type but are drawn from different classes.

2.3 Adaptive Margin Contrastive Loss

After selecting pairwise training data, it is essential to measure the quality of learned representations. Hence, we propose a novel loss function based on the contrastive loss in [4] and it is defined as the following:

$$\mathcal{L}_r(x_i, x_j, s_{i,j}) = \begin{cases} \mathcal{D}(x_i, x_j) & \text{if } s_{i,j} = 1 \\ max(0, m_{adapt} - \mathcal{D}(x_i, x_j)) & \text{if } s_{i,j} = 0 \end{cases},$$

where $\mathcal{D}(x_i, x_i) = \|x_i - x_j\|_2^2$. We denote x_i and x_j as the representations from image i and j respectively. $s_{i,j}$ equals to 1 if x_i and x_j are regarded as a similar pair, otherwise as a dissimilar pair, and m_{adapt} is our proposed adaptive margin. The physical meaning of adaptive margin contrastive loss is to make the representations of similar pairs closer and try to keep that of dissimilar pairs at least m_{adapt} away from each other. The illustration of adaptive margin contrastive loss function is shown in Figure 3. The idea of adaptive margin m_{adapt} is inspired by [7]. For each iteration, we calculate the pairwise distance $\mathcal{D}$ of all the similar and dissimilar pairs in

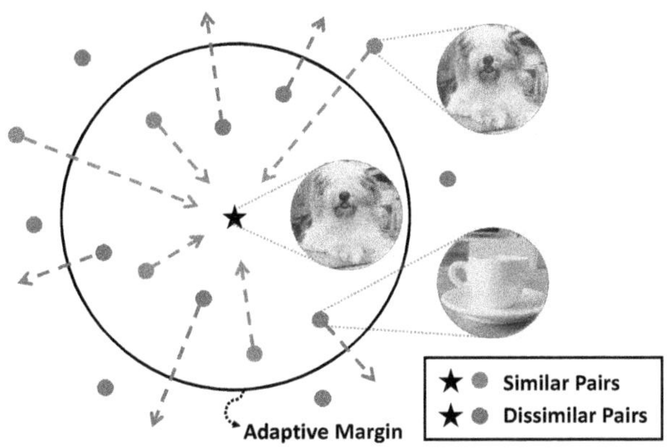

Figure 3: Illustration of adaptive margin contrastive loss. We visualize the relationship between sample point (star symbol), its corresponding similar pairs (orange points) and dissimilar pairs (blue points) on a 2D-plane. The idea is to encourage the similar pairs (generated from the same image but with different filter types) to be closer, and keep dissimilar pairs (drawn from different class but with same filter type) at least m_{adapt} apart from each other.

one batch. Then, we calculate the average pair distance between similar pairs as $mean_{sim}$, as well as $mean_{dis}$ for dissimilar pairs. After that, we set the adaptive margin m_{adapt} for each iteration as the following:

$$m_{adapt} = \frac{1}{2}(mean_{sim} + mean_{dis}).$$

The idea is to separate the representations of similar and dissimilar pairs to avoid confusing. By using adaptive margin rather than a fixed margin, we can get rid of the effort for tuning the margin parameter and adapt to datasets without any pre-processing. We apply two adaptive margin contrastive losses on both *pool5* and *fc7* layer since they are the last layer of the convolutional part and the fully-connected part respectively. Therefore, the final objective loss function of our proposed method is

$$\mathcal{L} = \mathcal{L}_c(X, Y) + \lambda \mathcal{L}_r(P, S).$$

We denote X as the training data, Y as the labels, $\mathcal{L}_c$ as classification loss and $\mathcal{L}_r$ means the adaptive margin contrastive loss we propose. P are the training pairs we sampled from X, and S are the collections of indicators for similar and dissimilar pairs. Hence, combining with the classification loss and the adaptive margin contrastive loss we added, we can learn a representation that is both semantic meaningful and filter-invariant.

2.4 Discriminative Pair Sampling

In the training phase, we may want to learn as many pairs as possible to avoid overfitting. However, the number of possible pairs increases quadratically with the number of selected filters, and makes it unrealistic to include all the possible pairs in training set since it will be computationally prohibitive. For instance, as described in Section 2.2, 50,000 original images with 5 types of filtered images in training set will result in more than 10 billions of possible pairs. Intuitively, we can use uniform sampling to limit the number of pairs in training data, but it will give a sub-optimal solution. Therefore, we propose a discriminative pair sampling method which tries to include as many informative pairs as possible in a given number of selection. The idea is to select similar pairs whose changes of the color and lighting are more drastic, which might be more informative for training. For every original image, we sample similar pairs with the probabilities proportional to the pairwise distance based on *fc7* layer representations. For instance, if we include original images and filtered images with N types of filter, we have all C_2^{N+1} possible similar pair combinations for every single image g, which is denoted as U. If we want to select k similar pairs from all possible combinations U with the representation on *fc7*, which is denoted as x. We sample similar pairs with the probabilities of each pair combination as the following:

$$Prob(g_{i,j}) = \frac{\mathcal{D}(x_i, x_j)}{\sum_{u,v \subset U} \mathcal{D}(x_u, x_v)},$$

where $g_{i,j}$ means the similar pair of image g with filter type i and j. By using this discriminative pair sampling method, we can learn in a more efficient and effective way.

3. EXPERIMENTS

Since we want to learn a both filter-invariant and semantic meaningful representation, we use zero-shot testing, in other words, test models on the validation images applied with filters which are unseen in training. Therefore, we can ensure we learned robust representations that are less vulnerable to different types of filters. In this section, we describe the details of the experiments we conducted.

3.1 Filter100

To generate a large scale dataset with filters, we randomly sample 100 classes from ILSVRC2012 [8] with 500 images per class. After that, we apply 18 types of popular filters available on Instagram to generate filtered images and finally form a dataset that contains 0.95M images (original images included) in total. We call this dataset **Filter100**.

For one single training set, we randomly select 5 types of filters and include the corresponding filtered images along with the 50,000 original images as training set, which contains 300,000 images in total. In validation, we use zero-shot testing, i.e., we use the filtered validation set only contains 13 unseen filters to evaluate the robustness of learned representations. There are total 65,000 images in a single validation set. We repeat the procedure 5 times on 5 different train/validation sets and report the average accuracy of the 5 sets to reduce the bias caused by the selection of filters.

3.2 Experiment Settings

For the implementation, we use Caffe [5] to implement our adaptive margin contrastive loss layer and the Siamese network structure as we illustrated in Figure 2. We sample 6 similar pairs and 6 dissimilar pairs from every original images, which results in 0.6M training pairs for each training set by using our discriminative pair sampling method. After that, we use the pre-trained Caffenet model as the initial weights in our fine-tuning process by using the CNN architecture we designed.

3.3 Experiment Results

Table 2 shows the result of pure AlexNet fine-tuned with only 50,000 original images in Filter100 and the performance degrades from around 80% (test on only validation images

Table 2: Our method outperforms all the other works, like pure AlexNet [6] fine-tuned on 100 classes subset of ILSVRC2012 without any filtered images and the one fine-tuned on Filter100, on all 5 train/test sets with different filter selections. Also, our work surpasses the state-of-the-art in domain adaptation [14] and implies that domain adaptation cannot adapt to such a "filter domain" and cannot relieve the filter bias problem.

	Set 1	Set 2	Set 3	Set4	Set5	Average
AlexNet [6] (fine-tuned without filtered images)	65.93%	66.96%	67.33%	67.93%	65.96%	66.82%
AlexNet [6] (fine-tuned on Filter100)	70.53%	70.69%	73.93%	73.22%	69.60%	71.59%
DDC [14]	70.42%	70.67%	73.55%	72.86%	68.93%	71.29%
Adaptive Margin Contrastive Loss + Uniform Sampling **(ours)**	71.55%	71.24%	74.70%	73.87%	70.01%	72.34%
Adaptive Margin Contrastive Loss + Discriminative Pair Sampling **(ours)**	**71.76%**	**71.65%**	**74.93%**	**74.19%**	**70.29%**	**72.56%**

with no filter) to around 67% (with filter) in all validation set, which is concurrent with the result in Table 1. Then, we compare with AlexNet fine-tuned with Filter100, and the result shows that the traditional data augmentation techniques reduce the performance degradation caused by filter bias. However, our work surpasses it by utilizing pairwise constraint. Furthermore, compare with uniform sampling, discriminative pair sampling effectively limits the pair number in training and further improves performance. In addition, we observe that the mean distance of similar pairs on the learned *fc7* representations in our work is much smaller than the one in other work, which is about 9 times smaller than the one in AlexNet fine-tuned on Filter100. That is to say, an image and its filtered images are more similar after considering pairwise constraint in the learning process, which is coincident with our intuition. We think it is one of the key points to learn filter-invariant representations.

Moreover, our work outperforms the state-of-the-art in domain adaptation, DDC [14]. We treat original images as source domain and both original and filtered images as target domain to do supervised domain adaptation. The results indicate that it might be hard to solve filter bias by simply adapting to such a big "filter domain." To sum up, we outperforms all of the literature aforementioned in all 5 train/validation set and achieves state-of-the-art performance in image classification on social media photos.

4. CONCLUSIONS AND FUTURE WORKS

We point out the problem of filter bias in image classification on social media photos and propose a novel CNN architecture leveraging the pairwise constraint to relieve this phenomenon. We propose an adaptive margin loss function which dynamically selects the most suitable parameter for different batches in the training process. Furthermore, the discriminative pair sampling method we propose effectively limits the pair number needed in training and improves the performance. To the best of our knowledge, this is the first work to deal with the problem of filter bias in CNN-based image classification and our work surpasses other works and achieve state-of-the-art performance.

Determining the optimal selection of filters included in training is still an issue. We will exploit more cues about how different types of filters affect the CNN model in our future work. Moreover, though the implementation of our architecture is based on AlexNet [6], the adaptive margin contrastive loss we propose is not limited to AlexNet. We will work on other state-of-the-art CNN architectures, like GoogLeNet [11] and VGG-Net [10] to find out a generic method that can learn a more filter-invariant and semantic meaningful representation to improve the performance of image classification on social media photos.

5. ACKNOWLEDGEMENTS

This work was supported in part by HTC and MediaTek.

6. REFERENCES

[1] J. Bromley, J. W. Bentz, L. Bottou, I. Guyon, Y. LeCun, C. Moore, E. Säckinger, and R. Shah. Signature verification using a "siamese" time delay neural network. *IJPRAI*, 1993.

[2] I. J. Goodfellow, J. Shlens, and C. Szegedy. Explaining and harnessing adversarial examples. *ICLR*, 2015.

[3] Z. Guo and Z. J. Wang. An adaptive descriptor design for object recognition in the wild. In *ICCV, 2013*.

[4] R. Hadsell, S. Chopra, and Y. LeCun. Dimensionality reduction by learning an invariant mapping. In *CVPR*, 2006.

[5] Y. Jia, E. Shelhamer, J. Donahue, S. Karayev, J. Long, R. Girshick, S. Guadarrama, and T. Darrell. Caffe: Convolutional architecture for fast feature embedding. In *ACM MM*, 2014.

[6] A. Krizhevsky, I. Sutskever, and G. E. Hinton. Imagenet classification with deep convolutional neural networks. In *NIPS*, 2012.

[7] J. Lin, O. Morère, V. Chandrasekhar, A. Veillard, and H. Goh. Deephash: Getting regularization, depth and fine-tuning right. *CoRR*, abs/1501.04711, 2015.

[8] O. Russakovsky, J. Deng, H. Su, J. Krause, S. Satheesh, S. Ma, Z. Huang, A. Karpathy, A. Khosla, M. Bernstein, A. C. Berg, and L. Fei-Fei. ImageNet Large Scale Visual Recognition Challenge. *IJCV*, 2015.

[9] K. Saenko, B. Kulis, M. Fritz, and T. Darrell. Adapting visual category models to new domains. In *ECCV*. 2010.

[10] K. Simonyan and A. Zisserman. Very deep convolutional networks for large-scale image recognition. *ICLR*, 2015.

[11] C. Szegedy, W. Liu, Y. Jia, P. Sermanet, S. Reed, D. Anguelov, D. Erhan, V. Vanhoucke, and A. Rabinovich. Going deeper with convolutions. *CVPR*, 2015.

[12] C. Szegedy, W. Zaremba, I. Sutskever, J. Bruna, D. Erhan, I. Goodfellow, and R. Fergus. Intriguing properties of neural networks. *ICLR*, 2014.

[13] Y. Taigman, M. Yang, M. Ranzato, and L. Wolf. Deepface: Closing the gap to human-level performance in face verification. In *CVPR*, 2014.

[14] E. Tzeng, J. Hoffman, N. Zhang, K. Saenko, and T. Darrell. Deep domain confusion: Maximizing for domain invariance. *CoRR*, abs/1412.3474, 2014.

Learning Multi-view Deep Features for Small Object Retrieval in Surveillance Scenarios

Haiyun Guo[1], Jinqiao Wang[1], Min Xu[2], Zheng-Jun Zha[3], and Hanqing Lu[1]
[1]National Laboratory of Pattern Recognition, Institute of Automation
Chinese Academy of Sciences, Beijing, China, 100190
[2]GBDTC, School of Computing and Communications, University of Technology, Sydney, Australia
[3]Institute of Intelligent Machines, Chinese Academy of Sciences, Hefei, China
{haiyun.guo, jqwang, luhq}@nlpr.ia.ac.cn, min.xu@uts.edu.au, junzzustc@gmail.com

ABSTRACT

With the explosive growth of surveillance videos, object retrieval has become a significant task for security monitoring. However, visual objects in surveillance videos are usually of small size with complex light conditions, view changes and partial occlusions, which increases the difficulty level of efficiently retrieving objects of interest in a large-scale dataset. Although deep features have achieved promising results on object classification and retrieval and have been verified to contain rich semantic structure property, they lack of adequate color information, which is as crucial as structure information for effective object representation. In this paper, we propose to leverage discriminative Convolutional Neural Network (CNN) to learn deep structure and color feature to form an efficient multi-view object representation. Specifically, we utilize CNN trained on ImageNet to abstract rich semantic structure information. Meanwhile, we propose a CNN model supervised by 11 color names to extract deep color features. Compared with traditional color descriptors, deep color features can capture the common color property across different illumination conditions. Then, the complementary multi-view deep features are encoded into short binary codes by Locality-Sensitive Hash (LSH) and fused to retrieve objects. Retrieval experiments are performed on a dataset of 100k objects extracted from multi-camera surveillance videos. Comparison results with several popular visual descriptors show the effectiveness of the proposed approach.

Categories and Subject Descriptors

I.4.10 [**Image Representation**]: Multidimensional; I.5.4 [**Applications**]: Signal processing

Keywords

Object retrieval; Object representation

MM'15, October 26–30, 2015, Brisbane, Australia.
© 2015 ACM. ISBN 978-1-4503-3459-4/15/10 ...$15.00.
DOI: http://dx.doi.org/10.1145/2733373.2806349.

1. INTRODUCTION

Nowadays an increasing number of surveillance cameras are installed in public places and produce massive video data every day. Therefore, efficiently retrieving objects of interest across large scale surveillance videos has become a hot spot of research. Although it has been studied for many years, small object retrieval in surveillance videos remains a challenging topic, primarily due to the following reasons. Firstly, the objects extracted from surveillance videos are usually of small size, even imprecise. Secondly, the image including object of interest also inevitably involves some background pixels. Thirdly, there are various complex conditions existing in surveillance areas, such as illumination changes, shadows, viewpoint shifts and partial occlusions.

Therefore, an efficient object representation is crucial to object retrieval in surveillance videos. Over the past few decades, a series of hand-crafted features have been proposed to bridge the semantic gap between image pixels and semantic concepts. One is global descriptor, which describes the coarse global color, texture or shape information distribution of input image. Yang and Yu [19] made use of color histograms and three different texture descriptors to real-time search eight kinds of clothes in surveillance videos. Calderara *et al.* [3] presented a global descriptor by estimating the color probability distribution with a mixture of Gaussians to conduct person retrieval in multi-camera surveillance scenarios. However, these global descriptors fail to distinguish between the object and unrelated pixels within image, thus introducing noise to object representation. Besides, they are not robust to some complex variations. Another is local descriptor such as SIFT [10] and GLOH [12], all of which are based on feature point detection. However, as mentioned before, the objects detected from surveillance videos are usually rather small, so there are often few even no feature points detected from an object. As a result, local descriptors extracted from small objects usually lack of adequate discrimination. Apart from the above descriptors, other researchers utilized various attributes to describe visual objects. Thornton *et al.*[16] proposed a generative model covering some attributes such as gender, hair/hat color, clothing color and bag position for person search. Although attribute features convey middle-level visual information, the extraction and fusion of various attributes are a very challenging task for small objects in surveillance videos.

With the rapid development of deep learning, it has been verified in [8, 20] that features learned by deep models are more efficient than traditional hand-crafted features. Hinton

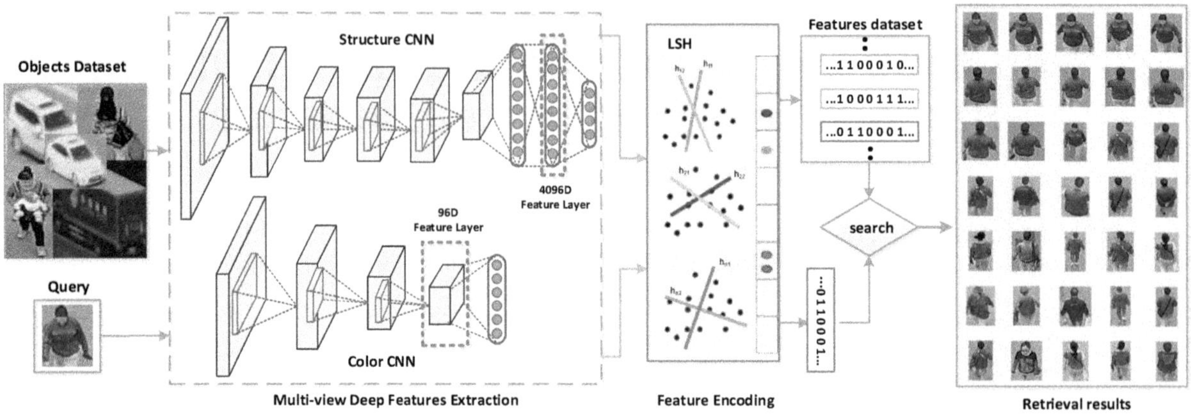

Figure 1: The overall framework of learning multi-view deep features for small object retrieval.

et al.[7] and Teng *et al.*[15] both applied features learned by deep auto-encoders to content-based similar image retrieval and obtained better retrieval performance than using pixel-based features. But as pointed out in [8], the retrieval results can have similar edge patterns but may not be semantically related. In contrast, deep representations learned by Convolutional Neural Network (CNN) conveyed rich semantic information and obtained state-of-the-art image retrieval performance in [13].

Structure and color attributes are two most crucial properties for effective object representation. In this paper, we leverage multi-view information abstracted with CNN models to jointly describe the structure and color properties of visual objects. The overall framework of the proposed approach is illustrated in Figure 1. Specifically, we take advantage of the CNN model trained on ImageNet [20] to extract deep feature from the view of structure. This kind of feature has two advantages: for one thing, it includes rich local structure information and is robust to pose change, object deformation as well as partial occlusion; for another, it delivers rich semantic information about object category. However, the above deep structure feature turns out to lack of adequate color information in retrieval experiments. Thus, we build a CNN model supervised by 11 color names [18] to abstract deep feature from the view of color, which could capture the common color property across different illumination conditions. Therefore, with discriminative CNN models, we can extract efficient and robust multi-view deep features for small objects. Furthermore, to accelerate the retrieval efficiency, the above two deep features are encoded into 256-bit binary codes by Locality Sensitive Hashing (LSH) [4] separately. Finally, we combine the complementary multi-view deep features using a late fusion strategy and obtain state-of-the-art performance for small object retrieval in surveillance scenarios.

2. MULTI-VIEW DEEP REPRESENTATION

Since introduced by LeCun [9] in the early 1990's, CNN has demonstrated record-beating performance at challenging tasks such as image classification, object detection and face recognition. Three crucial architectural ideas, local receptive fields, shared weights, and spatial or temporal subsampling, are responsible for the power of CNN. Usually,

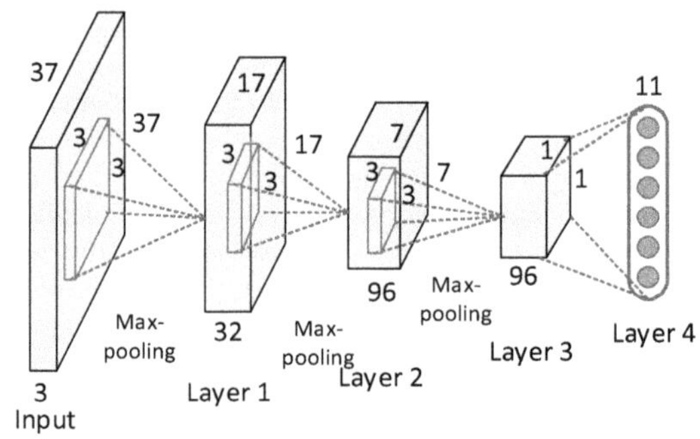

Figure 2: The structure of color CNN.

CNN-based deep feature learning pipeline has two stages. The first is to learn a CNN model in a supervised manner. The second is to extract deep feature from last several layers of CNN. Following this pipeline, we extract two deep features to jointly describe the object from the view of structure and color.

2.1 Deep Structure Feature

It has been verified that CNN model supervised by object categories can not only abstract rich semantic information but also capture local structure property of the object [20]. Since the 1000 object categories in ILSVRC12 dataset include person and vehicle, which are the most often retrieved objects in surveillance scenarios, we choose ILSVRC12 dataset to train a CNN model to extract rich semantic structure information. Specifically, we adopt the exact CNN architecture specified in [20] and train the model with the help of Caffe [6]. Considering higher layers in CNN models generally produce more discriminative features, we extract deep structure feature from the penultimate layer. During the image preprocessing in feature extraction phase, we first resize the input image to 225×225, then subtract the mean activity over the training set from each pixel.

2.2 Deep Color Feature

Although deep structure feature delivers rich semantic structure information, it does not contain enough color information, which is rather crucial in describing small objects. Therefore, inspired by [17], we build a CNN model to describe the object from the view of color. Based on the linguistic study of Berlin and Kay [2], we select 11 basic color terms of the English language: black, blue, brown, grey, green, orange, pink, purple, red, white and yellow, as the supervisory information when training CNN on Google color name set. By training CNN model to classify 11 color names, we can learn deep color representation which is robust to illumination change and color distortion across different scenes. The detailed architecture of the CNN model is shown in Figure 2. To comprehensively describe the spatial color distribution, we first preprocess the input image to be of 55×55 size and zero mean value, then divide it averagely into 16 overlapping 37×37 patches and send them into color CNN to get 16 96-d features, which are concatenated into 1536-d deep color feature. To test the discriminability of the deep color feature, we perform a classification experiment on Ebay dataset [18] and achieve an accuracy of 0.80, which is higher than that obtained by using traditional hand-crafted color features, such as color histogram.

2.3 Multi-view Deep Features Encoding

The above multi-view deep features are rather descriptive but not compact enough. For searching objects in large scale dataset, high dimensionality will significantly corrupt the retrieval efficiency. Due to the efficiency in both storage and speed, hashing based approximate nearest neighbor search methods have attracted much attention in the past years. Hashing converts all feature representation of images into binary codes and then conducts a bitwise XOR operation in very fast speed. LSH [4] is one of the most popular hashing algorithms. Using LSH, we encode each deep feature into one 256-bit binary code as a compact descriptor for visual object. The time cost is smaller for computing Hamming distance than Euclidean distance. Since in modern CPUs, it only takes one CPU cycle to compute Hamming distance for 128-bit hash code in Hamming space. To further improve retrieval accuracy, we combine the two compact descriptors with a late fusion strategy to obtain final retrieval results.

3. EXPERIMENTS

Since there is no available standard large scale database in the field of object retrieval in surveillance scenarios, we collect surveillance videos with HD cameras mounted at residential entrances inside university. We adopt background subtraction and object tracking [5] to extract moving objects, and build a dataset consisting of 100k objects. The dataset covers various weather conditions, light changes, poses, viewpoints, and partial occlusions. A total of 300 query objects, 100 vehicles and 200 persons, are selected to evaluate the retrieval performance. Mean average precision (MAP) is used to measure the retrieval performance of different methods.

3.1 Comparison with Hand-crafted Features

To show the effectiveness of the multi-view deep features, we compare them with some hand-crafted visual descriptors. The comparison results are demonstrated in Table 1. We calculate the MAP of top 10k returned objects for person and vehicle respectively. Six hand-crafted visual descriptors are used as comparison features. "ColorHist" is a 81-d color histogram in HSV space, while "ColorMoment [14]" is a 9-d feature obtained by calculating first, second and third moments of image pixels in LAB space. "GLCM [11]" is a 48-d texture feature based on gray-level co-occurrence matrix and "WaveletTransform" is a 20-d texture feature based on wavelet transform. "CannyEdgeHist" is a 64-d feature describing the edge information returned by canny edge detector, while "ShapeContext [1]" is a 72-d feature describing the local shape information of objects. It can be found that color descriptors are more useful than texture, edge and shape descriptors for small object retrieval.

Table 1: Comparison with hand-crafted features.

	MAP(person)	MAP(vehicle)
WaveletTransform	0.1801	0.1750
ShapeContext [1]	0.1978	0.1921
CannyEdgeHist	0.2119	0.1835
GLCM [11]	0.2390	0.2119
ColorMoment [14]	0.2825	0.2998
ColorHist	0.2876	0.3648
colCNN-LSH	0.4378	0.4113
strCNN-LSH	0.4729	0.3991
colCNN	0.5007	0.4609
strCNN	0.6122	0.4321
str+colCNN-LSH	0.5955	0.4732
str+colCNN	**0.6585**	**0.4893**

Table 2: Retrieval cost of different methods.

	Retrieval cost(s)
colCNN-LSH	0.935
strCNN-LSH	0.971
str+colCNN-LSH	1.243
ColorMoment [14]	1.861
WaveletTransform	1.871
GLCM	1.936
CannyEdgeHist	1.954
ColorHist	1.964
ShapeContext [1]	1.979
colCNN	5.758
strCNN	12.445
str+colCNN	18.109

For deep features extracted from CNN, "strCNN" is the 4096-d deep structure feature and "colCNN" is the 1536-d deep color feature, which describe the object from the view of structure and color respectively. "str+colCNN" indicates the late fusion of "strCNN" and "colCNN", which performs the best both in person and vehicle retrieval with a relative improvement of 7.56% and 6.16% in MAP than the best results achieved by single descriptor. "strCNN-LSH" and "colCNN-LSH" is the 256-bit compact feature encoded from "strCNN" and "colCNN" with LSH respectively. Although they achieve lower MAP than "strCNN" and "colCNN", they perform better than all of the remaining comparison features and save retrieval time greatly. By fusing "strCNN-LSH" and "colCNN-LSH", we get "str+colCNN-LSH", which reduces the retrieval time from about 18 seconds to 1 seconds, with only a little decrease in MAP compared with "str+colCNN".

3.2 Comparison of Retrieval Cost

As shown in Table 2, six hand-crafted features all cost less than 2 seconds in retrieval time due to the low dimensionality. And it is no surprise that the 4096-d deep structure feature costs the most retrieval time, which is then greatly

Figure 3: Comparison of the ranking examples.

reduced by encoding deep features into 256-bit binary codes with LSH. All the retrieval experiments are conducted on Intel i5-2400 CPU 3.1 GHz with 20 GB memory. Figure 3 shows some retrieval examples of our proposed approach as well as several comparison methods.

4. CONCLUSIONS

In this paper, we propose an effective multi-view deep features learning approach for small object retrieval in surveillance scenarios. For structure view, we train a CNN model for object category classification to extract deep structure feature. For color view, we propose a CNN model for color name classification to extract deep color feature. Then we use LSH to encode deep features into short binary codes to accelerate retrieval efficiency and fuse the compact deep features to increase retrieval accuracy. Compared with several popular visual descriptors, our proposed approach achieves the best performance.

5. ACKNOWLEDGMENTS

This work was supported by 863 Program 2014AA015104, and National Natural Science Foundation of China 61273034, and 61332016.

6. REFERENCES

[1] S. Belongie, J. Malik, and J. Puzicha. Shape matching and object recognition using shape contexts. *TPAMI*, 24(4):509–522, 2002.

[2] B. Berlin. *Basic color terms: Their universality and evolution.* Univ of California Press, 1991.

[3] S. Calderara, R. Cucchiara, and A. Prati. Multimedia surveillance: content-based retrieval with multicamera people tracking. In *IWVSSN*, pages 95–100. ACM, 2006.

[4] M. S. Charikar. Similarity estimation techniques from rounding algorithms. In *Symposium on Theory of computing*, pages 380–388. ACM, 2002.

[5] S. Chris and G. W. E. L. Adaptive background mixture models for real-time tracking. In *CVPR*, volume 2. IEEE, 1999.

[6] Y. Jia, E. Shelhamer, J. Donahue, S. Karayev, J. Long, R. Girshick, S. Guadarrama, and T. Darrell. Caffe: Convolutional architecture for fast feature embedding. *arXiv preprint arXiv:1408.5093*, 2014.

[7] A. Krizhevsky and G. Hinton. Using very deep autoencoders for content-based image retrieval. In *ESANN*. Citeseer, 2011.

[8] A. Krizhevsky, I. Sutskever, and G. Hinton. Imagenet classification with deep convolutional neural networks. In *NIPS*, pages 1097–1105, 2012.

[9] Y. LeCun, B. Boser, J. Denker, D. Henderson, R. Howard, W. Hubbard, and L. Jackel. Backpropagation applied to handwritten zip code recognition. *NC*, 1(4):541–551, 1989.

[10] D. Lowe. Object recognition from local scale-invariant features. In *CV*, volume 2, pages 1150–1157. Ieee, 1999.

[11] B. S. Manjunath and W. Y. Ma. Texture features for browsing and retrieval of image data. *PAMI*, 18(8):837–842, 1996.

[12] K. Mikolajczyk and C. Schmid. A performance evaluation of local descriptors. *PAMI*, 27(10):1615–1630, 2005.

[13] A. Razavian, H. Azizpour, J. Sullivan, and S. Carlsson. Cnn features off-the-shelf: an astounding baseline for recognition. *arXiv preprint arXiv:1403.6382*, 2014.

[14] S. M. Singh and K. Hemachandran. Image retrieval based on color moments. *Digital Image Processing*, 4(16):910–916, 2012.

[15] K. Teng, J. Wang, M. Xu, and H. Lu. Mask assisted object coding with deep learning for object retrieval in surveillance videos. In *MM*, pages 1109–1112. ACM, 2014.

[16] J. Thornton, J. Baran-Gale, D. Butler, M. Chan, and H. Zwahlen. Person attribute search for large-area video surveillance. In *HST*, pages 55–61. IEEE, 2011.

[17] Y. Wang, J. Liu, J. Wang, Y. Li, and H. Lu. Color names learning using convolutional neural networks. In *ICIP*. IEEE, 2015.

[18] J. V. D. Weijer, C. Schmid, and J. Verbeek. Learning color names from real-world images. In *CVPR*, pages 1–8. IEEE, 2007.

[19] M. Yang and K. Yu. Real-time clothing recognition in surveillance videos. In *ICIP*, pages 2937–2940. IEEE, 2011.

[20] M. Zeiler and R. Fergus. Visualizing and understanding convolutional neural networks. *arXiv preprint arXiv:1311.2901*, 2013.

Unsupervised Extraction of Human-Interpretable Nonverbal Behavioral Cues in a Public Speaking Scenario

M. Iftekhar Tanveer
ROC HCI
Electrical and Computer Eng.
University of Rochester
itanveer@cs.rochester.edu

Ji Liu
ROC HCI
Computer Science
University of Rochester
jliu@cs.rochester.edu

M. Ehsan Hoque
ROC HCI
Computer Science
University of Rochester
mehoque@cs.rochester.edu

ABSTRACT

We present a framework for unsupervised detection of nonverbal behavioral cues—hand gestures, pose, body movements, etc.—from a collection of motion capture (MoCap) sequences in a public speaking setting. We extract the cues by solving a sparse and shift-invariant dictionary learning problem, known as *shift-invariant sparse coding.* We find that the extracted behavioral cues are human-interpretable in the context of public speaking. Our technique can be applied to automatically identify the common patterns of body movements and the time-instances of their occurrences, minimizing time and efforts needed for manual detection and coding of nonverbal human behaviors.

Categories and Subject Descriptors

G.1 [**NUMERICAL ANALYSIS**]: Optimization; J.5 [**ARTS AND HUMANITIES**]: Performing arts

Keywords

Public Speaking; Action Recognition; Unsupervised Analysis; Sparsity; Shift-Invariant Sparse Coding

1. INTRODUCTION

Public speaking is a widely-used method for articulating ideas. Understanding the influence of nonverbal behaviors in a public speaking setting is an interesting research topic [6]. It might be possible to improve our understanding of such influence by using data analytic approaches over a large collection of public speaking data. Human *Activity* or *Action* Recognition is a growing field of research that is already aiming towards such analysis. However, this domain is mostly focused on supervised classification of body language [1, 4]. It is often necessary to utilize unsupervised approaches in order to extract common body movement patterns without prior knowledge. For example, if we want to know all the common fidgeting patterns in a public speaking setting, we need an unsupervised algorithm to find these patterns. With supervised approach, we would have to provide samples of the fidgeting behaviors as an input to the algorithm. This is infeasible due to the lack of prior knowledge.

We propose a framework[1] to automatically identify and localize the common *behavioral cues* [6] in a public speaking video. In order to track the body movements of the speaker, we use a Kinect skeleton tracker [12]. The tracker provides time dependent, three dimensional signal of 20 joint locations of the speaker—collectively known as Motion Capture (MoCap) signal. We apply *shift-invariant sparse coding (SISC)* [9, 5] to extract the behavioral cues that are manifested as small temporal patterns in the MoCap signal. SISC is formulated as an optimization problem for learning a dictionary of temporal patterns, where the patterns appear within the signal in a sparse manner. We notice that the learned set of patterns are human-interpretable. People can relate the extracted behavioral cues to real-life public speaking scenarios.

Our work has several future applications. For instance, it can be used to mine different types of behavioral patterns from time sequence data (e.g. variations in facial expressions, vocal characteristics, body language, etc.). As the patterns are human-interpretable, this technique can be used to build an ontological coding schema for behavioral cues by simultaneously learning and manually annotating meaningful labels. Finally, the behavioral cues learned from this process could be used as "features" to train supervised algorithms in order to predict human performance for public speaking or any other forms of human communications.

2. RELATED LITERATURE

Computational analysis of nonverbal behaviors [14, 8, 1] has recently received a considerable attention from the researchers. Metaxas et al. [8] summarized works that focus on sensing body movements and representing them as a sequence of numbers (facial point trackers represent facial movements as a sequence of landmark points, Kinect skeleton trackers [12] represent full body movements as a sequence of joint locations, etc.)

Researchers also work on holistically predicting the outcome of specific tasks through automated analysis of nonverbal behaviors—outcomes of dating [11], job interviews [10], public speaking [2], etc. Most of these works use a fixed taxonomy and summary statistics like mean, variance, minima, maxima, count. These features may not be granular enough to segment or detect nonverbal behavioral cues.

[1] A demo is available in http://hci.cs.rochester.edu

MM'15, October 26–30, 2015, Brisbane, Australia.
 ISBN 978-1-4503-3459-4/15/10 ...$15.00.
DOI: http://dx.doi.org/10.1145/2733373.2806350.

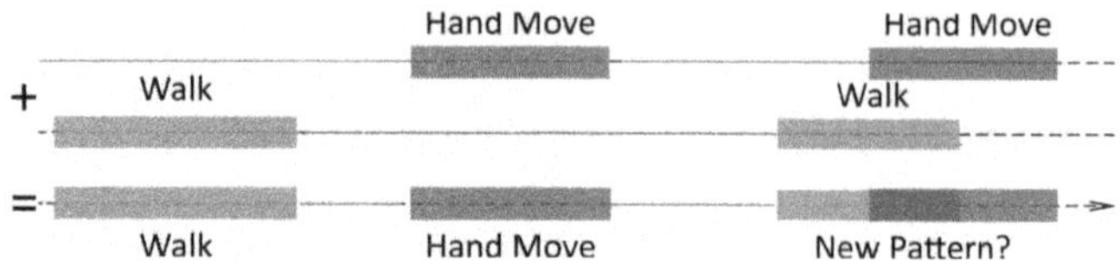

Figure 1: A simplified illustration of a problem that can be introduced from overlapping activities.

Activity analysis [1, 4] is another area related to nonverbal behavioral analysis. As Aggarwal et al. described [1], the focus of this type of work is to identify the activities (walking, jumping, talking, etc.) within a video, as well as to identify the start and end times of the segments. This domain is mostly focused on supervised classification approaches.

There exist a few unsupervised methods for activity analysis as well. Zhou et al. [15] proposed a method named Aligned Cluster Analysis (ACA) for simultaneously segmenting and clustering temporal sequences using Dynamic Time Warping (DTW) and k-means clustering. In this approach, the temporal segments are assumed to be non-overlapping. However, in real life, the segments might overlap depending on the signal representations. For example, if we consider only the three dimensional coordinates of a person's hand, it may appear as different patterns depending on whether the person is showing a hand gesture or physically moving about (Figure 1). Now, if the person performs both actions together, the resulting pattern will be overlapped. Many different spurious patterns may emerge depending on how they overlap—these are typically difficult to detect. Our model can address this issue.

Our work is inspired by the SISC model presented by Mørup et al. [9]. An optimization problem similar to SISC is applied by Li et al. [7] in the action recognition problems. However, they considered the input as a set of K independent 1D signals. On the other hand, we consider it as a multivariate signal with K components. For MoCap data, our model allows the temporal patterns to capture the interdependence among the body-joints. In addition, we solve the optimization problem using a Gradient Descent (GD) approach, as opposed to the Orthogonal Matching Pursuit (OMP) used by Li et al [7]. GD relaxes the requirement of specifying a maximum number of repetitions for the patterns within the signal.

3. NONVERBAL BEHAVIORAL CUES

Behavioral scientists define nonverbal behavioral cues as patterns observed in gestures, posture, touching behavior, facial expressions, eye behavior, vocal behavior, etc. [6]. Vinciarelli et al. [14] notes that "The term behavioural cue is typically used to describe a set of temporal changes in neuromuscular and physiological activity that last for short intervals of time (milliseconds to minutes)."

To capture the essence of this definition, we assume a specific structure for the behavioral (MoCap) signals, as illustrated in Figure 2. We model the signals to be composed of several small patterns (behavioral cues). These patterns get activated sparsely at various time-instances. This sparse activation ensures that a pattern is not distorted by overlapping with itself. However, different patterns are allowed to overlap. A mathematical formulation of this model is discussed in the following section.

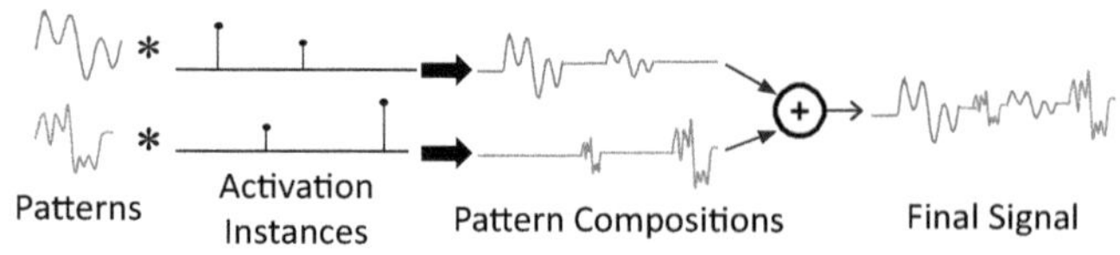

Figure 2: An assumption about the behavioral signal generation model.

4. PROBLEM FORMULATION

Let $\mathbf{f}[n]$ be a finite length multivariate behavioral signal with K elements. More specifically, it is the output of the skeleton tracker at every frame, representing the x, y, z coordinates of the body joints. The length of the signal is N; i.e. $0 \leq n < N$. The mathematical model of the behavioral signal, $\mathbf{f}_{\text{model}}[n]$, is as follows:

$$\sum_{d=0}^{D-1} \alpha_d[n] * \psi_d[m] = \sum_{d=0}^{D-1} \sum_{u=0}^{N-1} \alpha_d[u]\psi_d[n-u] \quad (1)$$

where, $\psi_d[m]$ denotes the dth pattern ($0 \leq d < D$, $0 \leq m < M$). In general, the patterns are short; i.e. $M \ll N$. The activation sequence, $\alpha_d[n]$, consists of sparse impulses. These impulses represent the locations where the pattern d appears in the signal. Length of $\alpha_d[n]$ is the same as the signal length, N. The convolution ($*$) of $\psi_d[m]$ with a single impulse of $\alpha_d[n]$ shifts the pattern d to the location of the impulse. We use this idea to make the behavioral cues *shift-invariant.*

To estimate the model parameters, $\psi_d[m]$ and $\alpha_d[n]$, we minimize the total squared difference between the actual signal and the model, $\mathbf{f}_{\text{model}}[n]$. As the behavioral cues activate sparsely over time, most of the elements of α should be zero. We enforce sparsity over the activation sequence by minimizing the ℓ_1 norm of α. In addition, we enforce non-negativity over α to avoid upside-down patterns. The overall optimization problem is shown in the Eq (2)

$$\hat{\psi}[m], \hat{\alpha}[n] = \underset{\psi,\alpha}{\operatorname{argmin}} \underbrace{\frac{1}{2}\left\|\mathbf{f}[n] - \mathbf{f}_{\text{model}}[n]\right\|^2}_{P(\psi,\alpha)} + \underbrace{\lambda\left\|\alpha\right\|_1}_{Q(\alpha)} \quad (2)$$
$$\text{s.t.} \quad \|\psi\|_F^2 \leq 1 \quad \text{and,} \quad \forall_n \alpha[n] \geq 0.$$

Here, $\|\alpha\|_1 := \sum_{d=0}^{D-1}\sum_{n=0}^{N-1}|\alpha_d[n]|$ represents the ℓ_1 norm of α. λ is the Lagrange multiplier controlling the weights imposed on the sparsity constraint of α. We also use a constraint $\|\psi\|_F^2 \leq 1$ to ensure that ψ is not affected by the values of λ.

5. OPTIMIZATION

The objective function shown in (2) is generally non-convex. However, when any one of the model parameters (α or ψ) is held fixed, it becomes convex over the other parameter. We use *alternating proximal gradient descent* approach to solve this optimization problem, as shown in Algorithm 1. In this approach, we alternatively update the parameters. For instance, we hold ψ fixed while updating α, and vice versa. It reduces the error after each iteration and guarantees to converge. However, there is no guarantee that it will converge to the global optimum. We rerun the algorithm multiple times with random initialization to make it likely to find the global optimum.

Algorithm 1: Learning the Behavioral Cues

Input: $\mathbf{f}[n]$, M, D and λ
Output: ψ, α
Initialize;
$i \leftarrow 0$;
$\alpha \leftarrow 0$, $\psi \leftarrow$ random;
while *not Converge* **do**
  Update ψ;
  reconstruct $\mathbf{f}_{model} \leftarrow \sum_{d=1}^{D-1} \alpha_d * \psi_d$;
  calculate $\nabla_\psi P$ using $\mathbf{f}, \mathbf{f}_{model}$ and α [Eq. (4)];
  $\psi^{(i+1)} \leftarrow$ **project**$(\psi^{(i)} - \gamma_\psi \nabla_\psi P)$;
  Update α;
  reconstruct $\mathbf{f}_{model} \leftarrow \sum_{d=1}^{D-1} \alpha_d * \psi_d$;
  calculate $\nabla_\alpha P$ using $\mathbf{f}, \mathbf{f}_{model}$ and ψ [Eq. (5)];
  $\alpha^{(i+1)} \leftarrow$ **shrink**$(\alpha^{(i)} - \gamma_\alpha \nabla_\alpha P)$ [Eq. (3)];
  $i \leftarrow i+1$

The objective function in (2) is a composite function with a smooth part, $P(\psi,\alpha)$, and a non-smooth part, $Q(\alpha)$. We use an *iterative soft-thresholding* approach for this minimization, as reviewed by Beck et al. [3]. We update α by the gradients of $P(\psi,\alpha)$, followed by a **shrink** operation, as shown in (3). This operation reduces each component of α towards zero and thus resulting in a sparse solution. We simultaneously project α to the set of positive numbers to enforce non-negativity.

$$\begin{aligned} \alpha[n] &\leftarrow \text{sgn}(\alpha[n])\max(0, |\alpha[n]| - \gamma\lambda) \quad \forall_{0\le n<N} \\ \alpha[n] &\leftarrow max(0, \alpha[n]) \quad \forall_{0\le n<N} \end{aligned} \tag{3}$$

The gradients of P with respect to ψ and α ($\nabla_\psi P$ and $\nabla_\alpha P$) are given by Eq (4) and (5), respectively.

$$\frac{\partial P}{\partial \psi_{d',k'}[m']} = \sum_{n=0}^{N-1} \{f_{\text{model},k'}[n] - f'_k[n]\}\alpha_{d'}[n-m'] \tag{4}$$

$$\frac{\partial P}{\partial \alpha_{d'}[n']} = \sum_{k=0}^{K-1}\sum_{n=0}^{N-1} \{f_{\text{model},k}[n] - f_k[n]\}\psi_{d',k}[n-m'] \tag{5}$$

In order to determine a correct learning rate γ_ψ or γ_α, we use a *backtracking line search* approach. We gradually decrease the learning rate until the objective function, $\mathcal{F}(x_i)$, satisfies $\mathcal{F}(x_{i+1}) \le \mathcal{M}_{x_i,\gamma_i}(x_{i+1})$, where, $\mathcal{M}_{x_i,\gamma_i}$ represents a function as defined in (6).

$$\begin{aligned} \mathcal{M}_{x_i,\gamma_i}(x_{i+1}) &:= \mathcal{F}(x_i) + \langle \nabla\mathcal{F}(x_i), x_{i+1} - x_i\rangle \\ &+ \frac{1}{2\gamma_i}\|x_{i+1} - x_i\|^2 + Q(\alpha). \end{aligned} \tag{6}$$

Here, x_i refers to the model parameters (ψ or α) in the ith iteration.

In the **project** procedure, we use (7) to project $\psi_d[m]$ on the set $\{\psi_d[m] \mid \|\psi_d[m]\|_F^2 \le 1\}$ at every iteration. This enforces the constraint $\|\psi_d[m]\|_F^2 \le 1$.

$$\psi_d[m] \leftarrow \min(\|\psi_d[m]\|_F, 1)\frac{\psi_d[m]}{\|\psi_d[m]\|_F} \tag{7}$$

We set the value of λ using the L-curve method, as described by Mørup et al. [9].

Figure 3: A sample frame from one of the videos in the public speaking dataset.

6. DATA

We applied this algorithm on two different types of datasets. The first type was a synthetically-formulated dataset with overlapping patterns. We used this data to empirically check if the algorithm could solve the problem described in Figure 1. The second type was a real dataset, collected in an actual public speaking scenario [13].

The public speaking dataset contained videos (Figure 3) and MoCap sequences of 55 public speeches given by 20 students—12 males and eight females. Each speech was approximately three minutes long. The MoCap sequences were captured by a Kinect skeleton tracker. All the sequences contained x, y, and z coordinates of 20 joints of the speaker's body. Therefore, each MoCap signal was a time-varying signal with 60 components.

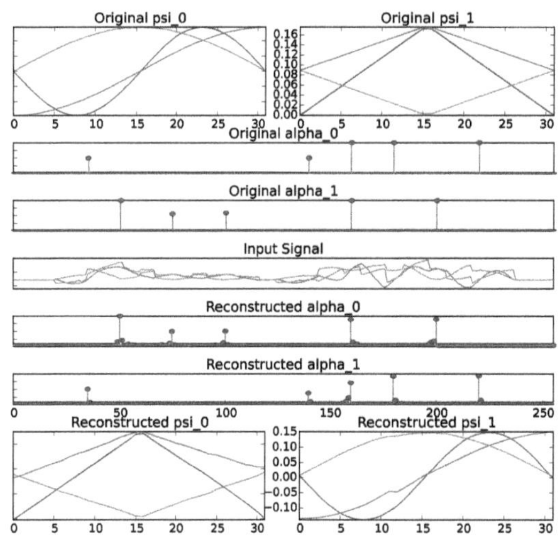

Figure 4: The test of SISC algorithm using synthetically-generated data.

7. RESULTS

The results of running the algorithm on both synthetic and real data are discussed below.

7.1 Synthetic Data

We illustrate a synthetically-generated data in Figure 4. The top row shows two patterns (ψ_0 and ψ_1) in a three dimensional signal (i.e. K = 3) that were used to construct the input data (row four). The second and the third row illustrate the activation sequences α_0 and α_1, respectively. We notice that the reconstructed patterns (row seven) are

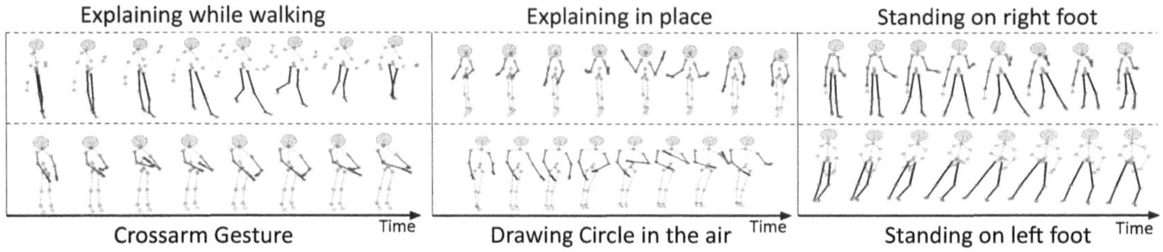

Figure 5: A few behavioral cues automatically extracted from the public speaking data. The length of each behavioral cue (M) was set to 2 seconds. We highlighted the bones showing large movements in time.

almost identical to the original patterns (row one), although their order is not same. Notice that the original activation sequences (second and third rows) contain an impulse at index 160, indicating an overlap of the patterns. The reconstructed plots of the activation sequences (fifth and sixth rows) show that this overlap was perfectly identified and decoupled. This shows that SISC can handle overlapping patterns. However, this is not true for all possible cases. For example, if the result of overlapping signals is orthogonal to any of its constituents, SISC will not be able to decouple them. Nevertheless, such orthogonality is not likely in practice.

7.2 Real Data

The algorithm was run individually on each public speaking MoCap sequence. A few behavioral cues captured by the algorithm are shown in Figure 5. Each sequence of the skeletons represents a single behavioral cue that the algorithm extracted automatically. The position of the skeleton represents different instances in time. We observed that, the patterns represent the most common body movements in the sequence. We say the behavioral cues are "human-interpretable" if we can associate the retrieved movement patterns of the skeleton with the actual body movements shown in the videos purely through visual observation. However, both the notion of interpretibility and the actual interpretation of the patterns are subjective and manually assigned by the authors.

The time length of the behavioral cues, M, was heuristically set to two seconds. If M is too small (< 0.5 sec), only short parts of the original sequence are captured. In that case, the captured patterns become difficult to interpret. On the other hand, increasing M (2 sec $< M < 5$ sec) does not seem to have much influence on the interpretibility of the patterns. However, we've noticed multiple patterns of body movements to be merged together when M is too large (e.g. $M > 8$ seconds).

The parameter D controls the maximum number of patterns to be extracted from the signal. The extracted patterns lose interpretibility if D is set too low (e.g. $D \leq 2$). On the other hand, setting D to a large value does not have any negative effect on the interpretibility. In that case, the additional patterns show up as a signal of all zeros. However, increasing D slows down the program linearly.

8. CONCLUSION

In this paper, we presented a mathematical framework for unsupervised extraction of body movement patterns. We used shift-invariant sparse coding to extract the patterns. We noticed that the extracted patterns are human-interpretable, that is, we could manually associate the patterns with the movements shown in the video. In the future, this framework could be used to mine common body movement patterns (e.g., fidgeting) in public speaking scenarios. We shall try to apply this framework to extract patterns from other behavioral signals (e.g., facial expressions, prosody, etc.). A demo of our framework is available in hci.cs.rochester.edu.

9. REFERENCES

[1] J. K. Aggarwal et al. Human activity analysis: A review. *ACM Computing Surveys (CSUR)*, 2011.

[2] L. Batrinca et al. Cicero-towards a multimodal virtual audience platform for public speaking training. In *Intelligent Virtual Agents*, 2013.

[3] A. Beck and M. Teboulle. A fast iterative shrinkage-thresholding algorithm for linear inverse problems. *SIAM journal on imaging sciences*, 2(1):183–202, 2009.

[4] G. Cheng et al. Advances in human action recognition: A survey. *arXiv preprint arXiv:1501.05964*, 2015.

[5] R. Grosse et al. Shift-invariant sparse coding for audio classification. In *UAI*, 2007.

[6] M. Knapp, J. Hall, and T. Horgan. *Nonverbal communication in human interaction.* Cengage Learning, 2013.

[7] Y. Li et al. Learning shift-invariant sparse representation of actions. In *CVPR*, 2010.

[8] D. Metaxas and S. Zhang. A review of motion analysis methods for human nonverbal communication computing. *Image and Vision Computing*, 2013.

[9] M. Mørup et al. Shift invariant sparse coding of image and music data. Technical Report IMM2008-04659, Technical University of Denmark, 2008.

[10] I. Naim et al. Automated prediction and analysis of job interview performance: The role of what you say and how you say it. In *FG'15*, 2015.

[11] R. Ranganath et al. It's not you, it's me: Detecting flirting and its misperception in speed-dates. In *EMNLP*, 2009.

[12] J. Shotton et al. Real-time human pose recognition in parts from single depth images. *Communications of the ACM*, 2013.

[13] M. I. Tanveer et al. Rhema: A real-time in-situ intelligent interface to help people with public speaking. In *IUI'15*, pages 286–295. ACM, 2015.

[14] A. Vinciarelli et al. Social signal processing: Survey of an emerging domain. *Image and Vision Computing*.

[15] F. Zhou et al. Aligned cluster analysis for temporal segmentation of human motion. In *FG'08*, 2008.

Exploiting Word and Visual Word Co-occurrence for Sketch-based Clipart Image Retrieval

Ching-Hsuan Liu, Yen-Liang Lin, Wen-Feng Cheng, and Winston H. Hsu
National Taiwan University, Taipei, Taiwan

ABSTRACT

As the increasing popularity of touch-screen devices, retrieving images by hand-drawn sketch has become a trend. Human sketch can easily express some complex user intention such as the object shape. However, sketches are sometimes ambiguous due to different drawing styles and inter-class object shape ambiguity. Although adding text queries as semantic information can help removing the ambiguity of sketch, it requires a huge amount of efforts to annotate text tags to all database clipart images. We propose a method directly model the relationship between text and clipart images by the co-occurrence relationship between words and visual words, which improves traditional sketch-based image retrieval (SBIR), provides a baseline performance and obtains more relevant results in the condition that all images in database do not have any text tag. Experimental results show that our method really can help SBIR to get better retrieval result since it indeed learned semantic meaning from the "word-visual word" (W-VW) co-occurrence relationship.

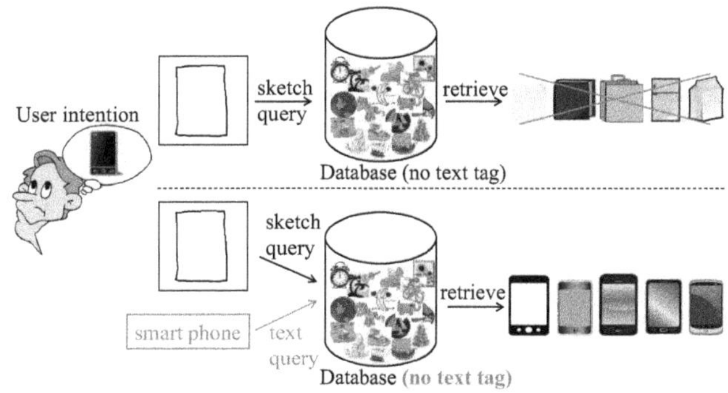

Figure 1: We propose a clipart image retrieval system which can support sketch and text query even all images in the database do not have any text tag. This example shows when hand-drawn sketch query is ambiguous, users can add text query to refine the retrieval list to find clipart images matching their intention.

Categories and Subject Descriptors

H.3.3 [**Information Storage and Retrieval**]: Information Search and Retrieval—*Retrieval models*

Keywords

sketch, co-occurrence

1. INTRODUCTION

Since the amount of online clipart images grows explosively, how to effectively and efficiently find the clipart images matching user's intention has become a strong need. Most of the existing clipart image search engines (e.g., openclipart) use text-based methods to search and thus require manually annotate text tags to each clipart image, which is time consuming and needs huge amount of human effort.

MM'15, October 26–30, 2015, Brisbane, Australia.
 ISBN 978-1-4503-3459-4/15/10 ...$15.00.
DOI: http://dx.doi.org/10.1145/2733373.2806351.

That is why the number of clipart images in clipart collection websites are far less than that in the whole web. Fortunately, due to the increasing popularity of touch-screen devices, and the advantage of that human sketch can easily express some complex user intention such as the object shape, sketch-based image retrieval (SBIR) has become a trend.

However, hand-drawn sketches are sometimes ambiguous, because of various drawing skills by different person, and the similar shape among different objects. Thus, adding text queries as semantic information to remove ambiguity is necessary. Since annotating text tags to clipart images is impractical, we desire a clipart image retrieval system which can support sketch and text query even all images in the database do not have any text tag (see Figure 1).

Most previous research of SBIR focused on extracting effective features to better match a hand-drawn sketch to natural images [3, 4, 1, 6]. Eitz *et al.* [4] designed new local shape features and use BoVW approach for search, Cao *et al.* [1] described a new kind of visual word using orientation and edge information, and Parui *et al.* [6] used contour chains to form a similarity (translation, scale and rotation) invariant descriptor. However, they only use one type of query (i.e., sketch) to retrieve images, thus cannot get satisfactory result when sketch query is ambiguous. Although Cao *et al.* [2] built a sketch-based multimodal search engine to support sketch, tag and color queries, they required

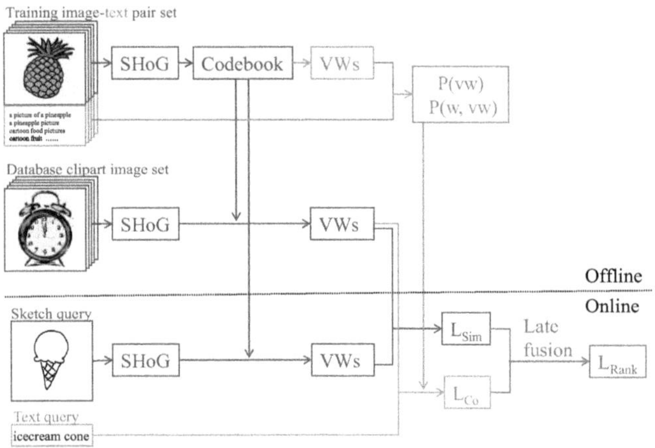

Figure 2: Framework: The blue part is the sketch-to-clipart-image process, the red part is the text-to-clipart-image process, and the green part is the fusion process of the previous two methods.

tag information in the database to support the text-based retrieval. In [7], they use hand-drawn sketch recognition results as text queries to improve the SBIR, but still need to search in the database with text information. Besides, if the sketch query is too ambiguous to recognize, the semantic information cannot be provided.

To build a clipart image retrieval system which can support sketch and text query even all images in the database do not have any text tag, we propose a "text-clipart image" co-occurrence probability model, which builds on existing sketch-based image retrieval method [4]. To our best knowledge, this is the first work to directly model the relationship between text and clipart images. We use a bunch of "clipart image-description text pairs" (in the rest of this paper, we abbreviate it as "image-text pairs") to learn the W-VW co-occurrence relationship, then utilize this relationship to estimate the co-occurrence score between text and clipart image. Users can query by either sketch or text first to express their intention, then adding another query type to enhance the retrieval results when they are not satisfied the original results.

2. METHODS

The framework of our proposed method is illustrated in Figure 2, which can be divided into three main parts: the sketch-to-clipart-image process (blue part), the text-to-clipart-image process (red part), and the fusion process of the previous two methods (green part). The sketch-to-clipart-image process produces a similarity score between the sketch query and each database clipart image by calculating the cosine value of their representation vectors. The text-to-clipart-image process produces a co-occurrence score between the text query and each database clipart image by estimating the probability of each database clipart image given the text query. The fusion process combines the two score lists by late fusion to obtain the final ranking list.

2.1 Sketch to Clipart Image

The sketch-to-clipart-image process in our framework uses the SBIR method in [4]. We learn the codebook from a set of training clipart images which is disjoint from the set of database clipart images. For each training clipart image, we extract $F(=500)$ sketched histogram of oriented gradients (SHoG) features, and perform hierarchical k-means (HKM) clustering on the feature set from all training clipart images to produce the codebook. We choose $K = 512$ (each level has 8 nodes, $k = 3$) as the codebook size by experiments[1]. Then we can extract SHoG features from database clipart images and user sketch query, quantize each SHoG feature into a visual word (VW) according to the codebook, and represent each database clipart image and the user sketch to bag-of-visual-word (BoVW) representation vectors. We denote each BoVW representation vector of database clipart image by $D_n = [db_{vw_1}(n), db_{vw_2}(n), ..., db_{vw_K}(n)]^T$, where $n = 1, 2, ..., N$, N is the number of database cilpart images, and $db_{vw_\cdot}(n)$ is the count of visual word $vw_\cdot$ in image n. The sketch query is denoted as $S = [sb_{vw_1}, sb_{vw_2}, ..., sb_{vw_K}]^T$, where $sb_{vw_\cdot}$ is the count of visual word $vw_\cdot$ in the sketch. Finally, we calculate the cosine value between sketch query S and each database clipart image D_n to obtain a similarity score $Sim(S, D_n) = \frac{S^T D_n}{\|S\|\|D_n\|}$, producing the similarity score list $L_{Sim} = \{Sim(S, D_1), Sim(S, D_2), ..., Sim(S, D_N)\}$.

2.2 Text to Clipart Image

Given a text query T:

$$T = \{w_{t(1)}, w_{t(2)}, ..., w_{t(M)}\}, \quad (1)$$

where M is the number of words in the text query, $t(\cdot)$ is the index in the word dictionary, and $w_{t(\cdot)}$ denotes the word corresponding to the index. In order to find those related database clipart images which do not have any text tag, we can choose those images having high $P(D_n|T)$, i.e., the co-occurrence probability of the database clipart image and the text query given the text query, as related images.

For derivation convenience, we rewrite the BoVW representation of database clipart images by listing all the visual words:

$$D_n = \{vw_{d(n,1)}, vw_{d(n,2)}, ..., vw_{d(n,F)}\}, \quad (2)$$

where F is the number of visual words in the clipart image, $vw_{d(n,\cdot)}$ denotes the visual word whose index is $d(n, \cdot)$ in the codebook. Then $P(D_n|T)$ can be represented to:

$$P(D_n|T) = P(vw_{d(n,1)}, vw_{d(n,2)}, ..., vw_{d(n,F)}|T). \quad (3)$$

We assume $vw_{d(n,1)}, vw_{d(n,2)}, ..., vw_{d(n,F)}$ are mutually independent given T, so Eq. (3) becomes:

$$P(D_n|T) = \prod_{i=1}^{F} P(vw_{d(n,i)}|T). \quad (4)$$

Then we apply Bayes' rule to Eq. (4), and replace T according to Eq. (1) to get:

$$P(D_n|T) = \prod_{i=1}^{F} \frac{P(vw_{d(n,i)})P(w_{t(1)}, w_{t(2)}, ..., w_{t(M)}|vw_{d(n,i)})}{P(T)}. \quad (5)$$

By assuming $w_{t(1)}, w_{t(2)}, ..., w_{t(M)}$ are mutually independent given $vw_{d(n,i)}$, Eq. (5) can be futher expressed as:

$$P(D_n|T) = \prod_{i=1}^{F} \frac{P(vw_{d(n,i)}) \prod_{j=1}^{M} P(w_{t(j)}|vw_{d(n,i)})}{P(T)}. \quad (6)$$

[1]We try $K = 5^3, 6^3, ..., 12^3$ and use nDCG to evaluate.

Since what we care is the relative score instead of exact value of $P(D_n|T)$, we take the logarithm of $P(D_n|T)$ to simplify the calculation (Eq. (7)), and remove the denominator of Eq. (6) because the given text query T is the same for every D_n (Eq. (8)). Therefore, our goal is formulated as:

$$D_n^* = \arg\max_{D_n \in \mathbf{D}} P(D_n|T) = \arg\max_{D_n \in \mathbf{D}} \log P(D_n|T) \quad (7)$$

$$= \arg\max_{n\in\{1,2,...,N\}} \log\{\prod_{i=1}^{F}[P(vw_{d(n,i)}) \prod_{j=1}^{M} P(w_{t(j)}|vw_{d(n,i)})]\} \quad (8)$$

$$= \arg\max_{n\in\{1,2,...,N\}} \sum_{i=1}^{F}\{\log P(vw_{d(n,i)}) \quad (9)$$

$$+ \sum_{j=1}^{M}[\log P(w_{t(j)}, vw_{d(n,i)}) - \log P(vw_{d(n,i)})]\},$$

where $\mathbf{D} = \{D_1, D_2, ..., D_N\}$. So the database clipart images which are related to the text query is those D_n^* with top K-maximal scores.

The text-to-clipart-image process in our framework is based on Eq. (9). We learn the $P(vw_{d(n,i)})$ and $P(w_{t(j)}, vw_{d(n,i)})$ from a set of training image-text pairs:

$$P(vw_p) = \frac{\sum_{t=1}^{R} C^t(vw_p)}{\sum_{t=1}^{R}\sum_{p'=1}^{K} C^t(vw_{p'})} \quad (10)$$

$$P(w_q, vw_p) = \frac{\sum_{t=1}^{R} C^t(vw_p) \times C^t(w_q)}{\sum_{t=1}^{R}\sum_{p'=1}^{K}\sum_{q'=1}^{V} C^t(vw_{p'}) \times C^t(w_{q'})}, \quad (11)$$

where R is the size of training set, V is the size of word dictionary, and $C^t(\cdot)$[2] denotes the occurrence count of the word/visual word in training data t. Then we can calculate the co-occurrence score $Co(T, D_n)$ between the text query T and each database clipart image D_n by calculating Eq. (9):

$$Co(T, D_n) = \sum_{i=1}^{F}\{\log P(vw_{d(n,i)}) \quad (12)$$

$$+ \sum_{j=1}^{M}[\log P(w_{t(j)}, vw_{d(n,i)}) - \log P(vw_{d(n,i)})]\},$$

producing the co-occurrence score list $L_{Co} = \{Co(T, D_1), Co(T, D_2), ..., Co(T, D_N)\}$.

2.3 Late Fusion

We combine the two score lists L_{Sim} and L_{Co}[3] by late fusion to obtain the final ranking list:

$$L_{Rank} = \alpha \cdot L_{Sim} + (1-\alpha) \cdot L_{Co}, \quad (13)$$

where $\alpha \in [0, 1]$. Then the top ranked database clipart images are the retrieval result of our system.

[2]We use atc-tfidf as smoothing to avoid zero value of $C^t(\cdot)$.
[3]Since all values in L_{Sim} is in $[0, 1]$, we also normalize all L_{Co} values to $[0, 1]$ before late fusion.

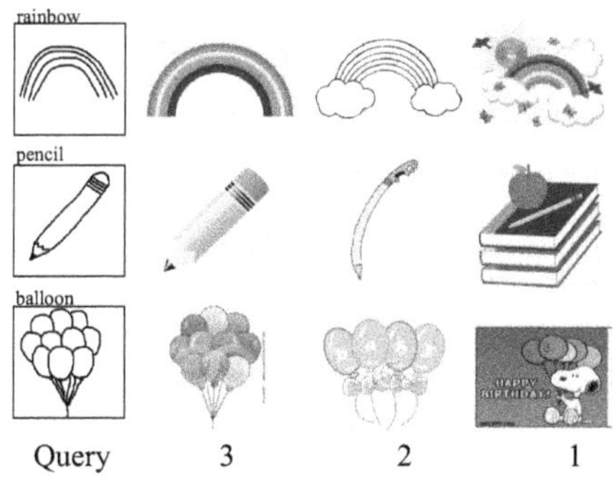

Figure 3: Text + sketch query and three related database clipart image with relevance value = 3, 2, and 1, respectively.

3. EXPERIMENTS

3.1 Dataset

In order to learn the co-occurrence relationship between clipart images and texts, we build our dataset from Clickture-Lite [5], which contains a subset of one-year click log (a.k.a. image-query pairs) of a commercial image search engine. Clickture-Lite consists of a big table of triads, a triad $< I, Q, C >$ means that the image I was clicked C times in the search results of text query Q in one year. We first remain those images whose text query Q contains keyword such as "clipart" or "cartoon", removing irrelevant images by browsing those images, then separate these images into two parts. In the first part, we construct a bunch of image-text pairs according to these images. Each description text of a clipart image I is formed by concatenating the text query Q[4] for C times of each related triads. Finally, we get the training set containing $R = 27,815$ image-text pairs. In the second part, we simply gather these images to form the database clipart image set with size $N = 6,954$. Besides, we self-produce 70 hand-drawn sketches and text pairs as the sketch and text queries.

3.2 Evaluation

We use normalized discounted cumulative gain (nDCG) to evaluate the performance of our proposed methods. For each sketch + text query, each database clipart image is assigned a relevance value on a scale of 3 (highly relevant) to 0 (irrelevant). Figure 3 shows some queries and their relevant images.

The late fusion results of similarity score list L_{Sim} and co-occurrence score list L_{Co} are shown in figure 4, evaluated by average $nDCG_{10}$ and average $nDCG_{50}$. We choose $\alpha = 0.3$ since it produces the best result. Although the performance of using only text query ($\alpha = 0$) is the worst, we can see that all late fusion results are better than using only sketch query ($\alpha = 1$), which means that the co-occurrence model for text-to-clipart-image really can help SBIR for user to find those images they want.

Figure 5 and 6 show some examples of the effectiveness of adding another query type to enhance the original retrieval result which uses only one query type. Although our original goal is to help SBIR to find related clipart images by adding text queries, our system can also support query by text directly. Figure 7 shows some impressive results of using only text to query the clipart image database which

[4]With text preprocessing such as stop words removal.

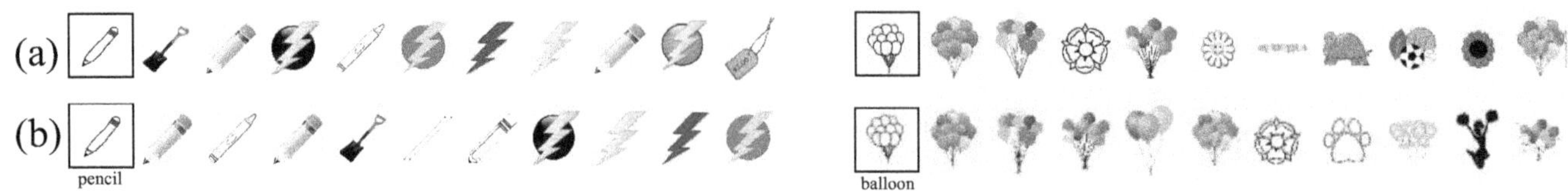

Figure 5: Examples of adding text queries helps the retrieval result. (a) is the retrieval result querying by only sketch, and (b) is the retrieval result querying by sketch + text.

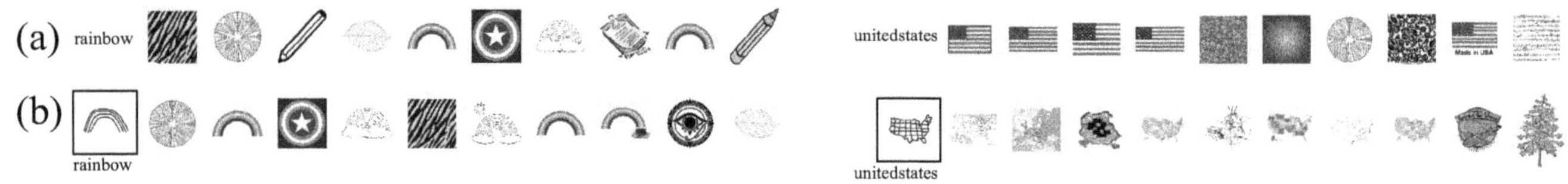

Figure 6: Examples of adding sketch queries helps the retrieval result. (a) is the retrieval result querying by only text, and (b) is the retrieval result querying by sketch + text.

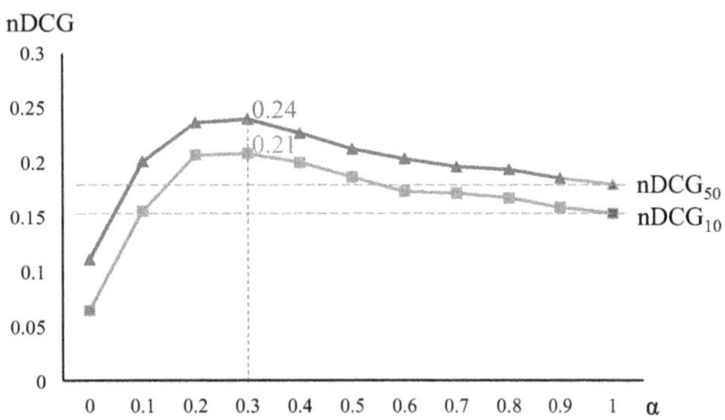

Figure 4: The late fusion results of similarity score list L_{Sim} and co-occurrence score list L_{Co} evaluated by nDCG. The blue dots ($\alpha = 1$) is the sketch-to-clipart-image results, the red dots ($\alpha = 0$) is the text-to-clipart-image results, and the green dots ($\alpha = 0.1, 0.2, ..., 0.9$) is the late fusion results. Results show that the co-occurrence model for text-to-clipart-image can benefit sketch-based clipart image retrieval, and alpha = 0.3 gives the best performance.

without any text tag. We can find that our method indeed learned semantic meaning from the W-VW co-occurrence relationship.

4. CONCLUSIONS

In this paper, we proposed a method to directly model the relationship between text and clipart images by W-VW co-occurrence relationship. This method allows user to query images by text in the condition that all images in the database do not have any text tag. By using late fusion to combine the retrieval results of SBIR and our method, experimental results showed that our method really can help SBIR to get better retrieval results since it indeed learned semantic meaning from the W-VW co-occurrence relationship, providing a baseline for future comparison. Besides, our text-clipart image co-occurrence model can build on any SBIR methods using BoVW representation, thus can easily embed into many existing SBIR systems to refine their retrieval results.

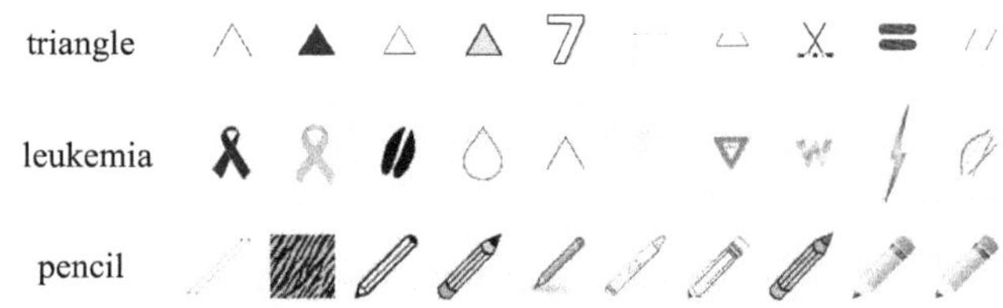

Figure 7: Examples of using only text to query the clipart image database whose images do not have any text tag. We can find that our method indeed learned semantic meaning from the W-VW co-occurrence relationship.

5. REFERENCES

[1] Y. Cao, C. Wang, L. Zhang, and L. Zhang. Edgel index for large-scale sketch-based image search. In *Computer Vision and Pattern Recognition (CVPR), 2011 IEEE Conference on*, pages 761–768. IEEE, 2011.

[2] Y. Cao, H. Wang, C. Wang, Z. Li, L. Zhang, and L. Zhang. Mindfinder: interactive sketch-based image search on millions of images. In *Proceedings of the international conference on Multimedia*, pages 1605–1608. ACM, 2010.

[3] M. Eitz, K. Hildebrand, T. Boubekeur, and M. Alexa. An evaluation of descriptors for large-scale image retrieval from sketched feature lines. *Computers & Graphics*, 34(5):482–498, 2010.

[4] M. Eitz, K. Hildebrand, T. Boubekeur, and M. Alexa. Sketch-based image retrieval: Benchmark and bag-of-features descriptors. *IEEE Transactions on Visualization and Computer Graphics*, 17(11):1624–1636, 2011.

[5] X.-S. Hua, L. Yang, M. Ye, K. Wang, Y. Rui, and J. Li. Clickture: A large-scale real-world image dataset. Technical report, Microsoft Research Technical Report MSR-TR-2013–75, 2013.

[6] S. Parui and A. Mittal. Similarity-invariant sketch-based image retrieval in large databases. In *Computer Vision–ECCV 2014*, pages 398–414. Springer, 2014.

[7] Z. Sun, C. Wang, L. Zhang, and L. Zhang. Query-adaptive shape topic mining for hand-drawn sketch recognition. In *Proceedings of the 20th ACM international conference on Multimedia*, pages 519–528. ACM, 2012.

Heterogeneous Graph-based Video Search Reranking using Web Knowledge via Social Media Network

Soh Yoshida, Takahiro Ogawa and Miki Haseyama
Graduate School of Information Science and Technology, Hokkaido University
{yoshida,ogawa}@lmd.ist.hokudai.ac.jp, miki@ist.hokudai.ac.jp

ABSTRACT

Graph-based reranking is effective for refining text-based video search results by making use of the social network structure. Unlike previous works which only focus on an individual video graph, the proposed method leverages the mutual reinforcement of heterogeneous graphs, such as videos and their associated tags obtained by social influence mining. Specifically, propagation of information relevancy across different modalities is performed by exchanging information of inter- and intra-relations among heterogeneous graphs. The proposed method then formulates the video search reranking as an optimization problem from the perspective of Bayesian framework. Furthermore, in order to model the consistency over the modified video graph topology, a local learning regularization with a social community detection scheme is introduced to the framework. Since videos within the same social community have strong semantic correlation, the consistency score estimation becomes feasible. Experimental results obtained by applying the proposed method to a real-world video collection show its effectiveness.

Categories and Subject Descriptors

H.3.3 [**Information Search and Retrieval**]: Retrieval models

General Terms

Algorithms; Performance

Keywords

Video search reranking; Social multimedia; Heterogeneous graph

1. INTRODUCTION

With the explosive growth of social media, massive numbers of videos are created and shared online everyday. For example, one of the most popular video sharing sites, YouTube, streams more than one billion videos a day[1]. Many techniques have been developed for multimedia search, and due to the success of information retrieval business, such as Google and Yahoo!, most search engines employ text-based search techniques. However, since textual information is sometimes noisy or unavailable, it cannot always describe the media content accurately.

To improve the text-based search performance, multimedia search reranking has attracted extensive attention [9]. It is an integrated framework that aims to obtain effective search results. A list of text-based search results is first returned by using textual information. Then visual information is applied to reorder the initial search result for refinement. In recent years, many methods have been proposed for graph-based multimedia search reranking targeting social media content [6, 12]. Although previous studies have shown promising performance, evaluations of the relative importance of multimedia contents have been carried out independently across different modalities. Thus, due to the complexity of real-world video contents, video search reranking using only visual information does not guarantee its accuracy. On the other hand, because of the various social activities, the video contains rich social media information such as tags, related videos, and social community, etc., which can provide meaningful contextual cues to understand its content. We call these cues Web knowledge. However, since the relations between videos and other information are not fully leveraged, the reinforcing dependency between them, which is beneficial to further improve reranking results, is not considered. Therefore, it is desirable to develop a novel algorithm that optimizes these heterogeneous contexts for better video search reranking.

In this paper, we propose a heterogeneous graph-based video search reranking method using Web knowledge obtained from social information. We adopt the following two procedures: (A) exploration of the mutual reinforcement between video and tag graphs through their combined graph, and (B) modeling graph-based reranking with a social community detection scheme using the modified video graph obtained in (A).

First, in (A), we explore the mutual reinforcement between videos and their associated tags by constructing three graphs: a video graph, a tag graph, and a bridging graph that combines the two graphs. Then, we adopt circular propagation [15] to the combined heterogeneous graph. This propagation iteratively refines the inter- and intra-relations of each heterogeneous graph through exchanging information across different graphs in a cyclic manner. From this procedure, we can obtain the modified video graph whose intra-relations are reinforced by information of a tag graph. Therefore, in (B), we model reranking using a graph. The basic assumption behind graph-based reranking methods is that neighboring nodes should have similar ranking scores, i.e., the ranking score is consistent over the graph topology. By modeling this assumption explicitly, the video search reranking is formulated from the probabilistic perspective in a Bayesian framework [12]. This reranking

[1]http://www.youtube.com/yt/press/en/statistics.html

MM'15, October 26–30, 2015, Brisbane, Australia.
© 2015 ACM. ISBN 978-1-4503-3459-4/15/10 ...$15.00.
DOI: http://dx.doi.org/10.1145/2733373.2806352.

method maximizes the ranking score consistency while minimizing the ranking distance, which represents the disagreement between the reranking result and the initial text-based ranking result. Furthermore, motivated by the work of community in network analysis structure [10], we derive a new local learning regularization with a community detection scheme to effectively model consistency over the graph. A community consists of a group of nodes that are densely connected to one another but sparsely connected to other dense groups. Since a community structure in networks usually reveals the common topic or interest, the consistency over a local area within a same community means that each sample has strong correlation with its neighbor. In our regularization, a local model is first trained for each sample with its neighbors to utilize community information by using the result of community detection scheme [3]. This model is then used to predict its consistent ranking score. Finally, by minimizing the difference between the objective ranking score and this locally predicted score, the desired consistency over the graph is guaranteed.

2. GRAPH CONSTRUCTION

This section explains how to construct heterogeneous graphs. We construct three types of graphs: a video graph, a tag graph, and a combined graph. Let G^k ($k = \{M, T\}$) denote the video graph and the tag graph, respectively, which is represented by $G^k = (V^k, E^k)$, where V^k and E^k are sets of nodes and edges. Specifically, $V^k = \{v_1^k, v_2^k, \ldots, v_{N_k}^k\}$, where N_k is the number of nodes in V^k, and each edge in E^k connects two nodes with weight function w^k. For instance, the weight function $w^k(i, j)$ measures the weight of the edge between v_i^k and v_j^k. We define the affinity matrix $\mathbf{W}^k$ by taking $w^k(i, j)$ as its (i, j)-th element.

2.1 Video Graph Construction

The proposed method constructs the video graph G^M by following social links, i.e. related video network, in the social media network. Specifically, our method is implemented by crawling videos from YouTube. First, for the video graph construction, we collect video sets $V^M = \{v_1^M, v_2^M, \ldots, v_{N_M}^M\}$ by adopting top-N_M videos, which are obtained by keyword search, as seeds of the related video search, and simply connect edges between the seed video and its related videos. Second, to model the relationship between the two videos, we extract low-level video features from these videos. Finally, we define the weight function w^M by calculating the video similarity between v_i^M and v_j^M.

2.1.1 Low-level feature extraction

In order to define the weight function of the video graph, we first extract low-level features. Let $\mathbf{s}_i = \{s_i^1, s_i^2, \ldots, s_i^{m_i}\}$ denote the shots in a video v_i^M by adopting the state-of-the-art shot segmentation technique [1], where m_i is the number of shots. Then the proposed method extracts three types of features from each shot s_i^h, including 1000-dimensional BOW [13] as object features, and 1600-dimensional HSV color histogram as color features, and 39-dimensional MFCC [5] as audio features, respectively. Note that we extract visual features from keyframes, and then, obtain keyframes among a shot by extracting top-three intermediate frames which are given as shot boundary candidates in [1].

2.1.2 Weight function calculation

The video weight function w^M in the video graph G^M between v_i^M and v_j^M is defined as follows:

$$w^M(i, j) = \sum_{l \in \mathcal{L}} \alpha_l \exp\left\{ -\frac{\min_{u \in \mathbf{s}_i, v \in \mathbf{s}_j} \mathrm{ED}(\mathbf{f}_u^l, \mathbf{f}_v^l)}{2\sigma_l^2} \right\}, \quad (1)$$

where $\mathcal{L} = \{BOW, HSV, MFCC\}$ is a set of features, $\mathbf{f}_u^l$ is a feature vector extracted from a shot s_i^u, $\mathrm{ED}(\cdot, \cdot)$ denotes the Euclidean distance, α_l is a weight parameter to combine different features, and σ_l is the positive radius parameter estimated by the median value of all the Euclidean distances.

2.2 Tag Graph Construction

Tags, supplied by users, describe the content of videos while providing additional contextual modalities about the videos. First, we collect N_T tags $V^T = \{v_1^T, v_2^T, \ldots, v_{N_T}^T\}$, which are associated with videos in the video graph G^M. As a preprocessing procedure, the standard stemming algorithm implemented by NLTK [2] and stop words[2] removal are applied. Then, since user-contributed tags are usually noisy and limited in terms of completeness, we adopt tag refinement algorithm in [7]. Second, in order to model the relations between tags, we assume there is a semantic relationship between two tags which are assigned to the same video, and then connect them with an edge. We calculate the tag distance using the concurrence similarity between tags based on their co-occurrence. Specifically, analogous to the principle of the Normalized Google distance (NGD) [4], we calculate $\mathrm{NGD}(v_i^T, v_j^T)$ between tags v_i^T and v_j^T as follows:

$$\mathrm{NGD}(v_i^T, v_j^T) = \frac{\max\{\log g(v_i^T), \log g(v_j^T)\} - \log g(v_i^T, v_j^T)}{\log N_g - \min\{\log g(v_i^T), \log g(v_j^T)\}}, \quad (2)$$

where N_g is the total number of pages on Google and $g(v_i^T)$, $g(v_j^T)$, and $g(v_i^T, v_j^T)$ denote the number of hit counts for tag v_i^T, v_j^T, and $v_i^T + v_j^T$ on Google, respectively. The weight function w^T in the tag graph G^T between tag v_i^T and v_j^T is calculated by

$$w^T(i, j) = \exp\left\{ -\frac{\mathrm{NGD}(v_i^T, v_j^T)}{2\sigma_{TAG}^2} \right\}, \quad (3)$$

where σ_{TAG} is the positive radius parameter, and it is also estimated by the median value of all the tag distances.

2.3 The Combined Heterogeneous Graph

To leverage mutual reinforcement between heterogeneous graphs, i.e., the video graph and the tag graph, we apply circular propagation [15] to the combined heterogeneous graph. This procedure can iteratively refine the inter- and intra-relations of each heterogeneous graph through exchanging information across these graphs in a cyclic manner. Let G^{MT} denote the combined heterogeneous graph, which is represented by $G^{MT} = \{V^{MT}, E^{MT}\}$. Specifically, $V^{MT} = \{V^M \cup V^T\}$ and E^{MT} denote the set of inter-edges which consists of edges connecting the two graphs (G^M and G^T) mutually. We link inter-edges between the video and its associated tags, and then we define inter-edge strength $\pi^{MT}(i, j)$ between video v_i^M and v_j^T as follows:

$$\pi^{MT}(i, j) = \begin{cases} \exp\left\{ -\frac{score(v_j^T, v_i^M)}{2\sigma_{MT}^2} \right\} & \text{if } v_j^T \in S^T(v_i^M) \\ 0 & \text{otherwise} \end{cases}, \quad (4)$$

where σ_{MT} is also the positive radius parameter, $S^T(v_i^M)$ denotes the subset of tags which are associated with video v_i^M, and we define the matrix $\mathbf{\Pi}^{MT}$ by taking $\pi^{MT}(i, j)$ as its (i, j)-th element. The function $score(v_j^T, v_i^M)$ computes a relevance score between the video v_i^M and the tag v_j^T. We adopt *tagRelevance* in [7] as an implementation of

[2][Online]. Available: http://bit.ly/8vBrVF

score function. Thus, we perform circular propagation as follows:

$$\begin{cases} \mathbf{W}^T_{(t)} = \theta_T \mathbf{\Pi}^{MT\prime} \mathbf{W}^M_{(t-1)} \mathbf{\Pi}^{MT} + (1-\theta_T)\mathbf{W}^T_{(0)} \\ \mathbf{W}^M_{(t)} = \theta_M \mathbf{\Pi}^{MT} \mathbf{W}^T_{(t-1)} \mathbf{\Pi}^{MT\prime} + (1-\theta_M)\mathbf{W}^M_{(0)} \end{cases}, \quad (5)$$

where $\mathbf{\Pi}^{MT\prime}$ represents the transposed matrix of $\mathbf{\Pi}^{MT}$, the subscript (t) denotes the iteration, the subscript (0) represents the initial state of iteration, and the trade-off parameter θ_M, θ_T $(0 \le \theta_M, \theta_T \le 1)$ weights the importance of the propagated and initial intra-relation of each heterogeneous graph. In this circular propagation, each row of $\mathbf{\Pi}^{MT}$ is normalized to 1 and we repeat the calculation C-times until the two affinity matrices converge as $(\mathbf{W}^M_{(C+1)} - \mathbf{W}^M_{(C)}) = 0$.

Therefore, for the proposed video retrieval, we adopt this well-propagated weight matrix $\mathbf{W}^M_{(C)}$ as an affinity matrix of the modified video graph. In the following section, we explain the details of the proposed video reranking by using this video graph.

3. HETEROGENEOUS GRAPH-BASED VIDEO SEARCH FRAMEWORK

As a result of the aforementioned procedure, we obtain the modified video graph which is mutually reinforced by the tag graph. This section explains a heterogeneous graph-based video search framework. In the proposed method, we introduce a Bayesian visual reranking framework to implement video search reranking based on this modified video graph. In other words, our method is an extension to the reranking method in [12]. Let $\bar{\mathbf{r}} = [\bar{r}_1, \bar{r}_2, \ldots, \bar{r}_{N_M}]'$ and $\mathbf{r} = [r_1, r_2, \ldots, r_{N_M}]'$ denote the initial ranking score list and the reranking score list, respectively, where $\bar{r}_i$ and r_i $(0 \le \bar{r}_i, r_i \le 1)$ are the relevance scores with respect to the query.

3.1 Reranking score list estimation

In this subsection, we explain the estimation of reranking score list. The problem of reranking in [12] is to model the textual and visual information from a probabilistic perspective. Supposing $\mathbf{r}$ is a random variable, reranking can be regarded as a process to derive the most probable score list given the initial one and the video content. Then this method formulates reranking as the following optimization problem:

$$\mathbf{r}^* = \frac{1}{2}(\mathbf{R} + \rho \mathbf{L_A})^{-1}\tilde{\rho}, \quad (6)$$

where ρ is a trade-off parameter, $\mathbf{L_A}$ is a Laplacian regularization matrix defined over the graph $G_\mathbf{A}$ which has the same structure of G^M with the weight between nodes v_i and v_j is $|\alpha_{ij}|$. The $\tilde{\rho} = 2\rho(\mathbf{Ae})$, where $\mathbf{e}$ is a vector with all elements equal to 1 and $\mathbf{A} = [\alpha_{ij}]_{N_M \times N_M}$ is an anti-symmetric matrix with $\alpha_{ij} = 1/(\bar{r}_i - \bar{r}_j)$. Note that the set of pairs (i, j) satisfies $\bar{r}_i > \bar{r}_j$. Furthermore, $\mathbf{R}$ is defined as the local learning regularization matrix, which balances the video graph consistency. We explain the details of this regularization matrix in the following subsection.

3.2 Local learning regularization

In graph-based video search reranking, visually similar videos among the local area are excepted to have close reranking scores. With this visual consistency assumption, we introduce the local learning regularization. First, by using the community detection method proposed in [3], we detect social communities among the video graph G^M. Next, for each node v_i, we extract its neighboring node set $\mathcal{N}(v_i) = \{(v_h^{(i)}, r_h^{(i)})\}_{h=1}^{n_i}$ based on the shortest path distance in the graph, where $v_h^{(i)}$ is the h-th nearest neighbor of v_i within the same community, $r_h^{(i)}$ is its score, and n_i is the total number of its neighbors. By using its neighboring node set $\mathcal{N}(v_i)$, the local learning regularization matrix in Eq.(6) is calculated as follows: $\mathbf{R} = (\mathbf{I} - \mathbf{B})'(\mathbf{I} - \mathbf{B})$, where $\mathbf{B} = [b_{ij}]_{N_M \times N_M}$ and b_{ij} equals to the corresponding element of $\boldsymbol{\beta}_i$ if $\mathbf{x}_j \in \mathcal{N}(\mathbf{x}_i)$, otherwise, $b_{ij} = 0$. Note that, $\boldsymbol{\beta}'_i = \mathbf{k}'(\lambda\mathbf{I}+\mathbf{K})^{-1}$, where λ is a parameter and $\mathbf{k}$ is a vector with $k_h = k(\mathbf{x}_i, \mathbf{x}_h^{(i)})$. Furthermore, $\mathbf{K}$ is a matrix with $k_{mn} = k(\mathbf{x}_m^{(i)}, \mathbf{x}_n^{(i)})$, where $\mathbf{x}_i$ is a feature vector extracted from v_i, and $k(\cdot, \cdot)$ is a kernel function. As for the kernel function, we implement the edge-weight function based on the Gaussian kernel in Eq.(1), and then use the shortest path weight between each pair of nodes, which is normalized by its path length, for the value of $k(\cdot, \cdot)$.

Table 1: 10 Event Queries.

Query
FIFA WorldCup 2014 highlights
Sochi 2014 Winter Olympics opening ceremony
NBA Finals 2014 highlights
New York Fashion Week 2014
Speech at Apec China 2014
2014 Hong Kong protests
2014 Israel Gaza Conflict air strikes
Malaysia Airlines Flight 17 crash moment
Flood in Indonesia 2014
Calbuco Volcano Eruption in Chile

4. EXPERIMENTAL RESULTS

In this section, we verify the effectiveness of our proposed method. We first describe the datasets collected from YouTube[3] and measurement of experiments. We then analyze the performance of our method on video search reranking.

4.1 Experimental Setup and Datasets

The used videos were crawled from YouTube by using event type of queries as shown in Table 1. These queries cover current topics of news from events, which were selected by reference to the categories "Categories:2014 or 2015" from Wikipedia[4]. For each query, we obtained max top-500 videos, and analyzed the related videos of each video by using YouTube API [5]. Furthermore, the associated contextual information such as tags, titles and descriptions were also crawled together with videos. By using these videos and tags, we constructed the initial video graph G^M, the tag graph G^T, and the combined heterogeneous graph G^{MT}, respectively.

The performance was measured by the widely used average precision (**AP**) which averages the precision obtained when each relevant video occurs. We average the APs over all queries to get mean AP (**MAP**) for an overall performance measurement. Then, to measure Web video search performance, the normalized discounted cumulative gain (**NDCG**) [8], which is a common measure used in information retrieval when relevance levels are more than two, is adopted. For a given query, the NDCG score at position d in the ranking list is calculated as follows;

$$\mathrm{NDCG}@d = Z_d \sum_{j=1}^{d} \frac{2^{t^j} - 1}{\log(1 + j)}, \quad (7)$$

where t^j is the degree of the j-th video in the ranking list and Z_d is a normalization constant which is chosen to guarantee that the perfect ranking's NDCG@d is 1. For each video, in this experiments, the relevance degree t^j was manually judged on three scales: "0:Irrelevant", "1:Fair", and "2:Relevant". To evaluate the overall per-

[3] http://www.youtube.com
[4] http://en.wikipedia.org/wiki/Category:2014 or 2015
[5] https://developers.google.com/youtube/v3/

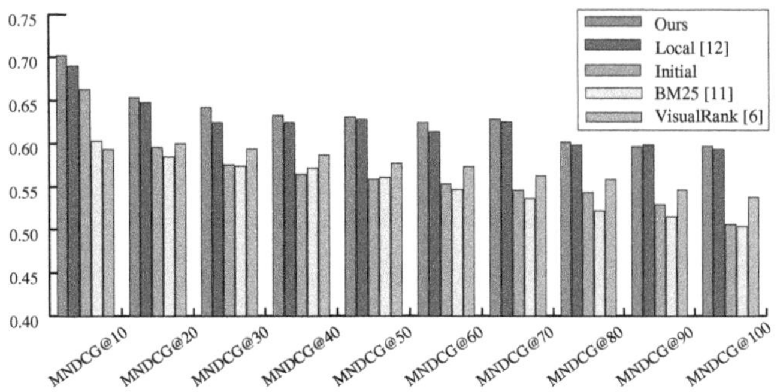

Figure 1: MNDCG Comparison of the Video Search Performance.

formance, we averaged the NDCGs over all queries to obtain the mean NDCG (**MNDCG**).

In the experimental settings, the parameters were empirically set as follows: α_l for multimodal feature fusion so that all weights are equal, $\theta_M = \theta_T = 0.2$, $\rho = 0.5$, and $\lambda = 0.01$. For the local learning regularization, the number of nearest neighbors was set to 20. Furthermore, for calculating initial ranking score, we adopt the rank method [8], which is widely used to estimate the samples' relevance probability. This method assigns the initial score $\bar{r}_i = N - \hat{r}_i$, where $\hat{r}_i$ is the rank of video v_i returned by the search engine and N is the number of videos to rerank.

4.2 Reranking Results

To evaluate the performance of the proposed regularization, we first compare the four methods derived under the Bayesian visual reranking framework. Table 2 shows the following results: Laplacian regularization (**Lap**), normalized Laplacian regularization (**N-Lap**) [14], local learning regularization (**Local**) [12], and local learning regularization with a community detection scheme (**Ours**). For comparison, we also showed the three results: the text-based search baseline based on BM25 formula (**BM25**) [11] using the associated contextual information of each video, the **VisualRank** [6], and the initial ranking score list (**Initial**). Note that, for VisualRank implementation, we used the same video graph and its affinity matrix as the proposed method. We can see that the use of the proposed regularization gives better performance than the other ones.

Next, in order to confirm the improvement by the mutual reinforcement between the two heterogeneous graphs, Table 2 also shows the two types of reranking results obtained by using the original video graph (**VG**) and the modified video graph (**MVG**), respectively. As shown in Table 2, we applied the proposed method to each regularization based reranking method. From the results, we can also see that the proposed method always gives a better performance.

Finally, we show the Web video retrieval results obtained by using the proposed method and other retrieval methods. Figure 1 shows the retrieval results in terms of MNDCG at each position. It can be also seen that the performance improvement is realized by introducing our method into visual reranking methods.

From the above results, we can verify the effectiveness of the proposed method. Therefore, the proposed method improve the performance of graph-based reranking for video search.

5. CONCLUSIONS

This paper has presented a method to improve performance of heterogeneous graph-based video search reranking. The proposed method is composed of two procedures. It first constructs the reinforced heterogeneous graphs, which are obtained by exchanging the information of inter and intra-relations among heterogeneous graphs. Second, by considering this graph consistency, video search reranking is formulated as an optimization problem. By using these procedures, we can obtain reinforced video graph and estimate the accurate renraking score list by the modified video graph. Consequently, the improvement of our method over the existing methods can be confirmed.

Table 2: MAP Comparison of each Regularization.

Method	MAP	
	VG	MVG
Ours	0.236	**0.239**
Local [12]	0.223	**0.227**
N-Lap [14]	0.206	**0.215**
Lap	0.202	**0.211**
Initial	0.196	
BM25 [11]	0.186	
VisualRank [6]	0.201	

6. ACKNOWLEDGMENTS

This work was partly supported by Grant-in-Aid for Scientific Research (B) 25280036, Japan Society for the Promotion of Science (JSPS).

7. REFERENCES

[1] E. Apostolidis and V. Mezaris. Fast Shot Segmentation Combining Global and Local Visual Descriptors. In *Proc. Int'l Conf. Acoust., Speech., Signal Process.*, pages 6583–6587, 2014.

[2] S. Bird, E. Klein, and E. Loper. *Natural language processing with Python*. O'Reilly, 2009.

[3] V. Blondel, J. Guillaume, R. Lambiotte, and E. Mech. Fast Unfolding of Communities in Large Networks. *J. Stat. Mech*, page P10008, 2008.

[4] R. Cilibrasi and P. Vitanyi. The Google Similarity Distance. *IEEE Trans. Knowledge and Data Engineering*, 19(3):370–383, 2007.

[5] N. Inoue and K. Shinoda. A Fast and Accurate Video Semantic-Indexing System Using Fast MAP Adaptation and GMM Supervectors. *IEEE Trans. Multimedia*, 14(4):1196–1205, 2012.

[6] Y. Jing and S. Baluja. VisualRank: Applying PageRank to Large-Scale Image Search. *IEEE Trans. Pattern Analysis and Machine Intelligence*, 30(11):1877–1890, 2008.

[7] X. Li, C. Snoek, and M. Worring. Learning social tag relevance by neighbor voting. *IEEE Trans. Multimedia*, 11(7):1310–1322, 2009.

[8] C. D. Manning, P. Raghavan, and H. Schütze. *Introduction to Information Retrieval*. Cambridge University Press, New York, NY, USA, 2008.

[9] T. Mei, Y. Rui, S. Li, and Q. Tian. Multimedia Search Reranking: A Literature Survey. *ACM Comput. Surv.*, 46(3):38:1–38:38, 2014.

[10] M. A. Porter, J.-P. Onnela, and P. J. Mucha. Communities in Networks. *Notices of the AMS*, 56(9):1082–1097, 2009.

[11] S. Robertson and H. Zaragoza. The Probabilistic Relevance Framework: BM25 and Beyond. *Found. Trends Inf. Retr.*, 3(4):333–389, 2009.

[12] X. Tian, Y. Yang, J. Wang, X. Wu, and X. S. Hua. Bayesian Visual Reranking. *IEEE Trans. Multimedia*, 13(4):639–652, 2011.

[13] J. Wang, J. Yang, K. Yu, F. Lv, T. Huang, and Y. Gong. Locality-constrained Linear Coding for Image Classification. In *Proc. IEEE Int'l Conf. Computer Vision and Pattern Recognition*, pages 3360–3367, 2010.

[14] M. Wu and B. Schölkopf. Transductive Classification via Local Learning Regularization. In *Proc. Int'l Conf. Artificial Intelligence and Statistics*, pages 628–635, 2007.

[15] T. Yao, C. W. Ngo, and T. Mei. Circular Reranking for Visual Search. *IEEE Trans. Image Processing*, 22(4):1644–1655, 2013.

Selective K-means Tree Search

Tuan Anh Nguyen, Yusuke Matsui, Toshihiko Yamasaki, Kiyoharu Aizawa
The University of Tokyo, Japan
{t_nguyen, matsui, yamasaki, aizawa}@hal.t.u-tokyo.ac.jp

ABSTRACT

In object recognition and image retrieval, an inverted indexing method is used to solve the approximate nearest neighbor search problem. In these tasks, inverted indexing provides a nonexhaustive solution to large-scale search. However, a problem of previous inverted indexing methods is that a large-scale inverted index is required to achieve a high search recall rate. In this study, we address the problem of reducing the time required to build an inverted index without degrading the search accuracy and speed. Thus, we propose a selective k-means tree search method that combines the power of both hierarchical k-means tree and selective nonexhaustive search. Experiments based on approximate nearest neighbor search using a large dataset comprising one billion SIFT features showed that the hierarchical inverted file based on the selective k-means tree method could be built six times faster, while obtaining almost the same recall and search speed as the state-of-the-art inverted indexing methods.

Categories and Subject Descriptors

H.3.3 [**Information Storage and Retrieval**]: Information Search and Retrieval—*Clustering, Retrieval Models, Search Process, Selection Process*

General Terms

Theory, Algorithms, Experimentation

Keywords

Approximate Nearest Neighbor Search, Hierarchical K-means Tree, Inverted Indexing, Product Quantization

1. INTRODUCTION

In most computer vision and image retrieval applications, approximate nearest neighbor (ANN) search is an important problem [7]. An inverted file is the most popular data structure employed during nonexhaustive search to improve the search speed in large-scale databases. In particular, Jégou et al. [4] proposed an inverted file with asymmetric distance computation (IVFADC) index by combining inverted files and product quantization. IVFADC outperforms previous methods [2, 4, 7] during ANN search in terms of the tradeoff between memory usage and accuracy. Recently, Babenko et al. [1] improved IVFADC by proposing the inverted multi-index (Multi-D-ADC). Both IVFADC and Multi-D-ADC are built using clustering processes. IVFADC performs clustering in the search space to create K codewords, whereas Multi-D-ADC performs clustering in multiple subspaces before combining multiple independent codewords based on the Cartesian product to yield K^m codewords, where m is the number of subspaces. Therefore, Multi-D-ADC has a dense space-partitioning form that accelerates the ANN search, while still achieving the same recall as IVFADC. The problem addressed in the present study is how to create a dense space partitioning for fast search to allow Multi-D-ADC to perform a large-scale indexing process. In previous studies [4, 1], the time required to build an inverted file was shown to be linear up to K.

The main contributions of this study are as follows. (1) To reduce the time required to build an inverted file, we propose the selective k-means tree method based on the hierarchical k-means tree [8]. (2) We obtain an inverted file structure (SKT-ADC), which combines the strength of the selective k-means tree and product quantization for use in ANN search. (3) The selective approach limits the search to highly likely candidates, thereby accelerating the search process in the selective k-means tree method.

Our experiments showed that Multi-D-ADC required a dense space partitioning (codebook size $K = 2^{14}$) to achieve fast search, whereas SKT-ADC achieved the same recall and runtime with a 16-times smaller codebook size, i.e., $K = 2^{10}$, where the inverted file-building process was six times faster (4 hours compared with 24 hours by Multi-D-ADC using SIFT1B data on the same machine). Our search method is fast (2 milliseconds for a single query). It is also simpler compared with the state-of-the-art search methods used with Multi-D-ADC.

MM'15, October 26–30, 2015, Brisbane, Australia.
© 2015 ACM. ISBN 978-1-4503-3459-4/15/10 ...$15.00.
DOI: http://dx.doi.org/10.1145/2733373.2806353.

2. PREVIOUS WORK

Inverted indexing: In [4], Jégou et al. proposed IVFADC, which comprises two components: (i) a *dictionary* (Figure 1) created by k-means [6]; and (ii) a *posting lists* containing the compressed versions of database vectors. The database vectors are compressed by product quantization to facilitate better memory usage. To create a dictionary, k-means is applied to a learning dataset $\mathcal{L}$, which creates K clusters in a d-dimensional space $\mathbb{R}^d$ with K codewords (clusters' centroids) $\mathbf{c}_1, \mathbf{c}_2, \ldots, \mathbf{c}_K$. Each vector $\mathbf{y}$ in the set of database of vectors $\mathcal{Y}$ is assigned to a cluster with its nearest codeword in $\mathbf{c}_1, \mathbf{c}_2, \ldots, \mathbf{c}_K$.

Data compression with product quantization: To avoid accessing the disk to obtain the vector data $\mathbf{y}$, a resid-

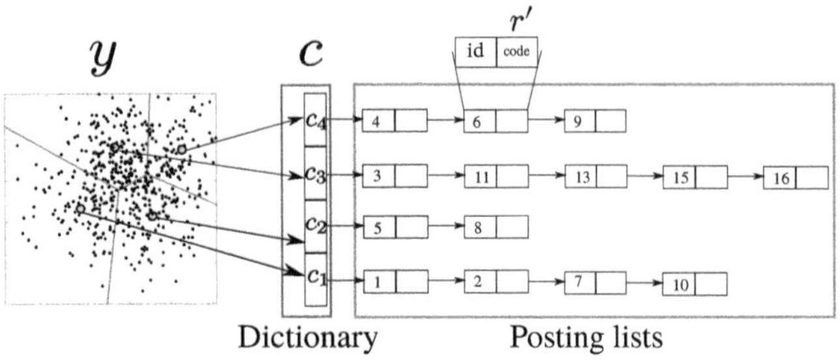

Figure 1: An inverted file with four clusters: k-means clustering is used to divide the search space into four parts, where each part represents a cluster (codeword vector c) in the inverted file. The database vectors y in each cluster are compressed and stored in the inverted file. Each compressed version (code r′) is associated with an identifier (id) to retrieve the original vector data y.

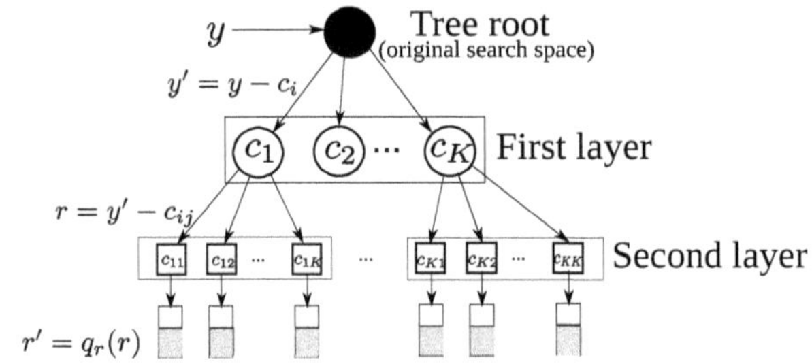

Figure 2: Our inverted file, SKT-ADC: the first layer contains K codewords that correspond to K subsearch spaces, where each codeword forms a new subsearch space by residual vector computation. Each subsearch space is then divided again into K clusters to form K child nodes for the codeword in the first layer. K^2 codewords are created to form the second layer. Finally, the database vectors are compressed by product quantization.

ual vector $\mathbf{r}$ between $\mathbf{y}$ and the nearest codeword in $\mathbf{c} \in \{\mathbf{c}_1, \mathbf{c}_2, \ldots, \mathbf{c}_K\}$ to $\mathbf{y}$ is computed and quantized by a product quantizer $q_r(.)$: $\mathbf{r} = \mathbf{y} - \mathbf{c} \xrightarrow{q_r(.)} \mathbf{r}' = q_r(\mathbf{r})$. A database vector $\mathbf{y}$ is approximated by the sum $\mathbf{c} + \mathbf{r}'$.

Multi-D-ADC: Multi-D-ADC [1] is an improved version of IVFADC. To build a dictionary, product quantization is used instead of single k-means clustering [6]. The total training time required by a product quantizer to build a codebook of K^2 codewords is almost the same as that needed to build a codebook of K codewords in IVFADC, i.e., $O(MKd)$, where M is the size of the learning dataset and d is the dimensionality.

Search methods: In both IVFADC and Multi-D-ADC, the search methods comprise two processes. (i) *Dictionary scanning* : a k nearest neighbor search is performed using the set of codewords to retrieve a list of candidate clusters. For Multi-D-ADC, a multisequence algorithm [1] was proposed to reduce the scanning time in two parallel sorted sequences. (ii) *Posting lists scanning*: the ANN is found by computing the distances between the query $\mathbf{q}$ and the compressed vectors $\mathbf{c} + \mathbf{r}'$. In the search method employed for Multi-D-ADC [1], all of the dot products and norms are precomputed to facilitate a faster search process. In this case, the approximated distance is computed in $O(m)$ time, where m is the number of divisions during product quantization.

3. SELECTIVE K-MEANS TREE SEARCH

In this section, we introduce our inverted file (SKT-ADC) based on a two-layer selective k-means tree (Figure 2). A general version with more than two layers is straightforward.

Building a dictionary: First, a learning dataset $\mathcal{L} = \{\mathbf{y} \in \mathbb{R}^d\}$ is divided into K clusters with K codewords $\mathbf{c}_1, \mathbf{c}_2, \ldots, \mathbf{c}_K$, where d is the dimensionality. Then, each cluster is again divided into K clusters with K codewords $\mathbf{c}_{i1}, \mathbf{c}_{i2}, \ldots, \mathbf{c}_{iK}$, $1 \le i \le K$. A product quantizer $q_r(.)$ is learned from the residual vectors of $\mathbf{y} - \mathbf{c}_i - \mathbf{c}_{ij}$, where $\mathbf{y}$ is a training vector, $\mathbf{c}_i$ is the nearest codeword of $\mathbf{y}$ in the first layer, and $\mathbf{c}_{ij}$ is the nearest codeword of $\mathbf{y} - \mathbf{c}_i$ in the second layer. Let M be the size of the learning dataset $\mathcal{L}$. The complexity of k-means [6] is linear with respect to the size of the training set, dimensionality, and the number of clusters, so we need $O(MKd)$ operations to construct the first layer. Let $M_1, M_2, \ldots, M_K$ be the number of learning vectors in each of the clusters in the first layer and the sum of all M_is equals M. Therefore, we need $O(\sum_{i=1}^{K} M_i Kd) = O(MKd)$ operations to construct the second layer. The time complexity of the dictionary-building process is $O(MKd)$.

Data indexing: After the codewords $\mathbf{c}_i, \mathbf{c}_{ij}$, $1 \le i \le K$, $1 \le j \le K$ have been computed, a database vector $\mathbf{y}$ is compressed according to the following steps (Figure 2). (i) *Step 1:* The nearest neighbor c_i of $\mathbf{y}$ in $\{\mathbf{c}_i\}_{i=1}^{K}$ is retrieved and the residual vector $\mathbf{y}' = \mathbf{y} - \mathbf{c}_i$ is computed. (ii) *Step 2:* The nearest neighbor $\mathbf{c}_{ij}$ of $\mathbf{y}'$ in $\{\mathbf{c}_{ij}\}_{j=1}^{K}$ is retrieved and the residual vector $\mathbf{r} = \mathbf{y}' - \mathbf{c}_{ij}$ is computed. (iii) *Step 3:* The residual vector $\mathbf{r}$ is compressed into an m-byte code by product quantization. The time complexity of the data-indexing process is $O(NKd)$ for a dataset of N vectors. Note that the time complexities required to build the dictionary and to perform data indexing for Multi-D-ADC are also $O(MKd)$ and $O(NKd)$, respectively.

Search method: We illustrate the search process in Figure 3. Let $\mathbf{q}$ be the query vector. Our search process comprises the following three steps. (i) *Step 1:* Compute all of the distances between $\mathbf{q}$ and the codewords in the first layer to find h nearest neighbor (h-NN) of $\mathbf{q}$ in the first layer. (ii) *Step 2:* In each cluster $\mathbf{c}_i$ corresponding to h-NN for $\mathbf{q}$ in the first layer, l-NN for $\mathbf{q} - \mathbf{c}_i$ in the set of codewords $\{\mathbf{c}_{ij}\}_{j=1}^{K}$ are computed. (iii) *Step 3:* In this step, we retrieve $h \times l$ selected clusters and from all of the candidate vectors in the $h \times l$ clusters after Step 2, a final list of candidates is obtained. We compute all of the approximated distances between $\mathbf{q}$ and all of the candidate vectors. The R smallest values and their corresponding identifiers are exported as the search results. When the length of the candidate list exceeds a predefined candidate list length T, the process in Step 2 is terminated. In our experiments, for SIFT1B when $K \le 2^{11}$, the setting values of $h = 32 \sim 128$ and $l = 8 \sim 16$ yielded an acceptable recall rate.

The main operations in Steps 1 and 2 are distance-computing operations. In Step 1, the distances between the query and all K of the codewords in layer 1 are computed in $O(Kd)$ operations. In Step 2, $O(Kd)$ operations are required for

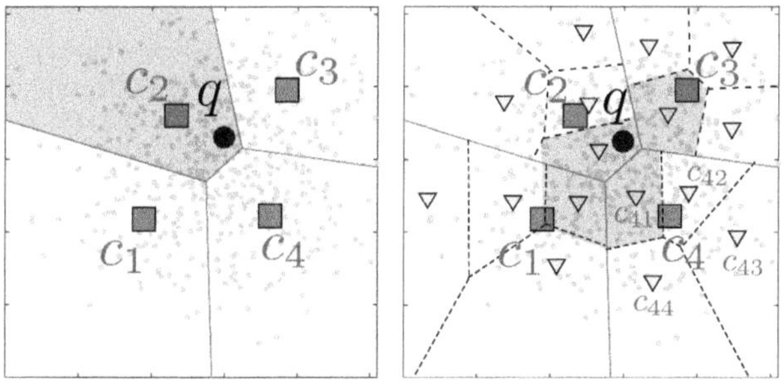

(a) Conventional search method (b) Our search method with $(h, l) = (4, 1)$

Figure 3: Our search method: the gray area is the search area corresponding to a query, q. (a) After assigning the query q to cluster c_2, all of the database vectors in this cluster are listed as candidates. The candidates in cluster c_3 and c_4 are missed. (b) In SKT-ADC, the tree structure allows the retrieval process to focus only on the nearby subclusters. The most likely possible candidates are scanned in all four clusters: c_1, c_2, c_3, c_4 (gray area).

each cluster retrieved after Step 1. In Steps 1 and 2, to improve the recall rate, h-NN (l-NN) are reranked by sorting the top h (l) smallest distances in ascending order. The number of reranking operations is low when $h, l \ll K \times d$ and h clusters are retrieved after Step 1; therefore, the total required for Steps 1 and 2 is $O(hKd)$ operations. In Step 3, as described in Section 2, with the precomputing processes, a single approximated distance-computing process requires $O(m)$ operations; therefore, the distance-computing tasks in Step 3 require $O(mT)$ operations in total. In summary, the search process using our inverted file requires $O(hKd+mT)$ operations for a single query.

4. EXPERIMENTS

4.1 Experimental setup

We conducted experiments using several publicly available datasets: SIFT1M [4] (1 million 128-dimensional SIFT features + 10000 queries), GIST1M [4] (1 million 960-dimensional GIST features + 1000 queries), and SIFT1B [5] (1 billion 128-dimensional SIFT features + 10000 queries). The search quality was measured based on the recall@R measure, i.e., the proportion of queries with nearest neighbor ranked in the first R positions in the final candidate list. We considered that recall rates where $R \leq 100$ were sufficient for a large scale ANN search [1]. All of the experiments using SIFT1B are conducted on a computer with 6-core Intel Xeon 3.50 GHz CPUs and 512 GB RAM. The search experiments were performed in the single-thread mode. All of the algorithms were implemented in C++ with BLAS instructions. For clustering tasks, we employed the k-means algorithm in [3].

4.2 Results

In this section, we describe the results obtained using SIFT1B. The results of the experiments using SIFT1M and GIST1M are described in the supplementary material.

Inverted file-building time: Table 1 shows the relationship between time required to build the inverted file and the search performances of IVFADC, Multi-D-ADC, and SKT-ADC with different codebook scales K. SKT-ADC with $K = 2^{10}$ achieved the same recall@100 as Multi-D-ADC with $K = 2^{14}$. The training times for both SKT-ADC and Multi-D-ADC were linear with respect to the codebook scale K, so SKT-ADC could achieve a good recall rate with only a short training time. In our experiments, to build a codebook with $K = 2^{10}$ for SKT-ADC using a 6-core computer, the training process required about 4 hours, whereas building Multi-D-ADC with $K = 2^{14}$ required about 24 hours and IVFADC with $K = 2^{13}$ required about 12 hours on the same computer.

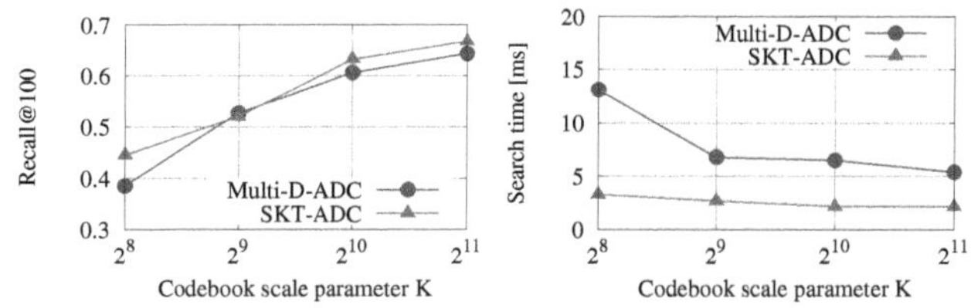

(a) Recall@100 for SKT-ADC and Multi-D-ADC (b) Search time for $T = 100K$

Figure 4: Search performance obtained by SKT-ADC and Multi-D-ADC using SIFT1B ($K = 2^8 \sim 2^{11}$, $T = 100K$), and by SKT-ADC with $(h, l) = (32, 16)$: (a) recall@100; (b) search time.

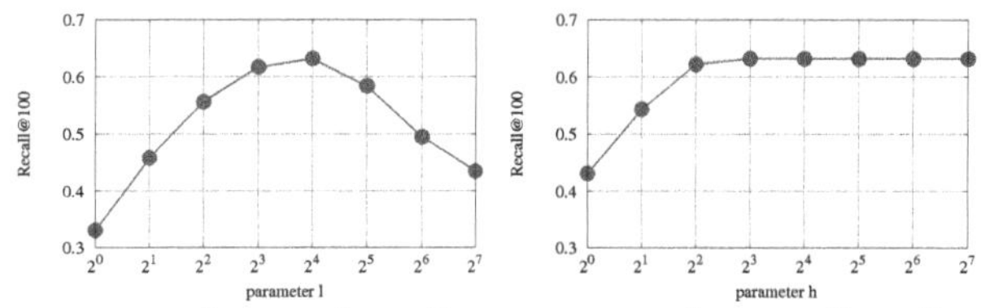

(a) $h = 2^7$, $l = 2^0 \sim 2^7$ (b) $l = 2^4$, $h = 2^0 \sim 2^7$

Figure 5: The recall@100 rate obtained by SKT-ADC varied with (h, l) using SIFT1B with $K = 2^{10}$: a) $h = 2^7$, $l = 2^0 \sim 2^7$; (b) $l = 2^4$, $h = 2^0 \sim 2^7$.

Search performance: With the same candidate list length $T = 100K$ and codebook scale $K = 2^{10}$, SKT-ADC also achieved the same recall rate as Multi-D-ADC, but the search was three times faster. Table 1 shows that SKT-ADC required 20 GB of memory while searching. These overheads are required because SKT-ADC must precompute more norms and dot products than Multi-D-ADC to perform an efficient search [1]. In our implementations, the memory overheads incurred were linear with respect to K for Multi-D-ADC and with respect to K^2 for SKT-ADC (please refer to the supplementary material for mathematical descriptions). Thus, the storage volume required for these computations was also larger than that for Multi-D-ADC.

Figure 4 shows the performance measures for SKT-ADC and Multi-D-ADC when scanning 100 K candidate vectors. Figure 4(a) shows that with the same K, SKT-ADC achieved a better recall than Multi-D-ADC, and Figure 4(b) shows that with the same codebook scale K, SKT-ADC performed a faster search than Multi-D-ADC. Our experiments showed that SKT-ADC was two times faster than Multi-D-ADC.

Table 1: Performance of the proposed method for SIFT1B (recall for top 1–100 + time in milliseconds). A vector was compressed to an 8-byte code. The search times are shown per query. For SKT-ADC, we set the codebook scale parameter $K = 2^{10}$ and $(h, l) = (32, 16)$ for SKT-ADC, $K = 2^{10}$, 2^{14} for Multi-D-ADC, and $K = 2^{13}$ for IVFADC. The candidate list length T ranged from 10 K to 1 M. The inverted files were built using a 6-core computer.

Method	K	T	R@1	R@10	R@100	Time [ms]	Memory [GB]	IVF building time [h]
IVFADC	2^{13}	1M	0.095	0.338	**0.652**	20.0	**12**	12
Multi-D-ADC	2^{14}	10K	**0.136**	**0.419**	0.631	2.3	**12**	24
Multi-D-ADC	2^{10}	100K	0.104	0.317	0.606	6.5	**12**	**2**
SKT-ADC	2^{10}	100K	0.099	0.315	0.632	**2.2**	20	4

Table 2: Number of nonempty clusters with each method using SIFT1B.

K	IVFADC	Multi-D-ADC	SKT-ADC
2^8	2^8	65,386	65,535
2^9	2^9	257,248	261,991
2^{10}	2^{10}	975,912	1,044,686
2^{11}	2^{11}	3,406,222	4,141,985

How dense is SKT-ADC? With the same codebook scale parameter K, IVFADC [4, 5] could create K clusters, whereas Multi-D-ADC [1] and SKT-ADC each created K^2 clusters. Table 2 shows the number of nonempty clusters, which varied with the codebook scale parameter K. SKT-ADC created more nonempty clusters than IVFADC and Multi-D-ADC in almost the same time $O(MKd)$, where M is the size of the learning dataset and d is the dimensionality. Multi-D-ADC creates the codewords based on the Cartesian product between two independent spaces, whereas SKT-ADC creates the codewords by performing k-means clustering recursively in the same space.

Selecting the parameters (h, l). Figure 5 shows the recall rates with different values for h, l. Figure 5(a) shows that when $h = 2^7$, the recall rate reached its maximal value at $l = 2^4$. Single k-means was performed to construct K codewords in the first layer of SKT-ADC. When K was small, k-means yielded an ANN search result with many noisy vectors. In our search method, the parameter l was set to filter these noisy vectors. To scan the candidate clusters in the first layer, SKT-ADC only searched the candidates in l nearest clusters. The distance between a query and a cluster was treated as the distance between the query and the codeword (the centroid of the cluster). In our experiments, SKT-ADC with $l = 2^4$ obtained the best filtering results with the highest recall. The candidate list length T was limited, so more noisy vectors were scanned and the recall was degraded when $l > 2^4$. In addition, as shown in Figure 5(b), SKT-ADC with $h \geq 2^3$ resulted in a high recall search. After increasing h while $l = 2^4$ remained fixed, the candidate list was unchanged after retrieving all T candidates; therefore, the recall rate was stable when $h \geq 2^3$.

5. CONCLUSION

In this study, we proposed a selective k-means tree search method, which is based on the hierarchical k-means tree [8] with a selective search approach. Our proposed inverted index SKT-ADC obtained almost the same recall and search speed, and the inverted file was built six times faster compared with the best conventional inverted index, i.e., Multi-D-ADC. With the same candidate list length T and codebook scale K, our method also achieved better recall rates than Multi-D-ADC. We also performed our experimental validations using small and large datasets. Our implementation is publicly available[1].

In our future research, we will investigate the following. (1) We will try to reduce the memory overheads incurred by SKT-ADC. The number of codewords in the selective k-means tree is linear with respect to K^2, so the storage required for precomputing is also linear with respect to K^2, thereby incurring large memory overheads. (2) Both Multi-D-ADC [1] and SKT-ADC produce good candidate lists, thereby facilitating high recall search, so combining these data structures will be an objective in our future works.

Acknowledgments: We would like to thank Krishna Onkar for his helpful comments. This work was partially supported by JSPS Grant-in-Aid for challenging Exploratory Research Grant Number 26540078 and the Strategic Information and Communications R&D Promotion Programme (141203018).

6. REFERENCES

[1] A. Babenko and V. Lempitsky. The inverted multi-index. *IEEE Trans. Pattern Anal. Mach. Intell.*, PP(99):1–1, 2014.

[2] M. Datar, N. Immorlica, P. Indyk, and V. S. Mirrokni. Locality-sensitive hashing scheme based on p-stable distributions. In *Proc. SCG*, pages 253–262. ACM, 2004.

[3] G. Hamerly. Making k-means even faster. In *SDM*, pages 130–140, 2010.

[4] H. Jégou, M. Douze, and C. Schmid. Product quantization for nearest neighbor search. *IEEE Trans. Pattern Anal. Mach. Intell.*, 33(1):117–128, 2011.

[5] H. Jégou, R. Tavenard, M. Douze, and L. Amsaleg. Searching in one billion vectors: Re-rank with source coding. In *Proc. ICASSP*, pages 861–864. IEEE, 2011.

[6] S. Lloyd. Least squares quantization in pcm. *IEEE Trans. Inf. Theory*, 28(2):129–137, 1982.

[7] M. Muja and D. Lowe. Fast approximate nearest neighbors with automatic algorithm configuration. In *Proc. VISAPP*, pages 331–340. IEEE, 2009.

[8] D. Nistér and H. Stewénius. Scalable recognition with a vocabulary tree. In *Proc. CVPR*, volume 2, pages 2161–2168. IEEE, 2006.

[1] https://github.com/marker68/skt

Predicting Continuous Probability Distribution of Image Emotions in Valence-Arousal Space

Sicheng Zhao, Hongxun Yao, Xiaolei Jiang

School of Computer Science and Technology, Harbin Institute of Technology, Harbin, China.
zsc@hit.edu.cn, h.yao@hit.edu.cn, xljiang@hit.edu.cn

ABSTRACT

Previous works on image emotion analysis mainly focused on assigning a dominated emotion category or the average dimension values to an image for affective image classification and regression. However, this is often insufficient in many applications, as the emotions that are evoked in viewers by an image are highly subjective and different. In this paper, we propose to predict the continuous probability distribution of dimensional image emotions represented in valence-arousal space. By the statistical analysis on the constructed Image-Emotion-Social-Net dataset, we represent the emotion distribution as a Gaussian mixture model (GMM), which is estimated by the EM algorithm. Then we extract commonly used features of different levels for each image. Finally, we formulize the emotion distribution prediction as a multi-task shared sparse regression (MTSSR) problem, which is optimized by iteratively reweighted least squares. Besides, we introduce three baseline algorithms. Experiments conducted on the Image-Emotion-Social-Net dataset demonstrate the superiority of the proposed method, as compared to some state-of-the-art approaches.

Categories and Subject Descriptors

H.3.1 [**Information storage and retrieval**]: Content Analysis and Indexing; J.5 [**Computer Applications**]: Arts and Humanities

General Terms

Algorithms, Human Factors, Experimentation, Performance

Keywords

Image Emotion Distribution; Valence-Arousal; Gaussian Mixture Model; Sparse Regression

1. INTRODUCTION

Images can convey rich semantics and evoke strong emotions in viewers. Understanding the perceived emotions in images has been widely studied recently due to its vital importance in many applications of various domains, ranging from entertainment to education and advertisement [1, 13, 3]. However, this is a non-trivial problem due to the great challenges of affective gap and subjective evaluation [13]. According to the emotion representation models, including categorical emotion states (CES) and dimensional emotion space (DES) [13], related works on image emotion analysis can be classified into three different tasks: affective image classification [11, 7, 4, 6, 1, 13, 3], regression [6, 13] and retrieval [15].

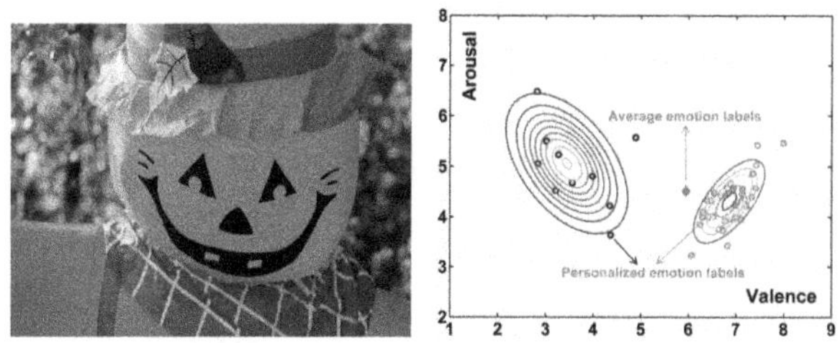

(a) (b)

Figure 1: The differences between affective image regression and emotion distribution prediction. (a) is the original image, (b) illustrates the differences, where the hollow points are the perceived emotion labels in VA space, the magenta diamond point is the predicted average VA scores by traditional affective image regression, while the contour lines of GMM are the predicted emotion distribution by the proposed method.

Existing works mainly focused on finding features that can express emotions better to bridge the affective gap. Based on the extracted features, state-of-the-art methods tried to assign a dominated emotion category or the average dimension values to an image for affective image classification and regression with CES and DES models, respectively. Holistic features including Wiccest features and Gabor features were extracted to classify image emotions in [11]. Machajdik *et al.* [7] extracted features inspired from psychology and art theory, such as *color*, *texture* and *composition*. Lu *et al.* [6] investigated the computability of emotion through *shape* features. Zhao *et al.* [13] proposed to extract more interpretable emotion features based on principles-of-art, such as *balance*, *contrast* and *variety*, which were demonstrated to have stronger link to emotions than the elements-of-art. Visual sentiment ontology and detectors are proposed to detect high-level adjective noun pairs (ANPs) based on large-scale social multimedia data [1, 3]. Yuan *et al.* [12] used mid-level scene attributes for binary sentiment classification. Simple social correlation features are explored for emotion classification of social network images [4].

However, just predicting the dominated emotion is insufficient in many applications, as the emotions that are evoked in different viewers by an image are highly subjective and different [14], due to the influence of social and cultural backgrounds [5]. For example, in a test of image emotions to personal interest estimation,

MM'15, October 26–30, 2015, Brisbane, Australia.
© 2015 ACM. ISBN 978-1-4503-3459-4/15/10 ...$15.00.
DOI: http://dx.doi.org/10.1145/2733373.2806354.

(a) Image examples in the Image-Emotion-Social-Net dataset

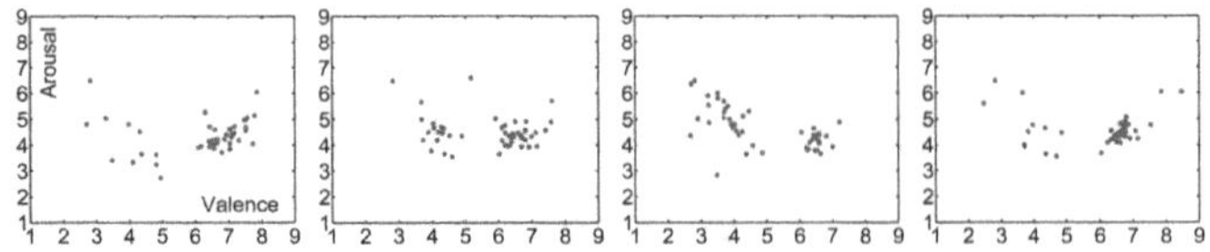

(b) Emotion distributions of personalized perceptions in VA space

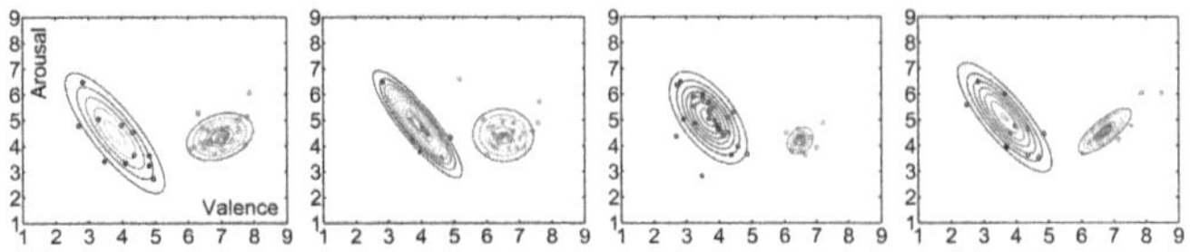

(c) The estimated GMM using specified EM algorithm

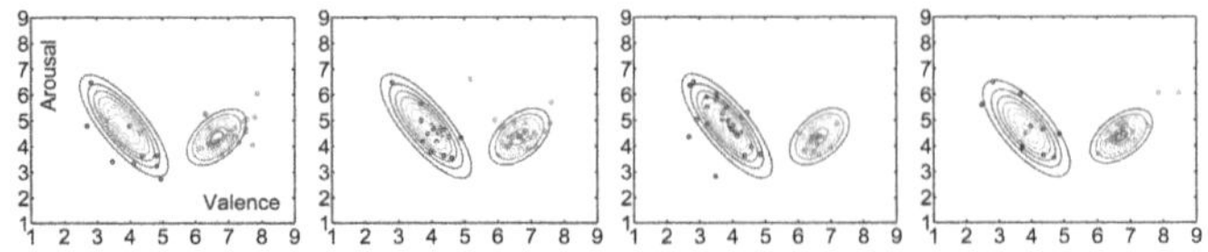

(d) The predicted GMM by KNNW ($K = 300$) using ANP features

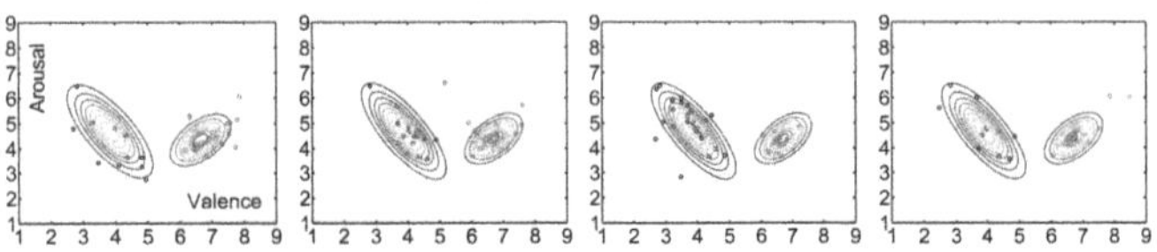

(e) The predicted GMM by SVR using Elements features

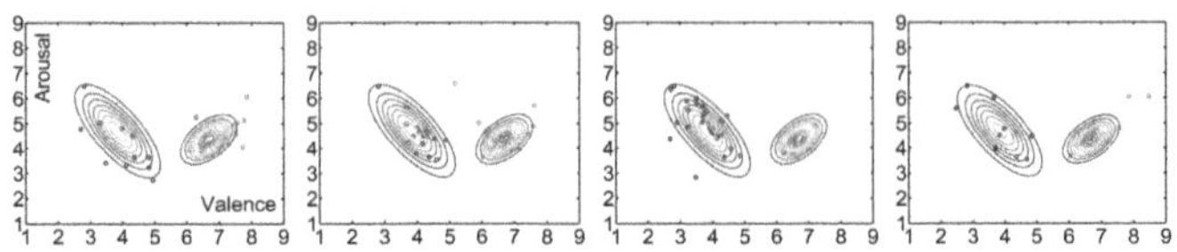

(f) The predicted GMM by MTSSR using ANP features

Figure 2: Image examples, related emotion labels and the predicted emotion distributions on the Image-Emotion-Social-Net dataset.

the personalized emotion perceptions are required. In such cases, we need to take the subjective evaluation into account. Therefore, predicting the probability distribution of image emotions becomes more reasonable and useful in practice. To our knowledge, there have been few works tackling the subjective evaluation challenge and predicting the probability distribution of image emotions.

In this paper, we make an initial attempt to predict the probability distribution of image emotions in DES form, as shown in Figure 1. By the statistical analysis of personalized emotion perceptions on the constructed Image-Emotion-Social-Net dataset, we observe that the valence-arousal emotion labels can be well represented by a mixture of bidimensional Gaussian distributions. The expectation-maximization (EM) algorithm with specified initializations is used to estimate the parameters of GMM. We formulize the emotion distribution prediction as a multi-task shared sparse regression (MTSSR) problem, which is optimized by iteratively reweighted least squares. Experiments are conducted on the Image-Emotion-Social-Net dataset to demonstrate the effectiveness of the proposed emotion distribution prediction method.

2. PROBLEM DEFINITION

As there is no public dataset on image emotion distribution in VA space, we set up a large-scale dataset, named Image-Emotion-Social-Net dataset, with over 1 million images downloaded from Flickr. To get the personalized emotion labels, firstly we use traditional lexicon-based methods to obtain the text segmentation results of the title, tags and descriptions from uploaders for expected emotions and the comments from viewers for actual emotions. Then we compute the average value of valence, arousal and dominance of the segmentation results as ground truth for dimensional emotion representation based on recently published VAD norms of 13,915 English lemmas [9].

Some image examples and related personalized emotion labels are shown in Figure 2(a) and 2(b), from which we have the following observations: (1) The emotions evoked by an image in different viewers are truly subjective and different; Just assigning the average dimensional values of valence and arousal to an image is obviously not enough; (2) Though highly different, the perceived emotions follow certain distributions, which can be clearly grouped into two clusters, corresponding to the positive and negative sentiments; In each cluster, the VA emotion values are relatively stable; (3) The VA emotion labels can be well modeled by a mixture of two bidimensional Gaussian distributions.

Based on these observations, we define the distribution of VA emotion labels as a GMM by

$$p(\mathbf{x};\boldsymbol{\theta}) = \sum_{l=1}^{L} \pi_l \mathcal{N}(\mathbf{x}|\boldsymbol{\mu}_l, \boldsymbol{\Sigma}_l), \tag{1}$$

where $\mathbf{x} = (v, a)$ is pair-wise VA emotion labels, $\boldsymbol{\mu}_l$ and $\boldsymbol{\Sigma}_l$ are the mean vector and covariance matrix of the lth Gaussian component, while π_l is the mixing coefficient, which satisfies $\pi_l \geq 0$ and $\sum_{l=1}^{L} \pi_l = 1$. In this paper, the number of Gaussian components is 2, i.e. $L = 2$ and $\boldsymbol{\theta} = (\boldsymbol{\mu}_1, \boldsymbol{\Sigma}_1, \boldsymbol{\mu}_2, \boldsymbol{\Sigma}_2, \pi_1, \pi_2)$. It should be noted that the number of Gaussian components L can be easily enlarged if more personalized emotion labels are obtained.

The EM algorithm is used to estimate the parameters of GMM. Specifically, the initializations are obtained by firstly partitioning the VA labels into two clusters based on whether valence is greater than 5 and then computing the mean vector $\boldsymbol{\mu}_l$ and covariance matrix $\boldsymbol{\Sigma}_l$ of each cluster. The mixing coefficients are set as the proportions of related VA labels in each cluster to the total labels. In experiment, the EM algorithm is converged in 6.28 steps on average. Some estimated results of GMM are shown in Figure 2(c).

Suppose we have N training images $\mathbf{f}_1, \cdots, \mathbf{f}_N$, the emotion distributions are $p_1(\mathbf{x};\boldsymbol{\theta}_1), \cdots, p_N(\mathbf{x};\boldsymbol{\theta}_N)$, where $\boldsymbol{\theta}_n = (\boldsymbol{\mu}_{n1}, \boldsymbol{\Sigma}_{n1}, \boldsymbol{\mu}_{n2}, \boldsymbol{\Sigma}_{n2}, \pi_{n1}, \pi_{n2})$ are the parameters of the nth emotion distribution ($n = 1, \cdots, N$). Similarly, suppose we have M test images $\mathbf{g}_1, \cdots, \mathbf{g}_M$ with ground truth emotion distributions $q_1(\mathbf{x};\boldsymbol{\vartheta}_1), \cdots, q_M(\mathbf{x};\boldsymbol{\vartheta}_M)$, where $\boldsymbol{\vartheta}_m (m = 1, \cdots, M)$ are the distribution parameters. Then our goal is to predict the emotion distribution parameters $\widehat{\boldsymbol{\vartheta}}_m$ based on $\{\mathbf{f}_n, \boldsymbol{\theta}_n\}_{n=1}^{N}$ for each $\mathbf{g}_m$. That is

$$f : (\{\mathbf{f}_n, \boldsymbol{\theta}_n\}_{n=1}^{N}, \mathbf{g}_m) \rightarrow \widehat{\boldsymbol{\vartheta}}_m. \tag{2}$$

3. EMOTION DISTRIBUTION PREDICTION ALGORITHMS

The emotion distribution prediction task of Equ. (2) can be viewed as a regression problem. In this section, we briefly introduce the extracted emotion features and detail the proposed MTSSR method together with several baseline algorithms.

As shown in [15], there are various types of features that may contribute to the perceptions of image emotions. Similar to [15], we extract commonly used emotion features of different levels and generalities for each image, including low-level GIST and elements-of-art [7], mid-level attributes [8] and principles-of-art [13], and high-level ANPs [1] and expressions [10]. The extracted features are abbreviated as GIST, Elements, Attributes, Principles, ANP and Expressions with dimension 512, 48, 102, 165, 1200 and 8, respectively. Please refer to [15] for details.

3.1 K-Nearest Neighbor Weighting

The emotion distribution parameters $\boldsymbol{\theta}_n (n = 1, \cdots, N)$ of all training images are considered as basis functions. K-nearest neighbor weighting (KNNW) selects the top K most similar training images and estimates $\widehat{\boldsymbol{\vartheta}}_m$ by weighting the selected basis functions

$$\widehat{\boldsymbol{\vartheta}}_m = \frac{\sum_{k=1}^{K} s_{t_k} \boldsymbol{\theta}_{t_k}}{\sum_{k=1}^{K} s_{t_k}}, \tag{3}$$

where $s_n = \exp(-\frac{d(\mathbf{g}_m, \mathbf{f}_n)}{\sigma})$ is the similarity between images $\mathbf{g}_m$ and $\mathbf{f}_n$, $d(\cdot,\cdot)$ is a specified distance function, σ is set as the average distance of all the training images, while $s_{t_1}, \cdots, s_{t_K}$ are the top K largest similarities. In experiment, the Euclidean distance is used for $d(\cdot,\cdot)$ and each $\boldsymbol{\theta}_n$, $\widehat{\boldsymbol{\vartheta}}_m$ is reshaped as a column vector for convenience.

3.2 Support Vector Regression

Support vector regression (SVR) aims to find support vectors which lie on the maximum margin hyperplanes in feature space and contribute to predictions. Training SVR means solving

$$\min \frac{1}{2}\|\boldsymbol{w}_i\|_2, s.t. \begin{cases} \theta_{ni} - \langle \boldsymbol{w}_i, \mathbf{f}_n \rangle - b \leq \epsilon, \\ \langle \boldsymbol{w}_i, \mathbf{f}_n \rangle + b - \theta_{ni} \leq \epsilon, \end{cases} \tag{4}$$

where the target value θ_{ni} is the ith component of $\boldsymbol{\theta}_n$ $(n = 1, \cdots, N)$, the inner product plus intercept $\langle \boldsymbol{w}_i, \mathbf{f}_n \rangle + b$ is the prediction for that sample, and ϵ is a free parameter that serves as a threshold. After optimization, we can predict $\widehat{\vartheta}_{mi}$ by $\widehat{\vartheta}_{mi} = \langle \boldsymbol{w}_i, \mathbf{g}_m \rangle + b$. We use the LIBSVM[1] toolbox with linear kernel (for fast speed) to implement SVR for emotion distribution prediction.

3.3 Shared Sparse Regression

Suppose $\mathbf{F} = [\mathbf{f}_1, \cdots, \mathbf{f}_N]$, $\boldsymbol{\Theta} = [\boldsymbol{\theta}_1, \cdots, \boldsymbol{\theta}_N]$. The basic idea of shared sparse regression (SSR) is that $\mathbf{g}_m$ and $\widehat{\boldsymbol{\vartheta}}_m$ can be written in terms of bases $\mathbf{F}$ and $\boldsymbol{\Theta}$ respectively, but with shared sparse coefficients $\boldsymbol{\phi}_m$. That is

$$\mathbf{g}_m = \mathbf{F}\boldsymbol{\phi}_m \quad \text{and} \quad \widehat{\boldsymbol{\vartheta}}_m = \boldsymbol{\Theta}\boldsymbol{\phi}_m, \tag{5}$$

where $\boldsymbol{\phi}_m$ is obtained by

$$\boldsymbol{\phi}_m^* = \underset{\boldsymbol{\phi}_m}{\operatorname{argmin}} \|\mathbf{F}\boldsymbol{\phi}_m - \mathbf{g}_m\|^2 + \eta\|\boldsymbol{\phi}_m\|_1, \tag{6}$$

where η is a regularization coefficient. Equ. (6) can be solved using iteratively reweighted least squares [2] (similar to Section 3.4).

3.4 Multi-Task Shared Sparse Regression

The above three baselines either model one test image or predict one target value each time, without jointly combining them together to explore the latent correlation. Multi-task shared sparse regression (MTSSR) utilizes this information. Suppose $\mathbf{G} = [\mathbf{g}_1, \cdots, \mathbf{g}_M]$, $\boldsymbol{\Omega} = [\widehat{\boldsymbol{\vartheta}}_1, \cdots, \widehat{\boldsymbol{\vartheta}}_M]$, MTSSR jointly predicts $\boldsymbol{\Omega}$ for $\mathbf{G}$ by letting the test features and the target values share the same coefficients $\boldsymbol{\Phi}$ on training data $\mathbf{F}$ and $\boldsymbol{\Theta}$ as follows

$$\mathbf{G} = \mathbf{F}\boldsymbol{\Phi} \quad \text{and} \quad \boldsymbol{\Omega} = \boldsymbol{\Theta}\boldsymbol{\Phi}. \tag{7}$$

$\boldsymbol{\Phi} \in \mathbb{R}^{N \times M}$ is obtained by solving the following convex optimization problem

$$\min_{\boldsymbol{\Phi}} \|\mathbf{F}\boldsymbol{\Phi} - \mathbf{G}\|^2 + \eta_1\|\boldsymbol{\Phi}\|_1 + \eta_2\|\boldsymbol{\Phi}\|_{2,1}, \tag{8}$$

where η_1 and η_2 are regularization coefficients, $\|\cdot\|_{2,1}$ denotes the $\ell_{2,1}$-norm of a matrix $\|\boldsymbol{\Phi}\|_{2,1} = \sum_{n=1}^{N}\sqrt{\sum_{m=1}^{M}\phi_{n,m}^2}$.

We employ the iteratively reweighted least squares [2] to optimize Equ. (8). The components of Equ. (8) are transformed by

$$\|\boldsymbol{\Phi}\|_1 = \sum_{n,m}|\phi_{n,m}| \simeq \sum_{n,m}\frac{\phi_{n,m}^2}{|\phi_{n,m}| + \varepsilon}, \tag{9}$$

$$\|\boldsymbol{\Phi}\|_{2,1} = \sum_{n}\sqrt{\sum_{m}\phi_{n,m}^2} \simeq \sum_{n}\left(\frac{\sum_m \phi_{n,m}^2}{\sqrt{\sum_m \phi_{n,m}^2 + \varepsilon}}\right). \tag{10}$$

Let $\varphi_{n,m} = \dfrac{1}{|\phi_{n,m}| + \varepsilon}$ and $\psi_n = \dfrac{1}{\sqrt{\sum_m \phi_{n,m}^2 + \varepsilon}}$, then the objective function of Equ.(8) is transformed to

$$\begin{aligned} \mathcal{J}(\boldsymbol{\Phi}) &\simeq \sum_m \|\mathbf{F}\boldsymbol{\phi}_m - \mathbf{g}_m\|^2 + \sum_{n,m}(\eta_1\varphi_{n,m} + \eta_2\psi_n)\phi_{n,m}^2 \\ &= \sum_m \|\mathbf{F}\boldsymbol{\phi}_m - \mathbf{g}_m\|^2 + \sum_m \boldsymbol{\phi}_m^{\mathrm{T}}\mathbf{W}_m\boldsymbol{\phi}_m, \end{aligned} \tag{11}$$

where $\mathbf{W}_m$ is a diagonal matrix with $\mathbf{W}_m(n,n) = \eta_1\varphi_{n,m} + \eta_2\psi_n$. $\min \mathcal{J}(\boldsymbol{\Phi})$ is a quadratic programming problem, which can be easily solved by off-the-shelf optimization methods. This process is iteratively updated until convergence.

4. EXPERIMENTS

To evaluate the effectiveness of the proposed method for continuous distribution prediction of dimensional image emotions, we carried out experiments on the Image-Emotion-Social-Net dataset (see Section 2). Totally we selected 18,700 images with more than 20 VA labels each for experiment. The data can be downloaded at `https://sites.google.com/site/schzhao/`.

4.1 Evaluation Criteria

The Kullback-Leibler divergence and the log likelihood (abbreviated as KL and LLH) are used as the evaluation metric. The KL divergence of the predicted distribution $\widehat{q}_m(\mathbf{x}; \widehat{\boldsymbol{\vartheta}}_m)$ from the ground truth distribution $q_m(\mathbf{x}; \boldsymbol{\vartheta}_m)$ is defined as

$$KL(q_m\|\widehat{q}_m) = -\int q_m(\mathbf{x}; \boldsymbol{\vartheta}_m)\ln\left\{\frac{\widehat{q}_m(\mathbf{x}; \widehat{\boldsymbol{\vartheta}}_m)}{q_m(\mathbf{x}; \boldsymbol{\vartheta}_m)}\right\}d\mathbf{x}. \tag{12}$$

In practice, $KL(q_m\|\widehat{q}_m)$ is approximated by a finite sum of the points $\{\mathbf{s}_1, \cdots, \mathbf{s}_S\}$ sampled following distribution $q_m(\mathbf{x}; \boldsymbol{\vartheta}_m)$ by

$$KL(q_m\|\widehat{q}_m) \simeq \frac{1}{S}\sum_{n=1}^{S}\left\{\ln q_m(\mathbf{s}_n; \boldsymbol{\vartheta}_m) - \ln \widehat{q}_m(\mathbf{s}_n; \widehat{\boldsymbol{\vartheta}}_m)\right\}. \tag{13}$$

The log likelihood metric is computed based on the actual VA labels $\{\mathbf{x}_{m1}, \cdots, \mathbf{x}_{mR_m}\}$ by

$$LLH(m) = \frac{1}{R_m}\log\prod_{r=1}^{R_m}\widehat{q}_m(\mathbf{x}_{mr}; \widehat{\boldsymbol{\vartheta}}_m) = \frac{1}{R_m}\sum_{r=1}^{R_m}\log\widehat{q}_m(\mathbf{x}_{mr}; \widehat{\boldsymbol{\vartheta}}_m). \tag{14}$$

[1]http://www.csie.ntu.edu.tw/~cjlin/libsvm/

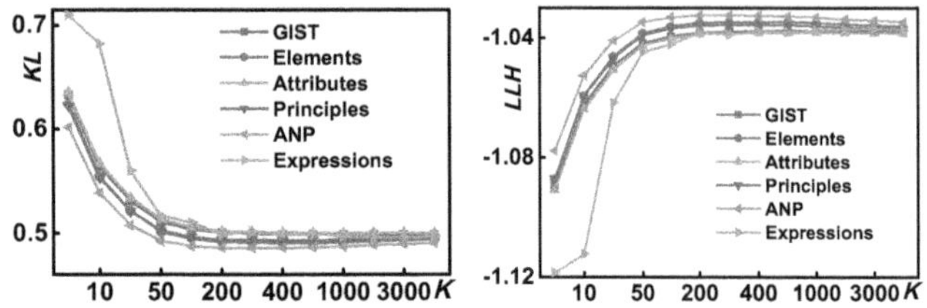

(a) KL divergence (b) Log likelihood

Figure 3: The influence of K in KNNW on continuous emotion distribution prediction using different features on measurement (a) KL divergence and (b) Log likelihood.

$KL \geq 0$ and lower value indicates better performance, while $LLH \leq 0$ and higher value represents better performance. In experiment, the data was separated into a training set and a test set using K-fold Cross Validation (K=5). We computed the average KL and LLH together with the standard deviation of the K folds.

4.2 Results and Discussions

Firstly, we investigated the influence of K in KNNW on emotion distribution prediction ($K = 5, 10, 20, 50, 100, 200, 300, 400, 500, 1000, 2000, 3000, 4000$). The results are illustrated in Figure 3. For clarity, the standard deviations are not shown. It is clear to see that the best K is dependent on the extracted features and is almost consistent on KL and LLH for each feature. $K = 4000$, 500, 1000, 400, 300 and 3000 perform best for features GIST, Elements, Attributes, Principles, ANP and Expressions, respectively. These Ks are selected as baselines for comparison with MTSSR.

The regularization parameters η and η_1, η_2 can influence the performance of SSR and the proposed MTSSR. In experiment, they are selected by grid search. Due to page limit, we do not show the detailed influences here. Using the best η and η_1, η_2 for each kind of features, we compared the performance of the proposed method with the three baselines on different features. The results measured by KL and LLH are illustrated in Figure 4. Some detailed prediction results of different methods using related best features are shown in Figure 2(d), 2(e) and 2(f).

From these results, we can find that (1) KL and LLH are dependent on both the features and the models; they are relatively consistent to measure the performance of distribution prediction; (2) For almost all the features, the proposed MTSSR model performs the best, which benefit from the exploration of latent information between different tasks; (3) The best features are ANP, Elements, Principles and ANP for KNNR, SVR, SSR and MTSSR, respectively; Generally, the low-level generic features perform the worst, which indicates that they cannot represent image emotions well because of the largest "affective gap"; Mid-level and the high-level features have stronger link to image emotions, which is consistent with the conclusions in [15]; (4) Though simple, the KNNW outperforms SVR on average in emotion distribution prediction.

5. CONCLUSION

In this paper, we proposed to predict the continuous probability distribution of image emotions represented in VA space, which can be viewed as an initial attempt to measure the subjective evaluation of human perceptions. We presented multi-task shared sparse leaning as the learning model and optimized it by iteratively reweighted least squares. Besides, we provided another three baseline algorithms. Experiments conducted on the Image-Emotion-Social-Net dataset demonstrated the effectiveness of the proposed method.

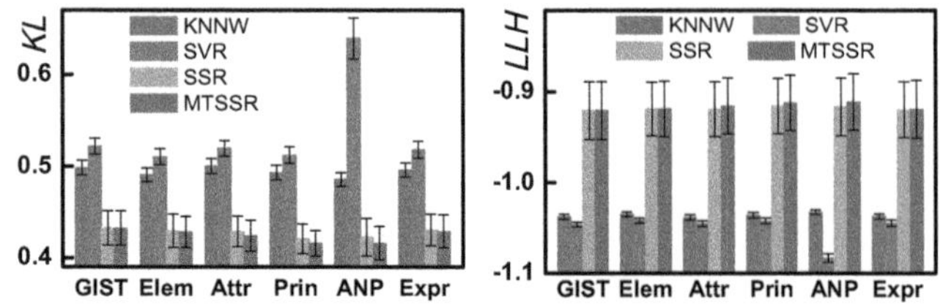

(a) KL divergence (b) Log likelihood

Figure 4: Performance comparison between the proposed method and the three baselines on emotion distribution predictioni using different features measured by KL and LLH.

The predicted emotion distribution can be explored in many applications, such as affective image retrieval and emotion transfer. For further studies, we will consider exploring social related factors for emotion distribution prediction. Consistently combining and fusing multi-modal features in MTSSR may further improve the prediction performance, which is also worth studying.

6. ACKNOWLEDGEMENTS

This work was supported by the National Natural Science Foundation of China (No. 61472103) and Key Program (No. 61133003).

7. REFERENCES

[1] D. Borth, R. Ji, T. Chen, T. Breuel, and S.-F. Chang. Large-scale visual sentiment ontology and detectors using adjective noun pairs. In *ACM International Conference on Multimedia*, pages 223–232, 2013.

[2] C. Chen, J. Huang, L. He, and H. Li. Preconditioning for accelerated iteratively reweighted least squares in structured sparsity reconstruction. In *IEEE Conference on Computer Vision and Pattern Recognition*, pages 2713–2720, 2014.

[3] T. Chen, F. X. Yu, J. Chen, Y. Cui, Y.-Y. Chen, and S.-F. Chang. Object-based visual sentiment concept analysis and application. In *ACM International Conference on Multimedia*, pages 367–376, 2014.

[4] J. Jia, S. Wu, X. Wang, P. Hu, L. Cai, and J. Tang. Can we understand van gogh's mood? learning to infer affects from images in social networks. In *ACM International Conference on Multimedia*, pages 857–860, 2012.

[5] D. Joshi, R. Datta, E. Fedorovskaya, Q.-T. Luong, J. Z. Wang, J. Li, and J. Luo. Aesthetics and emotions in images. *IEEE Signal Processing Magazine*, 28(5):94–115, 2011.

[6] X. Lu, P. Suryanarayan, R. B. Adams Jr, J. Li, M. G. Newman, and J. Z. Wang. On shape and the computability of emotions. In *ACM International Conference on Multimedia*, pages 229–238, 2012.

[7] J. Machajdik and A. Hanbury. Affective image classification using features inspired by psychology and art theory. In *ACM International Conference on Multimedia*, pages 83–92, 2010.

[8] G. Patterson and J. Hays. Sun attribute database: Discovering, annotating, and recognizing scene attributes. In *IEEE Conference on Computer Vision and Pattern Recognition*, pages 2751–2758, 2012.

[9] A. B. Warriner, V. Kuperman, and M. Brysbaert. Norms of valence, arousal, and dominance for 13,915 english lemmas. *Behavior research methods*, 45(4):1191–1207, 2013.

[10] P. Yang, Q. Liu, and D. N. Metaxas. Exploring facial expressions with compositional features. In *IEEE Conference on Computer Vision and Pattern Recognition*, pages 2638–2644, 2010.

[11] V. Yanulevskaya, J. Van Gemert, K. Roth, A.-K. Herbold, N. Sebe, and J.-M. Geusebroek. Emotional valence categorization using holistic image features. In *IEEE International Conference on Image Processing*, pages 101–104, 2008.

[12] J. Yuan, S. Mcdonough, Q. You, and J. Luo. Sentribute: image sentiment analysis from a mid-level perspective. In *ACM International Workshop on Issues of Sentiment Discovery and Opinion Mining*, page 10, 2013.

[13] S. Zhao, Y. Gao, X. Jiang, H. Yao, T.-S. Chua, and X. Sun. Exploring principles-of-art features for image emotion recognition. In *ACM International Conference on Multimedia*, pages 47–56, 2014.

[14] S. Zhao, H. Yao, X. Jiang, and X. Sun. Predicting discrete probability distribution of image emotions. In *IEEE International Conference on Image Processing*, 2015.

[15] S. Zhao, H. Yao, Y. Yang, and Y. Zhang. Affective image retrieval via multi-graph learning. In *ACM International Conference on Multimedia*, pages 1025–1028, 2014.

Towards Distributed Video Summarization

Shayok Chakraborty[1], Omesh Tickoo[2] and Ravishankar Iyer[2]
[1]Electrical and Computer Engineering, Carnegie Mellon University, Pittsburgh, USA
[2]Intel Labs, Oregon, USA

ABSTRACT

Video summarization is a fertile topic in multimedia research. While the advent of modern video cameras and several social networking and video sharing websites (like YouTube, Flickr, Facebook) has led to the generation of humongous amounts of redundant video data, video summarization has emerged as an effective methodology to automatically extract a succinct and condensed representation of a given video. The unprecedented increase in the volume of video data necessitates the usage of multiple, independent computers for its storage and processing. In order to understand the overall essence of a video, it is therefore necessary to develop an algorithm which can summarize a video distributed across multiple computers. In this paper, we propose a novel algorithm for distributed video summarization. Our algorithm requires minimal communication among the computers (over which the video is stored) and also enjoys nice theoretical properties. Our empirical results on several challenging, unconstrained videos corroborate the potential of the proposed framework for real-world distributed video summarization applications.

Categories and Subject Descriptors

I.4.9 [**Image Processing and Computer Vision**]: Applications; I.2.10 [**Artificial Intelligence**]: Vision and Scene Understanding—*Video Analysis*

Keywords

Video Summarization, Submodular Functions

1. INTRODUCTION

The progress of technology in leaps and bounds has led to the emergence and widespread deployment of inexpensive video cameras. These cameras have a high frame rate (typically, $25 - 30$ frames per second) and thus capture a humongous amount of data in a short duration. The captured data has high redundancy (due to the high frame rate) and also is also extremely unstructured and diverse (both in terms of contents and duration). Scanning through these staggering number of images manually entails significant human labor. This has set the stage for research in the field of video summarization, which automatically extracts the salient and informative frames from a video stream and enables a more efficient and engaging viewing experience [15]. It is extensively used as a preprocessing step in many video-based applications like indexing, retrieval and browsing. Common approaches of video summarization include shot boundary detection [17], motion-based sampling [12] and clustering [3]. Shroff *et al.* [14] proposed an iterative algorithm to select the exemplar frames from a given video sequence. Egocentric video summarization has recently gained attention to recognize important people and objects in a video [9].

Video data volumes are increasing faster than the ability of individual computers to store and process them. Consider a surveillance system where a video camera is installed in a public place to detect suspicious behaviors. The high frame rate and long duration of operation of the camera result in the generation of an enormous number of frames, which need to be stored across multiple machines. In order to detect unusual activities, it is necessary to generate a summary of the entire video stream. Further, it may be necessary to quickly sift through months of security video footage, stored across multiple computers, in order to recognize suspicious/anomalous behavior. Medical video analysis is another application where the informative frames need to be identified from vast amounts of a patient's video data, spread across multiple machines. Thus, there is a pressing need for an algorithm to summarize a video, which is distributed across multiple machines, with minimal interaction among them. Even though video summarization is extensively studied, distributed video summarization is much less explored. Ioannis *et al.* [8] proposed an unsupervised data reduction algorithm based on non-negative matrix factorization (NMF) to identify the summary frames in a distributed setting. The NMF algorithm is run separately on each machine to identify the representative frames and the results are merged to generate the final summary. To the best of our knowledge, this is the only published algorithm to summarize a video distributed across multiple computers. However, this method is heuristic in nature and also lacks any theoretical guarantees on the quality of the obtained solution. Other related efforts in this domain are all focused on speeding up the summarization process using multi-core CPUs, GPUs and parallelization schemes [2, 1], but the entire video is assumed to be present in a single computer.

In this paper, we propose a novel algorithm for distributed video summarization. We develop an optimization-based framework to identify the salient and informative frames distributed across multiple independent computers. Our algorithm requires minimal communication among the machines and the obtained solution can be theoretically guaranteed to be competitive with the centralized so-

MM'15 October 26-30, 2015, Brisbane, Australia
Copyright 2015 ACM ISBN 978-1-4503-3459-4/15/10 ...$15.00
DOI: http://dx.doi.org/10.1145/2733373.2806355.

lution (obtained when the entire video is present in a single computer). Although we focus on video summarization in this work, the proposed framework is generic and can be used in any application where the salient exemplars need to be identified from large amounts of redundant data distributed across multiple machines.

2. PROPOSED FRAMEWORK

2.1 Problem Formulation

Consider a distributed video summarization set-up, as shown in Figure 1. The video captured by the camera is discharged in computer C_0, which broadcasts the frames to m computers C_1 to C_m. Each computer (C_1 to C_m) processes its own chunk of the video stream and the results are broadcasted to a backend server (it is not possible to store the entire contents of C_1 to C_m in the backend, due to resource limitations). The objective is to select k summary frames from the entire video.

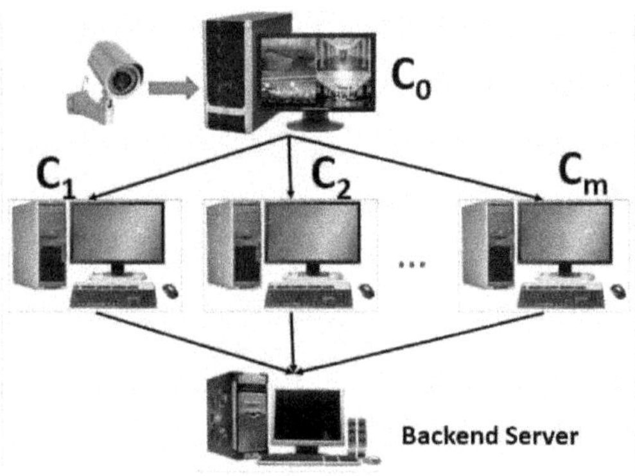

Figure 1: Distributed Video Summarization Setup

Summary Selection Criteria: Video streams have an inherent redundancy among them due to the high frame rate of video cameras. Thus, a good summarization technique should focus on identifying the critical events in a given video. However, if two summary frames separately furnish important, but duplicate information, then the net information gained by selecting both of them is not maximal. A metric computing the redundancy among a set of selected frames is therefore of paramount importance. We hence quantify the utility score of a set of summary frames in terms of the following two criteria:

- **Exhaustive**, which ensures that the summary captures a large portion of the events in the video
- **Mutually Exclusive**, which enforces the summary frames to be non-redundant (distinct from each other)

A summarization framework based on maximizing the exhaustive and mutually exclusive criteria ensures that the essence of the original video is captured well in the summary (exhaustive) and that there is minimal duplication of information (mutually exclusive). Such selection criteria are commonly used in selective sampling applications like active learning [13].

Formally, consider a video $V = \{v_1, v_2, \ldots v_n\}$ consisting of n frames and let S denote the set of frames selected in the summary. The exhaustive-ness of the summary can be quantified as:

$$E(S) = \frac{1}{|V|} \sum_{i \in V, j \in S} w_{ij} \tag{1}$$

where $w_{ij} \geq 0$ denotes the similarity between two frames v_i and v_j in the video sequence. Maximizing $E(S)$ ensures that the summary set S has maximal similarity to the ground set V.

The mutually exclusive-ness score of a frame is computed as its minimum distance from the set of already selected summary frames:

$$M(S) = \sum_{i \in S} \min_{j \in S: j < i} d_{ij} \tag{2}$$

where $d_{ij} \geq 0$ denotes the distance between two frames v_i and v_j. This is conceptually similar to the Hausdorff distance metric, commonly used for image matching [7]. Maximizing $M(S)$ avoids selection of duplicate information in the summary S. The net utility score of a summary set can be expressed as a weighted combination of $E(S)$ and $M(S)$:

$$Q(S) = E(S) + \lambda M(S) \tag{3}$$

where $\lambda \geq 0$ denotes the weight parameter. The summary selection can therefore be posed as the following optimization (k denotes the summary length):

$$\max_{S \subseteq V} Q(S)$$

$$\text{s.t.} \quad |S| = k \tag{4}$$

The search space being exponentially large, exhaustive search techniques are computationally prohibitive. We solve this problem using submodular optimization algorithms.

2.2 Submodular Optimization

Let N be a finite ground set and consider a function $f : 2^N \rightarrow \Re$, that returns a real value for any subset $S \subseteq N$. The function f is called submodular if for all $A \subseteq B \subseteq N$ and $x \in N \backslash B$,

$$f(A \cup \{x\}) - f(A) \geq f(B \cup \{x\}) - f(B) \tag{5}$$

This is called the diminishing returns property [6]. Further, f is called monotonically non-decreasing if $f(A) \leq f(B)$ whenever $A \subseteq B$.

THEOREM 1. *The objective function $Q(S)$ defined in Equation (3) is submodular.*

PROOF. From Equation (3), we get:

$$Q(S) = E(S) + \lambda M(S)$$
$$= \frac{1}{|V|} \sum_{i \in V, j \in S} w_{ij} + \lambda \sum_{i \in S} \min_{j \in S: j < i} d_{ij}$$

Consider an element $x \in V \backslash S$, we have

$$Q(S \cup \{x\}) - Q(S) = \frac{1}{|V|} \sum_{i \in V} w_{ix} + \lambda \min_{i \in S} d_{ix} \tag{6}$$

Now, consider two arbitrary summary sets S_1 and S_2 such that $S_1 \subseteq S_2$. We then have,

$$\min_{i \in S_2} d_{ix} \leq \min_{i \in S_1} d_{ix} \tag{7}$$

This holds since S_2 being a larger summary, it is possible to have an element in this superset, which is closer to the element x. The first term on the right side of Equation (6) does not depend on the set S; λ is a non-negative scalar. We therefore have,

$$Q(S_1 \cup \{x\}) - Q(S_1) \geq Q(S_2 \cup \{x\}) - Q(S_2)$$

$\forall S_1, S_2, S_1 \subseteq S_2$. Hence, $Q(S)$ is submodular. □

Further, since both the distance and similarity-based terms are non-negative, the objective $Q(S)$ is monotonically non-decreasing as addition of elements to the set S can only increase the value of $Q(S)$. The optimization in Equation (4) is therefore the maximization of a monotonically non-decreasing submodular function, subject to a cardinality constraint. This can be efficiently solved using the greedy algorithm proposed by Nemhauser *et al.* [11], which produces a solution guaranteed to be within $1 - \frac{1}{e}$ of the optimal.

2.3 Distributed Submodular Maximization

In the distributed video summarization setup (outlined in Figure 1), however, the entire video V is not present in a single machine, but is distributed across multiple machines. Our summary selection problem therefore reduces to maximizing a monotone submodular function in a distributed setting. Mirzasoleiman *et al.* [10] proposed the GREEDI framework for distributed submodular maximization under cardinality constraints. The algorithm first distributes the ground set uniformly at random across the m machines. It operates in two stages, where in the first round, each machine separately runs the standard greedy algorithm [11] on its local data samples and selects k exemplars. In the second step, the selected mk elements are merged in the backend server (Figure 1) and k final summary frames are selected using the same greedy algorithm on the mk samples.

The computation of the term $E(S)$ in our algorithm (Equation 1) requires the complete ground set V, while evaluation of $M(S)$ (Equation 2) requires only the elements of the set S. In the first step, $E(S)$ is evaluated in a particular machine with respect to the local data samples in that machine. According to our definition, $E(S)$ satisfies the definition of decomposable functions [10] and thus, in the second step, it can be evaluated with respect to a randomly chosen subset of the ground set, of size $\lceil n/m \rceil$, where n is the size of the ground set V. This distributed maximization algorithm has a concrete mathematical guarantee on the quality of the obtained solution with respect to that of the optimum centralized solution (the solution obtained when the entire video is present in a single machine). This is formalized in the following theorem [10] (we take $\kappa = l = k$, and follow the notations in the paper); f is the submodular function being used for sample selection ($f \equiv Q$, in our case):

THEOREM 2. *Let $A^c[k]$ denote the optimum centralized solution and $A^{gd}[m,k]$ denote the solution obtained using the distributed maximization algorithm. Let $\delta > 0, \epsilon < 1/4$ and let n_0 be an integer such that for $n \geq n_0$ we have $\ln(n)/n \leq \epsilon^2/(mk)$. For $n \geq \max(n_0, m\log(\delta/4m)/\epsilon^2)$, we have, with probability at least $1 - \delta$,*

$$f(A^{gd}[m,k]) \geq (1 - 1/e)^2 (f(A^c[k]) - 2\epsilon)$$

3. EXPERIMENTS AND RESULTS

Datasets and Feature Extraction: We conducted experiments on a wide range of videos from different application domains to validate the generalizability of our approach: (1) **The UT Egocentric Video dataset**, which contains videos captured by a subject under unconstrained natural settings, using a wearable camera [9], (2) **DARPA's VIVID video surveillance dataset**, which contains low resolution aerial videos captured by an unmanned aerial vehicle (UAV) [4] and (3) **The SFU Skating dataset**, which contains unconstrained images with real pan, tilt and zoom of the camera capturing rapid moves of a skater like jumps, spins, lifts and turns [16]. Each video was split into images and the histogram of oriented gradients (HOG) feature [5] was used as a descriptor of each frame. The distance d_{ij} between two frames was computed using the chi-squared distance between their color histograms; the cosine similarity metric was used to compute the similarity.

Experiment Set-up: The experimental set-up is outlined in Figure 1. Since this is our first effort to validate the proposed framework, we simulate the set-up in a single computer by partitioning the video data V into m segments (corresponding to the m machines) $V_1, V_2 \ldots V_m$, such that $V_i \cap V_j = \phi, \forall i, j, i \neq j$; no communication mechanism is assumed among the data in different segments (replicating the situation with m different machines). The outputs from the different segments are combined to select the final summary. Validation of the framework in a distributed infrastructure with multiple computers will be taken up as part of future research. The summary length k was taken as 50 and the number of machines m as 10 for the UT Egocentric and VIVID datasets; for the SFU Skating dataset, we take $k = 10$ and $m = 4$. The weight parameter λ was set as 5, based on preliminary experiments.

Comparison Baselines: We compare the proposed framework against the following two approaches for distributed summarization: (i) **Random**: in the first round, each machine selects k frames at random from its local contents and in the second round, k out of the mk frames are again selected at random in the final summary; (ii) **NMF**: the method proposed in [8] for distributed video summarization, where non-negative matrix factorization (NMF) is used in the first step to select k frames from each of the computers and the outputs are combined to select the final summary.

Evaluation Metric: To evaluate a video summary quantitatively, we compute the count of the number of frames whose reconstruction error using the summary is above a given threshold. The insight behind this metric is that a good summary is one where all the frames in the video lie in the space spanned by the linear combination of the exemplars; fewer the number of frames in the null-space of the exemplars, better the summary. Please refer [14] for details.

Experiment 1: Proposed against Baselines: The results comparing the proposed framework against the baselines are depicted in Figure 2, where the x-axis denotes the threshold and the y-axis denotes the number of frames with error above this threshold (lower the better). We note that for the proposed algorithm, the number of frames with reconstruction error above the threshold drops at the fastest rate with increasing values of this threshold; at any given threshold, it consistently has the lowest number of frames with error above that threshold. This corroborates the fact that our algorithm appropriately identifies the exemplar frames in a distributed setting and best captures the overall essence of a video. The improved performance is particularly evident for the SFU Skating video (Figure 2(c)), where a diverse variety of actions is performed by the skater. The images selected in the final summary by all the methods for this dataset are shown in Figure 3. Our method captures samples from a wide range of actions, thereby generating a more informative summary in a distributed setup, which accounts for its superior performance.

Experiment 2: Proposed vs. Centralized: We also compare the solution obtained by the proposed algorithm against the centralized solution that we would obtain if we had the resources to store the entire video in a single computer. The centralized solution is obtained by running the greedy algorithm (used in the first step of our framework) once on the entire video stream. Figure 4 reports the results on the VIVID dataset. We note that the performance of our algorithm is very close to the optimum centralized solution. This corroborates the fact that the proposed framework produces high quality solutions, even when the data is partitioned across multiple machines.

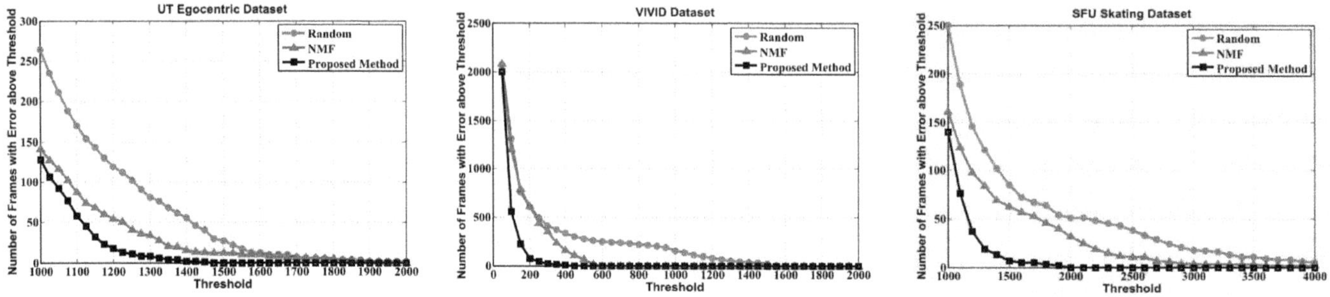

(a) UT Egocentric Dataset (b) VIVID Surveillance Dataset (c) SFU Skating Dataset

Figure 2: Comparison of the Proposed Method against the Baselines. Best viewed in color.

Figure 3: Images Selected in the Final Summary by all the Methods: SFU Skating Dataset

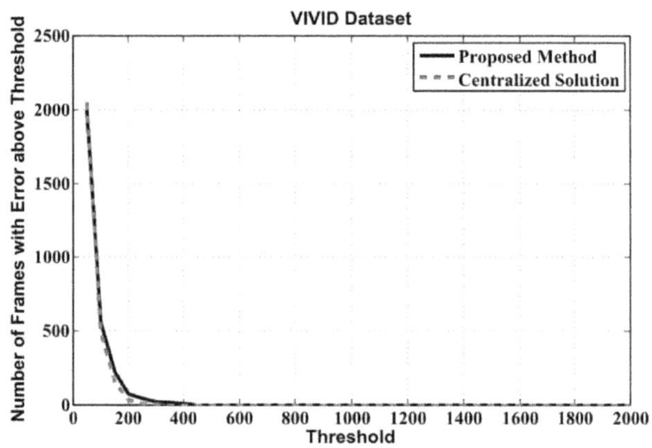

Figure 4: Comparison of the Proposed Framework against the Centralized Solution: VIVID Dataset. Best viewed in color.

4. CONCLUSION AND FUTURE WORK

In this paper, we proposed a novel algorithm for distributed video summarization. We exploited distributed submodular maximization techniques to identify a set of exemplar frames from a video distributed across multiple machines. Our empirical results demonstrate tremendous promise in identifying the useful and relevant information from a video in a distributed environment. As part of our future work, we plan to conduct extensive large scale experiments to validate the merit of our framework.

5. REFERENCES

[1] S. Almeida, E. Cahuina, A. Araujo, G. Chavez, and D. Menotti. GPUs and multicore CPUs implementations of a static video summarization. In *Progress in Pattern Recognition, Image Analysis, Computer Vision, and Applications*, 2014.

[2] S. Almeida, A. Nazare, A. Araujo, G. Chavez, and D. Menotti. Speeding up a video summarization approach using GPUs and multicore CPUs. In *International Conference on Computational Science*, 2014.

[3] S. Avila, A. Lopes, A. Luz, and A. Araujo. VSUMM: A mechanism designed to produce static video summaries and a novel evaluation method. In *Pattern Recognition Letters*, 2011.

[4] R. Collins, X. Zhou, and S. Teh. An open source tracking testbed and evaluation web site. In *IEEE International Workshop on Performance Evaluation of Tracking and Surveillance (PETS)*, 2005.

[5] N. Dalal and B. Triggs. Histograms of oriented gradients for human detection. In *CVPR*, 2005.

[6] S. Fujishige. Submodular functions and optimization. In *Elsevier Science*, 2005.

[7] D. Huttenlocher, G. Klanderman, and W. Rucklidge. Comparing images using the hausdorff distance. In *IEEE TPAMI*, 1993.

[8] K. Ioannis, S. Tsevas, I. Maglogiannis, and D. Iakovidis. Enabling distributed summarization of wireless capsule endoscopy video. In *International Conference on Imaging Systems and Techniques*, 2010.

[9] Y. Lee, J. Ghosh, and K. Grauman. Discovering important people and objects for egocentric video summarization. In *CVPR*, 2012.

[10] B. Mirzasoleiman, A. Karbasi, R. Sarkar, and A. Krause. Distributed submodular maximization: Identifying representative elements in massive data. In *NIPS*, 2013.

[11] G. Nemhauser, L. Wolsey, and M. Fisher. An analysis of approximations for maximizing submodular set functions. In *Mathematical Programming*, 1978.

[12] C. Ngo, Y. Ma, and H. Zhang. Automatic video summarization by graph modeling. In *ICCV*, 2003.

[13] D. Shen, J. Zhang, J. Su, G. Zhou, and C. Tan. Multi-criteria based active learning for named entity recognition. In *ACL*, 2004.

[14] N. Shroff, P. Turaga, and R. Chellappa. Video precis: Highlighting diverse aspects of videos. In *IEEE Transactions on Multimedia*, 2010.

[15] B. Truong and S. Venkatesh. Video abstraction: A systematic review and classification. In *ACM TOMCCAP*, 2007.

[16] Y. Wang, H. Jiang, M. Drew, Z. Li, and G. Mori. Unsupervised discovery of action classes. In *CVPR*, 2006.

[17] H. Zhang, J. Wu, D. Zhong, and S. Smoliar. An integrated system for content based video retrieval and browsing. *Pattern Recognition*, 1997.

Semantic Image Search From Multiple Query Images

Gonzalo Vaca-Castano
Center for Research in Computer Vision.
University of Central Florida
gonzalo@knights.ucf.edu

Mubarak Shah
Center for Research in Computer Vision.
University of Central Florida
shah@crcv.ucf.edu

ABSTRACT

This paper presents a novel search paradigm that uses multiple images as input to perform semantic search of images. While earlier focuses on using single or multiple query images to retrieve images with views of the same instance, the proposed paradigm uses each query image to discover common concepts that are implicitly shared by all of the query images and retrieves images considering the found concepts. Our implementation uses high level visual features extracted from a deep convolutional network to retrieve images similar to each query input. These images have associated text previously generated by implicit crowdsourcing. A Bag of Words (BoW) textual representation of each query image is built from the associated text of the retrieved similar images. A learned vector space representation of English words extracted from a corpus of 100 billion words allows computing the conceptual similarity of words. The words that represent the input images are used to find new words that share conceptual similarity across all the input images. These new words are combined with the representations of the input images to obtain a BoW textual representation of the search, which is used to perform image retrieval. The retrieved images are re-ranked to enhance visual similarity with respect to any of the input images. Our experiments show that the concepts found are meaningful and that they retrieve correctly 72.43% of the images from the top 25, along with user ratings performed in the cases of study.

1. INTRODUCTION

The goal of any Image Retrieval system is to retrieve images from a large visual corpus that are similar to the input query. To date, most Image Retrieval systems (including commercial search engines like Google[1]) base their search on a single image input query. Recently, multiple images as input queries have been proposed for image retrieval [1, 2]. In these cases, the objective of the multiple image inputs is to acquire different viewing conditions of the unique object or concept for the user.

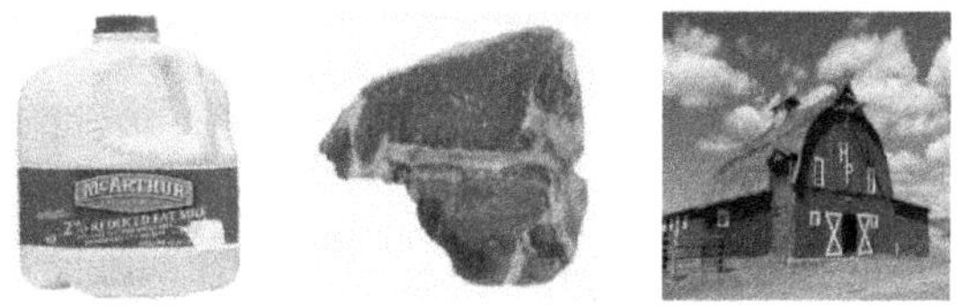

(a) Query Images

(b) Retrieved Images

Figure 1: Results of the proposed paradigm with three input images. a) Query images. b) Top retrieved images.

In this work, we follow a different approach for multiple query image inputs, since the input images are employed jointly to extract underlying concepts common to the input images. The input images do not need to be part of the same concept. In fact, different input image either enriches, amplifies, or reduces the importance of one descriptive aspect of the multiple significances that any image inherently has. Consider the example in Figure 1. Three input images are used to query the system. The first input image is a milk bottle, the second contains a piece of meat, and the third contains a farm. These three images are dissimilar from a visual point of view. However, conceptually, they could be linked by the underlying concept "cattle," since farmers obtain milk and meat from cattle. These types of knowledge-based conceptual relations are the ones that we propose to capture in this new search paradigm. Figure 1b shows the top retrieved images by our system.

The use of multiple images as input queries in real scenarios is straightforward, especially when mobile and wearable devices are the user interfaces. Consider for instance a wearable device. In this case, pictures can be passively sampled and used as query inputs of a semantic search to discover the context of the user. Once meaningful semantic concepts are found, many specific applications can be built,

[1] http://images.google.com/

MM'15, October 26–30, 2015, Brisbane, Australia.
© 2015 ACM. ISBN 978-1-4503-3459-4/15/10 ...$15.00.
DOI: http://dx.doi.org/10.1145/2733373.2806356.

including personalization of textual search, reduction of the search space for visual object detection, and personalization of output information such as suggestions, advertising, and recommendations.

The utility of the proposed search paradigm is enhanced when the user has constructed an unclear search or lacks the knoledge to describe it, but does have some idea of images of isolated concepts. For example, consider a user looking for ideas for a gift. While walking through the mall, the user adds some pictures of vague ideas for the gift. Based on the provided images, semantic concepts are found and used to retrieve images of gift suggestions. Another example of this type of application is retrieving image suggestions from a domain–specific knowledge area (painting, cooking, etc.), based on the user's more general visual inputs, where the user does not have specialized knowledge in the specific area. Hence, given a couple of paints that you like as input, the semantic search could find other images for you that share similar common concepts.

This paper presents a new Image Retrieval paradigm with the following novelties:

1) Multiple image queries are used as inputs.

2) The input images are used to retrieve the concepts that images represent, instead of merely visual similarities.

3) Implicit crowdsourcing is used to obtain textual descriptions of pictures that are less noisy than typical surrounding text of web images.

4) Text descriptors are used as operands to discover underlying concepts common to the input images. The retrieved images capture semantic similarity from knowledge gained via text concepts and visual similarity.

2. METHOD

The proposed method to retrieve images from multiple query input images is explained next. Initially, each one of the query images I_i is processed individually to retrieve candidate images, based on the visual similarity, from the retrieval dataset. Each query image I_i produces a set of k nearest neighbor candidates, denoted as C_{ij}, where j goes from $1 \ldots k$.

All of the images from the dataset used for retrieval are assumed to have a dual representation: a visual representation given by a global image descriptor and a textual descriptor represented by a histogram of all of the texts describing the image. Hence, every candidate image C_{ij} has an associated textual descriptor represented by a word histogram that serves to link the visual representation with the conceptual representation.

Candidate images that are visually closer to the query image have a higher impact in the text representation of the query image. The most representative text words that describes the query images, are processed using Natural Language Processing (NLP) techniques to discover new words that share conceptual similarity. Afterwards, the histogram summation of the weighted word representations of the candidate images C_{ij} and the aggregation of bins for the discovered words produces a histogram that represents the queries of the search jointly. Later, cosine distance between the tf–idf textual representation of the database images and the joint search representation is performed to retrieve images. Finally, a re-ranking is performed to privilege images with high visual similarity to any of the query images.

2.1 Visual Similarity

We use Convolutional Neural Network (CNN) to generate a high level visual representation of the images. The Convolutional Neural Network (CNN) presented by Krizhevsky et al. [5] contains eight layers with weights; the first five layers are convolutional and the last three layers are fully connected neural networks. The last layer contains 1000 output units fed to a softmax function that determines the class label output. Since we are interested in a high level representation of the image instead of a classifier, we remove the last layer of the network. Features are then calculated by forward propagation of a mean subtracted 224x224 RGB image over five convolutional layers and two fully connected layers. The result is a 4096 dimension vector that represents the image as a global descriptor.

Since our image descriptor is global, we perform Locality-Sensitive Hashing (LSH) to have fast approximated nearest neighbor retrieval of candidate images. The presented scheme produces retrievals that are similar in appearance, but also account for the meaning of the image as an object, which is one of the main goals of our proposed framework.

2.2 Textual Representation of Dataset Images

The images of the dataset are assumed to have a dual representation (visual / textual). In order to extract textual representation of an image, traditionally the text surrounding the images or associated meta-tags are used as text descriptors for the images. However, surrounding text is highly noisy, and meta-tags are frequently absent, incomplete, or inconsistent with other tasks. We believe that implicit crowdsourcing is a source for cleaner text descriptions. Implicit crowdsourcing engages users in an activity in order to gather information about another topic based on the user's actions or responses. The dataset provided for the Bing challenge [9] is an example of implicit crowdsourcing where text for the images were added by users after they clicked for the best results for their textual searches. Many phrases can describe a single image. Instead of deciding which text best represents the image, we represent the image as a Bag of Words representation of collected text.

2.3 Textual Representation of Query Images

The input to our retrieval system is a set of query images without tags, labels, text description, or metadata. In order to operate in the conceptual level, textual representation of the content of the query images must be generated. Textual representations of the top retrieved images from visual features are transferred to obtain a textual representation of each query image. The top retrieved candidates are weighted using a decreasing function of their visual distance to the query image. Hence, if a retrieved image matches exactly with the query image, it receives a maximum weight equal to one, while others receive lower weights. The textual representation of the query image is given by the weighted sum of retrieved textual representations.

2.4 Word Representation in Vector Space

The phrases that describe images are morphologically simple. The images in the dataset are fairly well described by a Bag of Words (BoW) textual representation. From a relatively broad vocabulary, only a small set of words are enough to describe the content of images. Hence, similarities be-

input :

- BoW representation of the N input images
- Index of the sorted columns of kernel K_{ij}

output: List of new words conceptually shared by the N input images

initialization;
while $size(ListNewWords) == 0$ **do**
  increase number T of words used to create N-tuples;
  increase number of sorted terms to be intercepted;
  for *All N-tuples from top ranked words* **do**
    $V \longleftarrow$ Intersection(current N-tuple);
    if $size(V) \neq 0$ **then**
      add V to ListNewWords
    end
  end
end

Algorithm 1: Algorithm to discover words conceptually shared by the input images from their textual representations.

tween pairs of words can be enough to capture semantic relations between images.

In the proposed multi-query input image retrieval system, we combine the text descriptor from each input image represented by a small set of words, to infer new words that capture the common meaning of inputs.

Discrete words can be represented in a continuous dense vector space that captures semantic knowledge learned in the text domain. The skip-gram and the Continuous Bag of Words (CBOW) model architectures proposed by Mikolov et al. [7,8] efficiently learn semantically meaningful float point representations of words from very large text datasets.

Cosine distance can be used in order to find the semantic similarity between two words of the vocabulary, by normalizing the vector representation of each word and computing the dot product between them.

A kernel K_{ij} that measures the similarity between any word i and any word j of the vocabulary is calculated during the training phase. The purpose of the kernel K_{ij} is to quickly find the similarity of any pair of words.

2.5 Concept Discovery

The representation of a query image is typically formed by only tens of words. If N is the number of query inputs and one word is selected from each query image, an N-tuple of words is formed. We want to examine the N words of the N-tuple to discover new words that relate them conceptually.

A word W_l is considered as a new word concept, when W_l has simultaneously high similarity to all the words of the N-tuple measured in the vector space.

The kernel K_{ij} enables finding the similarity between any pair of words of the vocabulary. A row (or column) q of the kernel matrix K_{ij} is the distance of the word indexed by q to any other word of the vocabulary. Performing a descend sort operation and taking their indices in the selected column q, gives the word indices that are conceptually closer to the word W_q.

Given an N-tuple, we can find the closest words for all the words that are part of the N-tuple. If a word W_l is found in the top positions of all the sorted lists of the N-tuple words, then the word W_l is declared as a new word conceptually shared by the N-tuple. We call this procedure "intersection."

There are many combinations of N-tuples that could be formed; however, the most interesting ones are the N-tuples created from words that have highest weights in the textual representation of each query image.

A small number T of words with higher weights are used to create the N-tuples. When no shared word is found in the given set of N-tuples, the number of words used to create N-tuples and the number of sorted terms to be intercepted is increased until at least one common word is found. Algorithm 1 summarizes this procedure.

2.6 Image Retrieval

Image retrieval is performed from a unique textual representation that accounts for all input images and the list of words conceptually shared by the input images. The textual representation of the joint query is the summation of the individual query input representations and the addition of new bins indexed by the list of words shared by the input images.

Image retrieval is performed based on the ranking score produced by the cosine scoring algorithm [6] between the joint search representation and the tf-idf representation of the images of the dataset.

Instead of comparing with the entire set of images of the dataset, we use a shorter number of possible outputs to calculate the score of the images. This subset of images is formed by all the images of the dataset that contain at least one word from either the list of words conceptually shared by the inputs or the most representative words of each query input. Hence, the number of images to evaluate reduces from one million to just a couple of thousand candidate images in the Bing dataset. The retrieved images are based on their conceptual ranking only. Therefore, a re-scoring of the retrieved images is performed based on the visual similarity to the input images. Images that are visually inconsistent with all the input images are penalized, and re-ranked to lower positions. The value of penalization is calculated using an inverse exponential function of the Euclidean norm of the difference between descriptors of the retrieved image and its most visual similar input image.

3. EXPERIMENTS

We use the public domain implementation and trained model available from the caffe library [4] to calculate our visual image representation. Image resizing and feature extraction of one million images can be performed in less than 24 hours in a regular Quad core personal computer.

The dataset [9] provided for the 2013 MSR-Bing Image Retrieval Challenge[2] was sampled from one-year click logs of the Microsoft Bing image search engine. We chose this dataset for image retrieval since the texts associated with the images are fairly accurate because they are built from user's search criteria and click preferences. The most important advantage is that the image labeling does not require humans dedicated to this activity and that is the product of

[2]http://acmmm13.org/submissions/call-for-multimedia-grand-challenge-solutions/msr-bing-grand-challenge-on-image-retrieval-scientific-track/

Table 1: Mean accuracy of the retrieved images according to user ratings in 101 pairs of query images. Results are showed at different top retrieval levels.

Method	Top 5	Top 10	Top 15	Top 20	Top 25
Baseline (Before visual re-ranking)	0.5058	0.4843	0.4823	0.4774	0.4784
Baseline (After visual re-ranking)	0.5549	0.5294	0.5124	0.5093	0.5011
Ours (Before visual re-ranking)	0.7509	0.7450	0.7327	0.7172	0.7098
Ours (After visual re-ranking)	**0.7765**	**0.7579**	**0.7490**	**0.7358**	**0.7243**

implicit crowdsourcing. The average number of queries per image is 23.1, consequently there is a significant amount of text describing each image.

A stop list is created to ignore frequent words in the dataset. Words that appear in over 50000 images are ignored since they correspond to non-discriminative words.

The resulting text representation of the images is very sparse since only a few tens of words describe each image. For this reason, text representation can be saved in a very compact way. In fact, the full dataset representation of one million images can be fully loaded in 51 Mb of memory.

For our experiments, we used vector representation of words trained on a part of the Google News dataset, which contains about 100 billion words.[3] The vocabulary size D of this model is 300.

3.1 Multiple Query Image Retrieval

We performed experiments to evaluate our system for a set of 101 pairs ($N = 2$) of image inputs. The definition of the input pairs of images was performed with the help of semantic maps downloaded from the internet.[4]

A semantic map is a visual strategy for vocabulary expansion and extension of knowledge by displaying words and their relations with other words [3]. Any person can define a semantic map about any topic; therefore, there is no "correct" semantic map. We chose several sets of pairs of words that were related according to the semantic maps found. Words that were not easily represented pictorially were discarded, and the remaining words were used to download example images and form query pairs of images conceptually related.

For each pair of available query images, we asked several users to rate the top 25 retrieved images of a pair of query images. They were then asked to provide a binary answer to the following question: Is the retrieved image conceptually similar to both input images or not?

Based on the user ratings, we calculated the mean accuracy of the retrieved images from the 101 pairs of query images. Accuracy is reported for the top X retrieved images, with X ranging from 5 to 25 in intervals of 5.

The baseline method is defined as the image retrieval performed from a joint search representation given by the summation of the individual input textual representations without the addition of words conceptually shared by the input images.

Table 1 presents the results of accuracy of our method and the baseline. For both methods we include the results before applying visual re-ranking. Our method clearly outperforms the baseline results by more than 22% in the proposed task. The visual re-ranking also helps to improve the ratings of the users. The improvement is more significant in the baseline case, where the retrieved images are worse in the task of retrieving shared concepts. The previous observation is an indication that some users tend to rate positively near identical images when the conceptual meaning of the query images cannot be clearly established.

[3]https://code.google.com/p/word2vec/

[4]http://www.bing.com/images/search?q=semantic+mapping

4. CONCLUSIONS

We have introduced a new search paradigm that leverages representations of multiple input images to infer concepts shared by all the input images. The retrieved images are conceptually and visually meaningful.

We presented a complete solution to the problem. Our solution includes novel visual and text representation of the images, exploiting a dataset with annotations obtained by implicit crowdsourcing, and operating a vector space that allows conceptually measuring the similarity between words.

The proposed approach achieved mean accuracy of 77.65% on the top 5 retrievals and 72.43% on the top 25, according to user ratings. The proposed approach outperforms the baseline by more than 22%, which shows that the method works very well in the proposed problem.

5. REFERENCES

[1] R. Arandjelovic and A. Zisserman. Multiple queries for large scale specific object retrieval. In *BMVC*, 2012.

[2] F. Basura and T. Tuytelaars. Mining multiple queries for image retrieval: On-the-fly learning of an object-specific mid-level representation. In *ICCV*, 2013.

[3] G. G. Duffy. *Explaining Reading, Second Edition: A Resource for Teaching Concepts, Skills, and Strategies.* Guilford Press, 2009.

[4] Y. Jia. Caffe: An open source convolutional architecture for fast feature embedding. In *http://caffe.berkeleyvision.org/*, 2013.

[5] A. Krizhevsky, I. Sutskever, and G. E. Hinton. Imagenet classification with deep convolutional neural networks. In *NIPS*, 2012.

[6] C. D. Manning, P. Raghavan, and H. Schtze. *Introduction to Information Retrieval.* Cambridge University Press New York, 2008.

[7] T. Mikolov, K. Chen, G. Corrado, and J. Dean. Efficient estimation of word representations in vector space. In *arXiv preprint arXiv:1301.3781*, 2013.

[8] T. Mikolov, W.-t. Yih, and G. Zweig. Linguistic regularities in continuous space word representations. In *Proceedings of NAACL-HLT*, 2013.

[9] MSR-Bing. Image retrieval challenge dataset. In *http://web-ngram.research.microsoft.com/GrandChallenge/Datasets.aspx.*

Geolocation with Subsampled Microblog Social Media

Miriam Cha
Harvard University

Youngjune Gwon*
Harvard University

H. T. Kung
Harvard University

ABSTRACT

We propose a data-driven geolocation method on microblog text. Key idea underlying our approach is sparse coding, an unsupervised learning algorithm. Unlike conventional positioning algorithms, we geolocate a user by identifying features extracted from her social media text. We also present an enhancement robust to erasure of words in the text and report our experimental results with uniformly or randomly subsampled microblog text. Our solution features a novel two-step procedure consisting of upconversion and iterative refinement by joint sparse coding. As a result, we can reduce the amount of input data required by geolocation while preserving good prediction accuracy. In the light of information preservation and privacy, we remark potential applications of these results.

Categories and Subject Descriptors

H.3.3 [**Information Storage and Retrieval**]: Information Search and Retrieval—*Clustering*; I.2.6 [**Artificial Intelligence**]: Learning—*Unsupervised feature learning*

Keywords

Geolocation; joint sparse coding; text subsampling; Twitter

1. INTRODUCTION

Traditionally, geolocation involves the detection and related computational processing of beacon signals used in a positioning system such as GPS. We consider a data-driven framework for geolocation that leverages the increased availability of geotagged social media data. In particular, we aim to develop an algorithm for estimating geocoordinates of a social network user by learning features from the user's social media text. We also extend the algorithm to take lossy, *subsampled* text data as input to geolocation prediction while preserving accurate geolocation estimates.

Geolocation information serves valuable context for social media. Recent research [1, 2] has experimented with latent variable models trained on the Twitter microblog text ("tweets") for geolocation. To achieve decent geolocation accuracy, a geographic topic model must be trained with a sufficient amount of labeled training examples. The fact that only 2.2% of tweets are geotagged [3] indicates the difficulty of supervised learning.

In this paper, we describe a model-free, geolocation method driven by a relatively small labeled dataset. Our key component is sparse coding, an unsupervised algorithm that learns a feature mapping for the raw text input. It is advantageous for prediction algorithms to operate on *sparse* (feature) representations of the raw data. We exploit the mapping to build a lookup table of reference geocoordinates and search it using the sparse feature vector computed on the text input. We apply k-Nearest Neighbor (k-NN) similarity matching in the feature domain for geolocation.

This paper also studies the preservation of geographic information after discarding words in the text. While the cause of such discarding could be unknown or randomly introduced, a purposeful usage would be to enhance privacy of a user, especially if the computing for geolocation is done remotely (*e.g.*, in the cloud). We demonstrate robustness of our approach by experimenting with uniformly and randomly subsampled tweet text. While subsampling is a simple method of dimensionality reduction, we face the difficulty unique for text data where information erasure is highly irregular depending on which word gets discarded.

To address this challenge, we propose a novel two-step procedure consisting of upconversion and refinement inspired by joint sparse coding for image super-resolution [4]. We will show that the refinement step can be iteratively repeated to produce better geolocation estimates.

Geolocation based on comprehending social media text is an ongoing, hard research problem [1, 2, 5]. Prediction with heavily subsampled text (*e.g.*, 50% of words in the text) is even more challenging. Our work here assesses the feasibility of a learning approach robust to subsampling. The results of this paper may be useful to develop secure applications for devices with limited computing power.

Rest of this paper is organized as follows. In Section 2, we describe our data-driven framework for text-based geolocation. Section 3 will present our approach based on subsampled text data. In Section 4, we discuss the results from an experimental evaluation on the CMU GeoText dataset [6], and Section 5 concludes the paper.

2. TEXT-BASED GEOLOCATION VIA SPARSE CODING

To alleviate the scarcity of labeled training examples in practice, we focus on unsupervised feature learning based on sparse coding and dictionary training.

*The author was a Ph.D. student at Harvard while the work was done. He now works for MIT Lincoln Laboratory in Lexington, MA.

MM'15, October 26–30, 2015, Brisbane, Australia.
© 2015 ACM. ISBN 978-1-4503-3459-4/15/10 ...$15.00.
DOI: http://dx.doi.org/10.1145/2733373.2806357.

2.1 Sparse coding for text data

We use sparse coding as the basic means to extract features from text. A text document, however, cannot be directly applied to sparse coding. Instead, we convert text to a numeric form in a procedure called "embedding." Let **vocab** denote a collection of unique words appearing in documents with size $V = |\texttt{vocab}|$. In *binary-bag-of-words* (BW) embedding scheme, a text document containing W words is represented as a bit vector $\mathbf{w}_{BW} \in \{0,1\}^V$. The ith element in $\mathbf{w}_{BW}$ is 1 if the word $\texttt{vocab}[i]$ has appeared in the text. We also use *word-sequence* (WS) embedding $\mathbf{w}_{WS} \in \{1,\dots,V\}^W$, where w_i, the ith element in $\mathbf{w}_{WS}$, represents $\texttt{vocab}[w_i]$. Sparse coding takes in an unit input vector called patch drawn from data. We denote patch $\mathbf{x} \in \mathbb{R}^N$, a consecutive subvector taken from $\mathbf{w}_{BW}$ or $\mathbf{w}_{WS}$ for an input to sparse coding.

Given an input $\mathbf{x} \in \mathbb{R}^N$, sparse coding solves for a representation $\mathbf{y} \in \mathbb{R}^K$ in the following optimization problem:

$$\min_{\mathbf{D},\mathbf{y}} \|\mathbf{x} - \mathbf{D}\mathbf{y}\|_2^2 + \lambda\psi(\mathbf{y}) \quad (1)$$

where input $\mathbf{x}$ is represented as a sparse linear combination of basis vectors in an overcomplete dictionary $\mathbf{D} \in \mathbb{R}^{N\times K}$ $(K > N)$. The solution $\mathbf{y}$ is the feature representation for $\mathbf{x}$. The system $\mathbf{x} = \mathbf{D}\mathbf{y}$ is underdetermined (*i.e.*, more unknowns than equations) and needs an extra constraint for assuring unique solution. As in the second term of Eq. (1), sparse coding regularizes on the ℓ_0- or ℓ_1-norm of $\mathbf{y}$ for $\psi(.)$ with $\lambda > 0$. Because the ℓ_0-norm of a vector is the number of nonzero elements, it can precisely serve the regularization purpose. Finding the sparsest ℓ_0-minimum solution in general, however, is known to be NP-hard. The ℓ_1-minimization with LASSO [7] or Basis Pursuit [8] is often preferred. Recently, it is known that the ℓ_0-based greedy algorithms such as Orthogonal Matching Pursuit (OMP) [9] can run fast.

Dictionary learning for sparse coding is done by an unsupervised, data-driven process incorporating two separate optimizations. It first computes sparse code for each training example using the current dictionary. Then, the reconstruction error from the computed sparse codes is used to update each basis vector in the dictionary. We use K-SVD algorithm [10] for dictionary learning.

2.2 Preprocessing patches

We can enhance the quality of unsupervised learning by preprocessing patches. For example, binary-bag-of-words embedding produces highly sparse bit vectors that are difficult for sparse coding to learn meaningful features. We can preprocess the patches of embedded text by removing the mean value and scaling with standard deviation. Another technique called whitening makes input data less redundant such that dictionary learning can be more effective. Combining these into one integrated procedure, we preprocess a batch of n input patches taken from embedded text vectors by whitening.

1. Remove mean $\mathbf{x}^{(i)} := \mathbf{x}^{(i)} - \frac{1}{n}\sum_{i=1}^{n}\mathbf{x}^{(i)}$;
2. Compute covariance matrix $\mathbf{C} = \frac{1}{n-1}\sum_{i=1}^{n}\mathbf{x}^{(i)}\mathbf{x}^{(i)\top}$;
3. Do eigendecomposition $\texttt{[U,}\boldsymbol{\Lambda}\texttt{] = eig(C)}$;
4. Compute $\mathbf{x}_{\text{white}} = (\boldsymbol{\Lambda}+\epsilon\mathbf{I})^{-1/2}\mathbf{U}^\top\mathbf{x}$, where ϵ is a small positive value for regularization.

2.3 Baseline geolocation method

Our baseline geolocation method consists of the following steps in the training phase.

1. (Text embedding) perform binary or word-sequence embedding of text data using **vocab**;
2. (Unsupervised learning) feed patches drawn from unlabeled embedded text vectors to sparse coding and learn basis vectors for dictionary $\mathbf{D}$;
3. (Feature extraction) using the dictionary $\mathbf{D}$ learned during unsupervised learning, for given labeled training patches $\{(\mathbf{x}^{(1)}, l^{(1)}), (\mathbf{x}^{(2)}, l^{(2)}), \dots\}$, perform sparse coding on $\{\mathbf{x}^{(1)}, \mathbf{x}^{(2)}, \dots\}$ and obtain sparse codes $\{\mathbf{y}^{(1)}, \mathbf{y}^{(2)}, \dots\}$ with their associated labels;
4. (Feature pooling) aggregate features by max pooling over a group of M sparse codes extracted from the same document and obtain pooled sparse code $\mathbf{z}$ such that the jth element in $\mathbf{z}$, $z_j = \max(y_{1,j}, y_{2,j}, \dots, y_{M,j})$ where $y_{i,j}$ is the jth element from $\mathbf{y}_i$, the ith sparse code in the pooling group;
5. (Tabularization of reference geocoordinates) build a lookup table of geocoordinates associated with pooled sparse codes $\mathbf{z}$ from labeled data patches.

Note that each label contains geocoordinates in the form $l^{(i)} = \{lat, lon\}$.

The baseline method works in the following manner for the testing phase. When text data (tweets) of unknown geocoordinates arrive, we perform preprocessing, feature extraction via sparse coding, and max pooling. Using the max-pooled sparse code of the tweets, we find the k pooled sparse codes from the lookup table that are closest in *cosine similarity*. We take the average geocoordinates of the k-NNs.

2.4 Grid-based voting scheme for k-NN

We accompany a simple voting scheme for k-NN. We lay out a grid over the all k-NN geocoordinates. Each k-NN casts a vote to its corresponding grid. We identify the grid that receives the most votes and take the average of geocoordinates in the selected grid as the final geolocation estimate.

3. GEOLOCATION FROM SUBSAMPLED TEXT

Using a linear subsampling matrix (*i.e.*, uniform or random), we consider two blind subsampling strategies. First, we subsample after binary-bag-of-words embedding. Secondly, we can subsample the raw text before embedding. Blind text subsampling concerns a tradeoff between amount of input data required for geolocation and prediction accuracy. This section proposes an enhancement robust to the effect of blind text subsampling on degradation of geolocation accuracy.

3.1 Subsampling binary-bag-of-words

Given $\mathbf{w}_{BW}$, we perform either uniform or random subsampling. For uniform subsampling, every αth component of $\mathbf{w}_{BW}$ is discarded for some integer α. Similarly, random subsampling discards the equivalent number of components randomly from $\mathbf{w}_{BW}$. As a result, the subsampled embedded vector has a smaller dimension than the original binary bag-of-words vector. Subsampling $\mathbf{w}_{BW}$ has an identical effect as embedding the raw text based on subsampled **vocab**.

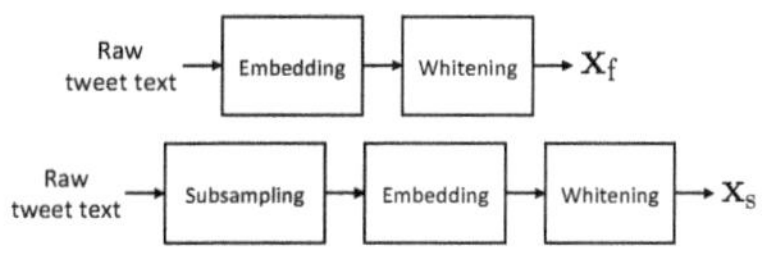

Figure 1: Patches $\{\mathbf{x}_f, \mathbf{x}_s\}$ from full and subsampled text

3.2 Subsampling raw text

Unlike $\mathbf{w}_{BW}$, $\mathbf{w}_{WS}$ converts text to a numeric form while retaining the ordering of words. Thus subsampling $\mathbf{w}_{WS}$ is subsampling raw text vector. Uniform subsampling discards every αth words, and random subsampling discards the same number of words randomly. The subsampled raw texts are embedded based on the binary-bag-of-words scheme, resulting the final subsampled vector of dimension V.

3.3 Joint sparse coding for upconversion and refinement

The effect of subsampling raw text is more devastating than subsampling binary-bag-of-words vectors. In this section, we propose a variation of joint sparse coding that can recover the original text and refine the recovery from the subsampled text for better geolocation performance.

Let us denote the pair $\{\mathbf{x}_f, \mathbf{x}_s\}$ patches drawn from the binary-bag-of-words vectors embedded on full and subsampled text, as seen in Figure 1. The sparse coding problems for $\mathbf{x}_f \in \mathbb{R}^N$ and its subsampled counterpart $\mathbf{x}_s \in \mathbb{R}^N$ are

$$\min_{\mathbf{D}_f, \mathbf{y}_f} \|\mathbf{x}_f - \mathbf{D}_f\mathbf{y}_f\|_2^2 + \lambda_f\|\mathbf{y}_f\|_1 \quad (2)$$

and

$$\min_{\mathbf{D}_s, \mathbf{y}_s} \|\mathbf{x}_s - \mathbf{D}_s\mathbf{y}_s\|_2^2 + \lambda_s\|\mathbf{y}_s\|_1 \quad (3)$$

where $\mathbf{D}_f$ and $\mathbf{D}_s$ are dictionaries from full and subsampled text, respectively. Image super-resolution [4] takes advantage of the shared sparse code between the high- and low-resolution pair of patches for the same image such that one can recover a high-resolution image from the low-resolution version. Similarly, if the sparse code for the full and subsampled is shared (*i.e.*, $\mathbf{y}_f = \mathbf{y}_s$), we can attempt to recover the full by using the subsampled. We formulate a new joint optimization that forces the sharing of the sparse code $\mathbf{v} = \mathbf{y}_f = \mathbf{y}_s$ between the full and subsampled pair of patches

$$\min_{\mathbf{D}_u, \mathbf{D}_d, \mathbf{v}} \|\mathbf{x}_f - \mathbf{D}_u\mathbf{v}\|_2^2 + \|\mathbf{x}_s - \mathbf{D}_d\mathbf{v}\|_2^2 + \lambda_v\|\mathbf{v}\|_1 \quad (4)$$

where $\mathbf{D}_u$ is the upconversion dictionary, and $\mathbf{D}_d$ for down-conversion.

In the unsupervised learning stage, we first solve for $\mathbf{D}_u$, $\mathbf{D}_d$, and $\mathbf{v}$ via joint sparse coding of Eq. (4). Using the learned $\mathbf{D}_u$, we obtain an upconversion estimate $\hat{\mathbf{x}}_f = \mathbf{D}_u\mathbf{v}$. We can refine $\hat{\mathbf{x}}_f$ in another joint optimization

$$\min_{\mathbf{D}_r, \mathbf{D}_q, \mathbf{w}} \|\mathbf{x}_f - \mathbf{D}_r\mathbf{w}\|_2^2 + \|\hat{\mathbf{x}}_f - \mathbf{D}_q\mathbf{w}\|_2^2 + \lambda_w\|\mathbf{w}\|_1. \quad (5)$$

Here, we explicitly look for $\mathbf{D}_r$ and $\mathbf{D}_q$ that make the refinement of $\hat{\mathbf{x}}_f$ possible. In the supervised learning stage, we perform sparse coding with (labeled) subsampled data patches using the learned $\mathbf{D}_d$ and yield joint sparse codes $\mathbf{v}$. The joint sparse codes are applied to feature pooling and tabularization of reference geocoordinates in steps 4 and 5 of baseline geolocation method.

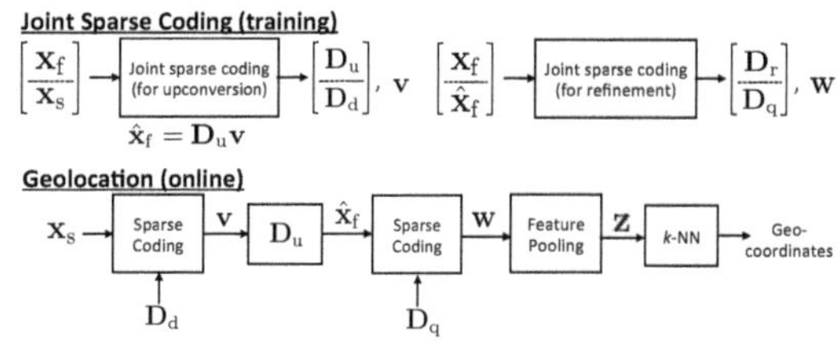

Figure 2: Full system pipelines

When subsampled tweets from unknown geocoordinates arrive, the geolocation pipeline consists of upconversion and refinement. We can iteratively repeat the refinement step. For enhanced geolocation with subsampled text, we use the refined feature vector $\mathbf{w}$. Figure 2 illustrates our full pipelines.

4. EVALUATION

In this section, we empirically evaluate the proposed approaches using the CMU geo-tagged microblog corpus [6]. We train our baseline geolocation method using the full data samples. We also train our method with uniformly and randomly subsampled raw text and binary-bag-of-words (embedded) text vectors to analyze the effect of subsampling on the accuracy degradation. We will discuss the improved geolocation performance by our joint sparse coding method for upconversion and refinement on subsampled text data.

4.1 Data

GeoText is a Twitter text dataset comprising 377,616 tweets by 9,475 users from 48 contiguous US states and Washington D.C. Each document in the dataset is concatenation of the entire tweets by a single user collected over one week. All documents include the user location information provided as GPS-assigned latitude and longitude values. The document is a sequence of integer numbers ranging 1 to 5,216, where each number represents the position in `vocab`.

4.2 Experimental methodology

For all our experiments, we have cut the dataset into five folds such that `fold=user_id%5`, following Eisenstein *et al.* [1]. Folds 1–4 are used for training, and fold 5 for testing. We have embedded the entire text data from each user to binary-bag-of-words and word-sequence vectors and applied uniform or random subsampling by $\alpha = 2, 3, 4$, and 6.

We precondition patches with PCA whitening before sparse coding. After numerous experiments, we have determined to use patch size $N = 64$. We have used OMP, a greedy-ℓ_0 sparse encoder, and K-SVD for dictionary learning. Other sparse coding parameters are also determined experimentally. We have used a dictionary size $K \approx 10N$, sparsity level S for $0.1N \leq S \leq 0.4N$ (S is number of nonzero elements in $\mathbf{y}$). We use max pooling factors M in 10s.

In supervised learning, we have built the table of reference geocoordinates for k-NN, using the max-pooled sparse code as the feature for lookup. This results in the lookup table of more than 7,500 entries. We have found good geolocation accuracy with $10 \leq k \leq 40$.

For the metric of performance evaluation, we use the median distance error between the predicted and ground-truth geocoordinates measured in kilometers. We note that related previous research has regarded median distance error more important than the mean. It is required to approximate the

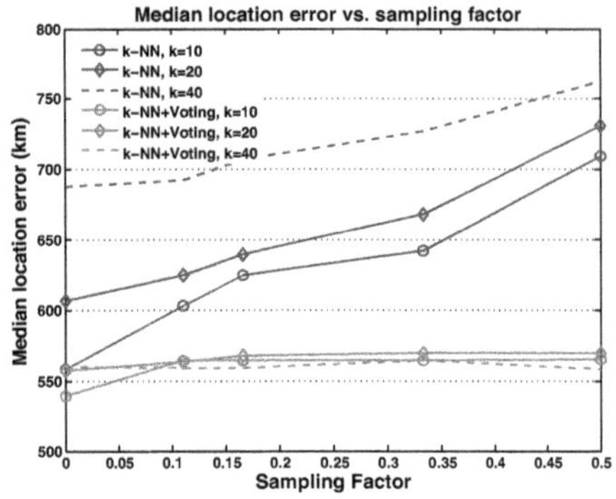

Figure 3: Median geolocation errors of subsampling binary-bag-of-words against various sampling factors

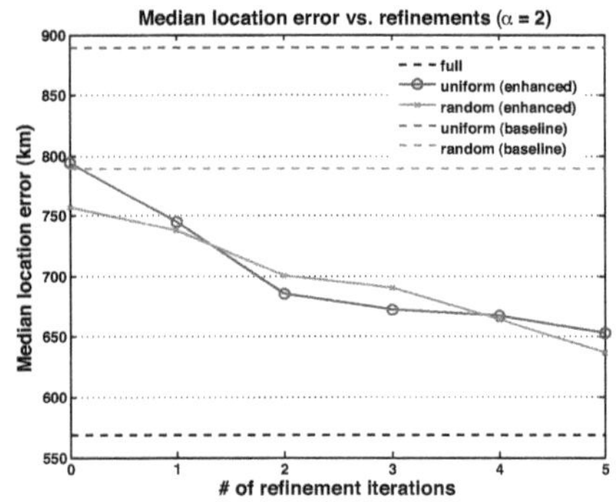

Figure 4: Median geolocation errors of uniform and random subsampling the raw text with $\alpha = 2$.

great-circle distance between any two locations on earth because of its round surface. We use the Haversine formula [11].

4.3 Results and discussion

In Figure 3, we present the effect of grid-based voting scheme on the geolocation errors using uniformly subsampled binary-bag-of-words text. Notice that the grid-based voting scheme is robust to subsampling binary-bag-of-words text. However, the effect of subsampling raw text is stronger than subsampling binary-bag-of-words vectors, and we have experienced that the grid-based voting scheme is not as effective when applied to subsampled raw text. Therefore we use our proposed upconversion and iterative refinement scheme by joint sparse coding that is robust to subsampling raw text. We present the median geolocation errors of uniform and random 2x subsampling (*i.e.*, $\alpha = 2$) on the raw text in Figure 4. We gradually increase the number of refinement steps to observe changes in the geolocation error. Applying our baseline geolocation method on full text gives 568 km error. As expected, discarding 50% of words significantly increases geolocation errors, 794 km for uniform subsampling and 757 km for random subsampling. Remarkably, multiple iterations of refinement step can help mitigate the geolocation error caused by heavy subsampling. After five iterations of refinement step, geolocation error for uniform subsampling decreases to 652 km and random subsampling to 636 km. Notice that these geolocation errors are only 84 km and 68 km higher than using the full text.

Figure 5 depicts the median geolocation errors against various uniform subsampling factors (in $1/\alpha$) for subsampling only, subsampling with enhancement by upconversion, and

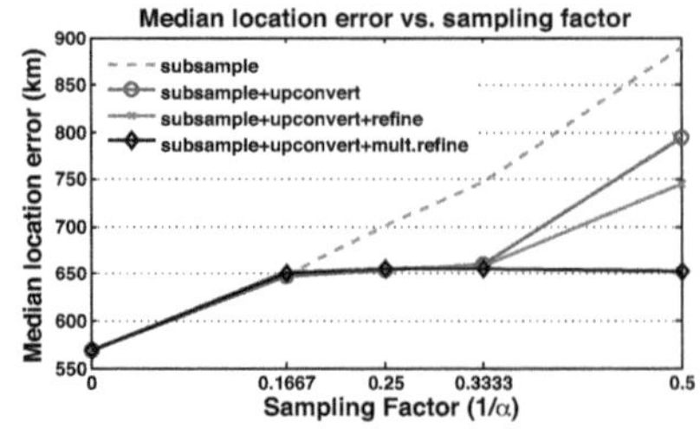

Figure 5: Median geolocation errors of uniform subsampling and enhancements against various sampling factors

subsampling with enhancements by both upconversion and single or multiple (5) iterations of refinement. As uniform and random subsampling results are comparable, we only report uniform subsampling results. Compared to subsampling only, upconversion and multiple iterations of refinement after subsampling is more robust to increased sampling factor.

5. CONCLUSION

We have presented a geolocation method based on sparse coding of microblog text data. We achieve the median geolocation errors of 568 km for full and 636 km even under 2x subsampling on the GeoText dataset. The proposed upconversion and iterative refinement scheme by joint sparse coding proves to be successful in drawing out the correlation between the full and subsampled text pair. The geolocation accuracy degradation is only by 12%, even if we have halved words in the text. The main contributions of this paper are the refinement scheme and its application to geolocation for subsampled microblog text. For future work, we plan to improve feature learning schemes by introducing hierarchy and evaluate our methods using both US and worldwide data.

Acknowledgments

This work is supported by the National Science Foundation Graduate Research Fellowship under Grant No. DGE1144152, the Naval Supply Systems Command award under the Naval Postgraduate School Agreement No. N00244-15-0050, and gifts from the Intel Corporation.

6. REFERENCES

[1] J. Eisenstein, B. O'Connor, N.A. Smith, and E.P. Xing. A Latent Variable Model for Geographic Lexical Variation. In *EMNLP*, 2010.

[2] L. Hong, A. Ahmed, S. Gurumurthy, A.J. Smola, and K. Tsioutsiouliklis. Discovering Geographical Topics in the Twitter Stream. In *WWW*, 2012.

[3] C. Weidemann. Social Media Location Intelligence: The Next Privacy Battle—An ArcGIS andd-in and Analysis of Geospatial Data Collected from Twitter.com. *Journal of Geoinfo.*, 2013.

[4] J. Yang, J. Wright, T.S. Huang, and Y. Ma. Image Super-Resolution via Sparse Representation. *IEEE Trans. on Image Processing*, 19(11):2861–2873, 2010.

[5] M. Cha, Y. Gwon, and H. T. Kung. Twitter Geolocation and Regional Classification via Sparse Coding. In *ICWSM*, 2015.

[6] GeoText. CMU Geo-tagged Microblog Corpus. `http://www.ark.cs.cmu.edu/GeoText/`, 2010.

[7] R. Tibshirani. Regression Shrinkage and Selection via the Lasso. *Journal of Royal Statistical Society, Series B*, 1994.

[8] S.S. Chen, D.L. Donoho, and M.A. Saunders. Atomic Decomposition by Basis Pursuit. *SIAM Rev.*, 2001.

[9] J.A. Tropp and A.C. Gilbert. Signal Recovery From Random Measurements via Orthogonal Matching Pursuit. *IEEE Trans. on Information Theory*, 2007.

[10] M. Aharon, M. Elad, and A. Bruckstein. K-SVD: An Algorithm for Designing Overcomplete Dictionaries for Sparse Representation. *IEEE Trans. on Sig. Proc.*, 54(11), 2006.

[11] R.W. Sinnott. Virtues of Haversine. *Sky and Telescope*, 1984.

Social Tag Relevance Estimation via Ranking-Oriented Neighbour Voting

Chaoran Cui[1], Jialie Shen[2], Jun Ma[1], and Tao Lian[1]
[1] School of Computer Science and Technology, Shandong University, Jinan, China
[2] School of Information Systems, Singapore Management University, Singapore
{bruincui, liantao1988}@gmail.com, jlshen@smu.edu.sg, majun@sdu.edu.cn

ABSTRACT

User-generated tags associated with social images are frequently imprecise and incomplete. Therefore, a fundamental challenge in tag-based applications is the problem of tag relevance estimation, which concerns how to interpret and quantify the relevance of a tag with respect to the contents of an image. In this paper, we address the key problem from a new perspective of learning to rank, and develop a novel approach to facilitate tag relevance estimation to directly optimize the ranking performance of tag-based image search. A supervision step is introduced into the neighbour voting scheme, in which tag relevance is estimated by accumulating votes from visual neighbours. Through explicitly modelling the neighbour weights and tag correlations, the risk of making heuristic assumptions is effectively avoided for conventional methods. Extensive experiments on a benchmark dataset in comparison with the state-of-the-art methods demonstrate the promise of our approach.

Categories and Subject Descriptors

H.3.1 [**Information Storage and Retrieval**]: Content Analysis and Indexing

Keywords

Tag-based image search; Tag relevance estimation; Learning to rank; Neighbour voting

1. INTRODUCTION

With the advent of Web 2.0 technology, we have witnessed an explosive growth of social images in recent years [1, 9]. This also raises an urgent demand for smart search technologies to explore large scale social image repositories, such as Flickr and Pinterest. Rather than simply providing the interfaces for image storage and sharing, these repositories allow users to label images with freely-chosen tags. Naturally, these tags can be used to index social images to facilitate the search process. As a result, tag-based image search has become the *de facto* way to access and browse resources in current social image repositories.

Despite the popularity of tag-based image search, its performance is still far from satisfactory due to the inferior quality of user-generated tags, which are often imprecise and incomplete for describing the image contents, and thus cannot be regarded as qualified indexing keywords for image search. Extensive research endeavours have been devoted to improving the descriptive capability of tags regarding the image contents [7, 8]. Although varying in terms of their targeted tasks and methodologies, these works all rely on the key functionality of tag relevance [6], i.e., estimating the relevance of a tag with respect to the visual content of an image, which is also referred to as the problem of *tag relevance estimation.*

Tag relevance estimation has been widely studied, however, there remains a common limitation in the literature. In essence, the aim of tag relevance estimation is to find out the tags that can be applied as content descriptors for the images, so that the accuracy of image search can be further improved by indexing the images with these reliable tags. However, existing studies generally perform tag relevance estimation without the explicit intention of promoting the performance of tag-based image search. In most cases, they estimate the tag relevance via heuristic rules [5], through optimizing the classification accuracy for specific tags [10], or by maximizing the likelihood of the annotations of training images [10]. We argue that these objectives are not directly related to the search performance, and optimizing them does not necessarily yield good search results.

In light of the above deficiency, in this paper, we investigate the problem from a new perspective of learning to rank, and perform tag relevance estimation to directly optimize the ranking performance of tag-based image search. Specifically, we introduce a supervision step into the neighbour voting scheme [5], in which the tag relevance is estimated by accumulating votes from the visual neighbours of the given image. Our approach explicitly models the neighbour weights and tag correlations, and thereby avoids the risk of making heuristic assumptions for conventional methods. Experimental results demonstrate the promise of our approach in both applications of tag-based image search and automatic tag recommendation.

2. TAG RELEVANCE FORMULATION

Our framework formulates a tag relevance function based on the neighbour voting scheme, where the relevance score

MM'15, October 26–30, 2015, Brisbane, Australia.
© 2015 ACM. ISBN 978-1-4503-3459-4/15/10 ...$15.00.
DOI: http://dx.doi.org/10.1145/2733373.2806358.

of a tag is inferred by the tagging information of the visual neighbours of the given image. While the standard neighbour voting algorithm [5] simply let the neighbours vote equally, efforts have been made to weight neighbours in terms of their importance. Typically, the weights are heuristically determined by the visual similarity [4], or in a soft manner that performs a random walk over the k-nearest neighbor graph [13]. However, the performance gain obtained by these heuristic weighting strategies appears to be limited [13]. In this paper, we propose to explicitly model the individual weight of each visual neighbour. Given a tag t_i and an image x, we define $r(t_i, x)$ as the relevance score of t_i with respect to x:

$$r(t_i, x) = \sum_{l=1}^{k} v_l \varphi(d_l^x, t_i) \ , \tag{1}$$

where d_l^x denotes the l-th nearest neighbour of x, $\mathbf{v} \in \mathbb{R}^{k\times 1}$ is a vector of parameters whose l-th element v_l indicates the weight of d_l^x, and k is the total number of the visual neighbours. Note that we treat an image itself as its first nearest neighbour, i.e., $d_1^x = x$. $\varphi(d_l^x, t_i)$ represents the confidence value that t_i is relevant to d_l^x, which is estimated by a multiple Bernoulli process with a beta prior:

$$\varphi(d_l^x, t_i) = \frac{\mu\delta_{d_l^x, t_i} + s_{t_i}}{\mu + s} \ , \tag{2}$$

where $\delta_{d_l^x, t_i}$ indicates the tagging observation on d_l^x, i.e., $\delta_{d_l^x, t_i} = 1$ if d_l^x is tagged with t_i in the image collection and zero otherwise. μ is a smoothing parameter associated with $\delta_{d_l^x, t_i}$. s_{t_i} denotes the number of images tagged with t_i, and s is the total number of images.

It has proven that the information of tag correlations is highly beneficial to many tag-based applications [7]. Motivated by this, we seek to incorporate the tag correlations to facilitate tag relevance estimation. Co-occurrence statistics and WordNet similarity are the most commonly used correlation measurements. However, these prior information may be unreliable when dealing with noisy social tags. More importantly, limited by their non-negative property, both co-occurrence statistics and WordNet similarity cannot capture the potential negative correlations among tags. Therefore, we propose to explicitly model the pairwise tag correlations and to reformulate the relevance function as follows:

$$r(t_i, x) = w_{ii} \sum_{l=1}^{k} v_l \varphi(d_l^x, t_i) + \sum_{j=1, j\neq i}^{m} w_{ij} \sum_{l=1}^{k} v_l \varphi(d_l^x, t_j) \ , \tag{3}$$

where $W \in \mathbb{R}^{m\times m}$ is a parameter matrix whose (i,j)-th entry w_{ij} represents the correlation between the tag t_i and the tag t_j, and m is the total number of unique tags. We assume that W is a symmetric matrix, i.e., $w_{ij} = w_{ji}$, and both positive and negative values are allowed in W. In Equation (3), we exploit not only the confidence score of t_i being relevant to the neighbours of x, but also the evidences provided by all the other tags. For the simplicity of the expression, we introduce a supplementary matrix $\Phi_x \in \mathbb{R}^{k\times m}$ whose (l,j)-th entry is equal to $\varphi(d_l^x, t_j)$. As a result, Equation (3) can be written in a concise form:

$$r(t_i, x) = \mathbf{e}_i{}^T W \Phi_x{}^T \mathbf{v} \ . \tag{4}$$

A potential problem with the above formulation is that it requires a large number of parameters to capture the correlation between each pair of tags. From the viewpoint of statistical learning theory, too many parameters may degrade the model stability and generalization in performance. In light of this, we further introduce a low-rank prior into the parameter W with $W = U^T U$, which results in the new formulation of the relevance function as follows:

$$r(t_i, x) = \mathbf{e}_i{}^T U^T U \Phi_x{}^T \mathbf{v} \ , \tag{5}$$

where $U \in \mathbb{R}^{p\times m}$ and p is the dimensionality of a latent space. Let $\mathbf{u}_i$ denote the i-th column of U, which corresponds to the representation vector of t_i in the latent space. The correlation w_{ij} is thus measured by the dot product of $\mathbf{u}_i$ and $\mathbf{u}_j$, which is commonly used to measure the matching between textual vectors. Because the intrinsic dimensionality of the latent space is typically much smaller than that of the original space (i.e., $p \ll m$), the number of parameters in Equation (5) is significantly reduced.

3. RANKING-ORIENTED LEARNING

Our framework seeks to learn the parameters $\mathbf{v}$ and U in a supervised fashion, and to facilitate tag relevance estimation to boost the accuracy of image search. To this end, we consider the relevance function r as a ranking criterion for tag-based image search, and approach the problem from a new perspective of learning to rank.

Without loss of generality, assume that a set of training instances for the first n tags is available:

$$\{(t_q, Y_q^*) \in \mathcal{T} \times \mathcal{Y} : q = 1, \ldots, n\} \ ,$$

where t_q is a query tag and Y_q^* is the true ranking of the images with respect to t_q. $\mathcal{T}$ is the tag vocabulary and $\mathcal{Y}$ is the set of all possible rankings over images. Similar to [11], we represent any ranking $Y \in \mathcal{Y}$ as a matrix of pair orderings, whose (i,j)-th entry $y_{ij} = +1$ if the image x_i is ranked ahead of the image x_j, $y_{ij} = -1$ if x_i is ranked behind x_j, and $y_{ij} = 0$ if x_i and x_j have equal rank. Note that Y_q^* is a weak ranking with only two relevance levels, i.e., relevant and irrelevant. We denote by $\mathcal{I}_{t_q}^+$ and $\mathcal{I}_{t_q}^-$ the sets of the relevant and irrelevant images with respect to t_q.

Our goal is transformed into learning a ranking hypothesis $h : \mathcal{T} \to \mathcal{Y}$. For the query tag t_q, $h(t_q)$ needs to correspond to the image ranking in descending order of $r(t_q, x)$. For this purpose, we first construct a compatibility function $f(t_q, Y)$ measuring how well a possible image ranking Y fits for t_q:

$$\begin{aligned} f(t_q, Y) &= \sum_{x_i \in \mathcal{I}_{t_q}^+} \sum_{x_j \in \mathcal{I}_{t_q}^-} y_{ij} \left(\frac{r(t_q, x_i) - r(t_q, x_j)}{|\mathcal{I}_{t_q}^+| \cdot |\mathcal{I}_{t_q}^-|} \right) \\ &= \sum_{x_i \in \mathcal{I}_{t_q}^+} \sum_{x_j \in \mathcal{I}_{t_q}^-} y_{ij} \left(\frac{\mathbf{e}_q{}^T U^T U (\Phi_{x_i} - \Phi_{x_j})^T \mathbf{v}}{|\mathcal{I}_{t_q}^+| \cdot |\mathcal{I}_{t_q}^-|} \right) . \end{aligned} \tag{6}$$

$h(t_q)$ is then defined by maximizing $f(t_q, Y)$ over $Y \in \mathcal{Y}$:

$$h(t_q) = \arg\max_{Y \in \mathcal{Y}} f(t_q, Y) \ . \tag{7}$$

Here, $f(t_q, Y)$ is decomposed into a series of pairwise components, i.e., $y_{ij}(r(t_q, x_i) - r(t_q, x_j))$. For the fixed $\mathbf{v}$ and U, $h(t_q)$ can be attained by maximizing each component individually: if $r(t_q, x_i) > r(t_q, x_j)$, y_{ij} is set to $+1$; otherwise, it is set to -1. Note that this is the same procedure as sorting the images by $r(t_q, x)$, and $h(t_q)$ proves to be equivalent to the ranking in descending order of $r(t_q, x)$.

With the set of training instances, we learn the ranking hypothesis $h(t_q)$ by minimizing the empirical ranking risk,

$$R_\Delta(h) = \frac{1}{n} \sum_{q=1}^{n} \Delta(Y_q^*, h(t_q)) \ , \tag{8}$$

where the loss function Δ quantifies the inconsistency between the derived ranking $h(t_q)$ and the true ranking Y_q^*. In our study, we define Δ based on AP score:

$$\Delta(Y_q^*, h(t_q)) = 1 - AP(Y_q^*, h(t_q)) \ . \tag{9}$$

As a result, minimizing $R_\Delta(h)$ is equivalent to directly optimizing MAP performance of tag-based image search.

We adopt the structural SVM [3] as the backbone of our learning algorithm. Specifically, we rewrite the compatibility function f as:

$$f(t_q, Y) = \left\langle U^T U \otimes \mathbf{v},\ \mathbf{e}_q \otimes \Psi(t_q, Y) \right\rangle_F , \tag{10}$$

$$\Psi(t_q, Y) = \sum_{x_i \in \mathcal{I}_{t_q}^+} \sum_{x_j \in \mathcal{I}_{t_q}^-} y_{ij} \frac{\Phi_{x_i} - \Phi_{x_j}}{|\mathcal{I}_{t_q}^+| \cdot |\mathcal{I}_{t_q}^-|} , \tag{11}$$

where $\otimes$ denotes the Kronecker product, and $\langle \cdot, \cdot \rangle_F$ denotes the Frobenius inner product. $\Psi(t_q, Y)$ encodes the *joint features* of the input-output pair $(t_q,\ Y)$. By representing f in such a form of a linear function of $\Psi(t_q, Y)$, the structural SVM can be employed to learn $\mathbf{v}$ and U through the following optimization problem [3]:

Optimization Problem 1.

$$\min_{V,U,\xi} \ \frac{\lambda}{2}\|V\|_2^2 + \frac{\lambda}{2}\|U\|_F^2 + \xi \tag{12}$$

$$s.t. \quad \forall (Y_1, \dots, Y_n) \in \mathcal{Y}^n :$$

$$\frac{1}{n}\sum_{q=1}^{n} \left[f(t_q, Y_q^*) - f(t_q, Y_q) \right] \geqslant \frac{1}{n}\sum_{q=1}^{n} \Delta(Y_q^*, Y_q) - \xi \ . \tag{13}$$

The main difficulty of Optimization Problem 1 is that there are as many as $|\mathcal{Y}|^n$ constraints to be considered. To solve it efficiently, we employ the cutting plane algorithm. The pseudo-code of the algorithm is presented in Algorithm 1. It starts with an empty working set $\mathcal{W}$ of active constraints (step 1). Then it iteratively finds the $\widehat{Y_q}$ which generates the most violated constraint for each t_q with current $\mathbf{v}$ and U (step 3-5). For our MAP-related loss, this step can be accomplished with the method presented in [11]. If the corresponding constraints are on average violated by more than the error tolerance ε, the algorithm adds $(\widehat{Y}_1, \dots, \widehat{Y}_n)$ into $\mathcal{W}$, and re-optimizes over the updated $\mathcal{W}$ (step 6-9). We implement a sub-gradient method to solve the problem at this step. The sub-gradients with respect to $\mathbf{v}$ and U can be computed in terms of the single constraint $(\widehat{Y}_1, \dots, \widehat{Y}_n)$ that achieves the current largest margin in $\mathcal{W}$:

$$\nabla_{\mathbf{v}} = \lambda \mathbf{v} - \frac{1}{n}\sum_{q=1}^{n} \delta\Psi(t_q, \widehat{Y}_q) U^T U \mathbf{e}_q$$

$$\nabla_{\mathrm{U}} = \lambda U - \frac{1}{n}\sum_{q=1}^{n} \Big(\mathbf{v}^T \delta\Psi(t_q, \widehat{Y}_q) \otimes \mathbf{u}_q \tag{14}$$

$$+ {\mathbf{e}_q}^T \otimes U \delta\Psi(t_q, \widehat{Y}_q)^T \mathbf{v} \Big)$$

where $\delta\Psi(t_q, \widehat{Y}_q) = \Psi(t_q, Y_q^*) - \Psi(t_q, \widehat{Y}_q)$. Algorithm 1 terminates when no constraints are added into $\mathcal{W}$ (step 10).

Algorithm 1 Cutting Plane Algorithm

Input: training instances $(t_1, Y_1^*), \dots, (t_n, Y_n^*)$, regularization trade-off λ, error tolerance ε

Output: model parameters $\mathbf{v}$ and U, slack variable ξ

1: Initialize $\mathcal{W} \leftarrow \emptyset$

2: **repeat**

3:   **for** $q = 1, 2, \dots, n$ **do**

4:     $\widehat{Y}_q \leftarrow \arg\max_{Y \in \mathcal{Y}} \Delta(Y_q^*, Y) + f(t_q, Y)$

5:   **end for**

6:   **if** $\frac{1}{n}\sum_{q=1}^{n} \Delta(Y_q^*, \widehat{Y}_q) - \frac{1}{n}\sum_{q=1}^{n} \left[f(t_q, Y_q^*) - f(t_q, \widehat{Y}_q) \right] > \xi + \varepsilon$ **then**

7:     $\mathcal{W} \leftarrow \mathcal{W} \cup \left\{ (\widehat{Y}_1, \dots, \widehat{Y}_n) \right\}$

8:     Optimize Equation (12) over $\mathcal{W}$

9:   **end if**

10: **until** $\mathcal{W}$ has no change during iteration

4. EXPERIMENTS

4.1 Data Collections

All the experiments are conducted on a benchmark image dataset collected from Flickr, i.e., NUS-WIDE-Lite (NUS for short hereafter) [2]. On NUS, the labelling ground-truth of the images for 75 *concepts* has been provided. These concepts are used as the query tags in the experiments.

Each image is represented with the same features as described in [2]. We use the Euclidean metric to measure the visual distance between images. Given an image, all images are ranked by their distance from it and the k nearest neighbours are subsequently discovered.

4.2 Evaluation Methodology

We compare our approach with several state-of-the-art methods on tag relevance estimation. Specifically, the competitors include: NVote [5], WVote [4], Graph [12], SVM [10] and TagProp [10]. We denote our approach as RankVote.

To conduct a comprehensive comparison, we first evaluate in the scenario of tag-based image search. Given a query tag, we sort images by descending the predicted tag relevance concerning each image. We study the performance of different methods with regard to the parameter k. We take half of the total concepts as query tags during training, and keep the rest for testing. We use MAP as the evaluation metric.

We also compare different methods in the scenario of automatic tag recommendation. Note that SVM is excluded from this evaluation because of its excessive computational cost in the need of learning a separate classifier for each tag. We randomly choose 1,000 images as the evaluation testbed. Given an image, all tags are ranked by their relevance values, and the top 10 results are added into the recommendation list. Three volunteers manually label each recommended tag with four relevance levels: Most Relevant (score 3), Relevant (score 2), Weakly Relevant (score 1) and Irrelevant (score 0). As the ground-truth tag ranking for a single image is not available, DCG is used to evaluate the quality of the recommendation list.

4.3 Experimental Results

4.3.1 Performance Comparison

Figure 1 shows the image search results of different methods. Clearly, RankVote consistently achieves the best performance in all cases, reaching at least 20% relative improvement over the other methods. Besides, RankVote is also more robust to the variation of k. Even though tested with only 10 neighbours, RankVote still remains a relatively high performance level of 49.9%. The results verify the promise of RankVote for tag-based image search.

Table 1 reports the empirical results for automatic tag recommendation. It is shown that RankVote outperforms

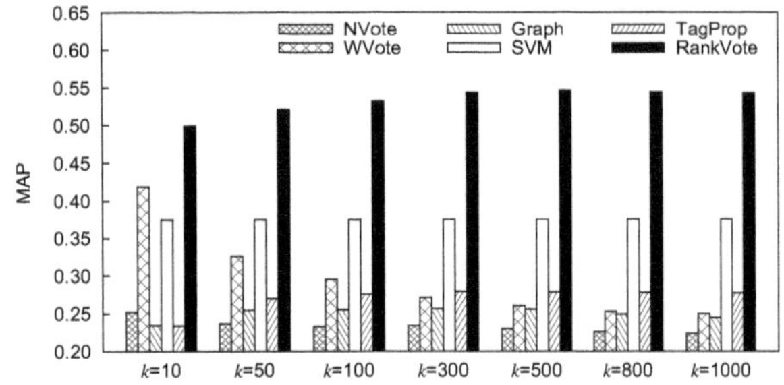

Figure 1: Performance comparison for image search.

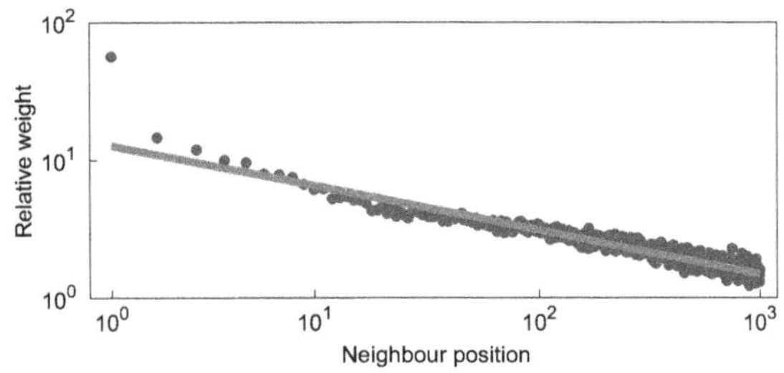

Figure 2: Illustration of neighbour weights.

the other approaches in both evaluation criteria. Especially, we find that the relative improvements on DCG@5 are more significant than those on DCG@10. It is a nice property as users are usually more interested in the top results in recommendation. The conclusion can thus be drawn that RankVote is an effective technique for tag recommendation.

4.3.2 *Illustration of Learned Parameters*

To the best of our knowledge, this is the first study that effectively estimates the tag relevance, while jointly learns the neighbour weights and tag correlations in a unified framework. Figure 2 plots the individual weight of each neighbour in the top 1,000 sequence on a log-log scale. We notice that the variation trend of neighbour weights is in accordance with the intuition that close neighbours are more important than those distant ones, and it can also be well fitted by a power-law relationship, which has been indicated by a red line. We believe this finding is valuable to guide the future research on neighbour voting.

Figure 3 illustrates the learned pairwise correlations a-

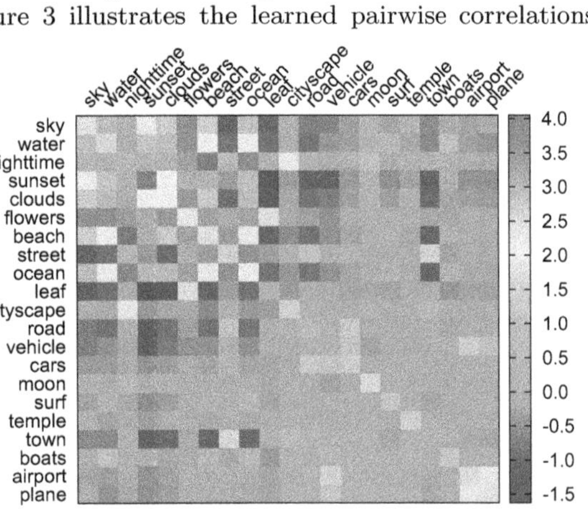

Figure 3: Illustration of tag correlations.

Table 1: Results for automatic tag recommendation.

	NVote	WVote	Graph	TagProp	RankVote
DCG@5	3.50	3.29	2.46	3.65	**4.43**
DCG@10	4.82	4.49	3.57	4.88	**5.72**

mong a group of frequent tags, where a colour map is used to indicate the magnitude of tag correlations. Among the pairwise elements, the higher correlations are assigned to the pairs of tags that commonly co-occur such as (sky, clouds), or the tags with the same or similar meanings such as (water, ocean). On the other hand, those rarely co-occurring tags like (sunset, leaf) and (ocean, town) are assigned with lower negative correlation values. This reveals that the learned correlations can properly encode the various kinds of relationships among tags.

5. CONCLUSIONS

In this paper, we investigate the problem of tag relevance estimation from a new perspective of learning to rank. A supervision step is introduced into the neighbour voting scheme, and both neighbour weights and tag correlations are explicitly modelled. Experimental results demonstrate the effectiveness of our approach in both scenarios of image search and tag recommendation. For future study, we plan to incorporate the distance metric learning techniques for discovering more accurate visual neighbours.

6. ACKNOWLEDGEMENTS

This work is supported by the Natural Science Foundation of China (61272240, 71402083, 61103151), the Doctoral Fund of Ministry of Education of China (20110131110028) and the Natural Science Foundation of Shandong province (ZR2012FM037). Dr. Jialie Shen was supported by Singapore Ministry of Education under Academic Research Fund Tier-2 (MOE Ref: MOE2013-T2-2-156) and the Microsoft Research Faculty Grant (FY14-RES-OPP-048).

7. REFERENCES

[1] Z. Cheng, J. Shen, and H. Miao. The effects of multiple query evidences on social image retrieval. *Multimedia Systems*, 2014.

[2] T.-S. Chua and J. Tang. Nus-wide: a real-world web image database from national university of singapore. In *CIVR*, 2009.

[3] T. Joachims, T. Finley, and C. Yu. Cutting-plane training of structural svms. *Machine Learning*, 2009.

[4] S. Lee and W. De Neve. Visually weighted neighbor voting for image tag relevance learning. *Multimed Tools Appl.*, 2014.

[5] X. Li, C. Snoek, and M. Worring. Learning social tag relevance by neighbor voting. *TMM*, 2009.

[6] X. Li, T. Uricchio, and L. Ballan. Socializing the semantic gap: A comparative survey on image tag assignment, refinement and retrieval. *arXiv preprint arXiv:1503.08248*, 2015.

[7] D. Liu, X. Hua, and H. Zhang. Content-based tag processing for internet social images. *Multimed Tools Appl.*, 2011.

[8] J. Shen, M. Wang, and T.-S. Chua. Accurate online video tagging via probabilistic hybrid modeling. *Multimedia Systems*, 2014.

[9] J. Shen, M. Wang, S. Yan, and X.-S. Hua. Multimedia tagging: past, present and future. In *MM*, 2011.

[10] J. Verbeek, M. Guillaumin, T. Mensink, and C. Schmid. Image annotation with tagprop on the mirflickr set. In *MIR*, 2010.

[11] Y. Yue, T. Finley, F. Radlinski, and T. Joachims. A support vector method for optimizing average precision. In *SIGIR*, 2007.

[12] D. Zhou, O. Bousquet, and T. Lal. Learning with local and global consistency. In *NIPS*, 2004.

[13] X. Zhu and W. Nejdl. An adaptive teleportation random walk model for learning social tag relevance. In *SIGIR*, 2014.

EMV-matchmaker: Emotional Temporal Course Modeling and Matching for Automatic Music Video Generation

Jen-Chun Lin
Academia Sinica
Taipei, Taiwan
jenchunlin@gmail.com

Wen-Li Wei
National Cheng Kung University
Tainan, Taiwan
lilijinjin@gmail.com

Hsin-Min Wang
Academia Sinica
Taipei, Taiwan
whm@iis.sinica.edu.tw

ABSTRACT

This paper presents a novel content-based emotion-oriented music video (MV) generation system, called EMV-matchmaker, which utilizes the emotional temporal phase sequence of the multimedia content as a bridge to connect music and video. Specifically, we adopt an emotional temporal course model (ETCM) to respectively learn the relationship between music and its emotional temporal phase sequence and the relationship between video and its emotional temporal phase sequence from an emotion-annotated MV corpus. Then, given a video clip (or a music clip), the visual (or acoustic) ETCM is applied to predict its emotional temporal phase sequence in a valence-arousal (VA) emotional space from the corresponding low-level visual (or acoustic) features. For MV generation, string matching is applied to measure the similarity between the emotional temporal phase sequences of video and music. The results of objective and subjective experiments demonstrate that EMV-matchmaker performs well and can generate appealing music videos that can enhance the viewing and listening experience.

Categories and Subject Descriptors

H.3.3 [**Information Storage and Retrieval**]: Information Search and Retrieval; H.5.1 [**Information Interfaces and presentation**]: Multimedia Information Systems

Keywords

Automatic music video generation, computational emotion model, cross-modal media retrieval.

1. INTRODUCTION

With the prevalence of mobile devices, video is widely used to record the memorable moments of our daily events such as wedding, graduation, and birthday parties. Websites such as YouTube or Vimeo have furthered the phenomenon as sharing becomes easy. In addition, people enjoy listening to music to release their emotions. In psychology, it is argued that a musical experience may evoke emotions when a listener conjures up images of things and events that have never occurred, in the absence of any episodic memory from a previous event in time [1]. Thus, music and video are often accompanied to complement each other to enhance emotional resonance in movie and television program. To enhance the entertaining quality and emotional resonance of user-generated videos (UGVs), accompanying a UGV with music is thus desirable. For example, a wedding video can accompany with romantic music to enhance a sweet atmosphere. Nevertheless, to select good music for a video, music professionals are required. With the rapid growth of music collections, matching a video with suitable music becomes ever difficult. The advent of an automatic music video (MV) generation system is foreseeable.

MM '15, October 26-30, 2015, Brisbane, Australia
© 2015 ACM. ISBN 978-1-4503-3459-4/15/10...$15.00
DOI: http://dx.doi.org/10.1145/2733373.2806359

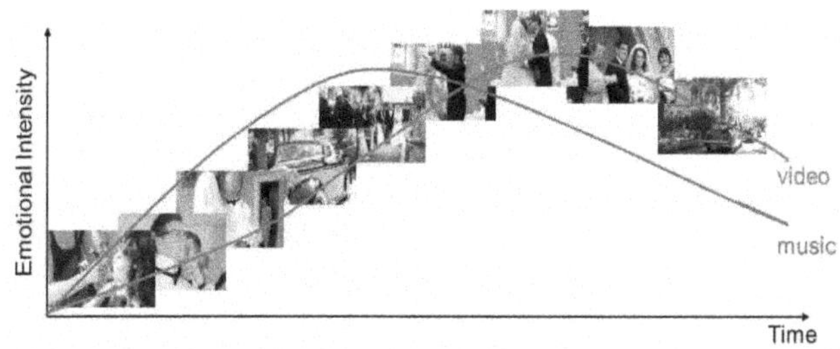

Figure 1. The mismatched temporal courses of emotional expression between music (green line) and video (red line); music reaches the emotional hot point (i.e., the vertex of the emotional curve) earlier than video.

In response to this trend, machine-aided automatic MV composition has been studied in the past decade [2–7]. However, the performance of existing systems is usually limited, because most of them only consider the relationship between the low-level acoustic features and visual features [3–5]. It is difficult to establish a direct relationship between the music and video modalities from low-level features. Moreover, there is a so-called semantic gap between the low-level acoustic (or visual) features and the high-level human perception. To narrow down such gap, motivated by the recent development in affective computing of multimedia signals, research has begun to map the low-level acoustic and visual features into the emotional space [6,7]. A music-accompanied video composed in this way is attractive, as the perception of emotion naturally occurs in video watching. However, most of the existing studies for MV generation [6,7] only model the relationship between the low-level features (i.e., acoustic or visual features) and the emotion labels, without considering the temporal course of emotional expression of music and video. Even the music and video are with the same emotional category, the nonsynchronous temporal courses of emotional expression may still result in bad viewing experience. Figure 1 shows an example of nonsynchronous temporal courses of emotional expression of video and music.

To handle the aforementioned problem, as shown in Figure 2, a novel emotion-oriented MV generation system called EMV-matchmaker is proposed in this paper. For a music (or video) clip,

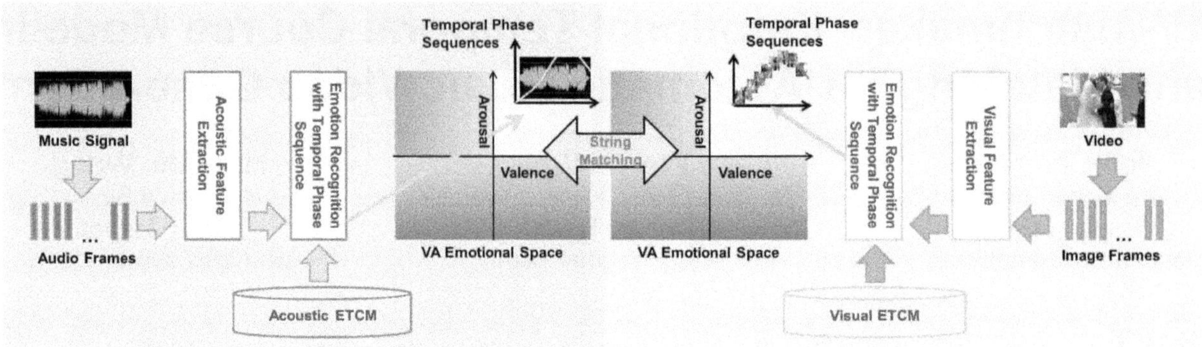

Figure 2. Illustration of the EMV-matchmaker framework.

an acoustic (or visual) emotional temporal course model (ETCM) is applied to predict its emotional temporal phase sequence in an emotional quadrant in the valence-arousal (VA) emotional space [8] from its low-level acoustic (or visual) features. For MV generation, the matching between music and video is based on whether they are located in the same emotional quadrant and the distance between their predicted emotional temporal phase sequences. The acoustic and visual ETCMs can be learned from an emotion-annotated MV corpus. To the best of our knowledge, this is the first attempt to consider the temporal structure of emotional expression for emotion-oriented MV generation.

2. RELATED WORK

Recent progress on video soundtrack recommendation and MV generation is overviewed here. Gillet et al. [3] employed the Pearson's correlation and mutual information to learn the correlation between the low-level acoustic and visual features, such as Mel-frequency cepstral coefficients, zero crossing rates, pitch, motion intensity, and color, from the music and video contents for MV generation; Similarly, Kuo et al. [5] employed multi-modal latent semantic analysis to learn the co-occurrence relationship between the low-level acoustic and visual features for video soundtrack recommendation, and Wu et al. [4] used multiple ranking canonical correlation analysis to learn such relationship for MV generation. To narrow down the semantic gap between the low-level features and the high-level human perception, Wang et al. [6] proposed an acoustic-visual emotion Gaussians (AVEG) model to respectively map the acoustic features and the visual features into the same VA emotional space to measure the distance between a music clip and a video clip for MV generation; Shah et al. [7] employed a support vector machine (SVM) to model the categorical emotion, such as sweet, funny, and sad, from the acoustic, visual, and geographic features for video soundtrack recommendation.

3. METHODOLOGY

In the proposed EMV-matchmaker system, as shown in Figure 2, an acoustic (or visual) ETCM is used to predict the emotional temporal phase sequence of a music (or video) clip in the VA emotional space. A string matching method is then used to match music and video based on the predicted emotional temporal phase sequences for MV generation.

3.1 Emotional Temporal Phase Sequence Prediction

The psychologist Ekman's research [9] demonstrated that the complete temporal course of an emotional expression can be divided into three sequential temporal phases, namely onset (application), apex (release), and offset (relaxation), considering the manner and intensity of the expression. To precisely model and predict the temporal course of an emotional expression, we adopt the ETCM, which was previously developed to model the temporal course of emotion from facial and speech expressions in [10,11]. We modified the ETCM to model the temporal course of emotional expression from MVs (including music and video contents). As shown in Figure 2, the EMV-matchmaker framework contains one acoustic ETCM and one visual ETCM for modeling music and video contents, respectively.

3.1.1 ETCM Derivation

In an ETCM, three emotional sub-states are defined to represent the temporal phases, namely onset, apex, and offset, of the emotional expression of a music clip (or a video clip), and a hidden Markov model (HMM) is used to model the temporal characteristics in an emotional sub-state.

Given an observation (i.e., acoustic or visual feature) sequence $O = o_1^T = o_1, o_2, ..., o_T$, the emotion recognition task is defined as selecting one among the three emotional quadrants $EQ \in \{EQ_1, EQ_2, EQ_3\}$ in the VA emotional space shown in Figure 2, i.e.,

$$EQ^* = \arg\max_{EQ} P(EQ \mid O). \quad (1)$$

For each emotional quadrant, $P(EQ \mid O)$ can be approximated as *a posteriori* probability of the best emotional sub-state (i.e., temporal phase) sequence $ES_{EQ} = es_{EQ}^1, es_{EQ}^2, ..., es_{EQ}^M$ as follows,

$$P(EQ \mid O) \approx \max_{ES_{EQ}} P(ES_{EQ} \mid O). \quad (2)$$

Therefore, the recognition problem is translated to finding out the emotional sub-state sequence that has the largest *a posteriori* probability over three emotional quadrants.

By using the Bayes' rule, the *a posteriori* probability $P(ES_{EQ} \mid O)$ can be decomposed as

$$P(ES_{EQ} \mid O) = P(O \mid ES_{EQ}) P(ES_{EQ}) / P(O), \quad (3)$$

where $P(O \mid ES_{EQ})$ is calculated by the corresponding emotional sub-state HMM sequence for the emotional quadrant *EQ*; $P(ES_{EQ}) = P(es_{EQ}^1, es_{EQ}^2, ..., es_{EQ}^M)$ is the *a priori* probability of the corresponding emotional sub-state sequence for the emotional quadrant *EQ*, which can be calculated according to a pre-defined grammar, as shown in Figure 3; $P(O)$ is identical for all possible emotional sub-state sequences, and thus can be omitted when (3) is applied in (1). Therefore, the task of emotion recognition with temporal phase sequence using ETCM can be expressed as

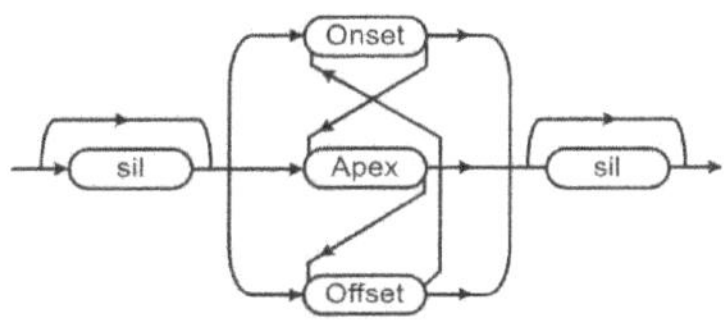

Figure 3. Recognition network based on the predefined grammar for characterizing an emotional quadrant expressed in a music or video clip.

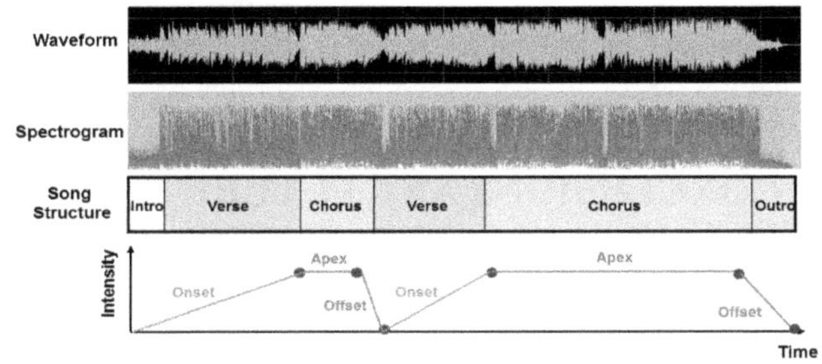

Figure 4. An example of annotated temporal phases of emotional expression of the song "Someone Like You" by Adele.

$$EQ^{*}=\arg\max_{EQ}\left[\max_{ES_{EQ}} P(O\mid ES_{EQ})P(ES_{EQ})\right]. \quad (4)$$

3.1.2 Emotional Temporal Phase Sequence Annotation and ETCM Training

We have collected a set of official music videos (OMVs) for training and testing. Since annotating the temporal course of emotional expression in an OMV is time-consuming, to accelerate the annotation process, two assumptions have been made. First, we assume that the temporal courses of emotional expressions for the music and video contents are the same in an OMV, since we believe that music and video are always highly synchronized and carefully composed to match each other in terms of emotion. Second, we assume that the temporal course of emotional expression in an OMV can be represented by a series of temporal phase (i.e., onset, apex and offset) combinations, since music is constructed based on a temporal structure consisting of intro, verse, chorus, bridge, and outro sections as well as optional repeats in order to over and over pave and express emotion. In our preliminary investigation, we observed that a complete emotional temporal phase sequence (i.e., onset-apex-offset) usually maps to a verse-chorus section in a song, as shown in Figure 4. We also observed that an apex phase is usually accompanied with more high frequency energy in the spectrogram. Based on these observations, to accelerate the annotation process, the temporal phases of each OMV in the training set were annotated according to the number of repetitions of verse-chorus sections by referring to the lyrics.

In acoustic ETCM training, for each emotional quadrant, we trained a set of HMMs (i.e., the acoustic emotional sub-state HMMs, including the onset HMM, the apex HMM, and the offset HMM) from the corresponding training OMVs together with the emotional temporal phase sequence annotation using the expectation-maximization (EM) algorithm. For each emotional sub-state HMM, a left-to-right HMM with three hidden states was used to model the emotional temporal characteristics. Similarly, we trained the visual emotional sub-state HMMs for constructing the visual ETCM. In addition, we also trained the sil HMMs (cf. Figure 3) to respectively absorb the black screen (for video) and the silence portion (for music) in the beginning and ending sections of an OMV, because these sections do not contain information of emotional expression. To permit the repetitions of emotional temporal phases in an OMV, an emotional temporal course grammar shown in Figure 3 was used to guide the recognition process by referring to the emotional temporal phases defined in [9]. All the temporal phase transition probabilities in the grammar were assumed uniformly distributed in this study.

3.2 MV Generation via String Matching

Given a queried video (or music) clip, the goal is to find a ranked list of music (or video) clips for the query. Specifically, the queried video (or music) clip is paired with each music (or video) clip from the target dataset to form a testing pair. The visual and acoustic ETCMs are then applied to predict the emotional temporal phase sequences $VES_{EQ}=(ves_{EQ,1},ves_{EQ,2},\ldots,ves_{EQ,T})$ and $MES_{EQ}=(mes_{EQ,1},mes_{EQ,2},\ldots,mes_{EQ,T})$ for the video and music clips by using (4), respectively. T is the length of the query. The similarity between the two emotional temporal phase sequences is evaluated by string matching as

$$S(VES_{EQ},\, MES_{EQ})=\frac{1}{T}\sum_{t=1}^{T} S(ves_{EQ,t},\, mes_{EQ,t}), \quad (5)$$

where $S(ves_{EQ,t},\, mes_{EQ,t})$ is defined as

$$S(ves_{EQ,t},\, mes_{EQ,t}) = \begin{cases} 4, & \textit{if the emotional quadrant and temporal phase are same} \\ 3, & \textit{if only the emotional quadrant is same} \\ 2, & \textit{if only the temporal phase is same} \\ 1, & \textit{otherwiese} \end{cases}, \quad (6)$$

based on whether video and music are in the same emotional quadrant and with the same emotional temporal phase at time t. A ranked list of music (or video) is generated in descending order of $S(VES_{EQ},\, MES_{EQ})$ (or $S(MES_{EQ},\, VES_{EQ})$) over all testing pairs, and the top one is regarded as the best recommendation for the queried video (or music) to generate the MV.

4. EXPERIMENTS

To evaluate the effectiveness of the proposed EMV-matchmaker framework, we performed experiments on a set of OMVs downloaded from YouTube according to the links provided in the DEAP database [12]. 65 complete OMVs were collected, with a total length of about 5 hours. Each OMV was assigned one (out of three) emotional quadrant based on the VA annotations provided in the DEAP database. The two emotional quadrants in the low arousal space were merged into one, as shown in Figure 2, since emotions mapped into the lower arousal space are difficult to differentiate [13]. For music, we used MIRToolbox to extract four types of frame-based acoustic features, namely dynamic, spectral, timbre, and tonal features [14,15]. For video, the frame-based color themes and motion intensities were extracted as the visual features [16,17].

In the experiments, two tasks were conducted: video retrieving music (i.e., the "V2M" task) and music retrieving video (i.e., the "M2V" task). We compared the proposed EMV-matchmaker framework with the state-of-the-art AVEG framework (k=32, iteration=12) [6,14,18], with 5-fold cross-validation. For the "V2M" task, the 65 videos were divided into 5 disjoint subsets. For each fold, each video of the testing subset was used in turn to search for the best matched music, and the videos in the

Table 1. Average ranking accuracy of the EMV-matchmaker and AVEG frameworks.

The "V2M" Task (Video Retrieving Music)		
	AVEG [6]	**EMV-matchmaker**
complete dataset	0.6401	0.6706
outliers removed	0.5434	0.7369
The "M2V" Task (Music Retrieving Video)		
	AVEG [6]	**EMV-matchmaker**
complete dataset	0.6797	0.5986
outliers removed	0.6253	0.6464

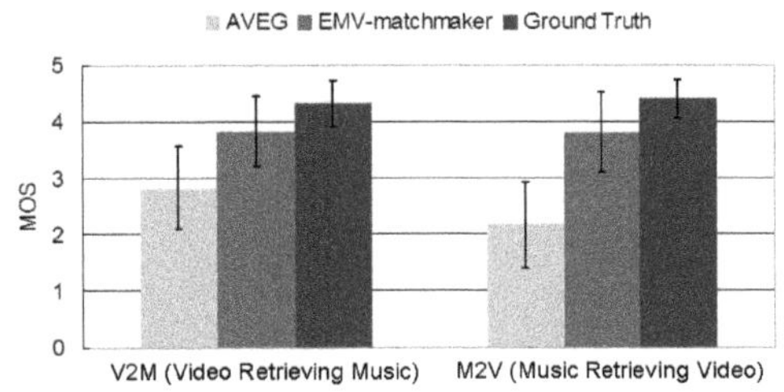

Figure 5. Results of the subjective MOS test.

remaining 4 subsets were used for training the visual ETCM to be used to generate the predicted emotional temporal phase sequence for the queried video. All the music tracks of the 65 OMVs were considered candidates and the one extracted from the test video was regarded as the ground truth. The ranking accuracy [5] defined as

$$Ranking\ Accuracy = 1 - \frac{rank(g) - 1}{|C| + 1}, \quad (7)$$

was adopted as the objective performance measure, where *rank(g)* is the rank of the ground truth *g*, and $|C|$ is the total number of music clips in the candidate set. We reported the average ranking accuracy over all folds. The "M2V" task adopts the same experimental setup as the "V2M" task.

As shown in the rows marked by "complete dataset" in Table 1, the proposed EMV-matchmaker framework slightly outperformed the AVEG framework in the "V2M" task, but performed worse in the "M2V" task, although it is expected that EMV-matchmaker should outperform AVEG in both tasks as EMV-matchmaker matches video and music based on the detailed emotional temporal phase sequences while AVEG matches them simply based on average emotional representations. One possible reason could be that the dataset contains several MVs that are composed from live concerts and singing contests, and the emotional expressions of the video parts of these MVs are actually not as matched to those of the music parts as they are in the remaining OMVs. There were 21 such MVs. Therefore, we also evaluated the retrieval performance only on the remaining 44 queried video (or music) clips. The results are shown in the rows marked by "outliers removed" in Table 1. We can see that EMV-matchmaker outperformed AVEG in both the "V2M" and "M2V" tasks, and its performance was improved a lot. Interestingly, the performance of AVEG degraded. We believe that it is also because AVEG did not consider the temporal course of emotional expression.

Subjective evaluation[1] in terms of 5-point mean opinion score (MOS) was conducted on 6 "V2M" MV sets generated by retrieving music for video and 6 "M2V" MV sets. Each "V2M" (or "M2V") MV set contains the original official MV (ground truth) and the MVs generated by EMV-matchmaker and AVEG. Each of the 36 MVs (including automatically generated MVs and original official MVs) was evaluated by sixteen subjects. Note that the MVs were randomly selected from the results of the "complete dataset" experiments, but none were outliers. The average MOS over all MVs and subjects is shown in Figure 5. It is clear that EMV-matchmaker achieved better MOS performance than AVEG. The results reveal that considering the temporal course of emotional expression in video and music matching can generate more attractive MVs to enhance subjects' viewing and listening experiences. The results also show that the MOS of the MVs generated by EMV-matchmaker is quite close to that of the ground truth MVs. In fact, we did find that some MVs generated by EMV-matchmaker are satisfactory.

[1] MOS results for individual MVs and a system demonstration video are available at https://sites.google.com/site/emvmatchmaker/home?pli=1.

5. CONCLUSIONS AND FUTURE WORK

We have presented a novel content-based emotion-oriented music video generation system called EMV-matchmaker that utilizes the emotional temporal phase sequence of the multimedia content as a bridge to connect music and video. The results of both subjective and objective evaluations have demonstrated that the proposed EMV-matchmaker framework outperforms the state-of-the-art AVEG framework, and can offer a satisfactory generated music video to enhance human viewing and listening experience. Personalization techniques can be applied to further address the subjectivity issue of automatic MV generation, which is important and will be studied in our future work.

6. ACKNOWLEDGMENTS

This work was supported by the Ministry of Science and Technology of Taiwan under Grant: NSC 102-2221-E-001-008-MY3. The first author would like to thank his best friend, Chao-Wei Chen, for his suggestion and encouragement.

7. REFERENCES

[1] P. N. Juslin and D. Västfjäll. Emotional responses to music: the need to consider underlying mechanisms. *Behav Brain Sci.*, 2008.

[2] D. A. Shamma et al. MusicStory: a personalized music video creator. In *ACM MM*, 2005.

[3] O. Gillet et al. On the correlation of automatic audio and visual segmentations of music videos. *IEEE TCSVT*, 2007.

[4] X. Wu et al. Automatic music video generation: cross matching of music and image. In *ACM MM*, 2012.

[5] F. F. Kuo et al. Background music recommendation for video based on multimodal latent semantic analysis. In *ICME*, 2013.

[6] J. C. Wang et al. The acousticvisual emotion Gaussians model for automatic generation of music video. In *ACM MM*, 2012.

[7] R. R. Shah et al. ADVISOR–personalized video soundtrack recommendation by late fusion with heuristic rankings. In *ACM MM*, 2014.

[8] R. E. Thayer. *The Biopsychology of Mood and Arousal*. New York: Oxford Univ. Press, 1989.

[9] P. Ekman. *Handbook of Cognition and Emotion*. Wiley, 1999.

[10] J. C. Lin et al. Emotion recognition of conversational affective speech using temporal course modeling. In *INTERSPEECH*, 2013.

[11] C. H. Wu et al. Two-level hierarchical alignment for semi-coupled HMM-based audiovisual emotion recognition with temporal course. *IEEE TMM*, 2013.

[12] S. Koelstra, et al. DEAP: a database for emotion analysis using physiological signals. *IEEE TAC*, 2012.

[13] M. Soleymani et al. A Bayesian framework for video affective representation. In *ACII*, 2009.

[14] J. C. Wang et al. The acoustic emotion Gaussians model for emotion-based music annotation and retrieval. In *ACM MM*, 2012.

[15] O. Lartillot and P. Toiviainen. A Matlab toolbox for musical feature extraction from audio. In *DAFx*, 2007.

[16] X. Wang et al. Affective image adjustment with a single word. *Vis. Comput.*, 2013.

[17] H. W. Chen et al. Action movies segmentation and summarization based on tempo analysis. In *MIR*, 2004.

[18] Tool of the AEG model: http://slam.iis.sinica.edu.tw/demo/aeg/

Scalable Multimedia Retrieval by Deep Learning Hashing with Relative Similarity Learning

Lianli Gao
University of Electronic Science and Technology of China.
lianli.gao@uestc.edu.cn

Jingkuan Song
University of Trento.
jingkuan.song@unitn.it

Fuhao Zou
Huazhong University of Science and Technology
fuhao_zou@hust.edu.cn

Dongxiang Zhang
National University of Singapore.
zhangdo@comp.nus.edu.sg

Jie Shao
University of Electronic Science and Technology of China.
shaojie@uestc.edu.cn

ABSTRACT

Learning-based hashing methods are becoming the mainstream for approximate scalable multimedia retrieval. They consist of two main components: hash codes learning for training data and hash functions learning for new data points. Tremendous efforts have been devoted to designing novel methods for these two components, i.e., supervised and unsupervised methods for learning hash codes, and different models for inferring hashing functions. However, there is little work integrating supervised and unsupervised hash codes learning into a single framework. Moreover, the hash function learning component is usually based on hand-crafted visual features extracted from the training images. The performance of a content-based image retrieval system crucially depends on the feature representation and such hand-crafted visual features may degrade the accuracy of the hash functions. In this paper, we propose a semi-supervised deep learning hashing (DLH) method for fast multimedia retrieval. More specifically, in the first component, we utilize both visual and label information to learn an relative similarity graph that can more precisely reflect the relationship among training data, and then generate the hash codes based on the graph. In the second stage, we apply a deep convolutional neural network (CNN) to simultaneously learn a good multimedia representation and hash functions. Extensive experiments on three popular datasets demonstrate the superiority of our DLH over both supervised and unsupervised hashing methods.

Categories and Subject Descriptors

H.3.3 [**Information Systems**]: INFORMATION STORAGE AND RETRIEVAL—*Search process*

Keywords

Image retrieval; hashing; deep learning

MM'15, October 26–30, 2015, Brisbane, Australia.
© 2015 ACM. ISBN 978-1-4503-3459-4/15/10 ...$15.00.
DOI: http://dx.doi.org/10.1145/2733373.2806360 .

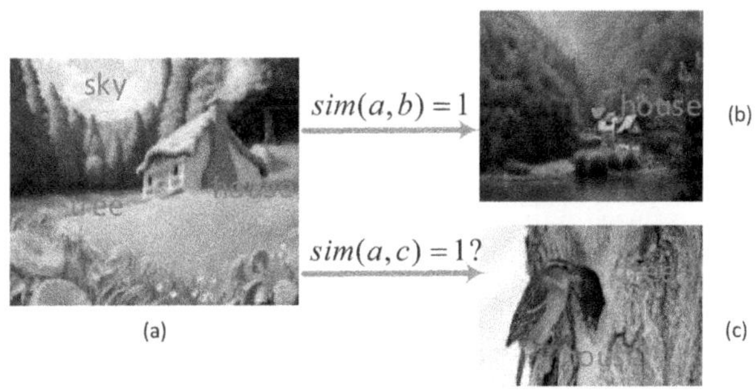

Figure 1: Purely using image labels to calculate the similarity between images is inaccurate. By using the widely-used similarity criteria stating that if two images have at least one common label, their similarity is defined as 1, $sim(a, b) = 1$ and $sim(a, c) = 1$. However, it is clear that (b) is closer to (a), both semantically and visually, compared with (c). Our main task is to learn a relative similarity between images by using visual and label information, based on which more accurate hash codes can be generated.

1. INTRODUCTION

With large image databases becoming a reality both in scientific and industrial domains, content-based image retrieval (CBIR) becomes an important research area in computer vision and it largely relies on extracting the appropriate characteristic quantities describing the desired contents of images. To date, there has been significant research within numerous domains that aims to improve the accuracy of CBIR and most of them are focusing on designing sophisticated low-level feature extraction algorithms to reduce the semantic gap between the visual features and the richness of human semantics. To conduct CBIR, image features can be either extracted from regions or from the entire image, thus successful scalable image retrieval algorithms can be divided into two categories: 1) quantized local features (e.g., BOW) [14] indexed by an inverted index; and 2) holistic features (e.g., GIST and HSV) indexed by compact hash codes [13]. More specifically, local features have been proved to be more close to human perception system, while global features based CBIR is relatively simpler. To make the CBIR truly scalable to large size of databases, hashing methods are usually adopted. In this way, images can be encoded by a small number of bytes using hashing methods [13, 3, 9, 11].

Although a variety of techniques have been proposed, image retrieval remains one of the most challenging problems. This is due to the fact that the global and local features have different strength and weakness, and specific search schemes have to be adopted based on different visual features. This motivates us to investigate how to find a more robust feature and an unified searching scheme for larger scale image retrieval. This arises several questions for scalable CBIR: Is there a generic feature extraction method that is robust on different image datasets? How to integrate this generic feature to existing searching schemes? Some recent efforts have been proposed to tackle these questions. In [13, 6], they proposed to utilize supervised deep learning to learn image representation and hash codes for image retrieval and promising results were obtained. Wan *et al.* [10] proposed a general framework by applying deep learning to CBIR. However, these methods use the label information only to identify the similarity between two data points, which is inaccurate in a lot of cases. For example, in Fig. 1, image (b) is more similar than (c) to the query (a). If we only use the label information, (b) and (c) will have the same similarity to (a). Therefore, it is necessary to learn a more accurate similarity between images by using visual and label information.

In this paper, we propose integrating a generic feature into a hashing search scheme. More specifically, we present a deep learning hashing (DLH), which integrates with semi-supervised graph construction to enhance the performance of hashing methods for scalable image retrieval. It is worth highlighting the following contributions: 1) We propose a framework to utilize the CNN-generated visual feature as a generic feature, and incorporate this feature into this hashing search scheme for efficient image retrieval on scalable datasets. 2) To infer the hash codes of the training set in both supervised and unsupervised settings, a novel semi-supervised graph construction approach is proposed and an efficient solution is devised. This graph reflect the relative similarity among data points. 3) We propose to simultaneously learn a good feature representation and a set of hash functions via CNN for new data points.

2. DEEP LEARNING HASHING WITH SEMI-SUPERVISED GRAPH CONSTRUCTION

In this section, we introduce our method. The learning process is decomposed into two stages: a hash code learning stage followed by a hash function inferring stage.

2.1 Semi-supervised hash codes learning

Suppose $\mathbf{X} = \{\mathbf{x}_1, \mathbf{x}_2, ..., \mathbf{x}_n\}$ represents a set of n images, and $\mathbf{F} = \{\mathbf{f}_1, \mathbf{f}_2, ..., \mathbf{f}_n\}$, where $\mathbf{f}_i = \{0,1\}^c$ is the label for the i-th image ($1 \le i \le n$), and c is the number of classes. The task is to learn the hash codes $\mathbf{Y}$ based on $\mathbf{X}$ and $\mathbf{F}$. Suppose $\mathbf{Y} = \{\mathbf{y}_1, \mathbf{y}_2, ..., \mathbf{y}_n\}$, where $\mathbf{y}_i = \{-1,1\}^L$ is the hash code for the i-th training image ($1 \le i \le n$), and L is the code length of the hash code. For supervised hashing methods, a good criteria for $\mathbf{Y}$ is that the similarity of a pair of hash codes $\mathbf{y}_i$ and $\mathbf{y}_j$ should be consistent with the similarity of their labels. For unsupervised hashing, $\mathbf{y}_i$ and $\mathbf{y}_j$ should be consistent with their similarity in their original space. They can be uniformly formulated as:

$$\min_{\mathbf{Y}} \sum_{ij} \left(sim_{i,j} - C \times sim_H\left(\mathbf{y}_i, \mathbf{y}_j\right)\right)^2 \tag{1}$$

where $sim_{i,j}$ for supervised hashing is usually defined as:

$$sim_{i,j} = \begin{cases} +1, \; if \; f_i f_j^T > 0, \\ -1, \; else \end{cases} \tag{2}$$

where $\mathbf{f}_i$, $\mathbf{f}_j$ are the labels for the i-th and j-th images, and C is a constant. For unsupervised hashing, $sim_{i,j}$ is usually defined as:

$$sim_{i,j} = \begin{cases} e^{-\|\mathbf{x}_i - \mathbf{x}_j\|_2^2 / 2\sigma^2}, & \begin{array}{l} if \; x_i \in \mathcal{N}_K(\mathbf{x}_j) \\ or \; x_j \in \mathcal{N}_K(\mathbf{x}_i) \end{array} \\ 0, \text{else} \end{cases} \tag{3}$$

where $\mathcal{N}_K(\cdot)$ is the K-nearest-neighbor set and $1 \le (i,j) \le n$.

For supervised hashing, the similarity between two data points is set to $+1$ or -1, which is too rigid. As is shown in Fig. 1, the image pair (a,b) has higher similarity than the pair (a,c), both visually and semantically. But they are assigned with the same value of similarity, which degrades the discriminative power of hashing. For unsupervised hashing methods, the variance σ will affect the performance significantly, and it is usually empirically tuned. In this work, we propose integrating supervised and unsupervised hashing into a single framework and automatically learning an optimal similarity graph by using both visual feature and image labels, which can more precisely encode the relationships between data points.

An optimal similarity graph $\mathbf{S}$ should be smooth on all these information cues, which can be formulated as:

$$\begin{aligned} &\min_{\mathbf{S},\mathbf{Y}} \mathbf{g}(\mathbf{F},\mathbf{S}) + \alpha \mathbf{h}(\mathbf{X},\mathbf{S}) + \beta \mathbf{r}(\mathbf{S}) \\ &+\gamma \sum_{ij} \left(\mathbf{s}_{ij} - C \times sim_H\left(\mathbf{y}_i, \mathbf{y}_j\right)\right)^2 \end{aligned} \tag{4}$$

where $\mathbf{g}(\mathbf{F},\mathbf{S})$ is the penalty function to measure the smoothness of $\mathbf{S}$ on the label information $\mathbf{F}$ and $\mathbf{h}(\mathbf{X},\mathbf{S})$ is the loss function to measure the smoothness of $\mathbf{S}$ on the feature $\mathbf{X}$. $\mathbf{r}(\mathbf{S})$ are regularizers defined on the target $\mathbf{S}$. α, β and γ are balancing parameters.

The penalty function $\mathbf{g}(\mathbf{F},\mathbf{S})$ and $\mathbf{h}\left(\mathbf{X}^t,\mathbf{S}\right)$ should be defined in the way such that close labels (data points) have high similarity and vice versa. In this paper, we define it as follows:

$$\begin{cases} \mathbf{g}(\mathbf{F},\mathbf{S}) = \sum_{ij} \|\mathbf{f}_i - \mathbf{f}_j\|_2^2 \mathbf{s}_{ij} \\ h(\mathbf{X},\mathbf{S}) = \sum_{ij} \|\mathbf{x}_i - \mathbf{x}_j\|_2^2 \mathbf{s}_{ij} \end{cases} \tag{5}$$

where $\mathbf{f}_i$ and $\mathbf{f}_j$ are the labels of data point $\mathbf{x}_i$ and $\mathbf{x}_j$. The regularizer term $\mathbf{r}(\mathbf{S})$ is defined as:

$$r(\mathbf{S}) = \|\mathbf{S}\|_F^2 \tag{6}$$

We then define

$$sim_H\left(\mathbf{y}_i, \mathbf{y}_j\right) = \frac{1}{L}\left(L - \|\mathbf{y}_i, \mathbf{y}_j\|_H\right) = \frac{1}{2L}\mathbf{y}_i\mathbf{y}_j^T + \frac{1}{2} \tag{7}$$

and we further constrain that $\mathbf{S} \ge 0$ and $\mathbf{S1} = \mathbf{1}$ (the sum of each row equals to 1). Then we can obtain the objective function for learning hash codes by replacing $g(\mathbf{F},\mathbf{S})$, $\mathbf{h}(\mathbf{X},\mathbf{S})$, $r(\mathbf{S},\alpha)$ and $sim_H\left(\mathbf{y}_i,\mathbf{y}_j\right)$ in (4) using (5), (6) and (7):

$$\begin{aligned} &\min_{\mathbf{S},\mathbf{Y}} \left(\sum_{ij} \|\mathbf{f}_i - \mathbf{f}_j\|_2^2 \mathbf{s}_{ij} + \alpha \sum_{ij} \|\mathbf{x}_i - \mathbf{x}_j\|_2^2 \mathbf{s}_{ij} \right. \\ &\left. +\beta \sum_{ij} \left(\mathbf{s}_{ij} - \tfrac{C}{2L} \times \mathbf{y}_i\mathbf{y}_j^T - \tfrac{C}{2}\right)^2 + \gamma \|\mathbf{S}\|_F^2 \right) \\ &s.t. \left\{ \; \mathbf{S} \ge 0, \mathbf{S1} = \mathbf{1}, \mathbf{Y} \in \{-1,1\}^{N \times L} \right. \end{aligned} \tag{8}$$

2.2 Iterative optimization

We propose an iterative method to minimize the above objective function (8) , as below:

2.2.1 *Update* S

By fixing $\mathbf{Y}$, we can obtain $\mathbf{S}$ by optimizing (8). It is equivalent to optimize the following objective function:

$$\begin{aligned}&\min_{\mathbf{S}} \sum_{ij} \|\mathbf{f}_i - \mathbf{f}_j\|_2^2 \mathbf{s}_{ij} + \alpha \sum_{ij} \|\mathbf{x}_i - \mathbf{x}_j\|_2^2 \mathbf{s}_{ij} \\ &+\beta \sum_{ij} \left(\mathbf{s}_{ij} - \tfrac{C}{2L} \times \mathbf{y}_i\mathbf{y}_j^T - \tfrac{C}{2}\right)^2 + \gamma \|\mathbf{S}\|_F^2 \\ &= \min_{\mathbf{S}} \sum_i \mathbf{tr}\left(\left(\mathbf{a}_i + \alpha\mathbf{b}_i\right)\mathbf{s}_i{}^T + \gamma\mathbf{s}_i\mathbf{s}_i{}^T\right) + \beta\|\mathbf{s}_i - \mathbf{d}_i\|^2 \\ &s.t. \mathbf{S} \geq 0, \mathbf{S1} = \mathbf{1}\end{aligned} \quad (9)$$

where $\mathbf{a}_i = \{\mathbf{a}_{ij}, 1 \leq j \leq n\}$ with $\mathbf{a}_{ij} = \|\mathbf{f}_i - \mathbf{f}_j\|_2^2$, $\mathbf{b}_i = \{\mathbf{b}_{ij}\}$ with $\mathbf{b}_{ij} = \|\mathbf{x}_i - \mathbf{x}_j\|_2^2$ and $\mathbf{d}_i = \{\mathbf{d}_{ij}, 1 \leq j \leq n\} \in \mathbb{R}^{1\times n}$ with $\mathbf{d}_{ij} = \frac{C}{2L} \times \mathbf{y}_i\mathbf{y}_j^T + \frac{C}{2}$.

Since d_i is a constant, (9) can be reformulated as:

$$\begin{aligned}&\min_{\mathbf{S}, \mathbf{S}\geq 0, \mathbf{S1}=\mathbf{1}} \sum_i \mathbf{tr}\left(\left(\beta+\gamma\right)\mathbf{s}_i\mathbf{s}_i{}^T + \left(\mathbf{a}_i + \alpha\mathbf{b}_i - 2\beta\mathbf{d}_i\right)\mathbf{s}_i{}^T\right) \\ &\Rightarrow \min_{\mathbf{S}, \mathbf{S}\geq 0, \mathbf{S1}=\mathbf{1}} \sum_i tr\left(\mathbf{s}_i\mathbf{s}_i{}^T + \tfrac{\mathbf{a}_i + \alpha\mathbf{b}_i - 2\beta\mathbf{d}_i}{2(\beta+\gamma)}\mathbf{s}_i{}^T\right)\end{aligned} \quad (10)$$

and it is equivalent to:

$$\min_{\mathbf{S}, \mathbf{S}\geq 0, \mathbf{S1}=\mathbf{1}} \sum_i \left\|\mathbf{s}_i + \frac{\mathbf{a}_i + \alpha\mathbf{b}_i - 2\beta\mathbf{d}_i}{2\left(\beta+\gamma\right)}\right\|_2^2 \quad (11)$$

The constraint in problem (11) is simplex [1]. Then each $\mathbf{s}_i$ can be efficiently solved, and we will get the updated graph S.

2.2.2 *Update* Y

By fixing $\mathbf{S}$, we can obtain $\mathbf{Y}$ by optimizing (8). It is equivalent to optimize the following objective function:

$$\begin{aligned}&\min_{\mathbf{Y}} \sum_{ij} \left(\tfrac{2L}{C}\left(\mathbf{s}_{ij} - \tfrac{C}{2}\right) - \mathbf{y}_i\mathbf{y}_j{}^T\right)^2 \Rightarrow \min_{Y} \|\bar{\mathbf{S}} - \mathbf{Y}\mathbf{Y}^T\|_F^2 \\ &s.t. \mathbf{Y} \in \{-1, 1\}^L\end{aligned} \quad (12)$$

This algorithm sequentially or randomly chooses one entry in $\mathbf{Y}$ to update while keeping other entries fixed. Let $\mathbf{Y} = [\mathbf{y}_{.1}, ..., \mathbf{y}_{.L}]$, where $\mathbf{y}_{.p} \in \mathbb{R}^{n\times 1}$ is the p-th column of $\mathbf{Y}$ (the p-th bit of all data). The objective function (12) can be rewritten as:

$$\min_{\mathbf{Y}} \left\|\bar{\mathbf{S}} - \sum_{l\neq p} \mathbf{y}_{.l}\mathbf{y}_{.l}^T - \mathbf{y}_{.p}\mathbf{y}_{.p}^T\right\|_F^2 = \min_{\mathbf{Y}} \sum_{i,j}^{n} \left(\mathbf{e}_{ij} - \mathbf{y}_{ip}\mathbf{y}_{jp}\right)^2 \quad (13)$$

where $\mathbf{E} = \bar{\mathbf{S}} - \sum_{l\neq p} \mathbf{y}_{.l}\mathbf{y}_{.l}^T$ and $\overline{\mathbf{s}_{ij}} = \frac{2L}{C}\left(\mathbf{s}_{ij} - \frac{C}{2}\right)$. Suppose we want to update $\mathbf{y}_{qp}$ by fixing the other hash codes. Optimizing (12) is equivalent to:

$$\min_{\mathbf{y}_{qp}} \sum_{i,j}^{n} \left(\mathbf{e}_{ij} - \mathbf{y}_{ip}\mathbf{y}_{jp}\right)^2 = \min_{\mathbf{y}_{qp}} \sum_{i,j}^{n} \left(-2\mathbf{e}_{ij}\mathbf{y}_{ip}\mathbf{y}_{jp} + const\right)$$

and it is equivalent to:

$$\begin{aligned}&\max_{\mathbf{y}_{qp}} \left(\mathbf{e}_{qq}\mathbf{y}_{qp}\mathbf{y}_{qp} + \sum_{j=1}^{n} \mathbf{e}_{qj}\mathbf{y}_{qp}\mathbf{y}_{jp} + \sum_{i=1}^{n} \mathbf{a}_{iq}\mathbf{y}_{ip}\mathbf{y}_{qp}\right) \\ &\Rightarrow \mathbf{y}_{qp}^* = \mathrm{sgn}\left(\sum_{j=1, j\neq q}^{n} \mathbf{e}_{qj}\mathbf{y}_{jp} + \sum_{i=1, i\neq q}^{n} \mathbf{e}_{iq}\mathbf{y}_{ip}\right)\end{aligned} \quad (14)$$

We update $\mathbf{S}$ and $\mathbf{Y}$ iteratively until (8) converges.

2.3 Supervised hash functions learning via CNN

In this section, we introduce hash functions learning via CNN, which consists of two stages: (i) feature extraction using CNN, (ii) hash functions learning on the features. Following [5], we use Caffe [4] for the implementation of deep CNN learning.

In general, the deep CNN consists of convolution/maxpooling layers, and fully connected/output layers. Specifically, the first layer is the input layer which adopts the mean-centered raw RGB pixels in intensity value. The first and the second convolution layers are followed by a response normalization layers and a max pooling layers, while the third, fourth, and fifth convolution layers are connected to each other without any intervening pooling or normalization. Following the convolutional layers, there are two more fully connected layers and the output layer.

We make use of the generated hash codes and discrete class labels of the training images for training. Specifically, for n training images in c classes (an image may belong to multiple classes), we define a $n \times c$ discrete label matrix $F \in \{0,1\}^{n\times c}$, where $F_{ij} = 1$ if the i-th training image belongs to the j-th class, otherwise $F_{ij} = 0$. For the output layer in our network, in addition to defining the L output units, we add c output units which correspond to the class labels of the training images. By incorporating the image class labels as a part in the output layer, we enforce the network to learn a shared image representation which matches both the approximate hash codes and the image labels. This can be regarded as a transfer learning case in which the incorporated image labels are expected to be helpful for learning a more accurate image representation (i.e. the hidden units in the fully connected layer). This image representation may be advantageous for hash functions learning. CNN automatically learns the image representation as well as a set of hash functions. In prediction, one can input a test image to the trained network and obtain the hash code from the values in the output layer.

3. EXPERIMENTS

We experimentally evaluate our algorithm on the task of high-dimensional approximate nearest neighbor (ANN) search.

3.1 Settings

We evaluate the proposed method on three benchmark datasets with different kinds of images: 1) AWA dataset consisting of 30,475 images of 50 animals classes with six pre-extracted feature representations for each image; 2) CIFAR consisting of 60,000 32 × 32 color tinny images which are categorized into 10 classes (6K images per class); and 3) The NUS-WIDE dataset with nearly 270,000 images. Each image is annotated with one or multiple tags from 81 concept tags. We utilize the features provided within the datasets. Specifically, each dataset is divided into three subsets: training set, testing set and query set. For CIFAR, the provided split is adopted. For AWA and NUSWIDE, 10,000 data points are randomly selected for training and the rest for testing.

The ANN search is conducted to evaluate our proposed approaches, and two indicators are reported, namely Recall and Mean Average Precision (MAP). We compare our DLH with other state-of-the-art supervised and unsupervised hashing algorithms, such as spectral hashing (SH) [12], iterative quantization (ITQ) hashing [2] and K-means Hashing (KMH) [3]. We also compare with two supervised hashing methods KSH [8] and FastH [7].

3.2 Results

We first tune the parameters of our method and then show the best results to compare with others. Note that the parameters are data-sensitive, and we omit the parameter tuning step here due to the page limit. Fig. 2(a)-2(f) show the comparison on the three datasets and Table 1 presents the MAP for the different hashing methods. We have tested L=32 and L=64. From these figures, we have the following observations: 1) Our method consistently outperforms other hashing methods in all datasets. FastH and KSH is competitive in most settings. However, great improvement of DLH over FastH is achieved on AWA dataset. This indicates that

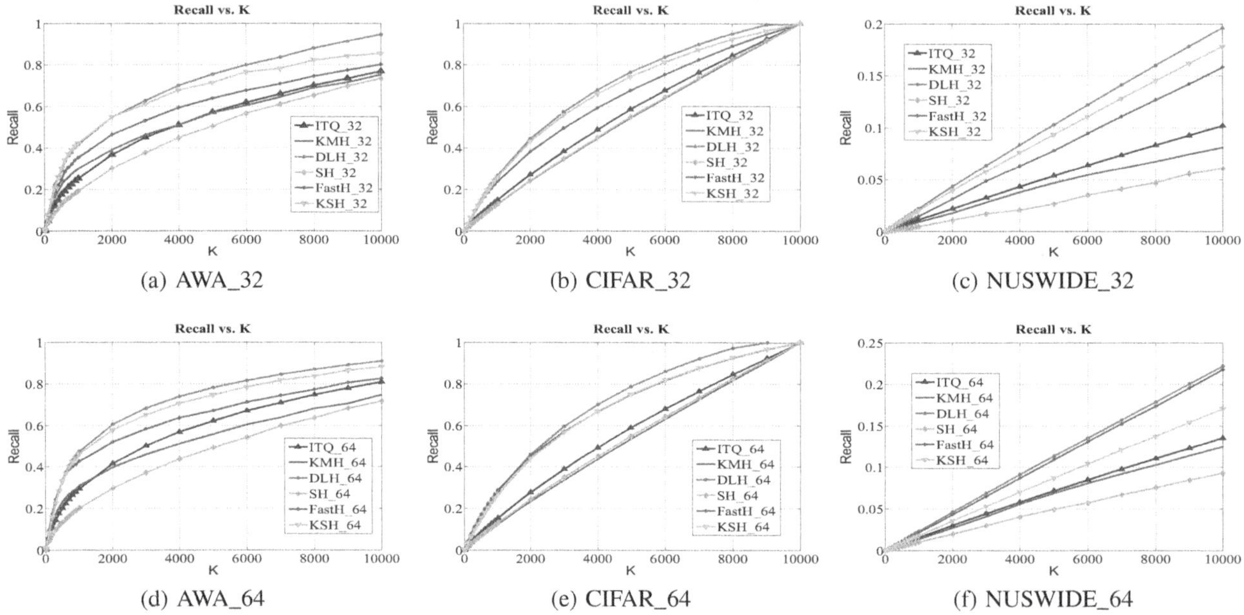

(a) AWA_32 (b) CIFAR_32 (c) NUSWIDE_32

(d) AWA_64 (e) CIFAR_64 (f) NUSWIDE_64

Figure 2: Comparison of six hashing methods on three datasets with code length 32 and 64

Table 1: MAP of different methods with code length 32 and 64 on different databases

Methods	AWA	CIFAR	NUSWIDE
ITQ_32	13.9	13.9	7.78
KMH_32	18.0	11.8	5.86
SH_32	9.24	12.0	5.12
FastH_32	21.1	22.3	11.6
KSH_32	27.5	24.2	14.7
DLH_32	**28.3**	**25.1**	**15.2**
ITQ_64	16.4	14.1	7.91
KMH_64	19.1	11.5	6.94
SH_64	9.80	12.1	7.81
FastH_64	30.2	27.8	12.1
KSH_64	29.3	27.4	15.2
DLH_64	**31.4**	**28.6**	**17.3**

a good image representation and the CNN-generated hash functions can improve the performance of hashing methods. 2) With the increase of code length, the performance of different hashing methods is improved accordingly. Generally, MAP improvements of supervised hashing methods are more significant than that of unsupervised hashing methods. 3) The supervised hashing methods outperform their unsupervised counterparts significantly. More specifically, the MAP gap between the best supervised and unsupervised hashing methods is 12%, 14% and 10% respectively, for AWA, CIFAR and NUSWIDE datasets, with $L = 64$. This indicates that exploiting the content information only cannot preserve the label-based similarity. 4) All the unsupervised methods have similar performance. In general, SH performs the worst while ITQ and KMH are comparable to each other.

4. CONCLUSIONS

In this paper, we propose a general framework for semi-supervised deep learning hashing (DLH) method for fast multimedia retrieval. We firstly utilize visual features and labels to learn an relative similarity graph, which reflects the relationship among training data more precisely. Based on this graph, the hash codes can be generated. Then, we apply deep learning to automatically learn hash functions for new data points. Experiments on three popular datasets demonstrate the superiority of our DLH compared to others.

5. ACKNOWLEDGMENTS

The work of Lianli Gao is supported by the Fundamental Research Funds for the Central Universities of China under grant No. ZYGX2014Z007 and No.ZYGX2014J063.

6. REFERENCES

[1] L. Gao, J. Song, F. Nie, Y. Yan, N. Sebe, and H. T. Shen. Optimal graph leaning with partial tags and multiple features. In *CVPR*, 2015.

[2] Y. Gong, S. Lazebnik, A. Gordo, and F. Perronnin. Iterative quantization: A procrustean approach to learning binary codes for large-scale image retrieval. *TPAMI*, 35(12):2916–2929, 2013.

[3] K. He, F. Wen, and J. Sun. K-means hashing: An affinity-preserving quantization method for learning binary compact codes. In *CVPR*, 2013.

[4] Y. Jia, E. Shelhamer, J. Donahue, S. Karayev, J. Long, R. Girshick, S. Guadarrama, and T. Darrell. Caffe: Convolutional architecture for fast feature embedding. *arXiv preprint arXiv:1408.5093*, 2014.

[5] A. Krizhevsky, I. Sutskever, and G. E. Hinton. Imagenet classification with deep convolutional neural networks. In *NIPS*, 2012.

[6] H. Lai, Y. Pan, Y. Liu, and S. Yan. Simultaneous feature learning and hash coding with deep neural networks. In *CVPR*, 2015.

[7] G. Lin, C. Shen, Q. Shi, A. van den Hengel, and D. Suter. Fast supervised hashing with decision trees for high-dimensional data. In *CVPR*, 2014.

[8] W. Liu, J. Wang, R. Ji, Y. Jiang, and S. Chang. Supervised hashing with kernels. In *CVPR*, 2012.

[9] J. Song, Y. Yang, Z. Huang, H. T. Shen, and R. Hong. Multiple feature hashing for real-time large scale near-duplicate video retrieval. In *ACM Multimedia*, 2011.

[10] J. Wan, D. Wang, S. C. H. Hoi, P. Wu, J. Zhu, Y. Zhang, and J. Li. Deep learning for content-based image retrieval: A comprehensive study. In *ACM Multimedia*, 2014.

[11] J. Wang, H. T. Shen, J. Song, and J. Ji. Hashing for similarity search: A survey. *CoRR*, abs/1408.2927, 2014.

[12] Y. Weiss, A. Torralba, and R. Fergus. Spectral hashing. In *NIPS*, 2008.

[13] R. Xia, Y. Pan, H. Lai, C. Liu, and S. Yan. Supervised hashing for image retrieval via image representation learning. In *AAAI*, 2014.

[14] S. Zhang, M. Yang, T. Cour, K. Yu, and D. N. Metaxas. Query specific fusion for image retrieval. In *ECCV*, 2012.

Image Popularity Prediction in Social Media Using Sentiment and Context Features

Francesco Gelli, Tiberio Uricchio, Marco Bertini, Alberto Del Bimbo
MICC, Università degli Studi di Firenze
Viale Morgagni 65 - 50134 Firenze, Italy
{name.surname}@unifi.it

Shih-Fu Chang
Columbia University
500 West 120th Street, New York, NY, USA
sfchang@ee.columbia.edu

ABSTRACT

Images in social networks share different destinies: some are going to become popular while others are going to be completely unnoticed. In this paper we propose to use visual sentiment features together with three novel context features to predict a concise popularity score of social images. Experiments on large scale datasets show the benefits of proposed features on the performance of image popularity prediction. Exploiting state-of-the-art sentiment features, we report a qualitative analysis of which sentiments seem to be related to good or poor popularity. To the best of our knowledge, this is the first work understanding specific visual sentiments that positively or negatively influence the eventual popularity of images.

Categories and Subject Descriptors

H.3.1 [**Information Storage And Retrieval**]: Content Analysis and Indexing

General Terms

Algorithms, Experimentation

Keywords

Image popularity; social networks; visual sentiment; affective computing

1. INTRODUCTION

In the last decade users of social networks such as Flickr and Facebook have uploaded tens of billions of photos, often adding accompanying metadata by tagging and by providing a short description. Users interact with each other by forming groups of shared interests, following the status streams of each other, and by commenting the photos that have been shared. Inevitably, in the huge quantity of available media, some of these images are going to become very popular, while others are going to be totally unnoticed and end up in oblivion. Often, media may be popular because it conveys sentiments or it has a rich meaning in the social context it is put. In fact, sentiments have been known to affect popularity of visual media since the widespread watch of television programs [8]. Also, it was recently found to be related to popularity in tweets [1]. Being able to predict the popularity of a media may have a profound impact on several essential applications such as content retrieval and annotation, but also in other fields such as advertising and content distribution [9].

MM'15, October 26–30, 2015, Brisbane, Australia.

ACM 978-1-4503-3459-4/15/10 ...$15.00.
DOI: http://dx.doi.org/10.1145/2733373.2806361 .

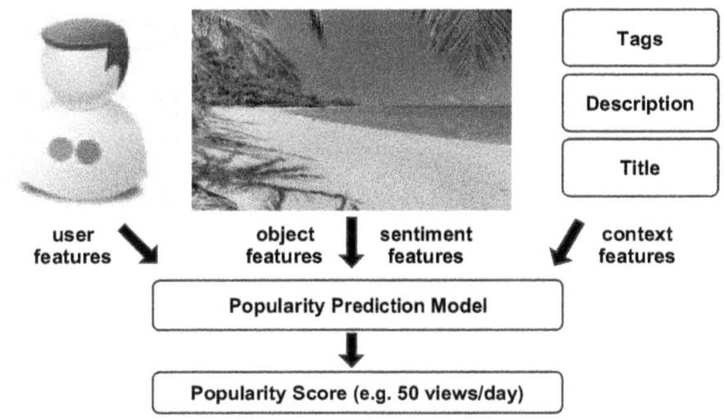

Figure 1: A schema of our approach to popularity prediction of images.

In this paper, we address the problem of predicting the popularity of an image posted in a social network, considering different scenarios that are typical of different situations. Despite the recent crop of literature that studies the question of what makes an image popular [12, 14, 16], none of these works addresses the question of how much the visual sentiment is influencing the popularity of media. As social context has been widely found important to predict media popularity [12], we show how to further improve popularity estimation by using a knowledge base to supplement the understanding of semantics in textual metadata.

The main contributions of this paper are:

- we propose to employ state-of-the-art visual sentiment features [2, 5] to perform image popularity prediction;
- we propose three new textual features based on a knowledge base, to better model the semantic description of an image, in addition to the social context features proposed in [12, 14];
- we show qualitative results of which sentiments seem to be related to a good or poor popularity.

To the best of our knowledge, this is the first work understanding specific visual concepts that positively or negatively influence the eventual popularity of images, beyond just numerical prediction of photo popularity.

Experiments performed on large scale datasets illustrate several benefits of the two types of proposed features, and show how their combination impacts effectively on the performance of popularity prediction.

2. RELATED WORK

Popularity Prediction. Recently, a significant effort has been spent on investigating popularity of social media content. Regarding image popularity, the majority of works agree that social features have the greatest predictive power [12, 14, 16]. Visual content features are less powerful than social ones in terms of predictive power, but they are useful when no user metadata is present (e.g. no tags or description) or to address scenarios such as the case in which no social interactions have been recorded before posting the image (e.g. because the user has just joined the social network). Previous works vary in terms of popularity score definition (e.g. image views, reshares, mean views over a period) but they all share the same basic pipeline: they extract several content and context related features and successively employ a regressor to compute the popularity score.

In [12], Khosla *et al.* investigate both low-level features such as color, GIST, LBP, and content features such as the object predictions and network activations of a state-of-the-art CNN image classifier [13]. Together with user and image context features, they show promising results. McParlane *et al.* [14] propose to use image content, context features and user context to predict popularity. Their analysis is limited to a cold start scenario, i.e. where there exist no or little textual or interaction data. Totti *et al.* [16] investigate the use of aesthetics features such as blur, aspect ratio and color channel statistics together with the output of 85 object classifiers as content features.

Visual Sentiment. A few works have addressed the problem of multimedia sentiment analysis of social network images. Starting from the 24 basic emotions of Plutchik's Wheel of Emotions [15], Borth *et al.* [2] have recently presented a large-scale visual sentiment ontology termed SentiBank. They train 3,244 detectors on pairs of nouns and adjectives (ANPs) based on a combination of global and local features. Based on the recent breakthrough of convolutional networks for classification [13], Chen *et al.* [5] used a CNN to replace SVM in the approach of Borth *et al.* [2], obtaining an improved accuracy on ANPs.

The authors in [6] proposed an hierarchical system able to handle sentiment concept classification and localization on objects. They found individual concept detector of SentiBank [2] less reliable for object-based concepts.

Chen *et al.* [7] studied the correlation between the intended publisher sentiment and the actual induced in the viewer ('viewer affect concept'). They aim to recommend appropriate images for the publisher by predicting in advance the induced sentiment in the viewer.

3. THE PROPOSED METHOD

Our proposed method is based on two hypotheses: *i)* the popularity of an image can be fueled by the inherent visual sentiments conveyed; *ii)* semantic descriptions of an image is also important for its popularity, since it makes it easier to be found or looked at.

3.1 Measuring Popularity

It is difficult to precisely define a single score as measure of popularity, and several ways have been proposed to measure it. Khoshla *et al.* [12] used the number of views on Flickr as the principal metric. McParlane *et al.* [14] consider both the number of views and the number of comments for each image as they have been found correlated in video popularity [4]. However they only aim to predict two classes of popularity: high or low.

In this work we follow Khoshla *et al.* [12] and consider the number of views on Flickr as popularity metric. To cope with the large variation of views, we divide the popularity metric by the difference of time between the user upload and our retrieval, then we apply the log function.

3.2 Visual Sentiment Features

To discover which visual emotions are roused from the visualization of an image, a visual sentiment concept classification is performed based on the Visual Sentiment Ontology (VSO). The ontology, consisting in a collection of 3,244 Adjective-Noun-Pairs (ANPs), has been defined by Borth *et al.* [2]. In particular we used DeepSentiBank [5]: a convolutional neural network pre-trained from [13] has been fine-tuned to classify images in one of a subset of 2,096 ANPs. Similarly to its previous version [2], this tool provides a mid-level representation of an image.

For each image we extract two descriptors that we term respectively SentANPs and FeatANPs: the ANPs prediction layer of 2,096d and the rectified activations of the 7th fully connected layer of 4,096d.

3.3 Object Features

Since image popularity is related also to the visual content of the image, we extract the convolutional neural networks features, initially proposed in [12]. A very deep CNN with 16 layers [3] was used to extract for each image the final output containing 1,000 objects from ILSVRC 2014 challenge (termed ObjOut) and the 4,096d representation of the 7th rectified fully connected layer (termed ObjFC7).

3.4 Context Features

Image context information such as tags and description contains important cues that may reflect on the number of views that an image obtains. Entities like people, locations or tourist attractions can affect popularity as *i)* people may be more interested in photographs referring some particular subject; *ii)* the presence of tags and description, the submission of a photo to some groups, etc. make it easier to be found by other users. The extraction of entities from image context strongly depends on the nature of the text, i.e. tags and textual description; due to the different nature of these channels, two different approaches are proposed.

Entity Extraction from Tags. Starting from image tags, we define two new context features that we term TagType and TagDomain. They both rely on Freebase, a large collaborative ontology containing millions of interconnected topics. Given a tag, a search for a *Freebase topic* is performed: if the tag is related to some topics, the most popular one is picked, according to Freebase popularity ranking. Meaningless tags that do not have a match in Freebase topics are ignored, thus they do not act as a nuisance. When a Freebase topic is retrieved, another query is performed to extract its *Freebase types* with the "notable" property and its *Freebase domain.* While *types* are mostly specific (e.g. Person, Author) *domains* cover broader areas (e.g. Film, Music).

Due to the vast number of types in the ontology, a smaller specific type knowledge base is introduced. We first randomly sampled 10k tags from MIR-Flickr dataset vocabulary [11] and used them to extract Freebase types. We select the 100 most frequent types as our specific knowledge base.

The extraction of TagType feature for an image is then straightforward: each tag is used to query Freebase for a notable type. We count the matches to the 100 selected types and obtain a 100d histogram as final feature.

Regarding the TagDomain feature, we take the full list of 78 domains pre-defined by Freebase curators and count the tag matches, similarly as TagType. Thus, the eventual TagDomain feature result in a 78d histogram.

Entity Extraction from description. Differently from the concise tags, image descriptions allow users to comprehensively detail their images in natural language. We seek to recognize subjects and objects of this text to detail context. Hence, we adopt a well known CRF-based language model to perform Named Entity Recognition (NER) [10]. We used the pre-trained 7-class model for MUC that is able to recognize Time, Location, Organization, Person, Money, Percent, Date. We count the occurrences for each class and build a 7d feature that we term NER_7.

3.5 User Features

Previous works have found that the number of views that a photograph is going to obtain depends not only on the image itself and its context information, but also on the author data. In this work we used the same user features proposed by Khosla *et al.* [12]: among these features the most related one to popularity is the mean views of the images of the user, as it represents the popularity of the user himself.

3.6 Popularity prediction

In order to predict popularity as a concise score, we used an off-the-shelf Support Vector Machine. As we are working with large-scale dataset, we used a L2 regularized L2 loss Support Vector Regression (SVR) from LIBLINEAR package due to its scalability with large sparse data and huge number of instances compared to a kernelized version.

4. EXPERIMENTS

As different scenarios show different aspects of popularity, we structure our experimental setups similarly to those of Khosla *et al.* [12], using Flickr social network. Two datasets were used to represent two different scenarios:

- *One-Per-User (OPU)*: we randomly selected 250k images from the VSO Flickr Dataset [2]. This dataset represents the scenario of a Flickr search, where images belong to different users.
- *User Specific (US)*: 25 users from the VSO Flickr Dataset are selected at random to constitute 25 different trials. For each one, 10k images are randomly selected. This dataset represent the scenario of a user that wants to select which of his pictures should be uploaded to attract the attention of other users.

In each experiment, we extract and concatenate the selected features. We freely provide the extracted features on our website. Multidimensional features are L2 normalized, while scalar attributes are scaled in the [0, 1] range. We split every dataset in training and evaluation: half was randomly chosen as training set, while the remaining images were equally split in validation and testing set. The C of SVM was set in the range $[0.001 - 100]$.

After the prediction, testing images are ranked in descending popularity scores and compared to the correct ranking obtained by the ground truth scores. The correlation between these two lists r and s is computed using *Spearman's rank correlation* that ranges in $[-1, 1]$:

$$\rho = \frac{\sum_i (r_i - \bar{r})(s_i - \bar{s})}{\sqrt{\sum_i (r_i - \bar{r})^2}\sqrt{\sum_i (s_i - \bar{s})^2}} \quad (1)$$

a score of 1 (or -1) corresponds to perfect (inverse) correlation, while 0 corresponds to random ranks.

4.1 Results

Experiments have been carried out for visual features, context ones and visual + context + user combination. We train a model with each single feature to show its predictive power. Then, we combine the features and compare a model with all of them against baselines implemented following the method of Khosla *et al.* [12] i.e. without our novel features. Results are reported in terms of *Spearman's rank correlation* and, for the User Specific dataset, the average scores between the 25 users are reported.

Visual Features. Visual content features include visual sentiment and object detections (Sec. 3.2, 3.3). The latter ones are used in this case as a baseline, including ObjOut and ObjFC7.

Dataset	SentANPs	FeatANPs	ObjOut	ObjFC7	Baseline	All
OPU	0.28	0.32	0.13	0.30	0.30	**0.36**
US	0.31	0.40	0.27	0.40	0.40	**0.43**

Table 1: Visual Features Results

Results are reported in Table 1: sentiment features are comparable with object features. As ANPs are learned starting from a similar network for classification, this suggests the existence of some correlation between them. Nevertheless, SentANPs is higher than ObjOut, suggesting that ANPs are better for popularity prediction than purely object classification. Our features are able to improve overall prediction in both scenarios.

Context Features. The performance of the proposed context features (Sec. 3.4) is compared with a baseline composed by the number of tags, the length of title and description (Table 2).

Dataset	TagType	TagDomain	NER_7	TagNum	TitleLen	DescLen	Baseline	All
OPU	0.42	0.36	0.50	0.55	0.22	0.48	0.61	**0.63**
US	0.44	0.37	0.13	0.23	0.17	0.20	0.33	**0.54**

Table 2: Context Features Results

Our features are comparable with other context-based ones in the OPU scenario. In the US scenario, all the features except TagType and TagDomain lose predictive power due to the limited context of a single user. This is because our features are able to better model semantically the single photos, regardless of the single user. When combined, our feature boost correlation to 0.54 from 0.33 of the baseline.

Visual + Context + User. In this experiment we combined visual, context and user features along with the total combination with and without our novel features. User features are added to resemble a state of the art pipeline. Each modality is singularly tested and finally combined together. Results are reported in Table 3. Note that User Features can't be used for the User Specific scenario as each model is trained for a single user.

User Features produce the highest correlation in the OPU scenario, confirming that popularity is highly related to the

Dataset	Method	Visual Content	Image Context	User Features	All
OPU	proposed	0.36	0.63	0.72	**0.76**
	baseline	0.30	0.61	0.72	0.74
US	proposed	0.43	0.54	n/a	**0.61**
	baseline	0.40	0.33	n/a	0.50

Table 3: Visual + Context + User Features Results

popularity of the author [12]. Despite this, the combination of the three modalities is helpful, boosting correlation from 0.72 to 0.74. Our features further improve upon this, bringing the value to 0.76. In the User Specific dataset, the improvement from the baseline is more pronounced, where a correlation of 0.61 vs 0.50 is obtained.

4.2 Qualitative Analysis

We investigate which specific ANP and semantic metadata correlated the most with the number of views of images. This analysis is performed for the One-Per-User scenario, as it aims to be as generic as possible. Fig. 2a shows the trained SVR weights for each of the 2089 ANPs, in descending order. According to the figure we split the visual sentiments in three categories.

A first group include those ANPs that have a positive impact on image popularity (e.g. *sexy legs*, *beautiful eyes*, *heavy rain*). The rapid drop evinces that a very short number of ANPs corresponds to strongly popular images in the training dataset. Then, we observe that some visual sentiments obtain very low weights, near zero: that ANPs are almost irrelevant to the number of views (e.g. *sunny trees*, *dry forest*). Finally a third group includes ANPs that are associated to a sufficiently negative score: the detection of those push an image towards unpopularity (e.g. *creepy eyes*, *silly clown*).

Extending our analysis to the 28 basic emotions of the Plutchick wheel, we found out that our model marked as unpopular those images that arouse emotions such as *annoyance* or *serenity*, while high scores are likely to be returned in case of sentiments as *amazement* or *ecstasy*. These last emotions derive from ANPs containing the adjective *sexy*, resulting in 10 occurrences in the top 35 visual emotions. A similar analysis on the 100 semantic entities is shown in Fig. 2b. This plot has a similar trend compared with that of visual sentiment, but for the extreme values: in this case the negatively weighted types (e.g. *religious practice* and *software genre*) have more prominent values than the positively weighted ones (e.g. *garment* and *film character*).

5. CONCLUSIONS

In this paper we proposed to employ state-of-the-art visual sentiment features and three new context features to address the problem of predicting whether an image posted on a social network may became popular. We are the first to show a qualitative analysis of which sentiments (as ANPs) are correlated to popularity. Our experiments suggest that some sentiments have a correlation with popularity, still smaller than user features. However, together with our novel context features, they have good prediction power, especially when user features are unavailable as in the User Specific scenario.

Acknowledgments. T. Uricchio is supported by Telecom Italia PhD grant funds and M. Bertini is partially supported by the "Social Museum and Smart Tourism" MIUR project (CTN01_00034_231545).

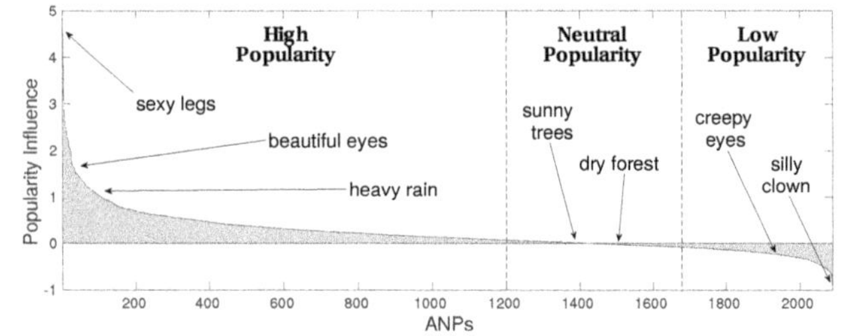

(a) Weights associated to the 2089 ANPs

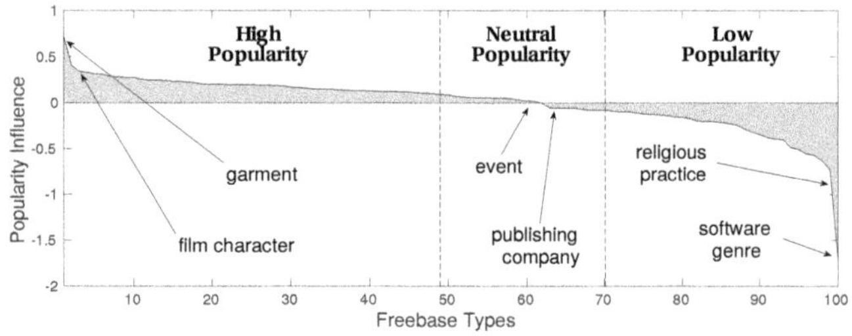

(b) Weights associated to the 100 Freebase Types

Figure 2: Influence of Multimedia Concepts on Popularity: weights of the 2089 ANP visual sentiment concepts *(top)*; weights of the 100 Freebase Types extracted from contextual image tags *(bottom)*.

6. REFERENCES

[1] Y. Bae and H. Lee. Sentiment analysis of Twitter audiences: Measuring the positive or negative influence of popular twitterers. *JASIST*, 63(12):2521–2535, 2012.

[2] D. Borth, R. Ji, T. Chen, T. Breuel, and S.-F. Chang. Large-scale visual sentiment ontology and detectors using adjective noun pairs. In *Proc. of ACM MM*, 2013.

[3] K. Chatfield, K. Simonyan, A. Vedaldi, and A. Zisserman. Return of the devil in the details: Delving deep into convolutional nets. In *Proc. of BMVC*, 2014.

[4] G. Chatzopoulou, C. Sheng, and M. Faloutsos. A first step towards understanding popularity in YouTube. In *Proc. of INFOCOM*, 2010.

[5] T. Chen, D. Borth, T. Darrell, and S.-F. Chang. DeepSentiBank: Visual sentiment concept classification with deep convolutional neural networks. *arXiv:1410.8586*, 2014.

[6] T. Chen, F. X. Yu, J. Chen, Y. Cui, Y.-Y. Chen, and S.-F. Chang. Object-based visual sentiment concept analysis and application. In *Proc. of ACM MM*, 2014.

[7] Y.-Y. Chen, T. Chen, W. H. Hsu, H.-Y. M. Liao, and S.-F. Chang. Predicting viewer affective comments based on image content in social media. In *Proc. of ICMR*, 2014.

[8] E. Diener and D. DeFour. Does television violence enhance program popularity? *JPSP*, 36(3):333, 1978.

[9] F. Figueiredo, J. M. Almeida, M. A. Gonçalves, and F. Benevenuto. On the dynamics of social media popularity: A YouTube case study. *TOIT*, 14(4):24, 2014.

[10] J. R. Finkel, T. Grenager, and C. Manning. Incorporating non-local information into information extraction systems by Gibbs sampling. In *Proc. of ACL*, 2005.

[11] M. Huiskes, B. Thomee, and M. Lew. New trends and ideas in visual concept detection: the MIR Flickr retrieval evaluation initiative. In *Proc. of ACM MIR*, 2010.

[12] A. Khosla, A. Das Sarma, and R. Hamid. What makes an image popular? In *Proc. of WWW*, 2014.

[13] A. Krizhevsky, I. Sutskever, and G. E. Hinton. Imagenet classification with deep convolutional neural networks. In *Proc. of NIPS*, 2012.

[14] P. J. McParlane, Y. Moshfeghi, and J. M. Jose. Nobody comes here anymore, it's too crowded; predicting image popularity on Flickr. In *Proc. of ACM ICMR*, 2014.

[15] R. Plutchik. The nature of emotions. *American Scientist*, 89(4):344–350, 2001.

[16] L. C. Totti, F. A. Costa, S. Avila, E. Valle, W. Meira Jr, and V. Almeida. The impact of visual attributes on online image diffusion. In *Proc. of WebSci*, 2014.

Subtle Facial Expression Recognition Using Adaptive Magnification of Discriminative Facial Motion

Sung Yeong Park
Image and Video Systems Lab
KAIST
Daejeon, Korea
clover200@kaist.ac.kr

Seung Ho Lee
Image and Video Systems Lab
KAIST
Daejeon, Korea
leesh09@kaist.ac.kr

Yong Man Ro*
Image and Video Systems Lab
KAIST
Daejeon, Korea
ymro@kaist.ac.kr

ABSTRACT

Recently, recognizing spontaneous facial expression has gained increasing attention in various emerging applications related to human affect. Generally, spontaneous facial expressions may have different temporal characteristics across subjects, emotion types, and so on. In this paper, we propose a facial expression recognition (FER) method, which adaptively magnifies a subtle facial motion based on its temporal characteristics. In the training stage, the relations between the temporal characteristics of facial motions and their corresponding discriminative temporal filters are learned. The learned model is used to automatically predict the most discriminative temporal filter, such that subtle facial motion can be magnified in a test sequence. Experimental results showed that the proposed FER using the adaptive motion magnification clearly performed better than a FER using non-adaptive motion magnification or a FER without motion magnification.

Categories and Subject Descriptors

I.4.9 [**Image Processing and Computer Vision**]: Applications

General Terms

Algorithms, Experimentation, Performance

Keywords

Subtle facial expression recognition (FER), adaptive motion magnification, facial dynamic

1. INTRODUCTION

Interpreting human facial expressions is the key to a wide range of applications related to human affect, as they constitute an important factor of communication, revealing cues about a person's mood, meaning, and emotion [6]. Previous works have made a great success in recognizing prototypical and deliberate (or posed) facial expressions captured under controlled conditions [7]. On the contrary, there have been relatively few attempts to recognize spontaneous facial expression. Nevertheless, it is becoming increasingly important because the current and future face-related applications lie in a more natural context [6][7] (e.g., replicating human-to-human communication to a large extent).

Spontaneous facial expression recognitions (FER) are significantly more challenging than posed ones [7]. In particular, subtle facial expressions appear on a small scale and are often difficult for human vision to perceive [3]. The subtlety of a facial expression makes the recognition less discriminative. Therefore, incorporating facial movement analysis is necessary for successful subtle FER, thus subtle expressions can be recognized in facial motion [1].

Recently, increasing research efforts have been made in subtle FER using facial dynamics [3][5]. The FER methods in [4][8] tried to improve subtle FER by exploiting a spatio-temporal descriptor such as the Local Binary Pattern Three Orthogonal Planes (LBP-TOP) [12]. However, as demonstrated in our experiment, such typical spatio-temporal descriptors are ineffective for subtle FER due to their low discriminating power in low intensity expression.

To obtain sufficient discriminative power in subtle facial dynamics, the methods in [3][5] have adopted a motion magnification scheme. In [5], the authors tried to emphasize the facial dynamic by magnifying feature point-region motion. In this method, a fixed universal magnification was applied to all feature point-region motions although subtle facial expressions have very different temporal characteristics due to their emotion type [11]. To address this issue, in [3], subtle expressions belonging to different emotion classes were magnified in different frequency bands pre-defined by the authors. In this method, the emotion class of a test sequence needs to be known prior to applying the motion magnification, which is not suitable for an automatic FER.

In this paper, we propose an automatic subtle FER method using adaptive magnification of discriminative facial motion. The main contribution of our paper is explained as follows.

Contribution: Considering that subtle expressions have various temporal characteristics, the proposed method learns the relation between the temporal characteristics of the facial expression and the frequency band needed for motion magnification. In the test stage, for a given test expression sequence, the learned model is used to adaptively select the most discriminative frequency band. The motion magnification within the selected frequency band can dominantly provide discriminative information (e.g., action unit [6] related information in Fig. 3), compared to the other frequency

*Corresponding author

MM '15, October 26–30, 2015, Brisbane, Australia

ACM 978-1-4503-3459-4/15/10 ...$15.00.
DOI: http://dx.doi.org/10.1145/2733373.2806362.

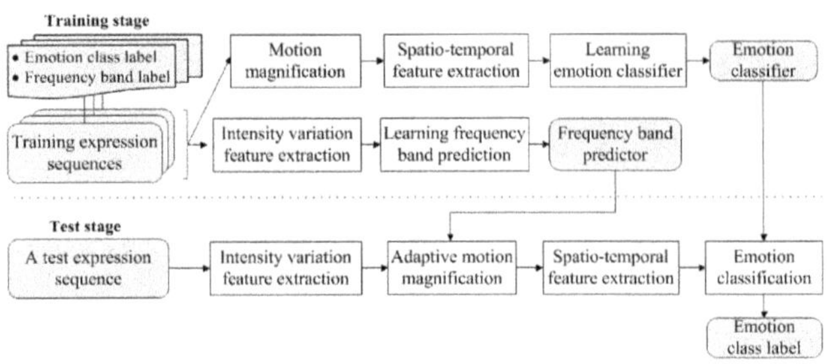

Figure 1: Overall framework of the proposed method

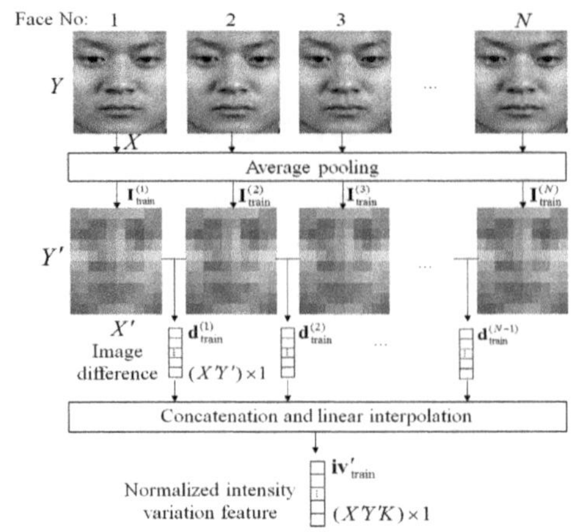

Figure 2: Intensity variation feature extraction for frequency band prediction

bands. Note that the proposed method does not require any prior knowledge for the test expression sequence. Thus, it can be suitable for an automatic subtle FER.

Through comparative experiments using CASME II database (DB) [10] consisting of spontaneous and subtle facial expression sequences, we observed that the proposed FER method using the adaptive motion magnification clearly performed better than the FER using a fixed (or non-adaptive) motion magnification as well as FER without motion magnification. In addition, we successfully verified that the proposed method yielded higher performance compared to other FER methods recently proposed for subtle FER.

The rest of this paper is organized as follows. Section 2 presents the proposed FER method, which consists of frequency band learning and FER using the selective motion magnification. Section 3 presents experimental setup and results. Conclusions of the paper are drawn in section 4.

2. PROPOSED METHOD

Fig. 1 shows the overall framework of the proposed subtle FER method. In the training stage, a frequency band predictor for the purpose of adaptive motion magnification is learned. The learning is performed using the intensity variation features and frequency band labels (pre-defined by the authors) of the training expression sequences. In addition, spatio-temporal features extracted from the training expression sequences are used for learning an emotion classifier. Before extracting the spatio-temporal features, the facial motions of the training expression sequences are magnified using the Eulerian motion magnification in [9].

In test stage, the learned frequency band predictor returns the discriminative frequency band label for a test sequence for the intensity variation feature of a test expression sequence. According to the predicted frequency band label, the facial motion of the test sequence is adaptively magnified, followed by a spatio-temporal feature extraction. The spatio-temporal feature is fed into the learned emotion classification, which yields an emotion class label (e.g., surprise). Detailed descriptions about learning the frequency band predictor and the emotion classification using the adaptive motion magnification are given in the following subsections.

2.1 Learning automatic frequency band prediction for adaptive motion magnification

This section describes the learning of automatic frequency band predictor using training expression sequences. Let $\mathbf{V}_{train} \in \Re^{X \times Y \times Z}$ denote the spatio-temporal volume of an expression sequence in the training set. Herein, X, Y, and N are the width, height, and the number of the faces in the spatio-temporal volume, respectively. To capture the temporal characteristics of the facial motion from the spatio-temporal volume $\mathbf{V}_{train}$, the intensity variation feature is obtained by calculating the difference between consecutive faces as illustrated in Fig. 2, in order to extract features related to the Eulerian motion [9]. To achieve robustness against face misalignments, each $X \times Y$ face is resized to $X' \times Y'$ pixels using an average pooling where $X > X'$ and $Y > Y'$. The m-th ($m = 1, ..., N$) resized face in the spatio-temporal volume $\mathbf{V}_{train}$ is denoted by $\mathbf{I}^{(m)}_{train} \in \Re^{X' \times Y'}$. To extract intensity variation information, the image difference ($\mathbf{D}^{(m)}_{train} \in \Re^{X' \times Y'}$) is computed between the consecutive faces ($\mathbf{I}^{(m+1)}_{train}$ and $\mathbf{I}^{(m)}_{train}$) as $\mathbf{D}^{(m)}_{train} = \mathbf{I}^{(m+1)}_{train} - \mathbf{I}^{(m)}_{train}$ ($m = 1, ..., N$). Then, the vectorized image difference $\mathbf{d}^{(m)}_{train} \in \Re^{(X'Y') \times 1}$ of $\mathbf{D}^{(m)}_{train}$ is obtained. After that, the vectorized image differences $\mathbf{d}^{(m)}_{train}$ ($m = 1, ..., N$) are concatenated to form an intensity variation feature $\mathbf{iv}_{train} \in \Re^{(X'Y'(N-1)) \times 1}$ for the spatio-temporal volume $\mathbf{V}_{train}$ as follows:

$$\mathbf{iv}_{train} = [(\mathbf{d}^{(1)}_{train})^T (\mathbf{d}^{(2)}_{train})^T ... (\mathbf{d}^{(N-1)}_{train})^T]^T. \quad (1)$$

Note that, in (1), the number of dimensions in $\mathbf{iv}_{train}$ may vary across training expression sequences due to the different number N of faces. To unify the number of dimensions of the feature, each $\mathbf{iv}_{train}$ is linearly interpolated such that we obtain a constant dimension $(X'Y'K) \times 1$ of the normalized intensity variation feature $\mathbf{iv}'_{train} \in \Re^{(X'Y'K) \times 1}$.

Once the normalized intensity variation feature is extracted from every training expression sequence, the frequency band predictor is learned as follows. We manually categorize each training expression sequence as one out of the five frequency bands defined in Table 1. To define them, each sequence was magnified with the five frequency bands. Accordingly, the frequency that corresponds to the most discriminative magnified motion appearance in terms of action unit (e.g., AU14 in Fig. 3(b)) is selected. Note that the highest frequency cutoff 10.0 Hz is determined based on the fact that a facial expression duration does not exceed 100 ms [11]. Using the pairs of the normalized intensity variation feature $\mathbf{iv}'_{train}$ and their frequency band labels, the relations between the temporal characteristics of the facial motion and their dominant temporal frequency are learned. To that end, we train a five-class support vector machine (SVM) classifier [2]. For training SVM classifier, radial basis function (RBF) kernel

Table 1: Five frequency bands used for motion magnification

frequency band label f	Frequency range(Hz)
$f = 1$	0.1-3.0
$f = 2$	1.0-4.5
$f = 3$	2.5-6.0
$f = 4$	4.0-7.5
$f = 5$	5.5-10.0

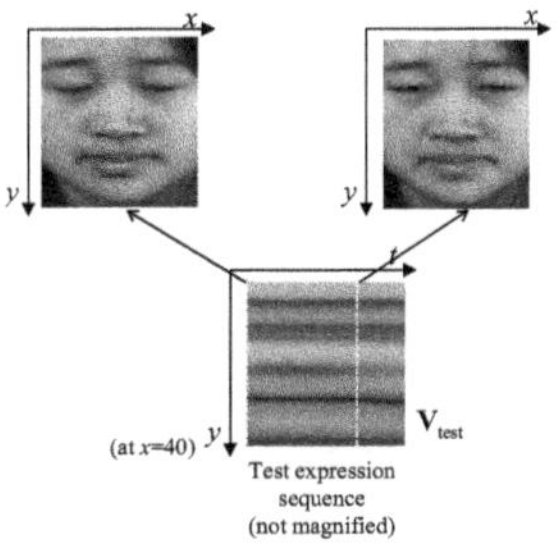

(a)

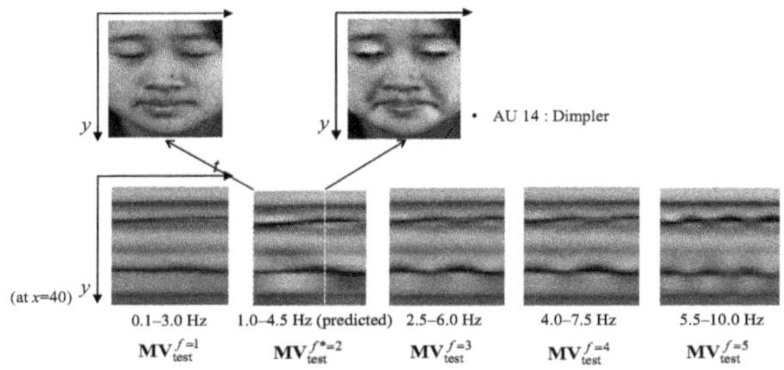

(b)

Figure 3: Effectiveness of the adaptive motion magnification. (a) Motion appearances without magnification. y-t planes at x=40 are illustrated as an example. Face image size is 134 (width) x 163 (height) pixels. (b) Motion appearances magnified in different frequency bands.

[2] is used. The SVM classifier is used as the frequency band predictor for adaptive motion magnification based emotion classification which will be explained in Section 2.2.

2.2 Emotion classification using adaptive motion magnification

In this section, we describe the prediction of the discriminative frequency band and the emotion classification based on the adaptive motion magnification for a test expression sequence. In an expression sequence, multiple action units can occur additively. Their intensities may vary simultaneously and can be confined in a particular frequency range. Hence, we select the most probable frequency band as follows. Let $\mathbf{V}_{test}$ denote the spatio-temporal volume of the test expression sequence. To predict the frequency band, the normalized intensity variation feature $\mathbf{iv}'_{test}$ is extracted from $\mathbf{V}_{test}$. The extraction of the intensity variation feature $\mathbf{iv}'_{test}$ is achieved in a similar way to $\mathbf{iv}'_{train}$. The trained frequency band predictor takes $\mathbf{iv}'_{test}$ as the input and selects the frequency band label(f^*) out of the five frequency band labels ($f = 1, ..., 5$):

$$f^* = \underset{f=1,\dots,5}{argmax} P_f(\mathbf{iv}'_{test}) \quad (2)$$

where $P_f(\mathbf{iv}'_{test})$ is a function that returns the SVM confidence score for the f-th frequency band.

Figure 4: Face images example of apex frames

The temporal bandpass filter associated with the selected frequency band f^* is utilized to amplify the discriminative facial motion in the spatio-temporal volume $\mathbf{V}_{test}$. For details on motion magnification using the selected frequency band, please refer to [9]. The magnified spatio-temporal volume for $\mathbf{V}_{test}$ is denoted by $\mathbf{MV}^{f^*}_{test}$. Fig. 3(b) shows examples of the motion appearance magnifications in five different frequency bands for a given test expression sequence in Fig. 3(a). As can be seen, the magnification in the predicted frequency band ($f^* = 2$, i.e., 1.0-4.5 Hz) can successfully emphasize the informative facial motion (related to AU 14: Dimpler). On the other hand, for the case of the other frequency bands, the magnification is not clearly visible (e.g., 0.1-3.0 Hz) or looks noisy (e.g., 5.5-10.0 Hz).

From the magnified spatio-temporal volume $\mathbf{MV}^{f^*}_{test}$, the spatio-temporal descriptor is extracted. The widely used LBP-TOP [12] is adopted for the spatio-temporal descriptor. The spatio-temporal descriptor is fed into another multiclass SVM classifier with an RBF kernel learned for emotion classification. The classifier determines the emotion class label of the spatio-temporal volume $\mathbf{V}_{test}$.

3. EXPERIMENT

To verify the proposed method, CASME II database (DB) [10] was utilized. The DB contains 247 spontaneous and subtle expression sequences of 26 subjects. Each expression sequence was categorized as one of five emotion classes (i.e., Happiness, Disgust, Repression, Surprise, and Others). In our experiment, we used the sequences of the cropped face images available in [10]. Each face image was resized to 134 (width)$\times$168 (height) pixels. As shown in Fig. 4, the face images contain very low expression intensities even at apex frames, which make the FER less discriminative. For the extraction of the intensity variation feature, each face image was resized to a 12$\times$12 face image (i.e., $X' = Y' = 12$). For the the extraction of spatio-temporal descriptor, the radius for each plane was set to 1, 1, and 4 as recommended in [10]. A one-versus-all SVM was used for the five-class emotion classifier. The magnification factor was set to 10.

In the first experiment, we aimed to verify the effectiveness of the adaptive motion magnification scheme for subtle FER. For comparison, three FER methods were presented: 1) Without MM: FER with LBP-TOP features extracted from the non-magnified spatio-temporal volume, 2) Non-adaptive MM: FER with LBP-TOP features extracted from the magnified spatio-temporal volume with a fixed frequency range from 0.1 to 10.0 Hz (that covers almost all of facial motion), and in five frequency ranges each of which corresponds to a frequency band label ($f = 1, ..., 5$), 3) Adaptive MM (proposed): FER with LBP-TOP feature extracted from the proposed magnified spatio-temporal volume with adaptively selected frequency bands. In this experiment, leave-one-subject-out cross validation was adopted for the subject-independent FER evaluation. The results are given in Table 2. We can see that the FER using motion magni-

Table 2: Comparison of recognition rate among three different kinds of motion magnification(MM) methods in Leave-one-subject-out method

FER Method	Recognition rate(%)
Without MM	44.12
Non-adaptive MM (0.1 - 10.0Hz)	48.99
Non-adaptive MM ($f = 1$)	46.15
Non-adaptive MM ($f = 2$)	45.75
Non-adaptive MM ($f = 3$)	46.15
Non-adaptive MM ($f = 4$)	42.92
Non-adaptive MM ($f = 5$)	45.75
Adaptive MM (proposed)	**51.91**

Table 3: Comparison with recently proposed subtle FER methods in Leave-one-sample-out method

FER Method	Recognition rate(%)
Method in [4]	66.40
Method in [8]	67.21
Without MM	60.73
Non-adaptive MM	66.80
Adaptive MM (proposed)	**69.63**

cation (e.g., Non-adaptive MM or Adaptive MM) is able to improve the performance of the FER without using motion magnification. This is because both temporal and spatial discriminating capabilities can be improved by magnifying spatio-temporal volume. We can also see that the proposed adaptive motion magnification is more effective than the non-adaptive motion magnification. FER using the motion magnification in the adaptively selected frequency band of f^* yields constantly higher recognition rates than FER using the motion magnification in one out of six frequency bands. This is due to the fact that the adaptive motion magnification is related to two characteristics of the facial motion. First, as shown in Fig. 3, the discriminative information of a facial motion can be confined within a particular narrow range (e.g., 1.0-4.5 Hz) of frequencies rather than a whole range of frequencies (e.g., 0.1-10.0 Hz). Second, discriminative frequency band is different across the facial motions. Indeed, the proposed method differently selected the discriminative frequency bands for obtaining the result in Table 2. The proportions of selected frequency bands $f = 1, 2, 3, 4, 5$ were 13.3%, 38.0%, 30.2%, 11.8%, 6.7%, respectively.

The goal of the second experiment was to compare the proposed FER method with recently proposed subtle FER methods. For fair comparisons, leave-one-sample-out cross validation was adopted as in [4] and [8]. For the comparison purposes, the performance of the methods in [4][8] were presented. In addition, FER without using motion magnification and FER with non-adaptive motion magnification were also presented as baselines. The comparison results are illustrated in Table 3. Compared to the competing subtle methods in [4][8], the proposed FER method yielded an improved and a feasible recognition rate of around 70%. Further, in comparison with the baseline methods, similar tendencies were obtained as in Table 2, demonstrating the effectiveness of the proposed adaptive motion magnification.

4. CONCLUSIONS

This paper proposed a dynamic based subtle facial expression recognition (FER) method. The proposed FER method made use of adaptive scheme to select the most discriminative temporal filter to magnify subtle facial motion to be recognized in the FER stage. To select the most discriminative temporal filter, the relations between appearance varying over time and its dominant frequency band were learned in advance. Experimental results on a subtle and spontaneous expression dataset showed that the proposed adaptive scheme was able to improve discriminating power of motion magnification. For future work, a more rigorous evaluation of the proposed method is to be conduct on additional datasets of spontaneous facial expression.

5. ACKNOWLEDGEMENTS

The authors would like to thank Wissam J. Baddar for his valuable comments and suggestions. This work was supported by the National Research Foundation of Korea (NRF) grant funded by the Korea government (MSIP) (No. 2015R1A2A2A01005724).

6. REFERENCES

[1] Z. Ambadar, J. W. Schooler, and J. F. Cohn. Deciphering the enigmatic face the importance of facial dynamics in interpreting subtle facial expressions. *Psychological Science*, 16(5):403–410, 2005.

[2] C. J. Burges. A tutorial on support vector machines for pattern recognition. *Data mining and knowledge discovery*, 2(2):121–167, 1998.

[3] S. Gogia and R. Liu. Motion magnification of facial micro-expressions. 2014.

[4] S.-T. Liong, J. See, R. C.-W. Phan, A. C. Le Ngo, Y.-H. Oh, and K. Wong. Subtle expression recognition using optical strain weighted features. In *Computer Vision-ACCV 2014 Workshops*, pages 644–657. Springer, 2014.

[5] S. Park and D. Kim. Subtle facial expression recognition using motion magnification. *Pattern Recognition Letters*, 30(7):708–716, 2009.

[6] G. Sandbach, S. Zafeiriou, M. Pantic, and D. Rueck. A dynamic approach to the recognition of 3d facial expressions and their temporal models. In *Automatic Face & Gesture Recognition and Workshops (FG 2011), 2011 IEEE International Conference on*, pages 406–413. IEEE, 2011.

[7] S. Wan and J. Aggarwal. Spontaneous facial expression recognition: A robust metric learning approach. *Pattern Recognition*, 47(5):1859–1868, 2014.

[8] Y. Wang, J. See, R. C.-W. Phan, and Y.-H. Oh. Lbp with six intersection points: Reducing redundant information in lbp-top for micro-expression recognition. In *Computer Vision–ACCV 2014*, pages 525–537. Springer, 2015.

[9] H.-Y. Wu, M. Rubinstein, E. Shih, J. V. Guttag, F. Durand, and W. T. Freeman. Eulerian video magnification for revealing subtle changes in the world. *ACM Trans. Graph.*, 31(4):65, 2012.

[10] W.-J. Yan, X. Li, S.-J. Wang, G. Zhao, Y.-J. Liu, Y.-H. Chen, and X. Fu. Casme ii: An improved spontaneous micro-expression database and the baseline evaluation. *PloS one*, 9(1), 2014.

[11] W.-J. Yan, Q. Wu, J. Liang, Y.-H. Chen, and X. Fu. How fast are the leaked facial expressions: The duration of micro-expressions. *Journal of Nonverbal Behavior*, 37(4):217–230, 2013.

[12] G. Zhao and M. Pietikainen. Dynamic texture recognition using local binary patterns with an application to facial expressions. *Pattern Analysis and Machine Intelligence, IEEE Transactions on*, 29(6):915–928, 2007.

"Clustering of Dancelets" – Towards Video Recommendation Based on Dance Styles

Tingting Han, Hongxun Yao, Xiaoshuai Sun, Yanhao Zhang, Sicheng Zhao, Xiusheng Lu, Yinghao Huang, Wenlong Xie
School of Computer Science and Technology, Harbin Institute of Technology, China.
{ttinghan,h.yao, xiaoshuaisun, yhzhang, zsc,xiusheng.lu}@hit.edu.cn

ABSTRACT

Dance is a special and important type of action, composed of abundant and various action elements. However, the recommendation of dance videos on the web are still not well studied. It is hard to realize it in the way of traditional methods using associated texts or static features of video content. In this paper, we study the problem focusing on extraction and representation of action information in dances. We propose to recommend dance videos based on the automatically discovered "Dance Styles", which play a significant role in characterizing different types of dances. To bridge the semantic gap of video content and mid-level concept, style, we take advantage of a mid-level action representation method, and extract representative patches as "Dancelets", a sort of intermediation between videos and the concepts. Furthermore, we propose to employ Motion Boundaries as saliency priors and sparsely extract patches containing more representative information to generate a set of dancelet candidates. Dancelets are then discovered by Normalized-cut method, which is superior in grouping visually similar patterns into the same clusters. For the fast and effective recommendation, a random forest-based index is built, and the ranking results are derived according to the matching results in all the leaf notes. Extensive experiments validated on the web dance videos demonstrate the effectiveness of the proposed methods for dance style discovery and video recommendation based on styles.

Categories and Subject Descriptors

H.3.3 [**Information storage and retrieval**]: Information Search and Retrieval; I.4.7 [**Image processing and computer vision**]: Feature Measurement

Keywords

Video Recommendation; Dance Style; Dancelets Mining; Normalized-cut; Random Forest-based Index

1. INTRODUCTION

Video recommendation is becoming a more and more important task with the explosive increase of video data on the Internet.

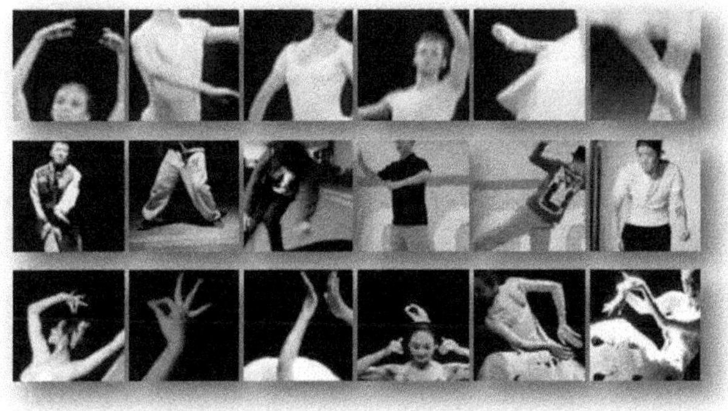

Figure 1: Illustration of dance styles. Top are the patches that reflect styles of Ballet. Middle are the symbolic actions of Popping Dance. Bottom are representative dance element of Chinese folk dance Peacock Dance.

Many existing algorithms for video recommendation tended to collectively model relevance of multimodal content and user feedback [6] [14]. Cui et al. [2] attempted to address the video recommendation by learning a common attributed representation for users and videos in social media with good interpretability. Although some of these methods take into consideration of video content, they use only static features but ignore motion information of videos. As a consequence, it is hard to realize recommendation of dance videos, where the motion components account for the most primary part in the way of traditional video recommendation methods. To this end, we aim to solve this problem by sufficiently exploiting the intrinsic action clues in dances video.

Each type of dances is usually composed of a series of unique and representative action elements. For example, as illustrated in Figure 1, we can easily name Ballet as we see the "tiptoes" or "arm positions", while Popping can be easily recognized by "robot-like actions" "body vibrations" generated by the quick contraction and relaxation of muscles. By contrast, "peacock-like hand gestures" is the most discriminative element in Chinese folk Peacock dance. Sometimes it is hard to describe these unique action elements by languages, but is easy to distinguish by visual content, and we name them "Dance Styles". Such a mid-level concept plays a vital role in distinguishing different types of dances. Therefore, in this paper, we first present an algorithm to automatically discover dance styles from user click videos. And then implement video recommendation based on the mined dance styles. To capture styles in dances, we employ a mid-level patch based representation to describe actions. On the one hand, compared with low-level STIP [5] or Dense Trajectory [11] based representations, it retains more visual con-

MM'15, October 26–30, 2015, Brisbane, Australia.
© 2015 ACM. ISBN 978-1-4503-3459-4/15/10 ...$15.00.
DOI: http://dx.doi.org/10.1145/2733373.2806363.

tent and semantic information. On the other hand, the relation to mid-level "style" concept can be built more easily compared with high-level action representation [8].

In view of above, our work (1) uses mid-level patches, named Dancelets, to build bridges between space-time visual content and mid-level semantic concept "styles". Instead of densely sampling, the dancelets candidates are sparsely extracted under guidance of motion boundary-based salient clues to reduce time complexity; (2) automatically discover representative dancelets from a small group of "user click videos" benefitting from an effective spectral clustering method; and (3) recommend style-specific dance videos based on a random forest-based index. The ranking results are generated by the voted scores of matchings in the leaves of the random forest, which has been proved to be efficient and effective.

2. METHOD

The framework of the proposed video recommendation method based on dance styles is shown in Figure 2. Firstly, we utilize motion boundary as a clue to detect dancelets candidates, and multiple features are used to describe these candidates. In the process of dance style mining, Normalized-cut is exploited to partition these candidates into multiple clusters with similar visual and motion patterns, based on which a set of dancelets are selected. To rank videos in database, a random forest-based index is build considering both effectiveness and time efficiency.

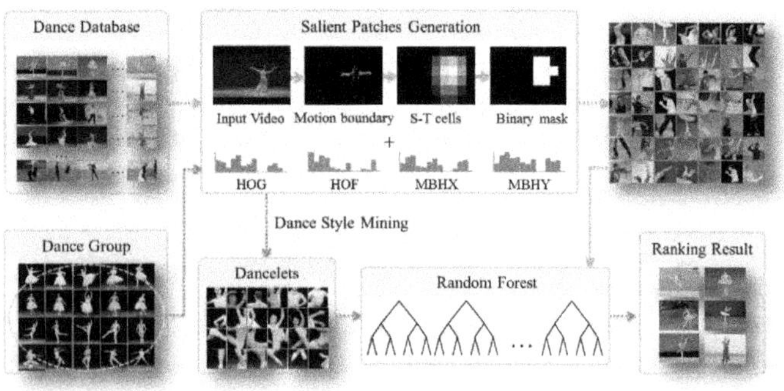

Figure 2: The framework of the proposed method.

2.1 Dancelet Candidates Generation

2.1.1 *Salient Patches Extraction*

The idea of exploiting motion boundary to guide the detection of salient regions in dance videos is motivated by the success of MBH descriptor in the task of action recognition [11] recently. It has been proved that motion boundary has superior capability in suppressing camera motion [11]. Besides, the sparse sampling based on motion boundary is conductive to improve time efficiency [7]. In our implementation, we fusion motion boundaries derived from two flow components F^x, F^y as the motion saliency map, M. Then, a grid of overlapping spatial-temporal cells was placed in the motion saliency map and the saliency value of a cell is calculated by summing all the values in the cell:

$$S(\Psi) = \frac{1}{\| \Psi \|} \sum_{(i,j,t \in \Psi)} M(i,j,t), \tag{1}$$

Based on that, a threshold δ was set to generate a binary mask:

$$B(\Psi) = \begin{cases} 1 & if\ S(\Psi) > \delta, \\ 0 & otherwise. \end{cases} \tag{2}$$

In this way, we obtain a set of salient spatial-temporal dancelet candidates. In practice, we set δ as 0.6 times of saliency maximum in the current temporal window. And the size of each cell is fixed to $80 \times 80 \times 20$ uniformly, with overlapping of 50, 50, 10 in three directions, respectively.

2.1.2 *Feature Representation*

We consider three descriptors to represent the extracted dancelet candidates, gradient and optical flow histograms(**HOG**, **HOF**)and motion boundary histograms(**MBH**), which have been widely used and proved to be effective on many datasets [5] [3] [11]. **HOG** abstracts appearance information including poses and clothes, meantime, **HOF** and **MBH** focus on the motion information of dance actions. Moreover, **MBH** has superior property of eliminating camera movements. In the implementation, we refer to the method and code proposed in [10]. But instead of using dense sampling, we extract features in the salient patches. In each patch, we further divide it into blocks of size $8 \times 8 \times 4$. Then for each descriptor, **HOG/HOF/MBHX/MBHY**, the magnitude is quantized in 8 orientations. Thus, the total dimension of feature in one dancelet candidate is 8192 (i.e. $8 \times 8 \times 4 \times 8 \times 4$). In the calculation of optical flow, the employed method is the classical Horn-Schunk algorithm [1].

2.2 Dance Style Mining

To discover dancelets from the set of candidates, we adopt a graph-based clustering method, named Normalized Cut(N-cut), to automatically cluster the candidates into K groups. Benefitting from its advantage of solving the clustering of non-convex sphere of sample spaces and obtaining the global optimal clustering. The N-cut algorithm treat all the dancelet candidates as a set of vertices V, the connection between any two vertices i, j is weighted by their similarity, which is given by the element (i,j) of similarity affinity matrix W. Here, W is obtained based on Euclidean distance.

Given the weighted undirected graph $G = (V, E, W)$, The K-way normalized cuts [13] aims to partition the vertices set V into K disjoint sets, i.e., $V = \cup_{l=1}^{K} V_l$ and $V_k \cap V_l = \phi, \forall k \neq l$. Then the K-way partitioning can be denoted by $\Gamma_V^K = \{V_1, \cdots, V_K\}$.

The partition is solved by a optimization problem, i.e. solving Equ. 3, where $linkratio(V_l, V \backslash V_l)$ measures how many links escape from V_l. Benefitting from N-cut, we get a clustering satisfying both tight connections within partitions and loose connections between partitions.

$$minimize = \frac{1}{K} \sum_{l=1}^{K} linkratio(V_l, V \backslash V_l). \tag{3}$$

Empirically, the parameter K is adjustable to control the amount of patches in each cluster to be about 100. After discarding clusters with very few patches, we randomly select l patches as dancelets in each group. These dancelets represent elements that commonly appear in dances videos and can be viewed as embodiments of a certain style. The discovered dancelets results in several Chinese folk dances are visually displayed in Figure 3.

2.3 Styles-based Dance Recommendation

Based on the dance styles discovered in Section 2.2, we rank the dance videos in the database according to the statistic scores of patches that match with the dancelets representing a specific style. In order to get this goal, a random forest based index construc-

Figure 3: Dancelets of four Chinese folk dances discovered by the proposed method. It can be seen that the dancelets of different types of dance indeed imply various "Style" concepts. As shown in Dai Dance, the "bend arms" and "twisted waist" are the most important characteristics. And the style of Mongolia Dance tend to be ebullience and magnanimous, characterized by actions such as "shoulder shaking" and "palming". Whereas, Uyghur Dance is consist of action elements such as "neck moving" and "filliping'. And rhythmical flexible body actions are the most representative style of Chinese Classical Dance.

Algorithm 1 Dance Style Indexing based on Random Forest.

Input: $S = \{x_i\}_{i=1}^{N_D}, K, R, MaxDepth;$
Output: Random forest $F = \{T\{1\}, C\{2\}, \cdots, T\{K\}\};$
for $t = 1 : K$ **do**
  initialize a tree $T\{t\}$ with only the root (S);
  for $d = 1 : MaxDepth$ **do**
    for $r = 1 : R$ **do**
      Generate the index of feature dimensions $e1$ and $e2$;
      Compute "feature difference" $D_r = x_i\{e_1\} - x_i\{e_2\}, i = 1, 2, \cdots, N_D$, and its variance;
    end for
    Set the mean of D_r' with the largest variance as the split criterion, and split the father nodes into two child nodes;
  end for
end for
return $F = \{T\{1\}, C\{2\}, \cdots, T\{K\}\}$.

---

tion[12][4] is adopted in consideration of both the effectiveness and time efficiency. The building process of random forest-based index is given by Algorithm 1. The algorithm treat the set of input dancelets S as the root and randomly generate splitting rules and partition the father node into two children nodes until reaching the maximum depth. The random splitting aims to select two dimensions on which the representations have the widest distribution and the most discrimination. Therefore, each splitting can be viewed as a partition of the feature space, and eventually results in leaves including patches with similar features.

Then, the discovered dancelets are put into the random forest to match their nearest neighbors in the feature space and vote the dances in the database according to the matching scores. Furthermore, we build multiple random trees to eliminate negative impact of random partition of feature space of one tree. In practice, the number of random trees, K, is set to 4, the random times, R, is set to 2000 taking the high dimension of the feature vector into account, and the parameter $MaxDepth$ is set according to the total number of extracted salient patches in the database. Based on the index, the rank score can be easily obtained by counting the matched patches with the dancelets of a group of user clicked dance videos. Note that, in the process of ranking database videos, factors such as various lengths of videos and uneven partition of feature space are considered and therefore a normalized voting are performed.

3. EXPERIMENTS

3.1 Data Collection and Evaluation Criteria

We have collected multiple dance videos from the Internet for dance style discovery, including Ballet [1], Street Dance and several kinds of Chinese folk dances (Dai Dance, Mongolia Dance, Uyghur Dance and Chinese Classical Dance). These dance groups are of small sizes with total lengths ranging from 5 to 15 minutes, because when the users are surfing on the searching web the recommender should give recommendation based on a small amount of video clicks. To validate the effectiveness of the proposed dance styles based video recommendation method, we collect another set of dance videos with various styles. All the videos are uniformly resized to 320×240 in the experiments.

We use Average Precision at N (AP@N) to evaluate the recommendation ranking results. It is commonly used in evaluating the ranking performance of information retrieval system. AP@N represents the average precision of a query, revealing its position-sensitive ranking precision within N^{th} position[9].

3.2 Results and Discussion

We mine dance styles from multi-group dance videos of different types and then perform recommendation based on the styles. The ranking results are further evaluated by AP@N. We compare normalized voting which taking inconsistent factors into consideration to common voting strategy and the quantitative AP@N curves for two types of dance groups are shown in Figure 4 and Figure 5, respectively. Figure 4 shows the results for Popping Dance. It is indicated that both two voting strategies recommend videos with related or similar dance style in top 6 returned results and therefore the AP@N values remain at 1. And the AP@12 for the these two strategies are 92.7% and 90.8%, respectively, which demonstrate the effectiveness of the proposed dance video recommendation method based on styles. Moreover, comparing the two voting strategies, it reveals that it is of great significance to exclude inconsistent factors and so the normalized voting get better results. Similar result is gained for Chinese folk Uyghur Dance, as shown in Figure 5, where both two voting strategies recommend style-related video in top 1 returned result and so both the AP@1 values stand at 1 at this point, and AP@12 are 57.2% and 53.0% for two voting strategies, respectively. It once again proves that normalized voting is more effective compared with common voting strategy.

[1]https://www.cs.sfu.ca/research/groups/VML/semilatent/

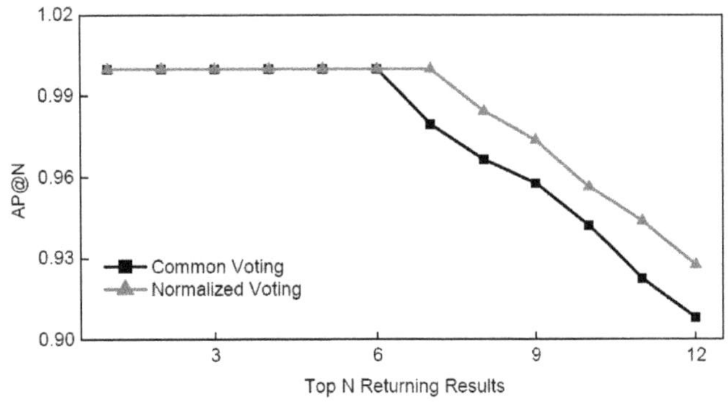

Figure 4: AP@N of recommendation result of Popping Dance.

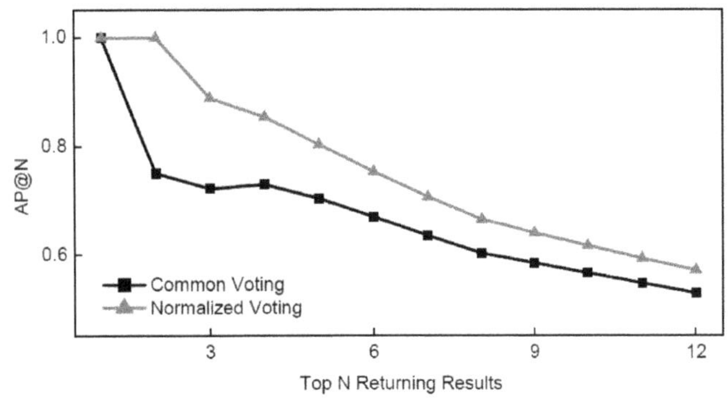

Figure 5: AP@N of recommendation result of Uyghur Dance.

The qualitative recommendation result of Popping Dance is shown in Figure 6, where the left is the set of dancelets discovered by the proposed style mining method from a small group of user click videos, and the right is the returned top 6 videos with normalized voting. It can be found that all the top 6 recommended videos share the same dance style with the query dances. Moreover, it proves that the proposed dancelets discovery method is capable to connect the spatial-temporal video data with the mid-level sementic concept "style" and can effectively mine representative and discriminative dacelets from raw videos.

To further demenstrate the effectiveness of the style mining, we also display several samples from multiple clusters generated by Normalized-cut in Figure7, from which it can be seen that patterns grouped into the same clusters usually have the same or similar visual and motion elements. For example, in Cluster #1, all the patches reflect actions of upper bodies, and patches in Cluster #K are all related with movement of feet.

4. CONCLUSION

In this paper, we have investigated the problem of dance video recommendation focusing on intrinsical action components in dance video data. We have proposed a mid-level semantic concept named "Dance Style", based on which the relevance of database videos to a group of user click videos are measured. Instead of enumerating all the possible styles potentially existing in vast and divergent dances, the styles are automatically discovered based on the Normalized-cut clustering method. Besides, a random forest-based index has been built and utilized to realize fast matching of styles and to get the ranking of videos. The experimental results show the effectiveness of the proposed method.

Figure 6: Illustration of top 6 video recommendation results (the right) based on the discovered dancelets (the left) from "Popping" dance.

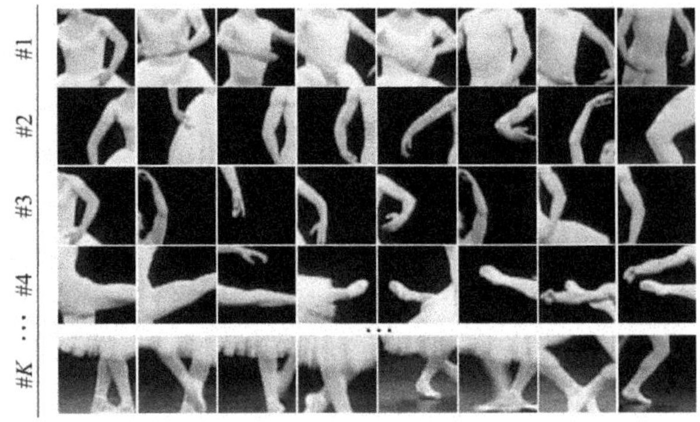

Figure 7: Demonstration of patches that are grouped into one clusters by Normalized-cut clustering method. Each row corresponds to one cluster.

5. ACKNOWLEDGMENTS

This work was supported by the National Natural Science Foundation of China (No. 61472103) and Key Program (No. 61133003).

6. REFERENCES

[1] H. B and S. B. Determining optical flow. *Artificial Intelligence*, 17:185–203, 1981.

[2] P. Cui, Z. Wang, and Z. Su. What videos are similar with you? learning a common attributed representation for video recommendation. In *MM*, 2014.

[3] N. Dalal, B. Triggs, and C. Schmid. Human detection using oriented histograms of flowand appearance. In *ECCV*, 2006.

[4] T. Han, H. Yao, Y. Zhang, and P. Xu. A spatial-temporal constraint-based action recognition method. In *ICIP*, pages 2767–2771, 2013.

[5] I. Laptev, M. Marszalek, C. Schmid, and B. Rozenfeld. Learning realistic human actions from movies. In *CVPR*, pages 1–8, 2008.

[6] T. Mei, B. Yang, X.-S. Huan, and S. Li. Contextual video recommendation by multimodal relevance and user feedback. *ACM Transactions on Information Systems*, 29:1–24, 2011.

[7] X. Peng, Y. Qiao, and Q. Peng. Motion boundary based sampling and 3d co-occurrence descriptors for action recognition. *Image and Vision Computing*, 32:616–628, 2014.

[8] S. Sadanand and J. Corso. Action bank: A high-level representation of activity in video. In *CVPR*, pages 1234–1241, 2012.

[9] X. Sun, R. Ji, H. Yao, P. Xu, T. Liu, and X. Liu. Place retrieval with graph-based place-view model. In *MIR*, pages 268–275, 2012.

[10] J. Uijlings, I. C. Duta, E. Sangineto, and N. Sebe. Video classification with densely extracted hog/hof/mbh features: an evaluation of the accuracy/computational efficiency trade-off. *International Journal of Multimedia Information Retrieval*, 4:33–44, 2015.

[11] Wang, Heng, A. Kläser, C. Schmid, and C.-L. Liu. Dense trajectories and motion boundary descriptors for action recognition. *International Journal of Computer Vision*, 103(1):60–79, 2013.

[12] G. Yu, J. Yuan, and Z. Liu. Unsupervised random forest indexing for fast action search. In *CVPR*, pages 865–872, 2011.

[13] S. X. Yu and J. Shi. Multiclass spectral clustering. In *ICCV*, pages 313–319, 2003.

[14] X. Zhao, J. Yuan, M. Wang, G. Li, R. Hong, Z. Li, and T.-S. Chua. Video recommendation over multiple information sources. *Multimedia Systems*, 19(1):3–15, 2013.

The Quest for Visual Interest

Mohammad Soleymani
Swiss Center for Affective Sciences
University of Geneva
Switzerland
mohammad.soleymani@unige.ch

ABSTRACT

In this paper, we report on identifying the underlying factors that contribute to the visual interest in digital photos. A set of 1005 digital photos covering different topics and of different qualities was collected from Flickr. Images were annotated by a pool of diverse participants on a crowdsourcing platform. 12 bipolar ratings were collected for each photo on 7-point semantic differential scale, including dimensions related to interest, emotions and image quality. Every image received 20 annotations from unique participants. The most important appraisals and visual attributes for visual interest in photos was identified. We found that intrinsic pleasantness, arousal, visual quality and coping potential are the most important factors contributing to visual interest in digital photos. We developed a system that automatically detects the important visual attributes from low level visual features and demonstrated their significance in predicting interest at individual level.

Categories and Subject Descriptors

H5.5 [**Information storage and retrieval**]: Content Analysis and Indexing

Keywords

Interest; emotion; appraisal; crowdsourcing; computer vision.

1. INTRODUCTION

Deciphering why a user is interested in one image over another can benefit image retrieval and recommendation engines. Users actively create, look at and share millions of images on platforms such as Flickr[1] and Pinterest[2] on a daily basis. Both users and content repositories will benefit from novel methods for both indexing the content and better understanding users' desires while interacting with the content delivery platforms. Interest is an affective state that drives users' attention, and in combination with users' intent, it constructs users' preference and shapes their behavior on multimedia delivery platforms.

1.1 Related work

In the last decades, psychologists increasingly supported the idea that interest is an emotion [14]. Appraisal theory is one of the most widely-accepted theories that explains the development of emotional experience. According to this theory, cognitive judgment about, or appraisal of, a situation is a key factor in the emergence of emotions. When an agent, in our case a person, faces a stimulus a series of concurrent evaluations or appraisals results in an emotional episode. The appraisals start with goal-relevance. If the stimulus is not relevant to the person, there is no further evaluation and therefore no emotion. If the stimulus is relevant to her, then further evaluations regarding its intrinsic pleasantness, the person's coping potential, novelty-complexity and its position to the norms and values of the person impacts the type of emotion she feels [13]. Silvia [14] has studied the appraisal mechanism of interest. He found novelty-complexity and coping potential to be the most important appraisals in the process of feeling interest. He has also identified that people with a higher level of familiarity with the subject have a higher level of interest in more complex forms of the stimuli. Therefore, comprehensibility and novelty both contribute to the feeling of interest. He later found that people can be categorized into different groups according to how much interest they feel towards an object or situation [14]. The first group, higher on curiosity and openness personality trait, is more likely to be interested by novel and more complex stimuli. For the second group, however, coping potential and comprehensibility was more important.

Gygli et al. and Grabner et al. [4, 3] demonstrated how the visual content features related to unusualness, aesthetics and general preference in images are important in predicting visual. However, the predicted interest does not take the personal differences into account and these different attributes are not separately learned. As a result their best performing results were obtained by combining all the visual features related to different attributes. Halonen et al. [5] identified a set of characteristics that are related to visual interestingness, including aesthetics, affect, colors, composition, genre, and personal connection.

1.2 Main contributions

In this paper, we are reporting a work in progress on identifying the underlying visual and personal factors contributing to the construction of visual interest as an emotion. To

[1]http://flickr.com
[2]http://www.pinterest.com

MM'15, October 26–30, 2015, Brisbane, Australia.

ACM 978-1-4503-3459-4/15/10 ...$15.00.
DOI: http://dx.doi.org/10.1145/2733373.2806364.

this end, following the work of Silvia and colleagues [14], we first identified the appraisals that are important for interest. Then, a set of ratings on 12 different scales was collected to identify the visual attributes relevant to image interestingness, e.g., quality and complexity [14, 5]. The visual attributes that are important for visual interest are identified and learned from low level visual features. An automatic person-specific interest detection is also implemented and presented. The major contributions of this work are as follows: first, the appraisal structure of interest is studied using a set of real-world digital photos; second, for the first time, the effect of visual attributes and appraisals on visual interest in photos are investigated; and third, a content-based visual interest prediction from visual attributes is presented and evaluated.

2. DATA COLLECTION

2.1 Image selection

We aimed to create a diverse set of images both in terms of topic and aesthetics. A set of queries was constructed from image titles in International Affective Picture System [9] and Kodak Lossless True Color Image Suite[3]. Chu et al. [1] showed person familiarity in images depicting people to be an important factor in their interestingness. Therefore, to add a set of familiar faces, the 20 most famous celebrities according to Forbes[4] were also added to the query terms. In total, 139 queries were chosen for image selection. To ensure the diversity of images in terms of quality and aesthetics, we tried to diversify the photos based on the cameras that captured them. Flickr API was used to collect images published under Creative Commons (CC) license[5]. First a list of all camera brands and their models were retrieved. At every step of querying Flickr, 15 different models of each brand were randomly selected and the top 4 images according to relevance and date-posted (ascending) were retrieved. We decided to avoid the Flickr interestingness sort option due to its bias towards more popular images and its undisclosed technical definition. To include the photos without EXIF metadata and known cameras, for each query, top 20 photos were also retrieved regardless of the cameras capturing them. To avoid bias from the shape of the image and its details during the annotations, only images with landscape orientation with the aspect ratio 4:3 were kept. Black and white images, photos with watermarks and photos depicting extreme nudity (depicting genitals) or extremely unpleasant images were removed from the dataset. The black and white images were discarded to have a more homogenous set. A significant number of queries, including most of the queries related to celebrities did not yield any relevant results. Therefore, a second round of photo collection was performed. In the second round, at each step 200 CC licensed images with the permission for derivation and no requirement regarding the camera were collected for the missing queries. In the second round, images that were not very far in shape from landscape orientation with 4:3 aspect ratio were cropped and added to the dataset after manual selection. We randomly subsampled the collected photos from the first round considering the presence of the results from all the queries. The photos relevant to the queries with a small number or no results in

[3]http://r0k.us/graphics/kodak/

[4]http://www.forbes.com/celebrities/list/

[5]http://creativecommons.org/licenses/

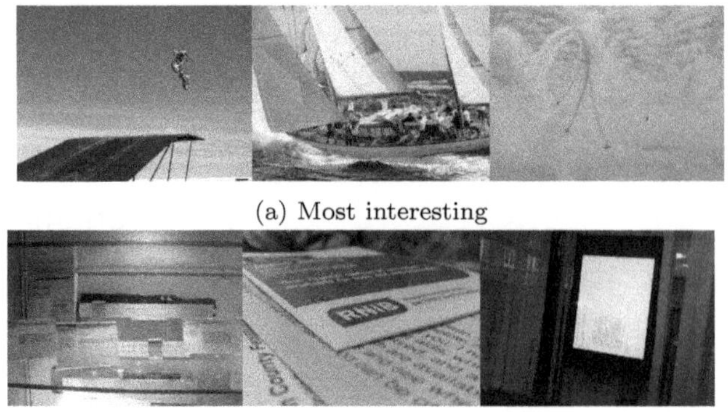

(a) Most interesting

(b) Least interesting

Figure 1: The most and least interesting images according to the average ratings given by workers.

the first round were manually selected from the results of the second round. In total 1005 photos were selected and resized to 600×400 pixels.

2.2 Labeling via crowdsourcing

In order to asses the Big-Five personality traits, we used the fake-proof personality questionnaire proposed by Hirsh and Peterson [6] in addition to a short version of IPIP test [2]. Similar to the work of Silvia et al. [14], the same personality questionnaires were used to assess the following traits: openness scale, sensation seeking, the tendency to seek new and varied experiences, curiosity, epistemic curiosity and perceptual curiosity. General interest in arts, sports, people, cars, celebrities, animals, scenery and food was also assessed using a 7-point Likert scale.

Crowdsourcing provides the scale and efficiency required for large scale data collection. Therefore, to collect annotations, we turned to Amazon Mechanical Turk[6]. It is essential to ensure the quality of labels collected through crowdsourcing. We followed a two-step strategy that we designed based on many current state-of-the-art crowdsourcing approaches [8]. The first step was a recruitment phase which included the personality, demography and general preference questionnaires in addition to annotating and describing one sample image. We were able to efficiently monitor the consistency of the responses by calculating the correlation between the Big-Five results of the IPIP test and the fake-proof test. Workers who randomly selected the responses were easily identified. We could also verify that the workers had a good knowledge of English by reading their description of the sample image. Moreover, we could verify that the scripts were properly working and compatible with the workers' browser. Two sets of qualifications were given to the workers who provided satisfactory responses to the qualification task. One set was given to the workers with a lower openness to experience score and one to the ones with the higher scores. For the second phase, image labeling, two identical batches that required 10 unique workers were published for these two groups. This way, we were sure to receive the same amount of labels from workers with different degree of openness to experience. Each Human Intelligence Task (HIT) in the second phase, consisted of providing 12 ratings on a 7-point semantic differential scale to 5 images. These scales were selected to identify the appraisals and visual attributes relevant to visual interest [14, 5]. A list of

[6]http://www.mturk.com

all the scales is available in Table 1. This dataset is freely available for academic research[7].

Table 1: The 12 bipolar scales and their inter-rater agreements are given; for α the higher the better.

Scale	Krippendorf's α
Complex - Simple	0.13
Low quality - High quality	0.23
Appealing - Unappealing	0.29
Natural - Staged	0.30
Pleasant - Unpleasant	0.24
Arousing - Soothing	0.31
Familiar - Unfamiliar	0.14
Easy - Hard (to understand)	0.18
Comprehensible - Incomprehensible	0.13
Coherent - Incoherent	0.11
Boring - Exciting	0.24
Interesting - Uninteresting	0.20

2.3 Analysis of annotations

The qualification HIT was initially published for 150 workers. No requirement such as HIT acceptance rate or the number of completed HITs was required to avoid shrinking the pool of eligible workers. We further extended the qualification HIT for 150 more workers due to the lack of workers with lower openness trait. In total, there were 300 workers who performed the qualification HIT. We extended the qualification of high and low openness to 52 and 43 workers respectively. The qualified workers were invited to participate in the main image labeling HITs via MTurk messaging. Out of the total of 95 qualified workers, 66 workers (69.5% of the invited workers) performed at least one of the main HITs. From 66 workers who participated in our main HITs, 39 were male and 27 were female and they were mostly from the USA. They were in average 36.0 ± 11.4 years old. The workers on average spent 11.49 seconds annotating every image on 12 different scales. The whole crowdsourcing campaign cost about $2'400.00 USD for performing 20'100 image labeling tasks and took 11 days to complete. The average effective hourly rate for the image labeling HITs was $5.74 USD. Krippendorf's alpha on ordinal scale was calculated for each scale and is listed in Table 1.

3. METHODS

3.1 Appraisal structure and relevant attributes

To study the effect of different attributes, including appraisals on interest, we used a mixed-effect linear model estimating the interest from the other ratings. Appraisal of coping potential was constructed by averaging the scores given to "easy to understand - hard to understand", "comprehensible - incomprehensible" and "coherent - incoherent" scales. Appraisal of novelty is related to both complexity and familiarity; however due to their low correlation ($\rho = -0.23$), we decided to keep them separate. Appraisal of intrinsic pleasantness was constructed by averaging pleasantness and aesthetics scores. Arousal, naturalness and quality were also added as fixed effect independent variables. Other ratings which can be associated with appraisals were set as fixed effect independent variables and images as a random effect covariate. A mixed-effect linear model enables us to model the between image variations in a random effect term while studying the effect of the independent variables on the dependent variable, i.e., interest. Interest scores were calculated by averaging the interest scale and reversed boring-exciting scale.

[7]http://cvml.unige.ch/databases/visInterest

3.2 Attribute learning and interest prediction

A set of attributes important to visual interest was identified. An automatic system that can identify these attributes will be useful for an interest-centered indexing scenario.

Gygli et al. [4] identified a set of features that are related to visual quality, aesthetics and general preference. Inspired by their findings, the following features were extracted from images: spatial pyramids of sift histograms [10] (as a general scene descriptor), jpeg compression rate from an uncompressed image (as an indicator of image complexity), the color histogram, contrast, naïve arousal score [11] and edge distribution [4]. Khosla et al. [7] identified a set of features that were effective in predicting memorability. Even though memorability and interestingness have inverse correlation [4], the features can be effective in capturing the semantic content of the image. The following features were extracted based on [7]: histogram of oriented gradients (HOG) at 2×2 and 3×3 cells which were max-pooled at 2 spatial pyramid levels; color name feature; local binary patterns (LBP) which is reduced by max pooling; and a bag of word representation of GIST descriptors using the dictionary size of 512. The features that are taken from [7] are extracted using the feature extraction toolbox[8].

Given the nature of the attributes, we used a regression with sparse approximation of data [12], which performed slightly better than Support Vector Regressor (SVR) with an RBF kernel with much lower processing time. The sparse representation of the dictionary (here the normalized training set) was calculated using the Spectral Projected Gradient Method for ℓ_1-minimization (SPGL1) [15]. A Principal Component Analysis (PCA) was used for dimensionality reduction. PCA was applied on the training set in each iteration of the cross-validation. After calculating the number of principal components that carry 95% of the variance, the corresponding mapping was used to reduce the dimensionality of the test set. A leave-one-out cross-validation strategy was used for the evaluation.

The most straightforward way of predicting users' interest given a set of images with ratings is to use the labeled images of each user as the training set. We implemented this baseline method using the same regressor explained in the previous section. In order to demonstrate the significance of the attributes, a second method is proposed that learns individual interest from the visual attributes learned from the ratings given by a larger population. To this end, we trained a linear regression that combines the visual attributes for each image and each user. Only the data from the 22 workers who annotated at least 400 images were processed for individual interest prediction.

4. EXPERIMENTAL RESULTS

4.1 Appraisal structure

The statistical analysis on the effect of appraisals and attributes was performed using a mixed-effect linear model. It was found that the most important attributes were intrinsic pleasantness and arousal which further justifies the

[8]https://github.com/adikhosla/feature-extraction

affective dimension of interest. Complexity and familiarity both contributed positively to higher interest whereas coping potential had a negative effect on average. Naturalness had the smallest effect in presence of the other factors. The coefficients of the fixed effects were as follows: arousal: 0.29, intrinsic pleasantness: 0.11, familiarity: 0.01, quality: 0.07, complexity: 0.02, coping potential: -0.08, and naturalness: 0.01.

The traits that are related to curiosity and openness were averaged to generate an openness score. The workers were divided into two groups of high and low openness and the previous model was fit on their annotations. Although the results were similar, for the groups with a higher openness personality trait, complexity coefficient was higher (0.17 vs. 0.13) and coping potential had a more negative effect (-0.09 vs. -0.04). This is in agreement with the findings of Silvia and colleagues [14] who observed that people with higher openness are interested in stimuli that is more difficult to understand and is more complex.

4.2 Attribute and interest detection

We attempted learning the attributes that are related to interest, namely, quality, familiarity, naturalness, coping potential, intrinsic pleasantness, arousal, complexity and general interest. All the labels were generated based on the averaged scores given by 20 participants. The scores were scaled between [-0.5 ,+0.5]. At every iteration of cross-validation, visual content features were normalized by subtracting the mean and dividing by the standard deviation of the feature values in the training set. The detection results are evaluated by r-squared (r^2) metric which adjusts for the random level (averaged score from the training set) and is roughly equivalent to the squared correlation. Root-mean-square error (RMSE) and Pearson correlation (ρ) are also reported. The results are shown in Table 2.

Table 2: Attribute detection results are given. The last two rows include the results for individual interest prediction. All attribute and interest scores are scaled between [-0.5 ,+0.5]; for RMSE $\in [0, 1]$ the lower the better; for r^2 and ρ the higher the better. Acronyms: Intr.: Intrinsic; Ind.: Individual, BL: Baseline, At. Attribute-based.

Attribute	r^2	ρ	$RMSE$
Quality	0.26	0.51	0.13
Coping potential	0.06	0.27	0.11
Naturalness	0.32	0.57	0.18
Intrinsic pleasantness	0.16	0.40	0.15
Familiarity	0.08	0.30	0.14
Arousal	0.37	0.14	0.09
Complexity	0.13	0.37	0.12
General interest	0.20	0.44	0.13
Ind. interest (At.)	**0.08**±0.00	0.27±0.08	0.24±0.07
Ind. interest (BL)	**0.03**±0.00	0.26±0.09	0.24±0.08

The evaluation based on r^2 demonstrates that for individual-specific interest prediction, the attribute-based method significantly outperforms the direct baseline approach (based on one tailed t-test on r^2; $p < 0.01$).

5. CONCLUSIONS

In this work, we investigated the underlying factors for visual interest. Affective content, quality, coping potential and complexity are shown to have a significant effect on visual interest in images. We demonstrated that using the visual attributes that are learned from a population, it is possible to detect individual interest. Content-based methods are however limited by their input. The first appraisal in an affective episode is goal-relevance which cannot be assessed only from the content without the knowledge of a user and the context. Therefore, having social information and personal connections, especially for photos depicting people, is very important. We also expect that some appraisal subcomponents that we did not consider in this study have to be identified; for example, there are different categories of intrinsic pleasantness and the role of aesthetics in cognitive appraisal theory is still unclear. In this paper, promising results are reported for detecting interest and its relevant attributes. In the future, the attributes can be learned from a larger set of images and public databases specific to image quality and aesthetics assessment.

6. ACKNOWLEDGMENTS

This work is supported by the Swiss National Science Foundation's Ambizione grant. We would like to thank Danny Dukes for helpful discussions.

7. REFERENCES

[1] S. L. Chu et al. The effect of familiarity on perceived interestingness of images. In *IS&T/SPIE EI*, 2013.
[2] L. R. Goldberg et al. The international personality item pool and the future of public-domain personality measures. *J. Res. Per.*, 40(1):84–96, 2006.
[3] H. Grabner et al. Visual interestingness in image sequences. In *ACM MM*, 2013.
[4] M. Gygli et al. The Interestingness of Images. In *IEEE ICCV*, 2013.
[5] R. Halonen et al. Naturalness and interestingness of test images for visual quality evaluation. In *SPIE IQSP*, 2011.
[6] J. B. Hirsh and J. B. Peterson. Predicting creativity and academic success with a "Fake-Proof" measure of the Big Five. *J. Res. Pers.*, 42(5):1323–1333, 2008.
[7] A. Khosla et al. Memorability of image regions. In *NIPS*, 2012.
[8] A. Kittur et al. Crowdsourcing user studies with Mechanical Turk. In *ACM CHI*, 2008.
[9] P. Lang et al. International affective picture system (IAPS): Affective ratings of pictures and instruction manual. Technical Report A-8, Univ. Florida, 2008.
[10] S. Lazebnik et al. Beyond bags of features: Spatial pyramid matching for recognizing natural scene categories. In *CVPR*, 2006.
[11] J. Machajdik and A. Hanbury. Affective image classification using features inspired by psychology and art theory. In *ACM MM*, 2010.
[12] P. Noorzad and B. L. Sturm. Regression with sparse approximations of data. In *EUSIPCO*, 2012.
[13] K. R. Scherer. Studying the emotion-antecedent appraisal process: An expert system approach. *Cogn Emot.*, 7(3):325–355, 1993.
[14] P. J. Silvia et al. Are the sources of interest the same for everyone? Using multilevel mixture models to explore individual differences in appraisal structures. *Cogn Emot.*, 23(7):1389–1406, 2009.
[15] E. van den Berg and M. Friedlander. Probing the pareto frontier for basis pursuit solutions. *SIAM J. Sci. Comput.*, 31(2):890–912, 2009.

How to Take a Good Selfie?

Mahdi M. Kalayeh[*] Misrak Seifu[○] Wesna LaLanne[◇] Mubarak Shah[*]

[*]Center for Research in Computer Vision at University of Central Florida

[○]Jackson State University [◇]University of Central Florida

mahdi@eecs.ucf.edu misrak.seifu@gmail.com wlalanne@knights.ucf.edu shah@crcv.ucf.edu

ABSTRACT

Selfies are now a global phenomenon. This massive number of self-portrait images taken and shared on social media is revolutionizing the way people introduce themselves and the circle of their friends to the world. While taking photos of oneself can be seen simply as recording personal memories, the urge to share them with other people adds an exclusive sensation to the selfies. Due to the Big Data nature of selfies, it is nearly impossible to analyze them manually. In this paper, we provide, to the best of our knowledge, the first selfie dataset for research purposes with more than 46,000 images. We address interesting questions about selfies, including how appearance of certain objects, concepts and attributes influences the popularity of selfies. We also study the correlation between popularity and sentiment in selfie images. In a nutshell, from a large scale dataset, we automatically infer what makes a selfie a *good selfie*. We believe that this research creates new opportunities for social, psychological and behavioral scientists to study selfies from a large scale point of view, a perspective that best fits the nature of the selfie phenomenon.

Categories and Subject Descriptors: I.4 [Image Processing and Computer Vision]: Applications

Keywords: Selfie; Social Media; Sentiment Analysis; Recommendation Models.

1. INTRODUCTION

According to the Oxford Dictionary, *Selfie is a photograph that one has taken of oneself, typically one taken with a smartphone or webcam and shared via social media.* In the past few years, taking selfies has become very popular. People from different socio-economic, gender, race and age groups take selfies in various occasions. Google recently reported[1] that there are 93 million selfies taken every day only on Android devices. These gigantic data can reveal interesting statistics about the preferences, moods and feelings of the members of our society, if it is properly analyzed. Due to the large scale and continuous growth of the data, it is appropriate to employ machine learning and computer vision techniques to study selfie images. We believe that when someone takes a selfie, he/she considers two major aspects among many possible others to make it a *good selfie*, popularity and sentiment. Popularity refers to the log_2 normalized *view* counts while sentiment indicates the feeling that viewers infer by looking at a selfie. Typically, a social media user desires to increase the popularity of his/her selfie and imply a positive sentiment. In this paper we are addressing the following questions: **(1)** How do different attributes, such as gender, race or hair color, influence the popularity of selfies? **(2)** How does the appearance of certain objects or particular concepts affect the popularity of selfies? **(3)** Is there a relationship between the sentiment inferred from a selfie and its popularity? **(4)** How does post-processing, such as applying different Instagram filters, influence the popularity of selfies?

Figure 1: Examples of images in the Selfie dataset.

Recently, Khosla et al. [1] proposed a framework to predict the popularity of a photograph before being uploaded on social media. They use about 2.3 million images from Flickr to predict the normalized number of views for images. Exploiting both visual content and social cues, Khosla et al. predict the popularity of an image with about 0.81 rank correlation to its ground truth. Borth et al. [2] have proposed sentiment prediction based on both visual content and tags associated to the images. They [2] use SentiBank, a library of visual concept detectors based on more than 2,000 Adjective Noun Pairs (ANP) to predict the implied emotion of a photograph. While these studies are valuable, they deal with photographs in general. We believe that studying selfies as the current most popular type of shared content on so-

[1]http://goo.gl/53Z0jG

MM'15, October 26–30, 2015, Brisbane, Australia.

DOI: http://dx.doi.org/10.1145/2733373.2806365.

cial media deserves an exclusive study. Knowing that photos with human faces are respectively 38% and 32% more likely to receive *likes* and *comments*, Bakhshi et al. [1], further demonstrate the importance of this work. Our study does not focus on improving the popularity score prediction or boosting the sentiment prediction performance. Instead, we are using state-of-the-art techniques in these areas to simply answer the four aforementioned questions. In the rest of this paper, we introduce our Selfie dataset in section 2. In section 3, we present an attribute prediction baseline. In section 4, we evaluate how does the appearance of different objects and concepts influence the popularity of selfies. In section 5, we answer the question of correlation between popularity and sentiment. Finally in section 6, we study whether applying different Instagram filters affects the popularity of selfies. We conclude the paper in section 7.

2. SELFIE DATASET

Due to the massive number of selfies being uploaded on social media every minute, any study aiming to provide insights about selfies has to be conducted on very large number of images to ensure that it sufficiently captures the variations in the data. To the best of our knowledge, there exists no selfie dataset publicly available for research purposes. Therefore, we collected our own dataset. We downloaded 85,000 images from `selfeed.com`, a real-time update of *#selfie* on Instagram. Despite being tagged with *#selfie*, we found that only 69,710 of those images are actually selfie images. The remaining 15,290 images were either completely irrelevant or general photographs of people. This is an interesting observation, since different social media usually report the number of selfies shared on their environment by counting the images tagged with *#selfie*. However, in our data collection, at least 18% of images tagged with *#selfie* are not, in fact, selfies. In preparation of the Selfie dataset, we made sure to discard any images that do not fall under the definition of *selfie*. Clearly this is a subjective judgment and different annotators may disagree in a few cases whether a photo is a selfie or not. In order to generate a uniform understanding of *selfie* among our annotators, we asked them to annotate a fixed set of images containing about 2,000 images. Then, the images with mixed votes where discussed and disagreement was resolved by clarifying the definition. About 32% of selfie images that we collected were showing multiple faces either in form of group selfies or collages. Excluding multiple-face images yields to a total number of 46,836 single-face selfies. Since we wanted to annotate selfies with attributes such as age, gender, hair color and etc., we were mostly interested in selfies that do not show multiple faces. Figure 1 shows some of the collected selfie images. We annotated 46,836 selfie images with 36 different attributes divided into several categories as follows: *Gender:* is female. *Age:* baby, child, teenager, youth, middle age, senior. *Race:* white, black, asian. *Face shape:* oval, round, heart. *Facial gestures:* smiling, frowning, mouth open, tongue out, duck face. *Hair color:* black, blond, brown, red. *Hair shape:* curly, straight, braid. *Accessories:* glasses, sunglasses, lipstick, hat, earphone. *Misc.:* showing cellphone, using mirror, having braces, partial face. *Lighting condition:* harsh, dim.

We asked annotators to look into a random subset (~3,000 images) of the Selfie dataset and create a list of attributes that they 1) frequently observe and 2) can easily detect. These two conditions assure enough positive samples for each attribute and an acceptable performance for the attribute detectors. Figure 2 shows the ground truth statistics of the collected Selfie dataset.

3. ATTRIBUTE PREDICTION BASELINE

To analyize selfie images outside our dataset, we have to be able to predict different attributes of interest with an acceptable precision. Therefore, we provide a baseline for attribute prediction along with introduction of our Selfie dataset. In our experimental setting, for every attribute, positive instances were randomly divided into 3 folds. We do the same for the negative instances. Training split for each attribute consists of 2 out of 3 folds from both positive and negative instances. The third folds from positive and negative instances, together create the testing split. For feature extraction from images, we use

SIFT: We densely extract SIFT descriptors from images at every 3 pixels and at 8 different scales. To encode these descriptors into a single feature vector, we employ VLAD [3] with a codebook size of 256.

HOG: We densely extract HOG descriptors from images with the cell size of 8 pixels. Descriptor encoding is the same as the one used for dense SIFT.

Deep Features: Using deep convolutional neural networks (CNN) [5] trained on ImageNet dataset [6], we extract 4096-D feature vectors from CNN's last fully connected layer. We also use final 1000-D classification layer as another feature representation. We employed the large network of OverFeat [7] to implement CNN.

SentiBank: Authors in [2] have trained 2,089 visual concept detectors based on a list of Adjective Noun Pairs (ANP). These ANPs are like *smiling boy, lovely dress, scary face* and etc. Using SentiBank, we generate a 2089-D vector for each image where every dimension is the detection score of its corresponding ANP concept detector.

We employed *one-vs-all* support vector machine (SVM) with linear kernel to train attribute detectors. The performance of detectors is measured via average precision (AP). Figure 3 shows the performance of different features for the task of attribute detection on the Selfie dataset. Deep features extracted from last fully connected layer of CNN perform better (29.51% vs 24.03% meanAP) than the 1000-D features from CNN's classification layer. Features obtained by applying SentiBank ANP concept detectors achieve the best performance with 31.97% meanAP among three different mid-level features. We expected to observe this since ANPs are very diverse and a very large portion of them are relevant to human attributes. Using SIFT and HOG (low-level features) with VLAD encoding results in 33.76% and 22.95% meanAP, respectively. We also fused 4096-D deep features, SentiBank features and SIFT via mean and max pooling their detection scores (late fusion). While max pooling was not helpful (32.49% meanAP), mean pooling further improved the attribute prediction baseline to 35.79% meanAP.

4. WHAT MAKES A SELFIE POPULAR?

In this section, we attempt to answer the second question that we proposed in the beginning of this paper. How does the appearance of certain objects or particular concepts

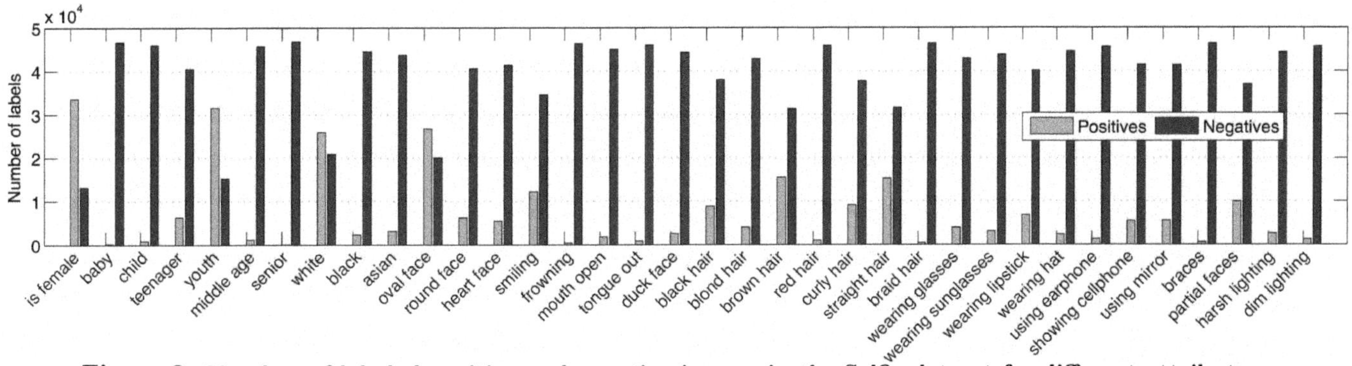

Figure 2: Number of labeled positive and negative images in the Selfie dataset for different attributes.

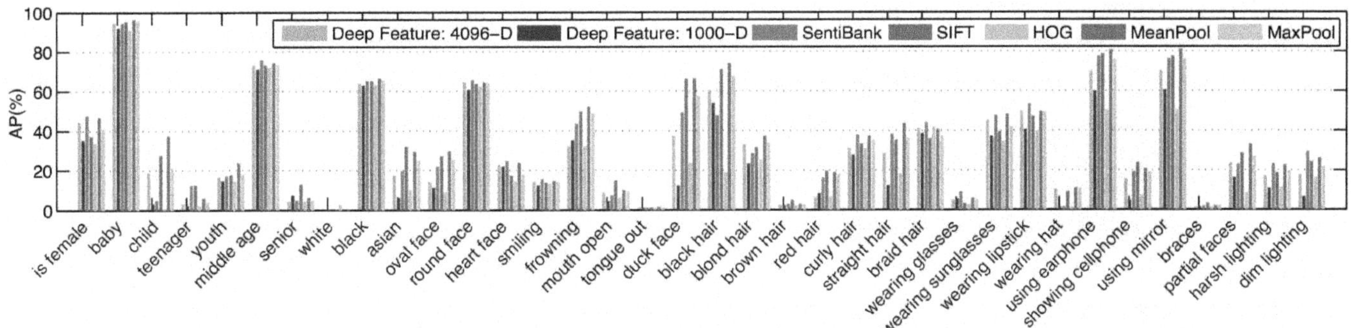

Figure 3: Attribute prediction performance of different features on the Selfie dataset.

influence the popularity of selfie images? We discuss the effect of attributes in section 6. Here we study object categories of ImageNet [6] and concepts associated with ANPs in SentiBank [2]. To evaluate the correlation of each object/concept with popularity of selfie images, we use 1000-D output of [7], pre-trained on ImageNet dataset, and 2089-D output of SentiBank ANP concept detectors as mid-level features. We then train an L_2-regularized support vector regression (SVR) to predict the popularity score of the images. Regression coefficients corresponding to different objects/concepts indicate their correlation to the popularity. We use object/concept detector responses with at least 0.5 confidence. This assures that we only consider images in which a particular object/concept is confidently detected. We observed that among ImageNet object categories: *maillot, lab coat, jersey, fur coat, brassiere, wig, abaya, hair spray, suit, sunglasses, and lipstick* (in decreasing order) are the most relevant objects to the popularity of selfies. Among different ANPs in SentiBank: *sexy dress, lovely dress, fancy dress, traditional tattoo, smiling baby, shiny hair, sexy girls, cute baby, strong legs, stupid hat and happy baby* (in decreasing order) are the most relevant concepts to the popularity score. Figure 4 illustrates the normalized regression coefficients (in decreasing order) obtained from training SVR.

Popularity Score Prediction: Observing the performance of different features in attribute prediction, we are also interested to see how they perform in predicting the popularity of selfie images. Thus, we randomly divided the entire Selfie dataset using 3-fold cross validation where 2 folds were used to train an L_2-regularized SVR and we tested on the third fold. We evaluate the quality of different features in terms of Spearman's rank correlation between the predicted and the actual popularity (generated by [4]). Using SIFT, we achieved 0.40 rank correlation. The 4096-D deep features and 2089-D SentiBank features resulted in 0.41 and 0.54 rank correlation, respectively. While max pooling of these features was not helpful (0.49 rank correlation), we observe that mean pooling can further boost the rank correlation to 0.55.

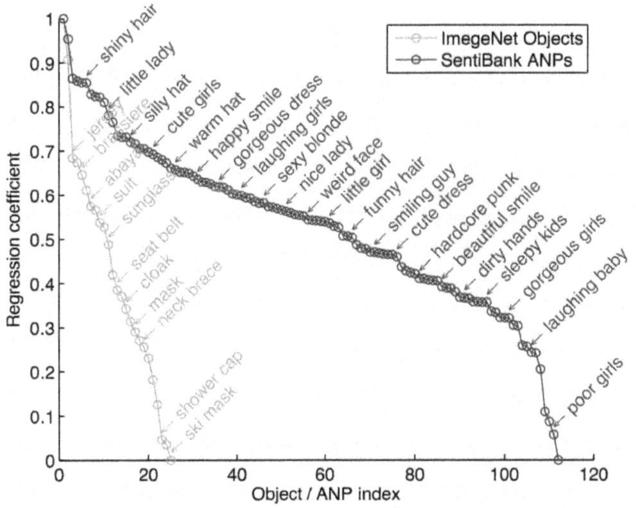

Figure 4: Normalized regression coefficients of SVR for popularity score prediction.

5. SENTIMENT-POPULARITY CORRELATION

In this section we explore the correlation between the popularity of selfie images and their implied sentiments. Each ANP in SentiBank is associated with a sentiment measure where negative, close to zero and positive numbers depict negative, neutral and positive sentiments, respectively. Out of 2,089 ANPs, we manually select 126 of them that are

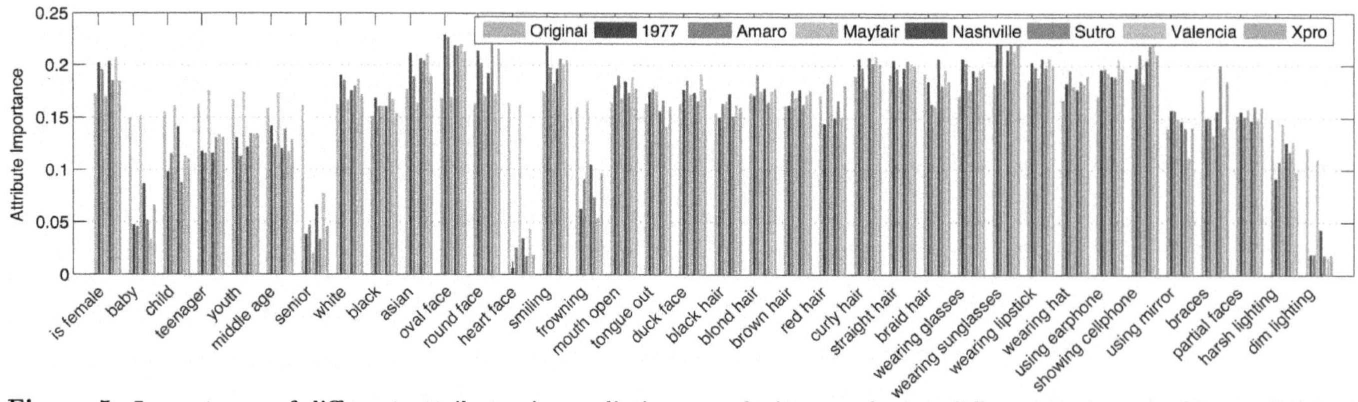

Figure 5: Importance of different attributes in predicting popularity, employing different Instagram filters. *Original* indicates no filter is applied.

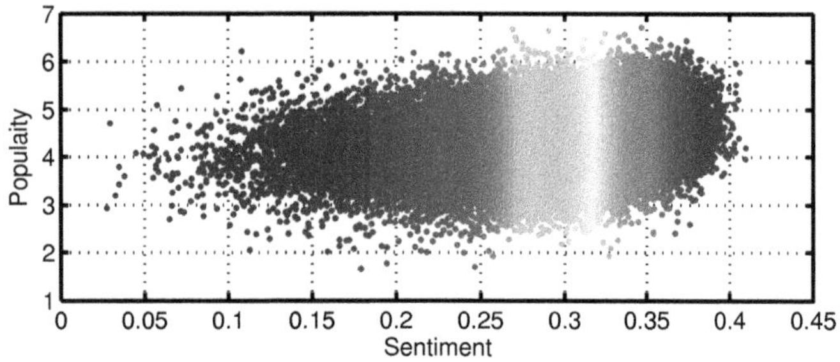

Figure 6: Sentiment-popularity scatter plot.

relevant to selfie images and their corresponding detectors have acceptable performance (AP$\geq$ 0.3). We compute implied sentiment of a selfie image I as $\mathcal{S}(I) = \sum_i \gamma_i s_i \omega_i^T x$, where γ_i, s_i and ω_i, respectively, represent the AP, sentiment measure and linear detector corresponding to the ith ANP. Given x as the feature representation of image I, $\omega_i^T x$ is the confidence score for which i^{th} ANP concept appears in the image I. We generate the scatter plot of the popularity versus sentiment using our entire dataset. Figure 6 illustrates the scatter plot in which a more positive sentiment, on average, results in a higher popularity. We observe, on average, up to 65% higher popularity comparing the two ends of the sentiment spectrum, shown in color. Another interesting observation is how the range of popularity changes as the sentiment measure increases. From bluish to green/yellow parts of the spectrum, increasing sentiment yields a larger range of popularity score (the blue cone). However, moving toward more reddish parts of the spectrum, the range of the popularity decreases. Therefore, we conclude that while at two ends of the sentiment spectrum there exist a direct correlation between sentiment and popularity, this is not true for the middle of the spectrum. In other words, unless the sentiment is too high or too low, one cannot estimate the popularity based on the sentiment with high precision.

6. EFFECT OF POST-PROCESSING ON POPULARITY

This section addresses the last question that we proposed in the beginning of this paper: How does post-processing, such as applying different Instagram filters, influence the popularity of selfies? We randomly select about 10,000 images from our Selfie dataset and apply 7 different Instagram filters to them. We observe that for a given selfie, applying some filters boosts the popularity while others have a counter-effect. We found that there is no definite ranking of filters in terms of improving the popularity, rather ranking varies from one image to another. Figure 5 shows the relevance of different attributes to popularity of selfies when various Instagram filters are applied. Therefore, the choice of the most effective filter varies according to the content of a selfie. We obtain the importance of different attributes using SVR in a similar strategy discussed in section 4.

7. CONCLUSION

In this work, for the first time, we address the Selfie phenomenon from a machine learning and computer vision perspective. We conduct a series of experiments addressing four distinct questions about selfie images. Our work sheds light on how to take a *good selfie*, a selfie that becomes popular and delivers a positive sentiment. We collected, to the best of our knowledge, the first Selfie dataset for research purposes with more than 46,000 images, annotated with 36 relevant attributes. Finally, we believe that our work creates novel opportunities for researchers in other disciplines to extend their studies on the selfie phenomenon to a larger scale.

8. REFERENCES

[1] S. Bakhshi, D. A. Shamma, and E. Gilbert. Faces engage us: Photos with faces attract more likes and comments on instagram. In *ACM CHI*, 2014.

[2] D. Borth, R. Ji, T. Chen, T. Breuel, and S.-F. Chang. Large-scale visual sentiment ontology and detectors using adjective noun pairs. In *ACM MM*, 2013.

[3] H. Jégou, M. Douze, C. Schmid, and P. Pérez. Aggregating local descriptors into a compact image representation. In *CVPR*, pages 3304–3311, 2010.

[4] A. Khosla, A. Das Sarma, and R. Hamid. What makes an image popular? In *ACM WWW*, 2014.

[5] A. Krizhevsky, I. Sutskever, and G. E. Hinton. Imagenet classification with deep convolutional neural networks. In *NIPS*, 2012.

[6] O. Russakovsky, J. Deng, H. Su, J. Krause, S. Satheesh, S. Ma, Z. Huang, A. Karpathy, A. Khosla, M. Bernstein, A. C. Berg, and L. Fei-Fei. ImageNet Large Scale Visual Recognition Challenge, 2014.

[7] P. Sermanet, D. Eigen, X. Zhang, M. Mathieu, R. Fergus, and Y. LeCun. Overfeat: Integrated recognition, localization and detection using convolutional networks. In *ICLR*, 2014.

R2P: Recomposition and Retargeting of Photographic Images

Hui-Tang Chang
Po-Cheng Pan
EE, National Taiwan University, Taipei, Taiwan
r02921089@ntu.edu.tw
b00901087@ntu.edu.tw

Yu-Chiang Frank Wang
Research Center for IT Innovation, Academia Sinica, Taipei, Taiwan
ycwang@citi.sinica.edu.tw

Ming-Syan Chen
Electrical Engineering, National Taiwan University, Taipei, Taiwan
mschen@cc.ee.ntu.edu.tw

ABSTRACT

In this paper, we propose a novel approach for performing joint recomposition and retargeting of photographic images (R2P). Given a reference image of interest, our method is able to automatically alter the composition of the input source image accordingly, while the recomposed output will be jointly retargeted to fit the reference. This is achieved by recomposing the visual components of the source image via graph matching, followed by solving a constrained mesh-warping based optimization problem for retargeting. As a result, the recomposed output image would fit the reference while suppressing possible distortion. Our experiments confirm that our proposed R2P method is able to achieve visually satisfactory results, without the need to use pre-collected labeled data or predetermined aesthetics rules.

Categories and Subject Descriptors

I.4.3 [**Image Processing & computer vision**]: Enhancement; I.4.9 [**Image Processing & computer vision**]: Applications; I.5.4 [**Pattern Recognition**]: Applications - Computer Vision

General Terms

Algorithms, Experimentation

Keywords

Photography Composition; Graph Matching; Image Aesthetics; Computational Photography

1. INTRODUCTION

Image enhancement aims at improving the visual quality of an image, which can be achieved by applying photographic techniques (e.g., high dynamic range (HDR) or auto white balance (AWB)) or image processing algorithms (e.g., denoising or deblurring). However the only thing which cannot be easily altered is the geometric structure of visual components, i.e., *composition*, of an image.

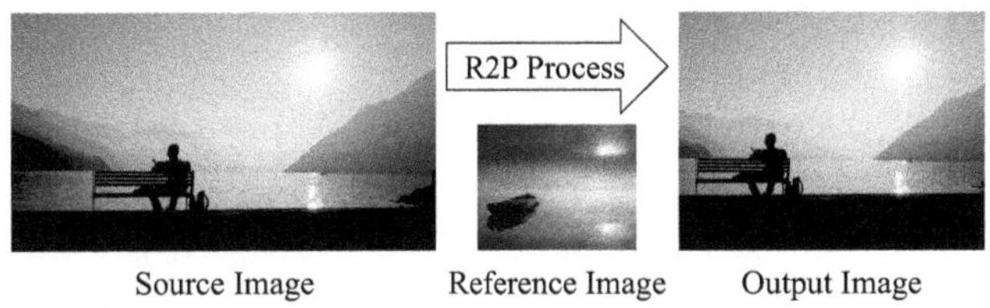

Figure 1: Example of a source image which is recomposed and retargeted to fit the reference image.

Improving image aesthetics is an alternative way to increase user satisfaction. Several computer vision and machine learning techniques have been applied to address this task. Since composition of an image has been viewed as a factor in assessing the image aesthetics, some researchers addressed the task of photographic composition [10, 9, 1, 6, 7]. Most of them aim at cropping the input image for satisfying particular rules of image aesthetics. For example, Nishiyama et al. [7] proposed sensation-based cropping for learning image aesthetics models. Santella et al. [8] utilized eye-tracking data, while Liu et al. [6] used pre-defined photography composition rules for image cropping. In addition to image cropping, Wong and Wong [9] proposed an algorithm to adjust the ratio of foreground/background regions. To perform recomposition, Bhattacharya et al. [1] trained their aesthetics models using pre-collected labeled (scored) image data, while Zhang et al. [10] further took the relationship between visual components into consideration.

Nevertheless, the above methods require pre-determined rules or pre-collected training data for performing photography recomposition. In practice, one cannot apply such rules to images taken in different scenarios. Thus, the robustness of such methods would not be sufficient. Recently, Chang et al. [2] proposed a transfer-learning based method for recompose a source image based on a reference image of interest. However, their approach applied image inpainting techniques which are computationally expensive. Moreover, they need to fine-tune their output image by post-processing the recomposed foreground regions.

Inspired by a mesh-based image retargetting work [5], we extend the work of [2] by integrating image retargeting and warping into a unified framework for image recomposition. As illustrated in Figure 1, we not only transfer the photo-

MM'15, October 26-30, 2015, Brisbane, Australia
 ISBN 978-1-4503-3459-4/15/10 ...$15.00.
DOI: http://dx.doi.org/10.1145/2733373.2806366.

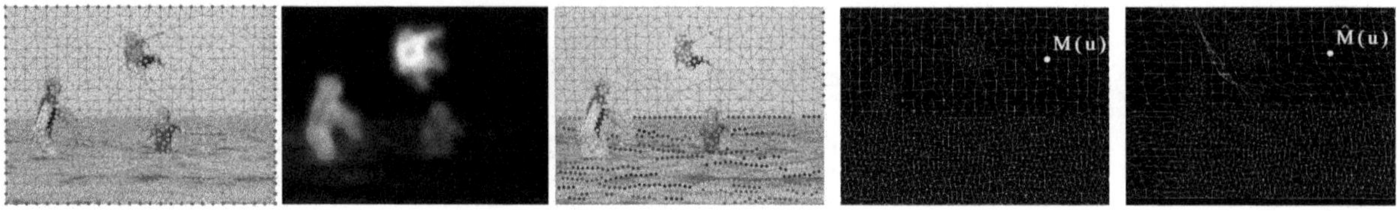

(a) Mesh Generation (b) Salience Map (c) Object Extraction (d) Initial Mesh (e) Recomposed Mesh

Figure 2: Illustration of foreground extraction and recomposition. Note that $M(u)$ and $\hat{M}(u)$ denote the source and recomposed locations of the uth mesh point in the background, respectively.

graphic composition from the reference to the source image, the output image will be simultaneously retargeted to fit the reference. Thus, we refer to our proposed methods as recomposition and retargeting of photographic images (R2P).

In Section 2, we will present the details of our proposed method for joint recomposition and retargeting. We will discuss that, while no user interaction or pre-collected labeled training data are required, why our method is able to preserve image context information after the R2P process without additional post-processing procedures. It is worth repeating that, our work focus on transferring the photography composition from a reference image to the source image, rather than improving image aesthetic scores for the input image by pre-determined rules or features.

The contributions of our work are highlighted below:

- Automatically transfer the photography composition from a reference to the source image by solving a graph-matching based optimization problem.
- With the observed composition information, we perform a joint recomposition and retargeting on the source image, so that it would visually fit the reference image.
- Our proposed method is fully automatic, without the need to use pre-collected labeled training data, pre-determine aesthetics rules, or user interaction.

2. OUR PROPOSED FRAMEWORK

2.1 Foreground Object Retrieval

Given a source and reference image pair, we first identify the foreground objects in both images. Prior works like [2] and [10] applied saliency detection and graph-cut for iteratively detect the foreground regions. For simplicity, we consider an one-pass algorithm as described below.

Inspired by a mesh-based image retargeting algorithm [5], we apply Canny edge detectors to detect the edges in an image, followed by sampling the pixels along the detected edges as the feature points. We note that, as depicted in Figure 2a, we mark the features points of detected edges and boundaries in green and blue, respectively. In order to describe smooth regions (e.g., sky in Figure 2a), we additionally add random feature points for collecting a sufficient number for representation purposes. Once such feature points are obtained, we utilize Delaunay triangulation algorithm to construct triangular meshes, as shown in Figure 2a.

Instead of iteratively applying saliency detection for determining possible foreground objects, our method directly combines the derived meshes and the saliency detection output of [4] (e.g., Figure 2b) for separating foreground and background regions, which is achieved by DB-scan clustering. Finally, N foreground objects set can be automatically observed. Also, we record all strong edges detected in the background regions (see Figure 2c), which will be crucial for the final stage of joint recomposition and retargeting.

2.2 Recomposition via Graph Matching

In our work, we apply a *composition graph* $G = (V, E, A)$ to describe each foreground object, and the recomposition can be performed by graph matching. For each graph, V and E denote the foreground objects and the edges connecting between them, respectively. We have A contain the attributes a_s for each vertex and $\mathbf{a}_l$ for each edge. That is, for $V_x \in V$, $a_s(x)$ indicates the area of that region. For each edge $e_{xy} \in E$, we have $\mathbf{a}_l(x, y)$ measuring the normalized Euclidean distance between the two vertices of edge e_{xy}.

To perform photography recomposition, we solve a graph-matching based optimization problem based on the observed affinity matrix $\mathbf{W}$ between the two composition graphs G^S and G^R, which are the constructed by source and reference images, respectively. The affinity matrix $\mathbf{W}$ is composed of the affinity between vertices and edges in the dimension of $|V^S||V^R| \times |V^S||V^R|$. In $\mathbf{W}$, each entry w is defined as:

$$w_{xm;yn} = \begin{cases} f(v_x^S, v_m^R) & \text{if } x = y,\ m = n \\ f(e_{xy}^S, e_{mn}^R) & \text{if } x \neq y,\ m \neq n \\ 0 & \text{otherwise,} \end{cases} \tag{1}$$

where the affinity functions are calculated as follows:

$$\begin{aligned} f(v_x^S, v_m^R) &= min[a_s(x), a_s(m)]/max[a_s(x), a_s(m)], \\ f(e_{xy}^S, e_{mn}^R) &= 1/\|\mathbf{a}_l^I(x, y) - \mathbf{a}_l^R(m, n)\|. \end{aligned} \tag{2}$$

Now, we convert the original recomposition problem into the task of determining an indicator matrix $\mathbf{Z} \in \{0, 1\}^{|V^S| \times |V^R|}$, where $z_{xm} = 1$ indicates a matching of foreground regions between V_x^S and V_m^R. For computation purposes, we make $\mathbf{Z}$ into a column vector $\mathbf{z} \in \{0, 1\}^{|V^S||V^R|}$, and apply the method of [3] for solve the following problem instead:

$$\max \left(\mathbf{z}^T \mathbf{W} \mathbf{z}\right), \text{s.t.} \sum_{k=1}^{|V^R|} z_{xk} \leq 1, \ \sum_{k=1}^{|V^I|} z_{km} \leq 1, \ \forall x, m. \tag{3}$$

The constraints in (3) enforces one-to-one matching between G^S to G^R. After solving (3), the locations of the foreground objects in the source image can be updated accordingly. As depicted in Figure 3, we denote the original location of objects in the source image as $\mathbf{S} = [\mathbf{s}_1, \mathbf{s}_2, ...\mathbf{s}_N] \in \mathbb{R}^{2 \times N}$, the estimated ones as $\mathbf{P} = [\mathbf{p}_1, \mathbf{p}_2, ...\mathbf{p}_N] \in \mathbb{R}^{2 \times N}$, and the final recomposed and retargeted ones as $\mathbf{Q} = [\mathbf{q}_1, \mathbf{q}_2, ...\mathbf{q}_N] \in \mathbb{R}^{2 \times N}$ (as detailed in the following subsection).

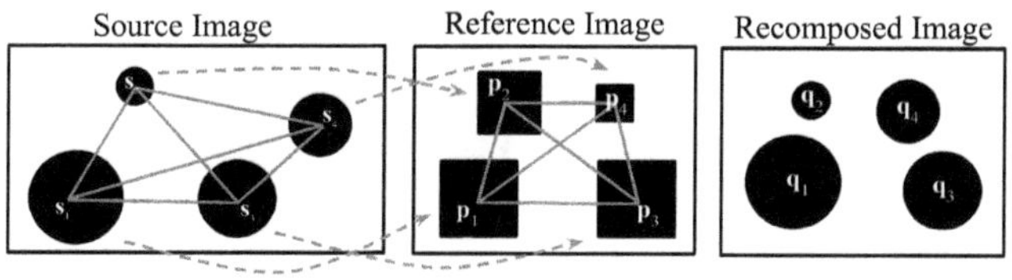

Figure 3: Graph matching for recomposition. The blue lines denote the *composition graphs*, and the red dotted lines associate the foreground objects across images. Note that $\mathbf{s}$, $\mathbf{p}$, and $\mathbf{q}$ denote the object locations in each image.

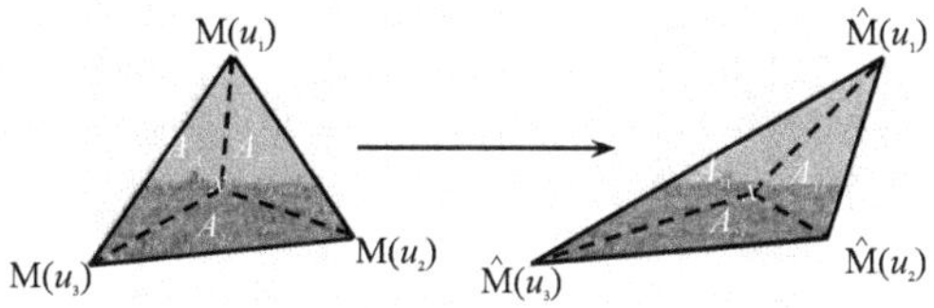

Figure 4: Illustration of mesh-based texture mapping.

2.3 Joint Recomposition and Retargeting

2.3.1 *Background Mesh Warping*

From Section 2.2, we estimate the new locations of the foreground objects in the source image for recomposition purposes. To complete the proposed R2P process, we propose to advance background warping for joint recomposition and retargeting. This allows us to move the foreground objects to the target locations without leaving any unfilled or distorted regions in the background.

We note that, the recent works of [2] and [10] apply image inpainting techniques for producing their recomposed outputs. Such techniques require the background regions to exhibit proper textural properties. Moreover, it is also computationally expensive to perform image inpainting (compared to our warping-based algorithm).

In [5], a uniform stretch method was considered to construct image meshes for image retargeting. Their goal was to minimize the predicted error of the recovered image with consistency in the observed boundaries and edges. Since their approach is not able to alter the composition of the input image (i.e., recomposition), we propose a novel mesh-warping algorithm for solving the tasks of recomposition and retargeting simultaneously.

To be more specific, our goal is to estimate the locations of foreground objects and the image cropping factor, which would that fulfill the following two requirements:

1. Recompose and retarget the input to fit the reference.
2. Minimize the *distortion* of the output image.

With the above two goals, our task is to determine the optimal locations Q for each foreground object and the image cropping factor $\mathbf{b}$, which are defined as follows:

$$\begin{aligned} Q &= [\mathbf{q}_1, \mathbf{q}_2, ...\mathbf{q}_N] \in \mathbb{R}^{2\times N} \\ \mathbf{b} &= [b_{top}, b_{bottom}, b_{left}, b_{right}] \in \mathbb{R}^{1\times 4}, \end{aligned} \tag{4}$$

where each b indicates the amount of the image boundary to be cropped (negative b values mean image stretching). Thus, the objective function to be optimized for joint recomposition and retargeting is:

$$[Q, \mathbf{b}] = \underset{Q,\mathbf{b}}{\operatorname{argmin}}\, D(Q, \mathbf{b})E(Q, \mathbf{b}). \tag{5}$$

Algorithm 1 Optimization for Background Mesh Warping

Sort O in decreasing order of object size.
for all $u \in M, n \in [1, N]$ **do**
  $c_n(u) = 1/distance(u, O_n)^2$.
end for
for all Possible decision of $\mathbf{b}$ **do**
  for $n = 1$ to N **do**
    for all $\mathbf{q_n}, \|\mathbf{q_n} - \mathbf{p_n}\| < r_{max}$ **do**

$$\hat{\mathbf{M}}_n(u) = \frac{c_n(u)\left[\mathbf{M}(u) + \mathbf{q}_n - \mathbf{s}_n\right] + \sum\limits_{k=1\to n-1} c_k(u)\hat{\mathbf{M}}_k(u)}{\sum\limits_{k=1\to n} c_k(u)}, \forall u$$

      Handle boundary constraint.
      Calculate $D(\mathbf{q_n}, \mathbf{b})$ and $E(\mathbf{q_n}, \mathbf{b})$.
    end for
    $\hat{\mathbf{q}}_n = \operatorname{argmin}_{\mathbf{q_n}} D(\mathbf{q_n}, \mathbf{b})E(\mathbf{q_n}, \mathbf{b})$
  end for
  $Q_\mathbf{b} = [\hat{\mathbf{q}}_1, \hat{\mathbf{q}}_2, ...\hat{\mathbf{q}}_N]$
end for
Find $\hat{B} = \operatorname{argmin}_\mathbf{b} D(Q_\mathbf{b}, \mathbf{b})E(Q_\mathbf{b}, \mathbf{b})$
return $\hat{Q} = Q(q_{\hat{\mathbf{b}}}, \hat{\mathbf{b}})$

The first objective function D jointly solve recomposition and retargeting as follows:

$$D(Q, \mathbf{b}) = \prod_{n\in[1,N]} (1 + \alpha\|\mathbf{q}_n - \mathbf{p}_n\|) \prod_{b_i\in\mathbf{b}} (1 + \beta\|b_i\|), \tag{6}$$

To avoid remarkable changes between the original and output images, we set the constraint of the foreground object locations in the output image as $\|\mathbf{q}_n - \mathbf{p}_n\| < r_{max}$. We also limit the cropping factor $\|b_i\| < b_{max}$. In our work, parameters r_{max} and b_{max} are set as 10% and 20% of the width of the source image, respectively.

On the other hand, the objective function E suppresses image distortion, which is determined by:

$$E(Q, \mathbf{b}) = (1 + \gamma F) \sum_{L_x\in L} \sum_{(u,v)\in L_x} \left\|\hat{\mathbf{M}}(u, v) - \mathbf{M}(u, v)\right\|^2, \tag{7}$$

where $\mathbf{M}$ and $\hat{\mathbf{M}}$ represent the 2D coordinates of source and recomposed mesh points (see Figure 2d and 2e for examples), and u and v denote the indices of the corresponding mesh points. Thus, $\mathbf{M}(u, v)$ represents the vector connecting points u and v. F is the proportion of flip-over triangle in the recomposed output, L denotes the set of strong edges (see Section 2.1).

To solve (5) for producing the final output image, we calculate the distances between each mesh point and the foreground objects, and update the locations of the mesh points $\hat{M}$ (via iterating between the calculation of $\mathbf{q}$ and $\mathbf{b}$). Note that, for display purposes, we show the recomposed but uncropped output in Figure 2e (i.e., no updates of $\mathbf{b}$). As for satisfying the boundary constraints to minimize image distortion, we uniformly stretch the background mesh grids to meet the nearest image boundary. The optimization process is summarized in Algorithm 1.

2.3.2 *Texture Mapping for Image Completion*

Once the locations of each mesh point in $\hat{\mathbf{M}}$ are determined, the remaining task is to render the final image output. This is achieved by texture mapping. That is, for each

Figure 5: Examples of photography recomposition and retargeting with different foreground object numbers.

triangle in $\mathbf{M}$, we calculate the areas A_{12}, A_{23} and A_{31} for each pixel $\mathbf{x}$ inside the triangular mesh (see Figure 4 for illustration). By barycentric interpolation, the pixels in $\hat{\mathbf{M}}$ can be computed as follows:

$$\hat{\mathbf{x}} = \left[A_{23}\hat{\mathbf{M}}(u_1) + A_{31}\hat{\mathbf{M}}(u_2) + A_{12}\hat{\mathbf{M}}(u_3)\right] / (A_{23}+A_{31}+A_{12}). \tag{8}$$

After all pixels are derived, the output will be the final recomposed and retargeted image.

3. EXPERIMENTS

We consider a variety of photographic images for evaluation. All the image data are collected from either those considered in related works or the Internet[1] . Figure 5 shows the results produced by our method. It can be seen that, given different reference images, our method successfully recomposed and retargeted images with single or multiple foreground objects. For example, we were able to transfer the composition and preserve the foreground-to-background relationships (see the shadow of the cat in Figure 5b and the grass regions in Figure 5c). As noted in [2], we can only provide qualitative evaluation for the effectiveness of recomposition, since no aesthetic scores can be calculated (we do not apply any predetermined aesthetic rules).

Compared to a recent work of [2], they required complex post-processing procedures to refine the recomposed outputs to avoid possible background mismatch. Moreover, they did not address the task of retargeting, so their outputs cannot fit the references well (see Figure 6 for example).

Finally, we present results in Figure 7 to show that our method can retarget the images, so that the outputs would fit the reference images with different aspect ratios. From the above experiments, we confirm the the effectiveness and robustness of our proposed method for joint recomposition and retargeting photographic images.

[1] Fig.1-s: CC Attribution, Thomas Leuthard; Fig.5a-r: hjjanisch @Flickr; Fig.5b-s, 5d-s: cited from [10]; Others: free or CC0 or public image from Internet.

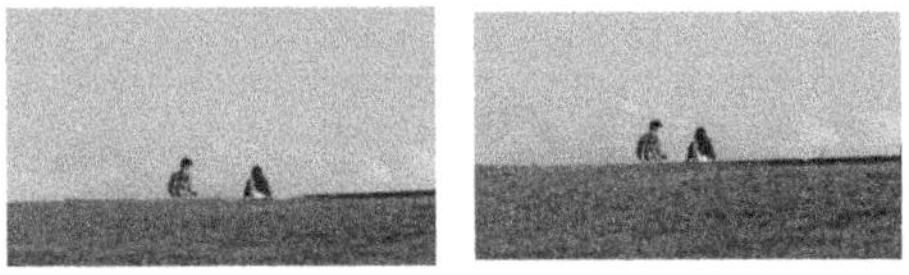

Figure 6: Comparison between [2] and our approach. Note that [2] simply performs image inpainting for recomposition, and thus its output does not fit the reference in Figure 5c.

Figure 7: Retargeted outputs of Figure 5d using reference images (in black and white) with different aspect ratios.

4. CONCLUSION

We presented an automatic framework to perform joint recomposition and retargeting of the input image for fitting the reference of interest. Unlike prior works requiring precollected data or predetermined aesthetics rules, our method applies graph matching to predict the locations of the foreground objects, while both foreground and background regions will be retargeted to fit the reference image. The above process is completed by solving a constrained mesh-warping based optimization problem, which minimizes both recovered errors and image distortion. Our experiments on several real-world photographic images with different foreground numbers verified the effectiveness of our method.

Acknowledgement This work is supported in part by the Ministry of Science and Technology of Taiwan via MOST104-3011-f-002-005 and MOST103-2221-E-001-021-MY2.

5. REFERENCE

[1] S. Bhattacharya, R. Sukthankar, and M. Shah. A framework for photo-quality assessment and enhancement based on visual aesthetics. In *ACM Multimedia*, 2010.
[2] H.-T. Chang, Y.-C. F. Wang, and M.-S. Chen. Transfer in photography composition. In *ACM Multimedia*, 2014.
[3] T. Cour et al. Balanced graph matching. In *NIPS*. 2007.
[4] S. Goferman, L. Zelnik-Manor, and A. Tal. Context-aware saliency detection. In *IEEE CVPR*, 2010.
[5] Y. Guo et al. Image retargeting using mesh parametrization. *IEEE Trans. Multimedia*, 2009.
[6] L. Liu, R. Chen, L. Wolf, and D. Cohen-Or. Optimizing photo composition. *Computer Graphics Forum*, 2010.
[7] M. Nishiyama, T. Okabe, Y. Sato, and I. Sato. Sensation-based photo cropping. In *ACM Multimedia*, 2009.
[8] A. Santella et al. Gaze-based interaction for semi-automatic photo cropping. In *SIGCHI*, 2006.
[9] L.-K. Wong and K.-L. Wong. Enhancing visual dominance by semantics-preserving image recomposition. In *ACM Multimedia*, 2012.
[10] F.-L. Zhang, M. Wang, and S.-M. Hu. Aesthetic image enhancement by dependence-aware object recomposition. *IEEE Trans. Multimedia*, 2013.

Egocentric Video Summarization of Cultural Tour based on User Preferences

Patrizia Varini, Giuseppe Serra and Rita Cucchiara
Dipartimento di Ingegneria "Enzo Ferrari", Università degli Studi di Modena e Reggio Emilia
Via Vivarelli, 10, Modena MO 41125, Italy
name.surname@unimore.it

ABSTRACT

In this paper, we propose a new method to obtain customized video summarization according to specific user preferences. Our approach is tailored on Cultural Heritage scenario and is designed on identifying candidate shots, selecting from the original streams only the scenes with behavior patterns related to the presence of relevant experiences, and further filtering them in order to obtain a summary matching the requested user's preferences. Our preliminary results show that the proposed approach is able to leverage user's preferences in order to obtain a customized summary, so that different users may extract from the same stream different summaries.

Categories and Subject Descriptors

I.4 [**Image processing and computer vision**]: Costumized egocentric video summarization; H.3.1 [**Information systems**]: Content analysis and indexing

General Terms

Algorithms, Design, Experimentation

Keywords

Video summarization, egocentric vision, wearable devices

1. INTRODUCTION

The increasingly popular life-logging streams, captured by head-mounted cameras, are claiming new techniques for automatic analysis, understanding and summarizing, being characterized by continuous changes of observer's focus, incessantly changing objects appearance and lack of hard cuts between scenes.

Lee *et al.* [4] show egocentric video summarization method that focuses on learning importance cues for each frame, such as objects and people the camera wearer interacts with, using features related with interaction distance, gaze, object-like appearance and motion and likelihood of a person's face within a region. Lu and Grauman [6] handle egocentric video summarization partitioning videos into sub-shots on the basis of motion features analysis, smooth the classification with a MRF and then select a chain of sub-shots choosing the ones in which they can detect the reciprocal influence propagation between important objects and characters, recovering their story. Yeung *et al.* [7] present techniques to evaluate video summarization through text, by measuring how well a video summary is able to retain the semantic information contained in its original stream. Although these summarization techniques deal with egocentric characteristics, they produce a univocal summary, not taking into account that different viewers, according to their own preferences, might prefer to retain some events rather than others. For instance, art lovers and fashion enthusiasts might want to extract different summaries from the same stream. In this paper we tackle customized ego-video summarization in a cultural heritage scenario, extracting from the streams only the scenes matching user's specific topic requests. In particular, to identify candidate relevant shots, we propose a behavior pattern detection classifier based on motion related features, as visual velocity, visual acceleration gradient and 3D GPS detected velocity. Due to user preferences heterogeneity, semantic classifiers for requested topics are built using a data-driven approach, that exploits geolocalization information and DBPedia knowledge. Experimental results show that our approach is able to achieve a customized summarization w.r.t. the user topic requests.

2. CUSTOMIZED SUMMARY

Our method takes a long first person video and user preferences as input and returns a customized short video summary as output. First, we identify the candidate subshots of video, discarding all the groups of frames whose motion based pattern cannot be put in relation with the presence of a relevant experience for the observer, for instance when he's changing his focus of attention. In particular our hypothesis relies on the assumption, tailored on a typical cultural experience scenario, that relevant scenes are associated to a camera's viewer behavior due to the presence of attention patterns. Discarding the non relevant subshots and limiting the analysis to keyframes, aims to reduce the computational overhead and to focus on the analysis of presumably relevant experiences. We assume that behavior patterns can be put in relation with user motion patterns, described by directly measurable features like frame visual assessment and apparent 2D and real 3D GPS measured motion. Thus we define a motion taxonomy, structured in two tiers, "Body in

MM'15, October 26–30, 2015, Brisbane, Australia.

DOI: http://dx.doi.org/10.1145/2733373.2806367.

motion" and "Body still". In "Body still" tier we find the classes "Static" (Body and head stand still) and "Looking around" (Body is still, head is moving). In the "Body in motion" tier we find "Walking" (Body is walking, head is approximately still), "Running" (Body running and Head in coherent motion), "On wheels" (Body and Head are still respect to a moving wheel mean of transport), "Wandering" (Body is in motion and head is rolling and/or pitching). To detect these classes, we analyze the aforecited features by partitioning frame in a 3×3 grid. Finally we smooth the motion classification with a Hidden Markov Model to shape, from the primitive motion classes, the behavior patterns defined as "Attention" (where user is paying attention to something), and the homonym w.r.t. motion classes "Looking around","Walking", "Running", "On wheels", "Wandering", filter the "Attention" behavior shots, that represent candidate shots, and extract the keyframes. In addition, we select from the candidate subshots only the ones that maximize the score of semantic relatedness to the user preferences and the visual diversity. Assuming that in Cultural Heritage scenario we usually deal with well localized classes of objects, we expect to enhance our performances leveraging GPS coordinates to gain context awareness. Thus, we build specific classifiers for the topics of interest using a data driven approach, to extract "on the fly" reliable image training, location relevant, samples from the web, evaluating importance on concept relatedness with user input using DBpedia semantic knowledge. Figure 1 synthesizes our method.

2.0.1 Visual Motion Descriptor

Visual motion feature is based on optic flow and acceleration gradient histograms estimated using the Farneback algorithm on frame sections using a 3×3 grid. Considering the optic flow computed for each couple of consecutive frames, the relative apparent velocity and acceleration gradient of each pixel is V_x, V_y, A_x and A_y. These values are expressed in polar coordinates as in the following:

$$M_V = \sqrt{V_x^2 + V_y^2} \qquad \theta_V = \arctan(V_y/V_x) \tag{1}$$

$$M_A = \sqrt{A_x^2 + A_y^2} \qquad \theta_A = \arctan(A_y/A_x) \tag{2}$$

Apparent velocity and acceleration gradients on x and y are computed for horizontal and vertical component. We compute the motion histogram by concatenating the apparent motion magnitudes M_V and M_A, with the orientations θ_V and θ_A, both quantized in eight bins for each frame section, weighting them by their magnitude respectively.

To assess the frame quality, we compute blur feature by using the method proposed by Roffet *et al.* [1]. The blurriness descriptor is obtained by concatenating sector features.

2.0.2 3D Motion Feature

Visitor's velocity and stops are a semantically relevant part of a touristic visit, being related to his intention and interests. Thus, collecting spatial coordinates via GPS tracking every second, allows to compute real velocity in three dimensions. Therefore visitor's trajectories are represented by movement tracks, consisting in the temporal sequence of the spatio-temporal points, meant as pairs compound with coordinate in space and in time $\{p_i = (x_i, y_i, z_i, t_i)\}$, where $(x_i, y_i, z_i) \in \mathcal{R}^3, t_i \in \mathcal{R}^+$ for $i = 0, 1, ..., N$ and $t_0 < t_i < t_N$. Even if trajectory is known, it does not entirely embed insight about stops and moves semantic information, in fact different visitors may have the same velocities in a number of subsequent points, but due to their different motion patterns, these points may have different classification outcomes for each of them. So we propose to adopt a spatio-temporal clustering algorithm to add the stop or move further information to our overall motion descriptor. K-means is a standard and efficient clustering algorithm, but needs to calculate the number of clusters, instead, we propose the use of a Shared Nearest Neighbor (SNN) density-based algorithm [2], whose extension in 4 spatio-temporal dimensions was first explored by [5], that is able to deal with noisy clusters of different densities, sizes and shapes. SNN relies on strength or similarity concept, evaluated on the number of nearest neighbors that couples of points, belonging to a set of N points in a metric space D, share. Therefore, our final overall 3D motion descriptor is obtained chaining the 3D real velocity components measured every second with a Boolean value that takes into account if the corresponding point must be regarded as a stop or a move.

2.0.3 Subshot Scoring

In order to reduce the jumpy values of motion measures due to meaningless head motion, the aforecited feature vector descriptors have been averaged over a window of 25 frames. This window corresponds to a duration of less than a second (acquiring at 29 FPs) and has been regarded to be a reasonable compromise to reduce randomness without information loss. In fact, the typical interval duration of head movement in the "paying attention" pattern has been put in relation to visual fixation, studied using gaze analysis, that is about 330 ms [3] but has a wide range of variation. Finally, we compose our overall feature vector concatenating the apparent motion histogram described in 2.0.1, averaged over the 1 sec window as described upper-line, with the three components of real velocity histogram and a Boolean value that indicates if the frame, within the window, belongs to a pattern of stop or of move of the visitor.

To speed up classification task, a linear multiclass SVM has been trained over the six identified motion classes and, using a Hidden Markov Model, the six behavior states are obtained from the six motion observables defined upper. Candidate relevant shots are finally identified as the ones associated with "Attention behavior" pattern.

2.1 Semantic classification and Shot chain

To identify the set of candidate shots that maximize the relatedness to the user's preferences extracted on input keywords, we build a visual recognition system based on discrete classifiers. Since topics of interest requested by the user can be potentially limitless, visual classification based on a number of rigidly defined classes may lead to poor results. To deal with this problem we proposed a data-driven approach that gathers 100 positive and negative training samples from the web, analyzing visual importance on semantic relatedness with user's preferences.

DBpedia is an important dataset in Linked Open Data, being provided with constantly updated semantic support structure, taxonomies (hyponyms, hyperonyms, synonyms, antonyms), cross references between related topics, disambiguation pages, ontology management and topic inference.

We regard Dbpedia as a undirected weighted graph $G = \{V, E\}$ where $V = \{1, ...n\}$ are the nodes representing con-

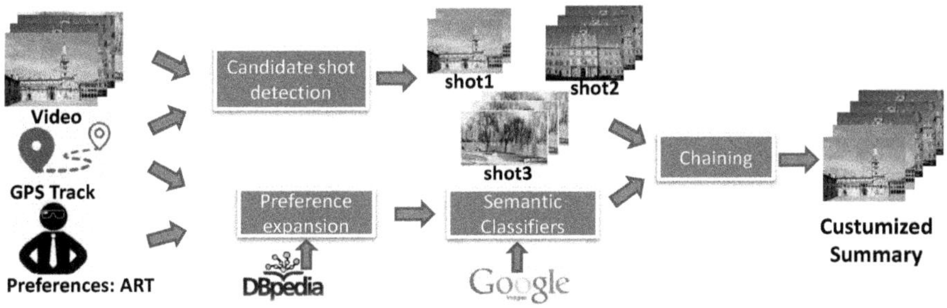

Figure 1: Schematization of the proposed method

cepts and $E \subset V \times V$ are the edges representing the links among nodes. To detect semantic community in DBpedia we use the recursive Girvan-Newman algorithm. The algorithm starts with computing the "betweenness" score for each of the edges ("betweenness" of an edge is the number of shortest paths between pairs of nodes that run along it). Then edges with the highest score are removed and the betweenness of all edges affected by the removal are computed. The last two steps are repeated until no edges remain.

At last for each detected semantic community including the user keywords and at most three related concepts, whose edge weight is over a threshold, we evaluate average of the shortest paths between communities members and the geolocalized place where the video has been captured, using Dijkstra algorithm. The basic intuition is that semantic concepts that are strictly related with user's preferences and visit location can improve the search terms for collecting training images, being Cultural Heritage items highly location-specific. Therefore positive samples are extracted from an image search on this set of terms, explicitly excluding all images labeled with semantic concepts or tags that have a shortest path distance from the preference cloud over a threshold. Negative samples are gathered using a search of semantic concepts reached moving on the graph from the expanded preference of N steps (empirically fixed to ten). Finally, starting from the positive and negative samples extracted, we build semantic classifiers using the Bag of Words approach (BOW). Relevance of each shots is computed taking into account classification scores (S) and visual diversity (D): $R(s) = w_1 S + w_2 D$. For each shot, S is computed as the sum of the scores obtained on each keyframe by all classifiers learned form the expanded preference communities and normalized by shot length. To measure visual diversity D, we represent a shot as a phrase (string) formed by the concatenation of the bag-of-words representations of consecutive characters (keyframes). To compare these phrases (or shots) we use the Needleman-Wunsch distance defined as the number of operations required to transform one string into the other. In particular, D is the normalized sum of the distances of the shot with respect to the adjacent ones. Based on preliminary experiments, we empirically fix the weighting coefficients w_1 and w_2.

3. EXPERIMENTAL RESULTS

To evaluate the performance of our approach we collected twelve videos captured by tourists that spend some time to visit cultural cities. Each video is about thirty minutes long and taken in a uncontrolled setting. They show the experience visitors such as a visit of cultural interest point (church, monument etc), shopping or walking. The camera is placed on the tourist's head and captures a 720×576, 25 frames per second RGB image sequence. A subset of 26100 annotated frames is used in order to test our methodology to recognize the motion classes belonging to the taxonomy cited above.

3.0.1 *Shot classification according to visual and motion pattern*

We examine the effectiveness of our feature vector representing frame quality assessment features and motion pattern, both apparent, due to first person capture, and absolute, measured by GPS. First, we compare our Visual motion descriptor (VMD), with a recent similar feature vector proposed by Lu *et al.* [6] that exploits HOF and Blur. As can be seen in Table 1, our VMD feature achieves a better performance. This may be mainly due to the presence of the acceleration gradient, that helps identify visual abrupt motion due to head movements. Moreover, we also present the performance of our final descriptor VMD-3DM (that includes 3D motion information). Figure 2 shows the confusion matrix for VMD and VMD-3DM features.

Visual descriptor	Accuracy
Lu *et al.* [6]	61.7
VMD	69.7
VMD-3DM	74.1

Table 1: Comparison of average class accuracy.

As can be seen, adding descriptors related to 3D motion can help to easily distinguish higher speed motions from wide head motion or sprawl movements. For this reason, among the classes that increase their accuracy, can be found found "Running" and above all "Moving on Wheels". The earning of "Looking around" class also may be due to the difficulty to discriminate steady head motion from sprawl behavior in motion in absence of measurements related to real motion.

3.0.2 *Keyframe classification according to relatedness to user preferences*

We evaluate the ability of our approach to collect reliable training set analyzing the semantic relatedness of user's preference with DBpedia knowledge structure. We show the results of three experiments, where the user's preferences are expressed by two groups of keywords: "Social" and "Clothes" for the first one, "Romanesque" and "Baroque" for the second and "Sport Cars" and "Gardens" for the third. To analyze our results we compare the performance obtained by

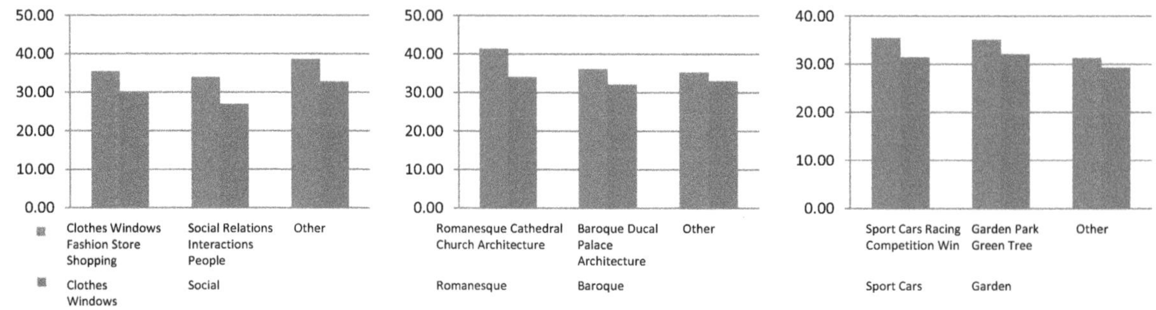

Figure 3: Keyframes classification accuracy with (blue) and without (red) semantic expansion

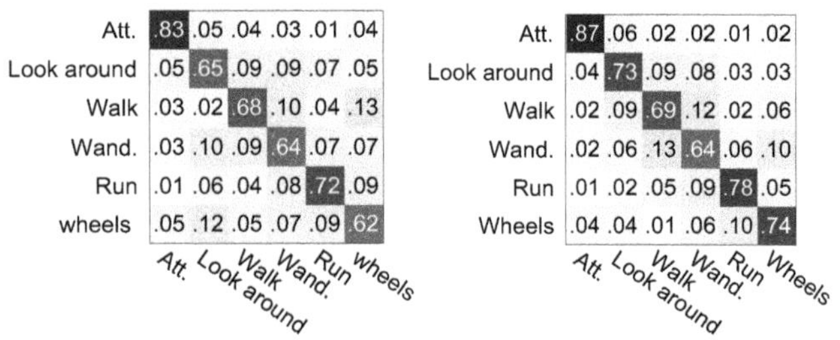

(a) (b)

Figure 2: Classification accuracy using different descriptors: a) feature vector based on visual features (Blur, Optical Flow and Acc. Gradient; b) our feature vector.

classifiers trained with web images extracted using the proposed geolocalization and semantic expansion with classifiers learned using only the user keywords. In particular, for each image we extract SIFT descriptors computed at four scales (4, 6, 8, and 10), over a dense regular grid with a spacing of 6 pixels. The codebook size is set to 2000. Images are hierarchically partitioned into 1×1, 2×2 and 4×4 blocks on 3 levels respectively. SVM classifiers have been trained on the collected images (60% for training and 40% validation and testing) and performance was evaluated using 10-fold cross-validation. Notice that in all cases classification performances outperform the baseline. In particular, we observe that the information about visit location can better restrict the visual appearances of the topics of interest requested by the user.

3.0.3 User experience

Finally, we perform a "blind taste test" in which, for each video of the dataset, the summarization based on our approach and a baseline are shown to six students, that have to report which summary best meets the user's preferences related to video. We first show to the students a browsable sped-up version of the entire original videos, and ask them to annotate the shots that they think are fitting the user's preferences. Afterward, for each original video, we show them two summaries: one is obtained with the proposed method, the other is from a baseline method in which a random selection of a fixed number of candidate shots are chained. We do not reveal the order as it is obtained randomly. After viewing both, each of them is asked to report which summary better matches the user's preferences in his opinion. We used a Likert scale with a score between 1 and 5, where 1 was "no good summarization" and 5 "perfect summarization". This test shows that 76% of the comparisons assigns a higher score to summaries obtained with our approach w.r.t. the baseline.

4. CONCLUSIONS

In this paper we have introduced a novel approach to obtain customized egocentric video summaries in Cultural Heritage scenario. The approach relied on detecting candidate shots, extracting from the original video the ones with a "paying attention" pattern, and further filtering them in order to obtain a summary matching the requested user preferences. Preliminary experiments show that our results are promising in enabling users to achieve personalized summary from visitor videos.

Acknowledgments

This work was partially supported by the Fondazione Cassa di Risparmio di Modena project "Vision for Augmented Experiences" and the PON R&C project DICET-INMOTO (Cod. PON04a2_D).

5. REFERENCES

[1] F. Crété-Roffet, T. Dolmiere, P. Ladret, M. Nicolas, et al. The blur effect: Perception and estimation with a new no-reference perceptual blur metric. In *Proc. of SPIE*, 2007.

[2] L. Ertöz, M. Steinbach, and V. Kumar. Finding clusters of different sizes, shapes, and densities in noisy, high dimensional data. In *Proc. of SDM*, 2003.

[3] J. M. Henderson. Regarding scenes. *Current Directions in Psychological Science*, 16(4):219–222, 2007.

[4] Y. J. Lee, J. Ghosh, and K. Grauman. Discovering important people and objects for egocentric video summarization. In *Proc. of CVPR*, 2012.

[5] Q. Liu, M. Deng, J. Bi, and W. Yang. A novel method for discovering spatio-temporal clusters of different sizes, shapes, and densities in the presence of noise. *International Journal of Digital Earth*, 7(2):138–157, 2014.

[6] Z. Lu and K. Grauman. Story-driven summarization for egocentric video. In *Proc. of CVPR*, 2013.

[7] S. Yeung, A. Fathi, and L. Fei-Fei. Videoset: Video summary evaluation through text. *CoRR*, abs/1406.5824, 2014.

A Novel Statistical Approach for Image and Video Retrieval and Its Adaption for Active Learning

Moitreya Chatterjee
USC Institute for Creative Technologies
Playa Vista, CA, USA
metro.smiles@gmail.com

Anton Leuski
USC Institute for Creative Technologies
Playa Vista, CA, USA
leuski@ict.usc.edu

ABSTRACT

The ever expanding multimedia content (such as images and videos), especially on the web, necessitates effective text query-based search (or retrieval) systems. Popular approaches for addressing this issue, use the query-likelihood model which fails to capture the user's information needs. In this work therefore, we explore a new ranking approach in the context of image and video retrieval from text queries. Our approach assumes two separate underlying distributions for query and the document respectively. We then, determine the extent of similarity between these two statistical distributions for the task of ranking. Furthermore we extend our approach, using Active Learning techniques, to address the question of obtaining a good performance without requiring a fully labeled training dataset. This is done by taking Sample Uncertainty, Density and Diversity into account. Our experiments on the popular TRECVID corpus and the open, relatively small-sized USC SmartBody corpus show that we are almost at-par or sometimes better than multiple state-of-the-art baselines.

Categories and Subject Descriptors

H.3.3 [**Information Search and Retrieval**]: Clustering, Retrieval Models; H.5.1 [**Multimedia Information Systems**]: Video (e.g., tape, disk, DVI)

Keywords

KL-Divergence; Active Learning; Clustering; Uncertainty

1. INTRODUCTION

The ever increasing volume of multimedia content (such as images, videos, etc.), thanks to the web, has necessitated effective multimedia search systems. The goal of these search (or retrieval) systems, is to be able to rank the content (multimedia samples) in order of relevance to a given text query by the user. The popular web-based image/video search systems, e.g. Google, Yahoo, etc. are common examples.

MM '15, October 26-30, 2015, Brisbane, Australia.

http://dx.doi.org/10.1145/2733373.2806368.

Conventional search systems typically, first automatically annotate the samples with multiple text labels (each typically one word long), specifying different objects, events, etc. called *concepts*. They then, treat every sample as simply a text document containing the labels and rank them based on the similarity of these labels with the user's query [11]. However the first step of automated annotation, tends to be noisy and introduces errors. Thus, these approaches are often not effective. Direct-retrieval approaches, inspired from cross-language retrieval techniques, bypass the task of annotation [5]. Such techniques treat the query to be coming from one language and the feature representations of the documents to be ranked, to be coming from some other.

For the task of ranking, many of these direct-retrieval systems [6, 9, 2], including the Continuous Relevance Model (CRM), uses query-likelihood as a ranking function [5]. The query-likelihood models assume a language model over the documents and the query to have been sampled out from that distribution. It then ranks the documents by computing the conditional probability of the query given a document. This style of modeling ignores the user's information need, since the query is assumed to be modeled by the document distribution [3]. This raises a central research question: Can there be a new way to rank the documents, without making such an assumption?

In this work, we address this fundamental issue by exploring a ranking function that captures the notion of relevance of the query and the document as a measure of distance.

Another major concern with these retrieval systems is that they require a large fully annotated training corpus for a good performance. The human-effort costs for doing this, is prohibitively high. This begs an answer to another research question: Can we achieve a good retrieval performance without requiring a fully annotated training data (i.e. would a partially annotated training dataset suffice)?

Active Learning addresses this issue by outputting an order of labeling the unlabeled training samples such that a good retrieval performance is achieved before all unlabeled data is queried for their labels. Typical active learning systems consists of a retrieval/classification engine and a sample selection engine, which ranks the unlabeled samples, typically by a measure of *informativeness* [11]. In our work, we determine this informativeness by combining measures of Sample Density and Diversity [2] with that of Sample Uncertainty, while the ranking function that we talked about is used for the retrieval engine. We call this system KLActive. Our experiments show that KLActive performs better than the state-of-the-art on the popular, large TRECVID corpus and almost at-par on the smaller USC SmartBody corpus.

2. BACKGROUND

2.1 Query-Likelihood and CRM

The research community has already explored retrieval of multimedia content using Query-Likelihood as a ranking function [6, 9, 4]. The idea behind query-likelihood is to compute the quantity $P(w|\mathbf{r_i})$, the conditional probability of the text query word w given a M-dimensional feature vector $\mathbf{r_i}$, of an image/video sample i. Assuming we have t samples to rank, we compute $P(w|\mathbf{r_i})$ for each $i = 1, 2, ..., t$ and then rank them based on their conditional probability scores. CRM, one such approach, proposes to compute this probability as follows: $P(w|\mathbf{r_i}) = P(w, \mathbf{r_i})/P(\mathbf{r_i})$ [4]. The joint-distribution is then estimated from the training data ($Train$) by

$$P(w, \mathbf{r_i}) = \sum_{J \in Train} (P(J)P(w|J) \prod_{s_k \in \mathbf{r_i}, k=1}^{M} P(s_k|J)) \quad (1)$$

2.2 CBIR Systems and KL-Divergence

Content-Based IR (CBIR) systems seek to rank the image/video samples just like conventional multimedia search systems, except here the query is in the form of an image/video rather than text. The research community has addressed this question by utilizing distance measures to compute similarity between the query and the sample to be ranked. One such popular distance measure is the Kullback-Leibler Divergence (KL-Divergence) [7, 10]. KL-Divergence between two continuous distributions P and Q (defined over the variable $\mathbf{r}$) is defined as :

$$D(P||Q) = \int_{\mathbf{r}} P(\mathbf{r}) \log(P(\mathbf{r})/Q(\mathbf{r}))d\mathbf{r} \quad (2)$$

CBIR systems, typically compute a language model (a Bag-of-Words) representation for both the query and the sample to be ranked and are thus able to compute a KL-Divergence based similarity between the two distributions.

2.3 Active Learning

Active Learning is a technique for determining an optimal order of labeling the unlabeled samples in the training data, such that a system achieves a good performance at the task of retrieval/classification on unseen test data, even before it has been trained with the fully annotated training dataset. This is typically done by ranking the unlabeled training samples by a measure of *informativeness* and labeling the samples with a higher score first and using them to train the retrieval/classification engine [11, 2]. This process is repeated in batches. CRMActive, a promising recent approach, computes this *informativeness* measure by combining quantities measuring Sample Uncertainty (how sure is the retrieval engine about the relevance of a query to the sample in question), Sample Density (does the sample chosen for labeling represent the population or is it an outlier) and Sample Diversity (how much do the samples chosen for labeling resemble each other) [2].

For computing Sample Uncertainty, CRMActive first uses Normalized CRM [4] for annotating the unlabeled samples with concepts from the vocabulary. Assuming a vocabulary $\mathcal{V}$ consisting of k concepts, it computes $P(w_i|\mathbf{r})$, $w_i \in \mathcal{V}$, $i = 1, 2, ..., k$ for the image/video described by the M-dimensional feature vector $\mathbf{r}$ and picks the top-n concepts, where $0 < n < k$, as relevant for the particular image/video (in decreasing order of relevance). Now, Sample Uncertainty of an unlabeled sample $\mathbf{x}$, $unct(\mathbf{x})$ is obtained by computing the difference between the conditional probabilities of the most relevant label, i.e. $i = 1$ and the first irrelevant one $i = n + 1$ [2].

For computing Sample Density and Diversity, CRMActive clusters the samples in the feature space, taking into account the agreement between the labels of the samples of a cluster.

Sample Density of an unlabeled sample $\mathbf{x}$ in cluster C is then computed by

$$den(\mathbf{x}) = \frac{p(\mathbf{x})}{\max_{\mathbf{x}_i \in Train} p(\mathbf{x}_i)},$$

where $Train$ is the training set and $p(\mathbf{x})$ is the standard Gaussian Kernel Density Estimate:

$$p(\mathbf{x}) = \frac{1}{|C|} \sum_{\mathbf{x}_i \in C} K_{Gauss}(\mathbf{x}, \mathbf{x}_i)$$

and $|C|$ is the total number of samples in cluster C. For two M-dimensional vectors $\mathbf{x}$, $\mathbf{y}$, $K_{Gauss}(\mathbf{x}, \mathbf{y})$ is defined by:

$$K_{Gauss}(\mathbf{x}, \mathbf{y}) = \prod_{i=1}^{M} (\frac{1}{\sqrt{2\pi}\sigma} \exp(-(x_i - y_i)^2/2\sigma^2)) \quad (3)$$

where σ controls the spread of the kernel.

Assuming there are T clusters, each "represented" by their respective centroids in set $\mathcal{S}$, $\mathcal{S} = \{rep(C_1), ..., rep(C_T)\}$, Sample Diversity of an unlabeled sample $\mathbf{x}$ is defined as:

$$div(\mathbf{x}) = 1 - \max_{\mathbf{x}_i \in \mathcal{S}} \frac{K_{Gauss}(\mathbf{x}, \mathbf{x}_i)}{\sqrt{K_{Gauss}(\mathbf{x}, \mathbf{x}) \times K_{Gauss}(\mathbf{x}_i, \mathbf{x}_i)}},$$

Finally, *informativeness* of an unlabeled sample $\mathbf{x}$ is defined as :

$$Info(\mathbf{x}) = \lambda_1 \times unct(\mathbf{x}) + \lambda_2 \times den(\mathbf{x}) + \lambda_3 \times div(\mathbf{x}), \quad (4)$$

where $\sum_{i=1}^{3} \lambda_i = 1$; $\forall i$, $\lambda_i \geq 0$.

3. PROPOSED APPROACH

CRM-based approaches use query-likelihood for ranking and assume the query to be sampled out from the distribution governing the documents. The query is not modeled directly, thereby ignoring the user's information needs. In order to mitigate this weakness, drawing inspiration from cross-language retrieval [3], we explore a model comparison based approach for ranking. Our approach assumes that there is a separate probability distribution governing both the query and the samples to be ranked. We now compare the similarity between the expected value of the query distribution and that of the sample distribution, using KL-Divergence. This permits the ranking of the samples.

Let θ_d be the distribution governing the samples to be ranked, $E_q\theta$ be the expected value of the query distribution and $\mathbf{r}$ be the random variable over which the distributions are defined. Then the KL-Divergence between these two distributions according to Equation 2 is proportional to:

$$-D(E_q\theta||\theta_d) \propto \int_{\mathbf{r}} E_q\theta(\mathbf{r}) \log \theta_d(\mathbf{r})d\mathbf{r}, \quad (5)$$

where both the query and the document distributions are approximated by kernels. θ_d is approximated by the Gaussian kernel (Equation 3) $K_{Gauss}(\mathbf{r}, \mathbf{r}_d)$, with $\mathbf{r_d}$ being the feature vector representing the document(d) to be ranked. However, different from CBIR approaches, our query distribution is not directly representable in terms of $\mathbf{r}$, since our queries are texts. Taking a cue from cross-language retrieval [3], we address this issue by the following mapping:

$$E_q\theta(\mathbf{r}) = \frac{\sum_{J \in Train} K_{Gauss}(\mathbf{r}, \mathbf{r}_J).\beta_J(q)}{\sum_{J \in Train} \beta_J(q)}, \quad (6)$$

where $\mathbf{r}_J$ is the feature vector of the current training image J, $Train$ is the training set, q is the query term and $K_{Gauss}(.,.)$ is the Gaussian kernel of Equation 3 and the query distribution, $\beta_J(q)$, has the following multinomial form:

$$\beta_J(q) = \lambda \frac{N_{q,J}}{N_J} + (1 - \lambda) \frac{N_q}{N} \quad (7)$$

where $N_{q,J}$ is the number of times q occurred in the annotation of image J, N_J is the number of annotation labels for image J, N_q is the total number of times q occurred in the training set, and N is the total length of all annotations across the training data. λ denotes a parameter that controls the degree of smoothing. Equation 6 computes the mapping statistic over the entire training set and is thus, in effect an expected value of the query distribution.

Note that the integral in Equation 5 is actually an integration over all M-dimensions of the features. Also, due to the limitation of expressing continuous integrals in computers, we approximate this representation by a sum over the corresponding feature values which occur in the dataset. This version of the Equation 5 constitutes our ranking function.

In order to extend this model for active learning, we compute measures of Sample Density and Sample Diversity following the cluster-refinement based approach proposed in CRMActive [2]. However, we determine Sample Uncertainty of an unlabeled sample $\mathbf{x}$ as follows:

$$unct(\mathbf{x}) = \frac{1}{-D(q_1||\mathbf{x}) - (-D(q_{k+1}||\mathbf{x}))}, \quad (8)$$

where $q_1, ..., q_k$ (in decreasing order of relevance) are the top-k most relevant labels assigned to $\mathbf{x}$ by our model. The denominator in Equation 8 gives a measure of the gap (distance) between the KL-Divergence measures of the most relevant label and the first irrelevant one with respect to the sample $\mathbf{x}$. This therefore points to the level of uncertainty the model has about the labels it assigns to $\mathbf{x}$. Now, we combine the three measures of Density, Diversity and Uncertainty using Equation 4. Thus, we have in place both the ranking system as well as the sample selection(order determining) system. We call this combined system KLActive.

4. EXPERIMENTS

4.1 Methodology

We conduct experiments to test the effectiveness of an algorithm at the task of retrieving relevant images/videos for a query concept and see how its performance evolves under an active learning setting. In our experiments, the goal of an algorithm is to rank the test samples by their similarity to a single word query without annotating the test samples, i.e. direct-retrieval. The algorithm starts with the initial training dataset, a small section of which is labeled and the rest being unlabeled. For each concept label in the vocabulary, the algorithm ranks the test samples by their similarity to the concept. It then selects a batch of K unlabeled training samples, we reveal the labels for these selected samples, and the algorithm repeats the ranking task. For each round, we compute precision scores of the algorithm for the top 5 retrieved images/videos per concept and report their average. We call this score (AP for the top 5 documents): P@5.

4.2 Datasets

TRECVID 2007: The portion of the TRECVID 2007 video corpus, which is annotated, has 110 short video clips, with a total of about 21,500 frames [1]. Each frame in every video is annotated with at most 16 concept labels selected from a set of 36 concepts such as "crowd", "building", "airplane", etc. that constitute the whole vocabulary. This corpus has been used extensively in video retrieval/annotation experiments [11, 2]. For every frame, a 225-dimensional feature vector (color moment, edge orientation histogram, wavelet PWTTWT texture) is computed, as described in Zha et al. [11]. The frames from 13 randomly selected videos constitute our test set for our experiments, while we use the rest of the data (frames from 97 videos) for training. We selected 4000 frames from the training data as the initial set of labeled samples, containing at least 1 positive example of every concept. We set the batch size (i.e. the number of samples which are annotated in every iteration), to be 2400.

USC SmartBody: SmartBody is an open virtual character animation platform. It ships with a library of 274 animation clips such as walking, hand beat gesture, pointing, etc. [8]. The animations are defined on a 3D skeleton consisting of 119 individual joints, the 3D coordinates of which are available from the SmartBody API. A dataset created with this software was recently made public [2]. Here, each video is annotated (not at the frame-level) using at most 6 concept labels from a vocabulary of 30 labels such as "Legs", "Arms", "Face", etc. The dataset along with the features - the differences between the minimum and the maximum values for the skeleton angles at 9 joints (neck, left(L)/right(R) shoulders, L/R elbows, L/R hip joints, and L/R knees)- is open to the research community. Using these features, we encode every video as a 9-dimensional feature vector. We randomly selected 24 videos for testing and used the rest of the data (250 animations) for training. We selected 40 animations from the training data as the initial set of labeled samples, containing at least one positive example of each concept. We now set, batch size (i.e. the number of samples which are annotated in every iteration), to be 23.

4.3 Baseline Systems

For the task of direct retrieval in an active learning context, we compare KLActive with three different approaches. The first and the second one being an active learning system that uses KL-Divergence based model comparison (KL-Random) and Normalized CRM (CRMRandom) as the retrieval engines respectively, while the samples are selected randomly in each batch of active learning. The results are averaged over 3 runs with different random seeds for both cases. The only prior approach that is known to us, that selects the samples non-randomly in this setting, is CRMActive [2]. We therefore, also compare our approach with theirs. For our experiments, the values of the parameters λ, σ and the validated parameters of the baseline approaches

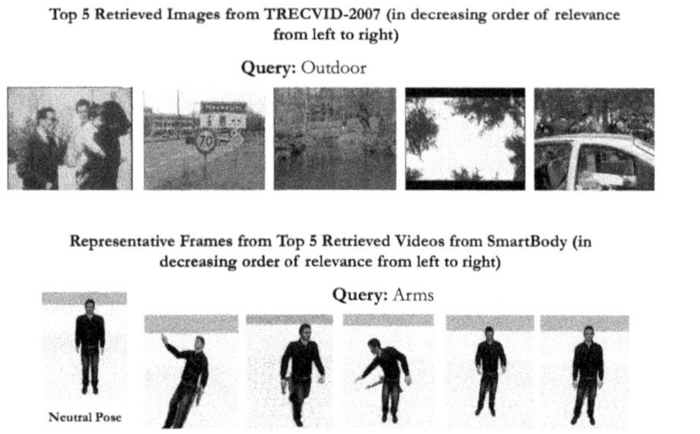

Figure 1: Example retrieval results by KLActive after Round 0 for TRECVID and SmartBody Datasets.

are all selected by performing 10-fold cross-validation on the first annotation batch. The values of all the parameters for the active-learning setup are reused from past work [2].

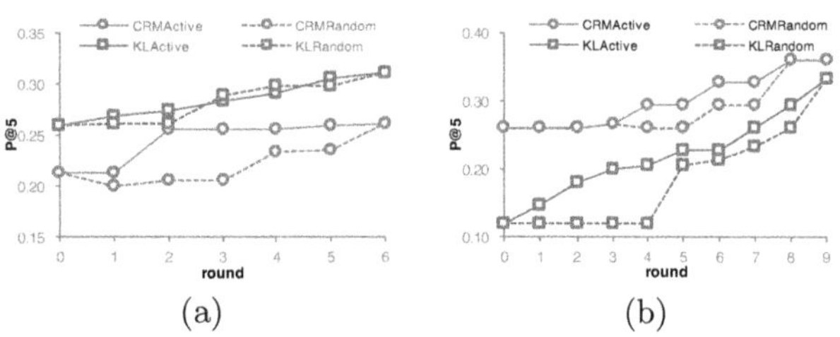

Table 1: AP scores for top-5 videos/images (on Y-axis) for retrieval on TRECVID (a), SmartBody (b).

4.4 Results and Discussion

Table 1 presents the retrieval results for the TRECVID Corpus and for the USC SmartBody corpus over different rounds of active learning. The first observation that stands out from the results is that all the models tend to improve their performance as successive rounds of active learning progress. This leads us to conclude that supplying more training data helps improve the performance. The next noteworthy observation is that for both the datasets the Active Learning version of both the CRM and KL-Divergence algorithms generally outperform their random counterparts. Thus it seems prudent, in the context of active learning, to label unlabeled samples based on a measure of sample *informativeness* rather than random sample selection.

However, the more interesting observation is a comparison of the two ranking schemes: KL-Divergence and query-likelihood based CRM. For TRECVID, clearly the KL- Divergence based approaches win while this is not the case for SmartBody. We hypothesize that this is primarily due to difference in dataset size. TRECVID is a much larger dataset compared to SmartBody. Further for the experiments, we start with much more samples in TRECVID (4000 as opposed to 40) and then in every pass we add more labeled samples (2400 as opposed to 23). Now recall that the idea in query-likelihood is to estimate the parameters of a distribution over the documents(θ_d) and the query is treated to be sampled out from this distribution. On the other hand in KL-divergence based model comparison, we assume separate distributions for the query(θ_q) and the documents(θ_d) and compare the two. This results in two fundamentally different ranking functions, Equation 1 for CRMActive and Equation 5 for KLActive. Due to the paucity of samples in SmartBody, KLActive fails to capture the true query distribution θ_q. This problem however, is less acute for TRECVID. Thus, the KL-Divergence based models do not perform as well on SmartBody as they do in TRECVID. This is also borne out by the fact that in SmartBody, the difference between the two approaches in terms of precision values at Round-0 (when there is less labeled training data) is much larger as compared to Round-9.

Figure 1 shows sample retrieval results for both SmartBody and TRECVID for sample queries in the first round using KLActive. The relevance of the retrieved results to the queries is very apparent, showing the model's effectiveness.

5. CONCLUSIONS

This work explores a novel ranking scheme for retrieval of multimedia content based on a statistical model comparison-based approach of query and document distributions. Furthermore, we extend the model in order to adapt it to an active learning setting. Experimental results show the effectiveness of our approach viz-a-viz other baselines. KLActive is a promising avenue to explore for future research.

Acknowledgements

The project or effort described here has been sponsored in part by the U.S. Army. Statements and opinions expressed do not necessarily reflect the position or the policy of the United States Government, and no official endorsement should be inferred.

6. REFERENCES

[1] TRECVID 2007: TREC Video Retrieval Evaluation. link: http://www-nlpir.nist.gov/projects/tv2007/tv2007.html.
[2] M. Chatterjee and A. Leuski. Crmactive: An active learning based approach for effective video annotation and retrieval. In *Proceedings of the 5th ACM ICMR*, 2015.
[3] V. Lavrenko. *A generative theory of relevance*. Springer Science & Business Media, 2008.
[4] V. Lavrenko, S. Feng, and R. Manmatha. Statistical models for automatic video annotation and retrieval. In *ICASSP*, 2004.
[5] V. Lavrenko, R. Manmatha, and J. Jeon. A model for learning the semantics of pictures. In *NIPS*, 2003.
[6] A. Llorente, R. Manmatha, and S. Rüger. Image retrieval using markov random fields and global image features. In *Proceedings of the ACM CIVR*, 2010.
[7] P. J. Moreno, P. P. Ho, and N. Vasconcelos. A Kullback-Leibler divergence based kernel for svm classification in multimedia applications. In *NIPS*, 2003.
[8] M. Thiebaux, S. Marsella, A. N. Marshall, and M. Kallmann. Smartbody: Behavior realization for embodied conversational agents. In *AAMAS*, 2008.
[9] M. Wang, X.-S. Hua, Y. Song, X. Yuan, S. Li, and H.-J. Zhang. Automatic video annotation by semi-supervised learning with kernel density estimation. In *14th ACM Multimedia*, 2006.
[10] X. Wu, W.-L. Zhao, and C.-W. Ngo. Near-duplicate keyframe retrieval with visual keywords and semantic context. In *Proceedings of the 6th ACM CIVR*, 2007.
[11] Z.-J. Zha et al. Interactive video indexing with statistical active learning. *Multimedia, IEEE Transactions on*, 14(1), 2012.

Automatically Stereoscopic Camera Control for 3D Animation Production

Dawei Lu, Huadong Ma, Zeyu Wang, Liang Liu, Huiyuan Fu
Beijing Key Laboratory of Intelligent Telecommunications Software and Multimedia
Beijing University of Posts and Telecommunications
Beijing, China
ludawei19@gmail.com, mhd@bupt.edu.cn, anitawangzy@gmail.com,
liangliu82@gmail.com, fhy@bupt.edu.cn

ABSTRACT

This paper proposes a novel approach for automatically controlling stereoscopic camera parameters that specifically addresses challenges in stereo 3D animation production process. Our proposed camera control method produces stereo contents with preferable depth perception and guarantees visual comfort by optimization of camera parameters. We introduce an attention tracking method to calculate convergence plane, avoiding window violation and minimizing visual conflict. Moreover, we derive an smoothing function on convergence plane that reduces depth jump over time. Then, we calculate the inter-axial separation using a perceived depth mapping. We describe how to implement our method on the Maya plug-in and test the stereo effect using professional stereo 3D animation scenes. The experimental results, including a user study, show that our method enhances the stereo effect. Our controller provides automatic camera control that can be helpful in creating comfortable and faster stereo 3D animations.

Categories and Subject Descriptors

I.3.7 [**Computer Graphics**]: Three-Dimensional Graphics and Realism—*animation*; H.5.1 [**Information Interfaces and Presentation**]: Multimedia Information Systems—*animations*

Keywords

Stereoscopic 3D; Disparity control; Animation; Attention tracking; Visual comfort

1. INTRODUCTION

Production and display of computer graphics (animation) have been studied for many years. Recent advances in stereoscopic displays make stereo 3D animation play a vital role in the movie and entertainment industry. The sources of stereo 3D animation are usually created by virtual stereo cameras that simulate human binocular vision. However, similar to realistic stereoscopic contents, there are several challenges in producing stereo 3D animations with comfortable view experience.

MM'15, October 26–30, 2015, Brisbane, Australia.
© 2015 ACM. ISBN 978-1-4503-3459-4/15/10 ...$15.00.
DOI: http://dx.doi.org/10.1145/2733373.2806369.

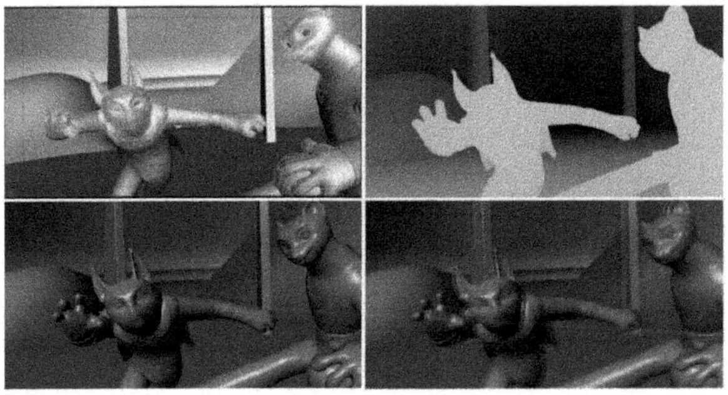

Figure 1: An example frame of a animation scene cut with our method. The top left is an animation scene and the top right is depth map of the scene. The bottom left shows the result of left view and the bottom right shows the red-cyan result.

The principal challenge is controlling the perceived depth of human visual system. Depth perception of a scene is achieved through differences between two views in the display screen. Unlike viewing in the realistic world, in order to ensure visual comfort the reconstructed depth in stereoscopic displays is limited in a certain range that depends on the display environment.The comfortable range of the perceived depth, also called the comfort zone, is controlled by stereoscopic camera parameters. In the past decades, a number of methods have been proposed for camera control of stereo contents based on stereoscopic geometry [2, 3, 8]. Zilly et al. [8] provided an overview of stereo content creation. However, the main concern of these researches are stereo camera control for realistic scenes. For virtual environments, Oskam et al. [5] presented a real-time stereo camera controller for interactive 3D applications. Recently, Celikcan et al. [1] also proposed an attention-aware camera control method for interactive 3D environments, they took the importance of scene elements into account to optimize camera parameters in real-time.

In the process of stereo 3D animation production, unlike interactive environments, the trajectories of camera position are predefined by directors similar to movie shooting. Thus, in order to create stereo animations with excellent view experience, the factors affecting stereo effect (including vergence-accommodation conflict, stereoscopic window

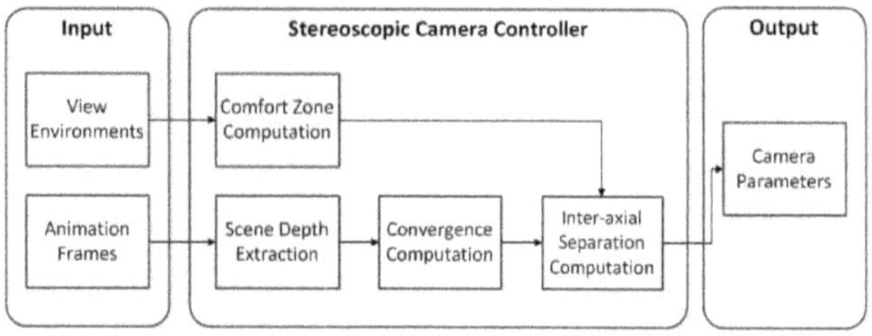

Figure 2: The flowchart of the automatically stereoscopic camera system.

violation, and perceived depth jump), all should be fully considered and handled. Even though previous works manage to control the perceived depth for visual comfort, the other factors also need be considered for optimization of stereoscopic camera parameters. In this paper, we propose a stereoscopic camera controller for 3D animation production that is able to automatically optimize camera parameters (Figure 1). Our method divides the convergence and inter-axial separation computation into two steps. Based on the scene depth we define the attention objects and introduce an attention tracking mechanism to initialize the convergence plane per frame. In this way, the accommodation-vergence conflict and stereo window violation can be avoided as much as possible. Moreover, the object motion and convergence sharply change always create depth jump over time which leads to visual fatigue. To solve the problem, we provide a smooth function to smooth the change in convergence planes. Then, based on the stereoscopic geometry, we define a mapping of the perceived depth to the comfort zone. At last we use the mapping and the optimized convergence to calculate the inter-axial separation.

Our automatic camera controller can assist producer to create stereo 3D animations more quickly and accurately. For the viewer our controller ensures that the animations are always comfortable to watch. The results of a user study show that our method is preferred over naive and previous camera control methods.

2. OUR APPROACH

Our goal is to automatically control camera convergence and inter-axial separation per frame in animations. In our system, we use off-axis camera model to avoid keystones and other distortions. Figure 2 shows the flowchart of our system.

2.1 Stereoscopic geometry

The binocular depth is created when two eyes of human view the world from different angles, and the depth is affected by interpupillary distance and vergence. Thus stereoscopic cameras simulate the human visual system to create stereo contents by two principal parameters: convergence distance Z_c and inter-axial separation s. Moreover, the two parameters are controlled by a mapping of the scene depth to the perceived depth, using relationship between projection plane disparity d and screen parallax p.

Fig 3 shows the geometry of off-axis camera model and the perceived depth of human eyes. The projection plane disparity of a point with the scene depth Z is defined by

$$d = (1 - \frac{Z_c}{Z})s. \tag{1}$$

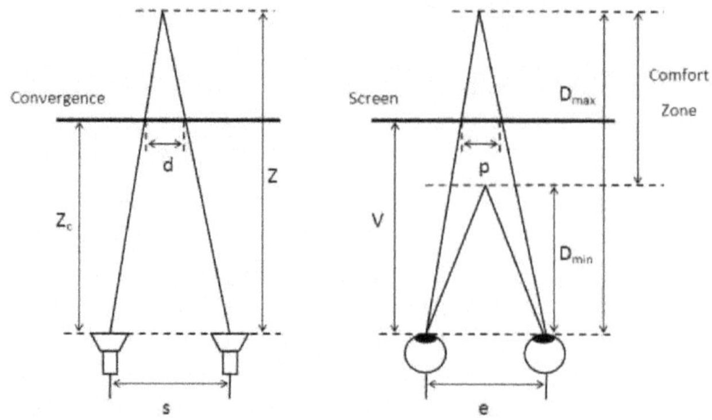

Figure 3: The geometry of stereoscopic vision. The left is a virtual camera setup with off-axis model and the right is a human perception of a stereoscopic 3D scene in the screen.

Given the scaling factor according to the screen width w_p and the projection plane width w_d, the screen parallax p can be defined by $p = d(w_p/w_d)$. Then the perceived depth of human is derived as

$$D = \frac{eV}{e - p}, \tag{2}$$

where V is the distance between the human eyes and the display screen and e is the human interpupillary distance (we use average 65 mm). Thus, using Eq.(1) and Eq.(2) we can define the mapping of the scene depth Z to the perceived depth D:

$$D = f(Z) = \frac{eV}{e - \frac{w_p}{w_d}(1 - \frac{Z_c}{Z})s}. \tag{3}$$

Moreover, given a viewing distance we can calculate the comfortable depth zone $\{D_{min}, D_{max}\}$. A number of studies have been proposed for defining the comfort zone [4, 6, 7] and the results have slightly differences. In our controller we use the comfort zone in [4] as default, which can be modified according to personal preferences.

For mapping the scene depth to the comfort zone, we extract the minimum scene depth Z_{min} and the maximum scene depth Z_{max}. In our method, the scene depth is the distance between a point of the scene and the camera. When the following equation is satisfied:

$$\frac{V - D_{min}}{D_{max} - V} = \frac{Z_c - Z_{min}}{Z_{max} - Z_c}, \tag{4}$$

the scene depth range can be mapped to all the comfort zone, which are defined as $D_{min} = f(Z_{min})$ and $D_{max} = f(Z_{max})$.

2.2 Convergence computation

In stereoscopic displays, visual comfort may decrease due to the accommodation-vergence conflict and stereo window violation [4]. In order to avoid these issues, we provide an attention tracking method to initialize the convergence plane. For a scene of an animation frame, we define the attention regions (components of attention objects) and extract scene depths of the regions$\{Z_1, Z_2, ..., Z_N\}$. In our method we use the geometry center of a region to extract the attention depth. Then for each frame, we initialize the depth of convergence plane Z_c by

$$Z_c = min(Z_1, Z_2, ..., Z_N). \tag{5}$$

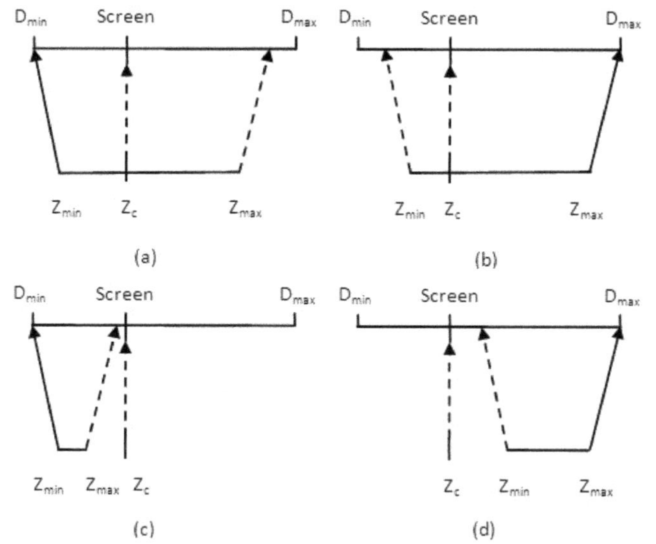

Figure 4: The depth mapping for covering comfort zone in different conditions.

The convergence plane that track the attention region in the minimum depth can guarantee visual comfort per frame. However, visual fatigue by depth jump in animations over time may be created due to object motions, interaction between the motions of different objects and convergence planes sharply change. Thus we use the least square method to smooth the convergence planes. For the trade-off between gliding property and locality we use 7 points linear smoothing with multi-iterations.

2.3 Inter-axial separation computation

Our method calculates convergence and inter-axial separation in two steps, therefore Eq.(4) is not satisfied for every frame. We define $\lambda_1 = (V - D_{min})/(D_{max} - V)$ and $\lambda_2 = (Z_c - Z_{min})/(Z_{max} - Z_c)$. For using the comfort zone as much as possible, we propose the following depth mapping strategies:

1) $\lambda_2 > \lambda_1 \geq 0$, we use the minimum depth mapping $D_{min} = f(Z_{min})$ and part of comfort zone behind the screen is not covered(Figure 4(a)). When $Z_c = Z_{max}$, we use the same mapping;

2) $\lambda_1 > \lambda_2 \geq 0$, we use the maximum depth mapping $D_{max} = f(Z_{max})$ and part of comfort zone in fornt of the screen is not covered(Figure 4(b));

3) $\lambda_2 \leq 0$, the situation may be created due to the convergence smoothing. Thus for $Z_c < Z_{min}$ we use the maximum depth mapping(Figure 4(c)), while the minimum depth mapping is used for $Z_c > Z_{max}$(Figure 4(d)).

Then given the depth mapping and the convergence plane, the inter-axial separation can be computed by Eq.(3).

3. EXPERIMENTAL EVALUATION

We have implemented the proposed method as Autodesk Maya plug-ins with C++ API. We used a graphics workstation with an E5-2620 2.00GH CPU and 8GB RAM for rendering and a 24 inch screen with a resolution of 1920×1200 for display.

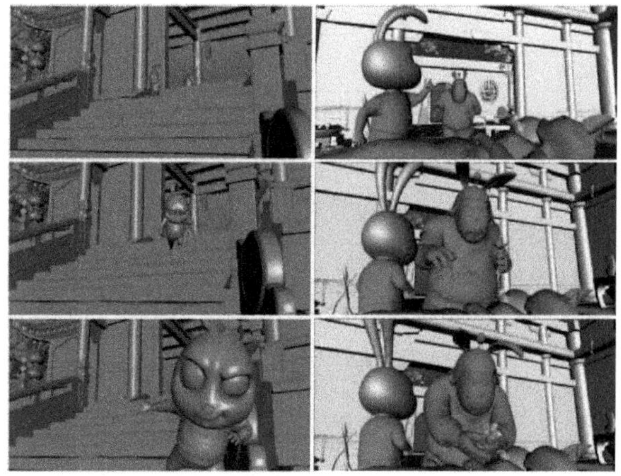

Figure 5: The scene cut in left column includes one attention object and the right column includes multiple attention objects (only three frames are shown for each cut).

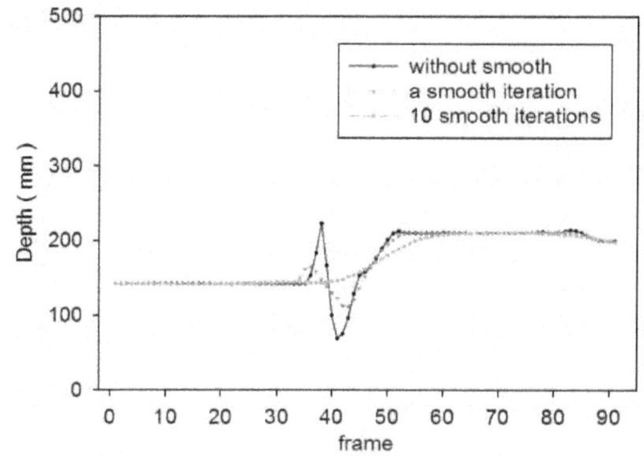

Figure 7: The convergence planes with different smoothing iterations.

In our experiments, we use 10 scene cuts of an 3D animation *Legend of a Rabbit: The Martial of Fire* [1] as the test data. In the animation production pipeline, stereoscopic contents are created and rendered before integral animation rendering. Thus, these test cuts only include the entire scene depth cues without color, textures and shadows. Figure 5 shows two examples of the animation cuts which use the center of two cameras as the viewpoint.

To evaluate the stereo quality of our method, we compare with a naive method (manual configuration) and DADC [1] by depth curve charts as in Figure 6. We show the maximum scene depth, the minimum scene depth, the minimum screen border depth and the convergence plane over frames. The results shows that the convergence planes in our method make the regions which mostly attract viewer close to the screen all the time for avoiding accommodation-vergence conflict. And we smooth the convergence planes to decrease depth jump by convergence sharply change, while in DADC this issue is not addressed. Note that due to the smooth process a few frames may create stereo window violations, however, in stereoscopic display the view experiences are not affected

[1]This chinoiserie animation movie was displayed in the 67th Festival de Cannes and received compliments of a Hollywood animation level for the delicate visual quality and vigorous plot

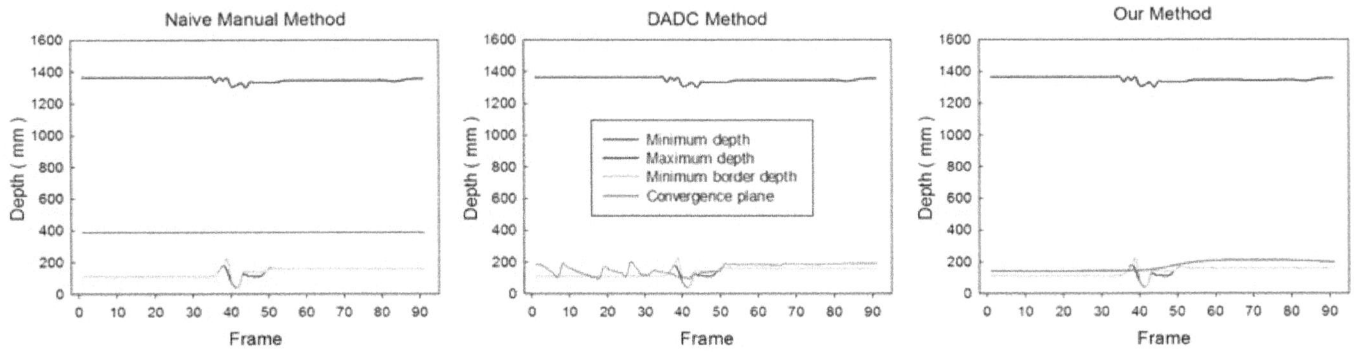

Figure 6: The depth comparison of the scene cut (Figure 1) with 90 frames. The left is naive method, the middle is DADC and the right is our method.

Table 1: The user study results for comparison of three methods

	Naive	DADC	Our	Not distinguish
Comfortable	19	55	90	36
Stereo effect	29	48	71	52

in most cases. Figure 7 shows that the original captured convergence planes and the results with one and ten iterations in our method. We can see that after multi-iterations the captured convergence planes can efficiently decrease depth jump.

User Study In order to further evaluate the applicability of our method we conducted a user study with 20 participants. The study compared our method to DADC and naive method with fixed camera convergence and inter-axial separation. The goal of this study was to evaluate the comfortable perception an the stereo effect of our method. Thus the participants had to answer two questions for every comparison: which one is more viewing comfortable and which one has better stereo effect. All the participants had experience of stereoscopic vision and did not participate in similar experiments. We rendered the 10 scene cuts with the camera parameters by three methods and displayed the 10 comparisons by a random order. The viewing distance was 700 mm. After the participants watched the result of a comparison, they either selected the scene cuts that were better or were unable to distinguish between the rendering results for each question. This study received 200 votes for each question when considering all the 10 scenes cuts and the subjective results are shown in Table 1.

The results illustrate that the stereoscopic camera parameters using our method create more comfortable animations with better effect for viewers than the parameters using naive method and DADC.

4. CONCLUSIONS

In this paper we have described a new solution to produce stereoscopic 3D animations before the integral rendering by automatically optimizing stereoscopic camera parameters. Our method calculates the convergence plane independently by considering the attention objects in the scene to avoid visual artifacts and automatically find the inter-axial separation for mapping the scene depth to the comfortable depth zone. Our method enables 3D animation producers to easily create 3D animation with high stereo quality. In the future, we will explore more visual distortions in the stereo displays and improve our approaches to address these issues.

5. ACKNOWLEDGMENTS

The research is supported the National Key Technology R&D Program of China under Grant No.2012BAH39F07; the Funds for Creative Research Groups of China under Grant No.61421061; the Cosponsored Project of Beijing Committee of Education; the National Natural Science Foundation of China under Grant No.61272517; Beijing Training Project For The Leading Talents in S&T under Grant No.ljrc201502.

6. REFERENCES

[1] U. Celikcan, G. Cimen, E. B. Kevinc, and T. Capin. Attention-aware disparity control in interactive environments. *The Visual Computer*, 29(6-8):685–694, 2013.

[2] S. Heinzle, P. Greisen, D. Gallup, C. Chen, D. Saner, A. Smolic, A. Burg, W. Matusik, and M. Gross. Computational stereo camera system with programmable control loop. *ACM Transactions on Graphics*, 30(4), 2011.

[3] G. Jones, D. Lee, N. Holliman, and D. Ezra. Controlling perceived depth in stereoscopic images. In *Stereoscopic Displays and Virtual Reality Systems VIII*, pages 42–53, 2001.

[4] M. Lambooij, M. Fortuin, I. Heynderickx, and W. IJsselsteijn. Visual discomfort and visual fatigue of stereoscopic displays: a review. *Journal of Imaging Science and Technology*, 53(3):30201–1–30201–14, 2009.

[5] T. Oskam, A. Hornung, H. Bowles, K. Mitchell, and M. Gross. Oscam-optimized stereoscopic camera control for interactive 3d. *ACM Transactions on Graphics*, 30(6), 2011.

[6] W. J. Tam, F. Speranza, S. Yano, K. Shimono, and H. Ono. Stereoscopic 3d-tv: visual comfort. *IEEE Transactions on Broadcasting*, 57(2):335–346, 2011.

[7] A. Woods, T. Docherty, and R. Koch. Image distortions in stereoscopic video systems. In *Electronic Imaging: Science and Technology*, pages 36–48, 1993.

[8] F. Zilly, J. Kluger, and P. Kauff. Production rules for stereo acquisition. *Proceedings of the IEEE*, 99(4):590–606, 2011.

Color Photo Makeover via Crowd Sourcing and Recoloring

Wengang Cheng[1,2] Ruru Jiang[1] Chang Wen Chen[2]
[1]North China Electric Power University, Beijing, China
[2]State University of New York at Buffalo, Buffalo, NY, USA
chengwg@buffalo.edu, rurjiang@gmail.com, chencw@buffalo.edu

ABSTRACT

It is not always easy for amateur photographers to capture photos with desired colors even on a classic hot spot as the appearance of color photo dependent on many factors. This paper proposes a novel approach to recolor given photos via a crowdsourcing based makeover scheme. When a user input a photo to be recolored, the proposed system will first conduct favorite exemplars suggestion from the images hosted by the social media sites, by jointly leveraging contextual and visual information associated with the images. The recommended exemplars shall reveal the scene and context dependent color compositions and provide users with diverse possible color styles. Then, a novel superpixel-based recoloring scheme, incorporating color statistics, texture characteristics and spatial constraints into soft matching, is applied to generate new photos of desired color. Experiments and a user study demonstrate that the proposed color photo makeover is able to achieve robust recoloring results for various outdoor photos.

Categories and Subject Descriptors

I.4.3 [**Image Processing and Computer Vision**]: Enhancement; I.4.9 [**Image Processing and Computer Vision**]: Applications

General Terms

Algorithms, Experimentation.

Keywords

Social media; image recommendation; image recoloring; contexts.

1. INTRODUCTION

For amateur photographers, it is usually difficult to capture perfect photos with desired color even on a classic hot spot, due to various constraints, including device setting limitations, undesired weather and lighting conditions, inconvenient time of the day, and sophisticated photography rules. Post processing has been frequently used to enhance some poorly captured photos. In recent years, photo editing packages (e.g., Adobe Photoshop Lightroom) and online photo sharing services (e.g., Instagram) have been able to offer various functions to adjust photo quality. However, these universal tools suffer from the inconsistency of users' manual adjustment skills and non-intuitive way of manipulation. Among automatic post processing methods, Cohen-Or et al. [1] presented an artistic technique to adjust color harmony in an image to enhance visual harmony. Lalonde et al. [2] proposed a scheme for assessing image realism by using color compatibility. While they are helpful for color enhancement, they offer no hint on a given image's color style. In fact, an intuitive color style is often needed for photography users, especially for amateurs. On the contrary, color transfer techniques take a given image as a reference and alters the source image's color palette to achieve color changes [3]. Ideally, the scheme can achieve different stylistic effects with different examples. A survey of these techniques can be found in [4]. Although it seems color transfer techniques are possibly suited for photo recoloring, it should be noted that they do not approach the problem of example providing. In addition, existing color transfer techniques, even more deliberate local ones, are far from well developed, e.g., some regions especially on the boundaries may be incorrectly colored and visual artifacts will occur [5].

MM'15, October 26-30, 2015, Brisbane, Australia

DOI: http://dx.doi.org/10.1145/2733373.2806370

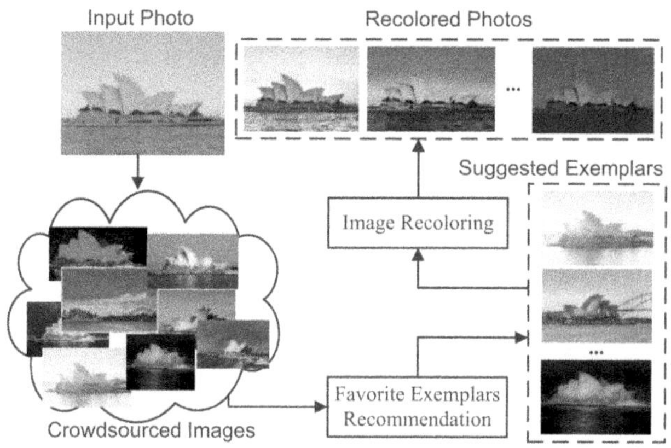

Figure 1. Overview of the proposed *color photo makeover* system.

Meanwhile, we observe that photography and editing rules are often dependent on scene and context. General processing without regard to specific contents and contexts may not ensure desired enhancement and realistic effects. Consider a similar example as in [2] which is used to exemplify the image realism. When making a decision to recolor an image of a forest scene, it might be better to look for different color styles of *forest* images rather than those *beach* images to make the recoloring results more realistic. Therefore, images similar in content and context should be good examples for recoloring problem of this research. Such an approach can be validated by several works using Internet photo collections to accomplish different tasks [6-8].

Based on the previous analysis, we attempt to design a photo post processing scheme called color photo makeover to recolor a given photo based on exemplars obtained from crowd sourcing of popular social media sites. This scheme consists of two steps. The first step is to recommend favorite exemplars, which are expected to reveal the scene and context dependent color compositions and to illustrate different popular color styles. We develop an approach of favorite exemplars suggestion by jointly leveraging contextual and visual information associated with the social images. The second step is to design an automatic scheme to recolor users' input photo by emulating color styles from suggested exemplars. A novel recoloring scheme is proposed. Specifically, we use the superpixel based representation to enforce the spatial and color coherence beyond what histogram and color cluster can do, which is more robust than semantic regions. Moreover, other than statistical color information (mean and variance) which were used by most existing color transfer methods, we incorporate texture characteristics and spatial constraints into a soft matching scheme to seek more precise correspondences, yielding robust and natural results. The proposed system is illustrated in Figure1.

2. COLOR PHOTO MAKEOVER

2.1 Favorite Exemplars Recommendation

Automatic selection of the exemplars should meet several criteria. First, these representative photos should effectively reveal the scene and context dependent color composition. Second, they should provide users with diverse but possible styles for reference. Third, they should be regarded as high quality, either by professional assessment or by popular crowd sourcing results. With these desired properties, such exemplars are expected to effectively assist users with possible processing options for the desired makeover. To satisfy these criteria, we first use the images similar in visual content and geo-location as the seed photo to build the specific "context". From the context, we choose from them by applying additional color and quality constraints as the final exemplars.

We first search similar images to build the context for the user's captured photo. We need an image representation scheme that is able to capture geometric patterns and scene structures as well as location related cues. GIST descriptor, which has been shown to be a good image representation for scene classification and matching, is used for visual representation. For the location clue, images captured in nearby location have a greater likelihood of sharing same content, which is often true for landscape photos especially in hot spots. Each image x can therefore be represented by a two-tuple $\{v, g\}$, where v denotes the image's visual content, and g its geo-location. In this research, GISTs are built from 4 scales with [8, 8, 8, 4] filter orientations at 4×4 spatial grid. Thus, the similarity index $Sim(x, y)$ between two image x and y can be calculated as:

$$Sim(x,y) = \exp\left(-\left(D_v(x,y) + w_g D_g(x,y)\right)\right) \quad (1)$$

where $D_v(x, y)$ and $D_g(x, y)$ are roughly calculated based on GIST and GPS using Euclidean distance, respectively. The balance parameter $w_g = 0$ when the GPS coordinates are unavailable for some images. The distances are normalized and w_g is simply set to 1 in the experiments based on the crawled dataset for this research. We shall adopt k-d tree based range searching to find the results.

The searching results cover diverse color patterns. However, for the suggested exemplars, we want each one to represent a typical color style. Therefore, color composition needs to be considered. We compare among several schemes, including block based HSV color histogram, block based CIE L*a*b* color statistics as well as dominant colors, with several different block sizes and combinations. The CIE L*a*b* first three order statistics at 8×8 spatial grid are finally chosen to represent an image's color style approximately, considering the trade-off between efficiency and performance.

Visual quality serves as another important criterion to determine an exemplar. Different from most existing photo aesthetics assessment approaches that focused on image content itself, we leverage photo associated contexts for photo aesthetic quality estimation, adopting the crowd sourcing based scheme reported in [7][8]. Specifically, Flickr's interestingness is a good index to decide which photos will be included in daily explore. However, it tends to give higher priority to newly uploaded photos than the old ones to keep fresh and diverse. To compensate for this bias, we refine the interestingness by enhancing several important factors and calculate image x's visual quality q_x as:

$$q_x = \exp(-r_x)(1 - \exp\{-(\alpha g_x + \beta f_x + \gamma v_x)\}) \quad (2)$$

where r_x is the normalized rank value based on interestingness in the range of similar image searching results. In Eqn. (2), g_x, f_x and v_x are the number of groups x belongs to, favorites, and views, respectively. They always take larger values for photos of high quality. These values are normalized and the three weighted parameters are set as 0.35, 0.35 and 0.30, respectively, in this research.

It is difficult to manually specify a predefined value for the number of exemplars considering the variety of photo content, which is often scene and context dependent. In addition, it is desired for those high quality photos to have higher priorities for selection as exemplars. Affinity propagation will be appropriate for the proposed task, in which preference vector is constructed by an array of normalized q_x according to Eqn. (2) and the distance matrix is calculated based on the Euclidean distance of color features. Consequently, each cluster yields an exemplar of a specific color style. Among these exemplars, users can choose one or more to emulate the desired makeover.

2.2 Photo Recoloring

The goal of recoloring is to modify the input image's color distribution D_s to match a target color distribution D_t. To obtain a desired color distribution, we use the superpixel based representation. It can keep the spatial and color coherence simultaneously beyond the historical histogram [9] and color cluster [2]. Moreover, such scheme is more robust than the scheme based on semantic regions [5] for precision concerns. In this research, the recommended exemplar shall define the color style. Soft assignment is then constructed for each superpixel by integrating color, texture and spatial differences into a new cost function. Finally, each pixel is recolored by considering color shifts of superpixel it belongs to and its nearest neighbors. All steps of processing shall be performed in the CIE L*a*b* color space.

As neighboring pixels often share color and spatial consistency, we attempt to group pixels into superpixel by jointly taking color and spatial information into consideration. The strategy of superpixel generation of SLIC [10] is consistent with the proposed research and is adopted in the implementation.

Most existing color transfer methods only rely on color mean and variance for image representation. As natural scenes are usually recognized via their textures, texture patterns should be an important clue for matching between landscape images in this research. In addition, local spatial smoothness can be exploited to preserve spatial coherence. Therefore, each superpixel, P_x, can be represented as:

$$P_x = < s_x, u_x, \sigma_x, t_x, IND_x, w_x > \quad (3)$$

where s_x is the position of the centroid; u_x and σ_x are the color mean and variance, respectively; t_x is the texton histogram of P_x; IND_x is a pixel's set belonging to P_x; w_x is its weight, computed as the percentage of pixels belonging to P_x. For the universal texture library, we first calculate oriented filter responses on each pixel giving rise to 32-dimensional vector [11] and then construct the texton dictionary by clustering on our 20,000 training images.

To get each superpixel's color shift, we need to compute the best assignment between superpixels of users' input and those of the exemplars. Each superpixel can be treated as a warehouse, so the assignment problem becomes a well-known transportation problem, which can be solved by the approach of Earth Mover's Distance [12]. The total goods flow from P_x to P_y, denoted as $f(x, y)$, is subject to constraints $\sum_y f(x,y) = w_x$ and $\sum_x f(x,y) = w_y$. The solution can be obtained by minimizing the transportation cost:

$$\min_f \sum_{x,y} f(x,y)c(x,y) \quad (4)$$

and the cost function is denoted as $c(x,y)$. In the previous works, only color difference is considered for this cost, while some regions especially boundaries of the regions may be incorrectly colored and visual artifacts can occur. Such a phenomenon is resulting partially from the fact that color statistics cannot fully guarantee precise correspondences. Considering the characteristics of landscape images, we incorporate texture features to improve matching. In addition, spatial smoothness constraint is also considered for spatial coherence of the recoloring results. The cost function is defined as:

$$c(x,y) = \exp(\tau_u d_u + \tau_s d_s + \tau_t d_t) \quad (5)$$

where d_u and d_s are color and spatial L_2 distance; d_t is the texton histograms χ^2 distance; τ_u, τ_s and τ_t are parameters to balance the distributions of corresponding features, respectively. We set τ_u=1.20, τ_s=0.45 and τ_t=1.0 as default.

Based on the soft assignment results, each superpixel of the input image is mapped into multiple superpixels of the exemplar image. In this way, color shifts for each superpixel are computed as a weighted average of distances to its assigned superpixels' color statistics, which can be calculated as:

$$\Delta u_x = \sum_y f(x,y)(u_y - u_x) / \sum_y f(x,y),$$
$$\Delta \sigma_x = \sum_y f(x,y)(\sigma_y - \sigma_x) / \sum_y f(x,y). \quad (6)$$

The color shifts for each pixel $I(i,j)$ in P_x can be computed as:

$$M^x_{I(i,j)} = \Delta\sigma_x / \sigma_x \, (I(i,j) - u_x) + \Delta u_x \quad (7)$$

To avoid boundary artifacts and to obtain more natural result, we take further processing for each pixel' color shifts. We also consider its neighboring superpixels' influence. The neighboring superpixels set is denoted as X and KNN is used to determine this set, where k is set to 35 for all the images in our experiments. Thus, the color shifts for each pixel are computed as a weighted combination of $M^x_{I(i,j)}(x \in X)$ in Eqn. (7), with weights inversely proportional to the pixel-superpixel distance:

$$M_{I(i,j)} = \sum_{x \in X} \varpi_x M^x_{I(i,j)} \quad (8)$$

where ϖ_x is the weight for how superpixel P_x impacts on $I(i,j)$. ϖ_x is measured by:

$$\varpi_x = \|I(i,j) - u_x\|^2 + \gamma\|(i,j) - s_x\|^2 \quad (9)$$

and then normalized by the total weights of every superpixel in X. We set γ=0.15 in the experiments.

Now every pixel can be recolored by adding the color shifts and the results are converted back to RGB for visualization.

3. EXPERIMENTS

To validate the proposed approach, we carried out experiments on a dataset of geo-tagged outdoor photos (~70,000) crawled from Flickr. It contains a variety of categories of scenes, such as "beach", "mountain", "forest", "lake", "waterfall" and "architecture". In each category, we collected more than 5 locations of hot spot places as subclasses. A set of 320 photos with relatively common color composition were selected manually and uniformly from all subclasses as the inputs such that the dataset were well-represented.

3.1 Evaluations for Recommendation

To speed up the searching, GIST and color statistics features were extracted offline. Input photos served as queries for searching similar images using a leave-one-out strategy. Although the average precision is not very high (63.36%, with subclasses' location names as labels), we find that the search results capture well the scene category and structure, which in turn will work well for the proposed task. Indeed, some are similar in visual content and structure but are retrieved from different locations. The searching results are used as the data source of clustering for exemplars suggestion.

It is difficult to objectively assess the recommended results. However, social rating itself is a very good quality indicator for evaluation. Therefore, we show the statistics of the numbers of favorites, views and groups belonging to, as summarized in Table 1. They are all presented in average values, which manifest the quality of the suggested exemplars. We carried out user studies for some samples and the results are consistent with the same trends as in Table 1. After eliminating overly small clusters, we obtain an average of 9.1 clusters for each input. Figure 2 (b) demonstrates the exemplars, i.e., the clustering outcome, for an input image in Figure 2 (a).

3.2 Evaluations for Recoloring

The proposed recoloring algorithm has been tested on the dataset we built. Figure 2 (c) gives an example. Furthermore, we also compare it with several commonly used color transfer schemes. Like existing approaches, we use the scheme of Reinhard [3] as the baseline approach. As a representative of local approaches, Lalonde's method [2] was also implemented, in which each color distribution is represented by a mixture of k spherical Gaussians. We set k=300, which can guarantee good results in the experiments. Besides, histogram reshaping [9] is a prominent global approach for creative color transfer as well as tone reproduction and the corresponding results are generated by the source code from the authors.

Results show that the proposed scheme is able to achieve better results at both global color patterns and local color shifts. Figure 3 shows several typical examples from different scene categories. For the input and the exemplar in the first row, comparative effects are obtained. In this case, color statistics or color histogram can ensure good mapping. Therefore, global ones can also work. Nevertheless, sky's blue distortion occurred in [2]'s result. In the second row, we observe that the baseline and the method of [9] did not catch the Statue of Liberty's color as that in the exemplar and failed at local color shifting. Results in third row show that the proposed scheme can find better correspondence with the aid of texture pattern and spatial constraints, while other schemes cannot. In the last row, we can see the exemplar image has three main color layers, green vegetation, gray mountain and white sky. Our method can preserve the spatial distribution of the exemplar's color style, while all the others failed. This is due the adoption of spatial constraints in the proposed scheme. Others can only make same color shifts for pixels of similar color without regard to their spatial locations.

We also performed a user study to compare the results generated by the proposed scheme. We randomly choose 32 sets of images (1 image pair from each subclasses) for comparisons. The input, the exemplar and randomly displayed recoloring results were showed to 30 participants of different profiles. Users were asked to select maximum 2 best images from the recoloring results of each group. The hit rates for each method are summarized in Table 2.

Table 1. Statistics of social rating for exemplars and others

Class	Favors	Views	Groups
Exemplars	142.2	11119.2	33.3
Others	31.9	2439.7	12.7

Table 2. User study of recoloring methods

[2]'s method	Ours	[3]'s method	[9]'s method
15.42%	56.77%	12.60%	28.13%

(*a*) An input (*b*) Recommended exemplars (*c*) Recolored results with corresponding exemplars of (*b*)

Figure 2. An example of exemplar recommendation results and the recolored results based on these suggested exemplars

(*a*) Input (*b*) An Exemplar (*c*) Result of [2] (*d*) Our Result (*e*) Result of [3] (*f*) Result of [9]

Figure 3. Comparison of recoloring results

4. CONCLUSIONS

We have presented in this paper a novel approach to color photo makeover by crowd sourcing and recoloring, in which the colors of user captured photos can be enhanced by referencing to the favorite photos obtained from the social media sites. By creative utilization of the crowdsourced photos and their associated social contexts, favorite exemplars are recommended for users' input to reveal the scene and context dependent color composition and styles. A superpixel based recoloring method, in combination with the color, texture and spatial coherence principles, is applied to recolor the input photo by utilizing the suggested exemplars as the targets. The approach has been validated by the experiments and user study.

The proposed scheme can be further improved. For image pairs with substantially different scene contents, the recoloring scheme may generate unnatural results in some cases. However, this can be partially compensated by using favorite exemplar recommendation results of the first step of the proposed scheme and these exemplars also provide users with proper targets to utilize other recoloring methods. This is one of the future works we plan to pursue. Other future works include additional processing based on the recoloring results because a perfect makeover needs more sophisticated and intelligent image processing strategies beyond simple recoloring.

5. ACKNOWLEDGMENTS

This work was supported by "the Fundamental Research Funds for the Central Universities".

6. REFERENCES

[1] D. Cohen-Or, O. Sorkine, R. Gal, T. Leyvand, and Y. Xu, Color harmonization. *ACM Trans. on Graphics* (*SIGGRAPH2006*), v.25 n.3, July 2006.

[2] J.-F. Lalonde and A. Efros, Using color compatibility for assessing image realism. In *Proc.of ICCV*, 2007.

[3] E. Reinhard, M. Ashikhmin, B. Gooch, and P. Shirley, "Color transfer between images," *IEEE Journal of Computer Graphics and Applications*, vol. 21, pp. 2-9, 2001.

[4] Hasan Sheikh Faridul, Tania Pouli, et al, A Survey of Color Mapping and its Applications. *Eurographics* 2014.

[5] F. Wu, W. Dong, et al. Content-based colour transfer. *Computer Graphics Forum*, vol.32, pp. 190-203, 2013.

[6] M. K. Johnson, K. Dale, et al. CG2Real: Improving the realism of computer-generated images using a large collection of photographs. *TR MIT-CSAIL-TR-2009-034,MIT,* 2009.

[7] W. Yin, T. Mei and C. W, Chen, "Assessing Photo Quality with Geo-Context and Crowdsourced Photos," *Proc. IEEE VCIP 2012*, Nov, 2012

[8] W. Yin, T. Mei, C. W. Chen and S. Li. Socialized Mobile Photography: Learning to Photograph with Social Context via Mobile Devices. *IEEE Trans. on Multimedia*, 16(1),2014.

[9] Tania Pouli, Erik Reinhard. Progressive Color Transfer for Images of Arbitrary Dynamic Range. *Computers and Graphics*,vol.35, pp.67-80, 2011.

[10] R. Achanta, A. Shaji, et al. SLIC Superpixels Compared to State-of-the-art Superpixel Methods. *TPAMI*, vol. 34, 2012.

[11] D. Martin and C. Fowlkes and D. Tal and J. Malik. A Database of Human Segmented Natural Images and its Application to Evaluating Segmentation Algorithms and Measuring Ecological Statistics. *Proc. of ICCV*, 2001.

[12] Y. Rubner, C. Tomasi and L. Guibas. The Earth Mover's Distance as a Metric for Image Retrieval. *IJCV*, v.40, 2000.

Multi-view Semi-supervised Learning for Web Image Annotation

Mengqiu Hu[†], Yang Yang[†], Hanwang Zhang[‡], Fumin Shen[†], Jie Shao[†], Fuhao Zou[§]
[†]University of Electronic Science and Technology of China
[‡]National University of Singapore
[§]Huazhong University of Science and Technology
{hmq.uestc, dlyyang, hanwangzhang, fumin.shen}@gmail.com; shaojie@uestc.edu.cn; fuhao_zou@hust.edu.cn

ABSTRACT

With the explosive increasing of web image data, image annotation has become a critical research issue for image semantic index and search. In this work, we propose a novel model, termed as *multi-view semi-supervised learning* (MVSSL), for robust image annotation task. Specifically, we exploit both labeled images and unlabeled images to uncover the intrinsic data structural information. Meanwhile, to comprehensively describe an individual datum, we take advantage of the correlated and complemental information derived from multiple facets of image data (i.e., multiple views or features). We devise a robust pair-wise constraint on outcomes of different views to achieve annotation consistency. Furthermore, we integrate a robust classifier learning component via $\ell_{2,1}$ loss, which can provide effective noise identification power during the learning process. Finally, we devise an efficient iterative algorithm to solve the optimization problem in MVSSL. We conduct extensive experiments on the NUS-WIDE dataset, and the results illustrate that our proposed approach is promising for large scale web image annotation task.

Categories and Subject Descriptors

H.3.1 [**Content Analysis and Indexing**]: Indexing methods; I.2.6 [**Learning**]: Concept learning

General Terms

Algorithm

Keywords

multi-view learning; semi-supervised learning; image annotation

MM'15, October 26–30, 2015, Brisbane, Australia.
© 2015 ACM. ISBN 978-1-4503-3459-4/15/10 ...$15.00.
DOI: http://dx.doi.org/10.1145/2733373.2806371.

1. INTRODUCTION

In recent years, with the explosive development of the progress of digital and Internet technologies, tremendously large numbers of images are available. Confronted with such situation, web image annotation [8] has become a critical research issue for image index and search [5,9]. Image annotation has become very popular in [6,7]. Most photo sharing sites give their users opportunity to label the images manually. The labels collected by that way, however, are usually very incomplete due to different backgrounds and cognitions of the people and most images are not properly labeled according to all the categories which they belong to. Among ever-increasing web images, many are mislabeled or unlabeled and many classes have relatively few representative examples. Image annotation is the procedure of automatically assigning labels to images, where the labels can reflect the semantic concepts of the contents of the images. Given an image, image annotation technique figures out what objects or things are within the images. With these labels we can further browse or search the relevant images in the database. Confronted with continuously explosive growth of the web images, how to automatically annotate these countless web images effectively and efficiently has become a critical research issue.

In the era of big data, we can get as many data as we want, nonetheless, how to leverage these precious resources to train an annotation model for achieving better prediction performance has been attracting extensive attention. For the task of image annotation, most photo sharing sites give their users the opportunity to assign some labels when uploading photos. The image collections together with their users' tags have some intrinsic properties that are significant for performance improvement when developing automatic annotation models. In many categories, the number of labeled samples is generally only small, while the number of unlabeled data seems "unlimited". Labeling such a large image collection is usually a tedious, time-consuming and labour-extensive task. Thus, how to leverage the limited labeled data together with unlabeled images to explore the underlying structural knowledge for boosting automatic image annotation is especially important. On the other hand, it is notable that images can be naturally represented by several distinct feature sets, or views, such as edge direction histogram, wavelet texture, and Decaf deep learning feature. These features are mutually complementary in terms of depicting an individual data point.

In this paper, we present an effective image annotation approach, termed as multi-view semi-supervised learning (MVSSL), which jointly explores intrinsic data structural knowledge as well as multi-faceted information embedded in the various features of data. Specifically, we employ graph-based semi-supervised learning to model local structure of image data. Meanwhile, we devise a multi-view constraint to enforce the outcomes of different views to be as consistent as possible. By doing so, we are able to effectively explore the correlated and complemental information from different views to comprehensively describe data. Moreover, in order to further handle the problem of unreliable labels, we develop a robust learning component which leverages $\ell_{2,1}$ loss function to effectively suppress the negative influence of noisy samples in the training set. We further design an effective iterative algorithm to solve the optimization. Extensive experiments are conducted on a large-scale web image dataset NUS-WIDE dataset [1], the promising results demonstrate that MVSSL is able to achieve better performance as compared to other methods.

The rest of the paper is organized as follows. Section 2 elaborates details of our proposed MVSSL model and its solution. Section 3 gives experimental results and analysis, followed by conclusions in Section 4.

2. THE PROPOSED APPROACH

In this section, we present Multi-view Semi-supervise Learning (MVSSL) algorithm. Firstly, we introduce graph Laplacian semi-supervised learning, then give the formulation of our MVSSL, followed by the optimized solutions of MVSSL.

2.1 Notations

Suppose we have a training dataset of n observations from m views. Denote $X_t = [x_1^{(t)}, x_2^{(t)}, \dots, x_l^{(t)}, x_{l+1}^{(t)}, \dots, x_n^{(t)}]$ as the t-th features of these samples, where $x_i^{(t)} \in \mathbb{R}^{d_t \times 1} (1 \leq i \leq n)$ is the t-th view feature of the i-th observation, where d_t is the dimensionality of the t-th feature space. Note that the first l samples in the datasets are associated with labels while the rest $n-l$ samples are unlabeled. Given the label matrix of the training dataset corresponding to the t-th view $Y_t = [y_1^{(t)}, y_2^{(t)}, \dots, y_l^{(t)}, y_{l+1}^{(t)}, \dots, y_n^{(t)}]^T \in \{-1, 0, 1\}^{n \times c}$, where c is the number of labels, $y_i^{(t)} \in \{-1, 1\}^c$ if $(1 \leq i \leq l)$ (i.e., labeled sample) and $y_i^{(t)}$ is all-zero vector if $(l+1 \leq i \leq n)$ (i.e., unlabeled sample). Let $y_{ij}^{(t)}$ denote the j-th class of the i-th datum corresponding to the t-th view, then $y_{ij}^{(t)} = 1$ if the i-th sample is in the j-th class, and $y_{ij}^{(t)} = -1$ otherwise. If the sample is unlabeled, $y_{ij}^{(t)}$ is set to zero. The objective of this work is to utilize multiple views of both the labeled and unlabeled data to learn robust classifiers for image annotation.

2.2 Graph-based Semi-Supervised Learning

Given a set of data samples, we can define a graph model S, whose element S_{ij} reflects the similarity between the i-th sample and the j-th sample on the graph. For the simplicity, we define S as below:

$$S_{ij} = \begin{cases} 1, & x_i \in \mathcal{N}_k(x_j) \text{ or } x_j \in \mathcal{N}_k(x_i); \\ 0, & \text{otherwise}, \end{cases} \tag{1}$$

where $\mathcal{N}_k(\cdot)$ denotes the set of k nearest neighbors of a datum. By defining a diagonal matrix D, whose i-th diagonal element is computed as $D_{ii} = \sum_{j=1}^n S_{ij}$, we have the graph Laplacian matrix $L = D - S$.

In order to exploit labeled and unlabeled data simultaneously, we define $F = [f_1, f_2, \cdots, f_n]^T \in \mathbb{R}^{n \times c}$ as a predicted label matrix for all the training data, where $f_i \in \mathbb{R}^c (1 \leq i \leq n)$ is the predicted label of the i-th sample. According to the idea of semi-supervised learning [10], F should simultaneously satisfy the smoothness on the ground truth labels of the training data and the graph model S. Hence, F can be obtained by minimizing the following objective function:

$$\min_F Tr(F^T LF) + Tr((F-Y)^T U(F-Y)), \tag{2}$$

where $U \in \mathbb{R}^{n \times n}$ is a diagonal matrix and named as a decision rule matrix, whose diagonal elements U_{ii} is a large number if the i-th data point is labeled and $U_{ii} = 1$ otherwise. This decision rule matrix U makes the predicted labels F consistent with the ground truth label matrix Y.

In order to learn a robust classifier, which should be tolerant to samples with noisy labels, we propose to integrate a robust loss function with adaptive power to different noise levels. To this end, we employ the generalized $\ell_{2,1}$ loss, then the graph-based semi-supervised classification learning framework can be rewritten as follows:

$$\begin{aligned} \min_{F,W,b} \; & Tr(F^T LF) + Tr((F-Y)^T U(F-Y)) \\ & + \mu(\|X^T W + \mathbf{1}_n b^T - F\|_{2,1} + \gamma \|W\|_F^2), \end{aligned} \tag{3}$$

where μ and γ are balance parameters. $W \in \mathbb{R}^{d \times c}$ is the mapping matrix and $b \in \mathbb{R}^c$ is the bias term. $\|W\|_F^2$ is the regularization term, $\mathbf{1}_n$ is an all-one vector. The $\ell_{2,1}$ norm of a matrix M is defined as

$$\|M\|_{2,1} = \sum_{i=1}^n \|M_i\|_2, \tag{4}$$

where M_i is the i-th row of M.

2.3 Multi-view Semi-supervised Learning

For the t-th view of the data, we can compute a view-depended Laplacian matrix L_t from the view feature X_t. Then we can calculate a view-depended predicted label matrix F_t from Eq. (3) accordingly. Thus we can introduce the idea of multi-view learning into the aforementioned graph-based semi-supervised classification learning to leverage the correlated and complemental information between different views for better performance. To this end, we propose to jointly minimize all the view-specific objective functions and restricting all view-specific F_t to be as closely as possible.

Therefore, the objective function of the multi-view semi-supervised learning (MVSSL) can be expressed as:

$$\begin{aligned} \min_{\{F_t, W_t, b_t\}|_{t=1}^m} & \sum_{t=1}^m \Big(Tr(F_t^T L_t F_t) + Tr((F_t - Y_t)^T U(F_t - Y_t)) \\ & + \mu(\|X_t^T W_t + \mathbf{1}_n b_t^T - F_t\|_{2,1} + \gamma \|W_t\|_F^2) \Big) + \lambda \sum_{t,s} \|F_t - F_s\|_{2,1}, \end{aligned} \tag{5}$$

where λ is a balance parameter. The above formulation benefits from multi-view learning together with graph-based semi-supervised learning. This model effectively utilizes the large amount of unlabeled data and complemental information from different views. The last term $\lambda \sum_{t,s} \|F_t - F_s\|_{2,1}$ is able to enforce the outcomes of all pairs of views to be as consistent as possible, thereby leading to better performance.

2.4 Solution

In this section, we propose an efficient iterative algorithm to solve our model. Note that it is non-trivial to directly solve the problem in Eq. (5) due to the non-convexity of the $\ell_{2,1}$ loss and the $\ell_{2,1}$ regularizer. To overcome this problem, we first transform the original formulation to the following alternative one:

$$\min_{\{F_t,W_t,b_t\}|_{t=1}^m} \sum_{t=1}^{m} \Big(Tr(F_t^T L_t F_t) + Tr((F_t - Y_t)^T U (F_t - Y_t)) + \mu Tr(X_t^T W_t + 1 b_t^T - F_t)^T D_t^{(l)} (X_t^T W_t + 1 b_t^T - F_t) + \mu\gamma \|W_t\|_F^2) + \lambda \sum_{t,k} Tr(F_t - F_s)^T D_{ts}^{(r)} (F_t - F_s), \quad (6)$$

where $D_t^{(l)}$ a diagonal matrix with its i-th diagonal element computed as

$$(D_t^{(l)})_{ii} = \frac{1}{2\|r_t^i\|_2}, \quad (7)$$

where r_t^i is the i-th row of the matrix $X_t^T W_t + \mathbf{1}_n b_t^T - F_t$. Similarly, $D_{ts}^{(r)}$ is diagonal and its diagonal element is calculated as

$$(D_{ts}^{(r)})_{ii} = \frac{1}{2\|r_{ts}^i\|_2}, \quad (8)$$

where r_{ts}^i is the i-the row of the matrix $F_t - F_s$.

Note that both $D_t^{(l)}$ and $D_{ts}^{(r)}$ are related to F_t W_t and/or b_t, which makes the problem in Eq.(6) hard to solve. Thus, we design an iterative method which uses fixed $D_t^{(l)}$ and $D_{ts}^{(r)}$ obtained in the previous iteration to bypass the obstacle. In this way, we can see that F_t, W_t and b_t can be solved from Eq. (6).

3. EXPERIMENTS

In this section, we conduct extensive experiments on the web image dataset NUS-WIDE to validate the performance of our proposed approach.

3.1 Dataset and setup

The NUS-WIDE dataset includes 269,648 real-world images with 81 concepts. The dataset is separated into two parts. The first part contains 161,789 images used for training while the second part contains 107,859 testing images. This collection provides six kinds of global visual features. Three of them are color based features: 1) color histogram, 2) a color auto-correlogram and 3) block-wise color moments. Using the texture-base technique, two other feature types have been extracted: 4) edge direction histogram and 5) wavelet texture. The last set of visual features in this collection is 6) bag of visual words, which is obtained by using the SIFT method [4]. In our experiments, we used two types of visual features including 73-dimension edge direction histogram (EDH) and 128-dimension wavelet texture (WT). In addition, we extracted a new set of features called Decaf which is 4096-dimension based on caffe [3].

In our experiment, we randomly sampled 2000 images from training part comprising our training set and the whole training part was used as testing set. Our training set included l labeled samples, where l was set to 50% of the total training set. To simulate a semi-supervised learning scenario, we randomly divided the training data into two subsets: one set was called labeled set whose labels are known,

Algorithm 1: Multi-View Semi-Supervised Learning.

Input : The training feature matrix of tth view $X_t \in \mathbf{R}^{d_t \times n}$; and the training labels matrix $Y \in \mathbf{R}^{n \times c}$;

Output: Optimized classification parameters matrix $W_t \in \mathbf{R}^{d_t \times c}$;

Randomly initialize F_t, W_t and b_t, $t = 1, 2, \ldots, m$;
Compute Laplacian matrix L_t of the t-th view according to Eq. (1);
repeat
  Compute $D_t^{(l)}$ and $D_{ts}^{(r)}$ according to Eq. (7) and Eq. (8), respectively;
  for $t = 1, 2, \ldots, m$ **do**
    Compute $H_t = I - \frac{1_n 1_n^T D_t^l}{1_n^T D_t^l 1_n}$;
    Compute $A_t = (X_t H_t^T D_t^l H_t X_t^T + \gamma I)^{-1} X_t H_t^T D_t^l H_t$;
    $M_t = (L_t + \mu(I - A_t^T X_t) H_t^T D_t^l H_t + U + \lambda \sum_{k=1,2,\ldots,t-1,t+1,\ldots,m} D_{tk}^r)^{-1}$;
    $Q_t = (UY_t + \lambda \sum_{k=1,2,\ldots,t-1,t+1,\ldots,m} D_{tk}^r F_t)$;
    Update $F_t = M_t Q_t$;
    Update $W_t = A_t F_t$;
    Update $b_t^T = \frac{1_n^T D_t^l (F_t - X_t^T W_t)}{1_n^T D_t^{(l)} 1_n}$;
  end
until *there is no change to* F_t, W_t *and* b_t, $t = 1, 2, \ldots, m$;
return F_t, W_t *and* b_t, $t = 1, 2, \ldots, m$;

the rest was called unlabeled set whose labels were hidden. To evaluate the annotation performance, we used the well known evaluation metric, namely Mean Average Precision (MAP), which has been widely used for multi-label classification tasks and image annotation. The number k of nearest neighbors for computing Laplacian matrix is set to 15.

We conducted extensive experiments to tune several parameters for better performance in our experiments. The balance parameters in all comparing methods (e.g., μ, γ, and λ in Eq.(5) were set in the range of $\{10^{-6}, 10^{-5}, \ldots, 10^{14}\}$. The parameters corresponding to the best results were used in our experiments.

3.2 Effects of Parameters

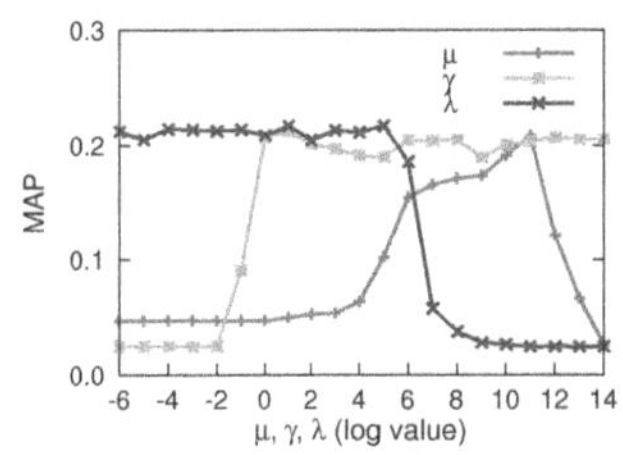

Figure 1: Effects of different parameters on image annotation performance.

In this part, we evaluate the effects of different parameters on our methods. Specifically, in order to simplify the tuning process, we report the effect of each individual parameter while keeping other parameters fixed. While Figure 1 shows the performance w.r.t. μ, γ and λ.

	Decaf	EDH+WT	EDH+Decaf	WT+Decaf	EDH+WT+Decaf
MVSSL	21.06%	4.95%	21.27%	21.39%	21.86%
SVM2K	-	4.20%	5.84%	5.74%	-

Table 1: Comparison of our approach and existing methods on different combinations of visual features.

From Figure 1, we can see that a totally different pattern for performance, i.e., three different trends. For instance, when μ varies from 10^{-6} to 10^{11}, the performance keeps going up; as μ keeps increasing, the performance becomes worse. Such phenomenon implies that either large or small value of balance parameters does not help to achieve the best results. We should choose a balancing point among these parameters. For parameter λ, the performance keeps little changed when λ varies from 10^{-6} to 10^{5}; as λ keeps increasing, the performance becomes worse sharply. Such phenomenon implies that too large value of parameter λ helps to achieve very poor results. As balance parameter λ controls the level of consistency between different views, the correlated and complemental information may become the same and disappear if the value of λ is too large.

Finally, we set all parameters to the values corresponding to the best performance for our experiments, i.e., $\mu = 10^{11}, \gamma = 10, \lambda = 10$.

3.3 Performance Evaluation

In this part, we evaluate the effectiveness of our proposed approach by comparing to other methods.

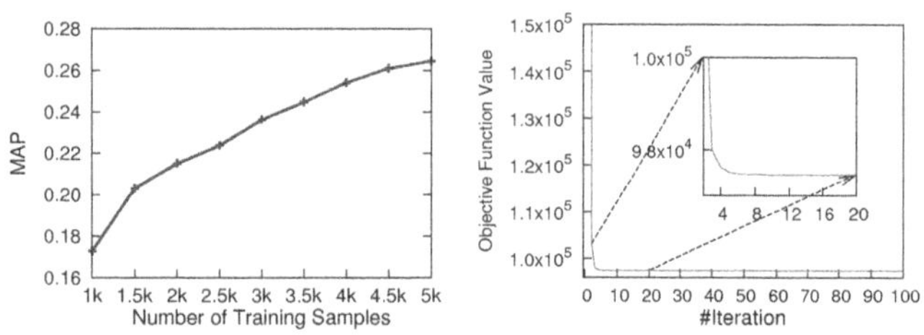

(a) (b)

Figure 2: (a) Effects of number of training data and (b) Convergence study.

We conducted experiment to explore how the number of training set can affect the effectiveness. We set the number to $\{1000, 1500, 2000, \ldots, 4000, 4500, 5000\}$. The results for this experiment are shown in Figure 2.(a), from which we can see that as the number increasing, we first observe an obvious increasing trend of the MAP performance, and then there is a gradually converging trend on the performance. For the rest experiments, we choose to use 2000 training samples since it can help to achieve reasonable performance while guaranteeing computational efficiency.

Figure 2.(b) illustrated the convergence analysis of our approach on NUS-WIDE. We fix all parameter to 1. We can see that our approach can converge very fast within only a few iterations, which indicates its efficiency for practical use.

Further, we compare the proposed MVSSL to one of the classic multi-view approaches, namely SVM2K [2]. We form three two-view combinations (i.e., EDH+WT, EDH+Decaf and WT+Decaf) from the three evaluated visual features. We also test and evaluate our proposed approach in three-view setting (i.e., EDH+WT+Decaf) and single-view setting (i.e., Decaf). The experimental results are shown in Table 1. From the table, it can be seen that MVSSL always gains better performance than SVM2K on all three two-view settings. For comparison of different settings in MVSSL, we observe that multi-view settings can consistently outperform single-view setting. Besides, EDH+Decaf and WT+Decaf significantly outperform EDH+WT. Even we employ three features, the performance still increases. All these observations reveal the strong representative power of Decaf feature.

4. CONCLUSIONS

In this paper, we proposed a new model for image annotation task, termed as Multi-view Semi-supervised Learning (MVSSL). It utilizes the correlated and complemental information from different views to comprehensively depict data, and explores underlying data structural knowledge to jointly boost image annotation performance. Pair-wise constraints were posed on MVSSL to guarantee consistency among different views. We further devised an effective iterative algorithm to optimize the model. Experiments conducted on a real-world image dataset NUS-WIDE dataset demonstrated the effectiveness of MVSSL.

5. REFERENCES

[1] T. Chua, J. Tang, R. Hong, H. Li, Z. Luo, and Y. Zheng. NUS-WIDE: a real-world web image database from national university of singapore. In *CIVR*, pages 48:1–48:9, 2009.

[2] J. D. R. Farquhar, D. R. Hardoon, H. Meng, J. Shawe-Taylor, and S. Szedmák. Two view learning: Svm-2k, theory and practice. In *NIPS*, pages 355–362, 2005.

[3] Y. Jia, E. Shelhamer, J. Donahue, S. Karayev, J. Long, R. B. Girshick, S. Guadarrama, and T. Darrell. Caffe: Convolutional architecture for fast feature embedding. In *ACM Multimedia*, pages 675–678, 2014.

[4] D. G. Lowe. Object recognition from local scale-invariant features. In *ICCV*, pages 1150–1157, 1999.

[5] A. W. M. Smeulders, M. Worring, S. Santini, A. Gupta, and R. Jain. Content-based image retrieval at the end of the early years. *TPAMI*, 22(12):1349–1380, 2000.

[6] Y. Yang, Y. Yang, Z. Huang, H. T. Shen, and F. Nie. Tag localization with spatial correlations and joint group sparsity. In *CVPR*, pages 881–888, 2011.

[7] Y. Yang, Z. Zha, Y. Gao, X. Zhu, and T. Chua. Exploiting web images for semantic video indexing via robust sample-specific loss. *TMM*, 16(6):1677–1689, 2014.

[8] D. Zhang, M. M. Islam, and G. Lu. A review on automatic image annotation techniques. *Pattern Recognition*, 45(1):346–362, 2012.

[9] H. Zhang, Z. Zha, Y. Yang, S. Yan, Y. Gao, and T. Chua. Attribute-augmented semantic hierarchy: towards bridging semantic gap and intention gap in image retrieval. In *ACM Multimedia*, pages 33–42, 2013.

[10] X. Zhu. Semi-supervised learning literature survey. 2005.

Tracking Cultural Differences in News Video Creation

Chun-Yu Tsai and John R. Kender
Dept. of Computer Science, Columbia University
chunyu@cs.columbia.edu, jrk@cs.columbia.edu

ABSTRACT

Many videos on the Web are created in different countries about the same international event. Their specialized video content, as well as their viewing and reposting rates, reflect different cultural interests. Effectively tracking cross-cultural visual memes of the same event, in online video repositories of different cultures, can provide users with a more comprehensive understanding of an international event. We propose a new way to use the PageRank algorithm to model cross-cultural visual meme influence, which more accurately captures the rates at which visual memes are re-posted in a specified time period in a specified culture.

Categories and Subject Descriptors

I.2.10 [**Artificial Intelligence**]: Vision and Scene Understanding—*Video analysis*

General Terms

Algorithms, Design, Experimentation, Human Factors, Performance

Keywords

Visual meme tracking, Visual meme influence and Cross-cultural visual meme analysis.

1. INTRODUCTION

News tracking (text-only, visual-only, or both) [2] [3] [4] has been an active research topic in recent years. In the literature, a "meme" is a frequently re-posted phrase, and a "visual meme" is a frequently re-posted video segment or image. They both act as signatures of topics and events, and their propagation and diffusion over the web has been widely used to monitor the lifespan of a news story. While some journalism research has (mostly manually) investigated the impact of cultural differences in meme analysis, visual meme analysis is still limited to approaches that are not culturally based. Additionally, IR researchers have found that the coverage of text-based news is known to be negatively influenced by the physical distance of consumers from the location of the event. But

MM'15, October 26–30, 2015, Brisbane, Australia.
 ISBN 978-1-4503-3459-4/15/10 ...$15.00.
DOI: http://dx.doi.org/10.1145/2733373.2806372.

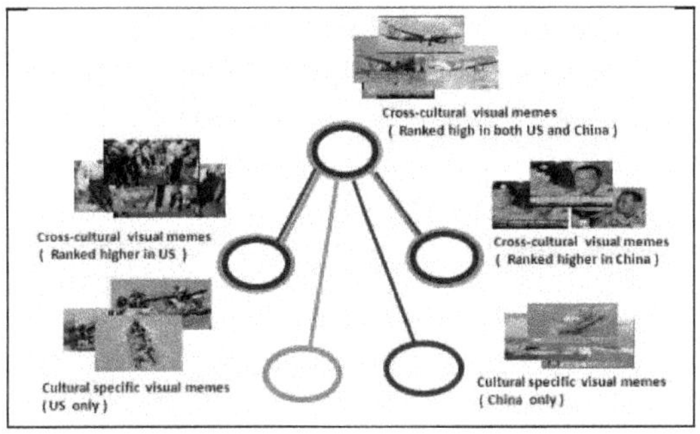

Figure 1: A partial illustration of a cross-cultural visual meme graph for the AirAsia Flight Q8501 event. Red nodes: visual memes occurring in U.S.. Blue nodes: visual memes in China. Red and blue nodes overlapping: visual memes in both countries.

visual information by its very nature is much less dependent on language, and therefore it is much more likely to become viral across cultures.

With the continued rapid growth of online video data, the common usage of only a few universal video sharing platforms (YouTube, Baidu), and the universal importance of human-interest international news events, it becomes imperative to understand how visual memes can cross cultural language barriers. Understanding these viral paths will enable users in a given culture to find more complete information about an international event by querying the search engines of another culture, particularly for those aspects of an event that are not in the news coverage of the user's culture. We have developed representations and methods to recognize, track, measure, and query these cross-cultural visual memes. These tools show interesting patterns of visual meme propagation not previously reported (Figure 1).

We propose a new way to use the PageRank algorithm to model cross-cultural visual meme influence, in order to capture the rates that a visual meme will be re-posted in a specific time period in a particular culture. We have collected videos from YouTube (the primary source for U.S. and European videos) and from Baidu (the primary source for Chinese videos). We use generic text queries as a pre-filter for content on a given topic, then build visual meme co-occurrence graphs to calculate cross-cultural visual meme influence. In this paper we specifically showcase two international events, the Ebola crisis and the AirAsia crash, from three viewpoints, showing the tracking of their memes, and discussing their cultural differences.

Prior literature such as [4] tracked the amounts of visual memes over time through YouTube. However, their analysis is based on

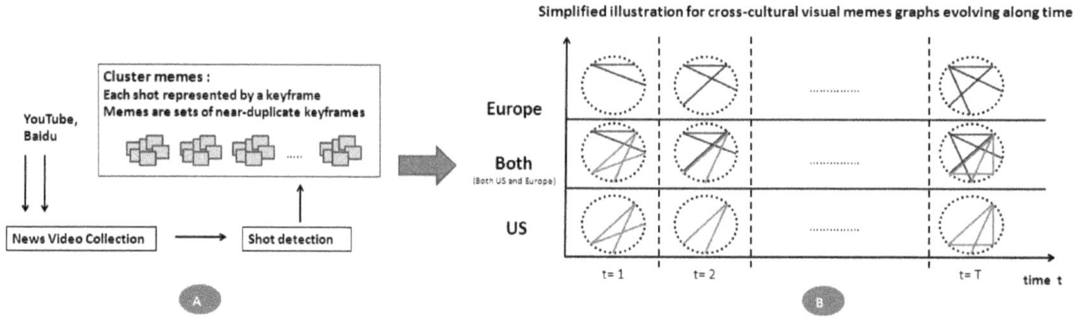

Figure 2: Pipeline for generating cross-cultural visual meme graphs. (A) Video preprocessing. We collect videos from YouTube and Baidu, detect shots in each video, then visually cluster these shots, with each shot represented by a keyframe. A visual meme is defined as a collection of two or more near-duplicate keyframes. (B) Simplified visualization of visual meme graphs for the Ebola event, in a culture-versus-time matrix. Each graph displays in a circle the same visual meme nodes, but with only the edges present in culture c at time t, illustrating differences and evolution.

video volumes and video relationship graphs, where the nodes were videos, and the edges indicate a shared visual meme. Videos are clustered using visual memes. Their primary concern was to determine the author's and the reposters' roles in visual meme diffusion.

In contrast, our analysis is based on a novel visual meme co-occurrence graph, which is a kind of dual to the previous graph. In our graph, the nodes are the visual memes themselves, and the edges indicate visual meme co-occurrence within the same video. Visual memes are clustered using videos. From this graph we can compute new measures of visual meme dynamics, which include, but are not limited to, the rate that a visual meme is re-posted, the relationship of visual meme influence on video composition versus the view counts of those videos, and a number of quantifications and visualizations of cross-cultural visual meme propagation.

2. CROSS-CULTURAL VISUAL MEME INFLUENCE

In this section, we present the pipeline for calculating cross-cultural visual meme influence. (Figure 2)

2.1 Visual meme clustering

We define a visual meme as a frequently re-posted video segment that starts and ends at shot boundaries. In order to find visual memes from our collected video repository, first we extract high-entropy I-frames from each video, perform shot detection over this reduced frame set, then select one keyframe to represent each shot. Then, we cluster these selected keyframes by near-duplicate matching, using SIFT-BoF and color histograms. Each visual meme is defined as consisting of a cluster with two or more keyframes.

2.2 Visual meme graph construction and influence calculation

We track the influence of visual memes as they change across two discrete dimensions: culture and time. We represent a culture as $c \in C = \{US, Europe, China\}$, and a time as $t = 1, 2, ..., T$. At each c and t we construct a visual meme influence graph, where the nodes are visual memes and the edges represent the degree to which the memes co-occur within the same video.

We first note that the total set of visual memes that occur across all cultures and all times can be represented by $M = \bigcup_i m_i$, where m_i is a visual meme. Each m_i carries a weight, w_i, defined as the number of videos that contain a near-duplicate shot of this visual meme; more viral visual memes have higher weights. We also note that any pair of visual memes m_i and m_j can be related by a weighted undirected edge s_{ij}, which counts the number of videos which share both memes; we let the set $S = \{s_{ij}\}$.

Now, at any given t, and any culture c, we can form a graph that represents the sharing of visual memes at that time and in that culture, $G_{ct} = (M_{ct}, S_{ct})$, where the nodes and edges are selected into G_{ct} from M and S in the obvious way. For example, the memes are m_{cti} and the edges are s_{ctij}. We can create $|C| * T$ such graphs.

We can apply the PageRank algorithm to each G_{ct}, computing for each visual meme $r(m_{cti})$, in the context of all visual memes in M, with $\epsilon = 0.15$:

$$r(m_{cti}) = (1 - \epsilon) \sum_{(m_{cti}, m_{ctj}) \in G_{ct}} \frac{r(m_{ctj})}{out(m_{ctj})} + \frac{\epsilon}{|M|} \quad (1)$$

However, because we have many such graphs G_{ct}, in some of these graphs there will be "dangling" visual memes, that is, visual memes of M that do not properly occur in M_{ct}. Let this set be $D_{ct} = \bigcup_k d_{ctk}$. Since this set varies over c and t, and since PageRank considers their effect in each graph G_{ct}, the values of individual PageRank scores, $r(m_{cti})$, are generally not comparable across different graphs. To normalize these scores, we borrow the idea in [1], which divides each score by a value l_{ct} that removes the varying effects of the D_{ct} as follows:

$$l_{ct} = \frac{1}{|M|}(\epsilon + (1 - \epsilon) \sum_{D_{ct}} r(d_{ctk})) \quad (2)$$

These normalized PageRank scores convey how much more likely a node is to be visited in a random walk, compared to a node having the least possible importance. Thus, we can compare these normalized PageRank scores across different graphs, and we are able to track the influence of a visual meme across cultures and along time.

3. DISCUSSIONS

In this paper, we examine two events. We collected about 2400 videos and their metadata in an approximate 3:1 (US:Europe) ratio for the Ebola news event, in a date range from 8/21/14 to 10/30/14. We collected about 1000 videos and their metadata in an approximate 1:1 (China:US) ratio for the AirAsia Flight 8501 event, in a date range from 12/28/14 to 1/15/15. Videos sourced from US and Europe were collected from YouTube, and we verified their posted

	Ebola	AirAsia
Europe only	88	
US-Europe both	65	
US only	273	96
US-China both		37
China only		48

Table 1: The average number of visual memes per day for Ebola and AirAsia news events.

location in the metadata. Videos sourced from China were collected from Baidu[1], the biggest Chinese video search engine in the world, which aggregates videos from Chinese online news channels and from Chinese video sharing websites.

We successfully extracted cross-cultural visual memes from our data set: 3969 distinct ones for Ebola and 553 distinct ones for AirAsia. (The number for Ebola is greater than that for AirAsia because the date range for Ebola is longer.) We found that less than 1% of the visual memes were isolated, that is, they did not co-occur with some other visual memes in at least one video; most re-postings involve multiple visual memes at once. In this paper, our analysis uses U.S., Europe, China, and "Both" cultures, where Both for Ebola means Europe and U.S. visual memes considered together, but for AirAsia it is China and U.S. together.

3.1 Visual meme coverage in different cultures

The average number of visual memes per day in each culture is shown in Table 1. For both events, US has more culturally-specific visual memes than the other two cultures. Aside from the fact that U.S. media dominate world media, this imbalance is partly caused by the large amount of videos remixed and uploaded by users from U.S. sources. The data also reflects the prevalence of more personal viewpoints in visual memes selection in the U.S. In general, there are very few personally edited videos from China, and even in those, the visual meme selection is not very different from those of the Chinese news video mainstream.

3.2 Visual meme influence correlation

We calculate Pearson and Spearman correlation coefficients between the normalized PageRank scores, for cross-cultural visual meme coverage along time:

$$\rho_{Pearson} = Pearson(r(t, c_1), r(t, c_2)) \quad (3)$$

$$\rho_{Spearman} = Spearman(r(t, c_1), r(t, c_2)) \quad (4)$$

where r refers to normalized PageRank score, t refers to timestamp, c_1 is U.S., and c_2 is Europe for Ebola but China for AirAsia. We display these correlation coefficients in Figure 3. We note that in general Pearson and Spearman are similar in shape, but the Spearman coefficient is always smaller. This is because visual meme influence is not uniformly distributed; most influence values are small, and are not shared across cultures. For example, one visual meme for Ebola scored a 8.34 PageRank in the U.S., but only scored 1.12 in Europe, which is near the normalized lower bound of 1. But we also note that a few visual memes scored very high in both cultures, showing to some degree a universal interest in specific visual memes.

We can interpret some cultural preferences from the ups and downs in the correlation curves. In the Europe-Both correlation curve for Ebola, we note that there are three peeks. The first peak (from 9/2 to 9/12) is due to news related to the Ebola survivor William Pooley (a

[1]http://v.baidu.com/

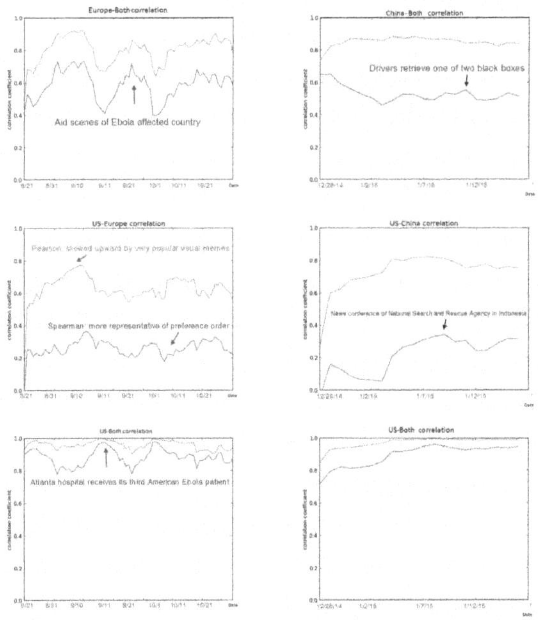

(a) Ebola (Europe and US) (b) AirAsia (China and US)

Figure 3: Cross-cultural visual meme influence correlation coefficients for different countries, for different news events, along time. Red curves are Pearson, blue curves are Spearman.

British nurse), and to a WHO conference discussing aid to Africa. During the second peak (from 9/22 to 9/30), European news focused on the reporting of the spread of Ebola in certain countries. Europe re-posted many aid scenes sourced from Reuters, and those memes were also re-posted by the U.S. The third peak (from 10/18 to 10/28) contains many small visual memes, some of them sourced from U.S. news. For example, they include the CDC announcement for Ebola care and the fourth U.S. patient's arrival at Atlanta. Other visual memes in this peak are again related to aid scenes in Ebola-affected countries.

In addition, we note that the China-Both Spearman correlation coefficient is much lower than its Pearson correlation coefficient. This is due to the large inconsistency of the ranks of visual memes between China and Both. Many China videos contained visual memes of a conference held by the National Search and Rescue Agency of Indonesia, which were not stressed in U.S. videos. So this particular visual meme ranks lower in Both than in China. Additionally, there were visual memes reporting on the Chinese navy joining the rescue, and some other videos with interviews of Chinese and Indonesian officials, also not covered in the U.S. And in general, U.S. visual meme influence is more consistent with Both visual meme influence, partly since the U.S. media dominates the world media, and partly since the U.S. media is more effective in reporting influential news events in other countries.

3.3 Single visual meme tracking

(A) U.S. ahead of Europe

We note that for some visual memes the peak of the U.S. curve of normalized PageRank score is ahead of Europe. For example, we note a particular Ebola subevent: the American Dr. Kent Brantly is released from an Atlanta hospital. Dr. Kent's recovery was important because it represented the success of the experimental drug, ZMapp. Therefore, this news became worldwide, but it originated

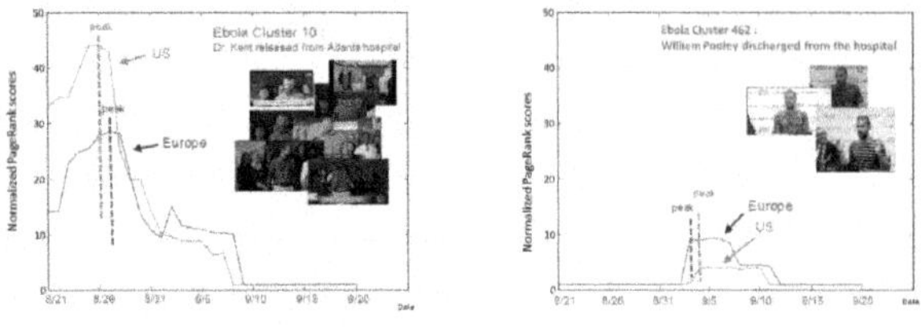

(a) (b)

Figure 4: Timing of visual meme propagation. (a) Coverage of American Dr. Kent Brantly: the peak of the U.S. curve is ahead of Europe. (b) Coverage of British nurse William Pooley: the peak of the European curve is ahead of the U.S.

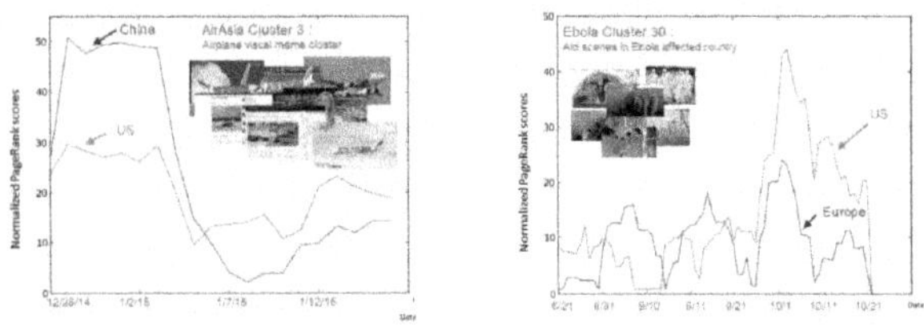

(a) (b)

Figure 5: Long-lasting visual meme clusters. (a) Airplane visual meme from AirAsia. (b) One of aid scenes from Ebola.

in the U.S. Following U.S. media, the European media also covered this news story. (Figure 4 (a))

(B) Europe ahead of U.S.

In other cases, the peak of the Europe curve is ahead of the U.S. We note another particular Ebola subevent: the British nurse William Pooley is discharged from the Royal Free hospital. However, we also notice that this visual meme was less influential than other memes in U.S., probably because at this same time there was also another Ebola case in U.S. (Rick Sacra, an American missionary doctor) and the U.S. media gave precedence to it. (Figure 4 (b))

(C) Visual memes with long lifespan

Some visual memes last much longer than others. They were continually re-posted throughout the entire news event lifetime, and became a type of signature for the event: for example, aid scenes for Ebola, and airplane images and water scenes for AirAsia. In Figure 5 (a), we note that the visual meme influence scores of airplane scenes in China were much higher than those in U.S., even from the very beginning, Nevertheless, these airplane visual memes were still highly ranked in U.S. news coverage, and they persisted over weeks in both. Figure 5 (b) shows one of visual meme clusters of aid scenes. Although its influence fluctuated over time for many weeks in both cultures (and at times was notably out of phase across them), they were always present during our tracking period.

3.4 Visual meme and view count correlation

We hypothesized that visual meme influence may be related to video view counts obtained from video metadata. Figure 6 plots, on a log-log scale, influence versus view count, for each visual meme in our system. Influence here is defined as the average influence during a visual meme's lifespan, and view count is defined as the average view count of videos containing this visual meme. The graph failed to support this hypothesis, as did its derived statistics.

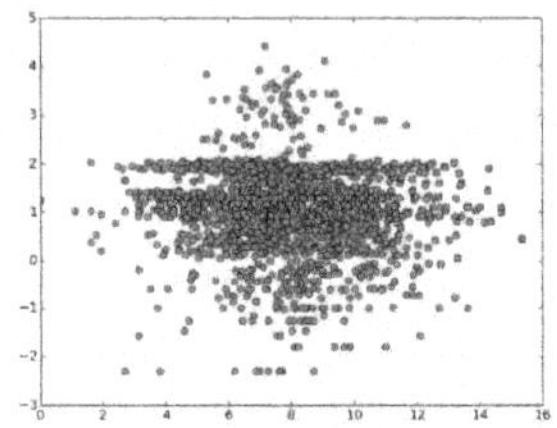

Figure 6: Log-log plot of visual meme influence versus view count, showing independence. Both influence and view count also follow log-normal distributions marginally.

We used the standard EM algorithm to fit a two-dimensional Gaussian distribution for the plot, starting with a random seed. The resulting μ and Σ are:

$$\mu = [8.4728, 1.6328], \;\; \Sigma = \begin{bmatrix} 4.0746 & -1.6245 \\ -1.6245 & 6.4940 \end{bmatrix} \qquad (5)$$

We believe the explanation is as follows. We note that influence is the result of a producer process, whereas view count is the result of a consumer process. In the real world, they do not appear to be strongly coupled to each other: a repeated visual meme is not necessarily viewed more because of the repetition. We note that not only is the covariance matrix nearly diagonal, suggesting independence, but also both processes are independently log-normal. Such distributions are typically the results of "multiplicative" processes, where several independent considerations must all occur together in order to achieve a maximum effect. Since the probabilities of these considerations multiply, their logs add, and approach a normal central limit. Visual memes appear to become influential when the several causes of virality (for example, emotional impact, good photographic properties, regional interest, etc.) all co-occur. Likewise, videos can appeal to viewers for many reasons (political alignment, novelty, the resolution of fear, etc.), but these reasons are not necessarily the same as the ones for the re-posting of individual visual memes. We plan to investigate these observations further.

4. FUTURE WORK

We observe that many visual memes tend to be re-posted only in videos on specific topics. For example, visual memes related to experimental drugs are re-posted most often in videos about different Ebola-infected people. However, it is hard to automatically analyze these relationships without additional semantic (textual) information. We therefore plan to fuse visual memes with their related tag information for further analysis.

In this paper we showcased cross-cultural visual meme tracking by using two specific cultures for each of two specific news events (Ebola and AirAsia), over a relatively short expanse of time. However, our proposed model is easily extended to multiple cultures and longer time ranges. We anticipate establishing additional interesting cultural-specific phenomena.

5. REFERENCES

[1] K. Berberich and others. Comparing apples and oranges: Normalized pagerank for evolving graphs. WWW, 2007.

[2] J. Leskovec, L. Backstrom, and J. Kleinberg. Meme-tracking and the dynamics of the news cycle. SIGKDD, 2009.

[3] T. M. Swit Phuvipadawat. Breaking news detection and tracking in twitter. WI-IAT, 2010.

[4] L. Xie, A. Natsev, X. He, J. Kender, et al. Visual memes in social media. ACM MM, 2011.

Click-through-based Deep Visual-Semantic Embedding for Image Search

Yuan Liu †, Zhongchao Shi †, Xue Li ‡, Gang Wang †
† Ricoh Software Research Center (Beijing) Co., Ltd., Beijing, China
‡ Ricoh Company, Ltd., Yokohama, Japan
{Yuan.Liu, Zhongchao.Shi, Gang.Wang}@srcb.ricoh.com; setsu.ri@nts.ricoh.co.jp

ABSTRACT

The problem of image search is mostly considered from the perspectives of feature-based vector model and image ranker learning. A fundamental issue that underlies the success of these approaches is the similarity learning between query and image. The need of image surrounding texts in feature-based vector model, however, makes the similarity sensitive to the quality of text descriptions. On the other, the image ranker learning can suffer from robustness problem, originating from the fact that human labeled query-image pairs do not always predict user search intention precisely.

We demonstrate in this paper that the above two issues can be well mitigated by jointly exploring visual-semantic embedding and the use of click-through data. Specifically, we propose a novel click-through-based deep visual-semantic embedding (C-DVSE) model for learning query and image similarity. The proposed model consists of two components: a deep convolutional neural networks followed by an image embedding layer for learning visual embedding, and a deep neural networks for generating query semantic embedding. The objective of our model is to maximize the correlation between semantic (query) and visual (clicked image) embedding. When the visual-semantic embedding is learnt, query-image similarity can be directly computed by cosine similarity on this embedding space. On a large-scale click-based image dataset with 11.7 million queries and one million images, our model is shown to be powerful for keyword-based image search with superior performance over several state-of-the-art methods.

Categories and Subject Descriptors

H.3.3 [**Information Storage and Retrieval**]: Information Search and Retrieval—*Retrieval models*

General Terms

Algorithms, Experimentation, Performance.

MM'15, Oct 26-30, 2015, Brisbane, Australia.
 ISBN 978-1-4503-3459-4/15/10 ...$15.00.
DOI: http://dx.doi.org/10.1145/2733373.2806373.

Keywords

Image search; similarity learning; deep convolutional neural networks; visual-semantic embedding; click-through data.

1. INTRODUCTION

The problem of retrieving images from textual queries is one of the key tasks in information retrieval. The objective is to output an image ranking list by sorting the images based on their similarities with the query. Therefore, similarity measure is the core to image search.

As textual queries and visual images are of two different views, they cannot be directly compared. As a result, a typical solution is to represent an image by a feature vector of its surrounding texts. The similarity between a query and an image is then defined based on their textual feature vectors. The classical feature-based vector models [7], e.g. Vector Space Model, BM25, and Language Models, can all be used as similarity functions. However, the text descriptions may not fully depict salient visual content, not to mention that some images do not even associate with any text. Consequently, the feature-based vector models do not always perform well. Another solution of similarity measure is to learn image rankers on query-image pairs which are usually labeled by human experts. Such labels are well known to be noisy due to the factors of ambiguous queries and unclear user search intention. Moreover, human labeling is expensive, making it hard to scale up.

Our similarity method tackles the two issues highlighted above as follows. First, inspired by the effectiveness of cross-view embedding such as Canonical Correlation Analysis (CCA) [3] and Polynomial Semantic Indexing (PSI) [11], a visual-semantic embedding is learnt to allow direct comparison between textual queries and visual images in the common embedding space. The image representations are visual features extracted from image content, rather than textual features. Second, by leveraging user click-through data from search engines, we alleviate the label noise problem and bridge the gaps between semantics and images, as well as search queries and user intention [5]. As most image search engines display results as thumbnails, the user can see the entire image before clicking on it. As such, barring intention changes, users predominantly tend to click on images that are relevant to their search queries. Therefore, the click-through data can serve as a reliable and implicit feedback for image search.

By jointly integrating cross-view embedding and click-through data, this paper presents a novel Click-through-based Deep Visual-Semantic Embedding (C-DVSE) model

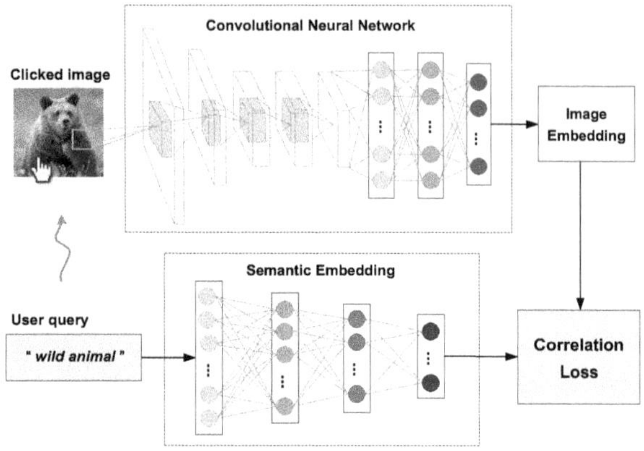

Figure 1: Click-through-based deep visual-semantic embedding.

for similarity learning, as shown in Figure 1. Specifically, the correspondences between original semantic (query) and visual (image) spaces are first established based on the click-through data collected from a commercial image search engine. Next, a deep convolutional neural networks (DCNN) is exploited for extracting image representation, followed by an image embedding layer for generating visual embedding. Similarly, a deep neural networks (DNN) is utilized for semantic embedding. The learning of visual-semantic embedding aims to maximize the correlation in between. After the optimization of visual-semantic embedding, the similarity between a query and an image in the original spaces can be directly computed by cosine similarity of their mappings in the embedding space.

2. CLICK-THROUGH-BASED DEEP VISUAL-SEMANTIC EMBEDDING

We begin this section by presenting the click-through bipartite graph that naturally encodes user actions in the query log, followed by the proposed deep visual-semantic embedding. Finally, the process for keyword-based image search is presented.

2.1 Notation

Let $\mathcal{G} = (\mathcal{V}, \mathcal{E})$ denote a click-through bipartite graph. $\mathcal{V} = Q \cup V$ is the set of vertices, which consists of a query set Q and an image set V. $\mathcal{E}$ is the set of edges between the query and image vertices. The number associated with an edge represents the number of times that an image is clicked given a query. Suppose there are n triads $\{q_i, v_i, c_i\}_{i=1}^{n}$ generated from the click-through bipartite in total, where c_i is the click counts of image v_i in response to query q_i. As the query q_i and image v_i may not be unique in each triad, we assume there are m unique images in the bipartite graph and let s_i be the set of queries which have the edges linked to the image v_i. Let $\mathbf{Q} = \{\mathbf{q}_{s_1}, \mathbf{q}_{s_2}, \ldots, \mathbf{q}_{s_m}\}^\top \in \mathbb{R}^{m \times d_q}$ and $\mathbf{V} = \{\mathbf{v}_1, \mathbf{v}_2, \ldots, \mathbf{v}_m\}^\top \in \mathbb{R}^{m \times d_v}$ denote the query and image feature matrix, where $\mathbf{q}_{s_i}$ and $\mathbf{v}_i$ are the textual and visual feature of query set q_{s_i} and image v_i, and d_q and d_v are the feature dimensionality, respectively.

2.2 Visual-Semantic Embedding

From the click-through bipartite, each query set establishes a link with each unique clicked image, which makes a natural one-to-one correspondence between query and image spaces. The similarity in between, nevertheless, could not be directly computed since the representations of query and image are absolutely heterogenous. One solution, that we pursue in this work, is to rely on cross-view learning [10], which assumes that a low-dimensional joint latent space exists for the representation of query and image. Inspired by the effectiveness of cross-view embedding in cross-modal retrieval [8] or multi-view embedding [3][12], we propose to use deep architecture to learn a visual-semantic embedding.

Visual Embedding. AlexNet [6], which is the recent advance image classification architecture, is first exploited for learning image representations. The AlexNet is pre-trained on the 1.2 million images of the ImageNet challenge dataset [2] and readers can refer to [6] for more technical details. We take the output of 1000-way fc8 classification layer of AlexNet as image representation, which is denoted by $\mathbf{V}$. Then, an image embedding layer is applied to map image representation into the embedding space as

$$\mathbf{V}_e = f_v(\mathbf{V}), \tag{1}$$

where $\mathbf{V}_e \in \mathbb{R}^{m \times d_e}$ denotes the image representation in the visual-semantic embedding space, d_e is the dimensionality of the embedding space and $f_v(\cdot)$ is the mapping function of the image embedding layer.

Semantic Embedding. We take the words in queries as "word features." With word features, each query is represented by a tf vector in the query space, represented as $\mathbf{q}_i$. Then, the feature of the query set s_i is given by

$$\mathbf{q}_{s_i} = \sum_{q_i \in s_i} c_i \mathbf{q}_i \Big/ \sum_{q_i \in s_i} c_i. \tag{2}$$

The resulting $\mathbf{Q}$ forms the input to a neural networks for generating the query semantic embedding as

$$\mathbf{Q}_e = f_q(\mathbf{Q}), \tag{3}$$

where $\mathbf{Q}_e \in \mathbb{R}^{m \times d_e}$ and $f_q(\cdot)$ is the output function for query semantic embedding. The neural networks here encodes both the syntactic and semantic meaning of the queries.

Correlation loss layer. To learn the whole architecture of our deep visual-semantic embedding, the objective is to maximize the correlations between the textual queries and their clicked visual images. One natural choice is to minimize the distance between their mappings in the embedding space as

$$\min_{\theta_v, \theta_q} \|\mathbf{V}_e - \mathbf{Q}_e\|_2^2 \quad s.t.\ \mathbf{V}_e{}^T\mathbf{V}_e = \mathbf{I},\ \mathbf{Q}_e{}^T\mathbf{Q}_e = \mathbf{I}, \tag{4}$$

where θ_v, θ_q are the layer parameters for image visual embedding and query semantic embedding, respectively. The mappings in the embedding space $\mathbf{V}_e$ and $\mathbf{Q}_e$ are designed to be orthogonal in order to make each dimension uncorrelated to each other, i.e. $\mathbf{V}_e{}^T\mathbf{V}_e = \mathbf{Q}_e{}^T\mathbf{Q}_e = \mathbf{I}$ where $\mathbf{I}$ is the identity matrix.

By relaxing the two constraints, the optimization problem in Eq.(4) can be rewritten as

$$\min_{\theta_v, \theta_q} \|\mathbf{V}_e - \mathbf{Q}_e\|_2^2 + \lambda_v \left\|\mathbf{V}_e{}^T\mathbf{V}_e - \mathbf{I}\right\|_2^2 + \lambda_q \left\|\mathbf{Q}_e{}^T\mathbf{Q}_e - \mathbf{I}\right\|_2^2, \tag{5}$$

where λ_v and λ_q are tradeoff parameters. Eq.(5) is the final loss function of the correlation loss layer and this loss layer does not have any parameters. During learning, it evaluates the distance between query semantic embedding and image visual embedding, and back-propagates the gradients to the lower layers so that the lower layers can adjust their parameters to minimize the correlation loss.

2.3 Keyword-based Image Search

After the optimization of the whole architecture, we can obtain the visual embedding and semantic embedding defined in Eq.(1) and Eq.(3), respectively. Next, given a test query and image pair $(\hat{q}, \hat{v})$, we compute the cosine similarity between their mappings in the visual-semantic embedding space as

$$sim(\hat{q}, \hat{v}) = \frac{f_v(\hat{v}) \cdot f_q(\hat{q})}{\|f_v(\hat{v})\| \, \|f_q(\hat{q})\|}. \quad (6)$$

This value reflects how relevant the given image could be in answering a query, with higher score indicating higher relevance. Thus, given a textual query, a rank list of images is produced by sorting the scores of query-image pairs.

3. EXPERIMENTS

We conducted our experiments on the Clickture dataset [5] and evaluated our approach on keyword-based image search.

3.1 Dataset

The dataset, Clickture, is a large-scale click-based image dataset [5]. It was collected from one year click-through data of one commercial image search engine. The dataset comprises two parts, i.e., the training and development (dev) sets. The training set consists of 23.1 million $\{query, image, click\}$ triads, where *query* is a textual word or phrase, *image* is a base64 encoded JPEG image thumbnail, and *click* is an integer of value no less than one. The training set contains 11.7 millions of distinct queries and 1.0 million unique images. The dev dataset contains 79,926 $\langle query, image\rangle$ pairs generated from 1,000 queries. The relevancy of each image to query was manually annotated on a three point ordinal scale: Excellent, Good, and Bad. In the experiments, the training set is used for learning the visual-semantic embedding, while the dev set is used for performance evaluation.

3.2 Experimental Settings

We investigate our visual-semantic embedding on keyword-based image search task. The task is to estimate the similarity of each query-image pair in the dev set, and then for each query, we order the images based on their similarities to the query.

Compared Approaches. We compare the following approaches for performance evaluation:

(1) Passive-Aggressive Model [4] (*PA*) measures the relevance between a query-image pair by projecting the query into the image space. The training procedure of the projection from query to image space is derived by adapting the Passive-Aggressive algorithm.

(2) Polynomial Semantic Indexing [11] (*PSI*) first learns an embedding space for query and image in a learning to rank framework, and then a polynomial model is taken to measure the relevance between query and image.

(3) Canonical Correlation Analysis [3][9] (*CCA*) explores the mapping matrices by maximizing the correlation between the projections of images and queries in the embedding space.

(4) Click-through-based Cross-view Learning [8] (*CCL*) learns the embedding space by minimizing the distance between the mappings of query and image in the embedding space, while preserving the structures in original spaces.

(5) Bag-of-Words based Deep Neural Networks [1] (*BoWD NN*) uses a deep neural networks to map images into bag-of-words representation space of queries and measures the query-image similarity by cosine similarity.

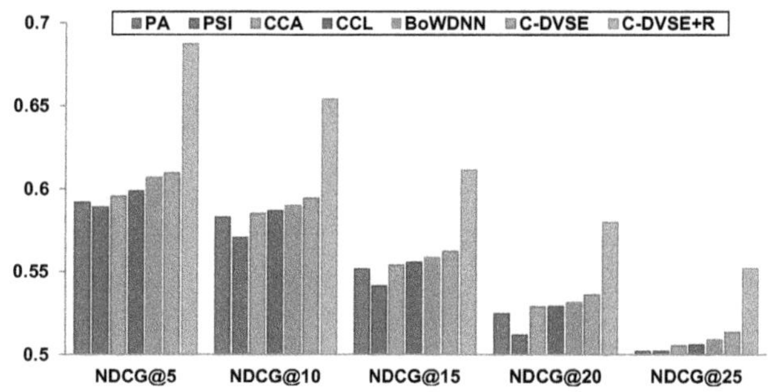

Figure 2: The NDCG of different approaches for keyword-based image search.

(6) Click-through-based Deep Visual-Semantic Embedding (*C-DVSE*) based on our proposal in Section 2. An enhanced version of *C-DVSE* is named as *C-DVSE+R*, which reorders the ranking list of *C-DVSE* by performing random walks on image similarity graph for each query.

Parameter Settings. *PA* directly projects query into image space and thus the dimension of embedding is equal to that of visual feature. *BoWDNN*, in contrast, maps image into query space and the dimension is that of query representation. For the other four embedding learning methods, the dimension d_e of the embedding space is in the range of $\{40, 60, 80, 100\}$. Following the setting in [1], we use the top 50,000 most frequent words as the word vocabulary for generating tf feature of query. The architecture of neural networks used for semantic embedding is $F50,000 - Fd_e - Fd_e - Fd_e$, which contains four fully-connected layers (denoted by F with the number of neurons). We set the two tradeoff parameters $\lambda_v = \lambda_q = 1.0$ in our approach based on a validation set.

Evaluation Metrics. For the evaluation of image search, we adopted Normalized Discounted Cumulative Gain (NDCG) as the performance metric. Given an image ranking list, the NDCG score at the depth of d in the ranking list is defined by: $NDCG@d = Z_d \sum_{j=1}^{d} \frac{2^{r^j}-1}{\log(1+j)}$, where $r^j = \{Excellent = 3, Good = 2, Bad = 0\}$ is the manually judged relevance for each image with respect to the query. Z_d is a normalizer factor to make the score for d Excellent results 1. The final metric is the average of NDCG@d for all the queries in the dev set.

3.3 Performance Comparison

Figure 2 shows the NDCG performances of seven approaches. It is worth noticing that *PA* and *BoWDNN* use image and query space as the embedding space, whose dimension is 1,000 and 50,000, respectively. For other four methods, the performances are given by choosing 80 as the dimension of the latent embedding space.

Overall, the results across different depths of NDCG consistently indicate that our *C-DVSE* outperforms others. In particular, the NDCG@25 of *C-DVSE* achieves 0.5135, which makes the improvement over *PA* by 2.3%. Furthermore, by performing random walks to reorder the results of *C-DVSE*, the NDCG@25 of *C-DVSE+R* can reach 0.5519, which is so far the highest performance reported on Clickture dataset. Compared to conventional cross-view embedding models of

Figure 3: Examples showing the top ten image search results by different methods of query "women looking up" (better viewed in color). The relevance scale is provided at the top left corner for each image.

PA, *PSI*, *CCA* and *CCL*, *BoWDNN* and *C-DVSE* using deep neural networks architecture exhibit better performances. The results basically indicate the advantage of exploiting neural networks for modeling the relationships between visual images and semantic queries. There is also a performance gap between *BoWDNN* and *C-DVSE*. Though both methods involve utilization of neural networks, they are different in the way that *BoWDNN* directly takes the original query space as the embedding space, while *C-DVSE* is by exploring a latent joint visual-semantic embedding. As indicated by our results, learning a joint embedding can better measure query-image similarity and constantly lead to better performance gain.

Figure 3 shows the top ten image search results by different approaches for the exemplary query "women looking up." We can see that the proposed *C-DVSE* method gets more satisfying ranking results and retrieves eight excellent images in the returned top ten images. The ranking could be further improved after reranking.

3.4 Effect of the Dimension of Embedding

In order to show the relationship between the performance and the dimension of the embedding space, we compared the results of the dimension in the range of 40, 60, 80, and 100. Note that only the four joint visual-semantic embedding learning methods are included in this comparison. The results are shown in Figure 4. Compared to the other three runs, performance improvement is consistently observed at each dimension of the latent embedding by our proposed *C-DVSE* method. Furthermore, *C-DVSE* achieves the best result at the latent embedding dimension of 80, and the results at other dimensions are close to the best one. This observation basically verifies that *C-DVSE* has a desirable property of being not sensitive to the change of dimension of the embdding space. In addition, the performance trends of NDCG at other depths are similar with that of NDCG@25.

4. CONCLUSIONS

We have presented click-through-based deep visual-semantic embedding which explores cross-view embedding and the use of click-through data for image search. Particularly, we establish the correspondences between original visual image and textual query spaces from image search click-through. To learn the visual-semantic embedding, a DCNN architecture with an image embedding layer is developed for visual embedding, while a DNN is devised for semantic embedding. On the top of the architecture, a correlation loss layer is employed to maximize the correlation between the mappings on the embedding space for optimizing the whole architecture. Experiments conducted on a large-scale click-based image dataset basically validate our proposal and analysis. Performance improvements are also observed when comparing to other cross-view embedding techniques and other DNN architecture on this task.

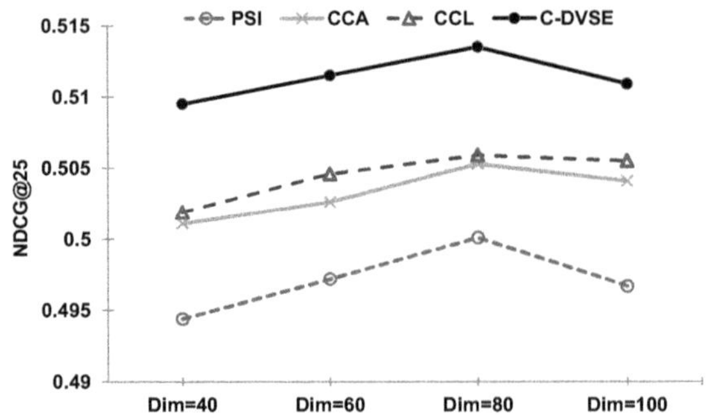

Figure 4: The NDCG@25 performance with different dimension of the embedding space.

5. REFERENCES

[1] Y. Bai, W. Yu, T. Xiao, C. Xu, K. Yang, W.-Y. Ma, and T. Zhao. Bag-of-words based deep neural network for image retrieval. In *ACM MM*, 2014.

[2] J. Deng, W. Dong, R. Socher, L.-J. Li, K. Li, and L. Fei-Fei. Imagenet: A large-scale hierarchical image database. In *CVPR*, 2009.

[3] Y. Gong, Q. Ke, M. Isard, and S. Lazebnik. A multi-view embedding space for modeling internet images, tags, and their semantics. *IJCV*, (106):210–233, 2014.

[4] D. Grangier and S. Bengio. A discriminative kernel-based model to rank images from text queries. *IEEE Trans. on PAMI*, 2008.

[5] X.-S. Hua, L. Yang, J. Wang, J. Wang, M. Ye, K. Wang, Y. Rui, and J. Li. Clickage: Towards bridging semantic and intent gaps via mining click logs of search engines. In *ACM MM*, 2013.

[6] A. Krizhevsky, I. Sutskever, and G. E. Hinton. Imagenet classification with deep convolutional neural networks. In *NIPS*, 2012.

[7] C. D. Manning, P. Raghavan, and H. Schütze. *Introduction to information retrieval*, volume 1. Cambridge university press Cambridge, 2008.

[8] Y. Pan, T. Yao, T. Mei, H. Li, C. W. Ngo, and Y. Rui. Click-through-based cross-view learning for image search. In *SIGIR*, 2014.

[9] Y. Pan, T. Yao, X. Tian, H. Li, and C. W. Ngo. Click-through-based subspace learning for image search. In *ACM MM*, 2014.

[10] C. Xu, D. Tao, and C. Xu. A survey on multi-view learning. *CoRR*, abs/1304.5634, 2013.

[11] T. Yao, T. Mei, C.-W. Ngo, and S. Li. Annotation for free: Video tagging by mining user search behavior. In *ACM MM*, 2013.

[12] T. Yao, Y. Pan, C.-W. Ngo, H. Li, and T. Mei. Semi-supervised domain adaptation with subspace learning for visual recognition. In *CVPR*, 2015.

Partially Common-Semantic Pursuit for RGB-D Object Recognition

Lu Jin
Nanjing University of Science and Technology
Nanjing, China 210094
jinlu_nj@hotmail.com

Zechao Li
Nanjing University of Science and Technology
Nanjing, China 210094
zechao.li@njust.edu.cn

Xiangbo Shu
Nanjing University of Science and Technology
Nanjing, China 210094
shuxb104@gmail.com

Shenghua Gao
ShanghaiTech University
Shanghai, China 200000
gaoshh@shanghaitech.edu.cn

Jinhui Tang*
Nanjing University of Science and Technology
Nanjing, China 210094
jinhuitang@njust.edu.cn

ABSTRACT

For the RGB-D object recognition task, the robust and rich representations can boost the performance. Most works employ feature learning approaches to learn specific representation for the RGB and depth modalities independently, while some directly learn common property. Different from them, this paper proposes a novel supervised feature learning method for RGB-D object recognition, named Partially Common-Semantic Learning (PCSL), which jointly captures the complementary and consistency semantic information from RGB and depth modalities. The complementary information is revealed by the individual modality, while the consistency is exploited by both modalities simultaneously. In PCSL, Reconstruction Independent Component Analysis (RICA) is extended to integrate the supervised information and learn both of the complementary and partially shared common semantic information. The proposed approach is evaluated on two public RGB-D datasets and achieves better performance than several state-of-the-art methods.

Categories and Subject Descriptors

I.4.8 [**Image Processing and Computer Vision**]: Scene Analysis — object recognition

Keywords

RGB-D object recognition; feature learning; RICA; deep networks

*Corresponding author.

MM'15, October 26–30, 2015, Brisbane, Australia.
© 2015 ACM. ISBN 978-1-4503-3459-4/15/10 ...$15.00.
DOI: http://dx.doi.org/10.1145/2733373.2806374.

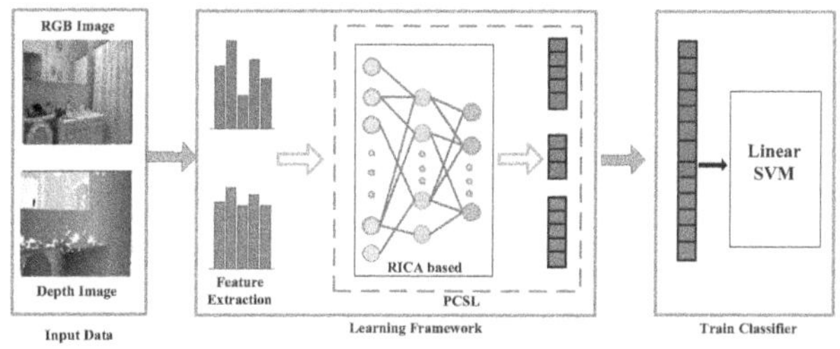

Figure 1: The flowchart of the proposed approach. The red and blue bins indicate the CNN features for RGB and depth images, respectively. In PCSL, we exploit the complementary information (e.g. red and blue square) and the consistency semantic property (e.g., purple square). (Better view in the color version)

1. INTRODUCTION

Object recognition is one of the fundamental research issues in computer version and multimedia areas. With the advanced sensing technology, such as Kinect style camera, the high quality RGB and depth images can be recorded synchronously, and the performance can be improved by jointly exploiting them. For example, the robots can understand indoor environment easier by employing the depth information for scene understanding and object inference. Consequently, it is necessary and challenging to jointly exploit the RGB and depth information for RGB-D object recognition [1].

For RGB-D based object recognition, robust image representation can boost the performance. These image representation methods can be mainly divided into two categories, one focuses on designing a feature extraction method and applying it on RGB and depth images separately, while the other devotes to capture unique characteristic from each modality. Bo *et. al.* [1] transformed pixel level attributes to patch level representation based on a set of kernel descriptors, which are employed to obtain feature representations for RGB and depth images independently. However, it just capture specific characteristic from each modality, with the shared information unexploited. Jhuo *et. al.* [4] employed the deep Reconstruction Independent Component Analysis network (RICA) [7] to encode the relationship between both modalities, while they ignored the complementary perspective of each modality. However, in fact, the RGB and depth modalities have not only the modality-specific information, but also the shared semantic information. Thus, it is necessary and reasonable to exploit them simultaneously.

Towards this end, we propose a novel supervised feature learning method, named Partially Common-Semantic Learning (PCSL), to jointly explore complementarity and consistency attributes for RGB and depth modalities, as illustrated in Figure 1. Firstly, we extract fixed-size CNN features, where the CNN is pre-trained on ImageNet for classification task and then fine-tuned on specific RGB-D object recognition task. In PCSL, RICA-based formulation is employed to learn compact latent representations which are assumed to be composed of some specific latent factors for each modality and partially common latent factors shared across both modalities. Besides that, we extend the RICA in a supervised manner by introducing a label consistent regularization which directly imposes the class information on the latent representations. The label consistent regularization guarantees that the input data from the same category have the same response, resulting in compact and discriminative data representation. Finally, the expected RGB-D image representations are obtained by concatenating the shared latent representations and the modality-specific latent representations. Extensive experiments on the 2D&3D object recognition dataset and NYU Depth V1 Scene Benchmark demonstrate the effectiveness of the proposed method compared with related works.

2. THE PROPOSED METHOD

2.1 Motivation

To learn robust image representation for RGB-D based object recognition, we mainly focus on three aspects, containing data reconstruction for both modalities, discriminative property and both of complementary and consistency components of RGB-D information. We define the latent representation as $H = [H^r; H^d]$, where H^r and H^d are the latent representation of RGB and depth modalities, respectively. We assume that there are two kinds of properties embodied in RGB and depth semantic contents: complementary and consistency. Thus, we divide the latent representation into two parts: $H_s = [H_s^r; H_s^d]$ and $H_c = [H_c^r; H_c^d]$, where H_s is the specific semantic contents of individual modality and H_c is the common semantic content. To effectively capture the partially shared common semantic information, we define

$$H_c^r = H_c^d \tag{1}$$

where H_c^r and H_c^d are common semantic content for RGB and depth, respectively. Noting that matrix superscript "^{r}" and "^{d}" is related to RGB and depth, respectively. Matrix subscript "$_s$" means that this matrix is corresponding to the specific part for the individual modality, while "$_c$" is corresponding to the common part for both modalities.

2.2 Representation Learning

Motivated by the success of the Reconstruction Independent Component Analysis (RICA) in object recognition task, we employ RICA for data reconstruction and representation learning. We denote $X = [X^r; X^d] \in R^{m \times n}$ as the input data.

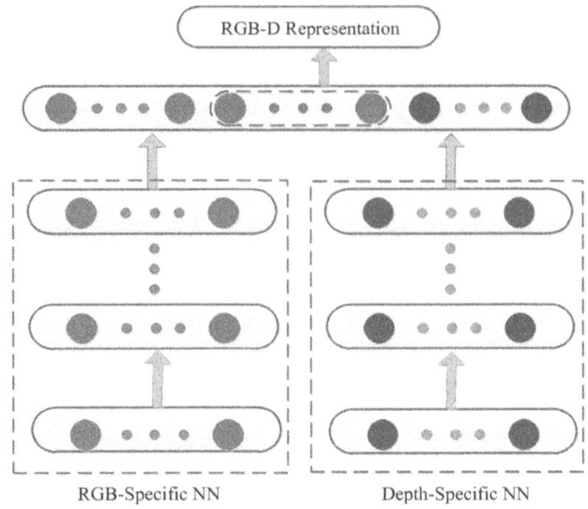

Figure 2: The architecture of our proposed deep neural networks. The red and blue nodes are the latent representations for RGB and depth images respectively, while the purple nodes in the top layer are the shared common latent representation of each modalities. (Better view in the color version)

To enhance the discriminative ability of feature representation, we leverage the class information of the input feature to learn a reconstructive and discriminative feature representation, employing a label consistent regularization by jointly incorporating the label information and feature learning [8]. We formulate the joint minimization of the reconstruction cost and label consistent regularization as the following problem:

$$\begin{aligned} \min_{W,T} & \left\|WW^TX - X\right\|_F^2 + \lambda f(W^TX) \\ & + \left\|TW^TX - Y\right\|_F^2 + \beta \left\|T\right\|_F^2 \end{aligned} \tag{2}$$

where $W = [W^r; W^d] \in R^{m' \times m}$ projects X into a m'-dimensional feature space. Thus, the latent representation is denoted as $H = W^TX \in R^{m' \times n}$, f is the smooth $L1$ penalty function [7]. According to the dividing of the latent representation H in section 2.1, we split the matrix W into two parts: $W_s = [W_s^r; W_s^d]$ and $W_c = [W_c^r; W_c^d]$. The matrix X can be also divided to $X_s = [X_s^r; X_s^d]$ and $X_c = [X_c^r; X_c^d]$. Furthermore, the latent representation H_c can be rewritten as $H_c = [H_c^r; H_c^d]$, where $H_c^r = (W_c^r)^T X_c^r$ and $H_c^d = (W_c^d)^T X_c^d$.

Since the training images of the same class lay in the same subspace, the ideal representation of training images should has classwise block-diagonal structure, we define Y as follows,

$$\begin{bmatrix} \overline{Y}_1^* & 0 & 0 \\ 0 & \ddots & 0 \\ 0 & 0 & \overline{Y}_C^* \end{bmatrix}$$

where each elements of $\overline{Y}_i^*$ equal to one, indicating that they belong to the same class. The subscript "i" is the label index and "C" is the total class number.

Table 1: Parameters Setting of The Used Datasets

Datasets	Neurons	λ	γ	β	η	α
2D&3D	2800-1400-1400	0.01	10	0.005	1.5	0.36
NYU	1200-1200-1200	0.005	5	0.5	0.001	0.25

In the third term of Eq. (2), T is a linear transformation matrix, which transform latent feature representations H to be most discriminative and compass in feature space $R^{m'}$.

2.3 PCSL

Different from exiting methods for RGB-D image representation, we propose to exploit properties of both complementary and consistency components of each modality simultaneously, as shown in Figure 2. However, the fact that each modality is embodied with intrinsically different structures causes the heterogeneity-gap between the modalities. We propose to employ independent column NN, (e.g., RGB-Specific NN in Figure 2), focusing on learning specific and complementary information from each modality. Then, the partially shared consistency latent representation is encoded across both modalities in the top layer of the network and a unified image representation is designed for RGB-D modalities. To address the problem in Eq. (1), we rewrite the proposed problem as follows:

$$(W_c^r)^T X^r = (W_c^d)^T X^d \tag{3}$$

The above equation is over-determined and always there is no exact solutions. Therefore, we relax it as the following problem:

$$\min_{W_c^r, W_c^d} \left\| (W_c^r)^T X^r - (W_c^d)^T X^d \right\|_F^2 \tag{4}$$

We define $S_c = \frac{1}{2}(H_c^r + H_c^d)$ as the common semantic contents, which is shared across RGB and depth information and reveals the consistency information. $S_s = [H_s^r; H_s^d]$ is the specific property for each modality, which carries the complementary information. Finally, we define $F = [S_c; S_s]$ as the feature representation of RGB-D pairs. In particular, we set a parameter $\alpha = \frac{N_c}{N_c + N_s}$ as the common factor ratio, where N_c is the shared common latent representation dimension and N_s is the specific latent representation dimension. The larger α indicates that the more significant role the consistency attribute plays.

By exploiting the above aspects simultaneously, we arrive at the object function as follows:

$$\begin{aligned} \min_{\theta} & \left\| WW^T X - X \right\|_F^2 + \lambda f(W^T X) \\ & + (\gamma \left\| TW^T X - Y \right\|_F^2 + \beta \left\| T \right\|_F^2) \\ & + \eta \left\| (W_c^r)^T X^r - (W_c^d)^T X^d \right\|_F^2 \end{aligned} \tag{5}$$

In Eq. (5), we need to optimize W and T jointly, which is not convex over all variables. Thus, we solve the problem by updating the two variables iteratively. Giving a input data X, we first fix T, W can be updated by minimize the object function, applying Broyden-Fletcher-Goldfarb-Shanno (BFGS) algorithm. With W fixed, T is obtained by solving the following convex optimization problem

$$\min_{T} \gamma \left\| TW^T X - Y \right\|_F^2 + \beta \left\| T \right\|_F^2. \tag{6}$$

which has a closed-form solution:

$$T = (W^T X (W^T X)^T + \beta I)^{-1} W^T X Y^T \tag{7}$$

3. EXPERIMENT

Datasets We evaluate the proposed method on one RGB-D object recognition dataset (e.g., 2D&3D object dataset (2D& 3D) [3]) and an indoor scene dataset (e.g., NYU Depth V1 indoor scene segmentation dataset [9]). 2D&3D object dataset is composed of 154 objects belonging to 18 distinct object categories. Following the experimental setting in [3], 6 objects are randomly selected from each category for training and the remaining objects are for testing. The indoor depth segmentation dataset is composed of 7 scene types and 64 instinct indoor environment, containing 108,617 unlabeled images. Following the experiment set in [9], we randomly split the training and testing set with the same number and repeat this procedure for five times.

Experimental setup In the CNN network training, we employ the AlexNet architecture [5]. The network is firstly pre-trained on ImageNet for image classification task and then adapts to the new target domain by applying domain specific fine-tuning on RGB-D datasets. All the CNN experiments are performed by the efficient Caffe [5] implementation. Finally, we extract the output of the seventh full connected layers (FC7) as the features, which are used for hierarchical representation learning.

In the proposed deep neural network, as shown in Figure 2, we set the depth of the network as 3 for all the datasets In all of our experiments, we preprocess the input data (CNN features) before supervised feature learning (e.g., feature normalization, zero mean and unit covariance operations). The parameters are same for each modality in each layer for the proposed deep network, as shown in Tab. 1. For test phrase, we only use the latent representations of the last layer as the RGB-D features. Furthermore, we employ a linear SVM classifier for object recognition evaluation.

Performance comparison We compare our PCSL method with the other state-of-the-art methods (e.g.,HMP-S [2], SP-M [6], RICA [7], R^2ICA [4]).

Tab. 2 reports the performance of PCSL and other comparative methods on the 2D&3D dataset, demonstrating that the proposed PCSL outperforms all the comparison models for RGB-D object recognition task. As shown in Tab. 2, the concatenation features of RGB and depth achieve better accuracy performance than that based on RGB only, which confirms the usefulness of depth information for object recognition. It can be seen that the proposed PCSL approach yields 93.6% accuracy for object recognition, which outperforms CNN, RICA and R^2ICA by 7.3%, 2.1% and 0.9%, respectively, verifying that the effectiveness of discovering consistent and complementary component is superior than that based on one aspect only.

Tab. 3 indicates the performance of different models on NYU Depth V1 indoor scene segmentation benchmark [9]. It is observed that PCSL achieves 74.3%, 65.5% and 76.8% recognition accuracy for RGB, depth and RGB-D, respectively. As shown in Tab. 3, although the individual modality achieves a slightly worse performance than that of RICA and R^2ICA, the concatenation representation of both modalities achieves significant improvement, outperforming all the comparable methods. The reasons may be as follows. Firstly, the label consistent regularization can enhance

Table 2: Accuracy Comparisons (%) on 2D&3D Dataset

Algorithms	RGB	Depth	RGB-D
Ev2D3D	66.6	74.6	82.8
SPM	60.7	75.2	78.3
RICA	85.1	87.3	91.5
R^2ICA	**87.9**	89.2	92.7
CNN	80.1	85.0	86.3
PSCL(Layer 3)	84.1	**90.6**	**93.6**

Table 3: Accuracy Comparisons (%) on NYU Depth V1 Dataset

Algorithms	RGB	Depth	RGB-D
SPM	52.8±3.2	53.2±2.7	63.4±2.9
RICA	74.5±2.9	64.7±2.1	74.5±3.5
HMP-S	72.6±2.8	63.9±2.6	72.8±3.1
R^2ICA	**75.9±2.9**	**65.8±2.7**	76.2±3.2
CNN	73.4±2.0	62.5±3.3	74.5±3.2
PSCL	74.3±3.0	65.5±4.4	**76.8±3.5**

the discriminative property by optimizing the discriminative distribution and latent representation jointly, and the both components boost each other. Secondly, the consistent and complementary attributes can compensate each other and benefit to boost the performance of the learning task. Finally, the CNN features transferred from auxiliary ImageNet are robust and general enough for high semantic component learning.

We also evaluate the performance of the proposed PCSL by comparing with the individual modality and common semantic content S_c as illustrated in Figure 3. The representation of individual modality reveals the specific semantic property, while the partially common semantic information is shared across both modalities. The proposed PCSL jointly discovers the specific and common semantic information of each modality. As can be seen in Figure 3, the PCSL, concatenation of specific and common semantic content, achieves the best accuracy performance, verifying the assumption that the performance can be guaranteed by jointly exploiting consistency and complementary properties of RGB and depth modality.

4. CONCLUSION

The main contributions of this paper include three aspects. Firstly, we extend the RICA model in a supervised fashion by incorporating a label consistent regularization, which can enhance the discriminative ability of latent representations. Secondly, we propose the PSCL approach to jointly encode the consistency and complementary semantic information of both modalities. Finally, to our knowledge, it is the first attempt in the direction of characterizing the independent specific and semantic information of RGB and depth images simultaneously. Furthermore, the performance can be boosted using the hierarchical feature representation of the stacked neural networks. Extensive experiments on two public RGB-D datasets demonstrate that the proposed method outperforms several existing state-of-the-art methods.

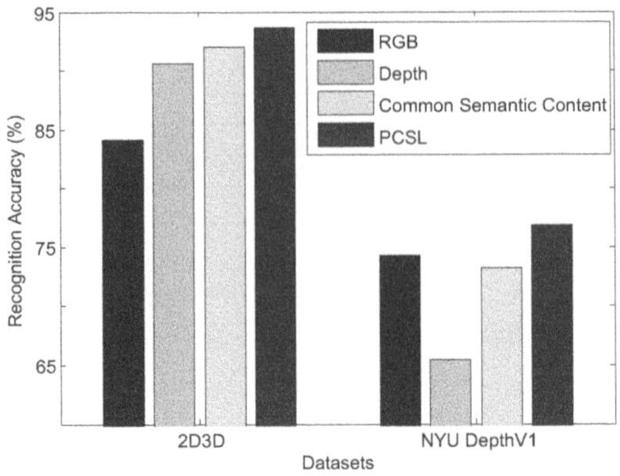

Figure 3: Performance of individual modality, common semantic content and PCSL on two datasets. This figure is better vies in color.

5. ACKNOWLEDGMENTS

This work was partially supported by the 973 Program (Project No. 2014CB347600), the National Natural Science Foundation of China (Grant No. 61402228), Natural Science Fund for Distinguished Young Scholars of Jiangsu Province under Grant BK2012033 and the Open Projects Program of National Laboratory of Pattern Recognition.

6. REFERENCES

[1] L. Bo, X. Ren, and D. Fox. Depth kernel descriptors for object recognition. In *IROS*, pages 821–826, 2011.

[2] L. Bo, X. Ren, and D. Fox. Unsupervised feature learning for rgb-d based object recognition. In *Experimental Robotics*, pages 387–402, 2013.

[3] B. Browatzki, J. Fischer, B. Graf, H. Bulthoff, and C. Wallraven. Going into depth: Evaluating 2d and 3d cues for object classification on a new, large-scale object dataset. In *ICCV Workshops*, pages 1189–1195, 2011.

[4] I.-H. Jhuo, S. Gao, L. Zhuang, D. T. Lee, and Y. Ma. Unsupervised feature learning for rgb-d image classification. In *ACCV*, pages 276–289, 2014.

[5] Y. Jia, E. Shelhamer, J. Donahue, S. Karayev, J. Long, R. Girshick, S. Guadarrama, and T. Darrell. Caffe: Convolutional architecture for fast feature embedding. *arXiv preprint arXiv:1408.5093*, 2014.

[6] S. Lazebnik, C. Schmid, and J. Ponce. Beyond bags of features: Spatial pyramid matching for recognizing natural scene categories. In *CVPR*, volume 2, pages 2169–2178, 2006.

[7] Q. V. Le, A. Karpenko, J. Ngiam, and A. Y. Ng. Ica with reconstruction cost for efficient overcomplete feature learning. In *NIPS*, pages 1017–1025, 2011.

[8] Z. Li, J. Liu, J. Tang, and H. Lu. Robust structured subspace learning for data representation. *IEEE Trans. on Pattern Analysis and Machine Intelligence*, 2015. Online Publication.

[9] N. Silberman and R. Fergus. Indoor scene segmentation using a structured light sensor. In *ICCV Workshops*, pages 601–608, 2011.

Pinterest Board Recommendation for Twitter Users

Xitong Yang
University of Rochester,
Rochester, NY 14623
xyang35@cs.rochester.edu

Yuncheng Li
University of Rochester,
Rochester, NY 14623
yli@cs.rochester.edu

Jiebo Luo
University of Rochester,
Rochester, NY 14623
jluo@cs.rochester.edu

ABSTRACT

Pinboard on Pinterest is an emerging media to engage online social media users, on which users post online images for specific topics. Regardless of its significance, there is little previous work specifically to facilitate information discovery based on pinboards. This paper proposes a novel pinboard recommendation system for Twitter users. In order to associate contents from the two social media platforms, we propose to use MultiLabel classification to map Twitter user followees to pinboard topics and visual diversification to recommend pinboards given user interested topics. A preliminary experiment on a dataset with 2000 users validated our proposed system.

Categories and Subject Descriptors

H.3.5 [**Online Information Services**]: We-based services

General Terms

Experimentation

Keywords

cross-network recommendation; multi-label classification

1. INTRODUCTION

Socially Curation Service [3], on which people can share and reshare online content that they found interesting, is becoming more and more popular. For example, Pinterest has successfully attracted more than 40 million monthly active users [1] to create pinboards and share online images. Social curation creates high quality contents for users to discover, search and follow what they are interested in. For example, Pinterest has already delivered better search results than Google for a number of segments, such as food recipes, fashion and DIY [2]. Pinboard, on which people can put together

[1]eMarketer, Feb 2015

[2]`http://goo.gl/PCWG3W`

MM'15, October 26–30, 2015, Brisbane, Australia.
© 2015 ACM. ISBN 978-1-4503-3459-4/15/10 ...$15.00.
DOI: http://dx.doi.org/10.1145/2733373.2806375.

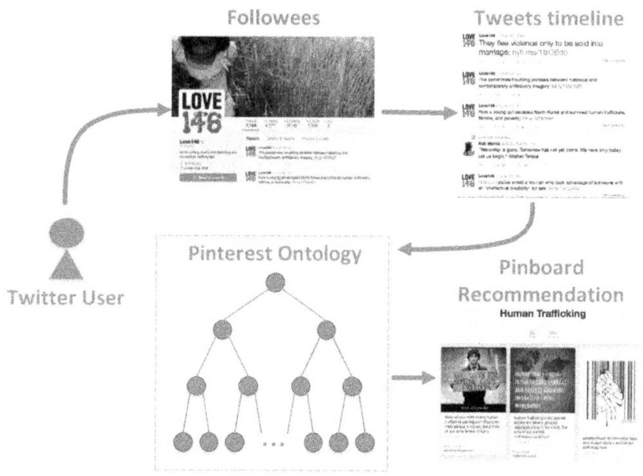

Figure 1: An illustrative example to recommend pinboards to a Twitter user "@xyz"

online images for specific topics to share with others, is the key element for Pinterest to engage users. Different from traditional photo albums, such as those on Facebook and Flickr, pinboards are not yet another way for people to organize images, but also encouraging users to carefully select images using their creativity. Also, in order to continuously attract followers, pinboard curators take efforts to keep up most recent contents, so pinboards give users a new way to follow most fresh updates on the topic they are interested in. As with other online systems, efficient information discovery is one of the major hurdles for continuous growth. In this paper, we propose a pinboard recommendation system to help users to discover interesting pinboards on Pinterest.

As a relatively new social media platform, Pinterest is still in its young age. Therefore, how to keep new users is an important topic, but recommendation for new users suffers cold start problem for the lack of activity history. We propose to leverage 3rd party social media platforms, such as Twitter, to solve the cold start problem for new Pinterest users. There are a number of reasons to use Twitter as an intermediate platform to recommend pinboards. First, Twitter is more mature and attracts even more active users, so it represents larger coverage for online users. Second, because most contents on Twitter are text based, it is much easier to find out interesting topics on Twitter than on Pinterest. Third, even though text based platform makes it easier to find interesting topics, image based pinboards, if

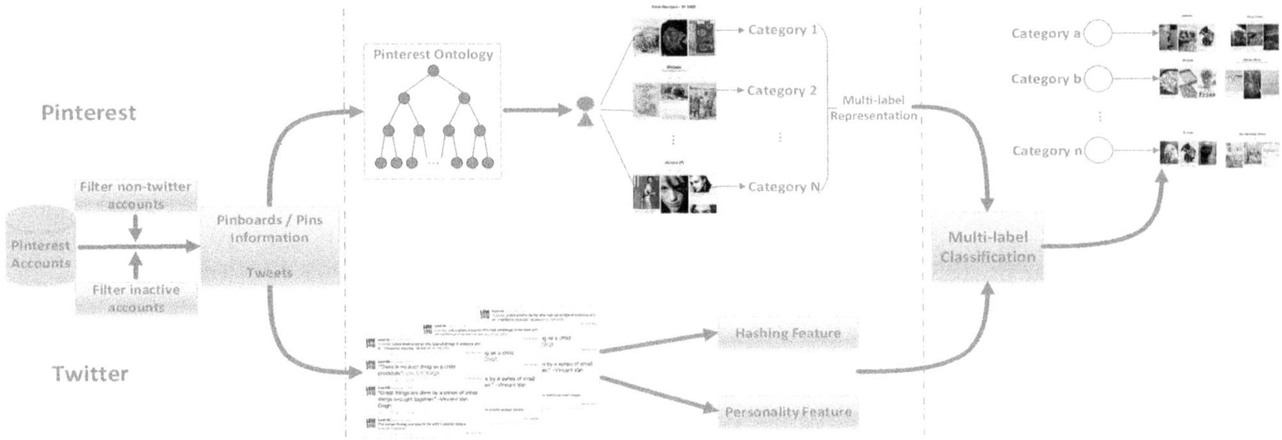

Figure 2: Overview of the proposed recommendation system. First, we align and filter the data from two different sources. After that, we collect multimedia contents, such as Pinboards and Pins information, and tweets from these active users. In the meanwhile, we build the pinboard topic ontology automatically, which is done by pruning an expert ontology such as Wikipedia. Second, we perform user modeling in two folds. For Pinterest, we obtain multi-label representation for each account by mapping their boards to the topics in Pinterest ontology. For Twitter, we extract both text feature and personality feature from user timeline. Third, we associate these two user models using multi-label classification, in which Twitter feature is used to predict the Pinterest category representation of each user. In the end, we recommend diverse Pinterest boards according to this prediction, where diversity is guaranteed by combining visual contents of the images in each board.

well aligned with the interests, provide better content for users to digest. For these reasons, recommending pinboards based on Twitter activity history is a perfect match.

We propose following procedure to recommend pinboards to Twitter users. (1) Given Twitter users, we extract their followees. We assume that the follower relationship represents user interests. (2) Using the proposed association method, we map the followees to pinboards topics, which represent what kind of boards the Twitter users will be interested in. The noise of individual followee can be reduced by aggregating all mapping results. (3) We choose a number of pinboards from the selected topics, and recommend these pinboards to the Twitter users.

Using the example in Fig. 1, we find that twitter user "@xyz" is following a twitter user "@love146". By collecting and classifying timeline of "@love146", we map the user "@love146" to one of the pinboard topics "anti human trafficking", so we assume that the target twitter user "@xyz" is interested in the boards about "anti human trafficking". Therefore, we select a number boards on this topic. We further improve the recommendation quality by a reranking method based on visual diversity analysis.

Since the followees can be extracted trivially from Twitter API, we solve the following two key problems in this paper, as illustrated in Fig. 2

Map user timeline to pinboard topics is an example of cross network analysis [10], and we build the association by mining users who are active on both Pinterest and Twitter. We crawl the timeline and pinboards associated with users that are active on both platforms. The pinboards are then mapped onto a predefined topic ontology using text based matching. After that, the users are associated with a twitter timeline and a distribution of pinboard topics. Then we learn a multi-label classifier to map user timeline to the pinboard topics. Using this multi-label classifier, we can map twitter followees without Pinterest account to pinboard topics.

Pinboard reranking is the process to recommend the best subset from the list of interested pinboards. We adapt a clustering based algorithm to perform this reranking, and the goal is to make sure that the recommended pinboards cover as much aspects as possible for the selected topics.

We make following contributions in this paper, (1) We present and release a linked dataset that associate pinboards and Twitter users. This will be of interests to broader research than cross network recommendation. (2) We propose a cross network recommendation method based on multi-label classification. (3) We propose a visual reranking method to diversify pinboard recommendation.

2. RELATED WORK

Our work is related to cross network analysis, user modeling and hierarchical multi-label classification. In this section, we highlight the novelty of our work by comparing with recent works on these related fields.

Cross network analysis aims to merge social signals from different network to increase online social media platform engagement. For example, in [10], Yan *et al.* proposed to identify the best Twitter accounts to promote YouTube videos, by mining the associations between topics learning from user tweets and their favorite YouTube videos.

User modeling is the foundation of personalized services, such as personalized recommendation, search engine reranking and advertisements targeting. One component of our Pinterest board recommendation system is based on Pinterest board ontology mapping, which is inspired from [2]. In this work, Geng *et al.* proposed a multi-task CNN to map pinterest images to fashion ontology and the classification results were sorted as user profiles for image recommendation. We adapt the idea that user interests can be represented by multiple nodes on ontology and further extend the on-

#	statistics
total nodes	471
root nodes	20
leaf nodes	440
least/largest depth	2 / 5

Table 1: Pinterest topic ontology Statistics

tology domain to 20 categories, including "Fashion", "Food" and "Wedding". In addition, instead of single label classification on images and aggregating the classification results to form user profile, we perform hierarchical multi-label classification on aggregated user tweets to figure out the user interests directly.

Hierarchical MultiLabel Classification is the problem of classifying data instances to multiple labels or attributes, in which the labels are structured in a hierarchical taxonomy. [7] proposed a hierarchical multi-label system to classify short texts (e.g., tweets). In this work, Ren *et al.* proposed to use text expansion, e.g., entity linking, to deal with the shortness and concept drift problem in short text classification. Our twitter user modeling is also based on hierarchical multi-label classification. However, instead of single tweet classification, we deal with the entire timeline of users, so that each user is modeled by a large number of tweets. In this paper, we adapt Randomized Labelsets [8] to efficiently model the hierarchical dependency automatically.

3. PINBOARD VISUAL DIVERSIFICATION

The goal of this stage is to recommend most relevant and diverse boards, given predicted categories and millions of board candidates sampled from Pinterest board pool. To guarantee the relevance, we map each board to the categories onto the topic ontology with the method described in Experiments Section 4, and also sort the boards of each category according to their popularity (e.g. followers). We then chose top k boards for each category as its preliminary candidates (we set $k = 10$ in our experiment).

To enhance diversity, we utilize the visual contents in Pinterest, that is, for each category, we cluster all pin images that belong to its preliminary board candidates, and then chose the boards that can maximize the coverage of these clusters. Specifically, we use deep Convolutional Neural Network (CNN) to learn useful features for the pin images (fc7 layer of the AlexNet [4]). After that, Affinity Propagation algorithm [1] is applied to cluster 4096D image features. After obtaining the clusters and assignment for each pin image, we can build a cluster distribution for each board. Then the board selection problem can be formalize as follows.

Denote the candidate set by $\mathcal{B}$, its subset by $B \subset \mathcal{B}$, a board in the subset by $b \in B$ and the cluster assignment distribution of the board by $\mathcal{P}_b \in R^C$. C is the number of clusters for all images in the pinboard candidates. Then, we define the set level entropy by,

$$T(B) = H\left(\frac{\sum_{b \in B} \mathcal{P}_b}{|B|}\right), \tag{1}$$

in which $H(x)$ is the entropy of a distribution x. Then, we select the best set of pinboards by $argmax_B\, T(B)$. We can prove that this is actually an NP-complete problem, so an approximation algorithm is needed, but in our experiments we just use brutal force to enumerate all possibilities by restricting the number of pinboard candidates $|\mathcal{B}|$ and the recommendation set $|B|$.

4. EXPERIMENTS

4.1 Data Collection

4.1.1 Pinterest ontology construction and refining

Ontology is a natural way to model the hierarchical structure of the categories in Pinterest, as is also used in [2] to organize items in fashion domain. To construct a full Pinterest ontology, we first build a preliminary ontology based on Wikipedia Categories, where the root nodes of it are 20 manually selected categories according to the 38 original categories given by Pinterest, such as "Fashion", "Food" and "Wedding". After that, we prune the ontology to adapt it to Pinterest user interest distribution. Basically, categories with low term frequency in board and pin information are removed. As board information and pin information share different weights for the ontology, we consider their pruning approaches separately, and the pruned ontology is obtained by uniting the results of two approaches. In addition, popularity metrics like the number of followers, likes, comments and repins are also considered as positive weighted metric while pruning. As a result, we obtain the refined Pinterest ontology and the statistics are shown in Table 1.

4.1.2 Map pinboards to topic ontology

With the refined Pinterest ontology, we can model a user's Pinterest profile by topic distribution. As users have their own boards, we can obtain this representation by mapping their boards to the categories in the ontology. For each board, this mapping approach takes three steps. First, we match board information to the categories, which can get a few or even no matches (but more accurate), as the board information is always rare. Second, we match all pins information under the board. Third, concatenate the result of previous two steps. After obtaining the categories mapping for each board, we can get the representation for the users through the union of the categories of their own boards.

4.1.3 Twitter timeline features

We extract two kinds of features to represent the tweets information for each user. First is the original text feature extraction, where feature hashing [9] and tf-idf term weighting are applied to reduce feature dimension and weight feature appropriately. Second, we also compute 64 LIWC features (e.g., word categories such as "social" and "work") to model the personality of each user [5]. These features may potentially reflect the distribution of their interest and user-curated data (e.g., Pinterest boards).

4.1.4 Data Statistics and Thresholds

In data preparation stage, we filter out those accounts that do not have twitter links or twitter activities are not active enough (number of tweets less than 200). Finally we get 2265 accounts from original 50000 sample Pinterest accounts. With these active accounts, we crawl 4.9 million tweets, 25.5 thousand boards and 2 million pins in total.

In ontology pruning stage, we set the threshold of term frequency for pins information to be 200 and the threshold for board information to be 1/100 of it, as the number of boards is nearly 1/100 of that of pins. After that we get 471 nodes in the ontology, as illustrated in Table 1.

In user modeling stage, for Pinterest data, we build up a multi-label representation for each user. Table 2 shows cer-

Examples	Attributes	Labels	Label Cardinality	Label Density
2265	5000+64	471	16.02	0.034

Table 2: Data Statistics

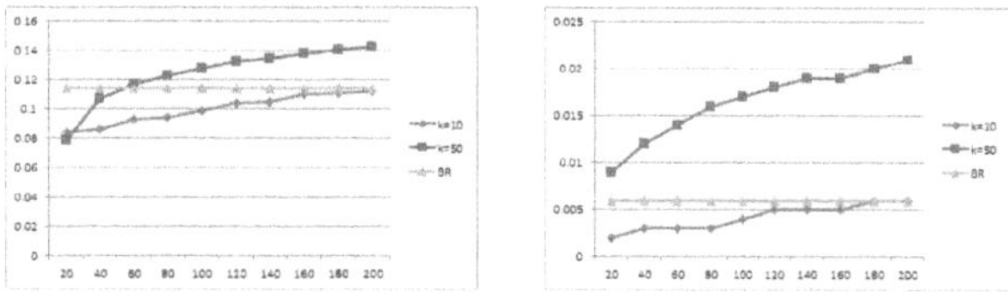

(a) F macro-ex. (b) F macro-label

Figure 3: Experiment results varying key parameters in RAkEL algorithm [8].

tain standard multi-label statistics of these representation, such as the number of labels, the label cardinality and the label density [8]. Label cardinality (LC) is the average number of labels per example, and label density is LC divided by the number of labels $|L|$. For Twitter data, we extract bag of words (BOW) text feature, and then apply feature hashing to get 5000 dimensional features. 64D LIWC feature is also extracted from the tweets via LIWC dictionary.

4.2 Preliminary Evaluation

We use *macro-F1*, a macro-averaged version of F-measure to measure our approaches, which is widely used in multi-label classification tasks[6]. Formally, we represent an association of labels v and its prediction $\hat{v}$ as two binary vectors $\{0,1\}^T$. Then F-measure (F1) can be used to measure the accuracy of the prediction, which is the harmonic mean of precision and recall and defined as follows: $F1(v,\hat{v}) = (2 \times precision \times recall)/(precision + recall)$, where *precision* is defined as $|v \wedge \hat{v}|/|\hat{v}|$, and *recall* is $|v \wedge \hat{v}|/|v|$.

For a multi-label classification task with N examples and L labels, we have two different ways to average the F1 scores: (1) *F1 macro-ex.* average F1 scores of N examples, which reflects example based evaluation. (2) *F1 macro-label:* average F1 scores of L labels, which reflects label based evaluation.

We compare two common multi-label classification methods: *Binary Relevance*(BR) and *Label Powerset*(LP)[6]. BR considers the prediction of each label as an independent binary classification task, while LP considers subset of labels as a single label to perform a multi-class classification task. For efficiency consideration, we adopt RAkEL[8] method, which is a variant of LP that ensemble different light LP classifiers trained by small random subsets of the set of labels.

In order to evaluate the effect of personality features, i.e., LIWC feature, in this user-interest relevant task, we compare following three cases: *Hashing feature only*, *LIWC feature only* and an *early fusion* of both features.

4.3 Experiment results and Conclusion

Figure. 3 present the comparison between BR and RAkEL while tuning the parameters k and M in RAkEL method.

Table 3 shows the full experiment results while comparing BR and LP using different kind of features. Through result above, we notice that LP based method can capture label dependencies and get better performance than BR method, especially when the subset size is large enough to contain sufficient labels. LIWC alone cannot get good result, which means that this personality feature cannot reflect one's interest distribution across different platforms.

	F1 macro-ex.		**F1 macro-label**	
	BR	LP	BR	LP
Hashing	0.114	0.143	0.006	0.021
LIWC	0.099	0.086	0.002	0.002
fusion	0.115	0.142	0.006	0.021

Table 3: Experiment results, comparing different feature schemes. Note that the total number of labels is 471, so these results are significantly better than random guess.

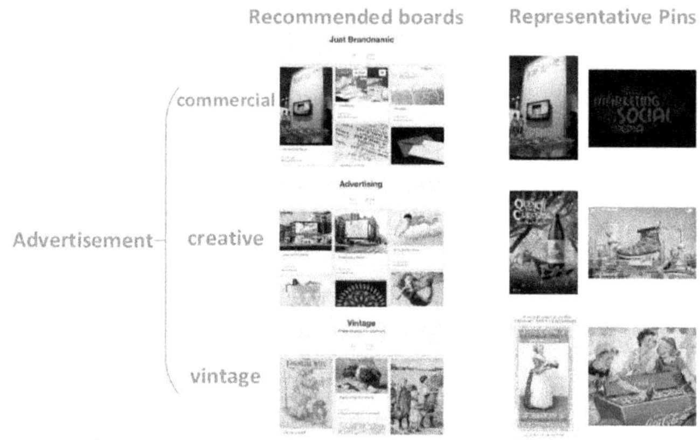

Figure 4: The recommended boards for the topic "Advertisement". Different kinds of advertisements are recommended, such as "commercial Ads", "creative" and "vintage".

We show diversification results qualitatively in Figure. 4. The preliminary results qualitatively validate our proposed system, and further research will work on improving each components and perform user study to prove the efficiency and effectiveness of the system, and also on how to model the dynamic nature of the user interests.

5. REFERENCES

[1] B. J. Frey and D. Dueck. Clustering by passing messages between data points. *Science*, 315:972–976, 2007.

[2] X. Geng, H. Zhang, Z. Song, Y. Yang, H. Luan, and T.-S. Chua. One of a kind: User profiling by social curation. MM'14.

[3] A. Kimura, K. Ishiguro, M. Yamada, A. Marcos Alvarez, K. Kataoka, and K. Murasaki. Image context discovery from socially curated contents. MM '13.

[4] A. Krizhevsky, I. Sutskever, and G. E. Hinton. Imagenet classification with deep convolutional neural networks. NIPS '12.

[5] J. Pennebaker, M. Francis, and R. Booth. *Linguistic inquiry and word count [computer software]*. Mahwah, NJ: Erlbaum Publishers, 2001.

[6] J. Read. Scalable multi-label classification. 2010.

[7] Z. Ren, M.-H. Peetz, S. Liang, W. van Dolen, and M. de Rijke. Hierarchical multi-label classification of social text streams. SIGIR '14. ACM.

[8] G. Tsoumakas and I. Vlahavas. Random k-labelsets: An ensemble method for multilabel classification. In *Machine Learning: ECML 2007*. Springer Berlin Heidelberg, 2007.

[9] K. Weinberger, A. Dasgupta, J. Langford, A. Smola, and J. Attenberg. Feature hashing for large scale multitask learning. ICML '09, New York, NY, USA. ACM.

[10] M. Yan, J. Sang, and C. Xu. Mining cross-network association for youtube video promotion. MM '14.

A Video Timeline with Bookmarks and Prefetch State for Faster Video Browsing

Axel Carlier
University of Toulouse
axel.carlier@enseeiht.fr

Vincent Charvillat
University of Toulouse
charvi@enseeiht.fr

Wei Tsang Ooi
National Univ. of Singapore
weitsang@nus.edu.sg

ABSTRACT

Reducing seek latency by predicting what the users will access is important for user experience, particularly during video browsing, where users seek frequently to skim through a video. Much existing research strived to predict user access pattern more accurately to improve the prefetching hit rate. This paper proposed a different approach whereby the prefetch hit rate is improved by biasing the users to seek to prefetched content with higher probability, through changing the video player user interface. Through a user study, we demonstrated that our player interface can lead to up to 4× more seeks to bookmarked segments and reduce seek latency by 40%, compared to a video player interface commonly used today. The user study also showed that the user experience and the understanding of the video content when browsing is not compromised by the changes in seek behavior.

Categories and Subject Descriptors: H.5.1 [Multimedia Information Systems]: Video

General Terms: Design, Human Factors, Performance

Keywords: Prefetching, Bookmarks, Video Browsing

1. INTRODUCTION

A tremendous amount of videos is uploaded and shared on the Internet. For instance, 5 hours worth of videos is uploaded to YouTube every second [2]; The amount of videos that appear in Facebook's news feed increases 3.6× year-over-year [1]. Presented with many videos to watch, and with limited time, users exhibit a behavior when watching videos on these social media web sites, known as *video browsing*, in which users quit watching a video frequently (if they find the video uninteresting) and seek frequently (to look for interesting content). Chen et al. conducted a study on video viewing behavior from 540 million sessions, and found that viewers do not complete watching the video in 80% of the sessions; Furthermore, users seek in 62.5% of the sessions, with an average of 9.36 seeks for movies and 4.75 seeks for music videos [5].

This new seeking behavior amplifies a challenge in ensuring the quality of experience (QoE) while viewing the video. A typical video player downloads and buffers the video segments immediately after the current playback point, as most of the time, a user watches the video linearly. Such *sequential* buffering mechanism ensures that, as long as the bandwidth does not drop unexpectedly, sufficient content is buffered for smooth playback without a freeze. Seeking, however, is a *non-linear* behavior that leads to a random access to a segment of video that may not be buffered, in which case, the playback freezes until (i) the target segment being seeked to is downloaded, and (ii) the player buffered enough subsequent segments to absorb the delay jitter. The time between the seek action and the playback of the target segment is called the *seek latency*.

To reduce the expected seek latency experienced, researchers have proposed to prefetch segments of videos beyond the current playback buffer in a non-contiguous manner, hoping that if and when the user seeks to the prefetched segment, zero seek latency is incurred. Such approach requires the system to predict the seek destinations. In this paper, we set out on a different path to reduce the seek latency: *instead of prefetching the segments that we predict the users would seek to, we bias the users to seek to the segments that we have prefetched.* Our idea is to show to the user, on the video timeline, the prefetched segments, i.e., segments that would lead to zero seek latency. We hypothesize that users would naturally prefer to seek to segments with zero seek latency, which would result in improving the overall video browsing experience.

We organize the rest of the paper into six sections. We start with an overview of the literature in Section 2. In Section 3, we explain the video timeline interface that we study in this paper. Section 4 explains how we setup the user studies. In Section 5, we present our results. Finally, we conclude in Section 6.

2. RELATED WORK

We now discuss related research in the literature and contrast our proposed video timeline with the existing work.

We found only few research efforts for which video user interfaces aim at optimizing system-centric criteria (such as network latency, cache hits etc.) as opposed to user-centric performance metrics. Dilip et al.[12] took advantage of the repeatability of user behaviors and proposed to reorder YouTube recommendations, such that the videos already in the cache are pushed to the top of the related list, to improve the performance of video caches.

Brampton et al. [3] showed that, in the context of football matches, bookmarking critical events can lead to three to four times more views of the bookmarked segments compared to non-bookmarked segments. They then proposed to prefetch segments of videos ahead of the bookmark points, and show that up to 38% of the seeks would result in zero seek latency. In our work, we assume that in a video browsing scenario, users are more interested in a quick overview of the video content than on actually understanding the video content.

MM'15, October 26–30, 2015, Brisbane, Australia.
© 2015 ACM. ISBN 978-1-4503-3459-4/15/10 ...$15.00.
DOI: http://dx.doi.org/10.1145/2733373.2806376.

Displaying prefetching state becomes then a strong bias towards seeking to the prefetched temporal regions.

Some work have studied optimal prefetching policies for non-linear access. Huang and Hsu [9] proposed a data mining-approach in which the seeking pattern of other users is used to predict the seek destinations. Similar approaches have been proposed in the context of peer-to-peer video on-demand systems [7, 18, 13] and mobile video streaming [11], where the seek latency could be significantly larger. Simpler approaches to prefetching, such as prefetching evenly-spaced segments, segments that correspond to scene changes, or segments that summarize the video, were mentioned by Uchihara et al. [17]. In our work, we choose to prefetch bookmarked segments.

Guiding the users towards important portions of the video with bookmarks, thumbnails, or recommendations can ease browsing tasks [15]. Many papers address the improvement of video players to facilitate searching and seeking. We categorize these research into content-based, user-based, and hybrid recommendations. For instance, the content-aware timeline [14] extracts keyframes with content analysis and plays a video snippet around these points when the user scrubs the timeline.

In the user-aware category, Syeda-Mahmood and Ponceleon interpret the video playback interactions in the temporal domain (play, fast-forward, pause) and infer the most interesting temporal segments from the video [16]. This pioneer work inspired many subsequent papers including the work by Gkonela et al. [8] that rethinks the underlying user models. Kim et. al [10] introduced a 2D video timeline with an innovative exploitation of collective navigation traces.

The current trend is to mix content-aware and user-aware recommendations. In [4], Carlier et al. proposed to compliment content analysis with implicit feedback of a community of users to recommend interesting video regions. A similar idea is used in the SmartPlayer [6], which adapts the playback speed from both the visual richness of the scene (estimated from content analysis) and the user preferences (learnt from their video interactions). In this work, we assume that such recommendations are available and can be strategically included in our video timeline as bookmarks.

3. VIDEO PLAYER UI

In this section, we present our approach to improve the predictability of user access patterns through a subtle change in the user interface of a video player. In particular, we propose to augment the video timeline with information about the prefetch buffer along with bookmarks.

Regular Video Timeline Interface. Figure 1(a) shows the video timeline of a typical video streaming player that can be found on many Web-based video hosting sites, such as YouTube or Vimeo. The timeline is divided into three sections, depicted in different colors in Figure 1(a). The left most section (in red) stretches from the beginning of the video to the current playback point. The middle section (light gray) shows the segments that has been buffered (sequentially prefetched ahead of the playback point). The right most section (in dark gray) shows the segments that have not been buffered. We denote this interface as the Regular interface.

Consider a user who wants to skip forward beyond the current playback point. If the user clicks on the timeline section that has been buffered, the playback can resume almost immediately with negligible seek delay, as the segment that the user wants to seek to has already been downloaded and buffered. On the other hand, if the user clicks on the timeline section that has not been buffered, the video player would pause the playback, until the segment that is seeked to has been downloaded and sufficient subsequent segments have been downloaded to absorb network jitter.

Video Timeline with Prefetching States. It is also common for a video timeline to display bookmarks. These bookmarks serve as annotations to important or interesting points in the video, such as commercial breaks, beginning of chapters, and critical events in the narration of the video. Figure 1(b) shows an example. These bookmarks can be determined manually by content provider, or automatically through content analysis or user behavior analysis [3, 19], to identify popular or semantically important points in the video content. Bookmarks can be annotated with text describing the content or images that depict the content of the videos (as shown in Figure 1(b)).

The UI we investigate in this paper not only shows (i) the playback point, (ii) bookmarks, (iii) thumbnails of the bookmarks which will become visible with mouse hover, and (iv) buffered segments ahead of the playback point, it also shows (v) the prefetched segments ahead of the bookmarks. Figure 1(b) shows a screenshot of this video timeline. Since users would experience zero seek latency when seeking to any of the prefetched segment, we hypothesize that, by depicting (v) in the video timeline, users would seek more frequently to prefetched segments than to non-prefetched segments. Combining features (i)-(v), this video timeline interface would therefore lead to more prefetching hits and lower seek delay, compared to a regular video timeline that depicts only (i) and (iv). Due to the additional information depicted in this video timeline, we denote this interface as Extra.

One question that arises is whether users would appreciate less the content of the videos if we nudge users to click on the bookmarked and prefetched segments more, especially for the case where the bookmarks are automatically generated and may not accurately cover all the key events or interesting segments in the videos. This is true in general, especially for video with informational content (documentary, news, lectures) or narrative entertainment (drama, sports). Research on automatically generating appropriate bookmarks is outside the scope of our work in this paper. We assume that bookmarks are manually generated. Furthermore, this work is done in the context of video browsing behavior on social video sharing sites, where videos tend to be short (less than 10 minutes) and placement of bookmarks does not affect the understanding of the video as much, as long as they are spread throughout the video so that the users get to sample a broad range of segments as they skim through the video.

4. USER STUDY

To evaluate the effectiveness of our proposed video timeline design, we conducted a user study, where each user viewed six videos using two different video timeline interfaces. The user seek actions while viewing the videos were then logged for analysis.

Videos Used: We chose six fairly similar videos depicting dance performances with the length of $5' \, 45''$, $5' \, 59''$, $7' \, 53''$, $7' \, 59''$, $8'$ and $8' \, 6''$ respectively for the user study. All videos are VBR encoded and segmented into 1-second chunks. For video timeline that requires bookmarks, we manually selected four bookmarks on each of these six videos that are reasonably spaced out, with different lighting and camera angle. It is our intention to choose videos where no particular chunk is more important or interesting than other chunks throughout the video, so that our bookmarking decisions do not affect the viewing experience. We also chose dance performances without a strong narrative, so that seeking does not interfere with the understanding of videos. Snapshots of two of the videos are shown in Figure 1.

(a) (b)

Figure 1: Video Timeline Interfaces: (a) A typical video player showing only playback point and sequentially buffered region; (b) A video player with timeline showing bookmarks and prefetched video segments.

Task: Since our experiment aims to learn how users behavior would change when presented with a different video timeline design, we designed a task that is doable without relying on specific user interaction, except play, pause, and seek. We showed six videos to each participant and asked if he/she likes each video, and whether he/she would recommend it to a friend. The videos were shown to the participant on a Web page, one after another, in randomized order, using one of two video timeline interfaces. The first three videos were shown with either the Regular interface or Extra interface, chosen randomly with uniform probability. The next three videos were shown with the other interface. We did not give specific instructions to the participants on how to use the video timeline (to avoid biasing them to seek), nor did we ask them to watch the video completely (to see if seeking behavior would arise naturally). The task mimics existing natural behavior when users watch videos online.

Setup: We developed an HTML5-based Web video player in which we can configure different video timeline design. The video player logs all user interactions with the video and relays it back to a backend server for logging and later analysis. Even though our user study targets a video streaming scenario, where chunks are downloaded while the video is being watched, our video player pre-loads the complete video before it allows the user to play. As the video plays, the player *simulates* buffering and prefetching of chunks, as well as the seek latency when the player seeks to a chunk that has not been downloaded according to the simulation. The player pauses for 2 seconds, before the playback continues.

There are two reasons why the videos are pre-loaded and the buffering, prefetching, and seek latency are simulated: (i) Different participants may experience different network conditions and thus the viewing experience and user behavior may be affected in an unpredictable way if our player actually downloads and plays the video simultaneously; (ii) By simulating the downloading process, our setup is predictable, reproducible, and controllable (e.g., we can tune the bandwidth allocated to prefetching).

The Regular video player has a simple prefetching policy that sequentially prefetch ahead of the current playback time. The video player with Extra interface (Figure 1(b)) prefetches the chunks according to the following algorithm: the chunks ahead of the current playback point have the highest priority of being prefetched. When the player has at least 5 seconds of data prefetched ahead of the current playback point, the algorithm starts to prefetch chunks after the bookmarks, in two phases. First, the algorithm fetches 5 seconds of chunks ahead of each bookmark, one bookmark after another, starting from the bookmarks closest to (and after) the playback point. Second, once at least 5 seconds of chunks are buffered after each bookmark, the algorithm prefetches one more chunk ahead of each bookmark, in a round-robin manner.

Our prefetch algorithm above arbitrarily assumes that a 5-second buffer is sufficient to absorb variations in network bandwidth. Further, the algorithm is not optimized (e.g., according to the probability of seek to a particular bookmark). Our goal is to study how user behavior differs under different video timeline interface, not the effects of prefetching algorithm. Varying the prefetching algorithms would introduce too many variations into our user study.

To reduce pre-loading time for low-bandwidth participants, we resample the videos to resolution 480×270. The video player has the size of 480×270 pixels as well and displays the videos without resizing. The video timeline has the size of 400×12.

5. RESULTS

A total of 21 participants participated in the user study. The result, summarized in Table 1, is consistent (or even better) with our hypothesis – 44% of seeks landed on bookmarks, and the average seek latency is reduced by 40%.

	Regular	Extra
% Seek to Bookmarks	12 %	44 %
Average Seek Latency	1.09s	0.65s

Table 1: Video Browsing Seeks and Hits

One could wonder why 12 % of the seeks landed on bookmarks even when the bookmarks are not displayed in the Regular UI. This number is actually very close to the expected percentage if the seeks landed randomly and uniformly along the timeline.

At the end of participation, we ask each participant to answer to a survey. The questions and results of the survey are summarized in Table 2. Note that we gave the participants three choices for each question: Extra, Regular, or the same[1].

Table 2 shows that, less than a quarter of the participants prefer Regular over Extra for browsing the video. No participant finds that Regular is more helpful than Extra to understand the content

[1]In the actual study, we named the interfaces A and B to avoid biasing the participants

of the video (about half feels that both UIs are equally helpful, the rest finds Extra more helpful). Finally, 14 out of 21 participants answered that Extra helps them scan through the videos faster.

In the quantitative comments, a participant who prefers Regular over Extra responds that Regular does not suggest to them where to click so he/she is free to click anywhere. Another participant with the same preference mentioned that the bookmarks remind him/her of advertisements.

Question	Regular	Extra
Which interface do you prefer to use to browse through the videos?	5	13
Which interface helps you more in understanding the content of the video?	0	11
Which interface helps you in scanning the content of the video faster?	2	14

Table 2: Video Browsing Survey Results

In summary, this user study shows that depicting the prefetch states of bookmarked segments can bias users to seek to the prefetched segments, reducing the average seek latency experience, and (ii) for a majority of participants, showing bookmarks and prefetch state is preferred, and helps to understand the video content as well as allow faster skimming through the video.

6. CONCLUSION AND FUTURE WORK

Researchers have been trying to reduce seek latency by predicting where a user would seek to when watching videos through content analysis and user behavior mining. In this paper, we show that, we can simply reduce seek latency by tweaking the user interface, therefore altering the user behavior. Instead of prefetching where we think the user would seek to, we show that it is possible to influence the user to seek to what we have prefetched. As a result, users' behaviors are more predictable, bringing lower seek latency. Our technique can complement existing prediction techniques to improve the user experience while browsing videos online. This question will be further studied in our future work.

7. REFERENCES

[1] Facebook video: New universal language. `http://insights.fb.com/2015/01/07/new-universal-language/`. posted January 7, 2015.

[2] YouTube statistics. `https://www.youtube.com/yt/press/statistics.html`. retrieved March 31, 2015.

[3] A. Brampton, A. MacQuire, M. Fry, I. A. Rai, N. J. Race, and L. Mathy. Characterising and exploiting workloads of highly interactive video-on-demand. *Multimedia Systems*, 15(1):3–17, 2009.

[4] A. Carlier, G. Ravindra, V. Charvillat, and W. T. Ooi. Combining content-based analysis and crowdsourcing to improve user interaction with zoomable video. In *Proceedings of the 19th ACM International Conference on Multimedia*, MM '11, pages 43–52, Scottsdale, AZ, USA, Nov. 2011.

[5] L. Chen, Y. Zhou, and D. M. Chiu. A study of user behavior in online VoD services. *Computer Communications*, 46:66–75, 2014.

[6] K.-Y. Cheng, S.-J. Luo, B.-Y. Chen, and H.-H. Chu. SmartPlayer: User-centric video fast-forwarding. In *Proceedings of the SIGCHI Conference on Human Factors in Computing Systems*, CHI'09, Boston, MA, USA, 2009.

[7] Y. Feng, B. Li, and B. Li. Peer-assisted VoD prefetching in double auction markets. In *Prceedings of the 18th IEEE International Conference on Network Protocols*, ICNP'10, pages 275–284, Kyoto, Japan, Oct. 2010.

[8] C. Gkonela and K. Chorianopoulos. VideoSkip: event detection in social web videos with an implicit user heuristic. *Multimedia Tools and Applications*, 69(2):383–396, 2014.

[9] C.-M. Huang and T.-H. Hsu. A user-aware prefetching mechanism for video streaming. *World Wide Web*, 6(4):353–374, 2003.

[10] J. Kim, P. J. Guo, C. J. Cai, S.-W. D. Li, K. Z. Gajos, and R. C. Miller. Data-driven interaction techniques for improving navigation of educational videos. In *Proceedings of the 27th Annual ACM Symposium on User Interface Software and Technology*, UIST'14, pages 563–572, Honolulu, HI, USA, 2014.

[11] C. Koch and D. Hausheer. Optimizing mobile prefetching by leveraging usage patterns and social information. In *Prceedings of the 22nd IEEE International Conference on Network Protocols*, ICNP'14, pages 293–295, Raleigh, NC, USA, Oct. 2014.

[12] D. K. Krishnappa, M. Zink, C. Griwodz, and P. Halvorsen. Cache-centric video recommendation: an approach to improve the efficiency of youtube caches. In *Proceedings of the 4th ACM Multimedia Systems Conference*, MMSys'13, pages 261–270, Oslo, Norway, February 2013.

[13] C. Lee, E. Hwang, and D. Pyeon. A popularity-aware prefetching scheme to support interactive P2P streaming. *IEEE Transactions on Consumer Electronics*, 58(2):382–388, 2012.

[14] S. Pongnumkul, J. Wang, G. Ramos, and M. Cohen. Content-aware dynamic timeline for video browsing. In *Proceedings of the 23nd Annual ACM Symposium on User Interface Software and Technology*, UIST'10, pages 139–142, New York, NY, USA, 2010.

[15] K. Schoeffmann and L. Boeszoermenyi. Video browsing using interactive navigation summaries. In *Proceedings of the 7th International Workshop on Content-Based Multimedia Indexing*, CBMI'09, pages 243–248, Chania, Crete, June 2009.

[16] T. Syeda-Mahmood and D. Ponceleon. Learning video browsing behavior and its application in the generation of video previews. In *Proceedings of the 9th ACM International Conference on Multimedia*, MM'01, pages 119–128, Ottawa, Canada, 2001.

[17] N. Uchihara, H. Kasai, Y. Suzuki, and Y. Nishigori. Asynchronous prefetching streaming for quick-scene access in mobile video delivery. *IEEE Transactions on Consumer Electronics*, 56(2):633–641, 2010.

[18] Z. Wang, L. Sun, S. Yang, and W. Zhu. Prefetching strategy in peer-assisted social video streaming. In *Proceedings of the 19th ACM International Conference on Multimedia*, MM'11, pages 1233–1236, Scottsdale, AZ, USA, Nov. 2011. ACM.

[19] Y. Zhao, Y. Tian, and Y. Liu. Extracting viewer interests for automated bookmarking in video-on-demand services. *Frontiers of Computer Science*, pages 1–16, 2014.

Giggler: An Intuitive, Real-Time Integrated Wireless In-Ear Monitoring and Personal Mixing System using Mobile Devices

Andries Valstar, Min-Chieh Hsiu, Te-Yen Wu, Mike Y. Chen
Mobile and HCI Research Lab, National Taiwan University
{valstarsander, teyanwu}@gmail.com, {r03922073, mikechen}@csie.ntu.edu.tw

ABSTRACT

For live music performances, current Wireless In-Ear Monitoring and Personal Mixing setups require a lot of equipment and wiring. This paper introduces Giggler, a system that makes a Wireless In-Ear Monitoring and Personal Mixing experience, easier to setup, easier to use, faster to control and more accessible for musicians than conventional systems by integrating all equipment into one mobile device per musician. The results of the two user studies that we conducted show that Giggler's User Interface performs up to more than twice as fast as a traditional mixer and indicate that Giggler outperforms a Physical mixer because visual features are added to streamline the channel identification process.

Categories and Subject Descriptors

J.5 [**Arts and Humanities**]: Performing arts; H.5.3 [**Group and Organization Interfaces**]: Computer-supported cooperative work

General Terms

Design, Human Factors, Experimentation, Performance

Keywords

Mobile Application; Live Music; Audio Streaming; Mixing

1. INTRODUCTION

When a band gives a music performance - a Gig - it is essential that all musicians can hear each other and themselves clearly so they feel that they are making a good sound [5]. To achieve this, there needs to be a monitoring system in place. There are different arrangements for these monitoring systems, including combinations of: Floor Monitors or In-Ear Monitors and a Sound Engineer controlled Monitor Mix or a Personally controlled Monitor Mix [3].

MM'15, October 26–30, 2015, Brisbane, Australia.
 ISBN 978-1-4503-3459-4/15/10$15.00.
DOI: http://dx.doi.org/10.1145/2733373.2806377.

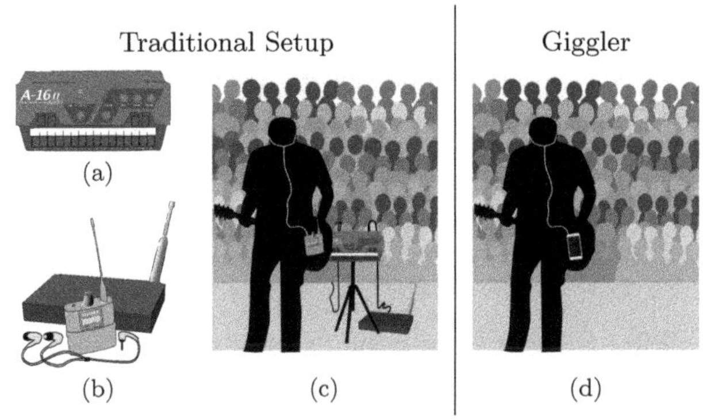

Figure 1:
(a): Aviom A-16II Personal Mixer (PM),
(b): Shure PSM300 In-Ear Monitor (IEM),
(c): Traditional Setup using a PM and an IEM,
(d): Giggler only requires a mobile device

All of the monitoring arrangements have their own disadvantages, such as Feedback, Audio Leaking, Communication Issues, Setup Issues and Volume Wars. The arrangements that are generally considered to be superior - In-Ear Monitors and Personal Mixing, as Shown in Figure 1(a), (b) and (c) - require professional audio equipment that is highly expensive, of considerable size, cumbersome to setup and difficult to operate for people without much experience [1]. For instance for a 5 person band, one would need to setup 5 PMs, 5 IEMs, an A/D Converter and a Distributor, all have to be connected with wires, all are highly expensive and all are of considerable size.

Hence one tends to only see these arrangements at professional concerts. Because of this inaccessible equipment, recreational and semi-professional bands are often found using Floor Monitors mixed by a Sound Engineer and have to deal with all of the disadvantages that come with this setup.

Therefore we present Giggler, an overall superior IEM and PM solution that makes it more accessible and more user friendly for musicians by integrating all the bulky and expensive equipment into a single mobile device which presents an intuitive interface and requires no wiring.

We conducted 2 user studies and found that Giggler performs up to more than 2 times faster than a Physical mixer while having a lower work load, especially for Channel Identification. As users indicated they used Pictures and Names to Identify a Channel on Giggler, we subscribe Gigglers advantages to these visual elements that are present in its interface.

2. RELATED WORK

As show in Figure 1 Giggler combines Wireless In-Ear Monitoring and Wireless Personal Mixing into one device which is both easy to setup and operate by the musician. Current systems provide parts of these functionalities, but not all together, which introduces specific issues in each case.

2.1 Floor Monitors

Traditionally floor monitors are used for live performances, while these are still widely used they come with a number of disadvantages. Floor monitors are highly vulnerable to feedback issues, audio quality strongly depends on the musicians position and the room acoustics, and finally they are likely to cause volume wars [5, 3]. Research has been done to try to deal with the musicians position issue [6].

2.2 In-Ear Monitors (IEMs)

IEMs were introduced to solve the problems of floor monitors, but they introduced new ones. Since IEMs produce such clear audio it is difficult for a sound engineer to configure them to the musician's desire, because with IEMs "the tiniest change on a fader can really throw a musician" - Professional Tourmanager Steve Down [1].

2.3 Sound Engineer (SE) Mixing

Because the SE never hears exactly what the musician hears it is extremely difficult for him to reach a desirable mix. Reaching a desiring mix requires a lot of communication between the musicians and the SE. As the SE is usually located in the back of the room, this complicates communication [5]. Previous work has been done to try to simplify this process by automated mixing [8]. Research has also found that a musician's desire is changing during the performance, which complicates things even more in case of a SE controlled monitor mix [2].

2.4 Personal Mixing (PM)

PM was introduced to solve the communication issues between musicians and sound engineers. With PM every musician has his own mixing board such as the Aviom in Figure 1. Downsides are that it requires a lot of extra hardware and wiring and when used in combination with floor monitors it is very likely to cause a volume war [5]. Recently there are some digital mixers available which provide a wireless "Stage Mixing" experience, these systems are not called PMs, because the number of musicians can easily exceed the number of monitor mixes provided by the mixer.

3. GIGGLER SYSTEM DESIGN

This section describes Gigglers design goals, hardware and software choices and interface design.

3.1 System Design Goals

We designed Giggler with the following goals:

1. A full PM and Wireless IEM experience
2. Mobile devices replacing audio equipment and wires
3. Faster setup time
4. More intuitive and faster interface

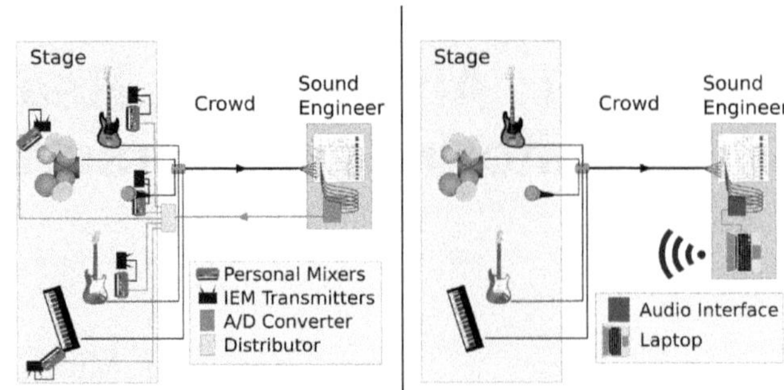

(a) Conventional IEM PM (b) Giggler Setup

Figure 2: The amount of hardware and wiring involved with a Conventional IEM + PM Setup compared to Giggler. Black Wires are Analog and Red Wires are Digital.

To demonstrate that Giggler requires considerably less hardware and wiring, we draw the hardware required for a Conventional IEM and PM Setup and compare this to a drawing for the same setup with Giggler.

For the illustrations in Figure 2 we assume a band of 5 musicians, which is a quite common number also for well known bands, for instance The Rolling Stones, Guns 'n Roses and Radiohead all have 5 musicians. When comparing the two illustrations one can see that where a conventional PM and IEM system requires a substantial number of extra pieces of specialized audio equipment - Personal Mixers, an Analog/Digital Converter, a Distributor and IEM Systems - Giggler requires only one extra piece of audio equipment - an Audio Interface - the rest of the hardware are mobile devices and a laptop, which are very common devices. This makes Giggler much more accessible to non-professional musicians.

Since Giggler works via WiFi, the setup requires considerably less wires, in case of this example with 5 musicians, the 6 digital and 5 analog cables for a conventional system are replaced by 1 digital cable for Giggler. This makes Giggler significantly easier to set up compared to a conventional system, as adding a musician to the server only takes a single tap on the screen of the mobile device as opposed to attaching more cables to more equipment on the stage for a conventional system.

3.2 Hardware and Software

We chose to implement Giggler for Apple devices which provide a native low audio latency library - called Core Audio - as opposed to for instance Windows and Android, which do not provide this functionality in their native libraries.

Giggler consists of a server application on the Mac and client applications on iOS Devices. The server application on the Mac receives audio from an Audio Interface - we use a Focusrite Scarlett 18i8 - and then creates and sends an individual monitor mix for every client. To ensure that the data flow over the network does not grow as one adds more channels, the server application mixes the monitor mix for every client to a stereo signal before sending it to the client. However, although the actual mixing happens on the server, the client applications are the ones that are in control of their own mix.

As Giggler requires extremely low latency, we use the User Datagram Protocol (UDP) for transmission of all data. UDP is known to provide very low latency because it gives no guarantees for package delivery as opposed to Transmission Control Protocol (TCP). The lossless and in-order nature of

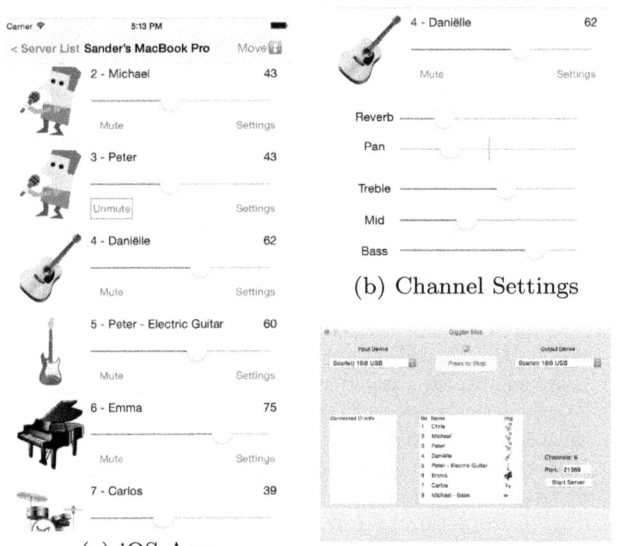

(a) iOS App (b) Channel Settings (c) Mac Server

Figure 3: The Giggler iOS App and Mac Server

TCP makes that it can block until a lost package has been retransmitted. In real-time streaming, such a block might lead to larger audio dropouts than skipping a package would have caused. UDP is therefore best suited for Giggler.

3.3 Interface Elements

We want to provide the same mixing functionality in Giggler that conventional PM systems provide as well. This includes, volume, mute, pan, reverb, bass, mid and treble for every channel. As displaying all of these controls for every channel would result in a clogged interface, we decide to only show the Volume control and Mute button for every channel, as can be seen in Figure 3(a), and place the rest of the functionality in a per channel "Settings" menu that appears under the channel, as shown in Figure 3(b), when "Settings" is tapped.

In contrast to conventional systems which only provide channel numbers, the usage of digital devices also opens the possibility to update the clients' interfaces dynamically from the server with pictures, names etc. We implement this functionality as shown in Figure 3(c).

Finally, we add a "Move ↕" button to the iOS App which, in combination with the swiping capabilities of touch screens, makes it very simple for the musician to reorder the list of channels by just dragging channels up and down.

4. EVALUATION

We evaluated Giggler's overall latency performance and did two user studies to find users' opinions and compare Giggler's user interface's performance to current systems.

4.1 Audio Latency

The overall delay of Giggler depends on audio hardware, operating system and networking delays. Audio hardware input/output latency in seconds can be computed using the following formula:

$$(BufferSize/SampleRate) * 2 \quad (1)$$

Hence, the performance of Giggler depends in part on the audio buffer size and sample rate used; the operating system and the network delays cannot be controlled. According to Schuett [7], the maximum allowed latency - "Ensemble Performance Threshold" - is between 20-30ms for impulsive, rhythmic music. We tested Giggler against this threshold by varying the buffer size and sample rate. For a Sample Rate of 96000 Hz and a buffer size of 64 frames we were able to reach overall delays as low as 20.5ms on average with a standard deviation of 5.7ms over 100 samples.

4.2 User Study

To evaluate the usability of Giggler we conducted two user studies. The first study was designed to test Giggler in a real world scenario with an actual band using it as IEM and PM system. The second study used a quantitative approach, designed to compare the performance and user task load of Giggler to a traditional hardware based mixer.

4.2.1 User Experience

We found a band of 5 people (4 male and 1 female) willing to try out Giggler. The band consisted of 2 singers (one also played rhythm guitar), 1 lead guitarist, 1 bass player and 1 drummer. We conducted a pre-study questionnaire to record their experience as musicians and their past experiences with monitors and monitor mixes.

Their ages ranged from 23 to 38 years old, experience as musician ranged from 6 to 20 years, their experience with playing in bands ranged from 2 to 10 years and the band practices and performs every week. The band normally uses Floor Monitors mixed by a Sound Engineer in the back of the room and they usually have 0 to 2 monitor mixes (0 meaning that the monitor mix is the same as the mix for the audience). None of them had used a PM before and only 1 of them used IEMs before.

At first the musicians were given some assignments to get familiar with all the functionality of the app. Two examples of these assignments: "Pan the Bass to the Right" and "Volume of the Drums to 0". After being familiarized with the functionalities, they played 3 songs of their own choice.

Finally the musicians filled out a post-study questionnaire. We found that musicians were pleasantly surprised about how easy to use Giggler was; 4 out of 5 band members mentioned easy to use or simple interface as its best feature and also mentioned this as the reason why they were interested in using Giggler if it was available. The 5th member found it the most useful that he could control every one's volume in his own mix and therefore hear himself better than usual.

4.2.2 Task Completion Time and Workload

This Quantitative Study was designed to measure the time performance and user load for tasks performed on Giggler compared to a physical Mixer. As baseline for this study we used the BOSS BX-60, a compact 6 channel Mixer. We conducted this study on 7 musicians (4 male and 3 female), ages ranged from 22 to 34 years old, music experience ranged from 7 to 16 years and band experience ranged from 1 to 10 years. Only 1 participant had used IEMs before and only 1 other participant had used a PM system before.

We let participants mix 3 multitrack songs of 6 tracks each on both Giggler and the Mixer. The order of the songs and which device was used first was changed for every participant. Participants were given Volume and Pan assignments similar to the ones described in the User Experience Study.

	Volume Assignments	
	Mixer	Giggler
Mean	5.92 s	2.54 s
SD	3.60 s	1.50 s

t-value = 8.47
p-value < 0.0001

	Panning Assignments	
	Mixer	Giggler
Mean	5.86 s	4.36 s
SD	2.99 s	5.32 s

t-value = 2.52
p-value = 0.0128

Table 1: Assignment Completion Time Results in Seconds

	Mixer		Giggler		t-test
	Mean	SD	Mean	SD	p-value
Finding Chan	3.86	1.52	2.40	1.36	0.0001
Changing Vol	2.98	1.65	1.93	1.42	0.0025
Changing Pan	3.24	1.78	2.62	1.38	0.0782

Table 2: Task Load Index, 7-Point Likert Scale Results

For the Mixer, participants were provided with a list indicating which Instrument corresponded to which Channel Number. The participants were recorded in order to measure the time it took for them to complete each assignment. For each device, after the assignments, participants filled out a 7 point Likert Scale Task Load Index questionnaire, with questions based on the NASA Task Load Index [4].

We performed a Two-Sample T-Test on the assignment completion times and as shown in Table 1 the p-values for both Volume and Pan assignments are lower than 0.05, indicating that the time participants spent to complete assignments on Giggler was significantly lower than on the Mixer, with Volume assignments being completed more than twice as fast on Giggler. Notable is that the Mean and SD for Volume and Pan assignments on the Mixer are statistically identical with a p-value of 0.91, whereas with a p-value of 0.0013, this is not the case for Giggler. We subscribe this difference to the fact that on Giggler - for the sake of keeping the interface clean - there is an extra tap on "Settings" required to access the panning functionality of a channel.

The NASA Task Load Index is designed to assess the workload required to complete a task on a system. It asks participants about the Mental and Physical Demand, Frustration experienced and more. On a 7-Point Likert Scale, 1 means very low workload and 7 means very high workload. The workload index results of the Mixer and Giggler, as presented in Table 2, show that the workload for both finding the right channel and changing volume was significantly lower for Giggler compared to the Mixer. The p-value for Changing Pan is just above 0.05, which indicates that the workload for the Mixer and Giggler was identical for the Panning assignments where participants had to click "Settings" first to access a channel's Pan setting on Giggler.

In a Post-Study Questionnaire we asked participants on a 5-Point Likert Scale how often they looked at Channel Pictures, Names and Numbers to identify a channel on Giggler, 1 indicating never and 5 indicating always. Our results show that participants preferred to look at the Channel Pictures with a score of 3.57, Names were second favorite with a score of 3.29. Participants mentioned that they often looked at both the pictures and the names when there were for instance two guitar channels. Numbers were never looked at for channel identification with a score of 1.29.

Therefore we subscribe the faster task completion times and lower workload found in our results for Giggler to the Pictures and Channel Names that are present in Giggler and empower the user to not have to search for numbers.

5. DISCUSSION

Gigglers limitations are all network related. Because UDP was used there can be audio-dropouts in case of an unstable WiFi connection with a lot of package loss. In our Real World Study the WiFi performance was less stable than in our lab and participants thus indicated that dropouts was what they disliked the most. This could be solved by repositioning the router, changing the frequency or using a safer protocol than UDP.

6. CONCLUSIONS

Giggler provides an IEM and PM setup that requires much less hardware and wiring and is therefore easier to setup and more affordable than current systems. Our User Experience Study indicates that Gigglers limitations are caused by the network performance, research has to be done to find out how this can be improved and also how many milliseconds of dropouts per minute is acceptable for musicians. The Task Completion and Workload study shows that mixer interfaces can perform more than two times faster on average when visual information in the form of pictures and text is provided to help users with identifying channels.

7. ACKNOWLEDGMENTS

We express our gratitude towards all the people in our lab and all the musicians who have helped us with our work.

8. REFERENCES

[1] J. Burton. An introduction to in-ear monitoring. Sound On Sound, `http://www.soundonsound.com/sos/feb13/articles/in-ear-monitors.htm`, February 2003. [accessed 14-April-2015].

[2] J. Federman and T. Ricketts. Preferred and minimum acceptable listening levels for musicians while using floor and in-ear monitors. *J Speech Lang Hear Res.*, 51:147–159, February 2008.

[3] G. Harrison. On-stage monitoring. Sound On Sound, `http://www.soundonsound.com/sos/mar04/articles/livesound.htm`, March 2004. [accessed 14-April-2015].

[4] S. G. Hart and L. E. Staveland. Development of nasa-tlx (task load index): Results of empirical and theoretical research. *Advances in psychology*, 52:139–183, 1988.

[5] D. Mellor. Stage monitoring & monitor mixing. Sound On Sound, `http://www.soundonsound.com/sos/dec05/articles/live_stagemonitoring.htm`, December 2005. [accessed 14-April-2015].

[6] J. Paloranta and I. Renström. Automized optimization of stage monitor hearing. KTH, 2012.

[7] N. Schuett. The effects of latency on ensemble performance. *Undergraduate Honors Thesis, Stanford CCRMA*, 2002.

[8] M. J. Terrell and J. D. Reiss. Automatic monitor mixing for live musical performance. *Journal of the AES*, 57(11):927–936, November 2009.

Dynamic Adjustment of Subtitles Using Audio Fingerprints

Lucas C. Villa Real
IBM Research
Sao Paulo - Brazil
lucasvr@br.ibm.com

Rodrigo Laiola Guimarães
IBM Research
Sao Paulo - Brazil
rlaiola@br.ibm.com

Priscilla Avegliano
IBM Research
Sao Paulo - Brazil
pba@br.ibm.com

ABSTRACT

Anyone who ever downloaded subtitle files from the Internet has faced problems synchronizing them with the associated media files. Even with the efforts of communities on reviewing user-contributed subtitles and with mechanisms in movie players to automate the discovery of subtitles for a given media, users still face lip synchronization issues. In this work we conduct a study on several subtitle files associated with popular movies and TV series and analyze their differences. Based on that, we propose a two-phase subtitle synchronization method that annotates subtitles with audio fingerprints, which serve as synchronization anchors to the media player. Preliminary results obtained with our prototype suggest that our technique is effective and has minimal impact on the extension of subtitle formats and on media playback performance.

Categories and Subject Descriptors

H.5.1 [**Information Interfaces and Presentation**]: Multimedia Information Systems—*Audio, Video*; I.7.2 [**Document and Text Processing**]: Doc. Preparation—*Format and notation, Languages and Systems, Multi/mixed media.*

General Terms

Measurement, Experimentation, Standardization, Languages.

Keywords

Captions; Subtitles; Timed-text; SRT; Audio fingerprinting; Synchronization.

1. INTRODUCTION

Captioning (or subtitling) enriches audiovisual content by providing speech information and description of representative events in a textual format. Captioning is especially important to include people with hearing loss or deafness, but its use is not limited to that domain. For instance, it is frequently the case that captions are necessary to watch a movie or TV show in a noisy environment (e.g., in an airplane) or when one is not familiar with the language or accent available in the audio streams. In fact, the benefits of captioning goes beyond the mere description of what is said or what is happening in the audiovisual content, and those benefits have been extensively reported in the research literature. The use of captioning for comprehension of a foreign language [8], vocabulary learning [6], and accessibility enhancement [5], are just some examples of these benefits.

MM'15, October 26–30, 2015, Brisbane, Australia.

ACM 978-1-4503-3459-4/15/10 ...$15.00.
DOI: http://dx.doi.org/10.1145/2733373.2806378

The lifecycle of captioning can be analyzed from different perspectives. In professional post-production, extensive support is typically available; professionals create and synchronize caption data alongside the audiovisual stream. Then, the final contents are normally encapsulated in a container format and distributed on DVDs[1], Blu-Rays, broadcast television, or video on-demand services. Given that this is a very controlled workflow, major synchronization problems are not expected during consumption. Alternatively, non-professional enthusiasts are *up to the task.* This is the case particularly for online TV series and movies that are shared online. The resulting captioning files are then shared on popular online databases in a wide range of languages.

But the abundance of user-generated subtitle files comes at a price: often multiple versions are available for the same audiovisual material, leading to difficulties in identifying which of the versions is the correct one to choose. The number of different captioned files can also reflect the various editions of the media files that may or may not include advertisements, scenes from the previous or the next episode, different frame rate settings, and so on. As a result, the synchronization of the media can be compromised by choosing the *wrong* captioned file: caption entries may be displayed on the screen earlier or later than the corresponding audio and video events, as illustrated in Figure 1.

In this context, we make the following contributions. First, we perform a qualitative analysis of subtitles available in an open multi-language captioning database. This study shows that there is a great number of captioning files for a given media and that they present considerable variation on their content. Second, we introduce a two-level mechanism to dynamically adjust the presentation time of captions based not only on the regular timestamps available in captioning files, but also on audio fingerprint annotations, that work as synchronization check-points. Whenever the media player identifies such audio fingerprints, it adjusts the temporal

[1]Due to space restrictions not all technologies mentioned in this paper are Web-referenced.

```
01. ...
02. 615
03. 00:50:02,280 --> 00:50:06,046
04. TYRION: I wish I had enough poison
05. for the whole pack of you.
06.
07. 616
08. 00:50:06,120 --> 00:50:10,489
09. TYRION: I would gladly give my life
10. to watch you all swallow it.
11.
12. 617
13. 00:50:10,693 --> 00:50:12,711
14. [crowd shouting]
15. ...
```

```
01. ...
02. 729
03. 00:48:25,351 --> 00:48:28,937
04. I wish I had enough poison
05. for the whole pack of you.
06.
07. 730
08. 00:48:28,971 --> 00:48:31,139
09. I would gladly give my life
10.
11. 731
12. 00:48:31,141 --> 00:48:33,475
13. to watch you all swallow it.
14. ...
```

Figure 1: Two distinct captioning files. Equivalent entries for the same video may differ not only in the synchronization offset (in red, left side of the '->' token), but also in the duration (in red, difference between the two) and textual content (in blue).

offset and reschedules subsequent caption entries, in order to provide a better viewing experience. Last, we present an extension to existing subtitle file formats to support our method.

This paper is organized as follows. In Section 2 we provide an overview of related work. Next, in Section 3 we motivate our work based on a qualitative analysis of non-professional subtitle content available in a popular online database. Then, Section 4 describes our approach to address the problem of having captioning files not well synchronized with the audiovisual material. Section 5 presents the enriched subtitle format that contemplates audio fingerprint annotations. Finally, Section 6 is dedicated to concluding remarks and future work.

2. RELATED WORK

A large body of research has been carried out to study captioning from different perspectives [3][4][6][8][9]. For example, Hong et al. [5] propose a dynamic captioning approach that explores a set of technologies including face detection and recognition, visual saliency analysis and text-speech alignment. The authors then investigate whether subtitles placed at suitable positions can help people with hearing loss to better recognize the speaking characters. Brown et al. [1] use eye-tracking data to investigate the effect of dynamic subtitles in the viewing experience of subjects with hearing loss. Our work is related, but we focus on a different challenge: we provide a general solution to adjust the synchronization of tens (or even hundreds) of subtitle files with displaced timestamps.

From the encoding point of view, Liu and Wang [7] propose a stroke-like edge detection method for extrating captions that are hard-coded in videos. More closely related to our scenario, Bulterman et al. [2] survey many public and proprietary formats for encoding subtitles and captions. Based on a careful analysis, they describe a timed-text format that balances the need for style formatting with the requirement for more structured representation that can be easily parsed and scheduled at runtime. Our work builds on this timed-text format by proposing a second level of synchronization adjustment for captions based on audio fingerprinting.

Some well-known media players, such as VLC, are able to automatically download SubRip Text (SRT) files, one of the most popular subtitle file formats. This is possible using VLSub[2], an extension that searches for the corresponding subtitle of the loaded media based on two different approaches. In the first, the media file name is used to query a remote subtitle server. If there is a match, the corresponding subtitle file is automatically downloaded and displayed with the media. In the second approach, a hash (checksum) of the loaded media file is computed and the resulting hash is used to query a remote subtitle server. Again, if there is a match, then the corresponding subtitle file is automatically downloaded. Some of the problems with these approaches are: (1) it is easy to have file name collisions; (2) users may no longer know the original file name due to file system name mangling or to renaming; and (3) changes to the original encoding settings, such as exporting an original file in H.264 format to a QuickTime .MOV format, will alter the hash of the file. In addition, the time that the subtitle should appear and disappear on the screen might still not match. In our work, we compute the signature of audio events alone. These are not likely to change drastically when the original audio is re-encoded with different settings. Thus, we propose the usage of an audio fingerprint to univocally determine the moment a check-point is achieved. Once this audio fingerprint is identified on the file, the temporal offset of all the subtitles entries are dynamically adjusted to the specific media file.

3. QUALITATIVE ANALYSIS

To get an understanding of the quality and differences among subtitle files available on the Internet, we picked a Top-5 movie ranked by IMDb and analyzed all of the corresponding subtitle files available for such movie at the OpenSubtitles.org[3] repository. Since movies are different from TV series in some ways (for instance, a TV series episode may start with scenes from the previous episode, and finish with a preview of what is coming in the next one), we also analyzed the subtitles of an episode of a popular TV series (according to IMDb).

For the movie, there were 193 subtitle files distributed across 33 different languages. The languages with the highest number of captioned files are English (35), followed by Brazilian Portuguese (18), and Spanish (16). Since these files often come with advertisements and credits that are introduced as actual caption entries[4], all files were sanitized

[2]https://github.com/exebetche/vlsub

[3]We used OpenSubTitles.org because it offers an open API

[4]Interestingly enough, it is not uncommon to find the very

Table 1: Analysis of captions for a popular movie. The duration is given by the difference between the last and first caption entries.

Language	Time at first caption	Total duration
English	26 ± 5 s	8781 ± 191 s
Brazilian Portuguese	14 ± 3 s	8960 ± 575 s
Spanish	15 ± 5 s	8779 ± 341 s
French	16 ± 12 s	8730 ± 275 s
Turkish	14 ± 7 s	8762 ± 184 s

before being properly analyzed.

Table 1 shows there are variations in the starting time and total duration covered by the captions even within the same language. The meta-data[5] of the movies associated with these subtitle files indicate that sometimes their duration also differs, since some are extracted from DVDs and Blu-Rays and some others are recorded from broadcast TV. Second, at times there is an offset between translated subtitles and subtitles in the original language (English). We found that this comes from audio differences in dubbed versions of the movie. The standard deviation is mostly caused by the use of audio-descriptions (i.e., caption entries describing audio events such as an opening door) and different reference times (e.g., some subtitle files have their first caption entry starting at time zero, even though the actual audio event happens only a few seconds from the start).

In our analysis of one episode of a popular TV series, a total of 170 subtitle files were collected, covering 38 languages. We inspected patterns from Brazilian Portuguese (19 subtitle files), English (13 files), and Spanish (11 files). In contrast to the movie file, the presence and absence of prologues and epilogues was often observed and caused a large standard deviation at the time of presentation of the first caption (45 seconds for an average of 88 seconds in Brazilian Portuguese). This is more clearly seen in Figure 2, which depicts the presentation time of caption entries of files with and without a prologue. Surprisingly, we have also noticed subtitle files with differing *pace*. That is, even when they are properly aligned at the first caption entry, they eventually get out of sync with each other. Our analysis found that the associated video files had different encoding settings (frame rate) which caused one of them to be played back quicker. This finding is shown in Figure 3.

This study reinforces that finding a subtitle file that will fit well with a given media can be a challenging task. The variations in the starting times and the problems caused by different encoding settings support our premise that a mechanism to automate the synchronization of such a large range of potential subtitle files is required.

4. OUR APPROACH

The golden standard for captioning is a file containing, essentially, the textual entries to be displayed (thereafter called subtitles) and the moment of that presentation. The media player, when playing back a multimedia file/stream, renders also the textual entries specified on the subtitle file for that moment.

same subtitles disguised in different file names but with different names listed in the credits. This suggests that ownership infringement could be a recurrent problem in subtitle sharing communities on the Internet.

[5]Information such as frame rate, resolution, and bit rate of the multimedia file.

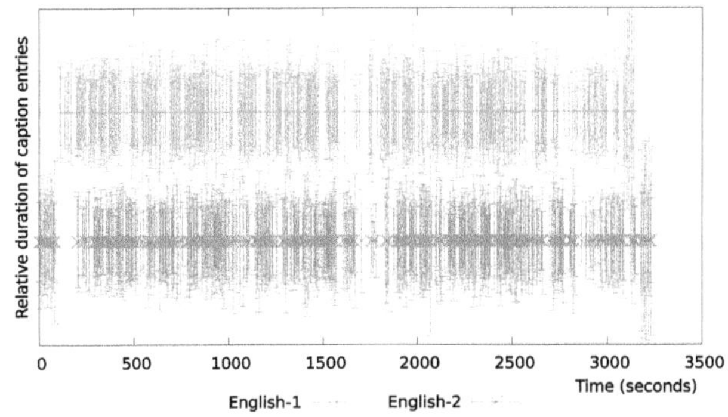

Figure 2: Caption entries for an episode of a TV series. The bottommost captions include a prologue.

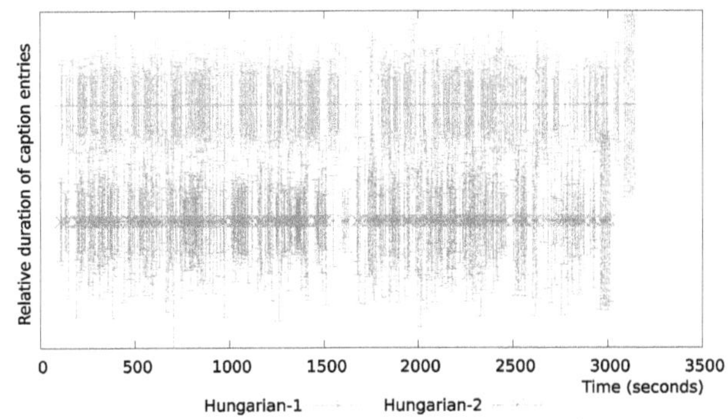

Figure 3: Caption entries for two videos encoded with different frame rates: differences begin small but increase over time (represented by the X axis).

Our method to dynamically synchronize a subtitle file with media streams works on two steps: (1) on the creation or modification of a subtitle file through an authoring software and (2) on the playback of that subtitle file along with its media streams.

The first step consists of electing subtitle entries as synchronization anchors. Ideally, each subtitle file has at least two anchors, chosen, preferably, from moments close to the begining and the ending of the file. The authoring software then takes short audio fingerprints that describe the main audio component of these anchors. In other words, it extracts the *signature* of the audio signal associated with each anchor. Next, all the fingerprints are added to the subtitle file with their corresponding offset time.

The second step of the synchronization happens on the playback of the media file. Essentially, it begins with the opening of the media streams and with the parsing of the subtitle file, from where the caption entries and the fingerprints are read. The media player seeks to the offsets of the first and last anchors and calculates the audio fingerprint of the media streams at these offsets. Subsequently, they are compared against the fingerprints specified on the subtitle file. The two media files are considered in perfect sync if the calculated and the reference fingerprints match.

If the fingerprints do not match, then the media player seeks to the beginning of the media file and computes its audio fingerprints until there is a match with the signature of the first anchor annotated on the subtitle file. The difference between the media player's time offset and the timestamp of the matched anchor is then propagated to all subsequent caption entries. A comparison between the last anchor's fingerprint is then performed to assure the correct synchronization. If discrepancies are still found, the media player moves back to the first anchor point and starts to search for the second anchor point, in order to correct the subsequent subtitles one more time. This process is repeated until the fingerprint of the last anchor matches the one from the file. Finally, the media player utilizes the updated caption timestamps to synchronize the playback.

A special case applies to non-seekable media streams (as is the case of broadcast and streaming services.) Since there is no indication of the beginning of the stream, the media player needs to continuously compute the audio fingerprints until a match is found. At that point in time, the subtitles can be put in sync with the media streams and the media player can start rendering them. This process can be performed at uniform intervals, to guarantee the synchronization throughout the playback.

5. ENRICHED SUBTITLE FORMAT

The method proposed in this paper has been prototyped with the VLC media player and Chromaprint[6], a library that implements a custom algorithm for extracting fingerprints from audio sources. Besides the purpose of validating the core idea, the prototype also helped us better understand the performance impacts of the fingerprinting process and to investigate how to integrate audio signatures into existing subtitle file formats.

Our prototype includes support for the SRT format, depicted in Figure 4, which is comprised of three elements: (1) the sequence number of the caption entry (lines 01 and 05), (2) the starting and ending times in which the caption entry must be presented on the screen (lines 02 and 06), and (3) the textual entries. To overcome the lack of support for including meta-data in SRT, we chose to represent fingerprints as caption entries with zero duration. The string **@fingerprint@** indicates the presence of the audio signature computed by the fingerprint library, as shown in Figure 4. Other subtitle file formats could embed the audio fingerprints as proper meta-data and a binary format would store the fingerprints more efficiently. Given the popularity of SRT, though, it is essential to include new features while maintaining backwards compatibility with that format.

```
01. 0
02. 00:00:00,000 --> 00:00:00,000
03. @fingerprint@ -177,-168,-167,...,934,934,904
04.
05. 1
06. 00:01:46,144 --> 00:01:48,831
07. - ( woman laughing )
```

Figure 4: Sample fingerprint anchored at time zero.

In our method, anchors do not necessarily need to be associated with actual captions or subtitles. It is perfectly possible to compute audio fingerprints from the very first seconds of the multimedia streams and annotate them as an empty caption entry, as shown in Figure 4 (line 02). By doing so, a minimal amount of fingerprint processing can be performed during playback.

[6]http://acoustid.org/chromaprint

6. CONCLUSION

In this paper we presented three contributions to the area. First, through a qualitative analysis of publicly available subtitles we identified sources of synchronization problems between captioned files and their corresponding media. Second, we developed a method to dynamically sychronize subtitles based on audio fingerprints. Third, we proposed an extension to the subtitle file formats currently in use so they can benefit from our dynamic synchronization method.

As future work, we intend to deepen the investigation on the causes of the discrepancies between subtitle files, in order to propose new or enhance our extension on subtitle files. Moreover, we would like to conduct an experiment to measure the sensitivity of users to subtitle's dyssynchrony. This information will be useful for the calculation of the optimized frequency of anchor points in subtitle files.

7. ACKNOWLEDGMENTS

This work has been partially funded by Brazilian's FINEP / MCTI under contract no. 03.11.0371.00.

8. REFERENCES

[1] A. Brown, R. Jones, et al. Dynamic subtitles: the user experience. In *Proceedings of the 2015 ACM International Conference on Interactive Experiences for TV and Online Video*. ACM, 2015.

[2] D. C. Bulterman, A. Jansen, et al. An efficient, streamable text format for multimedia captions and subtitles. In *Proceedings of the 2007 ACM symposium on Document engineering*, pages 101–110. ACM, 2007.

[3] C. Concolato and J. Le Feuvre. Live http streaming of video and subtitles within a browser. In *Proceedings of the 4th ACM Multimedia Systems Conference*, pages 146–150. ACM, 2013.

[4] M. Federico and M. Furini. An automatic caption alignment mechanism for off-the-shelf speech recognition technologies. *Multimedia tools and applications*, 72(1):21–40, 2014.

[5] R. Hong, M. Wang, et al. Dynamic captioning: video accessibility enhancement for hearing impairment. In *Proceedings of the international conference on Multimedia*, pages 421–430. ACM, 2010.

[6] G. Kovacs and R. C. Miller. Smart subtitles for vocabulary learning. In *Proceedings of the 32nd annual ACM conference on Human factors in computing systems*, pages 853–862. ACM, 2014.

[7] X. Liu and W. Wang. Robustly extracting captions in videos based on stroke-like edges and spatio-temporal analysis. *Multimedia, IEEE Transactions on*, 14(2):482–489, 2012.

[8] K. Rooney. The impact of keyword caption ratio on foreign language listening comprehension. *International Journal of Computer-Assisted Language Learning and Teaching (IJCALLT)*, 4(2):11–28, 2014.

[9] J. Tiedemann. Synchronizing translated movie subtitles. In *Proceedings of the 6th International Conference on Language Resources and Evaluation (LREC'2008)*, 2008.

Octave-dependent Probabilistic Latent Semantic Analysis to Chorus Detection of Popular Song

Sheng Gao, Haizhou Li
Institute for Infocomm Research, A*STAR, Singapore
{gaosheng,hli}@i2r.a-star.edu.sg

ABSTRACT

Content representation of music signal is an essential part of music information retrieval applications, e.g. chorus detection, genre classification, etc. In the paper, we propose the octave-dependent probabilistic latent semantic analysis (OdPlsa) to discover the latent audio patterns (or clusters) through spectral-temporal analysis. Then the audio content of each segment is characterized using the statistical pattern distribution. In OdPlsa, the latent pattern is modeled by multinomial distribution which characterizes the magnitude distribution of 12-dimensional pitch class profiles over a temporal window. It thus effectively models melody information as well as octave relations in music signal. Its efficiency as a feature extraction technique is evaluated on chorus detection of popular songs. In terms of multiple performance metrics such as boundary accuracy, precision, recall and F1, the proposed technique is much superior to the widely accepted chroma feature.

Categories and Subject Descriptors

H.5.5 [**Information Interfaces and Presentation**]: Sound and Music Computing

General Terms

Algorithms; Experimentation

Keywords

Probabilistic latent semantic analysis; Chroma; Chorus detection

1. INTRODUCTION

Music information retrieval (MIR), such as music search by a sample clip, cover song detection, genre classification, etc., has been investigated more than one decade. The community has organized benchmark evaluations on music information retrieval to promote the areas and technology adoption[1]. In recent years, smart phone is becoming pervasive. Music entertainment on the mobile becomes part of our everyday life, that gives rise to many music services (e.g. Apple iTunes store[2], SoundHound[3], Spotify[4], Baidu[5], etc.). They provide mobile products to give the users anywhere, anytime and personalized listening experiences so that the users can stick to their services. To facilitate the users searching and browsing millions of music recordings and making decision whether to buy a recording, music recommendation and preview are important functions. Recommendation in the current commercial products exploits the user profile, music metadata (e.g. title, artist, recording year), listening history, et al. They are categorized as the metadata-based method. However, the metadata approach cannot handle the cold start songs (less metadata available) in the web. In such scenario, audio similarity based on signal analysis will be a help.

Traditionally, many MIR studies resort to the feature extraction techniques in speech processing for the audio content representation (e.g. [4], [12], [15], [16], and [22]). A comprehensive survey can be found in [15]. Among many kinds of speech features, mel-frequency cepstral coefficient (MFCC) is found useful in various MIR tasks. For example, [2] exploits MFCC to measure audio similarity for music summary and it is used for chorus detection and emotion classification in [7]. However, MFCC is known sensitive to the changes of key or accompaniment. To address the issues, chroma (pitch class profile) feature is adopted. It is a 12-dimensional vector corresponding to 12 distinct semitones of the Western chromatic scale. It now becomes an effective representation for music signal and is successfully used in chorus detection, music segmentation, cover song detection, etc. [6][8][9][13][18-21].

Chroma characterizes the magnitude distribution in 12 semitones regardless of octave and temporal information. It is generally extracted by mapping the FFT frequency band to the octave and semitone, and, for each semitone, the magnitude in different octaves are (most of the times linearly) combined. The chroma feature does not model the frequency-temporal pattern, which plays the important role in music perception and discrimination. The structure of music signal means that the limited frequency-temporal patterns are enough to characterize the content of a song.

This observation motivates us to develop the octave-dependent probabilistic latent semantic analysis (OdPlsa) to analyze the magnitude distribution of semitones along the octave and temporal dimensions. OdPlsa is formulated to extract spectral (semitone)-temporal patterns through analyzing the magnitude distribution and then music content is represented in terms of the patterns.

OdPlsa is novel and different from the existing work on applying latent component analysis technique to audio signal analysis. For example, in [10], MFCC based frame feature is first tokenized

[1] http://www.music-ir.org/mirex/wiki/MIREX_HOME
[2] http://www.apple.com/itunes/
[3] https://www.soundhound.com/
[4] https://www.spotify.com
[5] http://music.baidu.com/

MM '15, October 26-30, 2015, Brisbane, Australia
© 2015 ACM. ISBN 978-1-4503-3459-4/15/10…$15.00
DOI: http://dx.doi.org/10.1145/2733373.2806379

using clustering algorithm and then Probabilistic Latent Semantic Analysis (PLSA) is applied to model the occurrence of audio tokens. It ignored the evidences from the octave, semitone and temporal. In [23], PLSA is used to model similar songs rather than the spectrum structure of music signal. The most similar work is [3], which proposed the shift-invariance PLSA to modeling the magnitude distribution at the 12-dimensional semitone and time axes. This model can solve the key change. But it discards the octave.

In the next section, we will discuss the detail of OdPlsa for extracting spatial-temporal pattern and its application for content representation. In Section 3, we will introduce the task of chorus detection, which is used to demonstrate the representation capability of OdPlsa. In Section 4, the experimental results on chorus detection are reported. Finally we summarize our work.

2. OCTAVE-DEPENDENT PLSA (OdPlsa)

2.1 Model of OdPlsa

OdPlsa is based on the FFT-based short-time spectrum. Frequency bands of FFT are mapped to their corresponding midi notes. The process is similar to [9]. A midi note is denoted with its octave level and semitone. Thus the FFT sequence in the midi space is denoted as $X(o,s,t)$. Here

o: the octave level

s: the semitone between $[0,11]$

t': the time stamp (the basic unit is frame) between $[0,T-1]$ with T being the sequence length

As the short-time frame feature is weak in discrimination, it is often to segment the sequence using a window having L continuous frames. Thus the sequence becomes to be the L-frame chunk sequence with the length, $ceil(T/L)$. For the *i-th* chunk, it is a sequence as: $X(o,s,t'_i), X(o,s,t'_i+1), \cdots, X(o,s,t'_i+L-1)$ with $t'_i=(i-1)*L$. So each component pattern models the magnitude distribution in both semitone and time dimensions (L-frame length). To simplify the notation, semitone and time are combined into a variable, f. Without any confusion, the chunk sequence is still noted as $X(o,f,t)$ (t: the *t-th* chunk. f: refer to a specific semitone and time location in the rectangle region 12*L.).

The occurrence probability of a particular spectrum at the *o-th* octave and *f-th* location for the *t-th* chunk, $P(o,f,t)$, is modeled by the following mixture models with K components as,

$$P(o,f,t) = P(o,t)\sum_{k=1}^{K} P(f|k)\,P(k|o,t). \quad (1)$$

In the model, $P(f|k)$ models the magnitude distribution of the *k-th* pattern, $P(k|o,t)$ tells us how the pattern is distributed across the octaves in each chunk, and $P(o,t)$ describes the importance of the octave in each chunk.

Thus the log-likelihood of the model to generate the observation sequence $X(o,f,t)$ is defined as,

$$L = \sum_{o,f,t} X(o,f,t) log P(o,f,t) \quad (2)$$

To estimate the pattern models, an auxiliary variable, $Q(k|o,f,t)$, is introduced into Eq.(2) (abbreviated as $Q(.)$). And we get

$$L = \sum_{o,f,t} X(o,f,t) log \sum_{k=1}^{K} P(f|k)P(k,o,t)Q(.)/Q(.) \quad (3)$$

According to the Jensen's inequality, we get the objective function as,

$$L^{+} = \sum_{o,f,t} X(o,f,t) \sum_{k=1}^{K} \begin{bmatrix} Q(.)log\big(P(f|k)P(t,o|k)P(k)\big) \\ -Q(.)logQ(.) \end{bmatrix}, \quad (4)$$

with the constraints on the parameters $P(f|k)$, $P(t,o|k)$, $P(k)$, and $Q(k|o,f,t)$ shown in Eq. (5),

$$\begin{cases} \sum_f P(f|k) = 1 \\ \sum_{t,o} P(t,o|k) = 1 \\ \sum_k P(k) = 1 \\ \sum_k Q(k|o,f,t) = 1 \end{cases}. \quad (5)$$

The traditional EM algorithm can be applied to estimate model parameters $P(f|k)$, $P(t,o|k)$, and $P(k)$.

In the E-step, $Q(k|o,f,t)$ is estimated as,

$$Q(k|o,f,t) = exp\Big(X(o,f,t)\log\big(P(f|k)P(t,o|k)P(k)\big)\Big)/\lambda_{oft}. \quad (6)$$

In Eq.(6), λ_{oft} is a constant to make , $Q(k|o,f,t)$ satisfies the constrain in Eq.(5).

In the M-step, the model parameters are estimated as,

$$P(f|k) = \sum_{t,o} X(o,f,t)Q(k|o,f,t)/\lambda_k \quad (7)$$

$$P(t,o|k) = \sum_f X(o,f,t)Q(k|o,f,t)/\lambda'_k \quad (8)$$

$$P(k) = \sum_{o,f,t} X(o,f,t)Q(k|o,f,t)/\lambda \quad (9)$$

Similar to Eq. (6), $\lambda_k, \lambda'_k, and\ \lambda$ in the above equations are constants in order to satisfy the conditions in Eq.(5).

2.2 Discussion on OdPlsa

The component pattern model is $P(f|k)$ in OdPlsa. It describes the magnitude distribution in 2-dimensional axes. In the current implementation, it is 12-dimensional semitones and L-frame time window. It is shared by the different octaves. We can imagine that the patterns are the most prominent information occurred in the music signal such as frequently repeated melody or chord.

From the learned models, we can know how the patterns distribute in the octaves, i.e. $P(k|o,t)$, according to the following equations.

$$P(k,o,t) = P(t,o|k)P(k) \quad (10)$$

$$P(o,t) = \sum_k P(k,o,t) \quad (11)$$

$$P(k|o,t) = P(k,o,t)/P(o,t) \quad (12)$$

For each chunk of music we can represent its content in the audio pattern space like as,

$$P(t|k,o) = P(k,o,t)/P(k,o) \quad (13)$$

If the octave size is O, then the feature dimension will be $K*O$. This representation depends on the octave. If we want to get an octave-invariance feature, we can sum up the pattern distribution over all octaves such as,

$$P(t|k) = \sum_o P(t,o|k) \quad (14)$$

3. CHORUS DETECTION

As discussed in the above, OdPlsa can find the latent audio patterns from music signal, help us understand how the pattern distributes in the different octave and give us a tool to represent audio features in the audio pattern space. In the paper, we will discuss its efficiency as a feature extraction tool in the chorus detection task.

Chorus sections are the most repeated and memorable portions of a song. Many papers have been published under the chorus detection or music structure detection [6-9], [11-15], [18-21]. Up to now, chroma feature dominates in the task. The general technique in chorus detection is to calculate the pair-wise similarity matrix based on the audio feature. When visualizing the similarity matrix, we observe a line for two similar segments along the diagonals. Based on this property, various heuristic algorithms are developed to find the most significant lines from the matrix [9, 18, 20].

In the paper we design the OdPlsa-based chorus detection system. For each song, its audio pattern is found by OdPlsa (See sec.2). Then each music segment is represented in the pattern space (See Eq.13), and pair-wise music segment similarity matrix is computed. Due to the limited space, we just list the important steps and operations in Table 1 for chorus detection (all parameters are heuristic setting using a few randomly selected songs such as 5.

Input: similarity matrix, A_{N*N} for a song (see Fig.1a). N: the size of audio chunk. $a_{i,j}$: *(i,j)-th* entry in A
Output: chorus sections

1. Find significant points with highly possibility lying in the similar segments and binarize A as following (μ: mean of similarity scores. σ: standard variance.)

$$a_{i,j} = \begin{cases} 1, & (a_{i,j} - \mu)/\sigma > th1 \\ 0, & otherwise \end{cases}$$

Here $th1$ is set to keep top 2% points. Only the 1-value points are considered in the next steps (see Fig.1b).

2. Find all lines from the diagonals with the conditions (see Fig.2b): a) if two neighbor points along the diagonal is less than smoothing threshold ($th_s = 1s$), then merge them with previous points; b) if the line length is less than a threshold ($th_l = 2s$), ignore it.

3. Merge overlapped lines from the line candidates and generate new lines. Only keep the *top-n (=30)* longest lines for the next step.

4. Get all segments from the above lines, and count the repetition number of each segment. Select the longest segments with repetition numbers more than 2 as chorus sections (each section is marked with its starting and ending timestamps) (see Fig.1c).

Table 1 Chorus detection algorithm

4. EXPERIMENTAL RESULTS

The evaluated music dataset contains 247 popular songs with large diversity in the styles, which is provided by our industry collaborator. For each song, the boundaries of all chorus sections are manually tagged. On average there are ~2.6 chorus per song.

4.1 Evaluation Metrics

The performance is evaluated using multiple metrics to reflect different aspects of the detection system.

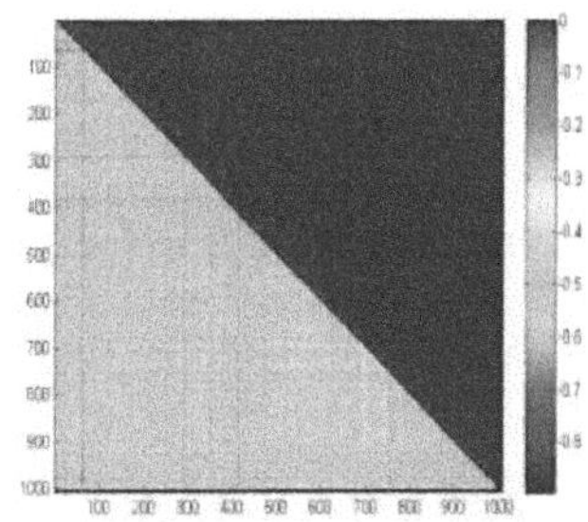

(a) Similarity matrix (only lower triangle part of matrix)

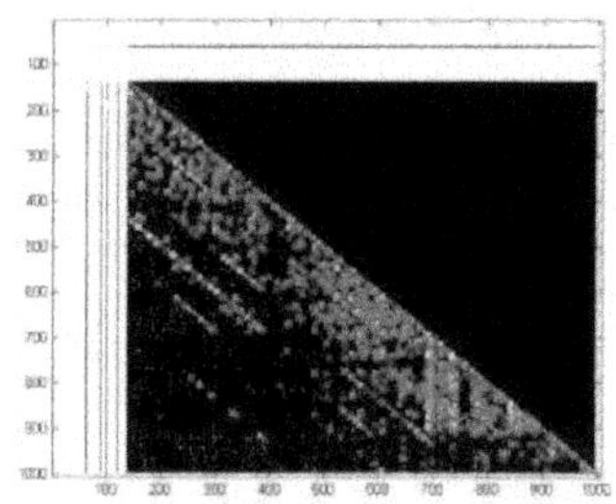

(b) Significant points (white dots) and detected lines (green) with red X marking starting and ending)

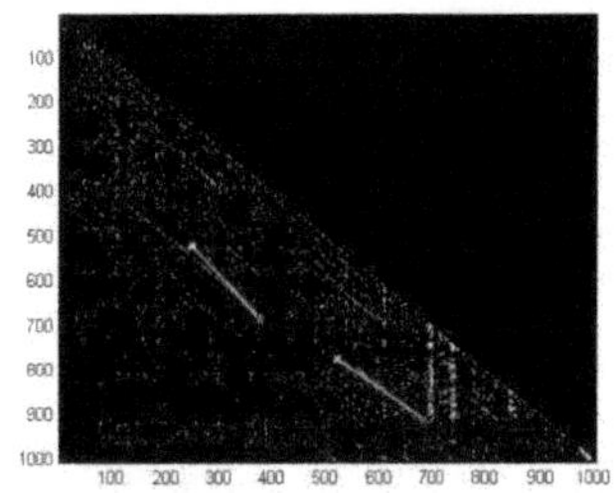

(c) Detected chorus sections (green lines)

Figure 1 Visualizing the process of chorus detection: from similarity matrix to chorus sections

a) **n-second staring time accuracy (M1)**: *if the absolute difference between any one of the detected starting times for a song and the ground-truth is less than n-second, then the chorus of the song is considered to be correct.*

b) **n-percent overlap accuracy (M2)**: *if the overlap between any one of the detected starting times and the ground-truth is more than n-percent of length of the ground-truth, then the song chorus is considered to be correct.*

c) **n-second staring time based precision, recall and F1 (M3)**: *it is based on the n-second starting time accuracy, from which we will know if the detected section is true positive or false positive. It gives us a complete image about the detected sections.*

4.2. Experimental Setup

Each song is 16bit/8kHz sample rate and mono channel. The 1024-point FFT (128ms frame length) spectrum is extracted with 112ms overlapping between the consecutive frames. We only consider FFT bands in the range between 32.7Hz (C1) and 4000Hz (B7) covering 7 octaves.

The OdPlsa based feature is extracted as in Section 2 (K=8) with a 20-frame (0.32s) audio chunk without any overlap. The benchmark system is based on the 12-dimensional chroma feature implemented as in [9]. In addition, the effect of the first-order difference feature, $\Delta X(t) = (X(t+1) - X(t-1))/2$, is also studied considering its success in speech recognition [16]. We segment the sequence into a 0.64s-length section with 0.32s overlap and calculate the pair-wise segment similarity scores (here similarity function is negative Euclidean distance). Then the chorus detection algorithm (see Table 1 in Section 3) is started to find all chorus sections.

4.3 Results

The results are reported in Figure 2 in terms of 1-second staring time accuracy (M1), 80% overlap accuracy (M2), and 1-second starting time F1 (M3). The relative gains reach up to 18.4% (M1), 34.4% (M2) and 39.8% (M3) respectively when comparing with the chroma-based benchmark system. OdPlsa-based feature significantly outperforms the popular chroma feature. The improvement is because OdPlsa feature characterizes the pattern distribution in both octave and temporal dimensions as well as the distribution of each frequency band in the song level. But chroma only describes the distribution along the frequency band. Our results demonstrate that OdPlsa is a powerful tool for the audio content representation.

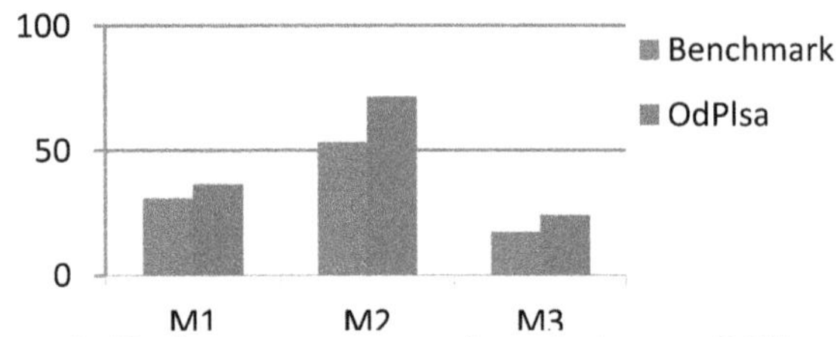

Figure 2 Performance comparison between OdPlsa and chroma

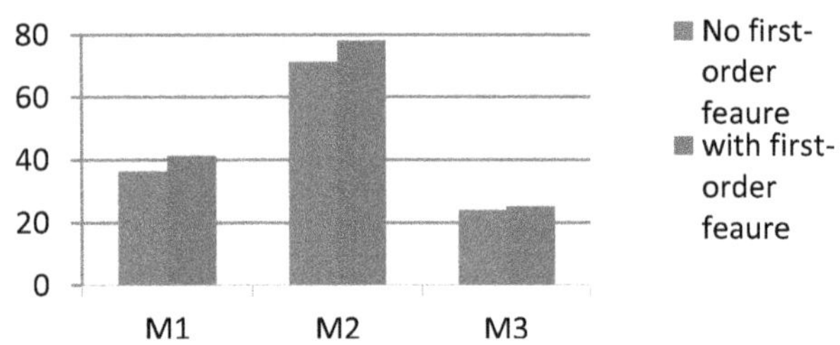

Figure 3 Effect of first-order feature on performance with OdPlsa

The effect of the first-order difference feature on the performance is shown in Figure 3. With the addition of first-order feature, the relative improvements are 13.3% (M1), 9.7% (M2) and 5.3% (M3). It demonstrates that the first-order OdPlsa-based feature is a good addition for chorus detection.

5. CONCLUSION

In the paper, the OdPlsa is presented to model the audio content in the spectral-temporal domain. It exploits the latent audio patterns occurred in the octaves, semitones and temporal and is used to characterize the audio content in the low-dimensional latent space. Its capability as the feature representation is demonstrated in the chorus detection, which significantly outperforms the popular chroma feature in terms of chorus detection performance. In the future, we will investigate its applications in other MIR tasks such as cover song detection.

6. ACKNOWLEDGEMENTS

We thank Lei Jia and Hui Song from Baidu Inc. for the support of the project and kindly providing the music dataset.

7. REFERENCES

[1] T. Hofmann, 1999. Probabilistic latent semantic indexing. In *Proc. of ACM SIGIR'99*, pp.50-57.

[2] M. Cooper and J. Foote, 2002. Automatic music summarization via similarity analysis. In *Proc. of ISMIR'02*, pp.81-85.

[3] R. J. Weiss and J. P. Bello, 2011. Unsupervised discovery of temporal structure in music. In *IEEE Journal of Selected Topics in Signal Processing,* 5(6):1240-1251.

[4] D. Turnbull, et al., 2007. A supervised approach for detecting boundaries in music using difference features and boosting. In *Proc. of ISMIR'07*, pp.42-49.

[5] J. Serra, et al., 2012. Unsupervised detection of music boundaries by time series structure features. In *Proc. of AAAI'12*, pp.1613-1619.

[6] J. V. Balen, et al., 2013. An analysis of chorus features in popular song. In *Proc. of ISMIR'13*, pp.107-112.

[7] C.-H. Yeh, et al., 2010. Popular music analysis: chorus and emotion detection. In *Proc. of APSIPA'10*, pp.907-910.

[8] A. Eronen, 2007. Chorus detection with combined use of MFCC and chroma features and image processing filters. In *Proc. of DAFx'07*.

[9] M. Goto, 2006. A chorus section detection method for musical audio signals and its application to a music listening station. In *IEEE Trans. on ASL*, Vol.14, No.5, pp.1783-1794.

[10] P. Smaragdis, et al., 2009. Topic models for audio mixture analysis. In *Proc. of NIPS Workshop on Applications for Topic Models: Text and Beyond*, pp.1-4.

[11] C. Burges, et al., 2005. Using audio fingerprinting for duplicate detection and audio thumbnails. In *Proc. of ICASSP'05*, pp.9-12.

[12] B. McFee and D. P.W. Ellis, 2014. Learning to segment songs with ordinal linear discriminant analysis. In *Proc. of ICASSP'14*, pp.5197-7201.

[13] M. Goto, 2003. SmartMusicKIOSK: music listening station with chorus-search function. In *Proc. of ACM Symposium on User Interface Software and Technology (UIST)*, pp.31-40.

[14] M. Muller, et al., 2011. A segment-based fitness measure for capturing repetitive structures of music recordings. In *Proc. of ISMIR'11*, pp.615-620.

[15] M. Schedl, et al., 2014. Music information retrieval: recent developments and applications. In *Foundations and Trends in Information Retrieval*, Vol.8, Issue 2-3, pp.127-261.

[16] L.R. Rabiner and B.-H. Juang, 1993. *Fundamentals of Speech Recognition*, Prentice Hall.

[17] A. Bosch, et al. 2006. Scene classification via pLSA. In *Proc. of ECCV'06*, pp.517-530.

[18] M. A. Bartsch and G.H. Wakefield, 2001. To catch a chorus: using chroma-based representations for audio thumbnailing. In *Proc. of IEEE Workshop on Applications of Signal Processing to Audio and Acoustics*, pp.15-18.

[19] J. Paulus, et al., 2010. Audio-based music structure analysis. In *Proc. of ISMIR'10*, pp.625-636.

[20] V. Mildner, et al., 2003. Chorus detection in songs of pop music. In *Proc. of ESSV'03*.

[21] N.C. Maddage, et al., 2004. Content-based music structure analysis with applications to music semantics understanding. In *Proc. of ACM MM'04*, pp.112-119.

[22] P. Golik, et al., 2012. Mobile music modeling, analysis and recognition. In *Proc. of ICASSP'12*, pp.2353-2356.

[23] J. Arenas-Garcia, et al., 2007. Unveiling music structure via PLSA similarity fusion. In *Proc. of IEEE Workshop on Machine Learning for Signal Processing*, pp.419-424.

Subjectivity in Aesthetic Quality Assessment of Digital Photographs: Analysis of User Comments

Won-Hee Kim
Yonsei Institute of Convergence Technology, Yonsei University
Incheon, Republic of Korea
wonheekim@yonsei.ac.kr

Jun-Ho Choi
School of Integrated Technology & Yonsei Institute of Convergence Technology, Yonsei University
Incheon, Republic of Korea
idearibosome@yonsei.ac.kr

Jong-Seok Lee
School of Integrated Technology & Yonsei Institute of Convergence Technology, Yonsei University
Incheon, Republic of Korea
jong-seok.lee@yonsei.ac.kr

ABSTRACT
While most of the existing work in aesthetic image quality assessment focuses on the overall (or average) opinion of users, this paper raises the issue of subjectivity (or taste) of aesthetic quality. We argue that subjectivity differs among different images, and investigate what causes such difference. We first analyze statistics of the user ratings of photos in a photo contest website, DPChallenge, in the viewpoint of average and standard deviation values of the ratings. Then, more importantly, we analyze the users' comments in order to identify sources contributing to subjectivity. When considering the importance of personalization in photo applications, we believe that our findings will be a valuable first step in the relevant future research.

Categories and Subject Descriptors
H.5.1 [**Information Interfaces and Presentation**]: Multimedia Information Systems

General Terms
Measurement, Experimentation, Human Factors

Keywords
Aesthetic quality assessment, subjectivity, user comments, digital photographic image

1. INTRODUCTION
With the rapid growth of the imaging and mobile technologies, taking digital photographs has become a daily life activity these days. The number of photographs possessed personally or available online has grown explosively. Accordingly, users' interests and demands toward aesthetically pleasing photographs have also increased significantly. People want to take, share, and view photographs that have high aesthetic quality. Therefore, automatic assessment of aesthetic quality of photographs is a promising technique in many applications related to production, enhancement, management, retrieval, and recommendation of photographs. In general, however, it is very challenging because different people have different aesthetic tastes and preferences.

Over the past decade, aesthetic image quality assessment has been studied by several researchers. Most conventional work used image features to measure the aesthetics of photos. The initial work concentrated on low level features. In the work by Tong *et al.* [1], a large set of general purpose low level features related to blurness, contrast, colorfulness, saliency, color, energy, texture, and shape is used to classify photos as professional or snap-shots. Most of these features are not designed particularly for measuring the aesthetic properties of photos, but for image classification such as indoor vs. outdoor images, city vs. landscape pictures, photos vs. paintings, etc. Therefore, they are not sufficient to accurately evaluate aesthetic photo quality.

To overcome this limitation, Ke *et al.* [2] proposed a photo quality assessment method using high level features that are designed to distinguish high and low quality photos, such as edge distribution, color distribution, hue count, and blurriness. Datta *et al.* [3] proposed an approach using high level features related to light, colorfulness saturation, hue, rule of thirds, familiarity, texture, size ratio, region composition, depth of field, and shape.

There exists some work on aesthetic quality assessment using other high level features. Wong and Low [4] used a set of salient features that characterize the subject and the subject-background relationship. Li *et al.* [5] represented the aesthetic quality of a photo with faces by using technical, perceptual, and social relationship features. Marchesotti *et al.* [6] used generic image descriptors such as bag-of-visual words, Fisher vector, and GIST. Zhang *et al.* [7] introduced photo aesthetics evaluation framework, focusing on learning the image descriptors that characterize local and global structural aesthetics from multiple visual channels.

These researches aimed at evaluating the level of aesthetic photo quality. Their main tasks are prediction and classification of average aesthetic scores. Therefore, they ignore the subjectivity in aesthetic quality. Recently, there have been a few attempts to understand the subjectivity of image assessment in the psychological perspective.

Fedorovskaya and De Ridder [8] showed the existence of subjectivity in assessment of image quality degradation. Palmer and Schloss [9] demonstrated that the gender, expertise, culture, and perceptual experience affect color preference of individuals. Chu *et al.* [10] showed that the familiarity exerts a major influence on determining the perceived interestingness of images. Fedrizzi [11] argued that the gender plays an important role in the aesthetic perception by examining the brain activity recorded

MM '15, October 26-30, 2015, Brisbane, Australia
© 2015 ACM. ISBN 978-1-4503-3459-4/15/10…$15.00
DOI: http://dx.doi.org/10.1145/2733373.2806380

using magnetoencephalography (MEG) and functional magnetic resonance imaging (fMRI).

These studies are limited in that they showed only the existence of subjectivity or examined effects of only certain factors on only certain aesthetic aspects. In this paper, we go one step further by considering more fundamental questions regarding subjectivity and examining much larger number of data, in order to obtain more comprehensive understanding about subjectivity in aesthetic photo quality assessment. We analyze of evaluations (ratings and comments given by online users) for a significantly large number of photos. We aim at answering questions such as which factors in photos contributes to aesthetic subjectivity, how the average aesthetic quality level is related to subjectivity, how the image content influences subjectivity, etc.

2. DATA SET DESCRIPTION

We use photo and comment data available in DPChallenge (http://www.dpchallenge.com), which is an online photograph community website. It hosts weekly digital photography contests called challenges for particular topics. Users of the community can rate a photo submitted to a challenge from 1 (worst) to 10 (best), and can also write comments. At the end of the week, the photos in the challenge are ranked by their mean rating values and the winner is announced. Naturally, photos submitted to a challenge significantly vary in terms of aesthetic quality. The characteristics of the users also vary significantly, i.e., from amateurs to professionals.

Total 307,132 photos and their ratings in 1,971 challenges (from January 2002 to August 2014) were collected for our study. Figure 1 shows the histogram of the mean rating scores, which is close to a normal distribution. The mean and standard deviation values of the distribution are 5.43 and 0.73, respectively; the minimum and maximum values are 1.81 and 8.60, respectively.

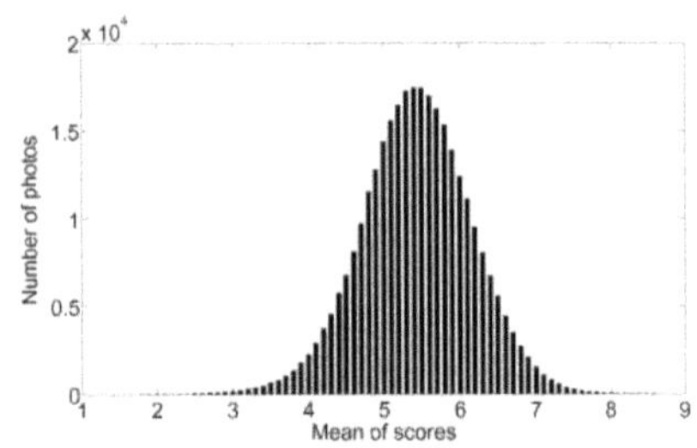

Figure 1. Histogram of the mean ratings

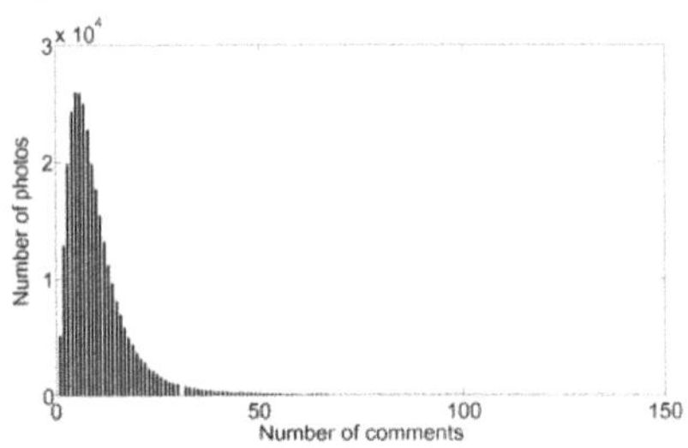

Figure 2. Histogram of the number of comments

In addition, the comments for the photos were collected. We considered only the comments made during the challenge period in our analysis, since comments after the challenge period may be biased due to the announced ranking result. The number of such valid comments was 2,828,525. The maximum number of comments per photo is 145, and the average number of comments per photo is 9.4. Figure 2 shows the histogram of the number of comments. 69.7% of the photos have less than 10 comments and 92.6% photos have less than 20 comments.

In order to analyze subjectivity based on the content of comments, we set six broad categories, each of which contains several challenges sharing the same topic. In total, 18,033 photos and the 182,368 comments for them are analyzed. Table 1 summarizes the statistics of each category, i.e., the number of photos, total number of comments, total number of words in the comments, average of mean ratings (***M***), and average of standard deviations of ratings (***S***).

Table 1. Summary of the data set used for comment analysis

category	#photos	#comments	#words	avg(*M*)	avg(*S*)
portrait	6374	80352	1339132	5.49	1.41
landscapes	3242	29257	460592	5.53	1.38
architecture	1335	9723	151708	5.52	1.38
animal	3665	37541	577239	5.58	1.35
plant	2135	14794	229205	5.44	1.31
street	1282	10701	176637	5.51	1.31

3. SUBJECTIVITY IN ASSESSMENT

The mean value of ratings (denoted as ***M***) of a photo, shown in Figure 1, represents the aggregated overall level of aesthetic quality of the photo. The standard deviation of ratings (denoted as ***S***), on the other hand, represents the level of disagreement or diversity in rating across users, which reflects subjectivity in aesthetic quality evaluation. A low value of ***S*** means agreement among raters about the aesthetic quality of the photo, whereas a large value of ***S*** indicates that some users rate the photo high and some other users rate it low, and thus individual preference significantly differs among them.

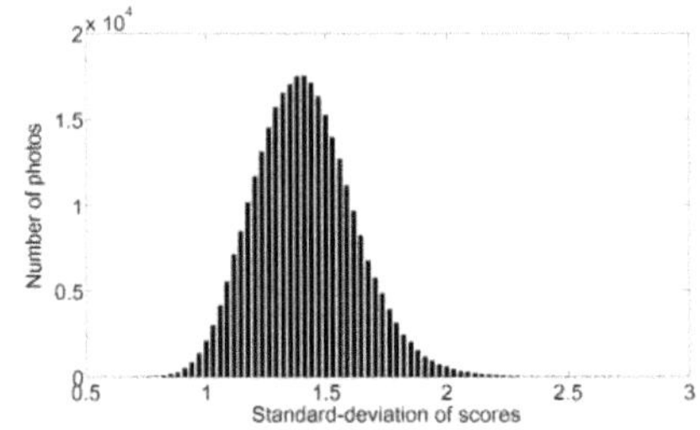

Figure 3. Histogram of the standard deviations of the ratings

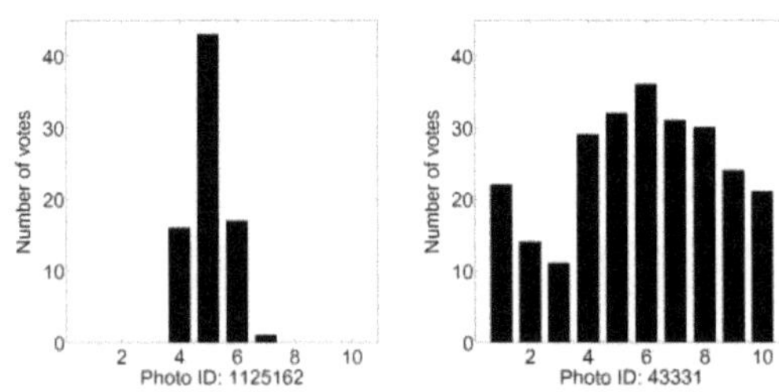

(a) **(b)**

Figure 4. Example histograms of ratings. (a) A case with low subjectivity (*S*=0.69) (b) A case with high subjectivity (*S*=2.62)

Figure 3 shows the histogram of ***S*** for the 307,132 photos. The mean and standard deviation values of the distribution are 1.41 and 0.21, respectively; the minimum and maximum values are 0.69 and 2.89, respectively. As in Figure 1, the histogram of ***S*** follows approximately a normal distribution. Figure 4 shows rating distributions of two particular photos, one with a low ***S*** value and another one with a high ***S*** value. In Figure 4(a), most of the ratings are concentrated between 4 and 6, but in Figure 4(b), the whole rating range (from 1 to 10) is used by raters.

We examine the correlation between ***M*** and ***S***, but they do not have significant correlation, with a Pearson correlation coefficient of 0.086.

4. ANALYSIS OF COMMENTS

In this section, aesthetic photo quality assessment and its subjectivity are analyzed based on the users' comments.

The relationship between the number of comments and the ratings is shown in Figures 5 and 6. Figure 5 presents the scatter plot of the number of comments with respect to ***M***. Overall, it is observed that photos having higher ***M*** values tend to have more comments. In addition, the distribution of the number of comments is rather uniform in the extremely low range of ***M*** (lower than 3), while it is concentrated in the low range (below about 30 comments) for the photos in the mid range of ***M*** (between 4 and 5). Therefore, it seems that the commenters are more interested in high or low quality photos than the mid-level quality photos.

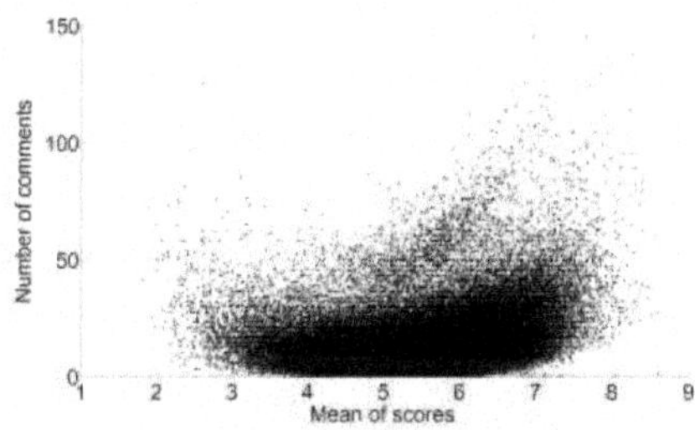

Figure 5. Scatter plot of the number of comments with respect to the mean rating values (*M*)

Figure 6 shows the scatter plot of the number of comments with respect to ***S***. A weak positive correlation is observed on the whole. It is also interesting to see that photos having extremely low ***S*** values (i.e., having almost perfect agreement among raters) received very low numbers of comments. Therefore, it can be said that photos incurring higher subjectivity tend to receive more comments.

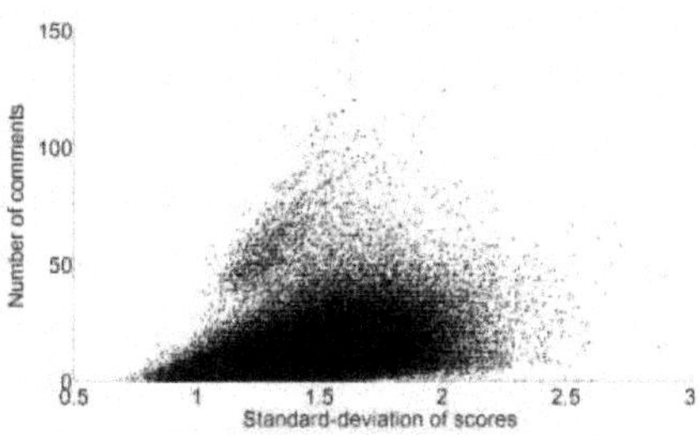

Figure 6. Scatter plot of the number of comments with respect to the standard deviation of ratings (*S*)

In order to analyze subjectivity from the content of comments, we identify words conveying users' opinions and categorize them into six groups as shown Table 2. The words were manually classified into six groups. The POSI group is composed of words representing positive feedback. Especially, the word 'ribbon' means the markers given to the photos ranked first, second, and third. The words in the CREA group evaluate the originality and creativity of photos. The NEGA group consists of words with negative and critical meanings. PERS is the group consisting of words used to describe personal and individual opinions. The words in the BOTH group indicate that the comments simultaneously include contrasting positive and negative opinions (for instance, "The photo has good color balance **but** the composition is poor."). Finally, the words in the ELEM group represent particular elements of photo aesthetics. For each photo, the frequency of the words listed in the table is counted for each of the six groups for further analysis.

Table 2. Word groups for comment analysis

group	words
POSI	amazing, beautiful, excellent, fabulous, fantastic, top, favorite, good, gorgeous, great, like, love, nice, perfect, please, sweet, wonderful, awesome, best, ribbon, well
CREA	creative, interesting, novel, origin, concept, idea, new, unique, unusual, not usual
NEGA	artifact, lack, miss, need, poor, require, bad, blurry, noise, sorry, why, out of focus
PERS	personal, taste, because, me, my, think, thought
BOTH	although, but, however, nevertheless, notwithstanding, nonetheless, though, despite that, even so, even though,
ELEM	align, balance, color, curve, detail, drama, emotion, expose, light, line, mood, object, rotation, simple, tone, texture, angle, background, brightness, composition, contrast, foreground, harmony, hue, perspective, pose, ratio, saturation, symmetry, viewpoint, depth of field

Table 3 shows the Pearson correlation coefficients between the total word frequencies and the mean rating values (***M***). The POSI group has a high correlation with ***M***, which is obviously expected. The ELEM group also has a relatively high correlation. The *portrait* category receives more influence of the words in the CREA group than any other categories. Since most people have seen a lot of portraits of many different kinds, originality and creativity tend to affect positively to evaluate the aesthetic quality. In contrast, CREA is not related to the evaluation of the *landscapes* and *animal* categories. It means that the assessment criteria of the categories are rather conservative and classical.

Table 3. Correlation coefficients for *M*

category	POSI	CREA	NEGA	PERS	BOTH	ELEM
portrait	0.656	0.202	-0.169	0.318	0.170	0.499
landscapes	0.663	0.039	-0.247	0.209	0.021	0.457
architecture	0.628	0.152	-0.186	0.353	0.088	0.483
animal	0.658	0.003	-0.205	0.276	-0.002	0.462
plant	0.711	0.027	-0.151	0.353	0.167	0.552
street	0.752	0.163	-0.130	0.483	0.209	0.502

Table 4 presents the Pearson correlation coefficients between the word frequencies and the standard deviation values of ratings (***S***). In comparison to Table 3, one can observe significantly increased correlations of ***S*** with the word frequencies in the CREA, PERS, and BOTH groups. Existence of the words in the CREA group indicates that the photo is unusual in aesthetic quality. The creativity and unusualness act positively to some users but negatively to some other users. When a commenter uses a word in the PERS group, he/she already knows that his/her opinion is subjective and thus may not be accepted by some users. Furthermore, use of a word in the BOTH group indicates mutually contradictory opinion within a comment; depending on personal preference, the positive or negative side plays a more important role, which results in subjectivity. The photos in *landscapes* show a relatively high correlation between the frequency of the ELEM words and ***S***. This means that subjectivity of the landscape photos is largely evaluated by low level aesthetic criteria (e.g., composition, color, and lighting) rather than high level perceptual aspects such as emotion and feeling. Exceptionally, the *street* category has low correlations for all groups. This is probably due to the fact that the photos in this category significantly vary in terms of their content, ranging from faces of people in streets, cars and buildings in streets, to landscapes containing streets.

Table 4. Correlation coefficients for *S*

category	POSI	CREA	NEGA	PERS	BOTH	ELEM
portrait	0.376	0.321	0.186	0.453	0.412	0.255
landscapes	0.514	0.325	0.219	0.456	0.442	0.458
architecture	0.495	0.326	0.186	0.465	0.412	0.392
animal	0.455	0.367	0.193	0.484	0.429	0.278
plant	0.507	0.322	0.107	0.429	0.391	0.367
street	0.379	0.223	0.091	0.346	0.361	0.246

Linear regression is performed to examine to which extent the overall aesthetic quality level (i.e., ***M***) and subjectivity (i.e., ***S***) are explained by the word frequencies of the six groups. The total word frequencies of the groups, X_i (i=1,…,6), are considered as independent variables. And, the dependent variable, Y, is ***M*** or ***S***. We aim to find the regression coefficients β_i for each X_i of the linear regression model given by

$$Y = \beta_0 + \beta_1 X_1 + \beta_2 X_2 + \beta_3 X_3 + \beta_4 X_4 + \beta_5 X_5 + \beta_6 X_6 + \varepsilon \qquad (1)$$

where ε means the prediction error. Table 5 shows the results of the regression analysis. For ***M***, the correlation coefficients are higher than 0.7 in most cases. A lower correlation for the *architecture* category is mainly due to a weak correlation of the POSI group in Table 3. For ***S***, correlation coefficients up to about 0.6 are obtained, while the category-dependence is higher than for ***M***. A lower correlation for the *street* category than the other categories is due to the low correlations shown in Table 4. The highest correlations are obtained for the *animal* and *landscape* categories (0.595 and 0.581, respectively). These observations indicate that the extent to which creativity and unusualness (CREA), personal preference (PERS), and simultaneous existence of aesthetically positive and negative aspects (BOTH) explain subjectivity depends on the image content.

Table 5. Regression results in terms of Pearson correlation coefficient

category	*M*	*S*
portrait	0.718	0.497
landscapes	0.744	0.581
architecture	0.684	0.560
animal	0.732	0.595
plant	0.739	0.578
street	0.761	0.448

5. CONCLUSION

In this paper, we investigated subjectivity in aesthetic photo quality assessment. By analyzing the words in users' comments for photos in DPChallenge, we investigated what contributes to aesthetic subjectivity. It was found that creativity/unusualness and simultaneous existence of positive and negative aspects are notable sources provoking subjectivity. It was also shown that the image content plays an important role in determining the acceptability of unusualness and the amount of influence of basic low level aesthetic elements to subjectivity.

6. ACKNOWLEDGMENTS

This research was supported by the MSIP (Ministry of Science, ICT and Future Planning), Korea, under the "IT Consilience Creative Program" (IITP-2015-R0346-15-1008) supervised by the IITP (Institute for Information & Communications Technology Promotion).

7. REFERENCES

[1] Tong, H., Li, M., Zhang, H. -J., He, J., and Zhang, C. 2005. Classification of digital photos taken by photographers or home users. In *Proceedings of Pacific Rim Conference on Advances in Multimedia Information Processing*, 198-205.

[2] Ke, Y., Tang, X., and Jing, F. 2006. The design of high-level features for photo quality assessment. In *Proceedings of IEEE Computer Society Conference on Computer Vision and Pattern Recognition*, 419-426.

[3] Datta, R., Joshi, D., Li, J., and Wang, J. 2006. Studying aesthetics in photographic images using a computational approach. In *Proceedings of European Conference on Computer Vision*, 288-301.

[4] Wong, L. -K. and Low, K. –L. 2009. Saliency-enhanced image aesthetics class prediction. In *Proceedings of IEEE International Conference on Image Processing,* 997-1000.

[5] Li, C., Andrew, G., Loui, A. C., and Chan, T. 2010. Aesthetic quality assessment of consumer photos with faces. In *Proceedings of IEEE International Conference on Image Processing,* 3221-3224.

[6] Marchesotti, L., Perponnin, F., Larlus, D., and Csurka, G. 2011. Assessing the aesthetic quality of photographs using generic image descriptors. In *Proceedings of IEEE International Conference on Computer Vision,* 1784-1791.

[7] Zhang, L., Gao, Y., Zimmermann, R., Tian, Q., and Li, X. 2014. Fusion of multichannel local and global structural cues for photo aesthetics evaluation. *IEEE Transactions on Image Processing, 23*, 3, 1419-1429.

[8] Fedorovskaya, E. A. and De Ridder, H. 2013. Subjective matters: from image quality to image psychology. In *Proceedings of IS&T/SPIE Electronic Imaging*, 86510O-1-86510O-11.

[9] Palmer, S. E. and Schloss, K. B. 2010. Human preference for individual colors. In *Proceedings of IS&T/SPIE Electronic Imaging*, 752718-1-752718-12.

[10] Chu, S. L., Fedorovskaya, E., Quek, F., and Snyder, J. 2013. The effect of familiarity on perceived interestingness of images. In *Proceedings of IS&T/SPIE Electronic Imaging*, 86511C-1-86511C-12.

[11] Fedrizzi, L. 2012. Beauty and its perception: historical development of concepts, neuroaesthetics, and gender-differences. *Rendiconti Lincei, 23*, 3, 259-269.

EEG Connectivity Analysis in Perception of Tone-mapped High Dynamic Range Videos

Seong-Eun Moon Jong-Seok Lee

School of Integrated Technology
& Yonsei Institute of Convergence Technology
Yonsei University
162-1 Sondo-dong, Yeonsu-gu
406-840 Incheon, Republic of Korea

{se.moon, jong-seok.lee}@yonsei.ac.kr

ABSTRACT

High dynamic range (HDR) imaging has attracted attention as a new technology for immersive multimedia experience. In comparison to conventional low dynamic range (LDR) contents, HDR contents are expected to provide better quality of experience (QoE). In this paper, we investigate implicit QoE measurement of tone-mapped HDR videos by using connectivity-based EEG features that convey information about simultaneous activations of different brain regions and thus can explain better the cognitive process than the conventional features using single channel powers. Through the experiment classifying EEG signals into tone-mapped HDR and LDR, it is shown that the connectivity features, particularly those representing directed information flows between brain regions, are effective in both subject-dependent and subject-independent scenarios.

Categories and Subject Descriptors

H.1.2 [**User/Machine Systems**]: Human information processing

Keywords

EEG, high dynamic range (HDR), quality of experience (QoE), brain connectivity

1. INTRODUCTION

When natural scenes are captured in the conventional imaging format, some of details that the human visual system (HVS) can capture are lost because of the limited dynamic range of the conventional low dynamic range (LDR) imaging. The high dynamic range (HDR) imaging is expected to reproduce natural lighting better than the LDR imaging and preserve fine details better using a higher dynamic range. Ultimately, the goal of the HDR imaging is to deliver better quality of experience (QoE) of visual contents to end-users. Therefore, it is important to understand and measure the perceptual quality of visual contents for QoE-optimized HDR imaging systems.

Methodologies of multimedia QoE measurement can be divided into two general categories: explicit approaches and implicit approaches. The former indicates the traditional subjective assessment, where users rate target contents explicitly. It has been adopted popularly for understanding QoE, however, in recent years implicit approaches are actively studied. Instead of asking users to rate perceived QoE, the implicit approaches monitor physiological signals changing due to the perceptual mechanism. Among various physiological signals, cerebral physiological signals, such as electroencephalography (EEG), functional magnetic resonance imaging (fMRI), and functional near-infrared spectroscopy (fNIRS), have been mainly studied because they contain high-level cognition information with high temporal and spatial resolutions in comparison to peripheral physiological channels such as galvanic skin response, body temperature, heart rate, etc.

In [9], EEG was used for evaluating the quality of JPEG images. It was shown that, the EEG channels in the occipital area respond to JPEG artifacts. The visual fatigue of 3D contents was investigated by using fMRI in [5]. A statistical test was conducted to evaluate the difference of brain activities for small and large visual depths, and statistical significance was observed in the frontal eye field.

These results are usually based on the signal power or activation of single brain regions. On the other hand, the microstate, also called connectivity, of the brain has been introduced in [8], which refers to functional connections between different brain regions. It is considered as the 'atom of thought', meaning that it represents a fundamental unit of cognition. In [7], it was shown that EEG connectivity features are useful for distinguishing different emotional responses.

Previously, the perceptual experience of tone-mapped HDR videos was investigated in comparison to LDR videos based on the EEG features representing signal powers in different frequency bands [10]. It was revealed that the power

MM'15, October 26–30, 2015, Brisbane, Australia.
© 2015 ACM. ISBN 978-1-4503-3459-4/15/10 ...$15.00.
DOI: http://dx.doi.org/10.1145/2733373.2806382.

of the gamma frequency band is particularly related to the perception of tone-mapped HDR videos.

In this paper, we pay attention to the connectivity between EEG electrode channels for implicit QoE measurement. Connectivity-based features are employed for classification between tone-mapped HDR and LDR videos in subject-dependent and subject-independent classification scenarios. Moreover, we discuss effective types of the connectivity features and frequency bands based on their classification performance.

2. DATA SET

The EEG data set constructed in [10] is employed for this study. It contains EEG data of five subjects, three males and two females, under the condition of watching tone-mapped HDR and LDR videos. The video stimuli consist of five pairs of tone-mapped HDR and LDR videos containing daily indoor and outdoor scenes. For the tone-mapping process, the video tone-mapping operator (TMO) by Boitard et al. [1] was employed with the photographic image TMO by Reinhard et al. [11]. All videos have a full HD resolution (1920×1080 pixels) with a frame rate of 30 fps. Their lengths range between 20 and 50 seconds. The EEG data was recorded by the 32-channel Biosemi ActiveTwo system. Additionally, four electrodes were used for rejecting eye blinking and eye movement artifacts. Baseline signals recorded during first 10 seconds with a gray screen are followed by stimulated signals.

3. METHODS

3.1 Pre-processing

The recorded EEG signals are downsampled to 256 Hz and band-pass filtered between 2-100 Hz. The Cz electrode is used as a scalp reference. Then, eye relevant artifacts and line artifacts are removed by using the independent component analysis. One-second EEG signals are removed from both at the beginning and end of each trial to acquire stabilized EEG signals only. Then, the resulting signals are divided into 10 second-long segments as in [10]. As a result, 28 EEG segments are obtained for each subject. Moreover, EEG signals in the frequency bands of theta (4-7 Hz), alpha (8-13 Hz), beta (14-29 Hz), and gamma (30-47 Hz) are extracted for the following feature extraction process. All pre-processing is implemented with the EEGlab ToolBox [3].

3.2 Feature Extraction

In this study, three types of connectivity-based features, namely, the Pearson correlation coefficient (PCC), directed transfer function (DTF), and phase locking value (PLV), are employed. These three types of features are extracted either from the entire EEG signals or for each frequency band.

Pearson correlation coefficient (PCC) is defined as follows:

$$PCC_{m,n} = \frac{1}{T}\sum_{i=1}^{T} \frac{cov_i(m,n)}{\sigma_{i,m}\sigma_{i,n}}, \tag{1}$$

where $cov_i(m,n)$ and $\sigma_{i,m}$ indicate the covariance of the signals of EEG channels m and n and the standard deviation of the signal of EEG channel m in the i-th time window, respectively. T represents the number of time windows. We use a non-overlapping time window having a length of 125 ms. Considering all pairwise combinations of the 31 EEG channels, total 465 ($= 31 \times 30/2$) PCC features are obtained for each segment.

Phase locking value (PLV) [6] indicates significance of the phase covariance between two signals, and can be described as

$$PLV_{m,n} = \frac{1}{T}\sum_{i=1}^{T} |\exp\{j(\phi_{i,m} - \phi_{i,n})\}| \tag{2}$$

where $\phi_{i,m}$ is the phase of EEG channel m in the i-th time window. Similarly to PCC, total 465 ($= 31 \times 30/2$) PLV features are acquired.

Directed transfer function (DTF) [4] is based on the multichannel auto-regressive (AR) model expressed as

$$\sum_{d=0}^{D} A_d x_{i-d} = e_i, \tag{3}$$

where $x_i = (x_{1,i}, x_{2,i}, ..., x_{k,i})$ is a vector of the EEG signals of k channels in the i-th time window, and $e_i = (e_{1,i}, e_{2,i}, ..., e_{k,i})$ is a vector of multivariate uncorrelated white noises in the i-th time window. A_d is a $k \times k$ matrix of AR model coefficients of the d-th order, and D is the model order determined empirically. The above equation can be expressed in the frequency domain with a transfer function $H(f)$ between signals and noises:

$$X(f) = H(f)E(f) \tag{4}$$

where $X(f)$ and $E(f)$ indicate transformed EEG signals and white noises of frequency f, respectively. The (m,n)-th element of the matrix $H(f)$, $H_{m,n}(f)$, indicates the connection between the m-th and n-th EEG channels. DTF is obtained from $H_{m,n}(f)$ via normalization over all channels and summation over the considered frequency range (F), i.e.:

$$DTF_{m,n} = \frac{1}{F}\sum_{f} \frac{|H_{m,n}(f)|}{\sqrt{\sum_{l=1}^{k} |H_{m,l}(f)|^2}} \tag{5}$$

Because DTF measures directional information flows, we obtain $31 \times 31 = 961$ DTF features for each segment.

3.3 Classification

Support vector machines (SVMs) with radial basis function (RBF) kernels are adopted as binary classifiers for tone-mapped HDR videos versus LDR videos classifications. Particularly, the LIBSVM package is used [2].

Two classification scenarios are considered: subject-dependent and subject-independent classification. In the former scenario, training and testing classifiers are done within each subject. Among the 28 segments obtained from the segmentation process, training and parameter optimization are conducted using 27 segments, and the remaining one segment is used for testing. This is repeated until all segments are tested. In the latter scenario, the data of one subject are used for testing, and the data of the remaining subjects are used for training and parameter optimization. This is also repeated until all subjects are tested.

Table 1: Classification accuracies of power-based and connectivity-based features [%]. For PCC, PLV, and DTF, the features are extracted either from the entire EEG signals (denoted as "All") or for each frequency band (denoted as "Alpha", "Beta", "Gamma", and "Theta").

		Subject-dependent classification	Subject-independent classification
Power [10]		82.14	42.86
PCC	All	92.14	50.00
	Alpha	73.57	51.43
	Beta	80.00	50.00
	Gamma	84.29	50.00
	Theta	70.00	50.00
PLV	All	86.43	50.00
	Alpha	55.71	64.29
	Beta	82.14	45.71
	Gamma	87.86	50.00
	Theta	62.86	46.43
DTF	All	93.57	55.71
	Alpha	80.00	55.00
	Beta	73.57	67.86
	Gamma	92.86	62.14
	Theta	73.57	57.14

The parameters of SVMs, i.e., the width of the RBF kernels, are optimized for each trial using a grid search in a leave-one-out cross-validation scheme. Among the training data, one segment is set aside for validation, and the validation is repeated until all segments are used for validation.

3.4 Results

The average classification accuracies of different features are shown in Table 1. The second row of Table 1 represents classification accuracies of power-based features selected by using Fisher's linear discriminant analysis in [10]. In the subject-dependent classification scheme, where the accuracy using the power-based features is 82.14%, higher classification accuracies are obtained using any of the three connectivity features extracted from the entire signals and gamma frequency band. However, using alpha, beta, or theta frequency bands, classification accuracies are similar to or lower than those by the power-based features. In the subject-independent classification scheme, all cases of the connectivity features yield higher classification accuracies than the power-based features.

It is noteworthy that the gamma frequency band, which was proved as important for classification in [10], also shows good performance in the subject-dependent classification based on the brain signal connectivity. The connectivity features of the gamma frequency band also exhibits better classification performance than the power-based features in the subject-independent classification scenario.

However, in the subject-independent classification, the other frequency bands show better performance than the gamma frequency band; PLV for the alpha frequency band and DTF for the beta frequency band outperform their counterparts for the gamma frequency band, respectively. This indicates that the connectivity of the gamma frequency band is a relatively individual representation of the perception of tone-mapped HDR videos.

The individual difference is one of the most challenging issues in implicit monitoring of perceptual responses. The perception of multimedia contents is usually highly individualized depending on personal past experience, environment, and so on. The significant decrease of accuracies in the subject-independent classification compared to the subject-dependent case is considered as an effect of such personalized factors.

Overall, the features based on connectivity achieve notable improvement in comparison to the power-based features, particularly for the subject-independent classification scheme. This implies that the connectivity of different brain regions conveys information that is more relevant and more general for classification of perceptual responses for tone-mapped HDR and LDR videos.

When the three types of connectivity features are compared, DTF exhibits best performance. PCC and PLV examine the undirected functional connectivity between brain regions, whereas DTF concerns directed causal dependencies of brain signals. That is, DTF contain additional cues of information flows. Thus, it can be concluded that capturing the causal relation between brain regions that evoked during video perception is beneficial for implicit QoE measurement.

To examine the difference of the connectivity patterns between tone-mapped HDR and LDR video stimuli, Figure 1 visualizes the average DTF values extracted from the entire signal among all subjects, where a darker line indicates a higher DTF value. Because DTF has directional information, the DTF values need to be disjointed depending on its direction. Therefore, the 31×31 DTF matrix is divided into upper and lower triangular parts for visualization. While the tone-mapped HDR and LDR videos exhibit similar patterns, the DTF values flowing to the F8 and Fz electrodes slightly decrease for the tone-mapped HDR videos in comparison to the LDR videos in the upper triangular parts. Instead, the DTF values to the Fp2 electrode become larger in the tone-mapped HDR case. When the lower triangular parts are examined, the DTF values from the T7 electrode decrease, and the DTF values from the F7 and to the P8 electrode increase in the case of tone-mapped HDR.

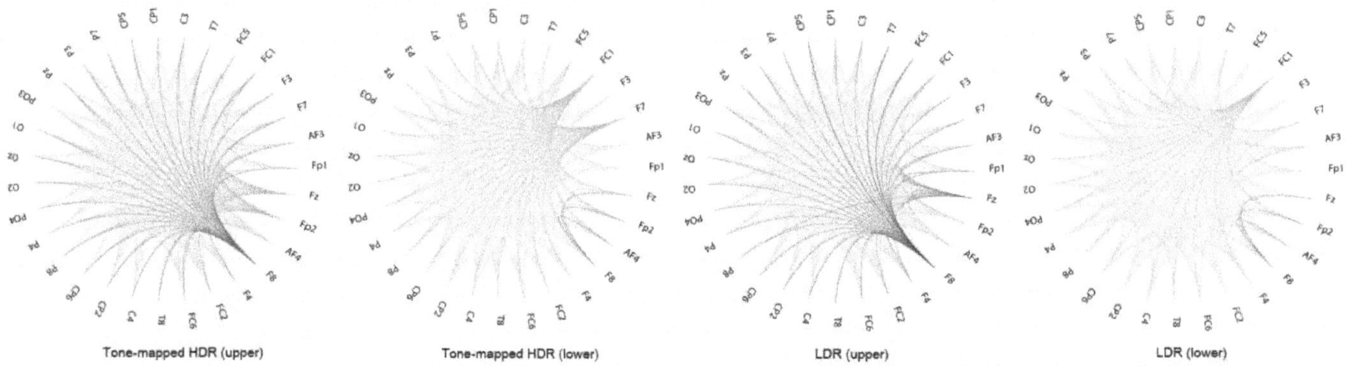

Figure 1: Visualizing information flows between pairs of electrodes in terms of DTF values of the entire signal. The upper (or lower) panels are for the upper (or lower) triangular parts of the DTF matrices.

4. CONCLUSION

In this paper, we have adopted connectivity-based EEG features to investigate the perceptual experience of tone-mapped HDR videos. A SVM classification system was constructed to examine the feasibility and effectiveness of the brain connectivity-based features as physiological cues of the perception of tone-mapped HDR videos. Higher classification accuracies were obtained in both the subject-dependent and the subject-independent classification schemes.

In addition, we obtained valuable findings regarding the EEG connectivity features. First, the gamma frequency band, which was significantly employed for classification in [10], consistently shows higher performance. Second, as shown by the significant increase of the classification accuracies in the subject-independent classification scenario, the connectivity-based features are more robust to individual differences than the power-based features. Third, the directed causal relation between brain regions contained in DTF is more effective than the undirected functional connectivity.

5. ACKNOWLEDGMENTS

This research was supported by the MSIP(Ministry of Science, ICT and Future Planning), Korea, under the "IT Consilience Creative Program" (IITP-2015-R0346-15-1008) supervised by the IITP(Institute for Information & Communications Technology Promotion), and by the Basic Science Research Program through the National Research Foundation of Korea funded by the MSIP (2013R1A1A1007822).

6. REFERENCES

[1] R. Boitard, K. Bouatouch, R. Cozot, D. Thoreau, and A. Gruson. Temporal coherency for video tone mapping. In *Proceedings of the SPIE Optical Engineering + Applications*, 2012.

[2] C.-C. Chang and C.-J. Lin. LIBSVM: A library for support vector machines. *ACM Transactions on Intelligent Systems and Technology*, 2:27:1–27, 2011.

[3] A. Delorme and S. Makeig. EEGLAB: an open source toolbox for analysis of single-trial EEG dynamics including independent component analysis. *Journal of Neuroscience Methods*, 134(1):9–21, 2004.

[4] M. J. Kaminski and K. J. Blinowska. A new method of the description of the information flow in the brain structures. *Biological Cybernetics*, 65(3):230–210, 1991.

[5] D. Kim, Y. J. Jung, E. Kim, Y. M. Ro, and H. Park. Human brain response to visual fatigue caused by stereoscopic depth perception. In *Proceedings of the 17th International Conference on Digital Signal Processing*, pages 1–5, 2011.

[6] J.-P. Lachaux, E. Rodriguez, J. Martinerie, and F. J. Varela. Measuring phase synchrony in brain signals. *Human Brain Mapping*, 8(4):194–208, 1999.

[7] Y.-Y. Lee and S. Hsieh. Classifying different emotional states by means of EEG-based functional connectivity patterns. *PloS One*, 9(4):e95415, 2014.

[8] D. Lehmann, W. Strik, B. Henggeler, T. Koenig, and M. Koukkou. Brain electric microstates and momentary conscious mind states as building blocks of spontaneous thinking: I. visual imagery and abstract thoughts. *International Journal of Psychophysiology*, 29(1):1–11, 1998.

[9] L. Lindemann and M. Magnor. Assessing the quality of compressed images using EEG. In *Proceedings of the International Conference on Image Processing*, pages 3109–3112, 2011.

[10] S.-E. Moon and J.-S. Lee. Classifying perceptual experience of tone-mapped high dynamic range videos through EEG. *Proceedings of the 1st International Workshop on Perception Inspired Video Processing*, pages 27–32, 2014.

[11] E. Reinhard, M. Stark, P. Shirley, and J. Ferwerda. Photographic tone reproduction for digital images. *ACM Transactions on Graphics*, 21(3):267–276, 2002.

Polyphonic Music Modelling with LSTM-RTRBM

Qi Lyu
qilyu.pub@gmail.com

Zhiyong Wu
zywu@se.cuhk.edu.hk

Jun Zhu
dcszj@tsinghua.edu.cn

Center for Bio-inspired Computing Research
State Key Lab of Intelligent Technology & Systems
Tsinghua National Lab for Information Science & Technology
Department of Computer Science & Technology, Tsinghua Univ., Beijing 100084, China

ABSTRACT

Recent interest in music information retrieval and related technologies is exploding. However, very few of the existing techniques take advantage of the recent advancements in neural networks. The challenges of developing effective browsing, searching and organization techniques for the growing bodies of music collections call for more powerful statistical models. In this paper, we present LSTM-RTRBM, a new neural network model for the problem of creating accurate yet flexible models of polyphonic music. Our model integrates the ability of Long Short-Term Memory (LSTM) in memorizing and retrieving useful history information, together with the advantage of Restricted Boltzmann Machine (RBM) in high dimensional data modelling. Our approach greatly improves the performance of polyphonic music sequence modelling, achieving the state-of-the-art results on multiple datasets.

Categories and Subject Descriptors

H.5.5 [**Sound and Music Computing**]: Modelling

General Terms

Algorithm

1. INTRODUCTION

Music is among the most widely consumed types of signal streams. Models for finding, extracting and reproducing musical temporal structure are of considerable interest. In particular, generative models for composing (good) music might have not only artistic value but also commercial potential. Besides that, in the same way that natural language models tremendously improve the performance of speech recognition systems, *musical language model* can also improve audio music recognition, i.e., the transcription of raw audio into symbolic notations [13]. Moreover, ad hoc music retrieval could be possible, e.g., by building a model for every piece of music in the collection and then ranking each piece according to the probability that model produces when a query is provided.

A generative theory of music can be constructed by explicitly coding music rules in some logic or formal grammar. This approach is sometimes called an expert or knowledge engineering system. Although these methods could achieve impressive results in some cases, they require extensive exploitation of musical knowledge, often specific to each composer or style. Another approach relies on statistical learning or empirical induction, such as hidden Markov models (HMMs) [1], Markov random fields (MRFs) [10], etc. These Markov models are statistical models of random sequences with the typical assumption that the probability for generating the next symbol depends only on a limited past. It is often hard to choose the order of Markov models because a small fixed order will certainly limit the representation ability, while a large one will result in a large number of parameters that are difficult to estimate, with no guarantee of better performance.

Non-symbolic approaches such as Recurrent Neural Networks (RNNs), which become popular with the recent breakthrough in deep learning, can also capture the knowledge of music. For example, the system in [5] could learn entire songs given a melody and the associated chord sequence, and the RNNs combined with restricted Boltzmann machines (RBMs) for feature representation [3] have showed the best results in music generation recently. However, the music composed by RNN-type models often suffers from a lack of global structure. Although networks can learn note-by-note transition probabilities and even reproduce phrases, the attempts to learn an entire musical form and to use that knowledge to guide composition have been unsuccessful. The reason for this failure seems to be that RNNs cannot keep track of temporally distant events that indicate global music structure. On the other hand, Long Short-term Memory (LSTM) [8] has succeeded in similar domains where other RNNs have failed, with state-of-the-art results in various sequence processing tasks, including speech recognition [7], handwriting recognition [6] and machine translation [17].

In this work, we present LSTM-RTRBM, a hybrid model for the notoriously tricky problem of capturing the long-term structure in polyphonic music. Our model embeds long-term memory into the

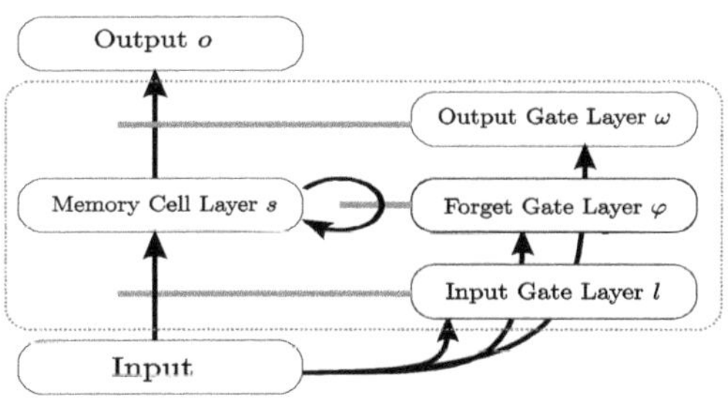

Figure 1: Layer-wise architecture of a LSTM block (peephole connections omitted) picture adapted from [11].

MM'15, October 26–30, 2015, Brisbane, Australia.

DOI: http://dx.doi.org/10.1145/2733373.2806383 .

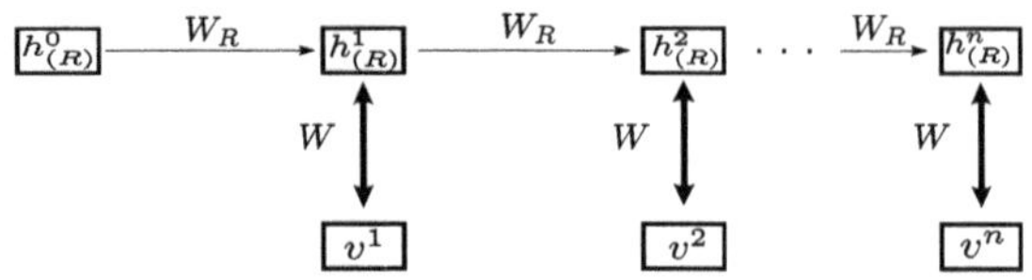

Figure 2: Structure of RTRBM.

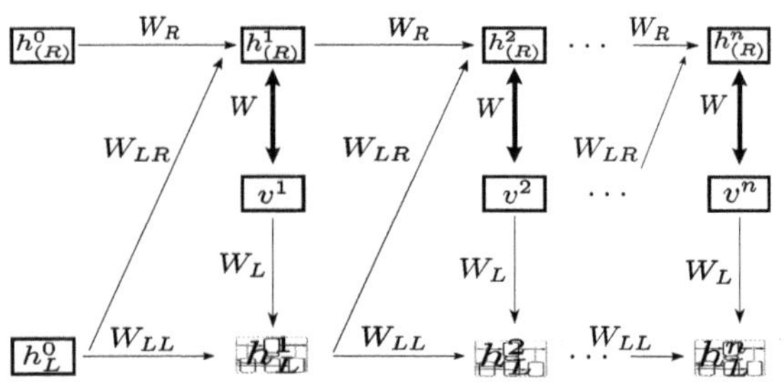

Figure 3: Structure of LSTM-RTRBM.

Recurrent Temporal RBM (RTRBM) [16], by increasing a bypassing channel from data source filtered by a recurrent LSTM layer. We show that our LSTM-RTRBM model increases performance and advances the state-of-the-art results even without additional optimizations used in the previous models.

The rest of the paper is organized as follows: In Section 2 we briefly introduce LSTM, RBM and RTRBM as background. In Section 3 we present our new model. We then validate our model on benchmark datasets in Section 4, and present our results on musical sequences in Section 5.

2. BACKGROUND

In this section, we briefly introduce the building blocks of our model. More details can be found in supplementary materials.

LSTM is a special kind of RNN that can store and retrieve information from input streams and do complicated tasks like classifying, processing and most importantly, predicting time series when there are very long time lags of an unknown size between important events. As illustrated in Fig. 1, LSTM is enabled to do so by utilizing memory cells that use logistic and linear units with multiplicative interactions with input and output gates. The information gets into (out of) the memory cell whenever a logistic input (output) gate is turned on. The memory cell state is kept from irrelevant information by keeping the input gate off, and its information stored can be later probed by turning the output gate on. Forget gates can reset the memory cell state for storage of new information, so that in continuous prediction the memory cells can keep the information when useful and forget the information when useless. With the extension of peephole connections, which are the direct connections from memory cell states to gates, the performance of LSTM is improved. The behavior of all these gates can be learned, rendering LSTM's ability in long term memory compared with simple recurrent networks without such kind of architecture.

The RBM is a typical kind of product-of-experts (PoE) model, which defines a probability distribution over the visible vector v (inputs) and the hidden vector h as:

$$P(v,h) = \exp(v^\top b_v + h^\top b_h + v^\top W h)/Z \tag{1}$$

where b_v, b_h are vectors of biases for the visible and hidden vectors respectively, W is the matrix of connection weights, Z is the usually intractable partition function that ensures $P(v,h)$ is a well-normalized probability distribution and $x^\top$ is the transpose of x while $v^T(h^T)$ is the entire sequence of $v^t(h^t)$ from start to time T.

The Recurrent Temporal RBM (RTRBM) [16] (See Fig. 2) is a sequence of conditional RBMs (one at each time step) whose parameters are time-dependent on the sequence history. Given previous hidden units h^{t-1} $(t > 1)$, the conditional distributions for current hidden units are factorized and takes the form:

$$P(h^t|v^t, h^{t-1}) = \sigma(W^\top v^t + W_R^\top h^{t-1} + b_h) \tag{2}$$

where $\sigma(x) = (1 + e^{-x})^{-1}$ is the element-wise logistic sigmoid function. To sample v^T from RTRBM, we can use the following:

$$\begin{aligned} P(v^t, h^t|h^{t-1}) = \exp((v^t)^\top b_v + (v^t)^\top W h^t + \\ (h^t)^\top (b_h + W_R h_R^{t-1}))/Z(h^{t-1}) \end{aligned} \tag{3}$$

The RTRBM is defined by its joint probability distribution:

$$P(v^T, h^T) = \prod_{t=2}^{T} P(v^t|h^{t-1}) P(h^t|v^t, h^{t-1}) \cdot P(v^1) P(h^1|v^1)$$

3. LSTM-RTRBM

Though previous models have merits in modelling different aspects of data, they cannot meet all the requirements on modelling music sequences. In this section, we present LSTM-RTRBM, a new model that conjoins the strengths of LSTM and RTRBM.

Specifically, the creation of music is a complicated mental activity and we would like our neural network model to mimic this process, especially from the information memorizing and retrieving perspective. Music feature extraction is a sort of perceptual categorization and grouping of music data. Music notes processed at this stage can activate those parts of long-term memory evoked by similar notes in the past. Activated long-term memory at this point forms a context for current awareness. Long-term memory of conceptual categories that reaches higher states of activation can then persist as current short-term memory while other *semi-activated* remains as context or degrades with time, and the information being circulated in short-term memory will cause modifications in permanent long-term memory [15]. For example, in order to complete a melody line, the beginning of the music sequence needs to be held in mind while the rest is played, a task which is carried out by the short-term memory. And the long-term memory will serve as the theme and emotion that will help maintain the global coherence of music. The existence of both the short-term and the long-term memory is vital for generating melodic and coherent music sequences.

Moreover, polyphonic music sequences are of high dimensions where simply predicting the expected value at the next time step for generating music sequences is not satisfying, since the conditional distribution is very often muti-modal. For example, it is obvious that the occurrence of a particular note at a particular time modifies considerably the probability with which other notes may occur at the same time. In other words, notes appear together in correlated patterns cannot be conveniently described by a normal RNN architecture designed for multi-class classification task, because enumerating all configurations of the variable to predict would be very expensive. This difficulty motivates energy-based models which allow us to express the log-likelihood of a given configuration by an arbitrary energy function, such as the RBM.

In this context, we wish to combine the ability of RBM to represent a complicated distribution for each time step, together with a temporal model in sequence. We consider both long-term memory and short-term memory in our design of guide and learning modules, by integrating LSTM with normal recurrent models, RTRBM in our case. Adding LSTM units to RTRBM is not trivial, considering RTRBM's hidden units and visible units are intertwined in inference and learning. The simplest way to circumvent this difficulty is to use bypass connections from LSTM units to the hidden units besides the existing recurrent connections of hidden units, as in LSTM-RTRBM (Fig. 3).

The recurrent hidden units ($h_{(R)}$s in Fig. 3) serves as the short-term memory and the LSTM units ($h_{(L)}$s) serves as the long-term memory. To sample v^T, we can simply use the following:

$$P(v^t, h^t|h^{t-1}) = \exp((v^t)^\top b_v + (v^t)^\top W h_t + (h^t)^\top (b_h + W_R h_R^{t-1} + W_L h_L^{t-1}))/Z(h^{t-1}) \quad (4)$$

By this means, there are two channels for temporal information flow, the direct connection (W_R) between the conditional RBM at each time step, and the connection (W_{LR}) from the recurrent LSTM units of previous time steps. The main computation complexity comes from the repeated sampling procedure of RBM learning and replacing some hidden units in RBM with LSTM units actually boosts learning speed. The inference and sampling procedure is roughly the same as in RTRBM while the Backpropagation Through Time (BPTT) procedure is a bit complex. Due to space limit, we defer the details to supplementary materials.

4. BASELINE EXPERIMENTS

Before presenting the music modelling experiments, we first compare the performance of our model with RTRBM on the human motion capture data experiment, a classic baseline experiment for evaluating sequence models. The human motion capture dataset[1] represents human motion by sequences of joint angles, translations, and rotations of the base of spine. This dataset is recorded on real persons and has more repeated patterns than normal music sequences, such as the half circular motion of arm and the alternative moving and static status of feet. Since the data consists of 49 real values per time step, we use the Gaussian RBM variant (see supplementary materials for details) for this task. The mean squared prediction error per dimension per time step is 0.32 for the RTRBM with 200 logistic hidden units and reduced to 0.13 by LSTM-RTRBM with 100 logistic hidden units and 100 LSTM units, and to 0.09 with twice as many units. It can be seen that with the inclusion of long-term information in LSTM-RTRBM, the prediction is significantly more accurate and stable.

5. MODELLING SEQUENCES OF POLYPHONIC MUSIC

In this section, we show results with the main application of interest: probabilistic modelling of sequences of polyphonic music. We conduct experiments on two music datasets of different styles: MuseData, an electronic library of orchestral and piano classical music from CCARH 4[2] and JSB chorales, the entire corpus of 382 four-part harmonized chorales by J. S. Bach with the split of [1].

Each dataset contains at least 7 hours of polyphonic music and the total duration is approximately 29 hours. The polyphony (number of simultaneous notes) varies from 0 to 15 and the average polyphony is 4.2. We use a completely general piano-roll representation with an input of 88 binary visible units that span the whole range of piano from A0 to C8 and temporally aligned on an integer fraction of the beat (quarter note). Consequently, pieces with different time signatures will not have their measures start at the same interval. Although it is not strictly necessary, learning is facilitated if the sequences are transposed in a common tonality (e.g. C major/minor) as preprocessing.

In addition to the models previously described, the results (taken from [3]) of the following commonly used methods are also listed for comprehensive comparison:

- The simplest baseline model is the Gaussian density model (PREVIOUS + GAUSSIAN) with the previous frame as mean value $u = v^{(t-1)}$ and learned covariance Σ.
- The neural autoregressive distribution estimator (NADE) [9] is a model inspired by the RBM, which decomposes the joint distribution of observations into tractable conditional distributions, and modelling each conditional using a non-linear function similar to a conditional of an RBM. Thus it is a tractable model and can be further optimized with its exact gradient.
- Other common methods include Gaussian mixture models (GMM), hidden Markov models (HMM) using GMM indices as their state, and multilayer perceptron (MLP) with the last n time steps as input.

We adopt the classic momentum training regime, with learning rate 0.01 and momentum 0.9. The learning starts with CD_{10} (10 steps of Contrastive Divergence) for the first 1000 weight updates, which then switches to CD_{25}. We use 88 hidden units and 88 LSTM units, the same number as the input and the output dimension, which is trained faster than using hundreds of hidden units in the RTRBM, for the main computation takes place in the CD steps (not needed if changed to LSTM units) . The partition function of conditional RBM at each time step is calculated with 100 run of annealed importance sampling [14] on GPU. The Log-likelihood and expected frame-level accuracy [2] are presented in Table 1. There are some key observations:

- It generally improves the performance of the model, to predict the parameters of the distribution of the data, i.e., the hid-

Table 1: Log-likelihood (LL) and expected frame-level accuracy (ACC%) for various musical models in the generation task. The double line separates frame-level models (above) and models with a temporal component (below).

MODEL	MUSEDATA		JSB CHORALES	
	LL	ACC%	LL	ACC%
RANDOM	-61.00	3.74	-61.00	4.42
GMM	-12.20	7.37	-11.90	15.84
NADE	-10.06	7.65	-7.19	17.88
RBM	-9.56	8.19	-7.43	4.47
PREVIOUS + GAUSSIAN	-12.90	25.93	-19.00	18.36
GMM+HMM	-11.17	13.93	-11.89	19.24
MLP	-7.94	25.68	-8.70	30.41
RNN	-8.13	23.25	-8.71	28.46
RNN(HF)	-7.19	30.49	-8.58	29.41
LSTM	-6.88	30.15	-7.92	30.07
RNN-NADE	-6.74	24.91	-5.83	32.11
RTRBM	-6.35	30.85	-6.35	30.17
RNN-RBM	-6.01	**34.02**	-6.27	33.12
RNN-NADE(HF)	**-5.60**	32.60	-5.56	32.50
LSTM-RTRBM	**-5.54**	**33.89**	**-4.72**	**35.22**

[1] people.csail.mit.edu/ehsu/work/sig05stf
[2] www.musedata.org

Figure 4: Slice of sample music generated by LSTM-RTRBM.

den units of RBM, rather than the raw data itself. However, LSTM or RBM alone only gives moderate performance; it is the combination of both the best recurrent model and the best static feature extraction model that gives the best performance.

- The combined RNN-NADE model with Hessian-free (HF) optimization [12] is a robust distribution estimator because the RNN part and the NADE part are optimized jointly, though frame-level NADEs are less powerful than RBMs. The use of HF optimization significantly helps the density estimation and prediction performance, although considerably increases the training time. On the other hand, the approximated gradient and iterative CD estimation process alienate models with RBM from optimization methods like HF.
- LSTM performs better than standard RNN with strong optimization method like HF generally, and the inclusion of LSTM units significantly improves the performance of the model (LSTM-RTRBM compared with RTRBM), achieving state-of-the-art result in these datasets. It can be conjectured that NADE combined with LSTM might give better result with the aid of HF optimization.

We also evaluate our models qualitatively by generating sample sequences (see Fig. 4 for a glimpse). The model has learned the chords (such as sequential D major triads in Fig. 4), local and global temporal coherence, melody lines and generate music that is harmonic and coherent. With the same configuration, LSTM-RTRBM could learn melody lines from both datasets while RTRBM generates inconsistent and unpleasant sample sequences. However, all the recurrent temporal model forms a closed loop that have no new incitations from outside, making the long piece of music dull. This can be solved with the technique of side-slipping [4], by playing out-of-key to produce a short sensation of surprise in a context deemed too predictable.

6. CONCLUSIONS

We investigate the problem of modelling long-term dependencies in high-dimensional polyphonic music sequences. We present a new neural network model for the problem of creating accurate yet flexible statistical models of polyphonic music, and conduct extensive experiments to evaluate the proposed model. Our model greatly improves the performance of polyphonic music modelling, achieving the state-of-the-art results on various datasets. For future work, we are interested in optimizing LSTM with hessian-free techniques for better results, and integrating side-slipping mechanism for more variable music generation.

7. ACKNOWLEDGEMENTS

Q.L and Z.W are supported by the National High Technology Research and Development Program of China (2015AA016305), the National NSF of China (61375027 and 61433018) and the Major Program for the National Social Science Foundation of China (13& ZD189). J.Z is supported by NSF of China Projects (61322308, 61332007) and Tsinghua Initiative Scientific Research Program (20121088071, 20141080934).

8. REFERENCES

[1] M. Allan and C. K. Williams. Harmonising chorales by probabilistic inference. *Advances in neural information processing systems*, 17:25–32, 2005.

[2] M. Bay, A. F. Ehmann, and J. S. Downie. Evaluation of multiple-f0 estimation and tracking systems. In *ISMIR*, pages 315–320, 2009.

[3] N. Boulanger-Lewandowski, Y. Bengio, and P. Vincent. Modeling temporal dependencies in high-dimensional sequences: Application to polyphonic music generation and transcription. In *Proceedings of the 29th International Conference on Machine Learning*, pages 1159–1166, 2012.

[4] J. Coker. *The complete method for improvisation*. Studio P/R, 1980.

[5] J. A. Franklin. Recurrent neural networks for music computation. *INFORMS Journal on Computing*, 18(3):321–338, 2006.

[6] A. Graves. *Supervised sequence labelling with recurrent neural networks*, volume 385. Springer, 2012.

[7] A. Graves, A.-r. Mohamed, and G. Hinton. Speech recognition with deep recurrent neural networks. In *International Conference on Acoustics, Speech and Signal Processing*, pages 6645–6649. IEEE, 2013.

[8] S. Hochreiter and J. Schmidhuber. Long short-term memory. *Neural computation*, 9(8):1735–1780, 1997.

[9] H. Larochelle and I. Murray. The neural autoregressive distribution estimator. *Journal of Machine Learning Research*, 15:29–37, 2011.

[10] V. Lavrenko and J. Pickens. Polyphonic music modeling with random fields. In *Proceedings of the eleventh ACM international conference on Multimedia*, pages 120–129. ACM, 2003.

[11] Q. Lyu and J. Zhu. Revisit long short-term memory: An optimization perspective. *Advances in neural information processing systems workshop on deep Learning and representation Learning*, 2014.

[12] J. Martens. Deep learning via hessian-free optimization. In *Proceedings of the 27th International Conference on Machine Learning*, pages 735–742, 2010.

[13] J. Nam, J. Ngiam, H. Lee, and M. Slaney. A classification-based polyphonic piano transcription approach using learned feature representations. In *ISMIR*, pages 175–180, 2011.

[14] R. Salakhutdinov and I. Murray. On the quantitative analysis of deep belief networks. In *Proceedings of the 25th International Conference on Machine learning*, pages 872–879. ACM, 2008.

[15] B. Snyder. *Music and memory: An introduction*. MIT press, 2000.

[16] I. Sutskever, G. E. Hinton, and G. W. Taylor. The recurrent temporal restricted boltzmann machine. In *Advances in Neural Information Processing Systems*, pages 1601–1608, 2008.

[17] I. Sutskever, O. Vinyals, and Q. V. Le. Sequence to sequence learning with neural networks. In *Advances in Neural Information Processing Systems*, pages 3104–3112, 2014.

Multi-Sensor Cello Recordings for Instantaneous Frequency Estimation

Fabian-Robert Stöter
International Audio
Laboratories Erlangen*
fabian-robert.stoeter@
audiolabs-erlangen.de

Michael Müller
Graz University of Technology
michael.g.mueller@
student.tugraz.at

Bernd Edler
International Audio
Laboratories Erlangen
bernd.edler@
audiolabs-erlangen.de

ABSTRACT

Estimating the fundamental frequency ($F0$) of a signal is a well studied task in audio signal processing with many applications. If the $F0$ varies over time, the complexity increases, and it is also more difficult to provide ground truth data for evaluation. In this paper we present a novel dataset of cello recordings addressing the lack of reference annotations for musical instruments. Besides audio data, we include sensor recordings capturing the finger position on the fingerboard which is converted into an instantaneous frequency estimate. In speech processing, the electroglottograph (EGG) is able to capture the excitation signal of the vocal tract, which is then used to generate a reference instantaneous $F0$. Inspired by this approach, we included high speed video camera recordings to extract the excitation signal originating from the moving string. The derived data can be used to analyze vibratos — a very commonly used playing style. The dataset is released under a Creative Commons license.

Categories and Subject Descriptors

H.5.5 [**Sound and Music Computing**]: Signal analysis, synthesis, and processing

Keywords

Cello; dataset; sensors; visual acoustics; fundamental frequency estimation

1. INTRODUCTION

Fundamental Frequency ($F0$) is used as the main cue of what humans perceive as pitch. The difficulty of obtaining $F0$ estimates depends on the signals complexity. If the signal is a perfectly periodic sine wave, an estimate is relatively simple to compute. In scenarios where the signal is part of a mixture, the problem of "Multi-Pitch estimation" [11] is challenging for machines. Even with monophonic signals, the problem can become rather difficult if the signal is non-stationary, meaning the fundamental frequency is being modulated over time, or in presence of noise or reverberation. Vibrato, a very common type of frequency modulation, can be generated both by humans as well as by many types of musical instruments. There is a large number of contributions addressing the problem of $F0$ estimation for audio signals, some of which are compared in [2], which shows that YIN [3] performs very good on speech and singing voice. An algorithm's performance is typically measured by comparing to a ground truth. There are several ways to obtain such a reference signal; some datasets like [6] include manual or supervised annotations. This is mostly done by overlaying the signal's spectrogram with a layer where the $F0$ contour is drawn on. This is not only a very time-consuming task, but is also prone to errors. Furthermore, the time and frequency resolution are mainly set by the resolution of the underlying spectrogram. Another method is to evaluate on synthesized data, generated from an artificial ground truth [17]. For speech signals, an EGG device (also known as laryngograph) captures the excitation of the human vocal tract. This signal is then processed by an $F0$ estimator to generate the ground truth. Such a method is accepted in published research [11, 2] because the EGG signal is considered to be easier to process than speech. To our knowledge, a similar method to evaluate $F0$ estimates on musical instrument signals does not exist. In this paper we present a novel test set consisting of violin cello tones

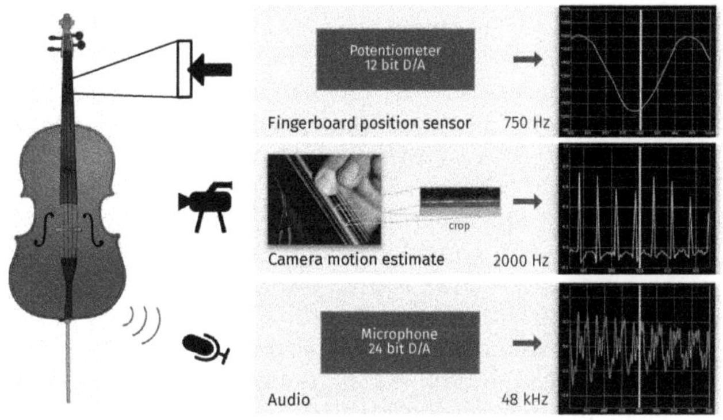

Figure 1: Overview of the multi-modal data recorded for the proposed dataset.

*The International Audio Laboratories Erlangen are a joint institution of the Friedrich-Alexander-Universität Erlangen-Nürnberg (FAU) and Fraunhofer - Institut für Integrierte Schaltungen (IIS)

MM'15, October 26–30, 2015, Brisbane, Australia.
© 2015 ACM. ISBN 978-1-4503-3459-4/15/10 ...$15.00.
DOI: http://dx.doi.org/10.1145/2733373.2806384.

in various expressions. We made use of multiple sensors to capture the most relevant processes involved in creating time-varying output signals, including video data to capture excitations from the bowed string at 2000 fps. By releasing this test set into public domain, our main contribution is to enable other researchers to improve the evaluation methods for $F0$ estimators. Also within the scope of this work, we introduce other applications of such data, useful for tasks in music information retrieval or source separation.

2. MULTI-SENSOR CELLO RECORDINGS

In this section we present our test set and describe how data from different domains was obtained. In the proposed test set we chose the violin cello for the following reasons: (1) vibrato is used as a common style for expression, (2) there is an observable physical relationship between frequency modulation and vibrato, and (3) the instrument is large enough to embed sensors to capture the vibrato. The properties of the cello are studied by research in acoustics [15, 16]. The aim of the multi-sensor recordings is to capture the major aspects of the cello while being played by a musician. We identify three main components: (1) The excitation caused by the moving bow; (2) the vibrating string, and (3) the finger, controlling the string length by rolling it on the fingerboard. The main focus of the recordings is set to analyze vibrato playing style. Since it is common that vibrato characteristics differ from musician to musician, all recordings were performed by two musicians. One is a professional cellist with 30 years of experience in a symphonic orchestra. The other musician is an amateur with less than 1 hour per week of practice. The recordings took place on a single day and were conducted on a mid-quality full-size cello equipped with sensors as described below. Due to the width of fingerboard sensors and the attached cables we were able to equip two strings (G and A) allowing to record pitches $G2, D3, D^\sharp 3, E3, A3, B3, C4, C^\sharp 4$ from both musicians. The resulting test set yields in 148 recorded notes after removal of some notes due to errors in the sensor recordings. The process for cleaning up the data is documented[1].

2.1 Audio

High-quality audio serves as the basis for this test set. The recordings took place in a professional recording studio. We used an AKG C414 condenser microphone placed at a distance of approx. 30 cm from the cello bridge. The audio was sampled by an RME MADIface A/D converter. The sample rate is 48000 kHz at 24 bit. All files are available as uncompressed PCM files.

2.2 High Speed Video Camera

Recently, Davis et. al. published a paper [4] about a visual microphone which is able to observe sound solely with a camera, pointing to objects in the sound field. In our scenario, we are interested in the excitation of the string by the bow, which is then transferred to the cello body by the bridge. The use of a camera to track the string motion is discussed in [13, 18]. By using a high speed camera focusing on the string, we are able to extract the movement pattern from the video signal. We used a professional high-speed camera and bright light sources specifically designed to minimize flicker present on the image when standard bulbs would be used. We recorded at 2000 fps at a resolution of 1024 by 786 pixels. Camera data is available as uncompressed raw video. To also be able to extract the slowly varying finger motion, we ensured the camera captured the finger movements as well as the moving string. One close-up video was made from each of the two players playing the $D^\sharp 3$ note. We decided not to include high speed camera videos for the complete test set, because of the loud noise emitted from the camera, as well as the bright set light which needs constant fan cooling.

2.3 Position and Acceleration Sensors

A vibrato on fretless instruments like a cello is different to a vibrato played on fretted instruments like a guitar, where it is induced by bending the string vertically with respect to the string axis. On the violin and violin cello it is typically played by moving or rolling the finger on the fingerboard along the string direction. By doing so the player dynamically changes the active length of the vibrating string. String length L is one of the parameters determining the frequency f of an ideal, flexible string:

$$f = \frac{1}{2L}\sqrt{\frac{T}{\rho_L}} \tag{1}$$

where ρ_L is the linear density in [kg/m], and T the string tension. Thus, assuming that a vibrato is mainly produced by varying the string length, which is set by the finger pressing the string against the fingerboard. To measure this position we used a linear membrane potentiometer. The base layer consists of material with length dependent resistance. The middle layer is made of highly conductive material. The sensor therefore acts as a resistance linearly dependent on the point where the circuit is shorted. The benefits of this sensor type are described in [8, 9]. We chose sensors of length 100 mm; a trade-off between the sensors linearity and convenience to capture multiple notes from a single finger position. The membrane sensor is thin enough to be attached on the fingerboard of the cello. Additionally the motion of the finger on the fingerboard was recorded using a 3-axis accelerometers (Texas Instruments LM335), taped on the players fingers. All sensor data was sampled by an Arduino Due microcontroller at 12 bit resolution.

2.4 Synchronization

Data synchronization is crucial in the context of high time resolution. Since manual alignment of the data is error prone, we made sure the different domains were already aligned during recording time. We therefore used a centralized ADAT clock available from the audio interface. The clock is then fed into the Arduino, sampling every 64 clock ticks effectively resulting in a sensor rate of 750 Hz. The camera could not be clocked externally. However, the high speed camera continuously records data into a fixed size ring buffer and could be triggered by an external signal. To minimize the input-output delay caused by the recording computer we used the audio interface's D/A converter to set the trigger at the audio output while recording the audio input. A 5 volt trigger signal was then fed into the Arduino and the high speed camera to trigger the recording process.

3. DERIVED DATA

In this section we present methods to derive data from the measurements targeted for $F0$ estimation purposes.

[1] `https://github.com/audiolabs/muserc`

3.1 Motion Analysis

When the bow excites the string next to the bridge position, it begins to vibrate. To analyze these displacements we use high frame rate video cropped to the region of interest. The cropped video is depicted by the light blue rectangle in Figure 1. The displacement of the string in the video image is then processed by calculating the dense optical flow [7] using an implementation in OpenCV. We then normalized the velocity vector. High-pass filtering to remove the DC component results in one-dimensional string motion $M(n)$ also plotted in Figure 1. The captured excitation shows high similarity with the slip-and-stick model typically used for simulations of bow excitations [15]. The resulting signal can then be processed like an audio signal.

3.2 Fingerboard Sensor to String Length

The fingerboard sensor produces a smooth and clean signal however, a small amount of crosstalk is present, originating from the vibrating body/string which is transferred to the finger and the sensor. Since the vibrato frequency is usually around 4–6 Hz, it is safe to low-pass filter the signal using a cutoff frequency of 50 Hz. In a small number of recordings, the fingerboard sensor was found to be erroneous in some parts because pressure from the finger was not high enough. To prepare the fingerboard sensor values to be used in Equation 1, the sensor readouts needs to be transferred into time dependent string length $L(n)$. This requires measuring the cellos geometry. Therefore we include the physical dimensions of the fingerboard, the bridge and the sensor positions in the test set.

The raw recordings and the derived data is available for download on the accompanying website[2]. The derived test set is split into a small set of two recordings including all sensor domains and a larger set including audio and fingerboard sensor data.

4. APPLICATIONS

In this section, we show how the derived data can be used for $F0$ estimation and other applications.

4.1 F0 Estimation

Both of the derived data $M(n)$ and $L(n)$ described in Section 3 can be used to compute a reference $F0$ signal. Since $M(n)$ can be processed like audio signals, $F0$ estimators can be used to extract the fundamental frequency of the signal. This procedure is related to EGG based-reference data used in speech. We found the MELODIA [12] algorithm to deliver satisfying results, possibly because the motion signal is very spiky, resulting in a very harmonic signal. When comparing the $F0$ estimation results on the motion signal with results on the pure audio signal, a phase shift is revealed. This is due to the fact that the string motion is not the signal which is captured by the microphone; the transfer function of the cello bridge and its body is not taken into account. Due to our time-synchronous recordings we are able to detect these delays by using a cross correlation function to shift the data. Since the delay is frequency-dependent this data can be used to compare group delays.
When generating a reference signal from the fingerboard

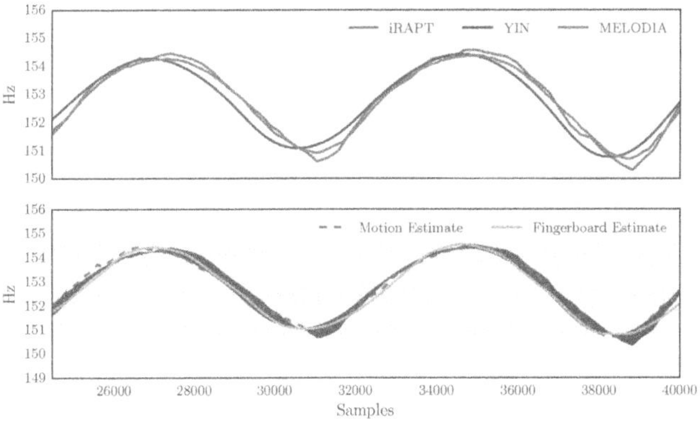

Figure 2: Excerpt of $F0$ estimates based on audio signal (upper plot). Estimates derived from the test set data (lower plot). Grey area shows min/max range of upper plot's estimators.

sensor, the string constants in Equation 1 need to be determined. One method is to do additional measurements as described in [16]. An approximation is calculated by taking the length of an open string and estimating its (stationary) frequency. This is feasible because $F0$ estimators tend to be accurate under these stable conditions. Now, assuming that the string tension is almost constant for neighbouring notes played on one string, this method allows to measure $\sqrt{\frac{T}{\rho_L}} = C$ to fit Equation 1. To improve the fitting we propose to use a non-linear least square algorithm to fit measurement data to the (non-shifted) $F0$ estimates derived from $M(n)$.

For evaluation we chose three estimators to process audio: **YIN** [3] is used as an FFT based implementation [5]; **iRAPT** [1] is an improved version of the RAPT framework. **MELODIA** [12] was not designed to be $F0$ estimator, but is also able to extract the *predominant* melody in a polyphonic mixture. We increase the bin resolution to 0.5 semitones. For the pitch estimators we used a frame length of 85 ms and a hop size of 2.6 ms. Figure 2 shows an excerpt of one of the cello notes and several fundamental frequency estimates. The fingerboard sensor based estimates were fitted as described above. One can see that the sensor estimate is very smooth and does not exhibit many deviations compared to the audio-based estimators. It is worth mentioning that this comparison is made under very good conditions in favor of the audio-based estimators. In a scenario where the audio signal includes additive noise, reverberation or other undesired signals, those estimates would become less reliable, whereas the video and sensor based estimates could still deliver good results.
In another baseline experiment focusing on the larger set which misses the video motion data, we evaluated the three estimators as follows: the (stable) middle third of each fingerboard sensor recording was fitted to each of the outputs of the $F0$ estimators using non-linear least square minimization. We used $\frac{a}{L(n)} + b$ as the model to match Equation 1. Figure 3 shows the root mean square errors after the fit. The results indicate that the YIN estimator is the closest to the sensor estimates.

[2]`https://www.audiolabs-erlangen.de/resources/muserc`

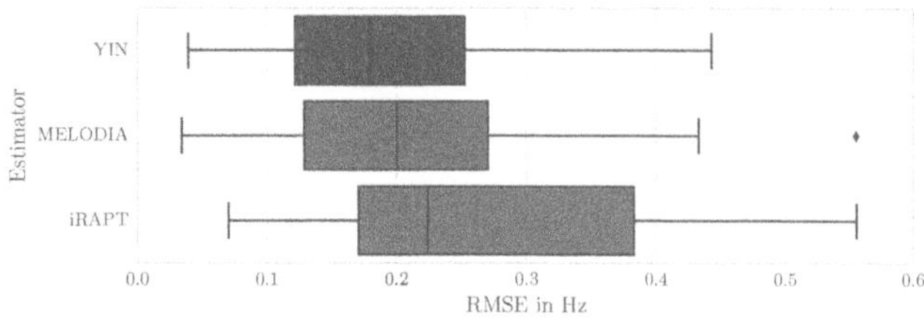

Figure 3: Boxplots of root mean square errors after fitting fingerboard sensor data to different F0 estimators

4.2 Time-Warping

Time warping is a technique based on non-linear resampling to stretch or shorten a signal with the aim to produce a signal with constant $F0$. In [14] a source separation system is described which benefits from time warping. The warping contour used to time-warp a signal does not require to include the absolute frequency values. Thus, a relative frequency contour like the one we derived from the fingerboard sensor can be used to reduce frequency modulation of the input signal.

4.3 Vibrato Analysis

Research aiming to analyze playing styles in recordings relies on conventional $F0$ estimators based on the audio signal [10]. By using sensor data samples from our test set researchers get more robust and detailed data to compute features like mean vibrato frequency. The data might also be targeted to reveal information about differences between musicans. Further it can be used for synthesizers to add a natural vibrato by using the sensor data as modulation source.

5. SUMMARY

In this work we propose a novel dataset of cello recordings accompanied by multi-sensor data. The data includes time synchronous fingerboard positions and high-speed camera recordings. Further in this work we show how to derive $F0$ estimates from the data which can be used to improve $F0$ estimators. The derived string motion estimate shows similarity to the EGG signals used in speech. The slowest feature rate of the set is 750 Hz, which enables to evaluate $F0$ estimators with high temporal resolution. We want to add more musical instruments to the data set in the future. By making this dataset public domain and including the raw recordings, we believe other researchers can benefit from the data and possibly generate their own derived data.

6. ACKNOWLEDGMENTS

This work has been supported by the German Research Foundation (INST 90/747-1 FUGG).

7. REFERENCES

[1] E. Azarov, M. Vashkevich, and A. Petrovsky. Instantaneous Pitch Estimation Based on RAPT Framework. In *Proc. EUSIPCO*, pages 2787–2791, 2012.

[2] O. Babacan, T. Drugman, N. d'Alessandro, N. Henrich, and T. Dutoit. A comparative study of pitch extraction algorithms on a large variety of singing sounds. In *Proc. ICASSP*, pages 7815–7819. IEEE, 2013.

[3] A. D. Cheveigné and H. Kawahara. YIN, a fundamental frequency estimator for speech and music. *Journal of the Acoustical Society of America*, 111(4):1917–1930, 2002.

[4] A. Davis, M. Rubinstein, N. Wadhwa, G. Mysore, F. Durand, and W. T. Freeman. The visual microphone: Passive recovery of sound from video. *Proc. SIGGRAPH*, 33(4):79:1–79:10, 2014.

[5] D. B. et. al. Essentia: An Audio Analysis Library for Music Information Retrieval. In *Proc. ISMIR*, pages 493–498, 2013.

[6] R. M. B. et al. MedleyDB: A multitrack dataset for annotation-intensive MIR research. In H. Wang, Y. Yang, and J. H. Lee, editors, *Proc. ISMIR*, pages 155–160, 2014.

[7] G. Farnebäck. Two-frame motion estimation based on polynomial expansion. In *Image Analysis*, pages 363–370. Springer, 2003.

[8] T. Grosshauser and G. Tröster. Finger position and pressure sensing techniques for strings and keyboard instruments. In *Proc. NIME*, pages 27–30, 2013.

[9] T. Grosshauser and G. Tröster. Musical instrument interaction: development of a sensor fingerboard for string instruments. In *Proc. Tangible, Embedded and Embodied Interaction*, pages 177–180. ACM, 2014.

[10] M. Mellody and G. H. Wakefield. The time-frequency characteristics of violin vibrato: Modal distribution analysis and synthesis. *Journal of the Acoustical Society of America*, 107(1):598–611, 2000.

[11] G. Pirker, M. Wohlmayr, S. Petrik, and F. Pernkopf. A pitch tracking corpus with evaluation on multipitch tracking scenario. In *Proc. INTERSPEECH*, pages 1509–1512, 2011.

[12] J. Salamon and E. Gómez. Melody extraction from polyphonic music signals using pitch contour characteristics. *IEEE TASLP*, 20(6):1759–1770, 2012.

[13] E. Schoonderwaldt, N. Rasamimanana, and F. Bevilacqua. Combining accelerometer and video camera: Reconstruction of bow velocity profiles. In *Proc. NIME*, pages 200–203. IRCAM, 2006.

[14] F.-R. Stöter, S. Bayer, and B. Edler. Unison source separation. In *Proc. DAFx*, 2014.

[15] J. Woodhouse and P. Galluzzo. The bowed string as we know it today. *ACTA Acustica united with Acustica*, 90(4):579–589, 2004.

[16] J. Woodhouse and A. Loach. Torsional behaviour of cello strings. *ACTA Acustica United with Acustica*, 85(5):734–740, 1999.

[17] C. Yeh, N. Bogaards, and A. Roebel. Synthesized polyphonic music database with verifiable ground truth for multiple f0 estimation. In *Proc. ISMIR*, pages 393–398, 2007.

[18] C.-Z. Zhang, G.-M. Zhang, B. Ye, and L. Liang. Three dimensional motion tracking of a point on a bowed violin string using high speed videography. *ACTA Acustica united with Acustica*, 100(3):574–582, 2014.

An Elicitation Study on Gesture Attitudes and Preferences Towards an Interactive Hand-Gesture Vocabulary

Haiwei Dong
University of Ottawa
800 King Edward Avenue
Ottawa, Canada
hdong@uottawa.ca

Nadia Figueroa
Swiss Federal Institute of Technology Lausanne (EPFL)
Route Cantonale
Lausanne, Switzerland
nadia.figueroafernandez@epfl.ch

Abdulmotaleb El Saddik
University of Ottawa
800 King Edward Avenue
Ottawa, Canada
elsaddik@uottawa.ca

ABSTRACT

With the introduction of new depth sensing technologies, interactive hand-gesture devices are rapidly emerging. However, the hand-gestures used in these devices do not follow a common vocabulary, making certain control command device-specific. In this paper we present an initial effort to create a standardized interactive hand-gesture vocabulary for the next generation of television applications. We conduct a user-elicitation study using a survey in order to define a common vocabulary for specific control commands, such as Volume up/down, Menu open/close, etc. This survey is entirely user-oriented and thus it has two phases. In the first phase, we ask open questions about specific commands. In the second phase, we use the answers suggested from the first phase to create a multiple choice questionnaire. Based on the results from the survey, we study the gesture attitudes and preferences between gender groups, and between age groups with a quantitative and qualitative statistical analysis. Finally, the hand-gesture vocabulary is derived after applying an agreement analysis on the user-elicited gestures. The proposed methodology for gesture set design is comparable with existing methodologies and yields higher agreement levels than relevant user-elicited studies in the field.

Categories and Subject Descriptors

H.5 [**Information Interfaces and Presentation**]: Multimedia Information Systems—*Evaluation/Methodology*; H.5.2 [**User Interfaces**]: Interaction Styles/Benchmarking

General Terms

Design

Keywords

Hand-gesture interaction; Kinect; preferences and attitudes

MM'15, October 26–30, 2015, Brisbane, Australia.
© 2015 ACM. ISBN 978-1-4503-3459-4/15/10$15.00
DOI: http://dx.doi.org/10.1145/2733373.2806385.

1. INTRODUCTION

Many Human-Computer-Interaction (HCI) systems such as surface, mobile and free-hand computing use gestures created by system designers which might be biased towards the recognition system's abilities instead of the comfort and preference of the users. Moreover, these gestures have to be learned by the non-expert user and sometimes it takes some time to get accustomed and become a frequent user of these technologies. In the following part, we present a comparison of user-elicited studies relevant to our research goals from the recent years targeted at gesture set design and their salient characteristics. We begin the study comparison with the work from [8], which introduced a user-elicited gesture set for surface computing applications, specifically using a Microsoft Surface prototype. In this study, they demonstrated that 3 HCI experts designing the same gesture set came up with only 60% of the user-elicited gestures, moreover 19.1% of the suggested gestures by the experts were never tried by the participants, thus it is clear that including the users in the development of interactive technologies is of great advantage. To corroborate these findings, Nacenta et al. conducted a comparative study between a user-defined versus pre-designed gesture sets, evaluating their memorability [3]. Indeed, one of their key findings is that user-defined gestures are more memorable than pre-designed gestures, another highly beneficial aspect of user-elicited studies.

Regarding other types of user interaction, Ruiz et al. proposed a user-defined gesture set for motion gestures with mobile devices (i.e. movements of the device to invoke specific commands like answer phone, ignore call, navigate mail, etc) [4]. Nevertheless, user-elicited studies have been successful for not only surface and mobile computing applications but also with free-hand interaction by means of gesture recognition using a Microsoft Kinect. Vatavu conducted the first study investigating users' preferences for the design of a gesture set for TV control tasks [5], which has the same goal as ours. We compare our results in Section 3 and show that our proposed gesture set has a higher level of agreement between the participants' preferences. Similarly, Morris studied user preferences by asking users to navigate web on a home TV (equipped with a Microsoft Kinect) with speech and gesture recognition [2]. They found that the participants were indeed enthusiastic with the idea of web browsing on the TV and that multiple modalities (i.e. gesture and speech) increased the guessability. More recently, research in the Augmented Reality community has adopted this methodol-

Group	Referents	Description
(i) Menu Navigation	Open	Open menu
	Up	Move up in menu
	Down	Move down in menu
	Enter Option	Enter option in menu
	Enter Submenu	Enter a submenu
(ii) Channel Surfing	Previous	Go to previous channel
	Next	Go to next channel
	Last	Go to last visited channel
(iii) Volume Control	Increase	Increase volume
	Decrease	Decrease volume
	Mute	Mute volume
(iv) Override	Shutdown	Shutdown

Table 1: Referents used for the design of our user-elicited gesture set for TV control

ogy. Vatavu developed interactive commands for a hybrid-physical augmented TV using a Wii remote control [6].

Most of the previously mentioned user-elicited studies have achieved good results and high agreement within suggested gesture categories. They all follow the same methodology, which we describe as demonstrative and was initially introduced by [7]. We introduce a new methodology which as can be seen later on in Section 3 yields to higher agreement rates than the presented related studies.

2. SURVEY

We have developed a questionnaire to target the user's preferences in terms of interactive hand-gesture vocabulary, using a set of control commands that can be applied to gaming consoles, televisions or digital displays. It is possible to observe that people adapt rapidly to technology interaction, similar to what is currently happening with touch-screen devices (e.g. smart phones and tablets). Users learn quickly and can easily adapt to the new ways of interaction, but doing so via gesture language is different. Despite the active research in gesture recognition and related user-elicited studies, higher requirements are still needed in the real-time processing of such recognition systems. Thus, we focus on building a vocabulary that is inferred by the user's preferences and can give us an indication of the level of complexity of the selected gestures. Following we describe how we designed the questionnaire and provide the tendencies and distributions of the answers for each question.

The questionnaire was elaborated as general as possible. It was designed in such a way, that we could achieve a hand-gesture set useful for a wide range of users (disregarding age, gender or technical background). Each participant was asked to complete an online questionnaire and choose gestures for defined control commands such as Next Channel, Volume Up, Return, etc. These control commands are actually the effect of a gesture, defined in linguistics as a referent, which is used in [8] and [5]. We elicit a set of 12 different referents (control commands) which are frequently used for television control (Table 1) and classify them into four groups: (i) Menu Navigation, (ii) Channel Surfing, (iii) Volume Control and (iv) Override.

The questionnaire was applied in two phases. In the first phase, we asked participants open-ended questions, to obtain a list of possible answers for each referent. We did not want the current state of gesture recognition technologies to influence the user's preferences and suggestions, this is called removing the gulf of execution, and is also considered in previous studies from [8] and [4], where they avoid giving any recognizer feedback. Furthermore, compared to these studies, our open-ended questions permit the user's imagination to flow without limiting to an example with a specific display or operating system.

Participants were encouraged to complete all questions. Incomplete and vague answers were dropped. The second phase was in multiple choice form, the options were extracted from the answers of the first phase. What we wanted to achieve was that no matter what the final results were, they would be completely user-oriented. We considered it important not to show any preferences for certain answers. For instance, when explaining how to complete the questionnaire, we did not provide any example. The range of sample participants also varied between the two phases. In the first phase, we targeted at the most general audience, such as our friends and acquaintances, to take the wide spectrum of backgrounds in consideration. In the second phase, we then targeted at the university members (students and faculty). This was done in order to obtain more intuitive final answers, since this demographic is more in contact with new technologies.

Regarding the questions (shown in Table 2), we can categorize them into three main groups (i) demographics, (ii) attitudes and (ii) preferences. In the demographics group Q(1-2) we collect data about age and gender which is typical for any survey. In the attitudes group Q(3-4,17-22), we collect data about attitudes towards gesture control of gaming and television commands, frequency of gaming and opinions towards hand-gesture interaction with digital devices. Finally, the preferences group Q(5-16), collects data towards more specific questions such as preferences of hand-gestures for television control (referents).

3. RESULTS

3.1 Answers and Demographics

The total number of participants in this study was 130, 49 in the first phase and 81 in the second phase. The two genders are divided into approximately 50-50: 44 men and 37 women (regarding the second phase). The surveyed participants in the first phase did not take part in the second phase, thus the learning and the training groups were completely independent. We provided 22 questions to the user (Table 2), with the multiple choice answers extracted from the first phase of the survey and the percentages of each answer from the second phase.

Most of the participants are from the younger age range (18 - 25), this is not surprising since the second phase was run in the university. An interesting observation is that there are more female users in that age range, contrary to the rest of the samples of the survey. It is worth mentioning that in the first phase, the age group with the largest population was 30 - 40, therefore the population of the older age range chose the answers for the second phase, and the youngest participants ratified them. Thus, we can corroborate that the chosen answers for the questionnaire encompass the preferences of participants from all ages.

Index	Question
Q1	Select the age range that you are in
Q2	Please select your gender
Q3	Do you usually play videogames?
Q4	How often do you play videogames in which the game control is made using body movements?
Q5	Your gestures: Next Channel
Q6	Your gestures: Previous Channel
Q7	Your gestures: Back to the last visited channel
Q8	Your gestures: More volume
Q9	Your gestures: Less volume
Q10	Your gestures: Open menu
Q11	Your gestures: Menu, enter a submenu
Q12	Your gestures: Menu, up in the menu
Q13	Your gestures: Menu, down in the menu
Q14	Your gestures: Menu, enter an option
Q15	Your gestures: Mute / Unmute
Q16	Your gestures: Shut down the TV
Q17	Do you prefer accuracy rather than speed (time response)?
Q18	Do you like the idea of a set of recognition gestures instead of conventional commands?
Q19	Would you remember a set of gestures for easy navigation on TV?
Q20	Would you find it more useful to have one gesture for each option (enter menu, enter volume options, enter channel options ...) and repeat the ones for up/down
Q21	Would you prefer a system controlled by gestures rather than a conventional remote control?
Q22	Why do you choose a particular gesture to an associated control command (e.g., Volume Up)?

Table 2: Questionnaire of interactive hand-gesture vocabulary

Regarding video game playing frequency, most of the users from the youngest age range (< 18 - 21) answered that they played sometimes, rarely (12.35%) or never (24.69%). We can find a small presence in the very frequent players (1.23%) and in those that play rarely (1.23%). The greatest presence is for those who never play (6.17%). Regarding gender, in both genders there are seldom users that play often or very often. In the case of the females, they mostly never play, and in the case of males it seems as if they only play sporadically. It is worth noting that in this second phase, the users were targeted among the people of the university, students and faculty. Thus, they are not only people from a technical background.

In summary, most of the participants are not frequent players, or at least don't play very often. We see this as a good sign, if the participants in our study were frequent players, they would be biased to some of the preferences since they are used to certain gestures for control commands.

3.2 Statistical Analysis on User Preferences and Attitudes

We used the independent-samples T-test for equality of means to measure the significance of the difference on gesture control attitude between the male and female group. We produces two tests of the difference between the two groups. The first test assumes that the variances of the two groups are equal. We use Levene's test for equality of variance to measure this assumption. Here, the significance value in Q(4, 17, 18, 19) is greater than 0.10, thus we can assume that the two groups in these questions have equal variances. Based on the results of the equality test of variances, we apply the T-test to find out if the two groups (male/female) have differences in attitude on gesture control. We found that in Q(4), the significance value of the test is less than 0.05, indicating that for Question 3 and 4, there is no difference between the male and female groups. I.e., the male play video games (especially that with gesture control) as frequently as the female. Moreover, the male group has more positive answer in the Question (17, 18, 19) indicating the male is more likely to try the gesture control.

Similarly, we compared the attitude difference between age groups. We divided the samples into two groups according to age: $\leq$25 years old (young group) and >25 years old (old group). The significance values of Q(17, 18, 19, 20, 21) are greater than 0.10 and thus pass Levene's test for Equality of variances. Hence, we finally obtained that there is no attitude difference in Q(21) on gesture control between the two age groups indicating both the age groups are optimistic in trying the gesture control compared with the conventional remote control. The young group has more positive answer in the Question (17, 19, 20) indicating that they prefer to remember more gesture control commands to increase control accuracy. Whereas, the old group is more optimistic in Question (18) which means the old people prefer the gesture vocabulary control idea more than the young group.

3.3 Gesture Agreement Analysis

We evaluate the elicited gestures for each referent by computing an agreement score A_r, which represents the level of consensus between the participants for a specific referent r. This agreement score was initially introduced by [7], for agreement scores of similar user-elicited studies. The agreement score A_r for a specific referent r is calculated as

$$A_r = \sum_{P_i \subset P_r} \left(\frac{|P_i|}{|P_r|} \right)^2 \quad (1)$$

where P_r is the set of proposed gestures for referent r and P_i is the subset of identical gestures within P_r. The value of A_r ranges between $|P_r|^{-1}$ and 1, where $|P_r|^{-1}$ represents no agreement at all and 1 is perfect agreement. Our study was run in a group of 130 people, 49 in the first phase and 81 in the second one. In this evaluation, P_r has the same value as the number of users in the second phase, because that is our training set value and we dismiss incomplete surveys [1].

The main comparisons and references in our study are [8, 5, 6]. When starting to analyze our results, we thought that we would find a higher divergence in the responses compared to the previously mentioned studies. This is due to two reasons. Firstly, our number of participants is much larger, around 4 times as large (81) compared to 20 in [8, 5, 6]. Secondly, we didn't provide any explanation on what where

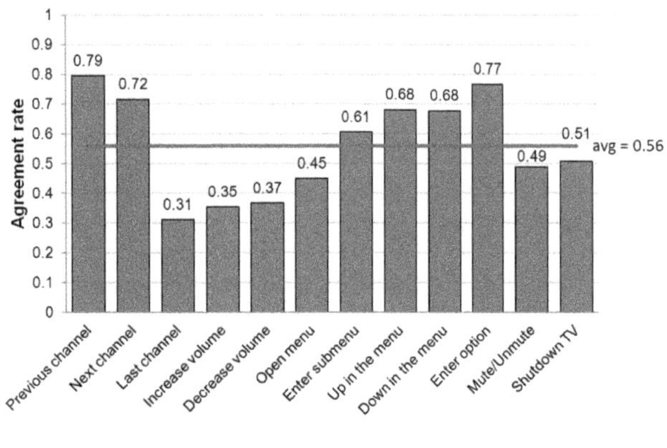

Figure 1: Agreement rates for user-elicited hand-gesture commands (Mean agreement rate is 0.56).

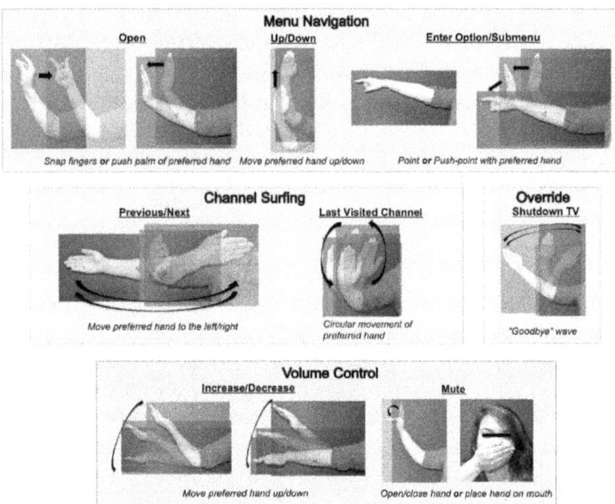

Figure 2: User-elicited hand-gesture vocabulary for interactive navigation. Referents are the underlined titles, suggested gestures are depicted as images and their description can be found below.

the effects of the referents are. Our elicitation method is based completely on the user preferences and imagination, both to propose the referents and to train them.

However, our results yield towards the opposite of our predictions, the mean agreement for our set is 0.56, compared to the agreement values obtained by [6] (0.53) for hand-held motion control within an augmented TV prototype, [5] (0.42) for free-hand TV control, [8] (0.32) for surface computing and [4] (0.28) for mobile phone interaction. We show the agreement rates for each suggested referent and the average agreement rate of our proposed vocabulary in Figure 1. The standard deviation is 0.12 (0.47 in [8] and 0.14 in [5]). If we focus on the graph, we can see that the gestures with highest agreement rate are the ones related to pointing and moving the hand sideways or up/down.

3.4 Interactive Hand-Gesture Vocabulary

Finally, we present our proposed interactive hand-gesture vocabulary for navigating through television and digital display menus using a 3D depth sensor, such as Kinect (Figure 2). For referents that have a specific button on a touchscreen device such as Mute/Unmute or Shutdown, the interactive hand-gestures suggested by the users are quite interesting, since they resemble body/sign language (i.e. hand on mouth for Mute/Unmute or goodbye gesture for Shutdown).

4. CONCLUSION

In this paper we present a study on gesture recognition, and an initial effort for creating an interactive hand-gesture vocabulary. We present a statistical analysis and we discuss several interesting points that appear in the survey. As a result of this study, we have learnt several interesting facts; for example, that smartphones have really taken their place in our society, and we, as users, have embraced their peculiarities. We could see it in one of the questions that very few of the users clearly notice that most of the hand-gestures they chose are very similar to those that use everyday with their smartphones. This paper has been a first approach to develop an interactive hand-gesture vocabulary that can be useful for a wide range of users and devices. As future work we wish to conduct a deeper study, focusing on hardware and targeting at specific kinds of users, for example aid handicapped people to control digital devices in a more natural way.

5. REFERENCES

[1] H. Dong, A. Danesh, N. Figueroa, and A. El Saddik. An elicitation study on gesture preference and memorability towards a practical hand-gesture vocabulary for smart televisions. *IEEE Access*, 3:543–555, 2015.

[2] M. Morris. Web on the wall: Insights from a multimodal interaction elicitation study. In *Proceedings of the ACM International Conference on Interactive Tabletops and Surfaces*, pages 95–104, 2012.

[3] M. Nacenta, Y. Kamber, Y. Qiang, and P. Kristensson. Memorability of pre-designed and user-defined gesture sets. In *Proceedings of the SIGCHI Conference on Human Factors in Computing Systems*, pages 1099–1108, 2013.

[4] J. Ruiz, Y. Li, and E. Lank. User-defined motion gestures for mobile interaction. In *Proceedings of the SIGCHI Conference on Human Factors in Computing Systems*, pages 197–206, 2011.

[5] R. Vatavu. User-defined gestures for free-hand TV control. In *Proceedings of the 10th European Conference on Interactive TV and Video*, pages 45–48, 2012.

[6] R. Vatavu. There's a world outside your TV: Exploring interactions beyond the physical TV screen. In *Proceedings of the 11th European Conference on Interactive TV and Video*, pages 143–152, 2013.

[7] J. Wobbrock, H. Aung, B. Rothrock, and B. Myers. Maximizing the guessability of symbolic input. In *Proceedings of CHI Extended Abstracts on Human Factors in Computing Systems*, pages 1869–1872, 2005.

[8] J. Wobbrock, M. Morris, and A. Wilson. User-defined gestures for surface computing. In *Proceedings of the SIGCHI Conference on Human Factors in Computing Systems*, pages 1083–1092, 2009.

Automated Video Editing for Aesthetic Quality Improvement

Jun-Ho Choi Jong-Seok Lee

School of Integrated Technology &
Yonsei Institute of Convergence Technology
Yonsei University
Incheon, Republic of Korea

{idearibosome, jong-seok.lee}@yonsei.ac.kr

ABSTRACT

In these days, a large number of videos is taken by various kinds of handheld devices, but many of them have poor aesthetic quality. In this paper, we present an automated video editing system that uses the shot length, camera motion, and color distribution as key aesthetic features. Given an amateur video, our system computes the original unrefined camera motion as homography and tries to remove some unreliable frames, which consequently splits the video into several shots. It then applies enhancement processes, including reconstruction of the overall camera motions and harmonization of color distributions. We apply our method to some amateur videos and evaluate the results through a subjective test. It is demonstrated that reducing the shot length in our method is a key point of editing that can lead enhanced satisfaction by viewers for the edited videos.

Categories and Subject Descriptors

I.4.3 [**Image Processing and Computer Vision**]: Enhancement; I.4.9 [**Image Processing and Computer Vision**]: Applications

Keywords

Aesthetics, video editing, shot segmentation, video stabilization, color harmonization

1. INTRODUCTION

Thanks to the advances in mobile technologies, tons of tiny cameras inside smartphones and other handheld devices take advantage of their connectivity to video streaming and social network services. Nowadays, it is very easy to take a video having a full HD resolution (1920×1080 pixels) and share it with friends within just a minute.

One of the problems is that those videos usually have lower aesthetic quality than professional videos. Niu and Liu [7] investigated differences between professional and amateur videos in various aspects. They found that most professional videos have only a few sets of colors, very smooth camera moves, and short shot lengths around 5.84 seconds, while amateur ones have a large number of colors, too shaky camera motions, and long-lasting shots having a median of 50.38 seconds in length.

There are many researches about enhancing aesthetic features of videos. For example, Gleicher and Liu [4] suggested a method to improve the overall camera motion to follow cinematic conventions. Sawant and Mitra [8] tried to refine colors in videos by using color harmonizing templates. These enhancement techniques can be part of a complete editing process chain to reinforce the overall quality of the videos.

One of the main features that are usually modified in the professional editing process is the shot length, which has been rarely considered in the previous research toward aesthetic enhancement. Experts in professional fields, especially in film making, usually shoot for a long time and exclude most part of the recorded video later during the editing [5]. Fortunately, because many amateur videos have sufficiently long shot lengths, this "cutting" operation can be also applied to them for achieving real video editing.

In this study, we present a novel automated video editing method that generates an edited version containing several improved scenes for a given original video. The system consists of well-organized procedures, including estimating camera motions via homography, dividing the video into appropriate number of shots, removing low quality shots, stabilizing camera motions of each shot, and improving the color distribution.

The rest of the paper is organized as follows. In Section 2, the details of our system are presented. Section 3 presents editing results with several amateur videos and evaluation results of a subjective test. Finally, we conclude our work in Section 4.

MM'15, October 26–30, 2015, Brisbane, Australia.
© 2015 ACM. ISBN 978-1-4503-3459-4/15/10 ...$15.00.
DOI: http://dx.doi.org/10.1145/2733373.2806386.

2. PROPOSED METHOD

2.1 Homography Computation

First, the camera motion of the source video is analyzed for further processing such as unstable frame removal and motion stabilization. Because camera movement results in moving both objects and background on the screen, estimating camera motion can be interpreted as calculating corresponding positions of pixels in a frame when they are on the coordinate system of another frame. This geometric connection between two frames can be estimated as a 2D transformation, referred to as homography, to reduce complexity of the calculation.

For arbitrary two frames F_a and F_b, the position of each pixel $(x_{b,a}, y_{b,a})$ in F_b on the coordinate system of F_a can be calculated by following transformation:

$$\begin{bmatrix} wx_{b,a} \\ wy_{b,a} \\ w \end{bmatrix} = \begin{bmatrix} c_{b,a,1} & c_{b,a,2} & c_{b,a,3} \\ c_{b,a,4} & c_{b,a,5} & c_{b,a,6} \\ c_{b,a,7} & c_{b,a,8} & c_{b,a,9} \end{bmatrix} \begin{bmatrix} x \\ y \\ 1 \end{bmatrix}$$

where (x, y) is the original position of each pixel in F_b. The 3×3 matrix having nine parameters from $c_{b,a,1}$ to $c_{b,a,9}$, defined as $\mathbf{H}_{b,a}$, is the homography of F_b corresponding to F_a.

If there are some frames between F_a and F_b, the homography can be calculated from the multiplication of temporally adjacent homography matrices between those frames as follows:

$$\mathbf{C}_{b,a} = \begin{cases} \prod_{k=a}^{b-1} \mathbf{H}_{k+1,k} & \text{if } a < b \\ \prod_{k=a-1}^{b} \mathbf{H}_{k+1,k}^{-1} & \text{if } a > b \\ \mathbf{I} & \text{if } a = b \end{cases}$$

where $\mathbf{I}$ is the 3×3 identity matrix. We name $\mathbf{C}_{b,a}$ as the cascaded homography of F_b corresponding to F_a.

Our method uses SIFT descriptors [6] to estimate parameters of each transformation. SIFT points of each frame are calculated and the best matching pairs of SIFT features are searched. Finally, the RANSAC method [3] is used to estimate parameters of the homography.

2.2 Shot Removal

Many amateur videos contain some types of aesthetic defects such as severe blurring caused by hand shaking and the appearance of an unknown person who passes in front of the camera. In such cases, the homography values may become unreliable due to lack of SIFT points matched between two frames. To deal with this issue, our method computes so-called unreliability score introduced by Gleicher and Liu [4].

The unreliability score of frame F_i is calculated from homography values related to its adjacent frames F_{i-1} and F_{i+1}. If F_i is unstable, the homography $\mathbf{H}_{i+1,i-1}$ and the cascaded homography $\mathbf{C}_{i+1,i-1}$ would become different. For that reason, the difference matrix $\mathbf{H}_{i+1,i-1}\mathbf{C}_{i+1,i-1}^{-1}$ is computed and the maximum displacement of pixels at the four corners of the image frame is regarded as the unreliability score.

Our system removes parts having high unreliability scores in the video in order to remove the aforementioned aesthetic defects and, at the same time, shorten each shot. First, the frame that has the maximum unreliability score is detected. Then, the nearest preceding and succeeding local minima of the unreliable score are detected and the corresponding frames are marked as the starting and ending frames to be removed. Eliminating this sequence of frames is the same to extracting two separate shots from the video. This process is repeated until all shots have lengths within $p_{shotLMin}$ to $p_{shotLMax}$ seconds. Also, shots having lengths shorter than $p_{shotLMin}$ are removed.

Those two parameters $p_{shotLMin}$ and $p_{shotLMax}$ are determined from the shot length distribution of professional videos. For ten movies, the shot segmentation algorithm proposed by Apostolidis et al. [1] is applied to obtain their shot length distribution. $p_{shortLMin}$ and $p_{shortLMax}$ are set as -1.5σ and +1.5σ values from the mean of the distribution, which are 1.08 and 6.46 seconds, respectively. Note that the values are similar to those found in the previous studies about the shot length distribution of professional videos [7, 9].

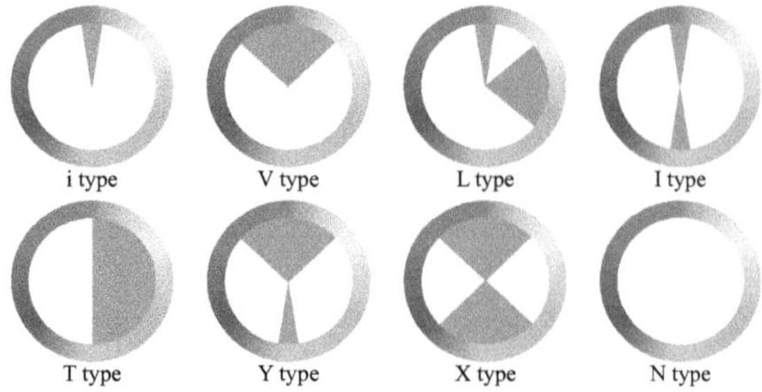

Figure 1: Hue templates proposed by Tokumaru et al. [10]. Each template can be rotated by any angle.

2.3 Motion Stabilization

After dividing the source video into several shots, our method breaks each shot into segments of three categories, namely, "static," "zoom," and "moving," based on the camera motion [4].

First, a sequence of frames having an amount of camera movements less than a threshold ($p_{staticMove}$) is considered as a static segment. The amount of camera movements is determined by the relative displacement (with respect to the image width) of the image center between adjacent frames based on their homography. Second, a zoom segment is a sequence of frames having zoom ratios larger than a threshold ($p_{zoomRatio}$). Zoom ratio is defined as a relative change of the perimeters of a pair of adjacent frames. Finally, the remaining parts are regarded as moving segments.

Once every shot is broken into several segments, different motion stabilization strategies are applied to each type of segment. For a static segment, by considering the middle frame as a reference, the rest frames are so moved that the camera is fixed through the whole segment. For a zoom segment, the size of each frame is changed so as to make zoom ratios between adjacent frames constant through the whole segment, which smoothes the zooming action. These two processes may produce frames having blank areas. To remove this artifact, all the image frames in the segment are enlarged until any blank areas are removed. However, excessive enlargement degrades the quality of the videos, so shots that have at least one segment enlarged by more than a scale factor threshold ($p_{segZoom}$) are removed. Because the camera motion is small for static segments and the zooming speed is limited in the camera, very few shots are removed in this step.

For a moving segment, the displacement of the image center from the first to last frames is calculated and the position of every frame is changed so as to simulate a consistent moving direction and speed. When this process creates blank parts in image frames, the frames are properly enlarged to remove the blank areas, as in the other types of segment. However, frames with various moving directions

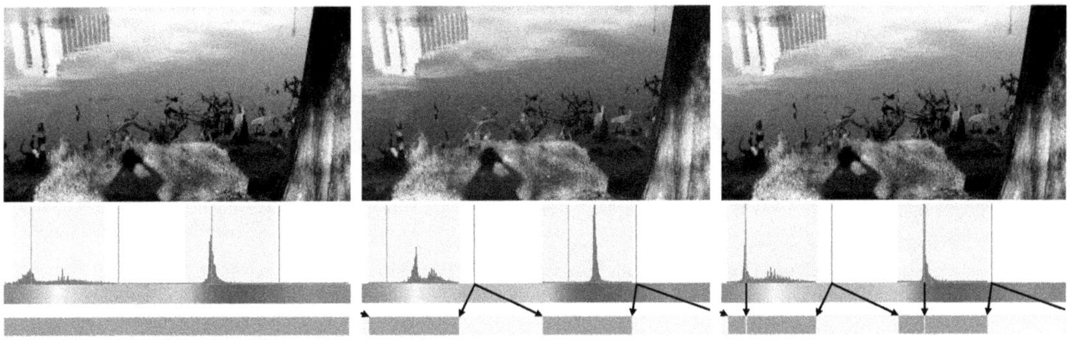

Figure 2: Color harmonization process. (a) The X type template is best suited for color distribution of the source frame. The gray areas in the distribution correspond to the gray areas in the template in Figure 1. (b) Linear contraction of hue with only the hue values for the minimum in the histogram outside the template (red lines) results in altering dominant colors. (c) Using the hue values for the maximum in the histogram inside the template (green lines) as boundaries of linear contraction prevents the change of dominant colors.

and speeds are immoderately magnified, which results in significant quality degradation. To resolve this issue, a segment having zoom ratio higher than $p_{segZoom}$ is split into two moving segments at the frame having the largest blank area, which are processed further separately.

2.4 Color Harmonization

Finally, a color enhancement process based on color harmonization is proceeded. Color harmonization refers to a color modification process by fitting colors of a given image into one of color harmonizing templates. Cohen-Or et al. [2] implemented image color harmonization using eight hue templates proposed by Tokumaru et al. [10] (Figure 1). Sawant and Mitra [8] extended this to color harmonization of videos by using linear contraction. However, their method also shifts hue values that are originally inside the template, which is subject to change dominant colors of the shot. Therefore, we propose a modified video color harmonization method that preserves main colors, which is illustrated in Figure 2.

For each frame in a shot, the hue histogram is calculated from only pixels whose saturation is greater than p_{colSat} and brightness is within $p_{colValMin}$ to $p_{colValMax}$. Then, the best matching template to the histogram is found. After that, hue values associated with the minimum number of pixels is selected for each region outside the template. These points are used in linear contraction of hue values to shift all colors into the template. Also, the dominant hue value that has the maximum number of pixels for each template region is used as the boundaries of linear contraction to prevent the change of dominant colors.

3. EXPERIMENT AND RESULTS

The proposed method is applied to 80 amateur videos having a full HD resolution (1920×1080 pixels) and a frame rate of 30 fps. Each video contains only one shot. They were recorded by five amateurs that have little knowledge of videography.

Before proceeding the experiment, the thresholding parameters of our system are configured. For the shot removal process, $p_{staticMove}$ and $p_{segZoom}$ are set to 0.08 and 1.5, respectively, and $p_{zoomRatio}$ is set to 1.015 as Gleicher and Liu [4] used. For the color harmonization process, p_{colSat}, $p_{colValMin}$, and $p_{colValMax}$ are set to 0.2, 0.15, and 0.95, respectively, as Niu and Liu [7] used in the computation of hue distributions.

We manually examined the resulting videos obtained by applying the proposed method, and found that the method is successful overall. Because of the blank area removing process in motion stabilization, the resolution of each edited video is reduced to HD (1280×720 pixels). The average duration of videos is also decreased from 53.9 to 28.5 seconds, due to the elimination of unreliable parts in the shot removal process, which made the videos more aesthetically pleasing, less boring, and more interesting.

Figure 3 shows an example of a source video and its edited version. The single-shot 28.0 second-long video is refined to a 11.4 second-long video having 3 shots. In this example, the source video contains uncomfortable scenes such as the appearance of videographer's fingers and abrupt camera shaking, especially between the first and second segments, which have been removed in the edited video. Also, the camera motion is smoothed and color distribution is enhanced.

To evaluate the proposed method, a subjective test was conducted. A total of 12 participants between 21 and 36 years old took part in the test. Five video pairs (unedited and edited) were used in the test. The average lengths of the unedited and edited videos are 53.0 and 25.9 seconds, respectively. The order of video pairs was shuffled for each subject. Each pair of edited and unedited videos were placed on the screen in a side-by-side manner, where the placement of them (left or right) was randomly selected. Subjects freely watched the two videos, and then were asked the following two questions:

1. Which one would you prefer if you are supposed to upload the video onto social network services, and why?
2. Which one would you prefer if you are supposed to watch these videos on social network services, and why?

Figure 4 shows the average number of votes in uploader's and viewer's perspectives. As shown in the graph, subjects picked the edited videos more than the unedited videos in both perspectives. Most of them indicated short shot lengths, conciseness of camera motion, and naturalness of

Figure 3: Example of a source video and its edited result.

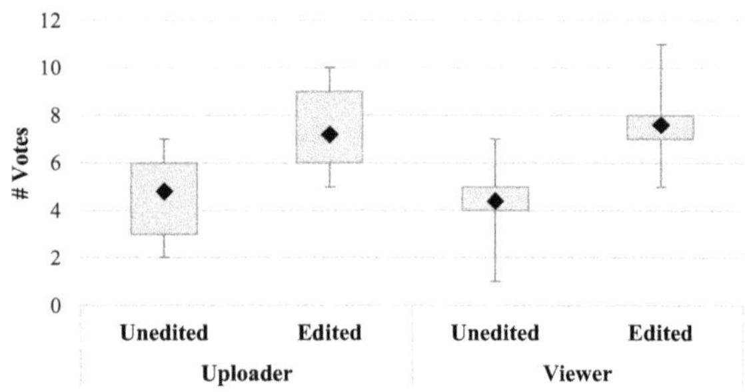

Figure 4: Subjective test results.

color as attractive aspects of the edited videos. In particular, removal of disturbing shots was mentioned frequently as the reason of choosing edited videos. It proves that limiting the shot length is one of the key points to improve aesthetic quality of amateur videos.

Although most subjects were satisfied with the edited videos, some participants sometimes preferred the unedited ones. They pointed out that some interesting shots were removed. This is because our method does not consider contextual information, which needs to be covered in our future work.

4. CONCLUSION

In this paper, we have presented a novel automated video editing method targeting amateur videos. Inspired from the professional video editing process, uncomfortable frames are excluded and long shots are divided into several short shots. In addition, camera motion stabilization for static, zooming, and moving shots is performed, and color harmonization preserving dominant colors is applied. The subjective test results proved the validity and effectiveness of the proposed method.

5. ACKNOWLEDGMENTS

This research was supported by the MSIP (Ministry of Science, ICT and Future Planning), Korea, under the "IT Consilience Creative Program" (IITP-2015-R0346-15-1008) supervised by the IITP (Institute for Information & Communications Technology Promotion).

6. REFERENCES

[1] E. Apostolidis and V. Mezaris. Fast shot segmentation combining global and local visual descriptors. In *Proceedings of the IEEE International Conference on Acoustics, Speech and Signal Processing*, pages 6583–6587, 2014.

[2] D. Cohen-Or, O. Sorkine, R. Gal, T. Leyvand, and Y.-Q. Xu. Color harmonization. *ACM Transactions on Graphics*, 25(3):624–630, 2006.

[3] M. A. Fischler and R. C. Bolles. Random sample consensus: a paradigm for model fitting with applications to image analysis and automated cartography. *Communications of the ACM*, 24(6):381–395, 1981.

[4] M. L. Gleicher and F. Liu. Re-cinematography: Improving the camerawork of casual video. *ACM Transactions on Multimedia Computing, Communications, and Applications*, 5(1):1–28, 2008.

[5] E. Laurier, I. Strebel, and B. Brown. Video analysis: Lessons from professional video editing practice. In *Forum Qualitative Sozialforschung / Forum: Qualitative Social Research*, volume 9, 2008.

[6] D. G. Lowe. Distinctive image features from scale-invariant keypoints. *International Journal of Computer Vision*, 60(2):91–110, 2004.

[7] Y. Niu and F. Liu. What makes a professional video? A computational aesthetics approach. *IEEE Transactions on Circuits and Systems for Video Technology*, 22(7):1037–1049, 2012.

[8] N. Sawant and N. J. Mitra. Color harmonization for videos. In *Proceedings of the 6th Indian Conference on Computer Vision, Graphics, and Image Processing*, pages 576–582, 2008.

[9] C. M. Taskiran and E. J. Delp. A study on the distribution of shot lengths for video analysis. In *Proceedings of the SPIE Conference on Storage and Retrieval for Media Databases*, pages 20–25, 2002.

[10] M. Tokumaru, N. Muranaka, and S. Imanishi. Color design support system considering color harmony. In *Proceedings of the IEEE International Conference on Fuzzy Systems*, volume 1, pages 378–383, 2002.

Multimodal Dataset for Assessment of Quality of Experience in Immersive Multimedia

Anne-Flore Perrin, He Xu, Eleni Kroupi, Martin Řeřábek, Touradj Ebrahimi
Multimedia Signal Processing Group (MMSPG)
Ecole Polytechnique Federale de Lausanne (EPFL)
Lausanne, Switzerland

ABSTRACT

This paper presents a novel multimodal dataset for the analysis of Quality of Experience (QoE) in emerging immersive multimedia applications. In particular, the perceived Sense of Presence (SoP) induced by one-minute long video stimuli is explored with respect to content, quality, resolution, and sound reproduction and annotated with subjective scores. Furthermore, a complementary analysis of the recorded physiological signals, such as EEG, ECG, and respiration is carried out, aiming at an alternative evaluation of human experience while consuming immersive multimedia content. Results confirm the value of the introduced dataset and its consistency for the purposes of QoE assessment for immersive multimedia. More specifically, subjective ratings demonstrate that the created dataset enables distinction between low and high levels of immersiveness, which is also confirmed by a preliminary analysis of recorded physiological signals.

Categories and Subject Descriptors

H.2.4 [**Information Systems**]: Database management—*Systems, Multimedia database*; H.5.1 [**Information Systems**]: Information Interfaces and presentation—*Multimedia Information Systems ; Evaluation/methodology, Video*

Keywords

Sense of Presence (SoP); Immersive multimedia; Quality of Experience (QoE); EEG; ECG; Respiration; Subjective assessment

1. INTRODUCTION

The Sense of Presence (SoP) also known as Immersiveness Levels (ILs) in this paper, is a desired quality metric for immersive environments [19]. According to [23], SoP refers to the subjective experience of "leaving" the intrinsic world and "being present" in a virtual environment. Detailed definition and description of SoP including its measurement can be found in [15, 23].

Multimedia technologies aim at providing higher Quality of Experience (QoE), through combination of sensory, in particular audio and visual information. For instance, audio-visual content in TV can be regarded as a limited virtual environment replicating physical reality. Indeed, sensory cues for virtual environments usually consist of visual but also audio information. Therefore, it is necessary to better investigate and understand the influence of both modalities and their impact on the QoE. The SoP, being the most significant quality metric of virtual environment, is then expected to be highly correlated to the QoE. Hence, the SoP is investigated here. Various studies in television services using subjective ratings as assessment of SoP are presented in [7].

Any explicit subjective assessment by human subjects is influenced by emotional, cultural, educational, and environmental differences across subjects [6, 8]. More importantly, explicit assessments can have an impact on the experience itself, and interfere with it. Therefore, implicit assessment based on subjects physiological signals is expected to provide additional and less biased information, when compared to explicit assessment. In [21], an objective measure of SoP using behavior or physiological responses is envisioned, nevertheless the authors used only subjective ratings. Electroencephalography (EEG) and peripheral physiological signals including Electrocardiography (ECG) and respiration have been used in various studies to assess the physiological responses to stimuli. In particular, in [12], 2D and 3D overall perceived quality is assessed using brain and peripheral signals, [11] concludes that perceived quality is related to emotional processes, whereas [10, 20] analyze emotional experiences as opposed to SoP. The authors of [1] present a similar sensor-based assessment of SoP using galvanic skin response, EEG, and facial motion tracking.

This paper presents a novel dataset that captures the differences in user experience during multimedia stimuli with various ILs. In this dataset the different ILs are induced by modifying the resolution, the amount of compression in the video, and sound reproduction. EEG and peripheral physiological signals including ECG and respiration, as well as subjective ratings are acquired during experiments.

Analysis of subjective ratings indicates that stimuli properties, such as presence of audio and its quality, are correlated with SoP. Additionally, proper application of classification algorithms can distinguish the various ILs, based on EEG and other peripheral physiological signals.

MM'15, October 26–30, 2015, Brisbane, Australia.
 ISBN 978-1-4503-3459-4/15/10 ...$15.00.
DOI: http://dx.doi.org/10.1145/2733373.2806387.

Parameters Setting	Immersiveness Levels (ILs)		
	Low	Middle	High
Audio	No Audio	Stereo	Surround
Quality (QP)	36	20	20
Resolution	SD	HD	UHD

Table 1: Parameters setting for different ILs

The remainder of this paper is organized as follows. The next section describes how we conducted experiments to collect subjective ratings and physiological responses. Section 3 presents the results of a subjective rating analysis and of the classification using physiological signals. Finally, conclusions are provided in Section 4.

2. DATA COLLECTION

Four uncompressed (FLAC, RAW YUV 4:2:0) audiovisual contents[1] from Blender open source project[2], two originally in HD (Big Buck Bunny and Elephant Dream) and two in UHD resolutions (Sintel and Tears of Steel), were used to extract ten one-minute audiovisual sequences. Nine of these sequences were used for test stimuli preparation, whereas one sequence was used for training stimuli creation. The audiovisual sequences were selected and cut from the original contents based on the audio energy level in surround channels, as well as on spatial and temporal properties of the video. More specifically, parts of the contents with the highest values of the above-mentioned properties were used, while the original movie scene editing was respected. Low, middle, and high ILs were defined for each audiovisual sequence by experts based on the exploited audio sound system (mono, stereo, and 5.1), the video quality/level of compression (high and low QP, using x264 encoding), and the resolution (UHD, HD, and SD). The Table 1 illustrates the characteristic settings for the three defined ILs. The combination of the nine video sequences with the three ILs leads to 27 video stimuli shown to each subject during each experiment.

The professional high-performance 4K/QFHD LCD reference 56-inch monitor Sony Trimaster SRM-L560 was used to display the video stimuli. As recommended in [16], the viewing distance was set at 1.6 times the height of the screen. The Altec Lansing 5.1 THX speaker system, super subwoofer was used as audio sound system. The laboratory setup provided a quiet environment and the ambient light was set in order to ensure subject comfort during bright and dark scenes, as well as during assessment and resting periods. To record the brain activity, a 256-electrodes net was placed at the standard position on the scalp. An EGI's Geodesic EEG System (GES) 300 was used to record, amplify, and digitize the EEG signals while the participants were watching the stimuli. The heart activity was recorded from two standard ECG electrodes placed on the lower left rib cage and the upper right clavicle. Two respiratory inductive plethysmography belts (thoracic and abdomen) were used to acquire the respiration. All signals were recorded at 250 Hz.

Eight female and twelve male subjects participated in the study. They were from 18 to 30 years old (23 in average with a 3.03 standard deviation). The 20 subjects were screened for correct visual acuity (no errors on 20/30 lines) and color vision using Snellen and Ishiara charts respectively. They all provided written consent forms. Before each experiment, oral instructions were provided to the participants to explain their tasks. Additionally, a training session was used to illustrate the low, middle, and high levels in SoP to guide subjects to bound their own perceived overall ratings.

The experiments consisted of three sessions intersected by ten-minute breaks in order to prevent subject fatigue and lack of attention. The audiovisual stimuli were displayed in low-middle-high IL, middle-low-high IL, and high-middle-low IL order during first, second, and third sessions, respectively. In order to avoid boredom or fatigue, the same audiovisual sequence was displayed only once during each session. Thus, nine audiovisual stimuli were presented in each session leading to a total of 27 audiovisual stimuli forming 27 trials.

Each trial consisted of a ten-second baseline period and a stimulus period. The physiological signals recorded during the baseline period were used to remove stimulus-unrelated variations from the signals obtained during the stimulus period. During the baseline periods, the subjects were instructed to remain calm and focus on a 2D white cross on a black background presented on the screen in front of them. Once this baseline period was over, a video stimulus was presented. After the video sequence was over, subject was asked to provide his/her self-assessed ratings for the particular video sequence without any restriction in time, following the Absolute Category Rating (ACR) evaluation methodology [9]. Once a trial was over, the next baseline period was recorded and the next video sequence, whose content was randomly selected, was presented. The procedure was repeated until all 27 video stimuli were presented and rated. Although the experiments lasted for almost two hours, including the training and the set up, the subjects did not report fatigue.

Regarding the self-assessed ratings, subjects were asked to evaluate the video sequences according to five different criteria, namely, interest in the video content, perceived video quality, interest in the audio content, level of immersiveness, and awareness of their surrounding. A 9-point rating scale was used ranging from 1 to 9, with 1 representing the lowest, and 9 the highest value of each criteria. In particular, the two extremes (1 and 9) correspond to "low" and "high" for interest in video and audio content as well as the perceived video quality, "no immersion" and "full immersion" for level of immersion and "no awareness of my environment" and "full awareness of my environment" for awareness of the surrounding. The dataset, including subjective ratings, as well as recorded physiological signals, is publicly available[3].

3. ANALYSIS AND RESULTS

To ensure that the ratings did not deviate significantly across subjects, detection and elimination of outliers was performed based on the scale of the IL ratings. The outliers detection was applied according to the guidelines described in Section 2.3.1 of Annex 2 of [4]. In this study, no outliers were detected.

[1] `http://media.xiph.org`

[2] `http://www.blender.org/foundation`

[3] `http://mmspg.epfl.ch/SoPMD`

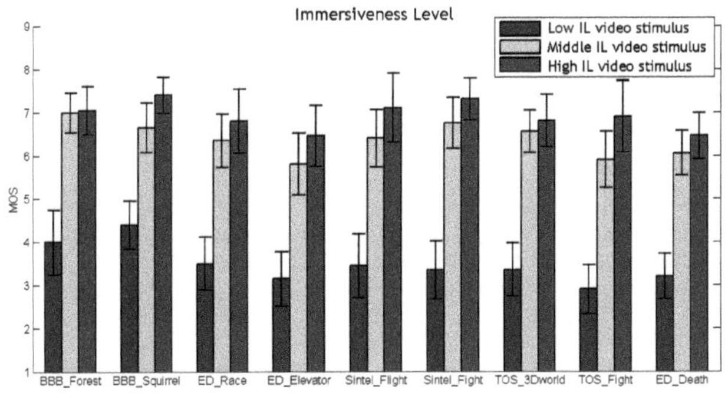

Figure 1: MOSs and CIs for the experienced IL.

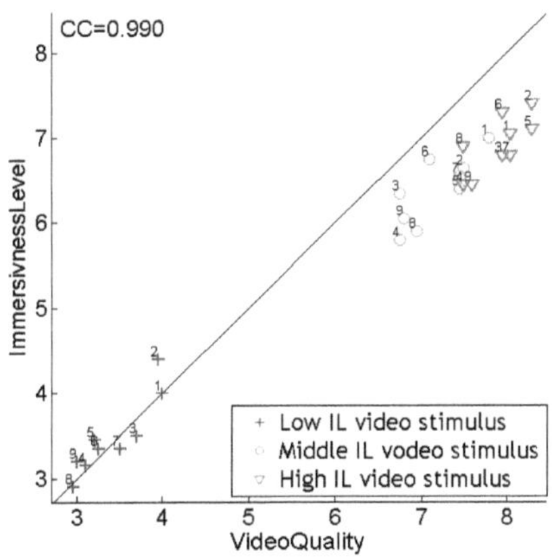

Figure 2: Correlation between the experienced SoP and the assessed quality of the video.

3.1 Subjective ratings analysis and results

The analysis conducted on the subjective ratings includes score distribution histograms, Mean Opinion Scores (MOSs) and associated 95% Confidence Intervals (CIs), as well as Pearson's correlations, assuming a Student's t-distribution of the subjective rates.

Figure 1 shows the resulting MOSs and CIs for the SoP experienced during stimuli for each content. The observed MOSs confirm that all ILs were experienced. In general, a higher IL provokes a better immersive experience as the average MOSs values show for low, middle, and high ILs corresponding to 4, 6.5, and 7, respectively. Moreover, the difference between the middle and high IL is not significant in any content as the CIs considerably overlap for all contents. However, the CIs attest that there is a significant difference between the low IL and the two other levels. These findings indicate that investigation of immersiveness is possible from this database.

To understand the impact of the sequence characteristics (interest in the video and the audio content, the quality, and resolution of the video) and verify that the awareness of surrounding is inversely related to IL, the correlation between the MOSs for all five criteria was measured using Pearson correlation coefficient. Figure 2 depicts the correlation between the MOSs rates given for the video quality and the SoP, and Table 2 presents the overall correlation coefficients. In Figure 2, the stimuli with the same number originate from the same content. This shows that, for each content, the higher the perceived quality of a video stimulus, the more

	Video Quality	Video Content Interest	Audio Content Interest	Surrounding Awareness
Immersiveness Level	**0.990**	**0.914**	**0.974**	**-0.986**
Video Quality	-	0.892	0.988	-0.987
Video Content Interest	-	-	0.857	-0.903
Audio Content Interest	-	-	-	-0.965

Table 2: Pearson correlation coefficients between the ratings of different perceptual criteria.

immersive is the experience. The correlation coefficient of IL and video quality is 0.99, meaning that these two criteria are highly correlated. A huge difference is observed between the low and middle/high classes, corroborating with the previous analysis. It also explains the high correlation results. It should be pointed out that each sequence provides a better immersive experience when its IL is increased. The Table 2 confirms the high correlation between IL and the perceived video quality (cc = 0.99), and shows the influence of sound (cc = 0.97). It also validates that the surrounding awareness is inversely related to the IL (cc = -0.99).

3.2 Physiological signal analysis and results

This section presents the pre-processing steps to remove the artifacts from recordings, the feature extraction methods and the classification results.

The pre-processing steps were inspired by [13]. Regarding the ECG signals, the Heart Rate Variability (HRV) was extracted. HRV is the physiological measurement of variation in the time interval between consecutive heart beats, i.e., the variation of R-R intervals, in beats per minute. Since the HRV is a time-series of non-uniform R-R intervals, the HRV was regularly resampled at a rate of 4 Hz. The obtained HRV sequences were used for feature extraction. Features extracted from the HRV signals include the mean and variance, the heart rate, the power of the low-frequency band (0.03 - 0.12 Hz), and the power of the high-frequency band (0.12 - 0.49Hz).

Both respiratory signals (abdomen and thoracic) were filtered using a wavelet multivariate de-noising [2]. Respiration rate and average power across 0.1 to 0.4 Hz frequency band were extracted as respiration features.

EEG signals were filtered by a fourth-order Butterworth filter between 3 and 47 Hz, in order to remove Electrooculogram (EOG) and Electromyogram (EMG) artifacts. Based on the international 10-20 system configuration, 19 channels were selected and processed from a total of 256 channels. Eye-movements and blinking artifacts were removed using Independent Component Analysis (ICA). We used the concept of functional connectivity to explore the EEG signals. Functional connectivity describes the dependence across various sub-regions of the brain [5]. In this study linear granger causality was applied to the pre-processed EEG data to estimate the functional connectivity between each pair of channels.

Previous studies have shown that the brain can be interpreted as a network [3], and that related features [18] can be extracted using granger causality estimated functional connectivity maps [17]. We extracted network features, such as characteristic path length [22], global efficiency [14], clustering coefficient [22], and local efficiency [14], from the estimated functional connectivity maps. Features for each trial are concatenated into one row for classification.

		Predicted IL			
		Low	Middle	High	Total
Actual IL	Low	110	0	70	180
	Middle	70	20	90	180
	High	11	0	169	180
	Total	191	20	329	540

Table 3: Confusion matrix of classification results between ILs. Numbers in the confusion matrix represents the resulting number of trials that are classified into each classes.

A 3-class Support Vector Machine (SVM) with a Gaussian radial basis function kernel was employed to classify between low, middle, and high ILs based on the physiological signals. The feature set was constructed from fusing all the features, i.e., concatenating all EEG and peripheral features in one feature vector. The whole feature set was split into ten folds. Moreover, a radial basis function kernel parameter was selected based on one-fold cross-validation. The confusion matrix was computed to evaluate the performance of the classifier(cf. Table 3). The three classes (low, middle, and high) of IL were equally balanced (i.e., 180 instances each), so the random classification accuracy is 33%.

The confusion matrix shows that it is easy to classify low and high IL with 61% and 94% accuracy, respectively. On the other hand, the middle IL classification accuracy is only 11%. The results are consistent with the subjective analysis, indicating that high and low ILs are easier to be identified, when compared to middle IL.

4. CONCLUSION

This paper introduces a publicly available dataset of immersive multimedia contents including corresponding subjective ratings, as well as recorded physiological signals. More specifically, the dataset comprises EEG, ECG, and respiration signals, as well as subjective ratings with respect to video quality, interest in video and audio content, and Immersiveness Level (IL).

A preliminary analysis based on the subjective ratings and the physiological signals was performed. The subjective ratings analysis demonstrated that various IL were experienced. A clear distinction between low and high IL was observed, whereas the differences between middle and high IL were not significant. The results also showed a high correlation between the Sense of Presence (SoP) and the quality of the stimuli. A classifier based on EEG and peripheral features enables the clear distinction between low and high IL, which is in line with subjective ratings analysis. This leads to the conclusion that this SoP dataset is consistent and can be valuable for further analysis.

5. ACKNOWLEDGMENTS

This work has been performed in the framework of the European Union's Horizon 2020 research and innovation programme under the Marie Sklodowska-Curie grant agreement No. 643072 – Network QoE-Net, SNF project No. 200020-149259 – LEADME, and EUROSTARS project No. E!8307 – TOFuTV.

6. REFERENCES

[1] M. K. Abadi, J. Staiano, A. Cappelletti, M. Zancanaro, and N. Sebe. Multimodal engagement classification for affective cinema. In *Affective Computing and Intelligent Interaction (ACII), 2013*, pages 411–416. IEEE, 2013.

[2] M. Aminghafari, N. Cheze, and J.-M. Poggi. Multivariate denoising using wavelets and principal component analysis. *Computational Statistics & Data Analysis*, 50(9):2381 – 2398, 2006.

[3] D. S. Bassett and E. Bullmore. Small-world brain networks. *The neuroscientist*, 12(6):512–523, 2006.

[4] I.-R. BT.500-13. Methodology for the subjective assessment of the quality of television pictures. *International Telecommunication Unio*, January 2012.

[5] A. A. Fingelkurts, A. A. Fingelkurts, and S. Kähkönen. Functional connectivity in the brain - is it an elusive concept? *Neuroscience & Biobehavioral Reviews*, 28(8):827–836, 2005.

[6] J. P. Forgas. On feeling good and being rude: Affective influences on language use and request formulations. *Journal of Personality and Social Psychology*, 76(6):928, 1999.

[7] J. Freeman, S. Avons, D. Pearson, and W. IJsselsteijn. Effects of sensory information and prior experience on direct subjective ratings of presence. *Presence*, 8(1):1–13, Feb 1999.

[8] X. Geng. Cultural differences influence on language. *Review of European Studies*, 2(2):p219, 2010.

[9] P. ITU-T RECOMMENDATION. Subjective video quality assessment methods for multimedia applications. *International Telecommunication Unio*, April 2008.

[10] S. Koelstra, C. Muhl, M. Soleymani, J.-S. Lee, A. Yazdani, T. Ebrahimi, T. Pun, A. Nijholt, and I. Patras. DEAP: A database for emotion analysis ;using physiological signals. *Affective Computing, IEEE Transactions on*, 3(1):18–31, Jan 2012.

[11] E. Kroupi, P. Hanhart, J.-S. Lee, M. Rerabek, and T. Ebrahimi. EEG correlates during video quality perception. In *Signal Processing Conference (EUSIPCO), 2014 Proceedings of the 22nd European*, pages 2135–2139, Sept 2014.

[12] E. Kroupi, P. Hanhart, J.-S. Lee, M. Rerabek, and T. Ebrahimi. Predicting subjective sensation of reality during multimedia consumption based on EEG and peripheral physiological signals. In *Multimedia and Expo (ICME), 2014 IEEE International Conference on*, pages 1–6, July 2014.

[13] E. Kroupi, P. Hanhart, J.-S. Lee, M. Rerabek, and T. Ebrahimi. User-independent classification of 2D versus 3D multimedia experiences through EEG and physiological signals. *8th International Workshop on Video Processing and Quality Metrics for Consumer Electronics-VPQM. 2014. No. EPFL-CONF-197071.*, 2014.

[14] V. Latora and M. Marchiori. Efficient behavior of small-world networks. *Physical review letters*, 87(19):198701, 2001.

[15] J. Lessiter, J. Freeman, E. Keogh, and J. Davidoff. A cross-media presence questionnaire: The ITC-sense of presence inventory. *Presence*, 10(3):282–297, June 2001.

[16] J. Li, Y. Koudota, M. Barkowsky, H. Primon, and P. Le Callet. Comparing upscaling algorithms from hd to ultra hd by evaluating preference of experience. In *The International Workshop on Quality of Multimedia Experience (QoMEX) 2014*, Singapore, Singapore, Sep 2014.

[17] W. Liao, J. Ding, D. Marinazzo, Q. Xu, Z. Wang, C. Yuan, Z. Zhang, G. Lu, and H. Chen. Small-world directed networks in the human brain: multivariate granger causality analysis of resting-state fmri. *Neuroimage*, 54(4):2683–2694, 2011.

[18] M. Rubinov and O. Sporns. Complex network measures of brain connectivity: uses and interpretations. *Neuroimage*, 52(3):1059–1069, 2010.

[19] M. Slater and S. Wilbur. A framework for immersive virtual environments (five), speculations on the role of presence in virtual environments. *Presence: Teleoperators and Virtual Environments*, 6(6):603–616, Dec. 1997.

[20] M. Soleymani, M. Pantic, and T. Pun. Multimodal emotion recognition in response to videos. *Affective Computing, IEEE Transactions on*, 3(2):211–223, April 2012.

[21] A. M. von der Pütten, J. Klatt, S. T. Broeke, R. McCall, N. C. Krämer, R. Wetzel, L. Blum, L. Oppermann, and J. Klatt. Subjective and behavioral presence measurement and interactivity in the collaborative augmented reality game timewarp. *Interacting with Computers*, 24(4):317 – 325, 2012. Special Issue on Presence and Interaction.

[22] D. J. Watts and S. H. Strogatz. Collective dynamics of "small-world" networks. *nature*, 393(6684):440–442, 1998.

[23] B. G. Witmer and M. J. Singer. Measuring presence in virtual environments: A presence questionnaire. *Presence: Teleoper. Virtual Environ.*, 7(3):225–240, June 1998.

MIL: Music Exploration and Visualization via Lyric and Image

Xixuan Wu[1], Yu Qiao[2], and Xiaoou Tang[1,2]
[1]Department of Information Engineering, The Chinese University of Hong Kong
[2]Shenzhen Institutes of Advanced Technology, Chinese Academy of Sciences, China
xixuan1124@gmail.com, yu.qiao@siat.ac.cn, xtang@ie.cuhk.edu.hk

ABSTRACT

In this paper, we introduce MIL: a music exploration prototype which integrates music (M), image (I), and lyrics (L), for efficiently visualizing and browsing music collections. MIL utilizes a novel structure, music semantic graph (MSG), to organize music collections in a hierarchical way by leveraging lyrics and acoustic cues of music. Each node of MSG corresponds to a music concept and is associated with a cluster of music tracks. MIL offers users a novel way to efficiently explore and scan music collections by using lyrics and image information. In addition, the proposed prototype supplies an easy-to-use interface to visualize MSG hierarchically. The user study shows that our prototype can effectively and efficiently help users to browse, search, and scan music collections.

Categories and Subject Descriptors

H.5.m. **[Information Interfaces and Presentation]**: Miscellaneous

Keywords

music semantic graph; lyric; image

1. INTRODUCTION

Along with the advance of Internet technology and the popularity of digital music devices, the ways users explore and enjoy music collection are also evolving rapidly. Huge research efforts [1, 2, 5, 8, 9, 11, 15] have been devoted to helping end-users to explore music collections by timbre, rhythm, artist, and derivative work. Various music-archive visualization tools like Islands of Music [7], SoniXplorer [4], 3D interactive environment [12], and Stober's music gallery [13] are also proposed to help user browsing music by navigating in geographic maps, walking in a musical 3D environment, or viewing music album covers. However, facing a new collection of music, users always need a way to quickly scan the collection and obtain the first emotional impressions of tracks. It takes a long time to listen to large number of tracks. Furthermore, for amateur users, acoustic musical features and complex metadata always seem to be too difficult and abstract to understand.

MM'15, October 26–30, 2015, Brisbane, Australia.
© 2015 ACM. ISBN 978-1-4503-3459-4/15/10 ...$15.00.
DOI: http://dx.doi.org/10.1145/2733373.2806388.

It is well known that first, lyric delivers meaningful message on emotional understanding of music. Secondly, human perceive music and image in a highly correlated way. Visual imagery is main yield useful cues to demonstrate the emotional parts of music [6, 3]. Furthermore, compared with music audio, text and image can be scanned in a more efficient way (reading and seeing is faster than listening). Inspired by these facts, this paper studies how to utilize lyric and image information for better browsing, visualizing, and scanning music collections. To our best knowledge, lyrics and images have not been introduced simultaneously to this task before.

The main objective of this paper is to develop a music exploration prototype, which integrates lyrics, visual and audio cues for effectively visualizing and scanning music collections. The key idea is to organize music collection in a hierarchical structure, called music semantic graph (MSG), which is constructed with lyrics and audio information. Each node of MSG corresponds to a semantic music concept and is associated with a cluster of music tracks, which share comparatively similar lyrics and audio features.

We propose our node expansion algorithm to construct the MSG. It is like building a forest. Once we decide the root nodes in MSG, the proposed node expansion algorithm can be used to expand them level by level, and finally construct different trees. In this work, we use lyrics as the source of all these nodes' concepts. But our node expansion algorithm do not limit the type of the nodes's concept in the forest (MSG), which can be lyrics, artists, or any other kinds of concepts. This new re-organization of music collection helps to show users different levels of lyric-based concepts and their accompanying music clusters. Moreover, single music in the collection is visualized by semantically-related images. Our contributions are summarized as follows:

First, we propose and construct a novel music semantic graph for organizing and further visualizing music collection. Both lyrics and audio information are used in our node expansion algorithm to construct the MSG. During the constructing process, we mine music concepts from the lyrics of the collection, and explore the cluster of tracks associated with each concept. Different clusters of tracks share similar rhythm and lyrics patterns.

Secondly, our prototype MIL allows user to quickly scan music with the help of mined concepts, lyrics, and images. We introduce a technique to visualize music tracks by a sequence of images searched from Internet, which can express the semantic meaning of the music. Since viewing image is much faster than listening to music, this function can significantly improve the efficiency of music browsing and exploring. User study shows that this also yields more fun and rich visual feedback during music listening.

Finally, MIL enable user to search music with lyric words. Different from existing lyric-based search, user can directly obtain high-level concepts for searching and navigating music tracks with

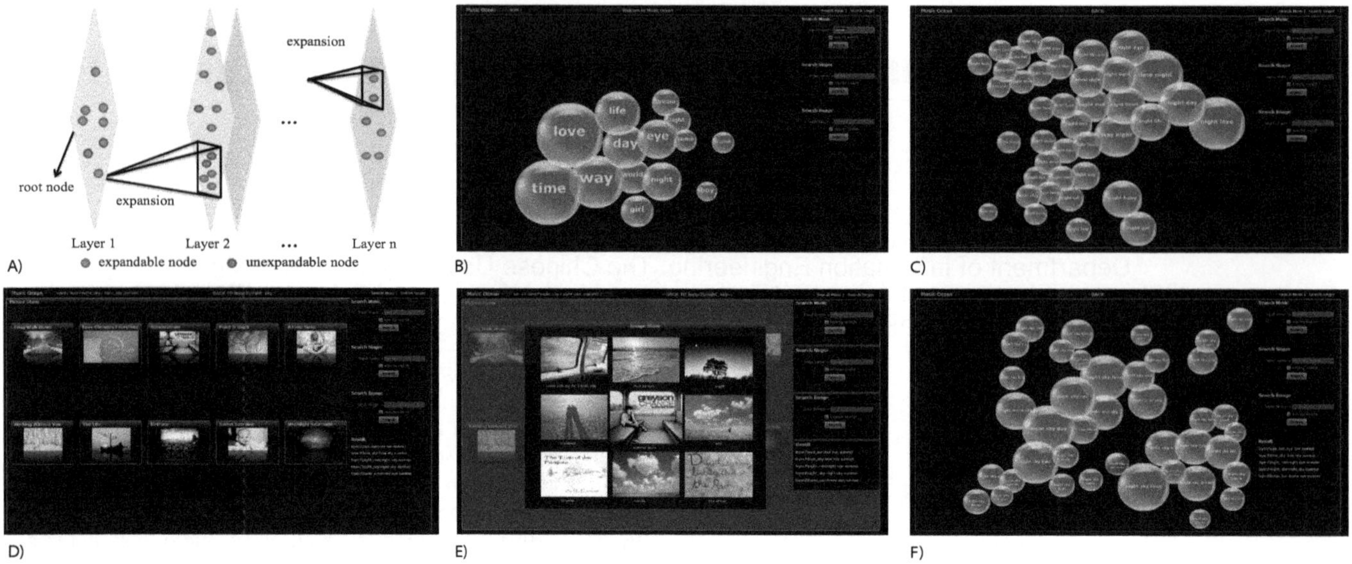

Figure 1: User interface: A). A brief illustration of our hierarchical graph structure; B). The first layer of node (root nodes); C). The second layer for node of label "night". The sub-concepts, like "night tear", represent a set of music whose lyrics include "night" and "tear", and also share similar melody; D). The interface after clicking a leaf node "night sky summer"; E). Music visualization by lyrics and images; F). The location of one of the searching result by using "summer" as searching input.

related concepts, instead of only obtaining a music list with query text in their lyrics.

2. DATA PREPROCESSING

To begin with, we introduce the two types of music features, lyrics and acoustic features. For the lyric of each music track, we use bag-of-words (BoW) representation where the dictionary consists of the most frequent 5, words extracted from musiXmatch dataset[1]. We also weight the terms with TF-IDF weights[10]. Furthermore, we utilize NTLK [2] to analyze the preliminary lexical classes (part-of-speech) of each word. Each word is given one of the following tags according to the lexical classes of their synsets: adjective (ADV), noun (NOUN), verb (VERB), adverb (ADV), and other (ADJ_SAT).

For audio part of each track, we first use Mel-Frequency Cepstral Coefficients (MFCC) vectors as our low-level features of music. In practise, the dimension of MFCC feature is 39 for a frame, which is composed by MFCC, MFCC-Delta, and MFCC-Delta Delta vectors. By sliding window along the audio file with half overlapping, we can obtain a long sequence of feature vectors (about $5,2$ per minute). Based on MFCCs, mixture hierarchies estimation (MHE) method [14] is adopted to estimate the posterior probabilities of 1 1 predefined semantic music attributes, which are collected from Google and Yahoo music, and categorized into nine types: Emotion, Instrument, Rhythm, Usage, Style, Genre, Region, Time, and Special Class. The acoustic feature vector of each track is composed of the estimated posterior probabilities of these attributes.

We calculate the distance between two tracks by a weighted combination of their lyric and acoustic distance. The lyric distance is defined as

$$d_l(l_1, l_2) \quad 1 - \frac{2\cos^{-1}(s_l(l_1, l_2))}{\pi}, \tag{1}$$

where

$$s_l(l_1, l_2) \quad \frac{\sum_i l_{1i} \times l_{2i}}{\sqrt{\sum_i (l_{1i})^2} \times \sqrt{\sum_i (l_{2i})^2}}, \tag{2}$$

and l_{1i}, l_{2i} are the i-th dimension of the lyric BoW vectors l_1, l_2 for two tracks.

The distance between two acoustic feature vectors v_1 and v_2 is calculated by

$$d_a(v_1, v_2) = KL(v_1, (v_1 + v_2)/2) + KL(v_2, (v_1 + v_2)/2), \tag{3}$$

where KL denotes KL-divergence.

2.1 Music Semantic Graph Construction

Once obtained lyrics and acoustic features of tracks, we build MSG for the music collection $\mathcal{C}$. MSG has a hierarchical structure with several layers, whose depth depends on the complexity of $\mathcal{C}$. Each layer is composed of a set of nodes. Each node corresponds to a lyric-based concept, which is also defined as the nodeąŕs label. Each node is associated with a cluster of tracks that share similar lyrics and audio features. In practise, we have 5, key words from our lyrics corpus, denoted as $\mathcal{W} \quad \{w_1, ..., w_{|W|}\}$. Lyric-based concept (node's label) can be a single word w_i or a group of words (a subset of $\mathcal{W}$). We use q and $L(q)$ to denote a node and the node's label (concept). Each node has an associated music set $T(q) \quad \{t_q^1, ..., t_q^{|T(q)|}\}$, which includes acoustically similar tracks whose lyrics contain the node's label. $|T(q)|$ refers to the size of a node (or the size of the node's label), which equals to the number of the tracks in its associated music set.

The layers in MSG $\mathcal{G}$ are denoted as L_1,L_2,...,L_n, where n is the number of layers. The nodes on the first layer are called root nodes (concepts). The nodes in i-th layer L_i are expanded from the nodes in upper layer L_{i-1}. Please be noted that not all nodes can be expanded. It depends on the complexity of the node's associate music set and the size of the node. A brief description of the MSG structure is shown in Fig. 1A. Generally, for building a MSG, we first detect a list of root concepts as our nodes in Layer L_1. Then iteratively, we examine whether the nodes in current layer L_i is expandable or not, and for every expandable node, we will do single node expansion to obtain its child nodes in layer L_{i+1}. In the next, we will introduce (i) how to determine the root nodes, and (ii) how to do single node expansion. Please note that we only need to manually choose the root nodes for MSG. Once they are decided,

[1]http://labrosa.ee.columbia.edu/millionsong/musixmatch
[2]http://nltk.org/

the following node expansions (the constructing process of MSG) can be automatically done by single node expansion algorithms.

Root Nodes: We identify the root concepts from 5, lyrics-based keywords by taking account of three factors: lexical classes (Secion 2), inverse document frequency (IDF), and the number of the tracks associated with the concept. First we remove words whose lexical classes are ADV, ADJ-SAT, and VERB since these classes usually do not correspond to meaningful concepts. Then we filter the meaningless words like "a" and "the" by limiting the IDF value of the remaining words to be larger than a given threshold. Finally, we obtain the first 15 nodes with the largest sizes as our root nodes.

Single Node Expansion: After obtaining root nodes in layer L_1, we conduct node expansion layer by layer. The key idea is to identify the sub-concepts (words) as those that appear frequently in the lyrics of the acoustically similar tracks. These words are regarded as more likely to be correlated with the audio part of tracks. Therefore, we develop a neighbor-voting algorithm for node expansion. The sub-concepts are voted out by the tracks that sounds similar. Specifically, given the label of a node q, we first scan its associate music set $T(q)$. For each track in $T(q)$, we get the lyrics of its nearest K acoustic neighbors, and weight the lyrics words according to their occurrences. Through this way, the words co-occurring most frequently in similar music will be extracted. We repeat the node expansion process until no node can be split. The loop terminates in two situations: the sizes of all leaf nodes are small enough or the expansion results show that all lyric words' co-occurrence are small enough. For completeness, the algorithm of node expansion is shown in Algorithm 1.

Please note that even though lyric is chosen as node concept in this work, other kinds of concepts can also be our options. When lyric is missing, or it does not represent solid emotional understanding of music, we can change the concept to artist or age, and the definition of $T(q)$ should be changed correspondingly. For example, The associated music set $T(q)$ of a singer node q can refer to the songs of this singer.

3. VISUALIZATION

In this section, we show how to visualize music in an user-friendly interface based on MSG (Fig. 1B-F).

3.1 Visualization for MSG

For visualizing music semantic graph, we adopt "bubble" to represent every node (concept) in our graph. Bubbles can be of different diameters and colors, which reflect the sizes of node, and the style of nodes. Basically, bubbles are blue. When the bubble is the user's searching goal, its color will changes to red.

The relative positions of the bubbles in the interface approximate the concept distances between nodes. The concept distance among nodes which share the same parent are calculated by combining lyric-based distances and acoustic distances among their associated tracks,

$$D(q_1, q_2) = (1-\omega)\cdot\sum_i\sum_j d_l(l_i, l_j) + \omega\cdot\sum_i\sum_j d_a(v_i, v_j), \quad (4)$$

where $\le \omega \le 1$, which balances two distance types, i and j represent the i-th and j-th track in $T(q_1)$ and $T(q_2)$, respectively.

Based on the inter-node distances, we map the nodes to 2D space using multidimensional scaling (MDS). For clear exhibition, we calculate the relative force between each node pair. It is large when two nodes are close, and disappear when the distance between two nodes is above a threshold. When two nodes are too close after MDS, they will be forced to stay away. If several nodes huddle together, each node will move due to the combination of forces.

Algorithm 1 Single Node Expansion

Input: Node q, music collection $\mathcal{C}$, Lyric word list $\mathcal{W}$ $\{w_1, w_2, ..., w_{|\mathcal{W}|}\}$

Output: Learned sub-node set $\mathcal{E}_q$ $\{e_i\}_{i=1}^{|\mathcal{E}_q|}$.

Get the associate music set $T(q)$
Initialization: $\mathcal{E}_q :\ \emptyset$, $r(w_i) :$.
for all track $t_q^i \in T(q)$ **do**
  Find the top K nearest neighbors of t_q^i using the distances of acoustic features, denoted as $\mathcal{N}(t_q^i)$ $\{t_q^{i1}, t_q^{i2}, ..., t_q^{ik}\}$
  Count the occurrences of words $o(w_1)$ to $o(w_{|\mathcal{W}|})$ in all the lyrics of $\mathcal{N}(t_q^i)$
  Let W_{qi} $\{w_{qi}^j\}_{j=1}^T$ be the T most frequent words in all the lyrics of $\mathcal{N}(t_q^i)$.
  Filter out words w_{qi}^j in W_{qi} that $IDF(w_{qi}) < \tau_{IDF}$
  for all word $w_{qi}^j \in W_{qi}$ **do**
    $r(w_{qi}^j) :\ r(w_{qi}^j)\ \ (T-i)$.
  end for
end for
filter all $r(w)$ that $r_w < r_{min}$, where r_{min} is the minimum co-occurrence requirement.
Combine q and top N_q words with largest $r(w)$ (if exist) to form $\mathcal{E}_q$.

3.2 Visualization for Music

Furthermore, our prototype offer user an efficient and new audio-visual perception by visualizing music via lyrics and images. When users step into a leaf node, which means it cannot be expanded, the interface will show all the tracks that share the same concept (node's label). Each track is first represented by a cover image. When users click the cover image, a sequence of images with their corresponding lyrics are shown for quick viewing. Users can immediately have a general image of the track without taking several minutes to pre-listen an unknown music.

Practically, we do not limit the scope of the representing images. Every music is visualized by a sequence of images which are searched from Internet. We use the lyrics word to first search images from Internet, and then match them to the music by features. The cover image of a music is not the cover image of the corresponding album. It is an image that has the highest matching score for the music among all the images used for visualizing this music. The detailed matching process is described below.

For each track, we first extract nine phrases in its lyrics which repeats most frequently $p_1 \sim p_9$, and cut out the corresponding audio part $a_1 \sim a_9$, associated with the lyric phrase.

For one leaf node in the MSG and a particular track that belongs to it, 9 candidate image sets are obtained by using the label of the leaf node and the 9 phrases as query inputs to search on the Internet. Then for each candidate image set and its corresponding audio part, we adopt music-image matching method [16] to estimate the matching degree between them, and select the images with the highest matching scores as the representing images for this track.

The cover image for this track is chosen as the one with the top matching score among the nine selected ones. Overall, we use lyric-based concepts and phrases in lyrics to limit the scope of the candidate image set, and utilize music-image matching approach to further take account of audio features. Users can scan the representing images and lyrics, and click any of the nine images to listen to the corresponding audio part (Fig. 1E). Through this procedure, our prototype provides an interesting and efficient way to scan music and music collection.

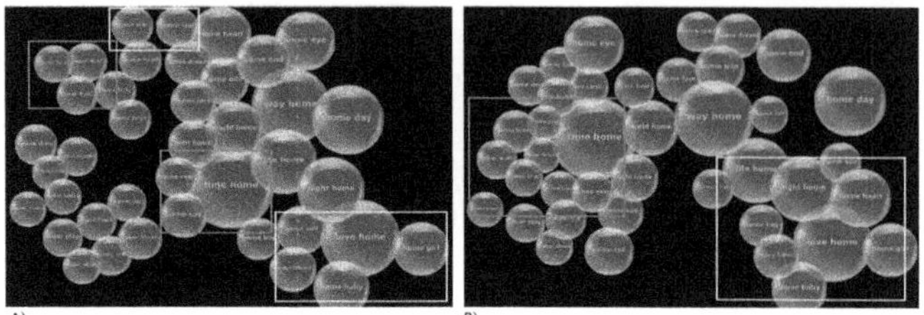

A) B)

Figure 2: A). The layout for ω (only lyric-based distance is considered); B). The layout for ω 1 (only acoustic distance is considered).

4. USER STUDY

Based on the track list musiXmatch dataset, we successfully collect about 8, songs from website to construct a MSG. We invite 16 volunteers who are all amateur of music with an average age of 2 .75 to try our system for about 15 minutes. Users are asked to try four functions: browsing concepts in MSG, evaluating the quality of the cover image for each track, estimating the quality of music visualization by images, and concept searching. After the trial, they are required to give marks between 1 (bad) and 5 (good) for a questionnaire of questions. The average scores for these questions are shown in Table 1. We summarize some of the qualitative findings.

semantic browsing and searching based on MSG: Most users think the minded lyric-based concepts are generally reasonable, but some of them are hard to understand. The easiest concept to understand is emotion-based concept ("happy","cry" and "pain") and the concepts which have specific imagination ("sky","summer", and "sun"). Users are interested in searching function, which provides the location of the query keyword in a hierarchical graph. They feel it is new and offers them a structured overview of searching input. For example, the lower right corner of Figure 1D shows the searching result of "summer". Previously, users can only get a list of songs whose lyrics include "summer". In our prototype, users can further decide which kinds of "summer" they want, for example, "rain summer" or "sun summer".

Visualization of MSG and music: Overall, the users think bubbles are clear enough for showing lyric-based concepts. Some of them noticed and tried different weights between lyric-based and acoustic distance (ω in Eq. 4). 75 of them recognize that the structure of graph is reasonably different for different ω. Figure 2 shows the different layouts when the weight is adjusted. We can find that when the effect of lyric (ω 1) is not considered, the positions of the concepts change: "home star" is a little far from "home sun", and "home tear" is changed to be near to "home year". For single music visualization, most users respond that multiple images and lyrics together can offer an overall and comparatively emotionally correct, but not an accurate impression of a track. It is reported that users only spend 1 s to have a first glance of a track with image visualization, but take 3 s to obtain a similar first impression of the track by listening from its start.

5. CONCLUSIONS

In this paper, we propose music semantic graph, a music browsing and scanning prototype, for organizing a music collection by utilizing lyrics and audio features. The MSG is constructed by node expansion algorithm, and furthermore, music collection and single music is visualized by leveraging lyrics and image information, which improve the efficiency of browsing and scanning music for amateur users. Based on our proposed MSG, we develop an user-friendly interface to present the hierarchical semantic structures among a music collection. As a first attempt on the construction of music semantic graph, there are still much to improve, such as introducing hyphenation into lyrics analysis, enlarging the music collection and dynamic adjusting the music graph. We hope this paper can inspire more future works along this line.

Score	1	2	3	4	5	Avg
Easiness of learning MIL	0	0	1	9	6	4.31
Quality of lyric-based concept	1	1	5	8	1	3.44
Quality of image-based visualization for music	2	1	2	9	2	3.5
Fun factor	0	0	1	8	7	4.44
Interest in future usage	0	0	4	4	8	4.25

Table 1: Evaluation results for MIL. The numbers of users who answered by choosing $1 \sim 5$ points, and the average scores for each question are shown.

6. ACKNOWLEDGMENTS

This work is partially supported by the research grants council of HK SAR through grant CUHK 16713, and partly supported by National Natural Science Foundation of China (9132 1 1, 61 72 1), Shenzhen Basic Research Program (JCYJ2 12 9 3 9 2 5 89 , JCYJ2 12 61711 61 38, JCYJ2 13 2113127 96), Guangdong Research Program (2 1 B 5 5 5 17), 1 Talents Program of CAS, and Guangdong Innovative Research Team Program (No.2 1 1D 1 6 828).

7. REFERENCES

[1] M. Goto and T. Goto. Musicream: Integrated music-listening interface for active, flexible, and unexpected encounters with musical pieces. *Journal of Information Processing*, 2009.

[2] M. Hamasaki and M. Goto. Songrium: A music browsing assistance service based on visualization of massive open collaboration within music content creation community. In *Int. Symposium on Open Collaboration*, 2013.

[3] P. N. Juslin and D. Västfjäll. Emotional responses to music: The need to consider underlying mechanisms. *Behavioral and brain sciences*, 2008.

[4] D. Lübbers. Sonixplorer: Combining visualization and auralization for content-based exploration of music collections. In *ISMIR*, 2005.

[5] D. O. Maidin and M. Fernström. The best of two worlds: Retrieving and browsing. In *DAFX-00, Verona, Italy*, 2000.

[6] I. R. Olson, J. C. Gatenby, and J. C. Gore. A comparison of bound and unbound audio–visual information processing in the human cerebral cortex. *Cognitive Brain Research*, 2002.

[7] E. Pampalk. Islands of music: Analysis, organization, and visualization of music archives. *Master's thesis, TUW, Vienna, Austria*, 2001.

[8] E. Pampalk, S. Dixon, and G. Widmer. Exploring music collections by browsing different views. *Computer Music Journal*, 2004.

[9] E. Pampalk and M. Goto. Musicsun: A new approach to artist recommendation. In *ISMIR*, 2007.

[10] G. Salton and C. Buckley. Term-weighting approaches in automatic text retrieval. *Information processing & management*, 1988.

[11] M. Schedl, C. Höglinger, and P. Knees. Large-scale music exploration in hierarchically organized landscapes using prototypicality information. In *ACM ICMR*, 2011.

[12] R. Stewart, M. Levy, and M. Sandler. 3d interactive environment for music collection navigation. *Proc. DAFx-08*, 2008.

[13] S. Stober and A. Nürnberger. A multi-focus zoomable interface for multi-facet exploration of music collections. In *Int. Symposium on CMMR*, 2010.

[14] D. Turnbull, L. Barrington, D. Torres, and G. Lanckriet. Semantic annotation and retrieval of music and sound effects. *IEEE Trans. on ASLP*, 2008.

[15] G. Tzanetakis and P. Cook. Marsyas3d: a prototype audio browser-editor using a large scale immersive visual and audio display. In *ICAD*, 2001.

[16] X. Wu, Y. Qiao, X. Wang, and X. Tang. Cross matching of music and image. *ACMMM*, 2012.

ESC: Dataset for Environmental Sound Classification

Karol J. Piczak
Institute of Electronic Systems
Warsaw University of Technology
Warsaw, Poland
K.Piczak@stud.elka.pw.edu.pl

ABSTRACT

One of the obstacles in research activities concentrating on environmental sound classification is the scarcity of suitable and publicly available datasets. This paper tries to address that issue by presenting a new annotated collection of 2 000 short clips comprising 50 classes of various common sound events, and an abundant unified compilation of 250 000 unlabeled auditory excerpts extracted from recordings available through the Freesound project. The paper also provides an evaluation of human accuracy in classifying environmental sounds and compares it to the performance of selected baseline classifiers using features derived from mel-frequency cepstral coefficients and zero-crossing rate.

Categories and Subject Descriptors

H.3.1 [**Information Systems**]: Content Analysis and Indexing; H.5.5 [**Information Systems**]: Sound and Music Computing

Keywords

environmental sound; classification; dataset

1. INTRODUCTION

Recent years have brought a steady stream of advances in machine perception. Computer systems undertake progressively more complex tasks, at times even surpassing human capabilities. A significant part of these spectacular achievements has come in visual recognition, with recent proliferation of successful deep learning approaches.

At the same time, research in auditory recognition tasks has been focusing mostly on speech and music processing. Analysis of environmental sounds (a very diverse group of everyday audio events which cannot be described as speech nor music) has lagged behind in applying those recent improvements, despite numerous possible applications in audio surveillance systems [9], hearing aids [2], smart room monitoring [16], and video content highlight generation [3].

MM'15, October 26–30, 2015, Brisbane, Australia.

ACM 978-1-4503-3459-4/15/10 ...$15.00.
DOI: http://dx.doi.org/10.1145/2733373.2806390.

One of the objective impediments to more active research in this field is strong fragmentation and difficulty in comparability and reproducibility. Most studies so far (Barchiesi et al. [4] and Chachada & Kuo [5] present recent surveys of this topic) have been conducted on datasets that are either very specific, small, or (semi-)proprietary [1, 7, 8, 10, 11, 13, 15, 17]. This scarcity of publicly available datasets[1] and difficulty in accessing the original code for study replication make research reproducibility efforts harder than they should be. That is in stark contrast to such fields as computer vision where corpora like MNIST[2] and CIFAR[3] have been prominently used as a de facto standard for baseline comparisons. Only in the recent months did initiatives such as the Urban Sound project [14] (a dataset of recordings concentrating on urban environments) bring some hope for a change in this matter. The situation, however, still remains rather bleak.

Therefore, the goal of this paper is to facilitate open research in the field of environmental sound classification by:

- contributing a publicly available dataset of environmental recordings,
- presenting estimates of human classification accuracy for this dataset,
- comparing these numbers with baseline performance of most common machine learning classifiers,
- providing a Jupyter (IPython) notebook with a more thorough analysis and code for easy replication of obtained results.

2. THE ESC DATASET

The presented compilation consists of three parts: the main labeled set comprising 50 classes of various environmental sounds, a small proof-of-concept subset of 10 classes selected from the main dataset - serving as a simplified benchmark - and a supplementary dataset of unlabeled excerpts suitable for unsupervised learning experiments.

All datasets consist of sound clips constructed from recordings available publicly through the Freesound project [6]. Classes included in the labeled part of the dataset were arbitrarily selected with the goal of maintaining balance between major types of sound events, all the while taking into consideration the limitations in the number and diversity of available source recordings, and subjectively assessed usefulness and distinctiveness of each class. The Freesound database of field recordings was queried for common terms

[1] Most datasets are listed on a website maintained by Toni Heittola: http://www.cs.tut.fi/~heittolt/datasets.html [*Accessed Aug. 5, 2015*]
[2] http://yann.lecun.com/exdb/mnist/ [*Accessed Aug. 5, 2015*]
[3] http://www.cs.toronto.edu/~kriz/cifar.html [*Accessed Aug. 5, 2015*]

related to the constructed classes. Search results were individually evaluated and verified by the author by annotating fragments containing events belonging to the given class. These annotations were then used to extract 5-second-long recordings of audio events (shorter events were padded with silence as needed). The extracted samples were reconverted to a unified format (44.1 kHz, single channel, Ogg Vorbis compression at 192 kbit/s). The labeled datasets were consequently arranged into 5 uniformly sized cross-validation folds, ensuring that clips originating from the same initial source file are always contained in a single fold.

The resulting dataset is available under a Creative Commons non-commercial license through the Harvard Dataverse project[4]. It is accompanied by an IPython notebook containing a more thorough analysis of the dataset than is possible in a short paper format, and the detailed results obtained along with source code for study replication[5].

2.1 ESC-50

The *ESC-50* dataset consists of 2 000 labeled environmental recordings equally balanced between 50 classes (40 clips per class). For convenience, they are grouped in 5 loosely defined major categories (10 classes per category):

- animal sounds,
- natural soundscapes and water sounds,
- human (non-speech) sounds,
- interior/domestic sounds,
- exterior/urban noises.

The goal of the extraction process was to keep sound events exposed in the foreground with limited background noise when possible. However, field recordings are far from sterile, thus some clips may still exhibit auditory overlap in the background.

The dataset provides an exposure to a variety of sound sources - some very common (*laughter*, *cat meowing*, *dog barking*), some quite distinct (*glass breaking*, *brushing teeth*) and then some where the differences are more nuanced (*helicopter* and *airplane* noise).

One of the possible deficiencies of this dataset is the limited number of clips available per class. This is related to the high cost of manual annotation and extraction, and the decision to maintain strict balance between classes despite limited availability of recordings for more exotic types of sound events. Nevertheless, it will, hopefully, be useful in its current form and is a concept that could be expanded on if sufficient interest is expressed.

2.2 ESC-10

The *ESC-10* is a selection of 10 classes from the bigger dataset, representing three general groups of sounds:

- transient/percussive sounds, sometimes with very meaningful temporal patterns (*sneezing*, *dog barking*, *clock ticking*),
- sound events with strong harmonic content (*crying baby*, *crowing rooster*),
- more or less structured noise/soundscapes (*rain*, *sea waves*, *fire crackling*, *helicopter*, *chainsaw*).

This subset should provide an easier problem to start with, and it was initially constructed as a proof-of-concept dataset. The task of classifying sounds from such a constrained set of classes, a trivial feat from a human perspective, sets the bar really high for accuracy expected from automatic sound recognition systems. Therefore, this subset presents a slightly different problem to tackle than the whole *ESC-50* dataset. The differences between classes are much more pronounced, with limited ambiguity, and as such it may favor a different kind of machine learning approaches.

2.3 ESC-US

Unfortunately, the limited number of instances available in the labeled part of the dataset makes it rather inadequate for more complex knowledge discovery approaches like learning representations from data. To mitigate this issue, an additional dataset of 250 000 recordings (extracted from Freesound files tagged as "field recording") is provided in the same short-clip (5-second-long) format. It should be more fitting for procedures involving unsupervised pre-training and generative models.

Although the *ESC-US* dataset should be treated as not hand-annotated and is presented as such, it does include the metadata (tags/sound descriptions) submitted for the original recordings. However, in contrast to the labeled part of the dataset, the metadata were not verified individually by the author, but rely solely on Freesound's quality control procedures through crowd moderation.

Therefore, the dataset, apart from clustering and manifold learning experiments, could be also used in weakly supervised learning regimes (classification with labels partially missing or not specific enough).

3. SOUND CLASSIFICATION

3.1 Human classification accuracy

The human auditory system has little problem recognizing a plethora of sound stimuli, even in very noisy conditions. Therefore, it is to be expected that, with such a limited challenge as presented by the dataset, proper recognition of sound events should not be difficult at all. The real question was: how easy is it? To answer this, numerous participants were asked through the CrowdFlower crowdsourcing platform to try their best at classifying sounds from the labeled datasets.

The experiment involved presenting a number of sound recordings to participants and asking them to choose a correct label from a list of 10 or, respectively, 50 categories. The participants were paid a flat fee per unit of work (classifying 10 recordings). Quality control was maintained through internal CrowdFlower's procedures (participant pre-screening and ongoing monitoring through randomly inserted test questions with an expected answer). The final results were further assessed by the author for potential outliers, and a small number of entries were eliminated this way. In total around 4 000 judgments were collected for each dataset (on average a dozen human classification entries per individual clip of *ESC-10* and two for *ESC-50*). Although it is hard to come up with formal statistical interpretation with such an experiment setup, it should nevertheless provide a rough estimate of human capabilities in recognizing everyday sounds.

The average accuracy achieved was 95.7% for the *ESC-10* dataset and 81.3% for *ESC-50*. Recall for individual classes varied greatly between types of sound events - from 34.1% for washing machine noise to almost 100% for crying babies

[4] http://dx.doi.org/10.7910/DVN/YDEPUT

[5] https://github.com/karoldvl/paper-2015-esc-dataset

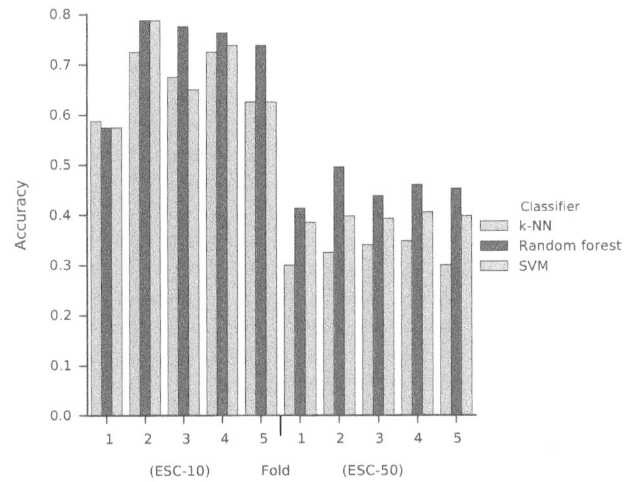

Figure 1: Comparison of classification accuracy between folds depending on the choice of classifier.

and barking dogs. Without going too much into details[6], sound events presented in the dataset can be divided into three groups based on their difficulty level:

- easy categories (most human sounds, animals, and some very distinct sound sources, like *siren*, *water drops*, *breaking glass*),
- average categories (everything in between the other two),
- difficult categories (mostly soundscapes and various mechanical noises).

One of the problems in such experiments is that with increasing number of categories, it becomes more difficult for untrained participants to mentally grasp all the possibilities and semantic differences. With 50 classes of sound events, it was still possible to provide them in one coherent view (divided into 5 major groups for faster orientation) without reaching for nested taxonomies, but it was on the verge of what is verifiable in such an experiment setup.

Nevertheless, based on these experiments, one can expect that trained and attentive listeners could score flawlessly on the smaller dataset and most probably achieve accuracy levels reaching 90% on the main dataset, with some room for error when classifying more ambiguous mechanical noises and soundscapes.

3.2 Baseline machine classification results

Having established an approximate figure on what is the desired target accuracy for a sound recognition system with near-human capacity, the second goal was to verify what can be achieved with some baseline approaches to machine classification of environmental sounds. The aim of this analysis was not to construct the most robust system possible, but to investigate what can be done with basic approaches, exploring potential pitfalls and intricacies of the dataset.

Two types of features were extracted from each clip: zero-crossing rate and mel-frequency cepstral coefficients (*MFCC*). The former is a very simple, yet useful feature, whereas the latter are ubiquitous in speech processing and analyzing

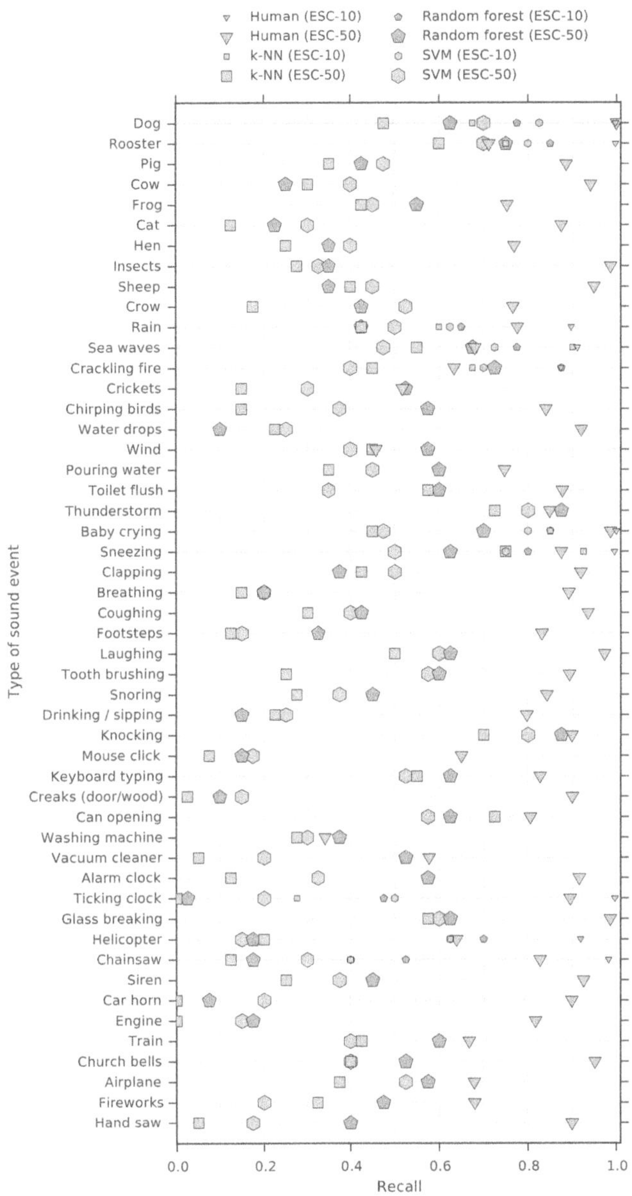

Figure 2: Category recall for different types of classifiers and human assessment.

harmonic content. MFCCs were computed using the librosa package[7] with default settings resulting in frame length of 11.6 ms. Discarding the 0th coefficient, first 12 MFCCs and zero-crossing rate were summarized for each clip with their mean and standard deviation across frames. Feature vectors created in this way were treated as input to three types of classifiers: k-nearest neighbors (*k-NN*), random forest ensemble and support vector machine (*SVM*) with linear kernel. Learning was performed on both datasets with a 5-fold cross-validation regime.

The *ESC-10* dataset had an average classification accuracy ranging from 66.7% for the k-NN classifier to 72.7% for the random forest ensemble, with SVM in the middle (67.5%). Some significant dispersion in results achieved could be seen

[6] Full experiment results are available as a spreadsheet supplementing the dataset, and a more thorough analysis is performed as part of the provided IPython notebook.

[7] *librosa: v0.3.1* library by B. McFee et al., DOI: http://dx.doi.org/10.5281/zenodo.12714 [*Accessed Aug. 5, 2015*]

between folds, owing to their small absolute size (see figure 1). The *ESC-50* dataset had less variability between folds when validating the models, but more pronounced outperformance by the random forest ensemble (44.3%) as compared to SVM (39.6%) or k-NN (32.2%).

One tendency that stands out when contrasting performance of different classifiers on both datasets is the pronounced drop in accuracy for the simplest (k-NN) model. It could indicate that the dependencies between features were more intricate in the bigger dataset, and they were better captured with more complex models.

In general, these rudimentary classification systems performed poorly when contrasted with their human counterparts, yet the difference is more pronounced for some groups of sounds than the others (see figure 2). For instance, lots of recordings in soundscape/background noise categories prove to be quite ambiguous for human listeners, a group which coincidentally scores quite high with automated systems.

The SVM classifier performed better for animal sounds than the random forest ensemble. Although a possible artifact of the data, it may also indicate that using more customized models for specific broader groups of sounds could be a viable option (creating a form of hierarchical multi-stage classification system).

It should be noted that the presented baseline classification methods are relatively simple. An evaluation of more robust approaches (based on convolutional neural networks) is performed in a more recent work of the author [12].

4. SUMMARY

The aim of this paper was to present a new compilation of environmental recordings that could enrich the research domain not so abundant with publicly available datasets. Hopefully, this material will help foster more open research efforts in analyzing environmental sounds.

There are numerous possible ways to expand on this topic, some of which include:

- compiling a fully replicable survey comparing various approaches utilized in past research papers,
- evaluating deep neural networks and other deep learning models in the context of environmental sound classification, e.g. with unsupervised pre-training using the *ESC-US* dataset,
- exploring the *ESC-US* dataset and the research possibilities it creates (clustering techniques, using available metadata in weakly-supervised setting or a hybrid machine-crowd annotation project, manifold learning etc.).

Acknowledgments

I would like to thank Frederic Font for his help in using the Freesound API and anonymous reviewers for their thorough and helpful comments.

5. REFERENCES

[1] BBC sound effects library. http://www.sound-ideas.com/sound-effects/bbc-sound-effects.html. (*Aug. 5, 2015*).

[2] E. Alexandre et al. Feature selection for sound classification in hearing aids through restricted search driven by genetic algorithms. *IEEE Transactions on Audio, Speech, and Language Processing*, 15(8):2249–2256, 2007.

[3] L. Ballan et al. Deep networks for audio event classification in soccer videos. In *Proceedings of the IEEE International Conference on Multimedia and Expo*, pages 474–477, 2009.

[4] D. Barchiesi et al. Acoustic scene classification: Classifying environments from the sounds they produce. *Signal Processing Magazine*, 32(3):16–34, 2015.

[5] S. Chachada and C.-C. J. Kuo. Environmental sound recognition: A survey. *APSIPA Transactions on Signal and Information Processing*, 3:e14, 2014.

[6] F. Font, G. Roma, and X. Serra. Freesound technical demo. In *Proceedings of the ACM International Conference on Multimedia*, pages 411–412. ACM, 2013.

[7] D. Giannoulis et al. Detection and classification of acoustic scenes and events: An IEEE AASP challenge. In *Proceedings of the IEEE Workshop on Applications of Signal Processing to Audio and Acoustics (WASPAA)*. IEEE, 2013.

[8] I. Lallemand, D. Schwarz, and T. Artieres. Content-based retrieval of environmental sounds by multiresolution analysis. In *Proceedings of the Sound and Music Computing conference*, 2012.

[9] K. Łopatka, P. Zwan, and A. Czyżewski. Dangerous sound event recognition using support vector machine classifiers. In *Advances in Multimedia and Network Information System Technologies*, pages 49–57. Springer, 2010.

[10] J. Maxime et al. Sound representation and classification benchmark for domestic robots. In *Proceedings of the IEEE International Conference on Robotics and Automation (ICRA)*, pages 6285–6292. IEEE, 2014.

[11] T. Nishiura and S. Nakamura. An evaluation of sound source identification with RWCP sound scene database in real acoustic environments. In *Proceedings of the IEEE International Conference on Multimedia and Expo*, volume 2, pages 265–268. IEEE, 2002.

[12] K. J. Piczak. Environmental sound classification with convolutional neural networks. In *Proceedings of the IEEE International Workshop on Machine Learning for Signal Processing (MLSP)*. IEEE, 2015. *In press.*

[13] A. Plinge et al. A bag-of-features approach to acoustic event detection. In *Proceedings of the IEEE International Conference on Acoustics, Speech and Signal Processing (ICASSP)*, pages 3704–3708. IEEE, 2014.

[14] J. Salamon, C. Jacoby, and J. P. Bello. A dataset and taxonomy for urban sound research. In *Proceedings of the ACM International Conference on Multimedia*, pages 1041–1044. ACM, 2014.

[15] D. Stowell and M. D. Plumbley. An open dataset for research on audio field recording archives: freefield1010. *arXiv preprint arXiv:1309.5275*, 2013.

[16] M. Vacher, J.-F. Serignat, and S. Chaillol. Sound classification in a smart room environment: an approach using GMM and HMM methods. In *Proceedings of the IEEE Conference on Speech Technology and Human-Computer Dialogue*, pages 135–146, 2007.

[17] M. van Grootel, T. Andringa, and J. Krijnders. DARES-G1: Database of annotated real-world everyday sounds. In *Proceedings of the NAG/DAGA International Conference on Acoustics*, 2009.

Improving Feature Aggregation for Semantic Music Retrieval

Zhouyu Fu
School of Computing, Engineering & Mathematics
University of Western Sydney
Penrith, NSW Australia
z.fu@uws.edu.au

ABSTRACT

Feature aggregation is an important step in semantic music retrieval that accumulates features obtained from local frames to produce a global song-level representation. A good aggregation scheme should capture both feature correlations and temporal information, while existing schemes only focus on one of the two respects and lack in the other. In this paper, we present a new feature aggregation scheme to model the dependencies in both feature and temporal domains. This is achieved by augmenting local feature vectors with second-order monomials that capture the correlations between different variables and performing temporal integration over the augmented features. To cope with increased feature dimensions, we further employ an embedded technique for feature selection by training an $\ell_{2,1}$ regularized linear classifier model for all label classes. The use of $\ell_{2,1}$ regularization produces a group sparse solution for classifier weight vectors, thus automatically eliminating irrelevant feature variables with varnishing weights. Our preliminary results demonstrate the effectiveness of the proposed feature aggregation scheme over existing aggregation schemes for large-scale music retrieval and annotation.

Categories and Subject Descriptors

H.5.5 [**Information Interfaces and Presentation**]: Sound and Music Computing

Keywords

Audio features; Music retrieval; Feature selection

1. INTRODUCTION

Audio features play a pivotal role in the design of content-based music retrieval systems. Since music signals are non-stationary in nature and occupy long durations, a localized approach is usually taken for audio feature extraction by splitting the raw signal into small frames and extracting local feature vectors from each frame that characterize the sound locally. To use the local feature vectors for song-level analysis , one needs to aggregate them to produce a single global feature representation for the entire song.

A standard approach for feature aggregation is to treat local feature vectors as a "bag of words" and model their distributions separately [5]. A simple yet effective technique for distribution modeling is to use summary statistics of local features for global representation, such as the widely used Mu-Var and Mu-Cov schemes [8, 6] that model the local features with a multivariate Gaussian distribution.

Distribution based schemes do not consider the temporal dependencies between neighboring frames. To overcome this limitation, various temporal modeling schemes were proposed that treat sequences of local feature variables as separate signals and apply spectral analysis techniques to capture the variations of the signals over time [9, 7, 4]. Nonetheless, existing temporal models only consider feature dependencies along the temporal axis disregarding the possible intra-feature correlations for features within the same frame, which are captured implicitly in distribution based schemes.

Hence, a good aggregation scheme should be able to capture both intra-feature and inter-feature (i.e. temporal) dependencies within and across local frames, while both distribution and temporal based aggregation schemes focus only on one of the above two respects. The first main contribution of the paper is a novel feature aggregation scheme capable of preserving both intra-feature and inter-feature information in the global representation. This is achieved by augmenting the local features with second-order variables that explain feature dependencies within each local frame and applying temporal modulation to the augmented local feature vectors. The proposed feature aggregation scheme establishes a more generic scenario that includes existing distribution and temporal based aggregation schemes as special cases, and provides richer information in the global feature representation that facilitates further semantic retrieval tasks.

Due to potentially large number of feature variables involved in the proposed aggregation scheme, we need to apply feature selection to avoid the curse of dimensionality. As the second main contribution, we employ an embedded feature selection scheme by casting retrieval as a classification problem and defining a $\ell_{2,1}$ regularized linear classification model for joint feature selection. $\ell_{2,1}$ regularization is well-known for producing a group sparse solution to classifier weights with zero-valued row norms, which enables implicit feature selection based on non-zero entries. The formulated optimization problems can be efficiently solved using the recent techniques for non-smooth optimization [3].

MM'15, October 26–30, 2015, Brisbane, Australia.
© 2015 ACM. ISBN 978-1-4503-3459-4/15/10 ...$15.00.
DOI: http://dx.doi.org/10.1145/2733373.2806391.

2. PROPOSED FEATURE AGGREGATION

In this section, we present the new feature aggregation scheme based on and generalizing the distribution based aggregation scheme of Mu-Cov [8, 6] and the temporal based scheme of Fluctuation Patterns (FP) [9, 7].

Let $\mathbf{S} = [\mathbf{s}_t]_{t=1}^{\mathcal{T}}$ be a matrix of local feature vectors obtained from different frames of an audio segment, where each column $\mathbf{s}_t \in \mathcal{R}^d$ denotes the feature vector for the tth frame. To produce a single feature vector for the whole segment, the Mu-Cov aggregation scheme [8, 6] takes the mean and covariance statistics of local features over all frames

$$\mathbf{x}_{mucov} = \left[\mu_s^T, svec\left(\mathbf{C}_s\right)^T\right]^T \quad (1)$$

$$\mu_s = \sum_{t=1}^{\mathcal{T}} \mathbf{s}_t/\mathcal{T}, \qquad \mathbf{C}_s = \sum_{t=1}^{\mathcal{T}} (\mathbf{s}_t - \mu_s)(\mathbf{s}_t - \mu_s)^T/\mathcal{T}$$

where μ_s and $\mathbf{C}_s$ denote the sample mean and covariance matrix of local feature vectors $\mathbf{s}_t$, T denotes transpose operator, *svec* is the vectorization operator for symmetric matrix that takes all lower triangular entries to form a column vector. The inclusion of covariance terms helps better model intra-feature dependencies between different feature variables in the same column of the feature matrix $\mathbf{S}$.

Alternatively, temporal based aggregation schemes such as variants of FP [9, 7] aim to capture the variation of local feature variables along the temporal axis by applying spectral analysis to separate sequences of local feature variables and accumulating the results into the global feature vector. This is equivalent to manipulating the rows of the feature matrix $\mathbf{S}$ and applying linear transformations to each row of $\mathbf{S}$ separately using different projection vectors

$$\mathbf{x}_{fp} = vec([\mathbf{Sb}_1, \ldots, \mathbf{Sb}_m]) \quad (2)$$

where $\mathbf{b}_j$ defines the jth projection vector for the linear transformation, *vec* is the vectorization operator that concatenates columns of the matrix into a single vector.

In practice, the projection vectors are derived from a set of orthonormal basis functions of a spectral transform such as the Fourier transform or the discrete Cosine transform that capture the temporal modulation of the underlying signal formed by the same feature variables across different frames. The first projection $\mathbf{b}_1 = \mathbf{1}_{\mathcal{T}}/\mathcal{T}$ is usually a scaled vector of all 1's that captures the DC component of the signal. Applying $\mathbf{b}_1$ to a signal is equivalent to taking the average of all samples. With this fact, we can connect the FP scheme with the Mu-Cov scheme in Eq. (1). Specifically, for each local feature vector $\mathbf{s}_t$, we define an augmented vector $\hat{\mathbf{s}}_t$ by

$$\mathbf{o}_t = [(s_{t,p} - \mu_{s,p})(s_{t,q} - \mu_{s,p})]_{p,q=1,p\neq q}^d \quad (3)$$

$$\hat{\mathbf{s}}_t = [\mathbf{s}_t^T, \mathbf{o}_t^T]^T \quad (4)$$

where $\mu_{s,p}$ is the pth component of the mean vector defined in Eq. (1), and $\mathbf{o}_t$ is a vector containing all second-order monomials for entries of $\mathbf{s}_i$ centralized to zero mean. The augmented feature vector $\hat{\mathbf{s}}_t$ is the concatenation of the original feature vector $\mathbf{s}_t$ and vector $\mathbf{o}_t$. It can be easily verified that the Mu-Cov scheme is equivalent to

$$\mathbf{x}_{mucov} = \hat{\mathbf{S}}\mathbf{b}_1 \quad (5)$$

where $\hat{\mathbf{S}} = [\hat{\mathbf{s}}_t]_{t=1}^{\mathcal{T}}$ denotes the new feature matrix by stacking the augmented feature vectors in columns.

Hence Mu-Cov can be seen as the special scenario of applying temporal integration to the augmented features preserving only the DC component. Although the FP scheme applies more basis vectors to capture the temporal information of local feature variables, it does not consider feature correlations. This motivates a new aggregation scheme that captures both inter-feature and intra-feature dependencies by applying the FP basis vectors to the augmented local feature vectors

$$\mathbf{x}_{afp} = vec\left([\hat{\mathbf{S}}\mathbf{b}_1, \ldots, \hat{\mathbf{S}}\mathbf{b}_m]\right) \quad (6)$$

The above augmented FP (AFP) aggregation scheme defines a generic form for global feature representation. It reduces to the Mu-Cov scheme if only the first column is kept in the feature matrix above, and to the FP scheme if only the first d rows are kept in the inside feature matrix.

Fig. 1 illustrates different processes for the three feature aggregation schemes discussed above. The augmented local feature matrix $\hat{\mathbf{S}}$ is shown on the left, which contains on top the raw feature matrix $\mathbf{S}$ consisting of input local feature vectors in columns. Global features are produced by applying linear transformations to the rows of the augmented feature matrix and displayed on the right half of Fig. 1, where each column corresponds to the results of transformation with a different projection vector $\mathbf{b}_j$. The Mu-Cov scheme only takes the first column from the global feature matrix, wheres the FP scheme takes all columns but are restricted to rows corresponding to the input $\mathbf{S}$. The proposed AFP scheme takes the whole matrix as the global feature representation and thus retains important information in both feature and temporal domains for further processing.

3. EMBEDDED FEATURE SELECTION

A major issue with the AFP aggregation scheme proposed above is the potential high dimension of the global feature vectors, which amounts to $D = md(d+3)/2$ global features with d local features and m projection vectors for temporal modulation. This is much larger than the feature dimensions of Mu-Cov ($d(d+3)/2$) and FP (md) schemes which only take subsets of all variables. Hence, feature selection is important to effectively leverage the proposed AFP aggregation scheme for music retrieval.

In this section, we present an embedded algorithm for feature selection. We cast retrieval into a multi-label learning problem [10], where each song is annotated with labels that describe the styles of the music. Songs with the same labels are treated as similar ones. A binary relevance strategy is adopted which learns a separate linear classifier for each binary problem defined on an individual label against all other labels. Let $(\mathbf{x}_n, (y_{n,j})_{j=1}^c)_{n=1}^l$ be the training dataset, where $\mathbf{x}_n$ denotes the global feature vector for the nth song produced from the AFS scheme and $y_{n,j} \in \{1, -1\}$ denotes its jth label value, l and c denote the number of training data and labels respectively. We then formulate the following optimization problem for both feature selection and classifier training

$$\min_{\mathbf{W}} \quad \ell(\mathbf{W}) + \eta\|\mathbf{W}\|_{2,1} \quad (7)$$

$$\ell(\mathbf{W}) = \sum_{n=1}^{l}\sum_{j=1}^{c}\left(1 - y_{n,j}\mathbf{w}_j^T\mathbf{x}_n\right)_+^2 \quad (8)$$

where $\mathbf{W} = [\mathbf{w}_j]_{j=1}^c \in \mathbb{R}^{D\times c}$ is the weight matrix holding c classifier weight vectors in columns. $\ell(\mathbf{W})$ defines the data term for the mis-classification cost on the training

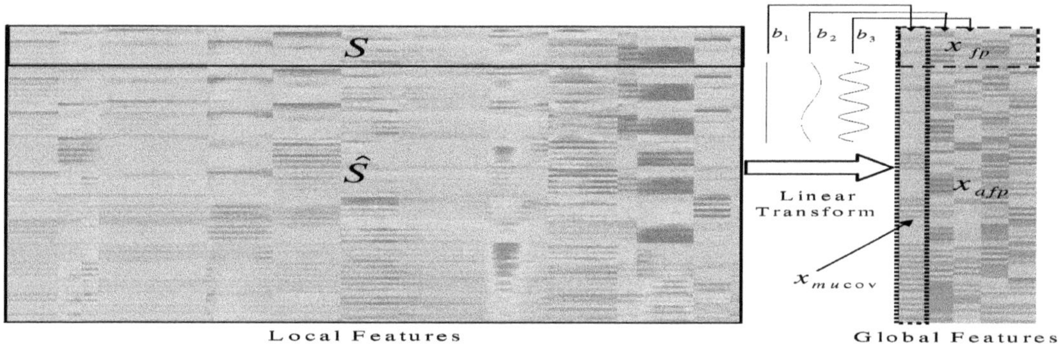

Figure 1: Illustration of the proposed feature aggregation scheme ($\mathbf{x}_{afp}$).

data for all c labels, where $(.)_+ = \max(0, v)$. We employed the squared Hinge loss function that has been widely used for training support vector machine (SVM) classifiers. It achieves the same large margin effects for classifier learning as the Hinge loss, but is numerically more stable due to its differentiability.

The second term on the right-hand-side of Eq. (7) is the regularization term on classifier weights. We have used a $\ell_{2,1}$ norm on the classifier weights for regularization, with $\|\mathbf{W}\|_{2,1} = \sum_{i=1}^{D} \|\mathbf{w}^i\|_2$ and $\mathbf{w}^i$ denotes the ith row of $\mathbf{W}$. The use of $\ell_{2,1}$-norm enforces group sparsity over row vectors and tends to produce a weight matrix with many zero-valued rows [1]. Thus it is particularly suited to joint feature selection for multiple tasks defined over different labels, where feature variables corresponding to zero-valued rows can be safely removed for all tasks, achieving implicit feature selection. Moreover, our formulation is different from existing $\ell_{2,1}$-norm based methods for feature selection [1] where the squared Hinge loss is used for the data term instead of standard square loss. Hence it provides an embedded solution to simultaneous feature selection and classifier learning, defined by a convex objective function leading to the globally optimal solution regardless of initialization.

The formulation in Eq. (7) can be solved by employing the alternating direction methods of multipliers (ADMM) [3]. We first reformulate the original problem in Eq. 7 into the equivalent constrained optimization problem below by introducing a surrogate variable $\mathbf{V}$

$$\min_{\mathbf{W},\mathbf{V}} \quad \ell(\mathbf{W}) + \eta\|\mathbf{V}\|_{2,1} + \frac{\rho}{2}\|\mathbf{W} - \mathbf{V}\|_2^2 \qquad (9)$$
$$s.t. \quad \mathbf{V} = \mathbf{W}$$

where ρ is a parameter that controls the strength of the last term. The Lagrangian of the above problem is given by

$$L(\mathbf{W}, \mathbf{V}, \mathbf{\Lambda}) = \ell(\mathbf{W}) + \eta\|\mathbf{V}\|_{2,1} + \frac{\rho}{2}\|\mathbf{W} - \mathbf{V}\|_2^2 + \mathbf{\Lambda}^T(\mathbf{W} - \mathbf{V}) \qquad (10)$$

where $\mathbf{\Lambda} \in \mathbb{R}^{D \times c}$ is a matrix of Lagrangian multipliers for the equality constraint. ADMM is an iterative optimization technique by repeating the following three steps in each iteration until convergence

- $\mathbf{W}^{(t+1)} = \arg\min_{\mathbf{W}} L(\mathbf{W}, \mathbf{V}^{(t)}, \mathbf{\Lambda}^{(t)})$
- $\mathbf{V}^{(t+1)} = \arg\min_{\mathbf{V}} L(\mathbf{W}^{(t+1)}, \mathbf{V}, \mathbf{\Lambda}^{(t)})$
- $\mathbf{\Lambda}^{(t+1)} = \arg\min_{\mathbf{\Lambda}} L(\mathbf{W}^{(t+1)}, \mathbf{V}^{(t+1)}, \mathbf{\Lambda})$

where the superscript indicates the iteration number. Basically, with each step, one fix the other two variables and optimize over the remaining variable.

There is no closed form solution for $\mathbf{W}$ in step 1. However, we can use the gradient descent method to solve each weight vector $\mathbf{w}_j$ separately due to the convexity of the problem. The gradient of L w.r.t. $\mathbf{w}_j$ is given by

$$\nabla_{\mathbf{w}_j} L(\mathbf{W}, \mathbf{V}, \mathbf{\Lambda}) = 2 \sum_{n \in SV_j} (\mathbf{w}_j^T \mathbf{x}_n - y_{n,j}) + \rho(\mathbf{w}_j - \mathbf{v}_j) + \mathbf{\Lambda}_j \qquad (11)$$

where $SV_j = \{n | y_n \mathbf{w}_j^T \mathbf{x}_n < 1\}$ indicates the set of support vectors for label j with non-zero losses.

Step 2 is equivalent to solving D independent problems below for each variable $\mathbf{v}^i$ taken from the ith row of $\mathbf{V}$

$$\min_{\mathbf{v}^i} \quad \eta \left\|\mathbf{v}^i\right\|_2 + \frac{\rho}{2}\left\|\mathbf{v}^i - \mathbf{w}^i - \frac{\mathbf{\Lambda}^i}{\rho}\right\|_2^2 \quad \forall i \in \{1, \ldots, D\} \qquad (12)$$

The above problem has a closed form solution by using the soft thresholding technique [3]

$$\mathbf{v}^i = \left(\mathbf{w}^i + \frac{\mathbf{\Lambda}^i}{\rho}\right)\left(1 - \frac{\eta}{\rho} \cdot \frac{1}{\|\mathbf{w}^i + \mathbf{\Lambda}^i/\rho\|_2}\right)_+ \qquad (13)$$

and the Lagrangian variables in the final step are updated by $\mathbf{\Lambda}^{(t+1)} = \mathbf{\Lambda}^{(t)} + \rho(\mathbf{w}^{(t+1)} - \mathbf{v}^{(t+1)})$.

It can be seen that the introduction of variable $\mathbf{V}$ in ADMM manages to separate the optimization routines for the smooth and non-smooth terms of the original problem, where each subproblem can be solved in an efficient manner.

4. RESULTS

In this section, we show some preliminary results of the proposed feature aggregation and selection scheme (AFP-S) against other aggregation schemes discussed in Section 2 for music retrieval and annotation, including the standard MuCov and FP schemes, as well as the proposed AFP scheme without feature selection. We used a subset of the MillionSong dataset [2] that contains 10,000 contemporary popular music tracks produced by 3,863 artists taken from different online sources. Each artist is annotated with ground truth labels that describe the style of the artist, and we take artist labels directly for song labels. Since some label classes only contain a limited number of positive examples, we have only learned the models for the top 42 labels to ensure that there are sufficient amount of training data for each model.

Method	Accuracy(%)	MAP	AUC	Macro-F1
AFP-S	**26.13 ± 0.54**	**0.492 ± 0.009**	**0.607 ± 0.013**	**0.368 ± 0.008**
Mu-Cov	23.61 ± 0.24	0.475 ± 0.003	0.584 ± 0.003	0.328 ± 0.014
FP	22.38 ± 0.74	0.460 ± 0.002	0.546 ± 0.003	0.216 ± 0.017
AFP	22.69 ± 0.56	0.462 ± 0.003	0.580 ± 0.001	0.317 ± 0.014

Table 1: Performance comparison of different feature aggregation schemes for music retrieval.

For feature extraction, we split each song into disjoint 23-ms frames and extracted the first 13 Mel-frequency cepstral coefficients from each frame as the local features. We then group every 512 frames into a segment and apply different feature aggregation schemes to compute segment-level feature vectors, which are then averaged across different segments to produce the song-level feature vectors. For each experiment, we randomly split the whole dataset into two equal subsets for training and testing the retrieval models. We trained a linear SVM classifier for different aggregation schemes, where the regularization parameter is chosen via 3-fold cross validation on the training dataset. Performances on the testing set were measured using four different metrics from multi-label learning [10], namely subset accuracy, mean average precision (mAP), Macro-F1 scores and areas under the ROC curve (AUC). Accuracy and mAP are calculated over the testing examples and measure the annotation performance. Macro-F1 and AUC values are calculated over different labels and measure the retrieval performance. We then repeated the above process five times for different random partitions of training and testing data, where the same partition is used for different methods in each round to ensure a fair performance comparison.

Tab. 1 shows the mean values and standard deviations of different performance metrics obtained by the four feature aggregation schemes over five rounds, with the best result for each metric highlighted in bold font. From the table of results, we can clearly see that AFP-S, the proposed embedded feature selection scheme on augmented local features, achieves the best overall performances for both annotation and retrieval. It gains a margin of advantage over all other schemes for all the metrics being evaluated. Using the augmented aggregation scheme alone without feature selection is not nearly as effective. This is demonstrated by the performance of AFP, which is on par with the performance of the standard Mu-Cov scheme. A possible reason is the large feature dimension involved with AFP, that inevitably contains many irrelevant and noisy feature variables, making it harder for the effective learning of retrieval models. FP obtains the poorest result among all aggregation schemes, an indication that feature correlations are probably more important than temporal relations for the particular application considered here.

To provide further details on the retrieval performance, we have also plotted the individual AUC scores against different label classes in Fig. 2, where the results for the four aggregation schemes tested are displayed in different line styles as marked on the plot. For visual clarity, we have ranked the label classes in decreasing order according to the AUC scores obtained by AFP-S. From the plot, we can see that AFP-S consistently outperforms all other aggregation schemes for all but one label classes in terms of higher AUC scores. The performance gaps are quite pronounced for some label classes, a further indication on the effectiveness of feature selection for the augmented feature. On the other hand, the performances of AFP and Mu-Cov are quite close overall despite variations for individual classes, indicated by the mixing of performance curves in the plot. The performance of FP is not as competitive as other schemes, with the AUC curve sitting on the bottom of the plot.

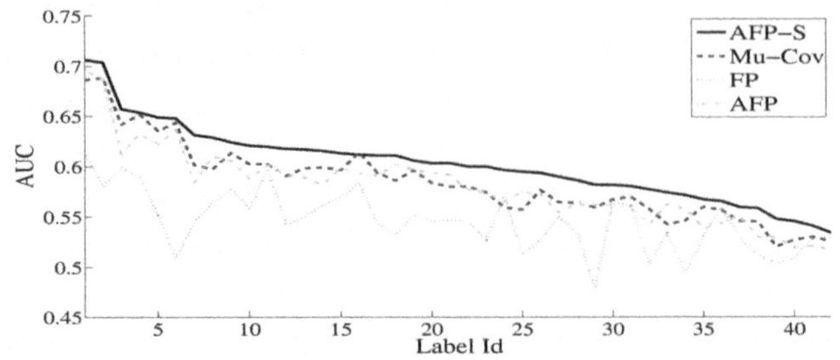

Figure 2: AUC scores for different label classes and feature aggregation schemes.

5. CONCLUSIONS

We proposed a new feature aggregation scheme which presents a richer song-level representation for music retrieval and annotation tasks. We also proposed an embedded feature selection scheme based on $\ell_{2,1}$ regularization of the classifier weights in training the classifier model for retrieval.

There are two important directions for future research. One possible direction is to investigate the similar idea of feature augmentation for other aggregation schemes, such as dictionary based bag-of-words representation [5] and the time series model for temporal analysis [4]. It would also be interesting to explore group sparsity for joint feature selection over multiple label groups in classifier learning.

6. REFERENCES

[1] A. Argyriou, T. Evgeniou, and M. Pontil. Multi-task feature learning. In *Adv. in Neural Info. Proc. Syst.*, 2006.

[2] T. Bertin-Mahieux, D. P. W. Ellis, B. Whitman, and P. Lamere. The million song dataset. In *Intl. Conf. Music Information Retrieval*, 2011. http://labrosa.ee.columbia.edu/millionsong.

[3] S. Boyd, N. Parikh, E. Chu, B. Peleato, and J. Eckstein. Distributed optimization and statistical learning via the alternating direction method of multipliers. *Foundations and Trends in Machine Learning*, 3(1):1Ű–122, 2011.

[4] E. Coviello, A. B. Chan, and G. Lanckriet. Time series models for semantic music annotation. *IEEE Trans. Audio, Speech, and Language Proc.*, 19(5):1343–1359, 2011.

[5] Z. Fu, G. Lu, K.-M. Ting, and D. Zhang. Music classification via the bag-of-features approach. *Pattern Recognition Letters*, 32(14):1768–1777, 2011.

[6] Z. Fu, G. Lu, K.-M. Ting, and D. Zhang. A survey of audio-based music classification and annotation. *IEEE Trans. Multimedia*, 13(2):303–319, 2011.

[7] C.-H. Lee, J.-L. Shih, K.-M. Yu, and H.-S. Lin. Automatic music genre classification based on modulation spectral analysis of spectral and cepstral features. *IEEE Trans. Multimedia*, 11(4):670–682, 2009.

[8] M. Mandel, G. Poliner, and D. Ellis. Support vector machine active learning for music retrieval. *Multimedia Systems*, 12(1):3–13, 2006.

[9] E. Pampalk, A. Flexer, and G. Widmer. Improvements of audio-based music similarity and genre classification. In *Intl. Conf. Music Info. Retrieval*, 2005.

[10] M.-L. Zhang and Z.-H. Zhou. A review on multi-label learning algorithms. *IEE Trans. Knowledge Data Engr.*, 2013.

Accelerating Large-scale Image Retrieval on Heterogeneous Architectures with Spark

Hanli Wang* Bo Xiao Lei Wang Jun Wu

Department of Computer Science and Technology, Tongji University, Shanghai, China
Key Laboratory of Embedded System and Service Computing, Ministry of Education,
Tongji University, Shanghai, China
{hanliwang,1314xiaobo,110_wangleixx,wujun}@tongji.edu.cn

ABSTRACT

Apache Spark is a general-purpose cluster computing system for big data processing and has drawn much attention recently from several fields, such as pattern recognition, machine learning and so on. Unlike MapReduce, Spark is especially suitable for iterative and interactive computations. With the computing power of Spark, a utility library, referred to as IRlib, is proposed in this work to accelerate large-scale image retrieval applications by jointly harnessing the power of GPU. Similar to the built-in machine learning library of Spark, namely MLlib, IRlib fits into the Spark APIs and benefits from the powerful functionalities of Spark. The main contributions of IRlib lie in two-folds. First, IRlib provides a uniform set of APIs for the programming of image retrieval applications. Second, the computational performance of Spark equipped with multiple GPUs is dramatically boosted by developing high performance modules for common image retrieval related algorithms. Comparative experiments concerning large-scale image retrieval are carried out to demonstrate the significant performance improvement achieved by IRlib as compared with single CPU thread implementation as well as Spark without GPUs employed.

Categories and Subject Descriptors

H.3.3 [**Information Search and Retrieval**]: Relevance feedback; H.3.4 [**Systems and Software**]: Distributed systems, Performance evaluation (efficiency and effectiveness)

*H. Wang is the corresponding author. This work was supported in part by the National Natural Science Foundation of China under Grant 61472281, the "Shu Guang" project of Shanghai Municipal Education Commission and Shanghai Education Development Foundation under Grant 12SG23, the Program for Professor of Special Appointment (Eastern Scholar) at Shanghai Institutions of Higher Learning (No. GZ2015005), and the Fundamental Research Funds for the Central Universities under Grant 0800219270.

MM'15, October 26–30, 2015, Brisbane, Australia
 ISBN 978-1-4503-3459-4/15/10$15.00
DOI: http://dx.doi.org/10.1145/2733373.2806392.

General Terms

System, Experimentation, Performance

Keywords

Heterogeneous Computing; Spark; Image Retrieval; Graphics Processing Units

1. INTRODUCTION

With the popularity of social networks and mobile multimedia applications, huge amounts of multimedia data are generated containing countless information to be mined and analyzed. Content-based image retrieval is such a golden example of applications for multimedia data mining. Most image retrieval systems are based on the model of Bag of Feature (BoF) [1], which represents images with sparse vectors by extracting salient local features from images and assigning them to the nearest visual word(s) in the vocabulary learned before. When the amount of images to be processed becomes larger and larger, the challenges including efficiency and accuracy arise from the huge computational demands produced by large-scale image retrieval.

To meet the escalating computational demands, scientists and engineers seek solutions from high performance computing communities. Meanwhile, there is a trend towards heterogeneity in the last decade since Graphics Processing Units (GPUs) have been developed into general-purpose coprocessors with the aid of the programming models and architectures, such as CUDA[1] and OpenACC[2]. GPU, usually manufactured with hundreds or even thousands of stream processors, is capable of invoking massive parallelization at fine grained level, which makes it ideal for executing data-intensive computations. As a consequence, such heterogeneous clusters, equipped with multiple GPUs on each computing node, are more powerful and environment friendly in comparison with traditional computer clusters.

Moreover, the development of distributed applications deployed on computer clusters has become much productivity and reliability since a wide range of programming paradigms, middle-wares and frameworks are developed. MapReduce [2], for instance, is such a popular programming paradigm proposed by Google, which applies the intuition that many large-scale workloads can be scaled out horizontally and ex-

[1]https://developer.nvidia.com/cuda-zone
[2]http://www.openacc-standard.org/

pressed with map and reduce operations. Apache Spark[3] is another famous and general-purpose cluster computing system for big data analysis and aims at improving the performance of iterative and interactive computations. Although the performance of the heterogeneous clusters is impressive and the distributed parallel frameworks continue to be prosperous and effective, it is challenging to utilize heterogeneous clusters for large-scale image retrieval with existed parallel frameworks.

To meet the huge computational demands for large-scale multimedia mining, several researchers propose to employ parallel frameworks. In [3], MapReduce is applied to multimedia data mining including K-Means clustering and background substraction. Shukla *et al.* [4] demonstrate how iterative computations can benefit from parallel execution on Spark and the results on Amazon EC2 clusters are presented. In [5], a framework, namely YAFIM, is proposed to parallelize frequent itemset mining with Spark and the experiments show that YAFIM achieves 18× speedup in average for various benchmarks as compared with MapReduce. In addition, a number of works are developed to achieve the maximum performance of the combined CPU+GPU system. In [6], StarPU is designed for numerical kernels to execute parallel tasks on a shared-memory machine of heterogeneous multicore architectures. He *et al.* [7] propose Mars, a GPU-based MapReduce framework to evaluate the benefits of co-operative usage of CPU and GPU on several traditional applications such as string matching, matrix multiplication, etc.

In this work, a utility library for Spark, namely IRlib, is designed aiming at accelerating large-scale image retrieval on heterogeneous clusters. IRlib fits into the Spark APIs and thus can be easily integrated into Spark as a built-in library. It enables dramatic increases of Spark in parallel computing performance by harnessing the power of GPUs. The rest of this paper is organized as follows. The proposed IRlib is introduced in Section 2. Evaluation results are shown in Section 3. Finally, Section 4 concludes this paper.

2. PROPOSED IRLIB IMPLEMENTATION

The design goal of IRlib is to make full use of the heterogeneous clusters and provide a uniform set of APIs which is compatible with that of Spark for large-scale image retrieval. A number of common image retrieval related algorithms are implemented, referred to as modules, to exploit the joint power of CPU and GPU. Each module contained in the IRlib is composed of two relatively independent parts, namely Module Driver and Algorithm Worker as depicted in Fig. 1.

As shown in Fig. 1, CUDA, which provides a comprehensive environment for GPU programming, is employed for developing the part of Algorithm Worker which is responsible for the implementation of the corresponding algorithm. The part of Module Driver which is programmed with Java language aims to interact with Spark engine and invoke Algorithm Worker. These two parts are communicated with each other by using the Java Native Interface (JNI). Although there are plenty of data structures provided by Spark, the exclusive data structures implemented by ProtocolBuffer[4], are developed for inner communication among the modules of IRlib so as to improve the performance of data serializa-

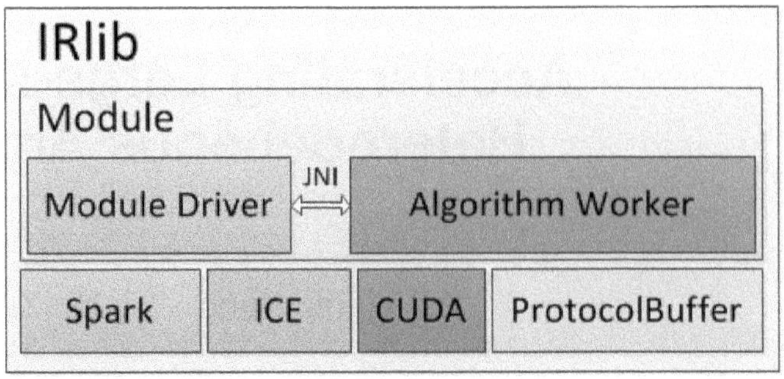

Figure 1: IRlib Overview.

tion and deserialization, which is suitable for handling the data of image retrieval such as feature vectors, visual dictionary vocabularies, BoF vectors, inverted file index and so on. These data structures can also be accessed by users for performance consideration. The Internet Communications Engine (ICE)[5], which is a fast and highly-scalable communication infrastructure, is utilized as Remote Procedure Call (RPC) service for building online retrieval applications.

Within the proposed IRlib, a number of image retrieval modules are realized, including feature extraction, K-Means clustering, BoF generation, similarity search, Hamming Embedding (HE) [8], Weak Geometric Consistency (WGC) [8], RANSAC [9] for homograph calculation, the Selective Match Kernel (SMK)/Aggregated Selective Match Kernel (ASMK) and their binary variants [10], etc. Due to the space limit, only the K-Means clustering module is discussed in detail to demonstrate the implementation of a module of IRlib.

As it is well known that K-Means clustering is an iterative and computationally laborious algorithm which aims to group a set of feature vectors (in the context of image retrieval) in such a way that the feature vectors belonging to one group are similar to each other than those in other groups. The Spark machine learning library MLlib[6] implements K-Means clustering and a significant improvement is achieved because the in-memory techniques are utilized as compared to the implementation with MapReduce. However, the power of GPUs can not be exploited by MLlib. Considering the fact that the most time-consuming calculations of finding the nearest object can be accelerated greatly when executed on GPUs, a K-Means clustering module is designed in IRlib which achieves high performances by dispatching computations onto GPUs. A comparative experiment of K-Means clustering provided by the two libraries of IRlib and MLlib will be described in Section 3.4.

Specifically, the API of K-Means clustering module is identical to that provided by the built-in MLlib, which means that it is easy for users to port the existed applications adopting K-Means clustering module in MLlib for usage of heterogeneous clusters. Firstly, the splits of input data scheduled by the Spark engine are received by the Module Driver in the format of ProtocolBuffer which have been serialized as binary streams. Then, after acquiring computational resources (*i.e.*, GPU), the proper data is transferred to the memory of GPU and the related processing is ex-

[3] http://spark.apache.org/

[4] https://developers.google.com/protocol-buffers/

[5] https://www.zeroc.com/

[6] http://spark.apache.org/mllib/

ecuted by Algorithm Worker on both CPU and GPU. In order to achieve coalesced read which can dramatically increase the efficiency of GPU, the centroid data is stored in column major in the global memory of GPU. The feature vector is cached into GPU shared memory when the calculation of locating the nearest centroid for a feature vector is executed by a thread block.

3. EXPERIMENTAL RESULTS

The computing performance of IRlib for large-scale image retrieval on heterogeneous clusters is evaluated by means of comparative experiments with applications running under a single CPU thread situation and these deployed on Spark without GPUs.

3.1 Experimental Setup

The experiments are carried out on a 12-node computer cluster equipped with multiple GPUs. Each node is running GNU/Linux Ubuntu 12.04 64-bit Desktop operating system and gigabit-nics are utilized among them for communication. The detailed configuration of the cluster is given in Table 1. In addition, a computer with middle-level performance as indicated as 'single*' in Table 1 is selected to run the single CPU thread version of all the following experiments.

Table 1: Hardware configuration of Spark cluster.

Hardware	Amount		
	2	6+1(single*)	4
CPU	Intel Core i5-3450	Intel Core i5-3470	Intel Core i5-4430
CPU Cores	4	4	4
Host Memory	24 GB	24 GB	24 GB
GPU	GTX 660Ti×2	GTX 660×2	GTX 760×2
CUDA Cores	1344×2	960×2	1152×2
GPU Memory	2 GB×2	2 GB×2	2 GB×2
Network	1Gbps LAN		

In order to verify the retrieval accuracy with the proposed IRlib, two benchmark works [11] and [10] are followed for guiding our implementation of image retrieval algorithms. Specifically speaking, the work of [11] is employed to demonstrate the performances of HE and WGC, where the Hessian-Affine detector [12] and SIFT descriptor [13] are used. On the other hand, the SMK/ASMK/ASMK-Binary algorithms are carried out according to [10], where the modified Hessian-Affine detector [14] and the Root-SIFT descriptor [15] are employed for feature detection and description. Several benchmark image datasets are utilized for experiments, including Oxford5K[7], Paris[8], Flickr100K[9] and MSR-Bing1M[10]. The information of these image datasets and the related descriptors is shown in Table 2.

3.2 Image Retrieval on Oxford5K

[7]http://www.robots.ox.ac.uk/~vgg/data/oxbuildings/
[8]http://www.robots.ox.ac.uk/~vgg/data/parisbuildings/
[9]http://www.robots.ox.ac.uk/~vgg/data/oxbuildings/flickr100k.html
[10]http://web-ngram.research.microsoft.com/GrandChallenge/Datasets.aspx

Table 2: Image datasets and the related descriptors.

Dataset	# images	# descriptors	descriptor size
Hessian-Affine detector [12] and SIFT descriptor [13]			
Oxford5K	5,063	18,190,561	11.2GB
Flickr100K	100,000	317,565,032	195.0GB
MSR-Bing1M	1,000,000	392,528,043	242.0GB
Modified Hessian-Affine detector [14] and Root-SIFT descriptor [15]			
Oxford5K	5,063	13,759,319	8.5GB
Paris	6,392	16,402,339	10.2GB

In this subsection, the Oxford5K dataset is used to evaluate the computational performance and the retrieval accuracy in terms of mean Average Precision (mAP) of the proposed IRlib, while the MSR-Bing1M dataset is used as distracting images and Flickr100K is employed as an independent dataset to train visual dictionary vocabularies. The speedup performance on K-Means clustering achieved by IRlib as compared to the single CPU thread version is listed in Table 3 where it can be easily seen that dramatic speedup performances can be obtained by IRlib and the speedup increases as the size of visual dictionary increases.

Table 3: Speedup of K-Means clustering on Flickr100K with different sized visual dictionaries.

Size	20K	200K	1M
Speedup	1,201.3	2,318.7	2,657.9

As shown in Table 4, the speedups of several representative IRlib modules are presented, including feature extraction (ImageProc), BoF calculation (BoF), HE model training (HETrain) and inverted file index generation (InvFlGen). The speedups of the ImageProc module in Table 4 remain the same under all test cases because this module is unrelated with the size of visual dictionary. In addition, as compared with other modules, the speedup of ImageProc is relatively low because it only owns CPU implementation at present.

Table 4: Speedup of image retrieval on Oxford5K retrieval with different sized visual dictionaries.

	20K	200K	1M
ImageProc	30.8	30.8	30.8
BoF	1,413.7	2,365.2	2,635.1
HETrain	502.1	650.5	713.1
InvFlGen	523.1	654.1	720.9

Table 5 shows the retrieval accuracy in terms of mAP for different sized vocabularies. As compared with [11], the mAP results are significantly better under all test conditions, with the minimum improvement of 0.03, maximum improvement of 0.16, and average improvement of 0.11. This improvement of mAP is mainly because much more images and feature vectors can be processed by using IRlib with Spark.

3.3 Extension with SMK/ASMK

In this subsection, the performances of the SMK module are presented by strictly following the benchmark work

Table 5: Retrieval accuracy in terms of mAP.

	20K		200K		1M
Distractors	0	1M	0	1M	0
Baseline	0.397	0.330	0.461	0.284	0.502
HE	0.588	0.448	0.625	0.383	0.612
WGC	0.533	0.363	0.542	0.266	0.544
HE+WGC	0.657	0.427	0.656	0.363	0.618

of [10] including the SMK, ASMK and ASMK-Binary algorithms. Two image datasets including Oxford5K and Paris are utilized for performance evaluation. As specified in [10], a 65K sized visual dictionary is generated by K-Means clustering. The visual dictionary trained on Paris is applied for Oxford5K image retrieval, and vice versa. The experimental results of speedup and mAP are listed in Table 6, where the mAP values in the parenthesis indicate the improvement of our implementation against that of [10]. Since our implementation follows [10], the mAP performances should be similar to each other, which is verified by the small mAP improvements as shown in the parenthesis in Table 6. As far as the computational performance is concerned, significant speedup ratios can be achieved by the SMK module for all test cases.

Table 6: Speedup and mAP performances achieved by the SMK module.

		ASMK	SMK	ASMK-Binary
Speedup	Oxford5K	340.9	372.3	401.7
	Paris	343.5	381.7	410.9
mAP	Oxford5K	0.817(0.000)	0.795(0.021)	0.800(-0.004)
	Paris	0.785(0.003)	0.744(0.026)	0.788(0.018)

3.4 Comparison with Spark MLlib

As aforementioned, MLlib is a built-in library of Spark for scalable machine learning consisting of common learning algorithms and utilities, including classification, clustering, etc. In this subsection, the comparison on K-Means clustering between IRlib and MLlib is carried out to verify the dramatic performance improvement of IRlib. The Flickr100K dataset is employed for testing with different sized visual dictionaries from 20K to 400K.

Table 7: Speedup of K-Means clustering achieved by IRlib over Spark MLlib with different sized visual dictionaries.

	20K	60K	120K	200K	400K
Speedup	26.3	42.4	50.0	56.3	65.9

As seen in Table 7, the performance improvement achieved by IRlib over Spark MLlib is significant because of the computing power of GPUs being harnessed by IRlib.

4. CONCLUSION

In this work, a utility library for Spark, namely IRlib, is designed to accelerate large-scale image retrieval by harnessing the computing power of GPU. In order to fully exploit the power of GPU and take the advantages of Spark, several techniques are employed for the development of IRlib. The experimental results demonstrate that a significant speedup can be achieved by the proposed IRlib as compared with both single CPU thread implementation and the Spark version without GPU. In the future, more research efforts and attempts will be put to enrich the utilities and functions of IRlib.

5. REFERENCES

[1] J. Sivic and A. Zisserman. Video google: A text retrieval approach to object matching in videos. *ICCV'03*, pages 1470–1477, Oct. 2003.

[2] J. Dean and S. Ghemawat. MapReduce: Simplified data processing on large clusters. *Comm. of the ACM - 50th anniversary issue: 1958-2008*, 51(1):107–113, Jan. 2008.

[3] B. White, T. Yeh, J. Lin, and L. Davis. Web-scale computer vision using MapReduce for multimedia data mining. In *MDMKDD'10*, pages 1–10, Jul. 2010.

[4] S. Shukla, M. Lease, and A. Tewari. Parallelizing ListNet training using Spark. In *ACM SIGIR'12*, pages 1127–1128, Aug. 2012.

[5] H. Qiu, R. Gu, C. Yuan, and Y. Huang. YAFIM: A parallel frequent itemset mining algorithm with Spark. In *PDPS'14*, pages 1664–1671, May 2014.

[6] C. Augonnet, S. Thibault, R. Namyst, and P.-A. Wacrenier. StarPU: A unified platform for task scheduling on heterogeneous multicore architectures. In *Euro-Par'09*, pages 863–874, Aug. 2009.

[7] B. He, W. Fang, Q. Luo, N. K. Govindaraju, and N. T. Wang. Mars: A MapReduce framework on graphics processors. In *PACT'08*, pages 260–269, Oct. 2008.

[8] H. Jégou, M. Douze, and C. Schmid. Hamming embedding and weak geometric consistency for large scale image search. In *ECCV'08*, pages 304–317, Oct. 2008.

[9] M. A. Fischler and R. C. Bolles. Random sample consensus: A paradigm for model fitting with applications to image analysis and automated cartography. *Comm. of the ACM*, 24(6):381–395, Jun. 1981.

[10] G. Tolias, Y. Avrithis, and H. Jégou. To aggregate or not to aggregate: Selective match kernels for image search. In *ICCV'13*, pages 1401–1408, Dec. 2013.

[11] H. Jégou, M. Douze, and C. Schmid. Improving Bag-of-Features for large scale image search. *IJCV*, 87(3):316–336, May 2010.

[12] K. Mikolajczyk and C. Schmid. Scale and affine invariant interest point detectors. *IJCV*, 60(1):63–86, Oct. 2004.

[13] D. Lowe. Distinctive image features from scale-invariant keypoints. *IJCV*, 60(2):91–110, Nov. 2004.

[14] M. Perd'och, O. Chum, and J. Matas. Efficient representation of local geometry for large scale object retrieval. In *CVPR'09*, pages 9–16, Jun. 2009.

[15] R. Arandjelovic and A. Zisserman. Three things everyone should know to improve object retrieval. In *CVPR'12*, pages 2911–2918, Jun. 2012.

Implementation of Face Recognition for Screen Unlocking on Mobile Devices

Chung-Hua Chu
Department of Multimedia Design
National Taichung University of Science and Technology
Taichung, Taiwan, ROC
chchu777@gmail.com

Shih-Ming Peng
Department of Multimedia Design
National Taichung University of Science and Technology
Taichung, Taiwan, ROC

ABSTRACT
Face recognition is a computer technique to capture the feature of the human face for user authentication. In the advanced mobile technology, mobile devices take the place of computers to become the major human-computer interaction. Related researches become more and more popular. This study discusses about the identification of users on the mobile devices. Recently, many users still use passwords for user authentication. However, such traditional password identification may not be secure since the passwords are easily intercepted. To solve this problem, this thesis adopts facial recognition for screen unlocking on the mobile devices.

Categories and Subject Descriptors
I.5.4 [**Pattern Recognition**]: Applications

General Terms: Algorithm

Keywords: Face recognition; mobile devices

1. INTRODUCTION
The User Authentication distinguishes whether the user is the legal owner, preventing the non-owners from operating the built-in system of mobile device directly. The system distinguishes the user depending on the unique identifier information of legal owner, so as to implement user authentication. The face recognition is a calculator technology extracting the "facial features" of face image as unique identifier information and using Pattern Recognition technology to process the biological feature information of face image. It is used very extensively for image information processing, including access control system, photographic surveillance system, and vehicle driving assistance At present, general mobile device users still use password authentication for user authentication, the "password" is used as the unique identifier information. This traditional authentication mode is extensively accepted by mobile device users for its familiar and convenient operation mode. However, it has operational issues, such as easy to forget, steal and input error, and there are information security vulnerabilities in standby mode setting. The system starts power saving mode and locks up the mobile device until the mobile device is not used for a long time to meet the preset stand-by time. However, the longer the preset stand-by time system.

This research subject is "face recognition for mobile device screen unlock", discussing the development of face recognition unlocking application by combining mobile devices with face recognition technique. First, the direction in the research is determined in the introduction, and related literatures and application studies are analyzed, so as to clarify current condition of face recognition technique and to determine the research items. Afterwards, the system is analyzed and the face recognition technique of mobile devices is designed to implement the face recognition authentication mechanism. Finally, the user test result of the completed system is compared with the application examples in literature review, so as to evaluate whether the utility meets the research objectives or not.

2. Proposed Methods
This section describes the system design and development of face recognition authentication mechanism. The present development conditions of mobile device platform and face recognition technique are known by literature review and clarifying the research motives and purpose stated in the introduction.

2.1 System Overview
This study proposes using two characteristics of face recognition technique to improve the usability and information security of password authentication: (1) use image capture to replace manual input for operation; (2) use facial feature to replace password as the unique identifier information. This study combines mobile devices with face recognition technique to develop face recognition authentication mechanism. The completed system is compared with the examples of application in literature review for analysis.

2.2 System Design
According to the discussion about face recognition technique and the example of face recognition, the face recognition authentication mechanism designed in this study has two major functions, which are face detection and face recognition. In terms of face detection function, in order to improve the range limited face detection of face recognition authentication on current market, the Haar-like feature is used to detect facial feature and look for face image automatically, so as to strengthen the automatic control of face recognition authentication. The face recognition function is designed aiming to reduce the

MM'15, October 26–30, 2015, Brisbane, Australia.
© 2015 ACM. ISBN 978-1-4503-3459-4/15/10...$15.00.
DOI: http://dx.doi.org/10.1145/2733373.2806393

consumption of system performance and the face recognition authentication execution time. The face image model is built by using global feature method and the feature points are matched by K neighbor points. Therefore, the face recognition authentication mechanism will be developed by Eigenface and Fisherface feature extraction methods respectively. Finally, in order to distinguish the difference between dissimilar face images, the histogram equalization is used to remove external ambient light source to enhance facial feature matching, and the secondary face images are matched for similarity

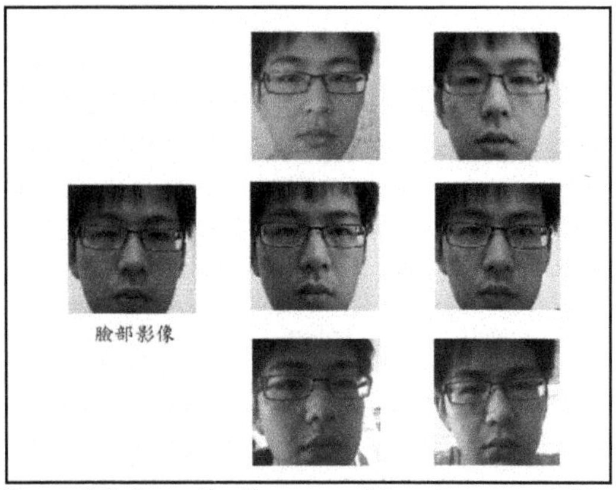

Figure 1 Schematic diagram of face image matching

2.3 System framework

When the user operates the mobile device, he can access the mobile device system until the face recognition authentication completes user authentication. The system framework is divided into three blocks, which are face detection, face recognition and face database. The functions of the blocks are described below:

1) Face detection: the front camera of mobile device detects face image and captures face image.
2) Face recognition: the face image is compared with the face samples of face database.
3) Face database: the captured face image is stored as face sample for matching.

2.4 System flow

In terms of the face recognition authentication mechanism of this study, the face detection function detects face image and extracts the facial feature of face image as the unique identifier information. The face recognition function matches the face image with the face samples in the face database for user authentication. The face detection and face recognition functions are described below:

1) Face detection function

   Step 1. The front camera of mobile device takes image and uses Haar-like feature to detect facial feature to judge if there is face image or not.

   Step 2. When the face image is detected, the face image is captured and stored.

   Step 3. Judge whether the face database has created the face sample. (If not, the face image is stored in face database and return to A-1)

2) Face recognition function

   Step 1. Use feature extraction method to extract facial feature and build face image model.

   Step 2. The feature points of face image are matched by KNN algorithm.

The face images are matched for similarity by histogram equalization.

3. Evaluation

This section describes the design of experiments for the face recognition authentication mechanism of this study. According to the aforesaid literature review and analysis of application research examples, this study proposes using face recognition authentication as password authentication to improve the user authentication of mobile devices. The developed face recognition unlocking application is compared with the face recognition unlock example in literature review, so as to evaluate the utility of the face recognition authentication mechanism of this study.

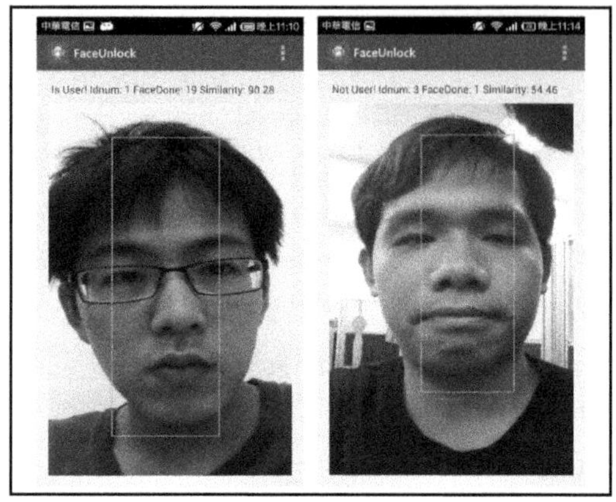

Figure 2 Success and failure in identity authentication

3.1 System Implementation

The test environment of this study is divided into hardware and site constraints according to the system development environment and experimental environment, described below:

1) Constraint of applicable hardware

   This study uses Android system platform to develop face recognition unlocking application, using Google Android SDK 4.0, OpenCV Android SDK 2.4.5 and JavaCV SDK 0.5 system development kits. The hardware for face recognition authentication is system platform above Android 4.0 and mobile devices supporting Android SDK and OpenCV SDK.

2) Constraint of applicable site

In order to evaluate the usability of this face recognition authentication mechanism in mobile devices, it is compared with the face recognition unlock example in literature review to evaluate the utility. The experiment has two test items, including the usability evaluation criteria of image recognition rate and authentication success rate and recording the time consumed by executive system. The authentication success rate is the success rate of test owners in passing face authentication mechanism, the recognition accuracy of the same face image (test image and face sample) is tested by image recognition rate to work out the correlation. The experimental process is described below:

Step 1. Description of experiment: explain research content, test process and system operation precautions.

Step 2. System test:

2.1 Execute face recognition authentication program: the subject clicks unlocking application in the standby menu to enter the face recognition authentication mechanism.
2.2 Enter unique identifier information: the front camera lens detects the subject's face image and captures face image as the unique identifier information.
2.3 Recognize user: compare the subject's face image with the face samples of face database, as shown in Figure 1. If the face image matching succeeds, the user authentication is completed, as shown in Figure 2. If the matching fails, return to 2.2 to capture the subject's face image again for matching. (system executes at most 3 times)

Record data: the system test ends, the test data are recorded, the experiment is finished.

Table 1 Face recognition evaluation criteria

Name of evaluation criteria	**Description**
Number of face samples	Number of face samples stored in face database.
Execution time (Sec)	Time consumed for executing face recognition authentication.
Recognition time (Sec)	Time consumed for recognizing face image.
Image similarity (%)	Similarity between face image and face sample.
Number of authentications	Number of recognitions through face recognition authentication.
Image recognition rate (%)	Success probability of face image matching.
Authentication success rate (%)	Success probability of the same face image passing face recognition authentication.
Authentication misrecognition rate (%)	Success probability of dissimilar face images passing face recognition authentication.

3.2 Evaluation Criteria

In order to improve the usability and information security of password authentication, this study proposes using face recognition technique to develop face recognition authentication for user authentication. The completed system is tested to evaluate the usability of face recognition unlocking application. After literature review [1, 2, 3, 4, 5], the following common test items are compiled as usability evaluation criteria, as shown in Table 1.

3.3 Simulation Analysis

. This section is the analysis of experimental result. There are 20 subjects for system test, and 5, 10, 15 and 20 face database samples are tested 30 times for face recognition authentication. There are 300 effective data. The average execution time of this face recognition authentication mechanism is 7.24 seconds, the average authentication success rate is 99%, the average number of authentications is 1.

Table 2 Effects of histogram equalization

	Without histogram equalization	**With histogram equalization**
Image recognition rate	100%	56.67%
Image similarity	42.36%	84.41%
Authentication success rate	99%	94.7%
Authentication misrecognition rate	56.67%	0%

According to the system test, the classification of face image by matching Kth-Nearest Neighbor with facial feature points of this face recognition authentication mechanism succeeds in the same face image matching, there is no authentication failure, but the difference between dissimilar face images cannot be distinguished effectively, the authentication misrecognition rate is about 57%. In order to reduce the authentication misrecognition rate, the histogram equalization is added in face recognition function to remove the external ambient light source to increase the facial feature contrast, and the secondary face image matching is implemented. The recognition is accepted until the image similarity is 90%, so as to distinguish the difference between dissimilar face images. Table 2 shows the differences in 5 face samples before and after histogram equalization.

After the secondary face image matching of histogram equalization, the image recognition rate with image similarity above 90% is screened, so that the number of successes in image matching is reduced greatly, the image recognition rate decreases to approximately 57%, even there are several authentication failure records in the system test process, the authentication success rate decreases to approximately 95%. However, the statistical result shows that the image similarity increases to 84%, and there is no authentication misrecognition record in the matching of dissimilar face images.

3.4 Performance Evaluation

This face recognition authentication mechanism is compared with the face recognition unlock example, as the face recognition authentication of mobile devices on current market is only provided for the system platform above Android 4.0, the mechanism continues the "Face Unlock" face recognition function of Galaxy Nexus, the usability and operation are almost identical. Therefore, the matching object is set as similar HTC Onc X. The research findings are shown in Table 3.

Table 3 Face recognition unlock results

	HTC One X with Face Identification	Face detection + Fisherface	Face detection + Eigenface
Number of face samples		20	
Face detection	Face detection (eyes)	Real-time face detection	Real-time face detection
Face recognition	Fisherface	Fisherface	Eigenface
Recognition time(Sec)	5.2	5.87	5.83
Execution time(Sec)	5.2	7.44	7.04
Authentication success rate	93%	99%	99%
Authentication misrecognition rate	0%	0%	0%
Number of authentications	2	1	1

The face detection of HTC One X uses range limited image capture and infrared eyeball reflection to locate the eyes to obtain the user's face image. In terms of face recognition, the Fisherface creates face image model and uses Kth-Nearest Neighbor and a few face database samples to match facial feature. As the face detection uses semiautomatic image capture and hardware-based facial feature location and one-off face recognition, the system processing procedure is reduced, and the average execution time is 5.2 seconds. However, there are several authentication failure records in the actual test process. The average authentication success rate is 93%, and the average number of authentications is 2.

4. Conclusion

This study discusses the user authentication of mobile devices, and proposes combining face recognition technique with mobile devices to develop face recognition authentication for improvement. The face recognition unlocking applications on current market are compared by the developed face recognition unlocking application and actual test, the result shows that the face recognition authentication can improve the operability of password authentication and strengthen the unique identifier information effectively. The face recognition authentication mechanism of this study replaces the range limited face detection by automatic face detection and uses three times of face image matching and image similarity matching of histogram equalization, the success rate of face recognition authentication is increased by about 6%. According to the test results of face recognition authentication mechanisms Face Detection+Fisherface and Face Detection+Eigenface, the maximum utility of feature extraction method in face database samples is determined. Based on 15±5 face database samples, the Fisherface feature extraction method shall be used when the number of face samples is smaller than 15, otherwise the Eigenface feature extraction method shall be used. In order to meet the research objective, consume less system performance and guarantee the success rate of face recognition authentication, this study uses Face Detection+Fisherface face recognition authentication mechanism as the representative face recognition authentication.

5. ACKNOWLEDGMENTS

The work was supported in part by the National Science Council of Taiwan, R.O.C., under Contracts NSC103-2221-E-025 -009.

6. REFERENCES

[1] M. Kirby and L. Sirovich, "Application of the Karhunen-Loeve procedure for the characterization of human faces," IEEE Transactions on Pattern Analysis and Machine Intelligence, vol. 12, no. 1, pp. 103-108, January 1990.

[2] W. D. Yang, A simple approach to a small-scaled face recognition system, Graduate Institute of Computer Science & Information Engineering, National Central University, 2007.

[3] R. L. Hsu, M. Abdel-Mottaleb and A. K. Jain, "Face detection in color images," IEEE Transactions on Pattern Analysis and Machine Intelligence, vol. 24, no. 5, pp. 696-706, May 2002.

[4] D. R. Kisku, M. Tistarelli, J. K. Sing and P. Gupta, "Face recognition by fusion of local and global matching scores using DS theory: An evaluation with uni-classifier and multi-classifier paradigm," in 2009 IEEE Computer Society Conference on Computer Vision and Pattern Recognition Workshops, Miami, FL, pp. 60-65, Jun 20-25, 2009.

[5] S A. Pentland, B. Moghaddam and T. Starner, "View-based and modular eigenspaces for face recognition," in 1994 IEEE Computer Society Conference on Computer Vision and Pattern Recognition, Seattle, WA, pp. 84-91, Jun 21-23, 1994.

Web-based Interactive Free-Viewpoint Streaming

A framework for high quality interactive free viewpoint navigation

Matthias Ueberheide[1], Felix Klose[1], Tilak Varisetty[2],
Markus Fidler[2] and Marcus Magnor[1]
[1]TU Braunschweig, Germany [2]Leibniz Universität Hannover, Germany
{ueberheide,klose,magnor}@cg.cs.tu-bs.de,
{tilak.varisetty,markus.fidler}@ikt.uni-hannover.de

ABSTRACT

Recent advances in free-viewpoint rendering techniques as well as the continued improvements of the internet network infrastructure open the door for challenging new applications. In this paper, we present a framework for interactive free-viewpoint streaming with open standards and software. Network bandwidth, encoding strategy as well as codec support for open source browsers are key constraints to be considered for our interactive streaming applications. Our framework is capable of real-time server-side rendering and interactively streaming the output by means of open source streaming. To enable viewer interaction with the free-viewpoint video rendering back-end in a standard browser, user events are captured with Javascript and transmitted using WebSockets. The rendered video is streamed to the browser using the FFmpeg free software project. This paper discusses the applicability of open source streaming and presents timing measurements for video-frame transmission over network.

Categories and Subject Descriptors

I.3.3 [**Computer Graphics**]: Picture/Image Generation-Miscellaneous; I.3.8 [**Computer Graphics**]: Applications; H.4 [**Multimedia Transport and Delivery**]: Miscellaneous

General Terms

Network, Streaming, Interactive, Free-Viewpoint Video

Keywords

Viewpoint; HTML5; Real-time streaming

1. INTRODUCTION

With the success of video platforms such as YouTube, video-on-demand services as Netflix and the increase in live streaming platforms such as Twitch, the internet infrastructure becomes ready for more involved media applications. Recently, interactive gaming services that enable server-side rendering of complex game graphics to thin-client consoles at home, started to appear. However, it is still extremely challenging to stream interactive applications due to the inherent constraints on low latency, network bandwidth and the requirement for real-time encoding. Existing frameworks and commercial products that enable applications such as Twitch, Gaikai, Sony Playstation NOW and Skype rely heavily on proprietary software and video codecs. In contrast, our goal in this paper is to evaluate and show the possibility of creating an interactive free-viewpoint experience using open standards and software. The client application runs completely inside a HTML5 compatible webbrowser and requires no further addons or plugins.

The main challenge in creating interactive video streaming applications, where the video content is directly controlled by the viewer, is keeping low latency response times. We explore different aspects of real-time, low latency streaming while only relying on open source APIs as backend and widely available consumer browsers as frontend.

Free-viewpoint video applications enable the viewer to interact with the video by freeing the camera from its usually fixed position and let the user explore the video [7]. The challenge in synthesizing new views from preprocessed data in real-time is the high volume of data required to represent the entire scene. Streaming these large volumes of input data to a client side renderer is impractical. Our system avoids high bandwidth data transfer by combining server-side rendering with low latency streaming.

We present an approach for image-based free-viewpoint rendering based on the work by Lipski et al. [2] and its implementation in a real-time rendering and real-world networking environment. We employ only open standardized protocols and open source codecs. This enables interactive video exploration in standard consumer browsers. The aim of this work is to demonstrate an interactive streaming application and implement a measurement technique to evaluate the performance of that application. The first contribution of this paper is to demonstrate an image based real time capable interactive free-viewpoint system. The second contribution of this paper is to give an overview of the challenges in real-time streaming using only open source software and provide results on the overall system performance in terms of delay. This work reflects the network characteristics of an interactive rendering application for Local Area Network environments.

MM'15, October 26–30, 2015, Brisbane, Australia.
© 2015 ACM. ISBN 978-1-4503-3459-4/15/10 ...$15.00.
DOI: http://dx.doi.org/10.1145/2733373.2806394.

Figure 1: (left),(right) Two input images and (middle) the generated in between view.

2. RELATED WORK

Video streaming over the internet can be categorized into two groups: VOD (video on demand) and live streaming [9]. One of the main differences is that for VOD it is possible for the client to buffer data to guarantee an uninterrupted playback while live streaming ideally requires no buffering at all. This requirement can be relaxed for live broadcasts that do not involve an interactive component, such as live sporting events. For interactive live streaming however, the video frames that are shown are generated in real-time and their content is influenced directly by the user. Well-known interactive systems are teleconferencing applications such as Skype, remote desktop sharing, and recently streamed gaming platforms such as Gaikai, Steam Homestreaming or Sony Playstation NOW. All of the named methods are only available commercially and heavily rely on proprietary software for encoding and display, which makes it difficult to use them in an open research environment.

Transmitting geometry and texture data required for a client to interactively render and show the information can be compressed efficiently for transmission [12]. However, this is mostly focused on sending static objects and scenes and is not suitable for continuous transmission of dynamic sequences.

Current research into interactive multi-view streaming [5, 13, 14] focuses on optimizing the encoding, storage and bandwidth requirements for transmitting and switching between multiple streams. The authors [1] have proposed a framework for streaming 3D objects to HTML5 browser without plugins. Our work focuses on streaming a single video generated interactively on the render-server side from multiple input videos of a scene containing arbitrary motion.

Shi et al. [10] propose a low latency remote rendering system that implements the real-time streaming of 3D data over the network to a mobile client.

Creating new viewpoints from multiple input streams is often referred to as free-viewpoint rendering. In the last years impressive results were created by depth-based rendering techniques such as [15] as well as purely image-based methods [3] that do not require explicit geometry. We base our free-viewpoint rendering on a hybrid approach presented recently by Lipski et al. [2] combining the strength of image-based and depth-based methods. While their rendering results have the high quality required, their system is not capable of creating interactive viewpoint changes in real-time. Video exploration of performances captured by multiple cameras has been done by Miller et al. [7]. They base view interpolation on proxy geometry from visual hulls of the captured object. First research into general scene interactive free-viewpoint video has been done by Meyer et al. [6], creating a desktop application for interactive free-viewpoint exploration.

To the best of our knowledge, the recent work does not illustrate the methodology for accurately mapping the video frame packets from the server to the client. We employ only open standardized protocols and open source codec implementations like the HTML5 video element, the Ogg Theora video codec and the WebSockets framework for user event transmission.

3. RENDERING PIPELINE

Image-based rendering relies directly on images to interpolate new views instead of modelling and subesequently rendering textured 3D geometry. For a new viewpoint of the scene a subset of the input frames is selected. These nearby frames are warped to the position of the desired view based on dense image correspondences and blended together for a convincing new virtual view [3]. The image correspondences are obtained automatically using a high quality image correspondence estimation method [4]. Dense correspondences additionally allow the computation of per pixel depth maps, with visible imperfections from incorrect correspondences. The hybrid approach by Lipski et al. [2] can be used to render consistent views despite the imperfections in scene depth. In this section we will give a short overview of the hybrid approach. The amount of data required by the renderer is discussed to motivate the use of server-side rendering.

3.1 Hybrid Approach

The hybrid free-viewpoint video approach relies on additionally available depth maps and uses 2D image correspondences to apply a warping in 3D space.

For every frame A the per-pixel depth D_A is known. Using the intrinsic parameters (e.g. focal length) and the extrinsic parameters as camera matrix M_A, each pixel X can be projected to its 3D space position x,

$$x = M_A^{-1}\left(\frac{r_f(X)}{||r_f(X)||}D_A(X)\right), \qquad (1)$$

where $r_f(X)$ denotes the ray through pixel X.

The image-space correspondence maps a pixel in one frame to a pixel position in a second frame. Since the 3D positions for both is known from the respective depth maps and camera positions, a 3D space mapping can be computed. Using this 3D mapping allows the warping and blending of images in 3D. The new 3D position x' of a pixel x in frame A, can be computed from the its 3D correspondence W_{AB} from source frame A to target frame B.

$$x' = x + c \cdot W_{AB}(X). \qquad (2)$$

The warp coefficient c determines how far the pixels from frame A are warped towards their positions in B. It can be obtained by an orthogonal projection of the virtual view position onto the source to target vector. The warps are applied and the 3D pixels reprojected respecting their depth. To allow for smooth blending between multiple views soft z-buffering is applied. For a more detailed description of the image synthesis process we refer to [2].

3.2 Bandwidth

Image-based free-viewpoint video requires a huge amount of data to be loaded for each rendered frame. In addition to the image color and depth data for all frames, the dense 2D image correspondences have to be stored for each image pair that shall be used for rendering later on. Assuming for one camera to have a neighboring camera above, below, to the left and to the right results in four image pairs per input frame. To enable temporal interpolation as well, we add the correspondences to the next frame in the same camera and therefore require five correspondence maps per input frame. The correspondence map is saved as a two-channel image with two bytes per channel resulting in approximately 16.5MB per warp for full HD images. Although that includes source and target images, which can be shared between warps with the same source or target, in the worst case the warps do not share any images. A small scene with 10 cameras, 100 frames per camera and dense correspondences from each frame to five of its neighbors can reach up to 80GB. Streaming this amount of data to the client on demand is impractical with current bandwidth limitations for network traffic. Rendering the scene on a server and just transmitting the video, however, reduces the required bandwidth and allows even small devices to present interactive free viewpoint video.

Rendering the free viewpoint video in real-time on the server remains a challenging task as the full scene does not fit into GPU or main memory. Scheduling is required to decide which parts of the data should be available in RAM or GPU memory and which parts of data should remain on disk. The typical exploration of free viewpoint video utilizes continuous camera paths which leads to continuous access to the camera data. Thus the current position is used as a predictor to preload images and correspondences from surrounding cameras. This applies for the frame and warp data; the intrinsic and extrinsic data are uploaded on demand per warp computation but can remain in main memory as their memory footprint is small.

Our rendering application is able to produce 30fps on a computer with an Intel i7 CPU 3.2GHz, a NVidia GeForce GTX TITAN Black GPU and 12GB RAM. However, the client side framerate is mostly limited by network bandwidth and buffering.

4. NETWORK PIPELINE

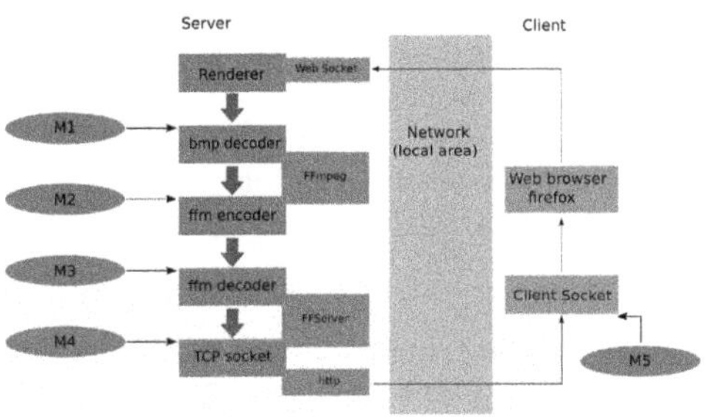

Figure 2: System overview

We developed a framework for streaming an image from the OpenGL-based renderer to a webbrowser-based client using the open source software ffmpeg and ffserver for encoding and streaming. The video stream is rendered in the browser using the HTML5 video element and WebSockets are used for the browsers communication with the server-side rendering application [8]. This allows us to perform our experiments in a Firefox browser without any modifications or plugins on the client side. In our experiments we run ffmpeg and ffserver in version 2.1, on the client side we performed our tests using Firefox 32.0 and Google Chrome 42.0.

Figure 2 illustrates the overall experimental set up. The OpenGL based renderer produces raw images which are transfered in memory to ffmpeg through the image2pipe interface. The very low overhead BMP format structure is used for the RGB frames before they are encoded in the ffm format used by the ffserver internally. The encoded stream is streamed via ffserver to the Firefox browser when the client connects via HTML5 video element to the ffserver feed. To avoid encoding delay, B-frames are disabled for the encoder. The user interaction, such as mouse and key events, is captured in Javascript and sent to the server using the WebSocket connection.

We rely completely on TCP/HTML streaming which has the advantage that TCP streaming over port 80 will not be blocked by typical firewall configurations. Streaming over TCP has other challenges in the form of the congestion control [11] and thus delays have to be expected.

To measure the delay introduced by every part of the pipeline each video frame is annotated with epoch times which are logged at each measurement point at the beginning of the components (see Figure 2).

The first measurement point $M1$ lies directly after the OpenGL renderer and before the encode image preprocessing. At the input of the ffm encoder component the frames and their timestamps are logged again at $M2$. The ffm encoded data stream is handed to the ffserver which has to decode the ffm format again after the third measurement point $M3$. Before the data is sent to the client via the TCP socket the delay is measured again at $M4$. Finally, the transmitted TCP packets are logged with the network analysis tool Wireshark on the client side. By logging the position from the OGG header on both, the sender and receiver side, each received packet can be matched to the timestamp when this particular frame was encoded. Comparing the sender side timestamps against the timestamps of the matching incomming packets on the client side, measured at measurement point $M5$, allows a fine granular delay measurement. To ensure the accuracy of this measurment the sytem clock of the client and server have been synchronized using NTP.

5. RESULTS

For the evaluation of our pipeline we measure the delay between the measurement points (see Figure 2). The experiment is performed over 100 Mbps link capacity over the LAN. Table 1 shows the average delay measured over 1000 frames per run.

The image preprocessing delay is calculated from $M1$ to $M2$ which includes the required image preprocessing (e.g. changes in color format for optimal encoding). Similarly the delay of the ffm encoder is measured from $M2$ to $M3$. The delay of ffm decoder includes the reinterpretation of the ffm container by the ffserver from $M3$ to $M4$. As buffering delay we measure time spent waiting for the next frame to fully load. The total delay is computed from $M1$ to $M5$.

We can observe that the delays remain constant over time, when we tested streaming large numbers of frames. However the buffered frames in the pipeline still constitute a significant part of the observable delay. Each individual part of the encoding and streaming pipeline keeps only approximately one frame in their buffers. Over the framework these sum

Run Nr	Img proc. delay [ms]	ffm en-coder [ms]	ffm de-coder [ms]	Buffer delay [ms]	Total delay [ms]
1	21	37	2	167	229
2	20	37	2	163	224
3	20	38	3	164	226
4	21	37	2	166	228
5	21	37	2	168	227
6	21	38	2	167	230
7	21	37	3	168	230
8	22	37	3	170	234
9	22	37	3	169	233
10	21	38	2	170	233

Table 1: Observed delay in our test system and network environment. Delays are average numbers over 1000 frames of video streamed in each test run

up to a total of 4-6 frames. At 30 frames per second each have a time impact of 33 ms for a total of the 165 ms which can be seen in Table 1. In comparison to the average buffering delay the delays introduced by decoding and encoding appear insignificant. The total delay through the complete pipeline, beginning with a rendered frame to the frame being shown in the browser, is given in the last column on table 1. While still allowing an interactive experience, much lower values are desired for realtime interaction.

6. CONCLUSION AND FUTURE WORK

We have presented a framework for real-time streaming of free-viewpoint renderings which relies solely on open standards and software. Our approach requires only a standard web browser which has to support the HTML5 video element for streaming the video data. A methodology to calculate the one way delay from the server to the client over a Local Area Network on a per frame basis has been demonstrated with insights into the application performance. In the future further investigation could be done on the buffering delays of the server component and optimizing the application performance in terms of delays to improve the interactive experience.

The recently standardized WebRTC is a promising alternative to the TCP/HTML video streams and we will investigate its application in open source based interactive streaming in the future.

7. ACKNOWLEDGMENTS

The research leading to these results has received funding from the European Union's Seventh Framework Programme FP7/2007-2013 under grant agreement no. 256941, Reality CG, and European Research Council StG 306644 for the project UnIQue.

8. REFERENCES

[1] K. Kapetanakis, S. Panagiotakis, and A. G. Malamos. Html5 and websockets; challenges in network 3d collaboration. In *Proc. 17th Panhellenic Conference on Informatics*, PCI '13, pages 33–38, New York, NY, USA, 2013. ACM.

[2] C. Lipski, F. Klose, and M. Magnor. Correspondence and depth-image based rendering: a hybrid approach for free-viewpoint video. *IEEE Trans. Circuits and Systems for Video Technology*, 24(6):942–951, June 2014.

[3] C. Lipski, C. Linz, K. Berger, A. Sellent, and M. Magnor. Virtual video camera: Image-based viewpoint navigation through space and time. *Computer Graphics Forum*, 29(8):2555–2568, Dec. 2010.

[4] C. Lipski, C. Linz, T. Neumann, M. Wacker, and M. Magnor. High resolution image correspondences for video post-production. *Journal of Virtual Reality and Broadcasting*, 9.2012(8):1–12, Dec. 2012.

[5] P. Merkle, A. Smolic, K. Muller, and T. Wiegand. Multi-view video plus depth representation and coding. In *Image Processing, 2007. ICIP 2007. IEEE International Conference on*, volume 1, pages I–201. IEEE, 2007.

[6] B. Meyer, C. Lipski, B. Scholz, and M. Magnor. Real-time free-viewpoint navigation from compressed multi-video recordings. In *Proc. 3D Data Processing, Visualization and Transmission*, pages 1–6, May 2010.

[7] G. Miller, A. Hilton, and J. Starck. Interactive free-viewpoint video. In *IEE European Conf. on Visual Media Production*, pages 50–59, 2005.

[8] D. Puranik, D. Feiock, and J. Hill. Real-time monitoring using ajax and websockets. In *Engineering of Computer Based Systems (ECBS), 2013 20th IEEE International Conference and Workshops on the*, pages 110–118, April 2013.

[9] A. Rao, Yeon-sup, Lim-Chadi, B. Arnaud, L. D. Towsley, and W. Dabbous. Network characteristics of video streaming traffic. In *Network Experiments and Technologies, ACMCoNEXT 2011 7th International Conference on*, December 2011.

[10] S. Shi. *A low latency remote rendering system for interactive mobile graphics*. PhD thesis, University of Illinois at Urbana-Champaign, 2012.

[11] H.-P. Shiang and M. van der Schaar. A quality-centric tcp-friendly congestion control for multimedia transmission. *Multimedia, IEEE Transactions on*, 14(3):896–909, June 2012.

[12] J. Sutter, K. Sons, and P. Slusallek. Blast: A binary large structured transmission format for the web. In *Proc. 9th International ACM Conference on 3D Web Technologies*, Web3D '14, pages 45–52, New York, NY, USA, 2014. ACM.

[13] X. Xiu, G. Cheung, and J. Liang. Frame structure optimization for interactive multiview video streaming with bounded network delay. In *Image Processing (ICIP), 2011 18th IEEE International Conference on*, pages 593–596, Sept 2011.

[14] G. C. Zhi Liu and Y. Ji. Optimizing distributed source coding for interactive multiview video streaming over lossy networks. *Circuits and Systems for Video Technology, IEEE Transactions on*, 23(10):1781–1794, Oct 2013.

[15] C. L. Zitnick, S. B. Kang, M. Uyttendaele, S. A. J. Winder, and R. Szeliski. High-quality video view interpolation using a layered representation. *ACM Trans. Graph.*, 23(3):600–608, 2004.

Distributed Bandwidth-efficient Packet Scheduling for Live Streaming with Network Coding

Shenglan Huang
Queen Mary
University of London, UK
s.huang@qmul.ac.uk

Ebroul Izquierdo
Queen Mary
University of London, UK
e.izquierdo@qmul.ac.uk

Pengwei Hao
Queen Mary
University of London, UK
p.hao@qmul.ac.uk

ABSTRACT

This paper proposed a distributed packet scheduling algorithm for live peer-to-peer streaming system, where network coding is extended to improve the efficiency in bandwidth utilization. A problem of superfluous packet transmission due to the lack of synchronization among peers is identified. This problem often leads to bandwidth inefficiencies. We solve the problem of finding a suitable asynchronous packet scheduling policy by posing and solving a bandwidth allocation problem. This proposed scheduling policy can reduce the superfluous packet transmission, thereby achieving a more efficient bandwidth usage and an improved quality of service in live streaming applications. Experimental results confirm that the proposed scheme demonstrates significantly better video quality, delivery ratio under different network size and different loss rate compared with other push-based schemes.

Categories and Subject Descriptors

C.2.4 [**Computer-Communication Networks**]: Distributed System - Distributed Applications

General Terms

Design

Keywords

P2P Network, Live Streaming, Network Coding, Packet Scheduling

1. INTRODUCTION

In recent years, multimedia communication has become a part of our everyday life. Many studies [1], [2] have been conducted in the multi-source streaming and scalable video streaming. According to the importance, timeliness and scarcity of packets [3], [4], the packet scheduling can be more specifically targeted. Comparatively, little attention has been given to improve bandwidth efficiencies through suitable packet scheduling schemes. In fact, improving bandwidth efficiency is necessary as a more effective bandwidth usage may lead to a better quality of service in media streaming applications. Therefore, this paper focuses on improving bandwidth efficiency in cooperative live streaming networks.

Network coding has demonstrated its benefits in the field of multimedia transmission in terms of reducing communication delay[5], [6], error-resilience[7], scalable transmitting [8], and quality optimization[9]. However, bandwidth efficiencies in combining network coding with multimedia transmission need further to be improved. In present push scheduling schemes, nodes actively push encoded packets to its neighbors until arrival of a stop message. Nevertheless, due to the lack of synchronization among peers, in some cases, some transmitted packets are received after the current content generation has already been decoded. In the sequel, we call that type of packets *uninformative*. In some other cases, available packets are not enough to decode the original content within the given time window. Let us term these packets *unrecoverable*. In conventional push-based schemes, it is impossible to avoid such superfluous transmissions, i.e., *uninformative* and *unrecoverable* packets. This is because fully synchronization needs enormous amounts of communication overheads and these overheads cannot be compensated by the gains achieved. Thus, it is critical to find a trade-off between improved transmission efficiencies and the information overheads needed to achieve it. To address this problem, a new transmission mechanism is proposed. In a nutshell, the idea behind the proposed approach is that sender nodes pre-calculate the number of packets that receivers need, then the sender nodes push packets to these receivers according to the pre-calculation results.

Some works have also been carried out in using NC to improve the bandwidth efficiency. For instance, work in [6] considers the sub-stream scheduling problem as a max-weighted bipartite matching problem (MWBM). Nevertheless, with network coding, the scheduling problem becomes a new more flexible and simpler problem. Another previous research [10] constructs the cost function for each possible transmitting policy. Nevertheless, it still cannot avoid communication overheads and the bandwidth inefficiencies caused by these *unrecoverable* packets.

MM'15, October 26–30, 2015, Brisbane, Australia.
 ISBN 978-1-4503-3459-4/15/10 ...$15.00.
DOI: http://dx.doi.org/10.1145/2733373.2806395.

2. SYSTEM MODEL

In this section, the overall system model is defined. The overall model includes a network encoded media streaming model, a network model and a loss compensation model of the network.

2.1 Network encoded media streaming and network model

The media stream distributed to the network nodes is modelled as a single dimensional array of generation. Each generation is identified within the media stream by a temporal index $g \in [1, G]$. Each generation g is subdivided into s_g blocks of symbols and all s_gs form the vector $\boldsymbol{s}$. Each generation has a same playback duration κ seconds. The average streaming rate is represented by S.

The network model is modelled as a swarm-push P2P streaming network. Three types of peers are defined in the system: *streaming source*, *tracker server*, and *client node*. Each peer contacts the tracker server to join the P2P network and form neighbor relationships. Some control information (e.g. information related to the upload bandwidth of neighbor nodes, video packets) is exchanged during the handshake procedure. The overlay of network nodes is represented as the graph ($\mathcal{N}$, ε) composed for nodes $\mathcal{N} = \{\mathcal{N}_1, ..., \mathcal{N}_N\}$ and the edge ε. Its upload ability of each client node is $U = \{U_1, ...U_N\}$ in κ seconds for $\mathcal{N} = \{\mathcal{N}_1, ..., \mathcal{N}_N\}$ respectively. For simplicity, the average upload ability in a generation duration in the network is represented by $U^{avg} = \sum_{i=2}^{i=N} U_i/N$. In these nodes, $\mathcal{N}_1$ represents the *tracker server* and $\mathcal{N}_2$ represents the *streaming source*. For any node $\mathcal{N}_j$, $A_j \subset \mathcal{N}$ is the neighborhood of $\mathcal{N}_j$. It is the set of sender nodes that transmit packets to node $\mathcal{N}_j$. $|A_i|$ is the size of neighborhood of $\mathcal{N}_i$.

Instead of transmitting raw video packets, the P2P network transmits network-encoded packets. A new network-encoded packet is generated by performing random network coding in a single generation in the Galois field of size $q = 2^8$. When a client node receives a packet, it checks if the packet is *uninformative* (linearly dependent to other received packets). If the packet is *uninformative*, it is discarded. Once a client node has collected enough informative packets in a generation before the playback deadline, it recovers this generation using the progressive Gauss-Jordan elimination. During the media streaming, only generations in the *priority period* are transmitted to guarantee a smooth low-delay playback. A *priority period* Γ is defined as a moving window next to the playback point.

2.2 Proposed Loss Compensation Model

The loss compensation model reduces unrecoverable transmissions due to the loss in the network. In a lossy network, the scheduled data rate needs to be more than the original media rate to compensate the impact of loss rate and inherit linear dependent rate, such that enough linear independent packets can be received by receivers. The loss compensation model is developed to find a trade-off between bandwidth efficiencies and the media quality.

To achieve a fluent playback, at any temporal index g, each node $\mathcal{N}_j$ needs to receive s_g linear independent packets to decode the original generation g. The number of scheduled packets sent from the senders is denoted as ς_g in generation g. To achieve recoverable transmissions, ς_g is defined as s_g over the successful transmission rate ϱ. ϱ is denoted as the probability that a linear independent packet is successfully received by a node. Therefore, the number of scheduled packets ς_g in generation g can be written as:

$$\varsigma_g = s_g/\varrho \tag{1}$$

ϱ is related to the loss rate θ and inherit linear dependent rate ρ of random network coding. A received packet is linear dependent to other received packets due to the property of random network coding. Randomly chosen coefficients may be the same as the coefficients in previously sent packets. According to the research in [11], the lower bound on this inherit linear independent probability ρ only depends on the size of the Galois Field, q, and $\rho \geq (1 - 2^{-q})$. Therefore, the lower bound of the probability of receiving a linear independent packet can be simply given as:

$$\begin{aligned} \varrho &= (1-\theta) * \rho \\ &\geq (1-\theta) * (1 - 2^{-q}) \end{aligned} \tag{2}$$

According to Eq.2, it can be concluded that the rate of receiving a linear independent packet is larger than the product of the loss rate and the linear dependent rate. It also means that when ς_g are pushed from the sender, more than s_g linear independent packet can be received by the receiver. Therefore, ς_g is chosen as the optimal trade-off between transmission efficiencies and the media quality.

3. DISTRIBUTED PACKET SCHEDULING

In this section, the details of the distributed bandwidth-efficient packet scheduling (DPS) algorithm are clarified. The main features of this algorithm are that 1) it builds a cooperation model among sender peers; 2) it calculates the decoding status and allocates senders' upload bandwidth to receiver nodes.

3.1 Handshake Procedure

In the handshake procedure, each sender node $\mathcal{N}_i$ decides its allocated upload bandwidth U_{ij} to receiver node $\mathcal{N}_j$. Firstly, when the receiver node $\mathcal{N}_j$ joins the network, it contacts with the tracker node to obtain a list of free sender peers $\mathcal{N}_i$ as its neighbor nodes A_i and become one of the client peer automatically. For each $\mathcal{N}_i \in A_j$, they are given an integer number i as its uniquely identification. Then, the tracker server calculates the amount of upload bandwidth U_{ij} that each sender $\mathcal{N}_i$ should contribute for supporting the full-rate delivery of this receiver node $\mathcal{N}_j$. The scheduled upload bandwidth U_{ij} from sender node $\mathcal{N}_i \in A_j$ to receiver node $\mathcal{N}_j$ is given as

$$U_{ij} = \frac{U_i}{\sum\limits_{\mathcal{N}_i \subset A_j} U_i} * \varsigma \tag{3}$$

After that, the scheduled upload bandwidth allocation U_{ij}s for $\forall \mathcal{N}_i \in A_j$ are stored into a vector following its identification order and sent to each parental node $\mathcal{N}_i \subset A_j$. At the same time, the tracker calculates the residual available upload bandwidth $U_i^{'}$ for each sender $\mathcal{N}_i \in A_j$ by $U_i^{'} = U_i - U_{ij}$. In this way, at the end of the handshake procedure, each sender $\mathcal{N}_i$ will get a list of cooperative senders $\mathcal{N}_i \in A_j$, and their corresponding allocated bandwidth U_{ij} for this receiver U_j.

3.2 Real-time Distributed Scheduling

The real-time distributed scheduler pre-calculates the scheduled number of packets d_{ij} from node $\mathcal{N}_i$ to $\mathcal{N}_j$ in any generation g. The transmission model in the local scheduling algorithm can be summarized as a multi-sender and single receiver relationship. A receiver node $\mathcal{N}_j$ has a set of parent nodes $\mathcal{N}_i$, where $\mathcal{N}_i \in A_j$. Allocated upload capacity of the link connecting peers $\mathcal{N}_i$ and $\mathcal{N}_j$ is denoted as U_{ij}. Each parent node $\mathcal{N}_i$ also keeps a list of all parent nodes and their corresponding allocated upload capacity U_{ij} for $\forall \mathcal{N}_i \in A_j$. For each generation g of Γ, each node U_i independently decides how many packets and to whom it will send. To achieve an accurate allocation, parent node U_i performs the real-time distributed scheduling algorithm to get the number of scheduled packets per generation. The number of scheduled packets d_{ij} for any generation g from sender $\mathcal{N}_i$ to receiver node $\mathcal{N}_j$ can be expressed as followed in Eq. 4:

$$\begin{aligned} d_{ij} &= round\left(\frac{U_{ij}}{\sum_{k=i}^{k=I} U_{kj}} \varsigma_r\right) \quad (a) \\ \varsigma_r &= \varsigma_g - \sum_{k=0}^{k=i-1} d_{kj} \quad (b) \end{aligned} \tag{4}$$

In Eq.4 (a), d_{ij} is calculated by the produce of the rate of ith allocated upload bandwidth over all allocated upload bandwidth from sender node U_i to the last sender node U_I in the sender list and the rest needed number of packets ς_r. 4 (b) means that the rest needed number of packets ς_r can be represented by the difference between the scheduled result ς_g and the number of scheduled results for sender node U_0 to U_{i-1}.

In general, the DPS algorithm performs the upload bandwidth allocation for each receiver based on the chronological order that the node U_i becomes the sender of the client node U_j. Each sender calculates the number of pending transmitting packets based on the pre-mentioned information. The algorithm achieves the bandwidth-efficient packet delivery without buffer-updating. This algorithm is simple to implement as it is only according to the ratio of upload bandwidth U_i over overall upload bandwidth.

4. PERFORMANCE EVALUATION

4.1 Experiment Settings

In our experiment, we only focus on the packet scheduling algorithm. To achieve a fair comparison, all the experiments use the same network construction: The network is implemented on the event-based network simulator. All end nodes independently choose its neighbors and then form a random connected network. The size of the default test network is setting to be 100 nodes and the default loss rate of the link is set to be 0.02.

The testing video streaming is the Paris sequence encoded with H.264/AVC. The bit rate of stream S is 116 Kbyte/s. The video quality achieved after the decoding of all packets is 40.12dB. Generation size κ is 8 frames, which correspond to a group of pictures covering 0.26 seconds of video. The size of priority period Γ_l is 8κ. It means that the *playback deadline* at each peer as 2.13 seconds and the packets need to arrive at each node in 2.13 second to not expire. The maximum upload bandwidth of streaming source U_2 is set to satisfy 10% end users. The actual size of the video block is 1024 Bytes. Coefficients of network-encoded packets are stored in the packet header and transmitted with the video

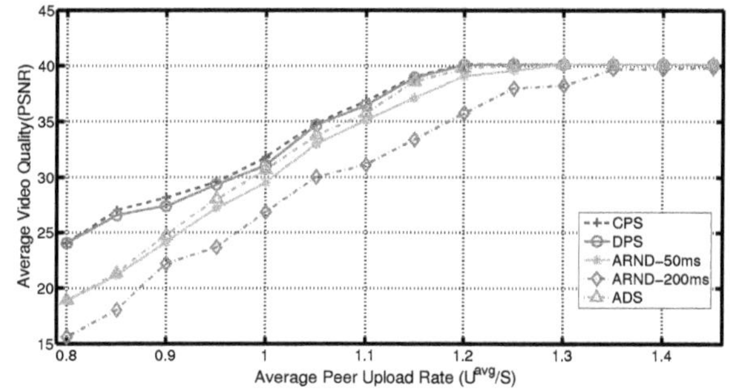

Figure 1: Performance comparison of the average media quality as a function of U^{avg}

packets as well, whose size depends on the number of encoding packets in the generation. In the simulation, the packet header (e.g. address of destination peer, and sequence number of video) is 150 Bytes and the average size of network coding coefficients is about 32 Byte per packet (1 Byte for the coding coefficient of each video packet in the generation). Theoretically, in such packet size settings, to achieve full rate streaming, the actual bandwidth demand U^d should be at least equal to 1.18 times ς.

4.2 Streaming Performance Comparison

In this section, we compare our proposed scheme with a centralized packet scheduler (CPS), an advanced version of the random-push reference scheme (ARND), and an asynchronous distributed scheduler (ADS) similar to [10]. CPS means a hypothesized central coordinator performs the centralized push scheduling algorithm. The ARND is an improved version of RND similar to [12]. In RND, each node randomly pushes its encoded packets to its neighbors according to the buffer-map of its neighbors. In ARND, generations which require more packets to decode the original data are given more chance to be chosen. The ARND-50ms and the ARND-200ms mean that the buffer-map which represents the data availability of its neighbor peers updates every 50ms or 200ms separately. The ADS selects push policy based on the time-weighted cost.

We first study the performance of average video quality of each method when U^{avg} ranging from 0.8S to 1.45S and the network is set as default configurations. The average video quality is measured by the peak signal-to-noise ratio (PSNR) at the receiver nodes. As depicted in Fig. 1, the DPS allows almost all clients to recover the media stream when the upload bandwidth is just enough to compensate for the actual bandwidth demand U^d. When $U^{avg} = U^d$, the CPS and the DPS can achieve over 40.12, 40.05dB respectively and the DPS curve almost overlaps the CPS curve over the whole range of U^{avg}. By contrast, when $U^{avg} = U^d$, the ADS, the ARND-50ms, and the ARND-200ms can only achieve 39.75dB, 39.06dB, and 35.76dB separately. Besides, when U^{avg} is $0.8S$, the DPS has more significant improvement(5.14dB, 5.16dB, 8.43dB)compared with ADS, ARND-50ms, and ARND-200ms algorithm separately, which proves that the DPS can achieve better quality of service through improving bandwidth efficiencies.

In Fig.2, the performances of the average delivery ratio are analysed as a function of the loss rate in the network. The delivery ratio is defined as the average received *informative*

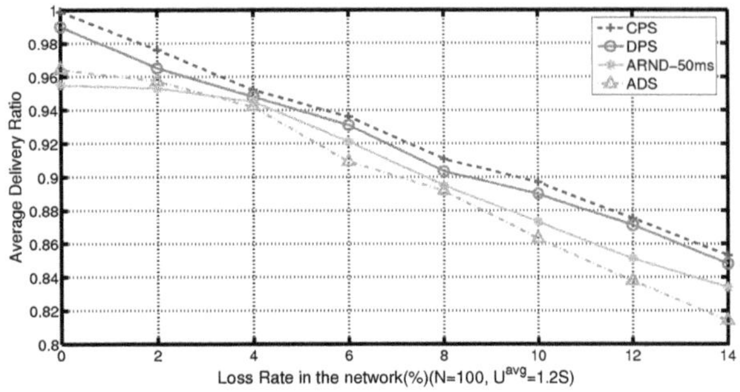

Figure 2: Performance comparison of the average delivery ratio as a function of network loss rate

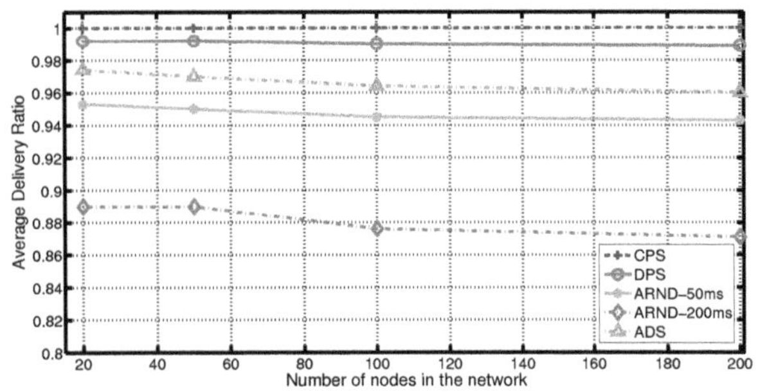

Figure 3: Performance comparison of the average delivery ratio as a function of network size

packet rate over the streaming packet rate. Average upload bandwidth of client node U^{avg} is set to be $1.2S$ and the network settings are the default settings. The results in Fig. 2 show that the proposed DPS algorithm outperforms the ARND-50ms and ADS algorithms and performs close to the CPS algorithm over the whole range of loss rate from 0% to 14%. It also shows that the DPS does not lose its advantages even when the loss rate increases to 14%.

In the last experiment, the average delivery ratio versus the number of peers is compared in Fig. 3. As depicted in Figure 3, the delivery ratio among these five methods is compared when the network size N is 20, 50, 100, 200 separately. Average node upload bandwidth U^{avg} is set to be $1.2S$. From the figure, we can see that the five methods are all scalable. Under such experimental setting, both CPS and DPS can achieve over 99% delivery ratio. Under different network size, the ADS and the ARND-50ms and the ARND-200ms can achieve about average 96.4%, 94.5%, 89% deliver ratio separately. In all, the DPS achieves similar delivery ratio as the CPS over the whole range of chosen network size. Because the DPS only transmits informative and recoverable packets, the performance of bandwidth utilization and delivery ratio is improved.

5. CONCLUSION

This paper proposes a distributed bandwidth-efficient packet scheduling algorithm which solves the asynchronous bandwidth allocation problem. The new approach reduces the typical source of *uninformative* video packets, *unrecoverable* video packets and control overhead, thereby achieving a more efficient network bandwidth utilization and better quality of service. Numerous experiments justify the robustness of our approach to link loss, different upload bandwidth and network scalability.

6. ACKNOWLEDGMENTS

This work is supported by the LASIE project with funding from the European Union's Seventh Framework Programme for research, technological development and demonstration under grant agreement nr. 607480.

7. REFERENCES

[1] T Zgaljic, N Sprljan, and E Izquierdo. Bitstream syntax description based adaptation of scalable video. In *Integration of Knowledge, Semantics and Digital Media Technology, 2005. EWIMT 2005. The 2nd European Workshop on the*, pages 173–178. IET, 2005.

[2] T. Zgaljic, N. Sprljan, and E. Izquierdo. Bit-stream allocation methods for scalable video coding supporting wireless communications. *Signal Processing: Image Communication*, 22(3):298–316, 2007.

[3] S. Huang, M. Sanna, E. Izquierdo, and P. Hao. Optimized scalable video transmission over p2p network with hierarchical network coding. In *Image Processing (ICIP), 2014 IEEE International Conference on*, pages 3993–3997. IEEE, 2014.

[4] N. Ramzan, S. Wan, and E. Izquierdo. Joint source-channel coding for wavelet-based scalable video transmission using an adaptive turbo code. *Journal on Image and Video Processing*, 2007(1):16–16, 2007.

[5] L. Cui, Y. Jiang, and J. Wu. Optimizing push scheduling algorithm based on network coding for mesh peer-to-peer live streaming. In *Communications (ICC), 2012 IEEE International Conference on*, pages 2075–2080. IEEE, 2012.

[6] K-HK Chan, S-HG Chan, and Ali C Begen. Spanc: Optimizing scheduling delay for peer-to-peer live streaming. *Multimedia, IEEE Transactions on*, 12(7):743–753, 2010.

[7] X. Guang, F.-W. Fu, and Z. Zhang. Construction of network error correction codes in packet networks. *Information Theory, IEEE Transactions on*, 59(2):1030–1047, 2013.

[8] N. Thomos, J. Chakareski, and P. Frossard. Prioritized distributed video delivery with randomized network coding. *Multimedia, IEEE Transactions on*, 13(4):776–787, 2011.

[9] Y. Zhang, S. Qin, and Z. He. Transmission distortion-optimized unequal loss protection for video transmission over packet erasure channels. In *Multimedia and Expo (ICME), 2011 IEEE International Conference on*, pages 1–6. IEEE, 2011.

[10] A. M. Sheikh, A. Fiandrotti, and E. Magli. Distributed scheduling for low-delay and loss-resilient media streaming with network coding. *Multimedia, IEEE Transactions on*, 2014.

[11] P. A Chou, Y. Wu, and K. Jain. Practical network coding. 2003.

[12] M. Wang and B. Li. R2: Random push with random network coding in live peer-to-peer streaming. *IEEE Journal on Selected Areas in Communications*, 25(9):1655–1666, 2007.

Vision-Inertial Hybrid Tracking for Robust and Efficient Augmented Reality on Smartphones

Xin Yang[1], Xun Si[1], Tangli Xue[1], Liheng Zhang[1], Kwang-Ting (Tim) Cheng[2]

[1]Huazhong University of Science and Technology, [2]University of California, Santa Barbara

ABSTRACT

This paper aims at robust and efficient pose tracking for augmented reality on modern smartphones. Existing methods, relying on either vision analysis or motion sensing, are either too computationally expensive to achieve real-time performance on a smartphone, or too noisy to achieve sufficient robustness. This paper presents a hybrid tracking system which can achieve real-time performance with high robustness. Our system utilizes an efficient featureless method based on pixel-based registration to track the object pose on every frame. The featureless tracking result is revised from time to time by a feature-based method to reduce tracking errors. Both featureless and feature-based tracking results are sensitive to large motion blurs. To improve the robustness, an adaptive Kamlan filter is proposed to fuse the visual tracking results with the inertial tracking results computed form phone's built-in sensors. Our hybrid method is evaluated on a dataset consisting of 16 video clips with synchronized inertial sensing data. Experimental results demonstrated the superior performance of our method to state-of-the-art visual tracking methods [5, 12] on smartphones. The dataset will be made publicly available with the publication of this paper.

Categories and Subject Descriptors: I.4.8 [Image Processing and Computer Vision]: Scene Analysis -Tracking.

General Terms

Algorithms, Performance, Experimentation, Verification

1. INTRODUCTION

Today's smartphones are equipped with powerful application processors, cameras, and inertial sensors, providing an attractive platform for mobile augmented reality (MAR). Acquiring the relative position and orientation between a moving camera and a static object, known as six degrees of freedom (6DOF) pose tracking, is a key task in an MAR system. Despite tremendous amount of research on this topic, robust, accurate and efficient pose tracking on a mobile phone remains challenging due to the limited computing power of mobile handheld devices and a wide range of environmental variations in a mobile scenario.

Features-based tracking [1, 2, 5, 8], which matches visual features between an object model and a current frame, has received high interests due to its impressive tracking accuracy and robustness to environmental changes, including occlusions, clutter, geometric changes, etc. However, extracting and matching visual features incur high computational complexity, and hence are difficult to achieve sufficient efficiency on a handheld mobile device. Several efforts have been made to address this problem. A notable result is Wagner et al.'s feature tracking system [8] which employs a feature, called SIFT and Ferns, heavily modified from existing state-of-the-art features. Several lightweight binary features, e.g. ORB [6] and LDB [1, 2], have been developed to facilitate efficient tracking. These lightweight features can be extracted and compared with high efficiency, but their robustness and distinctiveness are largely degraded. As a result, they usually fail to achieve satisfactory tracking performance, especially for objects with large motion blurs caused by fast movement and/or long exposure time of a camera, and for objects with little texture (e.g. sparse text and sketch images).

On the other hand, featureless tracking [12] which estimates homography between frames can bypass the feature extraction and matching process completely. Specifically, the homography parameters between frames are estimated by minimizing a global dissimilarity measure (e.g. SSD) based on an optimization algorithm (e.g. gradient descent [11] and Levenberg-Marquardt [11]). To speed up the optimizing process, homography between consecutive frames is estimated to take advantage of the fact that geometric changes between consecutive frames are usually very small and thus only a small number of iterations are demanded for optimizing homography parameters. The homography between an object model and the object on current frame is computed by multiplying all previous homography matrices. Featureless tracking has been demonstrated a faster speed than feature-based tracking in [12]; however, the result is sensitive to fast movement of a camera which could cause large errors in homography estimation. Such error accumulates from frame to frame, yielding a degradation of tracking accuracy over time.

Modern smartphones have been widely equipped with inertial sensors, including accelerometer and gyroscope, which can measure the angular velocity and translational acceleration of a camera at an ultrafast speed and with few restrictions on the object appearance. Several tracking systems have been developed based on inertial sensors [9, 10]. However, the tracking result solely relies on inertial sensing usually lacks of sufficient accuracy, especially as time increases the tracking error accumulates due to noises and bias in sensors. To address this problem, authors in [3, 4] utilized inertial sensing only as an assistance of a visual tracker to guide fast feature extraction and matching, and to take over the tracking task when the visual tracker fails due to severe occlusions and motion blurs. However, large inertial tracking errors, which do occur from time to time for today's smartphones, result in instability of their system due to the sole reliance on the inertial tracker to guide the subsequent vision-based tracking. In addition to the algorithm limitations, these hybrid approaches were evaluated using dedicated inertial sensors with higher accuracy than typical sensors available in today's smartphones and their results were reported only on their own dataset. To our best knowledge, fusing the measurements of the built-in sensors and the camera in a standard smartphone has not been successfully demonstrated to date.

This paper presents a novel vision-inertial hybrid tracking system which can run efficiently on today's smartphones and meanwhile achieve high robustness and accuracy even for challenging cases, e.g. objects with significant motion blurs and/or with sparse texture information. Our hybrid system combines a featureless method [12] and a state-of-the-art feature-based method [5] for an efficient and accurate visual tracker. Specially, the object pose is tracked by the featureless method on every frame. The tracking result is updated from time to time by the feature-based method [5]

MM'15, October 26–30, 2015, Brisbane, Australia.
© 2015 ACM. ISBN 978-1-4503-3459-4/15/10…$15.00.
DOI: http://dx.doi.org/10.1145/2733373.2806396

to avoid accumulated errors. To improve the robustness of the tracking system for cases when both featureless and feature tracking results contain large errors, an adaptive Kamlan filter is proposed to fuse the visual tracking results with the inertial tracking results computed form phone's built-in sensors. The adaptive Kalman filter dynamically adjusts the contributions of the visual and inertial tracking results for the final result according to the reliability of the visual and inertial tracker. We evaluate our method using current-generation smartphones and a dataset consisting of 16 video clips with synchronized inertial sensor data collected from the same smartphones used for capturing the videos. Experimental results demonstrated that, compared to a state-of-the-art visual tracking methods [5, 12], the hybrid method achieves up to a 2.3X speedup and 12% improvement in tracking accuracy.

2. OUR METHOD

The framework of our hybrid method (shown in Fig. 1) consists of three major modules: 1) a visual tracker based on featureless and feature-based tracking methods (Sec. 2.1); 2) an inertial tracker based on the measurements from built-in accelerometer and gyroscope of a smartphone (Sec. 2.2); and 3) an adaptive Kalman filter which fuses the visual and inertial results (Sec. 2.3). In the following, we provide details of each module.

2.1 Vision-based Tracking

2.1.1 Featureless Tracking

We utilize a highly efficient featureless method based on image registration to ensure a real-time performance of the visual tracker. Given two consecutive frames I_{t-1} and I_t, we estimate the homography matrix $H_{t|t-1}$ which maps I_{t-1} to I_t by minimizing a dissimilarity measure, i.e. sum square difference (SSD) between I_{t-1} and I_t, as shown in Eq. 1.

$$E_{SSD}(H_{t|t-1}) = \sum_i [I_t(H_{t|t-1}x_i) - I_{t-1}(x_i)]^2 \quad (1)$$

where x_i denotes pixel i on a frame. Minimizing Eq. 1 is solved using the Levenberg-Marquardt (LM) algorithm [11] in an iterative process. Specifically, in each iteration the $H_{t|t-1}$ is updated as $H_{t|t-1} \leftarrow H_{t|t-1} + \Delta H_{t|t-1}$ so that the value of $E_{SSD}(H_{t|t-1})$ is maximally reduced. According to Talyor expansion, expanding $E_{SSD}(H_{t|t-1} + \Delta H_{t|t-1})$ at $(H_{t|t-1} + \Delta H_{t|t-1})$ can be approximated as:

$$\begin{aligned} &E_{SSD}(H_{t|t-1} + \Delta H_{t|t-1}) \\ &\approx \sum_i [I_t(H_{t|t-1}x_i) + J_t(H_{t|t-1}x_i)\Delta H_{t|t-1} - I_{t-1}(x_i)]^2 \end{aligned} \quad (2)$$

where $J_t(H_{t|t-1}x_i)$ is the gradient of I_t at pixel $H_{t|t-1}x_i$. Calculating the derivative of Eq.2 and setting the derivative to 0 can derive $\Delta H_{t|t-1}$ which minimizes Eq.2. $H_{t|t-1}$ is then updated as $H_{t|t-1} + \Delta H_{t|t-1}$. This process iterates several times until $\Delta H_{t|t-1}$ is smaller than a threshold or a fixed number of iteration is reached.

As in our tracking task, we assume the interframe motion of a camera is usually very small, thus the object pose does not change too much between two consecutive frames. Based on this fact, we only iterate once in the LM optimization process and our extensive experimental results demonstrated that in most cases when the motion is small one iteration is sufficient to derive a correct homography matrix, yielding an ultra-fast tracking speed. The homography between the object model and the object on frame t (denoted as $H_{t|0}$) is calculated by multiplying homography matrices of all consecutive frames,

$$H_{t|0} = \prod_{i=0\sim t-1} H_{i+1|i} \quad (3)$$

2.1.2 Feature-based Tracking

Featureless tracking accumulates errors over time, yielding accuracy degradation as time increases. In addition, it is sensitive to fast camera movement which could result in large errors in homography estimation. To address these problems, we employ a feature-based tracking method based on online structure output learning (OSO) [5] as another solution for the visual tracker. Next, we provide the key idea of the OSO-based feature tracking followed by the method of fusing featureless and feature-based results in subsection 2.1.3.

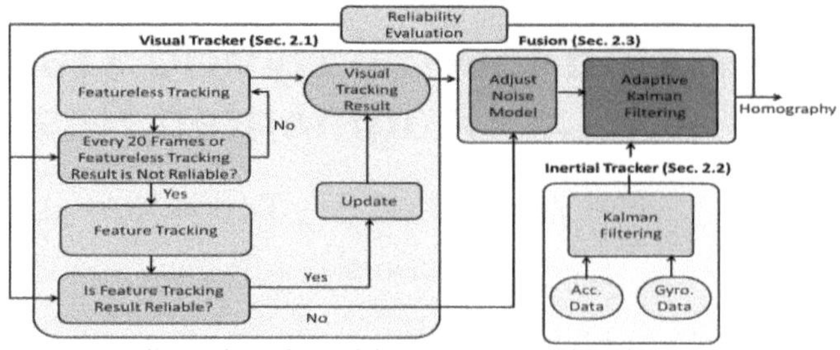

Fig. 1: Illustration of our vision-inertial hybrid tracking framework

The pipeline of OSO-based feature tracking proceeds as follows. First, an object to be tracked is specified by a user and a collection of local features are extracted from the object to construct an object model. In the tracking phase, the same type of local features are extracted from a video frame and then matched to the object model to construct correspondences. Possible transformations are derived from the correspondences and evaluated using the PROSAC [7] algorithm. The transformation with the highest PROSAC score is considered as the final homography between the object on the current frame and the object model (denoted as H^*). After that, the object model is updated so that the probability of obtaining an incorrect homography as the final tracking result in the next frame is minimized. This is achieved by identifying a set of feature descriptors $\{\boldsymbol{d'}\}$ which form false correspondences $\{\boldsymbol{m_f}\}$ that comply with the homography with the second highest scores (denoted as H'). These descriptors $\{\boldsymbol{d'}\}$ may facilitate generation of a false homograhy that very likely has the highest PROSAC score in the next frame, resulting in degradation of tracking accuracy. The model is adjusted to increase the distance between the revised model and the descriptors $\{\boldsymbol{d'}\}$ so that the chance of forming a wrong homography in the next frame is reduced.

2.1.3 Fusing Featureless and Feature-based Results

To achieve both efficiency and accuracy for the visual tracker, we combine the featureless and feature-based methods in a sequential way, as shown in Fig. 1. Specifically, featureless tracking is performed on every frame and its result is directly used as the visual tracking result when both the following two conditions meet: 1) for a small number of consecutive frames (i.e. 20 frames) as the accumulated error is small for a short period of time, and 2) if the featureless tracking result is reliable. If any of the two conditions is not satisfied, feature-based tracking is executed and visual tracking result is updated by the feature tracking result if it is reliable. In particular, the reliability of the tracking results for both featureless and feature-based methods is evaluated as follows. First, we select four points located at the four corners around the tracked object and track the locations of those four points in every video frame. We calculate an average translation of the four points between two consecutive frames t-1 and t, denoted as $T_{t|t-1}$. Then we compare $T_{t|t-1}$ with the M_{t-1}, the weighted mean of all the average translations $T_{2|1}, T_{3|2}, \ldots, T_{t-2|t-1}$ as denoted in Eq. (4),

$$\begin{aligned} M_{t-1} &= \left(1 - \frac{1}{|T_{t-1|t-2} - M_{t-2}| + 1}\right) M_{t-2} \\ &+ \frac{1}{|T_{t-1|t-2} - M_{t-2}| + 1} T_{t-1|t-2}, \quad (t > 2,\ M_1 = T_{2|1}) \end{aligned} \quad (4)$$

Consider the fact that the camera movement is always smooth and continuous during the tracking process, the translation $T_{t|t-1}$ is less

Fig. 2: Exemplar tracking results obtained from inertial sensors (denoted by blue quadrangles) and manual labels (denoted by red quadrangles). The rotation estimation is relatively accurate (i.e. the red quadrangles are almost parallel to the blue ones) and the translation error is large.

likely to become suddenly greater than previous cases, otherwise it is considered as an unreliable result. Therefore, if $T_{t|t-1}$ is significantly bigger than M_{t-1} (i.e. $|T_{t|t-1} - M_{t-1}| > \Delta$, Δ is set to 100 in our experiment), it is considered as an unreliable result. If both featureless and feature-based tracking results are unreliable, we updated parameters of the adaptive Kalman filter so that the importance of the visual tracking results is reduced. Details of how to update the adaptive Kalman filter is provided in Sec. 2.3.

2.2 Inertial-based Tracking

We track the camera motion based on gyroscope and accelerometer measurements. Specially, at time 0 when the object to be tracked is specified, the phone is almost static thus the accelerometer measurement includes only the gravity acceleration force of the phone, which can be used directly to derive an the initial camera orientation, denoted as $(\theta_x, \theta_y, \theta_z)_0$. During the tracking phase, gyroscope measures the angular velocity of the phone. By single integration of gyroscope measurements over time, the camera rotation with respect to three axes at time t can be obtained, denoted as $(\theta_x, \theta_y, \theta_z)_t$. The rotation matrix of the camera at time t is calculated by multiplying the thee rotation matrix $R(\theta_x)_t$, $R(\theta_y)_t$ and $R(\theta_z)_t$ as:

$$R_t = R(\theta_x)_t \times R(\theta_y)_t \times R(\theta_z)_t \tag{5}$$

3D translation of a phone (denoted as $T_{t|0}$) can be simply estimated by double integration of the motion-induced acceleration force measured from an accelerometer with time. The measurement from a built-in accelerometer consists of two parts: gravity acceleration force and motion-induced acceleration force. We decompose the motion-induced component by first deriving the gravity component based on the estimated phone orientation and then subtract it from the accelerometer measurement.

The homography between the object model and the object on current frame can be calculated based on the estimated 3D orientation and translation of the phone:

$$H^s_{t|0} = P \times V_t \times V_0^{-1} P^{-1} \tag{6}$$

where P is the projection matrix and we use the perspective projection in this work. V_t and V_0 are the transformation matrices consisting of rotation and translation matrices at time t and 0,

$$V_t = \left[R_t \;\; [x_0, y_0, z_0]^T + T_{t|0}\right],\; V_t = \left[R_t \;\; [x_0, y_0, z_0]^T\right] \tag{7}$$

where $[x_0, y_0, z_0]^T$ are the 3D coordinates of the object with respective to the camera coordinate system at time 0, indicating the initial depth between the object and the camera. This can be roughly estimated at time 0 by vision-based depth estimation.

Fig. 2 displays the estimated homography of two exemplar objects by inertial sensors and the true homography labelled manually. Results show that the rotation estimation is relatively accurate (i.e. the red quadrangles are almost parallel to the blue ones) and the translation error based on sensors is large due to large errors in depth estimation and translation estimation based on accelerometer measurements.

2.3 Vision-Inertial Hybrid Tracking based on Adaptive Kalman Filtering

We combine the visual and inertial tracking results based on an adaptive Kalman filter. Specifically, we define the filter's state vector x_k as a eight-element vector consisting of homography parameters $x_k = [R_1, R_2, R_3, R_4, R_5, R_6, T_1, T_2]^T$ where $R_1 \sim R_6$ are parameters related to rotation and scaling changes, and T_1 and T_2 represent translation changes in the x and y directions on a 2D image plane. The process model and measurement model are defined in Eqs. (8) and (9), respectively:

$$x_{t|t-1} = \Phi_2 \, x_{t-1|t-1} + \xi_t \tag{8}$$

$$V_t = \Gamma x_{t|t-1} + \eta_t \tag{9}$$

where Φ_2 is the state transition matrix and in our case it represents the homography transformation between two consecutive frames. We calculate the state transition matrix based on the inertial tracking results $H^s_{t|t-1}$,

$$H^s_{t|t-1} = \begin{bmatrix} \Delta R_1 & \Delta R_2 & \Delta x \\ \Delta R_3 & \Delta R_4 & \Delta y \\ \Delta R_5 & \Delta R_6 & 1 \end{bmatrix} = P \times V_t \times V_{t-1}^{-1} P^{-1} \tag{10}$$

ξ_t in Eq. (8) is the process noise which is drawn from a zero mean Gaussian distribution with covariance Q_t, $\xi_t \sim N(0, Q_t)$. Γ and η_k in Eq. (9) are the measurement matrix which is defined as $I_{8\times 8}$ in our case, and the measurement noise drawn from a zero mean Gaussian distribution with covariance R_t, $\eta_t \sim N(0, R_t)$. V_t is the estimated homography derived from visual tracking.

At time t we fuse the homography from the inertial tracker $H^s_{t|0}$ with the homography from the visual tracker $H^v_{t|0}$ using the proposed adaptive Kalman filter as follows:

1. Calculate the state transition matrix Φ_2.
2. Propagate the state vector from $x_{t-1|t-1}$ to $x_{t|t-1}$:

$$x_{t|t-1} = \Phi_2 x_{t-1|t-1} \tag{11}$$

3. Compute the state covariance matrix $P_{t|t-1}$:

$$P_{t|t-1} = \Phi_2 P_{t-1|t-1} \Phi_2^{\,T} + Q_2 \tag{12}$$

4. Check the reliability of the visual result according to the evaluation metric described in subsection 2.1.3: If if $T_{t|t-1}$ is significantly bigger than M_{t-1} (i.e. $|T_{t|t-1} - M_{t-1}| > \Delta$), we increase the Gaussian variance R_t of the noise model η_t in Eq. (9) by multiplying it with $(|T_{t|t-1} - M_{t-1}|/\Delta)$. By increasing the noise parameters when the result' reliability is low, the Kalman gain is adjusted adaptively to de-emphasize the unreliable visual result, which improve the robustness of the hybrid system; if $|T_{t|t-1} - M_{t-1}| \leq \Delta$, we set R_t to its initial value.
5. Update the Kalman gain K_t:

$$K_t = P_{t|t-1}(P_{t|t-1} + R_t)^{-1} \tag{13}$$

6. Update the state covariance matrix $P_{k|k-1}$:

$$P_{t|t} = P_{t|t-1} - K_t \cdot P_{t|t-1} \tag{14}$$

7. Update the state vector to obtain $x_{t|t}$:

$$x_{t|t} = x_{t|t-1} + K_t(V_t - x_{t|t-1}) \tag{15}$$

The state vector $x_{t|t}$ updated by Eq. (15) is the fusion result.

3. EXPERIMENTS

In this section, we describe the dataset, experimental setup and the measurement metrics used for our evaluation, followed by experimental results.

3.1 Dataset Collection

We collected four planar objects with different visual characteristics as the targets to be tracked: 1) "Cartoon" which contains homogeneous regions, 2) "Painting" which contains similar patterns, 3) "Map" and 4) "Paper" which contain sparse text, lines and figures. We fixed the targets on a wall and used the camera of a Samsung Galaxy S5 smartphone to record videos of the targets. For each target we recorded four videos, each of which was taken under different camera motions, including pan

Fig.3: Visualization of the tracking results on exemplar video frames from our dataset. The blue, red, green and yellow quadrangles denote the homography estimated by the ground truth, our hybrid method based on adaptive Kalman filtering, featureless tracking and feature-based tracking, respectively. Results demonstrate superior performance of hybrid method to the two vision-based methods.

Table 1. Tracking Accuracy Comparison (%)

Method	Cartoon	Painting	Map	Paper	Avg
Feature	98.5	97.8	85.4	75.8	89.4
Featureless	74.6	89.2	77.4	75.8	79.7
Our Method	98.2	97.4	90.4	83.9	92.5

Table 2. Comparison of Runtime (ms) on Samsung Galaxy S5

Method	Cartoon	Painting	Map	Paper	Avg
Feature	473.1	435.2	461.7	440.3	452.6
Featureless	150.7	155.5	151.9	152.2	152.4
Our Method	189.3	192.6	203.6	196.5	195.5

(~±60°), tilt (~±45°), in-plane rotation (±45°) and random movement, resulting in a total of 16 videos. The length of each video is about 20s. Exemplar frames of video are shown in Fig. 3.

To collect the ground truth describing the true homograph of the target in frames, we placed four black dots as tracking markers at the four corners around each planar target. We manually labeled the four dots on every frame and calculated the ground truth homography based on the manually labelled dots.

For each video clip, we recorded sensing data, synchronized with video frames, from the built-in inertial measurement unit (IMU) in the same smartphone used for capturing the videos based on an Android app which triggers the video recording and measurements from the IMU concurrently. For the IMU we recorded 3-axis accelerometer data, accelerometer timestamps, 3-axis gyroscope data and gyroscope timestamps.

3.2 Experimental Setup

In all experiments, we extract 500 features on every video frame and an object model using an ORB point detector [10] and a LDB feature descriptor [5]. The 8x8 covariance matrix Q_k of the process noise ξ_k in Eq. (8) is initially set to a diagonal matrix $diag(10^{-2},10^{-2},10^{-2},10^{-2},10^{-2},10^{-2},1,1)$, and the covariance matrix R_k is initially set to $diag(10^{-2},10^{-2},10^{-2},10^{-2},10^{-2},10^{-2},10^{-4},10^{-4})$. With these settings, the fusion result initially relies equally on the visual and inertial results for orientation estimation and more on the visual results for translation estimation.

Runtime was recorded by running the program on a Krait 400, 2.5GHz processor, in a Samsung Galaxy S5. We evaluate the tracking accuracy by computing the overlap between the two quadrangles, derived from an estimated homograhy and from the ground truth, divided by the union of the two quadrangles.

3.3 Experimental Results

Table 1 compares the accuracy of the three methods: feature-based tracking [5], featureless tracking [12] and our hybrid method. The 2nd ~ 5th columns of Table 1 show the average accuracy for each target category. Comparing to feature-based method, our method achieves comparable tracking accuracy for the "Cartoon" and "Painting" cases and much higher accuracy for challenging targets—"Map" and "Paper" which include sparse texture information. Our method significantly outperforms the featureless method for all cases. An average tracking accuracy of our method is 12% higher than that of the featureless method. Fig. 3 displays the tracking results on exemplar video frames from our dataset. Table 2 compares the runtime of the three methods. Comparing to feature-based method, our method achieves an average 2.3X speedup. Comparing to the featureless method, our method is only slightly slower (i.e. 1.3X slower) even though the computationally expensive feature-based method is performed from time to time in our method to ensure a high tracking accuracy and robustness.

4. CONCLUSIONS

This paper presents a hybrid tracking system which combines a visual tracker with an inertial tracker based on an adaptive Kamlan filter. The Kalman gain is adjusted adaptively to de-emphasize unreliable visual and inertial tracking result, improving the robustness and accuracy of the hybrid system. To improve the efficiency of the visual tracker and meanwhile maintain a satisfactory accuracy, an efficient featureless method is performed for pose tracking on every frame and a feature-based method is activated from time to time reduce tracking errors. Experimental results demonstrated superior performance of our method to the state-of-the-art methods [5, 12] relying on only vision analysis.

5. REFERENCES

[1] X. Yang, K.T. Cheng, LDB: An Ultrafast Feature for Scalable Augmented Reality on Mobile Devices, *In Proc. of ISMAR*, 2012.

[2] X. Yang, K.T. Cheng, Local Difference Binary for Ultrafast and Distinctive Feature Description, *TPAMI*, 36(1), 188-194, 2014.

[3] W.K. Obeidy, H. Arshad, S.A. Chowdhury, B. Parhizkar, J. Huang, Increasing the Tracking Efficiency of Mobile Augmented Reality Using a Hybrid Tracking Technique, *Advances in Visual Informatics*, 8237:447-457, 2013.

[4] M. Maidi, F. Ababsa, M. Mallem, Vision-Inertial Tracking System for Robust Fiducials Registration in Augmented Reality, *In Proc. of CIMSVP*, 83-90, 2009.

[5] S. Hare, A. Saffari, P.H.S. Torr. Efficient Online Structure Output Learning for Keypoint-based Object Tracking. In *Proc. of CVPR*, pp: 1894-1901, 2012.

[6] E. Rublee, V. Rabaud, K. Konolige, G. Bradski. ORB: an Efficient Alternative to SIFT or SURF. In *Proc. of ICCV*, 2011.

[7] O. Chum, J. Matas. Matching with PROSAC-Progressive Sample Consensus. In *Proc. of CVPR*, pp: 220-226, 2005.

[8] D. Wagner, G. Reitmayr, A. Mulloni, T. Drummond, D. Schmalstieg. Pose Tracking from Natural Features on Mobile Phones. In *Proc. of ISMAR*, pp: 125-134, 2008.

[9] N. Ozer, T. Erdem, A. O. Ercan, C. E. Erdem. Inertial Sensor Fusion for 3D Camera Tracking. In *Proc. of SIU*, pp: 1-4, 2012.

[10] D. L. Morgan. Improved Orientation Estimation for Smartphone Indoor Localization. *M.S. Thesis*, *UCSB*, 2014.

[11] W. H. Press, S. A. Teukolsky, W. T. Wetterling, and B. P. Flannery, Numerical Recipes, The Art of Scientific Computing (Cambridge University, 1992).

[12] F. Dornaika, F. Chakik. In Efficient Object Detection and Tracking in Video Sequences. In J. Opt. Soc. Am. A, 29(6), 2012.

An SDN Controller for Delay and Jitter Reduction in Cloud Gaming

Maryam Amiri
University of Ottawa
Mamir097@uottawa.ca

Hussein Al Osman
University of Ottawa
halosman@uottawa.ca

Shervin Shirmohammadi
University of Ottawa
shervin@site.uottawa.ca

Maha Abdallah
UPMC Univ. Paris 06
Maha.Abdallah@lip6.fr

ABSTRACT

Cloud gaming is an emerging service that has recently started to garner prominence in the gaming industry. Since the significant part of computational processing, including game rendering and video compression, is performed in data centers, controlling the transfer of information within the cloud has an important impact on the quality of cloud gaming services. In this paper, we make two contributions: we propose a design to apply the recent paradigm of Software Defined Networks (SDNs) to Cloud Gaming, and we propose an SDN controller that reduces end-to-end delay and delay variations experienced by players. Our SDN controller adaptively disperses the game traffic load among different network paths according to their corresponding end-to-end delays. Experimental results show that our proposed controller reduces end-to-end delay and delay variation by almost 9% and 50% respectively without engendering additional packet loss, compared to a representative conventional method: Open Shortest Path First (OSPF). These reductions lead to improvements in players' gaming experience.

Categories and Subject Descriptors

K.8.0 **[Personal Computing]**: General – games; C.2.4 **[Computer-Communication Networks]**: Distributed Systems - Client/server.

Keywords

Cloud gaming; Software Defined Network (SDN); Load sharing;

1. INTRODUCTION

Recent advances in cloud computing and data center deployment have led to numerous innovative services. Centralizing the resources and computational processes into data centers brings the ability of multiuser collaboration which is highly desired for multisource applications. Gaming is one such application that can benefit from cloud computing advancements. In fact, today's developments in cloud computing has introduced a new paradigm of online gaming, called Could Gaming [3]. Such cloud systems enable users to play graphically high-end games on various platforms, even tablets and smartphones, which have less computational and graphical processing resources than PCs and laptops, because all of the game logic processing and graphics rendering is done in the cloud: the result is simply a video that is streamed to the player. Cloud gaming also allows game developers to support more platforms, reduce the production costs, and increase their net revenues. In cloud gaming, players' commands are sent from their device (smartphone, tablet, gaming console, PC, etc.) to the cloud server, where appropriate actions are taken by the game engine to produce the resulting game scene, rendered by a GPU and encoded by a video codec, both in the cloud. Afterwards, the compressed video frames are sent to players through the network, and finally decoded and displayed on the players' devices. Although this significantly decreases the computation load at the client side, it adds additional latencies imposed by the network and the server. In fact it is known that today's cloud games introduce about 1.7 times higher latency than their console counterparts [8]. These latencies could adversely impact the players' Quality of Experience (QoE). This is a difficult challenge to overcome, because only 70% of end-users are able to meet the 80 ms latency target required for acceptable cloud gaming [4]. In addition to latency, the large amount of variation in latencies, known as jitter, has detrimental effects on gamers' QoE [4]. Moreover, [10] has shown that cloud games suffer from a much higher level of jitter compared to console games. Hence, new solutions to reduce the end-to-end delay and delay variation must be considered to overcome this challenge.

A variety of techniques have been proposed to address this challenge. Since we do not have any control over the Internet Service Provider (ISP) networks, these techniques mostly focus on the processing of games and forwarding of the gaming data within the cloud, and can be divided into two categories:

1. Processing techniques for the game engine and video encoder running on the servers.
2. Networking techniques for the distribution of the streamed gaming data within the data center.

Although most of the previous studies that deal with latency in cloud gaming focus on the game server side processing [13, 14], a handful of works have been proposed to cope with the delay and delay variation in cloud networks. For instance, Choy et al. [4] proposed a server selection method that takes into consideration the latency requirements of games running in the cloud in order to increase the players' coverage while ensuring lower network latency. Beskow et al [2] suggest a core selection method to find an optimal server to cover a group of players belonging to the same geographic region, with the goal of minimising latency in data transfer. Once the optimal server has been found, the game state will be migrated to that server.

In this paper we focus on the second type of techniques: network solutions, to reduce the delay and jitter in the cloud networks. We make two contributions: first, we show how the recent paradigm of SDN, as a novel approach in network management and network programmability, can be applied to cloud gaming systems. Second, we propose an SDN controller that optimizes the distribution of flows among the various redundant paths inside the cloud network to reduce the delay and jitter experienced by players.

MM'15, October 26–30, 2015, Brisbane, Australia.
© 2015 ACM. ISBN 978-1-4503-3459-4/15/10...$15.00.
DOI: http://dx.doi.org/10.1145/2733373.2806397

2. Cloud Gaming Data Center Architecture with SDN

Today's data centers typically consist of a core switch that dispatches client requests among aggregation switches, each of which further dispatches the request to a Top of Rack (ToR) switch, which finally dispatches the request to a processing node running multiple Virtual Machines (VM). In cloud gaming systems, since large amounts of video data are transmitted, the core switches are prone to congestion. So, some auxiliary network routes are employed as soon as the main paths are congested. Even though there are several methods to determine the optimal paths in the network, these methods usually select the best routes based on the link metrics provided at the setup time, and they often fail to take into consideration the current status of links (such as current available bandwidth) or the requirements of data flows passing through the network.

In traditional networks, although a router advertises its routing table to other neighboring routers, each router autonomously controls its own table using the highly localized network information it gathers. This makes distributed control inefficient. Furthermore, the routing protocols do not take into account the dynamic network conditions pertaining to bandwidth utilization, packet loss and delays. Therefore, SDNs were proposed as a new approach to traffic controlling through a centralized network controller [16]. Basically, SDN separates the network control and the forwarding planes to enable the optimization of each one separately. This results in a network that is more adaptable to different conditions and able to optimize QoS parameters. However, since most of the optimization methods are computationally costly, some predefined algorithms like load sharing are usually utilized. Even though such algorithms do not produce optimum traffic distribution, they are practical and computationally inexpensive.

Load sharing allows traffic to be dispersed among the different available paths between a source and a destination. As traffic is spread, the network load fluctuations are diminished and the corresponding end-to-end delay and jitter experienced by end users is decreased. As it can be seen in Figure 1, we propose an OpenFlow[12] based controller in a cloud gaming datacenter network which utilizes our proposed load sharing algorithm to decrease end-to-end delay as well as jitter. It is worth noting that in this work, we are focused on data centers dedicated solely to cloud gaming.

3. Proposed Load Sharing Algorithm

In our proposed controller, in order to provide efficient load sharing, when the core switch receives a packet without any matched entry in its own flow table, it sends the packet to the SDN controller, which then finds the optimum path; i.e., the path more suitable to forward this packet. Once the path is chosen, a new entry is created in the core switch's flow table for future packets of the same flow. Each player's session with a game is associated with one flow, and vice-versa.

Conventional SDN controllers usually find the optimum path in terms of different criteria (e.g., shortest delay, least hop-count etc...) to create a forwarding rule. Conversely, in our proposed method, first, all possible paths, from the requesting core switch to the Top of Rack (ToR) switches are identified by the controller. While this is an NP-problem, since the graphs constructed based on the current architectures of data centers (e.g. Fat-tree [1] and VL2 [6]) are simple, and the source (i.e. core switch) is fixed for all flows, the problem of finding all possible paths can be solved using Dijkstra's algorithm.

Next, the controller collects QoS statistics from the switches along the extracted paths using the OpenFlow protocol messages (STATISTICS_REQUEST, STATISTICS_REPLY,...), defined in the OpenFlow specification [7].

Given $P = (p_1, p_2, \cdots, p_N)$ and $L = (l_1, l_2, \cdots, l_N)$ denoting a set of N possible edge disjoint paths from core to a ToR switch and a set of associated end-to-end delays, respectively; these paths are available for the controller to disperse the incoming packets of the newly detected flow. p_j is a set of edges, with corresponding delays represented by $D_j = \left(d_{j1}, d_{j2}, \cdots d_{j|p_j|}\right)$. To measure the delay of each intermediate link of p_j, d_{jk} (where $1 \le k \le |p_j|$), the controller sends a message to each of the two switches directly connected to each other by that link and measures the RTT pertaining to each switch, i.e. RTT_{jk} and RTT_{jk+1}.

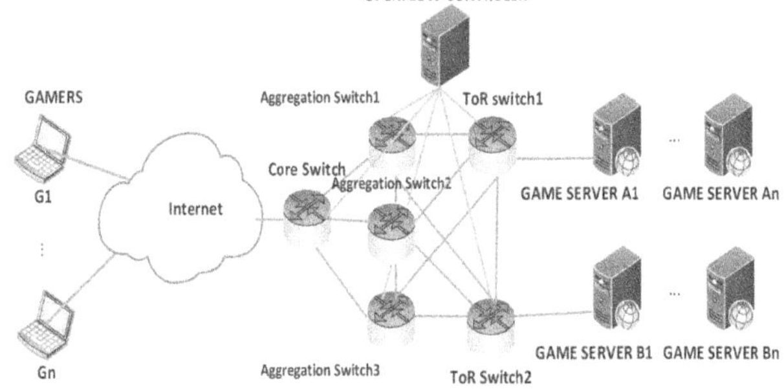

Figure 1. Cloud Gaming Architecture Using SDN

Having RTT_{jk+1} and RTT_{jk}, d_{jk} can then be calculated using equation (1).

$$d_{jk} = t_a - t_s - \tfrac{1}{2}(RTT_{jk+1} - RTT_{jk}) \qquad (1)$$

where t_a and t_s denote arrival and send time respectively.

Given D_j for j^{th}path, a corresponding end-to-end delay, l_j, is $\sum_{k=1}^{|p_j|} d_{jk}$. Consequently, a weight factor of path j, α_j, is obtained by equation (2).

$$\alpha_j = \frac{1}{l_j \sum_{j=1}^{N} \frac{1}{l_i}} \qquad (2)$$

The proposed controller splits the incoming packets, belonging to a flow, dynamically among different available paths directly proportional to the associated measured end-to-end delays. Also, since the aforementioned computation is conducted only once (when a new flow is detected by the controller), the proposed controlling method does not impose high computational costs on the controller. The controller first picks a path among the possible paths randomly to serve as a starting point, and then changes the path in a weighted round-robin fashion using the computed weight factor, α_j $(1 \le j \le N)$. It is worth noting that the random selection of the first path can reduce the creation of bias among different flows. The number of packets forwarded to each path is proportional to the weight factor which is computed for that path. Thus, the incoming traffic is fairly distributed among the alternative paths so that the network utilization is increased and consequently, traffic congestion is minimized.

The above proposed load sharing algorithm is detailed in Algorithm 1. As it will be shown in our Experimental Results section, this reduction in congestion level leads to the reduction in end-to-end delay as well as jitter which in turn increases the QoE of players in delay-sensitive cloud gaming systems. Furthermore, in the case of large scale DCs, the proposed method can be separately applied to switches within each pod.

Algorithm 1: Computation algorithm for available paths and the associated weighted factors (α_j)

Inputs:
$G(V, E)$: Data Center Topology Digraph
v_s: Source Vertex
v_d: Destination Vertex
$W = (w_1, w_2, \dots, w_{|E|})$: Weights of edges
Initialize $P = \emptyset$, $W = (1,1, \dots ,1)$
$p = Dijkstra(G, W, v_s, v_d)$
$\forall e_i \in p: w_i = w_i + |E|$
while(true) **do**
$p = Dijkstra(G, W, v_s, v_d)$
if $p \exists P$ { break;} // It means there are no new paths
$P \leftarrow P \cup \{p\}$
$\forall e_i \in p: w_i = w_i + |E|$
End while;
// $P = \{p_1, p_2, \dots, p_N\}$, All available edge disjoint paths from source to destination
for $p_j \in P$ **do**
$\forall e_k \in p_j$: compute the corresponding delay (d_{jk}) using equation (1)
Compute the weight factor of p_j (α_j) using equation (2)
End for

4. EXPERIMENTAL RESULTS

In this section, we provide the results of our experiments to evaluate the impact of the proposed controller on different types of games. We ran our experiments on an Ubuntu version 14.4 box and a Mininet emulator on the Oracle virtual box version 4.3. The Mininet emulator enabled us to create a realistic network experiment with OpenFlow and SDN. Figure 2 shows the details of the network topology utilized in all experiments. As we aimed to evaluate the performance of the proposed load sharing algorithm in highly utilized links [9], we assigned delays of 10 ms for all the links except L5 and L6 which were assigned delays of 15 ms and 20 ms respectively. This was done to have a variety of end-to-end delays between source and destination. Also, all links were assigned a bandwidth of 10 Mbps. We deployed the same custom topology which consists of five OpenFlow vSwitches (S1, S2, S3, S4, and S5) connected to four hosts (h1, h2, h3, h4) and an OpenFlow controller. In our setup, h1, h2 and h3 represent players and h4 represents a cloud server. We deployed the OpenFlow controller based on POX controller libraries. The application which is running on the controller manages network flows and tells the open vSwitches where to send the packets. Although all the hosts are running over one open terminal, we assigned distinct MAC addresses to them. In our scenario, we used Iperf to generate streams for the simulated gaming flows. We ran Iperf in server mode on h4 and client mode on (h1, h2, h3). Wireshark was used to monitor the OpenFlow messages, capture, and analyze the streamed packets. In order to evaluate the performance of the proposed controller, we have considered two scenarios. For each scenario, we tested both OSPF, as a representative conventional method [15], and our proposed SDN based method. For the conventional method, SDN is not used and the forwarding is entirely controlled by the switches. In the first scenario, three streams with the same throughput were generated for all players. Since the recommended range of bandwidth for cloud gaming is 2 Mb/s to 5 Mb/s [5] , we conducted this experiment for different Throughputs going from 1 Mb/s to 5Mb/s (with a step size of 1 Mb/s). Figures 3a and 3b show the delay variations and packet loss rate, measured for all players using proposed and conventional methods, respectively.

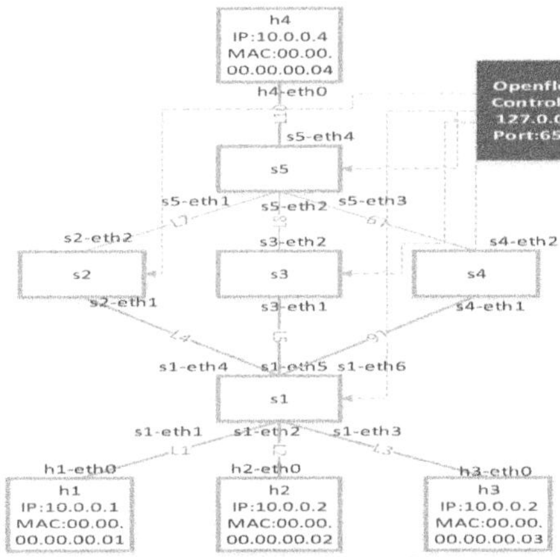

Figure 2.Experiment Setup

Figure 3a shows that when the network is under-utilized (1 Mb/s to 2 Mb/s), the amount of jitter is larger than when the network is more congested. On average, our proposed method reduces delay variations to almost half of that of the conventional method. It is worth noting that when we computed the aforementioned average, we did not consider the jitter corresponding to the lowest throughput (1 Mbps), since at that bandwidth the network is deemed to be under-utilized. Furthermore, Figure 3b shows that our method leads to 8% lower packet loss than the conventional method.

In the second scenario, three players played three different games (Crazytaxi, 4elements, pes2012), and we generate the traffic for these games based on the model in presented in [11]. The details of the network traffic parameters for these games are presented in Table 1.

The jitter obtained for the different types of games is illustrated in Figure 4a. The results show that the average of delay variation experienced by players using our proposed method is almost one third of the average jitter experienced in the conventional network. In addition to the significant improvement of jitter, figure 4b shows that the proposed method brings about around 9% reduction in the end-to-end delay compared to that of the conventional method. Both of these improvements stem from the fact that our proposed method selects the least congested paths on the network to forward new flows.

In order to evaluate the robustness of the proposed method, the packet loss rate is also shown in figure 4c. In this scenario, the proposed method achieves almost 10% lower packet loss than the conventional method. Based on these results, we can hypothesise that our proposed method decreases jitter without degrading packet delivery rate. Moreover, we can see that the impact of the proposed controller differs based on the type of the game. For instance, as shown in figure 4a, the jitter reduction resulting from our proposed method for Crazytaxi (Racing genre) and pes2012 (Sports genre) is approximately two times that of 4elements (Puzzle genre). The games with higher scene complexity and higher interaction level produce larger packet sizes and shorter departure-intervals respectively, which means that these games produce higher data rates. This results in more congestion on the network. Our proposed controller manages this congestion by distributing network flows among the available paths based on the overall current network condition. Conversely, conventional methods such as OSPF disregard such conditions. Therefore, our method supports games with higher data rates better than conventional methods.

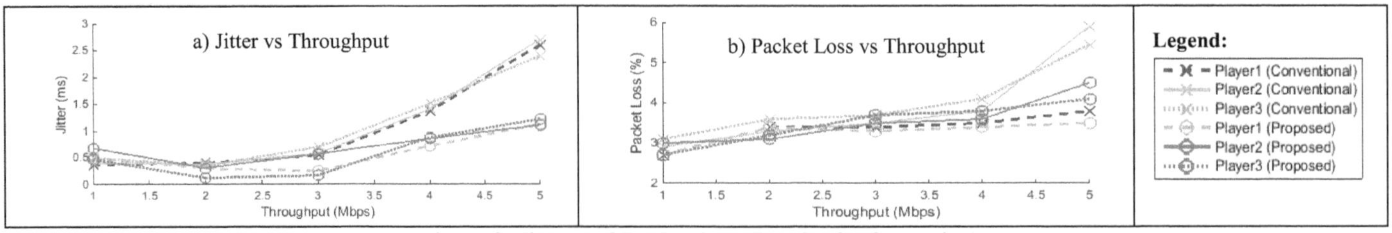

Figure 3. Jitter and Packet Loss Results for Scenario 1

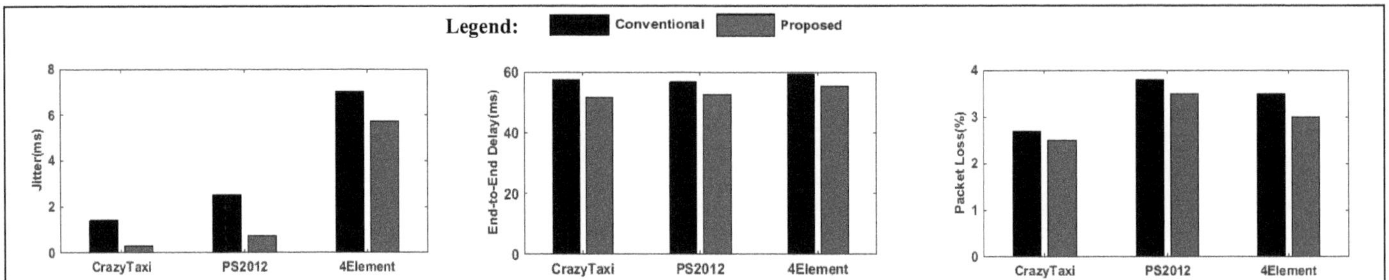

a) Jitter Measurement b) End-To-End Delay Measurement c) Packet Loss Rate

Figure 4. Jitter, Delay and Packet Loss Results for Scenario 2

Table 1. Network Traffic Parameters of three games

Games	Genre	Upstream traffic		Downstream traffic	
		Mean Packet Size (bytes)	Mean Inter-Departure time (ms)	Mean Packet Size (bytes)	Mean of Inter-Departure time (ms)
Crazytaxi	Racing	34.01	2.7	1,014.99	1.4
pes2012	Sports	35.86	2.8	915.57	1.6
4elements	Puzzle	62.72	1.6	722.58	2.1

5. CONCLUSION

In this paper, we presented a new SDN controller for cloud gaming data centers to improve latency. Our proposed algorithm detects all possible paths between the core and the ToR switches and adaptively distributes the traffic flows based on the end-to-end delay computed for all these paths. We have shown that our proposed method has several advantages over a representative conventional traffic forwarding method: OSPF. Since our proposed SDN controller shares the load among network paths, it tends to decrease traffic congestion, which consequently leads to a reduction in delay and jitter. This reduction in delay and jitter does not impose any additional packet loss, which has a significant impact on cloud players' QoE. For future work, we plan to augment the controller with capabilities to distinguish between various games and take their requirements into consideration.

6. REFERENCES

[1] Al-Fares, M., Loukissas, A. and Vahdat, A. A scalable, commodity data center network architecture. ACM SIGCOMM Computer Communication , (2008), 63-74.

[2] Beskow, P., Halvorsen, P. and Griwodz, C. Latency reduction in massively multi-player online games by partial migration of game state. In *Second International Conference on Internet Technologies and Applications,* (2007), 153-163.

[3] Cai, W., Chen, M. and Leung, V. Toward Gaming as a Service. Internet Computing, IEEE, 18, 3 (2014), 12-18.

[4] Choy, S., Wong, B., Simon, G. and Rosenberg, C. A hybrid edge-cloud architecture for reducing on-demand gaming latency. Multimedia Systems,Springer, (2014), 503-519.

[5] Claypool, M., Finkel, D., Grant, A. and Solano, M. Thin to win? Network performance analysis of the OnLive thin client game system. In *Network and Systems Support for Games (NetGames),* (2012), 1-6.

[6] Greenberg, A., Hamilton, J. R., Jain, N., Kandula, S., Kim, C., Lahiri, P., Maltz, D. A., Patel, P. and Sengupta, S. VL2: a scalable and flexible data center network. In *ACM SIGCOMM computer communication review*, (2009), 51-62.

[7] http://www.cs.princeton.edu/courses/archive/fall13/cos597E/papers/openflow-spec-v1.3.2.pdf.

[8] http://www.geforce.com/whats-new/articles/geforce-grid.

[9] Kandula, S., Sengupta, S., Greenberg, A., Patel, P. and Chaiken, R. The nature of data center traffic: measurements & analysis. In *Proceedings of the 9th ACM SIGCOMM conference on Internet measurement, (*2009), 202-208.

[10] Lampe, U., Wu, Q., Dargutev, S., Hans, R., Miede, A. and Steinmetz, R. Assessing Latency in Cloud Gaming. In *Cloud Computing and Services Science* , (2014), 52-68.

[11] Manzano, M., Urueña, M., Sužnjević, M., Calle, E., Hernandez, J. A. and Matijasevic, M. Dissecting the protocol and network traffic of the OnLive cloud gaming platform. Multimedia Systems,Springer, (2014), 451-470.

[12] McKeown, N., Anderson, T., Balakrishnan, H., Parulkar, G., Peterson, L., Rexford, J., Shenker, S. and Turner, J. OpenFlow: enabling innovation in campus networks. ACM SIGCOMM Computer Communication , (2008), 69-74.

[13] Semsarzadeh, M., Yassine, A. and Shirmohammadi, S. Video Encoding Acceleration in Cloud Gaming. Circuits and Systems for Video Technology, IEEE (2015).

[14] Wang, S. and Dey, S. Rendering adaptation to address communication and computation constraints in cloud mobile gaming. In *Telecommunications Conference*, (2010), 1-6.

[15] Wollman, W. V. and Barsoum, Y. Overview of open shortest path first, version 2 (OSPF V2) routing in the tactical environment. In *Military Communications Conference,* (1995).

[16] Yassine, A., Rahimi, H. and Shirmohammadi, S. Software defined network traffic measurement: Current trends and challenges. Instrumentation & Measurement Magazine, IEEE, 18, 2 (2015), 42-50.

The Invisible QR Code

Zhongpai Gao, Guangtao Zhai and Chunjia Hu
Institute of Image Communication and Information Processing
Shanghai Jiao Tong University
Shanghai, China
{gaozhongpai, zhaiguangtao, hcj-sjtu}@sjtu.edu.cn

ABSTRACT

QR (Quick Response) Codes are widely used as a convenient unidirectional communication channel to convey information, such as emails, hyperlinks, or phone numbers, from publicity materials to mobile devices. But the QR Code is not visually appealing and takes up valuable space of publicity materials. In this paper, we propose a new method to embed QR Code on digital screen via temporal psychovisual modulation (TPVM). By exploiting the difference between human eyes and semiconductor imaging sensors in temporal convolution of optical signals, we make QR Code perceptually transparent to human but detectable for mobile devices. Based on the idea of invisible QR Code, many applications can be implemented, e.g., "physical hyperlink" for something interesting on TV or digital signage , "invisible watermark" for anti-piracy in theater. A prototype system introduced in this paper serves as a proof-of-concept of the invisible QR Code and can be improved in future works.

Categories and Subject Descriptors

I.4.0 [**General**]: Image displays; H.1 [**Models and Principles**]: Miscellaneous; C.2.0 [**General**]: Open Systems Interconnection reference model (OSI)

General Terms

Design

Keywords

QR Code; temporal psychovisual modulation; invisible

Figure 1: Image formation via TPVM for HVS and imaging sensors. The display emits a pair of negative and positive QR Code embedded images alternately. Human eyes can just see the original image but imaging sensors get the image containing the QR Code that can be extracted by algorithms.

1. INTRODUCTION

The QR (Quick Response) Code is a two-dimensional (2-D) matrix code that belongs to barcodes [1]. Since introduced in 1994 by Denso Wave, the QR Code® has gained wide acceptance in such diverse industries as manufacturing, warehousing and logistics, retailing, healthcare, life sciences, transportation and office automation. Now with the explosive growth of smartphones, the QR Code is also being used in mobile marketing and advertising campaigns as a fast and effective way of connecting with customers and providing end-user content, including Web links, mobile coupons, airline boarding passes, etc [9]. QR codes serve as a convenient unidirectional communication channel from printed materials or display panels to a mobile computing device equipped with a camera.

QR Codes provide users with unique offline-to-online experience, but are often criticized for their dull black-and-white looks. The random appearance of QR codes is not visually appealing, and significantly distracts from the overall production quality of the advertisements. More importantly, QR codes are not visually significant, that is, without decoding with scanning software, the resemble random images do not make sense to the naked eye. Moreover, the codes take up valuable space in publicity materials. To improve the appearance of QR Code and encourage usages, there have been several efforts both from the academic and commercial sectors [5]. These methods can be classified in three main categories. First, many aesthetic/artistic barcodes are manually designed [6]. Second, this category corresponds to direct manipulation of QR modules (e.g., replacing the cen-

MM'15, October 26–30, 2015, Brisbane, Australia.
© 2015 ACM. ISBN 978-1-4503-3459-4/15/10 ...$15.00.
DOI: http://dx.doi.org/10.1145/2733373.2806398.

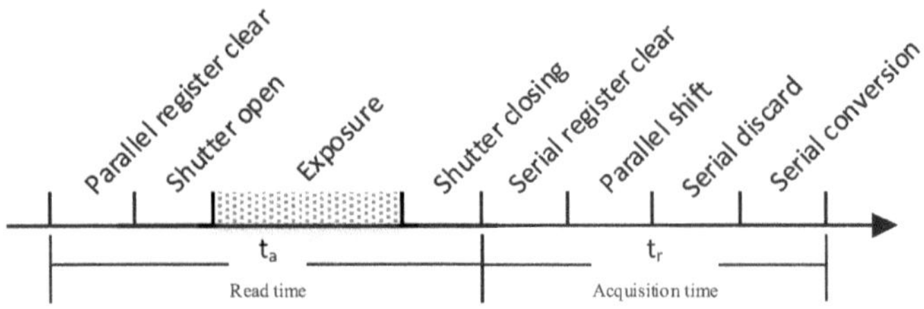

Figure 2: Time slices of one frame recorded by full frame CCD in digital cameras. The frame rate f of the digital cameras is determined by the frame acquisition time t_a and read time t_r as $f = 1/(t_a + t_r)$.

ter portion of the barcode by the intended logo) [7]. Third, this category of QR embedding algorithms is based on the modification of the luminance of individual pixels without altering the location of QR modules [2, 4]. Most of these methods deliberately use up some of the error budget provided in the code, that reduces the error-correction capability of QR Code. Also, they just improve the appearance of QR Codes and still take up the space of publicity materials.

This paper presents a new method that achieves the two conflicting objectives of QR Code completely: enhance visual appearance and maximize decoding robustness. In this method, by exploiting the difference of image formation mechanism between human eyes and imaging sensors, the QR Codes are perceptually transparent to human eyes (i.e., people cannot perceive the existence of QR Codes by naked eye, so the visual appearance does not need to be considered) but can be detected and recognized by mobile computing device with a camera when the codes are on screens (e.g., public billboards, TVs, and other digital displays). Here is the difference of the image formation mechanisms: in human visual system (HVS), a steady image is formed by continuous integration of light field, whereas semiconductor imaging sensors take discrete samples of continuous light source in time. CCD (charge-coupled device) and CMOS (complimentary metal oxide semiconductor) [8] are two commonly used types of sensors. Fig. 2 shows the time schedule of imaging process for a single frame by full frame CCD in digital cameras. The integration period of the sensors, i.e. the exposure time is only a portion of the total imaging time $(t_a + t_r)$. Therefore, the digital cameras cannot capture all the information on the screen due to the "blackout" period [11]. They are limited by CCD's working mechanism if the refresh rate of the screen is high enough. CMOS works much like CCD.

As analysis above, digital camera cannot fully record all the optical signals emitted from the screen. Therefore, human eyes and imaging sensors apply different temporal convolution kernels to light sources when forming images. Based on this difference, we can design optical signals in the way that human and imaging sensors perceive drastically different images. In this paper, for example, we can embed QR Codes in an image so that human eyes can just see the original image but the image taken by camera will contain the codes. The intriguing bifurcation can be realized by the recently proposed paradigm of information display technology, called temporal psychovisual modulation (TPVM) [10], as shown in Fig.1. The rationale behind TPVM is that, the HVS cannot detect quick temporal changes above the flicker fusion frequency (about 60 Hz) and yet modern display technologies offer much higher refresh rates. For example, active 3D displays support 120 Hz, BenQ DLP® Projector TH681 can support full HD resolution (1920×1080) with triple flash (144 Hz)[1], and for LED displays, refresh rate is possible to reach more than 1200 Hz at a moment.

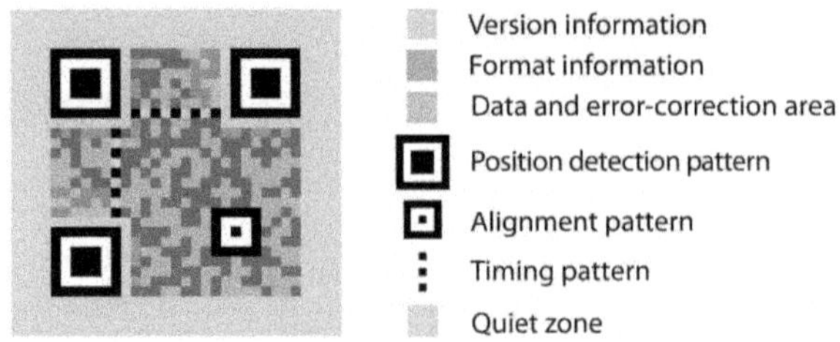

Figure 3: The QR Code structure

2. PHILOSOPHY AND MODEL

2.1 Philosophy

In the past decade, with the development of display technology, display devices make great changes in our modern life. Nowadays, lots of information is obtained through display device. However, we obtain the information through display device just by the visual system and yet modern display devices can offer much higher refresh rates than the flicker fusion frequency. That is, the modern display has extra capacity, i.e., psychovisual redundancy can be used. There are mainly two ways to utilize the extra capacity. First, the psychovisual redundancy of display device can be used to generate multiple visual percepts for different viewers introduced in [10]. Second, the redundancy can be used for data transmission to computing devices (i.e., visible light communication from display devices to computing devices). That means, while the display device emits images to people, it can transmit data to computing device as well. So there is a unidirectional communication channel from display device to computing device which can be widely used in many fields.

2.2 QR Code Symbol

There are many ways to transmit signals from display devices to computing device. For example, we can design some specific patterns and encode the signals with specific rules. Here we choose QR Code symbol as the communication channel from display device to computing device.

The QR Code can hold a large amount of data. In addition, an advanced error-correction method and other unique characteristics allow the QR Code to be read more reliably and at higher speeds than other codes [1], the structure of QR Code is shown in Fig. 3. The QR Code is a 2-D matrix code that conveys information by the arrangement of its dark and light elements, called "modules", in columns and rows. The QR Code modules perform several functions: Some contain the actual data itself, while others are grouped into various function patterns that improve reading performance and allow symbol alignment, error correction and distortion compensation. The timing pattern lets the scanning device know the size of the symbol. There is also a required "quiet zone", a four-module-wide buffer area containing no data, to ensure that surrounding text or markings are not mistaken for QR Code data. The QR Code has many unique

[1]DLP® Projector: http://benq.eu/product/projector/th681

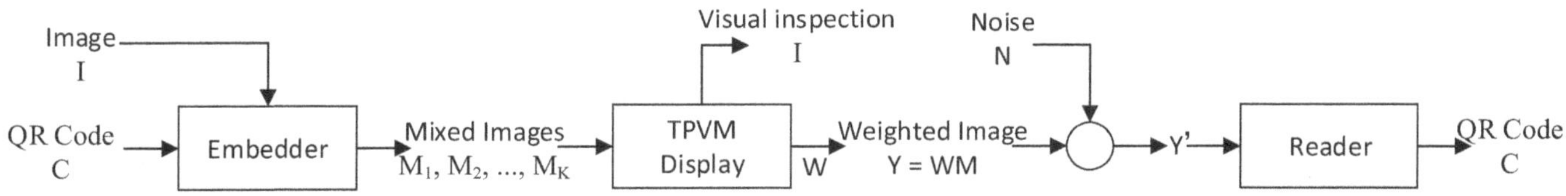

Figure 4: Communication model of QR Code based on temporal psychovisual modulation (TPVM).

advantages and benefits, including: 1) Fast and omnidirectional scanning; 2) High-capacity data storage up to 7089 numerals; 3) Small size; 4) Error correction up to 30% of data damaged; 4) Handle many types of data; 5) Distortion compensation; 6) Linkability (Structured Append); 7) Direct marking onto a part or product.

2.3 Communication model

Fig. 4 shows the communication model of QR Code based on TPVM technology. First, Let f_d be the flicker fusion frequency and $f_c = Kf_d$ be the refresh rate of a digital display. The embedder, taking an image $\mathbf{I} \in \mathbb{R}^L$ and a QR Code $\mathbf{C} \in \mathbb{R}^L$ as input (L is the resolution of $\mathbf{I}$ and $\mathbf{C}$ is padded with zeros to have the same size of $\mathbf{I}$), generates a set of mixed images $\mathbf{M}_1, \mathbf{M}_2, \cdots, \mathbf{M}_K$ which are subjected to $\sum_{i=1}^{K} \mathbf{M}_i = K\mathbf{I}$, where $K = f_c/f_d$. The high-speed TPVM display emits the mixed images sequentially. For human, the HVS integrates all of light field of the mixed images to form the complete image $\mathbf{I}$. But for imaging sensor, because of the "blackout" period, camera cannot receive all the optical signals emitted from screen, as shown in Fig. 2 and Fig. ??. That is, the mixed images are weighted to form the image $\mathbf{Y} = \mathbf{MW}$, where $\mathbf{Y} \in \mathbb{R}^L$, $\mathbf{W} \in \mathbb{R}^{K\times 1}$ and $\mathbf{M} \in \mathbb{R}^{L\times K}$ contains all $\mathbf{M}_i$'s as its columns. The channel from display device to the QR Code reader is noisy, e.g., because of the position and angle of camera are not certain, the image obtained by the camera might be rotated and distorted. Also, the luminance disturbances and other noise might impact the image. All these changes can be considered as noise $\mathbf{N}$. Under the influence of $\mathbf{N}$, the weighted image $\mathbf{Y}$ turns into $\mathbf{Y}'$. For a specific QR Code reader, we want to design an embedder that minimizes the visual distance between $\mathbf{C}$ and $\mathbf{Y}'$, and yet $\mathbf{C}$ can be successfully extracted and decoded with high probability.

3. SYSTEM DESIGN

In this paper, we build a prototype system of invisible QR Code based on TPVM using an LCD display with 120 Hz refresh rate, as shown in Fig. 5. The system is written in C++ language in Microsoft Visual Studio 2010. SDKs of NVIDIA 3D Vision, DirectX, CEGUI are used to fully realize of the application. Suppose the critical flicker frequency is 60 Hz, then the 120 Hz display is able to emit a pair of frames without causing flashing feeling of the HVS, as shown in Fig. 1. The proposed system can be separated into the following two steps.

3.1 Embed QR Code

The principle of the embedder is to minimize the visual distance between the QR Code $\mathbf{C}$ and the image $\mathbf{Y}'$, which is equivalent to minimize the visual distance between $\mathbf{C}$ and the weighted image $\mathbf{Y}$, as shown in Fig. 4. Here we just need to consider the square area of the QR Code. For an 120Hz LCD display, $K = 2$. So we need to design two mixed images $\mathbf{M}_1$ and $\mathbf{M}_2$ which are subjected to $\mathbf{M}_1 + \mathbf{M}_2 = 2\mathbf{I}$. Based on the TPVM technology as illustrated in subsection 2.3, $\mathbf{M}_1$ and $\mathbf{M}_2$ are emitted from the display alternately. It is important to mention that, the parameters of the camera (e.g., frame rate, shutter speed, exposure time) can be controlled in the computing device, that is, the weights $\mathbf{W}$ of camera can be determined freely. So support $\mathbf{W} = [1, 0]^T$, then $\mathbf{Y} = \mathbf{M}_1 \times 1 + \mathbf{M}_1 \times 0 = \mathbf{M}_1$. Now, we just need to design $\mathbf{M}_1$ that has the minimum visual distance to the QR Code $\mathbf{C}$.

Figure 5: Setup of the system. We can see the QR Code in the top right corner of the display because the picture is taken by camera, however it can hardly be seen by naked eye.

To make the QR Codes more detectable by smartphone, there are two points to be mentioned: 1) The pixels of M1 within the black modules of C should be as small as possible and within the white modules of C should be as large as possible, as just the opposite for M2. 2) To make the QR Code invisible, the computing of gray scale vales should be converted to brightness space because the correspondence between brightness and gray values are not linear for most display devices.

3.2 Read QR Code

Because the camera are not synchronized with the display, the luminance values of the QR Code in the obtained image $\mathbf{Y}'$ can change randomly. However, if we set the parameters of camera correctly, the obtained images are close to $\mathbf{M}_1$ or $\mathbf{M}_2$. To unify the $\mathbf{M}_1$-like images and $\mathbf{M}_2$-like images, we can inverse the $\mathbf{M}_2$-like images first. So we just need to consider the $\mathbf{M}_1$-like images. The QR Codes are extracted by the following two steps. First, color space transformation, we transform the image $\mathbf{Y}'$ from RGB space to YUV space to get the luma component $\mathbf{L}$. Second, image binaryzation, every pixel of $\mathbf{L}$ is binarized according the average of its neighbors. Fig. 6 shows the results of extracting QR

(a) (b) (c) (d) (e) (f)

Figure 6: Results of extracting the QR Codes. (a), (b), (c) are obtained by smartphone. (d), (e), (f) are extracted from (a), (b), (c) respectively. Although the QR Codes are not fully recovered. They all can be recognized by mobile devices because of the powerful error-correction capability of QR Code.

Codes. The codes can be detected by the scanner on mobile devices [3].

4. ANALYSIS AND FUTURE WORKS

Without extra help people are not aware of the existence of QR Codes. So the QR Codes are invisible to human eye. All the QR Codes in Fig. 6 can be recognized by mobile devices of three main platforms, IOS (iPhone 5S), Windows Phone (Lumia 520) and Android (Huawei Honor 6). This paper just presents a prototype system to implement invisible QR Code via TPVM. There are many aspects that can be refined and improved. First, in the future, we can develop the system on multiple mobile platforms, e.g., IOS, Windows Phone and Android. So that users with mobile devices can scan the invisible QR Codes on screen anytime and anywhere. Second, the method to read QR Code introduced in this paper is simple but not robust enough. In the future, the invisible QR Code recognition should be studied to make the recognition more reliably and at higher speeds. Third, based on the idea of invisible QR Code, many applications can be implemented. For example, in theater, we can embed QR Code in the movies. This not only can defeat piracy (the pirated movies will contain the QR Code which may flash all the time, that will make people feel objectionable and offensive.), but also can track the pirated movies that contain information of where and when the movies are pirated, etc. On TV or digital signages, through the invisible QR Codes, people can get more information about the things they are interested in (e.g., a coat on a movie star).

5. CONCLUSIONS

The paper proposes a new method to embed QR Code on digital screen via temporal psychovisual modulation (TPVM). By exploiting the difference between human eyes and semiconductor imaging sensors in temporal convolution of optical signals, we verify the feasibility of this method that QR Code is invisible to human but can be detected by computing device with camera. Based on the idea of invisible QR Code, there are many applications can be implemented, e.g., "physical hyperlink" for something interesting on TV or digital signages and "invisible watermark" for anti-piracy in theater. A prototype system presented in this paper serves as a proof-of-concept of the invisible QR Code and can be refined and improved in future works.

6. ACKNOWLEDGMENTS

This work was supported in part by NSFC (61422112, 61331014, 61371146).

7. REFERENCES

[1] D. ADC. QR Code essentials, 2011. Retrieved 12 March 2013.

[2] Z. Baharav and R. Kakarala. Visually significant QR Codes: Image blending and statistical analysis. In *Multimedia and Expo (ICME), 2013 IEEE International Conference on*, pages 1–6, July 2013.

[3] L. Belussi and N. Hirata. Fast QR Code detection in arbitrarily acquired images. In *Graphics, Patterns and Images (Sibgrapi), 2011 24th SIBGRAPI Conference on*, pages 281–288, Aug 2011.

[4] C. Fang, C. Zhang, and E.-C. Chang. An optimization model for aesthetic two-dimensional barcodes. In C. Gurrin, F. Hopfgartner, W. Hurst, H. Johansen, H. Lee, and N. O'Connor, editors, *MultiMedia Modeling*, volume 8325 of *Lecture Notes in Computer Science*, pages 278–290. Springer International Publishing, 2014.

[5] G. J. Garateguy, G. R. Arce, D. L. Lau, and O. Villareal. QR images: Optimized image embedding in QR Codes. 2014.

[6] J. Labs. QR Code art. [Online]. Available: http://jess3.com/qr-code-art/, 2014.

[7] S. Ono, K. Morinaga, and S. Nakayama. Two-dimensional barcode decoration based on real-coded genetic algorithm. In *Evolutionary Computation, 2008. CEC 2008. (IEEE World Congress on Computational Intelligence). IEEE Congress on*, pages 1068–1073, June 2008.

[8] S. A. Taylor et al. CCD and CMOS imaging array technologies: technology review. *Xerox Research Centre Europe, Technical Report EPC-1998-106*, pages 1–14, 1998.

[9] Wikipedia. QR code. [Online]. Available: http://en.wikipedia.org/w/index.php?title=QR_code, 2014.

[10] X. Wu and G. Zhai. Temporal psychovisual modulation: A new paradigm of information display [exploratory dsp]. *Signal Processing Magazine, IEEE*, 30(1):136–141, 2013.

[11] G. Zhai and X. Wu. Defeating camcorder piracy by temporal psychovisual modulation. *Display Technology, Journal of*, 10(9):754–757, Sept 2014.

3D Background Modeling in Multi-view RGB-D Video

Yung-Lin Huang [*], Ku-Chu Wei [†], Shao-Yi Chien [†]
[*] Graduate Institute of Networking and Multimedia
[†] Graduate Institute of Electronics Engineering and Department of Electrical Engineering
National Taiwan University, Taipei, Taiwan
{cary, kcwei, sychien}@media.ee.ntu.edu.tw

ABSTRACT

In this paper, we proposed a 3D background modeling system for multi-view 3D video. We first reconstructed a 3D model, and we updated the subsequent frames into it using our proposed updating strategy. The results show that dynamic objects in the model can be excluded, leaving behind a compact 3D background model.

Categories and Subject Descriptors

I.4.5 [**Image Processing and Computer Vision**]: Reconstruction; I.4.9 [**Image Processing and Computer Vision**]: Applications

Keywords

Multi-view 3D video, RGB-D video, 3D reconstruction, background modeling

1. INTRODUCTION

Recently, three-dimensional (3D) video has attained a high level of maturity in both capture and display devices. In addition to two-dimensional (2D) video, 3D video can provide viewers with depth impression of the captured scene. Moreover, to enable viewers to have a more immersive viewing experience, multiple cameras have been used to capture multi-view video.

These 3D techniques have benefited many studies on computer vision. For example, in augmented reality (AR), some researchers utilize 3D cameras to enhance the robustness when augmenting virtual objects [8]. This approach not only estimates the camera poses of the video, but also reconstructs the 3D model. Therefore, virtual objects can more easily be augmented because of the known 3D shape.

In this paper, we introduce 3D reconstruction into multi-view 3D video systems. We focus on static 3D background modeling, and using our proposed strategy, the 3D model can be updated by subsequent video frames. As a result, we reconstructed a compact 3D background model.

MM'15, October 26–30, 2015, Brisbane, Australia.
© 2015 ACM. ISBN 978-1-4503-3459-4/15/10 ... $15.00.
DOI: http://dx.doi.org/10.1145/2733373.2806399.

2. RELATED WORKS

In this section, we will discuss current 3D video technology and 3D scene reconstruction methods.

2.1 Multi-view 3D Video

One way to produce 3D video is to extract 3D information from 2D video using 2D-3D conversion techniques [10]. However, the retrieved 3D information may be inaccurate due to errors in the estimated depth. Recently, stereo cameras and camera arrays have become more widely used to capture 3D video [11]. These advanced devices have enabled us to simultaneously capture multiple viewpoints of real scenes, in the process preserving more 3D information than would have been possible before. In other words, the depth maps of each viewpoint can be estimated more robustly.

To achieve high performance in various video applications, many video codec standards have been developed. 3D video technology is also included in multi-view video coding (MVC) [12]. To encode efficiently the 3D information for free-viewpoint TV (FTV) application, the 3D information is recorded as a depth map along with each video frame [7]. This introduces multi-view video plus depth, and is referred to as multi-view 3D video or multi-view RGB-D video.

2.2 3D Scene Reconstruction

3D scene reconstruction techniques aim to capture the shapes and appearances of real scenes. These techniques have been a popular topic in the fields of computer vision, computer graphics, and robotics [3]. In this study, we focus on vision-based methods, which are more relevant to digital image and video systems.

Given an image collection taken from various camera viewpoints, the structure from motion (SfM) [9] is the approach used to reconstruct the 3D model and estimate the camera poses. To determine correspondence among images, feature detection and matching [6] are often employed.

In addition to 2D video, recently developed off-the-shelf depth cameras are capable of capturing depth video along with RGB color video. They are limited to indoor environments because of the requirements of the IR projector and camera, but they produce robust depth information considering these constraints. Therefore, 3D reconstruction using RGB plus depth (RGB-D) video has become more attractive recent times [8] [4] [5]. Most studies have assumed the presence of static scenes because dynamic 3D object reconstruction remains a challenging issue. In this paper, we focus on multi-view RGB-D video in FTV applications.

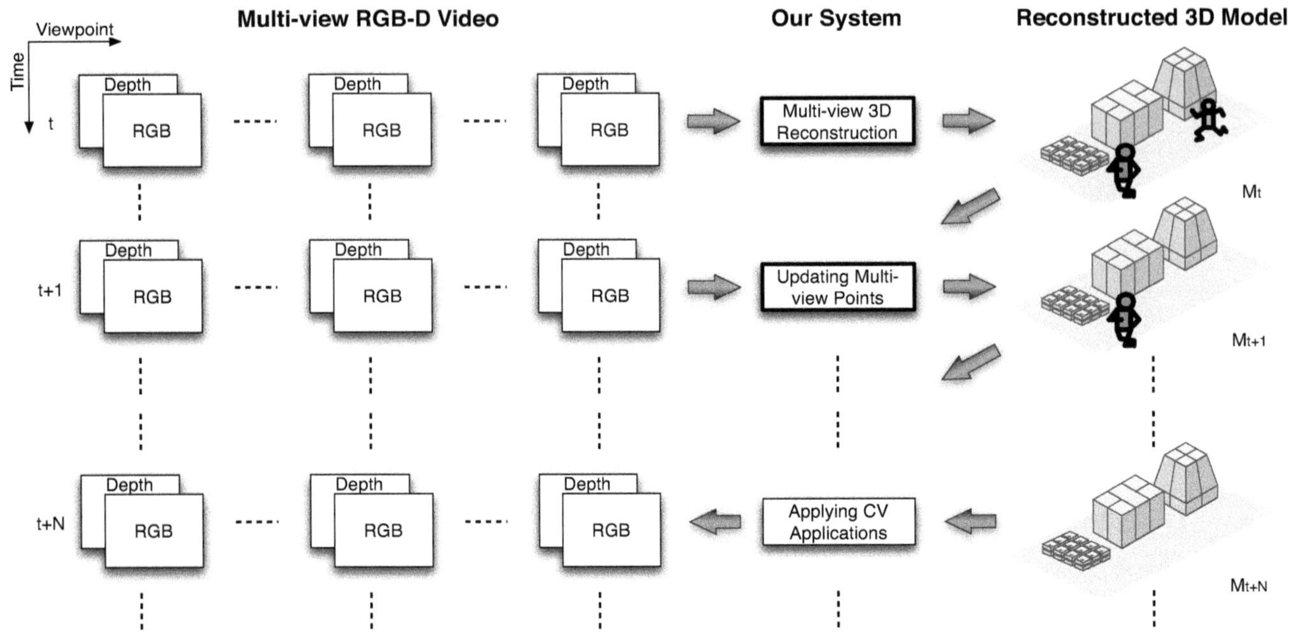

Figure 1: Illustration of our proposed system. Multi-view video frames with the same time stamp are processed simultaneously. Multi-view 3D reconstruction is employed for the first frames. The multi-view points are updated between the 3D model and the subsequent multi-view video frames. The 3D background model will be steadied automatically. It can then be applied to many computer vision applications.

3. SYSTEM OVERVIEW

An illustration of our proposed system is shown in Fig. 1. The input multi-view RGB-D video contains color images and the corresponding depth maps from multiple viewpoints. Given an arbitrary multi-view RGB-D video, the first frames of each viewpoint are all used to reconstruct a generic point-based 3D model. We used point primitive to represent the 3D model because it is more suitable for video [5] [13]. Hence, we updated the 3D model using the following multi-view video frames. After a certain number of frames, the 3D model will be steadied with only the static background remaining. Finally, the reconstructed 3D background model can be applied to computer vision applications such as AR and motion object segmentation.

4. MULTI-VIEW 3D RECONSTRUCTION

The first part of our proposed system is to reconstruct a point-based 3D model. The 3D reconstruction for a static scene is a well-studied issue, as explained in Sec. 2.2. In our system, the multi-view video frames having the same time stamp can also be treated as a static scene. Consequently, we generated the 3D models of each viewpoint, and then registered these 3D models into a generic one. Note that the 3D reconstruction was only performed at the first time stamp, and the following frames were subsequently updated.

4.1 Depth Map to 3D Space Projection

The relationship between the camera image plane and the world coordinate can be formulated as a camera intrinsic matrix $\mathbf{K}$. Given a 2D pixel $\boldsymbol{p} = (x, y)^T \in \mathbf{R}^2$, and its corresponding 3D point $\boldsymbol{P} \in \mathbf{R}^3$ can be determined uniquely as $\boldsymbol{P} = Z(\boldsymbol{p})\mathbf{K}^{-1}(\boldsymbol{p}^T, 1)^T$ with the aid of depth Z.

For the depth map in the 3D video, the real depth is usually non-linearly quantized into 256 levels to be stored as a depth image D. The real depth $Z(\boldsymbol{p})$ of a depth value $D(\boldsymbol{p})$ can be restored as $Z(\boldsymbol{p}) = 1/[\frac{D(\boldsymbol{p})}{255} \cdot (\frac{1}{z_{min}} - \frac{1}{z_{max}}) + \frac{1}{z_{max}}]$. Besides, the color information of each point can be directly derived from the corresponding color images.

4.2 3D Model Registration

The relationship between the data captured from different viewpoints can be formulated as a 6 degrees of freedom (6-DoF) rigid transformation. The transformation can be derived from the camera extrinsic matrices, which describe the 6-DoF rigid transformation, including the rotation $\mathbf{R}$ and the translation $\mathbf{t}$. On the other hand, if the extrinsic matrices are unknown, the registration techniques can be employed to derive the appropriate transformation.

A two-stage registration framework has often been used in previous works [4] [13]. The framework includes a global estimation method, followed by a local refinement. Moreover, an additional global optimization is required to handle the loop closure problem when reconstructing a large-scale scene using moving cameras. Nevertheless, for registration between different viewpoints in 3D video, the global estimation method can achieve acceptable results without further refinement. Even if the registration is not perfect without local refinement, the updating of our subsequent multi-view points can tolerate it. In addition, there is no loop closure problem among multiple viewpoints.

It is costly to match all points in the 3D model. In our system, SIFT feature points [6] are used to effectively reduce the search space. Also, to reduce the effect of incorrect correspondence caused by improper feature matching, we employed random sample consensus (RANSAC). We then computed the 3D transformation $[\mathbf{R}|\mathbf{t}]$ to obtain a least-square minimization between these feature pairs.

5. UPDATING MULTI-VIEW POINTS

Within the initial 3D model, we updated pixels from subsequent frames into the model using our proposed strategy. To steady the 3D model, we updated only static background pixels. On the contrary, we excluded dynamic object points in the 3D model.

The proposed updating strategy was inspired by [1], where the 3D model points were projected into images to determine whether the image pixels belong to the 3D model. However, their 3D model points could hardly be matched to image pixels because the model was reconstructed from a large image collection using SfM. In our system, the frames used for reconstructing the 3D model are highly correlated. Therefore, there were negligible variations in the color and illumination of points, enabling point-to-pixel matching.

5.1 3D Points Back-projection

To compare a 3D model point with an image pixel, we projected the 3D point back into the image as the inverse process of Sec. 4. We performed matching in the image space instead of the 3D space. Because the depth of 3D video is estimated by stereo matching, which operates in the image space, it is more appropriate to measure the re-projection error in the image space [4].

Fig. 1 shows that the 3D model needs to be matched to the subsequent frames of all the viewpoints. For one viewpoint i, Sec. 4.2 presents our estimation of the 3D transformation $[\mathbf{R}_i|\mathbf{t}_i]$ with respect to the 3D model. In addition, the camera motion $[\mathbf{R}_{t,t+1}|\mathbf{t}_{t,t+1}]$ between video frame t and t+1 can help the projection of the 3D model M_t to frame t+1. Thus, a point $\boldsymbol{P}$ in the 3D model M_t can be projected into the next frame, and is shown as $\boldsymbol{p} = \mathbf{K}_i[\mathbf{R}_{t,t+1}|\mathbf{t}_{t,t+1}][\mathbf{R}_i|\mathbf{t}_i]\boldsymbol{P}$. Finally, we compared the depth values to determine whether the projected point was the closest one.

5.2 Updating Strategy

After performing the 3D point back-projection procedure, the pixels to which no points were projected belong to appearing regions, and we then updated them into the new 3D model M_{t+1}. Nevertheless, most pixels have corresponding projected points. In other words, these pixels are likely to be similar to or in conflict with existing 3D points. To identify how these image pixels should be updated, we evaluated the background modeling cost function $F(\boldsymbol{p}, \boldsymbol{p}_{i,t+1})$ between each projected point $\boldsymbol{p}$ and its corresponding image pixel $\boldsymbol{p}_{i,t+1}$. The function can be expressed as

$$F(\boldsymbol{p}, \boldsymbol{p}_{i,t+1}) = \alpha Geo(\boldsymbol{p}, \boldsymbol{p}_{i,t+1}) + (1-\alpha) App(\boldsymbol{p}, \boldsymbol{p}_{i,t+1}) \quad (1)$$

where $Geo(\cdot,\cdot)$ measures the geometric constraint, $App(\cdot,\cdot)$ measures the appearance constraint, and α is an adaptive weighting.

Specifically, $Geo(\boldsymbol{p}, \boldsymbol{p}_{i,t+1}) = D(\boldsymbol{p}) - D(\boldsymbol{p}_{i,t+1})$, which performs the z-test using the depth values. In 3D video, the largest depth value 255 represents the closest distance. Hence, a positive $Geo(\cdot,\cdot)$ indicates that the 3D point is likely to have originated from a dynamic object because its projected point was closer than its corresponding pixel. This usually happens when the object was initially reconstructed in the 3D model, but subsequently moved away. We measured the appearance constraint using the L2 distance in the CIELAB space because it is more perceptually linear. Between the projected point and the pixel, the appearance constraint can be written as $App(\boldsymbol{p}, \boldsymbol{p}_{i,t+1}) = ||Lab(\boldsymbol{p}) - Lab(\boldsymbol{p}_{i,t+1})||$.

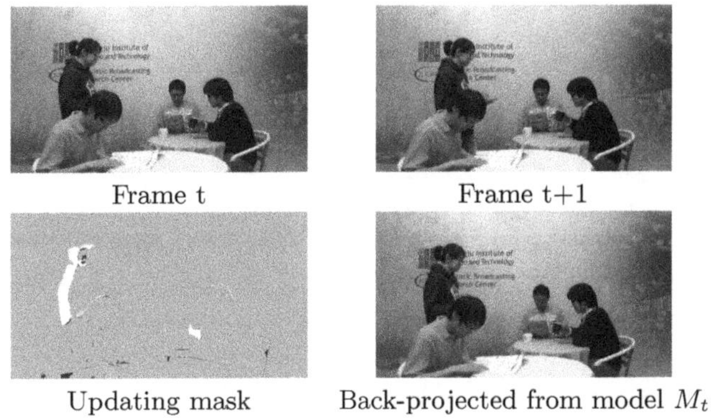

Figure 2: Sequence "Cafe": The updating mask enable us to visualize the result of the background modeling cost. Three colors are shown: white represents a pixel that should be updated, gray represents a pixel that is coherent with the 3D model, and black represents that no points were projected.

To better preserve the static points, we determined the adaptive weighting α by $Geo(\cdot,\cdot)$. In our system, $\alpha = 0$ when $Geo(\cdot,\cdot)$ is close to zero, otherwise $\alpha = 1$. That is, the appearance constraint is measured only when the geometric constraint gives an ambiguous result.

Now, given a 3D point, we can calculate the background modeling cost with respect to each viewpoint. The smaller the cost is, the point is more likely to belong to the static background. Therefore, for each viewpoint, we can distinguish 3D points from the static background by simply thresholding the cost.

We also employed a temporal multi-view voting strategy to increase the robustness. This means that the 3D point is allowed to be updated only when it is regarded as a dynamic point in all viewpoints during the period of time T_{upd}. The 3D point will be removed and its corresponding pixels in each view will be updated into the new 3D model M_{t+1}. Note that to keep the 3D model compact, the pixels with low background modeling costs will not be updated.

6. EXPERIMENTAL RESULTS

To demonstrate the results, we used MPEG 3D video sequences that are frequently shown in 3D video studies. We utilized the RGB color video, corresponding depth video and camera intrinsic parameters contained in these sequences.

An example of updating multi-view points is shown in Fig. 2. Because the girl is walking from left to right, the wall appears as shown in the white region of the updating mask. Most pixels are static, corresponding to the gray region of the mask, and will not be updated into the 3D model. In addition, our temporal multi-view voting strategy avoids updating those pixels near the object boundary because they are treated as noise. In this case, only the appearing region of the wall will be updated into the 3D model.

Fig. 3 shows the reconstruction results of the "Street" sequence in the Poznan multi-view video test sequences [2]. The camera motion matrices $[\mathbf{R}_{t,t+1}|\mathbf{t}_{t,t+1}]$ are first set to

Figure 3: Sequence "Street": Selected frames of middle viewpoint and the 3D model. In the first frame, the 3D model is reconstructed. In the updating stage, points belonging to dynamic objects are replaced by the static background. The background model can remain compact when new dynamic objects appear.

identity matrices because of the static camera array setting. Note that there are three viewpoints in the sequence, and we show the middle one as an example. The T_{upd} for the temporal multi-view updating strategy is arbitrarily set to 3, affecting only the speed to be realized by excluding dynamic objects; however, it remains robust. It shows that the 3D model is updated to the static background model after a specific number of frames.

7. CONCLUSIONS

In this paper, we proposed a 3D background modeling system for multi-view 3D video. We first reconstructed the point-based 3D model, after which we updated it into a static background model. We adapted the 3D reconstruction method to perform only a global estimation. Our proposed updating of the multi-view points enable us to evaluate whether the 3D model need to be updated using subsequent frames. The experimental results show that we successfully reconstructed the compact 3D background model, and the dynamic objects were excluded.

8. ACKNOWLEDGMENTS

Part of the work is supported by Himax Technologies, Inc.

9. REFERENCES

[1] R. Diaz, S. Hallman, and C. Fowlkes. Detecting dynamic objects with multi-view background subtraction. In *IEEE International Conference on Computer Vision (ICCV)*, pages 273–280, Dec. 2013.

[2] M. DomaÃśski, T. Grajek, K. Klimaszewski, M. Kurc, O. Stankiewicz, J. Stankowski, and K. Wegner. Poznan multiview video test sequences and camera parameters. In *ISO/IEC JTC1/SC29/WG11 MPEG 2009/M17050.*

[3] R. I. Hartley and A. Zisserman. *Multiple View Geometry in Computer Vision.* Cambridge University Press, ISBN: 0521540518, second edition, 2004.

[4] P. Henry, M. Krainin, E. Herbst, X. Ren, and D. Fox. RGB-D mapping: Using Kinect-style depth cameras for dense 3D modeling of indoor environments. *Int. J. Rob. Res.*, 31(5):647–663, Apr. 2012.

[5] M. Keller, D. Lefloch, M. Lambers, S. Izadi, T. Weyrich, and A. Kolb. Real-time 3D reconstruction in dynamic scenes using point-based fusion. In *International Conference on 3D Vision (3DV)*, pages 1–8, June 2013.

[6] D. G. Lowe. Distinctive image features from scale-invariant keypoints. *Int. J. Comput. Vision*, 60(2):91–110, Nov. 2004.

[7] K. Muller, P. Merkle, and T. Wiegand. 3-D video representation using depth maps. *Proceedings of the IEEE*, 99(4):643–656, Apr. 2011.

[8] R. A. Newcombe, S. Izadi, O. Hilliges, D. Molyneaux, D. Kim, A. J. Davison, P. Kohi, J. Shotton, S. Hodges, and A. Fitzgibbon. KinectFusion: Real-time dense surface mapping and tracking. In *IEEE International Symposium on Mixed and Augmented Reality (ISMAR)*, pages 127–136, Oct. 2011.

[9] N. Snavely, S. M. Seitz, and R. Szeliski. Photo tourism: Exploring photo collections in 3D. *ACM Trans. Graph.*, 25(3):835–846, July 2006.

[10] S.-F. Tsai, C.-C. Cheng, C.-T. Li, and L.-G. Chen. A real-time 1080p 2D-to-3D video conversion system. *IEEE Transactions on Consumer Electronics*, 57(2):915–922, May 2011.

[11] K. Venkataraman, D. Lelescu, J. Duparré, A. McMahon, G. Molina, P. Chatterjee, R. Mullis, and S. Nayar. PiCam: An ultra-thin high performance monolithic camera array. *ACM Trans. Graph.*, 32(6):166:1–166:13, Nov. 2013.

[12] A. Vetro, T. Wiegand, and G. Sullivan. Overview of the stereo and multiview video coding extensions of the H.264/MPEG-4 AVC standard. *Proceedings of the IEEE*, 99(4):626–642, Apr. 2011.

[13] K.-C. Wei, Y.-L. Huang, and S.-Y. Chien. Point-based model construction for free-viewpoint TV. In *IEEE International Conference on Consumer Electronics - Berlin (ICCE-Berlin)*, pages 220–221, Sept. 2013.

Audio Routing for Scalable Conferencing using AAC-ELD and Bit Stream Domain Energy Estimation

Iaroslav Kryvyi, Nikolaus Färber, Conrad Benndorf, Manfred Lutzky
Fraunhofer IIS, Erlangen, Germany
+49 9131 7766051, iaroslav.kryvyi, nikolaus.faerber, conrad.benndorf, manfred.lutzky@iis.fraunhofer.de

ABSTRACT

There is an increasing interest in multipoint conferencing but service providers face the challenge of complexity when scaling to thousands of users. This problem can be resolved by a scalable architecture based on central media routers, which allows for low complexity server components and therefore low operational cost. In this paper we describe an audio routing approach using advantages offered by the AAC-ELD bit stream structure. By estimating the signal energy in the bit stream domain, we can detect active speakers at low complexity, which results in substantial bitrate and complexity reduction. Subjective tests with mediated conversations among four participants are conducted to compare the perceived audio quality of the audio router to conventional mixing in a conference bridge. The results show a reduction of complexity by one order of magnitude while maintaining the same subjective audio quality when forwarding the two most active speakers on a 10 ms framing.

Categories and Subject Descriptors

H.4.3 [**Information Systems Applications**]: Communications Applications; F.2.2 [**Analysis of Algorithms and Problem Complexity**]: Non-numerical Algorithms and Problems

General Terms

Algorithms, Performance, Measurement, Experimentation

Keywords

Audio router, MPEG-4 AAC-ELD, active speaker selection, energy estimation, multipoint conferencing, complexity

1. INTRODUCTION

Multipoint conferencing has made huge progress in the recent years and has become more and more popular and easily accessible. The most prominent examples are Google Hangouts [1] and Skype [2]. In addition, the WebRTC project promises easy integration into web services by making real-time communication a part of web browsers and HTML5 [3]. Though WebRTC per se is only addressing point-to-point communication between two participants, it can also be extended to address multipoint communication as explained below. Since the number of users for web conferencing is increasing constantly, service providers face the problem of operational expenses.

Generally speaking, conferencing providers have to operate a service with many users in order to be successful. There are two challenges to this task: maximizing the number of simultaneous sessions and maximizing the number of participants in each session. The classic approach to this problem in telecommunication networks is a central Multipoint Control Unit (MCU), see Figure 2, which is used as a conference bridge to connect the participants. MCUs perform full decoding, mixing, and re-encoding; they are computationally very expensive and only a few tens of sessions can be run on each hardware unit. Hence, for thousands of users hundreds of MCUs have to be operated in a data center, which quickly becomes a critical part of the operational expenditure.

To address this problem, we have developed an alternative approach to multi-point conferencing, which drastically reduces the cost of operating such a service by reducing complexity of server side components while maintaining the same perceptual audio quality. Reasonable operational costs are especially important in web services like social networks where users are not willing to pay extra money for conferencing – if paying anything for any services at all.

In this paper, we focus on the underlying architecture for audio processing, i.e. media codec and transmission. In addition, we provide an analysis of perceptional audio quality as obtained from listening tests of the innovative audio routing technology. For the audio codec we focus on MPEG-4 AAC-ELD because it supports the full audio bandwidth of 20kHz providing CD-comparable communication quality at low delay and low bitrates [4].

2. CONFERENCING ARCHITECTURES

There are several approaches to enable multi-party conferencing that impose different requirements on the client, server and network infrastructure, see Figure 1. For example, clients can establish a fully meshed network in which each client establishes a peer-to-peer session with each of its N-1 remote participants. Although this approach does not require any server infrastructure (except for session setup) it puts a heavy load on the upload channel because each client has to send N-1 copies of his stream. In addition, each client has to decode N-1 streams and mix those before playout, which increases its complexity.

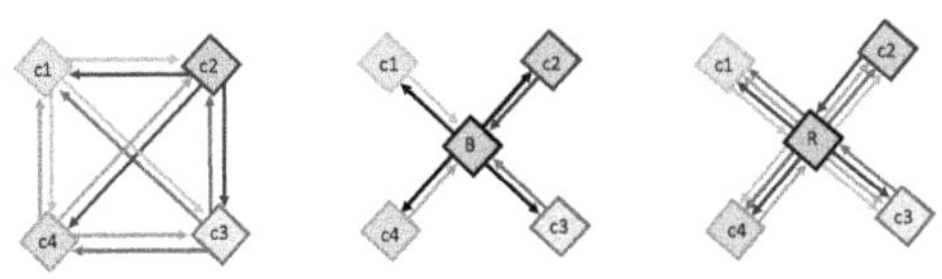

Figure 1: Architectures for audio conferencing

Another approach is an MCU, which acts as a central bridge in a star topology. This architecture is convenient for the client, because it can treat the MCU as a normal client and therefore establishes a normal point-to-point call. Therefore, only a single encoder and decoder instance is needed in the client-side and also the channel usage in the uplink- and downlink remains unchanged. The drawback of this architecture is the complex MCU, which has to do decoding, mixing, and re-encoding for each of the N clients. This is a problem for the operation of the

MM'15, October 26-30, 2015, Brisbane, Australia
© 2015 ACM. ISBN 978-1-4503-3459-4/15/10…$15.00
DOI: http://dx.doi.org/10.1145/2733373.2806401

platform as it becomes expensive to run, e.g. when each session requires its own dedicated hardware server.

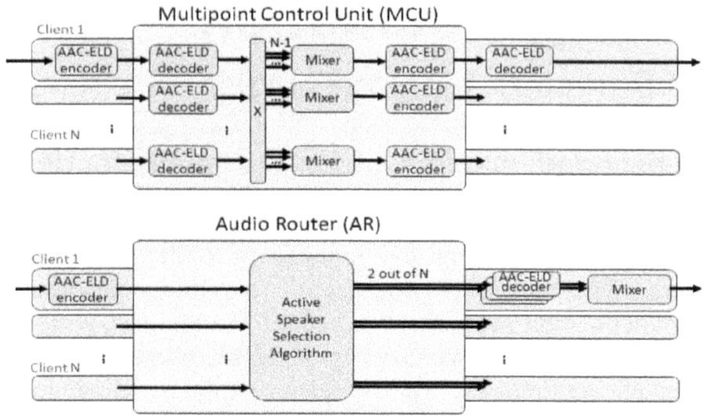

Figure 2: Architecture for classic Multipoint Control Unit (MCU, top) and Audio Router (AR, bottom).

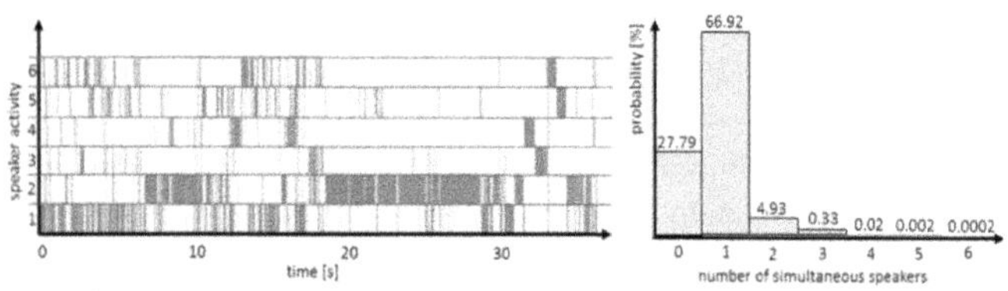

Figure 3: Temporal structure of a 6-party conversation (left, [13]) and probability distribution for the number of simultaneous speakers (right, [14])

A good compromise between these two architectures is a central Audio Router (AR), see Figure 2, which balances the requirements for the client and server in a pragmatic way. While maintaining a star topology, it replaces the bridge with a low complexity media router. Technically, this media router is implemented on the application layer and runs on a server with high bandwidth access. However, as the application running on this server is mainly forwarding packets, the term media router, or simply router, is used. The key benefit is that the complexity of the router is minimal compared to the bridge. The drawback is a higher downlink bitrate and higher client complexity because each client receives streams from N-1 participants and does decoding and playout similar to the peer-to-peer approach. However, it turns out that a higher download bitrate is often acceptable in practice because of the asymmetric requirements in Internet traffic. For example ADSL links often have a ten times higher downlink speed than uplink speed and also 3G/4G mobile networks are much more limited in the uplink than in the downlink. Besides, the additional client complexity of N-1 decoders is also acceptable, because decoding is significantly less complex than encoding and can be well handled by modern PCs or mobile phones. Hence, the central media router architecture makes pragmatic use of the available resources in the client CPU and downlink channel, while allowing low complexity server components as needed for cost effective operation for many users.

Given the advantages, the basic idea has already been proposed for audio conferencing earlier in 2003 by Prasad [5, 6]. The same approach can also be implemented in WebRTC when using special media routers [9, 10]. We have improved on it as described in the next sections.

Prototypes of both MCU and AR used for this paper have been developed from scratch as part of EU-funded research project Vconect [15].

3. DESCRIPTION OF TECHNOLOGY

3.1 Audio router

The proposed alternative to the MCU is a central AR, which optimizes the resources by selecting active speakers. While maintaining a star topology, the AR selects M out of N-1 audio streams to be forwarded to each client, where $M<N$ and typically set to M=2 or M=3. This follows the idea proposed in [5] in which it is observed that in a normal group conversation there are very seldom more than 3 participants speaking at the same time. This is a result of behavioral rules which are followed implicitly by humans in conversations. For example, if the current speaker is interrupted by another participant in the group, he will not continue to speak but give the other person a chance to take the floor (at least intermediately). As a result, the probability that more than 3 speakers are active at any given time is very low, as illustrated in Figure 3. Exploiting this behavior, the AR limits the audio bit rate on the downlink to M times the bit rate of a single stream. In order to select the M most active speakers, a low complexity energy estimation algorithm is used which does not require full decoding of the audio packets. Given the energy estimation of each audio frame, a selection algorithm is used which operates on multiple window sizes and uses hysteresis to avoid oscillations.

3.2 Energy estimation in AR

Conventional audio activity detection tools operate on raw audio samples; therefore, in the case of audio conferencing each audio frame of the bit stream has to be fully decoded to determine its energy in the time domain. This means that the complete workload-intense decoding process as well as audio activity detection is required for each incoming stream of the current conferencing session. In contrast, the Energy Estimation (EE) in the AR takes advantage of the MPEG-4 AAC-ELD bit stream structure. Estimation the AAC-frame's energy is done by decoding only few first bytes of compressed data. The processing delay of this calculation is below 1 ms and therefore negligible in comparison to the algorithmic delay of an audio encoder.

In theory, the frame's energy is calculated by building the sum of the energies of each spectral line. Having no access to those without decoding, the estimation is made by looking at the scale factors and Huffman codebook of all frequency groups. This information is packed in the beginning of the frame preceding spectral coefficients. The core of the estimation is the $E_{line}(cb,scf)$ function (2), which calculates the expected energy of a line for a given codebook (*cb*) and scale factor (*scf*). Codebook dimension (*cb_dim*) is the number of spectral lines in a given codebook (either two or four). Codebook size (*cb_size*) is the number of codewords in the codebook. It works by building the sum of the energies of each codeword of the line's codebook, multiplied by the respective probability of their occurrence *P(cw)*. The sum's value is divided by the codebook's dimension to obtain a per-line value, since the codeword actually encodes two or four lines. E_{cw} (1) provides the energy of a Huffman codeword. We are interested in the energy of the codeword, therefore summed values are raised to the power of two. E_{frame} (3) is then used to calculate the total frame's estimated energy. The result of (2) is multiplied by the number of spectral lines in the scale factor band (*band_lines*) and summed over the total number of scale factor bands (*bands*). While Eqn. (1) refers to Section 5.6.2 of [7] and Section 4.6.1.3 of [8], Eqn. (2) and (3) form an original contribution in this paper.

$$E_{cw}(cw, scf) = \sum_{i=1}^{cb\_dim} \left((\text{sign}(cw[i]) * |cw[i]|)^{\frac{4}{3}} * 2^{\frac{scf}{4}} \right)^2 \quad (1)$$

$$E_{line}(cb, scf) = \frac{\sum_{n=1}^{cb_{size}} E_{cw}(cb[n], scf) * P(cb[n])}{cb\_dim} \quad (2)$$

$$E_{frame} = \sum_{b=1}^{bands} E_{line}(band_{cb(b)}, band\_scf(b)) * bandlines(b) \quad (3)$$

3.3 Active speaker selection algorithm

The task of the algorithm is to pick M active speakers out of N-1 remote participants in the conference. The simple solution of comparing energies of each of the users and switching on a frame-by-frame basis proves to be inadequate since it switches too frequently in a random-like pattern resulting in poor audio quality. For instance, a burst of noise from one of the clients that is not speaking could result in the interruption of an actual active speaker. This indicates that the algorithm should take into account the energies of both current and previous frames to produce smoothed results. To improve the switching between users we therefore calculate a moving average (MA) on multiple windows of audio frames. Each decision window (DW) is assigned a weight coefficient α_i. The shorter window gets a higher weight to emphasize the importance of more recent activity. This approach facilitates short conversation interruptions from participants that were not previously speaking. The correct choice of values for the DW lengths and associated weights help to fine-tune the smooth turn taking. We have picked these values heuristically based on a limited survey conducted among beta users of our test platform. Thus, we have employed three overlapping DW with length L_1 = 200 ms, L_2 = 500 ms, and L_3 = 5000 ms. The MA is calculated on each DW and updated with every audio frame. In addition, the complete MA for the whole conversation for each user is used. The weight coefficients used are $\alpha_1 = 0.4$, $\alpha_2 = 0.3$, and $\alpha_3 = 0.3$ and the MA of the whole conversation is set to $\alpha_{complete} = 0.1$. After each new audio frame the energy level λ for each participant is calculated in real time as:

$$\lambda = a_1 * \text{MA}_1 + a_2 * \text{MA}_2 + a_3 * \text{MA}_3 + a_{complete} * \text{MA}_{complete}.$$

Finally, after each iteration of the algorithm, we pick the M participants with the highest λ. The parameter λ has some memory depending on the length of the windows. After one participant becomes silent another one can take its place among the M active participants. This mechanism also simulates a natural conversation where participants that want to be heard have to put some effort into getting the floor, i.e., they should be loud enough to attract attention of other speakers and keep trying for a short while. As explained below, we use a framing of approximately 10 ms for each audio frame.

4. EXPERIMENTS AND RESULTS

In order to verify the functionality of the AR we need to evaluate two main criteria: complexity and quality. As a baseline for comparison we use the MCU, which always mixes all participants and therefore has the best quality with respect to conversational interactivity. As a drawback, the MCU is more complex. We want to quantify the complexity reduction of the AR compared to the MCU. At the same time, we want to ensure that high quality is maintained.

The **computational complexity** is evaluated by executing the MCU and AR on a *c3.large* instance of the Amazon Elastic Cloud Compute (EC2) platform. The MCU and the AR were executed separately on the EC2 while the CPU usage was evaluated using the Unix tool *top*. The load was generated by initiating sessions with an increasing number of N = 1 … 10 clients. As can be seen from Figure 4, the CPU usage of the AR is reduced by a factor of more than 10 when compared to the MCU, i.e. by one order of magnitude. It should be noted that real-time performance can only be maintained up to a CPU usage of 60%, such that only 8 participants can be served safely by the MCU on a single c3.large instance. After this threshold, real-time performance cannot be maintained in each 10 ms time frame even though 40% CPU capacity is still available an average over a longer period of time.

The **conversational quality** is evaluated by conducting an experiment with test persons who evaluate the subjective quality on a 5-point, discrete quality scale (bad, poor, fair, good, excellent). The Audio Communication Engine (ACE) [16] was used as a basis for implementing the conferencing software. Six groups of participants with 4 participants per group were recruited from the research staff of Fraunhofer IIS (24 persons in total). Though the people are from the same division within Fraunhofer IIS they were not involved in the development of the AR. After a short introduction, the participants in the group were split into separate rooms and asked to wear a headset which was attached to a PC running the client software. The AR was running locally in the LAN, such that a relatively low end-to-end (mouth-to-ear, including sound card buffers and jitter buffers) delay of 70 ms was achieved. The client-side audio was encoded as mono with AAC-ELD at 64 kbit/s using a sampling rate of 44.1 kHz. As AAC-ELD uses 512 samples/frame, this results in a framing of about 10 ms (512/44100 ms to be exact). Each group evaluated three conditions:

- **MCU**: Client connected to MCU which mixes all remote participants. Hence, the received audio is a mix of all 3 other participants.
- **AR1**: Clients connect to AR, which forwards the most active speaker. The received audio is a selection of 1 out of 3 participants, possibly switched every 10 ms.
- **AR2**: Clients connect to AR, which forwards the 2 most active speakers. The received audio is a selection of 2 out of 3 participants, possibly switched every 10 ms.

The order in which the conditions were presented to the participants was randomized between the 6 groups. For each condition, the participants were asked to discuss a controversial topic for five minutes and evaluate the quality in a questionnaire directly afterwards. The experiment was controlled by the experimenter, who joined the session as a fifths participant but remained muted during the actual test periods. Before the test conditions were presented, a training session with MCU was conducted to familiarize the participant with the system and the expected best reference quality. Participants were explained that this test is not about audio quality as typically evaluated in audio coding (noise, bandwidth, ringing, warbling, pre-echo, etc.) but about conversational interactivity, i.e. the ability to interrupt each other and take turns in a discussion. This was found to be necessary, as a question about "audio quality" in general showed non-discriminatory results in preliminary-tests.

The results of the subjective tests are shown in Figure 5, which includes the mean and 95% confidence intervals of the three conditions. The results for the MCU should be considered as a baseline and upper anchor. As can be seen, forwarding only the single most active speaker does not achieve a sufficient quality (MCU vs. AR1). In this condition participants noticed missing audio during double talk situations and had the impression that people were "cut off". This impression improved significantly when adding a second stream, i.e. when forwarding the two most active streams. In this case, no difference to the MCU was perceived (MCU vs. AR2). This positive finding may be surprising at first but can be explained through the fast switching frequency operating on 10 ms time frames and the structure of natural conversations, see Figure 3.

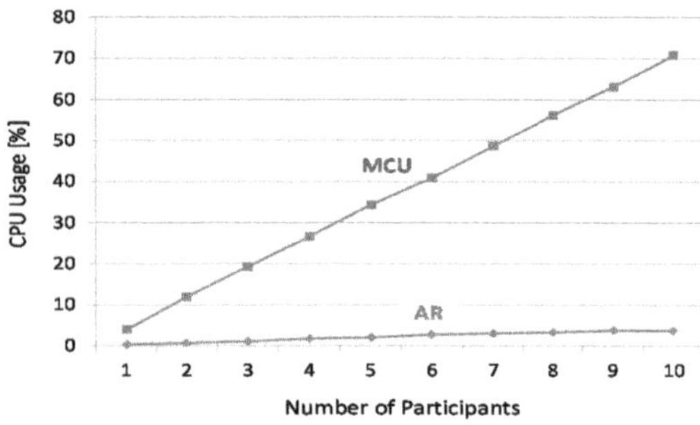

Figure 4: Evaluation of Audio Router (AR) and Multipoint Control Unit (MCU) in terms of complexity.

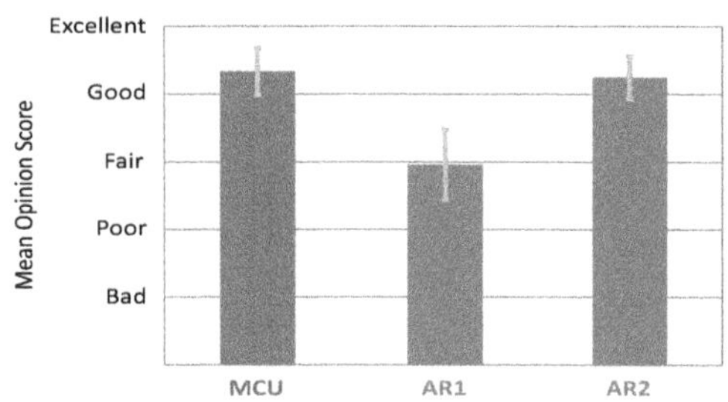

Figure 5: Evaluation of Audio Router (AR) and Multipoint Control Unit (MCU) in terms of quality.

In addition, mutual masking during highly active periods helps to conceal missing audio signals. When more than two participants speak at the same time with equal audio levels, the resulting general disturbance makes the missing audio less obvious.

In addition to the experiments described above, the AR was used and tested extensively in the EU-funded research project Vconect [15]. The reduced complexity did significantly ease the deployment, especially for the final trial in SAPO Campus [12] (the social network operated by Portugal Telecom Group). A more detailed description can be found in [11]. The requirement specification included support for up to 100 simultaneous users in up to 30 sessions with up to 30 participants per session. Meeting this goal would have required running a minimum of 30 servers in case of the MCU. While this would have been feasible for a medium-sized trial with limited life time, it became clear that it would pose a problem for commercial operation over a continuous period of time. Instead, by switching to AR for media distribution, the same requirements could be fulfilled with a single server. Hence, the reduced complexity already showed significant benefits in real-world service, even for a medium-sized web service.

5. CONCLUSION

The benefits of the presented audio routing approach to scalable conferencing with active speaker selection using bit stream domain energy estimation are proven by the results of the conducted subjective conversational tests. In our implementation audio routing reduces the complexity by one order of magnitude while maintaining the perceptual audio quality during conversations. The only drawback is the increase in downlink bit rate by a factor of two and higher complexity in the client. However, these drawbacks are acceptable in practice due to high-performance CPUs in modern devices (decoding an additional audio stream is computationally inexpensive) and sufficient downlink bitrate in access networks. Therefore, the overall trade-off makes such audio routing very attractive server side architecture for implementing audio conferencing for web services such as social networks. The low complexity significantly reduces operational expenses and enables scalable deployments to thousands of users. This benefit became apparent for conducting medium-sized trials in SAPO Campus which required up to 100 simultaneous users. It is even more obvious for large-scale services with thousands of users. We therefore believe that audio routing, and more generally media routing, will become the dominant architecture for multi-point communication systems in the web which have to scale to a high number of users.

6. ACKNOWLEDGMENTS

The research leading to these results has received funding from the European Community's Seventh Framework Program (FP7/2007-2013) under grant agreement no. ICT-2011-287760.

7. REFERENCES

[1] Home page of Google Hangouts, http://www.google.com/+/learnmore/hangouts/

[2] Home page of Skype, http://www.skype.com/en/

[3] Home page of WebRTC, http://www.webrtc.org/

[4] Markus Schnell et. al., "MPEG-4 Enhanced Low Delay AAC - a new standard for high quality communication", 125th AES convention, San Francisco CA USA, October 2008.

[5] R.V. Prasad, H.S. Jamadagni, and H. N. Shankar, "Number of Floors for a Voice-Only on Networks – A Conjecture," IEE Comm. Proc., Vol. 151, No. 3, pp. 287- 291, 25 2004.

[6] R.V. Prasad, R. Hurni, and H. S. Jamadagni, "A Scalable Distributed VoIP Conference Using SIP", in Proc. 8th IEEE International Symposium on Computers and Communications (ISCC'03), 2003.

[7] 3GPP TS 26.403. General Audio Codec audio processing functions. Technical specification v1.0.0. May 2004.

[8] ISO/IEC 14496-3:2009. Information technology – coding of audio-visual objects. ISO, Geneva:ISO.

[9] Home page of Licode, http://lynckia.com/licode/

[10] Home page of OpenTok, https://tokbox.com/opentok/

[11] N. Färber, Y. Kryvyi, and Vilmos Zsombori, "Multi-Party Videoconferencing for the Web", IEEE STCSN E-Letter, Vol. 2, No. 2, June 2014.

[12] Home page of SAPO Campus , http://campus.sapo.pt

[13] M. Galley et al., "Discourse Segmentation of Multi-Party Conversation", In: ACL ´03 Proc., 41st Annual Meeting on Assoc. for Computational Linguistics – Vol. 1., pp 562-569, July 2003.

[14] Laskowski et al., "On the Dynamics of Overlap in Multi-Party Conversation", In: Proc. Interspeech ´12. Portland, USA: ISCA.

[15] Home page of Vconect, http://www.vconect-project.eu/

[16] Fraunhofre IIS Audio Communication Engine, http://www.iis.fraunhofer.de/en/ff/amm/prod/kommunikation/komm/ace.html

EcoFlow: An Economical and Deadline-Driven Inter-Datacenter Video Flow Scheduling System

Yuhua Lin, Haiying Shen and Liuhua Chen
Department of Electrical and Computer Engineering, Clemson University
Clemson, South Carolina 29634
{yuhual, shenh, liuhuac}@clemson.edu

ABSTRACT

Cloud providers need to transfer video contents between different datacenters in order to provide scalable and consistent service to users across different geographical regions. These inter-datacenter transfers are charged by ISPs under the dominant percentile-based charging models. In order to minimize the payment costs, existing works aim to keep the traffic on each link under the charging volume. However, these methods cannot fully utilize each link's available bandwidth capacity, and may increase the charging volumes. To further reduce the bandwidth payment cost by fully utilizing link bandwidth, we propose an economical and deadline-driven video flow scheduling system, called EcoFlow. Considering different video flows have different transmission deadlines, EcoFlow transmits videos in the order of their deadline tightness and postpones the deliveries of later-deadline videos to later time slots so that the charging volume at current time interval will not increase. The flows that are expected to miss their deadlines are divided into subflows to be rerouted to other under-utilized links in order to meet their deadlines without increasing charging volumes. Experimental results on EC2 show that compared to existing methods, EcoFlow achieves the least bandwidth costs for cloud providers.

Categories and Subject Descriptors

I.6 [**Simulation And Modeling**]: Applications, Model Validation and Analysis

Keywords

Video streaming; Bandwidth cost; Inter-datacenter traffic; Percentile-based charging models

1. INTRODUCTION

Cloud providers (e.g., Amazon) offer various pay-as-you-use cloud based services (e.g., Amazon Web Services) to cloud customers (e.g., Netflix) [1, 2]. Cloud has proved to be an effective infrastructure to host video streaming services with many benefits [3]. In order to enhance service availability and scalability, cloud providers generally deploy a number of datacenters across different geographical regions, which are inter-connected by high-capacity links leased from internet service providers (ISPs). Both server-to-customer video dissemination and video replication lead to a substantial amount of inter-datacenter traffic. Cloud providers purchase transit bandwidth from ISPs based on certain pricing schemes, such as the 95th percentile charging model adopted by most ISPs [4]. In the 95th percentile charging model, the bandwidth cost is charged based on the 95th percentile value in all traffic volumes recorded in every 5-minute interval generated within a charging period (e.g., 1 month [4]). We refer the 95th percentile traffic volume from the beginning of the charging period up to current time as **charging volume**. Many previous studies [5, 6, 4, 7] focus on minimizing the bandwidth payment cost on inter-datacenter video traffic to ISPs.

The *store-and-forward* methods [5, 6] take advantage of the spatial and temporal features of the inter-datacenter video traffic. The spatial feature means that at a specific time, datacenters in different geographic areas exhibit different traffic loads and available bandwidth capacities. The temporal feature means that the traffic loads on a datacenter exhibit strong diurnal patterns that are correlated with the local time [8]. These methods predefine peak and off-peak hours for each datacenter based on its local time and geographic area, and then utilize the leftover traffic volume (which is the charging volume minus the actual traffic volume) during off-peak hours to transfer delay-tolerant data flows. However, the *store-and-forward* methods fail to fully utilize the available bandwidth capacities of the light-traffic links during the peak hours.

The optimal routing path [4, 7] optimize the routing paths for video flows to minimize the charging volume on each link. When the transmission of a video is expected to exceed the charging volume on a link, the video will be transferred over an alternating path to maximize the utilization of other links without increasing their charging volumes. However, these methods transmit each video immediately when the video transmission request arrives at the source datacenter regardless of their deadlines. So these methods can easily increase the charging volumes of some links when a large number of video transfer requests arrive simultaneously.

To handle the problems in previous methods, we propose EcoFlow: an economical and deadline-driven video flow scheduling system. As different applications from cloud cus-

MM'15, October 26–30, 2015, Brisbane, Australia.
© 2015 ACM. ISBN 978-1-4503-3459-4/15/10 ...$15.00.
DOI: http://dx.doi.org/10.1145/2733373.2806403.

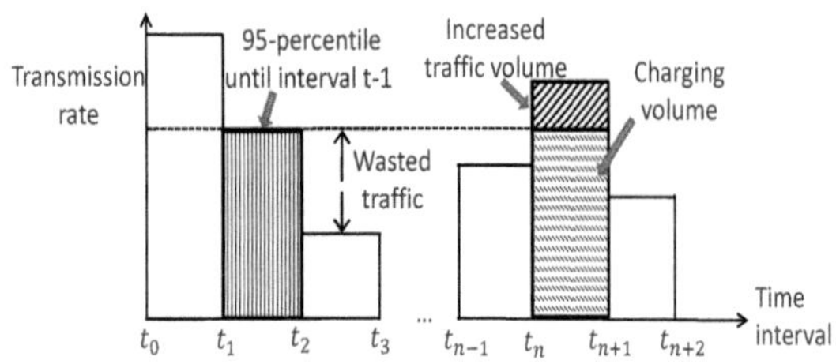

Figure 1: Bandwidth cost of inter-datacenter video traffic.

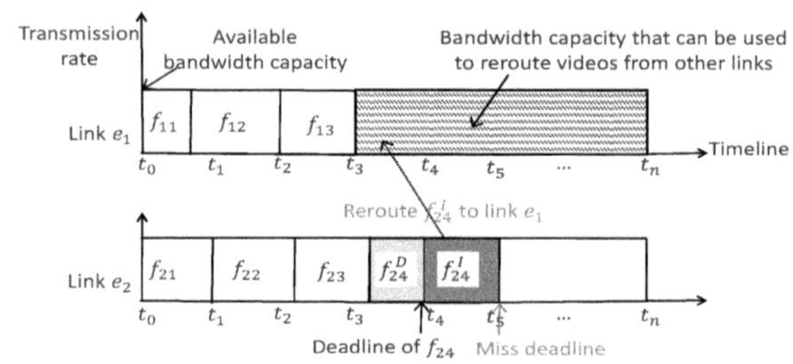

Figure 2: An overview of EcoFlow.

tomers have different service-level agreements (SLAs) that specify data Get/Put bounded latency [9] or a service probability [10] by ensuring a certain number of replicas in different locations [11]. The idea of EcoFlow is to postpone the transfers of delay-tolerant videos while still ensure their transmission within deadlines if the transmission of these videos will increase the current charging volume.

2. OVERVIEW OF ECOFLOW

Figure 1 shows an example of an inter-datacenter link's bandwidth cost under the 95th percentile charging model. The traffic volume in time interval $[t_1, t_2)$ is the 95th percentile value until time t_n, and is marked as the charging volume at t_n. When a larger traffic volume v_{ij} comes up in time interval $[t_n, t_{n+1})$, it becomes the new charging volume at time t_{n+1}. Then, from time t_0 to t_{n+1}, the unused bandwidth below v_{ij} is wasted, that is, the cloud provider does not fully utilized the charging volume. Given this observation, a feasible way to reduce bandwidth cost is to maximize the utilization of the charging volume at different time intervals. For example, the increased traffic volume in time interval $[t_n, t_{n+1})$ can be postponed to time interval $[t_{n+1}, t_{n+2})$.

Three steps of EcoFlow. We first briefly introduce the three steps using an example in Figure 2.

Step 1: **available bandwidth capacity estimation.** We use T_p to denote the time window used to estimate the available bandwidth capacity on each link, and use T_r ($T_r < T_p$) to denote the time window to record traffic volume in current charging model. Based on historical data, we estimate the total volume of video traffic needed to be transmitted on each link during time interval $[t_0, t_n)$, $t_n - t_0 = T_p$, denoted by $\tilde{v}(t_0, t_n)$. Assume link e_1's charging volume at time t_0 is $\hat{v}_1(t_0)$, it then can transfer a volume of $\hat{v}_1(t_0) \times T_p/T_r$ video during time interval $[t_0, t_n)$. We define **a link's available bandwidth capacity** as the maximum transmission rate that can be used to transfer videos without increasing the current charging volume during a certain time interval. We then calculate the available bandwidth capacity $\Delta c_1(t_0, t_n)$ on link e_1 during time interval $[t_0, t_n)$.

Step 2: **deadline-driven flow scheduling.** On each link, the pending video flows are scheduled on an earliest-deadline-first base. On link e_2, f_{24}'s expected transmission time is at t_5, which is later than its deadline. We divide f_{24} into two subflows: f_{24}^D and f_{24}^I. On link e_1, all pending videos are scheduled to finish transmission before t_3, its available capacity during $[t_3, t_n)$ is not utilized (highlighted in dashed fill). We call the available bandwidth capacity that are not utilized during $[t_3, t_n)$ **extra bandwidth capacity** ($\delta c_1(t_3, t_n)$), $\delta c_1(t_3, t_n) = \Delta c_1(t_0, t_n)$. We define the links with extra bandwidth capacity as the under-utilized links. The extra bandwidth capacity on link e_1 can be utilized to reroute subflow f_{24}^I from e_2 by its deadline.

Step 3: **routing path identification.** For the video rerouting, we identify an alternating path that has extra bandwidth capacity to transmit the video by its deadline.

3. SYSTEM DESIGN

3.1 Available Bandwidth Capacity Estimation

We first use Exponentially weighted moving average (EWMA) [12] to estimate the traffic volume during $[t_i, t_i + T_p]$ on link e_{ij} (denoted by $\tilde{v}_{ij}(t_i, t_i + T_p)$) based on the actual historical traffic volume. During time interval $[t_i, t_i + T_p)$, a total volume of $\hat{v}_{ij}(t_i) \times T_p/T_r$ video traffic can be transferred under the current bandwidth cost. Given estimated traffic volume $\tilde{v}_{ij}(t_i, t_i + T_p)$, we can calculate the available bandwidth capacity in time interval $[t_i, t_i + T_p)$:

$$\Delta c_{ij}(t_i, t_i + T_p) = \min\{c_{ij}, \hat{v}_{ij}(t_i)/T_r - \tilde{v}_{ij}(t_i, t_i + T_p)/T_p\}. \quad (1)$$

When $\Delta c_{ij}(t_i, t_i + T_p) > 0$, the current charging volume on link e_{ij} is larger than the expected traffic volume, and the available bandwidth capacity can be used to reroute video flows from other links.

3.2 Deadline-driven Flow Scheduling

Like existing work [7] that assumes the existence of a centralized server connecting to all datacenters that schedules the video flows in all datacenters, we first introduce EcoFlow in a centralized manner. The network scheduler maintains a sending queue $Q(t_i) = (< f_1, d_1, s_1 >, < f_2, d_2, s_2 >, \ldots < f_m, d_m, s_m >)$ to store all pending flows on each link e_{ij} at time t_i, which are ordered based on their deadlines. Note that flows on link e_{ij} includes all flows that are transmitted bidirectionally between datacenter i to j. Each triple $< f_k, d_k, s_k >$ in $Q(t_i)$ contains the flow information of f_k, where d_k and s_k are the deadline and size of f_k, respectively.

All pending videos in $Q(t_i)$ are sent out sequentially, and the flow transmission time for flow f_k can be computed as:

$$T_k = \mathcal{A}/\Delta c_{ij}(t_i, t_i + T_p). \quad (2)$$

$\mathcal{A} = \sum_{f_p \in F_{<k}} s_p$, where $F_{<k}$ is a subset of flows in $Q(t_i)$ that have earlier deadlines than flow f_k (including f_k), and $\Delta c_{ij}(t_i, t_i + T_p)$ is the estimated available bandwidth capacity on link e_{ij} in time interval $[t_i, t_i + T_p)$. The flow completion time for f_k is t_k^{end}:

$$t_k^{end} = \begin{cases} t_i + T_k & \text{If k=1} \\ t_{k-1}^{end} + T_k & \text{otherwise} \end{cases} \quad (3)$$

The flow start time for f_1 is t_i. For flow f_k ($k > 1$), the flow start time is the completion time of the previous flow, that is, $t_k^{start} = t_{k-1}^{end}$. d_k is the deadline of video f_k. When $t_k^{end} \leq d_k$, flow f_k is expected to finish transmission before its deadline, and we call it a **Direct Flow** (DF). When $t_k^{end} > d_k$, flow f_k is likely to miss the transmission deadline under the expected bandwidth capacity. Then, f_k can be split to two subflows: f_k^D and f_k^I. f_k^D is the volume with size s_k^D that can be transmitted directly on link e_{ij} before its deadline; while f_k^I is the residual volume with size s_k^I (s_k^I=$s_k - s_k^D$), which should be rerouted in an alternating path. We call f_k^I an **Indirect Flow** (IF).

$$s_k^D = max(0, d_k \times \Delta c_{ij}(t_i, t_i + T_p) - \mathcal{A}). \quad (4)$$

Using the alternating routing path identification method in Section 3.3, we identify alternating paths for each indirect flow f_k^I which can transmit f_k^I before its deadline.

Algorithm 1 Pseudocode for identifying alternating path for flow f_k^I.

```
1:  Input: G = (V, E); s_k, δc_ij(t_i, t_i + T_p), ∀ij ∈ E;
2:  Output: alternating path P from source i to destination j
3:    for each vertex u in V:
4:       rate[u] := 0   //Maximum transmission rate on each path
5:       pre[u] := null   //Record last hop on the path
6:       t_k^end[u] := t_i   //Transmission completion time
7:       Q+ = j   //Q is a temporal set
8:    end for
9:    rate[i] := infinity
10:   while Q is not empty do:
11:      u := vertex in Q with max rate[u]
12:      remove u from Q
13:      for each neighbor v of u with δc_uv(t_i, t_i + T_p) > 0 do:
14:        t_k^end[v]:=s_k^I/min{rate[u], δc_uv(t_i, t_i + T_p)} + t_i
15:        alt :=max{rate[v], δc_uv(t_i, t_i + t_k^end[v])}
16:        if alt ≥ rate[v]:  //A path with higher transmission rate
17:           rate[v] := alt
18:           pre[v] := u
19:        end if
20:      end for
21:   end while
22:   P := empty sequence
23:   while pre[j] is defined do:   //Construct the alternating path
24:      insert j at the beginning of P
25:      δc_{j,pre[j]}(t_i, t_i + t_k^end[j]) := 0
26:      j := pre[j]   // Traverse from destination to source
27:   end while
28:   if t^end[v]<d_k: Return P
29:   if t^end[v]>d_k:   //P cannot transmit f_k^I before its deadline
30:      split f_k^I into f_k1, f_k2
31:      Return P, f_k1, f_k2
32:   end if
```

3.3 Alternating Routing Path Identification

$F^I(t_i)$ denotes the set of all IFs in the network at time t_i, which are sorted by their deadlines in ascending order. Assume f_k^I is an IF from datacenter i to datacenter j, in this section, we describe how the scheduler identifies an alternating routing path P for f_k^I, $P = (v_1, v_2, \ldots, v_p)$.

When f_k^I is transmitted on path P, its transmission rate is the minimum extra bandwidth capacity on all P's constituent edges, that is $\min_{\forall i \in (1,p-1)}\{\delta c_{i,i+1}(t_i, t_i+T_p)\}$. f_k^I's transmission completion time t_k^{end} is calculated by:

$$t_k^{end} = s_k^I / \min_{\forall i \in (1,p-1)} \{\delta c_{i,i+1}(t_i, t_i + T_p)\} + t_i. \quad (5)$$

s_k^I denotes the flow size of f_k^I and $\delta c_{i,i+1}(t_i, t_i + T_p)$ denotes the extra bandwidth capacity on link $e_{i,i+1}$. We then express the requirement that the transmission of flow f_k^I on path P would be finished before its deadline by: $t_k^{end} \leq d_k$.

We develop a modified Dijkstra's algorithm shown in Algorithm 1 to identify an alternating routing path for f_k^I. In this algorithm, we input the flow information including its size, deadline, source datacenter and destination datacenter, together with network information including all link's extra bandwidth capacity. Algorithm 1 will return an alternating path P for f_k^I, and splits f_k^I into two parts if P cannot finish transmission before its deadline. If the identified path can transmit f_k^I before its deadline, alternating path P is returned (Line 23); otherwise f_k^I is split into f_{k1} and f_{k2} (Line 24-26). The simplest implementation of the Dijkstra's algorithm requires a running time of $O(|E| + |V|^2) = O(|V|^2)$.

If P cannot finish f_k^I's transmission before its deadline and f_k^I is split into f_{k1} and f_{k2}, we will use Algorithm 1 to identify an alternating path for f_{k2}. If the new identified alternating path cannot transmit f_{k2} before its deadline, f_{k2} is further split into two parts: f_{k2}^1 and f_{k2}^2. f_{k2}^1 is transmitted on the new alternating path and f_{k2}^2 is transmitted on e_{ij} by increasing the charging volume on e_{ij}. The new charging volume $\hat{v}_{ij}(t_i)$ at time t_i is calculated by:

$$\hat{v}_{ij}(t_i) = (\mathcal{A} - s_k + s(f_{k2}^2) \times T_r / (d_k - t_i). \quad (6)$$

Where $s(f_{k2}^2)$ is the size of f_{k2}^2. The flow start time and completion time of all flows on link e_{ij} will then be updated based on Equation (2), and the schedule table $S(t_i) =< f_k, S, D, t_k^{start} >$ will also be updated.

4. PERFORMANCE EVALUATION

We conducted experiments on Amazon EC2 platform [13], which has a total of 7 datacenters, the capacity and cost per traffic unit of each link are set according to the studies in [7]. We compare EcoFlow with three datacenter traffic scheduling strategies: 1) Direct transfer (denoted as Direct), which directly transfers video flows to the destination whenever the video transfer requests are initiated by the cloud provider without considering each link's charging volume; 2) JetWay [7] and 3) NetSticher [6]. We defined two types of videos: Standard Definition (SD) videos with sizes randomly selected in [500, 800] MB, and High Definition (HD) videos with sizes randomly selected in [2, 4] GB [7]. For simplicity, we assumed that 10-12am and 6pm-12am of a node's local time are peak hours. A datacenter transfers x and y videos per hour to all other datacenters during its peak hours and off-peak hours, respectively, where x and y were randomly selected from [2, 5] and [0, 1], respectively. The transfer request of each video is initiated at a random time during the selected hours, and its deadline is chosen in [30, 120] minutes after the transfer request's initiated time. We set T_p = 1 hour and T_r = 5 minutes. We set a 48 hour period as an independent charging period and calculated the bandwidth cost on each link at the end of the experiment. In EcoFlow, we had a 48 hour warmup period and used the traffic records to predict the traffic volume during the charging period.

We defined a metric of *bandwidth cost per link* as the sum of bandwidth payment cost on all links divided by the total number of links in the network. Figure 3(a) shows the average cost per link at different time intervals for the 95th percentile charging models. We see that the per link cost follows: EcoFlow<JetWay<NetSticher<Direct. Direct results in the highest bandwidth cost as it immediately transfers the video by using only the direct link between two datacenters without considering the current charging volume on

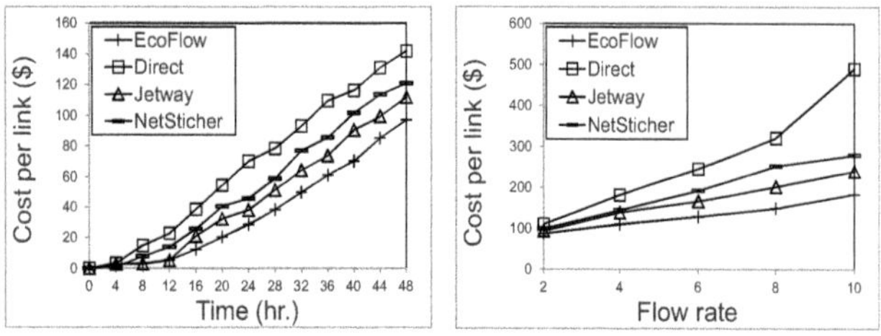

(a) Results at different time intervals. (b) Results at at different flow rates.

Figure 3: Average bandwidth cost.

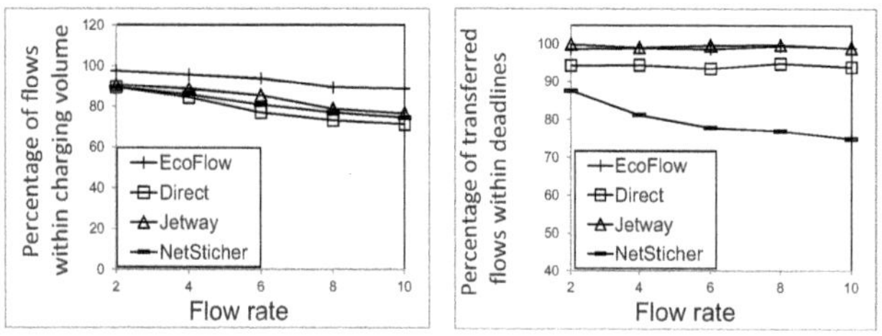

(a) Average percentage of flows transmitted within the charging volume. (b) Percentage of transferred flows within deadlines.

Figure 4: Results at at different flow rates.

the link. NetSticher postpones the transmission of delay-tolerant videos until both source datacenter and destination datacenter are during off-peak hours, so that the traffic load during peak hours is alleviated. However, as the available bandwidth capacity is not fully utilized during peak hours, there is still room for NetSticher to further reduce the bandwidth cost. JetWay is able to incur less bandwidth cost than NetSticher by controlling the transmissions of current videos within the charging volume. EcoFlow generates the least bandwidth cost among all comparison methods as it transmits each video with the link's available bandwidth capacity. Next, we changed the flow arrival rates during a link's peak hours from 2 to 10 flows per hour on each link. Figure 3(b) shows the average bandwidth cost per link at the end of the 48-hour charging period under different flow rates. The relative performance of different methods concurs that in Figure 3(a) due to the same reason.

Figure 4(a) shows the average percentage of flows transmitted within the charging volume at different flow rates. We see that performance of different methods with respect to average percentage of flows transmitted within the charging volume follows: EcoFlow>JetWay>NetSticher>Direct. Figure 4(b) show the percentage of video flows that are transferred within their deadlines at different flow rates. We see that the result follows: JetWay>EcoFlow>Direct> NetSticher. EcoFlow and JetWay generate comparably high percentage of transferred videos within the deadlines, as they both use the available bandwidth capacities from all links to finish the video's transmission before its deadline.

5. CONCLUSIONS

To provide video streaming services to users across different regions, cloud providers need to transfer video contents between different datacenters. Such inter-datacenter transfers are charged by ISPs under the percentile-based charging models. We take advantage of the particular characteristic of these models and propose EcoFlow to minimize cloud providers' payment costs on inter-datacenter traffics. It first calculates the under-utilized traffic volume on each link, then schedules video flows with the objective that these flows do not incur additional charges on the link and guaranteing that each video flow meets its transmission deadline. Finally, the under-utilized links with low traffic burden are used to build alternating paths for video flows that are estimated to miss their deadlines. Experimental results on EC2 show the effectiveness of EcoFlow in reducing bandwidth costs for inter-datacenter video transfers.

6. ACKNOWLEDGMENTS

This research was supported in part by U.S. NSF grants NSF-1404981, IIS-1354123, CNS-1254006, CNS-1249603, and Microsoft Research Faculty Fellowship 8300751.

7. REFERENCES

[1] M. Armbrust, A. Fox, R. Griffith, A. Joseph, R. Katz, A. Konwinski, G. Lee, D. Patterson, A. Rabkin, I. Stoica, and M. Zaharia. A view of cloud computing. *Commun. ACM*, 53(4):50–58, 2010.

[2] S. Rajani and T. Rajender. Literature review: Cloud computing-security issues, solution and technologie. *International Journal of Engineering Research*, 3(4):221–225, 2014.

[3] V. K. Adhikari, Y. Guo, F. Hao, M. Varvello, V. Hilt, M. Steiner, and Z. Zhang. Unreeling netflix: Understanding and improving multi-cdn movie delivery. In *Proc. of INFOCOM*, 2012.

[4] D. Goldenberg, L. Qiu, H. Xie, Y. Yang, and Y. Zhang. Optimizing cost and performance for multihoming. In *Proc. of SIGCOMM*, 2004.

[5] N. Laoutaris, G. Smaragdakis, P. Rodriguez, and R. Sundaram. Delay tolerant bulk data transfers on the internet. In *Proc. of SIGMETRICS*, 2009.

[6] L. Nikolaos, S. Michael, X. Yang, and R. Pablo. Inter-datacenter bulk transfers with netstitcher. In *Proc. of SIGCOMM*, 2011.

[7] Y. Feng, B. Li, and B. Li. Jetway: Minimizing costs on inter-datacenter video traffic. In *Proc. of Multimedia*, 2012.

[8] A. Greenberg, J. Hamilton, D. Maltz, and P. Patel. The Cost of a Cloud: Research Problems in Data Center Networks. *SIGCOMM Comput. Commun. Rev.*, 39(1):68–73, 2009.

[9] A. Hussam, P. Lonnie, and W. Hakim. Racs: A case for cloud storage diversity. In *Proc. of SoCC*, 2010.

[10] Service Level Agreements. http://azure.microsoft.com/en-us/support/legal/sla/, [Accessed in Apr, 2015].

[11] Amazon S3. http://aws.amazon.com/s3/, [Accessed in Apr. 2015].

[12] J. Lucas and M. Saccucci. Exponentially weighted moving average control schemes: Properties and enhancements. *Technometrics*, 32(1):1–29, 1990.

[13] Amazon Elastic Compute Cloud. http://aws.amazon.com/ec2/, [Accessed in Apr. 2015].

Ciphertext-Only Attack on an Image Homomorphic Encryption Scheme with Small Ciphertext Expansion

Yunyu Li, Jiantao Zhou, and Yuanman Li
Faculty of Science and Technology, University of Macau
{mb35468, jtzhou, mb25510} @umac.mo

ABSTRACT

The paper "*An Efficient Image Homomorphic Encryption Scheme with Small Ciphertext Expansion*" (*In Proc.* ACM MM'13, pp.803-812) presented a novel image homomorphic encryption approach achieving significant reduction of the ciphertext expansion. In the current work, we study the security of this cryptosystem under a ciphertext-only attack (COA). We show that our proposed COA is effective in generating a sketch of great fidelity of the original image. Experimental results are provided to verify the validity of the proposed attack strategy.

Categories and Subject Descriptors

H.4 [**Information Systems Applications**]: Information Systems Applications- Miscellaneous; K.6.5 [**Computing Milieux**]: Metrics—*Management of Computing and Information Systems–Security and Protection*

Keywords

Image homomorphic encryption, ciphertext expansion, ciphertext-only attack

1. INTRODUCTION

Signal processing over encrypted domain (SPED) has been receiving increasing attention in recent years, primarily driven by the various privacy-preserving applications and the wide adoption of cloud computing platforms [7, 2, 8]. Among the encryption solutions enabling SPED, homomorphic encryption is arguably the most popular one, as it provides a generic framework of performing basic algebraic operations over the encrypted domain [11, 10, 5, 6]. The existing homomorphic cryptosystems can be roughly classified into two categories: partially homomorphic schemes [5, 10] and fully homomorphic ones [6]. The partially homomorphic schemes support encrypted domain operations that correspond to the addition *or* multiplication in the plaintext domain, while the latter type allows both the addition *and* multiplication.

MM'15, October 26–30, 2015, Brisbane, Australia.
© 2015 ACM. ISBN 978-1-4503-3459-4/15/10 ...$15.00.
DOI: http://dx.doi.org/10.1145/2733373.2806406.

However, one of the major obstacles that precludes the widespread adoption of homomorphic encryption in practice is the huge expansion of the ciphertext. For instance, when the Paillier cryptosystem, with modulus being 1024 bits, is used to encrypt 8-bit image, the resulting encrypted file is 256 times larger than the original image [10]. For fully homomorphic cryptosystem, the ciphertext expansion is even much more prohibitive[6]. To deal with the ciphertext expansion problem, Trobcoso-Pastoriza proposed a packing scheme, in which several messages are packed as a word and encrypted together [12]. This scheme was later extended in [4] with generalized packing basis. However, such packing makes it impossible to process each message differently, and causes many operations, e.g., encrypted-domain DFT [3] and DWT [13], infeasible without interactive protocol. Recently, Zheng and Huang suggested a very promising approach for reducing the ciphertext expansion by indexing a sequence of ciphertexts produced by the scaled-down histogram of the image [14]. It was claimed that significant reduction of the ciphertext expansion can be achieved, while not affecting the security of the image encryption system.

In this work, we evaluate the security of the image homomorphic encryption scheme in [14] under a ciphertext-only attack (COA). We design a state set in which each element represents an encrypted (quantized) pixel, and model the image local smoothness property through a state transition matrix describing the correlation between different states. The statistical analysis of this transition matrix allows us to determine, with high accuracy, which locations share similar (even identical) pixel values, and which ones more likely lie in the edge regions. We also design a pixel value assignment strategy to further preserve image local smoothness and enlarge the image contrast, enabling us to obtain a sketch version of the original image of high quality. Experimental results are provided to verify the effectiveness of our proposed COA strategy.

The rest of this paper is organized as follows. Section 2 gives a concise introduction of the image homomorphic encryption scheme [14]. In Section 3, we present our proposed COA strategy. Experimental results are given in Section 4 to demonstrate the effectiveness of our method. We finally conclude in Section 5.

2. IMAGE HOMOMORPHIC ENCRYPTION SCHEME PROPOSED IN [14]

The idea of this image homomorphic encryption scheme is to first generate a pixel sequence $\mathbf{S} = (S_0, S_1, \cdots, S_{K-1})$ where K is smaller than the number of pixels in the input image, and then produce a map with each element being the index of the original pixel value relative to $\mathbf{S}$. The homomorphically encrypted sequence $[[\mathbf{S}]]$ and the index map in the plaintext serve as the ciphertext. In the sequel, we use $[[x]]$ to represent the element-wise, homomorphically encrypted version of x.

More specifically, let $\mathbf{I} = \{I(x, y)\}$ be the image to be encrypted, where $0 \leq x, y \leq M - 1$. If not otherwise specified, we assume images to be 8-bit and Paillier as the homomorphic cryptosystem [10]. Let also $\mathbf{n} = (n_0, n_1, \cdots, n_{255})^T$ be the associated histogram vector, where n_i denotes the number of pixel value i in $\mathbf{I}$. The sequence $\mathbf{S}$ is designed in such a way that 1) $0 \leq S_j \leq 255, \forall j$, 2) the associated histogram vector $\mathbf{v} = (v_0, v_1, \cdots, v_{255})^T$ is a scaled-down version of $\mathbf{n}$, namely

$$v_i = \lceil \frac{n_i}{Q} \rceil \tag{1}$$

where $Q > 1$ is a scaling factor; and 3) the order of placing all S_j is *randomly* determined. The sequence $\mathbf{S}$ is encrypted element-wise into $[[\mathbf{S}]] = ([[S]]_0, [[S_1]]_1, \cdots, [[S]]_{K-1})$, using a probabilistic homomorphic encryption scheme (Paillier), in which secret key is involved. This also implies that $[[S]]_j \neq [[S]]_k$ if $j \neq k$.

To produce the index map, the sequence $[[\mathbf{S}]]$ is divided into a series of sub-sequences $[[\mathbf{S}]](i)$, for $0 \leq i \leq 255$, each of which corresponds to the original pixel value i, i.e.

$$[[\mathbf{S}]](i) = \left\{ [[s]] \in [[\mathbf{S}]] \middle| \mathcal{D}([[s]]) = i \right\} \tag{2}$$

where $\mathcal{D}(\cdot)$ denotes the homomorphic decryption function. The input image $\mathbf{I}$ is then partitioned into non-overlapping blocks, and the index map generation is carried out in a block by block fashion. For each pixel value $I(x, y)$, one component from the sub-sequence $[[\mathbf{S}]](I(x, y))$ is selected sequentially and its index in the whole sequence $[[\mathbf{S}]]$ is recorded in the index map. In the case that all the elements in $[[\mathbf{S}]](I(x, y))$ are consumed, a randomly permuted $[[\mathbf{S}]](I(x, y))$ is used. Following the notation of [14], we use $\mathbf{P}([[\mathbf{I}]], [[\mathbf{S}]])$ to denote the index map relative to $[[\mathbf{S}]]$.

Eventually, the ciphertext is represented by $\{[[\mathbf{S}]], \mathbf{P}([[\mathbf{I}]], [[\mathbf{S}]])\}$, which can be transmitted to a third party, e.g., cloud server for outsourced computation. Prior to homomorphic operations, an element-wise, homomorphically encrypted image $[[\mathbf{I}]]$ can be calculated based on $[[\mathbf{S}]]$ and $\mathbf{P}([[\mathbf{I}]], [[\mathbf{S}]])$ in a straightforward and cost-effective way (simple lookup table process).

A very desirable feature of this image homomorphic encryption scheme is the significantly reduced ciphertext size. Assuming the modulus used in Paillier is of 1024 bits, the ciphertext size contributed by the encrypted sequence $[[\mathbf{S}]]$ is $2048 \cdot K$ bits. For the index map $\mathbf{P}([[\mathbf{I}]], [[\mathbf{S}]])$, it can be readily coded with fixed-length coding and the size can be determined by $M^2 \cdot \lceil \log_2 K \rceil$. Therefore, the size of the encrypted image becomes

$$2048 \cdot K + M^2 \cdot \lceil \log_2 K \rceil \tag{3}$$

The ciphertext expansion factor can then be given by

$$\gamma = \frac{256 \cdot K}{M^2} + \frac{\lceil \log_2 K \rceil}{8} \tag{4}$$

Typical values of K are 1024, 2048, and 4096 (corresponding Q values are 256, 128, and 64) for 512×512 sized images, which can lead to significant reduction of the ciphertext expansion [14]. In contrast, in the traditional image homomorphic encryption scheme, the ciphertext expansion factor is fixed to be 256 when the modulus is of 1024 bits. It was also claimed that high level of security can still be achieved. For more details, please refer to [14].

3. CIPHERTEXT-ONLY ATTACK

When evaluating the security of the image homomorphic encryption scheme in [14], we assume that the Paillier cryptosystem is secure. Following Kerckhoff's principle, the strength of a cryptosystem depends only on the key and, in particular, the security does not depend on keeping the encryption algorithm secret. This principle implies that the attacker knows the protocols and the overall system in which the cryptosystem is used, while only does not know the secret key. According to the information that is available to the attacker, the attacks can be classified into several types.

- A ciphertext-only attack (COA) is one where the attacker tries to deduce the secret key or the plaintext by only observing the ciphertext.
- A known-plaintext attack (KPA) is one where the attacker has a quantity of plaintext and the corresponding ciphertext
- A chosen-plaintext attack (CPA) is one where the attacker chooses plaintext and is then given the corresponding ciphertext
- A chosen-ciphertext attack (CCA) is one where the attacker can have access to the decoder, and thus can select ciphertext and obtain the corresponding plaintext

Though COA is the least effective attack type, it is of practical significance, as in many applications the ciphertext is the only information available to the attacker. As to be demonstrated shortly, the image encryption scheme [14] is vulnerable even under COA.

More specifically, the attacker can access the ciphertext composed of $[[\mathbf{S}]]$ and $\mathbf{P}([[\mathbf{I}]], [[\mathbf{S}]])$. Since Paillier is assumed to be secure, we cannot infer any useful information from $[[\mathbf{S}]]$. Our COA strategy instead exploits the information leaked from the index map $\mathbf{P}([[\mathbf{I}]], [[\mathbf{S}]])$, based on the following key observations: 1) identical encrypted pixel values can be observed in the encrypted image $[[\mathbf{I}]]$, and they must correspond to the same original pixel value; and 2) pixels that are close spatially should have similar or even identical original values, though the encrypted ones may differ significantly. The latter observation is due to the local smoothness property inherent to natural images.

With $[[\mathbf{S}]]$ and $\mathbf{P}([[\mathbf{I}]], [[\mathbf{S}]])$, the attacker can generate the encrypted image $[[\mathbf{I}]]$, as the cloud server does. To model the local smoothness of image signal in encrypted domain (as only encrypted signal is available), we define a state set

$$\mathcal{S} = \left\{ [[S]]_0, [[S]]_1, \cdots, [[S]]_{K-1} \right\} \tag{5}$$

where each distinct encrypted pixel value is regarded as a state. To further integrate the image local smoothness prior,

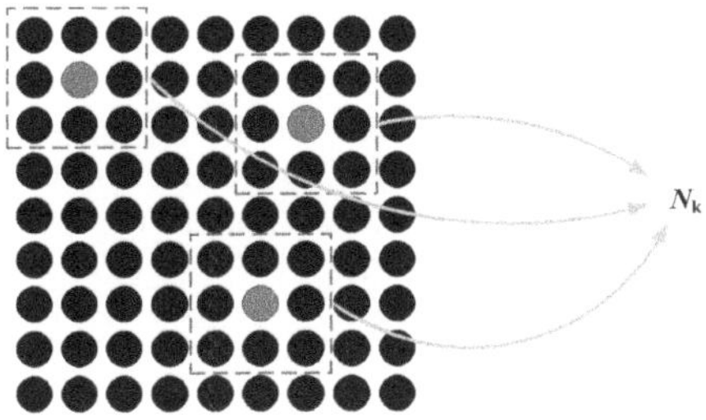

Figure 1: The process of generating $\mathcal{N}_k$. Here, red dots denote $[[S]]_k$.

we propose to quantize the state set $\mathcal{S}$ according to the spatial distribution of encrypted pixels. To this end, we localize $[[S]]_k$ in the encrypted image $[[\mathbf{I}]]$ (may have multiple locations, as $K < M^2$). We then construct a 3×3 sized patch centered by each localized $[[S]]_k$, and use $\mathcal{N}_k$ to denote the collection of patches ($[[S]]_k$ excluded), as demonstrated in Fig. 1. We randomly select τ elements from $\mathcal{N}_k$ and eliminate them from $\mathcal{S}$. A typical setting is $\tau = 3$. This is equivalent to quantize these τ elements into $[[S]]_k$. This process is repeated for all the remaining, unprocessed $[[S]]_k$, which eventually results in a quantized set

$$\mathcal{S}' = \left\{[[S]]'_0, [[S]]'_1, \cdots, [[S]]'_{K'-1}\right\} \tag{6}$$

where $K' = \lceil K/(\tau + 1)\rceil$. A state transition matrix $\mathbf{T}$ can then be defined to describe the relationship between different states of $\mathcal{S}'$

$$\mathbf{T} = \begin{bmatrix} T(0,0) & T(0,1) & \cdots & T(0,K'-1) \\ T(1,0) & T(1,1) & \cdots & T(1,K'-1) \\ \vdots & \vdots & \ddots & \vdots \\ T(K'-1,0) & T(K'-1,1) & \cdots & T(K'-1,K'-1) \end{bmatrix} \tag{7}$$

where the state transition probability $T(k,l)$ from state $[[S]]'_k$ to $[[S]]'_l$ can be calculated as follows. We first localize all $[[S]]'_k$ in the encrypted image $[[\mathbf{I}]]$, and form the set $\mathcal{N}'_k$ in a very similar way as Fig. 1 illustrates. $T(k,l)$ is then computed by

$$T(k,l) = \frac{\#[[S]]'_l \in \mathcal{N}'_k}{|\mathcal{N}'_k|} \tag{8}$$

where $|\cdot|$ denotes the cardinality of the corresponding set.

The state transition matrix $\mathbf{T}$ obtained completely in encrypted domain conveys important information about the original image. When $T(k,l)$ is large, it means that $[[S]]'_l$ appears in the neighboring region of $[[S]]'_k$ with high probability. Due to the local smoothness of image signal, the original pixel value S'_l and S'_k very likely are similar or even identical. On the other hand, when $T(k,l)$ is relatively small (but non-zero), e.g., median value among all $T(k,l)$, $0 \le l \le K'-1$, it implies that $[[S]]'_l$ appears in the neighboring region of $[[S]]'_k$ with non-negligibly small (not very high neither) probability. In this case, the original pixels S'_l and S'_k may reside in different sides of an edge, and should be remarkably different. Hence, if we assign identical values for those $[[S]]'_k$ and $[[S]]'_l$ with $T(k,l)$ being large, and sufficiently different values for those $[[S]]'_k$ and $[[S]]'_l$ with $T(k,l)$ being relatively small, then we can expect a sketch version of the original image. This is because natural images are primarily formed by smooth objects separated by boundaries and edges.

More specifically, we can employ the following **Algorithm 1** to reconstruct a sketch of the original image from the available encrypted image $[[\mathbf{I}]]$ and the pre-calculated state transition matrix $\mathbf{T}$. Here, the med($\cdot$) and AHE($\cdot$) denote the median function and the adaptive histogram equalization (AHE) function, respectively. The purpose of applying the AHE is to enhance the contrast of the resulting sketch image, making it visually more pleasing. It should be noted that we make the step size of updating the pixel values in the sketch image rather small ($m \leftarrow (m+1) \bmod 256$). This helps better preserve the image local smoothness characteristics, as we process the pixels in a raster-scan order and adjacent locations (except high-activity regions) should have similar pixel values.

Algorithm 1 Obtain a sketch image from the ciphertext and the state transition matrix

Input: $\mathbf{P}([[\mathbf{I}]], [[\mathbf{S}]])$, $[[\mathbf{S}]]'$, and $\mathbf{T}$
Output: The sketch image $\hat{\mathbf{I}} = \{\hat{I}_{x,y}\}$

Generate the encrypted image $[[\mathbf{I}]]$ according to $\mathbf{P}([[\mathbf{I}]], [[\mathbf{S}]])$ and $[[\mathbf{S}]]'$.
Initialization: $\hat{\mathbf{I}} \leftarrow [[\mathbf{I}]]$, $m \leftarrow 0$
for $x = 0$ to $M-1$ **do**
  for $y = 0$ to $M-1$ **do**
    if $\hat{I}_{x,y}$ has been filled in **then**
      continue
    end if
    Determine the state index k associated with $[[\mathbf{I}(x,y)]]$
    Computer two quantities

$$l_{\max} = \arg\max_{l} T(k,l) \tag{9}$$

$$l_{\text{med}} = \text{med}\left\{T(k,l)\right\}_{l=0}^{K'-1} \tag{10}$$

    Replace all $[[S]]'_{l_{\max}}$ in $\hat{\mathbf{I}}$ with pixel value m
    Replace all $[[S]]'_{l_{\text{med}}}$ in $\hat{\mathbf{I}}$ with pixel value $255 - m$
    Update $m \leftarrow (m+1) \bmod 256$
  end for
end for
$\hat{\mathbf{I}} \leftarrow \text{AHE}(\hat{\mathbf{I}})$

4. EXPERIMENTAL RESULTS

In this section, we experimentally evaluate the performance of the proposed attack strategy using two groups of test images. The first group consists of three images, two of which are from the MNIST image database [9], and the other one is a medical image. These three images are relatively simple with large portion of homogeneous regions. In Fig. 2, we show the quality of the sketch images, where the first column lists the original images, and the last three columns give the corresponding sketch images obtained by running the **Algorithm 1** when the scaling factor $Q = 2, 4, 6$, respectively. It can be seen that even when Q is rather small, e.g., $Q = 4$, the sketch images are of high quality. For instance, the digits 1 and 4 are largely recognizable. With the increasing of Q values, higher quality of the sketch images

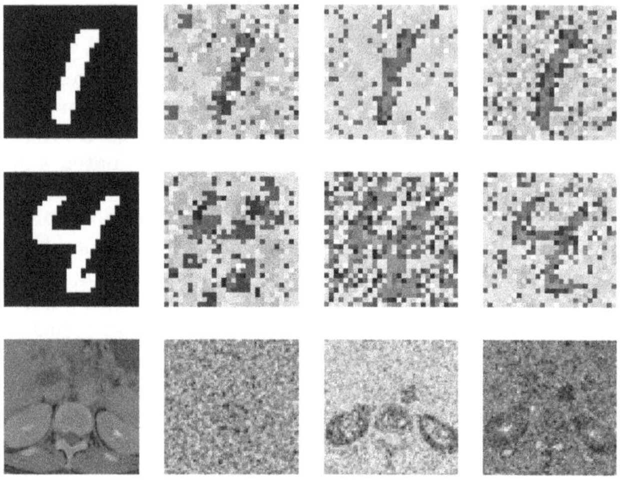

Figure 2: Reconstructed sketch images for `Digit 1` (first row), `Digit 4` (second row), and a medical image `Liver` (third row) when $Q = 2, 4, 6$, respectively.

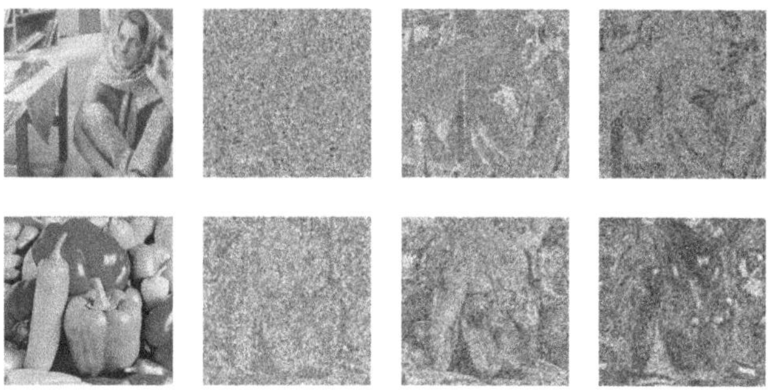

Figure 3: Reconstructed sketch images for `Barbara` (first row) and `Peppers` (second row) when $Q = 4, 6, 8$, respectively.

can be retained. This is due to the fact that more repeated encrypted pixel values would appear in $[[\mathbf{I}]]$, making the task of estimating the sketch images more effective.

The second test group is composed of two widely-used natural images selected from the CVG-UGR gray level image database [1]. The sketch images illustrated in the last three columns of Fig. 3 are retained when the scaling factor $Q = 4, 6, 8$, respectively. It can be observed that when $Q \geq 6$, rich amount of semantic information of the original image can be recovered. Further, the quality of the sketch images improves when Q becomes larger.

As a secure image encryption method should be successful in protecting *any* images, the above experimental results on a limited test set are sufficient to demonstrate the security vulnerability of the image encryption scheme in [14].

5. CONCLUSIONS

In this paper, we have analyzed the security problem of a recently published image homomorphic encryption scheme with small ciphertext expansion. We have shown that even under ciphertext-only attack (COA), the least effective attack type, the attacker can still recover a rich amount of semantic information from the encrypted images. Experimental results have been provided to validate our findings.

6. ACKNOWLEDGMENTS

This work was supported in part by the Macau Science and Technology Development Fund under grants FDCT/009/2013/A1 and FDCT/046/2014/A1, in part by the Research Committee at University of Macau under grants MRG007/ZJT/2015/FST, MRG021/ZJT/2013/FST, MYRG2014-00031-FST and MYRG2015-00056-FST, and in part by the National Science Foundation of China under grant 61402547.

7. REFERENCES

[1] CVG UGR image database. `http://decsai.ugr.es/cvg/dbimagenes/`.

[2] C. Aguilar Melchor, S. Fau, C. Fontaine, G. Gogniat, and R. Sirdey. Recent advances in homomorphic encryption: A possible future for signal processing in the encrypted domain. *IEEE Sig. Proc. Mag.*, 30(2):108–117, 2013.

[3] T. Bianchi, A. Piva, and M. Barni. On the implementation of the discrete fourier transform in the encrypted domain. *IEEE Trans. Inf. Forensics Security*, 4(1):86–97, 2009.

[4] T. Bianchi, A. Piva, and M. Barni. Composite signal representation for fast and storage-efficient processing of encrypted signals. *IEEE Trans. Inf. Forensics Security*, 5(1):180–187, 2010.

[5] T. ElGamal. A public key cryptosystem and a signature scheme based on discrete logarithms. *IEEE Trans. on Inf. Theory*, 31(4):469–472, 1985.

[6] C. Gentry. Fully homomorphic encryption using ideal lattices. In *Proc. 41st Annu. ACM Symp. Theory Comput. (STOC'09)*, pages 169–178, 2009.

[7] C.-Y. Hsu, C.-S. Lu, and S.-C. Pei. Image feature extraction in encrypted domain with privacy-preserving sift. *IEEE Trans. on Image Proc.*, 21(11):4593–4607, 2012.

[8] R. L. Lagendijk, Z. Erkin, and M. Barni. Encrypted signal processing for privacy protection: Conveying the utility of homomorphic encryption and multiparty computation. *IEEE Sig. Proc. Mag.*, 30(1):82–105, 2013.

[9] Y. LeCun. MNIST handwritten digit database. Available on the web at `http://www.research.att.com/yann/ocr/mnist/`.

[10] P. Paillier. Public-key cryptosystems based on composite degree residuosity classes. In *Advances in Cryptology (EUROCRYPT'99)*, pages 223–238. Springer, 1999.

[11] R. L. Rivest, L. Adleman, and M. L. Dertouzos. On data banks and privacy homomorphisms. *Foundations of Secure Computation*, 4(11):169–180, 1978.

[12] J. R. Troncoso-Pastoriza, S. Katzenbeisser, M. Celik, and A. Lemma. A secure multidimensional point inclusion protocol. In *Proc. 9th ACM Workshop on Multimedia and Security*, pages 109–120. ACM, 2007.

[13] P. Zheng and J. Huang. Discrete wavelet transform and data expansion reduction in homomorphic entrypted domain. *IEEE Trans. Image Proc*, 22(6):2455–2468, 2013.

[14] P. Zheng and J. Huang. An efficient image homomorphic encryption scheme with small ciphertext expansion. In *Proc. of the 21st ACM Int. Conf. on Multimedia (MM'13)*, pages 803–812. ACM, 2013.

Sense Beyond Expressions: Cuteness

Kang Wang*
Rensselaer Polytechnic Institute
wangk10@rpi.edu

Tam V. Nguyen*
Singapore Polytechnic
nguyen_van_tam@sp.edu.sg

Jiashi Feng
University of California, Berkeley
jshfeng@gmail.com

Jose Sepulveda
Singapore Polytechnic
sepulveda_jose@sp.edu.sg

ABSTRACT

With the development of Internet culture, *cute* has become a popular concept. Many people are curious about what factors making a person look cute. However, there is rare research to answer this interesting question. In this work, we construct a dataset of personal images with comprehensively annotated cuteness scores and facial attributes to investigate this high-level concept in depth. Based on this dataset, through an automatic attributes mining process, we find several critical attributes determining the cuteness of a person. We also develop a novel Continuous Latent Support Vector Machine (C-LSVM) method to predict the cuteness score of one person given only his image. Extensive evaluations validate the effectiveness of the proposed method for cuteness prediction.

Categories and Subject Descriptors

H.4 [**Information Systems Applications**]: Miscellaneous

General Terms

Algorithms, Experimentation

Keywords

Cuteness, Attribute, Continuous Latent SVM

1. INTRODUCTION

Cuteness describes a type of attractiveness commonly associated with youth and appearance, which activates in others the motivation to care [6]. Recent studies suggest that cute images stimulate the pleasure centers of the brain which is closely related with the positive emotion of human [3]. This explains why everybody prefers *cute* persons or stuff in social network, shopping, browsing images/videos on the web and so on. For example, some survey shows that women's fashions opt for the cute even over the sensible or glamorous[1]. This makes cuteness be a quite important factor to consider in product design, advertisement and so on.

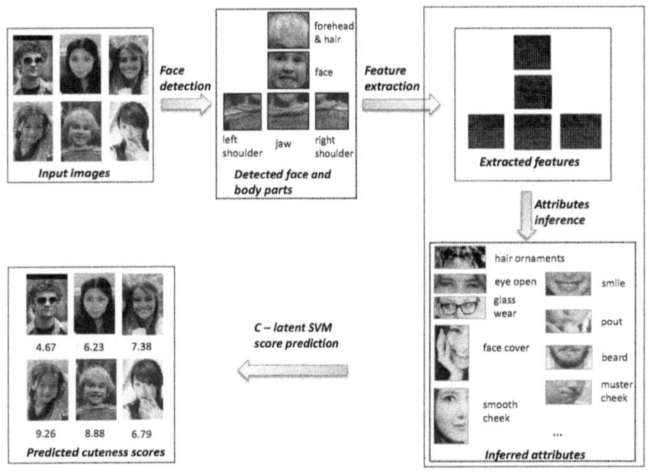

Figure 1: The framework of cuteness prediction. For each input image, we first detect the bounding box of the human faces and neighboring body parts, and then extract the appearance features accordingly. Based on the appearance features, we infer the underlying middle-level attributes and the cuteness score simultaneously.

Cuteness has received the attention of psychologists and neuroscientists for several years. For example, Kim *et al.* [4] conducted studies on why humans think certain animals are cute using functional magnetic resonance imaging (fMRI) to measure changes in human brain activity. Some evidence from this work suggests the brain activity is greater when the stimulus has juvenile characteristics – a button nose, big eyes, a large wobbly head, fat cheeks, *etc.*

Though it has been investigated by psychologists and neuroscientists, cuteness has not roused the attention of computer scientists yet. In computer vision and multimedia files, there are plenty of works focusing on recognizing ordinary expressions, *i.e.*, happiness and sadness. However, cuteness, which is beyond these traditional expressions and has higher-level semantics, is far more difficult to recognize. In this work, we explore the secrets of cuteness through the application of machine learning techniques. This is the first

*indicates the co-first authorship

MM '15, October 26-30, 2015, Brisbane, Australia
Copyright 2015 ACM ISBN 978-1-4503-3459-4/15/10$15.00
DOI: http://dx.doi.org/10.1145/2733373.2806283

[1] `http://www.nytimes.com/2006/01/03/science/03cute.html?pagewanted=all`

research attempt of computational analysis on what factors determine the cuteness, a high-level concept. We construct a model that learns from human images and their respective cuteness ratings to produce human-like evaluation of cuteness. Our work is based on the underlying theory that there are objective regularities in cuteness to be analyzed and learned. And in this work, we also provide a general framework for investigating and analyzing other high-level expressions, such as "funny" and "scary".

To investigate the factors determining the cuteness of a person, we construct a large dataset of human images with comprehensively annotated attributes and cuteness scores. In this work, the attributes are defined empirically and used as the middle-level descriptors of certain characteristic of the persons. For example, some of the attributes describe the facial appearance such as *skin smoothness* and *age*. And others describe the pose or expression of the human, such as *smile* and *face cover*. Based on this dataset, we propose a novel model to automatically learn which features and attributes determine the cuteness of persons. And we train the predictors on these features and attributes for predicting the cuteness score of a new person image. In previous works, latent SVM is a widely adopted method for the attributes mining and prediction [5, 10]. However, for the cuteness prediction problem, the annotations of the samples (cuteness scores) are continuous values. Thus, the traditional latent SVM, which can only handle discrete annotations, cannot be applied here. In this work, we propose a novel Continuous Latent SVM (C-LSVM) method, which can handle the continuous labels of the samples, to solve this issue. And we show that C-LSVM is a more general method than standard Latent SVM and has a great potential for solving many other problems involving predicting continuous variables.

Studying what makes person looks cute and how to predict cuteness from person images alone may have many useful applications. These applications include choosing a collection of cute clips from a video to generate the attractive video summarization, organizing photos in an album according to the cuteness, automatically retrieve the cute images in a large image set. Cuteness prediction and generation also benefit greatly the advertisement and production design.

2. DATASET CONSTRUCTION

Since none datasets exist for the cuteness research, in order to investigate this problem well, we collect a new dataset of personal images by ourselves. The images are crawled from the web and 4,800 images are collected in total. Most of these images contain the frontal face of the persons.

We invite 40 subjects to participate the annotation of the images' scores and attributes. To relieve the burden of the cuteness score annotation, in this work, we adopt a k-wise comparison to estimate the rank of the images and then automatically infer their absolute scores [7, 8]. In each round of annotation, the subjects are required to rank k images in a descend order of their scores. After they finish all the annotations, we estimate the absolute score of the cuteness based a rank SVM method, which maintains the rank of the photos annotated in each k-wise annotation. For the details please refer to [7, 8]. The cuteness degree of a person heavily depends on his appearance and pose. For example, a young and pretty girl pouting her mouth will look quite cute. In this work, we define following 19 attributes to comprehensively describe the ap-

Smile	√	√	x	√	√	√
Hair color	blonde	**black**	others	others	**black**	**black**
Skin color	**bright**	**bright**	**bright**	**bright**	**bright**	**dark**
Smooth cheek	√	√	x	x	√	x
Eye open	√	√	√	x	√	√
Visible teeth	√	√	x	√	√	√
Face cover	x	√	x	x	x	x
Hair ornaments	√	x	x	x	√	x
Glasses wear	x	x	√	x	√	x
...						
Cuteness	8.72	8.30	4.67	3.86	9.28	1.56

Figure 2: Examples of the collected photos with annotated attributes and cuteness scores.

pearance and pose of a person in a middle semantic level. The adopted attributes include Gender (Male, Female), Age (Young, Teen, Middle, Old), Eye (Open, Close), Mouth Variation, Mouth (Open, Close), Teeth (Visible, Invisible), Smile, Wearing Glasses, Beard, Skin Color (Bright, Dark), Hair Color (Black, Blonde, Other), Hair Ornaments, Face Cover, Skin Smoothness. For the attribute of mouth variation, we consider the poses such as pout, muster cheek having the value of 1. For the attribute of face cover, it includes finger touches lips, hand holds jaw and so on. Some examples of the above attributes are shown in Figure 1 and Figure 2. Most of the attributes admit two values and are represented by a binary variable.

3. C-LSVM FOR CUTENESS PREDICTION

3.1 Features

We first run Viola-Jones face detector [9] on the collected images to obtain bounding boxes for the human faces. Then we extract the appearance features from the face bounding box and the four spatially neighboring bounding boxes with the same size as shown in Figure 1. Here all of the bounding boxes are resized to 128×128 pixels. We extract Gabor, LBP [1], HOG [2] features within the bounding boxes to describe the pose and facial texture of persons. More specifically, for the Gabor feature, we extract the filter responses in 5 scales and 8 orientations and form a $128 \times 128 \times 5 \times 8$ feature vector for each bounding box. Then its feature dimension is reduced to 200 dimensions via PCA. Similarly, we extract HOG feature and reduce its dimensionality from 8,000 to 200 and LBP feature from 256 to 40. We experimentally find that reducing the feature dimensionality can enhance both the prediction performance and efficiency.

3.2 Prediction Model

We propose a continuous latent support vector machine (C-LSVM) for modeling the relationship between the raw feature with the attributes and cuteness score. In particular, we use three linear models to describe the relationship between raw feature $\mathbf{x}$ and attribute $\mathbf{a}$, raw feature $\mathbf{x}$ and cuteness score y, attributes $\mathbf{a}$ and cuteness score y respectively. For an image I_i, we extract the aforementioned features $\mathbf{x}_i$. The relationship of the attributes and cuteness score with the raw feature are modeled as follows:

$$\begin{aligned} y_i &= \mathbf{w}_{x,y}^T \mathbf{x}_i + b_{x,y}, \\ \mathbf{a}_i &= W_{x,a}^T \mathbf{x}_i + b_{x,a}, \\ y_i &= \mathbf{w}_{a,y}^T \mathbf{a}_i + b_{a,y}. \end{aligned}$$

Here $\mathbf{w}_{x,y}, b_{x,y}, W_{x,a}, b_{x,a}, \mathbf{w}_{a,y}, b_{a,y}$ are the parameters of the linear prediction models, which will be determined in the model learning process. In the proposed C-LSVM method, the cuteness score of an image is inferred by maximizing the following fitness function,

$$\begin{aligned} \mathcal{F} &= -\beta_1(\mathbf{w}_{x,y}^T \mathbf{x}_i + b_{x,y} - y)^2 - \beta_2(\mathbf{w}_{a,y}^T \mathbf{a} + b_{a,y} - y)^2 \\ &\quad -\|\Lambda(W_{x,a}^T \mathbf{x}_i + \mathbf{b}_{x,a} - \mathbf{a})\|^2 + \mathbf{a}^T(P \otimes M)\mathbf{a}. \qquad (1) \end{aligned}$$

The fitness function is a linear combination of the following three types of fitness, *i.e.*, score prediction from raw feature, score prediction from attributes, the attributes prediction from raw feature. And the last term accounts for the attributes correlation, which encourages the correlated attributes to be predicted simultaneously and can help improve the attributes prediction accuracy. The matrix M, constructed based on the statistics from the training data, is of size $n \times n$ and accounts for the attributes co-occurrence.

Besides the three linear models, there are also parameters trading-off the cost terms including $\beta_1, \beta_2, \Lambda, P$. Λ is a diagonal matrix with the size of $n \times n$. The ith element in the diagonal weights the prediction cost for the ith attribute, which in fact reflects the importance of the ith attribute in the cuteness score prediction. And P is a matrix with the same size as M, which weights the co-occurrence of each pair of attributes. All of these parameters, including β_1, β_2, Λ and P need to be determined in the learning process. Here we also employ a latent max-margin framework for the parameter learning and the details are provided in the following subsections.

3.3 Model Learning

In the learning process, we construct the following three prediction functions: the first one predicts the cuteness score from the raw feature, $\mathbf{w}_{x,y} : \mathbf{x} \to y$; the second one predicts the attributes from the raw feature, $W_{x,a} : \mathbf{x} \to \mathbf{a}$; the third one predicts the cuteness score from the attributes, $\mathbf{w}_{a,y} : \mathbf{a} \to y$. We adopt a max-margin regression scheme to learn the above three prediction functions individually.

$$\begin{aligned} &\min \frac{1}{2}\|\mathbf{w}_{x,y}\|^2 + C_{x,y}\sum_{i=1}^{m}(\xi_i + \xi_i^*) \\ \text{s.t.} \quad & y_i - \langle \mathbf{w}_{x,y}, x_i \rangle - b_{x,y} \le \varepsilon + \xi_i \qquad (2) \\ & \langle \mathbf{w}_{x,y}, x_i \rangle + b_{x,y} - y_i \le \varepsilon + \xi_i^* \\ & \xi_i, \xi_i^* \ge 0 \end{aligned}$$

After optimizing the above objective function via off-the-shelf solvers, we can obtain the parameters $\mathbf{w}_{x,y}, b_{x,y}$ of the prediction function $\phi_{x,y}$. The other two prediction functions, $W_{x,a}, b_{x,a}, \mathbf{w}_{a,y}, b_{a,y}$, can be obtained in a similar way.

For the parameters optimization, including $\beta_1, \beta_2, \lambda, P$, we propose the following C-LSVM method. The objective function is defined as:

$$\begin{aligned} &\min \frac{\gamma}{2}\|\mathbf{z}\|^2 + \sum_{i=1}^{m}\zeta_i \\ &\text{s.t.} \max_{a \in \mathcal{S}} \mathbf{z}^T\phi(\mathbf{x}_i, \mathbf{a}, y_i) \ge \max_{\substack{a \in \mathcal{S} \\ \bar{y} \in \mathcal{Y}_i}} \mathbf{z}^T\phi(\mathbf{x}_i, \mathbf{a}, \bar{y}) + \Delta(y_i, \bar{y}) - \zeta_i, \end{aligned}$$

where the set $\mathcal{Y}_i$ is defined as $\mathcal{Y}_i = \{y | y < y_i - \epsilon\} \cup \{y | y > y_i + \epsilon\}$ containing all of the incorrect cuteness scores. ϵ is a parameter to control the tolerance of the prediction error and is set as 0.5 throughout the experiments. And the set $\mathcal{A}$ is defined as $\mathcal{A} = \{\mathbf{a} | 0 \le a_i \le 1, \forall i = 1, \ldots, n\}$. Here the parameter $\mathbf{z}$ is the concatenation of $\beta_1, \beta_2, \lambda, P$. The potential function $\phi(\mathbf{x}_i, \mathbf{a}, y)$ is defined as:

$$\phi(\mathbf{x}_i, \mathbf{a}, y) = [\phi_{x,y}(\mathbf{x}_i, y); \phi_{a,y}(\mathbf{a}, y); \phi_{x,a}(\mathbf{x}_i, \mathbf{a}); \phi_{a,a}(\mathbf{a}, \mathbf{a})].$$

In particular, the contained four potential functions are defined as follows:

$$\begin{aligned} \phi_{x,y}(\mathbf{x}_i, y) &= -(\mathbf{w}_{x,y}^T \mathbf{x}_i + b_{x,y} - y)^2, \\ \phi_{a,y}(\mathbf{a}, y) &= -(\mathbf{w}_{a,y}^T \mathbf{a} + b_{a,y} - y)^2, \\ \phi_{x,a}(\mathbf{x}_i, \mathbf{a}) &= -(W_{x,a}^T \mathbf{x}_i + \mathbf{b}_{x,a} - \mathbf{a}) \otimes (W_{x,a}^T \mathbf{x}_i + \mathbf{b}_{x,a} - \mathbf{a}), \\ \phi_{a,a}(\mathbf{a}, \mathbf{a}) &= \mathbf{a}^T P \otimes M\mathbf{a}. \end{aligned}$$

The above optimization problem is equivalent to minimizing the following loss function:

$$\mathcal{L}(\mathbf{z}) = \frac{\gamma}{2}\|\mathbf{z}\|^2 + R(\mathbf{z}), \qquad (3)$$

where

$$R(\mathbf{z}) = \max_{\substack{a \in \mathcal{S} \\ \bar{y} \in \mathcal{Y}_i}} \mathbf{z}^T\phi(\mathbf{x}_i, \mathbf{a}, \bar{y}) + \Delta(y_i, \bar{y}) - \max_{a \in \mathcal{S}} \mathbf{z}^T\phi(\mathbf{x}_i, \mathbf{a}, y_i) \quad (4)$$

The subgradient for the above function can be calculated as follows,

$$\begin{aligned} \partial L(\mathbf{z}) &= \mathbf{z} + [\phi_{x,y}(\mathbf{x}, y); \phi_{a,y}(\mathbf{a}^*, y); \phi_{x,a}(\mathbf{x}, \mathbf{a}^*); \mathbf{m} \otimes \tilde{\mathbf{a}}] \\ &\quad -[\phi_{x,y}(\mathbf{x}, y); \phi_{a,y}(\mathbf{a}^\star, y); \phi_{x,a}(\mathbf{x}, \mathbf{a}^\star); \mathbf{m} \otimes \bar{\mathbf{a}}]. \end{aligned}$$

Here $\mathbf{a}^*$ and $\mathbf{a}^\star$ are obtained from solving the first and second maximizing problems in (4) respectively. Note that the optimization problems are standard quadratic programming and can be solved efficiently. Here $\mathbf{m}$ is the long vector formed by stacking the column vectors of matrix M. $\tilde{\mathbf{a}}$ and $\bar{\mathbf{a}}$ are formed by stacking the column of matrices $\mathbf{a}^*\mathbf{a}^{*T}$ and $\mathbf{a}^\star\mathbf{a}^{\star T}$. In the optimization, we alternatively solve the problems (2) and (3). In particular, the problem (2) can be solved via standard SVR solver and we can obtain the individual prediction model. Then the problem (3) is solved via standard quadratic programming and the estimation of the underlying attributes are updated. This procedure is repeated until convergence.

3.4 Inference

After learning the prediction functions and the model parameters, for a new image, its cuteness score can be inferred as follows,

$$\{\mathbf{a}, y\} = \arg\max_{\mathbf{a}, y} \mathbf{z}^T\phi(\mathbf{x}, \mathbf{a}, y).$$

In solving the above optimization problem, we first infer the attributes confidence vector $\mathbf{a}$. Then we binarize the elements in $\mathbf{a}$ via a fixed threshold 0.5[2]. After determining the

[2] It is widely used in applying regression for classification.

Table 1: MAE of the cuteness score prediction.

Method	NN	F-S	F-A-S	C-LSVM
MAE	1.92	1.49	1.35	**1.27**

attributes, we then infer the cuteness score y via solving a standard quadratic programming problem. This optimization procedure is inspired by the fact that a sparse attribute vector $\mathbf{a}$ generally produces better prediction result of the cuteness score. The rationale lies on that in the learning process, the attributes annotation associated with each sample are binary values. Thus the learned model prefers such sparse input attribute vectors.

4. EXPERIMENTS

In this section, we evaluate the proposed C-LSVM cuteness score prediction on the constructed dataset. In the experiments, 3,000 images from the dataset are used for training. We compare the C-LSVM method with the following three methods: the first one is based on constructing a feed forward neural network, which has been successfully applied in the beauty prediction [7]. The second one is to directly predict the cuteness score from the raw feature, where the prediction is based on a support vector regression model; and the third one is to predict the attributes at first and then predict the score from the estimated attributes based on two individual SVR models.

The accuracy of the cuteness score prediction is measured by the mean absolute error (MAE) in the evaluation. Note that the groundtruth score is ranged from 0 to 10. The evaluation results are presented in the Table 1. From the results, we can observe that the neural network method performs worst. Introducing the attributes will improve the results over only using raw feature by 0.14. And our proposed C-LSVM can further reduce the MAE by 0.08 and achieves the best result. Note that the MAE for the last three methods are quite small and such improvement is in fact significant. We also present some attributes inference results for the test samples in Figure 3. We can see that most of the attributes can be correctly inferred. While for the *cheek smoothness*, the accuracy is relatively low. The reason may be that the low-level feature we adopted are describing the whole face region, instead of only describing the cheek region. Thus some noise may contaminate the prediction for the smoothness. To more intuitively show how the defined attributes determine the cuteness of one person, we visualize the learned inference model $\mathbf{w}_{a,y}$ in Figure 4. We observe that the attribute *cheek smoothness* is most important for the cuteness of one person. And the attributes *age (young)* and *skin color* are also important. Meanwhile, the *age (old)* and *gender* attributes are least important for the cuteness.

5. CONCLUSIONS

In this work, we present the first research attempt of computational analysis on the cuteness, which is beyond the ordinary expressions such as happiness or sadness. We construct a large dataset of persons' images with well annotated cuteness scores and attributes. We propose the novel C-LSVM method which automatically mines the important features and attributes determining the cuteness of a person. Extensive evaluations show that our method can better capture the relationship between the raw feature, attributes and the cuteness score, over the traditional linear predictors.

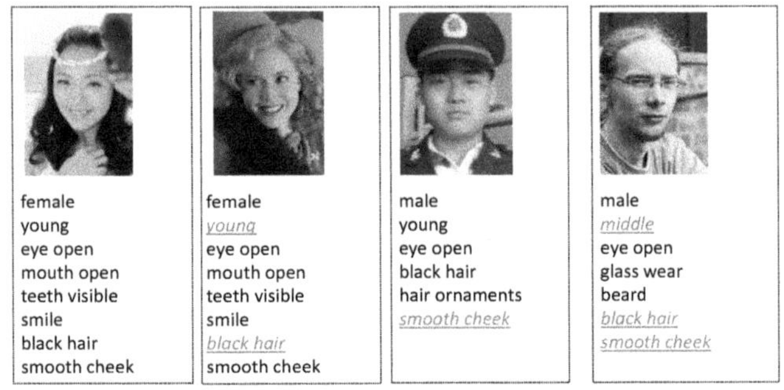

Figure 3: Examples of the inferred attributes. Most of the attributes can be inferred correctly. And the incorrect inferred attributes are highlighted by red color.

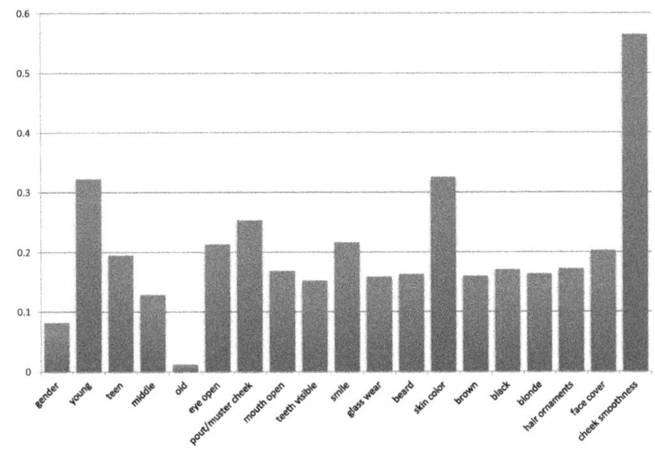

Figure 4: The mined weights of the attributes for cuteness prediction. The horizontal axis displays the attributes and the vertical axis shows the learned weights.

6. ACKNOWLEDGMENTS

This work was supported by Singapore Ministry of Education under research Grant MOE2014-TIF-1-G-007.

7. REFERENCES

[1] T. Ahonen, A. Hadid, and M. Pietikäinen. Face recognition with local binary patterns. In *ECCV*, pages 469–481, 2004.

[2] N. Dalal and B. Triggs. Histograms of oriented gradients for human detection. In *CVPR*, pages 886–893, 2005.

[3] M. L. Glocker, D. D. Langleben, K. Ruparel, J. W. Loughead, J. N. Valdez, M. D. Griffin, N. Sachser, and R. C. Gur. Baby schema modulates the brain reward system in nulliparous women. *Ethology*, pages 9115–9119, 2009.

[4] S. H. Kim and S. Hamann. Neural correlates of positive and negative emotion regulation. *J. Cognitve Neuroscience*, pages 776–798, 2007.

[5] S. Liu, T. Nguyen, J. Feng, M. Wang, and S. Yan. Hi, magic closet, tell me what to wear! In *ACM MM*, pages 1333–1334, 2012.

[6] K. Lorenz. Part and parcel in animal and human societies. *Studies in animal and human behavior*, 1971.

[7] T. Nguyen, S. Liu, B. Ni, J. Tan, Y. Rui, and S. Yan. Sense beauty via face, dressing, and/or voice. In *ACM MM*, 2012.

[8] T. Nguyen, S. Liu, B. Ni, J. Tan, Y. Rui, and S. Yan. Towards decrypting attractiveness via multi-modality cues. *TOMCCAP*, 9(4):28:1–28:20, 2013.

[9] P. Viola and M. J. Jones. Robust real-time face detection. *IJCV*, pages 137–154, 2004.

[10] Y. Wang and G. Mori. A discriminative latent model of object classes and attributes. *ECCV*, pages 155–168, 2010.

Joint Visual-Textual Sentiment Analysis with Deep Neural Networks

Quanzeng You and Jiebo Luo
University of Rochester
Rochester, NY 14623
{qyou, jluo}@cs.rochester.edu

Hailin Jin
Adobe Research
San Jose, CA 95110
hljin@adobe.com

Jianchao Yang
Snapchat Inc
Venice, CA 90291
jianchao.yang@snapchat.com

ABSTRACT

Sentiment analysis of online user generated content is important for many social media analytics tasks. Researchers have largely relied on textual sentiment analysis to develop systems to predict political elections, measure economic indicators, and so on. Recently, social media users are increasingly using additional images and videos to express their opinions and share their experiences. Sentiment analysis of such large-scale textual and visual content can help better extract user sentiments toward events or topics. Motivated by the needs to leverage large-scale social multimedia content for sentiment analysis, we utilize both the state-of-the-art visual and textual sentiment analysis techniques for joint visual-textual sentiment analysis. We first fine-tune a convolutional neural network (CNN) for image sentiment analysis and train a paragraph vector model for textual sentiment analysis. We have conducted extensive experiments on both machine weakly labeled and manually labeled image tweets. The results show that joint visual-textual features can achieve the state-of-the-art performance than textual and visual sentiment analysis algorithms alone.

Categories and Subject Descriptors

I.2 [**Artificial Intelligence**]: Vision and Scene Understanding; I.5.4 [**Pattern Recognition**]: Applications—*Computer vision*

General Terms

Algorithms, Experimentation, Application

Keywords

sentiment analysis, multimodality analysis, deep neural networks

1. INTRODUCTION

The increasing popularity of social networks attracts more and more people to share their experiences and to express their opinions on virtually all events and subjects in online social network platforms. Each day, billions of messages and posts are generated. In this study, we focus on deriving people's opinions or sentiments towards topics and events happening in real world. In other words, we are interested in automatic detection of sentiment from online user generated content.

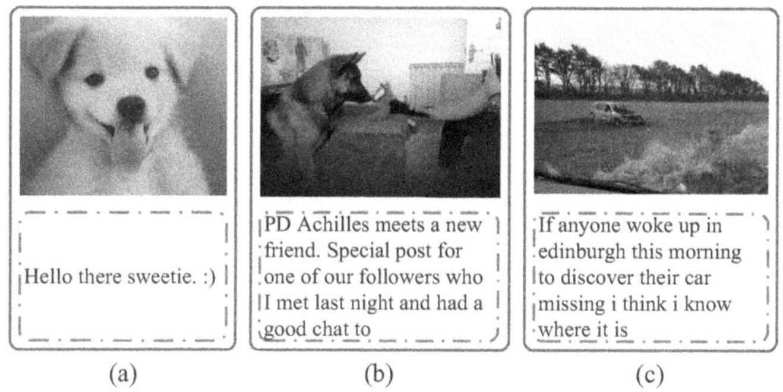

Figure 1: Examples of image tweets from Twitter.

Figure 1 shows several example image tweets from Twitter. Image tweets refer to those tweets that contain images. If we take a look at these three example image tweets, we can observe that in example (a), both image and the text indicate that this tweet carries a positive sentiment; in (b) while it is difficult to tell the sentiment from the image in the *middle* image tweet, however, we can tell that this tweet expresses positive sentiment from the text; in (c) on the contrary, it is hard to tell the sentiment from the text, however the worn-out car in the image suggest an overall negative sentiment. These examples explain the motivation for our work. We would like to learn people's overall sentiment over the same object from different modalities of the object provided by the user. In particular, we focus on inferring people's sentiment according to the available images and the short and informal text.

Many researchers have contributed to sentiment analysis. For instance, there are related works on detecting users' sentiment and applying sentiment analysis to predict political elections [14, 16]. However, current techniques are mostly based on the analysis of textual content to detect sentiment. On the other hand, visual content, including both images and videos, are becoming increasingly popular in all mainstream online social network platforms. For example, Twitter's support of image tweets and Vine as well as Facebook's

MM'15 October 26-30, 2015, Brisbane, Australia
ACM 978-1-4503-3459-4/15/10 ...$15.00.
DOI: http://dx.doi.org/10.1145/2733373.2806284 .

Instagram are all designed to support people to share and post more visual content.

To the best of our knowledge, little attention has been paid to the sentiment analysis of visual content as well as multi-modality sentiment analysis. Only a few recent works attempted to predict visual sentiment using features from images [15, 2, 1, 19] and videos [13]. Visual sentiment analysis is extremely challenging, as image sentiment involves a much higher level of abstraction and subjectivity in the human recognition process [8], on top of a wide variety of visual recognition tasks including object, scene, action and event recognition. However, Convolutional Neural Networks [11, 4, 9] have been proved to be very powerful in solving computer vision related tasks.

To that end, we address in this work two major challenges as follows: 1) we adopt Convolutional Neural Networks [9, 18] to visual sentiment analysis and employ the state-of-the-art distributed representation of documents [10] for textual sentiment analysis, and 2) we demonstrate the feasibility of using weakly labelled data for multi-modal sentiment analysis and how to easily transfer models from one domain to another domain.

2. RELATED WORK

For sentiment analysis of online user generated textual content, dictionaries based approaches [16, 5] have been widely used due to its efficiency and simplicity. Very recently, distributed representation of words started to attract research attention due to its ability in learning robust features for words [12]. Le and Mikolov [10] further proposed an approach to learn distributed representation for documents. They applied their document representations to sentiment analysis and achieve the best performance over existing competing algorithms.

There are also several recent works on visual sentiment analysis. The work in [15] is a machine learning algorithm to predict the sentiment of images using pixel-level color histogram and SIFT bag of words visual features. Motivated by the fact that sentiment involves high-level abstraction, which may be easier to explain by objects or attributes in images, both [1] and [19] proposed to employ visual entities or attributes as features for visual sentiment analysis. In [1], the responses from 1200 adjective noun pair (ANP) classifiers was considered as mid-level features and Yuan *et al.* [19] employed a similar mechanism but using 102 scene attributes instead. More recently, You *et al.* [18] proposed a progressively trained Convolutional Neural Network for visual sentiment analysis and achieved the state-of-the-art performance in predicting image sentiments.

There are only a few publications publications on analyzing sentiment using multi-modalities, such as text and images. Both [17] and [3] employed both text and images for sentiment analysis, where late fusion is employed to combine the prediction results of using n-gram textual features and mid-level visual features [1]. In addition, researchers have investigated cross-modal issues in other multimedia retrieval related tasks.

3. MULTI-MODALITY SENTIMENT ANALYSIS

In this section, we describe in details on how to apply the proposed model to multi-modality sentiment analysis. In particular, we focus on how to extract the state-of-the-art visual and textual features and apply them to the proposed model. Figure 2 shows the framework for multi-modality sentiment analysis. The recent developed Convolutional Neural Network (CNN) [9] has achieved the state-of-the-art performance on a wide range of vision tasks. You *et al.* [18] conducted experiments on deploying CNN for visual sentiment analysis and achieved better performance than both low-level [15] features and mid-level [1, 19] features. Inspired by their conclusions, we propose to use CNN for the extraction of visual features. In particular, we employ the pre-trained CNN model on imagenet [7] to fine-tune a CNN model for visual sentiment analysis. The details on how to fine-tune the CNN model will be discussed in the experimental section. Next, the fine-tuned CNN model is employed to extract visual features from the second to the last layer of the neural network.

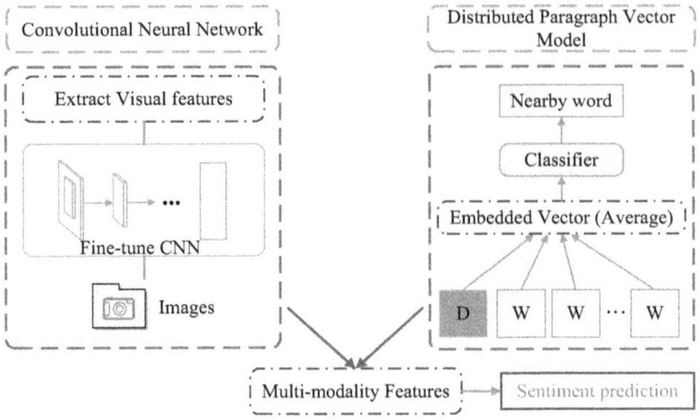

Figure 2: The framework for joint visual-textual sentiment analysis.

For textual features, Le and Mikolov [10] developed an unsupervised language model to learn distributed representations for documents and paragraphs. They applied the learned representations to analyze textual sentiment, which achieved the best performance compared with existing state-of-the-art textual sentiment analysis models on existing benchmark data sets. We train the model on the related descriptions and titles of images our crawled from Getty Images.

Given the visual and textual features, we are able to train a joint model for sentiment analysis. Meanwhile, the trained visual and textual model can extract visual and textual features for testing images and text individually, which next can be used to predict the sentiment distribution for the image and related text respectively. In our implementation, we tried both the early and late fusion to obtain the joint sentiment analysis results.

4. EXPERIMENTS

In this section, we conduct experiments to evaluate the performance different models on sentiment analysis. To train the visual and textual model in Figure 2, we choose to crawl data from Getty Images[1]. The main reasons to use Getty Images are its relatively formal descriptions of images and its convenient and powerful query based searching system.

[1]http://www.gettyimages.com

4.1 Training visual and textual models

To fine-tune the pre-trained CNN model for sentiment analysis, we need a relatively large labeled data set, which can cost huge human efforts. In our implementation, we use a list of keywords for both positive and negative sentiment.[2] We query Getty Images with these keywords and all the returned images are labeled using the sentiment labels of these keywords. In this way, we are able to collect a large weakly labeled data set consisting of both images and text, which is employed to fine-tune the CNN model and learn the paragraph vector for related text of each image. Table 1 summarizes the statistics of our collected data set from Getty Images. In total, there are 101 keywords. We collect a total of over half million weakly labeled images as well as their titles and descriptions.

Table 1: Summary of the dataset from Getty Image.

Sentiment	Num of Keywords	Num of Images
Positive	37	311,940
Negative	64	276,281
Sum	101	588,221

Given the above collected data set, we randomly split them into 80% for training and 20% for testing. We fine-tune the CNN model on the publicly available implementation Caffe [7]. For textual model, the title and description of each image are concatenated as a single *document*. We remove numbers and special characters. Then, we tokenize the text using the tokenizer model from NLTK (`http://www.nltk.org`). We also remove those words that appear less than 5 times in all the documents. We use the default settings in [10] to learn textual features. We reports both the performance of using visual features and textual features, which are state-of-the-art approaches on textual and visual sentiment analysis respectively [10, 18]. We also employ early fusion and late fusion to analyze the performance of joint visual-textual features [17, 3].

4.2 Performance on Getty Images testing data set

We extract visual features for the 20% testing images given the fine-tuned CNN model. In this paper, we use the second to the last layer to extract features, which has a total of 4096 features for each image. For textual features, since the training is unsupervised, all documents are given to the model to learn their features [10].

Table 2: Performance on the testing data set by different approaches.

Algorithm	Precision	Recall	F1	Accuracy
Textual	0.806	0.544	0.655	0.696
Visual	0.747	0.745	0.746	0.732
Early Fusion	0.778	0.769	0.774	0.763
Late Fusion	0.785	**0.775**	0.780	0.769

[2]`http://www.sci.sdsu.edu/CAL/wordlist/origwordlist.html`

Table 2 shows the performance of different approaches on the 20% weakly labeled testing data from Getty Images. The results show that visual features may have comparable precision and recall on these data. Textual features can achieve higher precision but lower recall. Both early fusion and late fusion can produce improved results over single modalities. However, both fail to improve the performance of precision than the single textual model.

4.3 Performance on Twitter data set

We employ the Twitter API to collect a large number of Tweets. The recent proposed rule based sentiment classifier VADER [6] is employed to weakly label the tweets. We filter out duplicates, low-quality, porn and all-text images. In total, we collect 31,584 *weakly* labeled image tweets, 16,844 of them are positive tweets and the rest are negative. We use these image tweets to fine-tune a CNN model and to learn distributional representations for each post of Tweets.

Meanwhile, we also employed crowd intelligence, Amazon Mechanical Turk (AMT), to generate sentiment labels for selected image tweets. We recruited 5 AMT workers for each of the candidate image tweet. We test the performance of different models on this manually labeled data using the previously fine-tuned models on the *weakly* labeled image tweets. After receiving the batch results from AMT, we keep those that have at least 4 agreements on the sentiment label. Eventually, we have 613 image tweets, of which 389 are labelled positive and 224 are labelled negative.

Table 3: Performance on the AMT manually labeled data set by different approaches.

Algorithm	Precision	Recall	F1	Accuracy
Textual	0.832	0.638	0.722	0.688
Visual	0.762	0.715	0.737	0.677
Early Fusion	0.776	**0.740**	0.758	0.700
Late Fusion	0.799	0.738	0.767	0.716

Table 3 gives the performance of different approaches. It is possible that the labels by AMT workers are biased compared with the weak labels given by VADER, causing relatively poor performance of both Early and Late Fusion.

In addition, we extract the most *confident* prediction examples of two approaches on the manually labeled image tweets by AMT workers. Figure 3 shows the top ranked 5 images of early fusion and late fusion on both positive and negative categories respectively (red circles indicate wrongly predicted samples). All the image tweets are ranked from left to right in a decreasing order. There are many common highly ranked examples between the two approaches. However, the two approaches have different ranking orders. In particular, the early fusion even has one positive example wrongly predicted.

5. CONCLUSIONS

Sentiment analysis, in particular visual sentiment analysis, is a challenging and interesting problem. In this work, we aim to analyze sentiment via both visual and textual content. The recently developed machine learning algorithms lead to the availability of robust visual and textual features for abstract tasks, such as sentiment analysis. Due to the largely easily accessible weakly labeled data, we can train

(a) Negative examples using early fusion

(b) Positive examples using early fusion

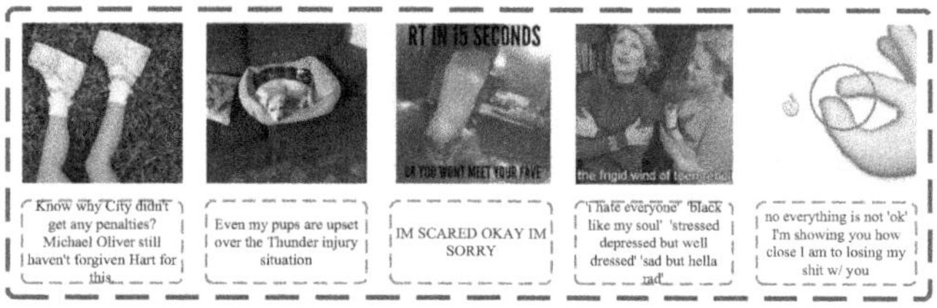

(c) Negative examples using late fusion

(d) Positive examples using late fusion

Figure 3: Examples of most confident image tweets of different approaches.

both visual and textual models to extract features for sentiment analysis. The experimental results suggest that the joint visual-textual model outperforms both the state-of-the-art single textual and visual sentiment analysis models. We hope our sentiment analysis results can encourage further research on online user generated multimedia content.

6. ACKNOWLEDGMENTS

This work was generously supported in part by Adobe Research.

7. REFERENCES

[1] D. Borth, T. Chen, R. Ji, and S.-F. Chang. Sentibank: large-scale ontology and classifiers for detecting sentiment and emotions in visual content. In *ACM MM*, pages 459–460, 2013.

[2] D. Borth, R. Ji, T. Chen, T. Breuel, and S.-F. Chang. Large-scale visual sentiment ontology and detectors using adjective noun pairs. In *ACM MM*, pages 223–232. ACM, 2013.

[3] D. Cao, R. Ji, D. Lin, and S. Li. A cross-media public sentiment analysis system for microblog. *Multimedia Systems*, pages 1–8, 2014.

[4] D. C. Cireşan, U. Meier, J. Masci, L. M. Gambardella, and J. Schmidhuber. Flexible, high performance convolutional neural networks for image classification. In *IJCAI*, pages 1237–1242, 2011.

[5] X. Hu, J. Tang, H. Gao, and H. Liu. Unsupervised sentiment analysis with emotional signals. In *WWW*, pages 607–618, 2013.

[6] C. Hutto and E. Gilbert. Vader: A parsimonious rule-based model for sentiment analysis of social media text. In *ICWSM*, 2014.

[7] Y. Jia, E. Shelhamer, J. Donahue, S. Karayev, J. Long, R. Girshick, S. Guadarrama, and T. Darrell. Caffe: Convolutional architecture for fast feature embedding. *arXiv preprint arXiv:1408.5093*, 2014.

[8] D. Joshi, R. Datta, E. Fedorovskaya, Q.-T. Luong, J. Z. Wang, J. Li, and J. Luo. Aesthetics and emotions in images. *IEEE Signal Processing Magazine*, 28(5):94–115, 2011.

[9] A. Krizhevsky, I. Sutskever, and G. E. Hinton. Imagenet classification with deep convolutional neural networks. In *NIPS*, pages 1097–1105, 2012.

[10] Q. Le and T. Mikolov. Distributed representations of sentences and documents. In *ICML*, 2014.

[11] Y. LeCun, L. Bottou, Y. Bengio, and P. Haffner. Gradient-based learning applied to document recognition. *Proceedings of the IEEE*, 86(11):2278–2324, 1998.

[12] T. Mikolov, I. Sutskever, K. Chen, G. S. Corrado, and J. Dean. Distributed representations of words and phrases and their compositionality. In *NIPS*, pages 3111–3119, 2013.

[13] L.-P. Morency, R. Mihalcea, and P. Doshi. Towards multimodal sentiment analysis: Harvesting opinions from the web. In *ICMI*, pages 169–176, 2011.

[14] B. O'Connor, R. Balasubramanyan, B. R. Routledge, and N. A. Smith. From tweets to polls: Linking text sentiment to public opinion time series. *ICWSM*, 11:122–129, 2010.

[15] S. Siersdorfer, E. Minack, F. Deng, and J. Hare. Analyzing and predicting sentiment of images on the social web. In *ACM MM*, pages 715–718. ACM, 2010.

[16] A. Tumasjan, T. O. Sprenger, P. G. Sandner, and I. M. Welpe. Predicting elections with twitter: What 140 characters reveal about political sentiment. *ICWSM*, 10:178–185, 2010.

[17] M. Wang, D. Cao, L. Li, S. Li, and R. Ji. Microblog sentiment analysis based on cross-media bag-of-words model. In *ICIMCS*, pages 76:76–76:80. ACM, 2014.

[18] Q. You, J. Luo, H. Jin, and J. Yang. Robust image sentiment analysis using progressively trained and domain transferred deep networks. In *AAAI*, 2015.

[19] J. Yuan, S. Mcdonough, Q. You, and J. Luo. Sentribute: image sentiment analysis from a mid-level perspective. In *WISDOM*, page 10, 2013.

Attribute Mining for Scalable 3D Human Action Recognition

Xingyang Cai
xycai@mail.ustc.edu.cn

Wengang Zhou
zhwg@ustc.edu.cn

Houqiang Li
lihq@ustc.edu.cn

Dept. of EEIS, University of Science and Technology of China
Hefei 230027, P. R. China

ABSTRACT

With the development of depth sensor, skeletal human action recognition from 3D video is paving the way for many practical applications. For most applications, scalable action recognition is desired to identify novel actions without rebuilding the system. To address this problem, a potential solution is to identify those intrinsic attributes which are semantic-aware and shared among known and novel actions. With such motivation, in this paper, we propose an attribute-based skeletal action recognition and explore the scalable action recognition. We first present a new skeletal feature with the representations of static pose and motion of human skeleton to support a comprehensive action attribute space. Then, a novel action attribute mining method is proposed to discover action attributes for each bone pair across action classes. Finally, we accomplish action recognition based on those mined attributes. Extensive experiments on MSRAction3D and UTKinect-Action demonstrate the effectiveness and superiority of our attribute-based action recognition approach over the existing methods.

Categories and Subject Descriptors

I.4.8 [**Image Processing and Computer Vision**]: Scene Analysis—*Motion*

Keywords

3D Video; Action Attributes; Scalable Action Recognition

1. INTRODUCTION

Recently, with the development of depth sensor, such as Microsoft Kinect and Nintendo Wii, 3D videos become increasingly popular in the area of multimedia. 3D videos not only record RGB information, but also capture depth clue of the scene in front of depth sensor, which greatly alleviates the difficulty in video understanding and readily paves the way for many commercial applications. Skeletal human action recognition is an important research topic in 3D video understanding. There are lots of potential interesting applications with skeletal human action recognition, such as gesture control, augmented reality gaming, *etc.* For those applications, it is highly desired to develop a scalable action recognition system to identify novel actions without rebuilding the system. For example, in gesture control or human-computer interaction, new instructions may need to define novel gestures. In augmented reality gaming, new game content may require adding novel actions. However, many existing methods [1, 6, 8, 9, 10] simply take skeletal action recognition as a conventional classification problem and model the discrimination of pre-defined action classes for classification, which are incapable of recognizing novel actions.

To address the problem of scalability to novel actions, discovery of action attributes on skeletal data is a promising solution. Here, action attributes refer to the "atoms" of human actions, which compose different actions. Thus different actions are likely to share same states on some part of the skeleton, which can be mined in a data-driven manner so as to represent human actions. The data-driven mining method from skeletal data ensures that attributes are sematic-aware and ready to represent novel actions. In fact, attributes mined from skeletal action are more close to the nature of action, considering the fact that the extracted features directly describe human joints or bones (here a bone is the line segment of two adjacent joints in a human skeleton) without complex background or camera motion (skeletons are easily fixed in the global coordinate). Therefore, the extracted features are semantic-aware for human action. Another reason is that for skeletal human action, an action is composed by some simple motions occurring on several bones. We regard those simple motions occurring on bone pairs as action attributes. This definition of attributes ensures that the representation of an action is compact and different actions will share the same attributes. In this paper, we prove the property of attribute sharing by recognizing one dataset based on attributes mined from another similar dataset.

The contribution of this work is three folds. First, we present an improved skeletal feature from [6] by including motion representation into the 3D geometric relationships of bone pairs. The improved feature describes human skeleton with both static pose and motion information to support a comprehensive action attribute space. Second, we propose a novel action attributes mining method. We define action attributes as the simple motions occurring on bone pairs. The mined attributes can be regarded as "atoms" of skeletal

MM'15, October 26–30, 2015, Brisbane, Australia.
 ISBN 978-1-4503-3459-4/15/10 ...$15.00.
DOI: http://dx.doi.org/10.1145/2733373.2806285.

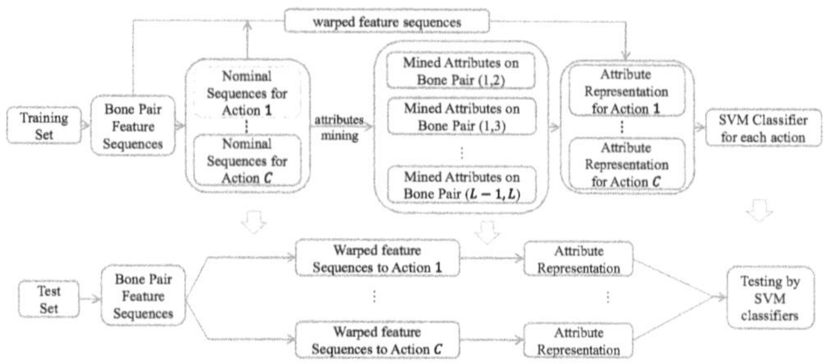

Figure 1: The framework of the proposed approach.

human actions. Third, we explore a scalable action recognition system based on attribute sharing.

2. PROPOSED APPROACH

In this section, we introduce the proposed attribute-based skeletal action recognition approach. We first introduce the skeletal feature extraction in Section 2.1, and explain the attribute mining method in Section 2.2.

2.1 Skeletal Feature Extraction

For skeletal human action recognition, the input data is human skeleton temporal sequence. In each frame, human skeleton is recorded as 3D positions of human joints. In this paper, we extract skeletal features from human skeleton in each frame and generate feature sequences. We extend the method of [6], by representing human skeleton from two aspects, *i.e.*, static pose and motion.

2.1.1 Representation of Static Pose

We first describe human skeleton with the relative geometry of a pair of bones. Compared with using joints individually, using relative pairs to describe human skeleton can avoid variances brought by coordinate axis translation, alleviate negative influence by noise and also give a more discriminative representation for skeleton sequences (*e.g.*, "bending" or "clapping"). Here we define a bone as a line segment connecting two adjacent joints in the skeleton. For a bone $\vec{l}_n$, we denote l_{n1} as its starting point and l_{n2} as its end point. Then we define a unit vector $\vec{e}_n$. The starting point of $\vec{e}_n$ is l_{n1} and $\vec{e}_n$ shares the same orientation with $\vec{l}_n$. Given a pair of bone $\vec{l}_m$ and $\vec{l}_n$, the relative geometry between them is computed using $\vec{e}_m$ and $\vec{e}_n$. The relative geometry from $\vec{e}_n(t)$ to $\vec{e}_m(t)$ in frame t is computed as:

$$\begin{bmatrix} \vec{e}_m(t) \\ 1 \end{bmatrix} = \begin{bmatrix} \mathbf{R_1}_{m,n}(t) & \vec{d}_{m,n}(t) \\ 0 & 1 \end{bmatrix} \begin{bmatrix} \vec{e}_n(t) \\ 1 \end{bmatrix} \quad (1)$$

where $\mathbf{R_1}_{m,n}(t)$ and $\vec{d}_{m,n}(t)$ are the rotation matrix and translation vector required to align $\vec{e}_n$ to coincide with $\vec{e}_m$. Symmetrically, we can also compute $\mathbf{R_1}_{n,m}(t)$ and $\vec{d}_{n,m}(t)$, which align $\vec{e}_m$ to coincide with $\vec{e}_n$.

We denote $\mathbf{T}_{m,n}(t) \in SE(3)$ as the 4×4 matrixes computed in Eq (1). $SE(3)$ is the special Euclidean group [5]. Then the matrixes are mapped to their Lie algebra $\mathfrak{se}(3)$, which is a vector space with six dimensions, because either rotation or translation has three degrees of freedom. For more details of Lie algebra map of $SE(3)$, please refer to [5]. Different with the representation proposed in [6], both $\mathbf{T}_{m,n}(t)$ and $\mathbf{T}_{n,m}(t)$ are computed in the global coordinate system. In

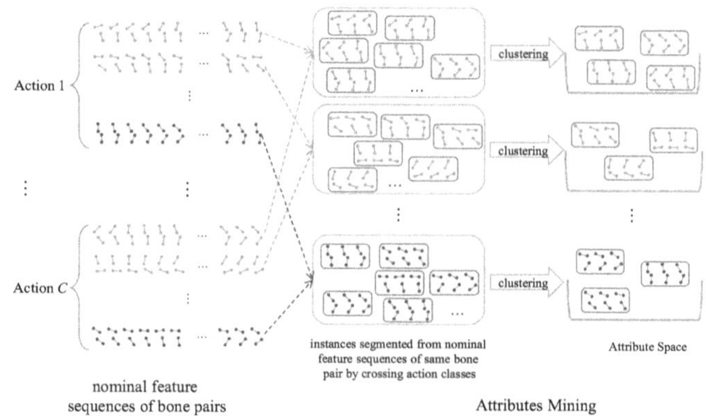

Figure 2: The procedure of attribute mining. We use same colors to represent same bone pairs in different actions.

this paper, we use $\mathbf{T}_{m,n}(t)$ to describe the relative geometry from $\vec{e}_n$ to $\vec{e}_m$. Features contain absolute positions and orientations of bones in the global coordinate can support a more comprehensive attribute space.

2.1.2 Representation of Motion

In this section, we introduce the representation of motion in the skeletal features. Besides extracting the relative geometry for the position and orientation of a bone pair, we also describe the bone pair from their motions. For motion representation, we denote $\vec{S}_n(t)$ as the motion vector of bone $\vec{l}_n$ in frame t. Given the motion vectors $\vec{S}_m$ and $\vec{S}_n$ occurring on the bone pair $\vec{l}_m$ and $\vec{l}_n$, respectively, we also compute the relative geometry between $\vec{S}_m$ and $\vec{S}_n$ as the representations of motion for this bone pair. Different from the representation of static pose, the translation of two motion vectors is ignored here since the translation is described in static pose. But the relationship between magnitudes of $\vec{S}_m$ and $\vec{S}_n$ is important for describing motions, so we extract it in the representation. Similar to 1, we also compute the rotation matrix $\mathbf{R_2}_{m,n}(t)$ and $\mathbf{R_2}_{n,m}(t)$ for motion vectors. We also map $\mathbf{R_2}_{m,n}(t)$ and $\mathbf{R_2}_{n,m}(t)$ to $\mathfrak{se}(3)$ and obtain a three dimensional vector.

For computing the magnitude relationship, we first translate $\vec{S}_m(t)$ and $\vec{S}_n(t)$ to locate their starting points at the origin of the global coordinate. We compute the proportion of $\|\vec{S}_m(t)\|$ and $\|\vec{S}_n(t)\|$ as the magnitude relationship $\lambda_{m,n}(t)$ and $\lambda_{n,m}(t)$ between the motion vectors.

We concatenate the representations of static pose and motion to generate skeletal features in each frame. For each bone pair, the dimensionality of the extracted skeletal feature is 20. Finally we represent a skeletal action as $B = L \times (L-1)/2$ feature sequences based on every bone pair, where L is the number of bones in a human skeleton. Here different from [6], we do not concatenate representations on all bone pairs to generate a vector for human skeleton. Instead, we represent human skeleton with action attributes, which are mined from the basic motions occurring on bone pairs.

2.2 Attributes Mining

In this section, we will introduce the attributes mining method based on the extracted skeletal features. Here, we mine simple motions occurring on bone pairs by collecting the feature instances segmented from the feature sequence of each bone pair. Since we need to segment feature sequences, we first adopt DTW [4] to address the problems of temporal misalignment and rate variations. Here DTW is used for warping sequences and measuring the distance of two sequences. To handle the noise problem in feature sequences, we compute the nominal sequence for each bone pair from the same action samples in the training set using the algorithm of computing a nominal curve [6]. Then there are B nominal feature sequences computed for each action, where B is the number of bone pairs. To mine simple motions occurring on bone pairs as action attributes, we collect instances segmented from nominal feature sequence of a same bone pair by crossing action classes. Here the instances contain features extracted from fixed-length successive frames. We assume that these instances present simple motions occurring on bone pairs. We segment these instances starting from each frame of feature sequences.

As human action is composed by some simple motions made by several bones and each bone is in limited states for the articulated skeleton, instances on a bone pair are redundant. We use clustering algorithm for the instances on each bone pair to reduce redundancy. Here clustering is computed inter-class to mine action attributes with the property of sharing and also let the attribute representation compact. Considering different attributes have unbalanced proportions in the collected instances and we do not know how many attributes each bone pair should have, we use affinity propagation [2] here. We utilize the average similarity as the preference of each instance for affinity propagation. The learned cluster centers are regarded as action attributes. They present simple but distinct motions occurring on some bone pair. These motions are the "atoms" of skeletal human action and describe some properties of actions. We cluster these action attributes by crossing action classes so that they can be shared among different actions. Figure 2 shows the procedure of attribute mining.

Finally, a skeletal human action video is represented by an attribute histogram vector which records the occurrence of each attribute. We train C one-vs-all linear SVM classifiers as final classification for C action classes. As shown in Figure 1, for a test sample, we first compute the representations of static pose and motion to extract skeletal feature sequence of each bone pair. Then for each action class c, we warp the feature sequence to the corresponding nominal feature sequence and segment the warped feature into instances. The similarities to attributes are accumulated as the occurrences and the test sample is represented by the histogram of attributes. The final recognition label is the one with highest prediction probability of SVM.

3. EXPERIMENTS

In this section, we will analyze the experimental results about our proposed approach. We first study the impact of some parameters. Then we compare our approach with the state-of-the-art methods on three public datasets. At last, we explore the scalable action recognition based on MSRAction3D and UTKinect datasets to justify the sharing property of mined attributes.

3.1 Impact of Parameters

In this section, we determine several key parameters in the proposed approach by experimental study. For the representation of motion, τ is the frame gap for computing motion vector and ε is the threshold for determining whether a motion vector is generated by noise or not. We use τ and ε to remove negative effects caused by noise. In addition, τ determines the granularity of motion described in the representation. Figure 3 gives the recognition accuracy under different parameter settings on MSRAction3D dataset. From the curves we can find that when frame gap $\tau = 2$, the representation is most discriminative. Large frame gap make the representation of motion miss key simple motions but small gap can not distinguish motion from noise effectively. Meanwhile, when $\varepsilon = 0.01$, noisy motions are suppressed most. We set $\tau = 2$ and $\varepsilon = 0.01$ in experiments.

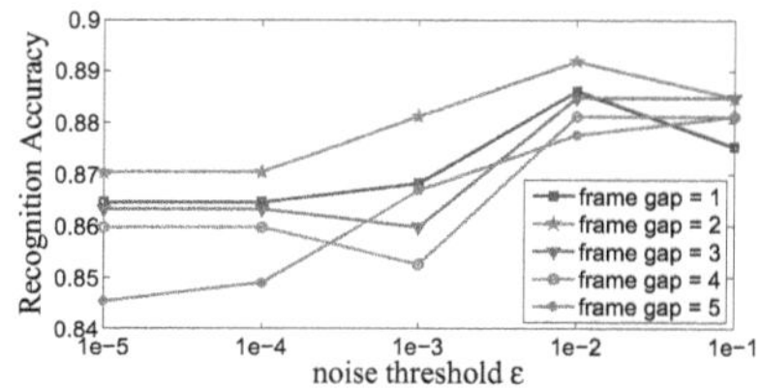

Figure 3: Comparison on the accuracies under different frame gaps τ and noise threshold ε.

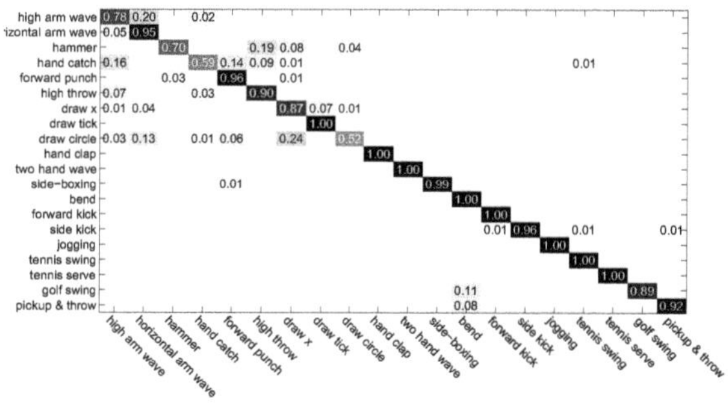

Figure 4: The confusion matrix of MSRAction3D dataset.

3.2 Skeletal Action Recognition Results

Table 1: Comparison with the state-of-the-art results on MSRAction-3D Dataset

MSR-Action3D dataset (protocol of [3])	
Histograme of 3D joints [8]	78.97
Lie Group SE(3) [6]	92.46
Proposed approach	**92.96**
MSR-Action3D dataset (protocol of [7])	
Actionlets[7]	88.20
Lie Group SE(3)[6]	89.48
The moving pose [9]	**91.70**
Proposed approach	89.19

We evaluate the proposed approach on MSRAction3D dataset with two kinds of protocols. In [3], actions in the dataset are splited into three subsets $AS1$, $AS2$ and $AS3$. Action recognition is evaluated in each subset. In [7], the whole dataset is used for action recognition. This dataset is very challenging because of many highly similar actions (*e.g.* "high arm wave" and "horizontal arm wave") and the similarities

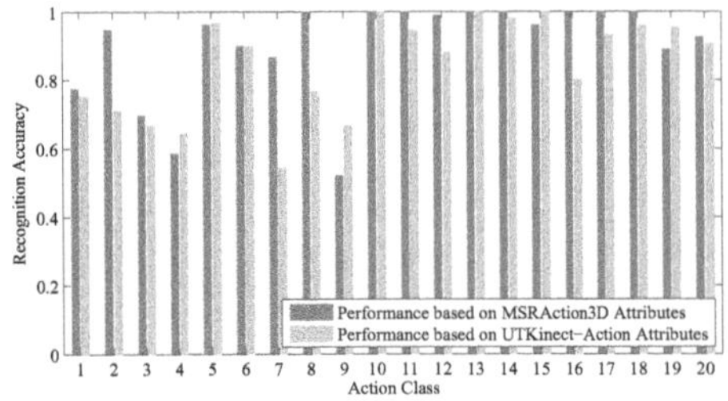

Figure 5: Comparison the performance of each action in MSRAction3D based on attributes mined from UTKinect-Action.

among actions are reduced in each subset. The two kinds of protocols both use the cross-subject test setting. Table 1 compares the proposed approach with several various state-of-the-art skeletal human action recognition approaches with these two protocols. In protocol of [3], our approach outperforms the state-of-the-art, while in protocol of [7], our approach is comparable with state-of-the-art. Since the mined attributes need to keep the property of sharing, attribute-based classification lose some abilities on distinguish similar actions. Figure 4 displays the confusion matrix from the proposed approach. Although most actions can be classified correctly, the accuracy is low for some highly similar actions. These actions share many attributes and we need to use more detailed representation to describe them, which is a trade-off to determine the granularity of feature representation and attribute mining.

We also evaluate the proposed approach on UTKinect-Action dataset. The proposed approach also gives the comparable results on this dataset. Table 2 lists the performances of proposed approaches and several various state-of-the-art skeletal recognition approaches. The proposed attribute-based recognition can achieve good performance when actions are composed with distinct attributes.

Table 2: Comparisons with the state-of-the-art results on UTKinect-Action Dataset

Histograme of 3D joints [8]	90.92
Lie Group SE(3)[6]	97.08
Proposed approach	**97.36**

3.3 Scalable Action Recognition Results

We evaluate the scalable action recognition system using MSRAction3D and UTKinect-Action. We demonstrate that the property of attribute sharing by mining attributes using UTKinect-Action but evaluate the attribute representation with MSRAction3D. Figure 5 compares the recognition accuracy of each action in MSRAction3D based on the MSRAction3D attributes and UTKinect-Action attributes. UTKinect-Action only contains 10 actions but MSRAction3D contains 20 actions. However, these actions overlap in some simple motions occurring on parts of human skeleton. From the results we can find that the accuracies of most actions based on UTKinect-Action are comparable with the accuracies based on the attributes mined from MSRAction3D, which has demonstrated that the mined attributes are general "atoms" of skeletal human action. Some actions such as "high arm wave", "horizontal arm wave" and "draw x" obtain lower accuracies because there are highly similar actions in MSRAction3D and the attributes mined from a dataset with less actions can not describe them well.

4. CONCLUSION

In this paper, we investigate scalable skeletal action recognition based on action attributes. We propose a new skeletal feature to describe the static pose and motion of human skeleton. Then, a novel attribute mining method is proposed to uncover action attributes for each bone pair with crossing action classes. We use the attribute representation to classify skeletal human actions. We also explore the scalable action recognition and demonstrate the property of attribute sharing. Extensive experiments demonstrate the effectiveness and robustness of our approach. In the future work, we will investigate the temporal dynamics of action attributes and build a temporal model to capture transitions of action attributes.

5. ACKNOWLEDGMENTS

This work was supported in part to Dr. Wengang Zhou by Anhui Provincial Natural Science Foundation under contract No. 1508085MF109, and in part to Prof. Houqiang Li by NSFC under contract No. 61325009.

6. REFERENCES

[1] C. Ellis, S. Z. Masood, M. F. Tappen, J. J. LaViola Jr, and R. Sukthankar. Exploring the trade-off between accuracy and observational latency in action recognition. *International Journal of Computer Vision*, 101(3):420–436, August 2012.

[2] B. J. Frey and D. Dueck. Clustering by passing messages between data points. *Science*, 315(5814):972–976, 2007.

[3] W. Li, Z. Zhang, and Z. Liu. Action recognition based on a bag of 3d points. In *IEEE CVPR Workshops*, pages 9–14, 2010.

[4] M. Müller. *Information retrieval for music and motion*, volume 2. Springer, 2007.

[5] R. M. Murray, Z. Li, S. S. Sastry, and S. S. Sastry. *A mathematical introduction to robotic manipulation*. CRC press, 1994.

[6] R. Vemulapalli, F. Arrate, and R. Chellappa. Human action recognition by representing 3d skeletons as points in a lie group. In *IEEE CVPR*, pages 588–595, 2014.

[7] J. Wang, Z. Liu, Y. Wu, and J. Yuan. Mining actionlet ensemble for action recognition with depth cameras. In *IEEE CVPR*, pages 1290–1297, 2012.

[8] L. Xia, C.-C. Chen, and J. Aggarwal. View invariant human action recognition using histograms of 3d joints. In *IEEE CVPR Workshops*, pages 20–27, 2012.

[9] M. Zanfir, M. Leordeanu, and C. Sminchisescu. The moving pose: An efficient 3d kinematics descriptor for low-latency action recognition and detection. In *IEEE ICCV*, pages 2752–2759, 2013.

[10] X. Zhao, Y. Liu, and Y. Fu. Exploring discriminative pose sub-patterns for effective action classification. In *Proceedings of ACM international conference on Multimedia*, pages 273–282, 2013.

Learning Features from Large-Scale, Noisy and Social Image-Tag Collection

Hanwang Zhang[†], Xindi Shang[†], Huanbo Luan[†§], Yang Yang[‡], Tat-Seng Chua[†]
[†]National University of Singapore
[‡]University of Electronic Science and Technology of China
[§]Tsinghua University
{hanwangzhang,xindi1992,luanhuanbo,dlyyang}@gmail.com;dcscts@nus.edu.sg

ABSTRACT

Feature representation for multimedia content is the key to the progress of many fundamental multimedia tasks. Although recent advances in deep feature learning offer a promising route towards these tasks, they are limited in application to domains where high-quality and large-scale training data are hard to obtain. In this paper, we propose a novel deep feature learning paradigm based on large, noisy and social image-tag collections, which can be acquired from the inexhaustible social multimedia content on the Web. Instead of learning features from high-quality image-label supervision, we propose to learn from the image-word semantic relations, in a way of seeking a unified image-word embedding space, where the pairwise feature similarities preserve the semantic relations in the original image-word pairs. We offer an easy-to-use implementation for the proposed paradigm, which is fast and compatible for integrating into any state-of-the-art deep architectures. Experiments on NUSWIDE benchmark demonstrate that the features learned by our method significantly outperforms other state-of-the-art ones.

Categories and Subject Descriptors

H.3.3 [**Information Search and Retrieval**]: Retrieval Model

Keywords

feature learning; visual-semantic embedding; multimodal analysis

1. INTRODUCTION

The progress in multimedia applications is largely due to the advances of feature representations for multimedia content. For example, over the past decades, we have witnessed the evolution of visual features from color histogram to SIFT interest points and to the recent deep learning features, that help to move a large varieties of multimedia applications

MM'15, October 26–30, 2015, Brisbane, Australia.
© 2015 ACM. ISBN 978-1-4503-3459-4/15/10 ...$15.00.
DOI: http://dx.doi.org/10.1145/2733373.2806286.

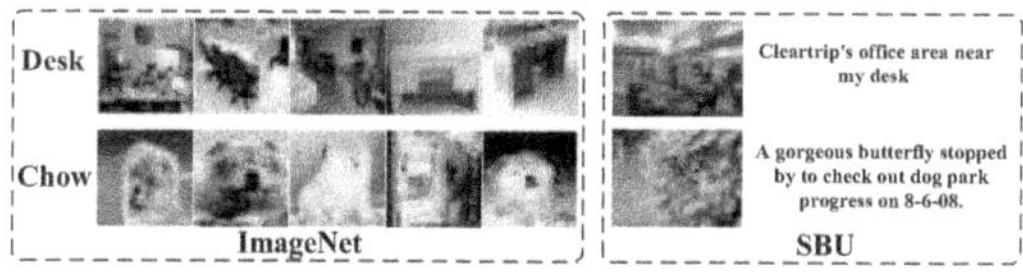

(a) Samples from ImageNet and SBU

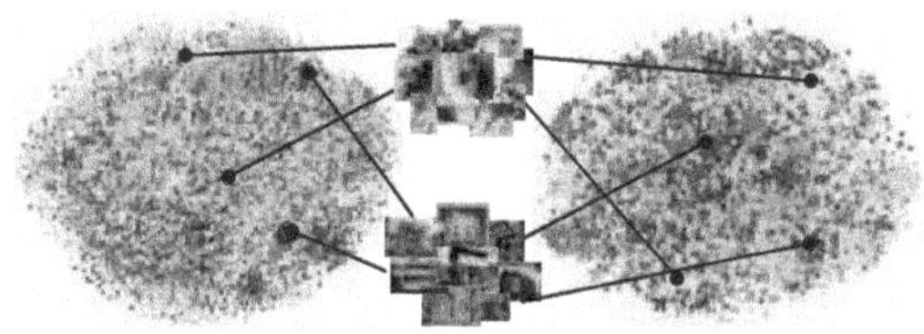

(b) Feature Visualization

Figure 1: t-SNE visualization for the features of a million SBU images from Flickr. Different colors represent different semantic categories. One of the distribution is learned by deep learning a million images across 1,000 categories from high-quality labeled ImageNet and the other is learned by a million images weakly-labeled by over 30,000 unique tags by SBU (cf. Section 3 for details). Both sides show that the features are representative. Can you tell which side is learned by SBU? (see answers below)

from academic prototypes into industrial products [14]. Today, a general consensus is that learning-based features by deep neural networks can outperform most hand engineered features and therefore free us to focus on designing algorithms and end applications.

In order to learn strong features, we need a large-scale and high-quality dataset. At this point, ImageNet with millions of human-labeled images across thousands of semantic categories has offered us a reliable incubator to develop features. However, this dataset is built by Web images five years ago and hence it lags behind the fast evolving semantic and visual diversities in real-world scenarios. For example, different emerging vertical domains like fashion (*e.g.*, Taobao and Amazon) would need different datasets in order to learn specific features for shoes and clothes domain. Moreover, videos from emerging popular social networks (*e.g.*, Snapchat and Vine) would love features different from what were learned from images. Building such datasets not only requires heavy and tedious labeling efforts but also expert domain knowledge, any of which is expensive. This awkward situation

[1]Left: ImageNet. Right: SBU.

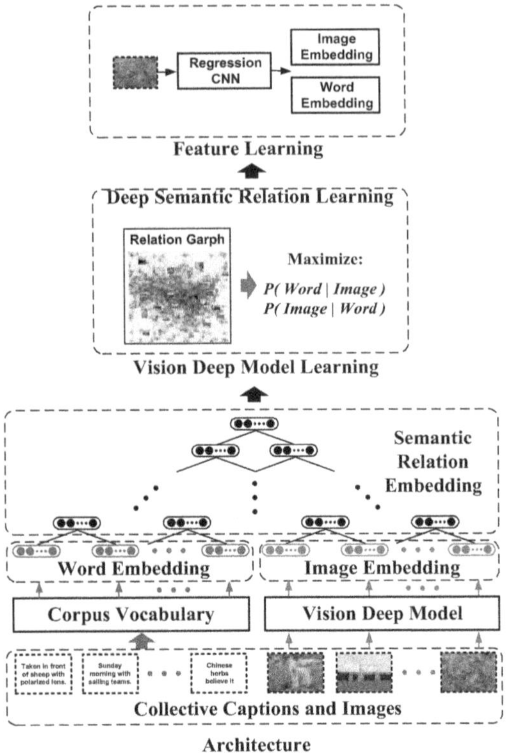

Figure 2: The overview of the proposed feature learning paradigm. Architecture: a hierarchical model that learns a unified vector space for words and images, which embeds the semantic relations. Feature Learning: After learning the embedded space by *Deep Semantic Relation Learning*, we learn a deep feature map from raw image pixels to the desired embedding vector by *Regression CNN*, which composes our *Vision Deep Model Learning.*

highlights the weakness of current feature learning methods: even though it requires no human expertise on feature engineering, it still needs a great labor intensity in building a good quality dataset as payoff.

In this paper, we propose a novel feature learning paradigm based on large, noisy and social image-tag collections which are ubiquitously accessible to us (*e.g.*, SBU in Figure 1(a)). The overview of our proposed feature learning paradigm is shown in Figure 2. The architecture is designed for mapping both images and words into the same embedding space of semantic relations, which are discovered from the large amount of social images and captions. The off-line feature learning includes two core components. The first is a deep relational learning method to learn the semantic relation embedding from the heterogeneous relation graph of images and words, which are noisy and sparse. In particular, we break down the topology of the graph into a tree-structured deep hierarchy, where the leaves are images and words. Each non-leaf node encodes the information about the semantic relations (*i.e.*, word-image, image-image and word-word) in terms of a feature vector. In order to generalize the learned collective intelligence to the content of images, the second component maps visual information into the semantic embedding. Our vision deep learning regresses images to the image embedding (by Regression CNN). So, our on-line feature extraction is simply to apply the learned deep vision model on an input image.

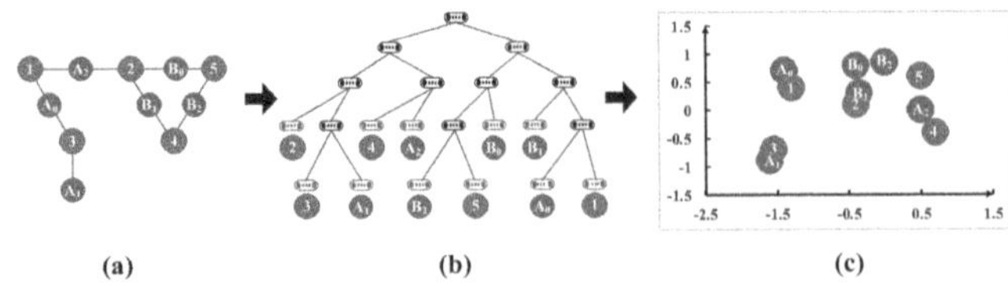

Figure 3: We want to transform the image-word graph into a continuous vector space. We take the graph (left) as the input to the tree-structured deep architecture (middle). It then learns the image and word feature representations (right) as the output. Here is a simple illustration on a toy graph: gray ones are words and red ones are items. We can see that the similarities between the learned features perserve the orginal graph topology.

We use a million-scale social media of Flickr images and captions: SBU dataset, as our source of collective intelligence. On the social image benchmark: NUSWIDE images, we conduct extensive experiments to show the effectiveness of the proposed feature learning paradigm in generating superior features. We believe that our work has a great potential in relieving human labor for feature learning.

2. RELATED WORK

Although deep learning features have been shown to outperform hand-engineered features on many vision benchmarks [3], there is limited research on how to further finetune the features for specific domains, especially for the social multimedia in the wild. One of the most probable reason might be the sparsity and noise in social media, which makes the problem very challenging. Zhang *et al.* [15] developed a multimodal autoencoder to discover the common patters of images and text and the binary classifier responses of the discovered patterns were considered as the semantic featuers. Gong *et al.* [6] used a large weakly annotated photo collection from Flickr (similar to SBU used in our work) to learn a generic image-sentence embeddings. The above methods lack a principled way to tackle the challenge of social media but generally resort to the deep architecture to discover the semantic relations between the noisy images and text. However, we specially propose to explicitly learn the inherent semantic relations embedded in social multimedia. This learning method is inspired by recent advances in social network learning [12] and natural language modeling [10] and has been shown to be robust to the sparse, diverse and noisy nature of data. In this way, our work is related to a latest work by Fang *et al.* [4], where they applied a matrix factorization method to learn the embeddings of images and users from a fashion collection. However, their method requires a reasonable measure for "negative" relations, which is not a generic solution for general social collections.

3. DEEP SEMANTIC RELATION LEARNING

Inspired by the recent advance in network topology learning [12], we first construct an image-word graph for social image-description collection and then introduce the deep architecture to learn the representations. We denote images as $\mathcal{I}$ and words as $\mathcal{W}$. So, a image-word relation graph is denoted as $\mathcal{G} = \{\mathcal{I}, \mathcal{W}, \mathcal{E}\}$, where $\mathcal{E} \subseteq \mathcal{U} \times \mathcal{I}$ is the set of edges that connect images and words. We define that image i connects to word w if and only if w is a word appeared in the description of i. Our goal is to learn vector representations for the symbolic vertices in the graph. We denote $\mathbf{x}_i \in \mathbb{R}^d$ and $\mathbf{x}_w \in \mathbb{R}^d$ as vectors in a d-dimensional space. In particular, we want the similarities between vectors $s_{iw} = \mathbf{x}_i^T \mathbf{x}_w$ to preserve the topology of the graph. That is, we expect $s_{iw} > s_{iw'}$ if i is connected to w but not w'. Also, we expect the intra-image/word similarities to have similar properties such that $s_{i_j i_k} > s_{i_j i_l}$ (or $s_{w_j w_k} > s_{w_j w_l}$) if i_j and i_k (or w_j and w_k) share more words (or images) than i_j and w_l (or w_j and w_l). Figure 3 illustrates a toy example of such properties. In order to capture the topology information of the graph, we explore a series of short random walks in the graph. Rooted from each vertex v (v can be i or w), we randomly choose K-length list $\{v_1, ..., v_K\}$ ($K = 5$ in our paper), where v_{k+1} is a vertex chosen at random from the neighbors of vertex v_k.

Specifically, they statistically preserve the frequencies of image-word co-occurrences, that is, the number of optimizations for frequent connections will be larger than that of rare ones. Therefore, the learned vectors will reveal the desired semantic relations. As a result, our learning objective is to maximize the similarities between the vertices within a random walk. A widely used objective function is the softmax that models the probability of vertices i and j within a random walk: $p(i|j) = exp\left(\mathbf{x}_i^T \mathbf{x}_j\right) / \sum_{i'} exp\left(\mathbf{x}_{i'}^T \mathbf{x}_j\right)$, where we discard the distinct notations of image and word vertices for simplicity. We deploy the Hierarchical Softmax [9] to implement the probability as in [12] for efficiency and robustness.

4. VISUAL DEEP LEARNING FOR IMAGE-WORD EMBEDDING

Recall that our goal is to learn image features from collective intelligence, here, the discovered image-word embeddings. Although the embeddings have successfully gained semantic relations, visual information of images are not taken into account. In this section, we first use deep vision model to transform images into the embeddings and then exploit the visual information to fine-tune them. As a result, we expect to obtain image features that are close to their semantically related words.

Suppose the core visual model (*i.e.*, usually a convolution neural network pretrained by ILSVRC dataset), with its prediction layer removed, is denoted as $f(i)$, where i is the input image. For example, if we use AlexNet, $f(i)$ will be a 4,096-D sparse nonnegative vector which is the ReLU ouput of the 7-th fully-connected layer. We want to map $f(i)$ into the same embedding space as learned above. In particular, we expect that a linear mapping $\mathbf{W}f(i)$ to be sufficiently as:

$$loss(i; \mathbf{W}) = \|\mathbf{W}f(i) - \mathbf{x}_i\|_1 \tag{1}$$

which is a simple regression task with ℓ_1-norm since ℓ_2-norm is sensitive to outliers. However, one could argue to use a more complex and discriminative loss function as in [5]:

$$loss(i; \mathbf{W}) = \sum_{j \neq i} \max\left(0, margin - \mathbf{x}_i^T \mathbf{W} f(i) + \mathbf{x}_j^T \mathbf{W} f(i)\right) \tag{2}$$

Unfortunately, in practice, we find that training a deep model with the loss in Eq. (2) is very tricky. First, it is difficult to define the negative samples of i. For millions or billions images, even maintaining a small set of margin-violating negative samples can take hours. Second, the negative samples are dependent on the learning of $f(i)$ and hence the training cannot be easily asynchronized. Third, the margin brings in additional hyperparameters which need to be tuned.

So far, we have incorporated visual information into the image-word embedding. After the learning process, at test time, we can extract features for newly arrived images from the fully connected layers before the loss function. Also, we find that the visually fine-tuned image-word embeddings has great potentials in some fundamental multimedia tasks such as key-word based image search and image annotation (see Figure 4).

5. EXPERIMENTS

5.1 Datasets

SBU: the SBU Captioned Photo Dataset, was originally used as a gallery for retrieval based image description generations [11]. It contains a million images with associated descriptive text. In this paper, we further removed stop-words like "is" and "that" and words with frequency less than 5 from the captions. This gives rises to a vocabulary of the size 3,0456. We used SBU as our social multimedia source.

NUSWIDE: it is a popular social image benchmark [1]. It contains 269,648 images across 81 general noun concepts. We followed the official "161,789/107,859" as the "tran/test" split.

5.2 Implementation Details

For the image-word graph deep learning method in Section 3, we used the source codes in [12] with minor modifications. We applied 5-step random walks with 5 repetitions and window-size of 5 for pair-wise optimization. We used 8 computing threads on a 8-core machine. It took about 10 minutes for a good solution.

For deep vision models used in Section 4, we depoyed Caffe framework [7] for CNN implementation on a NVIDIA Titan Z GPU. In particular, we used the well-known AlexNet architecture [8], which consists of 5 convolutional layers with max-pooling and 2 fully connected layers before the loss layer. We used the author provided ImageNet pretrained model (in Caffe format) as initializations for the proposed Regression CNN. The initial learning rate was set to $1e^{-4}$ with dynamic momentum. The size of the batch was 128 and it took 20 epochs to converge. Each epoch took about 90 mins. We used ℓ_2-norm weight decay with $5e^{-5}$ coefficient.

The choice of the embedding dimension is crucial. We tuned the values within $\{300, 400, ..., 2,000\}$ and found that 1,000 was the best choice for accuracy and efficiency.

For classification task, we used LIBLINEAR linear SVM toolbox[3] for classifier implementation. We ℓ_2-normalized all the input features and the trade-off parameter was tuned within $\{0.001, 0.01, 0.1, 1, 10\}$.

5.3 Results

Good features should perform well in classification task. We extracted two kinds of features by our method: 4,096-

[3]www.csie.ntu.edu.tw/ cjlin/liblinear/

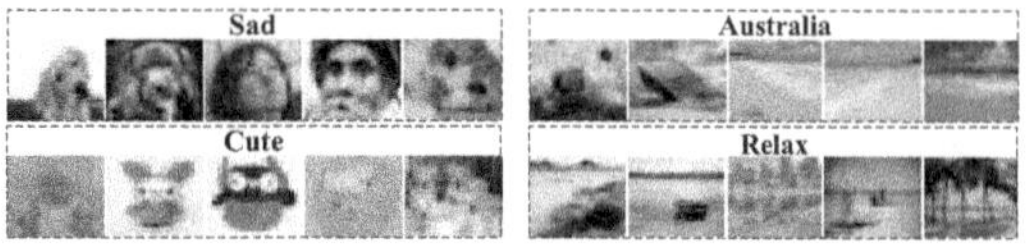

Figure 4: Examples of the 5 most similar images to those concepts that are not labeled in NUSWIDE. From collective intelligence, we can generalize visual properties to any word, even for those "words" that do not exist in the target domains. For example, there is no "relax"concept in NUSWIDE, but we can return "vocation" and "beach" concepts, which most relates to "relax".

Table 1: Performance (mAP%) of classification on NUSWIDE.

Dataset/Method	DeCAF	ICMAE	Ours-fc7
NUSWIDE	38.6	32.7	**39.1**

D **Ours-fc7**, which is the 7-th fully-connected layer output of our R-CNN. We compared our features with the following two strong baselines: **DeCAF** [3] , which is a 4,096-D feature from the 7-th fully-connected layer of AlexNet, and **ICMAE** [15], which is a 1,898-D feature learned from a million Flickr images with tags[5].

Table 1 lists the performance of classification using various features. On both datasets, we can see that our two methods considerably outperform DeCAF. This demonstrates the effectiveness of learning from large social collection. We note that ICMAE, which is also learned from social images, performs the worst. The reasons are two folds. First, the dimension is the lowest. Second, it does not explicitly tackle the sparsity and diversity in large but noisy social media. Note that sparse coding image embeddings in terms of word dictionaries performs the best. This is because as compared to the lower-level fc7 feature, the 4,000-D sparse codes endow higher-level semantic information. Moreover, we find that our feature learning framework can also learn useful image-tag embeddings which can be used for querying images out of the concept domain in a data collection (see Figure 4).

6. CONCLUSIONS

We presented a novel feature learning paradigm from large-scale but noisy social multimedia. Our key idea is to acquire collective intelligence from big multimedia data, which helps to better understand the semantic relations between images and words. In order to achieve this, we proposed a deep learning method to learn image-word embeddings from a million image-caption pairs of SBU dataset. Then, we proposed a visual deep learning method to map images into the embeddings. Experiments on NUSWIDE benchmark validated the effectiveness of our learned features. We believe that the proposed paradigm is of great practical use since it is effective, efficient and easy-to-use.

7. ACKNOWLEDGMENTS

This work was supported by NUS-Tsinghua Extreme Search (NExT) project under the grant No.: R-252-300-001-490 and the National Natural Science Foundation of China, No. 61303075.

[5]http://pub.nextcenter.org/deeplearning/modelParams.tar

8. REFERENCES

[1] T.-S. Chua, J. Tang, R. Hong, H. Li, Z. Luo, and Y. Zheng. Nus-wide: a real-world web image database from national university of singapore. In *CIVR*, 2009.

[2] J. Dean, G. Corrado, R. Monga, K. Chen, M. Devin, M. Mao, A. Senior, P. Tucker, K. Yang, Q. V. Le, et al. Large scale distributed deep networks. In *NIPS*, 2012.

[3] J. Donahue, Y. Jia, O. Vinyals, J. Hoffman, N. Zhang, E. Tzeng, and T. Darrell. Decaf: A deep convolutional activation feature for generic visual recognition. *arXiv preprint arXiv:1310.1531*, 2013.

[4] C. Fang, H. Jin, J. Yang, and Z. Lin. Collaborative feature learning from social media. In *CVPR*, 2015.

[5] A. Frome, G. S. Corrado, J. Shlens, S. Bengio, J. Dean, T. Mikolov, et al. Devise: A deep visual-semantic embedding model. In *NIPS*, 2013.

[6] Y. Gong, L. Wang, M. Hodosh, J. Hockenmaier, and S. Lazebnik. Improving image-sentence embeddings using large weakly annotated photo collections. In *ECCV*. 2014.

[7] Y. Jia, E. Shelhamer, J. Donahue, S. Karayev, J. Long, R. Girshick, S. Guadarrama, and T. Darrell. Caffe: Convolutional architecture for fast feature embedding. *arXiv preprint*, 2014.

[8] A. Krizhevsky, I. Sutskever, and G. E. Hinton. Imagenet classification with deep convolutional neural networks. In *NIPS*, 2012.

[9] T. Mikolov, K. Chen, G. Corrado, and J. Dean. Efficient estimation of word representations in vector space. In *ICLR*, 2013.

[10] T. Mikolov, I. Sutskever, K. Chen, G. S. Corrado, and J. Dean. Distributed representations of words and phrases and their compositionality. In *NIPS*, 2013.

[11] V. Ordonez, G. Kulkarni, and T. L. Berg. Im2text: Describing images using 1 million captioned photographs. In *NIPS*, 2011.

[12] B. Perozzi, R. Al-Rfou, and S. Skiena. Deepwalk: Online learning of social representations. In *KDD*, 2014.

[13] C. Szegedy, W. Liu, Y. Jia, P. Sermanet, S. Reed, D. Anguelov, D. Erhan, V. Vanhoucke, and A. Rabinovich. Going deeper with convolutions. *arXiv preprint*, 2014.

[14] O. Vinyals, A. Toshev, S. Bengio, and D. Erhan. Show and tell: A neural image caption generator. *arXiv preprint*, 2014.

[15] H. Zhang, Y. Yang, H. Luan, S. Yan, and T.-S. Chua. Start from scratch: Towards automatically identifying, modeling, and naming visual attributes. In *MM*, 2014.

Saliency Detection Based on Graph-Structural Agglomerative Clustering

Youbao Tang[†], Xiangqian Wu[†], Wei Bu[‡]

[†]School of Computer Science and Technology, Harbin Institute of Technology (HIT), Harbin, 150001 China

[‡]Department of New Media Technologies and Arts, HIT, Harbin, 150001 China

{tangyoubao, xqwu, buwei}@hit.edu.cn

ABSTRACT

This paper proposes a novel saliency detection method based on graph-structural agglomerative clustering (GSAC). In this method, a number of intermediate images with consecutive number of regions are firstly created by using GSAC to the input image with the maximum incremental path integral criterion. Then an initial salient map is computed based on the boundary connectivity of the regions in the intermediate images, with enforcing the early formed objects in the clustering process. Finally, the initial salient map is refined to get the final salient map by using the reconstruction errors of sparse coding and the object-bias prior. The experimental results demonstrate that the proposed method greatly outperforms the state-of-the-art approaches on two standard benchmark datasets.

Categories and Subject Descriptors

I.4.6 [**Computing Methodologies**]: Image Processing and Computer Vision – *Segmentation*; I.4.8 [**Computing Methodologies**]: Image Processing and Computer Vision – *Scene Analysis*

General Terms

Algorithms, Experimentation, Performance

Keywords

Saliency Detection; Graph-Structural Agglomerative Clustering; Boundary Connectivity; Sparse Coding; Object-Bias

1. INTRODUCTION

Automatic salient region detection, which aims to softly separate background and foreground or locate important objects in images, is a profound challenge in computer vision. With the salient map of an image, the performance of numerous image applications, including image segmentation [1], object detection [2], and image retrieve [3], etc. can be improved significantly. Therefore, saliency detection has attracted great attentions in recent years, and a number of approaches have been successfully proposed.

Some researchers [4-8] extract local and global features from pixels for saliency detection. Rosin [4] performs edge detection, distance transformation, and other pixel operations to detect salient regions. Achanta et al. [5] compute the salient map by using the pixel-wise color difference. Liu et al. [6] exploit the contrast, color, and spatial relationship between adjacent pixels to describe salient objects. Jiang et al. use manifold learning [7] and deep belief propagation [8] for saliency estimation. These approaches usually highlight high-contrast edges instead of the salient objects, or get a low contrast salient map, or poorly preserve boundaries of salient objects.

To efficient and effective to detect saliency, some researchers [9-15] estimate the salient maps from regions instead of pixels. Cheng et al. [9] evaluate global color differences and spatial weighted coherence scores of regions for salient object detection. Perazzi et al. [10] estimate the salient map by using high dimensional Gaussian filters. Li et al. [11] extract features of the regions at the image boundary as templates for densely and sparsely reconstruction of all image regions, and use the reconstruction errors to measure the saliency. Yang et al. [12] detect salient regions through manifold ranking. Margolin et al. [13] use PCA to represent image patches and employ this representation to compute salient maps. Kim et al. [14] represent a salient map as a linear combination of several high-dimensional color spaces. Zhu et al [15] present a boundary connectivity measure to detect the background with high accuracy and use the background to estimate saliency. But the efficiency and effectiveness of these approaches are heavily dependent on the number of segmented regions of the image. Since the size and the number of salient objects in different images are largely varying, it is difficult to accurately detect saliency by segmenting these images into the same number of regions. To deal with this problem, the hierarchical saliency detection approaches [16-19] hierarchically represent images with different number of regions, and then compute the salient map by using these hierarchical regions.

This work proposes a novel hierarchical saliency detection method by analyzing the human's visual process, in which the pixels of input image are gradually clustered to form salient regions and the earlier the regions are formed, the more salient they are. Motivated by this visual process, this work proposes a novel coarse-to-fine method of saliency detection. In this method, the pixels of the input image are agglomeratively clustered into continuous numbers of regions to generate a series of successive intermediate images. Then an initial salient map is computed by analyzing the boundary connectivity of the region and emphasizing the early formed regions during the clustering process. Finally, the initial salient map is further refined to form the final salient map. With the coarse-to-fine framework, the proposed saliency detection method achieves much better performance than the state-of-the-art approaches by using very simple features (color and position) on two standard benchmark datasets.

MM'15, October 26-30, 2015, Brisbane, Australia
© 2015 ACM. ISBN 978-1-4503-3459-4/15/10...$15.00
DOI: http://dx.doi.org/10.1145/2733373.2806287

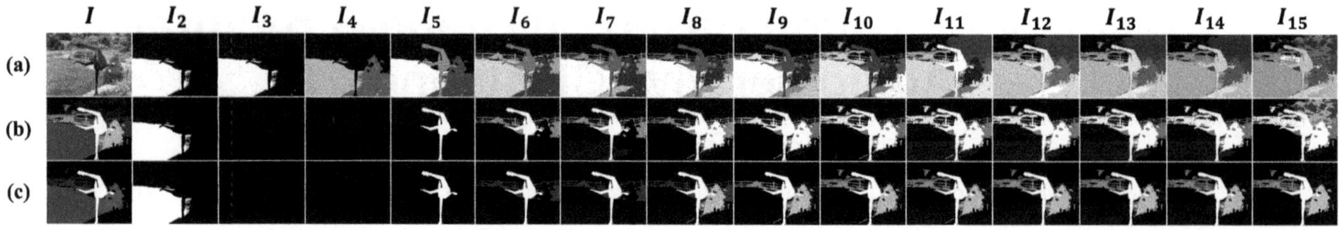

Figure 1. The process of initial saliency computation. (a) shows an input image I and its corresponding fourteen intermediate images $\{I_i|i = 2, 3, ..., 15\}$. (b) is the coarse salient maps M and S_i. (c) gives the initial salient maps *ISM* and S_i'. The first images in the last two rows are obtained according to the rest fourteen images in the same row.

2. GSAC-BASED SALIENCY DETECTION

In this paper, a graph-based algorithm, namely graph-structural agglomerative clustering (GSAC), which can handle the images at multi-levels and produce a hierarchy of regions, is employed for saliency detection. The proposed saliency detection method based on GSAC is a coarse-to-fine process and consists of three stages, i.e. graph construction and clustering, initial saliency computation, and saliency refinement.

2.1 Graph Construction and Clustering

Given an input image $I \in \mathbf{R}^{m*n}$, we construct a weighted directed graph from I, which is denoted as $G = (V, E, \mathbf{W})$, where V is a set of nodes, E is a set of edges connecting nodes, and $\mathbf{W}$ is a weighted adjacency matrix on edges.

In this work, the image I is firstly segmented into N regions or superpixels by using SLIC algorithm [20], which constitute the node set V of Graph G. The descriptor of a region R, denoted as f_R, is defined as its average colors in L*a*b color space and the average spatial coordinates. Each component of f_R is further normalized to the same range [0, 1]. The distance $dist(v_i, v_j)$ between nodes v_i, v_j is defined as the Euclidean distance of their descriptors.

For $\forall v_i \in V$, define K directed edges pointing from node v_i to its K nearest nodes. The edges of all nodes constitute the edge set E of graph G.

Let $\mathcal{N}_i^K$ be the K-nearest neighbor node set of v_i. The weighted adjacency matrix $\mathbf{W} = [w_{ij}]^{N\times N}$ is constructed as follows:

$$w_{ij} = \begin{cases} \exp\left(-\frac{dist(v_i, v_j)^2}{\sigma^2}\right), & if\ v_j \in \mathcal{N}_i^K \\ 0 \quad , & otherwise \end{cases} \tag{1}$$

where σ^2 controls the strength of the weight.

In this work, we set $\sigma^2 = \left[\sum_{i=1}^{N} \sum_{v_j \in \mathcal{N}_i^3} dist(v_i, v_j)^2\right]/(3N)$, $N = 800$, and $K = 30$. Here, σ^2 is set to the geometric mean of weights of the 3 shortest edges of each of N nodes, as done in [21].

Given a graph $G = (V, E, \mathbf{W})$ with N nodes, we present the process of graph clustering used in this work as follows. Each node and its nearest neighbor form a cluster, so there will be N clusters and each cluster has two nodes. Two clusters are merged if they share some nodes. This merging process is iteratively conducted until no more clusters can be merged. As a result, L clusters $RS = \{R_1, R_2, ... , R_L\}$ are obtained and L is much less than N. With the help of graph G, the next step is to cluster the regions in RS by using an agglomerative clustering strategy with the maximum incremental path integral criterion [21] until only two clusters are left. The detail of the clustering process can be found in Reference [21].

And after agglomerative clustering, $L - 1$ intermediate images are produced with the number of clusters from 2 to L. Through experiments, we find that the performance of the method varies little when the number of clusters is larger than 15. Therefore, we compute the salient map by using the last fourteen intermediate images, denoted as $\{I_i|i = 2,3, ... ,15\}$, where i is the number of clusters in the intermediate image.

2.2 Initial Saliency Computation

Given an image I (see the leftmost image in Figure 1(a)), the agglomerative clustering algorithm is used to generate its fourteen intermediate images $\{I_i|i = 2,3, ... ,15\}$ (see the right 14 images in Figure 1(a)). The initial salient map (ISM) of I will be computed based on these intermediate images.

In general, most portions of the image boundaries connect with the background, while none or very small portions of the boundary connect with the salient objects. Therefore, the boundary connectivity of a region in the intermediate images can reflect its saliency in the image. A robust boundary connectivity measure of a region R in I_i can be defined as follows [15]:

$$C_i(R) = \frac{\#(R \cap B)}{\sqrt{\text{area}(R)}} \tag{2}$$

where B is the set of image boundary pixels, $\#(X)$ is the number of elements in set X, and $\text{area}(R)$ is the area of region R.

After getting all regions' boundary connectivity values of I_i, the regional saliency of region R in I_i are computed by

$$S_i(R) = \frac{\max(C_i) - C_i(R)}{\max(C_i) - \min(C_i)} \tag{3}$$

where $\max(X)$ and $\min(X)$ are the operators to compute the maximum and minimum of set X, respectively.

Since none or very small portions of the salient objects connect with image boundaries, if R belongs to salient objects, $C_i(R)$ should be small. Therefore, in this work, the regional saliencies of the regions are set as 0 if their boundary connectivity measures are larger than 2, and we just use the boundary connectivity values which are equal or less than 2 to compute the maximum and minimum in Eq. (3). Further, since too small objects in an image cannot be salient, the regional saliencies of the regions are also set as 0 if their areas are less than $\frac{W\times H}{300}$, where W and H are the width and height of the image. The right 14 images in Figure 1(b) are the intermediate salient maps S_i of the intermediate images I_i ($i = 2,3, ... ,15$).

Then S_i of the intermediate images I_i ($i = 2,3, ... ,15$) are combined to form the coarse salient map M (see the leftmost image in Figure 1(b)) of I as follows:

$$M = \sum_{i=2}^{15} \frac{S_i^2}{\sqrt{i-1}} \tag{4}$$

$$M = \frac{M - \min(M)}{\max(M) - \min(M)} \tag{5}$$

According to the leftmost image in Figure 1(b), although the salient object has been highlighted, its contrast to the background is not strong. We should further enhance the salient objects.

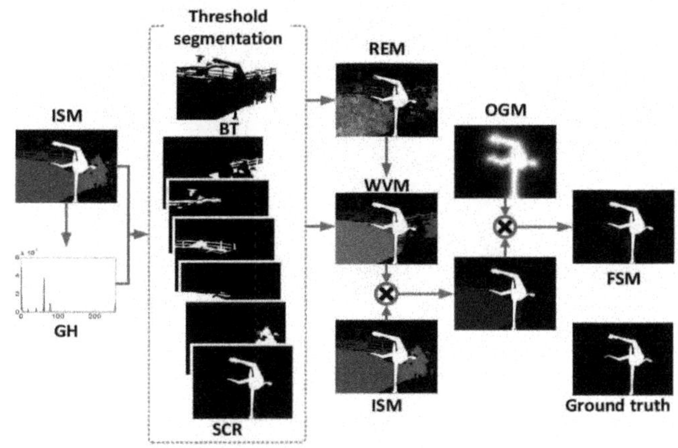

Figure 2. The process of saliency refinement.

In Eq. (3), $S_i(R)$, i.e. the regional saliency of region R, is computed by using only the boundary connectivity measure $C_i(R)$. Actually, the saliency of a region is also decided by some other factors (e.g. some priors) in original image. Suppose that these factors are represented by a guard map GM, with which a weight w_R and the weighted regional saliency $S'_i(R)$ of region R are computed as follows:

$$w_R = \frac{\sum_{(x,y)\in R} GM(x,y)}{\#(R)} \tag{6}$$

$$S'_i(R) = w_R S_i(R) \tag{7}$$

Then we replace S_i with S'_i in Eq. (4) and Eq. (5) to compute the initial salient map of the original image I, denoted as ISM.

The guard map GM can be some priors of the original image or a salient map computed by existing approaches. In this work, we use the coarse salient map M as the guard map GM to compute the ISM. Figure 1(c) shows the weighted saliencies of intermediate images (the right 14 images) and the ISM (the leftmost one).

2.3 Saliency Refinement

To further suppress the saliencies of background, we refine the initial salient map by employing the sparse coding technique and the object-bias prior. The whole process is given in Figure 2.

From the gray histogram in Figure 2, we can find that the gray values in the initial salient maps (ISMs) are sparse and in most case the backgrounds have small gray values. We segment the initial salient map into several regions by using multiple thresholds and take the region with smallest gray value as background templates. The rest regions except the background templates constitute the salient candidate regions. The regional descriptors of the superpixels constituting the background templates are employed to form a dictionary **A**, which is used for sparse coding the regional descriptors of superpixels in SCR.

Obviously, a region with large reconstruction error of sparse coding based on the dictionary **A** is more likely to be the foreground. The coefficient α_i of a salient candidate regional descriptor f_{R_i} is first computed by solving the following optimization problem [11]:

$$\alpha_i = \operatorname{argmin}_{\alpha_i} \left\| f_{R_i} - \mathbf{A}\alpha_i \right\|_2^2 + \gamma |\alpha_i|_1 \tag{8}$$

where the regularization coefficient γ is empirically set to 0.01 in this work as done in [11]. Then the sparse reconstruction error of f_{R_i} is computed as

$$\varepsilon_i = \left\| f_{R_i} - \mathbf{A}\alpha_i \right\|_2^2 \tag{9}$$

After processing all salient candidate regional descriptors, a reconstruction error map can be obtained. To make the saliency in a salient candidate region uniform, we assign all pixels in this region with the median value of reconstruction errors belonging to it, and get a weighted value map, WVM. Then we multiply ISM by WVM to get a new salient map, in which the background is further suppressed.

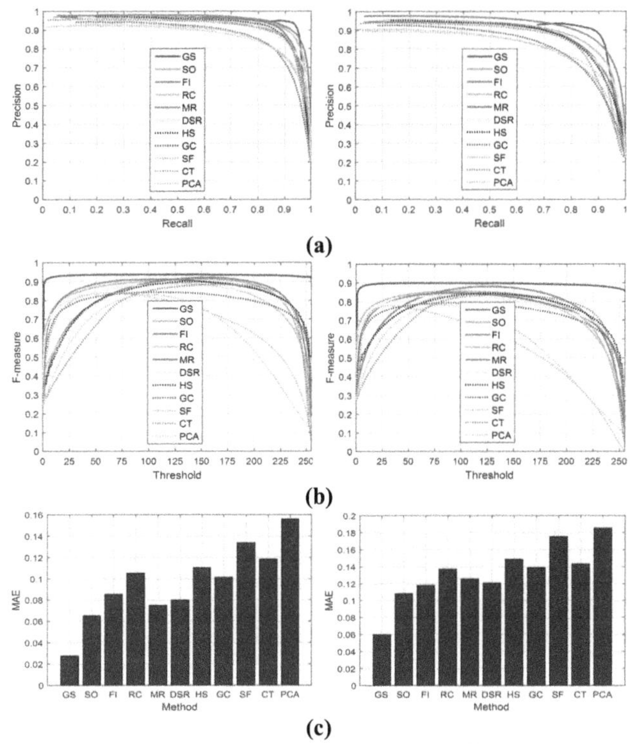

Figure 3. Results of all test approaches on two datasets, i.e. ASD (left column), and MSRA10K (right column), in terms of precision-recall curves (a), F-measures (b), and MAEs (c).

Then we use an object-bias prior to further suppress the background by considering that the pixels are closer to the salient object should be more important. We first binarize the new salient map with a threshold obtained by Otsu's algorithm, then get a distance map DM by performing the distance transformation on the binary image. The object-bias Gaussian map OGM is computed by

$$OGM(x,y) = \exp\left(-\frac{DM(x,y)}{\sigma^2}\right) \tag{10}$$

where the variance σ^2 is set to 15 in this work. With OGM, the final salient map FSM is computed by

$$FSM(x,y) = ISM(x,y) \times WVM(x,y) \times OGM(x,y) \tag{11}$$

3. Experiments

We evaluate the proposed method on two benchmark datasets: ASD [5] and MSRA10K [9]. ASD dataset [5] contains 1,000 images which is widely used in almost all approaches, and the images in this dataset are relatively simple. MSRA10K dataset [9] contain 10,000 images which is ten times bigger than ASD dataset. As done by other approaches [14, 15], the precision-recall (PR) curve, $F_{0.3}$-measure, and mean absolute error (MAE) are used as metrics to evaluate the performance of different saliency detection methods.

We evaluate the proposed method, denoted as GS, with comparison with ten state-of-the-art saliency detection approaches, i.e. SO [15], FI [18], RC [9], MR [12], DSR [11], HS [17], GC [16], SF [10], CT [14], PCA [13]. In this work, the source codes of these state-of-the-art approaches released by the authors are used for test.

Figure 3 gives the PR curves, F-measures, and MAEs of the proposed method and other state-of-the-art approaches. Figure 3(a) shows the PR curves of different approaches. From these curves, it

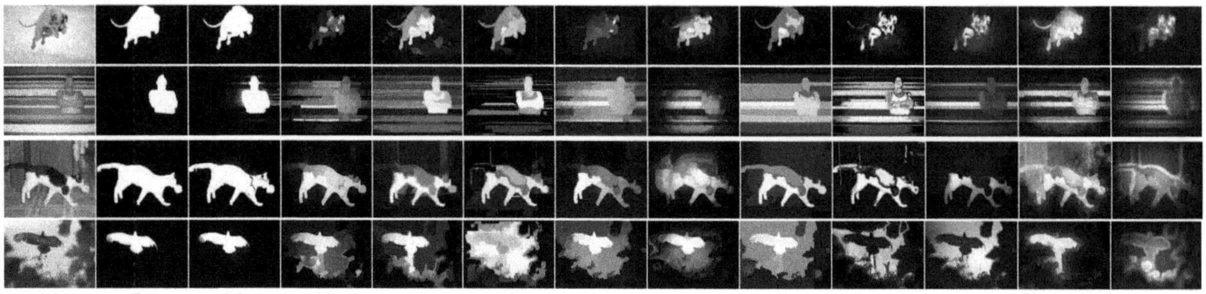

(a) (b) (c) (d) (e) (f) (g) (h) (i) (j) (k) (l) (m)

Figure 4. Visual Comparisons of different saliency detection approaches on two datasets. (a) Original images, (b) Ground truth, (c) GS (the proposed method), (d) SO, (e) FI, (f) RC, (g) MR, (h) DSR, (i) HS, (j) GC, (k) SF, (l) CT, (m) PCA.

can be seen that the least recall of the proposed method on ASD/MSRA10K dataset is 0.82/0.67, which is much larger than those of the other approaches. The precisions of all approaches drop when their recalls exceed some thresholds. The threshold of the proposed method on ASD/MSRA10K dataset is about 0.9/0.85, which is much larger than the thresholds of other approaches, and the precisions of the proposed method drop much faster than those of other approaches. Figure 3(b) shows the F-measures curves of different approaches, which illustrates the changing of F-measures with the changing of the thresholds. According to these curves, when the threshold increases from 0 to 250, the F-measures of the proposed method are always the largest and change least among all of these approaches. Figure 3(c) gives the MAEs of different approaches, from which it can be seen that the proposed method gets the smallest MAEs on two datasets. These demonstrate that the saliencies detected by the proposed method have higher contrast between salient objects and backgrounds, and are more uniform compared with other approaches, and are closer to the ground truth than those computed by other approaches.

We also provide the visual comparisons of different saliency detection approaches in Figure 4. As it can be seen, the proposed method produces nearly uniform salient maps, which are much closer to the ground truth than other approaches. For some simple background images, although the salient object has similar color with background, the proposed method still can get the salient maps nearly matching the ground truth, while some approaches (such as SO, SF) cannot highlight the salient object from the background, as shown in the 1th rows in Figure 4. For complex background images, the proposed method can effectively suppress the background and highlight the salient object, while some approaches (such as SO, DSR) almost lose the salient objects in their salient maps, as shown in the 2th row in Figure 4. These results further demonstrate the effectiveness of the proposed method.

4. Conclusion

In this paper, a novel saliency detection method based on graph-structural agglomerative clustering has been successfully proposed. This method can obtains a highly uniform salient map with high contrast which can nearly match the ground truth. The process of the initial salient map computation can well simulate the coarse-to-fine mechanism of human's visual attention and therefore can get a good initial salient map. The reconstruction errors of sparse coding and object-bias prior can effectively enhance the salient object and suppress the background. The proposed method outperforms ten state-of-the-art approaches on two benchmark datasets.

5. ACKNOWLEDGMENTS

This work was supported in part by the Natural Science Foundation of China under Grants 61350004 and 61472102, and in part by the Fundamental Research Funds for the Central Universities under Grants HIT.NSRIF.2013091 and HIT.HSS.201407.

6. References

[1] Jung, C. and Kim, C. A unified spectral-domain approach for saliency detection and its application to automatic object segmentation. *TIP*, 21(3): 1272-1283, 2012.

[2] Alexe, B., Deselaers, T. and Ferrari, V. What is an object? *CVPR*, 2010.

[3] Gao, Y., Wang, M., Zha, Z., Shen, J., Li, X., Wu, X. Visual-textual joint relevance learning for tag-based social image search. *TIP*, 22(1): 363-376, 2013.

[4] Rosin, P. A simple method for detecting salient regions. *PR*, 42(11): 2363-2371, 2009.

[5] Achanta, R., Hemami, S., Estrada, F., Susstrunk, S. Frequency-tuned salient region detection. *CVPR*, 2009.

[6] Liu, T., Yuan, Z., Sun, J., Wang, J., Zheng, N., Tang, X., Shum, H. Learning to detect a salient object. *TPAMI*, 33(2): 353-367, 2011.

[7] Jiang, R. and Crookes, D. Visual saliency estimation through manifold learning. *AAAI*, 2012.

[8] Jiang, R. and Crookes, D. Deep Salience: Visual salience modeling via deep belief propagation. *AAAI*, 2014.

[9] Cheng, M., Mitra, N., Huang, X., Torr, P., Hu, S. Global contrast based salient region detection. *TPAMI*, 37(3): 569-582, 2015.

[10] Perazzi, F., Krahenbuhl, P., Pritch, Y., Hornung, A. Saliency filters: contrast based filtering for salient region detection. *CVPR*, 2012.

[11] Li, X., Lu, H., Zhang, L., Ruan, X., Yang, M. Saliency detection via dense and sparse reconstruction. *ICCV*, 2013.

[12] Yang, C., Zhang, L., Lu, H. , Ruan, X., Yang, M. Saliency detection via graph-based manifold ranking. *CVPR*, 2013.

[13] Margolin, R., Tal, A. and Zelnik, M. What makes a patch distinct? *CVPR*, 2013.

[14] Kim, J., Han, D., Tai, Y., Kim, J. Salient region detection via high-dimensional color transform. *CVPR*, 2014.

[15] Zhu, W., Liang, S., Wei, Y., Sun. J. Saliency optimization from robust background detection. *CVPR*, 2014.

[16] Cheng, M., Warrell, J., Lin, W., Zheng,S., Vineet, V., Crook, N. Efficient salient region detection with soft image abstraction. *ICCV*, 2013.

[17] Yan, Q., Xu, L., Shi, J., Jia, j. Hierarchical saliency detection. *CVPR*, 2013.

[18] Jiang, H., Wang, J., Yuan, Z., Wu, Y., Zheng, N., Li, S. Salient object detection: a discriminative regional feature integration approach. *CVPR*, 2013.

[19] Felzenszwalb, P. and Huttenlocher, D. Efficient graph-based image segmentation. *IJCV*, 59(2): 169-181, 2004.

[20] Achanta, R., Shaji, A., Smith, K., Lucchi, A., Fua, P., Susstrunk, S. SLIC superpixels compared to state-of-the-art superpixel methods. *TPAMI*, 34(11): 2274-2282, 2012.

[21] Zhang, W., Zhao, D. and Wang, X. Agglomerative clustering via maximum incremental path integral. *PR* 46(11): 3056-3065, 2013.

Detecting Salient Objects via Spatial and Appearance Compactness Hypotheses

Ping Hu
University of Chinese Academy of Sciences
Beijing, China
huping13@mails.ucas.ac.cn

Weiqiang Wang
University of Chinese Academy of Sciences
Beijing, China
wqwang@ucas.ac.cn

Ke Lu
University of Chinese Academy of Sciences
Beijing, China
luk@ucas.ac.cn

ABSTRACT

Object-level saliency detection has been attracting a lot of attention,due to its potential enhancement in many high-level vision tasks. Many previous methods are based on the contrast hypothesis which regards the regions with high contrast in a certain context as salient. Although the contrast hypothesis is valid in many cases, it cannot handle some difficult cases. To make up for the weakness of contrast hypothesis, we propose a novel compactness hypothesis which assumes salient regions are more compact than background spatially and in appearance. Based on compactness hypotheses, we implement an effective object-level saliency detection method, which is demonstrated to be effective even in difficult cases. In addition, we present an adaptive multiple saliency maps fusion framework which can automatically select saliency maps of high quality according to three quality assessment rules. We evaluate the proposed method on four benchmark datasets and the comparable performance as the state-of-the-art methods has been achieved.

Categories and Subject Descriptors

I.2.10 [**Artificial Intelligence**]: Vision and Scene Understanding, Perceptual Reasoning; I.4.10 [**Image Processing and Computer Vision**]: Image Representation

General Terms

Algorithms, Performance, Design, Experimentation.

Keywords

Salient object, Saliency detection, Compactness

1. INTRODUCTION

Human visual system tends to preselect the most informative regions in a scene naturally. Accordingly, to model this mechanism, saliency detection has become an active research branch of computer area. The main task of saliency detection is to locate salient objects accurately, and this will paly an important role in many high-level vision tasks, e.g., image compression, image cropping, image retrieval, object tracking etc.

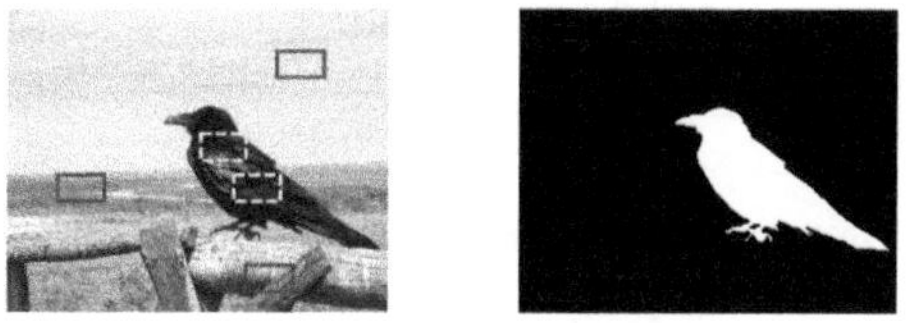

(a) (b)

Figure 1: The example of salient objects and groundtruth.

According to their mechanism, saliency detection methods can be categorized into the top-down and bottom-up approaches. The top-down methods are task-driven and the supervised learning is usually utilized. The bottom-up methods are data-driven, which relies on various visual low-level features and assumptions. Many saliency detection methods have been proposed and most of them can be theoretically traced to feature integration theory [1], which indicates that human vision is a process from low-level feature extraction to feature integration and object representation. Inspired by the observation that salient regions present high contrast in a certain context, Ma and Zhang [2] compute the center-surrounding color difference between each pixel and its neighbors directly. Harel *et al.* [3] propose a graph-based visual saliency model with Markovian approach. Goferman *et al.* [4] define the saliency as the contrast between a patch and its most similar K patches. Jiang *et al.* [5] integrate the region features of multi-scale segmentation by supervised learning. Fu *et al.* [6] propose a graph-based merging scheme to reassemble regions based on their shared contour strength. Taking global contrast in account, Cheng *et al.* [7] compute the uniqueness and spatial distribution based on color and position information. Perazzi *et al.* [8] analyze the saliency via the uniqueness and spatial distribution of color. Kim *et al.* [9] separate the salient region from background with a linear framework in a high-dimensional color space. Lu *et al.* [10] describe each region by a set of features and a large-margin framework is adopted to learn the weights.

In this paper we mainly focus on the object-level saliency detection in a bottom-up way. As shown in Figure 1, we found that the salient regions of a same object (yellow dash rectangles) have similar appearance and are spatially close to each other. For non-salient regions (blue solid rectangles), even if they also have similar appearance, they are loosely scattered in the images [11]. Based on this observation,

MM'15, October 26–30, 2015, Brisbane, Australia.
© 2015 ACM. ISBN 978-1-4503-3459-4/15/10 ...$15.00.
DOI: http://dx.doi.org/10.1145/2733373.2806288.

we propose an effective saliency detection method based on *spatial compactness* and *appearance compactness* hypotheses. The *spatial compactness* is intuitively measured by the appearance-similarity-weighted spatial distance between a given region and others. However, the spatial compactness hypothesis cannot work well when background regions are composed of some isolated regions which also show great spatial compactness or multiple similar salient objects are located far away from each other. At this moment, the *appearance compactness* is effective to characterize the saliency of a region. The *appearance compactness* is measured by the spatial-similarity-weighted appearance distance between a given region and others.These two hypotheses can nicely complement each others. Moreover, by combining the proposed compactness hypotheses with the center-surrounding hypothesis, the proposed method can achieve a better performance.

2. THE PROPOSED METHOD

In the proposed method, a given image is converted into CIE Lab color space and is segmented into a group of superpixels by the linear iterative clustering (SLIC) algorithm [12]. For each superpixel $v_i, i = 1, 2, \cdots, N$, where N is the number of superpixels, $\mathbf{r}_i$ and $\mathbf{p}_i$ denote the average color value and spatial coordinates of all pixels in it. Then, the spatial compactness value and the appearance compactness value are computed in each color channel as well as the whole color space to generate eight saliency maps. Finally, the candidates are integrated into the final saliency map based on their quality scores. In the following subsections, we will elaborate each step of the proposed method.

2.1 From Compactness to Saliency

The compactness is defined by the unified form of linear combination of distances weighted by similarity. Concretely, for computing the spatial compactness values, the spatial distance is weighted by the appearance similarity. For appearance compactness, the appearance distance is weighted by the spatial similarity.

When computing the distance factor, the appearance distance between superpixels i and j is measured by the Euclidean distance for individual channel and the whole color space, i.e.,

$$D_r(r_i^c, r_j^c) = ||r_i^c - r_j^c||_2. \tag{1}$$

where $c \in \{L, a, b, Lab\}$. When $c = Lab$, the distance is computed in the whole color space. Additionally, the spatial distance $D_p(\mathbf{p}_i, \mathbf{p}_j)$ between superpixels i and j is the coordinates distance and is measured by the infinite norm, i.e.,

$$D_p(\mathbf{p}_i, \mathbf{p}_j) = ||\mathbf{p}_i - \mathbf{p}_j||_\infty. \tag{2}$$

The two kinds of similarities, which act as the weight factor, are computed according to the Gaussian functions, i.e.,

$$W_r(r_i^c, r_j^c) = \frac{1}{\Omega_r^c} exp(-\frac{D_r(r_i^c, r_j^c)^2}{2(\sigma_r^c)^2}), \tag{3}$$

$$W_p(\mathbf{p}_i, \mathbf{p}_j) = \frac{1}{\Omega_p} exp(-\frac{D_p(\mathbf{p}_i, \mathbf{p}_j)^2}{2\sigma_p^2}), \tag{4}$$

where Ω_r^c and Ω_p are the normalization factors that make sure $\Sigma_{j=1}^N W_r(r_i^c, r_j^c)$ and $\Sigma_{j=1}^N W_p(\mathbf{p}_i, \mathbf{p}_j)$ to be 1. The parameters $\sigma_r = \frac{\max_{i,j} D_r(r_i^c, r_j^c)}{3}$ and $\sigma_p = \frac{\max_{i,j} D_p(\mathbf{p}_i, \mathbf{p}_j)}{3}$ adaptably control the strength of the weights.

2.1.1 Spatial compactness

In order to highlight the compact regions, we define the spatial compactness as the reciprocal of the sum of appearance-weighted spatial distances between current superpixel and all other superpixels. The spatial compactness of superpixel v_i for color channel c is defined as,

$$\theta_s^c(v_i) = \frac{1}{\Sigma_{j=1}^N D_p(\mathbf{p}_i, \mathbf{p}_j) W_r(r_i^c, r_j^c)} \tag{5}$$

where $C \in \{L, a, b, Lab\}$, $D_p(\mathbf{p}_i, \mathbf{p}_j)$ is the spatial distance between superpixel v_i and v_j, defined in Eq.(2), $W_r(r_i^c, r_j^c)$ is the appearance similarity weight defined in Eq.(3).

2.1.2 Appearance compactness

Appearance compactness is defined as the sum of the spatial-weighted appearance distance between current superpixel and all other superpixels. The appearance compactness of superpixel v_i for color channel c is defined as,

$$\theta_a^c(v_i) = \Sigma_{j=1}^N D_r(r_i^c, r_j^c) W_p(\mathbf{p}_i, \mathbf{p}_j), \tag{6}$$

where $c \in \{L, a, b, Lab\}$, $D_r(r_i^c, r_j^c)$ is the appearance similarity for color channel c defined by Eq.(1), and $W_p(\mathbf{p}_i, \mathbf{p}_j)$ is the spatial similarity weight defined in Eq.(4).

2.1.3 Candidate saliency maps

To reduce the impact of noises and improve the homogeneity of saliency maps, we employ a weighted sum of compactness values to define the saliency of superpixel v_i, i.e.,

$$S_h^c(v_i) = \Sigma_{j=1}^N f_j^c W_r(r_i^c, r_j^c) \theta_h^c(v_j) \tag{7}$$

where $c \in \{L, a, b, Lab\}$ denote the color channel and $h \in \{a, s\}$ denote the appearance compactness or the spatial compactness. f_j^c is used to suppress noises or small-scale high-contrast patterns in the background, and it is evaluated by

$$f_j^c = exp(-\frac{\delta_j^c}{2\sigma_s^2}), \tag{8}$$

where δ_j^c is the variance of intensities of superpixel v_j and its neighbors when c corresponds to individual channel, σ_s is a predefined parameter.

2.1.4 Further refinement of saliency map

We observe that salient objects are prone to locating in the central region of an image, while background generally shows high similarity to the boundary regions. We define a new metric to measure the confidence for a superpixel v_i to be background. First, let E_T, E_D, E_L, E_R denote four sets of superpixels which locate at top,down,left and right boundaries respectively, and e_i^n denotes the superpixel on the boundary $n \in \{T, D, L, R\}$ which is the most similar to v_i, i.e., $e_i^n = argmin_e ||r_i - e||, e \in E_n$. Then the similarity between superpixel v_i and a given boundary region is measured by

$$R^n(v_i) = exp(-\frac{||r_i - e_i^n||^2}{2\sigma_b^2}), \tag{9}$$

where σ_b is a predefined parameter and it is set as 0.125 in our system. Finally, the confidence of superpixel as non-background is measured by

$$W_b(v_i) = \prod_{l \in \{T,D,L,R\}} (1 - R^l(v_i)) \quad (10)$$

By incorporating this with Eq.(7), we get a new definition of saliency computation,

$$S_h^c(v_i) = W_b(v_i)\Sigma_{j=1}^{N} f_j^c W^{(r)}(r_i^c, r_j^c)\theta_h^c(v_j). \quad (11)$$

Finally we normalize the obtained saliency values to [0,1] by a linear stretch.

By now, we obtain eight superpixel-level saliency maps generated on different color channel and based on two kinds of compactness measures. Based on these superpixel-level saliency maps, the pixel-level saliency maps can be easily obtained by assigning the saliency value of a superpixel to the pixels within it.

2.2 Ultimate Saliency Map

The final saliency map is generated by integrating the candidate saliency maps above. For each saliency map, the quality evaluation is carried out to measure its reliability. Then those good-quality maps are identified and integrated into the final result.

2.2.1 *Measure the quality of saliency maps*

As discussed above, it is necessary to select out the saliency maps of good quality. In the proposed method, the quality of saliency maps is evaluated mainly based on the following three criterion.

Center-surround ratio: For a given pixel-level saliency map $S(i, j)$, with the center-bias prior, we define the ratio of average saliency value of the central region to that of surrounding region as center-surround ratio, denoted by $\varphi_c(S)$.

Distribution compactness: According to the proposed compactness hypotheses, salient regions are spatially compact. So pixels with high saliency values are also expected to be distributed close. We define the distribution compactness of a saliency map $S(i, j)$ as,

$$\varphi_d(S) = (\Sigma_{i=1}^{H}\Sigma_{j=1}^{W} S(i,j)((i-u_i)^2 + (j-u_j)^2))^{-1}, \quad (12)$$

where μ_i and μ_j denote the coordinates of the gravity center of saliency map $S(i, j)$.

Saliency variances: A lot of observations in the experiments show that the saliency map which is well consistent with the ground truth usually has a high pixel variance, so we employ the pixel variance of saliency map as one of assessment criteria, denoted by $\varphi_v(S)$

Based on the three rules above, the assessment score $\psi(S_h^c)$ is defined as,

$$\psi(S) = \frac{\varphi_c(S)}{\max(\varphi_c(S))} + \frac{\varphi_d(S)}{\max(\varphi_d(S))} + \frac{\varphi_v(S)}{\max(\varphi_v(S))}. \quad (13)$$

2.2.2 *Fusion of saliency maps*

After computing the quality evaluation score of each saliency map $S_k(i, j)$, some saliency maps with high scores are identified and then we combine those selected saliency maps in a linear weighted sum form. Formally, the ultimate saliency map is computed by,

$$\hat{S}(i,j) = \sum_k F(\psi(S_k)) \cdot S_k(i,j), \quad (14)$$

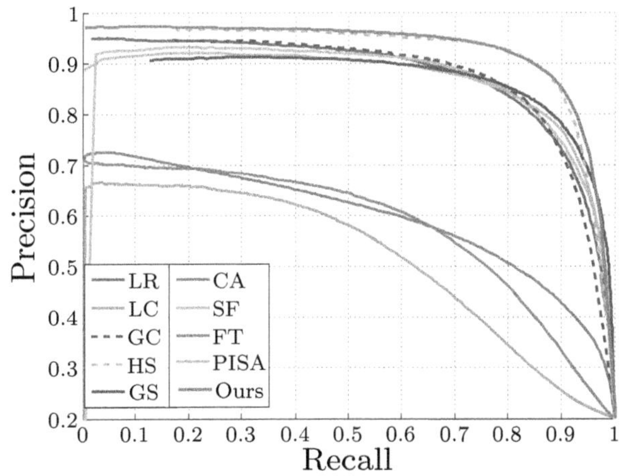

Figure 2: PR curves on the ASD dataset.

where $F(z)$ is a piecewise function and defined as,

$$F(z) = \begin{cases} 0, & z < \eta \max_k \psi(S_k) \\ z, & z \geq \eta \max_k \psi(S_k) \end{cases}, \quad (15)$$

Where $\eta = 0.667$ in our system.

Finally, we linearly stretch the final saliency values $\hat{S}(i, j)$ into [0,1] . It is worth mentioning that, with the fusion framework, we can also easily integrate new features and hypotheses.

3. EXPERIMENT

We evaluate the proposed method on four different types of public datasets. The first one is ASD dataset [13] containing 1000 images and groundtruth masks. The second is SED1 which consists of 100 natural images with single object. The third is SED2 which contains 100 two-object images. The SED1 and SED2 dataset both come from the SED dataset [14]. The last one is the SOD dataset [15],which is a more challenging dataset including complex objects and scenes.

For comparison, we employ the standard precision-recall curve and adaptive threshold F-measure to evaluate the method. With saliency value in the range [0,255], the curve is obtained by generating the binary map when the threshold varies from 0 to 255, and comparing the binary result with the ground-truth. The F-measure is the overall evaluation computed by the weighted harmonic mean of precision and recall,$F = \frac{(1+\beta^2)\cdot Precision\cdot Recall}{\beta^2 \cdot Precision + Recall}$ where β^2 is set to be 0.3. In all the computation of adaptive-threshold F-measure, we employ the adaptive threshold used in [13],which is defined as twice of the mean saliency.

Considering that PR curves are limited since it does not consider the the number of pixel correctly marked as non-salient. For a more balanced comparison, we employ the mean absolute error (MAE) [8] which computes the average per-pixel difference between saliency map S and the binary ground truth G, $MAE = \frac{1}{W \times H}\sum_{x=1}^{W}\sum_{y=1}^{H}|S - G|$, where W and H are again the width and the height of the respective saliency map and ground truth image.

We compare the proposed method with several state-of-the-art algorithms: GS [16], SF [8], CA [4], FT [13], LC [17], LR [18], and the recently proposed HS [19], GC [20], PSIA [21]. All the results are computed on saliency maps provided or generated by the author's code. For quantitative compari-

Table 1: **adaptive threshold F-measure of different methods.**

	SF	CA	FT	LC	LR	HS	GC	Ours
ASD	.83	.58	.59	.54	.81	.85	.83	**.88**
SED1	.69	.60	.48	.49	.59	.75	.73	**.80**
SED2	.73	.55	.65	.60	.50	.71	.67	**.77**
SOD	.50	.51	.40	.39	.46	.57	.50	**.63**

Table 2: MAE of different methods.

	SF	CA	FT	LC	LR	HS	GC	Ours
ASD	.13	.23	.22	.21	.18	.11	.10	**.10**
SED1	.22	.26	.28	.28	.27	**.16**	.18	.19
SED2	.17	.22	.19	.19	.24	.21	.17	**.15**
SOD	.27	.31	.32	.31	.26	.28	.27	**.25**

son, the result of PR-curve on the MSRA-1000 is shown in Figure. 2. The performance comparison based on adaptive threshold F-measure is summarized in Table 1 and MAE is summarized in Table 2. Some visual comparison results are shown in Figure. 3. Both qualitative and quantitative comparison results validate the performance of the proposed method.

4. CONCLUSION

In this paper, we propose a compactness hypothesis which assumes salient regions are more compact than background spatially and in appearance. The comprehensive experiments demonstrate the validation of the proposed compactness hypothesis. By incorporating both the popular background hypothesis and the effective compactness hypothesis, we implement an effective object-level saliency detection method. The experimental results show that the proposed method achieves the competitive performance compared with many art-of-the-state methods.

5. ACKNOWLEDGEMENT

This work was supported by the National Natural Science Foundation of China under Grant No. 61175115, No. 61232013, No. 61271434

6. REFERENCES

[1] A. M. Treisman and G. Gelade, "A feature-integration theory of attention," *Cognitive psychology*, vol. 12, no. 1, pp. 97–136, 1980.

[2] Y.-F. Ma and H.-J. Zhang, "Contrast-based image attention analysis by using fuzzy growing," in *ACM Multimedia*. ACM, 2003, pp. 374–381.

[3] J. Harel, C. Koch, and P. Perona, "Graph-based visual saliency," in *NIPS*, 2006, pp. 545–552.

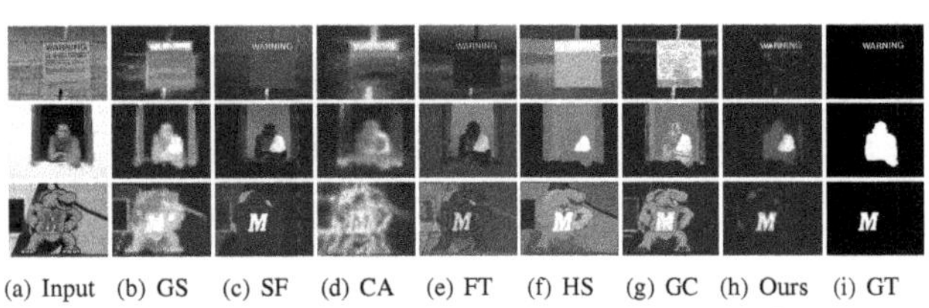

(a) Input (b) GS (c) SF (d) CA (e) FT (f) HS (g) GC (h) Ours (i) GT

Figure 3: Visual comparison of state-of-the-art algorithms with our methods.

[4] S. Goferman, L. Zelnik-Manor, and A. Tal, "Context-aware saliency detection," *TPAMI*, vol. 34, no. 10, pp. 1915–1926, 2012.

[5] H. Jiang, J. Wang, Z. Yuan, Y. Wu, N. Zheng, and S. Li, "Salient object detection: A discriminative regional feature integration approach," in *CVPR*. IEEE, 2013, pp. 2083–2090.

[6] K. Fu, C. Gong, Y. Yun, Y. Li, I. Y.-H. Gu, J. Yang, and J. Yu, "Adaptive multi-level region merging for salient object detection," in *BMVC*, 2014.

[7] M.-M. Cheng, G.-X. Zhang, N. J. Mitra, X. Huang, and S.-M. Hu, "Global contrast based salient region detection," in *CVPR*. IEEE, 2011, pp. 409–416.

[8] F. Perazzi, P. Krahenbuhl, Y. Pritch, and A. Hornung, "Saliency filters: Contrast based filtering for salient region detection," in *CVPR*. IEEE, 2012, pp. 733–740.

[9] J. Kim, D. Han, Y.-W. Tai, and J. Kim, "Salient region detection via high-dimensional color transform," in *CVPR*. IEEE, 2014, pp. 883–890.

[10] S. Lu, V. Mahadevan, and N. Vasconcelos, "Learning optimal seeds for diffusion-based salient object detection," in *CVPR*. IEEE, 2014, pp. 2790–2797.

[11] C. Zhang and W. Wang, "Object-level saliency detection based on spatial compactness assumption," in *ICIP*, 2013, pp. 2475–2479.

[12] R. Achanta, A. Shaji, K. Smith, A. Lucchi, P. Fua, and S. Süsstrunk, "Slic superpixels," *Ecole Polytechnique Fédéral de Lausssanne (EPFL), Tech. Rep*, vol. 2, p. 3, 2010.

[13] R. Achanta, S. Hemami, F. Estrada, and S. Susstrunk, "Frequency-tuned salient region detection," in *CVPR*. IEEE, 2009, pp. 1597–1604.

[14] S. Alpert, M. Galun, R. Basri, and A. Brandt, "Image segmentation by probabilistic bottom-up aggregation and cue integration," in *CVPR*. IEEE, 2007, pp. 1–8.

[15] D. Martin, C. Fowlkes, D. Tal, and J. Malik, "A database of human segmented natural images and its application to evaluating segmentation algorithms and measuring ecological statistics," in *ICCV*, 2001, vol. 2, pp. 416–423.

[16] Y. Wei, F. Wen, W. Zhu, and J. Sun, "Geodesic saliency using background priors," in *ECCV*. Springer, 2012, pp. 29–42.

[17] Y. Zhai and M. Shah, "Visual attention detection in video sequences using spatiotemporal cues," in *ACM Multimedia*. ACM, 2006, pp. 815–824.

[18] X. Shen and Y. Wu, "A unified approach to salient object detection via low rank matrix recovery," in *CVPR*. IEEE, 2012, pp. 853–860.

[19] Q. Yan, L. Xu, J. Shi, and J. Jia, "Hierarchical saliency detection," in *CVPR*. IEEE, 2013, pp. 1155–1162.

[20] M.-M. Cheng, J. Warrell, W.-Y. Lin, S. Zheng, V. Vineet, and N. Crook, "Efficient salient region detection with soft image abstraction," in *ICCV*. IEEE, 2013, pp. 1529–1536.

[21] K. Shi, K. Wang, J. Lu, and L. Lin, "Pisa: Pixelwise image saliency by aggregating complementary appearance contrast measures with spatial priors," in *CVPR*. IEEE, 2013, pp. 2115–2122.

A Probabilistic Approach for Image Retrieval Using Descriptive Textual Queries

Yashaswi Verma
CVIT, IIIT Hyderabad, India
yashaswi.verma@research.iiit.ac.in

C. V. Jawahar
CVIT, IIIT Hyderabad, India
jawahar@iiit.ac.in

ABSTRACT

We address the problem of image retrieval using textual queries. In particular, we focus on descriptive queries that can be either in the form of simple captions (e.g., "a brown cat sleeping on a sofa"), or even long descriptions with multiple sentences. We present a probabilistic approach that seamlessly integrates visual and textual information for the task. It relies on linguistically and syntactically motivated mid-level textual patterns (or *phrases*) that are automatically extracted from available descriptions. At the time of retrieval, the given query is decomposed into such phrases, and images are ranked based on their joint relevance with these phrases. Experiments on two popular datasets (UIUC Pascal Sentence and IAPR-TC12 benchmark) demonstrate that our approach effectively retrieves semantically meaningful images, and outperforms baseline methods.

Categories and Subject Descriptors

H.3.3 [**Information Search and Retrieval**]: Retrieval models; I.2.10 [**Computing Methodologies**]: Artificial Intelligence-Vision and Scene Understanding

General Terms

Algorithms, Experimentation, Measurement

Keywords

Image Retrieval, Descriptive Queries, Statistical Models

1. INTRODUCTION

Since the past decade, there has been an outburst of multimedia content, particularly in the form of digital photographs and videos. This has led to new challenges in accurate and efficient archiving as well as retrieval of this content. While most of this content is in free-form, a considerable portion of it is loosely linked with textual meta-data. This has made it feasible to study the associations between the two modalities, which in turn can be useful in semantic analysis of the unannotated visual data [14, 16, 18].

In this work, we address the problem of image retrieval using textual queries. In the conventional text-based image retrieval set-up, a query is usually a set of one or more labels. However, these labels carry minimal linguistic information (such as relationships among labels in terms of action and relative position). As a result, the retrieved images may not match the desired semantics. Hence it comes as a natural choice to develop approaches that can support image retrieval using descriptive queries (e.g., [14]). Such queries inherently carry information about the properties of individual objects as well as relationships among different objects, which can be useful in semantically coherent retrieval.

With this motivation, we present a probabilistic approach for image retrieval using queries that can be either in the form of simple captions, or even long descriptions. Our approach is motivated by the fact that available annotated images (i.e., images with corresponding descriptions) can be harvested to perform retrieval on unannotated images. Assuming a collection of annotated images, our goal is to rank unannotated (test) images based on their semantic similarity with a given query. This similarity seamlessly integrates both visual as well as linguistic aspects. The visual semantics of a test image are approximated based on its relevance with a subset of its most similar images retrieved from the annotated collection. The semantics of the query are determined based on its relevance with the descriptions of the retrieved subset of annotated images as above. One distinctive aspect of our approach is that rather than using either individual words from a query, or the full query as is, images are ranked based on their joint relevance with the *phrases* automatically extracted from the query. These phrases can be thought of as *mid-level textual patterns* corresponding to different visual aspects that may be depicted in an image (e.g., "person near car", "blue airplane", etc.). Experiments validate the intrinsic capacity of our approach in efficiently capturing the semantics of a query, and also demonstrate its superior performance compared to baseline techniques.

2. RELATED WORK

The problem of image retrieval is a well-studied topic in computer vision and multimedia [2]. Two popular streams in this field are: (a) content-based retrieval of images (e.g., retrieve images similar to a given query image [1]), and (b) directly retrieving images based on textual category [7]. In the first setting, the role of semantics of the query image is minimal, and retrieval is usually performed using a standard

MM'15, October 26–30, 2015, Brisbane, Australia
© 2015 ACM. ISBN 978-1-4503-3459-4/15/10 ...$15.00.
DOI: http://dx.doi.org/10.1145/2733373.2806289.

set of visual features (e.g., GIST). In the second setting, semantics get introduced in the form (textual) labels. Due to this, now it is possible to have two visually dissimilar images depicting the same concept.

The task of image retrieval gets semantically richer as more and more language aspects get introduced into the query. E.g., performing image retrieval for queries that are bigger than a single category label (say a pair of labels) may be more meaningful than a single-label query. This now requires to look for images containing all the concepts rather than just one or few of them. Image annotation methods such as [8, 4], that aim at associating a *set* of relevant labels with a given image, can be useful in multi-label image retrieval. However, one limitation of this setting is that it does not capture the relationships among the labels. E.g., the query "person, car" gives no clue about the relative position of "person" and "car". This gives rise to several possibilities, such as a "person" can be sitting inside a "car", standing near a "car", etc. This limitation was addressed in [15], where it was proposed that it is semantically more meaningful to learn complete phrases in the visual domain (e.g., "person sitting in car") rather than individual labels.

A complementary task to image retrieval is to associate an image with semantically meaningful text (say a group of labels, phrases, or captions). In order to get a deeper understanding of image semantics, it is desirable to associate images with language constructs that are even bigger than phrases (such as captions). With this motivation, several approaches have been proposed that are aimed at describing the content of an image, such as [6, 14, 16, 18]. These descriptions are usually in the form of simple captions containing few tens of words. Among these, there are two popular practices: either to *generate* a description given an image [6, 16, 17], or to *retrieve* one from a collection of available descriptions [11, 14, 18]. In the first setting, a new description is generated by combining visual clues using natural language generation (NLG) techniques. Whereas in the second setting, a description is retrieved by using either image-to-image similarity [11] or image-to-text similarity [14, 18]. The approaches that perform image-to-text similarity are cross-modal retrieval approaches, and have also been shown to be useful in retrieving images given a descriptive query. Lately, there have also been some attempts like [9] that address this task using deep learning models.

The motivation of our work is similar to cross-modal image retrieval approaches [14, 18]. However, one limitation of these is that they represent a complete description (query) using a single feature vector. Due to this, it becomes difficult to understand the impact of linguistic aspects of a query. As we will discuss in the next section, our approach in fact makes use of the linguistic structure of a query, and image retrieval is performed based on these properties. This in turn can be helpful in analyzing the interplay among the individual components of the query. Conceptually, our work closely relates with the image description generation methods [6, 17], and demonstrates their application to the image retrieval task given descriptive textual queries.

3. APPROACH

Our approach consists of two phases. In the first (training) phase, we extract a set of textual phrases from the descriptions of training images, and learn the parameters of our model. In the second (retrieval or testing) phase, we extract all the phrases from a given query, and rank the test images based on their joint relevance with these phrases.

3.1 Training Phase

3.1.1 Phrase Extraction

One of the most important components of our approach is to effectively harness the semantic information encoded in the available descriptions. Rather than considering objects, attributes, verb, preposition, etc. from a sentence in a piece-wise manner, we extract relation tuples or phrases [1]. These carry a bigger chunk of information compared to individual components of a sentence. To extract phrases, the available descriptions are parsed using the Stanford CoreNLP toolkit[2]. As suggested in [3], we use "collapsed-ccprocessed-dependencies" that are useful for extracting relations. From the parsed sentence, a set of phrases of the form $(subject, verb)$, $(verb, prep, object)$, etc. are extracted ("*prep*" stands for preposition). In practice, we extract nine types of phrases: $(subject)$, $(object)$, $(attribute, subject)$, $(attribute, object)$, $(subject, verb)$, $(object, verb)$, $(subject, prep, object)$, $(object, prep, object)$, and $(verb, prep, object)$. We consider two set-ups while extracting phrases: without synonyms and with synonyms. In the first set-up, we consider all the extracted phrases as is. However, in the second set-up, we consider synonyms by expanding each noun (object/subject) up to at most three hyponym levels using its WordNet synsets. This results into replacing a noun with its most popular synonym (e.g., replacing "pug" with "dog", "Ferrari" with "car", etc.).

3.1.2 Phrase Relevance Prediction Model

Let $\mathcal{T}_r$ be the collection of training images that are annotated with descriptions. As discussed above, we extract phrases from all the available descriptions, and then map each description to a set of phrases. Let $\mathcal{Y}$ denote the collection of all the extracted phrases. Then the training data takes the form $\mathcal{T}_r = \{(I_i, Y_i)\}$, where $Y_i \subseteq \mathcal{Y}$ is the set of phrases corresponding to image I_i. Each image is represented using a set of n features $\{f_1, \ldots, f_n\}$ such as colour histograms, texture features, etc. For parameter learning, the training set $\mathcal{T}_r$ is divided into disjoint training and validation sets $\mathcal{T}$ and $\mathcal{V}$ respectively. Now, given an image $I \in \mathcal{V}$, we compute the relevance of a phrase $y_i \in \mathcal{Y}$ with it using their joint probability score $P(y_i, I)$ defined as ([8]):

$$P(y_i, I) = \sum_{J \in \mathcal{T}_I^K} P_{\mathcal{T}}(J) P_{\mathcal{F}}(I|J) P_{\mathcal{Y}}(y_i|J) \quad (1)$$

Here, $\mathcal{T}_I^K \subset \mathcal{T}$ is the set of K nearest neighbours of I from $\mathcal{T}$. These neighbours are determined based on distance of I from the images in $\mathcal{T}$ in the feature space. Let J be an image from $\mathcal{T}$, then distance between I and J is defined as:

$$D_{I,J} = w_1 d^1_{I,J} + \ldots + w_n d^n_{I,J} = \mathbf{w} \cdot \mathbf{d}_{I,J} \quad (2)$$

Here $d^1_{I,J}, \ldots, d^n_{I,J}$ are distances between the corresponding features $f_1, \ldots, f_n$ of both the images computed using some specific distance metric (e.g., Manhattan or Euclidean distance), $w_1, \ldots, w_n$ are non-negative real-valued weights denoting linear distance combination, and $D_{I,J}$ is the actual distance between the two images I and J.

[1]For simplicity, we shall refer "relation tuples" as "phrases".
[2]http://nlp.stanford.edu/software/corenlp.shtml

As shown in Eq. 1, there are three components in our definition of joint probability. The first component $P_{\mathcal{T}}(J)$ denotes the probability of picking an image J from $\mathcal{T}_I^K$. Assuming that all the neighbouring images are equally likely, this is modeled as a uniform prior; i.e., $P_{\mathcal{T}}(J) = \frac{1}{K}$. The second component $P_{\mathcal{F}}$ denotes the likelihood of *seeing* image I given its neighbouring image J, and is defined as a function of distance between the two images:

$$P_{\mathcal{F}}(I|J) = \frac{\exp(-D_{I,J})}{\sum_{J' \in \mathcal{T}_I^K} \exp(-D_{I,J'})} \quad (3)$$

The above definition signifies that the weights will decay smoothly with distance, which in turn helps in adjusting the distance during parameter learning.

The last component in Eq. 1 denotes the probability of seeing the phrase y_i given image J, and is defined as [4]:

$$P_{\mathcal{Y}}(y_i|J) = \frac{\mu\delta_{y_i,J} + N_i}{\mu + N} = \frac{\nu\delta_{y_i,J} + (N_i/N)}{\nu + 1} \quad (4)$$

Here, $\nu = \frac{\mu}{N} \geq 0$ is a smoothing weight, N_i denotes Google count[3] of the phrase y_i, and N denotes the total Google count of all the phrases. Since our approach is data-driven, and the number of phrases is usually large, it is difficult to predict their general behaviour using only the available data. Hence, Google counts help in estimating the statistical behaviour of different phrases.

Let Y_J^t be the phrases in Y_J that are of the same *form* as that of y_i (e.g., say both are $(subject, verb)$). Then, $\delta_{y_i,J}$ in the above equation is given by:

$$\delta_{y_i,J} = U_{sim}(y_i, Y_J^t) = \max_{y_j \in Y_J^t} Z_{sim}(y_i, y_j) \quad (5)$$

where $Z_{sim}(y_i, y_j) \in [0, 1]$ denotes similarity between the phrases y_i and y_j. This is computed using the procedure described in [17], which is based on WordNet based similarity between the individual terms of the two phrases. The above definition denotes that if the phrase y_i is present in the ground-truth phrases of J, then $\delta_{y_i,J} = 1$. Otherwise, it will be the similarity score of y_i with the closest matching phrase in Y_J^t. Such a definition helps in considering semantic interdependence among phrases while predicting phrase relevance rather than just presence/absence.

From Eq. 1, we can observe that there are two types of parameters in our phrase relevance model: distance weights w_i and smoothing weight ν. Given an image $I \in \mathcal{V}$, and $Y_I \subset \mathcal{Y}$ being the phrases extracted from its descriptions, our goal is to learn the above parameters such that (a) the probability of predicting any phrase $y_j \notin Y_I$ should be small, and (b) the probability of predicting a phrase $y_i \in Y_I$ should be more than that of predicting any other phrase $y_j \notin Y_I$. With this goal, our loss function is defined as:

$$e = \sum_{I,y_j} P(y_j, I) + \lambda \sum_{(I,y_i,y_j) \in \mathcal{M}} \eta_{ij}(P(y_j, I) - P(y_i, I)) \quad (6)$$

where $\lambda > 0$ takes care of the trade-off between the two competing terms, $\eta_{ij} = 1 - Z_{sim}(y_i, y_j)$, and $\mathcal{M}$ is the set of triples (I, y_i, y_j) (with $y_i \in Y_I$ and $y_j \notin Y_I$) that violate the second constraint as discussed above. The significance of η_{ij} is that if two phrases are semantically similar (e.g., "bus on road" and "coach on highway"), then the penalty for giving higher score to the phrase not present in the ground-truth (y_j) should be small, and vice-versa. To optimize the parameters, we use a stochastic gradient descent method.

[3]The number of approximate search results obtained using Google search for an exact match query.

3.2 Retrieval Phase

In the previous section, we described the model for predicting the relevance of a phrase with a given image. This is done by combining the similarity of the given image with available images, and similarity of the given phrase with those in the ground-truth of available images. Here we describe how this model can be used for performing retrieval on an unannotated image collection given a descriptive query.

Let $\mathcal{T}_e$ be the collection of (unannotated) test images. These images constitute our retrieval set. To perform retrieval on this set, we make use of the available images with descriptions. Note that now we consider all the samples in $\mathcal{T}_r$, which was earlier partitioned into training and validation sets for parameter optimization.

During the retrieval phase, we are given a descriptive query Q, and our goal is to rank the images in $\mathcal{T}_e$ based on their relevance with the query. This is done based on the posterior $P(J|Q)$ of an image $J \in \mathcal{T}_e$ given the query Q:

$$P(J|Q) = \frac{P(Q, J)}{P(Q)} \propto P(Q, J) \quad (7)$$

To compute $P(Q, J)$, first we parse the query and extract all its phrases (Y_Q) as described in Section 3.1.1. Then for each phrase $y \in Y_Q$, we compute its relevance score with the given test image J. This score is the joint probability of associating y with J, and is obtained using Eq. 1. Here we consider the annotated images from $\mathcal{T}_r$ to compute the neighbouring images of J, and pick the K most similar images. These images are then used to compute the different components ($P_{\mathcal{F}}(\cdot)$ and $P_{\mathcal{Y}}(\cdot)$) of Eq. 1. After computing the relevance of all the phrases in Y_Q with J, we compute the joint relevance score of associating J and query Q as:

$$P(Q, J) = \prod_{y \in Y_Q} P(y, J) \quad (8)$$

Similarly, we compute the joint relevance scores for all the images in $\mathcal{T}_e$, and then rank them in the descending order of this score (higher score means more relevance).

It is worth noticing that the second term in Eq. 1 ($P_{\mathcal{F}}(\cdot)$) considers only visual similarity, i.e., query-independent. Hence, this needs to be computed just once for all the images in the retrieval set, and can be done off-line. In other words, we can pre-compute the K nearest neighbours $\mathcal{T}_J^K \subset \mathcal{T}_r$ of each test image J and store their indices and conditional probability scores. Then, during the retrieval phase, we need to compute just the relevance of the phrases in the given query with those of the images in $\mathcal{T}_J^K$ (using Eq. 4).

4. EXPERIMENTS

We evaluate and compare our approach on two popular image description datasets: (1) **UIUC Pascal Sentence:** This was introduced in [13], and is a de facto benchmark for evaluating image-caption associations [16, 6, 18]. It contains 1,000 images, each annotated with captions from 5 human-annotators. On an average, each description has around 10 words. (2) **IAPR-TC12 benchmark:** This was introduced in [5] for cross-language retrieval, and has 19,627 images. Each image is annotated with a long description of up

Dataset →	Pascal		IAPR-TC12	
Method ↓	BLEU-1	Rouge-1	BLEU-1	Rouge-1
CCA [14]	0.29	0.17	0.26	0.28
BITR [18]	0.31	0.21	0.27	0.26
Ours (syn.✗)	0.33	0.22	0.31	0.30
Ours (syn.✓)	0.36	0.24	0.35	0.33

Table 1: Comparison of our approach to the state-of-the-art methods using automatic evaluation.

Figure 1: Sample queries from the Pascal Sentence dataset along with the top two retrieved images.

to 5 sentences. Compared to Pascal Sentence dataset, this has more diverse object categories and complicated descriptions, thereby providing a challenging test-bed for evaluation. On an average, each description has around 25 words.

We represent each image using a set of global and local features similar to [6]. The global features include GIST, colour histograms in RGB and HSV colour spaces, and Gabor and Haar features. The local features include bag-of-words histogram using SIFT descriptor. Except GIST, we also compute other features over three vertical and horizontal partitions of an image and concatenate them. This helps in encoding the spatial layout of an image into the features. While computing distance between two images, Euclidean distance is used for GIST, Gabor and Haar features, Manhattan distance for colour histograms, and chi-square distance for bag-of-words histogram (of SIFT features).

4.1 Experimental Set-up and Comparisons

For evaluations, we partition each dataset into 45% training set, 45% retrieval set and 10% query set. The training set is used to learn the model parameters, the images in the retrieval set constitute the images on which we perform retrieval, and the descriptions in the query set are used for querying the retrieval set. This is repeated ten times in order to include all the descriptions in a dataset into the query set. While extracting phrases from available descriptions, we consider two set-ups, where (1) all the phrases are considered as such, and (2) each subject/object in a phrase is replaced by its synonym determined using WordNet synsets.

For evaluation, we consider BLEU [12] and Rouge [10] metrics. Following [18], for a given query, we average these scores over the top five retrieved images, by matching the query with their ground-truth descriptions. For both these measures, we report average unigram scores.

Since our work is closely related to cross-modal image retrieval methods, we compare with two such methods [14, 18]. Both these methods have been shown to perform well for image retrieval using descriptive queries, and cross-modal retrieval in general. To evaluate both these methods, we follow the same experimental set-up as described in [18].

4.2 Results and Discussion

In Table 1, we report the results for automatic evaluation. Evaluations using both the metrics confirm the superior performance of our approach compared to [14, 18]. This validates that during retrieval, it is better to consider meaningful chunks of a descriptive query (phrases in our case) rather than the whole query as is. The results also show that by considering synonyms, we are able to achieve better performance than without synonyms. This is because nouns play a central role in image retrieval. On replacing each noun with its synonym, the number of distinct phrases reduces. This results in lowering the competition among semantically similar phrases, and thus improves the chances of retrieving images that better match a query. Figure 1 shows the top two images retrieved for sample queries from the Pascal Sentence dataset. Here it can be observed that usually the retrieved images are quite relevant to a given query. E.g., in the third column, none of the retrieved images has a "blue *and* white airplane". However, there is either a blue or a white coloured airplane in each image, with a background depicting the other colour (white building or blue sky). This indicates that even when the image content does not completely match with the query, we are able to retrieve images that match its components.

Acknowledgement: Yashaswi Verma is partially supported by Microsoft Research India PhD fellowship 2013.

References

[1] R. Arandjelović and A. Zisserman. Three things everyone should know to improve object retrieval. In *CVPR*, 2012.
[2] R. Datta, D. Joshi, J. Li, and J. Wang. Image retrieval: Ideas, influences and trends of new age. *ACM Computing Surveys*, 2008.
[3] M.-C. de Marneffe and C. D. Manning. The stanford typed dependencies representation. In *COLING Workshop*, 2008.
[4] S. L. Feng, R. Manmatha, and V. Lavrenko. Multiple bernoulli relevance models for image and video annotation. In *CVPR*, 2004.
[5] M. Grubinger. *Analysis and Evaluation of Visual Information Systems Performance*. PhD thesis, 2007.
[6] A. Gupta, Y. Verma, and C. V. Jawahar. Choosing linguistics over vision to describe images. In *AAAI*, 2012.
[7] V. Jain and M. Varma. Learning to re-rank: Query-dependent image re-ranking using click data. In *WWW*, 2010.
[8] J. Jeon, V. Lavrenko, and R. Manmatha. Automatic image annotation and retrieval using cross-media relevance model. In *SIGIR*, 2003.
[9] A. Karpathy, A. Joulin, and L. Fei-Fei. Deep fragment embeddings for bidirectional image sentence mapping. In *NIPS*, 2014.
[10] C.-Y. Lin and E. Hovy. Automatic evaluation of summaries using n-gram co-occurrence statistics. In *NAACLHLT*, 2003.
[11] V. Ordonez, G. Kulkarni, and T. L. Berg. Im2Text: Describing images using 1 million captioned photographs. In *NIPS*, 2011.
[12] K. Papineni, S. Roukos, T. Ward, and W. Zhu. BLEU: A method for automatic evaluation of machine translation. In *ACL*, 2002.
[13] C. Rashtchian, P. Young, M. Hodosh, and J. Hockenmaier. Collective image annotation using amazon's mechanical turk. In *NAACLHLT Workshop*, 2010.
[14] N. Rasiwasia, J. C. Pereira, E. Coviello, G. Doyle, G. R. G. Lanckriet, R. Levy, and N. Vasconcelos. A new approach to cross-modal multimedia retrieval. In *ACM MM*, 2010.
[15] M. A. Sadeghi and A. Farhadi. Recognition using visual phrases. In *CVPR*, 2011.
[16] Y. Ushiku, T. Harada, and Y. Kuniyoshi. Automatic sentence generation from images. In *ACM MM*, 2011.
[17] Y. Verma, A. Gupta, P. Mannem, and C. V. Jawahar. Generating image descriptions using semantic similarities in the output space. In *CVPR Workshop*, 2013.
[18] Y. Verma and C. V. Jawahar. Im2Text and Text2Im: Associating images and texts for cross-modal retrieval. In *BMVC*, 2014.

Multi-cue Augmented Face Clustering

Chengju Zhou[1,2,3], Changqing Zhang[1,2], Huazhu Fu[3], Rui Wang[1]*, Xiaochun Cao[1]
[1]State Key Laboratory of Information Security, IIE, Chinese Academy of Sciences, Beijing 100093, China
[2]School of Computer Science and Technology, Tianjin University, Tianjin 300072, China
[3]School of Computer Engineering, Nanyang Technological University, Nanyang Avenue 639798, Singapore
chengjuzhou@outlook.com, zhangchangqing@tju.edu.cn, huazhufu@gmail.com,
wangrui@iie.ac.cn, caoxiaochun@iie.ac.cn

ABSTRACT

Face clustering is an important but challenging task since facial images always have huge variation due to change in facial expressions, head poses and partial occlusions, etc. Moreover, face clustering is actually an unsupervised problem which makes it more difficult to reach an accurate result. Fortunately, there are some cues that can be used to improve clustering performance. In this paper, two types of cues are employed. The first one is pairwise constraints: must-link and cannot-link constraints, which can be extracted from the temporal and spatial knowledge of data. The other is that each face is associated with a series of attributes (*i.e*, gender) which can contribute discrimination among faces. To take advantage of the above cues, we propose a new algorithm, Multi-cue Augmented Face Clustering (McAFC), which effectively incorporates the cues via graph-guided sparse subspace clustering technique. Specially, facial images from the same individual are encouraged to be connected while faces from different persons are restrained to be connected. Experiments on three face datasets from real-world videos show the improvements of our algorithm over the state-of-the-art methods.

Keywords

Face Clustering, Graph-guided, Sparse Representation

1. INTRODUCTION

Given a set of facial images, face clustering aims to separate them into different groups according to different individuals. This technique can be used in many fields, such as movie summation, content based image retrieval and automatic collection of large-scale face dataset, etc. General face clustering methods focus on how to separate faces only according to visual information. Most of them try to use the unlabeled facial images to obtain a good similarity representation [8, 9, 10, 6, 2, 15]. In [8], an affine invariant distance metric is proposed which is robust to different face poses and then [9] extends to Joint Manifold Distance (JMD) which represents a set of facial images of the same person detected in consecutive video frames as independent subspace. Hu et al. [10] introduces a between-set distance called Sparse Approximated Nearest Point (SANP) distance, where the dissimilarity of two sets is measured as the distance between their nearest points. In addition to the fully unsupervised clustering, there are also some methods with weak prior information. In [6], the scripts and subtitles are used to obtain cues as to which charactersare present. These weak cues for character presence are then combined with facial similarities to help the clustering. In [2], a multi-view clustering framework, called Diversity-induced Multi-view Subspace Clustering (DiMSC), is proposed to boost clustering performance by exploring the complementary information among multi-view features. Wolf et al. [15] proposes approach called Matched Background Similarity, in which can tell the differences between images with similar background, so that the similarities due to pose, lighting, and viewing conditions can be ignored.

An individual's facial images may have large variation due to change in facial expressions, head poses and partial occlusions, which make face clustering difficult for promising result. In some specific situation, some cues can be employed. For instance, in videos there are some inherent benefits: *faces in the same face track must be the same person while faces in the overlapped tracks can not belong to the same person*. This observation is referred as must-link and cannot-link constraints respectively and have been explored in [5, 16, 17, 19]. Cinbis and Verbeek [5] propose an unsupervised logistic discrinative metric learning (ULDML) method to learn a distance metric. The faces in the same track are pulled closer, while faces with the inter-track relation are pushed away from each other. Based on the Hidden Markov Random Fields (HMRF) model, a probabilistic constrained clustering method called HMRF-com [16] is proposed, in which the pairwise constraints, label-level and constraint-level local smoothness assumptions are incorporated together to guide the clustering process. The work in [19] proposes a video face clustering method which incorporates must-link and cannot-link constraints through constrained sparse representation. [17] develops a Weighted Block-Sparse Low Rank Representation (WBSLRR) to learn a more discriminative representation. However, these methods ignore the higher level attributes such as gender, skin color and hair style, etc. These attributes are consistent and robust in general. Some of these attributes are hard which means that they can not be changed. Therefore, the hard biometric attributes of facial images can be employed to guide the face clustering.

In this paper we explore the effectiveness of high level attributes for face clustering where the hard biometric attribute is employed to improve the clustering. We develop a novel face clustering method, Multi-cue Augmented Face Clustering (McAFC), in which the prior knowledge that can be represented as prior graphs (*i.e.*, pairwise

*Corresponding Author

MM'15, October 26-30, 2015, Brisbane, Australia ©2015 ACM.
ISBN 978-1-4503-3459-4/15/10 ... $15.00
DOI: http://dx.doi.org/10.1145/2733373.2806290

constraints and attribute information) is integrated through graph-guided sparse representation effectively. We compare the proposed method with the state-of-art methods and show its improvements on real-world datasets.

The remaining of this paper is structured as follows: In Section 2, the Multi-cue Augmented Face Clustering is detailed. Section 3 shows the face clustering experiments on three face datasets from real-world videos. Finally, we conclude our paper in Section 4.

2. PROPOSED METHOD

Given a set of facial images $\{f_1, f_2, ..., f_N\}$, where N is the number of faces. Each facial images is represented as a feature vector $\mathbf{x}_i \in \mathbb{R}^D$. Then the whole dataset can be represented as a feature matrix $\mathbf{X} = [\mathbf{x}_1, \mathbf{x}_2, ..., \mathbf{x}_N]$.

2.1 Attributes and Constraints

There are several attributes that can be integrated into our proposed method, such as gender and skin color. In this paper we focus on using the gender information. We employ [4] to extract the gender information from each facial image. Note that faces in a face track belong to a same person and should have same gender information. Hence, the gender of a track should be determined as the mode value of the gender information in this face track. To utilize this prior, we build up the attribute-link matrix $\boldsymbol{A} \in \mathbb{R}^{N\times N}$, where N is the number of total facial images. The attribute-link matrix is constructed from the attribute information, in which the indices of face pairs that are different in gender are set to a negative value while others are 0. For convenience, we define $\mathcal{A} = \{(\mathbf{x}_i, \mathbf{x}_j) \in \mathcal{A} | \boldsymbol{A}_{ij} \neq 0\}$ as the set of attribute-link information.

To describe the constraints of the video faces, we also build up two spatial-temporal constraint matrices: must-link matrix $\boldsymbol{M} \in \mathbb{R}^{N\times N}$ and cannot-link matrix $\boldsymbol{C} \in \mathbb{R}^{N\times N}$. The matrix $\boldsymbol{M}$ represents the must-link constraints, where the indices corresponding to the face pairs in the same track are set to 1 while others are set to 0. The matrix $\boldsymbol{C}$ represents the cannot-link constraints, the elements of which corresponding to the face pairs belonging to the overlapped tracks are set to -1 while others are set to 0. We also define $\mathcal{M} = \{(\mathbf{x}_i, \mathbf{x}_j) \in \mathcal{M} | \boldsymbol{M}_{ij} = 1\}$ and $\mathcal{C} = \{(\mathbf{x}_i, \mathbf{x}_j) \in \mathcal{C} | \boldsymbol{C}_{ij} = -1\}$ as the sets of the must-link and cannot-link constraints respectively.

2.2 Multi-cue Augmented Face Clustering

Ideally, the face $\mathbf{x}_i$ can be sparsely represented by small subset of faces from the same person [7] in the dataset. The relationship can be written as:

$$\mathbf{x}_i = \mathbf{X}\boldsymbol{\beta}_i \text{ s.t. } \boldsymbol{\beta}_{ii} = 0, i = 1, \dots, N \tag{1}$$

where $\boldsymbol{\beta}_i \triangleq [\boldsymbol{\beta}_{1i}, \boldsymbol{\beta}_{2i}, ..., \boldsymbol{\beta}_{Ni}]^\mathsf{T}$ is the sparse representation of face $\mathbf{x}_i$, and the constraint $\boldsymbol{\beta}_{ii} = 0$ eliminates the trivial solution of representing a face as itself. Ideally, the coefficient vector $\boldsymbol{\beta}_i$ should have non-zero entries for these few facial images from the same person while the coefficient corresponding to different persons are zeros. In other words, the matrix $\mathbf{X}$ is a *self-expressive* dictionary in which each face can be rewritten as a linear combination of other faces in $\mathbf{X}$. To find a non-trivial sparse representation of $\mathbf{x}_i$, the tightest convex relaxation of the ℓ_1-norm is often employed, i.e.,

$$\arg\min_{\boldsymbol{\beta}} \frac{1}{2} \left\|\mathbf{x}_i - \mathbf{X}\boldsymbol{\beta}_i\right\|^2 + \lambda \left\|\boldsymbol{\beta}_i\right\|_1 \text{ s.t. } \boldsymbol{\beta}_{ji} = 0, i = 1, \dots, N \tag{2}$$

where λ is regularization parameter which control the sparsity of $\boldsymbol{\beta}$. The optimization problem 2 can be solved efficiently using convex programming tools [1, 11].

2.2.1 Graph-guided Sparse Representation

Intuitively, the must-links can be regarded as a kind of positive prior that tell sparse representation which faces it should choose. On the contrary, the cannot-links and attribute-links can be referred as a kind of negative prior that indicates the sparse representation which faces it should not choose as its representation. Given these information, it is reasonable to assume that a sparse representation tends to choose the positive faces and neglect the negative ones. Therefore, we propose a graph-guided sparse representation as follows,

$$\begin{aligned}
&\arg\min_{\boldsymbol{\beta}} \frac{1}{2} \left\|\mathbf{x}_i - \mathbf{X}\boldsymbol{\beta}_i\right\|^2 + \lambda \left\|\boldsymbol{\beta}_i\right\|_1 \\
&+ \gamma_M \sum_{(i,j)\in\mathcal{M}} \tau(\boldsymbol{M}_{ij}) \sum_{k=1}^{K} |\boldsymbol{\beta}_{ki} - sign(\boldsymbol{M}_{ij})\boldsymbol{\beta}_{kj}| \\
&+ \gamma_C \sum_{(i,j)\in\mathcal{C}} \tau(\boldsymbol{C}_{ij}) \sum_{k=1}^{K} |\boldsymbol{\beta}_{ki} - sign(\boldsymbol{C}_{ij})\boldsymbol{\beta}_{kj}| \\
&+ \gamma_A \sum_{(i,j)\in\mathcal{A}} \tau(\boldsymbol{A}_{ij}) \sum_{k=1}^{K} |\boldsymbol{\beta}_{ki} - sign(\boldsymbol{A}_{ij})\boldsymbol{\beta}_{kj}| \\
&\text{s.t. } \boldsymbol{\beta}_{ii} = 0, i = 1, \dots, N
\end{aligned} \tag{3}$$

where $\lambda, \gamma_M, \gamma_C$ and γ_A are regularization parameters that control the complexity of the model. The third term tells which faces should tend to choose as its sparse representation. The last two terms show which faces should be avoided as its sparse presentation. The larger γ_M, γ_C and γ_A lead to a greater graph effect. In this paper, we use $\tau(r) = |r|$ [3]. Actually, any positive monotonically increasing function of the absolute value of correlations can be used. The $\tau(r)$ weights the fusion penalty for each face pairs such that β_{ki} and β_{kj} for highly correlated face pairs with large $|r|$ receive a greater graph effect than other pairs with weaker relationships. The $sign(r)$ indicates that two negatively correlated relationships are encouraged to have the same set of relevant representation coefficients with opposite sign. Note that the similarity coefficient used in spectral clustering should be non-negative. Therefore, we can approximately rewrite the optimization problem 3 as follows,

$$\begin{aligned}
&\arg\min_{\boldsymbol{\beta}} \frac{1}{2} \left\|\mathbf{x}_i - \mathbf{X}\boldsymbol{\beta}_i\right\|^2 + \lambda \left\|\boldsymbol{\beta}_i\right\|_1 \\
&+ \gamma \sum_{(i,j)\in\mathcal{Y}} \tau(\boldsymbol{Y}_{ij}) \sum_{k=1}^{K} |\boldsymbol{\beta}_{ki} - sign(\boldsymbol{Y}_{ij})\boldsymbol{\beta}_{kj}| \\
&\text{s.t. } \boldsymbol{\beta}_{ii} = 0 \quad \text{and} \quad \boldsymbol{\beta} \geq 0, i = 1, \dots, N
\end{aligned} \tag{4}$$

with

$$\boldsymbol{Y} = \gamma_M \boldsymbol{M} + \gamma_C \boldsymbol{C} + \gamma_A \boldsymbol{A}, \quad \mathcal{Y} = \{(\boldsymbol{x}_i, \boldsymbol{x}_j) \in \mathcal{Y} | \boldsymbol{Y}_{ij} \neq 0\}, \tag{5}$$

whereγ_M, γ_C and γ_A are the corresponding weight coefficients which can reveal effectiveness of different prior knowledge. Without loss of generality, we can rewrite the optmization problem 4 for all face $i = 1, \dots, N$ in matrix form as follows,

$$\begin{aligned}
&\arg\min_{\boldsymbol{B}} \frac{1}{2} \left\|\mathbf{X} - \mathbf{X}\boldsymbol{B}\right\|^2 + \lambda \left\|\boldsymbol{B}\right\|_1 \\
&+ \gamma \sum_{(i,j)\in\mathcal{Y}} \tau(\boldsymbol{Y}_{ij}) \sum_{k=1}^{K} |\boldsymbol{B}_{ki} - sign(\boldsymbol{Y}_{ij})\boldsymbol{B}_{kj}| \\
&\text{s.t. } \boldsymbol{B}_{ii} = 0 \quad \text{and} \quad \boldsymbol{B} \geq 0, i = 1, \dots, N
\end{aligned} \tag{6}$$

where $\boldsymbol{B} \triangleq \{\boldsymbol{\beta}_i, \dots, \boldsymbol{\beta}_N\} \in \mathbb{R}^{N\times N}$ is the sparse representation matrix, and the i-th column of which corresponds to the sparse representation of $\mathbf{x}_i$. $\boldsymbol{\beta}_i \in \mathbb{R}^N$ is the vector of elements of $\boldsymbol{B}$. The optimization problem 6 can be solved effectively utilizing [3].

2.2.2 *Constrained Spectral Clustering*

After solving the proposed optimization problem 6,we build a weighted graph $\mathcal{G} = (\mathcal{V}, \mathcal{E}, \mathbf{W})$, where $\mathcal{V}$ denotes the set of N nodes in graph $\mathcal{G}$ corresponding to the set of N faces, and $\mathcal{E}$ denotes the edges between nodes. $\mathbf{W} \in \mathbb{R}^{N\times N}$ is a symmetric non-negative similarity matrix representing the weights of the edges. Intuitively, an ideal similarity graph $\mathcal{G}$ should have connections corresponding to the same person and have no connections corresponding to different individuals. In the sparse representation solution $\boldsymbol{B}$, nonzero elements can be regarded as a measurement of the relationships between faces. This provides a choice of constructing the similarity matrix [7],

$$\mathbf{W} = \boldsymbol{B} + \boldsymbol{B}^{\mathsf{T}}, \tag{7}$$

where $\boldsymbol{B}$ is normalized as $\boldsymbol{\beta}_i \leftarrow \boldsymbol{\beta}_i/\|\boldsymbol{\beta}_i\|_\infty$ to make sure the weights in similarity graph are of the same scale. In this way, nodes in the graph are connected to each other with a same weight. Besides, the must-link faces should have a much higher weight coefficient than the cannot-links and faces with different hard biometric traits. In spectral clustering, we can also take advantages of the prior knowledge. A straightforward way is [19] as follows,

$$\mathbf{W}^{new} = \mathbf{W} + \eta_M \mathbf{M} + \eta_C \mathbf{C} + \eta_A \mathbf{A}, \tag{8}$$

where η_M, η_C and η_A are the corresponding weights and balance the effect of different kinds of prior knowledge in spectral clustering. In the clustering result, the faces belongs to must-links should be divided into a same cluster. This can be approximately reached by setting η_M with a value that is slighter larger than two which is the maximun value in weight matrix $\mathbf{W}$. The negative prior, attribute-links and cannot-links, means the corresponding face pairs should have a lower similarity coefficient. Therefore, a small value of η_C and η_A are taken for a lower coefficient while maintaining the nature of similarity matrix. Finally, the spectral clustering [13] is conducted on the new similarity matrix $\mathbf{W}^{new}$ to obtain the final clustering result.

3. EXPERIMENTS

3.1 Experimental Setting

Datasets: We conduct our experiments on three real-world datasets: Notting-Hill, TBBTS06E12 and YouTube_6. The Notting-Hill [16, 18] is extracted from the movie "Notting-Hill". Faces of 5 main casts are used, including 4660 faces in 76 tracks. The original dataset consists of the facial images with size of 120×150. The TBBTS06E12 is from the Season 6 Episodes 12 of TV series "The Big Bang Theory" [19]. The detected faces of 9 main casts are employed, including 17168 faces in 385 tracks. The third dataset is YouTube_6, which is a part of YouTube Face Dataset [15]. The facial images are derived from different videos and only face tracks are provided but no frame indices. Accordingly, there are no cannot-link constraints. We select the individuals of whom has at least 6 face tracks. Finally, we get 7266 facial images corresponding to 8 people, each of whom has 6 face tracks. Due to facial images from a face track belong to a same individual, we sample a part of faces from each track instead of using the whole track. The sample number are set 3, 3, 10 in three datasets respectively. We also downsample the original facial images to a corresponding size, which is 40×50, 50×50 and 50×50 for three datasets respectively and then vectorize the gray image as feature. These measurements can significantly reduce the computation complexity. In HMRFs, we follow [16] to use PCA to project the original gray scale feature space to a lower dimensional space which is equal to the number of casts.

Comparisons and Evaluation Criteria: In experiments, we compare our algorithm with some baselines and state-of-the-art methods: K-means [12], ULDML [5], HMRF-com [16], SSC [7], CS-VFC [19] and WBSLRR [17]. We also report the performance of method with only must-link and cannot-link constraints (McAFC$_c$), only attribute-links (McAFC$_a$) and both of prior knowledge above mentioned (McAFC$_{c\&a}$) respectively. To obtain a comprehensive comparison, two standard measurements are employed to evaluate the clustering result: Accuracy, and Rand Index (RI) [14]. The Accuracy is calculated based on confusion matrix, which is derived from the match between the predicted labels of all faces and the ground-truth labels. The Rand Index is a measure of the similarity between clustering results. It evaluates true positives within clusters and true negatives between clusters. For each of the metrics, the higher it is, the better the performance is.

3.2 Quantitative and Qualitative Results

The detailed quantitative results are shown in Table 1. First, our proposed methods (McAFC$_c$, McAFC$_a$, McAFC$_{c\&a}$) achieve much better performances in three datasets. In Notting-Hill, CS-VFC and WBSLRR achieve about 7% improvement over SSC while McAFC$_c$ obtains about a more 2% improvement in terms of accuracy. The McAFC$_a$ also reaches the same performance with CS-VFC. With attribute and pairwise constraint cues, McAFC$_{c\&a}$ reaches about 96%. In dataset TBBTS06E12, our proposed graph-guided approach makes a remarkable improvement. McAFC$_c$ acquires a better performanc than CS-VFC and WBSLRR at least 6% improvement. With pairwise constraints and attributes, McAFC$_{c\&a}$ achieves about 28% improvement than SSC. The dataset YouTube_6 is more challenging due to the faces are from different videos and have a larger variation. The CS-VFC and WBSLRR reach about 20% improvement over SSC while McAFC$_c$ obtains about 23% improvement. McAFC$_a$ also reaches about 45.83% which has about 14% improvement. With two kinds of prior knowledge used, the McAFC$_{c\&a}$ achieves about 58.33% which is a comparable performance considering the challenges in YouTube_6. One can observe that McAFC$_c$ always achieves a better performance than McAFC$_a$ in all cases despite that attribute-links is much larger than constraints in quantity. This is not surprise because McAFC$_a$ just utilize the negative representation cues while McAFC$_c$ not only uses negative cues but also positive ones simultaneously. Our McAFC$_c$ achieves a better result than CS-VFC in three datasets, which shows that our proposed graph-guided approach is more effective than utilizing pairwise constraints with simple manner (*i.e.*, setting indices of must-link and cannot-link constraints to zeros). To sum up, our method outperforms the comparisons thanks to the multiple cues. Moreover, according to the results, we can find that, both the pairwise constraints (*i.e.*, must-links and canot-links) and the high level attributes contribute to improve the clustering performance.

The groundtruth, similarity and confusion matrices of SSC and McAFC are shown in Fig. 1 and Fig. 2. In Fig. 1, with prior knowledge, the similarity matrix of McAFC is more clear than SSC and it reveals the underlying data structure better. This can be further verified in the corresponding confusion matrix in Fig. 2. From the confusion matrices, we can find that 11 instances are wrongly clustered by SSC while McAFC only have 6 ones, so the whole clustering accuracy raises from 85.52% up to 92.10%. This also proves that our proposed method can significantly improve the clustering performance with multiple cues.

Table 1: Results (Mean $\pm$ Standard) on Notting-Hill, TBBTS06E12 and YouTube_6

	Notting-Hill		TBBTS06E12		YouTube_6	
	Accuracy	RI	Accuracy	RI	Accuracy	RI
K-Means [12]	59.21 ± 8.40	77.18 ± 3.49	53.00 ± 4.64	82.38 ± 0.99	40.25 ± 3.83	80.64 ± 3.01
ULDML [5]	55.26 ± 2.78	74.50 ± 2.98	56.73 ± 5.93	82.67 ± 0.34	33.33 ± 3.62	69.29 ± 0.21
HMRF-com [16]	70.21 ± 0.99	83.19 ± 1.53	55.32 ± 0.96	83.23 ± 1.57	40.13 ± 1.01	80.41 ± 0.81
SSC [7]	85.52 ± 0.94	88.52 ± 0.36	52.99 ± 0.23	81.92 ± 0.34	31.63 ± 3.47	63.88 ± 6.79
CS-VFC [19]	92.11 ± 0.89	95.41 ± 0.67	72.47 ± 0.89	87.55 ± 0.56	51.10 ± 3.11	82.39 ± 1.43
WBSLRR [17]	92.11 ± 0.24	95.52 ± 0.27	69.09 ± 2.46	86.58 ± 1.42	52.08 ± 2.09	83.36 ± 1.76
McAFC$_c$	94.73 ± 0.74	$\mathbf{96.59 \pm 0.57}$	78.70 ± 0.23	90.52 ± 0.83	54.17 ± 3.45	83.64 ± 2.34
McAFC$_a$	92.10 ± 0.68	93.56 ± 0.31	56.36 ± 0.16	82.17 ± 0.23	45.83 ± 0.63	80.12 ± 0.56
McAFC$_{c\&a}$	$\mathbf{96.05 \pm 0.39}$	96.07 ± 0.28	$\mathbf{80.51 \pm 0.32}$	$\mathbf{91.44 \pm 0.12}$	$\mathbf{58.33 \pm 0.26}$	$\mathbf{84.86 \pm 0.19}$

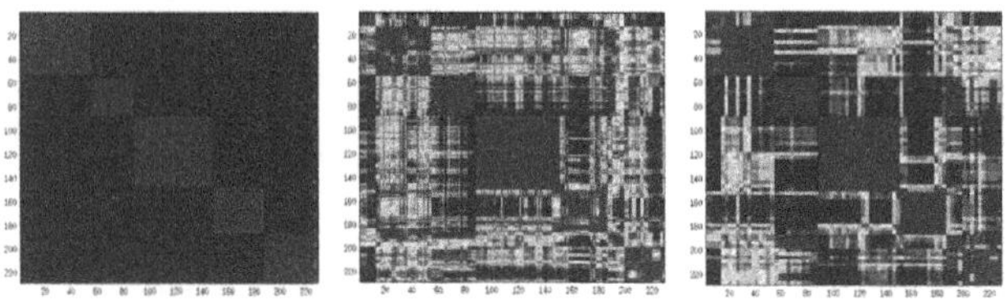

(a) Groundtruth (b) SSC (c) McAFC

Figure 1: Visualization of similarity matrices on Notting-Hill.

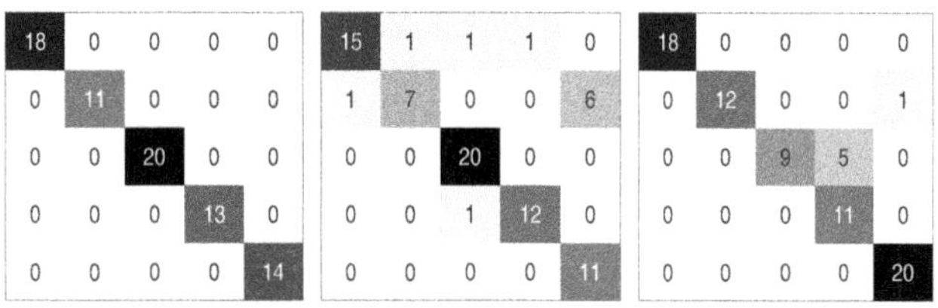

(a) Groundtruth (b) SSC (c) McAFC

Figure 2: Visualization of confusion matrices on Notting-Hill.

4. CONCLUSION

In this paper, we have proposed a face clustering approach, termed as Multi-cue Augmented Face Clustering (McAFC) to effectively take advantages of multiple cues. Specifically, the pairwise constraints, must-link and cannot-link constraints and face attributes knowledge, gender information, are effectively incorporated into the clustering process via graph-guided sparse representation to improve face clustering performance in two steps: sparse representation and spectral clsutering. The proposed approach is flexible to integrate prior knowledge for boosting the clustering performance. We have conducted experiments on three real-world video face datasets which demonstrate the effectiveness of our method. For future work, we hope to develop a framework to take advantage of multiple facial image attributes and explore how to utilize the relative attribute efficiently.

5. ACKNOWLEDGEMENT

This work was supported by National Natural Science Foundation of China (No. 61422213, 61332012,), 100 Talents Programme of The Chinese Academy of Sciences, and "Strategic Priority Research Program" of the Chinese Academy of Sciences (XDA06010-701).

6. REFERENCES

[1] S. P. Boyd and L. Vandenberghe. *Convex optimization*. Cambridge university press, 2004.

[2] X. Cao, C. Zhang, H. Fu, S. Liu, and H. Zhang. Diversity-induced multi-view subspace clustering. In *CVPR*, pages 586–594, 2015.

[3] X. Chen, Q. Lin, S. Kim, J. G. Carbonell, E. P. Xing, et al. Smoothing proximal gradient method for general structured sparse regression. *The Annals of Applied Statistics*, 6(2):719–752, 2012.

[4] W.-S. Chu, F. De la Torre, and J. F. Cohn. Selective transfer machine for personalized facial action unit detection. In *CVPR*, pages 3515–3522, 2013.

[5] R. G. Cinbis, J. Verbeek, and C. Schmid. Unsupervised metric learning for face identification in tv video. In *ICCV*, pages 1559–1566, 2011.

[6] T. Cour, B. Sapp, A. Nagle, and B. Taskar. Talking pictures: Temporal grouping and dialog-supervised person recognition. In *CVPR*, pages 1014–1021, 2010.

[7] E. Elhamifar and R. Vidal. Sparse subspace clustering: Algorithm, theory, and applications. *IEEE Transactions on PAMI*, 35(11):2765–2781, 2013.

[8] A. Fitzgibbon and A. Zisserman. On affine invariant clustering and automatic cast listing in movies. In *ECCV*, pages 304–320. 2002.

[9] A. W. Fitzgibbon and A. Zisserman. Joint manifold distance: a new approach to appearance based clustering. In *CVPR*, pages 19–26, 2003.

[10] Y. Hu, A. S. Mian, and R. Owens. Sparse approximated nearest points for image set classification. In *CVPR*, pages 121–128, 2011.

[11] S. J. Kim, K. Koh, S. Lustig, M. Byod, and D. Gorinevsky. An interior-point method for large-scale ℓ_1-regularized logistic regression. *JMLR*, 8(8):1519–1555, 2007.

[12] J. MacQueen et al. Some methods for classification and analysis of multivariate observations. In *Proceedings of the fifth Berkeley symposium on mathematical statistics and probability*, volume 1, pages 281–297. Oakland, USA., 1967.

[13] A. Y. Ng, M. I. Jordan, Y. Weiss, et al. On spectral clustering: Analysis and an algorithm. *NIPS*, 2:849–856, 2002.

[14] W. M. Rand. Objective criteria for the evaluation of clustering methods. *Journal of the American Statistical association*, 66(336):846–850, 1971.

[15] L. Wolf, T. Hassner, and I. Maoz. Face recognition in unconstrained videos with matched background similarity. In *CVPR*, pages 529–534, 2011.

[16] B. Y. Wu, Y. F. Zhang, B. G. Hu, and Q. Ji. Constrained clustering and its application to face clustering in videos. In *CVPR*, pages 3507–3514, 2013.

[17] S. Xiao, M. Tan, and D. Xu. Weighted block-sparse low rank representation for face clustering in videos. In *ECCV*, pages 123–138. 2014.

[18] Y. F. Zhang, C. S. Xu, H. Lu, and Y. Huang. Character identification in feature-length films using global face-name matching. *IEEE Transactions on Multimedia*, 11(7):1276–1288, 2009.

[19] C. Zhou, C. Zhang, X. Li, G. Shi, and X. Cao. Video face clustering via constrained sparse representation. In *ICME*, pages 1–6, 2014.

Robust Deep Auto-encoder for Occluded Face Recognition

Lele Cheng, Jinjun Wang, Yihong Gong, Qiqi Hou

Institute of Artificial Intelligence and Robotics, Xi'an Jiaotong University
28 Xianning West Road, Xi'an, Shaanxi, China

{ch_lele2012, houqiqi}@stu.xjtu.edu.cn,{jinjun, ygong}@mail.xjtu.edu.cn

ABSTRACT

Occlusions by sunglasses, scarf, hats, beard, shadow etc, can significantly reduce the performance of face recognition systems. Although there exists a rich literature of researches focusing on face recognition with illuminations, poses and facial expression variations, there is very limited work reported for occlusion robust face recognition. In this paper, we present a method to restore occluded facial regions using deep learning technique to improve face recognition performance. Inspired by SSDA for facial occlusion removal with known occlusion type and explicit occlusion location detection from a preprocessing step, this paper further introduces Double Channel SSDA (DC-SSDA) which requires no prior knowledge of the types and the locations of occlusions. Experimental results based on CMU-PIE face database have showed that, the proposed method is robust to a variety of occlusion types and locations, and the restored faces could yield significant recognition performance improvements over occluded ones.

Keywords

face recognition, occlusion, stacked sparse denoising auto-encoder, deep neural network

1. INTRODUCTION

Face recognition has long been a hot research topic in computer vision with a wide range of real-world applications. The recent development of local descriptors has led to further progress in recognition performance and robustness. On the other side, many existing systems exhibit noticeable performance decrease when applied to uncontrolled environment with occlusions, illumination changes, facial pose and expression variations. Although there exists a rich literature of researches focusing on face recognition with illuminations, poses and facial expression variations [1, 2], there is very limited work reported for occlusion robust face recognition.

Recent research have shown that non-linear deep models can achieve superior performance for image denoising [3, 4, 5]. To list some examples, Jain et al. [3], showed that using Convolutional Neural Networks (CNN) to remove images noise could achieve state-of-the-art performance but with less computational expens cost. As the image denoising problem can be regarded as to map from a noisy image to a noise-free image, Burger et al. [4] proposed to use Multi-layer Perceptron (MLP) to discover the mapping directly. Other deep structure such as pretrained denoising auto-encoder or Restricted Boltzmann Machine can also capture the complicated statistical patterns for the denoising tasks [5, 6]. In [7], Xie et al. proposed a SSDA for image denoising and blind inpainting, with satisfactory results reported. Similarly, Tang et al. [8] introduced a Robust Boltzmann Machine to distinguish between corrupted and uncorrupted and find latent representations of images. By pre-training on noise-free images followed by unsupervised fine tuning on noisy images, which can discover the structure of the noise to allows for better face denoising and recognition performance.

In this paper, we present Double Channel SSDA (DC-SSDA) to address the face occlusion removal problem. SSDA adopts greedy layer-wise algorithm to learn data representation, and the deep architecture of SSDA allows the learned features to be represented as the output of neuron from a previous layer. In DC-SSDA, we train one SSDA for noisy data and transfer the encoding parameters of this SSDA to another SSDA for clean data, to extract image features. In this way, the difference between the activation values of the two SSDAs becomes a good indicator of noise and clean image regions. In this way, without any prior knowledge of the type and location of the noise, i.e., the occlusion, DC-SSDA can accurately detect occlusion, such that by replacing the noise nodes' output with clean nodes' output, the effect of occlusion can be well reduced or removed. As can be seen from our experimental results in Section 3, the final reconstructed image will be occlusion-free.

2. ALGORITHM

This section first briefly revisits the SSDA algorithm [5] and then presents our DC-SSDA algorithm.

2.1 Stacked Sparse Denoising Auto-encoder (SSDA)

DA [5] is typically used to pre-train deep networks in order to overcome the difficulty in training multi-layers networks as a whole [9]. As shown in Fig. 1(a), SSDA consists of a serious of DAs where the hidden layer's activation of one DA is fed into the next DA. Typically, when training SSDA, only the clean data is provided while the noisy version of it

MM'15, October 26–30, 2015, Brisbane, Australia
© 2015 ACM. ISBN 978-1-4503-3459-4/15/10 ...$15.00.
DOI: http://dx.doi.org/10.1145/2733373.2806291.

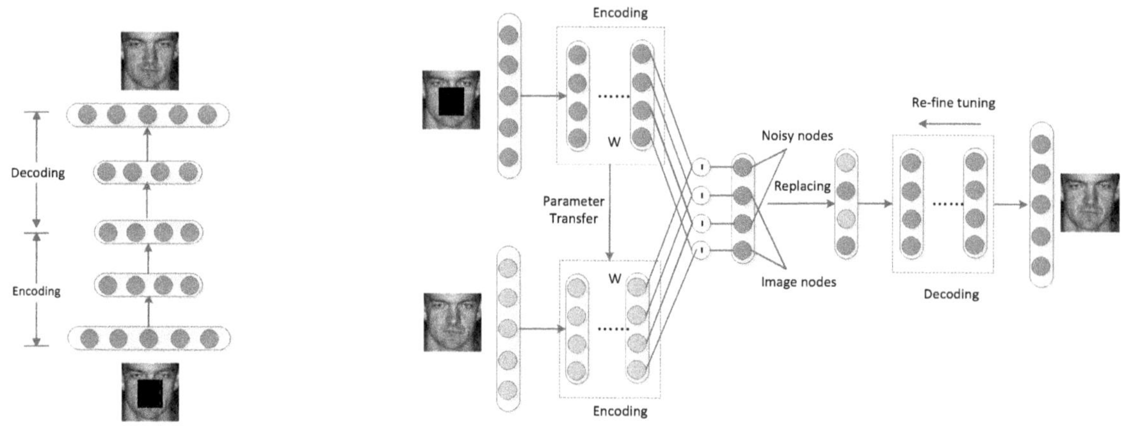

(a) SSDA (b) DC-SSDA

Figure 1: Illustration of DC-SSDA. (a) SSDA. (b) DC-SSDA. We calculate the relative difference of activation in the last encoding layer and replace the activations from noisy nodes with that from clean nodes. Then we re-fine tune the decoding weights such that the output of DC-SSDA becomes noise free.

is generated by adding random Gaussian or Salt-and-Pepper type noise. After training one layer, only the clean data is passed to the network to produce clean training data for the next layer, while the noisy data is discarded. The noisy training data for the next layer is similarly constructed by randomly corrupting the clean training data.

For the image occlusion removal task, however, the choices of clean and noisy input are straightforward: they are set to be the desired image after denoising and the observed noisy image respectively. In this paper, we follow [7] by reconstructing the clean image from noisy observation directly. After training of the first layer, the hidden layer's activations of both the noisy input and the clean input are calculated to serve as the training data of the second layer. It is shown in [7] that such modification allows SSDA to learn better presentations for denoising.

Specifically, for the ith image, the feedforward process of DA is:

$$h(x_i) = f(Wx_i + b)\,, \tag{1}$$

and the restored image is

$$\hat{y}(x_i) = g(W'h(x_i) + b')\,, \tag{2}$$

where $f(\cdot)$ and $g(\cdot)$ are respectively the encoding and decoding functions using sigmoid, $h(x_i)$ is the hidden layer's activation, $\hat{y}(x_i)$ is the reconstruction of the input (i.e., the DA's output), W and b are encoding weights and biases, and W' and b' are the decoding weights and biases.

When training the SSDA, we feed the hidden layer's activation of any previous DA layer as the input to the next DA layer. In our work, we pre-trained the deep network with K stacked DAs. Thus, the network has one input layer, one output layer, and 2K-1 hidden layers.

$$\hat{y}(x) = g_1 \circ g_2 \cdots g_K \circ f_K \cdots f_2 \circ f_1(x), \tag{3}$$

where f_i and g_i (i=1,2...K) are encoding functions and decoding functions respectively. The entire neural network is then trained again by back-propagation as fine-tuning stage to minimize the following loss, where the sparsity term is removed as it's already incorporated in the pre-training stage.

$$L_{SSDA}(D;\Theta) = \frac{1}{N}\sum_{i=1}^{N} \|y_i - \hat{y}(x_i)\|_2^2 + \frac{\lambda}{2}\sum_{l=1}^{2K} L \left\|W^l\right\|_F^2\,, \tag{4}$$

2.2 Double Channel SSDA (DC-SSDA)

The main idea of training SSDA is to map noisy images to images with lower/no noise. This is achievable through identifying which nodes encode image and noise contents in the last encoding layer of SSDA. Thus, we train one SSDA, as shown in Fig. 1(a), for noisy images, the input of which are noisy images and output are noiseless images. As shown in Fig. 1(b), after training, we transfer the encoding parameters of this SSDA to another SSDA for noiseless images, so the encoding parameters for noisy images and noiseless images are the same. As shown in Fig. 2, since most of the areas of input face images in two DDAEs are exactly the same except for the occlusion region, most of the activations of nodes in the last encoding layer of two DDAEs will be approximately equal except for the nodes corresponding to occlusion regions. As a result, we can use a criterion called relative difference of activation to detect noise and noiseless nodes in the last encoding layer. Relative difference of activation at each node is defined as the average difference between the activations resulting from feeding the network with noisy and its corresponding noiseless image (two images with same image contents but one is corrupted by noise). As a result, any node with high relative activation difference can be taken as noise node, and vise verse.

After training DC-SSDA, the average relative difference of activation AVG of each node can be obtained by averaging the activations of each node in the last encoding layer by

$$AVG[i] = \frac{1}{N}\sum_{j=1}^{N} \|f_{noise}^{(j)}(Wx_{noise}) - f_{clean}^{(j)}(Wx_{clean})\|, \tag{5}$$

where N is the number of images, $i = 1, 2, ..., K$, K is the number of neural nodes in the last encoding layer, W is the encoding parameter of DDAE, x_{noise} and x_{clean} are noise image and corresponding clean image, $f_{noise}^{(\cdot)}$ and $f_{clean}^{(\cdot)}$ are the activation of last encoding layer of SSDA for noisy im-

Noise Type	R-PCA[11]	SSDA[7]	RoBM[8]	Ours
occ1	18.47	27.45	27.32	28.74
occ2	15.23	25.87	25.65	28.13
occ3	13.68	26.25	24.73	27.68
sunglass	16.13	26.98	25.82	28.86
scarf	13.34	25.67	15.43	27.43

Table 1: PSNRs for previously added noises. The first column are different types of occlusion we added, and occ1∼occ3 represent 10%∼30% occlusion areas. The second to fourth column are PSNRs for R-PCA, SSDA, RoBM and our method respectively.

ages and noiseless images respectively. If the average relative activation difference of one node is high, we can take it as the noisy node, and replace its activations with corresponding clean node's activations to lower noisy nodes' activation or make them inactive. After this step, the decoding weights may deviate from the optimal values, so we keep the encoding weights unchanged and re-fine tune the decoding weights of noise channel,

$$\{g_1', g_2', g_K'\} = RFT\{g_1, g_2, g_K\}, \quad (6)$$

where RFT represent re-fine tuning, $g_1, g_2 ... g_K$ are the decoding parameters before re-fine tuning, $g_1', g_2' ... g_K'$ are the parameters after re-fine tuning. As a result,we can guarantee that the facial occlusion regions can be correctly mapped to feature region, and obtain the accurate decoding denoising image.

Since training image and testing image have the same type and location of occlusions, for example, training and testing images both have sunglass occlusion, the location and area of occlusion is the same, and it is assumed that any node been identified to encode noise content in training stage will always encode noise in testing stage. Thus, in testing stage, we replace the activations from noisy nodes with that from image nodes of training stage (i.e., average image's node) to reconstruct the final denoised image.

$$\hat{y}(x) = g_1' \circ g_2' \cdots g_K' \circ rep(f_K \cdots f_2 \circ f_1(x)), \quad (7)$$

where $f_1, f_2 ... f_K$ are the encodig weights of SSDA for noisy images before re-fine tuning, *rep* represent replacing the noisy nodes with clean nodes, and $g_1', g_2' ... g_K'$ are the decoding weights after re-fine tuning.

3. EXPERIMENTS

To assess the performance of our proposed DC-SSDA, we report a set of experiments on CMU-PIE face dataset [10]. The database contains 41,368 images of 68 people, each person under 13 different poses, 43 different illumination conditions, and with 4 different expressions. In order to eliminate the similarities between images, we selected a subset images, which contains 7480 frontal images of 68 persons, 110 images for every people, in our work. In the experiment, we select 77 images from every people for training and 33 images for testing, thus we got 5236 images for training and 2244 images for testing.

To obtain occluded/unoccluded image of the same person, we simulated three common types of noises, namely block occlusion, sunglass occlusion and scarf occlusion on the images. For block occlusion, different amount of occlusion by 10%, 20%, 30% of the entire image area were applied on images. For sunglass and scarf occlusions, they are positioned over the eye and mouth region respectively.

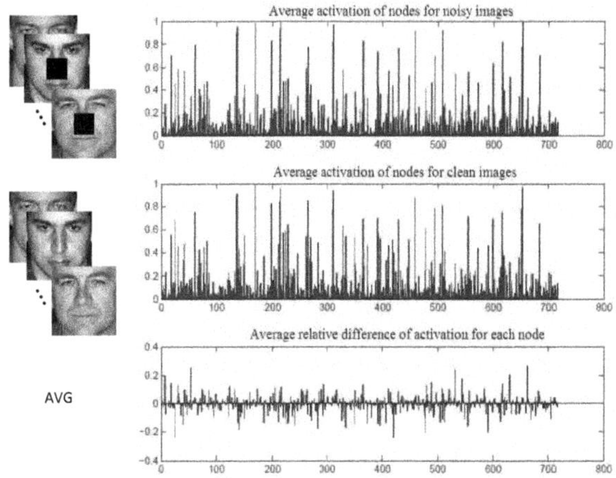

Figure 2: Average activations of the last encoding layer of SSDA for noisy and clean images respectively, the last row is the activation difference between noisy and clean images.

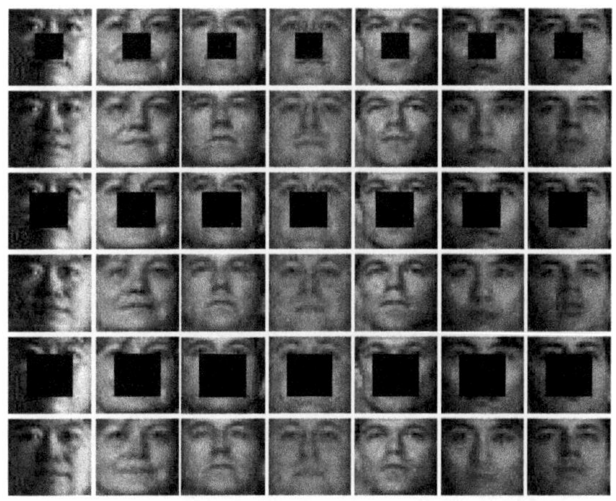

Figure 3: Results of DC-SSDA for face reconstruction with block occlusion. From up to bottom,the occlusion areas are respectively 10%,20%,30%,and images in adjacent rows are the reconstructive face images.

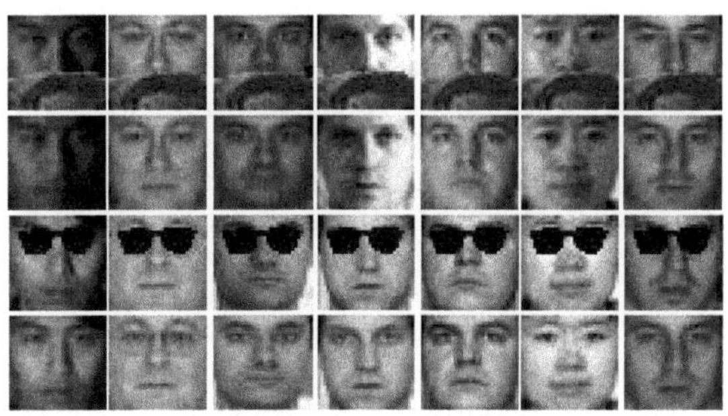

Figure 4: Results of DC-SSDA for face reconstruction with sunglass and scarf occlusion.

In the experiments,we cropped and resized each image to 32×32 pixels and trained a DC-SSDA with 3 hidden layers: 1024-800-717-800-1024 (number of neural nodes of each layer) on clean and noisy images respectively. To quantitatively measure our method, we employ PSNR to measure the denoising performance. PSNR is defined as $PSNR = 10log_{10}(p_{max}^2/\delta_e^2)$, where p_{max} is the maximum possible pixel value and δ_e^2 is the mean-square error between the noisy and original images.

The PSNRs for different type of occlusions are listed in Table 1. As can be observed, our proposed method DC-SSDA outperformed all other methods, and achieved better denoising result. Fig.3 and Fig.4 further illustrate some denoising results of DC-SSDA. As can be seen from the figure, our method performed well for all block, sunglass and scarf occlusions, and the restored image looks natural and realistic. In addition, comparisons between different amount of block occlusion, the restored images present only minor difference. The above experiments demonstrate that our proposed method,requires no prior knowledge of the types and locations of occlusions, is robust to different type and amount of occlusions.

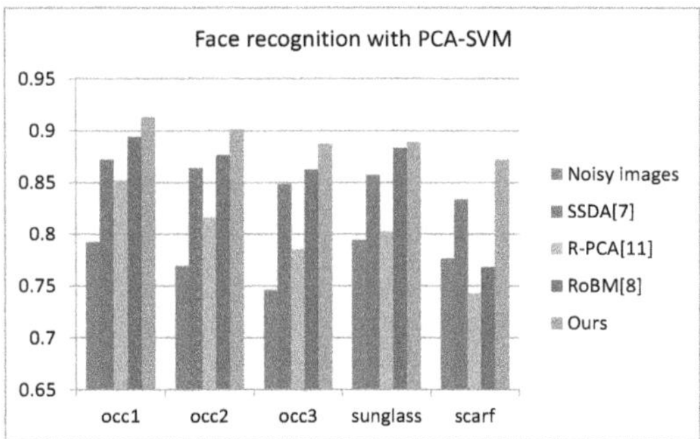

(a)

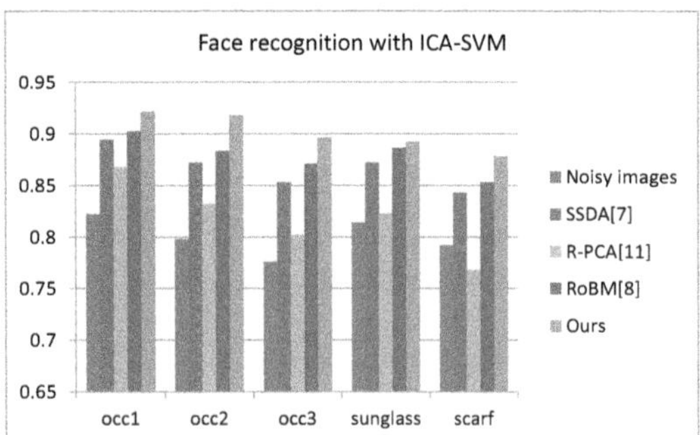

(b)

Figure 5: Face recognition with different denoising methods.We studied the recognition performance of (a) PCA-SVM and (b) ICA-SVM algorithm on noisy images and corresponding reconstructive images with SSDA, R-PCA, RoBM and our method.Noisy images represent occluded face images, occ1$\sim$occ3 represent 10%$\sim$30% block occlusion areas,and sunglass,scarf represent sunglass and scarf occlusions

Next and most importantly, we examined how much our proposed method can help improving face recognition performance. We test PCA and ICA based face recognition algorithm on the restored images with SSDA [7], R-PCA [11], RoBM [8] and DC-SSDA denoising methods respectively. PCA and ICA benchmark techniques were chosen because they have very limited capacity for processing occluded facial image as compared to other local and reconstructive methods which would otherwise complicate the analysis of our occlusion removal performance. The recognition results are showed in Fig.5. As we can see, the performances of R-PCA drops rapidly when the occlusion areas increase, and it performs poorly on sunglass and scarf occlusions. The SSDA method performs better than R-PCA, but is outperformed by our proposed DC-SSDA method. The results suggest that our DC-SSDA method can reliably improve classification performance without having to know the type and location of occlusion.

4. CONCLUSION

In this paper, we introduce the DC-SSDA, a novel technique of combining two SSDAs for facial image occlusion removal. We have demonstrated that DC-SSDA can robustly denoise images corrupted by different types of occlusions without prior knowledge of the occlusion type and location. With facial image restored by DC-SSDA, face recognition performance can be effectively improved.

5. ACKNOWLEDGEMENTS

This work is partially supported by the National Science Foundation of China under Grant No. 61473219, and the National High Technology Research and Development Program of China (863 Program) under Grant No. 2014AA015205 and No.2013AA014601.

6. REFERENCES

[1] X.D. Xie, K.M. Lam. Face recognition under varying illumination based on a 2D face shape model. Pattern Recognition, 2005.

[2] H. Li, G. Hua, Z. Lin, J. Brandt, J. Yang. Probabilistic Elastic Matching for Pose Variant Face Verification. CVPR, 2013

[3] V. Jain,H. Seung. Natural Image Denoising with Convolutional Networks. NIPS, 2008.

[4] H. C. Burger, C. J. Schuler, and S. Harmeling. Image denoising: Can plain neural networks compete with BM3D? CVPR, 2012.

[5] P. Vincent, H. Larochelle, I. Lajoie. Stacked Denoising Autoencoders : Learning Useful Representations in a Deep Network with a Local Denoising Criterion. In Journal of Machine Learning Research, 2010.

[6] M. Ranzato, J. Susskind, V. Mnih, and G. Hinton. On Deep Generative Models with Applications to Recognition. CVPR, 2011.

[7] J. Xie, L. Xu, and E. Chen. Image denoising and inpainting with deep neural networks. NIPS, 2012.

[8] Y. Tang, R. Salakhutdinov, G. Hinton. Robust Boltzmann Machines for Recognition and Denoising. CVPR, 2012.

[9] Bengio, Yoshua. Learning deep architectures for AI. Foundations and Trends in Machine Learning, 2009.

[10] T. Sim, S. Baker, and M. Bsat. The cmu pose, illumination, and expression database. PAMI, 2003.

[11] J. Wright, Y. Peng and Y. Ma. Robust Princ Component Analysis:Exact Recovery of Corrupted Low-Rank Matrices by Convex Optimization. NIPS, 2009.

Dissecting Urban Noises from Heterogeneous Geo-Social Media and Sensor Data

Hsun-Ping Hsieh
National Taiwan University
Taipei, Taiwan
d98944006@csie.ntu.edu.tw

Rui Yan
Baidu Inc.,
Beijing, China
yanrui02@baidu.com

Cheng-Te Li
Academia Sinica
Taipei, Taiwan
ctli@citi.sinica.edu.tw

ABSTRACT

Geo-social media services, such as Foursquare and Flickr, provide rich data that sensors various urban activities of human beings from geographical, mobility, visual, and social aspects. While noise pollution in modern cities is getting worse and sound sensors are sparse and costly, it is highly demanded to infer and analyze the noise at any region in urban areas. In this paper, we aim to leverage heterogeneous geo-social sensor data on Foursquare, Flickr, and Gowalla, to dissect urban noises for every regions in a city. Using NYC 311 noise complaint records as the approximation of urban noises generated by regions, we propose a novel unsupervised framework that integrates the extracted geographical, mobility, visual, and social features to infer the noise composition for regions and time intervals of interest in NYC. Experimental results show that our system can achieve promising results with substantially few training data, compared to state-of-the-art methods.

Categories and Subject Descriptors

H.2.8 [**Database Management**]: Database Applications—*Data Mining*; H.5.1 [**Information Systems Applications**]: Miscellaneous

General Terms

Algorithms, Performance, Experimentation

Keywords

noises; heterogeneous data; geo-social sensor

1. INTRODUCTION

With the prosperity of geo-social media, like Flickr, Facebook, Foursquare and Picasa, the volume of data that sensors and records the urban dynamics has increased dramatically. Geo-social media data is essentially *heterogeneous* since it is a mixture of geographical information (venue and location attributes), mobility footprints (check-in data), visual snapshots (consumer-contributed photos), and social interactions (social network). Data collected from geo-social media can be extensively considered as a kind of *sensors* that monitor urban human activities, and can be applied to urban-driven applications, such as detecting natural hazards events [9], tracking disease activities [11], and inferring air quality [14]. In current big cities like New York City, noise pollution had become a major problem [13] that affects the work efficiency and the sleep quality, and damages the mental health of people [1]. To tackle noise pollution of a certain urban region, the first step is to understand the elements and causes that produce the noise. If the composition of noise of any place in a city can be unveiled, such as "*in evening rush hour, 60% noise come from vehicle traffic, 30% from loud music of stores, and 10% from people' talking*" on weekdays at Time Square, the government agencies may make the policies to cope with the problems.

In this paper, we attempt to leverage heterogeneous geo-social sensor data to dissect the urban noises of regions in NYC. It is a challenging problem because both the magnitude and the composition of noise vary by places and change over time. One might think installing sound sensors everywhere in the city is an approach. However, sound sensors are costly, limited to very small areas, and hard to help diagnose the reasons that produce noises. Since it is infeasible to access the noise information of all the urban regions, we resort to use the noise complaint records of the 311 service in NYC, which is a platform allowing people to report the locations, time, and categories of their near-by annoyed

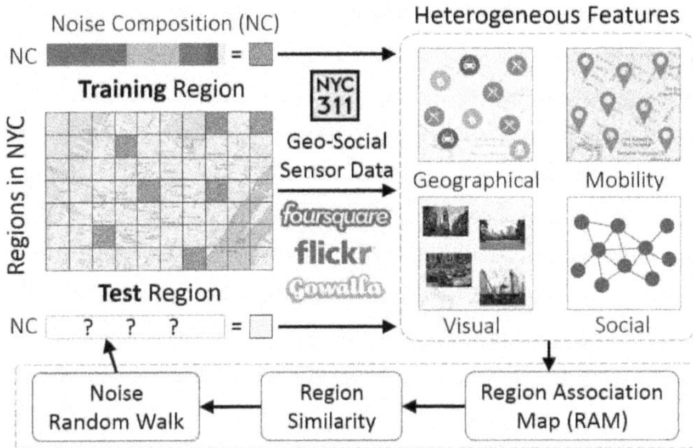

Figure 1: System Overview.

MM '15, October 26–30, 2015 Brisbane, Australia

DOI: http://dx.doi.org/10.1145/2733373.2806292.

events via phone calls, as an approximate of urban noises at some regions and time. Hence it is practicable and useful to analyze the noise composition of any region in a city.

Given the regions in NYC, in which some regions have sufficient noise composition information derived from 311 data, and the geo-social sensor data, collected from various sources, including Foursquare, Flickr, and Gowalla, we aim to infer the noise composition of the remaining regions. We devise a novel model, *Urban Noise Diagnotor* (UND) to deal with this task. A systematic overview of UND is shown in Figure 1. For each of the noise-labeled regions (marked ones) and the unlabeled regions, we use the geo-social sensor data to extract four heterogeneous features: geographical features from Foursquare, mobility features from Gowalla check-in data, visual features from Flickr geo-tagged photos, and social features from Gowalla location-based social network. Then a three-stage unsupervised method is devised: constructing *region association map* (RAM), modeling the region similarity, and a *noise random walk* algorithm to infer the noise composition of a region.

More Related Work. Recent studies have exhibited the potential of visualizing and exploiting different urban geo-social sensor data. CityBeat [12] used real-time geo-tagged photos to detect hyper-local trending activities. LiveHoods [5] employed check-in records to dynamically group and visualize locations with similar spatio-social characteristics. UrbanSound [10] classified urban sounds into a taxonomy to analyze urban events. Urban Tribes [8] detected the social intent of group photos to analyze the tribes in a city. While existing work unveiled urban informatics using a specific type of geo-social data, we collectively leverage heterogeneous geo-social media data to infer noise composition.

2. URBAN NOISE DIAGNOTOR

2.1 Geo-Social & NYC 311 Noise Datasets

We extract the noise complaint records from the open data of the NYC 311 service[1]. From Jan 2010 to Mar 2015, there are 196,631 complaint records of urban noise. The noise composition consists of 14 categories, in which the top-4 categories with the largest proportions are *Loud Music/Party*, *Construction*, *Loud Talking*, and *Vehicle*. On the other hand, we collect the check-in and the place data from the most well-known online geo-social media Foursquare[2] and the commonly-used location-based social network (LBSN) data Gowalla[3]. We focus on New York City where Foursquare was launched and thus had significantly more users than any city in the world. The collected data contains 47,581 geo-tagged venues. As for the Gowalla LBSN, which is collected by Cho et al. [4], there are totally 196,591 users, 950,327 social connections between users, and 6,442,890 check-in records. In addition, for the geo-tagged photos, we use Flickr tourist photos whose GPS coordinates are in New York City, collected by Chen and Grauman [3]. Totally there are 57,200 images. According to a well-known study of urban noise analysis [6], we partition the geographical area of NYC into a number of *regions*, in which the size of each region is 1 km × 1 km. Totally there are 560 regions in NYC.

[1]https://nycopendata.socrata.com/Social-Services/311-Service-Requests-from-2010-to-Present/erm2-nwe9
[2]https://foursquare.com/
[3]https://snap.stanford.edu/data/loc-gowalla.html

2.2 Heterogeneous Geo-Social Sensor Features

Geographical Features (G) are devised to describe the spatial and category distribution and the geographical interactions between venues because the type of noise can be related to the urban business environment. Regions with more/less venues or more/less venue categories can have different effects on the composition of noise. We extract two kinds of features for a region r.

- *Volume-based* features (**G-V**) use the *region density* and the *venue closeness* as the feature values. Region density $\mathcal{F}_d(r)$ is the number of venues in a region. Venue closeness $\mathcal{F}_{vc}(r)$ is the average geographical distance between venues in region r.
- *Category-based* features (**G-C**) consider the categories of venues, such as `food`, `shops`, `outdoors`, and `nightlife`, to characterize the activities of a region. We propose two category-based features. The first is *category entropy* measuring the diversity of a region, given by $\mathcal{F}_e(r) = -\sum_{a\in A} f_a \cdot \log(f_a)$, where a is a venue category, A is the set of all categories, and f_a is the fraction of venues with category a in region r. The second is *competitiveness* estimating the extent that venues with the same category gather in a region, given by $\mathcal{F}_b(r) = |\{l_i, l_j \in r : a(l_i) = a(l_j)\}|/\mathcal{F}_d(r)$, where l_i is a check-in venue, and $a(l_i)$ is the category of l_i.

Mobility Features (M) are developed to model the human moving dynamics among venues in a region. Regions with larger volume of visits, higher density of movement, and more incoming movements can produce more noises. Hence we use check-in data to propose the following features to characterize the human mobility.

- *Region Popularity* (**M-P**), denoted by $\mathcal{F}_p(r)$, is the number of check-ins in region r at a certain time.
- *Movement Density* (**M-D**) is the density of transitions between venues in region r. By denoting the set of consecutive check-ins from venue l_i and l_j in region r as TS_r, $(\langle l_i, l_j\rangle \in TS_r)$, the movement density $\mathcal{F}_{md}(r)$ is defined as the size of TS_r.
- *Incoming Flow* (**M-F**) estimates the transitions from venues outside r to venues in r. The incoming flow value of r is given by: $\mathcal{F}_{if}(r) = |\{\langle l_i, l_j\rangle \in TS : l_i \notin L(r) \text{ and } l_j \in L(r)\}|$, where TS is the set of all consecutive check-ins, $L(r)$ is the set of all venues in r.

Visual Features (V). We combine the global features of colors and texture and local geometric features to model the visual contents of photos. The global features capture the photographic visual composition while the local ones identify the actual structural elements of objects. Such mixed global and local features have been shown to provide significant complementary information in recognition tasks [2].

- *Global* (**V-G**). We extract color histograms $\mathcal{F}_{ch}(r)$ and color moments $\mathcal{F}_{cm}(r)$ as global features of photos to capture theirs visual and spatial color distributions. We also utilize the Gabor textures $\mathcal{F}_{gt}(r)$ to model the textural information. Feature vectors are produced for each photo by concatenating these features. The similarity between two photos is calculated according to normalized Euclidean distance.

- *Local* (**V-L**). We represent photos by local interest point descriptors, given by the scale-invariant feature transform (SIFT) with a Difference of Gaussian (DoG) process. Given two photos p_i and p_j with the descriptor vectors, $D_i = (d_i^1, d_i^2, ..., d_i^m)$ and $D_i = (d_j^1, d_j^2, ..., d_j^n)$, we define the similarity between two photos as the number interest points shared between two photos divided by their average number of interest points.

Social Features (**S**) are designed to characterize the social interactions for people who had ever been in the region. Some public regions are crowded while people who tend to be unacquainted with each other while other regions favor friends or family gathering together. Different social interactions can lead to various levels of noises with distinct compositions of noise. Therefore, we compute features from the location-based social network.

- *Centrality Metrics* (**S-C**). We employ network centrality metrics $\mathcal{F}_{cm}(r)$, including degree, closeness, betweenness, *PageRank*, and *SimRank*, and geo-social influence measures [7] $\mathcal{F}_{im}(r)$, including spatial degree, spatial closeness, node novelty, and geographic clustering coefficient, over users who had ever visit region r as feature values. The maximum, minimum, and average values for these nine features are computed.

- *Group Measures* (**S-G**). We characterize the extent of cohesion or separation for people who visit venues in region r, by modeling the structure connectivity of the graph $\mathbb{G}[r]$ induced by users who had ever visited venues in r. We compute the values of density, clustering coefficient, the number of communities, and the number of components in $\mathbb{G}[r]$ as group features $\mathcal{F}_g(r)$.

2.3 Region Association Map

We construct *Region Association Map* (RAM) to model the correlation between regions. We first introduce the noise composition and RAM, then describe how to exploit the extracted features to derive region similarities as edge weights.

The noise composition of a region r, denoted by $\mathbf{n}(r)$ is a vector, in which each element $n_c(r)$ is the percentage of a certain noise category c happening to region r. The dimension of $\mathbf{n}(r)$ is the number of noise categories, and $\sum_{c\in C} n_c(r) = 1$, where C is the set of all noise categories.

A *RAM* is a multi-layer weighted connected graph $G = \langle G^{t_1}, G^{t_2}, ..., G^{t_n}\rangle$, in which t is the total number of layers for time periods $t_1, t_2, ..., t_n$, and $G^{t_i} = (V, E, W)$ is the layer graph in at the t_i-th time period, where V is the set of regions, E is the set of edges between regions, and $W = W^{t_i} + W^{t_i,t_j}$ is the matrix representing edge weights, where W^{t_i} and W^{t_i,t_j} are edge weights learned from nodes within time period t_i and across time periods t_i and $t_j (i \neq j)$ respectively. The node set V consists of (a) regions whose noise compositions have known from NYC 311 noise complaint records, termed by **labeled nodes** $V_\bullet$, and (b) regions whose noise compositions are unknown, termed by **unlabeled nodes** $V_\circ$, where $V = V_\bullet \cup V_\circ$. Each labeled node $v_\bullet$ is associated with the corresponding noise composition $\mathbf{n}(v_\bullet)$, and the noise composition $\mathbf{n}(v_\circ)$ of each unlabeled node $v_\circ$ is initialized as a zero vector. The edge set E also consists of two parts: the set of edges $E_{\circlearrowleft}$ connecting nodes within each layer graph G^{t_i}, and the set of edges $E_{\frown}$ connecting the same nodes across different layer graphs G^{t_i} and $G^{t_j} (i \neq j)$,

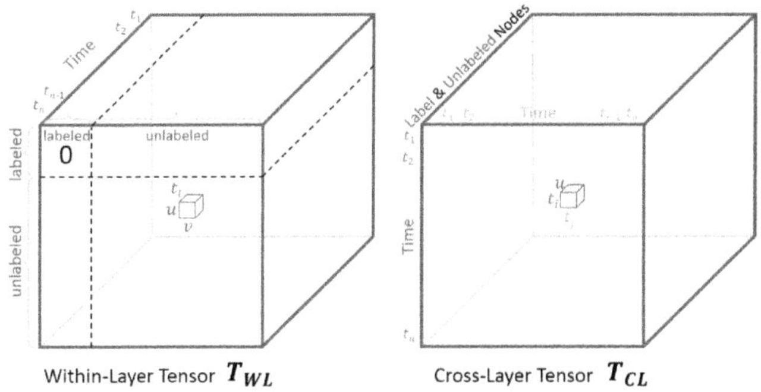

Figure 2: Tensor representation for RAM.

where $E = E_{\circlearrowleft} \cup E_{\frown}$. We use two tensors to represent a RAM. As illustrated in Figure, one is *Within-Layer Tensor* T_{WL} that records the edge weights in $E_{\circlearrowleft}$ while the other is *Cross-Layer Tensor* T_{CL} that keeps the edge weights in $E_{\frown}$. By combing T_{WL} and T_{CL}, we use a matrix $M(u, v, t_i, t_j)$ to represent RAM, given by:

$$M(u, v, t_i, t_j) = \begin{cases} T_{WL}(u, v, t_i) & \text{if } t_i = t_j \\ T_{CL}(u, t_i, t_j) & \text{if } u = v \end{cases}. \quad (1)$$

The construction of RAM consists of three parts. First, since we aim to infer the noise composition of unlabeled regions from labeled ones, we connect each $v_\circ \in V_\circ$ to all $u_\bullet \in V_\bullet$ in each layer graph. Second, owing to the fact that the noise composition of a region can be highly correlated to its history, we connect each $v_\circ$ within time period t_j to the corresponding unlabeled node at time period $t_i (i < j)$ whose noise composition had ever observed. Third, since the noise composition of near-by regions tends to be similar (due to sharing similar characteristics), each $v_\circ \in V_\circ$ is connected to the direct near-by $u_\circ \in V_\circ$.

2.4 Region Similarity

Learning edge weights in RAM from features plays a key role in the inference of noise compositions for unlabeled nodes. We model the similarity between regions as edge weights. The idea is that for a certain time period, if two regions with higher similarity in terms of features, they tend to have similar noise composition. While various features can contribute different degree of effect on the similarity for noise composition, the importance of each feature should be considered separately. Given a certain feature $\mathcal{F}_k$, we compute the corresponding individual region similarity $rs_{\mathcal{F}_k}(u(t_i), v(t_j))$ between nodes u and v in time periods t_i and t_j respectively from their feature difference $\Delta\mathcal{F}_k(u(t_i), v(t_j))$, where $\Delta\mathcal{F}_k$ is their feature difference, defined by $\Delta\mathcal{F}_k = \|\mathbf{f_k}(u(t_i)) - \mathbf{f_k}(v(t_j))\|$, and $\mathbf{f_k}(u(t_i))$ is $u(t_i)$'s feature vector of feature $\mathcal{F}_k$. Then, given a set of features $F = \{\mathcal{F}_1, \mathcal{F}_2, ..., \mathcal{F}_m\}$, we can derive the combined region similarity $rs(u(t_i), v(t_j))$ via the weighted sum of $rs_{\mathcal{F}_k}$, given by $rs(u(t_i), v(t_j)) = \exp(-\sum_{k=1}^{m} \pi_k \times rs_{\mathcal{F}_k}(u(t_i), v(t_j)))$, where π_k is the weight of feature $\mathcal{F}_k$. The combined region similarity is considered as the edge weight $M(u, v, t_i, t_j) = rs(u(t_i), v(t_j))$ between $u(t_i)$ and $v(t_j)$ ($(u(t_i), v(t_j)) \in E$). We will empirically learn the feature weight π_k from the validation set.

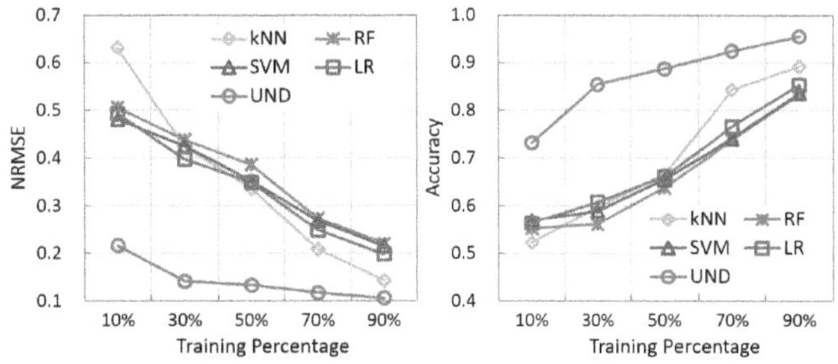

Figure 3: Results by varying training percentages.

2.5 Noise Random Walk in RAM

We infer the noise composition of each unlabeled region using RAM. The idea is to apply the random walk mechanism to iteratively update the noise composition $\mathbf{n}(v_\circ)$ of each unlabeled node $v_\circ$ until the change of its noise composition converges. The noise composition $\mathbf{n}(v_\circ)$ of $v_\circ$ is computed from its neighboring labeled or unlabeled nodes in RAM, given by:

$$n_c(v_\circ) = \sum_{u \in \Gamma(v_\circ)} w_{v_\circ,u} \times n_c(u), c \in C, \quad (2)$$

where $\Gamma(v_\circ)$ is the set of neighboring nodes in RAM. That said, we aggregate the noise composition of $v_\circ$'s neighbors via edge weights. Note that the noise composition for each labeled node $v_\bullet$ will not be updated (i.e., they are fixed). Since RAM provides the benefit on modeling the region similarities between nodes, a near-by region u with higher similarity with unlabeled node $v_\circ$ can contribute more weights on the propagation of noise to $v_\circ$.

3. EXPERIMENTS

The experiments consists of three parts: show the effectiveness of our UND model and understand the performance under time intervals. For the first part, we control the percentage of regions used as the training set from 10% to 90%, fix 5% as the validation set, and use the remaining as the test set. For the second part, we divide the regions according to two time scales: weekdays/weekends, and hour intervals (4 hours per unit). As for evaluation metrics, we use Normalization Root Mean Square Error (NRMSE) that measure the difference between ground-truth and inferred noise compositions, and Average Accuracy that is defined by whether the inferred noise category with the highest percentage of an unlabeled region is its corresponding ground-truth category in average. In addition, we compare our UND model with several typical supervised learning methods, including Support Vector Machine (SVM), Random Forest (RF), L_1 logistic regression (LR), and k-nearest neighbor (kNN) (averaging the noise composition from the top-k most similar labeled regions using features, $k = 5$).

The main results are shown in Figure 3. We can find that our UND model outperforms the competitors in every case, especially when the training percentage is higher than 50%. The best accuracy (around 0.95) exhibits that UND can accurately identify the major noise category of an unlabeled region. In addition, using UND, we report the performance of regions in different time intervals in Table 1. The results show that the noises of weekdays and daytime are easier to be inferred. We think it is because the human activities in

Table 1: Results of different days and hour intervals.

	Days		Hour Intervals					
	Weekday	Weekend	00-03	04-07	08-11	12-15	16-19	20-23
RMSE	0.118	0.159	0.167	0.061	0.081	0.075	0.106	0.219
Accuracy	0.909	0.858	0.853	0.923	0.904	0.911	0.895	0.836

such time intervals tend to be more regular and more energetic.

4. CONCLUSIONS

The contribution of this paper is three-fold. First, we extract a series of features from heterogeneous geo-social sensor data to characterize urban noise dynamics. Second, we develop the UND model that is validated to accurately infer the noise compositions of unlabeled regions. Third, we show that heterogeneous features in geo-social sensor data are collectively effective in inferring urban noises, and encourage future advanced analysis on this direction.

5. ACKNOWLEDGEMENTS

This work was sponsored by Ministry of Science and Technology of Taiwan under grant 104-2221-E-001-027-MY2. This work is also supported by Multidisciplinary Health Cloud Research Program: Technology Development and Application of Big Health Data, Academia Sinica, Taipei, Taiwan under grant MP10212-0318.

6. REFERENCES

[1] D. Butler. Noise management: Sound and vision. *Nature*, 2004.
[2] S. Chang, W. Hsu, L. Kennedy, L. Xie, A. Yanagawa, E. Zavesky, and D. Zheng. Columbia university trecvid-2005 video search and high-level feature extraction. In *NIST TRECVID Workshop*, 2005.
[3] C.-Y. Chen and K. Grauman. Clues from the beaten path: Location estimation with bursty sequences of tourist photos. In *IEEE CVPR*, 2011.
[4] E. Cho, S. A. Myers, and J. Leskovec. Friendship and mobility: user movement in location-based social networks. In *ACM SIGKDD*, 2011.
[5] J. Cranshaw, R. Schwartz, J. I. Hong, and N. M. Sadeh. The livehoods project: Utilizing social media to understand the dynamics of a city. In *AAAI ICWSM*, 2012.
[6] E. D'Hondt, M. Stevens, and A. Jacobs. Participatory noise mapping works! an evaluation of participatory sensing as an alternative to standard techniques for environmental monitoring. 2013.
[7] A. Lima and M. Musolesi. Spatial dissemination metrics for location-based social networks. In *ACM UbiComp*, 2012.
[8] A. Murillo, I. Kwak, L. Bourdev, D. Kriegman, and S. Belongie. Urban tribes: Analyzing group photos from a social perspective. In *IEEE CVPR*, 2012.
[9] T. Sakaki, M. Okazaki, and Y. Matsuo. Earthquake shakes twitter users: Real-time event detection by social sensors. In *WWW*, 2010.
[10] J. Salamon, C. Jacoby, and J. P. Bello. A dataset and taxonomy for urban sound research. In *ACM MM*, 2014.
[11] A. Signorini, A. M. Segre, and P. M. Polgreen. The use of twitter to track levels of disease activity and public concern in the u.s. during the influenza a h1n1 pandemic. *PLoS ONE*, 2011.
[12] C. Xia, R. Schwartz, K. Xie, A. Krebs, A. Langdon, J. Ting, and M. Naaman. Citybeat: Real-time social media visualization of hyper-local city data. In *WWW*, 2014.
[13] Y. Zheng, L. Capra, O. Wolfson, and H. Yang. Urban computing: concepts, methodologies, and applications. *ACM TIST*, 2014.
[14] Y. Zheng, F. Liu, and H.-P. Hsieh. U-air: When urban air quality inference meets big data. In *ACM SIGKDD*, 2013.
[15] D. Zhou, O. Bousquet, T. Navin Lal, J. Weston, and B. Scholkopf. Learning with local and global consistency. In *NIPS*, 2003.

Deep Multimodal Speaker Naming

Yongtao Hu
The University of Hong Kong
ythu@cs.hku.hk

Jimmy SJ. Ren
SenseTime Group Limited
rensijie@sensetime.com

Jingwen Dai
Xim Industry Inc.
dai@ximmerse.com

Chang Yuan
Lenovo Group Limited
yuanchang@lenovo.com

Li Xu
SenseTime Group Limited
xuli@sensetime.com

Wenping Wang
The University of Hong Kong
wenping@cs.hku.hk

ABSTRACT

Automatic speaker naming is the problem of localizing as well as identifying each speaking character in a TV/movie/live show video. This is a challenging problem mainly attributes to its multimodal nature, namely face cue alone is insufficient to achieve good performance. Previous multimodal approaches to this problem usually process the data of different modalities individually and merge them using handcrafted heuristics. Such approaches work well for simple scenes, but fail to achieve high performance for speakers with large appearance variations. In this paper, we propose a novel convolutional neural networks (CNN) based learning framework to automatically learn the fusion function of both face and audio cues. We show that without using face tracking, facial landmark localization or subtitle/transcript, our system with robust multimodal feature extraction is able to achieve state-of-the-art speaker naming performance evaluated on two diverse TV series. The dataset and implementation of our algorithm are publicly available online.

Categories and Subject Descriptors

H.3 [**Information Storage and Retrieval**]: Content Analysis and Indexing

Keywords

Speaker Naming; Multimodal; CNN; Deep Learning

1. INTRODUCTION

Identifying speakers, or speaker naming (SN), in movies, TV series and live shows is a fundamental problem in many high-level video analysis tasks, such as semantic indexing and retrieval [21] and video summarization [16], etc. As noted by previous authors [6], automatic SN is extremely challenging as characters exhibit significant variation of visual appearance due to changes in scale, pose, illumination, expression, dress, hair style, etc. Additional problems with video acquisition, such as poor image quality and motion blur, make the matter even worse. Previous studies using only a single visual cue, such as face features, failed to generate satisfactory results.

Real-life TV/movie/live show videos are all multimedia data consisting of multiple sources of information. In particular, audio provides reliable supplementary information for SN task because it is closely associated with the video. In this paper, we propose a novel CNN based learning framework to tackle the SN problem. Unlike previous methods which investigated different modalities individually, our method automatically learns the fusion function of both face and audio cues and outperforms other state-of-the-art methods without using face/person tracking, facial landmark localization or subtitle/transcript. Our system is also trained end to end, providing an effective way to generate high quality intermediate unified features to distinguish outliers.

Contributions. 1) a novel CNN based framework which automatically learns high quality multimodal feature fusion functions; 2) a systematic approach to reject outliers for multimodal classification tasks typified by SN, and 3) a state-of-the-art system for practical SN applications.

2. RELATED WORK

Automatic SN in TV series, movies and live shows has received increasing attention in the past decade. In previous works like [11], SN was considered as an automatic face recognition problem. Recently, more researchers have tried to make use of video context to boost performance. Most of these works focused on *naming face tracks*. In [6], cast members are automatically labelled by detecting speakers and aligning subtitles/transcripts to obtain identities. This approach had been adapted and further refined by [15]. Bauml *et al.* [2] use a similar method to automatically obtain labels for those face tracks that can be detected as speaking. However, these labels are typically noisy and incomplete (i.e., usually only 20-30% of the tracks can be assigned a name) [2]. That is mainly due to that speaker detection relies heavily on lip movement detection, which is not reliable for videos of low quality or with large face pose variation.

In [17], each TV series episode is modeled as a Markov Random Field, which integrates face recognition, clothing appearance, speaker recognition and contextual constraints in a probabilistic manner. The identification task is then formulated as an energy minimization problem. In [19, 20], person naming is resolved by a statistical learning or multiple instances learning framework. Bojanowski *et al.* [4] utilize scripts as weak supervision to learn a joint model of actors and actions in movies for character naming. Although

MM'15, October 26–30, 2015, Brisbane, Australia.
© 2015 ACM. ISBN 978-1-4503-3459-4/15/10 ...$15.00.
DOI: http://dx.doi.org/10.1145/2733373.2806293.

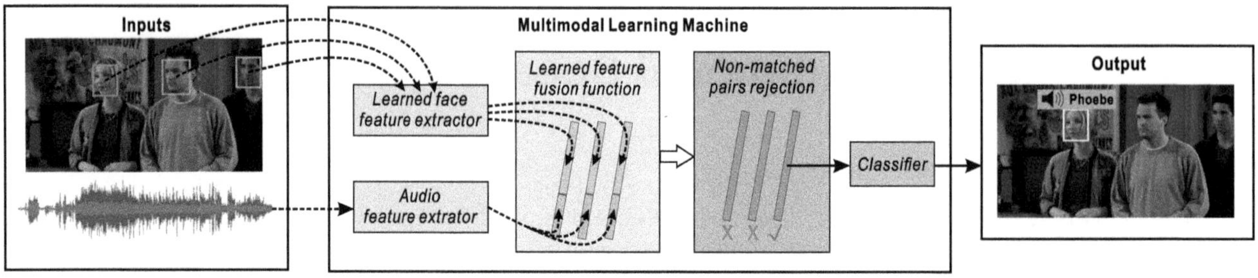

Figure 1: Multimodal learning framework for speaker naming.

these methods try to solve character naming or SN problem in new machine learning frameworks, they still heavily rely on accurate face/person tracking, motion detection, landmark detection and aligned transcripts or captions.

Unlike all these previous works, our approach does not rely on face/person tracking, motion detection, facial landmark localization or subtitle/aligned transcript as well as handcrafted features engineering. With only the input of cropped face regions and corresponding audio segment, our approach recognizes speaker in each frame in real-time.

3. MULTIMODAL CNN FRAMEWORK

Our approach is a learning based system in which we fuse the face and audio cues in the feature extraction level. The face feature extractor is learned from data rather than handcrafted. Then our learning framework is able to leverage both face and audio features and learns a unified multimodal feature extractor. This enables a larger learning machine to learn a unified multimodal classifier which takes both face image and speaker's sound track as inputs. The overview of the learning framework is illustrated in Figure 1.

3.1 Multimodal CNN Architecture

We adopted CNN [10] as the baseline model in our learning machine. As we will see shortly, CNN's architecture is inherently extensible. This makes our extension to multimodal learning concise, efficient but powerful.

The role of CNN in our framework is two-fold. Firstly, it learns a face feature extractor from face imagery data so that we have a solid face recognition baseline. Secondly, it combines both face feature extractor as well as the audio feature extractor and learns a unified multimodal classifier.

Figure 2 illustrates the design of our model. We will later show with insights that this model is very effective for SN tasks despite its conciseness.

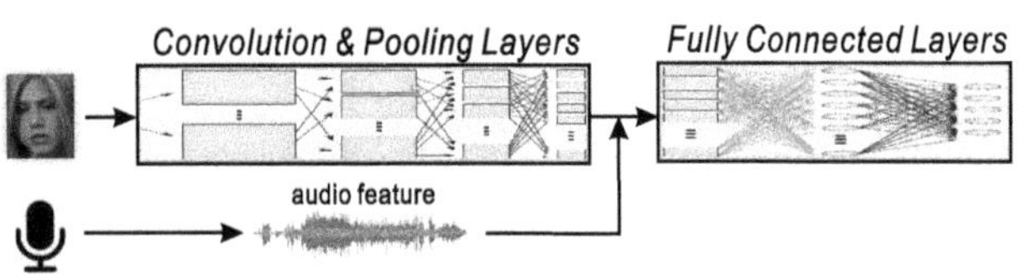

Figure 2: Multimodal CNN architecture.

In the trainable face feature extractor part, each layer of the network can be expressed as

$$N_c(\mathcal{I}) = \sigma(\mathcal{P}(\sigma(\mathcal{I} * K^l + b^l))),\ l = 1, 2, ..., n, \qquad (1)$$

where $\mathcal{I}$ is the input for each layer. $\mathcal{I}$ is usually a 3D image volume, namely 3-channel input images when $l = 1$, multi-channel feature maps when $1 < l \leq n$. K^l and b^l are the trainable convolution kernels and trainable bias term in layer l respectively. σ represents the nonlinearity in the network, which is modeled by a rectifier expressed as $f(x) = \max(0, x)$. $\mathcal{P}$ is a pooling function which subsamples the inputs by a factor of 2. Same nonlinearity is applied after the pooling function. When $l = n$ the output of $N_c(\mathcal{I})$ is a one dimensional high level feature vector.

For audio feature extraction, we use mel frequency cepstral coefficients (MFCCs) [14]. The MFCCs of one audio frame is also an one dimensional feature vector. This allows us to ensemble a unified multimodal feature by stacking $N_c(\mathcal{I})$ and MFCCs together.

It is worth noting that stacking of face feature and MFCCs in this stage is non-trivial in terms of classification. The reason is the ensuing trainable classifier essentially learns a higher dimensional nonlinear feature representation of the previous layer by mapping the stacked multimodal feature to a higher dimensional feature space. This is expressed as

$$N_f(\mathcal{F}) = \sigma(\mathcal{F} \cdot \mathcal{W}^l + b^l),\ l = n+1, n+2, ..., m, \qquad (2)$$

where $\mathcal{F}$ is the stack of face feature and MFCCs with layer $l = n + 1$. When $n + 1 < l < m$, we impose constraint $Dim(\mathcal{F}^{l-1}) < Dim(\mathcal{F}^l)$ where $Dim()$ denotes the dimension of the intermediate feature vector, which promotes the learning of higher dimensional feature mapping. Such feature mapping is realized by the trainable weights $\mathcal{W}$ and b as well as the nonlineary σ. The system outputs the decision values of each class label by going through a softmax layer when $l = m$. The cross-entropy error function $\sum_{i=0}^{n} \ln(o_i) \cdot t_i$ is used as the error function during training, where o_i is the i-th element in $N_f(\mathcal{F})$, t is the ground truth class label. Though the conciseness of the model, one key insight of this approach is the whole system is trained end to end such that the influence of face feature extractor and MFCCs to the whole network is interwinding through learning.

Multimodal Feature Extraction. One important character of the CNN based classifier is its intermediate layers are essentially high level feature extractors. Previous studies [12] showed that such high level features is very expressive and can be applied in tasks such as recognition and content retrieval. It was not clear if such high level feature extraction mechanism works well in the context of multimodal learning. We will show in our experiments that our method is able to generate high quality multimodal features which is highly expressive in distinguishing outlier samples. This discovery forms one of the most important building blocks of making our system superior for real-life SN applications.

4. EXPERIMENTS

Experimental Setup. We evaluate our framework on over three hours videos of nine episodes from two TV series, i.e. "Friends" and "The Big Bang Theory" ("BBT"). For "Friends", faces and audio from *S01E03* (Season 01, Episode 03), *S04E04*, *S07E07* and *S10E15* serve as the training set and those from *S05E05* as the evaluation set. Note that, the whole "Friends" TV series of ten seasons is taken over a large time range of ten years. To leverage such a long time span, we intentionally selected these five episodes that spans the whole range. For "BBT", as in [17], *S01E04*, *S01E05* and *S01E06* are for training and *S01E03* for testing. For these two TV series, we only report performance of the leading roles, including six ones of "Friends", i.e. *Rachel*, *Monica*, *Phoebe*, *Joey*, *Chandler* and *Ross*, and five ones of "BBT", i.e. *Sheldon*, *Leonard*, *Howard*, *Raj* and *Penny*.

We conduct three experiments in terms of 1) face recognition; 2) identifying non-matched face-audio pairs and 3) real world SN respectively. For face recognition using both face and audio information, we only identify matched face-audio pairs. We further show how our model be able to classify matched face-audio pairs from non-matched ones. It is worth noting that the first two experiments provide solid foundations towards achieving promising performance in our third real world SN experiment. It also justifies the effectiveness of the building blocks in our resulting system.

Our CNN's detailed setting is described as follows. The network has 2 alternating convolutional and pooling layers in which the sizes of the convolution filters used are 15×15 and 5×4 respectively. The connection between the last pooling layer and the fully connected layer uses filters of size 7×5. The number of feature maps generated by the convolutional layers are 48 and 256 respectively. For fully connected layers, the number of hidden units are $1,024$ and $2,048$ respectively. Such architecture requires more than 11 million trainable parameters. All the bias terms are initialized to 0.01 to prevent the dead unit caused by rectifier units during training. All other parameters are firstly initialized within the range of -1 to 1 drawn from a Gaussian distribution and then scaled by the number of fan-ins of hidden unit they connect to. Average pooling of factor 2 is used throughout the network.

4.1 Face Model

We evaluate our model for face recognition on "Friends" (all face images resized to 50×40). We also test four previous algorithms under the same setting, i.e. Eigenface [18], Fisherface [3], LBP [1] and OpenBR/4SF [9].

Accuracies of these four previous methods are 60.7%, 64.5%, 65.6% and 66.1% respectively. All four previous algorithms fail to work well (all $< 70\%$), on the other hand, our method works better for every subject and achieves an accuracy of 86.7%. The results are expected as previous algorithms either require alignment of the face images or detecting facial feature points or both. This makes them not able to work well in the small sized face images that are extracted from unconstrained videos, which has no guarantee of alignment of the images, challenging large variations in pose, illumination and aging, etc.

We further apply audio to fine-tune our face model. The weights in this extended network is initialized by the parameters in the face-alone network. For the newly introduced parameters by the audio inputs, they are initialized in the

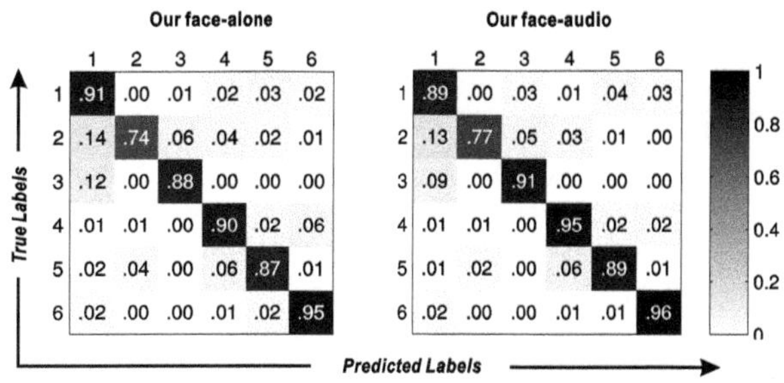

Figure 3: Confusion matrices of our face-alone and face-audio models for face recognition on "Friends". Labels 1-6 stand for the six subjects accordingly, i.e. *Rachel*, *Monica*, *Phoebe*, *Joey*, *Chandler* and *Ross*.

same way as presented before. Concerning audio features, a window size of 20ms and a frame shift of 10ms are used. We then select mean and standard deviation of 25D MFCCs, and standard deviation of 2-ΔMFCCs, resulting in a total of 75 features per audio sample. For each face, we catenate it with 5 audio samples of the same subject that are randomly selected to generate face-audio pairs.

Compared with previous face-alone model (acc: 86.7%), our face-audio model further improved this to 88.5% with corresponding confusion matrix shown in Figure 3. We can clearly see that, by adding audio information to the model, the accuracies of identifying all the subjects improve by 1-5% except a slight drop for *Rachel*.

4.2 Identifying Non-matched Pairs

In above experiments, all face-audio samples are matched pairs, i.e. belong to the same person. However, this condition cannot be fulfilled in practice. Consider a speaking frame, there are N faces, one of which is speaking, see Figure 1 as an example where $N = 3$. In order to find the correct speaker, we need to examine all face-audio pairs. All the pairs are non-matched except the one of the real speaker. And, it is almost impossible to train all possible non-matched pairs because new faces are unpredictable.

Thus, to identify non-matched pairs, a better way is to develop new strategies at the same time guarantee the quality of the face model. Instead of using the final output label of our face models, we explore the effectiveness of the features returned from the model in the last layer. As baseline, we train two binary supporting vector machines (SVM) [5]. One is trained on the 1024D fused feature that returned from our face-audio model and the other trained on 1024D face feature returned from our face-alone model concatenating with 75D audio feature (MFCC). We then train another SVM model using the same setting with the second SVM expect that we replace the 1024D face feature by the same dimensional fused feature from our face-audio model.

We test these three models on the evaluation video, which contains in total $17,131$ speaking frames. It will count as correct if the most confident face-audio pair matches, i.e. both from the same person. Two baseline SVMs achieve 82.2% and 82.9% respectively, whilst the third one can achieve 84.1%. Results clearly justify that the fused feature is more discriminative than the original face feature. On the other hand, we believe it also shows that the fused feature and MFCCs capture different but complimentary dimensions of the required information in distinguishing non-matched pairs.

Figure 4: Speaker naming result under various conditions, including pose (a)(c)(d), illumination (c)(d), small scale (b)(d), occlusion (a) and clustered scene (b)(d), etc (time stamp shown at the bottom left).

4.3 Speaker Naming

The goal of speaker naming is to identify the speaker in each frame, i.e. find out the matched face-audio pair and also identify it. It's worth noting that such a problem can be viewed as an extension of previous experiment of identifying non-matched pairs (reject all non-matched ones).

For the in total 17,131 speaking frames in the evaluation video *Friends.S05E05*, we applied the third SVM to reject all non-matched pairs. The remaining pair will be assigned with the label returned by our face-audio model. Under such setting, we can achieve the SN accuracy of 90.5%. Sample SN result can be viewed from Figure 4.

Compared with Previous Works. Previous works [2, 17] have addressed similar SN problem by incorporating face, facial landmarks, cloth features, character tracking and associated video subtitles/transcripts. They evaluated on "BBT" and achieved SN accuracy of 77.8% and 80.8% respectively (evaluation on *S01E03*). In comparison, we can achieve SN accuracy of 82.9% without introducing any face/person tracking, facial landmark localization or subtitle/transcript.

4.4 Applications

Speaking activity is the key of multimedia data content. With our system, detailed speaking activity can be obtained, including speakers' locations, identities and speaking time ranges, etc, which further enables many useful applications. We highlight two major applications in the following (please refer to our supplementary video for details):

Video Accessibility Enhancement. With speakers' locations, we can generate on-screen dynamic subtitles next to the respective speakers thus enhance video accessibility for the hearing impaired [7] and enhance the overall viewing experience as well as reduce eyestrain for normal viewers [8].

Multimedia Data Retrieval and Summarization. With the detailed speaking activity, we can further achieve some high-level multimedia data summarization tasks, including characters conversation information and scene changing information, etc, based on which fast video retrieval is possible. We highlight such information in Figure 5.

5. CONCLUSIONS

In this paper, we propose a CNN based multimodal learning framework to tackle the task of *speaker naming*. Our approach is able to automatically learn the fusion function of both face and audio cues. We show that our multimodal learning framework not only obtains high face recognition

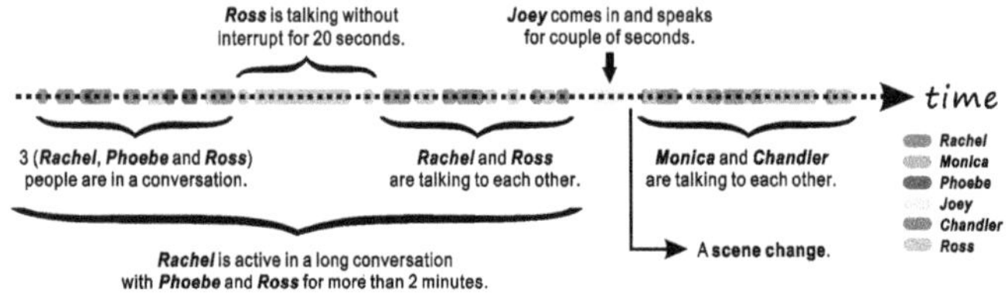

Figure 5: Speaking activity and video summarization for a 3.5 minutes video clip of *Friends.S05E05*.

accuracy but also extracts representative multimodal features which is the key to distinguish sample outliers. By combining the aforementioned capabilities, our system achieved state-of-the-art performance on two diverse TV series without introducing any face/person tracking, facial landmark localization or subtitle/transcript. The dataset and implementation of our algorithm, based on VCNN [13], are publicly available online at `http://herohuyongtao.github.io/research/publications/speaker-naming/`.

6. REFERENCES

[1] T. Ahonen, A. Hadid, and M. Pieti-kainen. Face description with local binary patterns: Application to face recognition. *TPAMI*, 2006.

[2] M. Bauml, M. Tapaswi, and R. Stiefelhagen. Semi-supervised learning with constraints for person identification in multimedia data. In *CVPR*, 2013.

[3] P. Belhumeur, J. Hespanha, and D. Kriegman. Eigenfaces vs. fisherfaces: Recognition using class specific linear projection. *TPAMI*, 1997.

[4] P. Bojanowski, F. Bach, I. Laptev, J. Ponce, et al. Finding actors and actions in movies. In *ICCV*, 2013.

[5] C. Chang and C. Lin. LIBSVM: A library for support vector machines. *TIST*, 2011.

[6] M. Everingham, J. Sivic, and A. Zisserman. "Hello! my name is... Buffy" – automatic naming of characters in TV video. In *BMVC*, 2006.

[7] R. Hong, M. Wang, M. Xu, S. Yan, and T. Chua. Dynamic captioning: Video accessibility enhancement for hearing impairment. In *MM*, 2010.

[8] Y. Hu, J. Kautz, Y. Yu, and W. Wang. Speaker-following video subtitles. *TOMM*, 2014.

[9] J. Klontz, B. Klare, S. Klum, A. Jain, and M. Burge. Open source biometric recognition. In *BTAS*, 2013.

[10] A. Krizhevsky et al. Imagenet classification with deep convolutional neural networks. In *NIPS*, 2012.

[11] C. Liu, S. Jiang, and Q. Huang. Naming faces in broadcast news video by image google. In *MM*, 2008.

[12] M. Oquab, L. Bottou, I. Laptev, and J. Sivic. Learning and transferring mid-level image representations using convolutional neural networks. In *CVPR*, 2014.

[13] J. Ren and L. Xu. On vectorization of deep convolutional neural networks for vision tasks. In *AAAI*, 2015.

[14] M. Sahidullah and G. Saha. Design, analysis and experimental evaluation of block based transformation in mfcc computation for speaker recognition. *SC*, 2012.

[15] J. Sivic et al. "Who are you?" - learning person specific classifiers from video. In *CVPR*, 2009.

[16] K. Takenaka, T. Bando, S. Nagasaka, et al. Drive video summarization based on double articulation structure of driving behavior. In *MM*, 2012.

[17] M. Tapaswi, M. Bauml, and R. Stie-felhagen. "Knock! Knock! Who is it?" probabilistic person identification in TV-series. In *CVPR*, 2012.

[18] M. Turk and A. Pentland. Eigenfaces for recognition. *JCN*, 1991.

[19] J. Yang and A. Hauptmann. Naming every individual in news video monologues. In *MM*, 2004.

[20] J. Yang, R. Yan, and A. Hauptmann. Multiple instance learning for labeling faces in broadcasting news video. In *MM*, 2005.

[21] H. Zhang, Z. Zha, Y. Yang, S. Yan, et al. Attribute-augmented semantic hierarchy. In *MM*, 2013.

Cross-Modal Image-Tag Relevance Learning for Social Images

Yong Cheng, Zhengxiang Cai, Rui Feng, Cheng Jin, Yuejie Zhang
School of Computer Science, Shanghai Key Laboratory of Intelligent Information Processing
Fudan University, Shanghai 200433, China
{13110240027, 14110240020, fengrui, jc, yjzhang}@fudan.edu.cn

Tao Zhang
School of Information Management and Engineering
Shanghai University of Finance and Economics
Shanghai 200433, China
taozhang@mail.shufe.edu.cn

ABSTRACT
A new algorithm is developed in this paper to support more effective cross-modal image-tag relevance learning for large-scale social images, which integrates the multimodal feature representation, multimodal relevance measurement, and cross-modal relevance fusion. The main contribution of our work is that we provide a more reasonable base to learn cross-modal relevance among social images, which can be acquired from integrating multimodal image and tag relevance with multiple features in different modalities. Very positive results were obtained in our experiments using a large quantity of public social image data.

Categories and Subject Descriptors
H.3.3 [**Information Storage and Retrieval**]: Information Search and Retrieval – *Search Process*.

Keywords
Cross-modal image-tag relevance learning; social image; multimodal feature representation; multimodal relevance measurement; cross-modal relevance fusion

1. INTRODUCTION
With the explosive growth of social images available on sharing websites such as *Flickr*, how to seamlessly handle the complex structures of social images to achieve more effective cross-media image retrieval has become an important research focus [1]. However, because of the semantic gap, there may exist huge uncertainty on the correspondence relationships among visual contents in images and semantic tags in annotations. The quality of tags is far from satisfactory due to the ambiguity, incompleteness and over-subjectivity [3]. Thus enabling the objective cross-modal image-tag relevance learning has become a critical issue for supporting cross-media image retrieval.

In recent years, there is some research work for multimodal relevance learning between visual contents and semantic tags in social images. Li *et al.* [2] proposed a neighbor voting algorithm for tag relevance learning and then extended their work using a variety of visual features. Liu *et al.* [3] proposed a social image "retagging" scheme that aimed at assigning images with better content descriptors. Zhuang *et al.* [4] overcame the challenge of social tag ranking for social images by proposing a two-view learning approach. Li *et al.* [5] proposed a nonlinear matrix factorization method to predict the tag relevance to visual contents. Gao *et al.* [6] proposed an approach that simultaneously utilized both visual and textual information to estimate the relevance of user tagged images. Lan *et al.* [7] proposed Max-Margin Riffled Independence Model for image tag ranking. Zhu *et al.* [8] cast the social tag relevance learning problem as an adaptive teleportation random walk process on the voting graph. To achieve cross-modal image-tag relevance learning, three inter-related issues should be addressed simultaneously: 1) multimodal analysis of social images to discover valuable multimodal features; 2) multimodal relevance measurement to model the objective criterion for image relevance and tag relevance; and 3) cross-modal relevance fusion to identify better cross-modal correlations between images and tags.

Based on the above observations, a novel scheme is developed in this paper to facilitate more effective cross-modal image-tag relevance learning for large-scale social images. Our scheme significantly differs from other earlier work in: a) The multimodal feature extraction and fusion are developed to construct better multimodal feature representations for multimodal contents in social images. b) An efficient measurement mechanism is established to achieve the objective decision-making for multimodal relevance. c) The cross-modal relevance fusion has the strong ability to achieve more precise characterization of multimodal correlations between visual images and semantic tags. d) A new cross-modal relevance learning framework is built by integrating the above representation, measurement and fusion mechanisms. The main contribution of our work is that we provide a more reasonable base to learn cross-modal relevance among social images, which can be acquired from integrating multimodal image and tag relevance with multiple features in different modalities. We have obtained very positive results in our experiments on a large number of public social image data.

2. MULTIMODAL FEATURE REPRESENTATION
Multimodal Feature Generation with LDA
Latent Dirichlet Allocation (LDA) aims at representing each document with a list of topic probabilities, and each word is generated from a single topic. To apply LDA to extract visual features of social images, we represent each social image as a visual document with "*visual words*", and these visual words are extracted based on *Classeme* which is a mid-level descriptor with the output of a large number of weakly trained object category classifiers. The obvious advantage of such visual words over others like the SIFT descriptor is that each visual word has the semantic meaning rather than merely visual information. Thus LDA can be applied to extract the visual features of social images based on visual words. While the textual annotation associated with a social image can be viewed as the semantic document, LDA can also be directly utilized to extract the semantic features.

In LDA, each document can be represented with a vector of probabilities on the directory of all the topics, and these vectors

MM '15, October 26-30, 2015, Brisbane, Australia.

DOI: http://dx.doi.org/10.1145/2733373.2806294

are adopted as the generated visual and semantic features to represent the social image. Let $SIMG$ be the set of social images that consists of N samples, TS_V is the set of hidden topics for visual images, and TS_A is the set of hidden topics for semantic annotations; for a social image $simg_i$ ($1 \le i \le N$), $simg_i^V$ is the visual document with all the visual words that have ever occurred in the visual image of $simg_i$, and $simg_i^A$ is the semantic document with all the tag words that have ever occurred in the annotation of $simg_i$; T_i^V is the topic sequence that generates $simg_i^V$, and T_i^A is the topic sequence that generates $simg_i^A$; TP_i^V is the topic probability distribution of $simg_i^V$ on TS_V, and TP_i^A is the topic distribution of $simg_i^A$ on TS_A. Thus for the image and annotation parts of $simg_i$, the joint probability distributions of topic sequence, visual/semantic document, and topic probability distribution are:

$$P\left(TP_i^V, T_i^V, simg_i^V \middle| \alpha_1, \beta_1\right) = P\left(TP_i^V \middle| \alpha_1\right) \prod_{j=1}^{\left|simg_i^V\right|} P\left(T_{ij}^V \middle| TP_i^V\right) P\left(simg_{ij}^V \middle| T_{ij}^V, \beta_1\right) \quad (1)$$

$$P\left(TP_i^A, T_i^A, simg_i^A \middle| \alpha_2, \beta_2\right) = P\left(TP_i^A \middle| \alpha_2\right) \prod_{j=1}^{\left|simg_i^A\right|} P\left(T_{ij}^A \middle| TP_i^A\right) P\left(simg_{ij}^A \middle| T_{ij}^A, \beta_2\right)$$

where α_1, α_2, β_1 and β_2 are four constant parameters for the Dirichlet distribution, and Markov Chain Monte Carlo (MCMC) is used to implement the parameter estimation. Finally TP_i^V and TP_i^A are used to represent the visual feature vector F_i^V and semantic feature vector S_i^V for each $simg_i$.

Multimodal Feature Fusion with CCA

Canonical Correlation Analysis (CCA) can provide a linear function learning method by projecting different types of data into a high dimension feature space. Thus CCA is introduced to make a better solution for multimodal feature fusion.

Assume for $SIMG$ with N samples, $V \in R^{|F^V|*N}$ and $S \in R^{|FA|*N}$ are the centered visual and semantic feature matrices, and $|F^V|$ and $|F^A|$ are the dimensionality values for these two matrices, generally $|F^V| \neq |F^A|$, the following projection can be considered:

$$CCA_{VV} = VV^T, \quad CCA_{SS} = SS^T, \quad (2)$$
$$CCA_{VS} = VS^T, \quad CCA_{SV} = SV^T$$

To find a projection relation between the visual feature space and semantic feature space that could maximize the correlation between different feature views, Formula (3) is adopted:

$$\underset{p \in R^{F^V}, q \in R^{F^A}}{\arg\max} \; p^T CCA_{VS} q, \quad (3)$$
$$s.t., \; p^T (CCA_{VV} + \upsilon I) p = 1, \; q^T (CCA_{SS} + \upsilon I) q = 1$$

where the small regularization factor υ is used to avoid the numerically ill-conditioned problem; p and q are the projection directions that force the data from V and S into the common space; and I denotes an identity matrix. Hence, we can obtain the set of the projection matrix $P=\{p_1, p_2, \ldots, p_R\}$ and $Q=\{q_1, q_2, \ldots, q_R\}$ by transforming it to a symmetric eigenvalue problem. The ith component p_i and q_i can be calculated by Formula (4).

$$(CCA_{VV} + \upsilon I)^{-1} CCA_{VS} (CCA_{SS} + \upsilon I)^{-1} CCA_{SV} p_i = \lambda_i^2 p_i \quad (4)$$
$$(CCA_{SS} + \upsilon I)^{-1} CCA_{SV} (CCA_{VV} + \upsilon I)^{-1} CCA_{VS} p_i = \varphi_i^2 q_i$$

where λ^2_i and φ^2_i represent the ith eigenvalue. We can project the feature vectors of V and S into a common space based on the matrices of $P \in R^{|F^V|*N}$ and $Q \in R^{|FA|*N}$. Thus we can embed the visual and semantic features into a subspace that can generate the final multi-modal feature MF in Formula (5).

$$MF = \gamma V^T * P + (1-\gamma) S^T * Q \quad (5)$$

where γ is a constant parameter in [0, 1]. Such a linear weighting can achieve the lower dimensional feature representation without the sacrifice of the relevance learning performance.

3. MULTIMODAL RELEVANCE MEASUREMENT

Hypergraph Model Construction

We utilize two hypergraphs to describe multimodal associations among images and tags from different perspectives of image and tag. In the image hypergraph, each image is taken as the vertex and the inter-tag relations are used to define the associations between two vertices. For an image hypergraph $IHG=\{IH\_V, IH\_E\}$, IH_V is the vertex set, $IH\_V=\{ih\_v|ih\_v \in SS\_I\}$, SS_I is the visual image part of the social image set; and IH_E is the hyper-edge set, $IH\_E=\{ih\_e|ih\_e \in SS\_T\}$, SS_T is the annotation tag part of the social image set. Each tag corresponds to a hyper-edge, and all the images with such a tag are regarded as the vertices connected to the hyper-edge. In the tag hypergraph, each tag is taken as the vertex and the inter-image relations are used to define the associations between two vertices. For a tag hypergraph $THG=\{TH\_V, TH\_E\}$, TH_V is the vertex set, $TH\_V=\{th\_v|th\_v \in SS\_T\}$; and TH_E is the hyper-edge set, $TH\_E=\{th\_e|th\_e \in SS\_I\}$. Each image associates with a hyper-edge, and all the related tags are taken as the vertices connected to the hyper-edge. An instantiation of hypergraph construction is shown in Figure 1.

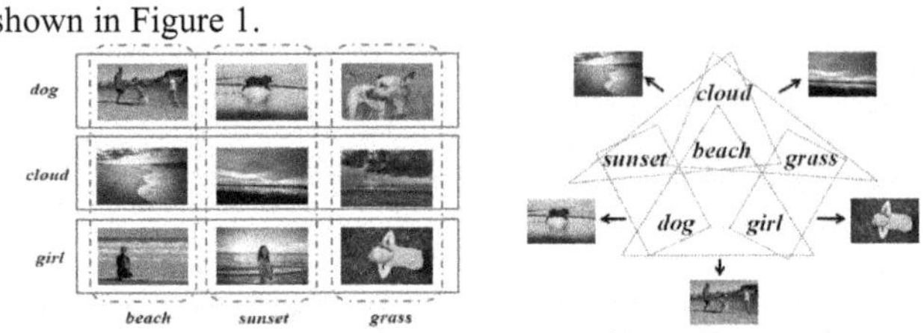

(a) Image Hypergraph (b) Tag Hypergraph

Figure 1. An instantiation of hypergraph construction.

In the image hypergraph, we consider the relevance for the images covered in the corresponding hyper-edge to each tag is the image relevance. For a given tag, all the images that contain this tag form a semantic space, in which each image is more or less related to the tag. Thus the image with higher density in the semantic space is more relevant to the corresponding tag. Similarly, the tag relevance in the tag hypergraph means that all the tags contained by the given image form a semantic space for this image and the tag with higher density should have the higher relevance.

Relevance Measurement via Random Walk

Since in the hypergraph each hyper-edge with the covered vertices forms a semantic space, the Random Walk (RW) is conducted to compute the vertex density for acquiring two relevance matrices of RM_I and RM_T, where $RM\_I \in R^{|SS\_T|*|SS\_I|}$, $RM\_I[t][i]$ is the relevance of the image $SS\_I[i]$ to the tag $SS\_T[t]$; and $RM\_T \in R^{|SS\_I|*|SS\_T|}$, $RM\_T[i, t]$ is the relevance of $SS\_T[t]$ to $SS\_I[i]$.

Algorithm 1: *RW_IHG*(Initial Value *RM_I*(0)) //RW on Image Hypergraph
1: **Initialize** *RM_I*=*RM_I*(0);
2: **for** t=1 **to** $|SS\_T|$ **do**
3: *Compute the transition probability* $P^V \in R^{|SS\_I|*|SS\_I|}$ *for the* t^{th} *tag* $SS\_T[t]$;
4: **while** *not converged* **do**
5: $RM\_I[t] = \theta_I RM\_I[t] \cdot P^V + (1-\theta_I) RM\_I(0)[t]$; //$\theta_I$ is a constant parameter
6: **return** *RM_I*;

Algorithm 2: *RW_THG*(Initial Value *RM_T*(0)) //RW on Tag Hypergraph
1: **Initialize** *RM_T*=*RM_T*(0);
2: **for** i=1 **to** $|SS\_I|$ **do**
3: *Compute the transition probability* $P^A \in R^{|SS\_T|*|SS\_T|}$ *for the* i^{th} *image* $SS\_I[i]$;
4: **while** *not converged* **do**
5: $RM\_T[i] = \theta_T RM\_T[i] \cdot P^A + (1-\theta_T) RM\_T(0)[i]$; //$\theta_T$ is a constant parameter
6: **return** *RM_T*;

The initial values for $RM\_I(0)$ and $RM\_T(0)$ are set as:

$$RM\_I(0)[t][i] = RM\_T(0)[i][t] = \begin{cases} \frac{KNN(SS\_I[i], SS\_T[t])/k - |IS(SS\_T[t])|/|SS|}{|IS(SS\_T[t])|/|SS|}, & iff(SS\_I[i] \in IS(SS\_T[t])) \\ 0, & Otherwise \end{cases} \tag{6}$$

$$1 \le i \le |SS\_I|, 1 \le t \le |SS\_T|$$

where $KNN(SS\_I[i], SS\_T[t])$ is the number of images labeled with the tth tag $SS\_T[t]$ of SS_T in the k-nearest-neighbor image set for the ith image $SS\_I[i]$ of SS_I; SS is the entire social image set; and $IS(SS\_T[t])$ is the set of images that have $SS\_T[t]$ as one of its annotation tags. The higher rate means the closer association between $SS\_I[i]$ and $SS\_T[t]$, and vice versa.

In the image hypergraph *IHG*, the transition probability P^V represents the jump possibility from one image vertex ih_v_{i1} (i.e., $SS\_I[i_1]$) to another ih_v_{i2} (i.e., $SS\_I[i_2]$) in the related hyper-edge to a certain tag $SS\_T[t]$, which can be obtained with the following semantic similarity between two images.

$$P^V[ih\_v_{i_1}][ih\_v_{i_2}] = P^V[SS\_I[i_1]][SS\_I[i_2]] = \begin{cases} \frac{Sim(SS\_I[i_1], SS\_I[i_2])}{\sum_{i=1}^{|SS\_I|} Sim(SS\_I[i_1], SS\_I[i])}, & iff\begin{pmatrix} (SS\_T[t] \in TS(SS\_I[i_1]) \\ \&\& SS\_T[t] \in TS(SS\_I[i_2]) \end{pmatrix} \\ 0, & Otherwise \end{cases} \tag{7}$$

$$Sim(SS\_I[i_1], SS\_I[i_2]) = \exp(-Dist(MF(SS\_I[i_1]), MF(SS\_I[i_2])))$$

$$1 \le i_1, i_2 \le |SS\_I|, 1 \le t \le |SS\_T|$$

where $Dist(MF(SS\_I[i_1]), MF(SS\_I[i_2]))$ denotes the Euclidean distance between two multimodal feature vectors for $SS\_I[i_1]$ and $SS\_I[i_2]$; and $TS(SS\_I[i_1])$ and $TS(SS\_I[i_2])$ are the annotation tag sets for $SS\_I[i_1]$ and $SS\_I[i_2]$. Similarly, in the tag hypergraph *THG* the transition probability between two tag vertices of th_v_{t1} (i.e., $SS\_T[t_1]$) and th_v_{t2} (i.e., $SS\_T[t_2]$) for a given image $SS\_I[i]$ (i.e., the related hyper-edge) can be computed through aggregating all the images that are labeled with these tags.

$$P^A[th\_v_{t_1}][th\_v_{t_2}] = P^A[SS\_T[t_1]][SS\_T[t_2]] = \begin{cases} \frac{Sim(SS\_T[t_1],[SS\_T[t_2]])}{\sum_{t=1}^{|SS\_T|} Sim(SS\_T[t_1], SS\_T[t])}, & iff\begin{pmatrix} (SS\_I[i] \in IS(SS\_T[t_1]) \\ \&\& SS\_I[i] \in IS(SS\_T[t_2]) \end{pmatrix} \\ 0, & Otherwise \end{cases} \tag{8}$$

$$Sim(SS\_T[t_1], SS\_T[t_2]) = \exp\left(-Dist\left(\frac{\sum_{i_1=1}^{|IS(SS\_T[t_1])|} MF(IS(SS\_T[t_1])[i_1])}{|IS(SS\_T[t_1])|}, \frac{\sum_{i_2=1}^{|IS(SS\_T[t_2])|} MF(IS(SS\_T[t_2])[i_2])}{|IS(SS\_T[t_2])|}\right)\right)$$

$$1 \le i \le |SS\_I|, 1 \le t_1, t_2 \le |SS\_T|$$

4. CROSS-MODAL RELEVANCE FUSION

For integrating the image and tag relevance into the cross-modal relevance, it aims at projecting the multimodal relevance into a common framework and making sure that the correlation between images and tags can be maximized. Since the base matrix RM_I means the image relevance to a certain tag, such image relevance is mainly used in image ranking (i.e., all the images labeled with this tag are ranked according to the relevance to the tag). Thus RM_I can be transformed into the confidence matrix CRM_I:

$$CRM\_I[t][i_1][i_2] = \frac{RM\_I[t][i_1] - RM\_I[t][i_2]}{\max(RM\_I[t]) - \min(RM\_I[t])} \tag{9}$$

$$1 \le i_1, i_2 \le |SS\_I|, 1 \le i \le |SS\_T|$$

where $CRM\_I[t][i_1][i_2] \in [-1, +1]$ denotes the confidence that the image $SS\_I[i_1]$ is more relevant than another $SS\_I[i_2]$ to the given tag $SS\_T[t]$, and the higher positive value means a higher confidence for the relevance between $SS\_I[i_1]$ and $SS\_T[t]$; the numerator denotes the difference for $SS\_I[i_1]$ and $SS\_I[i_2]$ in RM_I; and the denominator is a normalized factor.

Since the base matrix RM_T means the tag relevance to a certain image, such tag relevance are mainly used in tag ranking (i.e., all the tags labeled for this image are ranked according to the relevance to the image). RM_T can be transformed into CRM_T:

$$CRM\_T[i][t_1][t_2] = \frac{RM\_T[i][t_1] - RM\_T[i][t_2]}{\max(RM\_T[i]) - \min(RM\_T[i])} \tag{10}$$

$$1 \le i \le |SS\_I|, 1 \le t_1, t_2 \le |SS\_T|$$

where $CRM\_T[i][t_1][t_2] \in [-1, +1]$ denotes the confidence that the tag $SS\_T[t_1]$ is more relevant than another $SS\_T[t_2]$ to the given image $SS\_I[i]$, and the higher value means a higher confidence for the relevance between $SS\_I[i]$ and $SS\_T[t_1]$.

For fusing the multimodal image and tag relevance into cross-modal image-tag relevance, we consider reconstructing a syncretic relevance matrix $SRM\_IT \in R^{|SS\_I|*|SS\_T|}$ to integrate the relevance confidence in the above two confidence matrices. Such a syncretic relevance matrix cannot only keep the characteristics of the relevance base matrices for different modalities, but also be consistent with these base matrices as much as possible. Thus we can take full advantage of the specific relationship between the relevance measurements for different modalities to get better cross-modal relevance. The objective function for SRM_IT is:

$$OF(SRM\_IT) = \underset{SRM\_IT}{\operatorname{argmin}} \begin{pmatrix} \rho \sum_{t=1}^{|SS\_T|} \sum_{SS\_I[i_1] \in IS(SS\_T[t])} \sum_{SS\_I[i_2] \in IS(SS\_T[t])} \frac{CRM\_I[t,i_1,i_2]*(SRM\_IT[i_2,t] - SRM\_IT[i_1,t])}{|IS(SS\_T[t])|} + \\ (1-\rho) \sum_{i=1}^{|SS\_I|} \sum_{SS\_T[t_1] \in TS(SS\_I[i])} \sum_{SS\_T[t_2] \in TS(SS\_I[i])} \frac{CRM\_T[i,t_1,t_2]*(SRM\_IT[i,t_2] - SRM\_IT[i,t_1])}{|TS(SS\_I[i])|} \\ + \sum_{i=1}^{|SS\_I|} \sum_{t=1}^{|SS\_T|} SRM\_IT[i][t]^2 \end{pmatrix}$$

$$1 \le i_1, i_2 \le |SS\_I|, 1 \le t_1, t_2 \le |SS\_T| \tag{11}$$

where the former two terms aim to keep SRM_IT being consistent with CRM_I and CRM_T; the last is a regular term; and ρ is a constant parameter in [0, 1] to tune the weights of image and tag relevance. Since this function is convex, its partial derivative can be adopted to obtain the final cross-modal relevance $SRM\_IT[i][t]$ between an image $SS\_I[i]$ and a tag $SS\_T[t]$.

5. EXPERIMENT AND ANALYSIS

Our dataset is established based on two benchmark datasets of *Nus-Wide* and *MIR-Flickr25k*. To evaluate the effectiveness of our algorithm, the ground truth relevance is considered to measure the benchmark metrics of *Average Precision@k* (*AP@k*) and *Mean Average Precision* (*MAP*) for image ranking and another metric of *Average Rank Position Distance* (*ARPD*) for tag ranking.

$$AP@k = \frac{1}{|TTS| \cdot k} \sum_{i=1}^{|TTS|} \sum_{j=1}^{k} rel(TTS[i], img_j) \tag{12}$$

$$MAP = \frac{1}{|TTS|} \sum_{i=1}^{|TTS|} \frac{1}{|RIS(TTS[i])|} \cdot \sum_{j=1}^{RN_i} \frac{rn_j}{j} rel(TTS[i], img_j) \tag{13}$$

$$ARPD = \frac{1}{|TTS| * AAL} \sum_{i=1}^{|TTS|} \left(\frac{1}{|IIS(TTS[i])|} \cdot \sum_{j=1}^{|IIS(TTS[i])|} rp(TTS[i], img_j) - \frac{1}{|RIS(TTS[i])|} \cdot \sum_{k=1}^{|RIS(TTS[i])|} rp(TTS[i], img_k) \right) \tag{14}$$

where *TTS* is the testing tag/concept set; k represents the returned top-k results for each testing tag; *rel*(,) is a binarization function, $rel(TTS[i], img_j)=1$ when img_j is relevant to $TTS[i]$, otherwise 0; $RIS(TTS[i])$ and $IIS(TTS[i])$ are the relevant and irrelevant image sets for $TTS[i]$; RN_i is the number of returned results; rn_j is the number of relevant images in the top-j ranked image list; *AAL* is the average annotation length for images in the whole dataset; and $rp(TTS[i], img_j)$ is the rank position of $TTS[i]$ for img_j.

Our cross-modal image-tag relevance learning model is created by integrating Unimodal Image Relevance (UIR), Unimodal Tag Relevance (UTR), and Cross-modal Image-Tag Relevance (CITR). To show the effect of each part, we focus on investigating the whole performance of cross-modal relevance learning for image ranking and tag ranking. We compare the performance rising speeds for different settings of the important parameter ρ in Formula (11), which implies the effectiveness difference between the unimodal relevance (i.e., ρ=0 for *UTR* or ρ=1 for *UIR*) and our cross-modal relevance (i.e., 0<ρ<1 for *CITR*). The experimental results for cross-modal relevance learning are shown in Figure 2.

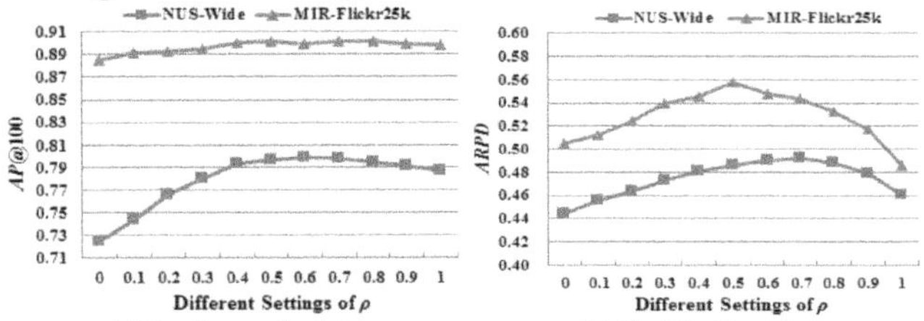

(a) For Image Ranking (b) For Tag Ranking

Figure 2. The experimental results for cross-modal relevance learning.

It can be seen from Figure 2(a) that for image ranking on *Nus-Wide* and *MIR-Flickr25k*, we can obtain the best *AP*@100 of 0.902 in the evaluation pattern of fusing unimodal image and tag relevance into cross-modal relevance. In comparison with the unimodal learning based on only image relevance (ρ=1), the performance could be greatly promoted by adding unimodal tag relevance based on cross-modal relevance fusion, which confirms the obvious advantage of our cross-modal relevance learning. Compared two models with unimodal tag relevance and cross-modal relevance, our cross-modal relevance learning can still gain the significant advantage for the performance on both *Nus-Wide* and *MIR-Flickr25k*. Compared the effectiveness of our relevance fusion on image ranking and tag ranking, we can find that the effect is more obvious on tag ranking, which implies that our cross-modal relevance learning can bring more image-tag association information gain for tag ranking. Compared the results on two different datasets, the results on *Nus-Wide* appear less performant due to the differences between these two datasets. *MIR-Flickr25k* is a small-scale refined dataset with relatively normative and consistent annotations and exhibits the relatively better image-tag relevance for limited testing tags/concepts, while *Nus-Wide* is a relatively large-scale dataset with more obvious characteristics of social images, such as noisy tag, redundant tag and missing tag, which may greatly affect the image-tag relevance for testing concepts. Compared the results for different settings of ρ, we can observe that with the appropriate setting for ρ in (0, 1) the pretty good performance can be obtained. These results are consistent with what we expect considering more valuable cross-modal relevance. As shown in Figure 2(b), the same conclusions as above can be drawn from *ARPD* on both *Nus-Wide* and *MIR-Flickr25k* for tag ranking, which show the consistence of our model on different indicators. All these observations indicate that the cross-modal relevance fusion has more positive effect on image-tag relevance learning for better description of social images, which can yield the significant performance improvement more than only considering unimodal relevance.

To give full exhibition to the superiority of our model, we have performed a comparison between our and the other classical approaches for the past few years from different aspects of image ranking and tag ranking. For image ranking, the conventional *tf-idf*-based method is adopted as the comparison baseline and Li *et al.* [2] (*Li*) and Zhu *et al.* [8] (*Zhu*) are analogous with ours, which were implemented on the same datasets of *Nus-Wide* and *MIR-Flickr25k*. The results are presented in Table 1. It can be found from Table 1 that the best performance can be acquired on *Nus-Wide* and *MIR-Flickr25k* by our approach. Although based on

Approach	*NUS-Wide*		*MIR-Flickr25k*	
	AP@10	*MAP*	*AP@10*	*MAP*
tf-idf-based	0.589	0.59	0.826	0.83
Li *et al.*'s (*Li*)	0.748	0.67	0.891	0.88
Zhu *et al.*'s (*Zhu*)	0.752	0.67	0.892	0.88
Our Approach	**0.799**	**0.71**	**0.897**	**0.89**

Table 1. The comparison among different approaches for image ranking.

our approach, the values of *AP*@100 and *MAP* on *MIR-Flickr25k* may exhibit the slight increase over those of *Li*/*Zhu*, we can observe that these values on *Nus-Wide* have been dramatically higher than those of *Li*/*Zhu*. Under such a complicated learning environment of *Nus-Wide*, our approach reveals more significant advantage. This implies that our model is exactly a better way for determining cross-modal associations.

For tag ranking, the conventional original rank method is adopted as the comparison baseline and Liu *et al.* [9] (*Liu*) and Zhuang *et al.* [4] (*Zhuang*) are analogous with ours, which were implemented on the same datasets of *Nus-Wide* and *MIR-Flickr25k*. The results are presented in Table 2.

Approach	*NUS-Wide*			*MIR-Flickr25k*		
	ARPD (TN<=5)	*ARPD (TN>5)*	*ARPD (All)*	*ARPD (TN<=5)*	*ARPD (TN>5)*	*ARPD (All)*
original-rank-based	0.005	0.219	0.200	0.059	0.398	0.229
Liu *et al.*'s (*Liu*)	0.043	0.474	0.385	0.11	0.558	0.378
Zhuang *et al.*'s (*Zhuang*)	0.021	0.307	0.257	0.081	0.625	0.33
Our Approach	**0.089**	**0.615**	**0.489**	**0.215**	**0.899**	**0.56**

Table 2. The comparison among different approaches for Tag ranking. (*TN* denotes the tag number for each image, and *All* refers to having no tag number limitation)

It can also be found from Table 2 that the best performance can be acquired on *Nus-Wide* and *MIR-Flickr25k* by our approach. Based on our approach, we can observe that the values of *ARPD*(*TN*<=5), *ARPD*(*TN*>5) and *ARPD*(*All*) on both two datasets have been dramatically higher than those of *Liu*/*Zhuang*. It means that for all the tags in an image, the relevant tags can get the higher rank than the irrelevant ones with the stronger learning ability for cross-modal image-tag relevance. This also confirms the prominent role of our cross-modal relevance learning once again.

6. CONCLUSIONS

A new framework is implemented to exploit multimodal correlations to enable cross-modal image-tag relevance learning, which contains the in-depth feature analysis for characterizing multimodal attributes, an efficient measurement for objective multimodal image and tag relevance, and a novel cross-modal relevance fusion for cross-modal relevance expressions. Our future work will focus on making our system available online, so that more Internet users can benefit from our research.

7. ACKNOWLEDGMENTS

This work is supported by National Natural Science Fund of China (61170095; 71171126), National Science & Technology Pillar Program of China (No. 2012BAH59F04), Shanghai Philosophy Social Sciences Planning Project (2014BYY009), and Zhuoxue Program of Fudan University. Cheng Jin is the corresponding author.

8. REFERENCES

[1] Wu, L., Jin, R., and Jain, A.K. 2013. Tag Completion for Image Retrieval. *IEEE Transactions on PAMI*, 35(3):716-727.

[2] Li, X.R., Snoek, C.G.M., and Worring, M. 2009. Learning Social Tag Relevance by Neighbor Voting. *IEEE Transactions on Multimedia*, 11(7):1310-1322.

[3] Liu, D., Hua, X.S., Wang, M., and Zhang, H.J. 2010. Image Retagging. In *Proceedings of MM 2010*, 491-500.

[4] Zhuang, J.F., and Hoi, S.C.H. 2011. A Two-View Learning Approach for Image Tag Ranking. In *Proceedings of WSDM 2011*, 625-634.

[5] Li, Z.C., Liu, J., and Lu, H.Q. 2013. Nonlinear Matrix Factorization with Unified Embedding for Social Tag Relevance Learning. *Neurocomputing*, 105(1):38-44.

[6] Gao, Y., Zha, Z.J., Shen, J.L., Li, X.L., and Wu, X.D. 2013. Visual-Textual Joint Relevance Learning for Tag-Based Social Image Retrieval. *IEEE Transactions on Image Processing*, 22(1):363-376.

[7] Lan, T. and Mori, G. 2013. A Max-Margin Riffled Independence Model for Image Tag Ranking. In *Proceedings of CVPR 2013*, 3103-3110.

[8] Zhu, X.F., Nejdl, W., and Georgescu, M. 2014. An Adaptive Teleportation Random Walk Model for Learning Social Tag Relevance. In *Proceedings of SIGIR 2014*, 223-232.

[9] Liu, D., Hua, X.S., Yang, L.J., Wang, M. and Zhang, H.J. 2009. Tag Ranking. In *Proceedings of WWW 2009*, 351-360.

Local Depth Patterns for Tracking in Depth Videos

Sari Awwad, Fairouz Hussein, Massimo Piccardi
Faculty of Engineering and IT
University of Technology, Sydney
{Sari.Awwad@student.,Fairouz.Hussein@student.,Massimo.Piccardi@}uts.edu.au

ABSTRACT

Conventional video tracking operates over RGB or grey-level data which contain significant clues for the identification of the targets. While this is often desirable in a video surveillance context, use of video tracking in privacy-sensitive environments such as hospitals and care facilities is often perceived as intrusive. Therefore, in this work we present a tracker that provides effective target tracking based solely on depth data. The proposed tracker is an extension of the popular Struck algorithm which leverages a structural SVM framework for tracking. The main contributions of this work are novel depth features based on local depth patterns and a heuristic for effectively handling occlusions. Experimental results over the challenging Princeton Tracking Benchmark (PTB) dataset report a remarkable accuracy compared to the original Stuck tracker and other state-of-the-art trackers using depth and RGB data.

Categories and Subject Descriptors

I.4.8 [IMAGE PROCESSING AND COMPUTER VISION]: Scene Analysis–depth cues, tracking.

Keywords

Depth videos; privacy; tracking; LDP features; Struck; Princeton Tracking Benchmark dataset.

1. INTRODUCTION AND RELATED WORK

In conventional video surveillance and multimedia applications, video tracking aims to extract detailed trajectory information from individuals' whereabouts. Given that tracking is typically performed on RBG or grey-level data, its natural by-product is rich appearance information about the tracked targets, often permitting their full identification. While this may be desirable in a video surveillance context, it is unacceptable in applications where privacy is paramount such as patient monitoring in hospitals. While it is in principle possible to apply post-processing to obfuscate faces, the availability of appearance data in the first instance poses a latent threat to privacy.

In recent years, the release of sensors such as Microsoft Kinect has made the availability of depth videos inexpensive and widespread.

MM'15, October 26-30, 2015, Brisbane, Australia.
© 2015 ACM ISBN 978-1-4503-3459-4/15/10 ...$15.00
DOI: http://dx.doi.org/10.1145/2733373.2806295.

A significant trend in tracking research has become the use of depth data in addition to RGB data to disambiguate occlusions and overcome illumination artifacts [2, 13, 16]. However, the possibility to track solely in depth videos has been largely unexplored to date. The challenge posed by depth tracking is major since conventional trackers rely on the targets' appearance and texture to provide correct data association. In this short paper, we investigate the possibility of providing effective tracking based on depth information alone. The motivation for this work comes mainly from hospital environments where it may be important to monitor contacts with patients, hand hygiene episodes, use of instrumentation and others while preventing subjects' identification for privacy reasons.

A tracking algorithm infers the location of a target from a sequence of measurements. In approaching tracking from depth data, the main challenge lies in the design of measurements, i.e., features, effective at tracking single targets through occlusions and in the presence of multiple targets. A common approach to the design of a depth tracker is to make use of skeletal models [15]. However, skeletal tracking is mostly designed to interact with co-operative users and is prone to fail in the presence of major view occlusions. For this reason, in this paper we approach depth tracking by features that do not require fitting of articulated pose models on the target. Our approach consists of extending a proven inferential engine - the Struck tracker of Hare *et al.* [8] - with dedicated local depth features extracted around the target hypothesis. In addition, we introduce heuristic rules leveraging depth information to improve data association. Experiments are carried out over two datasets: a simulated hospital environment dataset collected by these authors, and the recent Princeton Tracking Benchmark (PTB) dataset [16]. The first dataset consists of staged visits to a patient lying on a hospital bed. The second dataset consists of 95 videos varying in target type (humans, animals and non-deformable objects), scene type, presence of occlusion and bounding box distribution. Figure 1 displays samples of depth frames from these two datasets.

Since their inception, consumer depth cameras have found increasing adoption in multimedia and computer vision. For instance, [4] has used depth features in addition to appearance features for improved object recognition; [18] has approached human detection by fitting a 2-D head contour model and a 3-D head surface model over depth data; [9] has used leg history data for detecting human subjects from leg tracks. [6] used depth data to recognise human activities and apply adaptive data compression, winning the 3DLife Grand Challenge at ACM Multimedia 2013. In addition to these works, depth data have found significant use as an additional modality for tracking: [19] leverages point cloud clustering in depth data; [2, 13] use depth-based hierarchical clustering for tracking both individuals and groups; [16] designs dedicated features to resolve occlusions between targets. However, all of these

Figure 1: Depth frame examples from a simulated hospital scenario and the Princeton Tracking Benchmark dataset.

approaches rely on the availability of both appearance and depth data. To the best of our knowledge, this work is the first to attempt general tracking from depth data as the only modality.

2. DEPTH TRACKING

In this section, we provide a brief description of the Struck tracker that is used as the tracking engine, and present the proposed depth feature and occlusion handling procedure.

2.1 The Struck Tracker

The Struck tracker was proposed in [8] as a principled improvement to tracking-by-detection approaches. It leverages the framework of structural SVM [17] to provide a prediction for the displacement of a target from its previous position. By noting the displacement as y and the frame as x, Struck learns a predictive model by the following constrained minimisation:

$$\begin{aligned}&\underset{w,\xi}{\operatorname{argmin}} \frac{1}{2}\|w\|^2 + C\sum_{i=1}^{N}\xi_i \quad s.t.\\ &w^T\phi(x_i,y_i) - w^T\phi(x_i,y) \geq \Delta(y_i,y) - \xi_i,\\ &\quad i = 1\ldots N,\ \forall y \in Y\end{aligned} \tag{1}$$

The objective in (1) is the standard SVM objective balancing an upper bound over the empirical loss, $\sum_{i=1}^{N}\xi_i$, with a regularisation term, $\|w\|^2/2$. Feature function $\phi(x,y)$ computes a feature vector inside frame x centred on displacement y, and products $w^T\phi(x,y)$ assigns it a score. The constraints in (1) impose that the score assigned to the true displacement of the target, y_i, be greater than that assigned to any other displacement, $y \neq y_i$, by an amount decided by a chosen loss function, $\Delta(y^i,y)$. At its turn, the loss function is set to reflect the overlap between two bounding boxes centred, respectively, on target's location y_i and predicted location y:

$$\Delta(y_i,y) = 1 - overlap(y_i,y) \tag{2}$$

The challenges with the SVM problem in (1) are that the ground truth is unsupervised and that the model requires updating at every new frame. To this aim, Struck uses a number of heuristics to decide on "ground-truth" displacements and which samples to select for the updates [5,8].

Struck provides three options for feature vector $\phi(x,y)$:

- a 192-D Haar-like feature vector extracted from a grid centred at displacement y;
- a 256-D feature vector of spatially re-scaled raw pixels;
- a 480-D feature vector obtained from the concatenation of 16-bin intensity histograms computed on a four-level pyramid.

2.2 Local depth features for tracking

Many local features have been proposed for tracking in conventional video, including, amongst others, the popular spatio-temporal interest points (SIFT) [11], speeded-up robust features (SURF) [3] and local binary patterns (LBP) [14]. However, local features for tracking in depth video are still a subject of investigation. For this work, we have decided to explore a depth local feature recently proposed for activity recognition in depth video. The feature, called local depth pattern (LDP), resembles LBP in that it computes differences between cells of a local patch [21]. While this feature has proved effective for activity recognition, its performance for tracking cannot be anticipated since these two tasks rely on very different characteristics of the target.

To form our tracking feature (named LDP for tracking, or LDPT for short), we divide the target's bounding box into a $HD \times VD$ grid of LDPs. As values for HD and VD, we typically select 3 and 4, respectively. At its turn, each LDP contains a 3×3 grid of cells. Given that the bounding box has variable size, the size in pixels of the LDP and its cells has to adjust accordingly. The value of each LDP is obtained by concatenating the differences between the average depth of each of its cells with every other. Therefore, the total size of the LDPT feature is:

$$size(LDPT) = HD \times VD \times \binom{3*3}{2} \tag{3}$$

for a total of 432 dimensions. Algorithm 1 shows the detailed steps for computing an LDPT feature.

Algorithm 1 The algorithm for computing the LDPT feature.

Input: Bounding box
Output: LDPT feature
{initialises the LDPT feature to an empty set:}
$LDPT = \emptyset$
loop r = 1 : VD
  loop c = 1 : HD
    {initialises the LTD(r,c) descriptor to an empty set:}
    $LDP(r,c) = \emptyset$
    loop i = 1 : 9
      {loops over all cells in the LTD descriptor}
      loop j = i + 1 : 9
        {computes the difference with every other cell:}
        $diff(i,j) = |avgdepth(i) - avgdepth(j)|$
        $LDP(r,c) = concatenate(LDP(r,c), diff(i,j))$
      end loop
    end loop
    $LDPT = concatenate(LDP(r,c))$
  end loop
end loop

2.3 Occlusion Handling

View occlusions from static objects and other targets are likely the main challenge of tracking. While the weakness of depth data is

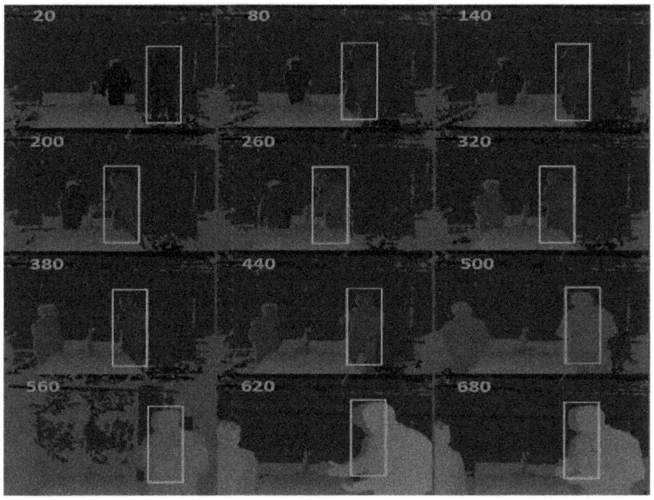

(a)

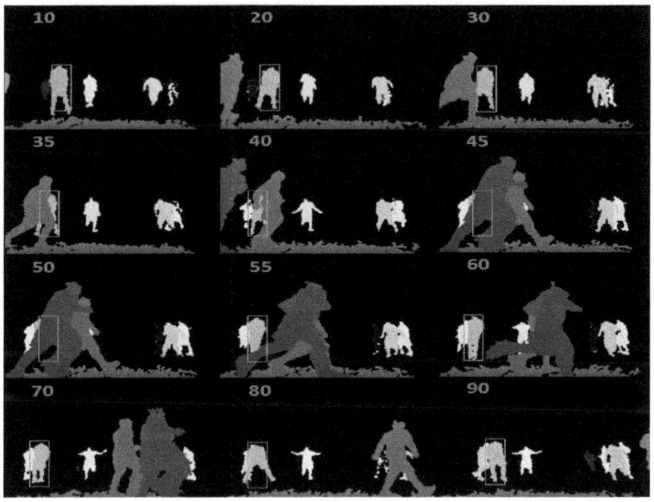

(b)

Figure 2: Examples of occlusion handling in a) the hospital simulation and b) PTB datasets.

their lack of appearance features, their strength is the possibility to provide reliable target discrimination based on their distance from the camera. Therefore, in the proposed tracker we have built an occlusion detector that flags an occlusion whenever the depth of the candidate target, d_t, differs from its historical average, d_{avg}, more than a given threshold θ. The measurements are computed at the centre of the respective bounding boxes and the historical average is maintained as a running average of update coefficient λ, updated only in the absence of detected occlusions:

$$occlusion = |d_t - d_{avg}| > \theta \qquad (4)$$

$$d_{avg}(updated) = \begin{cases} \lambda d_t + (1-\lambda) d_{avg} & \text{if } occlusion = 0 \\ d_{avg} & \text{otherwise} \end{cases} \qquad (5)$$

Figures 2.a and 2.b show examples of successful occlusion handling in a video from our hospital simulation dataset and a challenging basketball video from the PTB dataset. The videos with the full results are publicly downloadable from Dropbox [1].

3. EXPERIMENTS AND RESULTS

The proposed tracker has been evaluated both qualitatively and quantitatively using a hospital simulation dataset collected by these authors and the recent Princeton Tracking Benchmark (PTB) dataset [16]. Our hospital simulation dataset consists of 26 depth videos staging simulated visits to a patient lying on a hospital bed. These videos are characterised by ample back-and-forth target movement and static occlusions and have been used for qualitative evaluation only [2]. The PTB dataset was released as part of an ICCV 2013 publication to offer a unified, challenging benchmark for tracking in RGB and depth data. It consists of 95 videos varying in target type (humans, animals and substantially rigid objects such as toys and human faces), level of background clutter (plain living rooms, cafes, sport courts etc), and type of occlusions (different durations, appearance changes during occlusions, similarity between targets and occluders etc). The dataset comes accompanied by an evaluation website [3] managed by the benchmark's authors which allows for a blind and unbiased accuracy evaluation. The evaluation protocol considers three types of tracking errors: Type I errors occur when the target is visible, but the tracker's output is far off from the target (wrong detections); Type II errors occur when the target is invisible but the tracker still outputs a bounding box (false detections); Type III errors occur when the target is visible but the tracker fails to produce any output (missed detections). Accuracy figures are divided by target type, target size, movement, occlusion and motion type.

3.1 Experimental Results

Our experiments aim to compare the proposed tracker with the original Struck tracker and other state-of-the art trackers. The qualitative evaluation on the hospital simulation dataset is generally very positive, with the target (a visiting doctor or nurse) successfully tracked in all videos. The original Struck tracker instead tends to lose the target in the presence of large static occlusions.

The quantitative evaluation on the PTB dataset provides us with a test-bed for a rigorous and current performance analysis. Table 1, top part, reports the accuracy comparison for the proposed depth tracker against other trackers using only depth data. These include Struck with different types of features and a tracker based on HOG features [16]. The results in Table 1 show that the proposed tracker outperforms the other trackers in 8 categories out of 11. The inclusion of the occlusion handling module achieves an average accuracy improvement of over 2 percentage points compared to the same tracker without occlusion handling.

The bottom part of Table 1 reports the performance of trackers using RBG data for comparison. The proposed tracker outperforms Struck operating on RGB data in almost every category (10 out of 11). This result is impressive in that it shows that depth tracking with suitable features can outperform RGB tracking at a parity of targets and scenes. In turn, this proves that depth tracking is a viable approach to tracking under privacy-preserving operating conditions. It is also important to add that the performance of Struck on RGB data was reported in [16] as the best out of a pool of popular trackers including TLD [12], CT [20], MIL [1], semi-B [7] and VTD [10]. The only RGB tracker that outperforms our depth tracker in a few categories is the tracker proposed by the authors of the benchmark itself (*OF tracker*, Table 1). Remarked improvements over depth tracking alone is only achieved by fusion of depth and RGB information (*RGBD tracker*, Table 1).

[1] https://www.dropbox.com/s/8codeji5lnzkg22/hospital.avi?dl=0, https://www.dropbox.com/s/dzuock30489st1u/occlusion.avi?dl=0

[2] available at https://drive.google.com/file/d/0B9cAe42oTaT_aUs4ckVrazQ1OXM/

[3] http://tracking.cs.princeton.edu/submit.php

Table 1: **Accuracy comparison of the proposed tracker with the state of the art on the Princeton Tracking Benchmark.**

Algorithm	target type			target size		movement		occlusion		motion type	
	human	animal	rigid	large	small	slow	fast	yes	no	passive	active
Struck (Depth videos), Haar	0.31	0.32	0.36	0.29	0.36	0.36	0.32	0.21	0.49	0.36	0.32
Struck (Depth videos), raw pixels	0.34	0.44	0.42	0.37	0.41	0.44	0.37	0.29	0.54	0.43	0.37
Struck (Depth videos), histogram	0.38	0.46	0.44	0.45	0.40	0.51	0.39	0.31	0.57	0.52	0.38
HOG (Depth videos) from [16]	0.43	0.48	**0.56**	0.47	0.50	0.52	0.47	0.38	0.63	0.54	0.48
Proposed tracker (no occlusion handling)	0.39	**0.61**	0.54	0.46	0.51	**0.58**	0.45	0.32	**0.69**	**0.56**	0.46
Proposed tracker	**0.46**	0.59	0.54	**0.52**	**0.52**	0.56	**0.50**	**0.40**	0.68	**0.56**	**0.50**
Struck (RGB videos) from [16]	0.35	0.47	0.53	0.45	0.44	0.58	0.39	0.30	0.64	0.54	0.41
OF tracker (RGB videos) from [16]	0.47	0.47	0.63	0.47	0.47	0.57	0.52	0.47	0.62	0.63	0.49
RGBD tracker (RGB and depth) from [16]	0.74	0.63	0.78	0.78	0.70	0.76	0.72	0.72	0.75	0.70	0.82

4. CONCLUSION

In this paper, we have proposed a novel feature for effective tracking of people in depth videos. The feature, called local depth pattern for tracking (LDPT), extends a recently-proposed feature for activity recognition from depth data. The use of LDPT and the addition of an occlusion handling heuristic to a performing tracking engine, Struck [8], allows achieving remarkable accuracy in depth tracking. The experimental results over the current Princeton Tracking Benchmark show that:

- the lack of appearance information in depth videos is not a final impediment to tracking accuracy. Rather, tracking on depth data can outperform tracking from RGB data at a parity of targets and scene (Table 1);
- the proposed tracker based on the LDPT feature achieves a higher accuracy than existing results on depth data in 8 categories of the benchmark out of 11 (Table 1).

The depth frames displayed in Figs. 1 and 2 give visual evidence that depth data do not disclose identification clues of the targets. This allows adoption of depth tracking in privacy-sensitive contexts such as hospital environments and care facilities.

5. REFERENCES

[1] B. Babenko, Ming-Hsuan Yang, and S. Belongie. Visual tracking with online Multiple Instance Learning. In *CVPR Workshops*, pages 983–990, 2009.

[2] F. Basso, M. Munaro, S. Michieletto, E. Pagello, and E. Menegatti. Fast and robust multi-people tracking from rgb-d data for a mobile robot. In *Intelligent Autonomous Systems 12*, pages 265–276. Springer, 2013.

[3] H. Bay, A. Ess, T. Tuytelaars, and L. Van Gool. Speeded-up robust features (surf). *Comput. Vis. Image Underst.*, 110(3):346–359, June 2008.

[4] L. Bo, X. Ren, and D. Fox. Depth kernel descriptors for object recognition. In *IROS*, pages 821–826. IEEE, 2011.

[5] A. Bordes, L. Bottou, P. Gallinari, and J. Weston. Solving multiclass support vector machines with larank. In *24th International Conference on Machine Learning*, ICML '07, pages 89–96, 2007.

[6] S. Chen, P. Xia, and K. Nahrstedt. Activity-aware adaptive compression: A morphing-based frame synthesis application in 3dti. In *21st ACM International Conference on Multimedia*, MM '13, pages 349–352, 2013.

[7] H. Grabner, C. Leistner, and H. Bischof. Semi-supervised on-line boosting for robust tracking. In *10th European Conference on Computer Vision*, ECCV '08, pages I: 234–247, 2008.

[8] S. Hare, A. Saffari, and P. H. Torr. Struck: Structured output tracking with kernels. In *IEEE International Conference on Computer Vision (ICCV)*, pages 263–270, 2011.

[9] S. Koo and D.-S. Kwon. Multiple people tracking from 2d depth data by deterministic spatiotemporal data association. In *RO-MAN*, pages 656–661. IEEE, 2013.

[10] J. Kwon and K. M. Lee. Visual tracking decomposition. In *CVPR*, pages 1269–1276, 2010.

[11] D. G. Lowe. Distinctive image features from scale-invariant keypoints. *Int. J. Comput. Vision*, 60(2):91–110, Nov. 2004.

[12] M. Luber, L. Spinello, and K. O. Arras. People tracking in rgb-d data with on-line boosted target models. In *IROS*, pages 3844–3849, 2011.

[13] M. Munaro, F. Basso, and E. Menegatti. Tracking people within groups with rgb-d data. In *IROS*, pages 2101–2107. IEEE, 2012.

[14] M. Pietikäinen, G. Zhao, A. Hadid, and T. Ahonen. *Computer Vision Using Local Binary Patterns*. Number 40. Springer, 2011.

[15] J. Shotton, A. Fitzgibbon, M. Cook, T. Sharp, M. Finocchio, R. Moore, A. Kipman, and A. Blake. Real-time human pose recognition in parts from single depth images. In *IEEE Conference on Computer Vision and Pattern Recognition*, CVPR '11, pages 1297–1304, 2011.

[16] S. Song and J. Xiao. Tracking revisited using rgbd camera: Unified benchmark and baselines. In *IEEE International Conference on Computer Vision (ICCV)*, pages 233–240. IEEE, 2013.

[17] I. Tsochantaridis, T. Joachims, T. Hofmann, and Y. Altun. Large margin methods for structured and interdependent output variables. *Journal of Machine Learning Research*, pages 1453–1484, 2005.

[18] L. Xia, C.-C. Chen, and J. Aggarwal. Human detection using depth information by kinect. In *CVPR Workshops*, pages 15–22. IEEE, 2011.

[19] H. Yang, L. Shao, F. Zheng, L. Wang, and Z. Song. Recent advances and trends in visual tracking: A review. *Neurocomputing*, 74(18):3823–3831, 2011.

[20] K. Zhang, L. Zhang, and M.-H. Yang. Real-time compressive tracking. In *12th European Conference on Computer Vision*, ECCV'12, pages III: 864–877, 2012.

[21] Y. Zhao, Z. Liu, L. Yang, and H. Cheng. Combining rgb and depth map features for human activity recognition. In *APSIPA ASC*, pages 1–4, 2012.

ConvNets-Based Action Recognition from Depth Maps through Virtual Cameras and Pseudocoloring

Pichao Wang[1], Wanqing Li[1], Zhimin Gao[1], Chang Tang[2], Jing Zhang[1], and Philip Ogunbona[1]
[1]Advanced Multimedia Research Lab, University of Wollongong, Australia
[2]School of Electronic Information Engineering, Tianjin University, China
pw212@uowmail.edu.au, wanqing@uow.edu.au, zg126@uowmail.edu.au,
tangchang@tju.edu.cn, jz960@uowmail.edu.au, philipo@uow.edu.au

ABSTRACT

In this paper, we propose to adopt ConvNets to recognize human actions from depth maps on relatively small datasets based on Depth Motion Maps (DMMs). In particular, three strategies are developed to effectively leverage the capability of ConvNets in mining discriminative features for recognition. Firstly, different viewpoints are mimicked by rotating virtual cameras around subject represented by the 3D points of the captured depth maps. This not only synthesizes more data from the captured ones, but also makes the trained ConvNets view-tolerant. Secondly, DMMs are constructed and further enhanced for recognition by encoding them into Pseudo-RGB images, turning the spatial-temporal motion patterns into textures and edges. Lastly, through transferring learning the models originally trained over ImageNet for image classification, the three ConvNets are trained independently on the color-coded DMMs constructed in three orthogonal planes. The proposed algorithm was extensively evaluated on MSRAction3D, MSRAction3DExt and UTKinect-Action datasets and achieved the state-of-the-art results on these datasets.

Categories and Subject Descriptors

I.4.9 [**Computing Methodologies**]: Image Processing and Computer Vision—*Applications*

General Terms

Algorithms, Performance, Experimentation

Keywords

Action Recognition, ConvNets, Virtual Cameras, Pseudocoloring

1. INTRODUCTION

Action recognition has been an active research topic in computer vision due to its wide range of applications including intelligent surveillance and human-computer interactions. Recently, the release of the Microsoft Kinect Sensors opens up new opportunities in addressing the problem of action recognition. Depth maps have several advantages compared to traditional color images. For example, depth maps capture better geometric cues, which can often be more discriminative than color and texture for motion analysis and they are insensitive to changes in lighting conditions. Based on depth data, many works [6, 10, 7, 13] have been reported with respect to specific feature descriptors to take advantage of the properties of depth maps. However, all of them are based on hand-crafted features, which are often shallow and high-dimensional descriptions of local or global spatio-temporal information and their performance varies from dataset to dataset.

Different from these hand-designed features, Deep Convolutional Neural Networks (ConvNets) can automatically learn discriminative features from the raw data, instead of being devised specially. The key enabling factors behind these successes are techniques for scaling up the networks to millions of parameters and massive labelled datasets that can support the learning process. However, are the ConvNets suitable for action recognition using depth maps, where the training samples are relative very small? Can the available network architectures be employed directly without modifications? This paper provides answers to these questions. To address these practical issues in the context of action recognition from depth maps on relative small datasets, several strategies are proposed. Specifically, the 3D pointclouds constructed from the original depth data are rotated to mimic the different camera viewpoints, so that our algorithm becomes view-tolerant. Each rotated depth frame is first projected onto three orthogonal Cartesian planes, and then for each projected view, the absolute differences (motion energy) between consecutive frames are accumulated through an entire depth video sequence. To facility the transfer learning from trained ConvNets over ImageNets, the DMMs are encoded into Pseudo-RGB images in which the spatial-temporal motion patterns in videos can be effectively converted into spatial structures (edges and textures). Three ConvNets are trained on the three DMMs constructed from the projected Cartesian planes independently and fused lately to produce the final classification score.

2. RELATED WORK

Due to the success of deep learning approach, there are several attempts to apply deep architectures for 2D action recognition. In [2], 3D convolutional network is used to automatically learn spatio-temporal features directly from raw data. Recently, several ConvNet architectures for action recognition [4] are compared based on Sport-1M dataset, comprising 1.1 M YouTube videos of sports activities. The authors find that for a network, operating on individual video frames, performs similarly to the networks whose input is the stack of frames, which indicates that the learned spatio-temporal features do not capture the motion patterns effectively. In [8], spatial and temporal streams were proposed for action recogni-

MM'15 October 26-30 2015, Brisbane, Australia
© 2015 ACM. ISBN 978-1-4503-3459-4/15/10 ...$15.00.
DOI: http://dx.doi.org/10.1145/2733373.2806296.

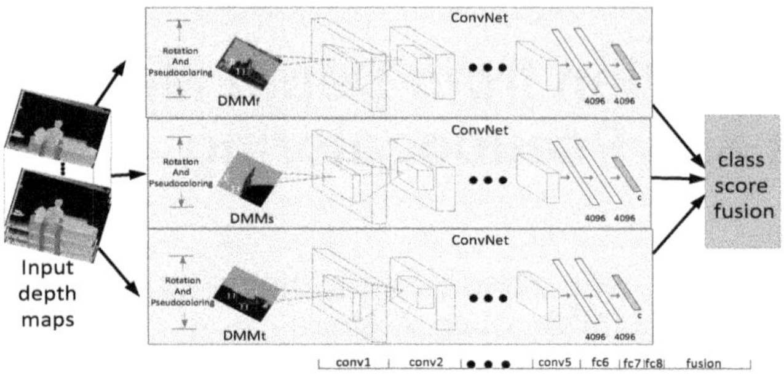

Figure 1: DMMs + 3ConvNets for depth-based action recognition.

tion. Two ConvNets are trained on the two streams and combined by late fusion. The spatial stream is comprised of individual frames while the temporal stream is stacked by optical flow. However, the best results of all the above deep learning methods can only match the state-of-the-art results achieved by hand-crafted features.

For depth-based action recognition, many works have been reported in the past few years. Li et al. [6] sample points from silhouette of a depth image to obtain a bag of 3D points which are clustered to enable recognition. Yang et al. [14] stack differences between projected depth maps as depth motion maps (DMM) and then use HOG to extract the features from the DMM. This method transforms the problem of action recognition from 3D space to 2D space. In [7], HON4D was proposed, in which surface normal is extended to 4D space and quantized by regular polychorons. Following this method, Yang and Tian [13] cluster hypersurface normals and form the polynormal which can be used to jointly capture the local motion and geometry information. Super Normal Vector (SNV) is generated by aggregating the low-level polynormals. However, all of these methods are based on carefully hand designed features, whose performance are often dataset and application dependent.

3. THE PROPOSED METHOD

The proposed method consists of two major components, as illustrated in Fig. 1, three ConvNets and construction of DMMs (calculated by accumulating the absolute difference between consecutive frames without any preprocessing but thresholding the depth values to get coarse foregrounds) from sequences of depth maps as the input to the ConvNets. Given a sequence of depth maps, 3D points are created and projected to the three orthogonal planes of the coordinates centred at the camera. Three DMMs are constructed in the three planes accordingly. Note that no preprocessing on the depth maps, such as filling of holes and missing values, is applied. Each DMM serves as an input to a ConvNet for classification. Final classification of the given depth sequence is obtained through a late fusion of the three ConvNets. Three strategies have been developed to deal with the challenges posed by small datasets. Firstly, more training data are synthesized by rotating the input 3D points to mimic different cameras; Secondly, the same ConvNet architecture as the one for ImageNet is adopted so that the model trained over ImageNet [5] can be adapted to our problem through transferring learning. Thirdly, each DMMs goes through a pseudo-color coding process to distinguish different motion patterns with enhancement into the Pseudo-RGB channels before being input to the ConvNets. In the rest of this section, rotation of the 3D points, Pseudo-color coding of DMMs, and training of the ConvNets are detailed.

3.1 Rotation to Mimic Virtual Cameras

Fig 2 (a) illustrates how to covert a pixel in a depth map into a 3D point by calculating its location(X, Y, Z) in the real-world coordinate system centred on the camera according to Eq. 1.

$$X = \frac{Z \cdot (U - C_x)}{f_x}; Y = \frac{Z \cdot (V - C_y)}{f_y}. \tag{1}$$

where (U, V) and Z denote screen coordinates and depth value respectively, C_x, C_y denote the center of a depth map, f_x and f_y are the focal lengths of the camera. For Kinect-v1 cameras, $f_x = f_y = 580$ [9].

The rotation of the 3D points can be performed equivalently by assuming a virtual RGB-D camera moves around and points at the subject from different viewpoints as illustrated in Fig. 2. Supposing the virtual camera moves from position P_o to P_d, it can be decomposed into two steps: first moves from P_o to P_t, with rotated angle denoted by θ and moves from P_t to P_d, with rotated angle denoted by β. The coordinates of subject with respect to the virtual camera can be computed by the transformation expressed in Eq. 2.

$$[X', Y', Z', 1]^{\mathrm{T}} = \mathbf{T}r_y \mathbf{T}r_x \, [X, Y, Z, 1]^{\mathrm{T}} \tag{2}$$

where X', Y', Z' represent the 3D coordinates with respect to the virtual camera system and $\mathbf{T}r_y$ denotes the transformation along Y axis (right-handed coordinate system) while $\mathbf{T}r_x$ denotes the transformation along X axis and they are:

$$\mathbf{T}r_y = \begin{bmatrix} \mathbf{R}_y(\theta) & \mathbf{T}_y(\theta) \\ \mathbf{0} & 1 \end{bmatrix}; \mathbf{T}r_x = \begin{bmatrix} \mathbf{R}_x(\beta) & \mathbf{T}_x(\beta) \\ \mathbf{0} & 1 \end{bmatrix} \tag{3}$$

where

$$\mathbf{R}_y(\theta) = \begin{bmatrix} 1 & 0 & 0 \\ 0 & cos(\theta) & -sin(\theta) \\ 0 & sin(\theta) & cos(\theta) \end{bmatrix} \mathbf{T}_y(\theta) = \begin{bmatrix} 0 \\ Z \cdot sin(\theta) \\ Z \cdot (1 - cos(\theta)) \end{bmatrix};$$

$$\mathbf{R}_x(\beta) = \begin{bmatrix} cos(\beta) & 0 & sin(\beta) \\ 0 & 1 & 0 \\ -sin(\beta) & 0 & cos(\beta) \end{bmatrix} \mathbf{T}_x(\beta) = \begin{bmatrix} -Z \cdot sin(\beta) \\ 0 \\ Z \cdot (1 - cos(\beta)) \end{bmatrix}.$$

After rotation, to generate the rotated depth map, rotated 3D pointclouds are projected back to the image plane by Eq. 4.

$$U' = \frac{X' \cdot f_x}{Z'} + C_x; V' = \frac{Y' \cdot f_y}{Z'} + C_y, \tag{4}$$

where U', V' and Z' denote the screen coordinates of the virtual camera and their corresponding depth value respectively.

Since RGB-D camera only captures $2\frac{1}{2}D$, not full $3D$, information, the movement of the virtual camera has to be within a range around the real camera such that the synthesized depth maps still capture sufficient spatial-temporal information of the actions. In other words, both θ and β have to be limited to a certain range. Fig.3 shows some examples of the synthesized depth maps and the original one. From the figure, it can be seen that even at relative large angle ($|\theta| = 45°, |\beta| = 45°$), the synthesized depth maps still capture the shape of the body well. In some extreme cases where θ and β become very large, the synthesized depth maps do not capture sufficient spatial information of the subject. Empirically, the useful range of the angles is between $(-60°, 60°)$ for both θ and β.

3.2 Pseudocoloring

Motivated by the work [1] where color-coding can harness the perceptual capabilities of the human visual system to extract more information from gray images and, hence, effectively to enhance

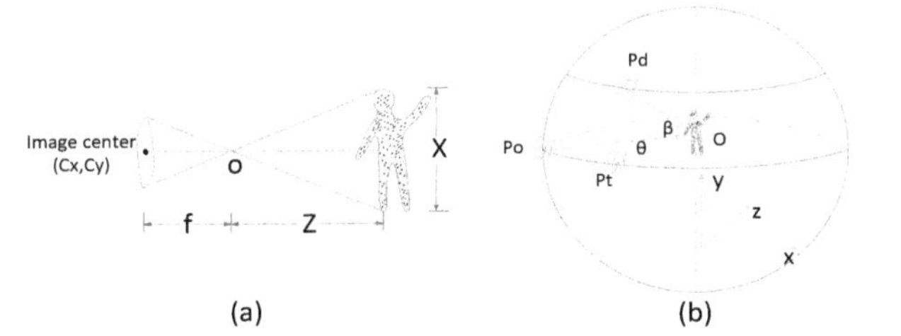

Figure 2: Illustration of 3D point rotation to mimic different camera viewpoints.

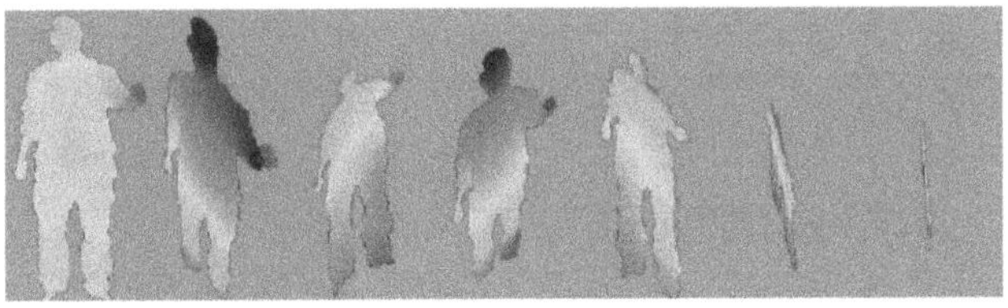

Figure 3: Example depth maps synthesized by the virtual RGB-D camera. From left to right: original depth maps, depth maps synthesized respectively with the parameters $(\theta = 45°, \beta = 45°)$, $(\theta = 45°, \beta = -45°)$, $(\theta = -45°, \beta = 45°)$,$(\theta = -45°, \beta = -45°)$,$(\theta = -75°, \beta = -75°)$, $(\theta = -85°, \beta = -85°)$.

the detailed texture patterns contained in the image, it is proposed in this paper to code a DMMs into a Pseudo-color image such that to effectively exploit/enhance the texture in the DMMs that corresponds to the motion patterns of actions. In this work, an improved rainbow transfrom is developed. The improved rainbow transform is expressed as

$$C_{i=1,2,3} = \{sin[2\pi \cdot (-I + \varphi_i) \cdot \frac{1}{2} + \frac{1}{2}]\}^2 \cdot f(I) \quad (5)$$

where $C_{i=1,2,3}$ presents the BGR channels, respectively; I is the normalized gray value; φ_i denotes the phase of the three channels; $f(I)$ is an amplitude modulation function which further increases the non-linearity; the added values, $\frac{1}{2}$ guarantee non-negativity. In our work, the $\varphi_{i=1,2,3}$ and $f(I)$ are set to $\frac{1}{5} - \frac{1}{2}\pi$, $\frac{1}{5} - \frac{1}{2}\pi - \frac{3}{14}$, $\frac{1}{5} - \frac{1}{2}\pi - \frac{6}{14}$, $\frac{1}{4} + \frac{3}{4}I$, respectively. To code DMMs, linear mapping is used to convert DMMs values to $I \in [0, 1]$.

Take the actions in MSRAction3D dataset as examples, as shown in Fig. 4, some actions appear similar in their DMMs, for example "forward kick" and "jogging", but the pseudo-color coding has highlighted the differences in texture and edges. As the texture and edges in DMMs are the accumulation of spatial and temporal information, thus, the DMMs and its pseudo-color coding can effectively embed the spatial-temporal information of actions and this has been verified empirically.

3.3 Network Training & Class Score Fusion

Three ConvNets are trained on thc pseudo-color coded DMMs constructed from both original and synthetic data in the three Cartesian planes. The layer configuration of the three ConvNets follows the one in [5]. The implementation is derived from the publicly available Caffe toolbox [3] based on one NVIDIA GeForce GTX680M card.

The training procedure is similar to the one in [5]. The network weights are learned using the mini-batch stochastic gradient descent with the momentum being set to 0.9 and weight decay being set to 0.0005. At each iteration, a mini-batch of 256 samples is constructed by sampling 256 shuffled training color-coded DMMs. All color-coded DMMs are resized to 256×256. The learning rate is initially set to 10^{-2} for directly training the networks from data and is set to 10^{-3} for fine-tuning with pre-trained models on ILSVRC-2012, and then it is decreased according to a fixed schedule, which is kept the same for all training sets. For each ConvNet the training undergoes 100 cycles and the learning rate decreases every 20 cycles. For all experiments, the dropout regularisation ratio was set to 0.5 in order to reduce complex co-adaptations of neurons in nets.

Given a testing depth video sequence (sample), only the DMMs that constructed from original non-rotated depth maps are used for testing. The final class score for a test sample are the averages of the outputs from the three ConvNets.

Figure 4: Examples of pseudocoloring for DMMs over MSRAction3D dataset. From top-left to bottom-right are encoded DMMs for actions performed by random subjects: "high arm wave", "horizontal arm wave", "hammer", "hand catch", "forward punch", "high throw", "draw X", "draw tick", "draw circle", "hand clap", "two hand wave", "side-boxing", "bend", "forward kick", "side kick", "jogging", "tennis swing", "tennis serve", "golf swing", "pick up & throw".

4. EXPERIMENTAL RESULTS

The proposed method was evaluated on two public benchmark datasets: MSRAction3D [6] and UTKinect-Action [12]. Moreover, an extension of MSRAction3D, called MSRAction3DExt Dataset, was used, which contains more than twice, i.e. 23, as many subjects as the previous one who performed the same set of actions.

4.1 MSRAction3D Dataset

The MSRAction3D Dataset [6] is composed of depth sequences captured by a MS Kinect-V1 camera. It contains 20 actions performed by 10 subjects facing the camera, with each subject performing each action 2 or 3 times. In order to facilitate a fair comparison, the same experimental setting in [10] is followed, namely, the cross-subjects settings: subjects 1, 3, 5, 7, 9 for training and subjects 2, 4, 6, 8, 10 for testing. For this dataset, θ varied in the range of $(-30^\circ : 15^\circ : 30^\circ)$ and β $(-5^\circ : 5^\circ : 5^\circ)$, thus, 15 times training data are synthesized.

4.2 MSRAction3DExt Dataset

The MSRAction3DExt Dataset is an extension of MSRAction3D Dataset with additional 13 subjects performing the same 20 actions 2 to 4 times in the same environment as MSRAction3D. Thus, there are 20 actions, 23 subjects and 1379 video clips. For this dataset, samples of odd-numbered subjects were used for training and samples of the even-numbered subjects were used for testing. The same setting of parameters as MSRAction3D Dataset was used for experiments. Table 1 shows the results for several training settings on MSRAction3D and MSRAction3DExt datasets.

Table 1: Comparison on different training settings for MSRAction3D and MSRAction3DExt datasets.

Training Settings	Accuracy	
	MSR-Action3D	MSR-Action3DExt
Original Samples	7.12%	10.00%
Synthesized Samples	34.23%	53.05%
Synthesized + Pre-trained + Fine-tuning	100%	100%

From Table 1, it can be seen that as the volume of dataset increases, directly training the nets from the original and synthesized samples, the performance was improved. However, the performance is not comparabe to the one obtained when the pre-trained model on ImageNet was used for initialization.

4.3 UTKinect-Action Dataset

The UTKinect-Action Dataset [12] was captured using a stationary Kinect sensor. There are 10 different subjects and each subject performs each action twice. This dataset is designed to investigate variations in the view point. For this dataset, θ varied in the range of $(-60^\circ : 15^\circ : 60^\circ)$ and β $(-15^\circ : 5^\circ : 15^\circ)$, thus, 63 times training data are synthesized. The cross-subject scheme as the one in [11] was adopted which is different from the one adopted in [12] where more subjects were used for training in each round. Table 2 compared the performance of the proposed method and that of the existing methods on the three datasets.

Table 2: Recognition accuracies of the exiting methods and proposed methods on the three datasets.

Methods	Datasets		
	MSR-Action3D	MSR-Action3DExt	UTKinect-Action
Bag of 3D Points [6]	74.70%	-	-
HOJ3D [12]	79.00%	-	90.91%
Actionlet Ensemble [10]	82.22%	-	-
Depth Motion Maps [14]	88.73%	-	-
HON4D [7]	88.89%	-	-
SNV [13]	93.09%	90.54%	88.89%
DSTIP+DCSF [11]	-	-	78.78%
Random Forests [15]	-	-	87.90%
Ours	**100%**	**100%**	**90.91%**

The proposed method did not achieve 100% accuracy on UTKinect-Action Dataset and one of the reasons is the background of this dataset is complicated which introduced much noise in the color-coded DMMs. However, the proposed method outperforms all of previous methods, and it verifies that our proposed three strategies for small datasets to use ConvNets are effective.

5. CONCLUSIONS

In this paper, a method for action recognition from depth map sequences using deep learning is proposed. The proposed method achieved state-of-the-art results on evaluated datasets. The experimental results have shown the strategies developed for applying ConvNets to small datasets worked effectively. Though the strategies are developed for depth based action recognition, the concept can be easily extended to action recognition based on skeleton data, RGB data or combination of them. Our experimental results have also shown dynamic background could adversely impact the recognition. The proposed method can benefit from any coarse segmentation of the subjects who perform the action in front of a dynamic or cluttered background.

6. REFERENCES

[1] B. R. Abidi, Y. Zheng, A. V. Gribok, and M. A. Abidi. Improving weapon detection in single energy X-ray images through pseudocoloring. *Systems, Man, and Cybernetics, Part C: Applications and Reviews, IEEE Transactions on*, 36(6):784–796, 2006.

[2] S. Ji, W. Xu, M. Yang, and K. Yu. 3D convolutional neural networks for human action recognition. *IEEE Trans. Pattern Anal. Mach. Intell.*, 35(1):221–231, Jan. 2013.

[3] Y. Jia, E. Shelhamer, J. Donahue, S. Karayev, J. Long, R. Girshick, S. Guadarrama, and T. Darrell. Caffe: Convolutional architecture for fast feature embedding. *arXiv:1408.5093*, 2014.

[4] A. Karpathy, G. Toderici, S. Shetty, T. Leung, R. Sukthankar, and L. Fei-Fei. Large-scale video classification with convolutional neural networks. In *CVPR*, 2014.

[5] A. Krizhevsky, I. Sutskever, and G. E. Hinton. Imagenet classification with deep convolutional neural networks. In *NIPS*, 2012.

[6] W. Li, Z. Zhang, and Z.Liu. Action recognition based on a bag of 3D points. In *CVPRW*, 2010.

[7] O. Oreifej and Z. Liu. HON4D: Histogram of oriented 4D normals for activity recognition from depth sequences. In *CVPR*, 2013.

[8] K. Simonyan and A. Zisserman. Two-stream convolutional networks for action recognition in videos. In *NIPS*, 2014.

[9] J. Smisek, M. Jancosek, and T. Pajdla. 3D with kinect. In *ICCVW*, 2011.

[10] J. Wang, Z. Liu, Y. Wu, and J. Yuan. Mining actionlet ensemble for action recognition with depth cameras. In *CVPR*, 2012.

[11] L. Xia and J. Aggarwal. Spatio-temporal depth cuboid similarity feature for activity recognition using depth camera. In *CVPR*, 2013.

[12] L. Xia, C.-C. Chen, and J. Aggarwal. View invariant human action recognition using histograms of 3D joints. In *CVPRW*, 2012.

[13] X. Yang and Y. Tian. Super normal vector for activity recognition using depth sequences. In *CVPR*, 2014.

[14] X. Yang, C. Zhang, and Y. Tian. Recognizing actions using depth motion maps-based histograms of oriented gradients. In *ACM MM*, 2012.

[15] Y. Zhu, W. Chen, and G. Guo. Fusing spatiotemporal features and joints for 3D action recognition. In *CVPRW*, 2013.

Spatio-Temporal Learning of Basketball Offensive Strategies

Ching-Hang Chen
Inst. of Information Science
Academia Sinica
Nankang, Taipei 115, Taiwan

Tyng-Luh Liu
Inst. of Information Science
Academia Sinica
Nankang, Taipei 115, Taiwan

Yu-Shuen Wang
Dept. of Computer Science
National Chiao Tung University
Hsinchu 300, Taiwan

Hung-Kuo Chu
Dept. of Computer Science
National Tsing Hua University
Hsinchu 300, Taiwan

Nick C. Tang
Inst. of Information Science
Academia Sinica
Nankang, Taipei 115, Taiwan

Hong-Yuan Mark Liao
Inst. of Information Science
Academia Sinica
Nankang, Taipei 115, Taiwan

ABSTRACT

Video-based group behavior analysis is drawing attention to its rich applications in sports, military, surveillance and biological observations. The recent advances in tracking techniques, based on either computer vision methodology or hardware sensors, further provide the opportunity of better solving this challenging task. Focusing specifically on the analysis of basketball offensive strategies, we introduce a systematic approach to establishing unsupervised modeling of group behaviors. In view that a possible group behavior (offensive strategy) could be of different duration and represented by dynamic player trajectories, the crux of our method is to automatically divide training data into meaningful clusters and learn their respective spatio-temporal model, which is established upon Gaussian mixture regression to account for intra-class spatio-temporal variations. The resulting strategy representation turns out to be flexible that can be used to not only establish the discriminant functions but also improve learning the models. We demonstrate the usefulness of our approach by exploring its effectiveness in analyzing a set of given basketball video clips.

Categories and Subject Descriptors

I.2.10 [**Artificial Intelligence**]: Vision and Scene Understanding—*video analysis*

Keywords

Group action recognition, machine learning

1. INTRODUCTION

Action/behavior analysis based on video content has been actively studied for decades. While quite a number of practical techniques are established mostly for dealing with single or two objects of concern, we focus especially on group behaviors involving multiple objects. Observe that the nature of this problem engages high-level semantics and reveals crucial information on the plan or goal of the associated group. For example, in the popular basketball sport, the coordination of players' movements on the court presents a well-thought-out pattern of group behavior, which is often regarded as a strategy. Analysis on these strategies helps the teams review the performance of their offense and defense executions, understand competitors' strategies, and highlight the weakness for future improvement reference. In addition, the discovered information would bring new insights into the game such as providing in-depth investigation on winning rate or evaluating value of certain players. However, the analysis typically requires onerous human labeling efforts, and expert knowledge on recognizing underlying strategies and interpreting the contents. Thanks to the advance in tracking techniques (vision-based or sensor-based), the activity of each individual can be extracted according to the intended features. Yet, even with the available data, group behavior analysis poses challenging tasks:

- The representation of a group behavior generally includes actions of multiple independent objects in terms of, *e.g.*, player trajectories. This could cause ambiguity in that their ordering might be randomly assigned, and needs to be addressed when evaluating the similarity with other data.
- To establish a robust description for a representative group behavior, we should find a way to account for the spatio-temporal variations of each involved individual among intra-class samples.
- Finally, to recognize the underlying group behaviors in a test video clip based on the learned representation models, designing the associated discriminant functions for classification is also a critical issue.

Existing relevant techniques for group behavior recognition are mostly model-based, and adopt, say, SVMs for classifications. Siddiquie *et al.* [11] consider *multiple kernel learning* with SVMs on football tactic classification. Ballan *et al.* [1] use SVMs with spatio-temporal features, generated from a *bag-of-words* model. In [15], Wang *et al.* instead employ SVMs with the designed motion descriptors. In addition to these efforts, probability-based approaches are also

MM'15, October 26–30, 2015, Brisbane, Australia.

DOI: http://dx.doi.org/10.1145/2733373.2806297.

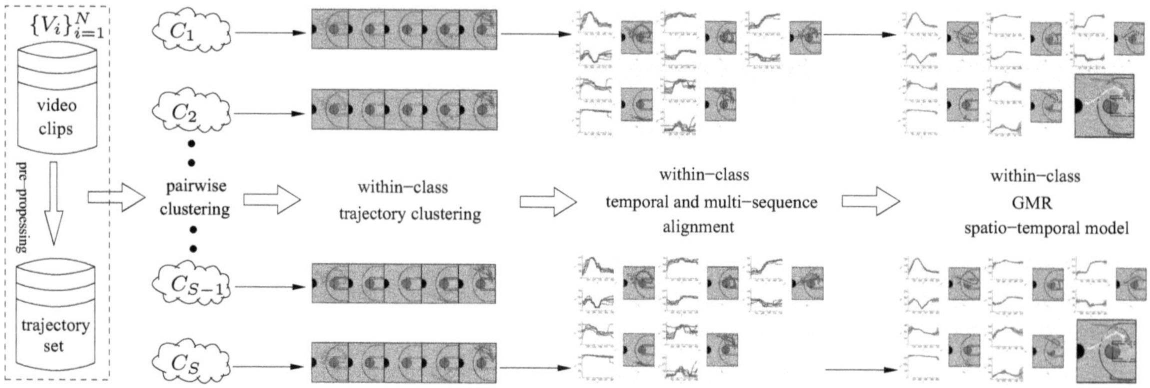

Figure 1: Flowchart of our method for learning the spatio-temporal models from given video clips.

popular. Li *et al.* [9] investigate *discriminative temporal interaction manifold* for football strategy recognition. Hu *et al.* [6] propose a *Dirichlet process mixture model* for trajectory analysis. Moreover, the Markov model is utilized in [13, 2, 12] for multi-trajectory behavior classification. The above-mentioned methods are implemented generally with supervised scenarios and thus require massive labeling efforts, while in our approach, models of group behavior can be learned in an unsupervised manner.

Figure 1 illustrates the steps of our method. We first represent each video clip in multi-trajectory form and measure pairwise trajectory-set distances by *dynamic time warping* (DTW) [7, 14, 16]. Leveraging with the pairwise clustering technique [10], we divide the data into clusters, each of which corresponds to a particular class of offensive strategy. On establishing the spatio-temporal models, we further partition each (strategy) cluster into (trajectory) sub-clusters, and perform temporal alignment as well as *Gaussian mixture regression* (GMR) [5] to complete the model learning. To accomplish classification, the learned GMR parameters can be incorporated into the resulting discriminant functions.

2. SPATIO-TEMPORAL LEARNING

We begin by proposing an efficient procedure to automatically divide a given collection of training video data into meaningful clusters. Denote the set of N video clips to be analyzed as $D = \{V_1, \ldots, V_N\}$ and assume they demonstrate totally S different offensive strategies. In case that the value of S is not available in training, our method can effectively overcome the difficulty by employing an iterative clustering scheme to yield a reasonable estimate. The goal of data clustering is then to divide D into S clusters so that our approach can establish their respective spatio-temporal model and discriminant function for classifying a test video clip.

2.1 Distance Measures

To accomplish the desired clustering, we first construct the representation of a basketball video clip and the distance measure. As each video records players' (half-court) actions during an interval of a basketball match, we pre-process the underlying image sequence using a *tracking by detection* [3] technique to obtain the players' trajectories of the offensive team. Specifically, we represent a video clip V, say, of F frames by $V = \{T_p\}_{p=1}^P$ where $P = 5$ reflects the number of players in an offensive team, and $T_p = \{\mathbf{x}_{p,f}\}_{f=1}^F \in \mathbb{R}^{d\times F}$ is the trajectory specified by the d-dimensional coordinates of player p at each image frame. Note that the exact ordering among the player trajectories is not specified as the ambiguity will be resolved via trajectory matching.

The trajectory-based representation implies that constructing a distance measure to correlate two video clips naturally relies on how the trajectory similarity is evaluated. For two arbitrary (player) trajectories $T \in \mathbb{R}^{d\times F}$ and $T' \in \mathbb{R}^{d\times F'}$, we take account that the two trajectories may not be of the same length, *i.e.*, $F \neq F'$, and exploit the DTW algorithm to define an appropriate distance function by

$$d_t(T, T') = \min_{W_T, W_{T'}} \frac{1}{\ell} \|TW_T - T'W_{T'}\|_F \quad (1)$$

where $\|\cdot\|_F$ is the Frobenius norm and ℓ, $W_T \in \{0,1\}^{F\times\ell}$, $W_{T'} \in \{0,1\}^{F'\times\ell}$ are the number of matchings and the warping matrices of a plausible dynamic-programming solution path. With (1), we set the distance function between two video clips, say, $V = \{T_p\}_{p=1}^P$ and $V' = \{T'_p\}_{p=1}^P$ as

$$d_c(V, V') = \min_{\pi(p)} \sum_{p=1}^{P} d_t(T_p, T'_{\pi(p)}) \quad (2)$$

where π is a permutation of $\{1, \ldots, P\}$.

2.2 Iterative Pairwise Clustering

We are to divide $D = \{V_1, \ldots, V_N\}$ into S clusters, each of which corresponds to a specific offensive strategy of basketball. As we prefer accommodating the situation that the exact value of S may not be known in advance, we consider the *dominant-set clustering* by Pavan and Pelillo [10]. In particular, we use (2) to yield the affinity matrix A and solve the following optimization problem:

$$\max_{\mathbf{y}} \mathbf{y}^T A \mathbf{y} \text{ subject to } \mathbf{y} \geq \mathbf{0} \in \mathbb{R}^N \text{ and } \mathbf{e}^T\mathbf{y} = 1 \quad (3)$$

where the (i,j)th entry of A is given by $\exp\{-d_c(V_i, V_j)/\sigma^2\}$ and $\sigma > 0$ is a scale parameter. Performing clustering with (3) is carried out iteratively. It starts by treating each V_i in D as a graph node and specifying a pre-determined positive threshold δ. Having solved (3), those nodes corresponding to positive components of the optimal $\mathbf{y}$ will be removed from the graph, and included in a new cluster if their value is larger than δ. With the updated graph, we repeat the above procedure until the algorithm uncovers S clusters, denoted as $C_1, \ldots, C_S$. If S is unknown, the iterative process can be terminated when reaching an empty graph. One notable advantage of the aforementioned clustering technique is that it provides a convenient way to exclude noisy data from corrupting the clustering result.

2.3 Spatio-temporal Representations

Our task now is to derive a spatio-temporal representation for each (strategy) cluster C. Suppose that C comprises Q video clips from D and thus has $P \times Q$ player trajectories. To yield an intra-cluster representation, we note that all the pairwise distances among player trajectories have already been evaluated when forming the affinity matrix A in (3). It follows that we can readily obtain the affinity matrix for the $P \times Q$ trajectories and again use dominant-set clustering to divide them into P (trajectory) clusters, upon which the strategy representation is established.

For each of the P clusters, let the underlying set of trajectories be $\{T_q\}_{q=1}^{Q}$ to reflect that they are from Q different video clips. We then carry out the following two steps.

1. We couple *multi-sequence* DTW [16] with *derivative* DTW [8] so that spatio-temporal relationships over sequences of different lengths can be more effectively explored. That is, we consider solving

$$\min_{\{W_q\}} Q \sum_{q=1}^{Q} \|\delta T_q W_q - \frac{1}{Q} \sum_{q'=1}^{Q} \delta T_{q'} W_{q'}\|_F \quad (4)$$

   where δT_q denotes the trajectory derivative and $\{W_q\}_{q=1}^{Q}$ are the warping matrices.

2. Assume that optimizing (4) results in q^* matchings between any two trajectories. We then apply Gaussian mixture regression to generate the mean trajectory $\boldsymbol{\mu} = [\mu_1, \ldots, \mu_{q^*}] \in \mathbb{R}^{d \times q^*}$ with the variance matrix $\boldsymbol{\sigma}^2 = [\sigma_1^2, \ldots, \sigma_{q*}^2] \in \mathbb{R}^{d \times q^*}$.

Finally, for each (strategy) cluster C, we can derive its spatio-temporal representation, denoted as $\{(\boldsymbol{\mu}_p, \boldsymbol{\sigma}_p^2)\}_{p=1}^{P}$.

2.4 Refinement and Discriminant Functions

Having established the spatio-temporal representations, we can define for each (strategy) cluster C its discriminant function f for classifying a new video clip, say, $V' = \{T'_p\}_{p=1}^{P}$ where trajectory $T'_p = \{\mathbf{x}'_{p,f}\}_{f=1}^{F'} \in \mathbb{R}^{d \times F'}$. Let the underlying spatio-temporal representation be $\{(\boldsymbol{\mu}_p, \boldsymbol{\sigma}_p^2)\}_{p=1}^{P}$. Then the discriminant function is defined by

$$f(V') = \min_{\pi(p)} \sum_{p=1}^{P} \tilde{d}_t(T'_{\pi(p)}, \boldsymbol{\mu}_p) \quad (5)$$

and

$$\tilde{d}_t(T'_{\pi(p)}, \boldsymbol{\mu}_p) = \min_{W_{T'} \in \{0,1\}^{F' \times q^*}} \|\frac{1}{\boldsymbol{\sigma}_p} \circ (T'_{\pi(p)} W_{T'} - \boldsymbol{\mu}_p)\|_F \quad (6)$$

where $\tilde{d}_t$ is a modified trajectory distance function weighted by taking Hadamard product with respect to the matrix $1/\boldsymbol{\sigma}_p$, whose (i,j)th entry is just the reciprocal of the (i,j)th entry of $\boldsymbol{\sigma}_p$, to account for the distribution assumption of a GMR representation. Having obtained all the discriminant functions $f_1, \ldots, f_S$ for clusters $C_1, \ldots, C_S$, respectively, we are ready to lay out the discriminant rule to decide which (strategy) cluster should V' be associated with:

$$V' \mapsto C_{s^*} \text{ if } s^* = \arg \min_{s \in \{1,\ldots,S\}} f_s(V'). \quad (7)$$

The discriminant rule in (7) is useful not just in testing but also in training. We can form an EM-like iterative training procedure to refine the spatio-temporal model. Specifically, we use the techniques just described to obtain the initial spatio-temporal representations and the discriminant functions. In the E-step, we use (7) to re-assign the training videos to their proper cluster. Then, in the M-step, we update each spatio-temporal model. We repeat the process until an M-step yields no re-clustering change.

So far, our proposed formulation is a fully unsupervised approach, but we indeed do not know what specific offensive strategies of basketball the S (strategy) clusters correspond to. To extend the usefulness of our method, we exploit *minimal* domain knowledge to label only S video clips, each of which is the one that has the least weighted distance, as in (6), to its cluster-wise mean trajectory. This way we could establish a classification framework for predicting the type of basketball offensive strategy without relying on manually labeling massive video clips.

3. EXPERIMENTAL RESULTS

To demonstrate the effectiveness of our method, we carry out experiments on modeling and classifying basketball offensive strategies. Specifically, we collect totally 134 video clips from NBA games, including ten different types of basketball offensive strategies. They are termed as `2-3 Flex`, `Elevator`, `Hawk`, `Pin-down`, `Princeton`, `Back-side pick and roll`, `Side-pick slip and pop`, `Single`, `Weave` and `Wing-wheel`. For simplicity, they are abbreviated by F23, EV, HK, PD, PT, RB, SP, WS, WV and WW, respectively. Each video clip yields one associated trajectory set containing five player trajectories from the offensive team on the court, and depicts the execution of a particular strategy out of the ten offensive types. (The ground-truth labels are annotated by experts.) Literatures such as [4] also propose to automatically acquire intended trajectory data in basketball games, though this aspect is beyond the focus of our discussion.

The spatio-temporal models are learned via unsupervised learning. To verify the advantage of the EM-like iterative training procedure described in Section 2.4, we use the resulting discriminant functions to categorize the training data and generate the confusion matrix. In Figures 2(a) and 2(b), we show the confusion matrices of the training procedures with and without using the EM iteration. There we can see that the EM-like approach can achieve an average accuracy of about 93.1%, which significantly improves the non-EM training result. We then split the set of video clips that 80% of them are randomly selected for training and the remaining 20% for testing. The test video clips are classified according to (7), where the respective discriminant functions are learned by our method with the EM-like procedure. To achieve a more reliable evaluation, we repeat the testing ten times (with different data splits), and obtain an average classification rate of 89.1%. (See the average confusion matrix in Figure 2(c).) The good performance indicates that the proposed spatio-temporal learning is promising for uncovering the subtle group behaviors behind the complex dynamics of a very active sports event, such as an NBA basketball game.

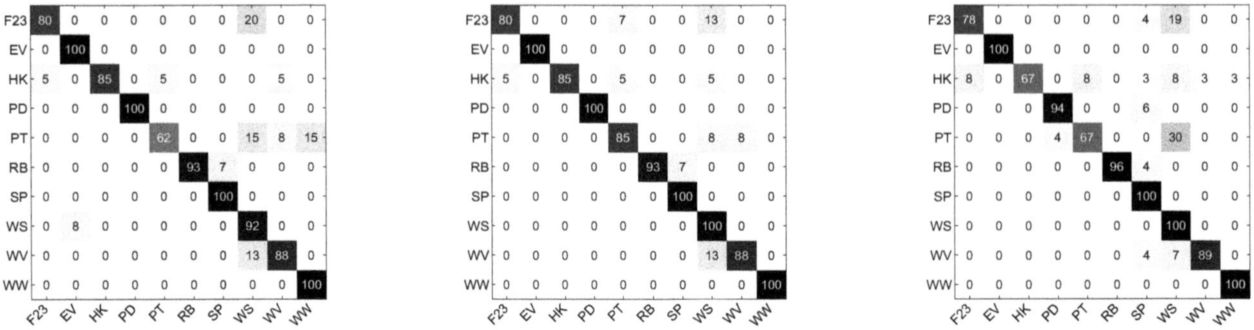

(a) Without EM (b) With EM (c) Testing result

Figure 2: Confusion matrices from training and testing: F23,EV,HK,PD,PT,RB,SP,WS,WV,WW represent the 10 different basketball offensive strategies. (a) Learning without EM refinement. (b) Learning with EM refinement. (c) Average confusion matrix of strategy classification from 80% (training) vs. 20% (testing) random split of the dataset.

4. CONCLUSIONS

Learning to understand group behaviors from video data is challenging. Our method starts with a succinct trajectory-based representation to encode the highly-dynamic player actions, and establish a DTW-based distance function to measure the closeness between two video clips. These enable dividing the dataset into clusters so that we can separately learn their spatio-temporal model. To accommodate the intra-class variations, we explore the GMR technique to boost the robustness of the learned discriminant functions. Our experimental results are encouraging and it is promising to extend the proposed formulation to address analyzing group behaviors of other forms. For future research efforts, it would be interesting to generalize our method to handle that the group size could vary in different video clips.

5. ACKNOWLEDGMENTS

This work was supported in part by MOST grants 103-2221-E-001-009-MY3, 102-2221-E-001-021-MY3, 102-2221-E-007-055-MY3 and 103-2221-E-007-065-MY3.

6. REFERENCES

[1] L. Ballan, M. Bertini, A. Del Bimbo, and G. Serra. Video event classification using string kernels. *Multimedia Tools and Applications*, 48(1):69–87, 2010.

[2] F. I. Bashir, A. A. Khokhar, and D. Schonfeld. Object trajectory-based activity classification and recognition using hidden markov models. *Image Processing, IEEE Transactions on*, 16(7):1912–1919, 2007.

[3] M. D. Breitenstein, F. Reichlin, B. Leibe, E. Koller-Meier, and L. Van Gool. Robust tracking-by-detection using a detector confidence particle filter. In *IEEE International Conference on Computer Vision*, pages 1515–1522, 2009.

[4] H.-T. Chen, C.-L. Chou, T.-S. Fu, S.-Y. Lee, and B.-S. P. Lin. Recognizing tactic patterns in broadcast basketball video using player trajectory. *Journal of Visual Communication and Image Representation*, 23(6):932–947, 2012.

[5] D. A. Cohn, Z. Ghahramani, and M. I. Jordan. Active learning with statistical models. *Journal of artificial intelligence research*, 1996.

[6] W. Hu, X. Li, G. Tian, S. Maybank, and Z. Zhang. An incremental DPMM-based method for trajectory clustering, modeling, and retrieval. *Pattern Analysis and Machine Intelligence, IEEE Transactions on*, 35(5):1051–1065, 2013.

[7] A. Kassidas, J. F. MacGregor, and P. A. Taylor. Synchronization of batch trajectories using dynamic time warping. *AIChE Journal*, 44(4):864–875, 1998.

[8] E. J. Keogh and M. J. Pazzani. Derivative dynamic time warping. In *SDM*, volume 1, pages 5–7. SIAM, 2001.

[9] R. Li, R. Chellappa, and S. K. Zhou. Learning multi-modal densities on discriminative temporal interaction manifold for group activity recognition. In *IEEE Conference on Computer Vision and Pattern Recognition*, pages 2450–2457, 2009.

[10] M. Pavan and M. Pelillo. Dominant sets and pairwise clustering. *Pattern Analysis and Machine Intelligence, IEEE Transactions on*, 29(1):167–172, 2007.

[11] B. Siddiquie, Y. Yacoob, and L. S. Davis. Recognizing plays in american football videos. Technical report, University of Maryland, 2009.

[12] G. Sukthankar and K. Sycara. Activity recognition for dynamic multi-agent teams. *ACM Transactions on Intelligent Systems and Technology (TIST)*, 3(1):18, 2011.

[13] J. Sun, X. Wu, S. Yan, L.-F. Cheong, T.-S. Chua, and J. Li. Hierarchical spatio-temporal context modeling for action recognition. In *IEEE Conference on Computer Vision and Pattern Recognition*, pages 2004–2011, 2009.

[14] M. Vlachos, G. Kollios, and D. Gunopulos. Discovering similar multidimensional trajectories. In *18th International Conference on Data Engineering*, pages 673–684. IEEE, 2002.

[15] H. Wang, A. Kläser, C. Schmid, and C.-L. Liu. Dense trajectories and motion boundary descriptors for action recognition. *International Journal of Computer Vision*, 103(1):60–79, 2013.

[16] F. Zhou and F. De la Torre. Generalized time warping for multi-modal alignment of human motion. In *IEEE Conference on Computer Vision and Pattern Recognition*, pages 1282–1289, 2012.

Weak Labeled Multi-Label Active Learning for Image Classification

Shiquan Zhao[1], Jian Wu[1,*], Victor S.Sheng[2], Chen Ye[1], PengPeng Zhao[1], Zhiming Cui[1]
[1]The Institute of Intelligent Information Processing and Application, Soochow University, Suzhou 215006,China
[2]Department of Computer Science, University of Central Arkansas
{20134227054,20134227041}@stu.suda.edu.cn, {jianwu,ppzhao,szzmcui}@suda.edu.cn, ssheng@uca.edu

ABSTRACT
In order to achieve better classification performance with even fewer labeled images, active learning is suitable for these situations. Several active learning methods have been proposed for multi-label image classification, but all of them assume that all training images with complete labels. However, as a matter of fact, it is very difficult to get complete labels for each example, especially when the size of labels in a multi-label domain is huge. Usually, only partial labels are available. This is one kind of "weak label" problems. This paper proposes an ingeniously solution to this "weak label" problem on multi-label active learning for image classification (called WLMAL). It explores label correlation on the weak label problem with the help of input features, and then utilizes label correlation to evaluate the informativeness of each example-label pair in a multi-label dataset for active sampling. Our experimental results on three real-world datasets show that our proposed approach WLMAL consistently outperforms existing approaches significantly.

Keywords
Multi-label active learning, weak label, multi-label image classification, label correlation, label dependence.

1. INTRODUCTION
In the field of traditional image classification, each image can only be classified into one class, which is well-known as single label classification, specifically including binary and multi-class classification [1]. However in the real world, images are always simultaneously associated with multiple labels according to their content [2]. For the sake of reducing the labeling effort and the corresponding cost, active learning methods have been widely used in this field. The main purpose of active learning is to obtain the best model with the least labeling effort and cost. There exist several researches on this topic [3,4,5]. Previous researches on multi-label active learning can be divided into two categories: example based sampling strategies and example-label pair based sampling strategies. The example based strategies take example as a sampling unit, but the example-label pair based strategies take example-label pair as a sampling unit, an intelligent example-label pair based sampling strategy is able to reduce the labeling effort to a great extent. Wu et al. [4] proposed a prototype of an example-label pair based batch mode active learning method for multi-label image classification. Li et al. [6] proposed two multi-label active learning strategies, a max-margin prediction uncertainty strategy and a label cardinality inconsistency strategy, and also integrated the two methods together by an adaptive way in order to obtain better results. Qi et al. [3] proposed a 2DAL method, in which the example-label pair is used as the sampling unit and the mutual information of the label in this example-label pair across all other labels is used to measure the informativeness of this example-label pair. Bang et al. [5] proposed a batch mode active learning method, which uses rule mining to explore global label correlation, and then select a batch of example-label pairs by incorporating label correlation with uncertainty in each iteration. Zhang et al. [7] proposed an example-label pairs based sampling approach by incorporating uncertainty with cross-label value of information based static given label constraints, but without label constraints updating during the active learning process. However, all of the previous studies are ignoring a grim fact: not all labels are available to all images, which is ubiquitous. In many cases, it is very difficult to provide all labels. Thus, only a portion of the labels are usually provided. In such a scenario, the training set contains many weak labeled images [8]. Unlike previous research, this paper will focus on the weak label issue in multi-label active learning for image classification. It will explore conditional label dependence in the weak label scenario of multi-label classification. Based on the conditional label dependence obtained, we will obtain a correlated label set for each label. The label correlation that will be integrated in the active learning process should be gained from its correlated label set. In order to estimate the conditional label dependence well, we will utilize the attributes of examples into the process of label correlation estimation, since examples with the similar features would share similar label correlations.

MM '15, October 26-30, 2015, Brisbane, Australia
© 2015 ACM. ISBN 978-1-4503-3459-4/15/10...$15.00
DOI: http://dx.doi.org/10.1145/2733373.2806298

2. LABEL DEPENDENCE EXPLORATION ON THE WEAK LABEL PROBLEM
We propose a novel example-label based active learning method for multi-label image classification with partial labels, which selects the most informative example-label pairs by integrating uncertainty with information gain over correlated labels, and the label correlation was obtained by exploiting conditional label dependence.

2.1 Conditional Label Dependence
Two different types of dependence should be distinguished when analyzing label dependence in multi-label classification [9], which

will be referred to as *conditional* and *unconditional* label dependence respectively. Unlike unconditional label dependence, which is a global statistical analysis results simply based on original label space, conditional label dependence is associated with not only external labels but also the inner feature space of examples, which have been used in a multi-label learning algorithm Classifier Chains [10]. In this paper, conditional label dependence is used to derive an correlated label set for each label in multi-label classification.

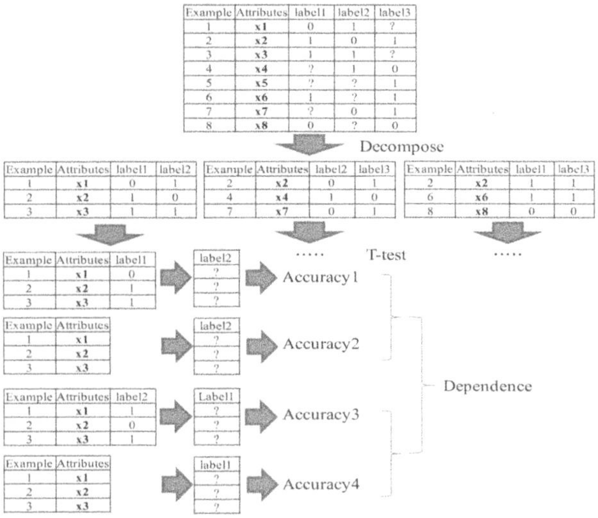

Figure 1. The illustration procedure of obtaining pair-wise conditional label dependence

The conditional dependence of each label pair of a multi-label dataset can be estimated by evaluating the gain of exploiting this dependence for binary classification of each label pair. To estimate the dependence of each pair of labels, four binary classifiers should be trained. Two classifiers are trained only on the original feature space with each label as the target respectively. Another two classifiers are trained on the original feature space augmented by each label and the other label as the target. Using k-fold cross-validation, we can obtain the accuracy of each classifier. Figure 1 illustrates the procedure of obtaining pair-wise conditional label dependence, using a multi-label dataset with three labels as an example. Obviously, if the accuracies of two augmented classifiers are significantly higher than original classifiers respectively, we think that the two labels are conditionally dependent. The statistical significance of the average accuracy difference between each pair of classifiers is determined using a paired t-test.

$$t = \frac{\bar{A}_1 - \bar{A}_2}{\sqrt{\frac{1}{2}(s_{\bar{A}_1}^2 + s_{\bar{A}_2}^2)} \times \sqrt{\frac{2}{n}}} \quad (1)$$

where $\bar{A}_i$ is the average accuracy of the each classifier, and $s_{\bar{A}_i}^2$ is the unbiased estimators of the variances of the two accuracies.

2.2 A Correlated Label Set for Each Label

As we know, a label may not correlate to all other labels but some partial labels in a multi-label dataset. We investigate the label dependence on multi-label image datasets and show our analysis on two datasets in Figure 2 respectively. The left sub-figure illustrates the dependence of all pairs of labels on the image dataset *scene* with 6 labels. The right shows the dependence of all pairs of the first 40 labels on the image dataset *NUS_WIDE*. Note that *NUS_WIDE* has 81 labels in total, in order to see the illustration clearly, we only show its label dependence of all pairs of its first 40 labels. Figure 2 shows that a label always correlated to partial labels. Among the correlated labels, the degree of the correlation is different. Thus, it is necessary to distinguish its significantly correlated labels for a specific label in a multi-label dataset. As shown in Figure 2. The deeper the color, the greater the dependence is.

Figure 2. The dependences for all pairs of the labels on the datasets *scene* and *NUS_WIDE* respectively.

In addition, when a multi-label dataset has a large number of labels, the computation cost for evaluating the effectiveness of each example-label pair is very high. In order to reduce the computational cost and improve the efficiency of multi-label active learning, it is necessary to choose a few significantly dependent labels as the correlated label set for each label in a multi-label dataset. The correlated label set for each label can be obtained by setting a threshold over the conditional dependence calculated following Equations (1) between this label with all others. The threshold can be set by looking up the t-Statistical table. As we know, the higher the threshold, the smaller the correlated label set is.

3. WEAK LABELED MULTI-LABEL ACTIVE LEARNING

After obtaining the correlated label sets for all labels in a multi-label dataset, we introduce information gain over correlated label sets for our multi-label active learning sampling process. Considering an active learning task, each image is associated with T labels. Our goal is to learn a classifier for each label: $p_i = p_i(y_i|x)$, $i=1,2,\dots,T$. During the active learning process, we need to evaluate the informativeness of each example-label pair. Before discussing the informative evaluation, we need to define a few notations. We use $UL(x_j)$ to denote the set of unknown labels of a specific example x_j, and use $L(x_j)$ to denote all labeled labels of this example x_j, and use $CL(y_i)$ to denote the correlated label set of the label y_i. We use KL divergence to represent information gain over the correlated label set $CL(y_i)$ for the unlabeled label y_i in $UL(x_j)$, which is defined as follows.

$$Info\_gain(x_j, y_i) = \sum_{y_l \in CL(y_i)} \sum_{l \in \{0,1\}} p_i(y_i = l|x_j) \ln \frac{p_i(y_i = l|x_j)}{p_l(y_l = l|x_j)} \quad (2)$$

where $p(y_i|x_j)$ denotes the posterior probability of label y_i of example x_j belonging to the positive or negative class produced by its multi-label learning model. As we said before, we will propose an example-label based multi-label active learning algorithm. That is, in each iteration of active learning, we need to choose the most informative example-label pairs to request labels from the oracle. How to evaluate the infomativeness of each example-label pair is the key of active learning for multi-label classification. It is obvious to us that both the uncertainty of an example-label pair and its information gain obtained from Equations (2) are the important factors for us to construct an evaluation criterion. Since entropy is a common method to measure the uncertainty, the informativeness for an example-label pair (x_j, y_i) can be represented as follows.

$$E_{x_{ji}} = -\sum_{l\in 0,1} p_i(y_i=l|x_j)\ln p_i(y_i=l|x_j) + \sum_{y_t\in CL(y_i)} \sum_{l\in 0,1} p_i(y_i=l|x_j)\ln \frac{p_i(y_i=l|x_j)}{p_t(y_t=l|x_j)} \quad (3)$$

Note that if the correlated label set $CL(y_i)$ of label y_i is empty, Equations (3) will reasonably degenerate to only consider uncertainty. After integrating the uncertainty and the information gain, we can use it as a selection criterion to select the most informative example-label pairs as follows, where UD denotes the unlabeled dataset.

$$x^*_{WLMAL} = \arg\max_{x_j\in UD, i\in[1,\dots,T]} E_{x_{ji}} \quad (4)$$

Now it is the time to show the complete framework of our algorithm WLMAL, shown in Algorithm 1, we briefly display the framework of our WLMAL.

Algorithm 1:WLMAL

Input:

The labeled example-label set LD, the unlabeled data set UD, the size of label set T.

Procedure:

Build multi-label classifier model θ based on LD;

Exploiting conditional label dependence on LD, derive correlated label sets CL for all labels;

while stopping criterion is not met

  for each example x_j in UD

    for each example-label pair x_{ji} of x_j

      Compute informativeness of x_{ji} by Equation. (3);

    end for

    Select the most informative example-label pair Ex_{ji} using Eq. (4), request the label for Ex_{ji};

    $UD=UD\backslash Ex_{ji}$; $LD=LD\cup Ex_{ji}$;

  End for

  Rebuild the classifier model θ based on LD;

  Update the conditional label dependence based on LD and then update CL for all labels;

End while

Output : The final classifier model θ ;

4. EXPERIMENTS

In this section, we evaluate our proposed WLMAL by conducting experiments on three image multi-label datasets (*scene*, *NUS-WIDE* and *corel5k*). All of these datasets are available in Mulan [11]. We will compare WLMAL with the following approaches in our experiments.

TDAL – a method proposed in [3], which selects the example-label pairs based on the informativeness measurement mutual information.

LMAL – the closest related method proposed in [4], which selects a batch of example-label pairs with the most uncertainty.

Adaptive – an adaptive method proposed in [6], which integrates the uncertainty and the label cardinality together.

MTAL – a method proposed in [7], which takes into account output constraints during the active sampling process.

4.1 Experiment Settings

In our experiments, BRkNN is used as the base learner, which is a typical model of *problem transformation* [12]. For each dataset, we first randomly divide an entire dataset into three partitions: an initial labeled set, an unlabeled pool and a test set. For each dataset, 30% instances are selected as the test set, and the rest works as its unlabeled pool after a few examples are chosen as its initial labeled set. For each image dataset, we random choose 10 examples as an initial training set. Considering the size of all datasets and the time consumption of our experiments, we set the number of active learning iterations as 400 for all datasets. For comparison purposes, we select T example-label pairs in each iteration for example-label pair based methods, and for the Adaptive method, we select one complete example to request all T labels in each iteration, T is the number of labels of each dataset. Three evaluation metrics are used in our experiments, i.e., Accuracy, Macro-F1 and Micro-F1. Each experiment repeats 10 times, and the average experimental results will show in following figures.

4.2 Experimental Results

The average experimental results of WLMAL and other four methods on three image datasets are shown in Figure 3 to 5 respectively, in terms of three evaluation metrics. From these figures, we can make following conclusions: (1) All example-label pair based methods perform better than the example based method in multi-label active learning, although the example based method Adaptive enhances the performance of multi-label classification. (2) Among the example-label pair based methods, the methods (i.e., WLMAL, MTAL, and TDAL) that take the label correlation into consideration during the active learning process perform better the one (LMAL) that ignores the label correlation. (3) Among the methods (i.e., WLMAL, MTAL, and TDAL), which consider label correlation in the active learning process, our method WLMAL always performs the best on all three datasets, in terms of the three evaluation metrics. This shows that considering information gain from correlated label sets during the active learning process, which is used in WLMAL, is more effective.

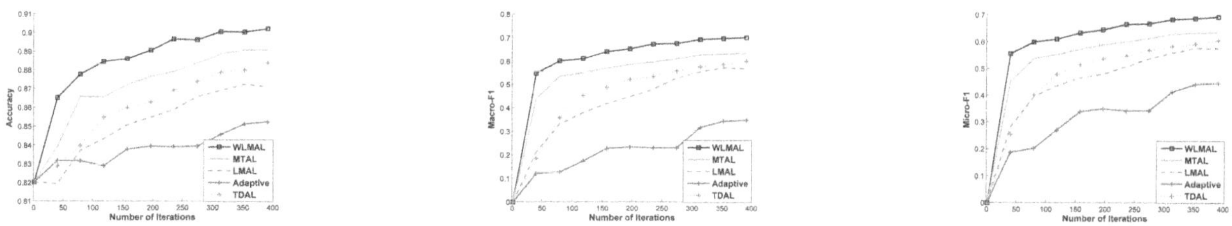

(a) Accuracy (b) Macro-F1 (c) Micro-F1

Figure 3. Average results over 10 runs in terms of three evaluations on the dataset scene.

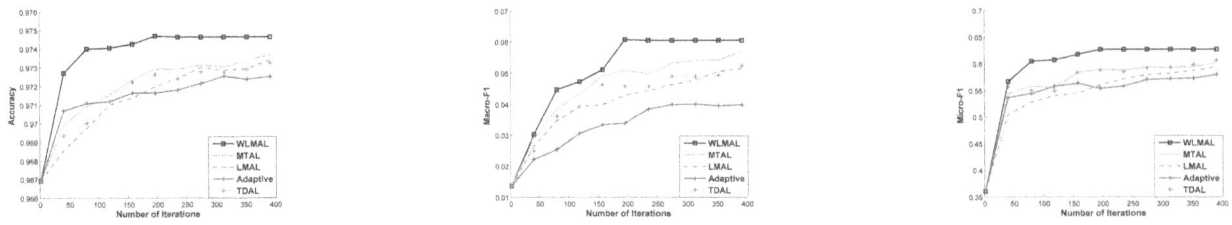

(a) Accuracy (b) Macro-F1 (c) Micro-F1

Figure 4. Average results over 10 runs in terms of three evaluations on the dataset NUS-WIDE.

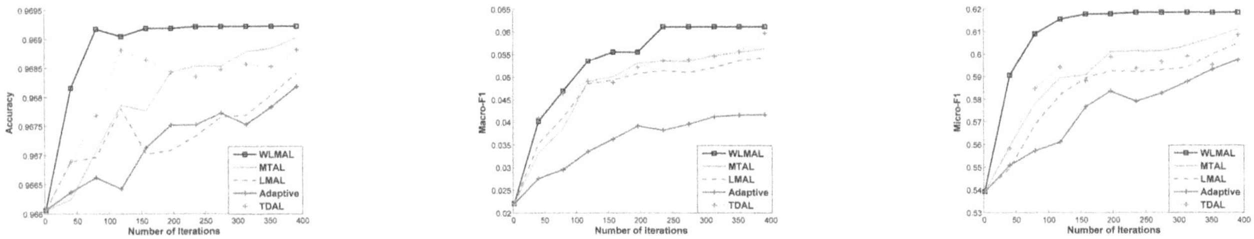

(a) Accuracy (b) Macro-F1 (c) Micro-F1

Figure 5. Average results over 10 runs in terms of three evaluations on the dataset corel5k.

5. CONCLUSIONS

In this paper, a novel active learning method (WLMAL) under the weak label scenario for multi-label image classification is proposed. WLMAL integrates uncertainty and information gain obtained from the correlated label sets together to select the most informative example-label pairs. Our experimental results show that WLMAL performs better than existing methods. Owing to the characteristic of conditional label dependence, there are two points need to pay attention to in the future. One is that the degrees of the dependences of a specific label with all other labels in its correlated label set are always different. Such differences should be reflected during the information measurement process when make active sampling. Another is the mutual assistant prediction of conditional label dependence in multi-label learning. In the future, we will investigate the mutual assistant prediction of conditional label dependence in multi-label classification, and further take advantage of conditional label dependence for predicting unlabeled examples during active learning process. Therefore, we can further reduce the cost of human annotations.

6. ACKNOWLEDGMENTS

This research was partially supported by the Natural Science Foundation of China under grant No. 61170020, 61402311 and 61440053, Jiangsu Province Colleges and Universities Natural Science Research Project under grant No. 13KJB520021, and the U.S. National Science Foundation (IIS-1115417).

7. EFERENCES

[1] Joshi, A. J., Porikli, F., & Papanikolopoulos, N. Multi-class active learning for image classification. Proceedings of the 22th IEEE Conference on Computer Vision and Pattern Recognition (CVPR), 2009, pp.2372-2379.

[2] Xu, X. S., Jiang Y., Peng L., Xue X., Zhou Z. H. Ensemble approach based on conditional random field for multi-label image and video annotation. Proceedings of the 19th ACM International Conference on Multimedia (ACM MM), 2011, pp.1377-1380.

[3] Qi, G. J., Hua, X. S., Rui, Y., Tang, J., & Zhang, H. J. Two-dimensional active learning for image classification. Proceedings of the 21th IEEE Conference on Computer Vision and Pattern Recognition (CVPR), 2008, pp.1-8.

[4] Wu, J., Sheng V.S., Zhang J., Zhao P. P., Cui Z. M. Multi-label Active Learning for Image Classification. Proceedings of the 18th IEEE International Conference on Image Processing (ICIP), 2014, pp.5227-5231.

[5] Bang Z., Yang W., Fang C. Multilabel image classification via high-order label correlation driven active learning. IEEE Transactions on Image Processing, 2014, 23(3): 1430-1441.

[6] Li X., Guo Y. Active learning with multi-label svm classification, Proceedings of the 23th International Joint Conference on Artificial Intelligence (IJCAI), 2013, pp. 1479-1485.

[7] Zhang, Y. Multi-Task Active Learning with Output Constraints, Proceedings of the 24th AAAI Conference on Artificial Intelligence (AAAI), 2010, pp.667-672.

[8] Sun, Y. Y., Zhang, Y., Zhou, Z. H. Multi-label learning with weak label. Proceedings of the 24th AAAI Conference on Artificial Intelligence (AAAI), 2010, pp.593-598.

[9] Dembczynski, K., Waegeman, W., Cheng, W., Hüllermeier, E. On label dependence in multi-label classification. Proceedings of the 2nd International Workshop on Learning from Multi-Label Data, 2010, pp.5-12.

[10] Read, J., Pfahringer, B., Holmes, G., Frank, E. Classifier chains for multi-label classification. Machine learning, 2011, 85(3), 333-359.

[11] Tsoumakas G, Spyromitros-Xioufis E, Vilcek J, et al. MULAN: A Java Library for Multi-Label Learning[J]. Journal of Machine Learning Research, 2011, 12(7):2411-2414.

[12] Spyromitros E., Tsoumakas G., Vlahavas I. An empirical study of lazy multi-label classification algorithms. Artificial Intelligence: Theories, Models and Applications, Springer Berlin Heidelberg, 2008, pp.401-406.

Probabilistic Semi-Canonical Correlation Analysis

Chie Kamada
Grad. School of Information Science and Technology
The University of Tokyo
kamada@mi.t.u-tokyo.ac.jp

Asako Kanezaki
Grad. School of Information Science and Technology
The University of Tokyo
kanezaki@mi.t.u-tokyo.ac.jp

Tatsuya Harada
Grad. School of Information Science and Technology
The University of Tokyo
harada@mi.t.u-tokyo.ac.jp

ABSTRACT

Canonical Correlation Analysis (CCA) requires paired multimodal data to ascertain the relation between two variables. However, it is generally difficult to collect a sufficient amount of paired data of two variables as training samples. This fact leads individual samples of unpaired variables to be additional resources for learning CCA, which are not only able to increase the number of training samples; they are also effective to remove the learning bias caused by the variables' missing patterns. As described in this paper, we propose a novel model of probabilistic CCA by considering the mechanism of data missing. Our method enables widespread applications such as semi-supervised learning via partially labeled training samples and analysis of sensory data which are lacking under certain circumstances. We demonstrate the superior performance of parameter estimation as well as an application of image annotation, compared with existing methods.

Categories and Subject Descriptors

G.3 [**Probability and statistics**]: Correlation and regression, Probabilistic algorithms

General Terms

Theory, Algorithms, Experimentation

Keywords

Canonical correlation analysis, Missing data, Image annotation

1. INTRODUCTION

Canonical correlation analysis (CCA) is a powerful tool applied in widely diverse areas such as pharmacy and economics. Typically in multimedia areas of study, CCA has been widely used for data compression, visualization, feature selection, and so on. One problem of learning models by CCA is that they require paired multimodal data, which are not always obtainable in perfect condition. In image annotation tasks, images annotated with labels should be collected manually as a training dataset. Moreover, sensory data such as time-series GPS data cannot be observed under a specific condition (e.g. inside a building). These problems can be resolved if unpaired data samples, which are missing a modality, can be managed in the analysis.

Several methods have been proposed to incorporate unpaired data samples in CCA. Kimura et al. [3] proposed a method which combines CCA and principal component analysis (PCA). This method was applied to semi-supervised learning of image annotation, where unlabeled images were used to achieve better performance. Zhang et al. [9] proposed a semi CCA method based on a probabilistic model, which is a mixed model of probabilistic CCA (pCCA) and probabilistic PCA (pPCA). Sun et al. [8] also proposed a method based on a probabilistic model. This method differs from that presented by Zhang et al. in the sense that it specifically examines a specific pattern of missing modality, which occurs because of the observational range limitation of sensor data.

Both Kimura et al. [3] and Zhang et al. [9] considered cases in which the missing data occur completely at random. However, Sun et al. [8] modeled the mechanism of data missing in a specific manner. Although this approach is effective if the mechanism is known, it is generally difficult to be modeled in advance. To deal with any type of the lack of real world data robustly, the analytical method should cover widely various missing data patterns.

According to Rubin et al. [6], the data missing mechanism is classified into the following three patterns.

- **Missing Completely At Random (MCAR)**
  Missing of data occurs completely at random.
- **Missing At Random (MAR)**
  The missing of one variable x depends on the other variable y.
- **Missing Not At Random (MNAR)**
  The missing of one variable x depends on x itself.

In the cases of MAR and MNAR, the pattern of data missing is biased because it depends on some variables. For instance, time-series GPS data belong to this family because they tend to become unobservable inside a building. Table 1 presents a comparison of methods related to the applicability of the mechanisms of data missing. It is noteworthy that no existing method can address both the cases of MCAR and MAR. We propose a novel method of semi-CCA based on the model of pCCA, which is able to address both the

MM'15, October 26–30, 2015, Brisbane, Australia.
© 2015 ACM. ISBN 978-1-4503-3459-4/15/10 ...$15.00.
DOI: http://dx.doi.org/10.1145/2733373.2806299.

Table 1: Comparison of methods related to the applicability of the mechanisms of data missing.

	Kimura et al.[3]	Zhang et al.[9]	Sun et al.[8]	pSemi-CCA
MCAR	✓	✓	✗	✓
MAR	✗	✗	✗	✓
MNAR	✗	✗	✓	✗

missing patterns of MCAR and MAR. Our method also performs well on MNAR due to its similarity to MAR. Main contributions of our manuscript are the following.

- Our method covers a wider range of the missing patterns than existing methods do.
- We showed superior performance of parameter estimation compared with existing methods.
- We demonstrated the effectiveness of our method on image annotation with unlabeled images.

2. PROBABILISTIC SEMI-CCA

In this section, we propose a novel model of pCCA by incorporating the mechanism of data missing. Actually, pCCA is a probabilistic interpretation of CCA. The pCCA model includes the assumption that latent variable $\boldsymbol{z}$ and the observation variables $\{\boldsymbol{x}_1, \boldsymbol{x}_2\}$ are generated as the following.

$$\begin{aligned} \boldsymbol{z} &\sim \mathcal{N}(0, I_{d_z}), min\{d_1, d_2\} \geq d_z \geq 1, \\ \boldsymbol{x}_1 | \boldsymbol{z} &\sim \mathcal{N}(W_1\boldsymbol{z} + \boldsymbol{\mu}_1, \Psi_1), \ W_1 \in \mathbb{R}^{d_1 \times d_z}, \ \Psi_1 \succeq 0, \\ \boldsymbol{x}_2 | \boldsymbol{z} &\sim \mathcal{N}(W_2\boldsymbol{z} + \boldsymbol{\mu}_2, \Psi_2), \ W_2 \in \mathbb{R}^{d_2 \times d_z}, \ \Psi_2 \succeq 0. \quad (1) \end{aligned}$$

Therein, $\boldsymbol{\mu}_m, W_m, \Psi_m$ respectively denote the mean, weight matrix, and noise of the m-th modality ($m = 1, 2$). Dimensions of $\boldsymbol{z}, \boldsymbol{x}_1, \boldsymbol{x}_2$ are denoted by d_z, d_1, d_2. Parameter estimation is performed by maximizing the log-likelihood function for pairs of variables $\{\boldsymbol{x}_1, \boldsymbol{x}_2\}$.

We reinterpret this pCCA model by considering the mechanism of data missing. When one considers a situation in which $\boldsymbol{x}_1$ of some training samples are missing, one can define the parameter of the mechanism as ϕ. In addition, one can introduce a binary variable r, which signifies that $\boldsymbol{x}_1$ is observed ($r = 1$) or missing ($r = 0$). The log-likelihood function $\mathcal{L}_i(\theta, \phi)$ of i-th training sample $\{*, \boldsymbol{x}_{2i}\}$ can be transformed as follows.

$$\begin{aligned} \mathcal{L}_i(\theta, \phi) &= \log \int_{\boldsymbol{x}_1} p(\boldsymbol{x}_1, \boldsymbol{x}_{2i}, r_i | \theta, \phi)\, d\boldsymbol{x}_1 \\ &= \log \int_{\boldsymbol{x}_1} p(\boldsymbol{x}_{2i}|\theta)\, p(\boldsymbol{x}_1|\boldsymbol{x}_{2i}, \theta)\, p(r_i|\boldsymbol{x}_1, \boldsymbol{x}_{2i}, \phi)\, d\boldsymbol{x}_1 \\ &= \log p(\boldsymbol{x}_{2i}|\theta) + \log \int_{\boldsymbol{x}_1} p(\boldsymbol{x}_1|\boldsymbol{x}_{2i}, \theta)\, p(r_i|\boldsymbol{x}_1, \boldsymbol{x}_{2i}, \phi)\, d\boldsymbol{x}_1. \quad (2) \end{aligned}$$

In cases of the missing data mechanism classified in MCAR or MAR, r_i is independent of the value of $\boldsymbol{x}_1$. In such a case, the log-likelihood function can be decomposed as shown below.

$$\begin{aligned} \mathcal{L}_i(\theta, \phi) &= \log p(\boldsymbol{x}_{2i}|\theta) + \log p(r_i|\boldsymbol{x}_{2i}, \phi) + \log \int_{\boldsymbol{x}_1} p(\boldsymbol{x}_1|\boldsymbol{x}_{2i}, \theta)\, d\boldsymbol{x}_1 \\ &= \log p(\boldsymbol{x}_{2i}|\theta) + \log p(r_i|\boldsymbol{x}_{2i}, \phi) \\ &= \mathcal{L}_i(\theta) + \mathcal{L}_i(\phi). \quad (3) \end{aligned}$$

When this decomposition is satisfied, the maximum likelihood estimation of θ can be performed even if ϕ is unknown. In other words, in the case of MCAR or MAR, it is possible to estimate θ without bias.

Algorithm 1 ECM algorithm for estimating θ.

Require: $X_1, X_2, d_z, threshold$
Ensure: parameter $\theta = \{\boldsymbol{\mu}_1, \boldsymbol{\mu}_2, W_1, W_2, \Psi_1, \Psi_2\}$.
  initialize $\boldsymbol{\mu}_1, \boldsymbol{\mu}_2$ with sample mean $\widetilde{\boldsymbol{\mu}}_1, \widetilde{\boldsymbol{\mu}}_2$
  initialize W_1, W_2, Ψ_1, Ψ_2 randomly
  $t \leftarrow 0$
  repeat
    /* E-Step */
    Calculate $\langle \boldsymbol{z}_i \rangle, \langle \boldsymbol{z}_i \boldsymbol{z}_i^T \rangle, (i = 1, \cdots, N)$ via (8) - (10).
    /* CM1-Step */
    Update W_1, W_2 via (12)
    Update Ψ_1, Ψ_2 via (13)
    /* E-Step */
    Calculate $\langle \boldsymbol{z}_i \rangle, \langle \boldsymbol{z}_i \boldsymbol{z}_i^T \rangle, (i = 1, \cdots, N)$ via (8) - (10).
    /* CM2-Step */
    Update $\boldsymbol{\mu}_1, \boldsymbol{\mu}_2$ via (11)
    Calculate $\mathcal{L}(\theta^{(t+1)})$.
    $t \leftarrow t + 1$.
  until $\left| \frac{\mathcal{L}(\theta^{(t)}) - \mathcal{L}(\theta^{(t-1)})}{\mathcal{L}(\theta^{(t)})} \right| \leq threshold$

The method of estimating θ is described below. The log-likelihood function $\mathcal{L}(\theta)$ for whole training data is definable as follows.

$$\mathcal{L}(\theta) = \mathcal{L}_1 + \mathcal{L}_2 + \mathcal{L}_3, \quad (4)$$

$$\mathcal{L}_1 = \sum_{i \in S_1} \log p(\boldsymbol{x}_{1i}|\theta), \quad (5)$$

$$\mathcal{L}_2 = \sum_{i \in S_2} \log p(\boldsymbol{x}_{2i}|\theta), \quad (6)$$

$$\mathcal{L}_3 = \sum_{i \in S_3} \log p(\boldsymbol{x}_{1i}, \boldsymbol{x}_{2i}|\theta). \quad (7)$$

Therein, S_1 is the set of samples including only $\boldsymbol{x}_1$, S_2 is the one including only $\boldsymbol{x}_2$, and S_3 is the other one including $\boldsymbol{x}_1$ and $\boldsymbol{x}_2$. The maximization of $\mathcal{L}(\theta)$ is performed by estimating latent variables $\boldsymbol{z}$ and θ alternately.

First, under $\theta^{(t)}$ as given, the expected value of $\boldsymbol{z}_i$ is calculable as follows.

For samples $i \in S_1$,

$$\begin{aligned} \langle \boldsymbol{z}_i \rangle &= \left(I + W_1^{(t)T}\Psi_1^{(t)-1}W_1^{(t)}\right)^{-1} W_1^{(t)T}\Psi_1^{(t)-1}\left(\boldsymbol{x}_{1i} - \boldsymbol{\mu}_1^{(t)}\right), \\ \langle \boldsymbol{z}_i\boldsymbol{z}_i^T \rangle &= \left(I + W_1^{(t)T}\Psi_1^{(t)-1}W_1^{(t)}\right)^{-1} + \langle \boldsymbol{z}_i \rangle \langle \boldsymbol{z}_i \rangle^T, \quad (8) \end{aligned}$$

for samples $i \in S_2$

$$\begin{aligned} \langle \boldsymbol{z}_i \rangle &= \left(I + W_2^{(t)T}\Psi_2^{(t)-1}W_2^{(t)}\right)^{-1} W_2^{(t)T}\Psi_2^{(t)-1}\left(\boldsymbol{x}_{2i} - \boldsymbol{\mu}_2^{(t)}\right), \\ \langle \boldsymbol{z}_i\boldsymbol{z}_i^T \rangle &= \left(I + W_2^{(t)T}\Psi_2^{(t)-1}W_2^{(t)}\right)^{-1} + \langle \boldsymbol{z}_i \rangle \langle \boldsymbol{z}_i \rangle^T, \quad (9) \end{aligned}$$

for samples $i \in S_3$

$$\begin{aligned} \langle \boldsymbol{z}_i \rangle &= \left(I + W_1^{(t)T}\Psi_1^{(t)-1}W_1^{(t)} + W_2^{(t)T}\Psi_2^{(t)-1}W_2^{(t)}\right)^{-1} \\ &\quad \times \left\{W_1^{(t)T}\Psi_1^{(t)-1}\left(\boldsymbol{x}_{1i} - \boldsymbol{\mu}_1^{(t)}\right) + W_2^{(t)T}\Psi_2^{(t)-1}\left(\boldsymbol{x}_{2i} - \boldsymbol{\mu}_2^{(t)}\right)\right\}, \\ \langle \boldsymbol{z}_i\boldsymbol{z}_i^T \rangle &= \left(I + W_1^{(t)T}\Psi_1^{(t)-1}W_1^{(t)} + W_2^{(t)T}\Psi_2^{(t)-1}W_2^{(t)}\right)^{-1} \\ &\quad + \langle \boldsymbol{z}_i \rangle \langle \boldsymbol{z}_i \rangle^T. \quad (10) \end{aligned}$$

Using $\langle \boldsymbol{z}_i \rangle, \langle \boldsymbol{z}_i\boldsymbol{z}_i^T \rangle$, the expected value of the complete data log-likelihood function $\mathcal{L}_c(\theta) = \log p(X_1, X_2, Z)$ can be calculated. The following equations can be acquired by taking the partial derivative of $\langle \mathcal{L}_c(\theta) \rangle$ with respect to each parameter.

$$\boldsymbol{\mu}_m = \frac{1}{N_m + N_3} \sum_{i \in S_m \cup S_3} (\boldsymbol{x}_{mi} - W_m \langle \boldsymbol{z}_i \rangle), \quad (11)$$

$$W_m = \{ \sum_{i \in S_m \cup S_3} (\boldsymbol{x}_{mi} - \boldsymbol{\mu}_m) \langle \boldsymbol{z}_i \rangle^T \} [\sum_{i \in S_m \cup S_3} \langle \boldsymbol{z}_i \boldsymbol{z}_i^T \rangle]^{-1}, \quad (12)$$

$$\Psi_m = \frac{1}{N_m + N_3} \sum_{i \in S_m \cup S_3} (\boldsymbol{x}_{mi} - \boldsymbol{\mu}_m - W_m \langle \boldsymbol{z}_i \rangle)(\boldsymbol{x}_{mi} - \boldsymbol{\mu}_m)^T. \quad (13)$$

Therein, $m = 1, 2$, and N_1, N_2, N_3 represent the numbers of samples included in S_1, S_2, S_3. To increase $\mathcal{L}_c(\theta)$, parameters should be updated to satisfy all of (11), (12), and(13).

In this problem, it is difficult to update and satisfy all equations because the parameters are mutually interdependent. Therefore, we use the framework called the Expectation Conditional Maximization (ECM) algorithm [4]. In the ECM algorithm, parameter θ is divided into several groups $\{\theta_1, \cdots, \theta_n\}$. The log-likelihood function can be increased by alternately updating the parameter group θ_k $(k = 1, \cdots, n)$ (CM-step), and latent variable (E-step) . In this case, the problem became easier by dividing parameter θ into two groups $\{\boldsymbol{\mu}_1, \boldsymbol{\mu}_2\}$ and $\{W_1, W_2, \Psi_1, \Psi_2\}$. In summary, the parameter estimation is conducted along with algorithm 1.

In this section, we demonstrated the model parameter θ can be estimated without bias if the missing data mechanism is classified in MCAR or MAR. The parameters can be estimated within the framework of the ECM algorithm.

3. EXPERIMENTS

3.1 Evaluation of artificial data

We evaluated the model parameter estimation accuracy of our method using artificially generated data. Training samples were generated randomly according to the pCCA model (1) with missing patterns of MCAR, MAR, and MNAR. The model parameters $\boldsymbol{\theta} = \{W_1, W_2, \boldsymbol{\mu}_1, \boldsymbol{\mu}_2, \Psi_1, \Psi_2\}$ were decided in each trial as follows. W_1 and W_2 were selected randomly so that each column has the normal distribution of $\mathcal{N}(0, I_{d_z})$. $\boldsymbol{\mu}_1$ and $\boldsymbol{\mu}_2$ respectively follow the normal distribution of $\mathcal{N}(0, I_{d_m})$, $(m = 1, 2)$. We used those for which $L2$ norms are greater than 1. The covariances of noise Ψ_1 and Ψ_2 are set as $\Psi_m = 0.1 \times (I_{d_m} + \sum_{j=1}^{\frac{d_z}{2}} \boldsymbol{u}_j \boldsymbol{u}_j^T)$, $(m = 1, 2)$, where $\boldsymbol{u}_j \sim \mathcal{N}(0, I_{d_m})$. The variable dimensions are set as $d_1 = 50$, $d_2 = 50$, and $d_z = 5$. We generated data missing at 20% of training samples. In the case of MCAR, we randomly selected a sample and removed its $\boldsymbol{x}_1$. In the case of MAR, we generated a d_2-dimensional vector $\boldsymbol{a}$ randomly and removed $\boldsymbol{x}_1$ of a sample if $\boldsymbol{a}^T \boldsymbol{x}_2$ is larger than a certain threshold. In the case of MNAR, we randomly generated a d_1-dimensional vector $\boldsymbol{a}$ and removed $\boldsymbol{x}_1$ of a sample if $\boldsymbol{a}^T \boldsymbol{x}_1$ is larger than a certain threshold.

For the evaluation, we used square errors of estimated parameters. The square error between the true mean $\boldsymbol{\mu}$ and the estimated mean $\hat{\boldsymbol{\mu}}$ is calculated as follows.

$$\boldsymbol{\mu}_{error} = \frac{(\boldsymbol{\mu} - \hat{\boldsymbol{\mu}})^T (\boldsymbol{\mu} - \hat{\boldsymbol{\mu}})}{\boldsymbol{\mu}^T \boldsymbol{\mu}}. \quad (14)$$

Letting $\boldsymbol{w}_i$ denote i-th row vector of W and $|\boldsymbol{w}_i|$ denote its norm, the square error between the true weight matrix W and the estimated weight matrix $\hat{W}$ is calculated as follows.

$$W_{error} = \frac{\sum_{i=1}^{d} (|\boldsymbol{w}_i| - |\hat{\boldsymbol{w}}_i|)^2}{\sum_{i=1}^{d} |\boldsymbol{w}_i|^2}. \quad (15)$$

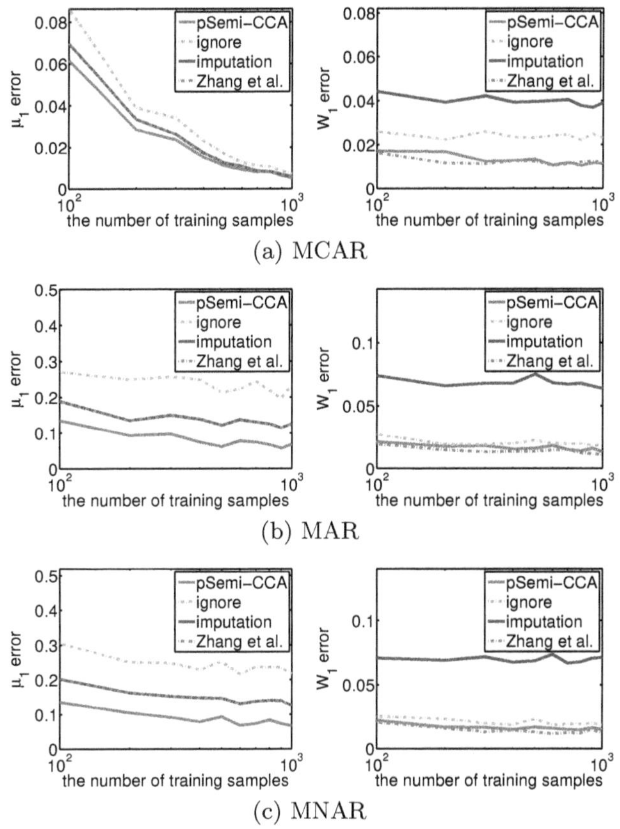

Figure 1: Estimation errors of the mean $\boldsymbol{\mu}$ (left) and weight matrix W (right) of artificial data.

In this experiment, we generated the training samples 50 times and estimated the parameters from each trial. Then we evaluated the mean errors of 50 trials in total.

For comparison with our method "pSemi-CCA", we tried a simple method "ignore", by which a sample with a missing variable is removed, as well as a method of "imputation", by which missing values are filled with the data mean, and a method reported by Zhang et al. [9].

Estimation errors of parameters versus the number of training samples are shown in Fig. 1. In the case of MCAR, the proposed method can estimate better parameters when the training samples are few, compared with other methods. In the case of MAR and MNAR, where the missing patterns are biased, our method provides more accurate estimation than other methods because of the bias relaxation.

3.2 Semi-supervised learning of image annotation

As an actual application of our method, we conducted an experiment of image annotation tasks. In general, the classifiers of image annotation are learned with a paired set of images and labels, but we also used unlabeled images to promote learning. Here we used Corel5k dataset [1], which includes images attached with multiple labels. We evaluated the accuracy of image annotation when we artificially removed labels of a part of training images. In the same manner as Section 3.1, we generated missing data according to the patterns of MCAR, MAR, and MNAR. We calculated the mean of F-measures of 100 trials for each miss-

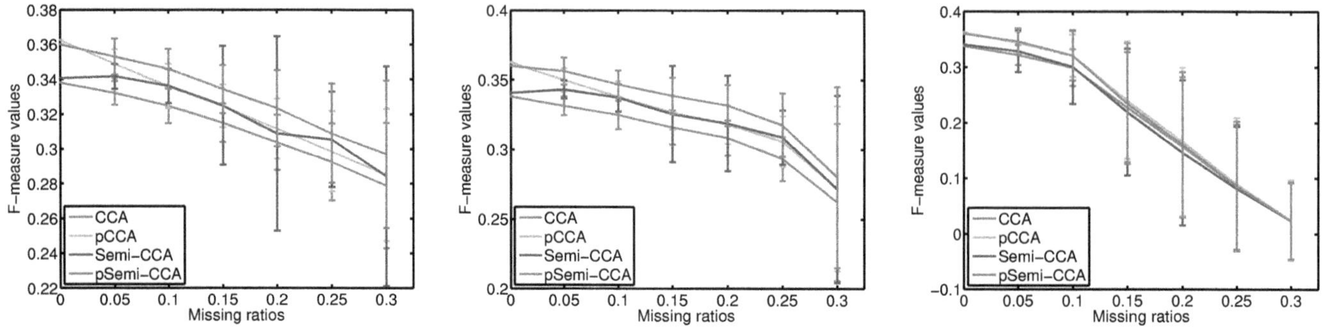

Figure 2: F-measures of image annotation. From left to right, the missing pattern is MCAR, MAR, and MNAR.

ing pattern. We used the Caffe library [2] to extract 4096-dimensional CNN-based features [7] learned on the ILSVRC dataset. The dimension of the image feature vectors was reduced to 309[1] by PCA with whitening. As label features, we used a binary vector for which the respective element represents the existence of each label: each element takes 1 if the corresponding label is attached to an image and takes 0 otherwise. The dimension of the label feature vectors is 260, which is the number of labels in this dataset.

Image annotation was conducted via Nakayama et al. [5]. This is a sample-based classification method working in a low-dimensional latent space, which is therefore fast and robust for increasing labels. In the training process, it calculates the low-dimensional space with the highest correlation values between image features and label features via pCCA. In the testing process, it outputs multiple labels by k nearest-neighbor search of the input image from the database in the low-dimensional space. Whereas Nakayama et al. used pCCA for dimension reduction and measuring sample distances, we substitute the proposed pSemi-CCA for pCCA and use unpaired (i.e. unlabeled) training images for learning. For comparison, we used CCA, pCCA [5], and Semi-CCA proposed by Kimura et al. [3]. We used both image features and label features to calculate sample distances in cases with pCCA and pSemi-CCA because they are based on probabilistic models. We used only image features to calculate sample distances in the cases with CCA and Semi-CCA. We set the dimension of latent space to 100.

F-measures versus ratios of unlabeled training images are shown in Fig. 2. When the training images are fully labeled, pCCA and pSemi-CCA are superior to CCA and Semi-CCA [3], probably because of the fact that pCCA and pSemi-CCA incorporate label features to measure sample distances. That fact indicates that the methods based on probabilistic models can measure distances of samples more properly. Moreover, the proposed pSemi-CCA demonstrated better performance than pCCA when unlabeled training images existed, demonstrating that the unpaired (or missing) samples were used effectively to learn better space for classification by our method. Semi-CCA [3] outperformed CCA when unlabeled training images existed because it also uses unpaired samples for learning. Semi-CCA [3] sometimes failed to learn the model when the ratio of unlabeled images was large, and thus the standard variation of its F-measures became large. [2]

[1]Here, the cumulative contribution ratio is 0.75.

[2]Large std. variation cause error bars passing below zero.

4. CONCLUSION

We proposed pSemi-CCA, a novel model of probabilistic CCA which can manage unpaired (or missing) samples in learning. We classified the mechanisms of data missing into MCAR, MAR, and MNAR, and demonstrated that our method covers a wider range of the missing patterns than existing methods do. In the experiments, we demonstrated the effectiveness of our method both with artificial data and with a real image annotation dataset. Our method is based on probabilistic models. Therefore, our future work shall include introduction of a prior probability distribution for increasing the stability of model estimation as well as the implementation of automatic model selection.

5. REFERENCES

[1] P. Duygulu, K. Barnard, J. F. de Freitas, and D. A. Forsyth. Object recognition as machine translation: Learning a lexicon for a fixed image vocabulary. In *ECCV*, 2002.

[2] Y. Jia, E. Shelhamer, J. Donahue, S. Karayev, J. Long, R. Girshick, S. Guadarrama, and T. Darrell. Caffe: Convolutional architecture for fast feature embedding. *arXiv preprint arXiv:1408.5093*, 2014.

[3] A. Kimura, H. Kameoka, M. Sugiyama, T. Nakano, E. Maeda, H. Sakano, and K. Ishiguro. SemiCCA: Efficient semi-supervised learning of canonical correlations. In *ICPR*, 2010.

[4] X.-L. Meng and D. B. Rubin. Maximum likelihood estimation via the ECM algorithm: A general framework. *Biometrika*, 80:267–278, 1993.

[5] H. Nakayama, T. Harada, and Y. Kuniyoshi. Canonical contextual distance for large-scale image annotation and retrieval. In *International Workshop on Large-Scale Multimedia Mining and Retrieval*, 2009.

[6] D. B. Rubin. Inference and missing data. *Biometrika*, 63:581–592, 1976.

[7] K. Simonyan and A. Zisserman. Very deep convolutional networks for large-scale image recognition. *arXiv preprint arXiv:1409.1556*, 2014.

[8] J. Sun and S. Keates. Canonical correlation analysis on data with censoring and error information. *Neural Networks and Learning Systems*, 24:1909–1919, 2013.

[9] B. Zhang, J. Hao, G. Ma, J. Yue, and Z. Shi. Semi-paired probabilistic canonical correlation analysis. In *ICIIP*, 2014.

Recognizing Human Activity in Still Images by Integrating Group-Based Contextual Cues

Zheng Zhou
Beijing Institute of Technology
zz24@bit.edu.cn

Kan Li
Beijing Institute of Technology
likan@bit.edu.cn

Xiangjian He
University of Technology, Sydney
xiangjian.he@uts.edu.au

ABSTRACT

Images with wider angles usually capture more persons in wider scenes, and recognizing individuals' activities in these images based on existing contextual cues usually meet difficulties. We instead construct a novel group-based cue to utilize the context carried by suitable surrounding persons. We propose a global-local cue integration model (GLCIM) to find a suitable group of local cues extracted from individuals and form a corresponding global cue. A fusion restricted Boltzmann machine, a focal subspace measurement and a cue integration algorithm based on entropy are proposed to enable the GLCIM to integrate most of the relevant local cues and least of the irrelevant ones into the group. Our experiments demonstrate how integrating group-based cues improves the activity recognition accuracies in detail and show that all of the key parts of GLCIM make positive contributions to the increases of the accuracies.

Categories and Subject Descriptors

U.3 [**Understanding**]: Multimedia and Vision

Keywords

activity recognition, context, group-based cue, Fusion-RBM, focal subspace measurement

1. INTRODUCTION

Image-based human activity recognition has attracted increasing research attention in very recent years. It is of great scientific importance and has useful applications in multimedia, such as image annotation, behavior based image retrieval, video frame reduction and human computer interaction. An activity contains a number of subsequent actions and gives an interpretation of the movement that is being performed [8]. Unlike video-based methods that model the subsequent actions by spatio-temporal features, image-based methods utilize contextual cues to help characterize an activity because there is no temporal information available in still images.

The existing popular contextual cues include action-related object cues, human-object interaction cues, and whole scene cues [5].

MM '15, October 26-30, 2015, Brisbane, Australia.
©2015 ACM. ISBN 978-1-4503-3459-4/15/10 ...$15.00.
DOI: http://dx.doi.org/10.1145/2733373.2806300.

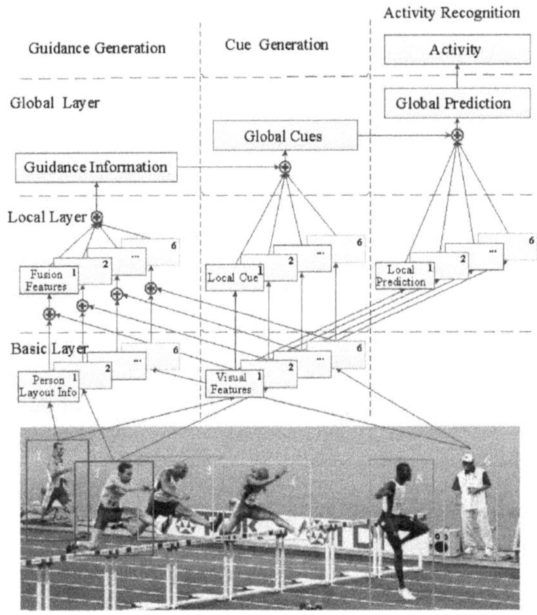

Figure 1: GLCIM for Human Activity Recognition.

Action-related object cues and human-object interaction cues work well when the "key object" can easily be found and recognized [9]. A scene cue models the occurrence of a scene, an object and an activity, and it is very suitable for the scene-specific activities [7]. However, for images with wider angles, taken in daily life and usually containing more persons, applying the above-mentioned three kinds of cues may lead to the difficulties as follows. "Key objects" are illegible and hard to be detected and recognized in a complex background, and the same scene contributes very little to discriminate persons with different activities in an image.

As a matter of fact, when humans see an image containing multiple persons, they confirm the activity of a certain person by referring to a group of persons who perform the same activity or related activities. In this paper, we try to model this biomimetic mechanism in computer vision and we call it a group-based contextual cue. For example, in Fig.1, person 1 is hurdling, but the action or pose of him looks more like running. If we apply a group-based cue by referring to persons 2-5, we will be sure of telling that person 1 is hurdling. An action-related object cue and a human-object interaction cue will work worse in this image because person 1 has no interaction with these hurdles. Scene cue will assertively tell that person 6 is hurdling too, but he is only a referee. This problem can also be solved in the following two procedures in theory: discovering groups and recognizing group activities. However, persons performing the same group activity may do different individual

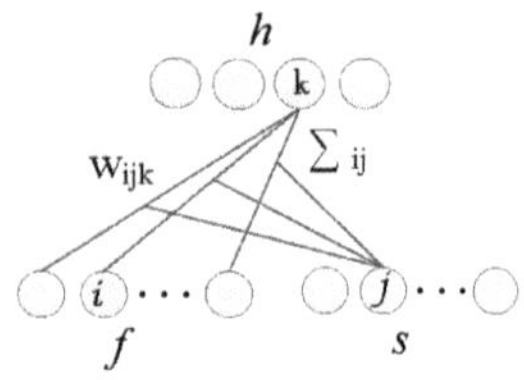

Figure 2: The Structure of FRBM.

activities. For example, two persons as a group working collaboratively to take photos may perform different individual activities, e.g., operating a camera and posing.

Two main challenges exist in generating group-based cues. One is taking full advantage of the relevant contextual information, and the other is minimizing the effect of the irrelevant or "misleading" contextual cues. In our global-local cue integration model, we design a series of methods and algorithms to select cues carried by suitable persons, including a fusion restricted Boltzmann machine (FRBM) to fuse features and a focal subspace measurement together with a global cue integration method based on entropy to integrate the most relevant local cues and stop the integrating process when misleading cues try to decrease the significance of the integrated global cues.

We highlight the main contributions of this paper as follows.

- We use a group-based cue to help human activity recognition in still images. It is for the first time that context carried by surrounding persons is formed as a contextual cue to do the activity recognition for a single person in an image.
- We develop a global-local cue integration model (GLCIM) for recognizing a human activity using a group-based cue. GLCIM can select suitable local cues to generate reasonable global cues which integrate least of the irrelevant context.
- We also propose a fusion restricted Boltzmann machine (FRBM) and a corresponding focal subspace measurement to estimate the interdependencies of persons. They play important roles in GLCIM and also allow the model to work well when the amount of training data is limited.

2. RELATED WORK

The existing and the most popular contextual cues for human activity recognition based on images are action-related object cues [9], human-object interaction cues [12], and whole scene cues [11]. An action-related object cue helps activity recognition by discovering objects that may relate to the activity. A human-object interaction cue further considers the relative position or relative angle between an object and a human to disambiguate some object-inferred activities. A scene cue utilizes the fact that some activities are happening in specific places. Some existing work jointly employs these cues. For example, Li et al. [7] combined object cues and scene cues to model sports events and Shapavolavo et al. [10] integrated all three kinds of cues to beat the state-of-the-art results on the PASCAL dataset. Unlike their approaches, which extract context from objects and scenes, we exploit the contextual information provided by surrounding persons instead, and our model can be easily extended to these three kinds of cues.

There is also a line of work on modeling group activities. Quite a proportion of them focus on video data [2]. Some of them also employ complex equipment, such as multiple cameras [13]. For the existing research on group activity recognition based on still images [1] [6], researchers pay much attention to how to model a group activity based on the activities of individual members. Moreover, all persons in one image share the same activity label in the group activity recognition. However, our work is to recognize the activities of individuals and the persons in one image can do different activities. A group-based cue is to find a group of persons that may provide useful and contextual information to the interested person. Persons doing the same activity may have other groups of persons that provide the cues.

3. GLOBAL-LOCAL CUE INTEGRATION MODEL

Global-local cue integration model (GLCIM) is proposed to select context carried by suitable persons and form a global cue based on the selected local cues to help the activity recognition.

3.1 Overview

The overview of GLCIM is shown in Fig.1. A local cue extracted from a surrounding person is a vector of probabilities that describe how much evidence that this surrounding person provides to infer an interested person doing potential activities. A global cue is generated by a combination of a group of selected local cues. Guidance information reflects the interdependencies of pairs of persons and determines which persons' local cues are selected. We assume the interdependencies are related to two key points: 1) the layout information of persons, and 2) the similarities in persons' visual features, such as clothes colors and poses. We design a fusion-restricted Boltzmann machine (FRBM) to form the fusion features based on the visual features extracted by a convolutional neural network (CNN) and the layout information. A focal subspace measurement is also developed to measure the relative distances between the fusion features of pairs of persons, and this allows the GLCIM to work with a limited amount of training data. With the guidance information, a proper group of local cues are chosen to form the global cue. Once the global cue for an interested person is generated, we can use it to improve the local activity recognition.

3.2 Fusion Restricted Boltzmann Machine

To fuse the visual features and the layout information, which are quite different in scale, we design a FRBM. The structure of the FRBM is shown in Fig.2. f and s are two visible layers standing for the visual features and the layout information respectively, and h is the hidden layer, in which the values are deemed as fusion features. FRBM is trained by minimizing the normalized reconstructing error of visible layers, so the generated fusion features are not influenced by the different scales of original features.

The energy function of FRBM capturing all possible correlations among the components of the visible f, s and the hidden h is given as:

$$E(f,s,h) = -\sum_{ijk} w_{ijk} f_i s_j h_k - \sum_i w_i^f f_i - \sum_j w_j^s s_j - \sum_k w_k^h h_k, \tag{1}$$

where $w_{ijk} \in W$ is the connection weight, $w_i^f \in W^f$ is the bias of layer f, $w_j^s \in W^s$ is the bias of layer s, and $w_k^h \in W^h$ is the bias of layer h. We define the parameter set $\theta := (W, W^f, W^s, W^h)$. Then, we have the joint probability distribution: $p(f,s,h) = \frac{e^{-E(f,s,h)}}{\sum_{f,s,h} e^{-E(f,s,h)}}$.

By maximizing the likelihood, we get the weight update rule: $\Delta\theta = \varepsilon \cdot \frac{\partial \ln p(f,s)}{\partial \theta}$, where ε is the learning rate. Then, for updating each parameter, we calculate the partial derivative of each component of θ. With these partial derivatives, we calculate the hidden values of h by Gibbs sampling as follows. First, the hidden units are sampled according to $p(h_k = 1|f,s) = sigmoid(\sum_{ij} w_{ijk} f_i s_j + w_k^h)$, and then the units of f and s are sampled through iteration between

$$\begin{cases} p(f_i = 1|s,h) = sigmoid(\sum_{jk} w_{ijk} s_j h_k + w_i^f) \\ p(s_j = 1|f,h) = sigmoid(\sum_{ik} w_{ijk} f_i h_k + w_j^s). \end{cases}$$

Figure 3: Examples in our dataset.

3.3 Focal Subspace Measurement

A FRBM can be regarded as a mapping that maps data points from original feature spaces to a unified fusion feature space. We need plenty of data to train the mapping between the spaces with large sizes. However, in GLCIM, we only need the relative distances from the surrounding persons to one certain interested person. Therefore, we propose the focal subspace measurement to give the relative distances. The focal subspace distance is defined as:

$$FSDis_{p_f}(p_i, p_j) = EuDis(Tran_{p_f}(p_i), Tran_{p_f}(p_j)), \qquad (2)$$

where p_f is the original data of the interested focal person, $Tran_{p_f}(p_i)$ means the hidden layer values when the data of the person p_i is run through the FRBM trained only by the data of p_f, and $EuDis(\cdot)$ stands for the Euclidean distance.

3.4 Global Cue Generation

A global cue is in the form of a vector of probabilities like a local cue. The guidance information is about the distances from the surrounding persons to the interested person measured by the focal subspace measurement, which reflects the possibilities of persons' doing the same or related activities. The higher possibility a surrounding person is with, the higher contribution he will make in deducing the activity of the interested person. Thus, we construct the global cue by accumulating the local cues one by one in the order of the possibilities from highest to lowest with the inverse of the entropies of local cues as weights, and we stop the accumulation when the significance of the accumulation result reaches the peak. The significance or stability of a set of possibilities is measured by its entropy, defined as: $Ent(P) = -\sum_P p \ln p$. In this way, the most relevant cues measured by the focal subspace measurement will be integrated and when irrelevant cues are going to cause the fall of the $Ent(P)$, the integrating process will stop.

Finally, the global prediction is given by:

$$GP(p_f) = C \cdot \left(\frac{LP(p_f)}{Ent(LP(p_f))} + \frac{GC(p_f)}{Ent(GC(p_f))}\right), \qquad (3)$$

where $C = \left(\frac{1}{Ent(LP(p_f))} + \frac{1}{Ent(GC(p_f))}\right)^{-1}$ is a normalization constant, and $LP(p_f)$ and $GC(p_f)$ are vectors of possibilities standing for the local prediction and the global cue of the focal person p_f respectively. $LP(p_f)$ can be obtained by any existing activity recognition method as long as the method can give the possibilities of the person performing the potential activities.

4. EXPERIMENTS

Many public datasets are available to validate human activity recognition methods based on still images. However, most of them are collected for classifying the activity of a single person. In datasets for pair of persons' interactions and collective activities of larger groups, only one group activity is label for each image. Each image in Structured Group Dataset (SGD) [3], a very recently proposed and challenging dataset, contains groups of persons, but only a small proportion of the images contain groups performing different activities. This dataset is not sufficient for our testing.

In this paper, we compile a new dataset with two characteristics described as follows. 1) Each image in the dataset contains several persons. 2) Persons in an image may execute different activities. Persons in this dataset are doing 8 activities: running, hurdling, playing soccer, playing basketball, dancing, singing, dining and watching. Watching is a relatively loose activity, and it can be an audience staring at a running race or a referee supervising a basketball game. We assign the watching label to the persons whose activities are different from the main activity in an image. In each activity category, there are about 2000 persons being detected. As shown in Fig.3, this dataset is a very challenging one and we highlight the difficulties as follows. 1) The activity classes are diverse, and some classes, such as singing and dancing, are hard to discriminate. 2) Within the same activity, the sizes and poses of person instances are very different. 3) The background of each image is highly cluttered and diverse. 4) Except the activity labels, no any other information, including basic segmentation, is given.

To prove that our GLCIM can improve the activity recognition performance by integrating a group-based cue and to validate the performance of select suitable local cue, we first need local predictions and local cues. Since no detailed segmentation is contained in our dataset, heavy pre-process is needed if we employ existing methods on recognizing the activity of a single person. Therefore, we choose feed-forward neural networks to give both the local cues and the local predictions. For the local cues, we train a neural network by the images in our dataset and the statistical data of activity labels. For the local prediction, tuning the amount of total number of the nodes in the neural network allows us to simulate local predictions with different accuracies. We employ the part-based deformable model [4] to detect the persons in an image and the C-NN to extract features from the detected persons. We implement the whole process from the raw images to the final prediction result automatically on this very challenging dataset. Our approach is a pioneering work working on the activity recognition of a person using the cues of other persons' activities in the same group and is very different from the existing methods, so it cannot be compared with the existing methods directly.

Table 1 shows the comparison of our activity recognition method with a group-based cue and the baseline without any cues at the 50% local prediction accuracy. We can see that except for the

Table 1: Comparison of Activity Recognition Accuracies.

	Without Cue	With Cue
total	50.83%	61.15%
running	49.56%	53.98%
hurdling	46.43%	57.14%
soccer	46.49%	50.00%
basketball	44.78%	59.70%
dancing	40.00%	60.00%
singing	48.28%	62.93%
dining	72.55%	87.25%
watching	60.47%	58.14%

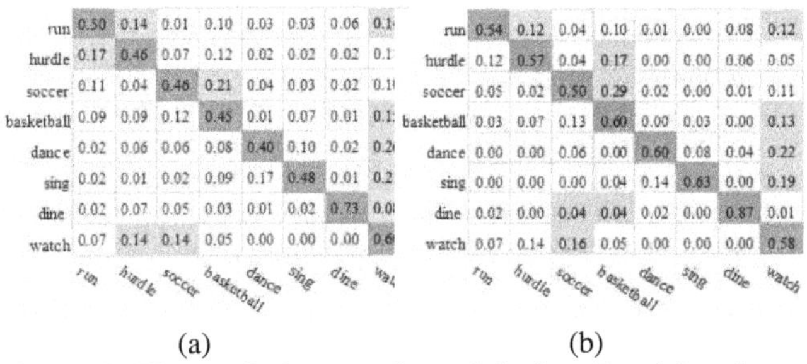

Figure 4: The confusion matrices of the baseline (a) and our method (b).

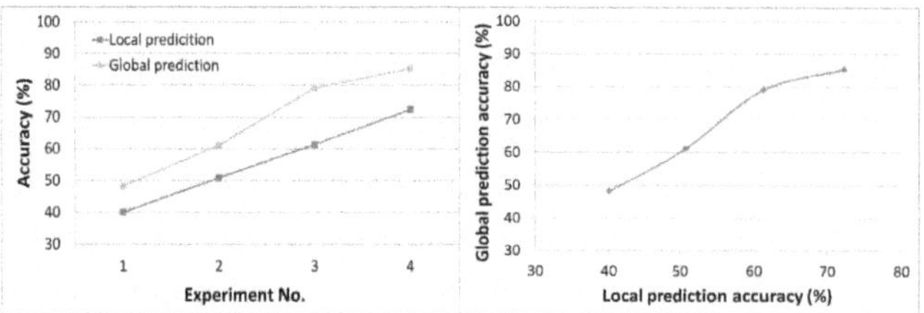

(a) (b)

Figure 5: The activity recognition accuracies of our activity recognition based on different local prediction accuracies.

watching activity, the accuracies of recognizing various activities increase between 3.51% to 20%. The confusion matrices in Fig.4 indicate the soundness of the increases, which benefit from 1) discriminating closer activities (referring to running and hurdling) and 2) removing unrelated activities (referring the increase of singing). For the case of watching activity, we see the decrease of accuracy as shown in Table 1. It is because, in some images as shown in Fig.1, the persons labeled watching are so isolated that all cues in the images have negative effects in recognizing the watching activities of the persons. GLCIM tries to select no local cues in this situation. Therefore, we have been happy enough to see this very small 2.33% decrease and it proves that GLCIM has integrated only very minimum number of mistaken local cues.

Fig.5 shows the activity recognition accuracies of GLCIM based on different local prediction accuracies. We can see that, for different local prediction results, we always achieve a significant improvement, and the increase of the global prediction accuracy shows an upward tendency.

Fig.6 shows a series of experiments to test the key parts in GLCIM. From (a), we see that the fusion features are a valid mix of the original features. From (b), we see that, with no extra training data, the focal subspace measurement outperforms the method of training a FRBM mapping for measurement. From (c), we see that, when many persons appear and interfere each other in one image, GLCIM achieves better performance than clustering the persons in their original feature spaces and combining all persons for a cue.

5. CONCLUSION

In this paper, we have presented a novel global-local cue to help recognize human's activities in still images. We have proposed a global-local cue integration model (GLCIM) to form the group-based cue based on context carried by suitable persons. We have also proposed a fusion restricted Boltzmann machine and a focal subspace measurement to estimate the interdependency between pairs of persons even if the amount of training data is limited. Our experimental results have demonstrated that the accuracies of recognizing human activities in still images are improved by integrating group-based cues and all key parts of GLICM contribute positively to the accuracy increases.

6. ACKNOWLEDGEMENTS

This work was supported by National High Technology Research and Development Program of China (No.2013CB329605) (973 Program) and Training Program of the Major Project of BIT.

References

[1] AMER, M. R., XIE, D., ZHAO, M., TODOROVIC, S., AND ZHU, S.-C. Cost-sensitive top-down/bottom-up inference for multiscale activity recognition. In *ECCV, 187-200, 2012.*

[2] CHENG, Z., QIN, L., HUANG, Q., YAN, S., AND TIAN, Q. Recognizing human group action by layered model with multiple cues. *Neurocomputing 136* (2014), 124–135.

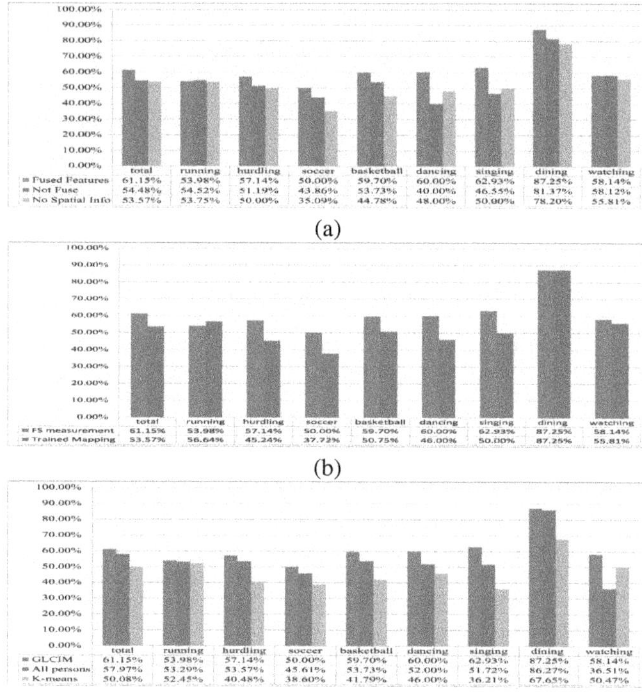

(a) (b) (c)

Figure 6: Experiments on the effect of the details in global cue generation. (a) Validation for FRBM. (b) Validation for focal subspace measurement. (c) Validation for local cue selecting algorithm.

[3] CHOI, W., CHAO, Y.-W., PANTOFARU, C., AND SAVARESE, S. Discovering groups of people in images. In *ECCV, 417-433, 2014.*

[4] FELZENSZWALB, P. F., GIRSHICK, R. B., MCALLESTER, D., AND RAMANAN, D. Object detection with discriminatively trained part-based models. *T-PAMI 32*, 9 (2010), 1627–1645.

[5] GUO, G., AND LAI, A. A survey on still image based human action recognition. *Pattern Recognition* (2014).

[6] LAN, T., WANG, Y., YANG, W., ROBINOVITCH, S. N., AND MORI, G. Discriminative latent models for recognizing contextual group activities. *T-PAMI 34*, 8 (2012), 1549–1562.

[7] LI, L.-J., AND FEI-FEI, L. What, where and who? classifying events by scene and object recognition. In *ICCV, 1-8, 2007.*

[8] MOESLUND, T. B., HILTON, A., AND KRÜGER, V. A survey of advances in vision-based human motion capture and analysis. *CVIU 104*, 2 (2006), 90–126.

[9] PREST, A., SCHMID, C., AND FERRARI, V. Weakly supervised learning of interactions between humans and objects. *T-PAMI 34*, 3 (2012), 601–614.

[10] SHAPOVALOVA, N., GONG, W., PEDERSOLI, M., ROCA, F. X., AND GONZÀLEZ, J. On importance of interactions and context in human action recognition. In *Pattern Recognition and Image Analysis*. 2011, pp. 58–66.

[11] VU, T.-H., OLSSON, C., LAPTEV, I., OLIVA, A., AND SIVIC, J. Predicting actions from static scenes. In *ECCV, 421-436, 2014.*

[12] YAO, B., AND FEI-FEI, L. Recognizing human-object interactions in still images by modeling the mutual context of objects and human poses. *T-PAMI 34*, 9 (2012), 1691–1703.

[13] ZHA, Z.-J., ZHANG, H., WANG, M., LUAN, H., AND CHUA, T.-S. Detecting group activities with multi-camera context. *T-CSVT 23*, 5 (2013), 856–869.

3D Person Tracking In World Coordinates and Attribute Estimation with PDR

Yuki Nagai Daisuke Kamisaka Naoya Makibuchi Jianfeng Xu
Shigeyuki Sakazawa

KDDI R&D Labs. Inc. 2-1-15 Ohara, Fujimino, Saitama, 356-8502 Japan
{yk-nagai, da-kamisaka, na-makibuchi, ji-xu, sakazawa}@kddilabs.jp

ABSTRACT

In this paper, we propose an online 3D person tracking method and an attribute estimation method with pedestrian dead reckoning (PDR). For person tracking, we employ a structured prediction approach, which extends the Struck algorithm. Although the main stream of visual object tracking, including Struck, utilizes only 2D information in image coordinates, it is difficult to track object correctly because of changes in the scale and angle of the target. In contrast, our classifier adaptively learns structural relationship in world coordinates and in image coordinates using Structured SVM. Furthermore, we combine visual tracking results and sensor trajectories based on PDR. Our method estimates a person attribute whether *insider* like a sales staff, or *outsider* like a customer. According to experimental results, the proposed method outperforms the existing methods regarding the quality of localization. In addition, experimental results show that our method can estimate the attribute at a ratio of 0.84.

Categories and Subject Descriptors

I.4.8 [**Image Processing and Computer Vision**]: Scene Analysis—*Tracking*

General Terms

Algorithms

Keywords

Person Tracking, Structured Prediction, Tracking-by-Detection

1. INTRODUCTION

Person tracking is one of the most fundamental and important problems in computer vision [15]. Although many person tracking technologies focus on estimating the position of the target person accurately, attribute information, such as *insider* who has been registered and permitted to enter the place on a daily basis or *outsider* who is not an insider, is also useful to understanding person behavior for surveillance systems, especially in buildings and shops. For example, whether an outsider interacts with an insider or not is one of the factors in finding suspicious persons.

In this paper, we propose a person tracking method with a calibrated camera and estimate the attributes of persons. Persons are classified into two categories; one is *insider* and the other is *outsider*. We employed pedestrian dead reckoning (PDR) [6] for the classification. PDR is a relative positioning technique that incrementally estimates current position upon a previously determined position, using motion sensors such as accelerometer and gyroscope embedded in smartphones. We identify anonymous trajectories detected in camera images as insiders or outsiders by evaluating similarity of trajectories of PDR and camera.

To adapt to gradual changes in object appearance, many studies employ the object tracking approach using a classifier to learn the appearance of tracking objects [7, 15]. These approaches consider object tracking as a continuous object detection problem. Such an approach is called *Tracking-By-Detection*. In online and single object tracking researches, Tracking-By-Detection is the recent mainstream framework [14, 9]. Existing algorithms [11, 3, 8, 13, 5] could be divided into a generative approach and a discriminative approach. While the generative approach does not explicitly separate the background, the discriminative approach considers object tracking as a binary classification problem to determine whether the target object is a real object or not. The Struck proposed by Hare [5] is one of the state-of-the-art algorithms of online object tracking. In experimental surveys [14, 9], Struck offers the best accuracy.

We extend Struck algorithm [5] to provide 3D world position for a following sensor fusion process. In our method, a classifier learns the structural relationship in world coordinates and in image coordinates with a calibrated camera.

The first contribution of our work is to propose an adaptive structured prediction method for online 3D person tracking in world coordinates. Although the main stream of visual object tracking, including Struck, utilizes only 2D information in image coordinates [7, 14], it is difficult to track object correctly because of changes in the scale and angle of the target. In addition, small changes in image coordinates causes a large change in world coordinates. Rapid changes in such trajectories are a particularly serious problem in matching the trajectories of the PDR. In contrast, with camera calibration information, we can track a person more precisely and stably. It is a realistic solution for person tracking by a

MM'15, October 26–30, 2015, Brisbane, Australia.

ISBN 978-1-4503-3459-4/15/10 ...$15.00.
DOI: http://dx.doi.org/10.1145/2733373.2806301.

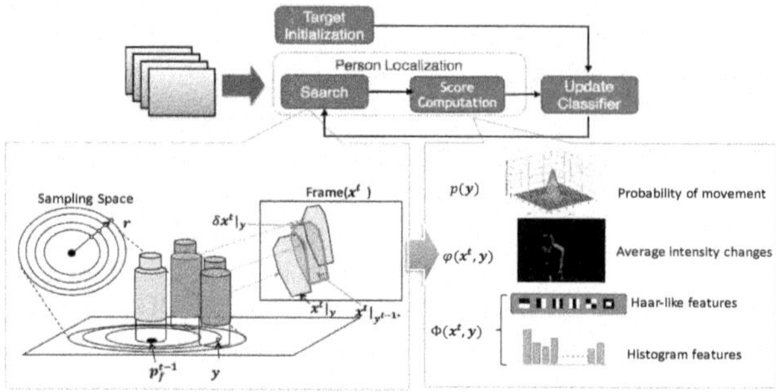

Figure 1: Framework of online tracking-by-detection

surveillance camera. Moreover, in consideration of cooperation with PDR, 3D trajectory in world coordinates is more essential than 2D trajectory in image coordinates. However, it is not clear how to exploit 3D information for a tracking method based on Tracking-By-Detection. Only a few 3D Tracking-By-Detection approach have been proposed [4]. Although PB-WVMF [4] employs a patch-based approach, we employ a discriminative approach because it is balanced in terms of accuracy and speed [14, 9]. Our classifier learns structural relationship in world coordinates and in image coordinates using Structured SVM, which is easy to incorporate motion and appearance features.

The second contribution is to propose an attribute estimation method that combines sensor data and visual tracking results. From the sensor data recorded by a smartphone that the insider has, we calculate the trajectories with the PDR technique. The attribute of a target person is estimated by matching the PDR trajectories and the visual tracking results.

2. ONLINE PERSON TRACKING BASED ON STRUCTURED PREDICTION

An overview of the proposed method is shown in Fig. 1. Given an initial location of a target person in image coordinates, our method tracks the target while attempting to learn the classifier to distinguish the target from its local background and searching the next location with the classifier.

Target Initialization

Given the bounding box of the target person, our method first creates and locates a 3D person model in world coordinates. We use a simple 3D person model that consists of two cylinders(see Fig. 1). Our method calculate appearance features of a 3D person model region in image coordinates with camera calibration parameters. We denote a position in world coordinates as $\boldsymbol{p} = (p_1, p_2, p_3)$, and each value is an element of the x-axis, y-axis, and z-axis. The initial foot position $\boldsymbol{p}_f = (p_{f1}, p_{f2}, 0)$ is calculated by projecting the center point of the bounding box base-line to the ground plane. This projection utilizes the camera projection matrix $\mathbf{P} \in \mathbb{R}^{3\times4}$. The head point of the target person $\boldsymbol{p}_h = (p_{h1}, p_{h2}, p_{h3})$ is estimated by projecting the center of the bounding box top-line to world coordinates with a constraint $(p_{h1}, p_{h2}) = (p_{f1}, p_{f2})$. The 3D person model is scaled to fit the target with the calculated height (p_{h3}) of the target.

Person Localization

Based on the previous person location in world coordinates, we predict the next location of the target by position translation. Then, corresponding areas in image coordinates are calculated by projecting a 3D person model onto the translation position.

Denote the set of input frames as $\mathcal{X} = \{x^0, ..., x^T\}$, and the set of candidate translations from the previous location as $\mathcal{Y} = \{(\Delta p_1, \Delta p_2) | \Delta p_1^2 + \Delta p_2^2 < r^2\}$, where T is the end frame number and r is the search radius . The prediction of the next person location becomes the task of correctly assigning the input $\boldsymbol{x} \in \mathcal{X}$ to the structured output $\boldsymbol{y} \in \mathcal{Y}$ based on a scoring function $F(\boldsymbol{x}, \boldsymbol{y}) = \langle \boldsymbol{w}, \Psi(\boldsymbol{x}, \boldsymbol{y}) \rangle$, where $\Psi : \mathcal{X} \times \mathcal{Y} \to \mathbb{R}^m$ is a joint feature function and $\boldsymbol{w}$ is the trained weight vector. The joint feature function Ψ extracts a feature vector from a pair of input and output sets.

We can formulate the problem of finding the best location translation as the Structured SVM [12]:

$$\boldsymbol{y}^* = \arg\max_{\boldsymbol{y}\in\mathcal{Y}} F(\boldsymbol{x}, \boldsymbol{y}). \tag{1}$$

With the best translation result $\boldsymbol{y}^{t*}$ at time t, the predicted location $\boldsymbol{p}_f^t$ is defined as $\boldsymbol{p}_f^t = \boldsymbol{p}_f^{t-1} + \boldsymbol{y}^{t*}$. We define scoring function F with input frame $\boldsymbol{x}^t$ at time t as

$$\begin{aligned} F(\boldsymbol{x}^t, \boldsymbol{y}) &= \langle \boldsymbol{w}, \Psi(\boldsymbol{x}^t, \boldsymbol{y}) \rangle \\ &= \langle \boldsymbol{w}_p, p(\boldsymbol{y}) \rangle \\ &\quad + \langle \boldsymbol{w}_\varphi, \varphi(\boldsymbol{x}^t, \boldsymbol{y}) \rangle \\ &\quad + \langle \boldsymbol{w}_\Phi, \Phi(\boldsymbol{x}^t, \boldsymbol{y}) \rangle, \end{aligned} \tag{2}$$

where $p(\boldsymbol{y})$ is a motion feature in world coordinates. $\varphi(\boldsymbol{x}^t, \boldsymbol{y})$ and $\Phi(\boldsymbol{x}^t, \boldsymbol{y})$ are appearance features in image coordinates.

We define the motion feature function p with a normal distribution $\mathcal{N}$ as

$$p(\boldsymbol{y}) = \alpha \mathcal{N}(\boldsymbol{y}; \boldsymbol{y}^{t-1*}, \Sigma), \tag{3}$$

where α and Σ are pre-defined parameters. α is the scaling parameter of this feature, and Σ is the variance-covariance matrix of distribution. We use $\alpha = 0.1$ and $\Sigma = [0.5, 0; 0, 0.5]$. This feature means the probability based on the previous movement in world coordinates. It provides smooth changes of motion in world coordinates.

Denote the region of the target person in image coordinates as $\boldsymbol{x}|_{\boldsymbol{y}}$. This region is obtained by calculating the convex region from the projected points of the 3D person model on the position determined by $\boldsymbol{y}$. $\varphi(\boldsymbol{x}^t, \boldsymbol{y})$ means an average change of pixel intensity in $\delta\boldsymbol{x}^t|_y$,where $\delta\boldsymbol{x}^t|_y$ is the difference set $\{\boldsymbol{u} | \boldsymbol{u} \in \boldsymbol{x}^{t-1}|_{\boldsymbol{y}^{t-1*}} \wedge \boldsymbol{u} \notin \boldsymbol{x}^t|_{\boldsymbol{y}}\}$. We formulate φ as

$$\varphi(\boldsymbol{x}^t, \boldsymbol{y}) = \begin{cases} 0 & (\delta\boldsymbol{x}^t|_y = \emptyset) \\ \beta \frac{\sum_{\boldsymbol{u}\in\delta\boldsymbol{x}^t|_y} \boldsymbol{x}^{t-1}|_{\boldsymbol{y}^{t-1*}}(\boldsymbol{u}) - \boldsymbol{x}^t|_{\boldsymbol{y}^t}(\boldsymbol{u})}{\sum_{\boldsymbol{u}\in\delta\boldsymbol{x}^t|_y} 1} & (\text{otherwise}), \end{cases} \tag{4}$$

where $\boldsymbol{x}^t|_{\boldsymbol{y}^t}(\boldsymbol{u})$ is intensity of a pixel at $\boldsymbol{u}$ in $\boldsymbol{x}^t|_{\boldsymbol{y}^t}$. β is a scaling parameter (we use 1.0). In the subtracted image which consists of $\boldsymbol{x}^{t-1}$ and $\boldsymbol{x}^t$, a pixel at which target appeared at time $t-1$ but the target does not appear at t has high value. Thus, $\varphi(\boldsymbol{x}^t, \boldsymbol{y})$ can be high if the projected region fitted to the pixel intensity changes.

For the appearance features $\Phi(\boldsymbol{x}^t, \boldsymbol{y})$, we utilize Haar-like features and histogram features, same as Struck [5]. We concatenate the features responses into a Haar-lile feature vector $\boldsymbol{h}$ and histogram feature vector $\boldsymbol{c}$. Haar-like features are arranged on a 2-scale grid on a 4 × 4 grid, resulting in 192 dimensional feature vector. Histogram features are obtained by concatenating 16-bin intensity histograms from

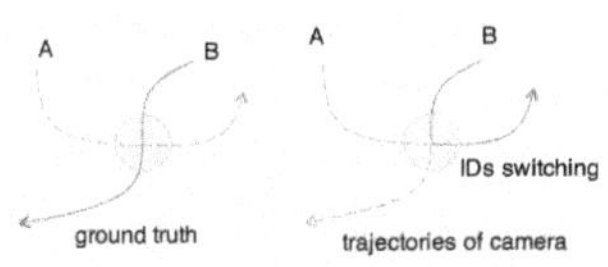

Figure 2: ID switching

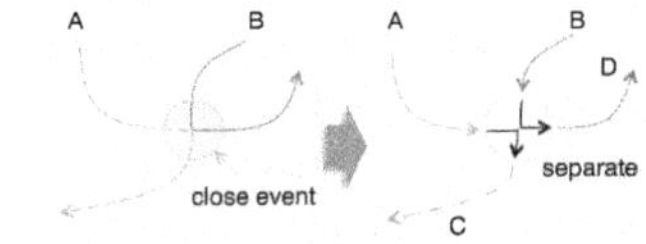

Figure 3: Separate trajectories

a spatial pyramid on 4 levels. At each level L, the patch is divided into $L \times L$ cells, resulting in a 480 dimensional feature vector. Then, the Haar-like feature vector is applied to a Gaussian kernel $k(\boldsymbol{h}, \bar{\boldsymbol{h}}) = \exp(-\sigma \parallel \boldsymbol{h} - \bar{\boldsymbol{h}} \parallel^2)$, with $\sigma = 0.2$, and the histogram feature vector is applied to intersection kernel: $k(\boldsymbol{c}, \bar{\boldsymbol{c}}) = \frac{1}{480}\sum_{l=1}^{480} \min(c_l, \bar{c}_l)$. We combine these two appearance feature vectors, resulting in 628 dimensional features.

Update Classifier

Now, the problem is how to train weight vector $\boldsymbol{w}$. For a set of training samples denoted by $(\boldsymbol{x}_i, \boldsymbol{y}_i) \in \mathcal{X} \times \mathcal{Y} (i = (1, ..., N)$, the Structured SVM solves the optimization problem to find weight vector $\boldsymbol{w}$, which is given by

$$\min_{\boldsymbol{w}} \frac{1}{2}||\boldsymbol{w}||^2 + C\sum_{i=1}^{N} \xi_i, \quad (5)$$

$$\text{s.t.} \forall i : \xi_i \geq 0$$

$$\forall i, \boldsymbol{y} \neq \boldsymbol{y}_i : \langle \boldsymbol{w}, \Psi(\boldsymbol{x}_i, \boldsymbol{y}_i) \rangle - \langle \boldsymbol{w}, \Psi(\boldsymbol{x}_i, \boldsymbol{y}) \rangle \geq \Delta(\boldsymbol{y}_i, \boldsymbol{y}) - \xi_i$$

where ξ_i is a slack variable and C is a constant(we use $C = 100$). $\Delta : \mathcal{Y} \times \mathcal{Y} \rightarrow \mathbb{R}$ is a loss function. In order to be able to asses the quality of prediction, an appropriate loss function Δ is necessary. The loss function $\Delta(\boldsymbol{y}_i, \boldsymbol{y})$ denotes the loss associated with a prediction $\boldsymbol{y}$ when the true value is $\boldsymbol{y}^*$. The loss should decrease as the prediction $\boldsymbol{y}$ approaches the ground truth $\boldsymbol{y}^*$, and $(\Delta(\boldsymbol{y}_i, \boldsymbol{y}) = 0$ iff $\boldsymbol{y} = \boldsymbol{y}^*)$. We define the loss function as

$$\Delta(\boldsymbol{y}_i, \boldsymbol{y}) = \gamma \parallel \boldsymbol{y}_i - \boldsymbol{y} \parallel + \{1 - \frac{|(\boldsymbol{x}|_{\boldsymbol{y}_i} \cup \boldsymbol{x}|_{\boldsymbol{y}})|}{|(\boldsymbol{x}|_{\boldsymbol{y}_i} \cap \boldsymbol{x}|_{\boldsymbol{y}})|}\}, \quad (6)$$

where γ is a pre-defined scaling parameter. The first term means the distance in world coordinates, and the second terms means an overlap ratio of the regions in image coordinates. This loss function can reflect both of errors in the world and the image in the optimization procedure.

In our approach, we adopt the *Larank* algorithm [2] for online optimization of Eq. (5) with large-margin duality techniques. Larank is simple to implement and efficient algorithm.

3. SENSOR FUSION FOR ATTRIBUTE ESTIMATION

We define the degree of coincidence timing of *start/stop* walking of each pair of trajectories as similarity criteria. Why we do not compare the position directly is that (i)PDR trajectories only know the relative position rather than the absolute position and (ii)both of visual tracking results and PDR trajectories have a potential to include errors. The similarity calculation is executed in the following steps:

1. Calculate the velocity $\boldsymbol{v}^t$ at time t.
2. Quantize the states at time t into the binary values $S(\boldsymbol{v}^t) = \{walking, stopping\}$ with a Schmitt trigger:

$$S(\boldsymbol{v}^t) = \begin{cases} walking & (||\boldsymbol{v}^t|| \geq \theta_H) \\ stopping & (||\boldsymbol{v}^t|| \leq \theta_L) \\ S(\boldsymbol{v}^{t-1}) & \text{(otherwise)}, \end{cases} \quad (7)$$

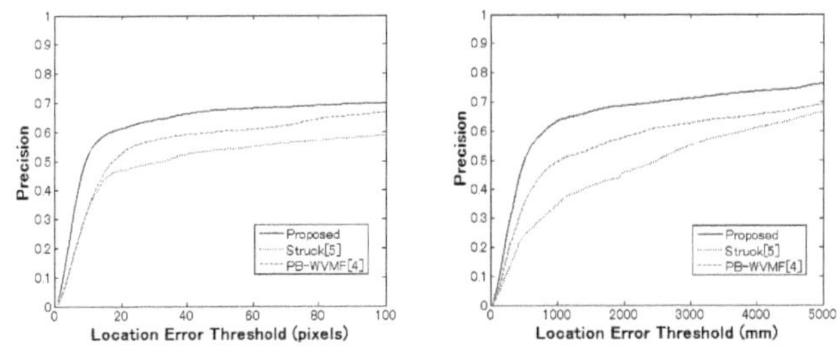

Figure 5: Location error (left: the centre position error in image coordinates, right: the foot position error in world coordinates)

where θ_H and θ_L are the thresholds.

3. Detect state change timings, i.e. walking to stopped and vice versa.
4. Calculate the similarity between a camera trajectory $\boldsymbol{\tau}_c$ and a sensor trajectory $\boldsymbol{\tau}_s$ as follows:

$$f(\boldsymbol{\tau}_c, \boldsymbol{\tau}_s) = \frac{2E_c E_s}{(E_c + E_s)}, \quad (8)$$

where E_c =(the number of state change events of PDR that match camera events)/(the number of state change events of camera), and E_s = (the number of state change events of PDR that match camera events)/(the number of state change events of PDR).

Tracking results sometimes include errors such as ID switching caused by well-known *drifting problems* [10] (see Fig. 2). Identifying such "patched" trajectory would be failed because it does not match any insider's trajectory of PDR. To address the ID switching problem, we separate trajectories when two persons' coordinates keeps in proximity for a certain period of time (see Fig. 3). The separated trajectories are treated as independent trajectories. Note that we can assign a consistent ID to the partial trajectories in this procedure. As a result, consistent ID for the detected person and its attribute for each trajectory can be obtained while preventing ID switching.

4. EXPERIMENTAL RESULTS

Visual Tracking Accuracy

Our first set of experiments aims to compare the results of the proposed approach with the state-of-the-art 2D and 3D tracking methods [5, 4]. We tested our method with the well-known dataset PETS 2009 (S2.L1)[1]. It is publicly available and has been commonly used for evaluating tracking algorithms [4, 14]. This dataset contains the calibration parameters of the camera and ground truth of person positions. Examples of tracking results are shown in Fig. 4. For each target person in the dataset, we set the tracking start to the first frame in which the person appears, and the tracking end to the last frame before the person disappears. We utilize the two metrics on tracking precision [14]. One is the centre location error of the person region (bounding box) in image coordinates, and the other is the location error of the person foot point in world coordinates. According to [14], we utilize the precision plot that shows the percentage of frames whose estimated location is within the given threshold distance of the ground truth. The precision plots are shown in Fig. 5. Table 1 shows the representative precision score for each tracker. We utilize the score for the

[1]`http://www.milanton.de/data/`

Figure 4: Example results: the top line is our results, the middle line is Struck [5] (without camera calibration parameter), and the bottom line is PB-WVMF [4] (with camera calibration parameter).

Figure 6: Experiment scene example of attribute estimation.

20 pixels [14] and the 500 mm [1]. As shown in Table 1, the proposed method obtains greater results than 8.5% and 14.7% in terms of the center error and the location error.

Table 1: The representative precision score.

	Struck [5]	PB-WVMF [4]	Proposed
center error (20 pixels)	0.468	0.527	0.612
foot error (500 mm)	0.241	0.349	0.496

Attribute Estimation Accuracy

The second set of experiments aims to show the attribute estimation results. In the experiment, we used two different sequences. There are four persons in each sequence, two of whom are insiders and the others are outsiders (see Fig. 6) . Each sequence consists of about 1,500 frames (480 × 270, 10fps). The sensor data is recorded by smartphones with the insiders. The start bounding box is manually labeled. Tracking is stopped when the confidence value is lower than 1.0, and restart as a different trajectory. The estimation accuracy is shown in Table 2. We estimated a label as insider or outsider for each tracking result trajectory. Accuracy is defined as the ratio that could estimate true attributes, obtained by dividing the number of success estimation by the number of all trajectories. Furthermore, we also estimated the person ID for each partial trajectory in the trajectories matching procedure. The success results of partial trajectories could be identified as each person ID.

Table 2: Accuracy of the attribute

	sequence1	sequence2	average
accuracy(success/all)	1.00(6/6)	0.714(5/7)	0.846(11/13)

5. CONCLUSIONS

In this paper, we proposed a person tracking method to estimate a person's position in world coordinates. In the method, we utilized the structured prediction approach for online person tracking. Our method identified the structural relationship in world coordinates and in image coordinates. We obtained comparable results that were higher than 8.5% and 14.7% in terms of the center error of pixel distance and the location error in world coordinates. In addition, experimental results show that our method could estimate the attribute at a ratio of 0.84.

6. REFERENCES

[1] K. Bernardin and R. Stiefelhagen. Evaluating multiple object tracking performance: The clear mot metrics. *J. Image Video Process.*, 2008:1:1–1:10, Jan. 2008.

[2] A. Bordes, L. Bottou, P. Gallinari, and J. Weston. Solving multiclass support vector machines with larank. In *Proc. of ICML*, pages 89–96, 2007.

[3] M. Donoser and H. Bischof. Efficient maximally stable extremal region (mser) tracking. In *Proc. of IEEE Conf. on CVPR*, volume 1, pages 553–560, June 2006.

[4] G. Fuhr and C. Jung. Robust patch-based pedestrian tracking using monocular calibrated cameras. In *Proc. of SIBGRAPI Conf. on SIBGRAPI*, pages 166–173, Aug 2012.

[5] S. Hare, A. Saffari, and P. Torr. Struck: Structured output tracking with kernels. In *Proc. of IEEE Conf. on ICCV*, pages 263–270, Nov 2011.

[6] D. Kamisaka, S. Muramatsu, T. Iwamoto, and H. Yokoyama. Design and implementation of pedestrian dead reckoning system on a mobile phone. *IEICE Trans.*, 94:1137–1146, 2011.

[7] X. Li, W. Hu, C. Shen, Z. Zhang, A. Dick, and A. V. D. Hengel. A survey of appearance models in visual object tracking. *ACM Trans. Intell. Syst. Technol.*, 4(4):58:1–58:48, Oct. 2013.

[8] G. Silveira and E. Malis. Real-time visual tracking under arbitrary illumination changes. In *Proc. of IEEE Conf. on CVPR*, pages 1–6, June 2007.

[9] A. Smeulders, D. Chu, R. Cucchiara, S. Calderara, A. Dehghan, and M. Shah. Visual tracking: An experimental survey. *IEEE Trans. Pattern Anal. Mach. Intell.*, 36(7):1442–1468, July 2014.

[10] S. Stalder, H. Grabner, and L. Van Gool. Beyond semi-supervised tracking: Tracking should be as simple as detection, but not simpler than recognition. In *Proc. of IEEE Conf. on ICCV Workshops*, pages 1409–1416, Sept 2009.

[11] S. Tran and L. Davis. Robust object trackinng with regional affine invariant features. In *Proc. of IEEE Conf. on ICCV*, pages 1–8, Oct 2007.

[12] I. Tsochantaridis, T. Joachims, T. Hofmann, and Y. Altun. Large margin methods for structured and interdependent output variables. *J. Mach. Learn. Res.*, 6:1453–1484, Dec. 2005.

[13] S. Wang, H. Lu, F. Yang, and M.-H. Yang. Superpixel tracking. In *Proc. of IEEE Conf. on ICCV*, pages 1323–1330, Nov 2011.

[14] Y. Wu, J. Lim, and M.-H. Yang. Online object tracking: A benchmark. In *Proc. of IEEE Conf. on CVPR*, pages 2411–2418, June 2013.

[15] A. Yilmaz, O. Javed, and M. Shah. Object tracking: A survey. *ACM Comput. Surv.*, 38(4), Dec. 2006.

Image Tagging via Cross-Modal Semantic Mapping

Zhi-Hong Deng*
zhdeng
@cis.pku.edu.cn

Hongliang Yu*
yuhongliang324
@gmail.com

Yunlun Yang
incomparable-lun
@pku.edu.cn

Key Laboratory of Machine Perception (Ministry of Education),
School of Electronics Engineering and Computer Science,
Peking University, Beijing 100871, China

ABSTRACT

Images without annotations are ubiquitous on the Internet, and recommending tags for them has become a challenging open task in image understanding. A common bottleneck of related work is the semantic gap between the image and text representations. In this paper, we bridge the gap by introducing a semantic layer, the space of word embeddings that represents the image tags as the word vectors. Our model first learns the optimal mapping from the visual space to the semantic space using training sources. Then we annotate test images by decoding the semantic representations of the visual features. Extensive experiments demonstrate that our model outperforms the state-of-the-art approaches in predicting the image tags.

Categories and Subject Descriptors

H.3.1 [**Information Storage And Retrieval**]: Content Analysis and Indexing—*indexing methods*

General Terms

Algorithms, Performance, Experimentation

Keywords

Cross-modal study, image tagging, semantic representation, optimization model, word embeddings

1. INTRODUCTION

With the rapid development of social networks and photo sharing sites, loads of untagged or partially tagged images spread throughout the internet. Automatically producing annotations for the images is an promising and challenging task of image understanding. Specifically, since most image search engines rely on text, image annotations improve the accessibility of the image collections.

Therefore, image annotation has become a hotspot in cross-modal study. [11] and [6] propose baselines for tag recommendation based on the tag transfer of visual neighbors. Similarly, [7] apply the idea of neighbor voting to large-scale dataset. In [13], the semi-supervised method is used in learning the annotation of images. Besides, some researchers ([1, 9, 15]) focus on the tag enrichment problem to improving the quality of original image tags. They argue that, although some images are annotated, most user-generated tags are noisy and incomplete.

However, there are some problems in general image tagging methods. Firstly, most models choose tags from a fixed tag set. [15] and [8] assume that the testing and training images share the same tag set. In online applications, on the contrary, the to-be-annotated images can be updated very fast. For example, Flickr share around 1 million photos every day. As a result, the tag set of new samples can hardly be predetermined. Secondly, in tag enrichment, synonyms of existing tags are likely to be selected due to their co-occurrence in other images (e.g. low-rank tag enrichment in [16]). Although the synonyms are "correct" tags, they do not provide additional textual information. Thirdly, since most tags in the training set only annotate a small number of images, the learned models tend to recommend frequently-used tags, which are only a small fraction of the tag set according to the power law. Moreover, text are mostly represented in "one-hot" form in which all words are independent. It obeys the commonsense that some words or phrases are semantically correlated.

To overcome the limitations of existing work, we study the problem of automatic image annotation using *word embeddings*, a distributed word representation scheme that associates each word to a vector. The dimensions of the word vector capture useful semantic properties [14]. In our model, both images and text are mapped to a common semantic space: the representation space of word vectors. In the training phase, we optimize the mapping function from visual features to the semantic space. At testing time, the target images are represented into the semantic space through the learned optimal function. The tags are subsequently predicted by a linear function mapping the semantic representation to the text space. In addition, we argue that similar images tend to share the same tags. Accordingly, a smoothness regularizer is introduced to our model. It is noteworthy that the training and testing tag sets are not restricted to be the same. Any tag having the word vector are accepted as the candidate regardless whether it appears in the training images.

To sum up, our contributions are: (1) We propose a novel optimization model based on semantic mapping for automatic image annotation. (2) The semantic space avoid di-

*These two authors contributed equally to this work.

MM'15, October 26–30, 2015, Brisbane, Australia.
© 2015 ACM. ISBN 978-1-4503-3459-4/15/10 ...$15.00.
DOI: http://dx.doi.org/10.1145/2733373.2806302.

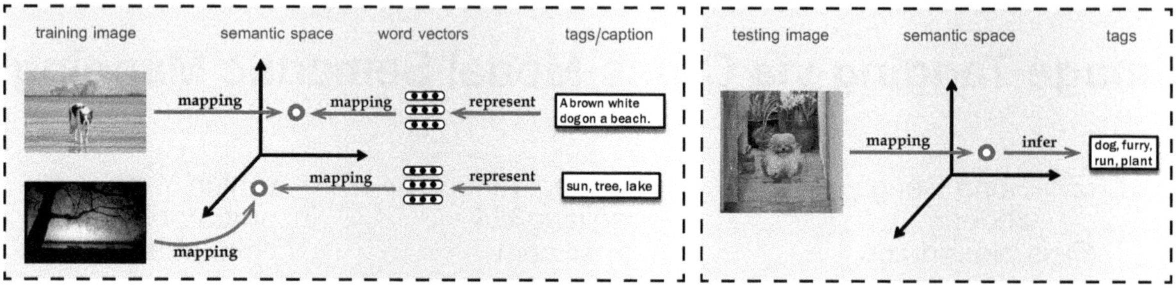

(a) Image semantic mapping (b) Tag inference

Figure 1: Illustration of framework.

rect cross-modal mapping which is always impractical to be constructed. Also, by introducing the word vectors, any tags are possible to be recommended including the ones not belonging to the training set. (3) Extensive experiments demonstrate our model outperforms the state-of-the-art algorithms.

2. PROPOSED MODEL

2.1 Preliminary

We formulate the problem of image annotation as follows. Let n and m be the number of training and testing images. Let the training set be denoted by $D_{train} = \{(\vec{x}_1, \vec{t}_1), \cdots, (\vec{x}_n, \vec{t}_n)\}$, where each vector $\vec{x}_i \in \mathbb{R}^F$ is the visual features of the i-th image and $\vec{t}_i$ represents its text component. Theoretically, the text component can be any text form, e.g. tags or captions. We propose to automatically annotate testing images, denoted by $D_{test} = \{(\vec{x}_{n+1}, \hat{t}_{n+1}), \cdots, (\vec{x}_{n+m}, \hat{t}_{n+m})\}$. $\hat{t}_i$ could be the incomplete tags given by users. Without loss of generality, the auxiliary text $\hat{t}_i$ is obligatory in our model, and $\hat{t}_i = \vec{0}$ if no textual annotation is provided.

2.2 Framework

The schematic illustration of the framework is shown in Figure 1. The model we proposed consists two steps: image semantic mapping and tag inference. They are the training and testing parts of our task.

Image Semantic Mapping We consider the K-dimensional space of word embeddings as the semantic space. At training time of image tagging, our model learns the mapping from the image space to the semantic space, denoted as $\mathbf{f} : \mathbb{R}^F \to \mathbb{R}^K$. To map the text description of each image to the semantic space, the word vectors of the tags are linearly combined. The optimal $\mathbf{f}^*$ is then obtained:

$$\mathbf{f}^* = \arg\min_{\mathbf{f}} \frac{1}{n} \sum_{i=1}^{n} E(\mathbf{f}(\vec{x}_i), \vec{t}_i) + \lambda \|\mathbf{f}\|^2, \quad (1)$$

where $E(\cdot)$ measures the difference between the projections of the image content $\mathbf{f}(\vec{x}_i)$ and the corresponding text description $\vec{t}_i$ on the semantic space. The L_2 penalty is imposed to control the complexity of $\mathbf{f}^*$ and avoid overfitting.

Tag Inference In Figure 1(b), our model predicts the image tags $\vec{t}_i$ for $i > n$. Using $\mathbf{f}^*$, our model maps the image to the semantic space. Similar to the training phase, we assume that the semantic representation of the image can be approximated by the word vectors of tags. Due to the observation that an image contains only a small number of tags, the sparsity constraint is imposed to control the nonzero entries of $\vec{t}_i$. For i-th image ($i > n$), we establish the initial model as:

$$\vec{t}_i^* = \arg\min_{\vec{t}_i} E(\mathbf{f}^*(\vec{x}_i), \vec{t}_i) + \omega \|\vec{t}_i\|_1. \quad (2)$$

Since some testing images have been annotated, we expect $\hat{t}_i$ can be utilized to infer more tags. We regard $\vec{t}_i$ as the completed and denoised version of the auxiliary text $\hat{t}_i$. Besides, we introduce the smoothness regularizer to capture the relevance of the image content. The objective function becomes:

$$\min_{\{\vec{t}_i\}_{i>n}} \frac{1}{m} \sum_{i=n+1}^{n+m} \Big(E(\mathbf{f}^*(\vec{x}_i), \vec{t}_i) + \omega \|\vec{t}_i\|_1 + \gamma \cdot \Omega(\vec{t}_i; \hat{t}_i) \Big) + \frac{1}{m^2} \rho \cdot S(\{\vec{t}_i\}_{i>n}). \quad (3)$$

$\Omega(\cdot)$ and $S(.)$ are the penalty terms on auxiliary text and smoothness.

2.3 Image Semantic Mapping

Before discussing our model, we represent the text on the semantic space. We collect all tags from the text component of training images to form the dictionary $\mathcal{V}$ with size V. For image i, The textual feature $\vec{t}_i \in \{0,1\}^V$ is thus defined as the apperance/absence of tags in $\mathcal{V}$.

Using word embeddings, we obtain the representation vector of words in each tag. In general, the representation of a tag is identical to the word vector if the tag contains only one word. In some special cases that the tag is a phrase with at least two words, the tag representation can be calculated by averaging the contained word vectors. We notate the tag representation as $\vec{b}_i \in \mathbb{R}^K$. In the semantic space, the text component of an image is the linear combination of all its tag representation vectors, i.e. $\mathbf{B}_{\mathcal{V}} \cdot \vec{t}_i$, where $\mathbf{B}_{\mathcal{V}} = [\vec{b}_1 | \cdots | \vec{b}_V] \in \mathbb{R}^{K \times V}$.

Now we expect the semantic representation of the image content to be consistent with $\mathbf{B}_{\mathcal{V}} \cdot \vec{t}_i$. So we have the following reconstruction error to measure the consistency as proposed in Formula (1):

$$E(\mathbf{f}(\vec{x}_i), \vec{t}_i) = \|\mathbf{f}(\vec{x}_i) - \mathbf{B}_{\mathcal{V}} \cdot \vec{t}_i\|_2^2. \quad (4)$$

Here we explicitly construct $\mathbf{f}(\cdot)$ through linear combination of the basis function $\psi(\cdot)$ of image features:

$$\mathbf{f}(\vec{x}_i) = \mathbf{M} \cdot \psi(\vec{x}_i), \quad \psi_j(\vec{x}_i) = \sigma\left(\frac{x_i(j) - \mu_j}{s}\right), \quad (5)$$

where $\mathbf{M} \in \mathbb{R}^{K \times F}$ is the mapping matrix, $\sigma(z) = \frac{1}{1+\exp(-z)}$ and $\mu_j = \frac{1}{n} \sum_{i=1}^{n} x_i(j)$. Therefore, the optimization problem in Formula (1) can be written as:

$$\mathbf{M}^* = \arg\min_{\mathbf{M}} \frac{1}{n}\sum_{i=1}^{n} \|\mathbf{M}\cdot\psi(\vec{x}_i) - \mathbf{B}_{\mathcal{V}}\cdot\vec{t}_i\|_2^2 + \lambda\|\mathbf{M}\|_F^2. \quad (6)$$

2.4 Tag Inference

When we obtain $\mathbf{M}^*$, any image $\vec{x}^{\text{new}}$ can be mapped to the semantic space by $\mathbf{M}^*\cdot\psi(\vec{x}^{\text{new}})$. In tag inference, we aim to find tags having similar descriptive power.

Unlike assumptions in traditional models, we do not specify the recommended tags to be from $\mathcal{V}$. Instead, we notate the testing dictionary as $\mathcal{U}$ with size U. Generally, $\mathcal{U} \supseteq \mathcal{V}$. In this setting, for testing images, $\vec{t}_i$ and $\hat{t}_i$ are U-dimensional vectors. Similar to Section 2.3, we denote the dictionary of candidate tags as $\mathbf{B}_{\mathcal{U}} \in \mathbb{R}^{K\times U}$. Consequently, the reconstruction error becomes:

$$E(\mathbf{f}^*(\vec{x}_i), \vec{t}_i) = \|\mathbf{f}^*(\vec{x}_i) - \mathbf{B}_{\mathcal{U}}\cdot\vec{t}_i\|_2^2. \quad (7)$$

Although the auxiliary tags might be noisy and incomplete, they provide prior knowledge for the optimization problem. The refined tag vector $\vec{t}_i$ should be similar to $\hat{t}_i$, especially on the non-zero entries. To exploit the auxiliary text, we prefer a solution with the constraint:

$$\Omega(\vec{t}_i;\hat{t}_i) = \|\mathbf{Z}_i\cdot(\vec{t}_i - \hat{t}_i)\|_2^2, \quad (8)$$

where $\mathbf{Z}_i$ is a diagonal matrix, and $(\mathbf{Z}_i)_{j,j} = I(\hat{t}_i(j) \neq 0)$. We can see that $\mathbf{Z}_i$ gives penalties to non-zero entries of observed tags.

Apart from supervised information, the distribution of image features can also be used in tag inference. Intuitively, an image strongly associated with its visual neighbors tends to contain similar tags. Based on this principle and motivated by [5], we define the smoothness regularizer as follows to transfer the relevance of image content to tags:

$$S(\{\vec{t}_i\}_{i>n}) = \sum_{i=n+1}^{n+m}\sum_{j=n+1}^{n+m} g_{ij}\|\vec{t}_i - \vec{t}_j\|_2^2, \quad (9)$$

where $g_{ij} = \exp\left(-\|\vec{x}_i - \vec{x}_j\|_2^2/\sigma^2\right)$ weighs the visual similarity of two images by Gaussian kernel. Substituting the above expressions into Formula (3), we get the objective function for tag inference:

$$\begin{aligned}\min_{\{\vec{t}_i\}_{i>n}} \mathcal{L} = \frac{1}{m}\sum_{i=n+1}^{n+m}\Big(&\|\mathbf{f}^*(\vec{x}_i) - \mathbf{B}_{\mathcal{U}}\cdot\vec{t}_i\|_2^2 + \omega\|\vec{t}_i\|_1 + \\ &\gamma\|\mathbf{Z}_i(\vec{t}_i - \hat{t}_i)\|_2^2\Big) + \frac{1}{m^2}\cdot\rho\sum_{i,j>n} g_{ij}\|\vec{t}_i - \vec{t}_j\|_2^2.\end{aligned} \quad (10)$$

2.5 Solution and Implementation

The loss function in Formula (6) is a standard ridge regression problem that can be effectively optimized by analytical solution. Assume $\mathbf{T}_{train} = \left[\vec{t}_1\middle|\cdots\middle|\vec{t}_n\right]^T \in \mathbb{R}^{n\times V}$ and $\mathbf{\Psi}_{train} = \left[\psi(\vec{x}_1)\middle|\cdots\middle|\psi(\vec{x}_n)\right] \in \mathbb{R}^{n\times F}$. The optimal solution is:

$$\mathbf{M}^* = \mathbf{B}_{\mathcal{V}}\mathbf{T}_{train}^T\mathbf{\Psi}_{train}\cdot(\mathbf{\Psi}_{train}^T\mathbf{\Psi}_{train} + n\lambda\mathbf{I})^{-1}. \quad (11)$$

Next, we relax the ℓ_1-norm $\omega\|\vec{t}_i\|_1$ to the ℓ_2-norm $\omega\|\vec{t}_i\|_2^2$ for efficiency reasons. Since the ℓ_1-norm is not differentiable, one can only adopt approximation techniques (e.g. subgradient descent [12]) which are always time-consuming and inaccurate. Specifically, the size of optimization variables is $O(m\times U)$, where m and U might reach the magnitude of 10^7 and 10^4 respectively in large-scale datasets. In comparison, the optimization with ℓ_2-norm is much easier to solve.

Take ℓ_2-norm into Formula (10), we calculate the gradient of $\mathcal{L}$ with respect to $\vec{t}_i$:

$$\begin{aligned}\nabla_i\mathcal{L} = \frac{2}{m}\Big[&\big(\mathbf{B}_{\mathcal{U}}^T\mathbf{B}_{\mathcal{U}} + (\omega + \frac{2\rho h_i}{m})\mathbf{I} + \gamma\mathbf{Z}_i^T\mathbf{Z}_i\big)\cdot\vec{t}_i \\ &- \big(\mathbf{B}_{\mathcal{U}}^T\mathbf{f}^*(\vec{x}_i) + \gamma\mathbf{Z}_i^T\mathbf{Z}_i\hat{t}_i + \frac{\rho}{m}\mathbf{T}_{test}^T\vec{g}_i\big)\Big].\end{aligned} \quad (12)$$

In Eq. (12) it is difficult to separate $\vec{t}_i$ from other optimization variables $\{\vec{t}_j\}_{j\neq i}$ which are included in $\mathbf{T}_{test}^T$. But when $\mathbf{T}_{test}^T$ is fixed, we can optimize $\vec{t}_i$ for all testing samples in turn. To be specific, in τ-th iteration, we set the gradient to zero and obtain:

$$\begin{aligned}\vec{t}_i^{(\tau)} = &\big(\mathbf{B}_{\mathcal{U}}^T\mathbf{B}_{\mathcal{U}} + (\omega + \frac{2\rho h_i}{m})\mathbf{I} + \gamma\mathbf{Z}_i^T\mathbf{Z}_i\big)^{-1}\cdot \\ &\big(\mathbf{B}_{\mathcal{U}}^T\mathbf{f}^*(\vec{x}_i) + \gamma\mathbf{Z}_i^T\mathbf{Z}_i\hat{t}_i + \frac{\rho}{m}(\mathbf{T}_{test}^{(\tau-1)})^T\vec{g}_i\big).\end{aligned} \quad (13)$$

The optimal tag vectors $\{\vec{t}_i^*\}_{i>n}$ are obtained until the convergence criterion $\|\mathbf{T}_{test}^{(\tau)} - \mathbf{T}_{test}^{(\tau-1)}\|_F \leq \varepsilon\|\mathbf{T}_{test}^{(\tau)}\|_F$ is met.

3. EXPERIMENTS

3.1 Experimental Setup

We use two standard datasets of image annotation, Corel5K [4] and NUS-WIDE [2]. Corel5K consists of 5,000 images in which each image is annotated with 1 to 5 words. In total, there are 260 keywords. We preprocess every image into a 2,000-dimensional feature vector. NUS-WIDE has 269,649 images consisting of 81 categories. We randomly separate each category into training, validation, testing set. The images are represented as the features in a bag-of-words format using 500 codewords. The number of distinctive tags in NUS-WIDE is 1,000.

We compare our proposed method to four baselines, *JEC* [11], *LSR* [8], *FastTag* [1], and *LR* (linear regression) implemented by [1]. In terms of semantic space, we use C&W embeddings [3] implemented by [14].

3.2 Image Annotation Test

We evaluate the quality of the top ranked tags on Corel5K and NUS-WIDE as shown in Table 1. On NUS-WIDE, every category is individually tested. We report the weighted average mean results based on the scales of the categories. In this experiment, we mainly focus on the performance of the algorithm instead of the effect of feature extraction. Thus, unlike previous work using at least 10 kinds of features, e.g. [1] and [8], we simply use SIFT descriptors [10] to form bag-of-words features.

For the first five algorithms, no tags are observed for test images. One can find that the task on NUS-WIDE is more difficult than Corel5K due to the size of the tag set. Our model outperforms other approaches in all measurements, indicating the effectiveness of our model. By contrast, JEC and LSR performs poorly: they depend on the tags of the visual neighbors but insufficient visual features might make it hard to accurately detect the neighbors. FastTag and LR are slightly better than JEC and LSR. Specially, LR is demonstrated better robustness than other baselines.

In the last two rows, we randomly remain 40% of the associated tags for testing images to perform "tag enrichment". Our model and LSR both gain remarkable improvement,

	Corel5K						NUS-WIDE					
	F1@5	P@5	R@5	F1@10	P@10	R@10	F1@5	P@5	R@5	F1@10	P@10	R@10
Ours	**0.359**	**0.306**	**0.435**	**0.296**	**0.200**	**0.567**	**0.170**	**0.211**	**0.142**	**0.169**	**0.147**	**0.200**
JEC	0.147	0.132	0.167	0.157	0.114	0.251	0.106	0.131	0.089	0.143	0.125	0.169
LSR	0.211	0.180	0.256	0.187	0.127	0.356	0.084	0.105	0.071	0.087	0.076	0.103
FastTag	0.242	0.207	0.294	0.212	0.143	0.415	0.103	0.129	0.086	0.111	0.097	0.129
LR	0.251	0.214	0.305	0.207	0.140	0.397	0.135	0.168	0.113	0.139	0.112	0.163
Ours w/ tags	**0.541**	**0.461**	**0.651**	**0.387**	**0.262**	**0.737**	**0.521**	**0.645**	**0.437**	**0.456**	**0.397**	**0.536**
LSR w/ tags	0.376	0.322	0.454	0.271	0.184	0.517	0.350	0.432	0.294	0.321	0.279	0.379

Table 1: Image Annotation. The first five methods use no tags of testing images, while the last two employ partial tags.

particularly on the larger dataset, NUS-WIDE. Moreover, our model has superior performance. From these experiments, we can infer that mapping from visual to semantic space of word embeddings could be more suitable than that to the text space because of the sparse text representation.

4. CONCLUSION

In this paper, we propose a novel optimization model for image tagging via cross-modal semantic mapping. The distinctive aspect of our work is introducing the word vector to bridge the semantic gap between image content and its text description. The experiments on benchmark datasets show that our model outperforms the state-of-the-art approaches. The robustness of our model can be seen by the fact that all good results are achieved using SIFT descriptor only.

In our future work, we expect to improve the model by taking into account other mapping methods and more powerful descriptors. Also, it would be of great interest to apply our idea of semantic mapping to more cross-modal studies.

5. ACKNOWLEDGMENTS

This work is partially supported by Project 61170091 supported by National Natural Science Foundation of China and Project 2015AA015403 supported by the National High Technology Research and Development Program of China (863 Program). We would also like to thank the anonymous reviewers for their helpful comments.

6. REFERENCES

[1] M. Chen, A. Zheng, and K. Weinberger. Fast image tagging. In *Proceedings of The 30th International Conference on Machine Learning*, pages 1274–1282, 2013.

[2] T.-S. Chua, J. Tang, R. Hong, H. Li, Z. Luo, and Y. Zheng. Nus-wide: a real-world web image database from national university of singapore. In *Proceedings of the ACM international conference on image and video retrieval*, page 48. ACM, 2009.

[3] R. Collobert and J. Weston. A unified architecture for natural language processing: Deep neural networks with multitask learning. In *Proceedings of the 25th international conference on Machine learning*, pages 160–167. ACM, 2008.

[4] P. Duygulu, K. Barnard, J. F. de Freitas, and D. A. Forsyth. Object recognition as machine translation: Learning a lexicon for a fixed image vocabulary. In *Computer Vision–ECCV 2002*, pages 97–112. Springer, 2002.

[5] C. Gong, D. Tao, K. Fu, and J. Yang. Relish: Reliable label inference via smoothness hypothesis. In *Twenty-Eighth AAAI Conference on Artificial Intelligence*, 2014.

[6] M. Guillaumin, T. Mensink, J. Verbeek, and C. Schmid. Tagprop: Discriminative metric learning in nearest neighbor models for image auto-annotation. In *Computer Vision, 2009 IEEE 12th International Conference on*, pages 309–316. IEEE, 2009.

[7] X. Li, C. G. Snoek, and M. Worring. Learning social tag relevance by neighbor voting. *Multimedia, IEEE Transactions on*, 11(7):1310–1322, 2009.

[8] Z. Lin, G. Ding, M. Hu, J. Wang, and X. Ye. Image tag completion via image-specific and tag-specific linear sparse reconstructions. In *Computer Vision and Pattern Recognition (CVPR), 2013 IEEE Conference on*, pages 1618–1625. IEEE, 2013.

[9] X. Liu, S. Yan, T.-S. Chua, and H. Jin. Image label completion by pursuing contextual decomposability. *ACM Transactions on Multimedia Computing, Communications, and Applications (TOMCCAP)*, 8(2):21, 2012.

[10] D. G. Lowe. Distinctive image features from scale-invariant keypoints. *International journal of computer vision*, 60(2):91–110, 2004.

[11] A. Makadia, V. Pavlovic, and S. Kumar. A new baseline for image annotation. In *Computer Vision–ECCV 2008*, pages 316–329. Springer, 2008.

[12] M. Schmidt, G. Fung, and R. Rosales. Fast optimization methods for l1 regularization: A comparative study and two new approaches. In *Machine Learning: ECML 2007*, pages 286–297. Springer, 2007.

[13] R. Socher and L. Fei-Fei. Connecting modalities: Semi-supervised segmentation and annotation of images using unaligned text corpora. In *Computer Vision and Pattern Recognition (CVPR), 2010 IEEE Conference on*, pages 966–973. IEEE, 2010.

[14] J. Turian, L. Ratinov, and Y. Bengio. Word representations: a simple and general method for semi-supervised learning. In *Proceedings of the 48th Annual Meeting of the Association for Computational Linguistics*, pages 384–394. Association for Computational Linguistics, 2010.

[15] L. Wu, R. Jin, and A. K. Jain. Tag completion for image retrieval. *Pattern Analysis and Machine Intelligence, IEEE Transactions on*, 2013.

[16] H. Yu, Z.-H. Deng, Y. Yang, and T. Xiong. A joint optimization model for image summarization based on image content and tags. In *Twenty-Eighth AAAI Conference on Artificial Intelligence*, 2014.

Predicting Image Memorability by Multi-view Adaptive Regression

Houwen Peng[1,2]*, Kai Li[1]*, Bing Li[1], Haibin Ling[2], Weihua Xiong[1], Weiming Hu[1]
[1]Institute of Automation, Chinese Academy of Sciences
[2]Department of Computer & Information Sciences, Temple University
{houwen.peng, kai.li, bli, wmhu}@nlpr.ia.ac.cn hbling@temple.edu

ABSTRACT

The images we encounter throughout our lives make different impressions on us: Some are remembered at first glance, while others are forgotten. This phenomenon is caused by the intrinsic memorability of images revealed by recent studies [5, 6]. In this paper, we address the issue of automatically estimating the memorability of images by proposing a novel *multi-view adaptive regression* (MAR) model. The MAR model provides an effective mapping of visual features to memorability scores by taking advantage of robust feature selection and multiple feature integration. It consists of three major components: an adaptive loss function, an adaptive regularization and a multi-view modeling strategy. Moreover, we design an alternating direction method (ADM) optimization algorithm to solve the proposed objective function. Experimental results on the MIT benchmark dataset show the superiority of the proposed model compared with existing image memorability prediction methods.

Categories and Subject Descriptors

I.5.1 [**Pattern Recognition**]: Models—*statistical*; I.2.10 [**Artificial Intelligence**]: Vision and Scene Understanding—*Modeling and recovery of physical attributes*

General Terms

Algorithms, Experimentation

Keywords

Image Memorability, Adaptive Regression, Multi-view Learning, Prediction

1. INTRODUCTION

Every day, we continuously encounter new photographs and images on social networks and in the media. While we may glance at them only once, some pictures stick in our minds whereas others fade away. Images are differentially memorable — not all are equal in our memory. This phenomenon demonstrates that memorability is an inherent property of individual images. It characterizes the probability that an observer will correctly recall a photograph after a period of time [6]. Predicting image memorability recently attracts lots of researchers' attention due to its promising applications in selecting magazine covers, designing logos, decorating websites and much more.

The prediction of an image's memorability is essentially a regression problem which maps an image (or its features) to a memorability score, where higher score indicates high memorability. Most existing prediction models are mainly based on support vector machine (SVM) technique. For example, Isola et al. [6, 5] propose to train support vector regression (SVR) on visual features and attributes to score the memorability of images. Khosla et al. [7] design a novel probabilistic process of memory forgetting, and exploit ranking SVM (RSVM) to sort the memorability of all images. To make use of attention mechanism, Celikkale et al. [2] introduce an attention-driven spatial pooling strategy for feature encoding and adopt SVR for prediction.

Although these existing SVM-based methods produce encouraging performance, two issues may prevent them from further improvement: (1) They combine multiple features through simple stacking or multiplication [6, 2], and feed them into regressors. Such combination schemes may not capture well the physical meaning of each feature and may cause information redundancy in learning. (2) They have

Figure 1: Sample images whose memorability scores are predicted by the proposed MAR method.

*H. Peng and K. Li contributed equally to this work.

MM'15, October 26–30, 2015, Brisbane, Australia.
© 2015 ACM. ISBN 978-1-4503-3459-4/15/10 ...$15.00.
DOI: http://dx.doi.org/10.1145/2733373.2806303.

limitations in automatic feature selection, which is crucial for image memorability prediction since it remains an open problem that what makes an image memorable.

To address these problems, we propose a novel multi-view adaptive regression (MAR) model, which consists of three components: (1) an adaptive loss function which smoothly interpolates between the traditional ℓ_1 and ℓ_2-norm, and is robust to noises and outliers, (2) an adaptive penalty term which automatically selects desirable features according to training data, and (3) a multi-view framework which regards each visual feature as an individual view for memorability prediction. The proposed model not only pursues a meaningful combination of multiple features, but also takes advantage of complementary characteristics of these features from multiple views, e.g., low-level gradient information and high-level object semantic. Compared with existing memorability prediction models, the proposed method is more effective and robust thanks to its adaptive feature selection and multi-view modeling.

2. MULTI-VIEW ADAPTIVE REGRESSION

For clarity, before presenting the proposed multi-view adaptive regression, we first give out the single-view case, namely the adaptive regression model.

2.1 Adaptive Regression (AR)

Given a feature vector $\mathbf{x} \in \mathbb{R}^p$ representing an image, the prediction of its memorability score $y \in \mathbb{R}$ is a standard regression problem formulated as $f(\mathbf{x}) \rightarrow y$, where f is the fitting model learned on the training samples. In this paper, we consider a linear regression model f formulated as follows:

$$y = \mathbf{w}^T \mathbf{x} + \varepsilon, \tag{1}$$

where $\mathbf{w} \in \mathbb{R}^p$ is the learned model's parameter, and ε is the residual error between the linear prediction and the true response. Given n training images with their feature representation $\mathbf{X} = (\mathbf{x}_1, \ldots, \mathbf{x}_n)^T \in \mathbb{R}^{n \times p}$ as well as corresponding memorability scores $\mathbf{y} = (y_1, \ldots, y_n)^T \in \mathbb{R}^n$, a common way to estimate the parameter vector $\mathbf{w}$ is to penalize the empirical risk minimization, which is defined as

$$\hat{\mathbf{w}} = \arg\min_{\mathbf{w}} L(\mathbf{y}, \mathbf{X}\mathbf{w}) + \lambda R(\mathbf{w}), \tag{2}$$

where $L(\cdot)$ is a loss function used to measure the error between the model's prediction and ground truth, $R(\cdot)$ is a regularization term to avoid overfitting through constraining the complexity of the model, and $\lambda > 0$ is a tradeoff parameter between the two items.

There exists a large body of loss functions and regularization alternatives in the community of statistics and machine learning. For the sake of stable feature selection and robust prediction, we propose a novel *adaptive regression* model which is composed of an adaptive loss and an adaptive regularization and formulated as:

$$\hat{\mathbf{w}} = \arg\min_{\mathbf{w}} \|\mathbf{y} - \mathbf{X}\mathbf{w}\|_\sigma + \lambda \|\mathbf{X}\mathrm{Diag}(\mathbf{w})\|_*. \tag{3}$$

Here, $\|\cdot\|_\sigma$ is the adaptive loss function with parameter σ computed as

$$\|\mathbf{a}\|_\sigma = \sum_{i=1}^{n} \frac{(1+\sigma)a_i^2}{|a_i| + \sigma}, \quad \text{where } \mathbf{a} = [a_1, \ldots a_n]^T, \tag{4}$$

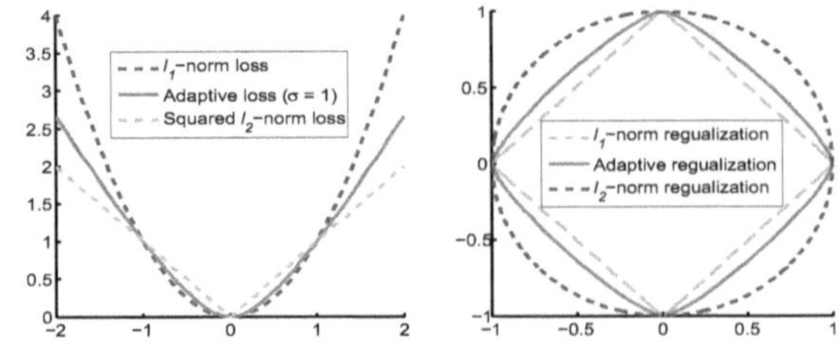

(a) Loss (b) Regularization

Figure 2: Illustration of the adaptive loss and regularization, both of which are between ℓ_1 and ℓ_2-norm.

$\|\cdot\|_*$ is the nuclear norm (the sum of singular values of a matrix), and $\mathrm{Diag}(\mathbf{w})$ converts the vector $\mathbf{w}$ into a diagonal matrix (the i-th diagonal entry is w_i). The adaptive regularization involves the sample matrix $\mathbf{X}$ and adaptively selects desirable feature subset for regression analysis according to the correlation information among samples [11].

The proposed regression model is adaptive because: (1) The loss function $\|\cdot\|_\sigma$ takes advantage of both ℓ_1-norm loss and squared ℓ_2-norm loss by smoothly interpolating between them as shown in Fig. 2(a). Thus it is robust to the data outliers (under Laplacian distribution) and efficient in learning the normal data (under Gaussian distribution) [12]. (2) The adaptive regularization, a.k.a. trace lasso [4], balances the ℓ_1 and ℓ_2-norm according to input samples (see Fig. 2(b)), and simultaneously groups correlated data together and performs automatic feature selection.

2.2 Multi-view Adaptive Regression (MAR)

Exploiting information from multiple sources can effectively improve the prediction performance as a result of their complementary characteristics. In this subsection, we extend the proposed adaptive regression model to multi-view setting that takes multiple visual features into account.

Contrary to the existing methods which simply concatenate multiple feature vectors into a single one [6, 2], our method jointly combines all residuals, which are derived from each individual features independently, to minimize the loss in learning via a weight β. Thus, the objective function Eq.(3) is extended to multi-view setting:

$$\begin{aligned} &\min_{\mathbf{w}^v, \beta^v} \sum_{v=1}^{M} \|\mathbf{y} - \beta^v \mathbf{X}^v \mathbf{w}^v\|_\sigma + \lambda \|\mathbf{X}^v \mathrm{Diag}(\mathbf{w}^v)\|_*, \\ &s.t. \sum_{v=1}^{M} \beta^v = 1, \quad \beta^v \geq 0. \end{aligned} \tag{5}$$

Here, $v \in \{1, \ldots, M\}$ indexes M types of features including color, texture, gradient, shape and semantics to be illustrated in Sec. 3. $\mathbf{X}^v$, $\mathbf{w}^v$ and β^v represent the feature matrix, model parameter and view weight corresponding to the v-th visual feature respectively. This multi-view extension not only preserves physical meaning of each feature, and also leverages their complementary characteristics for prediction.

2.3 Optimization

Considering the balance between efficiency and accuracy in practical applications, we adopt the well established alternating direction method (ADM) [10] to optimize the convex problem Eq.(5). (Eq.(3) can be viewed as a special case of Eq.(5)). We first introduce an auxiliary variable $\mathbf{H}^v$ to make

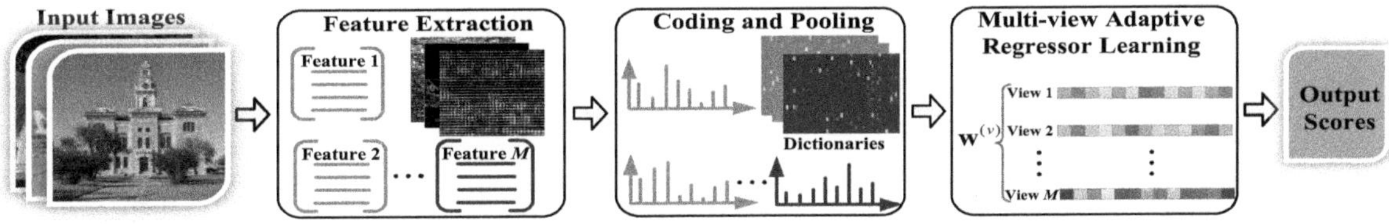

Figure 3: A flowchart to illustrate the proposed multi-view model for image memorability prediction.

the objective function Eq.(5) separable,

$$\min_{\mathbf{w}^v,\beta^v} \sum_{v=1}^{M} \|\mathbf{y} - \beta^v \mathbf{X}^v \mathbf{w}^v\|_\sigma + \lambda \|\mathbf{H}^v\|_*,$$
$$s.t.\ \ \mathbf{H}^v = \mathbf{X}^v \mathrm{Diag}(\mathbf{w}^v),\ \sum_{v=1}^{M} \beta^v{=}1,\ \beta^v \geq 0. \tag{6}$$

Now the problem Eq.(6) can be solved with the ADM, which minimizes the following augmented Lagrangian function:

$$L(\mathbf{H}^v, \mathbf{w}^v, \beta^v) = \sum_{v=1}^{M} \|\mathbf{y} - \beta^v \mathbf{X}^v \mathbf{w}^v\|_\sigma + \lambda \|\mathbf{H}^v\|_*$$
$$+ tr((\mathbf{\Phi}^v)^T (\mathbf{H}^v - \mathbf{X}^v \mathrm{Diag}(\mathbf{w}^v))) + \phi^v (\sum_{v=1}^{M} \beta^v - 1) \tag{7}$$
$$+ \tfrac{\mu}{2} \{\|\mathbf{H}^v - \mathbf{X}^v \mathrm{Diag}(\mathbf{w}^v)\|_F^2 + (\sum_{v=1}^{M} \beta^v - 1)^2\},$$

where $\mathbf{\Phi}^v \in \mathbb{R}^{n \times p}$ and $\phi^v \in \mathbb{R}$ are the Lagrange multipliers, and $\mu > 0$ is the penalty parameter for violation of the linear constraints. To solve Eq.(7), we search for the optimal $\mathbf{H}^v$, $\mathbf{w}^v$ and β^v iteratively as summarized in Algorithm 1. Specifically, Step 1 in Alg.1 can be optimized by the singular value thresholding operator [1], while Step 2 is solved via the iteratively re-weighted algorithm proposed in [12].

3. MAR-BASED IMAGE MEMORABILITY PREDICTION

Algorithm 1 Solving MAR via ADM.

Input: M types of feature matrices $\{\mathbf{X}^v\}_{v=1}^M \in \mathbb{R}^{n \times p}$, the memorability score $\mathbf{y} \in \mathbb{R}^n$, the parameters σ and λ .

Initialize: $\mathbf{H}^v, \mathbf{w}^v, \beta^v, \phi^v, \mathbf{\Phi}^v, \rho$, and $\mu_{\max}$.

While not converged **do**

1. Fix the others and update $\{\mathbf{H}^v\}_{v=1}^M$ by $\mathbf{H}^v{=}$ $\arg\min_{\mathbf{H}^v} \frac{\lambda}{\mu}\|\mathbf{H}^v\|_* + \frac{1}{2}\left\|\mathbf{H}^v - (\mathbf{X}^v \mathrm{Diag}(\mathbf{w}^v) - \frac{1}{\mu}\mathbf{\Phi}^v)\right\|_F^2.$
2. Fix the others and update $\{\mathbf{w}^v\}_{v=1}^M$ by $\mathbf{w}^v{=}\arg\min_{\mathbf{w}^v}$ $\|\mathbf{y} - \beta^v \mathbf{X}^v \mathbf{w}^v\|_\sigma + \frac{\mu}{2}\left\|\mathbf{X}^v \mathrm{Diag}(\mathbf{w}^v) - (\frac{1}{2}\mathbf{H}^v + \frac{1}{\mu}\mathbf{\Phi}^v)\right\|_F^2.$
3. Fix the others and update $\{\beta^v\}_{v=1}^M$ by $\beta^v =$ $((\mathbf{X}^v\mathbf{w}^v)^T \mathbf{D}^v \mathbf{X}^v \mathbf{w}^v + u/2)^{-1}[(\mathbf{X}^v\mathbf{w}^v)^T \mathbf{D}^v \mathbf{y} + (\mu - \phi^v)/2]$ where $\mathbf{D}^v = diag(d_1^v, ..., d_n^v)$ and $d_i^v = (1+\sigma)\frac{\left\|y_i - \beta^v (\mathbf{w}^{(v)})^T \mathbf{x}_i^{(v)}\right\|_2 + 2\sigma}{2(\left\|y_i - \beta^v (\mathbf{w}^{(v)})^T \mathbf{x}_i^{(v)}\right\|_2 + \sigma)^2}.$
4. Update the multipliers $\phi^v = \phi^v + \mu^v(\sum_{v=1}^{M} \beta^v - 1)$, $\mathbf{\Phi}^v = \mathbf{\Phi}^v + \mu^v(\mathbf{H}^v - \mathbf{X}^v \mathrm{Diag}(\mathbf{w}^v))$.
5. Update the parameter $\mu^v = \min(\rho\mu^v, \mu_{\max})$.
6. Check the convergence conditions $\mathbf{H}^v - \mathbf{X}^v \mathrm{Diag}(\mathbf{w}^v) \to 0$ and $\sum_{v=1}^{M} \beta^v - 1 \to 0$ for $v = 1, ..., M$.

End While

Output: The coefficients $\{\mathbf{w}^v\}_{v=1}^M$ and $\{\beta^v\}_{v=1}^M$.

This section elaborates on the prediction of image memorability using the proposed multi-view adaptive regression model. Our prediction method consists of three major stages as illustrated in Fig. 3. (1) We first extract features from each input image considering color, texture, gradient, etc. (2) For each type of feature, we build a dictionary using k-means and apply local-constraint linear coding (LLC) [16] to soft-encode each feature into some dictionary entries. Similar to [5], we perform max pooling with a spatial pyramid matching (SPM) [16] to obtain the final feature vector in each view of the input image. (3) Finally, we exploit the proposed MAR model to learn a regressor on the training data, and then conduct prediction on the testing data.

In more details, we extract five common features in terms of low, middle and high-level visual information to represent images. Considering the power of low-level features in human vision system, we extract the color, texture and gradient for our task. For color feature, we convert the image to color names [15], then learn a dictionary of size 128 and apply LLC at 2-level SPM to obtain the color descriptor. To encode visual texture perception information, we use the popular local binary pattern (LBP) [13] and perform a 2-level SPM of non-uniform LBP descriptors. For gradient information, we densely sample HOG [3] with a cell size of 2×2 and build a dictionary of size 256. The descriptors are max-pooled at 2-level SPM using LLC. We further exploit the mid-level shape feature to represent images. The shape is denoted as a histogram of local self-similarity geometric patterns (SSIM [14]) with the size of 256 pooled at 2-level SPM. Moreover, high-level semantic meaning has been verified to be strongly correlated to image memorability [6]. Similar to [7], we use the automatic object bank [9] feature to model the presence of various objects in the images.

4. EXPERIMENTS AND RESULTS

4.1 Experimental Setup

We use the MIT image memorability dataset [6] to evaluate the proposed prediction model. This dataset contains 2222 natural images associated with human-annotated memorability scores. For the quantitative analysis, we use Spearman's rank correlation ρ and the precision-recall curve introduced in [6] to measure the performance of models. Same as [6], we evaluate the performance over 25 random splits of the dataset with an equal number of images for training and testing (1111). These train and test splits have been scored by different halves of the participants, showing a human consistency of $\rho = 0.75$, which can be viewed as an upper bound in the performance of prediction methods.

The tradeoff parameter λ of the MAR model is tuned on a validation set using 5-fold cross validation and set to be 1 to balance the adaptive regularization and loss function.

	Color	LBP	HOG	SSIM	Semantic	All (**MAR**)	SVR-MGF[6]	RSVM[7]	SVR-SO[2]	SVR-WOA[8]	Human
Top 20	76%	79%	83%	82%	82%	85%	83%	85%	84%	85%	86%
Top 100	73%	76%	80%	79%	80%	83%	80%	81%	81%	81%	84%
Bottom 100	60%	57%	56%	59%	58%	56%	56%	55%	56%	55%	47%
Bottom 20	57%	55%	54%	53%	53%	51%	54%	52%	55%	52%	40%
ρ	0.26	0.37	0.45	0.44	0.46	**0.52**	0.46	0.50	0.47	0.49	0.75

Table 1: Comparison of predictions. Left: results produced by our method considering each individual features and their combination. Right: baselines and the human prediction.

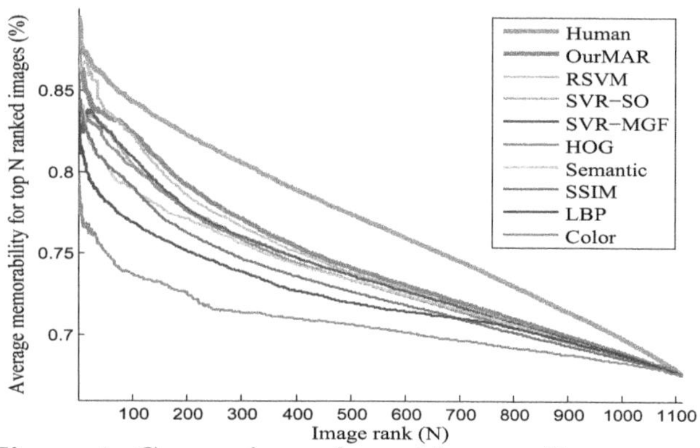

Figure 4: Comparison of precision-recall curves averaged across 25 random splits.

Upon our preliminary experiments, we empirically set the adaptive parameter as σ=0.1 in all experiments.

4.2 Results

We first compare the prediction performance of our MAR model with 4 other existing image memorability prediction methods on the MIT dataset. The baseline methods are SVR-MGF [6] which stacks multiple global features and uses SVR as the prediction model, RSVM [7] which fuses the results of ranking SVM learned on six common features independently, SVR-SO [2] which trains SVR over the combination of three groups of image features considering saliency and objectness, and SVR-WOA [8] which trains SVR on weighted object area features. Fig. 4 and Tab. 1 summarize the experimental results. It is observed that our method (MAR) outperforms SVR-MGF, SVR-SO and SVR-WOA by 10.8%, 8.7% and 4.3% respectively (see Tab. 1). This indicates the proposed multi-view learning model is more robust than the stereotyped regression methods at leveraging multiple features for image memorability prediction. Furthermore, our method achieves comparable performance compared to RSVM, and the average measured memorability of the 100 highest predicted images ("Top-100" shown in Tab. 1) of our method is superior. This may be caused by the fact that RSVM performs prediction by exploiting the ranking scheme, rather than the regression strategy used in our model. As shown in Fig. 4, the precision-recall curve of our method is also superior to others. Fig. 1 shows some sample images with their memorability scores predicted by our MAR method.

5. CONCLUSIONS

Predicting image memorability is a recent research topic which is crucial for the task of creating an image that a viewer will remember. In this paper, we propose a novel adaptive regression model to estimate image memorability. It is made up of an adaptive loss and an adaptive regularizer, and capable of selecting desirable features and robust to outliers. Moreover, we extend the regression model to multi-view case which effectively leverage multiple features for prediction. Extensive experiments show the superiority of our method compared with the state of the arts.

6. ACKNOWLEDGMENTS

This work is partly supported by the 973 basic research program of China (Grant No. 2014CB349303), NSFC (Grant No. 61472421, 61370038, 61202327, 61472227 and 61303086), the National 863 High-Tech R&D Program of China (Grant No. 2012AA012504), and the US NSF Grants US NSF Grants 1449860, IIS-1407156 and 1350521.

7. REFERENCES

[1] E. Candès, X. Li, Y. Ma, and J. Wright. Robust principal component analysis? *J. ACM*, 58(3):11, 2011.

[2] B. Celikkale, A. Erdem, and E. Erdem. Visual attention driven spatial pooling for image memorability. In *CVPRW*, pages 976–983, 2013.

[3] N. Dalal and B. Triggs. Histograms of oriented gradients for human detection. In *CVPR*, pages 886–893, 2005.

[4] E. Grave, G. Obozinski, and F. Bach. Trace lasso: a trace norm regularization for correlated designs. In *NIPS*, 2011.

[5] P. Isola, D. Parikh, A. Torralba, and A. Oliva. Understanding the intrinsic memorability of images. In *NIPS*, pages 2429–2437, 2011.

[6] P. Isola, J. Xiao, A. Khosla, A. Torralba, and A. Oliva. What makes a photograph memorable? *IEEE TPAMI*, 36(7):1469–1482, 2014.

[7] A. Khosla, J. Xiao, A. Torralba, and A. Oliva. Memorability of image regions. In *NIPS*, 2012.

[8] J. Kim, S. Yoon, and V. Pavlovic. Relative spatial features for image memorability. In *ACM Multimedia*, pages 761–764, 2013.

[9] L.-J. Li, H. Su, Y. Lim, and F.-F. Li. Object bank: An object-level image representation for high-level visual recognition. *IJCV*, 107(1):20–39, 2014.

[10] Z. Lin, R. Liu, and Z. Su. Linearized alternating direction method with adaptive penalty for low-rank representation. In *NIPS*, pages 612–620, 2011.

[11] C.-Y. Lu, J. Feng, Z. Lin, and S. Yan. Correlation adaptive subspace segmentation by trace lasso. In *ICCV*, 2013.

[12] F. Nie, H. Wang, H. Huang, and C. H. Q. Ding. Adaptive loss minimization for semi-supervised elastic embedding. In *IJCAI*, pages 1565–1571, 2013.

[13] T. Ojala, M. Pietikäinen, and T. Mäenpää. Multiresolution gray-scale and rotation invariant texture classification with local binary patterns. *IEEE TPAMI*, 24(7):971–987, 2002.

[14] E. Shechtman and M. Irani. Matching local self-similarities across images and videos. In *CVPR*, 2007.

[15] J. van de Weijer, C. Schmid, and J. J. Verbeek. Learning color names from real-world images. In *CVPR*, 2007.

[16] J. Wang, J. Yang, K. Yu, F. Lv, T. S. Huang, and Y. Gong. Locality-constrained linear coding for image classification. In *CVPR*, pages 3360–3367, 2010.

Spatio-Temporal Triangular-Chain CRF for Activity Recognition

Congqi Cao
National Laboratory of Pattern Recognition
Institute of Automation
Chinese Academy of Sciences
Beijing, China, 100190
congqi.cao@nlpr.ia.ac.cn

Yifan Zhang
National Laboratory of Pattern Recognition
Institute of Automation
Chinese Academy of Sciences
Beijing, China, 100190
yfzhang@nlpr.ia.ac.cn

Hanqing Lu
National Laboratory of Pattern Recognition
Institute of Automation
Chinese Academy of Sciences
Beijing, China, 100190
luhq@nlpr.ia.ac.cn

ABSTRACT

Understanding human activities in video is a fundamental problem in computer vision. In real life, human activities are composed of temporal and spatial arrangement of actions. Understanding such complex activities requires recognizing not only each individual action, but more importantly, capturing their spatio-temporal relationships. This paper addresses the problem of complex activity recognition with a unified hierarchical model. We expand triangular-chain CRFs (TriCRFs) to the spatial dimension. The proposed architecture can be perceived as a spatio-temporal version of the TriCRFs, in which the labels of actions and activity are modeled jointly and their complex dependencies are exploited. Experiments show that our model generates promising results, outperforming competing methods significantly. The framework also can be applied to model other structured sequential data.

Categories and Subject Descriptors

I.2.10 [**Artificial Intelligence**]: Vision and Scene Understanding

Keywords

Activity recognition, Hierarchical model, Joint learning, Spatio-temporal dependencies, Triangular-chain CRFs

1. INTRODUCTION

Activity recognition is one of the most popular research fields in computer vision which has spawned a rich literature [11, 4, 16, 3] due to its promising application in video monitoring, behavioral analysis and artificial intelligence. In real life, human activities are complex since humans are capable of performing multiple simple actions simultaneously. Complex human activities are composed of temporal and spatial arrangement of atomic actions and each atomic action is composed by a temporal arrangement of body poses [9]. Understanding such complex activities requires recognizing not only each individual action, but more importantly, capturing their spatio-temporal relationships.

Much of the initial work in activity recognition has been focused on analyzing either high-level coarse grained activities or mid-level fine grained actions. However, the recognition result of each level is useful in practice which allows multiple layers of abstraction. Besides, research in congnitive psychology has shown that human perceive activities as hierarchical structures [7]. Therefore it is necessary to recognize activities and actions jointly in a hierarchical model. Recently, there has been significant interest in it. [13] presented a framework for modeling complex composite activity using stochastic grammar. However, the grammar induction is very important for this model. It will be more robust and more flexible if the model could be learned from data fully automatically, instead of using expert's knowledge. [9] proposed a compositional hierarchical model to recognize human activities and actions by formulating an energy minimization problem which is similar to a latent structural SVM case. The energy terms are associated to the activity, actions and poses, as well as temporal transitions between actions and poses. However, the transitions between actions in [9] are independent of activity, and there is no energy terms to model the influence of pose observations to activity recognition. [7] trained a hierarchical model based on HMMs and a context-free grammar using HTK toolkit which is a speech recognition engine to model human activities as temporally structured processes. [7] demonstrated that applying techniques borrowed from speech recognition is feasible since human activities and speech have similar inherently hierarchical nature. The limitation of this model is that it can not capture spatial composition of actions. Besides, it is based on HMMs which make strong independence assumption of observations. Such assumption ignores the multiple interacting features and long-range dependencies of the observation [8].

Different from the existing deep learning methods [15, 12] which mainly focused on feature extraction and representation, our work aims at modeling spatial and temporal relationships of poses and actions in video. For modeling sequential data, [5] proposed TriCRFs shown in Figure 1, a unified probabilistic model jointly representing the sequence and meta-sequence labels. TriCRFs have been successfully used in named entity recognition and dialog act classification

MM'15, October 26–30, 2015, Brisbane, Australia.
© 2015 ACM. ISBN 978-1-4503-3459-4/15/10 ...$15.00.
DOI: http://dx.doi.org/10.1145/2733373.2806304.

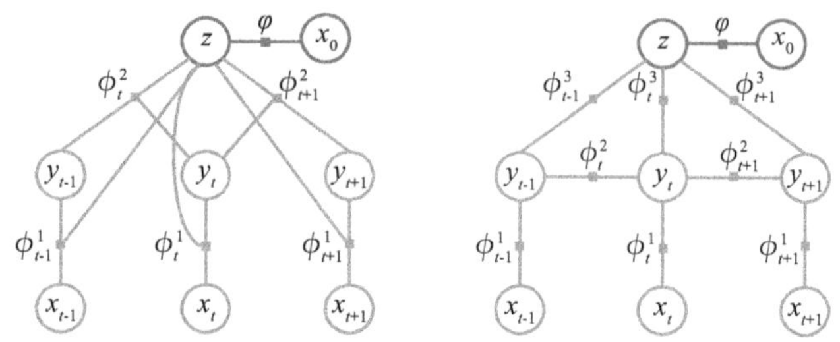

Figure 1: Two structures of triangular-chain CRFs. The transition potentials and observation potentials are dependent of z in the left structure and independent of z in the right structure.

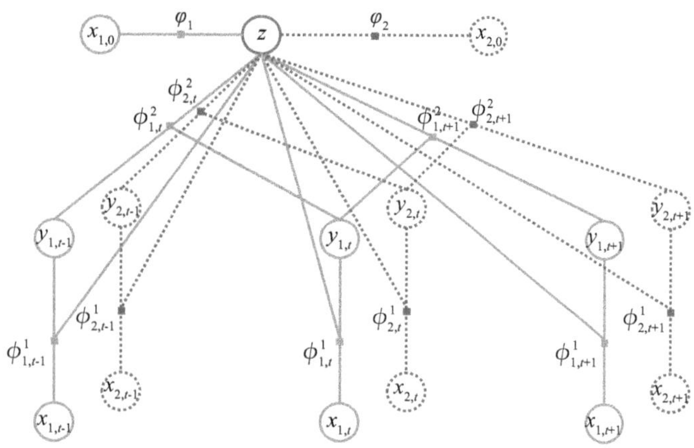

Figure 2: The structure of spatio-temporal triangular-chain CRFs which could capture spatial and temporal information in sequential data.

for spoken language understanding [5, 6, 14]. However, no applications on computer vision tasks have been observed.

As mentioned above, modeling complex human activity is still a challenging work because of its complicated spatio-temporal relationships and multiple variabilities among actions. In this paper, we propose a novel framework for activity and action recognition which could model the spatio-temporal relationships of multi-level labels jointly in a unified hierarchical model shown in Figure 2. Our model is based on triangular-chain CRFs. Furthermore, we expand traditional temporal TriCRFs to the spatial dimension. The model could both explicitly encode dependencies and preserves uncertainty between actions and activity. As far as we know, we are the first to utilize spatio-temporal TriCRFs in complex activity recognition. Experiments on composable human activity dataset show that our approach outperforms other methods which demonstrates the effectiveness of our framework for modeling spatio-temporal relationships in activity recognition. This model could also be applied to other structured sequential modeling problems.

2. FRAMEWORK

2.1 Background

Human activity, speech and natural language are all sequential data. Many problems of sequential data can be treated as sequential labeling or sequence classification [5]. More specifically, sequential labeling is a problem of predicting a sequence of label $\mathbf{y}$ given an input sequence of observations $\mathbf{x}$ which could be formulated as learning $p(\mathbf{y}|\mathbf{x})$. Sequence classification is a problem of predicting a single label z given $\mathbf{x}$, formulated as learning $p(z|\mathbf{x})$. TriCRFs solve the two correlated problems jointly by predicting the best labels $(\hat{\mathbf{y}}, \hat{z})$ using $p(\mathbf{y}, z|\mathbf{x})$ trained from data $(\mathbf{x}^{(n)}, \mathbf{y}^{(n)}, z^{(n)})_{n=1}^{N}$.

Linear-chain conditional random fields (CRFs) was proposed to segment and label data by Lafferty in 2001 [8]. As being discriminative that directly model the global conditional distribution, CRFs offer several advantages over generative models such as hidden Markov models and stochastic grammars which use non discriminant criterion, including the ability to relax strong independence assumptions. CRFs could also avoid the fundamental label bias limitation of maximum entropy Markov models (MEMMs) and other locally normalized discriminative models [8].

Spatio-temporal triangular-chain CRFs have all the advantages of CRFs. Besides, Spatio-temporal triangular-chain CRFs can capture the spatial and temporal relationships of atomic actions to model multi-level labels of activity at the same time. It could model the complex dependencies between activity, actions and pose observations. Especially, the transitions between actions are dependent of activity, and there is potential terms to model the influence of pose observations to activity recognition. Our model is shown in Figure 2. Let R be the number of spatial regions. For each region, the complex relationships between actions and activities are modeled by temporal tiangular-chain CRFs. Different regions are fused together in the activity level. The figure illustrates the $R = 2$ case.

2.2 Formulation

In order to take spatial information into account, we extend TriCRFs to spatial dimension. Spatio-temporal triangular-chain CRFs are defined as follows.

$$p_\lambda(\mathbf{y}, z|\mathbf{x}) = \prod_{r=1}^{R} p_{\lambda_r}(\mathbf{y}_r, z|\mathbf{x}_r) \quad (1)$$

where we assume that the probability $p_\lambda(\mathbf{y}, z|\mathbf{x})$ is proportional to the product of every region's probability $p_{\lambda_r}(\mathbf{y}_r, z|\mathbf{x}_r)$.

$$p_{\lambda_r}(y_r, z|x_r) = \frac{1}{Z(x_r)} \cdot \prod_{t=1}^{T} (\phi_{r,t}(z, y_{r,t}, y_{r,t-1}, x_r))\varphi_r(z, x_r) \quad (2)$$

where $\phi_{r,t}$ and φ_r are the potentials of spatio-temporal TriCRFs. $Z(\mathbf{x}_r)$ is for normalization which defined as follows.

$$Z(\mathbf{x}_r) \triangleq \sum_{\mathbf{y}_r, z} \prod_{t=1}^{T} \phi_{r,t}(z, y_{r,t}, y_{r,t-1}, \mathbf{x}_r)\varphi_r(z, \mathbf{x}_r) \quad (3)$$

As illustrated in Figure 2 and formulated with the equations, $\phi_{r,t}$ is time-dependent and φ_r is time-independent. Specifically, $\phi_{r,t}$ could be partitioned into z-dependent and z-independent factors. φ_r plays as a prior role.

$$\varphi_r(z, \mathbf{x}_r) = \exp(\sum_k \lambda_{r,k}^0 f_{r,k}^0(z, \mathbf{x}_{r,0})) \quad (4)$$

$$\phi_{r,t}(z, y_{r,t}, y_{r,t-1}, \mathbf{x}_r) = \phi_{r,t}^d(z, y_{r,t}, y_{r,t-1}, \mathbf{x}_r) \cdot \phi_{r,t}^i(y_{r,t}, y_{r,t-1}, \mathbf{x}_r) \quad (5)$$

where $\mathbf{x}_{r,0}$ is an observation feature vector for classifying z. $f_{r,k}$ stands for a real-valued feature function and $\lambda_{r,k}$ is a weight parameter.

z-dependent factor $\phi^d_{r,t}$ can be further partitioned into observation item and transition item dependent of z.

$$\phi^d_{r,t}(z, y_{r,t}, y_{r,t-1}, \mathbf{x}_r) = \phi^1_{r,t}(z, y_{r,t}, \mathbf{x}_r)\phi^2_{r,t}(z, y_{r,t}, y_{r,t-1}) \quad (6)$$

$$\phi^1_{r,t}(z, y_{r,t}\mathbf{x}_r) = \exp(\sum_k \lambda^1_{r,k} f^1_{r,k}(z, y_{r,t}, \mathbf{x}_r)) \quad (7)$$

$$\phi^2_{r,t}(z, y_{r,t}, y_{r,t-1}) = \exp(\sum_k \lambda^2_{r,k} f^2_{r,k}(z, y_{r,t}, y_{r,t-1})) \quad (8)$$

z-independent factor $\phi^i_{r,t}$ also can be partitioned into observation item and transition item independent of z.

$$\phi^i_{r,t}(y_{r,t}, y_{r,t-1}, \mathbf{x}_r) = \phi^1_{r,t}(y_{r,t}, \mathbf{x}_r)\phi^2_{r,t}(y_{r,t}, y_{r,t-1}) \quad (9)$$

$$\phi^1_{r,t}(y_{r,t}, \mathbf{x}_r) = \exp(\sum_k \lambda^1_{r,k} f^1_{r,k}(y_{r,t}, \mathbf{x}_r)) \quad (10)$$

$$\phi^2_{r,t}(y_{r,t}, y_{r,t-1}) = \exp(\sum_k \lambda^2_{r,k} f^2_{r,k}(y_{r,t}, y_{r,t-1})) \quad (11)$$

2.3 Inference and Parameter Estimation

Spatio-temporal TriCRFs have efficient training and decoding algorithms based on dynamic programming. And being a convex optimization problem, parameter estimation is guaranteed to find the global optimum.

For inference, the marginal probability distributions $p_{\lambda_r}(z, y_{r,t}|\mathbf{x}_r)$, $p_{\lambda_r}(z, y_{r,t}, y_{r,t-1}|\mathbf{x}_r)$, $p_{\lambda_r}(z|x_r)$ and the partition function $Z(\mathbf{x}_r)$ are calculated via the forward-backward algorithm introduced in [5]. The viterbi decoding algorithm for each chain is also the same as [5].

For parameter estimation, using conditional maximum log-likelihood criterion, the objective function is formulated as follows.

$$L(\lambda) = \sum_{r=1}^{R}\sum_{n=1}^{N}\sum_{t=1}^{T}\sum_{k=1}^{K} \lambda_{r,k} f_{r,k}(z^{(n)}, y^{(n)}_{r,t}, y^{(n)}_{r,t-1}, \mathbf{x}^{(n)}_r) - \sum_{r=1}^{R}\sum_{n=1}^{N} \log Z(\mathbf{x}^{(n)}_r) - \sum_{r=1}^{R}\sum_{k=1}^{K} \frac{\lambda^2_{r,k}}{2\sigma^2} \quad (12)$$

where the last term functions as a regularization term to avoid over-fitting.

The parameters are learned through differentiating the objective function. A limited memory version of the quasi-Newton method is used to optimize the parameters.

$$\frac{\partial L}{\partial \lambda_{r,k}} = \sum_{n=1}^{N}\sum_{t=1}^{T} f_{r,k}(z^{(n)}, y^{(n)}_{r,t}, y^{(n)}_{r,t-1}, \mathbf{x}^{(n)}_r) - \sum_{n=1}^{N}\sum_{t=1}^{T}\sum_{z', y_r, y'_r} f_{r,k}(z', y_r, y'_r, \mathbf{x}^{(n)}_r) p_{\lambda_r}(z, y_r, y'_r|\mathbf{x}^{(n)}_r) - \frac{\lambda_{r,k}}{\sigma^2} \quad (13)$$

The pseudo-likelihood parameters are used for initialization [1]. We modified the code published by Minwoo Jeong [5, 6] to construct our spatio-temporal TriCRFs by taking spatial information into account.

3. EXPERIMENTS

3.1 Composable Activity Dataset

We evaluate our method on Composable Activity dataset which is introduced by Ivan et al. in [9]. The dataset consists of 693 videos containing activities in 16 classes performed by 14 actors. Each activity is composed by spatio-temporal combinations of atomic actions. For instance, *composed activity 2* is composed by *walking*, *picking object*, *put an object*, *erasing board* in space and time. There are total 26 types of atomic actions. The dataset offers a global annotation at the activity level for each video, as well as per-frame annotations of the atomic actions with an array indicates the associated body region (right arm, left arm, right leg and left leg).

Table 1: Recognition accuracy of different R

Algorithm	Region number	Accuracy
Our method	1	0.759
Our method	2	**0.790**
Our method	4	0.772

Table 2: Recognition accuracy comparison

Algorithm	Codebook size	Accuracy
Our method	200(fixed)	**0.790**
BoW	200(fixed)	0.672
BoW	600(fixed)	0.623
H-BoW [9]	200(fixed)	0.742
H-BoW [9]	600(fixed)	0.716
HMM	200(fixed)	0.765
HMM	600(fixed)	0.723

3.2 Features

In order to facilitate a fair comparison, we follow the same experimental settings as [9]. Performance is evaluated in leave-one-subject-out experiment setup. Observed features are extracted using the method in [2, 10] from RGB-D videos which include relative location between body joints, angles between limbs and angles between limbs and plans spanned by body parts. Using the feature extraction code in [9], right arm, left arm, right leg and left leg are represented by a 21-dimension feature vector respectively. [9] quantized the observed features of each body part into M clusters of poses. The three techniques for comparison are a BoW representation plus a lineal SVM classifier (BoW-approach), a version of authors' hierarchical model without learning the pose dictionary (H-BoW approach), and a Hidden Markov Model approach (HMM approach). It is more equitable to compare our spatio-temporal model with the three techniques which also quantize the observations using k-means. The classification result of our model is higher than the other methods including the version of model in [9] with fixed pose dictionary. Experiments in [9] showed that jointly learning pose dictionary with actions and activities could improve the accuracy. Our model also can include a third semantic level. It is straightforward to add another layer in our model to represent pose and it is feasible to use other more appropriate methods to obtain a pose dictionary. The performance could probably be improved further.

3.3 Results and Analysis

We divide the whole body into R regions, where $R = \{1, 2, 4\}$. For the case $R = 4$, the body is divided into 4 regions which are right arm, left arm, right leg and left leg; There are 4 chains in spatio-temporal TriCRFs. For the case $R = 2$, the body is divided into upper body and lower body; The upper body is composed of right arm and left arm, while the lower body is composed of right leg and left leg; We concatenate the right arm observed features and left

Table 3: The comparison of robustness. The table lists the decreases of accuracies by randomly select a part to be occluded in every testing sequence.

Algorithm	Our method	Method in [9]	BoW	HMM
Decrease	**0.0527**	0.072	0.125	0.103

arm observed features together to represent the upper body part; The same setting is for the lower body part; There are 2 chains in spatio-temporal TriCRFs. For the case $R = 1$, the body is treated as a whole part and there is only one temporal TriCRFs chain.

For spatio-temporal TriCRFs, the accuracy of action labeling is 33.8%, 55.7%, 56.6% for R=1,2,4 respectively. The accuracies of activity recognition are shown in Table 1. Dividing the whole body into spatial regions does increase the recognition accuracies of actions and activities at the same time, which on the other side demonstrates that our spatio-temporal TriCRFs model captures the relationships in space successfully. The reason for why 2-region setting is better than 4-region setting is probably because the action labels are not fine-grained for each body part. In different actions, some body parts may show the same pose, resulting in that there is relatively small between-action-class distance, which is less discriminative to predict the action and activity label. The unsupervised clustering method used to quantize observations also should be improved.

As shown in Table 2. The accuracy of spatio-temporal TriCRFs shows clear improvement over the competing methods. The strength of our model can be measured against BoW, H-BoW and HMM with the same setting to obtain a fixed pose dictionary by k-means without dictionary learning. Our spatio-temporal TriCRFs model does better in modeling dependencies between multi-level labels. Adding pose learning method in our model with extra layer could probably further increase performance.

To evaluate the robustness, we randomly select a part to be occluded in every testing sequence. The accuracy of our model decreases by 5.27 %, while the method in [9] decreases by 7.2 %, BoW decreases by 12.5 % and HMM decreases by 10.3 % as shown in Table 3.

4. CONCLUSION

We have presented spatio-temporal triangular-chain CRF-s, a unified hierarchical model that is powerful in exploiting dependencies between multiple layers for complex activity recognition. Spatio-temporal TriCRFs could model the complex relationships between activity, actions and pose observations. Our model takes more information into account than other existing methods. The transitions between actions are dependent of activity, and there is potential terms to model the influence of pose observations to activity recognition. Furthermore, interactions between different spatial regions are included. Experiments demonstrates the effectiveness of our model. The framework is also applicable in other sequential modeling problems.

For future work, we consider to add another layer to learn pose representations jointly with actions and activity. We can add several constraints in inference to make sure action labels of different body parts are consistent with each other.

5. ACKNOWLEDGEMENTS

We thank the anonymous reviews for their valuable comments. This work was partly supported by 863 Program (2014AA015104) and National Natural Science Foundation of China (61332016, 61202325, 61379100).

6. REFERENCES

[1] J. Besag. Statistical analysis of non-lattice data. *Journal of the Royal Statistical Society. Series D (The Statistician)*, 24(3):pp. 179–195, 1975.

[2] C. Chen, Y. Zhuang, F. Nie, Y. Yang, F. Wu, and J. Xiao. Learning a 3d human pose distance metric from geometric pose descriptor. *IEEE Trans. Vis. Comput. Graph.*, 17(11):1676–1689, 2011.

[3] H. Chu, W. Lin, J. Wu, X. Zhou, Y. Chen, and H. Li. A new heat-map-based algorithm for human group activity recognition. In *Proceedings of the 20th ACM Multimedia Conference, October 29 - November 02, 2012*, pages 1069–1072. ACM, 2012.

[4] A. Fathi and J. M. Rehg. Modeling actions through state changes. In *CVPR 2013, June 23-28, 2013*, pages 2579–2586. IEEE, 2013.

[5] M. Jeong and G. G. Lee. Triangular-chain conditional random fields. *IEEE Transactions on Audio, Speech & Language Processing*, 16(7):1287–1302, 2008.

[6] M. Jeong and G. G. Lee. Multi-domain spoken language understanding with transfer learning. *Speech Communication*, 51(5):412–424, 2009.

[7] H. Kuehne, A. B. Arslan, and T. Serre. The language of actions: Recovering the syntax and semantics of goal-directed human activities. In *CVPR 2014, June 23-28, 2014*, pages 780–787. IEEE, 2014.

[8] J. D. Lafferty, A. McCallum, and F. C. N. Pereira. Conditional random fields: Probabilistic models for segmenting and labeling sequence data. In *ICML 2001, June 28 - July 1, 2001*, pages 282–289. Morgan Kaufmann, 2001.

[9] I. Lillo, A. Soto, and J. C. Niebles. Discriminative hierarchical modeling of spatio-temporally composable human activities. In *CVPR 2014, June 23-28, 2014*, pages 812–819, 2014.

[10] J. Shotton, A. W. Fitzgibbon, M. Cook, T. Sharp, M. Finocchio, R. Moore, A. Kipman, and A. Blake. Real-time human pose recognition in parts from single depth images. In *CVPR 2011, 20-25 June 2011*, pages 1297–1304. IEEE Computer Society, 2011.

[11] C. Sminchisescu, A. Kanaujia, and D. N. Metaxas. Conditional models for contextual human motion recognition. *Computer Vision and Image Understanding*, 104(2-3):210–220, 2006.

[12] D. Tran, L. D. Bourdev, R. Fergus, L. Torresani, and M. Paluri. C3D: generic features for video analysis. *CoRR*, abs/1412.0767, 2014.

[13] N. N. Vo and A. F. Bobick. From stochastic grammar to bayes network: Probabilistic parsing of complex activity. In *CVPR 2014, June 23-28, 2014*, pages 2641–2648. IEEE, 2014.

[14] P. Xu and R. Sarikaya. Convolutional neural network based triangular CRF for joint intent detection and slot filling. In *2013 IEEE Workshop on Automatic Speech Recognition and Understanding, December 8-12, 2013*, pages 78–83. IEEE, 2013.

[15] Z. Xu, Y. Yang, and A. G. Hauptmann. A discriminative CNN video representation for event detection. *CoRR*, abs/1411.4006, 2014.

[16] Y. Zhang, Y. Zhang, E. Swears, N. Larios, Z. Wang, and Q. Ji. Modeling temporal interactions with interval temporal bayesian networks for complex activity recognition. *IEEE Trans. Pattern Anal. Mach. Intell.*, 35(10):2468–2483, 2013.

Query-Adaptive Logo Search using Shape-Aware Descriptors

Sreyasee Das Bhattacharjee
Rapid Rich Object Search (ROSE) Lab
Nanyang Technological University
Singapore
dbhattacharjee@ntu.edu.sg

Junsong Yuan, Yap-Peng Tan
School of EEE
Nanyang Technological University
Singapore
jsyuan@ntu.edu.sg, eyptan@ntu.edu.sg

Lingyu Duan
School of EECS
Peking University
Beijing, China
lingyu@pku.edu.cn

ABSTRACT

We propose a graph-based optimization framework to leverage category independent object proposals (candidate object regions) for logo search in a large scale image database. The proposed contour-based feature descriptor EdgeBoW is robust to view-angle changes, varying illumination conditions and can implicitly capture the significant object shape information. Being equipped with a local descriptor, it can handle a fair amount of occlusion and deformation frequently present in a real-life scenario. Given a small set of initially retrieved candidate object proposals, a fast graph-based short-listing scheme is designed to exploit the mutual similarities among these proposals for eliminating outliers. In contrast to a coarse image-level pairwise similarity measure, this search focused on a few specific image regions provides a more accurate method for matching. The proposed query expansion strategy assesses each of the remaining better matched proposals against all its neighbors within the same image for a precise localization. Combined with an efficient feature descriptor EdgeBoW, a set of insightful edge-weights and node-utility measures can yield promising results, especially for object categories primarily defined by its shape. Extensive set of experiments performed on a number of benchmark datasets demonstrates its effectiveness and superior generalization ability in both clutter intensive real-life images and poor quality binary document images.

Categories and Subject Descriptors

H.4 [**Information Systems Applications**]: Miscellaneous; D.2.8 [**Image Processing, Computer Vision**]: [Scene Analysis, object recognition]

General Terms

Understanding

MM'15, October 26–30, 2015, Brisbane, Australia.
© 2015 ACM. ISBN 978-1-4503-3459-4/15/10 ...$15.00.
DOI: http://dx.doi.org/10.1145/2733373.2806305.

Keywords

Mobile Visual Search, Contour-based Descriptor, Localization, Graph-based Search

1. INTRODUCTION

A logo is a graphic object designed with colors, shapes, textures, perhaps as well as text also, following some specific spatial layout. It represents a product or an organization and can be treated as an object with a planer surface, which is extremely worthy in the premise of modern advertising, trademark registration, automatic logo annotation etc.

The most exploited feature color cannot be of much help for determining the unique identity of logos. In order to attract customers better, logos from the same brand can significantly vary in terms of their color/textures as well. In many cases, text occupies a significant portion of a logo. However, the text part is often modified deliberately to tempt the artistic senses of customers. On the other hand, logo images can also be blurred, or occupy only a small portion of the image with cluttered background and differ significantly in terms of affine distortion, noise and occlusion. All these pose a severe challenge for successful logo search and localization. Despite a significant success in the domain of image retrieval [1, 2, 3, 4], retrieving small and smooth (shape with less number of interest points, like Nike) objects like logos in cluttered environment is still critical.

The main contributions of this paper are as follows : (1) An integrated framework that leverages object proposals to solve the problem of logo search both in the real-life scenes as well as the poor quality binarized document images. (2) An effective short-listing and query expansion strategy exploit the mutual similarity between proposals to define various graphical models, apt at identifying the similar object instances in a cluttered background. (3) Unlike Dense-SIFT, the proposed shape-aware EdgeBoW as a group of EdgeWords can capture sufficient amount of global shape information in presence of varying image conditions. A robust local SIFT-like representation of its constituent EdgeWords is robust to occlusions and deformation. This helps the proposed method to offset the limitations of both global shape descriptors and local interest-point based descriptors. A diagram giving the overview of the entire method is shown in Figure 1.

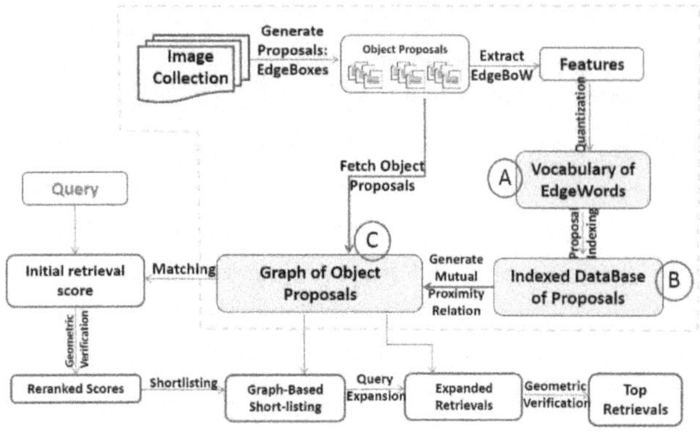

Figure 1: Method Overview. A, B and C show the database components. The portion of the work flow encapsulated with 'yellow' box can be performed a-priory while processing the database.

2. INITIAL SEARCH USING EDGEBOW

Given an image database $\mathcal{D} = \{I_i\}$ $(i \in \{1,..,M\})$ the task is to identify the subset $\{I_g\}$ of images having the similar instances as the query object Q and localize them within each I_g.

In order to achieve this, we identify only a smaller number of salient regions within an image for a more rigorous investigation. Over the past decade, the dominant approach to the problem of identifying potential interest regions in an image has been the sliding windows paradigm in which object classification is performed at every location and scale in an image. However, this is computationally expensive and an efficient alternative is to identify a smaller set of salient regions (candidate object proposals), which can then be explored for a more detailed search.

2.1 Identifying Salient Image Regions

We have adopted EdgeBox by Zitnick & Dollar [5] for generating some potential category independent object bounding box proposals from an underlying database image.

Given an image, any proposal with a skew ratio (defined as the ratio of the skew of the proposal and an average skew of the logo categories in the database) beyond a certain range is discarded. Given each bounding box, the associated 'objectness measure' quantifies its likelihood to contain an object. Only the top N ranked proposals per image are retained as the primary interest regions for further investigation. Based on the image types in a database, the value of N can be fixed experimentally. We will discuss more on this in the Section 4.

Thus, given a collection of M images, the database consists of $M \times N$ object proposals. This is denoted as $\mathcal{D} = \{P_i^j\}_{i\in\{1,..,M\}}^{j\in\{1,..,N\}}$, where P_i^j represents $j^{th}(j \leq N)$ object proposal generated from image I_i. Now onwards for simplicity sake, we accept a slight notational abuse to denote each P_i^j as just P_i. Hereafter, each such proposal will be treated as a separate image, on which the presence/absence of an object is to be determined.

2.2 EdgeBoW as the Proposal Representative

Each object proposal P_i is resized to a standard size while respecting its own aspect ratio. Given the edge map of P_i, each of its constituent contours C_j is uniformly sampled (at every 5th pixel) to identify a dense set of interest points $\mathcal{F}_i = \cup_{C_j \in P_i}\{p \in C_j\}$. Each $p \in \mathcal{F}_i$ at a co-ordinate location (p_x, p_y) is identified by a tuple $(p_x, p_y, \theta_p, s_p)$, where θ_p and s_p respectively represent the orientation and scale estimated by the multi-scale variant of Structured Edge detector [6] at p. The scale range is taken to be $[-2s_i, 2s_i]$, where s_i is the scale of $\mathcal{P}_i$. Given these estimates, each p is represented in terms of the 128 dimensional SIFT like descriptor [7] and each $\mathcal{P}_i$ can represented by a bag of SIFT descriptors $\{f_{i,j}\}_j$. Following the BoVW scheme, each local descriptor f is quantized to a visual word using a vocabulary of V words, represented as $w = (p, v)$, where $p = (p_x, p_y)$ is the location and $v \in \{1, ..., V\}$ is the corresponding index of the visual word. Using a stop list analogy, the most frequent visual words (top 10% as in our experiments) that occur in almost all images are discarded. All feature points are indexed by an inverted file so that only words that appear in the queries will be checked. Each word of the vocabulary is denoted as an EdgeWord. Thus the entire object proposal P_i is represented in terms of a Bag of EdgeWords, denoted as EdgeBoW $\mathcal{E}_i = \{w(= (p, v)),\ p \in \mathcal{F}_i\}$. $\mathcal{E}_i$ can then be characterized by a V-dimensional histogram h_i recording the word frequency of $\mathcal{E}_i$.

2.3 EdgeBoW Matching

Given a query Q, its similarity score $(s(Q, P_i))$ with an object proposal P_i is defined using the normalized histogram intersection $NHI(.)$ and computed as:

$$s(Q, P_i) = \frac{\sum_{j\in\mathcal{C}_i} NHI(h_Q, h_j)}{|\mathcal{C}_i|} \tag{1}$$

where $\mathcal{C}_i = \{j : \frac{\|(\mathcal{P}_i \cap \mathcal{P}_j)\|}{\|(\mathcal{P}_i)\|} > \tau\}$ and $|.|$ represents the cardinality of a set. In our experiment, we chose $\tau = 0.8$. As shown in [8] that such a cumulative voting strategy satisfies an asymptotic property and thereby ensures convergence. However, unlike [8], as illustrated in the step A ('Matching') of Figure 1, we use this coarse level similarity score only to extract some initial set of candidate matches, which is then used as an input to a more rigorous search. Unlike various sized random patches used in [8], the contour-based object proposals are more intuitive ensuring a semantically more meaningful structure of each EdgeBoW.

As such, this structural information implicitly captured within an EdgeBoW can be maximally exploited through a geometric verification (step B 'Validation' in Figure 1) for a more detailed validation. Therefore, a small set of top-K (we use $K = 100$) ranked retrievals obtained using the initial histogram-based matching score defined in equation (1), is then validated using second nearest neighbor test. The RANSAC inspired geometric verification re-ranks the matches in terms of a sorted list $\{P_i, s^Q(P_i)\}$, where $s^Q(P_i)$ based on the number of inlier matches $(s^Q(P_i))$ between the query Q and the ith proposal P_i. However, the geometric verification being time consuming prohibits its usability for validating a larger set of matches. Given this initial set of candidate matched proposals, we therefore propose a more principled approach for eliminating outliers, followed by a query expansion scheme to improve the localization performance.

3. SHORT-LISTING AND QUERY EXPANSION

A maximal-clique based graph search approach is proposed with an aim to identify a complete set of relevant proposals from the database, while minimizing the outliers at the same time.

3.1 Graph of Database Object Proposals

Given an indexed database $\{P_i\}$ of proposals, the k -neighborhood of P_i is defined as N_k^i, which is the set of all those images that are the top-k retrieved candidates using P_i as the query to the method proposed in Section 2.3. In order to exploit the mutual similarity between two images, the reciprocal neighborhood relation for P_i and P_j is defined as the Jaccard similaity coefficient:

$$R_k(P_i, P_j) = \frac{|N_k^i \cap N_k^j|}{|N_k^i \cup N_k^j|} \tag{2}$$

Given a suitable choice of k, the entire database $\mathcal{D}$ of $M \times N$ proposals can then be represented in terms of a database graph $G_\mathcal{D} = (\mathcal{V}_\mathcal{D}, E_\mathcal{D}, w_\mathcal{D})$, where each node represents a proposal in the database. Two proposals (P_i and P_j) are connected with an edge $(i, j) \in E_\mathcal{D}$ if they are reciprocal neighbors (i.e. $R_k(P_i, P_j) \neq 0$) to each other and the corresponding edge-weight $w_\mathcal{D}(i, j)$ is defined using its reciprocal neighborhood relation $R_k(P_i, P_j)$ defined as in equation (2).

The mutual similarity of the entire database $\mathcal{D}$ of $M \times N$ proposals can thus be represented in terms of an adjacency matrix, denoted as Database Adjacency Matrix, which can be computed a-priori. The choice of k is experimentally fixed to $k = \frac{K}{2}$.

3.2 Short-Listing Better Matched Proposals

Given a query Q, the set of initial top-K retrieved proposals can now be represented in terms of a query adaptive graph $G_Q = (\mathcal{V}_Q \cup \{Q\}, C_Q \cup e_Q, W_Q)$, where each $v \in \mathcal{V}_Q (\subseteq \mathcal{V}_\mathcal{D})$ represents one of the top-K retrievals using Q as a query. Therefore $\|\mathcal{V}_Q\| = K$. For any $v_i, v_j \in \mathcal{V}_Q$, $C_Q(i, j) = C_D(i, j)$. e_Q represents the set of unit-weight edges connecting the node Q to its top K similar proposals in the database, i.e. $\forall v_i \in \mathcal{V}_Q, C_Q(Q, i) = 1$ and $W_Q(Q, i) = 1$.

Each edge-weight between P_i and P_j in G_Q is computed as:

$$W_Q(i,j) = \begin{cases} (1 - O(i,j)) \times \frac{(\delta_Q^i, \delta_Q^j)}{2} \times R_k(P_i, P_j) & \text{if } P_i,\ P_j \text{ are from same image} \\ \frac{(\delta_Q^i, \delta_Q^j)}{2} \times R_k(P_i, P_j) & \text{otherwise} \end{cases} \tag{3}$$

where, $O(i, j)$ is the overlap-ratio between the proposals P_i and P_j originated from a same underlying image. δ_Q^i represents the shortest distance from Q to P_i in G_Q. In order to reduce the amount of redundancy among the top retrieved proposals (originating from the same underlying image), the edge-weight between them is penalized by a term inversely proportional to the amount of overlap. Given this graph structure, BronKerbosch algorithm is used to find the set of all maximally edge-weighted cliques R_Q. By maximally weighted cliques, we mean to identify those cliques within G_Q, which attain the maximum cumulative edge-weights.

3.3 Query Expansion

While the goal is to identify the best matched proposals to the query Q, usually there are multiple overlapped proposals originating from an image. The process described so far, ensures to identify R_Q as a set of good matches to Q. But, there is no assurance that each P appearing in R_Q will always be the best localization achievable from its parent image. This motivates us to expand each such P from the collection of all overlapped proposals to pick the best.

Now, given each $P \in R_Q$ originated from an underlying image I, the query expansion process follows a similar graph-based approach described in Section 3.2 by choosing the corresponding image specific similarity subgraph $G_I = (\mathcal{V}_I, C_I, w_I)$ of $G_\mathcal{D}$ such that each $v \in \mathcal{V}_I (\subseteq \mathcal{V}_\mathcal{D})$ represents on proposal from I. Hence, $\|\mathcal{V}_I\| = N$. For any $v_i, v_j \in \mathcal{V}_I$, $C_I(i, j) = C_\mathcal{D}(i, j)$ and $W_I(i, j) = W_\mathcal{D}(i, j)$.

The utility measure for each node $v_i \in V_I$ representing a proposal P_i is defined as:

$$C_i^I = \Big(1 - \frac{d(P, P_i)}{N_I}\Big) \times s(P, P_i) \tag{4}$$

where, $d(P, P_i)$ represents the Euclidean distance between the centroids of the proposals P and P_i. N_I represents the size of the image diagonal for I. A small set of good matches for P identified using the maximally node-weighted clique from each G_I, is augmented to R_Q to provide an expanded representation of P.

In order to minimize the number of outliers in the expanded list of retrievals, the newest entries in the expanded set R_Q is further validated using geometric verification. The entire re-ranked list R_Q is finally short-listed to retrieve the most similar proposals.

4. EXPERIMENTS

The proposed method for image search using EdgeBoW is evaluated and compared against multiple state-of-the art retrieval algorithms [8, 9, 10, 11, 12] in both recognition and retrieval scenario. The popular datasets like Belgalogo [13], Flickr27 [12] and Tobacco-800 are used as the testbed. Some sample results from Belgalogo, Flickr27 and Tobacco-800 [14] dataset are shown in the first, second and third row of Figure 2 respectively.

Given the 10000 entries of Belgalogo, 100 top-scoring proposals from each image are re-sized with a maximum value of height and width equal to 200 pixels. Nearly 20 million random EdgeWords are quantized into a large vocabulary of size 0.3M. The retrieval performance is evaluated by mean average precision (mAP), evaluated for all the queries in each class. As seen from the results in Table 1, the interest point based detectors ([1], [15]) often fail to represent smooth objects like 'Adidas', 'Nike'. Given the large intra-class variability observed in thousands of logo classes, methods (Yang & Bansal [10]) relying on color information may not be very stable always. In contrast, with an average mAP 45.75, the shape aware EdgeBoW accompanied by the proposed graph-based search strategy is more powerful and has outperformed others in 5 out of the 9 logo classes.

FlickrLogos-27 has been used to evaluate the generalization capability of our method in a recognition scenario. In an identical experimental protocol as in [12, 13], "training images" are used as reference logos per category. Each query is assigned the label corresponding to the reference image that

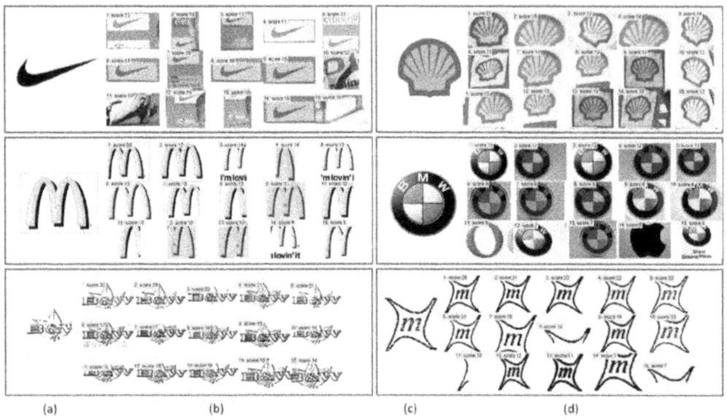

Figure 2: Some results of retrievals on Belgalogo dataset (First row), Flickr27 dataset (second row) and Tobacco-800 dataset (third row). Logos in (a) and (c) are taken as queries to obtain the results (top 15 retrieved object proposals) in (b) and (d) respectively.

Table 1: Performance of the proposed method with Generic Search by Tao et al. [1], RVP [8], ESR [9], the multi-feature fusion based logo retrieval model by Yang & Bansal [10], and the baseline approach [15] on the Belgalogo dataset using mAP-based measure. The performance rate for ESR was obtained from Jiang et al. [8]

Logo Class	[1]	[8]	[9]	[10]	[15]	Proposed Method
Adidas	15.4	-	-	-	7.8	**54.09**
Base	4.33	20.8	17.9	**52.4**	38.9	41.9
Bouigues	18.2	-	-	-	18.6	**65.7**
Dexia	20.6	24.1	11.7	24.1	29.3	**37.5**
Kia	56.8	50.6	49.7	41.2	**61.3**	46.7
Marcedes	10.7	21.5	18.0	11.0	18.5	**25.21**
Nike	10.2	-	-	-	1.4	**25.03**
President	**96.3**	67.5	44.6	76.4	64.3	71.2
Quick	**56.3**	-	-	-	39.0	44.5
Average	32.09	36.9	28.38	41.02	31.01	**45.75**

maximizes the similarity score. Table 2 shows the result.

Table 2: Performance of the proposed method with standard baseline Bag-of-Words [12], msDT [12] and CDS [13] on the Flickr-27 dataset using accuracy measure.

Images per class	[12]	[12]	[13]	Proposed Method
5	0.56	0.54	0.66	**0.68**
10	0.56	0.54	0.68	**0.81**
30	0.52	0.52	0.72	**0.81**

EdgeBoW is also evaluated in terms of its repeatability against SIFT. We follow the protocol provided by Lowe [7] and find that EdgeBoW has significantly more (around 60% on average) inlier correspondences throughout the view angle range $[0°, 60°]$. Although in terms of repeatability, SIFT is best for the affine distortion of angles upto $40°$, EdgeBoW dominates SIFT repeatability for larger tilts like $60°$.

The result using the mean average precision (mAP), averaged over queries across all 35 logo classes of the poor quality document images from UMD Tobacco-800 dataset is shown in Table 3. The significant performance improvement is attributed to the dense point-based feature-extraction stage with EdgeBoW, followed by an objectively defined short-list

Table 3: Performance of the proposed method with shape context based descriptor [16], SURF feature based method [17] and LSH [18] on the Tobacco-800 dataset using mAP.

	[16]	LSH [18]	[17]	proposed method
mAP	82.6	81.71	45	**92.69**

and expand scheme.

5. CONCLUSION

This work introduces a novel strategy for retrieving logos in a clutter intensive gray level as well as poor quality binary images in an integrated framework. EdgeBoW has worked well in such scenarios. The proposed graph-based search strategy can effectively identify the matched image regions, while ensuring a critical check on the number of outliers more accurately. Further extensions would include the application of this method to logo retrieval in videos and also investigating (and extending if required) the framework for non-logo generic objects.

6. ACKNOWLEDGMENTS

This research was carried out at the Rapid-Rich Object Search (ROSE) Lab at the Nanyang Technological University, Singapore. The ROSE Lab is supported by the National Research Foundation, Singapore, under its Interactive Digital Media (IDM) Strategic Research Programme.

7. REFERENCES

[1] R. Tao, E. Gavves, C. Snoek, and A. Smeulders, "Locality in generic instance search from one example," in *Proceedings of the Computer Vision and Pattern Recognition*, 2014.

[2] Y. Zhang, Z. Jia, and T. Chen, "Image retrieval with geometry-preserving visual phrases," in *Proceedings of the Computer Vision and Pattern Recognition*, 2011.

[3] J. Meng, J. Yuan, Y. Jiang, N. Narasimhan, V. Vasudevan, and Y. Wu, "Interactive visual object search through mutual information maximization," in *Proceedings of the ACM international conference on Multimedia*, 2010.

[4] Y. Jiang, J. Meng, and J. Yuan, "Grid-based local feature bundling for efficient object search and localization," in *IEEE Conference on Image Processing*, 2011.

[5] C. L. Zitnick and P. Dollár, "Edge boxes: Locating object proposals from edges," in *Proceedings of the European Conference on Computer Vision*, 2014.

[6] P. Dollár and C. L. Zitnick, "Structured forests for fast edge detection," in *Proceedings of the International Conference on Computer Vision*, 2013.

[7] D. G. Lowe, "Distinctive image features from scale-invariant keypoints," *International Journal of Computer Vision*, vol. 60, pp. 91–110, 2004.

[8] Y. Jiang, J. Meng, and J. Yuan, "Randomized visual phrases for object search," in *Proceedings of the Computer Vision and Pattern Recognition*, 2012.

[9] C. Lampert, "Detecting objects in large image collections and videos by efficient subimage retrieval," in *Proceedings of the International Conference on Computer Vision*, 2009.

[10] F. Yang and M. Bansal, "Feature fusion by similarity regression for logo retrieval," in *Winter Conference on Applications of Computer Vision*, 2015.

[11] H. Sahbi, L. Ballan, G. Serra, and A. Del Bimbo, "Context-dependent logo matching and recognition," *IEEE Transactions on Image Processing*, vol. 22, pp. 1018–1031, 2013.

[12] Y. Kalantidis, L. G. Pueyo, M. Trevisiol, R. van Zwol, and Y. Avrithis, "Scalable triangulation-based logo recognition," in *International Conference on Multimedia Retrieval*, 2011.

[13] P. Letessier, O. Buisson, and A. Joly, "Scalable mining of small visual objects," in *Proceedings of the ACM international conference on Multimedia*, 2012.

[14] G. Zhu and D. Doermann, "Automatic document logo detection," in *International Conference on Document Analysis and Recognition*, 2007.

[15] A. Joly and O. Buisson, "Logo retrieval with a contrario visual query expansion," in *Proceedings of the ACM International Conference on Multimedia*, 2009.

[16] G. Zhu and D. Doermann, "Logo matching for document image retrieval," in *International Conference on Document Analysis and Recognition (ICDAR 2009)*, 2009.

[17] Rajiv Jain and David Doermann, "Logo retrieval in document images," in *Document Analysis Systems*, 2012.

[18] M. Rusiñol and J. Lladós, "Efficient logo retrieval through hashing shape context descriptors," in *International Workshop on Document Analysis Systems*, pp. 215–222, 2010.

Hyperspectral Image Classification with Convolutional Neural Networks

Viktor Slavkovikj[1], Steven Verstockt[1], Wesley De Neve[1,2],
Sofie Van Hoecke[1], and Rik Van de Walle[1]

[1]Multimedia Lab, Department of Electronics and Information Systems, Ghent University-iMinds
B-9050 Ledeberg-Ghent, Belgium

[2]Image and Video Systems Lab, Korea Advanced Institute of Science and Technology (KAIST)
Yuseong-gu, Daejeon, 305-732, Republic of Korea

{viktor.slavkovikj, steven.verstockt, wesley.deneve, sofie.vanhoecke, rik.vandewalle}@ugent.be

ABSTRACT

Hyperspectral image (HSI) classification is one of the most widely used methods for scene analysis from hyperspectral imagery. In the past, many different engineered features have been proposed for the HSI classification problem. In this paper, however, we propose a feature learning approach for hyperspectral image classification based on convolutional neural networks (CNNs). The proposed CNN model is able to learn structured features, roughly resembling different spectral band-pass filters, directly from the hyperspectral input data. Our experimental results, conducted on a commonly-used remote sensing hyperspectral dataset, show that the proposed method provides classification results that are among the state-of-the-art, without using any prior knowledge or engineered features.

Categories and Subject Descriptors

I.5.1 [**Pattern Recognition**]: Models—*neural nets*; I.5.4 [**Pattern Recognition**]: Applications—*computer vision*; I.4.8 [**Image Processing and Computer Vision**]: Scene Analysis

Keywords

Classification, convolutional neural networks, deep learning, hyperspectral imaging

1. INTRODUCTION

Recent developments of imaging spectroscopy sensors have enabled acquisition of hyperspectral images with a high spatial resolution, a characteristic which was previously exclusive to standard electrooptical systems. However, unlike the standard color pictures, images acquired with hyperspectral sensors contain much higher spectral resolution. This is advantageous for image analysis, because each hyperspectral pixel comprises of a large number (in the order of hundreds) of measurements of the electromagnetic spectrum and carries more information as compared to color pixels, which provide data only from the visible range of the spectrum. As a result, hyperspectral image analysis has found numerous biomedical, forensic, and remote sensing applications [18, 5, 21].

One of the principal techniques in hyperspectral image analysis is image classification, where a label is assigned to each pixel based on its characteristics. Inference of class labels from hyperspectral data is challenging, however, since classification methods are affected by the curse of dimensionality (i.e., the Hughes effect[12]). That is, the classification accuracy is poor as the number of training samples required to populate the high-dimensional spectral space is limited. Therefore, many different feature extraction methods (see Section 2) have been proposed to tackle the classification problem in hyperspectral images. The goal of feature extraction is to reduce the dimensionality of the hyperspectral data while preserving as much of the discriminative information as possible, so that in a later stage a classifier can be trained on the extracted features. Since it is difficult to discern potentially relevant features from hyperspectral data, we approach hyperspectral image classification as an end-to-end learning [15, 25] task, where the assignment of class labels from hyperspectral input pixels is a single stage learning process, in which the intermediate feature representations are also learned. The contributions of our paper are twofold:

- We propose convolutional neural networks for hyperspectral image classification.
- We investigate hyperspectral data augmentation as a way of mitigating the problem of limited training samples in hyperspectral image classification.

The remainder of this paper is organized as follows. We discuss related work in hyperspectral image classification in Section 2. In Section 3, we present the architecture of the convolutional neural network that was used as basis for our

MM'15, October 26–30, 2015, Brisbane, Australia.
© 2015 ACM. ISBN 978-1-4503-3459-4/15/10 ...$15.00.
DOI: http://dx.doi.org/10.1145/2733373.2806306.

experiments. Section 4 describes hyperspectral data augmentation for alleviating the limited training samples problem. In Section 5, we report classification results obtained by the proposed method on a hyperspectral image dataset. Section 6 concludes the paper.

2. RELATED WORK

In the past, many different feature extraction and classification methods have been proposed for hyperspectral images. Some of the well-established feature extraction approaches are based on dimensionality reduction methods, such as principal component analysis (PCA) [11], or independent component analysis (ICA) [24]. These methods are aimed at projecting the hyperspectral data to a subspace, in which class separation is performed more effectively. Similarly, to be able to calculate coordinates of data in a lower-dimensional space, manifold learning methods [8, 7] try to estimate the intrinsic geometry of the manifold embedded in the high-dimensional hyperspectral data space. Discriminant analysis methods [1, 3] have been used to learn a projection matrix in order to maximize a separability criterion of the projected data. Morphological features [2], on the other hand, were introduced to take advantage of structural information present in the images. They have been successfully combined with support vector machines [6], which are known for their good generalization properties for high-dimensional data with lower effective dimensionality [19].

Recently, statistical learning models, such as neural networks, have also been investigated for the purpose of hyperspectral image classification. For instance, Li et al. [17] have proposed a deep belief network (DBN) approach for classification of hyperspectral images. The model is a stack of restricted Boltzmann machines, which are trained by greedy layer-wise unsupervised learning [9]. However, by reducing the data to the first three PCA components, the spectral characteristics of the images have not been used in a principal manner by the DBN model. Our proposed approach, by contrast, fully exploits the available spectral information in a hyperspectral image.

3. CNN ARCHITECTURE

Deep CNNs have been successfully applied in solving challenging tasks, such as image classification [13], speech recognition [16], music information retrieval [4], and text recognition [25]. However, to our knowledge, CNN models have not been studied in literature for the purpose of hyperspectral image classification.

Due to network generalization issues [10], deep CNNs for image classification tasks require a large number of images to prevent overfitting, and thus appear inadequate for the HSI classification problem, where a dataset typically consists of a single capture of a scene. Furthermore, the large number of bands in hyperspectral images pose a computational challenge for a straightforward application of a CNN model.

We propose a CNN architecture which integrates both spatial and spectral information for simultaneous spatial-spectral classification of hyperspectral images. The proposed architecture is visualized in Figure 1. The input to the network consists of the eight-connected neighborhood of a hyperspectral pixel, to account for the spatial information context. In order to exploit the original spectral information, all convolutional operations are performed across the spectral bands. The network consists of 5 layers: three convolutional layers with width 16, followed by two fully connected layers with 800 units each. Note that the size of the filters in the first convolutional layer is 9×16, where the first dimension accounts for the total number of pixels in the spatial neighborhood window of the input pixel, and the second dimension is the width of the filter. This allows for simultaneous learning from both the spatial and spectral domain.

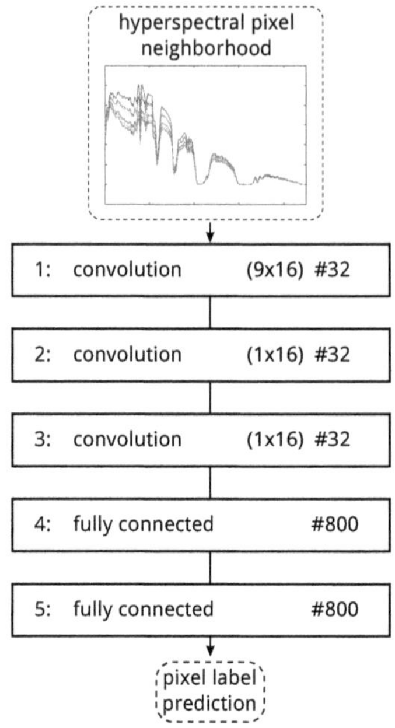

Figure 1: Diagram of the proposed convolutional neural network architecture for hyperspectral image classification. The size of the filters in the convolutional layers are indicated as $(h \times w)$, and # denotes the number of convolutional filters, as well as the number of hidden units in the fully connected layers.

In order to obtain the CNN architecture from Figure 1, we experimented with the number of layers, the number of hidden units in the fully connected layers, and the number and size of the filters in the convolutional layers. In addition, we tested several modifications of the original network. Namely, we experimented with max-pooling layers after the convolutional layers, and also with varying the stride of the convolutions. This worsened the classification results, which is indicative of non-stationarity of statistics across spectral bands. Testing the hyperbolic tangent activation function produced slightly better results than rectified linear units [20] activation. As a result, we used hyperbolic tangent activations in all layers exclusive of the last layer, where the softmax function was used. We also attempted dropout regularization [22] in the fully connected layers, however, this did not improve the classification results.

We trained the network using minibatch gradient descent and momentum [23], and we set the size of the minibatches to 50 samples. We evaluated the model on a held out validation set during training, and we report results on a separate test set for the model that achieved the best results on the validation set.

4. DATA AUGMENTATION

Identifying the classes of pixels from hyperspectral images to produce labeled training data is a manual task, which is expensive and time consuming. Therefore, available training samples for HSI classification are scarce. To try to alleviate this problem, we experimented with simple augmentation for hyperspectral data. For each class in the hyperspectral image dataset, we calculate the per-spectral-band standard deviation of the samples in the training set which belong to the class. Afterwards, we use the calculated vector of standard deviations σ as a parameter to a zero mean multivariate normal distribution $\mathcal{N}(0, \alpha\mathbf{\Sigma})$, where α is a scale factor, and $\mathbf{\Sigma}$ is a diagonal matrix containing σ along the main diagonal entries. Finally, the augmented samples for the class are generated by adding noise sampled from the distribution $\mathcal{N}$ to the original samples. We tried several values for the scaling factor in the set $\{1, 0.5, 0.33, 0.25, 0.125\}$, and fixed $\alpha = 0.25$ for the experiments. The goal of the proposed hyperspectral data augmentation is to prevent overfitting in cases where a low number of samples are used to train the network.

5. EXPERIMENTAL RESULTS

We tested our method on the commonly-used Indian Pines hyperspectral image dataset [14]. This dataset was acquired in June 1992 by NASA's Airborne Visible/Infrared Imaging Spectrometer (AVIRIS). The Indian Pines scene is a mixed forest and agricultural site in Northwest Indiana, captured at about 20 km altitude by the AVIRIS sensor. The hyperspectral image of the scene consists of 220 bands in the spectral range from 0.4 μm to 2.5 μm, with a spectral resolution of 10 nm. The whole scene consists of 145 $\times$ 145 pixels. There are in total 10,366 labeled samples. With a moderate geometrical resolution of 20 m per pixel, and 16 land cover classes, this dataset poses a challenging classification problem due to the unbalanced number of samples per class, and high inter-class similarity of samples in the dataset.

Table 1: AVIRIS Indian Pines dataset and per class training sets and corresponding test sets.

Class		Train set			Test set		
#	Name	5%	10%	20%	5%	10%	20%
1	Alfalfa	3	6	11	25	24	21
2	Corn-notil	72	144	287	681	645	573
3	Corn-min	42	84	167	396	375	333
4	Corn	12	24	47	111	105	93
5	Grass-pasture	25	50	100	236	223	198
6	Grass-trees	38	75	150	354	336	298
7	Grass-pasture-mowed	2	3	6	12	11	10
8	Hay-windrowed	25	49	98	232	220	195
9	Oats	1	2	4	9	9	8
10	Soybeans-notil	49	97	194	459	435	387
11	Soybeans-min	124	247	494	1,172	1,110	987
12	Soybeans-clean	31	62	123	291	276	245
13	Wheat	11	22	43	100	95	84
14	Woods	65	130	259	614	582	517
15	Bldg-grass-trees	19	38	76	180	171	152
16	Stone-steel-towers	5	10	19	45	42	38
Total		524	1,043	2,078	4,917	4,659	4,139

For our experiments, we evaluated the classification accuracy of the method using a balanced training set per class, with low number of training samples. We trained the network with 5%, 10%, and 20% of randomly selected labeled samples per class, and equally divided the remaining labeled samples into separate validation and test sets. In each case, we repeated the experiment with and without hyperspectral data augmentation.

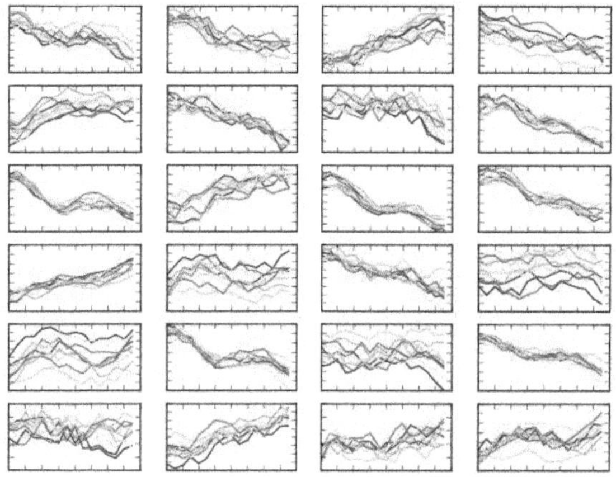

Figure 2: A subset of filters learned in the first convolutional layer of the network. Each subplot represents a (9×16) filter.

Table 2: Classification results for the Indian Pines image on the test sets.

Indian Pines		Test set		
		5%	10%	20%
Augmented	OCA(%)	86.54 ± 0.30	92.70 ± 1.00	96.58 ± 0.55
	F1 score	0.86 ± 0.00	0.93 ± 0.01	0.97 ± 0.01
Non-augment.	OCA (%)	85.46 ± 1.73	92.76 ± 0.93	96.54 ± 0.47
	F1 score	0.85 ± 0.02	0.93 ± 0.01	0.96 ± 0.00

The achieved classification results for each of the experiments are shown in Table 2. We performed 5 Monte Carlo runs, where for each run we selected a training set of 5%, 10%, and 20% of the labeled samples, as explained above, to train our model. In the cases with augmentation, we found 3 fold (per class) augmentation of the training data to give the best results. We report the average and standard error of the 5 Monte Carlo runs in terms of the overall classification accuracy (OCA), i.e., the number of correctly classified samples from the total number of samples in the test set, and the F1 score, which is weighted so that it accounts for the imbalance of the classes. From the results in Table 2, it can be seen that only when using a very low number of augmented labeled samples for training (5%), there is improvement in the classification scores over the non-augmented counterpart. However, we have observed that in all cases augmentation reduced the number of training iterations significantly, as compared with training with the corresponding non-augmented data.

We have visualized some of the learned filters from the first convolutional layer of the network in Figure 2. From the visualization, it is clear that the learned filters have a structured shape, and that some of the filters roughly resemble different spectral band-pass filters.

6. CONCLUSIONS

Due to the inherent nature of hyperspectral data, discernment of good features for hyperspectral image classification is difficult. Therefore, in this paper, we have presented a new approach towards hyperspectral image classification based on deep convolutional neural networks. To evaluate the effectiveness of the method, we performed experiments on a commonly-used hyperspectral image dataset. Our experimental results have shown that the neural network model can learn structured features resembling different spectral band-pass filters directly from the input data. These features prove useful for hyperspectral image classification, which makes end-to-end learning applicable to hyperspectral scene understanding.

7. ACKNOWLEDGMENTS

The research activities as described in this paper were funded by Ghent University and the Interdisciplinary Research Institute iMinds.

8. REFERENCES

[1] T. V. Bandos, L. Bruzzone, and G. Camps-Valls. Classification of hyperspectral images with regularized linear discriminant analysis. *IEEE Transactions on Geoscience and Remote Sensing*, 47(3):862–873, 2009.

[2] J. A. Benediktsson, J. A. Palmason, and J. R. Sveinsson. Classification of hyperspectral data from urban areas based on extended morphological profiles. *IEEE Transactions on Geoscience and Remote Sensing*, 43(3):480–491, 2005.

[3] D. Cai, X. He, and J. Han. Semi-supervised discriminant analysis. In *Proceedings of the International Conference on Computer Vision (ICCV)*, pages 1–7, Oct 2007.

[4] S. Dieleman and B. Schrauwen. End-to-end learning for music audio. In *Acoustics, Speech and Signal Processing (ICASSP), 2014 IEEE International Conference on*, pages 6964–6968, May 2014.

[5] G. Edelman, E. Gaston, T. van Leeuwen, P. Cullen, and M. Aalders. Hyperspectral imaging for non-contact analysis of forensic traces. *Forensic Science International*, 223(1-3):28–39, 2012.

[6] M. Fauvel, J. A. Benediktsson, J. Chanussot, and J. R. Sveinsson. Spectral and spatial classification of hyperspectral data using SVMs and morphological profiles. *IEEE Transactions on Geoscience and Remote Sensing*, 46(11):3804–3814, 2008.

[7] X. He, D. Cai, S. Yan, and H.-J. Zhang. Neighborhood preserving embedding. In *Proceedings of the International Conference on Computer Vision (ICCV)*, volume 2, pages 1208–1213, Oct 2005.

[8] X. He and P. Niyogi. Locality preserving projections. In *NIPS*, pages 153–160. MIT Press, 2004.

[9] G. E. Hinton, S. Osindero, and Y.-W. Teh. A fast learning algorithm for deep belief nets. *Neural Computation*, 18(7):1527–1554, July 2006.

[10] G. E. Hinton, N. Srivastava, A. Krizhevsky, I. Sutskever, and R. Salakhutdinov. Improving neural networks by preventing co-adaptation of feature detectors. *CoRR*, abs/1207.0580, 2012.

[11] H. Hotelling. Analysis of a complex of statistical variables into principal components. *Journal of Educational Psychology*, 24:417–441, 1933.

[12] G. Hughes. On the mean accuracy of statistical pattern recognizers. *IEEE Transactions on Information Theory*, 14(1):55–63, Jan 1968.

[13] A. Krizhevsky, I. Sutskever, and G. E. Hinton. Imagenet classification with deep convolutional neural networks. In *Advances in Neural Information Processing Systems 25*, pages 1097–1105. 2012.

[14] D. A. Landgrebe. *Signal theory methods in multispectral remote sensing*. Wiley series in remote sensing. Wiley, Hoboken, N.J., Chichester, 2003.

[15] Y. Lecun, U. Muller, J. Ben, E. Cosatto, and B. Flepp. Off-road obstacle avoidance through end-to-end learning. In *Advances in Neural Information Processing Systems 18*, pages 739–746, Cambridge, MA, 2006.

[16] H. Lee, P. Pham, Y. Largman, and A. Y. Ng. Unsupervised feature learning for audio classification using convolutional deep belief networks. In *Advances in Neural Information Processing Systems 22*, pages 1096–1104. 2009.

[17] T. Li, J. Zhang, and Y. Zhang. Classification of hyperspectral image based on deep belief networks. In *Image Processing (ICIP), 2014 IEEE International Conference on*, pages 5132–5136, Oct 2014.

[18] G. Lu and B. Fei. Medical hyperspectral imaging: a review. *Journal of Biomedical Optics*, 19(1):010901, 2014.

[19] F. Melgani and L. Bruzzone. Classification of hyperspectral remote sensing images with support vector machines. *IEEE Transactions on Geoscience and Remote Sensing*, 42(8):1778–1790, Aug 2004.

[20] V. Nair and G. E. Hinton. Rectified linear units improve restricted boltzmann machines. In *Proceedings of the 27th International Conference on Machine Learning (ICML-10), June 21-24, 2010, Haifa, Israel*, pages 807–814, 2010.

[21] A. Plaza, J. A. Benediktsson, J. W. Boardman, J. Brazile, L. Bruzzone, G. Camps-Valls, J. Chanussot, M. Fauvel, P. Gamba, A. Gualtieri, M. Marconcini, J. C. Tilton, and G. Trianni. Recent advances in techniques for hyperspectral image processing. *Remote Sensing of Environment*, 113, Supplement 1(0):S110–S122, 2009.

[22] N. Srivastava, G. Hinton, A. Krizhevsky, I. Sutskever, and R. Salakhutdinov. Dropout: A simple way to prevent neural networks from overfitting. *J. Mach. Learn. Res.*, 15(1):1929–1958, Jan. 2014.

[23] I. Sutskever, J. Martens, G. E. Dahl, and G. E. Hinton. On the importance of initialization and momentum in deep learning. In *Proceedings of the 30th International Conference on Machine Learning (ICML-13)*, volume 28, pages 1139–1147, May 2013.

[24] J. Wang and C.-I. Chang. Independent component analysis-based dimensionality reduction with applications in hyperspectral image analysis. *IEEE Transactions on Geoscience and Remote Sensing*, 44(6):1586–1600, 2006.

[25] T. Wang, D. Wu, A. Coates, and A. Ng. End-to-end text recognition with convolutional neural networks. In *Pattern Recognition (ICPR), 2012 21st International Conference on*, pages 3304–3308, Nov 2012.

Online Object Tracking Based on CNN with Metropolis-Hasting Re-Sampling

Xiangzeng Zhou and Lei Xie*
School of Computer Science
Northwestern Polythechnical University
Xi'an, P. R. China
xenuts@gmail.com, lxie@nwpu.edu.cn

Peng Zhang* and Yanning Zhang
School of Computer Science
Northwestern Polythechnical University
Xi'an, P. R. China
{zh0036ng, ynzhang}@nwpu.edu.cn

ABSTRACT

Tracking-by-learning strategies have been effective in solving many challenging problems in visual tracking, in which the learning sample generation and labeling play important roles for final performance. Since the concern of deep learning based approaches has shown an impressive performance in different vision tasks, how to properly apply the learning model, such as CNN, to an online tracking framework is still challenging. In this paper, to overcome the overfitting problem caused by straight-forward incorporation, we propose an online tracking framework by constructing a CNN based adaptive appearance model to generate more reliable training data over time. With a reformative Metropolis-Hastings re-sampling scheme to reshape particles for a better state posterior representation during online learning, the proposed tracking outperforms most of the state-of-art trackers on challenging benchmark video sequences.

Categories and Subject Descriptors

I.4.8 [**Image Processing and Computer Vision**]: Scene Analysis—*Tracking*

General Terms

Algorithm, Theory

Keywords

Object tracking, CNN, Metropolis-Hastings, Re-sampling

1. INTRODUCTION

Learning sample quality is an essential factor to robust online tracking, but this task is not easy because it is hard to manually intervene the sample generation and labeling when tracking is on-the-fly. Although different tracking strategies have tried various types of traditional models for sample generation[15], the descriptive capability of those online sample is still far from sufficient for object characteristic representation.

In order to exploit more descriptive training samples, nowadays, deep learning models, e.g. convolutional neural network (CNN) [16], have been successfully applied in a variety of audio and visual tasks such as speech recognition and image classification, and obtain a remarkable progress. But due to the requirement of a large number of training data and high computational cost, most of those studies approached their tasks with off-line learning process as presented in some recently proposed works [14, 11, 7]. Wang *et al.* [14] proposed an online tracking strategy based on a compact image representation learned from an off-line pre-trained deep neural network which requires large amounts of auxiliary images. Similarly, Hong *et al.* [7] carried out the learning of discriminative saliency using a CNN, but still demanded a pre-trained model. Different with [14] and [7], Li *et al.* [11] proposed a variation of CNN with truncated structural loss to construct an online tracker and showed promising performance. But it mainly focused on model reforming of CNN for online learning, and the sample generation problem is not addressed, which may lead to tracking failure in complicated scenarios. Thus, how to utilize the advantage of deep learning to generate more representative samples is a challenging problem in online tracking tasks, and this is also a motivation of this study.

Sample labeling is another challenge to properly utilize a CNN model as learning strategy for online tracking. This is because CNN is prone to overfitting to recent samples and is sensitive to mislabeled samples. Typically, a particle filter is used for efficiently conducting online object tracking by simulating object state's posterior with a finite set of weighted particles. However, it is difficult for the particles being used to carry out a self-repair without any prior knowledge when a specific error pattern arises. Such type of error may be caused by an incorrect object's interference due to dramatic appearance change or overfitting problem (e.g. CNN based appearance model). Therefore, an effective re-sampling process over particle filter may benefit the label assignment, providing more reliable labeled samples for the learning of CNN model. This is another motivation leading to this study.

In this work, we propose a robust online tracker by exploiting the strong learning capability of a CNN model with particle filtering framework. An overview of our tracking framework is shown in Fig. 1. The contributions of the proposed work are three folds. Firstly, we carry out an attempt by introducing a single convolutional neural network

*Corresponding author.

MM'15, October 26–30, 2015, Brisbane, Australia.
© 2015 ACM. ISBN 978-1-4503-3459-4/15/10 ...$15.00.
DOI: http://dx.doi.org/10.1145/2733373.2806307.

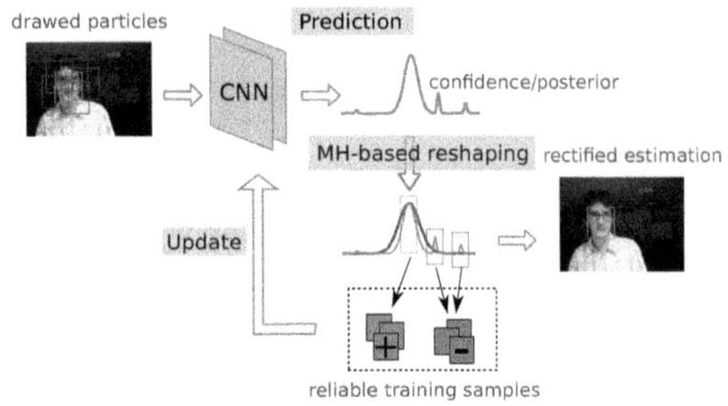

Figure 1: Our online tracking framework

for object appearance modeling and integrate it into particle filtering framework with online fashion. Secondly, a novel re-sampling scheme is proposed over particles based on the Metropolis-Hastings (MH) algorithm [5, 2] to obtain a set of more reliable positive and negative samples, which could conduct a more effective and robust training of CNN based appearance model. Thirdly, the proposed re-sampling method provides a way to apply a heuristic prior to reshape the drawn particles and gains a better object state posterior representation. Additionally, we apply an adaptive weighted approach with samples to feed CNN and a "lazy" training style is used.

The organization of the paper is as follows: Section 2 presents the single CNN architecture used in the proposed tracking framework. Section 3 and Section 4 elaborate our proposed Metropolis-Hastings based re-sampling method with an online robust tracking using CNN. Section 5 shows experimental demonstration and Section 6 draws conclusions.

2. APPEARANCE MODELING WITH CNN

In the proposed tracking framework (Fig. 1), we construct a single convolutional neural network (CNN) shown in Fig. 2, as an appearance model for object description, which consists of two convolutional layers with tanh as activation function and followed by max pooling operators. Then, there is a fully connected layer followed by a softmax classifier. The working mechanism of this model is: the input data is generated from gray-scale image and is locally normalized with $\sigma = 5$. Then, the image patches are normalized to size 40×40. The first convolution layer contains 10 kernels with size 3×3 followed by a max-pooling layer with size 2×2. The second convolution layer contains 20 kernels with size 3×3 as well as followed by a 2×2 max-pooling operation. The fully connected layer with size 500 is followed by a softmax classifier with cross-entropy loss function to produce confidence for each input patch.

The CNN is initially trained well in the first frame and is updated in a lazy manner only when the confidence of estimated object is lower than an empirical threshold $\mathcal{C} = 0.9$. In the updating phase, the training goal is to advance the confidence of each positive and negative sample above $\mathcal{C}$. Our CNN model allows to accept weighted training samples

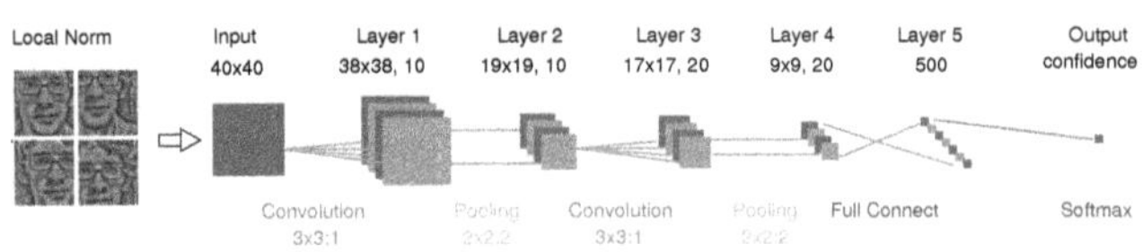

Figure 2: CNN architecture

as inputs. Inspired by the spirit of boosting, the weight of each sample is estimated according to the objective loss in former iteration. The process is beneficial to promote CNN's updating speed.

3. PARTICLE FILTERING WITH METROPOLIS-HASTINGS RE-SAMPLING

Particle filter has been widely used to conduct online tracking within a Bayesian framework of which a prediction of state $\mathbf{x}$ in time t is formulated as:

$$p(\mathbf{x}_t \mid \mathbf{y}_{1:t-1}) = \int p(\mathbf{x}_t \mid \mathbf{x}_{t-1}) p(\mathbf{x}_{t-1} \mid \mathbf{y}_{1:t-1}) d\mathbf{x}_{t-1}. \quad (1)$$

The key of particle filter is efficiently propagating the posterior $p(\mathbf{x}_t \mid \mathbf{y}_{1:t})$ using a finite set of N particles $\{\mathbf{x}_t^i\}$ attached with importance weights w_t^i that can be estimated as:

$$w_t^i = w_{t-1}^i \frac{p(\mathbf{y}_t \mid \mathbf{x}_t^i) \cdot p(\mathbf{x}_t^i \mid \mathbf{x}_{t-1}^i)}{q(\mathbf{x}_t \mid \mathbf{x}_{1:t-1}, \mathbf{y}_{1:t})}. \quad (2)$$

And importance distribution $q(\mathbf{x}_t \mid \mathbf{x}_{1:t-1}, \mathbf{y}_{1:t})$ is often simplified to $q(\mathbf{x}_t \mid \mathbf{x}_{t-1})$ with first-order Markov assumption.

Unfortunately, the particle filter framework does not supply a mechanism in nature to self-repair the mode drifting incurred by the accumulative error of observation model $p(\mathbf{y}_t \mid \mathbf{x}_t^i)$. The accumulative error is often caused by dramatic appearance change or the model's over-fitting problem. In practice, a heuristic assumption holds: the probability distribution of object's state should be a unimodal Gaussian distribution $\mathcal{P}(\mathbf{x} \mid \mathbf{y}) = \mathcal{N}(\mu, \sigma^2)$, of which we can take advantage to rectify the particles. Inspired by this, we propose a re-sampling method to reshape particles $\{w_t^i,\ \mathbf{x}_t^i\}$ using a variation of Metropolis-Hastings algorithm.

3.1 Reshape Particles by Metropolis-Hastings

The Metropolis-Hastings algorithm [5, 2] is a Markov chain Monte Carlo (MCMC) method for obtaining a sequence of random samples from a probability distribution for which direct sampling is difficult. A sketch of Metropolis-Hastings algorithm is shown in Algorithm 1.

Algorithm 1 Metropolis-Hastings Algorithm

1: Randomly choose a starting value $\mathbf{x}^0$.
2: At iteration m, draw a candidate $\hat{\mathbf{x}}$ from a proposal distribution $J(\hat{\mathbf{x}} \mid \mathbf{x}^{m-1})$.
3: Compute an acceptance ratio α (shown in Fig. 3).
4: Accept $\hat{\mathbf{x}}$ as $\mathbf{x}^m$ with a probability $\min(\alpha, 1)$, otherwise $\mathbf{x}^m = \mathbf{x}^{m-1}$.
5: Repeat step 2-4 until M samples are got.

The core step of the Metropolis-Hastings algorithm is to compute an *Acceptance Ratio* for m-th iteration as a fashion in Eq. 3.

$$\alpha = \frac{p(\hat{\mathbf{x}} \mid \mathbf{y}) \cdot J(\mathbf{x}^{m-1} \mid \hat{\mathbf{x}})}{p(\mathbf{x}^{m-1} \mid \mathbf{y}) \cdot J(\hat{\mathbf{x}} \mid \mathbf{x}^{m-1})} \quad (3)$$

In the m-th iteration, a sample candidate $\hat{\mathbf{x}}$ is generated by a proposal distribution $J(\hat{\mathbf{x}} \mid \mathbf{x}^{m-1})$. The sample candidate $\hat{\mathbf{x}}$ will be accepted as the m-th sample $\mathbf{x}^m$ with a probability $\min(\alpha, 1)$. In this work, the probability distribution we need to simulate is exactly the state posterior $p(\mathbf{x}_t \mid \mathbf{y}_{1:t})$.

For each time t, we conduct an M iterations Metropolis-Hastings sampling process over particles $\{w_t^i,\ \mathbf{x}_t^i\}$ by computing a new *Acceptance Ratio* as:

$$\alpha = \frac{\mathcal{P}(\hat{\mathbf{x}}_t \mid \mathbf{y}_{1:t}) \cdot J(\mathbf{x}_t^{m-1} \mid \hat{\mathbf{x}}_t)}{p(\mathbf{x}_t^{m-1} \mid \mathbf{y}_{1:t}) \cdot J(\hat{\mathbf{x}}_t \mid \mathbf{x}_t^{m-1})}, \quad (4)$$

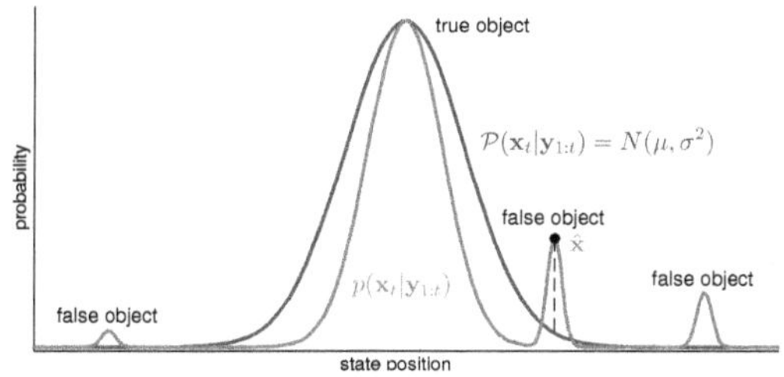

Figure 3: Reshaping posterior distribution

where $\mathcal{P}(\hat{\mathbf{x}}_t \mid \mathbf{y}_{1:t})$ is a Gaussian distribution that we want the particles to approach as far as possible, and $\hat{\mathbf{x}}_t$ is a sample candidate proposed by the proposal distribution $J(\hat{\mathbf{x}}_t \mid \mathbf{x}_t^{m-1})$ in time t. Fig. 3 shows us an illustration of this method in 2D space. For each sample candidate $\hat{\mathbf{x}}$, when it is situated in the neighborhood of the false object with a high probability, it will get a small acceptance ratio α. For another case, while a sample candidate is situated in the neighborhood of the true object, the value of α shall approach to 1, which means a high probability to be accepted.

Throughout this process, the higher the probability of particles belonging to a false object, the more heavily they will be penalized via acceptance ratio. The shape of rectified particles are more close to real posterior. Apart from this, the acceptance ratio α brings an extra profit. Particles with largest α are suggested as reliable positive samples, and those with lowest α then should be taken as negative samples which exactly identify some specific error patterns. Training samples obtained through this process put more focus on several notable error patterns and produce a more robust appearance model.

4. APPROXIMATE ESTIMATION

In the previous section, we present a Metropolis-Hastings based re-sampling method over particles to reshape a better posterior, and suggest a set of representative training samples at the same time. A remaining major problem is how to estimate the unknown target Gaussian distribution $\mathcal{P}(\mathbf{x} \mid \mathbf{y})$. In this section, we propose an approximate estimation algorithm, elaborated in Algorithm 2, to efficiently estimate the target distribution over time. We leave out the time subscript for the sake of brevity. At time t, Algorithm 2 is conducted over N particles $\{\mathbf{x}^i\}$ associated with confidence C^i estimated by a CNN based appearance model. $\mathcal{Q}$ is a First-Come-First-Served(FCFS) queue and F is a flag vector of length N, each of whose position is initialized as 0. This algorithm starts from an untagged particle $\hat{\mathbf{x}}$ with global maximum confidence and performs a top-down FCFS tagging process. In a ϵ-neighborhood of $\hat{\mathbf{x}}$, only particles with lower confidence C^k are accepted to put into queue $\mathcal{Q}$ and tagged with the same flag as $\hat{\mathbf{x}}$. Until the queue is empty, a segmentation of particles will be available by tracing the flag. The algorithm ends up with no more untagged particles left and K segments are eventually obtained. Please note that these segments may intersect with each other because no constraint of $F^k = 0$ is required in step 8. As shown in Fig. 4, a diagrammatic example of segmentation result is provided for better understanding. The right panel of Fig. 4 gives an insight on the result of segmentation from 3D viewpoint.

Algorithm 2 top-down Breadth-first Segmentation

1: **Init**: $\mathcal{Q} \leftarrow \emptyset$, $F^{1:N} \leftarrow 0$, $flag \leftarrow 1$, $K \leftarrow 1$
2: **while** $\exists F^i = 0$ **do**
3: $\quad \mathbf{x}^i \leftarrow \exists i, \forall j, C^i \geqslant C^j \wedge F^i = 0 \wedge F^j = 0$
4: $\quad F^i \leftarrow flag$
5: $\quad$ ENQUEUE($\mathcal{Q}$, $\mathbf{x}^i$)
6: $\quad$ **while** $\mathcal{Q} \neq \emptyset$ **do**
7: $\quad\quad \hat{\mathbf{x}} \leftarrow$ DEQUEUE($\mathcal{Q}$)
8: $\quad\quad \mathcal{X}_\epsilon = \{\mathbf{x}^k \mid \forall k, \|\hat{\mathbf{x}} - \mathbf{x}^k\|_2 \leq \epsilon \wedge C^k \leq \hat{C}\}$
9: $\quad\quad F_\epsilon \leftarrow flag$
10: $\quad\quad$ ENQUEUE($\mathcal{Q}$, $\mathcal{X}_\epsilon$)
11: $\quad$ **end while**
12: $\quad Seg_K = \{\mathbf{x}^k \mid \forall k, F^k = flag\}$
13: $\quad K \leftarrow K + 1$, $flag \leftarrow flag + 1$
14: **end while**

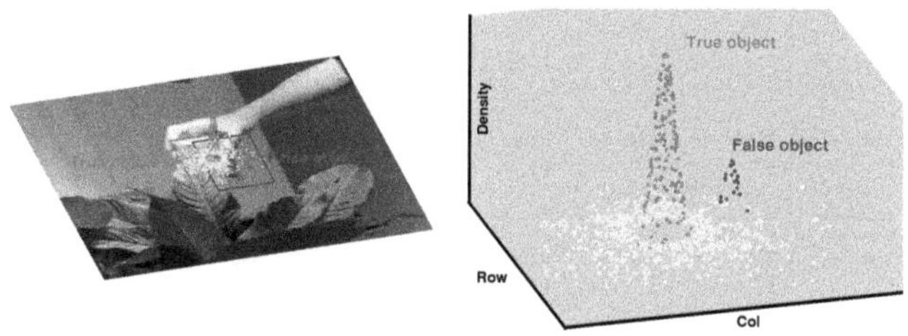

Figure 4: The top-down segmentation algorithm

Throughout this top-down segmentation process, we can easily achieve a rectified estimation of object's state in time t as:

$$\mathbf{x}_t^{est} = \arg\max_{\mathbf{x}^{k,i}} \max_{c^{k,i}} \{c^{k,i} \times Sup(Seg_k)\}, \ k \in [1, K] \tag{5}$$

where $Sup(Seg_k)$ is the size of support set of k-th segmentation. This estimation is more robust than a typical estimation method that selects the particle with highest confidence. After that, the support set of the selected segmentation can be utilized to estimate the target Gaussian distribution $\mathcal{P}(\mathbf{x} \mid \mathbf{y})$.

5. EXPERIMENTS

Experiment settings: We evaluate our proposed tracker with 20 video sequences from an online tracking benchmark [15] which covers most challenging tracking scenarios such as scale and illumination change, occlusion, fast movement, out of plane rotation and background clutters. We compare our method with 11 state-of-the-art tracking approaches: CSK [6], CT [17], CXT [3], IVT [13], LSK [12], MIL [1], SCM [18], Struck [4], TLD [8], VTD [9] and VTS [10]. The tracking performances are evaluated via average VOR (Pascal VOC overlap ratio) and average CLE (center location error) [15].

Comparison results: The elaborated quantitative results of VOR and CLE are shown in Table. 1, in which the Top-3 results are highlighted in red, blue and cyan, respectively. The overall satisfactory performance has confirmed that the proposed method can achieve more robust tracking in a variety of challenging scenarios with an average VOR of 95.67%. In addition, success-rate curves and precision curves are shown in Fig. 5 to demonstrate the general performance of all the tracking methods. We have also conducted the experiments based on CNN without Metropolis-Hastings (MH) re-sampling process and the obtained VOR has decreased to 66.47% in average, which demonstrated an essential role of the MH re-sampling in our tracking framework. The proposed work is mainly implemented by MATLAB, and the average speed is 2-3 fps without any code optimization.

Table 1: Comparison of 12 trackers on 20 video sequences. Upper panel: VOR, lower panel: CLE.

	Ours	CSK	CT	CXT	IVT	LSK	MIL	SCM	TLD	VTD	VTS	Struck
boy	99.3	84.2	68.8	49.7	32.6	*99.7*	38.5	43.9	93.5	78.6	79.6	*97.5*
car4	100	27.6	27.5	29.9	*100*	5.61	27.6	*97.3*	*78.1*	35.4	35.2	39.8
carDark	98.2	*99.2*	0.25	69.0	69.7	*100*	17.8	*99.7*	52.9	68.4	*100*	*100*
coke	85.9	*73.9*	9.28	59.1	13.1	16.2	11.7	33.7	28.9	13.7	14.4	*94.2*
crossing	100	31.7	*98.3*	34.2	24.2	11.7	*98.3*	*100*	51.7	41.7	40.0	*94.2*
david	92.4	23.6	42.7	83.4	79.4	58.6	22.9	*91.3*	*97.0*	67.7	73.0	23.6
deer	100	*100*	4.23	*91.5*	2.82	33.8	12.7	2.82	*73.2*	4.23	4.23	*100*
dudek	94.3	94.7	85.2	92.4	96.8	92.7	85.7	97.6	84.2	*100*	*99.6*	*98.0*
faceocc1	100	*100*	85.4	77.1	*97.5*	40.8	76.5	*100*	83.4	*92.5*	88.3	*100*
fish	100	4.20	88.9	*100*	*100*	33.2	38.7	86.3	*96.2*	64.3	*97.9*	*100*
girl	96.8	39.8	17.8	64.2	18.6	34.4	29.4	*88.2*	76.4	65.2	52.6	*98.0*
jumping	99.4	4.79	0.64	28.8	9.90	6.39	47.6	12.1	*84.7*	11.2	15.7	*79.9*
mhyang	100	*100*	73.0	*100*	*100*	*100*	38.9	*99.7*	89.3	94.8	*97.0*	*100*
mntBike	100	*100*	17.1	28.1	*98.2*	90.4	57.5	96.1	25.9	*100*	*99.6*	85.5
singer1	100	29.6	24.8	32.2	*48.1*	19.7	27.6	*100*	*99.1*	43.0	42.5	29.9
singer2	87.7	3.55	1.09	3.83	3.83	4.10	*47.5*	16.4	3.01	*45.1*	39.1	3.55
sylvester	83.6	71.7	82.8	74.7	67.6	26.3	54.6	*88.6*	*92.8*	80.4	80.7	*92.9*
trellis	95.3	59.1	35.0	80.8	30.9	*90.7*	24.4	*85.4*	47.3	50.1	49.0	78.4
walking2	100	38.8	38.4	39.8	*100*	*48.6*	38.0	*100*	34.0	40.2	40.4	*43.4*
woman	80.6	24.5	15.9	20.6	18.4	18.9	18.8	*85.8*	16.6	18.1	17.1	*93.5*
boy	2.23	20.1	9.03	7.39	91.3	*2.24*	12.8	51.0	4.49	7.57	7.27	*3.84*
car4	2.84	19.1	86.0	58.1	*2.15*	66.6	50.8	*4.27*	13.6	37.0	36.7	8.69
carDark	1.17	3.23	119	16.5	8.43	*1.29*	43.5	1.30	27.5	16.5	2.87	*0.95*
coke	14.4	*13.6*	40.5	25.7	83.0	55.0	46.7	56.8	25.1	68.7	62.5	*12.1*
crossing	1.76	8.96	3.56	23.4	*2.36*	54.8	3.18	*1.57*	24.3	26.1	43.1	2.81
david	5.64	17.7	10.5	6.05	*4.82*	12.0	16.9	*4.34*	*5.12*	11.6	10.2	42.8
deer	4.56	*4.97*	246	6.75	183	98.8	101	104	6.26	135	220	*5.27*
dudek	14.7	13.4	26.5	12.8	*9.62*	14.6	17.7	10.8	18.1	*10.3*	*9.85*	11.4
faceocc1	12.7	*11.9*	25.8	25.3	18.4	30.4	29.9	*13.0*	27.4	20.2	21.3	18.8
fish	4.19	41.2	10.7	6.25	*5.67*	50.8	24.1	8.54	6.57	16.8	7.21	*3.40*
girl	3.68	19.3	18.9	11.0	22.5	29.3	13.7	*2.60*	9.79	8.60	13.0	*2.57*
jumping	3.94	86.0	47.7	9.99	61.6	74.6	9.99	65.9	*5.94*	41.4	40.1	*6.55*
mhyang	2.39	3.61	13.3	3.97	*1.87*	3.43	20.4	*2.41*	9.51	4.36	4.07	2.59
mntBike	7.72	*6.51*	214	179	*7.66*	11.5	73.0	10.6	209	9.78	9.67	8.63
singer1	4.32	14.0	15.5	11.4	11.3	20.8	16.4	*2.72*	7.99	*4.19*	5.35	14.5
singer2	10.3	185	127	164	175	149	*22.5*	114	*8.47*	43.7	72.5	174
sylvester	13.2	9.92	8.56	14.8	34.2	68.4	15.2	*7.97*	*7.31*	19.6	19.4	*6.30*
trellis	3.73	18.8	41.7	7.01	120	*4.70*	71.5	7.01	31.6	32.3	24.3	*6.92*
walking2	3.35	17.9	58.5	34.7	*2.46*	18.9	60.6	*1.65*	52.5	46.2	54.0	11.2
woman	9.64	207	114	72.5	177	131	125	*7.88*	93.9	119	121	*4.17*

6. CONCLUSIONS

In this paper, we propose a robust online tracking approach for general objects with a convolutional neural network (CNN) based appearance model. To alleviate the problems incurred by direct use of CNN for online tracking task, we present a re-sampling method over particles with a variation of Metropolis-Hastings algorithm to gain better posteriors, and draw a set of more reliable training samples to feed CNN at the same time. With this proposed method, our tracker can employ CNN for online robust tracking task effectively and efficiently. Compared with several state-of-art trackers, the proposed tracker shows more satisfactory performance in various challenging scenarios.

7. ACKNOWLEDGMENT

This work is supported by the National Natural Science Foundation of China (61175018, 61301194, 61231016), Research Fund for the Doctoral Program of Higher Education of China (20126102120055), foundation grant from NWPU (3102014JSJ0014).

8. REFERENCES

[1] B. Babenko, M.-H. Yang, and S. Belongie. Visual tracking with online multiple instance learning. In *CVPR*, pages 983–990, June 2009.

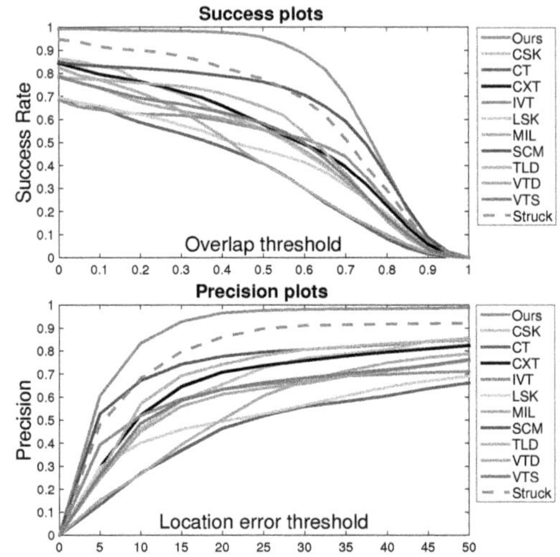

Figure 5: The success plots and precision plots

[2] R. Bardenet, A. Doucet, and C. Holmes. Towards scaling up markov chain monte carlo: an adaptive subsampling approach. In *ICML*, pages 405–413, 2014.

[3] T. B. Dinh, N. Vo, and G. Medioni. Context tracker: Exploring supporters and distracters in unconstrained environments. In *CVPR*, pages 1177–1184, 2011.

[4] S. Hare, A. Saffari, and P. Torr. Struck: Structured output tracking with kernels. In *ICCV*, pages 263–270, Nov 2011.

[5] W. K. Hastings. Monte carlo sampling methods using markov chains and their applications. *Biometrika*, 57(1):97–109, 1970.

[6] J. F. Henriques, R. Caseiro, P. Martins, and J. Batista. Exploiting the circulant structure of tracking-by-detection with kernels. In *ECCV*, 2012.

[7] S. Hong, T. You, S. Kwak, and B. Han. Online tracking by learning discriminative saliency map with convolutional neural network. *arXiv:1502.06796*, 2015.

[8] Z. Kalal, J. Matas, and K. Mikolajczyk. P-n learning: Bootstrapping binary classifiers by structural constraints. In *CVPR*, pages 49–56, June 2010.

[9] J. Kwon and K.-M. Lee. Visual tracking decomposition. In *CVPR*, pages 1269–1276, 2010.

[10] J. Kwon and K. M. Lee. Tracking by sampling trackers. In *ICCV*, pages 1195–1202, 2011.

[11] H. Li, Y. Li, and F. Porikli. Robust online visual tracking with a single convolutional neural network. In *ACCV*, pages 194–209, 2014.

[12] B. Liu, J. Huang, C. Kulikowski, and L. Yang. Robust visual tracking using local sparse appearance model and k-selection. *PAMI*, 35(12):2968–2981, Dec 2013.

[13] D. A. Ross, J. Lim, R.-S. Lin, and M.-H. Yang. Incremental learning for robust visual tracking. *IJCV*, 77(1-3):125–141, 2008.

[14] N. Wang and D.-Y. Yeung. Learning a deep compact image representation for visual tracking. In *NIPS*, pages 809–817, 2013.

[15] Y. Wu, J. Lim, and M.-H. Yang. Object tracking benchmark. *IEEE Transactions on Pattern Analysis and Machine Intelligence (T-PAMI)*, 2015.

[16] M. D. Zeiler and R. Fergus. Visualizing and understanding convolutional networks. In *ECCV*, pages 818–833. Springer International Publishing, 2014.

[17] K. Zhang, L. Zhang, and M.-H. Yang. Real-time compressive tracking. In *ECCV*, pages 864–877, 2012.

[18] W. Zhong, H. Lu, and M.-H. Yang. Robust object tracking via sparsity-based collaborative model. In *CVPR*, pages 1838–1845, June 2012.

Progressive Shape-Distribution-Encoder for 3D Shape Retrieval

Jin Xie[1,2] Fan Zhu[1,2] Guoxian Dai[1,2,3] Yi Fang[1,2*]

[1] NYU Multimedia and Visual Computing Lab
[2] Electrical and Computer Engineering, New York University Abu Dhabi
[3] Computer Science and Engineering, Polytechnic School of Engineering, New York University

ABSTRACT

In this paper, we propose a deep shape descriptor by learning the shape distributions at different diffusion time via a progressive deep shape-distribution-encoder. First, we develop a shape distribution representation with the kernel density estimator to characterize the intrinsic geometrical structure of the shape. Then, we propose to learn discriminative shape features through a progressive shape-distribution-encoder. Specially, the progressive shape-distribution-encoder aims at modeling the complex non-linear transform of the estimated shape distributions between consecutive diffusion time. Furthermore, in order to characterize the intrinsic structure of the shape more efficiently, we stack multiple proposed progressive shape-distribution-encoders to form a neural network structure. Finally, we concatenated all neurons in the hidden layers of the progressive shape-distribution-encoder network to form a discriminative shape descriptor for retrieval. The proposed method is evaluated on three benchmark 3D shape datasets and the experimental results demonstrate the superiority of our method to the existing approaches.

Categories and Subject Descriptors

H.3.3 [**Information Storage and Retrieval**]: Information Search and Retrieval-Retrieval models

General Terms

Algorithms, Performance, Experimentation

Keywords

3D shape retrieval; denoising auto-encoder; heat kernel signature; heat diffusion

1. INTRODUCTION

With the recent developments of 3D acquisition and printing technology, there is an increasing amount of 3D shapes in our daily life. The 3D shape retrieval has been receiving much more attention in a wide range of fields such as computer vision, mechanical engineering and molecular biology, etc. A key step in shape retrieval is to effectively develop shape descriptor that can capture the distinctive properties of shape[2, 3, 4, 17]. It is desirable that a shape descriptor is discriminative and insensitive to deformation and noise for retrieval.

Recently, inspired by the great success of the learning based features in image classification and retrieval, the learning based shape descriptors have been proposed. In [1], the authors proposed to apply the bag-of-features (BOF) paradigm to learn the shape descriptor, where the dictionary is first learned by the K-means clustering method from the training heat kernel signatures (HKSs)[13] and the spatially sensitive bag of features are then extracted as the shape descriptor. Tabia *et al.* [14] generalized the BOF paradigm to the Riemannian manifold of Symmetric Positive Definite matrices to learn a dictionary of words. By employing sparse coding to learn the dictionary, Litman *et al.* [7] proposed to use the histogram of encoded representation coefficients over the learned dictionary to represent shape for retrieval. Nonetheless, these sparse coding based shape descriptors are still the shallow feature representations, which cannot characterize the intrinsic structure of the shape well. By projecting the 3D model to 2D images, the stacked local convolutional auto-encoder [5] has been used to learn shape feature for retrieval.

In this paper, we propose a deep shape descriptor for retrieval by learning the discriminative shape distributions during the heat diffusion process. First, based on heat kernel, we develop a shape distribution representation with the kernel density estimation method. The developed shape distribution representation can efficiently characterize the intrinsic geometrical structure of the shape. Furthermore, inspired by the observations that the shape distributions change non-linearly but smoothly in the temporal domain, we model the complex non-linear change of the shape distributions between consecutive diffusion time through a deep network due to the favorable ability to model non-linearity [16]. Particularly, we restore denoising auto-encoder to propose a progressive shape-distribution-encoder to achieve this goal. Finally, we concatenate all neurons in the hidden layers of the progressive shape-distribution-encoder network, i.e., the discriminative shape distributions, to form a deep shape descriptor. The proposed deep shape descriptor is verified on the benchmark shape datasets and shows very promising performance.

The rest of the paper is organized as follows. Section 2 presents the shape descriptor with the proposed progressive shape-distribution-encoder. Section 3 performs extensive experiments and Section 4 concludes the paper.

*: Corresponding Author (Email: yfang@nyu.edu)

MM'15, October 26–30, 2015, Brisbane, Australia.
© 2015 ACM. ISBN 978-1-4503-3459-4/15/10 ...$15.00.
DOI: http://dx.doi.org/10.1145/2733373.2806308.

2. THE PROPOSED 3D SHAPE DESCRIPTOR

2.1 Heat Diffusion Based Shape Distribution Estimation

Shape distribution [8] refers to a probabilistic distribution sampled from a shape function describing the 3D model. Given a shape, we can define the probabilistic distribution of HKS at some diffusion time as the shape distribution. The heat kernel [13] controls the geometry dependent propagation of heat flow across the shape, which can be viewed as the quality of heat that passes from one vertex to another vertex within the time interval. Based on the heat kernel, heat kernel signature (HKS) [13] of vertex x at time t, $s_t(x)$, is defined as the diagonal value of the heat kernel of vertex x at time t. Since HKS is highly dependent of curvature of the meshed surface, heat diffusion based shape distribution can intrinsically characterize the geometric structure of the shape.

Suppose there are N vertices on the meshed surface of the shape. Given HKS at diffusion time t, $s_{i,t}(1), s_{i,t}(2), \cdots, s_{i,t}(N)$, the shape distribution of the ith shape, $p_{i,t}(s)$, can be estimated by the kernel density estimator. For simplicity, here we choose the Gaussian kernel to estimate the shape distribution:

$$p_{i,t}(s) = \frac{1}{N}\sum_{n=1}^{N}\frac{1}{(2\pi h_{i,t}^2)^{1/2}}e^{-\frac{\|s-s_{i,t}(n)\|_2^2}{2h_{i,t}^2}} \quad (1)$$

where $h_{i,t}$ denotes the bandwidth of the Gaussian kernel at diffusion time t. Since at different diffusion time the scales of HKSs are different, we employ the adaptive bandwidth selection method [12]:

$$h_{i,t} = 1.06\sigma_{i,t}N^{-1/5} \quad (2)$$

where $\sigma_{i,t}$ is the standard deviation of the HKS samples at diffusion time t. By parameterizing s, we can form a discrete shape distribution to represent the shape. Here we parameterize s by $s = s_{i,t}^{min} + u(s_{i,t}^{max} - s_{i,t}^{min})/l$, where $s_{i,t}^{min}$ and $s_{i,t}^{max}$ are the minimum and maximum of $s_{i,t}(1), s_{i,t}(2), \cdots, s_{i,t}(N)$, respectively, l is the dimension of the shape distribution and $u = 1, 2, \cdots, l$.

Fig. 1 shows the shape distributions of the Centaur and Wolf shapes during the diffusion process. From this figure, one can see that the shapes of different classes have different shape distributions (e.g., the shape distributions of Centaur model a and Wolf model c at $t = 3$) while the shapes of the same class have similar shape distributions (e.g., the shape distributions of Centaur models a and b at $t = 2$). Moreover, since the heat diffusion processes of the shapes from different classes are different, the changes of the shape distributions between consecutive diffusion time are different. In the next subsection, we model the change of shape distributions between consecutive diffusion time to learn the discriminative feature to represent the shape.

2.2 Progressive Shape-Distribution-Encoder

Assuming the shape distributions at diffusion time t and t' are $\boldsymbol{p}_{i,t}$ and $\boldsymbol{p}_{i,t'}$, we can formulate the change of the shape distributions at t and t':

$$\boldsymbol{p}_{i,t'} = \eta(\boldsymbol{p}_{i,t}) \quad (3)$$

where $\eta : \mathcal{R}^l \rightarrow \mathcal{R}^l$ is a non-linear transform. The denoising auto-encoder can model the non-linear transformation η by the encoder and decoder, where the input is the corrupted version of the original data and the output is the original data, the stochastic corruption can be viewed as a non-linear transform. And the output of the hidden layer is discriminative and usually used as the high-level feature.

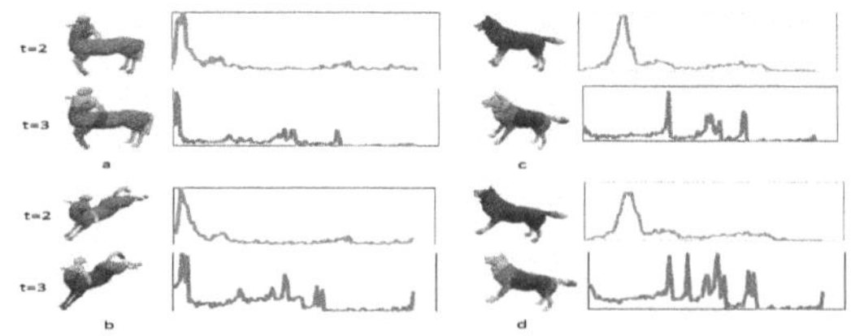

Figure 1: The first and third columns show the HKS maps of the Centaur and Wolf models while the second and fourth columns show the shape distributions of the corresponding HKS maps.

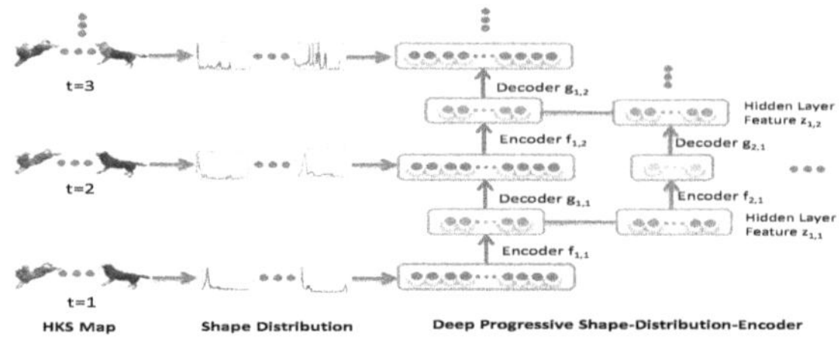

Figure 2: The framework of the proposed progressive shape-distribution-encoder.

Inspired by the denoising auto-encoder, we propose a progressive neural network to learn a discriminative shape descriptor by modeling the non-linearity between the shape distributions during the diffusion process. In the proposed progressive neural network structure, we specify the shape distributions at consecutive diffusion time as the input and output of the denoising auto-encoder, which is called the progressive shape-distribution-encoder. The progressive shape-distribution-encoder attempts to learn a discriminative shape distribution within a certain amount of diffusion time. In order to model the complex transform between the shape distributions during the diffusion process, the stacked progressive shape-distribution-encoder network with multiple input layers is preferred due to its discrimination ability. Thus, once the progressive shape-distribution-encoders in the current layer are trained, the outputs of the hidden layers can be fed into the progressive shape-distribution-encoders in the next layer to learn a deep feature. As shown in Fig. 2, the shape distributions at diffusion time $t = 1, 2, 3$ are used as the inputs and outputs of the first and second progressive shape-distribution-encoders in the first layer, respectively. Then the learned hidden layer representations $\boldsymbol{z}_{1,1}$ and $\boldsymbol{z}_{1,2}$ are fed into the first progressive shape-distribution-encoder in the second layer to learn a deep representation.

Suppose there are C shapes. Formally, the jth progressive shape-distribution-encoder in the first layer aims at mapping shape distribution $\boldsymbol{p}_{i,j}$ at diffusion time j to shape distribution $\boldsymbol{p}_{i,j+1}$ at diffusion time $j+1$, where $j = 1, 2, \cdots, T-1$. The cost function is formulated as follows:

$$argmin_{\boldsymbol{W}_{1,j},\boldsymbol{b}_{1,j}} \frac{1}{2}\sum_{i=1}^{C}\|\boldsymbol{p}_{i,j+1} - g_{1,j}(f_{1,j}(\boldsymbol{p}_{i,j}))\|_2^2 + \frac{1}{2}\lambda\|\boldsymbol{W}_{1,j}\|_F^2 \quad (4)$$

where $\boldsymbol{W}_{1,j}$ and $\boldsymbol{b}_{1,j}$ are the weight and bias matrices of the jth progressive shape-distribution-encoder in the first layer, $f_{1,j}$ and $g_{1,j}$ are the encoder and decoder. After the progressive shape-distribution-encoder is trained, we can obtain the output $\boldsymbol{z}_{1,j}^i$ of the hidden layer:

$$\boldsymbol{z}_{1,j}^i = f_{1,j}(\boldsymbol{p}_{i,j}) \quad (5)$$

Once the outputs of the hidden layers in the $T-1$ progressive shape-distribution-encoders, $\boldsymbol{z}_{1,1}^i, \boldsymbol{z}_{1,2}^i, \cdots, \boldsymbol{z}_{1,T-1}^i$, are obtained, we can feed these outputs to the $T-2$ progressive shape-distribution-encoders in the next layer for a deep shape representation. Thus, in the mth layer, the outputs $\boldsymbol{z}^i_{m,1}, \boldsymbol{z}^i_{m,2}, \cdots, \boldsymbol{z}^i_{m,T-m}$ can be used to represent the shape, where $m = 1, 2, \cdots, L$, L is the number of the layers.

In each progressive shape-distribution-encoder, the encoder $f_{m,j}$ maps the shape distribution $\boldsymbol{p}_{i,j}$ at diffusion time j to the hidden layer and the decoder $g_{m,j}$ maps the output of the hidden layer to the shape distribution $\boldsymbol{p}_{i,j+1}$ at diffusion time $j+1$. The output of the hidden layer, $\boldsymbol{z}^i_{m,j}$, can be viewed as a discriminative shape distribution at diffusion time j' ($j < j' < j+1$). The discriminative shape distribution $\boldsymbol{z}^i_{m,j}$ can be used to characterize the heat diffusion process from time j to time $j+1$. Thus, the outputs of the hidden layers of $T-m$ progressive shape-distribution-encoders, $\boldsymbol{z}^i_{m,1}, \boldsymbol{z}^i_{m,2}, \cdots, \boldsymbol{z}^i_{m,T-m}$, can describe the whole diffusion process to represent the ith shape.

2.3 3D Shape Descriptor

In this subsection, based on the proposed progressive neural network structure, we learn a deep 3D shape descriptor for retrieval. In order to efficiently characterize the complex variations of the shapes, we learn the descriptor from the multiple-layered progressive shape-distribution-encoder. That is, in the first layer, we can train $T-1$ progressive shape-distribution-encoders to learn $\boldsymbol{W}_{1,j}$ and $\boldsymbol{b}_{1,j}$, $j = 1, 2, \cdots, T-1$. Thus, the $T-1$ outputs of the hidden layers are used to train the $T-2$ progressive shape-distribution-encoders in the next layer. The procedure is repeated until the progressive shape-distribution-encoders in the Lth layer are trained.

Once the network with the L layers is trained, we can concatenate all activations of the hidden layers to form a deep shape descriptor. The shape descriptor of the ith shape, $\boldsymbol{\alpha}_i$, i.e., the activations in the hidden layers of the deep neural network, can be represented:

$$\boldsymbol{\alpha}_i = [\boldsymbol{z}^i_{1,1}; \boldsymbol{z}^i_{1,2}; \cdots; \boldsymbol{z}^i_{L,T-L}] \quad (6)$$

3. EXPERIMENTAL RESULTS

3.1 Experimental Settings

We define a time unit $\tau = 0.04$ and take 26 sampled time values to compute the HKS descriptor. And $l = 128$ is used to estimate the shape distribution, which results in a 128-dimensional input to the proposed progressive neural network. In the progressive neural network, the number of layers is set to 2, i.e., $L = 2$. And in each layer, the progressive denoising auto-encoder consists of an encoder with layers of 128-1000-500-250-30 and a decoder with layers of 30-250-500-1000-128. Moreover, in Eq. (4), λ is set to 0.005.

3.2 Evaluation of The Proposed Shape Descriptor

In our proposed shape descriptor, we use the estimated shape distribution as the input to the progressive shape-distribution-encoder. Learning deep feature from the estimated shape distribution with the progressive denoising auto-encoder can be viewed as enhancement of the estimated shape distribution. In order to demonstrate effectiveness of the proposed shape descriptor, we compare the proposed shape descriptor to the estimated shape distribution on the McGill shape dataset [11].

For shape distribution, we concatenate the 128-dimensional shape distributions at 26 sampled diffusion time values to form a 3328-dimensional vector to describe the shape. For a fair comparison, we use the single layered progressive shape-distribution-encoder network to learn the shape descriptor. Since the dimension of the hidden layer feature in each progressive shape-distribution-encoder is 30 and 25, a 750-dimensional shape descriptor is formed to represent the shape. Fig. 3 shows the precision-recall curves for shape distribution and the proposed shape descriptor. As can be seen in this figure, compared to the shape distribution without the progressive neural network structure, although the dimension of the learned descriptor is lower than that of the shape distribution, the proposed shape descriptor is much more discriminative and can significantly improve the retrieval performance.

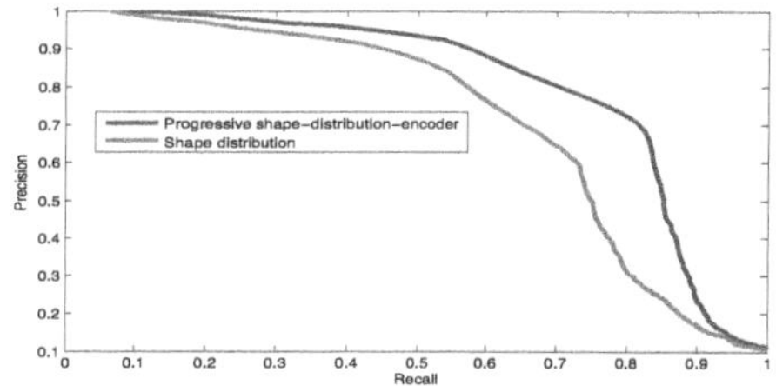

Figure 3: The precision-recall curves for the shape distribution and the proposed shape descriptor on the McGill shape dataset.

3.3 Comparison Evaluation

3.3.1 McGill Shape Dataset

In the McGill 3D shape dataset [11], there are 255 3D meshes with significant part articulations. Each class contains 3D shapes with large pose changes, which makes the McGill 3D shape dataset challenging. We denote our proposed shape-distribution-encoder based shape descriptor by SDESD. In our proposed SDESD method, 10 shapes per class are randomly chosen as the training samples and the remaining samples per class are used to test. And the experiments are repeated over 20 times. Four performance criteria, i.e., Nearest Neighbor (NN), the First Tier (1-Tier), the Second Tier (2-Tier) and the Discounted Cumulative Gain (DCG) are used to evaluate these methods. The retrieval performance of these methods is illustrated in Table 1. As can be seen in this table, compared to the state-of-the-art methods [9, 15, 14], the proposed SDESD method can achieve better performance on the four criteria. The large non-rigid deformations of the objects make the McGill shape dataset challenging. Nonetheless, due to the discriminative feature representation in the hidden layer of the proposed shape-distribution-encoder, SDESD is still robust to nonrigid deformations.

Table 1: Retrieval Results on The McGill Dataset.

Methods	NN	1-Tier	2-Tier	DCG
Covariance method [14]	0.977	0.732	0.818	0.937
PCA based VLAT [15]	0.969	0.658	0.781	0.894
Hybrid BOW [9]	0.957	0.635	0.790	0.886
SDESD	**0.984**	**0.783**	**0.841**	**0.941**

3.3.2 SHREC'10 ShapeGoogle Dataset

The SHREC'10 ShapeGoogle dataset [1] contains 1184 synthetic shapes, including 715 shapes from 13 classes generated by the five simulated transformations, i.e., isometry, topology, isometry+topology, partiality and triangulation, and 456 unrelated shapes. For the SHREC '10 ShapeGoogle dataset, we compared the proposed SDESD to the bag of feature descriptor based on standard vector quantization (VQ) [1] and unsupervised dictionary learning (UDL) [7] with sparse coding. It is noted that the supervised dictionary learning method (SDL) [7] with sparse coding is not involved to compare. This is because in the SDL method the positive samples from the same class and negative samples from the different classes are employed to learn the dictionary. Therefore, SDL is a supervised feature learning method while our proposed method is an unsupervised feature learning method. Comparison results with the mean average precision are listed in Table 2. From this table, one can see that our proposed SDESD is superior to the BOF descriptors based on VQ [1] and UDL [7] with sparse coding in the case of the isometry, isometry+topology and partiality transformations.

Table 2: Retrieval Results on The SHREC'10 ShapeGoogle Dataset.

Transformation	VQ [1]	UDL [7]	SDESD
Isometry	0.988	0.977	**1.000**
Topology	**1.000**	**1.000**	**1.000**
Isometry+Topology	0.933	0.934	**0.998**
Partiality	0.947	0.948	**0.983**
Triangulation	**0.954**	0.950	0.943

3.4 SHREC'14 Human Dataset

The SHREC'14 Human dataset [10] contains two sub-datasets. In the first sub-dataset, there are 15 synthetic human models, each having 20 different poses. The other one consists of 40 scanned human models, where there are 10 different poses for each human model. Following the setting in [7], all human shapes are re-scaled to 4500 triangles. The SHREC'14 Human dataset is an extremely challenging one because all human shapes have similar geometry information. For the synthetic and scanned human sub-datasets, we compare the proposed SDESD method to the recent shape retrieval methods [6, 18, 10, 1, 7]. For the synthetic sub-dataset, 12 shapes per class are used to train the progressive shape-distribution-encoder and the other shapes per class are used for testing. For the scanned sub-dataset, 6 shapes per class are used as the training samples and the rest of shapes are used to test. The mean average precision is reported by repeating the experiments over 20 times. The experimental results are listed in Table 3. Although the scanned sub-dataset is an extremely challenging one, compared to these methods [6, 18, 10, 1, 7], our proposed shape descriptor can obtain better performance. Nonetheless, for the synthetic sub-dataset, the mean average precision of our proposed method is lower than that of the ISPM method [6]. Since our proposed shape descriptor is learned in an unsupervised way, in this experiment, we did not compare our proposed descriptor to the supervised dictionary learning method [7].

Table 3: Retrieval Results on The SHREC'14 Human Dataset.

Method	Synthetic model	Scanned model
ISPM[6]	**0.92**	0.258
RBiHDM[18]	0.642	0.640
DBN[10]	0.842	0.304
VQ [1]	0.813	0.514
UDL [7]	0.842	0.523
SDESD	0.810	**0.651**

4. CONCLUSIONS

For 3D shape retrieval, we proposed a deep shape descriptor by developing a progressive shape-distribution-encoder network. During the diffusion process, the shape distributions at different diffusion time are estimated by the kernel density estimator. The stacked progressive shape-distribution-encoders are then proposed to describe the changes between the estimated shape distributions during the diffusion process. The hidden layer representations in the progressive neural network are extracted as the discriminative shape descriptor for shape retrieval. As evaluated, experimental results demonstrate that the proposed shape descriptor can improve the performance of shape retrieval and it is robust to deformation and noise.

5. REFERENCES

[1] A. M. Bronstein, M. M. Bronstein, L. J. Guibas, and M. Ovsjanikov. Shape google: Geometric words and expressions for invariant shape retrieval. *ACM Transactions on Graphics*, 30(1):1, 2011.

[2] Y. Fang, M. Sun, and K. Ramani. Temperature distribution descriptor for robust 3d shape retrieval. In *Computer Vision and Pattern Recognition Workshops (CVPRW), 2011 IEEE Computer Society Conference on*, pages 9–16. IEEE, 2011.

[3] Y. Fang, J. Xie, G. Dai, M. Wang, F. Zhu, T. Xu, and E. Wong. 3d deep shape descriptor. In *Proceedings of the IEEE Conference on Computer Vision and Pattern Recognition*, pages 2319–2328, 2015.

[4] K. Hu and Y. Fang. 3d laplacian pyramid signature. In *Computer Vision-ACCV 2014 Workshops*, pages 306–321. Springer, 2014.

[5] B. Leng, S. Guo, X. Zhang, and Z. Xiong. 3D object retrieval with stacked local convolutional autoencoder. *Signal Processing*, pages 119–128, 2015.

[6] C. Li and A. B. Hamza. A multiresolution descriptor for deformable 3d shape retrieval. *The Visual Computer*, 29(6-8):513–524, 2013.

[7] R. Litman, A. M. Bronstein, M. M. Bronstein, and U. Castellani. Supervised learning of bag-of-features shape descriptors using sparse coding. *Computer Graphics Forum*, 33(5):127–136, 2014.

[8] R. Osada, T. Funkhouser, B. Chazelle, and D. Dokin. Shape distributions. *ACM Transactions on Graphics*, 33:133–154, 2002.

[9] P. Papadakis, I. Pratikakis, T. Theoharis, G. Passalis, and S. J. Perantonis. 3D object retrieval using an efficient and compact hybrid shape descriptor. In *3DOR, Greece*, pages 9–16, 2008.

[10] D. Pickup, X. Sun, and P. L. Rosin. SHREC'14 track: Shape retrieval of non-rigid 3D human models. In *3DOR, France*, 2014.

[11] K. Siddiqi, J. Zhang, D. Macrini, A. Shokoufandeh, S. Bouix, and S. J. Dickinson. Retrieving articulated 3D models using medial surfaces. *Machine Vision Application*, 19(4):261–275, 2008.

[12] B. Silverman. *Density Estimation for Statistics and Data Analysis*. Wiley, 1998.

[13] J. Sun, M. Ovsjanikov, and L. Guibas. A concise and provably informative multi-scale signature based on heat diffusion. *Computer Graphics Forum*, pages 1383–1392, 2009.

[14] H. Tabia, H. Laga, D. Picard, and P. H. Gosselin. Covariance descriptors for 3D shape matching and retrieval. In *CVPR*, pages 4185–4192, 2014.

[15] H. Tabia, D. Picard, H. Laga, and P. H. Gosselin. Compact vectors of locally aggregated tensors for 3D shape retrieval. In *3DOR, Spain*, pages 17–24, 2013.

[16] P. Vincent, H. Larochelle, I. Lajoie, Y. Bengio, and P. Manzagol. Stacked denoising autoencoders: Learning useful representations in a deep network with a local denoising criterion. *Journal of Machine Learning Research*, 11:3371–3408, 2010.

[17] J. Xie, Y. Fang, F. Zhu, and E. Wong. Deepshape: Deep learned shape descriptor for 3d shape matching and retrieval. In *Proceedings of the IEEE Conference on Computer Vision and Pattern Recognition*, pages 1275–1283, 2015.

[18] J. Ye, Z. Yan, and Y. Yu. Fast nonrigid 3d retrieval using modal space transform. In *ICMR*, pages 121–126, 2013.

Cross-media Topic Detection with Refined CNN based Image-Dominant Topic Model

Zhiyi Wang[†♮], Liang Li[†♮], Qingming Huang[†‡♮]
[†]University of Chinese Academy of Sciences, China
[‡]Key Lab of Intell. Info. Process., Inst. of Comput. Tech., CAS, China
[♮]Key Laboratory of Big Data Mining and Knowledge Management, CAS, China
{zhiyi.wang, liang.li}@vipl.ict.ac.cn qmhuang@ucas.ac.cn

ABSTRACT

Online heterogenous data is springing up while the data has the rich auxiliary information (e.g. pictures and videos) around the text. However, traditional topic models are suffering from the limitations to discover the topics effectively from the cross-media data. Incorporating with the convolutional neural network (CNN) feature, we propose a novel image dominant topic model, which projects both the text modality and the visual modality into a semantic simplex. Further, an improved CNN feature is introduced to capture more visual details by fusing the convolutional layer and fully-connected layer. Experimental comparisons with state-of-the-art methods in the cross-media topic detection task show the effectiveness of our model.

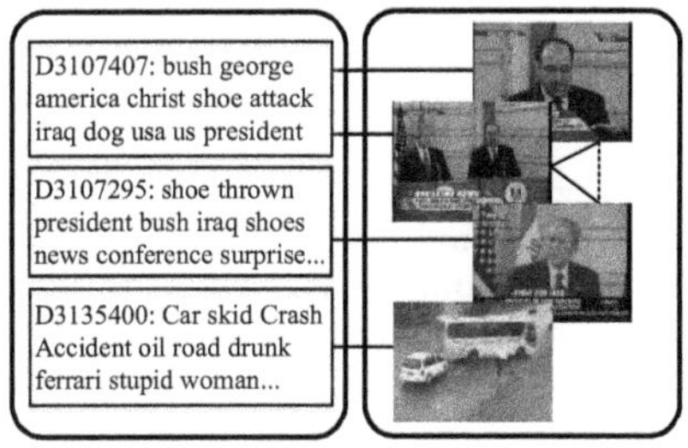

Figure 1: An illustration of semantic relationship in document. Explicit and potential relationships are drawn by solid and dotted lines respectively.

Categories and Subject Descriptors

H.3.1 [**Information Storage and Retrieval**]: Content Analysis and Indexing

General Terms

Experimentation, Theory

Keywords

Convolutional Neural Networks, Topic Model, Cross-media topic Detection

1. INTRODUCTION

Recently, social networks, video and content sharing websites burst to produce a large number of online multimedia data every day, and more and more people tend to share their moments with the heterogeneous information (text, image and video). In such expression of cross-media, the visual data usually delivers the more entitative content while the text data usually describes the emotion. Thus, how to use cross-media data properly and effectively is the key to detect the topics in the real networks.

The visual component of cross-media data plays an important role in providing the rich and useful information for the topic detection. Deep neural networks [8, 15] are the most popular models for the effective representation of the visual information. Since large convolutional network models have demonstrated impressive classification performance on the ImageNet benchmark [8], deep neural networks become newborn and popular methods to learn features, especially in the visual domain.

The topic model is widely used to solve the semantic-related tasks. Probabilistic topic models [2, 6] have been powerful methods of learning topic representation of document corpus. To treat the multi-modality information, [12] models the joint distribution of image content and class labels with supervised LDA. However, these topic models make the strong assumption of independent identical distribution of documents while they also ignore the hidden association among the cross-media data. To further solve this problem, Author Topic Model (ATM) [11] and Relational Topic Model (RTM) [4] are proposed to model the content of documents with link relationships. To model the cross-media data, Semi-supervised Relational Topic Model (ss-RTM) [10] incorporates image content, labels and relations into topic modeling. Hashtag Graph based Topic Model for Tweet Mining (HGTM) [13] introduces a hashtag relation graph as weakly-supervised information for effective tweet semantic modeling.

Although these methods have achieved some performance improvements, most previous works exploit document-oriented relationships to formulate the topic model. A beneficial fact is that more and more people express themselves by combining images and a few text in the social network and cross-media platforms. Obviously, straightforward and information-

MM'15, October 26–30, 2015, Brisbane, Australia.

DOI: http://dx.doi.org/10.1145/2733373.2806309.

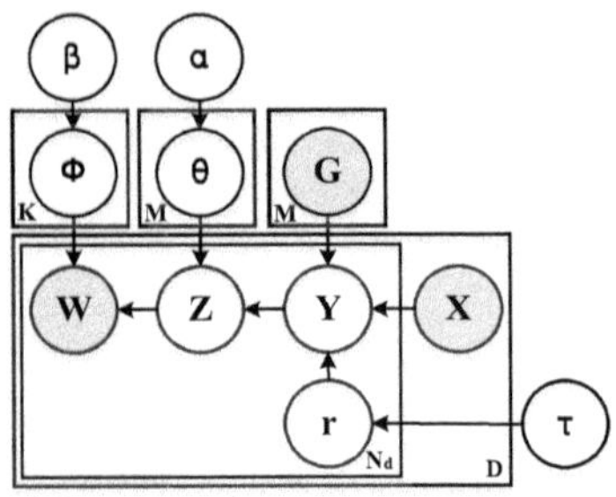

Figure 2: The graphical representation of IDTM.

rich images can reveal more relationships than the text. As shown in Figure 1, the images are weakly annotated in the social network, but the images of the same topic can enhance the latent relationships among the short and noisy documents.

Inspired by the above insights, incorporating with the deep feature of the visual information, this paper proposes an Image-Dominant Topic Model (IDTM), where the text is projected into semantic space by the latent features via the corresponding images. IDTM is a generative probabilistic model that incorporates weakly-supervised information based on a weighted image graph. By establishing the weighted image graph, IDTM can discover explicit text-image relationships and potential text-image relationships. Furthermore, we introduce a fuse mechanism of convolutional Layer 5 and fully-connected Layers 7 from the CNN feature based on the framework of Caffe [7], which is to capture more visual details and improve the generalization of the final visual representation. Finally, we evaluate the proposed method in the cross-media topic detection task and compare with several state-of-the-art methods to show its effectiveness.

The remainder of the paper is organized as follows. Section 2 describes IDTM for topic understanding and coarse-to-fine method. Section 3 analyzes the experimental results. Finally, Section 4 concludes this paper.

2. METHODOLOGY

The model for IDTM is shown in Figure 2. We define the number of documents and topics in a corpus as D and K. Suppose the document d corresponds to a word index $\mathbf{w}_d = \{w_{d1}, w_{d2}, \ldots, w_{dN_d}\}$, where N_d is the number of words in document d, and an image index $\mathbf{x}_d = \{x_{d1}, x_{d2}, \ldots, x_{dM_d}\}$, where M_d is the number of images in document d. We allocate a topic assignment z_{di} and an image assignment y_{di} for each w_{di} in the document d. Each topic by a Multinomial distribution over words as ϕ with β as the Dirichlet hyper-parameter. Similarly, each image by a Multinomial distribution over topics as θ with α as the Dirichlet hyper-parameter. τ is a Bernoulli variable to decide whether to assign images in the document d for current w_{di}. An image relation graph is an undirected graph, denoted as $G = (V, E)$ where nodes $V = \{m\}_{m=1}^{M}$ are images, and each edge e_{ij} of the similarity matrix $E = \{(e_{ij})\}_{i,j \in V, i \neq j}$ means the similarity between image i and image j. The shaded nodes indicate observations, while the others represent latent variables. The details of the generative process are as follows:

1. For each topic k: $\phi_k \sim Dirichlet(\beta)$
2. For each image x: $\theta_x \sim Dirichlet(\alpha)$
3. For each document $d \in D$

   For each word w_{di}, $i = 1 : N_d$

   a. Sample an image $y_{di}^1 \sim Uniform(\mathbf{x}_d)$

   b. Sample $r \sim Bernoulli(\tau)$

   c. If $r = 1$,

      sample $y_{di} = y_{di}^1$

      If $r = 0$,

      sample $y_{di} \sim Multinomial(norm(g_{y_{di}^1}))$

   d. Sample a topic $z_{di} \sim Multinomial(\theta_{y_{di}})$

   e. Sample a word $w_{di} \sim Multinomial(\phi_{z_{di}})$

$g_{y_{di}^1}$ denotes the image relation graph and is normalized by column. Hence, $norm(g_{y_{di}^1})$ represents the compactness of relationships between images and is an association probability vector, where the jth element is:

$$p(y_j|y_{di}^1) = \frac{g_{y_{di}^1, y_j}}{\sum_{j'} g_{y_{di}^1, y_{j'}}} \tag{1}$$

In the generative process, the key step is to sample a related image for the current word. Thus, we model the process by two steps: **1)** an image y_{di}^1 is sampled uniformly from $\mathbf{x}_d$; **2)** the parameter r is sampled from Bernoulli distribution to determine whether the current word is related to images $\mathbf{x}_d$. If related ($r = 1$), y_{di} equals to y_{di}^1; if not ($r = 0$), we sample y_{di} from the multinomial distribution of $norm(g_{y_{di}^1})$.

2.1 Inference and Parameter Estimation

In this section, we come to the learning strategy of our model. Words, images and image relationships are observed while the hidden variables are guided by latent distribution parameters. With the model defined, we turn to evaluate the posterior inference and parameter estimation. The probability of the whole corpus is:

$$p(\mathbf{w}|\theta, \phi, \mathbf{r}, \mathbf{x}, \mathbf{G}) = \prod_{d=1}^{D} p(\mathbf{w}_d|\theta, \phi, \mathbf{r}, \mathbf{x}_d, \mathbf{g}_{x_d}) \tag{2}$$

Assuming that "topic-word" distribution and "image-topic" distribution are conditionally independent, we have:

$$\begin{aligned} p(\mathbf{w}_d|\theta, \phi, \mathbf{r}, \mathbf{x}_d, \mathbf{g}_{x_d}) &= \prod_{i=1}^{N_d} p(w_{di}|\theta, \phi, \mathbf{r}, \mathbf{x}_d, \mathbf{g}_{x_d}) \\ &= \prod_{i=1}^{N_d} \sum_{s=1}^{M_d} \sum_{k=1}^{K} p(w_{di}, z_{di} = k, y_{di} = s|\theta, \phi, \mathbf{r}, \mathbf{x}_d, \mathbf{g}_{x_d}) \\ &= \prod_{i=1}^{N_d} \sum_{s=1}^{M_d} \sum_{k=1}^{K} p(w_{di}|z_{di} = k, \phi) p(z_{di} = k|y_{di} = s, \theta) \cdot \\ &\quad p(y_{di} = s|\mathbf{r}, \mathbf{x}_d, \mathbf{g}_{x_d}) \\ &= \prod_{i=1}^{N_d} \sum_{s=1}^{M_d} \sum_{k=1}^{K} \phi_{w_{di}k} \theta_{ks} p(y_{di} = s|\mathbf{r}, \mathbf{x}_d, \mathbf{g}_{x_d}) \end{aligned} \tag{3}$$

$p(y_{di} = s|\mathbf{r}, \mathbf{x}_d, \mathbf{g}_{x_d})$ indicates the probability of image assignment s conditioned on the current explicit images $\mathbf{x}_d$ and related potential images. Based on the Bernoulli distribution that we describe above, the probability that we assign images to words is:

$$\begin{aligned} & p(y_{di} = s|\mathbf{r}, \mathbf{x}_d, \mathbf{g}_{x_d}) \\ &= \left[p(y_{di}^1 = s|\mathbf{x}_d) p(y_{di} = s|y_{di}^1)\right]^r \cdot \\ & \left[\sum_{j=1}^{M_d} p(y_{di}^1 = x_{d,j}|\mathbf{x}_d) p(y_{di} = s|y_{di}^1 = x_{d,j}, g_{x_{d,j}})\right]^{1-r} \end{aligned} \tag{4}$$

$x_{d,j}$ is the jth image in document d. As the exact inference of the model is general intractable, some commonly used approximate methods are usually conducted in parameter inference as substitutes, such as variational inference[1], expectation propagation [9], or Gibbs sampling [5]. In this paper, we employ Gibbs sampling procedure to carry out approximated parameters for its simplicity and effectiveness and obtain the sample posterior distribution:

$$p(z_{di} = k, y_{di} = s, r_{di} = u | w_{di} = w, \mathbf{z}_{-di}, \mathbf{y}_{-di}, \mathbf{w}_{-di}, \mathbf{X}, \mathbf{G}, \alpha, \beta, \tau) \propto \frac{n_{k,w_{di}}^{-di} + \beta}{\sum_W n_{k,w}^{-di} + W\beta} \cdot \frac{n_{k,x_{di}}^{-di} + \alpha}{\sum_K n_{k,x}^{-di} + K\alpha} \cdot p(y_{di} = s | \mathbf{r}, \mathbf{x}_d, \mathbf{g}_{x_d}) \quad (5)$$

$n_{k,w_{di}}^{-di}$ is the occurrence number of word w_{di} assigned to topic k except for the current word while $n_{k,x_{di}}^{-di}$ is the occurrence number of topic assigned to image x_{di} except for the current word. W and K are the number of words and topics in whole corpus respectively. After iterative sampling, the probability reaches the convergence. ϕ and θ are:

$$\phi_k \propto \frac{n_{k,w_{di}} + \beta}{\sum_W n_{k,w} + W\beta}, \qquad \theta_s \propto \frac{n_{k,x_{di}} + \alpha}{\sum_K n_{k,x} + K\alpha} \quad (6)$$

According to the topic structure detected, IDTM can conclude distinguishable topics in real-world datasets and find out the representative words for each topic. Meanwhile, we can obtain the related images under each topic.

2.2 Coarse-to-fine Topic Detection

To capture more visual details, we employ deep neural networks in this paper. Based on the results shown in [14], the feature hierarchies become deeper, they learn increasingly powerful features. Thus, higher layers generally produce more discriminative and fine features. With the analysis of [14], Layer 5 and Layer 7 in Caffe [7] both have a steady improvement with SVM or Softmax. Ulteriorly, we explore how coarse or fine the features in Layer 5 and Layer 7 are and how to improve the performance by refining Layer 7. As far as we know, the features of Layer 7 are computed as follow:

$$v_1 = W_6 \cdot CNN_5 + B_6, \qquad v_2 = W_7 \cdot v_1 + B_7 \quad (7)$$

where W_i is the weights and B_i is the biases of each layer learnt by [7]. v_1 and v_2 are the features of Layer 6 and Layer 7 respectively.

Assuming Layer 5 can be regarded as coarse features and omits some detailed information, albeit with multi-iteration. We propose a coarse-to-fine method to optimize these features. From the weights of each layer, some absolute values of the weights are close to zero while their contiguous eight weights are not. Thus, it comes to us that the current weight may also contain information in spite of being set to zero after multi-iteration. Above all, we replace the current weight by the average of contiguous eight weights. Our weighted image relation graph is generated as Figure 3. Images are represented as a set of CNN features from Layer n and the weighted image relation graph will be built by calculating the similarities of features.

3. EXPERIMENTS AND ANALYSIS

3.1 Experiment Setting

In this section, we evaluate our method on a cross-media dataset, MCG-WEBV [3]. MCG-WEBV is built with the "Most viewed" videos of "This month" on YouTube from

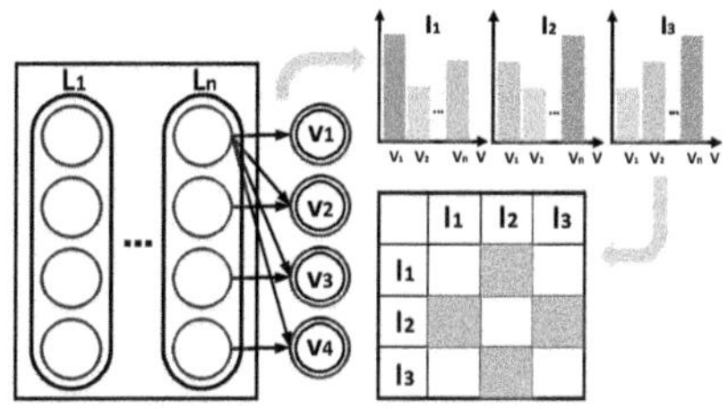

Figure 3: An illustration of generating weighted image relation graph.

Dec 2008 to Feb 2009. It contains 3282 web videos and 73 manually annotated ground truth topics. To compare our results with ground truth, we select the documents labeled from MCG-WEBV. Since the vocabulary has a very long tail word distribution, we filter out those words that occur less than or equal to 5 times. All text content is stemmed by portStemmer. Eventually, there are 832 documents, 22755 images and 4741 words in the collection.

In experiments, some preprocessing for establishing image relation graph is required. Firstly, to demonstrate the performance of the proposed method, we calculate cosine similarities on three kinds of features as comparisons: **1)** Bag of Visual Word features (abbreviated as BoVW). Each image is represented as a histogram of 128-codeword SIFT codebook; **2)** Original CNN features. We mainly analyze Layer 5 and Layer 7 of [7] (denote as CNN-5 and CNN-7); **3)** Coarse-to-fine CNN features (denote as CNN-7*). Secondly, we find out those images that have intense relationships (e.g. the value of cosine similarity ≥ 0.8) and set the other similarities to 0 to make the weighted image relation graph sparse. While preprocessing is relatively simple to deal with the relationships between images, it can reflect the potential relationships with different weights to some extent. We compare IDTM with two other models: **1)** LDA, which takes each text content as document; **2)** ATM, which treats images as "authors". In experiments, $\alpha = 50/K$ and $\beta = 0.01$ and Gibbs sampling is run for 1800 iterations.

3.2 Analysis of Our Approach

Here we analyze the quality of topics discovered by our model. Table 1 show examples of 2 topics out of 73 from MCG-WEBV dataset learnt by IDTM. We use the highest probability word to represent the topic.

Table 1: An illustration of 2 topics out of 73

Bush		Warcraft	
word	*prob*	*word*	*prob*
bush	0.16680	warcraft	0.03369
shoe	0.15164	ad	0.02379
president	0.09983	wow	0.02280
iraq	0.06193	paladin	0.02180
george	0.05940	tv	0.02081
iraqi	0.05561	commercial	0.01982
journalist	0.03918	pub	0.01784
throw	0.03413	spot	0.01685
conference	0.03160	ozzy	0.01685
press	0.02276	osbourne	0.01586

According to the results, the top-10 words and images are highly related to the specific topic. The corresponding top-

Figure 4: Image predictions by IDTM on topic Bush and Warcraft. The maximum and minimum probability of images is upper-left and lower-right respectively for each topic.

ic descriptions in [3] are "**Bush was attacked by shoes during press conference in Iraq**" and "**a popular online gaming world of warcraft (WOW in short), including the operate guides and ads**" respectively. The results denote that the top-5 words predicted by IDTM have explained the key information about the topic. For example, from "bush", "shoe", "president", "iraq", and "george", we might guess that topic is about "President George Bush" and "Iraq". The other words in top-10 may explain the information of where and who. Meanwhile, the top-10 images predicted by IDTM show the potential image relationship. As illustrated in Figure 4, images in the same topic are relative and gathered together, while they are in the separate documents beforehand. To demonstrate the performance of the proposed method, we compare the proposed model with ***F-Measure***. Table 2 shows the *F-Measure* of top-10 detected topics for all the test methods on MCG-WEBV dataset. ILDA and TLDA use Bag of visual Words of images and Bag of Words of documents as attributes respectively.

Table 2: *F-Measure* on MCG-WEBV

Method	IDTM			ATM	TLDA	ILDA
	$\tau = 0.8$	$\tau = 0.7$	$\tau = 0.6$			
BoVW	0.5244	0.5237	0.5184	0.4660	0.4565	0.1091
CNN-5	0.5499	0.5269	0.5317			
CNN-7	0.5486	0.5537	0.5255			
CNN-7*	0.5397	**0.5616**	0.5395			

From Table 2, the *F-Measure* of IDTM is significantly improved than other models no matter what hyper-parameter τ[1] or features we choose. The features in the first column are denoted in Section 3.1. Based on the method described in Section 2.2, we update W_6 to refine Layer 7. Since improved CNN feature shows better performance than BoVW and original CNN features generally, it convinces us that refining CNN feature by coarse-to-fine method indeed increases the discriminative power of images. Accordingly, the idea that combines text and image features together and builds topic model is meaningful and valuable.

4. CONCLUSIONS

In this paper, we propose a new deep image dominant topic model for cross-media topic detection. The model projects the text and the visual information into a semantic simplex. Compared to the traditional single document-oriented topic models, IDTM captures semantic relations between words by establishing weighted image relation graph and discovers more distinguishable topics than previous models. We introduce a fuse model of the convolutional layer and fully-connected layer in the CNN framework, which can obtain more visual details and improve the generalization of the final visual representation. In the future, we would like to explore image relationships with more robust methods and model emotional information among topics by image graph.

[1]In IDTM, hyper-parameter τ defines the possibility that image assignments are from images in the current document. The lower τ is, the higher randomness is, and vice versa.

5. ACKNOWLEDGMENTS

This work was supported in part by National Basic Research Program of China (973 Program): 2012CB316400 and 2015CB351802, in part by National Natural Science Foundation of China: 61332016, 61402431, and 61303154, in part by Project Funded by China Postdoctoral Science Foundation.

6. REFERENCES

[1] D. M. Blei and M. I. Jordan. Modeling annotated data. In *ACM SIGIR*, pages 127–134, 2003.

[2] D. M. Blei, A. Y. Ng, and M. I. Jordan. Latent dirichlet allocation. *JMLR*, 3:993–1022, 2003.

[3] J. Cao, Y. D. Zhang, Y. C. Song, Z. N. Chen, X. Zhang, and J. T. Li. Mcg-webv: A benchmark dataset for web video analysis. *Beijing: Institute of Computing Technology*, 10:324–334, 2009.

[4] J. Chang and D. M. Blei. Relational topic models for document networks. In *AISTATS*, pages 81–88, 2009.

[5] T. L. Griffiths and M. Steyvers. Finding scientific topics. *NAS*, 101(suppl 1):5228–5235, 2004.

[6] T. Hofmann. Probabilistic latent semantic indexing. In *ACM SIGIR*, pages 50–57, 1999.

[7] Y. Jia, E. Shelhamer, J. Donahue, S. Karayev, J. Long, R. Girshick, S. Guadarrama, and T. Darrell. Caffe: Convolutional architecture for fast feature embedding. In *ACM Multimedia*, pages 675–678, 2014.

[8] A. Krizhevsky, I. Sutskever, and G. E. Hinton. Imagenet classification with deep convolutional neural networks. In *NIPS*, pages 1097–1105, 2012.

[9] T. P. Minka. Expectation propagation for approximate bayesian inference. In *UAI*, pages 362–369, 2001.

[10] Z. X. Niu, G. Hua, X. B. Gao, and Q. Tian. Semi-supervised relational topic model for weakly annotated image recognition in social media. In *IEEE CVPR*, pages 4233–4240, 2014.

[11] M. Rosen-Zvi, T. Griffiths, M. Steyvers, and P. Smyth. The author-topic model for authors and documents. In *UAI*, pages 487–494, 2004.

[12] C. Wang, D. M. Blei, and F. F. Li. Simultaneous image classification and annotation. In *IEEE CVPR*, pages 1903–1910, 2009.

[13] Y. Wang, J. Liu, J. S. Qu, Y. L. Huang, J. M. Chen, and X. Feng. Hashtag graph based topic model for tweet mining. In *IEEE ICDM*, pages 1025–1030, 2014.

[14] M. D. Zeiler and R. Fergus. Visualizing and understanding convolutional networks. In *ECCV*, pages 818–833. 2014.

[15] Y. Zheng, Y. J. Zhang, and L. Hugo. A deep and autoregressive approach for topic modeling of multimodal data. *arXiv preprint:1409.3970*, 2014.

Human Action Recognition With Trajectory Based Covariance Descriptor In Unconstrained Videos

Hanli Wang* Yun Yi Jun Wu

Department of Computer Science and Technology, Tongji University, Shanghai, China
Key Laboratory of Embedded System and Service Computing, Ministry of Education, Tongji University, Shanghai, China
{hanliwang,13yunyi,wujun}@tongji.edu.cn

ABSTRACT

Human action recognition from realistic videos plays a key role in multimedia event detection and understanding. In this paper, a novel Trajectory Based Covariance (TBC) descriptor is proposed, which is formulated along the dense trajectories. To map the descriptor matrix to vector space and trim out the redundancy of data, the TBC descriptor matrix is projected to Euclidean space by the Logarithm Principal Components Analysis (LogPCA). Our method is tested on the challenging Hollywood2 and TV Human Interaction datasets. Experimental results show that the proposed TBC descriptor outperforms three baseline descriptors (*i.e.*, histogram of oriented gradient, histogram of optical flow and motion boundary histogram), and our method achieves better recognition performances than a number of state-of-the-art approaches.

Categories and Subject Descriptors

I.2.10 [**Artificial Intelligence**]: Vision and Scene Understanding

General Terms

Algorithms, Experimentation, Performance

Keywords

TBC Descriptor; Motion Trajectory; LogPCA; Covariance

*H. Wang is the corresponding author. This work was supported in part by the National Natural Science Foundation of China under Grant 61472281, the "Shu Guang" project of Shanghai Municipal Education Commission and Shanghai Education Development Foundation under Grant 12SG23, the Program for Professor of Special Appointment (Eastern Scholar) at Shanghai Institutions of Higher Learning (No. GZ2015005), and the Fundamental Research Funds for the Central Universities under Grant 0800219270.

MM'15, October 26–30, 2015, Brisbane, Australia
© 2015 ACM. ISBN 978-1-4503-3459-4/15/10$15.00
DOI: http://dx.doi.org/10.1145/2733373.2806310.

1. INTRODUCTION

The past few years have witnessed a great success of social networks and multimedia technologies, leading to the generation of vast amount of Internet videos. To well organize these videos and provide value-added services to users, it is increasingly important to automatically understand the human activities from videos. The success of many applications (*e.g.*, intelligent visual surveillance, human computer interaction, video retrieval and smart cameras) are conditioned on the accuracy of human action recognition. A number of research studies are focused on this challenging topic, such as [1, 2, 3], to name a few.

There are generally two main processing steps about a typical human action recognition algorithm. The first is feature extraction, in which the human action is described by feature vectors. The second is detection, in which the feature vectors are utilized for event classification. This paper focuses on the first step by describing human actions with dense trajectory and Riemannian manifolds.

The major contributions of this work are summarized as follows. First, a novel Trajectory Based Covariance (TBC) descriptor is proposed to describe human actions. Unlike other covariance descriptors, the TBC descriptor is formulated along the dense trajectories, which enhances the ability of describing human actions. Second, the TBC descriptor is projected to Euclidean space by the Logarithm Principal Components Analysis (LogPCA) to further improve its describing ability. The rest of this paper is organized as follows. The proposed TBC descriptor for human action recognition is introduced in Section 2. The experimental setup and results are presented in Section 3. Finally, Section 4 concludes this paper.

2. TBC DESCRIPTOR

2.1 Descriptor Formulation

As stated in [3], the dense trajectory based method with camera motion estimation is able to achieve excellent human action recognition performances on challenging datasets. Inspired by this, the proposed TBC descriptor is designed along dense trajectories. Given a video, it is firstly divided into N trajectories $\mathbb{T} = \{T_1, T_2, \cdots, T_N\}$, and a trajectory can be defined as

$$T_{n_\tau} = \{R_1(W, H), R_2(W, H), \cdots, R_L(W, H)\}, \quad (1)$$

where W and H are the width and height of the space region aligned with a trajectory, L is the trajectory length, and n_τ is the temporal grid number of the trajectory. An illustration of the proposed TBC descriptor is given in Fig. 1.

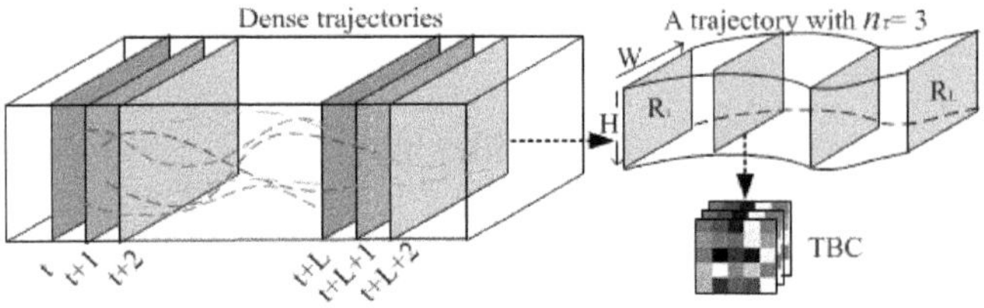

Figure 1: Illustration of TBC descriptor.

Let F be the $W \times H$ dimensional feature vector extracted from the region R, which can be given as

$$F(x, y) = \Phi(R, x, y), \qquad (2)$$

where the function Φ can be any mapping, *e.g.*, intensity, dense optical flow, etc. For a given region $R_i \subset T$, let $\mathbb{Z} = \{z_k\}_{k=1}^S$ be the d dimensional feature vector inside R_i. Each R_i can be represented with a $d \times d$ covariance matrix as

$$X_i = Cov(R_i) = \frac{1}{S-1}\Sigma_{k=1}^S (z_k - \mu)(z_k - \mu)^T, \qquad (3)$$

where S is the size of region R_i and μ is the mean of z.

Regarding the descriptor mapping $\phi = \{\Phi_1, \Phi_2, \cdots, \Phi_d\}$, it is defined as the following combination of dense optical flow based features being extracted along the trajectory:

$$\phi = [x, y, u, v, \sqrt{u^2+v^2}, \arctan\frac{u}{v}, u_x, u_y, v_x, v_y, \sqrt{u_x^2+u_y^2}, \sqrt{v_x^2+v_y^2}, \arctan\frac{u_x}{u_y}, \arctan\frac{v_x}{v_y}]^T, \qquad (4)$$

where x and y indicate the location of the dense optical flow, u and v are the horizontal and vertical components of the optical flow vector. In order, the follow-up optical flow based features include the magnitude of u and v, the orientation of u and v, the first order derivative of u with respect to x, the first order derivative of u with respect to y, the first order derivative of v with respect to x, the first order derivative of v with respect to y, the magnitude of u_x and u_y, the magnitude of v_x and v_y, the orientation of u_x and u_y, and the orientation of v_x and v_y. With the defined mapping in Eq. (4), the region R of a trajectory is represented with a $d = 14$ covariance matrix.

2.2 LogPCA

Tuzel *et al.* [4] argue that the Euclidean distance metric is not suitable for covariance, as they do not form a vector space. However, Log-covariance matrices form a vector space. To apply classical machine learning techniques, a region matrix X on the manifold can be mapped to an Euclidean space using the logarithm map operator. Let the eigenvalue decomposition of X be $X = VDV^{-1}$, in which each column of V is an eigenvector of X and D is a diagonal matrix whose diagonal elements are eigenvalues of X. Then, $\log(X) = VD'V^{-1}$, where D' is the diagonal matrix which is obtained from D by replacing D's diagonal entries with their logarithms.

Given N covariance descriptors $\mathbb{X} = \{X_1, X_2, \cdots, X_N\}$ from the Riemannian manifold $\mathcal{M}$, each covariance matrix X_i can be mapped to its corresponding Euclidean space vector Y_i as

$$Y_i = Vec(\log(X_i)), \qquad (5)$$

where $Vec(\cdot)$ transforms the upper triangular part of the input matrix into a vector.

As it is well known, the Principal Components Analysis (PCA) is a useful statistical technique to find patterns in data of high dimension. Accordingly, Algorithm 1 outlines the Logarithm PCA (LogPCA) on Riemannian manifold. The experimental results in Section 3.3 demonstrate that the LogPCA algorithm promotes the performance on two challenging datasets, as the data correlation is trimmed out.

Algorithm 1 Logarithm Principal Components Analysis.

Input:
Training set $\mathbb{X} = \{X_1, X_2, \cdots, X_N\}$.
Projection dimension p.

Output:
The projection matrix $\mathbb{A}$.

Processing:
1: Map each covariance matrix X_i to Euclidean space vector Y_i as Eq. (5) and then set $\mathbb{Y} = \{Y_1, Y_2, \cdots, Y_N\}$.
2: Calculate the covariance matrix and then set $\mathbb{C} = Cov(\mathbb{Y})$.
3: Perform eigenvalue decomposition of matrix $\mathbb{C}$.
4: Order eigenvectors by eigenvalues from highest to lowest.
5: Select the top p eigenvectors to form the projection matrix $\mathbb{A} = [A_1|A_2|\cdots|A_p]$.

Let $m = L/n_\tau$ be the region number of each temporal grid, then the temporal grid can be described as $G = \frac{1}{m}\sum_{i=1}^m Y_i$. According to the time sequence, the descriptor vectors of each temporal grid are concatenated to depict a trajectory. Let X_i be a $d \times d$ dimensional symmetric matrix, then the dimension of Y_i is $(d^2+d)/2$. Finally, the dimension of the TBC descriptor is $n_\tau \times (d^2+d)/2$, in which n_τ is the temporal grid number of trajectory as mentioned above.

2.3 Fast Computation and Complexity

Integral image has been widely used in computer vision, owing to its high efficiency of calculating the sum of an image patch. To fast calculate region covariances, the integral image is employed in this work to compute TBC descriptors. For a descriptor mapping function as defined in Eq. (4), its integral image can be written as

$$I(x', y') = \sum_{x \le x', y \le y'} \Phi(x, y). \qquad (6)$$

Let P be the $W \times H \times d$ tensor of the integral images as

$$P(x', y', i) = \sum_{x \le x', y \le y'} F(x, y, i), \qquad (7)$$

and Q be the $W \times H \times d \times d$ tensor of the second-order integral images as

$$Q(x', y', i, j) = \sum_{x \le x', y \le y'} F(x, y, i)F(x, y, j), \qquad (8)$$

where $i, j \in [1, d]$. As presented in [4], the covariance of the region $R(x', y'; x'', y'')$ can be computed as:

$$\begin{aligned} & C_{R(x',y';x'',y'')} = \\ & \frac{1}{S-1}[Q_{x'',y''} + Q_{x'-1,y'-1} - Q_{x'',y'-1} - Q_{x'-1,y''} \\ & -\frac{1}{S}(P_{x'',y''} + P_{x'-1,y'-1} - P_{x'-1,y''} - P_{x'',y'-1}) \\ & (P_{x'',y''} + P_{x'-1,y'-1} - P_{x'-1,y''} - P_{x'',y'-1})^T], \end{aligned} \tag{9}$$

where $S = (x'' - x' + 1) \cdot (y'' - y' + 1)$. Therefore, the covariance of any rectangular region can be computed in $O(d^2WH)$.

3. EXPERIMENTAL RESULTS

3.1 Experimental Setup

Three state-of-the-art descriptors including HOG [5], HOF [6] and MBH [7] are employed as the baseline descriptor, which are separately extracted from each trajectory with the same parameters (*i.e.*, $W = 32, H = 32, L = 15, n_\tau = 3$), and PCA is individually applied to each of these descriptor vectors for dimension reduction as in [3]. The TBC descriptor is also calculated with the same parameters, and LogPCA is utilized to reduce the dimensionality by a factor of two as the baseline descriptor.

Moreover, the Fisher vector [8] model is applied for codebook construction. For each descriptor, we compute one Fisher vector over the entire video, and apply the signed square root and ℓ_2 normalization. To achieve the balance of training samples, we weight positive and negative samples in an inverse manner as suggested in [9]. In the following experiments, the standard linear LIBSVM [10] is used with the penalty parameter C equal to 100 as in [3].

In order to evaluate the proposed TBC descriptor, two challenging human action video datasets, including Hollywood2 [11] and TV Human Interaction [12] are utilized for experiments. We follow the standard evaluation protocols by presenting mean Average Precision (mAP) over all classes on these two datasets.

3.2 Comparison with Baseline Descriptors

A number of experiments have been carried out to quantify the improvement obtained by our TBC descriptor as compared to three baseline descriptors (*i.e.*, HOG, HOF and MBH). For comparison in a fair manner, we use the implementation of improved dense trajectories in [3], and set the same parameters as presented in Section 3.1.

The summary of the comparison between our TBC descriptor and these three baseline descriptors is given in Table 1 on the Hollywood2 dataset. As observed in Table 1, the mAP results obtained by HOG, HOF, MBH and our TBC descriptor are 48.7%, 59.6%, 61.3% and 63.8%, respectively; as a consequence, the TBC descriptor outperforms HOG, HOF and MBH by 15.1%, 4.2% and 2.5%, respectively. For the 12 classes of events on Hollywood2, the TBC descriptor almost obtains the highest performance over other three descriptors, especially on '*GetOutCar*' and '*StandUp*'.

Table 2 shows the comparison between our TBC and the three baseline descriptors on the TV Human Interaction dataset. The mAP performances of HOG, HOF, MBH and our TBC descriptor are 63.4%, 75.0%, 75.6% and 78.1%, respectively; therefore, TBC outperforms HOG, HOF and MBH by 14.7%, 3.1% and 2.5%, respectively.

Table 1: mAP Comparison on Hollywood2.

	HOG	HOF	MBH	TBC
AnswerPhone	19.6%	19.0%	26.8%	27.1%
DriveCar	88.3%	93.7%	94.3%	94.5%
Eat	49.9%	69.8%	63.3%	65.2%
FightPerson	73.5%	81.9%	82.5%	86.4%
GetOutCar	47.4%	58.4%	59.3%	64.8%
HandShake	28.3%	29.6%	38.1%	39.2%
HugPerson	34.4%	41.6%	51.5%	54.9%
Kiss	58.6%	59.5%	62.0%	64.4%
Run	76.1%	84.8%	84.1%	84.4%
SitDown	40.0%	73.1%	76.0%	76.1%
SitUp	19.3%	31.9%	25.2%	30.1%
StandUp	49.5%	71.6%	72.0%	77.9%
mAP	48.7%	59.6%	61.3%	63.8%

Table 2: mAP Comparison on TV Human.

	HOG	HOF	MBH	TBC
Hand shake	56.0%	63.5%	64.8%	72.1%
High five	69.7%	83.9%	83.5%	84.1%
Hug	79.5%	86.1%	86.3%	88.1%
Kiss	48.4%	66.3%	67.7%	68.2%
mAP	63.4%	75.0%	75.6%	78.1%

As TBC captures more information of human actions than the baseline descriptors, it outperforms the baseline descriptors of HOG, HOF and MBH on both Hollywood2 and TV Human Interaction datasets. The experiments verify the covariance of optical flow based features along trajectories is more robust than histogram-based descriptors.

3.3 Evaluation of LogPCA

In order to evaluate the influence of the LogPCA algorithm, experiments have been performed with the results shown in Tables 3 and 4. We set the same experimental parameters as described in Section 3.1.

On Hollywood2, the mAP achieved by TBC with LogPCA enabled is 63.8%, which is 2.6% better than the test case with LogPCA disabled. For the 12 classes of events on Hollywood2, the method with LogPCA enabled generally obtains higher performances than that without LogPCA, except the '*AnswerPhone*' and '*Run*' events. On the TV Human Interaction dataset, the mAP obtained by the TBC descriptor with LogPCA enabled is 78.1%, which is 2.7% better than that with LogPCA disabled.

Therefore, on both Hollywood2 and TV Human Interaction datasets, the LogPCA approach is useful to improve the performance of human action recognition. Such an improvement is mainly due to the reason that LogPCA can decorrelate data and remove data noises.

3.4 Comparison with State-of-the-Arts

The proposed TBC based method is also compared with several state-of-the-art approaches with the results shown in Table 5, where 'Our Method' represents the method com-

Table 3: Evaluation of LogPCA on Hollywood2.

	without LogPCA	with LogPCA
AnswerPhone	31.2%	27.1%
DriveCar	93.2%	94.5%
Eat	61.5%	65.2%
FightPerson	83.7%	86.4%
GetOutCar	60.5%	64.8%
HandShake	34.9%	39.2%
HugPerson	51.6%	54.9%
Kiss	56.2%	64.4%
Run	84.6%	84.4%
SitDown	72.2%	76.1%
SitUp	28.8%	30.1%
StandUp	75.9%	77.9%
mAP	61.2%	63.8%

Table 4: Evaluation of LogPCA on TV Human.

	without LogPCA	with LogPCA
Hand shake	73.0%	72.1%
High five	87.4%	84.1%
Hug	87.1%	88.1%
Kiss	54.2%	68.2%
mAP	75.4%	78.1%

bining TBC with HOG, HOF and MBH descriptors. To combine the four descriptors, we employ early fusion strategy which linearly concatenates the feature vectors.

As far as Hollywood2 is concerned, Jain *et al.* [2] report the mAP of 62.5% by canceling the predominantly camera motion to stabilize dense trajectories. Oneata *et al.* [9] utilize the Fisher vector model to improve their results. Wang *et al.* [3] obtain the mAP of 64.3% by estimating camera motions. The proposed method achieves the best mAP of 66.8%, which is around 2.5% better than that of [3]. Regarding the TV Human Interaction dataset, the baseline result presented in [12] is 42.4%. Yu *et al.* [13] report 55.9% by employing propagative hough voting for activity analysis. Recently, Hoai *et al.* [14] achieve a better performance of 56.3% with upper-body track. We improve over their results by around 22%, reaching to the mAP of 78.2%.

Table 5: Comparison with state-of-the-art approaches.

Hollywood2	mAP	TV Human	mAP
Jain [2]	62.5%	Patron [12]	42.4%
Oneata [9]	63.3%	Yu [13]	55.9%
Wang [3]	64.3%	Hoai [14]	56.3%
TBC	63.8%	TBC	78.1%
Our Method	**66.8%**	Our Method	**78.2%**

4. CONCLUSION

In this paper, a novel TBC descriptor is designed for human action recognition, which is based on improved dense trajectories and Riemannian manifolds. TBC has shown to outperform several state-of-the-art descriptors (*i.e.*, HOG, HOF and MBH). Moreover, the LogPCA algorithm has been introduced to map the symmetric positive definite matrices to the Euclidean space and reduce the dimension of TBC descriptor. The experimental results demonstrate that the proposed approach combining TBC with HOG, HOF and MBH descriptors is superior to other state-of-the-art approaches for human action recognition. In the future, the data augmentation [15], spatial Fisher vector and spatio-temporal grid [9] approaches can also be used with the proposed TBC to further improve the performance, which will be one of our future research efforts.

5. REFERENCES

[1] Nicolas Ballas, Bertrand Delezoide, and Françoise Prêteux. Trajectory signature for action recognition in video. In *ACM MM'12*, pages 1429–1432, 2012.

[2] Mihir Jain, Hervé Jégou, and Patrick Bouthemy. Better exploiting motion for better action recognition. In *CVPR'13*, pages 2555–2562, 2013.

[3] Heng Wang and Cordelia Schmid. Action recognition with improved trajectories. In *ICCV'13*, pages 3551–3558, 2013.

[4] Oncel Tuzel, Fatih Porikli, and Peter Meer. Pedestrian detection via classification on riemannian manifolds. *IEEE Trans. Pattern Anal. Mach. Intell.*, 30(10):1713–1727, 2008.

[5] Navneet Dalal and Bill Triggs. Histograms of oriented gradients for human detection. In *CVPR'05*, pages 886–893, 2005.

[6] Ivan Laptev, Marcin Marszalek, Cordelia Schmid, and Benjamin Rozenfeld. Learning realistic human actions from movies. In *CVPR'08*, pages 1–8, 2008.

[7] Navneet Dalal, Bill Triggs, and Cordelia Schmid. Human detection using oriented histograms of flow and appearance. In *ECCV'06*, pages 428–441, 2006.

[8] Florent Perronnin and Christopher Dance. Fisher kernels on visual vocabularies for image categorization. In *CVPR'07*, pages 1–8, 2007.

[9] Dan Oneata, Jakob Verbeek, and Cordelia Schmid. Action and event recognition with fisher vectors on a compact feature set. In *ICCV'13*, pages 1817–1824, 2013.

[10] Rong-En Fan, Kai-Wei Chang, Cho-Jui Hsieh, Xiang-Rui Wang, and Chih-Jen Lin. LIBLINEAR: A library for large linear classification. *J. Machine Learning Research*, 9:1871–1874, 2008.

[11] Marcin Marszalek, Ivan Laptev, and Cordelia Schmid. Actions in context. In *CVPR'09*, pages 2929–2936, 2009.

[12] Alonso Patron-Perez, Marcin Marszalek, Ian Reid, and Andrew Zisserman. Structured learning of human interactions in TV shows. *IEEE Trans. Pattern Anal. Mach. Intell.*, 34(12):2441–2453, 2012.

[13] Gang Yu, Junsong Yuan, and Zicheng Liu. Propagative hough voting for human activity recognition. In *ECCV'12*, pages 693–706, 2012.

[14] Minh Hoai and Andrew Zisserman. Talking heads: Detecting humans and recognizing their interactions. In *CVPR'14*, pages 875–882, 2014.

[15] Minh Hoai and Andrew Zisserman. Improving human action recognition using score distribution and ranking. In *ACCV'14*, pages 3–20, 2014.

RECfusion: Automatic Video Curation Driven by Visual Content Popularity

Alessandro Ortis
Universitá degli Studi di Catania
Viale A. Doria 6, 95125
Catania, Italy
ortis@dmi.unict.it

Giovanni Maria Farinella
Universitá degli Studi di Catania
Viale A. Doria 6, 95125
Catania, Italy
gfarinella@dmi.unict.it

Valeria D'Amico
Telecom Italia
JOL WAVE - Viale A. Doria 6, 95125
Catania, Italy
valeria1.damico@telecomitalia.it

Luca Addesso
Telecom Italia
JOL WAVE - Viale A. Doria 6, 95125
Catania, Italy
luca.addesso@telecomitalia.it

Giovanni Torrisi
Telecom Italia
JOL WAVE - Viale A. Doria 6, 95125
Catania, Italy
giovanni.torrisi@telecomitalia.it

Sebastiano Battiato
Universitá degli Studi di Catania
Viale A. Doria 6, 95125
Catania, Italy
battiato@dmi.unict.it

ABSTRACT

The proliferation of mobile devices and the diffusion of social media have changed the communication paradigm of people that share multimedia data by allowing new interaction models (e.g., social networks). In social events (e.g., concerts), the automatic video understanding goal includes the interpretation of which visual contents are the most popular. The popularity of a visual content depends on how many people are looking at that scene, and therefore it could be obtained through the "visual consensus" among multiple video streams acquired by the different users devices. In this work we present RECfusion, a system able to automatically create a single video from multiple video sources by taking into account the popularity of the acquired scenes. The frames composing the final popular video are selected from the different video streams by considering those visual scenes which are pointed and recorded by the highest number of users' devices. Results on two benchmark datasets confirm the effectiveness of the proposed system.

Categories and Subject Descriptors

I.2.10 [**Artificial Intelligence**]: Vision and Scene Understanding—*Perceptual reasoning, Video Analysis*; I.4.9 [**Image Processing And Computer Vision**]: Applications

Keywords

Social Cameras, Video Curation, Summarization

MM'15, October 26–30, 2015, Brisbane, Australia.
© 2015 ACM. ISBN 978-1-4503-3459-4/15/10 ...$15.00.
DOI: http://dx.doi.org/10.1145/2733373.2806311.

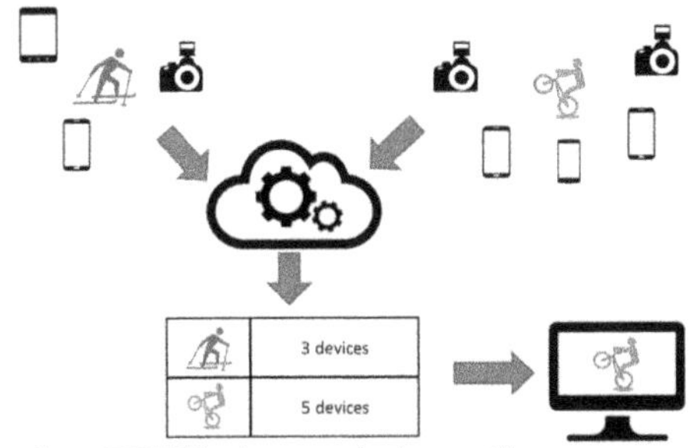

Figure 1: RECfusion - Automatic summarization of popular scenes of social events in a single video.

1. INTRODUCTION

In social events like a concert, a maratona or a car ride, the audience gathers multimedia information with mobile devices (e.g., images, video, geolocation, tags, etc.) related to what has captured their interest. Popular scenes (e.g., fireworks in a folkloristic event) are often observed and acquired simultaneously by multiple end-users with different devices. This redundancy in the video sequences can be exploited to infer which groups of people are interested to specific visual contents over time, and hence which scenes are the most popular.

This work proposes a system that automatically processes multiple video flows from different devices to understand the most popular scenes for a group of end-users. The scenes observed by the different devices are grouped by visual content. This allows an automatic video curation process to obtain a single video as output, by mixing the different inputs and taking into account the most popular scenes, i.e. those scenes acquired by many devices over time (Figure 1). Although much effort has been devoted to understand what is interesting in a scene [7], this problem is still unsolved. The task of establishing the popularity of a scene is challenging because of the variability of the visual content observed by multiple devices: different points of view, pose and scale of the objects, lighting conditions, occlusions, viewing quality, as well as different device models. The Imaging Generation Pipeline (IGP) can vary from device to device and even on an per-image basis [5]. The difference between responses depends essentially on the characteristics of the lenses, filters (e.g. Bayer pattern), sensors, and IGP algorithms [6].

The video curation system proposed in this paper works without specific priors on the input, as well as without knowledge of which and how many devices are involved in the curation process. A related work is described in [1], where a 3D reconstruction of the scene and the relative pose of the devices are exploited. However, the reconstruction of the whole scene is computationally expensive and the video curation algorithm in [1] can be applied only after such a preprocessing stage. In [10] it is proposed an approach which exploits multiple devices of the same model. Also in this case the algorithm needs a calibration phase to reconstruct the camera poses. The method proposed in [8] tries to create a single popular video of an event from multiple egocentric videos. All scenes were taken using the same camera model by different participants close each other (few meters). The approach assumes that the number of the different popular scenes and the number of the devices is known a priori. These information are used to recognize an exact number of regions of interest used as prototypes in the grouping phase. The algorithm proposed in [11] combines several videos of the same scene taken from different perspectives. Despite the final video is not based on the popularity (as in the case we are interested in) this framework is able to produce an unique final video related to the considered scenario. The main goal of the approach in [11] is to build an automatic system which tries to imitate a professional video editor by choosing automatically which shooting angle and distance should be used and how long the selected configuration should persists.

Differently than previous approaches, the method proposed in this paper combines several videos from unknown different devices based on the popularity of the acquired scenes without any prior knowledge or training stage.

2. PROPOSED SYSTEM

The multiple video streams acquired by the different devices are analysed by using two algorithms: one to segment the different scenes, transitions and the unstable intervals within each video (intraflow analysis), and the other one to perform the grouping of the involved devices over time by taking into account the visual content of the previously segmented video streams. The popularity of the obtained clusters over time is used to produce the final video.

2.1 Intraflow Analysis

During intraflow analysis each video is processed by comparing its frames in order to segment the video based on the visual content. For each frame selected by sampling the video, we extract keypoints using the well-known SIFT algorithm [9]. The set of SIFT features extracted from a frame are used as a template for the acquired scene. In our experiments we excluded the SIFT extracted near the border of the considered frames to make more robust the feature matching among frames. The intraflow analysis consists in the comparison of templates extracted from different frames of a video to split it in blocks by taking into account the visual content. During this process the system keeps a reference template regarding the last known scene (i.e., the last stable set of SIFT features extracted from the last detected scene) and compares this template with respect to the features extracted from the current frame under analysis. When a sensible variation of features is observed (i.e., low matching score), the algorithm refreshes the reference template and splits the video producing a new segment.

Given a frame, the number of matchings between its SIFT keypoints and the once of the reference template is considered as a similarity index between the involved scenes. To make the matching more reliable, we excluded the matchings where the keypoints are too far in terms of spatial coordinate by assuming smooth transition between frames (we used a threshold distance of 100 pixels for images with resolution 1280×720 or 1920×1080). In order to detect the sudden changes of the number of matchings we defined a slope function which is computed on a frame at time T as follows:

$$slope(T) = \frac{h}{w} = \frac{l \sin\theta}{l \sin\theta} = \tan\theta \quad (1)$$

This function represents the variation of the number of matchings h in a range interval w centered in a frame at time T. This value is related to the tangent of an angle θ which is proportional to the gradient of the matching curve. The algorithm asks for a new template (i.e., set of SIFT features) when the slope function has a peak greater than 10 (i.e., θ= 85°). In order to define only reliable templates the algorithm checks if the computed template is stable for at least 2 seconds (i.e., the number of matchings do not change too much). When a new stable template is defined, the algorithm compares it with respect to the past templates in order to understand if it regards a new scene or it is related to a known previously observed scene. This backward checking is done starting from the last found template. Two different templates of the same scene could be rather different due to the elapsed time between them. During this step, to check if two templates describe the same scene we use a geometric verification to exclude the spatial matchings with distance higher than one-third of the height of the image. Two templates are assigned to the same scene if the percentage of the matchings after the geometric verification is greater than 50% of the original matchings. Each reference template is assigned to a scene ID and all the video frames which achieve a robust match with a reference template are classified as of that scene. All the frames between the instant when a new scene template have to be upgraded by the system and the instant when that template is finally upgraded are classified as a transition interval.

Figure 2 shows an example of the result of the intraflow analysis applied on four input videos as a coloured chronogram: each scene is identified by a colour (red, blue and green in the figure), whereas the transition intervals and the unstable frames (e.g., shaking frames) are identified by black colour. The intraflow analysis allows an automatic segmentation of each video in several intervals depending on the visual content. It is also useful to correctly locate the transition intervals.

2.2 Interflow Analysis

Given two images acquired with different devices it is very challenging to understand if they are related to the same scene using only visual information [3, 4]. In our case, given frames of different videos which have been segmented as described in Section 2.1 we want to understand which of the different devices are looking at the same scene over time. The most popular scene over time is then used to produce the final video. In the interflow analysis we defined a frame descriptor based on a weighted colour histogram. In order

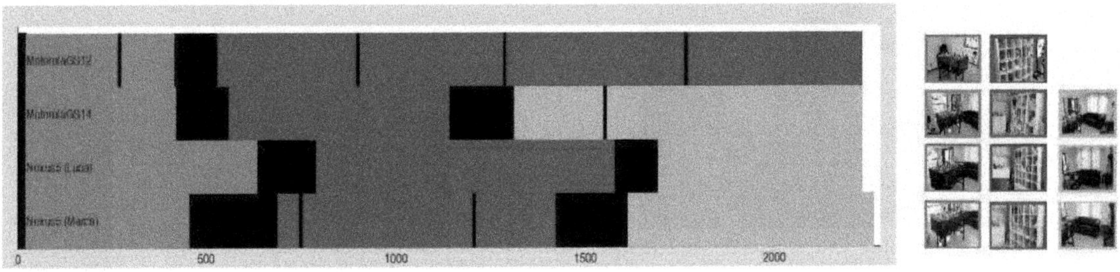

Figure 2: Output of the intraflow analysis.

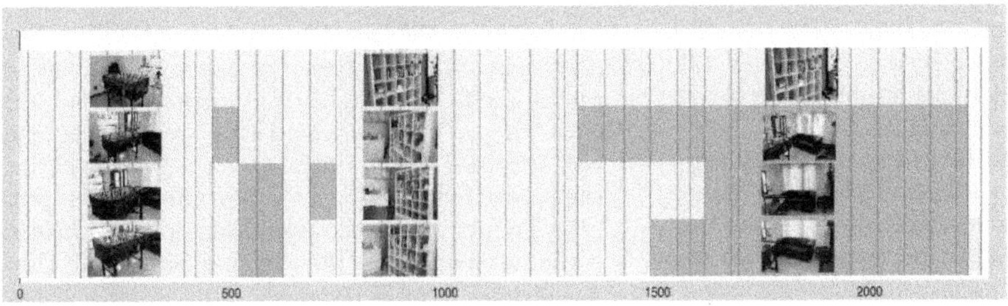

Figure 3: Clustering result applied on four devices. A vertical red line indicates when a clustering block is performed over time, this happens when one of the devices change his subject (e.g. in corrispondence of a intraflow change in Figure 2) or at most every 2 seconds.

to address the device invariance issue, we first apply the histogram equalization described in [5]. This method consists on the application of an histogram equalization to each RGB channel to reduce the variability introduced by the IGPs related to the different devices. After the equalization we compute a weighted colour histogram by quantizing the color space (8 color for each channel). The weights are obtained by using a gradient map as suggested in [2]. The gradient map highlights the structures of the objects involved in the scene making more robust the color-based descriptor. To compare histograms we use the same distance employed in [2]:

$$d(h_{D_a}, h_{D_b}) = \sum \frac{\sum (h_{D_a} - h_{D_b})^2}{\sum (h_{D_a})^2} \tag{2}$$

where h_{D_a} and h_{D_b} are the weighted histograms related to the two frames of two different devices D_a and D_b.

To cluster the devices accordingly to visual content at every instance of time, we first segment all the videos exploiting the intraflow analysis (Section 2.1), and then we use the weighted color histogram representation to compare the obtained video segments (Figure 3). Through the intraflow analysis we obtain the scene ID and a set of SIFT features used as scene template for each frame of the different videos. At each instant T, the set of frames of the different devices are clustered by taking into account the corresponding weighted histogram representation. The different scenes are considered as a complete graph where each node is a device and the arches are labelled with the interflow measure between the scenes taken by the devices (Equation 2). The interflow measures are used to establish similarity during the clustering of the devices. The final video produced as output by the proposed approach is obtained by considering the most popular cluster (i.e., the once with the highest number of devices). Specifically, for the output at each instant T we consider the video belonging to the most popular cluster which is closest to the cluster centroid (i.e., average among all histograms). The pseudocode to cluster the devices at each instant of time is reported in Algorithm 1.

Algorithm 1 Devices' clustering

1: **procedure**
2: Choose an unclustered device D.
3: Insert D in a new cluster C_d.
4: **for** each device $B \neq D$ **do**
5: **if** $d(h_D, h_B) < 1$ **then**
6: **if** B is unclustered **then**
7: Insert B in the cluster C_d.
8: **else**
9: Find the cluster containing B.
10: Compare B with the elements
11: of the two contending clusters.
12: Insert B in the closer cluster.
13: **if** all devices are clustered **then**
14: End procedure.
15: **else**
16: Return to 2.

3. EXPERIMENTAL RESULTS

To demonstrate the effectiveness of the proposed system we have performed experiments on a new benchmark dataset available at the URL http://iplab.dmi.unict.it/recfusion. The considered dataset includes different scenarios acquired with multiple devices of different models:

- Foosball - In this scenario each device takes a view of a Foosball room switching among three different regions of interest. This scenario is useful to highlights the behaviour of the system when the popularity of a scene leaves a subject advocating a new one.
- Meeting - There were four people sitting around a table. Each person records one of the participants using a mobile device (smartphone or tablet). One more device is placed in order to look constantly to a subject. We tested this scenario varying the number of the devices (2, 4 or 5 devices).
- SAgata - This set of videos have been taken in a real scenario during a folkloristic event (Saint Agata in Catania). Seven people recorded the event while the main subject (the Agata's statue) was carried along the city's streets.

Figure 4: Output video example. On the left and right the input videos, the final output at the center.

The aforementioned scenarios include challenging scenes with crowd, large perspective variation, occlusion, periods of tilt and shaking, etc. We have also tested the proposed approach on the benchmark dataset proposed in [8].

For testing purposes each video has been manually segmented. For each instant of time we known the exact number of clusters and the most popular scene. To evaluate the performances of the proposed method on each scenario we computed two measures obtained from the following scores calculated on each clustering over time:

- P_r: ground truth popularity score (number of cameras looking at the most popular scene) obtained from manual labelling;
- P_a: popularity score computed by our method (number of the elements in the popular cluster);
- P_g: number of correct videos in the popular cluster computed by our method.

From the above scores, we computed the weighted mean of the ratios P_a/P_r and P_g/P_r over all the segmented blocks of a video, where the weights are given by the length of the blocks (i.e., the number of frames). When P_a/P_r is close to 1, the popularity score computed by our method is similar to the ground truth popularity. When this number is greater than 1 it means that the most popular cluster obtained with our approach is affected by outliers, whereas when this number is less than 1 it means that our method missed some element of the ground truth popular cluster. Since P_a/P_r deal just with the number of video in the popular cluster, it is useful to look also at the ratio P_g/P_r. Indeed, P_g/P_r assesses the visual content of the videos in the popular cluster (i.e., true positive). This score have to be close to 1 to indicate accuracy in the popular cluster computed by our method.

Table 1 shows the obtained results. The first five rows are related to the scenarios of the proposed dataset, whereas the last three rows are related to the dataset proposed in [8]. The results show the effectiveness of our approach. Difficulties appear when some video regarding the most popular subject are taken with a quite different scale factors. This can be noted comparing the third and the fourth row in Table 1. In the meeting scenario (5 devices of different models) there is a huge difference in the scale of the acquired subjects in the scene. In the videos proposed in [8] the camera is constantly moving due to the shake induced by the natural head motion of the wearer. Despite we achieve good performances on wearable egocentric videos, we believe that there is still space for further improvements in such a video category (e.g., by filtering out the head motion).

In order to better asses the results obtained by the proposed system, the reader can perform a visual inspection of the videos produced by our approach at the following URL: http://iplab.dmi.unict.it/recfusion.

Table 1: Experimental Results

Scenario	Devices	Models	P_a/P_r	P_g/P_r
Foosball	4	2	1.02	1
Meeting	2	2	1.01	0.99
Meeting	4	4	0.99	0.95
Meeting	5	5	0.89	0.76
SAgata	7	6	1.05	1
Concert [8]	3	1	1.06	1
Lecture [8]	3	1	1.05	0.86
Seminar [8]	3	1	0.62	0.62

4. CONCLUSIONS

This work proposed an automatic video curation method driven by the popularity of the scenes acquired by multiple devices. Although some errors could occur during the clustering of the devices, the system rarely chooses outlier video frames as the output for the proposed dataset. When the algorithm works with a few number of input video these errors could affect the popularity of the clusters. However, if the number of the devices increases, then the effect of the clustering errors is reduced.

5. ACKNOWLEDGMENTS

This work has been performed in collaboration with Telecom Italia JOL WAVE in the project FIR2014-UNICT-DFA17D.

6. REFERENCES

[1] I. Arev, H. S. Park, Y. Sheikh, J. Hodgins, and A. Shamir. Automatic editing of footage from multiple social cameras. *ACM Transactions on Graphics*, 33(4):81, 2014.

[2] J. Domke and Y. Aloimonos. Deformation and viewpoint invariant color histograms. In *British Machine Vision Conference*, 2006.

[3] G. M. Farinella and S. Battiato. Scene classification in compressed and constrained domain. *IET Computer Vision*, 5(5):320–334, 2011.

[4] G. M. Farinella, D. Ravì, V. Tomaselli, M. Guarnera, and S. Battiato. Representing scenes for real-time context classification on mobile devices. *Pattern Recognition*, 48(4):1086–1100, 2015.

[5] G. Finlayson, S. Hordley, G. Schaefer, and G. Y. Tian. Illuminant and device invariant colour using histogram equalisation. *Pattern recognition*, 38(2):179–190, 2005.

[6] G. Finlayson and G. Schaefer. Colour indexing across devices and viewing conditions. In *Workshop on Content-Based Multimedia Indexing*, 2001.

[7] H. Grabner, F. Nater, M. Druey, and L. Van Gool. Visual interestingness in image sequences. In *ACM International Conference on Multimedia*, 2013.

[8] Y. Hoshen, G. Ben-Artzi, and S. Peleg. Wisdom of the crowd in egocentric video curation. In *IEEE Conference on Computer Vision and Pattern Recognition Workshops*, 2014.

[9] D. G. Lowe. Distinctive image features from scale-invariant keypoints. *International journal of computer vision*, 60(2):91–110, 2004.

[10] H. S. Park, E. Jain, and Y. Sheikh. 3d social saliency from head-mounted cameras. In *Advances in Neural Information Processing Systems*, 2012.

[11] M. K. Saini, R. Gadde, S. Yan, and W. T. Ooi. Movimash: online mobile video mashup. In *ACM International Conference on Multimedia*, 2012.

Gender Classification Using Pyramid Segmentation for Unconstrained Back-facing Video Sequences

Hao Tang, Hong Liu,* and Wei Xiao
Key Laboratory for Machine Perception (Ministry of Education)
Engineering Lab on Intelligent Perception for Internet of Things (ELIP)
Shenzhen Graduate School, Peking University, China
haotang@sz.pku.edu.cn; hongliu@pku.edu.cn; xiaoweipkusz@pkusz.edu.cn

ABSTRACT

This paper presents a pioneering study on gender classification from unconstrained back-facing video sequences in natural scenes. In many cases, classifying gender simply via faces or other biometric cues may fail when the video only contains back-facing people. To address this problem, we propose a novel approach to classify the gender according to back-facing video sequences. For this task, a novel Pyramid Segmentation approach is proposed to divide video sequence into a suite of equal time-length sleeves with different scales. Moreover, a heuristic approach is used to compute weights for different features from each sleeve. Finally, a framework of gender classification based on video sequences is presented. To validate our approach, we introduce a new dataset, called BackFacing dataset, featured by 720 annotated back-facing human video sequences. To our knowledge, this is the first dataset only containing back-facing video shots. Experiments demonstrate that the proposed approach achieves competitive results on VidTIMIT, Cohn-Kanade, CASIA Gait and BackFacing datasets.

Categories and Subject Descriptors

I.5.4 [**Computing Methodologies**]: Pattern Recognition Applications *Computer vision* ; I.4.9 [**Computing Methodologies**]: Image Processing and Computer Vision Applications

Keywords

gender classification; pyramid segmentation; back-facing; unconstrained video sequences

1. INTRODUCTION

Gender classification is one of the most interesting topics in pattern classification and computer vision. It aims at determining whether a given person in an image or video is male or female. This task has important applications, such as intelligent user interface, video surveillance, demographic statistics collection, people counting, etc. In video surveillance systems, gender classification is a challenging problem, e.g. people always appear in different scales, poses and viewpoints in uncontrolled environment, and frames usually contain back-facing people, low resolution, and variations in illumination and scale. Recent gender classification works are mainly based on face [1], gait [13, 23], iris, lip, posture [19], and age [6], etc. However, it is hard to obtain these discriminative cues due to illumination variation, occlusion and low resolution. Departing from previous works, this paper considers another situation where a video sequence only contains back-facing people. For video sequence, Zhao et al. propose a block-based method which divided face sequences into several non-overlapping block volumes (Below 'volumes' will be called directly) to deal with specific dynamic events (e.g. facial expressions analysis) [24]. The introduction of spatial feature within still images has also been primarily handled with spatial pyramids [10]. However, block-based method and spatial pyramids only provide a rough spatial description, because the pose of the person may vary significantly. To fix this problem, a semantic pyramid approach has recently been proposed for feature extraction [18]. Spatial pyramids can also be used in, for example, scenes categorization [12].

In this paper we propose a novel Pyramid Segmentation (PS) approach, which divides video sequence into a suite of equal time-length sleeves with different scales, show in Figure 2. The inspiration of PS approach comes from literatures of re-identification [21], dynamic texture recognition [24], and spatial pyramids [10, 18, 12]: different regions of the video sequence contain visually distinct feature repre-

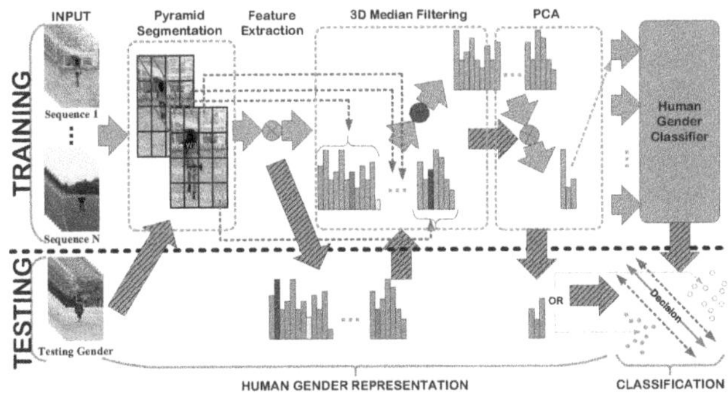

Figure 1: The proposed gender classification framework.

*Corresponding author.

MM'15, October 26-30, 2015, Brisbane, Australia.

DOI: http://dx.doi.org/10.1145/2733373.2806312.

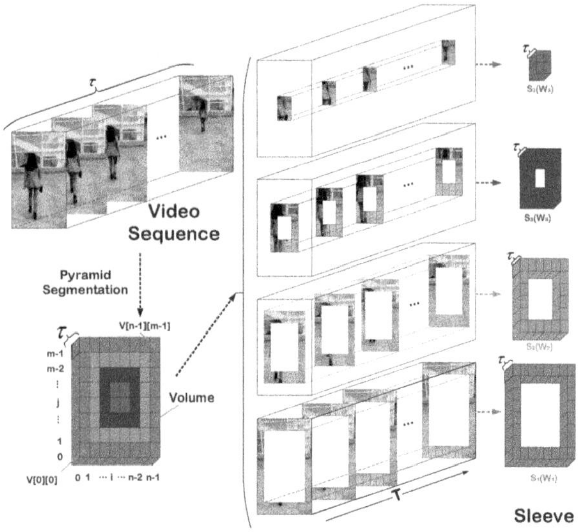

Figure 2: Pyramid segmentation for gender representation.

Algorithm 1 Pyramid segmentation and weights selection.

Require: N training video sequences, each sequence is divided into n by m volumes;
Ensure: The weight $W = \{W_1, W_2, ..., W_t\}$ for each pyramid sleeve $S = \{S_1, S_2, ..., S_t\}$;
1: **for** $t = 1$ to $min(\lceil \frac{n}{2} \rceil, \lceil \frac{m}{2} \rceil)$ **do**
2:   **for** $j = 0$ to $m - 1$ **do**
3:     $S_t.add(V[t-1][j])$, $S_t.add(V[n-t][j])$;
4:   **end for**
5:   **for** $i = 1$ to $n - 2$ **do**
6:     $S_t.add(V[i][t-1])$, $S_t.add(V[i][m-t])$;
7:   **end for**
8:   $m \leftarrow m - 1$, $n \leftarrow n - 1$;
9: **end for**
10: Obtain $S = \{S_1, S_2, ..., S_t\}$, features extracted from each sleeve, produce corresponding histogram $h = \{h_1, h_2, ..., h_t\}$, respectively;
11: By computing the classification rates for each histogram $h = \{h_1, h_2, ..., h_t\}$ separately, get t rates $R = \{R_1, R_2, ..., R_t\}$;
12: Using Formula (1) to normalize R;
13: Using Formula (2) to calculate W;
14: **return** W.

sentation. Some approaches use a single rectangle to capture the global appearance in still images [15], and others utilize more complicated structural representation [5]. Nevertheless, these approaches are applied to a still image of cropped body. Instead we choose a representation using PS to distinguish and reinforce the contributions of the features from each sleeve: the greater contribution it has, the higher weight it will be assigned. Those partitions with higher weight are considered as more important sleeves. For selecting the weights, we adopt the method in [24], which employs the weighted method to the three orthogonal planes of LBP-TOP [24]. Local Binary Patterns from Three Orthogonal Planes (LBP-TOP) [24] consists of three orthogonal planes: XY, XT and YT, and concatenates local binary pattern co-occurrence statistics in these three directions. However, in this paper, we apply the weighted method to each sleeve and use weighed sleeves to construct gender representation. The flowchart in Figure 1 shows the processing details of our gender classification framework based on video sequences.

2. PYRAMID SEGMENTATION AND GENDER CLASSIFICATION FRAMEWORK

We introduce a novel pyramid segmentation approach considering spatial feature in different area of video sequence, which divides video sequence into a suite of equal time-length sleeves with different scales. Assuming that a back-facing video sequence is divide into the n by m volumes evenly, as we can see from Figure 2, each unit volume denoted as $V[i][j]$, where $i = 0, 1, ..., n-1$ and $j = 0, 1, ..., m-1$. We concatenate the volumes which have the same scales as a sleeve, we denote each sleeve as S_t, where $t = min(\lceil \frac{n}{2} \rceil, \lceil \frac{m}{2} \rceil)$. Illustrated in Figure 2, video sequence is divided into 8 by 8 volumes, i.e. 64 volumes. Then $t = min(\lceil \frac{n}{2} \rceil, \lceil \frac{m}{2} \rceil) = 4$, we select $V[0][j]$, $V[7][j]$, $V[i][0]$ and $V[i][7]$, 28 volumes in total as the first sleeve, where $i = 1, 2, ..., 6$ and $j = 0, 1, ..., 7$. The second sleeve is consisted of $V[1][j]$, $V[6][j]$, $V[i][1]$ and $V[i][6]$, where $i = 2, 3, ..., 5$ and $j = 1, 2, ..., 6$, totally 20 volumes. The third sleeve is made up of 12 volumes, i.e. $V[2][j]$, $V[5][j]$, $V[i][2]$ and $V[i][5]$ (where $i = 3, 4$ and $j = 2, 3, ..., 5$). Finally, the last sleeve is composed of the last 4 volumes $V[3][j]$ and $V[4][j]$ (where $j = 3, 4$). Hence the video sequence is divided into 4 sleeves. Feature extracted from each sleeve. However different sleeves have different importance contributions for feature representation. Therefore, we assign different weights for different sleeves. For weights selection, we adopt the method proposed in [24], which assigns weights of three orthogonal planes (XY, XT and YT) in LBP-TOP [24]. In this paper, instead, we use this method for selecting the weights of different sleeves. First, by computing the classification rates for each sleeve separately, we obtain t rates $R = \{R_1, R_2, ..., R_t\}$. Based on the assumption that the higher the rate is, the better gender representation becomes, we compute the weights as follows:

$$T = \frac{R - min(R)}{(100 - min(R))/10}. \tag{1}$$

Finally, considering that the weight of the lowest rate is 1, the other weights can be obtained according to a linear relationship of their differences to that with the lowest rate. The final step is written as:

$$\begin{aligned} T1 &= round(T) \\ T2 &= \frac{T \times ((max(T1) - 1))}{max(T)} + 1 \\ W &= round(T2) \end{aligned} \tag{2}$$

in which W is the weight vector corresponds to each sleeve. Pyramid segmentation and weights selection is summarized in Algorithm 1. Given N video sequences for training, each sequence is divided into n by m volumes equally. The n by m volumes are partitioned t sleeves $\{S_1, S_2, ..., S_t\}$ (step 1 - 9). Then feature extracted from each sleeve S_t generate corresponding histogram h_t (step 10). Therefore, obtain t rates R_t via computing the classification rates of h_t respectively (step 11). Finally, using Formula (1) and (2) to calculate the W (step 12 and 13). In the end of the algorithm, return the weight vector W (step 14).

The gender classification framework is based on video sequence and composed of two parts, training and testing, which is summarized in Algorithm 2. During training stage,

Algorithm 2 Gender classification framework.

Require: N video sequences for training, corresponds to the gender label $N.Gender_{label}$ and each sequence divided into n by m volumes; Testing video sequences T;
Ensure: $T.Gender_{label}$;
1: TRAINING STAGE:
2: $W = \{W_1, W_2, ..., W_t\} \leftarrow$ Algorithm 1;
3: **for** $i = 1$ to N **do**
4: $h^i = \{h_1, h_2, ..., h_t\} \leftarrow$ from each sleeve $S = \{S_1, S_2, ..., S_t\}$ using LBP-TOP, respectively;
5: $h^i * W = \{W_1 * h_1, W_2 * h_2, ..., W_t * h_t\} \leftarrow$ weighted for each histogram;
6: Training gender descriptors $H^i = [W_1 * h_1, W_2 * h_2, ..., W_t * h_t]$ are constructed and concatenated from each sleeve $h^i * W$;
7: **end for**
8: Perform 3D median filtering operation of vector H;
9: Carried on the PCA to vector H;
10: SVM classifier $\leftarrow H \cup N.Gender_{label}$;
11: TESTING STAGE:
12: Obtain gender representation H_T for testing T use the same method as training stage;
13: Made a decision by classifier after calculation;
14: **return** $T.Gender_{label}$.

we first de-compose the training videos into frames, so that each training sample contains τ back-facing frames. Then we obtain weight W corresponds to the sleeve S using Algorithm 1 (step 2). Next we use LBP-TOP [24] to extract feature from each sleeve, producing the corresponding histogram h (step 4). Each histogram h is multiplied by their weights (step 5). Training descriptors H_i (where $i = 1, 2, ..., N$) are constructed and concatenated from each weighted histogram (step 6). In the end of the iteration, we get the training representation vector H (step 7). Therefore, we perform 3D median filtering for the vector H (step 8). It is time-consuming because H is a high-dimensional. Furthermore, we use the PCA [4] to reduce the dimension (step 9). Then H and corresponding labels are feed to a SVM classifier (step 10). During testing stage, testing gender representation is obtained in the same way as training stage (step 12). Thereby the trained classifier is used to predict the gender label $T.Gender_{label}$ (step 13).

3. EXPERIMENTS AND ANALYSIS

To our best knowledge, there is no publicly available dataset for gender classification based on video sequences of human back-facing. To bridge the gap between theoretical analysis and practical testing, a dataset of video sequences collected for further studying the problem of gender classification from back-facing sequences. This dataset named BackFacing which consists of 5760 video frames of 640 by 360 resolution from 720 video sequences, each of which recorded from a different subject (30 males and 30 females) in 12 different natural environment (room, corridor, elevator, stair, restaurant, supermarket, playground, parking, road, lawn, square and ATM). Challenging factors in this dataset is each video sequence is shotted under arbitrary illumination conditions and background clutter. Furthermore, people are completely free in their movements (walking or running), leading to arbitrary body scales, motion blur, and local or global occlusions. Figure 3 show two sample sequences of female and male walking on the corridor and lawn, respectively.

Figure 3: Back-facing video sequences.

$LBP\text{-}TOP_{8,8,8,1,1,1}$ [24] is used to extract feature from each sleeve. Note that this work does not focus on finding optimal features. Many other descriptors, e.g. EVLBP [7], 3D-SIFT [17] and VLBP [24] can be used as well, and may further improve performance. We use an RBF kernel binary SVM as the classifier and the implementation is provided by LIBSVM [3]. Specifically, we adopted a 5-fold cross validation test scheme by dividing the 720 sequences into five groups and using the data from four groups for training and the left group for testing. The sequence of a particular subject appear only in one group. We repeated this process ten times and report the average classification rates (A_{vg}). The implementation of 3D Median Filtering (3DMF) provided by Matlab is used. For PCA, we set the number of principle component coefficients retained as 90. Furthermore, LBP-TOP [24] + SVM is selected as the baseline method on BackFacing dataset.

3.1 Experiments on Public Datasets

To evaluate the performance of our gender classification framework, public datasets of face and gait video sequence, are adopted in our experiments.

VidTIMIT & Cohn-Kanade datasets. The VidTIMIT dataset [16] consists of face video sequence (with a resolution of 512×384 pixels) recordings of 43 people (19 female and 24 male), reciting short sentences selected from the N-TIMIT corpus. Cohn-Kanade dataset [9] is for research in automatic facial image analysis and synthesis and for perceptual studies. We randomly segment the datasets and extract over 6400 video shots of 8 frames each. Table 2 shows our approach has the best performance comparing with EVLBP + AdaBoost, LBP + SVM and Pixels + SVM [7] on the VidTIMIT and Cohn-Kanade datasets.

Table 2: Gender classification performance on VidTIMIT and Cohn-Kanade datasets.

ppr ac es	A_{vg} %	ppr ac es	A_{vg} %
LBP SV	91	EVLBP daB st	81 5
Pi e s SV	89 4	Ours	**97.92**

CASIA Gait Set B. The CASIA Gait Set B [22] is one of the largest gait datasets in the gait-research community currently. The dataset consists of 124 subjects aged between 20 and 30 years, of which 93 are male and 31 are female, and 123 are Asian and 1 is European. Three variations, namely view angle, clothing and carrying condition changes, are separately considered. We randomly select half of the dataset for training and half for testing when dividing the data into training and testing sets. Table 3 validates the superiority of our method on CASIA Gait Set B comparing with state-of-the-arts.

Table 1: . Gender classification rates on *BackFacing* dataset.

$n \times m$	ase i e	T_b s	P	3D teri	t	R	W	Wei ted	T_o s
1×1	69	52	64 31	76 11	1	76 11	1	76 11	235
2×2	74 22	1 776	71 51	85 64	1	85 64	1	85 64	288
3×3	76 4	4 634	75 14	87 51	2	86 71 81 44	3 1	9 31	429
4×3	77 91	9 221	77 94	89 1	2	88 64 85 98	2 1	91 18	57
4×4	78 6	1 27	77 27	9 3	2	88 3 84 6	2 1	91 35	63
5×4	78 49	19 153	78 44	9 14	2	86 92 89 5	1 2	**92.74**	647
5×5	77 34	21 674	8 14	9 2	3	88 32 88 77 8 65	4 4 1	91 69	7 9
6×5	76 56	32 151	78 49	89 15	3	87 89 89 1 84 43	2 3 1	91 7	735
6×6	76 3	37 253	79 55	88 94	3	91 18 88 58 88 6	3 1 1	91 52	819
7×6	77 6	52 936	**81.14**	9 9	3	88 6 9 83 89 45	1 2 2	91 14	852
7×7	79 7	59 567	8 69	89 76	4	75 43 76 82 76 13 6 38	4 4 4 1	9 14	926
8×7	77 85	78 772	8 67	**90.33**	4	91 35 9 66 88 41 83 56	5 5 3 1	92	981
8×8	76 82	87 376	79 74	9 22	4	88 43 85 29 9 87 83 91	3 2 5 1	91 83	**1.083**

Table 3: Classification results on CASIA dataset.

ppr ac es	Ours	13	11	23	2	8	14
A_{vg} %	**99.51**	98	93 3	95 79	96	98 39	98 4

3.2 Experiments on BackFacing Dataset

The results on BackFacing are shown in Table 1 and Figure 4 (a). The performance of the baseline can be noticeably improved by adding PCA, 3DME and Weight. t, R and W are mentioned in the Section 2. In our evaluation, Table 1 and Fig 4 (b) reports the average sum of training and testing time[1] per sequence. We can calculate that our approach is about 38 times faster than the baseline method on average. In addition we compare our approach with state-of-the-arts. The results, shown in Table 4, which indicate that our approach is superior to these approaches on BackFacing dataset. Finally, it is evident that our proposed PS approach and gender classification framework consistently outperforms other methods on there four datasets. The main reason lies in, PS strategy fully exploits the intrinsic feature of the video sequence, and further enhances its contribution by weighted.

Table 4: Comparison to state-of-the-arts on BackFacing dataset.

ppr ac es	A_{vg} %	ppr ac es	A_{vg} %
VLBP 24 SV	84 95	LD 2	67 82
LBP 1 SV	64 7	P 2 SV	79 98
a SV 6	79 4	P LD 2	59 6
LBP-TOP$_{[5,2,1]}$ 24	82 18	Ours	**92.74**

4. CONCLUSIONS

In this paper, we have addressed the relatively open problem of back-facing gender classification by proposing a novel Pyramid Segmentation approach based on video sequence that reinforces the weights of sleeve for the gender representation. Moreover, a framework of gender classification based on video sequence is presented. Experimental results show that the proposed approach is outperforms the competitive methods on VidTIMIT, Cohn-Kanade, CASIA Gait and BackFacing dataset.

5. ACKNOWLEDGMENTS

This work is supported by National Natural Science Foundation of China(NSFC, No.61340046), National High Technology Research and Development Program of China(863 Program, No.2006AA04Z247), Scientific and Technical Innovation Commission of Shenzhen Municipality (No. JCYJ20130331144631730).

[1]We run our experiments on a PC with 3.40 GHz four-Core CPU and 8 GB RAM.

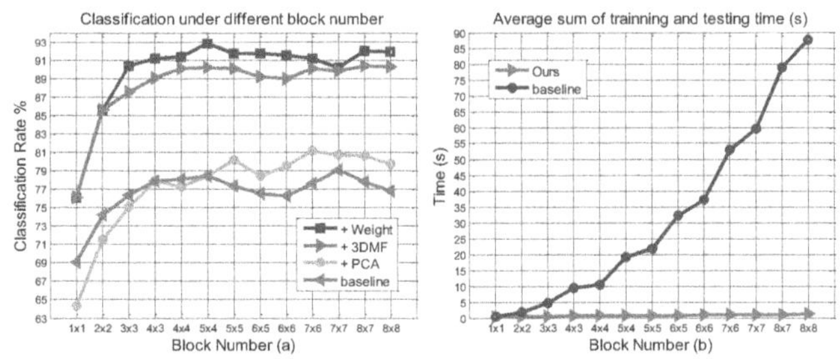

Figure 4: (a) Average gender classification rates (%) and (b) average sum of training and testing time (s) on BackFacing dataset.

6. REFERENCES

[1] T. Ahonen et al. Face description with local binary patterns: Application to face recognition. *IEEE TPAMI*, 2006.
[2] J. Bekios-Calfa et al. Revisiting linear discriminant techniques in gender recognition. *IEEE TPAMI*, 2011.
[3] C.-C. Chang and C.-J. Lin. Libsvm: a library for support vector machines. *ACM TIST*, 2011.
[4] S. Dupont and J. Luettin. Audio-visual speech modeling for continuous speech recognition. *IEEE TMM*, 2000.
[5] N. Gheissari et al. Person reidentification using spatiotemporal appearance. *in CVPR*, 2006.
[6] G. Guo et al. Is gender recognition affected by age? *in ICCVW*, 2009.
[7] A. Hadid and M. Pietikäinen. Combining appearance and motion for face and gender recognition from videos. *Elsevier PR*, 2009.
[8] M. Hu et al. Gait-based gender classification using mixed conditional random field. *IEEE TSMC Part B*, 2011.
[9] T. Kanade et al. Comprehensive database for facial expression analysis. *in FG*, 2000.
[10] F. S. Khan et al. Coloring action recognition in still images. *Springer IJCV*, 2013.
[11] W. Kusakunniran et al. Support vector regression for multi-view gait recognition based on local motion feature selection. *in CVPR*, 2010.
[12] S. Lazebnik et al. Beyond bags of features: Spatial pyramid matching for recognizing natural scene categories. *in CVPR*, 2006.
[13] J. Lu et al. Human identity and gender recognition from gait sequences with arbitrary walking directions. *IEEE TIFS*, 2014.
[14] D. S. Matovski et al. The effect of time on gait recognition performance. *IEEE TIFS*, 2012.
[15] B. Prosser et al. Multi-camera matching under illumination change over time. *in ECCVW*, 2008.
[16] C. Sanderson and K. K. Paliwal. Noise compensation in a person verification system using face and multiple speech features. *Elsevier PR*, 2003.
[17] P. Scovanner et al. A 3-dimensional sift descriptor and its application to action recognition. *ACM MM*, 2007.
[18] F. Shahbaz et al. Semantic pyramids for gender and action recognition. *IEEE TIP*, 2014.
[19] S. Wuhrer et al. Posture invariant gender classification for 3d human models. *in CVPRW*, 2009.
[20] D. Xu et al. Human gait recognition using patch distribution feature and locality-constrained group sparse representation. *IEEE TIP*, 2012.
[21] Y. Yang et al. Salient color names for person re-identification. *in ECCV*, 2014.
[22] S. Yu et al. A framework for evaluating the effect of view angle, clothing and carrying condition on gait recognition. *in ICPR*, 2006.
[23] S. Yu et al. A study on gait-based gender classification. *IEEE TIP*, 2009.
[24] G. Zhao and M. Pietikainen. Dynamic texture recognition using local binary patterns with an application to facial expressions. *IEEE TPAMI*, 2007.

Object Segmentation from Long Video Sequences

Bing Luo, Hongliang Li, Tiecheng Song, Chao Huang

University of Electronic Science and Technology of China, Chengdu, China
mathild1987@163.com, hlli@uestc.edu.cn, tggwin@gmail.com, huangues@gmail.com

ABSTRACT

Most existing video segmentation methods are focused on extracting the primary objects in test video sequences. They assumed that only one object appeared through the whole video sequences, which is impractical in many applications. In this paper, we focus on the object segmentation from the long video sequences which consist of many different scenes, shot cuts and various motion patterns, etc. In order to solve this problem, we propose a framework to segment the objects in relative video shots, while discarding the irrelative video shots. A graph is constructed to model the video object detection and final segmentation is obtained by getting the superpixels in the detection boxes. We also introduce a new long video segmentation dataset which corresponds to the pixel-wise ground truth. The experiments demonstrate that our proposed method can deal with the object segmentation in long video sequence.

Categories and Subject Descriptors

I.4.6 [**Image Processing and Computer Vision**]: Segmentation—*Video segmentation*

General Terms

Algorithms

Keywords

Long video sequence, Segmentation, Graph

1. INTRODUCTION

Video segmentation extracts the object through the whole videos with relative frames, which is widely used in action recognition, video analysis. Compared with the object segmentation from images, video segmentation utilizes not only the information in single frame but also the relationship between adjacent frames. Many existing methods have been proposed to obtain the foreground in video by extending the static and dynamic information, such as shortest path video segmentation [18, 19], key-segments video segmentation [8], maximum weight clique based video segmentation [12], and incremental learning based video segmentation [9].

Although these methods have successfully segmented the objects in the popular test sequences, such as SegTrack Dataset [15] and GaTech Segmentation Dataset [6], they assumed that the primary objects appeared in each frames and no shot cuts were present in these sequences. While this assumption is strong and impractical in many real applications, such as movies, long videos and edited videos. Many complex situations may frequently appear in these videos, such as suddenly scene change, multiple objects appearing across in different shot cuts, uncertain motion pattern, etc. When all the situations arise in a long video sequence, how to extract the object in the relevant video shots is challenge.

In order to declare our new problem for long video sequences object segmentation, we introduce a new benchmark video segmentation dataset, LongVideoSeg dataset. The LongVideoSeg dataset contains one video which consists of 10000 frames from various shot cuts with multiple objects and different scenes. All the video frames are annotated with pixel-wise groundtruth for specific classes by human. In order to get the specific-class objects prior information, few bounding boxes corresponding to class labels are provided with some noise data.

In this paper, we proposes a new framework to solve the long video sequence segmentation. We cluster the given bounding boxes and utilize the correlation among them to discard noisy boxes. The long video sequence is divided into shot cuts with consistent scene and the relevant shot cuts are found with the help of clustering object priority. We model the video object detection process as an energy minimization problem which is optimized via dynamic programming. Finally, some subjective and objective experiments validate our method on our new dataset.

2. RELATED WORK

Most existing video segmentation methods pay much attention to extracting primary object in single video sequence. Several methods proposed to segment the primary object by discovering the most objectness segments with appearance and motion information. Lee and Kim [8] firstly utilized spectrum clustering to discover the segments with the high static and dynamic scores and generate foreground prior for spatial-temporal graph cuts. Ma [12] utilized the spatial and temporal mutex constrain to model objects discovery as constrained maximum weight cliques. Zhang [19] constructed

MM'15, October 26–30, 2015, Brisbane, Australia.
© 2015 ACM. ISBN 978-1-4503-3459-4/15/10 ...$15.00.
DOI: http://dx.doi.org/10.1145/2733373.2806313.

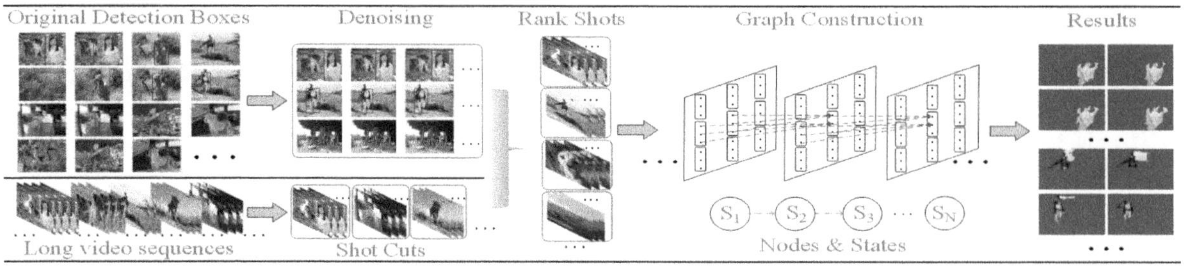

Figure 1: The flowchart of our proposed method.

directed acyclic graph to find the primary object regions based on appearance and motion similarity. These methods focus on single object appeared in each frames which are unsuitable for real unconstrained video sequences. Li [9] modeled the many figure-ground segments tracking as a incremental learning problem. Meanwhile, Banica [1] developed the multiple segments hypotheses as salient segment chain composition. These methods can deal with multiple objects in a successive video sequence.

Recently, in order to segment object in different video sequence, video cosegmentation is an alternative method to extract the common objects from two or multiple videos. Several methods [2, 14, 7] have been proposed to extract the common object from two or more videos, which assumed that the target object appeared in all videos. Liu [11] and Fu [5] proposed methods to solve the multiple foreground video cosegmentation. Their methods are constrained in the assumption that the common objects must appear in two or multiple videos. Zhang [20] proposed a maximum weight cliques based video cosegmentation to discard the assumption on the target objects appearance in all videos. Wang [17] presented an extremely weak supervision video cosegmentation to discover video object in relevant frames and cosegment in different videos.

3. PROPOSED METHOD

Given a long video sequence with a few specific-class bounding boxes, we present a new framework to solve the segmentation in a long video sequence. Fig. 1 overviews our proposed method. The framework consists of three steps: (1) We simultaneously cluster the given bounding boxes into subclasses and discard the noise boxes which are incorrect detection. (2) Given a long video sequence, we divide it into shot cuts and rank them by video-level class scores with the help of subclass bounding boxes to discover the relevant frames which the target object appears in them. (3) A graph is constructed to model the object detection process and the final segmentation is generated via these detection boxes.

3.1 Data Clustering and Denoising

Since the given specific-class bounding boxes are detected by DPM [3] and preserved upon a certain threshold, some noise data will be inevitably introduced into the class data. In this step, we avoid the noise data to contaminate the object prioriry. Firstly, we cluster the given bounding boxes via their height/width into K clusters. The noisy bounding boxes is independent of class information, so they are clustered into different subclasses which help us to prevent them into object trajectories. Secondly, for each subclass we calculate the correlative matrix in term of their corresponding overlap rate. We observe that the more overlap the adjacent bounding boxes have, the more likely the two boxes are a same object. So an object trajectory corresponds to the higher overlap rate and successive bounding boxes, the noisy data have lower overlap rate due to their independence, as show in Fig. 2. Hence, we generate object tracklets as the subclasses positive samples and discard the noise data.

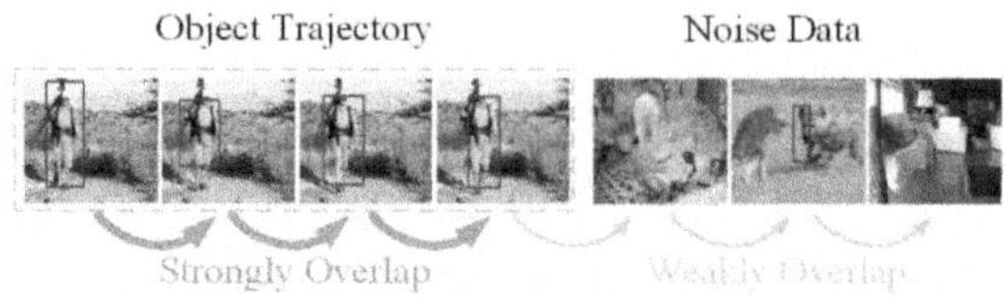

Figure 2: The object tracklet.

3.2 Generate and Identify Relevant Shot Cuts

Given a long video which is edited with many different shot cuts, we need to generate each single shot cut, i.e. identify the start and end points for a successive frame sequences. In general, a single shot cut is motion smoothness and object consistency, which is comfortable to handle with. We firstly identify the start and end point for the different shot cuts. Given a set of video frames $F = \{f_i, 1 \leq i \leq N\}$, where N is the frame number for the long video sequence. We denote $S = \{s_i, 1 \leq i \leq N-1\}$ as the inter-frame difference, i.e., $s_i = \frac{1}{\overline{N}} \sum_{x,y \in I}(f_{i+1} - f_i)$, where $\overline{N}$ is the pixel number in a frame, and x, y are the position in image I. We smooth s and add a threshold on it, and then the adjacent frames switched to different scene will yield a high response. The response points beyond the threshold are treated as the start and end points for the shot cuts.

After generating the shot cuts, we discovery the relevant shot cuts by matching the weighted histogram of shot cuts. We rank the matching distance and select the top N nearest shot cuts as the relevant shot cuts.

3.3 Video Object Detection

We treat the object detection as an optimization of model. A directed solution is to construct a graph such as Fig. 3. In this graph $\mathcal{G} = (\mathcal{V}, \mathcal{E})$, each node $v_i \in \mathcal{V}$ denotes a bounding box in corresponding frame and each edge $e_{ij} \in \mathcal{E}$ denotes the similarity between two bounding boxes in adjacent frames. In this model, the task is to obtain the state for each node, and the state space for each node $L = \{1 \leq l_i \leq \overline{N}, 1 \leq i \leq N\}$, is the bounding box position in current frame. Inspired by [4], our cost function is defined as:

$$E = \sum_{i \in \mathcal{V}} U_i(l_i) + \sum_{(i,j) \in \mathcal{E}} V_{i,j}(l_i, l_j) \quad (1)$$

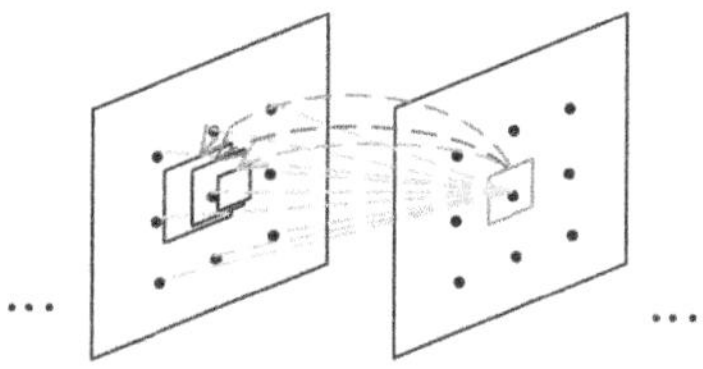

Figure 3: Connection of nodes in adjacent frames.

The energy function consists of unary terms $U_i(l_i)$ and pair-wise term $V_{i,j}(l_i, l_j)$, which represent the objectness scores of detected bounding box and smoothness between two bounding boxes in adjacent frames [10], respectively. $U_i(l_i)$ is calculated by $U_i(l_i) = \frac{B(l_i)}{Area(l_i)}$, where $Area(l_i)$ is the area of the l_i-th bounding boxes, and $B(l_i)$ is the score of the sliding windows detection. This unary term can preserve the tightness of the detection boxes. In order to obtain the objectness score, we train an appearance model for the target object via GMM in the color space, $O = \{\pi_o(k), \mu_o(k), \nu_o(k), o \in \{0,1\}, k \in \{1, ..., K\}\}$. Then frames in relevant shot cuts can be generated a pixel-wise foreground object likelihood. We use the integral image [16] to speed up the objectness scores calculation for unary terms. Hence, the unary term can be calculated in constant time. Then the pairwise terms are calculated the similarity of the normalized color histograms for adjacent nodes bounding boxes.

$$V_{i,j}(l_i, l_j) = 1 - exp\{-\chi^2(l_i, l_j)\} \tag{2}$$

Where $\chi^2(l_i, l_j) = \frac{1}{2}\sum_{b=1}^{N_d} \frac{(h_{l_i}(b) - h_{l_j}(b))^2}{h_{l_i}(b) + h_{l_j}(b)}$, h_{l_i} is the color histogram of bounding box l_i in frame i, and N_d is the number of histogram bins. Minimizing the cost function Eq. 1 will obtain the optimal state for each node, i.e., the optimal detection box for each frame.

In order to optimize Eq. 1, an optimization method via dynamic programming is summarized in Alg. 1. The algorithm finally outputs the optimal state for each node, i.e., the optimal center position Lab and scale S_{star} for detected bounding box. After obtaining the detected bounding boxes, we extract the superpixels in the detected bounding boxes as the final object segmentation.

4. EXPERIMENTS

In order to verify our proposed method, a new benchmark database, LongVideoSeg dataset, is introduced in this paper. The video sequence contains 10000 video frames with *people* and *cheetah* categories, which are annotated by pixel-wise groundtruth manually. Given by a few bounding boxes for above two categories with some noise detections, the task is to obtain the pixel-wise labels for the each object class.

We define the evaluation metrics in three situations:

(1) For the object class k, the groundtruth annotation and segmentation masks all exist in these frames. The evaluation score is calculated by intersection-over-union.

(2) The evaluation score is defined as zero if and only if one of groundtruth annotation and segmentation masks exists in the frames.

(3) The test frames don't contain the object and the segmentation masks also don't exist. We don't consider the evaluation into our scores.

Our evaluation metric is finally defined as follows:

Algorithm 1 Algorithm for Video Object Detection

Input:
Video shot cut $F = \{f_i, 1 \le i \le N\}$;
Foreground likelihood map, $M = \{m_i, 1 \le i \le N\}$;
Scale for sliding windows, $S = \{s_k, 1 \le s \le K\}$;
Output:
Detected bounding boxes $\{Lab(i), S_{star}(i), 1 \le i \le N\}$;

```
for i = 1 : N do
    for s = 1 : K do
        calculate U_i(l_i, s) by integral image, where l_i ∈ {1, ..., |L|} is the position for each node.
    end for
end for
for i = 2 : N do
    for l_i = 1 : |L| do
        calculate w_{l_i,s}(l_{i-1}, s) by Eq. 2, where l_{i-1} ∈ N(l_i)
        l*, s* ⟵ argmax_{l_{i-1}∈N(l_i), s∈{1,...,K}} (B(l_{i-1}, s) + w_{l_i,s}(l_{i-1}, s))
        B(l_i, s) = min_{l_{i-1}∈N(l_i), s∈{1,...,K}} (B(l_{i-1}, s) + w_{l_i,s}(l_{i-1}, s) + U_i(l_i, s))
        record the best child node for current position L(l_i) = l*
        record the best state of child node S(l_i, s) = s* for position l*
    end for
end for
trace back from i = N frame
l_*, s_* ⟵ argmax_{l_i∈L, s∈1,...,K} B(l_i, s)
Lab(N) = l_*, S_star(N) = s_*
for i = N − 1 : 1 do
    Lab(i) = L(Lab(i + 1))
    S_star(i) = S(Lab(i + 1), S_star(i + 1))
end for
```

$$Score = \begin{cases} \frac{M_i \bigcap G_i}{M_i \bigcup G_i} & \text{situation 1} \\ 0 & \text{situation 2} \\ not\ consider & \text{situation 3} \end{cases} \tag{3}$$

To our knowledge, there are no existing methods to perform multiple objects segmentation in long video sequences. We compare our proposed method with two baseline methods and FastVideoSeg [13]. In order to validate the first step, i.e., data clustering and denoising, Baseline1 is designed to directly model the foreground prior by GMM while step 2 and step 3 remain unchanged. This design evaluates the efficiency of the foreground map correctness by the noise data. The more correctly the foreground maps are generated, the higher accuracy our method gives. The second method Baseline2 is designed to randomly select the relevant shot cuts for step 2 and not to change other steps, which can evaluate the correctness of our step 2. Finally, [13] is used to compare with our step 3, i.e., detection and segmentation algorithm only on our detected relevant shot cuts.

Some subjective results are shown in Fig. 4 for our method and Baseline1. In this figure, our method generates more accurate foreground prior and leads to higher detection precision by eliminating the noise data than Baseline1. Specifically, the bounding box can detect the people more completely by our method. Cheetah detection by our method can locate the main object in these frames but Baseline1 loses the object due to the noise data. We also compare our

Figure 4: Comparison between our method and Baseline1. From top to bottom: original frames, foreground map by Baseline1, detection by Baseline1, our foreground map, our detection.

Table 1: IoU of our method and compared methods.

Class	Baseline1	Baseline2	[13]	Ours
people	38.62	9.27	20.38	**40.35**
cheetah	10.60	4.03	18.80	**24.97**

method with [13]. The subjective segmentation results are shown in Fig. 5. This figure shows that [13] only segments the face of the people and feet of the cheetah. The reason is that the performance of [13] seriously depends on optical flow, which is unreliable in many cases. In people shot cut, the person only twists her head. In cheetah shot cut, the optical flow calculation is inaccurate for the object. The above two situations will result in an error result by [13]. The results of our method don't utilize optical flow information and models the robust object detection as an energy minimization problem, which leads to the better performance.

Tab. 1 shows the results of our method and the compared methods. It can be seen that our method obtains 40.35% in people and 24.97% in cheetah, which outperforms other compared methods. From above experiments, the subjective and objective performance comparison demonstrates that our proposed method is effective.

5. CONCLUSIONS

In this paper, we propose a new framework to solve the long video sequence segmentation. We cluster the given bounding boxes and utilize the correlation among them to discard noisy boxes. The long video sequence is divided into shot cuts with consistent scene and the relevant shot cuts are found with the help of clustering object priority. We model the video object detection process as an energy minimization problem which is optimized via dynamic programming. Finally, a new database LongVideoSeg is introduced to evaluate our proposed method and some subjective and objective experiments validate our method.

6. ACKNOWLEDGMENTS

This work was supported in part by the National Basic Research Program of China (973 Program 2015CB351804), National Natural Science Foundation of China (No. 61271289), and by The program for Science and Technology Innovative Research Team for Young Scholars in Sichuan Province, China (No. 2014TD0006).

7. REFERENCES

[1] D. Banica, A. Agape, A. Ion, and C. Sminchisescu. Video object segmentation by salient segment chain composition. In *ICCVW*, 2013.

[2] D.-J. Chen, H.-T. Chen, and L.-W. Chang. Video object cosegmentation. In *ACM MM*, 2012.

Figure 5: Segmentation results of FastVideoSeg [13] (top two rows) and our method (bottom two rows).

[3] P. F. Felzenszwalb, R. B. Girshick, D. McAllester, and D. Ramanan. Object detection with discriminatively trained part-based models. *IEEE TPAMI*, 2010.

[4] P. F. Felzenszwalb and R. Zabih. Dynamic programming and graph algorithms in computer vision. *IEEE TPAMI*, 2011.

[5] H. Fu, D. Xu, B. Zhang, and S. Lin. Object-based multiple foreground video co-segmentation. In *CVPR*, 2014.

[6] M. Grundmann, V. Kwatra, M. Han, and I. Essa. Efficient hierarchical graph-based video segmentation. In *CVPR*, 2010.

[7] J. Guo, Z. Li, L.-F. Cheong, and S. Zhou. Video co-segmentation for meaningful action extraction. In *ICCV*, 2013.

[8] Y. J. Lee, J. Kim, and K. Grauman. Key-segments for video object segmentation. In *ICCV*, 2011.

[9] F. Li, T. Kim, A. Humayun, D. Tsai, and J. Rehg. Video segmentation by tracking many figure-ground segments. In *ICCV*, 2013.

[10] H. Li, F. Meng, Q. Wu, and B. Luo. Unsupervised multiclass region cosegmentation via ensemble clustering and energy minimization. *IEEE TCSVT*, 2014.

[11] X. Liu, D. Tao, M. Song, Y. Ruan, C. Chen, and J. Bu. Weakly supervised multiclass video segmentation. In *CVPR*, 2014.

[12] T. Ma and L. Latecki. Maximum weight cliques with mutex constraints for video object segmentation. In *CVPR*, 2012.

[13] A. Papazoglou and V. Ferrari. Fast object segmentation in unconstrained video. In *ICCV*, 2013.

[14] J. C. Rubio, J. Serrat, and A. López. Video co-segmentation. In *ACCV*. 2013.

[15] D. Tsai, M. Flagg, and J. Rehg. Motion coherent tracking with multi-label mrf optimization. *BMVC*, 2010.

[16] P. Viola and M. J. Jones. Robust real-time face detection. *IJCV*, 57(2):137–154, 2004.

[17] L. Wang, G. Hua, R. Sukthankar, J. Xue, and N. Zheng. Video object discovery and co-segmentation with extremely weak supervision. In *ECCV*. 2014.

[18] B. Zhang, H. Zhao, and X. Cao. Video object segmentation with shortest path. In *ACM MM*, 2012.

[19] D. Zhang, O. Javed, and M. Shah. Video object segmentation through spatially accurate and temporally dense extraction of primary object regions. In *CVPR*, 2013.

[20] D. Zhang, O. Javed, and M. Shah. Video object co-segmentation by regulated maximum weight cliques. In *ECCV*. 2014.

Summarization-based Video Caption via Deep Neural Networks

Guang Li*[1], Shubo Ma*[2], Yahong Han[1,3]
[1]School of Computer Science and Technology, Tianjin University, Tianjin, China
[2]School of Computer Software, Tianjin University, Tianjin, China
[3]Tianjin Key Laboratory of Cognitive Computing & Application, Tianjin University, Tianjin, China
lguang@live.cn, shuboma@tju.edu.cn, yahong@tju.edu.cn

ABSTRACT

Generating appropriate descriptions for visual content draws increasing attention recently, where the promising progresses were obtained owing to the breakthroughs in deep neural networks. Different from the traditional SVO (subject, verb, object) based methods, in this paper, we propose a novel framework of video caption via deep neural networks. For each frame, we extract visual features by a fine-tuned deep Convulutional Neural Networks (C-NN), which are then fed into a Recurrent Neural Networks (RN-N) to generate novel sentences descriptions for each frame. In order to obtain the most representative and high-quality descriptions for target video, a well-devised automatic summarization process is incorporated to reduce the noises by ranking on the sentence-sequence graph. Moreover, our framework owns the merit of describing out-of-sample videos by transferring knowledge from pre-captioned images. Experiments on the benchmark datasets demonstrate our method has better performance than the state-of-the-art methods of video caption in language generation metrics as well as SVO accuracy.

Categories and Subject Descriptors

H.3 [**INFORMATION STORAGE AND RETRIEVAL**]: Content Analysis and Indexing

Keywords

Video Caption, Summarization, Deep Learning, CNN, RNN

1. INTRODUCTION

Visual content understanding is an important subject in multimedia analysis and computer vision. The majority of previous works in this area has focused on labeling images or videos with a fixed set of visual categories, such as automatic image annotation, object recognition and action recognition. With great progresses made in related fields, some pioneering methods [7] [13] have been developed to address the challenge of generating natural language descriptions to visual content. In particular, a well description can not only caption the objects contained in visual content, but also narrate how these objects relate to each other as well as their attributes and the activities they are involved in [19]. In most cases, a well-devised language model is utilized to automatically generate sentences to the target visual content [15]. The typical practice is as follows: Firstly, a fixed tuple of role words, such as subject, verb, object and scene, are detected from the visual content. Then a pre-defined template is used to generate grammatical sentences. Their varieties, however, are always limited due to the fixed or predefined visual concepts and sentence template.

Inspirited by recent advances in machine translation, the Recurrent Neural Network (RNN), which is proved to be a powerful sequence model, shows the state-of-the-art performance in visual caption [4] [6]. Moreover, a fixed-length feature extracted by deep Convulutional Neural Networks (CNN) is fed into the RNN as input instead of the fixed word tuple. The combination of CNN and RNN has been shown to be a promising method in image caption [4] [6]. In this translation based model, an image (I) is treated as the source language and translated to the target language (S) by maximizing the likelihood $p(S|I)$ directly. However, because of the various temporal length of videos, it is difficult to obtain fix length CNN features for videos. Thus, the above translation based model can not be directly applied in video caption. As an alternative method, LSTM-YT [18] introduces a mean pooling operation to calculate a single mean vector of the extracted CNN features for video frames. Although LSTM-YT gains good performance, the mean vector of the CNN features may lose some key information in original extracted CNN features. Thus, the performance of LSTM-YT in video caption is restrained in situations where the scene changes fast and dramatically.

As each video clip can be taken as a spatial-temporal neighborhood, the characteristics of temporal consistency in videos may result in semantic consistency in the visual content of the sequential video frames. In this paper, we propose a novel framework of summarization-based video caption via deep neural networks. The proposed framework is illustrated in Fig. 1. Instead of trying to generate a fixed-length feature of video, our framework treats the target video clip as a a sequence of frames. We "translate" the frame sequence to the sentence sequence by the deep CNN and RNN. As is shown in Fig. 1, we develop a summarization process to generate the final description to the target video clip. In particular, we first construct an adjacency graph on the sentence sequence, in which each node denotes a sentence and the pairwise similarity is associated with each edge as the weight. After pruning the edges with small weights, we calculate the transitivity on the pruned graph until convergency. Finally, we output the top ranked sentence as the final video caption. Comparison results on the benchmark datasets demonstrate the better performance of our method.

*Equal contribution

MM'15, October 26-30, 2015, Brisbane, Australia
© 2015 ACM. ISBN 978-1-4503-3459-4/15/10 ...$15.00.
DOI: http://dx.doi.org/10.1145/2733373.2806314.

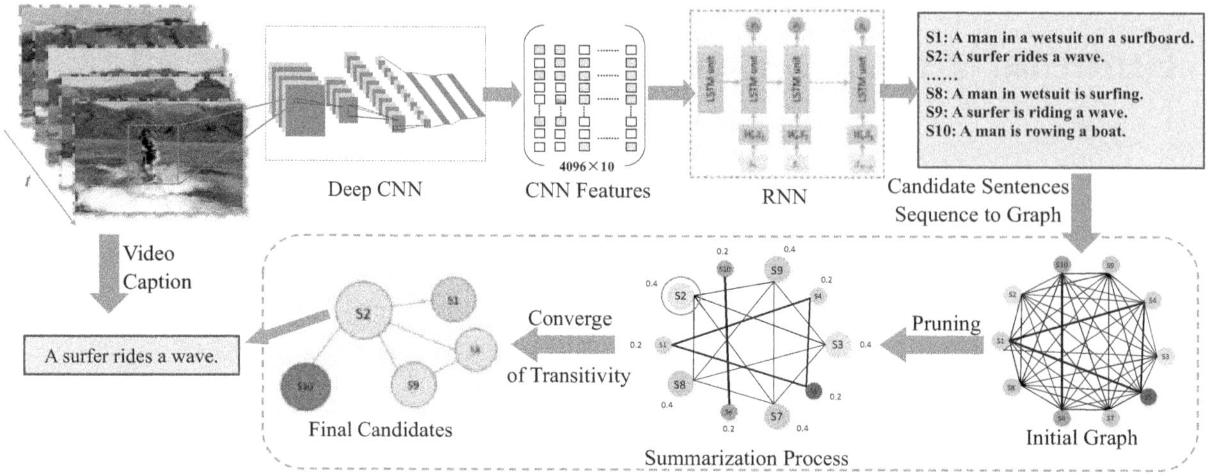

Figure 1: Flowchart of the proposed framework.

2. THE PROPOSED FRAMEWORK

Fig. 1 depicts our two-stage framework using neural and probabilistic approach and text analysis technique to generate descriptions from videos. For each video, we extract a number of frames by uniform sampling to form the sequence of representative video frames. In the first stage, a translation based natural language description generation process is constructed by deep CNN and RNN. Then, we develop an automatic summarization process to output the top ranked sentence as the final video caption.

2.1 Translation from Videos Frames to Sentences Sequence

Inspired by the principle of "translating" images [9], we maximize the log likelihood of the sentence S given the corresponding frame F and the model parameters θ,

$$\theta^* = \arg\max_{\theta} \sum_{(F,S)} \log p(S|F;\theta), \tag{1}$$

where S represents a sequence of words whose length is unbounded. By using the chain rule to model the joint probability over $S_{W_1}, ..., S_{W_n}$, Formula 1 can be expressed as:

$$p(S|F) = \sum_{t=0}^{N} \log p(S_{W_t}|F, S_{W_1}, ..., S_{W_{t-1}}), \tag{2}$$

where N is the total number of words in sentence S and S_{W_t} represents the $i-th$ word in sentence S. And for the sake of convenience we have dropped θ.

In order to get the conditional probabilities, RNN, parameterized by θ, is selected to model $p(S_{W_t}|F, S_{W_1}, ..., S_{W_{t-1}})$. The RNN expresses the previously seen words as a hidden state or memory h_{t-1}. After seen a new input x_t, the memory h_{t-1} is updated via a non-linear function f: $h_t = f_\theta(x_t, h_{t-1})$.

In our framework, we use a Long-Short Term Memory(LSTM) net [9], since it has shown state-of-the-art performance on sequence tasks such as machine translation and image captions [6][12][19].

For the encoding of images, we use a well-trained deep CNN model, which is pre-trained on ImageNet [3] and fine-tuned on the 200 classes of the ImageNet Detection Challenge [16]. In particular, we use Caffe [11] to extract CNN features.

2.2 LSTM-based Language Model

The basic unit of the LSTM is a memory cell c encoding knowledge at every time step of what inputs have been observed up to this step (see Fig. 2). The cell is controlled by three sigmoid functions, the first one managing whether to consider the current input x_t is named as input gate i, the second one allowing to forget its previous memory c_{t-1} is named as forget gate f, and third one deciding how much of the memory will transfer to next hidden state h_t is called output gate o. Such multiplicative gates makes it possible to train the LSTM robustly as these gates deal well with exploding and vanishing gradients. The detail of LSTM unit is described as follows:

$$i_t = \sigma\left(W_{ix}x_t + W_{im}m_{t-1}\right) \tag{3}$$

$$f_t = \sigma\left(W_{fx}x_t + W_{fm}m_{t-1}\right) \tag{4}$$

$$o_t = \sigma\left(W_{ox}x_t + W_{om}m_{t-1}\right) \tag{5}$$

$$c_t = f_t \odot C_{t-1} + i_t \odot h\left(W_{cx}x_t + W_{cm}m_{t-1}\right) \tag{6}$$

$$m_t = o_t \odot c_t, \quad p_t = Softmax\left(m_t\right) \tag{7}$$

where the weight matrices W are trained parameters, the non-linear functions (σ and h) are sigmoid and hyperbolic tangent respectively, and the $\odot$ represents the and operation with a gate value. The last equation will produce a probability distribution p_t over all words through a softmax function.

2.3 Summarization of Sentence Sequence

Inspired by the ranking based summarization method LexRank [5], we propose a summarization process to reduce outliers in sentences sequence that share little similarity with the others. The LexRank score is defined as follows:

$$LR(u) = (1-d) \sum_{v \in adj[u]} \frac{LR(v)}{deg(v)} + \frac{d}{N}, \tag{8}$$

where $LR(u)$ is the LexRank score of node u, $adj[u]$ is the set of nodes that are adjacent to u, and $deg(v)$ is the degree of the node v, N is the total number of nodes in the graph, and d is a "damping factor".

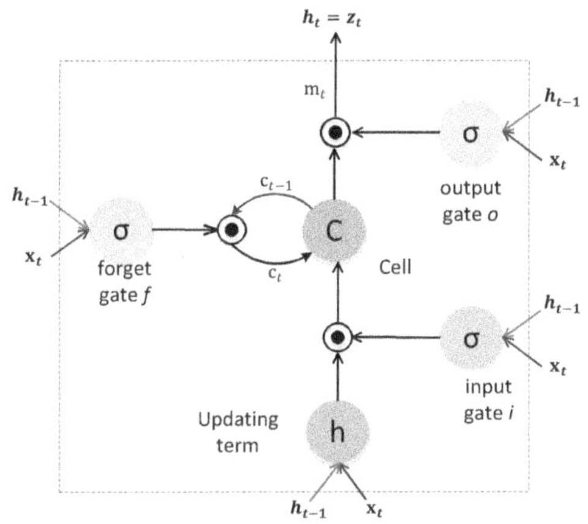

Figure 2: LSTM unit:the memory block contains a cell c controlled by three gates. The lines in blue show the recurrent connections - the output m at time $t-1$ is fed back to the memory at time t via the three gates.

As shown in Fig. 1, a graph is generated from these sentences with each sentence as a vertex. The similarity between the sentences are represented as edges, and we delete the edge between the sentences whose similarity is too small. The similarity is defined by the cosine between two corresponding sentences. Here we set the initial LexRank score as $\frac{d}{N}$, and then each vertex transfer their LexRank score to their adjacent vertex according to the similarity of each other. According to the convergence property of Markov chains, the algorithm is guaranteed to get an stationary distribution.

2.4 Transfer Caption from Images to Videos

In our framework, we treat the video as a sequence of frames, so it is natural to extend the training data by using some captioned images as auxiliary for the lack of video descriptions. In our experiments, the fc_7 layer features of video frames is extracted from the CNN, as well as captioned auxiliary images. The initial model is trained roughly with a relatively high learn rate (about 10^{-3}) on the mixed features of frames and images, then we fine-tune it on video frames with lower learn rate.

3. EXPERIMENTS

3.1 Datasets

We conduct our experiments on Microsoft Research Video Description Corpus [2], which consists of 1970 video clips collected from YouTube. Thus, we name the dataset by "YouTube" in the following. Each clip particularly contains a single action and lasts from 10 to 25 seconds. Each snippet has been aligned with a number of descriptions and we use roughly 40 available English descriptions per video. In our experiments, we follow the settings in [8] [17] to use 1200 videos as training data and 100 videos for validation and 670 videos for testing. For each video, we extract 10 frames by uniform sampling and select 5 sentences randomly for each frame.

In order to evaluate the performance of domain adaptation from images to video caption, we use a benchmark dataset Flickr8k [10] as the auxiliary training data, which is a subset of Flickr30k that consists of 8000 images. Each image is captioned with 5 sentences. We use 1000 images for validation and the rest images are combined with the video training set.

Table 1: Comparison results in terms of BLEU at 4 (combined n-gram 1-4) and METEOR. All values are reported as percentage(%).

	BLEU	METEOR
FGM-YT	13.68	23.9
LSTM-YT	31.19	26.87
OUR-YT	32.32	27.03
LSTM-YT$_{flickr}$	32.03	27.87
OUR-YT$_{flickr}$	**35.09**	**29.26**

Table 2: Comparison results in terms of SVO accuracy. All values are reported as percentage(%).

	S	V	O
HVC-YT	**76.57**	22.24	11.94
FGM-YT	76.42	21.34	12.39
LSTM-YT	71.19	19.4	9.7
OUR-YT	74.48	21.34	9.25
LSTM-YT$_{flickr}$	75.37	21.94	10.74
OUR-YT$_{flickr}$	74.33	**23.13**	**13.43**

3.2 Comparison Methods

We compare our framework (denote by OUR) with two state-of-the-art SVO-based methods HVC [17] and FGM [17]. In order to evaluate the effectiveness of the summarization process, we also compare with LSTM [18], which shows the best performance of video caption by the combination of deep CNN and RNN.

In the following, we let "-YT" denote the model is trained on the YouTube, for example OUR-YT and LSTM-YT, and "-YT$_{flickr}$" denote the model trained on YouTube and Flickr8k datasets, which means a transfer process of video caption from pre-captioned images, e.g., OUR-YT$_{flickr}$ and LSTM-YT$_{flickr}$.

3.3 Experimental Results

3.3.1 *Evaluation Metric*

To evaluate the generated sentences after summarization, we use the BLEU [14] and METEOR [1] as the criteria. As HVC [17] and FGM [17] used the SVO (subject, verb, object) accuracy, we also evaluate the results by the most frequent SVO accuracy.

3.3.2 *Comparison Results*

Firstly, we report the comparison results in Table 1 and 2. From the results we can see: (1) Comparing the results only trained on YouTube, our method obtains the best results in terms of BLEU and METEOR, see Table 1. (2) Comparing OUR-YT$_{flickr}$ with LSTM-YT$_{flickr}$, our method obtains better performance of transfer video caption. Moreover, by transferring knowledge from pre-captioned images, OUR-YT$_{flickr}$ obtains the best scores of BLEU and METEOR as well as the V and O scores of SVO, which further demonstrate the better performance of our method.

3.3.3 *Example Results of Transfer Caption*

In Fig. 3 we show some examples of video caption results. Four frames are extracted from a video clip. Note that there are some occlusions (dark noises) on the forth frame and thus the CNN-RNN generated sentence is not as accurate as the one obtained from a transfer caption process (see the sentence in green text). Furthermore, as there are some noises in the video frames, the output final video captions from FGM and LSTM are shown to be influenced by the noises, e.g., "A person playing the goal of the road" is not

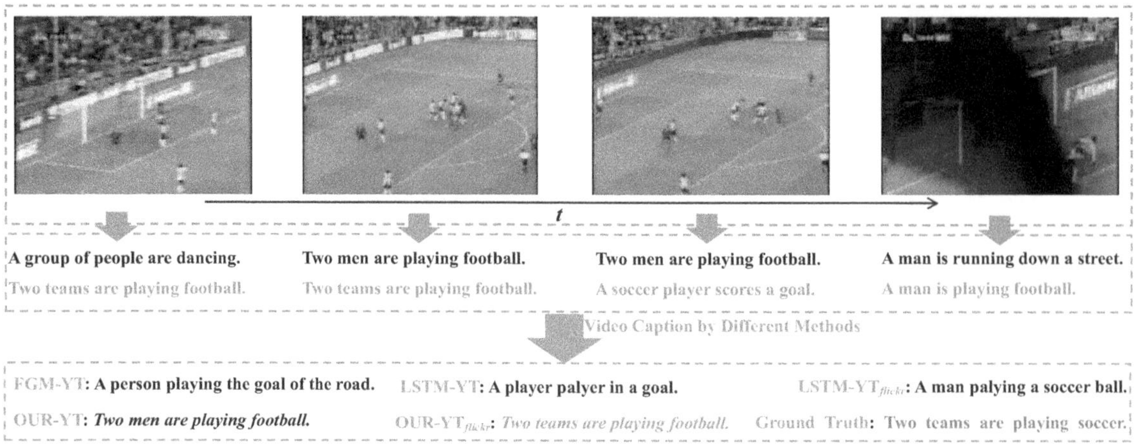

Figure 3: Example of video caption results. Sentences in dark text under each frame are generated by our CNN-RNN framework, whereas the sentences in green are obtained by the help of transferring knowledge from pre-captioned images in Flickr8K.

a correct sentence or some grammatical errors in "A player palyer in a goal". As our framework owns the merit of summarization and transferring caption, we generate sentences in better quality and are very close to the ground truth. Thus, these results further demonstrate the effectiveness of the proposed framework.

4. CONCLUSIONS

In this paper, we have proposed a framework of summarization-based video caption via deep neural networks. We translate the frame sequence to the sentence sequence by the deep CNN and RNN. To obtain the representative descriptions for video clip, we develop a summarization process to generate the final description to the target video clip. As shown in experimental results, our framework can generate better sentences than the state-of-the-art approaches, especially in noisy data. Moreover, the exploiting of pre-captioned images as auxiliary domain can help improve the performance of video caption. Future work includes utilizing the motion cue from videos to improve the prediction accuracy.

5. ACKNOWLEDGMENTS

This work was supported by NSFC (Grant 61202166, 61472276).

6. REFERENCES

[1] S. Banerjee and A. Lavie. Meteor: An automatic metric for mt evaluation with improved correlation with human judgments. In *Proceedings of the acl workshop on intrinsic and extrinsic evaluation measures for machine translation and/or summarization*, pages 65–72, 2005.

[2] D. L. Chen and W. B. Dolan. Collecting highly parallel data for paraphrase evaluation. In *Proc. of the 49th Annual Meeting of the Association for Computational Linguistics*, pages 190–200. Association for Computational Linguistics, 2011.

[3] J. Deng, W. Dong, R. Socher, L.-J. Li, K. Li, and L. Fei-Fei. Imagenet: A large-scale hierarchical image database. In *CVPR*, pages 248–255, 2009.

[4] J. Donahue, L. A. Hendricks, S. Guadarrama, M. Rohrbach, S. Venugopalan, K. Saenko, and T. Darrell. Long-term recurrent convolutional networks for visual recognition and description. *arXiv preprint arXiv:1411.4389*, 2014.

[5] G. Erkan and D. R. Radev. Lexrank: graph-based lexical centrality as salience in text summarization. *Journal of Artificial Intelligence Research*, pages 457–479, 2004.

[6] H. Fang, S. Gupta, F. Iandola, R. Srivastava, L. Deng, P. Dollár, J. Gao, X. He, M. Mitchell, J. Platt, et al. From captions to visual concepts and back. *arXiv preprint arXiv:1411.4952*, 2014.

[7] A. Farhadi, M. Hejrati, M. A. Sadeghi, P. Young, C. Rashtchian, J. Hockenmaier, and D. Forsyth. Every picture tells a story: Generating sentences from images. In *ECCV*, pages 15–29. 2010.

[8] S. Guadarrama, N. Krishnamoorthy, G. Malkarnenkar, S. Venugopalan, R. Mooney, T. Darrell, and K. Saenko. Youtube2text: Recognizing and describing arbitrary activities using semantic hierarchies and zero-shot recognition. In *ICCV*, pages 2712–2719, 2013.

[9] S. Hochreiter and J. Schmidhuber. Long short-term memory. *Neural computation*, 9(8):1735–1780, 1997.

[10] M. Hodosh, P. Young, and J. Hockenmaier. Framing image description as a ranking task: Data, models and evaluation metrics. *Journal of Artificial Intelligence Research*, pages 853–899, 2013.

[11] Y. Jia, E. Shelhamer, J. Donahue, S. Karayev, J. Long, R. Girshick, S. Guadarrama, and T. Darrell. Caffe: Convolutional architecture for fast feature embedding. *arXiv preprint arXiv:1408.5093*, 2014.

[12] A. Karpathy and L. Fei-Fei. Deep visual-semantic alignments for generating image descriptions. *arXiv preprint arXiv:1412.2306*, 2014.

[13] V. Ordonez, G. Kulkarni, and T. L. Berg. Im2text: Describing images using 1 million captioned photographs. In *NIPS*, pages 1143–1151, 2011.

[14] K. Papineni, S. Roukos, T. Ward, and W.-J. Zhu. Bleu: a method for automatic evaluation of machine translation. In *Proc. of the 40th annual meeting on association for computational linguistics*, pages 311–318, 2002.

[15] M. Rohrbach, W. Qiu, I. Titov, S. Thater, M. Pinkal, and B. Schiele. Translating video content to natural language descriptions. In *ICCV*, pages 433–440, 2013.

[16] O. Russakovsky, J. Deng, H. Su, J. Krause, S. Satheesh, S. Ma, Z. Huang, A. Karpathy, A. Khosla, M. Bernstein, A. C. Berg, and L. Fei-Fei. ImageNet Large Scale Visual Recognition Challenge. *IJCV*, 2015.

[17] J. Thomason, S. Venugopalan, S. Guadarrama, K. Saenko, and R. Mooney. Integrating language and vision to generate natural language descriptions of videos in the wild. In *COLING*, 2014.

[18] S. Venugopalan, H. Xu, J. Donahue, M. Rohrbach, R. Mooney, and K. Saenko. Translating videos to natural language using deep recurrent neural networks. *arXiv preprint arXiv:1412.4729*, 2014.

[19] O. Vinyals, A. Toshev, S. Bengio, and D. Erhan. Show and tell: A neural image caption generator. *arXiv preprint arXiv:1411.4555*, 2014.

A Multi-modal & Multi-view & Interactive Benchmark Dataset for Human Action Recognition

Ning Xu[1], Anan Liu[1*], Weizhi Nie[1], Yongkang Wong[2], Fuwu Li[1], Yuting Su[1]

[1]School of Electronic Information Engineering, Tianjin University, China

[2] Interactive & Digital Media Institute, National University of Singapore, Singapore

*Corresponding author: anan0422@gmail.com

ABSTRACT

Human action recognition is one of the most active research areas in both computer vision and machine learning communities. Several methods for human action recognition have been proposed in the literature and promising results have been achieved on the popular datasets. However, the comparison of existing methods is often limited given the different datasets, experimental settings, feature representations, and so on. In particularly, there are no human action dataset that allow concurrent analysis on three popular scenarios, namely single view, cross view, and cross domain. In this paper, we introduce a Multi-modal & Multi-view & Interactive (M^2I) dataset, which is designed for the evaluation of the performances of human action recognition under multi-view scenario. This dataset consists of 1760 action samples, including 9 person-person interaction actions and 13 person-object interaction actions. Moreover, we respectively evaluate three representative methods for the single-view, cross-view, and cross-domain human action recognition on this dataset with the proposed evaluation protocol. It is experimentally demonstrated that this dataset is extremely challenging due to large intraclass variation, multiple similar actions, significant view difference. This benchmark can provide solid basis for the evaluation of this task and will benefit advancing related computer vision and machine learning research topics.

Categories and Subject Descriptors

H.3.1 [**Information Storage and Retrieval**]: Content Analysis and Indexing-*Indexing methods*

General Terms

Experimentation

Keywords

human action recognition, multi-modal, multi-view

MM'15, October 26–30, 2015, Brisbane, Australia.

© 2015 ACM. ISBN 978-1-4503-3459-4/15/10 ...$15.00.

DOI: http://dx.doi.org/10.1145/2733373.2806315.

1. INTRODUCTION

Human action recognition has received increasing attention owing to its rich real-world applications, such as multimedia retrieval, human computer interaction, and video surveillance [1]. Depending on the environments, human actions may have different forms including atomic actions and interactions composed by person-object and person-to-person interactions. Existing action recognition dataset mainly focus on atomic actions (e.g., KTH [7], UCF50 [6], IXMAS [10], *etc.*), which limits the performance of video-based human activity recognition. Recently, researchers are engaging in person-person interaction actions and person-object interaction actions [2]. However, the current person-person interaction action dataset [3] and person-object interaction action dataset [5] only include limited action categories and video samples.

With the recent advancement of the cost-effective depth sensor (e.g., Kinect depth sensor), there is a significant attention of using depth data for various computer vision task in the research community. Multiple methods have been developed by leveraging RGB images and/or depth data on several popular RGB-D datasets (e.g., MSR Daily Activity [9], UTKinect [11], *etc.*). Until now the state-of-the-art approaches have achieved satisfactory performances on most of the public datasets [8].

Based on the evolution of human action datasets, it is necessary to prepare a challenging multi-modal & multi-view dataset with both person-person interaction and person-object interaction. To bridge the gap, we proposed a new video dataset which enumerate three major challenges to vision based on human action recognition. The first challenge is variation in modality, which contains RGB, depth and 3D body joints data captured simultaneously by Kinect sensors. The second challenge is variation in camera view, where the same actions can generate a different appearance from different perspectives. Moreover, double views is appropriate which is similar to the human physical features. The third challenge is the intra-class variability and inter-class similarity of actions. Individuals can perform an action in different directions with different characteristics of body part movements, and two actions may be only distinguished by very subtle spatio-temporal differences.

For human action recognition, there are three key tasks:

- *Single-view task*: The model learning and evaluation are independently conducted on two non-overlapping parts from the same dataset. One representative method was done by Wang *et al.*, which evaluated the bag of

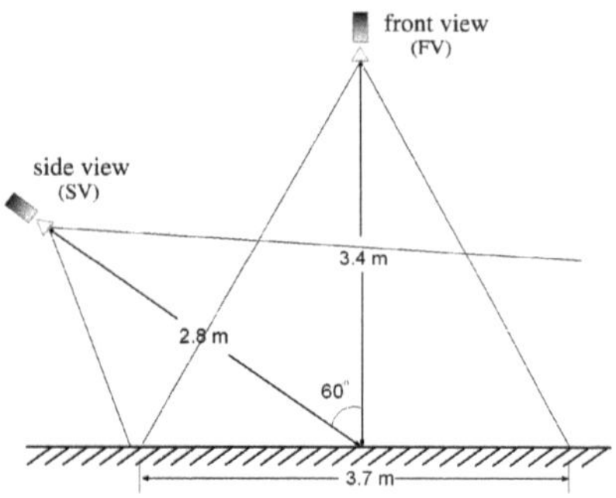

Figure 1: Camera configuration of the M^{2}I dataset.

visual word descriptor and SVM classifier on 9 popular datasets [11].

- *Cross-view task*: The model learning and evaluation are conducted on datasets with two overlapping views on the same observation. Transferable dictionary pair learning proposed by Zheng *et al.* [12] is a representative method. The basic philosophy is mapping the features from different views into the same feature space by the sparse representation framework to handle the cross-view action representation.

- *Cross-domain task*: It leverages a portion of the target dataset together with the auxiliary dataset for model learning and then evaluates on the remaining target dataset. Adaptive multiple kernel learning proposed by Xu *et al.* [4] is a representative method. It leverages fewer labeled data from the target domain and large-scale labeled data from the auxiliary domain together to augment the generalization ability of model learning.

However, there is lack of systematic evaluation of the representative methods under three scenarios on one benchmark dataset.

To tackle these problems, we benchmark a novel database for human action recognition. The major contributions are two-fold: (1) We contribute a Multi-modal & Multi-view & Interactive (M^{2}I) dataset[1] for human action recognition, which can be utilized for the evaluation of the three scenarios above. (2) We systematically evaluate three aforementioned representative methods (i.e., single-view, cross-view, and cross-domain scenarios) with the designed experimental protocol. Extensive experiments demonstrate that M^{2}I dataset is extremely challenging due to large intraclass variation, multiple similar actions, significant view difference. The details of the proposed new dataset is elaborated in Section 2, and the evaluation of the three experiment scenarios are shown in Section 3. Section 4 concludes the paper.

2. M^{2}I HUMAN ACTION DATASET

The proposed Multi-modal & Multi-view & Interactive (M^{2}I) dataset provide person-person interaction actions and person-object interaction actions. In this dataset, two static Kinect depth sensors were used to simultaneously capture the RGB image (320 × 240), depth image (320 × 240) and skeleton data (3D coordinates of 20 joints per frame) from both the front and side views. The dataset was recorded with 30 frames per second. The angle between the primary optical axes of two Kinects depth sensor was set with 60° to augment the view differences, which can further induce difficulty for shared knowledge discovery from multiple views. To increase the challenges, the layout of the indoor environment was set with cluttered background and illumination variation. The physical configurations of the data recording environment (indoor) is shown in Fig. 1.

Table 1: List of action categories of M^{2}I dataset.

Person-person Interaction		
1 Walk Together	2 Cross	3 Wait
4 Chat	5 Hug	6 Handshake
7 High Five	8 Bow	9 Box
Person-object Interaction		
10 Play Football	11 Pass Basketball	12 Carry Box
13 Throw Basketball	14 Bounce Basketball	15 Hula Hoop
16 Tennis Swing	17 Call Cellphone	18 Drink
19 Take Photo	20 Sweep Floor	21 Clean Desk
22 Play Guitar		

Compared against existing datasets, M^{2}I dataset contains most common person-person/person-object interaction actions and consequently has richer action diversity. It consists of 22 action categories (see Table 1) and a total of 22 unique individuals. Each action is performed twice by 20 groups (two persons in a group). In total, M^{2}I dataset contains 1760 samples (22 actions × 20 groups × 2 views × 2 run). All the RGB image, depth data, and skeleton data are preprocessed to remove noise. Furthermore, we implemented background modeling and foreground extraction to provide masks for individual frames. Totally, M^{2}I dataset contains the following information: RGB data (image sequence sample: 6.79G; video sample: 19.2G); Depth data (image sequence sample: 49.4G); mask (image sequence sample: 613M); 3D Skeleton data (53.9M). Image samples of selected action in the M^{2}I dataset is shown in Fig. 2.

For evaluation, all samples were divided with respect to the groups into a training set (8 groups), a validation set (6 groups) and a test set (6 groups). The classifiers are trained on the training set while the validation set is used to optimize the parameters. The final action recognition results are obtained with the test set.

3. EXPERIMENTS

We evaluated three representative methods under single-view, cross-view, and cross-domain scenarios on M^{2}I dataset.

3.1 Single-View Task

For single-view task, we respectively evaluated the BoW+SVM framework [8] on the front view and the side view of M^{2}I dataset in both RGB and depth. The popular dense trajectory+HOG&HOF spatiotemporal features were extracted. Then K-means was used to quantize them into visual words and a video is represented as the frequency histogram over the visual words. We empirically set the number of visual words with 1000. To limit the complexity, we cluster a subset of 100,000 randomly selected training features. Support vector machine (χ^2-kernel) was used for model learning. For multi-class classification, we applied the one-against-rest approach and selected the optimal parameters by cross validation. The split strategy was used for evaluation as [8] and

[1] http://media.tju.edu.cn/m2i.html

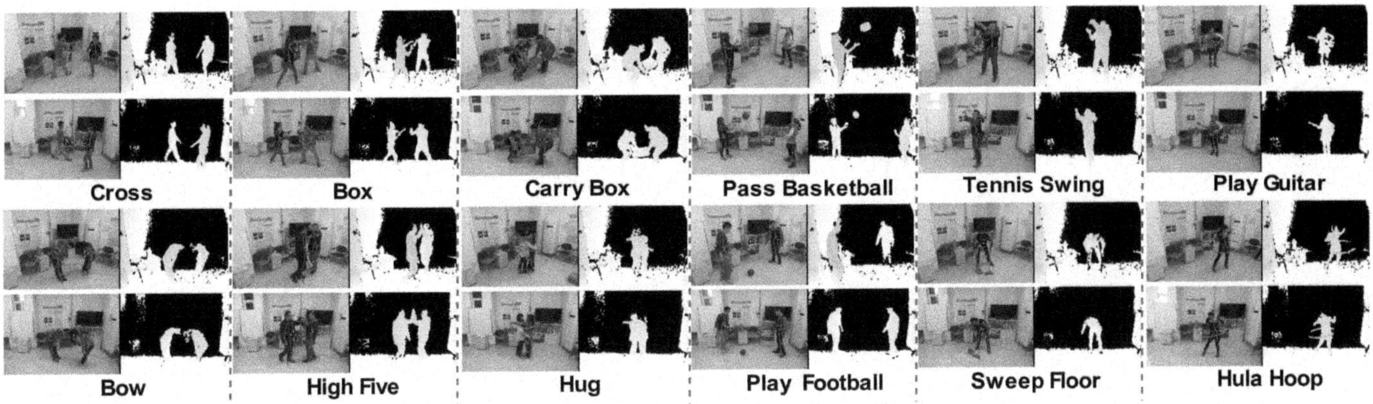

Figure 2: Image samples of selected action in the M^{2}I dataset. Each cell shows the front-view and side-view samples (RGB, depth, skeleton) of actions.

the model was trained on the training+validation data and tested on the test data.

We can achieve 75.7%/72.8% and 76.5%/75.4% on the front view and the side view of M^{2}I dataset in RGB/depth modality, respectively. With the category-wise comparison in Fig. 3, the performances in RGB modality can outperform most of those in depth modality with richer visual information and both modalities are complementary with each other. The low overall performances and multiple category-wise accuracy below 80% indicate that this dataset is very challenging with multiple similar actions (e.g., Wait & Chat, Handshake & High Five, *etc.*) and significant intraclass variation required when data capturing.

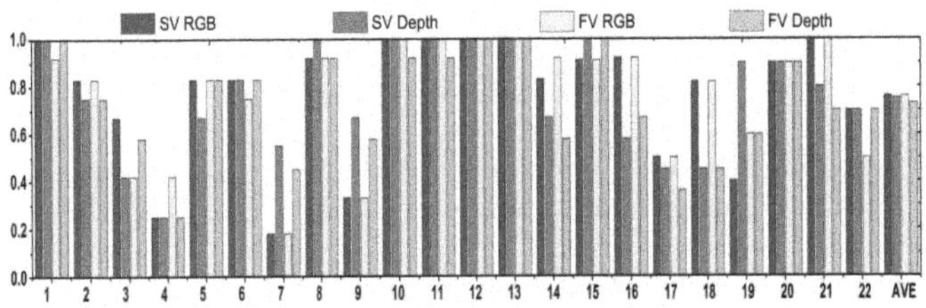

Figure 3: Category-wise accuracy and average accuracy on the RGB and Depth data under the single-view scenario. (SV: side view; FV: front view)

3.2 Cross-View Task

For feature representation, we respectively constructed the BoW features for individual views and individual modalities as introduced in Section 3.1. Then we implemented the transferable dictionary pair learning method [12] in both supervised (shared actions in both views are labeled) and unsupervised (shared actions in both views are not labeled) settings to transferring sparse feature representations of videos from the source to target view on the RGB and depth data of M^{2}I dataset, respectively. We varied the dictionary dimension and sparsity coefficient within [50, 100, 200, 300] and [10, 20, 30, 40, 50], respectively for the optimal performances. Then K-Nearest Neighbor (K=1) was utilized for action recognition. The leave-one-action-out strategy was used for evaluation as [12].

Fig. 4 shows: 1) In the RGB modality, learning in the side view to test in the front view can usually outperform learning in the from view to test in the side view; 2) In the depth modality, the conclusion is just the opposite since the front view usually has more significant depth variation; 3) The unsupervised learning case can outperform the supervised learning case by avoiding the confusion caused by the similar actions with different labels. The cross-view experiment also shows M^{2}I dataset is very challenging with significant view difference.

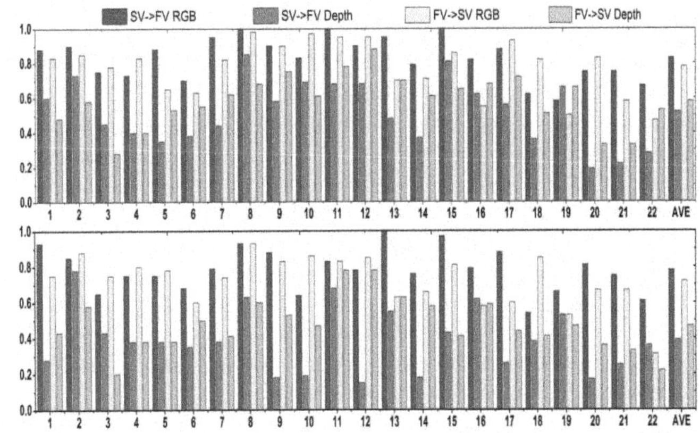

Figure 4: Category-wise accuracy and average accuracy on the RGB and Depth data under the cross-view scenario. The top bar figure corresponds to unsupervised approach and the bottom bar figure corresponds to supervised approach.

3.3 Cross-Domain Task

For cross-domain case, we selected one view as the target domain and the other as the auxiliary domain and mainly evaluated the Adaptive Multiple Kernel Learning (AMKL) method. As [4], we compared AMTL against the baseline by the single view-based method (SVM-T) introduced in Section 3.1 and four representative cross-domain learning methods, including DTSVM, MKL, FR, SVM-AT as [4]. Two different experiments for model learning were set: 1) Case 1: all the training+validation data of 14 persons in the auxiliary domain plus the data of N persons belonging to the training+validation part in the target domain; 2) Case 2: all the training+validation data of 14 persons in the target domain plus the data of N persons belonging to the training+validation part in the auxiliary domain. N was varied from 2 to 14. The front view and the side view were varied for the target domain and the auxiliary domain.

Fig. 5 shows that: 1) For Case 1, the performances of all methods can be monotonically increased by augmenting the

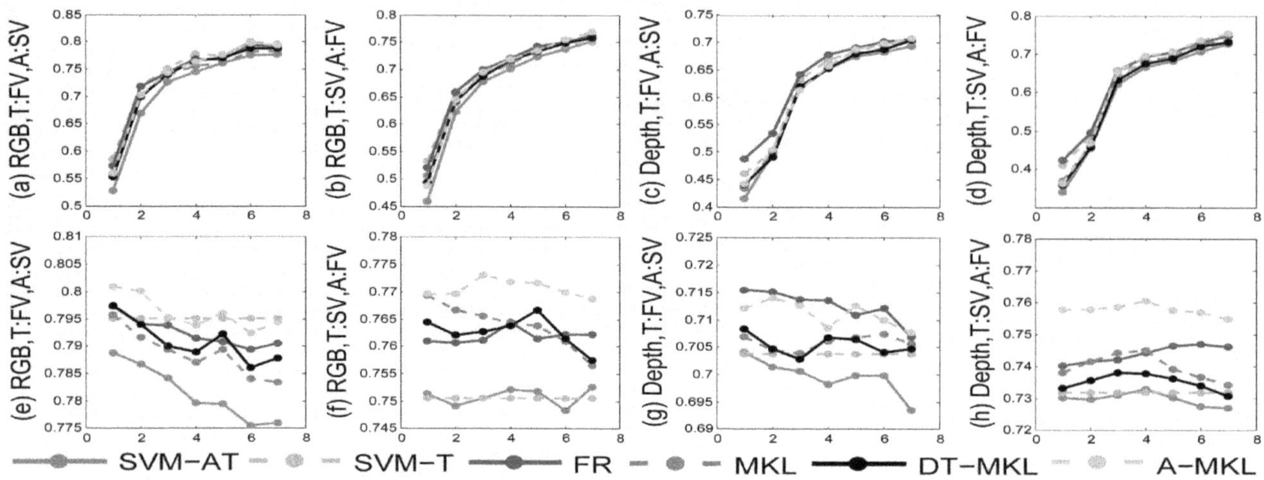

Figure 5: Overall accuracy on the RGB and Depth data under the cross-domain scenario. (a-d) Case 1; (e-h) Case 2. (T: target domain; A: auxiliary domain)

data from the target domain and AMKL can usually outperform the others by well leveraging the discovered knowledge from the auxiliary domain. 2) For Case 2, the performances can not be monotonically increased by augmenting the data from the auxiliary domain and it can even decrease since more samples in different feature space might have negative influence on useful knowledge transferring inbetween. This experiment further demonstrated that the dataset is extremely challenging with significant view differences.

4. CONCLUSIONS AND FUTURE WORK

In this paper, we introduce the Multi-modal & Multi-view & Interactive (M^2I) database for human action recognition. Moreover, we respectively evaluate three representative methods for the single-view, cross-view, and cross-domain human action recognition on this dataset. It is experimentally demonstrated that this dataset is extremely challenging due to large intraclass variation, multiple similar actions, and significant view difference. As the future work, we will evaluate more popular spatiotemporal features on this dataset and focus on multi-modal & multi-view information fusion to boost the performance.

5. ACKNOWLEDGMENT

This work was supported in part by the National Natural Science Foundation of China (61472275, 61303208), the Tianjin Research Program of Application Foundation and Advanced Technology (15JCYBJC16200), the grant of Elite Scholar Program of Tianjin University (2014XRG-0046).

6. REFERENCES

[1] J. K. Aggarwal and M. S. Ryoo. Human activity analysis: A review. *ACM Comput. Surv.*, 43(3):16, 2011.

[2] X. Chang, W. Zheng, and J. Zhang. Learning person-person interaction in collective activity recognition. *IEEE Transactions on Image Processing*, 24(6):1905–1918, 2015.

[3] W. Choi and S. Savarese. Understanding collective activities of people from videos. *IEEE Transactions on Pattern Analysis and Machine Intelligence*, 36(6):1242–1257, 2012.

[4] L. Duan, D. Xu, I. W. Tsang, and J. Luo. Visual event recognition in videos by learning from web data. *IEEE Trans. Pattern Anal. Mach. Intell*, 34(9):1667–1680, 2012.

[5] J. Hu, W. Zheng, J. Lai, S. Gong, and T. Xiang. Exemplar-based recognition of human-object interactions. *IEEE Transactions on Circuits and Systems for Video Technology*, 2015.

[6] K. K. Reddy and M. Shah. Recognizing 50 human action categories of web videos. *Mach. Vis. Appl.*, 24(5):971–981, 2013.

[7] C. Schüldt, I. Laptev, and B. Caputo. Recognizing human actions: A local SVM approach. In *17th International Conference on Pattern Recognition, ICPR 2004, Cambridge, UK, August 23-26, 2004.*, pages 32–36, 2004.

[8] H. Wang, A. Kläser, C. Schmid, and C. Liu. Dense trajectories and motion boundary descriptors for action recognition. *International Journal of Computer Vision*, 103(1):60–79, 2013.

[9] J. Wang, Z. Liu, Y. Wu, and J. Yuan. Mining actionlet ensemble for action recognition with depth cameras. In *2012 IEEE Conference on Computer Vision and Pattern Recognition, Providence, RI, USA, June 16-21, 2012*, pages 1290–1297, 2012.

[10] D. Weinland, E. Boyer, and R. Ronfard. Action recognition from arbitrary views using 3d exemplars. In *IEEE 11th International Conference on Computer Vision, ICCV 2007, Rio de Janeiro, Brazil, October 14-20, 2007*, pages 1–7, 2007.

[11] L. Xia, C. Chen, and J. K. Aggarwal. View invariant human action recognition using histograms of 3d joints. In *2012 IEEE Computer Society Conference on Computer Vision and Pattern Recognition Workshops, Providence, RI, USA, June 16-21, 2012*, pages 20–27, 2012.

[12] J. Zheng, Z. Jiang, P. J. Phillips, and R. Chellappa. Cross-view action recognition via a transferable dictionary pair. In *British Machine Vision Conference, BMVC 2012, Surrey, UK, September 3-7, 2012*, pages 1–11, 2012.

A Deep Siamese Network for Scene Detection in Broadcast Videos

Lorenzo Baraldi, Costantino Grana and Rita Cucchiara
Dipartimento di Ingegneria "Enzo Ferrari", Università degli Studi di Modena e Reggio Emilia
Via P. Vivarelli, 10, Modena MO 41125, Italy
name.surname@unimore.it

ABSTRACT

We present a model that automatically divides broadcast videos into coherent scenes by learning a distance measure between shots. Experiments are performed to demonstrate the effectiveness of our approach by comparing our algorithm against recent proposals for automatic scene segmentation. We also propose an improved performance measure that aims to reduce the gap between numerical evaluation and expected results, and propose and release a new benchmark dataset.

Categories and Subject Descriptors

H.3.1 [**Information Storage and Retrieval**]: Content analysis and indexing

Keywords

Deep Learning, Scene Segmentation, Video Re-use

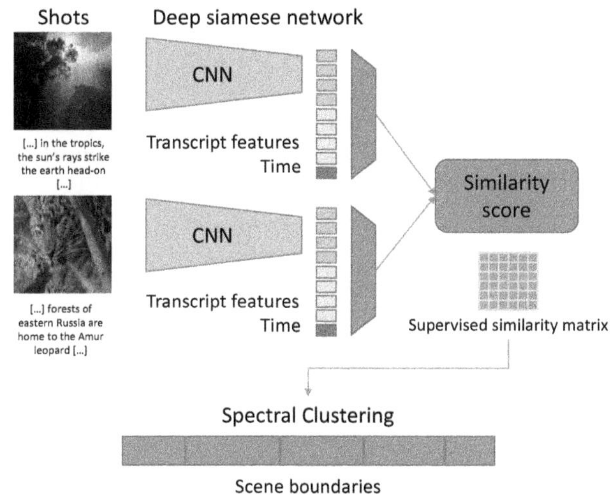

Figure 1: Our approach decomposes a video into coherent parts. A multimodal deep neural network learns a similarity score for each pair of shots, using visual and textual features. The resulting similarity matrix is used to cluster adjacent shots together.

1. INTRODUCTION

Scene detection is the task to automatically segment an input video into meaningful and story-telling parts, without any help from the producer, using perceptual cues and multimedia features extracted from data [10]. Therefore, it can be an effective tool to enhance video accessing and browsing; moreover, since each of the resulting parts could be automatically tagged, this kind of decomposition can enable a finer-grained search inside videos.

We address the problem of automatic scene detection in broadcast video. Differently from news videos, which present a well established structure, generic broadcast videos have different editing standards based on the specific style the director desires. This cue has been exploited in existing works: Liu *et al.* [6], for example, propose a probabilistic framework that imitates the authoring process and detects scenes by learning a scene model. Another solution is instead to disregard the structure, focusing only on similarities: in [2], shots are firstly clustered into symbolic groups, then, scene boundaries are detected by comparing successive non-overlapping windows of shot labels using a sequence alignment technique that considers the visual similarity of shot clusters and the frequency of sequential labels in the video.

An alternative view of the scenes structure is to arrange shots in a graph representation and then cluster them by partitioning the graph. Sidiropoulos *et al.* [9], for example, exploited the Shot Transition Graph method, where each node represents a shot and edges between shots are weighted by shot similarity. All these techniques rely on well established features such as histograms, bag-of-words representations, or MPEG-7 descriptors, extracted from one or multiple key frames; audio or transcript features have also been employed.

The task of scene detection requires good representations of the video content, specifically images and transcript. Recently, Convolutional Neural Networks have shown their powerful abilities on image representation [5]. In this paper we go beyond traditional hand-crafted features and apply the deep learning paradigm to scene detection, exploiting both visual and textual features from the transcript, that, when not directly available, can be obtained with automatic

MM'15, October 26–30, 2015, Brisbane, Australia.
© 2015 ACM. ISBN 978-1-4503-3459-4/15/10 ...$15.00.
DOI: http://dx.doi.org/10.1145/2733373.2806316.

speech recognition. Deeply learned features are then used together with a clustering algorithm to segment the video. To the best of our knowledge, this is the first attempt to use deep learning in this task.

As it usually happens in emerging topics, most works on scene detection conducted experiments on personal test sets, which are not publicly available, thus making it hard for others to reproduce or to compare the presented results. Evaluation measures were also sometimes not appropriate and did not reflect the quality perceived by the user. For these reasons, we propose a new dataset for scene detection, and we also try to tackle the problem of evaluation.

The main contributions of our work are:

- We propose a deep learning framework for segmenting videos into coherent scenes, which takes both visual and textual features as input and merges them to create similarity scores;
- A new benchmark dataset is proposed, and annotations are publicly released. To our knowledge, this is the biggest dataset for scene detection available.
- Lastly, we address the limitations of existing measures for scene detection evaluation, and propose an improved measure which solves frequently observed cases in which the numeric interpretation would be different from the expected results.

2. DEEPLY-LEARNED SCENE DETECTION

Given the nature of a broadcast video – i.e. a sequence of shots, and given that a shot usually has a uniform content, scene detection can also be viewed as the problem of grouping adjacent shots together, with the objective of maximizing the semantic coherence of the resulting segments. This implies a dimensionality reduction and poses scene detection as a clustering problem: our model, indeed, detects scenes by applying the spectral clustering algorithm to shots. Moreover, for the detected segmentation to be useful to the final user, we want it to be as close as possible to the desired output. For this reason, instead of applying pre-defined descriptors to build the similarity matrix the clustering algorithm needs, we couple the unsupervised clustering with a supervised deep neural network which learns similarities between shots.

The architecture of our neural network resembles that of a Siamese network [3] (see Fig. 1): it consists of two branches that share exactly the same architecture and the same weights. Each branch takes as input two distinct shots, and then applies a series of convolutional, ReLU and max-pooling layers. Branch outputs are then concatenated and given to a top network. Branch of the Siamese network can be seen as descriptor computation modules and the top network as a similarity function. At test time, similarity scores computed by the neural network are composed together to build a similarity matrix, which is then given to the spectral clustering algorithm to obtain the final scene boundaries.

2.1 Visual features

The first part of each branch consists of a Convolutional Neural Network (CNN) which takes the middle frame of a given shot, cropped and resized to fit the network input size. Using a single frame allows a complexity reduction while still allowing a good description.

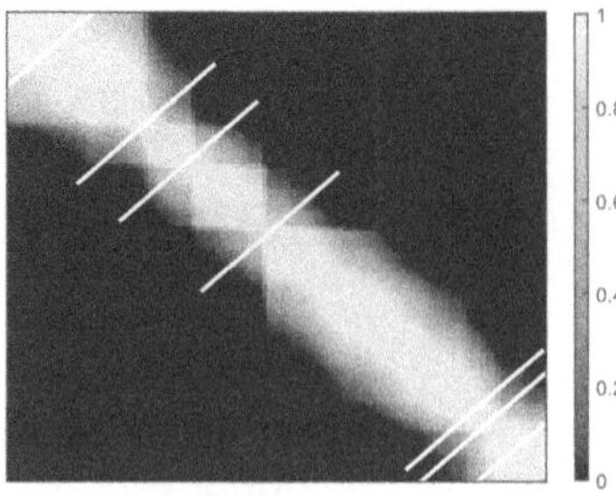

Figure 2: Detail of matrix W for the *From Pole to Pole* episode. Ground truth scene boundaries (white lines) correspond to low similarity areas.

We want to give the CNN the ability to recognize not only objects, animals and people, but indoor and outdoor places too, since a scene often takes place in a single location, and to be specific for the scene segmentation task. Therefore, we pre-train our CNN on 1.2 million images of the ImageNet dataset (ILSVRC 2012) [5], plus 2.5 million images from the Places dataset [11]. Finally, the CNN is fine-tuned using training shots.

The architecture of the CNN is the same as the one used in the Caffe reference network [4], and the visual representation of the shot is computed as follows:

$$r_{vis} = \sigma(\mathbf{w}_{vis}(CNN_{vis}(I)) + b_{vis} \quad (1)$$

where $\sigma(\cdot)$ is the ReLU activation function. The image CNN returns the 4096-dimensional activations of the fully connected layer immediately before the last ReLU layer. The matrix $\mathbf{w}_{vis}$ has dimension $d \cdot 4096$, and each image is thus represented as one d_{vis}-dimensional vector r_{vis}.

2.2 Textual features

Beside the visual content of a shot, we want to take into account the content of the transcript, while still keeping a shot-based representation. Given that a shot can contain a variable number of words, and a feed-forward neural network requires fixed size inputs, we exploit a variant of the bag-of-words approach that takes feature vectors obtained with Skip-gram models [7]: words in the transcript are represented using their Word2vec descriptors, and then clustered using k-means and the cosine distance between words.

Since shots can be very short, describing a brief shot using only the words it contains would result in a non-consistent descriptor. Therefore, for each shot we define a context window centered on the shot center frame, and with size $\max(w_s, W)$, where w_s is the shot duration and W is the minimum context window size. Words from each window are then represented with their bag-of-words vector, resulting in a d_{words}-dimensional vector r_{words} for each shot.

2.3 Similarity scores and clustering

In the last part of each branch, the visual representation r_{vis} is merged with the textual representation r_{words}; in addition, the resulting vector is concatenated with the index of the center frame of the shot, so that the network is aware of the temporal distance between two shots. A fully connected layer takes the joint representation and learns how to weight the components to get the final similarity scores.

The network is trained using a contrastive loss term and squared l_2-norm regularization, that leads to the following learning objective function:

$$L(\mathbf{w}) = \frac{\lambda}{2}\|\mathbf{w}\|_2^2 + \frac{1}{2N}\sum_{(i,j)\in\mathcal{D}} y_{ij}d_{ij}^2 + (1-y_{ij})\max(1-d_{ij}^2, 0) \tag{2}$$

where $\mathbf{w}$ are the weights of the neural network, $\mathcal{D}$ is the set of training shot pairs, d_{ij}^2 is the squared l_2-distance for shots i and j (computed between the two final layers of the Siamese network), and $y_{ij} \in \{0,1\}$ is the corresponding label (with 0 and 1 denoting a non-matching and a matching pair, respectively).

Finally, distances d_{ij} are turned into similarity scores by applying a Gaussian kernel, where bandwith σ is computed using a kernel density estimator. Similarity matrix W (see Fig. 2 for an example) is then used together with spectral clustering to group adjacent shots: final scene boundaries are placed between shots belonging to different clusters.

3. EXPERIMENTAL EVALUATION

Performance measures The problem of measuring scene detection performance is significantly different from that of measuring shot detection performance. Indeed, classical boundary detection scores, such as Precision and Recall, fail to convey the true perception of an error, which is different for an off-by-one shot or for a completely missed scene boundary.

In [10] the Coverage and Overflow measures were proposed to overcome this limitation. Coverage $\mathcal{C}$ measures the quantity of shots belonging to the same scene correctly grouped together, while Overflow $\mathcal{O}$ evaluates to what extent shots not belonging to the same scene are erroneously grouped together. Formally, given the set of automatically detected scenes $\mathbf{s} = [\mathbf{s}_1, \mathbf{s}_2, ..., \mathbf{s}_m]$, and the ground truth $\tilde{\mathbf{s}} = [\tilde{\mathbf{s}}_1, \tilde{\mathbf{s}}_2, ..., \tilde{\mathbf{s}}_n]$, where each element of $\mathbf{s}$ and $\tilde{\mathbf{s}}$ is a set of shot indexes, the coverage $\mathcal{C}_t$ of scene $\tilde{\mathbf{s}}_t$ is defined as:

$$\mathcal{C}_t = \frac{\max_{i=1...,m} \#(\mathbf{s}_i \cap \tilde{\mathbf{s}}_t)}{\#(\tilde{\mathbf{s}}_t)} \tag{3}$$

where $\#(\mathbf{s}_i)$ is the number of shots in scene $\mathbf{s}_i$. The overflow of a scene $\tilde{\mathbf{s}}_t$, $\mathcal{O}_t$, is the amount of overlap of every $\mathbf{s}_i$ corresponding to $\tilde{\mathbf{s}}_t$ with the two surrounding scenes:

$$\mathcal{O}_t = \frac{\sum_{i=1}^{m} \#(\mathbf{s}_i \setminus \tilde{\mathbf{s}}_t)\cdot \min(1, \#(\mathbf{s}_i \cap \tilde{\mathbf{s}}_t))}{\#(\tilde{\mathbf{s}}_{t-1}) + \#(\tilde{\mathbf{s}}_{t+1})} \tag{4}$$

The per-ground-truth-scene measures are aggregated for the entire video by averaging, weighting them by the number of shots in each scene. Finally, an F-Score measure, F_{co}, can be defined to combine Coverage and Overflow in a single measure, by taking the harmonic mean of $\mathcal{C}$ and $1 - \mathcal{O}$.

These measures, while going in the right direction, have a number of drawbacks, which may affect the evaluation. As also noted in [8], F_{co} is not symmetric, leading to unusual phenomena in which an early or late positioning of the scene boundary, of the same amount of shots, may lead to strongly different results. Moreover, the relation of $\mathcal{O}$ with the previous and next scenes creates unreasonable dependencies between an error and the length of a scene observed many shots before it. Finally, $\mathcal{C}$ only depends on the maximum overlapping scene, and does not penalize the other overlapping scenes in any way: any over-segmentation in the other overlapping scenes does not change the measure value.

We propose to use a symmetric measure based on intersection over union to assess the quality of detected scenes. For

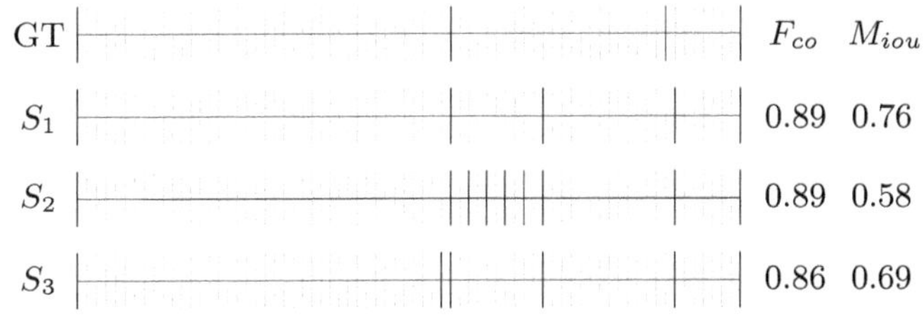

Figure 3: Values of F_{co} and M_{iou} for sample scene detections. Gray and black ticks represent shot and scene boundaries respectively.

each ground-truth scene, we take the maximum intersection-over-union with the detected scenes, averaging them on the whole video. Then the same is done for detected scenes against ground-truth scene, and the two quantities are again averaged. An important note is that both intersection and union are measured in terms of frame lengths for the shots, thus weighting the shots with their relative significance. The final measure is thus given by:

$$M_{iou} = \frac{1}{2}\left(\frac{1}{n}\sum_{i=1}^{n}\max_{j\in\mathbb{N}_m}\frac{\tilde{\mathbf{s}}_i \cap \mathbf{s}_j}{\tilde{\mathbf{s}}_i \cup \tilde{\mathbf{s}}_j} + \frac{1}{m}\sum_{j=1}^{m}\max_{i\in\mathbb{N}_n}\frac{\tilde{\mathbf{s}}_i \cap \mathbf{s}_j}{\tilde{\mathbf{s}}_i \cup \tilde{\mathbf{s}}_j}\right) \tag{5}$$

Figure 3 shows the behavior of the two measures in three synthetic cases. As it can be seen, M_{iou}, unlike F_{co}, penalizes over-segmentations and does not create dependencies between an error and previous scenes.

Experiments setting We evaluate our method on 11 episodes from the BBC educational TV series *Planet Earth*[1]. Each episode is approximately 50 minutes long, and the whole dataset contains around 4900 shots and 670 scenes. Shots and scenes of the entire dataset have been manually annotated by a set of human experts: annotations, as well as the Caffe [4] models of our network, are available at `http://imagelab.ing.unimore.it`.

To train our model, we employ Stochastic gradient descent with momentum 0.9 and weight decay $\lambda = 0.0005$. The learning rate is set to 0.001 for CNN neurons, and to 0.004 for the others. Parameters d_{vis}, d_{words} and W are set to 1183, 200 and 20 seconds, respectively, and the last fully connected layer of each branch is composed by 200 neurons. Training is done in mini-batches of size 128, and we shuffle and augment training data by flipping both shots horizontally and vertically. We also subtract from each frame the average frame computed over the training set.

The training set for a given video corresponds to all possible pairs of shots, most of them not belonging to the same scene, and it is therefore heavily unbalanced. To avoid the risk of having batches with only negative examples, and to balance the training phase, we artificially build batches using the same amount of positive and negative examples.

Evaluation We compare our model against two recent algorithms for scene detection: [9], which uses a variety of visual and audio features merged in a Shot Transition Graph (STG), and [2], that combines low level color features with the Needleman-Wunsh (NW) algorithm. We further include a baseline approach, which clusters shots using spectral clustering (SC) and three-dimensional color histograms and time

[1] `http://www.bbc.co.uk/programmes/b006mywy`

Table 1: Results on BBC *Planet Earth* series, using Intersection-over-union and Coverage-Overflow measures

Episode	M_{iou}				F_{co}			
	STG [9]	Color + NW[2]	Color + SC	Our method	STG [9]	Color + NW[2]	Color + SC	Our method
From Pole to Pole	0.42	0.35	0.43	**0.50**	0.47	0.39	0.48	**0.56**
Mountains	0.40	0.31	0.44	**0.53**	0.55	0.51	0.54	**0.63**
Fresh Water	0.39	0.34	0.48	**0.52**	0.56	0.53	0.50	**0.66**
Caves	0.37	0.33	0.44	**0.55**	0.46	0.39	0.42	**0.61**
Deserts	0.36	0.33	**0.46**	0.36	0.42	**0.56**	0.54	0.55
Ice Worlds	0.39	0.37	0.44	**0.51**	0.44	0.45	0.50	**0.64**
Great Plains	0.46	0.37	**0.48**	0.47	**0.65**	0.53	0.51	0.59
Jungles	0.45	0.38	**0.53**	0.51	0.63	0.45	0.60	**0.64**
Shallow Seas	0.46	0.32	0.47	**0.51**	0.61	0.36	0.55	**0.64**
Seasonal Forests	0.42	0.20	**0.43**	0.38	0.58	0.19	0.52	**0.64**
Ocean Deep	0.34	0.36	**0.48**	**0.48**	0.52	0.54	0.57	**0.64**
Average	0.41	0.33	0.46	**0.48**	0.54	0.45	0.52	**0.62**
Average with GT shots	–	0.39	0.47	**0.51**	–	0.55	0.50	**0.62**

as features. We use the executable of [9] provided by the authors and reimplemented the method in [2]. Training of the deep neural network was performed in a leave-one-out setup (ten videos for training and one for testing), and parameters of all methods were selected to maximize the performance on the training set. Since the performance of shot detection can condition the performance of scene detection, all experiments were carried out using the shot detector in [1], which is the same exploited by the executable of [9].

Table 1 shows experimental results on the *BBC Planet Earth* series, using both measures. Bottom line reports scene detection results when using ground truth shot boundaries instead of those obtained with [1]. Reported performances clearly show that color features, when used in combination with spectral clustering, can achieve good results according to both measures. The color histograms baseline, indeed, is superior or equivalent to the STG approach in [9] and to that of [2]. Our full model, which exploits both visual and textual learned features, shows consistent improvement over the baseline and over both the approaches it has been compared to.

4. CONCLUSIONS

We introduced a deep learning architecture that merges visual and textual data to partition broadcast videos into coherent parts. We showed that this model provides state of the art performance when compared to recent proposals for scene detection, both with classical performance measures, and with an improved proposal.

Acknowledgments

This work was carried out within the project "Città educante" (CTN01_00034_393801) of the National Technological Cluster on Smart Communities cofunded by the Italian Ministry of Education, University and Research - MIUR.

5. REFERENCES

[1] E. Apostolidis and V. Mezaris. Fast Shot Segmentation Combining Global and Local Visual Descriptors. In *IEEE Int. Conf. Acoustics, Speech and Signal Process.*, pages 6583–6587, 2014.

[2] V. T. Chasanis, C. Likas, and N. P. Galatsanos. Scene detection in videos using shot clustering and sequence alignment. *IEEE Trans. Multimedia*, 11(1):89–100, 2009.

[3] R. Hadsell, S. Chopra, and Y. LeCun. Dimensionality reduction by learning an invariant mapping. In *IEEE Int. Conf. Comput. Vis. Pattern Recognit.*, volume 2, pages 1735–1742. IEEE, 2006.

[4] Y. Jia, E. Shelhamer, J. Donahue, S. Karayev, J. Long, R. Girshick, S. Guadarrama, and T. Darrell. Caffe: Convolutional architecture for fast feature embedding. In *ACM Int. Conf. Multimedia*, pages 675–678. ACM, 2014.

[5] A. Krizhevsky, I. Sutskever, and G. E. Hinton. Imagenet classification with deep convolutional neural networks. In *Adv. Neural Inf. Process. Syst.*, pages 1097–1105, 2012.

[6] C. Liu, D. Wang, J. Zhu, and B. Zhang. Learning a Contextual Multi-Thread Model for Movie/TV Scene Segmentation. *IEEE Trans. Multimedia*, 15(4):884–897, 2013.

[7] T. Mikolov, I. Sutskever, K. Chen, G. S. Corrado, and J. Dean. Distributed representations of words and phrases and their compositionality. In *Adv. Neural Inf. Process. Syst.*, pages 3111–3119, 2013.

[8] P. Sidiropoulos, V. Mezaris, I. Kompatsiaris, and J. Kittler. Differential edit distance: A metric for scene segmentation evaluation. *IEEE Trans. Circuits Syst. Video Technol.*, 22(6):904–914, 2012.

[9] P. Sidiropoulos, V. Mezaris, I. Kompatsiaris, H. Meinedo, M. Bugalho, and I. Trancoso. Temporal video segmentation to scenes using high-level audiovisual features. *IEEE Trans. Circuits Syst. Video Technol.*, 21(8):1163–1177, 2011.

[10] J. Vendrig and M. Worring. Systematic evaluation of logical story unit segmentation. *IEEE Trans. Multimedia*, 4(4):492–499, 2002.

[11] B. Zhou, A. Lapedriza, J. Xiao, A. Torralba, and A. Oliva. Learning Deep Features for Scene Recognition using Places Database. *NIPS*, 2014.

Unsupervised Cosegmentation based on Global Graph Matching

Takanori Tamanaha
Grad. School of IST
The University of Tokyo
Tokyo, Japan
tamanaha@nlab.ci.i.u-tokyo.ac.jp

Hideki Nakamayama
Grad. School of IST
The University of Tokyo
Tokyo, Japan
nakayama@ci.i.u-tokyo.ac.jp

ABSTRACT

Cosegmentation is defined as the task of segmenting a common object from multiple images. Hitherto, graph matching has been known as a promising approach because of its flexibility in matching deformable objects and regions, and several methods based on this approach have been proposed. However, candidate foregrounds obtained by a local matching algorithm in previous methods tend to include false-positive areas, particularly when visually similar backgrounds (e.g., sky) commonly appear across images.

We propose an unsupervised cosegmentation method based on a global graph matching algorithm. Rather than using a local matching algorithm that finds a small common subgraph, we employ global matching that can find a one-to-one mapping for every vertex between input graphs such that we can remove negative regions estimated as background. Experimental results obtained using the iCoseg and MSRC datasets demonstrate that the accuracy of the proposed method is higher than that of previous graph-based methods.

Categories and Subject Descriptors

I.4.6 [Image Processing and Computer Vision]: Segmentation - *regiongrowing, partitioning*

General Terms

Algorithms

Keywords

Cosegmentation, Global Graph Matching, GrabCut

1. INTRODUCTION

Constructing a visual knowledge base for image recognition from Web data has been studied actively in the field of computer vision [1, 2]. While images on the Web relevant to a specific visual concept are usually collected via text-based image search engines, they often include miscellaneous backgrounds that hamper the construction of a visual knowledge base. Unsupervised cosegmentation is the technique of segmenting a common foreground (object region) from multiple images and can be used for removing backgrounds irrelevant to each visual concept to construct a high-quality knowledge base.

MM'15, October 26–30, 2015, Brisbane, Australia.

ACM 978-1-4503-3459-4/15/10 ...$15.00.
DOI: http://dx.doi.org/10.1145/2733373.2806317.

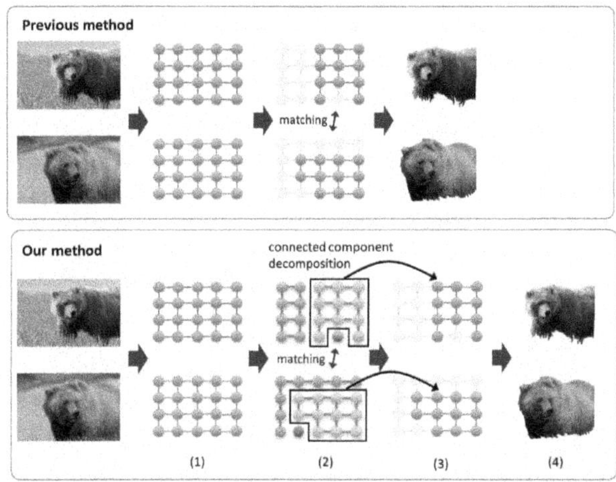

Figure 1: Process flows of previous typical methods (top) and the proposed method (bottom). Given two images, (1) each image is transformed into a graph composed of superpixels. (2) Visually similar regions (subgraphs) are paired by global graph matching and (3) the subgraph representing the foreground is extracted by connected component decomposition. Finally, (4) the foreground is refined by GrabCut using the subgraph as a seed.

Cosegmentation was first introduced by Rother et al. [3], and a number of methods have been proposed since then. Vicente et al. [4] proposed an unsupervised cosegmentation method in which the problem is formulated as an energy maximization problem that maximizes the similarity between candidate regions of the object in input images; they used random forest regression to obtain the similarity score. Meng et al. [5] also proposed an unsupervised cosegmentation method based on the shortest path problem. Hochbaum et al. [16] optimized an energy function in polynomial time using a maximum flow procedure. Rubio et al. [15] proposed a method based on Markov random fields to extract a common object from multiple images by

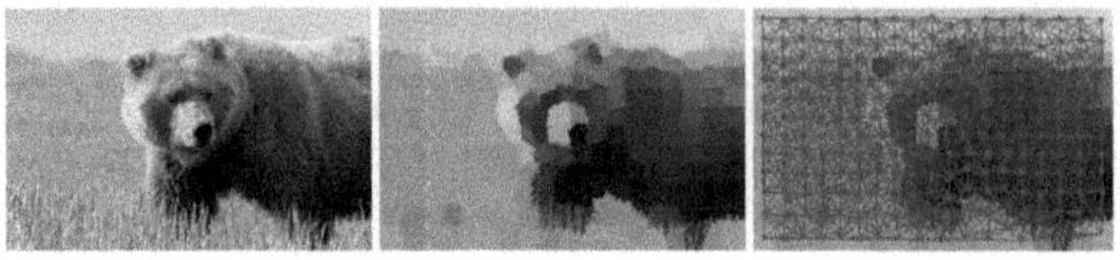

Figure 2: Illustration of the process to transform an image into the graph. First column, second column and third column show original images, superpixels obtained by SLIC and the resultant graph.

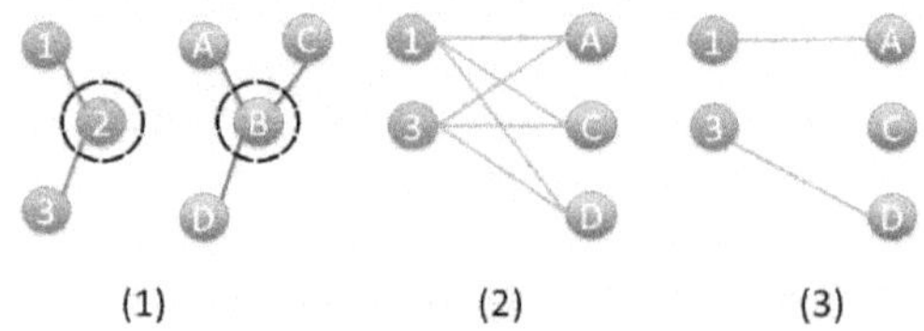

Figure 3: Coarse-grained phase process. (1) A vertex is chosen from each graph, and (2) the complete weighted bipartite graph is constructed from the neighbors of each vertex. (3) The maximum weighted matching score is considered as the similarity of these two vertices.

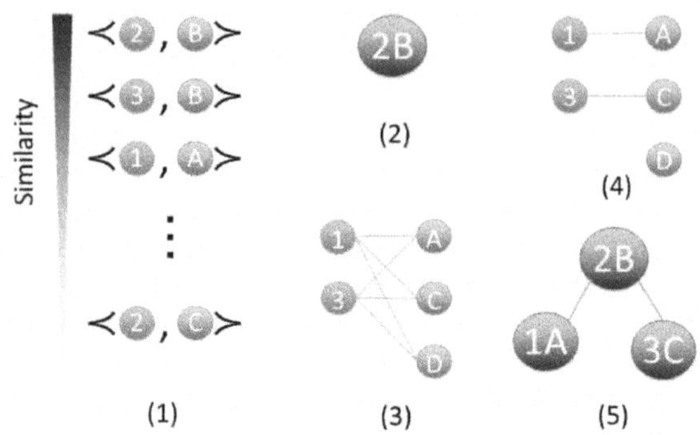

Figure 4: Fine-grained phase process. (1) Pairs of vertices are sorted in descending order of the similarity computed in the coarse-grained phase, and (2) the most similar pair is added to the alignment network. (3) The complete weighted bipartite graph is constructed from the neighbors of the vertices, and (4) the maximum weighted matching is computed. (5) The pairs of endpoints of the maximum weighted matching are added to the alignment network to increase the number of edges in E_{12}.

minimizing an energy function that includes an inter-image region matching term.

Among the many strategies for the cosegmentation problem, graph matching has been known as one of the best performing approaches because of its high flexibility in matching deformable objects and regions. Yu et al. [14] proposed a graph-matching-based approach that transforms each input image into a graph and obtains foreground regions by a local graph matching algorithm that computes matches with regard to only one common region from the input graphs. This appears conceptually reasonable for the cosegmentation problem; however, a candidate foreground region obtained by local matching tends to include background slightly. Specifically, when visually similar backgrounds (e.g., sky, sea and grass) commonly appear across images, they are also matched and may be included in the estimated foreground.

In this paper, we propose an unsupervised cosegmentation algorithm based on global graph matching. Using a global graph matching algorithm that can compute both a small common subgraph and one-to-one mapping for every vertex between input graphs, we can find all paired regions and remove ones those that seem to be background to obtain a more accurate foreground region. Specifically, the subgraph of a foreground region is selected from candidate subgraphs using an algorithm based on connected component decomposition.

2. PROPOSED METHOD

The proposed method consists of the following four steps illustrated in Figure 1 (bottom):

(1) Transform each image into a graph.

(2) Find matches between graphs.

(3) Extract the subgraph representing the foreground.

(4) Refine the foreground region.

We describe the detail of each step in the following.

2.1 Transform each image into a graph

To suppress the number of vertices in a graph, we employ superpixel representations. For this purpose, we use the SLIC [6] algorithm introduced by Achanta et al. SLIC is based on K-means; however, it differs from typical K-means-based clustering in some aspects. For example, it moves centroids to the lowest gradient position in the initialization step and reduces the search region for clustering each superpixel.

Thus, all input images are transformed into superpixels, each of which is considered as a vertex of the graph. Each vertex is connected to its neighbors within two steps. The dot product between the mean vectors of SIFT features extracted from each superpixel is employed as the similarity between a pair of vertices.

Figure 2 shows superpixels obtained by SLIC (middle) and the resultant graph (right) of an image in the iCoseg [10] dataset.

2.2 Find matches between graphs

We use the SPINAL algorithm [7] to find all matches from the graphs of a pair of images. SPINAL was originally proposed by Aladağ et al. to find matches between protein-protein interaction networks. In the field of bioinformatics, it has been suggested that SPINAL is more scalable than other algorithms such as IsoRank [8], MI-GRAAL [9], and NATALIE [17]. SPINAL is a global graph matching algorithm that computes one-to-one mapping for every vertex between two graphs.

Let $G_1 = (V_1, E_2)$ and $G_2 = (V_2, E_2)$ be two input graphs, where V and E represent their vertices and edges, respectively. To represent matches between graphs, alignment network $A_{12} = (V_{12}, E_{12})$ is defined. Each node of V_{12} represents a pair $\prec u_i, v_j \succ$, where $u_i \in V_1$ and $v_j \in V_2$. For any pair of vertices $\prec u_i, v_j \succ \in V_{12}$ and $\prec u'_i, v'_j \succ \in V_{12}$ it should be the case that $u_i \neq u'_i$ and $v_j \neq v'_j$. The edge set of the alignment network is defined as $(\prec u_i, v_j \succ, \prec u'_i, v'_j \succ) \in E_{12}$ if $(u_i, u'_i) \in E_1$ and $(v_j, v'_j) \in E_2$. The goal of SPINAL is to find the alignment network A_{12} that maximize the global network alignment score (GNAS), which is defined as follows;

$$GNAS(A_{12}) = \alpha|E_{12}| + (1-\alpha) \sum_{\forall \prec u_i, v_j \succ} seq(u_i, v_j), \quad (1)$$

where $|E_{12}|$ denotes the number of edges in E_{12}, and $seq(u_i, v_j)$ denotes the similarity between two vertices, where $u_i \in V_1$ and $v_j \in V_2$. Here $\alpha \in [0, 1]$ is a parameter to balance the network-topological similarity and the sequence similarities. We set $\alpha = 0.5$ for all experiments in this study.

Generally, finding the optimal solution for the above problem is NP-hard [7]. To relax the problem efficiently, SPINAL consists of two main phases: a coarse-grained phase that computes rough similarities of all pairs of vertices $u_i \in V_1$ and $v_j \in V_2$, and a fine-grained phase that constructs the alignment network.

Figure 3 shows the process of the coarse-grained phase. We denote the set of neighbors of u_i in G_1 as $N(u_i)$ and the set of neighbors of v_j in G_2 as $N(v_j)$. In the coarse-grained phase, the neighborhood bipartite graph ($\mathcal{NBG}$), a complete edge-weighted bipartite graph defined on the partitions $N(u_i)$ and $N(v_j)$, is constructed and the similarity between $N(u_i)$ and $N(v_j)$ is computed by the maximum weighted matching of $\mathcal{NBG}$. In this manner, initial matching scores are computed for all pairs $u_i \in V_1$ and $v_j \in V_2$.

Figure 4 shows the process of the fine-grained phase. In this phase, the most similar pair of vertices not contained in V_{12} is first added to V_{12}. Then, its $\mathcal{NBG}$ is constructed, and the maximum weighted matching is added to V_{12}. For the endpoints of an edge not contained in the matching, their $\mathcal{NBG}$s are repeatedly constructed. This process is repeated until there is no pair of vertices not contained in V_{12}.

2.3 Extract the subgraph representing the foreground

In this step, we extract the subgraph that represents the common foreground from the alignment network obtained by SPINAL. A depth-first search is applied to the alignment network to decompose the connected components, and each connected component is evaluated by the objective function (1) of SPINAL. The connected component with the highest score is considered as the subgraph that represents the foreground.

Although it is not guaranteed that a subgraph extracted in this approach always corresponds to the foreground in general cases, our assumption is that the foreground occupies large areas in images, which we consider reasonable for many practical situations.

2.4 Refine the foreground region

To extract the foreground more precisely, we use GrabCut [12] proposed by Rother et al. Given small portions of foreground and background annotations as seeds, GrabCut estimates their entire regions. In our pipeline, we use the region corresponding to the subgraph obtained in the previous step as the foreground seed. In this manner, the coarse foreground obtained by graph matching is refined at the pixel level.

Table 1: Cosegmentation accuracy on iCoseg (%).

iCoseg	GrabCut	Rubio+[15]	Yu+[14]	Ours
Alaskan bear	84.3	86.4	78.0	**86.7**
Red sox players	85.4	90.5	86.4	**95.5**
Stonehenge 1	78.0	87.3	**87.4**	87.2
Stonehenge 2	70.7	**88.4**	74.7	87.7
Liverpool	75.4	82.6	**82.9**	82.4
Ferrari	79.7	84.3	86.1	**91.5**
Taj Mahal	82.5	**88.7**	85.4	79.0
Elephants	84.7	75.0	82.2	**95.5**
Pandas	68.3	60.0	76.8	**85.8**
Kite	86.4	89.8	85.2	**92.6**
Kite Panda	73.0	78.3	80.1	**86.7**
Gymnastics	85.0	87.1	90.7	**96.6**
Skating	65.5	76.8	77.3	**78.4**
Hot Balloons	83.2	89.0	86.3	**91.8**
Liberty Statue	73.1	**91.6**	87.3	88.2
Brown Bear	70.7	80.4	81.5	**95.6**
Average	77.9	83.9	83.0	**88.8**

Table 2: Cosegmentation accuracy on MSRC (%).

MSRC	Images	GrabCut	Rubio+[15]	Ours
Cars (front)	6	75.9	65.9	**84.2**
Cars (back)	6	72.5	52.4	**81.1**
Face	30	67.8	76.3	**79.6**
Cow	30	83.9	80.1	**94.3**
Cat	24	81.3	77.1	**89.7**
Plane	30	81.3	77.0	**87.4**
Bike	30	71.5	62.4	**72.1**
Average	-	76.3	70.2	**84.1**

3. EXPERIMENTAL RESULTS

To evaluate the proposed method, we compared it with two state-of-the-art unsupervised graph-matching-based algorithms [15, 14] [1] on the widely used iCoseg [10] (38 object classes; approximately 17 images per class) and MSRC [11] (14 classes; approximately 30 images per class) datasets, equipped with pixel-level segmentation ground truth. To ensure fair comparison with previous methods, we used a subset that consists of 16 classes from iCoseg and 7 classes from MSRC. Segmentation accuracy was evaluated in terms of the ratio of the number of correctly labeled pixels to the total number of pixels in an image. For each class, we randomly paired all images to use them as testing queries and reported the average accuracy. Tables 1 and 2 show experimental results for iCoseg and MSRC, respectively.

Table 1 shows the experimental results for iCoseg. The second column shows the results obtained using GrabCut only, and the third and fourth columns show the results obtained using previous methods. The last column shows the results obtained using the proposal method. Table 2 shows results for MSRC (the second column shows the number of images).

These results demonstrate that the proposed method outperforms previous methods in nearly all classes. As discussed in the introduction, previous methods find matches for only one visually common region between images that often undesirably include background. On the other hand, the proposed method finds matches for all vertices and removes the connected components that are dissimilar to be

[1]Some recent work has achieved very good performance by simultaneously cosegmenting more than two images [13, 2]. Since this is not included in our current scope, we focus on those using only two images as input.

Figure 5: Cosegmentation results on the iCoseg (top) and MSRC (bottom) datasets. The results of each class consist of four images. The two left images show the original images and the two right images show the common object.

foreground. Therefore, the proposed method achieves much significantly higher accuracy than the previous methods.

Compared with the state-of-the-art method [2] with cosegmentating of more than two images simultaneously, the results show higher accuracy than the proposed method (89.6% iCoseg). However, we expect to improve the accuracy of the proposed method by extending it to enable cosegmentation of multiple images.

Figure 5 shows some examples of images from the iCoseg and MSRC datasets, as well as their foreground regions extracted by the proposed method. These results illustrate that the proposed method can obtain proper foregrounds under difficult conditions such as miscellaneous backgrounds, viewpoint and scale changes, and object deformation.

4. CONCLUSIONS

We have proposed a method of unsupervised object cosegmentation based on a global graph matching algorithm. A local graph matching algorithm has been applied to find a common region in previous methods; however, the proposed method exploits global graph matching that can find a one-to-one mapping for every vertex between input graphs to remove background regions more accurately. Experimental results obtained with the iCoseg and MSRC datasets demonstrate the effectiveness of the proposed metehod. In addition, experimental results indicate that the accuracy of the proposed method is higher than that of previous methods.

In future, we will extend the proposed method to enable cosegmentation of more than two images or image streams.

5. REFERENCES

[1] X. Chen et al. NEIL: Extracting visual knowledge from Web data. In Proc. of IEEE ICCV, 2013.

[2] M. Rubinstein et al. Unsupervised joint object discovery and segmentation in internet images. In Proc. of IEEE CVPR, 2013.

[3] C. Rother et al. Cosegmentation of image pairs by histogram matching - Incorporating a global constraint into MRFs. In Proc. of IEEE CVPR, 2006.

[4] S. Vicente et al. Object cosegmentation. In Proc. of IEEE CVPR, 2011.

[5] F. Meng et al. Object co-segmentation based on shortest path algorithm and saliency model. ACM Trans. Multimedia, vol. 14, no. 5, pp. 1429-1441, 2012.

[6] R. Achanta, A. Shaji, K. Smith, A. Luchi, P. Fua, and S. Susstrunk. SLIC: Superpixels compared to state-of-the-art superpixel methods. IEEE Trans. PAMI, vol. 34, no. 11, pp. 2274-2281, 2012.

[7] A. E. Aladağ et al. SPINAL: scalable protein interaction network alignment. Bioinformatics, vol. 29, no. 7, pp. 917-924, 2013.

[8] R. Singh et al. Global alignment of multiple protein interaction networks with application to functional orthology detection. Proc. Natl. Acad. Sci. USA, vol. 105, no. 35, pp. 12763-12768, 2008.

[9] O. Kuchaiev et al. Integrative network alignment reveals large regions of global network similarity in yeast and human. Bioinformatics, vol. 27, no. 10, pp. 1390-1396, 2011.

[10] D. Batra et al. iCoseg: Interactive co-segmentation with intelligent scribble guidance. In Proc. of IEEE CVPR, 2010.

[11] J. Winn et al. Object Categorization by Learned Universal Visual Dictionary. In Proc. of IEEE ICCV, 2005.

[12] C. Rother et al. "GrabCut" - Interactive foreground extraction using iterated graph cuts. In ACM Trans. Graphics, vol. 23, no. 3, pp. 309-314, 2004.

[13] A. Factor et al. Co-segmentation by composition. In Proc. of IEEE ICCV, 2013.

[14] H. Yu et al. Unsupervised cosegmentation based on superpixel matching and Fastgrabcut. In Proc. of IEEE ICME, 2014.

[15] J. C. Rubio et al. Unsupervised co-segmentation through region matching. In Proc. of IEEE CVPR, 2012.

[16] D. S. Hochbaum et al. An efficient algorithm for Co-segmentation. In Proc. of IEEE ICCV, 2009.

[17] G. W. Klau et al. A new graph-based method for pairwise global network alignment. BMC Bioinformatics, vol. 10, suppl. 1, S59, 2009.

Facial Age Estimation Based on Structured Low-rank Representation

Chenjing Yan
School of Computer and Information Technology
Beijing Jiaotong University,China
13120439@bjtu.edu.cn

Congyan Lang
School of Computer and Information Technology
Beijing Jiaotong University,China
cylang@bjtu.edu.cn

Songhe Feng
School of Computer and Information Technology
Beijing Jiaotong University,China
shfeng@bjtu.edu.cn

ABSTRACT

This paper presents an algorithm based on structured, low-rank representation for facial age estimation. The proposed method learns the discriminative feature representation of images with the constraint of the classwise block-diagonal structure to promote discrimination of representations for robust recognition. A block-sparse regularizer is introduced to exploit the similarity and structure information of class. Based on the new representation, we estimate the accurate age using a regression function. By subtly introducing the structured, low-rank representation, we achieve good age estimation performance. Experimental results on three well-known aging faces datasets have demonstrated that the proposed method is superior to the conventional approaches.

Categories and Subject Descriptors

I.4.5 [**Image Processing and Computer Vision**]: Reconstruction

Keywords

facial age estimation, classification and regression, low-rank representation, block-diagonal

1. INTRODUCTION

Age estimation has emerged as a hot topic in the field of face recognition due to its potential application in human-computer interaction and computer vision [7]. Generally speaking, the objective of age estimation is to estimate a person's accurate age or age group based on facial age images. Existing approaches usually formulate age estimation as a multi-class classification problem [7, 5] or a regression problem [12, 6]. Both of these methods have some problems. The classification approaches merely regard age labels independent to each other, but overlook the inter-relationship among the age values. And in the regression approaches, labels are treated as linearly increased values that cannot reflect the non-stationarity of human aging process. More recently, low-rank matrix recovery, which determines a low-rank matrix from corrupted input data, has been successfully applied to applications including salient object detection, segmentation and grouping, tracking. However, there is limited work using this technique for age estimation.

Figure 1: Facial age images in different age classes.

Motivated by the above observations, we propose a low-rank representation based approach for facial age estimation, by effectively exploiting the available class label information. Since aging is a continuous progress along time axis, instead of simply treating every single age as a class label, we assign facial age images with aging changes no more than 5 years as a class, as shown in Figure 1. Then we utilize the similarity and class structure to learn a low-rank representation of facial age images [15]. Specifically, we design a block-sparse regularizer on data representation to incorporate the class label information, so that the resultant data representation should be more discriminative. Moreover, the semi-supervised learning manner is utilized here to directly represent both training and testing images based on the given dictionary [8]. Finally, we realize accurate age estimation by regression function based on the labels and the low-rank representation. The experimental results show that the proposed method provides better results than traditional methods.

The rest of this paper is organized as follows. Section 2 reviews the related work on facial age estimation. In Section 3, we introduce the formulation details of the proposed framework and describe an efficient algorithm for computing the optimal solution. Experimental results on three different image datasets are reported and analyzed in Section 4. Finally, Section 5 concludes this work with future directions.

MM'15, October 26–30, 2015, Brisbane, Australia.
© 2015 ACM. ISBN 978-1-4503-3459-4/15/10 ...$15.00.
DOI: http://dx.doi.org/10.1145/2733373.2806318.

2. RELATED WORK

In the following, we give a brief review of the previous works in age estimation. Lanitis et al. [7] proposed the Active Appearance Models (AAM) [3], which extracts craniofacial growth and skin aging during childhood and adulthood. Different classifiers are compared when AAM is employed as the feature representation. Geng et al. proposed the aging pattern subspace (AGES) [5], which further considered the identity information and the ordinal relationship of ages during feature extraction. Moreover, Geng et al. [4] proposed a new age estimation approach based on label distribution. They regarded each image as an instance associated with a label distribution instead of considering each face image as an instance with one label (age). Guo et al. [6] used the SVR (Support Vector Regression) method to design a locally adjusted robust regressor for the prediction of human ages. Chang et al. [2] proposed an ordinal hyperplane ranking algorithm, which is based on the relative order information among the age labels. Human ages are inferred by aggregating a set of preferences from the ordinal hyperplanes with their cost sensitivities.

3. AGE ESTIMATION ALGORITHM

3.1 Learning Structured Sparse and Low-rank Representation

To use class label information, we study the discriminative, structured low-rank representation for facial age estimation.

Throughout the paper, symbols of training data and symbols of testing data are represented by notations with a wave and notations with a hat respectively. Given a feature matrix $X = \left[\tilde{X}, \hat{X}\right] \in R^{d \times N_{total}}$, where d is the dimension of facial features and N_{total} is the total number of samples. Training matrix $\tilde{X} = [X_1, X_2 \dots X_n]$ contains n classes where X_i is related to class i. As mentioned earlier, we assign the facial age images with aging changes no more than 5 years as a class. According to low-rank matrix recovery, we can decompose X, i.e. $X = DZ + E$, where $Z = \left[\tilde{Z}, \hat{Z}\right]$, Z is representation matrix of training images and testing images. Here we treat the whole training samples as the dictionary for simplity[8], i.e., $D = \tilde{X}$.

Taking into account the feature similarity in the same age group, we claim that the training images in the same age group should share similar structure. So the optimal representation of $\tilde{Z}$ should be block-diagonal [11] [9].

$$\tilde{Z} = \begin{pmatrix} Z_1^* & 0 & 0 & 0 \\ 0 & Z_2^* & 0 & 0 \\ 0 & 0 & \ddots & 0 \\ 0 & 0 & 0 & Z_n^* \end{pmatrix}$$

To reveal the structure information and class information by low-rankness and sparsity, the objective function can be formulated as:

$$\min_{Z,E} \|Z\|_* + \lambda \|E\|_1 + \beta \|Z\|_1 \ s.t\, X = DZ + E \quad (1)$$

where $\|\cdot\|_*$ reveals low-rankness, and $\|\cdot\|_1$ affects the sparsity, which is controlled by λ, β.

Inspired by [15], we assume Q is an ideal block-diagonal matrix, which is defined as $Q = [q_1, q_2, \dots q_{\tilde{n}}] \in R^{\tilde{N} * \tilde{N}}$. Here q_i is $[0, \dots 1, 1, 1, \dots, 0]^{\tilde{n}} \in R^{\tilde{N}}$ ($\tilde{N}$ is the number of training data and the number of 1 is the sample number of class i), which is corresponding to sample x_i . To guarantee the block-diagonal structure of Z, we add a regularization term $\left\|\tilde{Z} - Q\right\|_F^2$ in the formulation. The final objective formulation is defined as follow:

$$\begin{aligned} &\min_{Z,E} \|Z\|_* + \lambda \|E\|_1 + \beta \|Z\|_1 + \mu \left\|\tilde{Z} - Q\right\|_F^2 \\ &s.t\, X = DZ + E,\, D = \tilde{X} \end{aligned} \quad (2)$$

where μ makes contribution to the regularization term.

3.2 Optimization

We use linearized alternating direction method with adaptive penalty (LADMAP) [16] to solve this problem. By introducing a new auxiliary variable $J = \left[\tilde{J}, \hat{J}\right]$, where J is equal to Z, the problem is converted to the equal problem:

$$\begin{aligned} &\min_{Z,E} \|Z\|_* + \lambda \|E\|_1 + \beta \|J\|_1 + \mu \left\|\tilde{J} - Q\right\|_F^2 \\ &s.t\, X = DZ + E,\, J = Z \end{aligned} \quad (3)$$

We solve the problem by minimizing the following augmented Lagrangian function:

$$\begin{aligned} &L(Z, J, E, D, Y_1, Y_2, \alpha) \\ &= \|J\|_* + \lambda \|E\|_1 + \beta \|J\|_1 + \mu \left\|\tilde{J} - Q\right\|_F^2 \\ &+ tr\left(Y_1^T (X - DZ - E)\right) + tr\left(Y_2^T (Z - J)\right) \\ &+ \frac{\alpha}{2} \left(\|X - DZ - E\|_F^2 + \|Z - J\|_F^2\right) \\ &= \|J\|_* + \lambda \|E\|_1 + \beta \|J\|_1 + \mu \left\|\tilde{J} - Q\right\|_F^2 \\ &+ f(Z, J, E, D, Y_1, Y_2, \alpha) - \frac{1}{2\alpha} \left(\|Y_1\|_F^2 + \|Y_2\|_F^2\right) \end{aligned} \quad (4)$$

where $f(Z, J, E, D, Y_1, Y_2, \alpha)$

$$= \frac{\alpha}{2} \left(\left\|X - DZ - E + \frac{Y_1}{\alpha}\right\|_F^2 + \left\|Z - J + \frac{Y_2}{\alpha}\right\|_F^2 \right)$$

We minimized the function by updating J, Z, E respectively. Quadratic term f is replaced by its first order approximation at the previous iteration and then adding a proximal term [10]. So we get the updating scheme as follow:

$$\begin{aligned} Z_{i+1} = &\underset{Z}{argmin} \|Z\|_* \\ &+ tr\left(\left(\nabla_Z f(Z_i, J_i, E_i, Y_{1,i}, Y_{2,i}, \alpha_i)\right)^T (Z - Z_i)\right) \\ &+ \frac{\eta\alpha}{2} \|Z - Z_i\|_F^2 \end{aligned} \quad (5)$$

$$\begin{aligned} J_{i+1} = &\underset{J}{argmin} \beta \|J\|_1 + \mu \left\|\tilde{J} - Q\right\|_F^2 \\ &tr(Y_{2,i}^T (Z - J)) + \frac{\alpha}{2} \|Z_{i+1} - J\|_F^2 \end{aligned} \quad (6)$$

$$E_{i+1} = \underset{E}{argmin} \lambda \|E\|_1 + \frac{\alpha}{2} \|X - DZ_{i+1} - E + Y_{1,i}/\alpha_i\|_F^2 \quad (7)$$

where $\nabla_Z f$ is the partial differential of f with respect to Z, $\eta = \|D\|_2^2$. And the multipliers are updated, where $Y_{1,i+1} =$

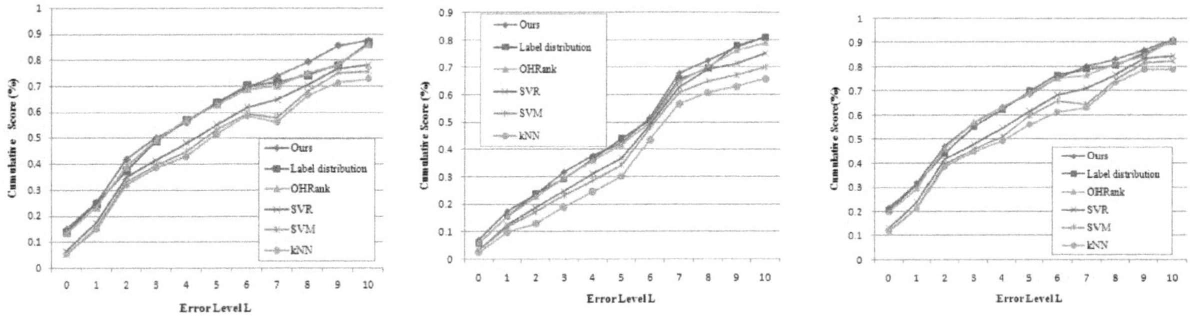

Figure 2: CS curves for different error levels on three different datasets.

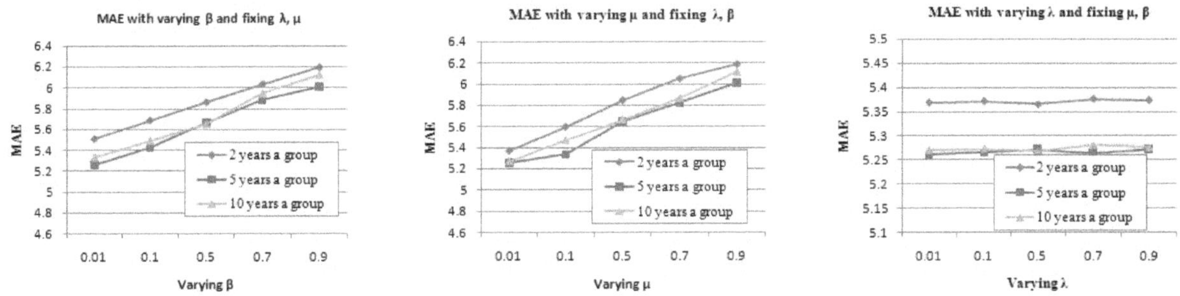

Figure 3: MAE of the proposed method for FG-NET dataset with varying age ranges and parameters.

Table 1: MAEs of the compared age estimation algorithms on three datasets.

Methods	FG-NET	MORPH-2	WebFace
SVM	8.53	8.78	8.35
SVR	6.74	6.93	6.50
kNN	8.96	10.26	8.77
OHRank	**5.05**	5.27	5.11
Label distribution	5.58	5.63	5.39
Proposed Method	5.25	**5.24**	**5.04**

$Y_{1,i} + \alpha(X - DZ_i - E_i)$, $Y_{2,i+1} = Y_{2,i} + \alpha(Z_i - J_i)$. By calculating this, we can get the optimal Z for regression.

3.3 Age estimation by regression function

After learning the new representation $Z = \left[\tilde{Z}, \hat{Z}\right]$, with each column is a sample, we design a regression function to estimate actual age. Specifically, we introduce label information to our algorithm. We say that $Y \in R^{L \times \tilde{N}}$ is a label information matrix of training data $\tilde{X}$, where $\tilde{N}$ is the number of training data and L is the number of labels. Accordingly, we formulate a regression function $\hat{W}$:

$$\hat{W} = \underset{W}{argmin} \left\|Y - W\tilde{Z}\right\|_F^2 + \|W\|_F^2 \quad (8)$$

Then we can get the label for a testing sample by:

$$k = \underset{k}{argmax}\,(l = \hat{W}\hat{z}_i) \quad (9)$$

where $\hat{z}_i$ is a column of testing data $\hat{Z}$, l is class label vector and k is related to the classifier with the largest output.

4. EXPERIMENT

4.1 Experiment setting

To evaluate the proposed algorithm for facial age estimation, we conduct extensive experiments on three benchmark datasets, including FG-NET [1], MORPH album 2 [14] and WebFace [12]. In FG-NET dataset, there are 1002 images from 82 person, ranging from 0 to 69 and each person has 6 to 18 images at different ages. Some facial age images of FG-NET are shown in Figure 1. The second dataset is MORPH album 2. It contains 55,608 facial images with about three images per person, ranging from 16 to 77. Among all the images, we select 5,492 Caucasian descent images to avoid the cross-race influence. The third dataset is WebFace dataset, which is obtained from web source. They crawlled images from Flickr and Google Image based on many age related queries for each year from 1 to 80, and 77021 images are selected, which is much larger than the other datasets.

The following approaches for age estimation are used as the baseline approaches in our evaluation: SVM [13], SVR, OHRank [2], kNN and label distribution [4]. We conduct experiments on FG-NET dataset by using the leave-one-person-out (LOPO) method. For the other two datasets, we randomly split the selected images into 4/5 for training and 1/5 for testing over 30 trails. We divide the training data of each dataset into different classes with 5 years age range in each class. Active Appearance Models (AAM)[3] is used to represent the facial features. LIBSVM is utilized to run the SVR and SVM algorithms. The k in kNN is empirically set 30.

We use two evaluation criteria to measure the performance of different methods. The first one is the mean absolute error (MAE): $MAE = \frac{1}{\hat{N}}\sum_{i=1}^{\hat{N}}|a_i - \hat{a_i}|$ where $\hat{N}$ is the total number of testing data, a_i is actual age and $\hat{a_i}$ is estimating age. Another is cumulative score (CS): $CS(e) = \frac{1}{\hat{N}}\sum_{i=1}^{\hat{N}} g(|a_i - \hat{a_i}| - e)$ where $g(\cdot)$ is a Boolean function $g(x) = 1$ if $x \leq 0$ and $g(x) = 0$ otherwise, and e donates the tolerant error level. In our experiments, we consider the error level from 0 to 10, because the estimation error larger than ten is usually unacceptable in real cases.

4.2 Experiment results

Table 1 shows the MAE results derived from the FG-NET, MORPH and WebFace datasets, respectively. We can see that the proposed method achieves good performance. In addition, Figure 2 shows the CS curves for different error levels on all three datasets. These figures demonstrate that our proposed method obtains the steepest curve and the highest accuracy at almost every error level.

We attribute the success of the proposed method to the special design of the discriminative feature representation with structured low-rank regularization. Specifically, we use the classwise structured information in our algorithm. Facial age images in any given classes are linearly represented by the facial age images from the same class, because we encourage the sparsity of blocks in the data representation. This makes the representation more discriminative. Secondly, representation of training and testing images are learned simultaneously, leveraging the global structure over the whole dataset. Finally, we utilize both the label information and structured low-rank representation to estimate one's actual age via a regression function. Thus, the proposed algorithm outperforms the other methods.

In addition, we examine the sensitivity of the proposed method to the age ranges and the critical parameters λ, β, μ. We conduct comparative trails with different age range and parameters on the FG-NET dataset. The influence of these factors can be revealed in Figure 3. The results indicate that by defining the age class with too large (10 years) or too small (2 years) age range achieves bad performances, because they cannot make use of the structure information properly. In addition, parameters β and μ are more sensitive than λ, which indicate that the structure information and low-rank representation are the key factors in our algorithm. We observe that the proposed method yields the best performance when the age range is defined as 5 years, while β and μ are setting around 0.01.

5. CONCLUSION

In this paper, a new facial age estimation approach based on structured low-rank representation is proposed. In contrast to the traditional methods which use the appearance-based feature representation (AAM or BIF), we try to incorporate the class label information and learn a more discriminative low-rank representation for images by designing a block-sparse regularizer. Then we estimate the actual age using this new representation by a regression function. Experiments show that our proposed algorithm achieves better performance than other age estimation algorithms. In future, we intend to make further researches on age estimation and try to improve the accuracy by considering the ranking information. We also hope to put our algorithm into some practical applications.

6. ACKNOWLEDGMENT

This work is supported by the Fundamental Research Funds for the Central Universities (No.2014JBM025), National Nature Science Foundation of China (No.61272352, No.61300071, No.61472028,No.61372148), Beijing Natural Science Foundation (No.4142045),Higher Education Young Elite Teacher Project (No.YETP0547), China Mobile research fund of Ministry of Education (No. MCM20130421).

7. REFERENCES

[1] Fg-net aging dataset. *http://sting.cycollege.ac.cy/alnantis/fgnetaging.html*, 2002.

[2] K. Chang, C. Chen, and Y. Hung. Ordinal hyperplanes ranker with cost sensitivities for age estimation. In *IEEE Conf. CVPR*, volume 42, pages 585–592, 2011.

[3] T. F. Edwards GJ and C. J. Taylor. Active appearance models. *IEEE Trans. on PAMI*, 23(6):681–685, 2001.

[4] X. Geng, C.Yin, and Z. Zhou. Facial age estimation by learning from label distributions. *IEEE Trans. on PAMI*, 35(10):1–12, 2014.

[5] X. Geng, Z. Zhou, and K. Smith-Miles. Automatic age estimation based on facial aging patterns. *IEEE Trans. on PAMI*, 29(12):2234–2240, 2007.

[6] G. Guo, Y. Fu, C. Dyer, and T. Huang. Image-based human age estimation by manifold learning and locally adjusted robust regression. *IEEE Trans. Image Processing*, 17(7):1178–1188, 2008.

[7] A. Lanitis, C. Draganova, and C. Christodoulou. Comparing different classifiers for automatic age estimation. *IEEE Trans. on SMC*, 34:621–628, 2004.

[8] Y. Li, J. Liu, Z. Li, Y. Zhang, H. Lu, and S. Ma. Learning low-rank representations with classwise block-diagonal structure for robust face recognition. In *AAAI 2014*, volume 9, pages 2810–2816, 2014.

[9] Y. Li, J. Liu, H. Lu, and S. Ma. Learning robust face representation with classwise block-diagonal structure. *IEEE Trans. on IFS*, 9(12):2051 – 2062, 2014.

[10] Z. Lin, R. Liu, and Z. Su. Linearized alternating direction method with adaptive penality for low rank representation. In *NIPS*, pages 612–620, 2011.

[11] G. Liu, Z. Liu, S. Yan, and J. Sun. Robust recovery of subspace structures by low-rank representation. *IEEE Trans. on PAMI*, 35(1):171–184, 2013.

[12] B. Ni, Z. Song, and S. Yan. Web image mining towards universal age estimator. In *ACM MM*, pages 85–94, 2009.

[13] Y. Pang, K. Zhang, Y. Yuan, and K. Wang. Distributed object detection with linear svms. *IEEE Trans. on Cybernetics*, 44(11):2122–2133, 2014.

[14] K. Ricanek and T. Tesafaye. Morph: A longitudinal image dataset of normal adult age-progression. In *IEEE CS*, pages 341–345, 2006.

[15] Y. Zhang, Z. Jiang, and D. L.S. Learning structured low-rank representations for image classification. In *IEEE Conf. CVPR*, volume 74, pages 1–21, 2013.

[16] L. Zhuang, H. Gao, Z. Lin, Y. Ma, X. Zhang, and N. Yu. Non-negative low rank and sparse graph for semi-supervised learning. *IEEE Conf. CVPR*, 157(10):2328–2335, 2012.

Semantic Segmentation based on Stacked Discriminative Autoencoders and Context-Constrained Weakly Supervised Learning

Xiwen Yao, Junwei Han*, Gong Cheng, Lei Guo
School of Automation
Northwestern Polytechnical University
127 West Youyi Road, Xi'an Shaanxi, 710072, P. R. China
{yaoxiwen517, junweihan2010, chenggong1119}@gmail.com, lguo@nwpu.edu.cn
* Corresponding author

ABSTRACT

In this paper, we focus on tacking the problem of weakly supervised semantic segmentation. The aim is to predict the class label of image regions under weakly supervised settings, where training images are only provided with image-level labels indicating the classes they contain. The main difficulty of weakly supervised semantic segmentation arises from the complex diversity of visual classes and the lack of supervision information for learning a multi-classes classifier. To conquer the challenge, we propose a novel discriminative deep feature learning framework based on stacked autoencoders (SAE) by integrating pairwise constraints to serve as a discriminative term. Furthermore, to mine effective supervision information, global context about co-occurrence of visual classes as well as local context around each image region is exploited as constraints for training a multi-class classifier. Finally, the classifier training is formulated as an ultimate optimization problem, which can be solved efficiently by an alternate iterative optimization method. Comprehensive experiments on the MSRC 21 dataset demonstrate the superior performance compared with several state-of-the-art weakly supervised image segmentation methods.

Categories and Subject Descriptors

I.4.6 [**Image Processing and Computer Vision**]: Segmentation *–pixel classification;* I.4.6 [**Image Processing and Computer Vision**]: Feature Measurement–*feature representation;*

General Terms

Algorithms, Experimentation, Performance.

Keywords

Semantic segmentation; Stacked autoencoders; Discriminative feature learning; Weakly supervised learning.

MM'15, October 26-30, 2015, Brisbane, Australia
© 2015 ACM. ISBN 978-1-4503-3459-4/15/10…$15.00
DOI: http://dx.doi.org/10.1145/2733373.2806319

1. INTRODUCTION

Weakly supervised semantic segmentation is a fundamental yet challenging task to segment an image into several regions of homogeneous texture or color and simultaneously recognize their associated semantic categories under weakly supervised settings, in which only image-level labels are provided for each training image, specifying the classes present in the image. Recently, many efforts have been contributed to this study [1-6].

How to describe the intrinsic representation of regions is the key to the success of semantic segmentation. HoG and SIFT features are exploited in [4, 6, 7]. However, such low-level features often fail to offer sufficient discriminative power. We argue that the usage of more semantically abstract features, such as high-level features learned by recent developed deep learning methods, may offer a promising venue to empower the model to handle intrinsically diverse and complex visual classes in natural images [8] and also remote sensing images [9], and hence to improve segmentation performance. In this paper, we propose a novel discriminative deep feature learning framework based on stacked autoencoders by integrating pairwise constraints to serve as a discriminative term. The pairwise constraints, including must-link constraints (indicating the semantic similarity between superpixels) and cannot-link constraints (indicating the semantic dissimilarity between superpixels), guarantee the ability of discriminative representation by keeping the superpixels connected by the must-link be close to each other in the learned feature space while ensuring the superpixels of cannot-link to be kept far away.

In contrast to full-supervised methods [10, 11], it is more challenging for weakly supervised segmentation methods to train region-level classifier with only image-level labels in the training set. Since there are no ground truth labels of superpixels in the training set, it is necessary to mine effective constraint information to supervise the classifier training. In [4, 12, 13], image-superpixel label inclusion information is exploited to directly infer the superpixel labels. However, only the label inclusion information does not effectively deal with regions that of similar appearances corresponding to distinct semantic concepts. For example, a smooth region in blue may be a part of sky or a part of water. It is even difficult for human observers to individually classify such regions without context. Contextual information plays a very important role to reduce semantic ambiguity. In this paper, we propose to incorporate both global and local semantic contextual constraint information, together with label inclusion information in a unified framework to provide supervision for training the multi-class classifier. The global semantic context describes the co-occurrence relationships of different concepts while the local context encourages neighboring superpixels with similar appearances within the same image to share the same concept label.

We evaluate the proposed approach on MSRC-21 dataset [14]. Experimental results show that the proposed algorithm outperforms state-of-the-art weakly supervised image segmentation methods, and its performance is even comparable to those of the fully supervised segmentation models.

2. THE PROPOSED METHOD

We start by setting up the problem and notations. Let $\mathrm{X} = \{X_1, \ldots X_m, \ldots X_M\}$ be the training set with corresponding image-level labels $G = [G_1, \ldots G_m, \ldots G_M]$, where $G_m = [g_m^1, \ldots g_m^c, \ldots g_m^C]^{\mathrm{T}}$ is the label indicator vector with $g_m^c = 1$ if the image containing class c and $g_m^c = 0$ otherwise. We oversegment an image X_m into n_m superpixels by an over-segmentation algorithm [15] and obtain the low-level feature data matrix $X_m = [x_{m,1}, \ldots x_{m,i}, \ldots x_{m,n_m}]$, where $x_{m,i}$ is the feature of ith superpixel and the associated label is denoted as $y_{m,i} = [y_{m,i}^1, \ldots y_{m,i}^c, \ldots y_{m,i}^C]$ with $y_{m,i}^c = 1$ if $x_{m,i}$ is assigned label c and $y_{m,i}^c = 0$ otherwise. For brevity, we denote $X = [x_1, \ldots x_n, \ldots x_N]$ as the training set and $Y = [y_1, \ldots y_n, \ldots y_N]$ as the corresponding label matrix, where $N = \sum_{m=1}^{M} n_m$ is the total number of superpixels in the training set. The task of weakly supervised semantic segmentation is to recover the latent label Y and simultaneously learn a classifier, which later help to predict superpixel labels in the new test images.

2.1 Stacked Discriminative Autoencoders

At the encoding part of autoencoder [16], an input vector x is mapped to the hidden representation h by a linear deterministic mapping and a nonlinear activation function $h = f(W_1 x + b_1)$, where W_1 is an encoding weight matrix, b_1 is encoding bias vector and $f(z)$ is the logistic sigmoid function. At the decoding part, hidden feature representation h is mapped back to a reconstruction $\hat{x}$ through $\hat{x} = f(W_2 h + b_2)$, where W_2 is an decoding weight matrix, b_2 is decoding bias vector. Weight matrices W_1 and W_2 and bias vectors b_1 and b_2 are learned by minimizing the cost function:

$$J = \frac{1}{2}\sum_{i=1}^{N} \| x_i - \hat{x}_i \|_2^2 + \frac{\lambda}{2}(\| W_1 \|_2^2 + \| W_2 \|_2^2) \tag{1}$$

We constructed must-link constraints P by selecting two superpixels with similarity larger than ξ from different images sharing common labels in condition that they are the most similar to each other in their respective images. We constructed cannot-link constraints D by simply selecting two superpixels with similarity larger than ξ from different images sharing no common labels.

To introduce pairwise constraints into autoencoders as a discriminative term, the learned latent features (h_i, h_j) of P are encouraged to be close in the learned latent feature space and of D are ensured to be kept far away, which can be formulated as minimizing the cost function:

$$J_{DAE} = J + \frac{\beta}{2}\sum_{i,j=1}^{N} (\| h_i - h_j \|_2^2 F_{ij}) \tag{2}$$

Parameter β controls the contribution of pairwise constraints, which are encoded in matrix F defined as:

$$F_{ij} = \begin{cases} +1, & \text{if}(x_i, x_j) \in \mathrm{P} \\ -1, & \text{if}(x_i, x_j) \in \mathrm{D} \\ 0, & \text{otherwise} \end{cases} \tag{3}$$

The gradient of the objective function J_{DAE} with respect to $\{W_1, W_2, b_1, b_2\}$ can be computed as follows:

$$\begin{aligned} \frac{\partial J_{DAE}}{\partial W_1} = & \frac{1}{N}\sum_{i=1}^{N} \Delta_i^{(1)} x_i^{\mathrm{T}} + \lambda W_1 \\ & + \beta \sum_{i,j=1}^{N} (((h_i - h_j) \odot f'(z_i^{(1)})) x_i^{\mathrm{T}} - ((h_i - h_j) \odot f'(z_j^{(1)})) x_j^{\mathrm{T}}) F_{ij} \end{aligned} \tag{4}$$

$$\frac{\partial J_{DAE}}{\partial W_2} = \frac{1}{N}\sum_{i=1}^{N} \Delta_i^{(2)} h_i^{\mathrm{T}} + \lambda W_2 \tag{5}$$

$$\frac{\partial J_{DAE}}{\partial b_1} = \frac{1}{N}\sum_{i=1}^{N} \Delta_i^{(1)} + \beta \sum_{i,j=1}^{N} ((h_i - h_j) \odot (f'(z_i^{(1)}) - f'(z_j^{(1)}))) F_{ij} \tag{6}$$

$$\frac{\partial J_{DAE}}{\partial b_2} = \frac{1}{N}\sum_{i=1}^{N} \Delta_i^{(2)} \tag{7}$$

where the operation $\odot$ denotes the element-wise multiplication, and $\Delta_i^{(1)}$ and $\Delta_i^{(2)}$ are defined as:

$$\Delta_i^{(1)} = W_2^{\mathrm{T}} \Delta_i^{(2)} \odot f'(z_i^{(1)}), \quad \Delta_i^{(2)} = -(x_i - \hat{x}_i) \odot f'(z_i^{(2)}) \tag{8}$$

Then the parameters $\{W_1, W_2, b_1, b_2\}$ can be learned by using the gradient descent method with learning rate μ .

However, due to the simple shallow structural characteristic, the representational power of a single layer discriminative autoencoder is limited. In this paper, we propose a stacked discriminative autoencoders (SDAE), in which DAE is used as a building block to learn discriminative high-level features from low-level ones as described in Section 3.1. The training of SDAE is performed in a greedy layer-wise learning manner introduced by Hinton *et al.*[17].

2.2 Context-constrained Weakly Supervised Learning

2.2.1 Constraint information

To perform segmentation, a neural network classifier is constructed by adding an additional classification layer on the top layer of SDAE described in the above subsection. Since there are not pixel-level labels, the following constraints information is taken into consideration to train the classifier.

2.2.1.1 Label inclusion constraint

The label inclusion constraint guarantees that there are no superpixels supporting an invalid label. That is, given an image X_m with image-level label $G_m = [g_m^1, \ldots g_m^c, \ldots g_m^C]^{\mathrm{T}}$ and its ith superpixel label $y_{m,i} = [y_{m,i}^1, \ldots y_{m,i}^c, \ldots y_{m,i}^C]$, $\max y_{m,i}^c$ should be close to zero, which is equal to minimize the objective function: $C_1 = \sum_m \sum_c (1 - g_m^c) \max_{x_{m,i} \in X_m} y_{m,i}^c$. We further give its matrix form $C_1 = \sum_m \sum_c (1 - g_m^c) h_c^T Y^T q_m$, where $h_c \in \mathrm{R}^C$ is an indicator vector with its all elements expect for the cth element are zeros. $q_m \in \mathrm{R}^N$ is a vector with its all elements except for those elements corresponding to the mth image are zeros.

2.2.1.2 Context constraints

We use the pairwise co-occurrence of concepts to capture the global context constraint. The element of reference co-occurrence matrix $A = \{a_{c_1 c_2}\} \in \mathrm{R}^{C \times C}$ is defined as the conditional probability of coincidence of concepts. To integrate the global contextual information into formulation, we introduce the following objective function:

$$C_{gc} = \frac{1}{2} \sum_{c_1, c_2}^{C} (A_{c_1 c_2} \| y_{c_1}^T - y_{c_2}^T \|_2^2) = Tr(Y L_{gc} Y^T) \tag{9}$$

where Laplacian matrix $L_{gc} = D_{gc} - A$ and D_{gc} is a diagonal matrix whose diagonal elements are the sums of the row elements of co-occurrence matrix A.

The local context can yield more semantically consistent segmentation results by imposing neighboring superpixels with similar appearances within the same image to share the same concept label. To model the local semantic context, we have the following equation to be minimized:

$$C_{lc} = \sum_{i,j=1}^{N} V_{ij} \| y_i - y_j \|^2 = Tr(Y^T L_{lc} Y) \tag{10}$$

where V encodes the interactions of superpixels in the adjacent set A, which is defined as:

$$V_{ij} = \begin{cases} \exp(-\| h_i - h_j \|^2 / \sigma^2), & \text{if} (h_i, h_j) \in \mathrm{A} \\ 0, & \text{otherwise} \end{cases} \tag{11}$$

Laplacian matrix $L_{lc} = D_{lc} - V$ and D_{lc} is a diagonal matrix whose diagonal elements are the sums of the row elements of matrix V.

2.2.2 Weakly supervised learning

Jointly considering the above constraints, the classifier training is formulated as optimizing the following objective function:

$$\min_{W_{nn}, Y} J_{NN}(Y, W_{nn}) + C(Y) \;\; s.t. Ye_1 = e_2, Y \geq 0 \tag{12}$$

where $J_{NN}(Y, W_{nn}) = \| h_{W_{nn}}(X) - Y \|_F^2 + \frac{\lambda}{2} \| W_{nn} \|_2^2$ is the loss function of neural network classifier with output $h_{W_{nn}}(X)$.

$C(Y) = \gamma_{gc} Tr(Y L_{gc} Y^T) + \gamma_{lc} Tr(Y^T L_{lc} Y) + \alpha \sum_m \sum_c (1 - g_m^c) h_c^T Y^T q$ is the constraint information. Constraint $Ye_1 = e_2$ is introduced to ensure the sum of each row in Y is equal to 1 with $e_1 = \mathbf{1}_{C \times 1}$ and $e_2 = \mathbf{1}_{N \times 1}$.

The minimization problem of (12) can be solved in the following two alternate optimization steps:

$$W_{nn}^* = \underset{W_{nn}}{argmin} J_{NN}(Y, W_{nn}) = \underset{W_{nn}}{argmin} \| h_{W_{nn}}(X) - Y^* \|_F^2 + \frac{\lambda}{2} \| W_{nn} \|_2^2 \tag{13}$$

$$Y^* = \underset{Y \geq 0}{argmin} \| h_{W_{nn}^*}(X) - Y \|_F^2 + C(Y) + \delta \| Ye_1 - e_2 \|_F^2 \; s.t. Y \geq 0 \tag{14}$$

The first subproblem is a standard neural network classifier training problem given Y^*, which can be solved by using back-propagation algorithm [18]. The second subproblem can be effectively solved by a nonnegative multiplicative updating procedure [19].

Therefore, considering the two alternate optimization steps together, after convergence, we can obtain superpixel labels Y and neural network classifier W_{nn}.

3. EXPERIMENT RESULTS

3.1 Experiment Setup

We evaluated our approach on the MSRC-21 dataset. This dataset contains 591 images of 21 visual classes with manually labeled object segmentation ground-truth [14]. Pixels on the boundaries of objects are usually labeled as background and are ignored during training and evaluation. For both datasets, we adopted the over-segmentation algorithm in [15] to obtain superpixels and described superpixel appearances with 980-dimimension low-level features including shape, location, histogram of texture, SIFT, and color. The proposed SDAE consists of 3 layers of discriminative autoencoders, which take the 980-dimimension low-level features as input and set the number of the first and hidden layer as 1960 and 1960, respectively and the number of the output layer is set to be 720. The performance was evaluated by average per-class accuracy, which measures the percentage of correctly classified pixels for an object class.

3.2 Parameters Analysis

In the implementation of SDAE, there are four parameters to be set: threshold ξ for pairwise constraints construction, weight decay cost parameter λ, discriminative parameter β and learning rate μ. For parameters λ and μ, we empirically set $\lambda = 0.001$, $\mu = 0.2$ based on the practical tricks introduced in book [20]. For parameters β and ξ, we varied the value of parameter ξ from 0.71 to 0.80 with a stride of 0.01 and set β with $\{0.001, 0.01, 0.1\}$. As shown in Fig.1 (a), we set $\xi = 0.72$ and $\beta = 0.001$ with the average accuracy reaching the peak point. In the classifier learning, parameters α, δ, γ_{gc} and γ_{lc} need to be set. Parameters α and δ are both set to be 1000 which is large enough to guarantee the label consistent constraint satisfied and to ensure the sum of each row in is equal to 1. Fig.1 (b) presents the accuracy with different values of γ_{gc} and γ_{lc}. Finally, we set $\gamma_{gc} = 10$ and $\gamma_{lc} = 100$.

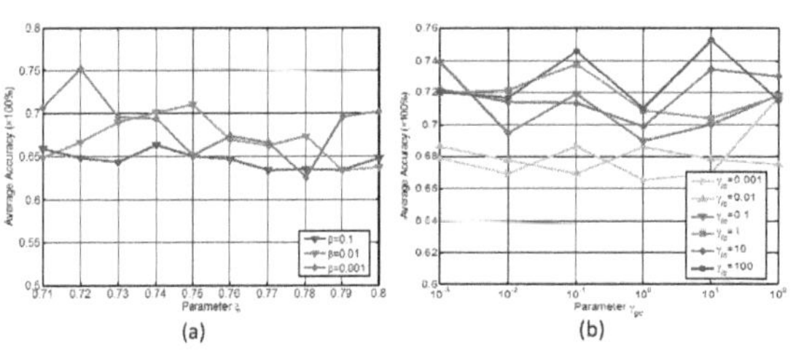

Fig.1 Average accuracy with different parameters.

3.3 Comparison with State-of-the-arts

Fig.2 shows some example results produced by our method in comparison with the ground-truth. Table 1 reports the average accuracy over all 21 object classes in comparison with state-of-the-art semantic segmentation methods, including both fully supervised (FS) [10, 11] and weakly supervised (WS) [4, 5]. As shown in Table 1, our method outperforms all other weakly supervised approaches and meanwhile is comparable to those of the fully supervised segmentation methods. Fig. 3 presents the per-class accuracy results on MSRC dataset. The class labels from 1 to 21 are assigned with building, grass, tree, cow, sheep, sky, aeroplane, water, face, car, bicycle, flower, sign, bird, book, chair, road, cat, dog, body and boat, respectively. Our method gets the best results on 10 out of 21 classes and especially works well on several confusing categories, such as aeroplane and boat, sky and water.

Table 1. Average accuracy (%) of our method and four comparison methods on MSRC-21 dataset.

	FS		WS		
Methods	[10]	[11]	[5]	[4]	Ours
Accuracy	75	76	69	71	**76**

Fig. 2 Some results of our method on MSRC-21 dataset.

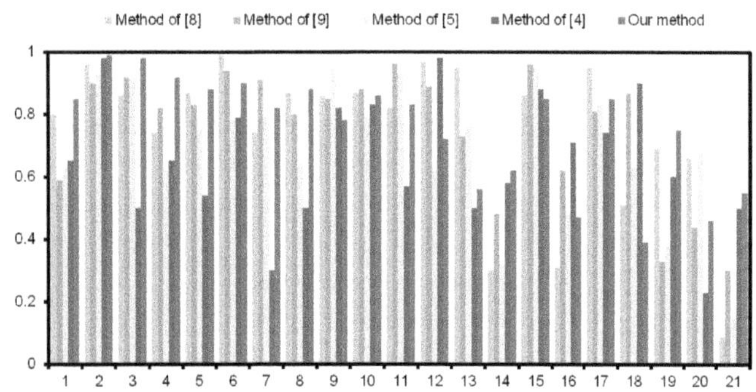

Fig.3 Per-class accuracy of our method and four comparison methods on MSRC-21 dataset.

4. CONCLUSIONS

In this paper, we proposed a coherent framework to perform semantic segmentation under weakly supervised settings. The framework includes two parts: a novel discriminative deep feature learning method based on stacked autoencoders with pairwise constraints and a context-constrained weakly supervised multi-class classifier learning method by employing both global and local semantic contextual information. Experiments on MSRC-21 dataset demonstrated the effectiveness of our proposed method, compared with several state-of-the-art full supervised and weakly supervised methods.

5. ACKNOWLEDGMENTS

This work was supported by the National Science Foundation of China under Grant 91120005 and 61473231, and Doctoral Fund of Ministry of Education of China under grant 20136102110037.

6. REFERENCES

[1] A. Vezhnevets, *et al.*, "Weakly supervised semantic segmentation with a multi-image model," in *ICCV*, 2011, pp. 643-650.

[2] A. Vezhnevets, *et al.*, "Active learning for semantic segmentation with expected change," in *CVPR*, 2012, pp. 3162-3169.

[3] A. Vezhnevets, *et al.*, "Weakly supervised structured output learning for semantic segmentation," in *CVPR*, 2012, pp. 845-852.

[4] Y. Liu, *et al.*, "Weakly-Supervised Dual Clustering for Image Semantic Segmentation," in *CVPR*, 2013, pp. 2075-2082.

[5] K. Zhang, *et al.*, "Sparse reconstruction for weakly supervised semantic segmentation," in *IJCAI*, 2013, pp. 1889-1895.

[6] Y. Liu, *et al.*, "Boosted MIML method for weakly-supervised image semantic segmentation," *Multimedia Tools and Applications*, pp. 1-17, 2014.

[7] L. Zhang, *et al.*, "Probabilistic graphlet cut: Exploiting spatial structure cue for weakly supervised image segmentation," in *CVPR*, 2013, pp. 1908-1915.

[8] R. Girshick, *et al.*, "Rich feature hierarchies for accurate object detection and semantic segmentation," in *CVPR*, 2014.

[9] J. Han, *et al.*, "Object detection in optical remote sensing images based on weakly supervised learning and high-level feature learning," *IEEE Trans. Geosci. Remote Sens.*, vol. 53, pp. 3325-3337, 2015.

[10] L. Ladicky, *et al.*, "Associative hierarchical crfs for object class image segmentation," in *ICCV*, 2009, pp. 739-746.

[11] A. Lucchi, *et al.*, "Structured image segmentation using kernelized features," in *ECCV*, 2012, pp. 400-413.

[12] S. Liu, *et al.*, "Weakly supervised graph propagation towards collective image parsing," *IEEE Trans. Multimedia*, vol. 14, pp. 361-373, 2012.

[13] W. Xie, *et al.*, "Weakly-Supervised Image Parsing via Constructing Semantic Graphs and Hypergraphs," in *ACM MM*, 2014, pp. 277-286.

[14] J. W. Shotton, *et al.*, "Textonboost: Joint appearance, shape and context modeling for multi-class object recognition and segmentation," in *ECCV*, 2006.

[15] G. Mori, "Guiding model search using segmentation," in *ICCV*, 2005, pp. 1417-1423.

[16] H.-C. Shin, *et al.*, "Stacked autoencoders for unsupervised feature learning and multiple organ detection in a pilot study using 4D patient data," *TPAMI*, vol. 35, pp. 1930-1943, 2013.

[17] G. E. Hinton and R. R. Salakhutdinov, "Reducing the dimensionality of data with neural networks," *Science*, vol. 313, pp. 504-507, 2006.

[18] M. T. Hagan and M. B. Menhaj, "Training feedforward networks with the Marquardt algorithm," *IEEE Trans. on Neural Networks*, vol. 5, pp. 989-993, 1994.

[19] X. Liu, *et al.*, "Unified solution to nonnegative data factorization problems," in *ICDM*, 2009, pp. 307-316.

[20] G. B. Orr and K.-R. Müller, *Neural networks: tricks of the trade*: Springer, 2003.

Deep Self-taught Hashing for Image Retrieval

Ke Zhou
Huazhong University of Science and Technology
k.zhou@hust.edu.cn

Yu Liu
Huazhong University of Science and Technology
lightyear416@163.com

Jinkuan Song
University of Trento
jingkuan.song@unitn.it

Linyu Yan
Hubei University of Technology
yanranyaya@hust.edu.cn

Fuhao Zou
Huazhong University of Science and Technology
fuhao_zou@hust.edu.cn

Fumin Shen
University of Electronic Science and Technology of China
fumin.shen@gmail.com

ABSTRACT

Hashing is a promising technique to tackle the problem of scalable retrieval, and it generally consists two major components, namely hash code generation and hash functions learning. The majority of existing hashing fall under the shallow model, which is intrinsically weak on mining robust visual features and learning complicated hash functions. In view of the superiority of deep structure, especially the Convolutional Neural Networks (CNNs), on extracting high level representation, we propose a deep self-taught hashing (DSTH) framework to combine deep structures with hashing to improve the retrieval performance by automatically learning robust visual features and hash functions. By employing CNNs, more robust and discriminative features of the images can be extracted to benefit the hash codes generation. Then, we apply CNNs and Multilayer Perceptron under deep learning scheme to learn hash function in supervised process by using the generated hash codes as labels. The experimental results have shown that the DSTH is superior to several state-of-the-art algorithms.

Categories and Subject Descriptors

H.3.3 [**Information Storage and Retrieval**]: Information Search and Retrieval; I.5.2 [**Pattern Recognition**]: Design Methodology; classifier design and evaluation

Keywords

Data Hashing; Deep Learning; Self-taught; Convolutional Neural Networks

1. INTRODUCTION

Hashing is a promising technique in terms of similarity search over large scale dataset. Actually, it is a special way of dimensionality reduction, mapping high dimensional feature to compact hash code. Since the Hamming distance between two binary hash codes can be computed efficiently by using bit XOR operation and counting the number of non-zero bits, an ordinary PC today would be able to do millions of Hamming distance computation in just a few milliseconds. As a result, hashing shows incomparable superiority in fast similarity search. Currently, the research on hashing confronts two challenge: first, how to precisely extract representative image features; second, how to tackle the problem of semantic gap, leading to accurate transformation from image feature to hash code.

Aiming at ensuring the effectiveness of hashing, hash code should preserve the property of discrimination, i.e., objects with similar semantic should be mapped into similar hash codes and vise versa. Several data-aware hashing methods have been proposed by introducing the machine learning tricks into the field of hashing to enhance the effectiveness of hash codes [2, 5, 10]. Self-taught hashing (STH) [7] is proposed and considered as one of state-of-the-art works. However, it suffers from overfitting problem since the operations of generating hash codes for training data and hash function for testing data are independently handled, which leads to poor generalization ability. Minimal loss hashing (MLH) [8] have shown higher search accuracy than unsupervised hashing approaches, but they all impose difficult optimization and slow training mechanisms. Spectral hashing (SpH) [6] uses a separable Laplacian eigenfunction (LE) formulation that ends up assigning more bits to directions along which the data has a greater variance. However, this approach is somewhat heuristic and relies on an unrealistic assumption that the data is uniformly distributed in a high-dimensional rectangle. To summarize, the majority of existing hashing fall under the shallow model, which perform poor in discovering semantic information. The drawback derives from two aspects: (1) For feature extraction, existing hashing methods are mainly based on hand-crafted feature, such as Color Histogram, GIST, SIFT, BoW, etc. However, those features are limited in aspect of reflecting image semantic information, because they represent the semantical content in just one aspect, either global or local view. (2) For semantic preservation, shallow model intrinsically could not explore the high level semantic information contained in feature data.

To avoid the shortcoming of hashing method of shallow model, a few deep hashing method have been proposed. Comparing to shallow learning based hashing, deep learning

MM'15, October 26-30, 2015, Brisbane, Australia.
© 2015 ACM. ISBN 978-1-4503-3459-4/15/10 ...$15.00.
DOI: http://dx.doi.org/10.1145/2733373.2806320.

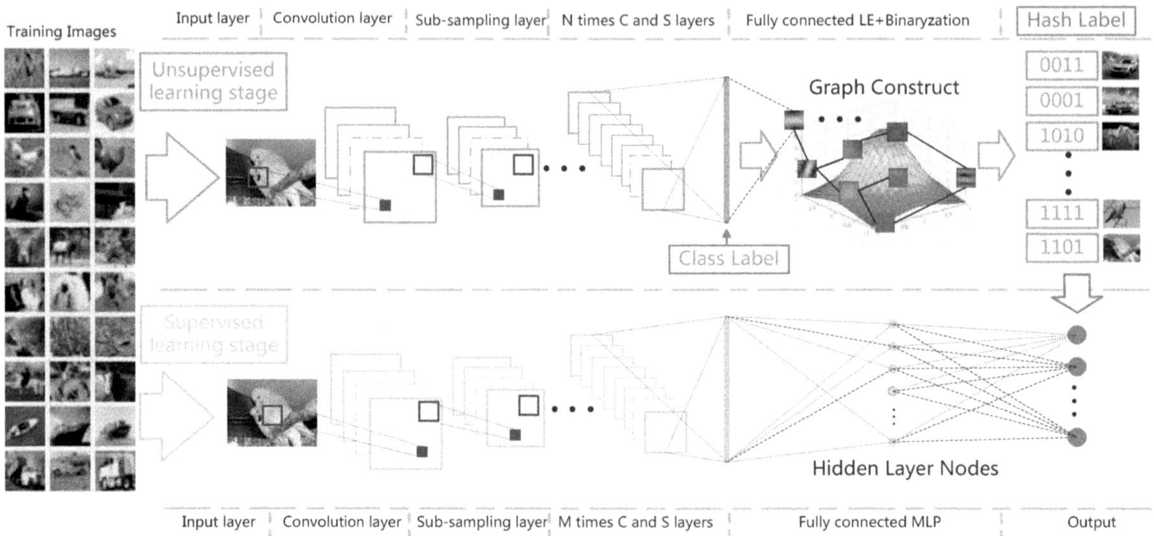

Figure 1: DSTH framework

has shown good performance on image applications. Convolutional neural networks(CNNs), have already achieved great success in various visual tasks such as image classification, retrieval and object detection [1] due to their powerful capability on mining high level semantic image representation. Through assuming the stationarity of statistics and the locality of pixel dependencies in images, CNNs have much fewer connections and parameters than standard deep neural networks, making it easier to train while the performance is nearly not affected. There are a few hashing methods that also use deep models. Given approximate hash codes learned from pairwise similarity matrix decomposition, Xia *et al.* [3] learn hash functions through using CNNs to fit the learned hash codes and class labels. Xia *et la.* [3] proposed a supervised hashing method, which firstly factorizes the pairwise semantic similarity matrix into approximate hash codes for the training images, and then trains a deep convolutional network with the approximate hash codes as well as the image tags. However, the in-sample hash codes are trained using the classification labels, which are coarse on measuring similarity among objects and makes the hashing model inaccurate for image representation.

Inspired by the successes of deep learning, in this paper, we explore deep learning techniques with application to image representation and establish a deep learning framework which learns hash functions by itself and yields accurate hash codes using extracted discriminative features. Meanwhile, we relate the hash value on each dimensional to representative features respectively. Although the framework seems similar to STH, we have two fundamental differences: (1) The image feature for training is automatically generated, while STH extracted hand-crafted visual features which do not necessarily preserve the accurate semantic relationship among images, degrading the performance of learning hashing model; (2) We learn hashing model by applying deep learning structure, while STH applied shallow SVM learning. The rest of this paper is organized as follows: In section 2, we illustrate our deep learning hashing framework. Extensive experimental results are presented in Section 3. Finally, we provide a conclusion in Section 4.

2. APPROACH

We propose an unsupervised and supervised learning algorithm under deep learning scheme, called deep self-taught hashing (DSTH), which is composed of unsupervised and supervised learning stages. The framework is shown in Fig. 1. In unsupervised learning stage, we adopt CNN and combination of LE and Binarization to learn hash labels with unsupervised constraints. In supervised learning stage, we use CNNs again with the hash labels acquired in the unsupervised learning stage, and apply Multi-layer Perceptron (MLP) to approximate acquired hash value. Finally, we get the hashing model learned from deep learning framework, aiming to efficiently map new images into hash codes for large scale image retrieval.

2.1 Unsupervised learning stage

In unsupervised learning stage, we mainly focus on generating hash labels. First, to capture discriminative fine features, we introduce CNNs to promote fine grained feature extraction with class labels. Second, we apply LE for dimension reducing and binaryzation for generating hash lables.

CNNs exploit spatially-local correlation by enforcing a local connectivity pattern between neurons of adjacent layers. Additionally, weight sharing increases learning efficiency by greatly reducing the number of free parameters to be learned. The constraints on the model enable CNNs to achieve better generalization on vision problems. In our algorithm, we adopt three layers, which contain convolution layer and subsampling layer respectively, to generate fine features.

After that, we use LE and binarization to transform the feature matrix consists of fully connected fine features to hash labels which retain relative distances among data from high dimension to low dimension. In practice, we collect n fully connected picture features as m-dimensional vectors $\{x_i\}_{i=1}^{n} \in \mathbb{R}^m$. We use x_i and y_i to represent ith sample and its hash label where $y_i \in \{-1, +1\}^l$ with l desired length of code. We set y_i^{ρ} is the ρ-th element of y_i where +1 if the ρ-th bit of code is on, or -1 otherwise.The hash code for the i-th image in n samples set can be represented as $[y_1, \ldots, y_n]^T$.

An excellent semantic hash for image retrieval should preserve Hamming distance of mapped codes to protect feature similarity from high dimension to low dimension. This method is based on graph structure and we focus on the local similarity one [9]. Therefore, we apply k-Nearest Neighbor (KNN) algorithm to construct data graph. Our $n \times n$ local similarity matrix W is

$$W_{ij} = \begin{cases} 0 & \text{if } N_k(x_i, x_j) \text{ is false,} \\ \dfrac{x_i^T x_j}{\|x_i\| \cdot \|x_j\|} & \text{otherwise.} \end{cases} \tag{1}$$

where $N_k(x_i, x_j)$ represents the ith and the jth samples are neighbours in k-nearest set. Furthermore, we apply diagonal matrix

$$D_{ii} = \sum_{j=1}^{n} W_{ij} \tag{2}$$

Meanwhile, we use the number of different bits for calculating Hamming distance between y_i and y_j as

$$H_{ij} = \|y_i - y_j\|^2 / 4 \tag{3}$$

As in SpH, we define an object function ζ to minimize the weighted average Hamming distance.

$$\zeta = \sum_{i=1}^{n} \sum_{j=1}^{n} W_{ij} H_{ij} \tag{4}$$

To calculate ζ, we transform it to $\xi = tr(Y^T LY)/4$, where $L = D - W$ is Laplacian matrix and $tr(\cdot)$ means trace of matrix. The last, we transform ξ to LapEig problem ψ with slacking constraint $y_i \in \{-1, +1\}^t$, and obtain the optimal t-dimensional real-valued vector $\tilde{y}$ to represent each sample. ψ is the following:

$$\psi = arg \min_{\tilde{Y}} \quad Tr(\tilde{Y^T} D \tilde{Y}) \quad s.t. \begin{cases} \tilde{Y^T} D \tilde{Y} = I \\ \tilde{Y^T} D1 \;\; = 0 \end{cases} \tag{5}$$

where $Tr(\tilde{Y^T} L \tilde{Y})$ gives the real relaxation of the weighted average Hamming distance $Tr(T^T LY)$. The solution of this optimisation problem is given by $\tilde{Y} = [v_1, \ldots, v_t]$ whose columns are the t eigenvectors corresponding to the smallest eigenvalues of following generalised eigenvalue problem. The solution of ψ can be transformed to

$$Lv = \lambda Dv \tag{6}$$

where vector v are the t eigenvectors corresponding to the smallest eigenvalues (nonzero) of it.

Then, we convert the t-dimensional real-valued vectors $\tilde{y_1}, \ldots, \tilde{y_n}$ into binary codes according to threshold. We set ε to present default threshold and y_i^p equivalent to p-th element of $\tilde{y_i}$. The value of y_i^p is

$$y_i^p = \begin{cases} +1 & y_i^p \geqslant \varepsilon, \\ -1 & \text{otherwise.} \end{cases} \tag{7}$$

2.2 Supervised learning stage

In supervised learning stage, we mainly focus on using the hash labels acquired in the unsupervised learning stage to get hashing model. First, using hash labels acquired in unsupervised learning stage, we employ CNNs again to receive fine grained features.

Then, we take advantage of single-hidden-layer MLP, which is an artificial neural network (ANN) and consists of input layer, hidden layer and output layer. It can adjust input to approximate output according to change weights on different nodes in hidden layer.

Formally, we set a function $f : \mathbb{R}^I \to \mathbb{R}^O$, where I is the size of input vector x and O is the size of the output vector $f(x)$. The formulation is

$$f(x) = b^{(2)} + W^{(2)} h(b^{(1)} + W^{(1)} x) \tag{8}$$

where b is bias vector, W is weight matrix and $h(x)$ is function in hidden layer. In addition, the core of $h(x)$ is logistic function $sigmoid(\alpha) = 1/(1 + e^{-\alpha})$.

In the learning process, MLP converges according to perceptron rules. We set trainset $D = \{(I_1, O_1), \ldots, (I_m, O_m)\}$, where I_i denotes ith input and O_i denotes ith objective output. The perceptron function is

$$E(W) = - \sum_{I_i \in M} (W^T I_i) O_i \tag{9}$$

where M is a set of input vectors who were classified wrong. Moreover, this function subjects to

$$O_i = \begin{cases} +1 & W^T I_i \geqslant 0, \\ -1 & W^T I_i \leqslant 0. \end{cases} \tag{10}$$

Therefore, $E(W)$ is summary of positive numbers. If all input vectors were classified correctly, $E(W) = 0$. In the practice, we use upper bound of $E(W)$ and times of iteration to control MLP convergence.

The reason why we select single-hidden-layer MLP to continue learning hash label after CNNs because CNNs is also a kind of transformation model of MLP. Therefore, we can construct integrate deep learning framework of ANN on the multi-output condition. However, single-hidden-layer MLP has a disadvantage of slow convergence rate and easy to fall into local optimum with effect to final result from initial condition. In the experiment, we will reset some cases by default condition to ensure computing efficiency. Sometimes, if we may never obtain W satisfied the upper bound of $E(W)$, we will stop iteration by default iteration times.

3. EXPERIMENT

To evaluate the retrieving performance of our approach DSTH, we test our approach and compare it with SpH, STH, ITQ and CNNH on the MNIST digit dataset and STL-10 dataset in this section. We use precision-recall curve to measure the performance of our approach. In addition,we choose 10 samples respectively and randomly in each category to calculate *precison* and select mean of their values of *precison* as final result. Meanwhile,we apply $k = 25$ for retrieving original nearest neighbours.

3.1 MNIST Digits

MNIST is a handwriting image set which contains 60000 training images and 10000 test images, each of size 28×28 pixels, with a label from 0 to 9. It is used as baseline for measurement. We randomly select 30,000 images and corresponding labels for establishing CNN models, then apply combination of LE and binarization to generate hash labels. After that, the hash labels are used to tune the CNN models and learn MLP mapping matrix. Finally, we map 10,000 test images into hash codes using the learned hash model, and evaluate the accuracy of retrieval. Figure 2 shows the 64-bit

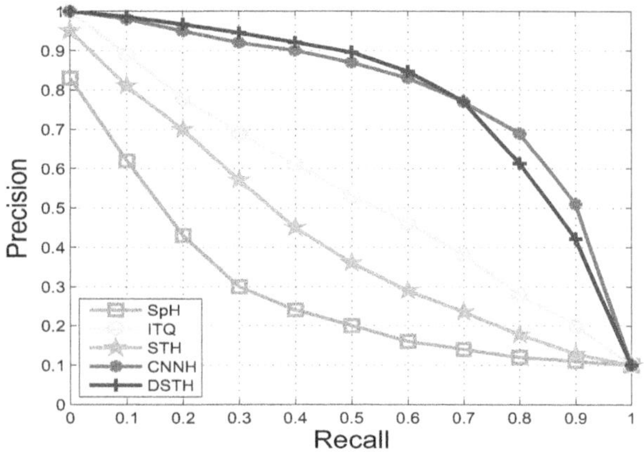

Figure 2: Precision-Recall curve of the comparative algorithm on MNIST with 64bits

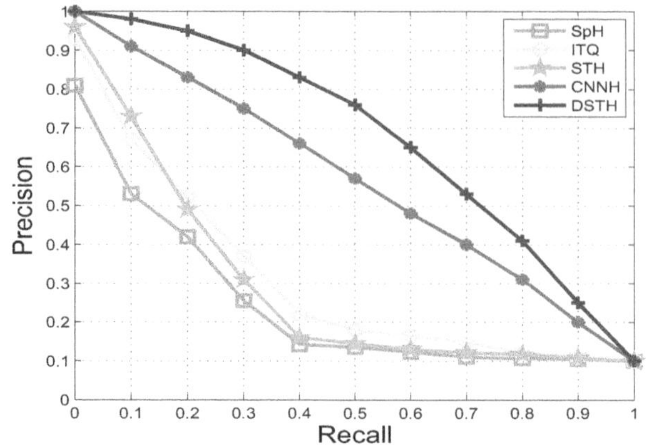

Figure 3: Precision-Recall curve of the comparative algorithm on STL-10 with 48bits

codes retrieving accuracy of our approach DSTH compared to other algorithms.

From Figure 2, it is obvious that DSTH and CNNH are better than other algorithms on P-R curve. The difference between them is whether using CNNs to extract feature. Meanwhile, we find that curves of DSTH and CNNH are twined, and the former is better until recall achieves 0.7. When the recall exceeds 0.7, both curves decrease dramatically. The superiority of our approach mainly derives from the fine grained analysis on images, which yields fine grained image representation. However,due to low dimension of MNIST, the structure of deep learning is not deep enough to get excellent hash labels, making the retrieval results not good enough. Therefore, we select another image set STL-10 with high resolution to highlight the capability of our approach.

3.2 STL-10 dataset

STL-10 is a sub-set of ImageNet dataset for image recognition, which consist of 5000 training images (500 images per class), 8000 test images (800 images per class) and 100000 unlabeled images, each of size 96×96 pixels, in 10 classes. We select 10000 of 100000 unlabeled images randomly to obtain hash model and test. We calculate 48 bits for comparison. Figure 3 shows the quantitative evaluation of different approaches with 48 bits.

According to the Figure 3, it can be observed that DSTH performs best over the STL-10 dataset(which have large size images) and the second is CNNH. The gain of performance maybe stem from two reasons: (1) The visual feature generated by CNN performs better than hand-crafted feature; (2) The deep hash function have superior generation ability than SVM shallow learning[4]. For image retrieval, the larger the image is, the more accurate the image feature should be. In our scheme, we promote deep CNNs layer architecture in both unsupervised learning and supervised learning to mine the high level semantic features, using fine grained hash labels to learn hashing model for image representation. In addition, using hash labels acquired in unsupervised stage to tune the deep neuron net yields accurate hashing models, which map new image samples to be precise hash codes.

4. CONCLUSION

In this paper, we propose Deep Self-taught Hashing(DSTH) learning algorithm on deep learning framework and introduce hash labels derived from image feature into hashing model learning. First, using CNNs in unsupervised learning stage to generate hash labels successfully maximized the value of image itself, leading to much more accurate image representation than hand-crafted extracted feature used in shallow model. Second, in terms of both feature extraction and hash label generation, utilizing deep architecture simultaneously to promote the hash models leads to excellent performance on big size images dataset.

5. ACKNOWLEDGEMENT

Thanks for the funding supported by the National Basic Research Program (973 Program) of China under Grant 2011CB302305, National Natural Science Foundation of China under Grant 61232004.

6. REFERENCES

[1] J. Wang, Y. Song, T. Leung, C. Rosenberg, and Y. Wu. Learning fine-grained image similarity with deep ranking. CVPR, 2014.

[2] Y. Yang, Y. Yang, Z. Huang, H. Shen and F. Nie. Tag Localization with Spatial Correlations and Joint Group Sparsity. CVPR, 2011.

[3] R. Xia, Y. Pan, H. Lai, C. Liu, S. Yan. Supervised Hashing for Image Retrieval via Image Representation Learning. AAAI, 2014.

[4] Bengio Y. Learning deep architecture for AI. Foundations and Trends in Machine Learning, 2009, 2(1): 1-127.

[5] J. Song, Y. Yang, Z. Huang, H. T. Shen, and R. Hong. Multiple feature hashing for real-time large scale near-duplicate video retrieval. In *ACM Multimedia*, 2011.

[6] Y. Weiss, A. Torralba, R. Fergus, Spectral hashing, NIPS, 2008.

[7] D. Zhang, J. Wang, D. Cai, J. Lu, Self-taught hashing for fast similarity search, SIGIR, 2010.

[8] M. E. Norouzi, D. J. Fleet, Minimal loss hashing for compact binary codes, ICML, 2011.

[9] L. Gao, J. Song, F. Nie, Y. Yan, N. Sebe, and H. T. Shen. Optimal graph leaning with partial tags and multiple features. In *CVPR*, 2015.

[10] J. Wang, H. T. Shen, J. Song, and J. Ji. Hashing for similarity search: A survey. *CoRR*, abs/1408.2927, 2014.

GPU Accelerated Generalised Subclass Discriminant Analysis for Event and Concept Detection in Video

Stavros Arestis-Chartampilas
CERTH-ITI
Thermi 57001, Greece
stav_ares@iti.gr

Nikolaos Gkalelis
CERTH-ITI
Thermi 57001, Greece
gkalelis@iti.gr

Vasileios Mezaris
CERTH-ITI
Thermi 57001, Greece
bmezaris@iti.gr

ABSTRACT

In this paper a discriminant analysis (DA) technique called accelerated generalised subclass discriminant analysis (AGSDA) and its GPU implementation are presented. This method identifies a discriminant subspace of the input space in three steps: a) Gram matrix computation, b) eigenvalue decomposition of the between subclass factor matrix, and c) computation of the solution of a linear matrix system with symmetric positive semidefinite (SPSD) matrix of coefficients. Based on the fact that the computationally intensive parts of AGSDA, i.e. Gram matrix computation and identification of the SPSD linear matrix system solution, are highly parallelisable, a GPU implementation of AGSDA is proposed. Experimental results on large-scale datasets of TRECVID for event and concept detection show that our GPU-AGSDA method combined with LSVM outperforms LSVM alone in training time, memory consumption, and detection accuracy.

Categories and Subject Descriptors

H.3.1 [**Information Storage and Retrieval**]: Content Analysis and Indexing; I.2.10 [**Artificial Intelligence**]: Vision and Scene Understanding

Keywords

GPU; discriminant analysis; nonlinear; large-scale data.

1. INTRODUCTION

Nonlinear discriminant analysis (NDA) approaches [6], which aim at identifying a discriminant subspace of the original high-dimensional input space, and GPU implementations of computationally intensive algorithms, are recently getting increasing attention in large-scale video analysis problems [1, 2, 7, 11]. For instance, generalised subclass discriminant analysis (GSDA) combined with linear support vector machines (LSVMs) achieved excellent performance in multimedia event detection [7], while in [1, 2] GPU accelerated machine learning algorithms are presented, obtaining substantial speedups. Motivated by the above developments, a new DA method, called accelerated GSDA (AGSDA), and its GPU implementation are presented. The proposed GPU-AGSDA is evaluated on large-scale video datasets of TRECVID for the tasks of event and concept detection, providing promising performance.

The rest of the paper is structured as follows. In Sections 2 and 3, AGSDA and its GPU implementation are presented, respectively. Experimental results are reported in Section 4, and Section 5 presents conclusions and future work.

MM'15, October 26–30, 2015, Brisbane, Australia.
© 2015 ACM. ISBN 978-1-4503-3459-4/15/10 ...$15.00.
DOI: http://dx.doi.org/10.1145/2733373.2806321.

2. ACCELERATED GSDA

Subclass NDA techniques combined with linear classifiers have resulted in improved classification accuracy as well as lower storage requirements. The major drawback of these approaches is the computational cost for learning the DA transformation matrix. Recent approaches, such as GSDA [7], have decreased the training times significantly; however, further improvements are still necessary to deal with large-scale problems. In this section, exploiting the NDA framework proposed in [8], AGSDA is presented, achieving significant speedups in training time.

Let $\mathbf{X} = [\mathbf{x}_1, \ldots, \mathbf{x}_N] = [\mathbf{X}_{1,1}, \ldots, \mathbf{X}_{\Omega,H_\Omega}] \in \mathbb{R}^{L \times N}$ be a subclass partition of an annotated training set of N observations $\mathbf{x}_r$, $r = 1, ..., N$, in the input space $\mathbb{R}^L$, where Ω is the number of classes, H_i is the number of subclasses of class i, $\mathbf{X}_{i,j} = [\mathbf{x}_{i,j}^1, \ldots, \mathbf{x}_{i,j}^{N_{i,j}}]$ is the subblock matrix containing the observations of the j-th subclass of class i, and $\mathbf{x}_{i,j}^n$, $N_{i,j}$ are the n-th observation and the number of observations of (i, j) subclass, respectively. Such a subclass partitioning can be easily created using an appropriate clustering algorithm, e.g. k-means. In order to deal with nonlinearly separable problems, a vector-valued function $\boldsymbol{\phi}(\cdot) : \mathbb{R}^L \rightarrow \mathbb{R}^F$, $\boldsymbol{\phi} = \boldsymbol{\phi}(\mathbf{x})$ may be used to map the partitioned training set $\mathbf{X}$ from the input space $\mathbb{R}^L$ to a higher- or infinite-dimensional space $\mathbb{R}^F$, where $\mathbf{\Phi} = [\boldsymbol{\phi}_1, \ldots, \boldsymbol{\phi}_N]$. It is also required that $\boldsymbol{\phi}(\cdot)$ is associated with a Mercer kernel evaluation function such that $\boldsymbol{\phi}_r^\top \boldsymbol{\phi}_q = k(\mathbf{x}_r, \mathbf{x}_q) = k_{rq}$. Assuming that in space $\mathbb{R}^F$ the data have zero mean, AGSDA seeks the column-orthogonal eigenvector matrix $\mathbf{\Gamma} \in \mathbb{R}^{N \times D}$ solving the following generalised eigenvalue problem (GEP) [7]

$$\mathbf{KAK\Gamma} = \mathbf{KK\Gamma\Delta}, \quad (1)$$

$$\mathbf{K} = \mathbf{\Phi}^\top \mathbf{\Phi}, \quad (2)$$

where $\mathbf{K}$ is the Gram matrix of the training set, $\mathbf{\Delta} \in \mathbb{R}^{D \times D}$ is the diagonal eigenvalue matrix with the real eigenvalues of the GEP in (1) along its diagonal ($D \ll F$). $\mathbf{A} \in \mathbb{R}^{N \times N}$

is the between subclass factor matrix, whose element $A_{r,q}$ corresponding to samples $\mathbf{x}_r \in \mathbf{X}_{i,j}$, $\mathbf{x}_q \in \mathbf{X}_{k,l}$ is defined as

$$A_{r,q} = \begin{cases} p_{i,j}(1-p_i)/(N_{i,j}N_{i,j}), & \text{if } (i,j)=(k,l), \\ 0 & \text{if } i=k, j\neq l, \\ -p_{i,j}p_{k,l}/(N_{i,j}N_{k,l}), & \text{otherwise}, \end{cases}$$

where p_i, $p_{i,j}$ are the estimated priors of the i-th class and (i,j) subclass respectively. Utilising the framework proposed in [8], the above problem may be solved in the following two steps: a) identifying the eigenpairs $(\mathbf{V},\mathbf{\Lambda})$, $\mathbf{V} \in \mathbb{R}^{N\times D}$, $\mathbf{\Lambda} \in \mathbb{R}^{D\times D}$ of $\mathbf{A}$, b) Obtaining $\mathbf{\Gamma}$ by solving the following linear matrix system

$$\mathbf{K\Gamma} = \mathbf{V}. \tag{3}$$

The eigenvector matrix $\mathbf{V}$ in the first step of AGSDA can be efficiently computed following [8].

3. GPU ACCELERATION OF AGSDA

The most computationally intensive parts of AGSDA training are the computation of the Gram matrix (2) and the solution of the linear matrix system (3). The above computations are highly parallelisable. To this end, we employ GPU hardware to accelerate these parts, achieving a significant overall speedup, as explained below.

3.1 Gram Matrix Computation

The naive computation of the training Gram matrix (e.g. see (4) below for Gaussian RBF kernel) for large-scale data problems is associated with high memory and computational time requirements. To alleviate these, a tiled general matrix multiplication (GEMM) algorithm is used in this work, exploiting the GEMM function of CUDA cuBLAS library and the concurrency capabilities of recent GPU architectures. In order to gain insight into our implementation, we provide an example of computing the Gram matrix using the Gaussian RBF kernel

$$k_{rq} = k(\mathbf{x}_r, \mathbf{x}_q) = \exp(-\|\mathbf{x}_r - \mathbf{x}_q\|^2/2\sigma^2), \tag{4}$$

where k_{rq} is the element of $\mathbf{K}$ at the r-th row and q-th column. Directly evaluating (4) for each pair of training observations is very costly due to many additions/subtractions, which do not fully exploit the potential GPU parallelism, and are additionally more susceptible to precision loss. Furthermore, no function is included in CUDA 7.0 toolkit that can directly perform this operation.

In matrix form, the Gram matrix can be computed as

$$\mathbf{K} = \exp(\mathbf{D}), \qquad \mathbf{D} = -\frac{(\mathbf{B}+\mathbf{C}-2\mathbf{X}^\top\mathbf{X})}{2\sigma^2}, \tag{5}$$

where $\mathbf{C} = \mathbf{B}^\top$with the elements of matrix $\mathbf{B}$ defined as $b_{rq} = \mathbf{x}_r^\top\mathbf{x}_r$, $\forall\, r,q$, and $\mathbf{B},\mathbf{C} \in \mathbb{R}^{N\times N}$. Utilising the matrix form, $\mathbf{D}$ can be computed in the GPU with a GEMM call as follows

$$\mathbf{D} = \alpha\mathbf{X}^\top\mathbf{X} + \beta\mathbf{E},$$

where $\mathbf{E} = \mathbf{B}+\mathbf{C}$, $\alpha = \frac{1}{\sigma^2}$, $\beta = \frac{-1}{2\sigma^2}$. Using the GEMM function, a large parallelisation with a respective speedup is achieved. However, GPU memory size is still the main restriction of this formulation.

To overcome the above limitation as well, a tiled GEMM was implemented, where the involved matrices are appropriately partitioned. For demonstration purposes we consider a 1×2 partition for the data matrix

$$\mathbf{X} = [\mathbf{X}_1, \mathbf{X}_2], \tag{6}$$

where $\mathbf{X}_1 = [\mathbf{x}_1,\ldots,\mathbf{x}_{N'}]$, $\mathbf{X}_2 = [\mathbf{x}_{N'+1},\ldots,\mathbf{x}_N] \in \mathbb{R}^{L\times N'}$, $N = 2N'$(and without loss of generality assuming that N is even). The overall problem is then formulated as

$$\begin{bmatrix} \mathbf{D}_{11} & \mathbf{D}_{12} \\ \mathbf{D}_{21} & \mathbf{D}_{22} \end{bmatrix} = \alpha \begin{bmatrix} \mathbf{X}_1^\top\mathbf{X}_1 & \mathbf{X}_1^\top\mathbf{X}_2 \\ \mathbf{X}_2^\top\mathbf{X}_1 & \mathbf{X}_2^\top\mathbf{X}_2 \end{bmatrix} + \beta \begin{bmatrix} \mathbf{E}_{11} & \mathbf{E}_{12} \\ \mathbf{E}_{21} & \mathbf{E}_{22} \end{bmatrix}.$$

Using the above fomulation and noting that $\mathbf{D}_{12} = \mathbf{D}_{21}^\top$, matrix $\mathbf{D}$ can be computed utilising three GEMM function calls as follows:

$$\mathbf{D}_{11} = \alpha\mathbf{X}_1^\top\mathbf{X}_1 + \beta\mathbf{E}_{11}, \tag{7}$$

$$\mathbf{D}_{21} = \alpha\mathbf{X}_2^\top\mathbf{X}_1 + \beta\mathbf{E}_{21}, \tag{8}$$

$$\mathbf{D}_{22} = \alpha\mathbf{X}_2^\top\mathbf{X}_2 + \beta\mathbf{E}_{22}. \tag{9}$$

The matrices involved in the above tiled GEMM function calls are considerably smaller in size compared to the full matrices in (5), thus alleviating the memory problem.

A further speedup can be achieved by exploiting the tiled GEMM procedure and properly pipelining GPU computations and CPU⇌GPU memory transactions (where ⇌ denotes a concurrent transaction), as shown in Fig. 1. In this figure, HD# and DH# denote Host-To-Device and Device-To-Host memory transactions respectively, K# denotes GPU computations, while CPU# denotes CPU computations. For instance, in our example, HD1 refers to the memory transactions to pass matrices $\mathbf{X}_1$ and $\mathbf{E}_{11}$ in the GPU RAM, K1 denotes the GEMM function (7), DH1 is the copying of the resulting matrix $\mathbf{D}_{11}$ back to CPU RAM and CPU1 denotes the calculation of $\mathbf{K}_{11}$ by exponentiating $\mathbf{D}_{11}$ according to the first part of (5). Using this notation for (7)-(9), and performing the pipelining described in Fig. 1, a 3–way concurrency is achieved in this example (and up to 4–way concurrency can be achieved in case of finer partitioning of the data matrix (6)).

We should also note that a formulation similar to the one described in this section can be used for computing the test-data kernel matrix, when applying the trained AGSDA method.

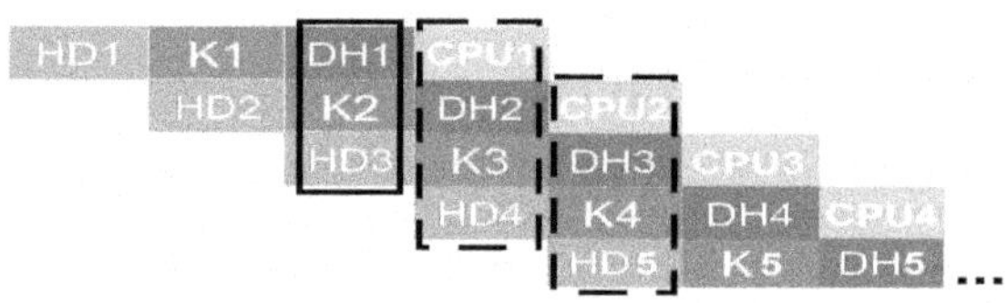

Figure 1: CPU⇌GPU concurrency.

3.2 Computation of Linear Matrix System Solution

Based on the fact that the Gram matrix is symmetric positive semi-definite (SPSD), the Cholesky factorisation is utilised to solve the linear system in (3) for $\mathbf{\Gamma}$

$$\mathbf{K\Gamma} = \mathbf{V} \Rightarrow \mathbf{LL}^\top\mathbf{\Gamma} = \mathbf{V} \Rightarrow \begin{aligned} \mathbf{L\Psi} &= \mathbf{V}, \\ \mathbf{L}^\top\mathbf{\Gamma} &= \mathbf{\Psi}, \end{aligned} \tag{10}$$

where $\mathbf{L} \in \mathbb{R}^{N\times N}$ is a lower triangular matrix, and $\mathbf{\Psi} \in \mathbb{R}^{N\times D}$ is an unknown intermediate matrix. The built-in dense linear solvers of CUDA 7.0 toolkit, namely cuSolver, are used. Specifically, the functions `cusolverDn<t>potrf()` and `cusolverDn<t>potrs()` are utilised to perform the Cholesky factorisation and the subsequent solution of the two linear matrix systems in (10) for $\mathbf{\Psi}$ and $\mathbf{\Gamma}$ respectively.

4. EXPERIMENTAL EVALUATION

In this section, GPU-AGSDA is evaluated in two different Nvidia graphic cards. Moreover, its performance is compared with the Matlab implementation of AGSDA and the C++ liblinear implementation of LSVM.

4.1 Datasets and Features

Three datasets are used for the experimental evaluation; specifically, we utilise subsets of the MED 2012 and SIN 2013 video corpora for event and concept detection:

MED-HBB: For event detection we used the publicly available partitioning of MED 2012 provided by the authors of [9]. It utilises a subset of the MED 2012 video corpus, comprising 25 target events and 13274 videos, and is divided to a training and evaluation set of 8824 and 4425 videos, respectively. We used improved dense trajectories (DT) to represent each video with a feature vector in $\mathbb{R}^{101376}$.

SIN13: For concept detection in video shots, 38 concepts of the SIN 2013 dataset are utilized. Two feature extraction procedures are used for representing the videos of the SIN dataset, as explained below:

a) *SIN13-LOCAL*: SIFT, SURF and ORB descriptors are applied to extract local features at keyframe-level. One keyframe per shot is used. The extracted features are encoded using VLAD, and compressed by utilizing a modification of the random projection matrix technique to provide a feature vector in $\mathbb{R}^{4000}$ for each keyframe [10].

b) *SIN13-CNN*: ConvNet network (CNN) features are employed for shot representation. Particularly, a 16-layer network [12] pre-trained using the 2009 ImageNet dataset [4] is employed. In our case, the last layer is utilized as output, providing a 1000-element vector representation for each keyframe. Again, one keyframe per shot is used.

4.2 Detection Approaches

We evaluated four different detection approaches. Specifically: GPU-AGSDA combined with LSVM running on two different Nvidia graphic cards, namely the low-end GeForce GTX 650 and the high-end Tesla K40; the Matlab implementation of AGSDA combined with LSVM; and the LSVM implementation of the C++ liblinear library [5]. In our AGSDA-based algorithms, the LSVM is implemented using the C++ libsvm library [3]. For convenience, we provide the following naming convention concerning the different algorithms, implementations and graphic cards used in the experiments:

a) AGSDA-1: GPU-AGSDA with LSVM, on GTX 650.
b) AGSDA-2: GPU-AGSDA with LSVM, on Tesla K40.
c) AGSDA-3: the Matlab version of AGSDA with LSVM.
d) LSVM: C++ liblinear implementation of LSVM, operating directly in the input space.

For all experiments we used Intel i7 3770K @3.5GHz, 32GB RAM machines with Win7 x64 OS. One set of parameters (Gaussian RBF parameter σ, LSVM parameter C) was estimated for each dataset using a grid search on a 3-fold cross-validation procedure, and the same parameter values were used for training all the detectors of the same detection approach. Moreover, the subclass parameters were set to $\mathrm{H}_1 = 2, \mathrm{H}_2 \in [1, 2]$, where $\mathrm{H}_1, \mathrm{H}_2$ refer to the number of subclasses for the target and rest-of-world classes, respectively.

4.3 Results

The detection results in terms of MXinfAP [13] for concept detection in SIN13-LOCAL and SIN13-CNN, and mean average precision (MAP) for event detection in MED-HBB for all approaches are shown in Fig. 2. In the same figure, the overall training and testing times along all concepts or events are reported. In Fig. 3 the distribution of the overall training and testing times of AGSDA-2 along its individual parts is shown. We observe the following:

■ As shown in Fig. 2, the detection performance between our Matlab (AGSDA-3) and GPU implementation (AGSDA-1,-2) is equivalent. In addition, a 1.4% to 2.5% improvement of AGSDA+LSVM over LSVM is achieved. Overall, AGSDA-LSVM provides better detection results than LSVM for 30 out of 38 concepts in SIN13-CNN.

■ Concerning training time, as shown in Fig. 2, GPU-AGSDA running on Tesla K40 (AGSDA-2) offers a significant speedup over both the LSVM of liblinear (which is a state-of-the-art LSVM implementation in terms of training time) and our Matlab implementation (AGSDA-3). Similarly, GPU-AGSDA running on GTX 650 (AGSDA-1) outperforms (MED-HBB, SIN13-CNN) or performs equivalently (SIN13-LOCAL) to our Matlab implementation. When compared to LSVM, it provides a 3$\times$ speedup in the MED-HBB dataset and an equivalent or slightly worse training time performance in the other two datasets.

■ In Fig. 3, we observe that for the SIN13-LOCAL and SIN13-CNN datasets, the most computationally intensive parts of AGSDA-2 are the computation of the Gram matrix, the Cholesky factorisation and the LSVM training, while for MED-HBB dataset, the computation time is dominated by the memory transactions of the sorting algorithm, followed by the computations of the Gram matrix. Thus, for the latter dataset (MED-HBB) the provision of sorted observations (e.g. sorting the observations during the feature extraction procedure) can considerably decrease the overall computation time. We should also note that the LSVM training time can be considerably reduced using a faster LSVM library such as liblinear. However, the libsvm library was preferred due to its better robustness in relation to generalisation performance. We finally observed that in the testing stage, the computation of Gram representations of test observations is the bottleneck of our algorithm; this could be alleviated by using faster Gram representation algorithms [11].

Additionally, comparison with the results reported in [7] reveals a one to two orders of magnitude training time improvement over GSDA. Specifically, the learning time for one event using a 5$\times$5 optimisation grid with GPU-AGSDA (on GTX 650) was approximately 5 minutes, while the reported time for the same experiment for GSDA [7] was above 50 minutes.

Further to the above, GPU-AGSDA also has lower memory requirements. Specifically, we observed that it required up to 8 times less memory than the corresponding Matlab implementation. This means, for instance, that on our hardware the GPU implementation avoided any use of HDD space as swap memory, in contrast to what the Matlab ver-

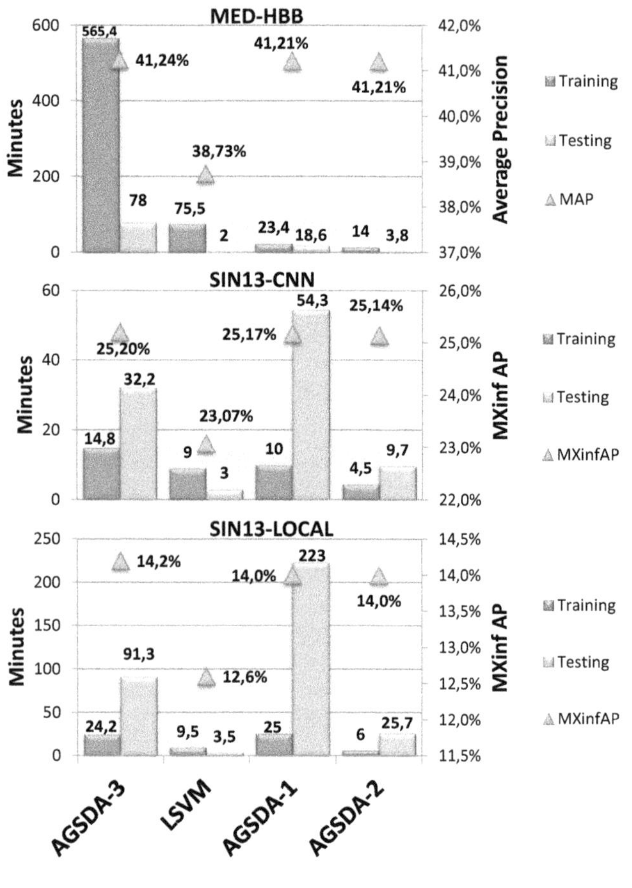

Figure 2: Experimental evaluation results.

sion of AGSDA did during the training part of the MED-HBB experiment.

5. CONCLUSIONS

In this paper a new efficient discriminant analysis method called accelerated generalized subclass discriminant analysis and its GPU implementation are presented. Specifically, a tiled GEMM procedure for the computation of the Gram matrix and the GPU implementation of Cholesky factorisation are exploited to further improve AGSDA in terms of training time and memory space requirements.

Future work directions include the investigation of a tiled linear matrix system solver, the exploitation of more efficient Gram matrix representation methods during the testing stage [11], and the porting of the proposed algorithm to Jetson TK1 embedded platform to achieve mobility and reduced power consumption.

6. ACKNOWLEDGEMENTS

This work was supported by the EC under contract FP7-600826 ForgetIT and by Nvidia corporation with the donation of a Tesla K40 GPU.

7. REFERENCES

[1] E. Agullo et al. Faster, cheaper, better – a hybridization methodology to develop linear algebra software for GPUs. *GPU Computing Gems*, 2, 2010.

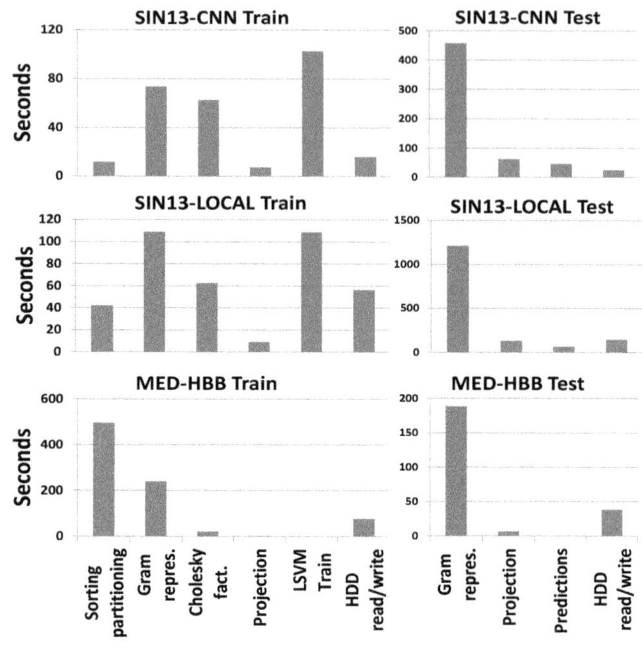

Figure 3: Bottlenecks of AGSDA on Tesla K40.

[2] A. Athanasopoulos et al. GPU acceleration for support vector machines. In *WIAMIS, Delft, NL, April 13-15*, 2011.

[3] C.-C. Chang and C.-J. Lin. LIBSVM: A library for support vector machines. *ACM Trans. Intell. Syst. Technol.*, 2(3):27:1–27:27, May 2011.

[4] J. Deng et al. Imagenet: A large-scale hierarchical image database. In *IEEE CVPR*, pages 248–255, 2009.

[5] R.-E. Fan et al. LIBLINEAR: A library for large linear classification. *J. Mach. Learn. Res.*, 9:1871–1874, June 2008.

[6] N. Gkalelis et al. Mixture subclass discriminant analysis link to restricted Gaussian model and other generalizations. *IEEE Trans. on Neural Netw. and Learning Sys.*, 24(1):8–21, 2013.

[7] N. Gkalelis and V. Mezaris. Video event detection using generalized subclass discriminant analysis and linear support vector machines. In *ACM ICMR*, 2014.

[8] N. Gkalelis and V. Mezaris. Accelerated nonlinear discriminant analysis. *arXiv preprint arXiv:1504.07000*, 2015.

[9] A. Habibian et al. Recommendations for video event recognition using concept vocabularies. In *ACM ICMR*, pages 89–96, 2013.

[10] F. Markatopoulou et al. Local features and a two-layer stacking architecture for semantic concept detection in video. *IEEE Trans. on Emerging Topics in Computing*, 3(2):193–204, June 2015.

[11] B. Schölkopf and A. J. Smola. *Learning with kernels.* MIT Press, Cambridge, MA, USA, 2001.

[12] K. Simonyan and A. Zisserman. Very deep convolutional networks for large-scale image recognition. *arXiv preprint arXiv:1409.1556*, 2014.

[13] Yilmaz et al. A simple and efficient sampling method for estimating AP and NDCG. In *ACM SIGIR*, pages 603–610, NY, USA, 2008.

Semi- and Weakly- Supervised Semantic Segmentation with Deep Convolutional Neural Networks

Yuhang Wang, Jing Liu, Yong Li and Hanqing Lu
The National Laboratory of Pattern Recognition, Institute of Automation,
Chinese Academy of Sciences, Beijing, China
{yuhang.wang, jliu, yong.li, luhq}@nlpr.ia.ac.cn

ABSTRACT

Successful semantic segmentation methods typically rely on the training datasets containing a large number of pixel-wise labeled images. To alleviate the dependence on such a fully annotated training dataset, in this paper, we propose a semi- and weakly-supervised learning framework by exploring images most only with image-level labels and very few with pixel-level labels, in which two stages of Convolutional Neural Network (CNN) training are included. First, a pixel-level supervised CNN is trained on very few fully annotated images. Second, given a large number of images with only image-level labels available, a collaborative-supervised CNN is designed to jointly perform the pixel-level and image-level classification tasks, while the pixel-level labels are predicted by the fully-supervised network in the first stage. The collaborative-supervised network can remain the discriminative ability of the fully-supervised model learned with fully labeled images, and further enhance the performance by importing more weakly labeled data. Our experiments on two challenging datasets, i.e, PASCAL VOC 2007 and LabelMe LMO, demonstrate the satisfactory performance of our approach, nearly matching the results achieved when all training images have pixel-level labels.

Categories and Subject Descriptors

I.2.10 [**Artificial Intelligence**]: [Vision and Scene Understanding]; H.3.1 [**Information Storage and Retrieval**]: Content Analysis and Indexing

Keywords

Semantic Segmentation; Semi-Supervised Learning; CNN

1. INTRODUCTION

Image semantic segmentation is a core problem in computer vision, aiming at parsing images into several semantic regions and labeling them with their concepts. It demands more fine-granular recognition of images, since pixel-wise classification is required along with understanding of various image contents. The restrictions of limited fine-annotated images and diversity of objects brings more challenges into this task.

In the past decades, numerous efforts have been paid on the task of semantic segmentation. According to the different levels of supervision, they can be roughly divided into two categories: fully-supervised and weakly-supervised. In the fully-supervised setting, CRF (Conditional Random Field) models are used typically and have lots of effective extensions [3]. Besides, the techniques of deep learning are applied to solve the problem of semantic segmentation effectively. Long *et.al* [8] proposed a fully convolutional network constrained by strong supervision of pixel labels and refined its results with a hierarchical structure. Although satisfactory segmentation performance of the fully-supervised solutions can be achieved when given a large amount of training data, the high cost on the pixel-level annotations is bound to restrict its extensive applications.

To alleviate the dependence on the fine-grained labeled data, weakly-supervised methods with only image-level labels available have emerged and attracted much attention [4, 6, 7]. Liu *et.al* [6] built a graph propagation model considering consistency of superpixels and weak supervision information simultaneously. Liu *et.al* [7] formulated the problem as a weakly-supervised dual clustering task to cluster superpixels and assign a suitable label to each cluster. And Xie *et.al* [15, 16] further improved the graph construction method of the model. Despite of largely decreasing requirement on training data, the weakly-supervised methods suffer a poor performance in discovering the object structure. To achieve the balance of the dependence on training data and the model performance, we turn to a semi- and weakly-supervised method in this paper, using mainly the image-level labeled images as training data and very few pixel-level labeled images for supplementary.

In this paper, we propose a two-stage Convolutional Neural Network (CNN) based framework to accomplish a coarse-to-fine learning process for image semantic segmentation. In the first stage, we build a pixel-level supervised network (PS-CNN), using only a small number of images with their pixel-level labels. The network predicts labels for each pixel of the input images and thus carries out a fine-grained learning on various object details. The prediction can indicate the differences between objects or object parts from different classes to some extent, but is too crude to ensure a satisfactory segmentation performance because of too limited training data explored in the first stage. Then, a collaborative-supervised

MM'15, October 26–30, 2015, Brisbane, Australia.
 ISBN 978-1-4503-3459-4/15/10 ...$15.00.
DOI: http://dx.doi.org/10.1145/2733373.2806322.

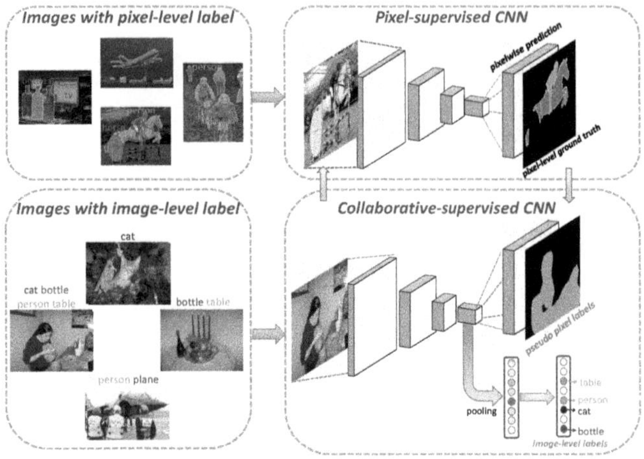

Figure 1: The overview of our approach. The upper and lower parts in the figure show the training process of the PS-CNN and CS-CNN respectively. During the training of CS-CNN, the response of its last convolutional layer is upsampled and averaged respectively and then supervised by the pixel-level and image-level labels collaboratively, which enhances the sensitivity of the model to both the object structures and the tiny objects.

network (CS-CNN) as the second stage is proposed to enhance the segmentation performance by making full use of two sides of information: one is the outputs of the first stage, the other is a large number of images associated with only image-level labels. Specifically, we build a two-head network to predict labels for each pixel and the entire image at the same time. Given a training image, the pseudo pixel labels obtained from the first stage and the image-level labels are used to supervise the two label prediction tasks respectively and the corresponding two loss functions are combined to contribute to updating the network. With such a collaborative-supervised network, we aim to refine the model by expanding the training scale with weakly labeled images, and better mask the object structure benefitting from the discriminative ability of the fully-supervised model learning with fully labeled images. Our experiments on two challenging datasets, i.e, PASCAL VOC 2007 dataset [1] and LabelMe LMO dataset [10], demonstrate the attractive performance of our approach, nearly matching the results achieved when all training images have pixel-level labels.

2. OUR APPROACH

Our approach consists of two stages of CNN training to progressively elaborate our model, of which one is a pixel-supervised CNN (PS-CNN) as a pre-trained model and the other is a collaborative-supervised CNN (CS-CNN) as a refined model. Both of the two networks are finetuned on the ImageNet-pretrained VGG 16-layer net [11], and the processes are implemented with Caffe [2]. An overview of our approach is shown in Figure 1.

2.1 Pixel-supervised CNN Model

In the first stage, we train a pixel-supervised CNN to learn the details of different objects, using few fully-supervised images. The model is built as a fully convolutional neural network referring to FCN [8]. The FCN model replaces the fully connected layers by convolutional ones with kernels covering their entire input regions, which further extends a convnet to adapt arbitrary-sized inputs and output a classification map. With this network structure, a feature map can be achieved from the last convolutional layer, of which each feature vector indicates the response of a receptive field in the input image. To connect the coarse output with the pixel-wise annotations, the feature map is then up-sampled with bilinear interpolation to the size of the input image . And classification is made on each pixel to make detailed segmentation.

The softmax loss function is used in this network for pixel-wise supervision and the averaged loss value of all the pixels in a training batch is used as the final loss. The loss function can be defined as follows,

$$Loss_1 = -\frac{1}{mn}\sum_{i=1}^{n}\sum_{j=1}^{m}\sum_{k=1}^{c} 1\{y_{ij} = k\} log(\hat{p}_{ij,k}^{pixel}) \quad (1)$$

$$\hat{p}_{ij,k}^{pixel} = \frac{exp(x_{ij,k}^{pixel})}{\sum_{l=1}^{c} exp(x_{ij,l}^{pixel})} \quad (2)$$

where n, m, c are the batchsize, pixel number in an image and the number of object classes, respectively. $\hat{p}_{ij,k}^{pixel}$ stands for the probability of the jth pixel in the ith image to be predicted to class k. x_{ij}^{pixel} stands for the feature vector of $pixel_{ij}$ given out by the last convolutional layer of the network and $x_{ij,k}^{pixel}$ is the value in its kth channel. y_{ij} is the groundtruth label of the $pixel_{ij}$ and $1\{y_{ij} = k\}$ is an indicator function judging whether the groundtruth label equals k.

2.2 Collaborative-supervised CNN Model

In this stage, more weakly-supervised images with only image-level labels are added to expand training scale and refine our model. To utilize them, we design a collaborative-supervised CNN model which takes both of the pixel-level and image-level information into consideration.

For the pixel-level loss term, we employ the same network structure as in the first stage and use pseudo pixel-level labels for the weakly-supervised images as supervision. The pseudo labels are pixel-wise prediction generated by the PS-CNN model achieved above. It is coarse because of the limited training data but already competent to distinguish most objects or their parts. So we use it here to maintain the discriminating ability of the network on different object details.

But as the pseudo pixel labels contain much noise and may be insensitive to tiny objects, we add an image-level loss term to alleviate the problem. We average the response of each receptive field as the response of the entire image and then make the image-level classification. As there are always more than one object in the image, we use KL-Divergence to formulate the loss function and assume that the prediction probability should distribute evenly on all the object classes existing in the image. That is, for an image containing q kinds of objects, we set $\frac{1}{q}$ as the groundtruth probability for the q classes while 0 for the others. In this way, we actually demand that every existing object should be given equal notice by the network. Therefore, some of the tiny objects or unconspicuous object parts will be forced to produce higher response to ensure that they are not ignored or mislabeled,

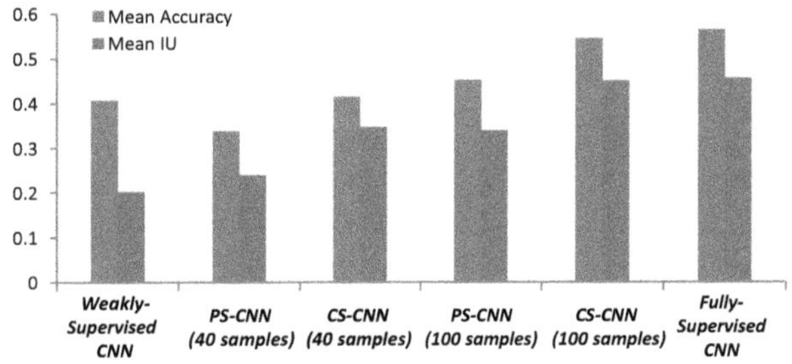

Figure 2: Performance of different CNN models on the PASCAL VOC 2007 dataset

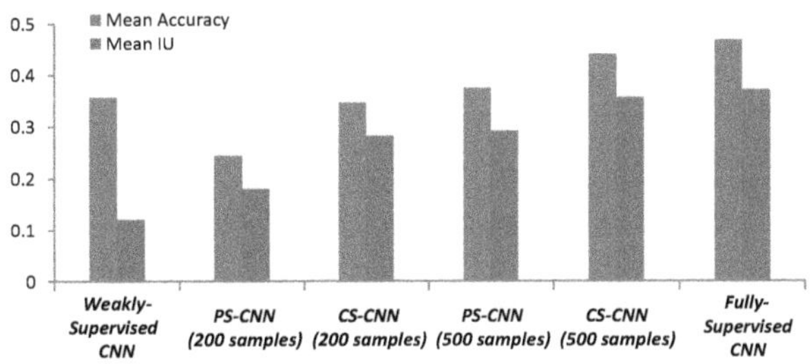

Figure 3: Performance of different CNN models on the LabelMe LMO dataset

which helps neutralizing the noise brought by the pseudo pixel labels. The loss function is as follows,

$$Loss_2 = -\frac{1}{n}\sum_{i=1}^{n}\sum_{k=1}^{c} p_{i,k}^{image} log(\hat{p}_{i,k}^{image}) \quad (3)$$

$$\hat{p}_{i,k}^{image} = \frac{exp(x_{i,k}^{image})}{\sum_{l=1}^{c} exp(x_{i,l}^{image})} \quad (4)$$

where $\hat{p}_{i,k}^{image}$ denotes the probability of $image_i$ to be predicted to class k. And $p_{i,k}^{image}$ denotes the groundtruth probability. x_i^{image} is the averaged feature vector of $image_i$.

Finally, we combine the two loss terms with a weighting parameter α and use them to constrain our model collaboratively. The final loss function is as follows,

$$Loss = Loss_1 + \alpha Loss_2 \quad (5)$$

3. EXPERIMENT

Extensive experiments are performed on PASCAL VOC 2007 dataset [1] and LabelMe Outdoor dataset [10], which are focused on object and scene segmentation, respectively. Both mean class accuracy and mean IU (intersection over union) are used as metrics to evaluate our model. Our approach is compared with several fully- and weakly- supervised methods and outperforms the state-of-the-art methods on both two datasets, which indicates the effectiveness of our approach. The results on different kinds of segmentation tasks also confirm the universality of our approach.

3.1 PASCAL VOC 2007 Dataset

The PASCAL VOC 2007 dataset consists of 422 training-validation images and 210 testing images belonging to 20 object classes. During the training process, we randomly sample a small percentage of images to train the PS-CNN with their pixel-level labels and the rest images are further added to train the CS-CNN with only image-level labels. The impact of the pixel-level labeled images is further evaluated by changing their numbers from 40 ($< 10\%$) to 100 ($< 25\%$). And the evaluations when the whole training set is pixel-level labeled (fully-supervised CNN, using only the pixel-level supervision) or image-level labeled (weakly-supervised CNN, using only the image-level supervision) are also performed for comparison.

Comparison between different settings are shown in Figure 2. It shows that, with both sampling rates, the proposed CS-CNN model outperforms the PS-CNN by about 10 percent on both the two evaluation metrics. It indicates the effectiveness of our semi-supervised approach which enhances the model with weakly-labeled images. Moreover, comparison between the results achieved with different sampling rates indicates the influence of the fully-supervised training data. Our results get an obvious improvement when the number of pixel-level labeled samples rises from 40 to 100. While compared with the weakly-supervised and fully-supervised CNN, the CS-CNN model always shows better results than the weakly-supervised CNN, by the reason of the few fully-supervised images. And it should be noticed that our CS-CNN model trained with only 100 ($< 25\%$) pixel-level labeled images already achieves very similar performance with the fully-supervised CNN using the whole training set with pixel-level annotations, which further comfirms the effectiveness of our approach.

Finally, results of our approach (semi-supervised, indicated as SS) and other fully-supervised (FS) or weakly-supervised (WS) methods are compared in Table 1. Our results are achieved using the CS-CNN model trained with 100 pixel-level labeled images. It can be seen that our approach shows better accuracy and robustness, which wins the highest accuracy in 8 classes among all of these methods and outperforms the state-of-the-art method [16] by 7 percent on mean accuracy.

3.2 LabelMe Outdoor Dataset

This dataset is a subset of LabelMe dataset [10] provided by [5]. It contains 2688 fully annotated images of 33 categories, of which 2488 images are for training and the rest for testing. Most of the images are outdoor scenes including sky, buildings and mountain. We continue to use the same settings as above and conduct our experiments with 200 ($< 10\%$) and 500 ($< 25\%$) pixel-level samples, respectively. The results are shown in Figure 3, which further verifies the above conclusion that our semi-supervised approach effectively enhances the model by exploiting more weakly-supervised images and is able to achieve similar performance with the fully-supervised CNN with only few pixel-level samples. Comparison with the state-of-the-art methods are shown in Table 2. Our result outperforms even the fully-supervised methods and exceeds the state-of-the-art method [9] by 12 percent on mean accuracy.

4. CONCLUSION

In this paper, we propose a semi- and weakly- supervised learning method for image semantic segmentation, which consists of two stages of CNN training. In the first stage, we train a pixel-supervised CNN to learn the discrimination between objects with very few pixel-level labeled images. In

Table 1: Semantic segmentation results on PASCAL VOC 2007 dataset.

Supervision	Method	plane	bike	bird	boat	bottle	bus	car	cat	chair	cow	table	dog	horse	motorbike	person	plant	sheep	sofa	train	tv	bkgd	mean
WS	[6]	28	20	52	28	46	41	39	60	25	68	25	35	17	35	56	36	46	17	31	20	65	38
	[18]	48	20	26	25	3	7	23	13	**38**	19	15	39	17	18	25	47	9	**41**	17	33	-	24
	[17]	65	25	39	8	17	38	17	26	25	17	47	41	44	32	59	34	36	23	35	31	-	33
	[15]	**85**	55	**87**	45	42	31	34	57	21	**81**	23	16	6	11	42	31	**72**	24	49	40	41	42
	[16]	77	48	**87**	**50**	**56**	48	44	60	27	76	18	38	25	31	52	38	59	31	51	34	41	47
FS	[3]	27	33	44	11	14	36	30	31	27	6	50	28	24	38	52	29	28	12	45	46	-	30
	[14]	19	21	5	16	3	1	**78**	1	3	1	23	**69**	44	42	0	**65**	30	35	**89**	**71**	-	31
SS	Ours	53	**66**	11	40	46	**69**	46	**94**	15	41	**67**	51	**56**	**74**	**87**	19	62	26	84	43	**93**	**54**

Table 2: Semantic segmentation results on LabelMe LMO dataset.

Supervision	FS			WS		SS
Method	[5]	[12]	[9]	[13]	[7]	Ours
Accuracy	24	29	32	21	26	**44**

the second stage, a collaborative-supervised CNN is designed to jointly perform the pixel-level and image-level classification tasks, given a large number of images with only image-level labels available. For the collaborative-supervised model training, the pixel-level labels are pseudo ones predicted by the fully-supervised network in the first stage. Our results on two commonly used datasets have proved that our model can achieve a result close to or better than the fully-supervised methods with the help of only a small amount of pixel-level labeled images. Experiments on larger external datasets will be implemented in the future to further confirm the effectiveness and scalability of our method.

5. ACKNOWLEGMENTS

This work was supported by 973 Program (2012CB316304) and National Natural Science Foundation of China (61332016, 61272329, and 61472422).

6. REFERENCES

[1] M. Everingham, L. Van Gool, C. K. Williams, J. Winn, and A. Zisserman. The pascal visual object classes (voc) challenge. *IJCV*, 88(2):303–338, 2010.

[2] Y. Jia, E. Shelhamer, J. Donahue, S. Karayev, J. Long, R. Girshick, S. Guadarrama, and T. Darrell. Caffe: Convolutional architecture for fast feature embedding. *arXiv preprint arXiv:1408.5093*, 2014.

[3] L. Ladicky, C. Russell, P. Kohli, and P. H. Torr. Associative hierarchical crfs for object class image segmentation. In *ICCV*, pages 739–746, 2009.

[4] Y. Li, J. Liu, Y. Wang, H. Lu, and S. Ma. Weakly supervised rbm for semantic segmentation. In *IJCAI*, 2015.

[5] C. Liu, J. Yuen, and A. Torralba. Nonparametric scene parsing: Label transfer via dense scene alignment. In *CVPR*, pages 1972–1979, 2009.

[6] S. Liu, S. Yan, T. Zhang, C. Xu, J. Liu, and H. Lu. Weakly supervised graph propagation towards collective image parsing. *TMM*, 14(2):361–373, 2012.

[7] Y. Liu, J. Liu, Z. Li, J. Tang, and H. Lu. Weakly-supervised dual clustering for image semantic segmentation. In *CVPR*, pages 2075–2082, 2013.

[8] J. Long, E. Shelhamer, and T. Darrell. Fully convolutional networks for semantic segmentation. *arXiv preprint arXiv:1411.4038*, 2014.

[9] H. Myeong and K. M. Lee. Tensor-based high-order semantic relation transfer for semantic scene segmentation, 2013.

[10] B. C. Russell, A. Torralba, K. P. Murphy, and W. T. Freeman. Labelme: a database and web-based tool for image annotation. *IJCV*, 77(1-3):157–173, 2008.

[11] K. Simonyan and A. Zisserman. Very deep convolutional networks for large-scale image recognition. *arXiv preprint arXiv:1409.1556*, 2014.

[12] J. Tighe and S. Lazebnik. Superparsing: Scalable nonparametric image parsing with superpixels. In *ECCV*, pages 352–365, 2010.

[13] A. Vezhnevets, V. Ferrari, and J. M. Buhmann. Weakly supervised structured output learning for semantic segmentation. In *CVPR*, pages 845–852, 2012.

[14] V. Viitaniemi and J. Laaksonen. Evaluation of techniques for image classification, object detection and object segmentation (technical report tkk-ics-r2). http://www.cis.hut.fi/projects/cbir/, 2008.

[15] W. Xie, Y. Peng, and J. Xiao. Semantic graph construction for weakly-supervised image parsing. In *AAAI*, 2014.

[16] W. Xie, Y. Peng, and J. Xiao. Weakly-supervised image parsing via constructing semantic graphs and hypergraphs. In *MM*, pages 277–286, 2014.

[17] K. Zhang, W. Zhang, S. Zeng, and X. Xue. Semantic segmentation using multiple graphs with block-diagonal constraints. In *AAAI*, 2014.

[18] K. Zhang, W. Zhang, Y. Zheng, and X. Xue. Sparse reconstruction for weakly supervised semantic segmentation. In *IJCAI*, pages 1889–1895, 2013.

Learning Pairwise Neural Network Encoder for Depth Image-based 3D Model Retrieval

Jing Zhu[1,3] Fan Zhu[1,2] Edward K. Wong[1,3] Yi Fang[1,2*]

[1] NYU Multimedia and Visual Computing Lab
[2] Electrical and Computer Engineering, New York University Abu Dhabi
[3] Computer Science and Engineering, Polytechnic School of Engineering, New York University

ABSTRACT

With the emergence of RGB-D cameras (e.g., Kinect), the sensing capability of artificial intelligence systems has been dramatically increased, and as a consequence, a wide range of depth image-based human-machine interaction applications are proposed. In design industry, a 3D model always contains abundant information, which are required for manufacture. Since depth images can be conveniently acquired, a retrieval system that can return 3D models based on depth image inputs can assist or improve the traditional product design process. In this work, we address the depth image-based 3D model retrieval problem. By extending the neural network to a neural network pair with identical output layers for objects of the same category, unified domain-invariant representations can be learned based on the low-level mismatched depth image features and 3D model features. A unique advantage of the framework is that the correspondence information between depth images and 3D models are not required, so that it can easily be generalized to large-scale databases. In order to evaluate the effectiveness of our approach, depth images (with Kinect-type noise) in the NYU Depth V2 dataset are used as queries to retrieve 3D models of the same categories in the SHREC 2014 dataset. Experimental results suggest that our approach can outperform the state-of-the-arts methods, and the paradigm that directly uses the original representations of depth images and 3D models for retrieval.

Categories and Subject Descriptors

H.3.3 [**Information Search and Retrieval**]: Retrieval models; I.5.4 [**Applications**]: Computer vision

Keywords

Neural network; cross-domain; depth image; retrieval

*: Corresponding Author (Email: yfang@nyu.edu)

MM'15, October 26–30, 2015, Brisbane, Australia.
 ISBN 978-1-4503-3459-4/15/10 ...$15.00.
DOI: http://dx.doi.org/10.1145/2733373.2806323.

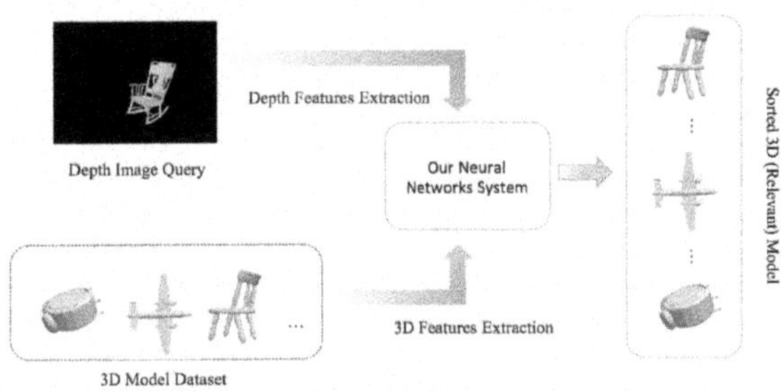

Figure 1: Framework of our proposed cross-domain 3D model retrieval based on depth image query.

1. INTRODUCTION

3D model retrieval has a wide range of applications in the industry, such as architecture and product design. Despite of extensive efforts on 3D model retrieval in recent years, strong requirements on the input queries (normally complete CAD models) have restricted the generalization of its applications. On the other hand, along with the increasing use of handy low-cost depth sensors such as Microsoft Kinect [14], RGBD images are becoming more popular, and as a consequence, large-scale depth images can be more easily accessible. Thus, a novel 3D model retrieval paradigm, depth image-based 3D model retrieval, is motivated and getting popularized in both computer vision and information management communities. A successful depth image-based 3D model retrieval has many potential applications, especially for product designs. While a traditional design process involves a digitization procedure that transforms early stage design drafts into producible CAD models, a depth image-driven retrieval system can avoid such a repetitive and time-consuming procedure by returning a set of relevant existing 3D models based on the depth scan of a query sample, so that designers can directly modify from the retrieved CAD models.

In our work, we exploit the Kinect-typed depth images as queries to retrieve visually similar 3D models from a large collection of 3D model database. In order to alleviate the discrepancy between highly diverged depth images and 3D models, we aim to build an effective cross-domain feature learning framework for depth image-based 3D model retrieval. The pipeline of our framework is shown in Figure 1.

We propose a neural network-based cross-domain feature learning technique by building a neural network pair for depth images and 3D models respectively. In order to reduce the cross-domain discrepancy, we force unique and identical vectors at the target layers of both neural networks in a supervised fashion for data of the same class. By connecting at the target layers of the neural network pair, data that share the same class label but come from diverged domains can be mapped to the same target vectors. When depth image and 3D model features pass through the neural network pair, values in the hidden layers of both networks are extracted as domain-invariant representations, which are used for depth image-based 3D model retrieval. We evaluate our method using two datasets: the 3D model database comes from SHREC 2014 Large Scale Sketch Track Benchmark [12] and depth images come from NYU Depth V2 dataset [17]. Experimental results demonstrate that our method can achieve outstanding performance. The main contributions of our work are as follows:

- ⋆ We address the challenging depth image-based 3D model retrieval problem with a novel neural network-based approach.
- ⋆ We propose a pairwise neural network technique (PNN) that significantly reduces the cross-domain divergence between depth image features and 3D model features.
- ⋆ The proposed method can achieve outstanding performance on the NYU Depth V2 dataset and the SHREC 2014 benchmark.

2. RELATED WORK

Based on the advancements of RGB-D cameras, depth images have been applied to many computer vision areas, such as object detection [8], gesture recognition, image segmentation, (etc. Saurabh et al.[8] proposed a decision forest approach to deal with the object detection problem in depth images. By cooperating RGB-D contours [2] with the popular convolutional neural networks (CNNs) [7], the proposed approach can achieve outstanding object detection performance. In addition to outputting object detection results at the bounding-box level, pixel-level object inferences are also provided. Wu et al. address the depth image-based gesture recognition problem in a one-shot-learning paradigm, where only one sample can be utilized for training in each gesture category. The NYU Depth v2 dataset [17] is a recently released RGBD dataset that provides diverse indoor scenes with detailed objects' location annotations. Rather than clean and single objects, NYU Depth v2 dataset aims to offer messy indoor scenes with the existence of multiple objects.

As a special machine learning paradigm, transfer learning tackles with the domain mismatch problem. Most existing transfer learning methods [10, 13, 21] operate at the feature learning level and aim to obtain a unified representation for two or multiple mismatched domains (e.g., sketch images vs. 3D shapes, and images vs. texts). Rasiwasia et al. [16] address the image-to-text and text-to-image retrieval problem by investigating the correlations between two modalities and the effectiveness of abstraction, where the canonical correlation analysis (CCA) and the use of abstraction are all proved to be effective. In order to validate the contributions of each separate component, three approaches correlation matching (CM), semantic matching (SM) and semantic correlations matching (SCM) are proposed for the correlation modeling, the abstraction method and the joint working mode of both approaches respectively.

While traditional 3D shape retrieval approaches [3, 11, 15, 19, 4] only consider the same domain data as the input queries, increasing attentions are being paid towards different domain queries. Gao et al. retrieve 3D object based on their 2D views by estimating Hausdorff distances [5] and constructing hypergraphs [6] between objects; Li et al. [12] organize a challenge along with a detailed summary on sketch-based 3D shape retrieval, where human freehand sketches are considered as inputs to the 3D shape retrieval system; Wang et al. [18] also consider using low-cost depth images as queries. In this work, we address the lattest challenge with a neural network-based transfer learning method, which brings two highly variant domains into a new feature space with a low cross-domain discrepancy.

3. APPROACH

We aim to learn pairwise neural networks, which can encode the depth image features and 3D model features respectively, and generate a smooth feature space[1] for both domains. Such pairwise neural networks can be obtained by independently optimizing two discriminative neural networks while connecting both networks at their target layers.

3.1 Discriminative Neural Networks

We consider a 3-layer neural network, which has an input layer, a hidden layer and a target layer. Without loss of generality, we denote $\boldsymbol{X} = \{\boldsymbol{x}^1, \boldsymbol{x}^2, \cdots, \boldsymbol{x}^M\} \in \mathbb{R}^{M\times D}$ as the input D-dimensional feature, $\boldsymbol{Y} = \{\boldsymbol{y}^1, \boldsymbol{y}^2, \cdots, \boldsymbol{y}^M\} \in \mathbb{R}^{M\times D'}$ as the D'-dimensional hidden layer features and $\hat{\boldsymbol{X}} = \{\hat{\boldsymbol{x}}^1, \hat{\boldsymbol{x}}^2, \cdots, \hat{\boldsymbol{x}}^P\} \in \mathbb{R}^{M\times D}$ be the D-dimensional target layer features for either depth images or 3D models. The structure of a single 3-layer neural network is illustrated in Figure 2 (Encoder-1 for example). In our implementation, the input layer features and the target layer features have an identical feature dimension. In the training stage, the weights on all neurons within the network are optimizing towards a minimum discrepancy between the input layer features $\boldsymbol{X}$ and the target layer features $\hat{\boldsymbol{X}}$. Once the weights are optimized, the hidden layer values $\boldsymbol{Y}$ can be extracted as encoded features. In order to enhance the extrapolation capability of the encoded features, we aim to train discriminative neural networks by forcing identical target vectors to instances that come from the same category at the target layer. Thus, the objective function for learning a discriminative neural network can be formulated as:

$$\arg\min_{\boldsymbol{W},\boldsymbol{b}} \frac{1}{D}\sum_{i=1}^{D}\|\hat{\boldsymbol{x}}^i - h_{\boldsymbol{W}^l,\boldsymbol{b}^l}(\boldsymbol{x}^i)\|_2^2 + \lambda\sum_{l=1}^{L}\|\boldsymbol{W}^l\|_F^2, \quad \text{s.t.} \quad \hat{\boldsymbol{x}}^i = \hat{\boldsymbol{x}}^j \quad \text{if} \quad q(\boldsymbol{x}^i) = q(\boldsymbol{x}^j) \tag{1}$$

where $\boldsymbol{W} = \{\boldsymbol{W}^1, \boldsymbol{W}^2, \cdots, \boldsymbol{W}^L\} \in \mathbb{R}^{M\times L}$ is the neuron parameters of the neural network and L is the number of layers, $q(\cdot)$ λ is the balancing parameter and W^l is the weight vector at layer l. The function $h_{W,b}(\boldsymbol{x}^p) = f(\sum_{k=1}^{K} w_k x_k^p + b)$ is a sigmoid function, where

$$f(z) = \frac{1}{1 + exp(-z)}. \tag{2}$$

[1]In a smooth feature space, feature points, which are close to each other, are more likely to share the same class label.

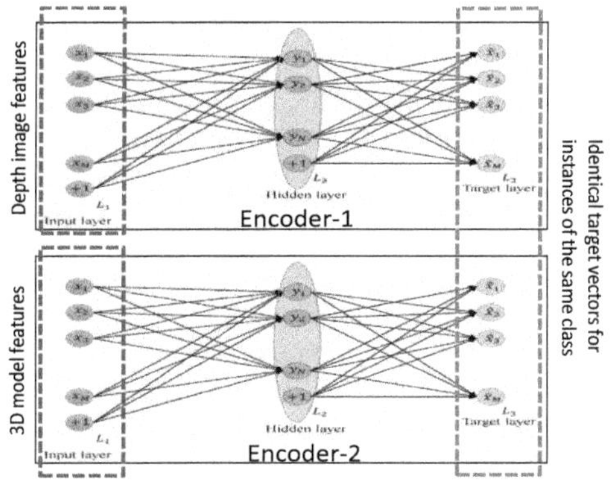

Figure 2: The structure of pairwise neural networks.

3.2 Pairwise Neural Networks

The discriminative neural network can improve the data smoothness in either the depth image domain or the 3D model domain. In order to minimize the data discrepancy between both domains, we use a structure that connects two discriminative neural networks at the target layers. Intuitively, since instances that come from the category are forced to possess identical features at the target ends, the pairwise neural networks are provided with the ability of encoding the same-category cross-domain instances towards similar representations at the hidden layers (see Figure 2). Let $\boldsymbol{X_d} = \{\boldsymbol{x_d^1}, \boldsymbol{x_d^2}, \cdots, \boldsymbol{x_d^{M_d}}\} \in \mathbb{R}^{M_d \times D_d}$ and $\boldsymbol{X_m} = \{\boldsymbol{x_m^1}, \boldsymbol{x_m^2}, \cdots, \boldsymbol{x_m^{M_m}}\} \in \mathbb{R}^{M_m \times D_m}$ be the depth and 3D model domain inputs, and $\boldsymbol{\hat{X}_d} = \{\boldsymbol{\hat{x}_d^1}, \boldsymbol{\hat{x}_d^2}, \cdots, \boldsymbol{\hat{x}_d^{M_d}}\} \in \mathbb{R}^{M_d \times D_d}$ and $\boldsymbol{\hat{X}_m} = \{\boldsymbol{\hat{x}_m^1}, \boldsymbol{\hat{x}_m^2}, \cdots, \boldsymbol{\hat{x}_m^{M_m}}\} \in \mathbb{R}^{M_m \times D_m}$ be the depth and 3D model domain target vectors, respectively, a unified objective function for learning the pairwise neural networks can be formulated as:

$$
\begin{aligned}
&\underset{\boldsymbol{W_d}, \boldsymbol{b_d}}{\arg\min} \frac{1}{M_d} \sum_{i=1}^{M_d} \|\boldsymbol{\hat{x}_d^i} - h_{\boldsymbol{W_d}, \boldsymbol{b_d}}(\boldsymbol{x_d^i})\|_2^2 + \lambda \sum_{l=1}^{L} \|\boldsymbol{W_d^l}\|_F^2, \\
&\underset{\boldsymbol{W_m}, \boldsymbol{b_m}}{\arg\min} \frac{1}{M_m} \sum_{j=1}^{M_m} \|\boldsymbol{\hat{x}_m^j} - h_{\boldsymbol{W_m}, \boldsymbol{b_m}}(\boldsymbol{x_m^j})\|_2^2 + \lambda \sum_{l=1}^{L} \|\boldsymbol{W_m^l}\|_F^2, \\
&\quad \text{s.t.} \quad \boldsymbol{\hat{x}_m^i} = \boldsymbol{\hat{x}_m^j} = \boldsymbol{\hat{x}_d^i} = \boldsymbol{\hat{x}_d^j} \\
&\quad \text{if} \quad q(\boldsymbol{x_m^i}) = q(\boldsymbol{x_m^j}) = q(\boldsymbol{x_d^i}) = q(\boldsymbol{x_d^j}),
\end{aligned} \tag{3}
$$

where W_d, b_d, W_m and b_m are parameters of the depth image network and the 3D model network respectively. Computing optimum parameters of the pairwise neural networks is a regression problem. The typical backpropagation algorithm [9], which can efficiently compute the partial derivatives, is applied to obtain the optimum parameters. Once we obtain the optimum $\boldsymbol{\hat{W}_d}$, $\boldsymbol{\hat{b}_d}$, $\boldsymbol{\hat{W}_m}$ and $\boldsymbol{\hat{b}_m}$, neuron values in L_2 layers are extracted as the representations when depth image and 3D model features pass through the networks.

4. EXPERIMENTS

The NYU Depth V2 dataset [17] contains frames of video sequences in a variety of indoor scenes, from where objects in depth images are extracted as queries in our experiments. The database is constructed by selecting 3D models in corresponding categories from the large-scale extended SHREC 2014 benchmark [12]. The numbers of samples in 7 categories (*bathtub, bathtub, bed, chair, desk, dresser, night stand, table*) of both datasets are given in Table 1. We follow the Sparse Coding Spatial Pyramid Matching (ScSPM) [20] framework for depth image representations, and extract Local Depth Scale-Invariant Features Transform (LD-SIFT) [1] features from 3D models and obtain 1000-dimensional 3D model histogram features by fitting LD-SIFT features to a Bag-of-Words (BoW) model.

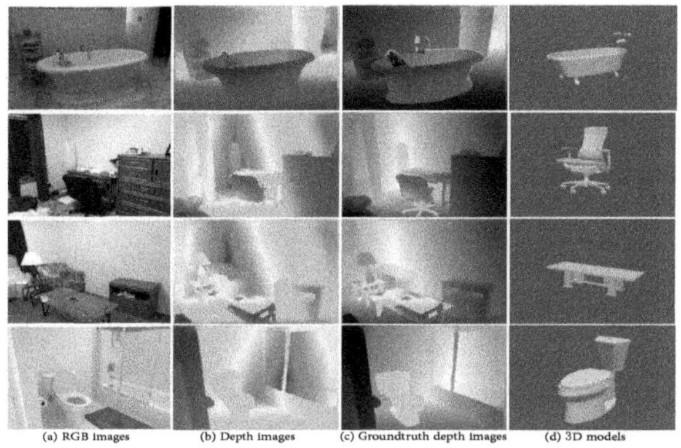

Figure 3: Examples of both the NYU Depth V2 dataset and the SHREC 2014 benchmark. In our experiments, groundtruth depth images (c) are used as queries and 3D models (d) are used as the database.

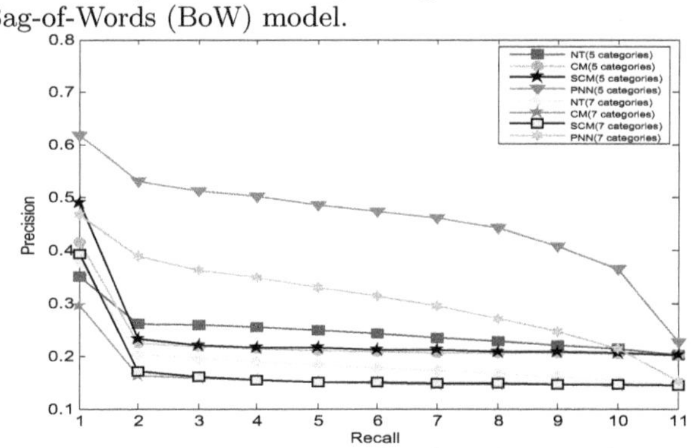

Figure 4: Precision-Recall plot for performance comparison.

We evaluate the proposed approach using 6 common evaluation metrics, Nearest Neighbor (NN), First Tier (FT), Second Tire (ST), E-Measure (E), Discounted Cumulated Gain (DCG) and Average Precision (AP). We conduct experiments using both 5 categories (the first 5 categories as displayed in Table 1) and 7 categories, and compare with the state-of-the-art transfer learning approaches CM and SCM. We also compare with the non-transfer (NT) approach, which directly utilizes the original depth image and 3D model representations for retrieval. Results are reported in Table 2, and the Precision-Recall (PR)-curves for both experiments are given in Figure 4. Experimental results suggest that the proposed PNN method consistently leads the best performance on different settings and evaluation metrics. We can also observe that the performance improvements of PNN over other methods are less significant on 7 categories than 5 categories. We conclude the cause of such performance degradation to the unbalanced numbers of samples across the depth image domain and the 3D model domain. When two domains are supplied with unbalanced numbers of samples for training, the learned neural networks become biased towards the domain with sufficient training samples.

Table 1: Numbers of samples in 7 categories of the NYU Depth V2 dataset and the SHREC 2014 benchmark.

Categories	bathtub	bed	chair	desk
Depth images	52	313	649	192
3D models	76	386	641	147
Categories	dresser	night stand	table	
Depth images	106	302	534	
3D models	140	149	520	

Table 2: Performance metrics comparison of depth image-based 3D model retrieval on the NYU Depth V2 dataset and the SHREC 2014 benchmark.

	NN	FT	ST	DCG	E	AP
7 categories						
NT	0.23	0.14	0.30	0.66	0.02	0.15
CM	0.14	0.14	0.27	0.65	0.02	0.15
SCM	0.14	0.14	0.27	0.65	0.03	0.15
PNN	**0.37**	**0.26**	**0.40**	**0.71**	**0.05**	**0.28**
5 categories						
NT	0.04	0.21	0.39	0.71	0.03	0.21
CM	0.12	0.19	0.39	0.71	0.03	0.20
SCM	0.20	0.18	0.38	0.70	0.02	0.20
PNN	**0.52**	**0.39**	**0.58**	**0.78**	**0.06**	**0.42**

5. CONCLUSIONS

In this work, we address the challenging depth image-based 3D model retrieval problem with a pairwise neural network approach. In order to minimize the discrepancy between highly diverged depth images and 3D models, we build a neural network pair for depth images and 3D models respectively, while enforcing identical target values at output layers of both networks. The proposed PNN method was successfully validated on the NYU Depth Dataset V2 and the extended SHREC 2014 3D shape retrieval benchmark, where the experimental results suggest that PNN can consistently outperform other methods. Moreover, since PNN does not require the correspondence information across different domains, it can be easily generalized.

6. REFERENCES

[1] T. Darom and Y. Keller. Scale-invariant features for 3-d mesh models. *Image Processing, IEEE Transactions on*, 21(5):2758–2769, 2012.

[2] P. Dollár and C. L. Zitnick. Structured forests for fast edge detection. In *International Conference on Computer Vision*, pages 1841–1848. IEEE, 2013.

[3] Y. Fang, M. Sun, and K. Ramani. Temperature distribution descriptor for robust 3d shape retrieval. In *Computer Vision and Pattern Recognition Workshops (CVPRW), 2011 IEEE Computer Society Conference on*, pages 9–16. IEEE, 2011.

[4] Y. Fang, J. Xie, G. Dai, M. Wang, F. Zhu, T. Xu, and E. Wong. 3d deep shape descriptor. In *Proceedings of the IEEE Conference on Computer Vision and Pattern Recognition*, pages 2319–2328, 2015.

[5] Y. Gao, M. Wang, R. Ji, X. Wu, and Q. Dai. 3-d object retrieval with hausdorff distance learning. *Industrial Electronics, IEEE Transactions on*, 61(4):2088–2098, 2014.

[6] Y. Gao, M. Wang, D. Tao, R. Ji, and Q. Dai. 3-d object retrieval and recognition with hypergraph analysis. *Image Processing, IEEE Transactions on*, 21(9):4290–4303, 2012.

[7] R. Girshick, J. Donahue, T. Darrell, and J. Malik. Rich feature hierarchies for accurate object detection and semantic segmentation. In *Computer Vision and Pattern Recognition*, pages 580–587. IEEE, 2014.

[8] S. Gupta, R. Girshick, P. Arbeláez, and J. Malik. Learning rich features from rgb-d images for object detection and segmentation. In *European Conference on Computer Vision*, pages 345–360. Springer, 2014.

[9] G. E. Hinton and R. R. Salakhutdinov. Reducing the dimensionality of data with neural networks. *Science*, 313(5786):504–507, 2006.

[10] K. Hu and Y. Fang. 3d laplacian pyramid signature. In *Computer Vision-ACCV 2014 Workshops*, pages 306–321. Springer, 2014.

[11] G. Leifman, R. Meir, and A. Tal. Semantic-oriented 3d shape retrieval using relevance feedback. *The Visual Computer*, 21(8-10):865–875, 2005.

[12] B. Li, Y. Lu, C. Li, A. Godil, T. Schreck, M. Aono, M. Burtscher, H. Fu, T. Furuya, H. Johan, et al. Shrec' 14 track: Extended large scale sketch-based 3d shape retrieval. In *Eurographics Workshop on 3D Object Retrieval 2014 (3DOR 2014)*, pages 121–130, 2014.

[13] W. Li, L. Duan, D. Xu, and I. W. Tsang. Learning with augmented features for supervised and semi-supervised heterogeneous domain adaptation. *Pattern Analysis and Machine Intelligence, IEEE Transactions on*, 36(6):1134–1148, 2014.

[14] Microsoft. Microsoft kinect description, 2015.

[15] M. Novotni and R. Klein. 3d zernike descriptors for content based shape retrieval. In *Proceedings of the eighth ACM symposium on Solid modeling and applications*, pages 216–225. ACM, 2003.

[16] N. Rasiwasia, J. Costa Pereira, E. Coviello, G. Doyle, G. R. Lanckriet, R. Levy, and N. Vasconcelos. A new approach to cross-modal multimedia retrieval. In *International Conference on Multimedia*, pages 251–260. ACM, 2010.

[17] N. Silberman, D. Hoiem, P. Kohli, and R. Fergus. Indoor segmentation and support inference from rgbd images. In *European Conference on Computer Vision*, pages 746–760. Springer, 2012.

[18] Y. Wang, J. Feng, Z. Wu, J. Wang, and S.-F. Chang. From low-cost depth sensors to cad: Cross-domain 3d shape retrieval via regression tree fields. In *European Conference on Computer Vision*, pages 489–504. Springer, 2014.

[19] J. Xie, Y. Fang, F. Zhu, and E. Wong. Deepshape: Deep learned shape descriptor for 3d shape matching and retrieval. In *Proceedings of the IEEE Conference on Computer Vision and Pattern Recognition*, pages 1275–1283, 2015.

[20] J. Yang, K. Yu, Y. Gong, and T. Huang. Linear spatial pyramid matching using sparse coding for image classification. In *Computer Vision and Pattern Recognition*, pages 1794–1801. IEEE, 2009.

[21] F. Zhu and L. Shao. Weakly-supervised cross-domain dictionary learning for visual recognition. *International Journal of Computer Vision*, 109(1-2):42–59, 2014.

Using the Eyes to "See" the Objects

Concetto Spampinato, Simone Palazzo, Francesca Murabito, Daniela Giordano
Department of Electrical, Electronics and Computeer Engineering
University of Catania
Viale Andrea Doria, 6 Catania - Italy
{cspampin, spalazzo, fmurabito, dgiordano}@dieei.unict.it

ABSTRACT

This paper investigates how to exploit eye gaze data for understanding visual content. In particular, we propose a human-in-the-loop approach for object segmentation in videos, where humans provide significant cues on spatio-temporal relations between object parts (i.e. superpixels in our approach) by simply looking at video sequences. Such constraints, together with object appearance properties, are encoded into an energy function so as to tackle the segmentation problem as a labeling one.

The proposed method uses gaze data from only two people and was tested on two challenging visual benchmarks: 1) SegTrack v2 and 2) FBMS-59. The achieved performance showed how our method outperformed more complex video object segmentation approaches, while reducing the effort needed for collecting human feedback.

1. INTRODUCTION

Object segmentation in videos is a fundamental upstream task for many computer vision applications, such as object tracking, behaviour understanding, event detection. While being a long-researched topic, so far no general solution exists, and current approaches are application domain–specific. Typical methods [3, 11] impose strict assumptions on objects' appearance, motion patterns and on the target videos, and none is able to effectively deal with background motion in complex situations (e.g. camera motion). One of the most recent trends in video object segmentation is to adopt superpixels [12, 7] to increase spatial coherency and the overall quality of the segmented objects. Still, these methods lack a deep understanding of visual content, and as a consequence they are very sensitive to false positives. A promising direction is to include humans in the loop, by having them select intrinsically or extrinsically object parts or attributes [4, 15]. However, it is known that providing human annotations, especially in videos, is a tedious, time-consuming and error-prone task and questions such as "what is the least intrusive way for humans to contribute automated visual tasks?" and "how can we effectively integrate humans' inputs in automated visual tasks?" have to be taken into account.

In this paper we aim at addressing these two questions by developing a human-in-the-loop video object segmentation approach where humans provide intrinsically feedback to the segmentation method by using their eyes, which a) greatly reduces the burden of providing annotations than clicking on frames and b) deals effectively with object motion. Acquiring accurate gaze data needs specific eye-tracking devices: while infrared systems still provide the highest accuracy, in the last years camera-based eye-tracking systems, built into mobile phones, have demonstrated good capabilities in assessing precisely the location of user eyes[1].

We argue that similarly to the rapid development of cameras embedded in mobile devices, more sophisticated eye-tracking tools might be integrated soon into consumer devices, enabling a new generation of human-centered applications supporting automated visual content analysis methods, e.g. having Youtube videos annotated or tagged while users watch them. Under this scenario, we propose an eye gaze–based approach for object segmentation in videos where segmentation is achieved by processing not only eye fixations (as most of the eye gaze–based methods already do) to select the most salient image regions but also saccades for identifying temporal constraints between neighbouring image parts. Our object segmentation method is able to effectively work with fast moving and multimodal backgrounds, highly deformable and/or articulated objects, slow motion and camera motion as demonstrated by the performance achieved on SegTrack v2 [6] and FBMS-59 [11].

2. RELATED WORK

The goal of our work is to perform video object segmentation based on spatio-temporal superpixel modeling [12], but our method is more inline with the new research trend of putting "humans in the loop" [4, 15]. In our approach, users identify moving objects by simply looking at video clips, and, contrary to other crowdsourcing approaches [5] it does not need 1) to check for annotation quality and 2) many users to perform the task, which usually requires complex annotation integration mechanisms. Our video segmentation approach is formulated as a superpixel labeling problem with two labels (foreground and background). In particular, eye gaze data is used to detect a small number of superpixels that are likely to be part of the foreground. These initial

MM'15, October 26–30, 2015, Brisbane, Australia.
© 2015 ACM. ISBN 978-1-4503-3459-4/15/10 ...$15.00.
DOI: http://dx.doi.org/10.1145/2733373.2806324.

[1] As an example, `http://www.samsung.com/us/support/faq/FAQ00053081/62452/SCH-R970ZWAUSC`

seeds, providing cues on salient visual regions, are then converted into spatio-temporal constraints for an energy-based minimization problem.

The way our approach is formulated makes it more similar to interactive segmentation or image annotation/tagging methods [15]. In particular, a few recent works have attempted to understand how humans perform recognition, e.g. by indicating background or foreground seed pixels [1], or by asking them to describe the differences between pairs of images [8]. All these methods employ user clicks to select image seeds; an adaptation of these approaches from static images to videos is found in [5], which uses an online game to gather user clicks for performing video object segmentation. However, processing user clicks in videos may be complex because 1) click speed is much lower than video frame rate, and 2) human reaction times introduce a delay between a click and the video frame it was meant for; as such, these methods need heavy post-processing steps to perform missing click interpolation and projection on the correct frames. A approach relevant to ours is presented in [10], where EEG maps are employed for the initialization of the popular GrabCut algorithm for interactive image segmentation. In recent years, eye gaze data has used with increasingly interest for supporting object segmentation (hence relevant to our work) [9, 13, 14]. However, these methods basically exploit eye fixations to provide priors for other methods, e.g. in [13] the authors use eye gaze data to accurately identity fixations within objects of interest (similarly to [10]), which are then used for object segmentation. Our work differs from the above ones by a) the way user input is provided, i.e. using their eyes, and b) how eye gaze data is used to drive object segmentation. Indeed, our method does not only use eye fixations but also exploits saccadic movements (enconded in our graph-based energy minimization problem) which provide important cues on object motion and on the spatial relations between object parts.

3. OUR METHOD

We pose our video object segmentation task as a three-dimensional (across consecutive frames) graph-based energy minimization problem, which enforces spatio-temporal continuity of visual features and includes constraints based on eye-tracking information: *eye fixations* (steadily maintaining the visual gaze on a single location) and *saccades* (quick movements between two fixations in the same direction).

Let $S_{t-n}, \ldots, S_{t+n}$ be the superpixel segmentations ($S_i = \{s_{i,1}, \ldots, s_{i,m}\}$)[2] of the frames at times $t-n, \ldots, t+n$, with t being the currently processed frame, and let $\mathcal{L}$ be an assignment of the *background* (0) or *foreground* (1) labels to all superpixels. The objective energy function is defined as:

$$E(\mathcal{L}) = \sum_{l_i} V_{a,g}(l_i) + \sum_{(l_i,l_j)\in\mathcal{N}_f} V_f(l_i,l_j) + \sum_{(l_i,l_j)\in\mathcal{N}_t\cup\mathcal{N}_s} V_t(l_i,l_j) \tag{1}$$

The unary potential $V_{a,g}$ defines the cost of assigning each superpixel to either background or foreground, based on the superpixel's appearance and on whether it is located close to *gaze points* (both fixations and saccades). It is computed from two terms, encoding the above information:

$$V_{a,g}(l_i) = -\log\left[\frac{1}{2}\left(a(l_i) + g(l_i)\right)\right] \tag{2}$$

In order to compute the appearance-related part of this cost, $a(l_i)$, we maintain a background model ψ_b and a foreground model ψ_f, both represented through Mixture of Gaussians (MoGs). At initialization, the foreground model ψ_f is computed by fitting a MoG to the pixel color values of all superpixels containing gaze points and their spatial neighbors; the background model ψ_b is similarly initialized from densely-sampled pixels which are distant from gaze points. After initialization, the background and foreground models at time t are computed from the segmentation maps obtained at $t-1$. For each superpixel s_i, we compute its *background likelihood* $p(s_i \mid \psi_b)$ and *foreground likelihood* $p(s_i \mid \psi_f)$, by averaging s_i's pixel likelihoods for the corresponding models. The value $a(l_i)$ is computed as:

$$a(l_i) = \begin{cases} \frac{p(s_i|\psi_f)}{p(s_i|\psi_b)+p(s_i|\psi_f)} & \text{if } l_i = 0 \\ \frac{p(s_i|\psi_b)}{p(s_i|\psi_b)+p(s_i|\psi_f)} & \text{if } l_i = 1 \end{cases} \tag{3}$$

Of course, $a(l_i)$ will be lower if l_i corresponds to the model which best describes s_i's appearance.

Closeness to gaze points is defined as:

$$g(l_i) = e^{-\frac{d^2(s_i,\hat{s}_{g,i})}{\sigma^2_{g,d}} - \frac{\hat{t}_{g,i}}{\sigma^2_{g,t}}} \tag{4}$$

where $d^2(s_i, \hat{s}_{g,i})$ is the squared distance between s_i's centroid and the centroid of its closest superpixel with gaze points, $\hat{s}_{g,i}$, and $\hat{t}_{g,i}$ is the longest eye fixation duration in $\hat{s}_{g,i}$, thus giving more importance to longer and more "reliable" fixations; $\sigma^2_{g,d}$ and $\sigma^2_{g,t}$ are two constants.

The binary potential V_f enforces spatial continuity of superpixel labels in a frame according to visual similarity. It is computed across the set $\mathcal{N}_f$ of all pairs of superpixels which are contiguous within each frame, and defines the cost of assigning two different labels to the superpixels in each pair: the cost should be high if the superpixels are visually similar, since they are likely to belong to the same object and should not be separated. $V_f(l_i, l_j)$ is computed as:

$$V_f(l_i,l_j) = e^{-\frac{d_{\chi^2}(H_i,H_j)}{\sigma^2_f}} \; [l_i \neq l_j] \tag{5}$$

where H_i and H_j are the color histograms of s_i and s_j, $d_{\chi^2}(\cdot,\cdot)$ is the chi-square distance, and the $[p]$ operator returns 1 if p is true and 0 otherwise, i.e. the cost is applied only if the assigned labels are different.

The binary potential V_t enforces temporal continuity of superpixel labels across consecutive frames, based on visual similarity and saccadic movements. It is computed across the set $\mathcal{N}_t$ of pairs of superpixels in two consecutive frames whose centroids are less than 10 pixels far apart, and the set $\mathcal{N}_s$ of pairs of superpixels in two consecutive frames which are linked by a saccadic movement:

$$V_t(l_i,l_j) = \left(e^{-\frac{d_{\chi^2}(H_i,H_j)}{\sigma^2_{t,H}} - \frac{d(s_i,s_j)}{\sigma^2_{t,d}}} + \beta_s \left[(s_i,s_j) \in \mathcal{N}_s\right] \right) \tag{6}$$

where $d(\cdot,\cdot)$ is the Euclidean distance between superpixel centroids, and $\sigma^2_{t,H}$, $\sigma^2_{t,d}$ and β_s are constants and $[l_i \neq l_j]$. In short, temporal superpixel edges are mainly computed

[2]For notation simplicity, we will drop the temporal index for superpixels when it is clear from the context whether two superpixels belong to the same frame or to different frames.

Figure 1: Example results on a slow motion video sequence (*cats01* of FBMS-59). First row: gaze data (fixations and saccades) of two users on two consecutive frames (first two columns), segmentation map not including temporal constraints (third column), and segmentation map when considering eye saccades (fourth column). For each user, there are multiple saccadic points since the Tobii T60 sample rate is higher than the video frame rate. Second row: user clicks (60 users) on the same frames and the related segmentation maps, excluding and including temporal constraints.

based on distance and similarity, but the cost of separating superpixel which also show saccadic movement is increased by β_s.

4. EXPERIMENTAL RESULTS

Experiment settings. We tested our method[3] using a Tobii T60 eye tracker (60 gaze points per second), which provides information on saccades and fixation duration while performing visual tests. We showed several video sequences to two participants and executed the method in Sect. 3. The participants were asked to look at videos without any instructions, in order to enforce bottom-up visual saliency. The method's parameters were identified by exhaustive search on the parameter space and set as follows: $n = 2$, $\sigma^2_{g,d} = \sigma^2_{t,d} = 10000$, $\sigma^2_{g,t} = \frac{1}{3}$, $\sigma^2_f = \sigma^2_{t,H} = \frac{1}{5}$, $\beta_s = 0.4$. Superpixel segmentation was carried out through SLIC [2] and superpixel size was set to 7×7, as a compromise between segmentation errors, sensitivity to noise, and processing speed.

Datasets and baselines. Performance evaluation was carried out on two common visual benchmarks for video object segmentation, SegTrack v2 [6] (containing 13 videos with all frames annotated) and FBMS-59 [11] (composed of 59 sequences and 720 annotated frames), with pixel-accurate segmentation of moving objects. Both datasets are known for being very challenging due to camera motion, slow object motion, object-background similarity, non-rigid deformations and articulated objects. As [12] is one of the first methods based on superpixel segmentation, it was used as the main baseline in all evaluations, using the public source code with default parameters (in order to avoid bias in the comparison). As additional baselines, we tested the approaches in [6, 11], and the approach in Sect. 3 when feedback was provided by clicks (60 users) as in [5]. We did not test the eye-tracking based approaches described in Sect. 2 because either the code was not publicly available [13] or they work only on still images [9].

	[12]	SPT+ CSI [6]	User click as in [5]	Eye Gaze
Bird of Paradise	75.6	**94.0**	81.6	88.6
Birdfall	0	62.5	48.1	**79.8**
BMX	59.5	55.1	58.1	**77.6**
Cheetah	40.6	39.1	33.9	**58.6**
Drifting Car	80.8	67.7	81.3	**82.6**
Frog	52.2	72.3	82.8	**86.1**
Girl	56.3	**89.2**	66.8	85.6
Hummingbird	48.7	63.3	72.6	**80.2**
Monkey	66.3	**84.8**	78.3	82.9
Monkeydog	40.3	45.1	48.4	**66.7**
Parachute	85.6	93.4	88.7	**96.8**
Soldier	44.6	**83.8**	64.7	81.5
Worm	67.6	82.8	72.1	**79.4**

Table 1: Results in terms of Jaccard score on SegTrack v2. The penguin video was discarded as only few penguins were segmented. The results of [12] on Birdfall were 0 as it was not able to fit Mixture of Gaussians for background/foreground models.

Results and discussion. Table 1 shows the achieved performance in terms of Jaccard index of our method compared to our baselines and the SPT+CSI method proposed in [6]. Table 2 shows pixelwise average precision, recall and F-measure achieved by our method, the baselines and [11] on the FBMS-59 dataset. The two tables clearly highlight how the proposed eye gaze–based method outperforms both our baselines and other state-of-the-art approaches on the two considered datasets. On video sequences with slow motion, e.g., *Monkey* or *Frog* (Segtrack v2), the performance of eye-gaze and user click–based method were comparable since

[3]Source code available at `http://perceive.dieei.unict.it/index-parallax.php?id=2015-using-the-eyes-to-see-objects`

Figure 2: Example results on a fast motion video sequence (*Cheetah*, SegTrack v2). Image layout as in Fig. 1.

	Precision	Recall	F-Measure
[12]	72.2	69.1	70.7
[11]	86.0	59.2	70.1
Click-based	77.8	62.3	69.2
Eye gaze–based	83.3	66.2	73.8

Table 2: Results on FBMS-59. Our method is compared to our baselines and [11] on both training and test video sequences.

user clicks were able to follow object motion, while in case of strong motion, e.g., *Cheetah* or *Monkeydog* (Segtrack v2), the user clicks failed to follow objects (see Fig. 2) and as such, segmentation results were sensibly lower.
The performance increase was, of course, much higher when compared to automated methods [12, 11], although there were cases, e.g., *Soldier* (Segtrack v2), where our method's performance was lower because participants were distracted by other salient areas in the videos.
Fig. 1 and 2 report some qualitative results on slow and strong motion video sequences of the eye gaze–based and user click–based methods: including temporal constraints (term V_t in Eq. 1) through saccades' analysis yields a significant performance increase.

The achieved results provide answers to the questions we raised in Sect. 1: 1) including humans in the automatic content analysis allows to obtain high quality video segmentations; 2) using the eyes is the least intrusive and most effective way to provide human feedback (only two users' eye gaze data achieved better performance than 60 users' clicks).

5. REFERENCES

[1] Image segmentation by iterated region merging with localized graph cuts. *Pattern Recognition 44*, 2527 – 2538.

[2] Achanta, R., Shaji, A., and Smith, K. SLIC superpixels compared to state-of-the-art superpixel methods. *IEEE PAMI 6*, 1 (2012), 1–8.

[3] Brutzer, S., Hoferlin, B., and Heidemann, G. Evaluation of background subtraction techniques for video surveillance. In *CVPR 2011*, pp. 1937–1944.

[4] Deng, J., Krause, J., and Fei-Fei, L. Fine-grained crowdsourcing for fine-grained recognition. In *CVPR 2013*, pp. 580–587.

[5] Kavasidis, I., Spampinato, C., and Giordano, D. Generation of ground truth for object detection while playing an online game: Productive gaming or recreational working? In *CVPRW 2013*, pp. 694–699.

[6] Li, F., Kim, T., Humayun, A., Tsai, D., and Rehg, J. M. Video segmentation by tracking many figure-ground segments. In *ICCV* (2013).

[7] Lim, J., and Han, B. Generalized background subtraction using superpixels with label integrated motion estimation. In *ECCV 2014*. 2014, pp. 173–187.

[8] Maji, S. Discovering a lexicon of parts and attributes. In *ECCV 2012 Workshops*. 2012, pp. 21–30.

[9] Mishra, A. K., and Aloimonos, Y. Active segmentation with fixation. In *ICCV* (2009).

[10] Mohedano, E., Healy, G., McGuinness, K., Giró-i Nieto, X., O'Connor, N. E., and Smeaton, A. F. Object segmentation in images using eeg signals. In *ACM MM '14* (New York, NY, USA), ACM, pp. 417–426.

[11] Ochs, P., Malik, J., and Brox, T. Segmentation of moving objects by long term video analysis. *IEEE PAMI 36*, 6, 1187–1200.

[12] Papazoglou, A., and Ferrari, V. Fast Object Segmentation in Unconstrained Video. *ICCV'13*, 1777–1784.

[13] Shanmuga Vadivel, K., Ngo, T., Eckstein, M., and Manjunath, B. Eye tracking assisted extraction of attentionally important objects from videos.

[14] Walber, T., Scherp, A., and Staab, S. Can you see it? two novel eye-tracking-based measures for assigning tags to image regions. In *Advances in Multimedia Modeling*, vol. 7732. 2013, pp. 36–46.

[15] Wu, J., Zhao, Y., Zhu, J.-Y., Luo, S., and Tu, Z. Milcut: A sweeping line multiple instance learning paradigm for interactive image segmentation. In *CVPR 2014*, pp. 256–263.

Discriminative Light Unsupervised Learning Network for Image Representation and Classification

Le Dong
Univ. of Electronic Science and Technology of China
ledong@uestc.edu.cn

Ling He
Univ. of Electronic Science and Technology of China
aleenheling@163.com

Qianni Zhang
Queen Mary Univ. of London
qianni.zhang@qmul.ac.uk

ABSTRACT

This paper proposes a discriminative light unsupervised learning network (DLUN) to counter the image classification challenge. Compared with the traditional convolutional networks learning filters by the time-consuming stochastic gradient descent, DLUN learns the filter bank from diverse image patches with the classical K-means, which significantly reduces the training complexity while maintains the high discriminative ability. Besides, we design a new pooling strategy named voting pooling which considers the contribution difference of the adjacent activations. In the output layer, DLUN computes histograms in the size-changed dense sliding windows, followed by a max pooling operation on histogram bins at different scales to obtain the most competitive features. The classification performance on two widely used benchmarks verifies that DLUN is competitive among some state-of-the-arts.

Categories and Subject Descriptors

I.4.10 [**Image Processing and Computer Vision**]: Image Representation—*Hierarchical*

General Terms

Algorithms, Experimentation, Performance

Keywords

Image Representation, Image Classification, Unsupervised learning network

1. INTRODUCTION

Image classification has long been a challenging task in vision community, especially when the image amount and intra-class variability get continually increasing. Numerous efforts have been made to counter this significant challenge, among which the convolutional neural networks (CNNs) have recently demonstrated impressive progress. The success of CNNs is attributed to their ability to learn rich mid-level image representations instead of hand-designed low-level features. Typically, filter bank learning plays a central role in CNNs. In general, previous CNNs optimize the filter bank by utilizing the stochastic gradient descent (SGD) method, which strictly relies on the expertise of parameter initiation and fine tuning.

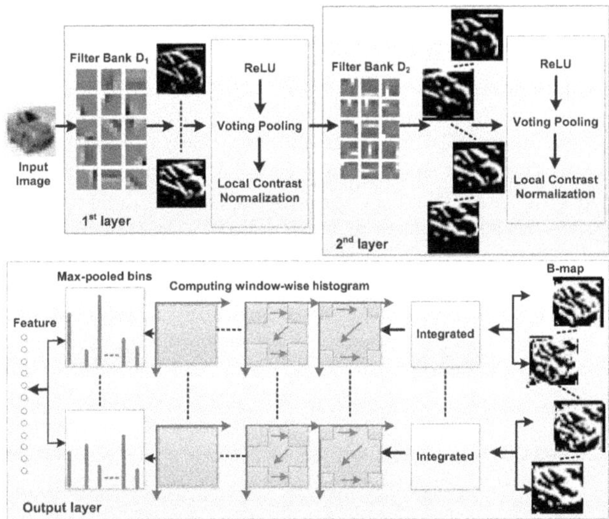

Figure 1: DLUN framework.

In this paper, we propose to address the image classification problem via a discriminative light unsupervised network (DLUN). Figure 1 illustrates the DLUN framework of two layers. Specifically, the system starts by using the classical K-means to learn the filter bank from the preprocessed image patches. K-means has been widely employed to gain a visual codebook [9] [8] in the vision community while seldom used to produce filters for convolution. After convolving the images to gain response maps, we maintain the Rectified Linear Units (ReLUs) to speed up subsequent training. Then, the proposed voting pooling is implemented, followed by the local contrast normalization among the feature maps. The second hidden layer is constructed in a similar manner, except that the filter banks are learned from feature map patches gained from the first layer. In the output layer, histograms are computed. To obtain the image spatial information, the histograms are computed in the dense size-changed sliding windows at different levels, which, however, might incur the high dimension and feature redundancy

MM '15 October 26-30, 2015, Brisbane, Australia.

DOI: http://dx.doi.org/10.1145/2733373.2806325.

issue. To resolve this issue, we implement max-pooling on histogram bins, which means that only the most competent activations are maintained for high discriminative ability.

The contributions of this paper can be concluded as follows: (1) the straightforward filter learning procedure bypasses the time-consuming tuning of millions of parameters and avoids falling into local optimum; (2) the proposed voting pooling considers the different contributions of all the activations in the pooling region, and thus improves the robustness to small image distortions; (3) computing histograms in dense size-changed sliding windows at different levels entails high discriminative ability of geometric variance.

2. DISCRIMINATIVE LIGHT UNSUPERVISED NETWORK

Suppose we are given N unlabeled input images $\{X_n\}_{n=1}^{N}$ of size $W \times H \times d$, where $d = 1$ for gray images and $d = 3$ for RGB ones. DLUN begins by extracting random patches from the train images in $\{X_n\}_{n=1}^{N}$. Each $w - by - h$ patch can be denoted as a vector in $\mathscr{R}$ of pixel intensity values, with $M = w \times h \times d$. Then, we can construct a dataset containing T randomly extracted patches, $P = \{p_1, \cdots, p_t, \cdots, p_T\}$, where $p_t \in \mathscr{R}$. Each patch p_t is normalized by subtracting the mean and dividing by the standard deviation of its elements. After normalizing each input vector, we apply the whitening operation over the whole dataset P. Then, we obtain the pre-processed input dataset $\bar{P} = \{\bar{p_1}, \cdots, \bar{p_2}, \cdots, \bar{p_T}\}$. Experimental results demonstrate that the filters gained from preprocessed data possess higher discriminative ability.

2.1 Unsupervised Feature Learning

Assuming that the number of filters in the first layer is K_1, we run K-means on $\bar{P}$ to get the clustering centroid denoted as $D_1 = \{d_1, \cdots, d_{k_1}, \cdots, d_{K_1}\} \in \mathscr{R}^{\times K_1}$ where each centroid d_{k_1} will act as a convolution filter in subsequent stages. We convolve each training image X_n with the K_1 filters:

$$O_n^1 = X_n \otimes D_1, n = 1, \cdots, N \tag{1}$$

where $O_n^1 = \left\{f_n^{1(1)}, \cdots, f_n^{1(k_1)}, \cdots, f_n^{1(K_1)}\right\}$ is the first layer's feature map set of X_n, $f_n^{1(k_1)}$ is the feature map of X_n convolved by the filter d_{k_1}, and $\otimes$ denotes the $2D$ convolution operation.

[7] has demonstrated that deep convolutional neural networks with ReLUs (Rectified Linear Units, the non-saturating nonlinearity $f(x) = max(0, x)$) train several times faster than their equivalents with tanh units $f(x) = tanh(x)$. Therefore, DLUN likewise adopts ReLUs to accomplish subsequent efficient processing.

2.1.1 *Voting pooling*

To build robustness to small distortions, we set the pooling layer after the activation layer just as most of the traditional CNN architectures do. Conventional pooling usually includes two popular choices, *i.e.* average pooling and max pooling. Max pooling captures the largest response values, which might lose the useful information of the small ones. As for average pooling, it aggregates local statistics information by preventing large response values taking over and small ones being removed out. However, since average pooling treats each neuron equally, the usefulness of each neuron's response might be confused. To this end, we propose a new pooling strategy named voting pooling, which considers each neuron's response as well as its response's contribution account in the whole neurons' responses. Suppose that the pooling window is of size $p_w - by - p_h$, the response value of each neuron is $a_{i,j}$, with $i = 1, \cdots, w; j = 1, \cdots, h$. Then, the pooling results of the $p_w - by - p_h$ window can be calculated according to Eq.(2):

$$P_{result} = \begin{cases} 0, if sum(a_{i,j}) = 0 \\ \sum_i \sum_j \frac{a_{i,j} \times a_{i,j}}{sum(a_{i,j})}, otherwise \end{cases} \tag{2}$$

where $sum(a_{i,j})$ is the sum of all the neurons' response value in the pooling window. Since that the pooling layer is set after ReLUs, the voting pooling can be directly implemented with no concern of negative activations. The proposed voting pooling will capture different proportion of local information of each neuron in the original feature map, thus leading to a better local representation.

2.1.2 *Local contrast normalization*

Given the pooled feature maps, we apply the local contrast normalization operation to enforce a sort of local competition among adjacent units in a feature map and among units at the same spatial location over a set of feature maps. Local contrast normalization is implemented among a set of feature maps corresponding to the K_L (L is the layer number, and the L-th layer has K_L filters) outputs of the filter bank D_L over an input. Taking the aforementioned $O_n^1 = \left\{f_n^{1(1)}, \cdots, f_n^{1(k_1)}, \cdots, f_n^{1(K_1)}\right\}$ for example, local contrast normalization performs local subtractive and divisive normalization over O_n^1. The subtractive normalization is computed according to:

$$a_{i,j}^{1(k_1)} = a_{i,j}^{1(k_1)} - \sum_{u,v} w_{u,v} \bullet w_{u,v}(a_{i,j}^{1(k_1)}) \tag{3}$$

where $a_{i,j}^{1(k_1)}$ is an unit in feature map $f_n^{1(k_1)}$, $w_{u,v}$ is a Gaussian window of size $u \times v$, $w_{u,v}(a_{i,j}^{1(k_1)})$ is the neighborhoods of $a_{i,j}^{1(k_1)}$ in the same region size as $w_{u,v}$. The divisive normalization is applied on the subtractive normalized feature maps:

$$a_{i,j}^{1(k_1)} = \frac{a_{i,j}^{1(k_1)}}{var(a_{i,j}^{1(1)}, a_{i,j}^{1(2)}, \cdots, a_{i,j}^{1(K_1)})}, k_1 = 1, \cdots, K_1 \tag{4}$$

where $var(a_{i,j}^{1(1)}, \cdots, a_{i,j}^{1(k_1)}, \cdots, a_{i,j}^{1(K_1)})$ is the variance of the unit $a_{i,j}^{1(k_1)} (k_1 = 1, \cdots, K_1)$ in the spatial position (i, j).

Thus, one layer of DLUN is accomplished, including four main stages: convolution, non-linear rectification, probabilistic pooling, and local contrast normalization. Note that the feature map size is maintained as the original input image, the convolution and pooling operations both pad the images (feature maps) with zeros. Subsequent hidden layers are in a similar formulation with the first layer.

2.2 Feature Extraction Beyond SPM

From the two-layer stacked DLUN presented in Figure 1, in the second layer, each of the K_1 feature maps $f_n^{1(k_1)}$ has K_2 outputs $F_n^2 = \left\{f_n^{2(1)}, f_n^{2(2)}, \cdots, f_n^{2(K_2)}\right\}$. First, each set of the K_2 feature maps are binary mapped, where each unit value is set as 1 if it is positive and 0 if non-positive. Thus, the feature maps are all composed of ones and zeros, and we call these B-maps. Obviously, such crude mapping inevitably loses some useful feature information. To obtain complementary feature information, we integrate the K_2 B-maps in F_n^2 into one integer-valued image:

$$I = \sum_{i=1}^{K_2} f_n^{2(i)} \tag{5}$$

[1] implements a similar integration with each feature map multiplied a coefficient $\lambda_i = 2^{i-1}$, which undoubtedly results in high dimension of features in subsequent histograms computing. Instead, we choose to learn more filters and still control the feature dimension in a reasonable scope.

For each group of K_1 feature maps in O_n^1 , we can obtain its corresponding image I_{k_1} with $k_1 = 1, \cdots, K_1$. Next, we simply compute the histogram of each I_{k_1} to gain the final image representation, just in the similar manner of [1]. Differently, considering the robustness that geometric invariance brings to image classification and matching of highly variable scenes, we propose to compute the histogram in a dense window-wise fashion. Previous works commonly adopt the SPM (Spatial Pyramid Matching) [4] model to gain geometric invariance, while we argue that the sparse partition of SPM still fails to capture enough local geometric invariance. To this end, we adopt a much denser partition to maximize the spatial information gained from the input image, which will help improve invariance to larger-scale and more global deformations. Specifically, a window of size $h_1 \times h_2$ slides over the whole image with stride s. When the window finishes sliding over the whole image, h_1 and h_2 are reset. Multiple level (assuming the total level number is W) of windows of different sizes are applied to accomplish the dense capture of the image's spatial information, and the last window size is the same as the original image, which ensures preserving the global spatial layout.

We simply compute the histogram over each window and concatenate all the histogram vectors to represent the original input image. To remove the feature redundancy, we pool these histograms gained from each level of windows [4]. In particular, we partition the image into $2^l \times 2^l$ blocks with $l = 0, 1, 2$, and pool the bins over one block in a max-pooling fashion. Thus, the dimension of the final image representation can be reduced to $[(W-1)\times 21\times(K_2+1)+(K_2+1)]\times K_1$ (the second (K_2+1) means that the bins gained at the W_{th} level, i.e. computing histograms over the whole image, need not be pooled). The representation is somewhat sparse due to the restricted number of bins in a single block.

3. EXPERIMENTAL EVALUATION

We evaluate the performance of DLUN on two benchmark datasets: STL-10 and MNIST. The networks used for the two datasets both consist of two stacked layers, followed by a linear SVM. More particular experimental settings are presented in subsequent sections.

3.1 Datasets

STL-10 consists of 96-by-96 pixels color images belonging to 10 different classes. Each class provides 500 training examples and 800 test examples. We downsampled the STL-10 images into 32×32 pixels for a simpler configuration. The standard MNIST consists of 28-by-28 greyscale images of handwritten digits 0-9, with 60,000 training and 10,000 test examples. The STL-10 dataset is used to verify our model's feasibility on small training data, and MNIST presents large training data.

3.2 Classification Performance

For STL-10, we learn $K_1 = 35$ and $K_2 = 30$ filters of size 5×5. Both the two layers set their voting pooling size as 2×2, and the pooling windows are overlapped with one pixel stride. The window-wise extraction is implemented at three levels: 8×8 with stride $s = 1$; 16×16 with $s = 1$; 32×32, exactly contains the whole image. The configuration of DLUN used for MNIST is different from that for STL-10 in two aspects: 1) the filter number is $K_1 = 25$ and $K_2 = 25$; 2) the dense window-wise extraction is similarly computed at three levels, while the window size is set as 7×7, 14×14, and 28×28, respectively.

Table 1: Comparison of error rate(%) of different methods on STL-10. $\oplus$ means with the operation and $\ominus$ means without.

Methods	Error rate(%)
DLUN $\oplus$ Voting pooling $\oplus$ whitening	41.36
DLUN $\oplus$ Voting pooling $\ominus$ whitening	54.64
DLUN $\oplus$ Max pooling $\oplus$ whitening	41.68
DLUN $\oplus$ Average pooling $\oplus$ whitening	41.75
2x PDL (1600 codes)[6]	41.72
Sparse TIRBM (combined) [10]	41.3
K-means(K=1600) [2]	48.5
VQ(K=1600) [3]	45.1
SC(K=1600) [3]	41

Table 2: Comparison of error rate(%) of different methods on standard MNIST. $\oplus$ means with the operation and $\ominus$ means without.

Methods	Error rate(%)
DLUN $\oplus$ Voting pooling $\oplus$ whitening	0.79
DLUN $\oplus$ Voting pooling $\ominus$ whitening	0.91
DLUN $\oplus$ Max pooling $\oplus$ whitening	0.82
DLUN $\oplus$ Average pooling $\oplus$ whitening	0.82
HSC [13]	0.77
DropConnect(relu)[12]	1.12
SOAE-σ [11]	0.75
Beyond Spatial Pyramids [5]	0.64

Table 1 gives the performance comparison of different methods on STL-10. With voting pooling and whitening, DLUN provides the most desirable result. When the voting pooling is replaced with max pooling or average pooling, the classification accuracy would decrease by 0.32% and 0.39%, respectively.

Table 2 presents the error rate of different works on MNIST. For fair comparison, we do not include the results of methods using augmented training samples. We observe that DLUN is comparable with the state-of-the-art methods on the standard MNIST benchmark. Since MNIST has many training samples, all methods perform very well and very close, thus, the subtle performance difference is not so statistically meaningful.

3.3 Impact of the number of filters

In this section, we conduct experiments to validate the impact of the number of filters on DLUN. For STL-10, we vary K_2 from 20 to 35 and fix $K_1 = 35$. For the simpler MNIST, we fix $K_1 = 25$ and vary K_2 from 15 to 30. The settings of voting pooling size and the dense window-wise extraction are the same as that stated in Subsection 3.2.

All the results provided in Figure 2(a) and Figure 2(b) are the average of five test runs. From Figure 2(a), we observe that STL-10 gains performance improvement when the filter number increases, and we get the lowest error when $K_2 = 30$. When K_2 is set larger than 30, the accuracy on STL-10 starts to show little change. Figure 2(b) shows similar trend with Figure 2(a). When the filter number K_2 is 25, MNIST achieves the lowest error rate, and likewise, the error rate shows little change if K_2 is larger than 25. From the aforementioned observation, more filters will certainly help improve the classification performance as expected. However, when the filter number achieves its saturation value, the classification performance will even decrease along with the increasing filters. We attribute such phenomenon to the useless duplicates of the filters. The repeated filters will contribute nothing and even drag down the final classification performance.

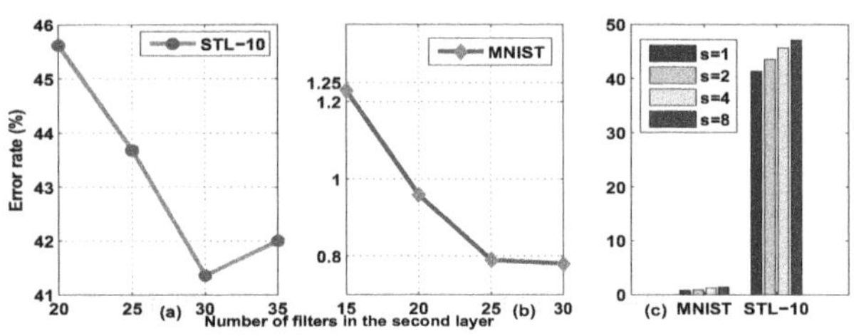

Figure 2: (a)-(b) Impact of the number of filters; (c) Impact of the window-wise extraction.

3.4 Impact of the window-wise extraction

In this part, we test the feasibility of our proposed window-wise extraction. For convenience, we padded the MNIST images with zeros to make them 32-by-32 pixels. The windows are extracted at three levels: $Level = 1$: the window size is 8×8; $Level = 2$: 16×16; $Level = 3$: 32×32. In the first round, we set the stride size between each 8×8 window as $s = 1$ pixel, and the same stride (*i.e.* one pixel) goes for the 16×16 windows. In the second and third turn, the stride size is set as $s = 2$ pixels and $s = 4$ pixels, respectively. In the fourth turn, the stride size is set as $s = 8$ pixels, which thus returns to the SPM model. Other settings of DLUN are the same as the previous subsections have discussed (*i.e.* those parameter settings make each dataset achieve the best performance).

Figure 2(c) illustrates the results comparison of different stride size on the four datasets. Likewise, all the results are the average of five test runs. From Figure 2(c), we observe that the classification performance will decrease at different extent when the stride size grows. For STL-10, the effect of the stride size on the final performance is obvious, while for MNIST, the effect is subtle. Thus, the spatial information is not very important for such dataset to accomplish recognition. However, STL-10 is a relatively complex dataset, containing different objects such as cars, dogs, *etc.* Hence, spatial information shows strong necessity to capture the mouth and the ears of a dog, or the wheels of a car. In practical applications, the dense window extraction level can be set larger, which we think is helpful for a relatively complicated dataset.

4. CONCLUSIONS

We proposed a new network DLUN for image classification in this paper. Pursuing the compactness without compromising the discriminative ability, some elegant strategies are designed to accomplish DLUN in a straightforward manner. Experiments demonstrate that DLUN can still show its competitiveness in the significant classification tasks. In future work, we would like to further simplify DLUN and make it feasible for more challenging benchmarks.

5. ACKNOWLEDGMENTS

This work was supported in part by NSFC 61370149, FRFCU (No.ZYGX2013J083), and SRF for ROCS, SEM (LXHG42DL).

6. REFERENCES

[1] T.-H. Chan, K. Jia, S. Gao, J. Lu, Z. Zeng, and Y. Ma. Pcanet: A simple deep learning baseline for image classification? *In arXiv:1404.3606v2.*, 2014.

[2] A. Coates, H. Lee, and A. Y. Ng. An analysis of single-layer networks in unsupervised feature learning. *In AISTATS 14*, 2011.

[3] A. Coates and A. Y. Ng. The importance of encoding versus training with sparse coding and vector quantization. *In ICML*, 2011.

[4] K. He, X. Zhang, S. Ren, and J. Sun. Spatial pyramid pooling in deep convolutional networks for visual recognition. *In ECCV*, 2014.

[5] Y. Jia, C. Huang, and T. Darrell. Beyond spatial pyramids: Receptive field learning for pooled image features. *In CVPR*, 2012.

[6] Y. Jia, O. Vinyals, and T. Darrell. Pooling-invariant image feature learning. *In arXiv:1302.5056v1*, 2013.

[7] A. Krizhevsky, I. Sutskever, and G. E. Hinton. Imagenet classification with deep convolutional neural network. *In NIPS*, 2012.

[8] D. Li, L. Yang, X.-S. Hua, and H.-J. Zhang. Large-scale robust visual codebook construction. *In ACM MM*, 2010.

[9] Y. Liang, L. Dong, S. Xie, N. Lv, and Z. Xu. Compact feature based clustering for large-scale image retrieval. *In ICME*, 2014.

[10] K. Sohn and H. Lee. Learning invariant representations with local transformations. *In ICML*, 2012.

[11] M. Thom and G. Palm. Sparse activity and sparse connectivity in supervised learning. *Journal of Machine Learning Research*, 14(3):1091–1143, 2013.

[12] L. Wan, M. Zeiler, S. Zhang, Y. LeCun, and R. Fergus. Regularization of neural networks using dropconnect. *In ICML*, 2013.

[13] K. Yu, Y. Lin, and J. Lafferty. Learning image representations from the pixel level via hierarchical sparse coding. *In CVPR*, 2011.

Ranking Optimization for Person Re-identification via Similarity and Dissimilarity

Mang Ye[1], Chao Liang[1,2,*], Zheng Wang[1], Qingming Leng[3], Jun Chen[1,2]

[1]National Engineering Research Center for Multimedia Software,
School of Computer, Wuhan University, Wuhan, 430072, China
{yemang,cliang,wangzwhu,chenj}@whu.edu.cn
[2]Collaborative Innovation Center of Geospatial Technology, Wuhan, China.
[3]School of Information Science & Technology, Jiujiang University, China
lengqingming@126.com

ABSTRACT

Person re-identification is a key technique to match different persons observed in non-overlapping camera views.Many researchers treat it as a special object retrieval problem, where ranking optimization plays an important role. Existing ranking optimization methods utilize the similarity relationship between the probe and gallery images to optimize the original ranking list in which dissimilarity relationship is seldomly investigated. In this paper, we propose to use both similarity and dissimilarity cues in a ranking optimization framework for person re-identification. Its core idea is based on the phenomenon that the true match should not only be similar to the strong similar samples of the probe but also dissimilar to the strong dissimilar samples. Extensive experiments have shown the great superiority of the proposed ranking optimization method.

Categories and Subject Descriptors

J.m [**Computer Applications**]: Miscellaneous;
H.3.3 [**Information Systems**]: INFORMATION STORAGE AND RETRIEVAL— *Retrieval models*

General Terms

Theory

Keywords

Person Re-identification, ranking optimization, similarity and dissimilarity

1. INTRODUCTION

In recent years, person re-identification (re-id) problem, namely matching people across disjoint camera views in a multi-camera system, has aroused an increasing interest in the multimedia analysis community [1]. The main challenges in person re-identification can be attributed to the significant visual changes in pose, illumination and viewpoint, making intra-personal variations even larger than that of inter-personal variations. Moreover, background clutters and occlusions cause additional difficulties.

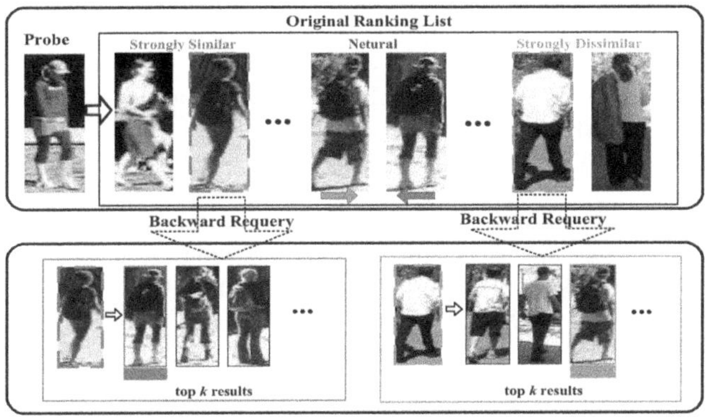

Figure 1: An illustration of our main idea. The first row is the original rank list, while the second row denotes some backward re-query top-k results of the new probes. The ones similar to the strongly similar samples are more likely to be the correct match and should be pulled, while the samples similar to strongly dissimilar samples are the wrong match and should be pushed.

To tackle the above problems, existing person re-id methods can be roughly divided into three categories [16]: appearance representation methods, metric learning methods, and ranking optimization methods. Appearance representation methods [2,4,11,19] aim to seek distinctive descriptions by utilizing the the structure and position of the human body. Metric learning methods [5,8,12,21] attempt to learn a proper distance metric to obtain an accurate similarity measurement to reduce the differences in disjoint camera images. Ranking optimization methods [6,7,9,13,17] try to refine the original ranking lists by establishing the similarity relationships lying in the identification results. While the ranking optimization methods based on ranking orders do not rely on the similarity scores, which own more flexibility and popularity, thus can be easily reproduced [10]. Therefore, we focus on order-based ranking optimization method in this paper.

Related ranking optimization methods can be categorized as automotive re-ranking and interactive relevance feedback. Li *et al.* [7] analyzed the commonness of the near neighbors

---

*indicates corresponding author

MM'15, October 26–30, 2015, Brisbane, Australia.

DOI: http://dx.doi.org/10.1145/2733373.2806326.

to optimize the issue. Leng *et al.* [6] proposed a automatic bidirectional ranking method based on content and context similarities. In this paper, we utilize the similarity relationships among samples to optimize the original ranking list with a common phenomenon. Both the similarity and dissimilarity cues are considered for person re-identification. A latent assumption is that true match should not only be similar to the strongly similar samples but also dissimilar to the strongly dissimilar samples of the probe person.

Motivated by the basic principles in social networks [6], good friends always trend to have more common friends. In other words, if a person is strongly similar to the friends (strongly similar samples) of the probe person, he will be more likely to be a friend of the probe, we name this phenomenon as *conductive similarity.* On the other hand, if a person is very similar to the strangers (strongly dissimilar samples) of the probe person, it is more prone to be a dissimilar sample of the probe person, we name it as *insulative dissimilarity.* An illustration example is shown in Fig.1. Furthermore, an objective statistic data is conducted by a preliminary experiment as shown in Fig.2, the top-10 results are treated as strongly similar samples while the bottom-10 as strongly dissimilar samples. As a reference, the neutral samples are denoted by the middle-10 samples. For each probe, we compute the pair-wise distance between the true match (groundtruth) and other gallery images. The average distance of the true match to the strongly similar samples is reported as "Avg_sim", while "Avg_neu" and "Avg_dis" represents the distance to neutral samples and strongly dissimilar samples, respectively. As can be seen from the figure, the true match are much likely to be similar to the strongly similar samples and dissimilar to strongly dissimilar samples. Therefore, it is reasonable to optimize the original ranking list based on the conductive similarity and insulative dissimilarity.

In this paper, a ranking optimization method for person re-identification is presented. More specifically, the quasi-similar samples (which are similar to strongly similar samples) are pulled while the quasi-dissimilar samples (which are similar to strongly dissimilar samples) are pushed to optimize the original ranking list. The main contribution of this paper can be summarized as follows: (1) We present a combination of similarity and dissimilarity cues while dissimilarity is seldom conducted in person re-identification. (2) The ranking optimization is conducted based on ranking orders which can be easily applied to other method. We have validated our approach on two public datasets, the VIPeR [3] and CUHK01 [14]. The experimental results illustrate the effectiveness of our method and the optimized results compare favorably with state-of-the-art methods.

2. OUR APPROACH

2.1 Similarity Ranking Optimization

Similarity ranking optimization is divided into three steps: First, the strongly similar samples are obtained by the top-k results achieved by an original method. Second, the strongly similar samples are treated as new probes to re-query in the original gallery set, named backward re-query [6]. For each strongly similar sample, the weighted Jaccard similarity coefficient of two neighborhood image sets is computed as the new similarity to the probe image. After that, those quasi-similar samples are pulled based on their frequencies and a

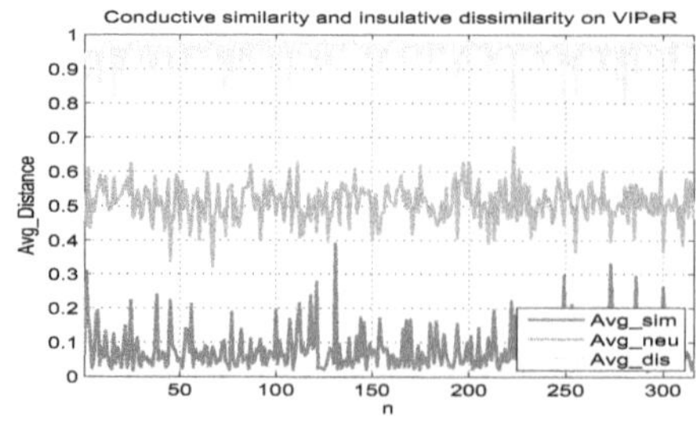

Figure 2: An illustration of our *conductive similarity* and *insulative dissimilarity.* The preliminary experiment is conducted by KISSME [5]. 316 image pairs are randomly selected from the VIPeR dataset [3] for testing. Note that the distances between true matches and the strongly similar samples are significantly lower than those of strongly dissimilar samples.

refined ranking list is generated. The details are discussed as follows.

In order to facilitate the following discussion, we denote the probe image as p and the gallery image set as $G = \{g_i \mid i = 1, 2, ..., n\}$, where n is the number of images in gallery set. An initial ranking list is achieved for a query p, and the top-k (k_+) matching results are defined as the strongly similar samples, $N_+(p) = \{g_+^j \mid j = 1, 2, ...k_+\}$.

After achieving k_+ strongly similar samples, we treat each g_+^j in $N_+(p)$ as a new probe to search in the original gallery set. A new ranking list is obtained for each g_+^j. Similar to [6], images of the same person are intended to have more common k-nearest neighbors than that of different persons. Therefore, a weighted Jaccard similarity between the neighborhoods of p and g_+^j is computed by:

$$Sim(p, g_+^j) = {w_0}^{r(p,g_+^j)} \frac{|N_+(p) \cap N_+(g_+^j)|}{|N_+(p) \cup N_+(g_+^j)|} \quad (1)$$

where $|\cdot|$ denotes the cardinality and $N_{k_+}(g_+^j)$ is the k-nearest neighbours of g_+^j achieved by the backward requery. And first item is a smoothing coefficient related to the original rank in $N_+(p)$. The decay factor is define as w_0 and we set $w_0 = 0.8$ as [18] in all experiments. $r(p, g_+^j)$ represents the rank of g_+^j in the original ranking list and expresses the original similarity.

Above procedure mainly focus on optimizing the ranking orders of the strongly similar samples, and then the whole ranking lists order can be revised via conductive similarity. The detail is shown as following, after the backward requery, we'll get k_+ ranking lists, and each top-k results of the backward ranking list is expressed by $N_{k_+}(g_+^j)$. The quasi-similar set $Q_+(p)$ is denoted by the union set of top-k results $Q_+(p) = \{N_{k_+}(g_+^j) \mid j = 1, 2, ...k_+\}$. The weighted penalization of each quasi-similar sample q_+ is denoted by $w_+^t(q_+)$, which is defined by its frequency and rank in $Q_+(p)$, which is formulated by:

$$w_+^t(q_+) = \sum_{k=1}^{k_+} log\{r(p, g_+^j) \cdot r(g_+^j, q_+)\} \quad (2)$$

where $r(p, g_+^j)$ denotes the original rank of g_+^j in the original ranking list and $r(g_+^j, q_+)$ represents the rank of q_+ in $N_{k_+}(g_+^j)$. Note that if q_+ is not an element of $N_{k_+}(g_+^j)$, we set $r(g_+^j, q_+)$ as k_+. Thus penalization can be extended to a general version for each g_i, the penalization of each gallery image g_i is rewritten as:

$$w_+^t(g_i) = \sum_{k=1}^{k_+} log\{r(p, g_+^j) \cdot r(g_+^j, g_i)\} \quad (3)$$

where $r(p, g_+^j)$ is set as k_+ if g_i is not a member of $Q_+(p)$. It can be seen that the one which is more likely to be the true match is assigned with a smaller penalization and vice versa. Therefore, the ranking list is refined by:

$$r'(g_i) = r(g_i) \cdot e^{w_+^t(g_i)} \quad (4)$$

where $r(g_i)$ denotes the rank of g_i after the second step re-ranking. In this way, the refined ranking list via *conductive similarity* is achieved.

2.2 Dissimilarity Ranking Optimization

The similarity ranking optimization do improve the quasi-similar samples' ranking orders. Then we penalize the quasi-dissimilar samples in dissimilarity ranking optimization. It also can be divided into three steps: First, the strongly dissimilar samples are achieved by the bottom-k (k_-) results of a baseline method. Second, the strongly dissimilar samples are treated as new probes to requery in the original gallery set. Third, a quasi-dissimilar set is achieved by backward requery of the strongly dissimilar samples, and then penalize the ranking orders of the quasi-dissimilar samples due to their frequency in the quasi-dissimilar set. The details are discussed as follows.

The bottom-k (k_-) farthest neighbours of the original method are defined as the strongly dissimilar samples of the probe, which is denoted as $G_-(p) = \{g_-^j \mid j = 1, 2, ...k_-\}$ as the strongly dissimilar samples of image p, k_- is the number of the strongly dissimilar samples. Similarly, the strongly dissimilar samples $G_-(p)$ are chosen for backward re-query. In other words, we treat each g_-^j in $G_-(p)$ as a new probe to search in the original gallery set. After the backward requery, we'll get k_- ranking lists, and each top-k of the backward ranking list can be expressed as $N_{k_+}(g_-^j)$. Take the quasi-dissimilar union set of top-k results $Q_-(p) = \{N_{k_+}(g_-^j) \mid j = 1, 2, ...k_-\}$. Similarly, the general penalization of each g_i is computed by:

$$w_-^t(g_i) = \sum_{k=1}^{k_-} log\{(r(p, g_-^j) - N + k_-)) \cdot (k_- - r(g_-^j, g_i)) + 1\} \quad (5)$$

Note that $r(g_-^j, g_i)$ is set as k_- if g_i is not a member of $N_{k_+}(g_-^j)$, and $r(p, g_-^j) = N - k_-$ if g_i is not an element of $Q_-(p)$. It can be seen that a higher penalization value is assigned for the one which is more likely to be wrong match. Therefore, the ranking list is refined by:

$$r^*(g_i) = r(g_i) \cdot e^{w_-^t(g_i)} \quad (6)$$

where $r(g_i)$ denotes the original rank of g_i. Specially, $r(g_i)$ can also be the revised ranking order after the similarity ranking optimization.

2.3 Complexity Analysis

Some implementation details are discussed in this subsection. As can be seen from above descriptions, the majority of the computation is spent on deriving the backward re-query ranking lists, which consist of mass pair-wise similarity computation between gallery images. In some special practical applications, e.g. surveillance video investigation, the gallery images can be obtained before querying the probe image. Therefore, the computation of our method is mainly spent off-line, where the similarity cues and dissimilarity cues can be computed offline together. In the offline part, all gallery images are mutually compared with a computation complexity $O(\frac{n(n-1)}{2})$ and a ranking complexity of $O(n^2 \log n)$. In the online portion, it only needs to compute the distance between the probe and every gallery image whose computation complexity is $O(n)$ and ranking complexity is $O(n \log n)$. With the above two-phrase implementation manner, the whole algorithm's complexity can be greatly reduced and its online part is only proportional to the size of the top-k and bottom-k, which is suitable in some practical applications.

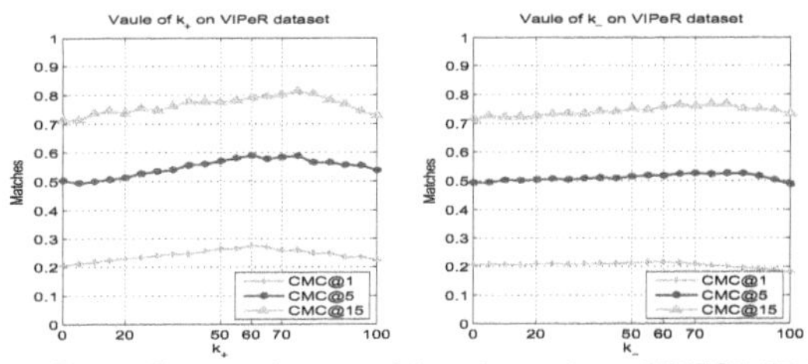

Figure 3: Different k_+s and k_-s based on KISSME [5] on VIPeR. k_+ refers to the similarity ranking optimization while k_- is for the dissimilarity ranking optimization.

3. EXPERIMENTAL RESULTS

3.1 Datasets and evaluation protocol

We evaluate our method on two publicly available datasets, the VIPeR dataset [3] and the CUHK01 dataset [14]. We chose these datasets that they provide many challenges faced in practical surveillance, *i.e.*, viewpoint, pose and illumination changes, different backgrounds, low image resolutions, occlusions, etc. The VIPeR dataset contains 632 person image pairs captured from two different static camera views in outdoor academic environment. The dataset is challenging due to the intensive viewpoint and illumination changes. All the images are normalized to 128×48 for experiments. The CUHK01 dataset is also obtained from two disjoint camera views in an outdoor campus environment. It contains 971 persons with 3,884 images, and each person has two images in each camera. The person images in camera A are mostly captured by frontal view or back views while camera B captures the side views. All the images are normalized to 160×60 for experiments.

All quantitative results are exhibited in Cumulated Matching Characteristics (CMC) curves [11]. The CMC curve is a plot of the recognition performance versus the rank score and represents the expectation of finding the correct match inside top k matches. Following the evaluation protocols described in [5,20], we randomly partition the dataset into two even parts, 50% for training and 50% for testing, without overlap on person identities. Especially, gave a comparison to two representative methods: multi-feature matching based on a classic metric learning method LMNN [15] and KISSME [5] as for its higher speed for testing.

3.2 Evaluation

Parameter Analysis Two important parameters k_+ and k_- are analyzed in this section. Note that the baseline method is the original KISSME [5] conducted on VIPeR dataset. And CMC@1, CMC@5 and CMC@15 are reported for different k_+s and k_-s as shown in Fig 3. Note that the number of selected image pairs is 316. For k_+, the peak is somewhere around $k_+ = 60$. It is evident from Section 2.1 that smaller value of k_+ indicates a slighter remodification with limited improvement, but when k_+ is too large which may lead unreliable strongly similar samples, thus caused negative effects. Moreover, the curves drops earlier for CMC@1 rather than CMC@15, it can further illustrate the conductive similarity. For k_-, different k_-s have slight

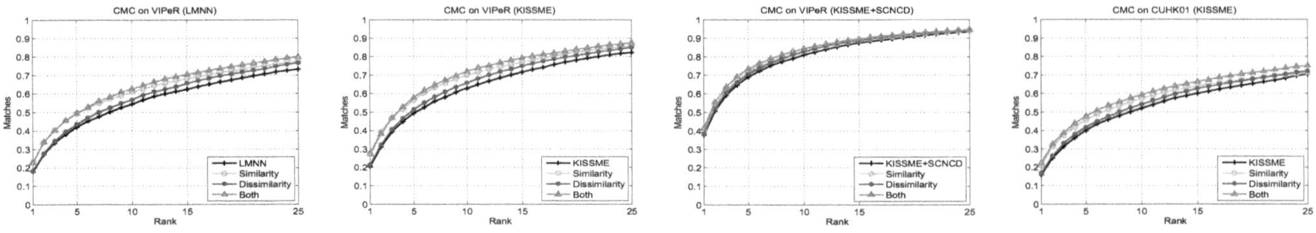

(a) (b) (c) (d)

Figure 4: Effectiveness of our method. "Similarity" and "Dissimilarity" denotes the similarity ranking optimization and dissimilarity ranking optimization respectively. "Both" indicates combine them together. (a) LMNN [15] on VIPeR; (b) Original KISSME [5] on VIPeR; (c) KISSME + SCNCD [16] on VIPeR; (d) KISSME on CUHK01 dataset.

Table 1: Top ranked matching rates [%] on VIPeR.

Rank →	$r = 1$	$r = 5$	$r = 15$	$r = 25$
ELF [4]	12.08	31.28	54.00	65.00
SDALF [2]	19.87	38.89	58.22	70.00
PRDC [21]	15.66	38.42	64.00	72.78
KISSME [5]	22.63	50.13	71.65	82.12
SalMatch [19]	30.16	52.00	73.41	*
MidFeat [20]	29.11	60.08	85.78	91.28
SCNCD [16]	37.72	68.45	87.06	93.80
Our_Both	**40.98**	**71.54**	**89.68**	**94.08**

influence on CMC@1 and CMC@5 due to the *insulative dissimilarity* mainly focus on improving the ranking orders of quasi-dissimilar samples. And the best choice for k_- is 60.

Effectiveness To verify the effectiveness of our proposed method, three baseline methods are conducted on VIPeR dataset as shown in Fig.4 (a-c) and another experiment on CUHK01 dataset is shown in Fig.4 (d). And the parameters are set $k_+ = 60$ and $k_- = 60$ in all the experiments. Several conclusions can be drawn from the above figures: (1) *Conductive similarity* can truly improve matching results by pulling the ranking orders of quasi-similar samples. As shown in the figures, our "Similarity" has 5-10% improvements compared to the baseline method. (2) *Insulative dissimilarity* ameliorates the results by pushing the ranking orders of quasi-dissimilar samples. Specially, according to the growth rate of the CMC curves, the "Similarity" mainly focus on the improving former part of the rank which corresponds to the quasi-similar samples, while the "Dissimilarity" focus on the middle part with a higher increasing speed which corresponds to the quasi-dissimilar samples. (3) Combination of the two cues truly improves the matching results further.

Moreover, we compare our performance (based on KISSME + SCNCD) in the range of first 25 ranks to some existing state-of-the-art methods as shown in Table 1. It indicates that our final results compare favorably with state-of-the-art methods.

4. CONCLUSION

In this paper, we address ranking optimization approaches for person re-identification problem, a novel and efficient ranking optimization method based on similarity and dissimilarity is conducted. The main idea is that the correct match should be similar to the probe's strongly similar samples and dissimilar to the strongly dissimilar samples, we pull the quasi-similar samples and push the quasi-dissimilar samples to optimize the ranking list. Extensive experiments without any parameters learning on two publicly data sets have validated the effectiveness. In the future, we will further estimate our method to combine multiple ranking lists and investigate intelligent ranking learning.

Acknowledgement. The research was supported by National Nature Science Foundation of China (61303114, 61231015, 61170023), the Specialized Research Fund for the Doctoral Program of Higher Education (20130141120024), the Technology Research Project of Ministry of Public Security (2014JSYJA016), the China Postdoctoral Science Foundation funded project (2013M530350), the major Science and Technology Innovation Plan of Hubei Province (2013AAA020), the Guangdong-Hongkong Key Domain Breakthrough Project of China (2012A090200007), and the Special Project on the Integration of Industry, Education and Research of Guangdong Province (2011B090400601).Nature Science Foundation of Hubei Province (2014CFB712).Jiangxi Youth Science Foundation of China(20151BAB217013).

5. REFERENCES

[1] R. Cucchiara. Multimedia surveillance systems. In *Proceedings of the third ACM international workshop on Video surveillance & sensor networks*. ACM, 2005.

[2] M. Farenzena, L. Bazzani, A. Perina, V. Murino, and M. Cristani. Person re-identification by symmetry-driven accumulation of local features. In *CVPR*, 2010.

[3] D. Gray, S. Brennan, and H. Tao. Evaluating appearance models for recognition, reacquisition, and tracking. In *PETS workshop*, 2007.

[4] D. Gray and H. Tao. Viewpoint invariant pedestrian recognition with an ensemble of localized features. In *ECCV*, 2008.

[5] M. Kostinger, M. Hirzer, and et al. Large scale metric learning from equivalence constraints. In *CVPR*, 2012.

[6] Q. Leng, R. Hu, C. Liang, and et al. Person re-identification with content and context re-ranking. In *MTAP*, 2014.

[7] W. Li, Y. Wu, M. Mukunoki, and et al. Common-near-neighbor analysis for person re-identification. In *ICIP*, 2012.

[8] C. Liu, S. Gong, and et al. Person re-identification: what features are important? In *ECCV*, 2012.

[9] C. Liu, C. C. Loy, S. Gong, and G. Wang. Pop: Person re-identification post-rank optimisation. In *ICCV*, 2013.

[10] X. Tian, L. Yang, and et al. Bayesian video search reranking. In *ACM Multimedia*, 2008.

[11] X. Wang, G. Doretto, T. Sebastian, J. Rittscher, and P. Tu. Shape and appearance context modeling. In *ICCV*, 2007.

[12] Y. Wang, R. Hu, C. Liang, C. Zhang, and Q. Leng. Camera compensation using feature projection matrix for person re-identification. In *TCSVT*, 2014.

[13] Z. Wang, R. Hu, and et al. Region-based interactive ranking optimization for person re-identification. In *PCM*, 2014.

[14] L. Wei and X. Wang. Locally aligned feature transforms across views. In *CVPR*, 2013.

[15] K. Weinberger and L. Saul. Fast solvers and efficient implementations for distance metric learning. In *ICML*, 2008.

[16] Y. Yang, J. Yang, J. Yan, and et al. Salient color names for person re-identification. In *ECCV*, 2014.

[17] M. Ye, J. Chen, and et al. Copuled-view based ranking optimization for person re-identification. In *MMM*, 2015.

[18] S. Zhang, M. Yang, T. Cour, and et al. Query specific fusion for image retrieval. In *ECCV*, 2012.

[19] R. Zhao, W. Ouyang, and X. Wang. Person re-identification by salience matching. In *ICCV*, 2013.

[20] R. Zhao, W. Ouyang, and X. Wang. Learning mid-level filters for person re-identfiation. In *CVPR*, 2014.

[21] W.-S. Zheng, S. Gong, and T. Xiang. Person re-identification by probabilistic relative distance comparison. In *CVPR*, 2011.

Leveraging Knowledge-based Inference for Material Classification

Jie Yu
Canon Innovation Center
3300 N. 1st Street
San Jose, CA 95134, USA
jyu@cusa.canon.com

Sandra Skaff
Canon Innovation Center
3300 N. 1st Street
San Jose, CA 95134, USA
sskaff@cusa.canon.com

Liang Peng
Canon Innovation Center
3300 N. 1st Street
San Jose, CA 95134, USA
plg519@gmail.com

Francisco Imai
Canon Innovation Center
3300 N. 1st Street
San Jose, CA 95134, USA
fimai@cusa.canon.com

ABSTRACT

Material classification is one of the fundamental problems for multimedia content analysis, computer vision and graphics. Existing efforts mostly focus on extracting representative visual features and training a classifier to recognize unknown materials. Compared with human visual recognition, automatic recognition cannot leverage common sense knowledge regarding material categories and contextual information such as object and scene. In this paper, we propose to first extract such knowledge on material, object and scene from heterogeneous sources, i.e. a public data set of 100 million Flickr images [13] and Bing search results. To improve the material classification task, the knowledge information is further exploited in a probabilistic inference framework. Our method is evaluated on OpenSurfaces [10], the largest public material data set which contains both visual features of physical properties as well as image context information. The quantitative evaluation demonstrates the superior performance of our proposed method.

Categories and Subject Descriptors

H.2.8 [**Database applications**]: Data Mining; I.5.4 [**Pattern Recognition**]: Application; H.3.1 [**Information Storage and Retrieval**]: Content Analysis and Indexing

General Terms

Algorithms, Performance, Experimentation, Measurement

Keywords

knowledge extraction; graphical model; material classification

1. INTRODUCTION

Material classification is one of the fundamental problems for multimedia content analysis, computer vision and computer graphics. A material surface/patch is defined as an image region that consists of homogenous material. In the human visual system, material classification is critical for object detection and scene understanding. Previous efforts on material classification mostly focus on extracting representative visual features and training a classifier to predict the category of a material surface. Specifically, researchers have spent tremendous efforts on designing texture features such as Textons [1] and Local Binary Patterns (LBPs) [2]. Popular selections of classifiers include AdaBoost, Support Vector Machine and Random Forest. Recently, deep learning based methods [3] have been proposed to integrate feature learning and classification into an end-to-end solution for image classification and object detection.

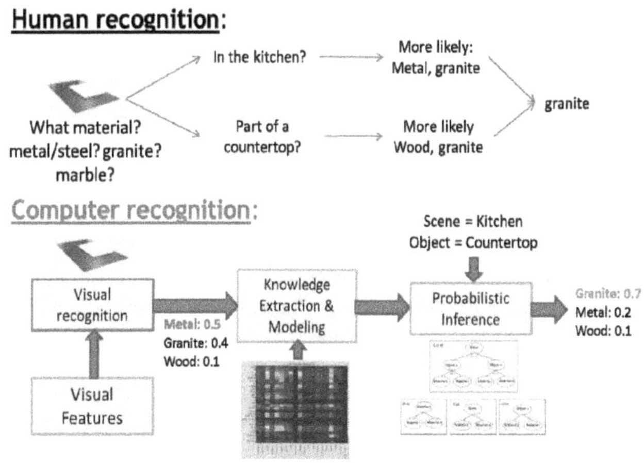

Figure 1. The framework of our proposed method.

Despite these advances, material classification systems still lack the capability of extracting and reasoning about common sense knowledge beyond a limited training data set. As illustrated in Figure 1, the visual recognition of the material surface shown is very challenging due to its resemblance to metal, granite and marble. However, if extra information is available, one can leverage common-sense knowledge to better infer the category of the material. For example, if the unknown material is part of a countertop, one can expect it to be more likely wood or granite. In combination with the visual recognition clues, the correct prediction of granite can be produced.

In this paper, we propose a novel method to harvest knowledge from heterogeneous sources and improve the material classification task by leveraging such knowledge in a probabilistic framework as illustrated in Figure 1.

2. RELATED WORK

Recently, leveraging contextual information has been studied for various computer vision applications. K. Murphy *et al.* proposed to model image scene context and objects in local patches using Conditional Random Fields and used the joint model to improve scene classification and object detection [4]. Similarly, D. Crandall *et al.* proposed to learn part-based spatial configurations of objects using a star topology for both the contextual and object components [5]. Instead of detecting objects within an image, J. Li *et al.* proposed to use object detection results for scene classification [6] and event categorization [7], respectively. Instead of using a topic model, Li *et al.* presented a method of

MM'15, October 26-30, 2015, Brisbane, Australia

DOI: http://dx.doi.org/10.1145/2733373.2806327

using chain-based probabilistic models to capture the co-occurrences of objects and scenes [8]. L. Xie et al. pioneered the work on mining robust knowledge from image tags using Inverse Random Walk and applied the learned knowledge on automatic picture annotation [9].

Compared with our work, existing methods which exploit the relationship of object, scene and/or events have the following drawbacks: (1) the existing methods focus on object detection, scene classification and/or scene categorization, which does not directly apply to material classification; (2) most graphical model based approaches learn the knowledge from the training data set, which greatly reduce the availability and reliability of the knowledge; and (3) current methods using external knowledge rely on single sources, such as ontology databases.

3. KNOWLEDGE-BASED INFERENCE

To overcome the aforementioned drawbacks of previous work, we propose a novel framework to extract knowledge on material, object and scene from heterogeneous sources and encode the knowledge using a probabilistic inference framework to improve the predictions of the materials of selected regions. Specifically, our framework consists of 4 modules as illustrated in Figure 1.

3.1 Segmentation and Feature Extraction

In general, the region of interest can be segmented automatically or via user interaction. Given the segmented region of a certain material, visual features are often extracted to represent the image patches in a compact feature space to overcome the curse of dimensionality. Although automatic segmentation and feature learning are important research areas, they are beyond the scope of this paper. For simplicity and fair benchmarking, we use the segmentation and visual features provided by the OpenSurfaces data set. Details are given in Section 4.1.

It is worth mentioning that our method has the flexibility to take arbitrary visual features as input, e.g. manually crafted features such as Textons, LBPs, and/or learning-based features.

3.2 Visual Recognition

In our framework, the visual recognition module takes the extracted feature of a material patch as input and uses a trained classifier to produce a confidence-rated initial prediction of the category of the material. Training of a classifier typically requires a set of material patches with known material types. Theoretically, our method can use an arbitrary classifier for an initial prediction. For evaluation purposes, we use AdaBoost to demonstrate the performance improvement introduced by our method in Section 4.

3.3 Knowledge Extraction and Modeling

To achieve automatic knowledge-based reasoning capability, we propose the following 2-stage method: automatic knowledge extraction and knowledge-based prediction inference.

3.3.1 Knowledge Extraction

Commonsense knowledge often refers to the collection of facts that an ordinary person should know. Constructing a complete knowledge database is extremely difficult and beyond the scope of our method. For the material classification task, we aim at leveraging the subset of common sense knowledge, such as the co-occurrences of materials, objects and scenes related to our task. Existing methods often learn such co-occurrences from a small set of training data, which greatly limit the availability and reliability of the knowledge model. In contrast, we propose to extract such knowledge from heterogeneous sources such as web image annotations and search results. Specifically, we extracted co-occurrence counts of all combinations of material, object and scene names from two sources: a public data set of annotations of 100 million Flickr images [13] and Bing search results. From a normalized co-occurrence matrix as shown in Figure 2, some common sense knowledge can be easily identified, e.g. the material "food" is likely to occur in the scene "kitchen".

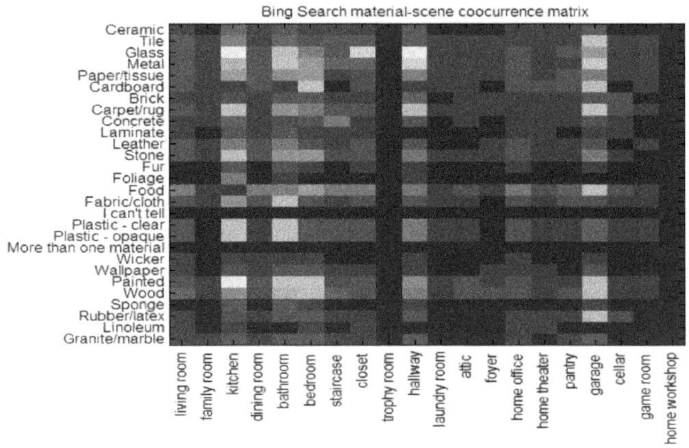

Figure 2. Co-occurrence counts of scenes and materials.

3.3.2 Material-Object-Scene Modeling

Although the common sense knowledge extracted as in the previous step reveals important non-visual context information, it could also be noisy and unreliable. To take such uncertainty into account, we propose to integrate it with the initial prediction from the visual recognition module in a probabilistic inference framework. Specifically, we model the material patches, the objects and scene of the same image as nodes in an undirected graph. In contrast to most existing work which models at the pixel level, our method models at the level of material patches and objects of images. Depending on the data and application, multiple graphical models can be configured to represent the inter-relationship of materials, objects and/or scenes. Figure 3 illustrates 4 typical configurations.

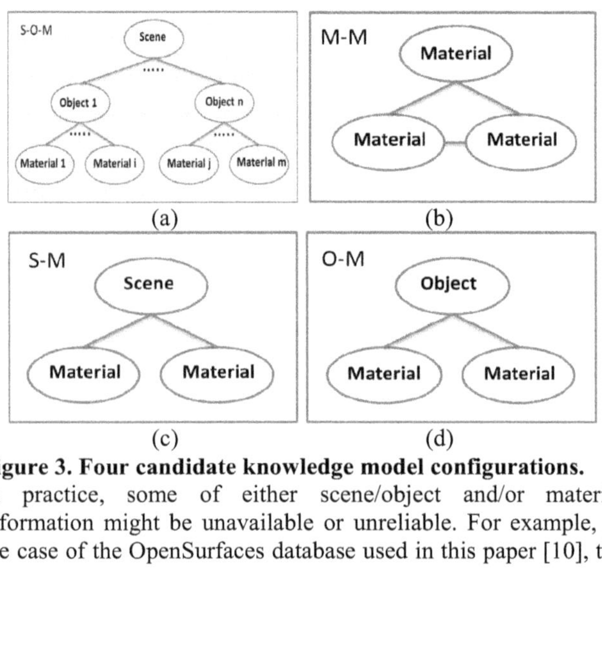

Figure 3. Four candidate knowledge model configurations.

In practice, some of either scene/object and/or material information might be unavailable or unreliable. For example, in the case of the OpenSurfaces database used in this paper [10], the object information is not reliable to build models as shown in Figures 3a and 3d. Therefore we use the alternate model configurations (shown in Figures 3b and 3c) to capture the partial relationships of material patches and/or scenes.

3.4 Probabilistic Inference

Direct learning of the model parameters from the training data set is impractical because the configuration of the model varies across images. Instead, we can exploit knowledge encoded in the co-occurrence counts of materials-scenes by using normalized correlation as priors. The prior of image patch with the *i-th* material category occurring in an image with the *j-th* scene category can be calculated as follows:

$$P(material_i \mid scene_j) = \frac{c_{ij}}{\sum_{m=1}^{M} c_{mj}},$$

where:

$$c_{i,j} = \text{co-occurrence counts of} < \text{material}_i, scene_j >$$

and M is the total number of material categories.

The initial confidence-based prediction from the visual recognition module can be used as the probability of each image patch belonging to a certain material category, i.e.

$$P(m_{ik} \mid v_k) = \frac{pred_{ik}}{\sum_{m=1}^{M} pred_{mk}},$$

where $pred_{i,k}$ is the prediction confidence of the *k-th* surface in an image belonging to the *i-th* material category based on visual feature v_k.

By jointly modeling material patches, objects and the scene of the image, we can obtain the final prediction of the category of a material patch using

$$\arg\max_i P(m_{ik} \mid v_1, .. v_k, s)$$

where s is the scene category information.

Inference of the graphical model depends on configuration as shown in Figure 3. For tree-structured models, such as (a), (c) and (d), exact inference can be obtained via the max-product algorithm [11]. For cyclic models, such as (b), approximate inference can be obtained via Loopy Label Propagation [12].

3.5 Multiple Model Integration

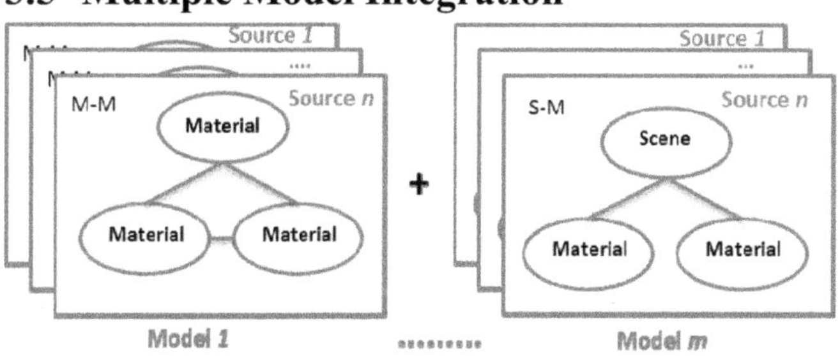

Figure 4. Integration of models and knowledge sources.

The combination of knowledge sources and graphical models poses a challenging problem of model selection, which is prone to overfitting. Instead of selecting a model and knowledge source, we propose to integrate multiple models and heterogeneous knowledge sources, which improve the robustness of knowledge-based inference. Specifically, our method combines the predictions based on the weights learned from the training data set as follows:

$$h = \sum_i \alpha_i h_i,$$

where

$$\alpha_i = \frac{\log\frac{1-e_i}{e_i} - \log(M-1)}{\sum_i (\log\frac{1-e_i}{e_i} - \log(M-1))}.$$

h_i is the refined prediction from the *i-th* model and e_i is the error rate of the *i-th* model on the training set.

Compared with the related work as described in Section 2, our method has the following advantages: (1) External knowledge is extracted from heterogeneous sources and exploited to improve material classification. (2) The material-object-scene models capture hierarchical relationships of semantic components. (3) Automatic integration of heterogeneous knowledge sources and multiple model configurations improves the robustness of the recognition task.

4. EXPERIMENTS AND ANALYSIS

To quantitatively evaluate the performance of the proposed method, we developed the algorithm and evaluated on the OpenSurfaces public material data set.

4.1 OpenSurfaces Data Set

OpenSurfaces is a large-scale database which contains both visual features of physical properties as well as image context information such as objects and scenes. It was constructed by researchers at Cornell University and initially published at SIGGRAPH 2013 [10]. The ground truth information of the material classes, object and scene categories were annotated by humans using Amazon Mechanical Turk. For our experiment, we filtered the OpenSurfaces data set based on availability of scene and object information and built a database of materials, the key information of which is listed in Table 1.

Table 1. Key information of the OpenSurfaces data set.

Material Surfaces	Images	Material Categories	Scene Categories	Visual Features
41611	13034	28	20	16

As explained in Section 3.2, the object information was not used because many of the object categories do not have enough material surfaces associated with them for learning an appropriate model.

4.2 Visual Features

Given a surface of certain material, our system can take arbitrary visual features to represent the material image in a compact feature space. For benchmarking, we used the physical property-based features provided in OpenSurfaces [10] and corresponding to the Visual Features column in Table 1, which included dominant RGB, RGB, specular RGB, diffuse RGB, LAB and Contrast.

4.3 Knowledge Extraction

To automatically extract knowledge for material classification, we investigated correlations of material and scene categories using the following two sources:

Bing search counts

Commercial web search engines, such as Google and Microsoft Bing, have crawled and indexed billions of web pages. Such web pages can be searched using one or multiple keywords. To quantitatively evaluate the relationships of materials and scenes, we searched all pair-wise combinations of their names. Instead of retrieving and analyzing the webpages directly, we used the "search count" to infer the correlations of a pair of names.

Flickr 100M image data set

Flickr is one of the most popular image sharing websites. In addition to storing images, it hosts rich context information such as textual annotations (tags), geographical locations (geo-tags) and comments of other users. Different from web search results, the textual annotations are often directly related to the content of the image(s). Recently, Flickr opened access to a public data set of over 100 million images for research purposes, which is the largest image data set by far [13]. Similarly to processing Bing search results, we extracted textual annotations and calculated co-occurrence counts of all pairwise combinations of the names of material, object and scene.

4.4 Performance and Analysis

After the co-occurrence-based knowledge information is extracted from the aforementioned sources, two types of graphical models, Material-Material (M-M, Figure 3(b)) and Scene-Material (S-M, Figure 3(c)), were developed and evaluated for each source. Integration of models (Integrated) was designed using the combinations of knowledge sources and models as proposed in Section 3.5. For comparison, the baselines of using only visual feature and the naïve combination of visual and scene category information were also implemented and tested.

The OpenSurfaces data set was randomly and evenly split into training and testing data sets. The AdaBoost was used as a baseline classifier. The training data set was used to build the initial classifier and calculate the weights for combining multiple models. The average prediction accuracies on the testing data sets are reported in Figure 4.

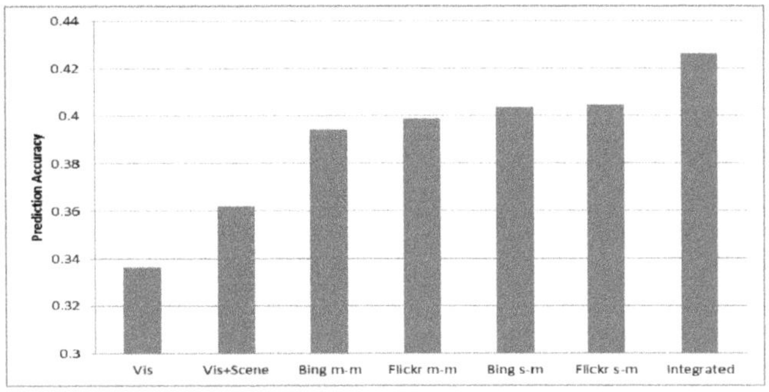

Figure 4. Average prediction accuracies.

The results show the improvement of the knowledge-based inference methods over the two baselines (Vis and Vis+Scene). However, there is no clear winner among individual knowledge sources (Bing m-m vs. Flickr m-m or Bing s-m vs. Flickr s-m), while there is a slight improvement in using an S-M model as compared with an M-M model configuration (Bing s-m vs. Bing m-m or Flickr s-m vs. Flickr m-m). Finally, the integrated model (Integrated) leverages the complementary property of multiple knowledge models and achieves the best prediction accuracy, which improves the Vis+Scene baseline model by 8.7%, a relative increase of 25.8%.

5. CONCLUSION

In this paper, we propose a new method to automatically extract and model knowledge information regarding material, object and scene and improve the material classification task. Compared with related work in the literature, our method has several advantages. Firstly, external knowledge can be extracted from heterogeneous sources and exploited to improve the general material recognition task. Secondly, the proposed models can capture multi-layer hierarchical relationships of semantic components in natural and man-made scenes. Finally, automatic integration of heterogeneous knowledge and multiple model configurations enhances the robustness of the recognition task and significantly improves the classification accuracy.

6. REFERENCES

[1] Leung, T. and Malik, J., 1999. Recognizing surface using three-dimensional textons, *International Conf. on Computer Vision.*

[2] Heikkilä, M. and Pietikäinen, M., 2006. A texture-based method for modeling the background and detecting moving objects, *IEEE Trans. Pattern Analysis and Machine Intelligence.*

[3] Li, W., and Fritz, M., 2014. Learning multi-scale representations for material classification, *arXiv preprint arXiv:1408.2938v1*

[4] Murphy, K., Torrolba, A., and Freeman, W., 2003. Using the forest to see the trees: a graphical model relating features, objects, and scenes, *Advances in Neural Information Processing Systems.*

[5] Crandall, D. and Huttenlocher, D., 2007. Composite models of objects and scenes for category recognition, *IEEE International Conf. on Computer Vision and Pattern Recognition.*

[6] Li, J., Su, H., Lim, Y., and Li, F., 2010. Objects as attributes for scene classification, *European Computer Vision Conference.*

[7] Li, J. and Li, F., 2007. What, where and who? Classifying events by scene and object recognition, *IEEE International Conf. on Computer Vision.*

[8] Li, X. and Guo, Y., 2012. An object co-occurrence assisted hierarchical model for scene understanding, *British Machine Vision Conference.*

[9] Xie, L., and He, X., 2013. Picture tags and world knowledge: Learning tag relations from visual semantic sources, *ACM International Conference on Multimedia.*

[10] Bell, S., Upchurch, P., Snavely, N., and Bala, K., 2013. OpenSurfaces: a richly annotated catalog of surface appearance, *ACM Transactions on Graphics.*

[11] Bishop, C., 2006. *Pattern Recognition and Machine Learning.*

[12] Weiss, Y. and Freeman, W., 2001. Correctness of belief propagation in Gaussian graphical models of arbitrary topology, *Neural Computation.*

[13] Thomee, B., Shamma, D., Friedland, G., Elizalde, B., Ni, K., Poland, D., Borth, D. and Li, J., 2015, The new data and new challenges in multimedia research, *arXiv preprint arXiv:1503.01817.*

Emotion Distribution Recognition from Facial Expressions

Ying Zhou, Hui Xue, Xin Geng*
MOE Key Laboratory of Computer Network and Information Integration
School of Computer Science and Engineering
Southeast University, Nanjing, China
{zhouying1, hxue, xgeng}@seu.edu.cn

ABSTRACT

Most existing facial expression recognition methods assume the availability of a single emotion for each expression in the training set. However, in practical applications, an expression rarely expresses pure emotion, but often a mixture of different emotions. To address this problem, this paper deals with a more common case where multiple emotions are associated to each expression. The key idea is to learn the specific description degrees of all basic emotions for each expression and the mapping from the expression images to the emotion distributions by the proposed emotion distribution learning (EDL) method. Experimental results show that EDL can effectively deal with the emotion distribution recognition problem and perform remarkably better than the state-of-the-art multi-label learning methods.

Categories and Subject Descriptors

I.2.6 [**Artificial Intelligence**]: Learning; I.4.8 [**Image Processing and Computer Vision**]: Scene Analysis

Keywords

Emotion distribution learning; facial expression recognition; description degree

1. INTRODUCTION

The increasing applications of facial expression recognition,especially those in human computer interaction, have attracted a great amount of interests in the past decade. There are many single-emotion learning methods that have been used, for example, neural-network-based methods [8], support vector machine (SVM) [14] and hidden markov model (HMM) [15]. As a single-emotion problem, satisfactory recognition accuracy has been reached in the previous research [10].

*Corresponding author.

MM'15, October 26–30, 2015, Brisbane, Australia.
© 2015 ACM. ISBN 978-1-4503-3459-4/15/10 ...$15.00.
DOI: http://dx.doi.org/10.1145/2733373.2806328.

However, according to Plutchik's wheel of emotions theory [11], there are a small number of basic emotions, and all the other emotions occur as combinations, mixtures or compounds of the basic emotions and can exist in varying degree of intensity or levels of arousal. So, the single-label learning methods used to recognize one basic emotion for each expression may not be suitable for the real-life facial expression recognition applications, where an expression rarely expresses only one basic emotion.

Fig. 1 gives three examples from the s-JAFFE database. The s-JAFFE database contains 213 facial expression images. Each image was rated by 60 persons. A five-level score is applied to each sample on the 6 basic emotions (happiness, sadness, surprise, anger, disgust and fear [3]), where 5 represents highest emotion intensity and 1 represents lowest emotion intensity. Then the average scores for each emotion on each expression image were obtained. From Fig. 1, we can see that each emotion in one expression image corresponds to a positive score, no matter it is high or low, which agrees with the Plutchik's theory that an expression can be viewed as a mixture of basic emotions [11].

Rudovic et al [13] proposed a multi-output Laplacian Dynamic Ordinal Regression method, which can output the probability of each emotion label and estimate intensity. However, it assumes only one correct emotion label for each expression and outputs the emotion with the highest probability as a result, which cannot match the mixture emotion cases in real life.

If each basic emotion is considered as a label, multi-label learning (MLL) [20] can be used to describe each expression image with several relevant emotions. However, MLL cannot learn the intensity of each emotion. MLL might first select a threshold, then the emotions with scores higher than the threshold are labeled as relevant emotions, while the others are labeled as irrelevant emotions. As in Fig. 1, the relevant emotions are set as +1 and the irrelevant emotions are set as -1. In such way, all the relevant emotions are deemed as equally important. As a result, the important information about the emotion intensity is lost.

To address the above problem, we propose an emotion distribution learning (EDL) algorithm in this paper. Different from the above algorithms, EDL considers that expressions are often the mixtures of basic emotions and allows different intensities in each emotion. Concretely, EDL uses a description degree d_x^y as a numerical indicator to measure the relationship of the emotion y to the expression x and indicate the relative emotion intensity. The sum of description degrees of all emotions for one expression is 1, meanwhile each description degree is between 0 and 1. For a particular expression, the description degrees of all the emotions have a similar data form to probability distribution. As a result, we termed it as emotion distribution. Then, a learning process is invoked to learn the mapping from the expression image to the emotion distribution, which aims to minimize the difference between the true distribution and the predicted distribution. Furthermore, both the single-label learning and MLL can be considered as special cases of EDL in facial expression recognition.

The rest of the paper is organized as follows. Section 2 proposes the method of emotion distribution learning. In section 3, the experimental results are reported. Finally, several conclusions are drawn in Section 4.

2. EMOTION DISTRIBUTION LEARNING

2.1 Emotion Distribution

The goal of EDL is to learn a mapping from an expression image space $\mathcal{X} = \mathbb{R}^m$ to the emotion distribution over a finite set of labels $\mathcal{Y} = \{y_1, y_2, ...y_c\}$. Each label represents one of the basic emotions. As discussed in Section 1, facial expression is often composed of one or more emotions, and each emotion has its own intensity. We use the description degree d_x^y to indicate the intensity of emotion y for the facial expression x, where $x \in \mathcal{X}$ and $y \in \mathcal{Y}$. Normalize the emotion intensity to make $d_x^y \in [0, 1]$, and $\sum_y d_x^y = 1$ to constitute the emotion distribution.

Fig. 1 shows some typical examples from the s-JAFFE database together with their multi-labels and emotion distributions. The threshold is chosen as 2.5 in MLL scenarios to illustrate the difference between MLL and EDL more clearly. The emotion distribution is represented by a curve. There are six values at the horizontal axis labeled by the six basic emotions. The values at the vertical axis represent the description degrees of each emotion. For Fig 1(a), the description degree of happiness is the highest, and all the other five emotions' description degrees are significantly lower. Happiness can be considered as the only relevant emotion. Single-emotion learning, MLL and EDL algorithms can all deal with such case well. In Fig 1(b), anger and disgust have similar emotion intensity and their description degrees are significantly higher than other emotions, which means that both anger and disgust might be the relevant emotions. In such case, single-emotion learning algorithms can no longer work. But both MLL and EDL algorithms can match such case well. In Fig 1(c), anger's description degree is the highest, while disgust's description degree is a little lower than that of anger but significantly higher than the other four emotions. In this case, both anger and disgust might be the relevant emotions, but they have different emotion intensity. For considering the relevant emotions as equally important, MLL might lose the important information about the intensity difference between the relevant emotions. Consequently, measuring emotion intensity is very important, as with emotion intensity one can know how much each emotion is and how many emotions are related to a particular expression.

2.2 Learning from Emotion Distribution

Given a training set $G = \{(x_1, E_1), (x_2, E_2), ..., (x_n, E_n)\}$, where $x_i \in \mathcal{X}$ is an expression instance and $E_i = \{d_{x_i}^{y_1}, d_{x_i}^{y_2}, ..., d_{x_i}^{y_c}\}$ is the emotion distribution associated with x_i. The goal of emotion distribution learning is to learn a conditional probability mass function $p(y|x)$ from G, where $x \in \mathcal{X}$ and $y \in \mathcal{Y}$. Assume that $p(y|x)$ is a parametric model $p(y|x;\theta)$, where θ is the model parameter vector.

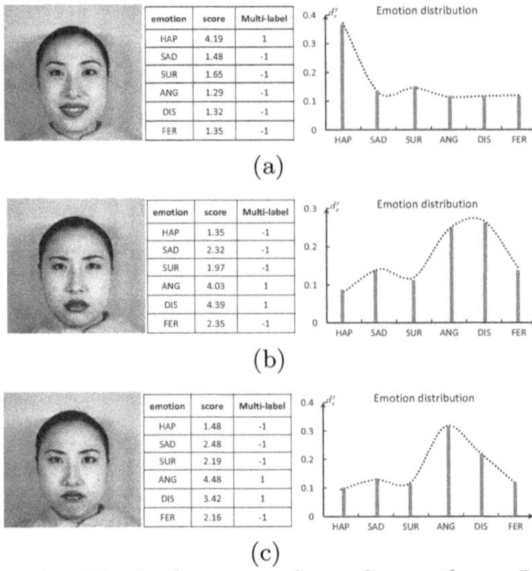

Figure 1: Typical expressions from the s-JAFFE database together with their scores, multi-labels, emotion distributions.

Many different criteria can be used to measure the distance between two distributions, such as Squared $\mathcal{X}^2$, Euclidean, Jeffery's divergence, Kullback-Leibler (K-L) divergence and so on. Here we use Jeffery's divergence defined by

$$D_J(Q_a||Q_b) = \sum_j (Q_a^j - Q_b^j) log \frac{Q_a^j}{Q_b^j}, \quad (1)$$

where Q_a^j and Q_b^j are the j-th element of the two distributions Q_a and Q_b, respectively. Jeffery's divergence is balanced, which makes $D_J(Q_a||Q_b)$ equal to $D_J(Q_b||Q_a)$.

The above formula calculates the sum of all the distances between the description degrees of the same emotion, i.e., the superscripts of Q_a and Q_b are the same (i.e., j). One possible problem of the definition in Eq. (1) is that the relationship among different emotions is not considered. In fact, some basic emotions often appear together, e.g., disgust and fear, and some often conflict to each other, e.g., happiness and sadness. Thus the weighted Jeffery's divergence is proposed here as

$$D_{wJ}(Q_a||Q_b) = \sum_{j,k} \lambda_{jk} (Q_a^j - Q_b^k) log \frac{Q_a^j}{Q_b^k}, \quad (2)$$

where the weight λ_{jk} models the relationship between the j-th emotion and the k-th emotion in the distribution, which can be calculated by

$$\lambda_{jk} = \begin{cases} \frac{1}{\Lambda_j}(\rho_{jk})^\eta & |\rho_{jk}| \geq \varepsilon \\ 0 & otherwise \end{cases} \quad (3)$$

where $\rho_{jk} = \frac{\sum_i (d_{x_i}^{y_j} - \overline{d_x^{y_j}})(d_{x_i}^{y} - \overline{d_x^{y}})}{\sqrt{\sum_i (d_{x_i}^{y_j} - \overline{d_x^{y_j}})^2}\sqrt{\sum_i (d_{x_i}^{y} - \overline{d_x^{y}})^2}}$ means correlation coefficient between the j-th emotion and the k-th emotion. $\Lambda_j = \sum_k (\rho_{jk})^\eta$ is a normalization factor that makes sure $\sum_k \lambda_{jk} = 1$. η is a positive odd number, which controls the degree the correlation coefficient works. ε is a threshold. If a couple of emotions have an absolute value of correlation coefficient smaller than ε, they are considered to have no relationship.

Then the optimal model parameter vector θ^* is determined by

$$
\begin{aligned}
\theta^* &= \arg\min_{\theta} \sum_i D_{wJ}(E_i||\hat{E}_i) \\
&\quad -\xi_1 \frac{1}{n}\sum_k \|\theta_k - \overline{\theta}\|_2^2 + \frac{1}{2}\xi_2 \sum_{k,r} \theta_{kr}^2 \\
&= \arg\min_{\theta} \sum_{i,j,k} \lambda_{ij}(d_{x_i}^{y_j} - p(y_k|x_i,\theta))(lnd_{x_i}^{y_j} - lnp(y_k|x_i,\theta)) \\
&\quad -\xi_1 \frac{1}{n}\sum_k \|\theta_k - \overline{\theta}\|_2^2 + \frac{1}{2}\xi_2 \sum_{k,r} \theta_{kr}^2,
\end{aligned} \tag{4}
$$

where E_i is the ground truth emotion distribution of the i-th example and the $\hat{E}_i$ is the predicted one by $p(y|x_i;\theta)$. The second term is a regularizer to prevent too smooth output to emphasize the important emotions, and the third term is another regularizer to prevent unstable output. ξ_1 and ξ_2 are the balance factors.

As to the form of $p(y|x;\theta)$, similar to the work of Geng et al [5], we assume it to be a maximum entropy model [2], i.e.,

$$
p(y_k|x_i;\theta) = \frac{1}{\mathcal{Z}_i}\exp(\sum_r \theta_{kr}x_i^r), \tag{5}
$$

where $\mathcal{Z}_i = \sum_k \exp(\sum_r \theta_{kr}x_i^r)$ is the normalization factor, x_i^r is the r-th feature of x_i, and θ_{kr} is an element in θ. Substituting Eq.(5) into Eq.(3) yields the target function of θ.

$$
\begin{aligned}
T(\theta) &= \sum_i \mathcal{Z}_i + \sum_{i,j,k} \lambda_{jk}[\frac{1}{\mathcal{Z}_i} exp(\sum_r \theta_{kr}x_i^r) \\
&\quad (\sum_r \theta_{kr}x_i^r - ln\mathcal{Z}_i - lnd_{x_i}^{y_j}) - d_{x_i}^{y_j}\sum_r \theta_{kr}x_i^r] \\
&\quad -\xi_1 \frac{1}{n}\sum_k \|\theta_k - \overline{\theta}\|_2^2 + \frac{1}{2}\xi_2 \sum_{k,r} \theta_{kr}^2.
\end{aligned} \tag{6}
$$

The minimization of the function $T(\theta)$ can be effectively solved by the limited-memory quasi-Newton method L-BFGS [7]. The computation of L-BFGS is mainly related to the first-order gradient of $T(\theta)$, which can be achieved by

$$
\begin{aligned}
\frac{\partial T(\theta)}{\partial \theta_{kr}} &= \sum_{i,j,k} \lambda_{jk}[p_{ik}x_i^k(1-p_{ik})(\sum_r \theta_{kr}x_i^r - ln\mathcal{Z}_i \\
&\quad -lnd_{x_i}^{y_j} + 1)] - \sum_i x_i^r(1-p_{ik}) - \xi_1\frac{1}{n}[(\theta_{kr} - \overline{\theta}_r) \\
&\quad -\frac{1}{c}\sum_k(\theta_{kr} - \overline{\theta}_r)] + \xi_2 \sum_{k,r}\theta_{kr},
\end{aligned} \tag{7}
$$

where $p_{ik} = \frac{1}{\mathcal{Z}_i}\exp(\sum_r \theta_{kr}x_i^r)$.

In order to compare with the multi-label learning methods, labels in the predicted distribution should be divided into two sets, i.e, the relevant and irrelevant sets. For this purpose, an extra virtual label y_0 is added into the label set, i.e., the extended label set $\mathcal{Y}' = \mathcal{Y} \cup \{y_0\}=\{y_0, y_1, y_2 \cdots y_c\}$. Using the new extended label set to do the training process, the optimal parameter vector θ^* is learned. As y_0 is the label that distinguishes the relevant and irrelevant emotions directly, it is initialized the same as the threshold used in MLL. Given a test image x', its emotion distribution is predicted by $p(y|x';\theta^*)$. The description degree of y_0 splits the predicted distribution into two sets. The emotions with the description degree higher than y_0's are regarded as the relevant emotions, and the rest emotions are regarded as irrelevant emotions. So that EDL can realize the function of MLL without setting the threshold manually.

3. EXPERIMENTS

To demonstrate the effectiveness of the proposed EDL algorithms, we have performed extensive experiments on two

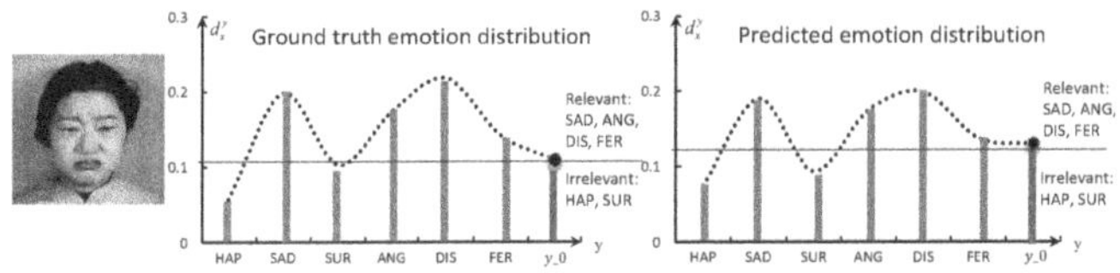

Figure 2: Typical example of the emotion distribution predicted by EDL.

widely used facial expression databases: s-JAFFE[9] and s-BU_3DFE [16], both of them are extended to the emotion distribution case proposal in this paper.

The s-JAFFE database contains 213 grayscale images posed by 10 Japanese female models. Each image is of the size 256 $\times$ 256 pixels and each model has 2-4 samples for each expression. The images are cropped manually so that the eyes are at the same positions, and then the cropped images are resized to 110 $\times$ 140 pixels. The features are extracted by the method of Local Binary Patterns (LBP) [1]. We set the diagram to 2 and the number of neighbours to 16. LBP histograms are then used as feature vectors. The dimensionality of each feature vector is eventually reduced to 243.

The s-JAFFE database is scored by 60 persons on the 6 basic emotions (i.e., happiness, sadness, surprise, fear, anger and disgust) with a 5 level scale (5 represents highest emotion intensity, while 1 represents lowest emotion intensity). The average score of each emotion is used to represent the specific emotion intensity.

The second database named s-BU_3DFE is much larger than s-JAFFE. There are 2500 examples in this database. 23 students are asked to score the s-BU_3DFE database by the same method of scoring s-JAFFE. The specific scores on each basic emotion are obtained and transferred into emotion distributions. We preprocessed the facial images and extracted the feature from s-BU_3DFE using the same method as s-JAFFE.

EDL is compared with four existing LDL methods and 7 widely used MLL methods. For each compared method, several parameter configurations are tested and the best performance is reported. The virtual label and the threshold value used in MLL are all set to 2.3. Besides, the η, ε, ξ_1 and ξ_2 are set as 5, 0.25, 0.0001, 0.001 respectively. For the LDL methods, k in AA-KNN is set to 6. Linear kernel is used in PT-SVM. The number of hidden-layer neurons for AA-BP is set to 60. For the MLL methods, the value of k is set to 6 in ML-KNN, ratio is 0.02 and μ is 2 in ML-RBF. Linear kernel is used in LIFT. Rank-SVM uses the RBF kernel with the width σ equals to 1. Ten-fold cross validation is conducted in each algorithm.

Fig. 2 gives one example from s-JAFFE database by EDL. The ground truth emotion distribution is obtained by normalizing the scores and the virtual label y_0. As can be seen, the curve of the predicted emotion distribution is very similar as the ground truth distribution, which demonstrates that EDL can learn the varying intensities of all the basic emotions well. Furthermore, the trained description degree of the virtual label y_0 can act as the threshold automatically rather than be set heuristically in MLL, which splits the predicted emotion distribution into relevant and irrelevant sets.

Table 1 reports the experimental results of EDL and several LDL algorithms. The best performance on each measure is highlighted by boldface. The two-tailed t-tests with 5% significance level are performed to see whether the dif-

Table 1: Experimental results of Label Distribution Learning Methods

database	Algorithm	Evaluation Criterion					
		Euclidean(↓)	Sϕrensen(↓)	Squared $\mathcal{X}^2$(↓)	K-L(↓)	Intersection(↑)	Fidelity(↑)
s-JAFFE	EDL	**0.0957±0.0068**	**0.1002±0.0059**	**0.0339±0.0043**	**0.0346±0.0045**	**0.8998±0.0059**	**0.9914±0.0011**
	AA-KNN [4]	0.1306±0.0117•	0.1273±0.0110•	0.0534±0.0086•	0.0556±0.0099•	0.8727±0.0110•	0.9863±0.0023•
	PT-Bayes [4]	0.1682±0.0219•	0.1644±0.0168•	0.0835±0.0215•	0.0916±0.0269•	0.8356±0.0168•	0.9784±0.0059•
	PT-SVM [4]	0.1696±0.0117•	0.1689±0.0099•	0.0812±0.0094•	0.0854±0.0110•	0.8311±0.0099•	0.9792±0.0025•
	AA-BP [4]	0.1908±0.0208•	0.1880±0.0195•	0.1139±0.0210•	0.1100±0.0273•	0.8120±0.0195•	0.9685±0.0058•
s-BU_3DFE	EDL	**0.1055±0.0023**	**0.1061±0.0025**	**0.0402±0.0017**	**0.0420±0.0020**	**0.8939±0.0043**	**0.9898±0.0046**
	AA-KNN [4]	0.1549±0.0036•	0.1464±0.0042•	0.0697±0.0036•	0.0743±0.0031•	0.8536±0.0008•	0.9821±0.0036•
	AA-BP [4]	0.1648±0.0076•	0.1595±0.0065•	0.0760±0.0061•	0.0808±0.0063•	0.8405±0.0017•	0.9804±0.0061•
	PT-Bayes [4]	0.1659±0.0044•	0.1606±0.0049•	0.0766±0.0039•	0.0830±0.0037•	0.8394±0.0010•	0.9803±0.0039•
	PT-SVM [4]	0.1701±0.0032•	0.1638±0.0047•	0.0799±0.0044•	0.0877±0.0029•	0.8362±0.0007•	0.9794±0.0044•

Table 2: Experimental results of Multi-label Learning Methods

database	Algorithm	Evaluation Criterion				
		Average Precision(↑)	Coverage(↓)	Hamming Loss(↓)	One Error(↓)	Ranking Loss(↓)
s-JAFFE	EDL	**0.9037±0.0300**	**2.6913±0.3680**	**0.2540±0.0352**	**0.1175±0.0687**	**0.1374±0.0316**
	ML-RBF [17]	0.8651±0.0738•	3.2675±0.4157•	0.2484±0.0810•	0.1810±0.1088•	0.2005±0.1085•
	ML-KNN [20]	0.8455±0.0605•	3.4310±0.3822•	0.2790±0.0617•	0.1976±0.0616•	0.2184±0.0878•
	LIFT [18]	0.8050±0.1042•	3.5397±0.3604•	0.3254±0.0777•	0.2690±0.1679•	0.2515±0.1268•
	Rank-SVM [20]	0.7516±0.0982•	3.9198±0.2844•	0.3356±0.1127•	0.3008±0.1390•	0.3276±0.1189•
	MLLOC [6]	0.7502±0.0998•	3.9127±0.2146•	0.5734±0.0639•	0.3214±0.1496•	0.3399±0.1275•
	BP-MLL [19]	0.7435±0.1009•	4.0786±0.2630•	0.3591±0.1133•	0.3444±0.1477•	0.3593±0.1210•
	ECC [12]	0.7380±0.0952•	3.9500±0.2305•	0.3591±0.1133•	0.3484±0.1130•	0.3424±0.1264•
s-BU_3DFE	EDL	**0.7861±0.0216**	**0.5236±0.0758**	**0.1167±0.0069**	**0.3667±0.0349**	**0.1761±0.0178**
	ML-RBF [17]	0.7157±0.0370•	0.6756±0.1139•	0.1271±0.0075•	0.4360±0.0559•	0.2165±0.0300•
	ML-KNN [20]	0.6224±0.0282•	0.9712±0.1103•	0.1387±0.0043•	0.5699±0.0362•	0.2947±0.0243•
	LIFT [18]	0.6062±0.0323•	1.0204±0.1225•	0.1443±0.0045•	0.5913±0.0413•	0.2515±0.0296•
	Rank-SVM [20]	0.6016±0.0321•	0.9876±0.1231•	0.2118±0.0164•	0.6101±0.0380•	0.3069±0.0338•
	MLLOC [6]	0.4970±0.0288•	1.4832±0.2538•	0.1453±0.0042•	0.7140±0.0247•	0.4352±0.0557•
	BP-MLL [19]	0.5367±0.0210•	1.1692±0.1043•	0.1817±0.0098•	0.7024±0.0280•	0.3480±0.0263•
	ECC [12]	0.4419±0.0185•	1.8396±0.0677•	0.1426±0.0046•	0.7484±0.0317•	0.5438±0.0105•

ferences between EDL and the baseline algorithms are statistically significant. The results of t-tests are given right after the performance of each method, where • indicates significance difference. As can be seen, EDL performs best on all criteria. The comparison results of EDL with seven multi-label classifiers are tabulated in Table 2. Similarly, EDL performs best on all evaluation measures. This implies that EDL can not only match more complex cases, but also perform better than MLL methods in the scenario of MLL, owing to the consideration in varying intensity of the basic emotions.

4. CONCLUSIONS

This paper presents the problem of emotion distribution recognition, and proposes to solve it by the algorithm of EDL. Different from the previous facial expression recognition methods, EDL can output the intensity of all the emotions, which well matches the reality that one facial expression is often the mixture of the basic emotions with different intensity. The experimental results show that EDL performs significantly better than some state-of-the-art multi-label algorithms and label distribution learning algorithms.

5. ACKNOWLEDGMENTS

This research was supported by the National Natural Science Foundation of China (61273300, 61232007, 61375057), Jiangsu Natural Science Funds for Distinguished Young Scholar (BK20140022), and Natural Science Foundation of Jiangsu Province of China (BK20131298).

6. REFERENCES

[1] T. Ahonen, A. Hadid, and M. Pietikainen. Face description with local binary patterns: Application to face recognition. *IEEE Transactions on Pattern Analysis and Machine Intelligence*, 28(12):2037–2041, 2006.

[2] A. L. Berger, V. J. D. Pietra, and S. A. D. Pietra. A maximum entropy approach to natural language processing. *Computational Linguistics*, 22(1):39–71, 1996.

[3] P. Ekman and W. V. Friesen. Constants across cultures in the face and emotion. *Journal of Personality and Social Psychology*, 17(2):124, 1971.

[4] X. Geng and R. Ji. Label distribution learning. In *Proceedings of the 13th IEEE International Conference on Data Mining Workshops*, pages 377–383, 2013.

[5] X. Geng, C. Yin, and Z.-H. Zhou. Facial age estimation by learning from label distributions. *IEEE Transactions on Pattern Analysis and Machine Intelligence*, 35(10):2401–2412, 2013.

[6] S.-J. Huang and Z.-H. Zhou. Multi-label learning by exploiting label correlations locally. In *Proceedings of the 26th AAAI Conference on Artificial Intelligence*, pages 949–955, Toronto, Canada, 2012.

[7] D. C. Liu and J. Nocedal. On the limited memory bfgs method for large scale optimization. *Mathematical Programming*, 45(1-3):503–528, 1989.

[8] P. Liu, S. Han, Z. Meng, and Y. Tong. Facial expression recognition via a boosted deep belief network. In *Proceedings of the IEEE Conference on Computer Vision and Pattern Recognition*, pages 1805–1812, Columbus, OH, 2014.

[9] M. J. Lyons, S. Akamatsu, M. Kamachi, J. Gyoba, and J. Budynek. The japanese female facial expression (JAFFE) database. http://www.kasrl.org/jaffe.html, 1998.

[10] V. J. Mistry and M. M. Goyani. A literature survey on facial expression recognition using global features. *International Journal of Engineering and Advanced Technology*, 2:653–657, 2013.

[11] R. Plutchik. A general psychoevolutionary theory of emotion. *Theories of emotion*, 1, 1980.

[12] J. Read, B. Pfahringer, G. Holmes, and E. Frank. Classifier chains for multi-label classification. *Machine Learning*, 85(3):333–359, 2011.

[13] O. Rudovic, V. Pavlovic, and M. Pantic. Multi-output laplacian dynamic ordinal regression for facial expression recognition and intensity estimation. In *Proceedings of the IEEE Conference on Computer Vision and Pattern Recognition*, pages 2634–2641, 2012.

[14] C. Song, W. Liu, and Y. Wang. Facial expression recognition based on hessian regularized support vector machine. In *Proceedings of the Fifth International Conference on Internet Multimedia Computing and Service*, pages 264–267. ACM, 2013.

[15] T.-H. Wang and J.-J. J. Lien. Facial expression recognition system based on rigid and non-rigid motion separation and 3d pose estimation. *Pattern Recognition*, 42(5):962–977, 2009.

[16] L. Yin, X. Wei, Y. Sun, J. Wang, and M. J. Rosato. A 3d facial expression database for facial behavior research. In *7th IEEE international conference on automatic face and gesture recognition*, pages 211–216, 2006.

[17] M.-L. Zhang. Ml-rbf: Rbf neural networks for multi-label learning. *Neural Processing Letters*, 29(2):61–74, 2009.

[18] M.-L. Zhang. Lift: Multi-label learning with label-specific features. In *Proceedings of the 22nd International Joint Conference on Artificial Intelligence*, pages 1609–1614, Barcelona, Spain, 2011.

[19] M.-L. Zhang and Z.-H. Zhou. Multilabel neural networks with applications to functional genomics and text categorization. *IEEE Transactions on Knowledge and Data Engineering*, 18(10):1338–1351, 2006.

[20] M.-L. Zhang and Z.-H. Zhou. A review on multi-label learning algorithms. *IEEE Transactions on Knowledge and Data Engineering*, 26(8):1819–1837, 2014.

Exclusive Constrained Discriminative Learning for Weakly-Supervised Semantic Segmentation

Peng Ying, Jing Liu, Hanqing Lu and Songde Ma
The National Laboratory of Pattern Recognition, Institute of Automation,
Chinese Academy of Sciences, Beijing, China
{peng.ying, jliu, luhq }@nlpr.ia.ac.cn, masd@most.cn

ABSTRACT

How to import image-level labels as weak supervision to direct the region-level labeling task is the core task of weakly-supervised semantic segmentation. In this paper, we focus on designing an effective but simple weakly-supervised constraint, and propose an exclusive constrained discriminative learning model for image semantic segmentation. To be specific, we employ a discriminative linear regression model to assign subsets of superpixels with different labels. During the assignment, we construct an exclusive weakly-supervised constraint term to suppress the labeling responses of each superpixel on the labels outside its parent image-level label set. Besides, a spectral smoothing term is integrated to encourage that both visually and semantically similar superpixels have similar labels. Combining these terms, we formulate the problem as a convex objective function, which can be easily optimized via alternative iterations. Extensive experiments on MSRC-21 and LabelMe datasets demonstrate the effectiveness of the proposed model.

Categories and Subject Descriptors

H.3.1 [**Information Storage and Retrieval**]: Content Analysis and Indexing; I.2.10 [**Artificial Intelligence**]: [Vision and Scene Understanding]

General Terms

Algorithms; Experimentation; Theory

Keywords

Semantic Segmentation; Weak Supervision

1. INTRODUCTION

Image semantic segmentation aims to collaboratively perform image segmentation and region-level label assignment. Simply, it is a task of region-level annotation. Semantic segmentation is a challenging and fundamental task in computer vision. An effective image semantic segmentation can facilitate many other vision tasks, such as scene understanding, object detection and region-based image retrieval.

MM'15, October 26–30, 2015, Brisbane, Australia.
© 2015 ACM. ISBN 978-1-4503-3459-4/15/10 ...$15.00.
DOI: http://dx.doi.org/10.1145/2733373.2806329.

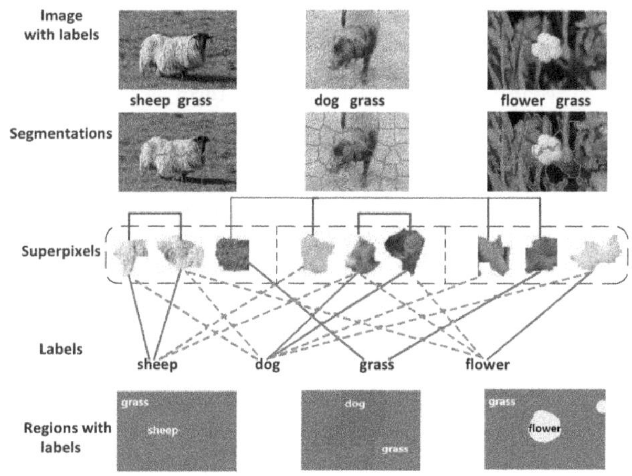

Figure 1: Overview of our model. The superpixels connected by purple lines are both visually and semantically similar. The mappings from superpixels to labels, denoted by red dash lines, are suppressed according to the exclusive constraint, while the mapping denoted by blue lines are expected.

Some typical image semantic segmentation methods are to train models on pixel-level annotated data [3, 5]. However, the obtainment of these pixel-level annotation costs much manpower and time. Fortunately, with the flourish of social media and the success of photo-sharing websites e.g. Flickr and Picasa, lots of images with user-contributed image-level annotation are easily to obtain. The online weakly labeled data allow us to deal semantic segmentation with weak supervision methods [16, 17, 15, 7]. For example, Liu et. al proposed to handle the image semantic segmentation problem with a weakly-supervised graph based algorithm [6]. In this algorithm, the process of label propagation from images to regions is bounded by weak supervision information. Y. Liu et. al proposed a weakly-supervised dual clustering approach to cluster the over-segmented regions and assign image-level tags to those regions simultaneously[8]. For the above weakly supervised approaches, they adopted the idea of multiple instance learning (MIL) to transfer the image-level labels to regions, i.e., the MIL-based models encourage maximum labeling responses of regions to be aligned with image-level labels. However, such a maximum optimization problem is non-convex and difficult to solve.

From the aforementioned approaches, we find the essence of weakly-supervised semantic segmentation is to learn the mapping from superpixels to labels while the co-occurrence of the labels and superpixels are also explored. Therefore, our work is motivated to find a well-optimized but effective form of weakly-supervised constraint to assist the labeling mapping for each superpixel in semantic segmentation task.

In this paper, we propose a novel discriminative classification with exclusive weakly-supervised constraint to perform superpixel classification and label propagation collaboratively. As shown in Fig. 1, we first over-segment images to obtain some image patches, i.e., superpixels, as the inputs of our model. Then, we employ a discriminative linear regression model to assign some subsets of superpixels with different labels. During the assignment, we expect the labeling responses of each superpixel are suppressed on the labels outside its parent image-level label set, and an exclusive weakly-supervised constraint term is formulated to implicitly import the image-level labels as weak supervision. Besides, a spectral smoothing term is integrated to encourage that both visually and semantically similar superpixels have similar labels, while the visual features and the labeling information of superpixels are jointly considered to contruct the similarity graph. Combining these terms, we formulate the problem as a convex objective function, which can be easily optimized via alternative iterations. Experimental results on two public datasets, MSRC and LabelMe, demonstrate that the proposed model outperforms some state-of-the-art methods.

2. THE PROPOSED MODEL

2.1 Problem Definition

Suppose we have a data collection $\chi = \{X_i\}_{i=1}^{I}$, where X_i indicates the i-th image. The images are from C classes and the image-level label information for all images is also given. That label information is represented symbolically by $G = [g_1, \ldots, g_i, \ldots, g_I]$, where $g_i = [g_i^1, \ldots, g_i^c, \ldots, g_i^C] \in \{0,1\}^C$ is the image-level label information for X_i and $g_i^c = 1$ if X_i has the c-th label and otherwise $g_i^c = 0$. After over-segmented, X_i are divided into a set of superpixels $\{x_{i1}, \ldots, x_{in_i}\}$, where x_{ik} indicates the k-th superpixel in the i-th image and its candidate label set is g_i. At superpixel-level, the data collection χ is also denoted by $\{x_1, \ldots, x_i, \ldots, x_N\}$, where $N = \sum_{i=1}^{I} n_i$. The exact label information for the superpixel x_i is marked as $y_i = [y_i^1, \ldots, y_i^c, \ldots, y_i^C] \in \{0,1\}^C$. In weakly-supervised semantic segmentation, $Y = [y_1, \ldots, y_n, \ldots, y_N] \in \{0,1\}^C$ is to be inferred with image label information G given.

2.2 Weakly-Supervised Discriminative learning

To deal with semantic segmentation task, we introduce the linear regression model with weak supervision constraint to mine the co-occurrence of superpixel-label pairs.

The linear regression is employed to model discriminative classification, which is formulated as

$$T_1 = \alpha \|X^T W - Y\|_F^2 + \beta \|W\|_F^2, \quad (1)$$

where $\|W\|_F^2$ is a regularization term and α and β are weight coefficients.

The mapping from superpixels to labels should be bounded by weak supervision information. In other words,label propagation should meet the constraint that the assigned label of the arbitrary superpixel should belong to the image-level label set. Besides, one superpixel can have and only one label. However, in consideration of the inevitable existence of noisy tags in training data for practical application, the constraint that one label has at least one superpixel mapped to it, is not required. In other words, non-image-level label should be suppressed [4]. To model the limitation on label propagation, we propose exclusive weakly-supervised constraint term:

$$\begin{aligned} T_2 &= \mathrm{Tr}[Y(P - [\underbrace{g_1, \ldots, g_1}_{n_1}, \ldots, \underbrace{g_i, \ldots, g_i}_{n_i}, \ldots, \underbrace{g_I, \ldots, g_I}_{n_I}])] \\ &= \mathrm{Tr}[Y M^T], \end{aligned} \quad (2)$$

where $P \in \{1\}^{C \times N}$, M is a binaryzation penalty matrix in which punishment or impunity is denoted by 1 or 0 respectively. If a superpixel x_{ij} is given a label outside its candidate set g_i, it will be punished; If x_{ij} maps to a label which belongs to g_i, it will not be punished. Moreover, the noisy tags in g_i are not required to have superpixels mapped to it. So the weakly-supervised discriminative classification is defined as minimizing the following equation:

$$\mathcal{F} = \alpha \|X^T W - Y\|_F^2 + \beta \|W\|_F^2 + \gamma \mathrm{Tr}[Y M^T] \quad (3)$$

It's worth mentioning that the proposed exclusive weak-supervised constraint term is a convex function and can be easily optimized.

2.3 Spectral Smoothing with Semantic Graph

The employment of spectral smoothing is based on the observation that the adjacent superpixels in feature space have good chance to share the same label. We adopt Euclidean distance to measure the similarity of superpixels. What's more, semantic information is also embed into the construction of the affinity graph, e.g. k-NN semantic graph. Unlike k-NN original graph, the k-nearest neighbors in k-NN semantic graph should be not only similar in feature space but also semantic relevant. For a specific image X_m, its image-level label set is denoted as $g_m = \{l_1, l_2, \ldots, l_n\}$, where n is the total numbers of labels for the image X_m. For a specific label $l_j \in g_m$ and superpixel x_{mi} from the $m-$th image, we select the k-NN superpixels of x_{mi} from the images with the specific label l_j and the selected superpixels corresponding to l_j is denoted as a set K_j^{mi}. Then we compute the average similarity A_j^{mi} between x_{mi} and the elements in K_j^{mi}:

$$A_j^{mi} = \sum_{a=1}^{k} \mathrm{Sim}(x_{mi}, x_{ja}) \quad s.t. \ x_{ja} \in K_j^{mi}, \quad (4)$$

where $\mathrm{Sim}(x_1, x_2) = \exp(-\|x_1 - x_2\|^2/t)$, t is a parameter controlling decay rate. The optimal k-NN superpixels K^{mi} of x_{mi} is decided by the following equation:

$$K^{mi} = \underset{K_j^{mi}}{\mathrm{argmax}} \{A_1^{mi}, \ldots, A_j^{mi}, \ldots, A_n^{mi}\} \quad (5)$$

The similarity between superpixels are formulated as a similarity matrix S

$$S_{pq} = \begin{cases} \exp(-\|x_p - x_q\|^2/t) & x_q \in K^p \text{ or } x_p \in K^q \\ 0 & \text{otherwise.} \end{cases} \tag{6}$$

Accordingly, the spectral smoothing term can be formulated as follows:

$$T_3 = \frac{1}{2}\sum_{p,q=1}^{N} S_{pq}\|\frac{y_p}{\sqrt{A_{pp}}} - \frac{y_q}{\sqrt{A_{qq}}}\|_2^2 = \text{Tr}[Y^T LY], \tag{7}$$

where $A = \sum_{p,q=1}^{N} S_{pq}$, and $L = A^{-1/2}(A - S)A^{-1/2}$.

2.4 Unified Objective Function

Combining the aforementioned items, the problem is formulated as a non-convex objective function as shown below:

$$\begin{aligned} \min_{Y,W} \mathcal{L} =& \alpha \left\|X^T W - Y\right\|_F^2 + \beta \|W\|_F^2 + \gamma \text{Tr}\left[YM^T\right] \\ &+ \text{Tr}\left[Y^T LY\right] \\ &s.t.\ Y^T Y = I_C,\ Y \geq 0. \end{aligned} \tag{8}$$

where α, β, γ are parameters controlling the weight of the three terms.

2.5 Optimization

We put the orthogonality constraint $\|Y^T Y - I_C\|_F^2$ into the objective function. So Eq. 5 is rewritten as:

$$\begin{aligned} \min_{Y,W} \mathcal{L} =& \alpha \left\|X^T W - Y\right\|_F^2 + \beta \|W\|_F^2 + \gamma \text{Tr}\left[YM^T\right] \\ &+ \text{Tr}\left[Y^T LY\right] + \frac{\mu}{2}\|Y^T Y - I_C\|_F^2 \\ &s.t.\ Y \geq 0. \end{aligned} \tag{9}$$

To solve the optimization problem, we propose an iterative optimization algorithm like in [10]. At r^{th} iteration:

1. Given Y, optimizing W: Fixing Y, let $\partial\mathcal{L}/\partial W = 0$ and we obtain

$$W = \alpha(\alpha XX^T + \beta I)^{-1} XY \tag{10}$$

2. Given W, optimizing Y: Fixing W, let $\partial\mathcal{L}/\partial Y = 0$ and we have

$$Y_{ij} \leftarrow Y_{ij} \frac{2(\mu Y)_{ij}}{(2PY + \gamma M + 2\mu YY^T Y)_{ij}} \tag{11}$$

where

$$P = L + \alpha(I_N - \alpha(\alpha XX^T + \beta I)^{-1} X) \tag{12}$$

Repeat step 1 to 2 until the objective function converges to a stable state.

3. EXPERIMENTS

We test our model on two frequently-used data in semantic segmentation field, e.g. MSRC-21 and LabelMe Outdoor(LMO). To evaluate the effectiveness, we compare the proposed model with several related works, including weakly-supervised approaches WSDC, MIM, MRF, MTL, GMIM and fully-supervised approaches HCRF, Texboost, THSR, Supix, LT. Methods are compared by computing the average per-class accuracy(percentage of pixels with agreement between the assigned label and groundtruth for a class, averaged on the whole classes).

Besides, to evaluate the robustness of our model, we conduct experiments on LabelMe in different noise polluted variety.

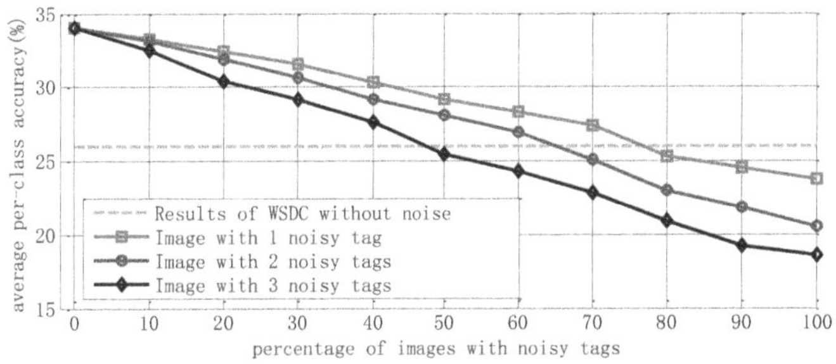

Figure 2: Average per-class accuracy with different percentage of images with 1,2 or 3 noisy tags on LabelMe dataset.

3.1 Experiments on MSRC-21

MSRC-21 dataset is widely used in image semantic segmentation field. There are 591 images with pixel-level ground truths in the dataset. The images are from 21 class and each image contains 3 labels on average. The dataset is standardly spilt into 276 images for training, 59 images for verification and 256 images for testing. The images are over-segmented into 40 superpixels per image on average via SLIC algorithm[1]. After over-segmentation, we employ SIFT as local descriptor and the standard bag-of-words model as representation of the superpixels. Besides, the parameters in formulation (9) are set as follows: $\alpha = 10000$, $\beta = 10000$, $\gamma = 100000$, $\mu = 10$.

Table 2 shows the experimental results of our approach and other comparison methods. From the experimental results, we have the following observations: (1) Our approach outperforms all the listed weakly-supervised methods and is close to some fully-supervised methods like HCRF. This clearly validate the effectiveness of our approach. (2) By comparing the results of ours and WSDC, we can see the proposed approach has enhanced the semantic segmentation accuracy 6 percentage points, which is largely due to the exclusive weakly-supervised constraint.

3.2 Experiments on LabelMe Outdoor

LabelMe Outdoor is a more challenging dataset for semantic segmentation, which consists of 2688 images from 33 classes. Each image contains around 5 labels and has pixel-level ground truths. It is randomly spilt into 2488 images for training and 200 images for testing. The parameters in this dataset are set as follows: $\alpha = 10000$, $\beta = 100$, $\gamma = 10000$, $\mu = 100$.

The experimental results of the proposed model and baseline algorithms are presented in Table 2. From the results, we can observe that our ECDL algorithm achieve the highest average per-class accuracy of 34 percent, which surpasses all the listed comparison methods. Specifically, compared with WSDC, our approach improves the accuracy by 8 percentage

Method	Texboost [11]	HCRF [2]	MTL [15]	MRF [14]	MIM [16]	WSDC [8]	ECDL
Supervision	FS	FS	WS	WS	WS	WS	WS
Accuracy	58	75	37	50	67	68	**74**

Table 1: Semantic segmentation results on MSRC dataset. WS denotes weak supervision, FS denotes full supervision.

Method	Texboost [12]	LT [5]	Supix [13]	THSR [9]	MIM [16]	GMIM [17]	WSDC [8]	ECDL
Supervision	FS	FS	FS	FS	WS	WS	WS	WS
Accuracy	13	24	29	32	14	21	26	**34**

Table 2: Semantic segmentation results on LabelMe dataset. WS denotes weak supervision, FS denotes full supervision.

points. The above comparisons show our method leads to a significant improvement over previous weakly-supervised approaches and even over some fully-supervised approaches.

To further explore the robustness of the proposed model to noisy tags, we perform experiments on LMO in different noise polluted variety. To be specific, the $p \in \{10, 20, \ldots, 100\}$ percentage images are randomly chosen and accordingly each chosen image is added $N \in \{1, 2, 3\}$ randomly chosen labels as noise. The experimental results are shown in Figure 2. From Fig. 2, we can find the accuracy reposefully descends with the increase of noisy tag number, which demonstrates to some extent our method are robust to noisy tags. Furthermore, with 70 percent images added one random noisy tag, our method can still achieve 27 percent accuracy, which is better than other weakly-supervised methods.

4. CONCLUSIONS

In this paper, we propose an exclusive weakly-supervised constraint with discriminative learning to collaboratively perform image segmentation and region-level annotation. We impose the exclusive constraint term on linear regression to construct a weakly-supervised discriminative classification model. To ensure that both visually and semantically similar superpixels have similar labels, a semantic graph based spectral smoothing term is integrated into the framework. Extensive experiments on two public datasets demonstrate the effectiveness of our approach.

5. ACKNOWLEDGEMENT

This work was supported by 863 Program (2014AA015104) and National Natural Science Foundation of China (61332016, 61272329, and 61472422).

6. REFERENCES

[1] R. Achanta, A. Shaji, K. Smith, A. Lucchi, P. Fua, and S. Susstrunk. Slic superpixels compared to state-of-the-art superpixel methods. *IEEE Transactions on Pattern Analysis and Machine Intelligence*, 34(11):2274–2282, 2012.

[2] L. Ladicky, C. Russell, P. Kohli, and P. H. Torr. Associative hierarchical crfs for object class image segmentation. In *ICCV, 2009*, pages 739–746, 2009.

[3] L.-J. Li, R. Socher, and L. Fei-Fei. Towards total scene understanding: Classification, annotation and segmentation in an automatic framework. In *CVPR 2009.*, pages 2036–2043. IEEE, 2009.

[4] Y. Li, J. Liu, Y. Wang, H. Lu, and S. Ma. Weakly supervised rbm for semantic segmentation. In *IJCAI*, pages 1888–1894, 2015.

[5] C. Liu, J. Yuen, and A. Torralba. Nonparametric scene parsing: Label transfer via dense scene alignment. In *CVPR 2009.*, pages 1972–1979. IEEE, 2009.

[6] S. Liu, S. Yan, T. Zhang, C. Xu, J. Liu, and H. Lu. Weakly supervised graph propagation towards collective image parsing. *IEEE Transactions on Multimedia.*, 14(2):361–373, 2012.

[7] X. Liu, S. Yan, J. Luo, J. Tang, Z. Huango, and H. Jin. Nonparametric label-to-region by search. In *CVPR, 2010*, pages 3320–3327. IEEE, 2010.

[8] Y. Liu, J. Liu, Z. Li, J. Tang, and H. Lu. Weakly-supervised dual clustering for image semantic segmentation. In *CVPR, 2013*, pages 2075–2082, 2013.

[9] H. Myeong and K. M. Lee. Tensor-based high-order semantic relation transfer for semantic scene segmentation. In *CVPR*, pages 3073–3080, 2013.

[10] S. Qiu, J. Cheng, X. Zhang, B. Niu, and H. Lu. Community discovering guided cold-start recommendation: A discriminative approach. In *Multimedia and Expo (ICME), 2014 IEEE International Conference on*, pages 1–6. IEEE, 2014.

[11] J. Shotton, J. Winn, C. Rother, and A. Criminisi. Textonboost: Joint appearance, shape and context modeling for multi-class object recognition and segmentation. In *ECCV 2006*, pages 1–15. 2006.

[12] J. Shotton, J. Winn, C. Rother, and A. Criminisi. Textonboost for image understanding: Multi-class object recognition and segmentation by jointly modeling texture, layout, and context. *IJCV*, 2009.

[13] J. Tighe and S. Lazebnik. Superparsing: scalable nonparametric image parsing with superpixels. In *ECCV 2010*, pages 352–365. Springer, 2010.

[14] J. Verbeek and B. Triggs. Region classification with markov field aspect models. In *CVPR,2007*, pages 1–8.

[15] A. Vezhnevets and J. M. Buhmann. Towards weakly supervised semantic segmentation by means of multiple instance and multitask learning. In *CVPR, 2010*, pages 3249–3256. IEEE, 2010.

[16] A. Vezhnevets, V. Ferrari, and J. M. Buhmann. Weakly supervised semantic segmentation with a multi-image model. In *ICCV*, pages 643–650, 2011.

[17] A. Vezhnevets, V. Ferrari, and J. M. Buhmann. Weakly supervised structured output learning for semantic segmentation. In *CVPR*, pages 845–852, 2012.

Multimedia Event Detection Using Event-Driven Multiple Instance Learning

Sang Phan*†, Duy-Dinh Le†§, Shin'ichi Satoh†
*The Graduate University for Advanced Studies (SOKENDAI), Japan
†National Institute of Informatics, Japan
§Multimedia Communications Lab, University of Information Technology, Vietnam
{plsang,ledduy,satoh}@nii.ac.jp

ABSTRACT

A complex event can be recognized by observing necessary evidences. In the real world scenarios, this is a difficult task because the evidences can happen anywhere in a video. A straightforward solution is to decompose the video into several segments and search for the evidences in each segment. This approach is based on the assumption that segment annotation can be assigned from its video label. However, this is a weak assumption because the importance of each segment is not considered. On the other hand, the importance of a segment to an event can be obtained by matching its detected concepts against the evidential description of that event. Leveraging this prior knowledge, we propose a new method, Event-driven Multiple Instance Learning (EDMIL), to learn the key evidences for event detection. We treat each segment as an instance and quantize the instance-event similarity into different levels of relatedness. Then the instance label is learned by jointly optimizing the instance classifier and its related level. The significant performance improvement on the TRECVID Multimedia Event Detection (MED) 2012 dataset proves the effectiveness of our approach.

Categories and Subject Descriptors

I.2.10 [**Artificial Intelligence**]: Vision and Scene Understanding—*Video analysis*

General Terms

Algorithms, Experimentation, Measurement

Keywords

Event Detection, Event-driven, Multiple Instance Learning

1. INTRODUCTION

The problem of recognizing complex event in videos has become a popular research topic due to the explosive growth of video data. A complex event can involve several actions or activities and happens in some particular settings. Therefore, recognizing complex event is more challenging than single action recognition. However, most complex detection systems are still based on the techniques that was developed for action recognition [6, 9]. These methods basically extract and aggregate local feature descriptors from the whole video to create a unique video representation. This strategy might be not effective for complex event detection because it treats different parts of the video equally. Therefore, it neutralizes the important local information of an event.

In practice, human can recognize a complex event by spotting several evidences in video [2]. This paper also demonstrated that better performance can be obtained by leveraging positive and negative visual cues selected by humans. Therefore, it is important to automatically detect key evidences for event detection. Several researchers have been working on this direction. Tang *et al.* [7] split the video into segments and models key segments and its duration as latent variables. Vahdat *et al.* [8] focus on intra-class variation by localizing only the most salient evidence using latent SVM. Lai *et al.* [5] detect salient instances in video based on a variant multiple instance learning. In another work [4], they represent static and dynamic instances as sparse features and adopt a learning-to-rank strategy to detect key evidence. In general, these approaches are based on the assumption that segment annotation can be obtained from its

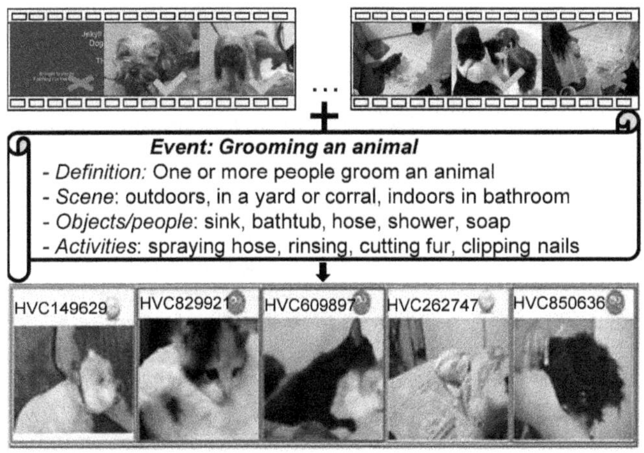

Figure 1: Event "Grooming an animal" in the TRECVID MED 2012 dataset. The event kit includes example videos and an event description which provides valuable cues to detect that event.

MM'15, October 26–30, 2015, Brisbane, Australia.
© 2015 ACM. ISBN 978-1-4503-3459-4/15/10 ...$15.00.
DOI: http://dx.doi.org/10.1145/2733373.2806330.

video label. However, this is a weak assumption because the importance of each segment is not taken into account.

On the other hand, the importance of a segment to an event can be obtained by matching its concept-based representation against the evidential description of that event. Some works have been using the event description for zero-shot event detection such as in [3, 10]. To the best of our knowledge, no work has taken into account this information for detecting key evidence in videos. However, the evidential description of an event provides valuable information to detect that event. Example of an event description (excerpted) is shown in Fig. 1.

Motivated by this observation, we propose a new method, Event-driven Multiple Instance Learning (EDMIL), to learn key evidences for complex event detection. We treat each segment as an instance and model it in a multiple instance learning framework [1], where each video is a "bag". The instance-event similarity is quantized into different levels of relatedness. Intuitively, the most (ir)relevant instances should have higher (dis)similarities. Therefore, we propose to learn the instance labels by jointly optimize the instance classifier and its related level. We evaluate our proposed method on the large scale TRECVID MED 2012 dataset. Comparing to other instance-based learning methods such as [1, 5], our method achieves a superior performance.

The remaining of this paper is organized as follows. In the next section, we present the method to calculate the instance-event similarity. Our proposed solution is introduced in Section 3. The experiments and results are shown in Section 4. Finally, Section 5 concludes the paper.

2. INSTANCE-EVENT SIMILARITY

In order to calculate the similarity between an instance and an event, we adopt a concept expansion strategy as in [3]. Our method is similar in spirit, however, we apply at instance level which is more accurate. The outline of our method is illustrated in Fig. 2 and it consists of four steps.

Step 1: Concept detection. We use the concept collection that proposed in [11] to cover a wide range of concept that can appear in realistic videos. This collection contains C = 1183 categories including 205 scene categories from the Places Database and 978 object categories from the ImageNet 2012. The concept detection part is done by using the provided pre-trained model[1]. To detect concept for the whole segment, we detect concept at sample frames and make the average aggregation.

Step 2: Event representation. We use standard natural language processing techniques to create the text-based event representation. At first, the event description is preprocessed by removing stop words and lemmatizing. It is then converted into a bag-of-words representation, where the dictionary is obtained from the English Wikipedia corpus. Tf-idf weighting scheme is also employed to put a higher weight on frequent as well as rare words.

Step 3: Concept-event similarity. To resolve the mismatch between words in the concept collection and event description, we adopt the concept expansion strategy [3]. For each concept category, we add the 10 most similar concepts obtained from word2vec model[2] to expand this category. It is then represented by a bag-of-words vector with

[1]http://places.csail.mit.edu

[2]https://code.google.com/p/word2vec

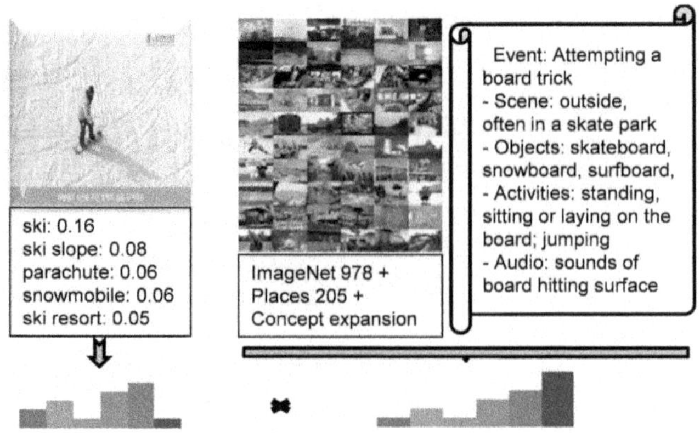

Figure 2: Outline of our method to calculate the instance-event similarity. Note that the concept expansion technique can bridge concept "ski" in the instance segment to the evidential description.

tf-idf weights. Based on this representation, we can calculate the cosine similarity s_c^e between each concept category and the event description. Table 1 shows top five most relevant concepts for some events on the MED 2012 dataset.

Step 4: Instance-event similarity. Having obtained the concept score x_c at each segment and the concept-event similarity as in Step 1 and Step 3, the instance-event similarity is calculated using the cosine similarity:

$$S_i^e = \frac{\sum_{c=1}^{C} s_c^e x_c}{\sqrt{\sum_{c=1}^{C}(s_c^e)^2}\sqrt{\sum_{c=1}^{C}(x_c)^2}}, \tag{1}$$

3. EVENT-DRIVEN MULTIPLE INSTANCE LEARNING

Problem Formalization. Suppose we have V training videos, and I_v instances in video v. We can calculate the similarity S_{iv}^e between an instance iv to a particular event e using Eq. (1). Suppose there is R level of relatedness from an instance to an event. We define two predict functions for positive and negative instances at level r as follows.

$$P_{pos}(S_{iv}^e, r) = \begin{cases} 1, & \text{if } Rank(S_{iv}^e) \le r \\ -1, & \text{otherwise} \end{cases}, \text{ and} \tag{2}$$

$$P_{neg}(S_{iv}^e, r) = \begin{cases} -1, & \text{if } Rank(S_{iv}^e) \le r \\ 1, & \text{otherwise} \end{cases}, \tag{3}$$

where $Rank(.)$ is the function to quantize a similarity into a related level. Note that smaller value of r results a higher confidence in the predict functions. We now learn the parameters of the instance classifier jointly with the related level r by optimizing the following objective function:

$$\begin{aligned} \min_{\mathbf{w},b,y,r} \frac{1}{2}\|\mathbf{w}\|^2 + C_f \sum_{v=1}^{V}\sum_{i=1}^{I_m} L_f\left(y_{iv}, \mathbf{w}^T\mathbf{x}_{iv} + b\right) \\ + C_p \sum_{v=1}^{V}\sum_{i=1}^{I_m} L_p\left(y_{iv}, P(S_{iv}^e, r)\right). \end{aligned} \tag{4}$$

C_f and C_p are cost parameters to control the influence of each loss function. Note that in the special case where

Table 1: **Top five concepts discovered by our system for the first 10 events in the MED 2012 dataset.**

Event ID	Event name	Concepts
E001	Attempting a board trick	Ski, slide rule, ski resort, ski mask, ice skating rink
E002	Feeding an animal	Meat loaf, white shark, food court, pop bottle, cleaver
E003	Landing a fish	Anemone fish, pole, raft, sturgeon, boat deck
E004	Wedding ceremony	Groom, bridegroom, banquet hall, gown, altar
E005	Working on a woodworking project	Jigsaw puzzle, bamboo forest, carpenter's kit, thatch, wooden spoon
E006	Birthday party	Table lamp, lampshade, torch, candle, custard apple
E007	Changing a vehicle tire	Recreational vehicle, car wheel, amphibian, scooter, sports car
E008	Flash mob gathering	Monitor, chime, bell, whistle, ballroom
E009	Getting a vehicle unstuck	Recreational vehicle, amphibian, tank, car wheel, motor scooter
E010	Grooming an animal	Nail, bathtub, shower, fur coat, washbashin

$C_p = 0$, the above formulation becomes a classic large-margin problem. $L_f(.)$ and $L_p(.)$ are two loss functions that will be jointly minimized. The first loss function minimizes the loss due to the classification mismatch based on the instance feature. The second one minimizes the loss due to the prediction obtained from the prior knowledge. Intuitively, when the related level r increases, the first loss will also tend to increase while the second loss will become smaller, and vice versa. $L_f(.)$ and $L_p(.)$ can be any loss function. Throughout this paper, we use the standard hinge-loss function for $L_f(.)$: $L_f\left(y_{iv}, \mathbf{w}^T\mathbf{x}_{iv} + b\right) = \max(0, 1 - y_{iv}(\mathbf{w}^T\mathbf{x}_{iv} + b))$, and the $L_p(.)$ function is defined so that it will penalize more on the high confident predictions: $L_p\left(y_{iv}, P(S^e_{iv}, r)\right) = \begin{cases} S^e_{iv}, & \text{if } P(S^e_{iv}, r) \neq y_{iv} \\ 0, & \text{otherwise} \end{cases}$.

Optimization Procedure. The optimization problem in Eq. (4) is a mixed-integer program which is not convex. In order to solve this problem, we apply the alternating optimization strategy to search for a suboptimal solution:

1. Fix instance labels y_{iv} and solve for $\mathbf{w}$ and b. By fixing y_{iv}, the optimization problem becomes a classic SVM: $\min_{\mathbf{w},b} \frac{1}{2}\|\mathbf{w}\|^2 + C_f \sum_{v=1}^{V}\sum_{i=1}^{I_v} L_f\left(y_{iv}, \mathbf{w}^T\mathbf{x}_{iv} + b\right)$. Thus it can be solved using a regular SVM solver.

2. Fix $\mathbf{w}$ and b, solve for r and update y_{iv}. The problem now becomes: $\min_{y,r} C_f \sum_{v=1}^{V}\sum_{i=1}^{I_v} L_f\left(y_{iv}, \mathbf{w}^T\mathbf{x}_{iv} + b\right)$ $+ C_p \sum_{v=1}^{V}\sum_{i=1}^{I_v} L_p\left(y_{iv}, P(S^e_{iv}, r)\right)$. We propose a greedy strategy to solve for this problem. At first, we iterate through all level of relatedness to search for the optimal r by finding the minimum total loss when updating y_{iv} using Eq. (2, 3). Because the most positive and negative instances will be selected first, there will be a higher possibility to correct mismatched labels that were learned in the previous step. Lastly we update instance labels using Eq. (2, 3) with the optimal r.

Because this is not a convex optimization problem, the initialized values of y_{iv} should be carefully selected. To this end, we use the same initilization method as in [1, 5], where instance labels are same with its "bag" (video) label.

It is also worth noted that the optimization framework only keeps updating the instance labels while the instance features are unchanged. Thus it is a good practice to use the pre-computed kernel technique for optimizing $\mathbf{w}$ and b. In fact, although our method is more complex, it only takes around 5 minutes for training one model, compared to 40 minutes that was reported in [5].

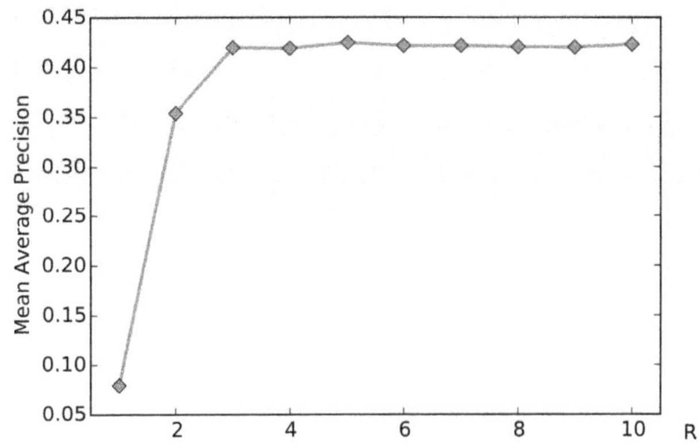

Figure 3: Optimal number of related levels.

4. EXPERIMENTS

Dataset. To evaluate our proposed method, we conducted experiments on the large scale TRECVID MED 2012 dataset[3]. This dataset provides the definition for 25 complex events. The first ten event names are listed in Table 1. We follow the setting by [5] to divide this video collection into training and testing parts. These parts contain 3,878 and 1,938 videos respectively.

Experimental setup. At first, original videos are scaled down to 320 x 240 with keeping the aspect ratio. Key frames are sampled at every 2 seconds from the resized video. The segment length is set to 8 seconds as suggested in [8]. To extract feature for each segment, we use the Improved Dense Trajectories feature proposed by Wang and Schmid [9]. Motion Boundary Histogram (MBH) is used to represent extracted trajectories because it can handle camera motion, which is prevalent in realistic videos. For learning, we use our framework jointly with the linear SVM. The cost parameters C_f and C_p are selected by cross-validation in the range of $\{0.1, 1, 10, 100\}$. At the testing step, video-level score is obtained by averaging over all instance scores. Finally we use the standard evaluation metric on MED, Mean Average Precision (mAP), to report the performance.

Baseline methods. To compare our methods with following baselines: miSVM, MISVM [1], VideoBOW and pSVM [5]. At first, because our method is based on the Multiple Instance Learning (MIL) framework, we evaluate two MIL solutions: miSVM and MISVM that were proposed by the

[3]http://www.nist.gov/itl/iad/mig/med12.cfm

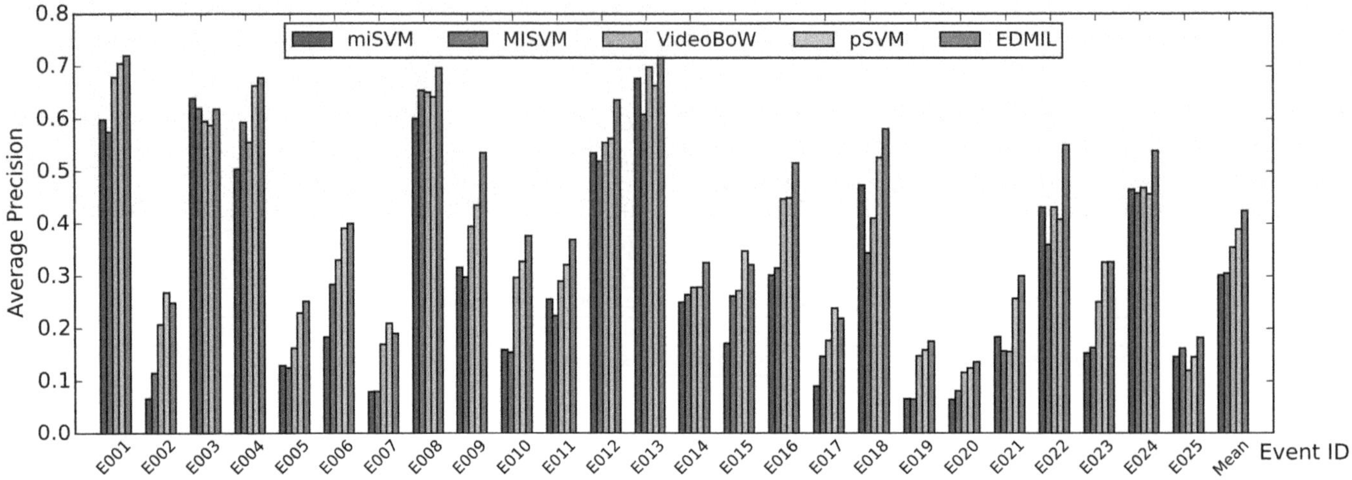

Figure 4: Evaluation results of 25 events in the TRECVID MED 2012 dataset. The mean APs are 0.3015 (miSVM), 0.3051 (MISVM), 0.3544 (VideoBOW), 0.3890 (pSVM) and 0.4246 (Ours).

Figure 5: The top 6 key evidences detected by our system for the event "Attempting board trick". The dominance of ski-related instances is reasonable.

authors in [1]. The VideoBOW method is the standard approach where local features are aggregated from the whole video. We also compare our method with the recently proposed pSVM which was adopted in [5] for TRECVID MED. For all the baseline methods, except VideoBOW, we utilize the codes provided by the authors to test with our features.

Experimental results. At first, we conduct experiments to find the optimal value of R. We select R in the range from 1 to 10. The overall performance is shown in Fig. 3. We obtain the peak performance with R around 5. Small values of R tend to get low performances. This indicates that the prediction of prior knowledge is not always good, and learning jointly with instance features is necessary. The performance becomes saturated when $R > 5$. Therefore, we fix the value of R to 5 for further experiments.

The performance of each baseline method as well as our method (EDMIL) are shown in Fig. 4. Our method significantly outperforms other baselines. For the best baseline, our method relatively outperforms by 10%. Our instance-based classifier can also provide key evidences for event detection. Example of key evidences detected by our system can be seen in Fig. 5.

5. CONCLUSIONS

We propose a new method to detect event in videos from its key evidences. Our method differs from others in that we utilize the evidential description provided for each event. Given this supportive information, we search for key evidences by jointly optimizing with instance feature in a variant of multiple instance learning framework. As a result, we obtained a superior event detection performance.

6. REFERENCES

[1] S. Andrews, I. Tsochantaridis, and T. Hofmann. Support vector machines for multiple-instance learning. In *NIPS*, pages 561–568, 2002.

[2] S. Bhattacharya, F. X. Yu, and S.-F. Chang. Minimally needed evidence for complex event recognition in unconstrained videos. In *ICMR*, 2014.

[3] J. Chen, Y. Cui, G. Ye, D. Liu, and S.-F. Chang. Event-driven semantic concept discovery by exploiting weakly tagged internet images. In *ICMR*, 2014.

[4] K.-T. Lai, D. Liu, M.-S. Chen, and S.-F. Chang. Recognizing complex events in videos by learning key static-dynamic evidences. In *ECCV*. 2014.

[5] K.-T. Lai, F. X. Yu, M.-S. Chen, and S.-F. Chang. Video event detection by inferring temporal instance labels. In *CVPR*, pages 2251–2258. IEEE, 2014.

[6] D. Oneata, J. Verbeek, and C. Schmid. Action and event recognition with fisher vectors on a compact feature set. In *ICCV*. IEEE, 2013.

[7] K. Tang, L. Fei-Fei, and D. Koller. Learning latent temporal structure for complex event detection. In *CVPR*, pages 1250–1257. IEEE, 2012.

[8] A. Vahdat, K. Cannons, G. Mori, S. Oh, and I. Kim. Compositional models for video event detection: A multiple kernel learning latent variable approach. In *ICCV*, pages 1185–1192. IEEE, 2013.

[9] H. Wang and C. Schmid. Action recognition with improved trajectories. In *ICCV*. IEEE, 2013.

[10] S. Wu, S. Bondugula, F. Luisier, X. Zhuang, and P. Natarajan. Zero-shot event detection using multi-modal fusion of weakly supervised concepts. In *CVPR*, pages 2665–2672. IEEE, 2014.

[11] B. Zhou, A. Lapedriza, J. Xiao, A. Torralba, and A. Oliva. Learning Deep Features for Scene Recognition using Places Database. *NIPS*, 2014.

Learning Semantic Correlation of Web Images and Text with Mixture of Local Linear Mappings

Youtian Du, Kai Yang
Ministry of Education Key Lab for Intelligent Networks and Network Security,
Xi'an Jiaotong University, Xi'an 710049, China
duyt@mail.xjtu.edu.cn, scfy.217@stu.xjtu.edu.cn

ABSTRACT

This paper proposes a new approach, called *mixture of local linear mappings* (*MLLM*), to the modeling of semantic correlation between web images and text. We consider that close examples generally represent a uniform concept and can be supposed to be locally transformed based on a linear mapping into the feature space of another modality. Thus, we use a mixture of local linear transformations, each local component being constrained by a neighborhood model into a finite local space, instead of a more complex nonlinear one. To handle the sparseness of data representation, we introduce the constraints of sparseness and non-negativeness into the approach. MLLM is with good interpretability due to its explicit closed form and concept-related local components, and it avoids the determination of capacity that is often considered for nonlinear transformations. Experimental results demonstrate the effectiveness of the proposed approach.

Categories and Subject Descriptors

H.3.3 [**Information Search and Retrieval**]: Retrieval models

General Terms

Theory

Keywords

Semantic correlation; heterogeneous modalities; cross-media retrieval

1. INTRODUCTION

There has been a massive explosion of multimedia contents on the web such as text, images and videos, which usually co-exist in a multimedia document and describe the similar semantic concepts. For example, an image can give us a vivid imagination but incomplete about a concept. In contrast, the text could accurately describe the details of a concept, but it is not intuitive enough. Consequently, it could make the content understanding more accurate to jointly exploit the full information from different modalities, and be significant to many applications such as image tagging [1, 2, 3] and cross-media retrieval [4, 5, 6]. However, the different representation and different ways of stimulating to human being's brains derived from heterogenous modalities lead to challenges of semantic correlation mining among the heterogenous modalities of medias [7].

The main related work can be categorized into three classes. 1) *Linear/nonlinear mapping*: The class of methods build a closed-form transformation between heterogeneous spaces [8, 9]. In general, complex models lead to high capacities but low generalization. A challenge in these methods is to choose the nonlinear model of a suitable capacity. 2) *Probabilistic models* such as probabilistic latent semantic analysis (PLSA) [10, 11]: These methods focus on the dominant global semantics of medias but ignore the direct relationship among the local components of documents, i.e., the textual words and local visual regions. 3) *Graph-based correlation propagation*: Graph-based methods, with documents as vertices and correlation as the weight of edges [4, 12], focus on the local structure of data distributions and are effective to the data with complicated distributions. The computational cost generally increases rapidly for a large scale of data.

This paper proposes a new approach to the analysis of semantic correlation between text and images based on *mixture of local linear mappings* (*MLLM*). We consider that data in a local region generally represent a uniform concept and can be supposed to be transformed based on a linear mapping into the feature space of another modality. Therefore, this work uses a mixture of local linear mapping, each local component being constrained by a neighborhood model into a finite local space, to substitute for a more complex nonlinear mapping between the feature spaces of textual and visual modalities. The MLLM model also considers the sparseness and non-negativeness and leads to the sparse output given a query, which is consistent with the true sparse representation in feature spaces of both text and images.

2. THE PROPOSED METHOD

2.1 Mixture of Local Linear Mapping

Since different representations tend to be adopted for images and text, there is typically no explicit correspondence between the representations, and it is difficult to construct a uniform correlated model over the whole distributions of

MM'15, October 26–30, 2015, Brisbane, Australia.

DOI: http://dx.doi.org/10.1145/2733373.2806331.

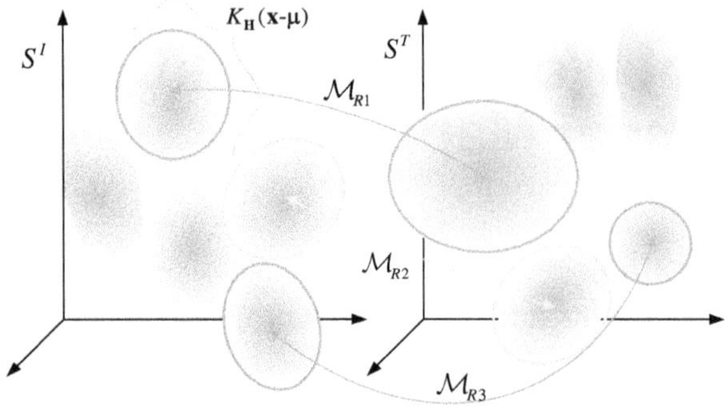

Figure 1: Illustration of the mixture of local linear mappings. The scale of darkness represents the distribution of data in feature space S^I and S^T, and the colored ellipses denote the local regions over which local linear mapping models are built.

images and text. Hence, in this work we present a mixture of local linear mappings (MLLM).

We assume that over a local region there exists a linear mapping model from textual (visual) space to visual (textual) space, and characterize this model by the concatenation of two matrices as follows:

$$\mathbf{y}_i = U \cdot W\mathbf{x}_i + \boldsymbol{\varepsilon}_i \tag{1}$$

where $\mathbf{x}_i$ denotes a query of d_q-dimensional vector, $\mathbf{y}_i$ is the d_o-dimensional example associated to query $\mathbf{x}_i$, $W \in \mathbf{R}^{K\times d_q}$ denotes the transformation from input space to a K-dimensional latent semantic space and $U \in \mathbf{R}^{d_o\times K}$ means that from the semantic space to output space, and $\boldsymbol{\varepsilon}_i$ is the fitness error. For simplicity, we let $\boldsymbol{\varepsilon}_i$ be a vector of independent and normally distributed elements with zero mean, i.e. $\Sigma_{\boldsymbol{\varepsilon}} = diag(\sigma_1^2, \sigma_2^2, \cdots, \sigma_{d_o}^2)$. The linear mapping in Eq.1 can be rewritten as the following probabilistic form:

$$\Pr(\mathbf{y}_i|\mathbf{x}_i, \mathcal{M}) = \frac{1}{(2\pi)^{\frac{d_o}{2}}|\Sigma_{\varepsilon_i}|^{\frac{1}{2}}} e^{-\frac{1}{2}\boldsymbol{\varepsilon}_i^T\Sigma_{\boldsymbol{\varepsilon}}^{-1}\boldsymbol{\varepsilon}_i} \tag{2}$$

where $\mathcal{M}$ denotes the model in Eq.1 that $\{\mathbf{x}_i, \mathbf{y}_i\}$ follows.

Intuitively, a set of close examples, denoted by $\mathcal{R}$, tend to have similar semantics and approximately follow the same cross-media mapping model. The data near the centroid of $\mathcal{R}$ follow the model with high confidence. In contrast, the data far away from the centroid follow the model with low confidence. Thus, we characterize the difference of confidence resulted from the location by introducing a neighborhood model $K_{\mathbf{H}}(\mathbf{x} - \boldsymbol{\mu})$ and a symmetric positive definite $d_q \times d_q$ bandwidth matrix $\mathbf{H}$. We choose Gaussian function as the neighborhood model:

$$K_{\mathbf{H}}(\mathbf{x}_i - \boldsymbol{\mu}) = \frac{1}{(2\pi)^{\frac{d_q}{2}}|\mathbf{H}|^{\frac{1}{2}}} e^{-\frac{1}{2}(\mathbf{x}_i-\boldsymbol{\mu})^T\mathbf{H}^{-1}(\mathbf{x}_i-\boldsymbol{\mu})} \tag{3}$$

where $\boldsymbol{\mu}$ denotes the centroid of set $\mathcal{R}$ that $\mathbf{x}_i$ belongs to. For simplicity, we assume that $\mathbf{H}$ is a diagonal matrix and $\mathbf{H} = diag(h_1, h_2, \cdots, h_{dq})$. $K_{\mathbf{H}}(\mathbf{x}_i - \boldsymbol{\mu})$ can be used to describe the probability (or confidence) of data that follow the mapping model, i.e. $\Pr(\mathbf{x}_i|\mathcal{M}_R)$.

Now, we define the following likelihood function for the pair $(\mathbf{x}_i, \mathbf{y}_i)$ given a specific local linear mapping $\mathcal{M}_R$:

$$\begin{aligned}\mathcal{L}_{F,i,m} &= \Pr(\mathbf{x}_i|\mathcal{M}_{Rm})\Pr(\mathbf{y}_i|\mathbf{x}_i, \mathcal{M}_{Rm}) \\ &= K_{\mathbf{H}}(\mathbf{x}_i - \boldsymbol{\mu}_m)\Pr(\mathbf{y}_i|\mathbf{x}_i, \mathcal{M}_{Rm}) \end{aligned}\tag{4}$$

Actually, due to the complicated data distribution and nonlinear mappings between textual and visual spaces, a unique linear model is of insufficient capacity in modeling the correlation between them. Consequently, we develop a mixture of local linear mappings to characterize the cross-media correlation as follows:

$$\begin{aligned}\mathcal{L}_F &= \prod_{i=1}^{N}\Pr(\mathbf{x}_i, \mathbf{y}_i) \\ &= \prod_{i=1}^{N}\sum_{m=1}^{M}\omega_m c_m e^{\sum_{j=1}^{d_q}\frac{-(\mathbf{x}_{i,j}-\boldsymbol{\mu}_{m,j})^2}{2h_{j,m}^2}} \cdot e^{\sum_{j=1}^{d_o}\frac{-\varepsilon_{i,m,j}^2}{2\sigma_{j,m}^2}} \end{aligned}\tag{5}$$

where M is the number of components of the mixture model, ω_m denotes the positive weight of the m-th component and $\sum_{m=1}^{K}\omega_m = 1$, c_m is a factor to normalize $\mathcal{L}_F$ to be a probability density function, $\mathbf{x}_{i,j}$ and $\boldsymbol{\mu}_{m,j}$ denote the j-th entry of $\mathbf{x}_i$ and $\boldsymbol{\mu}_m$, $\varepsilon_{i,m,j}$, $h_{j,m}$ and $\sigma_{j,m}$ are the j-th entry of $\boldsymbol{\varepsilon}_i$, $\mathbf{H}$ and $\Sigma_{\boldsymbol{\varepsilon}}$ corresponding to the model $\mathcal{M}_{Rm}$, respectively. In our mixture model in Eq.5, the first exponential term plays the role of making the dense points tend to share one model, and the second one focuses on modeling the correlation between two heterogeneous modalities.

2.2 Constraints to MLLP

In this section, we consider some extra constraints to the mixture of local linear mappings.

1) *Smoothness.* As mentioned above, close examples, with proper representation, tend to indicate the similar concept in both textual space and visual space. Hence, it is necessary to return the similar retrieved outputs for two close queries. We formulate the smoothness constraint as follows:

$$J_W = \sum\nolimits_{i\sim j}\|e_{ij}W(\mathbf{x}_i - \mathbf{x}_j)\|_2 \le \|D_X\|_F\|W\|_F \tag{6}$$

$$J_U = \sum\nolimits_{i\sim j}\|e_{ij}UW(\mathbf{x}_i - \mathbf{x}_j)\|_2 \le \|WD_X\|_F\|U\|_F \tag{7}$$

where $i \sim j$ means that $\mathbf{x}_i$ is the neighbor of $\mathbf{x}_j$, e_{ij} denotes the weight of the pair $\mathbf{x}_i$ and $\mathbf{x}_j$, and D_X is the matrix whose columns are vectors $\{\mathbf{x}_i - \mathbf{x}_j\}$ in a certain order for all $i \sim j$. We let $e_{ij} = 1$ for all i and j in Eqs.6 and 7 since we have no clear prior information to show which pair is more important. The neighbors of $\mathbf{x}_j$ is determined by choosing C-nearest points. Thus, we measure the smoothness of cross-media mappings with the following expression:

$$\begin{aligned}J_{sm}(U, W) &= J_W + J_U \\ &\triangleq \lambda_W\|W\|_F + \lambda_U\|U\|_F \end{aligned}\tag{8}$$

where λ_W and λ_U, which replace the coefficients on the right-hand side of Eqs.6 and 7 respectively, are used to control the importance of the two terms. The first term on the right-hand side of Eq.8 measures the distance in the concept space, and the second one measures the distance of two retrieved outputs. To obtain a smooth mapping model, $J_{sm}(U, W)$ needs to be constrained to a small value.

2) *Sparseness and Non-negativeness.* With the bag-of-word representation, both text and images are generally represented as the feature vectors of non-negative and sparse components. Take the mapping from textual space to concept space as example. When a document is mapped into the concept space, we expect that it corresponds to a few concepts that can describe its semantics. That is, the other components in the concept vector are zeros. Thus, the matrix W needs to be sparse. Further, we think every unit

appearing in a document supplies positive contribution to the corresponding concept. In other words, a whole concept is formed by combining a set of units and can be considered as the linear combination of elements. The non-negative constraint makes only additive combination be allowed.

Finally, we have the following optimization problem:

$$\min_{U_m \in \mathbf{R}^{d_o \times K}, W_m \in \mathbf{R}^{K \times d_q}} \mathcal{L}(U_m, W_m) \tag{9}$$

where

$$\mathcal{L}(U_m, W_m) = -\ln \mathcal{L}_F + \lambda_1 \sum_{m=1}^{M} J_{sm}(U_m, W_m) + \lambda_2 \sum_{m=1}^{M} J_{sp}(U_m, W_m)$$
$$S.t.\ U_m \geq 0, W_m \geq 0 \tag{10}$$

where $J_{sp}(U_m, W_m) \triangleq \|U_m\|_1 + \|W_m\|_1$ denotes the sparseness term, and λ_1 and λ_2 are used to control the balance between these terms.

2.3 Optimization Process

The optimization problem (9) is different from many regularization based learning because it contains some hidden information. More specifically, we don't know which local linear mapping that $(\mathbf{x}_i, \mathbf{y}_i)$ follows. We develop a sub-gradient descent approach under the framework of Expectation- Maximization. The parameter set is denoted by $\Theta = \{U_m, W_m, \omega_m, \mathbf{H}_m, \boldsymbol{\mu}_m, \Sigma_{\varepsilon,m}\}_{m=1}^{M}$.

1) *Initialization.* First, we use Kmeans clustering algorithm over training data $\{\mathbf{x}_i\}_{i=1}^{N}$ and achieve M clusters. Let the initial value of $\boldsymbol{\mu}_m$ and $\mathbf{H}_m$ (written as $\boldsymbol{\mu}_m^{(0)}$ and $\mathbf{H}_m^{(0)}$, respectively) equal the mean vector and covariance matrix of the m-th cluster; Initialize $U_m \in \mathbf{R}^{d_o \times K}$ and $W_m \in \mathbf{R}^{K \times d_q}$ with non-negative matrix.

2) *Determination of hidden information.* Given $\Theta^{(t-1)}$, we compute the probability that $(\mathbf{x}_i, \mathbf{y}_i)$ follows $\mathcal{M}_{Rm}$.

$$\Pr(\mathcal{M}_{Rm}|\mathbf{x}_i, \mathbf{y}_i, \Theta^{(t-1)}) = \frac{\Pr(\mathcal{M}_{Rm}, \mathbf{x}_i, \mathbf{y}_i|, \Theta^{(t-1)})}{\sum_{m=1}^{M} \Pr(\mathcal{M}_{Rm}, \mathbf{x}_i, \mathbf{y}_i|, \Theta^{(t-1)})} \tag{11}$$

where

$$\Pr(\mathcal{M}_{Rm}, \mathbf{x}_i, \mathbf{y}_i|\Theta^{(t-1)}) = \omega_m c_m e^{\sum_{j=1}^{d_q} \frac{-(\mathbf{x}_{i,j} - \boldsymbol{\mu}_{m,j})^2}{2h_{j,m}^2}} \cdot e^{\sum_{j=1}^{d_Q} \frac{-\varepsilon_{i,m,j}^2}{2\sigma_{j,m}^2}} \tag{12}$$

For simplicity, we rewrite $\Pr(\mathcal{M}_{Rm}|\mathbf{x}_i, \mathbf{y}_i, \Theta^{(t-1)})$ as $P_{i,m}^{(t-1)}$.

3) *Update.* The parameters of $\mathcal{M}_{Rm}$ are updated at t time sequentially by:

$$\omega_m^{(t)} = \frac{1}{N} \sum_{i=1}^{N} P_{i,m}^{(t-1)},\ \boldsymbol{\mu}_m^{(t)} = \sum_{i=1}^{N} \mathbf{x}_i P_{i,m}^{(t-1)} / \sum_{i=1}^{N} P_{i,m}^{(t-1)} \tag{13}$$

$${h_{j,m}^{(t)}}^2 = \sum_{i=1}^{N} (\mathbf{x}_{i,j} - \boldsymbol{\mu}_{m,j}^{(t-1)})^2 P_{i,m}^{(t-1)} / \sum_{i=1}^{N} P_{i,m}^{(t-1)} \tag{14}$$

For the update of the other parameters, we define another cost function based on problem (9):

$$\mathcal{Q}(U_m, W_m) = \sum_{m=1}^{M} (\sum_{i=1}^{N} (-\ln c_m - \sum_{j=1}^{d_o} \frac{\varepsilon_{i,m,j}^2}{2\sigma_{j,m}^2}) P_{i,m}^{(t-1)} + \lambda_1 J_{sm}(U_m, W_m) + \lambda_2 J_{sp}(U_m, W_m)) \tag{15}$$

Table 1: MAP scores (Top 50 retrieved examples).

	Corel5K		Wikipedia	
	T→I	I→T	T→I	I→T
CCA	0.1078	0.1725	0.2485	0.1646
KCCA	0.2115	0.1501	0.2807	0.2121
MLLM	**0.2787**	**0.2832**	**0.3581**	**0.2793**

Minimizing $\mathcal{Q}(U_m, W_m)$ subjected to $U_m \geq 0, W_m \geq 0$ with sub-gradient descent approaches can obtain the solution.

3. EXPERIMENTAL RESULTS

Two public real-world datasets are used in our experiments. 1) *Corel5K*: There are 50 categories in this dataset and each category is made up by 100 images. Each image has a caption of 1-5 keywords. We represent text and images of Corel5K by 374-dimensional and 500-dimensional bag-of-word feature vectors, respectively. We random choose 2/3 examples for training and the rest for test. 2) *Wikipedia dataset*: The set consists of 2,866 images, each with a paragraph of text to describe the image. We use the originally provided representation: 10-dimensional topic-based features for text and 128-dimensional SIFT feature for images, and the originally provided ratio 2173/693 (training/test). Each experiment is implemented 10 times independently.

We compare the proposed method to two previous representative methods, including 1) *Canonical Correlation Analysis* (*CCA*) [8]: The technique linearly transforms two kind of data from initial spaces to two new spaces respectively to achieve the largest relevance; 2) *KCCA* [8]: a non-linear version of CCA by introducing kernels. In this work, we employ the RBF kernel. We use two measures to evaluate the performance. 1) Percentage score: An image(or text) is considered correctly retrieved if it appears in the first t percent of the predicted list from its corresponding text (or image) query. 2) Mean average precision (MAP). Because users generally pay more attention to the front retrieved results, we only analyze the results of the first 50 returned samples in MAP analysis.

For parameter tuning, we split the training set into 5 folds and employ 5-fold cross-validation. For MLLM, we choose M and K as 50 and 15 for Corel5K, and 15 and 8 for Wikipedia. We search the other parameters over the grid: $\lambda_1, \lambda_2, \lambda_U, \lambda_W \in \{0.01, 0.1, 1, 10, 100\}$. In the implementation, we let $\lambda_U = \lambda_W$ for low complexity of search.

Fig.2 illustrates the average percentage score of 10 independent experiments over both datasets. For the often used percentage $t = 20\%$, MLLM achieves the precision of 0.561, 0.575, 0.452 and 0.421, which are clearly superior to the compared two methods. In some cases, we note that for large percentage t (e.g., $t > 70\%$), the precision of our method is similar with or slightly lower than CCA or KCCA. We consider that a highly possible reason is our method tends to describe the local property of data distribution over the similar data instead of the distribution over the whole space. Table 1 shows the MAP result, which measures whether the retrieved data belong to the same category as the query or not. Fig.3 shows an example of sparseness in the prediction of MLLM given a text query. Given the query including textual words "plane", "runway" and "boeing", the predicted visual words is highly correlated to the true ones of the image associated with the query, which means that MLLM method can predict the sparse output well given a query. In

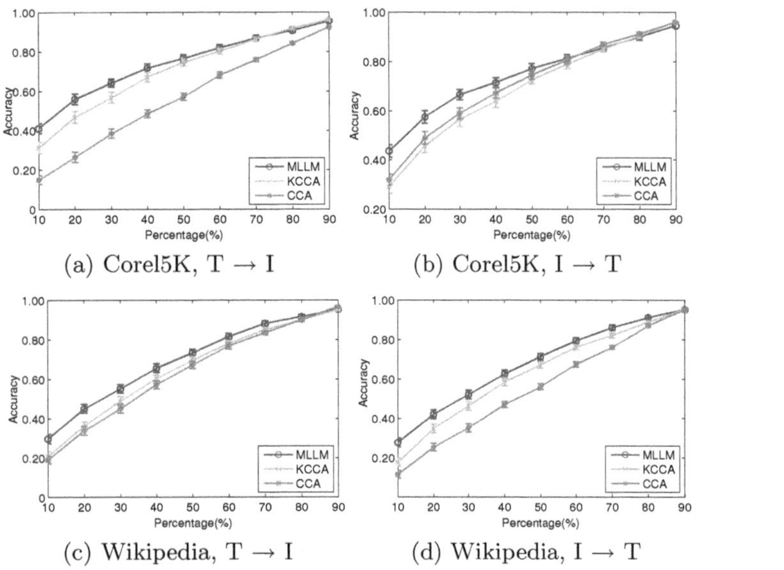

Figure 2: The percentage score evaluation on two sets. $T \rightarrow I$ and $I \rightarrow T$ denote text query and image query, respectively. The error bars indicate ± 1 standard error.

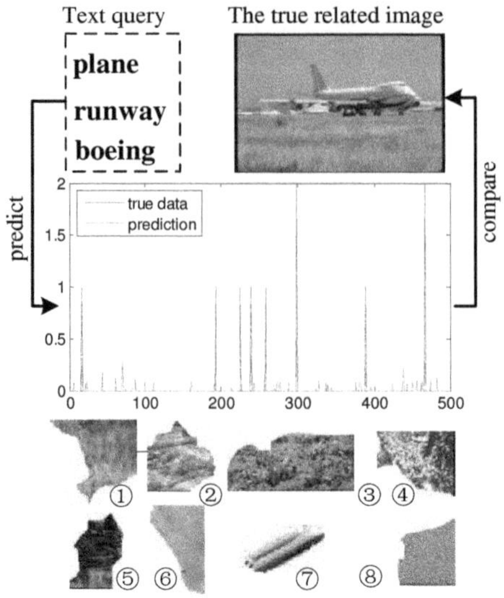

Figure 3: Illustration of sparseness. Small image patches 1-8 are those closest to the centers of the clusters corresponding orderly to the visual words indicated by blue vertical lines.

a majority of the data especially in Corel5K, we can find the results like this example.

4. CONCLUSIONS

In this paper, we proposes a new approach, named MLLM, to the modeling of semantic correlation between text and images. The close data in a local region can be supposed to be transformed based on a linear mapping into the feature space of another modality. Therefore, In the whole space, the correlation between heterogenous modalities can be modeled by a mixture of local linear mappings. We try to discover a transformation from one modality of information to the other based on mixture of local linear mapping that can replace and be superior to the more complex nonlinear transformation. Besides of the better performance shown in the experiments, our method also have some other advantages. It is with good interpretability due to its explicit closed form and concept-related local components. Moreover, it avoids the complicated analyse of the capacity that is often considered in nonlinear transformations.

5. ACKNOWLEDGMENTS

This work is supported in part by the National Natural Science Foundation (61375040, 61202392, 61175039, 61221063) of China.

6. REFERENCES

[1] J. Jeon, V. Lavrenko, and R. Manmatha. Automatic image annotation and retrieval using cross-media relevance models. In *ACM SIGIR*, pages 119–126. ACM, 2003.

[2] L. Wu, R. Jin, and A.K.Jain. Tag completion for image retrieval. *IEEE Transactions on Pattern Analysis and Machine Intelligence*, 35(3):716–727, 2013.

[3] M. Wang, B. Ni, X. Hua, and T. Chua. Assistive tagging: a survey of multimedia tagging with human-computer joint exploration. *ACM Computing Surveys*, 44(4):25–25, August 2012.

[4] Y. Zhuang, Y. Yang, and F. Wu. Mining semantic correlation of heterogeneous multimedia data for cross-media retrieval. *IEEE Transaction on Multimedia*, 10(2):221–229, 2008.

[5] Y. Gao, M. Wang, Z. Zha, J. Shen, X. Li, and X. Wu. Visual-textual joint relevance learning for tag-based social image search. *IEEE Transactions on Image Processing*, 22(1):363 – 376, 2013.

[6] Y. Zhuang, Y. Wang, F. Wu, Y. Zhang, and W. Lu. Supervised coupled dictionary learning with group structures for multi-modal retrieval. In *AAAI*, pages 1070–1076, 2013.

[7] X. Wu, Y. Qiao, X. Wang, and X. Tang. Cross matching of music and image. In *ACM Multimedia*, pages 837–840. ACM, 2012.

[8] J. Pereira, E. Coviello, G. Doyle, N. Rasiwasia, G. Lanckriet, R. Levy, and N. Vasconcelos. On the role of correlation and abstraction in cross-modal multimedia retrieval. *IEEE Transactions on Pattern Analysis and Machine Intelligence*, 36(3):521–535, 2014.

[9] T. Jiang and A. Tan. Learning image-text associations. *IEEE Transactions on Knowledge and Data Engineering*, 21(2):161–177, 2009.

[10] F. Monay and D.G.Perez. Modeling semantic aspects for cross-media image indexing. *IEEE Transactions on Pattern Analysis and Machine Intelligence*, 29(10):1802–1817, 2007.

[11] Y.Zhou, M. Liang, and J. Du. Study of cross-media topic analysis based on visual topic model. In *CCDC*, pages 3467–3470, 2012.

[12] X. Zhai, Y. Peng, and J. Xiao. Effective heterogeneous similarity measure with nearest neighbors for cross-media retrieval. In *MMM*, pages 312–322, 2012.

Learned vs. Hand-Crafted Features for Pedestrian Gender Recognition

Grigory Antipov, Sid-Ahmed Berrani
Orange Labs – France Telecom
35512 Cesson-Sévigné, France
{grigory.antipov, sidahmed.berrani}@orange.com

Natacha Ruchaud, Jean-Luc Dugelay
Eurecom
06410 Biot, France
{natacha.ruchaud, jean-luc.dugelay}@eurecom.fr

ABSTRACT

This paper addresses the problem of image features selection for pedestrian gender recognition. Hand-crafted features (such as HOG) are compared with learned features which are obtained by training convolutional neural networks. The comparison is performed on the recently created collection of versatile pedestrian datasets which allows us to evaluate the impact of dataset properties on the performance of features. The study shows that hand-crafted and learned features perform equally well on small-sized homogeneous datasets. However, learned features significantly outperform hand-crafted ones in the case of heterogeneous and unfamiliar (unseen) datasets. Our best model which is based on learned features obtains 79% average recognition rate on completely unseen datasets. We also show that a relatively small convolutional neural network is able to produce competitive features even with little training data.

Categories and Subject Descriptors

I.4.7 [**Feature Measurement**]: Feature representation.

Keywords

Pedestrian gender recognition; CNN; HOG; image features.

1. INTRODUCTION

An ability to profile people based on their gender is a very important issue which has obvious applications in video surveillance and multimedia retrieval systems. However, quite often it is not possible to get a clear close-shot of a person's face and the gender should be estimated having only a general silhouette of a body. In this work, we address the problem of the gender recognition from still images of pedestrians taken in adverse conditions.

The choice of features to describe an object is crucial in computer vision. Existing image features can be roughly divided into 2 categories: the hand-crafted and the learned ones. By hand-crafted features we understand those which are extracted from separate images according to a certain *manually predefined algorithm* based on the expert knowledge. LBP [16], SIFT [14] and HOG [4] features are commonly known examples of hand-crafted features. Contrary to hand-crafted image features, the learned ones are derived from an image dataset by a training procedure in order to fulfill a certain task (e.g. gender recognition). Convolutional Neural Networks (CNN) [13] are examples of deep neural networks which can be used to extract learned features.

We consider 4 types of features in this study: 2 examples per each considered category. We choose person re-identification [12] features and HOG as examples of hand-crafted features. In order to obtain learned features, we train 2 different CNN architectures.

The rest of the paper is organized as follows: the bibliography overview and motivations for the choice of features to compare are presented in Section 2; the chosen features are introduced in details in Section 3; the collection of datasets which we have used for experiments is described in Section 4; the performed experiments and obtained results are presented in Section 5 and the main conclusions are highlighted in Section 6.

2. RELATED WORK

To the best of our knowledge, PETA datasets collection [5] is the largest open-access collection of pedestrian images with gender annotation. Authors of PETA propose a universal way to recognize a number of attributes in pedestrian images. Gender is one of the attributes they have considered. In their algorithm, authors of PETA employ re-identification features which were originally described in [12] for the purpose of automatic re-identification of humans in CCTV videos. We use PETA collection of datasets in our experiments. Following the authors of PETA we also choose re-identification features for comparison in our work.[1]

In numerous works, authors have found Histogram of Oriented Gradients (HOG) features to be the most appropriate for pedestrian gender recognition. In particular, in [1] authors claim obtaining 76% recognition rate on MIT dataset, while in [3] authors claim obtaining 80% recognition rate on VIPeR dataset.[2] Hence, we include HOG features in our comparison as the 2nd example of hand-crafted features.

Due to their exceptional success in recent years, deep CNN have become the first-choice solution for supervised learning

MM'15, October 26–30, 2015, Brisbane, Australia.
© 2015 ACM. ISBN 978-1-4503-3459-4/15/10 ...$15.00.
DOI: http://dx.doi.org/10.1145/2733373.2806332.

[1] We use the re-identification features implementation which was kindly provided to us by authors of PETA.
[2] Both MIT and VIPeR datasets are included in PETA.

on image datasets [19, 6, 11]. In [15] authors employ a CNN for gender recognition on a tiny MIT dataset having only 900 images. They claim obtaining 80% recognition rate. In this work, we design a compact CNN architecture and corresponding learned features contribute to our comparison.

There are more and more examples ([2, 17]) where a CNN trained on a huge general-purpose dataset is successfully fine-tuned for a very specific classification task with little extra data. Some authors even claim that today fine-tuning of a pre-trained CNN is a must-try method in all image classification tasks [17]. In our work we fine-tune the model which was trained by Krizhevsky et al. [11] on the ILSVRC dataset [18] containing about 1.3 million images.

Contrary to previous works, we do not focus on a single dataset, we rather compare considered features on a versatile collection of pedestrian datasets. Moreover, besides evaluating performance of features on separate datasets, we also compare how well they generalize by applying them on unfamiliar (i.e. completely unseen) datasets.

3. FEATURE REPRESENTATIONS

Below we present features that are compared in this study.

3.1 Person re-identification features

Person re-identification features of an image [12] is a 2784-dimensional vector which contains low-level colour and texture information. The complete vector is composed of six 464-dimensional vectors each of which is extracted from 6 equal sized horizontal strips from the image. Each strip uses 8 colour channels (RGB, HSV and YCbCr) and 21 texture filters (Gabor, Schmid) derived from the luminance channel. We use a bin size of 16 to describe each channel.

3.2 HOG features

In order to extract HOG features, we use 8-by-8 square cells which are organized in 2-by-2 blocks. The number of histogram bins is set to 9. When an image of 50 pixels width and of 150 height is given as input (which is the case in our experiments), the resulting HOG features vector with the described parameters has the dimension 2448.

3.3 Features learned by Mini-CNN

In order to avoid ambiguity, in this section and below, we refer to the CNN which is designed by ourselves as *Mini-CNN*, whereas the term *AlexNet-CNN* is employed to refer to the CNN which is designed by Alex Krizhevsky.

The architecture of *Mini-CNN* is presented in Figure 1. *Mini-CNN* has 2 convolutional layers ($C1$ and $C2$) with 5x5 kernels, each of which is followed by max-pooling with a stride of 2 pixels ($P1$ and $P2$) and Rectified Linear Unit (ReLU) activations.[3] *Mini-CNN* is ended by 2 fully connected layers ($F1$ and $F2$). The $F2$ layer has 2 neurons (corresponding to the number of classes). The loss is computed by a softmax loss function. As it is depicted in Figure 1, *Mini-CNN* takes 3 $(50, 150)$-dimensional feature maps (red, green and blue channels of an image) as an input.[4] The 1st and 2nd convolutional layers $C1$ and $C2$ have $n1$ and $n2$ feature maps respectively. Values of $n1$ and $n2$ depend on

[3]We have also tried using sigmoid activations but ReLU activations proved to be much faster.

[4]Before being treated by *Mini-CNN*, all input images are rescaled to $(50, 150)$ size.

Figure 2: Examples of images from PETA.

the experiment: in the 1st experiment in Section 5.1 we use $n1 = n2 = 10$, while in the 2nd experiment in Section 5.2 we use a slightly bigger architecture with $n1 = n2 = 20$ (because in the 2nd experiment we have more training images). The number of neurons $n3$ in the last but one fully connected layer $F1$ also varies depending on the experiment: we have $n3 = 25$ and $n3 = 100$ for the 1st and for the 2nd experiments respectively. In order to augment the training data, we use each training image alongside with its mirrored copy. Parameters of *Mini-CNN* have been chosen by trying several architectures and by choosing the most possibly compact one so that performance is not sacrificed.

After training *Mini-CNN*, we use the obtained weights to calculate the values of neurons in the $F1$ layer for all testing images. These neuron values serve as *Mini-CNN* features for the testing images. Thus, *Mini-CNN* represents an image by either 25- or 100-dimensional vector (depending on the experiment), which is more than 100 times smaller than sizes of corresponding person re-identification or HOG vectors.

3.4 Features learned by AlexNet-CNN

The architecture of *AlexNet-CNN* is described in details in [11]. *AlexNet-CNN* is already a trained model. In our work, we only fine-tune it to recognize genders of pedestrians. After fine-tuning of *AlexNet-CNN* we use the weights from the last but one fully connected layer (which contains 4096 neurons) as features for input images. Thus, in the case of *AlexNet-CNN*, a features vector dimension is 4096.[5]

4. DATASETS

Originally, the PETA collection consists of 10 datasets of different sizes with a total amount of $19,000$ images. Appearances of images hugely vary between different datasets of PETA in terms of image resolutions (from 17x39 to 169x365 pixels), camera angles (pictures are taken either by ground-based cameras or by surveillance cameras which are set at a certain height) and environments (indoors or outdoors). Examples of PETA images are presented in Figure 2.

Authors of PETA perform series of experiments on prediction of gender on the whole collection of $19,000$ images [5] using re-identification features. They *randomly* split the total collection of images into $9,500$ for training, $1,900$ for validation and $7,600$ for testing. They report obtaining be-

[5]Training and fine-tuning of all CNNs in this work is performed using Caffe deep learning framework [9].

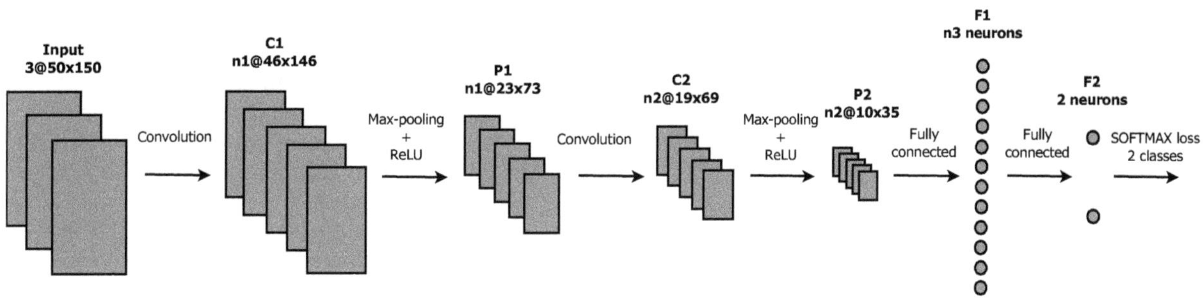

Figure 1: Architecture of *Mini-CNN*.

Dataset	Train size (♂+ ♀)	Test size (♂+ ♀)
CUHK	3432 = (2420 + 1012)	377 = (189 + 188)
PRID	942 = (449 + 493)	101 = (50 + 51)
GRID	928 = (531 + 397)	100 = (50 + 50)
MIT	792 = (532 + 260)	84 = (42 + 42)
VIPeR	1138 = (556 + 582)	120 = (60 + 60)
3DPeS	0	100 = (50 + 50)
CAVIAR	0	68 = (34 + 34)
i-LIDS	0	100 = (50 + 50)
SARC3D	0	41 = (21 + 20)
TownCentre	0	42 = (21 + 21)

Table 1: Training and testing parts per dataset.

tween 79.7% and 81.4% of male gender prediction rate (the results vary depending on the used classifier). We have successfully reproduced this result using several random splits of 19,000 images in the same proportions as it has been done by authors of PETA. However, the number of unique persons in the PETA collection is much smaller than 19,000 because PETA contains many images of the same persons which are taken few seconds away from each other by surveillance cameras. Images like that are almost identical and they can considerably bias the resulting prediction rates. After removal of all quasi-identical images from PETA the resulting prediction rates drop down to 63-65%.

This drastic drop in performance proves the importance of the manual filtering of PETA collection. Apart from filtering out images of the same people, we have also removed images with a very low resolution (height is less than 120 pixels or width is less than 40 pixels) and images where a person of interest is not clearly distinguishable (i.e. images of babies in strollers or images of several persons). Finally, we have been left with 8,365 images (see Table 1) which is less than half as many as the initial size of PETA.

5. EXPERIMENTS

In order to objectively compare the usefulness of considered features for the gender recognition problem and not to take into account a possible impact of a classifier on resulting prediction rates, we always use the same classifier for all considered features: the SVM classifier with a linear kernel.[6] Classification results are compared using Mean Average Precision (MAP) and Area Under ROC Curve (AUC) [7].[7]

[6]In particular, we use the publicly available SVM-light implementation of SVM [10].

[7]AUC is an important measure for us because of its invariance to the chosen decision threshold by an SVM-classifier.

Features	MAP		AUC	
	μ	σ	μ	σ
AlexNet-CNN	0.82	0.05	0.90	0.05
Mini-CNN	0.79	0.04	0.86	0.03
HOG	0.80	0.04	0.88	0.04
Re-identification	0.59	0.07	0.63	0.09

Table 2: Exp. 1: Results on 5 separate datasets (CUHK, PRID, GRID, MIT and VIPeR).

Features	Familiar		Unfamiliar	
	MAP	AUC	MAP	AUC
AlexNet-CNN	0.85	0.91	0.79	0.85
Mini-CNN	0.80	0.88	0.75	0.80
HOG	0.72	0.84	0.56	0.64
Re-identification	0.58	0.60	0.61	0.69

Table 3: Exp. 2: Results on "familiar" and "unfamiliar" datasets.

5.1 Exp. 1: evaluation on separate datasets

In the 1st experiment, we compare the performance of considered features on 5 separate datasets: CUHK, PRID, GRID, MIT and VIPeR. Sizes of training (which is used to train an SVM classifier) and testing parts for each of these datasets are given in Table 1. In the cases of *Mini-CNN* and *AlexNet-CNN* the features (i.e. CNN) are learned on the training images as well.

Results of the 1st experiment are summarized in Table 2. Mean values and standard deviations for 2 considered metrics are calculated over 5 datasets. Based on this experiment, we can conclude that re-identification features are hardly applicable for our problem. Successful results obtained by re-identification features in [5] might be explained by a significant number of quasi-identical images between training and testing datasets (as it is explained in Section 4). The other 3 features show very close performances and none of them can be favoured based only on the 1st experiment.

5.2 Exp. 2: evaluation of generalization

In the 2nd experiment, we evaluate the capability of compared features to generalize on heterogeneous and even completely unseen datasets.

Firstly, we train SVM classifiers with different features on the dataset which is composed of training parts of CUHK, PRID, GRID, MIT and VIPeR taken together. Then we test classifiers on the testing parts of the same datasets which are also taken together. Thus, we compare features on a single big dataset which is composed of non-homogeneous images (different camera angles, environments, etc.)

Results of this experiment are presented in Table 3 (in its "familiar" part). On one hand, we see that for learned features (i.e. *AlexNet-CNN* and *Mini-CNN*) both MAP and AUC metrics practically coincide with corresponding results in Table 2 (with respect to standard deviations). On the other hand, there is a significant drop of performance for HOG features. These results perfectly make sense because learned features have a possibility to adapt to the heterogeneity of the input data during the training phase, whereas HOG features are not trained and, therefore, less flexible. We do not consider re-identification features in the 2nd experiment due to their poor performance in the 1st one.

In the 2nd part of the 2nd experiment, we use the same SVM classifiers which have been trained on the collection of training images from CUHK, PRID, GRID, MIT and VIPeR but this time we apply them on the collection of images from completely unseen datasets: 3DPeS, CAVIAR, i-LIDS, SARC3D and TownCentre (see Table 1). In other words, classifiers are compared on "unfamiliar" datasets and, thus, we evaluate if they generalize well.

Results of this experiment are presented in Table 3 (in its "unfamiliar" part). *AlexNet-CNN* performs almost equally well as in Table 2 (with respect to standard deviations). *Mini-CNN* experiences a subtle drop in performance with respect to the 1st experiment. However, it still shows quite satisfactory recognition rate of 75% despite having only 100 features. The SVM-classifier learned on HOG features performs poorly on "unfamiliar" datasets showing results which are not so far away from random guessing.

6. CONCLUSIONS

In this work, we have compared 2 hand-crafted features (HOG and re-identification) and 2 learned features (obtained by *Mini-CNN* and by *AlexNet-CNN*) in the frame of pedestrian gender recognition problem. Our findings are:

1. On small-sized homogeneous datasets, HOG and learned features perform equally well. It complies with previous works ([1, 3, 15]) on pedestrian gender recognition.

2. Learned features *significantly* outperform HOG features in the case of heterogeneous data.

3. Contrary to hand-crafted features, *Mini-CNN* and *AlexNet-CNN* features generalize well to completely unseen datasets: MAPs of 75% and 79% respectively.

4. Even a relatively small CNN (like *Mini-CNN*) trained on little data is able to produce compact features which generalize almost as good as features produced by much bigger pre-trained networks (like *AlexNet-CNN*).

In our future work, different learned features will be tried in order to recognize other important attributes of soft biometrics (like age, clothing details etc.). Moreover, we would like to verify if our findings about learned and hand-crafted features hold in other domains of computer vision. Being encouraged by the results of this paper and by the recent work presented in [8], we are also planning to further investigate the possibility of approaching the expressiveness of complex models using architectures of moderate complexity.

7. REFERENCES

[1] L. Cao, M. Dikmen, Y. Fu, and T. S. Huang. Gender recognition from body. In *ACM MM*, Canada, 2008.

[2] K. Chatfield, K. Simonyan, A. Vedaldi, and A. Zisserman. Return of the devil in the details: Delving deep into convolutional nets. *CoRR*, abs/1405.3531, 2014.

[3] M. Collins, J. Zhang, P. Miller, and H. Wang. Full body image feature representations for gender profiling. In *ICCV*, Japan, 2009.

[4] N. Dalal and B. Triggs. Histograms of oriented gradients for human detection. In *CVPR*, USA, 2005.

[5] Y. Deng, P. Luo, C. C. Loy, and X. Tang. Pedestrian attribute recognition at far distance. In *ACM MM*, USA, 2014.

[6] I. J. Goodfellow, Y. Bulatov, J. Ibarz, S. Arnoud, and V. Shet. Multi-digit number recognition from street view imagery using deep convolutional neural networks. *CoRR*, abs/1312.6082, 2013.

[7] J. A. Hanley and B. J. McNeil. The meaning and use of the area under a receiver operating characteristic (roc) curve. *Radiology*, 1982.

[8] G. E. Hinton, O. Vinyals, and J. Dean. Distilling the knowledge in a neural network. In *NIPS Deep Learning Workshop*, Canada, 2014.

[9] Y. Jia, E. Shelhamer, J. Donahue, S. Karayev, J. Long, R. Girshick, S. Guadarrama, and T. Darrell. Caffe: Convolutional architecture for fast feature embedding. *CoRR*, abs/1408.5093, 2014.

[10] T. Joachims. Making large scale SVM learning practical. 1999.

[11] A. Krizhevsky, I. Sutskever, and G. E. Hinton. Imagenet classification with deep convolutional neural networks. In *NIPS*, USA, 2012.

[12] R. Layne, T. M. Hospedales, S. Gong, et al. Person re-identification by attributes. In *BMVC*, UK, 2012.

[13] Y. LeCun and Y. Bengio. Convolutional networks for images, speech, and time series. *The handbook of brain theory and neural networks*, 1995.

[14] D. G. Lowe. Object recognition from local scale-invariant features. In *ICCV*, Canada, 1999.

[15] C.-B. Ng, Y.-H. Tay, and B.-M. Goi. A convolutional neural network for pedestrian gender recognition. In *ISNN*. Springer, 2013.

[16] T. Ojala, M. Pietikäinen, and D. Harwood. A comparative study of texture measures with classification based on featured distributions. *Pattern recognition*, 1996.

[17] A. S. Razavian, H. Azizpour, J. Sullivan, and S. Carlsson. Cnn features off-the-shelf: an astounding baseline for recognition. *CoRR*, abs/1403.6382, 2014.

[18] O. Russakovsky, J. Deng, H. Su, J. Krause, and S. S. et al. ImageNet Large Scale Visual Recognition Challenge. *CoRR*, abs/1409.0575, 2014.

[19] Y. Taigman, M. Yang, M. Ranzato, and L. Wolf. Deepface: Closing the gap to human-level performance in face verification. In *CVPR*, USA, 2014.

Multi-Level Fusion for Person Re-identification with Incomplete Marks

Zheng Wang[1], Ruimin Hu[1,2,*], Yi Yu[3], Chao Liang[1,2], Wenxin Huang[1]

[1]National Engineering Research Center for Multimedia Software, Computer School of Wuhan Univ., China
{wangzwhu, hrm, cliang, wenxin.huang}@whu.edu.cn
[2]Collaborative Innovation Center of Geospatial Technology, China
[3]National Institute of Informatics, Japan
yiyu@nii.ac.jp

ABSTRACT

Most video surveillance suspect investigation systems rely on the videos taken in different camera views. Actually, besides the videos, in the investigation process, investigators also manually label some marks, which, albeit incomplete, can be quite accurate and helpful in identifying persons. This paper studies the problem of Person Re-identification with Incomplete Marks (PRIM), aiming at ranking the persons in the gallery according to both the videos and incomplete marks. This problem is solved by a multi-step fusion algorithm, which consists of three key steps: (i) The early fusing step exploits both visual features and marked attributes to predict a complete and precise attribute vector. (ii) Based on the statistical attribute dominance and saliency phenomena, a dominance-saliency matching model is suggested for measuring the distance between attribute vectors. (iii) The gallery is ranked separately by using visual features and attribute vectors, and the overall ranking list is the result of a late fusion. Experiments conducted on VIPeR [4] dataset have validated the effectiveness of the proposed method in all the three key steps. The results also show that through introducing marks, the retrieval accuracy is significantly improved.

Categories and Subject Descriptors

H.3.3 [**Information Systems**]: INFORMATION STORAGE AND RETRIEVAL—*Information Search and Retrieval*

Keywords

Person re-identification, Attributes, Fusion

1. INTRODUCTION

As the video surveillance system is widely constructed in the city, exploiting video surveillance system to find clues, track persons and re-identify criminal suspects, plays an increasingly important role in daily criminal investigation [3]. During the investigation processes, investigators are busy in browsing video records,

(a) An example of the manual mark

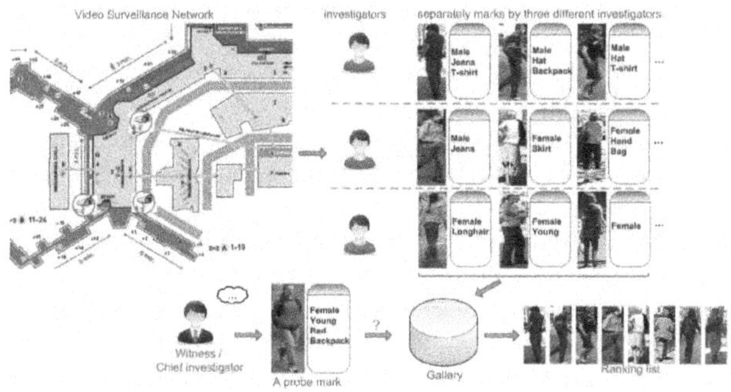

(b) The video surveillance suspect investigation system

Figure 1: (a) Once the investigator glimpses a person of interest, he should snap the frame of the watched video, indicate the image of the person, and describe some attributes of the person. Both the image and the marked attributes constitute an integral mark. (b) A large amount of marks labeled by different investigators make up a gallery. A ranking list can be generated in response to a probe mark.

marking the information they doubt, and matching these marks one by one. Fig.1(a) [1] illustrates what an investigator generally marks when he believes that a person appeared in the video would bring clues to a case. A manual mark includes the image of a person and some semantic descriptions in visual attributes. In this way, a number of investigators will make a huge number of marks, which are collected to a gallery. It is very time consuming to match these different marks by human labors, so a new video surveillance based suspect investigation system is needed to improve the retrieval efficiency. As illustrated in Fig.1(b), the chief investigator or the witness inputs an image and marked attributes, and then the marks in the gallery are ranked automatically by the investigation system.

*indicates corresponding author

[1]The example image is from the TV series "Person of Interest".

MM'15, October 26–30, 2015, Brisbane, Australia.
© 2015 ACM. ISBN 978-1-4503-3459-4/15/10 ...$15.00.
DOI: http://dx.doi.org/10.1145/2733373.2806400.

Actually, this kind of application is very similar to the person re-identification problem [2], which aims to show the images of the query person on the top of the ranking list, generated by various cameras configured in different places. However, different from the general person re-identification problem, which merely exploits the image features, this paper utilizes both image features and semantic attributes to retrieve the query person. In this problem, different investigators will select and annotate attributes separately, which cannot always cover all attributes in the attribute corpus. That is to say, the marked attributes attached to each image are incomplete. We define the new problem as Person Re-identification with Incomplete Mark (PRIM).

In addition to image features and incompletely marked attributes, integral attributes can also be learned from image features, in a similar way as in previous works [6, 1, 9]. Therefore, three kinds of information can be utilized in the PRIM problem. (1) **General low-level features**. As in general person re-identification research [2, 17, 15, 16, 7], a feature should be constructed to be robust and can easily distinguish different persons in various cameras. However, due to low resolution, partial occlusion, view change, and illumination variation in various cameras, designing a discriminative and robust feature is extremely challenging [18]. (2) **General high-level attributes**. The visual attributes, which cover the whole attribute corpus, are learned from the image content. These attributes, though complete, usually are imprecise, which are limited by the accuracy of attribute classifiers. (3) **Marked high-level attributes**. These attributes are incomplete but can be assumed precise.

The above three features have different characteristics, and are combined together in this paper to solve the PRIM problem. To this end, a multi-step fusion algorithm is proposed, which consists of three key steps: First, in the early fusing step, based on the hypothesis that the reconstructions should be consistent in both image feature and attribute levels [8], a complete and precise attribute vector is learnt. Second, based on the statistical attribute dominance and saliency phenomena (which will be illustrated in Section.2.3), a dominance-saliency matching model is suggested for measuring the distance between attribute vectors. Third, in the late fusing step, based on the assumptions that image features results are relatively precise but not robust to appearance changes, while attributes are relatively robust to appearance changes but may be imprecise or incomplete, the final ranking list is merged from the ranking lists generated by separately using image features and attributes. Experiments conducted on VIPeR [4] dataset have validated the effectiveness of the proposed method in all the three key steps.

2. THE PROPOSED METHOD

2.1 Feature and Attribute Vector

Once an investigator snaps an image of a person, and makes a mark, we extract the three kinds of description vectors.

(1) **The General Feature Vector**. The image is resized to 128 × 8. Following the model described in [14], the color and texture feature are extracted from overlapping blocks of size 16 × 16 and stride of 8 × 8. The color is encoded by RGB and HSV histograms with 24 bins, and the texture feature is encoded by LBP descriptors [10] with 59 bins. To accelerate the learning process and reduce noise, we apply principle component analysis (PCA) to obtain a low-dimension representation [5]. Then, the general feature vector f is constructed ($f \in \mathbb{R}^{N_f \times 1}$, N_f is the number of dimensions of the feature vector).

(2) **The General Attribute Vector**. An auxiliary person image dataset is exploited to train attribute classifiers. Attribute will be labeled 1, if it appears in the image, and -1 otherwise. We utilize the pre-labeled attributes contributed by [1]. For each kind of attribute, a linear SVM classifier is trained separately by adopting the software package Vlfeat [12][2]. It is assumed that the number of images in the auxiliary dataset is N, and the number of attributes in the attribute corpus is N_a. Then, for each input image, N_a values in the range of $[-1, \; 1]$ are predicted by attribute classifiers. These values constitute the general attribute vector a_g ($a_g \in \mathbb{R}^{N_a \times 1}$).

(3) **The Marked Attribute Vector**. The image is labeled by the investigator with some selected attributes with values 1 or -1, and the other unlabeled attributes in the attribute corpus will be vacant with the value . These values form the marked attribute vector a_m ($a_m \in \mathbb{R}^{N_a \times 1}$).

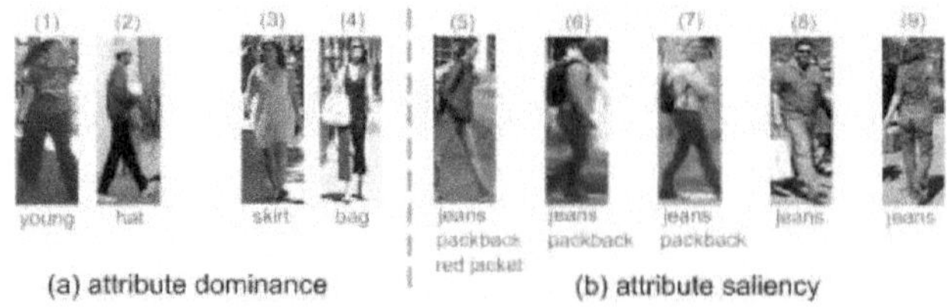

Figure 2: (a) The attributes are marked by investigators. Although the first two images both contain "blue", "young" dominates (1) but not (2), and "hat" dominates (2) not (1). In the same way, "skirt" dominates (3), while "bag" dominates (4). (b) Every person has the "jeans" attribute, so "jeans" has a low discriminative performance. While "packback" has a relatively higher discriminative capability. Specially, "red jacket" only appears once in these samples and has the highest discriminative performance.

2.2 Early Fusion

As is known, the general attribute vector is complete but imprecise, whereas the marked attribute vector is precise but incomplete. These two attribute vectors complement each other, and a combination of them can provide both complete and precise information. Therefore, it is reasonable to fuse a_g and a_m to obtain a complete and precise attribute vector. Inspired by [8], we exploit the cross-level sparse reconstruction consistency to do the early fusion work. Using the auxiliary dataset mentioned above, we can generate a feature dictionary D_f ($D_f \in \mathbb{R}^{N_f \times N}$) and an attribute dictionary D_a ($D_a \in \mathbb{R}^{N_a \times N}$). These two dictionaries are corresponding to each other in a way that each column of D_f or D_a is respectively extracted from or labeled on the same image. Then, the dictionary D_f is used to sparsely construct the feature vector f, and the reconstruction can be formulated as $\Theta_f \quad argmin_\alpha \|f - D_f\alpha\|_2^2 \quad \lambda\|\alpha\|_1$, where $\|\cdot\|_2$ and $\|\cdot\|_1$ are $L2$ norm and $L1$ norm respectively, α ($\alpha \in \mathbb{R}^{N \times 1}$) is the objective weighting vector for the reconstruction of f, and λ is a tuning factor. In the same way, the dictionary D_a is used to sparsely construct the general attribute vector a_g, and the reconstruction can be formulated as $\Theta_a \quad argmin_\beta \|a_g - D_a\beta\|_2^2 \quad \omega\|\beta\|_1$, where β ($\beta \in \mathbb{R}^{N \times 1}$) is another objective weighting vector for the reconstruction of a_g, and ω is another tuning factor.

The hypotheses is that reconstruction should be consistent in the feature and attribute levels (as the early fusion part in Fig.3 illustrates). Furthermore, we integrate both objective functions above into a unified optimization framework as follows

[2]It is available in http://www.vlfeat.org/

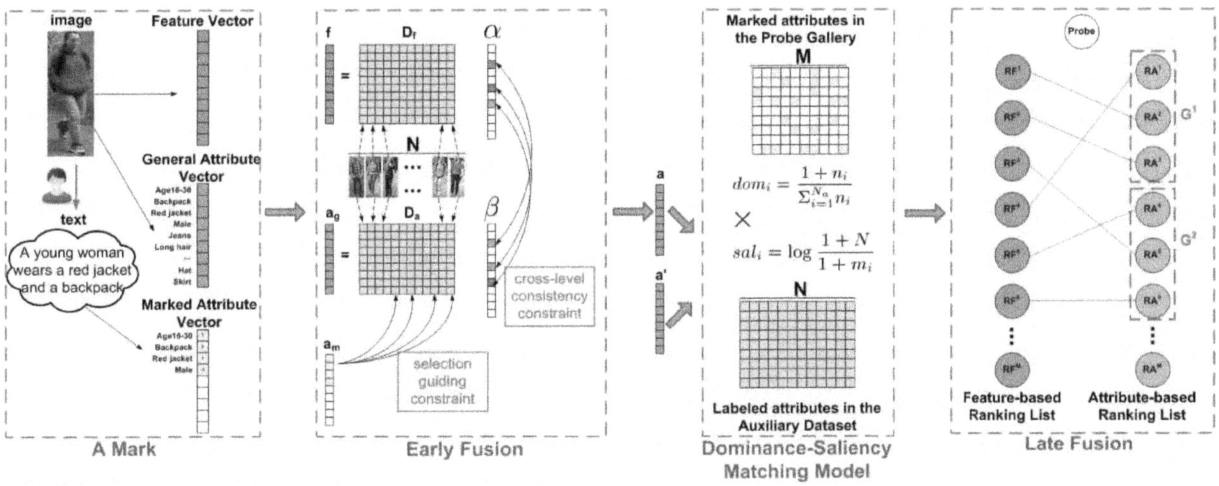

Figure 3: An overview of the proposed method, which includes three key steps. First, in early fusion step, a complete and precise attribute vector is obtained. Second, in dominance-saliency matching model step, the attribute-based ranking list is generated. Third, in late fusion step, together with the feature-based ranking list, the final ranking list is generated.

$$\Theta \quad argmin_{\alpha,\beta}\|f - D_f\alpha\|_2^2 \quad \lambda\|\alpha\|_1 \quad \mu(\|a_g - D_a\beta\|_2^2 \quad \omega\|\beta\|_1) \quad \nu\|\alpha-\beta\|_2^2 \quad \tau\|O(\beta|a_m)\|_2^2 \tag{1}$$

where $\|\alpha-\beta\|_2^2$ is the cross level consistency constraint. $\|O(\beta|a_m)\|_2^2$ is the selection guiding constraint, that corresponding non-zero elements of β will sum up, where the elements of the indicated column in D_a have different value from the elements of a_m. ν is a tuning factor for penalizing the difference between α and β, and τ is a tuning factor for the selection guiding constraint.

In this step, α and β are learnt, then a new attribute vector a is generated as $a \quad D_a\beta. * Not(a_m) \quad a_m$, where $Not(\cdot)$ means inverting the value of elements: if the value is not zero, it turns to zero, and one otherwise. The operation $.*$ indicates element-wise multiplication. Therefore, it means that generally a is equal to a_m (with high accuracy), but the incomplete items (zeros) of a_m are supplemented by those of $D_a\beta$.

2.3 Dominance-Saliency Matching Model

Measuring the distance between two feature vectors is well researched in traditional person re-identification problems, which often utilizes the Mahalanobis distance by metric learning methods [18, 5]. Similar to the feature vector, a fitable matching model for attribute vector is necessary. We find that there exist not only (i) attribute dominance (as Fig.2(a) illustrates): although some attributes are similar to different persons, some selected attributes are more dominant and make it easier to distinguish different persons, but also (ii) attribute saliency (as Fig.2(b) illustrates): if one attribute appears less often, it will hold more power of discrimination. Actually, attribute dominance and saliency are similar to the TF-IDF (term-frequency, inverse document frequency [11]) idea in information retrieval field. Using the TF-IDF idea, a dominance-saliency matching model is proposed to measure the attribute vectors a and a' (as the dominance-saliency matching model part in Fig.3 illustrates).

For each attribute i, the dominance, which originates in investigators' marks, indicates the importance and power of discriminating two different attribute vector. If an attribute is marked by more investigators, higher comparing weight should be used for this attribute. We denotes the dominance of attribute i as Eq.2, where n_i denotes the number of marks of the attribute i by investigators in the gallery.

$$dom_i \quad \frac{1 \quad n_i}{\Sigma_{i=1}^{N_a} n_i} \tag{2}$$

While, for each attribute i, the saliency, which originates in the auxiliary pre-labeled data set, indicates whether the attribute appears sparse statistically in the attribute set. If an attribute appears less, it means that more attention should be paid to the attribute and higher comparing weight should be used. We denotes the saliency of attribute i as Eq.3, where m_i denotes the number of label "+1" of the attribute i in the auxiliary data set.

$$sal_i \quad \log\frac{1 \quad N}{1 \quad m_i} \tag{3}$$

Furthermore, we integrate both dominance and saliency above into a comparing weight for the attribute i as $w_i \quad dom_i \times sal_i$. Then, the attribute distance is calculated by $d(a, a') \quad \Sigma_{i=1}^{N_a} w_i|a_i - a'_i|$.

2.4 Late Fusion

It is also a critical factor to find a suitable way to fuse the attribute-based results generated after the first two steps, and the feature-based results generated by existing methods in traditional person re-identification problem. It is assumed that the feature-based ranking list will be precise, if the person's appearance does not change a lot. It is also assumed that the attribute-based ranking list is robust to person's appearance change, but relatively imprecise. Base on these reasons, the late fusion ranking list should be generated by merging the fine-grained feature-based ranking list, and the coarse-grained attribute-based ranking list. For example, for a probe mark, with feature vectors and the learnt metric, a feature-based ranking list $RF \quad \{RF^1, RF^2, ..., RF \quad \}$ is generated, where M denotes the number of marks in the gallery, the superscript indicates the ranking number. Meanwhile, with the attribute vectors obtained in early fusion step and the matching model, an attribute-based ranking list $RA \quad \{RA^1, RA^2, ..., RA \quad \}$ is generated.

As the late fusion part in Fig.3 shows, each line connecting two elements in RF and RA indicates the same mark. We divide the

Table 1: CMC values (%) at different ranks on the VIPeR data set.

Method	rank@1	10	25	50
KISSME [5]	23.39	66.27	83.73	92.66
GA+L1	9.72	35.28	51.33	66.84
EF+L1	62.53	91.58	96.11	97.59
EF+DSM	**67.78**	96.20	98.73	99.40
EF+DSM+LF	60.70	**96.58**	**98.89**	**99.40**

list RA into multiple groups G $\{G^1, G^2, ..\}$. In coarse-grained consideration, the group ranking position will maintain in the finial ranking list. Then, with the list RF, we subtly adjust the ranking list in each group. As Fig.3 illustrates, the connected element pairs (RF^1, RA^2), (RF^2, RA^3), (RF^4, RA^1) will respectively rank number one to three in the final ranking list.

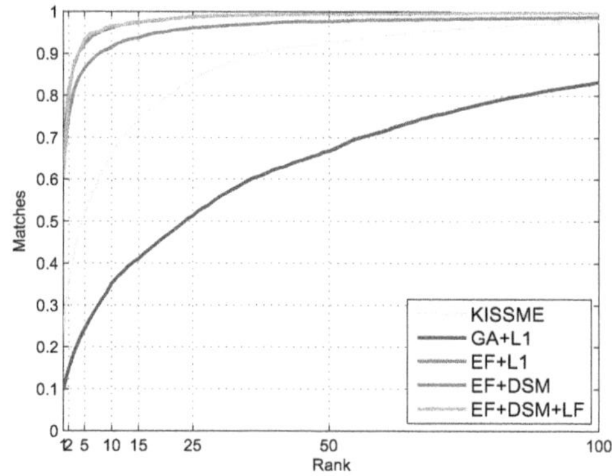

Figure 4: Comparative results on the VIPeR data set.

3. EXPERIMENT

Datasets and Evaluation. As most existing person re-identification researches did, the VIPeR dataset [4] was adopted to verify our approach. It contains 632 persons, each of which has two images with drastic appearance difference. The set of 632 image pairs were randomly split into two sets of 316 image pairs each, one for training and acting as the auxiliary dataset, while the other one for testing. The entire evaluation procedure was repeated 10 times. Cumulative Matching Characteristic (CMC) curves [13] were used to calculate the average performance, and the value of CMC@k indicates the percentage of the real match ranked in the top k.

Attributes. The attributes we adopted are derived from [1], i.e. PETA dataset. This dataset contains 105 attributes. Since some of the attributes are rarely used, we delete them and only 49 pre-defined attributes are kept, such as "personalFemale", "personLess30", "carryingBackpack" [3]. Therefore, the number of attributes in the attribute corpus is N_a 9. Five volunteers are invited for the marking job, acting as the investigators. They are asked to manually label the images with some of the attributes. The record shows that "carryingBackpack" is the most labeled attributes, which has the greatest dominance.

Methods Compared. To evaluate the effectiveness of the proposed method in each key step, we construct methods step by step, including the attribute-based method with General Attributes and L1 distance (GA+L1), the attribute-based method after Early-Fusion step and with L1 distance (EF+L1), the attribute-based method after Early-Fusion step and with Dominance-Saliency Matching model (EF+DSM), the feature-based method KISSME [5], and the Late-Fusion method (EF+DSM+LF). The results are presented in Fig.4, and Table.1 shows the performance of these approaches in the range of the first 50 ranks. The CMC results clearly show that the method in all key steps can improve the accuracy. The improvement is the most obvious in the early fusion step, while the improvement in the late fusion step is relatively limited. That is because the feature information has been exploited in the early fusion step, and it is re-exploited for the subtle adjustments in the late fusion step.

4. CONCLUSION

This paper investigates a new PRIM problem, which is solved by an effective multi-step fusion algorithm. It can be applied to video surveillance suspect investigation systems and improve the accuracy of investigation processes.

Acknowledgement. The research was supported by the National Nature Science Foundation of China (61231015, 61172173, 61303114, 61170023), the National High Technology Research and Development Program of China (2015AA016306), the Internet of Things Development Funding Project of Ministry of industry in 2013 (25), the Technology Research Project of Ministry of Public Security (2014JSYJA016), the Major Science and Technology Innovation Plan of Hubei Province (2013AAA020), the Nature Science Foundation of Hubei Province (2014CFB712), the Specialized Research Fund for the Doctoral Program of Higher Education (20130141120024), and the Fundamental Research Funds for the Central Universities(2042014kf0250).

5. REFERENCES

[1] Y. Deng, P. Luo, C. C. Loy, and X. Tang. Pedestrian attribute recognition at far distance. *ACM MM*, 2014.

[2] M. Farenzena, L. Bazzani, A. Perina, V. Murino, and M. Cristani. Person re-identification by symmetry-driven accumulation of local features. *CVPR*, 2010.

[3] R. Feris, R. Bobbitt, L. Brown, and S. Pankanti. Attribute based people search: Lessons learnt from a practical surveillance system. *ICMR*, 2014.

[4] D. Gray, S. Brennan, and H. Tao. Evaluating appearance models for recognition, reacquisition, and tracking. *PETS*, 2007.

[5] M. Kostinger, M. Hirzer, P. Wohlhart, P. M. Roth, and H. Bischof. Large scale metric learning from equivalence constraints. *CVPR*, 2012.

[6] R. Layne, T. M. Hospedales, S. Gong, and Q. Mary. Person re-identification by attributes. *BMVC*, 2012.

[7] Q. Leng, R. Hu, C. Liang, Y. Wang, and J. Chen. Person re-identification with content and context re-ranking. *MTAP*, 2014.

[8] Z. Lin, G. Ding, M. Hu, J. Wang, and X. Ye. Image tag completion via image-specific and tag-specific linear sparse reconstructions. *CVPR*, 2013.

[9] N.-B. Nguyen, V.-H. Nguyen, T. N. Duc, D.-D. Le, and D. A. Duong. Attrel: An approach to person re-identification by exploiting attribute relationships. *MultiMedia Modeling*, 2015.

[10] T. Ojala, M. Pietikainen, and T. Maenpaa. Multiresolution gray-scale and rotation invariant texture classification with local binary patterns. *IEEE T-PAMI*, 2002.

[11] G. Salton, A. Wong, and C.-S. Yang. A vector space model for automatic indexing. *Communications of the ACM*, 1975.

[12] A. Vedaldi and B. Fulkerson. Vlfeat: An open and portable library of computer vision algorithms. *ACM MM*, 2010.

[13] X. Wang, G. Doretto, T. Sebastian, J. Rittscher, and P. Tu. Shape and appearance context modeling. *ICCV*, 2007.

[14] Y. Wang, R. Hu, C. Liang, C. Zhang, and Q. Leng. Camera compensation using feature projection matrix for person re-identification. *IEEE T-CSVT*, 2014.

[15] Z. Wang, R. Hu, C. Liang, Q. Leng, and K. Sun. Region-based interactive ranking optimization for person re-identification. *PCM*, 2014.

[16] Y. Yang, J. Yang, J. Yan, S. Liao, D. Yi, and S. Z. Li. Salient color names for person re-identification. *ECCV*, 2014.

[17] R. Zhao, W. Ouyang, and X. Wang. Unsupervised salience learning for person re-identification. *CVPR*, 2013.

[18] W.-S. Zheng, S. Gong, and T. Xiang. Person re-identification by probabilistic relative distance comparison. *CVPR*, 2011.

[3] The details of the attribute corpus can be seen in the supplementary material.

Offloading Guidelines for Augmented Reality Applications on Wearable Devices

Bowen Shi, Ji Yang*, Zhanpeng Huang, Pan Hui
Department of Computer Science and Engineering,
The Hong Kong University of Science and Technology, Hong Kong
{bshiab, jyangaa}@connect.ust.hk, soaroc@ust.hk, panhui@cse.ust.hk

ABSTRACT

As Augmented Reality (AR) gets popular on wearable devices such as Google Glass, various AR applications have been developed by leveraging synergetic benefits beyond the single technologies. However, the poor computational capability and limited power capacity of current wearable devices degrade runtime performance and sustainability. Computational offloading strategy has been proposed to outsource computation to remote cloud for improving performance. Nevertheless, comparing with mobile devices, the wearable devices have their specific limitations, which induce additional problems and require new thoughts of computational offloading. In this paper, we propose several guidelines of computational offloading for AR applications on wearable devices based on our practical experiences of designing and developing AR applications on Google Glass. The guidelines have been adopted and proved by our application prototypes.

Categories and Subject Descriptors

H.5.1 [**Multimedia Information Systems**]: Augmented and virtual realities

General Terms

Design

Keywords

Offloading; Augmented reality; Wearable devices

1. INTRODUCTION

Nowadays, mobile devices, especially wearable devices such as Google Glass, have rapidly gained their popularity. In consequence, mobile computing and wearable computing have been attracting more attentions accompanied with various applications such as AR applications. Nevertheless, AR applications involve complex algorithms which require fast real-time processing and computation capability with power efficiency. Code offloading is one solution which utilizes nearby mobile devices and remote cloud for outstanding computations. A large amount of works [1, 2, 5, 7] have focused on designing offloading systems for mobile devices. However, wearable devices have their specific limitations. The computational capability, memory storage, and power capacity are more limited compared with mobile devices as illustrated in Table 1.

Category	Product	CPU	Memory	Battery
Wearable glass	Google Glass	OMAP 4430 SoC, dual-core @ 1GHz	1GB	570mAh
	VUZIX M100	OMAP4460 @ 1.2GHz	1G	600mAh
	Epson Moverio BT-200	1.2GHz dual-core TI OMAP 4480 CPU	1G	2720mAh#
	Meta Pro	i5 CPU	4G	1200mAh
	Icis Laforge	1GHz	500M	500mAh
Mobile device	Motorola s6	Quad-core 2.65GHz Krait	3G	3220mAh
	Samsung Galaxy S5	Quad-core 2.5GHz Krait 400 2G	2G	2800mAh
	Google Nexus 6	Quad-core 2.7GHz Snapdragon 3G	3G	3220mAh

Wired to a standalone control box

Table 1: Hardware comparison of mobile devices and wearable AR glasses in current market

Furthermore, wearable devices do not have keyboard or mouse inputs, so they usually take advantage of audio input and object or gesture recognition instead. These techniques require additional computations and lead more power consumption compared with traditional mobile devices. Even with the rapid development of hardware technology, hardware equipped on wearable devices is still too limited to meet the demand of compute-intensive applications.

Traditional offloading mainly outsources computation to remote cloud. It improves applications performance on mo-

*Contact author

MM'15, October 26–30, 2015, Brisbane, Australia.
© 2015 ACM. ISBN 978-1-4503-3459-4/15/10 ...$15.00.
DOI: http://dx.doi.org/10.1145/2733373.2806402.

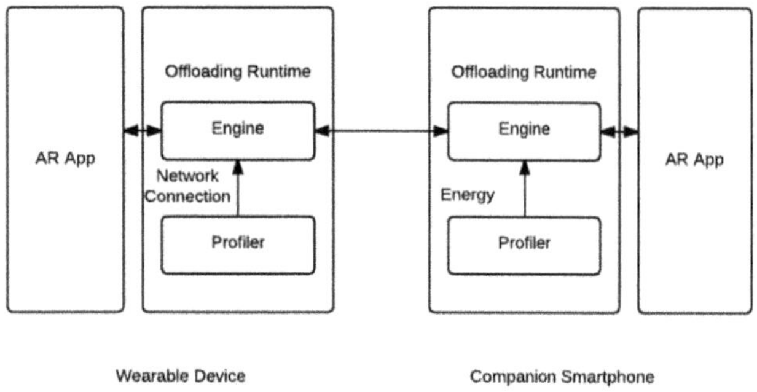

Figure 1: A simplified model of the adapted offloading system for AR applications on wearable devices

bile devices. However, the performance degenerates due to higher delay and possible failure of network connection. Since wearable devices usually work with companion mobile devices, it is possible to offload the computational tasks from wearable devices to the companion mobile devices.

In this paper, we propose several guidelines of computational offloading of AR application on wearable devices. These guidelines are designed based on our experience of designing and developing three AR applications on Google Glass. In the next section we will give detailed expatiation on these guidelines, followed by evaluation on the AR applications we have developed.

2. DESIGN GUIDELINES

In this section we present several guidelines for designing an offloading system specialized for AR applications on wearable devices. One of the most practical applications of offloading system is the Gabriel [6], a system for wearable cognitive assistance devices. In Gabriel, the so-called cloudlet is employed as an architecture element which is a 3-tier hierarchy: device-cloudlet-cloud. A cloudlet aims to bring the cloud closer. It can be a laptop or a notebook which the users usually carry with themselves. The applications on target device can be offloaded to either cloud or cloudlet. In cases when cloud is unavailable, the cloudlet will serve as the small data center to accelerate computing for wearable devices. Other work like Honeybee [4] and Misco [3] aims to design programming frameworks for smartphone device-to-device (D2D) offloading.

At present, the smartphone has become a powerful device, which is reliable enough to work as a data processing hub for offloaded tasks. In addition, users tend to carry smartphone meanwhile they take wearable device, so they can work as a pair. As the wearable device and smartphone are usually close to each other, there will be little network connection problem. In our system, the required augmented reality programs can be offloaded to smartphone rapidly.

The goal of offloading is minimizing the processing time and saving energy of wearable device as much as possible. Offloading system provides an environment where program developers only need to annotate the parts to be offloaded. When the program is invoked and the companion mobile device is available, the program will be offloaded to the mobile device automatically. Figure 1 shows the simplified model of our offloading system.

The whole system comprises two parts - one part on wearable devices and the other part on smartphones. On wearable device side, the offloading runtime consists of a proxy and a profiler. The proxy handles control and data transfer for offloaded methods. The profiler instruments the program and collects measurements of the wearable device, such as energy and storage. The profiler keeps detecting network conditions. When the bandwidth falls below a threshold b_0 or it cannot find a mobile device, it will choose to execute the program locally. On the smartphone side, the offloading system provides two similar components, a profiler and a server, which perform similar jobs with their wearable side counterparts. When the battery status of the smartphone falls below a threshold e_0, any offloading task will be refused at the smartphone side. Regarding network connection, both WiFi and Bluetooth can be employed to communicate between wearable device and smartphones. By default we choose WiFi for offloading because of its higher transmission speed. If WiFi is unaccessible, we will turn to Bluetooth.

One significant difference of the adapted offloading system from traditional ones is that it does not include any remote cloud. Computational tasks are only offloaded to the nearby mobile devices. On one hand, the computation capability of smartphones is adequate for AR applications on wearable devices, so offloading to remote cloud cannot largely enhance the performance. On the other hand, in order to minimize delays of real time tasks, the system will require high bandwidth for connection with remote cloud, which is hardly achievable under current situations. However the bandwidth will not be a problem if tasks are offloaded to nearby smartphones instead. Furthermore, privacy issue is another concern. It is common that the face of some person appears in the camera when wearable devices execute AR applications. There is potential danger that the privacy of the person is violated by a third party when the application is offloaded to remote cloud. If it is offloaded to the user's own smartphone, the privacy is well preserved.

In traditional offloading systems, there exists a solver or scheduler which can determine whether the method shall be executed remotely or locally. It aims to find a strategy to best partition the program in order to minimize the energy consumption on the offloader's side. MAUI [2] employs a linear programming model to make decision. When network conditions are not very good, the solver will select only methods which consume lots of computation to offload. The solver is no longer kept in our system for mainly three reasons. Firstly, augmented-reality applications are among the most energy-consuming applications. Being offloaded to mobile devices will certainly gain more than being executed locally. Secondly, the offloader (wearable device) and the offloadee (smartphone) are close to each other, so the network conditions do not pose a problem. Thirdly, the solver itself will consume time to get an optimal method of partitioning the program. Therefore it could lead to longer overhead and inevitably influence the user experience negatively.

Overall we give following guidelines of computational offloading for AR applications on wearable devices:

- Only offload programs to nearby companion mobile devices
- Consider all possible ways of communication, e.g. WiFi and Bluetooth

- Remove traditional scheduler: not using scheduler to decide whether the method should be offloaded
- Create a simplified mechanism at wearable device side to decide whether the method should be offloaded
- Create a simplified mechanism at mobile device side to decide whether to accept the offloaded method
- Offload all common recognition tasks, such as Optical Character Recognition (OCR), object recognition and object detection

3. CASE STUDY

In this section, we introduce three well designed experiments to test the performance of offloading system - AReader, SharpLens and Ubii. All of them are common and practical real-time augmented-reality applications based on Google Glass. The three applications involve computational intensive operations, for instance, image processing and OCR, which are widely used in AR applications.

3.1 SharpLens

SharpLens is an AR application which provides assistance for visually impaired people to access text information around them. It helps users retrieve text information from their view as shown in Figure 2(a). SharpLens contains four different modes: exploring mode, reading mode, meeting mode and driving mode. All detected sections containing text will be highlighted with a rectangle in exploring mode. The key component used in this mode is object recognition, which is the most exhaustive computational part. In reading mode texts will be amplified if they are pointed at by the user, where the key task is gesture recognition. In meeting mode, the application recognizes the text in certain area, in which the key part is OCR. Driving mode is designed for drivers to acquire brief text information of road signs when they are driving. OCR is used in this mode as well. The whole system uses voice command to start the application and switch modalities. For example, a short phrase "OK Glass, start SharpLens" will launch the SharpLens. Text To Speech (TTS) is another frequently-used functionality in SharpLens for speech synthesis. In summary, among all components employed in this application, the most computational intensive tasks are hand gesture detection, text recognition and speech synthesis.

3.2 AReader

AReader is a wearable system to digitally manipulate paper transcripts with Augmented Reality. It can assist users to perform virtual operations on the paper text like text amplification to improve user experience. All contents are shown on the AR overlay, which is over physical surface. Figure 2(b) presents one function mode (Amplification) of AReader. In this application, the main functional modes include text amplification, translation, glossary reference and text clipping. Voice command and finger touching can both be employed to switch between different modes. The text amplification is designed for reading small texts. The translation mode will be called when the finger moves around a word. The glossary reference and corresponding reference will be popped up just beside the finger. In text clipping mode, readers are able to clip, paste and save the contents.

In AReader, the most time-consuming tasks are image preprocessing, hand detection and text recognition. All images taken shall undergo preprocessing like Gaussian blurring to remove noise. Hand detection is one basic operation of the system. In each functional mode, we firstly need to detect the finger correctly in order to properly locate and amplify or translate the texts. Text recognition, namely OCR, is based on a tess-two library [8].

(a) (b) (c) (d)

Figure 2: (a) Text recognition with SharpLens (b) Text amplification with AReader (c) File copying between computers with Ubii (d) File pasting between computers with Ubii

3.3 Ubii

Ubii is short for Ubiquitous Interface and Interaction. It is an Graphical User Interface (GUI) where user can interact with physical objects such as computers, project screens and printers. Common operations include document copying, printing and displaying on a projector screen via hand gestures.

In Ubii, we leverage the hand gesture pinching to interact with objects. A series of pinching gestures are defined to represent different operations. Those gestures include picking, dropping, dragging, rotating and zooming. Picking, dropping, dragging are operated on selected items as their name imply. For example, zooming is for scaling up and down the item size and rotating is for file selection in a ring menu. A combination of different gestures can realize a complete function. Picking an image file from the computer, dragging and dropping it to the printer means to print the image. Figure 2(c) and Figure 2(d) illustrate the process of hand pinching and dragging to transmit a file between two computers. Ubii system can be regarded as a finite-state machine, where each operation is a state. Similar with SharpLens and AReader, the most computational intensive task is gesture recognition in Ubii.

4. EXPERIMENT RESULTS

Several experiments were designed to test the performance of offloading on the above three applications. To have a synthesized evaluation, we have conducted experiments on every mode in each application. For each mode the application is tested with and without offloading. The performance is measured in two aspects - energy consumption and execution time. Google Nexus 5 (2.26GHz CPU and 32GB ROM)

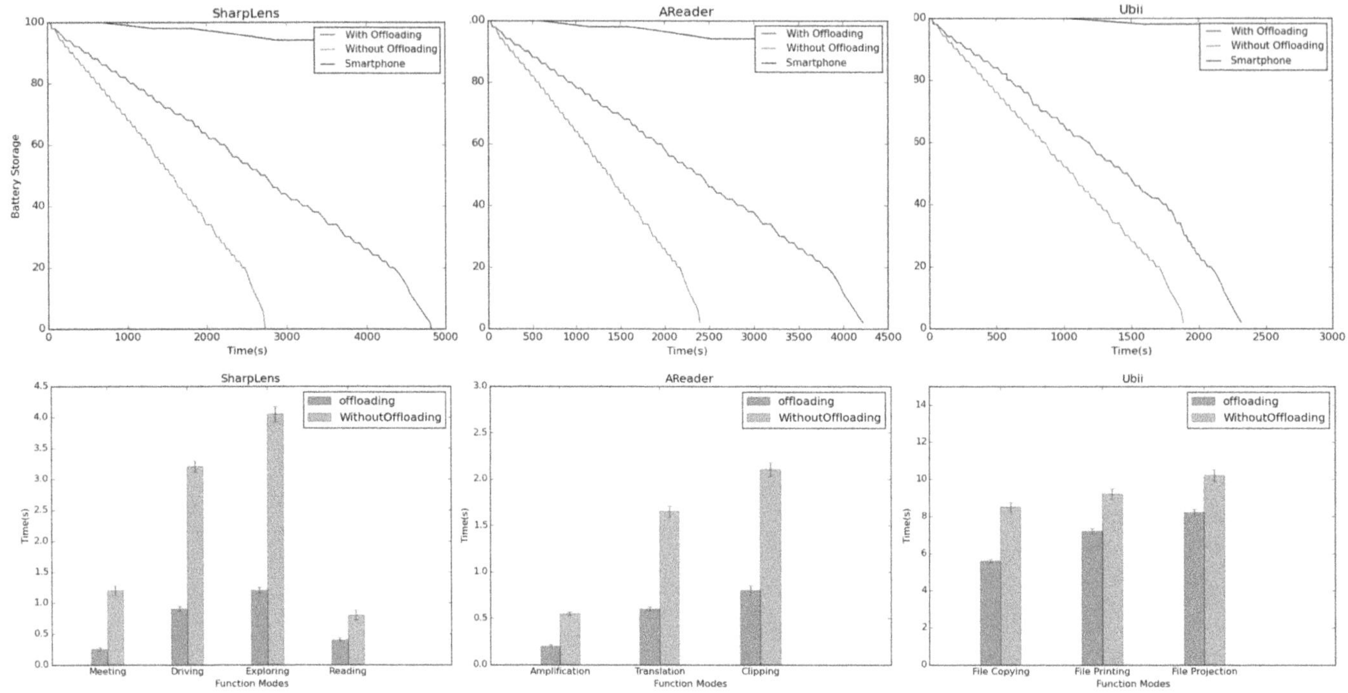

Figure 3: Time cost and energy consumption in different applications

is used as the smartphone to execute offloaded tasks. Data is transmitted via WiFi.

Figure 3 shows the time cost per frame of system and energy consumption in three experiments with and without offloading. In SharpLens and AReader, offloading helps to reduce the computation time to at least 50% in each mode with the battery endurance of Google Glass doubled. On smartphone side, about 6% to 8% of its electricity is consumed in order to do the offloaded computation as whole. The performance improvement by offloading in Ubii is not as prominent as SharpLens and AReader. Computation time is reduced by about 25% and battery life is prolonged by about 30%. The main reason is that there are not so many computational intensive tasks that can be offloaded in Ubii (i.e. gesture recognition) compared with the other two applications (i.e. OCR, finger detection, object recognition).

5. CONCLUSIONS

In this paper we propose several guidelines for designing AR applications on wearable devices and present an improved offloading system based on the guidelines. Our offloading system is lightweight and easy for programmers to offload computation intensive tasks. As we leverage the companion mobile device for offloading, multiple network connection methods can be employed. With experiments conducted on augmented reality applications on Google Glass, our offloading system and guidelines are proved promising. On average, it can achieve energy saving by 20% to 30% and reduce 50% computation time compared with local execution.

6. REFERENCES

[1] B. G. Chun, S. Ihm, P. Maniatis, M. Naik, and A. Patti. Clonecloud: elastic execution between mobile device and cloud. In *Proceedings of the sixth conference on Computer systems*, pages 301–314. ACM, 2011.

[2] E. Cuervo, A. Balasubramanian, D. Cho, A. Wolman, S. Saroiu, R. Chandra, and P. Bahl. Maui: making smartphones last longer with code offload. In *Proceedings of the 8th international conference on Mobile systems, applications, and services*, pages 49–62. ACM, 2010.

[3] A. Dou, V. Kalogeraki, D. Gunopulos, T. Mielikainen, and V. H. Tuulos. Misco: a mapreduce framework for mobile systems. In *Proceedings of the 3rd international conference on pervasive technologies related to assistive environments*, page 32. ACM, 2010.

[4] N. Fernando, S. W. Loke, and W. Rahayu. Honeybee: A programming framework for mobile crowd computing. In *Mobile and Ubiquitous Systems: Computing, Networking, and Services*, pages 224–236. Springer, 2013.

[5] M. S. Gordon, D. A. Jamshidi, S. A. Mahlke, Z. M. Mao, and X. Chen. Comet: Code offload by migrating execution transparently. In *OSDI*, pages 93–106, 2012.

[6] K. Ha, Z. Chen, W. Hu, W. Richter, P. Pillai, and M. Satyanarayanan. Towards wearable cognitive assistance. In *Proceedings of the 12th annual international conference on Mobile systems, applications, and services*, pages 68–81. ACM, 2014.

[7] C. Shi, K. Habak, P. Pandurangan, M. Ammar, M. Naik, and E. Zegura. Cosmos: computation offloading as a service for mobile devices. In *Proceedings of the 15th ACM international symposium on Mobile ad hoc networking and computing*, pages 287–296. ACM, 2014.

[8] Theis. R.tess-two. `https://github.com/rmtheis/tess-two`, 2011.

Real-Time Instant Event Detection in Egocentric Videos by Leveraging Sensor-Based Motion Context

Pei-Yun Hsu, Wen-Feng Cheng, Peng-Ju Hsieh, Yen-Liang Lin, Winston H. Hsu

National Taiwan University, Taipei, Taiwan

ABSTRACT

With rapid growth of egocentric videos from wearable devices, the need for instant video event detection is emerging. Different from conventional video event detection, it requires more considerations on real-time event detection and immediate video recording due to the computational cost on wearable devices (e.g., Google Glass). Conventional work of video event detection analyzed video content in an offline process and it is time-consuming for visual analysis. Observing that wearable devices are usually along with sensors, we propose a novel approach for instant event detection in egocentric videos by leveraging sensor-based motion context. We compute statistics of sensor data as features. Next, we predict the user's current motion context by a hierarchical model, and then choose the corresponding ranking model to rate the importance score of the timestamp. With importance score provided in real-time, camera on the wearable device can dynamically record micro-videos without wasting power and storage. In addition, we collected a challenging daily-life dataset called EDS (**E**gocentric **D**aily-life Videos with **S**ensor Data), which contains both egocentric videos and sensor data recorded by Google Glass of different subjects. We evaluate the performance of our system on the EDS dataset, and the result shows that our method outperforms other baselines.

Categories and Subject Descriptors

K.8.2 [**PERSONAL COMPUTING**]: [Hardware]

Keywords

Egocentric Video; Sensor; Wearable Device; Event Detection

1. INTRODUCTION

Due to the ubiquity of wearable devices (e.g., Google Glass, GoPro), there has been enormous growth in the number of egocentric videos. However, egocentric videos are often redundant and thus there is a strong need of efficiently extracting meaningful content for further browsing or indexing. Video summarization is an intuitive way to generate meaningful keyframes or short video clips of the original videos. Conventional works determined the score of the frames by visual attributes such as aesthetics and number of faces [2]. For egocentric videos, recent works used object-level features (e.g., faces, objects, and hands) [3, 4].

However, the above methods focused on visual features and required lots of computational cost. Other prior works claimed that with good computing resource (e.g., Intel Core i7 PC with 16 GB main memory [10]), they can speed up the processing time to quasi real-time. Although Wang et al. [6] proposed a real-time method (e.g., 10 secs for a 2 mins video), it still required offline processing. In addition, since wearable devices have limited storage, battery capacity and computing power, it is impractical to record whole video sequences and perform summarization on the wearable devices. A better strategy to address the aforementioned limi-

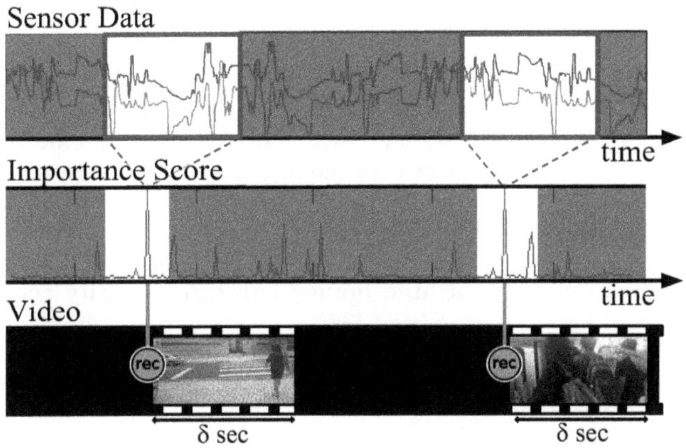

Figure 1: For instant event detection, it is impractical to analyze video content as conventional video event detection. Hence, we propose a method that uses sensor data for real-time instant event detection. Top row represents the sensor statistics. Middle row shows the importance score calculated by our method. We determine whether to record a micro-video by the scores and thus can save storage usage and power consumption, which is especially important for wearable devices.

MM'15, October 26–30, 2015, Brisbane, Australia.
© 2015 ACM. ISBN 978-1-4503-3459-4/15/10 ...$15.00.
DOI: http://dx.doi.org/10.1145/2733373.2806404.

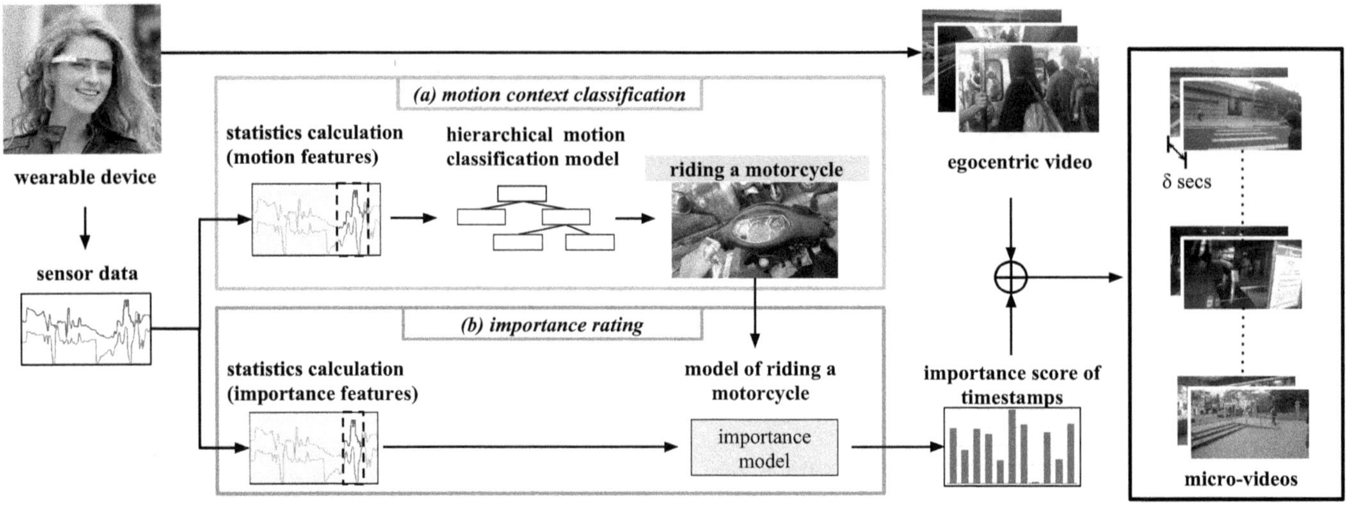

Figure 2: System Overview. Our approach can be divided into two parts: motion context classification (Sec. 2.3) and importance rating (Sec. 2.4). We use statistics of sensor data as features. (a) motion context classification: We use a hierarchical model trained by SVM to classify the subjects' current motion context into 6 classes. (b) importance rating: We train 6 ranking models for rating the importance of current timestamps according to the results from (a). With (a) and (b) providing importance score in real-time, camera on the wearable device can dynamically record micro-videos without wasting power and storage.

tation of wearable devices would be determining whether to record immediately on the wearable devices.

Subjects can decide whether to record a video for continuous events, while for instant events, we need an efficient way to capture them. Xiong et al. [8] used a web photo prior to detect snap points; however, in this way, the camera should be turned on all the time, which would lead to more power consumption. In addition, wearable devices are often equipped with sensors, and the advantages of sensors are low power and compact size. Thus, rather than exploit visual features, we propose to leverage sensor-based motion context to real-time detect instant events, as shown in Figure 1.

Our method predicts subjects' current motion context (e.g., walking, riding a bike) by sensor data, which is inspired by [5], and then applies different ranking models according to the predicted context to rate the importance of the timestamp. Finally, we select the timestamps with higher scores as the initial points of short videos called **micro-videos**, and output the micro-videos with length δ seconds (see Figure 1). In short, our system determines whether to record a micro-video immediately, and thus saves power and storage. Meanwhile, the micro-videos are suitable for users to share on social media (e.g., Vine) which only allows videos with few seconds. In order to evaluate our proposed method, we collect a daily-life dataset called EDS dataset (**E**gocentric **D**aily-life Videos with **S**ensor Data), which contains both egocentric videos and sensor data recorded by Google Glass of different subjects.

To sum up, our contribution includes:

- We propose a real-time system for instant event detection in egocentric videos by leveraging sensor-based motion context.
- The EDS dataset. We collect a challenging daily-life egocentric video dataset with head-mounted sensor data recorded by Google Glass.

2. SYSTEM DESIGN

2.1 System Overview

For instant event detection, we investigate sensor data for achieving low cost computing on wearable devices and real-time event detection. As shown in Figure 2, our approach can be divided into two parts: motion context classification and importance rating. We compute statistics of sensor data as features. To realize the motion context information from sensor data, we propose a hierarchical structure for motion context classification. Then, we can choose the corresponding ranking model to rate the importance score of the timestamp. The hierarchical model and the importance rating model are illustrated in Sec. 2.3 and Sec. 2.4. Finally, our system generates a micro-video with current timestamp as the initial point if the importance rating result is high.

2.2 Sensor Features

The sensor data contains three-axis accelerometer, three-axis gyroscope, three-axis gravity sensor, three-axis magnetometer (compass) and light sensor. The accelerometer is related to the forward motion that can be used to distinguish from stationary and moving. The gyroscope measures the rate of rotation around three axes, and abrupt change of orientation may imply some important events. The magnetometer provides information of users' absolute orientation and light sensor implies current locations (e.g., indoors or outdoors) and time of day. Therefore, we believe that these features can help both classify the motion context and rate the importance.

2.3 Motion Context Classification

In our work, we try to classify the user's motion context into six classes by leveraging sensor data. As motion features, we compute the statistics of sensor data such as mean, variance, skewness, kurtosis, and Fast Fourier Transform

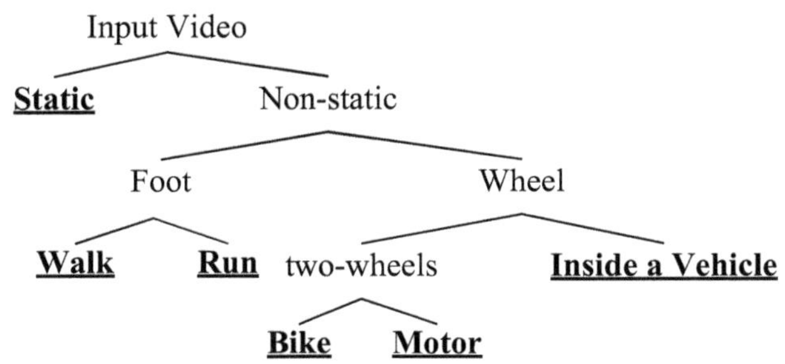

Figure 3: Based on the observation of egocentric videos, we propose a hierarchical structure with 6 motion context. We basically design the branches according to the motion speed and means of transportation.

(FFT) values in the window of size $wsize$ and $2 * wsize$ before current timestamp, and got a 72-dimension motion feature denoted as F_motion. For normalization, we scaled the features to zero mean and unit variance along the same dimension.

However, due to the dynamic natural head motion, it is hard to neglect the effects. By observing egocentric videos of daily life activities, we find that we can separate the motion of the subjects into 6 different types with hierarchical structure, which is also inspired by [5]. As Figure 3 shows, this hierarchical structure was designed according to physical meanings. For example, **static** is the motion context with the least movement, and thus we chose it as the first leaf node. Also, moving by foot or wheels is different in speed and vertical movement. We train SVM classifiers by LIBSVM [1] with polynomial kernel for each binary classification in the proposed hierarchical structure.

2.4 Importance Rating

After obtaining the motion context information, we can integrate those predicted models (e.g., riding a motorcycle as shown in Figure 2) with additional sensor data for important timestamp measurement. To rate the importance of a timestamp, we extract importance features from sensor data similar to F_motion (2.3), denoted as F_impo. While importance rating focused on instant events, we choose smaller window size (i.e., 1 second) for extracting features. Since the importance of the timestamp is not a binary case but a relative concept, we do not classify the timestamps into important or unimportant. In the training phase, we train 6 ranking models by AdaRank algorithm [9] by F_impo according to the manually labeled motion context and importance scores (i.e., 0 to 2). We try to model the relation between motion patterns and initial points of importance events.

3. EXPERIMENT

3.1 Dataset

We collect a challenging daily-life dataset called **EDS** (**E**gocentric **D**aily-life Videos with **S**ensor Data), which contains both egocentric videos and sensor data recorded by Google Glass of different subjects. The videos were recorded at the rate of 30 frames per second, and the sensor data was obtained from the built-in sensors of Google Glass, such as three-axis accelerometer, three-axis gyroscope, three-axis gravity sensor, three-axis magnetometer (compass) and light sensor. We ask 10 people to do their daily-life activities without any instruction of the events (e.g., walking a dog, riding bicycle, riding motorcycle, and taking a bus), as shown in Figure 4. Each video length varied from few minutes to hours, and the total length was about 11 hours.

Figure 4: Example video frames of EDS dataset. From left to right is walking a dog, riding bicycle, riding motorcycle, and taking a bus).

In addition, we manually labeled the motion context and importance score of every timestamp. Motion context contains 6 classes: **inside a vehicle**, **walk**, **bike**, **motor**, **static** and **run**. A timestamp is labeled as one specific motion context if the subject has maintained the motion in the past 5 seconds. For example, if a person drives for 5 minutes, stops at the traffic lights for 10 seconds and then drives for another 5 minutes, the ground truth would be **inside a vehicle-static-inside a vehicle**. To score the importance of the timestamps, we let the subjects annotate the importance score (i.e., 0 to 2) of every timestamp in the videos by themselves, since only the subjects themselves know the best of memorable or important parts in their own daily-life videos.

3.2 Evaluation

We used the 7 longest videos in the EDS dataset, which are longer than 22 minutes, as the testing set and others as the training set.

3.2.1 Motion Context Classification

Unlike [7], we use only sensor data instead of visual attributes, and we choose only six general motion class. In the experiment, we set the $wsize$ from 1 to 5 seconds, and $wsize = 3$ get the best result. Table 1 shows the classification performance at the leaf nodes of the hierarchical system. The average precision of our classifier is about 0.73. Since the sensors were mounted on head, it is hard to neglect the effect of natural head motion. We observed that **Inside a vehicle** is the most confusing class among all motion context since it is often involved in mixed actions, such as being stuck in a traffic jam. Therefore, the motion context would be confusing since the car repeats moving and stopping in a short period.

3.2.2 Importance Rating

Since we want to capture the initial points of important events instantly, we set the $wize$ to 1 second, which is smaller than the size we used in motion context classification. Previous works of video summarization evaluated the results by a **blind taste test** in which users choose which summary is the best [4], but it is time-consuming and the results may not be consistent with the subjects who recorded the videos. Other work [10] quantitatively determined the overlap between the generated summary and groundtruth. However, in our case, since we generate micro-videos with fixed length

Table 1: Confusion matrix of motion context classification results. Rows are groundtruth and columns are predicted classes. We can achieve 73% precision on the average.

	Inside a vehicle	Walk	Bike	Motor	Static	Run
Inside a vehicle	**62.5%**	5%	6.5%	0.5%	25.5%	0%
Walk	4%	**78%**	8.7%	0.3%	8.5%	0.5%
Bike	10.4%	9.4%	**70.5%**	3.1%	6.5%	0.1%
Motor	0.3%	5%	10%	**77.5%**	7.2%	0%
Static	10.5%	7%	5.5%	1%	**75.9%**	0.1%
Run	1.5%	20%	3%	0%	3.2%	**72.3%**

δ and choose the important events by online algorithm, previous evaluation methods would not be suitable.

We propose a new **weighted-hit** evaluation method, which measures the quality of choosing the timestamp as the micro-video's initial point. For each timestamp t_i in the full-length video, we give it a quality score $q(t_i)$:

$$q(t_i) = \sum_{t=t_i}^{t_{i+\delta-1}} \frac{O_t}{\delta} \quad (1)$$

$$O_{t_i} = \begin{cases} 1, & if \quad t_i \in T_G \\ 0, & otherwise \end{cases},$$

where T_G denotes the set of timestamps of groundtruth (i.e., importance score > 0) and O_{t_i} indicates whether t_i is in groundtruth. For example, if $q(t_i) = 1$, it indicates that the micro-video starting with timestamp t_i captures the groundtruth. Next, we sort all timestamps by the scores given by the importance ranking models, denote the jth timestamp in the sorted ranking list as t_j^*. Then we calculate $Q(j)$, which denotes the **quality** of the top j scores in the ranking list.

$$Q(j) = \frac{\sum_{k=1}^{j} q(t_j^*)}{Top_j} \quad (2)$$

$$Top_j = \sum_{k=1}^{j} qs_k$$

where qs_k denotes the top kth score in the sorted quality list and Top_j is for normalizing $Q(j)$. Finally, we compare our results to **Oracle**, **Motion Baseline** and **Random** by $Q(j)$ with $j = 5, 10, 20$. **Oracle** is the upper bound of our method (i.e., we give correct motion context to the ranking model). **Motion Baseline** chooses the timestamps with larger standard deviation in accelerometer and gyroscope, since the abrupt change of motion could imply some events. We choose $\delta = 6$, which is the same as the length constraint of videos uploaded to the Vine platform[1]. Table 2 shows the average performance $Q(j)$ of 7 videos with 4 different methods, and our method outperforms other baselines. The oracle case is much better than baselines, which can infer that the motion context helps detect instant events.

[1]http://vine.co

Table 2: Performance of our methods and other baselines. Oracle is the upper bound of our method (i.e., we give correct motion context to the ranking model). Motion Baseline chooses the timestamps with larger standard deviation in accelerometer and gyroscope, since the abrupt change of motion could imply some events.

	Oracle	Ours	Motion Baseline	Random
Q(5)	0.2234	0.1905	0.1147	0.005
Q(10)	0.2186	0.1655	0.1081	0.0033
Q(20)	0.1957	0.1144	0.12	0.0048

4. CONCLUSION

In this paper, we propose an online method for instant event detection by leveraging sensor-based motion context. Therefore, we can easily save power and storage due to the sensor-based method's advantages of low power and low computational cost. The system has two parts: motion context classification and importance rating. We predict the subject's current motion context by head-mounted sensor data and rate importance scores of current timestamp by corresponding ranking model. We also propose a new **weighted-hit** evaluation method, which measures the quality of choosing the timestamp as the micro-video's initial point, and our method outperforms other baselines. In addition, we collect a challenging daily-life dataset called **EDS** containing both egocentric videos and sensor data.

For future work, we will try to improve the performance of motion context classification and investigate the fusion of vision and sensor features.

5. REFERENCES

[1] C.-C. Chang and C.-J. Lin. Libsvm: a library for support vector machines. *ACM Transactions on Intelligent Systems and Technology (TIST).*

[2] M. Gygli, H. Grabner, H. Riemenschneider, and L. Van Gool. Creating summaries from user videos. In *ECCV 2014.*

[3] Y. J. Lee, J. Ghosh, and K. Grauman. Discovering important people and objects for egocentric video summarization. In *CVPR 2012.*

[4] Z. Lu and K. Grauman. Story-driven summarization for egocentric video. In *CVPR 2013.*

[5] Y. Poleg, C. Arora, and S. Peleg. Temporal segmentation of egocentric videos. In *CVPR 2014.*

[6] X. Wang, Y.-G. Jiang, Z. Chai, Z. Gu, X. Du, and D. Wang. Real-time summarization of user-generated videos based on semantic recognition. In *ACMMM*, 2014.

[7] J. Windau and L. Itti. Situation awareness via sensor-equipped eyeglasses. In *Intelligent Robots and Systems (IROS), 2013.*

[8] B. Xiong and K. Grauman. Detecting snap points in egocentric video with a web photo prior. In *ECCV 2014.*

[9] J. Xu and H. Li. Adarank: a boosting algorithm for information retrieval. In *SIGIR 2007.*

[10] B. Zhao and E. P. Xing. Quasi real-time summarization for consumer videos. In *CVPR 2014.*

Modeling Temporal Effects in Re-captured Video

Philipp Schaber, Sally Dong, Benjamin Guthier,
Stephan Kopf, and Wolfgang Effelsberg
Department of Computer Science IV, University of Mannheim, Germany
{schaber|guthier|kopf|effelsberg}@informatik.uni-mannheim.de
sally.dong@uwaterloo.ca

ABSTRACT

The re-capturing of video content poses significant challenges to algorithms in the fields of video forensics, watermarking, and near-duplicate detection. Using a camera to record a video from a display introduces a variety of artifacts, such as geometric distortions, luminance transformations, and temporal aliasing. A deep understanding of the causes and effects of such phenomena is required for their simulation, and for making the affected algorithms more robust. In this paper, we provide a detailed model of the temporal effects in re-captured video. Such effects typically result in the re-captured frames being a blend of the original video's source frames, where the specific blend ratios are difficult to predict. Our proposed parametric model captures the temporal artifacts introduced by interactions between the video renderer, display device, and camera. The validity of our model is demonstrated through experiments with real re-captured videos containing specially marked frames.

Categories and Subject Descriptors

I.4.1 [**Image Processing and Computer Vision**]: Digitization and Image Capture—*Sampling*

General Terms

Algorithms, Experimentation

Keywords

Frame blending; Temporal distortion; Camcorder copy

1. INTRODUCTION

Live video streaming software such as Twitter's *Periscope* makes it possible to set up a camera or a smartphone in front of a TV and illegally stream pay-per-view video content to a public audience. Digital copy-protection mechanisms, like watermarks that are embedded in the content, may be destroyed as a consequence of the artifacts introduced in the re-capturing process. Making copy-protection and related techniques such as automatic near-duplicate detection, biometric authentication, and video forensics robust to re-captured video requires a deep understanding of the extrinsic visual effects.

From the various artifacts introduced by the re-capturing of video, the aspect of luminance transformation has been covered in the work of Zid et al [2]. In another publication on the forensic characterization of pirated movies, the authors mention temporal aliasing effects caused by frame rate differences between the display and the camera [4]. However, no deeper analysis is provided in that paper. In the context of frame blending as an attack on watermarking systems, Hernandez et al. simulate a simple form of frame blending, by sliding a window of fixed size temporally across the video. The frames of the source video within the sliding window are averaged to compute a simulated blended frame [5]. In the field of video forensics, the work by Bestagini et al. identifies re-captured video based on frame blending [3]. However, their frame ghosting model is limited to equal blends of two neighboring source frames. In previous work we presented *CamMark*, a camcorder copy simulation, which considers realistic frame blending as part of its simulation [6]. A specially prepared marker video is used to extract the actual frame blending values for each frame of a re-captured copy. The extracted blends can then be applied directly to the frames of a simulated video. However, a precise simulation is only possible for videos with identical setups. Since there is no underlying *model* for the temporal distortion, each parameter change requires a repetition of the capturing of the marker video.

This paper contributes a parametric model which explains all temporal effects that result from re-capturing a video from a display. It enables a realistic, parameter-based simulation of the frame blending process. Our model is a concatenation of individual temporal effects and their respective parameters. The effects are: frame rate difference between the source and recording, exposure, rolling shutters, video playback and display refresh rate synchronization effects. We verify our model by analyzing ground truth frame blending values obtained by an actual re-capturing of specially marked videos. The proposed model has now been integrated in our open-source simulation tool CamMark [6].

2. MODEL

The main reason for temporal distortion in re-captured copies is the lack of synchronization between the playback of the frames of the source video, the screen refresh of the display device and the exposure of the camera during the

MM'15, October 26–30, 2015, Brisbane, Australia.

ACM 978-1-4503-3459-4/15/10 ...$15.00.
DOI: http://dx.doi.org/10.1145/2733373.2806405.

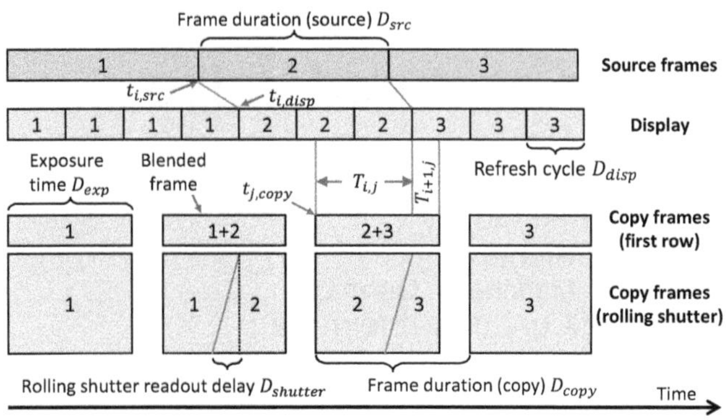

Figure 1: Overview of our model of temporal effects.

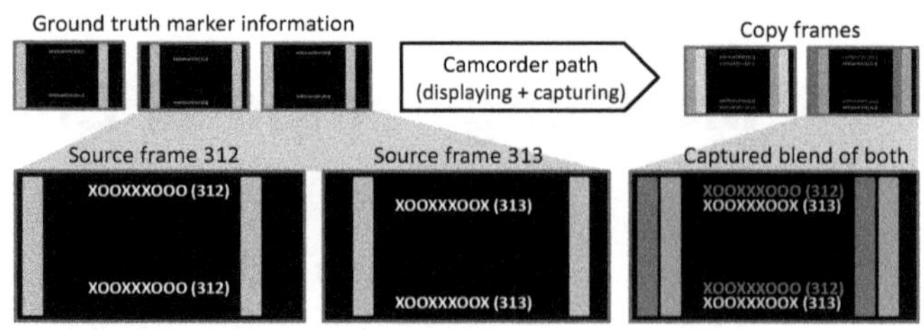

Figure 2: The source frames of our video contain markers that allow an unambiguous identification of blend ratios in the copy frames.

recording process, which all work in discrete units of time. This results in temporal aliasing and sampling effects as illustrated in Figure 1. The figure outlines our temporal model, with the horizontal axis representing time, and the path from the source video to the copy visualized from top to bottom. At the very top, the individual frames of the source video are shown. To play back a video, the video renderer needs to present each frame for the constant duration of D_{src} seconds, so that source frame i begins playing at time $t_{i,src} = i \cdot D_{src}$. The frame rate of the source video is then $\frac{1}{D_{src}}$ Hz. However, most video renderers only present new frames when the display signals a new refresh cycle, in order to avoid screen tearing. The duration of a refresh cycle is D_{disp} seconds, which is equivalent to a screen refresh rate of $\frac{1}{D_{disp}}$ Hz. The actual time at which a video frame is presented is thus $t_{i,disp} = \lceil \frac{t_{i,src}}{D_{disp}} \rceil \cdot D_{disp}$. This is visualized in the second row of the figure. If the frame duration D_{src} is an *exact* multiple of D_{disp}, frames can be presented at their intended time. If D_{src} is not a multiple of D_{disp}, but there exist small integers m and n such that $m \cdot D_{src} = n \cdot D_{disp}$, then the presented frame duration still equals D_{src} *on average*. In this case, aliasing effects create a pattern of shorter and longer source frame durations, resulting in an offset between the intended and the actual frame presentation times. This offset becomes zero every $m \cdot D_{src}$ seconds. In practice, display refresh rates are often non-integer values, so that a drift slowly accumulates over time. As soon as it exceeds the duration of a refresh cycle, a single source frame will be shown for D_{disp} seconds shorter or longer to reduce the error. Depending on the exact values of D_{src} and D_{disp}, this may occur once every several hundred frames.

The next aspect in our model is the discrete re-sampling introduced by the camera. At time $t_{j,copy} = j \cdot D_{copy}$ the camera begins capturing copy frame j. This is equivalent to a frame rate of the camera of $\frac{1}{D_{copy}}$ Hz. A shutter mechanism determines the periods in which the sensor is exposed to incident light. In our model, we call this parameter the exposure time D_{exp}. Due to read-out delays, the exposure time is always shorter than the full frame duration D_{copy}. Because the shutter of the camera is not synchronized to the display device, frame blending occurs. Several consecutive source frames may be accumulated into one copy frame, since a new frame may be presented while the shutter of the camera is still open. The variable $T_{i,j}$ denotes the time for which source frame i is recorded during the exposure period for copy frame j. It is calculated as $T_{i,j} = min(t_{i,src} + D_{src}, t_{j,copy} + D_{exp}) - max(t_{i,src}, t_{j,copy})$, which is the difference between the earliest ending time and the latest starting time of the two pertinent frames. When put in relation to the exposure time D_{exp}, a time ratio $R_{i,j} = \frac{T_{i,j}}{D_{exp}} \in [0, 1]$ can be calculated. $R_{i,j}$ indicates the share of the total exposure time of copy frame j that is taken up by the ith source frame.

If light from more than one source frame gets accumulated by the camera's sensor, the pixel values in the copy frame are a blend of the original source frames' pixel values. The larger a source frame's R_i, the brighter its pixels appear in the recording. However, the luminance transfer is not entirely linear due to non-linear steps such as gamma correction in both display and camera, and the camera response function. As a result, the pixel blending ratios change non-linearly with changes in time ratios. This is not straightforward to model mathematically, but the relation can be determined empirically (see Section 3) or approximated linearly.

The last effect considered in our model is the rolling shutter, which stops the exposure and reads out the sensor values for each row individually, while subsequent rows are still being exposed. The exposure time D_{exp} is still constant for all rows. The result, however, is that different rows of a frame are representations of different points in time. The time required to scan through the sensor from top to bottom is the rolling shutter readout delay $D_{shutter}$. The start time of a copy frame $\hat{t}_{j,copy}(v)$ then becomes a function of the vertical row position $v \in [0, 1]$: $\hat{t}_{j,copy}(v) = t_{j,copy} + v \cdot D_{shutter}$.

3. EVALUATION

To validate our model and to justify its parameters, we analyzed the temporal effects in real camera-capture set-ups. We used a specially prepared marker video as ground truth, which is displayed and captured in different set-ups. The markers in the video allow us to accurately identify blended source frames in each copy frame. Our analysis starts from the copy frame, i.e., the observed ground truth, and backtracks the frame formation process to show the individual temporal effects that cause each distortion.

Figure 2 illustrates this idea. Since our CamMark simulation tool [6] already provides a temporal marker solution, we use it as our marker mechanism. Frame blending in each copy frame is detected by two types of markers. First, machine-readable frame numbers are positioned at the top and bottom of a frame. An 8-bit CRC code is appended to their 24-bit binary representation, to detect incorrect readouts. For consecutive frames of the marker video, their embedding location alternates between three different neighboring but non-overlapping positions, so that the frame numbers of blended frames can still be read. The

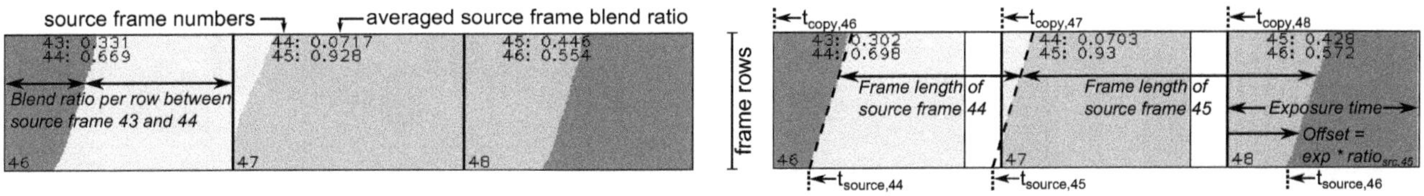

(a) Source frame *blend*-ratios per copy frame and row. (b) *Time*-ratios and inferred source frame start times.

Figure 3: Three resulting frames from recording a 24 fps marker video with 25 fps, exposure time of 1/30 s, represented as blend ratios (a) and time ratios (b).

second type of markers are vertical, uniform gray bars from the top to the bottom of the frame. They are embedded on the left and right side of each frame. In the same way as the frame number markers, they alternate between three different positions. In order to spatially locate both types of markers, the beginning of the marker video shows a spatial synchronization pattern that allows for the compensation of any perspective transformations as well as lens distortions.

The vertical marker bars indicate the relative visibility of source frames in a copy frame. Since the marker bars are constant in brightness and spatially non-overlapping, their relative brightness represents the blend ratio of source frames in each copy frame. To account for the effect of a rolling shutter, this ratio is individually calculated from top to bottom of a copy frame, so that vertical changes of the blend ratio can be detected. To accommodate for global illumination and the inability of displays to show true black, the value of a reference black marker can be subtracted before the ratio calculation.

3.1 Effects from Capturing

In our first set of experiments, a 24 fps marker video was played at a refresh rate of 60 Hz and recorded at 25 frames per second with an exposure time of 1/30 seconds. Figure 3(a) shows a visualization of the extracted marker data for three consecutive copy frames. A color scheme is used to represent the relative contribution of the different source frames to each of the three copy frames 46, 47, and 48. As a first observation, the frame blending is clearly visible, as each copy frame contains influences from more than one source frame. Their blend ratio changes vertically, which reflects the effect of the rolling shutter scanning the scene from top to bottom. Also, on the bottom of copy frame 47, no blending occurs. It seems as if the rolling shutter skips to the bottom of the frame instantaneously. This is an example of the artifacts that are introduced by sampling in discrete units of time, i.e., once every D_{copy} seconds, but only for the duration of the exposure, which is always less than D_{copy}.

To continue the investigation, the cause of the frame blending is examined. Frames are blended due to the different fractions of *time* during which each source frame is recorded by the camera. To be able to derive time ratios from the marker data, we conducted the following experiment: a static marker frame was recorded using different exposure times. This is equivalent to different fractions of time during which a marker may be recorded. For each exposure time, we extracted the resulting marker brightness in the copy, and obtained an exposure-to-brightness function, shown in Figure 4(a). To adopt to non-uniform screen brightnesses, we created this mapping for each row of the marker bars separately. By inverting this function, a look-up table was created that maps brightness values to exposure times. This table now allows us to calculate exposure time ratios R_i from the measured frame blend ratios.

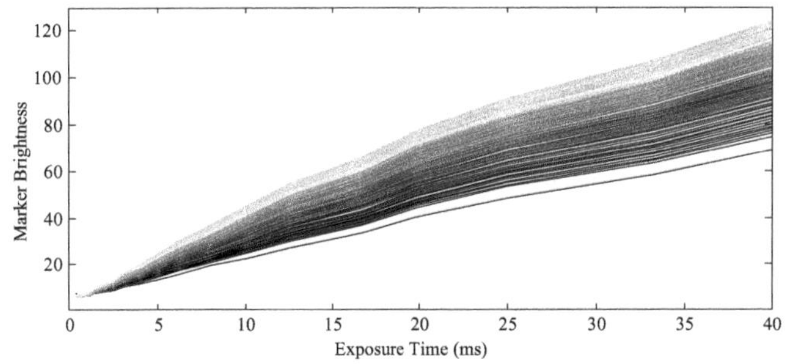

(a) Mapping the extracted marker brightness to the exposure time. Each line represents a different row of the frame.

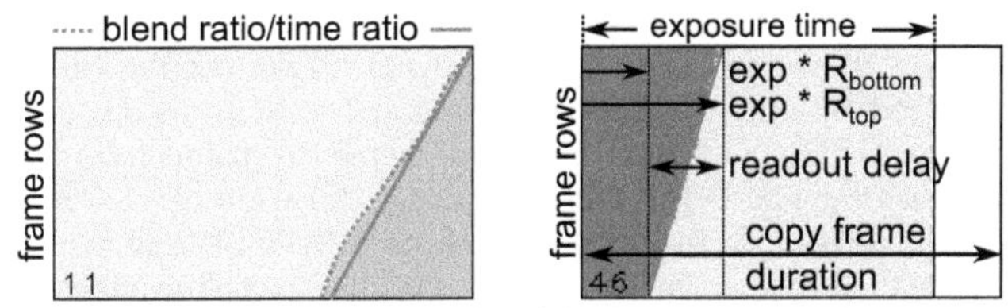

(b) Blend ratio (non-linear) versus time ratio (linear). (c) Calculating the rolling shutter readout delay.

Figure 4: Calculating time ratios from blend ratios.

When plotting both time- and blend ratios, it can be seen that the non-linear vertical gradient of blend ratios now results in a linear vertical gradient of time ratios (Figure 4(b)). This is supported by the fact that the relative acquisition delay for every row is constant [1], which means that the speed in which the rolling shutter moves vertically is constant, thus creating the linear gradient. On the other hand, this supports our model in the non-linearity of the blend ratios. To calculate the rolling shutter readout delay $D_{shutter}$, the time that passes between the corresponding top and bottom time ratios needs to be determined. This is depicted in Figure 4(c). By multiplying these two time ratios with the copy frame's exposure time and calculating the difference, an absolute time value can be extracted.

3.2 Effects from Playback

We now analyze how the video renderer and the display affect the timing of the source frames. Our model assumes that the source frame start times are modified due to aliasing effects caused by the display's refresh rate. To prove this, the source frame start times are inferred from the previously determined source frame time ratios. Using these ratios, we calculate time offsets from the start of each copy frame. The offset is the time that passed until the next source frame be-

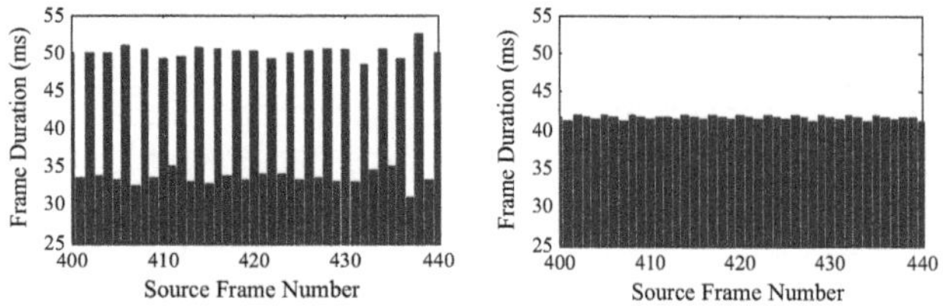

(a) 60 Hz refresh rate. (b) 120 Hz refresh rate.

Figure 5: Source frame durations when playing a 24 fps source video with different display refresh rates.

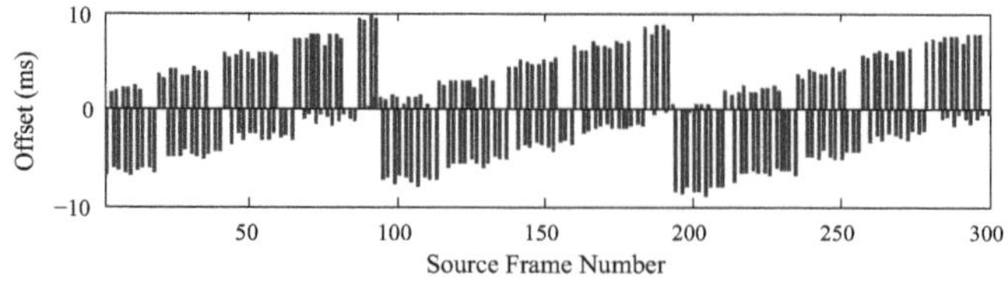

Figure 6: Aliasing effects in frame timing due to a 59.89 Hz display refresh rate for a 24 fps video.

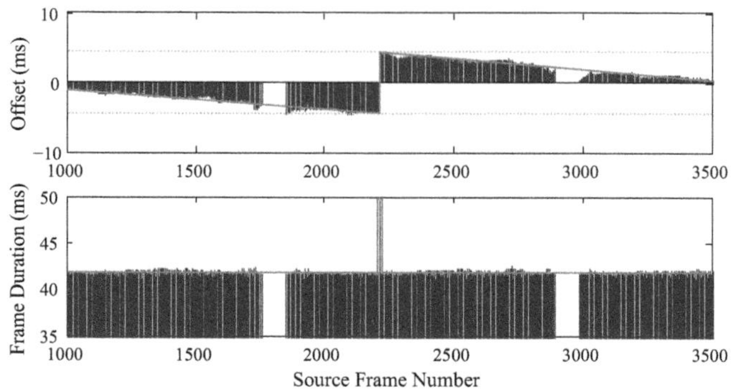

Figure 7: Long-term frame timing drift for a theoretically perfect 24 fps/120 Hz setup (blank parts fell inside periods without exposure).

comes visible in the copy. Since the exact copy frame start times are known, we can add these offsets to them, resulting in the inferred source frame start times. Figure 3(b) visualizes this approach. When consolidating the results from all copy frames, we can recreate the source video as it has been played, knowing the start and end times for all source frames, except the ones that start or end completely within a period without exposure.

Figure 5 shows the detected source frame durations of our marker video for two different display refresh rates. The intended constant frame duration is $D_{src} = \frac{1}{24}$ s $= 41.\bar{6}$ ms, which can be seen clearly in (b). For the 60 Hz refresh rate (a), frame durations exhibit a high-frequency oscillation between approximately 33 and 50 ms. This oscillation is predicted by our model: For $m = 2$ and $n = 5$, $m \cdot D_{src}$ is equal to $n \cdot D_{disp}$. Thus, the actual frame durations follow a pattern that yields the correct average duration of $41.\bar{6}$ ms. After n refresh cycles, exactly m frames have been shown.

When looking at the timing offset of the source frames over the course of 300 frames in Figure 6, it can be seen that the intended frame duration pattern exhibits an increasing drift over time. This is also explained by our model: if $m \cdot D_{src}$ does not exactly equal $n \cdot D_{disp}$, then the offset drifts and gets adjusted periodically. In our experiment, this is the case, because the *true* refresh rate of our Samsung monitor is 59.89 Hz.

Lastly, we analyze frame timing offsets for theoretically perfect set-ups where there are no drifts. To accomplish this, the 24 fps marker video was shown on a monitor with a refresh rate of *exactly* 120 Hz. Ideally, each frame should now be presented for $120/24 = 5$ refresh cycles. Figure 7 reveals that an offset slowly accumulates over time. The cause for this is clock drift between the different clocks that are used by the systems. If the system clock is chosen as the reference clock for the video playback, its difference to the video clock results in the same effect as the video clock not running exactly at the the specified rate. The offset accumulates to one refresh cycle $D_{disp} = \frac{1}{120}$ s $= 8.\bar{3}$ ms over a period of roughly 3800 frames or approximately 158 seconds, which corresponds to a clock drift of 0.00526%. This effect can be modeled as a slightly higher refresh rate parameter to yield the exact same result.

4. CONCLUSION

We presented a model of the temporal effects that occur when re-capturing a video using a camera. With the proposed set of parameters, any frame blending that occurs as a direct result of temporal distortions can be described accurately and can thus be simulated. The identified temporal parameters are the source video's and camera's frame rate, the exposure time, usage of a rolling shutter, rolling shutter readout time, and exact display refresh rate. Better results are achieved if information about the luminance transfer is available. The resulting error when neglecting the luminance transfer, however, is typically tolerable. In an experimental analysis, we verified our model and its parameters by separating the artifacts measured from the frame blending of a real camera into individual temporal effects. Each aspect of our model was thus verified separately.

5. REFERENCES

[1] S. Baudry, B. Chupeau, M. Vito, and G. Doerr. Modeling the flicker effect in camcorded videos to improve watermark robustness. In *Information Forensics and Security (WIFS)*, pages 42–47, 2014.

[2] C. Ben Zid, S. Baudry, B. Chupeau, and G. Doerr. A sneak peek into the camcorder path. *Proc. SPIE*, 8665:86650E–86650E–10, 2013.

[3] P. Bestagini et al. Video recapture detection based on ghosting artifact analysis. In *IEEE Int. Conf. on Image Processing (ICIP)*, pages 4457–4461, 2013.

[4] B. Chupeau, S. Baudry, and G. Doerr. Forensic characterization of pirated movies: digital cinema cam vs. optical disc rip. In *Information Forensics and Security (WIFS)*, pages 155–160, 2014.

[5] P. Hernandez-Avalos et al. Towards the construction of a benchmark for video watermarking systems: Temporal desynchronization attacks. In *Circuits and Systems (MWSCAS)*, pages 628–631, 2010.

[6] P. Schaber, S. Kopf, S. Wetzel, T. Ballast, C. Wesch, and W. Effelsberg. Cammark: Analyzing, modeling, and simulating artifacts in camcorder copies. *ACM Trans. Multimedia Comput. Commun. Appl.*, 11(2s):42:1–42:23, 2015.

On the Benefit of Synthetic Data for Company Logo Detection

Christian Eggert Anton Winschel Rainer Lienhart
Multimedia Computing and Computer Vision Lab
University of Augsburg
Universitätsstr. 6a, 86153 Augsburg, Germany
{ christian.eggert, anton.winschel, rainer.lienhart } @ informatik.uni-augsburg.de

ABSTRACT

In this paper we explore the benefits of synthetically generated data for the task of company logo detection with deep-learned features in the absence of a large training set. We use pre-trained deep convolutional neural networks for feature extraction and use a set of support vector machines for classifying those features. In order to generate sufficient training examples we synthesize artificial training images. Using a bootstrapping process, we iteratively add new synthesized examples from an unlabeled dataset to the training set. Using this setup we are able to obtain a performance which is close to the performance of the full training set.

Categories and Subject Descriptors

I.5 [**Pattern Recognition**]: Miscellaneous; I.4.3 [**Image Processing and Computer Vision**]: Enhancement

General Terms

Algorithms, Experimentation, Performance

Keywords

Logo detection, Logo classification, Synthetic training data, Dataset augmentation

1. INTRODUCTION

It is in the nature of machine learning algorithms to generalize previously seen training examples to unknown instances. For a robust prediction it is vital for the classifier to have access to a large variety of training examples. However, building a dataset can be a slow and tedious task and training examples are hard to come by for some machine learning problems.

Usually there are two approaches to tackle this problem: One way is to augment the training set by generating synthetic variations of the collected examples. Another approach is to use the already collected examples to search for related examples on a large unstructured dataset, browsing through the suggestions and deciding which ones to add to the training set. The problem with the latter approach is located in the second step, since related examples usually mean small variety.

MM'15, October 26–30, 2015, Brisbane, Australia.

ACM 978-1-4503-3459-4/15/10 ...$15.00.
DOI: http://dx.doi.org/10.1145/2733373.2806407 .

Figure 1: A suggestion (red) for user feedback generated by our bootstrapping process.

For the task of company logo detection it is compelling to use both approaches to reinforce each other. Company logos are a special case because typically, only the context in which a logo appears changes strongly while the actual logos themselves usually have relatively uniform appearances. Context is comparatively easy to synthesize as we will describe in section 2. Due to the uniformity of the company logos, similarity search has a good chance of success - especially when used in conjunction with high-level feature representations like features extracted from deep convolutional neural networks (DCNNs).

DCNNs have revolutionized many areas of computer vision. Typically, the convolutional layers of such a network learn a feature representation while the last layers - usually fully connected - are responsible for classification. Being a data driven approach, DCNNs typically require a large number of labeled instances to train. However, it has been found [3] that the features extracted by the convolutional layers generalize well to other computer vision tasks on different datasets. In order to repurpose a DCNN for a different task, the last layers tend to be discarded and the output of the previous layers are used as input for a different classifier, such as support vector machines (SVMs) or random forests.

In this paper we apply the principles mentioned above to the problem of company logo detection and recognition in the absence of a large dataset. For our scenario we will as-

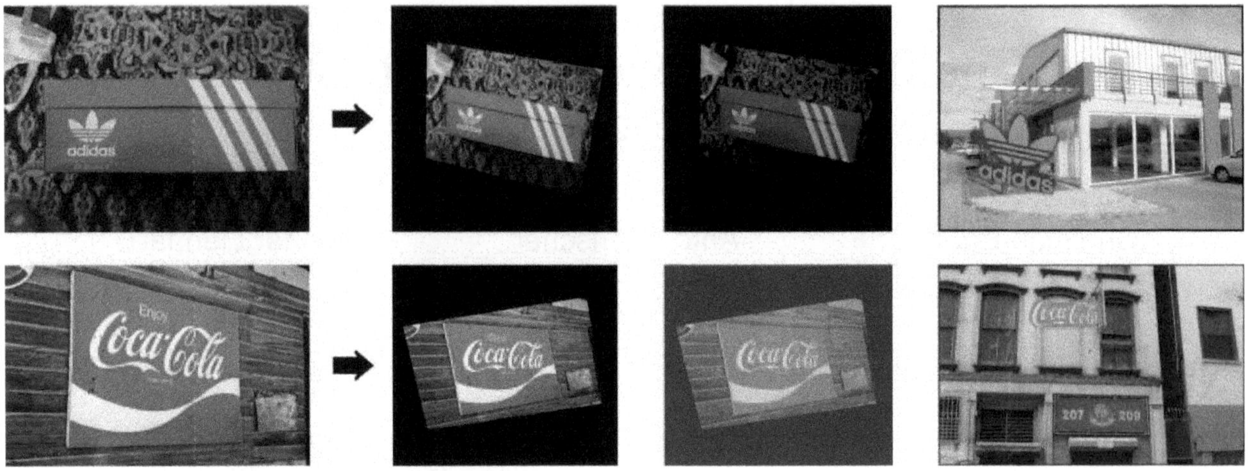

Figure 2: Two examples of synthetically generated images. Starting from a base image, a random perspective transform is applied, followed by gaussian blur (not shown), color augmentation (exaggerated for viewing purposes) and background replacement.

sume a limited number of labeled training examples with pixel-level annotations and an unlabeled number of images, some of which may contain additional instances of the logo. This could for example be achieved by downloading a set of images from an online photo-sharing website using the logo names as keywords. Furthermore, we require a set of images that is most likely free of the logos that we are attempting to detect. Again, this could be achieved by searching an online photo-sharing site with random keywords such as "landscape".

Our contributions are as follows:

1. We show that by training a classifier from synthetic training examples alone we are able to obtain a performance that is comparable to a classifier trained from real images.

2. We show that in a single-shot scenario synthetic training examples can be beneficial to boost the effectiveness of bootstrapping.

2. SYNTHETIC DATA GENERATION

Since we are using DCNNs solely as feature extractors and assume them to come pre-trained, we are only left to train the SVMs used for classifying the DCNN features. In the absence of a large database, we turn to synthetically generated training images. The generation process is depicted in figure 2.

For every class we start off with a small number b of base images from which the synthetic images are to be derived. For every base image we synthesize artificial training images in the following way:

1. We select a random perspective transform and warp both image and mask accordingly. The transformation is given by

$$\boldsymbol{M} = \boldsymbol{P}\boldsymbol{T}\boldsymbol{R_x}\boldsymbol{R_y}\boldsymbol{R_z} \tag{1}$$

where the image is regarded to be on a 3d-plane translated from the origin by $\boldsymbol{T}$ while $\boldsymbol{R_x}$, $\boldsymbol{R_y}$ and $\boldsymbol{R_z}$ represent the rotations of this plane around the coordinate axis associated with the angles Θ_x, Θ_y and Θ_z. $\boldsymbol{P}$ defines a perspective projection. For reasonably large, yet not extreme variations, we limit the allowed angles to the range $-50° \leq \Theta_x \leq 50°$, $-50° \leq \Theta_y \leq 50°$ and pick $\Theta_z \in \{0°, 90°, 180°, 270°\}$ from a uniform distribution.

2. In order to generate a larger visual variety, we modify the color of the warped image by using the approach of [2]. We calculate the eigenvalues $\alpha_i, i = 1, 2, 3$ and the corresponding eigenvectors $\boldsymbol{p_i}$ on the covariance matrix of RGB values in the original base image. For each image we draw three random numbers γ_i distributed according to $\mathcal{N}(0, 0.5)$ and add to each pixel $[I^R_{x,y}, I^G_{x,y}, I^B_{x,y}]^T$ a linear combination of the eigenvectors, given by

$$\sum_{i=1...3} \gamma_i \alpha_i \boldsymbol{p_i} \tag{2}$$

3. The logo is randomly blurred by convolution with a gaussian kernel $G(x, y, \sigma)$ to simulate different scales. This is done by picking $\sigma \in \{0, 0.5, 1.0, 1.5\}$ from a uniform distribution.

4. We remove the background of the logo using the pixel-level annotations of the training set and copy the warped and color-modified logo into a new image which contains no logos. This is done to prevent the classifier from adapting to features extracted from the background since the DCNN only processes rectangular bounding boxes.

On the synthesized images, we apply selective search [7] in order to obtain candidate regions. The candidate regions are split into positive and negative examples as described in section 3. Finally, we extract the DCNN features for the image patches defined by the selective search windows.

3. CLASSIFICATION PIPELINE

For our experiments we use the following classification pipeline: We are using selective search [7] to generate up to 2000 bounding boxes with object proposals per image. Images are limited to a maximum side length of 1024 pixels and are rescaled if necessary. Each bounding box defines an image patch which is resized to match the input dimensions of the neural network and is propagated through the DCNN. For our experiments, we use the 16-layer very deep architecture by [5].

We use the DCNN output after the first fully connected layer[1] without applying the ReLU [2] or employing the dropout. We have found the 4096-dimensional features extracted by this configuration to yield the best results. One exception is the output of the last pooling layer which delivers slightly better results but are impractical to use due to their high dimensionality.

The extracted features are L_2 -normalized and used as input for a series of linear SVMs. We train a separate SVM for every class. Each candidate region is classified according to the SVM which yields the highest score. We require a confidence of at least 0.5 for a positive classification. If no SVM yields a score greater than 0.5, the candidate region is classified as negative. A positive classification for the image is given by the predicted class of the highest-scoring candidate region.

For the initial training, we select candidate regions C whose overlap – calculated using intersection over union (IoU) – with the groundtruth annotation G is $\text{IoU}(C, G) \geq 0.7$ as positive examples for the SVM. As negative examples we choose candidate boxes with an overlap between $0.1 \leq \text{IoU}(C, G) \leq 0.3$. Since the number of negative examples typically is a lot higher than the number of positive examples, we only use a random subset of the negative examples for training.

4. MINING NEW TRAINING EXAMPLES

It is possible to train a decent classifier on purely synthetic data (see section 5). In this section we investigate a bootstrapping process which uses a rudimentary classifier - trained only from a few real images - to mine new training examples from a dataset containing unlabeled instances of company logos. The newly found real training examples can then be used as a basis to synthesize more training images.

Starting with a set of pre-trained SVMs - e.g. from a previous training run on synthetic images - we use our classifier to predict the class labels of object proposals on a previously unlabeled set of images as described in section 3. Typically, the number l of instances a user is willing to label is limited. In order to extract the number of training examples that are likely to be maximally beneficial to the performance of the classifier, we follow the idea of version space bisection by [6]. We select $l = 5$ training examples which are located closest to the decision surface of each SVM for the user to classify. Intuitively, this approach provides the classifier with labels to instances it is most uncertain about. In manually labeling these examples, the classifier is therefore provided with the currently most informative labels.

If classified as a positive example by the user, we generate synthetic versions of this example as described in section 2. We extract DCNN features from both the original example as well as from the synthetic variations. If classified as a logo by the user, the features are added as positive examples to the corresponding SVM responsible for this class. To all other SVMs the example is added as a negative example.

Additionally we make use of the set of logo-free images, which is used to replace the background of synthesized logo images (see section 2), for mining hard negatives. For this purpose, we select at most one candidate box per image that is classified as positive with the highest confidence on the logo-free dataset and add them as negative examples to the SVM which classified this image as positive.

[1]This layer is called FC6 in the CAFFE [1]-Model provided by [5]

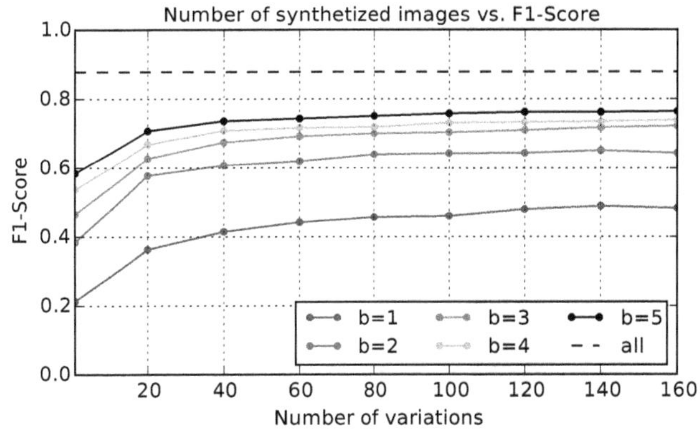

Figure 3: Influence of the number of variations on the recognition performance for different numbers of base images. The dotted line indicates the performance when trained with all training examples (no synthetic images)

5. EXPERIMENTS

We conduct our experiments on the FlickrLogos-32 dataset [4] which consists of 4280 training and validation images and 3960 test images containing both images of 32 logo classes and images containing no logos. The training set contains 10 examples per class while both the validation and the test set contain 30 positive examples each. Additionally, the validation set contains 3000 non-logo images.

First we establish the baseline for our logo recognition system by combining the positive examples from both training and validation set and use them for training. Using the training process described in section 3 and after two rounds of hard negative mining on the non-logo part of the validation set, we obtain a precision of 0.996, a recall of 0.786 and a F1-Score of 0.879.

In our first experiment we evaluate the performance of the classifier when trained on a purely synthetic training set using a fixed amount of base images. This will help us to determine a reasonable number of synthetic images to generate per real example and will serve as a baseline to evaluate the impact of the bootstrapping procedure. We start with a single base image per class $b = 1$ and progressively generate more synthetic images from each base image. Figure 3 shows the F1-Score for the logo recognition system as a function of the number of variations v. Remarkably, only a few base images are required to achieve a performance which is close to the performance of the recognition system trained with the full training set. Unsurprisingly the influence of synthetic training examples diminishes as the number of base images b increases, since the base images can already provide enough variation for the SVMs.

In our second experiment we use the classifiers trained in the first experiment as a starting point for the bootstrapping process described in section 4 (synth). For comparison we use the same bootstrapping process without dynamically synthesizing new training examples (w/o synth).

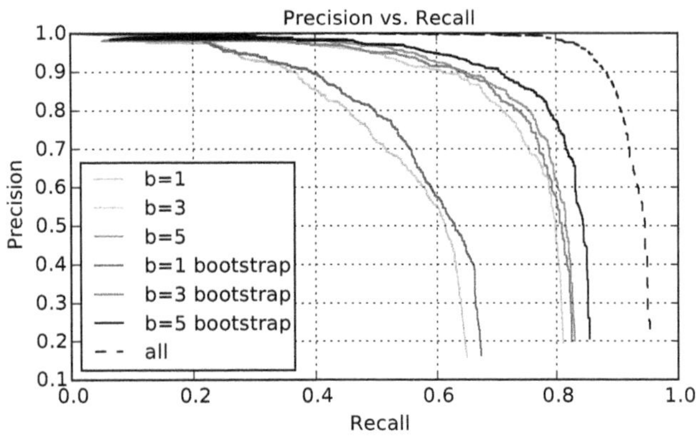

Figure 4: Precision-Recall curve for synthesized training sets with $b = 1$, $b = 3$ and $b = 5$. The dotted line indicates the performance when training with all examples (no synthetic images). In the case of synthetic training data, the number of variations is $v = 40$. Three learning rounds were performed for bootstrapping.

Learning rounds	b	1	2	3	4
synth	1	0.483	0.632	0.646	0.681
synth	3	0.730	0.791	0.795	0.807
synth	5	0.770	0.803	0.815	0.819
w/o synth	1	0.515	0.517	0.514	0.517
w/o synth	3	0.730	0.748	0.751	0.759
w/o synth	5	0.770	0.791	0.792	0.790

Table 1: Influence of the number of learning rounds ($l = 5$) on the performance of the classifier for different number of base images given as F1-Score. The initial classifiers were trained with $v = 40$.

In order to simulate a user providing input, we use the annotations provided from the FlickrLogos validation set. In each training round we select $l = 5$ examples from each SVM which are classified according to the overlap with the groundtruth.

While this approach for simulating user input yields reproducible results, it does have the weakness that it relies on the assumption that all logo instances in the dataset have been labeled. Clearly this is not always the case. In the process, we noticed some limitations in the annotations of the FlickrLogos dataset: One such example is shown in figure 1. The bounding box around the groundtruth annotations is shown in green which is a typical annotation for this particular class. The bounding box marked in red shows a suggestion for a new training example as generated by our bootstrapping process. Despite clearly being an instance of the company logo used in a different context, this example will be classified as a negative example during the bootstrapping process since instances like this are not annotated in the dataset, possibly confusing the classifier.

Table 1 shows the results of this experiment in terms of the F1-Score. While in every scenario synthetic training images are beneficial to the bootstrapping process, the effects are most strongly pronounced when the number of initial training images is small. This is especially obvious in the case of a single training image. As the initial training set grows larger the effects of bootstrapping diminishes as well as the effect of synthetic images. However, using this bootstrapping strategy we are still able to achieve 91% of the performance of the original dataset while using only 8% of the original training images in the case of $b = 3$.

Figure 4 shows the effect of mining new training examples in terms of precision and recall. We show the performance of classifiers trained from synthetic data and compare it with the performance of the classifier that has been subjected to three rounds of bootstrapping with synthesizing from newly mined training examples.

6. CONCLUSION

We have shown that training sets for company logo classification can be successfully enhanced with synthetic images when little training data is available. This is especially true when used in conjunction with a bootstrapping strategy. In this work we have exclusively used pre-trained DCNNs for feature extraction. We expect strong performance gains for DCNNs that have been specifically adapted to the task of logo detection. We imagine that synthetic images could also be beneficially employed in this regard which we will investigate in future works.

7. ACKNOWLEDGMENTS

This work was funded by GfK Verein (`www.gfk-verein.org`). The authors would like to thank Carolin Kaiser, Holger Dietrich and Raimund Wildner for the fruitful discussions about the application perspective of company logo detection.

8. REFERENCES

[1] Y. Jia, E. Shelhamer, J. Donahue, S. Karayev, J. Long, R. Girshick, S. Guadarrama, and T. Darrell. Caffe: Convolutional architecture for fast feature embedding. *CoRR*, "abs/1409.1556", 2014.

[2] A. Krizhevsky, I. Sutskever, and G. E. Hinton. Imagenet classification with deep convolutional neural networks. In *Neural Information Processing Systems (NIPS)*, pages 1097–1105. 2012.

[3] A. Razavian, H. Azizpour, J. Sullivan, and S. Carlsson. Cnn features off-the-shelf: An astounding baseline for recognition. In *IEEE Computer Vision and Pattern Recognition Workshops (CVPRW)*, pages 512–519, June 2014.

[4] S. Romberg, L. Pueyo, R. Lienhart, and R. van Zwol. Scalable logo recognition in real-world images. In *ACM International Conference on Multimedia Retrieval (ICMR)*, pages 25:1–25:8, 2011.

[5] K. Simonyan and A. Zisserman. Very deep convolutional networks for large-scale image recognition. In *International Conference on Learning Representations*, 2015.

[6] S. Tong and D. Koller. Support vector machine active learning with applications to text classification. In *International Conference on Machine Learning (ICML)*, pages 999–1006, Stanford, California, June 2000.

[7] J. Uijlings, K. van de Sande, T. Gevers, and A. Smeulders. Selective search for object recognition. *International Journal of Computer Vision*, 104(2):154–171, 2013.

Retrieving Unfamiliar Faces: Towards Understanding Human Performance

Xu Zhou
Arizona State University
Tempe, Arizona, USA
xzhou50@asu.edu

Baoxin Li
Arizona State University
Tempe, Arizona, USA
baoxin.li@asu.edu

ABSTRACT
Face image retrieval is to find from a dataset all images containing the same person in the query image. Automatic face retrieval has seen fast development in recent years, although humans still appear to be the better performer on this task. This paper reports a study towards understanding human performance on retrieving unfamiliar faces. Wild Web face images are utilized in the study, and two experiments are designed to assess human performance and behavior on the retrieval task. The experiments help to identify a set of important features and also to understand how human behaved when facing the task of retrieving unfamiliar faces. Such observations/conclusions may provide guidelines for improving existing automated algorithms.

Categories and Subject Descriptors
H.1.2 **[Information Systems]**: User/Machine Systems –*Human factors*, *Human information processing.*

General Terms
Human information processing.

Key words
Face image retrieval; Human performance

1. INTRODUCTION
Face retrieval is defined as given a query face image, to find the images containing the same person as in the query image from a large image dataset. The task is in general different from, although related to, face recognition in that it is not necessary to assume a finite set of identities (i.e., subjects) for a given dataset, and the retrieval is done only with respect to the given query image.

In recent years, many face retrieval algorithms have been proposed. Wu and Ke proposed a face image retrieval system [8] using a scalable face representation, where a multi-reference distance approach related to Pseudo-Relevance Feedback (PRF) [11] was used to rank the candidate images using the Hamming signature. In [1], a method using soft biometrics was described, which employs demographic information and facial marks for improving face image matching and retrieval. In [2], SIFT features were used for initial retrieval, followed by a relevance feedback strategy. There are also efforts dealing with feature selection for face retrieval [3]. In general, existing automatic algorithms are either still under-performing or yet to be evaluated on more challenging datasets with images from uncontrolled imaging conditions, indicating much more room for improvement on developing face retrieval approaches.

In the meantime, there have been efforts reported in the literature, attempting to understand human performance on face retrieval or recognition, as it appears human does a better job on such tasks. For example, in [4] and [6], human performance on face recognition was compared to automatic algorithms, both drawing the conclusion that human is more accurate than existing automatic algorithms. The study of [10] showed that faces of the same race are easier to recognize by human; and sex effect is studied in [9], with the conclusion that women are better at recognizing female faces. Nevertheless, little was revealed on how and why people obtained better performance, and thus it is difficult to derive principles for improving automated approaches.

In this paper, we set out to explore human performance on the task of retrieving unfamiliar faces. We consider only the task of retrieval of unfamiliar faces (as opposed to face recognition), since such a task would require a subject to derive all the necessary information from a given query image. This would presumably help us to avoid the complicating factors such as memorized identity in the task of recognizing a known person. Hence the study would potentially reveal the types of information that may be employed by an automated system, which would in general perform the retrieval task with information derived only from the query image. To the best of our knowledge, this is a novel problem that has received little attention in the literature. In our study design, to make the retrieval task even more challenging, we employ wild Web face images (as opposed to standard datasets that were used in most existing work). We also design two types of experiments, intended to assess the conscious and unconscious thinking process of the subjects respectively in performing the retrieval task.

2. METHOD
Recognizing that a subject may or may not be able to explicitly describe how he/she actually performed the task for a given query image, our basic strategy is to rely on two types of experiments: one mainly based on questionnaire to the subjects to collect their self-reported conscious thinking process during making the query (Experiment 1), and one mainly based on an eye-tracking system for capturing their unconscious search of the visual field of view during making the query (Experiment 2). We elaborate below the experimental protocols and the images used in the experiments.

2.1 Dataset Design
The face images in our experiments were selected from the Face In the Wild Database [5], a database of face photographs designed for studying the problem of unconstrained face recognition, which

MM'15, October 26–30, 2015, Brisbane, Australia.
 ISBN 978-1-4503-3459-4/15/10…$15.00.
DOI: http://dx.doi.org/10.1145/2733373.2806381

contains more than 13,000 images of faces collected from the web. These faces have been automatically labeled using the system described in [7]. Since the dataset has 1680 people who have two or more images, we were able to select the images that suit our needs in this study. In particular, we avoid images of well-known celebrities since our goal is to study human performance on retrieving "unfamiliar faces". Twenty query images of 20 different people, 10 female and 10 male respectively, were selected for the first experiment; and 40 query images (20 female and 20 male) were used for the second experiment. All selected images were later examined to see if it is unfamiliar before it is used in the analysis (see Section 2.2).

Additional care was taken in selecting the candidate images for any query image, so as to make the task more challenging. First, people appearing in these images belong to the same gender of the query. Second, we made sure that the candidate images do not have similar clothing style or background to the query image. On the other hand, to ensure the task is better-defined and to support better eye-tacking-based analysis, we also ensured that most of the images have only one dominant face in it.

Figure 1. Illustrating the interface: the query image shown on the right and the candidate images displayed on the left.

2.2 Design of the Experiments

A software utility was built for the experiments. Each subject who participated in the experiments was asked to log into the study via an interface. After that, the subject can click a menu button to start the experiment, then a query image is shown along with an array of $N \times N$ candidate images, as illustrated in Figure 1. N is either 4 or 5 in our experiment. The subject then needs to find out which face image (i.e., the "target image") in the array belongs to the same person in the query image (making the selection is a simply click of mouse, which takes little time). After that, the subject can click a button to move on to the next query image.

In Experiment 1, after recording the subject's query results (his/her response to each query image, including the time spent on each query image), we asked each subject a set of pre-defined questions and recorded their answers. The questionnaire contains two parts. Part 1 is to confirm the unfamiliarity of the query image. If a subject feels any of the query images have "familiar faces", then all the results related to these query images are not considered when we evaluate his/her performance metrics.

In Part 2, the following three questions are presented to each subject after the retrieval task is completed:

Question 1: "Do you think color images give more information than grey scale images when you do the retrieval task?"

Question 2: "What kind of features do you use or rely on when you retrieve a face?"

Question 3: "Rank the importance of the following features in your retrieval: a. Hair style; b. Skin tone; c. Facial features; d. Clothing style; e. Race; f. Age"

In Experiment 2, an eye-tracking system was deployed, which records the eye fixation points of a subject doing the retrieval task. The eye-tracking data were time-stamped and thus were later synchronized with the sequence of queries made and thus we can analyze a subject's unconscious search of the visual field for any given query image.

2.3 Experimental Procedure

We recruited 11 and 9 subjects for Experiment 1 and Experiment 2 respectively. The age range is from 24 to 31, 2 of them are female and the remaining are male. None of them had prior knowledge about what the query experiments were about and they were trained to perform the task right before the experiments. Each subject was asked to finish 80 sessions of face retrieval in the first experiment. Each query image was shown 4 times in random order, each time with a different candidate set. The 4 candidate sets are: 1. Color images with one and only one frontal face image (target image) belonging to the same person as the query image; 2. Color images with one and only one off-frontal face image belongs to the same person as the query image; 3.Grey scale version of set 1; 4. Grey scale version of set 2.

The sequence of these 80 sessions is completely random and within each session, the position of the 25 candidate images is randomized too. Additional care was taken to avoid positioning the target image on some special spots (e.g., the top row, where it may be too obvious, or the right-most row, where it is too close to the equerry image on the interface).

In Experiment 2, considering the resolution of the eye tracker, instead of playing 25 images at a time, we reduced the number to 16. After the observations from the first experiment that color images are more supportive to the retrieval task, in the second experiment we used only color images. Hence a total of 40 sessions of face retrieval tasks were done by each of the 9 subjects.

3. RESULTS AND ANALYSIS

We now report the experimental results, which are presented in three different groups: objective performance metrics (Sect. 3.1), subjective/qualitative responses from the participants (Sect. 3.2), and eye-tracking-based experiment and analysis (Sect. 3.3).

3.1 Objective performance metrics in Experiment 1

For each subject, we computed the hit rate and the average time spent on dealing with different types of images, as elaborated below. (For computing the average time spent on certain type of images, we only use results when the query is correctly done.)

Overall hit rate: The overall hit rate indicates that the subjects' performances are not ideal. The hit rates fall in to a range from 57.5%~97.5%, with the average of 78.64%.

Frontal vs. off-frontal faces: The majority (8 out of 11) spent longer time when dealing with off-frontal faces. The average time on frontal faces is 15.2s with STD of 5.2s while it is 17.4s on off-frontal faces with STD of 5.3s. This indicates that pose is an influential factor in face retrieval. An automated algorithm may need to explicitly handle the pose for improved performance.

Color vs. greyscale faces: The average time spent on color image is 16.0s with STD of 5.6s, while on greyscale image it is 17.4s with STD of 5.5s. 6 out of 11 subjects spent shorter time on color images. This indicates that color images are easier to retrieve than greyscale images. We note that most existing face recognition system actually use only greyscale images.

Male vs. female faces: The average time spent on male faces is 15.1s with STD of 5.0s, and 19.1s on female faces with STD of 6.6s. 26% more time is spent when dealing with female faces and all the subjects except one spent longer time on female faces than male faces. This indicates that female faces are harder to retrieve. One possible reason is the appearance of a female may change dramatically (e.g., due to new hair style or make-up), as illustrated in Figure 2. This suggests that, features that are invariant to common appearance changes in female images should be considered for improving an automated approach.

Figure 2. Drastic appearance changes in female face images. (a) and (b) belong to the same person, so as (c) and (d).

Hit rate vs. time spent: As shown above, the hit rate is only 78.64%. Intuitively we may think that the more time people spend on looking at the images, the higher chance that they can select the correct target image. However, interestingly, plotting the average time spent vs the hit rate reveals a wide scatter without any obvious positive correlation among these two metrics.

3.2 Subjective responses

The subjective responses to the questionnaire reveal additional information that either confirms or deepens the understanding of what observed in Sect. 3.1. For Question 1: "Do you think color images give more information than grey scale images when you do retrieval?", 10 out of 11 subjects responded "yes", only one responded "no" with the explanation that he only looked at facial features. This correlates well with the results of Sect. 3.1.

In asking Question 2: "What features did you use or rely on when retrieving a face?" we intended to learn specific features that human uses on retrieval. Figure 3 depicts all features mentioned by subjects and the corresponding number of times they are mentioned. Synonyms are merged. Frequently-mentioned features are: hair, mustache, eye glasses, face shape, nose and mouth. This open question gives us some important hints. For example, most existing automatic face retrieval algorithms do not use hair or mustache as one of the features, while more attention is given to facial components like eyes, nose, and mouths.

For Question 3: "Rank the importance of the following features in your retrieval: a. hair style, b. skin tone, c. facial features, d. clothing style, e. race, f. age", ranking scores are from 1-6 while 1 indicates most important and 5 indicates least important. Table 1 shows the average ranking scores of these features, lower scores indicate higher priority. Based on these ranking scores, the ranking of the 6 features are: facial features, skin tone, race, hair style, age, and clothing style.

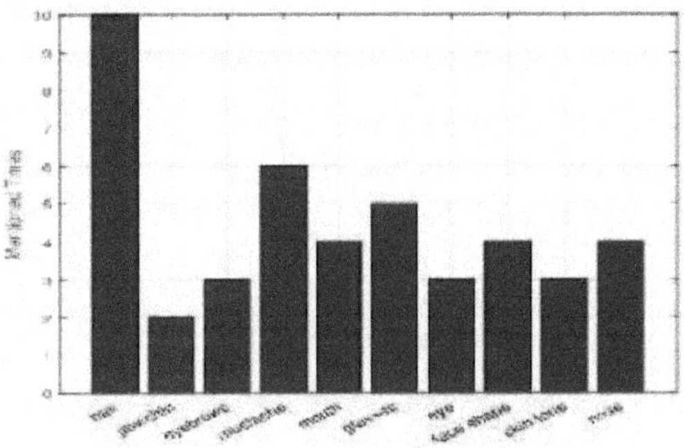

Figure 3. Relative frequency of features mentioned by the subjects, from left to right: hair, jaw/chin, eyebrows, mustache, mouth, glasses, eye, face shape, skin tone, nose.

Table 1. Average ranking scores.

Feature	a	b	c	d	e	f
Score	3.36	2.91	2.73	5.55	3.00	3.45

3.3 Experiment with eye-tracking

Experiment 1 provided some holistic understanding of human performance in retrieving unfamiliar faces, mostly in terms of accuracy (hit rate), time spent, and self-reported important factors. Recognizing the fact that a subject may employ some unconscious process that is not realized by the subject him/herself, we employed eye-tracking in Experiment 2 in order to learn the search behavior of the subjects in retrieving the images. Such experiment may also provide additional data for verifying the self-reported behaviors. In this experiment, an eye tracker tracks the eye fixation and gaze points during the retrieving actions of a subject. The recorded data include: eye gaze points, eye fixation points (duration >=0.1s), duration of each gaze or fixation points, and special events (when the subject advances to the next query).

The raw data from the eye tracker is the gaze point positions. The gaze points are sampled at a frequency of 100HZ which is dense enough to record accurate eye movement. This high sampling rate also caused crowded gaze points at some positions and thus care needs to be taken to make use of the noisy data. So based on the raw data, fixation points are generated in the following way: in a small radius if the difference of the time stamp of the first gaze point and the last point is more than 0.1s, then the mean position of these points is recorded as a fixation point.

We use both gaze points and fixation points for objective analysis. The candidates that received the least numbers of gaze points are those that were quickly discounted by the subjects. By analyzing such images, we came to the observation that hair color, skin tonc and eye glasses contributed to such quick elimination. More specifically, for the 40 sessions, choosing the 5 images with the least gaze points, a total of 5*40=200 images were identified (100 from female candidates and 100 from male candidates). Among these, hair color is the most distinguishing: 64% (female) and 61% (male) rejected candidates having a different hair color than the query image. For female sessions, skin tone is also distinctive:

63% of the candidates have a different skin tone than the query. We also observed 22% of the female candidates are persons wearing eye glasses while the query image does not (or vice versa). For male sessions, the percentages are 41% for the skin tone difference and 45% for with/without eye glasses, respectively.

We can plot the "heat map", which shows where the subject looked at during performing the task. Figure 4 is a sample heat map for one session, in which we observe that the searching is focused on only a few candidates. The subjects also performed intensive comparisons between query image and candidates. For all the 40 query images, we got 719 fixation points in total, among which 107 points are located around the eyes, 226 around the nose and 386 around the mouth. Surprisingly, we see that eyes are less important than nose and mouth in this searching stage.

Figure 4. Sample heat map of one query image. The fixations of one subject are visualized: red/yellow/green regions respectively receive many/fewer/least fixations.

Considering both the hit rate and the average time spent on a particular session, we may further define "easy cases" and "difficult cases" by thresholding these metrics. With this, we also looked into the "comparison behavior" of a subject. This behavior is defined as sweeping between the query and candidate images. We found that there is a correlation between the number of sweeps in one session and the difficulty level of the session. The average number of sweeps performed in one session is 56.72. For easy/difficult cases, the average numbers of sweeps are 33.6 and 98 respectively. It is obvious that in the difficult cases, the subjects needed to do more localized checking more often. Figure 5 shows a sample from the difficult cases.

Finally, we noticed that not all the candidates in one session received equal comparisons, and the variation can be dramatic. This suggests that most candidates are eliminated quickly by some semi-global features; then intensive comparison is done on a few candidates using more localized feature, and in this stage the nose and mouth are dominant factors that influence the final decision. Such a finding may lead to a staged design of new automated retrieval approaches: semi-global-feature-based elimination followed by localized-feature-directed refined comparison.

4. CONCLUSION

We carried out experiments to understand human performance in retrieving unfamiliar faces. In addition to measuring the hit rate while documenting other performance metrics, we employed eye-tracking to capture the search patterns of the subjects. The results, while confirming some intuitions, also revealed new clues as to what are important in human's retrieving action, providing insights into new ways of improving automated approaches.

Figure 5. A difficult case: the busy gaze trajectories suggest intensive comparisons between the query image and candidates were performed. Easy cases have much simpler trajectories.

Acknowledgement: The work was supported in part by a grant (#1135616) from the National Science Foundation. Any opinions expressed in this material are those of the authors and do not necessarily reflect the views of NSF.

6. REFERENCES

[1] Unsang Park; Jain, A.K. 2010. Face Matching and Retrieval Using Soft Biometrics, *Information Forensics and Security, IEEE Transactions on* , vol.5, no.3, pp.406-415

[2] B. Hu; Bijuan Weng; Shumin Ruan. 2012. Face recognition and retrieval based on feedback log information, *Computer Science and Automation Engineering (CSAE), IEEE International Conference on* , vol.1, no., pp.578-584, 25-27

[3] W. Dai; Y. Fang; B. Hu, Feature selection in interactive face retrieval, *Image and Signal Processing (CISP), 2011 4th International Congress on* , vol.3, no., pp.1358-1362

[4] Hancock, P. J.B.; Bruce, V.; Burton, A. M. 2000. Recognition of unfamiliar faces, *Trends in cognitive sciences*, volume 4 issue 9 pp.330 – 337.

[5] Gary B. Huang; Manu Ramesh; Tamara Berg; and Erik Learned-Miller. 2007. Labeled Faces in the Wild: A Database for Studying Face Recognition in Unconstrained Environments, *Univ. Mass., Amherst, Tech. Report 07-49*

[6] Adler, A.; Schuckers, M.E. 2007. Comparing Human and Automatic Face Recognition Performance, *Systems, Man, and Cybernetics, Part B: Cybernetics, IEEE Tran. on*, vol.37, no.5, pp.1248-1255

[7] Tamara L. Berg; Alexander C. Berg; Jaety Edwards; David A. Forsyth. 2004. Whos's in the Picture, *Neural Information Processing Systems (NIPS)*

[8] Z. Wu, Q. Ke, J. Sun, H. Shum, Scalable Face Image Retrieval with Identity-Based Quantization and Multireference Reranking, *Pattern Analysis and Machine Intelligence, IEEE Trans. on*, vol.33, no.10, pp.1991-2001

[9] C. L. Herlitz. 2002. Sex differences in face recognition—Women's faces make the difference, *Brain Cogn.*, vol. 50, no. 1, pp. 121–128

[10] N. Furl, A. J. O'Toole, and P. J. Phillips. 2002. Face recognition algorithms as models of the other race effect, *Cogn. Sci.*, vol. 96, pp. 1–19

[11] C.D. Manning, P. Raghavan, and H. Schu¨ tze. 2008. Relevance Feedback and Query Expansion, *Introduction to Information Retrieval*, pp. 177-194, Cambridge Univ. Press.

Acoustic Scene Classification based on Sound Textures and Events

Jiaxing Ye, Takumi Kobayashi, Masahiro Murakawa, Tetsuya Higuchi
National Institute of Advanced Industrial Science and Technology (AIST)
{jiaxing.you, takumi.kobayashi, m.murakawa, t-higuchi}@aist.go.jp

ABSTRACT

Semantic labelling of acoustic scenes has recently emerged as active topic covering a wide range of applications, e.g. surveillance and audio-based information retrieval. In this paper, we present an effective approach for acoustic scene classification through characterizing both background sound textures and acoustic events. The work takes inspiration from the psychoacoustic definition of acoustic scenes, that is, 'skeleton of (acoustic) events on a bed of (sound) texture'. In detail, we firstly employ distinct models to exploit sound textures and events in acoustic scenes, individually. Subsequently, based on fact that the perceptual importance of two parts will vary with respect to different scene categories, we develop favourable class-conditional fusion scheme to aggregate two-channel information. To validate proposed approach, we conduct extensive experiments on Rouen dataset which includes 19 categories of daily acoustic scenes with 3026 real-world recordings, and the proposed approach outperforms state-of-the-art methods by a large margin.

Categories and Subject Descriptors

H.2 [**Experience**]: Music, Speech and Audio Processing in Multimedia

Keywords

acoustic scene classification, constant-Q transform , Histogram of Gradients, model aggregation

1. INTRODUCTION

Motivated by various real-world applications, such as machine listening and surveillance, acoustic scene classification (ASC) has become a popular topic lately [1]. ASC aims to assign a semantic label to an input audio clip indicating the environment where it has been recorded. Unlike in conventional sound processing that speech and music are main objectives, ASC deals with comprehensive acoustics in daily life, such as sound of motor, footsteps and wind. Therefore,

MM'15, October 26-30, 2015, Brisbane, Australia
©2015 ACM. ISBN 978-1-4503-3459-4/15/10...$15.00
DOI: http://dx.doi.org/10.1145/2733373.2806389

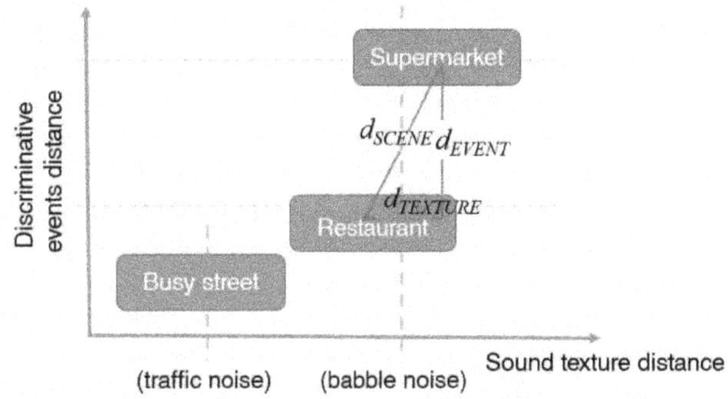

Figure 1: Illustration of conceptual psychoacoustic model for acoustic scene classification

due to the complexity in environmental sound composition, conventional sound analysis schemes, such as the ones developed for automatic speech recognition and music information retrieval, are not well suited to ASC [1].

ASC is quite a broad problem with all kinds of sounds in life involved. In order to design effective ASC scheme, it is critical to clarify the ASC task as well as to point out its distinction from other closely related problems, e.g. acoustic event detection (AED). In this regard, we introduce psychoacoustic definition of acoustic scenes, that is, "skeleton of (acoustic) events on a bed of (sound) texture" [7]. Clearly, there are two channels of information that contribute to acoustic scene perception, namely, sound textures which present high temporal homogeneity nature of environmental sound and acoustic events which are superimposed on the background. In Fig. 1 we present a conceptual chart for psychoacoustic model for ASC. And three major findings could be drawn from the chart:

† Perceptual distance between acoustic scenes should be obtained via characterizing both sound textures and key events [7].

† It is evident that AED is one sub-problem of ASC, which partially contributes to ASC analysis.

† The contributions for acoustic scene cognition of sound textures and events are anticipated to vary with respect to distinct scene classes.

Conventional studies on ASC mainly focus on sound texture information which is characterized by summary statistics over acoustic features. Various features have been evaluated for ASC, e.g. zero-cross rate (ZCR), MFCC and Gammatone filters [1, 10, 2]. Due to the high temporal homogeneity in sound textures, descriptive statistics, such as average and 1st/2nd order differential derivatives, are commonly adopted to build global textural feature [10]. Subsequently, various statistical models are employed to perform scene classification in a supervised manner. Compared with generative models like Gaussian mixture models (GMMs) and Hidden Markov model (HMM) [1], discriminative models, i.e. support vector machines (SVM), usually achieve superior results for ASC using multiple acoustic features with high dimension [4, 10]. It is noteworthy that bag-of-(acoustic)features (BoF) model has been regarded as standard model for ASC, however, latest investigation revealed its inefficiency in handling complex ASC with high within-class sound variability [5].

In this paper, we develop effective computational framework that approximates psychoacoustic auditory scene cognition to incorporate sound textures and events information for ASC. We firstly define general fusion rule of complementary information through convex combination as follows:

$$d_{SCENE} = \alpha_c \times d_E + (1 - \alpha_c) \times d_T,\ 0 \leq \alpha_c \leq 1\ , \quad (1)$$

where d_T and d_E denote perceptual distance for sound textures and acoustic events, respectively. α_c is the contribution weight with respect to certain sound scene class (indexed by c). Now the ASC task is decomposed into two sub-problems: sound texture analysis and acoustic event investigation. For the first sub-problem, we introduce effective acoustic features for sound texture extraction, subsequently probabilistic SVM (ProbSVM) is adopted to generate d_T in a supervised manner; for the latter sub-problem, BoF model is introduced to generate mid-level features representing acoustic events. Similarly, ProbSVM is applied again to the mid-level (event-based) features for estimating d_E. To fuse the two-way information , we adopt linear blending scheme on validation set to infer the optimal α_c. The main contributions of this paper can be outlined as follows:

- We propose an effective computational framework that characterizes both sound textures and acoustic events for ASC. The proposed approach outperformed state-of-the-art results by a big margin.
- To incorporate sound textures and acoustic events information logically, we explore varying (relative) contributions of complementary components with respect to different scene categories.
- We introduce the effective acoustic features for characterizing environmental sounds and the superiority of the proposed feature has been validated through experimental comparisons.

2. THE PROPOSED APPROACH

In this section, we present the proposed approach in a top-down design. To approximate the acoustic scene perceptual distance with a statistical learning formulation, we introduce probabilistic estimates to rewrite (1) as:

$$S^c_{SCENE} = \alpha_c \times S^c_E + (1 - \alpha_c) \times S^c_T,\ 0 \leq \alpha_c \leq 1\ , \quad (2)$$

where S^c_T, S^c_E and S^c_{SCENE} denote class scores (membership probabilities) to c-category of scene which are derived from sound textures, acoustic events and both components, respectively. In this part, we explain how to estimate the scene-conditional fusion weights of α_c and the class scores of S^c_E, S^c_T as follows.

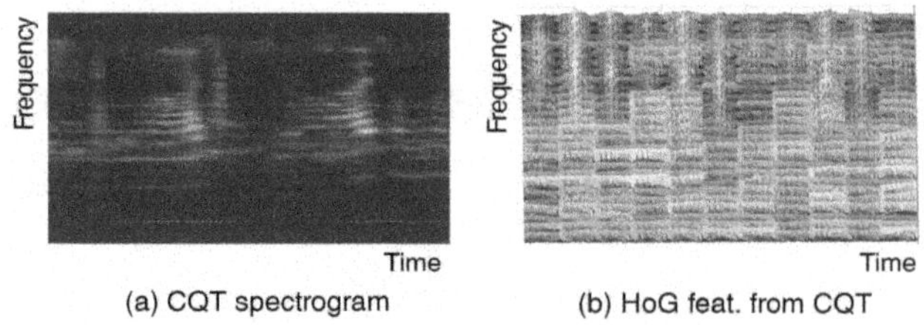

Figure 2: Acoustic features demonstration

2.1 Acoustic feature extraction

To characterize wide spectro-temporal dynamics in environmental sounds, some recent works attempt to adopt image features, such as Local Binary Patterns (LBP) and Histogram of oriented Gradients (HoG), to extract acoustic feature for ASC in a two-dimensional manner and achieved favourable results [4, 9]. Some adjustments, such as pre- and post- processing, are commonly applied to make image descriptors better suit for ASC.

In a similar setting, we introduce acoustic features through extracting HoG patterns from Constant-Q transform (CQT) time-frequency representations (TFR). CQT increases time resolution towards higher frequencies, it is therefore preferred for describing environmental sounds [11]. To encode rich spectro-temporal patterns, we adopt HoG descriptors which effectively characterize 2-dimensional variations with cumulative oriented gradients over all local regions in spectrogram. In Fig.2, we show both CQT spectrogram (a) and HoG representation (b) of *cafe* scene, and from the charts, we see predominant spectro-temporal patterns are well retained by HoG. Meanwhile, the feature dimension of HoG is much lower compared to that of CQT spectrogram. Notably, acoustic features used in [9] is most close to ours, yet the key difference is, they added a preprocessing stage to resize CQT spectrogram to 512 × 512, hence discarding much detail time-frequency information. On the contrary, we directly apply HoG to CQT spectrogram and thus precise local information can be characterized for ASC.

2.2 Sound textures analysis

In this section, we present our path to characterize sound textures in acoustic scene.

2.2.1 Sound textures feature extraction

Recent study in neuroscience reveals that auditory system summarizes temporal details of sounds using time-averaged statistics for auditory scene cognition [6]. Grounded on such finding, we extract sound textures by performing average pooling along time on all acoustic feature vectors $[\mathbf{x}_1, ..., \mathbf{x}_N]$ from a sound scene:

$$\mathbf{x}_{texture} = \frac{1}{N}\sum_{i=1}^{N}\mathbf{x}_i, \quad 1 \leq i \leq N\ , \quad (3)$$

where $\mathbf{x}_i$ is the ith (in time sequence) extracted HoG feature (from CQT spectrogram). $\mathbf{x}_{texture}$ denotes global sound textures of input acoustic scene.

2.2.2 Class score estimation

To estimate class score S^c_T in (2) based on textures information, we employ probabilistic SVM that estimates proba-

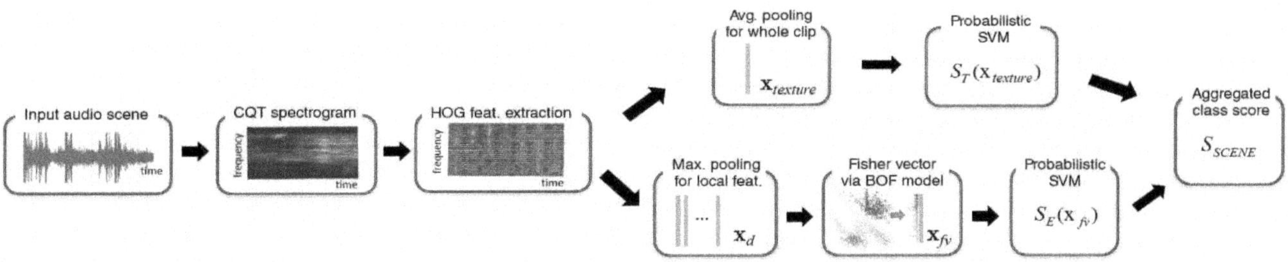

Figure 3: Overview of the proposed acoustic scene classification scheme

bility by investigating distance between input data and hyperplane in the (kernel) feature space. The formulation can be expressed as:

$$\min_{A,B} \frac{1}{M} \sum_{m=1}^{M} \log\left(1 + \exp\left(-y_m(A(\mathbf{w}'_{svm}\Phi(\mathbf{x}_m) + b_{svm}) + B)\right)\right) , \quad (4)$$

where $\{\mathbf{x}_m, y_m\}$ are training data and label. Parameters of $\mathbf{w}_{svm}$ and b_{svm} can be determined by quadratic programming, and logistic regression can be performed to compute A, B accordingly. Finally, we can derive class score $S^c_{texture}$ for input feature:

$$S_T(\mathbf{x}_{texture}) = \text{sigmoid}(A_T(\mathbf{w}'_T\Phi_T(\mathbf{x}_{texture}) + b_T) + B_T) \quad (5)$$

where subscript T denotes parameters are derived from sound texture information.

2.3 Acoustic events analysis

Bag-of-feature (BoF) model is efficient to build (content-based) mid-level representation from low-level features. In sound processing, the BoF model has been widely studied for both ASC and AED [1, 8]. Latest studies revealed that BoF model is preferred for acoustic event detection [8], rather than for sound scene classification [5]. In this study, we employ BoF model to generate mid-level features that encode key events in auditory scenes.

(1) Low-level (dense) feature extraction. Given the waveform of acoustic signal, we firstly apply 1-second sliding window with half overlapping to segment data into slices. For each slice, we perform CQT transform and further extract HoG features. Finally, we perform max. pooling along time to enhance low-level feature for describing events and one vector can be obtained for each slice.

(2) Codebook generation. We employ Gaussian mixture model (GMM) to characterize distribution of input features:

$$p(\mathbf{x}_d; \theta) = \sum_{k=1}^{K} \pi_k \mathcal{N}(\mathbf{x}_d; \mu_k, \Sigma_k) \quad (6)$$

where $\mathbf{x}_d$ denotes acoustic feature, K is number of mixtures, and $\theta = \{\pi_k, \mu_k, \Sigma_k\}$ are parameters for GMM. Expectation maximization (EM) algorithm is applied to fit GMM model to given features.

(3) Encoding feature with codebook. Fisher vector (FV) delivers more robust performance for modelling patterns with noise [3], and hence, we employ FV to generate mid-level representation for acoustic events and it can be computed as follows:

$$\mathcal{G}^{\mathbf{x}_d}_{\mu,k} = \frac{1}{\sqrt{\pi_k}}\gamma_k\left(\frac{\mathbf{x}_d - \mu_k}{\sigma_k}\right), \; \mathcal{G}^{\mathbf{x}_d}_{\sigma,k} = \frac{1}{\sqrt{\pi_k}}\gamma_k\left[\frac{(\mathbf{x}_d - \mu_k)^2}{\sigma_k^2} - 1\right], \quad (7)$$

where γ_k is the weight of feature $\mathbf{x}_d$ to k-th Gaussian mixture. FV is obtained by concatenating these two gradients: $\mathbf{x}_{fv} = \left[\mathcal{G}^{\mathbf{x}}_{\mu,1}, \mathcal{G}^{\mathbf{x}}_{\sigma,1}, ..., \mathcal{G}^{\mathbf{x}}_{\mu,k}, \mathcal{G}^{\mathbf{x}}_{\sigma,k}\right]$, and then L_2 normalization is applied to facilitate classification. In the same vein as in 2.2.2, we fit ProbSVM model to FV features for estimating class score as follows:

$$S_E(\mathbf{x}_{fv}) = \text{sigmoid}(A_E(\mathbf{w}'_E\Phi_E(\mathbf{x}_{fv}) + b_E) + B_E) , \quad (8)$$

where subscript E indicates sound event information.

2.4 Class score aggregation for ASC

Having computed class scores of $S_E(\mathbf{x}^{cj}_{fv})$ and $S_T(\mathbf{x}^{cj}_{texture})$, we further estimate optimal scene class-conditional fusion weights α_c via cross-validation. The objective function is defined as:

$$\min_{\alpha_c} \sum_{c=1}^{C}\sum_{j=1}^{N_c}\left(y_{cj} - (\alpha_c S_E(\mathbf{x}^{cj}_{fv}) + (1-\alpha_c)S_T(\mathbf{x}^{cj}_{texture}))\right)^2 \quad (9)$$

where C is number of scene classes and cj denotes jth sample in cth class. α_c can be solved analytically, and overall class score S^c_{SCENE} can be computed through (2). Finally, class label is derived by $\text{argmin}_c(-S^c_{SCENE})$. To summarize whole process, a flow chart is presented in Fig. 3.

3. EXPERIMENTS

To validate the proposed scheme, we conduct experiments on Litis Rouen Dataset [9], which consists of 19 classes of real-world audio scenes with 3026 samples with 30 sec length. 20-fold splits are provided to partition data into 80%-training/20%-test sets. Within a training set, learning and validation sets are also prepared with 50%-50%.

In our experiments, we set number of bins per octave for CQT transform to be 48. In HoG extraction, local region size, number of orientations were set to 8 × 8 and 8, respectively. For codebook generation in BoF model, we used 256 GMM models (K = 256 in (6)) and Gaussian kernel was applied in ProbSVM.

3.1 Acoustic feature evaluation

In first test, we drew comparison between proposed features with Fourier transform(FT) and MFCC. In FT, we set analysis window to 30ms with half overlapping and for MFCC, 1st and 2nd order differential derivatives are also extracted and dimension was 39. We extracted sound textures

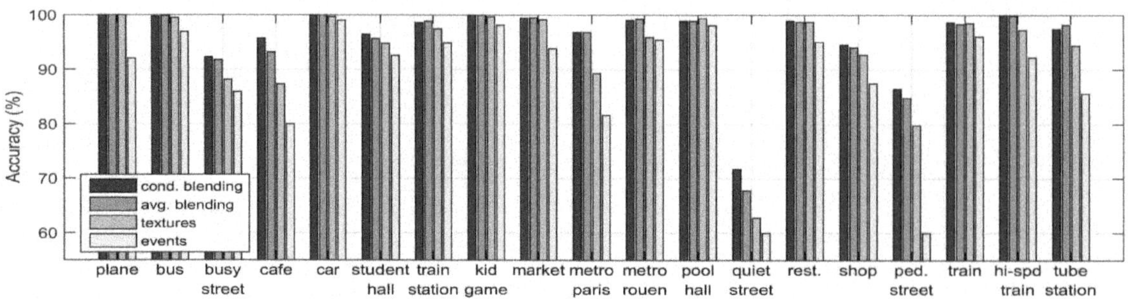

Figure 4: Classification experimental results comparison for whole Rouen dataset

Table 1: ASC accuracy for features test (%)

	MFCC	FFT	CQT
w/o HoG	70.9	81.84	88.68
w/ HoG	77.22	92.15	94.62

Table 2: Averaged ASC accuracy comparison (%)

Events	Textures	Avg. blend	Cond. blend	[9]'s
90.51	94.62	95.52	96.08	91.14

from all candidate features via time-averaging (3). Moreover, to clarify effectiveness of HoG features, we further compared cases of with/without HoG extraction. Results shown in Tab.1 brought us following conclusions: 1. CQT renders time-frequency representation that is well suited to ASC. 2. Over all three tests, HoG features contributed over 7.5% in accuracy on an average, hence its significance is evident.

3.2 Framework evaluation

We further conducted experiment to validate the proposed scheme, and results were summarized in Fig. 4 and Tab. 2. Three major conclusions can be drawn by examining the results: 1. Comparing to events, sound textures carry predominant scene information and thus exhibited higher classification accuracy. 2. Sound textures and events can compensate each other for achieving better ASC precision. 3. The proposed class-conditional fusion scheme had been validated and it always generated better results compared with average blending ($\alpha_c = 0.5$). Finally, the proposed approach achieved 96.08% average accuracy for Rouen dataset and outperformed previous method that presented average precision of 91.4% [9]

4. CONCLUSIONS

In this paper, we presented a novel framework for acoustic scene classification which imitates psychoacoustic auditory scene cognition process through characterizing both sound textures and events. Effective acoustic features are employed for describing sound textures and events, and we further incorporate the two-channel information with respect to their importance for scene classification. The framework achieved superior results in real data evaluation. Grounded on proposed formulation for ASC, various modifications can be made, such as extracting multi-resolution features and employing non-linear blending to fuse two-way information of textures and events. Those will be our future work.

5. ACKNOWLEDGEMENTS

This study was partly supported by Cross-ministerial Strategic Innovation Promotion Program (SIP) / Technologies for maintenance, renewal, and management for infrastructure, and supported by the New Energy and Industrial Technology Development Organization (NEDO), Japan.

6. REFERENCES

[1] D. Barchiesi, D. Giannoulis, D. Stowell, and M. Plumbley. Acoustic scene classification: Classifying environments from the sounds they produce. *Signal Processing Magazine, IEEE*, 32(3):16–34, May 2015.

[2] J. Chen, Y. Wang, and D. Wang. A feature study for classification-based speech separation at low signal-to-noise ratios. *IEEE TASLP*, 22(12):1993–2002, Dec. 2014.

[3] H. Jegou, M. Douze, C. Schmid, and P. Perez. Aggregating local descriptors into a compact image representation. In *Computer Vision and Pattern Recognition (CVPR), 2010 IEEE Conference on*, pages 3304–3311, June 2010.

[4] T. Kobayashi and J. Ye. Acoustic feature extraction by statistics based local binary pattern for environmental sound classification. In *IEEE ICASSP*, pages 3052–3056, May 2014.

[5] M. Lagrange, G. Lafay, B. Defreville, and J.-J. Aucouturier. The bag-of-frames approach: a not so sufficient model for urban soundscapes. *CoRR*, abs/1412.4052, 2014.

[6] J. H. McDermott, M. Schemitsch, and E. P. Simoncelli. Summary statistics in auditory perception. *Nature Neuroscience.*, 16:493 – 498, Apr. 2013.

[7] I. Nelken and A. de Cheveigne. An ear for statistics. *Nature Neuroscience.*, 16:381 – 382, Apr. 2013.

[8] A. Plinge, R. Grzeszick, and G. Fink. A bag-of-features approach to acoustic event detection. In *IEEE ICASSP*, pages 3704–3708, May 2014.

[9] A. Rakotomamonjy and G. Gasso. Histogram of gradients of time-frequency representations for audio scene classification. *IEEE TASLP*, 23(1):142–153, Jan 2015.

[10] J. Salamon, C. Jacoby, and J. P. Bello. A dataset and taxonomy for urban sound research. In *22th ACM Int. Conf. on Multimedia*, Nov 2014.

[11] C. Schörkhuber and A. Klapuri. Constant-q transform toolbox for music processing. In *7th Sound and Music Computing Conf.*, July 2010.

Coupled Support Vector Machines for Supervised Domain Adaptation

Hemanth Venkateswara*, Prasanth Lade†, Jieping Ye‡, Sethuraman Panchanathan*
*Center for Cognitive Ubiquitous Computing, Arizona State Univeristy
† Bosch Research and Technology Center, Palo Alto ‡ University of Michigan, Ann Arbor
hemanthv@asu.edu, prasanth.lade@us.bosch.com, jpye@umich.edu, panch@asu.edu

ABSTRACT

Popular domain adaptation (DA) techniques learn a classifier for the target domain by sampling relevant data points from the source and combining it with the target data. We present a Support Vector Machine (SVM) based supervised DA technique, where the similarity between source and target domains is modeled as the similarity between their SVM decision boundaries. We couple the source and target SVMs and reduce the model to a standard single SVM. We test the Coupled-SVM on multiple datasets and compare our results with other popular SVM based DA approaches.

Categories and Subject Descriptors

H.2.8 [**Database Management**]: Database Applications—*Data mining*

General Terms

Algorithms

Keywords

Supervised Domain Adaptation; Coupled SVM

1. INTRODUCTION AND MOTIVATION

Supervised learning algorithms often make the implicit assumption that the test data is drawn from the same distribution as the training data. These algorithms become ineffective when such assumptions regarding the test data are violated. *Transfer learning* techniques are applied to address these kinds of problems. Transfer learning involves extracting knowledge from one or more tasks or domains and utilizing (transferring) that knowledge to design a solution for a new task or domain [2]. Domain adaptation (DA) is a special case of transfer learning where we handle data from different, yet correlated distributions. DA techniques transfer knowledge from the *source* domain (distribution) to the *target* domain (distribution), in the form of learned models and efficient feature representations, to learn effective classifiers on the target domain. In this work we consider the problem of supervised DA where we use labeled samples from the source domain along with a limited number of labeled samples from the target domain, to learn a classifier for the target domain. We propose a Coupled linear Support Vector Machine (C-SVM) model that simultaneously estimates linear SVM decision boundaries $\mathbf{w}_s$ and $\mathbf{w}_t$, for the source and target training data respectively. Using a technique termed as *instance matching*, researchers sample source data points such that the difference between the means of the sampled source and target data is minimized [4], [10]. Our intuition behind the C-SVM is along similar lines, where we penalize the difference between $\mathbf{w}_s$ and $\mathbf{w}_t$. Since the SVM decision boundaries are a linear combination of the data points, penalizing the difference between $\mathbf{w}_s$ and $\mathbf{w}_t$, can be viewed as penalizing the difference between the weighted means of the source and target data points.

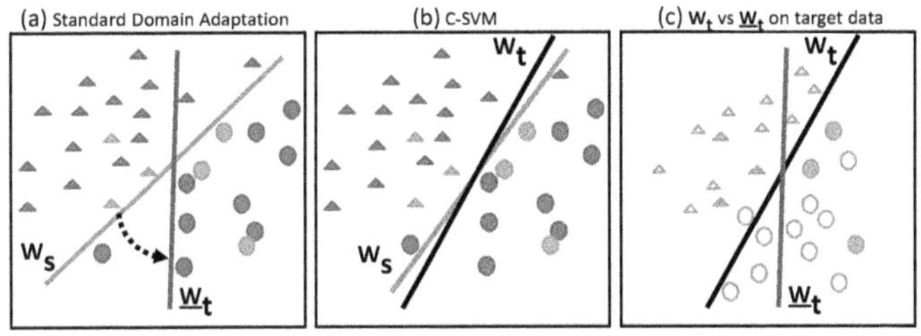

Figure 1: (a) Standard SVM based DA. The source SVM $\mathbf{w}_s$ is perturbed to get $\underline{\mathbf{w}}_t$. (b) C-SVM, $\mathbf{w}_s$ and $\mathbf{w}_t$ are learned together. Training error could be high. (c) The C-SVM does not over fit. *Red* is source and *Green* is target data. Filled unfilled objects are train and test data respectively.

Figure(1a), illustrates standard SVM based DA where $\mathbf{w}_s$ is first learned on the source and is subsequently perturbed to obtain the target ($\underline{\mathbf{w}}_t$). The perturbed SVM $\underline{\mathbf{w}}_t$ could be very different from $\mathbf{w}_s$ and can overfit the target training data. Figure(1b), depicts the C-SVM, where $\mathbf{w}_s$ and $\mathbf{w}_t$, are learned simultaneously. The source SVM $\mathbf{w}_s$, provides an anchor for the target SVM $\mathbf{w}_t$. The difference between $\mathbf{w}_s$ and $\mathbf{w}_t$ is modeled based on the difference between the source and target domains. In addition, the C-SVM trades training error for generalization as illustrated in Figure(1c). In this paper, we formulate a coupled SVM problem to estimate $\mathbf{w}_s$ and $\mathbf{w}_t$ and reduce it to a single SVM problem that can be solved with standard quadratic optimization. We test our model and report recognition accuracies on various datasets of objects, hand-written digits, facial expressions and activities.

MM'15, October 26–30, 2015, Brisbane, Australia.
 ISBN 978-1-4503-3459-4/15/10 ...$15.00.
DOI: http://dx.doi.org/10.1145/2733373.2806334.

2. RELATED WORK AND OUR METHOD

In this section we will discuss some of the SVM based DA techniques closely related to the C-SVM. Support Vector Machines have been extensively used for DA in the past. Daumé [3], modeled augmented features with a heuristic kernel. Bruzzone and Marconcini [2], proposed an unsupervised method (DASVM) to adapt a SVM learned on the source domain to the unlabeled data in the target domain in an iterative manner. Adapt-SVM is another technique closely related to our method, where Yang et al. [17] and Li [9], learn a SVM on the target by minimizing the classification error on the target data while also reducing the discrepancy between the source and target SVMs. We differ from this method by learning the source and target SVMs simultaneously. Aytar and Zisserman [1], extend this framework to the Projective Model Transfer SVM that relaxes the transfer induced by the Adapt-SVM. Hoffman et al. (MMDT) [6], learn a single SVM model for the source and the transformed target data. The target data is transformed by a transformation matrix that is learned in an optimization framework along with the SVM. Duan et al. (AMKL) [4] implement a multiple kernel method where multiple base kernel classifiers are combined with a pre-learned average classifier obtained from fusing multiple nonlinear SVMs. Unlike in C-SVM where the similarity between source and target is learned by the model, Widmer et al. [16] use a similar approach to solve multitask problems using graph Laplacians to model task similarity. We believe the C-SVM holds a unique position in this wide array of SVM solutions for DA. The C-SVM trains a linear SVM for both the source and target domains simultaneously, thereby minimizing the chances of over-fitting, especially when there are very few labeled samples from the target domain.

3. PROBLEM SPECIFICATION

We outline the problem as follows. Let $\{(\mathbf{x}_i^s, y_i^s)\}_{i=1}^{N_s} \subset \mathscr{S}$, where $\mathscr{S}$ is the *source domain*, $\mathbf{x}_i^s \in \mathbb{R}^d$, are data points and $y_i^s \in \{-1, +1\}$, are their labels. Along similar lines, $\{(\mathbf{x}_i^t, y_i^t)\}_{i=1}^{N_t} \subset \mathscr{T}$, where $\mathscr{T}$ is the *target domain.*

3.1 Coupled-SVM Model

The goal is to learn a target classifier f_t, that generalizes to a larger subset of $\mathscr{T}$ and does not over fit the target training data $\{(\mathbf{x}_i^t, y_i^t)\}_{i=1}^{N_t}$. The catch here is that the number of labeled target data points is small and $N_t \ll N_s$. We therefore incorporate the source data and learn the source classifier $f_s(\mathbf{x}) = \mathbf{w}_s^\top \mathbf{x} + b_s$ to provide an anchor point for $f_t = \mathbf{w}_t^\top \mathbf{x} + b_t$. The source and target SVM decision boundaries are $\{\mathbf{w}_s, b_s\}$ and $\{\mathbf{w}_t, b_t\}$ respectively. To simplify notation we re-define, $\mathbf{w}_s \leftarrow [\mathbf{w}_s^\top, b_s]^\top$ and $\mathbf{w}_t \leftarrow [\mathbf{w}_t^\top, b_t]^\top$ and account for the bias by re-defining, $\mathbf{x}_i^s \leftarrow [\mathbf{x}_i^{s\top}, 1]^\top$ and $\mathbf{x}_i^t \leftarrow [\mathbf{x}_i^{t\top}, 1]^\top$. Incorporating these definitions, the Coupled-SVM can be detailed as follows,

$$\begin{aligned}\{\mathbf{w}_s^*, \mathbf{w}_t^*\} = \underset{\mathbf{w}_s, \mathbf{w}_t}{\text{argmin}} \; & \frac{1}{2}\lambda||\mathbf{w}_s - \mathbf{w}_t||_2^2 + \frac{1}{2}||\mathbf{w}_s||_2^2 + \frac{1}{2}||\mathbf{w}_t||_2^2 \\ & + C_s\sum_i^{N_s} \xi_i^s + C_t \sum_i^{N_t} \xi_i^t \\ \text{s.t.,} \;\; & y_i^s(\mathbf{w}_s^\top \mathbf{x}_i^s) \geq 1 - \xi_i^s, \; \xi_i^s \geq 0, \;\; i \in [1, \ldots, N_s] \\ & y_i^t(\mathbf{w}_t^\top \mathbf{x}_i^t) \geq 1 - \xi_i^t, \; \xi_i^t \geq 0, \;\; i \in [1, \ldots, N_t] \end{aligned} \tag{1}$$

Equation (1) is a variation of a standard linear SVM with two decision boundaries and an additional term relating the two boundaries. The first term captures the similarity(dissimilarity) between the source and target domains as the difference between the decision boundaries. λ controls the importance of this difference. The 2nd and 3rd term are the SVM regularizers. The 4th and 5th terms capture training loss, where C_s and C_t control the importance of the source and target misclassification respectively.

3.2 Solution

To simplify notation, we define a new set of variables based on the earlier ones. We concatenate the two SVM boundaries into a single variable, $\mathbf{w} \in \mathbb{R}^{2(d+1)}$ defined as, $\mathbf{w} \leftarrow [\mathbf{w}_s^\top, \mathbf{w}_t^\top]^\top$. The individual SVMs $\mathbf{w}_s$ and $\mathbf{w}_t$ can be extracted from $\mathbf{w}$ using permutation matrices $I_s \in \mathbb{R}^{(d+1)\times 2(d+1)}$ and $I_t \in \mathbb{R}^{(d+1)\times 2(d+1)}$, where I_s and I_t are binary matrices such that, $I_s\mathbf{w} = \mathbf{w}_s$ and $I_t\mathbf{w} = \mathbf{w}_t$. For example, let $\mathbf{v}_1 = [a, b]^\top$, $\mathbf{v}_2 = [c, d]^\top$ and $\mathbf{v} \leftarrow [\mathbf{v}_1^\top, \mathbf{v}_2^\top]^\top$. Then the permutation matrices I_{v_1} and I_{v_2} such that, $I_{v_1}\mathbf{v} = \mathbf{v}_1$ and $I_{v_2}\mathbf{v} = \mathbf{v}_2$, are given by, $I_{v_1} = [\begin{smallmatrix}1&0&0&0\\0&1&0&0\end{smallmatrix}]$, and $I_{v_2} = [\begin{smallmatrix}0&0&1&0\\0&0&0&1\end{smallmatrix}]$. We also define new variables $(\mathbf{x}_i, y_i, c_i), i \in \{1, \ldots, (N_s + N_t)\}$, where, $\mathbf{x}_i \in \mathbb{R}^{2(d+1)}$ and $y_i \in \{-1, +1\}$ are the new data points and $c_i \in \{C_s, C_t\}$,

$$\mathbf{x}_i \leftarrow \begin{cases} [\mathbf{x}_i^{s\top}, \mathbf{0}^\top]^\top & 1 \leq i \leq N_s \\ [\mathbf{0}^\top, \mathbf{x}_{i-N_s}^{t\top}]^\top & (N_s + 1) \leq i \leq (N_s + N_t) \end{cases} \tag{2}$$

where, $\mathbf{0} \in \mathbb{R}^{d+1}$ is a vector of zeros. Similarly,

$$\{y_i, c_i\} \leftarrow \begin{cases} \{y_i^s, C_s\} & 1 \leq i \leq N_s \\ \{y_{i-N_s}^t, C_t\} & (N_s + 1) \leq i \leq (N_s + N_t) \end{cases} \tag{3}$$

For ease of derivation, we consider the linearly separable SVM and get rid of c_i (we will re-introduce it later). The minimization problem in Equation(1) can now be re-formulated as,

$$\begin{aligned}\{\mathbf{w}^*\} &= \underset{\mathbf{w}}{\text{argmin}} \; \frac{1}{2}\lambda||I_{st}\mathbf{w}||_2^2 + \frac{1}{2}||\mathbf{w}||_2^2 \\ \text{s.t.,} \;\; & y_i(\mathbf{w}^\top \mathbf{x}_i) \geq 1 \quad i \in \{1, \ldots, (N_s + N_t)\} \end{aligned} \tag{4}$$

where we have defined, $I_{st} \leftarrow (I_s - I_t)$ and used $I_s\mathbf{w} = \mathbf{w}_s$, $I_t\mathbf{w} = \mathbf{w}_t$ for the first term. For the second term, we have used $\frac{1}{2}||\mathbf{w}_s||_2^2 + \frac{1}{2}||\mathbf{w}_t||_2^2 = \frac{1}{2}||\mathbf{w}||_2^2$. We introduce Lagrangian variables $\{\alpha_i\}$ to solve the problem,

$$L(\mathbf{w}, \boldsymbol{\alpha}) = \frac{1}{2}\lambda||I_{st}\mathbf{w}||_2^2 + \frac{1}{2}||\mathbf{w}||_2^2 - \sum_i^{N_s+N_t} \alpha_i\big(y_i(\mathbf{w}^\top \mathbf{x}_i - 1)\big) \tag{5}$$

We need to minimize the Lagrangian w.r.t $\mathbf{w}$ and maximize w.r.t to $\boldsymbol{\alpha}$. We optimize first w.r.t $\mathbf{w}$ by setting the derivative $\frac{\partial L(\mathbf{w},\boldsymbol{\alpha})}{\partial \mathbf{w}} = 0$ and get, $\mathbf{w} = D\sum_i^{N_s+N_t} \alpha_i y_i \mathbf{x}_i$ where, I is an identity matrix and, $D = (I + \lambda I_{st}^\top I_{st})^{-1}$. By the nature of our permutation matrices I_s and I_t, $(I + \lambda I_{st}^\top I_{st})$ is full rank and therefore, D exists. We define $\mathbf{v} \leftarrow \sum_i^{N_s+N_t} \alpha_i y_i \mathbf{x}_i$ and substitute for $\mathbf{w}$ in Equation(5) to arrive at the SVM dual form which we need to maximize,

$$\{\alpha^*\} = \underset{\alpha}{\text{argmax}}\ \frac{1}{2}\mathbf{v}^\top D^\top I_{st}^\top I_{st} D\mathbf{v} + \frac{1}{2}\mathbf{v}^\top D^\top D\mathbf{v} - \mathbf{v}^\top D\mathbf{v} + \mathbf{1}^\top \alpha$$
$$= \underset{\alpha}{\text{argmax}}\ \mathbf{v}^\top (\frac{1}{2}D^\top (I + I_{st}^\top I_{st})D - D)\mathbf{v} + \mathbf{1}^\top \alpha$$
$$= \underset{\alpha}{\text{argmin}}\ \frac{1}{2}\mathbf{v}^\top D\mathbf{v} - \mathbf{1}^\top \alpha \quad (D \text{ is symmetric})$$
$$= \underset{\alpha}{\text{argmin}}\ \frac{1}{2}\alpha^\top \mathcal{Q}\alpha - \mathbf{1}^\top \alpha \qquad (6)$$

Equation(6) is the standard SVM dual where $\mathcal{Q}_{ij} = y_i y_j \mathbf{x}_i^\top D\mathbf{x}_j$ and $\mathbf{1}$ is a vector of 1s. To use any of the standard SVM libraries, we can set $\tilde{\mathbf{x}}_i = D^{1/2}\mathbf{x}_i$. Then $\mathcal{Q}_{i,j} = y_i y_j \tilde{\mathbf{x}}_i^\top \tilde{\mathbf{x}}_j$. The decision boundary in the space of $\tilde{\mathbf{x}}_i$, is given by, $\tilde{\mathbf{w}} = \sum_i \alpha_i y_i \tilde{\mathbf{x}}_i$. The decision boundary in the space of $\mathbf{x}_i$ is given by $\mathbf{w} = D\sum_i \alpha_i y_i \mathbf{x}_i$. Therefore $\mathbf{w} = D^{1/2}\tilde{\mathbf{w}}$. We re-introduce the slack variables as constraints $0 \leq \alpha_i \leq c_i$. We can easily extend the algorithm to the multi-class setting using one-vs-one or one-vs-all settings. Once $\mathbf{w}$ is estimated, $I_s\mathbf{w} = \mathbf{w}_s$ and $I_t\mathbf{w} = \mathbf{w}_t$ is used to get the source and target SVMs.

4. EXPERIMENTS

In this section we discuss the extensive experiments we conducted to study the C-SVM model. We first outline the different datasets and their domains. We then outline the DA algorithms we compare against. Finally, we report the experimental details and our results.

4.1 Data Preparation

For our experiments, we consider multiple datasets from different applications and also test the C-SVM with different kinds of features. For all the experiments (except *Office-Caltech*) we use the following setting. For the training data, we sample 20 examples from the source domain and 3 examples from the target domain from every category. The test data is the remaining examples in the target domain not used for training.

***Office-Caltech* datasets**: For this experiment we borrow the dataset and the experimental setup outlined in [5]. The *Office* dataset consists of three domains, `Amazon`, `Dslr` and `Webcam`. The *Caltech256* dataset has one domain, `Caltech`. All the domains consist of a set of common categories viz., {*back-pack, bike, calculator, headphones, computer-keyboard, laptop, monitor, computer-mouse, coffee-mug, video-projector*}. We use the 800 dimension SURF-BoW features that are provided by[5] for our experiments. We follow the experimental setup outlined in [5]. For the training data, we sample 8 examples from the source domain (for `Amazon` we use 20) and 3 examples from the target domain.

***MNIST-USPS* datasets**: The *MNIST* and *USPS* datasets are benchmark datasets for handwritten digit recognition. These datasets contain gray scale images of digits from 0 to 9. For our experiments, we have considered a subset of these datasets (2000 images from *MINST* and 1800 images from *USPS*) based on [10]. We refer to these domains as `MNIST` and `USPS` respectively. The images are resized to 16×16 pixels and represented as vectors of length 256.

***CKPlus-MMI* dataset**: The *CKPlus*[11] and *MMI*[12] are benchmark facial expression recognition datasets. We select 6 categories viz., {*anger, disgust, fear, anger, happy, sad,* and *surprise*}, from frames with the most intense expression (peak frames) from every facial expression video sequence to get around 1500 images for each dataset with around 250 images per category. We refer to these domains as `CKPlus` and `MMI`. We extract deep convolutional neural network based generic features which have shown astounding results across multiple applications [13]. We therefore decided to use an 'off-the-shelf' feature extractor developed by Simonyan and Zisserman [15]. We used the output of the first fully connected layer from the 16 weight layer model as features with dimension 4096 which were then reduced to 100 using PCA.

***HMDB51-UCF50* dataset**: We pooled 11 common categories of activity from *HMDB51*[8] and *UCF50*[14]. The categories from *UCF50* are, {*BaseballPitch(throw), Basketball(shoot_ball), Biking(ride_bike), Diving(dive), Fencing (fencing), GolfSwing(golf), HorseRiding(ride_horse), PullUps (pullup), PushUps(pushup), Punch(punch), WalkingWithDog (walk)*}. The category names from *HMDB51* are in parenthesis. We refer to these domains as `HMDB51` and `UCF50`. We extract state-of-the-art **HOG**, **HOF**, **MBHx** and **MBHy** descriptors from the videos according to [7]. We pool the descriptors into one grid **1x1x1**, and estimate Fisher Vectors with $K = 256$ Gaussians. The dimension of these Fishers Vectors is $202,752$. We apply PCA and reduce the dimension to 100.

4.2 Existing Methods

We compare our method with existing supervised DA techniques based on SVMs. **SVM(T)** (Linear SVM with training data from target domain), **SVM(S)** (Linear SVM with training data from source domain), **SVM(S+T)** (Linear SVM with union of source and target domain training data), **MMDT** (The Max-Margin Domain Transform [6]), **AMKL** (The Adaptive Multiple Kernel Learning [4]), and **C-SVM** (Coupled SVM algorithm).

4.3 Experimental Details and Results

We conducted 18 experiments with different combinations of datasets. Table(1) depicts the results comparing multiple algorithms. For the *Office-Caltech* dataset, the results are averaged across 20 splits of data and 100 splits for the rest of the experiments. The results for SVM(S) demonstrate the fact that although the datasets consist of the same categories, the domains have different distributions of data points. This is also highlighted by the success of SVM(T) even with few labeled training data points. The naive union of the source and target training data is in some cases beneficial but not always, as illustrated by SVM(S+T). Amongst the algorithms we have compared with, AMKL is on par with C-SVM in terms of performance. There is little to choose in terms of performance accuracies between the two. However, C-SVM is the easier and simpler solution as it is a standard linear SVM unlike AMKL, which is a multiple kernel based method. In all of these experiments we apply leave-one-out cross validation across the training target data to determine the best values of the parameters $\{C_s, C_t, \lambda\}$. We also studied the C-SVM by varying the number of samples available for training. We dropped the `Webcam` and `Dslr` datasets as they have fewer number of data points. Figure(2a) illustrates that increasing the number of source training data points, does not affect the test accuracies. The SVM relies on support vectors to estimate the source decision boundary, and additional source training data does not modify the source boundaries by much. The effect of

Expt.	SVM(T)	SVM(S)	SVM(S+T)	MMDT	AMKL	C-SVM
A→ W(1)	56.06±0.95	37.36±1.19	51.26±1.19	64.87±1.26	67.85±1.06	66.40±1.09
A→ D(2)	43.15±0.78	37.64±0.96	47.56±0.99	54.41±1.00	56.22±0.89	57.13±0.98
W→ A(3)	44.39±1.18	32.03±0.90	44.87±0.59	50.54±0.82	52.96±0.57	53.97±0.42
W→ D(4)	45.20±1.34	61.06±0.86	65.39±0.89	62.48±0.98	75.95±0.94	68.27±0.86
D→ A(5)	42.17±1.03	31.48±0.65	46.17±0.44	50.45±0.75	52.36±0.57	54.10±0.55
D→ W(6)	54.91±0.80	69.81±1.06	76.19±0.64	74.34±0.66	85.94±0.44	77.17±0.46
A→ C(7)	26.62±0.60	38.61±0.50	42.46±0.39	39.67±0.50	44.92±0.46	44.74±0.57
W→ C(8)	25.82±0.78	26.67±0.59	34.53±0.76	34.86±0.79	39.20±0.57	39.77±0.59
D→ C(9)	26.88±0.74	25.74±0.47	34.68±0.67	35.82±0.75	41.12±0.44	41.27±0.51
C→ A(10)	43.52±1.07	36.22±0.82	47.75±0.60	51.10±0.76	55.98±0.58	55.56±0.76
C→ W(11)	55.49±1.02	29.72±1.54	51.28±1.23	62.94±1.11	68.70±1.07	67.74±1.05
C→ D(12)	43.07±1.47	32.56±1.03	47.68±1.17	52.56±0.97	58.82±0.83	59.72±1.01
M→ U(13)	70.73±0.41	38.89±0.61	64.36±0.41	68.96±0.43	79.56±0.30	76.02±0.34
U→ M(14)	58.23±0.39	21.67±0.33	38.43±0.36	48.29±0.32	63.80±0.32	63.25±0.31
K→ I(15)	33.31±0.27	13.30±0.15	25.83±0.31	18.28±0.42	31.87±0.29	33.10±0.29
I→ K(16)	45.65±0.47	19.47±0.55	25.63±0.35	21.33±0.81	43.59±0.50	48.54±0.47
H→ F(17)	28.94±0.26	17.45±0.17	23.00±0.19	29.05±0.23	33.06±0.23	35.89±0.25
F→ H(18)	18.64±0.19	16.99±0.16	19.58±0.17	22.28±0.18	24.28±0.16	24.41±0.19

Table 1: Recognition accuracies (%) on the object, digit, facial expression abd activity datasets across multiple algorithms. {Amazon(A), Webcam(W), Dslr(D), Caltech(C), MNIST(M), USPS(U), CKPlus(K), MMI(I), HMDB51(H), UCF50(F)}. A→W implies A is source domain and W is target domain. The best results are highlighted in red.

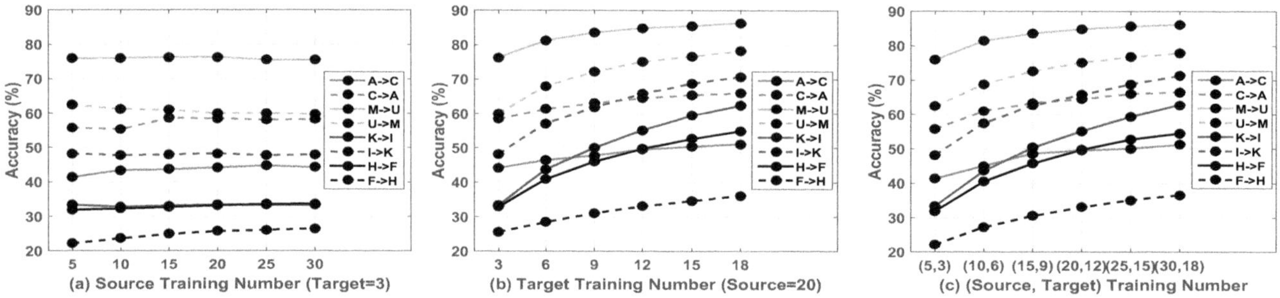

Figure 2: Average recognition accuracy (%) across different experiments varying number of training examples in source and target.

additional target training data is comparatively more pronounced in Figure(2b) which is intuitive. By far, the most interesting is Figure(2c). Increasing both source and target training data numbers is nearly comparable to increasing only the number of target training data points. Source training data does not contribute to the target SVM after a threshold number of training data points.

5. CONCLUSIONS

The C-SVM is elegant, efficient and easy to implement. We plan to extend this work to study nonlinear adaptations in the future. We would like to model classifier similarity in an infinite dimensional (kernel) space and also contemplate on the idea of unsupervised DA.

6. ACKNOWLEDGMENTS

This material is based upon work supported by the National Science Foundation (NSF) under Grant No:1116360. Any opinions, findings, and conclusions or recommendations expressed in this material are those of the authors and do not necessarily reflect the views of the NSF.

7. REFERENCES

[1] Y. Aytar and A. Zisserman. Tabula rasa: Model transfer for object category detection. In *IEEE ICCV*, 2011.

[2] L. Bruzzone and M. Marconcini. Domain adaptation problems: A dasvm classification technique and a circular validation strategy. *IEEE, PAMI*, 32(5):770–787, 2010.

[3] H. Daumé III. Frustratingly easy domain adaptation. In *Association of Computational Linguistics*, 2007.

[4] L. Duan, I. W. Tsang, and D. Xu. Domain transfer multiple kernel learning. *IEEE PAMI*, 34(3):465–479, 2012.

[5] B. Gong, Y. Shi, F. Sha, and K. Grauman. Geodesic flow kernel for unsupervised domain adaptation. In *IEEE CVPR*, 2012.

[6] J. Hoffman, E. Rodner, J. Donahue, K. Saenko, and T. Darrell. Efficient learning of domain-invariant image representations. In *Int'l Conference on Learning Representations (ICLR)*, 2013.

[7] V. Kantorov and I. Laptev. Efficient feature extraction, encoding, and classification for action recognition. In *IEEE CVPR*, 2014.

[8] H. Kuehne, H. Jhuang, E. Garrote, T. Poggio, and T. Serre. HMDB: a large video database for human motion recognition. In *IEEE ICCV*, 2011.

[9] X. Li. *Regularized adaptation: Theory, algorithms and applications.* PhD thesis, University of Washington, 2007.

[10] M. Long, J. Wang, G. Ding, J. Sun, and P. S. Yu. Transfer joint matching for unsupervised domain adaptation. In *IEEE CVPR*, 2014.

[11] P. Lucey, J. F. Cohn, T. Kanade, J. Saragih, Z. Ambadar, and I. Matthews. The extended cohn-kanade dataset (ck+): A complete dataset for action unit and emotion-specified expression. In *IEEE (CVPRW), 2010.*

[12] M. Pantic, M. Valstar, R. Rademaker, and L. Maat. Web-based database for facial expression analysis. In *IEEE ICME 2005.*

[13] A. S. Razavian, H. Azizpour, J. Sullivan, and S. Carlsson. Cnn features off-the-shelf: an astounding baseline for recognition. In *IEEE (CVPRW), 2014*, pages 512–519.

[14] K. K. Reddy and M. Shah. Recognizing 50 human action categories of web videos. *Machine Vision and Applications*, 24(5):971–981, 2013.

[15] K. Simonyan and A. Zisserman. Very deep convolutional networks for large-scale image recognition. *arXiv preprint arXiv:1409.1556*, 2014.

[16] C. Widmer, M. Kloft, N. Görnitz, G. Rätsch, P. Flach, T. De Bie, and N. Cristianini. Efficient training of graph-regularized multitask svms. In *ECML 2012.*

[17] J. Yang, R. Yan, and A. G. Hauptmann. Adapting svm classifiers to data with shifted distributions. In *Data Mining Workshops, IEEE ICDM*, pages 69–76, 2007.

Deep People Counting in Extremely Dense Crowds

Chuan Wang[1], Hua Zhang[1], Liang Yang[1,2], Si Liu[1], Xiaochun Cao[1*]
[1]State Key Laboratory of Information Security, Institute of Information Engineering,
Chinese Academy of Sciences.
[2]School of Information Engineering, Tianjin University of Commerce.
{wangchuan, zhanghua, yangliang, liusi, caoxiaochun}@iie.ac.cn

ABSTRACT

People counting in extremely dense crowds is an important step for video surveillance and anomaly warning. The problem becomes especially more challenging due to the lack of training samples, severe occlusions, cluttered scenes and variation of perspective. Existing methods either resort to auxiliary human and face detectors or surrogate by estimating the density of crowds. Most of them rely on hand-crafted features, such as SIFT, HOG *etc*, and thus are prone to fail when density grows or the training sample is scarce. In this paper we propose an end-to-end deep convolutional neural networks (CNN) regression model for counting people of images in extremely dense crowds. Our method has following characteristics. Firstly, it is a deep model built on CNN to automatically learn effective features for counting. Besides, to weaken influence of background like buildings and trees, we purposely enrich the training data with expanded negative samples whose ground truth counting is set as zero. With these negative samples, the robustness can be enhanced. Extensive experimental results show that our method achieves superior performance than the state-of-the-arts in term of the mean and variance of absolute difference.

Categories and Subject Descriptors

I.4.8 [**Image Processing and Computer Vision**]: Scene Analysis

Keywords

People counting; convolutional neural networks(CNN); crowd analysis;

1. INTRODUCTION

Crowd analysis, *e.g.*, estimating the number of people in the crowd, is becoming one of the most important and challenging problems in the field of multimedia and computer vision. The recurrent tragic stampedes at New Year's Eve or pilgrimages and terrorist attacks at the marathon or squares have shown great significance of crowd analysis on abnormal states alarm. Hence we urgently require powerful and sophisticated approaches for visual analysis of dense crowds. Besides, crowd analysis is useful in arrangement, modification and expansion of traffic facilities (tunnels, overpasses and traffic lights), as well. It can also be used to detect, track and manage crowd events like marathons, protests, and rallies that all may gather hundreds of people. A lot of works on crowd analysis are proposed including crowd detection [1], crowd segmentation [7], and collective motion learning for anomaly detection.

In recent years, great efforts have been made for counting people in natural scenes [2, 3], which can be divided into two categories: direct and indirect estimation. Direct methods are mostly based on human detection achieved by face or parts filters of people [2]. Indirect ones always obtain the number of people by estimating crowd density ranges. The general strategy is to learn a regression model between density and low level features belonging to corresponding region. Although the traditional methods have achieved much success, most of them verifies on low or medium density crowds. However, in particular scenes like concerts, rallies and protests, thousands of people may exist and each person may merely be represented by no more than 10 of pixels in photo records. These situation will certainly make traditional methods failed. With increase of density, decrease of number of pixels each person occupies or existence of severe occlusion among people, crowd counting becomes more difficult and most of existing techniques may degrade

Figure 1: Extremely dense crowd samples.

*Corresponding author

MM'15, October 26-30, 2015, Brisbane, Australia.

DOI: http://dx.doi.org/10.1145/2733373.28063370-12345-67-8/90/01.

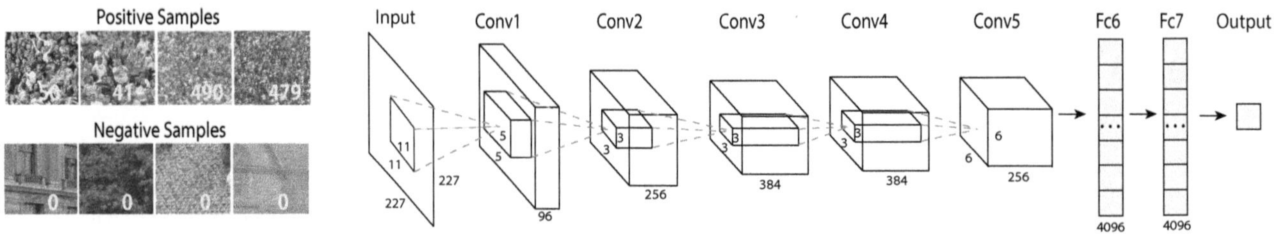

Figure 2: Deep model architecture. We feed this deep network with the patches of crowd images and negative sample images, and its output is the estimated people counts in the input patch.

or fail. Moreover, traditional methods rely on hand-crafted features, such as SIFT and HOG, which are turned to be sub-optimal for this task. Since cluttered scene, perspective distortion, or even environment factors like illumination can provide misleading information and lead traditional features based human detection methods, *e.g.*, Deformable Part Models (DPMs), invalid and prevent people counting from making success.

Recently, deep models especially convolutional neural networks have been widely applied to many computer vision problems like image classification, object detection and face recognition [9]. Girshick *et al.* [4] points out that features extracted from convolutional neural networks [8] trained for classification are sometimes more effective than hand-crafted features and can be reusable to broader tasks. Effectiveness of leveraging convolutional neural networks in people counting task has not been fully explored.

In this paper we develop a deep regression model for counting people in extremely dense crowd images using deep convolutional neural networks (CNN). Firstly, we adopt CNN as our basic framework to learn efficient features for counting and thus develop an end-to-end system. Secondly, we feed the CNN with expanded negative samples to reduce false alarms caused by specific factors caused by dense crowds like cluttered scenes. We collect a few images without people and set their regression score as 0, which makes our method more robust.

2. METHOD

We firstly describe the data collection and preparation in Section 2.1. Then we detail the adopted deep model in Section 2.2. Finally we present how we obtain negative samples in Section 2.3.

2.1 Data Collection and Preparation

Due to the requirement of large number of training data announced by CNN, we collect a set of images from publicly available websites, such as Google and Flickr, and mark people using a manually designed dotting tool. This set consists of 51 images each of which has 731 people on average. The counts range from 95 to 3714 as shown in Figure 3. These images cover various events including stadiums, concerts, rallies and Color Run *etc.*

Perspective effects can induce large variation of people, which means some people may merely occupy a few pixels whereas others may take a large regions separately. Consequently when cropping images with larger image size and lower density of people, operation with fixed and uniform size, which consisted with that employed on dense crowds, may result in a lot of samples with partial face or body across the full patches and hence loss representation power of cropped patches. Besides, we prefer to pay more attention on counting on extremely dense crowds in which bodies of most people may not been seen literally. Thus partial samples cropped by uniform size is definitely profitable, they may insufficient and make little effects on learning model for regression. To alleviate influence of partially cropping, we manually pick out images which may need multi-scale crop size and operate crop step with other size. Most of these pairs are cropped with fixed top left points and side length as 672 and 896, respectively. Totally we get a number of 5,705 training samples.

Firstly, we warp the cropped gray-scale patches with 227×227 pixels. Secondly we randomly crop 224×224 patches at four corners and the center over input patches and horizontally flipped for data augmentation. Finally the warped augmented mean-subtracted patches with a total number of 6,414 are fed to CNN and a 1-dimensional feature vector is inferred by forward propagating.

2.2 Convolutional Neural Network for Regression

Considering the excellent performance of CNN performs in most of computer vision tasks, we employ a CNN architecture as our base framework. This architecture consists of five convolutional, some of which are followed by pooling layers, and three fully connected layers. A schematic diagram of this architecture is presented in Fig. 2.

Convolutional layer. It convolves the input images with linear sliding filters to generate response maps. If $\mathbf{X}_i$ is the feature map of input or output of ith layer, this convolutional operation can be denoted as

$$\mathbf{X}_i = \mathbf{W}_i \otimes [\mathbf{X}_{i-1}, 1]^T$$

where $\mathbf{W}_i = [\mathbf{W}_{i1}, \mathbf{W}_{i2}, ..., \mathbf{W}_{ik}, \mathbf{b}_i]$ indicates filters' parameters of the ith layer, $\otimes$ indicates the convolution operation and $\mathbf{b}_i$ indicates the bias.

Pooling layer. Similar to Bag-of-Words (BoW) [10] and spatial pyramid [5] operated behind extracted encoded SIFT vectors, the deep convolutional features obtained by convolving can be pooled in a analogous way. Pooling layer down-samples the convolutional features non-linearly in a pattern of maximum or average over sliding-window subregions. It can significantly reduce the number of network parameters;

Fully-connected layer. It can be computed as

$$\mathbf{y}_{im} = \mathbf{W}_{im}\mathbf{X}_{(i-1)} + \mathbf{b}_m$$

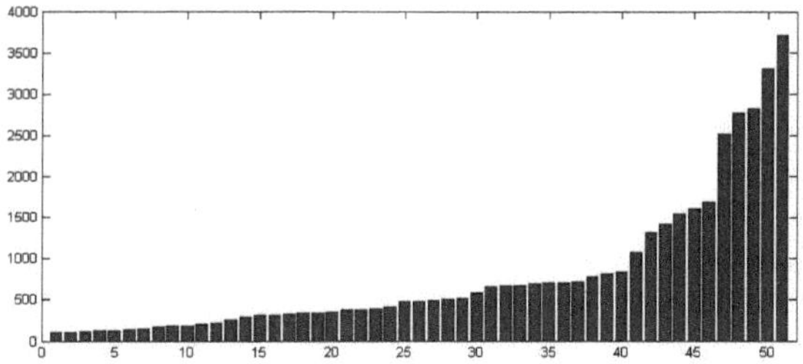

(a) Statistics of collected dataset

(b) Least GroundTruth: 95 (c) Most GroundTruth: 3714

Figure 3: Statistics and samples of the collected dataset. The statistics information is shown in (a). X-axis and y-axis denote the image id and the number of annotated person in the corresponding image, respectively. (b) and (c) demonstrate the images containing the least and the most people.

where $\mathbf{W}_{im}$ denotes the mth filter of the ith layer. This layer requires fixed number of inputs and outputs to convert response maps as close to the ground truth;

Neuron layer. It applies nonlinear activations, such as hyperbolic tangent function or rectified linear unit, between a neuron's output and the input of next layer.

Loss layer. For regression problem, the loss function is defined as the sum of squares of differences between the ground truth and prediction,

$$LOSS = \frac{1}{2N}\sum_{j=1}^{N}\left(p^j - g^j\right)^2,$$

where p^j and g^j are the predicted and ground truth numbers of people in patch j, respectively.

It has been proved that network trained for image classification [8] can also be effective on other visual computing tasks. Thus, we replace the last fully-connected layer consisted of 4096 items with that consisted of 1 item that means the predicted number of people. Then we use the pre-trained parameters of five convolutional layers and two fully-connected layers and fine-tune the model by the following collected crowd images.

2.3 Negative Samples

Our framework is an end-to-end system which automatically obtains the high responses around the crowds instead of resorting to auxiliary human or face detectors. Since we don't employ any human appearance or localization relevant information, some specific regions without person would also get high responses, such as tall lush trees, buildings with plenty of windows, decorative patterns *etc.* These high responses cause a lot of false alarms and seriously affect the performance. The main reason may be the similar appearance between objects and these crowds.

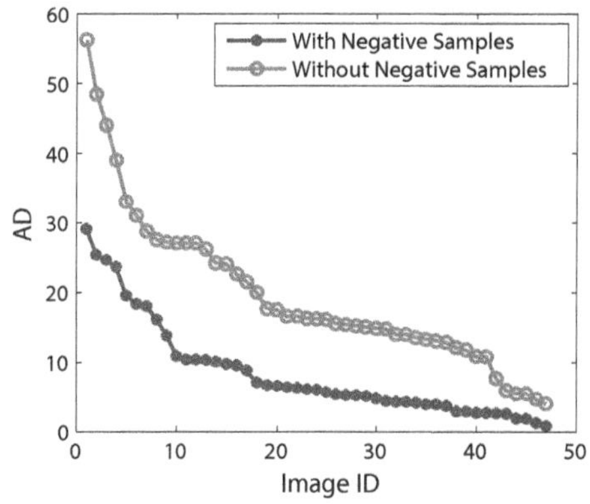

Figure 4: The impact of negative samples on performance. X-axis indicates image IDs rearranged from large AD to small. By feeding the deep model with negative samples, the mean value of AD can carry out a significant decrease.

Therefore we expand our training data by adding a number of samples with zero label containing the above mentioned factors. We add 709 negative samples, which do not contain any person, to the training set, including lush trees, buildings and some natural scene images.

Table 1: Quantitative Comparison on UCFCC.

Methods	AD	NAD
Fourier[6]	13.8±21.3	96.4±200.4
F+confidence[6]	11.0±19.7	58.7±74.9
Fc+Head[6]	11.1±19.3	63.3±84.0
FHc+SIFT[6]	10.2±18.9	53.3±69.5
traditional CNN	13.9±19.9	74.1±151.4
Our method	**8.5±15.0**	**38.9±63.1**

3. EXPERIMENTS

We use standard evaluation criteria, mean and deviation of Absolute Difference (AD) and these of Normalized Absolute Difference (NAD), to quantify the performance. NAD can be obtained by normalizing AD with the ground truth count for each patch or image. For comparison, we evaluate the performance of our method on one public people counting dataset UCFCC [6]. It consists of 50 images with a total number of 61,396 people with and count of each image ranges among 94 and 4,543. The number of average people per image could achieve 1,306 which surpass the existing crowd datasets.

In this paper we develop a deep regression model for counting people in extremely dense crowd images using deep model. To verify the influence of negative samples, we compare the performance with and without negative samples. As shown in Figure 4, by feeding CNN with negative samples, it is obvious that robustness is significantly improved with almost 50% decrease on mean value of AD. Besides, we also show mean and deviation of AD and NAD generated by CNN and our method in Table 1, and it also achieves almost 50% improvement on mean of AD and NAD by applying expanded negative samples.

Extensive experimental results show that, compared with the state-of-the-arts, our method achieves superior perfor-

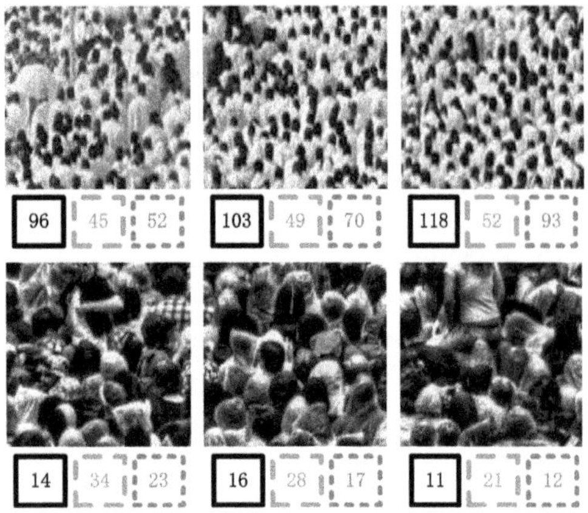

Figure 5: Quantitative comparison on 6 patches of UCFCC dataset. The numbers in black boxes are the ground truth of people in the patches, while the numbers in blue and red dashed boxes are the estimated numbers from Haroon et al. [6] and our framework respectively. It is obvious that the results of our algorithm are closer to the ground truth.

mance both in terms of mean and variance of absolute difference. For comparison, we use methods of Haroon Idrees [6] which obtain the-state-of-the-art on UCFCC dataset. We report our quantitative results both in Table 1 and Figure 5, which shows that our proposed method achieves superior performances. The first four rows in Table 1 show the improvements of gradually integrating a set of different factors including Fourier Analysis, Head detection and SIFT feature. Finally it gives best result with AD as 10.2 and NAD as 53.3. The last two rows show excellent performance of our deep model, with comprehensive large decrease of mean and deviation of AD and NAD, a descend of 16.7% and 27.0% to mean of AD and NAD, respectively. In Figure 5 we present 6 selected patches from UCFCC dataset and show improving results leading by our method. We display ground truth, estimation made by [6] and estimation made by our method in black, blue and red box, separately. Our method can deal with not only scenes available to head detection (the below row) but also the dotted ones lacking of human appearance (the upper one). Besides, we present AD and NAD of patches in Figure 6, respectively. The mean AD and NAD of patches per test image is shown with red diamond, deviation with red var, and ground truth with blue dot. It can be seen that although the ground truth increases, mean ADs change in a small region and NADs are almost stable except for ones in region 4 to 15 since less people exist in images.

4. CONCLUSION

In this paper we develop a deep regression model for counting people in extremely dense crowd images. We adopt CNN as our basic framework to learn efficient features for counting. By feeding the deep model with negative samples, the robustness is significantly improved and false alarms are remarkably suppressed. Extensive experimental results show that, compared with the state-of-the-arts, our method achieve superior performance in term of the mean and variance of absolute difference.

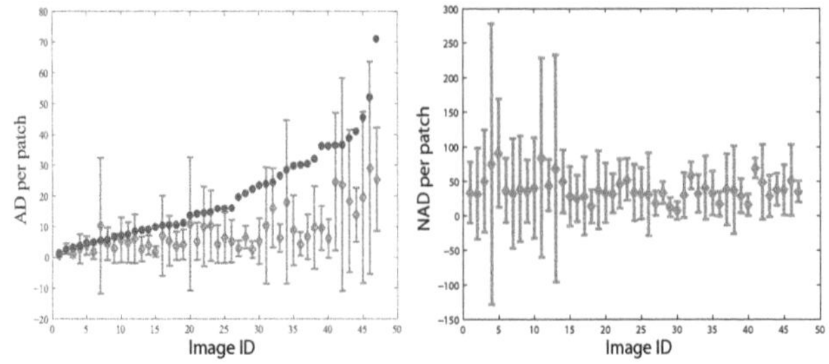

(a) AD an UCFCC (b) NAD on UCFCC

Figure 6: Patch estimation performance on UCFCC dataset. The x-axis shows the image IDs along with ascending ground truth counts. The means and standard deviations are shown in red asterisk and bar, while the ground truth counts in blue dot.

5. ACKNOWLEDGMENTS

This work was supported by National Natural Science Foundation of China (No. 61422213, 61332012,), 100 Talents Programme of The Chinese Academy of Sciences, "Strategic Priority Research Program" of the Chinese Academy of Sciences (XDA06010701), in part by the Foundation for the Young Scholars by the Tianjin University of Commerce under Grant 150113, and in part by the National Training Programs of Innovation and Entrepreneurship for Undergraduates under Grant 201410069040.

6. REFERENCES

[1] O. a. Arandjelovic. Crowd detection from still images. In *BMVC*, pages 53.1–53, 2008.

[2] P. F. Felzenszwalb, R. B. Girshick, D. A. McAllester, and D. Ramanan. Object detection with discriminatively trained part-based models. *TPAMI*, 32(9):1627–1645, 2010.

[3] W. Ge and R. Collins. Marked point processes for crowd counting. In *CVPR 2009*, pages 2913–2920, 2009.

[4] R. B. Girshick, J. Donahue, T. Darrell, and J. Malik. Rich feature hierarchies for accurate object detection and semantic segmentation. In *CVPR 2014*, pages 580–587, 2014.

[5] K. Grauman and T. Darrell. The pyramid match kernel: Discriminative classification with sets of image features. In *ICCV 2005*, pages 1458–1465, 2005.

[6] H. Idrees, I. Saleemi, C. Seibert, and M. Shah. Multi-source multi-scale counting in extremely dense crowd images. In *CVPR 2013*, pages 2547–2554, 2013.

[7] K. Kang and X. Wang. Fully convolutional neural networks for crowd segmentation. *CoRR*, abs/1411.4464, 2014.

[8] A. Krizhevsky, I. Sutskever, and G. E. Hinton. Imagenet classification with deep convolutional neural networks. In *NIPS 2012*, pages 1097–1105, 2012.

[9] S. Liu, X. Liang, L. Liu, X. Shen, J. Yang, C. Xu, L. Lin, X. Cao, and S. Yan. Matching-cnn meets KNN: quasi-parametric human parsing. *CoRR*, abs/1504.01220, 2015.

[10] J. Sivic and A. Zisserman. Video Google: A text retrieval approach to object matching in videos. In *ICCV*, pages 1470–1477, 2003.

Gyro-based Camera-Motion Detection in User-Generated Videos

Sophia Bano*†, Andrea Cavallaro*, Xavier Parra†
*Centre for Intelligent Sensing, Queen Mary University of London, United Kingdom.
†Technical Research Centre for Dependency Care & Autonomous Living,
Universitat Politècnica de Catalunya, Spain.
{s.bano, a.cavallaro}@qmul.ac.uk; xavier.parra@upc.edu

ABSTRACT

We propose a gyro-based camera-motion detection method for videos captured with smartphones. First, the delay between the acquisition of video and gyroscope data is estimated using similarities induced by camera motion in the two sensor modalities. Pan, tilt and shake are then detected using the dominant motions and high frequencies in the gyroscope data. Morphological operations are applied to remove outliers and to identify segments with continuous camera motion. We compare the proposed method with existing methods that use visual or inertial sensor data.

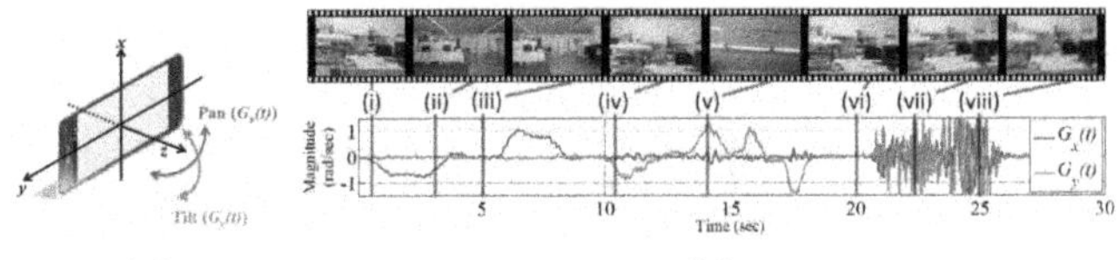

(a) (b)

Figure 1: (a) Definition of a device reference coordinates, pan $G_x(t)$ and tilt $G_y(t)$ signals. (b) A sample multi-modal video containing pan, tilt and shake: (i) and (ii): pan; (iv) and (v): tilt; (vii) and (viii): shake.

Categories and Subject Descriptors

I.2.10 [**Artificial Intelligence**]: Vision and Scene Understanding—*Video analysis, Motion*

Keywords

Gyroscope sensor, Visual sensor, User-generated videos, Camera motion, Detection, Synchronization

1. INTRODUCTION

Camera-Motion Detection (CMD) helps video summarization, composition, shot detection, segmentation and content analysis [1, 3, 4, 12]. When available, inertial sensors complement visual data and can support video-quality analysis with modest memory and battery consumption. We are interested in detecting camera motion that a user introduces while recording a video with a hand-held camera.

Most CMD methods analyze visual content, for example using template matching [1, 8], optical flow [2, 9, 10] or Luminance Projection Correlation (LPC) [4, 11]. Template matching can be applied to estimate the horizontal, vertical and zoom motion combined with a support vector machine [1, 8]. Optical flow-based methods classify frames into stationary or moving frames based on the magnitude of motion vectors. Moving frames are then classified into pan, tilt or zoom frames based on the dominant orientation or template matching [2, 9, 10]. LPC [11] correlates the horizontal and vertical projections of consecutive frames to compute pan and tilt [3, 4, 12, 13]. Existing methods are generally computationally expensive and can be corrupted by moving objects and brightness changes. Inertial sensors can help overcome these problems.

Cricri *et al.* [5] use inertial sensor data for event understanding in User-Generated Videos (UGVs). Low-Pass Filtered (LPF) compass data (sampled at $10Hz$) are used to detect pan by calculating the angular speed of the camera; the tilt angle is computed from unfiltered accelerometer data (sampled at $40Hz$); and High-Pass Filtered (HPF) accelerometer data are analyzed to detect shake. However, compass is sensitive to drift and errors induced by nearby magnetic objects, and unfiltered accelerometer data can be affected by noise that reduces the detection accuracy.

Unlike accelerometer and compass, a gyroscope is neither affected by gravity nor magnetic field. A gyroscope measures the angular velocities around the device's x, y and z axes (Fig. 1(a)). These velocities correspond to camera pan, tilt and roll, respectively. A high correlation on the motion of a device exists between visual and gyroscope data captured from the same device.

In this paper, we propose a gyro-based method for CMD. To the best of our knowledge, this is the first method that uses the output of a gyroscope to detect pan, tilt and shake in UGVs. We exploit the tri-axial gyroscope data captured along with the video to identify visual frames with motion. Because visual data logged with an inertial sensor have un-

S. Bano was supported by the EACEA Agency of the European Commission under EMJD ICE FPA n° 2010-0012. A. Cavallaro acknowledges the support of the UK Engineering and Physical Sciences Research Council (EPSRC), under grant EP/K007491/1.

MM'15, October 26–30, 2015, Brisbane, Australia.
© 2015 ACM. ISBN 978-1-4503-3459-4/15/10 ...$15.00.
DOI: http://dx.doi.org/10.1145/2733373.2806336.

known delay due to the time taken for the camera initialization, we synchronize video and gyroscope data using similarities induced by the camera motion itself. Dominant motions of the LPF gyroscope data in polar coordinates are utilized for pan and tilt detection, whereas dominant high-frequency motions are considered for shake detection. We further apply morphology to remove outliers and to identify segments with the same camera-motion type.

2. PROPOSED METHOD

Let $C(t) = \{V(t), D(t)\}$ be the multi-modal data of a UGV captured with a hand-held device. $V(t)$ is the visual data sampled at V_r frames per second (*fps*) and $D(t)$ represents the inertial data stream sampled at f_r *Hz*. $D(t)$ contains tri-axial gyroscope data $G(t) = (G_x(t), G_y(t), G_z(t))$ logged *simultaneously* with $V(t)$.

We aim to estimate the delay $\hat{t}$ for gyro-visual synchronization, and then to detect pan $P_d(t)$, tilt $T_d(t)$ and shake $S_d(t)$ using gyroscope data only. We assume that the gyroscope is auto-calibrated such that $G_x(t)$, $G_y(t)$ and $G_z(t)$ are zero at steady state and the gyroscope data are free from offset error.

2.1 Gyro-visual synchronization

The magnitude of $G(t)$ for a smartphone video captured without a tripod is affected by involuntary human body movements. Even in the absence of intentional camera motion, this low-magnitude motion due to involuntary body movement is sufficient for gyro-visual data synchronization. The frequency of involuntary human body movements when holding a device lies within $f_i = 20Hz$ [7]. Inertial sensors are logged and analyzed at $f_r = 50Hz > 2f_i$, thus satisfying the Nyquist theorem [6].

We correlate gyroscope and visual data to determine the recording delay between the two modalities. Firstly, LPC [11] (detailed in [13]) is used to compute the horizontal $L_x(t)$ and vertical $L_y(t)$ displacements from $V(t)$. $L_x(t)$ and $L_y(t)$ are the video-based pan and tilt, and correspond to the gyroscope $G_x(t)$ and $G_y(t)$ signals, respectively.

Let $I(t,i,j)$ be the grayscale value of pixel (i,j) at time t, and $I_y(t,i)$ and $I_x(t,j)$ its horizontal and vertical projections, respectively. These projections are computed as

$$I_y(t,i) = \frac{1}{h}\sum_{j=1}^{h} I(t,i,j)\ , \quad I_x(t,j) = \frac{1}{w}\sum_{i=1}^{w} I(t,i,j), \quad (1)$$

where h is the height and w is the width of the frame.

$L_x(t)$ and $L_y(t)$ (Fig. 2(a)(b)) are then computed as

$$L_x(t) = arg\ \min_{\delta p} \sum_{i=1+\delta p_1}^{w-\delta p_2} D_{I_y}(t,i,\delta p), \quad (2)$$

$$L_y(t) = arg\ \min_{\delta p} \sum_{j=1+\delta p_1}^{h-\delta p_2} D_{I_x}(t,j,\delta p), \quad (3)$$

where $\delta p \in [-20, 20]$. When $\delta p < 0$ then $\delta p_1 = 0$, $\delta p_2 = \delta p$, whereas when $\delta p \geq 0$ then $\delta p_1 = \delta p$, $\delta p_2 = 0$. $D_{I_x}(t,j,\delta p)$ and $D_{I_y}(t,i,\delta p)$ are computed as follows:

$$D_{I_x}(t,j,\delta p) = (I_x(t,j) - I_x(t+1, j-\delta p))^2,$$
$$D_{I_y}(t,i,\delta p) = (I_y(t,i) - I_y(t+1, i-\delta p))^2,$$

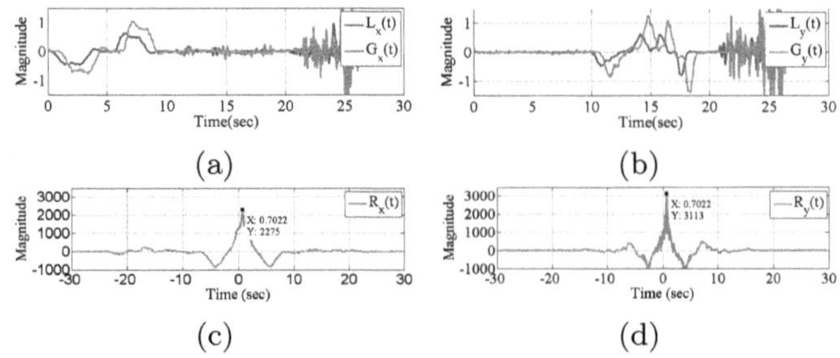

Figure 2: Gyro-visual synchronization. (a) LPC pan $L_x(t)$ and gyroscope $G_x(t)$, (b) LPC tilt $L_y(t)$ and gyroscope $G_y(t)$. Correlation (c) $R_x(t)$ and (d) $R_y(t)$.

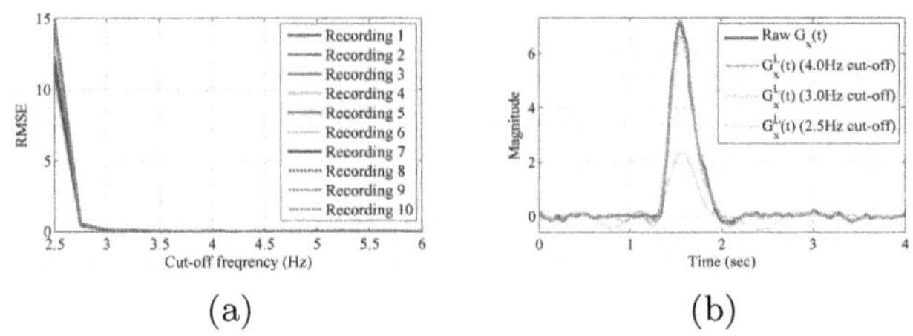

Figure 3: Analysis of f_c for the LPF. (a) The RMSE between the $G_x(t)$ and $G_x^L(t)$ for 10 recordings containing fast pan for varying values of f_c. (b) The raw $G_x(t)$ (for the fast pan) for one of the recording and its LPF signals with varying f_c.

where $D_{I_x}(.)$ and $D_{I_y}(.)$ are the projection distances between two consecutive frames in the horizontal and vertical direction, respectively.

We downsample $G(t)$ to have the same sampling rate as $V(t)$ and compute the pan cross-correlation

$$R_x(t) = \sum_{k=-\infty}^{\infty} G_x(k) L_x(k+t). \quad (4)$$

The correlation peak is $\hat{e}_x = \max_t R_x(t)$ and the estimated delay is $\hat{t}_x = \text{argmax}_t R_x(t)$. Likewise, $R_y(t)$, $\hat{t}_y$ and $\hat{e}_y$ are computed from the tilt signals. The overall estimated delay $\hat{t}$ is selected as

$$\hat{t} = \begin{cases} \hat{t}_x & if\ \hat{e}_x \geq \hat{e}_y, \\ \hat{t}_y & if\ \hat{e}_y > \hat{e}_x. \end{cases} \quad (5)$$

Figure 2(c)(d) shows an example of cross correlations $R_x(t)$ and $R_y(t)$, and their corresponding peaks.

2.2 Gyro-based camera-motion detection

Panning produces higher magnitudes of $G_x(t)$ whereas tilting produces higher magnitudes of $G_y(t)$. We low-pass filter the signals to obtain $G_x^L(t)$ and $G_x^L(t)$ using a cut-off frequency $f_c = 4Hz$ (Fig. 3).

We then jointly analyze $G_x^L(t)$ and $G_y^L(t)$ in polar coordinates with radial value $G_r^L(t) = \sqrt{G_x^L(t)^2 + G_y^L(t)^2}$ and angular value $G_\theta^L(t) = \arctan\left(\frac{G_y^L(t)}{G_x^L(t)}\right)$ (Fig. 4).

Pan, $P(t)$, is detected as

$$P(t) = \begin{cases} +1 & if\ 0 - \alpha \leq G_\theta^L(t) \leq 0 + \alpha, \\ -1 & if\ 180 - \alpha \leq G_\theta^L(t) \leq 180 + \alpha, \\ 0 & otherwise, \end{cases} \quad (6)$$

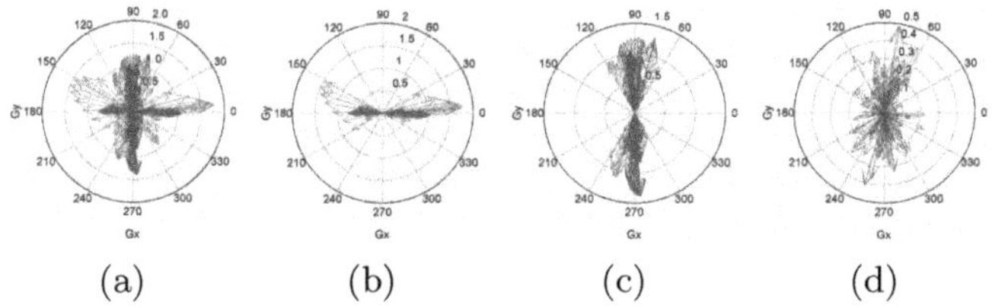

Figure 4: Analysis of $G_x(t)$ and $G_y(t)$ in polar coordinate. (a) $G_r^L(t)$ and $G_\theta^L(t)$, detected (b) pan and (c) tilt vectors, (d) $G_r^H(t)$ and $G_\theta^H(t)$ for shake detection are shown.

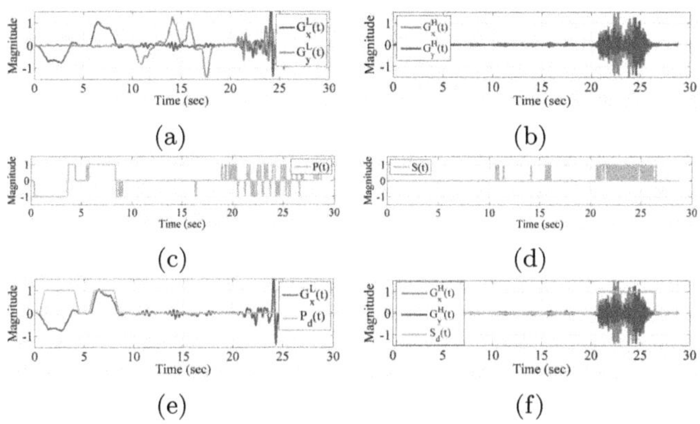

Figure 5: Camera-motion detection. For pan, (a) $G_x^L(t)$ and $G_y^L(t)$, (c) $P(t)$, (e) $P_d(t)$, and for shake, (b) $G_x^H(t)$ and $G_y^H(t)$, (d) $S(t)$, (f) $S_d(t)$ are shown.

where α (*degrees*) is a tolerance angle, and $+1$ and -1 denote pan left and right, respectively (Fig. 5c). Similarly, tilt $T(t)$ is detected as

$$T(t) = \begin{cases} +1 & \textit{if } 90 - \alpha \leq G_\theta^L(t) \leq 90 + \alpha, \\ -1 & \textit{if } 270 - \alpha \leq G_\theta^L(t) \leq 270 + \alpha, \\ 0 & \textit{otherwise}, \end{cases} \quad (7)$$

where $+1$ and -1 denote tilt down and up, respectively. The value of α should facilitate the detection of horizontal and vertical motions. Because freehand pan is not strictly along the x-axis in real-world scenarios, a higher magnitude of $G_x(t)$ is also associated to a non-zero value of $G_y(t)$ while panning with a smartphone. We therefore empirically set $\alpha = 30^o$ (Fig. 6(a)).

For shake detection, we obtain $G_r^H(t)$ and $G_\theta^H(t)$ after high-pass filtering $G_x^H(t)$ and $G_y^H(t)$ (Fig. 4(d)). $G_r^H(t)$ is used to classify shake camera motion as

$$S(t) = \begin{cases} 1 & \textit{if } G_r^H(t) > \beta, \\ 0 & \textit{otherwise}. \end{cases} \quad (8)$$

$G_r^H(t)$ ranges from 0 to 0.5. We selected $\beta = 0.06$ empirically (Fig. 6(b)) to remove the influence of involuntary body movement in freehand recordings.

$|P(t)|$, $|T(t)|$ and $S(t)$ give binary signals for samples with detected pan, tilt and shake motions (Fig. 5(c-d)). As we have not yet considered time continuity, false camera motion can be detected in few samples. To remove these outliers and to identify time-continuous camera-motion segments, we apply morphological operations to the binary signals [6]. In particular, we apply *opening* to $|P(t)|$ and $|T(t)|$ to remove false detection by erosion, followed by dilation to detect continuous segments, and to obtain the final motion-detection results $P_d(t)$ and $T_d(t)$ (Fig. 5(e)). To detect continuous segments of shake, we apply *closing* that performs dilation to connect discontinuous segments followed by erosion to maintain the original length of the shake detected segments. Segments that are shorter than 0.25 seconds are considered as outliers, and are removed to obtain the final shake detection signal $S_d(t)$ (Fig. 5(f)).

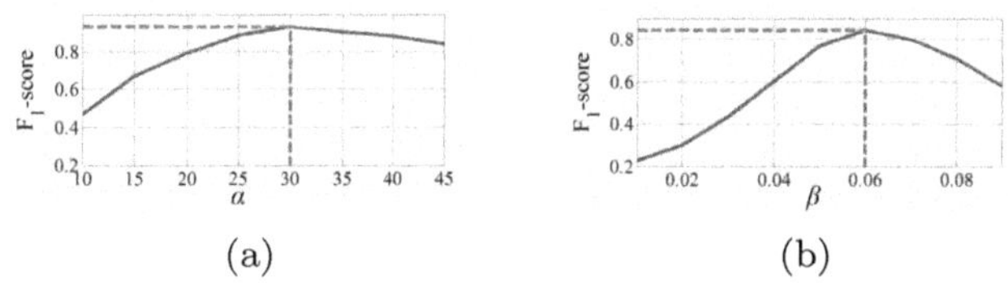

Figure 6: F_1-score of the proposed CMDG method with respect to the varying values of (a) α and (b) β for the captured multi-modal dataset.

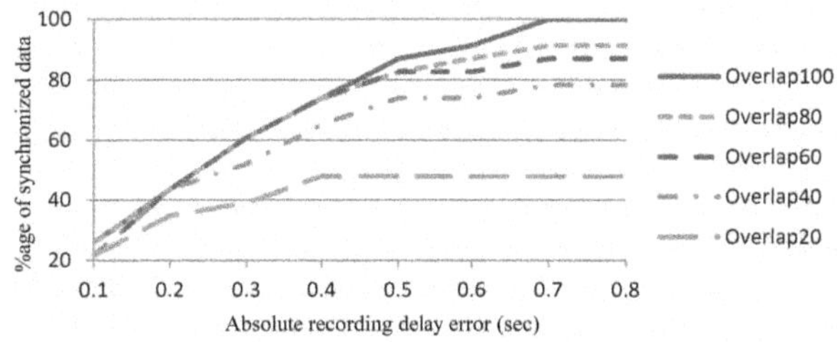

Figure 7: Gyroscope-visual synchronization result for 24 multi-modal UGVs. %age of synchronized data *w.r.t* the absolute delay error for varying Overlap$N$.

3. EXPERIMENTAL EVALUATION

To evaluate the proposed method, CMDG, we recorded multi-modal data in several scenarios such as concerts, parades, festivals and firework display, using Cellbots Data Logger[1] and compared with an existing visual [13, 4] (referred as VISUAL) and inertial sensor-based [5] (referred as ISENSOR) method.

We captured 24 UGVs for a total duration of 70 *mins* in High Brightness (HB) and Low Brightness (LB) scenarios (e.g. day and night-time). This collected dataset is available for downloading[2] and it contains single camera recordings at distinct timings and locations, changing lights and varying camera motions. The Ground-Truth (GT) delay is obtained by observing a pan/tilt/shake motion simultaneously in the gyro-visual data. Each captured video was manually annotated to get labels for camera motions for each second.

Figure 7 shows the results for gyro-visual synchronization for the captured multi-modal dataset. Acceptable delays are obtained for all UGVs with an absolute error of 0.7*sec* between GT and estimate. This error is mainly due to the imprecise GT labels as it was difficult to manually observe a coherent motion both in the video and gyroscope data. By

[1] `https://cellbots.googlecode.com/files/CellbotsDataLogger_v1.1.0_full.apk` (Last accessed: 30/07/2015). Note that the video frame rate and frame size varied depending on the brightness of the recorded scene due to the programmed settings of the App.

[2] `http://www.eecs.qmul.ac.uk/~andrea/cmdg`

Table 1: Results for CMDG and its comparison with a VISUAL [13, 4] and ISENSOR [5] method. Key: HB: high brightness recordings; LB: low brightness recordings; TP: true positive; FP: false positive; P: precision; R: recall; F_1: F_1-score.

		Pan						Tilt						Shake					
Method	Type	GT	TP	FP	P	R	F_1	GT	TP	FP	P	R	F_1	GT	TP	FP	P	R	F_1
CMDG	HB	294	272	11	0.96	0.93	**0.94**	36	29	6	0.83	0.81	**0.82**	389	365	129	0.74	0.94	**0.83**
VISUAL [13, 4]			217	64	0.77	0.74	0.75		19	42	0.31	0.53	0.39		260	118	0.69	0.67	0.68
ISENSOR [5]			175	52	0.77	0.60	0.67		14	46	0.23	0.39	0.29		188	93	0.67	0.48	0.56
CMDG	LB	123	117	12	0.91	0.95	**0.93**	49	41	7	0.85	0.84	**0.85**	272	235	37	0.86	0.86	**0.86**
VISUAL [13, 4]			31	44	0.41	0.25	0.31		10	48	0.17	0.20	0.19		200	606	0.25	0.74	0.37
ISENSOR [5]			44	40	0.52	0.36	0.43		23	24	0.49	0.47	0.48		213	129	0.62	0.78	0.69

jointly visualizing the synchronized data, we cross-validated the correctness of the obtained results. Acceptable delay is achieved even in the presence of slight camera motion. Although the illumination is extremely low in some LB recordings (e.g. fireworks) that resulted in low magnitude of $L_x(t)$ and $L_y(t)$ and inaccurate CMD, correlation existed between the gyro-visual data. A slight clue of brightness (e.g. an exploding firework) is sufficient to establish the correlation.

To investigate the robustness of gyro-visual synchronization, we changed the overlap duration between the gyroscope and visual data for the whole dataset. Overlap$N$ denotes that complete visual data and only N% of the duration of the gyroscope data are used. For Overlap80, Overlap60, Overlap40 and Overlap20, the percentage of synchronized recordings are 91%, 87%, 78% and 48%, respectively (Fig. 7). Note that the visual quality and frame rate are low in some of the night-time recordings: this affects $L_x(t)$ and $L_y(t)$, and decreases the performance when the overlap decreases.

For the evaluation of the proposed CMDG, we analyze its performance with respect to the GT and compared with alternative approaches (Table 1). To have a fair comparison, the parameters within the VISUAL and ISENSOR are adjusted to give the best possible results. To select α and β for pan, tilt and shake detection, we analyzed the effect of varying these parameters on the detection results (Fig. 6), for the captured multi-modal dataset. At $\alpha = 30^o$, the best F_1-score of 0.94 for pan and tilt, and at $\beta = 0.06$, the best F_1-score of 0.85 for shake were achieved and selected for the experimentation. In order to investigate their performance, we divided the UGVs into HB and LB recordings having total durations of 30 *mins* and 40 *mins*, respectively. In our dataset, most events of interest existed in the latitudinal plane (e.g. singer, crowd, parade), with the exception of few that existed in the longitudinal plane (e.g. fireworks, flying balloons), resulting in fewer tilt samples (Table 1). CMDG outperformed the existing methods giving the F_1-score of 94%, 82% and 83% for $P_d(t)$, $T_d(t)$ and $S_d(t)$, respectively, for the HB recordings, and 93%, 85% and 86% for the LB recordings. VISUAL and ISENSOR are the second best for the HB and LB recordings, respectively.

VISUAL is affected by the motion of objects and light conditions, thus reducing its performance in LB recordings compared to CMDG and ISENSOR, which are independent of these factors. ISENSOR uses compass and accelerometer, and is affected by magnetic noise, low sampling rate and unfiltered processing, resulting in false detections. CMDG is a more desirable solution for CMD because of the use of a more accurate sensor (gyroscope), and inclusion of the post-processing stage that suppresses outliers. Pan signals from CMDG and VISUAL are comparable in HB recordings. However, ISENSOR is less accurate due to the lower sampling rate ($10Hz$) of the compass [5]. Increasing the sampling rate to $50Hz$ increases the effect of noise that affects the derivative of the compass signal.

4. CONCLUSION

We proposed a method for camera-motion detection using gyroscope data for user-generated videos. The method aligns multi-modal data and uses the tri-axial gyroscope data captured simultaneously with the video to detect pan, tilt and shake. Our proposed method outperformed existing approaches with a collective F_1-score of 89% for pan, tilt and shake.

As future work, we are interested in developing a real-time application of the proposed method and in analyzing translational motion generated when users change their position while recording.

5. REFERENCES

[1] G. Abdollahian, C. Taskiran, Z. Pizlo, and E. Delp. Camera motion-based analysis of user generated video. *IEEE Transactions on Multimedia*, 12:28–41, 2010.

[2] J. Almeida, R. Minetto, T. A. Almeida, R. S. Torres, and N. J. Leite. Robust estimation of camera motion using optical flow models. In *Springer Advances in Visual Computing*, pages 435–446. 2009.

[3] S. Bano and A. Cavallaro. Vicomp: composition of user-generated videos. *Multimedia tools and applications*, in press, 2015.

[4] M. Campanella, H. Weda, and M. Barbieri. Edit while watching: home video editing made easy. In *SPIE Multimedia Content Access*, 2007.

[5] F. Cricri, K. Dabov, I. Curcio, S. Mate, and M. Gabbouj. Multimodal extraction of events and of information about the recording activity in user generated videos. *Multimedia tools and applications*, 70:119–158, 2012.

[6] R. Gonzalez and R. Woods. *Digital Image Processing, Chap. 4 and 9.* Pearson Education, 2008.

[7] D. M. Karantonis, M. R. Narayanan, M. Mathie, N. H. Lovell, and B. G. Celler. Implementation of a real-time human movement classifier using a triaxial accelerometer for ambulatory monitoring. *IEEE Trans. Inf. Technology in Biomedicine*, 10:156–167, 2006.

[8] D. Lan, Y. Ma, and H. Zhang. A systemic framework of camera motion analysis for home video. In *IEEE International Conference on Image Processing*, 2003.

[9] A. Mahabalagiri, K. Ozcan, and S. Velipasalar. Camera motion detection for mobile smart cameras using segmented edge-based optical flow. In *IEEE International Conference on Advanced Video and Signal Based Surveillance*, 2014.

[10] V. Makkapati. Robust camera pan and zoom change detection using optical flow. In *National Conference on Computer Vision, Pattern Recognition, Image Processing and Graphics*, 2008.

[11] A. Nagasaka and T. Miyatake. Real-time video mosaics using luminance-projection correlation. *IEICE Transactions on Information and Systems*, 1999.

[12] M. Saini, R. Gadde, S. Yan, and W. T. Ooi. Movimash: online mobile video mashup. In *ACM Multimedia*, 2012.

[13] K. Uehara, M. Amano, Y. Ariki, and M. Kumano. Video shooting navigation system by real-time useful shot discrimination based on video grammar. In *IEEE International Conference on Multimedia and Expo*, 2004.

Human Activity Recognition using Wearable Sensors by Deep Convolutional Neural Networks

Wenchao Jiang
Department of Computer Science
Missouri University of Science and Technology
wjm84@mst.edu

Zhaozheng Yin
Department of Computer Science
Missouri University of Science and Technology
yinz@mst.edu

ABSTRACT

Human physical activity recognition based on wearable sensors has applications relevant to our daily life such as healthcare. How to achieve high recognition accuracy with low computational cost is an important issue in the ubiquitous computing. Rather than exploring handcrafted features from time-series sensor signals, we assemble signal sequences of accelerometers and gyroscopes into a novel activity image, which enables Deep Convolutional Neural Networks (DCNN) to automatically learn the optimal features from the activity image for the activity recognition task. Our proposed approach is evaluated on three public datasets and it outperforms state-of-the-arts in terms of recognition accuracy and computational cost.

Categories and Subject Descriptors

I.2 [**Computing Methodologies**]: Artificial Intelligence; F.1.1 [**Theory of Computation**]: Models of Computation—*Self-modifying machines*

Keywords

Wearable Computing, Activity Recognition, Deep Convolutional Neural Networks, Activity Image.

1. INTRODUCTION

Human physical activity is defined by bodily states such as walking and standing, the recognition of which can be applied to many application fields such as human-computer interaction and surveillance [1][2]. Especially, activity recognition based on wearable sensors is directly related to our daily lives such as healthcare and workout monitoring [3][4]. This paper focuses on activity recognition using ubiquitous wearable devices (e.g., smart phones, smart watches and sport bracelets) which embed accelerometers and gyroscopes.

1.1 Related Work

Generally, sensor-based activity recognition methods are evaluated in two aspects: recognition accuracy and computational cost. To improve the accuracy, the pervious work tried to extract effective handcrafted features from tri-axis signals of accelerometers and gyroscopes [1] or explored different classifiers including Support Vector Machine [5], Random Forest [6] and Hidden Markov Model [7]. To decrease the computational cost, researchers performed feature selection [4], sensor selection [8], contextual prediction [9] and sample frequency reduction [10].

However, in most cases, the improvement of accuracy is at the expense of increasing the computational cost [11]. This paper aims to develop an accurate and efficient approach for activity recognition using wearable devices.

MM'15, October 26–30, 2015, Brisbane, Australia.
 ISBN 978-1-4503-3459-4/15/10 ...$15.00.
DOI: http://dx.doi.org/10.1145/2733373.2806333.

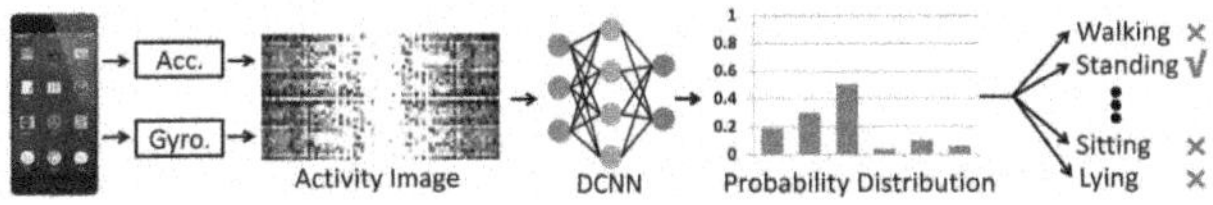

Figure 1: Overview of recognizing query signals.

1.2 Our Proposal

In the previous work, features used for activity recognition are usually extracted independently from multiple time-series sensor signals in a handcrafted way [1]. The correlation among different signals are usually overlooked. We propose to transfer all time-series signals from the accelerometer and gyroscope into a new *activity image* which contains hidden relations between any pair of signals.

As one of the most effective deep learning models, Deep Convolutional Neural Networks (DCNN) achieved the superior performance in speech recognition [12] and image classification [13]. Our novel 2D activity image enables DCNN to automatically learn the best discriminative features suited for activity recognition, rather than defining the features manually. In the DCNN framework, low- and high-level features are extracted from the newly-defined activity image, providing extra contextual information between signals compared with the statistics on the individual time-series signal.

1.3 Algorithm Overview

Fig.1 shows the flowchart to recognize query signals. With the activity image generated from sensor signals as input, DCNN outputs a probability distribution over activity categories, based on which the human activity is determined.

The paper is organized as follows. Section 2 and 3 introduce the activity image and DCNN architecture, respectively. Section 4 presents the complete activity recognition procedure. Experimental results on three public datasets are described in Section 5.

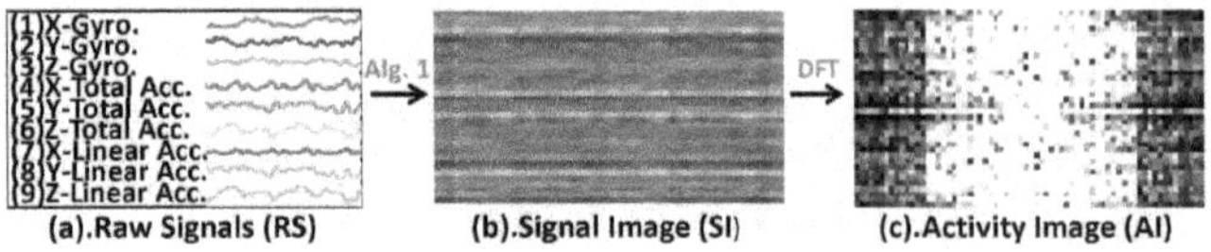

Figure 2: Flowchart to generate an activity image.

2. ACTIVITY IMAGE

The Inertial Measurement Unit in wearable devices includes an accelerometer and a gyroscope, measuring the strength of tri-axis acceleration and angular velocity, respectively. The combination of accelerometer and gyroscope achieves better results than accelerometer only [1]. Furthermore, the total acceleration can be separated into two components: linear acceleration (body motion) and gravity.

We propose a novel *activity image* based on signals of gyroscope, total acceleration and linear acceleration. Firstly, raw signals (Fig.2 (a)) are stacked row-by-row into a signal image (Fig.2 (b)) based on Algorithm 1. In the signal image, every signal sequence has the chance to be adjacent to every other sequence, which enables DCNN to extract hidden correlations between neighboring signals.

Then, 2D Discrete Fourier Transform (DFT) is applied to the signal image and its magnitude is chosen as our activity image (Fig.2 (c)). Fig.3 shows a few activity images corresponding to different activities. The visual difference in these activity images indicates their potential for DCNN to extract discriminative image features for activity recognition.

Figure 3: Samples of activity images.

Before introducing the DCNN architecture, we point out some engineering details. Given 9 signal sequences, the size of our signal image is $37 \times L_s$ based on Algorithm 1, where L_s is the time length of signal sequences. Since different devices may have different sampling rates, we interpolate all raw signals in the same time length (e.g., 1 second) with 68 signal samples. $L_s = 68$ will facilitate the design of our DCNN architecture. In addition, we delete the last row of the signal image generated by Algorithm 1, so each signal occurs four times in the revised signal image. The size of our signal image and consequent activity image is finalized as 36×68.

3. DCNN ARCHITECTURE

The architecture of our proposed DCNN is summarized in Fig.4. The first convolutional layer filters the 36×68 input activity image with 5 kernels of size 5×5, followed by 4×4 subsampling. The second convolutional layer takes the output of the first subsampling layer as input and filters it with 10 kernels of size 5×5, followed by 2×2 subsampling. The full connected layer vectorizes the output of the second subsampling layer into a 120-dimensional feature vector.

Each convolutional layer performs 2D convolution on its input maps. The output maps are generated as:

$$y_j = (1 + exp(b_j + \sum_i k_{ij} * x_i))^{-1} \tag{1}$$

Algorithm 1 Raw Signals → Signal Image

Notations:
- Signal Image (SI): a 2D array to store permutated raw signals.
- Signal Index String (SIS): a string to store signal indices, whose length is N_{SIS}.

Intput: N_s signal sequences. *// As shown in Fig.2(a), each signal is label with a sequence number. The number of signal sequences* $N_s = 9$.

Loops:

$i = 1; j = i + 1;$
SI is initialized to be the i-th signal sequence;
SIS is initialized to be $'i'$; N_{SIS}=1;
while $i \neq j$ **do**
  if $j > N_s$ **then**
    $j = 1;$
  else if $'ij' \not\subset SIS$ && $'ji' \not\subset SIS$ **then**
    Append the j-th signal sequence to the bottom of SI;
    Append $'j'$ to SIS; $N_{SIS} = N_{SIS} + 1;$
    $i = j; j = i + 1;$
  else
    $j = j + 1;$
  end if
end while

Output: SI.

// The final SIS is '1234567891357924681471582593694837261' with $N_{SIS} = 37$, *when* $N_s = 9$.

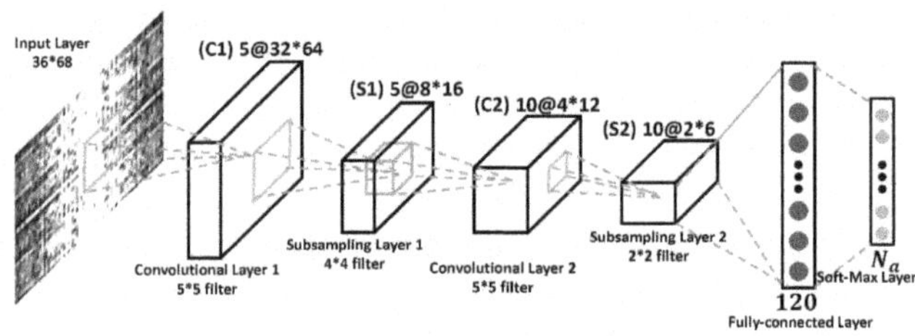

Figure 4: The proposed DCNN architecture.

where $*$ denotes the convolutional operator. k_{ij} is the convolutional kernel on the i-th input map x_i to generate the j-th output map y_j. b_j a bias term.

Mean-pooling is adopted as the subsampling method. The output map y_i is achieved by computing mean values over non-overlapping regions of the input map x_i with a square filter $m \times m$:

$$y_i(r, c) = \frac{\sum_{p=1}^{m} \sum_{q=1}^{m} x_i(r \cdot m + p, c \cdot m + q)}{m^2} \tag{2}$$

where $y_i(r, c)$ denotes the pixel value of y_i at location (r, c).

After fully connecting the output of the second subsampling layer into a 1D feature vector f_i, N_a-way softmax function is applied to obtain a probability distribution over N_a classes, where N_a denotes the number of activities to be recognized:

$$p(s) = \frac{g_s}{\sum_{j=1}^{N_a} g_j}, \text{ where } g_j = max(0, \sum_i f_i \cdot w_{ij} + h_j) \tag{3}$$

where $p(s)$ is the probability of an activity belonging to the s-th class. w_{ij} and h_j are coefficients in the softwmax function.

Fig.5 shows some output maps extracted by DCNN. From the training data, deep learning is able to automatically learn from low-level to high-level features as the layer goes deeper. The parameters such as k_{ij}, b_j, w_{ij} and h_j are updated by stochastic gradient descent where the gradient is obtained by back-propagation.

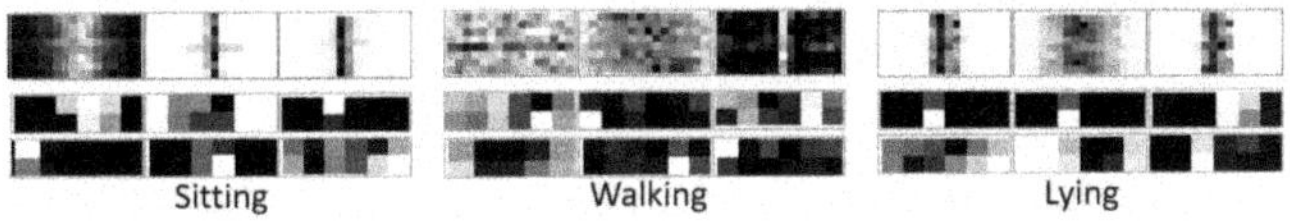

Figure 5: Examples of output maps in each layer. Maps in red boxes are the output of the first subsampling layer and maps in green boxes are the output of the second subsampling layer.

4. ACTIVITY RECOGNITION

With the activity image built from raw sensor signals as input, DCNN outputs a probability distribution over N_a activities. Fig.6 shows two distribution examples over N_a activities. In Fig.6(a), the probability of "Walking Downstairs (W.D.)" is overwhelmingly higher than the others, thus it is confident to determine the user's activity is walking downstairs. However, in Fig.6(b), although the probability of "Walking Downstairs" is still the highest, it's close to "Walking" and "Standing", thus the activity recognition is not confident.

We train pair-wise SVM classifiers to mitigate the uncertainty. For $N_a = 6$, 15 bi-class SVM classifiers are trained based on the statistic features from [1]. Then we compare each two activities in the descending order of their probability values. As shown in Fig.6(a), the result is determined by the activity with the highest probability, when the ratio between the highest probability and the second highest is higher than a threshold T

$$T = \frac{\sum_{i=1}^{N_{train}} \frac{1}{var(p_i(s), s \in [1, N_a])}}{N_{train}}, \quad (4)$$

which is the mean of the variance's reciprocal. N_{train} is the number of training cases. $p_i(s)$ denotes the probability of the i-th training case's activity belonging to the s-th class.

However, in Fig.6(b), the ratios are less than T in the first two iterations, so bi-class SVM is applied to find the optimal activities. In the third iteration, the ratio is larger than T, so we consider the activity with the higher probability as the final result. SVM is incorporated here because the handcrafted features complement the automatically learned features by DCNN and SVM has shown its effectiveness on bi-class classification [14].

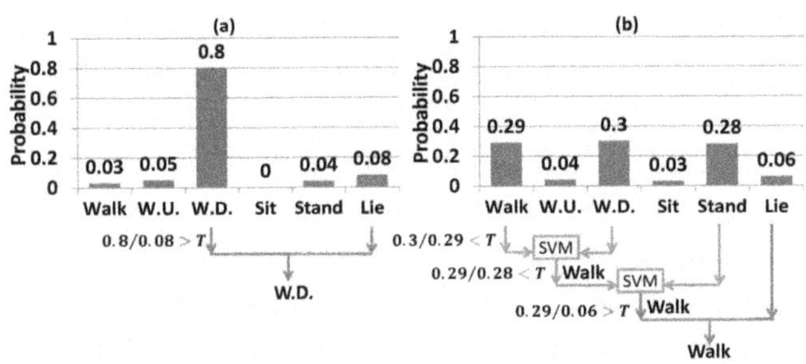

Figure 6: Two probability distribution examples by DCNN.

In summary, our activity recognition procedure consists of three steps: (1) generate an activity image from raw signals; (2) apply DCNN to the activity image and produce the probability distribution over all activities; and (3) if there is a sharp peak in the distribution, the activity categorization is confidently determined. Otherwise, bi-class SVM classifier will be applied to classify uncertain classes.

5. EXPERIMENTAL RESULTS

We validate our method on three public datasets whose information is summarized in Table 1. All our experiments are conducted in Matlab 2014 on an ordinary computer with a 2.6GHZ CPU and 8GB memory. Two quantitative metrics are used to evaluate different methods: (1) **Accuracy**, which is defined as the correctly recognized samples divided by the total number of testing samples and (2) **Computational cost**, which is defined as the average time used to recognize each testing sample.

Table 1: DATASET INFORMATION

Dataset	Number of Activity	Sensor Position	Sampling Rate	Number of Volunteers	Volunteers Age Range	Number of Training Samples	Number of Testing Samples
UCI[1]	6	Waist	50HZ	30	19~48	7352	2947
USC[2]	11	Hip	100HZ	14	21~49	7156	3414
SHO[3]	7	Wrist	50HZ	10	25~30	6826	2904

5.1 Evaluating the Design of Activity Image

Table 2 shows the accuracy of DCNN method with various designs of input activity images. The proposed activity image (Row 3) achieves the highest recognition accuracy. The accuracy decreases when we use the signal image directly (Row 1) or replace the Discrete Fourier Transform with the wavelet transform (Row 2). DFT improves the recognition performance because it increases the visual appearance difference of activity images (Fig.3), making it easier for DCNN to learn discriminative features.

Table 2: DCNN ACCURACY vs. INPUT IMAGES *

Input Image Design	DCNN Architecture	DCNN Accuracy (%)		
		UCI[1]	USC[2]	SHO[3]
RS $\xrightarrow{Alg.1}$ SI	Fig.4	88.87	94.11	96.76
RS $\xrightarrow{Alg.1}$ SI $\xrightarrow{2D\ Wavelet}$ AI	Fig.4	91.38	93.03	95.52
RS $\xrightarrow{Alg.1}$ SI $\xrightarrow{DFT}$ AI (Fig.2)	Fig.4	**95.18**	**97.01**	**99.93**

*Raw Signals (RS); Signal Image (SI); Activity Image (AI).

5.2 Evaluating the Design of DCNN Architecture

Although it is infeasible to evaluate all possible DCNN architectures, we compare four representative DCNN designs with an increasing number of layers (Table 3). For our activity recognition task, two convolutional layers combined with two subsampling layers achieve the best accuracy. If the convolutional neural network is too shallow, high-level features are not be able to be learned. If the network is too deep, useful features may be filtered out during the convolutional and subsampling processes.

Table 3: DCNN ACCURACY vs. ARCHITECTURE *

Input Image	DCNN Architecture	DCNN Accuracy (%)		
		UCI[1]	USC[2]	SHO[3]
Fig.2	3C21×21–S8×8	86.70	79.97	96.45
Fig.2	5C5×5–S4×4–10C5×5–S2×2 (Fig.4)	**95.18**	**97.01**	**99.93**
Fig.2	5C5×5–S2×2–8C5×5–S2×2–10C5×5–S2×2	94.77	96.60	99.59
Fig.2	5C3×3–S2×2–7C2×2–S2×2–9C3×3–S2×2–11C2×2–S2×2	90.43	88.61	99.04

*"C" and "S" denote convolutional layer and subsampling layer, respectively. The architecture is described as "{the number of output maps}C{kernel size}-S{kernel size}".

5.3 Quantitative Comparison

We compare our proposed methods, DCNN and DCNN+ (the DCNN method with the aid from SVM for uncertain cases), with two other state-of-the-arts: (1) SVM method [1], which extracts 561 handcrafted features from signals of accelerometers and gyroscopes and utilizes the SVM classifier; (2) Feature selection method [4], the aim of which is to reduce computational cost by selecting the most useful features. In [4], the feature importance is estimated by random forest which measures the increase of prediction error when a feature is permuted out.

The quantitative comparison on three public datasets in terms of recognition accuracy and computational cost is summarized in Table 4. The threshold T in DCNN+ method is computed by Eq.4, which is 43, 4, 2, respectively for the three datasets. The proposed DCNN+ and DCNN methods achieve the best performance in accuracy and computational cost, respectively. The SVM method [1] gets the second best accuracy but its computational cost is much higher. In contrast, the feature selection method [4] has the second lowest computational cost but its accuracy is the lowest among the four methods. Thus, there is a trade-off between accuracy and computational cost. Compared with the methods proposed in [1] and [4], the DCNN+ and DCNN methods achieve a good balance between accuracy and efficiency (high accuracy and low computational cost).

Table 4: PERFORMANCE COMPARISON

Dataset	Accuracy (%)				Computational Cost (ms)			
	DCNN+	DCNN	SVM[1]	Feature Selection[4]	DCNN+	DCNN	SVM[1]	Feature Selection[4]
UCI[1]	**97.59**	95.18	96.40	91.31	3.85	**1.56**	10.06	1.81
USC[2]	**97.83**	97.01	97.28	96.77	2.66	**1.54**	11.78	1.86
SHO[3]	**99.93**	99.93	99.93	99.58	1.56	**1.53**	9.87	1.56

5.4 Accuracy vs Computational Cost

Fig.7 shows the recognition accuracy and computational cost on the testing datasets if we gradually increase the threshold T in DCNN+ method. The green dots denote the accuracy corresponding to the T set by Eq.4 and the red dots denote the maximal accuracy achievable by DCNN+. They are very close to each other, which means T learnt from the training datasets by Eq.4 is effective on the testing datasets. On the UCI dataset (Fig.7(a)), when T increases, SVM classifier can assist DCNN on some uncertain cases. The accuracy curve increases and then levels off when $T = 50$, which means SVM cannot help solve uncertain cases anymore when $T > 50$. On the USC dataset (Fig.7(b)), the accuracy curve has the peak around $T = 4$, and then decreases a little bit. It indicates that handcrafted features overall can aid automatically learned feature for activity recognition, but there is possibly a small percentage of cases which are correctly recognized by DCNN while falsely classified by SVM if we choose T larger than 4. Accuracy curve on the SHO dataset (Fig.7(c)) is flat since our DCNN method only classifies 2 samples incorrectly out of total 2904 testing samples and the SVM classifier cannot solve these two samples either. Note that for all three datasets, time cost increases when T increases because more bi-class SVM classifications are applied when T increases.

6. CONCLUSION

This paper attacks the problem of accurate and efficient human activity recognition based on wearable sensors. To

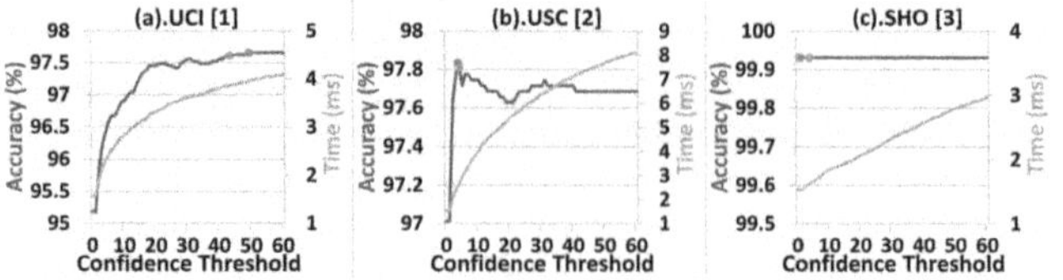

Figure 7: The recognition performance (accuracy and computational cost) regarding to different confidence thresholds. The green dots denote the accuracy corresponding to the T set by Eq.4 and the red dots denote the maximal accuracy achievable by DCNN+.

effectively learn discriminative features automatically, we propose a novel activity image as the input of DCNN. Raw sensor signals from accelerometers and gyroscopes are permutated and stacked in a signal image, the Discrete Fourier Transform of which is the newly-defined activity image. A DCNN architecture is designed to learn low-level to high-level features from the activity image for effective activity recognition. We compared our method with state-of-the-arts on three public datasets. The proposed two methods (DCNN+ and DCNN) achieve superior performance in terms of recognition accuracy and computational cost.

7. ACKNOWLEDGEMENT

This work was supported by NSF grants CNS-1205695 and IIP-1521289.

8. REFERENCES

[1] Davide Anguita, et al., "A public domain dataset for human activity recognition using smartphones," in European Symposium on Artificial Neural Networks, Computational Intelligence and Machine Learning, ESANN, 2013.

[2] Mi Zhang and Alexander A Sawchuk, "Usc-had: a daily activity dataset for ubiquitous activity recognition using wearable sensors," in ACM Conference on Ubiquitous Computing, 2012.

[3] Muhammad Shoaib, et al., "Fusion of smartphone motion sensors for physical activity recognition," Sensors, 2014.

[4] Pierluigi Casale, et al., "Human activity recognition from accelerometer data using a wearable device," in Pattern Recognition and Image Analysis, 2011.

[5] Davide Anguita, et al., "Human activity recognition on smartphones using a multiclass hardware-friendly support vector machine," in Ambient Assisted Living and Home Care, 2012.

[6] Toma Ât's Peterek, et al., "Comparison of classification algorithms for physical activity recognition," in Innovations in Bio-inspired Computing and Applications, 2014.

[7] Charissa Ann Ronao and Sung-Bae Cho, "Human activity recognition using smartphone sensors with two-stage continuous hidden markov models," in International Conference on Natural Computation, 2014.

[8] Piero Zappi, et al., "Activity recognition ÂÍ from on-body sensors: accuracy-power trade-off by dynamic sensor selection," in Wireless Sensor Networks, 2008.

[9] Dawud Gordon, et al., "Energy-efficient activity recognition using prediction," in International Symposium on Wearable Computers, 2012.

[10] Zhixian Yan, et al., "Energy-efficient continuous activity recognition on mobile phones: An activity-adaptive approach," in International Symposium on Wearable Computers, 2012.

[11] Jian Cui and Bin Xu, "Cost-effective activity recognition on mobile devices," in International Conference on Body Area Networks, 2013.

[12] Abdel-rahman Mohamed, et al., "Investigation of fullsequence training of deep belief networks for speech recognition.," in INTERSPEECH, 2010.

[13] Alex Krizhevsky, et al., "Imagenet classification with deep convolutional neural networks," in Advances in Neural Information Processing Systems, 2012.

[14] Shigeo Abe, Support vector machines for pattern classification, vol. 53, Springer, 2005.

Image2Emoji: Zero-shot Emoji Prediction for Visual Media

Spencer Cappallo[†] Thomas Mensink[†] Cees G. M. Snoek[†‡]
[†]University of Amsterdam [‡]Qualcomm Research Netherlands
{cappallo, tmensink, cgmsnoek}@uva.nl

ABSTRACT

We present *Image2Emoji*, a multi-modal approach for generating emoji labels for an image in a zero-shot manner. Different from existing zero-shot image-to-text approaches, we exploit both image and textual media to learn a semantic embedding for the new task of emoji prediction. We propose that the widespread adoption of emoji suggests a semantic universality which is well-suited for interaction with visual media. We quantify the efficacy of our proposed model on the MSCOCO dataset, and demonstrate the value of visual, textual and multi-modal prediction of emoji. We conclude the paper with three examples of the application potential of emoji in the context of multimedia retrieval.

1. INTRODUCTION

Visual classification and retrieval models traditionally rely on a limited set of pre-defined concepts, which are frequently trained on millions of photos and require a costly re-training process to adapt to new concepts, *e.g.* [1, 6]. Furthermore, at the end of this process, the model only outputs a list of concepts and their likelihood, which must be translated in some way to a more digestible form for an end user. To address these limitations, we suggest the use of ideograms as a final representation for concepts, and propose an approach to predict any arbitrary set of ideograms without re-training the visual classifier.

Ideograms maintain a visual grammar of interaction, limiting the semantic gap between a query and the returned media, and allow for language-independent, youth-friendly user interfaces which adapt seamlessly to a touchscreen saturated world. This work uses emoji as a candidate set of ideograms for visual search. Emoji are a set of over 700 ideograms, which is widely prevalent and supported natively by most smartphones, as well as many major websites such as Facebook and Twitter. Their widespread use suggests that, as a set of ideograms, emoji have sufficiently broad semantic coverage as to be interesting. See Figure 1 for examples of images with emoji predicted by our model.

MM'15, October 26–30, 2015, Brisbane, Australia.
 ISBN 978-1-4503-3459-4/15/10 ...$15.00.
DOI: http://dx.doi.org/10.1145/2733373.2806335.

Figure 1: Emoji predictions for three input images.

To avoid costly data annotation and training steps, and to be applicable to any arbitrary set of ideograms, our proposed approach for emoji labeling is zero-shot, relying on a previously-learned semantic embedding space to translate visual concept detections and user text into the target labels. We see several opportunities for the use of ideograms and emoji within the multimedia community. As a pre-defined set of queries, they hold advantages over text lists (see Figure 2) for retrieval or exploration tasks. As clear iconography they present opportunities as a means for interaction on small screens such as smart watches. They also suggest possibilities for description and summarization tasks, for example when describing image collections and videos.

The task we have chosen resembles that of zero-shot concept detection. In particular, our model's treatment of the visual modality is similar to that of [5]. In [5], a semantic embedding predicts unseen ImageNet classes from a classifier's probability outputs for known classes by finding the distance between the high-probability known concepts and the unseen concepts in a vector space. In both [5] and our work, the semantic embedding is generated using word2vec [4]. We differentiate our work from [5] through the introduction of a second, textual modality to the model; the motivated use of a significantly different training corpus for learning our semantic embedding; and an overall focus on the prediction of emoji labels, which is a multi-label setting in contrast to their single-label scenario. We call our approach *Image2Emoji* and detail its technicalities next.

2. IMAGE2EMOJI

Image2Emoji combines visual concepts and user text to predict unseen emoji labels in a zero-shot manner.

The problem can be formalized thus: The objective is to predict a target set of ideogram labels, $\mathcal{Z}$, by relying on a set of input concepts, $\mathcal{Y}$, where we assume $\mathcal{Z} \cap \mathcal{Y} = \emptyset$. Our input concepts are comprised of visual concepts from a pre-trained classifier, $\mathcal{Y}_v$, and textual concepts extracted

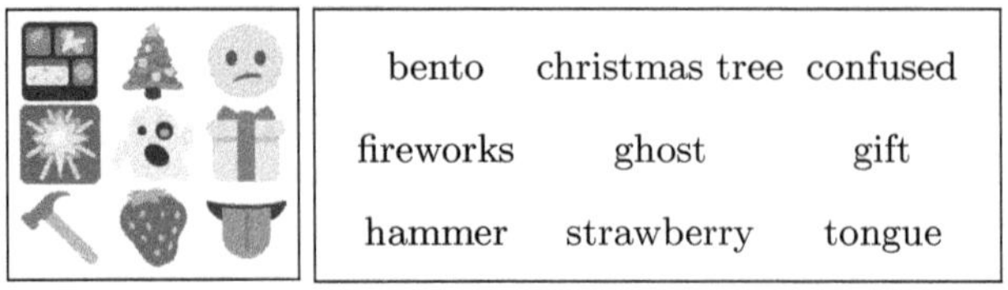

Figure 2: Comparison of emoji concepts presented as ideograms (L) and as text (R).

from user text, $\mathcal{Y}_t$, s.t. $\mathcal{Y}_v, \mathcal{Y}_t \in \mathcal{Y}$. To accomplish this without training, we rely on an intermediary vector space where semantic relationships between known labels $\mathcal{Y}$ and target labels $\mathcal{Z}$ can be exploited to score the emoji concepts. See Figure 3.

2.1 Semantic Embedding

Image2Emoji uses a word2vec vector representation [4] as a semantic embedding space. The embedding space is designed to minimize the distance between the vectors of semantically similar words. The word2vec model consists of a neural network with a single hidden layer. When given as input a token t_i, the network tries to predict n tokens from surrounding context on each side, $\{t_{i-n}, ..., t_{i-1}, t_{i+1}, ..., t_{i+n}\}$, which is known as a skip-gram model. Once trained, the d node-values of the hidden layer are used as a projection into the learned d-dimensional semantic vector space. These vector representations are normalized when calculating semantic similarity.

Our semantic embedding is a 500-dimensional word2vec model, which is trained on the title, description, and tag text from the 100M Flickr photos in the YFCC100M dataset [7]. An 11% increase in mean average precision for our task was observed by using the text from Flickr, compared against training the model on the text of Wikipedia, as used in [5]. We expect this increase is due to the language on Flickr being more closely tied to visual discussion than the language used on Wikipedia.

The semantic embedding space is denoted as $\mathcal{S}$, and a function w is defined which returns the vector representation of a given token within the space $\mathcal{S}$, namely $w : \mathcal{Y}, \mathcal{Z} \rightarrow \mathcal{S}$. By placing an input label $y \in \mathcal{Y}$ and target label $z \in \mathcal{Z}$ in a single vector space, their semantic closeness can be found by calculating the Cosine Similarity between their normalized vector representations. The combined operation of embedding the labels in the semantic space and finding their similarity is denoted by $cos(z, y) = w(z) \cdot w(y)$.

2.2 Emoji Scoring

For a given input image x_v, the visual classifier produces probabilities $p(y_v|x_v)$ across the set of visual concepts $y_v \in \mathcal{Y}_v$. For a given target label, $z \in \mathcal{Z}$, the influence of a given visual concept, y_v, is found through the product of their similarity in the semantic embedding space and the probability output of the classifier. The contribution of the visual modality to the target label prediction is the sum of these products for every $y_v \in \mathcal{Y}_v^*$, where $\mathcal{Y}_v^* \subset \mathcal{Y}_v$ consisting of the N_v labels with the highest probabilities for the given input image x_v. The scoring function for emoji labels based on the visual modality is labeled as S_v:

$$S_v(z, x_v) = \sum_{y_v \in \mathcal{Y}_v^*} cos(z, y_v) \cdot p(y_v|x_v) \quad (1)$$

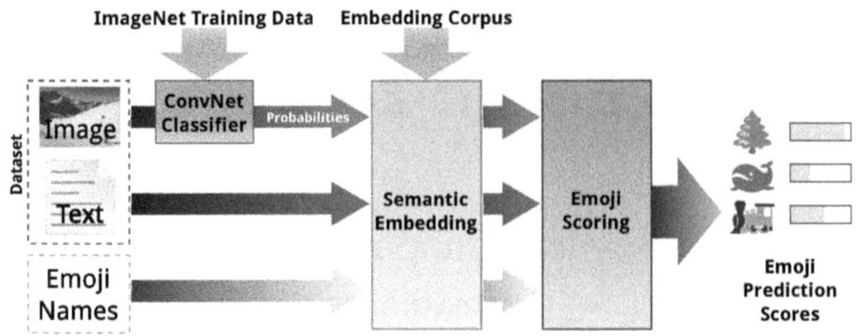

Figure 3: Data flow within Image2Emoji. Probability scores of visual classes along with the image's accompanying text are mapped to the semantic vector space, and their similarity to the emoji label names are used to score the emoji. Both modules are detailed in Section 2.

The predictions based on the text modality follow a similar pattern. However, due to the discrete nature of the text input and the fact that the probabilities $p(y_t|x_t)$ for a given text input x_t and text label $y_t \in \mathcal{Y}_t$ are restricted to being either 1 or 0 (present in the text or not), the maximum of the product is used instead of the sum. The scoring function based on the text modality is given as S_t:

$$S_t(z, x_t) = \max_{y_t \in \mathcal{Y}_t} cos(z, y_t) \cdot p(y_t|x_t) \quad (2)$$

To combine the predictions from the modalities, we employ a late-fusion strategy with a weighting factor α that is restricted to the range $[0, 1]$. The full scoring function is found through combining 1 and 2:

$$S(z, x_v, x_t) = \alpha S_v(z, x_v) + (1 - \alpha) S_t(z, x_t) \quad (3)$$

for a target label $z \in \mathcal{Z}$, an input image x_v, and accompanying user text x_t.

The value of α can be discovered through validation on known annotations, or simply left as 0.5 for an equal weighting of input modalities. Though our approach focuses on visual and text modalities, it is trivially adaptable to any number of input modalities, provided they can be mapped to the semantic embedding space.

Since the proposed method forgoes a costly training stage, it is computationally lightweight. Calculating the cosine similarity matrix needs only be done once per set of target labels and input modality, and has a complexity of $\mathcal{O}(N_{\mathcal{Y}} N_{\mathcal{Z}} D)$, where $N_{\mathcal{Y}}$ is the number of input labels, $N_{\mathcal{Z}}$ the number of target labels, and D is the dimensionality of the semantic embedding. Predicting an emoji representation for a given input has complexity $\mathcal{O}(N_T N_{\mathcal{Z}})$ per input image and modality, where N_T is the number of input labels selected ($N_T = N_v$ in the visual modality, and in the textual modality $N_T = \#$ of words.)

3. EXPERIMENTS

Dataset Although there is no existing dataset with emoji annotations, we wish to quantitatively evaluate the efficacy of our zero-shot approach before demonstrating its performance on emoji. To do this, we test our model on the train set of MSCOCO [3]. MSCOCO is selected for this task because 37 out of its 80 label categories correspond to concepts present within the set of emoji. The MSCOCO train data consists of 83k images with multi-label annotations in 80 classes and Mechanical Turk provided captions.

	im-mAP	mAP
Random lower bound	0.086	0.037
Image2Emoji-visual	0.460	0.355
Supervised upper bound	0.750	0.562

Table 1: Image2Emoji performance using only the visual modality. For context, upper and lower bounds are also reported in the form of a supervised SVM approach and random rankings. Our zero-shot approach is nearer the performance of the supervised upper bound than the lower bound.

Implementation details Our visual classifier is a deep convolutional network in the style of GoogLeNet [6], trained on ImageNet data [2] to classify 15,293 concepts – the number of concepts with at least 200 positive images in the dataset. To ensure that the evaluation remains zero-shot, 110 of these visual concepts are excluded due to their class names overlapping with any of the 80 MSCOCO classes, resulting in a total of 15,183 visual concepts.

Results are reported for two different sources of text. One is text source is the first listed caption per image from the high-quality Mechanical Turk annotations. Out of concern that these descriptions are not representative of user text under normal circumstances, we also collect the title, description, and tag information from Flickr. Results are also reported for this second, more realistic text source.

Evaluation criteria To demonstrate the relative performance of the text and visual modalities within our model, the two are evaluated individually without contribution from the other. Following this, we report the change in performance when both modalities are combined, with varying values of the fusion weighting parameter α. Two evaluation metrics are reported for each test. The first, corresponding to a retrieval task, is the mean average precision when ranking images for target labels, which we denote with 'mAP'. Also reported is the mean average precision *per image*, which corresponds to the success of ranking emoji labels for describing or summarizing a given input, and which we refer to as '*image*-mAP' or '*im*-mAP'.

4. RESULTS

Visual Prediction We first evaluate the performance of the model when relying solely on visual input. This corresponds to removing the blue arrows from the diagram in Figure 3. To provide context to our results, we provide upper and lower bound results.

To establish the upper bound, a supervised method is tested. A linear SVM is trained via a one-vs-rest paradigm to predict the 80 MSCOCO labels. The 15k concept probabilities are used as the feature representation, and the model is trained on the 40k images of MSCOCO's validation set. The performance of the supervised approach along with the performance of random predictions can be seen in Table 1. Encouragingly, our zero-shot approach is closer to the performance of the supervised upper bound than the random lower bound. These values also motivate the inclusion of a text modality in a zero-shot approach, in contrast to using only visual concepts as in [5].

	Captions		Flickr Text	
	im-mAP	mAP	*im*-mAP	mAP
Baseline	0.337	0.288	0.380	0.342
Image2Emoji-text	0.647	0.536	0.604	0.555

Table 2: Results of Image2Emoji using only the text modality. Two text sources are tested: Mechanical Turk-provided descriptions, and user text harvested from Flickr. Results are compared to a simple baseline that omits a semantic embedding in favor of a direct mapping. Our model outperforms the baseline, performing well even with the Flickr text.

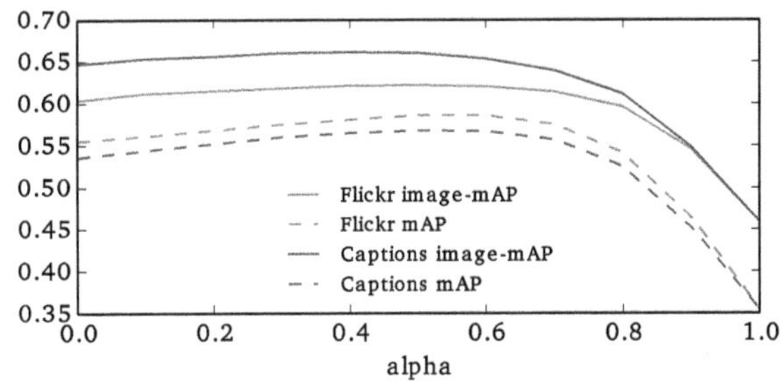

Figure 4: Effect of the modality-weighting parameter α. Peak performance occurs near $\alpha = 0.5$, where Image2Emoji has mAPs of 0.586 and 0.568, and *im*-mAPs of 0.622 and 0.660 for the Flickr text and the captions, respectively. In the mAP setting, our zero-shot, multi-modal model actually outperforms the visual-only supervised upper bound.

Textual Prediction Image2Emoji using solely the text modality is evaluated. This corresponds to removing the red arrows of the visual modality from the diagram in Figure 3.

We compare the text portion of our model against a simple zero-shot baseline. This baseline matches directly the terms in the input text with the target labels. In Table 2, results are presented for both the high-quality captions and the noisier Flickr text. Our model, utilizing an intermediary semantic embedding, outperforms the simple, direct baseline. This reflects the more complete relationships between words which are captured by the embedding. It is worth noting that our method yields roughly similar results for both the captions and the Flickr text. Despite the noise inherent to the Flickr text, it is usually longer than the single-sentence captions provided by Mechanical Turk users, which provides a greater number of semantic data points.

Fusion Prediction Lastly, we combine the predictions. This corresponds to the full diagram in Figure 3, containing both the text and visual modalities. The performance of Image2Emoji for varying values of α, and using either the caption text or Flickr text, are in Figure 4. Notably, when using the Flickr text, the mAP performance of the model for predicting labels actually exceeds that of the supervised visual baseline (0.586 to 0.562). Furthermore, the performance discrepancy with varying values of α is very small around the optimal selection. This suggests that selecting a suboptimal α should have only marginal effects on the overall performance.

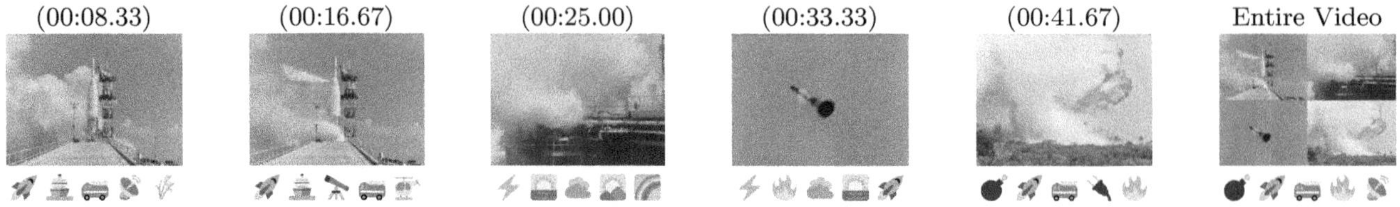

Figure 5: The five highest scoring emoji for frames at regular intervals across a video. Emoji predictions from frame-level visual detections were combined with the video's user-provided title. The emoji representation for the entire video is also shown.

Figure 6: Top images for queries of the *sheep*, *foggy*, and *credit card* emoji. *Credit card* performs poorly, perhaps due to a lack of credit cards in the dataset.

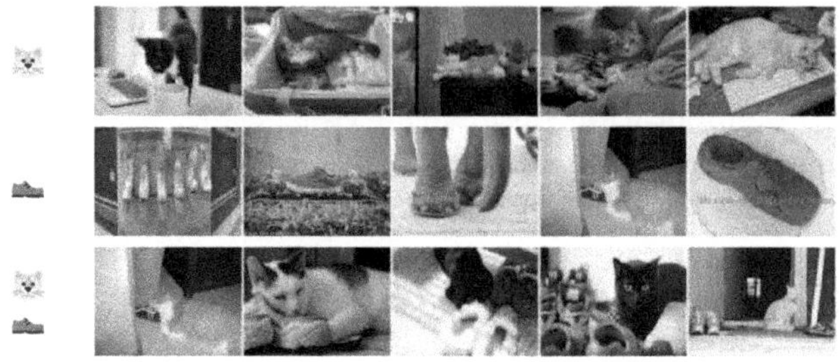

Figure 7: Example of composition with emoji concepts to create more nuanced queries. *Shoe* and *cat* are combined to retrieve images containing both.

5. APPLICATION POTENTIAL

Following the numerical evaluation of the proposed model, we showcase some possible applications of Image2Emoji. All examples presented in this section use a subset comprised of 385 emoji. These have been manually selected by removing emoji which were not pictographs and therefore not clearly tied to a visual concept (such as *abcd* or *left-right arrow*) and also removing those characters which repeat a concept already represented by another, very similar, character (e.g., *pig face* and *pig*).

Query-by-emoji The focus of the proposed model is to use emoji as a means for retrieval and exploration of visual data. Three examples of the top-ranked images for a given emoji query are shown in Figure 6. It is worth noting that *foggy* returns very sensible results, despite the concept of 'foggy' being very distant from the collection of concrete nouns used as concepts for the visual modality. The text modality is likely crucial in capturing this meaning. The query *credit card* performs very poorly, which we suspect is due to a lack of credit cards in the MSCOCO dataset we tested on. Also shown is an example of query composition in Figure 7, where the top images for *cat*, *shoe*, and *cat* + *shoe* are listed. The combination of emoji can allow for more specific or nuanced queries to be constructed from a limited concept set.

Emoji ranking In Figure 1, we show results of our model for the task of ranking descriptive emoji for a given visual input. Worth noting is the presence of multiple concepts that share similar semantics in the embedding space, such as *old man* and *old woman*. The training process for the semantic embedding will assign similar vector directions to tokens which are used in a similar manner, resulting in similar scores.

Emoji summarization Representational or descriptive emoji are most useful for describing collections of images or video. For this reason, Image2Emoji applied to a video is shown in Figure 5. The top-scoring emoji for five frames evenly distributed throughout the video are displayed, along with an emoji representation for the entire video using the average across all frames. The video-level title text from YouTube was used for the text modality, with a large α used for the frame-level predictions to emphasize the more local, visual information. In this example, the emoji summary gives a compelling summary of the video contents.

In this paper, we have proposed and evaluated a multi-modal, zero-shot approach to generating ideogram labels for visual media, and have investigated several uses of emoji for exploration and representation purposes.

Acknowledgments This research is supported by the STW STORY project and the Dutch national program COMMIT.

6. REFERENCES

[1] D. Borth, R. Ji, T. Chen, T. Breuel, and S.-F. Chang. Large-scale visual sentiment ontology and detectors using adjective noun pairs. In *MM*, 2013.

[2] J. Deng, W. Dong, R. Socher, L.-J. Li, K. Li, and L. Fei-Fei. Imagenet: A large-scale hierarchical image database. In *CVPR*, 2009.

[3] T.-Y. Lin, M. Maire, S. Belongie, J. Hays, P. Perona, D. Ramanan, P. Dollár, and C. L. Zitnick. Microsoft coco: Common objects in context. In *ECCV*, 2014.

[4] T. Mikolov, I. Sutskever, K. Chen, G. S. Corrado, and J. Dean. Distributed representations of words and phrases and their compositionality. In *NIPS*, 2013.

[5] M. Norouzi, T. Mikolov, S. Bengio, Y. Singer, J. Shlens, A. Frome, G. S. Corrado, and J. Dean. Zero-shot learning by convex combination of semantic embeddings. In *ICLR*, 2014.

[6] C. Szegedy, W. Liu, Y. Jia, P. Sermanet, S. Reed, D. Anguelov, D. Erhan, V. Vanhoucke, and A. Rabinovich. Going deeper with convolutions. In *CVPR*, 2015.

[7] B. Thomee, D. A. Shamma, G. Friedland, B. Elizalde, K. Ni, D. Poland, D. Borth, and L.-J. Li. The new data and new challenges in multimedia research. *arXiv:1503.01817*, 2015.

Rich Image Description Based on Regions

Xiaodan Zhang[†§], Xinhang Song[‡], Xiong Lv[‡], Shuqiang Jiang[‡], Qixiang Ye[†], Jianbin Jiao[†]
[†]University of Chinese Academy of Sciences, Beijing 101408, P. R. China
[‡]Institute of Computing Technology, Chinese Academy of Sciences, Beijing 100190, P. R. China
[§]City University of Hong Kong, Kowloon, Hong Kong
zhangxiaodan10@mails.ucas.ac.cn; {xinhang.song, xiong.lv}@vipl.ict.ac.cn;
sqjiang@ict.ac.cn; {qxye, jiaojb}@ucas.ac.cn

ABSTRACT

Automatically describing the content of an image is a fundamental problem in artificial intelligence that connects computer vision and natural language processing. In contrast to the previous image description methods that focus on describing the whole image, this paper presents a method of generating rich image descriptions from image regions. First, we detect regions with R-CNN (regions with convolutional neural network features) framework. We then utilize the RNN (recurrent neural networks) to generate sentences for image regions. Finally, we propose an optimization method to select one suitable region. The proposed model generates several sentence description of regions in an image, which has sufficient representative power of the whole image and contains more detailed information. Comparing to general image level description, generating more specific and accurate sentences on the different regions can satisfy more personal requirements for different people. Experimental evaluations validate the effectiveness of the proposed method.

Categories and Subject Descriptors

I.4.8 [**Image Processing And Computer Vision**]: Scene Analysis — Object recognition; I.2.10 [**Artificial Intelligence**]: Vision and Scene Understanding — perceptual reasoning

Keywords

Image Description; Object Detection; Region Optimization; Convolutional Neural Networks; Recurrent Neural Networks

1. INTRODUCTION

An image contains a lot of information from various aspects. Automatically describing the content of an image using natural language is a challenging task which should on the one hand accurately provide the object and activity information to avoid delivering the wrong message; on the other hand, the description should be as more coverage as possible to avoid miss important information. Compared with conventional image classification and object recognition tasks, which have been studied for a long time in the multimedia and computer vision community, an image description should capture not only the objects contained in an image, but it also must express how these objects relate to each other, as well as how their attributes and the activities are involved in. Moreover, the above semantic knowledge (e.g. objects, attributes, activities) has to be expressed in a natural language like English, which means that a language model is required in addition to visual understanding. Image description has many important application requirements. For example, it can help visually impaired people better understand the content of the image content. The vivid and informative image description is also helpful to satisfy our daily needs such as image searching, human-to-machine interaction, and mobile visual assistance.

Recently, some works [2, 1, 14, 7] have been proposed to generate image descriptions with natural sentences. M.

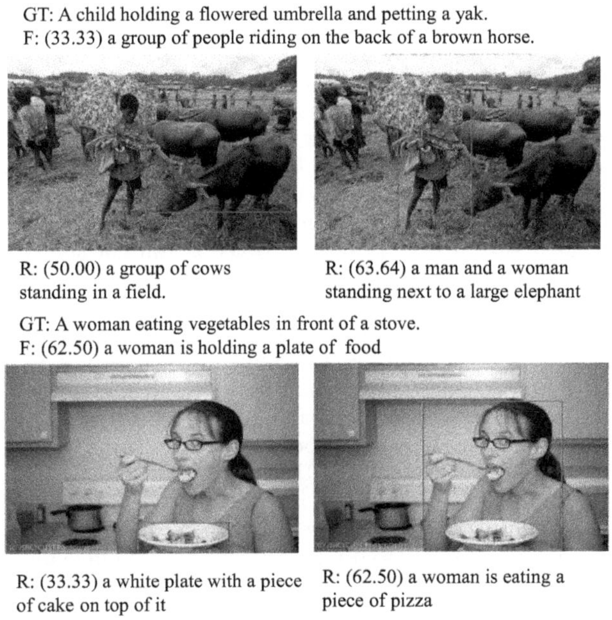

Figure 1: Image description based on regions, compared to full image description. GT: ground truth. F: full image description. R: region based description

MM'15, October 26–30, 2015, Brisbane, Australia.
© 2015 ACM. ISBN 978-1-4503-3459-4/15/10 ...$15.00.
DOI: http://dx.doi.org/10.1145/2733373.2806338.

Mitchell et al. [2] introduce a novel system by leveraging syntactically informed word co-occurrence statistics and generating syntactic trees from visual methods, which composes human-like descriptions of images. Socher et al. [1] introduce a max-margin structure based predicting architecture, which is recovered by recursive neural networks both in complex scene images and sentences. Oriol Vinyals et al. [14] present a novel model training recurrent neural networks (RNN) model base on the convolutional neural networks (CNN) features to generate natural sentences for describing images. Girish Kulkarni et al. [7] present a system to automatically generate natural language descriptions for images, which exploits statistics gleaned from parsing large quantities of text data and image recognition algorithms.

However, most of the existing works only focus on image description of the whole image, which is limited to represent the the rich information in the image content and are deficiency on personalized applications. For example, when someone wants to get the detailed information of specific position in front of a camera or Google glass, the full image description will be insufficient. Kapathy and Li [6] present a model that generates free-form natural language description of image regions. However, their region descriptions are only annotated with lists of keywords, which is still not suitable enough for practical applications. Detailed image description on image regions to acquire rich visual explanations with sentences have not been investigated yet.

In this paper, we focus on describing images with regions obtained from object detection, aiming to fill the gap and conquer the problem mentioned above. In the proposed approach, an object detection procedure is firstly used to generate candidate regions. An RNN is then trained to learn the describing models between image regions and sentences. Finally, all the regions are used for generating the image descriptions. Region based image description can give more informative representation of an image, which includes some descriptions even the ground truth sentences of benchmark datasets have not recorded. As is shown in Figure 1, where GT means ground truth image description, values like 33.33 are evaluation scores of the corresponding descriptions. The region description can generate sentences like, 'a group of cows standing in a field', 'a white plate with a piece of cake on top of it'. Note that the description of the two regions in the images are not appeared in ground truth sentences. From the experimental analysis, it can be observed that description of regions can be better than or comparable to full image description.

The rest of the paper is structured as follows. In Section 2, the proposed framework is described in detail. Evaluation and experimental results are provided in Section 3. Finally, Section 4 concludes our paper.

2. PROPOSED FRAMEWORK

2.1 Overview

In this paper, we proposed a visual to semantic framework to conduct detailed image description, which aims to generate rich image descriptions through object detection and sentence generation. The architecture of proposed system is shown in Figure 2. Firstly, R-CNN [3], the state-of-the-art object detection method, is adopted to detect image regions of objects. Then a 16 layers convolutional neural network model (VGG) [12] is used to extract visual features for each region. Finally, the language model of RNN [9] is used to generate the sentences for image regions. In addition, we propose an optimization method to select the optimal region to generate sentence.

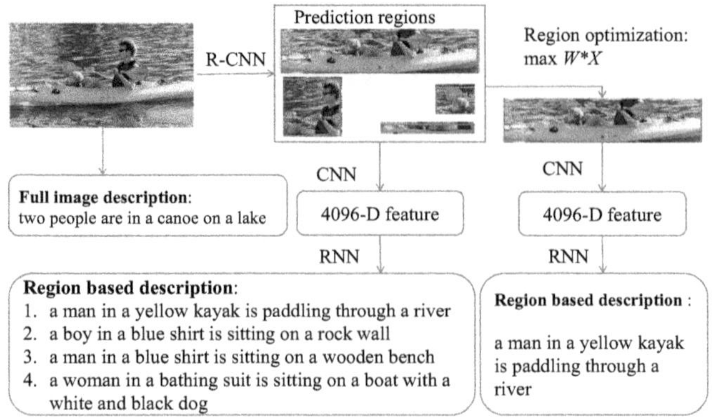

Figure 2: The framework of our region based image description model

2.2 Object Detection

Object detection has been extensively studied in the last decade. Currently, R-CNN [3] based method is the state-of-the-art framework, which uses selective search [13] to find candidate object window proposals, then extracts CNN features for detection.

In this paper, the R-CNN model [3] trained on the 200-category ILSVRC2014 detection challenge dataset is utilized to detect objects and generate image regions. As the corresponding regions of detected objects represent the prominent and significant area of an image, the image description based on these regions can be meaningful and informative.

2.3 Region Optimization

Although R-CNN is the state-of-the-art object detection methods, it can not guarantee the perfect performance in our task. On one hand, the detection results may contain some fault objects. On the other hand, even the right detection objects may contribute little to the final image description.

To reduce the number of the useless detection regions, we define $X = \{x_1, x_2, x_3, x_4\}$ to be the four cues of region selection, x_1: "size: area ratio", x_2: "location: coordinate center position ratio", x_3: "the universality of label", x_4: "prediction score" , and $W = \{w_1, w_2, w_3, w_4\}$ be the optimization parameter. The objective function is: $Y = max\, W * X$, and Y is the final description score of regions.

2.4 Image Description

For image description, the RNN model [6] trained on Flickr8K and MSCOCO datasets are adopted for our image description task. First, the 16-layers CNN network (VGG) [12] trained on the ImageNet dataset [11], is utilized for feature extraction. Then the RNN model is adopted to generate sentence descriptions for image regions. The core of RNN model is Long-Short Term Memory (LSTM) [4], which has shown state-of-the-art performance on sequence tasks such as translation.

The RNN takes the region pixels R and a sequence of input vectors $(x_1, ..., x_T)$. It then computes a sequence of hidden states $(h_1, ..., h_t)$ and a sequence of outputs $(y_1, ..., y_t)$ by iterating the following recurrence relation for $t = 1$ to N:

$$x_{-1} = VGG(R),$$
$$h_t = LSTM\,(h_{t-1},\, x_{t-1}),\ t \in \{1, ..., N\},$$
$$y_t = softmax\,(h_t,\, x_t),\ t \in \{1, ..., N\}.$$

With the raw generated regions for an image by object detection, there will be several sentences, which contain more detailed and informative contents of the image. And through our region optimization method, there will be one final region and a sentence description for an image, which is comparable with the conventional full image description. Both of the results will be described in our experiments to validate the effectiveness of our method.

2.5 Evaluation Metrics

The most commonly used metric so far in the image description literature is the BLEU score [10], which evaluates a candidate sentence by measuring the fraction of n-grams that appear in a set of references. So we evaluate our method with the BLEU score.

GT: A man and a baby are in a yellow kayak on water
F: (66.67) two people are in a canoe on a lake

(29.41) a woman in a bathing suit is sitting on a boat with a dog

(50.00) a man in a blue shirt is sitting on a wooden bench

(50.00) a boy in a blue shirt is sitting on a rock wall

(63.64) a man in a yellow kayak is paddling through a river

Figure 3: Visual display of the result. GT: ground truth sentence. F: full image description. The numbers indicate the BLEU1 score of sentences.

3. EXPERIMENTS

3.1 Image Datasets

We evaluate the proposed methods on two datasets: Flickr8K [5] and MSCOCO [8]. Flickr8K consists of 8091 images and 5 ground truth sentence descriptions for each image, and we follow the common train/test split. For the MSCOCO dataset, we use 80k images and corresponding sentence descriptions for training and 1k images for testing. For each dataset, we run two experiments for comparison: one is the conventional full image description, the other is the proposed region based rich image description, and both methods use the same CNN and RNN model.

3.2 Image Description of Regions

Through RCNN, each image proposes an average of 4 regions (range from 1 to 9). Then a 16-layers VGG net is adopted to extract features of the regions. At last the 4090-D features are imported to the LSTM model for sentence generation and there will be several sentences for each image. These sentences can be totally different from ground truth sentences. As are shown in Figure 1 and Figure 3 .We can generate more specific sentences from the different regions in the image, while the ground truth sentence only focus on the whole image.

We also use the region optimization method described in section 2.3 to select one best region for evaluation. And the reason why we choose the four cues as the region evaluation criteria is that, in experiment it is observed that regions with bigger size and closer to the image center perform well in image description, which is also unsurprising with the truth that salient region with large area and close to the center of image can represent the whole image. In addition, regions with universal label such as person, animal, fruit, furniture are also more representative. Finally, sentence score of region is also an important index to evaluate description performance.

To make comparison of our method and the conventional full image description, we also exert the full image description use the same CNN and RNN model, except the detection procedure.

Table 1: Result of Flickr8K dataset

Types	BLEU1	BLEU2	BLEU3	BLEU4
ID	51.9873	30.7134	13.6014	5.9712
IDR(mean)	46.6835	25.327	10.2291	4.0732
IDR(max)	52.5900	32.1969	15.0766	6.2731
ID+IDR	62.2139	42.7559	23.9343	11.3113

3.3 Evaluation Results

As the most commonly used metric so far in the image description literature is the BLEU score, we choose four indicators, BLEUn (n={1, 2, 3, 4}), as the evaluation metrics. And the bigger the values of BLEU1, BLEU2, BLEU3, BLEU4 are, the better.

Table 1 and Table 2 illustrate the comparison results of Flickr8K and MSCOCO datasets, respectively.

ID indicates the baseline image description method which generate sentence from the whole image. IDR is our approach of image description based on regions, and IDR (mean) is the mean value of BLEU score of all regions, IDR (max) is the max value of the regions score can be. ID+IDR means the combination of full image description and region based image description, and the value is the max BLEU score it can be. Experiments on the two datasets demonstrate that image description based on regions can contain more content than full image description.

To display the effectiveness of our region optimization method, we compare the results of different methods as shown in Figure 4. IDR-O is our approach with region opti-

Table 2: Result of MSCOCO dataset

Types	BLEU1	BLEU2	BLEU3	BLEU4
ID	57.2717	36.1942	17.5965	7.8787
IDR(mean)	50.6205	27.4891	10.7494	4.6179
IDR(max)	59.2985	38.5430	18.8187	8.9793
ID+IDR	64.0047	44.5745	24.8785	12.5477

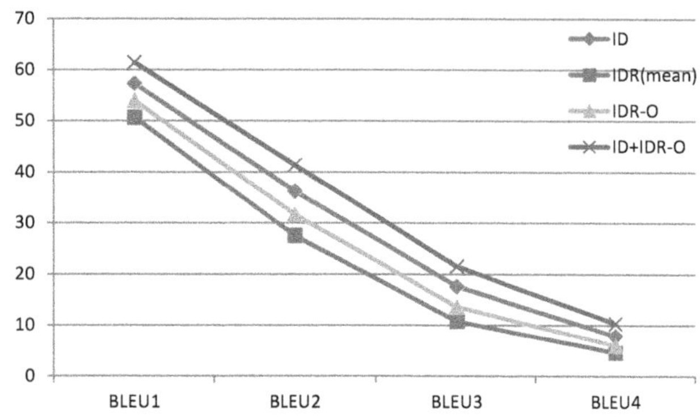

Figure 4: Comparison of IDR-O and ID for MSCOCO dataset.

mization. ID+IDR-O means the combination of full image description and our method with region optimization. It can be seen that our region optimization method can generate a comparable sentence as full image description, which demonstrate that image can be described by representative regions. Image description with region optimization (IDR-O) is better than the mean of region descriptions (IDR-mean), which is due to the reduction of noisy regions of images. And the the combination of two methods(ID+IDR-O) achieves the best performance. It is worth mentioning that for some pure scene image without significant objects, the region based description may degrade severely. So the combination of full image description and region based description gets the best performance.

4. CONCLUSIONS

In this paper, we propose a method to generate rich descriptions for image regions. In the proposed model, three deep neural networks are adopted to generate image regions (R-CNN), extract features (VGG) and generate descriptive sentences (RNN). The experimental results on Flickr8K and MSCOCO datasets verify the effectiveness of the proposed method. We showed that image description based on regions can represent the whole image sufficiently to a great extent, even contains more detailed information out of the ground truth sentences. The proposed region optimization method can select a suitable region for an image and achieve comparable descriptive effect to the full image description. And the full image description and region based description can be complementary.

5. ACKNOWLEDGMENTS

This work was supported in part by the National Basic Research Program of China (973 Program) under Grant 2011CB706900 and Grant 2012CB316400, in part by the National Science Foundation of China under Grant 61271433, Grant 61202323 and Grant 61322212, and in part by National Hi-Tech Development Program (863 Program) of China under Grant 2014AA015202. This work is also funded by Lenovo Outstanding Young Scientists Program (LOYS).

6. REFERENCES

[1] Richard Socher andCliff Chiung-Yu Lin, Andrew Y. Ng, and Christopher D. Manning. Parsing natural scenes and natural language with recursive neural networks. In *ICML*, 2011.

[2] Walter Daelemans, Mirella Lapata, and Lluís Màrquez, editors. *EACL 2012, 13th Conference of the European Chapter of the Association for Computational Linguistics, Avignon, France, April 23-27, 2012*. The Association for Computer Linguistics, 2012.

[3] Ross B. Girshick, Jeff Donahue, Trevor Darrell, and Jitendra Malik. Rich feature hierarchies for accurate object detection and semantic segmentation. In *2014 IEEE Conference on Computer Vision and Pattern Recognition, CVPR 2014, Columbus, OH, USA, June 23-28, 2014*, pages 580–587, 2014.

[4] Sepp Hochreiter and Jürgen Schmidhuber. Long short-term memory. *Neural Computation*, 9(8):1735–1780, 1997.

[5] Micah Hodosh, Peter Young, and Julia Hockenmaier. Framing image description as a ranking task: Data, models and evaluation metrics. *J. Artif. Intell. Res. (JAIR)*, 47:853–899, 2013.

[6] Andrej Karpathy and Fei-Fei Li. Deep visual-semantic alignments for generating image descriptions. *CoRR*, abs/1412.2306, 2014.

[7] G. Kulkarni, V. Premraj, V. Ordonez, S. Dhar, Siming Li, Yejin Choi, A.C. Berg, and T.L. Berg. Babytalk: Understanding and generating simple image descriptions. *TPAMI*, 2013.

[8] Tsung-Yi Lin, Michael Maire, Serge Belongie, Lubomir D. Bourdev, Ross B. Girshick, James Hays, Pietro Perona, Deva Ramanan, Piotr Dollár, and C. Lawrence Zitnick. Microsoft COCO: common objects in context. *CoRR*, abs/1405.0312, 2014.

[9] Tomas Mikolov, Martin Karafiát, Lukás Burget, Jan Cernocký, and Sanjeev Khudanpur. Recurrent neural network based language model. In *INTERSPEECH 2010, 11th Annual Conference of the International Speech Communication Association, Makuhari, Chiba, Japan, September 26-30, 2010*, pages 1045–1048, 2010.

[10] Kishore Papineni, Salim Roukos, Todd Ward, and Wei-Jing Zhu. Bleu: A method for automatic evaluation of machine translation. In *Proceedings of the 40th Annual Meeting on Association for Computational Linguistics*, ACL '02, pages 311–318, Stroudsburg, PA, USA, 2002. Association for Computational Linguistics.

[11] Olga Russakovsky, Jia Deng, Hao Su, Jonathan Krause, Sanjeev Satheesh, Sean Ma, Zhiheng Huang, Andrej Karpathy, Aditya Khosla, Michael S. Bernstein, Alexander C. Berg, and Fei-Fei Li. Imagenet large scale visual recognition challenge. *CoRR*, abs/1409.0575, 2014.

[12] Karen Simonyan and Andrew Zisserman. Very deep convolutional networks for large-scale image recognition. *CoRR*, abs/1409.1556, 2014.

[13] Jasper R. R. Uijlings, Koen E. A. van de Sande, Theo Gevers, and Arnold W. M. Smeulders. Selective search for object recognition. *International Journal of Computer Vision*, 104(2):154–171, 2013.

[14] Oriol Vinyals, Alexander Toshev, Samy Bengio, and Dumitru Erhan. Show and tell: A neural image caption generator. *CoRR*, abs/1411.4555, 2014.

VM Hub: Building Cloud Service and Mobile Application for Image/Video/Multimedia Services

Jin Li, Microsoft
One Microsoft Way, Bld. 99, Redmond, WA 98052

Abstract

In this tutorial, we will teach how to use VM Hub (Visual Media Hub), an open multimedia hub with most of the code in the open source space, to convert a multimedia application to a cloud service, and to build mobile applications that consumes the cloud service. The tutorial also covers the architecture and design consideration of VM Hub.

Categories and Subject Descriptors D.1.3 [**Concurrent Programming**]: Distributed programming; D.4.7 [**Organization and Design**]: Distributed systems, interactive systems; H.5.1 [**Multimedia Information Systems**].

Keywords VM Hub; cloud services; image recognition; video recognition; multimedia services; mobile applications.

1. Introduction

With the rapid evolution of cloud computation, GPGPU and cluster based machine learning, and the availability of datasets such as ImageNet and Clickture, the dawn of fast development of image/video multimedia technologies has come. Developers and researchers around the globe are working feverishly to invent on new multimedia services, with new technologies, algorithms, and platforms being developed constantly. Innovative multimedia applications, such as SnapChat, Instagram, and How-Old, are also being rapidly deployed, and are catching worldwide attention.

So far, a majority of the multimedia services are confined to university and corporate labs, accessible only in the form of research publications. Only a tiny percentage of them make it to cloud services that can be easily consumed in the form of mobile Apps or web site by a large number of users. It is a non-trivial obstacle for multimedia developers to turn a multimedia application from running on a single machine into a cloud service, with fail over support and scale-out capability. It also requires tremendous effort and a highly prized skillset to build an online multimedia service that can be operated 24x7, with high performance and low cost of operation. The required engineering resource and technical know-how is usually not accessible to ordinary multimedia developers.

VM Hub aims to bridge this gap and to build an open multimedia hub that allows the entire multimedia/vision community to easily build cloud services. VM Hub also include tools that allow developers to easily build mobile multimedia applications that can easily consume the cloud services, either built by themselves or built by third parties. From the ground up, VM Hub is built as a central hub that supports multiple cloud service providers, with different schemas and operating domains, and possibly multiple versions of cloud services in each domain and for each provider. VM Hub is a managed cloud service, which offers the following benefits to multimedia service developers and application developers.

Multimedia Service Developers: VM Hub makes it easier for the multimedia service developers to build distributed multimedia systems and deploy the systems in cloud. VM Hub includes an open sourced Client Library, toolkit and sample code that allows a multimedia developer to quickly turn his/her multimedia application into a hosted multimedia service endpoint with less than one day of programming work (estimated). Once the multimedia application is turned into a service endpoint, it has the following benefits:

- The multimedia application becomes accessible as a cloud service, and can be consumed all over the world, by applications (on Windows/Linux platform), or by mobile applications.
- The developers can launch more than one instance of service endpoints, either on a local machine, on a set of local computer cluster, or in a public cloud.
- Automatic load balancing among service endpoints is provided by VM Hub.
- If one or more service endpoints fail, VM Hub will automatically route the request to another live endpoint.
- The developer may implement multiple versions of the same multimedia service. The newer version of the service may run concurrently with the old version of the service. This allows the developer to seamlessly test, upgrade and migrate his/her multimedia applications to newer versions without service disruption during the upgrade.

Multimedia Application and Mobile Application Developers: VM Hub turns multimedia service call into standard RESTful web service [1] that is accessible globally from a wide range of platforms, including both desktop applications (on Windows, Linux, Mac platform) and mobile Apps (on Windows Phone, Android, and iOS). For ease to develop against, we include a VM Hub Application Library that implements the consumption of RESTful services in the form of a Portable Class Library, which can be used by both Windows Phone, Windows Store Apps, and desktop application on Windows and Linux (via Mono). It can also be used via Xamarin Suite to develop Android and iOS Apps. With VM Hub, the Multimedia Application developers can quickly develop their own apps across different mobile platforms (Windows Phone, Android and iOS) against either their own multimedia services or third party multimedia services in the cloud.

MM'15, October 26-30, 2015, Brisbane, Australia
ACM 978-1-4503-3459-4/15/10.
http://dx.doi.org/10.1145/2733373.2807416

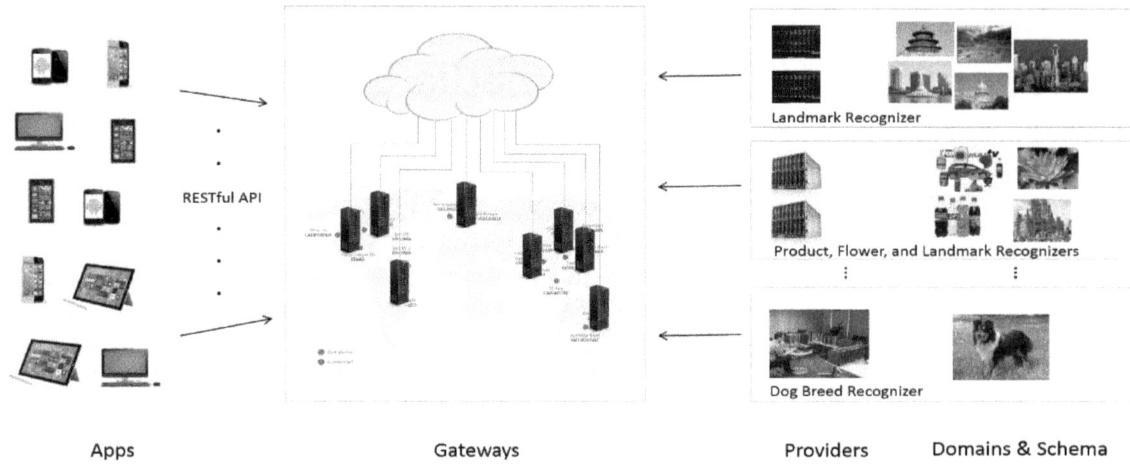

Figure 1 VHub architecture diagram: Apps, gateways, providers, domains and schema.

2. VM HUB Component

2.1 VM Hub Gateways

VM Hub runs a managed global cluster of gateways, with servers at different geographic location (the blue dot in Fig. 1). VM Hub gateways are centrally managed to make sure that the gateway service is available 24x7, with a reliable service level that can be consumed.

2.2 VM Hub: Service Endpoint.

VM Hub leverages Prajna, an open sourced distributed functional programming platform to turn any single-machine multimedia service (be it on GPU or CPU) into a cloud service. We will teach the steps to wrap an existing multimedia service into a service endpoint, so that it can be deployed in multiple nodes with failover support over either public cloud and/or private server. The programming steps include:

- Prepare a remote execution roster: For managed code, VM Hub can automatically traverse the code and figure out the .Net assemblies needed to execute the code. If the application calls unmanaged DLLs or executables, or use data file (e.g., machine learning models), the developer need to provide a roster of files (or directory) to be included for execution.
- Remote instance: The developer will need to extend a remote instance class that runs the functionality of the service endpoint. The developer also needs to register each multimedia service with its schema and the domains as a callback function. When the gateway receives a cloud service call of the associated multimedia service, the callback function will be invoked to service the request.
- Deployment: We provide scripts to deploy the resultant recognizer to either Azure VM (Microsoft provides an educational program that allows you to run free cloud service in Azure). Alternatively, you can deploy the recognizer on a group of server that you own.
- Failover Support: VM Hub is resilient to failure of either front end gateway and/or back end recognizer servers. We will teach the failover mechanism implemented and teach how the developers can take advantage of them.
- Telemetry and Monitoring: We will discuss tools that are included in VM Hub to provide real-time telemetry of the operation of the service endpoints. The default monitored information include: network roundtrip time to each front end gateway, the collection of domains that are being recognized, the average, medium, 90-percentile and 99.9-percentile latency of serving a request, and the average, medium, 90-percentile and 99.9-percentile latency of the request staying in queue waiting to be serviced.

3. Course outline

The outline of the course is as follows:

1. Introduction
2. VM Hub Cloud Architecture (1.5 hours)
2.1 Domain & recognition provider (5 min)
2.2 VM Hub gateways (10 min)
  Life cycle of a VHub Request
  Distribution policy
  Aggregation policy
2.3 VM Hub back end recognizers (75 min)
  Turn an application into a cloud based service
  Remote execution roster
  Remote instance
  Deployment script
  Failover support
  Telemetry and monitoring service
3. VM Hub Apps (1.5 hour)
  VHub API and client library (40 min)
  Cross platform app development by Xamarin (5 min)
  Windows phone app development (15 min)
  Android app development (15 min)
  iOS app development (15 min)
4. Summary

4. References

[1]. Richardson, Leonard, and Sam Ruby. RESTful web services." O'Reilly Media, Inc.", 2008.

[2]. https://msdn.microsoft.com/en-us/library/gg597391(v=vs.110).aspx

Interactive Video Search

Klaus Schoeffmann
Klagenfurt University
Universitätsstr. 65-67,
A-9020 Klagenfurt, Austria
ks@itec.aau.at

Frank Hopfgartner
University of Glasgow
11 University Gardens, Glasgow G12
8QH, UK
frank.hopfgartner@glasgow.ac.uk

ABSTRACT

With an increasing amount of video data in our daily life, the need for content-based search in videos increases as well. Though a lot of research has been spent on video retrieval tools and methods which allow for automatic search in videos through content-based queries, still the performance of automatic video retrieval is far from optimal. In this tutorial we discussed (i) proposed solutions for improved video content navigation, (ii) typical interaction of content-based querying features, and (iii) advanced video content visualization methods. Moreover, we discussed interactive video search systems and ways to evaluate their performance.

Categories and Subject Descriptors

H.4 [**Information Systems Applications**]: Miscellaneous

General Terms

Experimentation

Keywords

Interactive Video Retrieval; Search; Tutorial

1. INTRODUCTION

Over the last two decades, there has been a lot of research on content-based video retrieval to solve the task of finding the proper scene of interest in a large video archive. However, there are still well-known limitations with video retrieval applications. First, there is the *usability gap*. A user is often not able to express his/her needs and thoughts through text, a challenge that is already apparent for an image ("*An image is worth a thousand words.*") but much worse for a video segment consisting of many images. Additionally, the issue of *polysemy* is a challenging problem in text-based search, which can only be partially solved through relevance feedback. Similarly, an automatic retrieval tool cannot easily determine the user-dependent relative importance (i.e., weight) of a query term and hence often returns too many irrelevant results. Finally, there is another challenging problem that affects the content-based indexing phase, namely the *semantic gap*, which is the discrepancy between the semantics a user can derive from an image and the information a computer can extract from pixel values [15]. The semantic gap seriously limits the achievable performance of visual information retrieval tools.

There is consensus in the multimedia community that content-based retrieval approaches should have a stronger focus on the human behind the retrieval application [4, 16]. Instead of making small improvements in the field of content-based indexing and retrieval, video search tools should aim at more intense integration of the user into the search process, focusing on interactive video search [2, 3, 7, 8] rather than automatic querying. Interactive video search follows this idea of intense user integration with advanced content interaction and provides a powerful alternative to the common video retrieval approach [12]. It is known as the process of interactive video content exploration with the help of content navigation [9], summarization [1], on-demand querying [14], and browsing of querying results or filtered content [5]. In contrast to typical video retrieval, such interactive video search tools give more control to the user and provide flexible search and browsing features instead of focusing on the *query-and-browse-results* approach. Hence, even if the performance of content analysis is not optimal, there is a chance that a smart user could compensate shortcomings through clever use of available features.

Interactive video search tools support *directed* and *undirected* search scenarios. In the first scenario, users have a clear information need and want to find a specific target segment in the video (e.g., the weather forecast in a news show); such a search is also known as *known-item search* or *target search*. In the second scenario, users have no concrete search goal but want to explore the content in order to learn or find something interesting (e.g., a violent scene in surveillance videos); such a search scenario is known as *exploratory search*. Users need exploratory search when they cannot sufficiently describe the desired content, e.g., through a query in a video retrieval tool, or when they just want to browse instead of search (i.e., without a concrete desired scene).

Over the years many tools for interactive video search (often known as video browsing or video exploration tools) have been proposed in the literature (see [12, 13] for a survey), and it has been shown that these tools can effectively help users find desired content in videos (e.g., [1, 14]). Some of these tools combine sophisticated content analysis methods controlled by the user for their personal needs [10]. Some

MM'15, October 26–30, 2015, Brisbane, Australia
ACM 978-1-4503-3459-4/15/10.
DOI: http://dx.doi.org/10.1145/2733373.2807417.

others provide rather simple content navigation features but give the users more interactivity to allow them to effectively take advantage of their knowledge about the content and the content structure [11]. Interestingly, it has been shown that tools of the latter kind can even outperform tools of the first kind for some search tasks [10].

2. LEARNING OBJECTIVE

This tutorial gave a broad overview of solutions in two areas: (1) video retrieval, and (2) interactive video search. We discussed state-of-the-art approaches, but also the current shortcomings and outlined important research tasks for the future of multimedia search and retrieval. Our discussion also covered tools and methods that originate from the Human-Computer-Interaction (HCI) community, which many people in the multimedia community might not be aware of yet. The tutorial provided the basis to elevate research on video retrieval to the next level.

Target audience were researchers and practitioners in the field of multimedia analysis and information access. The participants learned best practice on how to interact with multimedia content and should be able to apply this knowledge in their own project upon completion of the tutorial.

Following an introduction of the subject matter, we highlighted the need for interactive video search and outlined well-known issues and current research areas. Then, we presented different graphical user interfaces that are designed to address these challenges. We started by presenting commercial and academic video search systems that represent the state-of-the-art in video search. In order to illustrate the limitations of video search, we began with an introduction to video content analysis. In particular, we focused on the segmentation of videos into different units of retrieval (i.e., video shots and semantically coherent scenes), argued for the selection of appropriate keyframes and explained how to index these video materials. Then, we overviewed methods for video content presentation, namely abstraction, summarization, and visualization of video content. After that, we introduced different methods to interact with video content. We showcased the advantages of browsing and exploration of video content, methods to navigate through the content, querying and sketching interfaces. Following this session, the participants learned how to evaluate the performance of video search engines. We introduced the de-facto standard evaluation protocol that is applied for scientific performance evaluation. Furthermore, we introduced popular Academic evaluation campaigns, namely the Known-Item search task promoted by TRECVid and the Video Browser Showdown. As an outlook in upcoming research challenges, we introduced a special case of multimedia search, namely access to visual lifelogs [6]. With the ever increasing amount of wearable devices that are released nowadays, people have the opportunity to capture vast amount of heterogeneous data (e.g., images, sensor readings, videos) that depict aspects of their personal lives. In the last part of the tutorial, we introduced approaches to access and display these "lifelogs".

Acknowledgments

This work was funded by the Austrian Federal Ministry for Transport, Innovation and Technology (bmvit), Austrian Science Fund (FWF): TRP 273-N15, and the ERDF.

3. REFERENCES

[1] B. Adams, S. Greenhill, and S. Venkatesh. Towards a video browser for the digital native. In *ICMEW'12*, pages 127–132, July 2012.

[2] M. Christel, C. Huang, N. Moraveji, and N. Papernick. Exploiting multiple modalities for interactive video retrieval. In *ICASSP'04*, volume 3, pages iii–1032, May 2004.

[3] M. G. Christel and R. Yan. Merging storyboard strategies and automatic retrieval for improving interactive video search. In *CIVR'07*, pages 486–493, New York, NY, USA, 2007. ACM.

[4] R. Datta, D. Joshi, J. Li, and J. Z. Wang. Image retrieval: Ideas, influences, and trends of the new age. *ACM Computing Surveys*, 40(2):5:1–5:60, May 2008.

[5] A. Girgensohn, F. Shipman, and L. Wilcox. Adaptive clustering and interactive visualizations to support the selection of video clips. In *ICMR '11*, pages 34:1–34:8, New York, NY, USA, 2011. ACM.

[6] C. Gurrin, A. F. Smeaton, and A. R. Doherty. Lifelogging: Personal big data. *Foundations and Trends in Information Retrieval*, 8(1):1–125, 2014.

[7] F. Hopfgartner. *Understanding Video Retrieval*. VDM Verlag, 2007.

[8] F. Hopfgartner, J. Urban, R. Villa, and J. M. Jose. Simulated testing of an adaptive multimedia information retrieval system. In *CBMI'07*, pages 328–335, 2007.

[9] J. Huber, J. Steimle, and M. Mühlhäuser. Toward more efficient user interfaces for mobile video browsing: An in-depth exploration of the design space. In *MM'10*, pages 341–350, New York, NY, USA, 2010.

[10] K. Schoeffmann, D. Ahlström, W. Bailer, C. Cobârzan, F. Hopfgartner, K. McGuinness, C. Gurrin, C. Frisson, D.-D. Le, M. Del Fabro, H. Bai, and W. Weiss. The video browser showdown: a live evaluation of interactive video search tools. *IJMIR*, 3(2):113–127, 2014.

[11] K. Schoeffmann and L. Boeszoermenyi. Video browsing using interactive navigation summaries. In *CBMI'09*, pages 243–248, Chania, Crete, June 2009.

[12] K. Schoeffmann, F. Hopfgartner, O. Marques, L. Boeszoermenyi, and J. M. Jose. Video browsing interfaces and applications: a review. *SPIE Reviews*, 1(1):1–35(018004), 2010.

[13] K. Schoeffmann, J. Huber, and M. A. Hudelist. Video interaction tools: A survey of recent work. *ACM Computing Surveys*, pages 1–36, 2015. Accepted for publication.

[14] K. Schoeffmann, M. Taschwer, and L. Boeszoermenyi. The video explorer: A tool for navigation and searching within a single video based on fast content analysis. In *MMSys'10*, pages 247–258. ACM, 2010.

[15] A. W. M. Smeulders, M. Worring, S. Santini, A. Gupta, and R. Jain. Content-based image retrieval at the end of the early years. *TPAMI*, 22(12):1349–1380, Dec 2000.

[16] M. Worring, P. Sajda, S. Santini, D. A. Shamma, A. F. Smeaton, and Q. Yang. Where is the user in multimedia retrieval? *IEEE MultiMedia*, 19(4):6–10, 2012.

Learning Knowledge Bases for Multimedia in 2015

Lexing Xie
Australian National University
Canberra, Australia
lexing.xie@anu.edu.au

Haixun Wang
Facebook Inc.
Mountain View, CA, USA
haixun@gmail.com

ABSTRACT

Knowledge acquisition, representation, and reasoning has been one of the long-standing challenges in artificial intelligence and related application areas. Only in the past few years, massive amounts of structured and semi-structured data that directly or indirectly encode human knowledge became widely available, turning the knowledge representation problems into a computational grand challenge with feasible solutions in sight. The research and development on knowledge bases is becoming a lively fusion area among web information extraction, machine learning, databases and information retrieval, with knowledge over images and multimedia emerging as another new frontier of representation and acquisition. This tutorial aims to present a gentle overview of knowledge bases on text and multimedia, including representation, acquisition, and inference. In particular, the 2015 edition of the tutorial will include recent progress from several active research communities: web, natural language processing, and computer vision and multimedia.

Category and Subject Descriptors I.2.6 ARTIFICIAL INTELLIGENCE Learning — Knowledge acquisition

Keywords knowledge graph, multimedia, learning.

1. INTRODUCTION

Knowledge is one of the key resources for processing noisy, ambiguous, and scarce input of multiple types – those commonly found in problems concerning multimedia. The challenges lie in every aspect of knowledge acquisition, representation, and inference. much recent progress has been made on knowledge intensive text and multimedia processing. This tutorial will survey recent advances on this topic, and discuss fundamental problems, techniques as well as open issues in this vibrant area.

In 2014–2015 there has been a number of new developments in constructing knowledge bases from text and images, and in different application areas. In this tutorial we will cover a unified view of relation learning [18], as well as a comprehensive benchmark on knowledge acquisition from the web and knowledge base completion [7]. In application areas related to multimedia, we will discuss a few new systems for image captioning [23, 4, 9, 6] and the emerging application of automatically composing and answering questions about images [1, 20, 10].

MM'15, Oct, 2015, Brisbane, Australia.
ACM 978-1-4503-3459-4/15/10.
http://dx.doi.org/10.1145/2733373.2807418 .

2. TUTORIAL OVERVIEW

This tutorial is structured in three main parts. The first part introduces the background and foundations of knowledge bases, the second part focuses on knowledge acquisition from text and hyper-text data, the third part discusses acquiring and applying knowledge for image and multimedia collections.

Introduction and foundations

- A brief history of knowledge bases. We will present a brief historic note contracting knowledge bases from the mid-1980s, from Cyc [14], Wordnet [17], to other manually curated sources such as ConceptNet [16].
- Introduction to knowledge representation. We will discuss the basic representation of knowledge as multi-relational graphs, and compare-and-contrast example contemporary knowledge bases that possess rich node structure, rich edge information, and their different uses.
- The cognitive science of knowledge structure and representation. This part will present relevant literature in cognitive science about the foundation of knowledge structure. We will discuss Rosch's theory of categorization, as well as work in the macroscopic structure of semantic networks [2], and predicting human memory search [11].

Knowledge acquisition, representation and inference for text

Language is the primary medium for encoding and disseminating knowledge. The representation of real-world knowledge in multimedia is tightly connected to, and often grounded in textual representations. This section covers fundamental and frontier techniques web-scale knowledge bases, and paves the way for discussing research challenges on multimedia knowledge.

- Information extraction from web-scale text. We will introduce systems such as YAGO [22], NELL [3], ReVerb [8], Probase [24] that focus on acquiring knowledge from text. We will also discuss core challenges such as bias from syntactic patterns, and how to evaluate the quality of acquired knowledge.

- Building a data driven semantic network. We will discuss how to score the data using measures such as typicality, basic level of categorization, similarity.
- The conceptualization mechanism. We will discuss how inferencing using the semantic network benefits semantic text processing.
- Applications of knowledge graphs.

Knowledge acquisition and applications for multimedia

- Knowledge and relations in computer vision and image understanding. We will discuss a set of diverse set of approaches to represent and acquire knowledge in computer vision, including Visipedia [19], attribute-based visual recognition, and image understanding with knowledge from WordNet.
- Learning knowledge graphs for multimedia. We will discuss a set of diverse set of approaches for constructing knowledge graphs from images and multimedia, from learning relationships within the visual modality [5], to grounding a textual databases to image instances, to learning knowledge graphs from parallel corpora of media and text.
- Embedding and recommendation models for relationship learning. We take a closer look at several mathematical models for learning knowledge relations from rich media, from relation learning as recommendation [21], to inverse random walk approaches [25].
- Application of multimedia knowledge. We will discuss classical and emerging applications, such as natural language generation [13, 12], video question-answering [15], and others.

We conclude the tutorial with a view to the open research and application challenges. Tutorial materials and an annotated bibliography will be released online. The audience of this tutorial will take away in-depth knowledge on the construction and application of knowledge graphs, acquire a crucial understanding in the technical challenges in designing and using a knowledge graph, and develop an appreciation to state-of-the-art tools and techniques at the frontiers of this area.

Acknowledgments This work was supported in part by the Australian Research Council under project DP140102185.

3. REFERENCES

[1] S. Antol, A. Agrawal, J. Lu, M. Mitchell, D. Batra, C. L. Zitnick, and D. Parikh. Vqa: Visual question answering. *arXiv preprint arXiv:1505.00468*, 2015.

[2] J. Borge-Holthoefer and A. Arenas. Semantic networks: Structure and dynamics. *Entropy*, 12(5):1264–1302, 2010.

[3] A. Carlson, J. Betteridge, B. Kisiel, B. Settles, E. R. Hruschka Jr, and T. M. Mitchell. Toward an architecture for never-ending language learning. In *AAAI*, 2010.

[4] X. Chen and C. Lawrence Zitnick. Mind's eye: A recurrent visual representation for image caption generation. In *The IEEE Conference on Computer Vision and Pattern Recognition (CVPR)*, June 2015.

[5] X. Chen, A. Shrivastava, and A. Gupta. Neil: Extracting visual knowledge from web data. ICCV, 2013.

[6] J. Donahue, L. A. Hendricks, S. Guadarrama, M. Rohrbach, S. Venugopalan, K. Saenko, and T. Darrell. Long-term recurrent convolutional networks for visual recognition and description. In *CVPR*, June 2015.

[7] X. Dong, E. Gabrilovich, G. Heitz, W. Horn, N. Lao, K. Murphy, T. Strohmann, S. Sun, and W. Zhang. Knowledge vault. In *Proceedings of the 20th ACM SIGKDD international conference on Knowledge discovery and data mining - KDD '14*, pages 601–610, 2014.

[8] O. Etzioni, M. Banko, S. Soderland, and D. S. Weld. Open information extraction from the web. *Communications of the ACM*, 51(12):68–74, 2008.

[9] H. Fang, S. Gupta, F. Iandola, R. K. Srivastava, L. Deng, P. Dollar, J. Gao, X. He, M. Mitchell, J. C. Platt, C. Lawrence Zitnick, and G. Zweig. From captions to visual concepts and back. In *The IEEE Conference on Computer Vision and Pattern Recognition (CVPR)*, June 2015.

[10] H. Gao, J. Mao, J. Zhou, Z. Huang, L. Wang, and W. Xu. Are you talking to a machine? dataset and methods for multilingual image question answering. *arXiv preprint arXiv:1505.05612*, 2015.

[11] T. L. Griffiths, M. Steyvers, and A. Firl. Google and the mind: Predicting fluency with pagerank. *Psychological Science*, 18(12):1069–1076, 2007.

[12] M. Hodosh, P. Young, and J. Hockenmaier. Framing image description as a ranking task: Data, models and evaluation metrics. *Journal of Artificial Intelligence Research*, pages 853–899, 2013.

[13] G. Kulkarni, V. Premraj, S. Dhar, S. Li, Y. Choi, A. C. Berg, and T. L. Berg. Baby talk: Understanding and generating simple image descriptions. In *CVPR*, pages 1601–1608. IEEE, 2011.

[14] D. B. Lenat. Cyc: A large-scale investment in knowledge infrastructure. *Communications of the ACM*, 38(11):33–38, 1995.

[15] G. Li, Z. Ming, H. Li, and T.-S. Chua. Video reference: question answering on youtube. MM '09, pages 773–776, 2009.

[16] H. Liu and P. Singh. ConceptNet – a practical commonsense reasoning tool-kit. *BT technology journal*, 22(4):211–226, 2004.

[17] G. Miller. WordNet: a lexical database for English. *Communications of the ACM*, 38(11):39–41, 1995.

[18] M. Nickel, K. Murphy, V. Tresp, and E. Gabrilovich. A review of relational machine learning for knowledge graphs: From multi-relational link prediction to automated knowledge graph construction. *arXiv preprint arXiv:1503.00759*, 2015.

[19] P. Perona. Vision of a visipedia. *Proceedings of the IEEE*, 98(8):1526–1534, 2010.

[20] M. Ren, R. Kiros, and R. Zemel. Image question answering: A visual semantic embedding model and a new dataset. *arXiv preprint arXiv:1505.02074*, 2015.

[21] S. Riedel, L. Yao, A. Mccallum, and B. M. Marlin. Relation Extraction with Matrix Factorization and Universal Schemas. In *HLT-NAACL '13*, 2013.

[22] F. M. Suchanek, G. Kasneci, and G. Weikum. Yago: A Core of Semantic Knowledge. In *WWW '07*, 2007.

[23] O. Vinyals, A. Toshev, S. Bengio, and D. Erhan. Show and tell: A neural image caption generator. In *The IEEE Conference on Computer Vision and Pattern Recognition (CVPR)*, June 2015.

[24] W. Wu, H. Li, H. Wang, and K. Q. Zhu. Probase: a probabilistic taxonomy for text understanding. SIGMOD, 2012.

[25] L. Xie and X. He. Picture tags and world knowledge: Learning tag relations from visual semantic sources. In *ACM Multimedia*, October 2013.

Image Tag Assignment, Refinement and Retrieval

Xirong Li*
Renmin University of China
xirong@ruc.edu.cn

Tiberio Uricchio*
University of Florence
tiberio.uricchio@unifi.it

Lamberto Ballan
University of Florence &
Stanford University
lballan@cs.stanford.edu

Marco Bertini
University of Florence
marco.bertini@unifi.it

Cees G.M. Snoek
University of Amsterdam &
Qualcomm Research
Netherlands
cgmsnoek@uva.nl

Alberto Del Bimbo
University of Florence
alberto.delbimbo@unifi.it

ABSTRACT

This tutorial focuses on challenges and solutions for content-based image annotation and retrieval in the context of online image sharing and tagging. We present a unified review on three closely linked problems, i.e., tag assignment, tag refinement, and tag-based image retrieval. We introduce a taxonomy to structure the growing literature, understand the ingredients of the main works, clarify their connections and difference, and recognize their merits and limitations. Moreover, we present an open-source testbed, with training sets of varying sizes and three test datasets, to evaluate methods of varied learning complexity. A selected set of eleven representative works have been implemented and evaluated. During the tutorial we provide a practice session for hands on experience with the methods, software and datasets. For repeatable experiments all data and code are online at `http://www.micc.unifi.it/tagsurvey`.

Categories and Subject Descriptors

H.3.3 [**INFORMATION STORAGE AND RETRIEVAL**]: Information Search and Retrieval; H.3.1 [**INFORMATION STORAGE AND RETRIEVAL**]: Content Analysis and Indexing—*Indexing Methods*

General Terms

Algorithms, Experimentation, Performance

Keywords

Content-based image retrieval, social tagging, tag relevance, tag assignment, tag refinement, tag retrieval

*Equal contribution and corresponding authors.

MM'15 October 26-30, 2015, Brisbane, Australia.
ACM 978-1-4503-3459-4/15/10.
DOI: http://dx.doi.org/10.1145/2733373.2807419.

1. TUTORIAL DESCRIPTION

Several technological developments have spurred the sharing of images in unprecedented volumes. The first is the ease with which images can be captured in a digital format by cameras, cellphones and other wearable sensory devices. The second is the Internet that allows transfer of digital image content to anyone, anywhere in the world. Finally, and most recently, the sharing of digital imagery has reached new heights by the massive adoption of social network platforms. All of a sudden images came with tags, and tagging, commenting, and rating of any digital image has become a common habit. Despite this downpour of images and tags, the problem of annotating and searching a particular image is still largely unsolved. It has instead dilated the problem with the demand of reliable and objective image tags.

In this tutorial we focus on challenges in content-based image annotation and retrieval in the context of social image sharing and tagging, with a unified review on three closely linked problems in the field, i.e., image tag assignment, tag refinement, and tag-based image retrieval.

Existing works in tag assignment, refinement, and retrieval vary in terms of their targeted tasks and methodology, making it non-trivial to interpret them within a unified framework. We reckon that all works rely on the key functionality of *tag relevance*, i.e., estimating the relevance of a specific tag with respect to the visual content of a given image. Given such a tag relevance function, one can perform tag assignment and refinement by sorting tags in light of the function, and retrieve images by sorting them accordingly. We present a taxonomy, which structures the rich literature along two dimensions, namely *media* and *learning*. The media dimension characterizes what essential information the tag relevance function exploits, while the learning dimension depicts how such information is exploited. With this taxonomy, we discuss connections and difference between the many methods, their advantages as well as limitations.

Comparative evaluation of methods and systems is imperative to appreciate progress. In spite of the growing literature in the field, there is a lack of consensus on the performance of the individual methods. This is largely due to the fact that existing works either use homemade data, which are not publicly accessible, or use selected subsets of benchmark data. Consequently we present an open-source test bed, with training sets of different sizes to evaluate methods of varied learning complexity, and three test sets contributed

Table 1: Methods evaluated in this tutorial. The media column characterizes what essential information a specific method exploits, while the learning SemanticField depicts how such information is exploited.

Method	Media	Learning	Code
SemanticField [11]	tag	Instance based	Python
TagCooccur [9]	tag	Instance based	Python
TagRanking [6]	tag + image	Instance based	Python
KNN [7]	tag + image	Instance based	C + Python
TagVote [4]	tag + image	Instance based	C + Python
TagCooccur+ [4]	tag + image	Instance based	Python
TagProp [2]	tag + image	Model based	C + Matlab + Python
TagFeature [1]	tag + image	Model based	C + Python
RelExample [3]	tag + image	Model based	C + Python
RobustPCA [10]	tag + image	Transduction based	C + Matlab + Python
TensorAnalysis [8]	tag + image + user	Transduction based	–[1]

by various research groups. A selected set of eleven representative works, i.e., SemanticField [11], TagRanking [6], KNN [7], TagVote [4], TagProp [2], TagCooccur [9], TagCooccur+ [4], TagFeature [1], RelExample [3], RobustPCA [10], TensorAnalysis [8], have been implemented and evaluated on the test bed for tag assignment, refinement, and/or retrieval. An overview of the methods is given in Table 1. The interested reader is referred to [5] for a comprehensive comparison between these methods.

During the tutorial, we also provide a practice session for hands on experience with the methods, software, and datasets. For each method a front-end pipeline is implemented, allowing users to conduct tag relevance learning from scratch, obtain tag ranks and image ranks accordingly, and report multiple performance metrics including image-centric Mean image Average Precision (MiAP), tag-centric Mean Average Precision (MAP), and Normalized Discounted Cumulative Gain (NDCG). In addition, Python wrappers for C and Matlab code are given for the ease of cross-platform use.

We conclude the course with our perspective on the many challenges and opportunities ahead for the multimedia community.

A survey paper entitled "Socializing the Semantic Gap: A Comparative Survey on Image Tag Assignment, Refinement and Retrieval" (`http://arxiv.org/abs/1503.08248`) [5] completes the material given to the attendees.

Acknowledgments. This research is supported by Natural Science Foundation of China (No. 61303184), the Fundamental Research Funds for the Central Universities and the Research Funds of Renmin University of China (No. 14XNLQ01), SRFDP (No. 20130004120006), the Dutch national program COMMIT, the STW STORY project, Telecom Italia PhD grant funds, and the AQUIS-CH project granted by the Tuscany Region (Italy). L. Ballan acknowledges also the support of the EC's FP7 under the grant agreement No. 623930 (Marie Curie IOF).

2. REFERENCES

[1] L. Chen, D. Xu, I. Tsang, and J. Luo. Tag-based image retrieval improved by augmented features and group-based refinement. *IEEE Transactions on Multimedia*, 14(4):1057–1067, 2012.

[2] M. Guillaumin, T. Mensink, J. Verbeek, and C. Schmid. TagProp: Discriminative metric learning in nearest neighbor models for image auto-annotation. In *Proc. of ICCV*, 2009.

[3] X. Li and C. Snoek. Classifying tag relevance with relevant positive and negative examples. In *Proc. of ACM Multimedia*, 2013.

[4] X. Li, C. Snoek, and M. Worring. Learning social tag relevance by neighbor voting. *IEEE Transactions on Multimedia*, 11(7):1310–1322, 2009.

[5] X. Li, T. Uricchio, L. Ballan, M. Bertini, C. Snoek, and A. Del Bimbo. Socializing the semantic gap: A comparative survey on image tag assignment, refinement and retrieval. *CoRR*, abs/1503.08248, 2015.

[6] D. Liu, X.-S. Hua, L. Yang, M. Wang, and H.-J. Zhang. Tag ranking. In *Proc. of WWW*, 2009.

[7] A. Makadia, V. Pavlovic, and S. Kumar. Baselines for image annotation. *International Journal of Computer Vision*, 90(1):88–105, 2010.

[8] J. Sang, C. Xu, and J. Liu. User-aware image tag refinement via ternary semantic analysis. *IEEE Transactions on Multimedia*, 14(3):883–895, 2012.

[9] B. Sigurbjörnsson and R. van Zwol. Flickr tag recommendation based on collective knowledge. In *Proc. of WWW*, 2008.

[10] G. Zhu, S. Yan, and Y. Ma. Image tag refinement towards low-rank, content-tag prior and error sparsity. In *Proc. of ACM Multimedia*, 2010.

[11] S. Zhu, Y.-G. Jiang, and C.-W. Ngo. Sampling and ontologically pooling web images for visual concept learning. *IEEE Transactions on Multimedia*, 14(4):1068–1078, 2012.

[1]Results provided by the method developers.

Tutorial on Emotional and Social Signals for Multimedia Research

Hayley Hung*
TU Delft
The Netherlands
h.hung@tudelft.nl

Hatice Gunes*
Queen Mary University of London
London, United Kingdom
h.gunes@qmul.ac.uk

Categories and Subject Descriptors

H.1.2 [**Models and Principles**]: User/Machine Systems Human Information Processing; H.3.1 [**Information Storage and Retrieval**]: Content Analysis and Indexing Methods; I.2.10 [**Vision and scene understanding**]: Video analysis; I.5.2 [**Design Methodoloy**]: Features evaluatio nand selection, Classifier design and evaluation; I.5.4 [**Applications**]: Signal processing

Keywords

Social signal processing; Human-centred Multimedia; Affective Computing; Audio/Visual emotion recognition; Personality computing

1. MOTIVATION

In 2006, Jaimes et al. [3] wrote about the role of human-centered computing (HCC) for Multimedia, finally devising a research agenda for Human-centered multimedia (HCM). Since then, the importance of humans in all aspects of multimedia research has increased significantly leading to an explosion in multimedia computing that exploits data coming from online social multimedia such as tags, social networks, etc. However, as the area grows and the research links between multimedia systems and humans become closer, theories and practices from other domains (namely social, behavioural, and emotional psychology, social signal processing, and affective computing) need to be more fully integrated into multimedia computing practices.

In 2014, ACM MM launched a new area on emotional and social signals in multimedia that received many submissions and had a full session during the conference. Concurrently to this, a panel discussion was held at the conference organised by ourselves, Lexing Xie, and Bjoern Schuller to discuss the state of play for emotional and social signals in Multimedia research. By the end of the panel a number of clear challenges to integrate emotional and social signals into core multimedia research domains became apparent as clear multimedia concerns, which we summarised later in [1].

A challenge for human-centred multimedia is the analysis of human communicative behaviour in multimedia content when considering especially the spontaneous non-verbal signals that are generated by humans when interacting with each other. These signals require a slightly different approach to multimedia computing where the methods developed need findings from other disciplines such as social and behavioural psychology, affective computing or social signal processing. Considering the shift of much of the multimedia community towards the close-captioning of images and video, the next step is clearly to consider both the social and affective content of these videos or images. Moreover, as much of multimedia content creation shifts towards portable mobile devices, we must also start to consider the role of other signals coming from mobile and wearable devices in enriching multimedia content creation, retreival, and consumption.

It is clear that there are many gaps in understanding between the affective computing, social signal processing, and multimedia community that prohibit a significant push towards more synergistic research in the present as well as the future. Understanding about the nature of emotional and social signals, the existing theories and practices that surround these two fields, and finally thinking about how to bring these two domains into closer contact with core multimedia concerns will certainly help to accelerate this process.

To address this gap we have written an article in IEEE Multimedia Magazine April 2015 edition [1] that summarises the findings of the panel but also tries to piece together and find structure in the gaps between the three domains. During the writing of this article, it became clear that how to dissect and fill the gap was something that was not immediately obvious to us. By using this article as an accompanying text for the tutorial, we will dive deeper into the issues initially described there. We therefore encourage the attendees (and the readers of this tutorial abstract) to read the article [1] prior to attending the tutorial.

2. AIM

This tutorial is aimed at researchers of all levels. Our aim for this tutorial is to help researchers to be able to understand more clearly where the gaps in knowledge lie, know the key references that provide foundations for research on emotional and social signals, and to avoid the pitfalls of ill-informed experimental assumptions or design. Moreover, the interleaved breakout sessions will encourage attendees to continuously reflect individually and collectively on the tutorial material so as to understand better how the gap can be closed in a practical manner.

We have seen often that experimental design choices can seriously compromise whether papers are accepted - while the technical contribution and experimental evaluation are sufficient, the understanding of how to handle the human element can often be over-simplified, without any reference to prior work from other disciplines. In an emerging domain, this can be extremely dangerous. On the one hand, work can be accepted to stimulate the commu-

*H. Hung and H.Gunes contributed equally to this tutorial.

MM'15, October 26–30, 2015, Brisbane, Australia.
ACM 978-1-4503-3459-4/15/10.
http://dx.doi.org/10.1145/2733373.2807420 .

nity while still containing flawed experimental design and debate. On the other hand, once accepted, these works become exemplars for others who then follow the same ill-informed choices as the accepted papers. We hope that this kind of cycle can be minimised by this tutorial and also provide awareness to the attendees of where pitfalls can be.

3. OUTLINE

The half-day tutorial on Analysis of Emotions for Multimedia Applications at ACM Multimedia 2012 [2], by one of the organisers, demonstrated the need for interactivity and discussions in such multidisciplinary tutorials. Therefore the aim of this tutorial is to disseminate basic foundational concepts in emotional and social signal research in a very practical and interactive manner. The interactive component is very important to us and thus the day will be interleaved with lectures and breakout sessions and discussions in smaller groups where attendees will be able to discuss the information they have learned in the first half and relate it back to their own research work.

Break out sessions will be followed by reporting to the entire class where the tutors will coordinate and summarise findings to help attendees understand how to break down tasks involving emotional and social signals, and multimedia into more easily manageable assignments. This could include discussions related to specific research directions, experimental design procedures, the appropriate use of theories from the social and affective sciences, or multimedia computing ethos etc.

The one day tutorial is broken down into the following themes and activities:

1. Preliminaries: This will cover an introduction to affective signals and social signals as well as discussions about where emotional and social signals are in multimedia data and multimedia computing in general.

2. Group Discussion and Reflection: Based on the tutorial material, each attendee summarises their research to each other in small groups and discusses ways in which their research is currently related to, or could integrate more, social and emotional signals research. Discussions will be summarised and discussed further with the class.

3. Putting it all together: State of the art research that considers emotional and/or social signals and multimedia will be described. A few selected papers will be used as case studies to discuss the strengths and weaknesses of the work with respect to multimedia computing as well as affective computing and social signal processing.

4. Closing the gap: Based on the tutorial material, in small groups, each attendee summarises their research to each other and discusses ways in which their research is related to, or could integrate more, social and emotional signals research (for people working mostly on multimedia) or multimedia research (for those working more on affective of social signals research). All discussions will be sumarised and shared with the class.

5. Wrap-up and Discussion: The tutors summarise the discussions in relation to the themes of the tutorial and ask attendees to reflect on what they have learned and what action points they might take as a result of the tutorial.

4. BIOGRAPHIES

Hatice Gunes is a Senior Lecturer (Associate Professor) at Queen Mary University of London, leading the Affective and Human Computing Lab. Her research interests lie in the multidisciplinary areas of affective computing and social signal processing, focusing on automatic analysis of emotional and social behavior and human aesthetic canons, multimodal interaction, computer vision, machine learning, and human-computer and human-robot interactions. She published over 75 technical papers in these areas (Google scholar citations>1700, H-index=20) and was a recipient of awards for Outstanding Paper (IEEE FG'11), Quality Reviewer (IEEE ICME'11) and Best Demo (IEEE ACII'09). She serves as Associate Editor of IEEE Transactions on Affective Computing, on the Management Board of Association for the Advancement of Affective Computing, and the Steering Committee of IEEE Transactions on Affective Computing. She has also served as a Guest Editor of Special Issues in Int'l J. of Synthetic Emotions, Image and Vision Computing, and ACM Transactions on Interactive Intelligent Systems, and member of the Editorial Advisory Board for the Affective Computing and Interaction Book (IGI Global, 2011), co-founder and main organizer of the EmoSPACE Workshops at IEEE FG'15, FG'13 and FG'11, workshop chair of MAPTRAITS'14, HBU'13 and AC4MobHCI'12, and area chair for ACM Multimedia'15, ACM Multimedia'14, IEEE ICME'13, ACM ICMI'13 and ACII'13. She has been involved as PI and Co-I in several projects funded by the Engineering and Physical Sciences Research Council UK (EPSRC) and the British Council.

Hayley Hung is an Assistant Professor and Delft Technology Fellow in the Pattern Recognition and Bioinformatics group at TU Delft, The Netherlands, since 2013. Between 2010-2013, she held a Marie Curie Intra-European Fellowship at the Intelligent Systems Lab at the University of Amsterdam. Between 2007-2010, she was a post-doctoral researcher at Idiap Research Institute in Switzerland. She obtained her PhD in Computer Vision from Queen Mary University of London, UK in 2007 and her first degree from Imperial College, UK in Electrical and Electronic Engineering. Her research interests are in social computing, social signal processing, machine learning, and ubiquitous computing. She is local arrangements chair for ACM MM 2016, Workshop co-chair ACM ICMI 2015, area chair of the area on emotional and social signals at ACM MM (2014-2015), co-panel organiser for the panel on Emotional and Signals in Multimedia (ACM MM 2014), Doctoral Symposium co-chair ACM MM (2013). She has organized workshops on human behavior understanding (InterHUB (AmI 2011), Measuring Behaviour in open spaces (MB 2012), HBU (ACM MM 2013). She is also a special issue guest editor for ACM Transactions on Interactive Intelligent Systems. She has received first prize in the IET Written Premium competition 2009, was nominated for outstanding paper at ICMI 2011, and was named outstanding reviewer at ICME 2014.

5. REFERENCES

[1] H. Gunes and H. Hung. Emotional and social signals: A neglected frontier in multimedia computing? *MultiMedia, IEEE*, 22(2):76–85, Apr 2015.

[2] H. Gunes and B. Schuller. Dimensional and continuous analysis of emotions for multimedia applications: a tutorial overview. In *Proc. of ACM International Conference on Multimedia*, pages 1531–1532. ACM, 2012.

[3] A. Jaimes, N. Sebe, and D. Gatica-Perez. Human-centered computing: a multimedia perspective. In *Proc. of ACM International Conference on Multimedia*, pages 855–864. ACM, 2006.

An Introduction to Arts and Digital Culture Inside Multimedia

David A. Shamma
Yahoo Labs
110 5th Street
San Francisco, CA 94103 USA
aymans@acm.org

Daragh Byrne
School of Design
Carnegie Mellon University
Pittsburgh, PA 15213 USA
daraghb@andrew.cmu.edu

ABSTRACT

The Arts and Digital Culture program has offered a high quality forum for the presentation of interactive and arts-based multimedia applications at the annual ACM Multimedia conference for over a decade. This tutorial will explore the evolution of this program as a guide to new authors considering future participation in this program. By surveying both past technical and past exhibited contributions, this tutorial will offer guidance to artists, researchers and practitioners on success at this multifaceted, interdisciplinary forum at ACM Multimedia.

Categories and Subject Descriptors

J.5 [**Computer Applications**]: Arts and Humanities—*Fine arts, performing arts*; H.5.2 [**Information Systems**]: Information Interfaces and Presentation: User Interfaces—*Theory and methods*

Keywords

Tutorial, art, culture, multimedia, preservation

1. INTRODUCTION

In 2004, ACM Multimedia began its Interactive Arts program as a joint technical track and associated gallery track. The goal was to offer a high quality publication venue for interactive and artistic multimedia systems as well as bring greater socio-cultural awareness into the conference. In 2011, the Arts papers became part of the official Technical Program for Multimedia and in 2012 the best student paper was an Arts submission in Nara Japan. As the area and track grows, we aim for the how and why of the Arts program to reach to new community members as well as begin interoperation with other ACM Special Interest Groups. The purpose of this tutorial is to serve as an introduction to the Interactive Arts and Digital Culture track at ACM MM for both those actively engaged in the Arts as well as those with no previous technical arts engagement.

MM'15, October 26–30, 2015, Brisbane, Australia.
ACM 978-1-4503-3459-4/15/10.
DOI: http://dx.doi.org/10.1145/2733373.2807421.

2. MOTIVATIONS IN ART AND MM

The ACM SIG Multimedia Arts and Digital Culture Track aims to demonstrate new research opportunities for the multimedia community at large by highlighting innovative artistic or cultural applications of multimedia tools and applications. Over the past ten years, 234 contributions from 577 individuals have been featured in this forum. This includes 70 exhibited works, 58 full paper and 80 short paper contributions along with 8 demonstrations, 17 poster and 1 video submission. 49 authors have presented more than 2 technical (full or short paper) contributions and 8 of which have presented more than 3 technical contributions. Growing from 7 initial contributions in 2004 to a peak of 32 papers in 2007 programmed within the technical track, it has added an average of 15.33 new multidisciplinary and applied reflections on multimedia systems to the discourse featured at ACM Multimedia each year. Complimented by an exhibit, the program has become a strong venue where the role of the aesthetic, humanistic and reflexive perspectives offered by the arts in enriching multimedia systems research.

Jaimes et al. posit art as "one of the most exciting application areas" for human centered multimedia noting the wide variety of ways in which tools and applications for computer vision, content analysis, media representation and beyond may be leveraged in these contexts [1]. As growing track within the Multimedia conference, the Arts and Digital Culture program most clearly articulates this agenda by providing a venue to highlight "innovative use of digital technology in the creation, analysis or critique of cultural artifacts, environments and processes." In so doing it offers a needed forum where practitioners, researchers and artists may intermingle to discuss use of multimedia technology in practice, *in the wild* and in applied arts or cultural contexts. This provides a place to chart not only the reach of multimedia beyond technical or scholarly research but new and emerging areas for multimedia exploration.

While the arts are recognized a key field of applied exploration for multimedia as it often "pushes multimedia software and hardware to limits and in unexpected ways" [2, 1], the integration of multiple cohorts, perspectives and systems scenarios into this applied, interdisciplinary track presents some challenges. The Arts program aims to engage multidisciplinary cohorts, some of which are not versed in research reporting or methodologies in presenting technical contributions of broad relevance to the multimedia community. Moreover, there can exist a two-culture paradigm that can create perceived tensions between the role of arts and the sciences in advancing multimedia systems and in expressing the value of practice-oriented aesthetic or reflexive contributions within the context of scholarly multimedia discourse [3]. This motivates the need for clearer articulation of the value of incorporating multidisciplinary knowledge and arts insights into computational frameworks. Additionally, the program is designed to craft a porous space for interdisciplinary exchange where art, design, and culture intersect with traditional engineering and computer science explorations. Encompassing qualitative and quantitative evaluations, applied explorations, systems, methodologies, case studies and reflections, it produces a complex multifaceted space that can be difficult for a novice author to navigate or enter successfully, especially for those uninitiated individuals with no previous technical arts engagement. This tutorial intends to directly address these challenges by offering guidance to existing and prospective authors in preparing new high quality contributions and in interrogating the lineage of Arts at ACM Multimedia.

Such a tutorial is particularly timely given the increasing interest in integrative explorations that bridge interactive systems with aesthetic and design and arts perspectives. We see a growing body of practitioners, researchers, and artists are working within multidisciplinary contexts including performance, installation artworks, digital narrative, media composition and game design [4]—creating solutions to large scale or 'grand challenges' and in delivering innovative outcomes that can have considerable impact.

The Arts program plays an integral role in consolidating the knowledge produced for multimedia research. Reflecting on a decade of the Digital Arts and Culture program at ACM Multimedia, this tutorial will serve multiple needs both for the program and for potential future contributors to it. First, it hopes to foster support for the Arts program by developing a deepened understanding of the value, role and relationship of arts in multimedia systems exploration among participants. By exploring significant contributions to the program, we hope to encourage multimedia researchers, artists and practitioners to consider and communicate the broader cultural, societal or global significance and impact of their work. The intention is to disambiguate the approaches for presenting high-quality outcomes that reflect research and emerging areas of practice. This hopes to develop participants' knowledge and expertise in reporting on multidisciplinary outcomes.

3. TUTORIAL OUTLINE

The tutorial will provide a tour of the past ten years of the Arts and Digital Culture program as a learning opportunity for those interested in future participation.

1. *Introduction to the Arts program (30 mins):* The workshop will begin with an introduction to the purpose, goals and intent of the Arts program. To achieve this, the past decade of organization, history and contributions to the program will be briefly surveyed. This introduction will emphasize the nature and range of contributions that the program seeks to solicit and their relationship to the broader goals of ACM Multimedia.

2. *Selected works explained (1 hr):* A handful of Arts pieces will be highlighted to explore the variety of successful approaches to presenting high-impact art integrative multimedia work as technical track content at ACM Multimedia. Additionally, they will be used to explore and discuss the relationship between these contributions and the state-of-the-art.

3. *The gallery explained (30 mins):* Beyond providing a night's entertainment at the conference, the gallery is coordinated with the technical program. In this module we will discuss its role within the Arts program and feature successful examples of past exhibitions.

4. *Writing a successful arts program paper (45 mins):* Here we will decompose what makes a great Arts technical paper (and what makes a bad one). This module will aim to demystify the process of writing and Arts paper and provide insight into what program chairs look for, what reviewers examine contributions on and what they often strike against.

5. *Open Discussion:* While we will open the floor for discussion at the end of each module, we will also set aside time at the end of the tutorial for people to dive into their own work and questions as they relate to the Arts and Digital Culture section at SIGMM.

4. MATERIALS

The half-day tutorial will present a series of selected readings that provides an overview of the past 10 years of the Arts and Digital Culture program in addition to selected review of works through available online content[1] and multimedia collateral. These will be assembled and accessible to participants as a website prepared by the tutorial leads. This site will also offer an overview of the tutorial objectives and auxiliary materials. Materials will be cross-listed and posted in the Arts and Digital Culture section of the ACM SIGMM website. Along with an annotated slide-deck and other materials, it is expected that outcomes of the tutorial, discussion points and other participant feedback will be also captured within this site to serve as a resource for the community and in particular those interested in learning more about or participating in the Arts and Digital Culture program in the future.

5. REFERENCES

[1] A. Jaimes, N. Sebe, and D. Gatica-Perez. Human-centered computing: A multimedia perspective. In *Proceedings of the 14th Annual ACM International Conference on Multimedia*, MULTIMEDIA '06, pages 855–864, New York, NY, USA, 2006. ACM.

[2] A. Jaimes, A. Senior, and W. Muench. Acm multimedia interactive art program: An introduction to the presence/absence exhibition. In *Proceedings of the 13th Annual ACM International Conference on Multimedia*, MULTIMEDIA '05, pages 1051–1052, New York, NY, USA, 2005. ACM.

[3] F. J. Lapoint. A sead network analysis of white papers, sead network white papers. http://seadnetwork.wordpress.com, 2012.

[4] S. Wilson. *Art+ Science Now.* Thames & Hudson, 2010.

[1]See: http://bit.ly/artsmmtutorial

Human-centric images and videos analysis

Si Liu[1], Bingbing Ni[2], Liang Lin[3]
[1]State Key Laboratory of Information Security, Institute of Information Engineering, Chinese Academy of Sciences
[2]Department of Electronic Engineering, Shanghai Jiaotong University
[3]School of Advanced Computing, Sun Yat-Sen University
liusi@iie.ac.cn, nibingbing1983@gmail.com, linliang@ieee.org

ABSTRACT

This article summarizes the corresponding half-day tutorial at ACM Multimedia 2015. This tutorial reviews recent progresses in human-centric images and videos analysis: 1) fashion analysis: parsing, attribute prediction and retrieval; 2) action analysis: discriminative feature selection, pooling and fusion; 3) person verification: cross-domain person verification via learning a generalized similarity measure, and bit-scalable deep hashing with regularized similarity learning.

Categories and Subject Descriptors

H.3.3 [**Information Search and Retrieval**]: Retrieval models

Keywords

fashion analysis; action analysis; person verification

1. INTRODUCTION

Human-centric image and video analysis is important in the computer vision field and real application. For example, with the emergence of many E-commerce companies, researchers put more and more efforts studying the clothes attribute prediction, human parsing problem, which can benefit the automatic tagging for the E-commerce websites.

Video based human action recognition and detection has many potential applications including smart surveillance and assisted living. However, to accurate recognize and detect human actions and interactions is very challenging due to large variations of human appearance/posture/movement, significant background/irrelevant motions, view point, scale and illumination changes etc. Research focus on how to discriminative motion feature extraction, selection, pooling and multimodal feature fusion is highly demanded.

In the research of Multimedia, there is a particular interest on developing such intelligent systems of human centric applications, e.g., intelligent surveillance, image/video content-based retrieval, social relation mining. On the other hand, the past decade has witnessed the rapid development of feature representation learning (e.g., deep neural networks, dictionary learning, sparse coding) and distance metric learning (e.g., Mahalanobis distance). These emerging techniques have effectively improved the system performances to achieve the goals against real challenges. Moreover, the more large-scale databases (e.g., millions of images in the ImageNet) and multi-modal collections (e.g., theFlickr) are available for model training and evaluations. It is hence expected that the current research could lead to applicable systems or we could discover new approaches or identify new problems in the related topics.

MM'15, October 26–30, 2015, Brisbane, Australia.
ACM 978-1-4503-3459-4/15/10.
DOI: http://dx.doi.org/10.1145/2733373.28063370-12345-67-8/90/01.

2. FASHION ANALYSIS

Fashion parsing aims to predict the label for each pixel in a fashion image. The performance of traditional fashion parsers are constrained by the limited training data, and thus cannot well parse the fashion images which contain human bodies in arbitrary, even exaggerated poses and various views. In this tutoiral, three fashion parsing works will be introduced. The first work utilizes the video context to solve the problem of insufficient training samples, and assist the fashion parsing. The other two works are deep learning based methods, including a parametric framework namely active template regression and a non-parametric framework called Matching-CNN. About fashion attribute prediction, I shall introduce a new framework to jointly estimate the fashion attribute and infer their corresponding semantic regions. Great performances have been achieved by the proposed methods in different aspects of fashion analysis.

We also investigate the attribute prediction problem, which is very applicable in the quickly developed E-commerce these days. Considering that many product attributes (such as collar shape, shoes heel length etc) are usually location-aware, we propose a method to predicting attribute with semantic area inference, which jointly localize the semantic area w.r.t. each attribute and predict the attribute value. PASTA enjoys many nice properties. First, it put semantic area inference and attribute prediction in an end-to-end framework, where their mutual relationships are fully explored. Second, by making use of the almost zero-cost, large-scale product images and labels crawled from the Internet, PASTA requires minimum extra annotation (besides the attribute labels crawled together with the images) and thus is applicable. Third, the semantic areas, such as their total number, aspect ratios, sizes etc, are adaptive to the attributes. Therefore, no redundant or useless semantic area are included. Fourth, the semantic areas are discriminative for the attribute prediction. To fulfill these properties, we construct a Convolutional Neural Network (CNN) to predict the attributes of the product. Inside the CNN flow, the location, aspect ratio, size of the semantic areas are estimated for each attribute.

Next, we consider a more interesting and practical fashion retrieval: given a human photo captured on street or saw occasionally, finding similar clothing from online street snap online store. To solve the problem of lack of labeling data, we propose a computational model for attribute prediction with video context. When very few image instances of a new concept are given, an initial attribute predictor is built by a CNN. Then, the well designed tracking solution is then used to discover more diverse instances from the massive online unlabeled videos. Then the attribute predictor can be fine-tuned based on these new tracked instances.

3. ACTION ANALYSIS

The first problem is how to effectively select *good* features for action representation. We introduce a *Motion Part Regularization* framework to mine for discriminative groups of dense trajectories which form important motion parts. First, motion part candidates are generated by spatio-temporal grouping of densely extracted trajectories. Second, an objective function which encourages sparse selection for these trajectory groups is formulated together with an action class discriminative term. Then, we propose an alternative optimization algorithm to efficiently solve this objective function by introducing a set of auxiliary variables which correspond to the discriminativeness weights of each motion part (trajectory group). These learned motion part weights are further utilized to form a discriminativeness weighted Fisher vector representation for each action sample for final classification.

The second problem is how to effectively pool local features to achieve a global representation. We propose an adaptive motion feature pooling scheme that utilizes human key poses as side information. Such key poses can be detected for instance in assisted living and indoor smart surveillance scenarios. Taking both video sub-volumes for pooling and human key pose types as hidden variables, we formulate the motion feature pooling problem as a latent structural learning problem where the relationship between the optimal pooling video sub-volumes and the key pose types is learned.

The third problem is how to effectively fuse data from different modalities for better recognition. We propose a framework which fuses information from both grayscale and depth image channels at multiple levels of the video processing pipeline. In the individual visual feature detection level, depth based filters are applied to the detected human/object rectangles to remove false detections. In the next level of interaction modeling, three dimensional spatial and temporal contexts among human subjects or objects are extracted by integrating information from both grayscale and depth images. Depth information is also utilized to distinguish different types of indoor scenes. Finally, a latent structural model is developed to integrate the information from multiple levels of video processing for activity detection.

4. PERSON VERIFICATION

Person verification is an important problem with many applications. Modern systems of image retrieval are often developed to verify whether input photos contain the same person or the same object. Person verification gains increasing attentions for building an intelligent video surveillance system, which are able to identify the same individual across different videos. In the applications of social networks, it is also highly preferred to correctly assign personal photos to users. Two main visual clues for person verification are widely studied: human body figures and face images.

In this tutorial, two works in the related topics of person verification will be introduced. The first work presents a pairwise similarity model for cross-domain visual matching. Conventional approaches to cross-domain visual matching usually involves two steps: i) projecting samples of different domain into a common space, and ii) computing (dis)similarity in this space based on a certain distance. our model advances existing models by i) expanding traditional linear projections into affine transformations and ii) fusing Mahalanobis distance and Cosine distance by a data-driven combination. Moreover, we unify our similarity metric with feature representation learning via deep convolutional neural networks. Specifically, we incorporate the similarity measure matrix into the deep architecture, enabling an end-to-end way of model optimization.

In the second work, we present a supervised hashing framework to generate compact and bit-scalable hashing codes. We pose hashing learning as a problem of regularized similarity learning. Specifically, we organize the training images into a batch of triplet samples, each sample containing two images with the same class label (i.e. person ID) and one with a different label. With these triplet samples, we maximize the margin between matched pairs and mismatched pairs in the Hamming space. Meanwhile, a regularization term is introduced to enforce the adjacency consistency, i.e. images of similar appearances should have similar codes. The deep convolutional neural network is utilized to train the model in an end-to-end fashion, where discriminative image features and hash functions are simultaneously optimized. Furthermore, each bit of our hashing codes is unequally weighted so that we can manipulate the code lengths by truncating the insignificant bits.

5. TUTORIAL OUTLINE

Fashion Analysis: Parsing, Attribute Prediction and Retrieval

- Deep Human parsing techniques: a parametric and a non-parametric way
- Deep Human attribute prediction with Video Context
- PASTA: Predicting Attribute with Semantic Area Inference

Action Analysis: Discriminative Feature Selection, Pooling and Fusion

- Action Recognition with Motion Part Selection
- Action Detection with Pose Adaptive Motion Feature Pooling
- Fine-grained Action Recognition with Context Fusion

Person Verification: Deep Representation Learning with Relative Distance Comparison

- Cross-Domain Person Verification via Learning A Generalized Similarity Measure
- Bit-Scalable Deep Hashing with Regularized Similarity Learning and Its Application to Person Re-identification

User-centric Cross-OSN Multimedia Computing

Jitao Sang
National Lab of Pattern Recognition, Institute of Automation
Chinese Academy of Sciences, Beijing 100190, China
jtsang@nlpr.ia.ac.cn

ABSTRACT

This article summarizes the corresponding half-day tutorial at ACM Multimedia 2015. This tutorial is divided into two parts as (1) User-centric Social Multimedia Computing; and (2) Cross-OSN Multimedia Computing.

Categories and Subject Descriptors

H.4.m [**Information Systems Applications**]: Miscellaneous

General Terms

Algorithms, Experimentation, Performance

Keywords

Social Media; Social Multimedia Computing; Cross-OSN

1. USER-CENTRIC SOCIAL MULTIMEDIA COMPUTING

Social media has exploded beyond anyone's wildest imagination. With the ubiquitous presence of capturing devices, multimedia has become the major sharing and interacting medium for information access and communication and contributed significantly to the prosperity of social media. Taking YouTube for example, there were in total two billion videos on this website by the end of 2013 with more than 100 hours of new videos being uploaded every minute.

The multimedia data generated and consumed under social media circumstances is referred to as social multimedia. The emergence of social multimedia has brought challenges as well as opportunities to computing. Social multimedia computing, a multidisciplinary research and application field, has been developed to understand social multimedia content and connect the social multimedia content with users by exploiting the various social interactions. The potential applications range from information service, communication, entertainment, to healthcare, security, etc. Thanks to the wide prevalence of social multimedia data and the increasing demands for social multimedia services, there has been a growing number of research on social multimedia computing, evidenced by the volume of papers produced, and many related tracks and special issues in prestigious multimedia conferences and journals.

Social multimedia computing is very different from traditional and web multimedia computing. Web multimedia computing is heavily related to the WEB1.0 environment, which is dominated by broadcast media developed by professional designers for passive users. In traditional multimedia computing, the analysis focus is the multimedia content, and the goal is content understanding and application, e.g., media content analysis, semantic classification and annotation, structured media authoring. On the contrary, social multimedia computing has an obvious **user-centric characteristic**: (1) User is the basic data collection unit. Viewing each user as a data sensor, social multimedia is constituted by what users see, listen, think, feel and speak. Moreover, user bridges multimedia network and social network, contributing to most of the social interactions in social multimedia. (2) User is the ultimate information service target. As discussed above, social multimedia services are user-oriented and have a customized trend. Understanding the personalized demands is critical to most social multimedia computing problems.

In the first part of this tutorial, I introduce the user-centric research paradigm for social multimedia computing [1], and organize the related work into two basic tasks of "From users, and For users": (1) **From users**: user-perceptive multimedia content analysis. Users' social interactions capture what they perceive the multimedia content and can be exploited towards multimedia content analysis [2, 3, 4, 5]. For example, user-contributed picture tags indicate user-perceived visual semantics, user browsing behaviors, such as pause, fast-forward, indicate video structure information. (2) **For users**: user modeling and customized multimedia applications. Online activities reveals important clues of user background information and are utilized for user modeling of demographic facts [6], personal interests [7], social network status [8], mobility patterns [9], consuming patters, emotional orientation, etc. Given results from user-perceptive multimedia content analysis and user modeling, customized multimedia services are developed to satisfy personalized needs [10, 11].

2. CROSS-OSN MULTIMEDIA COMPUTING

The explosion of social media has led to various Online Social Networking (OSN) services. Today's typical netizens are

MM'15, October 26–30, 2015, Brisbane, Australia.
© 2015 ACM. ISBN 978-1-4503-3459-4/15/10.
DOI: http://dx.doi.org/10.1145/2733373.2807423.

using a multitude of OSN services. For example, the same individual may communicate with his/her friends on Facebook, follow real-time hot events on Twitter, subscribe and watch videos on YouTube, share and discuss favorite restaurants on Yelp, etc. These activities conducted on different OSNs by the same individual are called cross-OSN activities, which together record people's integral online footprint and reflect the physical world at the same time. Moreover, the data involved in these cross-OSN activities are way beyond the traditional multi-modality, e.g., videos and photos in media sharing YouTube and Flickr, information stream in microblogging Twitter and Tumblr, social communication in private/professional social networks Facebook and LinkedIn, location and POI in check-in networks Foursquare and Yelp.

Exploring the cross-OSN heterogeneous data is critical to connect between the separated data island and facilitate value mining from big social multimedia. (1) From the perspective of content analysis, understanding the association among heterogeneous cross-OSN data is fundamental to advanced social media analysis and applications. For example, collective understanding of social streams, online comments, and user-generated images and videos will enable comprehensive tracking to social event progress and evolution. (2) From the perspective of user modeling, exploiting the available user data on different OSNs contributes to an integrated online user profile and thus improved customized social media services. For example, connecting between users' video watching pattern and consuming history will lead to advanced user modeling and facilitate cross-OSN targeted advertising.

Correspondingly, two basic tasks of cross-OSN multimedia computing are summarized as cross-OSN knowledge mining and cross-OSN user modeling. In the second part of this tutorial, I use several pilot works to introduce the very recent progresses on cross-OSN multimedia computing, following the above user-centric paradigm: (1) From users: cross-OSN knowledge association mining. Analogous to cross-media analysis, the fundamental problem in cross-OSN computing is to mine the association among different OSNs. While, different from cross-media analysis, it is difficult to mine the association in a bottom-up fashion based on the low-level features. Some pioneering works have addressed the new problem via the user-perceptive supervisions, i.e., aggregating user-contributed cross-OSN activities to mine cross-network knowledge association [12, 13]. (2) For users: cross-OSN user modeling and collaborative applications. Users' behaviors across different OSNs reflect their demographics, as well as interests from a variety of perspectives, which provide important complementary information that are unavailable in single-OSN scenarios [14, 15, 16]. Work along this line aims to leverage the user data distributed in disparate OSNs for comprehensive user modeling to facilitate personalized social media information recommendation services.

This tutorial focuses on introducing the important general concepts and themes of this timely topic, and not go deep into the algorithm details. The only prior knowledge expected for the audience is a familiarity with basic machine learning models, e.g., matrix factorization, collaborative filtering, probabilistic density estimation. The target audiences of the tutorial include both graduate students and senior researchers working in the field of multimedia and/or social computing, as well as industry practitioners who are working in the field of image/video processing, social applications, search engine development, developers of video/image sharing social platforms, advertising and recommendation systems, and so on.

3. REFERENCES

[1] Jitao Sang. *User-centric Social Multimedia Computing*. Springer, 2014.

[2] Jitao Sang, Changsheng Xu, and Jing Liu. User-aware image tag refinement via ternary semantic analysis. *TMM*, 14(3):883–895, 2012.

[3] Jitao Sang and Changsheng Xu. Browse by chunks: Topic mining and organizing on web-scale social media. *TOMM*, 7(1):30, 2011.

[4] Jitao Sang and Changsheng Xu. Faceted subtopic retrieval: Exploiting the topic hierarchy via a multi-modal framework. *Journal of Multimedia*, 7(1):9–20, 2012.

[5] Quan Fang, Jitao Sang, Changsheng Xu, and Ke Lu. Paint the city colorfully: Location visualization from multiple themes. In *Advances in Multimedia Modeling*, pages 92–105. 2013.

[6] Quan Fang, Jitao Sang, Changsheng Xu, and M Shamim Hossain. Relational user attribute inference in social media. *TMM*, 17(7):1031, 2015.

[7] Jitao Sang, Dongyuan Lu, and Changsheng Xu. A probabilistic framework for temporal user modeling on microblogs. In *CIKM*, 2015.

[8] Quan Fang, Jitao Sang, Changsheng Xu, and Yong Rui. Topic-sensitive influencer mining in interest-based social media networks via hypergraph learning. *TMM*, 16(3):796–812, 2014.

[9] Jitao Sang, Tao Mei, and Changsheng Xu. Activity sensor: Check-in usage mining for local recommendation. *ACM Transactions on Intelligent Systems and Technology (TIST)*, 6(3):41, 2015.

[10] Jitao Sang and Changsheng Xu. Right buddy makes the difference: An early exploration of social relation analysis in multimedia applications. In *ACM Multimedia*, pages 19–28, 2012.

[11] Jitao Sang, Changsheng Xu, and Dongyuan Lu. Learn to personalized image search from the photo sharing websites. *TMM*, 14(4):963–974, 2012.

[12] Ming Yan, Zhengyu Deng, Jitao Sang, and Changsheng Xu. User-oriented social analysis across social media sites. In *ICIAP*, pages 482–490, 2013.

[13] Ming Yan, Jitao Sang, and Changsheng Xu. Mining cross-network association for youtube video promotion. In *ACM Multimedia*, pages 557–566, 2014.

[14] Ming Yan, Jitao Sang, Tao Mei, and Changsheng Xu. Friend transfer: Cold-start friend recommendation with cross-platform transfer learning of social knowledge. In *ICME*, pages 1–6, 2013.

[15] Zhengyu Deng, Ming Yan, Jitao Sang, and Changsheng Xu. Twitter is faster: Personalized time-aware video recommendation from twitter to youtube. *TOMM*, 11(2):31, 2014.

[16] Ming Yan, Jitao Sang, and Changsheng Xu. Unified youtube video recommendation via cross-network collaboration. In *ICMR*, pages 19–26, 2015.

AVEC 2015 – The 5th International Audio/Visual Emotion Challenge and Workshop

Fabien Ringeval
University of Passau
Chair of Complex & Intelligent Systems
Passau, Germany

Björn Schuller*
University of Passau
Chair of Complex & Intelligent Systems
Passau, Germany

Michel Valstar
University of Nottingham
Mixed Reality Lab
Nottingham, UK

Roddy Cowie
Queen's University Belfast
School of Psychology
Belfast, UK

Maja Pantic†
Imperial College London
Intelligent Behaviour Understanding Group
London, UK

ABSTRACT

The fifth Audio-Visual Emotion Challenge and workshop AVEC 2015 was held in conjunction ACM Multimedia'15. Like the previous editions of AVEC, the workshop/challenge addresses the detection of affective signals represented in audio-visual data in terms of high-level continuous dimensions. A major novelty was further introduced this year by the inclusion of the physiological modality – along with the audio and the video modalities – in the dataset. In this summary, we mainly describe participation and its conditions.

Categories and Subject Descriptors

I [**Pattern Recognition**]: Applications

General Terms

Theory

Keywords

Affective Computing, Multimodality, Challenge

1. INTRODUCTION

This year's Audio-Visual Emotion Challenge and workshop (AVEC 2015) has been organised in conjunction with the 23rd ACM International Conference on Multimedia, held in Brisbane, Australia, 26 – 30 October 2015 (ACM-MM'15).

*The author is further affiliated with Department of Computing, Imperial College London, London, UK.

†The author is further affiliated with Twente University, EEMCS, Twente, The Netherlands.

MM'15, October 26–30, 2015, Brisbane, Australia
ACM 978-1-4503-3459-4/15/10.
http://dx.doi.org/10.1145/2733373.2806408.

The AVEC 2015's theme is 'Uniting Audio, Video and Physiological Data' and it is the fifth competition event aimed at comparison of multimedia processing and machine learning methods for automatic audio, visual and – for the first time ever – physiological emotion analysis, with all participants competing under strictly the same conditions in this first of its kind series [6, 5, 8, 9]. However, further similar endeavours are to be noted in the meanwhile, e.g., [1, 7].

The goal of the Challenge is to provide a common benchmark test set for multimodal information processing and to bring together the audio, video and physiological emotion recognition communities, to compare the relative merits of the three approaches to emotion recognition under well-defined and strictly comparable conditions and establish to what extent fusion of the approaches is possible and beneficial. A second motivation is the need to advance emotion recognition systems to be able to deal with fully naturalistic behaviours in large volumes of un-segmented, non-prototypical and non-preselected data, as this is exactly the type of data that both multimedia and human-machine/human-robot communication interfaces have to face in the real world.

We were calling for teams to participate in a Challenge of fully-continuous emotion detection from audio, or video, or physiological data, or any combination of these three modalities. As benchmarking database the RECOLA multimodal corpus of remote and collaborative affective interactions was used [4]. Even though this database does not feature human-machine but rather human-human interaction, we strongly believe that the latter is the most interesting type of communication to study for the development of systems that will interact with humans, as we want such systems achieving realistic human like behaviours in the near future. Emotion needed to be recognised in terms of continuous time, continuous valued dimensional affect in two dimensions: arousal and valence.

Besides participation in the Challenge we were calling for papers addressing the overall topics of this workshop, in particular works that address the differences between audio, video and physiological processing of emotive data, and the issues concerning combined audio-visual-physiological emotion recognition.

In the following sections, we will describe the participation in this year and outline the conditions for participation in particular in the competitive challenge event. We further acknowledge those that helped turn AVEC 2015 into reality.

2. PARTICIPATION

The call for participation and papers attracted registrations of 31 teams and 136 team members from all over the world. 13 teams submitted results for the emotion recognition challenge – overall, at the moment of writing over 38 submissions of results to the challenge were received. Finally, 15 paper submissions were received. AVEC 2015 reviewing was double blind, and acceptance was based on relevance to the workshop, novelty, and technical quality. The programme committee accepted 9 papers in addition to the baseline paper as oral presentation (the acceptance rate thus equalling 60%), which were assigned three reviewers, each, and reviewed independently. We hope that these proceedings will serve as a valuable reference for researchers and developers in the area of multimodal emotion recognition.

3. CHALLENGE CONDITIONS

A baseline paper explaining the dataset, the challenge evaluation procedure, baseline features and baseline results was made available during the ongoing challenge [3]. In order to ensure the correct use of the recordings provided in the RECOLA database, in compliance with the European and Swiss federal laws for data privacy and ethics, participants were required to sign an end user license agreement (EULA). Data were stored on a secured server (https) and a unique combination of user name and password was provided to each registered team, upon reception and validation of the completed EULA. After downloading the data participants could directly start their own experiments with the train and development sets. Once they found their best method they should write a paper for the Workshop. At the same time they could compute their results per instance of the test set. Participants' results needed to be sent as a single packed file to the organisers by email and scores were returned within 24 hours during typical working days.

Each participant had up to five submission attempts for both arousal and valence. Badly formatted results were not counted towards one of these five submissions. Further, the top-two performers of the Challenge were asked to submit their program to the organisers at University of Passau to verify the results, both on the original test set and extra hold-out data. Delivery was as an executable or, e. g., encrypted Matlab or similar code, and they were asked to work with the organisers in validating their results. The organisers provided for each dimension (i. e., arousal and valence) and data partition (i. e., train and development) the root mean squared error (RMSE), the Pearson's correlation coefficient and the concordance correlation coefficient (CCC) [2], which is used to rank participants. Predictions returned on the individual sequences of a same data partition were concatenated before computing the correlation based coefficients. Ranking of the participants was obtained by averaging the best CCC achieved on arousal and valence, independently of their submission.

4. PROGRAM AND COMMITTEE

The workshop is a full-day event held on 26 October 2015 starting with a keynote speech by Roland Goecke of University of Canberra, followed by an introduction to the challenge, a series of paper presentations (oral), a demo session, a panel discussion and finally an overview of the challenge results and an announcement of the winners of the Challenge. The organisers – the authors of this summary – would like to thank all participants and in particular also the highly dedicated program committee of this year: *Felix Burkhardt*, Deutsche Telekom, Germany, *Rama Chellappa*, University of Maryland, USA, *Fang Chen*, NICTA, Australia, *Mohamed Chetouani*, UPMC, France, *Jeffrey Cohn*, University of Pittsburgh, USA, *Laurence Devillers*, LIMSI-CNRS, France, *Julien Epps*, UNSW, Australia, *Anna Esposito*, Second University of Naples, Italy, *Roland Goecke*, University of Canberra, Australia, *Jarek Krajewski*, University of Wuppertal, Germany, *Marc Méhu*, Webster Vienna Private University, Austria, *Louis-Philippe Morency*, USC, USA, *Stefan Scherer*, USC, USA, *Stefan Steidl*, University of Erlangen-Nuremberg, Germany, *Jianhua Tao*, Chinese Academy of Science, China, *Matthew Turk*, University of California, USA and *Stefanos Zafeiriou*, Imperial College London, UK.

Acknowledgments

The research leading to these results has received funding from the EC's Seventh Framework Programme through the ERC Starting Grant No. 338164 (iHEARu), and the EU's Horizon 2020 Programme through the Innovative Action No. 644632 (MixedEmotions), No. 645094 (SEWA) and the Research Innovative Action No. 645378 (ARIA-VALUSPA). The authors would further like to thank the sponsors of the challenge, the Association for the Advancement of Affective Computing (AAAC) and the audEERING UG. The responsibility lies with the authors.

5. REFERENCES

[1] A. Dhall, R. Goecke, J. Joshi, K. Sikka, and T. Gedeon. Emotion Recognition In The Wild Challenge 2014: Baseline, Data and Protocol. In *Proc. ICMI*, pages 461–466, Istanbul, Turkey, November 2014. ACM.

[2] L. Li. A concordance correlation coefficient to evaluate reproducibility. *Biometrics*, 45(1):255–268, March 1989.

[3] F. Ringeval, B. Schuller, M. Valstar, S. Jaiswal, E. Marchi, D. Lalanne, R. Cowie, and M. Pantic. AV+EC 2015 – The First Affect Recognition Challenge Bridging Across Audio, Video, and Physiological Data. In *Proceedings of the 5th International Workshop on Audio/Visual Emotion Challenge (AVEC), ACM MM*, Brisbane, Australia, October 2015.

[4] F. Ringeval, A. Sonderegger, J. Sauer, and D. Lalanne. Introducing the RECOLA Multimodal Corpus of Remote Collaborative and Affective Interactions. In *Proc. FG*, Shanghai, China, April 2013.

[5] B. Schuller, M. Valstar, F. Eyben, R. Cowie, and M. Pantic. AVEC 2012 – The Continuous Audio/Visual Emotion Challenge. In *Proc. ICMI*, pages 449–456, Santa Monica (CA), USA, October 2012. ACM.

[6] B. Schuller, M. Valstar, F. Eyben, G. McKeown, R. Cowie, and M. Pantic. AVEC 2011 - The First International Audio/Visual Emotion Challenge. In *Proc. ACII 2011*, volume II, pages 415–424, Memphis (TN), USA, October 2011. Springer.

[7] M. Sjöberg, Y. Baveye, H. Wang, V. Quand, B. Ionescu, E. Dellandréa, M. Schedl, C.-H. Demarty, and L. Chen. The MediaEval 2015 Affective Impact of Movies Task. In *Proc. MediaEval 2015 Workshop*, Wurzen, Germany, 2015.

[8] M. Valstar, B. Schuller, J. Krajewski, R. Cowie, and M. Pantic. Workshop summary for the 3rd international audio/visual emotion challenge and workshop (AVEC'13). In *Proc. MM*, pages 1085–1086, Barcelona, Spain, October 2013. ACM.

[9] M. Valstar, B. Schuller, J. Krajewski, R. Cowie, and M. Pantic. AVEC 2014: the 4th international audio/visual emotion challenge and workshop. In *Proc. MM*, pages 1243–1244, Orlando (FL), USA, November 2014. ACM.

Multimedia COMMONS – Community-Organized Multimodal Mining: Opportunities for Novel Solutions (MMCommons Workshop 2015)

Gerald Friedland
International Computer Science Institute
Berkeley, CA, USA
fractor@icsi.berkeley.edu

Chong-Wah Ngo
VIREO Research Group
City University of Hong Kong
Hong Kong
cscwngo@cityu.edu.hk

David Ayman Shamma
Yahoo Labs
San Francisco, CA, USA
aymans@acm.org

ABSTRACT

The Multimedia COMMONS workshop laid the groundwork for developing a research community around the Multimedia Genome Project (MMGP), an initiative initially focused on annotation of—and research using—the 99.2 million images and nearly 800,000 videos in the Yahoo Flickr Creative Commons 100 Million dataset (YFCC100M). Current and potential users of the YFCC100M presented new research and systems that used this unprecedentedly large, unprecedentedly open-source dataset; discussed ideas for future data challenges and new benchmarking tasks that would not previously have been possible; and suggested priorities and plans for annotation and distribution based on community needs and interests.

Categories and Subject Descriptors

H.3.3 [**Information Storage and Retrieval**]: Information Search and Retrieval; H.3.7 [**Information Storage and Retrieval**]: Digital Libraries

Keywords

multimedia corpora; annotation; multimedia retrieval

1. MOTIVATION AND GOALS

Building flexible, accurate multimedia analysis and retrieval systems requires massive amounts of annotated data as ground-truth input. The Multimedia COMMONS workshop kicked off the development of a research community around the Multimedia Genome Project (MMGP), an initiative initially focused on annotation of the 99.2 million images and nearly 800,000 videos in the Yahoo Flickr Creative Commons 100 Million dataset (YFCC100M[1]) released in 2014 [3].

[1]`http://webscope.sandbox.yahoo.com/catalog.php?datatype=i&did=67`

MM'15, October 26–30, 2015, Brisbane, Australia.
ACM 978-1-4503-3459-4/15/10.
DOI: http://dx.doi.org/10.1145/2733373.2806409 .

This freely available dataset is already being used as the basis for several derived corpora and related tools, including a public-domain corpus of computed audio, visual, and motion features (the YLI Corpus[2]) [2], a set of preliminary public-domain annotations for multimedia event detection (YLI-MED[3]) [1], and a visual search index[4].

MMCommons offered an opportunity for researchers currently using the YFCC100M and the existing sets of derived features and annotations to present their work. However, it also accomplished much more, providing a forum for the community of current and potential users of the YFCC100M to:

- Explore the possibilities for novel research offered by this unprecedentedly large and open-source dataset;
- Lay the groundwork for future data challenges and new benchmarking tasks that would not previously have been possible;
- Kick off a "What's your ground truth?" process, encouraging researchers to define and generate small annotation sets for others to test against and expand on;
- Discuss priorities, methods, and plans for full-corpus annotation and distribution, based on the needs and research interests of a diverse set of multimedia researchers.

Because of its size and openness, the YFCC100M is already a distinct resource, inspiring a variety of researchers to consider new directions of research that could advance the state of the art. MMCommons enabled interested researchers to collaborate on leveraging this resource for the maximal benefit of the community.

2. SCOPE AND THEMES

What the Human Genome Project and the Music Genome Project have accomplished for their realms of big data, we anticipate the Multimedia Genome Project will do for consumer produced images and videos: foster a fundamental understanding of the major underlying structures by amassing and analyzing detailed information about the building

[2]`http://www.yli-corpus.org/computed-features`
[3]`http://www.yli-corpus.org/the-yli-med-corpus`
[4]`http://mklab.iti.gr/project/visual-features-and-search-index-flickr-100m-corpus`

blocks. The Multimedia COMMONS workshop was a first step toward this ambitious effort to describe what consumer-produced images and videos typically contain, how they are usually structured, and what visual and acoustic characteristics make them searchable.

In laying the groundwork for focused collaborations around an open, shared dataset, we hope to inspire participation from a diverse set of multimedia researchers working on a diversity of tasks. We particularly hope to encourage research that ties together multiple research threads or approaches questions from multiple perspectives.

Major themes of the MMCommons workshop included:

- Methods and best practices for annotating and analyzing large multimedia corpora;
- Comparative research using different datasets (especially YFCC100M, YLI, and related corpora, but also other datasets for multimedia benchmarks such as MediaEval);
- Connecting information about small-scale and large-scale structure (for example, audio features to localized audio concepts/objects to semantic events);
- New approaches to integrating modalities;
- Leveraging high-performance computing and cloud computing for processing, manipulating, moving, storing, and accessing corpus data;
- Innovative methods for generating subcorpora and bootstrapping annotations, for example using feature similarity;
- Interdisciplinary collaboration towards applications of content-based retrieval (e.g., medicine, social sciences, economics, meteorology, intelligence, journalism...).

In addition to work and work-in-progress based on the YFCC100M, YLI, YLI-GEO[5], and YLI-MED corpora, other highly relevant research was presented.

3. PROGRAM

The papers presented at the Multimedia COMMONS workshops addressed the challenges of working with large datasets from several angles – and likewise, found a diversity of ways to take advantage of the size of the YFCC100M and its derivatives. Submissions included research on on classifying images and videos by objects, events, and social meaning; examination of user-supplied tags and their value for retrieval and training; and the development of additional features and tools for using the dataset.

In addition, MMCommons included presentations by the participants in one of this year's Grand Challenges: to automatically detect, analyze the structure of, and summarize events in the YFCC100M dataset. This Grand Challenge (presented by Yahoo) has provided an early taste of how having a large new open dataset can stimulate new approaches and allow new tasks to be tackled.

Leveraging the dataset to stimulate new research directions through challenges and benchmarks from the dataset YFCC100M was, in fact, the focus of a panel discussion during the workshop. The panel discussed new tasks as well as potential applications, focusing on the need for multi-scale multi-modal feature representations that can provide a foundation for applied research that goes beyond multimedia (e.g., anthropology or medicine).

MMCommons also included a special session on annotation and potential collaborative models for developing the Multimedia Genome Project. Organizers and participants discussed potential annotation schemes, collection methods, and distribution mechanisms, in relation to the current needs and priorities of the multimedia research community.

4. ACKNOWLEDGMENTS

The chairs would like to thank the Multimedia COMMONS Steering Committee for their efforts in organizing the workshop: Martha Larson at Technische Universiteit Delft, Netherlands; Doug Poland at Lawrence Livermore National Laboratories, USA; Bart Thomee at Yahoo Labs, USA; Julia Bernd at International Computer Science Institute, USA; Damian Borth at German Research Center for Artificial Intelligence (DFKI), Germany; and Benjamin Elizalde at International Computer Science Institute, USA. We would also like to thank the patient and generous Program Committee. Finally, we would like the thank the presenters and participants at the Multimedia COMMONS workshop, for sharing their enthusiasm and creativity.

5. REFERENCES

[1] J. Bernd, D. Borth, B. Elizalde, G. Friedland, H. Gallagher, L. Gottlieb, A. Janin, S. Karabashlieva, J. Takahashi, and J. Won. The YLI-MED corpus: Characteristics, procedures, and plans (ICSI Technical Report TR-15-001). *arXiv:1503.04250*, 2015.

[2] J. Choi, B. Thomee, G. Friedland, L. Cao, K. Ni, D. Borth, B. Elizalde, L. Gottlieb, C. Carrano, R. Pearce, and D. Poland. The Placing Task: A large-scale geo-estimation challenge for social-media videos and images. In *Proceedings of the ACM Multimedia 2014 Workshop on Geotagging and Its Applications in Multimedia (GeoMM '14)*, Orlando, FL, November 2014. Association for Computing Machinery.

[3] B. Thomee, D. A. Shamma, G. Friedland, B. Elizalde, K. Ni, D. Poland, D. Borth, and L.-J. Li. YFCC100M: The new data in multimedia research. *Communications of the ACM*, 2015. To appear.

[5] `https://sites.google.com/a/yli-corpus.org/intro/mediaeval-2014-placing-task-dataset`

ImmersiveMe'15: 3rd ACM International Workshop on Immersive Media Experiences

Teresa Chambel
LaSIGE, Faculdade de Ciências
Universidade de Lisboa
Portugal
tc@di.fc.ul.pt

Paula Viana
Polytechnic of Porto and INESC TEC
Porto, Portugal
paula.viana@inesctec.pt

V. Michael Bove
MIT Media Lab
Cambridge, MA, USA
vmb@media.mit.edu

Sharon Strover
University of Texas at Austin
Austin, TX, USA
sharon.strover@austin.utexas.edu

Graham Thomas
BBC, UK
graham.thomas@bbc.co.uk

ABSTRACT
This ACM International Workshop on Immersive Media Experiences is in its 3rd edition. Since 2013 in Barcelona, it has been a meeting point of researchers, students, media producers, service providers and industry players in the area of immersive media environments, applications and experiences. After the successful first edition at ACM Multimedia 2013 and the consolidation of the theme and the team at Orlando in 2014, ImmersiveMe'15 aims at bringing to the stage new ideas and developments that keep this topic as appealing as in the previous editions. ImmersiveMe'15 will now take place in Brisbane and, again, it will be a platform to present interesting and out-of-the-box new work that contributes to make the world more interactive, immersive and engaging.

Categories and Subject Descriptors
H.5.1 [**Information Interfaces and Presentation**]: Multimedia Information Systems; I.2.10 [**Artificial Intelligence**]: Vision and Scene Understanding; H.3.3 [**Information Storage and Retrieval**]: Information Search and Retrieval

Keywords
Immersive media; perceptual immersion; multisensory interaction; participatory and affective media experiences; augmented reality and virtual environments.

1. INTRODUCTION
Immersive Media is related with aspects that have a direct impact in the viewers' experience and on their conscious feeling of being inside the virtual or surrounding world. Immersion may be determined by sensory modalities and surround effect as well as by participation and social immersion in the media chain, increasing the sense of belonging. It has an impact on the users and may benefit from personalized and context-aware environments and content. This interdisciplinary and transversal emerging field has the potential for strong impact on users' emotions, their sense of presence and engagement.

New approaches for capturing, producing, sharing and accessing information from users' perspectives and experiences, over the Internet, in social media, and through video on demand services offer tremendous opportunities for immersion, user participation and personalization. By using different media formats, including 3D content, panoramic displays, multiple views, as well as the possibility of delivering and accessing content through different communication methods, promote the development of a new participatory paradigm and enable new perceptual user experiences that provide more realistic, engaging and immersive involvement.

The workshop goal is to bring together researchers and practitioners in this field, and to foster discussion of ongoing work and future directions of related topics by providing a forum for focused exchanges on new ideas, developments, and results.

2. TOPICS OF INTEREST
The workshop covers a broad set of topics related to the concept of Immersive Media Experiences. Researchers were invited to contribute in the following areas:

- Perceptual Immersion and multisensory interaction and communication (including smell, taste and touch)
- Audiovisual Immersion: 3D, panoramic, multiview and holographic video, spatial and stereoscopic audio
- Augmented reality enhancing current perception of immersion
- Immersive TV, film and cinema
- Participatory media experiences including user generated content, collaborative scenarios and crowdsourcing
- Personalization and context-aware adaptation in immersive scenarios
- Emotions and affective interaction for immersive media
- Social aspects in new media services
- Novel rich media content production, distribution and consumption paradigms
- Enabling technologies and formats: new interaction devices, environments, modalities, and media formats
- Immersive media applications: culture, entertainment, education, art, health, personal media, etc.

MM'15, October 26-30, 2015, Brisbane, Australia
ACM 978-1-4503-3459-4/15/10.
http://dx.doi.org/10.1145/2733373.2806410

- Field trials, user studies and quality of experience in immersive media
- Design and evaluation of immersive media experiences

3. WORKSHOP CONTRIBUTIONS

As in the past, this third edition of the ACM ImmersiveMe workshop managed to attract a considerable number of high quality submissions. Accepted papers cover a broad number of relevant aspects including approaches for panoramic image capture, coding and streaming; distributed and collaborative augmented reality and live event management; impact of immersive environments in digital humanities; and human responses to stimulus. The workshop was also enriched by an invited talk by Pablo Cesar, leader of the Distributed and Interactive Systems group at CWI. His talk about Immersive Shared Experiences was grounded on the current scenario of confluence of social networking, multimedia, and computer-mediated interaction and presented ongoing work and challenges with a special focus on performing arts and personal communication.

4. WORKSHOP CHAIRS

Dr. Teresa Chambel is a professor at Faculty of Sciences, University of Lisbon (FCUL) in Portugal, and a senior researcher of the Human Computer Interaction and Multimedia group at the Lasige Lab. Her research interests include multimedia and hypermedia, with a special emphasis on video and hypervideo, human-computer interaction (HCI), creativity, immersion, visualization, accessibility, cognition and emotions, interactive TV, e-learning, digital talking books and digital art. In these areas, she has been working in research projects, authored around 125 conference or journal papers and book chapters, and also participated in the organization and program committees of workshops, conferences and journals, mainly in HCI and Multimedia.

Dr. Paula Viana is a Coordinator Professor at the Polytechnic of Porto and a Senior Researcher at INESC TEC, a research institute with more than 25 years of research results in the area of Telecommunications and Multimedia Services. She has authored papers in the areas of Digital TV, Multimedia Information Systems and Content Management. Her long collaboration with broadcasters and Industries enables an integrated vision of both future research topics as well as new applications for finished research. She has been serving as an expert for the European Commission on the evaluation of research proposals and on the assessment of project results.

Dr. V. Michael Bove, Jr. holds a Ph.D. in Media Technology, from MIT, where he is head of the Object-Based Media Group at the Media Lab, and co-directs the Center for Future Storytelling and the consumer electronics working group CE2.0. He has authored papers on digital TV systems, video processing HW/SW design, multimedia, scene modeling, visual display technologies, and optics. He holds patents relating to video recording, hardcopy, iTV, and medical imaging. He is co-author with the late Stephen A. Benton of the book Holographic Imaging (Wiley, 2008). He is on the Board of Editors of the SMPTE Journal, served as associate editor of Optical Engineering and is a fellow of SPIE and of the Institute for Innovation,Creativity, and Capital. He was a founder of and technical advisor to WatchPoint Media, Inc. and served as technical advisor to OneLaptopPerChild.

Dr. Sharon Strover is the Philip G. Warner Regents Professor in Communication at the University of Texas where she teaches communications and telecommunications courses and directs the Telecommunications and Information Policy Institute. Her research investigates the relationship between economic outcomes, policy and investments in digital media programs; social media; the digital divide; rural broadband deployment; e-government; and market structure and policy issues for international audiovisual industries. She has worked with several government agencies on telecommunications policy matters. She recently stepped down from chairing her Department, to work on a national broadband infrastructure program with the federal government in Washington, D.C.

Prof. Graham Thomas leads Immersive & Interactive Content Section at BBC R&D. Whilst the current work in his section spans both audio and video, his background is in image processing, computer vision and their application to 3D virtual graphics. He has played a key role in many EU and UK-funded research projects, e.g. on real-time image-based camera tracking, and model-based 3DTV. He was the main inventor in a number of projects that have gone on to commercial success, e.g. the *free-d* camera tracking system, retro-reflective chroma-key cloth, and sports graphics systems. Prior to 3D graphics, he worked on video compression, PAL coding, and motion estimation based on phase correlation (in his PhD), commercialized in a standards converter, which won an Emmy award and a Queen's Award to Industry. Graham holds over 20 patents and has published widely in the areas of image processing and computer vision for programme production. He is a Visiting Professor at the University of Surrey.

5. PROGRAMME COMMITTEE

Adrian Cheok, City University London, UK
Anthon Nijholt, Twente University, The Netherlands
Cha Zhang, Miscrosoft Research, Redmond, USA
George Lekakos, Athens Univ. of Econ. and Business, Greece
João Magalhães, New University of Lisbon, Portugal
Letizia Jaccheri, Norwegian Univ. of Science and Techn., Norway
Marc Cavazza, Teesside University, UK
Maria da Graça Pimentel, Universidade de São Paulo, Brazil
Marianna Obrist, University of Sussex, UK
Mario Montagud, CWI, The Netherlands
Matthew Davis, INESC TEC, Portugal
Nelson Zagalo, University of Minho, Portugal
Nimesha Ranasinghe, National University of Singapore
Nuno Correia, New University of Lisbon, Portugal
Omar A. Niamut, TNO, Delft, The Netherlands
Pablo Cesar, CWI, The Netherlands
Rene Kaiser, Joanneum Research, Graz, Austria
Ryohei Nakatsu, National University of Singapore
Santosh Basapur, Institute of Design, IIT, USA
Teresa Andrade, University of Porto and INESC TEC, Portugal
Teresa Romão, New University of Lisbon, Portugal
Thibault Langlois, LaSIGE, Fac. Ciências, Univ. Lisboa, Portugal

6. ACKNOWLEDGMENTS

This workshop was partially supported by: the Portuguese Foundation for Science and Technology through LaSIGE Strategic Project, ref. PEst-OE/EEI/UI0408/2014; and the Media, Arts and Technologies Project "NORTE-07-0124-FEDER-000061" funded by the North Portugal Regional Operational Programme (ON.2-O Novo Norte), under the National Strategic Reference Framework (NSRF), through the European Regional Development Fund (ERDF), and national funds, through the Portuguese funding agency, Fundação para a Ciência e a Tecnologia (FCT).

CrowdMM15 – Fourth International ACM Workshop on Crowdsourcing for Multimedia

Judith Redi
Delft University of Technology
Mekelweg 4
Delft, the Netherlands
j.a.redi@tudelft.nl

Stevan Rudinac
University of Amsterdam
Science Park 904
Amsterdam, The Netherlands
s.rudinac@uva.nl

ABSTRACT

Crowdsourcing has the potential to address key challenges in multimedia research. Multimedia evaluation, annotation, retrieval and creation can be obtained at a low time and monetary cost from the contribution of large crowds and by leveraging human computation. In fact, the applicative frontiers of this potential are yet to be discovered. And yet, challenges already arise as to how to cautiously exploit it. The crowd, as a users (workers) community, is a complex and dynamic system highly sensitive to changes in the form and the parameterization of their activities. Issues concerning motivation, reliability, and engagement are being more and more often documented, and need to be addressed. Since 2012, the International ACM Workshop on Crowdsourcing for Multimedia *CrowdMM* has welcomed new insights on the effective deployment of crowdsourcing towards boosting Multimedia research. On its fourth year, CrowdMM15 focuses on contributions addressing the key challenges that still hinder widespread adoption of crowdsourcing paradigms in the multimedia research community: identification of optimal crowd members (e.g., user expertise, worker reliability), providing effective explanations (i.e., good task design), controlling noise and quality in the results, designing incentive structures that do not breed cheating, and tackling privacy issues in data collection.

Categories and Subject Descriptors

H.1.2 [**User/Machine Systems**]: [Human Factors, Human information processing]

General Terms

Crowdsourcing, Evaluation and Methodology, Human-Computer Interaction

Keywords

Crowdsourcing, Multimedia evaluation, Human Computation, Multimedia Annotation, Human Factors

MM'15, October 26–30, 2015, Brisbane, Australia.
ACM 978-1-4503-3459-4/15/10.
DOI: http://dx.doi.org/10.1145/2733373.2806411 .

1. INTRODUCTION

Crowdsourcing is expected to change the face of Multimedia in the coming years. Multimedia research is inextricably tied to humans: not only they create media; they are the recipient of the technologies we research on, and their appreciation for the experience that is delivered is the ultimate measure of the goodness of a multimedia system or application. For this reason, humans (users) need to be kept in the loop in multimedia research, for technology evaluation, identification of human factors and requirements, for the annotation of ground truth, and, of course, content creation and curation.

Crowdsourcing is a booster for the human-centric development of multimedia. Technological advances have created new opportunities to leverage human effort to address limitations of current automation or to enhance current systems capabilities. The further enhancement of human intelligence attainable when contributions from multiple individuals are combined ("wisdom of the crowds") has just begun to give indications of greater potential for the multimedia field. Applications range from the exploitation of unsolicited user contributions, such as using tags to aid understanding of the visual content of yet-unseen images, to utilizing crowdsourcing platforms and marketplaces like Amazon Mechanical Turk and CrowdFlower, which micro-outsource tasks such as semantic video annotation to a large population of workers. Further, crowdsourcing offers a time- and resource-efficient tool for collecting large volumes of input for system design and evaluation, making it possible to optimize multimedia systems more rapidly and to address human factors more effectively.

On the other hand, there many challenges still prevent crowdsourcing from being widely (and successfully) adopted in multimedia research. The crowd in charge of carrying out research-related tasks has a dynamic, volatile nature. As a result, if measures for workers engagement and motivation are not taken, and methods for reliability control are not implemented, the risk of obtaining noisy output is high.

The aim of the fourth International ACM Workshop on Crowdsourcing for Multimedia (CrowdMM15) is to introduce and explore novel approaches for exploiting crowdsourcing methodologies at their full potential in the full range of multimedia research topics of interest for ACM Multimedia 2015. The core topic of this workshop concentrates around one issue: *How to advance the use of crowdsourcing to the next level for the state-of-the-art in multimedia research?*

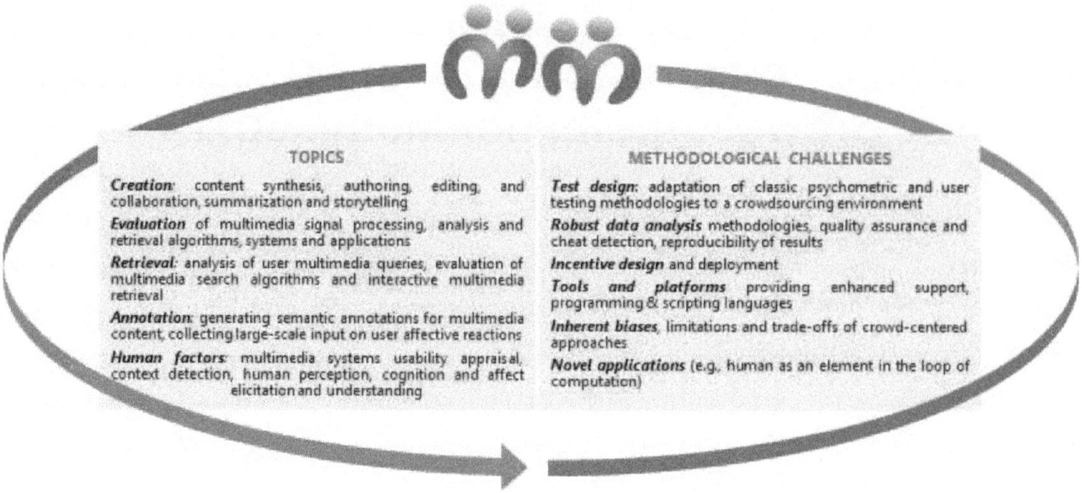

Figure 1: Topics and Methodological challenges addressed in CrowdMM15

2. OBJECTIVE

Crowdsourcing is a young technology that could prove invaluable for advancing the multimedia research and much work still has to be done to discover its full potential. However, being a problem solving tool rather than a goal in itself, crowdsourcing often requires a significant amount of exploratory work, in constant progress. For this reason, a workshop format, where fresh, new ideas and work in progress can be presented and discussed, is the most effective setup to push forward the use of Crowdsourcing for Multimedia Research, and solving the multitude of questions and challenges that are still open. Specifically, in its 2015 edition, CrowdMM focuses on addressing the methodological challenges listed in section 3 of this paper. Crowdsourcing cannot be considered as a mature technology for multimedia research if the results it produces are not reliable and repeatable. Hence, the goal of the workshop is to determine best practices for test and incentive schemes design, as well as robust data analysis and quality control techniques, along with eliciting new ideas for application areas in Multimedia where crowdsourcing may be a game-changer.

3. TOPICS

CrowdMM15 focuses on theoretical, methodological and applicative developments advancing the reliability and deployability of crowdsourcing for multimedia research. We explicitly called for submissions that (1) would employ crowdsourcing, wisdom of the crowd, games with a purpose, or human computation in different and new areas in multimedia topics (such as retrieval, evaluation and creation; see figure 1) and (2) would propose innovative solutions with respect to the methodological challenges that still justify skepticism around the widespread adoption of crowdsourcing, as indicated in figure 1.

4. PROGRAM

The workshop program includes oral presentations, invited keynote presentations, and a fishbowl discussion. Prof. Shih-Fu Chang, Richard Dicker Professor and senior Vice Dean of the School of Engineerign and Applied Sciences at Columbia University, joined CrowdMM15 as keynote speaker, addressing insights into the use of Crowdsourcing for video event detection, sentiment analysis and user intent modelling. CrowdMM14 also featured a "CrowdKeynote", during which all CrowdMM15 authors, and community members at large, gave their view on the future and the Challenges that Crowdsourcing has still ahead.

CrowdMM received a total of 12 submissions. Of these, three were accepted as oral presentations (25%) and another four as poster presentations. All papers received at least three double blind reviews, and 3.5 reviews on average. The organizers are grateful to the Program Committee members[1] and additional reviewers for their efforts in reviewing and for their insightful comments.

5. ORGANIZERS

- Judith Redi, Dept. Intelligent Systems, Delft University of Technology, The Netherlands [2]
- Stevan Rudinac, Intelligent Systems Lab Amsterdam, University of Amsterdam, The Netherlands [3]

6. STEERING COMMITTEE

The former workshop chairs are committed to CrowdMM and since 2014 have formed a steering committee to oversee and counsel on the integrity of the overall vision and goals of the workshop. The CrowdMM15 steering committee was:

- Kuan-Ta Chen, Academia Sinica, Taiwan.
- Martha Larson, Delft University of Technology, The Netherlands
- Tobias Hoßfeld, University of Wuerzburg, Germany
- Wei-Ta Chu, National Chung Cheng University, Taiwan
- Mathias Lux, Klagenfurt University, Austria

[1] `http://www.crowdmm.org/committees/`
[2] `http://www.mmi.tudelft.nl/~judith/`
[3] `https://staff.fnwi.uva.nl/s.rudinac/index.html`

2nd Workshop on Computational Models of Social Interactions: Human-Computer-Media Communication

Mohamed R. Amer
SRI International
201 Washington Rd.
Princeton, NJ, USA
mohamed.amer@sri.com

Ajay Divakaran
SRI International
201 Washington Rd.
Princeton, NJ, USA
ajay.divakaran@sri.com

Shih-Fu Chang
Colombia University
500 West 120th Street
New York, NY, USA
shih.fu.chang@columbia.edu

Nicu Sebe
University of Trento
via Sommarive 9
Povo, Trento, Italy
sebe@disi.unitn.it

ABSTRACT

Communicating ideas and information from and to humans is a very important subject. In our daily life, human interact with variety of entities, such as, other humans, machines, media. Constructive interactions are needed for good communication, which would result in successful outcomes, such as answering a query, learning a new skill, getting a service done, and communicating emotions. Each of these entities invokes a set of signals. Current research has focused on analyzing one entity's signals with no respect to the other entities in a unidirectional manner. The computer vision community focused on detection, classification and recognition of humans and their poses and gestures progressing onto actions, activities, and events but it does not go beyond that. The signal processing community focused on emotion recognition from facial expressions or audio or both combined. The HCI community focused on making easier interfaces for machines to ease their usage. The goal of this workshop is to bring multiple disciplines together, to process human directed signals holistically, in a bidirectional manner, rather than isolation. This workshop is positioned to display this rich domain of applications, which will provide the necessary next boost for these technologies. At the same time, it seeks to ground computational models on theory that would help achieve the technology goals. This would allow us to leverage decades of research in different fields and to spur interdisciplinary research thereby opening up new problem domains for the multimedia community.

MM'15, October 26–30, 2015, Brisbane, Australia.
© 2015 ACM. ISBN 978-1-4503-3459-4/15/10 ...$15.00.
DOI: http://dx.doi.org/10.1145/2733373.2806412.

Categories and Subject Descriptors

H.1.2 [**Information Systems Applications**]: User/Machine Systems| Human information processing; I.2.10 [**Artificial Intelligence**]: [Vision and Scene Understanding]

Keywords

Human Centric Computing, Human Computer Interaction, Human Media Interaction, Social Interaction

1. INTRODUCTION

Modeling human centric computing is anticipated to be a rewarding and challenging area of research. It would require modeling of a variety of contexts and interactions, each involving two or more entities with their context-dependent goals, emotions, affects and behavioral modes; and modeling of the interaction between them. The scope of the workshop covers the spectrum of Human-Human, Human-Machine, and Human-Media Interactions.

Human-Human Interactions: humans form a multitude of social groups through their life and regularly interact with other humans in these groups producing social behavior. Social behavior is behavior that is socially relevant or is situated in an identifiable social context. Interacting or observant humans sense, interpret, and understand these behaviors mostly using aural and visual sensory stimuli.

Human-Machine Interactions: aims to improve the interactions between users and computers by making interfaces more usable and receptive to users' needs by developing descriptive and predictive models and theories of interaction.

Human-Media Interactions: propaganda evokes strong emotions for or against a cause. Modern multimodal content is known to evoke much stronger emotions than textual content. The focus of human-media interaction is therefore on the analysis of the audience's affective response to social media content. Fine-grained assessment is essential to understand the affective impact of multimedia content.

These posit many unaddressed challenges for the signal processing, computer vision, machine learning, and human-computer interaction research communities. New systems and approaches will be needed to for real-time solutions for media analysis, interface adaptation, gaze, gesture, body affect, face affect, engagement, and joint attention detection.

2. SCOPE

This year's workshop continues its tradition of being the premier forum for presentation of research results and experience reports on leading edge issues of social interactions ranging from dyadic to multi-personal, including models, systems, applications, and theory spanning multipleâĂŞpertinent disciplines such as multimedia content analysis, social network analytics, behavior science and neuro-science among others. The mission of the workshop is to share novel approaches to social interaction modeling and systems that fulfill the needs of interactive applications and environments and identify new directions for future research and development. HCMC gives researchers and practitioners a unique opportunity to share their perspectives with others interested in the various aspects of computational models of social interaction. The workshop will address all aspects of the above research including the following topics of interest:

- Novel human-computer models for accessing media content, including multimodal and emotionally sensitive.
- Multimodal approaches to audio and video analysis, indexing, search, and retrieval.
- Modeling, prediction and forecasting collective behavior in social media.
- Human social, emotional, and/or affective cue extraction.
- Socially interactive and/or emotional multimedia content tagging.
- Multimedia tools for affective or interactive social behavior analysis.
- Dyadic or small-group interaction analysis in multimedia.
- Multimodal approaches to temporal or structural analysis of multimedia data.
- Machine learning for multimodal human behavior analysis.

3. SPEAKERS

We also host a set of keynote talks and paper presentations that will be valuable and insightful. We hope they will guide us to a better understanding of the future of Human-Computer-Media Communication. The keynote talks will be presented by:

- Lexing Xie "Can a video be promoted? a generative model for social media popularity"
- Alberto Del Bimbo "Natural Interaction Metaphors for Personalized Multimedia Museum Experiences"
- Ajay Divakaran "Human Social Interaction Sensing and Modeling"
- Vivek Singh "Sensing and Shaping Human Behavior using Multimodal Signals"
- Mohan Kankanhalli "Social Interactions and Presentation Analytics"

4. ORGANIZERS

Dr. Mohamed R. Amer (general co-chairs), SRI International, USA, is a Computer Scientist at SRI International. His main research focus is on human activity recognition, classification in Videos. His interest is in modeling context and interactions with goal event detection and video understanding. He has done some work on 2D to 3D conversion in images, and recently, he has done some work on the problem of Multimodal Event Detection for Affect Analysis. He received his B.S., M.S., and PhD at Oregon State University.

Dr. Ajay Divakaran (general co-chairs), SRI International, USA, is a Technical Manager at SRI International Sarnoff. Dr. Divakaran has developed several innovative technologies for multimodal systems for both commercial and government programs over the past 16 years. He currently leads SRI projects on Modeling and Analysis of Human Behavior for the DARPA SSIM project, Army "Master Trainer" intelligent tutoring project, audio concept detection Open Source Video for IARPA ALADDIN as well as DARPA SMISC. He worked at Mitsubishi Electric Research Labs for ten years.

Prof. Shih-Fu Chang (general co-chairs), Columbia University, USA, is the Director of the Digital Video and Multimedia Lab, and Senior Vice Dean of Engineering School at Columbia University. Prof. Chang is an active researcher leading development of innovative technologies for multimedia information extraction and retrieval, while contributing to fundamental advances of the fields of machine learning, computer vision, and signal processing.

Prof. Nicu Sebe (general co-chairs), University of Trento, Italy, is the dean of the doctoral school in ICT and leads the research in the areas of multimedia information retrieval and human-computer interaction in computer vision applications. Prof. Sebe was involved in the organization of the major conferences and workshops addressing the computer vision and human-centered aspects of multimedia information retrieval.

Prof. Lai-Tee Cheok (panel and publicity Chair), Singapore Managment University, Singapore, is an assistant professor in the school of information systems. Her research interests include: Mobile Computing (Mobile Search, Mobile Shopping), Data analytics for e-Commerce applications, Video Content Analysis, Machine Learning and Data Mining Applications for Video Surveillance, Optimization of resources for Video Streaming, Optimizing Machine Learning and Data Mining Methods.

5. CONCLUSION

We hope that you will find this program interesting and thought-provoking and that the workshop will provide you with a valuable opportunity to share ideas with other researchers and practitioners from institutions around the world.

Acknowledgments

We are grateful for the guidance of Dr. Brian Lande, and Dr. Rand Waltzman for their research insights and direction. We would like to also thank all the authors, reviewer, program committee members, and keynote speakers for their efforts and contributions.

About Events, Objects, and their Relationships: Human-centered Event Understanding from Multimedia

Ansgar Scherp
ZBW – Leibniz Information Centre for Economics and Kiel University
Kiel, Germany
asc@informatik.uni-kiel.de

Vasileios Mezaris
Centre for Research and Technology Hellas
Thessaloniki, Greece
bmezaris@iti.gr

Bogdan Ionescu
University Politehnica of Bucharest
Bucharest, Romania
bionescu@imag.pub.ro

Francesco De Natale
University of Trento
Trento, Italy
francesco.denatale@unitn.it

ABSTRACT

HuEvent'15 is a continuation of previous year's successful workshop on events in multimedia. It focuses on the human-centered aspects of understanding events from multimedia content. This includes the notion of objects and their relation to events. The workshop brings together researchers from the different areas in multimedia and beyond that are interested in understanding the concept of events.

1. INTRODUCTION

Events can be found from life-log applications to emergency response systems as well as in domains like cultural heritage, news, sports, and surveillance. Thus, we can understand events as natural abstraction of human experience [7]. The different applications and domains make use of different methods and approaches for detecting, representing, and using events. However, they share the common notion of considering events as important entities.

Events are generally understood as perduring entities that unfold over time. They are occurrences in which humans participate and may be subject to discussions and interpretations by humans. In contrast, objects are enduring entities that unfold over space. While some consider objects as 4D entities, i.e., extending across time just as they do in space, others consider both events and objects as first class entities that require each other.

Key research questions of the workshop series are:

HuEvent'15, October 30, 2015, Brisbane, Australia.
ACM 978-1-4503-3748-9/15/10.
DOI: http://dx.doi.org/10.1145/2733373.2806413.

- Discovering events and/or objects from media assets;
- Understanding objects' role in events;
- Understanding objects' interconnectivity through events;
- Understanding peoples' actions during events;
- Analysis of humans' reactions/emotions/comments to events and/or objects;
- Understanding humans' event interaction and its evolution in time;
- Analysis of human opinion and bias on event perception;
- Analysis of human factors for event evolution, spreading, and interpretation;
- Use of human behaviors for event prediction and trend analysis ("in" and "on" the event);
- Multiple views and multiple user event analysis;
- Time synchronization of multi-user event media;
- Multimedia event detection and recounting;
- Deep learning for multimedia event analysis and mining;
- Event-based processing and analysis of Big Multimedia Data;
- Event-based multimedia organization, clustering, summarization, and storytelling;
- Multimedia for human-centered event understanding;
- Novel applications of events and multimedia.

2. WORKSHOP GOAL

The goal of this workshop is to present and discuss the human-centered understanding of different aspects and notions of events and objects. This includes methods for detecting activities and low-level events and objects from media content and other sensory data. It also targets solutions and approaches for detecting and modeling the relationships between events and objects, as well as for organizing media according to events.

We aim to bring together researchers from the different areas in multimedia and beyond that are interested in understanding the concept of events. We invite original work in the areas of event modeling, detection of events from multimedia data, processing of events, organization of multimedia data using events as unifying mechanism, and applications of these techniques.

3. WORKSHOP HISTORY

The 2nd ACM International Workshop on Human-centered Event Understanding from Multimedia[1] (HuEvent'15) at the 23rd ACM Multimedia Conference in Brisbane, Australia is a continuation of a successful series of previous events. Most notably, it is a successor of the 1st Workshop on Human-centered Event Understanding from Multimedia[2] (HuEvent'14) that was co-located with ACM Multimedia in Orlando, Florida, USA [7].

However, the workshop finds its roots in earlier activities: There have been three successful Events in Multimedia (EiMM) workshops that were held in conjunction with the previous editions of ACM Multimedia in Beijing, China (2009) [3], Florence, Italy (2010) [5], and Scottsdale, AZ, USA (2011) [2]. In those editions, the focus was on events only and not on an a human-centered approach of event understanding that also includes the notion of objects and their relation to events - as it is pursued in this workshop. The Workshop on Event-based Media Integration and Processing[3] held in 2013 at ACM Multimedia in Barcelona is also related but focused on events and their extraction from multimedia content.

From these activities, also different special issues on the topic of events and objects in multimedia emerged [1, 4]. Finally, we released an extensive survey on modeling and indexing events in multimedia [6].

4. WORKSHOP PROGRAMME

This year's workshop programme is organized into a keynote, a set of paper presentations, and a final discussion.

The keynote is held by Cees Snoek[4] on the topic of "Recognizing events in videos without examples". The talk presents recent progress on recognizing events in videos, without the need for examples. The key to event recognition in such a challenging setting is to have a lingual video representation. Three lingual representations for zero-example event recognition are highlighted: covering concept, tag, and sentence embedding.

The accepted research papers at the workshop are continuing the discussions focusing on the following topics: The first paper, "Using Photo Similarity and Weighted Graphs for the Temporal Synchronization of Event-Centered Multi-User Photo Collections", addresses the issue of temporal synchronization of photo collections that have been created during the same event by different users using different (unsynchronized) devices. The method proposed by the authors employ multiple similarity measures to identify pairs of similar photos and then temporally align the photo collections by traversing a graph, whose nodes represent the collections, and edges represent the similar photo pairs between collections.

The second paper, "Media Synchronization and Sub-Event Detection in Multi-User Image Collections", continues the idea of media synchronization by conducting a thorough evaluation of the performance of several visual-based image synchronization techniques; but goes beyond and applies it to sub-event detection. Common clustering techniques are experimented for the detection of sub-events in the presence of synchronization misalignment.

Finally, the paper "Discovering Commonness and Specificness for Human Action Recognition" brings into discussion another dimension of human-centered event understanding, namely human action recognition. A discriminative dictionary, learning-based method that is specifically adapted to recognize commonness and specificness among different action classes is introduced. Experimental validation on standard benchmarking datasets show promising results for this approach.

Like in the previous year, the workshop programme is a kick-off for a final discussion. Topics addressed are among others the different understandings of events and objects, approaches for harmonization, and future research.

[1]http://huevent15.uni-kiel.de/en
[2]http://huevent14.uni-kiel.de/en
[3]http://ebmip.disi.unitn.it
[4]http://www.ceessnoek.info/

5. REFERENCES

[1] V. Mezaris, A. Scherp, R. Jain, and M. S. Kankanhalli. Real-life events in multimedia: detection, representation, retrieval, and applications. *Multimedia Tools Appl.*, 70(1):1–6, 2014.

[2] V. Mezaris, A. Scherp, R. Jain, M. S. Kankanhalli, H. Zhou, J. Zhang, L. Wang, and Z. Zhang. Modeling and representing events in multimedia. In K. S. Candan, S. Panchanathan, B. Prabhakaran, H. Sundaram, W. chi Feng, and N. Sebe, editors, *Proc. of the 19th Int. Conf. on Multimedia 2011, Scottsdale, AZ, USA, November 28 - December 1, 2011*, pages 613–614. ACM, 2011.

[3] A. Scherp, R. Jain, and M. S. Kankanhalli. Events in multimedia. In W. Gao, Y. Rui, A. Hanjalic, C. Xu, E. G. Steinbach, A. El-Saddik, and M. X. Zhou, editors, *Proc. of the 17th Int. Conf. on Multimedia 2009, Vancouver, British Columbia, Canada, October 19-24, 2009*, pages 1147–1148. ACM, 2009.

[4] A. Scherp, R. Jain, and M. S. Kankanhalli. Introduction to the special issue of the multimedia tools and applications journal on events in multimedia. *Multimedia Tools Appl.*, 57(1):127–129, 2012.

[5] A. Scherp, R. Jain, M. S. Kankanhalli, and V. Mezaris. Modeling, detecting, and processing events in multimedia. In A. D. Bimbo, S.-F. Chang, and A. W. M. Smeulders, editors, *Proc. of the 18th Int. Conf. on Multimedia 2010, Firenze, Italy, October 25-29, 2010*, pages 1739–1740. ACM, 2010.

[6] A. Scherp and V. Mezaris. Survey on modeling and indexing events in multimedia. *Multimedia Tools Appl.*, 70(1):7–23, 2014.

[7] A. Scherp, V. Mezaris, B. Ionescu, and F. G. B. D. Natale. Huevent'14: 2014 workshop on human-centered event understanding from multimedia. In K. A. Hua, Y. Rui, R. Steinmetz, A. Hanjalic, A. Natsev, and W. Zhu, editors, *Proc. of the ACM Int. Conf. on Multimedia, MM '14, Orlando, FL, USA, November 03 - 07, 2014*, pages 1253–1254. ACM, 2014.

Overview of the 2015 Workshop on Speech, Language and Audio in Multimedia

Guillaume Gravier
CNRS
IRISA & Inria Rennes
guig@irisa.fr

Gareth J.F. Jones
Dublin City University
School of Computing
gareth.jones@computing.dcu.ie

Martha Larson
Delft Univ. of Technology
Multimedia Computing Group
m.a.larson@tudelft.nl

Roeland Ordelman
Univ. of Twente & Netherlands
Institute for Sound and Vision
roeland.ordelman@utwente.nl

ABSTRACT

The Workshop on Speech, Language and Audio in Multimedia (SLAM) positions itself at at the crossroad of multiple scientific fields—music and audio processing, speech processing, natural language processing and multimedia—to discuss and stimulate research results, projects, datasets and benchmarks initiatives where audio, speech and language are applied to multimedia data. While the first two editions were collocated with major speech events, SLAM'15 is deeply rooted in the multimedia community, opening up to computer vision and multimodal fusion. To this end, the workshop emphasizes video hyperlinking as an showcase where computer vision meets speech and language. Such techniques provide a powerful illustration of how multimedia technologies incorporating speech, language and audio can make multimedia content collections better accessible, and thereby more useful, to users.

Categories and Subject Descriptors

H.3.1 [**Information Systems**]: Information Storage and Retrieval—*Content Analysis and Indexing*

Keywords

Multimedia, Audio, Speech, Language

1. INTRODUCTION

The workshop on Speech, Language and Audio in Multimedia (SLAM) aims at bringing together researchers working in the fields of speech, language and audio processing with application to the analysis of, indexing of and access to multimedia data. In the context of SLAM, we define multimedia data as content captured, and often also edited, to create a message intended for humans, often combining multiple modalities. Typical data containing audio or language and fitting this definition are broadcast videos, video lectures, music and clips, or social media data. Note that in most cases, speech, language and audio are important carriers of semantics in multimedia content. In particular, language is of utmost importance for understanding the nature of the message. Yet these sources of information are often overlooked, or remain poorly exploited by researchers working to develop new multimedia technologies.

SLAM is by nature interdisciplinary, existing at the intersection of multiple scientific communities, including the research area of multimedia. Apart from traditional workshop objectives of sharing scientific results and visions, one of the goal of SLAM is to establish and make visible a cross-domain scientific community. To this end, SLAM gathers players from the fields of speech and audio processing, of natural language processing and of multimedia to share recent research results, discuss ongoing and future projects, explore potential areas for interdisciplinary collaboration or sharing or ideas, and develop new benchmarking initiatives of mutual interest to multimedia and language researchers.

SLAM'15 is the third edition of the workshop. The workshop series was initiated in 2013 by the Intl. Speech Communication Association (ISCA) Special Interest Group on Speech and Language in Multimedia[1], with support from the IEEE Special Interest Group on Audio and Speech Processing in Multimedia[2]. Previous editions [1, 6] were collocated with Interspeech, the premier international conference on speech communication yearly organized by ISCA. However, the long-term goal is to establish SLAM as a regular workshop, collocating in alternance with major multimedia conferences and major speech and language conferences, as a bridge between these domains.

Organizing SLAM'15 as an ACM Multimedia event is thus in logical continuation from the preceding editions. Previous efforts to highlight the importance of SLAM-related topics at ACM Multimedia include the workshop on Searching Spontaneously Conversational Speech [5] and the workshop on Audio and Multimedia Methods for Large-Scale Video Analysis [4]. SLAM transcends these efforts because it emphasizes language and audio in addition to speech, goes beyond the application of search and the large-scale issues, and

MM'15 October 26-30, 2015, Brisbane, Australia
ACM 978-1-4503-3459-4/15/10.
DOI: http://dx.doi.org/10.1145/2733373.2806414.

[1] `http://slim-sig.irisa.fr`
[2] `http://www.computer.org/portal/web/tcmc/SIGASP`

also puts an explicit focus on work in which speech, language or audio is *one* or multiple modalities.

In order to emphasize its connection with the multimedia community, SLAM'15 features a special focus on video hyperlinking, a multimedia task that was recently introduced in international benchmarks, where computer vision and image processing meets speech, language and audio. Details on the video hyperlinking session are given in Sec. 4.

2. WORKSHOP SCOPE AND GOALS

Multimedia data are available in enormous volumes in a wide variety of formats and qualities, from professional content to user-generated ones: Lectures, meetings, interviews, debates, conversational broadcast, podcasts, social videos on the Web, etc. A large number of those sources include audio, speech and language, which are considered as key modalities for structuring and understanding, e.g., speaker turns, topic segmentation, entities and keywords. Analyzing audio, speech and language in multimedia data raises specific challenges that arise both from the nature of the data (e.g., semantics, variety, variability, multimodality) and from the typical use-cases considered in multimedia applications. Typical challenges specific to the nature of multimedia data include robustness in face of high variability in quality, efficiency to handle very large amounts of data, semantics shared across modalities, or potentially high error rates in transcription affecting spoken language processing. An important set of challenges also arises from the application scenarios in which users make use of multimedia. User needs evolve rapidly, often during the experience of interacting with multimedia data, and users have a difficult time expressing their own needs concretely, or formulating them explicitly in a way that can be directly exploited by a system. All of these factors may also make it difficult to create the large and representative data sets needed in order to develop solutions to multimedia challenges.

Worldwide, several national and international research projects are focusing on audio analysis of multimedia data. Similarly, various benchmark initiatives have devoted effort to offering tasks related to multimodal multimedia challenges (e.g., TRECVid, CLEF, MediaEval). The aim of the workshop is to support these efforts by drawing attention to their importance, and to the variety of interdisciplinary solutions that are needed in order to address current challenges in multimedia.

3. TOPICS

The workshop embraces a broad range of contributions including research work, project descriptions, evaluation initiatives, demonstrations and applications. The common denominator is that each emphasizes the added value of speech and/or language and/or audio for multimedia technology.

This year the workshop includes papers that address a wide variety of topics. Examples include: the exploitation of the structure or music, the challenge processing of spoken clinical reports, in a way that combines speech recognition and human checks, the use of multimodal data in training systems that are capable of detecting spoken words, and finally, how audio information can be integrated into an overall visual object retrieval system. A large portion of the workshop is devoted to the showcase of the task of video hyperlinking, which we turn to next.

4. VIDEO HYPERLINKING CASE STUDY

A key feature of SLAM'15 is the focus on video hyperlinking, with a dedicated session and round-table. Video hyperlinking is the task of organizing a collection of videos with (hyper)links from segments of interest, also know as *anchors*, to relevant segments within the collection. The video hyperlinking task was recently introduced in the MediaEval international benchmarking initiative [3, 2], moving to TRECVid in 2015.

Interestingly in the context of SLAM, accurate video hyperlinking approaches require the integration of multiple modalities, in particular image and language, where language sources are typically automatic transcripts, subtitles or program synopsis. The multimodal nature of the video hyperlinking task makes it an emblematic case study where the speech and language modalities are perfectly complemented by audio and vision. The workshop program features a number of contributions where audio and natural language processing are used for video hyperlinking, possibly in conjunction with images. A panel discussion focused on discussing the past, present and future of hyperlinking will conclude the workshop. The panel will aim at an understanding of which approaches are most promising and how they can be evaluated. The goal is to shape research directions at the crossroad of the scientific communities involved in SLAM and nurturing future implementations of video hyperlinking benchmarks.

5. ACKNOWLEDGEMENTS

We would like to thank the authors, presenters, and reviewers, whose efforts made the workshop possible.

6. REFERENCES

[1] F. Bechet and G. Gravier, editors. *Proceedings of the 1st IEEE/ISCA International Workshop on Speech, Language and Audio in Multimedia*, 2013.

[2] M. Eskevich, R. Aly, D. N. Racca, R. Ordelman, S. Chen, and G. J. F. Jones. The Search and Hyperlinking task at MediaEval 2014. In *Working Notes Proc. of the MediaEval Workshop*, 2014.

[3] M. Eskevich, G. J. Jones, R. Aly, R. J. Ordelman, S. Chen, D. Nadeem, C. Guinaudeau, G. Gravier, P. Sébillot, T. de Nies, P. Debevere, R. Van de Walle, P. Galuscakova, P. Pecina, and M. Larson. Multimedia information seeking through search and hyperlinking. In *Proc. ACM Intl. Conf. on Multimedia Retrieval*, pages 287–294, 2013.

[4] G. Friedland, D. Ellis, and F. Metze, editors. *Proceedings of the 2012 ACM International Workshop on Audio and Multimedia Methods for Large-scale Video Analysis*, 2012.

[5] M. Larson, R. Ordelman, F. de Jong, J. Köhler and W. Kraaij, editors. *Proceedings of the 3rd Workshop on Searching Spontaneous Conversational Speech*, 2009.

[6] T.-P. Tan, G. Gravier, and K. M. Siti, editors. *Proceedings of the 2nd IEEE/ISCA International Workshop on Speech, Language and Audio in Multimedia*, 2014.

ASM'15: The 1st International Workshop on Affect and Sentiment in Multimedia

Mohammad Soleymani
Swiss Center for Affective Sciences
University of Geneva
Geneva, Switzerland
mohammad.soleymani@unige.ch

Yi-Hsuan Yang
Research Center for IT Innovation
Academia Sinica
Taipei, Taiwan
yang@citi.sinica.edu.tw

Yu-Gang Jiang
School of Computer Science
Fudan University
Shanghai, China
ygj@fudan.edu.cn

Shih-Fu Chang
Dept. of Electrical Engineering
Columbia University
New York, USA
sfchang@ee.columbia.edu

Categories and Subject Descriptors

H3.1 [**Content Analysis and Indexing**]: Indexing methods; H.1.2 [**User/Machine Systems**]: Human factors

Keywords

Emotion; affect; sentiment; multimedia

1. SUMMARY

In recent years, there has been a dramatic proliferation of research on multimedia retrieval and indexing based on highly subjective concepts such as emotion, sentiment, preference and aesthetics [1, 2, 4, 5]. These retrieval methods are considered human-centered, intuitive, and beyond the conventional keyword- or object-based retrieval paradigm. In addition, the problem is considered challenging because it requires multidisciplinary understanding of human behavior and perception as well as multimodal integration of different modalities (music, image, video, text) for better performance. The challenges in affective multimedia analysis are not limited to the technical problems but also to the way we use and assess emotional concepts, representations and responses. Therefore, research in affective analysis should pay a careful attention to the definitions, limitations and the developments in the psychology of emotions [3].

ASM workshop provides a forum to present and discuss the emerging field of affect and sentiment analysis in multimedia. Unlike the affect and social signal processing track at the main conference, we focus mainly on multimedia content analysis and its applications for automatic sentiment and affective analysis. Being a workshop, we also provide more space for focused discussions.

MM'15, October 26–30, 2015, Brisbane, Australia.
© 2015 ACM. ISBN 978-1-4503-3459-4/15/10 ...$15.00.
DOI: http://dx.doi.org/10.1145/2733373.2806415.

In response to an open call for contributions, we originally received 18 original submissions from which we accepted 9 high quality submissions, taking into account the reviewers' feedback and relevance to the topics of interest. The contributions featured at this workshop include content-based affective understanding of music, video and text; multimedia sentiment analysis, multimedia affective applications and affect-based multimedia retrieval systems. In addition to the contributions from the authors, the workshop will include two keynote talks from Dr. Nicole Nelson (University of Queensland) and Dr. Shlomo Berkovsky (Commonwealth Scientific and Industrial Research Organisation, or CSIRO), who are leading experts in the psychology of emotions and recommendation systems. The keynote talks enrich the discussions at the workshop bringing in experts with different perspectives, namely, affective and social sciences and recommendation systems.

We hope this workshop serves its purpose in advancing the analysis of affect and sentiment in multimedia.

2. ACKNOWLEDGMENTS

We thank the program committee members for their invaluable contribution in reviewing the submissions.

3. REFERENCES

[1] D. Borth, R. Ji, T. Chen, T. Breuel, and S.-F. Chang. Large-scale visual sentiment ontology and detectors using adjective noun pairs. In *Proc. ACM Int. Conf. Multimedia (MM)*, pages 223–232, 2013.

[2] Y.-G. Jiang, B. Xu, and X. Xue. Predicting emotions in user-generated videos. In *Proc. AAAI Conf. Artificial Intelligence*, pages 73–79, 2014.

[3] A. Kappas. Smile when you read this, whether you like it or not: Conceptual challenges to affect detection. *Affective Computing, IEEE Transactions on*, 1(1):38–41, Jan 2010.

[4] M. Soleymani, M. Larson, T. Pun, and H. Alen. Corpus development for affective video indexing. *IEEE Transactions on Multimedia*, 16(4):1075–1089, 2014.

[5] Y.-H. Yang and H. H. Chen. *Music Emotion Recognition.* CRC Press, Boca Raton, Florida, 2011.

Author Index

www.ingramcontent.com/pod-product-compliance
Ingram Content Group UK Ltd.
Pitfield, Milton Keynes, MK11 3LW, UK
UKHW051420290926
15471UKWH00009B/1695

9 781450 341127